# A Concordance to The Poetical Works of John Milton

BY

JOHN BRADSHAW

ARCHON BOOKS

HAMDEN, CONNECTICUT

1965

FIRST PUBLICATION 1894
REPRINTED 1965 BY ARRANGEMENT WITH
GEORGE ALLEN AND UNWIN, LTD.
IN AN UNALTERED AND UNABRIDGED EDITION

LIBRARY OF CONGRESS CATALOG CARD NUMBER: 65-25397
PRINTED IN THE UNITED STATES OF AMERICA

# PREFACE.

THE only Concordance to Milton's Poetical Works that has yet appeared is that by the late Mr. Guy Lushington Prendergast of the Madras Civil Service, published at Madras in 1857. The edition was small, and it has long been out of print. Unfortunately, too, the editing seems to have been left to the printers, who apparently cut off from either end of a quotation such words as would not fit into a line of the *Concordance*, thus rendering it necessary for one consulting the work to refer in most cases to the passage in Milton; there are also many errors in it owing to the fact that to copyists as well as to compositors English was a foreign language.

In 1867 Mr. C. D. Cleveland, of Philadelphia, published in England a small work entitled "A Complete Concordance to the Poetical Works of John Milton" (London, Sampson Low), but it was merely a verbal index, a first edition of which had appeared in Cleveland's edition of Milton's Poetical Works, published in America in 1854. Previous to this there was Todd's Verbal Index, appended to his edition of Milton's Poetical Works in 1809; but in it, according to Cleveland, there are over three thousand mistakes.

In the present *Concordance* I have followed the text of the new Aldine Edition of Milton's Poetical Works, edited by me this year for Messrs. George Bell & Sons, which was carefully revised from my edition of Milton's Poetical Works, published by W. H. Allen & Co. in 1877 and 1885.

It would be well if the spelling in the Poems were fixed, or more uniformity observed; words are spelled differently not only in different editions but even in the same edition; thus we have 'frenzy' and 'phrenzy', 'inactive' and 'unactive', 'inrolled' and 'enrolled', and other words beginning with 'in', 'en' etc., and in the same edition 'dropt' and 'dropped', 'swoln' and 'swollen', also some editors print as compounds words that others treat as separate words.

All the Poems are included in this *Concordance* except the *Psalms* and the Translations in the Prose works; and all the words are given with the exception of some of the pronouns, conjunctions, adverbs and prepositions; but any of these used peculiarly are given, and it is hoped that the present work will be found useful not only by the student of Milton but by the grammarian and the philologist.

I have to thank Major General Prendergast for supplying me with a copy of his father's *Concordance* and for allowing me to make use of it in the preparation of this; and to Mr. K. Deighton, M.A., late Principal of Agra College, my special thanks are due for kindly reading a portion of the proofs, as the printing of the work did not commence until I had left England.

MADRAS:

December 1893.                                                JOHN BRADSHAW.


Since the lamented death of Dr. BRADSHAW in January 1894, the revision of the proofs has been kindly undertaken by his father, the Rev. W. H. BRADSHAW, A.M., Booterstown, Dublin.

S. S. & Co.

# A

# CONCORDANCE

TO

# MILTON'S

# POETICAL WORKS

**Aaron.**—P. L. 3, 598. in *A.'s* breast-plate
P. L. 12, 170. Moses and *A.*
P. R. 3, 15. oraculous gems on *A.'s* breast
**Abaddon.**—P. R. 4, 624. in all her gates *A.*
**Abandon.**—P. L. 6, 494. *a.* fear
**Abandoned.**—P. L. 6, 134. *a.* at the terror
P. L. 10, 717. to sorrow *a.* but worse felt
S. A. 120. as one past hope *a.*
**Abarim.**—P. L. 1, 408. southmost *A.*
**Abashed.**—P. L. 1, 331. they heard and were *a.*
P. L. 4, 846. *a.* the devil stood
P. L. 8, 595. half *a.* Adam replied
P. L. 9, 1065. not less than Eve *a.*
P. L. 10, 161. thus *a.* replied
P. R. 2, 224. every sudden slighting quite *a.*
P. R. 4, 195. the fiend with fear *a.*
**Abassin.**—P. L. 4, 280. where *A.* kings
**Abate.**—P. R. 2, 455. *a.* her edge
**Abated.**—P. L. 11, 841. the flood which now *a.*
**Abbana.**—P. L. 1, 469. *A.* and Pharphar
**Abdiel.**—P. L. 5, 805. *A.* than whom none
P. L. 5, 896. seraph *A.* faithful found
P. L. 6, 111. *A.* that sight endured not
P. L. 6, 171. thus *A.* stern replied
P. L. 6, 369. nor stood unmindful *A.* to annoy
**Abhor.**—P.L. 4, 392.though damned, I should *a.*
P. L. 5, 120. thou didst *a.*
P. L. 11, 686. who of themselves *a.* to join
P. R. 4, 172. now both *a.*
**Abhorred.**—P. L. 2, 659. far less *a.* than these
P. L. 6, 607. to return they worse *a.*
P. L. 2, 8. in this *a.* deep
P. L. 2, 577. *a.* styx, the flood of deadly hate
P. R. 4, 191. to me my own, on such *a.* pact
C. 535. doing *a.* rites to Hecate
L. 75. comes the blind Fury with the *a.* shears
F. of C. 4. whose sin ye envied not *a.*
**Abhorrest.**—P.L. 12, 79. justly thou *a.*that son
**Abide.**—P. L. 1, 385. and durst *a.* Jehovah
P. L. 4, 87. how dearly I *a.* that boast
P. L. 5, 609. under his great vicegerent reign *a.*
S. A. 922. *a.* with me where my redoubled love
S. A. 136. where strength can least *a.*
C. 951. all the swains that there *a.*
H. 225. longer dare *a.*
P. 20. yet more the stroke of death he must *a.*
**Abides.**—P. L. 3, 388. effulgence of his glory *a.*
P. L. 11, 292. where he *a.*

**Ability.**—S. A. 743. if aught in my *a.* may serve
**Abject.**—P. L. 1, 312. *a.* and lost lay these
P. L. 1, 322. or in this *a.* posture
P. L. 9, 572. of *a.* thoughts and low
S. A. 169. to lowest pitch of *a.* fortune
P. L. 11, 520. so *a.* is their punishment
**Abjure.**—P. L. 8, 480. and other pleasures all *a.*
P. R. 1, 474. feign, flatter, or *a.*
**Able.**—P. L. 3,211. some other *a.* and as willing
P. L. 4, 155. *a.* to drive all sadness but despair
P. L. 5, 70. *a.* to make gods of men
P. L. 10, 819. I, were I *a.* to waste it all myself
P. L. 10, 950. ill *a.* to sustain his full wrath
P. L. 12, 491. with spiritual armour *a.* to resist
P. R. 3, 365. found *a.* to annoy
S. M. 4. with imbreathed sense *a.* to pierce
**Abler.**—P. R. 1, 151. far *a.* to resist
**Abode.**—P. L. 3, 734. Adam's *a.*
P. L. 4, 939. in hope to find better *a.*
P. L. 7, 553. Heaven of Heavens, his high *a.*
C. 693. was this the cottage and the safe *a.*
H. 18. to welcome him to this his new *a.*
D. F. I, 60. and after short *a.* fly back with speed
**Abolish.**—P. L. 2, 370. *a.* his own works
P. L. 3, 163. wilt thou *a.* thy creation
P. L. 9, 947. yet would be loth us to *a.*
**Abolished.**—P. L. 2, 93. we should be quite *a.*
**Abominable.**—P. L. 2, 626. *a.*, inutterable
P. L. 10, 465. *a.* accursed, the house of woe
P. R. 4, 173. the *a.* terms, impious condition
S. A. 1359. a Nazarite in place *a.*
**Abominations.**—P. L. 1, 389. their shrines *a.*
P. R. 3, 162. foul affronts, *a.* rather
**Abortive.**—P. L. 2, 441. in that *a.* gulf
P. L. 3, 456. *a.*, monstrous, or unkindly mixed
P. L. 11, 769. gaining birth *a.*
P. R. 4, 411. *a.* poured fierce rain
S. A. 1576 *a.* as the first-born bloom of spring
**Above.**—There are 63 instances of *above* as a
prep., and the following:
P. L. 2, 172. or from *a.* should intermitted
P. L. 2, 351. him who rules *a.*
P. L. 2, 731. him who sits *a.* and laughs
P. L. 2, 814. he who reigns *a.*
P. L. 2, 856. what owe I to his commands *a.*
P. L. 3, 56. the Almighty Father from *a.*
P. L. 4, 860. awe from *a.* had quelled his heart
P. L. 5, 363. descending from the thrones *a.*

B

P. L. 7, 118. commission from *a*. I have
P. L. 7, 268. from those *a*. dividing
P. L. 8, 168. leave them to God *a*.
P. L. 8, 318. Author of all thou seest *a*.
P. L. 10, 549. his will who reigns *a*.
P. L. 10, 2. from the mercy-seat *a*.
P. L. 11, 138. strength added from *a*.
P. L. 11, 232. of the thrones *a*.
P. L. 11, 668. peace and judgment from *a*.
P. R. 1, 274. which I believed was from *a*.
P. R. 1, 496. permission from *a*. thou canst
P. R. 4, 289. light from *a*.
S. A. 99. my vessel trusted to me from *a*.
S. A. 664. some source of consolation from *a*.
S. A. 1052. most is acceptable *a*.
L. 178. there entertain him all the saints *a*.
Il P. 152. sweet music breathe *a*., about
H. 4. our great redemption from *a*. did bring
Cir. 18. were lost in death till he that dwelt *a*.
C. 1003. far *a*. in spangled sheen
**Abound.**—P. L. 6, 502. if malice should *a*.
P. L. 12, 478. over wrath grace shall *a*.
**Abounded.**—P. L. 3, 312. love hath *a*.
**Abounds.** — P. L. 3, 312. more than glory *a*.
**About.**—There are 43 instances of *about*, as a
 prep., and the following :
P. L. 10, 420. and all *a*. found desolate
S. A. 530. I walked *a*. admired of all
S. A. 675. wandering loose *a*.
A. 58. haste I all *a*.
Il P. 152. sweet music breathe above, *a*.
**Abraham.**—P. L. 12, 152. faithful *A*.
P. L. 12, 260. to the land promised to *A*.
P. L. 12, 268. so call the third from *A*.
P. L. 12, 273. which concern just *A*.
P. L. 12, 328. foretold to *A*.
P. L. 12, 447. not only to the sons of *A.'s* loins
P. L. 12, 449. but to the sons of *A.'s* faith
P. R. 3, 434. remembering *A*.
S. A. 29. or benefit revealed to *A.'s* race
S. A. 465. prefering before the God of *A*.
**Abroad.**—P. L. 2, 463. while I *a*. through all
P. R. 4, 414. rushed *a*. from the four hinges
S. A. 809. whole to myself unhazarded *a*.
S. A. 919. eyesight exposes daily men *a*.
S. A. 160. all *a*. was rumoured that this day.
**Abrupt.**—P. L. 2, 409. over the vast *a*.
**Abruptly.**—P. R. 2, 10. so *a*. gone
**Absence.**—P. L. 5, 110. in her *a*. mimic fancy
P. L. 7, 107. we can bid his *a*.
P. L. 9, 248. to short *a*. I could yield
P. L. 9, 294. do I dissuade thy *a*.
P. L. 9, 861. pain of *a*. from thy sight
P. R. 2, 100. much more his *a*. now thus long
S. A. 806. wailing thy *a*. in my widowed bed
**Absent.**—P. L. 3, 261. long *a*. and return
P. L. 8, 229. I that day was *a*. as befell
P. L. 10, 82. the third best *a*. is condemned.
P. R. 4, 400. privation mere of light and *a*. day
P. R. 4, 440. was *a*. after all his mischief
S. A. 1604. not to be *a*. at that spectacle
L. 35. from the glad sound would not be *a*. long
**Absents.**—P. L. 9, 372. not free *a*. thee more
P. L. 10, 108. what change *a*. thee
**Absolve.**—P. L. 3, 291. shall *a*. them who
P. L. 10, 829. him after all disputes forced I *a*.
**Absolved.**—P. L. 7, 54. how soon *a*.
**Absolute.**—P. L. 2, 560. foreknowledge *a*.
P. L. 3, 115. disposed by *a*. decree
P. L. 4, 301. declared *a*. rule
P. L. 8, 421. through all numbers *a*.
P. L. 8, 547. so *a*. she seems
P. L. 10, 483. of *a*. perfection
P. L. 11, 311. prayer against his *a*. decree
P. L. 12, 68. dominion *a*.
P. R. 2, 138. perfections *a*. graces divine
S. A. 1405. to such as owe them *a*. subjection
**Absolutely.**—P. L. 9, 1156. command me *a*.
**Abstain.**—P. L. 4, 748. who bids *a*.
P. L. 7, 120. beyond *a*. to ask
P. L. 10, 557. could not *a*.

P. L. 10, 993. to *a*. from love's due
P. R. 2, 269. though ravenous taught to *a*.
**Abstained.**—P. L. 9, 1022. while we *a*.
**Abstaining.**—P. R. 3, 192. suffering, *a*.
**Abstemious.**—S. A. 637. *a*. I grew up
**Abstinence.**—P. L. 9, 924. sacred to *a*.
C. 709. praising the lean and sallow *a*.
**Abstract.**—P. L. 8, 462. *a*. as in a trance
**Abstracted.**—P. L. 9, 463. Evil One *a*. stood
**Abstruse.**—P. L. 8, 40. studious thoughts *a*.
S. A. 1064. be less *a*. my riddling days are past
**Abstrusest.**—P. L. 5, 712. *a*. thoughts
**Absurd.**— S. A. 1337. such *a*. commands
**Abundance.**—P. L. 4, 730. *a*. wants partakers
P. L. 5, 315. pour *a*. fit to honour
P. L. 9, 620. in such *a*. lies our choice
C. 764. should be riotous with her *a*.
**Abundant.**—P. L. 5, 72. more *a*. grows
P. L. 7, 388. reptile with spawn *a*.
**Abundantly.**—P. L. 8, 220. *a*. his gifts
**Abuse.**—P. L. 4, 204. best things to worst *a*.
P. L. 5, 800. to the *a*. of those imperial titles
P. R. 455. no more shalt thou by oracling *a*.
S. A. 76. to daily fraud, contempt, *a*. and wrong
S. A. 1354. shall I *a*. this consecrated gift
**Abused.**—P. L. 1, 479. *a*. fanatic Egypt
**Abyss.**—P. L. 1, 21. on the vast *a*.
P. L. 1, 658. the *a*. long under darkness
P. L. 2, 405. the dark unbottomed infinite *a*.
P. L. 2, 518. the hollow *a*. heard far and wide
P. L. 2, 910. into this wild *a*.
P. L. 2, 917. into this wild *a*. the wary fiend
P. L. 2, 956. Spirit of the nethermost *a*.
P. L. 2, 969. Spirits of this nethermost *a*.
P. L. 2, 1027. over the dark *a*.
P. L. 3, 83. the main *a*. wide interrupt
P. L. 4, 936. to wing the desolate *a*. and spy
P. L. 7, 211. vast immeasurable *a*.
P. L. 7, 234. darkness profound covered the *a*.
P. L. 10, 314. over the vexed *a*.
P. L. 10, 371. bridge the dark *a*.
P. L. 10, 476. forced to ride the untractable *a*.
P. L. 10, 842. O Conscience! into what *a*. of fears
P. L. 12, 555. beyond is all *a*.
S. A. 501. to their *a*. and horrid pains confined
**Academe.**—P. R. 4, 244. grove of *A*.
**Academics.**—P. R. 4, 278. the schools of *A*.
**Acanthus.**—P. L. 4, 696. *a*. and each odorous
**Accaron.**—P. L. 1, 466. *A*. and Gaza's
**Accent.**—P. L. 2, 118. with persuasive *a*.
P. L. 9, 321. with *a*. sweet renewed.
S. 13, 3. to span words with just note and *a*.
**Accept.**—P. L. 2, 58. *a*. this dark den
P. L. 2, 425. so hardy as to proffer or *a*. alone
P. L. 2, 452. refusing to *a*. as great a share
P. L. 3, 302. who when they may *a*. not grace
P. L. 4, 380. yet such *a*. your Maker's work
P. L. 9, 629. if thou *a*. my conduct
P. L. 10, 758. thou didst *a*. them
P. L. 11, 37. *a*. me and in me from these
P. L. 11, 505. would either not *a*. life offered
P. R. 2, 398. why should'st thou not *a*. it
S. A. 1179. he will *a*. thee to defend his cause
S. A. 1255. whether he durst *a*. the offer or not
S. A. 1460. to *a*. of ransom for my son
**Acceptable.**—S. A. 1052. most is *a*. above
P. L. 10, 139. so fit, so *a*., so divine
**Acceptance.**—P. L. 5, 531. finds no *a*. nor can
P. L. 8, 435. freedom and *a*. found
P. L. 10, 972. restored to place of **new** *a*.
P. L. 11, 457. found from heaven *a*.
P. L. 12, 305. to free *a*. of large grace
P. R. 2, 388. where no *a*. it can find
**Accepted.**—P. L. 5, 465. yet *a*. so
P. L. 6, 804. faithful and of God *a*.
P. L. 11, 46. thy request for man, *a*. Son obtain
**Accepting.**—P. R. 4, 497. that I *a*. at least
**Accepts.**—S. A. 510. approves and more *a*.
**Access.**—P. L. 1, 761. all *a*. was thronged
P. L. 2, 130. render all *a*. impregnable
P. L. 4, 137. grotesque and wild, *a*. denied

P. L. 9, 310. receive *a.* in every virtue
P. L. 9, 511. as one who sought *a.* but feared
P. L. 9, 810. and givest *a.* though secret
P. L. 12, 239. to God is no *a.* without mediator
P. R. 1, 492. disdain not such *a.* to me
**Accessible.**—P. L. 4, 546. *a.* from earth
**Accessories.**—P. L. 10, 520. *a.* to his bold riot
**Accident.**—P. R. 2, 39. what *a.* hath rapt him
S. A. 1519. some dismal *a.* it needs must be
S. A. 1552. the *a.* was loud and here before thee
V. Ex. 74. shall subject be to many an *a.*
**Accidents.**—S. A. 612. all his fierce *a.*
**Acclaim.**—P. L. 2, 520. returned them loud *a.*
P. L. 3, 397. with loud *a.* thee only extolled
P. L. 10, 455. loud was the *a.*
P. R. 2, 235. heard their grant in loud *a.*
**Acclamation.**—P. L. 7, 558. followed with *a.*
**Acclamations.**—P. L. 6, 23. joy and *a.* loud
**Accompanied.**—P. L. 4, 600. silence *a.*
P. L. 5, 352. without more train *a.*
P. L. 8, 428. although alone best with thyself *a.*
P. L. 10, 88. *a.* to Heaven-gate
P. L. 10, 848. with black air *a.*
P. R. 1, 300. with such thoughts *a.*
**Accomplish.**—P. R. 2, 113. how to *a.* best
P. R. 2, 452. as soon *a.* what they did perhaps
**Accomplished.**—P. L. 3, 160. revenge *a.*
P. L. 4, 660. daughter of God and man, *a.* Eve
P. L. 7, 550. even and morn *a.* the sixth day
S. A. 230. that specious monster, my *a.* snare
**Accomplishing.**—P.L. 129, 567. *a.* great things
**Accomplishment.**—P. R. 2, 207. *a.* of greatest
**Accord.**—P. L. 2, 36. firm faith, and firm *a.*
P. L. 2, 503. which might induce us to *a.*
P. R. 3, 9. thy actions to thy words *a.*
S. A. 1643. now of my own *a.* such other trial
**According.**—P. L. 6, 816. *a.* to his will
P. L. 10, 517. he sinned *a.* to his doom
P. L. 10, 806. *a.* still to the reception
C. 766. that live *a.* to her sober laws
**Accost.**—P. L. 4, 822. unmoved with fear, *a.* him
**Accosts.**—P. L. 3, 653. him Satan thus *a.*
P. R. 3, 6. with soothing words him thus *a.*
**Account.**—P. L. 3, 238. *a.* me Man
P. L. 4, 235. whereof here needs no *a.*
P. L. 4, 622. God takes no *a.*
P. L. 4, 841. shalt give *a.* to him who sent us
P. L. 6, 726. this I my glory *a.*, my exaltation
P. L. 10, 501. ye have the *a.* of my performance
P. R. 2, 193. made small *a.* of beauty present
S. 19, 6. my true *a.*
**Accountable.**—P. L. 2, 255. to none *a.*
P. L. 10, 29. *a.*, made haste, to make appear
**Accursed.**—P. L. 2, 1055. *a.*, and in a cursed
P. L. 4, 69. be then his love *a.*
P. L. 5, 877. O alienate from God, O Spirit *a.*
P. L. 6, 850. pernicious fire among the *a.*
P. L. 10, 168. justly then *a.* as vitiated
P. L. 10, 175. thou art *a.* above all cattle
P. L. 10, 465. abominable, *a.*, the house of woe
P. L. 10, 723. become *a.* of blessed
P. L. 12, 413. a shameful and *a.*
P. R. 4, 179. to worship thee *a.* now more *a.*
S. A. 930. nor think me so unwary or *a.*
**Accusation.**—P. L. 9, 1187. in mutual *a.*
**Accuse.**—P. L. 3, 112. nor can justly *a.*
P. L. 4, 67. whom hast thou or what to *a.*
P. L. 8, 561. *a.* not Nature
P. L. 9, 1186. his weak indulgence will *a.*
P. L. 10, 127. to *a.* my other self
P. L. 12, 37. though of rebellion others he *a.*
P. R. 4, 316. rather *a.* him under usual names
A. 10. we may justly now *a.*
**Accused.**—P. L. 10, 164. the *a.* Serpent
P. L. 10, 852. oft *a.* of tardy execution
**Accuser.**—P. L. 4, 10. the tempter ere the *a.*
P. L. 9, 1182. thou the *a.*
**Accustomed.**—P. L. 4, 779. at the *a.* hour
P. L. 11, 285. *a.* to immortal fruits
Il P. 60. gently o'er the *a.* oak
**Acheron.**—P. L. 2, 578. sad *A.* of sorrow

C. 604. under the sooty flag of *A.*
**Achieve.**—P. L. 12, 234. *a.* mankind's deliverance
P. R. 1, 68. to *a.* things highest.
**Achieved.**—P. L. 2, 21. hath been *a.* of merit
P. L. 2, 723. and now great deeds had been *a.*
P. L. 2, 363. some advantageous act may be *a.*
P. L. 10, 368. thou hast *a.* our liberty
P. L. 10, 469. with peril great *a.*
P. L. 11, 698. thus fame shall be *a.*
P. L. 11, 792. and *a.* thereby fame in the world
P. R. 2, 411. wherewith to be *a.*
S. A. 1492. all those high exploits by him *a*
**Achieving.**—P. L. 9, 696. deterred not from *a.*
**Achilles.**—P. L. 9, 15. the wrath of stern *A.*
**Acknowledge.** P. L. 5, 172. *a.* none
P. L. 7, 512. grateful to *a.* whence his good
P. L. 8, 574. the more she will *a.* thee her head
P. L. 12, 573. whom I now *a.* my Redeemer
P. R. 2, 376. and *a.* thee their Lord
S. A. 1170. *a.* them from God inflicted
S. A. 448. Father, I do *a.* and confess
S. A. 735. I cannot but *a.*
**Acknowledged.**—P. L. 4, 956. the *a.* power
P. L. 10, 939. peace obtained from fault *a.*
P. L. 11, 612. but they his gifts *a.* none
P. R. 2, 83. full grown to man, *a.*, as I hear
S. A. 245. *a.* not or not at all considered
**Acquaint.**—P. L. 10, 395. them to *a.*
M. W. 72. like fortunes may her soul *a.*
**Acquainted.**—P. R. 1, 400. nearer *a.*
S. A. 1755. new *a.* of true experience
**Acquist.**—S. A. 1755. new *a.* of true experience
**Acquit.**—S. A. 897. to *a.* themselves
**Acquittance.**—P. L. 10, 53. forbearance no *a.*
**Acquitted.**—P. L. 10, 827. then *a.* stand
**Act.**—P. L. 2, 109. Belial, in *a.* more graceful
P. L. 2, 363. some advantageous *a.*
P. L. 4, 94. by *a.* of grace
P. L. 7, 172. goodness which is free to *a.* or not
P. L. 9, 190. inspired with *a.* intelligential
P. L. 9, 668. comely and in *a.* raised
P. L. 9, 674. each *a.*, won audience
P. L. 10, 163. the heinous and despiteful *a.*
P. L. 10, 334. saw his guileful *a.*
P. L. 10, 390. triumphal with triumphal *a.*
P. L. 10, 807. according to ... matter *a.*
P. L. 11, 256. one bad *a.*
P. L. 12, 427. this godlike *a.* annuls thy doom
P. L. 12, 429. this *a.* shall bruise the head
P. L. 12, 517. feigning still to *a.* by spiritual
P. R. 4, 475. each *a.* is rightliest done
S. A. 28. from some great *a.* or benefit revealed
S. A. 231. I thought it lawful from my former *a.*
S. A. 503. but *a.* not in thy own affliction, son
S. A. 1362. what *a.* more execrably unclean
S. A. 1389. by some great *a.*
C. 465. most by lewd and lavish *a.* of sin
**Action.**—P. L. 4, 401. by word or *a.* marked
P. L. 9, 460. her every air of gesture or least *a.*
P. R. 4, 215. by that early *a.* may be judged
**Actions.**—P. L. 8, 602. all her words and *a.*
P. L. 9, 559. in their *a.* oft appears
P. L. 10, 608. his looks, words, *a.*, all infect
P. R. 2, 411. high designs, and high *a.*
P. R. 3, 9. thy *a.* to thy words accord
P. R. 3, 239. things that to greatest *a.* lead
P. R. 4, 266. high *a.* and high passions
S. A. 1440. thy wondrous *a.* hath been seen
**Active.**—P. L. 5, 477. in their several *a.* spheres
P. L. 9, 96. power *a.* within
P. R. 2, 239. to unfold some *a.* scene
P. R. 4, 371. life contemplative or *a.*
**Activity.**—S. A. 1328. sport with blind *a.*
**Acts.**—P. L. 5, 593. *a.* of zeal and love
P. L. 6, 264. these *a.* of hateful strife
P. L. 6, 377. wondrous and in *a.* of war
P. L. 6, 883. eye-witnesses of his almighty *a.*
P. L. 7, 176. immediate are the *a.* of God
P. L. 7, 601. creation, and the six days' *a.*
P. L. 8, 600. those graceful *a.*
P. L. 10, 1026. such *a.* of contumacy
P. L. 11, 789. in *a.* of prowess eminent

P. R. 1, 216. victorious deeds, heroic *a.*
P. R. 2, 412. great *a.* require great means
P. R. 3, 24. wonder at thy *a.*
S. A. 243. great *a.* which God had done
S. A. 527. after some proof of *a.* indeed heroic
S. A. 1101. highest name for valiant *a.*
S. A. 1210. and did hostile *a.*
S. A. 1368. outward *a.* defile not
S. A. 1736. *a.* enrolled in copious legend
S. 8, 6. that call fame on such gentle *a.*
P. 24. his god-like *a.* and his temptations fierce
**Actual.**—P. L. 10, 587. once *a.* now in body
**Adam.**—P. L. 3, 285. in *A.'s* room the head of
　all mankind, though *A.'s* son
P. L. 3, 734. *A.'s* abode, those lofty shades
P. L. 4, 323. *A.* the goodliest man
P. L. 4, 408. *A.* first of men
P. L. 4, 610. when *A.* thus to Eve
P. L. 4, 742. nor turned, I ween, *A.*
P. L. 5, 3. when *A.* waked, so customed
P. L. 5, 27. but with startled eye on *A.*
P. L. 5, 94. thus *A.* answered sad
P. L. 5, 230. converse with *A.*
P. L. 5, 299. *A.* discerned as in the door he sat
P. L. 5, 302. more warmth than *A.* needs
P. L. 5, 307. to whom thus *A.* called
P. L. 5, 321. *A.,* earth's hallowed mould
P. L. 5, 358. nearer his presence *A.*
P. L. 5, 372. *A.* I therefore came
P. L. 5, 453. sudden mind arose in *A.*
P. L. 5, 469. O *A.* one Almighty is
P. L. 5, 561. *A.* made request, and Raphael
P. L. 5, 751. to which all thy dominion *A.* is
P. L. 7, 42. had forewarned *A.* by dire example
P. L. 7, 45. the like befall in Paradise to *A.*
P. L. 7, 59. whence *A.* soon repealed the doubts
P. L. 7, 109. *A.* his illustrious guest besought
P. L. 7, 524. he formed thee, *A.,* thee, O man
P. L. 8, 51. in *A.'s* ear so charming left his voice
P. L. 8, 51. *A.* relating, she sole auditress
P. L. 8, 64. Raphael to *A.'s* doubt proposed
P. L. 8, 179. to whom thus *A.* cleared of doubt
P. L. 8, 296. thy mansion wants thee. *A.,* rise
P. L. 8, 401. in the choice of thy associates, *A.*
P. L. 8, 437. to try thee, *A.,* I was pleased
P. L. 8, 595. thus, half abashed, *A.* replied
P. L. 8, 644. whom *A.* followed
P. L. 8, 953. *A.* to his bower
P. L. 9, 205. *A.,* well may we labour
P. L. 9, 226. mild answer *A.* thus returned
P. L. 9, 289. *A.,* misthought of her to thee so
P. L. 9, 290. with healing words *A.* replied
P. L. 9, 318. so spake domestic *A.* in his care
P. L. 9, 342. to whom thus *A.* fervently replied
P. L. 9, 591. require thy utmost reach or *A.'s*
P. L. 9, 816. to *A.* in what sort shall I appear
P. L. 9, 828. and *A.* wedded to another Eve
P. L. 9, 831. *A.* shall share with me in bliss
P. L. 9, 838. *A.* the while, waiting desirous
P. L. 9, 856. hast thou not wondered, *A.*
P. L. 9, 888. *A.,* soon as he heard
P. L. 9, 960. so *A.;* and thus Eve to him replied
P. L. 9, 965. how shall I attain *A.*
P. L. 9, 988. on my experience *A.* freely taste
P. L. 9, 1004. *A.* took no thought, eating his fill
P. L. 9, 1016. *A.* thus gan Eve to dalliance move
P. L. 9, 1065. *A.* not less than Eve abashed
P. L. 9, 1132. *A.* estranged in look and altered
P. L. 9, 1144. *A.* severe
P. L. 9, 1162. then first incensed, *A.* replied
P. L. 10, 102. God, approaching, to *A.* called
P. L. 10, 103. where art thou, *A.,* wont with joy
P. L. 10, 115. *A.,* faltering long, answered
P. L. 10, 124. thus *A.,* sore beset, replied
P. L. 10, 197. on *A.* last thus judgment
P. L. 10, 715. growing miseries which *A.* saw
P. L. 10, 736. for this we may thank *A.*
P. L. 10, 845. thus *A.* to himself lamented loud
P. L. 10, 914. forsake me not thus, *A.*
P. L. 10, 939. in *A.* wrought commiseration
P. L. 10, 967. *A.!* by sad experiment I know

P. L. 10, 1010. *A.,* with such counsel
P. L. 11, 114. reveal to *A.* what shall come
P. L. 11, 136. when *A.* and first matron Eve
P. L. 11, 191. *A.* observed, and, with his eye
P. L. 11, 212. fear that day dimmed *A.'s* eye
P. L. 11, 223. *A.* sheltered, took his way
P. L. 11, 224. not unperceived of *A.*
P. L. 11, 249. *A.* bowed low
P. L. 11, 251. *A.!* Heaven's high behest
P. L. 11, 263. for *A* at the news heart-struck
P. L. 11, 293. *A.,* by this from the cold
P. L. 11, 335. *A.* thou know'st Heaven his
P. L. 11, 370. *A.* gratefully replied
P. L. 11, 383. our second *A.*
P. L. 11, 412. Michael from *A.'s* eyes
P. L. 11, 419. *A.,* now enforced to close his eyes
P. L. 11, 423. *A.* now ope thine eyes
P. L. 11, 448. *A.,* in his heart dismayed
P. L. 11, 454. these two are brethren, *A.*
P. L. 11, 495. *A.* could not, but wept
P. L. 11, 526. I yield it just, said *A.*
P. L. 11, 596. of *A.,* soon inclined to admit
P. L. 11, 628. thus *A.,* of short joy bereft
P. L. 11, 674. *A.* was all in tears
P. L. 11, 754. how didst thou grieve, then, *A.*
P. L. 11, 868. the heart of *A.,* erst so sad
P. L. 12, 4. if *A.* aught perhaps might interpose
P. L. 12, 63. *A.,* fatherly displeased
P. L. 12, 270. here *A.* interposed
P. L. 12, 372. discerning *A.* with such joy
P. L. 12, 552. thus *A.* last replied
P. L. 12, 607. *A.* to the bower where Eve lay
P. L. 12, 624. *A.* heard well pleased
P. R. 1, 51. *A.* and his facile consort Eve
P. R. 1, 102. to find out and ruin *A.*
P. R. 1, 115. had thrived in *A.'s* overthrow
P. R. 2, 133. when I dealt with *A.,* first of men
P. R. 2, 134. *A.* by his wife's allurement fell
P. R. 4, 607. thou hast avenged supplanted *A.*
P. R. 4, 614. for *A.* and his chosen sons
**Adamant.**—P. L. 2, 436. gates of burning *a.*
P. L. 6, 110. armed in *a.* and gold
P. L. 6, 255. of tenfold *a.* his ample shield
P. L. 10, 318. with pins of *a.* and chains
P. R. 4, 534. as a rock of *a.*
**Adamantean.**—S. A. 134. frock of mail *a.* proof
**Adamantine.**—P. L. 1, 48. in *a.* chains
P. L. 2, 646. three iron, three of *a.* rock
P. L. 2, 853. to unlock these *a.* gates
P. L. 6, 542. let each his *a.* coat gird well
A. 66. and turn the *a.* spindle round
**Add.**—P. L. 2, 700. to thy speed *a.* wings
P. L. 4, 36. and *a.* thy name, O sun
P. L. 4, 950. and couldst thou faithful *a.*
P. L. 5, 152. than needed lute or harp to *a.*
P. L. 8, 109. could *a.* speed
P. L. 9, 821. so to *a.* what wants in female sex
P. L. 12, 581. only *a.* deeds to thy knowledge
P. L. 12, 582. *a.* faith, *a.* virtue, *a.* love
P. R. 4, 113. though thou shouldst *a.* to tell
S. A. 290. of such examples *a.* me to the roll
S. A. 1121. *a.* thy spear a weaver's beam
S. A. 1357. and *a.* a greater sin
C. 859. and *a.* the power of some adjuring verse
Il P. 49. and *a.* to these retired leisure
**Added.**—P. L. 4, 845. *a.* grace invincible
P. L. 7, 484. snaky folds and *a.* wings
P. L. 10, 753. why hast thou *a.* the sense
P. L. 10, 909. he *a.* not and from her turned
P. L. 11, 138. found strength *a.* from above
P. L. 11, 263. he *a.* not for Adam at the news
P. R. 1, 497. he *a.* not and Satan bowing low
P. R. 4, 550. and *a.* thus in scorn
M. W. 5. *a.* to her noble birth
**Adder.**—P. L. 9, 625. to whom the wily *a.*
S. A. 936. so much of *a.'s* wisdom I have learned
**Addicted.**—P. R. 4, 213. *a.* more to contemplation
**Adding.**—S. A. 1351. by *a.* fuel to the flame
**Addition.**—P. L. 5, 116. with *a.* strange
P. L. 7, 555. the *a.* of his empire
**Address.**—P. L. 5, 868. we intend *a.*

S. A. 731. but now again she makes a. to speak
**Addressed.**—P. L. 6, 296. both a. for fight
P. L. 9, 496. toward Eve a. his way
P. L. 9, 672. to some great cause a.
P. L. 9, 855. she thus a
P. L. 11, 295. his humble word a.
P. R. 2, 301. these words to him a.
C. 272. that is a. to unattending ears
S. A. 729. and words a. seem into tears dissolved
**Ades.**—P. L. 2, 964. Orcus and A.
**Adhere.**—P. L. 2, 906. to whom these most a.
P. L. 8, 498. and to his wife a.
**Adherents.**—P. L. 6, 266. thyself and thy a.
P. L. 10, 622. the prince of Hell and his a.
**Adiabene.**—P. R. 3, 320. plains of A.
**Adjoined.**—P. L. 9, 449. villages and farms a.
P. R. 1, 403. small consolation then were man a.
**Adjourn.**—P. L. 12, 264. night's due course a.
**Adjudged.**—P. L. 3, 223. a. to death
P. L. 4, 823. those rebel spirits a. to hell
P. L. 10, 377. as battle hath a.
S. A. 288. without reprieve a. to death
**Adjure.**—F. of C. 3. dare ye for this a. the sword
**Adjured.**—S. A. 853. a. by all the bonds of civil duty
**Adjuring.**—C. 859. the power of some a. verse
**Admiration.**—P. L. 3, 271. a. seized all heaven
P. L. 3, 672. with secret gaze or open a.
P. L. 7, 52. was filled with a. and deep muse
P. L. 9, 872. reasoning to a.
P. R. 2, 221. in the a. only of weak minds
P. R. 4, 228. write and teach to a.
**Admire.**—P. L. 1, 690. let none a. that riches
P. L. 8, 25. I oft a. how nature wise and frugal
P. L. 8, 75. who ought rather a.
P. R. 1, 326. I ask the rather, and the more a.
P. R. 1, 380. to love at least contemplate and a.
P. R. 1, 482. most men a. virtue who follow not
P. R. 2, 222. cease to a. and all her plumes fall flat
P. R. 3, 52. they a. they know not what
**Admired.**—P. L. 2, 677. what this might be a.; a., not feared
P. L. 6, 498. the invention all a.
P. L. 9, 444. much he the place a.
P. L. 9, 542. best beheld where universally a.
P. L. 9, 746. and worthy to be a.
P. L. 11, 689. in those days might only shall be a.
P. R. 1, 214. and was a. by all
S. A. 530. I walked about a. of all
**Admires.**—P. R. 3, 39. now all the world a.
**Admirest.**—P. L. 8, 567. for what a. thou
**Admiring.**—P. L. 1, 681. a. more the riches
P. L. 1, 731. the hasty multitude a. entered
P. L. 9, 524. but as in gaze a. oft he bowed
P. L. 9, 1178. I also erred in overmuch a.
P. L. 10, 352. long he a. stood
P. R. 1, 169. and all heaven a. stood a space
P. R. 2, 175. doat'st on womankind, a. their shape
**Admit.**—P. L. 8, 637. free will would not a.
P. L. 10, 763. wouldst thou a. for his contempt
P. L. 11, 141. Eve, easily may faith a.
P. L. 11, 596. soon inclined to a. delight
S. A. 605. from these thy friends a.
L'A. 38. mirth a. me of thy crew
**Admits.**—P. R. 1, 95. which a. no long debate
**Admitting.**—P. L. 8, 115. a. motion
**Admonish.**—P. L. 11, 813. shall them a.
**Admonished.**—P. L. 3, 647. a. by his ear
P. L. 9, 1171. I warned thee, I a. thee
**Admonishment.**—P. L. 7, 77. his a. receive
**Adonis.**—P. L. 1, 450. while smooth A.
P. L. 9, 440. revived A. or renowned Alcinous
C. 999. where young A. oft reposes
**Adopted.**—P. L. 5, 218. the a. clusters
**Adoration.**—P. L. 3, 351. with solemn a.
P. L. 4, 737. but a. pure which God likes best
P. L. 5, 800. to be our Lord and look for a.
P. L. 8, 315. in a. at his feet I fell submiss
C. 452. with sudden a. and blank awe
**Adore.**—P. L. 1, 323. to a. the conqueror
P. L. 1, 373. and devils to a. for deities

P. L. 1, 475. and a. the gods
P. L. 3, 342. a. him, who to compass all this dies; a. the way
P. L. 4, 89. they a. me on the throne of hell
P. L. 7, 514. directed in devotion to a.
P. L. 8, 280. how may I know him, how a.
P. L. 8, 360. how may I a. thee
P. L. 8, 647. whose sovran goodness I a.
P. L. 9, 540. thy celestial beauty a.
P. L. 11, 333. and far off his steps a.
S. A. 1177. whom I with Israel's sons a.
A. 37. whom with low reverence I a. as mine
**Adored.**—P. L. 1, 384. gods a. among the nations
P. L. 4, 721. under open sky a. the God
P. L. 4, 959. cringed, and servilely a.
P. L. 5, 805. none with more zeal a. the Deity
P. L. 9, 547. a. and served by angels
P. R. 2, 189. lay'st thy scapes on names a.
P. R. 2, 212. queen a. on Beauty's throne
**Adorers.**—P. L. 9, 143. left the throng of his a.
P. R. 1, 451. thou shalt say to thy a.
**Adoring.**—P. L. 5, 144. lowly they bowed a.
**Adorn.**—P. L. 5, 218. to a. his barren leaves
P. L. 8, 576. made so a. for thy delight the more
P. L. 9, 840. a garland to a. her tresses
**Adorned.**—P. L. 1, 371. a. with gay religions
P. L. 2, 446. a. with splendour
P. L. 2, 1049. and battlements a.
P. L. 3, 550. with spires and pinnacles a.
P. L. 4, 634. Eve with perfect beauty a.
P. L. 6, 474. spacious heaven a.
P. L. 7, 87. with moving fires a.
P. L. 7, 384. then first a.
P. L. 8, 482. such as I saw her in my dream a.
P. L. 9, 393. to Pales, or Pomona, thus a.
P. L. 9, 1030. a. with all perfections
P. L. 10, 151. a. she was indeed and lovely
P. L. 11, 280. thee lastly nuptial bower by me a.
P. R. 2, 137. from Heaven a.
P. R. 4, 35. on seven small hills with palaces a.
S. A. 357. as a blessing with such pomp a.
S. A. 679. with gifts and graces eminently a
P. L. 4, 713. brought in naked beauty more a.
**Adorns.**—P. L. 7, 445. whose gay train a. him
**Adramelec.**—P. L. 6, 365. vanquished A.
**Adria.**—P. L. 1, 520. fled over A.
**Adrift.**—P. L. 11, 832. verdure spoilt and trees a.
**Advance.**—P. L. 2, 682. a. thy miscreated front
P. L. 5, 191. rising or falling still a. his praise
P. L. 6, 234. expert when to a. or stand
P. L. 8, 163. from west her silent course a.
P. L. 9, 148. to a. into our room a creature
P. L. 10, 616. these dogs of Hell a.
P. L. 12, 215. from the shore a.
P. R. 1, 88. what will he not do to a. his Son
P. R. 3, 143. who a. his glory, not their own
P. R. 3, 144. them he himself to glory will a.
**Advanced**—P. L. 1, 119. in foresight much a.
P. L. 1, 536. which, full high a.
P. L. 1, 563. a. in view they stand
P. L. 4, 90. with diadem and sceptre high a.
P. L. 4, 359. into our room of bliss thus high a.
P. L. 5, 588. ensigns high a.
P. L. 5, 744. far was a. on winged speed
P. L. 6, 109. with vast and haughty strides a.
P. L. 6, 299. in cubic phalanx firm, a. entire
P. L. 6, 884. with jubilee a.
P. L. 7, 626. whom God hath thus a.
P. L. 12, 632. in front a. the brandished sword
P. R. 2, 69. I to sorrows am no less a.
S. A. 136. insupportably his foot a.
S. A. 450. a. his praises high among the heathen
C. 1004. celestial Cupid, her famed son, a.
**Advancing.**—P. L. 5, 2. Morn, ... a.
**Advantage.**—P. L. 1, 327. discern the a.
P. L. 2, 35. with this a. then to union
P. L. 2, 987. yours be the a. all
P. L. 8, 122. and no a. gain
P. L. 9, 258. to find his wish and best a.
P. L. 9, 718. and that a. use on our belief
P. R. 2, 234. I shall let pass no a.

S. A. 1118. or rather flight no great *a.* on me
S. A. 1259. if they intend *a.* of my labours
**Advantaged.**—P. R. 4, 208. me nought *a.*
S. A. 255. what *a.* best.
**Advantageous.**—P. L. 2, 363. some *a.* act
**Advantages.**—P. L. 6, 401. such high *a.*
P. L. 12, 510. to their own vile *a.* shall turn
S. A. 1401. yet knowing their *a.* too many
**Adventure.**—P. L. 2, 474. not more the *a.*
P. L. 2, 571. on bold *a.* to discover wide
P. L. 10, 468. by my *a.* hard with peril great
**Adventurer.**—P. L. 10, 440. their great *a.*
**Adventures.**—S. A. 1740. to matchless valour
and *a.* high
**Adventurous.**—P. L. 1, 13. my *a.* song
P. L. 2, 615. the *a.* bands with horror pale
P. L. 6, 66. breathed heroic ardour to *a.* deeds
P. L. 9, 921. thou hast presumed *a.* Eve
P. L. 10, 255. let us try *a.* work
C. 79. to pass through this *a.* glade
**Adversary.**—P. L. 2, 629. the *a.* of God
P. L. 3, 81. what rage transports our *a.*
P. L. 3, 156. shall the *a.* thus obtain his end
P. L. 6, 282. to whom thus the *a.*
P. L. 9, 947. lest the *a.* triumph and say
P. L. 10, 906. wedlock-bound to a fell *a.*
P. L. 12, 312. who shall quell the *a.* Serpent
P. R. 1, 33. that heard the *a.* who roving still
P. R. 4, 527. to understand my *a.*
**Adverse.**—P. L. 1, 103. with *a.* power.
P. L. 2, 77. descent and fall to us is *a.*
P. L. 2, 259. useful of hurtful, prosperous of *a.*
P. L. 6, 206. nor stood at gaze the *a.* legions
P. L. 6, 490. o'erwhelm whatever stands *a.*
P. L. 7, 239. infernal dregs, *a.* to life
P. L. 10, 289. two polar winds blowing *a.*
P. L. 10, 701. with *a.* blast upturns them
P. L. 11, 364. prosperous or *a.*
P. R. 3, 189. in humble state and things *a.*
S. A. 192. but in *a.* withdraw their head
S. A. 1040. in his way to virtue, *a.* and turbulent
**Adversities.**—P. R. 4, 479. dangers and *a.*
**Advice.**—P. L. 2, 197. by my *a.*
P. L. 5, 889. yet not for thy *a.* or threats I fly
P. R. 1, 394. oft my *a.* by presages and signs
P. R. 3, 364. the Parthian first by my *a.*
C. 108. and *A.* with scrupulous head
**Advise.**—P. L. 2, 42. who can *a.* may speak
P. L. 2, 283. ye have what I *a.*
P. L. 2, 376. *a.* if this be worth attempting
P. L. 5, 234. as may *a.* him of his happy state
P. L. 5, 729. let us *a.* and to this hazard draw
P. L. 5, 888. well thou didst *a.* yet not for thy
P. L. 9, 212. thou therefore now *a.,* or hear
P. L. 12, 611. dreams *a.*
P. R. 4, 211. I shall no more *a.* thee
S. A. 328. *a.* forthwith how thou oughtst receive
S. 17, 7. then to *a.* how war may best upheld
**Advised.**—P. L. 5. 523. be *a.*
P. L. 6, 674. and permitted all *a.*
P. R. 2, 152. and thus *a.* set women in his eye
C. 755. think what, and be *a.*
**Advising.**—P. L. 2, 292. *a.* peace
**Adulterous.**—P. L. 4, 753. *a.* lust
**Adultery.**—P. L. 11, 717. rape or *a.*
**Advocate.**—P. L. 11, 33. his *a.* and propitiation
**Adust.**—P. L. 12, 635. the Libyan air *a.*
**Adusted.**—P. L. 6, 514. concocted and *a.*
**Ægean.**—P. L. 1, 746. on Lemnos, th' *Æ.* isle
P. R. 4, 238. on the *Æ.* shore a city stands
**Ænon.**—P. R. 2, 21. *Æ.,* and Salem old
**Æolian.**—P. R. 4, 257. *Æ.* charms
**Ætna.**—P. L. 1, 233. thundering *Æ.*
P. L. 3, 470. leaped fondly into *Æ.* flames
**Aereal.**—P. L. 5, 548. *a.* music send
P. L. 7, 442. tower the mid *a.* sky
P. L. 10, 667. through the dark *a.* hall
P. L. 3, 445. up hither like *a.* vapours flew
C. 3. of bright *a.* spirits live insphered
**Aery** or **Airy.**—P. L. 1, 430. their *a.* purposes
P. L. 1, 775. so thick the *a.* crowd swarmed

P. L. 2, 407. spread his *a.* flight
P. L. 2, 536. prick forth the *a.* knights
P. L. 3, 741. flight in many an *a.* wheel
P. L. 4, 568. and marked his *a.* gait
P. L. 5, 105. she forms imaginations, *a.* shapes
P. L. 5, 481. from thence the leaves more *a.*
P. L. 6, 283. with wind of *a.* threats to awe
P. L. 7, 246. to journey through the *a.* gloom
P. L. 7, 428. and set forth their *a.* caravan
P. L. 11, 185. stooped from his *a.* tour
P. R. 4, 57. I have disposed my *a.* microscope
P. R. 4, 402. after his *a.* jaunt
S. A. 974. greatest names in his wild *a.* flight
C. 208. and *a.* tongues that syllable men's names
C. 231. that livest unseen within thy *a.* shell
Il P. 148. wave at his wings in *a.* stream
H. 103. the *a.* region thrilling
**Aery-light.**—P. L. 5, 4. his sleep was *a.-l.*
**Afer.**—P. L. 10, 702. Notus, and *A.* black
**Affable.**—P. L. 7, 41. Raphael, the *a.* archangel
P. L. 8, 648. gentle to me and *a.* hath been
**Affairs.**—P. L. 1, 775. confer their state *a.*
P. L. 10, 408. the *a.* of Hell no detriment need fear
P. R. 1, 50. in manner at our will the *a.* of Earth
P. R. 1, 132. on Earth with man or men's *a.*
P. R. 4, 462. like turbulencies in the *a.* of men
**Affect.**—P. L. 6, 421. but what we more *a.*
P. L. 10, 653. as might *a.* the earth with cold
P. R. 3, 45. nor empire to *a.* for glory's sake,
S. A. 1030. but oftest to *a.* the wrong
**Affecting.**—P. L. 3, 206. *a.* Godhead
P. L. 5, 763. *a.* all equality with God
P. L. 12, 81. *a.* to subdue rational liberty
P. R. 3, 22. *a.* private life
**Affection.**—S. A. 739. conjugal *a.*
**Affects.**—P. L. 5, 97. this night in sleep *a.* me
C. 386. that musing meditation most *a.*
**Affirm.**—P. L. 5, 107. what we *a.* or what deny
P. L. 8, 117. not that I so *a.,* though so it seem
U. C. II, 13. nor were it contradiction to *a.*
**Affirming.**—P. R. 1, 253. *a.* it thy star
**Afflict.**—P. R. 1, 425. cruelly to *a.* him
S. A. 114. their daily practice to *a.* me more
S. A. 914. nor still insist to *a.* thyself in vain
S. A. 1252. yet further to *a.* thee
**Afflicted.**—P. L. 1, 186. our *a.* powers
P. L. 4, 939. my *a.* powers to settle here
P. L. 6, 852. exhausted, spiritless, *a.,* fallen
P. L. 10, 863. thus *a.* when sad Eve beheld
P. R. 2, 93. *a.* I may be, it seems, and blest
S. A. 660. with the *a.* in his pangs
**Afflicting.**—P. L. 2, 166. heaven's *a.* thunder
**Affliction.**—P. L. 1, 57. huge *a.* and dismay
S. A. 113. who come to stare at my *a.*
S. A. 457. which is my chief *a.,* shame and sorrow
S. A. 503. but act not in thy own *a.,* son
S. A. 1257. much more *a.* than already felt
**Afflictions.**—P. R. 2. 92. exaltation to *a.* high
**Afflicts.**—P. L. 11, 315. this most *a.* me
S. A. 195. which was the worst now least *a.* me
**Afford.**—P. L. 4, 46. to *a.* him praise
P. L. 5, 316. well we may *a.* our givers
P. L. 9, 912. and I another rib *a.*
P. L. 10, 271. but *a.* thee equal aid
S. A. 910. *a.* me place to show what recompense
S. A. 1109. your honourable lords *a.* me
H. 16. *a.* a present to the infant God
**Affords.**—P. L. 9, 968. good proof this day *a.*
**Affright.**—P. L. 4, 987. our number may *a.*
C. 356. what if in wild amazement and *a.*
**Affrighted.**—P. L. 6, 869. would have fled *a.*
**Affrights.**—H. 194. *a.* the flamens at service
**Affront.**—P. L. 1, 391. durst *a.* his light
P. L. 9, 302. if such *a.* I labour to avert
P. R. 4, 444. rather by this his last *a.* resolved
S. A. 531. on hostile ground, none daring my *a.*
**Affronts.**—P. L. 9, 328. *a.* his foul esteem
P. R. 3, 161. with foul *a.* abominations rather
**Afield.**—L. 27. we drove *a.*
**Afloat.**—P. L. 1, 305. or scattered sedge *a.*
**Afraid.**—P. L. 2, 759, back they recoiled *a.*

P. L. 10, 117. of thy voice *a.*, being naked
P. L. 12, 493. against them, not *a.*
**Afresh.**—P. L. 2, 801. bursting forth *a.*
**Afric.**—P. L. 1, 585. sent from *A.* shore
P. R. 2, 347. Lucrine bay, and *A.* coast
**Africa.**—P. R. 2, 199. how he surnamed of *A.*
C. 606. 'twixt *A.* and Ind
**African.** P. R. 3, 101. if young *A.* for fame
S. 17, 4. the fierce Epirot and the *A.* bold
**After-bands.**—P. L. 9, 761. bind us with *a.-b.*
**Afternoon's.**—P. L. 9, 403. or *a's* repose
**After-times.**—P. L. 3, 529. that of *a.-t.*
**Against.**—There are 95 instances of *against*,
   and the following:
P.R. 1,317.which might serve *a.*a winter's day
P. R. 2, 90. and to a sign spoken *a.*
   See also under *proof*
**Agape.**—P. L. 5, 357. sets them all *a.*
**Agate.**—C. 893. thick set with *a.* and the azure
**Age.**—P. L. 1, 698. what in *a.* they
P. L. 9, 44. unless an *a.* too late,or cold climate
P. L. 11, 538. this is old *a.*
P. L. 11, 665. of middle *a.* one rising
P. L. 11, 809. the only son of light in a dark *a.*
P. L. 12, 243. all the prophets in their *a.*
P. R. 1, 16. unrecorded left through many an *a.*
P. R. 1, 209. that ere yet my *a.* had measured
P. R. 2, 209. of this *a.* the wonder
P. R. 4, 380. now at full *a.*, fulness of time
S. A. 69. dungeon, or beggary, or decrepit *a.*
S. A. 336. cast back with *a.* came lagging after
S. A. 572. to a contemptible old *a.* obscure
S. A. 580. unemployed, with *a.* outworn
S. A. 700. in crude old *a.*
S. A. 925. may ever tend about thee to old *a.*
S. A. 1487. wont to nurse their parents in old *a*
S. A. 1488.in old *a.* car'st how to nurse thy son
S. A. 1489. made older than thy *a.*
C. 40. and here their tender *a.* might suffer peril
C. 59. who ripe and frolic of his full grown *a.*
C 109. strict *A.* and sour Severity
Il P. 101. or what though rare of later *a.*
Il P. 167. and may at last my weary *a.*
S. 11, 12. thy *a.*, like ours, O soul of Sir John
S.12,1.I did but prompt the *a.* to quit their clogs
S. 13, 7. to after *a.* thou shalt be writ the man
H.135.time will run back and fetch the *a.* of gold
W. S. 2. the labour of an *a.* in piled stones
V. Ex. 69. a Sibyl old, bow-bent with crooked *a.*
**Aged.**—P. R. 1, 314. an *a.* man in rural weeds
S. A. 1568. hitting thy *a.* ear
C. 835. bearing her straight to *a.* Nereus' hall
L. A. 82. from betwixt two *a.* oaks
H. 160. the *a.* earth aghast
**Agents.**—P. L. 9, 683. the ways of highest *a.*
**Ages.**—P. L. 2, 186. *a.* of hopeless end
P. L. 3, 328. the cited dead of all past *a.*
P. L. 7, 191. to worlds and *a.* infinite
P. L. 10, 647. shall to the *a.* rise
P. L. 10, 733. who of all *a.* to succeed
P. L. 11, 326. in memory or monument to *a.*
P. L. 11, 767. the burden of many *a.*
P. L. 12, 549. *a.* of endless date
P. R. 1, 48. how many *a.* as the years of men
P. R. 2, 441. sat so many *a.*
P. R. 3, 294. now some *a.* past
S. A. 765. as I by thee, to *a.* an example
S. A. 1707. a secular bird, *a.* of lives
**Aggravate.**—P. L. 3, 524. *a.* his sad exclusion
P. L. 10, 549. to *a.* their penance
P. R. 3, 218. rather than *a.* my evil state
S. A. 1000. to debase me, and *a.* my folly
**Aggravations.**—S. A. 769. *a.* not surcharged
**Aggregated.**—P. L. 10, 293. the *a.* soil
**Aghast.**—P. L. 2, 616. pale, and eyes *a.*
P. R. 1, 43. with looks *a.* and sad
H. 160. the aged earth *a.*
**Agitation.**—P. L. 9, 637. kindled through *a.*
**Agony.**—P. L. 2, 861. here in perpetual *a.*
P. L. 9, 858. *a.* of love till now not felt
P. L. 11, 482. qualms of heart-sick *a.*

**Agra.**—P. L. 11, 391. thence to *A.* and Lahor
**Agreeable.**—S. A. 1506. *a.* to a father's love
**Agrican.**—P. R. 3, 338. *A.* with all his powers
**Ahab.**—P. R. 1, 372. to draw the proud king *A.*
**Ahaz.**—P. L. 1, 472. *A.* his sottish conqueror
**Aialon.**—P. L. 12, 266. in the vale of *A.*
**Aid.**—P. L. 1, 13. I thence invoke thy *a.*
P. L. 1, 38. by whose *a.* aspiring
P. L. 1, 235. *a.* the winds
P. L. 3, 232. he her *a.* can never seek
P. L. 3, 727. her *a.* timely interposes
P. L. 4, 927. in battle to thy *a.*
P. L. 6, 119. trusting in th' Almighty's *a.*
P. L. 6, 294. join him named Almighty to thy *a.*
P. L. 6, 335. on all sides to his *a.* was run
P. L. 7, 140. by whose *a.* this inaccessible
P. L. 8, 459. called by nature as in *a.*
P. L. 8, 642. no outward *a.* require
P. L. 9, 208. till more hands *a.* us
P. L. 9, 260. speedy *a.* might lend
P. L. 9, 308. nor think superfluous others' *a.*
P. L. 10, 271. afford thee equal *a.*
P. L. 10, 919. thy gentle looks, thy *a.*
P. L. 10, 944. his counsel, his *a.*
P. L. 11, 651. call in *a.* which makes
P. L. 11, 800. found no *a.*
P. L. 12, 542. so lately promised to thy *a.*
P. R. 1, 393. lend them oft my *a.*, oft my advice
P. R. 2, 148. was assured their utmost *a.*
P. R. 3, 302. to her *a.* he marches now in haste
P. R. 4, 377. nicely or cautiously my offered *a.*
P. R. 4, 468. offered with my *a.*
P. R. 4, 493. obtrudest thy offered *a.*
S. A. 1146. go to his temple, invocate his *a.*
C. 90. likeliest and nearest to the present *a.*
C. 856. and will be swift to *a.* virgin
V. Ex. 14. I pray thee then, deny me not thy *a.*
**Aided.**—P. L. 6, 38. *a.* by this host of friends
**Aidless.**—C. 574. the *a.* innocent lady
**Aids.**—P. R. 3, 392. of *a.*, battles and leagues
**Aim.**—P. L. 1, 41. and with ambitious *a.*
P. L. 1, 168. counsels from their destined *a.*
P. L. 2, 28. to stand against the Thunderer's *a.*
P. L. 2, 128. as the scope of all his *a.*
P. L. 2, 712. levelled his deadly *a.*
P. R. 4, 105. *a.* at no less than all the world
P. R. 4, 106. *a.* at the highest
S. A. 1464. their *a.* private reward
**Aimed.**—P. L. 6, 317. one stroke they *a.*
P. L. 9, 173. I reck not, so it light well *a.*
P. R. 2, 202. *a.* not beyond higher design
P. R. 4, 208. missing what I *a.*
**Aims.**—P. L. 4, 808. vain *a.*, inordinate desires
**Aimest.**—P. L. 11. 884. dextrously thou *a.*
**Air.**—P. L. 1, 226. incumbent on the dusky *a.*
P. L. 1, 516. ruled the middle *a.*
P. L. 1, 545. banners rise into the *a.*
P. L. 1, 595. through the horizontal misty *a.*
P. L. 1, 767. both on the ground and in the *a.*
P. L. 2, 309. summer's noontide *a.*
P. L. 2, 400. the soft delicious *a.*
P. L. 2, 528. in the *a.* sublime
P. L. 2, 540. and ride the *a.* in whirlwind
P. L. 2, 594. the parching *a.* burns frore
P. L. 2, 663. riding through the *a.* she comes
P. L. 2, 718. dark encounter in mid *a.*
P. L. 2, 842. wing silently the buxom *a.*
P. L. 2, 912. neither sea, nor shore, nor *a.*
P. L. 2, 1045. emptier waste, resembling *a.*
P. L. 3, 72. in the dun *a.* sublime.
P. L. 3, 76. uncertain which, in ocean or in *a.*
P. L. 3, 254. through the ample *a.*
P. L. 3, 429. of glimmering *a.*
P. L. 3, 489. into the devious *a.*
P. L. 3, 564. through the pure marble *a.*
P. L. 3, 619. the *a.* no where so clear
P. L. 3, 715. earth, flood, *a.*, fire
P. L. 4, 153. of pure now purer *a.*
P. L. 4, 432. that possess earth, *a.*, and sea
P. L. 4, 558. vapours fired impress the *a.*
P. L. 4, 682. celestial voices to the midnight *a.*

P. L. 4, 722. the God that made both sky, a.
P. L. 4, 818. inflames the a.
P. L. 4, 940. to settle here on earth, or in mid a.
P. L. 4, 1000. earth with balanced a.
P. L. 5, 79. sometimes in the a., as we
P. L. 5, 180. a., and ye elements
P. L. 5, 270. winnows the buxom a.
P. L. 5, 417. earth and the sea feed a.; the a.
P. L. 5, 590. stream in the a.
P. L. 6, 72. the passive a. upbore
P. L. 6, 244. tormented all the a.; all a. seemed
P. L. 6, 304. in the a. made horrid circles
P. L. 6, 349. no more than can the fluid a.
P. L. 6, 536. and in mid a. aloud thus cried
P. L. 6, 587. with outrageous noise the a.
P. L. 6, 654. which in the a. came shadowing
P. L. 6, 664. amid the a. encountered hills
P. L. 7, 14. drawn empyreal a., thy tempering
P. L. 7, 89. the ambient a. wide interfused
P. L. 7, 241. and between spun out the a.
P. L. 7, 265. transparent, elemental a. diffused
P. L. 7, 421. and soaring the a. sublime
P. L. 7, 431. the a. floats as they pass
P. L. 7, 447. and the a. with fowl
P. L. 7, 502. a., water, earth, by fowl, fish, beast
P. L. 7, 521. over the fish and fowl of sea and a.
P. L. 7, 533. fowl of the a.
P. L. 7, 560. the earth, the a. resounded
P. L. 7, 629. on earth, in sea, or a.
P. L. 8, 141. the wide transpicuous a.
P. L. 8, 166. soft with the smooth a. along
P. L. 8, 284. from where I first drew a.
P. L. 8, 301. over fields and waters, as in a.
P. L. 8, 341. in sea or a., beast, fish, and fowl
P. L. 8, 348. to draw the thinner a.
P. L. 8, 370. the a. replenished
P. L. 8, 476. from her a. inspired the spirit of love
P. L. 8, 626. easier than a. with a.
P. L. 9, 446. sewers annoy the a.
P. L. 9, 459. her every a. of gesture
P. L. 9, 530. or impulse of vocal a.
P. L. 9, 658. of all in earth or a.
P. L. 10, 185. prince of the a.
P. L. 10, 188. captive through the a.
P. L. 10, 212. naked to the a.
P. L. 10, 280. into the murky a.
P. L. 10, 400. dominion exercise and in the a.
P. L. 10, 666. confound sea, a., and shore
P. L. 10, 847. with black a. accompanied
P. L. 10, 1073. grind the a. attrite to fire
P. L. 10, 1090. our sighs the a. frequenting
P. L. 10, 1102. their sighs the a. frequenting
P. L. 11, 53. a distemper gross, to a. as gross
P. L. 11, 183. bird, beast, a., a. suddenly eclipsed
P. L. 11, 202. flight pursued in the a.
P. L. 11, 284. how shall we breathe in other a.
P. L. 11, 337. land, sea, and a.
P. L. 11, 542. for the a. of youth
P. L. 12, 76. thin a. above the clouds
P. L. 12, 452. triumphing through the a.
P. L. 12, 454. the serpent, Prince of a.
P. L. 12, 579. heaven, a., earth, or sea
P. L. 12, 635. vapour as the Libyan a. adust
P. R. 1, 39. in mid a. to council summons
P. R. 1, 44. O ancient Powers of A.
P. R. 1, 45. for much more willingly I mention A.
P. R. 1, 63. this fair empire won of earth and a.
P. R. 1, 366. range in the a.
P. R. 1, 499. into thin a. diffused
P. R. 2, 74. to shelter him or me from the bleak a.
P. R. 2, 117. up to the middle region of thick a.
P. R. 2, 124. powers of fire, a., water
P. R. 2, 374. all these are spirits of a.
P. R. 4, 41. vision, multiplied through a.
P. R. 4, 201. Tetrarchs of fire, a., flood
P. R. 4, 239. pure the a. and light the soil
P. R. 4, 542. bore through the a. sublime
P. R. 4, 568. throttled at length in the a.
P. R. 4, 585. through the blithe a.
S. A. 8. scarce freely draw the a, imprisoned also
S. A. 176. their sense the a. dissolves unjointed

S. A. 628. nor breath of vernal a. from snowy Alp
S. A. 1240. or swing thee in the a.
S. A. 1621. the people with a shout rifted the a.
C. 4. in regions mild of calm and serene a.
C. 133. and makes one blot of all the a.
C. 154. my dazzling spells into the spongy a.
C. 247. with these raptures moves the vocal a.
C. 481. some far-off halloa break the silent a.
C. 550. filled the a. with barbarous dissonance
C. 557. stole upon the a., that even Silence
C. 730. the winged a. darked with plumes
C. 757. unlocked my lips in this unhallowed a.
C. 928. summer drouth, or singed a.
C. 980. there I suck the liquid a.
L. 98. the a. was calm, and on the level brine
Il P. 77. if the a. will not permit
Il P. 94. in fire, a., flood, or under ground
S. 8, 12. the repeated a. of sad Electra's poet
S. 13, 8. with smooth a. couldst humour best
S. 20, 12. warble immortal notes and Tuscan a.
H. 38. she wooes the gentle a.
H. 99. the a., such pleasure loth to lose
H. 164. in middle a. shall spread his throne
P. 2. wherewith the stage of a. and earth did ring
D. F. I. 16. empire of the freezing a.
V. Ex. 41. and misty regions of wide a.
**Airs.**—P. L. 4, 264. a., vernal a.
P. L. 8, 515. gentle a. whispered it
P. L. 9, 200. prime for sweetest scents and a.
P. L. 10, 93. gentle a., due at their hour
P. R. 2, 362. harmonious a. were heard
L'A. 136. lap me in soft Lydian a.
P. 27. me softer a. befit, and softer strings
**Alabaster.**—P. L. 4, 544. it was a rock of a.
P. R. 4, 548. like a mount of a.
C. 660. your nerves are all chained up in a.
**Alack.**—D. F. I. 28. a., that so to change thee
**Alacrity.**—P. L. 2, 1012. with fresh a.
**Aladule.**—P. L. 10, 435. the realm of A.
**Alarm.**—P. L. 2, 103. perpetual inroads to a.
P. L. 6, 549. without disturb they took a.
P. L. 10, 491. without our hazard, labour, or a.
**Alarmed.**—P. L. 4, 985. Satan a.
P. L. 12, 217. entering on the Canaanite a.
**Alarms.**—C. 364. if they be but false a. of fear
**Alas.**—P. L. 10, 949. all on thyself; a.!
P. L. 11, 461. a.! both for the deed
P. R. 2, 30. a.! from what high hope
P. R. 2, 348. a.! how simple
P. R. 4, 309. a.! what can they teach
S. A. 162. a.! puts forth no visual beam
S. A. 368. a.! methinks whom God hath chosen
C. 609. a.! good vent'rous youth, I love thy
L. 64. a.! what boots it with incessant care
Cir. 12. a.! how soon our sin
D. F. I. 7. thought to kiss, but killed, a.!
M. W. 8. a.! too soon
U. C. I. 2. here, a.! hath laid him
**Albracca.**—P. R. 3, 339. besieged A.
**Alcairo.**—P. L. 1, 718. Babylon, nor great A.
**Alcestis.**—S. 23, 2. like A., from the grave
**Alchemist.**—P. L. 5, 440. the empiric a.
**Alchymy.**—P. L. 2, 517. the sounding a.
**Alcides.**—P. L. 2, 542. as when A.
P. R. 4, 565. in Irassa strove with Jove's A.
**Alcinous.**—P. L. 5, 341. where A. reigned
P. L. 9, 441. renowned A.
V. Ex. 49. in solemn song as at king A. feast
**Ale.**—L'A. 100. then to the spicy nut-brown a.
U. C. II. 16. nor would with a. be quickened
**Aleian.**—P. L. 7, 19. on th' A. field I fall
**Alexander.**—P. R. 4, 252. who bred great A.
**Algarsife.**— Il P. 111. of Camball and of A
**Algiers.**—P. L. 11, 404. Morocco and A.
**Alien.**—P. L. 4, 571. his looks a. from heaven
**Alienate.**—P. L. 5, 877. O a. from God
**Alienated.**—P. L. 1, 457. of a. Judah
P. L. 9, 9. on the part of heaven now a.
P. L. 10, 378. by his own doom a.
**Alighted.**—P. L. 3, 422. Satan a. walks
**Alights.**—P. L. 4, 396. down he a.

**Alike.**—P. L. 2, 187. *a.* my voice dissuades
P. L. 2, 453. due *a.* to him who reigns.
P. L. 3, 593. but all *a.* informed
P. L. 4, 70. to me *a.* it deals eternal woe
P. L. 4, 640. all please *a.*
P. L. 5, 407. food *a.* those pure intelligential
P. L. 6, 123. in both disputes *a.* victor
P. L. 6, 847. distinct *a.* with multitude of eyes
P. L. 8, 389. but soon prove tedious *a.*
P. L. 10, 520. all transformed *a.* to serpents all
P. L. 10, 598. *a.* is Hell, or Paradise, or Heaven
P. L. 10, 888. *a.* destroys all hope of refuge
P. L. 11, 350. will be found *a.* present
P. L. 12, 519. promised *a.* and given to all
P. R. 3, 214. and will *a.* be punished
S. A. 703. just or unjust, *a.* seem miserable
S. A. 704. oft *a.* both come to evil end
S. A. 1074. or peace or not, *a.* to me he comes
**Alimental.**—P. L. 5, 424. *a.* recompense
**Alive.**—P. L. 11, 818. the one just man *a.*
S. A. 645. reserved *a.* to be repeated
**(At) All.**—P. L. 2, 48. cared not to be at *a.*
P. L. 9, 757. is as not had at *a.*
P. L. 11, 89. evil not at *a.*
S. A. 245. or not at *a.* considered
S. A. 295. who think not God at *a.*
S. A. 381. this well I knew, nor was at *a.*
  surprised
S. A. 1082. if thou at *a.* art known
**Allay.**—P. L. 10, 564. to *a.* their appetite
S. A. 582. thy thirst to *a.* after the brunt
C. 96. his glowing axle doth *a.*
**Allayed.**—P. L. 7, 67. yet scarce *a.*, still eyes
P. L. 8, 7. who thus largely hast *a.* the thirst
P. R. 2, 160. with mild and sweet *a.*
**Allaying.**—S. A. 550. *a.* thirst
**All-bearing.**—P. L. 5, 338. Earth, *a.-b.* mother
**All-bounteous.**—P. L. 5, 640. the *a.-b.* King
**All-cheering.**—P. L. 3, 581. his *a.-c.* lamp
**All-conquering.**—P. L. 10, 591. *a.-c.* Death
**Allege.**—S. A. 1253. he must *a* some cause
**Alleged.**—P. L. 4, 921. hadst thou *a.* this cause
**Allegiance.**—P. L. 3, 104. of true *a.*
P. L. 4, 956. to dissolve *a.*
**Allegoric.**—P. R. 4, 390. real or *a.*
**Alley.**—C. 311. each lane, and every *a.* green
**Alleys.**—P. R. 2, 293. walks beneath, and *a.*
  brown
P. L. 4, 626. yonder *a.* green
C. 990. about the cedared *a.*
**All-giver.**—C. 723. the *A.-g.* would be un-
  thanked
**All-judging.**—L. 82. witness of *a.-j.* Jove
**All-knowing.**—P. L. 10, 227. though *a.-k.*
**Allotted.**—P. L. 8, 148. for some to eat *a.* there
P. R. 2, 123. from the element each of his
  reign *a.*
**Allow.**—P. L. 6, 158. can *a.* omnipotence
**Allowance.**—S. A. 770. or else with just *a.*
C. 308. in such a scant *a.* of star-light
**All-powerful.**—P. L. 2, 851. *a.-p.* King
**All-ruling.**—P. L. 1, 212. of *a.-r.* Heaven
P. L. 2, 264. Heaven's *a.-r.* Sire.
**All-seeing.**—P. L. 10, 163. the eye of God *a.-s.*
**All-too.**—C. 380. were *a.-t.* ruffled
**Allure.**—P. R. 1, 179. seduce, *a.*, or terrify
P. R. 4, 112. *a.* mine eye
S. A. 546. *a.* thee from the cool crystalline
**Allured.**—P. L. 1, 447. *a.* the Syrian damsels
P. L. 3, 573. the golden sun, *a.* his eye
P. L. 5, 709. his countenance *a.* them
P. L. 11, 718. where passing fair *a.* them
**Allurement.**—P. L. 11, 810. against *a.*
P. R. 2, 134. Adam by his wife's *a.* fell
P. R. 2, 409. no *a.* yields to appetite
**Alluring.**—P. L. 9, 588. that *a.* fruit
C. 882. sleeking her soft *a.* locks
**Allusion.**—P. L. 10, 425. so by *a.* called
**All-worshipped.**—C. 719. the *a.-w.* ore
**Almansor.**—P. L. 11, 403. of *A.*, Fez and Sus
**Almighty.**—P. L. 1, 44. the *A.* Power

P. L. 1, 144. whom I now of force believe *a.*
P. L. 1, 259. the *A.* hath not built
P. L. 1, 623. matchless, but with the *A.*
P. L. 2, 65. the noise of his *a.* engine
P. L. 2, 144. we must exasperate the *A.* Victor
P. L. 2. 192. not more *a.* to resist our might
P. L. 2, 769. to our *A.* Foe clear victory
P. L. 2, 915. unless the *A.* Maker them ordain
P. L. 3, 56. now had the *A.* Father from above
P. L. 3, 273. but soon the *A.* thus replied
P. L. 3, 344. no sooner had the *A.* ceased
P. L. 3, 386. the *A.* Father shines
P. L. 4, 566. to know more of the *A.'s* works
P. L. 5, 154. Parent of good! *A.*
P. L. 5, 469. O Adam, one *A.* is, from whom
P. L. 5, 585. innumerable before the *A.'s* throne
P. L. 5, 676. the lips of heaven's *A.*
P. L. 5, 868. begirt the *A.* throne
P. L. 6, 119. trusting in the *A.'s* aid
P. L. 6, 294. join him named *A.* to thy aid
P. L. 6, 316. with next to *a.* arm
P. L. 6, 671. had not the *A.* Father
P. L. 6, 713. my *a.* arms gird on
P. L. 6, 883. eye witnesses of his *a.* acts
P. L. 7, 11. in presence of the *A.* Father
P. L. 7, 112. to recount *a.* works what words
P. L. 7, 174. so spake the *A.*
P. L. 7, 181. the Almighty's will
P. L. 7, 339. again the *A.* spake
P. L. 7, 398. whereto the *A.* answered
P. L. 9, 137. what he, *A.* styled
P. L. 10, 387. antagonist of Heaven's *A.* King
P. L. 10, 613. which the *A.* seeing
P. L. 11, 83. the *A.* thus pronounced his sovran
**Almost.**—P. L. 7, 620. of amplitude *a.* immense
P. L. 8, 110. could add speed *a.* spiritual
S. A. 91. and *a.* life itself, if it be true
H. 104, now was *a* won
**Alms.**—S. 14, 5. thy works, and *a.*
**Aloft.**—P. L. 1, 226. he steers his flight *a.*
P. L. 2, 938. hurried him as many miles *a.*
P. L. 3, 357. and flowers *a.* shading the fount
P. L. 3, 493. all these upwhirled *a.*
P. L. 4, 1014. knew his mounted scale, *a.*
P. L. 6, 252. two-handed sway, brandished *a.*
P. L. 6, 776. *a.* by angels borne
P. L. 9, 500. his head crested *a.*
L. 81. lives and spreads *a.* by those pure eyes
**Alone.**—P. L. 2, 426. or accept *a.* the dreadful
P. L. 2, 509. and seemed *a.* the antagonist
P. L. 2, 778. pensive here I sat *a.*
P. L. 2, 975. *a.*, and without guide
P. L. 3, 169. Son, who art *a.* my word
P. L. 3, 441. the fiend walked up and down *a.*
P. L. 3, 441. *a.*, for other creature
P. L. 3, 667. *a.* thus wandering
P. L. 3, 684. invisible, except to God *a.*
P. L. 3, 699. from thy empyreal mansion thus *a.*
P. L. 4, 129. then *a.*, as he supposed
P. L. 4, 202. so little knows any, but God *a.*
P. L. 4, 340. in happy nuptial league, *a.* as they
P. L. 4, 491. which *a.* is truly fair
P. L. 4, 689. hand in hand *a.* they passed
P. L. 4, 917. but wherefore thou *a.*
P. L. 4, 935. I therefore, I *a.* first undertook
P. L. 5, 50. methought, *a.* I passed
P. L. 5, 876. fearless, though *a.*
P. L. 6, 145. not visible, when I *a.*
P. L. 6, 420. found worthy not of liberty *a.*
P. L. 6, 820. they all, or I *a.* against them
P. L. 7, 28. yet not *a.*, while thou visitest
P. L. 8, 57. not words *a.* pleased her
P. L. 8, 89. when she *a.* receives the benefit
P. L. 8, 365. who can enjoy *a.*
P. L. 8, 405. who am *a.* from all eternity
P. L. 8, 427. although *a.*, best with thyself
P. L. 8, 438. thee knowing, not of beasts *a.*
P. L. 8, 445. knew it not good for man to be *a.*
P. L. 9, 105. light above light, for thee *a.*
P. L. 9, 303. I labour to avert from thee *a.*
P. L. 9, 336. love, virtue, unassayed *a.*

P. L. 9, 457. Eve thus early, thus *a.*
P. L. 9, 480. behold *a.* the woman
P. L. 9, 736. which to behold might tempt *a.*
P. L. 9, 766. for us *a.* was death invented
P. L. 9, 978. I would sustain *a.* the worst
P. L. 11, 222. he *a.* took his way
P. L. 12, 404. though love *a.* fulfil the law
P. R. 1, 189. one day forth walked *a.*
P. R. 1, 285. in whom *a.* he was well pleased
P. R. 3, 141. to God *a.* of right belongs
P. R. 3, 372. which *a.* can truly re-install thee
P. R. 4, 217. thou went'st *a.* into the temple
S. A. 20. no sooner found *a.*
S. A. 989. thou *a.* couldst hate me thy husband
C. 583. weakness of one virgin, *a.* and helpless
C. 1019. love Virtue, she *a.* is free
A. 17. this, this is she *a.*
A. 42. which I full oft, amidst these shades *a.*
H. 107. she knew such harmony *a.*
T. 18. of him to whose happy-making sight *a.*

**Along.**—P. L. 2, 574. *a.* the banks
P. L. 6, 275. hence then, and evil go with thee *a.*
P. L. 7, 166. might with thee I send *a.*
P. L. 8, 166. with the smooth air *a.*
P. L. 10, 250. must with me *a.*
S. A. 1316. rise therefore with all speed, come *a.*
S. A. 1384. I with this messenger will go *a.*
S. A. 1413. your company *a.* I will not wish
C. 295. that crawls *a.* the side of yon small hill
C. 844. visits the herds *a.* the twilight meadows
C. 984. *a.* the crisped shades and bowers
L. 174. where other groves and other streams *a.*
Il. P. 55. and the mute Silence hist *a.*
Cir. 4. so sweetly sung your joy the clouds *a.*
V. Ex. 94. his thirty arms *a.* the indented meads

**Aloof.**—P. L. 1, 380. stood yet *a.*
P. L. 3, 577. *a.* the vulgar constellations thick
P. R. 1, 313. the lion and fierce tiger glared *a.*
S. A. 135. but safest he who stood *a.*
S. A. 1611. I among these *a.* obscurely stood

**Aloud.**—P. L. 1, 126. vaunting *a.*, but racked
P. L. 4, 2. heard cry in Heaven *a.*
P. L. 4, 481. thou following criedst *a.*, return
P. L. 4, 865. from the front thus called *a.*
P. L. 6, 536. and in mid air *a.* thus cried
P. L. 8, 490. I overjoyed could not forbear *a.*
P. L. 10, 102. to Adam called *a.*
S. A. 1639. at last with head erect, thus cried *a.*

**Alp.**—P. L. 2, 620. many a fiery *A.*
S. A. 628. breath of air, from snowy *A.*

**Alpheus.**—A. 30. divine *A.*, who by secret sluice
L. 132. return *A.*, the dread voice is past

**Alpine.**—S. 18, 2. on the *A.* mountains cold

**Already.**—P. L. 6, 20. found *a.* known
P. L. 7, 151. in the harm *a.* done
P, L. 8, 85. *a.* by the reasoning this I guess
P. L. 8, 420. propagate *a.* infinite
P. L. 10, 50. which he presumes *a.* vain
P. L. 10, 716. miseries which Adam saw *a.*
P. L. 10, 905. *a.* linked and wedlock-bound
P. L. 10, 929. on me *a.* lost
S. A. 481. I *a.* have made way to some Philistian
S. A. 707. how hast thou dealt *a.*
S. A. 1092. dost thou *a.* single me?
S. A. 1257. much more affliction than *a.* felt
C. 573. *a.* ere my best speed could prevent

**Also.** There are 49 instances of *a.*

**Altar.**—P. L. 1, 384. their altars by his *a.*
P. L. 1, 434. and unfrequented left his righteous *a.*
P. L. 1, 473. whom he drew God's *a.* to disparage
P. L. 1, 493, to him no temple stood or a. smoked
P. L. 2, 244. his *a.* breathes ambrosial odours
P. L. 9, 195. from the Earth's great *a.* send up
P. L. 11, 18. where the golden *a.* fumed
P. L. 11, 432. in the midst an *a.* as the landmark
P, L. 12, 354. men who attend the *a.*
P. R. 1, 257. before the *a.* and the vested priest
P. R. 1, 489. about his *a.*, handling holy things
S. A. 26. from off the *a.*, where an offering burned
II P. 48. aye round about Jove's *a.* sing
H. 28. from out his secret *a.* touched with fire

**Altars.**—P. L. 1, 494, in temples and at *a.*
P. L. 11, 323. so many grateful *a.* I would rear
H. 192. in urns, and *a.* round

**Alter.**—P. L. 10, 953. if prayers could *a.* high

**Alteration.**—P. L. 2, 1024. strange *a.*
P. L. 9, 599. ere long I might perceive strange *a.*

**Altered.**—P. L. 5, 385. *a.* her cheek
P. L. 9, 1132. estranged in look and *a.* style
P. L. 10, 171. nor *a.* his offence

**Altern.**—P. L. 7, 348. the less by night, *a.*

**Alternate.**—P. L. 5, 657. *a.* all night long

**Although.**—P. L. 8, 427. *a.* alone
S. A. 1338. *a.* their drudge to be their fool

**Always.**—P. L. 1, 681. *a.* downward bent
P. L. 3, 517. nor stood there *a.*
P. L. 3. 704. *a.* with delight
P. L. 6. 724. thou *a.* seek'st to glorify thy Son,
   I *a.* thee
P. L. 9, 467, the hot hell that *a.* in him burns
P. L. 12, 84. which *a.* with right reason dwells
P. R. 3, 48. if *a.* praise unmixed
P. R. 3, 159. nor is *a.* ruled with temperate
S. A. 814. yet *a.* pity or pardon hath obtained

**Amain.**—P. L. 2, 165. when we fled *a.*
P. L. 2, 1024. Sin and death *a.* following
P. L. 10, 675. down *a.* by Leo and the Virgin
P. L. 11, 742. sent up *a.*
P. R. 2, 430. thrive in wealth *a.*
S. A. 637. abstemious I grew up and thrived *a.*
S. A. 1304. comes on *a.*, speed in his look
L, 111. the golden opes, the iron shuts *a.*

**Amalthea.**—P. L. 4, 278. old Cham hid *A.*
P. R. 2, 356. fruits and flowers from *A.'s* horn

**Amara.**—P. L. 4, 281. Mount *A.*

**Amarant.**—P. L. 3, 352. *a.* and gold immortal *a.*

**Amaranthine.**—P. L. 11, 78. of *a.* shade

**Amaranthus.**—L. 149. bid *A.* all his beauty shed

**Amaryllis.**—L. 68. to sport with *A.* in the shade

**Amaze.**—P. L. 6, 646. *a.*, be sure, and terror
P. L. 12, 496. and oft supported so as shall *a.*
P. R. 2, 38. into perplexity and new *a.*
S. A. 1645. as with *a.* shall strike all who behold
S. 15, 3. and all her jealous monarchs with *a.*
H. 69. the stars with deep *a.*

**Amazed.**—P. L. 1, 281. astounded and *a.*
P. L. 4, 820. those two fair angels half *a.*
P. L. 9, 614. and Eve yet more *a.* unwary
P. L. 9, 640. misleads the *a.* night-wanderer
P. L. 9, 889. *a.*, astonied stood and blank
P. L. 10, 452. all *a.* at that so sudden blaze
S. A. 1286. lose their defence, distracted and *a.*
C. 565. *a.* I stood, harrowed with grief and fear

**Amazement.**—P. L. 1, 313. under *a.*
P. L. 2, 758. *a.* seized all the host of heaven
P. L. 6, 198. *a.* seized the rebel thrones
P. R. 1, 107. impression left of much *a.*
P. R. 4, 562. but Satan, smitten with *a.* fell
C. 356. what if in wild *a.*, and affright

**Amazonian.**—P. L. 9, 1111. broad as *A.* targe

**Amber.**—P. L. 3, 359. her *a.* stream
P. L. 6, 759. inlaid with pure *a.*
P. R. 3, 288. Susa by Choaspes, *a.* stream
S. A. 720. an *a.* scent of odorous perfume
C. 333. thy pale visage through an *a.* cloud
L'A. 61. robed in flames and *a.* light

**Amber-dropping.**— C. 863. thy *a.-d.* hair

**Ambient.**—P. L. 6, 481. the *a.* light
P. L. 7, 89. the *a.* air wide interfused

**Ambiguous.**—P. L. 5, 703. *a.* words
P. L. 6, 568. so scoffing in *a.* words he scarce
P. L. 7, 473. *a.* between sea and land
P. R. 1, 435. dark *a.* and with double sense

**Ambition.**—P. L. 1, 262 to reign is worth *a.*
P. L. 2, 485. close *a.* varnished o'er with zeal
P. L. 4, 40. pride and worse *a.* threw me down
P. L. 4, 61. no unbounded hope had raised *a.*
P. L. 4, 92. such joy *a.* finds
P. L. 9, 168. what will not *a.* and revenge
P. L. 12, 38. he with a crew, whom like *a.* joins
P. L. 12, 511. of lucre and *a.*
P. R. 3, 90. without *a.*, war, or violence

S. A. 247. used no *a.* to commend my deeds
**Ambitious.**— P. L. 1, 41. and with *a.* aim
P. L. 2, 34. that with *a.* mind will covet more
P. L. 6, 160. *a.* to win from me some plume
P. L. 12, 25. till one shall rise of proud *a.* heart
P. R. 4, 137. first *a.* grown of triumph
P. R. 4, 495. *a.* spirit
V. Ex. 11. thou needest not be *a.* to be first
**Ambrosia.**—P. L. 5, 57. distilled *a.*
**Ambrosial.**—P. L. 2, 245. breathes *a.* odours
and *a.* flowers, our servile offerings
P. L. 3, 135. *a.* fragrance filled all heaven
P. L. 4, 219. blooming *a.* fruit of vegetable gold
P. L. 5, 427. the trees of life *a.* fruitage bear
P. L. 5, 642. when *a.* night with clouds
P. L. 6, 475. with plant, fruit, flower *a.*
P. L. 9, 852. and *a.* smell diffused
P. L. 11, 279. and water from the *a.* fount
P. R. 4, 589. celestial food, divine *a.* fruits
P. R. 4, 590. and from the fount of life *a.* drink
C. 16. I would not soil these pure *a.* weeds
C. 840. dropt in *a.* oils, till she revived
**Ambush.**—P. L. 2, 344. *a.* from the deep
P. L. 9, 408. such *a.* hid among sweet flowers
**Amends.**—P. L. 8, 491. this turn hath made *a.*
P. L. 10, 1032. piteous *a.*
S. A. 9. but here I feel *a.*, the breath of heaven
S. A. 745. thy mind with what *a.* is in thy power
**Amerced.**—P. L. 1, 609. *a.* of Heaven
**American.**—P. L. 9, 1116. the *A.* so girt
**Amiable.**—P. L. 4, 250. whose fruit, hung *a.*
P. L. 8, 484. to make her *a.*
P. L. 9, 899. holy, divine, good *a..* or sweet
**Amiable.**—P. L. 4, 479. less *a.* mild
**Amice.**—P. R. 4, 427. in *a.* gray
**Amid.**—P. L. 4, 186. *a.* the field secure
P. L. 4, 218. all *a.* them stood the tree of life
P. L. 4, 578. *a.* the sun's bright circle
P. L. 6, 664. so hills *a.* the air encountered hills
P. L. 7, 48. so easily obeyed *a.* the choice of all
P. L. 7, 262. let there be firmament *a.* the waters
P. L. 8, 326. *a.* the garden, by the tree of life
P. L. 9, 401. returned by noon *a.* the bower
P. L. 9, 594. *a.* the tree now got
P. L. 11, 671. unseen *a.* the throng
S. A. 80. O dark, dark, dark, *a.* the blaze of noon
**Amidst.**—P. L. 1, 71. *a.* the hall
P. L. 2, 263. how oft *a.* thick clouds and dark
P. L. 2, 896. *a.* the noise of endless wars
P. L. 3, 376. invisible *a.* the glorious brightness
P. L. 5, 264. or pilot, from *a.* the Cyclades
P. L. 5, 598. the Son *a.*, as from a flaming mount
P. L. 5, 903. from *a.* them forth he passed
P. L. 7, 132. brighter once *a.* the host
P. L. 9, 502. erect *a.* his circling spires
P. L. 9, 661. fruit of this fair tree *a.* the garden
P. L. 10, 33. from his secret cloud *a.*
P. L. 11, 820. from *a.* a world devote
P. R. 1, 42. a gloomy consistory; and then *a.*
P. R. 2, 149. when from *a.* them rose Belial
P. R. 4, 439. *a.* this joy and brightest morn
P. R. 4, 570. fresh assaults *a.* his pride
S. A. 443. by the idolatrous rout *a.* their wine
S. A. 683. *a.* their height of noon
C. 254. *a.* the flowery-kirtled Naiades
C. 549. the wonted roar was up *a.* the woods
C. 747. *a.* his gorgeous feast
C. 981. all *a.* the gardens fair
A. 42. which I full oft, *a.* these shades alone
**Amiss.**—C. 177. thank the gods *a.*
**Amity.**—P. L. 4, 376. and mutual *a.* so straight
P. L. 8, 426. collateral love and dearest *a.*
P. L. 10, 248. to unite with secret *a.*
**Ammiral.**—P.L.1, 294. the mast of some great *a.*
**Ammon.**—P. L. 4, 277. whom Gentiles *A.* call
**Ammonian.**—P. L. 9, 508. *A.* Jove
**Ammonite.**—P.L. 1, 396. him the *A.* worshipped
S. A. 285. defended Israel from the *A.*
**Ammunition.**—S. A. 1277. he all their *a.*
**Among.** occurs 81 times in P. L. and P. R.
**Amongst.**—P. L. 3, 565. *a.* innumerable stars

C. 1, 189. *a.* the enthroned gods on sainted
C. 629. *a.* the rest a small unsightly root
**Amorous.**—P. L. 1, 449. in *a.* ditties
P. L. 4, 311. sweet reluctant *a.* delay
P. L. 4, 603. all night long her *a.* descant sung
P. L. 8, 477. the spirit of love and *a.* delight
P. L. 8, 518. disporting till the *a.* bird of night
P. L. 9, 1035. glance or toy of *a.* intent
P. L. 9, 1045. wearied with their *a.* play
P. L. 11, 584. they sung soft *a.* ditties
P. L. 11, 586. in the *a.* net fast caught
P. R. 2, 158. expert in *a.* arts
P. R. 2, 162. hearts, tangled in *a.* nets
S. A. 393. prayers and sighs and *a.* reproaches
S. A. 1007. secret sting of *a.* remorse
S. 1, 8. linked that *a.* power to thy soft lay
H. 50. with turtle wing the *a.* clouds dividing
D. F. I. 9. for he being *a.* on that lovely dye
**Amours.**—P. L. 4, 767. nor in court *a.*
**Amphisbæna.**—P. L. 10, 524. asp and *a* dire
**Amphitrite.**—C. 921. to wait in *A.'s* bower
**Ample.**—P. L. 1, 725. within her *a.* spaces
P. L. 3, 254. I through the *a.* air in triumph high
P. L. 3, 389. transfused on thee his *a.* Spirit rests
P. L. 4, 413. and for us this *a.* world
P. L. 5, 393. her *a.* square from side to side
P. L. 6, 255. his *a.* shield
P. L. 7, 577. a broad and *a.* road
P. L. 8, 258. and gazed awhile the *a.* sky
P. R. 2, 339. in *a.* space under the broadest
P. R. 4, 82. in *a.* territory, wealth, and power
**Ampler.**—P. L. 9, 876. dilated spirits, *a.* heart
**Amplest.**—P. L. 11, 330. the *a.* reach of prospect
S. A. 1011. comeliness of shape, or *a.* merit
**Amplier.**—P. L. 12, 544. now *a.* known
**Amplitude.** P. L. 7, 620. of *a.* almost immense
P. R. 2, 139. and *a.* of mind to greatest deeds
**Amply.**—P. L. 10, 388. *a.* have merited of me
P. L. 8, 362. so *a.*, and with hands so liberal
**Amram.**—P. L. 1, 339. potent rod of *A.'s* son
**Amused.**—P. L. 6, 581. within our thoughts *a.*
P. L. 6, 623. we might perceive *a.* them all
**Amymone.**—P. R. 2, 188. or *A.*, Syrinx
**Anak.**—S. A. 528. far beyond the sons of *A.*
S. A. 1080. of stock renowned as Og or *A.*
**Anarch.**—P. L. 2, 988. him thus the *a.* old
**Anarchy.**—P. L. 2, 896. hold eternal *a.*
P. L. 6, 873. in their fall through his wild *a.*
P. L. 10, 283. into the waste wide *a.* of Chaos
P. R. 2, 471. subject himself to *a.* within
**Ancestor.**—P. L. 4, 659. our general *a.* replied
P. L. 10, 735. ill fare our *a.* impure
P. L. 11, 546. to whom our *a.*: henceforth I fly
**Ancestors.**—P. L. 2, 895. Night and Chaos,
*a.* of Nature
**Anchises.**—C. 923. sprung of old *A.*' line
**Anchor.**—P. L. 1, 206. fixed *a.* in his scaly rind
**Anchors.**—P. L. 2, 289. *a.* in a craggy bay
**Ancient.**—P. L. 1, 200. by *a.* Tarsus held
P. L. 1, 789. or unadored in *a.* Greece
P. L. 2, 346. if *a.* and prophetic fame in heaven
P. L. 2, 394. in spite of fate, nearer our *a.* seat
P. L. 2, 591. and ruin seems of *a.* pile
P. L. 2, 970. Chaos and *a.* Night
P. L. 2, 986. erect the standard there of *a.* Night
P. L. 3, 464. from the *a.* world those giants came
P. L. 11, 10. when the *a.* pair in fables old
P. L. 11, 862. the *a.* sire descends
P. R. 1, 44. O *a.* Powers of air
P. R. 1, 305. under the covert of some *a.* oak
P. R. 2, 121. Princes Heaven's *a.* sons
P. R. 2, 435. those *a.* empires of the earth
P. R. 3, 270. Assyria and her empire's *a.* bounds
P. R. 3, 428. freed as to their *a.* patrimony
P. R. 4, 251. then view the schools of *a.* sages
P. R. 4, 368. those *a.* whose resistless eloquence
S. A. 653. in *a.* and in modern books enrolled
C. 314. my daily walks and *a.* neighbourhood
S. 12, 2. by the known rules of *a.* liberty
S. 18, 6. who were thy sheep and in their *a.* fold
V. Ex. 98. or coaly Tyne, or *a.* hallowed Dee

P. R. 3, 281. as *a.*, but rebuilt by him who twice
P. L. 11, 11. less *a.* yet than these
**Anciently.**—P. L. 5, 723. what *a.* we claim
**Andrew.**—P. R. 2, 7. I mean *A.* and Simon
**Andromeda.**—P. L. 3, 559. that bears *A.*
**Angel.**—P. L. 1, 125. so spake the apostate *A.*
P. L. 1, 301. *a.* forms who lay entranced
P. L. 2, 689. art thou that Traitor. *a.*, art thou he
P. L. 2, 991. that mighty leading *a.*
P. L. 3, 622. saw within ken a glorious *a.* stand
P. L. 3, 645. the *a.* bright, ere he drew nigh
P. L. 3, 682. neither man nor *a.* can discern
P. L. 3, 694. fair *a.*, thy desire, which tends
P. L. 4, 59. ordained me some inferior *a.*
P. L. 4, 320. nor shunned the sight of God or *a.*
P. L. 4, 712. what day the genial *a.*
P. L. 4, 902. the warlike *a.*
P. L. 4, 926. insulting *a.*! well thou know'st
P. L. 4, 946. the warrior *a.* soon replied
P. L. 5, 385. on whom the *a.* Hail bestowed
P. L. 5, 404. to whom the *a.*
P. L. 5, 435. nor seemingly the *a.* nor in mist
P. L. 5, 519. to whom the *a.*: Son of Heaven
P. L. 5, 328. to entertain our *a.* guest
P. L. 5, 849. so spake the fervent *a.*
P. L. 6, 1. all night the dreadless *a.*, unpursued
P. L. 6, 92. that *a.* should with *a.* war
P. L. 6, 152. seditious *a.*
P. L. 6, 594. *a.* on Archangel rolled
P. L. 7, 110. the godlike *a.* answered mild.
P. L. 8, 51. the *a.* ended, and in Adam's ear
P. L. 8, 53. she preferred before the *a.*
P. L. 8, 72. the rest from man or *a.*
P. L. 8, 181. pure intelligence of Heaven, *a.* serene
P. L. 8, 560. to whom the *a.* with contracted brow
P. L. 8, 618. the *a.* with a smile that glowed
P. L. 8, 652. so parted they; the *a.* up to heaven
P. L. 9, 1. where God or *a.* guest with man
P. L. 9, 276. from the parting *a.* overheard
P. L. 9, 1081. of God or *a.*
P. L. 10, 327. Satan, in likeness of an *a.* bright
P. L. 10, 442. in show plebeian *a.* militant
P. L. 11, 286. the *a.* interrupted mild
P. L. 11, 421. him the gentle *a.* by the hand
P. L. 11, 449. thus in haste to the *a.* cried
P. L. 11, 598. prime *a.* blest
P. L. 11, 635. said the *a.*
P. L. 11, 759. gently reared by the *a.*
P. L. 11, 762. scarce to the *a.* utter'dst thus
P. L. 12, 201. though present in his *a.*
P. L. 12, 259. conducted by his *a.*
P. L. 12, 364. his place of birth, a solemn *a.* tells
P. L. 12, 485. be sure they will, said the *a.*
P. L. 12, 574. the *a.* last replied
P. L. 12, 637. the hastening *a.* caught
P. R. 2, 274. and by the *a.* was bid rise and eat
P. R. 2, 310. relief by a providing *a.*
P. R. 3, 352. though foretold by prophet or by *a.*
S. A. 24. from Heaven foretold twice by an *a.*
S. A. 361. for this did the *a.* twice descend
S. A. 1431. send thee the *a.* of thy birth, to stand
C. 214. thou hovering *a.*, girt with golden wings
C. 658. and some good *a.* bear a shield before us
L. 163. look homeward, *a.* now
H. 27. and join thy voice unto the *a.* choir
**Angelic.**—P. L. 4, 550. chief of the *a.* guards
P. L. 4, 977. the *a.* squadron bright
P. L. 5, 74. fair *a.* Eve, partake
P. L. 5, 251. the *a.* choir on each hand parting
P. L. 5, 371. the *a.* Virtue answered
P. L. 5, 535. all the *a.* host, that stand
P. L. 5, 650. the *a.* throng, dispersed in bands
P. L. 5, 834. or all *a.* nature joined in one
P. L. 6, 308. the *a.* throng
P. L. 6, 898. among the *a.* powers
P. L. 7, 560. harps that tuned *a.* harmonies
P. L. 8, 559. as a guard *a.* placed
P. L. 9, 142. well nigh half the *a.* name
P. L. 9, 458. her heavenly form *a.*
P. L. 10, 18, the *a.* guards ascended mute
P. L. 11, 76. the *a.* blast filled all the regions

P. R. 4, 593. as he fed *a.* choirs sung heavenly
P. R. 4, 505. *a.* song in Bethlehem field
H. 132. make up full consort to the *a.* symphony
S. A. 672. not evenly as thou rul'st the *a.* orders
**Angelica.**—P. R. 3, 341. the fairest of her sex *A.*
**Angelical.**—P. L. 2, 548. sing with notes *a.*
P. L. 3, 462. betwixt the *a.* and human kind
**Angels.**—P. L. 1, 38. with all his host of rebel *a.*
P. L. 1, 59. at once as far as *a.* ken
P. L. 1, 344. so numberless were those to *a.* seen
P. L. 1, 620. tears such as *a.* weep burst forth
P. L. 1, 734. sceptred *a.* held their residence
P. L. 2, 68. shot with equal rage among his *a.*
P. L. 2, 413. stations thick of *a.* watching round
P. L. 2, 1033. God and good *a.* guard
P. L. 3, 331. thou shalt judge bad men and *a.*
P. L. 3, 345. all the multitude of *a.*
P. L. 3, 396. o'er the necks of warring *a.*
P. L. 3, 511. Jacob saw *a.* ascending
P. L. 3, 521. sailing arrived, wafted by *a.*
P. L. 3, 533. on high behests his *a.* to and fro
P. L. 4, 161. back stepped those two fair *a.*
P. L. 5, 161. ye sons of light, *a.*
P. L. 5, 283. all the bands of *a.*
P. L. 5, 465. food not of *a.*, yet accepted so
P. L. 5, 494. when men with *a.* may participate
P. L. 5, 584. the empyreal host of *a.*
P. L. 5, 600. hear, all ye *a.*, progeny of light
P. L. 5, 633. on a sudden piled with *a.*' food
P. L. 6, 220. fierce encountering *a.* fought.
P. L. 6, 281. so spake the prince of *a.*
P. L. 6, 298. with the tongue of *a.*
P. L. 6, 336. by *a.*, many and strong
P. L. 6, 375. *a.*, contented with their fame
P. L. 6, 411. Michael and his *a.* prevalent
P. L. 6, 638. God hath in his mighty *a.* placed
P. L. 6, 776. aloft by *a.* borne
P. L. 6, 802. here stand, ye *a.* armed
P. L. 7, 133. brighter once amidst the host of *a.*
P. L. 7, 605. from the giant *a.*
P. L. 9, 146. failed more *a.* to create
P. L. 9, 308. who could seduce *a.*
P. L. 9, 392. had formed, or *a.* brought
P. L. 9, 548. served by *a.* numberless
' P. L. 9, 937. but to be gods, or *a.*, demigods
P. L. 10, 34. assembled *a.*, and ye powers
P. L. 10, 650. calling forth by name his mighty *a.*
P. L. 10, 668. he bid his *a.* turn askance
P. L. 10, 893. with men, as *a.*
P. L. 11, 70. with peccant *a.* late they saw
P. L. 11, 213. when the *a* met
P. L. 12, 367. squadroned *a.* hear this carol
P. R. 1, 129. who, in full frequence bright of *a.*
P. R. 1, 131. all *a.* conversant on earth
P. R. 1, 163. that all the *a.* and ethereal powers
P. R. 1, 237. *a.* and sons of men
P. R. 1, 243. at thy nativity, a glorious *a.*
P. R. 1, 371. when to all his *a.* he proposed
P. R. 1, 447 but from him, or his *a.* president
P. R. 2, 385. swift flights of *a.* ministrant
P. R. 3, 63. through heaven to all his *a.*
P. R. 3, 113. by all his *a.* glorified
P. R. 4, 197. sons of God both *a.* are and men
P. R. 4, 200. from men and *a.* I receive
P. R. 4, 474. for *a.* have proclaimed it
P. R. 4, 557. concerning thee to his *a.*
P. R. 4, 582. a fiery globe of *a.* on full sail
S. A. 343. who with a strength equivalent to *a.*
C. 455. a thousand liveried *a.* lackey her
H. 244. *a.* sit in order serviceable
P. 4. my muse with *a.* did divide to sing
**Angel-trumpets.**—S. M. 11. loud uplifted *a.-t.* blow
**Angel-wings.**—P. L. 9, 155. subjected *a.-w.*
**Anger.**—P. L. 2, 90. the vassals of his *a.*
P. L. 2, 158. end them in his *a.*, whom his *a.* saves
P. L. 2, 211. may much remit his *a.*
P. L. 3, 237. on me let thine *a.* fall
P. L. 3, 263. no cloud of *a.* shall remain
**P. L. 4.** 916. no pain can equal *a.* infinite

P. L. 9, 10. *a.* and just rebuke
P. L. 9, 300. scorn and *a.* wouldst resent
P. L. 9, 1123. high passions, *a.*, hate, mistrust
P. L. 10, 114. *a.* and obstinacy, and hate
P. L. 10, 802. draw out, for *a.'s* sake
P. L. 10, 945. as one disarmed, his *a.* all he lost
P. L. 11, 878. and all his *a.* to forget
P. R. 1, 466. inly stung with *a.* and disdain
S. A. 818. in uncompassionate *a.* do not so
S. A. 1, 963, thy *a.*, unappeasable, still rages
C. 667. here dwell no frowns, nor *a.*
S. 1, 8. no *a.* find in thee, but pity and ruth

**Angola.**—P. L. 11, 401. of Congo and *A.*
**Angry.**—P. L. 1, 169. but see! the *a.* Victor
P. L. 1. 741. thrown by *a.* Jove
P. L. 2, 152. whether our *a.* foe can give it
P. L. 10, 1095. when *a.* most he seemed
P. L. 11, 330. for though I fled him *a.*

**Anguish.**—P. L. 1, 558. *a.* and doubt, and fear
P. L. 2, 567. charm pain for a while or *a.*
P. L. 6, 340. gnashing for *a.* and despite
P. L. 9, 62. thence full of *a.*
P. L. 10, 1018. but *a.* and regret
P. L. 11, 778. famine and *a.* will at last consume
P. R. 4, 576. struck with dread and *a.*
S. A. 1, 458. the *a.* of my soul, that suffers not
S. A. 1, 600. from *a.* of the mind and humours
P. 6, 42. in pensive trance, and *a.*

**Animal.**—P. L. 4, 805. the *a.* spirits
P. L. 5, 484. to *a.*, to intellectual
**Animals.**—P. L. 4, 621. *a.* unactive range
**Animate.**—P. L. 8, 151. which two great sexes *a.*
P. L. 9, 112. of creatures *a.* with gradual life
**Anna.**—P. R. 1, 255. Simeon and prophetic *A.*
**Annexed.**—P. L. 12, 99. some fatal curse *a.*
**Annihilating.**—P. L. 6, 347. by *a.* die
**Announced.**—P. R. 4, 504. *a.* by Gabriel,
**Annoy.**—P. L. 6, 369. to *a.* the atheist crew
P. L. 9, 446. sewers *a.* the air
P. R. 3, 365. by invasion to *a.* thy country
S. A. 1 578. given thee to *a.* them
**Annual.**—P. L. 1, 447. *a.* wound in Lebanon
P. L. 7, 431. her *a.* voyage
P. L. 10, 576. to undergo this *a.* humbling
S. A. 987. with odours visited and *a.* flowers
**Annulled.**—S. A. 72. objects of delight *a.*
**Annuls.**—P. L. 12, 428. godlike act *a.* thy doom
**Anointed.**—P. L. 3, 317. *a.* universal king
P. L. 5, 605. and on this holy hill Him have *a.*
P. L. 5, 664. and proclaimed Messiah King *a.*
P. L. 5, 777. under the name of King *A.*
P. L. 5, 870. these tidings carry to the *a.* King
P. L. 6, 676. to honour his *a.* Son
P. L. 6, 718. Messiah his *a.* King
P. L. 12, 359. that the true *a.* King Messiah
P. R. 2, 50. sent his *A.*, and to us revealed him
**Anon.**—P. L. 1, 325. till *a.* his swift pursuers
P. L. 1, 549. *a.* they move in perfect phalanx
P. L. 1, 710. *a.* out of the earth a fabric huge
P. L. 1, 759, they *a.* with hundreds
P. L. 6, 360. but *a.* down cloven to the waist
P. L. 6, 564. heaven, witness thou *a.*, while
P. L. 11, 433. thither *a.* a sweaty reaper
P. L. 11, 661, *a.* gray-headed men and grave
P. L. 11, 861. *a.* dry ground appears
P. L. 12, 150. *a.* plainlier shall be revealed
P. L. 1, 304. *a.* in shady vale
P. R. 2, 285. up to a hill *a.* his steps he reared
L. 169. and yet *a.* repairs his drooping head
L'A. 131. then to the well-trod stage *a.*
**Another.**—P. L. 2, 292. such *a.* field
P. L. 2, 347. *a.* world, the happy seat
P. L. 2, 570. *a.* part, in squadrons
P. L. 2, 1004. Heaven and Earth, *a.* world
P. L. 4, 257. *a.* side, umbrageous grots and caves
P. L. 4, 459. that to me seemed *a.* sky
P. L. 4, 506. imparadised in one *a.'s* arms
P. L. 5, 310. seems *a.* morn risen on mid-noon
P. L. 5, 569. unfold the secrets of *a.* world
P. L. 5, 775. *a.* now hath to himself engrossed
P. L. 6, 604. stood ranked of seraphim *a.* row

P. L. 7, 155. and in a moment will create *a.* world
P. L. 7, 617. this new-made world, *a.* Heaven
P. L. 9, 828. and Adam, wedded to *a.* Eve
P. L. 9, 911. *a.* Eve, and I *a.* rib afford
P. L. 11, 555. now prepare thee for *a.* sight
P. L. 11, 637. now prepare thee for *a.* scene
P. L. 11, 756. thee *a.* flood of tears and sorrow
P. L. 11, 877. to raise *a.* world from him
P. L. 12, 528. their own faith not *a.'s*
P. R. 3, 149. yet of *a.* plea bethought him soon
P. R. 4, 540. *a.* method I must now begin
P. R. 4, 27. *a.* plain, long, wide
S. A. 330. ay me! *a.* inward grief, awaked
S. A. 507. let *a.* hand, not thine, exact
S. A. 559. against *a.* object more enticing
S. A. 561. at *a.* to let in the foe
S. A. 1063. this *a.* kind of tempest brings
S. A. 1352. expect *a.* message more imperious
C. 682. in *a.* country, as he said
C. 754. there was *a.* meaning in these gifts
V. Ex. 54. expectance calls thee now *a.* way

**Answer**—P. L. 3, 693. *a.* thus returned
P. L. 1, 265. made *a.*:—Migthy Father
P. L. 7, 119. to *a.* thy desire of knowledge
P. L. 8, 285. when *a.* none returned
P. L. 8, 436. which gained this *a.*
P. L. 9, 226. mild *a.* Adam thus returned
P. L. 9, 552. not unamazed, she thus in *a.* spake
P. L. 10, 862. I taught your shades to *a.*
P. R. 1, 467. and this *a.* smooth returned
P. R. 2, 172. quick *a.* Satan thus returned
P. R. 3, 146. and here again Satan had not to *a.*
P. R. 3, 181. our Saviour *a.* thus returned
P. R. 3, 442. made *a.* meet
S. A. 1090. if thy appearance *a.* loud report
S. A. 1220. these shifts refuted, *a.* thy appellant
S. A. 1236. this insolence other kind of *a.* fits
S. A. 1322. this *a.*, be assured, wil not content
C. 276. to give me *a.* from her mossy couch
L. 96. sage Hippotades their *a.* brings
S. M. 18. may rightly *a.* that melodious noise

**Answerable.**—P. L. 9, 20. if *a.* style
P. L. 12, 582. add deeds to thy knowledge *a.*
S. A. 615. with *a.* pains, but more intense

**Answered.**—P. L. 1, 127. and him thus *a*
P. L. 1, 272. him Beëlzebub thus *a.*
P. L. 2, 816. thus *a.* smooth:—Dear daughter
P. L. 2, 990. him the Anarch old, . . . *a.*
P. L. 4, 924. to which the fiend thus *a.*
P. L. 5, 94. thus Adam *a.* sad
P. L. 5, 371. whom thus the Angelic Virtue *a.*
P. L. 5, 877. thus *a.* bold
P. L. 6, 150. with scornful eye askance, thus *a.*
P. L. 7, 110. and thus the godlike angel *a.* mild
P. L. 8, 217. Raphael *a.* heavenly meek
P. L. 8, 398. whereto the Almighty *a.*
P. L. 8, 412. he ceased; I lowly *a.*
P. L. 8, 620. *a.*: Let it suffice thee
P. L. 10, 67. and thus divinely *a.* mild
P. L. 10, 115. Adam, faltering long, thus *a.*
P. L. 10, 264. the meagre shadow *a.* soon
P. L. 10, 383. the prince of darkness *a.* glad
P. L. 10, 596. the sin-born monster *a.* soon
P. L. 11, 515. their Maker's image, *a.* Michael
P. L. 12, 625. Adam heard, but *a.* not.
P. R. 1, 357. *a.* the arch-fiend, now undisguised
P. R. 2, 322. as I like the giver, *a.* Jesus
P. R. 2, 392. to whom thus *a.* Satan malcontent
P. R. 3, 386. to whom our Saviour *a.* thus
P. R. 4, 170. our Saviour *a.* with disdain
P. R. 4, 485. but in brief him *a.* thus
C. 888. till thou our summons *a.* have

**Answering.**—P. L. 4, 464. with *a.* looks
P. L. 4, 834. Zephon, *a.* scorn with scorn
P. L. 6, 450. cloudy in aspect, thus *a.* spake
P. L. 6, 722. the filial Godhead *a.* spake
P. L. 7, 557. how fair, *a.* his great idea
H. 97. *a.* the stringed noise

**Answers.**—P. R. 1, 395. *a.* oracles, portents
P. R. 1, 434. what have been thy *a.*
**Antæus.**—P. R. 4, 563. when Earth's son, *A.*

**Antagonist.**—P. L. 2, 509. alone the *a*. of Heaven
P. L. 10, 387. *a*. of Heaven's Almighty King
S. A. 1628. none daring to appear *a*.
**Antarctic.**—P. L. 9, 79. downward as far *a*.
**Anthems.**—P. R. 4, 594. sung heavenly *a*.
Il P. 163. in service high and *a*. clear
H. 219. in vain with timbreled *a*. dark
**Antics.**—S. A. 1325. dancers, *a*., mummers
**Antigonus.**—P. R. 3, 367. *A*. and old Hyrcanus
**Antioch.**—P. R. 3, 297. kings of *A*.
**Antiochus.**—P. R. 3, 163. as did once *A*.
**Antiopa.**—P. R. 2, 187. Daphne, or Semele, *A*.
**Antipater.**—P. R. 2, 423. *A*. the Edomite
**Antipathy.**—P. L. 10, 709. fierce *a*.
**Antique.**—L'A.128. with mask and *a*. pageantry
H. 158. with *a*. pillars massy-proof
**Antiquity.**—C. 439. *a*. from the old schools
**Anubis.**—H. 212. Isis, and Orus, and the dog *A*.
**Anxious.**—P. L. 8, 185. all *a*. cares
S. A. 659. lenient of grief and *a*. thought
**Any.**—P. L. 1, 185. if *a*. rest can harbour
P. L. 2, 438. these passed if *a*. pass the void
P. L. 2, 572. if *a*. clime perhaps might yield
P. L. 4, 117. if *a*. eye beheld
P. L. 4, 202. so little knows *a*. but God alone
P. L. 5, 212. where *a*. row of fruit-trees
P. L. 9, 417. where *a*. tuft of grove
P. L. 9, 972. one guilt, one crime, if *a*. be
P. R. 2, 82. little suspicious to *a*. king
P. R. 4, 558. lest at *a*. time thou chance
S. A. 4. there I am wont to sit when *a*. chance
S. A. 296. if *a*. be they walk obscure
S. A. 1018. if *a*. of these or all the Timnian bride
C. 78. therefore when *a*. favoured of high Jove
C. 244. can *a*. mortal mixture of Earth's mould
C. 273. not *a*. boast of skill but extreme shift
C. 392. or do his gray hairs *a*. violence
C. 497. hath *a*. ram slipped from the fold
D. F. I. 55. or *a*. other of that heavenly brood
U. C. I. 7. for he had *a*. time this ten years full
U. C. I. 17. if *a*. ask for him it shall be said
**Aonian.**—P. L. 1, 15. above the *A*. mount
**Apace.**—P. L. 12, 17. and multiply *a*.
C. 657. Thyrsis lead on *a*., I'll follow thee
L. 129. daily devours *a*. and nothing said
**Apart.**—P. L. 2, 557. others *a*. sat on a hill
P. R. 1, 229. inly rejoiced and said to me *a*.
S. A. 65. each *a*. would ask a life to wail
**Apathy.**—P. L. 2, 564. passion and *a*.
**Ape.**—P. L. 8, 396. converse nor with the ox the *a*.
**Apes.**—S. 12, 4. cuckoos, asses, *a*. and dogs
**Apocalypse.**—P. L. 4, 2. who saw the *A*
**Apollo.**—P. R. 2, 190. *A*., Neptune, Jupiter
C. 478. musical as is *A*.'s lute
C. 662. as Daphne was, root-bound, that fled *A*.
H. 176. *A*. from his shrine
D. F. I. 23. for so *A*., with unweeting hand
V. Ex. 37. listening to what unshorn *A*. sings
**Apology.**—P. L. 9, 854. and *a*. too prompt
**Apostasy.**—P. L. 7, 43. to beware *a*.
P. R. 1, 146. to the throng of his *a*.
**Apostate.**—P. L. 1, 125. so spake the *a*. angel
P. L. 5, 852. the *a*. and more haughty, thus replied
P. L. 6, 100. the *a*. in his sun-bright chariot sat
P. L. 6, 172. *a*., still thou errest
P. L. 7, 610. easily the proud attempt of spirits *a*.
P. L. 7, 44. by what befell in heaven to those *a*.
**Apostles.**—P. L. 12, 498. poured first on his *a*.
**Appaid.**—P. L. 12, 401. high justice rest *a*.
**Apparent.**—P. L. 4, 608. at length, *a*. queen
P. L. 10, 112. *a*. guilt, and shame
P. R. 2, 397. chose to impart to thy *a*. need
**Apparition.**—P. L. 8, 293. *a*. gently moved
P. L. 11, 211. a glorious *a*., had not doubt
C. 641. or ghastly furies' *a*.
**Appear.**—P. L. 2, 15. will *a*. more glorious
P. L. 2, 113. the worse *a*. the better reason
P. L. 2, 257. will *a*. then most conspicuous
P. L. 2, 643. at last *a*. hell bounds, high reaching
P. L. 2, 890. in sudden view *a*. the secrets
P. L. 3, 324. shalt in the sky *a*.

P. L. 3, 380. with excessive bright thy skirts *a*
P. L. 4, 964. within these hallowed limits thou *a*
P. L. 7, 284. into one place, and let dry land *a*.
P. L. 7, 285. immediately the mountains huge *a*.
P. L. 7, 578. as stars to thee *a*.
P. L. 9, 817. but to Adam in what sort shall I *a*.
P. L. 10, 29. accountable, made haste, to make *a*.
P. L. 11, 231. all places else inhospitable *a*.
P. L. 11, 475. a monstrous crew before thee shall *a*
P. L. 11, 610. they *a*. of arts that polish life
P. L. 11, 852. the tops of hills, as rocks, *a*.
P. L. 12, 437. to *a*. to his disciples
P. L. 12, 540. till the day of respiration
P. R. 1, 98. ere in the head of nations he *a*.
P. R. 2, 238. to be at hand, and at his beck *a*.
P. R. 3, 308. see how in warlike muster they *a*.
S. A. 902. bare in thy guilt, how foul must thou *a*
S. A. 1318. to *a*., as fits, before th'illustrious lords
S. A. 1628. none daring to *a*. antagonist
C. 166. I shall *a*. some harmless villager
C. 867. *a*. to us, in name of great Oceanus
L'A. 125. there let Hymen oft *a*.
H. P. 122. till civil-suited morn *a*.
S. 7, 7. inward ripeness doth much less *a*.
S. 22, 4. nor to their idle orbs doth sight *a*.
H. 83. he saw a greater sun *a*.
**Appearance.**—P. L. 9, 413. mere serpent in *a*.
P. R. 2, 41. will he now retire after *a*.
S. A. 1090. if thy *a*. answer loud report
**Appearances.**—P. L. 8, 82. to save *a*.
P. L. 11, 329. seek his bright *a*.
**Appeared.**—P. L. 1, 320. and such *a*. in hue
P. L. 1, 476. after these *a*. a crew
P. L. 1, 523. yet such wherein *a*.
P. L. 1, 548. thronging helms *a*.
P. L. 1, 592. nor *a*. less than archangel ruined
P. L. 2, 418. awaiting who *a*. to second
P. L. 3, 105. what they needs must do, *a*.
P. L. 3, 141. divine compassion visibly *a*.
P. L. 3, 239. patron or intercessor none *a*.
P. L. 3, 504. far more rich, *a*. the work
P. L. 4, 149. and fruits at once of golden hue *a*.
P. L. 4, 461. a shape within the watery gleam *a*.
P. L. 5, 586. from all the ends of Heaven, *a*.
P. L. 6, 79. far in the horizon to the north *a*.
P. L. 6, 319. *a*. in might or swift prevention
P. L. 6, 524. fair morn orient in Heaven *a*.
P. L. 6, 556. suddenly at head *a*. Satan
P. L. 6, 585. obscured with smoke all Heaven *a*.
P. L. 7, 8. before the hills *a*., or fountain flowed
P. L. 7, 193. on his great expedition now *a*.
P. L. 7, 278. embryon immature involved, *a*. not
P. L. 7, 383. *a*. spangling the hemisphere
P. L. 7, 463. now half *a*. the tawny lion
P. L. 7, 489. swarming next *a*. the female bee
P. L. 8, 313. from among the trees *a*.
P. L. 9, 1189. of their vain contest *a*. no end
P. L. 10, 106. duty ere-while *a*. unsought
P. L. 10, 450. head and shape star-bright *a*.
P. L. 11, 216. which on the flaming mount *a*.
P. L. 11, 320. on this mount he *a*.
P. L. 11, 478. before his eyes *a*., sad, noisome
P. L. 11, 589. evening star, love's harbinger, *a*.
S. A. 1256. that he durst not, plain enough *a*.
L. 25. together both, ere the high lawns *a*.
**Appearing.**—P. L. 5, 265. Delos or Samos first *a*.
P. R. 1, 249. a star, not seen before, in heaven *a*.
P. R. 4, 99. *a*., and beginning noble deeds
P. R. 4, 547. far off *a*. like a mount of alabaster
**Appears.**—P. L. 2, 223. since our present lot *a*.
P. L. 2, 533. war *a*. waged in the troubled sky
P. L. 2, 1035. the sacred influence of light *a*.
P. L. 3, 636. now a stripling cherub he *a*.
P. L. 4, 232. from his darksome passage now *a*.
P. L. 8, 30. to this one use, for aught *a*.
P. L. 9, 110. their known virtue *a*.
P. L. 9, 559. in their actions oft *a*.
P. L. 10, 885. bent as now *a*. more
P. L. 11, 861. anon dry ground *a*.
P. L. 12, 300. so law *a*. imperfect
S. A. 822. by this *a*.

**Appearest.**—P. R. 4, 193. plain thou now *a*.
**Appease.**—P. L. 3, 186. to *a*. betimes
P. L. 3, 406. to *a*. thy wrath
P. L. 5, 846. to *a*. the incensed Father
P. L. 10, 79. fully satisfied, and thee *a*.
P. L. 10, 792. let this *a*. the doubt
P. L. 11, 149. the offended Deity to *a*.
P. L. 12, 298. which the law cannot *a*.
S. A. 744. and *a*. thy mind with what amends
**Appeased.**—P. L. 10, 226. to him *a*.
P. L. 11, 257. well may then thy Lord *a*.
P. L. 11, 880. as the brow of God *a*.
**Appellant.**—S. A. 1220. answer thy *a*.
**Appertain.**—P. L. 12, 230. as *a*. to civil justice
P. L. 6, 815. kingdom, and power, and glory *a*.
**Appetence.**—P. L. 11, 619. lustful *a*.
**Appetite.**—P. L. 4, 330. and *a*. more grateful
P. L. 5, 85. so quickened *a*.
P. L. 5, 305. of taste to please true *a*.
P. L. 7, 49. of all tastes else to please their *a*.
P. L. 7, 127. temperance over *a*.
P. L. 7, 546. beware, and govern well thy *a*.
P. L. 8, 308. stirred in me sudden *a*. to pluck
P. L. 9, 580. grateful to *a*.
P. L. 9, 740. an eager *a*., raised by the smell
P. L. 9, 1129. in subjection now to sensual *a*.
P. L. 10, 565. to allay their *a*. with gust
P. L. 11, 517. to serve ungoverned *a*.
P. R. 2, 247. human food nor tasted, nor had *a*.
P. R. 2, 264. dreamed as *a*. is wont to dream
P. R. 2, 409. for no allurement yields to *a*.
C. 705. to a well-governed and wise *a*.
**Appian.**—P. R. 4, 68. on the *A*. road.
**Applauded.**—P. L. 6, 26. led him high *a*.
**Applause.**—P. L. 2, 290. such *a*. was heard
P. L. 5, 873. echoed to his words *a*.
P. L. 10, 505. universal shout and high *a*.
P. L. 10, 545. the *a*. they meant
P. R. 3, 63. who with true *a*. recount his praises
C. 259. and fell Charybdiș murmured soft *a*.
S. 21, 1. with no mean *a*. pronounced
**Apple**—P. L. 10, 487. with an *a*.
P. R. 2, 349. that crude *a*. that diverted Eve
**Apples.**—P. L. 9, 585. tasting those fair *a*.
**Applied.**—P. L. 5, 580. for time, *a*. to motion
P. L. 6, 583. *a*. with nicest touch
P. L. 10, 172. to Satan, first in sin, his doom *a*.
**Apply.**—P. L. 4, 264. the birds their choir *a*.
P. L. 9, 1019. since to each meaning savour we *a*
**Appoint.**—P. L. 5, 606. your head I him *a*.
S. A. 373. *a*. not heavenly disposition
**Appointed.**—P. L. 3, 720. each had his place *a*.
P. L. 4, 619. daily work of body or mind *a*.
P. L. 4, 726. we in our *a*. work employed
P. L. 6, 565. ye, who *a*. stand
P. L. 7, 167. within *a*. bounds
P. L. 10, 421. those, *a*. to sit there, had left
P. L. 11, 550. till my *a*. day of rendering
S. A. 1197. *a*. to await me thirty spies
**Appointment.**—S. A. 1, 643. by his *a*. had
**Appoints.**—P. L. 6, 808. whose he sole *a*.
**Apprehend.**—P. L. 5, 518. can seek or *a*.
P. L. 12, 280. this yet I *a*. not
S. A. 1028. to *a*. or value what is best in choice
C. 784. thou hast nor ear, nor soul, to *a*.
**Apprehended.**—P. L. 9, 574. *a*. nothing high
**Apprehension.**—P. L. 8, 354. my sudden *a*.
P. L. 11, 775. in *a*. than in substance feel
**Apprehensive.**—S. A. 1, 624. *a*., tenderest parts
**Approach.**—P. L. 3, 42. the sweet *a*. of even
P. L. 3, 382. that brightest seraphim *a*. not
P. L. 4, 154. now purer air meets his *a*.
P. L. 4, 363. no evil thing *a*. or enter in
P. L. 4, 624. streak the east with first *a*. of light
P. L. 5, 359. with submiss *a*. and reverence meek
P. L. 6, 256. at his *a*., the great Archangel
P. L. 7, 173. necessity and chance *a*. not me
P. L. 8, 546. yet when I *a*. her loveliness
P. L. 9, 191. waiting close the *a*. of morn
P. L. 9, 535. displeased that I *a*. thee thus
P. L. 11, 121. all *a*. far off to fright

P. L. 12, 206. his *a*. darkness defends between
P. R. 1, 319. he saw *a*. who first with curious eye
P. R. 1, 384. to see thee and *a*. thee
P. R. 1, 449. disdaining to *a*. thy temples
P. R. 2, 160. sweet allayed yet terrible to *a*.
P. R. 2, 281. to descry the morn's *a*.
S. A. 951. let me *a*. at least, and touch thy hand
C. 616. how durst thou then thyself *a*. so near
A. 83. *a*. and kiss her sacred vesture's hem
**Approached.**—P. L. 4, 874. those two *a*.
P. L. 5, 627. evening now *a*.
P. L. 9, 491. not *a*. by stronger hate
P. L. 10, 458. congratulant *a*. him
P. L. 11, 225. while the great visitant *a*.
**Approaches.**—P. L. 4, 367. your change *a*.
**Approaching.**—P. L. 6, 552. the foe *a*. gross
P. L. 8, 242. long ere our *a*. heard within
P. L. 8, 350. *a*. two and two
P. L. 10, 102. God *a*. thus to Adam called
P. L. 10, 864. desolate where she sat *a*. nigh
H. 20. hath took no print of the *a*. light
**Approbation.**—P. R. 3, 61. *a*. marks the just
**Appropriating.**—P. L. 12, 518. *a*. the Spirit
of God
**Approve.**—P. L. 4, 880. who *a*. not to transgress
P. L. 8, 611. *a*. the best and follow what I *a*.
P. [L. 9, 367. wouldst thou *a*. thy constancy,
*a*. first thy obedience
P. L. 9, 1140. to *a*. the faith they owe
P. L. 9, 1159. didst permit *a*. and fair dismiss
**Approved.**—P. L. 6, 36. to stand *a*.
P. L. 8, 509. with obsequious majesty *a*.
P. L. 10, 31. their utmost vigilance and easily *a*.
P. L. 11, 458. other's faith *a*. lose no reward
S. A. 421. rather *a*. them not
**Approves.**—S. A. 510. who ever more *a*.
**April.**—C. 671. *A*. buds in primrose season
**Apt.**—P. L. 8, 188. *a*. the mind or fancy is
S. A. 184. *a*. words have power to swage
P. R. 2, 454. more *a*. to slacken virtue
P. R. 3, 248. of thyself so *a*. in regal arts
P. 28. more *a*. for mournful things
**Apter.**—P. L. 4, 672. *a*. to receive perfection
**Aqueducts.**—P. R. 4, 36. theatres, baths. *a*.
**Aquilo.**—D. F. I. 8. grim *A*. his charioteer
**Arabian.**—P. L. 3, 537. on Egypt and the *A*.
P. R. 2, 364. *A*. odours fanned
P. R. 3, 274. and inaccessible, the *A*. drouth
S. A. 1700. in the *A*. woods embost
**Arable.**—P. L. 11, 430. a field part *a*. and tilth
**Araby.**—P. L. 4, 163. shores of *A*. the Blest
**Arachosia.**—P. R. 3, 316. from *A*.
**Araxes**—P. R. 3, 271. *A*. and the Caspian
**Arbiter.**—P. L. 2, 909. next him high *a*.
P. L 9, 50. short *a*. 'twixt day and night
**Arbitrary.**—P. L. 2, 334. *a*. punishment
**Arbitrate.**—C. 411, does *a*. the event
**Arbitrator.**—P. L. 2, 359. Heaven's high *A*.
**Arbitrement.**—P. L. 8, 641. in thine own *a*.
**Arbitress.**—P. L. 1. 785. the moon sits *a*.
**Arborets.**—P. L. 9, 437. thick-woven *a*.
**Arborous.**—P. L. 5, 137. shady *a*. roof
**Arbour.**—P. L. 5, 378. like Pomona's *a*.
P. L. 9, 216. the woodbine round this *a*.
**Arbours.**—P. L. 4, 626. yon flowery *a*.
**Arcadia.**—A. 95. all *A*. hath not seen
**Arcadian.**—P. L. 11, 132. charmed with *A*. pipe
**Arcady.**—C. 344. thou shalt be our star of *A*.
A. 28. of famous *A*. ye are
**Arch.**—P. L. 6, 759. and colours of the showery *a*.
**Archangel.**—P. L. 1, 243. the lost *A*.
P. L. 1, 593. nor appeared less than *A*. ruined
P. L. 1, 600. yet shone above them all the *A*.
P. L. 3, 648. the *A*. Uriel, one of the seven, who
P. L. 5, 660. he of the first if not the first *A*.
P. L. 5, 694. so spake the false *A*. and infused
P. L. 6, 203. Michael bid sound the *a*. trumpet
P. L. 6, 257. the great *A*. from his warlike toil
P. L. 6, 594. angel on *A*. rolled.
P. L. 7, 41. the affable *A*. had forewarned Adam.
P. L. 11, 238. the *A*. soon drew nigh

P. L. 11, 884. to whom the *A.*
P. L. 12, 2. so here the *A.* paused
P. L. 12, 466. so spake the *A.* Michael
**P. L. 12, 626.** for now too nigh the *A.* stood
**Archangelic.**—P. L. 11, 126. the *a.* power
**Archangels.**—P. L. 3, 325. the summoning *a.*
**Arch-chemic.**—P. L. 3. 609. the *a.-c.* sun
**Arched.**—P L. 1, 726. from the *a.* roof
P. L. 7, 438. the swan with *a.* neck
S. A. 1634. that to the *a.* roof gave main support
Il P. 133. bring to *a.* walks of twilight groves
H. 175. runs through the *a.* roof
**Arch-enemy.**—P. L. 1, 81. to whom the *a.-e.*
**Archers.**—P. R. 3, 330. with towers of *a.*
S. A. 1619. *a.* and slingers, cataphracts and spears
**Arch-felon.**—P. L. 4, 179. when the *a.-f.* saw
**Arch-fiend.**—P. L. 1, 156. the *a.-f.* replied
P. L. 1, 209. the *a.-f.* lay chained
P. R. 1, 357. the *a.-f.* now undisguised
**Arch-foe.**—P. L. 6, 259. the *a.-f.* subdued
**Archimedes.**—S. 21, 7. let *A.* pause
**Architect.**—P. L. 1, 732. and some the *a.*
P. L. 5, 256. the sovran *a.* had framed
P. L. 8, 72. the great *a.* did wisely to conceal
P. L. 10, 356. their author and prime *a.*
**Architects.**—P. R. 4, 52. skill of noblest *a.*
**Architrave.**—P. L. 1, 715. with golden *a.*
**Arcs.**—P. R. 4, 37. trophies and triumphal *a.*
**Arctic.**— P. L. 2, 710. huge in the *a.* sky
**Ardent.**—P. L. 9, 397. long with *a.* look
**Ardour.**—P. L. 6, 66. breathed heroic *a.*
P. L. 9, 1032. with *a.* to enjoy thee
**Ardours.**—P. L. 5, 249. celestial *a.*
**Arethuse.**—A. 31. under seas to meet his *A.*
L. 85. O fountain *A.*, and thou honoured flood
**Argent.**—P. L. 3, 460. those *a.* fields
**Argestes.**—P.L. 10, 699. Caecias and *A.* loud
**Argo.**—P. L. 2, 1017. when *A.* passed
**Argob.**—P. L. 1, 398. in *A.*, and in Basan
**Argue.**—P. L. 4, 931. *a.* thy inexperience
P. L. 10, 1014. to *a.* in thee something
P. L. 12, 283. so many laws *a.* so many sins
P. R. 2, 94. I will not *a.* that nor will repine
S. 22, 6 yet　I *a.* not against Heaven's hand
**Argued.**—P. L. 2, 562. much they *a.* then
P. L. 6, 238. no unbecoming deed that *a.* fear
S. A. 1193. I chose a wife which *a.* me no foe
**Argues.**—P. L. 2, 234. *a.* as vain the latter
P. L. 4, 830. *a.* yourselves unknown
P. L. 4, 949. *a.* no leader but a liar traced
P. L. 8, 21. for such their distance *a.*
S. A. 514. which *a.* over-just, and self-displeased
**Arguing.**—P. L. 6, 508. none *a.* stood
P. R. 3, 4. convinced of his weak *a.*
**Argument.**—P. L. 1, 24. this great *a.*
P. L. 5, 809. O *a.* blasphémous, false and proud
P. L. 6, 84. with boastful *a.* portrayed
P. L. 9, 13. yet *a.* not less, but more heroic
P. L. 9, 28. hitherto the only *a.* heroic deemed
P. L. 9, 42. higher *a.* remains
P. L. 10, 800. as *a.* of weakness, not of power
P. R. 1, 172. sung with the voice, and this the *a.*
P. R. 3, 46. by all thy *a.*
P. R. 3, 401. *a.* of human weakness, rather than
S. A. 283. who by *a.* not worse than
S. A. 658. consolatories writ with studied *a.*
S. A. 903. in *a.* with men a woman ever
**Arguments.**—S. A. 862. oppose against such *a.*
C. 760. I hate when vice can bolt her *a.*
**Argus.**—P. L. 11, 131. those of *A.*
**Ariel.**—P. L. 6, 371. *A.* and Arioch
**Aries.**—P. L. 10, 329. while the sun in *A.* rose
**Aright.**—P. L. 6, 470. which thou *a.* believest
P. L. 10. 156. hadst thou known thyself *a.*
P. L. 11, 578. to worship God *a.*
P. R. 2, 475. knowing worship God *a.*
P. R. 4, 348. where God is praised *a.*
S. A. 1547. to have guided me *a.*, I know no
**Arimaspian.**—P. L. 2, 945. pursues the *A.*
**Arioch.**—P. L. 6, 371. Ariel, and *A.*
**Arise.**—P. L. 1, 330. awake, *a.*

P. L. 4, 805. from pure blood *a.*
P. L. 8, 200. may *a.* of something
P. L. 12, 531. persecution shall *a.* on all
P. R. 2, 47. *a.* and vindicate thy glory
S. A. 467. but will *a.* and his great name assert
S. 16, 11. new foes *a.*, threatening to bind our
V. Ex. 91. Rivers *a.*, whether thou be the son
**Arises.**—P. L. 5, 170. while day *a.*
**Ark.**—P. L. 1, 458. when the captive *a.*
P. L. 11, 813. shall build a wondrous *a.*
P. L. 11, 823. shall in the *a.* be lodged
P. L. 11, 840. saw the *a.* hull on the flood
P. L. 11, 850. the *a.* no more now floats
P. L. 11, 855. forthwith from out the *a.*
P. L. 11, 861. from his *a.* the ancient sire
P. L. 12, 102. son of him who built the *a.*
P. L. 12, 251. an *a.*, and in the *a.* his testimony
P. L. 12, 333. the clouded *a.* of God
P. L. 12, 340. his holy *a.*
H. 220. bear his worshipped *a.*
**Arm.**—P. L. 1, 113. the terror of this *a.* so late
P. L. 2, 173. intermitted vengeance *a.* again
P. L. 2, 318. beyond his potent *a.*
P. L. 2, 568. *a.* the obdured breast
P. L. 4, 973. feel from my prevailing *a.*
P. L. 5, 64. with venturous *a.* he plucked
P. L. 6, 222. *a.* him with the force
P. L. 6, 239. as only in his *a.* the moment lay
P. L. 6, 316. with next to almighty *a.*
P. L. 6, 466. *a.* ourselves.
P. L. 6, 537. *a.*, warriors, *a.* for fight
P. L. 9, 583. much less *a.* thy looks
P. L. 10, 634. at one sling of thy victorious *a.*
P. L. 12, 490. also *a.* with spiritual armour
P. R. 3, 387. much ostentation vain of fleshy *a.*
S. A. 689. above the nerve of mortal *a.*
C. 600. against the opposing will and *a.*
C. 781. to him that dares *a.* his profane tongue
**Armed.**—P. L. 1, 101. force of Spirits *a.*
P. L. 1, 305. when with fierce winds Orion *a.*
P. L. 1, 676. with spade and pickaxe *a.*
P. L. 1, 764. where champions bold wont ride
P. L. 2, 61. *a.* with hell-flames and fury
P. L. 2, 447. *a.* with power
P. L. 2, 652. a serpent *a.* with mortal sting
P. L. 2, 757. a goddess *a.*,
P. L. 2, 825. that, in our just pretences *a.*
P. L. 4, 65. to all temptations *a.*
P. L. 4, 779. stood *a.* to their night-watches
P. L. 6, 110. *a.* in adamant and gold
P. L. 6, 168. such hast thou *a.*
P. L. 6, 364. in a rock of diamond *a.*
P. L. 6, 400. invulnerable, impenetrably *a.*
P. L. 6, 430. less firmly *a.*
P. L. 6, 655. and oppress'd whole legions *a.*
P. L. 6, 688. when two such foes met *a.*
P. L. 6, 697. with mountains, as with weapons
P. L. 6, 737. *a.* with thy might
P. L. 6, 760. he, in celestial panoply all *a.*
P. L. 6, 802. here stand, ye angels *a.*
P. L. 9, 390. with bow and quiver *a.*
P. L. 10, 9. with free-will *a.*
P. L. 10, 697. *a.* with ice
P. L. 10, 1023. God hath wiselier *a.* his
P. R. 3, 331. with spades and axes *a.*
S. A. 20, that, like a deadly swarm of hornets *a.*
S. A. 347. to save himself against a coward *a.*
S. A. 623. *a.* with deadly stings
S. A. 1134. *a.* thee or charmed thee strong_
S. A. 1280. celestial vigour *a.*
S. A. 1494. that of a nation *a.* the strength
P. L. 1, 567. he through the *a.* files darts
P. L. 2, 130. filled with *a.* watch
P. L. 6, 47. lead forth my *a.* saints
P. L. 6, 127. from his *a.* peers
P. L. 6, 231. in strength each *a.* hand a legion
S. A. 1190. went up with *a.* powers
S. A. 1617. on each side went *a.* guards
H. 58. the trumpet spake not to the *a.* throng
**Armies.**—P. L. 1, 272. leader of those *a.* bright
P. L. 2, 534. *a.* rush to battle in the clouds

P. L. 2, 594. where _a_. whole have sunk
P. L. 6, 44. go, Michaël, of celestial _a_. prince
P. L. 6, 138. have raised incessant _a_.
P. L. 6, 204. the faithful _a_. rung Hosanna
P. L. 7, 295. _a_. at the call of trumpets, for of _a_.
P. L. 10, 276. to a field where _a_. lie encamped
S. A. 129. ran on embattled _a_. clad in iron
S. A. 345. duelled their _a_. ranked in proud array
**Arming.**—P. L. 1, 553. heroes old _a_. to battle
P. L. 11, 374. _a_. to overcome by suffering
**Armoric.**—P. L. 1, 581. British and _A_. knights
**Armour.**—P. L. 1, 6, 209. arms on _a_. clashing
P. L. 6, 334. his _a_. stained erewhile so bright
P. L. 6, 389. with shivered _a_. strown
P. L. 6, 656. their _a_. helped their harm
P. L. 7, 409. in jointed _a_. watch
P. L. 12, 491. and also arm with spiritual _a_.
**Armouries.**—S. A. 1281. their _a_. and magazines
**Armoury.**—P. L. 4, 553. celestial _a_., shields
P. L. 6, 321. from the _a_. of God
P. L. 7, 200. chariots winged from the _a_. of God
**Arms.**—P. L. 1, 49. defy the Omnipotent to _a_.
P. L. 1, 94. the force of those dire _a_.
P. L. 1, 119. in _a_. not worse
P. L. 1, 269. with rallied _a_. to try what may be
P. L. 1, 325. with scattered _a_. and ensigns
P. L. 1, 539. seraphic _a_. and trophies
P. L. 1, 564. of dreadful length, and dazzling _a_.
P. L. 1, 667. fierce with grasped _a_.
P. L. 2, 55. millions that stand in _a_.
P. L. 2, 63. turning our tortures into horrid _a_.
P. L. 2, 124. who most excels in fact of _a_.
P. L. 2, 164. thus consulting, thus in _a_.
P. L. 2, 395. whence with neighbouring _a_.
P. L. 2, 513. horrent _a_.
P. L. 2, 537. with feats of _a_.
P. L. 2, 691. in proud rebellious _a_.
P. L. 2, 812. invulnerable in those bright _a_.
P. L. 4, 506. imparadised in one another's _a_.
P. L. 4, 1008. to boast what _a_. can do
P. L. 5, 217. twines her marriageable _a_.
P. L. 5, 722. with what _a_. we mean to hold what
P. L. 6, 17. chariots, and flaming _a_.
P. L. 6, 32. in word mightier than they in _a_.
P. L. 6, 50. them with fire and hostile _a_.
P. L. 6, 123. should win in _a_.
P. L. 6, 136. against the Omnipotent to rise in _a_.
P. L. 6, 209. _a_. on armour clashing
P. L. 6, 247. and met in _a_. no equal
P. L. 6, 302. in stature, motion, _a_.
P. L. 6, 361. with shattered _a_.
P. L. 6, 418. now known in _a_.
P. L. 6, 433. perhaps more valid _a_.
P. L. 6, 449. his riven _a_. to havoc hewn
P. L. 6, 454. against unequal _a_. to fight in pain
P. L. 6, 525. _a_. the matin trumpet sung, in _a_.
P. L. 6, 595. the sooner for their _a_. unarmed
P. L. 6, 635. found them _a_.
P. L. 6, 639. their _a_. away they threw
P. L. 6, 662. to like _a_. betook them
P. L. 6, 713. my almighty _a_. gird on
P. L. 9, 1103. in Malabar or Deccan spreads her _a_.
P. L. 10, 512. his _a_. clung to his ribs
P. L. 10, 541. down their _a_., down fell both spear
P. L. 11, 240. over his lucid _a_. a military vest
P. L. 11, 641. concourse in _a_., fierce faces
P. L. 11, 643. part wield their _a_.
P. L. 11, 654. with carcases and _a_.
P. L. 12, 222. untrained in _a_.
P. L. 12, 431. Sin and Death, his two main _a_.
P. L. 12, 644. and fiery _a_.
P. R. 1, 174. entering his great duel, not of _a_.
P. R. 3, 20. against thy few in _a_.
P. R. 3, 156. from possession won with _a_.
P. R. 3, 166. retired into the desert, but with _a_.
P. R. 3, 305. steel bows and shafts their _a_.
P. R. 3, 888. and fragile _a_.
P. R. 4, 83. civility of manners, arts, and _a_.
P. R. 4, 112. more than of _a_. before
P. R. 4, 235. error by his own _a_. is best evinced
P. R. 4, 368. _a_. or arts

P. R. 4, 405. whose branching _a_.
S. A. 131. weaponless himself, made _a_.
S. A. 137. in scorn of their proud _a_.
S. A. 1038. far within defensive _a_.
S. A. 1096. with other _a_.
S. A. 1119. then put on all thy gorgeous _a_.
S. A. 1130. thou durst not thus disparage _a_.
S. A. 1226. no man of _a_. will deign
S. A. 1633. his _a_. on those two massy pillars
S. A. 1636. which when Samson felt in his _a_.
C. 33. an old and haughty nation, proud in _a_.
C. 440. to testify the _a_. of Chastity
C. 612. far other _a_. and other weapons must
L'A. 123. and judge the prize of wit or _a_.
S. 8, 1. Captain, or Colonel, or Knight in _a_.
S. 15, 1. whose name in _a_. through Europe rings
S. 17, 3. gowns, not _a_., repelled the fierce Epirot
V. Ex. 94. his thirty _a_. along indented meads
**Army.**—P. L. 4, 953. _a_. of fiends
P. L. 6, 224. _a_. against _a_. numberless to raise
P. L. 6, 778. his _a_.. circumfused on either wing
P. L. 12, 76. to sustain himself and his rash _a_.
P. R. 4, 606. from Heaven cast with all his _a_.
S. A. 346. himself an _a_., now unequal match
**Arnon.**—P. L. 1, 399. to the stream of utmost _A_.
**Aroer.**—P. L. 1, 407. from _A_. to Nebo
**Arose.**—P. L. 5, 452. sudden mind _a_. in Adam
P. L. 7, 60. the doubts that in his heart _a_.
P. L. 7, 449. the sixth, and of creation last, _a_.
P. L. 7, 582. the seventh evening _a_. in Eden
P. L. 8, 644. so saying, he _a_.; whom Adam thus
**Around.**—P. L. 2, 900. _a_. the flag of each
H. 54. was heard the world _a_.
**Arraigned.**—P. L. 3, 331. they _a_. shall sink
**Array.**—P. L. 1, 548. shields in thick _a_.
P. L. 2, 887. chariots ranked in loose _a_.
P. L. 6, 74. in orderly _a_. on wing
P. L. 6, 106. presented stood in terrible _a_.
P. L. 6, 356. pierced the deep _a_. of Moloch
P. L 6, 801. stand still in bright _a_., ye saints
P. L. 10, 595. in station stood, or just _a_.
P. L. 11, 644. single or in _a_. of battle ranged
P. L. 12, 627. all in bright _a_.
P. R. 2, 219. and put to rout all her _a_.
P. R. 3, 17. might require the _a_. of war
S. A. 345. duelled their armies ranked in proud _a_.
V. Ex. 26. hast decked them in thy best _a_.
**Arrayed.**—P. L. 6, 13. _a_. in gold
P. R. 2, 386. _a_. in glory, on my cup to attend
H. 111. the shame-faced night _a_.
**Arraying.**—P. L. 4, 596. _a_. with reflected purple
P. L. 10, 223. with his robe of righteousness _a_.
**Arreed**—P. L. 4, 962. mark what I _a_. thee now
**Arrive.**—P. L. 2, 409. ere he _a_. the happy isle
P. L. 2, 979. thither to _a_. I travel this profound
P. L. 3, 197. and, to the end persisting, safe _a_.
P. R. 2, 426. if at great things thou wouldst _a_.
**Arrived.**—P. L. 3, 520. sailing _a_.
P. L. 4, 720. at their shady lodge _a_.;
P. L. 4, 792. from the sun's decline _a_.
P. L. 5, 254. till, at the gate of heaven _a_.
P. L. 6, 835. full soon among them he _a_.
P. L. 7, 587. the Filial Power _a_.
P. L. 8, 112. ere mid-day _a_. in Eden
P. L. 10, 22. from earth _a_., at heaven-gate
P. L. 10, 26. about the new-_a_. in multitudes
P. L. 10, 586. the hellish pair too soon _a_.
S. 2, 6. that I to manhood am _a_. so near
**Arrives.**—S. A. 1075. he now _a_.
**Arrogate.**—P. L. 12, 27. will _a_. dominion
P. R. 4, 315. to themselves all glory _a_.
**Arrow.**—P. L. 2, 811. shun his deadly _a_.
**Arrows.**—P. L. 6, 546. _a_. barbed with fire
P. L. 6, 845. tempestuous fell his _a_.
C. 422. like a quivered nymph with _a_. keen
**Arrowy.**—P. R. 3, 324. sleet of _a_. showers
**Arsaces.**—P. R. 3, 295. by great _A_. led
**Arsenal.**—P. R. 4, 270. shook the _a_.
**Art.**—P. L. 1, 696. strength, _a_. are easily outdone
P. L. 1, 703. a second multitude with wondrous _a_.
P. L. 2, 272. nor want we skill, or _a_.

c

P. L. 2, 410. what *a.* can then suffice
P. L. 3, 602. though by their powerful *a.*
P. L. 4, 236. rather to tell how if *a.* could tell
P. L. 4, 241. nice *a.* in beds and curious knots
P. L. 4, 801. assaying by his devilish *a.* to reach
P. L. 5, 297. above rule or *a.* enormous bliss
P. L. 5, 770. with calumnious *a.*
P. L. 6, 513. with subtle *a.* concocted
P. L. 9, 391. such gardening tools as *a.*, yet rude
P. L. 10, 312. by wondrous *a.* pontifical
P. R. 2, 295. it seemed nature taught *a.*
S. A. 1133. some magician's *a.* armed thee
S.A. 1399. I could be well content to try their *a.*
C. 63. excels his mother at her mighty *a.*
C. 149. for so I can distinguish by mine *a.*
C. 309. would overtask the best land-pilot's *a.*
L.121. that to the faithful herdman's *a.* belongs
W. S. 9. to the shame of slow-endeavouring *a.*
**Artaxata.**—P. R. 3, 292. *A.*, Teredon
**Artaxerxes.**—P. R. 4, 271. Macedon and *A.*
**Artful.**—P. R. 4, 335. with *a.* terms inscribed
C. 494. Thyrsis? whose *a.* strains have oft
S. 20, 11. the lute well touched or *a.* voice
**Articulate.**—P. L. 9, 557. all *a.* sound
**Artifice.**—P. L. 9, 39. the skill of *a.*
**Artificer.**—P. L. 4, 121. *a.* of fraud
**Artificers.**—P. R. 4, 59. the hand of famed *a.*
**Artillery.**—P.L. 2, 715. with heaven's *a.* fraught
**Artist.**—P. L. 1, 288. through optic glass the
Tuscan *a.* views
**Artists.**—S. A. 1324. of gymnic *a.*, wrestlers
**Arts.**—P. L. 11, 610. *a.* that polish life
P. R. 2, 158. expert in amorous *a.*
P. R. 3, 248. so apt, in regal *a.*
P. R. 4, 83. civility of manners, *a.*, and arms
P. R. 4, 240. the eye of Greece, mother of *a.*
P. R. 4, 338. Greece from us these *a.* derived
P. R. 4, 368. nor honour, arms, or *a.*
S. A. 748. thy wonted *a.*
S. A. 749 *a.* of every woman
S. A. 1139. I know no spells, use no forbidden *a.*
**Ascalon.**—P. L. 1, 465. in Gath and *A.*
S. A. 1187. those thirty men at *A.*
**Ascalonite.**—S. A. 138. the bold *A.* fled
**Ascend.**—P. L. 2, 56. wait the signal to *a.*
P. L. 2, 75. that in our proper motion we *a.*
P. L. 4, 140. as the ranks *a.*
P. L. 5, 80. sometimes *a.* to heaven
P. L. 5, 198. that singing up to heaven-gate *a.*
P. L. 5, 498. winged *a.* ethereal
P. L. 5, 512. by steps we may *a.* to God
P. L. 6, 711. *a.* my chariot
P. L. 7, 287. their tops *a.* the sky
P. L. 8, 592. to heavenly love thou mayst *a.*
P. L. 11, 143. from us aught should *a.*
P. L. 11, 366. *a.* this hill
P. L. 11, 371. *a.*; I follow thee
P. L. 11, 376. so both *a.* in the visions of God
P. L. 12, 369. he shall *a.* the throne hereditary
P.L. 12, 451. to the heaven of heavens he shall *a.*
S.A. 1518. from slaughter of one foe could not *a.*
**Ascended.**—P. L. 6, 762. *a.*; at his right hand
P. L. 7, 564. while the bright pomp *a.* jubilant
P. L. 10, 18. the angelic guards *a.*
P. L. 10, 445. invisible *a.* his high throne
S. A. 25. all in flames *a.* from off the altar
**Ascending.**—P. L. 1, 722. the *a.* pile stood fixed
P. L. 2, 489. the dusky clouds *a.*
P. L. 2, 930. *a.*, rides audacious
P. L. 3, 502. *a.* by degrees magnificent
P. L. 3, 511. as whereon Jacob saw angels *a.*
P. L. 4, 354. in the *a.* scale of heaven the stars
P. L. 7, 574. so sung the glorious train *a.*
P. R. 4, 101. in his place *a.*
**Ascends.**—P. L. 1, 499. the noise of riot *a.*
P. L. 4, 650. *a.* with charm of earliest birds
**Ascension.**—P. L. 10, 187. with *a.* bright
**Ascent.**—P. L. 2, 81. the *a.* is easy then
P. L. 3, 486. now at foot of heaven's *a.*
P.L. 3, 524. whether to dare the fiend by easy *a.*
P. L. 4, 172. the *a.* of that steep savage hill

P. L. 4, 545. winding with one *a.* accessible
P. L. 9, 936. tasting to attain proportional *a.*
P. L. 10, 224. with swift *a.* he up returned
**Ascribe.**—P. L. 8, 131. which else.. thou must *a.*
**Ascribest.**—P. R. 1, 453. to thyself *a.* the truth
**Asdod.**—S. A. 981. in Ecron, Gaza, *A.*
**Ashamed.**—P. R. 2, 332. nature *a.*
**Ashes.**—P. L. 3, 334. from her *a.* spring
P. L. 10, 566. instead of fruit chewed bitter *a.*
S. A. 1691. from under *a.* into sudden flame
S. 18, 10. their martyred blood and *a.* sow
**Ashore.**—C. 932. may thy billows roll *a.*
**Ashy.**—S. A. 1703. from out her *a.* womb
**Ashtaroth.**—P. L. 1, 422. Baalim and *A.*
**Astoreth.**—P. L. 1, 438. in troop came *A.*
P. R. 3, 417. Baal next and *A.*
S. A. 1242. by *A.*, ere long thou shalt lament
H. 200. and mooned *A.*
**Asia.**—P. L. 10, 310. Europe with *A.* joined
P. R. 3, 33. won *A.*, and the throne of Cyrus
**Asian.**—P. R. 4, 73. from the *A.* kings
**Aside.**—P. L. 4, 502. *a.* the devil turned
P. L. 11, 630. should turn *a.* to tread paths
C. 168. but here she comes, I fairly step *a.*
H. 12. that glorious form he laid *a.*
**Ask.**—P. L. 2, 957. to *a.* which way
P. L. 4, 632. *a.* riddance
P. L. 4, 832. why *a.* ye
P. L. 4, 908. who *a.* what boldness brought
P. L. 7, 69. to *a.* his heavenly guest
P. L. 7, 95. not to explore the secrets, *a.*
P. L. 7, 121. abstain to *a.*
P. L. 8, 53. of him to *a.* chose rather
P. L. 8, 66. to *a.* or search, I blame thee not
P. L. 8, 201. of something not unseasonable to *a.*
P. L. 8, 614. if lawful what I *a.*
P. R. 1, 326. I *a.* the rather
P. R. 4, 552. to stand upright will *a.* thee skill
S.A. 40. *a.* for this great deliverer now and find
S. A. 66. each apart would *a.* a life to wail
S. 19, 8. I fondly *a.*
S. 22, 9. what supports me dost thou *a.*
V. Ex. 7. here I salute thee and thy pardon *a.*
U. C. I. 17. if any *a.* for him it shall be said
**Askance.**—P. L. 4, 504. eyed them *a.*
P. L. 6, 149. with scornful eye *a.*, thus answered
P. L. 10, 668. he bid his angels turn *a.*
**Asked.**—P. L. 2, 685. without leave *a.* of thee
P. L. 3, 217. he *a.*, but all the heavenly
P. L. 4, 887. this question *a.* puts me in doubt
P. L. 4, 899. thus much what was *a.*
P. L. 7, 111. with caution *a.*, obtain
P. L. 7, 635. that *a.* how first this world
P. R. 1, 436. who *a.* have seldom understood
P. R. 3, 67. he *a.* thee, 'Hast thou seen
C. 575. who gently *a.* if he had seen such two
L. 91. he *a.* the waves, and *a.* the felon winds
**Asks.**—P. R. 2, 253. hath need of what she *a.*
**Asleep.**—P. L. 4, 791. now laid perhaps *a.*
P. L. 5, 14. whether waking or *a.*
P. L. 5, 92. fell *a.*; but O how glad I waked
P. L. 12, 614. wearied I fell *a.*
L'A. 116. by whispering winds soon lulled *a.*
**Aslope.**—P. L. 10, 1053. the curse *a.* glanced
**Asmodai.**—P. L. 6, 365. Adramelech and *A.*
P. R. 2, 151. and after *A.* the fleshliest Incubus
**Asmodeus.**—P. L. 4, 168. than *A.*
**Asp.**—P. L. 10, 524. scorpion and *a.*
S. 11. 13. not learning worse than toad or *a.*
**Aspect.**—P. L. 2, 301. with grave *a.* he rose
P. L. 3, 266. his meek *a.* silent yet spake
P. L. 4, 541. right *a.* against the eastern
P. L. 5, 733. the Son with calm *a.* and clear
P. L. 6, 81. stretched in battailous *a.*
P. L. 6, 313. two planets rushing from *a.* malign
P. L. 6, 450. cloudy in *a.*, thus answering
P. L. 7, 379. she needed none in that *a.*
P. L. 8, 336. but soon his clear *a.* returned
P. L. 10, 454. bent their *a.*
P. R. 3, 217. from that placid *a.*
**Aspects.**—P. L. 10, 658. motions, and *a.*

C. 694. what grim *a.* are these

**Asperses.**—P. L. 9. 296. in vain, at least *a.*

**Asphaltic.**—P. L. 1, 411. to the *A.* pool
P. L. 10, 298. and with *a.* slime

**Asphaltus.**—P. L. 1, 729. Naphtha and *A.*

**Asphodel.**—P. L. 9, 1040. *a.*, and hyacinth
C. 838, in nectared lavers strewed with *a.*

**Aspire.**—P. L. 5, 484. to vital spirits *a.*
P. L. 12, 64. so to *a.* above his brethren
P. L. 12, 560. beyond which was my folly to *a.*
P. R. 2, 417. which way,.. dost thou *a.*
C. 12. yet some there be that by due steps *a.*
D. F. I. 63. scorn the world and unto Heaven *a.*

**Aspired.**—P. L. 4, 62. as great might have *a.*
P. L. 9, 167. that to the height of Deity *a.*
P. R. 1, 215. yet this not all to which my spirit *a.*

**Aspirer.**—P. L. 6. 90. the proud *a.*

**Aspires.**—P. L. 2, 7. *a.* beyond thus high
P. L. 6, 383. yet to glory *a.* vain-glorious
P. L. 9, 169. who *a.* must down as low as high
P. R. 2, 469, who attains not ill a. to rule

**Aspiring.**—P. L. 1, 38. by whose aid, *a.*
P. L. 3, 392. the *a.* Dominations
P. L. 4, 526. *a.* to be such, they taste and die
P. L. 6, 132. the height of thy *a.* unopposed
P. L. 6, 793. *a.* to his height
P. L. 6, 899. fall of those too high *a.*

**Aspramont.**—P. L. 1, 583. jousted in *A.*

**Ass.**—S. A. 143. the jaw of a dead *a.*
S. A. 1095. such wonders with an *a.'s* jaw
S. A. 1097. where the *a.* lay thrown

**Assail.**—S. A. 756. which way to *a.*
S. A. 1165. no worthy match for valour to *a.*
S. A. 1396. we shall find such engines to *a.*

**Assailant.**—S. A. 1693. *a.* on the perched roosts
C. 589. virtue may be *a.*, but never hurt

**Assailed.**—P. L. 10, 417. bars *a.*

**Assassinated.**—S. A. 1109. *a.* and betrayed

**Assassin-like.**—P. L. 11, 219. *a.-l.*, had levied

**Assault.**—P. L. 2, 343. fear no *a.* or siege
P. L. 4, 190. fear no *a.*
P. L. 6, 51. fearless *a.*
P. L. 6, 216. with ruinous *a.*
P. L. 7, 214. surging waves, as mountains, to *a.*
P. L. 9, 256. work us woe and shame by sly *a.*
P. L. 9, 305. first on me the *a.* shall light
P. R. 3, 74. great battles win great cities by *a.*
P. R. 4, 19. the *a.* renew
S. A. 331. renews the *a.*
C. 589. boldly *a.* the necromancer's hall

**Assaulted.**—S. A. 365. ensnared, *a.*, overcome

**Assaulting.**—P. L. 11, 657. scale, and mine, *a.*

**Assaults.**—P. L. 1, 277. in all *a.*
P. L. 2, 953. *a.* his ear with loudest vehemence
P. L. 10, 882. proof against all *a.*
P. L. 12, 492. able to resist Satan's *a.*
P. R. 2, 195. scorned all her *a.*
P. R. 4, 570. renewing fresh *a.*, amidst his pride
S. A. 403. with blandished parleys, feminine *a.*
S. A. 845. hear what *a.* I had, what snares

**Assay.**—P. L. 3, 90. with purpose to *a.*
P. L. 6, 153. the first *a.* of this right hand
P. L. 9, 747. at first *a.* gave elocution
P. R. 1, 143. now *a.* his utmost subtlety
P. R. 1, 264. through many a hard *a.*
P. R. 2, 234. and his strength as oft *a.*
P. R. 4, 478. many a hard *a.* of dangers
A. 80. I will *a.*, her worth to celebrate

**Assayed.**—P. L. 1, 619. thrice he *a.*
P. L. 10, 567. oft they *a.*
P. L. 10, 865. to his fierce passion she *a.*
S. A. 392. thrice she *a.*, with flattering prayers
S. A. 1625. which might be *a.*

**Assaying.**—P. L. 4, 801. *a.*, by his devilish art

**Assays.**—P. L. 4, 932. from hard *a.*
C. 972. sent them here through hard *a.*

**Assemble.**—P. L. 5, 683. *a.* thou
P. L. 11, 663. gray-headed men .. *a.*

**Assembled.**—P. L. 3, 330. all thy saints *a.*
P. L. 5, 767. for thither he *a.* all his train

P. L. 10, 34. *a.* Angels, and ye Powers returned

**Assemblies.**—P. L. 11, 722. frequented their *a.*

**Assembly.**—P. L. 2, 285. murmur filled the *a.*
P. L. 2, 749. when at the *a.*
P. L. 6, 446. he sat and in the *a.* next upstood
P. R. 1, 34. at that *a.* famed would not be last
S. A. 1315. to honour .. this great *a.*
V. Ex. 28. fly swiftly to this fair *a.'s* ears

**Assent.**—P. L. 2, 388. with full *a.* they vote

**Assenting.**—P. L. 5, 562. *a.* thus began

**Assert.**—P. L. 1, 25. I may *a.*
P. L. 5, 801. titles which *a.*
P. L. 6, 157. in synod met their deities to *a.*
S. A. 467. but will arise, and his great name *a.*

**Asses.**—P. R. 3, 242. seeking *a.*, found a kingdom
S. A. 1162. among the slaves and *a.*
S. 12, 4. of owls and cuckoos, *a.*, apes, and dogs

**Assessor.**—P. L. 6, 679. the *A.* of his throne

**Assiduous.**—P. L. 11, 310. with my *a.* cries

**Assigned.**P. L. 5, 477. active spheres *a.*
P. L. 6, 817. their doom he hath *a.*
P. L. 9, 231. work which here God hath *a.* us
P. L. 10, 926. by doom express *a.* us
S. A. 1116. without feigned shifts, let be *a.*
S. A. 1217. I was to do my part from Heaven *a.*

**Assimilate.**—P. L. 5, 412. digest, *a.*

**Assist.**—P. L. 9, 247. ere long *a.* us
P. R. 2, 145. with hand or counsel to *a.*

**Assisting.**—S. A. 1720. *a.* to the end

**Associate.**—P. L. 5, 696. the breast of his *a.*
P. L. 9, 227. sole Eve, *a.* sole
P. L. 10, 395. to my *a.*Powers, them to acquaint

**Associates.**—P. L. 1, 265. *a.* and co-partners
P. L. 8, 401. in the choice of thy *a.*

**Assuage.**—S. A. 627. or med'cinal liquor can *a.*

**Assume.**—P. L. 1, 424. can either sex *a.*, or both
P. L. 2, 450. wherefore do I *a.* these royalties
P. L. 3, 303. descending to *a.* man's nature
P. L. 3, 318. reign for ever, and *a.* thy merits
P. L. 5, 794. who can in reason then, or right, *a.*
P. L. 6, 353. colour, shape, or size *a.*
P. L. 6, 730. sceptre and power, thy giving, I *a.*
P. L. 10, 214. the form of servant to *a.*
P. R. 2, 483. far more magnanimous, than to *a.*

**Assuming.**—P. L. 12, 65. *a.*authority usurped

**Assure.**—P. L. 5, 553. assured me, and still *a.*

**Assured.**—P. L. 2, 40. prosperity could have *a.*
P. L. 2, 685. be *a.* without leave asked of thee
P. L. 3, 263. but peace *a.* and reconcilement
P. L. 5, 262. the glass of Galileo, less *a.*
P. L. 5, 553. my constant thoughts *a.* me
P. L. 8, 449. that shall please thee, be *a.*
P. L. 9, 981. chiefly *a.* remarkably
P. L. 11, 872. *a.* that man shall live
P. R. 2, 148. was *a.* their utmost aid
S. A. 739. though my pardon no way *a.*
S. A. 800. I was *a.* by those who tempted me
S. A. 1322. this answer, be *a.* will not content

**Assures.**—P. L. 11, 157. yet now *a.* me thus

**Assyria.**—P. L. 1, 721. Egypt with *A.* strove
P. R. 3, 270. *A.* and her empire's bounds

**Assyrian.**—P. L. 4, 126. and on the *A.*
P. L. 4, 285. this *A.* garden, where the Fiend
P. R. 3, 436. cleave the *A.* flood
C. 1002. sadly sits the *A.* queen

**Astarte.**—P. L. 1, 439. *A.*, queen of Heaven

**Asthmas.**—P. L. 11, 488. dropsies, and *a.*

**Astonied.**—P. L. 9, 890. amazed, *a.* stood

**Astonished.**—P. L. 1, 266. lie thus *a.*
P. L. 2, 423. read his own dismay, *a.*
P. L. 6, 838. they, *a.*, all resistance lost

**Astonishment.**—P. L. 1, 317. if such *a.* as this
C. 157. and my quaint habits breed *a.*
W. S. 7. thou, in our wonder and *a.*

**Astound.**—C. 210. startle well, but not *a.*

**Astounded.**—P. L. 1, 281. *a.* and amazed

**Astracan.**—P. L. 10, 432. by *A.* retires

**Astray.**—Il P, 69. like one that had been led *a.*

**Astrea.**—P. L. 4. 998. yet seen betwixt *A.*

**Astronomer.**—P. L. 3, 589. *a.* .. never saw

**Asunder.**—P. L. 9, 258. best advantage, us *a.*
  V. Ex. 77. that cannot live from him *a.*
**Atabalipa.**—P. L. 11, 409. seat of *A.*
**Atheist.**—P. L. 1, 495. when the priest turns *a.*
  P. L. 6, 370. Abdiel to annoy the *a.* crew
**Atheists.**—P. L. 11, 625. smiles of these fair *a.*
  S. A. 453. oped the mouths of idolists and *a.*
**Athenian.**—S. 8, 14. power to save the *A.* walls
  D. F. I. 9. by boisterous rape the *A.* damsel
**Athens.**—P. L. 9, 671. in *A.*, or free Rome
  P. R. 4, 240. *A.*, the eye of Greece, mother of arts
**Atheous.**—P. R. 1, 487. hypocrite or *a.* priest
**Athwart.**—P. L. 2, 688. *a.* my way
**Atlantean.**—P. L. 2, 306. with *A.* shoulders
**Atlantic.**—P. L. 3, 559. far off *A.* seas
  P. L. 10, 674. the seven *A.* Sisters
  P. R. 4, 115. on citron tables or *A.* stone
  C. 97. in the steep *A.* stream
**Atlas.**—P. L. 4, 987. *A.* unremoved
  P. L. 11, 402. from Niger flood to *A.* mount
**Atom.**—P. L. 8, 18. a grain, an *a.*
**Atoms.**—P. L. 2, 900. bring their embryon *a.*
**Atonement.**—P. L. 3, 234. *a.* for himself
**Atropatia.**—P. R. 3, 319. from *A.* and the
**Atrophy.**—P. L. 11, 486. pining *a.*
**Atropos.**—M. W. 28. *A.* for Lucina came
**Attached.**—P. L. 11, 595. *a.* the heart
**Attack.**—P. L. 6, 248. through the dire *a.*
  S. A. 1113. close-banded, durst *a.* me
**Attain.**—P. L. 3, 196. they shall *a.*
  P. L. 7, 115. yet what thou canst *a.*
  P. L. 8, 70. this to *a.*
  P. L. 8, 412. to *a.* the height and depth
  P. L. 9, 726. thus *a.* to know
  P. L. 9, 935. to *a.* proportional ascent
  P. L. 9, 964. how shall I *a.*
  P. L. 11, 376. if so I may *a.*
  P. R. 1, 265. ere I the promised kingdom can *a.*
  P. R. 1, 485. though I despair to *a.*
  P. R. 3, 211. the end I would *a.*, my final good
  Il P. 173. till old experience do *a.*
**Attained.**—P. L. 9, 689. more perfect have *a.*
  P. L. 12, 575. thou hast *a.* the sum
  P. R. 2, 437. endued with these have oft *a.*
  P. R. 3, 89. it may by means far different be *a.*
  P. R. 4, 106. without the highest *a.*
**Attains.**—P. L. 8, 34. *a.* her end without least
  P. L. 9, 724. forthwith *a.* wisdom
  P. L. 12, 135. Canaan he now *a.*
  P. R. 2, 468. every wise and virtuous man *a.*
  P. R. 2, 469. who *a.* not ill aspires to rule
**Attempt.**—P. L. 1, 44. battle proud with vain *a.*
  P. L. 1, 642. which tempted our *a.*
  P. L. 2, 420. or undertake the perilous *a.*
  P. L. 2, 610. and to oppose the *a.*
  P. L. 4, 15. begins his dire *a.*
  P. L. 7, 609. the proud *a.* of Spirits apostate
  P. L. 8, 237. they durst without his leave *a.*
  P. L. 9, 295. to avoid the *a.* itself
  P. L. 9, 978. ensue this my *a.*
  P. L. 9, 1149. or here the *a.*
  P. L. 9, 1180. I thought no evil durst *a.* thee
  P. L. 10, 8. hindered not Satan to *a.*
  P. R. 1, 113. whose *a.* at first against mankind
  P. R. 2, 205. but he whom we *a.* is wiser far
  P. R. 4, 180. now more accursed for this *a.*
  P. R. 4, 625. Abaddon rues thy bold *a.*
  S. A. 1267. draw their own ruin who *a.*
  C. 406. *a.* the person of our unowned sister
**Attempted.**—P. L. 2, 357. how *a.* best, by force
  P. L. 9, 369. not seeing thee *a.*
  S. A. 1457. I have *a.*, one by one, the lords
**Attempter.**—P. R. 4, 603. against the *a.*
**Attempting.**—P. L. 2, 377. if this be worth *a.*
  P. L. 2, 450. could deter me from *a.*
**Attempts.**—P. L. 9, 481. opportune to all *a.*
  P. R. 3, 26. reward that sole excites to high *a.*
  S. A. 1221. by his blindness maimed for high *a.*
**Attend.**—P. L. 3, 658. his sons thy embassy *a.*
  P. L. 4, 597. on his western throne *a.*
  P. L. 5, 520. Son of Heaven and Earth, *a.*

  P. L. 7, 407. in their pearly shells at ease, *a.*
  P. L. 8, 247. but thy relation now; for I *a.*
  P. L. 11, 551. patiently *a.* my dissolution
  P. L. 12, 12. give due audience, and *a.*
  P. L. 12, 354. men who *a.* the altar
  P. R. 2, 386. arrayed in glory, on my cup to *a.*
  S. A. 1731. to fetch him hence, solemnly *a.*
  C. 85. are coming to *a.* their father's state
  A. 81. so *a.* ye toward her glittering state
**Attendance.**—P. L. 10, 80. *a.* none
  C. 315. if your stray *a.* be yet lodged
**Attendant.**—P. L. 7, 205. *a.* on their Lord
  P. L. 7, 547. black *a.* death
  P. L. 8, 149. with their *a.* moons
**Attended.**—P. L. 1, 761. trooping came *a.*
  P. L. 3, 323. when thou, *a.* gloriously
  P. L. 6, 767. *a.* with ten thousand
  C. 211. the virtuous mind, that ever walks *a.*
**Attending.**—P. R. 1, 53. with dread *a.*
  H 242. with handmaid lamp *a.*
**Attends.**—P. L. 3, 270. he *a.* the will
  P. L. 8, 223. all comeliness and grace *a.* thee
  P. L. 9, 638. they say, some evil spirit *a.*
  P. L. 10, 239. success *a.* him
  P. R. 4, 387. *a.* thee, scorns, reproaches
  S. 9, 9. thy care is fixed, and zealously *a.*
**Attent.**—P. R. 1, 385. to hear *a.* thy wisdom
**Attention.**—P. L. 1, 618. *a.* held them mute
  P. L. 2, 308. his look drew audience and *a.* still
  P. L. 9, 529. he, glad of her *a.* gained
  P. L. 9, 566. for such wonder claims *a.* due
  P. L. 10, 459. with these words *a.* won
  P. L. 11, 422. his *a.* thus recalled
  C. 258. chid her barking waves into *a.*
**Attentive.**—P. L. 5, 545. thy words *a.*
  P. L. 7, 51. the story heard *a.*, and was filled
  P. L. 10, 1011. his more *a.* mind raised
**Attest.**—P. L. 2, 495. herds *a.* their joy
  P. L. 9, 369. not seeing thee attempted, who *a.*
  P. R. 1, 37. to whom such high *a.* was given
**Attested.**—P. R. 1, 122. *a.* Son of God
**Attic.**—P. R. 4, 245. the *A.* bird trills
  Il P. 124. with the *A.* boy to hunt
  S. 20, 10. light and choice, of *A.* taste
**Attire.**—P. L. 7, 501. earth in her rich *a.*
  S. 20, 7. clothe in fresh *a.* the lily and rose
  V. Ex. 21, 196. richest robes and gayest *a.*
**Attired.**—T. 21. *a.* with stars
**Attract.**—P. L. 10, 152. to *a.* thy love
**Attracted.**—P. L. 5, 47. with ravishment *a.*
**Attraction.**—P. L. 4, 498. eyes of conjugal *a.*
  P. L. 10, 263. this new-felt *a.*
**Attractive.**—P. L. 2, 762. with *a.* graces
  P. L. 4, 298. for softness she and sweet *a.* grace
  P. L. 8, 124. by his *a.* virtue and their own
  P. L. 8, 587. *a.*, human, rational
  P. R. 2, 176. their colour, and *a.* grace
**Attracts.**—P. R. 2, 476. this *a.* the soul
**Attribute.**—P. L. 8, 107. those circles *a.*
**Attributed.**—P. L. 8, 12. with glory *a.*
  P. L. 9, 320. who thought less *a.* to her faith
  P. R. 3, 69. *a.* to things not glorious
**Attributes.**—P. L. 11, 836. God *a.* to place
**Attributing.**—P. L. 8, 565. by *a.* overmuch
**Attrite.**—P. L. 10, 1073. grind the air *a.* to fire
**Attune.**—P. L. 4, 265. *a.* the trembling leaves
**Audacious.**—P. L. 1, 400. *a.* neighbourhood
  P. L. 2, 931. ascending rides *a.*
**Audible.**—P. L. 11, 266. with *a.* lament
**Audibly.**—P. L. 7, 518. thus to his Son *a.* spake
  P. R. 1, 284. *a.* heard from heaven
**Audience.**—P. L. 2, 308. his look drew *a.*
  P. L. 2, 555. the thronging *a.*
  P. L. 5, 804. without control had *a.*
  P. L. 7, 31. fit *a.* find, though few
  P. L. 7, 105. and the moon haste to thy *a.*
  P. L. 9, 674. each act won *a.* ere the tongue
  P. L. 10, 641. the heavenly *a.* loud
  P. L. 12, 12. thou therefore give due *a.*
**Auditress.**—P. L. 8, 51. she sole *a.*
**Aught.**—P. L. 1, 159. to do *a.* good

P. L. 1, 683. than *a*. divine or holy else enjoyed
P. L. 1, 748. nor *a*. availed him now
P. L. 2, 447. if *a*. proposed and judged
P. L. 2, 657. if *a*. disturbed their noise
P. L. 2, 837. be this or *a*. than this more secret
P. L. 3, 121. or *a*. by me immutably foreseen
P. L. 3, 592. compared with *a*. on earth
P. L. 4, 419. nor can perform *a*.
P. L. 5, 207. if the night have gathered *a*. of evil
P. L. 5, 905. nor of violence feared *a*.
P. L. 6, 121. nor is it *a*. but just that he
P. L. 6, 545. if I conjecture *a*.
P. L. 7, 640. if else thou seek'st *a*.
P. L. 8, 30. to this one use, for *a*. appears
P. L. 8, 358. or *a*. than mankind higher
P. L. 8, 583. if *a*. therein enjoyed were worthy
P. L. 8, 596. nor *a*. in procreation
P. L. 8, 636. to do *a*. which else free will would
P. L. 9, 115. if I could joy in *a*.
P. L. 9, 347. or *a*. that might his happy state
P. L. 9, 573. nor *a*. but food discerned, or sex
P. L. 9, 969. death, or *a*. than death
P. L. 10, 962. if *a*. I see
P. L. 11, 143. from us *a*. should ascend
P. L. 12, 4. if Adam *a*. might interpose
P. R. 1, 333. where *a*. we hear
P. R. 1, 402. nor lightens *a*. each man's peculiar
P. R. 2, 456. to do *a*. may merit praise
P. R. 3, 88. but if there be in glory *a*. of good
P. R. 3, 100. *a*. be done, *a*. suffered
P. R. 3, 399. on my part *a*. endeavouring
P. R. 4, 345. with *a*. of profit or delight
P. R. 4, 369. nor *a*. by me proposed
P. R. 4, 382. if I read *a*. in heaven, *a*. of fate
P. R. 4, 592. what hunger, if *a*. hunger
S. A. 274. if he *a*. begin, how frequent to him
S. A. 376. if *a*. seem vile
S. A. 743. if *a*. in my ability may serve
S. A. 888. if *a*. against my life
S. A. 1387. if there be *a*. of presage in the mind
S. A. 1420. if *a*. religion seem concerned
L. 120. *a*. else the least that to the
Il. P. 116. if *a*. else great bards beside
**Augment.**—P.L. 2, 386. still serves his glory to *a*.
P. L. 2, 605. their sorrow to *a*.
P. L. 7, 367. or reflection they *a*. their small
P. L. 10, 964. a long day's dying, to *a*. our pain
P. R. 3, 88. quench not thirst of glory, but *a*.
**Augmented.**—P. L. 6, 280. with *a*. pain
P. L. 9, 985. not death, but life *a*., opened eyes
**Auran.**—P. L. 4, 211. from *A*. eastward
**Aurora.**—P. L. 5, 6. *A.'s* fan
L'A. 19. Zephyr, with *A*. playing
**Ausonian.**—P. L. 1, 739. in *A*. land
**Austere.**—P. L. 9, 272. sweet *a*. composure
S. A. 815. not *a*. as thou art strong
**Austerely.**—P. L. 4. 744. hypocrites *a*. talk
**Austerity.**—C. 450. but rigid looks of chaste *a*.
**Authentic.**—P. L. 3, 656. his great *a*. will
P. L. 4, 719. on him who had stole Jove's *a*. fire
**Author.**—P. L. 2, 381. but from the *a*. of all ill
P. L. 2, 864. thou art my father, thou my *a*.
P. L. 3, 374. eternal King; thee, *A*. of all being
P. L. 4, 635. my *a*. and disposer
P. L. 5, 73. the *a*. not impaired
P. L. 5, 188. in honour to the world's great *A*.
P. L. 5, 397. when thus began our *a*.
P. L. 6, 262. *a*. of evil, unknown till thy revolt
P. L. 7, 591. *A*. and End of all things
P. L. 8, 317. *A*. of all this thou seest above
P. L. 8, 360. *A*. of this universe
P. L. 9, 771. *a*. unsuspect, friendly to man
P. L. 10, 236. our great *a*.
P. L. 10, 356. thou art their *a*.
S. A. 376. sole *A*. I, sole cause
**Authority.**—P. L. 4, 295. whence true *a*. in men
P. L. 8, 554. *a*. and reason on her wait
P. L. 12, 66. to himself assuming *a*. usurped
P. R. 1, 289. the *a*. which I derived from Heaven
P. R. 2, 5. on that high *a*. had believed
P. R. 2, 418. whence *a*. derivest

S. A. 868. with grave *a*. took full possession
**Authors.**—P. L. 3, 122. *a*. to themselves in all
**Autumn.**—P. L. 4, 557. a shooting star in *a*.
P. L. 5, 394. from side to side all *a*. piled
P. L. 5, 394. spring and *A*. here danced
**Autumnal.**—P. L. 1, 302. thick as *a*. leaves
P. R. 4, 619. like an *a*. star, or lightning
**Auxiliar.**—P. L. 1, 579. mixed with *a*. gods
**Avail.**—P. L. 1, 153. what can it then *a*.
P. L. 6, 789. convince the proud what signs *a*.
P. L. 7, 85. what may no less perhaps *a*.
P. L. 12, 515. to *a*. themselves of names
**Availed.**—P. L. 1, 748. nor aught *a*. him now
S. A. 558. but what *a*. this temperance
**Avails.**—P. L. 6, 456. for what *a*. valour
P. L. 11, 312. no more *a*. than breath
P. R. 2, 66. O, what *a*. me now that honour high
**Avarice.**—S. 15, 14. *A*. and Rapine share the land
**Avaunt.**—P. L. 4, 962. *A*. fly thither
**Avenge.**—S. 18, 1. *a*., O Lord, thy saints
**Avenged.**—P. L. 4, 718. to be *a*.
P. L. 6, 676. to honour his anointed Son *a*.
P. L. 9, 143. he, to be *a*.
P. L. 10, 374. fully *a*. our foil in Heaven
P. L. 11, 458. the bloody fact will be *a*.
P. R. 4, 606. hast *a*. supplanted Adam
**Avengers.**—P. L. 10, 241. driven by his *a*.
**Avenging.**—P. L. 6, 278. this *a*. sword
P. L. 7, 184. glory to him, whose just *a*. ire
**Aver.**—S. A. 323. though reason here *a*.
**Averse.**—P. L. 8, 138. with her part *a*.
P. L. 2, 763. attractive graces won the most *a*.
P. L. 9, 67. on the coast *a*. from entrance
S. A. 1461. some much *a*. I found
**Aversion.**—P. R. 2, 457. with like *a*. I reject
**Avert.**—P. L. 9, 302. I labour to *a*. thee alone
P. L. 12, 108. *a*. his holy eyes
S. A. 519. offerings to *a*. his further ire
**Avoid.**—P. L. 1, 505. to *a*. worse rape
P. L. 9, 294. but to *a*. the attempt itself
P. L. 9, 364. which to *a*. were better
S. A. 505. if the punishment thou canst *a*.
C. 363. run to meet what he would most *a*.
**Avoided.**—P. L. 10, 691. *a*. pinching cold
S. A. 495. and *a*. as a blab
**Avon.**—V. Ex. 97. or rocky *A*., or of sedgy Lea
**Avow.**—S. A. 1151. the power of Israel's God *a*.
**Await.**—S. A. 1197. appointed to *a*. me spies
**Awaited.**—P. R. 2, 108. *a*. the fulfilling
**Awaiting.**—P. L. 1, 566. *a*. what command
P. L. 2, 418. *a*. who appeared to second
P. L. 4, 550. chief of the angelic guards, *a*. night
P. L. 4, 864. *a*. next command
**Awaits.**—P. L. 11, 193. some farther change *a*.
P. L. 11, 710. what reward *a*. the good
S. 15, 9. O, yet a nobler task *a*. thy hand
**Awake.**—P. L. 1, 330. *a*., arise or be for ever
P. L. 1, 334. bestir themselves ere well *a*.
P. L. 5, 17. *a*., my fairest, my espoused
P. L. 5, 20. my ever new delight! *a*.
P. L. 5, 40. that now *a*. tunes sweetest
P. L. 8, 464. still glorious before whom *a*.
C. 275. compelled me to *a*. the courteous Echo
**Awaked.**—P. L. 2, 171. *a*., should blow them
P. L. 4, 450. when from sleep I first *a*.
P. L. 6, 59. reluctant flames, the sign of wrath *a*.
P. R. 2, 272. *a*., he found his supper
S. A. 330. ay me! another inward grief, *a*.
**Awakened.**—P. R. 1, 197. at once *a*. in me swarm
**Awakening.**—P. L. 5, 672. subordinate *a*.
**Awakes.**—A. 57, 325. *a*. the slumbering leaves
**Aware.**—P. L. 4, 119. whereof he soon *a*.
P. L. 6, 547. so warned he them, *a*. themselves
**Awe.**—P. L. 4, 705. such was their *a*. of man
P. L. 4, 860. *a*. from above had quelled his
P. L. 5, 135. pious *a*. that feared
P. L. 6, 283. with wind of aery threats to *a*.
P. L. 8, 314. rejoicing, but with *a*.
P. L. 8, 558. and create an *a*. about her
P. L. 9, 703. why, but to *a*. why, but to keep
P. L. 10, 712. nor stood much in *a*. of man

P. R. 1, 22. to his great baptism flocked with *a.*
P. R. 2, 220. or turn to reverent *a.*
P. R. 4, 625. hereafter learn with *a.* to dread
S. A. 1055. power over his female in due *a.*
C. 32. has in his charge, with tempered *a.* to
C. 452. with sudden adoration and blank *a.*
H. 32. nature in *a.* to him
**Awed.**—P. L. 5, 358. though not *a.*
P. L. 12, 198. *a.* by the rod of Moses so to stand
S.A.847. which might have *a.* the best-resolved
**Awful**—P. L. 1, 753. with *a.* ceremony
P. L. 2, 478. they bend with *a.* reverence prone
P. L. 4, 847. felt how *a.* goodness is
P. L. 4, 960. adored heaven's *a.* monarch
P.L. 8, 577. so *a.*, with honour thou mayest love
P. L. 9, 537. thy *a.* brow, more *a.* thus
P. R. 1, 19. more *a.* than the sound of trumpet
H. 59. kings sat still with *a.* eye
**Awhile.**—P. L. 3, 280. to save, by losing thee *a.*
P. L. 5, 364. thou hast deigned *a.* to want
P. L. 5, 395. *a.* discourse they hold
P. L. 6, 556. at interview both stood *a.*
P. L. 6, 634. they stood *a.* in trouble
P. L. 8, 2. that he *a.* thought him speaking
P. L. 8, 258. gazed *a.* the ample sky
P. L. 9, 744. pausing *a.*, mused
P. L. 10, 447. down *a.* he sat
P. L. 10, 504. so having said, *a.* he stood
P. R. 1, 37. *a.* surveyed with wonder

P. R. 3, 2. and Satan stood *a.*, as mute
S. A. 115. this, this is he; softly *a.*
S. A. 1632. as over-tired to let him lean *a.*
S. A. 1636. with head *a.* inclined and eyes fixed
S. 11, 3. the subject new, it walked the town *a.*
**Awry.**—P. L. 3, 488. ten thousand leagues *a.*
P. R. 4, 313. they talk but all *a.*
S. A. 1041. by her charms draws him *a.*
**Axe.**—Il P. 136. the rude *a.* with heaved stroke
**Axes.**—P. R. 3, 331. with spades and *a.* armed
**Axle.**—P. L. 2, 926. mutiny had from her *a.* torn
P. L. 7, 381. revolved on heaven's great *a.*
P. L. 8, 165. that spinning sleeps on her soft *a.*
P. L. 10, 670. from the sun's *a.*
C. 96. his glowing *a.* doth allay
**Axle-tree.**—H. 84. burning *a.* could bear
**Ay me!** P. L. 10, 813. *a.* me! that fear comes
P. L. 4, 86. *a.* me! they little know how
**Aye.**— Il P. 48. *a.* round about Jove's altar
S. M. 7. *a.* sung before the throne
**Azazel.**—P. L. 1, 534. *A.* as his right
**Azores.**—P. L. 4, 592. now fallen beneath th' *A.*
**Azotus.**—P. L. 1, 464. temple high reared in *A.*
**Azure.**—P. L. 1, 297. those steps on heaven's *a.*
P. L. 7, 479. with spots of gold and purple, *a.*
P. L. 9, 429. *a.* or specked with gold
**Azurn.**—C. 893. agate and the *a.* sheen
S. 14, 11. with purple beams and *a.* wings
**Azza.**—S. A. 147. the gates of *A.*

# B

**Baal.**—P. R. 3, 417. the deities of Egypt, *B.*
**Baalim,**—P. L. 1, 422. *B.* and Ashtaroth
H. 197. Peor and *B.*
**Baal-zebub.**—S.A. 1231. O *B.!* can my ears hear
**Babble.**—C. 807 this is mere moral *b.*
**Babe.**—H. 151. the *B.* yet lies in smiling
H. 227. our *B.*, to show his Godhead true
H. 238. hath laid her *B.* to rest
M. W. 31. the hapless *b.*, before his birth
**Babel.**—P. L. 1, 694. and wondering tell of *B.*
P. L. 3. 466. the builders next of *B.*
**Babels.**—P. L. 3, 468. new *B. . . .* build
**Babylon.**—P. L. 1, 717. *B.*, nor great Alcairo
P. L. 12, 343. left in confusion *B.* thence called
P. L. 12, 348. returned from *B.*
P. R. 3, 280. there *B.*, the wonder of all tongues
P. R. 4, 336. in *B.* that pleased so well
**Babylonian.**—S. 18, 14. may fly the *B.* woe
**Bacchus.**—P. L. 4, 279. her florid son, young *B.*
P. L. 7, 33. of *B.* and his revellers the race
C. 46. *B.*, that first from out the purple grape
C. 522. of *B.* and of Circe born, great Comus
L'A. 16. to ivy-crowned *B.* bore
**Back.**—P. L. 1, 171. *b.* to the gates of heaven
P. L. 2, 603. thence hurried *b.* to fire
P. L. 2, 699. *b.* to thy punishment false fugitive
P. L. 2, 789. *b.* resounded Death
P. L. 3, 397. *b.* from pursuit thy powers
P. L. 3, 624. his *b.* was turned
P. L. 4, 17. and like a devilish engine *b.* recoils
P. L. 4, 462. I started *b.*, it started *b.*
P. L. 4, 480. *b.* I turned
P. L. 4, 820. *b.* stepped those two fair angels
P. L. 4, 914. and scourge that wisdom *b.*
P. L. 4, 965. *b.* to the infernal pit I drag thee
P. L. 5, 906. his *b.* he turned
P. L. 6, 39. *b.* on thy foes more glorious
P. L. 6, 194. ten paces huge he *b.* recoiled
P. L. 6, 338. bore him on their shields *b.*
P. L. 6, 534. *b.* with speediest sail
P. L. 9, 172. bitter ere long *b.* on itself recoils
P. L. 9, 410. or send thee *b.*
P. L. 9, 784. *b.* to the thicket slunk
P. L. 10, 252. the difficulty of passing *b.*
P. L. 10, 749. desirous to resign and render *b.*
P. L. 10, 814. that fear comes thundering *b.*

P. L. 11, 313. blown stifling *b.* on him
P. L. 12, 172. with glory and spoil *b.*
P. L. 12, 219. fear return them *b.* to Egypt
P. L. 12, 641. they looking *b.*, all the eastern side
P. R. 1, 153. and drive him *b.* to hell
S. A. 1137. that ridge the *b.* of chafed wild boars
C. 593. but evil on itself shall *b.* recoil
C. 958. *b.*, shepherds *b.*; enough your play
**Backed.**—P. R. 4, 29. *b.* with a ridge
P. R. 4, 448. *b.* on the north and west
**Backs.**—P. L. 7, 286. broad bare *b.* upheave
S. A. 140. old warriors turned their plated *b.*
**Backside.**—P. L. 3, 494. the *b.* of the world
**Backward.**—P. L. 1, 223. the flames driven *b.*
P. L. 6, 863. struck them with horror *b*
C. 817. and *b.* mutters
**Bactra.**—P. R. 3, 295. there thou seest, and *B.*
**Bactrian.**—P. L. 10, 433. *B.* Sophi
**Bad.**—P. L. 1, 348. numberless were *b.* angels
P. L. 2, 6. by merit raised to that *b.* eminence
P. L. 2, 483. lest *b.* men should boast
P. L. 2, 849. no less rejoiced his mother *b.*
P. L. 3, 331. thou shalt judge *b.* men and angels
P. L. 4, 795. on errand *b.* no doubt
P. L. 5, 695. infused *b.* influence
P. L. 9, 495. enclosed in serpent, inmate *b.*
P. L. 9, 1073. *b.* fruit of knowledge
P. L. 9, 1091. but let us now as in *b.* plight
P. L. 10, 41. he should prevail speed on his *b.*
P. L. 10, 837. divided with that *b.* woman
P. L. 11, 256. one *b.* act with many deeds
P. L. 11, 358. good with *b.* expect to hear
P. L. 11, 685. where good with *b.* were matched
P. L. 12, 106. still tend from *b.* to worse
P. L. 12, 336. part good, part *b.*; of *b*
P. L. 12, 538. to *b.* men benign
P. R. 3, 114. from all men, good or *b.*
P. R. 4, 1. troubled at his *b.* success
S. A. 211. by *b.* women been deceived
S. A. 1537. of good or *b.* so great, of *b.*
T. 9. when as each thing *b.* thou hast entombed
**Bade.**—C. 639. and *b.* me keep it
**Baffled.**—S. A. 1237. go, *b.* coward!
**Bait.**—P. L. 10, 551. the *b.* of Eve
P. R. 2, 204. to the *b.* of women lay exposed
S. A. 1066. nor fear the *b.* of honied words

**Baited.**—C. 162. *b.* with reasons not unplausible
**Baits.**—S. A. 1538. good news *b.*
C. 537. yet have they many *b.* . . guileful spells
C. 700. with lickerish *b.*, fit to ensnare a brute
P. L. 12, 1. in his journey *b.* at noon
**Balaam.**—P. R. 1, 491. to *B.* reprobate
**Balance.**—P. L. 1, 349. in even *b.*
P. L. 3, 482. whose *b.* weighs the trepidation
**Balanced.**—P. L. 4, 1000. earth with *b.* air
**Baleful.**—P. L. 1, 56. round he throws his *b.*
P. L. 2, 576. burning lake their *b.* streams
C. 255. culling their potent herbs, and *b.*
**Ball.**—P. L. 4, 768. wanton mask or midnight *b.*
S. A. 94. to such a tender *b.* as the eye
**Balls.**—P. L. 6, 518. *b.* of missive ruin
**Balm.**—P. L. 1, 774. new rubbed with *b.*
P. L. 2, 402. shall breathe her *b.*
P. L. 4, 248. wept odorous gums and *b.*
P. L. 5, 293. cassia, nard, and *b.*
P. L. 9, 629. blowing myrrh and *b.*
P. L. 11, 546. and last consume the *b.* of life.
S. A. 186. as *b.* to festered wounds
S. A. 651. the close of all my miseries, and the *b.*
C. 674. with spirits of *b.*
**Balmy.**—P. L. 4. 159. they stole those *b.* spoils
P. L. 5, 23. what the *b.* reed
P. L. 8, 255. I found me laid, in *b.* sweat
P. L. 11, 706. wrapt in a *b.* cloud
C. 991. nard and cassia's *b.* smells
**Balsara.**—P. R. 3, 321. to *B.*'s haven
**Ban.**—P. L. 9, 925. under *b.* to touch
**Band.**—P. L. 1, 356. every squadron, and each *b.*
P. L. 1, 758. their summons called from every *b.*
P. L. 9, 431. upstays gently with myrtle *b.*
P. L. 11, 646. one way a *b.* select
P. R. 2, 236. a chosen *b.* of spirits
S. A. 1753. and all that *b.* them to resist
C. 904. to undo the charmèd *b.*
**Banded.**—P. L. 2, 320. *b.* against his throne
P. L. 5, 717. were *b.* to oppose his high decree
P. L. 6, 85. the *b.* powers of Satan
P. L. 6, 528. refulgent host soon *b.*
**Bandit.**—C. 426. no savage fierce, *b.*
**Bands.**—P. L. 1, 675. as when *b.* of pioneers
P. L. 2, 570. in squadrons and gross *b.*
P. L. 2, 615. *b.*, with shuddering horror pale
P. L. 2, 997. her victorious *b.* pursuing
P. L. 3, 511. angels ascending and descending, *b.*
P. L. 4, 684. oft in *b.* while they keep watch
P. L. 5, 287. all the *b.* of angels
P. L. 5, 651. dispersed in *b.* and files
P. L. 11, 208. for by this the heavenly *b.*
H. 228. can in His swaddling *b.* control
**Bane.**—P. L. 1, 692. best deserve the precious *b.*
P. L. 2, 808. a bitter morsel, and his *b.*
P. L. 4, 167. who came their *b.*
P. L. 9, 123. all good to me becomes *b.*
P. L. 10, 412. spreading their *b.*
S. A. 63, suffices that to me strength is my *b.*
S. A. 351. but often proved our woe, our *b.*
**Baneful.**—C. 525. gives his *b.* cup
**Banish.**—C. 413. and gladly *b.* squint suspicion
**Banished.**—P. L. 4, 317. *b.* from man's life
P. L. 4, 573. one of the *b.* crew I fear
P. L. 12, 619. who for my wilful crime art *b.*
C. 692. that thou hast *b.* from thy tongue
**Banishment.**—P. L. 11, 108. thence perpetual *b.*
**Bank.**—P. L. 4, 262. *b.* with myrtle crowned
P. L. 4, 334. *b.* damasked with flowers
P. L. 4, 458. laid me down on the green *b.*
P. L. 7, 408 *b.* the mid sea, part single
P. L. 8, 286. on a green shady *b.*
P. L. 9, 438. imbordered on each *b.*
P. L. 9, 1037. to a shady *b.*
P. R. 2, 25. then on the *b.* of Jordan
P. R. 4, 587. set him down on a green *b.*
S. A. 3. *b.* hath choice of sun or shade
C. 353. perhaps some cold *b.* is her bolster
C. 543. I sat me down to watch upon a *b.*
C. 890. by the rushy-fringèd *b.* where grows
**Banks.**—P. L. 1, 468. the fertile *b.* of Abbana

P. L. 2, 574. along the *b.* of four infernal
P. L. 7, 305. all but within those *b.*
P. R. 4, 32. of whose *b.* on each side
S. A. 1610. on *b.* and scaffolds under sky
C. 936. and here and there thy *b.* upon
C. 993. waters the odorous *b.*, that blow
A. 97. by sandy Ladon's lilied *b.*
M. W. 59. sent thee from the *b.* of Came
**Bannered.**—P. L. 2, 885. a *b.* host
**Banners.**—P. L. 1, 545. ten thousand *b.* rise
P. L. 5, 687. all who under me their *b* wave
**Banquet.**—P. L. 10, 688. from Thyestean *b.*
**Banquets.**—C. 701. Juno when she *b.*
**Baptism.**—P. R. 1, 21. to his great *b.* flocked
P. R. 1, 273. as all others to his *b.* came
P. R. 1, 278. refused on me his *b.* to confer
P. R. 2, 61. others returned from *b.*
**Baptist.**—P. R. 1, 25. him the *B.* soon descried
P. R. 1, 270. the *B.* of whose birth I oft had
P. R. 2, 2. remained at Jordan with the *B.*
P. R. 2, 84. I hear by John the *B.*
P. R. 4, 511. flocked to the *B.* I among the rest
**Baptized.**—P. L. 1, 582. *b.* or infidel
P. L. 12, 500. then on all *b.*
P. R. 1, 21. nigh at hand to all *b.*
P. R. 1, 29. on him *b.* heaven opened
P. R. 1, 76. himself among them was *b.*
P. R. 1, 184. in Bethabara, where John *b.*
P. R. 4, 512. though not to be *b.*
**Baptizing.**—P.L.12, 442. *b.* the profluent stream
P. R. 1, 328. whom late our new *b.* prophet
**Bar.**—P. L. 2, 877. *b.* of massy iron
P. L. 4, 585. spiritual substance corporeal *b.*
P. L. 4, 897. let him surer *b.* his iron gates
S. A. 147. the gates of Azza, post, and massy *b.*
S. 21, 3. which others at their *b.* so often
**Barbaric.**—P. L. 2, 4. showers on her kings *b.*
**Barbarous.**—P. L. 1, 353. when her *b.* sons
P. L. 7, 32. but drive far off the *b.* dissonance
P. R. 3, 119. or *B.*, nor exception hath declared
P. R. 4, 86. two thrones except, the rest are *b.*
C. 550. and filled the air with *b.* dissonance
S. 12, 3. when straight a *b.* noise environs me
**Barbed.**—P. L. 6, 546. arrows *b.* with fire
**Barber's.**—S. A. 1167. by the *b.*'s razor
**Barca.**—P. L. 2. unnumbered as the sands of *B.*
**Bard.**—P. L. 2, 909. that tore the Thracian *b.*
C. 45. from old or modern *b.*
**Bards.**—L. 53. your old *b.*, the famous Druids
Il P. 116. and if aught else great *b.* beside
**Bare.**—P. L. 1, 379. he stood on the *b.* strand
P. L. 1, 614. their stately growth, though *b.*
P. L. 3, 74. on the *b.* outside of this world
P. L. 7, 286. and their broad *b.* backs upheave
P. L. 7, 313. the *b.* earth, till then desert
P. L. 7, 314. till then desert and *b.* unsightly
P. L. 9, 1062. destitute and *b.* of. . their virtue
P. L. 10, 317. to the outside *b.* of this world
S. A. 902. *b.* in thy guilt
C. 614. he with his *b.* wand
S. 8, 14. to save the Athenian walls from ruin *b.*
**Bark.**—P. L. 2, 288. whose *b.* by chance or pinnace
P. L. 10, 1076. gummy *b.* of fir or pine
C. 354. or against the rugged *b.* of broad elm
L. 100. it was that fatal and perfidious *b.*
**Barked.**—P. L. 2, 654. hounds never ceasing *b.*
P. L. 2, 658. there still *b.* and howled
**Barking.**—C. 258. chid her *b.* waves
**Barn-door.**—L'A. 51. the stack or the *b-d.*
**Barons.**—L'A. 119. knights and *b.* bold.
**Barred.**—P. L. 2, 437. *b.* over us, prohibit all
P. L. 4, 967. the facile gates of hell too slightly *b.*
P. L. 9, 80. to the ocean *b.* at Darien
P. L. 12, 360. might be born *b.* of his right
C. 343. or if our eyes be *b.*
**Barren.**—P. L. 3, 437. lights on the *b.* plains
P. L. 5, 219. to adorn his *b.* leaves
P. L. 8, 94. the sun that *b.* shines
P. R. 1, 354. wandered this *b.* waste
P. R. 3, 264. was room for *b.* desert
L'A. 73. mountains on whose *b.* breast

**Barrenness** —P. L. 10, 1042. wilful *b.*
  S. A. 352. and thought *b.* in wedlock a reproach
  M. W. 64. who after years of *b.*
**Barricadoed.**—P. L. 8, 241. gates and *b.* strong
**Bars.**—P. L. 3, 82. no *b.* of Hell
  P. L. 4, 795. escaped the *b.* of Hell
  P. L. 8, 625. joint or limb, exclusive *b.*
  P. L. 10, 417 the *b.* assailed
**Basan.**—P. L. 1, 398. in Argob, and in *B.*
**Base.**—P. L. 9, 498. circular *b.* of rising folds
  P. R. 4, 132. that people.. now vile and *b.*
  S. A. 414. the *b.* degree
  S. A. 415. is not yet so *b.* as was my former
  C. 599. and earth's *b.* built on stubble
  C. 698. vizored falsehood and *b.* forgery
  C. 778. but with besotted *b.* ingratitude
**Base.**—H. 130. *b.* of Heaven's deep organ
  P. L. 9, 150. exalted from so *b.* original
**Baser.**—P. L. 2, 141. and purge off the *b.* fire
**Bases.**—P. L. 9, 36. *b.* and tinsel trappings
**Basest.**—P. L. 9, 171. obnoxious to *b.* things
**Basis.**—P. L. 6, 712. that shake Heaven's *b.*
  P. R. 4, 456. or to the Earth's dark *b.*
**Basks.**—L'A. 112. *b.* at the fire his strength
**Bastards.**—C. 727. and live like nature's *b.*
**Bate.**—S. 22, 7. nor *b.* a jot of heart or hope
**Bathe.**—C. 812. will *b.* the drooping spirits
**Bathed.**—P. L. 7, 437. on silver rivers *b.*
**Bathing.**—P. L. 2, 660. Scylla, *b.* in thee
**Baths.**—P. R. 4, 36. theatres, *b.,* aqueducts
**Battailous.**—P. L. 6, 81. in *b.* aspect
**Battalion.**—P. L. 1, 569. the whole *b.* views
  P. L. 6, 534. in slow but firm *b.*
**Battening.**—L. 29. *b.* our flocks
**Battering.**—P. L. 2, 923. with her *b.* engines
**Battery.**—P. L. 11, 656. by *b.,* scale, and mine
  P. R. 4, 20. (vain *b* !) and in froth or bubbles end
**Battle.**—P. L. 1, 43. war in heaven, and *b.* proud
  P. L. 1, 104. in dubious *b.*
  P. L. 1, 277. on the perilous edge of *b.*
  P. L. 1, 319. after the toil of *b.* to repose
  P. L. 1, 436. as low bowed down in *b.*
  P. L. 1, 553. heroes old arming to *b.*
  P. L. 2, 107. and *b.* dangerous to less than gods
  P. L. 2, 535. and armies rush to *b.* in the clouds
  P. L. 2, 550. and hapless fall by doom of *b.*
  P. L. 2, 899. to *b.* bring their embryon atoms
  P. L. 4, 12. his loss of that first *b.*
  P. L. 4, 927. when in *b.* to thy aid
  P. L. 5, 728. to try in *b.* what our power is
  P. L. 6, 46. lead forth to *b.* these my sons
  P. L. 6, 97. but the shout of *b.* now began
  P. L. 6, 108. on the rough edge of *b.*
  P. L. 6, 202. and fierce desire of *b.*
  P. L. 6, 235. or turn the sway of *b.*
  P. L. 6, 246. long time in even scale the *b.* hung
  P. L. 6, 386. the *b.* swerved
  P. L. 6, 798. to final *b.* drew disdaining flight
  P. L. 6, 802. this day from *b.* rest
  P. L. 6, 819. in *b.* which the stronger proves
  P. L. 10, 275. against the day of *b.*
  P. L. 10, 377. sway as *b.* hath adjudged
  P. L. 11, 644. single or in array of *b.* ranged
  P. L. 11, 691. to overcome in *b.* and subdue
  P. L. 11, 800. in sharp contest of *b.*
  P. R. 3, 20. subsist in *b.* though against thy few
  P. R. 3, 322. he saw them in their forms of *b.*
  S. A. 287. in that sore *b.* when so many died
  S. A. 583. thirst to allay after the brunt of *b.*
  S.A.1131. which greatest heroes have in *b.* worn
  C. 654. fierce sign of *b.* make
  H. 53. no war, or *b.'s* sound
**Battles.**—P. L. 4, 1002. all events, *b.* and realms
  P. L. 6, 216. together rushed both *b.* main
  P. L. 9, 31. fabled knights in *b.* feigned
  P. L. 12, 261. how many *b.* fought
  P. R. 3, 73. in field great *b.* win
  P. R. 3, 392. of enemies of aids, *b.* and leagues
**Battlements.**—P. L. 1, 742. the crystal *b.*
  P. L. 2, 1049. and *b.* adorned of living sapphire
  P. R. 4, 53. with gilded *b.,* conspicuous far

L'A. 77. towers and *b.* it sees
**Baulk.**—F. of C. 17. *b.* your ears
**Bawl.**—S. 12, 9. that *b.* for freedom
**Bay.**—P.L.2, 289. pinnace anchors in a craggy *b.*
  P. L. 7, 399. each creek and *b.*
  P. R. 2, 347. Pontus and Lucrine *b.*
  P. R. 3, 273. to south the Persian *b.*
  L.191.and now was dropped into the western *b.*
**Bayona's**—L. 162. Namancos and *B's* hold
**Bays.**—M. W. 57. some flowers and some *b.*
**Beach.**—P. L. 1, 299. *b.* of that inflamed sea
  P. L. 10, 299. the gathered *b.* they fastened
**Beads.**—P. L. 3, 491. *b.,* indulgences, dispenses
  C. 391. his few books or his *b.,* or maple dish
**Beaked.**—P. L. 11, 746. with *b.* prow rode tilting
  L. 94. that blows from off each *b.* promontory
**Beaks.**—P. R. 2, 267. ravens with their horny *b.*
**Beam.**—P. L. 2, 399. the brightening orient *b.*
  P. L. 2, 493. sweet extend his evening *b.*
  P. L. 3, 2. or of the eternal co-eternal *b.*
  P. L. 3, 583. or are turned by his magnetic *b.*
  P. L. 4, 590. returned on that bright *b.*
  P. L. 4, 1004. quick up flew, and kicked the *b.*
  P. L. 8, 139. part averse from the sun's *b.*
  S. A. 83. O first-created *b.*
  S. A. 163. puts forth no visual *b.*
  S. A. 1122. add thy spear, a weaver's *b.*
  C. 98. and the slope sun his upward *b.*
  C. 460. begin to cast a *b.* on the outward shape
**Beaming.**—P. L. 3, 625. of *b.* sunny rays
**Beams.**—P. L. 1, 596. shorn of his *b.*
  P. L. 3, 361. locks inwreathed with *b.*
  P. L. 3, 378. shadest the full blaze of thy *b.*
  P. L. 3, 551. rising sun gilds with his *b.*
  P. L. 3, 616. as when his *b.* at noon culminate
  P. L. 4, 37. to tell thee how I hate thy *b.*
  P. L. 4, 150. sun more glad impressed his *b.*
  P. L. 4, 644. he spreads his orient *b.*
  P. L. 6, 15. shot through with orient *b.*
  P. L. 6, 82. bristled with upright *b.* innumerable
  P. L. 7, 363. firm to retain her gathered *b.*
  P. L. 8, 97. his *b.,* unactive else
  P. L. 8, 255. with his *b.* the sun soon dried
  P. L. 9, 106. concentring all their precious *b.*
  P. L. 10, 1070. how we his gathered *b.* reflected
  P. R. 4, 432. with more effectual *b.*
  A. 16. shooting her *b.* like silver threads
  L.170. tricks his *b.,* and with new-spangled ore
  Il P. 132. the sun begins to fling his flaring *b.*
  S. 14, 10. with purple *b.* and azure wing
  H. 111. with long *b.* the shame-faced night
**Bear.**—P. L. 2, 209. if we can sustain and *b.*
  P. L. 2, 306. fit to *b.* the weight
  P. L. 2, 411. or what evasion *b.* him safe
  P. L. 3, 652. down to the earth *b.* his swift
  P. L. 4, 422. that *b.* delicious fruit
  P. L. 4, 473. to him shalt *b.* multitudes
  P. L. 5, 199. *b.* on your wings his praise
  P. L. 5, 427. ambrosial fruitage *b.*
  P. L. 5, 592. glittering tissues *b.* emblazed
  P. L. 5, 664. could not *b.* through pride that
  P. L. 6, 34. far worse to *b.* than violence
  P. L. 8, 375. find pastime and *b.* rule
  P. L. 8, 614. *b.* with me then if lawful
  P. L. 9, 104. *b.* their bright officious lamps
  P. L. 10, 155. unseemly to *b.* rule
  P. L. 10, 726. would *b.* my own deservings
  P. L. 10, 835. heavier than the earth to *b.*
  P. L. 10, 916. reverence in my heart I *b.* thee
  P. L. 10, 950. *b.* thine own first
  P. L. 11, 363. by moderation either state to *b.*
  P. L. 11, 766. each day's lot enough to *b.*
  P. L. 11, 776. grievous to *b.*
  P. L. 11, 804. earth shall *b.* more than enough
  P. R. 1, 13. and *b.* through height or depth
  P. R. 1, 135. that she should *b.* a son
  S. A. 190. who friends *b.* in their superscription
  S.A.913. what remains past cure *b.* too sensibly
  S. A. 1353. more.. than thou well wilt *b.*
  C. 70. into some brutish form of wolf or *b.*
  C. 658. and some good angel *b.* a shield before us

Il P. 87. where I may oft outwatch the *B.*
S. 19, 11. who best *b.* his mild yoke
H. 84. or burning axle-tree could *b.*
H. 220. sable-stoled sorcerers *b.* his worshipt
P. 39. to *b.* me where the towers of Salem stood
Cir. 6. if sad share with us to *b.*
S. A. 150. whom the Gentiles feign to *b.*
S. A. 239. **I *b.* thee witness.**
S. 22, 8. but still *b.* up and steer
**Bearded.**—P. L. 4, 982. her *b.* grove of ears
P. L. 5, 342. *b.* husk, or shell
C. 71. ounce or tiger, hog, or *b.* goat
**Bearers.** U. C. II. 20. to make six *b.*
**Bearest.**—P. L. 10, 952. my displeasure *b.* so ill
P. R. 4, 199. thou *b.* that title
S. A. 430. and thou *b.* enough, and more
S. A. 1100. of whom thou *b.* the highest name
**Bearing.**—P. L. 12, 311. his name and office *b.*
S. A. 655. and to the *b.* well of all calamities
S. A. 947. *b.* my words and doings to the lords
C. 835. *b.* her straight to aged Nereus' hall
**Bears.**—P. L. 3, 558. star that *b.* Andromeda
P. L. 4, 344. *b.* tigers, ounces, pards
P. L. 5, 368. what the garden choicest *b.*
P. L. 8, 166. and *b.* thee soft
P. L. 12, 241. now Moses in figure *b.*
P. R. 2, 466. all this weight he *b.*
P. R. 4, 517. which *b.* no single sense
S. A. 57. to subserve where wisdom *b.*
S. A. 755. how far urged his patience *b.*
S. A. 974. *b.* greatest names in his wild flight
S. A. 1303. a sceptre or quaint staff he *b.*
**Bearth.**—P. L. 9, 624. disburden nature of her *b.*
**Beast.**—P. L. 4, 177. all path of man or *b.*
P. L. 4, 600. *b.* and bird
P. L. 4, 704. bird, *b.,* insect, or worm
P. L. 7, 452. *b.* of the earth
P. L. 7, 457. the wild *b.,* where he wons
P. L. 7, 495. subtlest *b.* of all the field
P. L. 7, 503. by fowl, fish, *b.,* was flown
P. L. 7, 522. *b.* of the field, and over all
**P. L. 8** 341. in sea or air. *b.,* fish and fowl
P. L. 8, 342. in sign whereof, each bird and *b.*
P. L. 8, 349. each bird and *b.* behold
P. L. 8. 395. bird with *b.,* or fish with fowl
P. L. 8. 397. worse, then, can man with *b.*
P. L. 8, 582. vouchsafed to cattle and each *b.*
P. L. 9, 86. subtlest *b.* of all the field
P. L. 9, 165. am now constrained into a *b.*
P. L. 9, 521. from every *b.,* more duteous
P. L. 9, 560. subtlest *b.* of all the field
P. L. 9, 691. to the *b.* is open
P. L. 9, 769. that one *b.* which first hath
P. L. 10, 176. each *b.* of the field
P. L. 10, 604. on each *b,* next and fish
P. L. 10, 710. *b.* now with *b.* gan war
P. L. 11, 183. gave signs impressed on bird, *b.*
P. L. 11, 187. the *b.* that reigns
P. L. 11, 733. provisions for man and *b.*
P. L. 11, 734. every *b.* and bird and insect
P. L. 11, 822. man and *b.* select for life
P. L. 11, 895. with man therein or *b.*
P. L. 12, 67. over *b.,* fish, fowl, dominion
P. R. 4, 461. on man, *b,* plant
S. A. 37. strength, put to the labour of a *b.*
S. A. 127. or fiercest wild *b.* could withstand
S. A. 1403. through their streets like a wild *b*
C. 528. and the inglorious likeness of a *b.*
**Beasts.**—P. L. 4, 341. all *b.* of the earth
P. L. 8, 438. knowing not of *b.* alone
P. L. 8, 594. among the *b.* no mate for **thee**
P. L. 9, 94. which, in other *b.* observed
P. L. 9, 543. in this enclosure wild, these *b.*
P. L. 9, 556. I thought denied to *b.,* whom God
P. L. 9, 571. I was at first as other *b.* that graze
P. L. 9, 592. all other *b.* that saw
P. L. 9, 768. for *b.* reserved? for *b.* it **seems**
P. L. 10, 217. with skins of *b.*
P. L. 10, 221. with the skins of *b.*
P. L. 12, 30. and men, not *b.* shall be his game
**P. R. 1,** 310. hungered .. among wild *b.*

P. R. 1, 502. and now wild *b.* came forth
P. R. 2, 342. *b.* of chase, or fowl of game
P. R. 4, 140. fighting *b.,* and men to *b.* exposed
**Beat.**—P. L. 2, 588. *b.* with perpetual storms
P. L. 11, 446. with a stone that *b.* out life
P. R. 4, 17. *b.* off returns as oft with humming
C. 143. come knit hands, and *b.* the ground
**Beaten.**—P. L. 2, 1026. a broad and *b.* way
**Beatific.**—P. L. 1, 684. enjoyed in vision *b.*
**Beatitude.**—P. L. 3, 62 received *b.*
**Beauteous.**—P. L. 4, 697. each *b.* flower
P. L. 11, 613. a *b.* offspring shall beget
P. L. 6. 481. so *b.,* opening to the ambient light
**Beauties.**—P. R. 2, 197. all the *b.* of the east
D. F. I. 31. or that thy *b.* lie in wormy bed
**Beauty.**—P. L. 4, 490. how *b.* is excelled
P. L. 4, 498. in delight both of her *b.*
P. L. 4, 634. Eve, with perfect *b.* adorned
P. L. 4, 713. in naked *b.* more adorned
P. L. 4, 845. severe in youthful *b.*
P. L. 5, 14. *b.,* which, whether waking or asleep
P. L. 5. 47. attracted by thy *b.* still to gaze
P. L. 8, 533. the charm of *b.'s* powerful glance
P. L. 9, 491. though terror be in love and *b.*
P. L. 9, 540. thy celestial *b.*
P. L. 9, 607. and in thy *b.'s* heavenly ray united
P. L. 9, 1029. never did thy *b.,* since the day
P. L. 11, 539. thy strength, thy *b.*
P. R. 2, 186. to way-lay some *b.* rare
P. R. 2, 194. made small account of *b.*
P. R. 2, 212. queen ador'd on *B.'s* throne
P. R. 2, 220. *B.* stands in the admiration
S. A. 1003. *B.* hath strange power
C. 393. but *B.* like the fair Hesperian tree
C. 739. *b.* is Nature's coin, must not be hoarded
C. 745. *b.* is Nature's brag, and must be shown
L. 149. bid Amaranthus all his *b.* shed
L'A. 79. where perhaps some *b.* lies
Il P. 20. to set her *b.'s* praise above
**Became.**—P. L. 11, 165. *b.* thy snare
P. L. 11, 420. all his spirits *b.* entranced
**Becamest.**—P. L. 2, 765. *b.* enamoured
P. L. 7, 528. and thou *b.* a living soul
**Because.**—P. L. 3, 305. *b.* thou hast
P. L. 3, 311. *b.* in thee love hath abounded
P. L. 5, 539. freely we serve, *b.*
P. L. 6, 814. all their rage, *b.* the Father
P. L. 7, 168. *b.* I am who fill infinitude
P. L. 9, 280. *b.* we have a foe
P. L. 10, 51. vain and void, *b.* not yet inflicted
P. L. 10, 175. *b.* thou hast done this
P. L. 10, 198. *b.* thou hast hearkened
P. L. 11, 197. *b.* from death released
P. R. 1, 144. *b.* he boasts
P. R. 2, 174. *b.* of old thou thyself doatest
P. R. 4, 156. how slight thou valuest, *b.* offered
S. A. 1265. yet so it may fall out, *b.* their end
S. A. 1402. *b.* they shall not trail me
**Beck.**—P. R. 2, 238. at his *b.* appear
**Beckoning.**—C. 207. *b.* shadows dire
**Becks.**—L'A. 28. nods and.. *b.* and wreathed smiles
**Become.**—P. L. 2, 275. *b.* our elements
P. L. 2, 445. but I should ill *b.* this throne
P. L. 9, 716. that man may not *b.* as they
P. L. 9, 869. and is *b.,* not dead
P. L. 9, 1181. that error, .. which is *b.* my crime
P. L. 10, 120. now *b.* so dreadful to thee
P. L. 10, 722. who now *b.* accursed of blessed
P. L. 11, 84. O sons, like one of us man is *b.*
P. L. 12, 275. what would *b.* of me and all mankind
S. A. 73, inferior to the vilest now *b.*
S. A. 155. thou art *b.* (O worst imprisonment)
**Becomes.**—P. L. 5, 843. thus reduced *b.*
P. L. 9, 122. all good to me *b.* bane
P. L. 11, 61. *b.* his final remedy
P. L. 12, 409. his obedience, imputed, *b.* theirs
P. R. 1, 288, but openly begin, as best *b.*
P. R. 3, 103. the deed *b.* unpraised
**Bed.**—P. L. 4, 710. decked first her nuptial *b.*
P. L. 4, 761. whose *b.* is undefiled
P. L. 7, 290. capacious *b.* of waters

P. L. 8, 598. higher of the genial *b.* by far
S. A. 806. wailing thy absence in my widowed *b.*
S. A. 1021. successor in thy *b.*
C. 107. rigour now is gone to *b.*
C. 886. from thy coral-paven *b,*
L. 168. so sinks the day-star in the ocean *b.*
L'A. 115. thus done the tales, to *b.* they creep
L'A. 146. from golden slumber on a *b.*
H. 229. so when the sun in *b.*
D. F. I. 13. of long uncoupled *b.* and childlesseld
D. F. I. 31. or that thy beauties lie in wormy *b.*
M. W 42. sideways as on a dying *b.*
U. C. I. 18. Hobson's newly gone to *b.*
U. C. II. 17. on his swooning *b.* outstretched
Vac. Ex. 63. and sweetly singing round thy *b.*
**Bedecked.**—S. A. 712. that so *b.,* ornate, and gay
**Bed-rid.**—S. A. 579. better at home lie *b.-r.*
**Bedropt.**—P. L. 10, 527. the soil *b.* with blood
**Beds.**—P. L. 2, 600. from *b.* of raging fire
P. L. 4, 242. in *b.* and curious knots
C. 998. *b.* of hyacinth and roses
L'A. 21. there, on *b.* of violets blue
**Bedward.**—P. L. 4, 352. or *b.* ruminating
**Bee.**—P. L. 5, 24. how the *b.* sits on the bloom
P. L. 7, 490. next appeared the female *b.*
Il P. 142. while the *b,* with honied thigh
**Beëlzebub.**—P. L. 1, 81. and named *B.*
P. L. 1, 271. and him *B.* thus answered
P. L. 2, 299. which when *B.* perceived
P. L. 2, 378. thus *B.* pleaded his devilish counsel
**Beërsaba.**—P. L. 3, 536. Jordan's flood to *B.*
**Bees.**—P. L. 1, 768. as *b.* in spring time
P. R. 4, 248. *b.'* industrious murmur
**Beeves.**—P. L. 11, 647. a herd of *b.,* fair oxen
**Befall.**—P. L. 4, 127. more than could *b.*
P. L. 7, 44. lest the like *b.* in Paradise to Adam
P. L. 9, 252. lest harm *b.* thee, severed from me
P. L. 9, 1182. thus it shall *b.* him
P. L. 10, 896. and more that shall *b.*
P. L. 11, 771. what shall *b* him or his children
P. L. 12, 444. and in mind prepared, if so *b.*
**Befallen.**—P. L. 2, 821. dire change *b.* us
P. L. 9, 771. brings with joy the good *b.* him
P. L. 10, 895. this mischief had not then *b.*
P. L. 10, 928. thy hatred for this misery *b.*
P. L. 11, 450. mischief hath *b.* to that meek
S. A. 374. nothing of all these evils hath *b.* me
S. A. 447. *b.* thee and thy father's house
**Befell.**—P. L. 6, 897. the discord which *b.*
P. L. 7, 43. by what *b.* in heaven
P. L. 8, 229. for I that day was absent as *b.*
P. L. 10, 28. to hear and know how all *b.*
P. L. 11, 716. marrying or prostituting, as *b.*
**Befit.**—P. 27. me softer airs *b.* and softer strings
**Befits.**—P. L. 10, 868. that name best *b.* thee
A. 92. clad in splendour as *b.* her deity
**Beforehand.**—P. R. 4, 8. *b.* had no better
P. R. 4, 526. if I *b.* seek to understand
**Befriend.**—C. 135. *b.* us thy vowed priests
P. 29. *b.* me, Night. best patroness of grief
V. Ex. 59. good luck *b.* thee, son
**Beg.**—P. L. 10, 918. thy suppliant I *b.* and clasp
P. L. 10, 1089. confess and pardon *b.*
P. L. 11, 506. or soon *b.* to lay it down
P. R. 4, 630. *b.* to hide them in a herd of swine
S. A. 707. what do I *b.,* how hast thou dealt
C. 623. and oft would *b.* me sing
**Began.**—P. L. 1, 83. breaking silence, thus *b.*
P. L. 1, 798. the great consult *b.*
P. L. 2, 118. and with persuasive accent thus *b.*
P. L. 2, 680. with disdainful look, thus first *b.*
**P. L. 3.** 355. fast by the tree of life *b.* to bloom
P. L. 4, 31. tnen much revolving, thus in sighs *b.*
P. L. 4, 537. and *b.,* through wood
P. L. 4, 560. he thus *b.* in haste
P. L. 4, 979. and *b.* to hem him round
P. L. 5, 144. lowly they bowed adoring, and *b.*
P. L. 5, 152. they thus *b.*
P. L. 5, 369. when thus *b.*
P. L. 5, 562. after short pause assenting, thus *b.*
P. L. 6, 56. and clouds *b.* to darken all the hill

P. L. 6, 97. but the shout of battle now *b.*
P. L. 6, 261. and visage all inflamed, first thus *b.*
P. L. 6, 406. now Night her course *b.*
P. L. 6, 417. in the midst, thus undismayed *b.*
P. L. 6, 679. Assessor of his throne, he thus *b.*
P. L. 6, 748. the third sacred morn *b.*
P. L. 7, 63. earth conspicuous first *b.*
P. L. 7, 86. how first *b.* this heaven
P. L, 7, 246. through the aery gloom *b.*
P. L. 7, 636. world and face of things *b.*
P. L. 8, 250. for man to tell how human life *b.*
P. L. 9, 192. whenas sacred light *b.* to dawn
P. L. 9, 204. Eve first to her husband thus *b.*
P. L. 9, 531. his fraudulent temptation thus *b.*
P. L. 9, 675. *b.,* as no delay of preface brooking
P. L. 9, 678. the Tempter all impassion'd thus *b.*
P. L. 9, 794. thus to herself she pleasingly *b.*
P. L. 9, 1014. on Eve *b.* to cast lascivious
P. L. 9, 1123. high winds worse within *b.*
P. L. 10, 234. who thus now to death *b.*
P. L. 10, 590. to whom sin thus *b.*
P. L. 10, 706. *b.* outrage from lifeless things
P. L. 11, 21. thus to intercede *b.*
P. L. 11, 729. *b.* to build a vessel of huge bulk
P. L. 12, 636. *b.* to parch that temperate clime
P. R. 1, 499. now *b.*... with her sullen wing
P. R. 2, 11. *b.* to doubt and doubted many
P. R. 2, 120. solicitous and blank, he thus *b.*
P. R. 3, 266. and new train of words *b*
P. R. 4, 311. how the world *b.*
C. 545. *b.,* wrapped in a pleasing fit
H. 63. his reign of peace upon the earth *b.*
**Beget.**—P. L. 8, 423. to *b.* like of his like
P. L. 9, 95. doubt might *b.* of diabolic power
P. L. 10, 728. or shall *b.,* is propagated curse
P. L. 10, 762. retort wherefore didst thou *b.*
P. L. 11, 613. a beauteous offspring shall *b.*
C. 669. that fancy can *b.* on youthful thoughts.
**Beggary.**—S. A. 69. *b.,* or decrepit age
**Begged.**—P. L. 10, 1101. pardon *b.*
**Begging.**—P. L. 4, 104. *b.* peace
**Begin.**—P. L. 4, 832. *b.* your message
P. L. 6, 278. avenging sword *b.* thy doom
P. L. 8, 162. from the east his flaming road *b.*
P. L. 9, 669. some great matter to *b.*
P. L. 9, 1142. conclude they then *b.* to fail
P. L. 10, 213. disdained not to *b.*
P. L. 11, 633. from woman to *b.*
P. L. 12, 6. thus thou hast seen one world *b.*
P. R. 1, 132. I *b.* to verify that solemn message
P. R. 1, 186. the mighty work he might *b.*
P. R. 1, 288. but openly *b.,* as best becomes
P. R. 2, 113. how to *b.,* how to accomplish best
P. R. 3, 185. so, when *b.* the Father
P. R. 3, 198. what concerns it thee when I *b.*
P. R. 4, 540. another method I must now *b.*
P. R. 4, 635. now enter and *b.* to save mankind
S. A. 225. I might *b.* Israel's deliverance
S. A. 274. if he aught *b.*
S. A. 1381. I *b.* to feel some rousing motions.
C. 125. come, let us our rites *b.*
C. 206. a thousand fantasies *b.* to throng
C. 460. *b.* to cast a beam on the outward
L. 15. b. then, Sisters of the sacred well
L. 17. *b.,* and somewhat loudly
L'A. 41. to hear the lark *b.* his flight
Cir. 13. our sin sore doth *b.*
**Beginning.**—P. L. 1, 9. in the *b.*
P. L. 3, 633. his journey's end, and our *b.*
P. L. 7, 638. done from the *b.*
P. L. 8, 251. for who himself *b.* knew
P. L. 9, 26. long choosing and *b* late
P. R. 1, 408. composed of lies from the *b.*
P. R. 4, 99. appearing, and *b.* noble deeds
P. R. 4, 392. as without end, without *b.*
**Begins.**—P. L. 2, 1037. here Nature first *b.*
P. L. 4, 15. *b.* his dire attempt
P. L. 5, 559. and scarce *b.* his other half
P. L. 10, 1064. the sky with various face *b.*
P. L. 11, 174. *b.* her rosy progress
P. L. 11, 634. man's effeminate slackness it *b.*

P. R. 3, 179. the happier reign the sooner it *b.*
L'A. 60. where the great sun *b.* his state
Il P. 132. and when the sun *b.* to fling
H. 167. but now *b.*, for from this happy day
**Begirt.**—P. L. 1, 581. *b.* with British
P. L. 5, 868. and to *b.* the almighty throne
P. R. 2, 213. with all her winning charms *b.*
**Begot.**—P. L. 2, 794. *b.* these yelling monsters
P. L. 5, 603. this day I have *b.* whom I declare
P. L. 10, 765. natural necessity *b.*
P. L. 12, 286. among them, as of thee *b.*
P. R. 2, 181. coupled with them, and *b.* a race
**Begotten.**—P. L. 2, 782. thine own *b.*
P. L. 3, 80. only *b.* Son seest thou what rage
P. L. 3, 384. *b.* Son, divine similitude
P. L 5, 835. equal to him *b.* Son
P. L. 7, 163. and thou my word, *b.* Son by thee
P. L. 10, 983. our own *b.*
**Beguiled.**—P. L. 1, 445. *b.* by fair idolatresses
P. L. 3, 689. which now for once *b.* Uriel
P. L. 9, 905. enemy hath *b.* thee
P. L. 10, 162. the serpent me *b.*, and I did eat
P. L. 10, 880. fooled and *b.*
P. R. 2, 169. women *b.* the heart
S. A. 759. that wisest and best men, full oft *b.*
P. 54. grief is easily *b.*
**Begun.**—P.L.7,93.the work *b.*,how soon absolved
P. L. 8, 311. here had new *b.* my wandering
P. L. 9, 224. brought to little, though *b.* early
P. L. 10, 811. which I feel *b.* both in me
**Behalf.**—P. L. 3, 218. on man's *b.*
P. L. 11, 102. or in *b.* of man, or to invade
**Beheld.**—P. L. 1, 309. *b.* from the safe shore
P. L. 1, 607. far other once *b.* in bliss
P. L. 3, 64. he first *b.* our two first parents
P. L. 3, 554. at sight of all this world *b.* so fair
P. L. 4, 117. if any eye *b.*
P. L. 4, 723. earth and heaven, which they *b.*
P. L. 5, 13. *b.* beauty
P. L. 5, 87. underneath *b.* the earth
P. L. 5, 219. *b.* heaven's high king
P. L. 6, 607. Satan *b.* their plight
P. L. 6, 681. invisible is *b.* visibly
P. L. 6, 825. too severe to be *b.*
P. L. 7, 137. from his throne *b.* their multitude
P. L. 7, 255. exhaling first from darkness they *b.*
P. L. 8, 284. I first drew air and first *b.*
P. L. 9, 541. beauty adore with ravishment *b.*
P. L. 9, 541. best *b.*, where universally admired
P. L. 9, 608. united I *b.*
P. L. 9, 1082. with joy and rapture so oft *b.*
P. L. 10, 454. and whom they wished *b.*
P. L. 10, 863. when sad Eve *b.*
P. L. 11, 429. his eyes he opened, and *b.* a field
P. L. 12, 641. all the eastern side *b.*
P. R. 1, 295. looking round, on every side *b.*
P. R. 2, 31. our eyes *b.* Messiah
P. R. 2, 338. our Saviour lifting up his eyes *b.*
S.A.1543. which erst my eyes *b.*, and yet behold
S. A. 1642. not without wonder or delight *b.*
**Beheldest.**—P. L. 11, 700. whom thou *b.*
P. L. 11, 819. a wondrous ark as thou *b.*
**Behemoth.**—P.L. 7,471 *B.*, biggest born of earth
**Behest.**—P. L. 5, 311. some great *b.* from heaven
P. L. 11, 99. this my *b.* have thou in charge
P. L. 11, 251. Heaven's high *b.* no preface
**Behests.**—P. L. 3, 533. on high *b.* his angels
P. L. 6, 185. his divine *b.* obey
P. L. 8, 238. us he sends upon his high *b.*
**Behind.**—P. L. 1, 286. his shield,... *b.* him cast
P. L. 1, 446. Thammuz came next *b.*
P. L. 1, 596. or from *b.* the moon
P. L. 2, 120. as not *b.* in hate
P. L. 3, 626. nor less his locks *b.* illustrious
P. L. 5, 119. and leave no spot or blame *b.*
P. L. 6, 578. at each *b.* a seraph stood
P. L. 6, 864. but far worse urged them *b.*
P. L. 9, 277. as in a shady nook I stood *b.*
P. L. 10, 266. I shall not lag *b.*
P. L. 10, 588. *b.* her Death
P. L. 12, 205. remove *b.* them

P. R. 2, 46. and *b.* them cast all fear of thee
P. R. 3, 78. who leave *b.* nothing but ruin
P. R. 3, 323. and flying *b.* them shot sharp sleet
P. R. 3, 423. a race *b.* like to themselves
P. R. 4, 193. get thee *b.* me
S. A. 360. draw a scorpion's tail *b.*
S. A. 721. a damsel train *b.*
S.A.858.the priest was not *b.*,but ever at my ear
S. A. 1300. yet, perhaps, more trouble is *b.*
S. A. 1375. and man prefer, set God *b.*
S.A.1618. both horse and foot,before him and *b.*
S. 14, 6. stayed not *b.*
**Behold.**—P.L.1,605.to *b.* the fellows of his crime
P. L. 1, 777. till the signal given, *b.* a wonder!
P. L. 2, 959. straight, *b.* the throne of Chaos
P. L. 2, 1046. at leisure to *b.*
P. L. 3, 78. wherein past, .. her *b.*
P. L. 3, 236. *b.* me then, me for him
P. L. 3, 387. whom else no creature can *b.*
P. L. 3, 672. gaze or open admiration, him *b.*
P. L. 4, 105. *b.*, instead of us outcast, exiled
P. L. 4, 358. what do mine eyes with grief *b.*
P. L. 4, 679. with ceaseless praise his works *b.*
P. L. 4, 821. so sudden to *b.* the grisly king
P. L. 5, 45. whom to *b.* but thee
P. L. 5, 161. angels, for ye *b.* him
P. L. 5, 308. and worth thy sight, *b.*
P. L. 5, 605. whom ye now *b.* at my right hand
P. L. 5, 719. Son, thou in whom my glory I *b.*
P. L. 5, 866. then thou shalt *b.*
P. L. 6, 550. when, *b.* not distant far
P. L. 6, 637. *b.* the excellence, the power
P. L. 6, 810. and *b.* God's indignation
P. L. 7, 86. this heaven, which we *b.*
P. L. 7, 222. to *b.* creation, and the wonders
P. L. 7, 539. delectable both to *b.* and taste
P. L. 7, 549. and *b.*, all was entirely good
P. L. 7, 554. thence to *b.* this new-created world
P. L. 8, 15. when I *b.* this goodly frame
P. L. 8, 342. each bird and beast *b.*
P. L. 8, 349. each bird and beast *b.* approaching
P. L. 8, 481. when out of hope, *b.* her not far off
P. L. 8, 529. transported I *b.*, transported touch
P. L. 8, 605, harmony to *b.* in wedded pair
P. L. 9, 455, pleasure took the serpent to *b.*
P. L. 9, 480, *b.* alone the woman
P. L. 9, 576. a goodly tree far distant to *b.*
P. L. 9, 735. which to *b.* might tempt alone
P. L. 9, 1080. how shall I *b.* the face of God
P. L. 10, 81. none are to *b.* the judgment
P. L. 10, 326. *b.* Satan in likeness of an angel
P. L. 10, 724. whom to *b.* was then my height
P. L. 11, 110. for I *b.* them softened
P. L. 11, 332. I now gladly *b.* though but his
P. L. 11, 423. now ope thine eyes, and first *b.*
P. L. 11, 464. foul and ugly to *b.*
P. L. 11, 495. what heart of rock.. dry-eyed *b.*
P. L. 11, 581. when from the tents *b.* a bevy
P. L. 11, 711. direct thine eyes and soon *b.*
P. L. 11, 754. to *b.* the end of all thy offspring
P. L. 11, 839. what farther shall ensue, *b.*
P. L. 12, 142. each place *b.* in prospect
P. R. 1, 130. this day by proof, thou shalt *b.*
P. R. 1, 269. when *b.* the Baptist
P. R. 1, 386. to hear attent thy wisdom, and *b.*
P. R. 2, 44. *b.* the kings of the earth
P. R. 2, 331. *b.*, Nature ashamed
P. R. 3, 293. with easy eye thou may'st *b.*
P. R. 4, 26. whence he might *b.* another plain
P. R. 4, 57. thou may'st *b.*, outside and inside
P. R. 4, 237. much nearer by south-west, *b.*
P. R. 4, 435. all things now *b.* more fresh
S.A.206. immeasurable strength they might *b.*
S. A. 339. as erst in highest *b.* him where he lies
S. A. 708. *b.* him in this state calamitous
S. A. 741. desirous to *b.* once more thy face
S. A. 1473. doubtless the people shouting to *b.*
S. A. 1543. erst my eyes beheld, and yet *b.*
S. A. 1608. of sort might sit in order to *b.*
S. A. 1645. with amaze shall strike all who *b.*
C. 672. *b.* this cordial julep here

C. 968. here *b.* so goodly grown
A. 40. where ye may more near *b.*
Il. P. 67. to *b.* the wandering moon
**Beholders.**—P. L. 9, 544. among *b.* rude
**Beholdest.**—P. R. 3, 269. here thou *b.* Assyria
P. R. 4, 162. which in a moment thou *b.*
**Beholding**—P. L. 3, 77. him God *b.* from
P. L. 5, 329. as he *b.* shall confess that here
P. L. 12, 50. them *b.* soon, comes down
**Beholds.**—P. L. 1, 323. who now *b.* cherub
P. L. 3, 78. wherein past, present, future, he *b.*
P. L. 6, 472. who *b.* the bright surface
P. L. 11, 864. over his head *b.* a dewy cloud
**Behoof**—P. L. 2, 982. brings it to your *b.*
D. F. I. 45. careful Jove in Nature's true *b.*
**Behoves**—P. L. 2, 942. *b.* him now both ear
P. L. 4, 931. what *b.*, from hard assays
**Being.**—P. L. 2, 98. to have eternal *b.*
P. L. 2, 147. who would lose this intellectual *b.*
P. L. 2, 440. with utter loss of *b.* threatens him
P. L. 2, 865. thou my *b.* gavest me
P. L. 3, 374. thee Author of all *b.*
P. L. 4, 483. *b.* I lent out of my side
P. L. 4, 455. of their *b.* who dwell in heaven
P. L. 5, 487. reason is her *b.*
P. L. 5, 825. and circumscribed their *b.*
P. L. 5, 858. while the Maker gave thee *b.*
P. L. 8, 174. what concerns thee and thy *b.*
P. L. 8, 294. to believe I yet had *b.*
P. L. 9. 266. faithful side that gave thee *b.*
P. L. 10, 747. as my will concurred not to my *b.*
P. L. 10, 988. to *b.* yet unbegot
P. L. 11, 769. to torment me ere their *b.*
P. L. 12, 85. that no dividual *b.*
P. R. 1, 62. and our *b.* in this fair empire won
C. 8. to keep up a frail and feverish *b.*
C. 469. the divine property of her first *b.*
**Belated.**—P.L. 1, 783. *b.* peasant sees or dreams
**Belched.**—P. L. 1, 671. *b.* fire and rolling smoke
P. L. 6, 586. from those deep-throated engines *b.*
**Belching.**—P. L. 10, 232. *b.* outrageous flame
**Beldam.**—V. Ex. 46. *b.* Nature in her cradle was
**Belial.**—P. L. 1, 490. *B.* came last, than when
P. L. 1, 502. then wander forth the sons of *B.*
P. L. 2, 109. *B.* in act more graceful
P. L. 2, 226. *B.* with words clothed in reasons
P. L. 6, 620. *B.* in like gamesome mood
P. R. 2, 150. when from amidst them rose *B.*
P. R. 2, 173. *B.*, in much uneven scale
**Belief.**—P. L. 8, 136. which needs not thy *b.*
P. L. 9, 719. advantage use on our *b.*
S. A. 117. O change beyond report thought, or *b.*
S. A. 1535. would fain subscribe and tempts *b.*
P. 31. work my flattered fancy to *b.*
**Believe.**—P. L. 1, 144. I now of force *b.* almighty
P. L. 1, 631. who can yet *b.* though after loss
P. L. 8, 294. moved my fancy to *b.* I yet had
P. L. 9, 684. do not *b.* those rigid threats
P. L. 11, 146. hard to *b.* may seem
P. L. 11, 355. which that thou may'st *b.*
P. L. 12, 116. O that men (canst thou *b.*) should
P. L. 12, 407. life to all who shall *b.*
P. L. 12, 441. them who shall *b.* baptizing
S. A. 599. *b.* not these suggestions
S. A. 830. weakness is thy excuse, and I *b.* it
C. 216. I see ye visibly, and now *b.*
C. 438. do ye *b.* me yet or shall I call
V. Ex. 12. *b.* me I have thither packed
**Believed.**—P. R. 1, 274. I *b.* was from above
P. R. 2, 5. and on that high authority had *b.*
**Believers.**—P. L. 12, 520. given to all *b.*
**Believes.**—P. L. 12, 127. yet firm *b.*
**Believest.**—P. L. 6, 471. thou aright *b.*
**Believing.**—P. L. 10, 42. *b.* lies against his Maker
**Belike.**—P. L. 2, 156. *b.* through impotence
**Bellerophon.**—P. L. 7, 18. as once *B.*
**Bellerus.**—L. 160. sleepest by the fable of *B.* old
**Bellies.**—L. 114. such for their *b.'* sake
**Bellman's**—Il P. 83. the *b.'s* drowsy charm
**Bellona.**—P. L. 2, 922. than when *B.* storms
**Bellow.**—P. L. 1, 177. to *b.* through the vast

**Bellowing.**—P. L. 6, 362. fled *b.*
**Bells.**—L. 135. and bid them hither cast their *b.*
L'A. 93. when the merry *b.* ring round
**Belly.**—P. L. 10, 177. upon thy *b.* grovelling
P. L. 10, 514. on his *b.* prone
**Belong.**—P. L. 5, 167. if better thou *b.* not to the
P. L. 11, 163. ill-worthy I such title should *b.* to
**Belonged.**—P. L. 3, 111. as to right *b.*
**Belongs.**—P. L. 6, 807. to other hand *b.*
P. L. 10, 84. conviction to the serpent none *b.*
P. L. 10, 496. that which to me *b.* is enmity
P. L. 11, 166. to me reproach rather *b.*
P. R. 3, 135. to whom nothing *b.*
P. R. 3, 141. to God alone of right *b.*
C. 84. that to the service of this house *b.*
L. 121. that to the faithful herdman's art *b.*
**Beloved.**—P. L. 6 680. Son *b.!* Son
P. L. 10, 70. in me, thy Son *b.*
P. L. 10, 489. given up both his *b.* man
P. L. 12, 308. though of God highly *b.*
P. R. 1, 32. pronounced, him his *b.* Son
P. R. 1, 85. this is my Son *b.*, in him am pleased
P. R. 1, 285. me his *b.* Son, in whom alone
P. R. 1, 379. lost to be *b.* of God, I have not lost
P. R. 4, 513. thee pronounced the Son of God *b.*
**Below.**—P.L. 3, 600. or like to that, which here *b.*
P. L. 11, 368. here sleep *b.*, while thou to
C. 734. that they *b.* would grow inured to light
Il P. 162. to the full-voiced **choir** *b.*
H. 90. was kindly come to live with them *b.*
D. B. 49. amongst us here *b.*
D. F. I. 64. O why didst thou not stay here *b.*
V. Ex. 80. being above them, he shall be *b.*
**Belus.**—P. L. 1, 720. *B.* or Serapis, their gods
**Bench.**—S. 21, 1. the royal *b.* of British Themis
**Bend.**—P. L. 1, 616. doubled ranks they *b.*
P. L. 2, 354. thither let us *b.* all our thoughts
P. L. 2, 477. they *b.* with awful reverence
P. L. 2, 573. *b.* four ways their flying march
P. L. 2, 729. *b.* that mortal dart against
P. L. 5, 787. and choose to *b.* the supple knee
P. L. 5, 817. in heaven shall *b.* the knee
P. L. 11, 30. *b.* thine ear to supplication
C. 1015. where the bowed welkin slow doth *b.*
A. 6. to whom our vows and wishes *b.*
**Bended.**—P. L. 6, 194. *b.* knee his massy spear
P. L. 7, 410. and *b.* dolphins play
P. L. 9, 1105. the *b.* twigs take root
**Bending.**—P. L. 4, 462. *b.* to look on me
P. L. 11, 152. placable and mild, *b.* his ear
H. 71. *b.* one way their precious influence
**Bends.**—P. L. 3, 573 thither his course he *b.*
P. L. 4, 981. waving *b.* her bearded grove
C. 899. that *b.* not as I tread
**Beneath.**—P. L. 1, 115. *b.* this downfall
P. L. 1, 355. *b.* Gibraltar to the Lybian sands
P. L. 2, 1003. stretching far and wide *b.*
P. L. 3, 30. and the flowery brooks *b.*
P. L. 3, 332. shall sink *b.* thy sentence
P. L. 3, 526. which opened from *b.*
P. L. 3, 739. and toward the coast of earth *b.*
P. L. 4, 83. among the Spirits *b.*
P. L. 4, 205. *b.* him with new wonder
P. L. 4, 303. but not *b.* his shoulders broad
P. L. 4, 592. sun now fallen *b.* the Azores
P. L. 6, 342. so far *b.* his confidence
P. L. 6, 510. and saw *b.* the originals of nature
P. L. 8, 318. above or round about thee, or *b.*
P. L. 8, 382. and these inferior far *b.* me set
P. L. 8, 411. *b.* what other creatures are to thee
P. L. 9, 1129. who from *b.*, usurping
P. L. 10, 687. and south as far *b.* Magellan
P. R. 2, 124. Air, Water, and Earth *b.*
P. R. 2, 293. and walks *b.*, and alleys brown
P. R. 4, 203. this World invoked and World *b.*
P. R. 4, 356. to our prophets far *b.*
S. A. 1469. misery *b.* their fears
S. A. 1652. upon the heads of all who sat *b.*
L. 16. that from *b.* the seat of Jove doth spring
L. 167. sunk though he be *b.* the watery floor
**Benediction.**—P. L. 8, 645. followed with *b.*

P. L. 12, 125. shower his *b*.
P. R. 3, 127. glory and *b*. that is thanks
**Benefactors.**—P. R. 3, 82. great *B*. of mankind
**Beneficence.**—P. R. 3, 133. so much *b*.
**Benefit**—P. L. 8, 90. she alone receives the *b*.
P. L. 12, 426. and the *b*. embrace by faith
S. A. 29. or *b*. revealed to Abraham's race
**Benefits.**—P. R. 3, 137. many *b*. received
**Benevolent.**—P. L. 8, 65. *b*. and facile
**Bengala.**—P. L. 2, 638. close sailing from *B*.
**Benighted.**—C. 150. *b*. in these woods
C. 384. *b*. walks under the mid-day sun
**Benign.**—P. L. 8, 492. creator bounteous and *b*.
P. L. 11, 334. thus Michaël with regard *b*.
P. L. 12, 538. to good malignant, to **bad men** *b*.
**Benison.**—C. 332. to love the traveller's *b*.
**Bent.**—P. L. 1, 681. were always downward *b*.
P. L. 2, 923. battering engines *b*. to rase some
P. L. 3, 58. *b*. down his eye
P. L. 3, 84. *b*. he seems on desperate revenge
P. L. 3, 441. alone *b*. on his prey
P. L. 4, 188. *b*. to unhoard the cash
P. L. 4, 460. *b*. down to look just opposite
P. L. 4, 568. *b*. all on speed
P. L. 4, 794. seen hitherward *b*.
P. L. 5, 829. *b*. rather to exalt our happy state
P. L. 6, 112. *b*. on highest deeds
P. L. 6, 506. on war and mutual slaughter *b*.
P. L. 6, 826. and full of wrath *b*. on his enemies
P. L. 9, 55. *b*. on man's destruction
P. L. 9, 384. so *b*., the more shall shame him
P .L. 10, 454. *b*. their aspect
P. L. 10, 885. crooked by nature,—*b*.
P. L. 11, 190. to the eastern gate was *b*.
P. L. 11, 548. *b*. rather how I
P. L. 11, 577. their study *b*. to worship God
P. L. 11, 597. admit delight, the *b*. of nature
P. L. 12, 2. baits at noon though *b*. on speed
P. R. 2, 291. thither he *b*. his way
P. R. 4, 424. some *b*. at thee their fiery darts
P. R. 4, 465. at this desert most was *b*.
S. A. 1148. thou for thy son art *b*. to lay out all
V. Ex. 55. it must be now thy only *b*.
S. 19, 4. my soul more *b*. to serve
**Benumb.**—P. L. 2, 74. lake *b*. not still
**Benumbed.**—P. L. 10, 1069. our limbs *b*.
**Benumbing.**—S. A. 630. death's *b*. opium
**Bereave.**—P. L. 10, 918. *b*. me not
**Bereaved.**—P. L. 6, 903. *b*. of happiness
P. L. 9, 461. with rapine sweet *b*. his fierceness
S. A. 85. why am I thus *b*. thy prime decree
S. A. 1294. sight *b*. may chance to number thee
**Bereaving.**—P. L. 10, 810. one stroke .. *b*. sense
W. S. 13. then thou our fancy of itself *b*.
**Bereft.**—P. L. 11, 628. of short joy *b*.
S. A. 48. how easily *b*. me
C. 277. what chance, good lady, hath *b*. you thus
S. 22, 3. *b*. of light, their seeing have forgot
**Berries.**—C. 55. with ivy *b*. wreathed
C. 186. to bring me *b*., or such cooling fruit
L. 3. I come to pluck your *b*.
**Berry.**—P. L. 5, 307. milky stream, *b*. or grape
P. L. 5, 307. milky stream *b*. or grape
P. L. 5, 346, and meaths from many a *b*.
**Beryl.**—P. L. 6, 756. with eyes the wheels of *b*.
C. 933. the *b*. and the golden ore
**Beseech.**—P. L. 12, 236. they *b*. that Moses
S. A. 751. as repentant, to submit, *b*.
**Beseeching.**—P. L. 5, 869. *b*. or besieging
P. L. 10, 1082. praying, and of grace *b*. him
**Beseem.**—Il P. 18. Memnon's sister might *b*.
**Beseeming.**—C. 769. a moderate and *b*. share
**Beseems.**—P. L. 2, 869. as *b*. thy daughter
P. L. 4, 338. as *b*. fair couple
P. R. 2, 335. to treat thee as *b*., and as her Lord
**Beset.**—P. L. 2, 1016. harder *b*. and more
P. L. 10, 124. thus Adam, sore *b*., replied
P. L. 11, 702. therefore so *b*. with foes
S.A. 257. prevent the harass of their land, *b*. me
**Beside.**—P. L. 5, 54. *b*. it stood one shaped
P. L. 6, 763. *b*. him hung his bow and quiver

C. 287. imports their loss *b*. the present need
C. 950. *b*., all the swains that there abide
H. 224. nor all the gods *b*.
Cir. 23. and the full wrath *b*.
**Besides.**—P. L. 1, 32. lords of the world *b*.
P. L. 1, 194. his other parts *b*., prone on the flood
P. L. 1, 298. smote on him sore *b*.
P. L. 2, 20. with what *b*., in counsel or in fight
P. L. 2, 221. *b*. what hope the never-ending
P. L. 2, 504. man had not hellish foes enow *b*.
P. L. 3, 598. and a stone *b*. imagined
P. L. 6, 626. this gift they have *b*.
P. L. 7, 125. enough is left *b*. to search
P. L. 8, 25. in all their vast survey useless *b*.
P. L. 10, 737. *b*. mine own that bide upon me
P. L. 11, 300. what *b*. of sorrow
P. L. 11, 527. but is there yet no other way, *b*.
P. R. 2, 408. thy temperance invincible *b*.
P. R. 3, 419. *b*. their other worse
P. R. 4, 55. many a fair edifice *b*., more like
P. R. 4, 150. all monarchies *b*.
P. R. 4, 202. nations *b*. from all the winds
S. A. 214. who hast of sorrow thy full load *b*.
S. A. 441. *b*. whom is no god
S. A. 845. hear what assaults I had .. *b*.
C. 18. *b*. the sway of every salt flood
L. 128. *b*. what the grim wolf
M. W. 4. *b*. what her virtues fair
M. W. 53. here *b*. the sorrowing
**Besiege.**—D. F. I, 47. earth's sons *b*. the wall
**Besieged.**—P. R. 3, 339. *b*. Albracca
**Besieging.**—P. L. 5, 869. beseeching or *b*.
**Besmeared.**—P. L. 1, 392, Moloch *b*. with blood
P. L. 5, 356. and grooms *b*. with gold
**Besotted.**—C. 778. *b*. base ingratitude
**Besought.**—P. L. 2, 166. *b*. the deep to shelter
P. L. 5, 848. pardon may be found, in time *b*.
P. L. 7, 109. thus Adam his illustrious guest *b*.
P. L. 9, 1135. as I *b*. thee, when that strange
P. L. 10, 912. embracing them, *b*. his peace
P. L. 12, 238. he grants what they *b*.
P. R. 3, 421. *b*. the God of their forefathers
**Bespake.**—P. L. 2. 849. and thus *b*. her sire
P. L. 4, 1005. thus *b*. the fiend
P. R. 1, 43. aghast and sad, he thus *b*.
L. 112. and stern *b*.
H. 76. until their Lord himself *b*.
**Best.**—P. L. 1, 247. farthest from him is *b*.
P. L. 1, 691. that soil may *b*. deserve
P. L. 1, 765. defied the *b*. of Panim chivalry
P. L. 2, 40. and by what *b*. way
P. L. 2, 230. if war be *b*.
P. L. 2, 280. how in safety *b*. we may compose
P. L. 2, 357. how attempted *b*., by force or
P. L. 2, 458. what *b*. may ease the present misery
P. L. 4, 203. perverts *b*. things to worst abuse
P. L. 4, 309. by her yielded by him *b*. received
P. L. 4, 398. as their shape served *b*. his end
P. L. 4, 738. as adoration which God likes *b*.
P. L. 4, 770. sings to his proud fair *b*.
P. L. 4, 852. if I must contend, *b*. with the *b*.
P. L. 5, 19. heaven's last, *b*. gift
P. L. 5, 95. *b*. image of myself and dearer half
P. L. 5, 160. speak ye who *b*. can tell
P. L. 5, 333. for delicacy *b*.
P. L. 5, 574. as may express them *b*.
P. L. 5, 779. only to consult, how we may *b*.
P. L. 6, 353. size assume, as likes them *b*.
P. L. 6, 724. first Highest, Holiest, *b*.
P. L. 7, 115. which *b*. may serve to glorify
P. L. 8, 106. for uses to his Lord *b*. known
P. L. 8, 169. as him pleases *b*., wherever placed
P. L. 8, 428. *b*. with thyself accompanied
P. L. 8, 550. wisest, virtuousest, discreetest, *b*.
P. L. 8, 611. approve the *b*., and follow
P. L. 9, 178. spite then with spite is *b*. repaid
P. L. 9, 201. they *b*. may ply their growing work
P. L. 9, 230. how we might *b*. fulfil the work
P. L. 9, 249. solitude sometimes is *b*. society
P. L. 9, 258. his wish and *b*. advantage

P. L. 9, 317. *b.* witness of thy virtue tried
P. L. 9, 343. *b.* are all things as the will of God
P. L. 9, 402. and all things in *b.* order
P. L. 9, 433. from her *b.* prop so far
P.L. 9,541.*b.* beheld where universally admired
P. L. 9. 745. great are thy virtues.. *b.* of fruits
P. L. 9, 808. experience to thee I owe, *b.* guide
P. L. 9, 896. last and *b.* of all God's works
P. L. 9, 995. such recompence *b.* merits
P. L. 9, 1092. what *b.* may for the..
P. L. 10, 82. those two; the third *b.*
P. L. 10, 173. judged as then *b.*
P. L. 10, 599. there *b.,* where most with ravin
P. L. 10, 651. as sorted *b.* with present things
P. L. 10, 867. serpent! that name *b.* befits thee
P. L. 11, 54. as may dispose him *b.*
P. L. 11, 365. and *b.* prepared endure
P. L. 11, 438. choicest and *b.*
P. L. 11, 497. compassion quelled his *b.*
P. L. 11, 603. judge not what is *b.* by pleasure
P. L. 12, 561. I learn that to obey is *b.*
P. R. 1, 105. induces *b.* to hope
P. R. 1, 186. how *b.* the mighty work begin
P. R. 1, 288. begin, as *b.* becomes
P. R. 2, 113. how to accomplish *b.*
P. R. 2, 382. when and where likes me *b.*
P. R. 3, 8. what *b.* to say canst say
P. R. 3, 174. rather are occasion *b.*
P. R. 3, 177. so shalt thou *b.* fulfil, *b.* verify
P. R. 3, 182. things are *b.* fulfilled in their due
P. R. 3, 194. who *b.* can suffer *b.* can do
P. R. 3, 195.*b.* reign who first well hath obeyed
P. R. 3, 224. thy feet so slow to what is *b.*
P. R. 3, 238. *b.* school of *b.* experience
P. R. 3. 250. know how *b.* their opposition
P. R. 3, 433. time to himself *b.* known
P. R. 4, 235. by his own arms is *b.* evinced
P. R. 4, 262. teachers *b.* of moral prudence
P. R. 4, 266. high passions *b.* describing
P. R. 4, 364. our Law, *b.* form a king
P. R. 4, 381. prophecies of thee are *b.* fulfilled
P. R. 4, 476. when it may be *b.*
P. R. 4, 524. all *b.* conjectures, I collect
P. R. 4, 553. and highest placed, highest is *b.*
S. A. 255. what advantaged *b.*
S. A. 314. he can *b.* dispense
S. A. 511. *b.* pleased with humble
S. A. 759. that wisest and *b.* men
S. A. 908. would have succeeded *b.*
S. A. 1029. to apprehend or value what is *b.*
S. A. 1034. to wisest men and *b.*
S. A. 1061. but had we *b.* retire?
S. A. 1167. by the barber's razor *b.* subdued
S. A. 1264. to me the *b.*
S. A. 1429. may serve his glory *b.*
S. A. 1521. *b.* keep together here
S. A. 1718. and, which is *b.* and happiest
S. A. 1745. all is *b.,* though we oft doubt
S. A. 1748. and ever *b.* found in the close
C. 28. the greatest and the *b.*
C. 171. my *b.* guide now
C. 309. the *b.* land-pilot's art
C. 377. where with her *b.* nurse
C. 487 *b.* draw and stand upon our guard
C. 573. ere my *b.* speed could prevent
C. 908. my office *b.* to help ensnared
S. 13, 8. could'st humour *b.* our tongue
S. 14, 9. Faith, who knew them *b.*
S. 17, 7. how war may *b.* upheld
S. 19, 10, 11. who *b.* bear his yoke serve him *b.*
P. 29. befriend me, Night, *b.* patroness of grief
D. F. 70. canst *b.* perform that office
V. Ex. 26. thy *b.* array
**Bested.**—Il P. 3. how little you *b.*
**Bestial.**—P. L. 1, 435. down to *b.* gods
P. L. 2, 873. rolling her *b.* train
P. L. 4, 754. among the *b.* herds to range
P. L. 9, 165. and mixed with *b.* slime
**Bestir.**—P. L. 1, 334. *b.* themselves
**Bestirs.**—P. L. 5, 337. *b.* her then
**Bestow.**—P. L. 5, 317. gifts, and large *b.*

P. L. 8, 483. earth or heaven could *b.*
**Bestowed.**—P. L. 3, 673. creator hath *b.* worlds
P. L. 5, 318. and large bestow from large *b.*
P. L. 5, 386. on whom the angel hail *b.*
P. L. 8, 537. on her *b.* too much of ornament
P. R. 2, 395. what I might have *b.*
**Best-resolved.**—S. A. 847, the *b.-r.* of men
**Bestrown.**—P. L. 1, 311. so thick *b.,* abject
P. L. 4, 631. that lie *b.,* unsightly
**Bestuck.**—P. L. 12, 536. truth shall retire *b.*
**Bestud.**—C. 734. and so *b.* with stars
**Betake.**—P. L. 10, 922. whither shall I *b.* me
C. 351. whither *b.* her
**Betakes.**—C. 61. *b.* him to this ominous wood
**Bethabara.**—P. R. 1, 184. *B.,* where John
P. R. 2, 20. nigh to *B.,* in Jericho
**Bethel.**—P. L. 1, 485. in *B.* and in Dan
P. R. 3, 431. and to their gods perhaps of *B.*
**Bethink.**—P. L. 2, 73. let such *b.* them
C. 820. now I *b.* me, some other
**Bethlehem.**— P. R. 1, 243. in the fields of *B.*
P. R. 2, 78. the streets of *B.*
P. R. 4, 505. the angelic song in *B.* field
H. 223. the rays of *B.* blind
**Bethought.**—P. R. 3, 149. another plea *b.*
**Betide.**—P. L. 12, 480. what will *b.* the few
**Betides.**—P. R. 4, 451. fair morning yet *b.*
**Betimes.**—P. L. 3, 186. appease *b.* incensed deity
S. 21, 9. to measure life learn thou *b.*
**Betokening.**—P. L. 11, 867. *b.* peace
P. R. 4, 490. as signs *b.* or ill-boding
**Betook.**—P. L. 6, 663. to like arms *b.* them
P. L. 9, 388. *b.* her to the groves
P. L. 10, 610. they both *b.* them several ways
P. R. 4, 403. *b.* him to his rest
**Betray.**—S. A. 383. Timna first *b.* me
S. A. 399. she purposed to *b.* me
S. A. 750. all vows, deceive, *b.*
S. A. 946. how again *b.* me
**Betrayed.**—P. L. 4, 116. *b.* him counterfeit
S. A. 33. *b.,* captived, and both my eyes put out
S. A. 379. *b.* it to a woman
S. A. 840. I must, by thee *b.*
S. A. 1109. assassinated and *b.*
C. 697. *b.* my credulous innocence
**Better.**—P. L. 1. 263. *b.* to reign in hell
P. L. 1, 645. our *b.* part remains
P. L. 1, 688. for treasures *b.* hid
P. L. 2, 114. worse appear the *b.* reason
P. L. 2, 196. *b.* these than worse
P. L. 3, 680. to serve him *b.*
P. L. 4, 167. though with them *b.* pleased
P. L. 4, 385. if no *b.* place, thank him
P. L. 4, 915. which taught thee yet no *b.*
P. L. 4, 939. hope to find *b.* abode
P. L. 5, 167. *b.* thou belong not to the dawn
P. L. 5, 785. if *b.* counsels might erect
P. L. 6, 30. well hast thou fought the *b.* fight
P. L. 6. 440. may serve to *b.* us
P. L. 7, 189. a *b.* race to bring
P. L. 8, 83. that *b.* might with far less compass
P. L. 9, 31. the *b.* fortitude of patience
P. L. 9, 102. what God after *b.* worse would build
P. L. 9, 365. which to avoid were *b.*
P. L. 9, 998. to eat against his *b.* knowledge
P. L. 10, 593. not *b.* far than still
P. L. 10, 1011. to *b.* hopes his more attentive
P. L. 10, 1068. some *b.* shroud, some *b.* warmth
P. L. 10, 1086. what *b.* can we do
P. L. 11, 42. to *b.* life shall yield him
P. L. 11, 502. *b.* end here unborn
P. L. 11, 599. much *b.* seems this vision
P. L. 11, 635. who should *b.* hold his place
P. L. 11, 763. *b.* had I lived ignorant
P. L. 12, 302. up to a *b.* covenant
P. R. 1, 190. the *b.* to converse
P. R. 1, 248. for in the inn was left no *b.* room
P. R. 2, 258. fed with *b.* thoughts
P. R. 2, 332. or, *b.* to express, troubled
P. R. 2, 486. a sceptre oftest *b.* missed
P. R. 3, 180. reign then; what canst thou *b.* do

P. R. 3, 397. for thee were *b.* farthest off
P. R. 4, 8. had no *b.* weighed the strength
P. R. 4, 357. divinely taught, and *b.* teaching
P. R. 4, 445. desperate of *b.* course
S. A. 182. if *b.* counsel or consolation we may
S. A. 579. *b.* at home lie bed-rid
S. A. 585. wherewith to serve Him *b.*
S. A. 797. no *b.* way I saw
S. A. 1163. no *b.* service
C. 123. night hath *b.* sweets to prove
C. 775. the giver would be *b.* thanked
A. 101. a *b.* soil shall give ye thanks
L. 67. *b.* done, as others use
S. 9, 5. the *b.* part with Mary and Ruth
S. 17, 2. a *b.* senator never held
S. 22, 14. had I no *b.* guide
**Between.**—P. L. 1, 387. *b.* the cherubim
P. L. 2, 726. with hideous outcry rushed *b.*
P. L. 3, 70. surveyed hell and the gulf *b.*
P. L. 4, 699. their flourished heads *b.*
P. L. 5, 268. sails *b.* worlds and worlds
P. L. 5, 307. of nectarous draughts *b.*
P. L. 5, 702. suggested cause, and casts *b.*
P. L. 6, 162. this pause *b.*
P. L. 6, 441. what *b.* us made the odds
P. L. 6, 756. and careering fires *b.*
P. L. 7, 201. myriads, *b.* two .. mountains
P. L. 7, 241. and *b.* spun out the air
P. L. 7, 439. arched neck *b.* her white wings
P. L. 7, 473. ambiguous *b.* sea and land
P. L. 9, 237. whether food or talk *b.*
P. L. 9, 1107. and echoing walks *b.*
P. L. 9, 1151. no ground of enmity *b.* us known
P. L. 10, 179. *b.* thee and the woman
P. L. 10, 362. though distant from thee worlds *b.*
P. L. 10, 497. he will put *b.* me and mankind
P. L. 10, 924. *b.* us two let there be peace
P. L. 11, 639. towns, and rural works *b.*
P. L. 12, 197. *b.* two crystal walls
P. L. 12, 207. darkness defends *b.*
P. L. 12,253. *b.* the wings of two bright cherubim
P. R. 3, 219. *b.* me and thy Father's ire
P. R. 3, 256. and left *b.* fair champaign
P. R. 3, 361. *b.* two such enclosing enemies
S. A. 1630. they led him *b.* the pillars
H. 144. mercy will sit *b.*
**Betwixt.**—P. L. 2, 593. *b.* Damiata
P. L. 2, 1018. Bosporus *b.* the justling rocks
P. L. 3, 462. *b.* the angelical and human kind
P. L. 4, 252. *b.* them lawns, or level downs
P. L. 4, 549. *b.* these rocky pillars Gabriel sat
P. L. 4, 998. seen *b.* Astrea and the Scorpion
P. L. 10, 328. *b.* the Centaur
P. L. 12, 3. *b.* the world destroyed and world
L'A. 82. from *b.* two aged oaks
U. C. I. 8. *b.* Cambridge and the Bull
**Bevy.**—P. L. 11, 582. a *b.* of fair women
**Bewail.**—S. A. 151. which shall I first *b.*
S. A. 182. to visit or *b.* thee
S. A. 955. *b.* thy falsehood
**Bewailed.**—D. F. I. 7. and then *b.* his fatal bliss
**Bewailing.**—P. L. 11, 111. and with tears *b.*
S. A. 1742. only *b.* his lot unfortunate
**Beware.**—P. L. 4. 559. from what point to .. *b.*
P. L. 5, 237. warn him to *b.* he swerve not
P. L. 6, 894. that thou mayst *b.*
P. L. 7, 42. by dire example to *b.*
P. L. 7, 545. death is the penalty imposed, *b.*
P. L. 8, 638. the weal or woe in thee .. *b.*
**Beyond.** There are about 43 instances of *beyond.*
**Bickering.**—P. L. 6, 766. smoke and *b.* flame
**Bid.**—P. L. 1, 246. can dispose and *b.*
P. L. 2, 514. their session ended they *b.* cry
P. L. 6, 176. God and nature is the same
P. L. 6, 202. *b.* sound the archangel trumpet
P. L. 7, 107. *b.* his absence, till thy song end
P. L. 7, 166. *b.* the deep within appointed
P. L. 7, 304. ere God had *b.* ground be dry
P. L. 8, 185. God hath *b.* dwell
P. L. 8, 519. and *b.* haste the evening-star
P. L. 9, 353. but *b.* her well be ware

P. L. 10, 668. he *b.* his angels turn askance
P. L. 10, 672. the sun was *b.* turn reins
P. L. 11, 590. and *b.* invoke Hymen
P. R. 1, 495. I *b.* not, or forbid
P. R. 2, 274. was *b.* rise and eat
P. R. 2, 326. nor to stay till *b.*
S. A. 967. *b.* go with evil omen
S. A. 1310. our lords thus *b.* me say
S. A. 1392. to thee I am *b.* say
C. 400. and *b.* me hope
A. 13. *b.* conceal the rest
L. 22. and *b.* fair peace
L. 134. and *b.* them hither cast
L. 149. *b.* Amaranthus all his beauty shed
L'A. 46. at my window *b.* good morrow
Il P. 105. *b.* the soul of Orpheus sing
S. 8, 10. Emathian conqueror *b.* spare
S. 14, 13. who thenceforth *b.* thee rest
H. 76. bespake, and *b.* them go
H. 124. *b.* the weltering waves
**Bidden.**—L. 118. the worthy *b.* guest
**Biddest.**—P. L. 4, 635. *b.* unargued I obey
**Bidding.**—P. L. 3, 712. at his second *b.*
P. L. 11, 112. patiently thy *b.* they obey
P. L. 11, 314. to his great *b.* I submit
S. 19, 12. thousands at his *b.* speed
**Bide.**—P. L. 3, 321. them that *b.* in heaven
P. L. 10, 738. mine own that *b.*
P. R. 1, 59. must *b.* the stroke
P. L. 2, 304. so long should *b.*
**Biding-place.**—D. F. I. 21. from her fair *b.-p.*
**Bids.**—P. L. 2, 733. whate'er his wrath .. *b.*
P. L. 4, 633. night *b.* us rest
P. L. 4, 748. our Maker *b.* increase, who *b.*
P. L. 10, 1067. *b.* us seek some better shroud
P. R. 1, 377. for what he *b.* I do
S. A. 505. self-preservation *b.*
C. 93. the star that *b.* the shepherd fold
**Bier.**—L. 12. he must not float upon his watery *b.*
**Biggest.**—P. L. 7,471. Behemoth, *b.* born of Earth
**Bigness.**—P. L. 1, 778. in *b.* to surpass
P. L. 2, 1052. in *b.* as a star
**Bill.**—P. L. 11, 859. in his *b.* an olive-leaf
S. 1, 6. the shallow cuckoo's *b.*
**Billows.**—P. L. 1, 224. and rolled in *b.*
C. 932. thy *b.* roll ashore
**Bind.**—P. L. 3, 361. *b.* their resplendent locks
P. L. 3, 602. they *b.* volatile Hermes
P. L. 5, 819. unjust to *b.* with laws the free
P. L. 9, 210. or prune, or prop, or *b.*
P. L. 9, 760. such prohibitions *b.* not
P. L. 9, 761. if death *b.* us
P. L. 11, 881. as a flowery verge, to *b.*
P. L. 12, 525. and *b.* his consort Liberty
S. A. 309. who made our laws to *b.* us
L'A. 88. to *b.* the sheaves
S. 16, 12. threatening to *b.* our souls
**Bird.**—P. L. 3, 38. as the wakeful *b.* sings
P. L. 4, 600. silence accompanied, beast and *b.*
P. L. 4, 648. with this her solemn *b.*
P. L. 4, 655. with this her solemn *b.*
P. L. 4, 704. other creature here, *b.,* beast
P. L. 5, 40. the night-warbling *b.*
P. L. 5, 272. as that sole *b.*
P. L. 7, 394. and every *b.* of wing
P. L. 8, 342. each *b.* and beast behold
P. L. 8, 349. *b.* and beast beheld approaching
P. L. 8, 351. each *b.* stooped on his wing
P. L. 8, 395. much less can *b.* with beast
P. L. 8, 518. till the amorous *b.* of night
P. L. 11, 183. impressed on *b.,* beast, air
P. L. 11, 185. in her sight the *b.* of Jove
P. L. 11, 734. of every beast, and *b.*
P. R. 4, 245. the Attic *b.* trills her ... notes
S. A. 1699. that self-begotten *b.*
S. A. 1707. a secular *b.*
Il P. 61, 79. sweet *b.,* that shunn'st the noise
S. 1, 9. ere the rude *b.* of hate
**Birds.**—P. L. 2, 494. the *b.* their notes renew
P. L. 4, 264. the *b.* their choir apply
P. L. 4, 642. charm of earliest *b.*

P. L. 4, 651. charm of earliest *b.*
P. L. 5, 8. and the shrill matin song of *b.*
P. L. 5, 197. join voices all living souls, ye *B.*
P. L. 6, 74. *b.*, in orderly array
P. L. 7, 433. the smaller *b.* with song solaced
P. L. 8, 265. *b.* on the branches warbling
P. L. 8, 515. joyous the *b.*
P. L. 8, 528. walks, and the melody of *b.*
P. L. 11, 186. two *b.* of gayest plume
P. R. 2, 290. with chant of tuneful *b.*
P. R. 4, 434. the *b.*, who all things now behold
H. 68. *b.* of calm sit brooding

**Birth.**—P. L. 3, 285 by wondrous *b.*
P. L. 4, 15. nigh the *b.*, now rolling boils
P. L. 5, 180. the eldest *b.* of nature's womb
P. L. 5, 862. *b.* mature of this our native
P. L. 7, 102. the rising *b.* of nature
P. L. 7, 454. her fertile womb teemed at a *b.*
P. L. 9, 111. nobler *b.* of creatures animate
P. L. 10, 207. know thy *b.*, for dust thou art
P. L. 11, 768. gaining *b.* abortive
P. L. 12, 360. his *b.* a star unseen before
P. L. 12, 364. his place of *b.*
P. R. 1, 66. his *b.* to our just fear
P. R. 1, 141. show him worthy of his *b.* divine
P. R. 1, 238. from God foretold thy *b.*
P. R. 1, 270. of whose *b.* I oft had heard
P. R. 2, 71. other women, by the *b.* I bore
P. R. 2, 413. unfriended, low of *b.*
P. R. 4, 503. thy *b.*, at length announced
S. A. 23. my *b.* from heaven foretold
S. A. 171. whom long descent of *b.*
S. A. 525. of *b.* from heaven foretold
S. A. 1135. at thy *b.* was given thee
S. A. 1431. send thee the Angel of thy *b*
L'A. 14. whom lovely Venus at a *b.*
P. 3. heavenly Infant's *b.*
M. W. 5. added to her noble *b.*
M. W. 15. her high *b.*, and her graces sweet
M. W. 31. the hapless babe before his *b.*
M. W. 67. at her next *b.* much like thee
V. Ex. 59. for at thy *b.*

**Birthday.**—P. L. 7, 256. *b.* Heaven and Earth
**Birth-night.**—P. R. 4, 506. on thy *b.-n.*
**Birthright.**—P. L. 1, 511. *b.* seized by younger
P. L. 3, 309. by merit more than *b.*, Son of God

**Births.**—P. L. 11, 687. produce prodigious *b.*
**Biserta.**—P. L. 1, 585. whom *B.* sent
**Bites.**—A. 53. with cankered venom *b.*
**Bitter.**—P. L. 2, 598. the *b.* change
P. L. 2, 808. I should prove a *b.* morsel
P. L. 4, 24. wakes the *b.* memory
P. L. 8, 328. and shun the *b.* consequence
P. L. 9, 172. revenge at first though sweet, *b.*
P. L. 10, 566. instead of fruit chewed *b.* ashes
S. A. 823. *b.* reproach, but true
L. 6. *b.* constraint and sad
H. 152. that on the *b.* cross
C. 365. how *b.* is such self-delusion

**Bitterly.**—S. A. 432. *b.* hast thou paid
**Bitterness.**—P. L. 11, 157. *b.* of death is past
**Bituminous.**—P. L. 10, 562. that *b.* lake
P. L. 12, 41. a black *b.* gurge boils out

**Bizance.**—P. L. 11, 395. or the sultan in *B.*
**Blab.**—S. A. 495. avoided as a *b.*
**Blabbing.**—C. 138. the *b.* eastern scout
**Black.**—P. L. 1, 405. and *b.* Gehenna called
P. L. 2, 67. *b.* fire and horror shot
P. L. 2, 578. sad Acheron, of sorrow, *b.* and deep
P. L. 2, 670. *b.* it stood as night
P. L. 2, 714. *b.* clouds
P. L. 3, 475. White, *B.* and Grey
P. L. 7, 238. the *b.*, tartareous
P. L. 7, 547. her *b.* attendant, Death
P. L. 9, 180. like a *b.* mist low-creeping
P. L. 10, 702. *b.* with thunderous clouds
P. L. 10, 847. with *b.* air accompanied
P. L. 11, 738. south wind .. and with *b.* wings
P. L. 12, 41. *b.* bituminous gurge boils out
S. A. 600. anguish of the mind, and humours *b.*
S. A. 622. to *b.* mortification

S. A. 973. one *b.*, the other white
S. A. 1133. spells and *b.* enchantments
C. 62. in thick shelter of *b.* shades embowered
C. 337. with *b.* usurping mists
Il P. 16. o'erlaid with *b.*, staid wisdom's hue
Il P. 17. *b.*, but such as in esteem
P. 34. the leaves should all be *b.*
D. F. I. 67. swift-rushing *b.* perdition

**Blackest.**—P. L. 2, 136. *b.* insurrection
P. L. 6, 515. *b.* grain, and into store conveyed
L'A. 2. of Cerberus and *b.* Midnight born
H. 207. his burning idol all of *b.* hue

**Blackmoor.**—P. R. 4, 72. to the *B.* sea
**Blade.**—C. 651. brandished *b.*
**Blains.**—P. L. 12, 180. botches and *b.*
**Blame.**—P. L. 3, 697. excess that reaches *b.*
P. L. 4, 758. that I should write thee sin or *b.*
P. L. 5, 119. leave no spot or *b.* behind
P. L. 8, 66. to ask or search I *b.* thee not
P. L. 9, 292. from sin and *b.* entire
P. L. 9, 1143. soon moved with touch of *b.*
P. L. 10, 130. conceal, and not expose to *b.*
P. L. 10, 833. all the *b.* lights due
P. L. 10, 958. no more contend, nor *b.* each other
S. A. 848. have yielded without *b.*
S. A. 1723. no contempt, dispraise, or *b.*
C. 509. to tell thee sadly, Shepherd, without *b.*
H. 41. pollute with sinful *b.*
M. W. 27. whether by mischance or *b.*

**Blamed.**—P. L. 10, 959. *b.* enough elsewhere
**Blamest.**—P. L. 8, 612. to love thou *b.* me not
**Blanc.**—P. L. 10, 656. to the *b.* moon her office
**Bland.**—P. L. 5, 5. and temperate vapours *b.*
P. L. 9, 855. with *b.* words at will
P. L. 9, 1047. that with exhilarating vapour *b.*
**Blandished.**—S. A. 403. with *b.* parleys
**Blandishment.**—P. L. 8, 351. with *b.*
**Blank.**—P. L. 3, 48. a universal *b.*
P. L. 9, 890. astonied stood and *b.*
P. R. 2, 120. solicitous and *b.*
S. A. 471. with confusion *b.*
C. 452. adoration and *b.* awe

**Blasphemed.**—P. L. 3, 166. questioned and *b.*
P. L. 12, 411. he shall live hated, be *b.*
S. A. 442. *b.* and had in scorn
**Blasphemes.**—C. 779, *b.* his Feeder
**Blasphemous.**—P. L. 5, 809. *b.*, false, and proud
P. L. 6, 360. refrained his tongue *b.*
P. R. 4, 181. more *b.*

**Blast.**—P. L. 1, 708. from one *b.* of wind
P. L. 10, 693. *b.*, vapour and mist
P. L. 10, 701. with adverse *b.* upturns
P. L. 11, 76. the angelic *b.* filled all the regions
S. A. 972. with contrary *b.* proclaims
C. 640. mildew, *b.* or damp
L. 97. not a *b.* was from his dungeon
H. 161. terror of that *b.*

**Blasted.**—P. L. 1, 615. on the *b.* heath
P. L. 6, 372. scorched and *b.*
P. L. 10, 412. the *b.* stars looked wan
D. F. I, 1. no sooner blown but *b.*

**Blasting.**—P. L. 4, 928. the *b.* volleyed thunder
A. 49. and *b.* vapours chill

**Blasts.**—P. R. 4, 31. from cold Septentrion *b.*
P. R. 4, 418. loaden with stormy *b.*
C. 845. helping all urchin *b.*

**Blaze.**—P. L. 1, 665. *b.* far round illumined hell
P. L. 3, 378. the full *b.* of thy beams
P. L. 4, 818. with sudden *b.* diffused
P. L. 6, 18. *b.* on *b.* first met his view
P. L. 9, 1083. their *b.* insufferably bright
P. L. 10, 453. at that so sudden *b.*
P. R. 3, 47. for what is glory but the *b.* of fame
S. A. 80. dark, amid the *b.* of noon
A. 2. sudden *b.* of majesty
A. 74 music worthiest were to *b.*
L. 74. burst out into sudden *b.*
H. 9. that far beaming *b.* of majesty

**Blazed.**—P. L. 1, 194. eyes that sparkling *b.*
P. L. 6, 306. their shields *b.* opposite
P. L. 6, 775. the great ensign of Messiah *b.*

**P. L.** 10, 65. *b.* forth unclouded deity
**P. L.** 12, 633. sword of God before them *b.*
**S. A.** 528. famous now and *b.*
**Blazing.**—P. L. 1, 728. lamps and *b.* cressets
**P. L.** 5, 757. high on a hill, far *b.*
**P. L.** 7, 575. opened wide her *b.* portals
**P. L.** 9, 639. *b.* with delusive light
**P. L.** 11, 229. I descry from yonder *b.* cloud
**M. W.** 70. *b.* Majesty and Light
**Bleak.**—P. R. 2, 74. shelter .. from the *b.* air
**C.** 269. every *b.* unkindly fog
**D. F. I.** 4. *b.* Winter's force
**Blear.**— C. 155. to cheat the eye with *b.* illusion
**Bleating.**—P. L. 1, 489. all her *b.* gods
**P. L.** 2, 494. and *b.* herds attest their joy
**P. L.** 7, 472. *b.* rose, as plants
**P. L.** 11, 649. ewes and their *b.* lambs
**Bleed.**—P. L. 6, 333. celestial Spirits may *b.*
**S.** 15, 13. in vain doth Valour *b.*
**Bleeds.**—Cir. 11. now *b.* to give us ease
**Blemish.**—S. 22, 2. view of *b.* or of spot
**Bless.**—P. L. 10, 821. how would you *b.* me
**A.** 60. murmurs made to *b.*
Il P. 84. to *b.* the doors from nightly harm
**S.** 11, 5. cries the stall-reader, *B.* us
**H.** 126. *b.* our human ears
**D. F. I.** 65. *b.* us with thy loved innocence
**Blessed.**—P. L. 2, 847. and *b.* his maw
**P. L.** 3, 136. the *b.* spirits elect
**P. L.** 5, 613. cast out from God and *b.* vision
**P. L.** 6, 267. disturb'd Heaven's *b.* peace
**P. L.** 7, 395. saw that it was good, and *b.*
**P. L.** 7, 530. *b.* mankind, and said, 'Be fruitful
**P. L.** 7, 592. *b.* and hallowed the seventh Day
**P. L.** 10, 723. now become accursed of *b.*
**P. L.** 11, 317. his *b.* countenance
**P. L.** 12, 148. shall in his seed be *b.*
**H.** 25. lay it lowly at his *b.* feet
**Blessedness.**—P. L. 7, 59. to mix with t.
**Blessing.**—S. A. 357. *b.* with pomp adorned
**M. M.** 8. hill and dale doth boast thy *b.*
**Blessings.**—C. 772. nature's full *b.*
**V. Ex.** 64. *b.* on thy sleeping head
**Blest.**—P. L. 3, 149. resound thee ever *b.*
**P. L.** 4, 163. spicy shore of Araby the *B.*
**P. L.** 3, 347. *b.* voices, uttering joy
**P. L.** 4, 774. *b.* pair, and O yet happiest
**P. L.** 5, 387. *B.* Mary second Eve
**P. L.** 6, 184. God ever *b.*
**P. L.** 8, 640. I shall rejoice and all the *B.*
**P. L.** 9, 796. of operation *b.* to sapience
**P. L.** 11, 67. call to synod all the *B.*
**P. L.** 11, 598. prime Angel *b.*
**P. L.** 12, 126. in his seed all nations shall be *b*
**P. L.** 12, 151. this patriarch *b.*
**P. L.** 12, 277. in whom all nations shall be *b.*
**P. L.** 12, 450. in his seed all nations shall be *b.*
**P. L.** 12, 553. thy prediction, Seer *b.*
**P. L.** 12, 573. my Redeemer ever *b.*
**P. R.** 2, 56. mock us with his *b.* sight
**P. R.** 2, 68. among women *b.*
**P. R.** 2, 94. afflicted I may be, it seems, and *b.*
**L.** 177. in the *b.* kingdoms
**C.** 268. by *b.* song forbidding
**C.** 329. eye me *b.* Providence
**H.** 237. but see the Virgin *b.*
**S. M.** 1. *b.* pair of Sirens
**D. F. I.** 36. O Soul, most surely *b.*
**Blew.**—P. L. 11, 73. he *b.* his trumpet
**Blind.**—P.L. 3, 35. *b.* Thamyris, and *b.* Mæonides
**P. L.** 3, 200. *b.* be blinded more
**P. L.** 3, 452. superstition and *b.* zeal
**P. R.** 4, 259. *b.* Melesigenes
**S. A.** 68. *b.* among enemies
**S. A.** 366. captive, poor and *b.*
**S. A.** 438. bound and *b.*
**S. A.** 563. now *b.,* disheartened, shamed
**S. A.** 941. how wouldst thou use me now, *b.*
**S. A.** 1106. combat with a *b.* man
**S. A.** 1328. make them sport with *b.* activity
**S. A.** 1474. captive and *b.* before them

**S. A.** 1687. though *b.* of sight
**C.** 181. the *b.* mazes of this tangled wood
**C.** 519. but unbelief is *b.*
**L.** 75. comes the *b.* Fury
**L.** 119. *b.* mouths! that scarce know how
**S.** 22, 14. though *b.,* had I no better guide
**H.** 223. *b.* his dusky eyn
**Blinded.**—P. L. 3, 200. blind be *b.* more
**Blindness.**—S. A. 196. now least afflicts me, *b.*
**S. A.** 418. that *b.* worse than this
**S. A.** 1221. by his *b.* maimed
**S. A.** 1686. with *b.* internal struck
**Bliss.**—P. L. 1, 607. (far other once beheld in *b.*)
**P. L.** 2, 86. to dwell here, driven out from *b.*
**P. L.** 2, 375. frail original, and faded *b.*
**P. L.** 2, 832. a place of *b.* in the purlieus
**P. L.** 2, 867. that new world of light and *b.*
**P. L.** 3, 305. though throned in highest *b.*
**P. L.** 3, 358. and where the river of *b.*
**P. L.** 3, 408. regardless of the *b.* wherein he sat
**P. L.** 3, 525. exclusion from the doors of *b.*
**P. L.** 4, 359. into our room of *b.*
**P. L.** 4, 508. shall enjoy their fill of *b.* on *b.*
**P. L.** 4, 728. love, the crown of all our *b.*
**P. L.** 4, 884. God hath planted here in *b.*
**P. L.** 5, 241. from like state of *b.*
**P. L.** 5, 297. rule or art, enormous *b.*
**P. L.** 5, 517. measure of what *b.*
**P. L.** 5, 543. O fall from what high state of *b.*
**P. L.** 5, 597. by whom, in *b.* embosomed
**P. L.** 6, 52. from God and *b.*
**P. L.** 6, 273. Heaven, the seat of *b.*
**P. L.** 6, 729. which to fulfil is all my *b.*
**P. L.** 6, 892. he sits at the right hand of *b.*
**P. L.** 7, 55. the peace of God in *b.*
**P. L.** 8, 299. thy guide to the garden of *b.*
**P. L.** 8, 522. the sum of earthly *b.*
**P. L.** 9, 263. perhaps no *b.* enjoyed
**P. L.** 9, 411. of innocence, of faith, of *b.*
**P. L.** 9, 831. Adam shall share with me in *b.*
**P. L.** 9, 879. for *b.,* as thou hast part, to me is *b.*
**P. L.** 9, 916. never shall be parted, *b.* or woe
**P. L.** 9. 1166. lived and joyed immortal *b.*
**P. L.** 10, 25. pity, violated not their *b.*
**P. L.** 10, 399. dwell, and reign in *b.*
**P. L.** 10, 503. enter now into full *b.*
**P. L.** 11, 43. may dwell in joy and *b.*
**P. L.** 11, 708. in salvation and the climes of *b.*
**P. L.** 12, 462. and receive them into *b.*
**P. L.** 12, 551. joy and eternal *b.*
**P. R.** 1, 361. driven with them from *b.*
**P. R.** 1, 419. lost to thee no more
**P. R.** 4, 597. throned in the bosom of *b.*
**P. R.** 4, 612. that seat of earthly *b.* be failed
**C.** 263. certainty of waking *b.*
**C.** 741. in mutual and partaken *b.*
**C.** 813. beyond the *b.* of dreams
**S.** 9, 13. passes to *b.* at the mid-hour of night
**S.** 14, 8. to joy; and *b.* for ever
**H.** 165. then at last our *b.*
**D. F. I.** 7. bewailed his fatal *b.*
**T.** 11. eternity shall greet our *b.*
**Cir.** 19. throned in secret *b.*
**Blissful.**—P. L. 1, 5. and regain the *b.* seat
**P. L.** 3, 69. unrivalled love in *b.* solitude
**P. L.** 3, 527. the *b.* seat of Paradise
**P. L.** 4, 208. *b.* Paradise of God
**P. L.** 4, 690. passed on to their *b.* bower
**P. L.** 5, 292. come into the *b.* field
**P. L.** 10, 225. into his *b.* bosom
**P. L.** 11, 77. from their *b.* bowers
**C.** 1010. two *b.* twins
**H.** 98. their souls in *b.* rapture took
**V. Ex.** 35. see each *b.* deity
**Blithe.**—P. L. 9, 625. wily Adder, *b.* and glad
**P. L.** 9, 886. with countenance *b.*
**P. L.** 11, 615. so *b.,* so smooth, so gay
**P. R.** 4, 585. through the *b.* air
**C.** 55. and his *b.* youth
**L'A.** 24. buxom, *b.,* and debonair
**L'A.** 65. the milkmaid singeth *b.*

D

**Blood.**—P. L. 1, 392. besmeared with *b.*
P. L. 1, 451. supposed with *b.* of Thammuz
P. L. 2, 664. lured with the smell of infant *b.*
P. L. 4, 805. from pure *b.* arise
P. L. 10, 527. bedropt with *b.* of Gorgon
P. L. 11, 447. with gushing *b.* effused
P. L. 11, 543. in thy *b.* will reign
P. L. 11, 791. who, having spilt much *b.*
P. L. 12, 176. to *b.* unshed the rivers
P. L. 12, 292. the *b.* of bulls and goats
P. L. 12, 293. *b.* more precious must be paid
P. R. 2, 78. with infant *b.*
P. R. 4, 139. by their sports to *b.* inured
S. A. 1513. *b.*, death, and deathful deeds
S. A. 1726. soaked in his enemies' *b.*
C. 670. when the fresh *b.* grows lively
C. 810. settlings of a melancholy *b.*
S. 12, 14. this waste of wealth and loss of *b.*
S. 16, 7. with *b.* of Scots imbrued
S. 18, 10. their martyred *b.* and ashes sow
H. 57. unstained with hostile *b.*
P. 40. now sunk in guiltless *b.*
**Bloody.**—P. L. 10, 278. in *b.* fight
P. L. 11, 457. the *b.* fact will be avenged
P. L. 11, 651. aid which makes a *b.* fray
S. 18, 7. slain by the *b.* Piemontese
**Bloom.**—P. L. 3, 43. or sight of vernal *b.*
P. L. 3, 355. the tree of life, began to *b.*
P. L. 5, 25. sits on the *b.* extracting liquid sweet
P. L. 8, 45. how they prospered, bud and *b.*
S. A. 1576. the first-born *b.* of spring
**C.** 289. of manly prime, or youthful *b.*
**Blooming.**—P. L. 4, 219. *b.* ambrosial fruit
C. 394. laden with *b.* gold
**Bloomy.**—S. 1, 1. on yon *b.* spray
**Blossom.**—S. 2, 4. spring no bud or *b.* sheweth
D. F. I. 4. that made thy *b.* dry
M. W. 41. the fair *b.* hangs the head
**Blossoms.**—P. L. 4, 148. *b.* and fruits at once
P. L. 4, 630. those *b.* also and . . dropping gums
P. L. 7, 326. gemmed their *b.*
C. 396. save her *b.*, and defend her fruit
**Blot.**—P. L. 11, 891. not to *b.* out mankind
P. L. 12, 188. and *b.* out three days
S. A. 411. O *b.* to honour and religion
S. A. 978. the *b.* of falsehood
C. 133. makes one *b.*
D. F. I. 12. to wipe away the infamous *b.*
**Blotted.**—P. L. 1, 362. *b.* out and rased
**Blow.**—P. L. 2, 171. *b.* them into sevenfold
P. L. 2, 717. till winds the signal *b.*
P. L. 4, 161. north-east winds *b.* Sabæan odours
P.L. 5, 192. ye Winds, that from four quarters *b.*
P. L. 6, 60. trumpet from on high gan *b.*
P. L. 6, 140. at one *b.* unaided
P. L. 6, 370. but with redoubled *b.*
P. L. 10, 1066. the winds *b.* moist and keen
P. R. 1, 317. when winds *b.* keen
C. 993. *b.* flowers of more mingled hue
Il. P. 161. let the pealing organ *b.*
H. 130. heaven's deep organ *b.*
S. M. 11. angel-trumpets *b.*
**Blowing.**—P. L. 1, 540. *b.* martial sounds
P. L. 9, 629. *b.* myrrh and balm
P. L. 10, 289. when two polar winds, *b.* adverse
P. L. 11, 842. *b.* dry, wrinkled the face of deluge
S. A. 10. the breath of heaven fresh *b.*
**Blown.**—P. L. 4, 809. *b.* up with high conceits
P. L. 7, 319. and these scarce *b.*
P. L. 9, 579. a savoury odour *b.*
P. L. 11, 16. by envious winds *b.* vagabond
P. L. 11, 313. *b.* stifling back on him
S. A. 1070. what wind hath *b.* him hither
Il P. 128. when the gust hath *b.*
D. F. I. 1. no sooner *b.* but blasted
**Blows.**—P. L. 3, 488. *b.* them transverse
P. L. 5, 22. how *b.* the citron grove
L. 48. when first the white-thorn *b.*
L. 94. *b.* from off each beaked promontory
**Blue.**—P. L. 11, 206. the *b.* firmament
C. 434. *b.* meagre hag

C. 894. of turkis *b.*, and emerald green
A. 51. the harms of thwarting thunder *b.*
L. 192. twitched his mantle *b.*
L'A. 21. on beds of violets *b.*
H. 210. dance about the furnace *b.*
**Blue-haired.**—C. 29. his *b.-h.* deities
**Blush.**—P. L. 11, 184. short *b.* of morn
**Blushing.**—P. L. 8, 511. I led her *b.* like the morn
P. L. 9, 426. the roses *b.* round about her glowed
**Bluster.**—P. L. 10, 665. with *b.* to confound
**Blustering.**—P. L. 2, 286. *b.* winds
P. L. 3, 426. Chaos *b.* round
**Board.**—P. L. 5, 343. on the *b.* heaps
**Boars.**—S. A. 1138. of chafed wild *b.*
**Boast.**—P. L. 1, 693. who *b.* in mortal things
P. L. 2, 52. of wiles, more unexpert, I *b.* not
P. L. 2, 483. lest bad men should *b.*
P. L. 4, 14. nor with cause to *b.*
P. L. 4, 87. how dearly I abide that *b.*
P. L. 4, 1008. to *b.* what arms can do
P. L. 6, 163. unanswered lest thou *b.*
P. L. 9, 965. from whose dear side I *b.* me
P. L. 11, 86. but let him *b.* his knowledge
P. R. 2, 119. without sign of *b.*
P. R. 4, 307. his tedious talk is but vain *b.*
S.A. 1104. *b.* not of what thou wouldst have done
S. A. 1127. to *b.* again in safety
C. 75. *b.* themselves more comely
C. 273. not any *b.* of skill
C. 662. fool, do not *b.*
M. M. 8. hill and dale doth *b.* thy blessing
**Boasted.**—P. L. 1, 510. their *b.* parents
S. A. 470. all these *b.* trophies
**Boaster.**—S.A. 1227. camest thou for this, vain *b.*
**Boast'st.**—P. R. 1, 409. who *b.* release
**Boastful.**—P. L. 6, 84. with *b.* argument
**Boasting.**—P. L. 4, 85. *b.* I could subdue
**Boasts.**—P. R. 1, 144. because he *b.*
P. R. 4, 306. when he lists, he leaves, or *b.* he can
**Bocchus.**—P. R. 4. 72. the realm of *B.*
**Bodies.**—P. L. 5, 497. your *b.* may at last turn
P. L. 6, 574. *b.* made of oak or fir
P. L. 6, 754. *b.* all and wings
P. L. 7, 354. of celestial *b.*, first the Sun
P. L. 8, 28. so many nobler *b.*
P. L. 8, 87. *b.* bright and greater
P. L. 10, 1072. by collision of two *b.*
**Boding.**—See *ill-boding.*
**Body.**—P. L. 3, 619. shadow from *b.* opaque
P. L. 4, 618. man hath his daily work of *b.*
P. L. 4, 953. army of fiends, fit *b.* to fit head
P. L. 5, 478. till *b.* up to spirit work
P. L. 8, 622. thou in the *b.* enjoy'st
P. L. 9, 779. at once both *b.* and mind
P. L. 10, 587. now in *b.*, and to dwell
P. L. 10, 791. the *b.* properly hath neither
P. L. 11, 687. births of *b.* or mind
P. R. 2, 256. without this *b.'s* wasting
P. R. 2, 478. other o'er the *b.* only reigns
S. A. 18. ease to the *b.* some
S. A. 52. O impotence of mind in *b.* strong
S. A. 159. in real darkness of the *b.*
S. A. 607. to the *b.'s* wounds and sores
S. A. 1706. though her *b.* die
S. A. 1725. find the *b.* where it lies
C. 473. loth to leave the *b.* that it loved
**Bog.**—P. L. 2, 592. that Serbonian *b.*
P. L. 2, 948. o'er *b.*, or steep, through strait
**Boggy.**—P. L. 2, 939. quenched in a *b.* Syrtis
**Bogs.**—P. L. 2, 621. *b.*, dens, and shades of death
P. L. 9, 641. to *b.* and mires
**Boiled.**—P. R. 2, 343. from the spit, or *b.*
**Boiling.**—P. L. 1, 706. and from the *b.* cells
P. L. 2, 183. yon *b.* ocean wrapped in chains
P. L. 2, 1027. whose *b.* gulf tamely endured
**Boils.**—P. L. 4, 16. now rolling, *b.*
P. L. 12, 42. *b.* out from under ground
**Boisterous.**—S. A. 1164. with those thy *b.* locks
S. A. 1273. *b.* force of violent men
D. F. I. 9. by *b.* rape
**Bold.**—P. L. 1, 82. with *b.* words

P. L. 1, 127. thus answered soon his *b.* compeer
P. L. 1, 470. against the house of God was *b.*
P. L. 1, 763. champions *b.* wont ride in armed
P. L. 2, 204. those who at the spear are *b.*
P. L. 2, 386. the *b.* design pleased highly
P. L. 2, 571. on *b.* adventure to discover
P. L. 2, 751. in *b.* conspiracy
P. L. 4, 13. though *b.* far off
P. L. 4, 854. thy fear, said Zephon *b.*
P. L. 4, 882. question thy *b.* entrance
P. L. 5, 66. *b.* words vouched with a deed so *b.*
P. L. 5, 803. thus far his *b.* discourse
P. L. 5, 876. thus answered *b.*
P. L. 8, 235. incensed at such eruption *b.*
P. L. 9, 304. though *b.* will hardly dare
P. L. 9, 436. then voluble and *b.*
P. L. 9, 664. when now more *b.* the tempter
P. L. 9, 921. *b.* deed thou hast presumed
P. L. 10, 161. *b.* or loquacious
P. L. 10, 521. as accessories to his *b.* riot
P. L. 11, 642. giants of mighty bone and *b.*
P. R. 2, 312. prophet *b.*, native of Thebez
P. R. 4, 625. Abaddon rues thy *b.* attempt
S. A. 138. the *b.* Ascalonite fled
S. A. 1152. to combat thee his champion *b.*
C. 397. the rash hand of *b.* Incontinence
C. 610. I love thy courage yet, and *b.* emprise
L'A. 119. throngs of knights and barons *b.*
Il P. 110. the story of Cambuscan *b.*
S. 17, 4. the fierce Epirot and the African *b.*
Brut. 14. conquer nations *b.*
**Bolder.**—P. L. 3, 13. I revisit now with *b.* wing
P. L. 9, 523. he, *b.* now. uncalled
P. L. 11, 93. lest therefore his now *b.* hand
P. R. 4, 180. *b.* than that on Eve
**Boldest.**—P. L. 6, 118. weakest prove where *b.*
**Boldly.**—P. L. 2, 968. Satan, turning *b.*, thus
P. L. 4, 891. and *b.* venture
C. 649. *b.* assault the necromancer's hall
**Boldness.**—P. L. 4, 908. what *b.* brought him
**Bolster.**—C. 353. some cold bank is her *b.*
**Bolt.**—P. L. 2, 877. *b.* and bar of massy iron
P. L. 6, 491. his only dreaded *b.*
C. 445. the frivolous *b.* of Cupid
C. 760. when vice can *b.* her arguments
**Bolted.**—P. L. 4, 190. cross-barred and *b.* fast
S. A. 1696. his cloudless thunder *b.*
**Bond.**—P. L. 9, 956. I feel the *b.* of nature
**Bondage.**—P. L. 1, 658. celestial Spirits in *b.*
P. L. 2, 321. remain in strictest *b.*
S. A. 152. thy *b.* or lost sight
S. A. 270. to love *b.* more than liberty
S. A. 271. *b.* with ease than strenuous liberty
**Bonds**—P. L. 2, 207. exile, or ignominy, or *b.*
P. L. 7, 465. then springs, as broke from *b.*
S. A. 42. in *b.* under Philistian yoke
S. A. 853. the *b.* of civil duty
**Bondslave.**—S. A. 38. lower than *b.*
S. A. 411. yoked her *b.*
**Bond-woman.**—P. R. 2, 308. fugitive *b.-w.*
**Bone.**—P. L. 4, 483. his flesh, his *b.*
P. L. 8, 495. I now see *b.* of my *b.*
P. L. 9, 915. *b.* of my *b.* thou art
P. L. 11, 642. giants of mighty *b.*
S. A. 143. his sword of *b.*
**Bones.**—P. L. 1, 427. the brittle strength of *b.*
S. A. 1142. all my sinews, joints, and *b.*
L. 155. where'er thy *b.* are hurled
S. 18, 1. thy slaughtered saints, whose *b.*
W. S. 1. Shakespeare for his honoured *b.*
**Book.**—P. L. 1, 363. from the *b.* of life
P. L. 3, 47. the *b.* of knowledge
P. L. 8, 67. for heaven is as the *b.* of God
C. 367. unprincipled in virtue's *b.*
S. 11, 1. a *b.* was writ of late
S. 18, 5. in thy *b.* record their groans
W. S. 11. the leaves of thy unvalued *b.*
**Bonnet.**—L. 104. his *b.* sedge
**Books.**—P. R. 4, 321. many *b.* are wearisome
P. R. 4. 327. deep-versed in *b.*
S. A. 653. in modern *b.* enrolled

C. 391. his few *b.* or his beads
**Boon.**—P. L. 4, 242. but nature *b.* poured forth
P. L. 9, 793. jocund and *b.*
**Boots.**—S. A. 560. what *b.* it at one gate
L. 64. alas! what *b.* it with incessant care
U. C. I. 16. pulled off his *b.*
**Booty.**—P. L. 11, 650. over the plain, their *b*
**Border.**—P. L. 2, 361. the utmost *b.*
P. L. 4, 131. to the *b.* comes of Eden
**Bordering.**—P. L. 1, 419. the *b.* flood
P. L. 2, 131. oft on the *b.* deep
P. L. 2, 959. lies *b.* on light
P. R. 1, 193. the *b.* Desert wild
S. A. 976. in Judah, and the *b.* tribes
**Borders.**—P. L. 3, 537. Land *b.* on Egypt
P. L. 7, 328. with *b.* long the rivers
S. A. 730. wetting the *b.* of her silken veil
**Bore.**—P. L. 1, 528. *b.* semblance of worth
P. L. 4, 591. *b.* him slope downward
P. L. 6, 337. *b.* him on their shields
P. L. 6, 485. *b.* with touch of fire dilated
P. L. 6, 646. *b.* them in their hands
P. L. 7, 470. *b.* up his branching head
P. L. 9, 509. with her who *b.* Scipio
P. L. 9, 1175. confidence then *b.* thee on
P. R. 1, 26. and witness *b.*
P. R. 2, 71. by the birth I *b.*
P. R. 3, 314. prancing their riders *b.*
P. R. 4, 542. *b.* through the air
S. A. 146. *b.* the gates of Azza
S. A. 1752. *b.* witness gloriously
C. 633. *b.* a bright golden flower
L. 58. the muse herself that Orpheus *b.*
L. 110. two mossy keys he *b.*
L'A. 16. to ivy-crowned Bacchus *b.*
Il P. 24. to solitary Saturn *b.*
Cir. 24. vengeful justice *b.*
M. W. 65. highly-favoured Joseph *b.*
**Boreas.**—P. L. 10, 699. *B.*, and Cæcias
**Born.**—P. L. 2, 797. hourly *b.* with sorrow
P. L. 2, 860. and heavenly-*b.*
P. L. 3, 463. sons and daughters *b.*
P. L. 4, 323. the goodliest man of men since *b.*
P. L. 7, 471. Behemoth, biggest *b.*
P. L. 10, 584. Jove was *b.*
P. L. 10, 980. be *b.* to certain woe
P. L. 11, 496. not of woman *b.*
P. L. 12, 359. be *b.* barred of his right
P. R. 1, 65. late of woman *b.*
P. R. 1, 140. *b.* and now upgrown
P. R. 1, 205. I thought *b.* to that end, *b.* to
P. R. 1, 245. Messiah now was *b.*
P. R. 1, 254. knew thee King of Israel *b.*
P. R. 1, 341. to such misery and hardship *b.*
P. R. 2, 72. in such a season *b.*
P. R. 3, 152. to a Kingdom thou art *b.*
P. R. 4, 506. sung thee Saviour *b.*
S. A. 11. with day-spring *b.*
C. 522. of Bacchus and of Circe *b.*
C. 1010. blissful twins are to be *b.*
L'A. 2. blackest Midnight *b.*
S. 10, 9. though later *b.*
H. 3. Virgin-Mother *b.*
D. F. I. 25. on Eurotas' strand
······ 13. kings be *b.* of thee
**Borne.**—P. L. 2, 953. *b.* through the hollow dark
P. L. 3, 16. through middle darkness *b.*
P. L. 6, 33. the testimony of truth hast *b.*
P. L. 6, 544. shield, *b.* even or high
P. L. 6, 776. aloft by angels *b.*
P. L. 7, 431. her annual voyage, *b.* on winds
P.L.11, 764. *b.* my part of evil only, each day's lot
P. R. 3, 93. thy wrongs with saintly patience *b.*
**Borrow.**—Cir. 8. burn in your sighs, and *b.*
**Borrowed.**—P. L. 1, 483. their *b.* gold
P. L. 3, 730. with *b.* light
P. L. 4, 116. marred his *b.* visage
**Borrower.**—C. 683. deal like an ill *b.*
**Borrowing.**—P. L. 7, 377. *b.* her light
**Bosky.**—C. 313. every *b.* bourn
**Bosom.**—P. L. 2, 1036. the *b.* of dim night

P. L. 3, 169. Son of my *b.*
P. L. 3, 239. I for his sake will leave thy *b.*
P. L. 3, 279. for him I spare thee from my *b.*
P. L. 7, 319. made gay her *b.*, smelling sweet
P. L. 10, 225. into his blissful *b.*
P. R. 4, 597. throned in the *b.* of bliss
S. A. 763. a poisonous *b.* snake
C. 23. the unadorned *b.* of the deep
M. W. 69. far within the *b.* bright
**Bosomed.**—P. L. 5, 127. their choicest *b.* smells
L'A. 78. high *b.* in tufted trees
**Bosoms.**—C. 368. peace that goodness *b.* ever
**Bosporus.**—P. L. 2, 1018. *B.*, betwixt the rocks
**Bossy.**—P. L. 1, 716. with *b.* sculptures graven
**Botches.**—P. L. 12, 180. *b.* and blains
**Both.**—occurs frequently, both pronoun and conj.
**Bottom.**—P. L. 1, 236. leave a singèd *b.*
P. L. 1, 329. transfix us to the *b.* of this gulf
P. L. 2, 882. the lowest *b.* shook of Erebus
P. L. 4, 19. from the *b.* stir the hell within him
P. L. 6, 649. the *b.* of the mountains
P. L. 7, 213. up the *b.* turned by furious winds
P. L. 7, 289. a hollow *b.*, broad and deep
P. L. 11, 753. all left in one small *b.*
P. R. 2, 289. in a *b.* saw a pleasant grove
C. 833. the water nymphs, that in the *b.* played
L. 158. the *b.* of the monstrous world
C. 532. that brow this *b.* glade
**Bottomless.**—P. L. 1, 47. to *b.* perdition
P. L. 6, 866. burned after them to the *b.* pit
P. R. 1, 361. from bliss to the *b.* Deep
**Bough.**—P. L. 5, 8. birds on every *b.*
P. L. 5, 326. from each *b.* and brake
P. L. 9, 851. in her hand a *b.*
P. L. 9, 995. from the *b.* she gave **him**
**Boughs.**—P. L. 4, 332. compliant *b.*
P. L. 5, 214. their pampered *b.*
P. L. 5, 428. from off the *b.* each morn
P. L. 9, 579. from the *b.* a savoury odour blown
P. L. 9, 1089. ye cedars, with innumerable *b.*
C. 349. close dungeon of innumerous *b.*
A. 50. from the *b.* brush off the evil dew
**Bought.**—P. L. 4, 102. short intermission *b.*
P. L. 4, 222. knowledge of good *b.* dear
P. L. 4, 765. not in the *b.* smile of harlots
**Bound.**—P L. 2, 236. within Heaven's *b.*
P. L. 2, 892. ocean without *b.*
P. L. 3, 256. the Powers of darkness *b.*
P. L. 3, 539. *b.* the ocean wave
P. L. 4, 171. to Egypt, there fast *b.*
P. L. 4, 181. at one slight *b.* high overleaped all *b.*
P. L. 5, 290. message high they guessed him *b.*
P. L. 6, 358. at his chariot-wheels to drag him *b.*
P. L. 6, 870. too fast had *b.*
P. L. 7, 21. *b.* within the visible diurnal spheres
P. L. 7, 608. can impair thee, mighty King or *b.*
P. L. 8, 230. *b.* on a voyage uncouth and obscure
P. L. 10, 297. look *b.* with Gorgonian rigour
P. L. 11, 265. all his senses *b.*
P. L. 11, 291. husband; him to follow thou art *b.*
P. L. 12, 370. *b.* his reign with earth's
P. R. 3, 315. from *b.* to *b.*
P. R. 3, 367. Antigonus and old Hyrcanus, *b.*
P. R. 4, 632. *b.*, and to torment sent
S. A. 261. *b.* with two cords
S. A. 365. assaulted, overcome, led *b.*
S. A. 438. delivered thee Samson *b.*
S. A. 715. for the isles of Javan
S. A. 1184. delivered *b.* into our hands
S. A. 1209. gave up *b.*
C. 816. snatched his wand, and *b.* him fast
H. 169. in straiter limits *b.*
P. 23. to this horizon is my Phœbus *b.*
**Boundless.**—P. L. 1, 177. the vast and *b.* deep
P. L. 3, 423. seems a *b.* continent
P. L. 7, 168. *b.* the deep
**Bounds.**—P. L. 1, 466. Gaza's frontier *b.*
P. L. 1, 518. through all the *b.*
P. L. 2, 644. hell *b.*, high reaching
P. L. 2, 976. where your gloomy *b.*
P. L. 3, 81. whom no *b.* prescribed

P. L. 3, 432. the roving Tartar *b.*
P. L. 3, 538. where *b.* were set
P. L. 4, 583. o'erleaped these earthly *b.*
P. L. 4, 878. why hast thou, Satan, broke the *b.*
P. L. 4, 897. object his will who *b.* us
P. L. 4, 909. his *b.* in hell prescribed
P. L. 5, 478. *b.* proportioned to each kind
P. L. 5, 639. full measure only *b.* excess
P. L. 6, 716. from all heaven's *b.*
P. L. 6, 859. the *b.* and crystal wall of heaven
P. L. 7, 120. desire of knowledge within *b.*
P. L. 7, 167. within appointed *b.*
P. L. 7, 230. thus far extend, thus far thy *b.*
P. L. 8, 338. not only these fair *b.*
P. L. 10, 365. hold us in her *b.*
P. L. 10, 380. by the empyreal *b.*
P. L. 11, 68. through Heaven's wide *b.*
P. L. 11, 341. to these narrow *b.* confined
P. L. 11, 828. to usurp beyond all *b.*
P. L. 11, 894. nor let the sea surpass his *b.*
P. L. 12, 187. overshadow all his *b.*
P. L. 12, 371. with earth's wide *b.*
P. R. 1, 13. height or depth of Nature's *b.*
P. R. 3, 270. her empire's ancient *b.*
S. A. 1714. through all Philistian *b.*
C. 673. dances in his crystal *b.*
S. 17, 12. the *b.* of either sword
**Bounteous.**—P. L. 5, 205. Lord! be *b.* still
P. L. 8, 492. Creator *b.* and benign
C. 176. they praise the *b.* Pan
M. M. 5. hail *b.* May that dost inspire
**Bounties.**—P. L. 5, 330. dispensed his *b.*
P. L. 5, 398. please to taste these *b.*
C. 710. pour her *b.* forth
C. 987. thither all their *b.* bring
**Bounty.**—P. L. 4, 437. extol his *b.*
P. L. 5, 430. God hath here varied his *b.* so
P. L. 9, 1033. *b.* of this virtuous tree
P. L. 10, 54. not return as *b.* scorned
P. R. 3, 142. so much *b.* is in God
**Bourn.**—C. 313. every bosky *b.*
**Bout.**—L'A. 139. many a winding *b.*
**Bow.**—P. L. 1, 111. *b.* and sue for grace
P. L. 3, 321. all knees to thee shall *b.*
P. L. 3, 350. towards either throne they *b.*
P. L. 4, 151. fair evening cloud, or humid *b.*
P. L. 5, 607. have sworn to him shall *b.*
P. L. 6, 713. bring forth all my war, my *b.*
P. L. 6, 763. beside him hung his *b.*
P. L. 9, 390. with *b.* and quiver armed
P. L. 11, 865. in the cloud a *b.*
P. L. 11, 897. his triple-coloured *b.*
P. R. 2, 171. *b.* to the gods of his wives
C. 441. hence had the huntress Dian her dread *b.*
C. 992. Iris there with humid *b.*
**Bow-bent.**—V. E. 69. *b.-b.* to with crooked age
**Bowed.**—P. L. 1, 436. *b.* down in battle
P. L. 5, 144. lowly they *b.* adoring
P. L. 9, 524. oft he *b.* his turret crest
P. L. 11, 249. Adam *b.* low
P. R. 4, 418. sturdiest oaks *b.*
S. A. 1646. all his nerves, he *b.*
C. 1015. where the *b.* welkin slow doth bend
Il P. 71. as if her head she *b.*
**Bowels.**—P. L. 1, 687. the *b.* of their mother
P. L. 2, 800. gnaw my *b.*
P. L. 2, 863. that on my *b.* feed
**Bower.**—P. L. 3, 734. those lofty shades, his *b.*
P. L. 4, 690. on to their blissful *b.*
P. L. 4, 705. in shadier *b.*
P. L. 4, 738. into their inmost *b.*
P. L. 4, 798. these to the *b.* direct
P. L. 5, 230. in what *b.* or shade
P. L. 5, 300. of his cool *b.*
P. L. 5, 367. in yonder shady *b.* to rest
P. L. 5, 375. where thy *b.* o'ershades
P. L. 8, 510. to the nuptial *b.* I led her
P. L. 8, 653. Adam to his *b.*
P. L. 9, 401. by noon amid the *b.*
P. L. 9, 417. in *b.* and field he sought
P. L. 11, 280. nuptial *b.*, by me adorned

P. L. 12, 607. the *b.* where Eve lay sleeping
C. 45. in hall or *b.*
C. 921. wait in Amphitrite's *b.*
A. 45. live in oaken *b.*
L'A. 87. in haste her *b.* she leaves
Il P. 104. raise Musæus from his *b.*
S. 8, 9. against the Muses' *b.*
**Bowers.**—P. L. 4, 246. the noontide *b.*
P. L. 8, 305. with walks and *b.*
P. L. 9, 244. these paths and *b.*
P. L. 10, 860. hillocks, dales, and *b.*
P. L. 11, 77. their blissful *b.* of amarantine
C. 536. obscured haunts of inmost *b.*
C. 984. along the crisped shades and *b.*
Il P. 27. in glimmering *b.* and glades
**Bowing.**—P. L. 3, 736. Satan *b.* low
P. L. 1, 434. *b.* lowly down
P. L. 5, 360. as to a superior nature *b.* low
P. L. 6, 746. so said, he, o'er his sceptre *b.*, rose
P. R. 1, 497. Satan *b.* low his gray dissimulation •
**Bows.**—P. R. 3, 305. steel *b.* and shafts
**Bow'st.**—S. A. 698. thou *b.* thee down
**Boy.**—Il P. 124. with the Attic *b.* to hunt
**Brace.**—P. L. 11, 188. pursued a gentle *b.*
**Brag.**—C. 745. beauty is nature's *b.*
**Braid.**—C. 105. *b.* your locks with rosy twine
**Braided.**—P. L. 4, 349. his *b.* train
**Braids.**—C. 862. in twisted *b.* of lilies
**Brain.**—Il P. 5. dwell in some idle *b.*
**Brains.**—S. A. 1241. to the hazard of thy *b.*
**Brake.**—P. L. 4, 175. as one continued *b.*
P. L. 5, 326. from each bough and *b.*
P. L. 7, 458. in thicket, *b.*, or den
P. L. 9, 160. pry in every bush and *b.*
**Brakes.**—C. 147. within these *b.* and trees
**Branch.**—P. L. 7, 433. from *b.* to *b.*
**Branches.**—P. L. 4, 627. with *b.* overgrown
P. L. 6, 575. with *b.* lopt
P. L. 7, 325. their *b.* hung with copious fruit
P. L. 8, 265. birds on the *b.* warbling
P. L. 9, 590. the *b.* would require
P. L. 9, 802. ease of thy full *b.*
C. 969. three fair *b.*
**Branching.**—P. L. 4, 139. fir, and *b.* palm
P. L. 6, 885. shaded with *b.* palm
P. L. 7, 470. bore up his *b.* head
P. L. 9, 1104. spreads her arms *b.*
P. R. 4, 405. whose *b.* arms thick intertwined
S. A. 1735. ever green, and *b.* palm
A. 89. *b.* elm star-proof
**Brand.**—P. L. 12, 643. that flaming *b.*
S. A. 967. the *b.* of infamy
S. 15, 12. cleared from the shameful *b.*
**Brandished.**—P. L. 6, 252. *b.* aloft
P. L. 12, 633. the *b.* sword of God
C. 651. hardihood and *b.* blade
**Brandishing.**—P. L. 2, 786. *b.* his fatal dart
**Brass.**—P. L. 2, 645. three folds were *b.*
P. L. 6, 576. *b.*, iron, stony mould
P. L. 11, 565. two massy clods of iron and *b.*
S. A. 1120. helmet and brigandine of *b.*
Il P. 114. the wondrous horse of *b.*
**Braveries.**—S. A. 1243. shalt lament these *b.*
**Bravery.**—S. A. 717. with all her *b.* on
**Brayed.**—P. L. 6, 209. *b.* horrible discord
**Brazen.**—P. L. 1, 724. opening their *b.* folds
P. L. 6, 211. the madding wheels of *b.* chariots
P. L. 7, 201. between two *b.* mountains lodged
P. L. 7, 496. with *b.* eyes
P. L. 10, 697. bursting their *b.* dungeon
P. L. 11, 713. the *b.* throat of war
S. A. 35. grind in *b.* fetters
S. A. 132. *b.* shield and spear
**Breach.**—P. L. 6, 879. her mural *b.*
P. L. 9, 6. *b.* disloyal on the part of man
**Bread.**—P. L. 10, 205. thou shalt eat *b.*
P. L. 10, 1055. I must earn my *b.*
P. L. 12, 78. famish him of breath, if not of *b.*
P. R. 1, 343. stones be made thee *b.*
P. R 1, 347. think'st thou such force in *b.*
P. R. 1, 349. man lives not by *b.* only

S. A. 573. drudge, and earn my *b.*
**Breadth.**—P. L. 2, 893. length, *b.*, and height
P. L. 3, 561. from pole to pole he views in *b.*
P. L. 10, 673. like distant *b.*
P. L. 11, 730. length, and *b.*, and height
P. R. 4, 27. in *b.* not wide
**Break.**—P. L. 2, 134. or could we *b.* our way
P. L. 3, 545. by *b.* of cheerful dawn
P. L. 4, 889. *b.* loose from hell
P. L. 5, 887. an iron rod to bruise and *b.*
P. L. 9, 412. since first *b.* of dawn
S. A. 116. let us not *b.* in upon him
S. A. 750. to *b.* all faith, all vows
S. A. 1349. whether to hold or *b.*
S. A. 1626. to heave, pull, draw, or *b.*
C. 145. *b.* off, *b.* off; I feel the different pace
C. 481. *b.* the silent air
C. 651. *b.* his glass
**Breaking.**—P. L. 1, 83. *b.* the horrid silence
P. L. 2, 782. *b.* violent way
S. A. 1115. *b.* her marriage faith
S. 10, 5. *b.* of that parliament
**Breaks.**—P. L. 3, 204 *b.* his fealty
P. L. 5, 612. *b.* union
C. 435. *b.* his magic chains
S. A. 1050. *b.* through all opposition
**Breast**—P. L. 2, 568. arm th' obdurèd *b.*
P. L. 4, 16 boils in his tumultuous *b.*
P. L. 4, 495. half her swelling *b.* naked met his
P. L. 5, 279. came mantling o'er his *b.*
P. L. 5, 695. influence into the unwary *b.*
P. L. 6, 560. with open *b.* stand ready
P. L. 6, 612. with open front and *b.*
P. L. 7, 438. bathed their downy *b.*
P. L. 9, 288. how found they harbour in thy *b.*
P. L. 9, 1131. from thus distempered *b.*
P. L. 10, 975. what thoughts in my unquiet *b.*
P. L. 11, 154. peace returned home to my *b.*
P. L. 11, 374. to the evil turn my obvious *b.*
P. R. 1, 185. much revolving in his *b.*
P. R. 1, 301. lodged in his *b.*
P. R. 2, 63. within her *b.* though calm, her *b.*
P. R. 2, 167. the manliest, resolutest *b.*
P. R. 3, 15. those oraculous gems on Aaron's *b.*
S. A. 609. in heart, head, *b.*, and reins
S. A. 1722. nothing to wail or knock the *b.*
C. 246. something holy lodges in that *b.*
C. 381. within his own clear *b.*
C. 911. I sprinkle on thy *b.* drops
L'A. 73. mountains on whose barren *b.*
**Breastplate.**—P. L. 3, 598. Aaron's *b.*
**Breasts.**—P. L. 9, 730. in heavenly *b.*
S. A. 1739. from his memory inflame their *b.*
**Breath.**—P. L. 2, 170. the *b.* that kindled
P. L. 2, 214. if his *b.* stir not their flames
P. L. 4, 641. sweet is the *b.* of Morn
P. L. 4, 650. neither *b.* of Morn
P. L. 7, 526. breathed the *b.* of life
P. L. 10, 784. that pure *b.* of life
P. L. 10, 789. it was but *b.* of life
P. L. 11, 147. one short sigh of human *b.*
P. L. 11, 312. *b.* against the wind
P. L. 12, 78. famish him of *b.*
P. R. 4, 258. who gave them *b.*
S. A. 10. the *b.* of heaven
S. A. 628. nor *b.* of vernal air
S. A. 905. lack of *b.*
S. A. 1126. while *b.* remains thee
S. A. 1555 but I recover *b.*
A. 56. ere the odorous *b.* of morn
M. W. 9. after so short time of *b.*
U. C. II. 12. put him out of *b.*
U. C. II. 25. that ev'n to his last *b.*
**Breathe.**—P. L. 2, 402. shall *b.* her balm
P. L. 3, 607. forth elixir pure
P. L. 5, 193. *b.* soft or loud
P. L. 9, 194. all things that *b.*
P. L. 9, 447. issuing on a summer's morn to *b.*
P. L. 11, 284. *b.* in other air less pure
C. 245. *b.* such divine enchanting ravishment
Il P. 151. as I wake, sweet music *b.*

**Breathed.** 25.—P. L. 1, 554. deliberate valour *b.*
P. L. 3, 267. *b.* immortal love
P. L. 6, 65. instrumental harmony that *b.*
P. L. 7, 525. *b.* the breath of life
P. L. 9. 193. *b.* their morning incense
P. L. 11, 5. sighs now *b.* unutterable
P. L. 12, 374. which these he *b.*
H. 179. no nightly trance or *b.* spell

**Breathes.**—P. L. 1, 709. the sound-board *b.*
P. L. 2, 244. his altar *b.* ambrosial odours
P. L. 5, 16. as when Zephyrus on Flora *b.*
P. L. 5, 482. spirits odorous *b.*
P. L. 11, 313. back on him that *b.* it forth
L'A. 18. the frolic wind that *b.*

**Breath'st.**—P. L. 2, ,697. *b.* defiance here

**Breathing.**—P. L. 1, 560. they *b.* united force
P. L. 4, 265. *b.* the smell of field and grove
A. 32. the *b.* roses of the wood
U. C. II. 12. too much *b.* put him out of breath

**Breaths.**—P. L. 4, 806. like gentle *b.*

**Bred.**—P. L. 2, 799. into the womb that *b.*
P. L. 3, 431. as when a vulture on Imaus *b.*
P. L. 5, 4. from pure digestion *b.*
P. L. 9, 1050. *b.* of unkindly fumes
P. L. 11, 276. *b.* up with tender hand
P. L. 11, 414. clearer sight had *b.*
P. L. 11, 618. *b.* only and completed to the taste
P. L. 12, 115. *b.* up in idol-worship
P. R. 2, 300. in city or court or palace *b.*
P. R. 2, 415. *b.* up in poverty and straits
P. R. 4, 251. *b.* great Alexander
P. R. 4, 509. though yet in private *b.*
Il P. 2, without father *b.*

**Breed.**—C. 157. quaint habits *b.* astonishment
C. 266. these rough shades did never *b.*
S. 15, 10. but endless war still *b.*
D. F. I. 61. what creatures heaven doth *b.*

**Breeding.**—P. L. 9, 1010. divinity .. *b.* wings
S. A. 30. why was my *b.* ordered and prescribed

**Breeds.**— P. L. 2, 624. death lives, and nature *b.*

**Brethren.**—P. L. 3, 297. raise his *b.*
P. L. 11, 454. these two are *b.*
P. L. 11, 680. but of their *b.*, men of men
P. L. 12, 28. dominion undeserved over his *b.*
P. L. 12, 65. to aspire above his *b.*
P. L. 12, 169. two *b.* call Moses and Aaron
P. R. 3, 374. deliverance of thy *b.*
P. R. 3, 403. my *b.*, as thou call'st them
S. A. 332. *b.*, and men of Dan
S. A. 1413. *b.*, farewell
S. A. 1445. peace with you, *b.*
P. 21, 169. fast by his *b.*'s side
V. Ex. 75. o'er all his *b.* he shall reign

**Brewed.**—C. 696. thy *b.* enchantments

**Briareos.**—P. L. 1, 199. *B.* or Typhon

**Brick.**—P. L. 12, 43. of *b.*, and of that stuff

**Bridal.**—P. L. 8, 520. to light the *b.* lamp
S. A. 1196. *b.* friends and guests

**Bride.**—S. A. 320. that fallacious *b.*
S. A. 1018. the Timnian *b.*
S. A. 1198. constrained the *b.*
C. 1008. make her his eternal *b.*

**Bridegroom.**—S. 9, 12. *B.* with his friends

**Bridge.**—P. L. 2, 1028. tamely endured a *b.*
P. L. 10, 301. a *b.* of length prodigious
P. L. 10, 351. at sight of that stupendous *b.*
P. L. 10, 371. overlay with this portentous *b.*

**Bridges.**—P. R. 3, 334. overlay with *b.*

**Bridging.**—P. L. 10, 310. *b.* his way

**Bridle.**—C. 887. *b.* in thy headlong wave

**Brief.**—P. L. 4, 875. and *b.* related
P, L. 6, 171. in *b.* thus Abdiel stern replied
P. L. 9, 664. she scarce had said, though *b.*
P. L. 10, 115. thus answered *b.*
P. R. 4, 264. received in *b.* sententious precepts
P. R. 4, 485. in *b.* him answered
S. A. 1570. take then the worst, in *b.*

**Brieny.**—P. L. 6, 566. *b.* touch what we
C. 512. prithee *b.* show

**Brigad**—P. L. 1, 675. a numerous *b.* hastened

**Brigads.**—P. L. 2, 532. or fronted *b.* form

**Brigandine.**—S. A. 1120. *b.* of brass

**Bright.**—P. L. 1, 87. myriads though *b.*
P. L. 1, 272. leader of those armies *b.*
P. L. 1, 429. *b.* or obscure
P. L. 1, 440. to whose *b.* image
P. L. 1, 737. the Orders *b.*
P. L. 2, 395. in view of those *b.* confines
P. L. 2, 513. with *b.* emblazonry
P. L. 2, 756. to thee in shape and countenance *b.*
P. L. 2, 812. invulnerable in those *b.* arms
P. L. 3, 6. *b.* effluence of *b.* essence
P. L. 3, 362. the *b.* pavement, that like a sea
P. L. 3, 380. dark with excessive *b.*
P. L. 3, 512. bands of guardians *b.*
P. L. 3, 518. underneath a *b.* sea
P. L. 3, 587. wondrously was set his station *b.*
P. L. 3, 591. beyond expression *b.*
P. L. 3, 645. the Angel *b.*, ere he drew nigh
P. L. 3, 655. God's high throne, gloriously *b.*
P. L. 4, 44. in that *b.* eminence
P. L. 4, 361. to heavenly Spirits *b.* little inferior
P. L. 4, 578. amid the sun's *b.* circle
P. L. 4, 590. returned on that *b.* beam
P. L. 4, 977. the angelic squadron *b.*
P. L. 5, 169. the smiling morn with thy *b.* circlet
P. L. 5, 274. his relics in the sun's *b.* temple
P. L. 5, 481. last the *b.* consummate flower
P. L. 5, 587. under their hierarchs in orders *b.*
P. L. 5, 838. created in their *b.* degrees
P. L. 6, 16. thick embattled squadrons *b.*
P. L. 6, 64. moved on in silence their *b.* legions
P. L. 6, 334. his armour stained erewhile so *b.*
P. L. 6, 472. beholds the *b.* surface
P. L. 6, 801. stand still, in *b.* array
P. L. 6, 885. with branching palm, each order *b.*
P. L. 7, 222. followed in *b.* procession
P. L. 7, 372. invested with *b.* rays
P. L. 7, 375. sweet influence. Less *b.* the moon
P. L. 7, 385. adorned with their *b.* luminaries
P. L. 7, 564. the *b.* pomp ascended jubilant
P. L. 8, 87. bodies *b.* and greater
P. L. 8, 88. should not serve the less not *b.*
P. L. 8, 91. great or *b.* infers not excellence
P. L. 8, 98. not to earth are those *b.* luminaries
P. L. 8, 367. the Vision *b.* as with a smile
P. L. 9, 104. their *b.* officious lamps
P. L. 9, 1084. their blaze insufferably *b.*
P. L. 10, 63. unfolding *b.* toward the right hand
P. L. 10, 187. and with ascension *b.*
P. L. 10, 327. in likeness of an Angel *b.*
P. L. 10, 426. that *b.* star to Satan paragoned
P. L. 10, 615. those *b.* Orders uttered
P. L. 11, 73. the *b.* minister that watched
P. L. 11, 127. cohort *b.* of watchful Cherubim
P. L. 11, 215. pavilioned with his guardians *b.*
P. L. 11, 221. in their *b.* stand there
P. L. 11, 329. seek his *b.* appearances
P. L. 12, 254. the wings of two *b.* Cherubim
P. L. 12, 627. all in *b.* array
P. R. 1, 128. who in full frequence *b.*
P. R. 1, 252. by whose *b.* course led on
S. A. 1674. in Silo, his *b.* sanctuary
C. 3. *b.* aërial spirits
C. 382. enjoy *b.* day
C. 633. bore a *b.* golden flower
C. 966. noble Lord and Lady *b.*
A. 18. sitting like a god-less *b.*
A. 27. I see *b.* honour sparkle through your eyes
L. 30. the star that rose at evening, *b.*
L'A. 121. with store of ladies, whose *b.* eyes
S. 8, 8. the sun's *b.* circle warms
Il P. 13. whose saintly visage is too *b.*
H. 21. keep watch in squadrons *b.*
H. 84. his *b.* throne or burning axle-tree
Cir. 1. wingèd warriors *b.*
M. M. 1. now the *b.* Morning-star
S. M. 10. where the *b.* Seraphim
D. F. I. 38. tell me, *b.* spirit
M. W. 61. thou *b.* Saint, high sitt'st in glory
M. W. 69. far within the bosom *b.*

**Brightened.**—P. L. 8, 368. with a smile more *b.*

**Brightening.**—P. L. 2, 399. *b.* orient beam
**Brightens.**—P. L. 9, 634. joy *b.* his crest
**Brighter.**—P. L. 7, 132. *b.* once amidst the host
P. L. 10, 450. star-bright appeared, or *b.*
**Brightest.**—P. L. 3, 134. mercy .. shall *b.* shine
P. L. 3, 381. *b.* Seraphim approach not
P. L. 3, 667. *b.* Seraph, tell
P. L. 4, 606. the starry host, rode *b.*
P. L. 5, 644. the face of *b.* heaven had changed
P. R. 4, 439. amidst this joy and *b.* morn
C. 910. *b.* Lady, look on me
**Bright-haired.**—Il P. 23. *b-h.* Vesta
**Bright-harnessed.**—H. 244. *b.-h.* angels
**Brightness.**—P. L. 1, 86. transcendent *b.*
P. L. 1, 592. not lost all her original *b.*
P. L. 3, 376. invisible amidst the glorious *b.*
P. L. 3, 624. but not his *b.* hid
P. L. 4, 836. or undiminished *b.* to be known
P. L. 5, 599. whose top *b.* had made invisible
P. R. 1, 378. my native *b.*
**Brimmed.**—C. 924. thy *b.* waves
**Brimming.**—P. L. 4, 336. scoop the *b.* stream
**Brimstone.**—P. L. 1, 350. light on the firm *b.*
**Brinded.**—P. L. 7, 466. shakes his *b.* mane
C. 443. she tamed the *b.* lioness
**Brine.**—L. 98. on the level *b.*
**Bring.**—P. L. 2, 222. future days may *b.*
P. L. 1, 163. out of our evil seek to *b.* forth good
P. L. 1, 217. all his malice served but to *b.* forth
P. L. 2, 639. merchants *b.* their spicy drugs
P. L. 2, 840. *b.* ye to the place
P. L. 2, 866. *b.* me soon to that new world
P. L. 2, 899. and to battle *b.*
P. L. 3, 158. thy goodness *b.* to nought
P. L. 3, 190. *b.* obedience due
P. L. 3, 235. hath none to *b.*
P. L. 3, 657. through highest Heaven to *b.*
P. L. 4, 38. *b.* to my remembrance
P. L. 4, 470. follow me, and I will *b.* thee
P. L. 4, 796. seize fast, and hither *b.*
P. L. 5, 314. *b.* forth and pour
P. L. 5, 233. such discourse *b.* on
P. L. 5, 335. *b.* taste after taste
P. L. 6, 471. to our success, I *b.*
P. L. 6, 712. *b.* forth all my war
P. L. 7, 105. night with her will *b.* silence
P. L. 7, 189. a better race to *b.*
P. L. 7, 451. let the earth *b.* forth
P. L. 8, 216. *b.* to their sweetness no satiety
P. L. 8, 343. I *b.* them to receive
P. L. 8, 449. what next I *b.* shall please thee
P. L. 9, 49. whose office is to *b.* twilight
P. L. 9, 162. the dark intent I *b.*
P. L. 9, 630. I can *b.* thee thither soon
P. L. 9, 715. no worse than this can *b.*
P. L. 10, 194. children thou shalt *b.* in sorrow
P. L. 10, 203. thistles it shall *b.* thee forth
P. L. 10, 655. to *b.* solstitial summer's heat
P. L. 10, 677. to *b.* in change of seasons
P. L. 10, 983. *b.* into this cursed world
P. L. 11, 25. I thy Priest before thee *b.*
P. L. 11, 302. thy tidings *b.*
P. L. 11, 428. to *b.* forth more violent deeds
P. L. 11, 473. shall *b.* diseases dire
P. L. 11, 477. Eve shall *b.* on men
P. L. 11, 692. and *b.* home spoils
P. L. 12, 312. *b.* back through the world's
P. L. 12, 551. to *b.* forth fruits
P. R. 1, 64. this ill news I *b.*
P. R. 1, 336. will *b.* me hence
P. R. 2, 394. I *b.* thee voluntary
P. R. 3, 244. but I will *b.* thee where
P. R. 3, 435. some wondrous call may *b.* them
S. A. 183. consolation we may *b.*
S. A. 277. to my remembrance *b.*
S. A. 519. where thou mayst *b.* thy offerings
S. A. 931. *b.* my feet again into the snare
S. A. 1536. will *b.* some notice hither
S. A. 1234. *b.* up thy van
C. 186. to *b.* me berries
C. 305. would *b.* me to that place

C. 987. thither all their bounties *b.*
A. 91. I will *b.* you where she sits
A. 103. *b.* your flocks, and live with us
L. 142. *b.* the rathe primrose
L'A. 25. *b.* with thee jest and .. jollity
Il P. 51. chiefest, with thee *b.*
Il P. 132. *b.* to arched walks
Il P. 166. *b.* all Heaven before mine eyes
H. 4. our great redemption from above did *b.*
M. W. 54. thy noble house doth *b.*
V. Ex. 18. *b.* thy chiefest treasure
V. Ex. 72. what future days should *b.* to pass
**Bringing.**—P. L. 10, 1052. *b.* forth soon
P. L. 12, 414. slain for *b.* life
P. R. 2, 268. food to Elijah *b.*
S. A. 1444. *b.* to us some glad news
**Brings.**—P. L. 1. 252. one who *b.* a mind
P. L. 2, 981. no mean recompense it *b.*
P. L. 4, 21. within him hell he *b.*
P. L. 5, 217. and with her *b.* her dower
P. L. 5, 312. to us perhaps he *b.*
P. L. 5, 583. as Heaven's great year *b.* forth
P. L. 8, 323. whose operation *b.* knowledge
P. L. 9, 47. who *b.* it nightly to my ear
P. L. 9, 770. but *b.* with joy
P. L. 10, 900. some misfortune *b.* him
P. L. 11, 860. in his bill an olive-leaf he *b.*
P. L. 11, 895. when he *b.* over the earth
P. L. 12, 345. *b.* them back remembering mercy
P. L. 12, 355. their strife pollution *b.*
P. R. 2, 422. money *b.* honour, friends
P. R. 2, 460. *b.* dangers, troubles, cares
P. R. 4, 323. *b.* not a spirit and judgment
P. R. 4, 325. what he *b.* what needs
S. A. 1063. but this another kind of tempest *b.*
S. A. 1747. Highest Wisdom *b.* about
L. 96. Hippotades their answer *b.*
S. 15, 5. unshaken virtue ever *b.* victory
V. Ex. 38. Hebè *b.* immortal nectar
**Brink.**—P. L. 2, 609. so near the *b.*
P. L. 2. 918. stood on the *b.* of Hell
P. L. 10, 347. at the *b.* of Chaos
**Brisk.**—C. 671. *b.* as the April buds
**Bristled.**—P. L. 6, 82. *b.* with upright beams
**Bristles.**—S. A. 1137. all thy hairs were *b.*
**British.**—P. L. 1, 581. *B.* and Armoric knights
P. R. 4, 77. Gades, and the *B.* west
S. 21, 2. the royal bench of *B.* Themis
**Brittle.**—P. L. 1, 427. the *b.* strength of bones
**Broad.**—P. L. 1, 286. the *b.* circumference
P. L. 2, 1026. a *b.* and beaten way
P. L. 3, 495. a Limbo large and *b.*
P. L. 4, 303. not beneath his shoulders *b.*
P. L. 5, 279. the pair that clad each shoulder *b.*
P. L. 6, 305. two *b.* suns their shields
P. L. 7, 286. their *b.* bare backs upheave
P. L. 7, 289. a hollow bottom, *b.* and deep
P. L. 7, 462. in *b.* herds upsprung
P. L. 7, 577. a *b.* and ample road
P. L. 9, 1087. their umbrage *b.* and brown
P. L. 9, 1095. *b.* smooth leaves together sewed
P. L. 9, 1104. branching so *b.* and long
P. L. 9, 1111. *b.* as Amazonian targe
P. L. 10, 298. *b.* as the gate
P. L. 10, 304. a passage *b.*, smooth, easy.
P. L. 10, 473. a *b.* way now is paved
P. R. 2, 23. the *b.* lake Genezaret
S. A. 1120. thy *b.* habergeon, vant-brace
C. 354. the rugged bark of some *b.* elm
C. 979. in the *b.* fields of the sky
L. 80, in *b.* rumour lies
S. 9, 2. wisely hast shunned the *b.* way
**Broadest.**—P. R. 2, 339. under the *b.* shade
**Broidered.**—P. L. 4, 702. with rich inlay *b.*
**Broils.**—P. L. 2, 837. to move new *b.*
P. L. 2, 1001. through your intestine *b.*
P. L. 6, 277. there mingle *b.*
P. L. 11, 718. from cups to civil *b.*
**Broke.**—P. L. 2, 690. *b.* peace in Heaven
P. L. 3, 87. through all restraint *b.* loose
P. L. 4, 878. why hast thou, Satan, *b.*

P. L. 4, 918. came not all Hell *b.* loose
P. L. 6, 311. nature's concord *b.*
P. L. 7, 465. then springs, as *b.* from bonds
P. L. 9, 895. he inward silence *b.*
P. L. 10, 353. thus the silence *b.*
P. L. 10, 1008. despair *b.* off the rest
P. L. 11, 827. all fountains of the deep, *b.* up
P. L. 11, 869. thus his joy *b.* forth
P. R. 4, 43. the tempter thus his silence *b.*
P. L. 4, 611. his snares are *b.*
S. A. 1189. when thou hadst *b.* the league
S. 10, 6. breaking of that Parliament *b.* him
S. M. 21. with harsh din *b.* the fair music
U. C. I. Death hath *b.* his girt
**Broken.**—P. L. 1, 311. *b.* chariot wheels
P. L. 2, 78. hung on our *b.* rear
P. L. 2, 1039. a *b.* foe
P. R. 1. 61. by the head *b.*
S. A. 1335. think me so *b.*, so debased
S. 15, 8. the false North displays her *b.* league
**Brood.**—P. L. 1, 511. his enormous *b.*
P. L. 1, 576. all the giant *b.* of Phlegra
P. L. 2, 863. mine own *b.*
P. L. 7, 418. their *b.* as numerous hatch
S. A. 1247. all his giant *b.*
Il P. 2. the *b.* of Follywithout father bred
D. F. I. 55. that heavenly *b.*
**Brooding.**—P. L. 1, 21. dove-like sat'st *b.*
P. L. 7, 235. his *b.* wings
L'A. 6. where *b.* Darkness spreads
H. 68. birds of calm sit *b.* on the charmed wave
**Brook.**—P. L. 1, 11. Siloa's *b.* that flowed
P. L. 1, 420. the *b.* that parts
P. L. 9, 1184. restraint she will not *b.*
P. L. 11, 325. every stone of lustre from the *b.*
P. R. 2, 266. by the *b.* of Cherith stood
P. R. 2, 345. freshet or purling *b.*
S. A. 557. only from the liquid *b.*
C. 119. by dimpled *b.* and fountain-brim
C. 495. have oft delayed the huddling *b.*
Il P. 139. in close covert by some *b.*
**Brooking.**—P. L. 9, 676. no delay of preface *b.*
**Brooks.**—P. L. 1, 302. the *b.* in Vallombrosa
P. L. 3, 30. and the flowery *b.* beneath
P. L. 4, 237. that sapphire fount the crispèd *b.*
P. L. 6, 274. *b.* not the works of violence
S. A. 1344, *b.* no delay
L. 137. wanton winds, and gushing *b.*
L'A. 76. shallow *b.*, and rivers wide
**Brother.**—P. L. 4, 757. of father, son, and *b.*
P. L. 11, 456. his *b.'s* offering found
P. L. 11, 609. his race who slew his *b.*
P. L. 11, 679. the sin of him who slew his *b.*
C. 359. peace, *b.*, be not over-exquisite
C. 407. I do not, *b.*, infer
C. 420. 'tis chastity, my *b.*, chastity
C. 493. O *b.*, 'tis my father's shepherd sure
C. 584. is this the confidence you gave me *b.*
**Brothers.**—C. 182. my *b.*, when they saw me
C. 226. I cannot halloa to my *b.*
C. 288. no less than if I should my *b.* lose
V. Ex. 82. on his *b.* shall depend for clothing
**Brought.**—P. L. 1, 3. *b.* death into the world
P. L. 1, 100. to the fierce contention *b.* along
P. L. 2, 598. all the damned are *b.*
P. L. 3. 606. hath *b.* me from the choirs
P. L. 3, 707. that *b.* them forth
P. L. 4, 452. whence thither *b.* and how
P. L. 4, 713. to our sire *b.* her
P. L. 4, 717. *b.* by Hermes
P. L. 4, 875. whom they *b.*, where found
P. L. 4, 908. what boldness *b.* him hither
P. L. 5, 51. that *b.* me on a sudden
P. L. 5, 667. on the dusky hour
P. L. 6, 267. into nature *b.* misery
P. L. 6, 395. to such evil *b.* by sin
P. L. 7, 315. *b.* forth the tender grass
P. L. 7, 537. he *b.* thee into this delicious grove
P. L. 8, 36. such a sunless journey *b.*
P. L. 8, 447. for trial only *b.* to see
P. L. 8, 500. though divinely *b.*

P. L. 8, 521. *b.* my story to the sum
P. L. 9, 11. *b.* into this world
P. L. 9, 224. our day's work, *b.* to little
P. L. 9, 392. or angels *b.*
P. L. 9, 462. the fierce intent it *b.*
P. L. 9, 475. forget what hither *b.* us
P. L. 10, 99. by soft winds *b.* to their ears
P. L. 10, 312. now had they *b.* the work
P. L. 10, 734. feeling the evil on him *b.*
P. L. 10, 1037. death *b.* on ourselves
P. L. 11, 168. I who first *b.* death on all
P. L. 11, 347. *b.* down to dwell on even ground
P. L. 11, 434. from his tillage *b.* first-fruits
P. L. 11, 837. if none be thither *b.* by men
P. L. 12, 81. such trouble *b.*
P. L. 12, 472. *b.* forth light out of darkness
P. L. 12, 504. the tidings *b.* from heaven
P. R. 1, 321. what ill chance hath *b.* thee
P. R. 1, 335. who *b.* me hither
P. R. 2, 269. taught to abstain from what they *b.*
P. R. 3, 34. *b.* down the Carthaginian pride
P. R. 3, 265. the Tempter *b.*
P. R. 3, 350. to what end I have *b.* thee
P. R. 3, 389. soon to nothing *b.*
P. R. 4, 22. to shameful silence *b.*
P. R. 4, 25. he *b.* our Saviour
P. R. 4, 396. *b.* back the Son of God
P. R. 4, 398. *b.* in louring night
P. R. 4, 553. I to thy Father's house have *b.*
P. R. 4, 577. *b.* joyless triumphals
P. R. 4, 688. *b.* on his way with joy
S. A. 269. by their vices *b.* to servitude
S. A. 375. I myself have *b.* them on
S. A. 449. I this pomp have *b.*
S. A. 451. to God have *b.* dishonour
S. A. 453. have *b.* scandal to Israel
S. A. 820. malice not repentance *b.* thee
S. A. 875. *b.* forth other deeds
S. A. 956. the pious works it hath *b.* forth
S. A. 1094. O that fortune had *b.* me
S. A. 1585. *b.* him so soon at variance
S. A. 1601. Samson should be *b.* forth
S. A. 1615. as a public servant *b.*
C. 58. whom therefore she *b.* up
C. 506. this my errand, and the care it *b.*
C. 619. *b.* to my mind
C. 967. I have *b.* ye new delight
S. 23, 2. *b.* to me, like Alcestis
S. 23. 14. day *b.* back my night
**Brought'st.**—P. R. 1, 10. *b.* him thence
**Brow.**—P. L. 3, 546. *b.* of some high climbing
P. L. 4, 885. with contemptuous *b.*
P. L. 6, 51. to the *b.* of Heaven pursuing
P. L. 8, 560. the Angel, with contracted *b.*
P. L. 9, 537. thy awful *b.*
P. L. 11, 880. the *b.* of God appeased
P. R. 1, 493. with unaltered *b.*
P. R. 2, 164. smooth the rugged'st *b.*
P. R. 2, 216. one look from his majestic *b.*
P. R. 3, 215. to that gentle *b.*
P. R. 4, 367. with stern *b.*, replied
S. A. 1073. his *b.* defiance
C. 532. the hilly crofts that *b.*
Il P. 58. smoothing the rugged *b.* of night
**Brown,**—P. L. 9, 1088. *b.* as evening
P. R. 2, 293. and alleys *b.*
P. R. 3, 326. cast a gleaming *b.*
L. 2. ye myrtles *b.*, with ivy never sere
Il P. 134. shadows *b.*, that Sylvan loves
**Brows.**—P. L. 1. 602. *b.* of dauntless courage
C. 38. nodding horror of whose shady *b.*
C. 736. to gaze upon the sun with shameless *b.*
**Bruise.**—P. L. 5. 887. an iron rod to *b.*
P. L. 10,181. her seed shall *b.* thy head, thou *b.*
P. L. 10, 191. who now foretold his fatal *b.*
P. L. 10, 498. I am to *b.* his heel
P. L. 10, 499. shall *b.* my head
P. L. 10, 500. not purchase with a *b.*
P. L. 10, 1031. thy seed shall *b.* the serpent's
P. L. 11, 155. thy seed shall *b.* our foe
P. L. 12, 149. who shall *b.* the Serpent's head

P. L. 12. 233. destined seed to *b.* the Serpent
P. L. 12, 383. the Serpent now his capital *b.*
P. L. 12, 385. what stroke shall *b.*
P. L. 12, 391. a deadlier *b.*
P. L. 12, 430. this act shall *b.* the head of Satan
P. L. 12, 433. shall *b.* the victor's heel
**Bruised.**—P. L. 6, 656. crushed in and *b.*
**Brunt.**—S. A. 583. the *b.* of battle
**Brush.**—P. L. 5, 428. we *b.* mellifluous dews
A. 50. from the boughs *b.* off the evil dew
**Brushed.**—P. L. 1, 768. *b.* with the hiss
**Brutal.**—P. L. 9, 188. his *b.* sense
P. L. 9, 565. above the rest of *b.* kind
**Brute.**—P. L. 1, 371. the image of a *b.*
P. L. 1, 459. the captive ark maimed his *b.* image
P. L. 7, 507. not prone and *b.* as other creatures
P. L. 8, 391. wherein the *b.* cannot
P. L. 8, 441. my image not imparted to the *b.*
P. L. 9, 96. beyond the sense of *b.*
P. L. 9, 240. to *b.* denied
P. L. 9, 554. pronounced by tongue of *b.*
P. L. 9, 712. I, of *b.*, human
P. L. 10, 165. Serpent, though *b.*, unable
P. L. 10, 495. the *b.* Serpent
P. R. 1, 219. quell o'er all the earth *b.* violence
S. A. 673. creatures mute irrational and *b.*
S. A. 1273. the *b.* and boisterous force
C. 451. grace that dashed *b.* violence
C. 700. liquorish baits, fit to ensnare a *b.*
C. 797. the *b.* Earth would lend her nerves
C. 828. had the sceptre from his father *B.*
**Brutish.**—P. L. 1, 481. disguised in *b.* forms
P. L. 6, 124. though *b.* that contest
P. L. 11, 518. a *b.* vice
P. R. 3, 86. scarce men, rolling in *b.* vices
P. R. 4, 128. expel a *b.* monster
C. 70. some *b.* form of wolf, or bear, or ounce
H. 211, the *b.* gods of Nile
**Bubbles**—P. R. 4, 20. in froth or *b.* end
**Bud.**—P. L. 8. 45. they prospered, *b.* and bloom
P. L. 11, 277. the first opening *b.*
S. 2. 4. my late spring no *b.* or blossom sheweth
M. W. 22. ye might discern a cypress *b.*
**Budge.**—C. 707. those *b.* doctors of the Stoic fur
**Buds.**—C. 671. brisk as the April *b.*
**Buffet.**—S. A. 1239. one *b.* lay thy structure low
**Build.**—P. L. 1, 401. to *b.* his temple
P. L. 1, 751. with his industrious crew to *b.*
P. L. 2, 314. *b.* up here a growing empire
P. L. 3, 468. wherewithal, would *b.*
P. L. 4, 521. laid whereon to *b.* their ruin
P. L. 7, 92. so late to *b.* in Chaos
P. L. 7, 424. cedar-tops-their eyries *b.*
P. L. 8, 81. how *b.*, unbuild
P. L. 8, 558. their seat *b.* in her loveliest
P. L. 9, 102. after better, worse would *b.*
P. L. 11, 729. began to *b.* a vessel
P. L. 11, 819. shall *b.* a wondrous ark
P. L. 12. 43. they cast to *b.* a city-and tower
P. R. 2, 170. made him *b.*
S. A. 1733. there I will *b.* him a monument
L. 11. to sing and *b.* the lofty rhyme
**Builded.**—P. L. 10, 373. what thy hands *b.* not
**Builders.**—P. L. 3, 466. *b.* next of Babel
P. L. 12, 57. the *b.*; each to other calls
**Building.**—P. L. 12, 61. the *b.* left ridiculous
S. A. 1605. the *b.* was a spacious theatre
**Builds.**—P. L. 7, 491. *b.* her waxen cells
**Built.**—P. L. 1, 259. hath not *b.* here
P. L. 1, 443. *b.* by that uxorious king
P. L. 1, 713. *b.* like a temple
P. L. 1, 749. to have *b.* in Heaven
P. L. 3, 449. *b.* their fond hopes
P. L. 4, 212. Seleucia, *b.* by Grecian kings
P. L. 7, 270. for as earth, so he the world *b.*
P. L. 8, 101. who *b.* so spacious
P. L. 9, 100. *b.* with second thoughts
P. L. 9, 152. for him *b.* magnificent
P. L. 9, 485. of limb heroic *b.*
P. L. 12, 102. son of him who *b.* the ark
P. L. 12, 527. his living temples *b.* by faith

P. R. 2, 343. fowl of game in pastry *b.*
P. R. 3, 276. *b.* by Ninus old
P. R. 3, 290. *b.* by Emathian
P. R. 4, 239. nobly, pure the air
P. R. 4, 292. fancies *b.* on nothing firm
C. 599. the earth's base *b.* on stubble
L. 101. *b.* in the eclipse
W. S. 8. hast *b.* thyself a live-long monument
**Bulk.**—P. L. 1, 196. in *b.* as huge
P. L. 7, 410. huge of *b.*, wallowing unwieldy
P. L. 11, 729. a vessel of huge *b.*
S. A. 1238. *b.* without spirit vast
**Bull.**— U. C. I. 8. betwixt Cambridge and The *B.*
**Bullion.**—P. L. 1, 704. the *b.* dross
**Bullock.**—P. L. 12, 20. *b.*, lamb, or kid
**Bulls.**—P. L. 3, 492. dispenses, pardons, *b.*
P. L. 12, 292. the blood of *b.* and goats
S. A. 1671. fat regorged of *b.* and goats
**Bulwark.**—P. L. 2,29. Thunderer's aim your *b.*
**Burden.**—P. L. 2, 767. a growing *b.*
P. L. 4, 57. what *b.* then
P. L. 9, 801. the fertile *b.* ease
P. L. 10, 835. *b.*, heavier than the earth
P. L. 10, 961. lighten each other's *b.*
P. L. 11, 767. the *b.* of many ages
P. R. 2, 462. on his shoulders each man's *b.* lies
S. A. 431. the *b.* of that fault
S. 21, 13. with superfluous *b.* loads the day
**Burdened.**—P. L. 5, 452. not *b.* nature
**Burdenous.**—S. A. 567. a *b.* drone
**Burdensome.**—P. L. 4, 53. so *b.* still paying
S. A. 54. unwieldy, *b.*
U. C. II. 24. lack of load made his life *b.*
**Burgher.**—P. L. 4, 189. the cash of some rich *b.*
**Burial.**—S. A. 104. by privilege of death and *b.*
M. W. 32. had *b.* yet not laid in earth
**Buried.**—P. L. 6, 652. *b.* deep
S. A. 101. a living death, and *b.*
S. A. 103. *b.*, yet not exempt by privilege
**Burn.**—P. L. 1. 474. whereon to *b.*
P. L. 3, 334. the world shall *b.*
P. L. 5, 713. the golden lamps that *b.*
P. L. 9, 1015. in lust they *b.*
P. L. 12, 254. before him *b.* seven lamps
P. R. 3, 75. *b.*, slaughter, and enslave
Cir. 8. *b.* in your sighs
**Burned.**—P. L. 1, 228. land that ever *b.*
P. L. 2, 708. like a comet *b.*
P. L. 6, 866. eternal wrath to *b.* after them
S. A. 26. off the altar where an offering *b.*
**Burning.**—P. L. 1, 210. chained on the *b.* lake
P. L. 1, 296. over the *b.* marle
P. L. 2, 169. chained on the *b.* lake
P. L. 2, 436. gates of *b.* adamant
P. I. 2, 576. disgorge into the *b.* lake
P. L. 6, 832. under his *b.* wheels
H. 84. his bright throne or *b.* axle-tree
H. 207. left in shadows dread his *b.* idol
S. M. 10. the bright Seraphim in *b.* row
**Burnished.**—P. L. 4, 249. *b.* with golden rind
P. L. 9, 501. *b.* neck of verdant gold
**Burns.**—P. L. 2, 538. the welkin *b.*
P. L. 2, 595. the parching air *b.* frore
P.L. 9,467. but the hot hell that always in him *b.*
C. 130. the secret flame of midnight torches *b.*
**Burnt.**—P. L. 1, 562 o'er the *b.* soil
**Burs.**—C. 352. among rude *b.* and thistles
**Burst.**—P.L. 1,620. tears, such as angels weep, *b.*
P. L. 10, 632. gorged, nigh *b.*
P. R. 1, 170. into hymns *b.* forth
S. A. 1555. it would *b.* forth
S. A. 1651. with *b.* of thunder
L. 74. and think to *b.* out into sudden blaze
**Bursting.**—P. L. 7, 419. *b.* with kindly rupture
P. L. 2, 800. *b.* forth afresh
P. L. 9, 98. his *b.* passion
P. L. 10, 697. to their brazen dungeon
**Bush.**—P. L. 7, 323. *b.* with frizzled hair
P. L. 9, 160. pry in every *b.*
P. R. 4, 437. their choicest notes in *b.* and spray
**Bushes.**—P. L. 4, 176. tangling *b.*

**Bushy.**—P. L. 4, 696. each odorous *b.* shrub
  C. 312. dingle, or *b.* dell
**Busied.**—P. L. 4, 876. how *b.*, in what form
  P. L. 9, 518. she, *b.*, heard the sound
**Busiest.**—P. L. 11, 490. tended the sick *b.*
**Business.**—P. L. 1, 150. whate'er his *b.* be
  P. L. 4, 943. whose easier *b.* were to serve
  P. R. 2, 99. went about his Father's *b.*
  C. 169. hearken, if I may her *b.* hear

V. Ex. 57. quick about thy purposed *b.* come
**Busiris.**—P.L.1,307. whose waves overthrew *B.*
**Buskined.**—Il P. 102. the *b.* stage
**Bustle.**—C. 379. the various *b.* of resort
**Busy.**—L'A. 118. the *b.* hum of men
  H. 92. silly thoughts so *b.* keep
**Buxom.**—P. L. 2, 842. the *b.* air, embalmed
  P. L. 5, 270. winnows the *b.* air
  L'A. 24. so *b.*, blithe, and debonair

# C

**Cabined.**—C. 140. from her *c.* loop-hole
**Cadence.**—P. L. 2, 287. with hoarse *c.* lull
  P. L. 10, 92. the sun in western *c.* low
**Cadmus.**—P. L. 9, 506. Hermione and *C.*
**Cæcias.**—P. L. 10, 699. Boreas, and *C.*
**Cæsar.**—P. R. 3, 385. *C.* not need fear
**Calabria.**—P. L. 2, 661. the sea that parts *C.*
**Calamities.**—S. A. 655. bearing well of all *c.*
  S. A. 1331. or make a game of my *c.*
**Calamitous.**—P. L. 10, 132. *c.* constraint
  S. A. 708. in this state *c.*
  S. A. 1480. in that *c.* prison
**Calamity.**—P. L. 1, 189. this dire *c.*
  P. L. 10, 907. infinite *c.* shall cause
**Calculate.**—P. L. 8, 80. *c.* the stars
**Cales.**—P. R. 4, 117. *C.*, and Falerne
**Calf.**—P. L. 1, 484. the *c.* in Oreb
**Calisto.**—P. R. 2, 186. *C.*, Clymene
**Call.**—P. L. 1, 267. *c.* them not to share
  P. L. 1, 378. their great Emperor's *c.*
  P. L. 3, 185. the rest shall hear me *c.*
  P. L. 3, 603. *c.* up unbound
  P. L. 4, 35. to thee I *c.*
  P. L. 4, 277. whom Gentiles **Ammon** *c.*
  P. L. 5, 48. rose as at thy *c.*
  P. L. 5, 107. *c.* our knowledge or opinion
  P. L. 5, 658. so *c.* him now
  P. L. 5, 760. so *c.* that structure
  P. L. 7, 5. the meaning, not the name I *c.*
  P. L. 7, 132. so *c.* him, brighter once
  P. L. 7, 295. at the *c* of trumpets
  P. L. 7, 498. obedient at thy *c.*
  P. L. 9, 521. at her *c.*, than at Circean *c.*
  P. L. 9, 1020. palate *c.* judicious
  P. L. 10, 462. I *c.* ye and declare ye **now**
  P. L. 10, 654. *c.* decrepit winter
  P. L. 10, 858. Death comes not at *c.*
  P. L. 11, 67. let us *c.* to synod
  P. L. 11, 411. Geryon's sons *c.* El **Dorado**
  P.L. 11, 651. *c.* in aid which makes a bloody **fray**
  P. L. 11, 660. the sceptred heralds *c.*
  P. L. 11, 898. *c.* to mind his covenant
  P. L. 12. 121. vouchsafes to *c.* by vision
  P. L. 12, 140. things by their names I *c.*
  P. L. 12, 152. due time shall *c.*
  P. L. 12, 169. *c.* Moses and Aaron
  P. L. 12, 267. so *c.* the third
  P. L. 12, 310. whom the Gentiles **Jesus** *c.*
  P. R. 2, 27. no greater men them *c.*
  P. R. 2, 385. *c.* swift flights of angels
  P. R. 3, 434. by some wondrous *c.*
  S. A. 43. let me not rashly *c.* in doubt
  S. A. 836. *c.* it furious rage
  S. A. 1079. men *c.* me Harapha
  S. A. 1311. that ne'er art *c.*
  S. A. 1678. to *c.* in haste
  C. 6, this dim spot which men *c.* **earth**
  C. 438. or shall I *c.*
  C. 588. that power which erring men *c.* Chance
  L. 134. *c.* the vales
  S. 8, 13. *c.* thee his mate
  S. S. 6. that *c.* fame on such gentle acts
  H. 209. they *c.* the grisly king
  T. 2. *c.* on the lazy leaden-stepping hours
  F. of C. 12. What d'ye *c.*
  Il P. 109. *c.* up him that left half-told

**Called.**—P. L. 1, 82. in heaven *c.* Satan
  P. L. 1, 300. *c.* his legions angel forms
  P. L. 1, 314. he *c.* so loud
  P. L. 1, 340. up *c.* a pitchy cloud
  P. L. 1, 405. and black Gehenna *c.*
  P. L. 1, 438. whom the Phœnicians *c.* Astarte
  P. L. 1, 740. men *c.* him Mulciber
  P. L. 5, 179. out of darkness *c.* up light
  P. L. 1, 757. their summons *c.* from every band
  P. L. 2, 312. *c.* princes of hell
  P. L. 2, 348. some new race *c.* man
  P. L. 2, 667. if shape it might be *c.*
  P. L. 2, 669. substance might be *c.*
  P. L. 2, 760. *c.* me Sin
  P. L. 3, 495. *c.* the Paradise of Fools
  P. L. 3, 727. so *c.* that opposite fair star
  P. L. 4, 474. *c.* mother of human race
  P. L. 4, 514. of knowledge *c.*
  P. L. 4, 786. two strong and subtle Spirits he *c.*
  P. L. 4, 865. from the front thus *c.* aloud
  P. L. 5, 36. one *c.* me forth to walk
  P. L. 5, 220. to him *c.* Raphael
  P. L. 5, 307. Adam *c.*, haste hither Eve
  P. L. 5, 584. by imperial summons *c.*
  P.L. 5, 766. the Mountain of the Congregation *c.*
  P. L. 6, 416. his Potentates to council *c.*
  P. L. 6, 608. to his mates thus in derision *c.*
  P. L. 7, 2. if rightly thou art *c.*
  P. L. 7, 308. congregated waters he *c.* Seas
  P. L. 8, 283. while thus I *c.* and strayed
  P. L. 8, 298. *c.* by thee, I come thy guide
  P. L. 8, 458. *c.* by nature as in kind
  P. L. 10, 102. thus to Adam *c.* aloud
  P. L. 10, 425. so by allusion *c.*
  P. L. 10, 580. the Serpent whom they *c.* Ophion
  P. L. 10, 629. know not that I *c.*
  P. L. 11, 159. Eve rightly *c.*
  P. L. 11, 690. valour and heroic virtue *c.*
  P. L. 11, 697. destroyers rightlier *c.*
  P. L. 12, 134. God, who *c.* him
  P. L. 12, 156. a land hereafter *c.* Egypt
  P. L. 12, 343. Babylon thence *c.*
  P. L. 12, 378. *c.* the Seed of Woman
  P. L. 12, 584. love by name to come *c.* charity
  P. R. 1, 136. *c.* the Son of God
  P. R. 1, 166. by merit *c.* my Son
  P. R. 1, 329. *c.* thee Son of God
  P. R. 2, 3, expressly *c.* Jesus Messiah
  P. R. 2, 123. rightlier *c.* powers of Fire, **Air**
  P. R. 4, 111. luxury though *c.* magnificence
  P. R. 4, 259. Melesigenes, thence Homer *c.*
  P. R. 4, 301. by him *c.* virtue
  P. R. 4, 516. thou art *c.* the Son of God
  S. A. 226. the work to which I was divinely *c.*
  C. 131. that ne'er art *c.*
  C. 638. he *c.* it hæmony, and gave it me
  S. 11, 1. writ of late *c.* 'Tetrachordon'
  S. 14, 4. this earthly load of death *c.* life
**Call'st.**—P. L. 2, 742. thou *c.* me father
  P. L. 6, 289. the strife which thou *c.* evil
  P. L. 8, 369. what *c.* thou solitude?
  P. L. 9, 1146. if wandering as thou *c.* it
  P. R. 3, 403. my brethren as thou *c.* them
**Calling.**—P. L. 10, 649. *c.* forth by name
  P. L. 10, 1030. *c.* to mind with heed
  C. 207. *c.* shapes and beckoning

C. 485. some roving robber *c.* to his fellows
**Callow**.—P. L. 7, 420. their *c.* young
**Calls**.—P. L. 2, 92. *c.* us to penance
P. L. 2, 733. his wrath which he *c.* justice
P. L. 5, 21. the fresh field *c.* us
P. L. 5, 696. together *c.*, or several, one by one
P. L. 11, 172. the field to labour *c.* us now
P. L. 12, 57. each to other *c.* not understood
M. W. 26. *c.* Lucina to her throes
V. Ex. 54, expectance *c.* thee now another way
**Calm**.—P. L. 3, 574. the *c.* firmament
P. L. 4, 120. smoothed with outward *c.*
P. L. 5, 210. and wonted *c.*
P. L. 5, 733. the Son with *c.* aspect
P. L. 7, 234. on the watery *c.*
P. L. 7, 270. built on circumfluous waters *c.*
P. L. 9, 920. thus in *c.* mood
P. L. 9, 1125. *c.* region once
P. R. 2, 63. within her breast though *c.*
P. R. 2, 81. unactive, *c.*, contemplative
P. R. 4, 425. *c.* and sinless peace
S. A. 604. meanwhile be *c.*
S. A. 1758. and *c.* of mind, all passion spent
C. 371. stir the constant mood of her *c.* thoughts
L. 98. the air was *c.*
Il P. 45. join with thee *c.* peace and quiet
H. 68. birds of *c.* sit brooding
**Calmed**.—P. L. 12, 595. gentle dreams have *c.*
S. A. 964. eternal tempests, never to be *c.*
**Calmer**.—P. L. 2, 1042. wafts on the *c.* wave
P. R. 1, 103. *c.* voyage now will waft me
**Calmest**.—P. L. 6, 461. live content, the *c.* life
**Calmly**.—P. R. 3, 43. our Saviour *c.* thus replied
**Calved**.—P. L. 7, 463. the grassy clods now *c.*
**Calves**.—P. R. 3, 416. to worship *c.*
**Calumnious**.—P. L. 5, 770. with *c.* art
**Camball**.—Il P. 111. *C.*, and of Algarsife
**Cambalu**.—P. L. 11, 388. walls of *C.*
**Cambridge**.—S. 11, 14. when thou taught'st *C.*
U.C.I. 8. dodged with him betwixt *C.* and the Bull
**Cambuscan**.—Il P. 110. the story of *C.* bold
**Came**.—P. L. 1, 354. *c.* like a deluge
P. L. 1, 379. as next in worth *c.* singly
P. L. 1, 419. with these *c.* they
P. L. 1, 438. with these in troop *c.* Astoreth
P. L. 1, 446. Thammuz *c.* next behind
P. L. 1, 457. next *c.* one who mourned
P. L. 1, 490. Belial *c.* last
P. L. 1, 522. all these and more *c.* flocking
P. L. 1, 760. thousands trooping *c.*
P. L. 2, 507. forth in order *c.*
P. L. 2, 508. midst *c.* their mighty Paramount
P. L. 2, 675. the monster moving onward *c.*
P. L. 3, 464. from ancient world those Giants *c.*
P. L. 3, 469. others *c.* single
P. L. 3, 520. who after *c.* from earth
P. L. 3, 709. this world's material *c.* to a heap
P. L. 4, 4. *c.* furious down
P. L. 4, 9. inflamed with rage, *c.* down
P. L. 4, 167. the fiend who *c.* their bane
P. L. 4, 469. with thee it *c.* and goes
P. L. 4, 555. thither *c.* Uriel, gliding
P. L. 4, 564. *c.* to my sphere a Spirit
P. L. 4, 598. now *c.* still evening
P. L. 4, 918. with thee *c.* not all Hell
P. L. 5, 279. *c.* mantling over his breast
P. L. 5, 372. I therefore *c.*
P. L. 5, 378. to the sylvan lodge they *c.*
P. L. 5, 756. into the limits of the North they *c.*
P. L. 6, 75. *c.* summoned o'er Eden
P. L. 6, 110. *c.* towering, armed
P. L. 6, 252. *c.* down, wide-wasting
P. L. 6, 536. *c.* flying, and in mid air
P. L. 6, 655. in the air *c.* shadowing
P. L. 6, 768. he onward *c.*
P. L. 7, 203. now *c.* forth spontaneous
P. L. 7, 475. *c.* forth whatever creeps
P. L. 7, 583. twilight from the east *c.* on
P. L. 8, 277. tell, if ye saw, how *c.* I thus
P. L. 8, 295. one *c.*, methought, of shape divine
P. L. 8, 484. on she *c.*, led by her Maker

P. L. 9, 197. forth *c.* the human pair
P. L. 9, 854. in her face excuse *c.* prologue
P. L. 10, 96. *c.*, the mild Judge
P. L. 10, 109. he *c.*, and with him Eve
P. L. 10, 309. *c.* to the sea
P. L. 10, 330. disguised he *c.*
P. L. 10, 349. to meet him *c.*, his offspring dear
P. L. 11, 19. *c.* in sight
P. L. 11, 436. unculled, as *c.* to hand
P. L. 11, 437. *c.* with the firstlings of his flock
P. L. 11, 584. in dance *c.* on
P. L. 11, 719. a reverend sire among them *c.*
P. L. 11, 735. *c.* sevens and pairs, and entered in
P. R. 1, 22. with them *c.* from Nazareth
P. R. 1, 24. to the flood Jordan *c.*
P. R. 1, 246. to thee they *c.*
P. R. 1, 273. I, as all others, to his baptism *c.*
P. R. 1, 297. the way he *c.* not having marked
P. R. 1, 368. I *c.* among the sons of God
P. R. 1, 502. wild beasts *c.* forth
P. R. 4, 427. Morning fair *c.* forth
P. R. 4, 442. to our Saviour *c.*
S. A. 142. with what trivial weapon *c.* to hand
S. A. 258. *c.* into their hands
S. A. 337. cast back with age *c.* lagging after
S. A. 733. I *c.*, still dreading thy displeasure
S. A. 851. princes of my country *c.* in person
S. A. 1449. I heard all as I *c.*
S. A. 1624. *c.* to the place
S. A. 1650. he shook, till down they *c.*
S. A. 1692. as an evening dragon *c.*
C. 191. why they *c.* not back
C. 292. from the furrow *c.*
C. 502. I *c.* not here on such a trivial toy
C. 510. we lost her as we *c.*
C. 647. and yet *c.* off
L. 108, last *c.* and last did go
S. 23, 9. *c.* vested all in white
H. 47. crowned with olive green, *c.* softly sliding
M. W. 19. he at their invoking *c.*
M. W. 28. Atropos for Lucina *c.*
M. W. 59. sent thee from the banks of *C.*
V. Ex. 45. secret things that *c.* to pass
**Camel**.—P. R. 1, 340. more than the *c.*
**Camels**.—P. R. 3, 335. *c.* and dromedaries
**Camest**.—P. L. 9, 563. how *c.* thou speakable
S. A. 1227. *c.* thou for this, vain boaster
S. A. 1332. return the way thou *c.*
C. 497. how *c.* thou here, good swain?
D. F. I. 52. *c.* again to visit us once more
**Camp**.—P. L. 1, 677. forerun the royal *c.*
P. L. 5, 651. their *c.* extend by living streams
P. L. 11, 217. covered with a *c.* of fire
P. R. 3, 337. so wide a *c.*
S A. 1087. in *c.* or listed field
S. A. 1436. the *c.* of Dan
S. A. 1497. about him like a *c.*
**Camus**.—L. 103. next *C.*, reverend sire
**Can**. — P. L. 11, 388. seat of Cathaian *C.*
**Canaan**.—P. L. 12, 135. *C.* he now attains
P. L. 12, 156. increased, departs from *C.*
P. L. 12, 215. safe towards *C.*
P. L. 12, 269. who thus shall *C.* win
P. L. 12, 309. his people into *C.* lead
P. L. 12, 315. they in their earthly *C.* placed
**Canaanite**.—P. L. 12, 217. entering on the *C.*
S. A. 380. a *C.*, my faithless enemy
**Canace**.—Il P. 112. who had *C.* to wife
**Cancelled**.—P. L. 6, 379. *c.* from Heaven
**Candaor**.—P. R. 3, 316. from *C.* east
**Canker**.—L. 45. as killing as the *c.* to the rose
**Cankered**.—A. 53. with *c.* venom bites
**Canon-laws**.—C. 808. against the *c.-l.*
**Canopied**.—C. 544. upon a bank with ivy *c.*
**Canopy**.—P. L. 3, 556. above the circling *c.*
**Cany**.—P. L. 3, 439. their *c.* waggons light
**Capable**.—P. L. 8, 49. not *c.* her ear
P. L. 9, 283. not *c.* of death or pain
**Capacious**.—P. L. 7, 290. *c.* bed of waters
P. L. 9, 603. with *c.* mind considered all things
**Capacity**.—S. A. 1028. *c.* not raised

**Caparisons.**—P. L. 9, 35. impresses quaint, *c.*
**Cape.**—P. L. 2, 641. to the *C.* ply, stemming
 P. L. 4, 160. beyond the *C.* of Hope
 P. L. 8, 631. beyond the Earth's green *C.*
**Caphtor.**—S. A. 1713. the sons of *C.*
**Capital.**—P. L. 1, 756. the high *c.* of Satan
 P. L. 2, 924. bent to rase some *c.* city
 P. L. 11, 343. this had been perhaps thy *c.* seat
 P. L. 12, 383. the Serpent now his *c.* bruise
 S. A. 394. my *c.* secret, in what part my strength
 S. A. 1225. due by the law to *c.* punishment
**Capitol.**—P. R. 4, 47. the *C.* thou seest
**Capitoline.**—P. L. 9, 508. *C.,* was seen
**Capreæ.**—P. R. 4, 92. retired to *C.*
**Capricorn.**—P L. 10, 677. as deep as *C.*
**Captain.**—S.8, 1. *c.,* or colonel, or knight in arms
**Captains.**—S. A. 1653. lords, ladies, *c.*
**Captive.**—P. L. 1, 458. the *c.* ark
 P. L. 2, 323. his *c.* multitude
 P. L. 3, 255. in triumph high shall lead Hell *c.*
 P. L. 4, 970. when I am thy *c.* talk of chains
 P. L. 6, 260. the Arch-foe subdued, or *c.*
 P. L. 10, 188. captivity led *c.* through the air
 P. R. 1, 411. as a poor miserable *c.*
 P. R. 2, 222. weak minds led *c.*
 P. R. 3, 77. made *c.,* yet deserving freedom
 P. R. 3, 283. led *c.,* and Jerusalem laid waste
 P. R. 3, 366. *c.* lead away her kings
 P. R. 3, 414. those *c.* tribes
 S. A. 335. my son, now *c.*
 S. A. 366. thy foes' derision *c.,* poor, and blind
 S. A. 426. to make thee their *c.*
 S. A. 1393. art thou our slave, our *c.*
 S. A. 1474. *c.* and blind before them
 S. A. 1603. I sorrowed at his *c.* state
**Captived.**—S. A. 33. if I must die betrayed, *c.*
 S. A. 694. to dogs and fowls a prey, or else *c.*
**Captivity.**—P. L. 10, 188. *c.* led captive
 P. L. 12, 344. in *c.* he lets them dwell
 P. R. 3, 279. Israel in long *c.* mourns
 P. R. 3, 415. wrought their own *c.*
 P. R. 3, 420. in the land of their *c.*
 S. A. 108. life in *c.* among inhuman foes
 S. A. 1744. *c.* and loss of eyes
 V. Ex. 52. in willing chains and sweet *c.*
**Car.**—P. L. 9, 65. the *c.* of night
 C. 95. the gilded *c.* of day
 H. 241. fixed her polished *c.*
 D. F. I. 15. mounting up in icy-pearled *c.*
**Caravan.**—P. L. 7, 428. set forth their aery *c.*
 P. R. 1, 323. in troop or *c.*
**Carbuncle.**—P. L. 3, 596. if stone, *c.*
 P. L. 9, 500. *c.* his eyes
**Carcase.**—P. L. 3, 259. his *c.* glut the grave
 P. R. 1, 325. dropt not here his *c.*
 S. A. 1097. or left thy *c.* where the ass lay
**Carcases.**—P. L. 1, 310. their floating *c.*
 P. L. 10, 277. lured with scent of living *c.*
 P. L. 11, 654. scattered lies with *c.* and arms
 S. A. 693. their *c.* to dogs and fowls
**Care.**—P. L. 1, 601. *c.* sat on his faded cheek
 P. L. 2, 48. that *c.* lost went all fear
 P. L. 2, 303. deliberation sat, and public *c.*
 P. L. 4, 575. him thy *c.* must be to find
 P. L. 6, 35. for this was all thy *c.*
 P. L. 6, 822. nor *c.* who them excels
 P. L. 9, 318. Adam in his *c.*
 P. L. 9, 799. henceforth my early *c.*
 P. L. 9, 813. other *c.,* perhaps
 P. L. 10, 37. your sincerest *c.*
 P. L. 10, 979. *c.* of our descent perplex us
 P. L. 10, 1057. his timely *c.*
 P. L. 11, 776. that *c.* now is past
 P. R. 1, 111. they all commit the *c.*
 P. R. 2, 18. with *c.* sought lost Elijah
 S. A. 602. must not omit a father's timely *c.*
 S. A. 918. exempt from many a *c.*
 S. A. 923. my redoubled love and *c.*
 S. A. 928. of my condition take no *c.*
 C. 6. men call earth, and with low-thoughted *c.*
 C. 506. my errand, and the *c.* it brought

 C. 617. *c.* and utmost shifts
 L. 64. with incessant *c.*
 L. 116. other *c.* they little reckoning make
 L'A. 31. sport that wrinkled *C.* derides
 S. 9, 9. thy *c.* is fixed
 S. 21, 12. disapproves that *c.*
 D.F. I. 18.ended was his quest, there ceased his *c.*
 M. W. 36. saved with *c.* from winter's nip
**Cared.**—P. L. 2, 48. *c.* not to be at all
**Career.**—P. L. 1, 766. mortal combat, or *c.*
 P. L. 4, 353. with prone *c.*
 Il. P. 121. Night, oft see me in thy pale *c.*
 S. 2, 3. days fly on with full *c.*
**Careering.**—P. L. 6, 756. *c.* fires between
**Careful.**—P. L. 4, 983. the *c.* ploughman
 P. L. 10, 438. reduced in *c.* watch
 S. A., 327. thy reverend sire with *c.* steps
 D. F. I. 45. *c.* Jove in Nature's true behoof
**Careless.**—P. R. 4, 299. and *c.* ease
 P. R. 4, 450. in a *c.* mood
**Carelessly.**—S. A. 118. *c.* diffused
**Cares.**—P. L. 8, 185. all anxious *c.*
 P. R. 2, 64. motherly *c.* and fears got head
 P. R. 2, 460. dangers, troubles, *c.*
 P. R. 4, 96. all public *c.*
 S. A. 805. I at home sat full of *c.*
 L'A. 135. against eating *c.*
**Caresses.**—P. L. 8, 56. conjugal *c.*
**Carest.**—S. A. 1488. *c.* how to nurse thy son
**Carmel.**—P. L. 12, 144. on the shore, Mount *C.*
**Carnage.**—P. L. 10, 268. a scent I draw of *c.*
**Carnal.**—P. L. 8, 593. not sunk in *c.* pleasure
 P. L. 9, 1013. *c.* desire inflaming
 P. L. 11, 212. *c.* fear that day
 P. L. 12, 521. by *c.* power shall force
 C. 474. by *c.* sensuality
**Carnation.**—P. L. 9, 429. gay *c.*
 M. W. 37. the pride of her *c.* train
**Carol.**—P. L. 12, 367. hear his *c.* sung
 C. 849. at their festivals *c.* her goodness
**Carpathian.**—C. 872. the *C.* wizard's hook
**Carpenter.**—P. R. 2, 414. a *c.* thy father
**Carriage.**—U. C. I. 10. his weekly course of *c.*
**Carrier.**—U. C. II. 20. one *c.* put down
 U. C. II. 28. he had been an immortal *c.*
**Carries.**—S. A. 1073. his habit *c.* peace
**Carry.**—P. L. 5, 870. these tidings *c.*
 P. L. 12, 621. yet secure I *c.* hence
 U. C. II. 18. if I mayn't *c.*
**Carrying.**—S. A. 385. professed, *c.* it straight
**Cart.**—U. C. II. 22. his *c.* went light
**Carthaginian.**—P. R. 3, 35. the *C.* pride
**Carved.**—P. R. 4, 59. pillars and roofs *c.* work
**Casbeen.**—P. L. 10, 436. Tauris or *C.*
**Casella.**—S. 13, 13. his *C.,* whom he wooed
**Cash.**—P. L. 4, 188. to unhoard the *c.*
**Casius.**—P. L. 2, 593. mount *C.* old
**Casket.**—P. 44. that was the *c.*
**Caspian.**—P. L. 2, 716. over the *C.*
 P. R. 3, 271. Araxes and the *C.* lake
**Cassia.**—P. L. 5, 293. *c.,* nard, and balm
 C. 991. *c.'s* balmy smells
**Cast.**—P. L. 1, 37. had *c.* him out from Heaven
 P. L. 1, 286. behind him *c.*
 P. L. 1, 526. on his countenance *c.*
 P. L. 1, 604. *c.* signs of remorse
 P. L. 1, 678. to trench a field, or *c.* a rampart
 P. L. 2, 122. *c.* ominous conjecture on the whole
 P. L. 2, 714. such a frown each *c.* at the other
 P. L. 2, 889. *c.* forth redounding smoke
 P. L. 3, 351. down they *c.* their crowns
 P. L. 5, 613. *c.* out from God and blessèd vision
 P. L. 5, 786. teach us to *c.* off this yoke
 P. L. 6, 869. *c.* too deep her dark foundations
 P. L. 9, 1014. began to *c.* lascivious eyes
 P. L. 10, 547. triumph to shame, *c.* on themselves
 P. L. 12, 43. and of that stuff, they *c.* to build
 P. R. 1, 228. words at times *c.* forth
 P. R. 2, 46. and behind them *c.* all fear of thee
 P. R. 2, 180. *c.* wanton eyes on the daughters
 P. R. 3, 326. the field all iron *c.* a gleaming

P. R. 4, 61. to the gates c. round thine eye
P. R. 4, 555. c. thyself down safely if Son of God
P. R. 4, 575. c. herself headlong
P. R. 4, 605. down from Heaven c. with all his
C. 360. to c. the fashion of uncertain evils
C. 460. begin to c. a beam on the outward shape
L. 134. and bid them hither c. their bells
Il P. 43. with a sad leaden downward c.
H. 123. and c. the dark foundations deep
S. A. 336. mine c. back with age came lagging
S. A. 641. but now hath c. me off as never known
**Castalian.**—P. L. 4, 274. C. spring
**Casting.**—Il P. 160. c. a dim religious light
S. 12, 8. but this is got by c. pearl to hogs
**Casts.**—P. L. 1, 183. c. pale and dreadful
P. L. 3, 634. first he c. to change his proper
P. L. 5, 702. c. between ambiguous words
P. L. 6, 272. Heaven c. thee out
C. 225. and c. a gleam over this tufted grove
H. 170. not half so far c. his usurpèd sway
**Casual.**—P. L. 4, 767. unendeared, c. fruition
P. L. 9, 223. object new c. discourse draw on
P. L. 11, 566. where c. fire had wasted woods
**Cataphracts.**—S. A. 1619. c. and spears
**Cataracts.**—P. L. 2, 176. spout her c. of fire
P. L. 11, 824. but all the c. of Heaven set open
**Catarrhs.**—P. L. 11, 483. epilepsies, fierce c.
**Catch.**—P. L. 12, 88. upstart passions c.
C. 953. we shall c. them at their sport
**Catched.**—P. L. 10, 544. c. by contagion
**Cateress.**—C. 764. she, good c., means her
**Cates.**—P. R. 2, 348. to these c. compared
**Cathaian.**—P. L. 10, 293. the rich C. coast
P. L. 11, 388. of Cambalu seat of C. Can
**Cattle.**—P. L. 7, 452. c. and creeping things
P. L. 7, 460. the c. in the fields and meadows
P. L. 8, 582. think the same vouchsafed to c.
P. L. 10, 176. accursed above all c.
P. L. 11, 558. herds of c. grazing
P. L. 11, 653. where c. pastured late
P. L. 12, 179. his c. must of rot and murrain die
**Caucasus.**—P. R. 3, 318. cliffs of C.
**Caught.**—P. L. 2, 180. c. in a fiery tempest
P. L. 11, 587. till, in the amorous net fast c.
P. L. 12, 637. the hastening angel c. our
P. R. 2, 14. and for a time c. up to God
P. R. 4, 541. so saying, he c. him up
S. A. 932. where once I have been c.
L'A. 69. straight mine eye had c.
**Cause.**—P. L. 1, 28. say first, what c.
P. L. 4, 14. nor with c. to boast begins, his
P. L. 4, 922. this c. of flight
P. L. 5, 702. tells the suggested c., and casts
P. L. 6, 31. the c. of truth
P. L. 6, 67. in the c. of God and his Messiah
P.L. 6, 442. if other hidden c. left them superior
P. L. 7, 64. for what c.
P. L. 7, 90. what c. moved the Creator
P. L. 8, 270. where, or from what c.
P. L. 8, 417. the c. of his desire by conversation
P. L. 8, 497. for this c. he shall forego father
P. L. 8, 593. for which c.
P. L. 9, 650. if c. of such effects
P. L. 9, 672. to some great c. addressed
P. L. 9, 862. strange hath been the c.
P. L. 9, 1140. needless c. to approve the faith
P. L. 9, 1168. am I now upbraided as the c.
P. L. 10, 907. which infinite calamity shall c.
P. L. 10, 935. on me, sole c. to thee of all
P. L. 10, 982. to be to others c. of misery
P. L. 11, 382. for different c., the Tempter set
P. L. 11, 461. both for the deed and for the c.
P. L. 12, 604. sad, with c., for evils past
P. R. 1, 66. our just fear gave no small c.
P. R. 2, 239. if c. were to unfold some
P. R. 2, 323. why should that c. thy refusal
P. R. 4, 375. thou shalt have c. to wish
S. A. 157. oft without c. complain
S. A. 234. she was not the prime c., but I myself
S. A. 316. nor in respect of the enemy just c.

S. A. 376. sole author I, sole c.
S. A. 472. with c. this hope relieves thee
S. A. 584. c. light again within thy eyes
S. A. 904. goes by the worse, whatever be her c.
S. A. 1179. He will accept thee to defend His c.
S. A. 1253. he must allege some c.
S. A. 1321. for that c. I cannot come
S. A. 1347. perhaps thou shalt have c. to sorrow
S. A. 1379. for some important c. thou needest
S. A. 1584. what c. brought him so soon
S. A. 1586. inevitable c.
S. A. 1709. nor much more c.
C. 489. defence is a good c., and Heaven be for us
C. 794. uncontrolled worth of this pure c.
**Caused.**—P. L. 4, 216, he c. to grow all trees
P. L. 5, 400. for delight hath c. the earth
S. A. 581. God, who c. a fountain at thy prayer
S. A. 793. what if love.. c. what I did
**Causeless.**—S. A. 701. yet c. suffering
**Causes.**—P. L. 2, 913. their pregnant c. mixed
P. L. 3, 707. but hid their c. deep
P. L. 9, 682. to discern things in their c.
P. L. 9, 731. and many more c. impart
P. L. 10, 806. nature's law by which all c. else
**Causey.**—P. L. 10, 415. the c. to Hell-gate
**Caution.**—P. L. 5, 513. what meant that c.
P. L. 5, 523. this was that c. given thee
P. L. 7, 111. thy request, with c. asked
**Cautious.**—P. L. 9, 59. c. of day
S. A. 757. with more c. and instructed skill
**Cautiously.**—P. R. 4, 377. thus nicely or c.
**Cave.**—P. L. 4, 454. waters issued from a c.
P. L. 6, 4. there is a c. within the mount
P. L. 11, 469. the ways that lead to his grim c.
P. L. 11, 568. gliding hot to some c.'s mouth
P. R. 1, 307. harboured in one c.
S. A. 89. hid in her vacant interlunar c.
C. 239. if thou have hid them in some flowery c.
L'A. 3. in Stygian c. forlorn, 'mongst horrid
**Caverns.**—C. 429. by grots and c. shagged
**Caves.**—P. L. 2, 621. rocks, c., lakes, fens, bogs
P. L. 2, 789. sighed from all her c.
P. L. 4, 257. grots and c. of cool recess
P. L. 7, 417. meanwhile the tepid c., and fens
P. L. 9, 118. rocks, dens, and c.
P. R. 4, 414. the winds within their stony c.
L. 39. thee the woods, and desert c.
**Cavil.**—P. L. 10, 759. c. the conditions
**Cease.**—P. L. 2, 100. and cannot c. to be
P. L. 2, 159. wherefore c. we, then
P. L. 3, 27. not the more c. I to wander
P. L. 5, 845. c. then this impious rage
P. L. 11, 309. I would not c. to weary him
P. L. 12, 238. to them his will, and terror c.
P. R. 2, 222. c. to admire
P. R. 4, 14. still tempting.. and never c.
H. 45. but he, her fears to c., sent down the
D. F. I. 72. her false-imagined loss c. to lament
V. Ex. 86. devouring war shall never c. to roar
**Ceased.**—P. L. 1, 283. he scarce had c.
P. L. 2, 43. he c.; and next him Moloch
P. L. 2, 845. he c., for both seemed highly
P. L. 2, 1010. he c.; and Satan stayed not
P. L. 3, 344. no sooner had the Almighty c.
P. L. 7, 436. the solemn nightingale c. warbling
P. L 8, 412. he c.; I lowly answered
P. L. 10, 910. with tears that c. not flowing
P. L. 11, 126. he c.; and the archangelic
P. L. 11, 713. throat of war had c. to roar
P. L. 11, 726. when he saw, he c. contending
P. L. 11, 780. when violence was c. and war
P. L. 12, 372. he c., discerning Adam
P. R. 1, 456. henceforth oracles are c.
P. R. 2, 235. he c., and heard their grant
P. R. 4, 507. seldom have I c. to eye
C. 551. at which I c., and listened them a while
D. F. I. 18. there ended was his quest, there c.
U. C. II. 10. his principles being c., he ended
**Ceaseless.**—P. L. 2, 795. with c. cry
P. L. 4, 679. all these with c. praise
P. L. 5, 183. let your c. change vary to our

P. L. 10, 573. worn with famine, long and c.
**Ceases.**—P. L. 1, 176. and c. now to bellow
**Ceasing.**—P. L. 2, 654. never c. barked
**Cedar.**—P. L. 4, 139. c., and pine, and fir
P. L. 9, 435. c., pine, or palm
P. L. 12, 250. of c., overlaid with gold
P. R. 1, 306. covert of some ancient oak or c.
P. R. 4, 60. artificers in c.
**Cedarn.**—C. 990. about the c. alleys
**Cedars.**—P. L. 5, 260. with c. crowned
P. L. 9, 1089. ye c., with innumerable boughs
**Cedar-tops.**—P. L. 7, 424. on cliffs and c.-t.
**Ceiling.**—P. L. 11, 743. like a dark c.
**Celebrate.**—P. L. 2, 241. to c. his throne
P. L. 11, 345. to c. and reverence thee
S. A. 435. a popular feast here c. in Gaza
A. 80. I will assay, her worth to c.
**Celebrated.**—P. L. 6, 888. he, c., rode
S. A. 866. c. in the mouths of wisest men
**Celestial.**—P. L. 1, 245. that c. light
P. L. 1, 658. shall never hold c. Spirits
P. L. 2, 15. from this descent c. Virtues rising
P. L. 3, 51. c. Light shine inward
P. L. 3, 364. impurpled with c. roses smiled
P. L. 3, 638. youth smiled c.
P. L. 4, 553. c. armoury, shields, helms
P. L. 4, 682. have we heard c. voices
P. L. 4, 812. touch of c. temper
P. L. 4, 1011. and read thy lot in yon c. sign
P. L. 5, 249. among thousand c. Ardours
P. L. 5, 403. that one c. Father gives to all
P. L. 5, 654. c. tabernacles where they slept
P. L. 6, 44., Michaël, of c. armies prince
P. L. 6, 333. such as c. Spirits may bleed
P. L. 6, 510. turned wide the c. soil
P. L. 6, 760. in c. panoply all armed
P. L. 7, 12. pleased with thy c. song
P. L. 7, 203. harnessed at hand, c. equipage
P. L. 7, 254. nor unsung by the c. choirs
P. L. 7, 354. of c. bodies, first the Sun
P. L. 8, 455. in that c. colloquy sublime
P. L. 8, 619. a smile that glowed c. rosy red
P. L. 9, 21. my c. patroness
P. L. 9, 540. thy c. beauty adore
P. L. 10, 24. did not spare .. c. visages
P. L. 11, 239. not in his shape c.
P. L. 11, 296. c.! whether among the thrones
P. L. 11, 785. unfold, c. Guide
P. R. 1, 170. in c. measures moved
P. R. 4, 588. a table of c. food
S. A. 1280. c. vigour armed their armouries
C. 1004. c. Cupid, her famed son, advanced
A. 63. then listen I to the c. Sirens' harmony
H. 145. throned in c. sheen, with radiant feet
S. M. 27. to his c. consort us unite, to live with
**Cell.**—P. L. 5, 109. retires into her private c.
P. L. 8, 460. but open left the c. of Fancy
C. 387. the pensive secrecy of desert c.
L'A. 5. find out some uncouth c.
Il P. 169. the hairy gown and mossy c.
H. 180. pale-eyed priest from the prophetic c
**Cells.**—P. L. 1, 700. many c. prepared
P. L. 1, 706. and from the boiling c.
P. L. 7, 491. her waxen c. with honey stored
**Celtic.**—P. L. 1, 521. o'er the C. roamed
C. 60. roving the C. and Iberian fields
**Censer.**—P. L. 11, 24. in this golden c.
**Censers.**—P. L. 7, 600. fuming from golden c:
**Censure.**—S. A. 787. that men may c.
**Censuring.**—S. A. 948. c., frown or smile
**Centaur.**—P. L. 10, 328. betwixt the C.
**Centre.**—P. L. 1, 74. from the c. thrice to the
P. L. 1, 686. ransacked the c.
P. L. 3, 575. by c. or eccentric, hard to tell
P. L. 5, 510. from c. to circumference
P. L. 5, 579. upon her c. poised
P. L. 6, 219. all Earth had to her c. shook
P. L. 7, 215. and with the c. mix the pole
P. L. 7, 242. self-balanced, on her c. hung
P. L. 8, 123. what if the sun be c. to the world
P. L. 9, 108. as God in heaven is c.

P. L. 10, 740. as on their natural c.
P. R. 4, 534. as a c., firm
C. 382. may sit in the c., and enjoy bright day
A. 19. goddess bright, in the c. of her light
H. 162. shall from the surface to the c. shake
**Centred.**—P. L. 7, 228. one foot he c.
**Centric.**—P. L. 8, 83. c. and eccentric
P. L. 10, 671. pushed oblique the c. globe
**Centring.**—P. L. 9, 109. so thou, c., receivest
**Cerastes.**—P. L. 10, 525. C. horned
**Cerberean.**—P. L. 2, 655. wide C. mouths
**Cerberus.**—L'A. 2. of C. and blackest Midnight
**Ceremonies.**—P. L. 12, 297. c. cannot appease
**Ceremony.**—P. L. 1, 753. with awful c.
**Ceres.**—P. L. 4, 271. cost C. all that pain
P. L. 4, 981. a field of C. ripe for harvest
P. L. 9, 395. or to C. in her prime
**Certain.**—P. L. 2, 470. c. to be refused
P. L. 2, 597. at c. revolutions all the damned
P. L. 3, 119. which had no less proved c.
P. L. 9, 907. c. my resolution is to die
P. L. 9, 953. c. to undergo like doom
P. L. 10, 576. c. numbered days
P. L. 10, 980. which must be born to c. woe
P. L. 12, 437. c. times to appear to his disciples
S. A. 474. nothing more c.. will not long defer
S. A. 723. no other c. than Dalila thy wife
S. A. 1102. that honour, c. to have won
C. 266. whom, c., these rough shades
C. 482. for c., either some one like us
C. 572. for so by c. signs I knew
C. 619. brought to my mind a c. shepherd lad
**Certainly.**—P. R. 2, 32. beheld Messiah c.
**Certainty.**—C. 263. such sober c.
**Chæronea.**—S. 10, 7. at C., fatal to liberty
**Chafe.**—S. A. 1246. in a sultry c.
**Chafed.**—S. A. 1138. c. wild boars
**Chaff.**—P. L. 4, 985. lest his sheaves prove c.
P. L. 2, 1005. linked in a golden c.
P. L. 2, 105¹ fast by hanging in a golden c.
**Chained.**—P. L. 1, 210. c. on the burning lake
P. L. 2, 169. when we lay c. on the burning lake
P. L. 4, 965. to the infernal pit I drag thee c.
P. L. 6, 589. c. thunder bolts and hail of iron
S. A. 7. where I, a prisoner c., scarce freely draw
C. 660. your nerves are all c. in alabaster
**Chains.**—P. L. 1, 48. adamantine c. ;
P. L. 2, 183. wrapped in c.; there to converse
P. L. 2, 196. to suffer here c. and these torments
P. L. 3, 82. no bars of Hell, nor all the c.
P. L. 4, 970. when I am thy captive talk of c.
P. L. 6, 186. c. in Hell, not realms, expect
P. L. 6, 260. captive dragged in c.
P. L. 6, 739. to c. of darkness and the undying
P. L. 10, 319. with pins of adamant and c.
P. L. 12, 454. drag in c., through all his realm
S. A. 68. blind among enemies, O worse than c.
S. A. 1238.lest I run upon thee, though in these c.
C. 435. breaks his magic c. at curfew time
C. 804. speaks thunder and the c. of Erebus
L'A. 143. untwisting all the c. that tie
S. 16, 12. to bind our souls with secular c.
V. Ex. 52. in willing c. and sweet captivity
**Chair.**—P. L. 1, 764. and at the Soldan's c.
P. L. 2, 930. as in a cloudy c., ascending rides
P. R. 4, 219. points and questions fitting Moses' c.
C. 134. stay thy cloudy ebon c.
D. F. I. 19. he descended from his snow-soft c.
**Chaldæa.**—P. L. 12, 130. Ur of C.
**Challenge.**—S. A. 1151. c. Dagon to the test
**Challenged.**—P. R. 4, 260. Phœbus c.
**Chalybean.**—S. A. 133. C.- tempered steel
**Cham.**—P. L. 4, 276. where old C.
**Chamber.**—C. 101. his c. in the east
**Chamber-ambushes.**—S. A. 1112. with c.-a.
**Chamberlin.**—U. C. I. 14. office of a c.
**Chambers.**—P. R. 2, 183. regal c.
**Champaign.**—P. L. 4, 134. the c. head
P. L. 6, 2. heaven's wide c. held his way
P. R. 3, 257. fair c., with less rivers
**Champing.**—P. L. 4, 859. c. his iron curb

**Champion.**—S. A. 705. once thy glorious *c*. this
S. A. 1152. offering to combat thee, his *c*. bold
S. A. 1751. and to His faithful *c*. hath in place
C. 212. a strong-siding *c*., Conscience
**Champions.**—P. L. 1, 763. where *c*. bold
P. L. 2, 424. those Heaven-warring *c*.
P. L. 2, 898. moist, and dry, four *c*. fierce
**Chance.**—P. L. 1, 133. *c*., or fate
P. B. 2, 222. what *c*. what change
P. L. 2. 233. shall yield to fickle *C*.
P. L. 2, 288. whose bark, by *c*., or pinnace
P. L. 2, 396. we may *c*. re-enter Heaven
P. L. 2, 492. if *c*. the radiant sun
P. L. 2, 551. to Force or *C*. their song was partial
P. L. 2, 910. high arbiter, *c*. governs all
P. L. 2, 935. had not, by ill *c*., the strong rebuff
P. L. 2, 965. Rumour next, and *C*. and tumult
P. L. 4, 403. who by *c*. hath spied
P. L. 4, 530. a *c*. but *c*. may lead
P. L. 7, 172. Necessity and *C*. approach not me
P. L. 9, 452. if *c*., with nymph-like step
P. L. 10, 108. what *c*. detains?
P. L. 10, 428. solicitous what *c*. might intercept
P. R. 1, 321. what ill *c*. hath brought thee
P. R. 4, 265. of fate, and *c*., and change
P. R. 4, 559. *c*. to dash thy foot against a stone
S. A. 4. there I am wont to sit, when any *c*.
S. A. 918. exempt from many a care and *c*.
S. A. 1076. I come not, Samson, to condole thy *c*.
S. A. 1295. may *c*. to number thee with those
C. 277. what *c*., good Lady, hath bereft you thus
C. 508. how *c*. she is not in your company
C. 588. or that power which erring men call *C*.
S. 8, 2. *c*. on these defenceless doors may seize
T. 22. triumphing over Death and *C*. and thee
**Chanced.**—P. L. 9, 423. what so seldom *c*.
P. L. 9, 575. on a day, roving the field, I *c*.
S. A. 1202. as on my enemies, wherever *c*.
**Chances.**—S. A. 656. all *c*. incident
C. 79. *c*. to pass through this adventurous glade
**Change.**—P. L. 1, 96. do I repent, or *c*.
P. L. 1, 244. that we must *c*. for Heaven
P. L. 1, 313. under amazement of their hideous *c*.
P. L. 1, 598. with fear of *c*. perplexes monarchs
P. L. 1, 625. and this dire *c*., hateful to utter
P. L. 2, 222. what *c*. worth waiting
P. L. 2, 598. the bitter *c*. of fierce extremes
P. L. 2, 599. extremes by *c*. more fierce
P. L. 2, 820. through dire *c*. befallen us
P. L. 3, 125. I else must *c*. their nature
P. L. 3, 634. but first he casts to *c*.
P. L. 4, 23. can fly by *c*. of place
P. L. 4, 367. how nigh your *c*. approaches
P. L. 4, 640. all seasons, and their *c*.
P. L. 4, 892. hope to *c*. torment with ease
P. L. 5, 89. *c*. to this high exaltation
P. L. 5, 183. let your ceaseless *c*. vary
P. L. 5, 336. upheld with kindliest *c*.
P. L. 5, 629. for *c*. delectable, not need
P. L. 5, 902. *c*. his constant mind, though single
P. L. 8, 347. they cannot *c*. their element
P. L. 8, 525. works in the mind no *c*.
P. L. 9, 5. I now must *c*. those notes
P. L. 9, 70. sin, not time, first wrought the *c*.
P. L. 9, 818. make known as yet my *c*.
P. L. 10, 107. or what *c*. absents thee
P. L. 10, 213. that now must suffer *c*.
P. L. 10, 273. the smell of mortal *c*. on earth
P. L. 10, 548. sprung up with this their *c*.
P. L. 10, 677. to bring in *c*. of seasons
P. L. 10, 693. like *c*. on sea and land
P. L. 11, 193. further *c*. awaits us nigh
P. L. 11, 308. to *c*. the will of him
P. L. 11, 539. which will *c*.
P. L. 11, 794. shall *c*. their course to pleasure
P. R. 2, 86. I looked for some great *c*.
P. R. 3, 197. my exaltation without *c*. or end
P. R. 4, 265. fate, and chance, and *c*.
P. R. 4, 442. would also seem of this fair *c*.
S. A. 117. O *c*., beyond report, thought, or belief
S. A. 340. O miserable *c*.! is this the man

S. A. 695. to the unjust tribunals, under *c*. of times
S. A. 753. confess, and promise wonders in her *c*.
S. A. 1406. for a life who will not *c*.
C. 10. after this mortal *c*. to her true servants
C. 328. I cannot be that I should fear to *c*.
C. 596. it shall be in eternal restless *c*.
C. 841. underwent a quick immortal *c*.
L. 37. oh, the heavy *c*., now thou art gone
D.F. I. 28. alack! that so to *c*. thee Winter had no
**Changed.**—P. L. 1, 84. how *c*. from him
P. L. 1, 97. though *c*. in outward lustre
P. L. 1, 253. mind not to be *c*. by place or time
P. L. 2, 217. or, *c*. at length
P. L. 2, 276. our temper *c*. into their temper
P. L. 4, 115. thrice *c*. with pale, ire, envy
P. L. 4, 224. nor *c*. his course
P. L. 5, 644. the face of brightest Heaven had *c*.
P. L. 6, 613. straight they *c*. their minds
P. L. 6, 824. into terror *c*. his countenance
P. L. 7, 160. and Earth be *c*. to Heaven
P. L. 9, 505. in Illyria *c*. Hermione
P. L. 11, 712. the face of things quite *c*.
C. 69. the express resemblance of the gods is *c*.
**Changes.**—P. L. 4, 405. then rising *c*.
P. L. 10, 692. these *c*. in the heavens
**Changest.**—S. A. 684. *c*. thy countenance
**Changing.**—P. L. 2, 312. and, *c*. style
P. L. 10. 333. *c*. shape to observe the sequel
P. L. 10, 541. they felt themselves now *c*.
**Channel.**—C. 895. that in the *c*. strays
H. 124. weltering waves their oozy *c*. keen
**Channels.**—P. L. 7, 303. deep *c*. wore
**Chant.**—P. R. 2, 290. *c*. of tuneful birds
**Chaos.**—P. L. 1, 10. rose out of *C*.
P. L. 1, 543. frighted the reign of *C*.
P. L. 2, 233. *C*. judge the strife
P. L. 2, 895. Night and *C*., ancestors
P. L. 2, 907. *C*. umpire sits
P. L. 2, 960. behold the throne of *C*.
P. L. 2, 970. *C*. and ancient Night
P. L. 2, 1038. *C*. to retire
P. L. 3, 18. sung of *C*. and eternal Night
P. L. 3, 421. *C*. and the inroad of Darkness
P. L. 3, 426. ever-threatening storms of *C*.
P. L. 5, 577. *C*. wild reigned
P. L. 6, 55. opens wide his fiery *c*.
P. L. 6, 871. confounded *C*. roared
P. L. 7, 93. so late to build in *C*.
P. L. 7, 220. *C*., and the world unborn, for *C*.
P. L. 7, 272. the loud misrule of *C*.
P. L. 10, 233. far into *C*.
P. L. 10, 283. into the waste wide anarchy of *C*.
P. L. 10, 317. from out of *C*.
P. L. 10, 347. at the brink of *C*.
P. L. 10, 416. disparted *C*. overbuilt exclaimed
P. L. 10, 477. Night and *C*. wild
P. L. 10, 636. through *C*. hurled
C. 334. and disinherit *C*., that reigns here
**Character.**—P. L. 8, 545. expressing the *c*.
**Charactered.**—C. 530. *c*. in the face
**Characters.**—P. R. 4, 384. single *c*.
P. 49. they would fitly fall in ordered *c*.
**Charge.**—P. L. 2, 775. with *c*. to keep
P. L. 3, 628. on some great *c*. employed
P. L. 3, 688. and to Simplicity resigns her *c*.
P. L. 4, 421. this one, this easy *c*.
P. L. 4, 562. thy course by lot hath given *c*.
P. L. 4, 589. Uriel to his *c*. returned
P. L. 4, 787. and gave them thus in *c*.
P. L. 4, 842. whose *c*. is to keep
P. L. 4, 879. and disturbed the *c*. of others
P. L. 5, 248. after his *c*. received
P. L. 6, 566. do as you have in *c*.
P. L. 8, 246. so we had in *c*.
P. L. 9, 157. to watch and tend their earthy *c*
P. L. 9, 399. oft he to her his *c*.
P. L. 10, 35. returned from unsuccessful *c*.
P. L. 10, 123. whereof I gave thee *c*.
P. L. 10, 421. had left their *c*.
P. L. 10, 650. gave them several *c*.
P. L. 11, 99. my behest have thou in *c*.

P. L. 11, 549. this cumbrous c.
P. L. 12, 439. to them shall leave in c.
P. R. 1, 376. to his destruction, as I had in c.
S.A.849.it was not gold, as to my c. thou layest
C. 32. has in his c. with tempered awe to guide
C. 762. do not c. most innocent nature
F. of C. 19. they shall read this clearly in your c.
**Charged.**—P. L. 7, 46. c. not to touch
P. L. 10, 200. I c. thee, saying
**Chariot.**—P. L. 3, 522. rapt in a c.
P. L. 6, 100. in his sun-bright c. sat
P. L. 6, 338. back to his c., where it stood
P. L. 6, 390. c. and charioteer lay overturned
P. L. 6, 711. ascend my c.
P. L. 6, 750. the c. of paternal Deity
P. L. 6, 829. and the orbs of his fierce c. rolled
P. L. 6, 881. his triumphal c. turned
P. L. 7, 197. about his c. numberless
C. 892. my sliding c. stays
H. 56. the hooked c. stood unstained
P. 36. see the c., and those rushing wheels
**Charioteer.**—P. L. 6, 390. chariot and c.
D. F. I. 8. for since grim Aquilo, his c.
**Charioting.**—S. A. 27. a fiery column c.
**Chariots.**—P. L. 2, 887. with horse and c.
P. L. 6, 17. c., and flaming arms
P. L. 6, 211. wheels of brazen c. raged
P. L. 6, 770. c. of God, half on each hand
P. L. 7, 199. winged Spirits, and c. winged
P.R. 3, 329. c., or elephants indorsed with towers
**Chariot-wheels.**—P. L. 1, 311. and broken c.-w.
P. L. 3, 394. thy flaming c.-w.
P. L. 6, 358. at his c.-w.
P. L. 12, 210. and craze their c.-w.
**Charities.**—P. L. 4, 756. the c. of father
**Charity.**—P. L. 3, 217. c. so dear
P. L. 12, 584. by name to come called c.
**Charlemain.**—P. L. 1, 586. C. with all his
P. R. 3, 343. both Paynim. and the peers of C.
**Charm.**—P. L. 1, 787. music c. his ear
P. L. 2, 460. if there be cure or c.
P. L. 2, 566. c. pain for a while
P. L. 4, 642. with c. of earliest birds
P. L. 4, 651. with c. of earliest birds
P. L. 8, 533. weak against the c. of beauty's
P. L. 9, 999. fondly overcome with female c.
C. 758. to c. my judgment, as mine eyes
C. 853. she can unlock the clasping c.
Il P. 83. or the bellman's drowsy c.
**Charmed.**—P. L. 1, 561. c. their painful steps
P. L. 11, 132. more wakeful than to drowse, c.
S. A. 1134. armed thee or c. thee strong
C. 51. whose c. cup
C. 904. to undo the c. band of true virgin
H. 68. birds of calm sit brooding on the c. wave
**Charming.**—P. L. 3, 368. c. symphony
P. L. 5, 626. smoothes her c. tones
P. L. 8, 2. in Adam's ear so c. left his voice
P. L. 11, 595. c. symphonies
P. R. 2, 363. or c. pipes
C. 476. how c. is divine philosophy
**Charms.**—P. L. 2, 556. song c. the sense
P. L. 2, 666. labouring moon eclipses at their c.
P. L. 4, 498. her beauty and submissive c.
P. R. 2, 213. with all her winning c. begirt
P. R. 4, 257. Æolian c. and Dorian lyric odes
S. A. 427. over-potent c.
S. A. 934. fair enchanted cup, and warbling c.
S. A. 1040. by her c. draws him awry enslaved
C. 150. now to my c., and to my wily trains
C. 613. those that quell the might of hellish c.
C. 664. the freedom of my mind with all thy c.
S. 8, 5. he can requite thine, for he knows the c.
**Charnel.**—C. 471. oft seen in c. vaults
**Charybdis.**—P. L. 2, 1020. shunned C.
C. 259. fell C. murmured soft applause
**Chase.**—P. L. 1, 557. c. anguish, and doubt
P. L. 4, 341. and of all c. in wood
P. L. 6, 288. and with threats to c.
P. L. 11, 191. with his eye the c. pursuing
P. R. 2, 342. beasts of c., or fowl of game

P. R. 4, 627. shall c. thee with the terror
**Chased.**—P. R. 4, 429. c. the clouds
**Chaste.**—P. L. 4, 761. and c. pronounced
P. L. 11, 12. Deucalion and c. Pyrrha
C. 146. some c. footing near about this ground
C. 442. fair silver-shafted queen for ever c.
C. 450. but rigid looks of c. austerity
C. 918. touch with c. palms moist and cold
**Chastening.**—P. L. 11, 373. however c.
**Chastity.**—C. 215. unblemished form of C.
C. 420. 'tis c., my brother, c.
C. 425. through the sacred rays of c.
C. 440. to testify the arms of c.
C. 453. so dear to Heaven is saintly c.
C. 782. against the sun-clad power of C.
C. 909. 'tis my office best to help ensnared c.
**Chatting.**—H. 87. sat simply c.
**Chaunting.**—S. A. 1672. c. their idol
**Chauntress.**—Il P. 63. c., oft the woods among
**Cheap.**—P. L. 2, 472. winning c.
**Cheat.**—C. 155. of power to c. the eye
**Chebar.**—P. 37. whirled the prophet up at C.
**Check**—P. L. 5, 214. needed hands to c.
P. R. 1, 477. endure c. or reproof
C. 761. virtue has no tongue to c. her pride
**Checked.**—P. L. 6, 853. c. his thunder
**Checks.**—P. L. 3, 732. c. the night
Il P. 59. while Cynthia c. her dragon yoke
**Cheek.**—P. L. 1, 602. his faded c.
P. L. 3, 641. curls on either c. played
P. L. 5, 10. glowing c.
P. L. 5, 385. no thought infirm altered her c.
P. L. 9, 887. but in her c. distemper
P. R. 4, 344. laid as varnish on a harlot's c.
L'A. 29. such as hang on Hebe's c.
Il P. 107. drew iron tears down Pluto's c.
D. F. I. 6. that did thy c. envermeil
S. 11, 12. O soul of Sir John C.
**Cheeks.**—P. L. 10, 1009. as dyed her c.
C.750. coarse complexions, and c. of sorry grain.
**Cheer.**—P. L. 6, 496. their drooping c.
S. A. 1613. with mirth. high c. and wine
C. 955. their mirth and c.
**Cheered.**—P. L. 4, 165. c. with the grateful
P.L.5, 129. so c. he his fair spouse and she was c.
P. L. 12, 604. much more c. with meditation
P. R. 4, 433. had c. the face of earth
S. A. 926. with all things grateful c.
**Cheerful.**—P. L. 2, 490. Heaven's c. face
P. L. 3, 46. the c. ways of men cut off
P. L. 3, 545. at last, by break of c. dawn
P. L. 5, 123. looks that wont to be more c.
P. L. 11, 543. the air of youth hopeful and c.
C. 388. far from the c. haunt of men and herds
S. 21, 14. when God sends a c. hour
**Cheering.**—C. 348. some little c.
**Cheerly.**—L'A.54. c.rouse the slumbering morn
**Cheers.**—S. A. 545. or taste that c. the heart
**Chemos.**—P. L. 1, 406. next C., the obscene
**Chequered.**—L'A. 96. dancing in the c. shade
**Cherish.**—P. L. 10, 1068. to c. our limbs
S. A. 958. c. thy hastened widowhood
**Cherishing.**—P. L. 8, 569. worthy well thy c.
**Cherith.**—P. R. 2, 266. by the brook of C.
**Chersonese.**—P. L. 11, 392. the golden C.
P. R. 4, 74. from India and the golden C.
**Cherub.**—P. L. 1, 157. fallen C.
P. L. 1, 324. C. and Seraph rolling in the flood
P. L. 1, 534. Azazel as his right, a C. tall
P. L. 3, 636. now a stripling C. he appears
P. L. 4, 844. so spake the C. and his grave rebuke
P. L. 4, 971. proud limitary C.
P. L. 6, 771. on the wings of C. rode sublime
P. L. 7, 198. C. and Seraph, potentates
Il P. 54. the C. Contemplation
P. 38. my spirit some transporting C. feels
**Cherubic.**—P. L. 5, 547. c. songs by night
P. L. 6, 413. c. waving fires
P. L. 6, 753. four c. shapes
P. L. 9, 68. or c. watch
P. L. 11, 120. c. watch

S. M. 12, the *c.* host, in thousand choirs
**Cherubim.**—P. L. 1, 387. between the *c.*
P. L. 1, 665. the thighs of mighty *C.*
P. L. 1, 794. the Great Seraphic lords and *C.*
P. L. 2, 516. the four winds four speedy *C.*
P. L. 3, 666. me from the choirs of *C.*
P. L. 4, 778. and from their ivory port the *C.*
P. L. 6, 102. flaming *C.* and golden shields
P. L. 6, 535. Zophiel, of *C.* the swiftest wing
P. L. 7, 218. but, on the wings of *C.*
P. L. 9, 61. entrance, and forewarned the *C.*
P. L. 11, 100. take to thee from among the *C.*
P. L. 11, 128. the cohort bright of watchful *C.*
P .L. 12, 254. between the wings of two bright *C.*
P. L. 12, 628. in bright array the *C.* descended
H. 112. the helmèd *C.*, and sworded Seraphim
**Chest.**—H. 217. within his sacred *c.*
**Chew.**—P. L. 4, 335. the savoury pulp they *c.*
**Chewed.**—P. L. 10, 566. *c.* bitter ashes
**Chewing.**—C. 540. the *c.* flocks
**Chid.**—C. 258. *c.* her barking waves
**Chide.**—S. 19, 6. lest he, returning, *c.*
**Chief.**—P. L. 1, 128. O *C.* of many
P. L. 1, 381. the *c.* were those who, from the
P. L. 1, 524. have found their *c,* not in despair
P. L. 1, 566. what command their mighty *C.*
P. L. 1, 762. but *c.* the spacious hall
P. L. 2, 469. others among the *c.* might offer
P. L. 2, 487. rejoicing in their matchless *c.*
P. L. 2, 527. till his great *C.* return
P. L. 3, 29. but *c.* thee, Sion
P. L. 3, 168. in whom my soul hath *c.* delight
P. L. 3, 664. Man, his *c.* delight and favour
P. L. 4, 550. *c.* of angelic guards
P. L. 4, 864. to whom their *C.*, Gabriel
P. L. 4, 920. courageous *c.!* the first in flight
P. L. 5, 102. faculties, that serve reason as *c.*
P. L. 5, 684. which we lead the *c.*
P. L. 6, 233. single as in *c.*
P. L. 6, 745. and I among them *c.* so said
P. L. 7, 515. who made him *c.* of all his works
P. L. 9, 29. *c.* mastery to dissect ›
P. L. 10, 455. beheld, their mighty *C.*
P. L. 10, 537. issuing forth their glorious *C.*
P. L. 11, 493. as their *c.* good and final hope
P. L. 11, 617. honour and *c.* praise
P. R. 2, 464. virtue, merit, and *c.* praise
S. A. 66. but *c.* of all, O loss of sight
S. A. 457. my *c.* affliction, shame and sorrow
S. A. 554. our *c.* support of health
S. A. 754. but *c.* to try her husband
S. A. 1440. all of gigantic size, Goliath *c.*
S. 16, 1. Cromwell, our *c.* of men
D. F. I. 3. summer's *c.* honour, if thou hadst
U. C. II. 21, 201. ease was his *c.* disease
**Chiefest.**— II P. 51. first and *c.*, with thee bring
V. Ex. 18. from thy wardrobe bring thy *c.*
**Chiefly.**—P. L. 1, 17. *c.* thou, O spirit
P. L. 2, 763. the most averse, thee *c.*
P. L. 3, 663. but *c.* Man, his chief delight
P. L. 4, 445. I *c.*, who enjoy so far
P. L. 4, 566. Almighty's works and *c.* man
P. L. 4, 790. but *c.* where those two
P. L. 4, 849. *c.* to find here observed
P. L. 9, 379. *c.* by what thy own last reasoning
P. L. 9, 878. which for thee *c.* I sought
P. L. 9, 981. pernicious to thy peace, *c.*
P. L. 10, 401. *c.* on Man, sole lord of all
P. L. 12, 272. *c.*, which concern just Abraham
P. L. 12, 599. *c.* what may concern
P. R. 1, 263. *c.*, that my way must lie
P. R. 3, 123. though *c.* not for glory
S. A. 1452. *c.* to give ye part with me what
**Child.**—P. R. 1, 201. when I was yet a *c.*
S. A. 942. in most things as a *c.* helpless
L'A. 133. sweetest Shakespeare, Fancy's *c.*
H. 30. the Heaven-born, and all meanly
D. F. I. 71. the mother of so sweet a *c.*
**Child-bearing.**—P. L. 10, 1051. *c.-b.* were
**Child-bed.**—S. 23, 5. from spot of *c.-b.*
**Childhood.**—P. R. 4, 220. the *c.* shows the

P. R. 4, 508. thy infancy, thy *c.*, and thy youth
**Childish.**—P. R. 1, 201. no. *c.* play to me
V. Ex. 3. mad'st imperfect words with *c.*
**Childless.**—P. L. 10, 989. *c.* thou art; *c.*
P. L. 10, 1037. or *c.* days
D. F. I. 13. of long-uncoupled bed and *c.* eld
**Children.**—P. L. 1, 395. their *c.'s* cries
P. L. 10, 194. *c.* thou shalt bring in sorrow
P L. 10, 330. disguised he came; but those his *c.*
P. L. 11, 761. his *c.* all in view destroyed
P. L. 11, 772. befall him or his *c.*
P. R. 4, 330. as *c.* gathering pebbles
S.A. 352. I prayed for *c.*, and thought barrenness
C. 720. and precious gems to store her *c.* with
C. 763. as if she would her *c.* should be riotous
**Chill.**—P. L. 9, 890. while horror *c.*
C. 352. from the *c.* dew
A. 49. winds and blasting vapours *c.*
H. 195. and the *c.* marble seems to sweat
**Chilled.**—P. L. 5, 65. damp horror *c.*
**Chilling.**—P. L. 11, 264. with *c.* gripe
**Chimæras.**—P. L. 2, 628. and *c.* dire
C. 517. of dire *C.* and enchanted isles
**Chime.**—P. L. 11, 559. made melodious *c.*
C. 1021. higher than the sphery *c.*
H. 128. and let your silver *c.* move in melodious
S. M. 20. jarred against Nature's *c.*
**Chiming.**—P. R. 2, 363. of *c.* strings
**Chimney.**—L'A. 81. hard-by a cottage *c.* smokes
L'A. 111. stretched out all the *c.'s* length
**Chin.**—H. 281. pillows his *c.* upon an orient wave
**Chineses.**—P. L. 3, 438. where *C.* drive
**Chios.**—P. R. 4, 118. *C.*, and Crete, and how
**Chivalry.**—P. L. 1, 307. his Memphian *c.*
P. L. 1, 765. defied the best of Panim *c.*
P. R. 3, 344. such and so numerous was their *c.*
**Choaspes.**—P. R. 3, 288. *C.*, amber stream
**Choice.**—P. L. 1, 261. and in my *c.* to reign
P. L. 1, 653. whom his *c.* regard should favour
P. L. 1, 759. by place or *c.* the worthiest
P. L. 2, 19. first create your leader, next, free *c.*
P. L. 2, 415. we now no less *c.* in our suffrage
P. L. 2, 423. none, among the *c.* and prime
P. L. 2, 524. pursues, as inclination or sad *c.*
P. L. 3, 108. and reason, (reason also is *c.*)
P. L. 3, 534. and his eye with *c.* regard
P. L. 3, 670. shining orbs his *c.* to dwell
P. L. 4, 434. and *c.* unlimited of manifold
P. L. 5, 327. will pluck such *c.* to entertain
P. L. 5, 333. what *c.* to choose for delicacy best
P. L. 5, 499. ethereal, as we, or may, at *c.*
P. L. 7, 48. so easily obeyed, amid the *c.*
P. L. 8, 335. though in my *c.* not to incur
P. L. 8, 400. in the *c.* of thy associates, Adam!
P. L. 9, 214. thou, where *c.* leads thee
P. L. 9, 620. in such abundance lies our *c.*
P. L. 9, 992. as of *c.* to incur divine displeasure
P. L. 10, 766. God made thee of *c.* his own
P. L. 10, 904. or his happiest *c.* too late
P. L. 10, 978. as in our evils, and of easier *c.*
P. L. 11, 101. thy *c.* of flaming warriors
P. R. 3, 314. flower and *c.* of many provinces
P. R. 4, 329. for *c.* matters, worth a sponge
S. A. 3. for yonder bank hath *c.* of sun or shade
S. A. 311. to exempt whom it pleases Him by *c.*
S. A. 555. made *c.* to rear his mighty champion
S. A. 633. his nursling once and *c.* delight
S. A. 1030. or value what is best in *c.*
S. A. 1654. their *c.* nobility and flower
S. A. 1743. his lot unfortunate in nuptial *c.*
S. 20, 9. neat repast shall feast us, light and *c.*
**Choicest.**—P. L. 5, 127. *c.* bosomed smells
P. L. 5, 368. and what the garden *c.* bears
P. L. 9, 840. had wove of *c.* flowers
P. L. 11, 438. firstlings of his flock, *c.* and best
P. R. 1, 302. such solitude before *c.* society
P. R. 2, 334. from all the elements her *c.* store
P. R. 4, 437. cleared up their *c.* notes
S. A. 264. with a trivial weapon felled their *c.*
V. Ex. 22. which deepest spirits and *c.* wits
**Choir.**—P. L. 3, 217. the heavenly *c.* stood

E

P. L. 4, 264. the birds their *c.* apply
P. L. 9, 198. vocal worship to the *c.* of creatures
P. L. 12, 366. and by a *c.* of squadroned
P. R. 1, 242. at thy nativity a glorious *c.* of
C. 112. imitate the starry *c.*
Il P. 162. to the full-voiced *c.* below
S. 13, 10. to honour thee, the priest of Phœbus' *c.*
H. 27. and join thy voice unto the angel *c.*
H. 115. harping in loud and solemn *c.*
M. W. 17. the virgin *c.* for her request

**Choirs.**—P. L. 3, 666. from the *c.* of Cherubim
P. L. 4, 711. and heavenly *c.* the hymenæan
P. L. 5, 251. the angelic *c.* on each hand
P. L. 7, 254. nor unsung by the celestial *c.*
P. R. 4, 593. and as he fed Angelic *c.* sung
S. M. 12. the cherubic host, in thousand *c.*

**Choose.**—P. L. 1, 428. what shape they *c.*
P. L. 2, 60. let us rather *c.* armed with hell
P. L. 2, 265. all-ruling Sire *c.* to reside
P. L. 3, 123. what they judge and what they *c.*
P. L. 5, 333. what choice to *c.* for delicacy best
P. L. 5, 534. by destiny, and can no other *c.*
P. L. 5, 787. and *c.* to bend the supple knee
P. L. 9, 221. our task we *c.*, what wonder
P. L. 9, 316. thy trial *c.* with me
P. L. 12, 225. and their great Senate *c.*
P. L. 12, 646. before them, where to *c.*
P. R. 3, 370. *c.* which thou wilt
S. A. 1478. rather I shall *c.* to live the poorest
Il. P. 176. and I with thee will *c.* to live
V. Ex. 29. yet I had rather, if I were to *c.*

**Chooses.**—S. A. 513. self-rigorous, *c.* death as due
**Choosing.**—P. L. 9, 26. pleased me, long *c.*
P. L. 10, 1005. ways to die the shortest *c.*
P. L. 12, 219. return them back to Egypt, *c.*

**Choral.**—P. L. 5, 162. and *c.* symphonies
P. L. 7, 599. intermixed with voice *c.* or unison
**Chords.**—P. L. 11, 561. and *c.* was seen.
**Chorus.**—P. L. 7, 275. even and morning *c.*
P. R. 4, 262. in *c.* or iambic

**Chose.**—P. L. 4, 72. *c.* freely what it now
P. L. 4, 406. *c.* his ground whence rushing
P. L. 8, 54. and of him to ask *c.* rather
P. L. 9, 88. his final sentence *c.* fit vessel
P. L. 9, 1100. there soon they *c.* the fig-tree
P. L. 9, 1167. *c.* rather death with thee
P. L. 11, 587. they liked, and each his liking *c.*
P. R. 1, 165. what consummate virtue I have *c.*
P. R. 2, 397. *c.* to impart to thy apparent need
S. A. 877. *c.* thee from among my enemies
S. A. 985. *c.* above the faith of wedlock bands
S. A. 1193. *c.* a wife, which argued me no foe
H. 14. *c.* with us a darksome house of mortal

**Chosen.**—P. L. 1, 8. first taught the *c.* seed
P. L. 1, 318. or have ye *c.* this place
P. L. 3, 183. some I have *c.* of peculiar grace
P. L. 4, 691. a place *c.* by the Sovran Planter
P. R. 1, 427. the other service was thy *c.* task
P. R. 2, 45. how they oppress thy *C.*
P. R. 2, 236. a *c.* band of spirits likest
P. R. 4, 614. now for Adam and his *c.* sons
S. A. 368. alas! methinks whom God hath *c.* once
S. 9, 6. with Mary and with Ruth *c.* thou hast

**Christ.**—F. of C. 6. our consciences that *C.* set free
**Chrysolite.**—P. L. 3, 596. *c.*, ruby or topaz
**Church.**—P. L. 4, 193. so since into his *C.*
**Cimmerian.**—L'A. 10. dark *C.* desert
**Cincture.**—P. L. 9, 1117. with feathered *c.*
**Cinders.**—P. L. 10, 570. with soot and *c.* filled
**Cinnamon.**—C. 937. groves of myrrh and *c.*
**Circe.**—C. 50. on *C.'s* island fell
C. 153. fair a herd as grazed about my mother *C.*
C. 253. my mother *C.* with the Sirens three
C. 522. of Bacchus and of *C.* born, great Comus
**Circean.**—P. L. 9, 522. than at *C.* call
**Circle.**—P. L. 4, 578. the sun's bright *c.*
P. L. 5, 163. day without night, *c.* his throne
P. L. 5, 182. perpetual *c.*, multiform
A. 15. in *c.* round her shining throne
S. 8, 8. whatever clime the sun's bright *c.* warms
**Circled.**—P. L. 3, 626. *c.* his head

P. L. 5, 862. fatal course had *c.* his full orb
P. L. 9, 65. thrice the equinoctial line he *c.*
**Circles.**—P. L. 5, 631. all in *c.* as they stood
P. L. 6, 305. and in the air made horrid *c.*
P. L. 8, 107. the swiftness of those *c.*
P. L. 10, 681. to those beyond the polar *c.*
**Circlet.**—P. L. 5, 169. with thy bright *c.*
**Circling.**—P. L. 2, 647. impaled with *c.* fire
P. L. 3, 556. so high above the *c.* canopy
P. L. 4, 146. a *c.* row of goodliest trees
P. L. 6, 3. till Morn waked by the *c.* Hours
P. L. 6, 743. far separate, *c.* thy holy mount
P. L. 7, 342. seasons, and for days, and *c.* years
P. L. 7, 580. which nightly, as a *c.* zone
P. L. 9, 502. erect amidst his *c.* spires
P. R. 1, 57. too soon for us, the *c.* hours
P. R. 1, 171. *c.* the throne and singing
S. A. 871. where all thy *c.* wiles would end
**Circuit.**—P. L. 2, 1048. extended wide in *c.*
P. L. 3, 721. in *c.* walls this universe
P. L. 4, 586. but if within the *c.*
P. L. 4, 784. our *c.* meets full west
P. L. 5, 287. heavenly fragrance filled the *c.*
P. L. 5, 595. of *c.* inexpressible they stood
P. L. 7, 266. in *c.* to the uttermost convex
P. L. 7, 301. under ground, or *c.* wide
P. L. 8, 100. and for the heaven's wide *c.*
P. L. 8, 304. a *c.* wide, enclosed
P. L. 9, 323. in narrow *c.*, straitened by a foe
P. R. 3, 254. outstretched in *c.* wide
**Circular.**—P. L. 9, 498. *c.* base of rising
H. 110. a globe of *c.* light, that with long
**Circumcised.**—S. A. 975. among the *c.*
**Circumcision.**—P. R. 3, 425. by *c.* vain
**Circumference.**—P. L. 1, 286. broad *c.*
P. L. 2, 353. that shook Heaven's whole *c.*
P. L. 5, 510. nature set from centre to *c.*
P. L. 6, 256. his ample shield, a vast *c.*
P. L. 7, 231. this be thy just *c.*, O world
**Circumfluous.**—P. L. 7, 270. *c.* waters
**Circumfused.**—P. L. 6, 778. his army, *c.*
P. L. 7, 624. earth with her nether ocean *c.*
**Circumscribe.**—P. L. 7, 226. to *c.* this
**Circumscribed.**—P. L. 5, 825. *c.* their being
**Circumspection.**—P. L. 2, 414. need all *c.*
P. L. 4, 537. but with sly *c.*
P. L. 6, 523. with silent *c.* unespied
**Circumstance.**—S. A. 1557. the *c.* defer
**Circumvent.**—P. L. 9, 259. to *c.* us joined
S. A. 1115. breaking her marriage faith, to *c.* me
**Circumvented.**—P. L. 3, 152. fall *c.*
**Citadel.**—P. L. 1, 773. their straw-built *c.*
P. R. 4, 49. on the Tarpeian rock, her *c.*
**Cited.**—P. L. 3, 327. and forthwith the *c.* dead
**Cities.**—P. L. 1, 498. and in luxurious *c.*
P. L. 2, 533. as when, to warn proud *c.*
P. L. 11, 640. *c.* of men with lofty gates
P. R. 2, 470. to rule *c.* of men
P. R. 3, 74. win great *c.* by assault
P. R. 3, 261. huge *c.* and high towered
P. R. 4, 363. ruins kingdoms, and lays *c.* flat
L'A. 117. towered *c.* please us then
**Citron.**—P. L. 5, 22. how blows the *c.* grove
P. R. 4, 115. on *c.* tables or Atlantic stone
**City.**—P. L. 2, 924. to rase some capital *c.*
P. L. 9, 445. as one who, long in populous *c.*
P. L. 10, 424. Pandemonium, *c.* and proud seat
P. L. 11, 386. wherever stood *c.* of old
P. L. 11, 410. whose great *c.* Geryon's sons
P. L. 11, 655. to a *c.* strong lay siege
P. L. 12, 44. a *c.* and tower whose top may
P. L. 12, 51. comes down to see their *c.*
P. L. 12, 340. their *c.*, his temple, and his
P. L. 12, 342. scorn and prey to that proud *c.*
P. R. 2, 21. Bethabara, in Jericho, *c.* of palms
P. R. 2, 22. and each town or *c.* walled
P. R. 2, 300. as one in *c.* or court
P. R. 3, 285. Persepolis, his *c.*, there thou
P. R. 3, 311. the *c.* gates outpoured
P. R. 3, 340. the *c.* of Gallaphrone
P. R. 4, 44. the *c.* which thou seest

P. R. 4, 238. on the Ægean shore a c. stands
P. R. 4, 243. c. or suburban, studious walks
P. R. 4, 545. the Holy C. lifted high her towers
S. A. 1194. and in your c. held my nuptial feast
S. A. 1449. I heard all as I came, the c. rings
S. A. 1561. the desolation of a hostile c.
S. A. 1596. occasions drew me early to this c.
S. A. 1655. each Philistian c. round
**City-gates.**—P. L. 11, 661. in the c.-g.
**Civil.**—P. L. 6, 667. war seemed a c. game
P. L. 11, 718. thence from cups to c. broils
P. L. 12, 231. such as appertain to c. justice
P. R. 4, 358. the solid rules of c. government
S. A. 853. adjured, by all the bonds of c. duty
S. A. 1367. of those who have me in their c.
S. A. 1467. more generous far and c.
S. 17, 10. spiritual power and c., what each means
F. of C. 5, dare ye for this adjure the c. sword
**Civility.**—P. R. 4, 83. c. of manners
**Civil-suited.**—Il P. 122. c.-s. Morn appear
**Clad.**—P. L. 1, 410. of Sibma c. with vines
P. L. 4, 599. with native honour c.
P. L. 4, 599. in her sober livery all things c.
P. L. 5, 278. that c. each shoulder broad
P. L. 7, 315. c. her universal face
P. L. 10, 216. he c. their nakedness with skins
P. L. 10, 450. c. with what permissive glory
P. L. 11, 17. c. with incense, where the golden
P. L. 11, 240. but as man c. to meet man
P. R. 2, 65. she in sighs thus c.
P. R. 2, 299. rustic as before, but seemlier c.
P. R. 2, 352. youths rich-c., of fairer hue
P. R. 3, 313. in mail their horses c.
S. A. 129. ran on embattled armies c. in iron
S. A. 1317. I will see thee heartened and fresh c.
S. A. 1616. in their state livery c.
C. 421. she that has c. in complete steel
A. 92. c. in splendour as befits her deity
S. 14, 10. c. them o'er with purple beams
D. F. I. 58. who having c. thyself in human weed
M. W. 73. with thee there c. in radiant sheen
**Claim.**—P. L. 2, 32. will c. in hell precedence
P. L. 2, 38. to c. our just inheritance of old
P. L. 4, 487. I seek thee, and thee c.
P. L. 5, 723. to hold what anciently we c.
P. L. 11, 258. from Death's rapacious c.
P. L. 12, 170. from God to c. his people
**Claimed.**—P. L. 1, 533. honour c. Azazel
P. L. 9, 1130. Reason, c. superior sway
**Claimest.**—P. L. 2, 817. c. me for thy sire
**Claiming.**—P. L. 12, 35. c. second sovranty
**Claims.**—P. L. 9, 566. c. attention due
**Clamorous.**—P. L. 10, 479. with c. uproar
**Clamour.**—P. L. 6, 208. and c. such as
P. L. 7, 36. the savage c. drowned both harp
P. L. 11, 853. with c. thence the rapid currents
P. R. 2, 148. with c. was assured
**Clamouring.**—S. A. 1621. c. their god
**Clamours.**—P. L. 2, 862. with c. compassed
**Clang.**—P. L. 7, 422. with c. despised
P. L. 11, 835. and orcs, and sea-mews' c.
H. 157. such a horrid c. as on mount Sinai
**Clans.**—P. L. 2, 901. their several c.
**Clarion.**—P. L. 7, 443. whose c. sounds
**Clarions.**—P. L. 1, 532. trumpets loud, and c.
**Clashed.**—P. L. 1, 668. c. on their sounding
**Clashing.**—P. L. 6, 209. on armour c.
**Clasp.**—P. L. 10, 918. and c. thy knees
**Clasping.**—P. L. 9, 217. direct the c. ivy
C. 853. she can unlock the c. charm
**Classic.**—F. of C. 7. with a c. hierarchy
**Clattered.**—S. A. 1124. on thy c. iron
**Clay.**—P. L. 9, 176. this man of c.
P. L. 10, 743. from my c. to mould me man
P. R. 1, 501. fowls in their c. nests
C. 339. from the wicker hole of some c.
H. 14. with us a darksome house of mortal c.
**Cleansing.**—S. A. 1727. and c. herbs
**Clear.**—P. L. 2, 770. c. victory, to our
P. L. 3, 28. c. spring, or shady grove
P. L. 3, 188. for I will c. their senses dark

P. L. 3, 595. part seemed gold, part silver c.
P. L. 3, 620. the air no where so c.
P. L. 4, 119. from distempers foul are ever c.
P. L. 4, 458. to look into the c. smooth lake
P. L. 5, 733. with calm aspect and c.
P. L. 7, 619. on the c. hyaline, the glassy sea
P. L. 8, 336. but soon his c. aspect returned
P. L. 9, 681. thy power within me c.
P. L. 9, 706. your eyes that seem so c.
P. L. 11, 844. and the c. sun on his wide
P. L. 12, 376. now c. I understand
S. A. 550. I drank from the c. milky juice
C. 381. he that has light within his own c. breast
C. 457. and in c. dream, and solemn vision
C. 722. feed on pulse, drink the c. stream
L. 70. fame is the spur that the c. spirit doth raise
L'A. 126. in saffron robe, with taper c.
Il P. 163. in service high and anthems c.
S. 22, 1. c., to outward view, of blemish
S. 23, 12. so c. as in no face with more delight
**Cleared.**—P. L. 5, 136. so all was c.
P. L. 8, 179. thus Adam, c. of doubt, replied
P. L. 9, 708. your eyes be then opened and c.
P. R. 4, 437. c. up their choicest notes
S. 15, 12. and public faith c. from the shameful
**Clearer.**—P. L. 11, 413. c. sight had bred
**Clearest.**—P. L. 11, 379. in c. ken
**Clearly.**—F. of C. 19. when they shall read this c.
**Cleave.**—P. R. 3, 436. c. the Assyrian flood
**Cleaving.**—S A. 1039. c. mischief
**Cleft.**—P. L. 11, 440. on the c. wood
P. R. 3, 438. Jordan once he c.
**Cleombrotus.**—P. L. 3, 473. C., and many more
**Cliff.**—P L. 1, 517. the Delphian c.
P. L. 4, 547. the rest was craggy c.
P. L. 5, 275. on the eastern c. of Paradise
P. L. 12, 639. and down the c. as fast to the
**Cliffs.**—P. L. 7, 424. c. and cedar tops
P. R. 3, 317. Margiana, to the Hyrcanian c.
**Climate.**—P. L. 9, 45. cold c., or years
P. L. 11, 274. never will in other c. grow
**Climb.**—P. L. 4, 193. lewd hirelings c.
P. L. 4, 548. still as it rose, impossible to c.
P. L. 9, 217. the clasping ivy where to c.
L. 115. creep, and intrude, and c. into the fold
T. 19. our heavenly-guided soul shall c.
**Climbest.**—P. L. 5, 173. when thou c.
**Climbing.**—P. L. 10, 559. up the trees c.
**Climbs.**—P. L. 4, 191. in at the window c.
P. L. 11, 119. up from Eden easiest c.
**Clime.**—P. L. 1, 242. this the soil, the c.
P. L. 1, 297. the torrid c. smote on him
P. L. 2, 572. if any c., perhaps might yield
P. L. 5, 1. her rosy steps in the eastern c.
P. L. 7, 18. Bellerophon, though from a lower c.
P. L. 10, 678. change of seasons to each c.
P. L. 12, 636. to parch that temperate c.
C. 1020. she can teach ye how to c.
A. 24, 324. who had thought this c. had held
S. 8, 8. whatever c. the sun's bright circle
**Climes.**—P. L. 11, 708. the c. of bliss
C. 977. and those happy c. that lie
**Clip.**—F. of C. 17. c. your phylacteries
**Clod.**—P. L. 10, 786. this corporeal c.
**Clods.**—P. L. 7, 463. the grassy c. now calved
P. L. 11, 565. two massy c. of iron
**Clogs.**—S. 12, 1. the age to quit their c.
**Cloisters.**—Il P. 156. the studious c., pale
**Clomb.**—P. L. 4, 192. so c. this first
**Close.**—P. L. 1, 646. to work in c. design
P. L. 1, 795. in c. recess and secret conclave sat
P. L. 2, 485. or c. ambition varnished o'er
P. L. 2, 537. till thickest legions c.
P. L. 2, 638. c. sailing from Bengala
P. L. 2, 1053. c. by the moon
P. L. 4, 347. c. the serpent sly, insinuating
P. L. 4, 376. so straight, so c., that I with
P. L. 4, 405. straight couches c.
P. L. 4, 708. here, in c. recess, with flowers
P. L. 4, 800. c. at the ear of Eve
P. L. 5, 36. c. at mine ear

P. L. 5, 673. what sleep can c. thy eyelids
P. L. 6, 235. open when, and when to c.
P. L. 9, 191. waiting c. the approach of morn
P. L. 10, 589. c. following pace for pace
P. L. 11,419. Adam now enforced to c. his eyes
P. R. 2, 28. c. in a cottage low together got
S. A. 8. c. and damp, unwholesome draught
S. A. 651. speedy death the c. of all my miseries
S. A. 1748. and ever best found in the c.
C. 197. in thy dark lantern thus c. up the stars
C. 349. in this c. dungeon of innumerous boughs
C. 548. ere a c. the wonted roar was up
Il P. 139. there in c. covert by some brook
S. 1, 5. thy liquid notes that c. the eye of day
S. 11,2. and woven c.,both matter form and style
H. 100. still prolongs each heavenly c.
**Close-banded.**—S. A. 1113. c.-b. durst attack
**Close-curtained.**—C. 554. c.-c. Sleep
**Closed.**—P. L. 3, 144. c. thy sovran sentence
P. L. 6, 330. the ethereal substance c.
P. L. 6, 875. and on them c.
P. L. 8, 459. and c. mine eyes
P. L. 8,460. mine eyes he c., but open left
P. R. 4, 481. c. thee round, so many terrors
L. 51. c. o'er the head of your loved Lycidas
**Closing.**—P. L. 4, 863. and c. stood
P. L. 6. 436. pierced with wound, soon c.
**Clothe.**—P. L. 10, 219. c. his enemies
S. 20, 7. and c. in fresh attire the lily and rose
V. Ex. 32. before thou c. my fancy in fit sound
**Clothed.**—P. L. 1, 86. c. with transcendent
P. L. 2, 226. with words c. in reason's garb
P. L. 10, 1059. and his hands c. us unworthy
**Clothing.**—V. Ex. 82. shall depend for c.
**Clotted.**—S. A. 1728. wash off the c. gore
C. 467. the soul grows c. by contagion
**Cloud.**—P. L. 1, 340. a pitchy c. of locusts
P. L. 2, 936. some tumultuous c.
P. L. 3, 45. but c. instead, and ever-during
P. L. 3, 263. wherein no c. of anger shall
P. L. 3, 378. and through a c. drawn round
P. L. 3, 385. without c. made visible
P. L. 4, 151. in fair evening c., or humid bow
P. L. 5, 122. nor c. those looks, that wont
P. L. 5, 257. from hence no c., or, to obstruct
P. L. 5. 686. her shadowy c. withdraws
P. L. 6, 28. from midst a golden c.
P. L. 6, 539. so thick a c. he comes
P. L. 7, 247. sphered in a radiant c.
P. L. 7, 422. despised the ground, under a c.
P. L. 9, 425. veiled in a c. of fragrance
P. L. 10, 32. from his secret c. amidst
P. L. 10, 449. as from a c., his fulgent head
P. L. 11, 45. whom the Father, without c.,serene
P. L. 11, 205. more orient in yon western c.
P. L. 11, 229. from yonder blazing c.
P. L. 11, 670. had not a c. descending
P. L. 11, 706. rapt in a balmy c.
P. L. 11, 865. a dewy c., and in the c. a bow
P. L. 11, 882. of that same watery c.
P. L. 11, 896. he brings over the earth a c.
P. L. 12, 185. a darksome c. of locusts
P. L. 12. 202. who shall go before them in a c.
P. L. 12,203. by day a c., by night a pillar of fire
P. L. 12, 208. the fiery pillar and the c.
P. L. 12, 256. over the tent a c. shall rest
P. R. 3, 222. interposition, as a summer's c.
P. R. 4, 321. an empty c.
C. 221. was I deceived, or did a sable c.
C. 333. thy pale visage through an amber c.
Il P. 72. stooping through a fleecy c.
Il P. 125. but kerchiefed in a comely c.
S. 16, 1. who through a c. not of war only
P. 56. a race of mourners on some pregnant c.
**Clouded.**—P. L. 4, 607. in c. majesty
P. L. 12,333. the c. ark of God, till then in tents
**Cloudless.**—S. A. 1696. c. thunder
**Clouds.**—P. L. 2. 264. amidst thick c.
P. L. 2, 488. the dusky c. ascending
P. L. 2, 535. to battle in the c.
P. L. 2, 637. hangs in the c.

P. L. 2, 714. as when two black c.
P. L. 4, 500. when he impregns the c.
P. L. 4, 544. of alabaster, piled up to the c.
P. L. 4, 597. the c. that on his western throne
P. L. 5, 86. up to the c. with him I flew
P. L. 5. 189. whether to deck with c.
P. L. 5, 642. ambrosial night, with c. exhaled
P. L. 6, 56. and c. began to darken
P. L. 7, 287. upheave into the c.
P. L. 7, 599. of incense c.
P. L. 8, 146. as c., and c. may rain
P. L. 10, 702. with thunderous c.
P. L. 10, 1073. as late the c. justling
P. L. 11, 739. all the c. together drove
P. L. 11, 841. the c. were fled, driven by a keen
P. L. 12, 77. where thin air above the c.
P. L. 12, 545. last, in the c., from Heaven
P. R. 1, 41. within thick c. and dark tenfold
P. R. 1, 81. the c. unfold her crystal doors
P. R. 3, 327. nor wanted c. of foot
P. R. 4, 410. the c. from many a horrid rift
P. R. 4, 429. chased the c.,and laid the winds
P. R. 4, 619. shall not long rule in the c.
C. 301. and play in the plighted c.
L'A. 62. the c. in thousand liveries dight
L'A. 74. the labouring c. do often rest
H. 50. with turtle wing the amorous c.
H. 146. with radiant feet the tissued c.
H. 159. and smouldering c. outbrake
Cir. 4. so sweetly sung your joy the c. along
**Cloudy.**—P. L. 2, 930. as in a c. chair
P. L. 5, 266. a c. spot, down thither prone
P. L. 6, 107. the c. van, on the rough edge
P. L. 6, 409. her c. covert both retired
P. L. 6, 450. c. in aspect, thus answering spake
P. L. 7, 248. she in a c. tabernacle
P. L. 7, 360. transplanted from her c. shrine
C. 134. stay thy c. ebon chair
H. 230. curtained with c. red, pillows his chin
D. F. I. 56. let down in c. throne
**Clouted.**—C. 635. with his c. shoon
**Cloven.**—P. L. 6. 361. c. to the waist
L. 34. Satyrs danced, and Fauns with c. heel
**Clung.**—P. L. 10, 512. c. to his ribs
**Clustering.**—P. L. 4, 303. hung c.
P. L. 7, 320. the c. vine
S. A. 569. c. down, vain monument of strength
C. 54. this Nymph that gazed upon his c. locks
**Clusters.**—P. L. 1, 771. about the hive in c.
P. L. 5, 218. her dower, the adopted c.
C. 296. plucking ripe c. from the tender shoots
**Clymene.**—P. R. 2, 186. Calisto, C.
**Coal.**—P. L. 5, 440. if by fire of sooty c.
**Coals.**—P. R. 2, 273. supper on the c.
**Coaly.**—V.Ex.98. or c.Tyne, or ancient hallowed
**Coarse.**—C. 749. c. complexions and cheeks
**Coast.**—P. L. 1, 306. hath vexed the Red Sea c.
P. L. 1, 340. waved round the c.
P. L. 1, 464. through the c. of Palestine
P. L. 2, 633. the right hand c.
P. L. 2, 958. the nearest c. of darkness
P. L. 3, 487. cross wind from either c.
P. L. 3, 739. toward the c. of earth
P. L. 4, 782. half these draw off, and c. the
P. L. 5, 340. in Pontus, or the Punic c.
P. L. 6, 529. looked round, and scouts each c.
P. L. 9, 67. on the c. averse from entrance
P. L. 10, 89. Eden and all the c.
P. L. 10, 293. to the rich Cathaian c.
P. R. 1, 119. the c. of Jordan he directs
P. R. 2, 347. Lucrine bay, and Afric c.
**Coasting.**—P. L. 3, 71. c. the wall of Heaven
C. 49. c. the Tyrrhene shore, as the winds listed
**Coasts.**—P. L. 2, 464. through all the c.
P. L. 8, 245. we returned up to the c. of light
**Coat.**—P. L. 5, 341. in c. rough
P. L. 6, 542. let each his adamantine c.
P L. 10, 218. with youthful c. repaid
**Coats.**—P. L. 7, 406. their waved c.
P. R. 3, 312. in c. of mail and military pride
**Cock.**—P. L. 7, 443. the crested c.

C. 346. or village *c.* count the night watches
L'A. 49. while the *c.*, with lively din
L'A. 114. ere the first *c.* his matin rings
**Cocytus.**—P. L. 2, 579. *C.*, named
**Co-eternal.**—P. L. 3, 2. *c.-e.* beam
**Coffers.**—V. Ex. 31. may make thee search thy *c.*
**Cogitation.**—P. L. 3, 629. *c.* deep
**Cohort.**—P. L. 11, 127. the *c.* bright
**Cohorts.**—P. R. 4, 66. legions and *c.*
**Coin.**—S. A. 189. how counterfeit a *c.*
S. A. 1204. to pay my underminers in their *c.*
C. 739. beauty is Nature's *c.*, must not be hoarded
**Cold.**—P. L. 1, 516. of *c.* Olympus
P. L. 2, 595. and *c.* performs the effect of fire
P. L. 2, 898. for Hot, *C.*, Moist, and Dry
P. L. 7, 238. the black, tartareous, *c.*
P. L. 9, 44. an age too late, or *c.* climate
P. L. 9, 636. and the *c.* environs round
P. L. 10, 294. *c.* and dry
P. L. 10, 653. *c.* and heat scarce tolerable
P. L. 10, 686. the snow from *c.* Estotiland
P. L. 10, 691. pinching *c.* and scorching heat
P. L. 10, 851. on the *c.* ground
P. L. 10, 1056. and, lest *c.* or heat
P. L. 10, 1070. leave *c.* the night
P. L. 11, 293. *c.* sudden damp recovering
P. L. 11, 544. *c.* and dry, to weigh
P. R. 4, 31. from *c.* Septentrion blasts
P. R. 4, 403. hungry and *c.*, betook him
C. 353. perhaps some *c.* bank is her bolster now
C. 802. a *c.* shuddering dew dips me all o'er
C. 918. I touch with chaste palms moist and *c.*
S. 18, 2. lie scattered on the Alpine mountains *c.*
**Cold-kind.**—D. F. I., 9. with his *c.-k.* embrace
**Colic.**—P. L. 11, 484. and ulcer, *c.* pangs
**Colkitto.**—S. 11, 9. *C.*, or Macdonald
**Collateral.**—P. L. 8, 426. *c.* love
P. L. 10, 86. of high *c.* glory
**Colleague.**—P. L. 10, 59. *c.* with justice
**Collect.**—P. R. 4, 524. I *c.* thou art to be
**Collected.**—P. L. 6, 581. *c.* stood
P. L. 9, 673. stood in himself *c.*
**Collecting.**—P. L. 4, 986. *c.* all his might
P. R. 3, 5. at length *c.* all his serpent wiles
P. R. 4, 328. *c.* toys and trifles
**Collision.**—P. L. 10, 1072. by *c.* of two bodies
**Colloquy.**—P. L. 8, 455. in that celestial *c.*
**Colonel.**—S. 8, 1. Captain or *C.* or Knight-in-arms
**Colour.**—P. L. 3, 612. *c.* glorious
P. L. 6, 352. and *c.*, shape, or size
P. L. 10, 870. shape like his, and *c.*
P. R. 2, 176. their *c.*, and attractive grace
**Coloured.**—P. L. 3, 642. a *c.* plume
P. L. 4, 702. more *c.* than with stone
P. L. 7, 445. *c.* with the florid hue
P. L. 11, 879. what mean those *c.* streaks
P. 32. that heaven and earth are *c.* with my woe
**Colours.**—P. L. 1, 546. with orient *c.* waving
P. L. 4, 149. with gay enamelled *c.* mixed
P. L. 5, 24. how nature paints her *c.*
P. L. 5, 283. and *c.* dipped in heaven
P. L. 6, 759. *c.* of the showery arch
P. L. 7, 318. opening their various *c.*
P. L. 9, 577. loaden with fruit of fairest *c.*
P. L. 11, 866. three listed *c.* gay
S. A. 901. these false pretexts and varnished *c.*
C. 300. that in the *c.* of the rainbow live
**Columbus.**—P. L. 9, 1116. such of late *C.*
**Column.**—S. A. 27. as in a fiery *c.* charioting
**Colure.**—P. L. 9, 66. traversing each *c.*
**Comb.**—C. 880. and fair Ligea's golden *c.*
**Combat.**—P. L. 1, 766. to mortal *c.*
P. L. 6, 315. in mid sky should *c.*
S. A. 1106. to *c.* with a blind man I disdain
S. A. 1152. offering to *c.* thee, his champion bold
S. A. 1176. by *c.* to decide whose god is God
**Combatant.**—S. A. 344. single *c.*
**Combatants.**—P. L. 2, 719. the mighty *c.*
**Combated.**—S. A. 864. and *c.* in silence
**Combined.**—P. L. 2, 750. with thee *c.*
P. L. 8, 394. in pairs thou hast *c.*

P. L. 9, 339. as not secure to single or *c.*
**Combines.**—S. A. 1048. that in domestic good *c.*
**Combustible.**—P. L. 1, 233. *c.* and fuelled
**Combustion.**—P. L. 1, 46. ruin and *c.*
P. L. 6, 225. dreadful *c.* warring
**Come.**—P. L. 2, 715. *c.* rattling on
P. L. 2, 822. *c.* no enemy, but set free
P. L. 2, 970. I *c.* no spy, with purpose to
P. L. 4, 580. *c.* well known from heaven
P. L. 4, 841. but *c.*, for thou be sure
P. L. 4, 923. hadst not *c.* sole fugitive
P. L. 5, 118. may *c.* and go, so unapproved
P. L. 5, 138. they forth were *c.* to open sight
P. L. 5, 291. *c.* into the blissful field
P. L. 5, 298. the spicy forest onward *c.*
P. L. 5, 493. time may *c.*, when men
P. L. 5, 770. thither to *c.* and with calumnious
P. L. 6, 609. O friends! why *c.* not on
P. L. 8, 79. when they *c.* to model heaven
P. L. 8, 298. I *c.* thy guide to the garden
P. L. 8, 372. to *c.*, and play before thee
P. L. 8, 414. all human thoughts *c.* short
P. L. 9, 366. trial will *c.* unsought .
P. L. 9, 413. in appearance, forth was *c.*
P. L. 9, 610. to *c.* and gaze and worship thee
P. L. 9, 1027. but *c.*, so well refreshed
P. L. 10, 38. what would *c.* to pass
P. L. 10, 107. or *c.* I less conspicuous
P. L. 10, 108. what chance detains? *c.* forth!
P. L. 10, 276. *c.* flying, lured with scent
P. L. 11, 114. what shall *c.* in future days
P. L. 11, 260. to remove thee I am *c.*
P. L. 11, 344. had hither *c.* from all the ends
P. L. 11, 357. to show thee what shall *c.*
P. L. 11, 454. and to *c.* out of thy loins
P. L. 11, 528. how we may *c.* to Death
P. L. 11, 704. that God would *c.* to judge
P. L. 11, 815. wrath to *c.* on their impenitence
P. L. 12, 11. what is to *c.* I will relate
P. L. 12, 258. and at length they *c.*
P. L. 12, 361. in heaven, proclaims him *c.*
P. L. 12, 458. shall *c.*, when this
P. L. 12, 584. add love, by name to *c.*
P. L. 12, 600. by her seed to *c.*
P. R. 1, 75. all *c.*, and he himself among them
P. R. 1, 138. should *c.* the Holy Ghost
P. R. 1, 181. machinations, *c.* to nought
P. R. 1, 271. now *c.*, who was to *c.*
P. R. 1, 300. of things past and to *c.*
P. R. 1, 331. *c.* forth to town or village
P. R. 1, 409. leave to *c.* into the Heaven
P. R. 1, 484. to hear thee when I *c.*
P. R. 2, 17. to Heaven yet once again to *c.*
P. R. 2, 32. Messiah certainly now *c.*
P. R. 2, 43. send thy Messiah forth, the time is *c.*
P. R. 2, 112. his great work to *c.* before him
P. R. 2, 375. *c.* to pay thee homage
P. R. 3, 204. let that *c.* when it comes
P. R. 3, 397. is not yet *c.*
P. R. 4, 615. *c.* down to reinstall
S. A. 112. who *c.* to stare at my affliction
S. A. 180. we *c.*, thy friends and neighbours
S. A. 205. how well are *c.* upon him his deserts
S. A. 444. to have *c.* to pass by means of thee
S. A. 704. for oft alike both *c.* to evil end
S. A. 725. my wife! my traitress! let her not *c.*
S. A. 785. weakness then with weakness *c.*
S. A. 1076. I *c.* not, Samson .. thy chance
S. A. 1088. now am *c.* to see of whom such noise
S. A. 1229. *c.* nearer; part not hence
S. A. 1262. but *c.* what will my deadliest foe
S. A. 1316. rise therefore with all speed, and *c.*
S. A. 1321. for that cause I cannot *c.*
S. A. 1332. the way thou camest; I will not *c.*
S. A. 1380. how thou wilt here *c.* off
S. A. 1395. *c.* without delay
S. A. 1397. and hamper thee, as thou shalt *c.*
S. A. 1404. master's commands *c.* with a power
S. A. 1448. to *c.* and play before them
S. A. 1566. to utter what will *c.* at last too soon
S. A. 1681. their own destruction to *c.* speedy

S. A. 1708. *c.*, *c.*, no time for lamentation now
C. 125. *c.*, let us our rites begin, 'tis only
C. 143. *c.*, knit hands, and beat the ground
C. 491. *c.* not too near, you fall on iron stakes
C. 599. but *c.*, let's on!
C. 735. and *c.* at last to gaze upon the sun
C. 806. *c.*, no more! this is mere moral babble
C. 938. *c.*, Lady, while heaven lends us grace
C. 943. till we *c.* to holier ground
C. 956. *c.*, let us haste, the stars grow high
L. 3. I *c.* to pluck your berries harsh and crude
L'A. 11. but *c.*, thou Goddess fair and free
L'A. 33. *c.* and trip it, as you go, on the light
L'A. 45. then to *c.*, in spite of sorrow
L'A. 97. and young and old *c.* forth to play
Il P. 31. *c.*, pensive Nun, devout and pure
Il P. 37. *c.*, but keep thy wonted state
Il P. 98. in sceptred pall *c.* sweeping by
H. 90. was kindly *c.* to live with them below
V. Ex. 9. that thence can *c.* unto thee
V. Ex. 57. about thy purposed business *c.*
V. Ex. 62. *c.* tripping to the room
U. C. I. 12. his journey's end was *c.*
U. C. II. 23. his time was *c.*
**Comeliness.**—P. L. 8, 222. all *c.* and grace
S.A.1011. strength, *c.* of shape or amplest merit
**Comely.**—P. L. 9, 668. yet *c.*, and in act
S. A. 1268. O how *c.* it is, and how reviving
Il P. 125. but kerchiefed in a *c.* cloud
C. 75. but boast themselves more *c.*
**Comes.**—P. L. 1, 66. hope never *c.*, that *c.* to all
P. L. 2, 663. riding through the air she *c.*
P. L. 3, 231. and to all *c.* unprevented
P. L. 4, 131. and to the border *c.* of Eden
P. L. 4, 869. and with them *c.* a third
P. L. 5, 310. what glorious shape *c.* this way
P. L. 5, 645. for night *c.* not there in darker
P. L. 6, 540. so thick a cloud he *c.*
P. L. 9, 225. and the hour of supper *c.*
P. L. 10, 813. that fear *c.* thundering
P. L. 10, 854. why *c.* not Death?
P. L. 10, 858. but Death *c.* not at call
P. L. 11, 366. mortal passage when it *c.*
P. L. 11, 785. how *c.* it thus?
P. L. 12, 51. *c.* down to see their city
P. L. 12, 160. to sojourn in that land he *c.*
P. L. 12, 393. he who *c.* thy Saviour
P. R. 1, 199. from without *c.* often to my ears
P. R. 1, 412. *c.* to the place where he
P. R. 1, 484. when I come (since no man *c.*)
P. R. 3, 204. when it *c.* All hope is lost
P. R. 3, 398. when that *c.*, think not thou
P. R. 4, 146. when my season *c.* to sit
S. A. 326. but see, here *c.* thy reverend sire
S. A. 713. *c.* this way, sailing like a stately ship
S.A.1070. *c.* he in peace? What wind hath blown
S. A. 1074. or peace; or not, alike to me he *c.*
S. A. 1304. *c.* on amain, speed in his look
S. A. 1441. wherefore *c.* old Manoah in such
C. 168. but here she *c.*; I fairly step aside
C. 488. if he be friendly, he *c.* well
L. 75. *c.* the blind Fury with the abhorred
M. M. 2. *c.* dancing from the east, and leads
**Comest.**—P. L. 4, 824. *c.* thou, escaped
P. L. 6, 159. but well thou *c.* before thy
P. R. 1, 410. thou *c.*, indeed, as a poor
P. R. 3, 298. and just in time thou *c.*
**Comet.**—P. L. 2, 708. like a *c.* burned
P. L. 12, 634. fierce as a *c.*, which with torrid
**Comfortable.**—P. L. 10, 1077. a *c.* heat
**Comforter.**—P. L. 12, 486. a *C.* will send
**Comfortless.**—P. L. 11, 760. though *c.*
**Comforts.**—C. L. 10, 1084. with many *c.*
**Coming.**—P. L. 3, 232. happy for Man so *c.*
P. L. 4, 7. warned the *c.* of their secret foe
P. L. 4, 471. where no shadow stays thy *c.*
P. L. 4, 646. the *c.* on of grateful evening
P. L. 5, 781. *c.* to receive from us
P. L. 6, 610. erewhile they fierce were *c.*
P. L. 6, 648. when, *c.* towards them
P.L. 6, 768. far off his *c.* shone

P. L. 7, 209. *c.* to create new worlds
P. L. 8, 46. they at her *c.* sprung
P. L. 9, 647. have spared our *c.* hither
P. L. 10, 104. with joy to meet my *c.*
P. L. 11, 233. such majesty invests him *c.*
P. L. 11, 250. but his *c.* thus declared
P. L. 12, 405. shall endure, by *c.* in the flesh
P. R. 1, 71. great Prophet, to proclaim his *c.*
P. R. 1, 494. thy *c.* hither, though I know
P. R. 4, 204. whose *c.* is foretold to me
S. A. 187. your *c.*, friends, revives me
S. A.1395. dispute thy *c.*? Come without delay
S. A. 1452. but that which moved my *c.*
C. 35. are *c.* to attend their father's state
C. 954. and our sudden *c.* there will double
**Command.**—P. L. 1, 566. awaiting what *c.*
P. L. 1, 752. by *c.* of sovran power
P. L. 2, 851. and by *c.* of Heaven's
P. L. 3, 94. transgress the sole *c.*
P. L. 3, 650. stand ready at *c.*, and are his eyes
P. L. 4, 864. in squadron joined, awaiting next *c.*
P. L. 5, 551. whose *c.* single is yet so just
P. L. 5, 685. tell them that by *c.*
P. L. 6, 61. at which *c.* the powers militant
P. L. 6, 781. which at *c.* the uprooted hills retired
P. L. 7, 47. transgress, and slight that sole *c.*
P. L. 7, 294. such flight the great *c.* impressed
P. L. 8, 232. (such *c.* we had), to see that
P. L. 8, 329. my sole *c.* transgressed inevitably
P. L. 8, 371. and all these at thy *c.*
P. L. 8, 635. and keep his great *c.*
P. L. 9, 652. God so commanded, and left that *c.*
P. L. 9, 1156. *c.* me absolutely not to go
P. L. 10, 430. gave *c.*, and they observed
P. L. 11, 385. his eye might there *c.*
P. L. 11. 818. by his *c.* shall build
P. L. 12, 210. by *c.*, Moses once more his
P. R. 1, 342. but if thou be the Son of God, *c.*
P. R. 2, 149. their utmost aid at his *c.*
P. R. 2, 382. likes me best, I can *c.*
P. R. 2, 384. *c.* a table in this wilderness
P. R. 4, 556. He will give *c.* concerning thee
P. R. 4, 631. *c.* them down into the Deep
S. A. 57. to subserve where wisdom bears *c.*
S.A.1212. and *c.* from Heaven to free my country
S. A. 1371. the Philistian lords *c.*
S. A. 1394. and darest thou at our sending and *c.*
C. 41. but that by quick *c.* from sovran Jove
**Commanded.**—P. L. 5, 768. *c.* to consult
P. L. 9, 652. God so *c.* and left that command
S. A. 852. solicited, *c.*, threatened, urged
**Commander.**—P. L. 1, 358. their great *C.*
P. L. 1, 589. yet observed their dread *C.*
**Commanding.**—P. L. 5, 699. Most High *c.*
P. L. 6, 557. and thus was heard *c.* loud
P. L. 12, 265. adjourn, man's voice *c.*
**Commandments.**—P. R. 4, 176. of all *c.*
**Commands.**—P. L. 1, 531. then strait *c.*
P. L. 2, 856. his *c.* above, who hates me
P. L. 3, 614. far and wide his eye *c.*
P. L. 4, 524. envious *c.*, invented with design
P. L. 4, 747. and *c.* to some
P. L. 5, 691. the great Messiah, and his new *c.*
P. L. 5, 806. the deity, and divine *c.* obeyed
S. A. 1337. will condescend to such absurd *c.*
S. A.1372. *c.* are no constraints; if I obey them
S. A. 1404. masters' *c.* come with a power
S. A. 1640. hitherto, lords, what your *c.* imposed
**Command'st.**—P. L. 9, 570. what thou *c.*
**Commend.**—S. A. 247. to *c.* my deeds
L'A. 124. to win her grace whom all *c.*
**Commended.**—C. 831. *c.* her fair innocence
**Commends.**—P. L. 9, 754. *c.* thee more
**Commercing.**—Il P. 39. looks *c.* with the skies
**Commiseration.**—P. L. 10, 940. wrought *c.*
**Commission.**—P. L. 7, 118. such *c.* from above
**Commit.**—P. L. 8, 26. could *c.* such
P. R. 1, 111. unanimous they all *c.* the care
P. R. 2, 233. the rest *c.* to me; I shall let pass
**Commits.**—C. 25. by course *c.* to several

**Committed.**—P. L. 10, 957. to me *c.*
S. A. 47. who this high gift of strength *c.* to me
S. A. 1000. and aggravate my folly, who *c.*
S.A.1185. for hadst thou not *c.* notorious murder
**Committing.**—P. R. 4. 95. *c.* to a wicked
S. 13, 4. with Midas' ears *c.* short and long
**Commodiously.**—P. L. 10, 1083. to pass *c.*
**Common.**—P. L. 2, 371. surpass *c.* revenge
P. L. 4, 752. of all things *c.* else
P. L. 5, 435. the *c.* gloss of theologians
P. L. 7, 426. in *c.,* ranged in figure
P. L. 8, 583. would not be to them made *c.*
P. L. 8, 597. in procreation, *c.* to all kinds
P. L. 9, 931. made *c.* and unhallowed
S. A. 6. daily in the *c.* prison
S. A. 674. nor do I name of men the *c.* rout
S. A. 777. to publish them, both *c.* female faults
S. A. 856. how glorious to entrap a *c.* enemy
S. A. 1161. and fettered send thee into the *c.*
S. A. 1416. of a *c.* enemy. so dreaded once
**Commonalty.**—P. L. 7. 489. tribes of *c.*
**Commotion.**—P. L. 4, 992. in this *c.*
P. L. 6, 310. unsafe within the wind of such *c.*
P. L. 6, 706. and this perverse *c.* governed thus
P. L. 8, 531. here passion first I felt, *c.* strange
**Commune.**—P. L. 9, 201. then *c.* how that
**Communed.**—P. R. 2, 261. the Son *c.*
**Communicable.**—P. L. 7, 124. to none *c.*
P. R. 1, 419. lost bliss, to thee no more *c.*
P. R. 3, 125. and impart his good *c.*
**Communicated.**—P. L. 5, 72. the more *c.*
P. L. 9, 755. infers the good by thee *c.*
**Communicating.**—P. L. 8, 150 *c.* male
**Communication.**—P. L. 8, 429. social *c.*
**Communion.**—P. L. 5, 637. and in *c.* sweet
P. L. 8, 431. thou wilt of union or *c.*
**Compact.**—P. L. 9, 635. *c.* of unctuous
**Companion.**—P. L. 5, 673, *c.* dear
P. L. 6, 907. thee once to gain *c.* of his woe
**Companions.**—P. L. 1, 76. the *c.* of his fall
P. L. 6, 419. not to be over-powered, *c.* dear
P. R. 1, 398. to gain *c.* of my misery and woe
**Company.**—P. L. 8, 446. and no such *c.*
S. A. 1413. your *c.* along I will not wish
C. 274. how to regain my severed *c.*
C. 508. how chance she is not in your *c.*
**Compare.**—P. L. 1, 588. beyond *c.*
P. L. 2, 921. to *c.* great things with small
P. L. 3, 138. beyond *c.* the Son of God
P. L. 5, 432. as may *c.* with heaven
P. L. 5, 467. yet what *c.*?
P. L. 6, 705. all may know .. thy power above *c.*
P. L. 9, 228. to me beyond *c.* above all living
P. R. 4, 346. unworthy to *c.*
P. R. 4, 563. to *c.* small things with greatest
S. A. 556. his mighty champion strong above *c.*
**Compared.**—P. L. 3, 592. *c.* with aught
P. L. 6, 170. their deeds *c.* this day shall prove
P. L. 8, 18. an atom, with the firmament *c.*
P. L. 10, 306. if great things to small may be *c.*
P. R. 1, 200. ill sorting with my present state *c.*
P. R. 2, 348. alas! how simple to these cates *c.*
S. A. 441. *c.* with idols, disglorified, blasphemed
S. A. 1020. thy paranymph, worthless to thee *c.*
**Comparing.**—S. A. 464. his deity *c.*
**Comparison.**—P. L. 8, 92. in *c.* of Heaven
**Compass.**—P. L. 3, 342. to *c.* all this
P. L. 4, 559. what point of his *c.* to beware
P. L. 8, 33. that better might with far less *c.*
P. R. 4, 51. the imperial palace, *c.* huge
S. A. 1477. if my whole inheritance may *c.* it
V. Ex. 56. to keep in *c.* of thy predicament
**Compassed.**—P.L.2,862. with clamours *c.* round
P. L. 7, 27. with dangers *c.*
P. R. 1, 58. this dreaded time have *c.*
**Compasses.**—P. L. 7, 225. the golden *c.*
**Compassing.**—P. L. 9, 59. *c.* the earth
P. L. 11, 352. following thee, still *c.* thee round
**Compassion.**—P. L. 3, 141. *c.* visibly appeared
P. L. 11, 496. *c.* quelled his best of man
**Compeer.**—P. L. 1, 127. his bold *c.*

**Compeers.**—P. L. 4, 974. with thy *c.*
**Compel.**—P. L. 6, 619. we should *c.* them
**Compelled.**—P. L. 9, 609. *c.* me thus
P. L. 12, 175. must be *c.* by signs
C. 275. *c.* me to awake the courteous Echo
C. 643. till now that this extremity *c.*
**Compels.**—P. L. 4, 391. *c.* me now
L. 7. *c.* me to disturb your season due
**Competition.**—S. A. 476. against all *c.*
**Complacence.**—P. L. 3, 276. my sole *c.*
P. L. 8, 433. nor in their ways *c.* find
**Complain.**—P. L. 2, 550. *c.* that Fate
S. A. 46. whom have I to *c.* of but myself
S. A. 67. O loss of sight, of thee I most *c.*
S.A.157.men enjoying sight oft without cause *c.*
**Complaint.**—P. L. 10, 131. by my *c.*
P. L. 10, 719. to disburden sought with sad *c.*
S. A. 662. and of dissonant mood from his *c.*
**Complete.**—P. L. b, 352. with his own *c.*
P. L. 8, 548. she seems, and in herself *c.*
P. L. 10,10. *c.* to have discovered and repulsed
P. R. 4, 283. will render thee a king *c.*
S. A. 558. what availed this temperance, not *c.*
C. 421. she that has that is clad in *c.* steel
M. W. 12. as *c.* as was her praise
**Completed.**—P. L. 11, 618. *c.* to the taste
**Completing.**—P. L. 9, 1003. *c.* of the mortal
**Complexions.**—C. 749. coarse *c.* and cheeks
**Compliance.**—P. L. 8, 603. sweet *c.*
S. A. 1411. by this *c.* thou wilt win the lords
**Compliant.**—P. L. 4, 332. the *c.* boughs
**Complicated.**—P. L. 10, 523. *c.* monsters
**Compliments.**—P. R. 4, 124. hollow *c.*
**Comply.**—S. A. 1408. be sure in nothing to *c.*
A. 38. and with all helpful service will *c.*
**Compose.**—P. L. 2, 281. me may *c.*
**Composed.**—P. L. 1, 483. borrowed gold *c.*
P. L. 2, 111. for dignity *c.,* and high exploit
P. L. 6, 469. with look *c.,* Satan replied
P. L. 12, 596. her spirits *c.* to meek submission
P. R. 1, 407. deservedly thou grievest, *c.* of lies
P. R. 2, 108. meekly *c.* awaited the fulfilling
**Composition.**—P. L. 6, 613. terms of *c.*
P. R. 4, 529. parle or *c.,* truce, or league
**Composure.**—P. L. 6, 560. peace and *c.*
P. L. 9, 272. with sweet austere *c.*
**Comprehend.**—P. L. 3, 705. can *c.*
P. L. 5, 505. this happy state can *c.*
P. L. 7, 114. or heart of man suffice to *c.*
P. R. 4, 224. in knowledge; all things in it *c.*
**Compulsion.**—P. L. 2, 80. with what *c.*
P. L. 9, 474. what sweet *c.* thus transported
A. 68. such sweet *c.* doth in music lie
**Compute.**—P. L. 3, 580. numbers that *c.*
P. L. 6, 685. as we *c.* the days of Heaven
P. L. 8, 16. and *c.* their magnitudes
**Comrades.**—S. A. 1162. slaves and asses, thy *c.*
**Comus.**—C. 58. she brought up, and *C.* named
C. 522. of Bacchus and of Circe born, great *C.*
**Concave.**—P. L. 1, 542. that tore Hell's *c.*
P. L. 2, 635. up to the fiery *c.,* towering high
**Conceal.**—P. L. 4, 123. deep malice to *c.*
P. L. 8, 73. the great Architect did wisely to *c.*
P. L. 10, 130. I should *c.,* and not expose
P. L. 10, 136. wouldst easily detect what I *c.*
A. 13. envy bid *c.* the rest
**Concealed.**—P. L. 1, 641. his strength *c.*
P. L. 2, 187. war therefore, open or *c.,* alike
P. L. 4, 312. mysterious parts were then *c.*
P. L. 5, 207. have gathered aught of evil, or *c.*
S. A. 998. discovered in the end, till now *c.*
C. 142. the tell-tale sun descry our *c.* solemnity
**Concealing.**—P. R. 4, 474. *c.* the time
**Conceals.**—P. L. 9, 751. *c.* not from us
P. R. 2, 96. some great intent *c.* him
**Conceits.**—P. L. 4, 809. with high *c.*
P. R. 4, 295. next to fabling fell and smooth *c.*
**Conceive.**—P. L. 7, 281. mother to *c.*
**Conceived.**—P. L. 2, 627. or fear *c.*
P. L. 2, 766. that my womb *c.* a growing
P. L. 2, 796. hourly *c.,* and hourly born

P. L. 9, 945. not well *c.* of God
P. R. 1, 239. thy birth *c.* in me a virgin
P. R. 2, 67. have *c.* of God, or that salute
S. A 390. by the scent *c.* her spurious firstborn
S. A. 1506. *c.,* agreeable to a father's love
S. A. 1574. what windy joy this day had I *c.*
**Conceives.**—P. L. 9, 449. *c.* delight
**Conceiving.**—P. L. 1, 234. *c.* fire
P. L. 5, 666. deep malice thence *c.* and disdain
P. L. 6, 787. hope *c.* from despair
P. R. 4, 598. and light of light *c.*
W. S. 14. dost make us marble with too much *c.*
**Concent.**—S. M. 6. undisturbed song of pure *c.*
**Concentring.**—P. L. 9, 106. in thee *c.*
**Conception.**—P. L. 6, 512. their crude *c.*
P. L. 10, 194. I will greatly multiply by thy *c.*
P. L. 10, 987. yet ere *c.,* to prevent the race
S. A. 1434. after his message told of thy *c.*
**Concern**—P. L. 7, 62. might *c.* him
P. L. 8, 196. renders us, in things that most *c.*
P. L. 11, 144. to *c.* the mind of God
P. L. 12, 272. chiefly, which *c.* just Abraham
P. L. 12, 599. may *c.* her faith to know
**Concerned.**—P. L. 7, 82. which yet *c.*
P. L. 10, 170. more to know *c.* not man
P. R. 1, 440. to fly or follow what *c.* him most
S. A. 1420. with zeal, if aught religion seem *c.*
S. A. 1551. so in the sad event too much *c.*
**Concerning.**—P. L. 10, 199. *c.* which
P. R. 1, 261. what was writ *c.* the Messiah
P. R. 4, 557. command *c.* thee to his angels
**Concernments.**—S. A. 969. thy *c.* I desist
**Concerns.**—P. L. 5, 721. now *c.* us
P. L. 8, 174. only what *c.* thee and thy being
P. R. 1, 293. for what *c.* my knowledge
P. R. 3, 198. but what *c.* it thee when I begin
P. R. 4, 205. to me most fatal, me it most *c.*
S. A. 1148. how highly it *c.* his glory now
**Conclave.**—P. L. 1, 795. and secret *c.* sat
**Conclude.**—P. L. 9, 1142. *c.* they then
P. L. 12, 292. they may *c.* some blood more
**Concludes.**—P. L. 10, 839. and *c.* thee
**Concludest.**—P. R. 2, 317. what *c.* thou
**Concoct.**—P. L. 5, 412. tasting *c.,* digest
**Concocted**—P. L. 6, 514. *c.* and adusted
**Concoctive.**—P. L. 5, 437. and *c.* heat
**Concord.**—P. L. 2, 497. firm *c.* holds
P. L. 3, 371. such *c.* is in heaven
P. L. 6, 311. if, Nature's *c.* broke
P. L. 12, 29. and quite dispossess *c.*
S. A. 1008. love-quarrels oft in pleasing *c.* end
**Concourse.**—P. L. 11, 641. *c.* in arms
P. R. 4, 404. under some *c.* of shades
**Concubine.**—S. A. 537. lap of a deceitful *c.*
**Concupiscence.**—P. L. 9, 1078. foul *c.*
**Concurred.**—P. L. 10, 747. my will *c.* not
**Concurring.**—P. L. 2, 831. by *c.* signs
P. L. 10, 44. no decree of mine *c.*
**Condemn.**—P. L. 5, 813. *c.* the just decree
S. A. 500. a sin that Gentiles in their parables *c.*
**Condemnation.**—P. R. 3, 136. *c.,* ignominy
S. A. 696. *c.* of the ingrateful multitude
**Condemned.**—P. L. 1, 607. *c.* for ever
P. L. 2, 86. *c.* in this abhorred deep
P. L. 2, 694. *c.* to waste eternal days
P. L. 10, 82. the third best absent is *c.*
P. L. 10, 823. man's fault, thus guiltless be *c.*
P. L. 12, 412. by force judged, and to death *c.*
P. R. 3, 213. my crime .. whatever for itself *c.*
S. A. 1224. with thee, a man *c.,* a slave enrolled
**Comdemning.**—S. A. 844. to thy own *c.*
**Condemns.**—P. L. 2, 29. and *c.* to greatest
**Condense.**—P. L. 6, 353. *c.* or rare
**Condensed.**—P. L. 1, 429. dilated or *c.*
**Condenses.**—P. L. 9, 636. the night *c.*
**Condescend.**—S. A. 1337. will *c.* to such
**Condescension.**—P. L. 8, 9. this friendly *c.*
P. L. 8, 649. affable hath been thy *c.*
**Condition.**—P. L. 3, 181. his fallen *c.*
P. L. 8, 176. in what state, *c.,* or degree
P. L. 9, 322. if this be our *c.,* thus to dwell

P. R. 4, 166. on this *c.,* if thou wilt fall down
P. R. 4, 173. abominable terms, impious *c.*
S. A. 928. of my *c.* take no care
C. 685. scorning the unexempt *c.*
**Conditions.**—P. L. 10, 759. cavil the *c.*
S. A. 258. on some *c.* came into their hands
**Condole.**—S. A. 1076, to *c.* thy chance
**Conduct.**—P. L. 1, 130. under thy *c.*
P. L. 6, 777, under whose *c.* Michael soon
P. L. 9, 630. accept my *c.,* I can bring thee
P. R. 3, 18. thy skill of *c.* would be such
C. 319. I can *c.* you.. to a low but loyal cottage
**Conducted.**—P. L. 12, 259. *c.* by his Angel
**Cone.**—P. L. 4, 776. with her shadowy *c.*
**Confer.**—P. L. 1, 774. expatiate and *c.*
P. R. 1, 278. refused on me his baptism to *c.*
**Conference.**—P. L. 5, 454. this great *c.*
**Conferred.**—P. L. 4, 430. *c.* upon us
S. A. 993. *c.* upon me for the piety
**Confess.**—P. L. 5, 329. beholding shall *c.*
P. L. 5, 608. and shall *c.* him Lord
P. L. 5, 818. *c.* him rightful King
P. L. 8, 523. and must *c.* to find in all things
P. L. 10, 1088. *c.* humbly our faults
P. R. 4, 532. and *c.* have found thee proof
S. A. 448. I do acknowledge and *c.* that I this
S. A. 753. *c.,* and promise wonders in her change
S. A. 829. and much rather *c.* it feigned
**Confessed.**—P. L. 1, 509. yet *c.* later
P. L. 10, 1100. and both *c.* humbly their faults
P. R. 1, 431. and what *c.* more true
S. A. 1183. their magistrates *c.* it when they
S. A. 1467. who *c.* they had enough revenged
**Confessing.**—P. L. 10, 160. *c.* soon
**Confide.**—P. L. 11, 235. should much *c.*
**Confidence.**—P. L. 6, 343. beneath his *c.*
P. L. 6, 651. all their *c.* under the weight
P. L. 9, 1056. just *c.,* and native righteousness
P. L. 9, 1175. but *c.* then bore thee on
P. R. 2, 140. lest *c.* of my success
S. A. 1174. in *c.* whereof I once again
C. 583. is this the *c.* you gave me, brother
**Confident.**—P. R. 2, 211. should she *c.*
**Confine.** P. L. 2, 977. *c.* with heaven
S. A. 307. as if they would *c.* the Interminable
P. 22. these latest scenes *c.* my roving verse
**Confined.**—P. L. 2, 859. here *c.*
P. L. 3, 711. stood vast infinitude *c.*
P. L. 5, 78. not to earth *c.,* but sometimes
P. L. 10, 368. *c.* within Hell-gates till now
P. L. 11, 341. to these narrow bounds *c.*
P. R. 1, 362. not so *c.* by rigour unconniving
S. A. 94. to such a tender ball as the eye *c.*
S. A. 501. to their abyss and horrid pains *c.*
S. A. 606. Oh that torment should not be *c.*
C. 7. with low-thoughted care, *c.*
**Confines.**—P. L. 2, 395. those bright *c.*
P. L. 6, 273. casts thee out from all her *c.*
P. L. 10, 321. the *c.* met of empyrean heaven
**Confirm.**—P. L. 1, 663. and to *c.* his words
**Confirmed.**—P. L. 2, 353. circumference, *c.*
P. L. 9, 830. *c.* then I resolve
P. L. 11, 71. though firm, stood more *c.*
P. L. 11, 355. and be *c.* ere thou from hence
**Conflagrant.**—P. L. 12, 548. the *c.* mass
**Conflict.**—P. L. 4, 995. violence of this *c.*
P. L. 6, 212. dire was the noise of *c.*
**Conflicting.**—P. L. 6, 245. *c.* fire
**Conflux.**—P. R. 4, 62. what *c.* issuing forth
**Conformed.**—P. L. 2, 217. to the place *c.*
**Conformity.**—P. L. 11, 606. *c.* divine
**Confound.**—P. L. 2, 136. to *c.* heaven's
P. L. 2, 382. to *c.* the race of mankind
P. L. 6, 315. and their jarring spheres *c.*
P. L. 10, 665. to *c.* sea, air, and shore
P. L. 10, 908. and household peace *c.*
**Confounded.**—P. L. 1, 53. *c.* though immortal
P. L. 2, 996. confusion worse *c.*
P. L. 6, 871. *c.* Chaos roared
P. L. 9, 1064. in face *c.* long they sat
P. L. 12, 455. and there *c.* leave

P. R. 3, 2. stood a while as mute, c. what to say
H. 43. c., that her Maker's eyes
**Confused.**—P. L. 2, 615. in c. march
P. L. 2, 952. sounds and voices all c.
P. L. 6, 249. attack of fighting Seraphim c.
P. R. 3, 49. and what the people but a herd c.
S. A. 165. for had I sight, c. with shame
**Confusedly.**—P. L. 2, 914. mixed c.
**Confusion.**—P. L. 1, 220. treble c.
P. L. 2, 372. interrupt his joy in our c.
P. L. 2, 897. and by c. stand
P. L. 2, 966. Tumult and C. all imbroiled
P. L. 2, 996. c. worse confounded
P. L. 3, 710. c. heard his voice and wild
P. L. 6, 668. horrid c. heaped upon c.
P. L. 6, 872. felt tenfold c. in their fall
P. L. 7, 56. with such c.
P. L. 10, 472. unbounded deep of horrible c.
P. L. 12, 62. and the work C. named
P. L. 12, 343. left in c., Babylon thence called
S. A. 471. and with c. blank his worshippers
S. A. 1058. so shall he least c. draw
S. A. 1593. while things yet are in c.
**Confuted.**—P. R. 3, 3. what to reply, c.
**Congealed.**—C. 449. freezed her foes to c. stone
**Conglobed.**—P. L. 7, 239. then founded, then c.
**Conglobing.**—P. L. 7, 292. drops on dust c.
**Congo.**—P. L. 11, 401. to the realm of C.
**Congratulant.**—P. L. 10, 458. with like joy c.
**Congregated.**—P. L. 7, 308. of c. waters
**Congregation.**—P. L. 5, 766. C. called
**Conjecture.**—P. L. 2, 123. ominous c.
P. L. 6, 545. will pour down, if I c. aught
P. L. 8, 76. or if they list to try c.
P. L. 10, 1033. whom I c., our grand foe
S. A. 1071. I less c. than when first I saw
**Conjectures.**—P. R. 4, 292. c. fancies
P. R. 4, 524. where, by all best c. I collect
**Conjoined.**—S. A. 1666. whose law in death c.
**Conjugal.**—P. L. 4, 493. eyes of c. attraction
P. L. 8, 56. with c. caresses
P. L. 9, 263. to disturb c. love
S. A. 739. c. affection, prevailing over fear
**Conjunction.**—P. L. 10, 898. strait c.
P. R. 4, 385. in their c. met, give me to spell
**Conjured.**—P. L. 2. 693. c. against
**Connatural.**—P. L. 10, 246. some c. force
P. L. 11, 529. and mix with our c. dust
**Connexion.**—P. L. 10, 359. in c. sweet
**Connive.**—S. A. 466. c., or linger thus provoked
**Conniving.**—P. L. 10, 624. c., seem to gratify
**Connubial.**—P. L. 4, 743. c. love refused
**Conquer.**—P. R. 1, 159. to c. sin and death
P. R. 1, 222. winning words to c. willing hearts
S. 16, 10. yet much remains to c. still
**Conquered.**—P. L. 11, 797. the c. also
P. R. 4, 134. c. well, but govern ill
S. A. 1207. is well ejected when the c. can
**Conquering.**—P. L. 4, 391. by c. this
**Conqueror.**—P. L. 1, 143. he our C.
P. L. 1, 323. have ye sworn to adore the C.?
P. L. 1, 472. Ahaz, his sottish c., whom he drew
P. L. 2, 208. the sentence of their c.
P. L. 2, 338. the C. least may reap his conquest
P. R. 2, 196. that Pellean c.
P. R. 3, 85. till c. Death discover them
S. 8, 10. the great Emathian c. bid spare
**Conquerors.**—P. L. 11, 695. great c.
P. R. 3, 78. more than those their c.
P. R. 3, 99. equal in fame to proudest c.
S. A. 244. singly by me against their c.
**Conquest.**—P. L. 2, 339. reap his c.
P. L. 2, 543. crowned with c.
P. L. 6, 37. the easier c. now remains thee
P. R. 1, 46. this our old c., than remember
P. R. 1, 154. winning by c. what the first man
P. R. 2, 422. money brings honour, friends, c.
P. R. 3, 72. to subdue by c. far and wide
P. R. 3, 370. choose which thou wilt, by c.
P. R. 4, 609. frustrated the c. fraudulent
S. A. 1206. it was the force of c.

**Conscience.**—P. L. 3, 195. my umpire C.
P. L. 4, 23. c. wakes despair that slumbered
P. L. 8, 502. the c. of her worth
P. L. 10, 842. O C., into what abyss of fears
P. L. 10, 849. which to his evil c. represented
P. L. 12, 297. and peace of c., which the law
P. L. 12, 522. shall force on every c.
P. L. 12, 529. against faith and c. can be heard
P. R. 4, 130. his tormentor, C., find him out
S. A. 1334. my c., and internal peace
C. 212. by a strong-siding champion C.
S. 16, 13. help us to save free c. from the paw
S. 22, 10. the c., friend, to have lost them
**Consciences.**—C. 6, our c. that Christ set free
**Conscious.**—P. L. 2, 429. c. of highest worth
P. L. 2, 801. with c. terrors vex me round
P. L. 6, 521. under c. night
P. L. 9, 1050. with c. dreams encumbered
**Consecrated.**—P. R. 1, 72. the c. stream
S. A. 1354. shall I abuse this c. gift of strength
H. 189. in c. earth, and on the holy hearth
**Consent.**—P. L. 1, 640. c. or custom
P. L. 2, 24. yielded with full c.
P. L. 5, 121. waking thou never wilt c. to do
P. L. 5, 555. more desire to hear, if thou c.
P. R. 3, 358. by free c. of all
C. 1007. till free c. the gods among
II P. 95. whose power hath a true c.
**Consented.**—S. A. 846. girt me round, ere I c.
**Consenting.**—P. R. 2, 130. with the vote c.
**Consequence.**—P. L. 8, 328. the bitter c.
P. L. 10, 364. such fatal c. unites us three
**Consider.**—P. L. 8, 90. c. first, that great
P. R. 1, 197. while I c. what from within
P. R. 3, 231. c. thy life hath yet been private
S. A. 1348. c., Samson, matters now are strained
S. 19, 1. when I c. how my light is spent
**Considerate.**—P. L. 1, 603. c. pride
**Considered.**—P. L. 9, 84. c. every creature
P. L. 9, 604. c. all things visible in heaven
S. A. 245. acknowledged not, or not at all c.
**Consist.**—P. L. 5, 793. but well c.
**Consisted.**—S. A. 780. wherein c. all thy
**Consistence.**—P. L. 2, 941. the crude c.
**Consisting.**—P. L. 8, 16. of heaven and earth c.
**Consistory.**—P. R. 1, 42. a gloomy c.
**Consists.**—P. L. 8, 589. love c. not
P. L. 11, 616. wherein c. woman's domestic honour
C. 741. c. in mutual and partaken bliss
**Consolation.**—P. L. 11, 304. only c. left
P. L. 12, 620. this further c. yet secure
P. R. 1, 403. small c., then, were man adjoined
S. A. 183. if better, counsel or c. we may bring
S. A. 664. some source of c. from above
S. A. 1757. with peace and c. hath dismissed
**Consolations.**—P. L. 12, 495. inward c.
**Consolatories.**—S. A. 657. c. writ with studied
**Consort.**—P. L. 2, 963. c. of his reign
P. L. 4, 448. like c. to thyself canst nowhere find
P. L. 4, 610. fair c., the hour of night
P. L. 7, 529. male he created thee, but thy c. female
P. L. 8, 392. the brute cannot be human c.
P. L. 9, 954. if death c. with thee
P. L. 12, 526. and bind his c. Liberty
P. R. 1, 51. since Adam and his facile c. Eve
II P. 145. with such c. as they keep
H. 132. make up full c. to the angelic symphony
S. M. 27. to his celestial c. us unite
**Consorted.**—P. L. 7, 50. he with his c. Eve
**Conspicuous.**—P. L. 2, 258. will appear then
P. L. 3, 385. c. countenance
P. L. 4, 545. piled up to the clouds, c. far
P. L. 6, 299. to what things liken on earth c.
P. L. 7, 63. heaven and earth c. first began
P. L. 10, 107. come I less c., or what change
P. L. 11, 866. a bow c. with three listed colours
P. R. 4, 56. with gilded battlements, c. far
**Conspiracy.**—P. L. 2, 751. bold c.
**Conspired.**—P. L. 11, 426. the snake c.
**Conspiring.**—S. A. 892. of men c. to uphold
**Constancy.**—P. L. 9, 367. approve thy c.

P. R. 2, 226. we must try his c.
S. A. 1032. of c. no root infixed
**Constant.**—P. L. 3, 104. c. faith or love
P. L. 4, 764. here lights his c. lamp
P. L. 5, 552. my c. thoughts assured me
P. L. 5, 902. or change his c. mind
P. L. 10, 882. imagined wise, c., mature
P. R. 1, 148. whose c. perseverance overcame
C. 371. could stir the c. mood of her thoughts
**Constantest.**—S. A. 848. of men the c.
**Constellations.**—P. L. 3, 577. c. thick
P. L. 6, 312. among the c. war were sprung
P. L. 7, 562. the heavens and all the c. rung
P. L. 8, 512. happy c., on that hour shed
P. L. 10, 411. through thickest c. held
H. 121. his c. set, and the well balanced world
**Constrained.**—P. L. 9, 164. am now c.
P. L. 9, 1066. gave utterance to these words c.
P. R. 1, 331. c. by want, come forth
S. A. 836. but love c. thee!
S. A. 1198. threatening cruel death, c. the bride
**Constraining.**—P. L. 10, 568. thirst c.
**Constrains.**—S. A. 1369. where outward force c.
S. A. 1370. but who c. me to the temple of Dagon
**Constraint.**—P. L. 2, 972. by c.
P. L. 10, 132. calamitous c.
L. 6. bitter c. and sad occasion dear
**Constraints.**—S. A. 1372. commands are no c.
**Consult.**—P. L. 1, 187. c. how we may
P. L. 1, 798. and the great c. began
P. L. 5, 768. pretending so commanded to c.
P. L. 5, 779. this only to c. how we may
P. R. 3, 12. nations from thy mouth c.
**Consultation.**—P. L. 6, 445. search and c.
**Consultations.**—P. L. 2, 486. doubtful c.
**Consulted.**—S. A. 1546. scarce c.
**Consulting.**—P. L. 2, 164. thus c.
P. L. 6, 673. c. on the sum of things
P. L. 10, 456. in haste the great c. peers
P. R. 1, 438. who ever, by c. at thy shrine
P. R. 4, 577. and to his crew, that sat c.
**Consume.**—P. L. 2, 96. quite c. us
P. L. 11, 545. and last c. the balm of life
P. L. 11, 778. famine and anguish will at last c.
S. A. 575. the draff of servile food, c. me
**Consumed.**—P. L. 11, 442. fire from Heaven c.
T. 10. and last of all thy greedy self c.
**Consumes.**—P. L. 5, 325. superfluous moist c.
**Consummate.**—P. L. 5, 481. c. flower
P. L. 7, 502. earth in her rich attire c. lovely
P. L. 8, 556. to c. all
P. R. 1, 165. what c. virtue I have chose
**Contagion.**—P. L. 5, 880. c. spread
P. L. 10, 544. the dire form catched by c.
C. 467. the soul grows clotted by c.
L. 127. rot inwardly and foul c. spread
**Contagious.**—P. L. 9, 1036. c. fire
**Contain.**—P. L. 5, 314. what thy stores c.
P. L. 5, 362. Heaven such glorious shape c.
P. L. 5, 409. and both c. within them
P. L. 7, 128. what the mind may well c.
P. L. 8, 93. may of solid good c. more plenty
P. L. 12, 559. what this vessel can c.
**Contained.**—P. L. 8, 473. in her c.
S. A. 1494. that of a nation armed the strength c.
**Contains.**—P. R. 3, 11. thy heart c. of good
**Contemn.**—P. L. 9, 306. false guile c.
P. R. 2, 390. thy pompous delicacies I c.
P. R. 2, 448. could c. riches
P. R. 4, 490. betokening or ill-boding I c.
**Contemned.**—P. L. 6, 432. known, as soon c.
P. R. 4, 537. have been before c.
S. A. 279 their great deliverer c.
S. A. 943. helpless, hope easily c. and scorned
**Contemning.**—P. R. 4, 304. c. all wealth
**Contemns.**—P. L. 10, 1015. thy mind c.
S. A. 1281. their armouries and magazines c.
**Contemplate.**—P. R. 1, 380. c. and admire
**Contemplation.**—P. L. 4, 297. for c. he
P. L. 5, 511. whereon in c. of created things
P. R. 4, 214. c. and profound dispute

C. 377. where, with her best nurse, C.
Il P. 54. the cherub C.
**Contemplative.**—P. R. 2, 81. calm, c.
P. R. 4, 370. by me proposed in life c.
**Contempt.**—P. L. 4, 180. and in c.
P. L. 10, 763. admit for his c. of thee
P. L. 10, 1013. thy c. of life and pleasure
P. L. 10, 1018. implies not thy c., but anguish
P. R. 3, 131. would likeliest render c. instead
S. A. 76. to daily fraud, c., abuse, and wrong
S. A. 400. with what c. she sought to make me
S. A. 494. how deserving c. and scorn of all
S. A. 1342. yet on me joined with extreme c.
S. A. 1722. no weakness, no c., dispraise, or blame
**Contemptible.**—S. A. 572. to a c. old age
S. A. 1361. besides, how vile, c., ridiculous
**Contemptibly.**—P. L. 8, 374. reason not c.
**Contempts.**—P. R. 3, 191. c., and scorns
**Contemptuous.**—P. L. 4, 885. with c. brow
P. L. 5, 671. unobeyed, the throne supreme, c.
S. A. 1462. c. proud, set on revenge and spite
C. 781. arm his profane tongue with c. words
**Contend.**—P. L. 1, 99. raised me to c.
P. L. 2, 529. upon the wing, or in swift race c.
P. L. 2, 687. not to c. with spirits of Heaven
P. L. 4, 851. if I must c., said he, best with
P. L. 6, 169. servility with freedom to c.
P. L. 10, 958. let us no more c. nor blame
L'A. 123. while both c. to win her grace
**Contended.**—P. L. 9, 163. c. with gods
**Contending.**—P. L. 2, 203. so great a foe c.
P. L. 11, 359. c. with sinfulness of men
P. L. 11, 727. when he saw, he ceased c.
**Contends.**—P. R. 3, 443. with truth falsehood c.
**Content.**—P. L. 1, 399. nor c. with such
P. L. 5, 727. nor so c, hath in his thought
P. L. 6, 461. but live c., which is the calmest
P. L. 11, 180. though in fallen state, c.
P. L. 12, 25. not c. with fair equality
P. R. 2, 256. without this body's wasting, I c. me
P. R. 3, 112. nor c. in heaven
P. R. 3, 170. and her suburbs once c.
S. A. 1322. this answer, be assured, will not c.
S. A. 1399. I could be well c. to try their art
S. A. 1403. like a wild beast, I am c. to go
S. 10, 4. and left them both, more in himself c.
S. 22, 14. c., though blind, had I no better guide
**Contented.**—P. L. 3, 701. c. with report
P. L. 6, 375. angels, c. with their fame
P. L. 8, 177. c. that thus far hath been
**Contention.**—P. L. 1, 100. the fierce c.
**Contentment.**—P. L. 8, 366. what c. find
P. L. 10, 973. the sole c. of my heart
**Contents.**—P. L. 6, 622. of hard c.
**Contest.**—P. L. 4, 872. hence without c.
P. L. 6, 124. though brutish that c. and foul
P. L. 9, 1189. of their vain c. appeared no end
P. L. 10, 756. to say truth, too late I thus c.
P. L. 11, 800. in sharp c. of battle found no aid
S. A. 461. all the c. is now 'twixt God and Dagon
S. A. 865. combated.. with hard c.
**Contiguous.**—P. L. 6, 828. shade c.
P. L. 7, 273. fierce extremes c. might distemper
**Continent.**—P. L. 2, 587. a frozen c.
P. L. 3, 423. now seems a boundless c.
P. L. 5, 422. her moist c. to higher orbs
P. L. 6, 474. this c. of spacious heaven adorned
P. L. 10, 392. and this world, one realm, one c.
**Continual.**—P. L. 9, 814. from c. watch
**Continue.**—P. L. 2, 314. here to c.
P. L. 4, 371. ill secured long to c.
S. A. 592. nor the other light of life c. long
**Continued.**—P. L. 2, 1029. from Hell c.
P. L. 4, 175. as one c. brake, the undergrowth
P. L. 9, 63. of seven c. nights
P. L. 9, 138. six nights and days c. making
P. L. 11, 744. c. till the earth no more was seen
**Continues.**—S. A. 588. his might c. in thee
S. A. 1516. Oh! it c.; they have slain my son
**Continuest.**—P. L. 5, 521. that thou c.
**Contracted.**—P. L. 8, 560. with c. brow

S. A. 1062. fair days have oft c. wind and rain
**Contraction.**—P. L. 6, 597. by quick c.
**Contradict.**—P. R. 4, 158. still to c.
**Contradicting.**—S. A. 301. found c.
**Contradiction.**—P. L. 6, 155. inspired with c.
P. L. 10, 799. that were to make strange c.
S. A. 898. the c. of their own deity
U. C. II. 13. nor were it c. to affirm too long
**Contraries.**—P. L. 9, 122. siege of c.
**Contrarious.**—S. A. 669. or might I say c.
**Contrary.**—P. L. 1, 161. as being the c.
P. L. 8, 132. moved c. with thwart obliquities
P. L. 10, 506. when, c., he hears on all sides
P. R. 1, 126. but, c., unweeting he fulfilled
P. R. 4, 382. now, c.—if I read aught in Heaven
S. A. 972. and with c. blast proclaims most deeds
S. A. 1037. once joined, the c. she proves
**Contribute.**—P. L. 8, 155. yet scarce to c.
**Contrite.**—P. L. 10, 1091. from hearts c.
P. L. 10, 1103. c., in sign of sorrow
P. L. 11, 90. repents, and prays c.
S. A. 502. be penitent, and for thy fault c.
**Contrition.**—P. L. 11, 27. sown with c.
**Contrive.**—P. L. 2, 53. let those c.
P. L. 8, 81. c. to save appearances
**Contrived.**—P. L. 5, 334. so c. as not
P. L. 10, 1034. the serpent hath c. against us
P. L. 11, 732. and in the side a door c.
**Contriving.**—P. L. 2, 54. while they sit c.
P. L. 9, 139. how long before had been c.
**Control.**—P. L. 5. 803. discourse without c.
H. 228. can in His swaddling bands c.
**Controversy.**—C. 409. all doubt or c.
**Contumacy.**—P. L. 10, 1027. such acts of c.
**Convenient.**—S. A. 1471. some c. ransom
**Conversant.**—P. R. 1, 131. c. on earth
**Conversation.**—P. L. 8, 418. by c. with
P. R. 4, 232. or they with thee hold c.
**Converse.**—P. L. 2, 184. there to c.
P. L. 5, 230. as friend with friend c. with Adam
P. L. 7, 9. thou with eternal Wisdom didst c.
P. L. 8, 252. desire with thee still longer to c.
P. L. 8, 396. so well c., nor with the ox the ape
P. L. 8, 408. have I then with whom to hold c.
P. L. 9, 247. if much c. perhaps thee satiate
P. L. 9, 909. how forgo thy sweet c.
P. R. 1, 190. the better to c. with solitude
P. R. 4, 229. with Gentiles much thou must c.
C. 459. till oft c. with heavenly habitants
**Conversed.**—P. R. 2, 52. we have c.
**Conversing.**—P. L. 4, 639. with thee c.
P. L. 8, 432. I, by c., cannot these erect
P. L. 10, 993. c., looking, loving
**Conversion.**—P. L. 11, 724. preached c.
**Convert.**—P. L. 5, 492. but c., as you
**Converts.**—S. A. 1564. and c. it nigh to joy
**Convey.**—P. L. 12, 75. what food will he c.
**Conveyance.**—P. L. 1, 707. strange c.
P. L. 8, 628. nor restrained c. need
P. L. 10, 249. things of like kind by secretest c.
**Conveyed.**—P. L. 6, 515. into store c.
P. L. 8, 156. a glimpse of light c.
**Convex.**—P. L. 2, 434. this huge c. of fire
P. L. 3, 419. whose first c. divides the luminous
P. L. 7, 266. in circuit to the uttermost c.
**Convict.**—P. L. 10, 83. c. by flight
**Conviction.**—P. L. 10, 84. c. to the serpent
P. L. 10, 831. lead me still but to my own c.
P. R. 4, 308. or subtle shifts c. to evade
**Convince.**—P. L. 6, 789. c. the proud
**Convinced.**—P. R. 3, 3. c. of his weak
C. 792. thou art not fit to hear thyself c.
**Convolved.**—P. L. 6, 328. to and fro c.
**Convoy.**—C. 81. from Heaven to give him safe c.
**Convoyed.**—P. L. 6, 752. c. by four cherubic
**Convulsion.**—S. A. 1649. horrible c. to and fro
**Convulsions.**—P. L. 11, 483. c., epilepsies
**Cool.**—P. L. 4, 258. of c. recess, o'er which
P. L. 4, 329. to recommend c. Zephyr
P. L. 5, 39. now is the pleasant time, the c.
P. L. 5, 300. as in the door he sat of his c. bower

P. L. 5, 370. and the sun more c. decline
P. L. 5, 396. no fear lest dinner c.
P. L. 5, 655. they slept fanned with c. winds
P. L. 9, 1109. shunning heat, shelters in c.
P. L. 10, 95. c., when he, from wrath more c.
P. L. 10, 847. c., and mild, but with black air
P. R. 3, 221. a shelter, and a kind of shading c.
S. A. 546. allure thee from the c. crystalline
C. 282. i' the valley some c. friendly spring
C. 678. to life so friendly, or so c. to thirst
C. 861. under the glassy, c., translucent wave
**Cooled.**—P. L. 11, 801. therefore, c. in zeal
**Cooling.**—S. A. 626. which no c. herb or
C. 186. to bring me berries, or such c. fruit
**Copartner.**—P. L. 9, 821. without c.
P. R. 1, 392. with them dwell c. in these regions
**Copartners.**—P. L. 1, 265. c. of our loss
**Cope.**—P. L. 1, 345. under the c. of Hell
P. L. 4, 992. the starry c. of heaven
P. L. 6, 215. under fiery c. together rushed
P. R. 4, 9. the strength he was to c. with
**Copious.**—P. L. 3, 413. the c. matter
P. L. 5, 641. who showered with c. hand
P. L. 7, 325. their branches hung with c. fruit.
S. A. 1737. in c. legend, or sweet lyric song
**Copses.**—L. 42. and the hazel c. green
**Coral.**—P. L. 7, 405. through groves of c. stray
**Coral-paven.**—C. 886. thy c.-p. bed
**Cordial.**—P. L. 5, 12. with looks of c. love
P. L. 8, 466. a rib, with c. spirits warm
C. 672. and first behold this c. julep here
**Cords.**—S. A. 261. bound with two c., but c. to me
**Cormorant.**—P. L. 4, 196. sat like a c.
**Corn.**—P. L. 12, 19. c., wine, and oil
P. R. 3, 259. fertile of c. the glebe
L'A. 108. his shadowy flail hath threshed the c.
**Corner.**—P. L. 4, 529. and no. c. leave unspied
C. 717. that no c. might be vacant of her plenty
**Corners.**—P. L. 10, 665. they set their c.
C. 1017. to the c. of the moon
**Cornice.**—P. L. 1, 716. c. or frieze
**Corny.**—P. L. 7, 321. upstood the c. reed
**Coronet.**—P. L. 3, 640. under a c.
**Corporal.**—P. L. 5, 496. c. nutriments
P. L. 5, 573. by likening spiritual to c. forms
P. R. 4, 299. in c. pleasure he, and careless ease
S. A. 616. though void of c. sense
S. A. 1336. so debased with c. servitude
C. 664. although this c. rind thou hast
**Corporeal.**—P. L. 4, 585. c. bar
P. L. 5, 413. and c. to incorporeal turn
P. L. 8, 109. to c. substances could add speed.
P. L. 10, 786. perish with this c. clod
**Corpse.**—P. L. 10, 601. unhidebound c.
**Corpulence.**—P. L. 7, 483. in length and c.
**Correspond.**—P. L. 7, 511. c. with heaven
P. L. 9, 875. also found the effects to c.
**Corrosive.**—P. L. 2, 401. these c. fires
**Corrupt.**—P. L. 10, 695. c. and pestilent
P. L. 10, 825. what can proceed, but all c.
P. L. 11, 784. peace to c. no less than war
S. A. 268. but what more oft in nations grown c.
**Corrupted.**—P. L. 1, 368. mankind they c.
P. L. 3, 162. race of mankind, by him c.
P. L. 11, 57. and of incorrupt c.
S. A. 386. to them who had c. her, my spies
**Corrupting.**—P. L. 11, 889. all flesh c.
**Corruption.**—P. L. 3, 249. ever with c.
P. L. 10, 833. source and spring of all c.
P. L. 11, 428. yet from that sin derive c.
**Corrupts.**—D. F. I. 30. or that thy corse c.
**Corse.**—D. F. I. 30. or that thy c. corrupts
**Corydon.**—L'A. 83. where C. and Thyrsis met
**Cost.**—P. L. 1, 414. rites, which c. them woe
P. L. 4, 271. which c. Ceres all that pain
P. R. 2, 421. thou canst feed them on thy c.
P. R. 3, 410. which c. the lives of threescore
S. A. 933. thy trains, though dearly to my c.
**Costliest.**—P. L. 4, 703. of c. emblem
**Cotes.**—P. L. 4, 186. in hurdled c.
C. 344. folded flocks penned in their wattled c.

**Cottage.**—P. R. 2, 28. close in a c. low
P. R. 2, 287. if c. were in view
P. R. 2, 288. but c., herd, or sheep-cote
C. 320.I can conduct you.. to a low but loyal c.
C. 693. was this the c. and the safe abode
L'A. 81. hard by, a c. chimney smokes
**Cotytto.**—C. 129. dark-veiled C.
**Couch.**—P. L. 1, 377. on that fiery c.
P. L. 2, 536. prick forth the aery knights, and c.
P. L. 4, 601. they to their grassy c., these to
P. L. 9, 1039. flowers were the c.
P. L. 11,490. tended the sick busiest from c. to c.
P. R. 2, 282. from his grassy c. up rose
P. R. 4, 585. and upbore, as on a floating c.
C. 276. to give me answer from her mossy c.
**Couchant.**—P. L. 4, 406. his c. watch
**Couched.**—P. L. 4, 123. c. with revenge
P. L. 4, 351. others on the grass c.
P. L. 4, 876. in what form and posture c.
P. R. 1, 501. in their clay nests were c.
P. R. 4, 225. knowledge is not c. in Moses' law
**Couches.**—P. L. 4, 405. straight c. close
**Council.**—P. L. 1, 755. a solemn c.
P. L. 2, 20. what besides, in c. or in fight
P. L. 2, 506. the Stygian c. thus dissolved
P. L. 6,416. his Potentates to c. called by night
P. L. 6, 507. from c. to the work they flew
P. L. 10, 428. in c. sat, solicitous what chance
P. L. 11, 661. the sceptred heralds call to c.
P. R. 1, 40. to c. summons all his mighty peers
P. R. 2, 118. where all his Potentates in c. sat
S. 10. 2. of England's C. and her treasury
**Council-table.**—H. 10. Heaven's high c.-t.
**Counsel.**—P. L. 1, 660. c. must mature
P. L. 2, 160. say they who c. war
P. L. 2, 304. princely c. in his face yet shone
P. L. 2, 379. pleaded his devilish c., first
P. L. 6, 494. to strength and c. joined
P. L. 10, 920. thy c. in this uttermost distress
P. L. 10, 944. his c., whom she had displeased
P. L. 10, 1010. with such c. nothing swayed
P. R. 1, 127. he fulfilled the purposed c.
P. R. 2, 145. with hand or c. to assist
P. R. 3, 13. thy c. would be as the oracle
S.A.183.if better,c. or consolation we may bring
S. A. 497. but I God's c. have not kept
S. A. 1251. and with malicious c. stir them up
S. 17. 1. Vane, young in years, but in sage c. old
**Counselled.**—P. L. 2, 227. c. ignoble ease and
P. L. 9, 1099. so c. he, and both together.
**Counsellors.**—S. A. 1653. c. or priests
**Counsels.**—P. L. 1, 88. thoughts and c.
P. L. 1, 168. his inmost c. from their destined
P. L. 1, 636. if c. different or dangers shunned
P. L. 2, 115. to perplex and dash maturest c.
P. L. 2, 125. in what he c. and in what excels
P. L. 2, 279. all things invite to peaceful c.
P. L. 5, 681. new c., to debate what doubtful
P. L. 5, 785. if better c. might erect our minds
P. L. 7, 610. their c. vain thou hast repelled
**Count.**—P. L. 5, 833. dost thou c.
P. L. 8, 319. paradise I give thee, c. it thine
P. R. 2, 248. to virtue I impute not, or c. part
P. R. 2, 391. and c. thy specious gifts
P. R. 3, 71. they err who c. it glorious
S. A. 250. to c. them things worth notice
S. A. 949. this jail I c. the house of liberty
S. A. 991. nor shall I c. it heinous to enjoy
C. 347. or village cock c. the night watches
**Countenance.**—P. L. 1, 526. on his c. cast
P. L. 2, 422. each in other's c. read his own
P. L. 2, 756. to thee in shape and c. bright
P. L. 3, 385. in whose conspicuous c.
P. L. 3,730. with borrowed light her c. triform
P. L. 5, 708. his c., as the morning star
P. L. 6, 825. and into terror changed his c.
P. L. 8, 39. by his c. seemed entering
P. L. 9, 886. thus Eve, with c. blithe
P. L. 10, 713. with c. grim, glared on him
P. L. 11, 317. deprived his blessed c.
S. A. 684. changest thy c. and thy hand

C. 68. soon as the potion works, their human c.
**Counterfeit.**—P. L. 4, 117. betrayed him c.
P. L. 9, 1069. taught to c. man's voice
S. A. 189. how c. coin they are
Il P. 80. teach light to c. a gloom
**Counterfeited.**—P. L. 5, 771. of c. truth
**Counterpoise.**—P. L. 4, 1001. air in c.
**Counterpoised.**—S. A. 770. just allowance c.
**Counterview.**—P. L. 10, 231. in c. within
**Countries.**—P. R. 3, 73. to over-run large c.
**Country.**—P. L. 4, 235. realm and c.
P. R. 3,102. his wasted c. freed from Punic rage
P. R. 3, 176. duty to free thy c. from her
P. R. 3, 366. by invasion to annoy thy c.
P. R. 4, 355. and lovers of their c.
S. A. 238. the Philistine, thy c.'s enemy
S. A. 518. to return thee home to thy c.
S. A. 851. and princes of my c. came in person
S. A. 884. then, as since then, thy c.'s foe
S. A. 886. thou wast to leave parents and c.
S.A.889.thy c. sought of thee, it sought unjustly
S. A. 891. no more thy c., but an impious crew
S. A. 894. for which our c. is a name so dear
S. A. 980. but in my c., where I most desire
S. A. 985. to save her c. from a fierce destroyer
S. A. 994. to my c. I was judged to have shown
S. A. 1208. whom my c. as a league-breaker
S.A.1213. command from Heaven, to free my c.
C. 1167. whom thrift keeps up about his c. gear
C. 632. but in another c., as he said
L'A. 85. of herbs and other c. messes
**Countrymen.**—S. A. 1549. my c.
**Counts.**—P. L. 10, 91. time c. not
**Couple.**—P. L. 4, 339. as beseems fair c.
**Coupled.**—P. R. 2, 181. and c. with them
**Courage.**—P. L. 1, 108. c. never to submit
P. L. 1, 279. they will soon resume new c.
P. L. 1, 530. gently raised their fainting c.
P. L. 1, 603. but under brows of dauntless c
P. L. 2, 126. grounds his c. on despair
P. L. 6, 839. all resistance lost, all c.
P. L. 9, 484. of c. haughty, and of limb
S. A. 524. and great in hopes, with youthful c.
S. A. 1381. be of good c.; I begin to feel some
S. A. 1716. find c. to lay hold on this occasion
C. 610. I love thy c. yet
**Courageous.**—P. L. 4, 920. c. chief
**Course.**—P. L. 1, 349. to direct their c.
P. L. 1, 786. wheels her pale c.
P. L. 2, 944. with winged c., o'er hill or moory
P. L. 2, 980. direct my c.
P. L. 3, 573. thither his c. he bends
P. L. 3, 720. his place appointed, each his c.
P. L. 4, 164. slack their c., and many a league
P. L. 4, 224. nor changed his c., but through
P. L. 4, 561. to thee thy c. by lot hath given
P. L. 4, 661. those have their c. to finish
P. L. 5, 173. in thy eternal c., both when thou
P. L. 5, 655. save those, who, in their c.
P. L. 5, 861. when fatal c. had circled
P. L. 6, 406. now Night her c. began
P. L. 7, 501. first wheeled their c.
P. L. 8, 126. their wandering c., now high
P. L. 8, 163. from west her silent c. advance
P. L. 10, 411. their c. through thickest
P. L. 10, 689. turned his c. intended
P. L. 11, 794. shall change their c. to pleasure
P. L. 11, 900. shall hold their c., till fire purge
P. L. 12, 264. night's due c. adjourn
P. R. 1, 252. by whose bright c. led on
P. R. 4, 445. desperate of better c., to vent
S. A. 670. thy providence through his short c.
C. 25. by c. commits to several government
C. 159. for that's against my c.
C.832.stayed her flight with his cross-flowing c.
U.C.I.10. had not his weekly c. of carriage failed
U. C. II. 30. he spent his date in c. reciprocal
**Court.**—P. L. 1, 792. that infernal c.
P. L. 4, 767. nor in c. amours, mixed dance
P. R. 2, 300. as one in city or c. or palace bred
C. 1. before the starry threshold of Jove's c.

C. 962. such c. guise as Mercury did first devise
**Courted.**—S. A. 719. c. by all the winds
**Courteous.**—C. 275. to awake the c. Echo
**Courtesy.**—C. 161. words of glozing c.
C. 322. and trust thy honest-offered c.
**Courtly.**—H. 243. and all about the c. stable
**Courts.**—P. L. 1, 497. in c. and palaces
P. L. 5, 650. the c. of God
P. L. 6, 889. into the c. and temple of his
P. R. 1, 488. tread his sacred c., and minister
P. R. 2, 183. in c. and regal chambers
P. R. 3, 237. monarchs and their radiant c.
C. 325. than in tapestry halls and c. of princes
C. 746. in c., at feasts, and high solemnities
H. 13. forsook the c. of everlasting day
**Covenant.**—P. L. 11, 116. intermix my c.
P. L. 11, 867. peace from God, and c. new
P. L. 11, 892. makes a c. never to destroy
P. L. 11, 898. and call to mind his c.
P. L. 12, 252. the records of his c.
P. L. 12, 302. up to a better c.
P. L. 12, 346. and his c. sworn to David
Cir. 21. that great c. which we still transgress
**Covenants.**—C. 682. but you invert the c.
**Cover.**—P. L. 1, 659. under darkness c.
P. L. 9, 1088. as evening! c. me ye pines
P. L. 9, 1096. on our loins, may c. round
P. L. 11, 257. many deeds well done may'st c.
S. A. 841. thou striv'st to **c.** shame with shame
**Covered.**—P. L. 1, 763. though like a c. field
P. L. 5, 430. the ground c. with pearly grain
P. L. 6, 16. c. with thick embattled squadrons
P. L. 7, 234. darkness profound c. the abyss
P. L. 9, 1058. he c., but his robe uncovered more
P. L. 9, 1120. thought their shame in part c.
P. L. 10, 223. of righteousness arraying, c.
P. L. 11, 217. in Dothan, c. with a camp of fire
P. L. 11, 749. sea c. sea, sea without shore
**Covering.**—P. L. 1, 312. c. the flood
P. L. 9, 1113. vain c., if to hide their guilt
C. 712. c. the earth with odours, fruits and flocks
**Covers.**—P. L. 2, 267. c. his throne
**Covert.**—P. L. 2, 41. open war, or c. guile
P. L. 3, 39. and in shadiest c. hid
P. L. 4, 693. of thickest c., was inwoven shade
P. L. 6, 409. under her cloudy c. both retired
P. L. 9, 435. stateliest c., cedar, pine, or palm
P. R. 1, 305. under the c. of some ancient oak
P. R. 2, 262. under the hospitable c. nigh
C. 945. through this gloomy c. wide
Il P. 139. there in close c. by some brook
**Covertures.**—P. L. 10, 337. sought vain c.
**Covet.**—P. L. 2, 35. will c. more
P. L. 10, 1020. or, if thou c. death
**Coveting.**—P. L. 9, 923. had it been only c.
**Coward.**—S. A. 347. against a c. armed
S. A. 1237. go, baffled c., lest I run upon thee
**Cowering.**—P. L. 8, 350. these c. low
**Cowls.**—P. L. 3, 489. c., hoods, and habits
**Cowslip.**—C. 898. o'er the c.'s velvet head
M. M. 4. the yellow c. and the pale primrose
**Cowslips.**—L. 147. with c. wan that hang
**Coy.**— P. L. 4, 310. with c. submission
C. 737. list, Lady, be not c. and be not cozened
L. 18. hence with denial vain, and c. excuse
**Cozened.**—C. 737. be not coy, and be not c.
**Crab.**—P. L. 10, 675. up to the tropic C.
**Crabbed.**—C. 477. not harsh and c. as dull fools
**Cradle.**—V. Ex. 46. when .. Nature in her c. was
**Craft.**—P. R. 1, 432. that hath been thy c.
**Craggy.**—P. L. 2, 289. in a c. bay
P. L. 4, 547. the rest was c. cliff, that overhung
**Crammed.**—P. L. 10, 632. c. and gorged
**Crams.**—C. 779. c., and blasphemes his Feeder
**Crane.**—P. L. 7, 430. the prudent c.
**Cranes.**—P. L. 1, 576. warred on by c.
**Cranks.**—L'A. 27. Quips and C.
**Crawls.**—C. 295. that c. along the side
**Craze.**—P. L. 12, 210. c. their chariot-wheels
S. A. 571. and sedentary numbness c. my limbs
**Cream-bowl.** L'A. 106. to earn his c.-b.

**Creams.**—P. L. 5, 347. she tempers dulcet c.
**Create.**—P. L. 1, 652. intended to c.
P. L. 2, 19. did first c. your leader
P. L. 2, 260. prosperous of adverse, we can c.
P. L. 2, 916. his dark materials to c. more worlds
P. L. 7, 154. in a moment will c. another world
P. L. 7, 188. ordained good out of evil to c.
P. L. 7, 209. coming to c. new worlds
P.L.7, 606. to c. is greater than created to destroy
P. L. 8, 28. so many nobler bodies to c.
P. L. 8, 558. and c. an awe about her
P. L. 9, 146. now failed more angels to c.
P. L. 9, 911. should God c. another Eve
P. L. 10, 403. and c. plenipotent on earth
P. L. 10, 890. c. at last this novelty on earth
C. 561. might c. a soul under the ribs of death
**Created.**—P. L. 1, 202. of all his works c.
P. L. 1, 573. for never since c. man
P. L. 2, 349. about this time to be c. like to us
P. L. 2, 623. which God by curse c.
P. L. 2, 679. c. thing nought valued he
P. L. 2, 832. ere now c. vast and round
P. L. 3, 100. such I c. all the ethereal Powers
P. L. 3, 112. so were c., nor can justly accuse
P. L. 3, 278. nor Man the least, though last c.
P. L. 3, 391. by thee c., and by thee threw
P. L. 3, 679. c. this new happy race of Men
P. L. 3, 705. but what c. mind can comprehend
P. L. 4, 43. from me, whom he c. what I was
P. L. 4, 107. mankind c., and for him this world
P. L. 4, 999. all things c. first he weighed
P. L. 5, 100. in thee can harbour none, c. pure
P. L. 5, 373. nor art thou such c., or such place
P. L. 5, 414. for know, whatever was c. needs
P. L. 5, 471. c. all such to perfection
P. L. 5, 511. in contemplation of c. things
P. L. 5, 549. both will and deed c. free
P. L. 5, 838. by him c. in their bright degrees
P. L. 5, 894. then who c. thee lamenting learn
P. L. 7, 64. when and whereof c., for what cause
P. L. 7, 227. this universe, and all c. things
P. L. 7, 232. thus God the heaven c.
P. L. 7, 391. and God c. the great whales
P. L. 7, 527. in his own image he c. thee
P. L. 7, 529. male he c. thee, but thy consort
P. L. 7, 535. wherever thus c., for no place
P. L. 7, 607. to create is greater than c. to destroy
P. L. 7, 627. whom God hath thus advanced, c.
P. L. 8, 623. and pure thou wert c.
P. L. 9, 147. if they at least are his c.
P. L. 9, 346. of all that he c., much less man
P. L. 9, 557. on their creation day c. mute
P. L. 9, 799. fruit let hang, as to no end c.
P. L. 9, 942. for us c., needs with us must fail
P. L. 10, 618. which I so fair and good c.
P. L. 11, 58. with two fair gifts c. him
P. L. 11, 508. the image of God in man c.
P. L. 11, 605. c. as thou art, to nobler end
P. R. 2, 324. hast thou not right to all c. things
**Createst.**—P. L. 7, 616. thence c. more good
**Creating.**—P. L. 9, 344. his c. hand
**Creation.**—P. L. 2, 365. his whole c.
P. L. 3, 163. thyself abolish thy c.
P. L. 3, 383. Thee next they sang, of all c. first
P. L. 3, 661. to visit oft this new c. round
P. L. 5, 857. who saw when this c. was
P. L. 6, 690. equal in their c. they were formed
P. L. 7, 223. to behold c., and the wonders
P. L. 7, 449. the sixth, and of C. last, arose
P. L. 7, 601. c. and the six days' acts they sung
P.L.8, 236. destruction with c. might have mixed
P. L. 9, 896. O fairest of c., last and best
P. L. 9, 946. though his power c. could repeat
P. L. 10, 168. polluted from the end of his c.
P. L. 10, 852. and oft cursed his c.
P. L. 12, 472. by c. first brought forth light
**Creation-day.**—P. L. 9, 556. on their c.-d.
**Creator.**—P. L. 1, 31. fall off from their c.
P. L. 1, 369. to forsake God their C.
P. L. 2, 385. done all to spite the great C.
P. L. 3, 167. to whom the great C. thus replied

P. L. 3, 673. on whom the great *C.* hath
P. L. 4, 684. singing their great *C.!* Oft in bands
P. L. 7, 91. moved the *C.* in his holy rest
P. L.7, 259.God and his works ;*C.* him they sung
P. L. 7, 551. yet not till the *C.,* from his work
P.L. 7, 567. the great *C.* from his work returned
P. L. 8, 13. with glory attributed to the high *C.*
P. L. 8, 492. thou hast fulfilled thy words, *C.*
P. L. 9, 196. send up silent praise to the *C.*
P. L. 9, 938. *C.* wise, though threatening
P. L. 10, 486. I have seduced from his *C.*
P. L. 10, 649. while the *C.*
P.L.10.889.Oh! why did God, *C.* wise, that peopled
H. 120. while the *C.* great his constellations set
**Creature.**—P. L. 3, 151. thy *c.* late so loved
P. L. 3, 387. whom else no *c.* can behold
P. L. 3, 442. for other *c.* in this place living
P. L. 4, 468. what there thou seest, fair *c.*
P. L. 4, 582. and since meridian hour no *c.*
P. L. 4, 703. other *c.* here, bird, beast, insect
P. L. 5, 74. here happy *c.,* fair angelic Eve
P. L. 7, 506. the end of all yet done, a *c.,* who
P. L. 8, 430. canst raise thy *c.* to what height
P. L. 8, 470. under his forming hands a *c.* grew
P. L. 9, 84. inspection deep considered every *c.*
P. L. 9, 149. into our room a *c.* formed of earth
P. L. 9, 897. *c.* in whom excelled whatever
P. L. 10, 943. *c.* so fair his reconcilement seeking
P. R. 2, 406. hunger, that each other *c.* tames
**Creatures.**—P. L. 2, 355. to learn what *c.*
P. L. 2, 498. men only disagree of *c.* rational
P. L. 2, 834. placed a race of upstart *c.*
P. L. 3, 230. to visit all thy *c..* and to all
P. L. 4, 287. living *c.* new to sight and strange
P. L. 4, 360. *c.* of other mould, earth-born
P. L. 4, 431. over all other *c.* that possess
P. L. 4, 616. other *c.* all day long rove idle
P. P. 4, 677. millions of spiritual *c.* walk
P. L. 4, 790. where those two fair *c.* lodge
P. L. 5, 164. on Earth join all ye *c.* to extol
P. L. 7, 413. leviathan, hugest of living *c.*
P. L. 7, 455. innumerous living *c..* perfect forms
P. L. 7, 507. not prone and brute as other *c.*
P. L. 8, 169. of other *c.* as him pleases best
P. L. 8, 175. of other worlds, what *c.* there live
P. L. 8, 264. by these, *c.* that lived and moved
P. L. 8, 276. ye that live and move, fair *c.,* tell
P. L. 8, 370. the earth with various living *c.*
P. L. 8, 409. save with the *c.* which I made
P. L. 8, 411. beneath what other *c.* are to thee
P. L. 8, 546. that dominion given o'er other *c.*
P. L. 9, 112. of *c.* animate with gradual life
P. L. 9, 199. to the choir of *c.* wanting voice
P. L. 9, 228. above all living *c.* dear
P. L. 9, 612. of right declared sovran of *c.*
P. L. 9, 940. us his prime *c.,* dignified so high
P. L. 10, 871. to warn all *c.* from thee henceforth
P. L. 11, 873. with all the *c.,* and their seed
P. R. 2, 157. like to goddesses than mortal *c.*
P. R. 2, 325. owe not all *c.,* by just right
S. A. 672. inferior *c.* mute, irrational and brute
C. 299. of some gay *c.* of the element
S. M. 21. broke the fair music that all *c.* made
D. F. I. 61. as if to show what *c.* heaven doth
**Credit.**—P. L. 9, 649. the *c.* of whose virtue
P. R. 4, 12. to salve his *c.,* and for very spite
**Credulous.**—P. L. 9, 644. our *c.* mother
P. R. 2, 166. draw out with *c.* desire
C. 697. hast thou betrayed my *c.* innocence
**Creek.**—P. L. 7, 399. each *c.* and bay
P. R. 2, 25. then on the bank of Jordan, by a *c.*
**Creep.**—P. L. 2, 656. when they list, would *c.*
P. L. 5, 201. and stately tread, or lowly *c.*
S.A.75.they *c.,* yet see; I, dark in light, exposed
L. 115. *c.,* and intrude, and climb into the fold
L'A. 115. thus done the tales, to bed they *c.*
**Creeping.**—P. L. 7, 452. cattle, and *c.* things
P. L. 7, 523. and every *c.* thing that creeps
**Creeps.**—P. L. 2, 950. or wades, or *c.,* or flies
P. L. 4, 259. and gently *c.* luxuriant
P. L. 7, 475. came forth whatever *c.* the ground

P. L. 7, 523. creeping thing that *c.* the ground
**Cremona.**—P. 26. o'er the rest *C.'s* trump doth
**Crept.**—P. L. 7, 320. forth *c.* the swelling
P. L. 7, 392. each soul living, each that *c.*
P. L. 7, 484. first *c.* the parsimonious emmet
**Crescent.** P. L. 1, 439. with *c.* horns
P. L. 10, 434. from the horns of Turkish *c.*
**Cressets.**—P. L. 1, 728. *c.* fed with naphtha
**Crest.**—P. L. 4, 988. on his *c.* sat horror
P. L. 6, 188. on thy impious *c.* receive
P. L. 6, 191. on the proud *c.* of Satan
P. L. 9, 525. bowed his turret *c.* and sleek
P. L. 9, 634. and joy brightens his *c.*
**Crested.**—P. L. 7, 443. the *c.* cock
P. L. 9, 500. his head *c.* aloft
S. A. 141. or, grovelling, soiled their *c.* helmets
**Crest-fallen.**—S. A. 1244. somewhat *c.-f.*
**Crete.**—P. L. 1, 514. in *C.* and Ida known
P. R. 4, 118. wines of Setia .. Chios and *C.*
**Crew.**—P. L. 1, 51. he with his horrid *c.*
P. L. 1, 477. after these appeared a *c.*
P. L. 1, 688. soon his *c.* opened into the hill
P. L. 1, 751. his industrious *c.,* to build in Hell
P. L. 4, 573. one of the banished *c.,* I fear
P.L.4,952.faithful to whom? to thy rebellious *c.*
P. L. 5, 879. and thy hapless *c.* involved in this
P. L. 6, 49. to that godless *c.* rebellious
P. L. 6, 277. thy wicked *c.!* there mingle broils
P. L. 6, 370. Abdiel to annoy the atheist *c.*
P. L. 6, 806. of this cursèd *c.* the punishment
P. L. 11, 474. a monstrous *c.* before thee
P. L. 12, 38. he with a *c.,* whom like ambition
P. R. 1, 107. amazement to the infernal *c.*
P. R. 2, 178. thou, with thy lusty *c.*
P. R. 4, 577. and to his *c.,* that sat consulting
S. A. 891.impious *c.* of men conspiring to uphold
C. 653. though he and his cursed *c.*
C. 805. to some of Saturn's *c.*
L'A. 38. Mirth admit me of thy *c.*
H. 228. control the damnèd *c.*
**Cricket.**—ll P. 82. save the *c.* on the hearth
**Cried.**—P.L.2,727.what intends thy hand? she *c.*
P. L. 2, 787. I fled and *c.* out, Death
P. L. 3, 515. and waking *c.,* This is the gate
P. L. 6, 536. and in mid air aloud thus *c.*
P. L. 11, 449. thus in haste to the Angel *c.*
P. R. 1, 19. the great Proclaimer .. *c.* repentance
S. A. 1639. at last, with head erect, thus *c.* aloud
U. C. II. 26. pressed to death, he *c.,* More weight
**Criedst.**—P. L. 4, 481. thou following *c.* aloud
**Cries.**—P. L. 1, 395. their children's *c.* unheard
P. L. 10, 859. slowest pace for prayers or *c.*
P. L. 10, 933. there with my *c.* importune
P. L. 11, 310. weary him with my assiduous *c.*
S. 11, 5. *c.* the stall-reader, Bless us,
**Crime.**—P. L. 1, 79. and next in *c.*
P.L.1,606.fellows of his *c.,* the followers rather
P. L. 3, 215. to redeem man's mortal *c.*
P. L. 3, 290. his *c.* makes guilty all his sons
P. L. 5. 881. both of thy *c.* and punishment
P. L. 6, 268. uncreated till the *c.* of thy rebellion
P. L. 9, 971. with me one guilt, one *c.*
P. L. 10, 127. undergo myself the total *c.*
P. L. 10, 545. like in punishment as in their *c.*
P. L. 10, 841. both *c.* and doom
P. L. 11, 424. thy original *c.* hath wrought
P. L. 12, 619. who for my wilful *c.* art banished
P. R. 3. 212. was my error, and my *c.* my *c.*
S. A. 490. and expiate, if possible, my *c.*
S. A. 842. or by evasions thy *c.* uncoverest more
U. C. II. 7. without a *c.* 'gainst old truth
**Crimes.**—P L. 1, 214. with reiterated *c.*
P. R. 3, 419. other worse than heathenish *c.*
**Cringe.**—P.—L. 4, 945. to *c.,* not fight
**Cringed.**—P.—L. 4, 959. once fawned, and *c.*
**Crisped.**—P.—L. 4, 237. the *c.* brooks
C. 984. along the *c.* shades and bowers
**Crocodile.**—P. L. 7, 474. and scaly *c.*
**Crocus.**—P.—L. 4, 701. violet, *c.,* and hyacinth
**Crofts.**—C. 531. my flocks hard by i' the hilly *c.*

**Cromwell.**—S. 16, 1. *C.,* our chief of men
**Cronian.**—P. L. 10, 290. upon the *C.* sea
**Crooked.**—P. L. 10, 885. all but a rib *c.*
   V. Ex. 69. a Sibyl old, bow-bent with *c.* age
**Crop.**—P. L. 12, 18. and reaping plenteous *c.*
   M. W. 39. who only thought to *c.* the flower
**Crop-full.**—L'A. 113. and *c.-f.* out of doors
**Cropped.**—P. L. 5, 68. much more sweet thus *c.*
**Cross.**—P. L. 2, 920. no narrow frith he had to *c.*
   P. L. 3, 487. violent *c.* wind from either coast
   P. L. 12, 413. nailed to the *c.* by his own nation
   P. L. 12, 415. to the *c.* he nails thy enemies
   A. 52. or what the *c.* dire-looking planets smites
   H. 152. that on the bitter *c.* must redeem our loss
   U. C. II. 19. the *c.* doctors all stood hearers
**Cross-barred.**—P. L. 4, 190. doors, *c.-b.*
**Crossed.**—P. L. 9, 65. four times *c.* the car
   P. L. 10, 39. first this Tempter *c.* the gulf
**Cross-flowing.**—C. 832. with his *c.-f.* course
**Crowd**—P. L. 1, 380. promiscuous *c.* stood
   P. L. 1, 775. so thick the aery *c.* swarmed
   P. L. 5, 357. dazzles the *c.* and sets them all
   P. L. 10, 538. a *c.* of ugly serpents
**Crowded.**—P. L. 10, 287. together *c.* drove
**Crown.**—P. L. 2, 673. of a kingly *c.* had on
   P. L 4, 728. mutual love, the *c.* of all our bliss
   P. L. 9, 841. and her rural labours *c.*
   P. R. 2, 458. a *c.* golden in show is but a
   P. R. 3, 169. obtained, though priests. the *c.*
   P. R. 4. 213. inclined than to a worldly *c.*
   S. A. 1296. whom patience finally must *c.*
   S. A. 1579. death to life is *c.* or shame
   C. 9. unmindful of the *c.* that virtue gives
   C. 973. with a *c.* of deathless praise
**Crowned.**—P. L. 2, 542. *c.* with conquest
   P. L. 3, 365. then, *c.* again, their golden harps
   P. L. 4, 32. that with surpassing glory *c.*
   P. L. 4, 262. the fringed bank with myrtle *c.*
   P. L. 5, 260. garden of God, with cedars *c.*
   P. L. 5, 445. cups with pleasant liquors *c.*
   P. L. 5, 636. and with fresh flowerets *c.*
   P. L. 5, 839. *c.* them with glory
   P. L. 7, 194. with radiance *c.* of majesty divine
   P. L. 7, 326. with high woods the fields were *c.*
   P. L. 7, 386. and glad morn *c.* the fourth day
   P. L. 9, 117. now sea and shores with forest *c.*
   P. L. 11, 781. peace would have *c.* with length
   S. A. 175. universally *c.* with highest praises
   C. 984. may thy lofty head be *c.* with many
   L. 86. smooth-sliding Mincius *c.* with vocal reeds
   H. 47. she *c.* with olive green, came softly sliding
   D. F. 1. 54. that *c.* Matron, sage white-robed Truth
   S. 16. 5. and on the neck of *c.* Fortune proud
**Crowns.**—P. L. 3, 352. they cast their *c.*
   P. L. 4, 133. *c.* with her enclosure green
   C. 26. gives them leave to wear their sapphire *c.*
**Crownest.**—P. L. 5, 168. *c.* the smiling morn
**Crow-toe.**—L. 143. tufted *c.-t.* and pale jessamine
**Crucified.**—P. L. 12, 417. with him there *c.*
**Crude.**—P. L. 2, 941. the *c.* consistence
   P. L. 6, 478. materials dark and *c.*
   P. L. 6, 511. nature in their *c.* conception
   P. R. 2, 349. that *c.* apple that diverted Eve
   P. R. 4. 328. *c.* or intoxicate, collecting toys
   S. A. 700. in *c.* old age
   C. 480. where no *c.* surfeit reigns
   L. 3. I come to pluck your berries harsh and *c.*
**Cruel.**—P. L. 1, 604. *c.* his eye, but cast signs
   P. L. 2, 501. and levy *c.* wars, wasting the earth
   P. L. 6, 448. he stood escaped from *c.* fight
   P. L. 10, 782. torment me with *c.* expectation
   P. L. 10, 927. that *c.* Serpent
   P. L. 11, 652. *c.* tournament the squadrons join
   P. R. 1, 149. his *c.* malice could invent
   P. R. 4, 139. then *c.,* by their sports to blood
   P. R. 4, 388. and stripes, and lastly *c.* death
   S. A. 642. and to those *c.* enemies
   S. A. 784. ere I to thee, thou to thyself wast *c.*
   S. A. 1198. threatening *c.* death, constrained
   C. 679. why should you be so *c.* to yourself
**Cruelly.**—P. R. 1, 425. then *c.* to afflict

**Cruelties.**—P. L. 12, 494. against such *c.*
**Cruelty.**—S. A. 646. their *c.* or scorn
   M. W. 29. and with remorseless *c.*
**Crumble.**—C. 615. and *c.* all thy sinews
**Crumbled.**—P. L. 7, 468. the *c.* earth above
**Crush.**—P. L. 10, 1035. to *c.* his head
   P. L. 12, 430. bruise head of Satan, *c.* his strength
**Crushed.**—C. 47. *c.* the sweet poison of misused
   P. L. 6, 656. *c.* in and bruised
**Crushes.**—P. L. 5, 345. the grape she *c.*
**Cry.**—P. L. 2, 514. session ended they bid *c.*
   P. L. 2, 654. a *c.* of Hell-hounds never ceasing
   P. L. 2, 795. with ceaseless *c.* surround me
   P. L. 4, 2. heard *c.* in heaven aloud
   S. A. 1524. from whom could else a general *c.*
   S. A. 1553. with rueful *c.* yet what it was we hear
   S. 12, 11. license they mean when they *c.* liberty
**Crystal.**—P. L. 1, 742. sheer o'er the *c.*
   P. L. 4, 263. her *c.* mirror holds
   P. L. 5, 133. stood each in their *c.* sluice
   P. L. 6, 757. over their heads a *c.*
   P. L. 6, 860. the bounds and *c.* wall of heaven
   P. L. 7, 293. part rise in *c.* wall, or ridge direct
   P. L. 12. 197. dry land between two *c.* walls
   P. R. 1, 82. above the clouds unfold her *c.* doors
   P. R. 4, 119. quaff in gold, *c.,* and myrrhine
   C. 65. his orient liquor in a *c.* glass
   C. 673. that flames and dances in his *c.* bounds
   C. 931. thy molten *c.* fill with mud
   H. 125. ring out, ye *c.* Spheres
**Crystalline.**—P. L. 3, 482. *c.* sphere
   P. L. 6, 772. on the *c.* sky, in sapphire throned
   P. L. 7, 271. in wide *c.* ocean
   S. A. 546. allure thee from the cool *c.* stream
**Ctesiphon.**—P. R. 3, 292. Teredon, *C.*
   P. R. 3, 300. in *C.* hath gathered all his host
**Cube.**—P. L. 6, 552. in hollow *c.* training
**Cubic.**—P. L. 6, 399. in *c.* phalanx firm
**Cubit.**—P. L. 11, 730. measured by *c.,* length
**Cuckoo.**—S. 1, 6. before the shallow *c.'s* bill
**Cuckoos.**—S. 12, 4. of owls and *c.,* asses, apes
**Cuirass.**—S. A. 132. the hammered *c.,* Chalybean
**Cuirassiers.**—P. R. 3, 328. *c.* all in steel
**Cull.**—V. Ex. 21. but *c.* those richest robes
**Culled.**—C. 630. but of divine effect. he *c.* me out
**Culling.**—C. 255. *c.* their potent herbs
**Culminate.**—P. L. 3, 617. *c.* from the equator
**Cumbered.**—C. 730. the earth *c.,* and the winged
**Cumbersome.**—P. R. 3, 400. or that *c.*
**Cumbrance.**—P. R. 2, 454. the wise man's *c.*
**Cumbrous.**—P. L. 1, 428. like *c.* flesh
   P. L. 3, 715. the *c.* elements, earth, flood
   P. L. 11, 549. fairest and easiest, of this *c.* charge
   P. L. 12, 131. after him a *c.* train of herds
**Cunning.**—P. R. 1, 145. great *c.* to the throng
   P. R. 4, 11. in *c.,* over-reached where least
   L'A. 141. with wanton heed, and giddy *c.*
**Cunningly.**—S. A. 818. how *c.* the sorceress
**Cup.**—P. R. 2, 386. arrayed in glory, on my *c.*
   S. A. 934. fair enchanted *c.,* and warbling charms
   C. 51. whose charmèd *c.* whoever tasted lost his
   C. 525. by sly enticement gives his baneful *c.*
**Cupid.**—C. 445. the frivolous bolt of *C.*
   C. 1004. celestial *C.* her famed son advanced
**Cups.**—P. L. 5, 444. their flowing *c.*
   P. L. 11, 718. thence from *c.* to civil broils
   P. R. 4, 119. crystal, and myrrhine *c.*
   L. 150. and daffadillies fill their *c.* with tears
**Curb.**—P. L. 2, 322. under the inevitable *c.*
   P. L. 2, 531. part *c.* their fiery steeds
   P. L. 4, 859 champing his iron *c.*
   P. L. 11, 643. part *c.* the foaming steed
   C. 825. that with moist *c.* sways the smooth
   D. F. I. 73. and wisely learn to *c.* thy sorrows wild
**Cure.**—P. L. 2. 145. that must be our *c.*
   P. L. 2, 460. if there be *c.* or charm to respite
   P. L. 9, 776. here grows the *c.* of all, this fruit
   P. L. 10, 1079. what may else be remedy or *c.*
   S. A. 630. benumbing opium as my only *c.*
   S. A. 912. remains past *c.* bear not too sensibly
   C. 811. but this will *c.* all straight

C. 913. I have kept of precious *c.*
**Curfew.**—C. 435. his magic chains at *c.* time
Il P. 74, I hear the far-off *c.* sound
**Curiosity.**—S. A. 775. *c.*, inquisitive, importune
**Curious.**—P. L. 4, 242. in beds and *c.* knots
P. R. 1, 319. who first with *c.* eye perused him
P. R. 1, 333. and *c.* are to hear what happens
P. R. 4, 42. glass of telescope, were *c.* to inquire
C. 714. but all to please and sate the *c.* taste
**Curius.**—P. R. 2, 446. Fabricius, *C.*, Regulus
**Curl.**—A. 46. the saplings tall, and *c.* the grove
**Curled.**—P. L. 9, 517. *c.* many a wanton wreath
P. L. 10, 560. than the snaky locks that *c.*
**Curls.**—P. L. 3, 641. in *c.* on either cheek
P. L. 4, 307. waved as the vine *c.* her tendrils
C. 608. or drag him by the *c.* to a foul death
**Current.**—P. L. 4, 227. upon the rapid *c.*
P. L. 5, 808. the *c.* of his fury thus opposed
P. L. 7, 67. yet scarce allayed, still eyes the *c.*
S. A. 547. wherever fountain or fresh *c.* flowed
C. 740 must not be hoarded, but must be *c.*
**Currents.**—P. L. 11, 853. the rapid *c.* drive
**Curse.**—P. L. 2, 374. shall *c.* their frail
P. L. 2, 622. God by *c.* created evil
P. L. 10, 174. Serpent thus his *c.* let fall
P. L. 10. 640. till then the *c.* pronounced
P. L. 10, 729. or shall beget, is propagated *c.*
P. L. 10, 734. will *c.* my head
P. L. 10, 922. you bless me now your *c.*
P. L. 10, 1053. on me the *c.* aslope glanced
P. L. 12. 99. justice and some fatal *c.* annexed
P. L. 12, 103. this heavy *c.*, servant of servants
**Cursed.**—P. L. 1, 389. with *c.* things
P. L. 2, 1055. in a *c.* hour, he hies
P. L. 4, 71. nay, *c.* be thou
P. L. 6, 650. till on those *c.* engines' triple row
P. L. 6, 806. this *c.* crew the punishment
P. L. 9, 904. some *c.* fraud of enemy
P. L. 10, 201. *c.* is the ground for thy sake
P. L. 10, 818. in me all posterity stands *c.*
P. L. 10, 852. oft *c.* his creation, Death as oft

P. L. 10, 984. to bring into this *c.* world
P. L. 12, 406. to a reproachful life and *c.* death
C. 609. to a foul death, *c.* as his life
C.653.seize his wand, though he and his *c.* crew
C. 989. let us fly this *c.* place
**Curses.**—P. L. 10, 732. but *c.* on my head
L.101. built in the eclipse and rigged with *c.* dark
**Curtained.**—H. 230. *c.* with cloudy red
**Cusco.**—P. L. 11, 408. and *C.* in Peru
**Custody.**—P. L. 2, 333. but *c.* severe
P. L. 2, 946. had from his wakeful *c.* purloined
S. A. 802. against thee but safe *c.*, and hold
**Custom.**—P. L. 1, 640. consent or *c.*
P. L. 11, 810. against allurement, *c.*, and a world
**Customed.**—P. L. 5, 3. so *c.*, for his sleep
**Cut.**—P. L. 3, 47. the cheerful ways of men *c.* off
P. L. 6, 325. and in half *c.* sheer
P. L. 9, 1110. at loop-holes *c.* through
P. R. 3, 269. *c.* shorter many a league
S. A. 764. if not by quick destruction soon *c.* off
S. A. 1157. thee he regards not, owns not, hath *c.*
**Cuts.**—P. L. 10, 1043. that *c.* us off from hope
**Cybele.**—A. 21. or the towered *C.*
**Cyclades.**—P. L. 5, 264. amidst the *C.*
**Cycle.**—P. L. 8, 84. *c.* and epicycle, orb in orb
**Cyllene.**—A. 98. on old Lycæus, or *C.* hoar
**Cymbals.**—H. 208. in vain with *c's.* ring
**Cynic.**—C. 708. their precepts from the *C.* tub
**Cynosure.**—C. 342. Arcady, or Tyrian *c.*
L'A. 80. the *c.* of neighbouring eyes
**Cynthia.**—Il P. 59. while *C.* checks her dragon
H. 103. of *C.'s* seat, the airy region thrilling
**Cypress.**—C. 521. immured in *c.* shades
Il P. 35. and sable stole of *c.* lawn
M. W. 22. ye might discern a *c.* bud
**Cyrene.**—P. L. 2, 904. Barca or *C.'s* torrid
**Cyriack.**—S. 21, 1. *C.*, whose grand-sire on the
S. 22, 1. *C.*, this three years day these eyes
**Cyrus.**—P. R. 3, 33. the throne of *C.* held
P. R. 3, 284. till *C.* set them free
**Cytherea's.**—P. L. 9, 19. *C's.* son

# D

**Daffadillies.**—L. 150. *d.* fill their cups with tears
**Daffodils.**—C. 851. pinks, and gaudy *d.*
**Dagon.**—P. L. 1, 462. *D.* his name, sea monster
S. A. 13. to *D.* their sea-idol
S. A. 437. and praises loud to *D.* as their god
S. A. 440. so *D.* shall be magnified
S. A. 450. I this pomp have brought to *D.*
S. A. 462. twixt God and *D.*, *D.* had presumed
S. A. 468. *D.* must stoop, and shall ere
S. A. 478. whether God be Lord, or *D.*
S. A. 861. an irreligious dishonourer of *D.*
S. A. 1145. for proof hereof, if *D.* be thy god
S. A. 1151. avow, and challenge *D.* to the test
S. A. 1311. this day to *D.* is a solemn feast
S. A. 1360. my strength in honour to their *D.*
S. A. 1370. who constrains me to the temple of *D.*
S. A. 1463. most reverenced *D.*
**Daily.**—P. L. 4, 445. and *d.* thanks
P. L. 4, 618. man hath his *d.* work of body
P. L. 8, 193. that which before us lies in *d.* life
P. L. 8, 601. that *d.* flow from all her words
P. L. 9, 548. by angels, numberless, thy *d.* train
P. L. 9, 565. of brutal kind that *d.* are in sight
P. R. 4, 142. and from the *d.* scene effeminate
S. A. 6. *d.* in the common prison else enjoined me
S. A. 76. to *d.* fraud, contempt, abuse, and wrong
S. A. 114, their *d.* practice to afflict me more
S. A. 919. to which eyesight exposes, *d.*, men
S. A. 1261. with no small profit *d.* to my owners
C. 314. my *d.* walks and ancient neighbourhood
C. 635. treads on it *d.* with his clouted shoon
L. 129. *d.* devours apace, and nothing said
**Daintiest.**—V. Ex. 14. the *d.* dishes shall be
**Dainty.**—C.680.those *d.*limbs which Nature lent

**Dairy.**—P. L. 9, 451. or *d.*, each rural sight
**Daisies.**—C. 120. decked with *d.* trim
L'A. 75, meadows trim, with *d.* pied
**Dale.**—P. L. 1, 410. the flowery *d.* of Sibma
P. L. 2, 944. o'er hill or moory *d.* pursues
P. L. 4, 243. on hill,' and *d.*, and plain
P. L. 4, 538. o'er hill, o'er *d.*, his roam
P. L. 6. 641. of pleasure situate in hill and *d.*
P. L. 8, 262. I saw hill, *d.*, and shady woods
P. R. 3, 267. we speeded, and o'er hill and *d.*
C. 496. and sweetened every muskrose of the *d.*
L'A. 68. under the hawthorn in the *d.*
H. 184. from haunted spring and *d.*
M. M. 8. hill and *d.* doth boast thy blessing
**Dales.**—P. L. 8, 275. ye hills and *d.*, ye rivers
P. L. 10, 860. O fountains, hillocks, *d.* and bowers
P. R. 3, 318. and dark Iberian *d.*
**Dalila.**—P. L. 9, 1061. harlot lap of Philistéan *D.*
S. A. 229. in the vale of Sorec, *D.*
S. A. 724. no other certain than *D.* thy wife
S. A. 1072. the sumptuous *D.* floating this way
**Dalliance.**—P. L. 2, 819. pledge of *d.*
P. L. 4, 338. nor youthful *d.* as beseems
P. L. 9, 443. held *d.* with his fair Egyptian
P. L. 9, 1016. Adam thus gan Eve to *d.* move
**Dally.**—L. 153. let our frail thoughts *d.* with
**Dam.**—C. 498. or young kid lost his *d.*
**Damage.**—P. L. 7, 152. my *d.* fondly deemed
**Damasco.**—P. L. 1, 584. *D.* or Morocco
**Damascus.**—P. L. 1, 468. seat was fair *D.*
**Damasked.**—P. L. 4, 334. *d.* with flowers
**Dame.**—P. L. 9, 612. of creatures, universal *D.*
C. 130. mysterious *d.* that ne'er art called
**Dames.**—C. 347. night watches to his feathery *d.*

L'A. 52. stoutly struts his *d.* before.
**Damiata.**—P. L. 2, 593. *D.* and mount Casius
**Dammed.**—C. 336. your influence be quite *d.* up
**Damnation.**—P. L. 1, 215. on himself *d.*
**Damned.**—P. L. 2, 482. the Spirits *d.* lose all
  P. L. 2, 496. O shame to men! devil with devil *d.*
  P. L. 2, 597. at certain revolutions all the *d.*
  P. L. 4, 392. though *d.,* I should abhor
  P. R. 4, 194. that Evil One, Satan for ever *d.*
  C. 571. where that *d.* wizard, hid in sly disguise
  C. 602. but for that *d.* magician, let him be girt
  H. 228. control the *d.* crew
**Damœtas.**—L. 36. and old *D.* loved to hear
**Damp.**—P. L. 1, 523. with looks downcast and *d.*
  P. L. 5, 65. me *d.* horror chilled at such bold
  P. L. 9, 45. or years *d.* my intended wing
  P. L. 10, 283. wide anarchy of Chaos, *d.*
  P. L. 11, 293. the cold sudden *d.* recovering
  P. L. 11, 544. will reign a melancholy *d.*
  S. A. 8. the air, imprisoned also, close and *d.*
  C. 470. are those thick and gloomy shadows *d.*
  C. 640. all enchantments, mildew blast, or *d.*
**Damps.**—P. L. 10, 848. with *d.* and dreadful
  P. R. 4, 406. from dews and *d.* of night
**Damsel.**—S. A. 721. her harbinger, a *d.* train
  C. 158. and put the *d.* to suspicious flight
  C. 829. she, guiltless *d.,* flying the mad pursuit
  D.F.I. 9. by boisterous rape the Athenian *d.* got
**Damsels.**—P. L. 1, 448. the Syrian *d.* to lament
  P. R. 2, 359. of faery *d.* met in forest wide
**Dan.**—P. L. 1, 485. that sin in Bethel and in *D.*
  P. R. 3, 431. perhaps of Bethel and of *D.*
  S. A. 332. brethren, and men of *D.*
  S. A. 976. in *D.,* in Judah, and the bordering
  S. A. 1436. rushed on thee in the camp of *D.*
**Danaw.**—P. L. 1, 353. to pass Rhene or the *D.*
**Dance.**—P. L. 1, 786. mirth and *d.* intent
  P. L. 2, 664. to *d.* with Lapland witches
  P. L. 3, 580. move their starry *d.* in numbers
  P. L. 4, 267. Graces and the Hours in *d.*
  P. L. 4, 768. mixed *d.,* or wanton mask
  P. L. 5, 178. move in mystic *d.* not without song
  P. L. 5, 619. in song and *d.* about the sacred
  P. L. 5, 620. mystical *d.,* which yonder starry
  P. L. 5, 630. forthwith from *d.* to sweet repast
  P. L. 6, 615. vagaries fell, as they would *d.*
  P. L. 6, 615. for a *d.* they seemed somewhat
  P. L. 7, 324. rose, as in *d.,* the stately trees
  P. L. 8, 125. incited, *d.* about him various rounds
  P. L. 8, 243. noise, other than the sound of *d.*
  P. L. 11, 584. amorous ditties, and in *d.* came on
  P. L. 11, 619. of lustful appetence, to sing. to *d.*
  P. L. 11, 715. to luxury and riot, feast and *d.*
  C. 104. tipsy *d.,* and jollity
  C. 176. in wanton *d.* they praise the bounteous
  C. 883. by all the nymphs that nightly *d.*
  C. 952. with jigs and rural *d.* resort
  C. 974. to triumph in victorious *d.*
  A. 96. nymphs and shepherds *d.* no more
  H. 210. in dismal *d.* about the furnace blue
**Danced.**—P. L. 5, 395. here *d.* hand in hand
  P. L. 7, 374. before him *d.,* shedding sweet
  P. L. 9, 103. terrestrial Heaven, *d.* round by
  L. 34. Satyrs *d.,* and Fauns with cloven heel
  V. Ex. 60. the faery ladies *d.* upon the hearth
**Dancers.**—S. A. 1325. jugglers, and *d.,* antics
**Dances.**—C. 673. that flames and *d.* in his crystal
**Dancing.**—S. A. 543. nor did the *d.* ruby
  L'A. 96. *d.* in the chequered shade
  M. M. 2. comes *d.* from the east, and leads
**Dandled.**—P. L. 4, 344. in his paw *d.* the kid
**Danger.**—P. L. 2, 421. pondering the *d.*
  P. L. 2, 449. in the shape of difficulty or *d.*
  P. L. 2, 1008. much the nearer *d.* go and speed
  P. L. 3, 635. which else might work him *d.*
  P. L. 4, 934. through ways of *d.* by himself
  P. L. 5, 239. tell him, withal, his *d.,* and from
  P. L. 6, 418. O now in *d.* tried, now known
  P. L. 9, 267. the wife, where *d.* or dishonour
  P. L. 9, 349. within himself the *d.* lies
  P. L. 9, 864. is not, as we are told, a tree of *d.*

P. L. 9, 1157. going into such *d.,* as thou saidst
P. L. 9, 1172. foretold the *d.* and the lurking
P. L. 9, 1176. secure either to meet no *d.,* or to
P. R. 1, 94. ye see our *d.* on the utmost edge
S. A. 529. fearless of *d.,* like a petty god
S. A. 1522. we, unawares, run into *d's* mouth
C. 370. not being in *d.* (as I trust she is not)
C. 401. bid me hope *D.* will wink on Opportunity
**Dangerous.**—P. L. 2, 107. and battle *d.*
  P. L. 2, 342. with *d.* expedition to invade
  P. L. 6, 698. wild work in heaven, and *d.* to the
  P. L. 10, 382. try thee now more *d.* to his throne
  P. R. 4, 455. as *d.* to the pillared frame
**Dangers.**—P. L. 1, 275. in fears and *d.*
  P. L. 1, 636. or *d.* shunned by me
  P. L. 2, 444. remains him less than unknown *d.*
  P. L. 7, 27. in darkness, and with *d.* compassed
  P. R. 2, 460. brings *d.,* troubles, cares
  P. R. 4, 479. many a hard assay of *d.*
  P. 11. *d..* and snares, and wrongs, and worse
**Daniel.**—P. R. 2, 278. with *D.* at his pulse
  P. R. 2, 329. those young *D.* could refuse
**Danite.**—P. L. 9, 1059. so rose the *D.* strong
**Dank.**—P. L. 7, 441. yet oft they quit the *d.*
  P. L. 9, 179. through each thicket *d.* or dry
  C. 891. where grows the willow and the osier *d.*
  S. 20, 2. now that the fields are *d.,* and ways are
**Dante.**—S. 13, 12. *D.* shall give Fame leave
**Danubius.**—P. R. 4, 79. beyond *D.* to the
**Daphne.**—P. L. 4, 273. of *D.* by Orontes
  P. R. 2, 187. *D.,* or Semele, Antiopa
  C. 661. you a statue; or as *D.* was, rootbound
**Dapper.**—C. 118. faeries and the *d.* elves
**Dappled.**—L'A. 44. till the *d.* dawn doth rise
**Dare.**—P. L. 3, 523. whether to *d.* the fiend
  P. L. 4, 942. and thy gay legions *d.*
  P. L. 9, 304. enemy though bold will hardly *d.*
  P. R. 4, 610. he never more henceforth will *d.*
  S. A. 1254. and offered fight will not *d.* mention
  C. 427. will *d.* to soil her virgin purity
  H. 225. nor all the gods beside longer *d.* abide
  F. of C. 5. *d.* ye for this adjure the civil sword
**Dared.**—P. L. 9, 922. who thus hast *d.*
  P. R. 4, 172. since thou hast *d.* to utter the
**Dares.**—P. R. 3, 57. lot who *d.* be singularly
  C. 780. to him that *d.* arm his profane tongue
  A. 23. Juno *d.* not give her odds
**Darest.**—P. L. 2, 682. that *d.,* though grim
  P. L. 6, 182. yet lewdly *d.* our ministering
  P. R. 4, 178. and *d.* thou to the Son of God
  S. A. 1394. and *d.* thou, at our sending and
**Darien.**—P. L. 9, 81. the ocean barred at *D.*
**Daring.**—P. L. 6, 129. met his *d.* foe
  P. L. 9, 305. or *d.,* first on me the assault
  P. L. 11, 703. beset with foes, for *d.* single
  S. A. 531. on hostile ground, none *d.* my affront
  S. A. 1628. none *d.* appear antagonist
**Dark.**—P. L. 1, 22. what in me is *d.* illumine
  P. L. 1, 213. left him at large to his own *d.*
  P. L. 1, 456. his eye surveyed the *d.* idolatries
  P. L. 2. 58. accept this *d.* opprobrious den
  P. L. 2, 264. how oft amidst thick clouds and *d.*
  P. L. 2, 405. the *d.,* unbottomed, infinite abyss
  P. L. 2, 464. through all the coasts of *d.*
  P. L. 2, 486. doubtful consultations *d.* ended
  P. L. 2, 588. a frozen continent lies *d.* and wild
  P. L. 2, 618. through many a *d.* and dreary vale
  P. L. 2, 718. their *d.* encounter in mid air
  P. L. 2, 823. from out this *d.* and dismal house
  P. L. 2, 891. a *d.* illimitable ocean
  P. L. 2, 916. them ordain his *d.* materials
  P. L. 2, 953. borne through the hollow *d.*
  P. L. 2, 960. and his *d.* pavilion spread wide
  P. L. 2, 1027. over the *d.* Abyss, whose boiling
  P. L. 3, 11. rising world of waters *d.* and deep
  P. L. 3, 20. to venture down the *d.* descent
  P. L. 3, 45. and ever-during *d.* surrounds me
  P. L. 3, 188. for I will clear their senses *d.*
  P. L. 3, 380. *d.* with excessive bright thy skirts
  P. L. 3, 424. *d.,* waste, and wild, under the
  P. L. 3, 498. all this *d.* globe the Fiend found

F

P. L. 3, 544. through d. and desert ways
P. L. 3, 611. here in the d. so many precious
P. L. 4, 609. and o'er the d. her silver mantle
P. L. 4, 899. if he intends our stay in that d.
P. L. 5, 208. as now light dispels the d.
P. L. 6, 380. in d. oblivion let them dwell
P. L. 6, 415. far in the d. dislodged
P. L. 6, 478. d. and crude of spiritous and fiery
P. L. 6, 482. these, in their d. nativity, the deep
P. L. 6, 870. cast too deep her d. foundations
P. L. 7, 212. outrageous as a sea, d., wasteful
P. L. 8, 478. she disappeared, and left me d.
P. L. 9, 90. and his d. suggestions hide
P. L. 9, 162. to hide me, and the d. intent
P. L. 10, 283. anarchy of Chaos, damp and d.
P. L. 10, 371. this portentous bridge, the d.
P. L. 10, 438. many a d. league, reduced in
P. L. 10, 457. raised from their d. divan
P. L. 10, 594. at Hell's d. threshold to have sat
P. L. 10, 667. with terror through the d.
P. L. 11, 478. appeared, sad, noisome, d.
P. L. 11, 743. the thickened sky like a d. ceiling
P. L. 11, 809. the only son of light in a d. age
P. R. 1, 41. thick clouds and d. tenfold involved
P. R. 1, 194. with d. shades and rocks
P.R. 1,434. thy answers, what but d., ambiguous
P. R. 3, 318. of Caucasus, and d. Iberian dales
P. R. 4, 456. the earth's d. basis underneath
S. A. 2. lend thy guiding hand to these d. steps
S. A. 75. d. in light, exposed to daily fraud
S. A. 80. O d., d., d., amid the blaze of noon
S. A. 86. the sun to me is d. and silent as the
S. A. 154. prison within prison inseparably d.
S. A. 591. that these d. orbs no more shall treat
C. 197. in thy d. lantern thus close up the stars
C. 383. he that hides a d. soul and foul thoughts
C. 500. how couldst thou find this d. sequestered
L. 101. the eclipse, and rigged with curses d.
L'A. 10. in d. Cimmerian desert ever dwell
S. 19, 2. half my days in this d. world
H. 123. and cast the d. foundations deep
H. 219. in vain with timbreled anthems d.
P. 7. swallowed up in d.
P. 33. my sorrows are too d. for day to know
D. F. I. 30. corse corrupts in earth's d. womb
V. Ex. 71. in Time's d. prospective glass
**Darked.**—C. 730. the winged air d. with plumes
**Darken.**—P. L. 6, 57. and clouds began to d.
**Darkened.**—P. L. 1, 343. and d. all the land
P. L. 1, 599. d. so, yet shone above them all
P. L. 2, 491. scowls o'er the d. landscape snow
P. L. 9, 1054. and their minds how d.
**Darkens.**—P. L. 1, 501. and when night d.
**Darker.**—P. L. 2, 720. grew d. at their frown
P. L. 5, 646. night comes not there in d. veil
**Darkest.**—Il P. 33. all in a robe of d. grain
**Darkish.**—C. 631. the leaf was d. and had
**Darkling.**—P. L. 3, 39. the wakeful bird sings d.
**Darkness.**—P. L. 1, 63. no light, but rather d.
P. L. 1, 72. in utter d.; and their portion set
P. L. 1, 391. and with their d. durst affront
P. L. 1, 659. nor the Abyss long under d. cover
P. L. 2, 220. this horror will grow mild, this d.
P. L. 2, 263. this deep world of d. do we dread
P. L. 2, 266. and with the majesty of d. round
P. L. 2, 269. as he our d., cannot we his light
P. L. 2, 377. attempting; or to sit in d. here
P. L. 2, 754. in d., while thy head flames thick
P. L. 2, 958. which way the nearest coast of d.
P. L. 2, 984. to her original d. and your sway
P. L. 3, 16. through utter and through middle d.
P. L. 3, 256. and show the Powers of D. bound
P. L. 3, 421. from Chaos and the inroad of D.
P. L. 3, 539. where bounds were set to d.
P. L. 3, 712. till at his second bidding d. fled
P. L. 4, 665. lest total d. should by night regain
P. L. 5, 179. who out of d. called up light
P. L. 5, 614. falls into utter d., deep ingulfed
P. L. 6, 6. where light and d., in perpetual
P. L. 6, 10. at the other door obsequious d.
P. L. 6, 11. though d. there might well seem

P. L. 6, 142. and whelmed thy legions under d.
P. L. 6, 407. inducing d., grateful truce imposed
P. L. 6, 715. pursue these sons of d.
P. L. 6, 739. to chains of d. and the undying
P. L. 7, 27. in d., and with dangers compassed
P. L. 7, 233. d. profound covered the abyss
P. L. 7, 250. light from d. by the hemisphere
P. L. 7, 251. Light the Day, and D. Night
P. L. 7, 255. exhaling first from d. they beheld
P. L. 7, 352. and light from d. to divide
P. L. 9, 64. continued nights he rode with d.
P. L. 10, 383. thus the Prince of D. answered
P. L. 10, 394. descend through d., on your road
P. L. 10, 745. I solicit thee from d. to promote
P. L. 11, 204. why in the east d. ere day's
P. L. 12, 187. d. must overshadow all his
P. L. 12, 188. palpable d., and blot out three days
P. L. 12, 207. d. defends between till morning
P. L. 12, 271. from Heaven, enlightener of my d.
P. L. 12, 473. first brought forth light out of d.
P. R. 4, 397. d. now rose, as daylight sunk
P. R. 4, 441. mischief done, the Prince of D.
S. A. 99. as in the land of d. yet, in light
S. A. 159. in real d. of the body dwells
S. A. 593. but yield to double d. nigh at hand
C. 132. of Stygian d. spets her thickest gloom
C. 194. and envious d., ere they could return
C. 204. yet nought but single d. do I find
C. 252. the raven-down of D. till it smiled
C. 278. dim d., and this leafy labyrinth
C. 335. in double night of d., and of shades
L'A. 6. where brooding D. spreads his jealous
L'A. 50. scatters the rear of d. thin
M. W. 10. to house with d., and with death
**Darksome.**—P. L. 2, 973. this d. desert
P. L. 4, 232. which from his d. passage
P. L. 5, 225. scaped through the d. gulf
P. L. 12, 185. a d. cloud of locusts swarming
H. 14. chose with us a d. house of mortal clay
**Dark-veiled.**—C. 129. d.-v. Cotytto! to whom
**Darling.**—P. L. 2, 373. when his d. sons
P. L. 2, 870. thy d., without end
**Dart.**—P. L. 2, 672. and shook a dreadful d.
P. L. 2, 702. or with one stroke of this d.
P. L. 2, 729. that mortal d. against thy father's
P. L. 2, 786. brandishing his fatal d.
P. L. 2, 854. ready stands to interpose his d.
P. L. 11, 491. triumphant Death his d. shook
P L. 11, 658. defend with d. and javelin
**Darted.**—P. L. 9, 1036. of Eve, whose eye d.
**Darts.**—P. L. 1, 568. d. his experienced eye
P. L. 6, 213. the dismal hiss of fiery d.
P. L. 8, 62. and from about her shot d. of desire
P. L. 12, 492. and quench his fiery d.
P. L. 12, 536. bestuck with slanderous d.
P. R. 4, 366. (for all his d. were spent)
P. R. 4, 424. some bent at thee their fiery d.
**Darwen.**—S. 16, 7. while D. stream, with blood
**Dash.**—P. L. 2, 114. to perplex and d.
P. L. 6, 488. mischief as shall d. to pieces
P. L. 10, 577. to d. their pride and joy
P. R. 4. 149. or as a stone that shall to pieces d.
P. R. 4, 559. thou chance to d. thy foot
S. A. 1240. or swing thee in the air, then d. thee
**Dashed.**—P. R. 4, 19. though all to shivers d.
C. 451. and noble grace that d. brute violence
**Date.**—P. L. 12, 549. ages of endless d.
P. R. 4, 392. for no d. prefixed directs me
C. 362. what need a man forestall his d. of grief
U.C. II. 29. obedient to the moon he spent his d.
**Daughter.**—P. L. 2, 817. dear d., since thou
P. L. 2, 870. beseems thy d. and thy darling
P. L. 4, 660. d. of God and man
P. L. 9, 291. d. of God and man, immortal Eve
P. L. 9, 653. and left that command sole d.
P. L. 10, 353. till Sin, his fair enchanting d.
P. L. 10, 384. d., and thou son and grandchild
P. L. 10, 708. but Discord first, d. of Sin
P. R. 3, 342. his d., sought by many prowest
S.A. 221. that I sought to wed the d. of an infidel
C. 51. who knows not Circe, the d. of the Sun

C 241. sweet Queen of Parley, *d.* of the Sphere
C. 827. whilom she was the *d.* of Locrine
C. 922. virgin, *d.* of Locrine, sprung of old
L'A. 23. filled her with thee, a *d.* fair
Il P. 25. his *d.* she; in Saturn's reign
S. 10, 1. *d.* to that good Earl, once President
M. W. 3. a Viscount's *d.*, an Earl's heir
**Daughters.**—P. L. 1, 453. infected Sion's *d.*
P. L. 3, 463. of ill-joined sons, and *d.* born
P. L. 4, 324. the fairest of her *d.*, Eve
P. L. 9, 1105. *d.* grow about the mother-tree
P. R. 2, 154. among *d.* of men the fairest found
P. R. 2, 180. cast wanton eyes on the *d.* of men
S. A. 876. I, before all the *d.* of my tribe
S. A. 1192. among the *d.* of the Philistines
C. 837. and gave her to his *d.* to imbathe
C. 982. his *d.* three that sing about the golden
A. 69. to lull the *d.* of Necessity
**Daunt.**—II P. 137. never heard the Nymphs to *d.*
S. 15, 4. and rumours loud that *d.* remotest kings
**Dauntless.**—P. L. 1, 603. *d.* courage
P. L. 9, 694. not praise rather your *d.* virtue
C. 650. where if he be, with *d.* hardihood
**David.**—P. L. 12, 326. the royal stock of *D.*
P. L. 12, 347. and his covenant sworn to *D.*
P. L. 12, 357. and regard not *D.'s* sons
P. R. 1, 240. be great and sit on *D.'s* throne
P. R. 3, 153. thy father *D.'s* throne
P. R. 3, 169. the crown, and *D.'s* throne
P. R. 3, 282. and all thy father *D.'s* house
P. R. 3, 353. endeavour, as thy father *D.* did
P. R. 3, 357. thou wert possessed of *D.'s* throne
P. R. 3, 373. in *D.'s* royal seat, his true successor
P. R. 3, 383. on the throne of *D.* in full glory
P. R. 3, 405. if I mean to reign *D.'s* true heir
P. R. 3, 408. for Israel, or for *D.*, or his throne
P. R. 4, 108. on *D.'s* throne, prophesied
P. R. 4, 147. on *D.'s* throne, it shall be like
P. R. 4, 379. on *D.'s* throne, or throne of all
P. R. 4, 471. gaining *D.'s* throne
P. R. 4, 500. hear, O Son of *D.*, virgin-born
**Dawn.**—P. L. 2, 1037. a glimmering *d.*
P. L. 3, 24. thy piercing ray, and find no *d.*
P. L. 3, 545. by break of cheerful *d.*
P. L. 5, 167. thou belong not to the *d.*
P. L. 6, 492. yet ere *d.*, effect shall end our wish
P. L. 7, 374. the grey *d.* and the Pleiades
P. L. 9, 192. whenas sacred light began to *d.*
P. L. 9, 412. for now, and since first break of *d.*
L'A. 44. till the dappled *d.* doth rise
H. 86. on the lawn, or ere the point of *d.*
**Dawning.**—P. L. 3, 500. a gleam of *d.* light
P. L. 4, 588. by morrow *d.* I shall know
P. L. 6, 528. others from the *d.* hills looked
P. L. 6, 749. morn began to shine, *d.* through
P. L. 12, 421. ere the third *d.* light return
P. L. 12, 423. fresh as the *d.* light
**Day.**—P. L. 1, 50. that measures *d.* and night
P. L. 1, 339. in Egypt's evil *d.*, waved round
P. L. 1, 449. amorous ditties, all a summer's *d.*
P. L. 1, 744. noon to dewy eve, a summer's *d.*
P. L. 2, 178. hideous fall one *d.* upon our heads
P. L. 2, 505. *d.* and night, for his destruction
P. L. 2, 734. wrath, which one *d.* will destroy
P. L. 3, 42. but not to me returns *d.*, or the
P. L. 3, 198. this my long sufferance and my *d.*
P. L. 3, 392. thou that *d.* thy Father's dreadful
P. L. 3, 725. the seat of Man; that light his *d.*
P. L. 4, 284. a whole *d.'s* journey high
P. L. 4, 449. that *d.* I oft remember
P. L. 4, 564. this *d.*, at height of noon, came
P. L. 4, 613. God hath set labour and rest, as *d.*
P. L. 4, 616. other creatures all *d.* long rove
P. L. 4, 680. works behold both *d.* and night
P. L. 4, 712. what *d.* the genial Angel to our
P. L. 4, 725. Omnipotent! and thou the *d.*
P. L. 5, 33. works of *d.* past, or morrow's
P. L. 5, 53. fairer to my fancy than by *d.*
P. L. 5, 162. symphonies, *d.* without night
P. L. 5, 168. sure pledge of *d.*, that crownest
P. L. 5, 170. while *d.* arises, that sweet hour

P. L. 5, 229. half this *d.* as friend with friend
P. L. 5, 313. and will vouchsafe this *d.* to be
P. L. 5, 558. and we have yet large *d.*
P. L. 5, 579. when, on a *d.*, for time though
P. L. 5, 582. on such *d.* as Heaven's great year
P. L. 5, 603. this *d.* I have begot whom I declare
P. L. 5, 612. and that *d.*, cast out from God
P. L. 5, 618. that *d.*, as other solemn days
P. L. 5, 662. that *d.* honoured by his great
P. L. 6, 8. grateful vicissitude, like *d.* and night
P. L. 6, 87. weened that selfsame *d.*, by fight
P. L. 6, 170. both their deeds compared this *d.*
P. L. 6, 246. till Satan, who that *d.* prodigious
P. L. 6, 423. who have sustained one *d.*
P. L. 6, 424. and if one *d.*, why not eternal days?
P. L. 6, 539. this *d.*; fear not his flight
P. L. 6, 544. for this *d.* will pour down
P. L. 6, 802. this *d.* from battle rest
P. L. 6, 809. number to this *d.'s* work
P. L. 7, 98. and the great light of *d.* yet wants
P. L. 7, 202. against a solemn *d.*, harnessed at
P. L. 7, 251. Light the *D.* and Darkness Night
P. L. 7, 252. thus was the first *D.* even and morn
P. L. 7, 275. morning chorus sung the second *D.*
P. L. 7, 338. and morn recorded the third *D.*
P. L. 7, 341. to divide the *d.* from night
P. L. 7, 347. the greater to have rule by *d.*
P. L. 7, 350. and rule the *d.* in their vicissitude
P. L. 7, 371. glorious lamp was seen, regent of *d.*
P. L. 7, 386. glad morn crowned the fourth *D.*
P. L. 7, 448. and morn solemnized the fifth *D.*
P. L. 7, 504. and of the sixth *D.* yet remained
P. L. 7, 544. thou may'st not; in the *d.*
P. L. 7, 550. and morn accomplished the sixth *D.*
P. L. 7, 592. blessed and hallowed the seventh *D.*
P. L. 7, 593. resting on that *d.* from all his work
P. L. 7, 605. these that *d.* thy thunders
P. L. 8, 24. one *d.* and night in all their vast
P. L. 8, 31. revolution *d.* by *d.* repeated
P. L. 8, 136. above all stars, the wheel of *d.*
P. L. 8, 137. industrious of herself, fetch *d.*
P. L. 8, 143. enlightening her by *d.* as she by
P. L. 8, 206. and *d.* is not yet spent
P. L. 8, 229. for I that *d.* was absent, as befell
P. L. 8, 329. the *d.* thou eat'st thereof
P. L. 8, 331. from that *d.* mortal, and this happy
P. L. 9, 51. short arbiter 'twixt *d.* and night
P. L. 9, 59. cautious of *d.*, since Uriel
P. L. 9, 136. in one *d.* to have marred
P. L. 9, 201. how that *d.* they best may ply
P. L. 9, 209. what we by *d.* lop overgrown
P. L. 9, 220. near each other thus all *d.*
P. L. 9, 224. which intermits our *d.'s* work
P. L. 9, 575. till on a *d.*, roving the field
P. L. 9, 705. he knows that in the *d.* ye eat
P. L. 9, 762. in the *d.* we eat of this fair fruit
P. L. 9, 968. whereof good proof this *d.* affords
P. L. 9, 1021. praise yield thee, so well this *d.*
P. L. 9, 1029. thy beauty since the *d.* I saw
P. L. 9, 1102. but such as, at this *d.*, to Indians
P. L. 10, 49. death denounced that *d.*
P. L. 10, 53. no acquittance ere *d.* end
P. L. 10, 99. brought to their ears, while *d.*
P. L. 10, 125. O Heaven! in evil straight this *d.*
P. L. 10, 210. stroke of death, denounced that *d.*
P. L. 10, 275. against the *d.* of battle
P. L. 10, 278. designed for death the following *d.*
P. L. 10, 681. to them *d.* had unbenighted
P. L. 10, 773. what his decree fixed on this *d.*
P. L. 10, 811. endless misery from this *d.*
P. L. 10, 854. denounced the *d.* of his offence
P. L. 10, 962. since this *d.'s* death denounced
P. L. 10, 964. a long *d.'s* dying to augment
P. L. 10, 1050. was meant by death that *d.*
P. L. 11, 177. where'er our *d.'s* work lies
P. L. 11, 178. enjoined laborious, till *d.* droop
P. L. 11, 204. east darkness ere *d.'s* mid-course
P. L. 11, 212. fear that *d.* dimmed Adam's eye
P. L. 11, 272. the respite of that *d.* that must
P. L. 11, 550. must keep till my appointed *d.*
P. L. 11, 765. each *d.'s* lot enough

P. L. 11, 826. shall pour rain d. and night
P. L. 11, 898. d. and night, seed time
P. L. 12, 203. by d. a cloud, by night a pillar
P. L. 12, 242. whose d. he shall foretell
P. L. 12, 257. a cloud shall rest by d.
P. L. 12, 264. mid heaven stand still a d. entire
P. L. 12, 277. I see his d., in whom all nations
P. L. 12, 446. shall teach; for, from that d.
P. L. 12, 539. till the d. appear of respiration
P. R. 1, 130. Gabriel, this d., by proof, thou shalt
P. R. 1, 189. one d. forth walked alone
P. L. 1. 317. winter's d., when winds blow keen
P. R. 4, 221. as morning shows the d.
P. R. 4, 400. mere of light and absent d.
S. A. 12. this d. a solemn feast the people hold
S. A. 82. total eclipse without all hope of d.
S. A. 145. in Ramath-lechi, famous to this d.
S. A. 265. had Judah that d. joined, or one whole
S. A. 404. she surceased not, d. nor night
S. A. 434. this d. the Philistines a popular feast
S. A. 794. feared lest one d. thou wouldst
S. A. 807. I should still enjoy thee, d. and night
S. A. 1016. in one d. or seven though one should
S. A. 1216. the unworthier they: whence to this d
S. A. 1297. this idol's d. hath been to thee no d.
S. A. 1299. more than the working d. thy hands
S. A. 1311. this d. to Dagon is a solemn feast
S. A. 1388. this d. will be remarkable in my life
S. A. 1574. what windy joy this d. had I
S. A. 1600. all abroad was rumoured that this d.
C. 95. and the gilded car of d. his glowing axle
C. 382. may sit in the centre, and enjoy bright d.
C. 569. paths and turnings often trod by d.
C. 688. that have been tired all d. without repast
C. 978. where d. never shuts his eye
Il P. 141. hide from d.'s garish eye
S. 1, 5. thy liquid notes that close the eye of d.
S. 20, 4. and by the fire help waste a sullen d.
S. 21, 13. with superfluous burden loads the d.
S. 22, 1. Cyriack, this three years' d. these eyes
S. 23, 14. I waked, she fled, and d. brought back
H. 13. forsook the courts of everlasting d.
H. 78. had given d. her room, the sun himself
H. 140. her dolorous mansions to the peering d.
H. 167. from this happy d. the old Dragon
P. 33. my sorrows are too dark for d. to know
M. M. 1. now the bright morning-star, d.'s
Cir. 26. with wounding smart, this d.
**Day-labour.**—P. L. 5, 232. respite his d.-l.
S. 19, 7. doth God exact d.-l., light denied?
**Day-labourers.**—L'A. 109. that ten d.-l.
**Daylight.**—P. R. 4, 398. now rose, as d. sunk
C. 126. 'tis only d. that makes sin, which these
L'A. 99. till the livelong d. fail
**Days.**—P. L. 2, 222. of future d. may bring
P. L. 2, 695. waste eternal d. in woe and pain
P. L. 3, 337. see golden d., fruitful of golden
P. L. 3, 581. in numbers that compute d.
P. L. 5, 618. that day, as other solemn d. they
P. L. 6, 424. if one day, why not eternal d.
P. L. 6, 502. future d., if malice should abound
P. L. 6, 684. two d. are passed, two d. as we
P. L. 6, 699. two d. are therefore passed
P. L. 6, 871. nine d. they fell; confounded
P. L. 7, 25. on evil d., on evil d. brought fallen
P. L. 7, 342. for seasons, and for d., and circling
P. L. 7, 568. his six d'. work, a world!
P. L. 7, 601. creation and the six d'. acts
P. L. 8, 69. his seasons, hours, or d., or months
P. L. 9, 137. six nights and d. continued making
P. L. 10, 178. dust shalt eat all the d. of thy life
P. L. 10, 202. shalt eat thereof all the d.
P. L. 10, 576. humbling certain numbered d.
P. L. 10, 680. equal in d. and nights
P. L. 10, 1037. or childless d. resolved
P. L. 11, 39. at least his d. numbered
P. L. 11, 114. what shall come in future d.
P. L. 11, 198. from death released some d.
P. L. 11, 254. defeated of his seizure many d.
P. L. 11, 357. what shall come in future d.
P. L. 11, 600. and more hope of peaceful d.

P. L. 11, 689. for in those d. might only
P. L. 11, 782. crowned with length of happy d.
P. L. 12, 22. shall spend their d. in joy
P. L. 12, 188. and blot out three d.
P. L. 12, 347. stablished as the d. of heaven
P. L. 12, 465. of Eden, and far happier d.
P. L. 12, 602. which will be many d.
P. R. 1, 183. yet some d. lodged in Bethabara
P. R. 1, 303. full forty d. he passed
P. R. 1, 309. nor hunger felt, till those d. ended
P. R. 1, 352. Moses was forty d., nor eat
P. R. 1, 353. and forty d. Elijah without food
P. R. 2, 11. to doubt, and doubted many d.
P. R. 2, 12. and, as the d. increased, increased
P. R. 2, 243. forty d., fasting had remained
P. R. 2, 245. four times ten d. I have passed
P. R. 2, 276. whereof sufficed him forty d.
P. R. 2, 315. of thee these forty d., none hath
P. R. 3. 234. once a year Jerusalem. few d.
P. R. 3, 276. within her wall several d.' journey
P. R. 3, 412. by three d.' pestilence
S. A. 191. in prosperous d. they swarm
S. A. 702. suffering the punishment of d.
S. A. 762. are drawn to wear out miserable d.
S. A. 1062. fair d. have oft contracted wind and
S. A. 1064. be less abstruse; my riddling d.
S. A. 1389. by some great actor of my d. the last
S. A. 1741. the virgins also shall, on feastful d.
L. 72. to scorn delights, and live laborious d.
S. 7, 2. my hasting d. fly on with full career
S. 10, 9. later born than to have known the d.
S. 19, 2. ere half my d. in this dark world
M. W. 11. yet, had the number of her d.
V. Ex. 72. foresaw what future d. should bring
**Day-spring.**—P. L. 5, 139. d.-s. and the sun
P. L. 6, 521. so all ere d.-s., under conscious
S. A. 11. pure and sweet, with d.-s born
**Day-star.**—L. 168. so sinks the d.-s. in the ocean
**Dazzle.**—P. L. 3, 381. appear, yet d. Heaven
P. L. 9, 1083. those heavenly shapes will d.
**Dazzled.**—P. L. 8, 457. d. and spent
**Dazzles.**—P. L. 5, 357. d. the crowd
**Dazzling.**—P. L. 1, 564. length, and d. arms
P. L. 4, 798. his radiant files d. the moon
C. 154. my d. spells into the spongy air
C. 791. that hath so well been taught her d. fence
**Dead.**—P. L. 3, 233. once d. in sins and lost
P. L. 3, 327. the cited d. of all past ages
P. L. 3, 477. to seek in Golgotha him d.
P. L. 9, 870. and is become not d., as we
P. L. 12, 190. first-born of Egypt must lie d.
P. L. 12, 460. to judge both quick and d.
P. L. 12, 461. to judge the unfaithful d.
P. R. 2, 77. the murderous king were d.
S. A. 79. half I seem to live, d. more than
S. A. 100. to live a life half d., a living death
S. A. 143. the jaw of a d. ass, his sword of bone
S. A. 984. living and d. recorded
S. A. 1570. then the worst in brief, Samson is d.
C. 879. by d. Parthenope's dear tomb
L. 8. for Lycidas is d., d. ere his prime
L. 166. for Lycidas your sorrow is not d.
S. M. 4. d. things with inbreathed sense able to
D. F. I. 29. yet can I not persuade me thou art d.
**Deadlier.**—P. L. 12, 391. a d. bruise
**Deadliest.**—P. R. 4, 622. last and d. wound
S. A. 1262. my d. foe will prove my speediest
**Deadly.**—P. L. 2, 577. the flood of d. hate
P. L. 2, 712. at the head levelled his d. aim
P. L. 2, 811. forewarn thee, shun his d. arrow
P. L. 3, 221. draw the d. forfeiture
P. L. 4, 99. where wounds of d. hate have
P. L. 9, 982. nor yet on him found d., he yet lives
P. L. 11, 446. and d. pale groaned out his soul
S. A. 19. like a d. swarm of hornets armed
S. A. 623. my tormentors, armed with d. stings
C. 567. sweet thou sing'st; how near the d. snare
H. 6. that he our d. forfeit should release
**Deaf.**—S. A. 249. but they persisted d.
S. A. 960. more d. to prayers than winds and seas
**Deafening.**—P. L. 2, 520. with d. shout

**Deal.**—P. L. 6, 125. hath to *d.* with force
P. L. 11, 676. who thus *d.* death inhumanly
P. L. 12, 483. will they not *d.* worse with his
S. A. 705. so *d.* not with this once thy glorious
C. 683. and harshly *d.* like an ill borrower
**Dealing.**—S. A. 1529. *d.* dole among his foes
**Deals.**—P. L. 4, 70. it *d.* eternal woe
**Dealt.**—P. L. 4, 68. love *d.* equally to all
P. L. 12, 484. followers than with him they *d.*
P. R. 2, 133. than when I *d.* with Adam
S. A. 283. had *d.* with Jephthah, who by
S. A. 707. what do I beg? how hast thou *d.*
**Dear.**—P. L. 2, 817. *d.* daughter! since thou
P. L. 2, 818. the *d.* pledge of dalliance had
P. L. 3, 216. dwells in all Heaven charity so *d.*
P. L. 3, 276. well thou knowest how *d.*
P. L. 3, 297. ransomed with his own *d.* life
P. L. 3, 403. no sooner did thy *d.* and only Son
P. L. 3, 531. the Promised Land to God so *d.*
P. L. 4, 101. so should I purchase *d.*
P. L. 4, 222. of good bought *d.* by knowing ill
P. L. 4, 486. henceforth an individual solace *d.*
P. L. 4, 756. relations *d.*, and all the charities
P. L. 5, 673. companion *d.?* Whatsleep can close
P. L. 6, 419. to be overpowered, companions *d.*
P. L. 8, 580. seem such *d.* delight beyond all
P. L. 9, 228. above all living creatures *d.*
P. L. 9, 289. misthought of her to thee so *d.*
P. L. 9, 832. so *d.* I love him, that with him all
P. L. 9, 965. from whose *d.* side I boast
P. L. 9, 970. separate us, linked in love so *d.*
P. L. 10, 238. provides for us his offspring *d.*
P. L. 10, 330. but those his children *d.*
P. L. 10, 349. to meet him came, his offspring *d.*
C. 564. of my most honoured Lady, your *d.* sister
C. 790. enjoy your *d.* wit, and gay rhetoric
C. 864. listen for *d.* honour's sake
C. 879. by dead Parthenope's *d.* tomb
C. 902. goddess *d.*, we implore thy ... hand
C. 1005. holds his *d.* Psyche sweet entranced
L. 6. bitter constraint, and sad occasion *d.*
L. 173. through the *d.* might of Him that walked
W. S. 5. *d.* son of memory, great heir of fame
S. A. 894. for which our country is a name so *d.*
C. 453. so *d.* to Heaven is saintly chastity
**Dear-bought.**—P. L. 10, 742. Paradise, *d.-b.*
**Dearer.**—P. L. 4, 412. of all these joys, *d.*
P. L. 5, 95. best image of myself, and *d.* half
**Dearest.**—P. L. 3, 226. his *d.* mediation
P. L. 8, 426. collateral love, and *d.* amity
L. 107. who hath reft, quoth he, my *d.* pledge
P. 10. which on our *d.* Lord did seize ere long
**Dearly.**—P. L. 3, 300. so *d.* to redeem what hellish
P. L. 4, 87. they little know how *d.* I abide
P. L. 9, 909. converse, and love so *d.* joined
S. A. 933. though *d.* to my cost
**Dearly-bought.**—S. A. 1660. O *d.-b.* revenge
**Dearly-loved.**—V. Ex. 24. did slay his *d.-l.* mate
**Dearth.**—P. L. 8, 322. fear here no *d.*
P. L. 12, 161. in time of *d.*, a son whose worthy
**Death.**—P. L. 1, 3. brought *d.* into the world
P. L. 1, 555. with dread of *d.* to flight or foul
P. L. 2, 621. bogs, dens, and shades of *d.*
P. L. 2, 622. a universe of *d.*, which God
P. L. 2, 624. all life dies, *d.* lives, and nature
P. L. 2, 787. I fled, and cried out, *D.*
P. L. 2, 789. and back resounded *D.*
**P. L. 2, 804. grim *D.* my son and foe**
P. L. 2, 840. thou and *D.* shall dwell at ease
P. L. 2, 845. and *D.* grinned horrible
P. L. 2, 854. *D.* ready stands to interpose
P. L. 2, 1024. sin and *d.* amain following
P. L. 3, 212. the rigid satisfaction, *d.* for *d.*
P. L. 3, 223. adjudged to *D.* and Hell
P. L. 3, 241. on me let *D.* wreak all his rage
P. L. 3, 245. though now to *D.* I yield
P. L. 3, 252. *D.* his *d.'s* wound shall then
P. L. 3, 259. *D.* last, and with his carcase
P. L. 3, 299. giving to *d.*, and dying to redeem
P. L. 4, 197. but sat devising *d.* to them
**P. L. 4, 221. and next to life, our *d.***

P. L. 4, 425. so near grows *d.* to life
P. L. 4, 427. God hath pronounced it *d.*
P. L. 4, 518. can it be sin to know? can it be *d.*
P. L. 7, 545. *d.* is the penalty imposed
P. L. 7, 547. and her black attendant *D.*
P. L. 9, 12. and her shadow *D.*, and Misery, *D.'s*
P. L. 9, 283. as we, not capable of *d.* or pain
P. L. 9, 685. those rigid threats of *d.*
P. L. 9, 695. *d.* denounced, whatever thing *d.*
P. L. 9, 702. your fear itself of *d.* removes
P. L. 9, 714. *d.* to be wished, though threatened
P. L. 9, 760. but if *d.* bind us with after-bands
P. L. 9, 767. for us alone was *d.* invented?
P. L. 9, 775. of God or *d.*, of law or penalty
P. L. 9, 792. and knew not eating *d.*
P. L. 9, 827. and *d.* ensue?
P. L. 9, 830. a *d.* to think!
P. L. 9, 901. deflowered, and now to *d.* devote
P. L. 9, 953. if *d.* consort with thee. *d.* is to me
P. L. 9, 969. rather than *d.*, or aught than *d.*
P. L. 9, 977. were it I thought *d.* menaced
P. L. 9, 984. not *d.*, but life augmented
P. L. 9, 989. and fear of *d.* deliver to the winds
P. L. 9, 993. displeasure for her sake, or *d.*
P. L. 9, 1167. willingly chose rather *d.* with
P. L. 10, 49. *d.* denounced that day
P. L. 10, 210. and the instant stroke of *d.*
P. L. 10, 230. the gates of Hell sat Sin and *D.*
P. L. 10, 234. who thus now to *D.*
P. L. 10, 251. for *D.* from Sin no power can
P. L. 10, 269. and taste the savour of *d.*
P. L. 10, 278. designed for *d.* the following day
P. L. 10, 294. the aggregated soil *D.* with his
P. L. 10, 304. now fenceless world, forfeit to *d.*
P. L. 10, 407. through Sin to *D.* exposed
P. L. 10, 473. by Sin and *D.* a broad way now
P. L. 10, 490. to Sin and *D.* a prey and so to us
P. L. 10, 588. behind her *D.* close following
P. L. 10, 591. Satan sprung, all-conquering *D.*
P. L. 10, 635. both Sin and *D.* and yawning
P. L. 10, 709. the irrational *D.* introduced
P. L. 10, 731. now *d.* to hear! for what can
P. L. 10, 774. why am I mocked with *d.*
P. L. 10, 788. knows but I shall die a living *d.*
P. L. 10, 797. without end on Man, whom *d.*
P. L. 10, 798. can he make deathless *d.?*
P. L. 10, 809. but say that *d.* be not one stroke
P. L. 10, 815. both *D.* and I am found eternal
P. L. 10, 852. cursed his creation; *D.* as oft
P. L. 10, 854. why comes not *D.*, said he
P. L. 10, 858. but *D.* comes not at call
P. L. 10, 962. since this day's *d.* denounced
P. L. 10, 981. devoured by *d.* at last
P. L. 10, 989. so *D.* shall be deceived his glut
P. L. 10, 1001. let us seek *D.*, or he not found
P. L. 10, 1004. fears that show no end but *d.*
P. L. 10, 1008. so much of *d.* her thoughts
P. L. 10, 1020. covet *d.*, as utmost end of misery
P. L. 10, 1024. much more I fear lest *d.*
P. L. 10, 1028. to make *d.* in us live
P. L. 10, 1037. will be lost by *d.*
P. L. 10, 1050. was meant by *d.* that day
P. L. 11, 36. and for these my *d.* shall pay
P. L. 11, 40. though sad, till *d.* his doom
P. L. 11, 61. I provided *d.*; so *d.* becomes
P. L. 11, 157. the bitterness of *d.* is past
P. L. 11, 168. that I, who first brought *d.*
P. L. 11, 197. from *d.* released some days
P. L. 11, 252. and *D.*, then due by sentence
P. L. 11, 258. redeem thee quite from *D.'s*
P. L. 11, 268. stroke worse than of *d.*
P. L. 11, 462. but have I now seen *D.*
P. L. 11, 466. *D.* thou hast seen in his first
P. L. 11, 468. shapes of *D.*, and many are the
P. L. 11, 491. triumphant *D.* his dart
P. L. 11, 529. to *D.*, and mix with our
P. L. 11, 537. not harshly plucked, for *d.*
P. L. 11, 547. I fly not *d.*, nor would prolong
P. L. 11, 601. those were of hate and *d.*, or pain
P. L. 11, 676. *D.'s* ministers, .. who thus deal *d.*
P. L. 11, 709. climes of bliss, exempt from *d.*

P. L. 12, 392. to give thee thy *d*.'*s* wound
P. L. 12, 398. penalty of *d*., and suffering *d*.
P. L. 12, 406. a reproachful life and cursed *d*.
P. L. 12. 412. judged, and to *d*. condemned
P. L. 12, 420. *D*. over him no power shall long
P. L. 12, 424. man from *d*. redeems, his *d*.
P. L. 12, 428. the *d*. thou shouldst have died
P. L. 12, 431. defeating Sin and *D*. his two
P. L. 12, 433. than temporal *d*. shall bruise
P. L. 12, 434. a *d*., like sleep, a gentle wafting
P. L. 12, 445. *d*. like that which the Redeemer
P. L. 12, 494. not afraid, though to the *d*.
P. L. 12, 571. to the faithful, of the life gate *d*.
P. R. 1 159. to conquer Sin and *D*. the two
P. R. 1, 264. hard assay, even to the *d*.
P. R. 3, 85. till conqueror *D*. discover them
P. R. 3, 87. violent or shameful *d*. their due
P. R. 3, 98. for truth's sake suffering *d*.
P. R. 4, 305. pain or torment, and life
P. R. 4, 388. and stripes, and lastly cruel *d*.
S. A. 100. to live a life half dead, a living *d*.
S. A. 104. by privilege of *d*. and burial
S. A. 138. spurned them to *d*. by troops
S. A. 288. without reprieve, adjudged to *d*.
S. A. 485. by pains and slaveries, worse than *d*.
S. A. 575. oft-invocated *d*. hasten the welcome
S. A. 630. to *d*.'*s* benumbing opinion as my only
S. A. 650. speedy *d*., the close of all my miseries
S. A. 1198. threatening cruel *d*., constrained
S. A. 1232. these dishonours, and not render *d*.
S. A. 1263. my speediest friend, by *d*. to rid me
S. A. 1513. blood, *d*., and deathful deeds, are in
S. A. 1572. but *d*., who sets all free, hath paid
S. A. 1579. *d*. to life is crown or shame
S. A. 1581. glorious hand gave Samson his *d*.'*s*
S. A. 1666. whose law in *d*. conjoined thee with
S. A. 1724. what may quiet us in a *d*. so noble
C. 562. might create a soul under the ribs of *D*.
C. 608. to a foul *d*., cursed as his life
S. 14, 3. this earthly load of *d*. called life
S. 19, 3. and that one talent which is *d*. to hide
S. 23, 4. rescued from *d*. by force, though pale
P. 20. yet more the stroke of *d*. he must abide
M. W. 10. to house with darkness and with *d*.
Cir. 18. were lost in *d*., till He, that dwelt above
T. 22. triumphing over *D*. and Chance, and thee
U. C. I. 1. here lies old Hobson; *D*. hath broke
U. C. I. 6. *D*. was half glad when he had got him
U. C. I. 9. and surely *D*. could never have
U. C. II. 11. gives all men life, gave him his *d*.
U. C. II. 26. were pressed to *d*. he cried more
V. Ex. 96. or Severn swift, guilty of maiden's *d*.
**Deathful.**—S. A. 1513. blood, death, and *d*.
**Deathless.**—P. L. 10, 775. to *d*. pain
P. L. 10, 798. can he make *d*. death?
C. 973. with a crown of *d*. praise
**Deaths.**—P. L. 9, 832. with him all *d*.
**Debar.**—P. L. 9, 236. as to *d*. us when we
**Debase.**—S. A. 999. God sent her to *d*. me
**Debased.**—P. L. 9, 487. so much hath Hell *d*.
P. L. 11, 510. to such unsightly sufferings be *d*.
S. A. 37. *d*. lower than a bond-slave
S. A. 1335. so *d*. with corporal servitude
**Debate.**—P. L. 2, 42. we now *d*.; who can
P. L. 2, 390. have ye judged, well ended long *d*.
P. L. 5, 681. new counsels to *d*. what doubtful
P. L. 6, 122. that he, who in *d*. of truth hath
P. L. 9, 87. him, after long *d*., irresolute
P. R. 1, 95. which admits no long *d*.
S. A. 863. only my love of thee held long *d*.
**Debel.**—P. R. 4, 605. of old thou didst *d*.
**Debonair.**—L'A. 24. so buxom, blithe, and *d*.
**Debt.**—P. L. 3, 246. yet that *d*. paid
P. L. 4, 52. in a moment quit the *d*. immense
S. A. 313. without taint of sin, or legal *d*.
S. A. 509. God will ... quit thee all His *d*.
**Decay.**—U. C. II. 5. sphere-metal, never to *d*.
**Decayed.**—P. L. 11, 843. face of deluge, as *d*.
**Deccan.**—P. L. 9, 1103. in Malabar or *D*.
**Deceit.**—P. L. 5, 243. but by *d*. and lies

P. L. 9, 772. to man, far from *d*. or guile
P. L 10, 1035. contrived against us this *d*.
**Deceitful.**—S. A. 202. of God to a *d*. woman
S. A. 537. in the lascivious lap of a *d*. concubine
**Deceivable.**—S. A. 350. O what not in man *d*.
S. A. 942. blind, and thereby *d*., in most things
**Deceive.**—P. L. 2, 189. or who *d*. his mind
P. L. 2, 461. to respite, or *d*., or slack the pain
P. L. 10, 6. or *d*. his heart omniscient
P. R. 2, 142. *d*. ye to persuasion over-sure
S. A. 750. to break all faith, all vows, *d*., betray
S. 2, 5. perhaps my semblance might *d*. the
**Deceived.**—P. L. 1, 35. *d*. the mother
P. L. 3, 130. man falls *d*. by the other first
P. L. 9, 404. O, much *d*., much failing, hapless
P. L. 9, 998. not *d*., but fondly overcome
P. L. 10, 496. in whose shape man I *d*.
P. L. 10, 564. not the touch, but taste *d*.
P. L. 10, 917. have offended, unhappily *d*.
P. L. 10, 990. so death shall be *d*. his glut
P. L. 11, 783. but I was far *d*., for now I see
P. R. 1, 52. lost paradise, *d*. by me
S. A. 211. erred, and by bad women been *d*.
C. 221. was I *d*., or did a sable cloud
**Deceiver.**—C. 696. enchantments, foul *d*.
**Deceiving.**—H. 175. in words *d*.
**Decencies.**—P. L. 8, 601. those thousand *d*.
**Decent.**—P. L. 3, 644. before his *d*. steps
Il P. 36. over thy *d*. shoulders drawn
**Deception.**—P. L. 9, 362. and fall into *d*.
**Decide.**—P. L. 6, 303. fit to *d*. the empire
S. A. 1176. by combat to *d*. whose god is God
**Decision.**—P. L. 2, 908. by *d*. more embroils
**Deck.**—P. L. 5, 189. whether to *d*. with clouds
C. 717. the smooth-haired silk to *d*. her sons
**Decked.**—P. L. 4, 710. espoused Eve *d*.
P. L. 5, 379. with flowerets *d*. and fragrant
P. L. 7, 478. in all the liveries *d*. of summer's
L. 120. the wood-nymphs, *d*. with daisies trim
V. Ex. 26. till thou hast *d*. them in thy best
**Declare.**—P. L. 5, 158. *d*. thy goodness
P. L. 5, 603. whom I *d*. my only Son
P. L. 6, 677. and to all power on him
P. L. 8, 603. which *d*. unfeigned union of mind
P. L. 10, 462. *d*. ye now, returned successful
P. R. 1, 445. among them to *d*. his providence
P. R. 4, 337. *d*. that rather Greece from us
**Declared.**—P. L. 4, 300. *d*. absolute rule
P. L. 5, 765. Messiah was *d*. in sight of heaven
P. L. 7, 181. when such was heard *d*. the
P. L. 9, 611. and worship thee of right *d*.
P. L. 9, 658. yet lords *d*. of all in earth
P. L. 10, 401. chiefly on man, sole lord of all *d*.
P. L. 11, 250. but his coming thus *d*.
P. R. 1, 385. whom I know *d*. the Son of God
P. R. 2, 4. Jesus, Messiah, Son of God, *d*.
P. R. 3, 119. nor exception hath *d*.
P. R. 4, 520. in some respect far higher so *d*.
**Declares.**—P. L. 4, 619. which *d*. his dignity
P. L. 4, 746. as impure what God *d*. pure
P. R. 2, 252. which *d*. nature hath need
**Declarest.**—P. L. 6, 728. well pleased, *d*.
**Declaring.**—P. L. 9, 968. *d*. thee resolved
**Decline.**—P. L. 4, 792. the sun's *d*. arrived
P. L. 5, 370. the sun more cool *d*.
P. L. 12, 97. yet sometimes nations will *d*.
**Declined.**—P. L. 4, 353. for the sun, *d*.
P. L. 10, 99. brought to their ears, while day *d*.
S. A. 727. with head *d*., like a fair flower
**Decree.**—P. R. 2, 198. and omnipotent *d*.
P. L. 3, 115. disposed by absolute *d*., or high
P. L. 3, 126. revoke the high *d*. unchangeable
P. L. 3, 659. here art likeliest by supreme *d*.
P. L. 5, 602. hear my *d*., which unrevoked
P. L. 5, 674. remember'st what *d*. of yesterday
P. L. 5, 717. banded to oppose his high *d*.
P. L. 5, 774. not merely titular, since by *d*.
P. L. 5, 814. condemn the just *d*. of God
P. L. 6, 683. whose hand what by *d*. I do

P. L. 10, 43. no *d.* of mine concurring
P. L. 10, 68. Father Eternal, thine is to *d.*
P. L. 10, 772. to execute what his *d.* fixed
P. L. 11, 47. all thy request was my *d.*
P. L. 11, 96. to remove him I *d.*, and send him
P. L. 11, 311. prayer against his absolute *d.*
S. A. 85. why am I thus bereaved thy prime *d.*?
**Decreed.**—P. L. 2, 160. we are *d.*, reserved
P. L. 3, 116. they themselves *d.* their own
P. L. 3, 172. all as my eternal purpose hath *d.*
P. L. 9, 151. what he *d.*, he effected
P. R. 3, 186. the Father in his purpose hath *d.*
P. R. 3, 188. what if he hath *d.* that I shall
**Decrees.**—P. L. 5, 884. other *d.* against thee
P. L. 10, 644. righteous are thy *d.*
P. L. 10, 953. if prayers could alter high *d.*
P. R. 1, 55. long the *d.* of heaven delay
**Decrepit.**—P. L. 10, 655. to call *d.* winter
S. A. 69. dungeon, or beggary, or *d.* age
**Dee.**—V. Ex. 98. Tyne, or ancient hallowed *D.*
**Deed.**—P. L. 5, 66. vouched with a *d.* so bold
P. L. 5, 549. to be, both will and *d.*, created free
P. L. 6, 237. no unbecoming *d.* that argued
P. L. 9, 921. bold *d.* thou hast presumed
P. L. 10, 142. her doing seemed to justify the *d.*
P. L. 11, 461. for the *d.* and for the cause
P. R. 3, 103. the *d.* becomes unpraised
S. A. 826. I give my folly, take to thy wicked *d.*
S. A. 1267. their own ruin who attempt the *d.*
L. 83. as he pronounces lastly on each *d.*
S. 8, 3. if *d.* of honour did thee ever please
**Deeds.**—P. L. 1, 130. and in dreadful *d.* fearless
P. L. 2, 116. but to nobler *d.* timorous
P. L. 2, 484. men should boast their specious *d.*
P. L. 2, 549. their own heroic *d.* and hapless fall
P. L. 2, 722. now great *d.* had been achieved
P. L. 2, 739. tell thee yet by *d.* what it intends
P. L. 3, 292. both righteous and unrighteous *d.*
P. L. 3, 337. golden days, fruitful of golden *d.*
P. L. 3, 454. fit retribution, empty as their *d.*
P. L. 4, 26. of worse *d.* worse sufferings
P. L. 4, 394. excused his devilish *d.*
P. L. 4, 990. dreadful *d.* might have ensued
P. L. 5, 113. ill matching words and *d.*
P. L. 5, 865. shall teach us highest *d.*
P. L. 6, 66. heroic ardour to adventurous *d.*
P. L. 6, 112. the mightiest, born on highest *d.*
P. L. 6, 170. as both their *d.* compared this day
P. L. 6, 240. *d.* of eternal fame were done
P. L. 6, 283. threats to awe whom yet with *d.*
P. L. 6, 354. in other parts like *d.* deserved
P. L. 10, 354. these are thy magnific *d.*
P. L. 11, 256. one bad act with many *d.*
P. L. 11, 428. to bring forth more violent *d.*
P. L. 11, 659. slaughter and gigantic *d.*
P. L. 11, 796. raise, out of friendship, hostile *d.*
P. L. 12, 161. a son whose worthy *d.* raise him
P. L. 12, 322. for piety renowned and puissant *d.*
P. L. 12, 582. only add *d.* to thy knowledge
P. R. 1, 14. to tell of *d.* above heroic
P. R. 1, 215. victorious *d.* flamed in my heart
P. R. 1, 233. by matchless *d.* express thy
P. R. 1, 386. and behold thy godlike *d.*
P. R. 2, 139. amplitude of mind to greatest *d.*
P. R. 2, 438. in lowest poverty to highest *d.*
P. R. 3, 16. to *d.* that might require the array
P. R. 3, 91. by *d.* of peace, by wisdom eminent
P. R. 4, 99. appearing, and beginning noble *d.*
S. A. 247. used no ambition to commend my *d.*
S. A. 248. *d.* themselves though mute
S. A. 276. to heap ingratitude on worthiest *d.*
S. A. 369. God hath chosen once to worthiest *d.*
S. A. 372. but for honour's sake of former *d.*
S. A. 638. he led me on to mightiest *d.*
S. A. 875. brought forth other *d.*
S. A. 893. worse than hostile *d.*, violating
S. A. 898. but by ungodly *d.*, the contradiction
S. A. 973. with contrary blast proclaims most *d.*
S. A. 1043. folly and shameful *d.*
S. A. 1513. death, and deathful *d.* are in that
S. 9, 10. to fill thy .. lamp with *d.* of light

**Deem.**—P. L. 6, 429. of future we may *d.* him
P. L. 8, 599. with mysterious reverence, I *d.*
P. L. 12, 534. will *d.* in outward rites
P. R. 3, 150. glory as thou wilt, said he, so *d.*
P. R. 4, 44. city which thou seest no other *d.*
**Deemed.**—P. L. 2, 46. eternal to be *d.* equal
P. L. 2, 748. once *d.* so fair in heaven
P. L. 3, 469. he, who to be *d.* a god, leaped
P. L. 7, 152. my damage fondly *d.*, I can repair
P. L. 9, 29. the only argument heroic *d.*
P. L. 9, 683. highest agents, *d.* however wise
P. L. 12, 567. by things *d.* weak subverting
P. R. 1, 23. from Nazareth the son of Joseph *d.*
S. A. 1705. vigorous most when .. unactive *d.*
**Deeming.**—P. L. 1, 205. *d.* some island
**Deep.**—P. L. 1, 28. nor the *d.* tract of Hell
P. L. 1, 126. but racked with *d.* despair
P. L. 1, 152. or do his errands in the gloomy *D.*
P. L. 1, 177. through the vast and boundless *d.*
P. L. 1, 314. the hollow *d.* of hell resounded
P. L. 1, 601. but his face *d.* scars of thunder
P. L. 2, 12. for, since no *d.* within her gulf can
P. L. 2, 79. and pursued us through the *d.*
P. L. 2, 87. this abhorred *d.* to utter woe
P. L. 2, 131. oft on the bordering *d.* encamp
P. L. 2, 167. and besought the *d.* to shelter us
P. L. 2, 262. *d.* world of darkness do we dread?
P. L. 2, 267. from whence *d.* thunders roar
P. L. 2, 302. *d.* on his front engraven
P. L. 2, 344. or siege, or ambush from the *d.*
P. L. 2, 382. could spring so *d.* a malice
P. L. 2, 392. which from the lowest *d.*
P. L. 2, 421. pondering the danger with *d.*
P. L. 2, 431. with reason hath *d.* silence
P. L. 2, 578. Acheron of sorrow, black and *d.*
P. L. 2, 591. *d.* snow and ice, a gulf profound
P. L. 2, 634. with level wing the *d.*; then soars
P. L. 2, 773. of heaven down into this *D.*
P. L. 2, 829. to tread the unfounded *d.*
P. L. 2, 891. the secrets of the hoary *d.*
P. L. 2, 934. ten thousand fathom *d.*
P. L. 2, 961. spread wide on the wasteful *d.*
P. L. 2, 994. silence through the frighted *D.*
P. L. 3, 11. world of waters dark and *d.*
P. L. 3, 586. invisible virtue even of the *d.*
P. L. 3, 629. or fixed in cogitation *d.*
P. L. 3, 707. and hid their causes *d.*
P. L. 4, 76. and in the lowest *d.*, a lower *d.*
P. L. 4, 99. deadly hate have pierced so *d.*
P. L. 4, 123. *d.* malice to conceal, couched with
P. L. 4, 574. hath ventured from the *d.*, to raise
P. L. 4, 674. though unbeheld in *d.* of night
P. L. 5, 614. falls into utter darkness, *d.*
P. L. 5, 666. *d.* malice thence conceiving
P. L. 5, 872. and as the sound of waters *d.*
P. L. 6, 326. *d.* entering, shared all his right
P. L. 6, 356. pierced the *d.* array of Moloch
P. L. 6, 478. *d.* under ground, materials dark
P. L. 6, 482. these, in their dark nativity. the *d.*
P. L. 6, 554. with shadowing squadrons *d.*
P. L. 6, 652. the weight of mountains buried *d.*
P. L. 6, 716. Heaven's bounds into the utter *d.*
P. L. 6, 862. disclosed into the wasteful *d.*
P. L. 6, 869. cast too *d.* her dark foundations
P. L. 6, 898. and the *d.* fall of those too high
P. L. 7, 52. filled with admiration and *d.* muse
P. L. 7, 103. nature from the unapparent *d.*
P. L. 7, 134. through the *d.* into his place
P. L. 7, 166. and bid the *d.* within appointed
P. L. 7, 168. boundless the *d.*, because I am
P. L. 7, 216. ye troubled waves, and thou *D.*
P. L. 7, 245. sprung from the *d.*, and from her
P. L. 7, 289. a hollow bottom, broad and *d.*
P. L. 7, 303. and on the washy ooze, *d.* channels
P. L. 7, 413. the *d.* stretched like a promontory
P. L. 9, 83. and with inspection *d.*
P. L. 9, 602. to speculations high or *d.*
P. L. 10, 245. beyond this *d.*; whatever draws
P. L. 10, 299. *d.* to the roots of Hell
P. L. 10, 301. over the foaming *d.* high-arched
P. L. 10, 471. vast, unbounded *d.* of horrible

P. L. 10, 677. as *d*. as Capricorn
P. L. 10, 844. from *d*. to deeper plunged
P. L. 11, 417. so *d*. the power of these
P. L. 11, 489. dire was the tossing, *d*. the groans
P. L. 11, 749. their pomp *d*. under water rolled
P. L. 11, 826. all fountains of the *d*. broke up
P. L. 11, 848. stole with soft foot towards the *d*.
P. L. 12, 578. all secrets of the *d*., all nature's
P. R. 1, 90. fierce thunder drove us to the *D*.
P. R. 1, 108. surprised with *d*. dismay
P. R. 1, 190. and his *d*. thoughts, the better to
P. R. 1, 361. from bliss to the bottomless *D*.
P. R. 3, 227. perhaps thou linger'st in *d*.
P. R. 3, 391. and projects *d*. of enemies of aids
P. R. 4, 417. pines though rooted *d*. as high
P. R. 4, 631. command them down into the *D*.
S. A. 1568. should pierce too *d*.
C. 23. the unadorned bosom of the *d*.
C. 523. *d*. skilled in all his mother's witcheries
C. 733. would so imblaze the forehead of the *d*.
C. 1000. waxing well of his *d*. wound
A. 61. but else in *d*. of night when drowsiness
L. 50. when the remorseless *d*.
S. 21, 5. to-day *d*. thoughts resolve with me
H. 69. the stars, with *d*. amaze, stand fixed
H. 123. and cast the dark foundations *d*.
H. 130. let the base of Heaven's *d*. organ blow
H. 156. must thunder through the *d*.
Cir. 9. seas wept from our *d*. sorrow
W. S. 12. those Delphic lines with *d*.impression
V. Ex. 33. such where the *d*.transported mind
**Deeper.**—P. L. 3, 201. stumble on, and *d*. fall
P. L. 10, 844. I find no way, from deep to *d*.
P. L. 12, 432. fix far *d*. in his head their stings
**Deepest.**—P. L. 3, 678. rebel foes to *d*. Hell
P. L. 5, 542. and so from Heaven to *d*. Hell
V. Ex. 22. which *d*. spirits and choicest wits
**Deep-throated.**—P. L. 6, 586. *d.-t.* engines
**Deep-vaulted.**—P. R. 1, 116. Hell's *d.-v.* den
**Deep-versed.**—P. R. 4, 327. *d.-v.* in books
**Defaced.**—P. L. 9, 901. *d*., deflowered
P. L. 11, 522. his likeness, by themselves *d*.
**Defamed.**—S. A. 977. all posterity may stand *d*.
**Defaming.**—P. L. 4, 746. *d*. as impure
**Default.**—P. L. 9, 1145. to my *d*., or will
S. A. 45. fulfilled but through mine own *d*.
**Defeat.**—P. L. 1, 135. overthrow and foul *d*.
P. L. 6, 138. have raised incessant armies to *d*.
**Defeated.**—P. L. 6, 606. back *d*. to return
P. L. 11, 254. *d*. of his seizure many days
P. R. 1, 6. in all his wiles, *d*. and repulsed
S. A. 1571. Oh, all my hopes *d*. to free him hence
**Defeating.**—P. L. 12, 431. *d*. Sin and Death
**Defeats.**—S. A. 1278. feats of war *d*.
**Defect.**—P. L. 10, 891. this fair *d*. of nature
**Defective.**—P. L. 8, 425. in unity *d*.
**Defects.**—P. L. 8, 419. to help or solace his *d*.
**Defence.**—P. L. 2, 362. to their *d*. who hold
P. L. 3, 166. and blasphemed without *d*.
P. L. 5, 731. and all employ in our *d*.
P. L. 6, 337. and strong, who interposed *d*.
P. L. 6, 467. or arm ourselves with like *d*.
P. L. 9, 325. we not endued single with like *d*.
S. A. 560. what boots it at one gate to make *d*.
S. A. 1286. who, surprised, lose their *d*.
C. 42. I was despatched for their *d*. and guard
C. 489. *d*. is a good cause, and Heaven be for us
S. 22, 11. in Liberty's *d*., my noble task
**Defenceless.**—P. L 10, 815. my *d*. head
C. 414. my sister is not so *d*. left as you imagine
S. 8, 2. whose chance on these *d*. doors may seize
**Defend.**—P. L. 2, 1000. which is left so to *d*.
P. L. 7, 37. nor could the Muse *d*. her son
P. L. 11, 657. from the wall *d*. with dart
P. L. 12, 483. shall guide his people, who *d*.
P. R. 1, 306. to *d*. him from the dew
S. A. 1179. he will accept thee to *d*. His cause
C. 396. to save her blossoms, and *d*. her fruit
**Defended.**—P. L. 11, 86. of that *d*. fruit
S. A. 235. *d*. Israel from the Ammonite
**Defends.**—P. L. 12, 207. darkness *d*. between

P. R. 2, 370. *d*. the touching of these viands
**Defensive.**—P. L. 6, 393. host, *d*. scarce
S.A.1038.far within *d*.arms a cleaving mischief
**Defer.**—P. L. 9, 586. I resolved not to *d*.
S. A.474. will not long *d*. to vindicate the glory
S. A. 1557. tell us the sum, the circumstance *d*.
**Defiance.**—P. L. 1, 669. *d*. toward the vault
P. L. 2, 697. and breath'st *d*. here and scorn
P. L. 4, 873. stand firm, for in his look *d*. lours
P. L. 12, 74. his tower intends siege and *d*.
S. A. 1073. his habit carries peace, his brow *d*.
V. Ex.44. in Heaven's *d*.mustering all his waves
**Deficience.**—P. L. 8, 416. is no *d*. found.
**Deficient.**—P. L. 9, 345. imperfect or *d*. left
**Defied.**—P. L. 1, 765. *d*. the best of Panim
P. L. 6, 130. and thus securely him *d*.
P. L. 6, 357. Moloch, furious king, who him *d*.
**Defies.**—S. A. 1222. who now *d*. thee thrice
**Defile.**—S. A. 1368. joins not, outward acts *d*.
**Defilement.**—C. 466. lets in *d*. to the inward
**Deflowered.**—P. L. 9, 901. defaced, *d*.
**Deform.**—P. L. 2, 706. more dreadful and *d*.
P. L. 11, 494. sight so *d*. what heart of rock
**Deformed.**—P. L. 6, 387. *d*. rout entered
P. R. 3, 86. brutish vices, and *d*.
S.A.699.painful diseases and *d*., in crude old age
**Deformities.**—P. L. 11, 513. such *d*. be free
H. 44. should look so near upon her foul *d*.
**Defy.**—P. L. 1, 49. who durst *d*. the Omnipotent
S. A. 1175. *d*. thee to the trial of mortal fight
**Degenerate.**—P. L. 11, 806. shall turn *d*.
P. R. 4, 144. thus *d*., by themselves enslaved
C. 475. to a *d* and degraded state
**Degenerately.**—S. A. 419. how *d*. I served
**Degrade.**—P. L. 3, 304. lessen or *d*. thine own
S. A. 687. not only dost *d*. them, or remit
**Degraded.**—P. L. 8, 552. her presence falls *d*.
P. L. 11, 501. mankind, to what fall *d*.
P. R. 4, 312. *d*. by himself, on grace depending
C. 475. to a degenerate and *d*. state
**Degree.**—P. L. 5, 490. differing but in *d*.
P. L. 5, 707. and high was his *d*. in heaven
P. L. 8, 176. in what state, condition, or *d*.
P. L. 8, 417. not so is man, but in *d*. the cause
P. L. 9, 599. to *d*. of reason in my inward
P. L. 9, 883. different *d*. disjoin us
P. L. 9 934. higher *d*. of life
P. R. 4, 516. in what *d*. or meaning thou art
S. A. 414. the base *d*. to which I now am fallen
S. A. 1607. seats where all the lords, and each *d*.
**Degrees.**—P. L. 3, 502. ascending by *d*.
P. L. 5, 473. with various forms, various *d*.
P. L. 5, 591. of hierarchies, of orders, and *d*.
P. L. 5, 750. and Thrones in their triple *d*.
P. L. 5, 792. for orders and *d*. jar not with
P. L. 5, 838. by him created in their bright *d*.
P. L. 7, 157. till, by *d*. of merit raised, they open
P. L. 10, 669. the poles of earth twice ten *d*.
C. 462. and turns it by *d*. to the soul's essence
**Deified.**—P. L. 8, 431. union, or communion, *d*.
**Deify.**—P. L. 1, 112. and *d*. his power
**Deign.**—P. L. 7, 84. *d*. to descend now lower
P. L. 7, 569. will *d*. to visit oft the dwellings
P. L. 12, 281. among whom God will *d*.
P. R. 2, 336. only *d*. to sit and eat
S. A.1226. fight with thee no man of arms will *d*.
Il P. 56. 'less Philomel will *d*. a song
**Deigned.**—P. L. 5, 221. that *d*. to travel
P. L. 5, 364. thou hast *d*. awhile to want
P. L. 8, 202. sufferance and thy wonted favour *d*.
**Deigns.**—P. L. 5, 59. *d*. none to ease thy load
P. L. 9, 21. who *d*. her nightly visitation.
**Deities.**—P. L. 1, 373. devils to adore for *d*.
P. L. 2, 11. Powers and Dominions, *D*. of heaven
P. L. 6, 157. in synod meet their *d*.
P. R. 3, 416. the *d*. of Egypt, Baal next
P. R. 4, 340. the vices of their *d*., and their own
C. 29. he quarters to his blue-haired *d*.
**Deity.**—P. L. 3, 187. the incensed *D*., while
P. L. 5, 724. what anciently we claim of *d*.
P. L. 5, 806. with more zeal adored the *D*.

P. L. 6, 682. is beheld visibly, what by *D.* I am
P. L. 6, 750. the chariot of paternal *D.*
P. L. 7, 142. the seat of *D.* supreme
P. L. 9, 167. that to the height of *d.* aspired
P. L. 9, 885. and I then too late renounce *d.*
P. L. 10, 65. blazed forth unclouded *D.*
P. L. 11, 149. by prayer the offended *D.*
P. L. 12, 15. in their minds fearing the *D.*
S. A. 464. his *d.* comparing and preferring
S. A. 899. the contradiction of their own *d.*
A. 25. this clime had held a *d.* so unparalleled
A. 93. clad in splendour as befits her *d.*
D. F. I. 10. he thought it touched his *d.* full near
V. Ex. 35 look in and see each blissful *d.*

**Deject.**—P. R. 2, 219. her female pride *d.*
S. A. 213. *d.* not, then, so overmuch thyself
**Dejected.**—S. A. 338. now in low *d.* state
**Dejection.**—P. L. 11, 301. *d.* and despair
**Delay.**—P. L. 2, 60. who reigns by our *d.*
P. L. 3, 635. might work him danger or *d.*
P. L. 4, 163. with such *d.* well pleased
P. L. 4, 311. and sweet, reluctant, amorous *d.*
P. L. 7, 101. and longer will *d.* to hear thee tell
P. L. 9, 675. as no *d.* of preface brooking
P. L. 10, 163. Lord God heard, without *d.*
P. L. 12, 223. also shall they gain by their *d.*
P. L. 12, 615. but now lead on, in me is no *d.*
P. R. 1, 56. long the decrees of Heaven *d.*
S. A. 1344. my message … brooks no *d.*
S. A. 1395. come without *d.*
**Delayed.**—P. L. 5, 247. nor *d.* winged saint
P. L. 9, 844. in her return, so long *d.*
P. L. 11, 492. shook, but *d.* to strike, though oft
C. 494. whose artful strains have oft *d.*
**Delays.**—P. L. 1, 208. and wished morn *d.*
P. L. 10, 771. why *d.* his hand to execute
P. R. 2, 95. but where *d.* he now ? some great
**Delectable.**—P. L. 5, 629. change *d.*, not need
P. L. 7, 539. *d.* both to behold and taste
**Delia.**—P. L. 9, 387. or Dryad, or of *D.'s*
P. L. 9, 388. but *D.'s* self in gait surpassed
**Deliberate.**—P. L. 1, 554. instead of rage *d.*
**Deliberation.**—P. L. 2, 303. engraven *d.*
**Delicacies.**—P. L. 8, 526. these *d.* I mean
P. R. 2, 390. thy pompous *d.* I contemn
**Delicacy.**—P. L. 5, 333. choose for *d.* best
C. 681. for gentle usage, and soft *d.*
**Delicious.**—P. L. 2, 400. the soft *d.* air
P. L. 4, 132. where *d.* Paradise, now nearer
P. L. 4, 251. if true, here only, and of *d.* taste
P. L. 4, 422. in Paradise that bear *d.* fruit
P. L. 4, 729. this *d.* place
P. L. 5, 635. fruit of *d.* vines, the growth of
P. L. 7, 537. he brought thee into this *d.* grove
P. L. 9, 439. spot more *d.* than those gardens
P. L. 9, 1028. as meet is, after such *d.* fare
P. L. 10, 746. or here place in this *d.* garden
S. A. 541. desire of wine and all *d.* drinks
C. 704. and that which is not good is not *d.*
**Deliciously.**—P. L. 7, 491. feeds her husband *d.*
**Delight.**—P. L. 1, 11. Sion Hill *d.* thee more
P. L. 1, 160. but ever to do ill our sole *d.*
P. L. 2, 247. our task in Heaven, this our *d.*
P. L. 3, 168. in whom my soul hath chief *d.*
P. L. 3, 664. but chiefly Man, his chief *d.*
P. L. 3, 704. in remembrance always with *d.*
P. L. 4, 106. his new *d.*, mankind created
P. L. 4, 155. heart inspires vernal *d.* and joy
P. L. 4, 206. to all *d.* of human sense exposed
P. L. 4, 286. saw, undelighted all *d.*, all kind
P. L. 4, 497. he, in *d.* both of her beauty
P. L. 4, 894. soonest recompense dole with *d.*
P. L. 5, 19. last best gift, my ever new *d.*
P. L. 5, 400. for food and for *d.* hath caused
P. L. 6, 727. my exaltation, and my whole *d.*
P. L. 7, 330. might dwell or wander with *d.*
P. L. 8, 11. now heard with wonder, but *d.*
P. L. 8, 384. what harmony or true *d.*
P. L. 8, 391. fit to participate all rational *d.*
P. L. 8, 477. the spirit of love and amorous *d.*
P. L. 8, 524. find in all things else *d.* indeed

P. L. 8, 576. so adorn for thy *d.*
P. L. 8, 580. such dear *d.* beyond all other
P. L. 9, 114. with what *d.* could I have walked
P. L. 9, 242. to *d.*, he made us. and *d.* to reason
P. L. 9, 419. tendance or plantation for *d.*
P. L. 9, 449. each thing met conceives *d.*
P. L. 9, 454. and in her look sums all *d.*
P. L. 9, 468. mid Heaven, soon ended his *d.*
P. L. 9, 787. such *d.* till then, as seemed
P. L. 10, 272. so saying with *d.* he snuffed
P. L. 10, 941. his life so late and sole *d.*
P. L. 11, 533. nourishment, not gluttonous *d.*
P. L. 11, 596. Adam, soon inclined to admit *d.*
P. L. 12, 245. such *d.* hath God in men
P. R. 1, 208. made it my whole *d.*
P. R. 1, 481. what wonder, then, if I *d.* to hear
P. R. 2, 192. but these haunts *d.* not all
P. R. 2, 373. with sweet restorative *d.*
P. R. 2, 480. reigning can be no sincere *d.*
P. R. 3, 54. and what *d.* to be by such extolled
P. R. 4, 263. with *d.* received in brief
P. R. 4, 331. if I would *d.* my private hours
P. R. 4, 345. sown with aught of profit or *d.*
S. A. 71. and all her various objects of *d.*
S. A. 633. I was his nurseling once, and choice *d.*
S. A. 1490. it shall be my *d.* to tend his eyes
S. A. 1642. not without wonder or *d.* beheld
C. 262. but such a sacred and home-felt *d.*
C. 812. will bathe the drooping spirits in *d.*
C. 967. I have brought ye new *d.*
L'A. 91. sometimes, with secure *d.*
S. 23, 12. so clear, as in no face with more *d.*
V. Ex. 20. which takes our late fantastics with *d.*
**Delighted.**—P. L. 5, 545. with more *d.* ear
P. L. 5, 627. that God's own ear listens *d.*
P. L. 7, 571. the dwellings of just men *d.*
P. L. 8, 49. as not with such discourse *d.*
P. L. 9, 398. ardent look his eye pursued *d.*
**Delightful.**—P. L. 1, 467. whose *d.* seat
P. L. 4, 437. following our *d.* task to prune
P. L. 4, 643. when first on this *d.* land
P. L. 4, 652. nor rising sun on this *d.* land
P. L. 4, 692. all things to man's *d.* use
P. L. 9, 1023. we abstained from this *d.* fruit
**Delightfully.**—P. L. 10, 730. heard *d.*
**Delights.**—P. L. 4, 367. when all these *d.*
P. L. 4, 435. choice unlimited of manifold *d.*
P. L. 5, 431. varied his bounty so with new *d.*
P. L. 8, 600. so much *d.* me, as those graceful
S. A. 916. where other senses want not their *d.*
C. 846. that the shrewd meddling elf *d.* to make
L. 72. to scorn *d.*, and live laborious days
L'A. 151. these *d.*, if thou canst give
S. 20, 13. he who of those *d.* can judge and spare
**Delineate.**—P. L. 5, 572. I shall *d.* so
**Deliver.**—P. L. 4, 368. will vanish and *d.* ye
P. L. 9, 989. and fear of death *d.* to the winds
P. R. 3, 380. this offer sets before thee to *d*
P. R. 3, 404. I must *d.*, if I mean to reign
S. A. 39. should Israel from Philistian yoke *d.*
**Deliverance.**—P. L. 2, 465. seek *d.* for us
P. L. 3, 182. and to me owe all his *d.*
P. L. 6, 468. deserves no less than for *d.*
P. L. 12, 235. he shall achieve mankind's *d.*
P. L. 12, 600. the great *d.* by her seed to come
P. R. 2, 35. now, now, for sure, *d.* is at hand
P. R. 3, 374. or of thy brethren, those Ten
S. A. 225. I might begin Israel's *d.*
S. A. 246. *d.* offered
S. A. 292. but God's proposed *d.* not so
S. A. 603. to prosecute the means of thy *d.*
**Delivered.**—S. A. 437. as their god, who hath *d.*
S. A. 1158. and *d.* up into thy enemies' hand
S. A. 1184. and *d.* bound into our hands
U. C. II, 33. his letters are *d.* all and gone
**Deliverer.**—P. L. 6, 451. *d.* from new lords
P. L. 12, 149. that seed is meant thy great *D.*
P. L. 12, 479. but say, if our *D.* up to heaven
S. A. 40. ask for this great *d.* now, and find him
S. A. 274. His special favour raised as their *d.*
S. A. 279. their great *d.* contemned

S. A. 1214. me, their *d.* sent, would not receive
S. A. 1270. when God into the hands of their *d.*
S. A. 1289. making them each his own *d.*
**Deliverers.**—P. R. 3, 82. of mankind, *D.*
**Delivery.**—S. A. 1505. nor seem vain of his *d.*
S. A. 1575. hopeful of his *d.*, which now proves
**Dell.**—C. 312. bushy *d.* of this wild wood
**Delos.**—P. L. 5, 265. *D.* or Samos first
P. L. 10, 296. and fixed as firm as *D.*, floating
**Delphian.**—P. L. 1, 517. or on the *D.* cliff
**Delphic.**—W. S. 12. those *D.* lines with deep
**Delphos.**—P. R. 1, 458. at *D.* or elsewhere
H. 178. hollow shriek the steep of *D.* leaving
**Delude.**—P. L. 10, 557. though to *d.* them
P. L. 11, 125. man once more to *d.*
**Deluded.**—S. A. 396. thrice I *d.* her and turned
**Deluding.**—P. R. 1, 435. with double sense *d.*
Il P. 77. hence, vain *d.* joys, the brood of
**Deluge.**—P. L. 1, 68. and a fiery *d.*
P. L. 1, 354. came like a *d.* on the South
P. L. 11, 843. wrinkled the face of *d.*
**Delusion.**—P. R. 1, 443. given.. up to thy *d.*
P. R. 4, 319. or, by *d.* far worse
**Delusive.**—P. L. 9, 639. blazing with *d.* light
P. L. 10, 563. this, more *d.*, not the touch
**Demeanour.**—P. L. 4, 129. and mad *d.*
P. L. 4, 871. and fierce *d.* seems the Prince
P. L. 8, 59. with goddess-like *d.* forth she went
P. L. 11, 162. to whom thus Eve, with sad *d.*
**Demi-gods.**—P. L. 1, 796. a thousand *d.*
P. L. 9, 937. but to be Gods or Angels, *D.*
**Democracy.**—P. R. 4, 269. that fierce *d.*
**Demodocus.**—V. Ex. 48. such as the wise *D.*
**Demogorgon.**—P. L. 2, 965. name of *D.*
**Demoniac.**—P. L. 11, 485. *d.* phrenzy
P. R. 4, 628. from thy *d.* holds, possession foul
**Demonian.**—P. R. 2, 122. *d.* Spirits now
**Demons.**—Il P.93. and of those *d.* that are found
**Demur.**—P. L. 2, 431. and *d.* seized us
P. L. 9, 558. the latter I *d.*, for in their looks
**Demure.**—S. A. 1036. soft, modest, meek, *d.*
Il P. 32. sober, steadfast, and *d.*, all in robe
**Demurring.**—P. R. 1, 373. *d.*, I undertook
**Den.**—P. L. 1, 199. whom the *d.* by ancient
P. L. 2, 58. accept this dark opprobrious *d.*
P. L. 4, 342. in wood, or wilderness, forest, or *d.*
P. L. 7, 458. forest wild, in thicket, brake, or *d.*
P. L. 9, 185. yet in horrid shade or dismal *d.*
P. R. 1, 116. from Hell's deep-vaulted *d.*
C. 399. of miser's treasure by an outlaw's *d.*
**Denial.**—L. 18. with *d.* vain, and coy excuse
**Denied.**—P. L. 4, 137. and wild, access *d.*
P. L. 9, 240. from reason flow to brute *d.*
P. L. 9, 555. first at least of these I thought *d.*
P. L. 9, 767. or to us *d.* this intellectual food
L. 159. or whether thou, to our moist vows *d.*
S. 19, 7. doth God exact day labour, light *d.*
**Denies.**—P. L. 12, 173. lawless tyrant, who *d.*
**Denounce.**—P. L. 11, 106. and *d.* to them
**Denounced.**—P. L. 2, 106. and his look *d.*
P. L. 9, 695. of death *d.*, whatever thing death
P. L. 10, 49. death *d.* that day
P. L. 10, 210. the instant stroke of death, *d.*
P. L. 10, 853. since *d.* the day of his offence
P. L. 10, 962. since this day's death *d.*
S. A. 968. brand of infamy upon my name *d.*
**Denouncing.**—P. L. 11, 815. *d.* wrath
**Dens.**—P. L. 2, 621. caves, lakes, fens, bogs, *d.*
P. L. 9, 118. with forest crowned, rocks, *d.*
**Dense.**—P. L. 2, 948. through strait, rough, *d.*
**Deny.**—P. L. 5, 107. what we affirm or what *d.*
S. A. 881. who could *d.* thee nothing
C. 559. and wished she might *d.* her nature
V. Ex. 15. I pray thee then *d.* me not thy aid
**Depart.**—P. L. 6, 40. scorned thou didst *d.*
P. L. 8, 632. my signal to *d.*
P. L. 11, 356. confirmed ere thou from hence *d.*
P. L. 12, 192. submits to let his sojournats *d.*
P. L. 12, 557. instructed I shall hence *d.*
**Departed.**—P. L. 4, 839. *d.* from thee
**Departing.**—P. L. 10, 430. so he *d.* gave

P. L. 11, 315. afflicts me, that, *d.* hence
**Departs.**—P. L. 12, 155. *d.* from Canaan
**Departure.**—P. L. 11, 303. *d.* from this
**Depend.**—P. L. 12, 564. and on him sole *d.*
V. Ex. 82. on his brothers shall *d.* for clothing
**Dependent.**—P. L. 9, 943. must fail, *d.* made
**Depending.**—P. R. 4, 312. on grace *d.*
**Depends.**—P. L. 10, 406. kingdom all *d.*
**Deplore.**—P. L. 8, 479. for ever to *d.* her loss
A. 100. though Erymanth your loss *d.*
**Deplored.**—P. L. 10, 939. acknowledged and *d.*
**Depopulation.**—P. L. 11, 756. so sad, *d.*
**Deport.**—P. L. 9, 389. and goddess-like *d.*
P. L. 11, 666. eminent in wise *d.*, spake much
**Deposed.**—P. R. 1, 413. now *d.*, ejected
**Deposited.**—S. A. 499. trust of silence *d.*
**Depraved.**—P. L. 5, 471. if not *d.* from good
P. L. 10, 825. both mind and will *d.*
P. L. 11, 806. so all shall turn degenerate, all *d.*
P. L. 11, 886. late repenting him of man *d.*
S. A. 1042. his sense *d.* to folly and shameful
**Depravest.**—P. L. 6, 174. unjustly thou *d.*
**Deprecation.**—P. L. 8, 378. and humble *d.*
**Depressed.**—P. L. 9, 46. my intended wing *d.*
S. A. 1698. *d.* and overthrown, as seemed
**Deprive.**—P. R. 3, 23. wherefore *d.* all Earth
**Deprived.**—P. L. 9, 857. thought it long, *d.*
P. L. 11, 316. *d.* his blessed countenance
**Deprives.**—P. L. 12, 100. *d.* them of their
**Depth.**—P. L. 1, 549. of *d.* immeasurable
P. L. 1, 627. from the *d.* of knowledge
P. L. 2, 324. for he, be sure, in height or *d.*
P. L. 8, 413. the height and *d.* of thy eternal
P. R. 1, 13. and bear through height or *d.*
**Derided.**—P. L. 6, 633. and all his host *d.*
P. L. 11, 817. of them *d.*, but of God observed
**Derides.**—P. L. 2, 191. motions vain sees and *d.*
P. L. 9, 211. with wanton growth *d.*
L'A. 31. Sport that wrinkled Care *d.*
**Derision.**—P. L. 5, 736. justly hast in *d.*
P. L. 6, 608. and to his mates thus in *d.* called
P. L. 12, 52. and in *d.* sets upon their tongues
S. A. 366. thy foes' *d.*, captive, poor, and blind
**Derive.**—P. L. 11, 427. yet from that sin *d.*
P. L. 12, 36. account from rebellion shall *d.*
**Derived.**—P. L. 9, 837. sciential sap, *d.*
P. L. 10, 965. to our seed (O hapless seed!) *d.*
P. R. 1, 289. authority which I *d.* from heaven
P. R. 4, 338. Greece from us these arts *d.*
**Derivest.**—P. R. 2, 418. whence authority *d.*
**Descant.**—P. L. 4, 603. amorous *d.* sang
S. A. 1228. *d.* on my strength, and give thy
**Descend.**—P. L. 7, 1. *d.* from Heaven, Urania
P. L. 7, 84. deign to *d.* now lower and relate
P. L. 8, 198. from this high pitch let us *d.*
P. L. 9, 169. will not ambition and revenge *d.*
P. L. 10, 337. saw *d.* the Son of God to judge
P. L. 10, 394. *d.* through darkness, on your road
P. L. 10, 398. right down to Paradise *d.*
P. L. 12, 588. let us *d.* now therefore from this
P. L. 12, 606. he ended; and they both *d.*
P. R. 1, 83. thence on his head a perfect dove *d.*
S. A. 361. for this did the angel twice *d.*
**Descended.**—P. L. 4, 541. sun slowly *d.*
P. L. 10, 90. down he *d.* straight
P. L. 11, 75. when God *d.*, and perhaps once
P. L. 11, 576. down to the plain *d.*
P. L. 12, 607. *d.*, Adam to the bower where Eve
P. L. 12, 628. in bright array the Cherubim *d.*
P. R. 1, 31. in likeness of a dove the Spirit *d.*
P. R. 1, 282. the Spirit *d.* on me like a dove
P. R. 2, 111. into himself *d.*, and at once
P. R. 4, 273. from Heaven *d.* to the low-roofed
Il P. 22. yet thou art higher far *d.*
D. F. I. 19. down he *d.* from his snow-soft chair
**Descending.**—P. L. 1, 327. and *d.* tread us
P. L. 3, 303. nor shalt thou, by *d.*, to assume
P. L. 3, 511. saw angels ascending and *d.*
P. L. 5, 363. since by *d.* from the Thrones

P. L. 6, 325. with steep force to smite *d*.
P. L. 11, 3. prevenient grace *d*. had removed
P. L. 11, 670. a cloud *d*. snatched him thence
P. L. 12, 228. he *d*., will himself in thunder
S. A. 635. by heavenly message twice *d*.
**Descends.**—P. L. 5, 399. unmeasured out, *d*.
P. L. 7, 513. to acknowledge whence his good *d*.
P. L. 11, 142. which we enjoy from Heaven *d*.
P. L. 11, 207. and slow *d*., with something
P. L. 11, 862. the ancient sire *d*.
P. L. 12, 48. but God, who oft *d*. to visit men
**Descent.**—P. L. 2, 14. from this *d*. celestial
P. L. 2, 76. *d*. and fall to us is adverse
P. L. 3, 20. to venture down the dark *d*.
P. L. 9, 163. foul *d*.! that I who erect contended
P. L. 10, 979. if care of our *d*. perplex us most
P. L. 11, 127. power prepared for swift *d*.
P. L. 12, 269. his whole *d*., who thus shall
S. A. 171. whom long *d*. of birth, or the sphere
L. 31. toward Heaven's *d*. had sloped his
**Descents.**—P. L. 8, 410. infinite *d*. beneath
**Describe.**—P. L. 8, 38. to *d*. whose swiftness
P. L. 9, 33. or to *d*. races and games
**Described.**—P. L. 4, 567. I *d*. his way
**Describing.**—P. R. 4, 266. passions best *d*.
**Descried.**—P. L. 2, 636. a fleet *d*. hangs
P. L. 9, 60. Uriel, regent of the sun, *d*. his
P. L. 10, 325. their way to Earth they had *d*.
P. R. 1, 26, but him the Baptist soon *d*.
**Descries.**—P. L. 3, 501. far distant he *d*.
**Descry.**—P. L. 1, 290. or in Valdarno, to *d*.
P. L. 6, 530. to *d*. the distant foe
P. L. 8, 149. their attendant moons, thou wilt *d*.
P. L. 11, 228. for I *d*., from yonder blazing
P. R. 2, 280. high towering to *d*. the morn's
S. A. 1301. for I *d*. this way some other tending
C. 141. and to the tell-tale sun *d*. our concealed
A. 3. is that which we from hence *d*.
**Desert.**—P. L. 2, 270. this *d*. soil wants
P. L. 2, 973. wandering this darksome *d*.
P. L. 3, 544. through dark and *d*. ways
P. L. 5, 515. his love *d*., who formed
P. L. 7, 314. till then *d*. and bare, unsightly
P. L. 8, 154. by living soul, *d*. and desolate
P. L. 10, 437. left *d*. utmost Hell many a dark
P. L. 11, 779. wandering that watery *d*.
P. L. 12, 139. Hamath northward to the *D*.
P. L. 12, 216. advance through the wild *D*.
P. R. 1, 9. into the *d*., his victorious field
P. R. 1, 193. he entered now the bordering *D*.
P. R. 1, 296. pathless *d*., dusk with horrid
P. R. 1, 501. sullen wing to double-shade the *d*.
P. R. 2, 109. while her Son, tracing the *d*. wild
P. R. 2, 241. then to the *d*. takes with these
P. R. 2, 271. Prophet also, how he fled into the *d*.
P. R. 2, 416. lost in a *d*. here and hunger-bit
P. R. 3, 166. he indeed retired into the *d*.
P. R. 3, 264. and there was room for barren *d*.
P. R. 4, 465. this tempest at this *d*. most was
S. A. 275. if he aught begin, how frequent to *d*.
C. 209. sands and shores and *d*. wildernesses
C. 387. the pensive secrecy of *d*. cell
L. 39. shepherd, thee the woods and *d*. caves
L'A. 10. in dark Cimmerian *d*. ever dwell
**Deserted.**—P. L. 4, 922. alleged to thy *d*.
P. L. 9, 980. rather die *d*. than oblige thee
P. L. 11, 655. and arms the ensanguined field *d*.
P. R. 2, 316. forty and more *d*. here indeed
**Desertion.**—S. A. 632. and sense of Heaven's *d*.
**Deserts.**—P. L. 8, 563. she *d*. thee not, if thou
S. A. 88. as the moon, when she *d*. the night
S. A. 205. how well are come upon him his *d*.
**Deserve.**—P. L. 1, 692. that soil may best *d*.
P. R. 4, 169. for what can less so great a gift *d*.?
S. A. 489. as I *d*., pay on my punishment
S. A. 1169. from thine, these evils I *d*. and more
S. A. 1366. by labour, honest, and lawful to *d*.
**Deserved.**—P. L. 4, 42. ah, wherefore? he *d*.
P. L. 6, 354. in other parts like deeds *d*.
P. L. 6, 709. by sacred unction, thy *d*. right
P. L. 10, 16. and manifold in sin, *d*. to fall

P. L. 10, 726. I *d*. it, and would bear my
P. R. 3, 106. as vain men seek, oft not *d*.
D. F. I. 69. to stand 'twixt us and our *d*. smart?
**Deservedly.**—P. R. 1, 407. *d*. thou grievest
P. R. 4, 133. *d*. made vassal—who, once just
**Deserves.**—P. L. 6, 467. to me *d*. no less
**Deserving.**—P. L. 5, 446. O innocence *d*.
P. L. 11, 171. far other name *d*.
P. R. 3, 77. made captive, yet *d*. freedom more
S. A. 493. how *d*. contempt and scorn of all
**Deservings.**—P. L. 10, 727. my own *d*.
**Design.**—P. L. 1, 646. to work in close *d*.
P. L. 2, 386. the bold *d*. pleased
P. L. 2, 630. thoughts inflamed of highest *d*.
P. L. 3, 467. and still with vain *d*.
P. L. 4, 521. invented with *d*. to keep them
P. L. 5, 33. of day past, or morrow's next *d*.
P. L. 9, 261. whether his first *d*. be to withdraw
P. R. 2, 203. aimed not beyond higher *d*.
**Designed.**—P. L. 2, 838. now *d*., I haste
P. L. 10, 60. man's friend, his Mediator, his *d*.
P. L. 10, 277. *d*. for death, the following day
S. A. 32. separate to God, *d*. for great exploits
S. A. 801. that nothing was *d*. against thee
**Designing.**—P. L. 2, 179. while we, perhaps, *d*.
P. L. 9, 213. to his own dark *d*.
**Designs.**—P. L. 5, 227. how he *d*. in them at once
P. L. 5, 737. secure, laugh'st at their vain *d*.
P. R. 2, 410. and all thy heart is set on high *d*.
**Desirable.**—P. L. 8, 505. but retired, the more *d*.
S. A. 358. why are his gifts *d*.
**Desire.**—P. L. 2, 295. and no less *d*. to found
P. L. 3, 662. unspeakable *d*. to see and know
P. L. 3, 694. fair Angel, thy *d*., which tends
P. L. 4, 466. and pined with vain *d*.
P. L. 4, 509. neither joy, nor love, but fierce *d*.
P. L. 4, 523. excite their minds with more *d*.
P. L. 5, 45. to behold but thee nature's *d*.
P. L. 5, 555. more *d*. to hear, if thou consent
P. L. 6, 201. presage of victory, and fierce *d*.
P. L. 7, 61. and now led on, yet sinless, with *d*.
P. L. 7, 119. to answer thy *d*. of knowledge
P. L. 8, 62. and from about her shot darts of *d*.
P. L. 8, 252. *d*. with thee still longer to converse
P. L. 8, 417. the cause of his *d*. by conversation
P. L. 8, 451. thy wish exactly to thy heart's *d*.
P. L. 8, 526. mind no change, nor vehement *d*.
P. L. 9, 584. to satisfy the sharp *d*. I had
P. L. 9, 592. with like *d*. longing and envying
P. L. 9, 741. with *d*. inclinable, now grown
P. L. 9, 1013. carnal *d*. inflaming
P. L. 9, 1136. that strange *d*. of wandering
P. L. 10, 995. with *d*. to languish without hope
P. L. 10, 997. languishing with like *d*.
P. R. 1, 383. what can be then less in me than *d*.
P. R. 2, 166. draw out with credulous *d*.
P. R. 2, 211. will vouchsafe an eye of fond *d*.
S. A. 541. *d*. of wine and all delicious drinks
S. A. 980. but in my country, where I most *d*.
S. A. 1677. and urged them on with mad *d*.
M. M. 6. mirth, and youth, and warm *d*.
V. Ex. 22. deepest spirits and choicest wits *d*.
**Desires.**—P. L. 3, 177. to foul exorbitant *d*.
P. L. 4, 808. vain hopes, vain aims, inordinate *d*.
P. L. 5, 518. human *d*. can seek or apprehend
P. L. 12, 87. inordinate *d*. and upstart passions
P. R. 2, 230. lawful *d*. of nature
P. R. 2, 467. and rules passions, *d*. and fears
**Desirest.**—P. L. 10, 837. thus what thou *d*.
P. L. 10, 948. *d*. the punishment all on thyself
**Desiring.**—P. L. 8, 628. of pure with pure *d*.
P. L. 9, 398. delighted, but *d*. more her stay
**Desirous.**—P. L. 5, 631. repast they turn *d*.
P. L. 9, 839. waiting *d*. her return
P. L. 10, 749. *d*. to resign and render back
P. L. 10, 947. unwary, and too *d*., as before
S. A. 741. *d*. to behold once more thy face
**Desist.**—P. R. 4, 497. *d*., thou art discerned
S. A. 969. to mix with thy concernments I *d*.
**Desisting.**—P. L. 7, 552. *d*., though unwearied
**Desolate.**—P. L. 4, 936. to wing the *d*. abyss

P. L. 8, 154. by living soul, desert and *d.*
P. L. 10, 420. and all about found *d.*
P. L. 10, 864. *d.* where she sat, approaching
P. L. 11, 306. inhospitable appear, and *d.*
**Desolation.**—P. L. 1, 181. the seat of *d.*
S. A. 1561. the *d.* of a hostile city
C. 428. yea, there, where very *d.* dwells
**Despair.**—P. L. 1, 126. but racked with deep *d.*
P. L. 1, 191. if not what resolution from *d.*
P. L. 1, 525. to have found their chief not in *d.*
P. L. 2, 6. and, from *d.* thus high uplifted
P. L. 2, 45. in heaven, now fiercer by *d.*
P. L. 2, 126. grounds his courage on *d.*
P. L. 2, 143. repulsed, our final hope is flat *d.*
P. L. 4, 23. now conscience wakes *d.*
P. L. 4, 74. wrath and infinite *d.*
P. L. 4, 115. with pale, ire, envy, and *d.*
P. L. 4, 156. able to drive all sadness but *d.*
P. L. 6, 787. insensate, hope conceiving from *d.*
P. L. 10, 113. shame and perturbation, and *d.*
P. L. 10, 1007. she ended here, or vehement *d.*
P. L. 11, 139. new hope to spring out of *d.*
P. L. 11, 301. of sorrow, and dejection, and *d.*
P. L. 11, 489. *D.* tended the sick busiest
P. R. 1, 485. talk at least, though I *d.* to attain
S. A. 631. thence faintings, swoonings of *d.*
S. A. 1171. justly, yet *d.* not of his final pardon
**Despaired.**—P. L. 1, 660. peace is *d.*
P. L. 6, 495. nothing hard, much less to be *d.*
**Despairing.**—P. L. 9, 255. and of his own *d.*
**Despatch** *etc. vide* **Dispatch**
**Desperate.**—P. L. 2, 107. *d.* revenge
P. L. 3, 85. so bent he seems on *d.* revenge
P. R. 4, 23. yet gives not o'er, though *d.*
P. R. 4, 445. *d.* of better course, to vent his rage
**Desperation.**—P. R. 4, 579. ruin and *d.*
**Despicable.**—P. L. 1, 437. spear of *d.* foes
P. L. 11, 340. no *d.* gift
**Despise.**—P. L. 6, 717. as likes them, to *d.*
P. L. 9, 878. without thee can *d.*
P. R. 3, 28. who all pleasures else *d.*
S. A. 272. and to *d.*, or envy, or suspect
**Despised.**—P. L. 2, 481. he *d.* his own
P. L. 5, 60. is knowledge so *d.*
P. L. 6, 602. would render them yet more *d.*
P. L. 6, 812. but me, they have *d.*, yet envied
P. L. 7, 422. with clang *d.* the ground
P. R. 2, 218. *d.* and put to rout all her array
S. A. 1688. *d.*, and thought extinguished quite
C. 724. not half his riches known, and yet *d.*
**Despite.**—P. L. 6, 340. for anguish, and *d.*
P. L. 6, 906. as a *d.* done against the Most High
P. L. 9, 176. this man of clay, son of *d.*
P. L. 10, 1044. and pride, impatience and *d.*
P. L. 12, 34. as in *d.* of Heaven, or from Heaven
P. R. 4, 446. and mad *d.* to be so oft repelled
**Despiteful.**—P. L. 10, 1. heinous and *d.* act
**Despoil.**—S. A. 469. quite *d.* him of all these
**Despoiled.**—P. L. 3, 109. of freedom both *d.*
P. L. 9, 411. *d.* of innocence, of faith, of bliss
P. L. 9, 1138. not as now *d.* of all our good
P. R. 3, 139. and so of all true good himself *d.*
S. A. 539. then turned me out ridiculous, *d.*
**Despotic.**—S. A. 1054. *d.* power over his female
**Destined.**—P. L. 1, 168. from their *d.* aim
P. L. 2, 161. reserved, and *d.* to eternal woe
P. L. 2, 848. and blessed his maw *d.* to that
P. L. 7, 622. every star perhaps a world of *d.*
P. L. 10, 62. and *d.* Man himself to judge
P. L. 10, 646. next to the Son *d.* Restorer
P. L. 11, 387. from the *d.* walls of Cambalu
P. L. 12, 233. by types and shadows of that *d.*
P. R. 1, 65. *d.* to this, is late of woman born
P. R. 4, 469. with my aid to win thy *d.* seat
S. A. 634. his *d.* from the womb, promised by
L. 20. with lucky words favour my *d.* urn
**Destiny.**—P. L. 4, 58. Oh ! had his powerful *d.*
P. L. 5, 534. but what they must by *d.*
U. C. II. 3. so hung his *d.*, never to rot
**Destitute.**—P. L. 9, 1062. they *d.* and bare
P. R. 2, 305. should bide, of all things *d.*

**Destroy.**—P. L. 2, 502. each other to *d.*
P. L. 2, 734. his wrath, which one day will *d.*
P. L. 2, 787. his fatal dart made to *d.*
P. L. 3, 91. to assay if him by force he can *d.*
P. L. 6, 226. disturb, though not *d.* their happy
P. L. 6, 855. not to *d.*, but root them out
P. L. 7, 607. is greater than created to *d.*
P. L. 9, 477. all pleasure to *d.*, save what is in
P. L. 9, 989. will in earnest so *d.* us his prime
P. L. 10, 611. both to *d.*, or unimmortal make
P. L. 10, 1006. destruction with destruction to *d.*
P. L. 11, 892. makes a covenant never to *a*
P. R. 3, 80. the flourishing works of peace *d*
S. A. 1587. at once both to *d.* and be destroyed
**Destroyed.**—P. L. 2, 85. to be worse *d.*
P. L. 2, 92. more *d.* than thus we should
P. L. 3, 301. what hellish hate so easily *d.*
P. L. 9, 130. him *d.*, or won to what may
P. L. 11, 761. children all in view *d.* at once
P. L. 11, 875. of wicked sons *d.*
P. L. 12, 3. the world *d.* and world restored
P. L. 12, 262. kings *d.*, and kingdoms won
S.A. 856. who had *d.* such numbers of our nation
S. A. 1587. at once both to destroy and be *d.*
**Destroyer.**—P. L. 4, 749. our *d.*, foe to God
S. A. 685. to save her country from a fierce *d.*
S. A. 1678. to call in haste for their *d.*
**Destroyers.**—P. L. 11, 697. *d.* rightlier
**Destroying.**—P. L. 9, 129. only in *d.*
P. L. 9, 478. to destroy save what is in *d.*
P. L. 12, 394. not by *d.* Satan, but his works
**Destroys.**—P. L. 3, 301. and still *d.* in those
P. L. 10, 838. alike *d.* all hope of refuge
P. R. 2, 372. but life preserves, *d.* life's enemy
**Destruction.**—P. L. 1, 137. in horrible *d.*
P. L. 2, 84. his wrath may find to our *d.*
P. L. 2, 464. through all the coasts of dark *d.*
P. L. 2, 505. that day and night, for his *d.* wait
P. L. 3, 208. but, to *d.* sacred and devote
P. L. 5, 907. on those proud towers to swift *d.*
P. L. 6, 162. thy success may show *d.* to the rest
P. L. 6, 253. such *d.* to withstand he hasted
P. L. 8, 236. *d.* with creation might have mixed
P. L. 9, 56. bent on man's *d.*, maugre what
P. L. 9, 134. that *d.* wide may range
P. L. 10, 612. and for *d.* to mature
P. L. 10, 1006. *d.* with *d.* to destroy
P. R. 1, 376. glibbed with lies to his *d.*
P. R. 3, 202. and my promotion will be thy *d.*
S. A. 764. if not by quick *d.* soon cut off
S. A. 1514. ruin *d.* at the utmost point
S. A. 1658. pulled down the same *d.* on himself
S.A. 1681. unweetingly importuned their own *d.*
**Detain.**—P. L. 8, 207. how subtly to *d.* thee
P. L. 10, 367. *d.* from following thy illustrious
**Detained.**—P. L. 3, 14. though long *d.*
P. R. 3, 227. thou linger'st in deep thoughts *d.*
**Detains.**—P. L. 10, 108. or what chance *d.*
**Detect.**—P. L. 10, 136. wouldst easily *d.*
**Deter.**—P. L. 2, 449. or danger could *d.*
**Determine.**—P. L. 6, 318. that might *d.*
P. L. 11, 227. which perhaps of us will soon *d.*
**Determined.**—P. L. 2, 330. war hath *d.* us
P. L. 5, 879. I see thy fall *d.*, and my hapless
P. L. 9, 148. *d.* to advance
P. R. 2, 291. *d.* there to rest at noon
**Determinest.**—S. A. 843. thou *d.* weakness
**Deterred.**—P. L. 9, 696. *d.* not from
**Detestable.**—P. L. 2, 745. sight more *d.*
**Detraction.**—A. 11. of *d.* from her praise
**Detractions.**—S. 16, 2. not of war only but *d.*
**Detriment.**—P. L. 7, 153. I can repair that *d.*
P. L. 10, 409. the affairs of hell no *d.* need fear
**Deucalion.**—P. L. 11, 12. *D.* and chaste
**Deva.**—L. 55. where *D.* spreads her wizard
**Device.**—P. R. 4, 443. yet with no new *d.*
C. 941. with some other new *d.*
**Devil.**—P. L. 2, 496. *d.* with *d.* damned
P. L. 3, 613. here matter new to gaze the *D.*
P. L. 4, 502. aside the *D.* turned for envy
**P. L. 4** 846. abashed the *D.* stood and felt

P. L. 9, 188. in at his mouth the *D.* entered
P. L. 10, 878. be seen though by the *D.* himself
P. R. 4, 129. expel a *D.* who first made him
**Devilish.**—P. L. 2, 379. his *d.* counsel
P. L. 4, 17. and like a *d.* engine back recoils
P. L. 4, 394. tyrant's plea, excused his *d.* deeds
P. L. 4, 801. assaying, by his *d.* art, to reach
P. L. 6, 504. or inspired with *d.* machination
P. L. 6, 553. training his *d.* enginery
P. L. 6, 589. disgorging foul their *d.* glut
P. R. 1, 181. *d.* machinations come to nought
**Devils.**—P. L. 1, 373. and *d.* to adore for deities
**Devious.**—P. L. 3, 489. into the *d.* air
**Devise.**—P. L. 6, 504. might *d.* like instrument
P. L. 8, 207. how subtly to detain thee I *d.*
P. L. 9, 1091. let us now as in bad plight, *d.*
C. 963. such court guise as Mercury did first *d.*
**Devised.**—P. L. 2, 379. counsel first *d.* by Satan
P. L. 5, 780. what may be *d.* of honours new
**Devising.**—P. L. 4, 197. but sat *d.* death
**Devoid.**—P. L. 2, 151. *d.* of sense and motion
**Devolved.**—P. L. 10, 135. be all *d.*
**Devote.**—P. L. 3, 208. sacred and *d.*
P. L. 9, 901. deflowered, and now to death *d.*
P. L. 11, 821. a world *d.* to universal wrack
**Devoted.**—P. L. 5. 890. these wicked tents *d.*
M. W. 60. *d.* to thy virtuous name
**Devotion.**—P. L. 7, 514. eyes directed in *d.*
P. L. 11, 452. is piety thus and pure *d.* paid
S. A. 1147. with solemnest *d.*, spread before him
A. 35. was all in honour and *d.* meant
**Devour.**—P. L. 2, 435. outrageous to *d.*
P. L. 2, 805. his parent, would full soon *d.*
P. L. 4, 77. threatening to *d.* me
P. L. 10, 606. the scythe of Time mows down *d.*
**Devoured.**—P. L. 10, 712. *d.* each other
P. L. 10, 980. *d.* by death at last
P. R. 4, 573. and him who solved it not *d.*
**Devouring.**—P. L. 5, 893. *d.* fire
P. L. 12, 183. and wheel on the earth, *d.*
V. Ex. 86. *d.* war shall never cease to roar
**Devours.**—P. L. 12, 184. what it *d.* not
L. 129. daily *d.* apace, and nothing said
T. 4. and glut thyself with what thy womb *d.*
**Devout.**—P. L. 11, 14. of Themis stood *d.*
P. L. 11, 863. with uplifted hands and eyes *d.*
Il P. 31. come, pensive Nun, *d.* and pure
S. M. 15. hymns *d.* and holy psalms
**Dew.**—P. L. 4, 614. and the timely *d.* of sleep
P. L. 4, 645. glistering with *d.*
P. L. 4, 653. fruit, flower, glistering with *d.*
P. R. 1, 306. to defend him from the *d.*
S. A. 728. like a fair flower surcharged with *d.*
C. 352. from the chill *d.*, among rude burs
C. 802. yet a cold shuddering *d.* dips me all o'er
C. 996. and drenches with Elysian *d.*
A. 50. and from the boughs brush off the evil *d.*
L'A. 22. and fresh-blown roses washed in *d.*
Il P. 172. and every herb that sips the *d.*
M. W. 43. and those pearls of *d.* she wears
**Dew-besprent.**—C. 542. of knot-grass *d.-b.*
**Dewed.**—P. L. 12, 373. grief been *d.* in tears
**Dew-drops.**—P. L. 5, 746. stars of morning, *d.-d.*
**Dews.**—P. L. 1, 771. among fresh *d.* and flowers
P. L. 5, 212. among sweet *d.* and flowers
P. L. 5, 429. we brush mellifluous *d.*, and find
P. L. 5, 646. and roseate *d.* disposed all
P. L. 11, 135. and with fresh *d.* embalmed
P. R. 4, 406. from *d.* and damps of night
L. 29. battening our flocks with the fresh *d.*
**Dewy.**—P. L. 1, 743. from noon to *d.* eve
P. L. 5, 56. his *d.* locks distilled ambrosia
P. L. 5, 141. parallel to the earth his *d.* ray
P. L. 7, 333. but from the earth a *d.* mist
P. L. 9, 1044. till *d.* sleep oppressed them
P. L. 11, 865. a *d.* cloud, and in the cloud a bow
**Dewy-feathered.**—Il P. 146. *d.-f.* Sleep
**Dextrous.**—P. L. 5, 741. whether I be *d.*
**Dextrously.**—P. L. 11, 884. *d.* thou aim'st
**Diabolic.**—P. L. 9, 95. beget of *d.* power
**Diadem.**—P. L. 4, 90. with *d.* and sceptre

P. R. 2, 461. to him who wears the regal *d.*
**Dialect.**—P. L. 5, 761. *d.* of men interpreted
**Diamond.**—P. L. 3, 506. frontispiece of *d.*
P. L. 4, 554. with *d.* flaming and with gold
P. L. 5, 634. in pearl, in *d.*, and massy gold
P. L. 5, 759. and towers from *d.* quarries
P. L. 6, 364. though huge, and in a rock of *d.*
C. 881. wherewith she sits on *d.* rocks
**Diamonds.**—S. M. 732. and the unsought *d.* would
**Dian.**—C. 441. hence had the huntress *D.* her
**Diana.**—P. R. 2, 355. nymphs of *D.'s* train
**Diapason.**—S. M. 23. motion swayed in perfect *d.*
**Dictæan.**—P. L. 10, 584. *D.* Jove was born
**Dictate.**—P. L. 9, 355. *d.* false, and misinform
C. 767. and holy *d.* of spare Temperance
**Dictates.**—P. L. 9, 23. *d.* to me slumbering
P. R. 1, 482. to hear her *d.* from thy mouth
**Dictator.**—P. R. 1, 113. to him their great *D.*
**Die.**—P. L. 3, 209. must *d.*; *d.* he or justice
P. L. 3, 240. and for him lastly *d.* well pleased
P. L. 3, 246. am his due, all that of me can *d.*
P. L. 3, 295. be judged and *d.*, and dying rise
P. L. 3, 409. offered himself to *d.* for man's
P. L. 4, 527. to be such, they taste and *d.*
P. L. 6, 347. but by annihilating *d.*
P. L. 8, 330. inevitably thou shalt *d.*
P. L. 9, 663. nor shall ye touch it, lest ye *d.*
P. L. 9, 685. ye shall not *d.*; how should ye?
P. L. 9, 713. so shall ye *d.* perhaps by putting
P. L. 9, 763. our doom is, we shall *d.*
P. L. 9, 907. certain my resolution is to *d.*
P. L. 9, 928. perhaps thou shalt not *d.*
P. L. 9, 979. rather *d.* deserted than oblige thee
P. L. 10, 783. lest all I cannot *d.*
P. L. 10, 788. who knows but I shall *d.*
P. L. 10, 792. all of me then shall *d.*
P. L. 10, 1005. of many ways to *d.* the shortest
P. L. 11, 459. though here thou see him *d.*
P. L. 11, 471. by violent stroke shall *d.*
P. L. 12, 179. cattle must of rot and murrain *d.*
P. L. 12, 507. they *d.*; but in their room
S. A. 32. if I must *d.* betrayed, captived
S. A. 1706. though her body *d.*, fame
H. 137. will sicken soon and *d.*
U. C. II. 2. he could never *d.* while he could
W. S. 16. for such a tomb would wish to *d.*
**Died.**—P. L. 12, 428. death thou shouldst have *d.*
P. L. 12, 445. like that which the Redeemer *d.*
P. R. 3, 422. but so *d.* impenitent, and left
S. A. 287. in that sore battle when so many *d.*
S. A. 1579. how *d.* he; death to life is crown or
U. C. II. 16. fainted and *d.* nor would with ale
U. C. II. 22. he *d.* for heaviness that his cart
**Dies.**—P. L. 2, 624. where all life *d.*, death lives
P. L. 3, 342. him, who to compass all this *d.*
P. L. 9, 766. how *d.* the Serpent? he hath eaten
P. L. 10, 790. what *d.* but what had life
P. L. 12, 163. there he *d.*, and leaves his race
P. L. 12, 419. so he *d.*, but soon revives
L. 142. bring the rathe primrose that forsaken *d.*
**Diest.**—P. L. 7, 544. the day thou eat'st, thou *d.*
**Diet.**—P. L. 5, 495. no inconvenient *d.*
Il P. 46. spare Fast, that oft with gods doth *d.*
**Dieted.**—P. L. 9, 803. till *d.* by thee, I grow
**Difference.**—P. R. 3, 115. no *d.*
**Different.**—P. L. 1, 636. if counsels *d.*
P. L. 8, 130. insensibly three *d.* motions move
P. L. 8, 471. manlike, but *d.* sex, so lovely fair
P. L. 9, 888. lest thou not tasting, *d.* degree
P. L. 11, 382. whereon, for *d.* cause, the Tempter
P. L. 11, 574. a *d.* sort from the high
P. R. 3, 89. it may by means far *d.* be attained
C. 145. I feel the *d.* pace of some chaste footing
**Differing.**—P. L. 5, 490. *d.* but in degree
P. L. 7, 71. far *d.* from this world
**Difficult.**—P. L. 2, 71. seems *d.* and steep
P. L. 10, 598. though earned with travail *d.*
P. L. 10, 992. but if thou judge it hard and *d.*
P. R. 1, 298. return was *d.*, by human steps
P. R. 2, 428. not *d.*, if thou hearken to me
P. R. 4, 157. nothing will please the *d.* and nice

**Difficulty.**—P. L. 2, 449. in the shape of *d.*
P. L. 2, 1021. so he with *d.* and labour
P. L. 10, 252. but, lest the *d.* of passing back
**Diffidence.**—S. A. 454. *d.* of God
**Diffident.**—P. L. 8, 562. be not *d.* of Wisdom
P. L. 9, 293. not *d.* of thee do I dissuade thy
**Diffuse.**—P. L. 7, 190. and thence *d.* his good
**Diffused.**—P. L. 3, 137. new joy ineffable *d.*
P. L. 3, 639. suitable grace *d.*, so well he feigned
P. L. 4, 818. with sudden blaze *d.*, inflames
P. L. 7, 265. transparent, elemental, air *d.*
P. L. 9, 852. gathered, and ambrosial smell *d.*
P. R. 1, 499. disappeared into thin air, *d.*
P. R. 2, 351. the wine that fragrant smell *d.*
S. A. 96. and not as feeling, through all parts *d.*
S. A. 118. see how he lies at random, carelessly *d.*
S. A. 1141. this strength *d.* no less through all
**Digest.**—P. L. 5, 412. tasting concoct, *d.*
**Digestion.**—P. L. 5, 4. from pure *d.* bred
**Digged.**—P. L. 1, 690. and *d.* out ribs of gold
P. L. 6, 516. part hidden veins *d.* up
**Dight.**—L'A. 62. clouds in thousand liveries *d.*
Il P. 159. and storied windows richly *d.*
**Dignified.**—P. L. 9, 940. creatures *d.* so high
S. A. 682. yet toward these, thus *d.*, thou oft
**Dignities.**—P. L. 1, 359. *d.* and powers
P. R. 3, 30. *d.* and powers
**Dignity.**—P. L. 2, 25. Heaven, which follows *d.*
P. L. 2, 111. he seemed for *d.* composed
P. L. 4, 619. declares his *d.*, and the regard
P. L. 5, 827. and of our good and of our *d.*
P. L. 8, 489. in every gesture *d.* and love
P. L. 10, 151. far excelled hers in all real *d.*
**Digressions.**—P. L. 8, 55. intermix grateful *d.*
**Dilated.**—P. L. 1, 429. *d.* or condensed
P. L. 4, 986. collecting all his might, *d.* stood
P. L. 6, 486. with touch of fire *d.* and infuriate
P. L. 9, 876. mine eyes dim erst, *d.* spirits
**Diligence.**—P. R. 2, 387. obtrude this *d.*
S. A. 924. with nursing *d.*, to me glad office
**Dim.**—P. L. 1, 597. *d.* eclipse, disastrous twilight
P. L. 2, 753. *d.* thine eyes, and dizzy swum
P. L. 2, 1036. far into the bosom of *d.* Night
P. L. 3, 26. or *d.* suffusion veiled
P. L. 5, 685. yet *d.* Night her shadowy cloud
P. L. 5, 700. ere *d.* night had disencumbered
P. L. 9, 707. that seem so clear, yet are but *d.*
P. L. 9, 876. mine eyes *d.* erst, dilated spirits
P. L. 10, 23. *d.* sadness did not spare that time
C. 5. above the smoke and stir of this *d.* spot
C. 278. *d.* darkness, and this leafy labyrinth
L. 105. inwrought with figures *d.*, and on the
Il P. 160. casting a *d.* religious light
H. 198. forsake their temples *d.*
**Dimension.**—P. L. 2, 893. without *d.*
**Dimensionless.**—P. L. 11, 17. passed *d.*
**Dimensions.**—P. L. 1, 793. in their own *d.*
P. L. 7, 480. these, as a line, their long *d.* drew
**Diminish.**—P. L. 7, 612. thought thee to *d.*
**Diminished.**—P. L. 4, 35. hide their *d.* heads
**Diminution.**—P. L. 7, 369. with *d.* seen
S. A. 303. regardless of His glory's *d.*
**Dimly.**—P. L. 5, 157. to us invisible or *d.* seen
**Dimmed.**—P. L. 4, 114. each passion *d.* his face
P. L. 11, 212. carnal fear that day *d.* Adam's
**Dimple.**—L A. 30. and love to live in *d.* sleek
**Dimpled.**—C. 119. by *d.* brook
**Din.**—P. L. 1, 668. sounding shields the *d.* of war
P. L. 2, 1040. and with less hostile *d.*
P. L. 6, 408. silence on the odious *d.* of war
P. L. 10, 521. dreadful was the *d.* of hissing
P. L. 12, 61. hubbub strange and hear the *d.*
L'A. 49. while the cock, with lively *d.*
S. M. 20. and with harsh *d.* broke the fair
**Dingle.**—C. 312. *d.*, or bushy dell of this wild
**Dinner.**—P. L. 5, 304. hour prepared for *d.*
P. L. 5, 396. no fear lest *d.* cool
L'A. 84. are at their savoury *d.* set
**Dint.**—P. L. 2, 813. for that mortal *d.*
**Dipped.**—P. L. 5, 283. and colours *d.* in heaven
**Dips.**—C. 803. cold shuddering dew *d.* me all

**Dipsas.**—P. L. 10, 526. and ellops drear, and *d.*
**Dipt.**—P. L. 11, 244. Iris had *d.* the woof
**Dire.**—P. L. 1, 94. the force of those *d.* arms
P. L. 1, 134. too well I see and rue the *d.* event
P. L. 1, 189. how overcome this *d.* calamity
P. L. 1, 624. though the event was *d.*
P. L. 1, 625. and this *d.* change. hateful to
P. L. 2, 128. of all his aim, after some *d.*
P. L. 2, 589. storms of whirlwind and *d.* hail
P. L. 2, 628. hydras, and chimæras *d.*
P. L. 2, 820. through *d.* change befallen us
P. L. 4, 15. with cause to boast, begins his *d.*
P. L. 6, 211. *d.* was the noise of conflict
P. L. 6, 248. ranging through the *d.* attack
P. L. 6, 665. to and fro with jaculation *d.*
P. L. 6, 766. bickering flame, and sparkles *d.*
P. L. 7, 42. had forewarned Adam by *d.*
P. L. 9, 643. so glistered the *d.* Snake, and into
P. L. 10, 524. and asp, and amphisbæna *d.*
P. L. 10, 543. *d.* hiss renewed, and the *d.* form
P. L. 11, 248. hung the sword, Satan's *d.* dread
P. L. 11, 474. the earth shall bring diseases *d.*
P. L. 11, 489. *d.* was the tossing, deep the
P. L. 12, 175. by signs and judgments *d.*
P. R. 4, 431. the Son of God with terrors *d.*
S. A. 626. *d.* inflammation, which no cooling
S. A. 1544. for *d.* imagination still pursues me
S. A. 1666. but tangled in the fold of *d.* necessity
C. 207. shapes and beckoning shadows *d.*
C. 517. of *d.* Chimæras and enchanted isles
**Direct.**—P. L. 1, 348. waving to *d.* their course
P L. 2. 980. *d.* my course, directed no mean
P. L. 3, 526. *d.* against which opened from
P. L. 3, 618. as they now shot upward, still *d.*
P. L. 3, 631. in hope to find who might *d.* his
P. L. 4, 798. these to the bower *d.* in search
P. L. 5, 301. shot down *d.* his fervid rays
P. L. 5, 508. way that might *d.* our knowledge
P. L. 6, 719. on his son with rays *d.* shone full
P. L. 7, 293. part rise in crystal wall, or ridge *d.*
P. L. 7, 576. led to God's eternal house *d.*
P. L. 9, 216. or *d.* the clasping ivy where to
P. L. 9, 974. for of good still good proceeds, *d.*
P. L. 11, 190. *d.* to the eastern gate was bent
P. L. 11, 711. which now *d.* thine eyes
P. L. 12, 639. to the eastern gate led them *d.*
P. R. 1, 396. whereby they may *d.* their future
C. 807. this is mere moral babble, and *d.* against
**Directed.**—P. L. 2. 981. direct my course, *d.*
P. L. 5, 49. to find thee I *d.* then my walk
P. L. 7, 514. with heart, and voice, and eyes, *d.*
P. R. 1, 247. *d.* to the manger, where thou lay'st
**Directly.**—P. L. 3, 89. *d.* towards the
S. A. 1250. he will *d.* to the lords I fear
**Directs.**—P. R. 1, 119. he *d.* his easy steps
P. R. 4, 393. for no date prefixed *d.* me
**Direful.**—C. 357. within the *d.* grasp of savage
**Dire-looking.**—A. 52. or what the cross *d.-l.*
**Dirt.**—U. C. I. 2. here alas hath laid him in the *d.*
**Dis.**—P. L. 4, 270. by gloomy *D.* was gathered
**Disabled.**—P. L. 12, 392, *d.* not to give thee
S. A. 1219. if my known offence had not *d.* me
**Disadvantage.**—P. L. 6, 431. some *d.*
**Disagree.**—P. L. 2, 497. men only *d.*
**Disallied.**—S. A. 1022. nor both so loosely *d.*
**Disappear.**—P. R. 4, 397. feigning to *d.*
**Disappeared.**—P. L. 6, 414. rebellious *d.*
P. L. 8, 478. she *d.*, and left me dark ; I waked
P. L. 12, 640. to the subjected plain; then *d.*
P. R. 1, 498. bowing low his gray dissimulation, *d.*
**Disapprove.**—S. A. 970. too much *d.* my own
**Disapproves.**—S. 21, 12. and *d.* that care
**Disarmed.**—P. L. 3, 253. of his mortal sting *d.*
P. L. 6, 490. that they shall fear we have *d.*
P. L. 9, 465. of enmity *d.*, of guile, of hate
P. L. 10, 945. as one *d.* his anger all he lost
S. A. 540. shaven, and *d.* among mine enemies
**Disarrayed.**—P. L. 3, 396. warring Angels *d.*
**Disastrous.**—P. L. 1, 597. *d.* twilight sheds
**Disband.**—P. L. 2, 523. the ranged Powers *d.*
**Disburden.**—P. L. 9, 624. help to *d.* Nature

P. L. 10, 719. thus to *d*. sought with sad
**Disburdened.**—P. L. 6, 878. *d*. heaven
**Disburdening.**—P. L. 5, 319. and by *d*. grows
**Discern.**—P. L. 1, 326. from Heaven-gates *d*.
P. L. 3, 682. neither Man nor Angel can *d*.
P. L. 4, 867. by glimpse *d*. Ithuriel and Zephon
P. L. 9, 544. and shallow to *d*. half what
P. L. 9, 681. only to *d*. things in their causes
P. R. 1, 164. they now, and men hereafter, may *d*.
P. R. 1, 348. I *d*. thee other than thou seem'st
P. R. 4, 390. real or allegoric, I *d*. not
S. A. 1305. by his habit I *d*. him now
M. W. 22. ye might *d*. a cypress bud
**Discerned.**—P. L. 3. 407. in thy face *d*.
P. L. 4, 570. *d*. his looks alien from Heaven
P. L. 5, 299. Adam *d*., as in the door he sat
P. L. 9, 573. nor aught but food *d*. or sex
P. L. 9, 1149. thou couldst not have *d*. fraud
P. L. 10, 331. parent soon *d*., though in disguise
P. R. 4, 497. thou art *d*., and toil'st in vain
**Discerning.**—P. L. 12, 372. *d*. Adam with
**Discerns.**—P. L. 1, 78. he soon *d*.
P. L. 5, 711. whose sight *d*. abstrusest thoughts
P. L. 9, 765. and speaks, and reasons, and *d*.
**Discharge.**—P. L. 6, 564. we *d*. freely
P. L. 11, 196. secure of our *d*. from penalty
S. A. 1573. hath paid his ransom now and full *d*.
**Discharged.**—P. L. 4, 57. indebted and *d*.
**Disciples.**—P. L. 12, 438. to appear to his *d*.
**Discipline.**—P. L. 4, 954. was this your *d*.
**Disciplined.**—P. L. 12, 302. *d*. from shadowy
**Disclose.**—P. L. 6, 445. consultation will *d*.
P. L. 8, 607. to thee *d*. what inward
**Disclosed.**—P. L. 6, 861. a spacious gap *d*.
P. L. 7, 419. with kindly rupture, forth *d*.
**Discomfit.**—S. A. 469. ere long receive such a *d*.
**Discomposed.**—P. L. 5, 10. with tresses *d*.
P. L. 10, 110. discountenanced both, and *d*
**Disconsolate.**—P. L. 11, 113. *d*., reveal to
**Discontented.**—P. L. 4, 807. *d*. thoughts
**Discontinuous.**—P. L. 6, 329. *d*. wound
**Discord.**—P. L. 2, 967. *D*. with a thousand
P. L. 6, 210. clashing brayed horrible *d*.
P. L. 6, 897. the *d*. which befell, and war in
P. L. 7, 217. the omnific word your *d*. end !
P. L. 9, 1124. hate, mistrust, suspicion, *d*.
P. L. 10, 707. but *D*. first, daughter of Sin
**Discountenance.**—P. R. 2, 218. *d*. her
**Discountenanced.**—P. L. 8, 553. loses *d*.
P. L. 10, 110. *d*. both and discomposed
**Discourse.**—P. L. 2, 555. in *d*. more sweet
P. L. 5, 233. such *d*. bring on, as may advise
P. L. 5, 395. a while *d*. they hold
P. L. 5, 488. *d*. is oftest yours, the latter most
P. L. 5, 803. thus far his bold *d*. without
P. L. 8, 48. as not with such *d*. delighted
P. L. 8, 211. and sweeter thy *d*. is to my ear
P. L. 8, 552. Wisdom in *d*. with her loses
P. L. 9, 5. permitting him the while venial *d*.
P. L. 9, 223. or object new casual *d*. draw on
P. L. 10, 343. sat in their sad *d*. and various
**Discoursed.**—P. R. 1, 479. *d*. pleasing, to the
**Discourtesy.**—C. 281. by falsehood, or *d*.
**Discover.**—P. L. 1, 64. served only to *d*.
P. L. 1, 724. *d*., wide within, her ample spaces
P. L. 2, 571. on bold adventure to *d*. wide
P. L. 12, 290. when they see law can *d*. sin
P. R. 3, 85. till conqueror death *d*. them
**Discovered.**—P. L. 4, 814. up he starts, *d*.
P. L. 6, 571. to our eyes *d*., new and strange
P. L. 10, 10. complete to have *d*. and repulsed
P. L. 11, 267. *d*. soon the place of her retire
P. R. 4, 3. *d*. in his fraud, thrown from his hope
S. A. 998. *d*. in the end, till now concealed
**Discovering.**—P. L. 5, 142. *d*. in wide
**Discovers.**—P. L. 3, 547. which to his eye *d*.
**Discreet.**—P. R. 2, 157. graceful and *d*.
**Discreetest.**—P. L. 8, 550. virtuousest, *d*.
**Discursive.**—P. L. 5, 488. *d*. or intuitive
**Disdain.**—P. L. 1, 98. and high *d*. from sense
P. L. 4, 82. and that word *d*. forbids me

P. L. 4, 770. proud fair, best quitted with *d*.
P. L. 5, 666. malice thence conceiving and *d*.
P. L. 9, 534. the heaven of mildness, with *d*.
P. R. 1, 466. inly stung with anger and *d*.
P. R. 1, 492. *d*. not such access to me
P. R. 4, 170. our Saviour answered with *d*.
S. A. 1106. to combat with a blind man I *d*.
**Disdained.**—P. L. 4, 180. due entrance he *d*.
P. L. 6, 367. that to be less than gods *d*.
P. L. 10, 213. *d*. not to begin thenceforth
P. L. 10, 876. and *d*. not to be trusted
**Disdainful.**—P. L. 2, 680. and, with *d*. look
**Disdainfully.**—P. L. 4, 903. moved, *d*.
**Disdaining.**—P. L. 6, 798. drew, *d*. flight
P. R. 1, 448. who themselves *d*. to approach
**Disease.**—S. A. 618. pain me as a lingering *d*.
S. A. 698. with sickness and *d*. thou bow'st them
U. C. II. 21. ease was his chief *d*. and to
**Diseased.**—P. L. 11, 480. numbers of all *d*.
**Diseases.**—P. L. 11, 474, shall bring *d*. dire
S. A. 699. painful *d*. and deformed
**Disencumbered.**—P. L. 5, 700. *d*. Heaven
**Disenthrone.**—P. L. 2, 229. either to *d*.
**Disespoused.**—P. L. 9, 17. for Lavinia *d*.
**Disfigured.**—P. L. 4, 127. saw him *d*.
**Disfigurement.**—C. 74. perceive their foul *d*.
**Disfiguring.**—P. L. 11, 521. *d*. not God's
**Disglorified.**—S. A. 442. with idols, *d*.
**Disgorge.**—P. L. 2, 575. that *d*. into the
**Disgorging.**—P. L. 6, 588. *d*. foul their
P. L. 12, 158. see where it flows, *d*. at seven
**Disguise.**—P. L. 10, 331. though in *d*.
C. 571. where that damned wizard, hid in sly *d*.
A. 26. stay gentle swains, for, though in this *d*.
P. 19. Oh, what a mask was there, what a *d*.!
**Disguised.** — P. L. 1, 481. wandering gods *d*.
P. L. 3, 480. or in Franciscan think to pass *d*.
P. L. 9, 522. at Circean call the herd *d*.
P. L. 10, 330. *d*. he came but those his children
C. 645. I knew the foul enchanter, though *d*.
**Disguises.**—P. L. 4, 740. troublesome *d*.
**Dish.**—C. 391. books, or his beads, or maple *d*.
**Disheartened.**—P. L. 5, 122. be not *d*.
P. R. 1, 268. yet neither thus *d*. or dismayed
S. A. 563. now blind, *d*., shamed, dishonoured
**Dishes.**—P. R. 2, 341. *d*. piled and meats
V. Ex. 14. the daintiest *d*. shall be served up last
**Dishevelled.**—P. L. 4, 306. tresses wore *d*.
**Dishonest.**—P. L. 4, 313, shame, *d*. shame
S. 10, 6. as that *d*. victory at Chæronea
**Dishonour.**—P. L. 9, 267. danger or *d*. lurks
P. L. 9, 297. asperses the tempted with *d*. foul
P. L. 9, 330. his foul esteem sticks no *d*.
P. R. 3, 131. render contempt instead, *d*.
S. A. 452. to God have brought *d*., obloquy
S. A. 1385. nothing to do, be sure, that may *d*.
**Dishonourable.**—P. L. 4, 314. honour *d*.
S. A. 1424. nothing *d*., impure, unworthy
**Dishonoured.**—S. A. 563. shamed, *d*., quelled
**Dishonourer.** S. A. 861. an irreligious *d*.
**Dishonours.**—S. A. 1232. hear these *d*.
**Disinherit.**—C. 334. and *d*. Chaos, that reigns
**Disinherited.**—P. L. 10, 821. so *d*.
**Disjoin.**—P. L. 3, 415. thy Father's praise *d*.
P. L. 9, 884. not tasting, different degree *d*. us
**Disjoining.**—P. L. 5, 106. joining or *d*.
**Dislike.**—P. L. 1, 102. that durst *d*. his reign
P. L. 8, 443. thou freely shouldst *d*.
P. L. 11, 720. and of their doings great *d*.
**Dislodge.**—P. L. 5, 669. all his legions to *d*.
P. L. 6, 7. in perpetual round, lodge and *d*.
**Dislodged.**—P. L. 6, 415. far in the dark *d*.
**Dislodging.**—P. L. 3, 433. *d*. from a region
**Disloyal.**—P. L. 3, 204. man disobeying, *d*.
P. L. 9, 7. and breach *d*., on the part of man
**Dismal.**—P. L. 1. 60. the *d*. situation waste
P. L. 2, 572. to discover wide that *d*. world
P. L. 2, 823. from out their dark and *d*. house
P. L. 6, 212. over head the *d*. hiss of fiery darts
P. L. 6, 666. underground they fought in *d*.
P. L. 8, 241. fast we found, fast shut the *d*. gates

P. L. 9, 185. not yet in horrid shade or *d.* den
P. L. 10, 508. a *d.* universal hiss, the sound
P. L. 10, 787. in the grave, or in some other *d.*
P. L. 11, 469. that lead to his grim cave, all *d.*
P. R. 1, 101. sole undertook the *d.* expedition
P. R. 4, 452. after a *d.* night. I heard the wrack
S. A. 1519. some *d.* accident it needs must be
H. 210. in *d.* dance about the furnace blue
V. Ex. 68. for once it was my *d.* hap to hear
**Dismay.**—P. L. 1, 57. huge affliction and *d.*
P. L. 2, 422. countenance read his own *d.*
P. L. 9, 917. as one from sad *d.* recomforted
P. L. 11, 156. which, then not minded in *d*
P. R. 1, 108. and surprised with deep *d.*
P. R. 4, 579. ruin, and desperation, and *d.*
**Dismayed.**—P. L. 2, 792. his mother, all *d.*
P. L. 4, 861. had quelled his heart, not else *d.*
P. L. 10, 35. from unsuccessful charge, be not *d.*
P. L. 11, 449. was Adam in his heart *d.*
P. R. 1, 268. yet, neither thus disheartened or *d.*
S. A. 1060. swayed by female usurpation, or *d.*
**Dismiss.**—P. L. 7, 108. and *d.* thee ere
P. L. 8, 564. deserts thee not, if thou *d.* not her
P. L. 9, 1159. didst permit, approve, and fair *d.*
P. L. 11, 113. *d.* them not disconsolate
**Dismissed.**—P. L. 10, 410. so saying, he *d.*
P. L. 11, 507. glad to be so *d.* in peace
P. L. 12, 195. pursuing whom he late *d.*
P. R. 2, 199. *d.*, in his prime youth, the fair
S. A. 1757. with peace and consolation hath *d.*
**Dismissing.**—P. L. 2, 282. *d.* quite all thoughts
**Dismission.**—S. A. 688. which were a fair *d.*
**Dismounted.**—P. L. 7, 19. *d.*, on the Aleian
**Disobedience.**—P. L. 1, 1. of man's first *d.*
P. L. 5, 541. and some are fallen,—to *d.*
P. L. 5, 888. iron rod to bruise and break thy *d.*
P. L. 6, 396. to such evil brought by sin of *d.*
P. L. 6, 911. terrible example, the reward of *d.*
P. L. 9, 8. revolt and *d.*
P. R. 1, 2. by one man's *d.*
**Disobedient.**—P. L. 6, 687. tame these *d.*
P. L. 10, 761. if thy son prove *d.*, and, reproved
**Disobeyed.**—P. L. 6, 403. not to have *d.*
**Disobeying.**—P. L. 3, 203. man *d.*, disloyal
**Disobeys.**—P. L. 5, 611. who *d.*, Me *d.*. breaks
**Disorder.**—P. L. 3, 713. from *d.* sprung
P. L. 6, 388. deformed rout entered, and foul *d.*
**Disordered.**—P. L. 6, 696. and to *d.* rage
P. L. 10, 911. all *d.*, at his feet fell humble
**Disordinate.**—S. A. 701. though not *d.*, yet
**Disparage.**—P. L. 1, 473. God's altar to *d.*
S. A. 1130. thou durst not thus *d.* glorious arms
**Disparity.**—P. L. 8, 386. but, in *d.*, the one
**Disparted.**—P. L. 7, 241. to several place *d.*
P. L. 10, 416. on either side *d.* Chaos over-built
**Dispatch.**—P. L. 5, 436. but with keen *d.*
P. L. 9, 203. outgrew the hands' *d.* of two
**Dispatched.**—C. 42. I was *d.* for their defence
S. A. 1599. little had I *d.*
**Dispatchful.**—P. L. 5, 331. with *d.* looks
**Dispelled.**—P. L. 1, 530. and *d.* their fears
**Dispels.**—P. L. 5, 208. now light *d.* the dark
**Dispensation.**—S. A. 61. of highest *d.*
**Dispense.**—P. L. 4, 157. *d.* native perfumes
S. A. 314. for with His own laws He can find
S. A. 1377. yet that He may *d.* with me or thee
**Dispensed.**—P. L. 5, 330. God hath *d.*
P. L. 5, 571. yet for thy good this is *d.*
P. L. 11, 766. *d.* the burden of many ages
C. 772. nature's full blessings would be well *d.*
**Dispenses.**—P. L. 3, 492. indulgences, *d.*
P. L. 3, 579. *d.* light from far
**Dispeopled.**—P. L. 7, 151. to have *d.* Heaven
**Disperse.**—P. L. 3, 54. thence purge and *d.*
P. L. 5, 208. *d.* it, as now light dispels the dark
**Dispersed.**—P. L. 4, 261. *d.*, or in a lake
P. L. 5, 7. lightly *d.*, and the shrill matin song
P. L. 5, 651. the angelic throng, *d.* in bands
P. L. 10, 578. however, some tradition they *d.*
P. L. 12, 45. get themselves a name, lest far *d.*
P. R. 3, 376. Habor, and among the Medes *d.*
**Displace.**—P. L. 1, 473. *d.* for one of Syrian

**Displaced.**—C. 560. still to be so *d.* I was all ear
**Displayed.**—P. L. 2, 10. imaginations thus *d,*
P. L. 7, 390. *d.* on the open firmament of heaven
P. L. 9, 1012. far other operation first *d.*
Il P. 149. of lively portraiture *d.*
H. 114. are seen in glittering ranks with wings *d.*.
**Displaying.**—P. R. 1, 67. *d.* all virtue, grace
**Displays.**—S. A. 819. *d.* her own
S. 15, 7. and the false North *d.* her broken
**Displease.**—S. A. 1373. to *d.* God for the fear
**Displeased.**—P. L. 8, 398. answered, not *d.*
P. L. 9, 535. heaven of mildness, with disdain, *d.*.
P. L. 10, 22. *d.* all were who heard; dim sadness
P. L. 10, 944. his counsel whom she had *d.*
P. L. 12, 63. whereto thus Adam, fatherly *d.*
S. A. 1084. in this *d.*, that I was never present
**Displeasure.**—P. L. 9, 993. incur divine *d.*
P. L. 10, 952. and my *d.* bear'st so ill
P. L. 10, 1094. will relent, and turn from his *d.*.
S. A. 733. I came still dreading thy *d.*, Samson
**Displode.**—P. L. 6, 605. in posture to *d.*
**Disport.**—P. L. 9, 520. as used to such *d.*
P. L. 9, 1042. their fill of love and love's *d.*
**Disporting.**—P. L. 8, 518. *d.*, till the amorous
**Disposal.**—S. A. 210. tax not divine *d.*,
S. A. 506. or the execution leave to high *d.*
**Dispose.**—P. L. 1, 246. now is Sovran can *d.*
P. L. 8, 170. let him *d.*, joy thou in what he
P. L. 11, 54. as may *d.* him best for dissolution
P. R. 2, 400. these things others quickly will *d.*
P. R. 3, 34. the throne of Cyrus held at his *d.*
P. R. 3, 369. to render thee the Parthian at *d.*.
S. A. 1382. which *d.* to something extraordinary
S. A. 1746. what the unsearchable *d.* of Highest
**Disposed.**—P. L. 3, 115. *d.* by absolute decree
P. L. 5, 646. and roseate dews *d.* all but the
P. L. 12, 349. kings their lords, whom God *d.*
P. R. 4, 56. well I have *d.* my aery microscope
**Disposer.**—P. L. 4, 635. my author and *d.*
P. R. 1, 393. if not *d.*—lend them oft my
**Disposition.**—S. A. 373. appoint not heavenly *d.*.
**Dispossess.**—P. L. 4, 961. to *d.* him
P. L. 12, 28. quite *d.* concord
**Dispossessed.**—P. L. 7, 142. us *d.*, he trusted
**Dispraise.**—P. L. 6, 382. nought merits but *d.*
P. L. 11, 166. distrust and all *d.*
S. A. 1723. no weakness, no contempt, *d.*, or blame
**Dispraised.**—P. R. 3, 56. of whom to be *d.*
**Disproportioned.**—S. M. 19. we did, till *d.* sin
**Disproportions.**—P. L. 8, 27. such *d.*
**Disputant.**—P. R. 4, 218. gravest Rabbies, *d*
**Dispute.**—P. L. 5, 822. shalt thou *d.* with him
P. L. 8, 55. and solve high *d.* with conjugal
P. L. 8, 158. back to them, is obvious to *d.*
P. R. 4, 214. to contemplation and profound *d.*
S. A. 1395. sending and command, *d.* thy coming
**Disputes.**—P. L. 6, 123. in both *d.* alike.
P. L. 8, 77. of the heavens hath left to their *d.*
P. L. 10, 828. Him, after all *d.*, forced I absolve
**Disrelish.**—P. L. 5, 305. and not *d.* thirst
P. L. 10, 569. hatefullest *d.* writhed their jaws
**Dissect.**—P. L. 9, 29. chief mastery to *d.*
**Dissemble.**—C. 805. I must *d.*, and try her net
**Dissembled.**—P. R. 1, 467. anger and disdain, *d.*.
**Dissembler.**—P. L. 3, 681. the false *d.*
**Dissension.**—P. L. 12, 353. the priests *d.*
**Dissent.**—P. L. 5, 679. can now thy sleep *d.*
P. L. 6, 146. seemed in thy world erroneous to *d.*
P. L. 9, 1160. been firm and fixed in thy *d.*
**Dissevering.**—C. 817. mutters of *d.* power
**Dissimulation.**—P. R. 1, 498. his gray *d.*
**Dissipation.**—P. L. 6, 598. but now foul *d.*
**Dissolve.**—P. L. 4, 955. to *d.* allegiance
P. L. 8, 291. insensible, and forthwith to *d.*
P. L. 11, 883. lest it again *d.* and shower
P. L. 12, 546. to *d.* Satan, with his perverted
P. R. 2, 165. and with voluptuous hope *d.*
S. A. 1149. to frustrate and *d.* these magic
Il P. 165. through mine ear, *d.* me into ecstasies
**Dissolved.**—P. L. 2. 506. council thus *d.*
P. L. 3, 457. *d.* on earth, fleet hither

P. R. 2, 436. of all their flowing wealth *d.*
**Dissolves.**—S. A. 177. their sense the air *d.*
**Dissolute.**—P. L, 11, 803. worldly or *d.*
S. A. 702. suffering the punishment of *d.* days
**Dissolutest.**—P. R. 2, 150. the *d.* Spirit
**Dissolution.**—P. L. 2, 127. and utter *d.*
P. L. 3, 458. till final *d.,* wander here
P. L. 10, 1049. we expected immediate *d.*
P. L. 11, 55. as may dispose him best for *d.*
P. L. 11, 552. and patiently attend my *d.*
P. L. 12, 459. when this world's *d.* shall be ripe
**Dissonance.**—P. L. 7, 32. the barbarous *d.*
C. 550. and filled the air with barbarous *d.*
**Dissonant.**—S. A. 662. and of *d.* mood from
**Dissuade.**—P. L. 2, 122. did not *d.* me most
P. L. 9, 293. not diffident of thee do I *d.*
**Dissuades.**—P. L. 2, 188. alike my voice *d.*
**Distance.**—P. L. 3, 578. his lordly eye keep *d.*
P. L. 7, 379. and still that *d.* keeps till night
P. L. 8, 21. for such their *d.* argues
P. L. 8, 113. *d.* inexpressible by numbers
P. L. 9, 9. now alienated, *d.* and distaste
P. L. 10, 247. powerful at greatest *d.* to unite
P. L. 10, 683. the low sun, to recompense his *d.*
S. A. 954. at *d.* I forgive thee; go with that
S. A. 1550. as at some *d.* from the place of
**Distances.**—P. L. 4, 945. and practised *d.*
**Distant.**—P. L. 3, 428. though *d.* far some
P. L. 3, 501. far *d.* he descries, ascending
P. L. 3, 566. that shone stars *d.,* but nigh
P. L. 3, 621. his visual ray to objects *d.* far
P. L. 4, 453. *d.* far from thence a murmuring
P. L. 6, 530. to descry the *d.* foe, where lodged
P. L. 6, 551. not *d.* far with heavy pace the foe
P. L. 7, 87. *d.* so high, with moving fires adorned
P. L. 9, 576. a goodly tree far *d.* to behold
P. L. 10, 362. though *d.* from thee worlds
P. L. 10, 673 like *d.* breadth
P. R. 2, 353. *d.* more under the trees
P. R. 4, 454. would mingle; but myself was *d.*
**Distaste.**—P. L. 9, 9. distance and *d.*
**Distemper.**—P. L. 7, 273. contiguous might *d.*
P. L. 9, 887. in her cheek *d.* flushing glowed
P. L. 11, 53. as a *d.,* gross, to air as gross
**Distempered.**—P. L. 4, 807. raise at least *d*
P. L. 9, 1131. from thus *d.*
P. L. 11, 56. wrought by sin that first *d.*
**Distempers.**—P. L. 4, 118. from such *d* foul
**Distended.**—P. L. 11, 880. in Heaven, *d.*
**Distends.**—P. L. 1, 572. and now his heart *d.*
**Distil.**—Cir. 7. your fiery essence can *d.* no tear
**Distilled.**—P. L. 5, 56. his dewy locks *d.*
C. 556. rose like a steam of rich *d* perfumes
**Distinct.**—P. L. 6, 846. *d.* with eyes
P. L. 6, 847. *d.* alike with multitude of eyes
P. L. 7, 536. for no place is yet *d.* by name
P. L. 9, 812. to see from thence *d.* each thing
S. A. 1595. relation more particular and *d.*
**Distinction.**—P. L. 5, 590. and for *d.* serve
**Distinguish.**—P. L. 5, 892. lest the wrath... *d.* not
C. 149. for so I can *d.* by mine art
**Distinguishable.**—P. L. 2, 668. none *d.*
P. R. 3, 424. *d.* scarce from Gentiles
**Distorted.**—P. L. 2, 784. fear and pain *d.*
**Distract.**—P. L. 4, 18. horror and doubt *d.*
S. A. 1556. sense *d.,* to know well what I utter.
**Distracted.**—P. R. 1, 108. *d.* and surprised
S. A. 1286. who surprised lose their defence, *d.*
**Distress.**—P. L. 10, 920. in this uttermost *d.*
P. L. 10, 942. now at his feet submissive in *d.*
P. L. 12, 613. since with sorrow and heart's *d.*
S. A. 1330. on my refusal, to *d.* me more
**Distressed.**—C. 905. of true virgin here *d.*
**Distrust.**—P. L. 9, 6. foul *d.,* and breach
P. L. 11, 166. reproach rather belongs, *d.*
P. R. 1, 355. dost thou, then, suggest to me *d.*
P. R. 3, 193. without *d.* or doubt that, he may
**Disturb.**—P. L. 1, 167. if I fail not, and *d.*
P. L. 2, 102. we feel our power sufficient to *d.*
P. L. 2, 971. with purpose to explore or to *d.*
P. L. 6, 225. and *d.,* though not destroy
P. L. 6, 549. instant without *d.* they took alarm

P. L. 9, 262. or to *d.* conjugal love, than which
L. 7. compels me to *d.* your season due
**Disturbance.**—P. L. 2, 873. joy upraise in his *d.*
**Disturbances.**—P. L. 10, 897. *d.* on earth
**Disturbed.**—P. L. 2, 657. aught *d.* their noise
P. L. 4, 879. and *d.* the charge of others
P. L. 4, 994. *d.* and torn with violence
P. L. 5, 226. and how *d.* this night the human
P. L. 6, 266. how hast thou *d.* Heaven's
P. L. 9, 191. but his sleep *d.* not, waiting close
P. L. 9, 668. to passion moved, fluctuates *d.*
P. L. 9, 918. after thoughts *d.*
P. R. 4, 409. and soon with ugly dreams *d.*
S. A. 1546. reason though *d.,* and scarce
C. 820. yet stay, be not *d.,* now I bethink me
**Ditties.**—P. L. 1, 449. in amorous *d.*
P. L. 11, 584. harp they sung soft amorous *d.*
L. 32. meanwhile the rural *d.* were not mute
**Divan.**—P L. 10, 457. raised from their dark *d.*
**Diverse.**—P. L. 4, 234. runs *d.,* wandering
P. L. 10, 284. flew *d.,* and with power
**Diverted.**—P. L. 9, 814. may have *d.* from
P. R. 2, 349. was that crude apple that *d.* Eve
**Divide.**—P. L. 4, 688. their songs *d.* the night
P. L. 7, 262. let it *d.* the waters from the waters
P. L. 7, 340. to *d.* the day from night.
P. L. 7, 352. and light from darkness to *d.*
P. L. 9, 214. let us *d.* our labours, thou, where
P. L. 10, 379. monarchy with thee *d.*
C. 279. *d.* you from near-ushering
P. 4. my Muse with Angels did *d.* to sing
**Divided.**—P. L. 4, 111. *d.* empire with
P. L. 4, 233. now *d.* into four main streams
P. L. 6, 230. each *d.* legion might have seemed
P. L. 6, 381. for strength from truth *d.*
P. L. 6, 570. to right and left the front *d.*
P. L. 7, 251. darkness by the hemisphere *d.*
P. L. 10, 836. though *d.* with that bad woman
P. L. 12, 157. called Egypt, *d.* by the river Nile
P. L. 12, 199. *d.* till his rescued gain..shore
P. R. 4, 32. thence in the midst *d.* by a river
**Divides.**—P. L. 3, 419. whose first convex *d.*
P. L. 6, 70. wood nor stream *d.* their...ranks
P. R. 1, 401. that fellowship in pain *d.* not smart
**Dividing.**—P. L. 7, 269. from those above *d.*
H. 50. with turtle wing the amorous clouds *d.*
**Dividual.**—P. L. 7, 382. lesser lights *d.* holds
P. L. 12, 85. from her hath no *d.* being
**Divine.**—P. L. 1, 683. than aught *d.* or holy
P. L. 2, 99. or if our substance be indeed *d.*
P. L. 3, 44. flocks, or herds, or human face *d.*
P. L. 3, 141. and in his face *d.* compassion
P. L. 3, 225. whom the fulness dwells of love *d.*
P. L. 3, 384. begotten Son, *D.* Similitude
P. L. 3, 411. nowhere to be found less than *D.*
P. L. 4, 291. for in their looks *d.* the image
P. L. 4, 364. so lively shines in them *d.*
P. L. 5, 67. O fruit *d.,* sweet of thyself
P. L. 5, 159. beyond thought, and power *d.*
P. L. 5, 256. as by work *d.* the sovran architect
P. L. 5, 278. to shade his lineaments *d.*
P. L. 5, 458. *d.* effulgence, whose high power
P. L. 5, 546. *d.* instructor, I have heard
P. L. 5, 625. and in their motions harmony *d.*
P. L. 5, 734. lightning *d.,* ineffable, serene
P. L. 5, 806. and *d.* commands obeyed
P. L. 6, 101. idol of majesty *d.*
P. L. 6, 158. they feel vigour *d.* within them
P. L. 6, 184. and his *d.* behests obey
P. L. 6, 780. Power *D.* his way prepared
P. L. 7, 2. whose voice *d.* following
P. L. 7, 72. *d.* Interpreter by favour sent
P. L. 7, 195. radiance crowned of majesty *d.*
P. L. 8, 6. *d.* historian, who thus largely hast
P. L. 8, 215. thy words, with grace *d.,* imbued
P. L. 8, 295. one came, methought, of shape *d.*
P. L. 8, 314. the trees appeared, presence *D.*
P. L. 8, 436. answer from the gracious Voice *D.*
P. L. 9, 606. all that fair and good in thy *d.*
P. L. 9, 776. the cure of all, this fruit *d.*
P. L. 9, 845. oft his heart, *d.* of something ill

G

P. L. 9, 865. but of *d.* effect, to open eyes
P. L. 9, 899. holy, *d.*, good, amiable, or sweet!
P. L. 9, 986. so *d.* that what of sweet before
P. L. 9, 993. of choice to incur *d.* displeasure
P. L. 10, 139. so fit, so acceptable, so, *d.*
P. L. 10, 857. Justice *d.* not hasten to be just
P. L. 10, 858. Justice *d.* mends not her slowest
P. L. 11, 319. where he vouchsafed presence *D.*
P. L. 11, 354. and of his steps the track *d.*
P. L. 11, 512. retaining still *d.* similitude
P. L. 11, 606. holy and pure, conformity *d.*
P. L. 12, 9. objects *d.* must needs impair
P. R. 1, 35. with the voice *d.* nigh thunder-struck
P. R. 1, 141. to show him worthy of his birth *d.*
P. R. 2, 138. perfections absolute, graces. *d.*
P. R. 4, 588. celestial food, *d.* ambrosial fruits
S. A. 44. not rashly call in doubt *d.* prediction
S. A. 210. tax not *d.* disposal, wisest men
S. A. 422. but thou didst plead *d.* impulsion
S. A. 526. full of *d.* instinct, after some proof
S. A. 1683. fallen into wrath *d.*, as their own ruin
C. 245. breathe such *d.* enchanting ravishment
C. 469. the *d.* property of her first being
C. 476. how charming is *d.* philosophy
C. 630. but of *d.* effect, he culled me out
A. 4. too *d.* to be mistook
A. 30. *d.* Alpheus, who by secret sluice
Il P. 100. the tale of Troy *d.*
H. 177. Apollo from his shrine can no more *d.*
D. F. I. 35. mortality, that showed thou wast *d.*
T. 15. and perfectly *d.*, with truth, and peace
S. M. 3. wed your *d.* sounds, and mixed power
**Divined.**—P. L. 10, 357. in my heart *d.*
**Divinely.**—P. L. 6, 761. work *d.* wrought
P. L. 8, 500. though *d.* brought, yet innocence
P. L. 9, 489. she fair, *d.* fair, fit love for gods
P. L. 10, 67. and thus *d.* answered mild
P. R. 1, 26. but him the Baptist soon descried, *d.*
P. R. 4, 357. as men *d.* taught, and better
S. A. 226. the work to which I was *d.* called
**Divinely-warbled.**—H. 96. *d.-w.* voice
**Divinest.**—Il P. 12. hail. *d.* melancholy
**Divinity.**—P. L. 9, 1010. *d.* within them
**Divisible.**—P. L. 6, 331. closed, not long *d.*
**Diurnal.**—P. L. 4, 594. *d.*, or this less
P. L. 7, 22. within the visible *d.* sphere
P. L. 8, 22. and their swift return *d.*
P. L. 8, 134. nocturnal and *d.* rhomb supposed
P. L. 10, 1069. ere this *d.* star leave cold
**Divulge.**—P. L. 8, 73. and not *d.* his secrets
S. A. 1248. though fame *d.* him father of five sons
**Divulged.**—P. L. 8, 583. and *d.*, if aught
S. A. 204. have *d.* the secret of God
**Divulges.**—P. R. 3, 62. and *d.* him through
**Dizzy.**—P. L. 2, 753. dim thine eyes, and *d.*
P. R. 2, 420. or at thy heels the *d.* multitude
**Do.**—P. L. 1, 149. or *d.* him mightier service
P. L. 1, 152. *d.* his errands in the gloomy deep
P. L. 1, 159. to *d.* aught good never will be
P. L. 1, 160. but ever to *d.* ill our sole delight
P. L. 1, 414. to *d.* him wanton rites
P. L. 2, 199. to suffer, as to *d.*, our strength
P. L. 3, 105. only what they needs must *d.*
P. L. 4, 392. compels me now to *d.* what else
P. L. 4, 475. what could I *d.* but follow
P. L. 4, 855. save us trial what the least can *d.*
P. L. 4, 1008. then to boast what arms can *d.*
P. L. 5, 121. thou never wilt consent to *d.*
P. L. 6, 566. *d.* as you have in charge
P. L. 6, 600. what should they *d.*?
P. L. 6, 683. in whose hand what by decree I *d.*
P. L. 6, 695. had performed what war can *d.*
P. L. 8, 549. that what she wills to *d.* or say
P. L. 8, 562. hath done her part *d.* thou but
P. L. 8, 636. to *d.* aught which else free will
P. L. 9, 356. to *d.* what God expressly hath
P. L. 9, 375. hath done his part, *d.* thine
P. L. 9, 944. frustrate, *d.*, undo, and labour lose
P. L. 10, 69. both in Heaven and Earth to *d.*
P. L. 10, 826. not to *d.* only, but to will the
P. L. 10, 1086. what better can we *d.*, than to

P. L. 12, 493. what man can *d.* against them
P. L. 12, 501. to speak all tongues, and *d.*
P. R. 1, 75. or rather to *d.* him honour as their
P. R. 1, 80. I saw the Prophet *d.* him reverence
P. R. 1, 88. and what will he not *d.* to advance
P. R. 1, 203. and thence to *d.* what might be
P. R. 1, 223. and make persuasion *d.* the work
P. R. 1, 377. for what he bids I *d.*
P. R. 1, 423. or pleasure to *d.* ill excites
P. R. 1, 495. bid not or forbid. *D.* as thou findest
P. R. 2, 259. more to *d.* my Father's will
P. R. 2, 389. my hunger what hast thou to *d.*
P. R. 2, 399. but I see what I can *d.* or offer
P. R. 2, 448. who could *d.* mighty things
P. R. 2, 456. prompt her to *d.* aught may merit
P. R. 3, 8. best to say canst say, to *d.* canst *d.*
P. R. 3, 74. what *d.* these worthies but rob
P. R. 3, 180. what canst thou better *d.*
P. R. 3, 195. who best can suffer best can *d.*
P. R. 4, 489. they can *d.* as signs betokening
S. A. 1104. but *d.* what thou wouldst
S. A. 1217. to *d.* my part from Heaven assigned
S. A. 1385. nothing to *d.*, be sure, that may
C. 122. what hath night to *d.* with sleep
C. 373. Virtue could see to *d.* what Virtue would
C. 392. or *d.* his gray hairs any violence
C. 611. but here thy sword can *d.* thee little stead
**Doatest.**—P. R. 2, 175. *d.* on womankind
**Doctor.**—S. A. 299. and no man therein *d.*
**Doctors.**—C. 707. those budge *d.* of the Stoic fur
U. C. II. 19. though the cross *d.* all stood hearers
**Doctrine.**—P. L. 5, 856. *d.* which we would
P. L. 12, 506. their *d.* and their story written
P. R. 2, 474. saving *d.*, and from error lead
P. R. 4, 290. no other *d.* needs, though granted
S. A. 297. for of such *d.* never was there school
C. 787. the sage and serious *d.* of Virginity
**Dodged.**—U. C. I. 8. *d.* with him betwixt
**Dodona.**—P. L. 1, 518. Delphian cliff, or in *D.*
**Doer.**—S. A. 248. though mute, spoke loud the *d.*
**Doff.**—S. A. 1410. *d.* these links
**Doffed.**—H. 33. had *d.* her gaudy trim
**Dog.**—C. 405. I fear the dread events that *d.* them
H. 212. Isis, and Orus, and the *d.* Anubis, haste
**Dogs.**—P. L. 10, 616. these *d.* of Hell advance
S. A. 694. their carcasses to *d.* and fowls a prey
S. 12, 4. of owls and cuckoos, asses, apes, and *d.*
**Doing.**—P. L. 1, 158. to be weak is miserable, *d.*
P. L. 2, 162. whatever *d.*, what can we suffer
P. L. 2, 340. and may least rejoice in *d.* what
P. L. 10, 142. her *d.* seemed to justify the deed
P. R. 3, 97. he taught, and suffered for so *d.*
C. 535. *d.* abhorred rites to Hecate
**Doings.**—P. L. 4, 622. of their *d.* God takes no
P. L. 11, 720. and their *d.* great
P. L. 12, 50. walks to mark their *d.*
P. R. 1, 469. with *d.* which not will, but misery
S. A. 947. bearing my words and *d.* to the lords
U. C. II. 27. but had his *d.* lasted as they were
**Dole.**—P. L. 4, 894. and soonest recompense *d.*
S. A. 1529. he now be dealing *d.* among his foes
**Doleful.**—P. L. 1, 65. of sorrow, *d.* shades
**Dolorous.**—P. L. 2, 619. many a region *d.*
P. L. 6, 658. pain implacable, and many a *d.*
P. R. 1, 364. but that off leaving my *d.* prison
H. 140. leave her *d.* mansions to the peering day
**Dolphins.**—P. L. 7, 410. and bended *d.* play
L. 164. and, O ye *d.*, waft the hapless youth
**Domain.**—P. R. 4, 81. whose wide *d.*
**Domestic.**—P. L. 4, 760. fountain of *d.* sweets
P. L. 9, 318. so spake *d.* Adam, in his care
P. L. 11, 617. woman's *d.* honour and chief
S. A. 917. at home, in leisure and *d.* ease
S. A. 1048. that in *d.* good combines
**Dominations.**—P. L. 3, 392. the aspiring *D.*
P. L. 5, 601. Thrones, *D.*, Princedoms, Virtues
P. L. 5, 772. Thrones, *D.*, Princedoms, Virtues
P. L. 5, 840. Thrones, *D.*, Princedoms, Virtues
P. L. 10, 87. Princedoms and *D.* ministrant
P. L. 10, 460. Thrones, *D.*, Princedoms, Virtues
**Dominic.**—P. L. 3, 479. put on the weeds of *D.*

**Dominion.**—P. L. 2, 978. from your *d.* won
P. L. 3, 732. in her pale *d.* checks the night
P. L. 4, 33. lookest from thy sole *d.* like the God
P. L. 4, 430. *d.* given over all other creatures
P. L. 5, 751. which all thy *d.*, Adam, is no more
P. L. 6, 422. honour, *d.* glory, and renown
P.L. 6, 887. Son, Heir, and Lord, to him *d.* given
P. L. 7, 532. subdue it, and throughout *d.* hold
P. L. 8, 545. expressing the character of that *d.*
P. L. 10, 244. and *d.* given me large beyond
P. L. 10, 400. thence on the earth *d.* exercise
P. L. 12, 27. will arrogate *d.* undeserved
P. L. 12, 68. over beast, fish, fowl, *d.* absolute
P. R. 2, 434. to gain *d.*, or to keep it gained
P. R. 3, 296. under his *d.* holds
**Dominions.**—P. L. 2, 11. Powers and *D.*
P. L. 3, 320. Thrones, Princedoms, Powers, *D.*
**Donation.**—P. L. 12, 69. right we hold by his *d.*
P. R. 4, 184. other *d.* none
**Done.**—P. L. 2, 384. *d.* all to spite the great
P. L. 3, 203. yet all is not *d.* Man disobeying
P. L. 5, 462. favour in this honour *d.* to man
P. L. 5, 844. all honour to him *d.* returns our
P. L. 6, 29. servant of God well *d.*! well hast
P. L. 6, 241. deeds of eternal fame were *d.*
P. L. 6, 805. as ye have received, so have ye *d.*
P. L. 6, 906. despite *d.* against the most High
P. L. 7, 65. what within Eden or without was *d.*
P. L. 7, 151. exalt him in the harm already *d.*
P. L. 7, 164. speak thou, and be it *d.*
P. L. 7, 506. master-work, the end of all yet *d.*
P. L. 7, 637. and what, before thy memory, was *d.*
P. L. 8, 203. I have heard relating what was *d.*
P. L. 8, 561. accuse not Nature, she hath *d.*
P. L. 9, 199. that *d.*, partake the season
P. L. 9, 375. for God towards thee hath *d.*
P. L. 9, 835. low reference *d.*, as to the Power
P. L. 9, 889. the fatal trespass *d.* by Eve
P. L. 9, 926. past who can recall, or *d.* undo
P. L. 10, 2. despiteful act of Satan *d.* in Paradise
P. L. 10, 158. what is this which thou hast *d*?
P. L. 10, 175. because thou hast *d.* this, thou art
P. L. 10, 470. what I have *d.*, what suffered
P. L. 11, 694. and for glory *d.* of triumph
P. L. 11, 791. and *d.* much waste, subduing
P. L. 12, 103. for the shame *d.* to his father
P. L. 12, 475. repent me now of sin by me *d.*
P. R. 1, 15. above heroic, though in secret *d.*
P. R. 2, 444. unknown what hath been *d.*
P. R. 2, 482. greater and nobler *d.*
P. R. 3, 100. if for fame and glory aught be *d.*
P. R. 4, 168. (easily *d.*) and hold them all of me
P. R. 4, 440. after all this mischief *d.*
P. R. 4, 475. rightliest *d.* not when it must
S. A. 243. those great acts which God had *d.*
S. A. 478. but for thee what shall be *d.*
S. A. 1104. of what thou wouldst have *d.*
S. A. 1128. in safety what thou wouldst have *d.*
S. A. 1594. of what first or last was *d.*
C. 137. till utmost end of all thy dues be *d.*
C. 431. be it not *d.* in pride or in presumption
C. 1012. but now my task is smoothly *d.*
L. 57. for what could that have *d.*?
L. 67. were it not better *d.*, as others use
L'A. 115. thus *d.* the tales, to bed they creep
H. 105. to think her part was *d.*
**Doom.**—P. L. 1, 53. but his *d.* reserved him
P. L. 2, 209. this is now our *d.*; which if we can
P. L. 2, 550. and hapless fall by *d.* of battle
P. L. 3, 159. return, though to his heavier *d.*
P. L. 3, 224. to Death and Hell by *d.* severe
P. L. 3, 328. of all past ages, to the general *d.*
P. L. 3, 401. thou didst not *d.* so strictly
P. L. 3, 404. perceive thee purposed not to *d.*
P. L. 4, 840. thy sin and place of *d.* obscure
P. L. 6, 278. this avenging sword begin thy *d.*
P. L. 6, 378. nor of renown less eager. yet by *d.*
P. L. 6, 385. therefore eternal silence be their *d.*
P. L. 6, 692. for I suspend their *d.*
P. L. 6, 817. to me their *d.* he hath assigned
P. L. 9, 763. we eat of this fair fruit, our *d.*

P. L. 9, 953. certain to undergo like *d.*
P. L. 10, 76. that I may mitigate their *d.*
P. L. 10, 172. Satan, first in sin, his *d.* applied
P. L. 10, 344. thence gathered his own *d.*
P. L. 10, 378. retiring, by his own *d.* alienated
P. L. 10, 517. he sinned, according to his *d.*
P. L. 10, 769. be it so for I submit; his *d.* is fair
P. L. 10, 841. only like, both crime and *d.*
P. L. 10, 926. a foe by *d.* express assigned us
P. L. 10, 1026. from the pain we are by *d.* to
P. L. 11, 40. till death, his *d.*
P. L. 11, 76. once more to sound at general *d.*
P. L. 12, 428. this godlike act annuls thy *d.*
S. 1, 10. foretell my hopeless *d.*, in some grove
H. 156. the wakeful trump of *d.* must thunder
Cir. 17. for we, by rightful *d.* remediless
D. F. I. 33. could Heaven ... thee so strictly *d.*?
**Doomed.**—P. L. 2, 316. King of Heaven hath *d.*
P. L. 4, 890. from Hell, though thither *d.*
P. L. 5, 907. towers to swift destruction *d.*
P. L. 10, 796. Man is not so, but mortal *d.*
L. 92. what hard mishap hath *d.* this swain
**Door.**—P. L. 1, 504. when the hospitable *d.*
P. L. 5, 299. in the *d.* he sat of his cool bower
P. L. 6, 9. at the other *d.* obsequious darkness
P. L. 10, 389. so near Heaven's *d.*, triumphal
P. L. 10, 443. the *d.* of that Plutonian hall
P. L. 11, 731. and in the side a *d.* contrived
P. L. 11, 737. and God made fast the *d.*
L. 130. but that two-handed engine at the *d.*
V. Ex. 5. driving dumb Silence from the portal *d.*
V. Ex. 34. and at Heaven's *d.* look in
V. Ex. 85. yet shall he live in strife, and at his *d.*
**Doors.**—P. L. 1, 723. straight the *d.*, opening
P. L. 2, 881. infernal *d.* and on their hinges
P. L. 3, 525. his sad exclusion from the *d.*
P. L. 4, 189. whose substantial *d.*, cross-barred
P. L. 7, 566. open, ye heavens, your living *d.*!
P. L. 11, 17. dimensionless through heavenly *d.*
P. R. 1, 82. the clouds unfold her crystal *d.*
P. R. 1, 281. Heaven opened her eternal *d.*
S. A. 77. within *d.*, or without, still as a fool
S. A. 950. whose *d.* my feet shall never enter
L'A. 113. and crop-full out of *d.* he flings
Il P. 84. to bless the *d.* from nightly harm
S. 8, 2. whose chance on these defenceless *d.*
**Dorado.**—P. L. 11, 411. sons call El *D.*
**Dorian.**—P. L. 1, 550. to the *D.* mood of flutes
P. R. 4, 257. Æolian charms and *D.* lyric odes
**Doric.**—P. L. 1, 519. all the bounds of *D.* land
P. L. 1, 714. and *D.* pillars overlaid
L. 189. with eager thought warbling his *D.* lay
**Dost.**—P. L. 8, 588. in loving thou *d.* well
**Dotage.**—S. A. 1042. enslaved with *d.*
**Dothan.**—P. L. 11, 217. appeared in *D.*
**Double.**—P. L. 4, 102. bought with *d.* smart
P. L. 5, 783. too much to one, but *d.* how endured
P. L. 9, 332. who rather *d.* honour gain
P. L. 10, 850. represented all things with *d.* terror
P. L. 10, 1040. shall *d.* ours upon
P. L. 11, 129. four faces each had, like a *d.*
P. L. 11, 201. else this *d.* object in our sight
P. R. 1, 435. dark, ambiguous, and with *d.* sense
S. A. 53. without a *d.* share of wisdom
S. A. 593. but yield to *d.* darkness nigh at hand
C. 335. in *d.* night of darkness and of shades
C. 955. will *d.* all their mirth and cheer
**Doubled.**—P. L. 1, 485. *d.* that sin in Bethel
P. L. 1, 616. whereat their *d.* ranks they bend
P. L. 4, 1009. though *d.* now to trample thee
P. L. 6, 602. and indecent overthrow *d.*
**Double-faced.**—S. A. 971. if not *d.-f.*
**Double-formed.**—P. L. 2, 741. thus *d.-f.*
**Double-founted.**—P. L. 12, 144. the *d.-f.*
**Double-mouthed.**—S. A. 971. fame ... is *d.-m.*
**Double-shade.**—P. R. 1, 500. to *d.-s.* the desert
**Doubt.**—P. L. 1, 558. anguish and *d.* and fear
P. L. 2, 94. what *d.* we to incense his utmost ire
P. L. 4, 18. horror and *d.* distract his troubled
P. L. 4, 426. some dreadful thing no *d.*
P. L. 4, 795. on errand bad, no *d.*

P. L. 4, 888. this question asked puts me in *d*.
P. L. 4, 890. thou wouldst thyself, no *d*.
P. L. 4, 907. gravely in *d*. whether to hold
P. L. 5, 554. some *d*. within me move
P. L. 6, 563. but that I *d*.; however witness
P. L. 6, 630. thoughts beyond all *d*. of victory
P. L. 8, 13. something yet of *d*. remains
P. L. 8, 64. and Raphael now to Adam's *d*.
P. L. 8, 116. show invalid that which thee to *d*.
P. L. 8, 179. to whom thus Adam, cleared of *d*.
P. L. 8, 568. an outside fair, no *d*., and worthy
P. L. 9, 95. which, in other beasts observed, *d*.
P. L. 9, 244. *d*. not but our joint hands
P. L. 9, 251 other *d*. possesses me, lest harm
P. L. 9, 257. watches, no *d*., with greedy hope
P. L. 9, 279. shouldst my firmness therefore *d*.
P. L. 9, 615. in *d*. the virtue of that fruit
P. L. 10, 782. yet one *d*. pursues me still
P. L. 10, 793. let this appease the *d*.
P. L. 10, 1022. *d*. not but God hath wisely
P. L. 11, 211. a glorious apparition, had not *d*.
P. L. 11, 349. *d*. not but in valley and in plain
P. L. 12, 285. *d*. not but that sin will reign
P. L. 12, 473. full of *d*. I stand, whether
P. R. 1, 79. thenceforth the nations may not *d*.
P. R. 2, 11. began to *d*., and doubted many days
P. R. 2, 12. days increased, increased their *d*.
P. R. 2, 383. I can at will, *d*. not, as soon as thou
P. R. 3, 193. distrust or *d*., that He may know
P. R. 4, 473. what thou art ordained, no *d*.
P. R. 4, 501. for Son of God to me is yet in *d*.
S. A. 43. not rashly call in *d*. divine prediction
S. A. 300. there be who *d*. his ways not just
S. A. 454. *d*. in feeble hearts, propense enough
S. A. 740. prevailing over fear and timorous *d*.
S. A. 905. for want of words no *d*., or lack
S. A. 1379. important cause, thou need'st not *d*.
S. A. 1534. He can, I know, but *d*. to think he will
S. A. 1745. all is best, though we oft *d*.
C. 409. secure without all *d*. or controversy
**Doubted.**—P. L. 1, 114.·*d*. his empire
P. R. 2, 11. began to doubt and *d*. many days
P. R. 4, 296. a third sort *d*. all things
**Doubtest.**—P. R. 2, 377. what *d*. thou
**Doubtful.**—P. L. 1, 527. like *d*. hue
P. L. 2, 154. how he can is *d*.; that he never will
P. L. 2, 203. contending, and so *d*. what might
P. L. 2, 486. thus they their *d*. consultations
P. L. 5, 682. to debate what *d*. may ensue
P. L. 6, 423. have sustained one day in *d*. fight
S. A. 477. nor will long endure it *d*.
S. A. 732. with *d*. feet and wavering resolution
**Doubting.**—P. L. 4, 983. ploughman *d*. stands
P. R. 1, 137. then told'st her, *d*. how these things
P. R. 2, 147. so spake the old Serpent, *d*.
S. A. 920. not *d*. their favourable ear
**Doubtless.**—P. L. 2, 315. *d*.! while we dream
P. L. 9, 745. great are thy virtues, *d*., best
S. A. 1473. *d*., the people shouting to behold
**Doubts.**—P. L. 7, 60. soon repealed the *d*.
P. R. 2, 368. what *d*. the Son of God to sit
**Dove.**—P. L. 11, 857. the surer messenger, a *d*.
P. R. 1, 30. and in likeness of a *d*.
P. R. 1, 81. thence on his head a perfect *d*.
P. R. 1, 282. spirit descended on me like a *d*.
**Dove-like.**—P. L, 1, 21. *d*.-*l*. sat'st brooding
**Dower.**—P. L. 5, 218. with her brings her *d*.
**Down.**—P. L. 1, 46. *d*. to bottomless perdition
P. L. 1, 349. in even balance *d*. they light
P. L. 2, 771. *d*. they fell, driven head long
P. L. 2, 772. pitch of Heaven, *d*. into this deep
P. L. 3, 19. the heavenly muse to venture *d*.
P. L. 3, 528. a passage *d*. to the earth
P. L. 3, 562. *d*. right into the world's
P. L. 3, 574. up or *d*., by centre or eccentric
P. L. 3, 651. or *d*. to the Earth bear his swift
P. L. 3, 740. *d*. from the ecliptic, sped with
P. L. 4, 125. whose eye pursued him *d*.
P. L. 4, 261. waters fall *d*. the slope hills
P. L. 4, 304. as a veil, *d*. to the slender waist
P. L. 4, 396. *d*. he alights among the sportful

P. L. 5, 266. *d*. thither prone in flight he speeds
P. L. 6, 361. but anon, *d*. cloven to the waist
P. L. 6, 593. but *d*. they fell by thousands
P. L. 7, 15. with like safety guided *d*.
P. L. 8, 157. conveyed so far *d*. to his habitable
P. L. 9, 169. *d*. as low as high he soared
P. L. 10, 305. smooth, easy, inoffensive, *d*. to
P. L. 10, 398. all yours, right *d*. to Paradise
P. L. 10, 447. *d*. awhile he sat, and round about
P. L. 10, 513. supplanted, *d*. he fell
P. L. 10, 541. *d*. their arms, *d*. fell both spear
P. L. 10, 648. or *d*. from Heaven descend
P. L. 10, 675. thence *d*. amain by Leo
P. L. 11, 187. *d*. from a hill the beast that
P. L. 11, 209. *d*. from a sky of jasper lighted
P. L. 11, 282. and whither wander *d*. into
P. L. 11, 392. *d*. to the golden Chersonese
P. L. 11, 568. *d*. to the veins of earth
P. L. 11, 576. *d*. to the plain descended
P. L. 11, 743. *d*. rushed the rain impetuous
P. L. 11, 833. *d*. the great river to the opening
P. L. 12, 185. cloud of locusts swarming *d*.
P. L. 12, 639. and *d*. the cliff as fast to the
P. R. 2, 128. our expulsion *d*. to Hell
P. R. 4, 631. lest he command them *d*.
S. A. 322. *d*. reason, then . . vain reasonings *d*.
S. A. 327. with careful step, locks white as *d*.
S. A. 1478. willingly be paid and numbered *d*.
S. A. 1650. he tugged, he shook, till *d*. they came
C. 251. at every fall smoothing the raven *d*.
D. F. I. 56. let *d*. in cloudy throne to do the world
**Downcast.**—P. L. 1, 523. *d*. and damp
**Downfall.**—P. L. 1, 116. beneath this *d*.
**Downs.**—P. L. 4, 252. or level *d*., and flocks
C. 505. doth enrich these *d*. is worth a thought
**Downward.**—P. L. 1, 463. and *d*. fish
P. L. 1, 681. thoughts were always *d*. bent
P. L. 3, 722. look *d*. on that globe
P. L. 4, 591. bore him slope *d*. to the sun
P. L. 7, 237. but *d*. purged the black, tartareous
P. L. 9, 79. *d*. as far antarctic
C. 53. and *d*. fell into a grovelling swine
Il P. 43. with a sad leaden *d*. cast
**Downy.**—P. L. 4, 334. on the soft *d*. bank
P. L. 5, 282. his loins and thighs with *d*. gold
P. L. 7, 438. bathed their *d*. breast
P. L. 9, 851. of fairest fruit that *d*. smiled
**Draff.**—P. L. 10, 630. lick up the *d*. and filth
S. A. 574. or the *d*. of servile food, consume me
**Drag.**—P. L. 4, 965. to the infernal pit I *d*. thee
P. L. 6, 358. and at his chariot wheels to *d*. him
P. L. 12, 454. *d*. in chains through all his realm
C. 608. or *d*. him by the curls to a foul death
**Dragged.**—P. L. 6, 260. captive *d*. in chains
**Dragging.**—S. A. 1371. not *d*.
**Dragon.**—P. L. 4, 3. the *D*. put to second rout
P. L. 10, 529. now *d*. grown, larger than whom
S. A. 1692. and as an evening *d*. came
C. 131. when the *d*. womb of Stygian darkness
Il P. 59. while Cynthia checks her *d*. yoke
H. 168. the old *D*. under ground
**Dragon-watch.**—C. 395. the guard of *d*.-*w*.
**Drained.**— P. L. 3, 605. *d*. through a limbec
P. L. 6, 851. their wonted vigour left them *d*.
P. L. 11, 570. the liquid ore he *d*. into fit moulds
P. R. 2, 346. for which was *d*. Pontus and Lucrine
**Drank.**—P. R. 1, 352. nor eat nor *d*.
S. A. 550. I *d*., from the clear milky juice allaying
**Draught.**—S. A. 9. unwholesome *d*.; but here
C. 701. were it a *d*. for Juno when she banquets
**Draughts.**—P. L. 5, 306. thirst of nectarous *d*.
**Draw.**—P. L. 2, 25. *d*. envy from each inferior
P. L. 3, 161. and to Hell *d*. after him
P. L. 3, 220. *d*. the deadly forfeiture
P. L. 4, 532. *d*. what further would be learned
P. L. 4, 782. Uzziel! half these *d*. off, and coast
P. L. 5, 729. let us advise, and to this hazard *d*.
P. L. 7, 306. and perpetual *d*. their humid train
P. L. 7, 365. their golden urns *d*. light
P. L. 8, 348. to *d*. the thinner air
P. L. 9, 223. object new casual discourse *d*. on

P. L. 9, 822. more to *d*. his love, and render me
P. L. 9, 914. the link of nature *d*. me
P. L. 9, 956. bond of nature *d*.me to my own
P. L. 10, 267. such a scent I *d*. of carnage
P. L. 10, 801. will he *d*. out, for anger's sake
P. R. 1, 372. *d*. the proud king Ahab into fraud
P. R. 2, 161. skilled to retire, and in retiring *d*.
P. R. 2, 166. *d*. out with credulous desire
S. A. 7. scarce freely *d*. the air, imprisoned also
S. A. 178. he speaks, let us *d*. nigh
S. A. 360. *d*. a scorpion's tail behind
S. A. 804. *d*. thee forth to perilous enterprises
S. A. 1058. so shall he least confusion *d*.
S. A. 1267. it may with mine *d*. their own ruin
S. A. 1626. to heave, pull, *d*., or break, he still
C. 487. best *d*., and stand upon our guard
C. 554. that *d*. the litter of close-curtained Sleep
A. 71. and the low world in measured motion *d*.
L. 126. and the rank mist they *d*.
**Draw'st.**—P. L. 4, 975. *d*. his triumphant
**Drawn.**—P. L. 1, 664. *d*. from the thighs
P. L. 3, 379. *d*. round about thee like a
P. L. 3, 509. by model, or by shading pencil *d*.
P. L. 3, 517. but *d*. up to heaven sometimes
P. L. 3, 522. rapt in a chariot *d*. by fiery steeds
P. L. 4, 63. though mean, *d*. to his part
P. L. 4, 228. with kindly thirst up-*d*.
P. L. 7, 14. and *d*. empyreal air, thy tempering
P. L. 10, 262. I miss the way so strongly *d*.
P. L. 10, 511. his visage *d*. he felt to sharp
P. L. 10, 886. the part sinister, from me *d*.
S. A. 762. are *d*. to wear out miserable days
Il P. 36. over thy decent shoulders *d*.
L'A. 140. of linked sweetness long *d*. out
**Draws.**—P. L. 7, 416. *d*. in, and at his trunk
P. L. 10, 245. whatever *d*. me on, or sympathy
P. L. 11, 205. that *d*. o'er the blue
P. R. 2, 168. as the magnetic hardest iron *d*.
S. A. 1041. or by her charms *d*. him
S. A. 1067. a rougher tongue *d*. hitherward
S. 21, 6. in mirth that after no repenting *d*.
**Dread.**—P. L. 1, 333. by whom they *d*.
P. L. 1, 406. the obscene *d*. of Moab's sons
P. L. 1, 555. firm and unmoved with *d*. of death
P. L. 1, 589. yet observed their *d*. Commander
P. L. 1, 644. or *d*. new war, provoked
P. L. 2, 16. glorious and more *d*.
P. L. 2, 263. deep world of darkness do we *d*.
P. L. 2, 510. nor less than Hell's *d*. Emperor
P. L. 3, 326. to proclaim thy *d*. tribunal
P. L. 4, 82. my *d*. of shame among the Spirits
P. L. 6, 59. nor with less *d*. the loud ethereal
P. L. 6, 648. towards them so *d*. they saw
P. L. 9, 158. the vigilance I *d*.; and to elude
P. L. 9, 969. or aught than death more *d*.
P. L. 10, 998. less than none of what we *d*.
P. L. 11, 248. hung the sword, Satan's dire *d*.
P. L. 12, 14. and while the *d*. of judgment
P. R. 1, 53. with *d*. attending when that fatal
P. R. 3, 220. whose ire I *d*. more than the fire
P. R. 3, 306. of equal *d*. in flight or in pursuit
P. R. 4, 576. so struck with *d*. and anguish
P. R. 4, 626. hereafter learn with awe to *d*.
S. A. 342. *d*. of Israel's foes, who with a strength
S. A. 1247. I *d*. him not, nor all his giant brood
S. A. 1474. great *d*., captive and blind
S. A. 1673. before our Living *D*. who dwells
C. 405. I fear the *d*. events that dog them both
C. 441. hence had the huntress Dian her *d*. bow
L. 132. return, Alpheus, the *d*. voice is past
H. 206. Moloch, fled, hath left in shadows *d*.
**Dreaded.** P. L. 1, 464. *d*. through the coast
P. L. 2, 293. for such another field they *d*.
P. L. 2, 474. they *d*. not more the adventure
P. L. 2, 964. and the *d*. name of Demogorgon
P. L. 4, 929. seconded thy else not *d*. spear
P. L. 6, 491. the Thunderer of his only *d*. bolt
P. L. 9, 1114. to hide their guilt and *d*. shame
P. R. 1, 58. the circling hours this *d*. time
S. A. 530. and *d*. on hostile ground, none daring
S. A. 1417. so *d*. once, may now exasperate them

H. 222. the *d*. Infant's hand
**Dreadful.**—P. L. 1, 130. and in *d*. deeds
P. L. 1, 183. casts pale and *d*.
P. L. 1, 564. of *d*. length, and dazzling arms
P. L. 2, 426. or accept, alone, the *d*. voyage
P. L. 2, 672. and shook a *d*. dart
P. L. 2, 706. grew tenfold more *d*. and deform
P. L. 3, 393. thy Father's *d*. thunder didst not
P. L. 4, 426. some *d*. thing no doubt
P. L. 4, 990. now *d*. deeds might have ensued
P. L. 6, 105. space was left, a *d*. interval
P. L. 6, 225. *d*. combustion warring
P. L. 6, 828. with *d*. shade contiguous
P. L. 8, 335. resounds yet *d*. in mine ear
P. L. 10, 121. how is it now become so *d*. to thee
P. L. 10, 521. *d*. was the din of hissing
P. L. 10, 779. his *d*. voice no more would
P. L. 10, 814. comes thundering back with *d*.
P. L. 10, 848. with damps and *d*. gloom
P. L. 12, 236. voice of God to mortal ear is *d*.
P. L. 12, 644. the gate with *d*. faces thronged
S. A. 1591. a *d*. way thou took'st to thy revenge
S. A. 1622. who had made their *d*. enemy
H. 164. the *d*. Judge in middle air
**Dreading.**—S. A. 733. *d*. thy displeasure
**Dreadless.**—P. L. 6, 1. the *d*. angel unpursued
**Dream.**—P. L. 2, 315. doubtless! while we *d*.
P. L. 5, 93. glad I waked to find this but a *d*.
P. L. 5, 98. I like this uncouth *d*. of evil spring
P. L. 5, 115. last evening's talk in this thy *d*.
P. L. 5, 120. in sleep thou did'st abhor to *d*.
P. L. 7, 39. for thou art heavenly, she an empty *d*.
P. L. 8, 175. *d*. not of other worlds, what creatures
P. L. 8, 292. when suddenly stood at my head a *d*.
P. L. 8, 310. all real as the *d*. had lively shadowed
P. L. 8, 482. such as I saw her in my *d*. adorned
P. L. 11, 95. for ever, *d*. at least to live for ever
P. L. 12, 386. to whom thou Michael *d*.
P. R. 2, 264. dreamed as appetite is wont to *d*.
P. R. 2, 283. and found all was but a *d*.
P. R. 2, 337. he spake no *d*.
C. 457. and in clear *d*. and solemn vision
L. 56. Ay me! I fondly *d*.
L'A. 129. such sights as youthful poets *d*.
Il P. 147. and let some strange mysterious *d*.
**Dreamed.**—P. L. 5, 31. have *d*., if *d*., not as I oft am wont
P. R. 2, 264. he slept, and *d*.
**Dreaming.**—P. L. 3, 514. *d*. by night
**Dreams.**—P. L. 1, 784. belated peasant sees, or *d*.
P. L. 4, 803. phantasms, and *d*.
P. L. 5, 112. work produces oft, and most in *d*.
P. L. 9, 1050. with conscious *d*. encumbered
P. L. 12, 595. with gentle *d*. have calmed
P. L. 12, 611. God is also in sleep and *d*. advise
P. R. 1, 395. answers, oracles, portents, and *d*.
P. R. 4, 291. these are false, or little else but *d*.
P. R. 4, 408. with ugly *d*. disturbed his sleep
C. 813. in delight beyond the bliss of *d*.
Il P. 9. or likest hovering *d*.
**Drear.**—P. L. 10, 525. hydrus, and ellops *d*.
C. 37. the perplexed paths of this *d*. wood
Il P. 119. of forests and enchantments *d*.
H. 193. a *d*. and dying sound
**Dreary.**—P. L. 1, 180. see'st thou yon *d*. plain
P. L. 2, 618. many a dark and *d*. vale they passed
**Dregs.**—P. L. 7, 238. tartareous, cold, infernal *d*.
**Drench.**—P. L. 2, 73. if the sleepy *d*.
S. 21, 5. deep thoughts resolve with me to *d*.
**Drenched.**—P. L. 11, 367. I have *d*. her eyes
**Drenches.**—C. 996. and *d*. with Elysian dew
**Dress.**—P. L. 9, 205. we labour still to *d*.
P. L. 11, 583. in gems and wanton *d*.
P. L. 11, 620. to *d*., and troll the tongue
**Dresses** —L'A. 86. the neat-handed Phillis *d*.
**Dressing.**—M. M. 7. woods and groves are of thy *d*.
**Drest.**—S. 14, 11. that up they flew so *d*.
**Drew.**—P. L. 1, 472. whom he *d*.
P. L. 2, 308. his look *d*. audience and attention
P. L. 2, 692. *d*. after him the third part
P. L. 2, 874. the huge portcullis high up-*d*.

P. L. 3, 645. he *d.* not nigh unheard
P. L. 3, 646. the angel bright, ere he *d.* nigh
P. L. 4, 861. now *d.* they nigh the western point
P. L. 5, 82. he *d.* nigh, and to me held
P. L. 5, 710. *d.* after him the third part
P. L. 6, 798. to final battle *d.*, disdaining flight
P. L. 7, 144. *d.* many whom their place knows
P. L. 7, 480. as a line, their long dimension *d.*
P. L. 8, 284. I first *d.* air, and first beheld
P. L. 9, 434. nearer he *d.*, and many a walk
P. L. 9, 578. I nearer *d.* to gaze, when from
P. L. 9, 739. the hour of noon *d.* on, and waked
P. L. 10. 629. know not that I called and *d.*
P. L. 11, 238. and the Archangel soon *d.* nigh
P. L. 11, 845. of the fresh wave largely *d.*
S. A. 736. though the fact more evil *d.*
S. A. 1596. occasions *d.* me early to this city.
S. A. 1650. he shook, till down they came, and *d*
Il P. 107. *d.* iron tears down Pluto's cheek
**Dried.**—P. L. 8, 256. his beams the sun soon *d.*
P. R. 4, 433. *d.* the wet from drooping plant
**Drift.**—P. R. 3, 4. weak arguing and fallacious *d.*
S. 17, 6. the *d.* of states hard to be spelled
**Drink.**—P. L. 5, 344. for *d.* the grape she
P. L. 5, 637. they *d.*, and in communion
P. L. 7, 362. made porous to receive and *d.*
P. L. 9, 838. derived from nectar, *d.* of gods
P. L. 10, 728. all that I eat or *d.* or shall beget
P. R. 1, 340. and to *d.* go far
P. R. 3, 289. amber stream, the *d.* of none
P. R. 4, 590. the fount of live ambrosial *d.*
S. A. 557. whose *d.* was from the liquid brook
C. 722. *d.* the clear stream
S. 14, 14. *d.* thy fill of pure immortal streams
**Drinks.**—P. L. 2, 584. whereof who *d.*
P. L. 5, 451. thus when with meats and *d.*
P. L. 11, 473. intemperance more in meats and *d.*
P. R. 2, 265. meats and *d.*, nature's refreshment
S. A. 541. desire of wine and all delicious *d.*
S. A. 554. and strongest *d.* our chief support
C. 527. the visage quite transforms of him that *d*
**Drinkest.**—P. L. 11, 532. thou eat'st and *d.*
**Drive.**—P. L. 1, 260. will not *d.* us hence
P. L. 2, 366. and *d.*, as we were driven
P. L. 2, 367. if not *d.*, seduce them to our party
P. L. 3, 438. where Chineses *d.* with sails
P. L. 4, 155. able to *d.* all sadness but despair
P. L. 6, 52. *d.* them out from God and bliss
P. L. 6, 715. these sons of darkness *d.* them out
P. L. 7, 32. but *d.* far off the dissonance
P. L. 10, 290. together *d.* mountains of ice
P. L. 11, 105. remorse *d.* out the sinful pair
P. L. 11, 853. thence the rapid currents *d.*
P. R. 1, 153. and *d.* him back to Hell
D. F. I. 68. or *d.* away the pestilence
U. C. II. 15. to *d.* the time away he sickened
**Driven.**—P. L. 1, 223. the flames *d.* backward
P. L. 2, 86. to dwell here, *d.* out from bliss
P. L. 2, 366. and drive, as we were *d.*
P. L. 2, 772. *d.* head-long from the pitch
P. L. 3, 677. justly hath *d.* out his rebel foes
P. L. 4, 753. by thee adulterous lust was *d.*
P. L. 6, 738. to their prepared ill mansion *d.*
P. L. 7, 57. but the evil, soon *d.* back, redounded
P. L. 7, 185. *d.* out the ungodly from his sight
P. L. 9, 62. full of anguish, *d.* the space of seven
P. L. 10, 240. he had returned, with fury *d.*
P. L. 10, 583. thence by Saturn *d.* and Ops
P. L. 10, 843. fears and horrors hast thou *d.*
P. L. 10, 1075. whose thwart flame *d.* down
P. L. 11, 842. *d.* by a keen north wind
P. R. 1, 360. but was *d.* with them from bliss
**Drives.**—P. L. 4, 184. whom hunger *d.* to seek
P. L. 11, 646. from forage *d.* a herd of beeves
**Driving.**—V. Ex. 5. *d.* dumb Silence from
C. 456. *d.* far off each thing of sin and guilt
**Drizzling.**—P. L. 6, 545. no *d.* shower
**Dromedaries.**—P. R. 3, 335. camels and *d.*
**Drone.**—P. L. 7, 490. feeds her husband *d.*
S. A. 567. a burdenous *d.*
**Droop.**—P. L. 11, 178. laborious, till day *d.*

S. A. 594. so much I feel my genial spirits *d.*
**Drooping.**—P. L. 1, 328. tread us down thus *d.*
P. L. 6, 496. their *d.* cheer
P. L. 9, 430. hung *d.* unsustained
P. R. 4, 434. from *d.* plant or *d.* tree
C. 812. will bathe the *d.* spirits in delight
L. 169. and yet anon repairs his *d.* head
**Drop.**—P. L. 2, 607. with one small *d.* to lose
P. L. 3, 25. so thick a *d.* serene hath quenched
P. L. 11, 535. thou *d.* into thy mother's lap
**Dropped** or **Dropt.**—P. L. 1, 745. *d.* from the
P. L. 2, 113. though his tongue *d.* manna
P. L. 6, 839. down their idle weapons *d.*
P. L. 7, 406. waved coats *d.* with gold
P. L. 9, 893. the garland ... down *d.*
P. L. 12, 645. tears they *d.*, but wiped them
P. R. 1, 324. and *d.* not here his carcase
C. 840. *d.* in ambrosial oils till she revived
L. 191. now was *d.* into the western bay
P. 16. *d.* with odorous oil down his fair eyes
**Dropping.**—P. L. 4, 630. and those *d.* gums
P. L. 9, 582. of ewe or goat *d.* with milk
C. 106. *d.* odours, *d.* wine
**Drops.**—P. L. 2, 933. *d.* ten thousand fathom
P. L. 5, 23. what *d.* the myrrh
P. L. 5, 132. other precious *d.* that ready stood
P. L. 7, 292. *d.* on dust conglobing from the dry
P. L. 9, 1002. sad *d.* wept at completing
P. L. 11, 416. from the web of life three *d.*
C. 912. *d.* that from my fountain pure
Il P. 130. with minute-*d.* from off the eaves
**Dropsies.**—P. L. 11, 488. *d.* and asthmas
**Dross.**—P. L. 1, 704. and scummed the bullion *d.*
P. R. 3, 29. treasures and all gain esteem as *d.*
T. 6. and merely mortal *d.*
**Drossiest.**—P. L. 5, 442. *d.* ore to perfect gold
**Drouth.**—P. L, 7, 66. whose *d.* yet scarce allayed
P. R. 1, 325. pined with hunger and with *d.*
P. R. 3, 274. and inaccessible, the Arabian *d.*
C. 66. to quench the *d.* of Phœbus
C. 928. summer *d.* or singed air
**Drove.**—P. L. 1, 418. *d.* theme thence to hell
P. L. 4, 169. the fishy fume that *d.* him
P. L. 6, 831. his impious foes right onward *d.*
P. L. 6, 858. *d.* them before him thunderstruck
P. L. 10, 287. together crowded *d.*
P. L. 11, 186. birds of gayest plume before him *d.*
P. L. 11, 739. all the clouds together *d.*
P. R. 1, 90. his fierce thunder *d.* us to the deep
S. A. 209. proportioned ill, *d.* me transverse
C. 115. with all their finny *d.*
L. 27. we *d.* afield, and both together heard
**Drovest.**—P. L. 3, 396. o'er the necks thou *d.*
**Drown.**—P. L. 11, 894. nor rain to *d.* the world
**Drowned.**—P. L. 7, 36. *d.* both harp and voice
P. L. 11, 13. to restore the race of mankind *d.*
P. L. 11, 757. and sorrow a flood, thee also *d.*
**Drowse.**—P. L. 11. 131. wakeful than to *d.*
**Drowsed.**—P L. 8, 289. seized my *d.* sense
**Drowsiness.**—A. 61. when *d.* hath locked up
**Drowsy.**—C. 553. gave respite to the *d.* frighted
Il P. 83. or the bellman's *d.* charm
V. Ex. 61. thy *d.* nurse hath sworn
**Drudge.**—P. L. 2, 732. ordained his *d.*
S. A. 573. here rather let me *d.* and earn
S. A. 1338. although their *d.*, to be their fool
S. A. 1393. at the public mill our *d.*
**Drudging.**—L'A. 105. how the *d.* goblin sweat
**Drudged.**—P. L. 10, 568. *d.* as oft with
**Drugs.**—P. L. 2, 640. bring their spicy *d.*
C. 255. culling their potent herbs and *d.*
**Druids.**—L. 53. your old bards, the famous *D.*, lie
**Drums.**—P. L. 1, 394. though for the noise of *d.*
**Drunk.**—S. A. 1670. *d.* with idolatry, *d.* with
**Dry.**—P. L. 1, 227. till on *d.* land he lights
P. L. 2, 898. for hot, cold, moist, and *d.*
P. L. 2, 940. neither sea, nor good *d.* land
P. L. 3, 652. moist and *d.*, o'er sea and land
P. L. 7, 284. and let *d.* land appear
P. L. 7, 292. on dust conglobing, from the *d.*
P. L. 7, 304. ere God had bid the ground be *d.*

P. L. 7, 307. the *d.* land, earth
P. L. 9, 179. through each thicket dank or *d.*
P. L. 10, 294. his mace petrific, cold and *d.*
P. L. 11, 544. a melancholy damp of cold and *d.*
P. L. 11, 842. a keen north wind, .. blowing *d.*
P. L. 11, 861. anon *d.* ground appears
P. L. 12, 197. lets pass, as on *d.* land
P. R. 3, 264. barren desert, fountainless and *d.*
S. A. 582. from the *d.* ground to spring
Il P. 66. on the *d.* smooth-shaven green
D. F. I. 4. winter's force made thy blossom *d.*
**Dryad.**—P. L. 9, 387. Oread or *D.*
**Dryades.**—C. 964. with the mincing *D.*
**Dry-eyed.**—P. L. 11, 495. long *d.-e.* behold
**Dubious.**—P. L. 1, 104. in *d.* battle on the
P. L. 2, 1042. wafts on the calmer wave by *d.*
**Duck.**—C. 960. without *d.* or nod
**Due.**—P. L. 1, 569. their order *d.*
P. L. 2, 453. *d.* alike to him who reigns
P. L. 2, 850. the key of this infernal pit, by *d.*
P. L. 3, 190. repent, and bring obedience *d.*
P. L. 3, 191. repentance, and obedience *d.*
P. L. 3, 245. to death I yield, and am his *d.*
P. L. 3, 578. his lordly eye keep distance *d.*
P. L. 3, 738. where honour *d.* and reverence
P. L. 4, 48. and pay him thanks? how *d.*
P. L. 4, 180. *d.* entrance he disdained
P. L. 5, 303. and Eve within, *d.* at her hour
P. L. 5, 817. and in that honour *d.* confess him
P. L. 6, 445. *d.* search and consultation
P. L. 7, 149. with ministeries *d.* and solemn
P. L. 8, 11. with wonder, but delight, and, as is *d.*
P. L. 8, 385. mutual, in proportion *d.* given
P. L. 9, 566 such wonder claims attention *d.*
P. L. 9, 800. each morning, and *d.* praise
P. L. 10, 93. gentle airs *d.* at their hour to fan
P. L. 10, 833. corruption, all the blame lights *d.*
P. L. 10, 994. from love's *d.* rites
P. R. 11, 253. then *d.* by sentence
P. L. 11, 440. and all *d.* rites performed
P. L. 11, 533. from thence *d.* nourishment
P. L. 12, 12. give *d.* audience, and attend
P. L. 12, 152. whom faithful Abraham *d.*
P. L. 12, 264. night's *d.* course adjourn
P. L. 12, 399. to thy transgression *d.*
P. R. 3, 10. thy large heart give utterance *d.*
P. R. 3, 87. shameful death their *d.* reward
P. R. 3, 182. fulfilled in their *d.* time
P. R. 3, 440. *d.* time and providence I leave
S. A. 513. who, self-rigorous, chooses death as *d.*
S. A. 1055. power over his female in *d.* awe
S. A. 1225. *d.* by the law to capital punishment
C. 12. yet some there be that by *d.* steps aspire
C. 199. with everlasting oil, to give *d.* light
C. 306. *d.* west it rises from this shrubby point
C. 776. better thanked, his praise *d.* paid
L. 7. compels me to disturb your season *d.*
L'A. 37. and if I give thee honour *d.*
Il P. 155. but let my *d.* feet never fail
**Duel.**—P. L. 12, 387. their fight as of a *d.*
P. R. 1, 174. entering his great *d.*, not of arms
S. A. 1102. have won by mortal *d.* from thee
**Duelled.**—S. A. 345. *d.* their armies ranked
**Dues.**—C. 137. till . . . . all thy *d.* be done
**Dulcet.**—P. L. 1, 712. of *d.* symphonies
P. L. 5, 347. she tempers *d.* creams
**Dulcimer.**—P. L. 7, 596. and *d.*, all organs of
**Dull.**—C. 477. not harsh and crabbed, as *d.* fools
C. 634. and the *d.* swain treads on it daily
L'A. 42. and singing, startle the *d.* night
**Duly.**—P. L. 5, 145. each morning *d.* paid
L'A. 106. to earn his cream-bowl *d.* set
**Dumb.**—P. L. 9, 527. his gentle *d.* expression
C. 796. *d.* things would be moved to sympathize
H. 173. the oracles are *d.*
V. Ex. 5. driving *d.* Silence from the portal door
**Dun.**—P. L. 3, 72. in the *d.* air sublime
C. 127. which these *d.* shades will ne'er report
V. Ex. 92. of utmost Tweed, or Ouse, or gulfy *D.*
**Dunbar.**—S. 16, 8. *D.* field resounds thy praises
**Dungeon.**—P. L. 1, 61. a *d.* horrible

P. L. 2, 317. hath doomed this place our *d.*
P. L. 2, 1003. your *d.*, stretching far and wide
P. L. 10, 466. the house of woe, and *d.*
P. L. 10, 697. bursting their brazen *d.* armed
S. A. 69. *d.*, or beggary, or decrepit age
S. A. 156. (O worst imprisonment) the *d.*
S. A. 367. into a *d.* thrust, to work with slaves
C. 349. in this close *d.* of innumerous boughs
C. 385. himself is his own *d.*
L. 97. that not a blast was from his *d.* strayed
**Durable.**—P. L. 5, 581. all things *d.*
P. L. 10, 320. too fast they made and *d.*
**Durance.**—P. L. 4, 899. stay in that dark *d.*
**Durst.**—P. L. 1, 49. who *d.* defy the Omnipotent
P. L. 1, 102. thus *d.* dislike his reign
P. L. 1, 382. *d.* fix their seats
P. L. 1, 385. and *d.* abide Jehovah
P. L. 1, 391. their darkness *d.* affront his light
P. L. 3, 220. less that *d.* upon his own head
P. L. 4, 704. insect, or worm, *d.* enter none
P. L. 4, 829. there sitting where ye *d.* not soar
P. L. 6, 155. *d.* oppose a third part of the gods
P. L. 8, 237. they *d.* without his leave attempt
P. L. 9, 1180. that I thought no evil *d.* attempt
P. R. 1, 100. I, when no other *d.*, sole undertook
P. R. 1, 324. for single none *d.* ever
P. R. 4, 580. who *d.* so proudly tempt the Son
S. A. 1110. who *d.* not with their whole united
S. A. 1113. close-banded, *d.* attack me
S. A. 1130. *d.* not thus disparage glorious arms
S. A. 1255. whether he *d.* accept the offer or not
S. A. 1256. that he *d.* not, plain enough appeared
C. 577. longer I *d.* not stay, but soon I guessed
C. 616. how *d.* thou then thyself approach
**Dusk.**—P. L. 11, 741. exhalation *d.* and moist
P. R. 1, 296. a pathless desert, *d.* with horrid
P. R. 4, 76. *d.* faces with white silken turbants
**Dusky.**—P. L. 1, 226. incumbent on the *d.* air
P. L. 2, 488. from mountain tops the *d.* clouds
P. L. 5, 186. hill or steaming lake, *d.* or gray
P. L. 5, 667. the *d.* hour friendliest to sleep
P. L. 6, 58. and smoke to roll in *d.* wreaths
C. 99. shoots against the *d.* pole
H. 223. the rays of Bethlehem blind his *d.* eyn
**Dust.**—P. L. 4, 416. that raised us from the *d.*
P. L. 5, 516. who formed us from the *d.*
P. L. 7, 292. as drops on *d.* conglobing
P. L. 7, 525. O man, *d.* of the ground
P. L. 7, 577. and ample road, whose *d.* is gold
P. L. 9, 178. to spite, his Maker raised from *d.*
P. L. 10, 178. and *d.* shalt eat all the days
P. L. 10, 208. *d.* thou art, and shalt to *d.* return
P. L. 10, 748. and equal to reduce me to my *d.*
P. L. 10, 770. *d.* I am, and shall to *d.* return
P. L. 10, 805. extend his sentence beyond *d.*
P. L. 10, 1085. end in *d.*, our final rest
P. L. 11, 199. or more than this, that we are *d.*
P. L. 11, 460. see him die, rolling in *d.* and gore
P. L. 11, 463. I must return to native *d.*
P. L. 11, 529. and mix with our connatural *d.*
S. A. 141. soiled their crested helmets in the *d.*
C. 165. hath met the virtue of this magic *d.*
Cir. 19. for us frail *d.* emptied his glory
**Duteous.**—P. L. 9, 521. more *d.* at her call
**Duty.**—P. L. 1, 333. men wont to watch on *d.*
P. L. 10, 106. where obvious *d.* erewhile
P. R. 2, 326. by just right, to thee *d.* service
P. R. 3, 172. and *d.*, zeal and *d.*, are not slow
P. R. 3, 175. zeal of thy father's house, *d.*
S. A. 853. adjured by all the bonds of civil *d.*
S. A. 870. as I thought, truth, *d.*, so enjoining
**Dwarfs.**—P. L. 1, 779. less than smallest *d.*
**Dwell.**—P. L. 1, 47. to *d.* in adamantine chains
P. L. 1, 66. where peace and rest can never *d.*
P. L. 2, 86. to *d.* here, driven out from bliss
P. L. 2, 398. *d.*, not unvisited of heaven's fair
P. L. 2, 841. where thou and death shall *d.*
P. L. 3, 249. with corruption there to *d.*
P. L. 3, 335. wherein the just shall *d.*
P. L. 3, 670. these shining orbs his choice to *d.*
P. L. 4, 377. that I with you must *d.*

P. L. 5, 373. or such place hast here to d.
P. L. 5, 456. of their being who d. in Heaven
P. L. 5, 500. in heavenly Paradises d.
P. L. 6, 292. however, to d. free, if not to reign
P. L. 6, 380. in dark oblivion let them d.
P. L. 6, 788. in spirits could such perverseness d.
P. L. 7, 156. there to d., not here, till by degrees
P. L. 7, 329. a seat where gods might d.
P. L. 7, 627. created in his image there to d.
P. L. 8, 185. God hath bid d. far off all anxious
P. L. 9, 125. here seek I, no, nor in heaven to d.
P. L. 9, 322. if this be our condition. thus to d.
P. L. 9, 729. can envy d. in heavenly breasts
P. L. 10, 399. there d., and reign in bliss
P. L. 10, 492. to d., and over man to rule
P. L. 10, 587. and to d. habitual habitant
P. L. 11, 43. redeemed may d. in joy and bliss
P. L. 11, 48. but longer in that Paradise to d.
P. L. 11, 178. while here we d., what can be
P. L. 11, 259. but longer in this Paradise to d.
P. L. 11, 348. to d. on even ground now with
P. L. 11, 608. wherein shall d. his race
P. L. 11, 838. who there frequent or therein d.
P. L. 11, 901. earth wherein the just shall d.
P. L. 12, 22. and d. long time in peace
P. L. 12, 146. but his sons shall d. to Senir
P. L. 12, 248. Holy One with mortal men to d.
P. L. 12, 281. God will deign to d. on Earth
P. L. 12, 316. long time shall d. and prosper
P. L. 12, 344. there in captivity he lets them d.
P. L. 12, 487. who shall d.. his Spirit within
P. R. 1, 116. from hell's deep-vaulted den to d.
P. R. 1, 331. for we sometimes who d. this wild
P. R. 1, 391. and with them d. copartner
P. R. 1, 462. his Spirit of Truth henceforth to d.
P. R. 4, 616. where they shall d. secure
C. 667. here d. no frowns nor anger, from these
L'A. 10. in dark Cimmerian desert ever d.
Il P. 5. d. in some idle brain, and fancies fond

S. 14, 2. had ripened thy just soul to d. with God
**Dwellest.**—P. L. 7, 7. top of old Olympus d.
P. R. 4, 466. for only thou here d.
C. 268. d. here with Pan or Silvan
**Dwelling.**—P. L. 4, 378. my d. haply may not
P. L. 4, 884. whose d. God hath planted here
P. L. 8, 118. who hast thy d. here on earth
P. R. 2, 80. in Nazareth hath been our d.
**Dwelling-place.**—P. L. 2, 57. and for their d.-p.
P. L. 7, 625. d.-p. thrice
**Dwellings.**—P. L. 7, 183. in their d. peace
P. L. 7, 570. to visit oft the d. of just men
P. L. 11, 747. all d. else flood overwhelmed
**Dwells.**—P. L. 1, 250. where joy for ever d.
P. L. 3, 216. d. in all heaven charity so dear
P. L. 3, 225. in whom the fullness d. of love
P. L. 8, 103. that man may know he d. not in
P. L. 12, 84. which always with right reason d.
S. A. 159. in real darkness of the body d.
S. A. 1673. before our Living Dread, who d.
C. 428. yea, there where very desolation d.
C. 521. in cypress shades, a sorcerer d.
C. 988. there eternal summer d.
**Dwelt.**—P. L. 3, 5. d. from eternity, d. then
P. L. 3, 570. but who d. happy there he stayed
P. L. 4, 214. the sons of Eden long before d.
P. L. 9, 836. as to the Power that d. within
Cir. 18. were lost in death, till He, that d. above
**Dye.**—D. F. I. 5. being amorous on that lovely d.
**Dyed.**—P. L. 10, 1009. as d. her cheeks with pale
**Dying.**—P. L. 3, 296. and d., rise, and rising
P. L. 3, 299. giving to death, and d. to redeem
P. L. 3, 479. d. put on the weeds of Dominic
P. L. 10, 964. a long day's d., to augment
P. L. 10, 974. living or d., from thee I will
S. A. 1661. living or d. thou hast fulfilled
H. 193. a drear and d. sound
M. W. 42. sideways, as on a d. bed

# E

**Each.**—P. L. 1, 222. on e. hand the flames
P. L. 1, 356. from every squadron and e. band
P. L. 1, 578. on e. side mixed with auxiliar gods
P. L. 1, 704. severing e. kind
P. L. 1, 707. strange conveyance filled e. hollow
P. L. 1, 737. e. in his hierarchy
P. L. 2, 26. might draw envy from e. inferior
P. L. 2, 181. e. on his rock transfixed
P. L. 2, 421. danger with deep thought; and e.
P. L. 2, 502. wasting the earth, e. other to
P. L. 2, 523. and wandering, e. his several way
P. L. 2, 535. e. van prick forth the aery knights
P. L. 2, 670. for e. seemed either, black it stood
P. L. 2, 711. e. at the head levelled his deadly
P. L. 2, 714. such a frown e. cast at the other
P. L. 2, 901. around the flag of e. his faction
P. L. 3, 516. e. stair mysteriously was meant
P. L. 3, 584. and to e. inward part with gentle
P. L. 3, 720. e. had his place appointed
P. L. 4, 114. thus while he spake, e. passion
P. L. 4, 120. e. perturbation smoothed with
P. L. 4, 240. visiting e. plant
P. L. 4, 408. griped in e. paw
P. L. 4, 683. responsive e. to other's note
P. L. 4, 696. and e. odorous bushy shrub
P. L. 4, 697. e. beauteous flower
P. L. 4, 1003. sequel e. of parting and of fight
P. L. 5, 133. that ready stood e. in their crystal
P. L. 5, 145. their orisons e. morning duly paid
P. L. 5, 252. angelic choirs on e. hand parting
P. L. 5, 279. the pair that clad e. shoulder broad
P. L. 5, 326. from e. bough and brake e. plant
P. L. 5, 337. and from e. tender stalk
P. L. 5, 429. from off the boughs e. morn
P. L. 5, 477. e. in their several active spheres
P. L. 5, 479. in bounds proportioned to e. kind
P. L. 5, 576. therein e. to other like

P. L. 6, 98. ended soon e. milder thought
P. L. 6, 230. as e. divided legion might have
P. L. 6, 231. in strength e. armed hand a legion
P. L. 6, 233. led in fight, yet leader seemed e.
P. L. 6, 238. e. on himself relied, as only in his
P. L. 6, 307. from e. hand with speed retired
P. L. 6, 362. on e. wing Uriel and Raphael
P. L. 6, 498. the invention all admired, and e.
P. L. 6, 529. and scouts e. coast light-armed
P. L. 6, 541. let e. his adamantine coat gird
P. L. 6, 578. at e. behind a seraph stood
P. L. 6, 753. four faces e. had wondrous
P. L. 6, 770. chariots of God, half on e. hand
P. L. 6, 782. e. to his place; they heard his voice
P. L. 6, 885. with branching palm e. order
P. L. 7, 327. the valleys and e. fountain-side
P. L. 7, 334. watered all the ground, and e. plant
P. L. 7, 391. and e. soul living, e. that crept
P. L. 7, 399. sounds and seas, e. creek and bay
P. L. 7, 453. beast of the earth, e. in their kind
P. L. 8, 152. stored in e. orb perhaps with some
P. L. 8, 156. to contribute e. orb a glimpse
P. L. 8, 223. and e. word, e. motion forms
P. L. 8, 306. e. tree, loaden with fairest fruit
P. L. 8, 342. in sign whereof e. bird and beast
P. L. 8, 349. he spake, e. bird and beast behold
P. L. 8, 351. with blandishment, e. bird
P. L. 8, 393. they rejoice e. with their kind
P. L. 8, 514. gave sign of gratulation, and e. hill
P. L. 8, 582. vouchsafed to cattle and e. beast
P. L. 9, 66. pole to pole, traversing e. colúre
P. L. 9, 179. through e. thicket dank or dry
P. L. 9, 220. while so near e. other thus all day
P. L. 9, 259. where e. to other speedy aid might
P. L. 9, 428. to support e. flower of tender stalk
P. L. 9, 438. imbordered on e. bank, the hand
P. L. 9, 449. e. thing met conceives delight,

P. L. 9, 451. *e.* rural sight, *e.* rural sound
P. L. 9, 660. *e.* tree in the garden we may eat
P. L. 9, 673. *e.* part, motion, *e.* act, won audience
P. L. 9, 800. not without song, *e.* morning
P. L. 9, 813. distinct *e.* thing on earth
P. L. 9, 1019. to *e.* meaning savour we apply
P. L. 9, 1052. and, *e.* the other viewing
P. L. 9, 1093. the parts of *e.* from other
P. L. 10, 112. either to God or to *e.* other
P. L. 10, 176. all cattle, *e.* beast of the field
P. L. 10, 235. why sit we here *e.* other viewing
P. L. 10, 288. from *e.* side shoaling towards the
P. L. 10, 324. in sight, to *e.* of these
P. L. 10, 440. *e.* hour their great adventurer
P. L. 10, 513. entwining *e.* other till supplanted
P. L. 10, 604. on *e.* beast next, and fish
P. L. 10, 678. in change of seasons to *e.* clime
P. L. 10, 712. leaving devoured *e.* other
P. L. 10, 959. nor blame *e.* other
P. L. 10, 961. lighten *e.* other's burden
P. L. 11, 128. four faces *e.* had, like a double
P. L. 11, 587. they liked, and *e.* his liking chose
P. L. 11, 659. on *e.* hand slaughter and gigantic
P. L. 11, 765. my part of evil only, *e.* day's lot
P. L. 11, 889. all flesh corrupting *e.* their way
P. L. 12, 57. the builders; *e.* to other calls
P. L. 12, 142. yonder sea; — *e.* place behold
P. L. 12, 503. *e.* nation to receive with joy
P. R. 1, 304. shady vale, *e.* night
P. R. 1, 349. but *e.* word proceeding from the
P. R. 1, 402. aught *e.* man's peculiar load
P. R. 2, 19. so in *e.* place these
P. R. 2, 22. Machærus, and *e.* town or city
P. R. 2, 123. from the element *e.* of his reign
P. R. 2, 155. many are in *e.* region passing fair
P. R. 2, 240. of various persons, *e.* to know his
P. R. 2, 406. *e.* other creature tames
P. R. 2, 462. on his shoulders *e.* man's burden
P. R. 3, 327. clouds of foot, nor, on *e.* horn
P. R. 4, 33. whose banks on *e.* side an imperial
P. R. 4, 475. *e.* act is rightliest done
S. A. 65. so many, and so huge, that *e.* apart
S. A. 397. *e.* time perceiving how openly
S. A. 1087. we might have tried *e.* other's force
S. A. 1089. *e.* limb to survey, if thy appearance
S. A. 1289. making them *e.* his own deliverer
S. A. 1599. festival proclaimed through *e.* high
S. A. 1607. all the lords, and *e.* degree
S. A. 1617. on *e.* side went armed guards
S. A. 1655. but *e.* Philistian city round
C. 19. of every salt flood and *e.* ebbing stream
C. 311. I know *e.* lane, and every alley green
C. 456. driving far off *e.* thing of sin and guilt
C. 839. through the porch and inlet of *e.* sense
L. 83. as he pronounces lastly on *e.* deed
L. 94. that blows from off *e.* beaked promontory
S. 15, 2. filling *e.* mouth with envy or praise
S. 17, 10. what *e.* means, what severs *e.*
H. 100. echoes still prolongs *e.* heavenly close
H. 196. while *e.* peculiar power foregoes
H. 234. *e.* fettered ghost
T. 9. whenas *e.* thing bad thou hast entombed
W. S. 10. easy numbers flow, and that *e.* heart
V. Ex. 35. look in and see *e.* blissful deity
**Eager.**—P. L. 6, 378. nor of renown less *e.*, yet
P. L. 9, 740. *e.* appetite, raised
L. 189. with *e.* thought warbling his Doric lay
**Eagerly.**—P. L. 2, 947. so *e.* the Fiend
**Eagle.**—P. L. 7, 423. the *e.* and the stork
S. A. 1695. but as an *e.* his cloudless thunder
**Eagles.**—P. L. 5, 271. within soar of towering *e.*
**Eagle-winged.**—P. L. 6, 763. Victory sat *e-w.*
**Ear.**—P. L. 1, 787. jocund music charm his *e.*
P. L. 2, 117. yet he pleased the *e.*
P. L. 2, 920. was his *e.* less pealed with noises
P. L. 2, 953. his *e.* with loudest vehemence
P. L. 3, 193. mine *e.* shall not be slow
P. L. 3, 647. admonished by his *e.*
P. L. 4, 410. all *e.* to hear new utterance flow
P. L. 4, 800. like a toad, close at the *e.* of Eve
P. L. 5, 36. close at mine *e.* one called me forth

P. L. 5, 545. with more delighted *e.*
P. L. 5, 626. God's own *e.* listens delighted
P. L. 5, 810. no *e.* ever to hear in Heaven
P. L. 6, 350. live all head, all eye, all *e.*
P. L. 8, 1. and in Adam's *e.* so charming left
P. L. 8, 49. not capable her *e.* of what was high
P. L. 8, 211. sweeter thy discourse is to my *e.*
P. L. 8, 335. resounds yet dreadful in mine *e.*
P. L. 8, 606. harmonious sound to the *e.*
P. L. 9, 47. who brings it nightly to my *e.*
P. L. 9, 1067. in evil hour thou didst give *e.*
P. L. 10, 506. high applause to fill his *e.*
P. L. 10, 1060. we pray him, will his *e.* be open
P. L. 11, 30. bend thine *e.* to supplication
P. L. 11, 152. placable and mild, bending his *e.*
P. L. 11, 435. the green *e.* and the yellow sheaf
P. L. 12, 236. to mortal *e.* is dreadful
P. R. 1, 479. pleasing to the *e.*
P. R. 3, 390. and in my *e.* vented much policy
P. R. 4, 272. to sage Philosophy next lend thine *e.*
P. R. 4, 337. that pleased so well our victor's *e.*
S. A. 177. dissolves, unjointed, ere it reach my *e.*
S. A. 858. priest was not behind, but ever at my *e.*
S. A. 921. not doubting their favourable *e.*
S. A. 937. to fence my *e.* against thy sorceries
S. A. 1172. whose *e.* is ever open, and his eye
S. A. 1568. thy aged *e.*, should pierce too deep
C. 170. this way the noise was, if mine *e.* be true
C. 203. was rife and perfect in my listening *e.*
C. 458. tell her of things that no gross *e.* can hear
C. 560. I was all *e.*, and took in strains
C. 570. till guided by mine *e.* I found the place
C. 784. thou hast nor *e.*, nor soul to apprehend
A. 73. of human mould with gross unpurged *e.*
L. 49. such Lycidas, thy loss to shepherd's *e.*
L'A. 148. as would have won the *e.* of Pluto
Il P. 120. where more is meant than meets the *e.*
Il P. 164. may with sweetness, through mine *e.*
Cir. 3. heard by happy watchful shepherds' *e.*
**Earl.**—S. 10, 1. daughter to that good *E.*
M. W. 3. a Viscount's daughter an *E.'s* heir
**Earlier.**—L'A. 89. or if the *e.* season lead
**Earliest.**—P. L. 4, 642. charm of *e.* birds
P. L. 4, 651. she ascends with charm of *e.* birds
P. R. 2, 365. and Flora's *e.* smells
**Early.**—P. L. 9, 225. to little, though begun *e.*
P. L. 9, 457. sweet recess of Eve thus *e.*
P. L. 9, 799. my *e.* care, not without song
P. L. 11, 275. *e.* visitation, and my last at even
P. R. 4, 215. as by that *e.* action may be judged
S. A. 1596. occasions drew me *e.* to this city
A. 56. and *e.* ere the odorous breath of morn
S. 18, 14. who having learned thy way, *e.* may fly
M. M. 9. thus we salute thee with our *e.* song
M. W. 23. once had the *e.* matrons run
**Earn.**—P. L. 2, 473. hazard huge must *e.*
P. L. 10, 1054. with labour I must *e.* my bread
P. L. 11, 375. and *e.* rest from labour won
P. R. 1, 167. to *e.* salvation for the sons of men
S. A. 573. rather let me drudge, and *e.* my bread
L'A. 106. to *e.* his cream-bowl duly set
**Earned.**—P. L. 10, 592. *e.* with travail difficult
P. R. 2, 401. whose pains have *e.* the far-fet spoil
**Earnest.**—P. L. 1, 458. who mourned in *e.*
P. L. 9, 939. will in *e.* so destroy us his prime
P. L. 10, 553. *e.* eyes they fixed
S. A. 359. to tempt our *e.* prayers
**Earnestly.**—P. L. 9, 1141. *e.* they seek such
P. R. 2, 367. his invitation *e.* renewed
**Earns.**—S. A. 1260. which *e.* my keeping
**Ears.**—P. L. 4, 982. her bearded grove of *e.*
P. L. 5, 771. thus held their *e.*
P. L. 7, 35. woods and rocks had *e.* to rapture
P. L. 7, 70. full of wonder in our *e.*
P. L. 7, 177. to human *e.* cannot without process
P. L. 9, 736. in her *e.* the sound yet rung
P. L. 10, 99. brought to their *e.*, while day
P. L. 10, 780. no more would thunder in my *e.*
P. R. 1, 199. from without comes often to my *e.*
S. A. 1231. O Baal-zebub! can my *e.* unused
C. 272. that is addressed to unattending *e.*

C. 706. O foolishness of men! that lend their *e*.
C. 997. list, mortals, if your *e*. be true
L. 77. Phœbus replied, and touched my *e*.
S. 13, 4. with Midas' *e*. committing short and
H. 94. their hearts and *e*. did greet
H. 126. once bless our human *e*.
F. of C. 17. though baulk your *e*.
V. Ex. 28. fly swiftly to this fair assembly's *e*.
**Earth.**—P. L. 1, 9. how the heavens and *e*.
P. L. 1, 365. till wandering o'er the *e*.
P. L. 1, 382. roaming to seek their prey on *e*.
P. L. 1, 509. confessed later than heaven and *e*.
P. L. 1, 687. rifled the bowels of their mother *e*.
P. L. 1, 710. anon out of the *e*. a fabric huge
P. L. 1, 778. in bigness to surpass *E.'s* giant sons
P. L. 1, 785. to the *e*. wheels her pale course
P. L. 2, 383. *e*. with hell to mingle
P. L. 2, 484. their specious deeds on *e*.
P. L. 2, 502. wasting the *e*. each other
P. L. 2, 927. from her axle torn the steadfast *e*.
P. L. 2, 1004. heaven and *e.,* another world
P. L. 3, 64. on *e*. he first beheld our two first
P. L. 3, 133. both through heaven and *e*.
P. L. 3, 146. heaven and *e*. shall high extol
P. L. 3, 274. O thou in heaven and *e*. the only
P. L. 3, 283. be thyself man among men on *e*.
P. L. 3, 322. in heaven, or *e.,* or under *e*. in hell
P. L. 3, 335. new heaven and *e.,* wherein the
P. L. 3, 444. but store hereafter from the *e*.
P. L. 3, 451. all who have their reward on *e*.
P. L. 3, 457. dissolved on *e.,* fleet hither.
P. L. 3, 508. the portal shone, inimitable on *e*.
P. L. 3, 520. whereon who after came from *e*.
P. L. 3, 528. a passage down to the *e*.
P. L. 3, 592. compared with aught on *e*.
P. L. 3, 651. or down to the *e*. bear his swift
P. L. 3, 685. through heaven and *e*.
P. L. 3, 715. the cumbrous elements, *e.,* flood
P. L. 3, 724. that place is *e.,* the seat of man
P. L. 3, 731. fills and empties, to enlighten the *e*.
P. L. 3, 739. toward the coast of *e*. beneath
P. L. 4, 5. 'woe to the inhabitants on *e*.!'
P. L. 4, 152. when God hath showered the *e*.
P. L. 4, 208. a heaven on *e*.
P. L. 4, 228. of porous *e*. with kindly thirst
P. L. 4, 341. all beasts of the *e.,* since wild
P. L. 4, 432. that possess *e.,* air, and sea
P. L. 4, 540. with *e*. and ocean meets
P. L. 4, 546. accessible from *e.,* one entrance
P. L. 4, 594. or this less voluble *e*.
P. L. 4, 645. fragrant the fertile *e*. after soft
P. L. 4, 661. round the *e.,* by morrow evening
P. L. 4, 672. on *e.,* made hereby apter to
P. L. 4, 677. spiritual creatures walk the *e*.
P. L. 4, 722. God that made both sky, air, *e*.
P. L. 4, 733. to fill the *e.,* who shall with us
P. L. 4, 940. to settle here on *e.,* or in mid air
P. L. 4, 1000. the pendulous round *e*.
P. L. 5, 2. advancing, sowed the *e*. with orient
P. L. 5, 78. not to *e*. confined, but sometimes
P. L. 5, 88. underneath beheld the *e*.
P. L. 5, 141. parallel to the *e*. his dewy ray
P. L. 5, 164. on *e*. join all ye creatures to extol
P. L. 5, 190. or wet the thirsty *e*. with falling
P. L. 5, 201. that walk the *e.,* and stately tread
P. L. 5, 224. thou hear'st what stir on *e*.
P. L. 5, 260. *e.,* and the garden of God
P. L. 5, 302. to warm *e.'s* inmost womb
P. L. 5, 321. Adam, *e.'s* hallowed mould
P. L. 5, 329. shall confess that here on *e*.
P. L. 5, 338. whatever *E.,* all-bearing mother
P. L. 5, 401. and for delight hath caused the *e*.
P. L. 5, 416. *e*. the sea, *e*. and the sea feed air
P. L. 5, 519. Son of heaven and *e*.
P. L. 5, 574. though what if *e*. be but the
P. L. 5, 576. each to other like, more than on *e*.
P. L. 5, 578. where *e*. now rests upon her
P. L. 5, 649. than all this globous *e*. in plain
P. L. 5, 752. this fair *e*. to all the *e*.
P. L. 6, 195. as if on *e.,* winds under ground
P. L. 6, 218. and had *e*. been then, all *e*. had

P. L. 6, 299. or to what things liken on *e*.
P. L. 6, 374. their names eternize here on *e*.
P. L. 6, 516. nor hath this *e*. entrails unlike
P. L. 6, 640. *e*. hath this variety from heaven
P. L. 6, 893. things in heaven by things on *e*.
P. L. 7, 23. standing on *e.,* not rapt above
P. L. 7, 63. heaven and *e*. conspicuous first began
P. L. 7, 90. embracing round this florid *e*.
P. L. 7, 124. communicable in *e*. or heaven
P. L. 7, 160. *e*. be changed to heaven and … to *e*.
P. L. 7, 167. appointed bounds be heaven and *e*.
P. L. 7, 232. the *e.,* matter unformed and void
P. L. 7, 242. *e.,* self-balanced, on her centre
P. L. 7, 256. birthday of heaven and *e*.
P. L. 7, 269. for as *e.,* so he the world built
P. L. 7, 276. the *e*. was formed, but in the womb
P. L. 7, 278. over all the face of *e*. main ocean
P. L. 7, 307. dry land, *e*. and the great receptacle
P. L. 7, 309. let the *e*. put forth the verdant grass
P. L. 7, 312. whose seed is in herself upon the *e*.
P. L. 7, 313. the bare *e.,* till then desert and bare
P. L. 7, 328. that *e*. now seemed like to heaven
P. L. 7, 332. God had yet not rained upon the *e*.
P. L. 7, 333. from the *e*. a dewy mist went up
P. L. 7, 335. ere it was in the *e*.
P. L. 7, 345. to give light on the *e*.
P. L. 7, 350. to illuminate the *e*.
P. L. 7, 389. let fowl fly above the *e*. with wings
P. L. 7, 398. let the fowl be multiplied on the *e*.
P. L. 7, 451. let the *e*. bring forth soul living
P. L. 7, 452. creeping things, and beast of the *e*.
P. L. 7, 453. the *e*. obeyed, and straight opening
P. L. 7, 468. the crumbled *e*. above them threw
P. L. 7, 471. Behemoth, biggest born of *e*.
P. L. 7, 501. *e*. in her rich attire
P. L. 7, 502. air, water, *e.,* by fowl, fish, beast
P. L. 7, 522. and over all the *e*.
P. L. 7, 531. be fruitful, multiply, and fill the *e*.
P. L. 7, 534. living thing that moves on the *e*.
P. L. 7, 541. all sorts are here that all the *e*. yields
P. L. 7, 560. the *e.,* the air resounded
P. L. 7, 581. and now on *e*. the seventh evening
P. L. 7, 624. among these the seat of men, *e*.
P. L. 7, 629. his works on *e.,* in sea, or air
P. L. 8, 16. this world of heaven and *e*. consisting
P. L. 8, 17. this *e.,* a spot, a grain, an atom
P. L. 8, 23. officiate light round this opacous *e*.
P. L. 8, 32. the sedentary *e*.
P. L. 8, 70. whether heaven move or *e*.
P. L. 8, 89. *e*. sitting still
P. L. 8, 91. the *e.,* though in comparison
P. L. 8, 96. in the fruitful *e*.
P. L. 8, 98. not to *e*. are those bright luminaries
P. L. 8, 99. officious but to thee *e.'s* habitant
P. L. 8, 118. who hast thy dwelling here on *e*.
P. L. 8, 120. placed heaven from *e*. so far
P. L. 8, 120. the planet *e.,* so steadfast
P. L. 8, 137. if *e.,* industrious of herself, fetch day
P. L. 8, 144. she by night this *e.,* reciprocal
P. L. 8, 161. rise on the *e.,* or *e*. rise on the sun
P. L. 8, 178. not of *e*. only, but of highest heaven
P. L. 8, 224. think we in heaven of thee on *e*.
P. L. 8, 274. thou enlightened *e.,* so fresh and gay
P. L. 8, 306. what I saw of *e*. before
P. L. 8, 338. the *e*. to thee and to thy race I give
P. L. 8, 369. the *e*. with various living creatures
P. L. 8, 483. what all *e*. or heaven could bestow
P. L. 8, 513. the *e*. gave sign of gratulation
P. L. 8, 631. beyond the *e.'s* green Cape
P. L. 9, 50. twilight upon the *e.,* short arbiter
P. L. 9, 59. returned from compassing the *e*.
P. L. 9, 99. O *e.,* how like to heaven
P. L. 9, 149. a creature formed of *e*.
P. L. 9, 153. this world, and *e*. his seat
P. L. 9, 195. breathe from the *e.'s* great altar
P. L. 9, 273. Heaven and *E.,* and all *E.'s* Lord
P. L. 9, 605. visible in heaven, on *e.,* or middle
P. L. 9, 658. lords declared of all in *e*. or air
P. L. 9, 752. this fair *e*. I see
P. L. 9, 782. she plucked, she eat, *e*. felt the wound
P. L. 9, 813. thence distinct each thing on *e*.

P. L. 9, 1000. *e.* trembled from her entrails
P. L. 9, 1011. wings, wherewith to scorn the *e.*
P. L. 9, 1041. *e.'s* freshest, softest lap
P. L. 10, 22. news from *e.* arrived at heaven-gate
P. L. 10, 36. troubled at these tidings from the *e.*
P. L. 10, 57. whether in heaven, or *e.,* or hell
P. L. 10, 69. in heaven and *e.,* to do thy will
P. L. 10, 72. judge on *e.* these thy transgressors
P. L. 10, 94. airs due at their hour to fan the *e.*
P. L. 10, 229. was sinned and judged on *e.*
P. L. 10, 273. the smell of mortal change on *e.*
P. L. 10, 325. their way to *e.* they had descried
P. L. 10, 360. that thou on *e.* hadst prospered
P. L. 10, 399. on the *e.* dominion exercise
P. L. 10, 404. create plenipotent on *e.*
P. L. 10, 638. *e.* renewed, shall be made pure
P. L. 10, 647 and *E.* shall to the ages rise
P. L. 10, 653. as might affect the *e.* with cold
P. L. 10, 669. the poles of *e.* twice ten degrees
P. L. 10, 679. spring perpetual smiled on *e.*
P. L. 10, 776. my sentence, and be *e.* insensible
P. L. 10, 835. heavier than the *e.* to bear
P. L. 10, 891. this novelty on *e.,* this fair defect
P. L. 10, 897. disturbances on *e.* through female
P. L. 11, 22. what first-fruits on *e.* are sprung
P. L. 11, 66. resigns him up with heaven and *e.*
P. L. 11, 136. with fresh dews embalmed the *e.*
P. L. 11, 335. know'st Heaven his, and all the *e.*
P. L. 11, 339. all the *e.* he gave thee to possess
P. L. 11, 345. come from all the ends of the *e.*
P. L. 11, 379. hemisphere of *E.* in clearest ken
P. L. 11, 384. to show him all *e.'s* kingdoms
P. L. 11, 473. on the *e.* shall bring diseases dire
P. L. 11, 568. down to the veins of *e.*
P. L. 11, 698. shall be achieved, renown on *e.*
P. L. 11, 744. till the *e.* no more was seen
P. L. 11, 780. violence was ceased and war on *e.*
P. L. 11, 804. for the *e.* shall bear more than
P. L. 11, 825. on the *e.* shall pour rain
P. L. 11, 883. again dissolve and shower the *e.*
P. L. 11, 888. the whole *e.* filled with violence
P. L. 11, 893. never to destroy the *e.* again
P. L. 11, 896. he brings over the *e.* a cloud
P. L. 11, 901. both heaven and *e.,* wherein the
P. L. 12, 29. and law of nature from the *e.*
P. L. 12, 147. that all nations of the *e.*
P. L. 12, 183. and wheel on the *e.,* devouring
P. L. 12, 281. God will deign to dwell on *e.*
P. L. 12, 371. with *e.'s* wide bounds
P. L. 12, 437. longer on *e.* than certain times
P. L. 12, 463. bliss whether in heaven or *e.*
P. L. 12, 463. then the *e.* shall all be paradise
P. L. 12, 528. for on *e.* who against faith
P. L. 12, 549. new heavens, new *e.,* ages of
P. L. 12, 579. of God in heaven, air, *e.,* or sea
P. R. 1, 50. ruled ... the affairs of *E.*
P. R. 1, 63. in this fair empire won of *e.* and air
P. R. 1, 99. their leader, and supreme on *e.*
P. R. 1, 125. end his reign on *e.* so long enjoyed
P. R. 1, 131. and all angels conversant on *e.*
P. R. 1, 218. to subdue and quell, o'er all the *e.*
P. R. 1, 237. all heaven and *e.,* angels and sons
P. R. 1, 365. liberty to round this globe of *e.*
P. R. 2, 44. behold the kings of the *e.,* how they
P. R. 2, 114. his end of being on *e.,* and mission
P. R. 2, 124. powers of fire, air, water, and *e.*
P. R. 2, 179. titled sons of God, roaming the *e.*
P. R. 2, 435. those ancient empires of the *e.*
P. R. 3, 24. wherefore deprive all *e.* her wonder
P. R. 3, 61. looking on the *e.,* with approbation
P. R. 3, 65. his fame through heaven and *e.*
P. R. 3, 68. famous he was in heaven, on *e.*
P. R. 3, 246. monarchies of the *e.,* their pomp
P. R. 4, 30. that screened the fruits of the *e.*
P. R. 4, 45. and glorious Rome, queen of the *e.*
P. R. 4, 148. and overshadowing all the *e.*
P. R. 4, 201. of fire, air, flood, and on the *e.*
P. R. 4, 433. had cheered the face of *e.*
P. R. 4, 453. as *e.* and sky would mingle
P. R. 4, 456. or to the *e.'s* dark basis
P. R. 4, 563. as when *E.'s* son, Antæus

P. R. 4, 566. from his mother *E.* new strength
S. A. 165. since man on *e.,* unparalleled
S. A. 174. might have subdued the *e.*
S. A. 1272. to quell the mighty of the *e.*
C. 6. of this dim spot, which men call *e.*
C. 244. can any mortal mixture of *e.'s* mould
C. 599. and *e.'s* base built on stubble
C. 712. covering the *e.* with odours
C. 730. the *e.* cumbered and the winged air
C. 797. and the brute *e.* would lend her nerves
C. 1014. quickly to the green *e.'s* end
Il P. 44. thou fix them on the *e.* as fast
S. 20, 7. till Favonius reinspire the frozen *e.*
H. 63. his reign of peace upon the *e.* began
H. 108. hold all heaven and *e.* in happier union
H. 160. the aged *e.* aghast
H. 189. in consecrated *e.*
P. 2. the stage of air and *e.* did ring
P. 32. heaven and *e.,* are coloured with my woe
M. W. 6. more than she could own from *e.*
M. W. 32. had burial, yet not laid in *e.*
S. M. 17. that we on *e.,* with undiscording voice
D. F. I. 30. thy corse corrupts in *e.'s* womb
D. F. I. 47. or did of late *e.'s* sons besiege the wall
D. F. I. 51. forsook the hated *e.,* O, tell me sooth
D. F. I. 59. to *e.* from thy prefixed seat didst post
**Earth-born.**—P. L. 1, 198. Titanian, or *e-b.*
P. L. 4, 360. creatures of other mould, *e-b.*
V. Ex. 93. who, like some *e-b.* giant
**Earthly.**—P. L. 5, 464. these *e.* fruits to taste
P. L. 7, 14. heavens I have presumed, an *e.* guest
P. L. 7, 82. to impart things above *e.* thought
P. L. 7, 179. so told as *e.* notion can receive
P. L. 8, 120. heaven from earth so far that *e.* sight
P. L. 8, 453. my *e.,* by his heavenly, over-powered
P. L. 8, 522. my story to the sum of *e.* bliss
P. L. 9, 1083. shapes will dazzle now this *e.*
P. L. 12, 315. they, in their *e.* Canaan placed
P. R. 4, 612. for, though that seat of *e.* bliss
H. 138. and leprous sin will melt from *e.* mould
**Earth-shaking.**—C. 869. by the *e.-s* Neptune's
**Earthy.**—P. L. 4, 583. o'er-leaped these *e.*
P. L. 9, 157. tend their *e.* charge
S. 14, 3. meekly thou didst resign this *e.* load
T. 20. then all this *e.* grossness quit
**Ease.**—P. L. 1, 320. for the *e.* you find
P. L. 2, 227. counselled ignoble *e.,* and peaceful
P. L. 2, 261. and work *e.* out of pain
P. L. 2, 458. best may *e.* the present misery
P. L. 2, 521. thence more at *e.* their minds
P. L. 2, 841. thou and death shall dwell at *e.*
P. L. 2, 868. among the gods who live at *e.*
P. L. 2, 878. of massy iron, or solid rock, with *e.*
P. L. 2, 1041. with less toil, and now with *e.*
P. L. 3, 563. and winds with *e.* through
P. L. 4, 96. *e.* would recant vows made in pain
P. L. 4, 187. leaps o'er the fence with *e.*
P. L. 4, 329. and made *e.* more easy
P. L. 4, 632. if we mean to tread with *e.*
P. L. 4, 893. to change torment with *e.*
P. L. 5, 59. *e.* thy load and taste thy sweet
P. L. 5, 439. transpires through spirits with *e.*
P. L. 7, 407. in their pearly shells at *e.* attend
P. L. 9, 129. for only in destroying I find *e.*
P. L. 9, 245. will keep from wilderness with *e.*
P. L. 9, 801. and the fertile burden *e.*
P. L. 9, 1120. but not at rest or *e.* of mind
P. L. 10, 394. darkness on your road with *e.*
P. L. 10, 622. that with so much *e.* I suffer
P. L. 11, 536. with *e.* gathered not harshly
P. L. 11, 794. change their course to pleasure, *e.*
P. R. 2, 201. for Solomon, he lived at *e.*
P. R. 4, 97. with what *e.* endued with regal
P. R. 4, 299. pleasure he, and careless *e.*
P. R. 4, 378. set thee in short time with *e.*
S. A. 17. to find some *e.,* *e.* to the body some
S. A. 271. with *e.* than strenuous liberty
S. A. 917. at home, in leisure and domestic *e.*
C. 687. refreshment after toil, *e.* after pain
L. 152. for so to interpose a little *e.*
Cir. 11. now bleeds to give us *e.*

U. C. II. 21. *e.* was his chief disease
**Eased.**—P. L. 4, 739. and *e.* the putting off
P. L. 12, 274. and my heart much *e.*
S. A. 72. which might in part my grief have *e.*
**Easier.**—P. L. 2, 345. some *e.* enterprize
P. L. 2, 573. might yield them *e.* habitation
P. L. 4, 943. whose *e.* business were to serve
P. L. 6, 37. the *e.* conquest now remains thee
P. L. 6, 286. *e.* to transact with me
P. L. 8, 626. *e.* than air with air, if spirits
P. L. 9, 699. why not known, since *e.* shunned
P. L. 10, 978. of *e.* choice
S. A. 772. the *e.* towards me, or thy hatred less
**Easiest.**—P. L. 4, 47. the *e.* recompense
P. L. 8, 183. taught to live the *e.* way
P. L. 11, 119. where entrance up from Eden *e.*
P. L. 11, 549. and *e.* of this cumbrous charge
P. R. 3, 128. slightest, *e.,* readiest recompense
P. R. 4, 361. plainest taught, and *e.* learnt
**Easily.**—P. L. 1, 696. are *e.* out-done
P. L. 3, 94. and *e.* transgress the sole command
P. L. 3, 301. what hellish hate so *e.* destroyed
P. L. 6, 596. have *e.,* as spirits, evaded swift
P. L. 7, 48. so *e.* obeyed, amid the choice of all
P. L. 7, 609. *e.* the proud attempt of spirits
P. L. 10, 31. their utmost vigilance, and *e.*
P. L. 10, 136. wouldst *e.* detect what I conceal
P. L. 11, 141. Eve, *e.* may faith admit that all
P. R. 1, 471. where *e.* canst thou find one
P. R. 2, 194. *e.* scorned all her assaults
P. R. 3, 156. not part *e.* from possession won
P. R. 4, 126. of the emperor, how *e.* subdued
P. R. 4, 168. *e.* done, and hold them all of me
S. A. 48. in what part lodged, how *e.* bereft me
S. A. 291. me *e.,* indeed, mine may neglect
S. A. 409. might *e.* have shook off all her snares
S. A. 943. *e.* contemned and scorned
S. A. 1005. nor can be *e.* repulsed
S. A. 1466. both God and State they *e.* would set
P. 54. and I (for grief is *e.* beguiled)
**Easing.**—P. L. 7, 430. mutual wing *e.* their flight
P. L. 10, 260. *e.* their passage hence
**East.**—P. L. 2, 3. or where the gorgeous *E*
P. L. 4, 178. there only was, and that looked *e.*
P. L. 4, 209. by him in the *e.* of Eden planted
P. L. 4, 595. by shorter flight to the *e.,* had
P. L. 4, 623. streak the *e.* with first approach
P. L. 5, 142. in wide landscape all the *e.*
P. L. 5, 339. India *e.,* or west, or middle shore
P. L. 7, 130. when morn purples the *e.*
P. L. 7, 245. and from her native *e.* to journey
P. L. 7, 370. in his *e.* the glorious lamp was seen
P. L. 7, 380. then in the *e.* her turn she shines
P. L. 7, 583. sun was set, and twilight from the *e.*
P. L. 8, 138. herself fetch day travelling *e.*
P. L. 8, 162. he from the *e.* his flaming road
P. L. 10, 685. not known or *e.* or west
P. L. 11, 118. and on the *e.* side of the garden
P. L. 11, 203. why in the *e.* darkness ere day's
P. L. 12, 141. from Hermon *e.* to the great
P. R. 1, 250. the wise men thither from the *e.*
P. R. 2, 197. how all the beauties of the *e.* he
P. R. 3, 272. as far as Indus *e.,* Euphrates west
P. R. 3, 316. from Arachosia, from Candaor *e.*
C. 101. of his chamber in the *e.*
M. M. 2. comes dancing from the *e.,* and leads
**Eastern.**—P. L. 1, 341. on the *e.* wind
P. L. 3, 557. from *e.* point of Libra to the fleecy
P. L. 4, 542. against the *e.* gate of Paradise
P. L. 5, 1. her rosy steps in the *e.* clime
P. L. 5, 275. at once on the *e.* cliff of Paradise
P. L. 11, 190. direct to the *e.* gate was bent their
P. L. 12, 362. guides the *e.* sages, who inquire
P. L. 12, 638. and to the *e.* gate led them direct
P. L. 12, 641. they, looking back, all the *e.* side
S. A. 548. against the *e.* ray, translucent, pure
C. 138. ere the blabbing *e.* scout
L'A. 59. right against the *e.* gate
H. 22. see how from far upon the *e.* road
**Eastward.**—P. L. 4, 211. from Auran *e.* to
P. L. 5, 309. and worth thy sight, behold, *e.*

P. L. 10, 292. imagined way beyond Petsora *e.*
P. L. 12, 145. stream, Jordan, true limit *e.*
**Easy.**—P. L. 2, 81. the ascent is *e.* then the
P. L. 2, 256. preferring hard liberty before the *e.*
P. L. 2, 1031. with *e.* intercourse pass to and
P. L. 3, 524. to dare the fiend by *e.* ascent
P. L. 4, 330. and made ease more *e.*
P. L. 4, 421. to keep this one, this *e.* charge
P. L. 4, 433. not think hard one *e.* prohibition
P. L. 6, 437. so small, as *e.* think the remedy
P. L. 6, 499. so *e.* it seemed once found
P. L. 6, 632. inventions they presumed so *e.*
P. L. 7, 304. *e.,* ere God had bid the ground be
P. L. 9, 24. inspires *e.* my unpremeditated verse
P. L. 9, 569. *e.* to me it is to tell thee all
P. L. 9, 734. into her heart too *e.* entrance won
P. L. 10, 58. *e.* it may be seen that I intend
P. L. 10, 305. smooth, *e.,* inoffensive, down to
P. L. 10, 393. one continent, of *e.* thoroughfare
P. R. 1, 120. he directs his *e.* steps girded
P. R. 3, 293. turning with *e.* eye thou mayst
S. A. 95. so obvious and so *e.* to be quenched
S. A. 583. as *e.* cause light again within
C. 286. how *e.* my misfortune is to hit
W. S. 10. thy *e.* numbers flow
**Easy-hearted.**—C. 163. into the *e.-h.* man
**Eat.**—P. L. 5, 637. they *e.,* they drink
P. L. 8, 147. for some to *e.* allotted there
P. L. 8, 309. sudden appetite to pluck and *e.*
P. L. 8, 320. till and keep, and of the fruit to *e.*
P. L. 8, 322. that in the garden grows *e.* freely
P. L. 9, 595. to pluck and *e.* my fill I spared not
P. L. 9, 657. these garden trees ye shall not *e.*
P. L. 9, 660. each tree in the garden we may *e.*
P. L. 9, 662. God hath said, Ye shall not *e.*
P. L. 9, 706. in the day ye *e.* thereof
P. L. 9, 762. in the day we *e.* of this fair fruit
P. L. 9, 781. she plucked, she *e.*
P. L. 9, 997. he scrupled not to *e.*
P. L. 10, 123. whereof ... thou shouldst not *e.*
P. L. 10, 143. she gave me of the tree, and I did *e.*
P. L. 10, 162. me beguiled and I did *e.*
P. L. 10, 178. and dust shalt *e.* all the days
P. L. 10, 200. saying, Thou shalt not *e.* thereof
P. L. 10, 202. thou in sorrow shalt *e.* thereof
P. L. 10, 204. *e.* the herb of the field
P. L. 10, 205. sweat of thy face shalt thou *e.*
P. L. 10, 728. all that I *e.* or drink
P. L. 11, 94. reach also of the tree of life, and *e.*
P. L. 12, 186. locusts swarming down must *e.*
P. R. 1, 352. Moses was forty days nor *e.*
P. R. 2, 274. rise and *e.,* and *e.* the second time
P. R. 2, 314. by a voice inviting him to *e.*
P. R. 2, 321. wouldst thou not *e.*
P. R. 2, 336. only deign to sit and *e.*
P. R. 2, 368. the Son of God to sit and *e.*
P. R. 2, 377. sit down and *e.*
L'A. 102. how Fairy Mab the junkets *e.*
**Eaten.**—P. L. 9, 764. he hath *e.* and lives
P. L. 9, 869. not obeying hath *e.* of the fruit
P. L. 10, 122. hast thou *e.* of the tree whereof
P. L. 10, 199. and *e.* of the tree concerning
**Eatest.**—P. L. 7, 544. in the day thou *e.*
P. L. 8, 329. the day thou *e.* thereof
P. L. 11, 532. in what day *e.* and drink'st
**Eating.**—P. L. 9, 792. and knew not *e.* death
P. L. 9, 1005. Adam took no thought, *e.* his fill
L'A. 135. and ever, against *e.* cares
**Eats.**—P. L. 9, 724. that whoso *e.* thereof
**Eaves.**—Il P. 130. minute-drops from off the *e.*
**Ebb.**—P. L. 11, 847. standing lake to tripping *e.*
**Ebbing.**—C. 19. salt flood and each *e.* stream
**Ebon.**—C. 134. stay thy cloudy *e.* chair
L'A. 8. under *e.* shades and low-browed rocks
**Ecbatan.**—P. L. 11, 393. the Persian in *E.*
**Ecbatana.**—P. R. 3, 286. *E.* her structure vast
**Eccentric.**—P. L. 3, 575. by centre, or *e.*
P. L. 5, 623. mazes intricate, *e.* intervolved
P. L. 8, 83. with centric and *e.* scribbled o'er
**Echo.**—P. L. 10, 861, other *e.* late I taught
C. 230. sweet *E.* sweetest nymph

C. 275.compelled me to awake the courteous E.
**Echoed.**—P. L. 5, 873. hoarse murmur e. to
**Echoes.**—L. 41. and all their e. mourn
H. 100. thousand e. still prolongs
P. 53. would soon unbosom all their e. mild
**Echoing.**—P. L. 4, 681. from the steep of e. hill
P. L. 9, 1107. and e. walks between
L'A. 56. through the high wood e. shrill
**Eclipse.**—P. L. 1, 597. the moon, in dim e.
P. L. 10, 413. planet-struck, real e. then suffered
S. A. 81. irrecoverably dark, total e.
L. 101. built in the e., and rigged with curses
**Eclipsed.**—P. L. 5, 776. and us e.
P. L. 11, 183. air suddenly e.
**Eclipses.**—P. L. 2,666. moon e. at their charms
**Ecliptic.**—P. L. 3, 740. down from the e., sped
**Ecron.**—S. A. 981. in E., Gaza, Asdod, and in
**Ecstasies.**—Il P. 165. dissolve me into e.
**Ecstasy.**—C. 625. and hearken even to e.
**Ecstatic.**—P. 42. and anguish, and e. fit
**Eden.**—P. L. 1, 4. with loss of E.
P. L. 4, 27. E., which now in his view lay
P. L. 4, 132. and to the border comes of E.
P. L. 4, 210. east of E. planted, E.
P. L. 4, 218. the sons of E. long before dwelt
P. L. 4, 223. through E. went a river
P. L. 4, 275. with this Paradise of E. strive
P. L. 4, 507. the happier E.
P. L. 4, 569. the mount that lies from E. north
P. L. 5, 143. of Paradise and E.'s happy plains
P. L. 6, 75. came summoned over E. to receive
P. L. 7, 65. within E. or without was done
P. L. 7, 582. the seventh evening arose in E.
P. L. 8, 113. and ere midday arrived in E.
P. L. 9, 54. the threats of Gabriel out of E.
P. L. 9, 77. from E. over Pontus
P. L. 9, 193. light began to dawn in E.
P. L. 9, 341. and E. were no E. thus exposed
P. L. 10, 89. from whence E. and all the coast
P. L. 11, 119. where entrance up from E.
P. L. 11, 342. bounds confined of Paradise or E.
P. L. 12, 40. marching from E. towards the west
P. L. 12, 465. far happier place than this of E.
P. L. 12, 649. took their solitary way
P. R. 1, 7. and E. raised in the waste wilderness
**Edge.**—P. L. 1, 276. and on the perilous e.
P. L. 1, 460. on the grunsel e.
P. L. 6, 108. the rough e. of battle ere it joined
P. L. 6, 252. the horrid e. came down
P. L. 6, 323. keen nor solid might resist that e.
P. R. 1, 94. danger on the utmost e. of hazard
P. R. 2, 455. to slacken virtue and abate her e.
L. 105. and on the e., like to that sanguine flower
**Edged.**—H. 185. e. with poplar pale
**Edict.**—P. L. 5, 798. can introduce law and e.
**Edicts.**—S.A.301. his own e. found contradicting
**Edifice.**—P. L. 8, 104. an e. too large for him
P. R. 4, 55. many a fair e. besides
S. A.1588. the e., where all were met to see him
**Edomite.**—P. R. 2, 423. raised Antipater the E.
**Edwards.**—F. of C. 12. by shallow E. and Scotch
**E'er.**—C. 823. the soothest shepherd that e. piped
**Effect.**—P. L. 2, 595. cold performs the e.
P. L. 3, 612. of colour glorious and e. so rare
P. L. 6, 493. ere dawn, e. shall end our wish
P. L. 7, 175. the filial Godhead gave e.
P. L. 8, 95. whose virtue on itself works no e.
P. L. 9, 865 but of divine e. to open eyes
P. R. 2, 215. once wrought that e. on Jove
S. A. 681. which in part they e.
C. 630. unsightly root, but of divine e.
**Effected.**—P. L. 1, 647. what force e. not
P. L. 9, 152. what he decreed, he e.
**Effects.**—P. L. 9, 650. if cause of such e.
P. L. 9, 875. also found the e. to correspond
P. L. 11, 424. the e., which thy original crime
**Effectual.**—P. L. 3, 170. and e. might
P. R. 4, 432. the sun with more e. beams
**Effeminacy.**—S. A. 410. but foul e. held me
**Effeminate.**—P. L. 11, 634. e. slackness
P. R. 4, 142. and from the daily scene e.

**Effeminately.**—S. A. 562. e. vanquished
**Efficacious.**—S. A. 1437. be e. in thee now at
**Efficacy.**—P. L. 10, 660. of noxious e.
**Effluence.**—P. L. 3, 6. bright e. of bright
**Effulgence.**—P. L. 3, 388. e. of his glory
P. L. 5, 158. divine e., whose high power so far
P. L. 6, 680. e. of my glory, Son beloved
**Effused.**—P. L. 11, 447. with gushing blood e.
**Effusion.**—P. L. 6, 765. fierce e. rolled of smoke
**Egg.**—P. L. 7, 418. hatch from the e., that soon
**Eglantine.**—L'A. 48. or the twisted e.
**Egress.**—P. L. 2, 437. prohibit all e.
**Egypt.**—P. L. 1, 339. in E.'s evil day
P. L. 1, 421. that parts E. from Syrian ground
P. L. 1, 480. abused fanatic E. and her priests
P. L. 1, 488. when he passed from E. marching
P. L. 1, 721. when E. with Assyria strove
P. L. 3, 537. the Holy Land borders on E.
P. L. 4, 171. sent from Media post to E.
P. L. 12, 157. called E., divided by the river Nile
P. L. 12, 190. all the first-born of E. must lie dead
P. L. 12, 219. fear return them back to E.
P. R. 2, 76. soon enforced to fly thence into E.
P. R. 2, 79. from E. home returned in Nazareth
P. R. 3, 379. their fathers in the land of E.
P. R. 3, 384. from E. to Euphrates and beyond
P. R. 3, 417. to worship calves, the deities of E.
C. 676. in E. gave to Jove-born Helena
**Egyptian.**—P. L. 5, 274. to E. Thebes he flies
P. L. 9, 443. held dalliance with his fair E. spouse
P. L. 12, 182. must rend the E. sky
**Eject.**—P. L. 11, 52. e. him tainted now
**Ejected.**—P. R. 1, 414. deposed, e., emptied
S. A. 1207. is well e when the conquered can
**Eight.**—M.W.7. summers three times e. save one
**Eighth.**—P. L. 9, 67. on the e. returned
**Either.**—P. L. 1, 424. can e. sex assume
P. L. 1, 644. so as not e. to provoke
P. L. 2, 96. will e. quite consume us
P. L. 2, 229. e. to disenthrone the king
P. L. 2, 364. e. with hell fire to waste his whole
P. L. 2, 538. from e. end of heaven the welkin
P. L. 2, 649. on e. side a formidable shape
P. L. 2, 670. each seemed e.,—black it stood
P. L. 2, 721. never but once more was e. like
P. L. 3, 350. towards e. throne they bow
P. L. 3, 487. a violent cross wind from e. coast
P. L. 3, 641. flowing hair in curls on e. cheek
P. L. 4, 695. on e. side Acanthus and each
P. L. 5, 131. tear let fall from e. eye
P. L. 5, 284. shadowed from e. heel with
P. L. 6, 214. and, flying, vaulted on e. host with fire
P. L. 6, 221. angels fought on e. side
P. L. 6, 570. and to e. flank retired
P. L. 6, 778. his army circumfused on e. wing
P. L. 6, 800. all his host on e. hand thus spake
P. L. 6, 844. nor less on e. side tempestuous fell
P. L. 8, 388. cannot well suit with e., but soon
P. L. 9, 284. can e. not receive, or can repel
P. L. 9, 407. found'st e. sweet repast or sound
P. L. 9, 1176. bore thee on, secure e. to meet
P. L. 10, 111. love was not in their looks, e. to
P. L. 10, 126. e. to undergo myself the total
P. L. 10, 415. on e. side disparted Chaos overbuilt
P. L. 10, 898. e. he never shall find out fit mate
P. L. 11, 363. by moderation e. state to bear
P. L. 11, 505. would e. not accept life offered
P. L. 12, 637. in e. hand the hastening angel
P. R. 4, 409. and e. tropic now gan thunder
S. A. 1033. that e. they love nothing, or not long
S. A. 1292. e. of these is in thy lot, Samson
**Elaborate.**—P. L. 8, 539. in outward show e.
**Eld.**—D. F. I. 13. uncoupled bed and childless e.
**Eldest.**—P. L. 2, 894. are lost; where e. Night
P. L. 2, 962. e. of things, the consort of his
P. L. 5, 180. thee e. birth of nature's womb
S. 17, 14. in peace, and reckons thee her e. son
**Eleäle.**—P. L. 1, 411. and E., to the asphaltic
**Elect.**—P. L. 3, 136. the blessed spirits e.
P. L. 3, 184. chosen of peculiar grace, e. above
P. L. 3, 360. the spirits e. bind

P. L. 6, 374. but those e. angels contented with
P. L. 12, 214. the race e. safe towards Canaan
**Elected.**—S. A. 678. thou hast solemnly e.
**Election.**—P. L. 10, 764. yet him not thy e.
**Electra.**—S. 8, 13. repeated air of sad E.'s poet
**Elegant.**—P. L. 9, 1018. exact of taste and e.
**Element.**—P. L. 2, 490. the louring e.
P. L. 7, 16. return me to my native e.
P. L. 8, 348. since they cannot change their e.
P. R. 2, 122. the e. each of his reign allotted
C. 299. of some gay creatures of the e.
Il P. 96. with planet, or with e.
**Elemental.**—P. L. 7, 265. transparent, e. air
**Elements.**—P. L. 2, 275. in .. time become our e.
P. L. 2, 925. and these e. in mutiny
P. L. 2, 1015. through the shock of fighting e.
P. L. 3, 715. the cumbrous e., earth, flood, air
P. L. 4, 993. the e. at least had gone to wrack
P. L. 5, 180. ye e., the eldest birth of nature's
P. L. 5, 415. of e. the grosser feeds the purer
P. L. 6, 222. of whom could wield these e.
P. L. 11, 50. those pure immortal e. that know
P. R. 2, 334. from all the e. her choicest store
**Elephant.**—P. L. 4, 345. the unwieldy e.
**Elephants.**—P. R. 3, 329. chariots or e.
**Elevate.**—P. L. 2, 558. in thoughts more e.
P. R. 4, 34. and temples proudly e.
**Elevates.**—P. L. 9, 633. hope e., and joy
**Elf.**—C. 846. shrewd meddling, e. delights
**Eli.**—P L. 1, 495. as did E.'s sons who filled with
**Elijah.**—P. R. 1, 353. forty days E. without food
P. R. 2, 19. sought lost E. so in each place these
P. R. 2, 268. food to E. bringing even and morn
P. R. 2, 277. sometimes that with E. he partook
**Elixir.**—P. L. 3, 607. breathe forth e. pure
**Ellops.**—P. L. 10, 525. hydrus, and e. drear
**Elm.**—P. L. 5, 216. the vine to wed her e.
C. 354. gainst the rugged bank of some broad e.
A. 89. of branching e. star-proof
**Elms.**—L'A. 58. by hedge-row e., on hillocks
**Elocution.**—P. L. 9, 748. gave e. to the
**Eloquence.**—P. L. 2, 556. for e. the soul
P. L. 5, 149. prompt e. flowed from their lips
P. L. 9, 671. where e. flourished, since mute
P. R. 4, 241. Greece, mother of arts and e.
P. R. 4, 268. those ancient whose resistless e.
P. R. 4, 354. extoll'st, as those the top of e.
**Eloquent.**—S. 10, 8. that old man e.
**Elsewhere.**—P. L. 1, 656. thither or e.
P. L. 3. 599 imagined rather oft than e. seen
P. L. 10, 959. each other, blamed enough e.
P. R. 1, 458. shalt bo inquired at Delphos or e.
P. R. 4, 325. he brings what needs he e. seek
**Elude.**—P. L. 9, 158. and to e., thus wrapped
**Elves.**—P. L. 1, 781. fairy e. whose midnight
C. 118. trip the pert fairies and the dapper e.
**Elysian.**—P. L. 3, 359. rolls o'er E. flowers
C. 996. and drenches with E. dew
L'A. 147. on a bed of heaped E. flowers
D. F. I. 40. or in the E. fields (if such there were)
**Elysium.**—P. L. 3, 472. to enjoy Plato's E.
C. 257. take the prisoned soul and lap it in E.
**Emathian.**—P. R. 3, 290. built by E. or by
S. 8, 10. the great E. conqueror bid spare
**Embalmed.**—P. L. 11, 135. dews e. the earth
**Embassies.**—P. R. 4, 67. or e. from regions
P. R. 4, 121. then e. thou show'st from nations
**Embassy.**—P. L. 3, 658. his sons thy e. attend
**Embattled.**—P. L. 6, 16. thick e. squadrons
P. L. 6, 550. onward moved e.
P. L. 7, 322. e. in her field
P. L. 12, 213. on their e. ranks the waves
S. A. 129. ran on e. armies clad in iron
**Embers.**—Il P. 79. where glowing e. through
**Emblem.**—P. L. 4, 703. stone of costliest e.
**Emboldened.**—P. L. 8, 434. thus I e. spake
**Emboss.**—P. L. 12, 180. must all his flesh e.
**Embossed.**—P. L. 4, 119. cups e. with gems
**Embost.**—S. A. 1700. in the Arabian woods e.
**Embowed.**—Il P. 157. and love the high e. roof
**Embowelled.**—P. L. 6, 587. e. with outrageous
**Embowered.**—P. L. 9. 1038. verdant roof e.

**Embrace.**—P. L. 8, 626. if spirits e.
P. L. 12, 426. and the benefit e. by faith
S. 23, 13. but, oh! as to e. me she inclined
D. F. I. 20. with his cold-kind e., unhoused
**Embraced.**—P. L. 9, 990. she e. him, and for
**Embraces.**—P. L. 2, 793. and, in e. forcible
P. L. 4, 322. that ever since in love's e. met
P. L. 4, 471. thy coming, ard thy soft e.
P. L. 5, 215. hands to check fruitless e.
P. L. 10, 994. love's due rites, nuptial e. sweet
S. A. 389. who also in her prime of love, spousal e.
**Embracing.**—P. L. 4, 771. e. slept
P. L. 5, 27. whom e., thus she spake
P. L. 7, 90. air wide interfused, e. round
P. L. 10. 912. and, e. them, besought his peace
**Embroidery.**—L. 148. that sad e. wears
**Embroils.**—P. L. 2, 908. more e. the fray
**Embryon.**—P. L. 2, 900. their e. atoms
P. L. 7, 277. e. immature, involved, appeared not
**Embryos.**—P. L. 3, 474. e. and idiots, eremites
**Emerald.**—C. 894. of turkis blue, and e. green
**Emergent.**—P. L. 7, 286. huge appear e.
**Emims.**—S. A. 1080. E. old that Kiriathaim held
**Eminence.**—P. L. 2, 6. raised to that bad e.
P. L. 4, 44. created what I was in that bright e.
P. L. 8, 624. (thou wert created), we enjoy in e.
**Eminent.**—P. L. 1, 590. and gesture proudly e.
P. L. 4, 219. high e., blooming, ambrosial fruit
P. L. 5, 594. acts of zeal and love recorded e.
P. L. 11, 665. of middle age one rising, e. in wise
P. L. 11, 789. first seen in acts of prowess e.
P. R. 2, 70. and fears as e. above the lot of other
P. R. 3, 91. by deeds of peace, by wisdom e.
**Eminently.**—P. L. 9, 976. so e. never had been
S. A. 679. with gifts and graces e.
S. 9, 3. and with those few art e. seen
**Emmet.**—P. L. 7, 485. the parsimonious e.
**Empedocles.**—P. L. 3, 471. into Ætna flames, E.
**Emperor.**—P. L. 1, 378. their great e.'s call
P. L. 2, 510. than hell's dread e.
P. L. 10, 429. might intercept their e. sent so
P. R. 4, 81. to Rome's great e. whose wide
P. R. 4, 90. this e. hath no son, and now is old
P. R. 4, 126. of the e., how easily subdued
**Empire.**—P. L. 1, 114. doubted his e.
P. L. 2, 296. no less desire to found this nether e.
P. L. 2, 315. and build up here a growing e.
P. L. 2, 327. but over hell extend his e.
P. L. 2, 974. lies through your spacious e. up
P. L. 4, 111. divided e. with heaven's King I
P. L. 4, 145. his nether e. neighbouring round
P. L. 4, 390. honour and e., with revenge
P. L. 5, 724. anciently we claim of deity or e.
P. L. 6, 303. fit to decide the e. of great heaven
P. L. 7, 96. the secrets ask of his eternal e.
P. L. 7, 555. created world, the addition of his e.
P. L. 7, 609. thee, mighty king, or bound thy e.
P. L. 10, 389. of all the infernal e.
P. L. 10, 592. what think'st thou of our e. now
P. L. 11, 387. the seat of mightiest e.
P. L. 11, 397. the e. of Negus to his utmost port
P. L. 12, 32. subjection to his e. tyrannous
P. L. 12, 581. and all the rule, one e.; only add
P. R. 1, 63. in this fair e. won of earth and air
P. R. 3, 45. to seek wealth for e.'s sake
P. R. 3, 45. nor e. to affect for glory's sake
P. R. 3, 270. Assyria, and her e.'s ancient
P. R. 3, 296. who founded first that e.
P. R. 4, 222. as thy e. must extend so let
P. R. 4, 284. thyself much more with e. joined
P. R. 4, 369. kingdom nor e., pleases thee
D. F. I. 16. through middle e. of the freezing air
**Empires.**—P. L. 2, 378. here hatching vain e.
P. R. 2, 435. witness those ancient e. of the
P. R. 3, 237. e., and monarchs, and their radiant
**Empiric.**—P. L. 5, 440. fire of sooty coal the e.
**Employ.**—P. L. 5, 730. all e. in our defence.
S. M. 3. divine sounds, and mixed power e.
**Employed.**—P. L. 3, 628. on some great charge e.
P. L. 4, 726. which we, in our appointed work e.
P. L. 4, 883. e., it seems, to violate sleep

P. L. 5, 219. them thus *e.* beheld with pity
P. L. 9,229. well thy thoughts *e.* how we might
**Employments.**—P. L. 5, 125. our fresh *e.*
**Employs.**—P.L.4,763. Love his golden shafts *e.*
**Empress.**—P. L. 9, 568. *e.* of this fair world
P. L. 9, 626. *e.,* the way is ready and not long
**Emprise.**—P. L. 11, 642. bone and bold *e.*
C. 610. I love thy courage yet, and bold *e.*
**Emptied.**—P. L. 1, 633. whose exile hath *e.*
P. R. 1,414. ejected, *e.,* gazed, unpitied,shunned
Cir. 20. *e.* his glory, even to nakedness
**Emptier.**—P. L. 2, 1045. or in the *e.* waste
**Empties.**—P. L. 3, 731. and *e.,* to enlighten
**Emptiness.**--P. L. 8, 195. fume, or *e.,* or fond
**Empty.**--P. L. 3, 454. *e.* as their deeds
P. L. 7, 39. thou art heavenly,she an *e.* dream
P. L. 11,616. yet *e.* of all good wherein consists
P. R. 4, 321. resemblance only meets an *e.*
**Empty-vaulted.**--C. 250. the *e.-v.* night
**Empyreal.**—P. L. 1, 117. this *e.* substance
P. L. 2, 430. O progeny of heaven, *e* thrones
P. L. 2, 1047. far off the *e.* heaven, extended
P. L. 3, 699. from thy *e.* mansion thus alone
P. L. 5, 253. through all the *e.* road
P. L. 5, 460. thus to the *e.* minister he framed
P. L. 5, 583. the *e.* host of angels
P. L. 6, 14. highest heaven arrayed in gold *e.*
P. L. 6, 433. since now we find this our *e.* form
P. L. 7, 14. and drawn *e.* air, thy tempering
P. L. 10, 380. of all th¹ngs, parted by the *e.*
**Empyrean.**—P. L. 2, 771. through all the *e.*
P. L. 3, 57. from the pure *e.* where he sits
P. L. 6, 833.the steadfast *E.*shook throughout
P. L. 7, 73. down from the *e.* to forewarn us
P. L. 7, 633. so sung they, and the *e.* rung
P. L. 10, 321. the confines met of *e.* heaven
**Emulate.**—P. L. 9, 963. engaging me to *e.*
**Emulation.**—P. L. 2, 298. in *e.* opposite
**Emulous.**—P. L. 6, 822. excellence not *e.*
**Enamelled.**—P. L. 4, 149. with gay *e.* colours
P. L. 9, 525. and sleek *e.* neck fawning
A. 84, o'er the smooth *e.* green
L. 139. all your quaint *e.* eyes
**Enamour.**—P. R. 2, 214. charms begirt to *e.*
**Enamoured.**—P. L. 2, 765. becam'st *e.*
P. L. 4, 169. that drove him, though *e.*
P. L. 5, 13. of cordial love hung over her *e.*
P. L. 5,448. sons of God excuse to have been *e.*
**Encamp.**—P. L. 2, 132. on the deep *e.*
**Encamped.**—P. L. 10, 276. where armies lie *e.*
P. L. 11, 656. to a city strong lay siege, *e.*
P. L. 12, 591. the guards by me *e.* on yonder
**Encamping.**—P. L. 6, 412. angels prevalent *e.*
**Enchanted.**—S. A. 934. thy fair *e.* cup
C. 517. of dire chimeras and *e.* isles
**Enchanter.**—C. 645. I knew the foul *e.*
C. 814. what! have you let the false *e.* scape?
C. 907. through the wile of unblest *e.* vile
**Enchanting.**—P. L. 10, 353. his fair *e.*
P. R. 2, 158. expert in amorous arts, *e.*
S. A. 1065. look now for no *e.* voice, nor fear
C. 245. breathe such divine *e.* ravishment
L. 59. the Muse herself, for her *e.* son
**Enchantments.**—S. A. 1133. and black *e.*
C. 640. 'gainst all *e.,* mildew blast, or 'damp
C. 696. hence with thy brewed *e.* foul deceiver
Il P. 119. of forests, and *e.* drear
**Enclosed.**—P. L. 4, 283. *e.* with shining rock
P. L. 6, 101. *e.* with flaming cherubim
P. L. 7, 486. in small room large heart *e.*
P.L. 8,304. circuit wide, *e.,* with goodliest trees
P. L. 9, 494. enemy of mankind, *e.* in serpent
P. L. 9,722. who *e.* knowledge of good and evil
S. A. 1117. let be assigned some narrow place *e.*
**Enclosing.**—P. R. 3, 361. such *e.* enemies
**Enclosure.**—P. L. 4, 133. with her *e.* green
P. L. 9,543. in this *e.* wild, these beasts among
**Encompassed.**—P. L. 3, 149. thy throne *e.*
P. L. 5, 876. *e.* round with foes, thus answered
**Encounter.**—P. L. 2, 718. join their dark *e.*
**Encountered.**—P. L. 6, 664. the air *e.* hills

**Encountering.**—P. L. 6, 220. *e.* angels
**Encounters.**—S. A. 1086. of those *e.,* where we
**Encroached.**—P. L. 2, 1001. *e.* on still
**Encroachment.**—P. L. 12, 72. his *e.* proud
**Encumbered.**—P. L. 9, 1051. *e.,* now had left
C. 774. and she no whit *e.* with her store
**End.**—P. L. 1, 67. torture without *e.* still urges
P. L. 1, 164. labour must be to pervert that *e.*
P. L. 2,89. must exercise us, without hope of *e.*
P. L. 2, 145. and that must *e.* us, that must be
P.L. 2,157. to give his enemies their wish,and *e.*
P. L. 2, 186. unreprieved, ages of hopeless *e.*
P. L. 2,538. from either *e.* of heaven the welkin
P. L. 2, 561. and found no *e.,* in wandering
P. L. 2, 807. that he knows his *e.* with mine
P. L. 2, 870. and thy darling, without *e.*
P. L. 3, 142. love without *e.*
P. L. 3, 157. the adversary thus obtain his *e.*
P. L. 3,197. and, to the *e.* persisting, safe arrive
P. L. 3, 406. he to appease thy wrath, and *e.*
P. L. 3, 633. his journey's *e.,* and our beginning
P. L. 4, 398. as their shape served best his *e.*
P. L. 4, 442. and without whom am to no *e.*
P. L. 4, 833. like to *e.* as much in vain
P. L. 5, 165. him midst, and without *e.*
P. L. 5, 615. without redemption, without *e.*
P. L. 6, 137. smallest things, could without *e.*
P. L. 6, 172. nor *e.* wilt find of erring
P. L. 6, 258. as hoping here to *e.* intestine war
P. L. 6, 288. err not, that so shall *e.* the strife
P. L. 6, 493. yet ere dawn effect shall *e.* our
P. L. 6, 703. since none but thou can *e.* it
P. L. 6, 731. shall resign, when in the *e.*
P. L. 7, 79. his sovran will, the *e.* of what we
P. L. 7,108. can bid his absence, till thy song *e.*
P. L. 7, 161. joy and union without *e.*
P. L. 7, 217. your discord *e.*
P.L. 7,505. wanted yet the master-work, the *e.*
P. L. 7,542. the earth yields variety without *e.*
P. L. 7, 591. author and *e.* of all things
P. L. 8, 35. attains her *e.* without least motion
P. L. 8, 189. and of her roving is no *e.*
P. L. 8, 540. in the prime *e.* of Nature
P. L. 9, 51. from *e.* to *e.* night's hemisphere
P. L. 9, 241. the lowest *e.* of human life
P. L. 9, 798. thy fair fruit let hang, as to no *e.*
P. L. 9, 1189. vain contest appeared no *e.*
P. L. 10, 53. no acquittance ere day *e.*
P. L. 10, 167. and polluted from the *e.* of his
P. L. 10,446. upper *e.* was placed in regal lustre
P. L. 10, 720. miserable of happy! is this the *e.*
P. L. 10, 725. well, if here would *e.* the misery
P. L. 10, 797. can he exercise wrȧth without *e.*
P. L. 10, 797. on Man, whom death must *e.*
P. L. 10, 856. thrice acceptable stroke to *e.* me
P. L. 10, 977. some relief of our extremes, or *e.*
P. L. 10, 1004. under fears that show no *e.*
P. L. 10,·1020. if thou covet death, as utmost *e.*
P. L. 11, 1084. till we *e.* in dust, our final
P. L. 11, 300. and in performing *e.* us
P. L. 11, 502. better *e.* here unborn
P. L. 11, 605. created, as thou art, to nobler *e.*
P. L. 11,755. the *e.* of all thy offspring, *e.* so sad
P. L. 11, 786. here the race of man will *e.*
P. L. 12, 6. hast seen one world begin and *e.*
P. L. 12, 330. that his reign shall be no *e.*
P. L. 12,556. eternity, whose *e.*no eye can reach
P. L. 12, 605. with meditation on the happy *e.*
P. R. 1, 125. to *e.* his reign on earth so long
P. R. 1, 205. myself I thought born to that *e.*
P. R. 1,241. thy kingdom there should be no *e.*
P. R. 1, 408. and in lies wilt *e.*
P. R. 2, 114. his *e.* of being on earth
P. R. 2, 245. where will this *e.*?
P. R. 2, 442. and reign in Israel without *e.*
P. R. 3, 123. chiefly not for glory as prime *e.*
P. R. 3, 185. hath told that it shall never *e.*
P. R. 3, 197. exaltation without change or *e.*
P. R. 3, 211. the *e.* I would attain, my final
P. R. 3, 350. to what *e.* I have brought thee

P. R. 4, 20. and in froth or bubbles *e.*
P. R. 4, 151. my kingdom there shall be no *e.*
P. R. 4, 391. as without *e.* without beginning
S. A. 232. from my former act, and the same *e.*
S. A. 461. that the strife with me hath *e.*
S. A. 522. to what *e.* should I seek it?
S. A. 576. hasten the welcome *e.* of all my pains
S. A. 704. for oft alike both come to evil *e.*
S. A. 709. labours, for thou canst, to peaceful *e.*
S. A. 871. where all thy circling wiles would *e.*
S. A. 1008. love-quarrels in pleasing concord *e.*
S. A. 1265. their *e.* is hate, not help to me
S. A. 1720. but favouring and assisting to the *e.*
A. 7. here our solemn search hath *e.*
C. 136. till utmost *e.* of all thy dues be done
C. 196. shouldst thou, but for some felonious *e.*
C. 783. would I something say, yet to what *e.*
C. 1014. quickly to the green earth's *e.*
L'A. 109. that ten day-labourers could not *e.*
D. F. I. 77. that till the world's last *e.*
U. C. I. 12. thinking his journey's *e.* was come
**Endangered.**—P. L. 1, 131. *e.* heaven's king
P. L. 2, 1017. more *e.* than when Argo passed
**Endangering.**—S. A. 1009. treachery *e.* life
**Endear.**—S. A. 796. how to *e.,* and hold thee
**Endearing.**—P. L. 4, 337. nor *e.* smiles
**Endeavour.**—P. L. 12, 355, most *e.* peace
P. R. 3, 353. *e.* as thy father David did
S. A. 766. not that I *e.* to lessen or extenuate
S.14, 5.thy works, and alms, and all thy good *e.*
**Endeavoured.**—P. L. 3, 192. but *e.* with
**Endeavouring.**—P. L. 8, 260. thitherward *e.*
P. R. 3, 399. on my part aught *e.,* or to need
V. Ex. 2. didst move my first *e.* tongue to speak
**Ended.**—P. L. 2, 106. he *e.* frowning
P. L. 2, 291. applause was heard as Mammon *e.*
P. L. 2, 390. well have ye judged, well *e.* long
P. L. 2, 487. consultations dark *e.,* rejoicing
P. L. 2, 514. of their session *e.* they bid cry
P. L. 2, 651. but *e.* foul in many a scaly fold
P. L. 3, 266. his words here *e.,* but his meek
P. L. 4, 874. he scarce had *e.,* when those two
P. L. 6, 98. sound of onset *e.* soon each milder
P. L. 6, 296. they *e.* parle, and both addressed
P. L. 6, 496. he *e.,* and his words their drooping
P. L. 6, 569. he scarce had *e.,* when to right and
P. L. 8, 1. the angel *e.* and in Adam's ear
P. L. 8, 452. he *e.* or I heard no more, for now
P. L. 9, 468. though in mid heaven, soon *e.* his
P. L. 9, 733. he *e.,* and his words replete with
P. L. 10, 641. he *e.,* and the heavenly
P. L. 10, 937. she *e.* weeping, and her lowly
P. L. 10, 1007. she *e.* here, or vehement despair
P. L. 11, 72. he *e.,* and the Son gave signal high
P. L. 11, 137. had *e.* now their orisons
P.L. 11, 238. he *e.,* and the archangel soon drew
P. L. 11, 246. prime in manhood, where youth *e.*
P. L. 12, 552. he *e.,* and thus Adam last replied
P. L. 12, 606. he *e.;* and they both descend the
P.R. 1, 106. he *e.,* and his words impression left
P. R. 1, 309. nor hunger felt till those days *e.*
P. R. 1, 346. he *e.,* and the Son of God replied
D. F. I. 18. there *e.* was his quest
U. C. II. 10. his principles being ceased, he *e.*
**Ending.**—P. L. 3, 729. still *e.,* still renewing
P. L. 6, 702. may be thine of *e.* this great war
Il P. 129. *e.* on the rustling leaves
H. 226. not Typhon huge *e.* in snaky twine
H. 239. is our tedious song should here have *e.*
**Endless.**—P.L. 1, 142. swallowed up in *e.* misery
P.L. 2, 30. condemns to greatest share of *e.* pain
P. L. 2, 159. whom his anger saves to punish *e.*
P. L. 2, 897. amidst the noise of *e.* wars
P. L. 4, 52. the debt immense of *e.* gratitude
P. L. 6, 694. fight they needs must last *e.*
P. L. 10, 754. thou added the sense of *e.* woes
P. L. 10, 810. but *e.* misery from this day
P. L. 12, 549. new earth, ages of *e.* date
P. R. 3, 178. who sung thy *e.* reign
S. 15, 10. for what can war, but *e.* war still breed
S. M. 28. and sing in *e.* morn of light

**Endow.**—P. L. 9, 149. and him *e.,* exalted
**Endowed.**—P. L. 4, 715. whom the gods *e.*
P. L. 11, 58. with two fair gifts created him *e.*
**Ends.**—P. L. 5, 586. forthwith from all the *e.*
P. L. 11, 345. come from all the *e.* of the earth
P. L. 11, 602. nature seems fulfilled in all her *e.*
P. R. 4, 410. and both *e.* of heaven
S. A. 62. haply had *e.* above my reach to know
S. A. 893. the *e.* for which our country is
S. A. 1043. shameful deeds, which ruin *e.*
C. 160. I, under fair pretence of friendly *e.*
**Endue.**—P. L. 12, 500. with wondrous gifts *e.*
**Endued.**—P. L. 2, 356. how *e.,* and what their
P. L. 5, 473. *e.* with various forms, various
P. L. 5, 815. by right *e.* with regal sceptre
P. L. 7, 507. but *e.* with sanctity of reason
P. L. 8, 353. with such knowledge God *e.* my
P. L. 9, 324. we not *e.* single with like defence
P. L. 9, 561. but not with human voice *e.*
P. L. 9, 871. thenceforth *e.* with human voice
P. R. 2, 437. but men *e.* with these have oft
P. R. 4, 98. *e.* with regal virtues as thou art
P. R. 4, 602. with godlike force *e.* against the
S. A. 1293. with might *e.* above the sons of men
**Endurance.**—P. L. 2, 262. labour and *e.*
**Endure.**—P. L. 2, 206. to *e.* exile, or ignominy
P. L. 4, 811. for no falsehood can *e.*
P. L. 4, 920. or thou than they less hardy to *e.*
P. L. 4, 925. not that I less *e.,* or shrink
P. L. 9, 833. with him all deaths I could *e.*
P. L. 11, 365. and best prepared *e.* thy mortal
P. L. 12, 324. his regal throne for ever shall *e.*
P. L. 12, 405. thy punishment he shall *e.*
P. R. 1, 476. thee I can and must, submiss, *e.*
P. R. 2, 251. what praise is it to *e.*
P. R. 4, 174. I *e.* the time, till which expired
S. A. 477. nor will long *e.* it doubtful
**Endured.**—P. L. 1, 299. nathless he so *e.*
P. L. 2, 1028. whose boiling gulf tamely *e.*
P. L. 5, 783. too much to one, but double how *e.*
P. L. 6, 111. Abdiel that sight *e.* not
P. L. 6, 431. some disadvantage we *e.* and pain
**Endures.**—P. L. 9, 269. with her the worst *e.*
**Endueth.**—S. 2, 8. more timely-happy spirits *e.*
**Enemies.**—P. L. 2, 157. to give his *e.* their wish
P. L. 6, 466. may offend our yet unwounded *e.*
P. L. 6, 677. anointed Son avenged upon his *e.*
P. L. 6, 826. and full of wrath bent on his *e.*
P. L. 10, 219. thought not much to clothe his *e.*
P. L. 10, 625. to gratify my scornful *e.*
P. L. 12, 318. provoking God to raise them *e.*
P. L. 12, 415. but to the cross he nails thy *e.*
P. L. 12, 482. the unfaithful herd, the *e.* of truth
P. R. 3, 361. between two such enclosing *e.*
P. R. 3, 392. of *e.,* of aids, battles
P. R. 4, 432. no; let them serve their *e.*
S. A. 34. made of my *e.* the scorn and gaze
S. A. 68. blind among *e.,* O worse than chains
S. A. 112. perhaps my *e.,* who come to stare
S. A. 540. shaven, and disarmed among mine *e.*
S. A. 640. against the uncircumcised, our *e.*
S. A. 642. and to those cruel *e.,* whom I by his
S. A. 782. but I to *e.* revealed, and should not
S. A. 878. chose thee from among my *e.*
S. A. 1159. and delivered up into thy *e.*' hand
S. A. 1202. as on my *e.,* wherever chanced
S. A. 1582. unwounded of his *e.* he fell
S. A. 1711. on his *e.* fully revenged
S. A. 1726. where it lies soaked in his *e.*' blood
**Enemy.**—P. L. 1, 188. most offend our *e.*
P. L. 2, 137. yet our great *e.,* all incorruptible
P. L. 2, 785. but he, my inbred *e.,* forth issued
P. L. 2, 822. I come no *e.,* but to set free
P. L. 4, 825. why sat'st thou, like an *e.* in wait
P. L. 5, 239. what *e.,* late fallen himself
P. L. 8, 234. or *e.,* while God was in his work
P. L. 9, 274. that such an *e.* we have, who seeks
P. L. 9, 304. the *e.,* though bold will hardly
P. L. 9, 494. so spake the *e.* of mankind
P. L. 9, 905. cursed fraud of *e.* hath beguiled
P. L. 9, 1172. the danger and the lurking *e.*

P. L. 12, 390. with more strength to foil thy *e*.
P. R. 2, 126. such an *e*. is risen to invade us
P. R. 2, 330. nor proffered by an *e*.—though
P. R. 2, 372. but life preserves, destroys life's *e*.
P. R. 4, 525. thou art to be my fatal *e*.
S. A. 238. the Philistine, thy country's *e*.
S. A. 316. nor in respect of the *e*. just cause
S. A. 380. a Canaanite, my faithless *e*.
S. A. 856. how glorious to entrap a common *e*.
S. A. 882. yet now am judged an *e*.
S. A. 1416. as of a common *e*., so dreaded once
S. A. 1622. had made their dreadful *e*. their thrall
**Enerve.**—P. R. 2, 165. and with voluptuous
**Enfeebled.**—P. L. 9, 488. and pain *e*. me
**Enforce.**—S. A. 1223. enterprize of small *e*.
**Enforced.**—P. L. 11, 419. that Adam now *e*.
P. R. 1, 472. and not *e*. oft-times to part from
P. R. 2, 75. yet soon *e*. to fly thence into Egypt
**Engage.**—P. R. 3, 347. I seek not to *e*.
**Engaged.**—P. L. 4, 954. discipline and faith *e*.
P. L. 9, 400. she to him as oft *e*. to be returned
C. 193. they had *e*. their wandering steps too far
**Engaging.**—P. L. 9, 963. *e*. me to emulate
**Engine.**—P. L. 2, 65. noise of his almighty *e*.
P. L. 4, 17. and like a devilish *e*. back recoils
L. 130. but that two-handed *e*. at the door
U. C. II. 9. like an *e*. moved with wheel
**Enginery.**—P. L. 6, 553. his devilish *e*.
**Engines.**—P. L. 1, 750. scape by all his *e*.
P. L. 2, 923. with all her battering *e*.
P. L. 6, 484. which, into hollow *e*. long
P. L. 6, 518. their *e*., and their balls of missive
P. L. 6, 586. from those deep-throated *e*.
P. L. 6, 650. till on those cursed *e*. triple row
S. A. 1396. or we shall find such *e*. to assail
**England's.**—S. 10, 2. President of *E's*. Council.
**English.**—S. 13, 2. first taught our *E*. music
**Engrave.**—P. L. 12, 524. shall on the heart *e*.
**Engraven.**—P. L. 2, 302. on his front *e*.
**Engrossed.**—P. L. 5, 775. *e*. all power
**Enjoined.**—P. L. 9, 207. pleasant task *e*.
P. L. 10, 575. *e*., some say, to undergo
P. L. 11, 177. though now *e*. laborious, till day
S. A. 6. in the common prison else *e*. me
**Enjoinest.**—P. L. 5, 563. high matter thou *e*.
**Enjoining.**—S. A. 870. truth, duty, so *e*.
**Enjoins.**—P. L. 9, 357. but tender love *e*.
**Enjoy.**—P. L. 3, 471. and he who, to *e*.
P. L. 4, 433. who *e*. free leave so large
P. L. 4, 445. I chiefly, who *e*. so far the happier
P. L. 4, 472. him thou shalt *e*. inseparably
P. L. 4, 507. shall *e*. their fill of bliss on bliss
P. L. 4, 534. yet happy pair! *e*., till I return
P. L. 5, 503. meanwhile *e*. your fill what
P. L. 8, 365. what happiness, who can *e*. alone
P. L. 8, 523. the sum of earthly bliss which I *e*.
P. L. 8, 623. we *e*. in eminence
P. L. 9, 1032. my sense with ardour to *e*. thee
P. L. 10, 758. wilt thou *e*. the good
P. L. 11, 142. good which we *e*. from heaven
P. L. 11, 804. their lords shall leave them to *e*.
P. R. 1, 364. I *e*. large liberty to round this
P. R. 2, 203. higher design than to *e*. his state
P. R. 3, 360. how couldst thou hope long to *e*.
P. R. 4, 94. his horrid lusts in private to *e*.
S. A. 807. I should still *e*. thee day and
S. A. 991. nor shall I count it heinous to *e*.
C. 382. may sit in the centre and *e*. bright day
C. 790. *e*. your dear wit, and gay rhetoric
**Enjoyed.**—P. L. 1, 683. divine or holy else *e*.
P. L. 8, 584. therein *e*. were worthy to subdue
P. L. 9, 264. perhaps no bliss *e*. by us excites
P. R. 1, 125. to end his reign on earth, so long *e*.
S. A. 915. life yet hath many solaces, *e*.
**Enjoyedst.**—P. L. 12, 580. of this world *e*.
**Enjoyest.**—P. L. 8, 622. thou in the body *e*.
**Enjoying.**—P. L. 3, 306. and equally *e*.
P. L. 4, 446. so far the happier lot, *e*. thee
P. L. 8, 366. or ail *e*., what contentment find
P. L. 9, 829. shall live with her *e*., I extinct
S. A. 157. which men *e*. sight oft without cause

**Enjoyment.**—P. L. 6, 452. leader to free *e*.
C. 742. unsavoury in the *e*. of itself
**Enjoyments.**—P. L. 8, 531. in all *e*. else
**Enlarged.**—P. L. 4, 390. with revenge *e*.
**Enlarges.**—P. L. 8, 590. thoughts and heart *e*
**Enlighten.**—P. L. 3, 731. to *e*. the earth
P. L. 4, 668. which these soft fires not only *e*.
P. L. 11, 115. as I shall thee *e*.
**Enlightened.**—P. L. 6, 497. drooping cheer *e*.
P. L. 8, 274. fair light, and thou *e*. earth
**Enlightener.**—P. L. 12, 271. from heaven, *e*.
**Enlightening.**—P. L. 8, 143. *e*. her by day
**Enmity.**—P. L. 1, 431. works of love or *e*. fulfil
P. L. 2, 500. yet live in hatred, *e*., and strife
P. L. 9, 465. of *e*. disarmed, of guile, of hate
P. L. 9, 1151. no ground of *e*. between us known
P. L. 10, 180. thee and the woman I will put *e*.
P. L. 10, 497. that which to me belongs is *e*.
P. L. 10, 925. *e*. against a foe by doom express
S. A. 1201. when I perceived all set on *e*.
V. Ex. 88. to harbour those that are at *e*.
**Enna.**—P. L. 4, 269. not that fair field of *E*.
**Ennobled.**—P. L. 9, 992. his love had so *e*.
S. A. 1491. and view him sitting in the house *e*.
Il P. 102. *e*. hath the buskined stage
**Enormous.**—P. L. 1, 511. with his *e*. brood
P. L. 5, 297. wild above rule or art, *e*. bliss
P. L. 7, 411. *e*. in their gait, tempest the ocean
**Enough.**—P. L. 4, 124. yet not *e*. had practised
P. L. 7, 125. *e*. is left besides to search and know
P. L. 8, 535. not proof *e*. such object to sustain
P. L. 8, 537. took perhaps more than *e*.
P. L. 9, 1169. *e*. severe, it seems, in thy restraint
P. L. 10, 959. each other, blamed *e*. elsewhere
P. L. 11, 766. each day's lot *e*. to bear
P. L. 11, 805. earth shall bear more than *e*.
S. A. 431. thou bearest *e*., and more, the burden
S. A. 455. in feeble hearts, propense *e*. before
S. A. 1468. who confessed they had *e*. revenged
S. A. 1592. more than *e*. we know
C. 780. shall I go on, or have I said *e*.
C. 958. back, shepherds, back! *e*. your play
S. 13, 6. with praise *e*. for envy to look wan
**Enow.**—P. L. 2, 504. man had not hellish foes *e*.
L. 114. *e*. of such, as for their bellies' sake
**Enrage.**—P. L. 2, 698. and to *e*. thee more
**Enraged.**—P. L. 1, 216. and *e*. might see
P. L. 2, 95. which, to the height *e*., will either
C. 830. of her *e*. stepdame, Guendolen
**Enrich.**—C. 505. that doth *e*. these downs
**Enriched.**—P. R. 4, 46. and with the spoils *e*.
**Ensanguined.**—P. L. 11, 654. the *e*. field
**Enshrine.**—P. L. 5, 273. to *e*. his reliques in
P. L. 12, 334. shall in a glorious temple *e*.
**Enshrined.**—P. R. 4, 598. from heaven, *e*.
**Ensign.**—P. L. 1, 536. unfurled the imperial *e*.
P. L. 6, 775. the great *e*. of Messiah blazed
**Ensigns.**—P. L. 1, 325. scattered arms and *e*.
P. L. 2, 886. under spread *e*. marching
P. L. 5, 588. thousand *e*. high advanced
P. L. 6, 356. and with fierce *e*. pierced the deep
P. L. 6, 533. under spread *e*. moving nigh
P. R. 4, 65. and rods, the *e*. of their power
**Enslaved.**—P. L. 2, 333. be given to us *e*.
P. L. 11, 797. the conquered also, and *e*. by war
P. R. 4, 144. thus degenerate, by themselves *e*.
S. A. 1041. or by her charms draws him awry *e*.
**Ensnare.**—S. A. 860. it would be to *e*.
C. 700. with liquorish baits fit to *e*. a brute
**Ensnared.**—P. L. 4, 717. she *e*. mankind
S. A. 365. *e*., assaulted, overcome, led bound
C. 909. 'tis my office best to help *e*. chastity
**Ensue.**—P. L. 4, 26. worse sufferings must *e*.
P. L. 4, 527. taste and die. What likelier can *e*.
P. L. 5, 682. to debate what doubtful may *e*.
P. L. 6, 456. which evil ruin must needs *e*.
P. L. 9, 827. death *e*.? then I shall be no more
P. L. 9, 977. I thought death menaced would *e*.
P. L. 9, 1185. left to herself, if evil thence *e*.
P. L. 11, 839. what further shall *e*., behold
P. L. 12, 331. first a long succession must *e*.

**Enrolled**—*see* **Inrolled**

H

**Ensued.**—P. L. 4, 991. deeds might have *e.*
P. L. 7, 40. what *e.* when Raphael the affable
**Entangled.**—S. A. 763. *e.* with a poisonous
**Enter.**—P. L. 3, 261. shall *e.* heaven
P. L. 4, 563. no evil thing approach or *e.* in
P. L. 4, 704. beast, insect, or worm, durst *e.*
P. L. 5, 464. to *e.*, and these earthly fruits
P. L. 9, 90. fittest imp of fraud in whom to *e.*
P. L. 10, 503. but up and *e.* now into full bliss
P. L. 10, 623. I suffer them to *e.* and possess
P. L. 12, 456. then *e.* into glory and resume
P. R. 4,635. now *e.*, and begin to save mankind
S. A. 463. me overthrown, to *e.* lists with God
S. A. 950. whose doors my feet shall never *e.*
**Entered.**—P. L. 1, 731. multitude admiring *e.*
P. L. 4, 373. such a foe as now is *e.*
P. L. 6, 388. deformed rout *e.*, and foul disorder
P. L. 9, 188. in at his mouth the devil *e.*
P. L. 11, 630. who to live well *e.* so fair
P. L. 11, 735. and *e.* in, as taught their order
P. R. 1, 193. he *e.* now the bordering desert
P. R. 2, 292. and *e.* soon the shade high roofed
S. A.252.with gathered powers,*e.* Judea,seeking
S. A. 1597. as the gates I *e.* with sunrise
C. 646. *e.* the very lime-twigs of his spells
P. 17. poor fleshly tabernacle *e.*
Cir. 11. he who whilere *e.* the world now bleeds
**Entering.**—P. L. 6, 326. deep *e.*, shared all
P. L. 8, 40. seemed *e.* on studious thoughts
P. L. 12, 217. lest. *e.* on the Canaanite alarmed
P. R. 1, 174. now *e.* his great duel, not of arms
P. R. 4, 62. what conflux issuing forth, or *e.* in
**Enterprise.**—P. L. 1, 89. in the glorious *e.*
P. L. 2, 345. what if we find some easier *e.*
P. L. 2, 465. this *e.* none shall partake with me
P. R. 1, 112. and management of this main *e.*
P. R. 2, 412. acts require great means of *e.*
P. R. 3, 228. of the *e.* so hazardous and high
S. A. 1223. as a petty *e,* of small enforce
**Enterprises.**—S. A. 804. forth to perilous *e.*
**Enterprisest.**—P. L. 10, 270. work thou *e.*
**Enters.**—P. L. 6, 10, obsequious darkness *e.*
**Entertain.**—P. L. 2, 526. and *e.* the irksome
P. L. 4, 382. to *e.* you two, her widest gates
P. L. 5, 328. will pluck such choice to *e.*
P. L. 5, 383. stood to *e.* her guest from heaven
P. L. 6, 611. to *e.* them fair with open front
L. 178. there *e.* him all the saints above
**Entertained.**—P. L. 4, 166. so *e.* those
P. L. 10, 105. not pleased, thus *e.* with solitude
P. L. 10, 1009. of death her thoughts had *e.*
**Entertainment.**—P. L. 5, 690. *e.* to receive
**Enthral.**—P. L. 3, 125. they *e.* themselves
P.L. 12, 94. undeservedly *e.* his outward freedom
**Enthralled.**—P. L. 3, 176. forfeit and *e.*
P. L. 6, 181. thyself not free, but to thyself *e.*
C. 590. unjust force but not *e.*
**Enthralment.**—P. L. 12, 171. people from *e.*
**Enthroned.**—P. L. 2, 961. with him *e.* sat
P. L. 5, 536. that stand in sight of God *e.*
C. 11, amongst the *e.* gods on sainted seats
**Entice.**—C. 940. lest the sorcerer us *e.*
Il P. 146. *e.* the dewy feathered sleep
**Enticed.**—P. L. 1, 412. when he *e.* Israel
**Enticement.**—C. 525. by sly *e.* gives his baneful
**Enticing.**—P. L. 9, 996. of that fair *e.* fruit
S. A. 559. another object more *e.*
**Entire.**—P. L. 1, 146. spirit and strength *e.*
P.L. 1,671. the rest *e.* shone with a glossy scurf
P. L. 3, 265. but in thy presence joy *e.*
P. L. 5, 502. retain unalterably firm his love *e.*
P. L. 5, 753. from one *e.* globose stretched into
P. L. 6, 399. cubic phalanx firm, advanced *e.*
P. L. 6, 741. whom to obey is happiness *e.*
P. L. 9, 292. thou art, from sin and blame *e.*
P. L.10, 9. with strength *e.*, and free will armed
P. L. 12, 264. in mid heaven stand still a day *e.*
**Entirely.**—P. L. 7, 549. and, behold, all was *e.*
Cir. 22. which we still transgress *e.* satisfied
**Entitle.**—P. L. 11, 170. to *e.* me vouchsafest
**Entombed.**—T. 9. each thing bad thou hast *e.*

**Entrails.**—P. L. 1, 234. and fuelled *e.* thence
P. L. 2,788. tore through my *e.*, that, with fear
P. L. 6, 346. not as frail man, in *e.*, heart, or
P. L. 6, 517. nor hath this earth *e.* unlike
P. L. 6, 588. and all her *e.* tore
P. L. 9, 1000. earth trembled from her *e.*
P. L. 12, 77. will pine his *e.* gross, and famish
S. A. 614. as on *e.*, joints, and limbs
**Entrance.**—P. L. 3, 50. wisdom at one *e.*
P. L. 4, 180. due *e.* he disdained
P. L. 4, 546. one *e.* high, the rest was craggy
P. L. 4, 882. to question thy bold *e.* on this place
P. L. 9, 61.Uriel, regent of the sun, descried his *e.*
P. L. 9, 68. and on the coast averse from *e.*
P. L. 9, 734. into her heart too easy *e.* won
P. L. 10, 21. how the subtle fiend had stolen *e.*
P. L. 11, 119. where *e.* up from Eden easiest
P. L. 11, 470. more terrible at the *e.* than
C. 518. and rifted rocks whose *e.* leads to hell
S. 9, 14. hast gained thy *e.*,Virgin wise and pure
**Entranced.**—P. L. 11, 420. spirits became *e.*
C. 1005. holds his dear Psyche sweet *e.*
**Entrap.**—S. A. 855. how glorious to *e.* a common
**Entwined.**—P. L. 4, 174. so thick *e.*; as one
**Entwining.**—P. L. 10, 512. his legs *e.* each
**Envenomed**—P. L. 2, 543. felt the *e.* rope
**Envermeil.**—D. F. I. 6. that did thy cheek *e.*
**Envied.**—P. L. 2, 244. lordly sits our *e.* Sovran
P. L. 6, 813. but me they have despised, yet *e.*
S. A. 551. nor *e.* them the grape
F.of C.4.from them whose sin ye *e.*, not abhorred
**Envier.**—P. L. 6, 89. to set the *e.* of his state
**Envies.**—P. L. 6, 900. he, who *e.* now thy state
P. L. 9, 770. which first hath tasted *e.* not
S. A. 995. at this whoever *e.* or repines
**Enviest.**—P. L. 8, 494. of all thy gifts ! nor *e.*
**Envious.**—P. L. 4, 524. to reject *e.* commands
P. L. 7, 139. at least our *e.* foe hath failed
P. L. 11, 15. by *e.* winds blown vagabond
C. 194. and *e.* darkness, ere they could return
T. 1. fly, *e.* Time, till thou run out thy race
**Environed.**—P. L. 2, 1016. *e.*, wins his way
P. R. 1, 194. dark shades and rocks *e.* round
P. R. 4, 423. and hellish furies round *e.* thee
**Environs.**—P. L. 9, 636. and the cold *e.*
S. 12, 3. when straight a barbarous noise *e.* me
**Envy.**—P. L. 1, 35. with *e.* and revenge
P. L. 1, 260. hath not built here for his *e.*
P. L. 2, 26. might draw *e.* from each inferior
P. L. 2, 27. but who here will *e.* whom the
P. L. 3, 553. but much more *e.* seized
P. L. 4, 115. with pale, ire, *e.*, and despair
P. L. 4, 503. aside the devil turned for *e.*
P. L. 4, 517. why should their Lord *e.* them
P. L. 5, 61. or *e.*, or what reserve, forbids
P. L. 5, 662. yet fraught with *e.* against the
P. L. 6, 793. see his glory, at the sight took *e.*
P. L. 9, 175. who next provokes my *e.*
P. L. 9, 264. bliss enjoyed by us excites his *e.*
P. L. 9, 466. of guile, of hate, of *e.*, of revenge
P. L. 9, 729. or is it *e.*? and can *e.* dwell
P. L. 9, 805. though others *e.* what they
P. L. 11, 456. for *e.* that his brother's offering
P. R. 1, 38. then, with *e.* fraught and rage
P. R.1,397. *e.*, they say, excites me, thus to gain
S. A. 272. and to despise, or *e.*, or suspect
A. 13. *e.* bid conceal the rest
S. 13, 6. with praise enough for *e.* to look wan
S. 15, 2. filling each mouth with *e.* or with praise
**Envying.**—P. L. 9, 254. what malicious foe, *e.*
P. L. 9, 593. longing and *e.* stood
**Enwrap.**—H. 134. *e.* our fancy long
**Ephraim.**—S. A. 282. and how ingrateful *E.*
S. A. 988. less renowned than in mount *E.* Jael
**Epicurean.**—P. R. 4, 280. and the sect *E.*
**Epicycle.**—P. L. 8, 84. cycle and *e.*, orb in orb
**Epidaurus.**—P. L. 9, 507. or the god in *E.*
**Epilepsies.**—P. L. 11, 483. *e.*, fierce catarrhs
**Epirot.**—S. 17, 4. the fierce *E.* and the African
**Epithets.**—P. R. 4, 343. swelling *e.*, thick laid
**Equal.**—P. L. 1, 88. *e.* hope and hazard

P. L. 1, 91. now misery hath joined in e. ruin
P. L. 1, 292. his spear, to e. which the tallest pine
P. L. 1, 654. favour e. to the sons of heaven
P. L. 2, 47. with the Eternal to be deemed e.
P. L. 2, 67. shot with e. rage among his angels
P. L. 2, 200. our strength is e., nor the law unjust
P. L. 2, 479. extol him e. to the Highest
P. L. 3, 306. throned in highest bliss, e. to God
P. L. 4, 296. both not e., as their sex not e.
P. L. 4, 526. whom knowledge might exalt e.
P. L. 4, 916. that no pain can e. anger infinite
P. L. 5, 726. to erect his throne e. to ours
P. L. 5, 791. and if not e. all, yet free equally
P. L. 5, 797. and splendour less, in freedom e.
P. L. 5, 820. and e. over equals to let reign
P. L. 5, 832. that e. over equals monarch reign
P. L. 5, 835. e. to him, begotten Son by whom
P. L. 5, 866. by proof to try who is our e.
P. L. 6, 49. e. in number to that godless crew
P. L. 6, 248. and met in arms no e.
P. L. 6, 343. beneath his confidence to e. God
P. L. 6, 441. or e. what between us made the
P. L. 6, 690. e. in their creation they were
P. L. 8, 6. sufficient, or what recompense e.
P. L. 8, 228. and set on man his e. fear
P. L. 8, 407. second to me or like, e. much less
P. L. 9, 286. which plain infers thy e. fear
P. L. 9, 823. and render me more e.
P. L. 9, 881. e. lot may join us, e. joy, as e. love
P. L. 10, 147. superior, or but e., that to her
P. L. 10, 271. but afford thee e. aid
P. L. 10, 680. e. in days and nights
P. L. 10, 748. it were but right and e. to reduce
P. R. 2, 146. who erst thought none my e.
P. R. 3, 99. lives now e. in fame to proudest
P. R. 3, 306. of e. dread in flight or in pursuit
P. R. 4, 29. to e. length backed with a ridge
P. R. 4, 303. and all possessing, e. to God
P. R. 4, 324. a spirit and judgment e.
C. 410. yet where an e. poise of hope and fear
**Equality.**—P. L. 5, 763. affecting all e.
P. L. 7, 487. pattern of just e. perhaps hereafter
P. L. 12, 26. who not content with fair e.
**Equalled.**—P. L. 1, 40. to have e. the most
P. L. 1, 248. whom reason hath e.
P. L. 1, 488. e. with one stroke both her
P. L. 1, 719. e. in all their glories, to enshrine
P. L. 3, 33. those other two e. with me in fate
P. L. 3, 34. so were I e. with them in renown
**Equally.**—P. L. 3, 306. and e. enjoying
P. L. 4, 68. but heaven's free love dealt e. to all
P. L. 5, 97. this night in single affects me e.
P. L. 5, 792. e. free; for orders and degrees
P. L. 11, 362. e. inured by moderation either
**Equals.**—P. L. 1, 249. supreme above his e.
P. L. 5, 796. over such as live by right his e.
P. L. 5, 820. and equal over e. to let reign
P. L. 5, 832. that equal over e. monarch reign
**Equator.**—P. L. 3, 617. culminate from the e.
**Equinoctial.**—P. L. 2, 637. by e. winds
P. L. 9, 64. thrice the e. line he circled
P. L. 10, 672. bid turn reins from the e. road
**Equipage.**—P. L. 7, 203. at hand, celestial e.
P. R. 3, 304. in what martial e. they issue forth
S. 17, 9. in all her e.; besides, to know
**Equity.**—P. R. 1, 220. and e. restored
**Equivalent.**—P. L. 9, 609. to thine e.
S. A. 343. who with a strength e. to angels'
**Ercoco.**—P. L. 11, 398. to his utmost port E.
**Ere.**—P. L. 1, 334. themselves e. well awake
P. L. 2, 409. e. he arrive the happy isle
P. L. 2, 831. by concurring signs, e. now created
P. L. 3, 646. the angel bright, e. he drew nigh
P. L. 4, 10. the tempter e. the accuser
P. L. 4, 113. as man, e. long, and this new world
P. L. 4, 623. to-morrow, e. fresh morning
P. L. 4, 971. but e. then far heavier load
P. L. 5, 133. he e. they fell kissed as the
P. L. 5, 685. that by command, e. yet dim night
P. L. 5, 699. now e. night, now e. dim night
P. L. 5, 871. and fly, e. evil intercept thy flight

P. L. 6, 108. rough edge of battle, e. it joined
P. L. 6, 278. e. this avenging sword begin
P. L. 6, 492. yet, e. dawn, effect shall end
P. L. 6, 521. all e. day-spring, under conscious
P. L. 6, 659. e. they could wind out of such
P. L. 7, 108. dismiss thee e. the morning shine
P. L. 7, 304. e. God had bid the ground be dry
P. L. 7, 335. which, e. it was in the earth, God
P. L. 8, 112. and e. mid-day arrived in Eden
P. L. 8, 204. what was done e. my remembrance
P. L. 8, 242. but, long e. our approaching heard
P. L. 8, 246. up to the coasts of light e. sabbath
P. L. 8, 444. e. thou spakest, knew it not good
P. L. 9, 172. bitter e. long, back on itself recoils
P. L. 9, 246. till younger hands e. long assist us
P. L. 9, 674. act won audience e. the tongue
P. L. 9, 931. and unhallowed e. our taste
P. L. 10, 53. find forbearance no acquittance e.
P. L. 10, 229. meanwhile, e. thus was sinned
P. L. 10, 240. mishap, e. this he had returned
P. L. 10, 584. e. yet Dictæan Jove was born
P. L. 10, 846. not now as e. man fell wholesome
P. L. 10, 987. yet e. conception, to prevent the
P. L. 10, 1069. e. this diurnal star leave cold
P. L. 11, 29. produced, e. fallen from innocence
P. L. 11, 204. why in the east darkness e. day's
P. L. 11, 356. and be confirmed e. thou from
P. L. 11, 769. to torment me, e. their being
P. L. 12, 51. to see their city, e. the tower
P. L. 12, 421. e. the third dawning light return
P. R. 1, 98. e. in the head of nations he appear
P. R. 1, 158. e. I send him forth to conquer sin
P. R. 1, 209. e. yet my age had measured
P. R. 1, 265. e. I the promised kingdom can
P. R. 3, 32. e. these won Asia, and the throne
P. R. 3, 195. just trial e. I merit my exaltation
P. R. 4, 236. look once more, e. we leave this
P. R. 4, 480. e. thou of Israel's sceptre get fast
P. R. 4, 621. for proof, e. this thou feel'st thy
S. A. 177. dissolves, unjointed, e. it reach my ear
S. A. 784. e. I to thee, thou to thyself wast cruel
S. A. 824. I to myself was false, e. thou to me
S. A. 846. sieges girt me round, e. I consented
S. A. 1578. e. I give the reins to grief, say, first
C. 56. had by him, e. he parted thence, a son
C. 138. e. the blabbing eastern scout
C. 151. I shall e. long be well stocked with as fair
C. 194. and envious darkness e. they could return
C. 317. I shall know e. morrow wake
C. 548. till fancy had her fill; but e. a close
C. 558. was took e. she was ware, and wished she
C. 573. already, e. my best speed could prevent
C. 920. and I must haste e. morning hour
A. 56. and early e. the odorous breath of morn
L. 8. for Lycidas is dead, dead e. his prime
L. 25. together both, e. the high lawns appeared
L'A. 107. when in one night, e. glimpse of morn
L'A. 114. e. the first cock his matin rings
S. 1, 9. now timely sing, e. the rude bird of hate
S. 19, 2. e. half my days in this dark world
**Erebus.**—P. L. 2, 883. bottom shook of E.
C. 804. speaks thunder and the chains of E.
**Erect.**—P. L. 2, 986. e. the standard there
P. L. 4, 288. e. and tall, godlike e.
P. L. 5, 725. who intends to e. his throne
P. L. 5, 785. better counsels might e. our minds
P. L. 7, 508. might e. his stature, and upright
P. L. 8, 432. cannot these e. from prone
P. L. 9, 353. bid her well be ware, and still e.
P. L. 9, 501. burnished neck of verdant gold, e.
P. L. 11, 509. created once so goodly and e.
S. A. 1639. at last, with head e., thus cried aloud
**Erected.**—P. L. 1, 679. the least e. spirit that
P. R. 3, 27. of most e. spirits, most tempered
**Eremite.**—P. R. 1, 8. who led'st this glorious e.
**Eremites.**—P. L. 3, 474. idiots, e., and friars
**Erewhile.**—P. L. 2, 83. as we e.
P. L. 6, 334. all his armour stained, e. so bright
P. L. 6, 610. victors proud? e.
P. L. 10, 106. where obvious duty e. appeared
P. L. 12, 275. e. perplexed with thoughts

P. R. 1, 1. who *e.* the happy garden sung
S. A. 1442. much livelier than *e.* he seems
S. A. 1702. and lay *e.* a holocaust
P. 1. *e.* of music and ethereal mirth
**Err.**—P. L. 2, 347. if prophetic fame in heaven *e.*
P. L. 5, 799. who without law *e.* not
P. L. 6, 148. may know, when thousands *e.*
P. L. 6, 288. *e.* not, that so shall end the strife
P. L. 8, 121. earthly sight, if it presume, might *e.*
P. L. 9, 1049. inmost powers made *e.*
P. L. 10, 266. nor *e.* the way, thou leading
P. R. 3, 71. they *e.* who count it glorious to
S. A. 369. if he through frailty *e.*
C. 223. I did not *e.*, there does a sable cloud
**Errand.**—P. L. 2, 827. go this uncouth *e.* sole
P. L. 4, 795. escaped the bars of hell, on *e.* bad
P. L. 10. 41. prevail and speed on his bad *e.*
S. A. 1285. he executes his *e.* on the wicked
C. 15. to such my *e.* is, and but for such
C. 506. to this my *e.*, and the care it brought
**Errands.**—P. L. 1, 152. *e.* in the gloomy deep
P. L. 3, 652. bear his swift *e.* over moist and
P. L. 7, 573. his winged messengers on *e.*
**Erred.**—P. L. 9, 1178. and perhaps I also *e.*
P. L. 11, 208. he *e.* not, for by this the heavenly
S. A. 211. have *e.*, and by bad women been
**Errest.**—P. L. 6, 172. still thou *e.*, nor end
**Erring.**—P. L. 1, 747. thus they relate *e.*
P. L. 6, 173. thou errest, nor end wilt find of *e.*
P. R. 1, 224. at least to try and teach the *e.* soul
C. 588. or that power which *e.* men call chance
**Erroneous.**—P. L. 6, 146. *e.* to dissent from
P. L. 7, 20. *e.* there to wander and forlorn
P. L. 10, 969. so *e.*, thence by just event
**Error.**—P. L. 4, 239. with mazy *e.* under
P. L. 7, 302. with serpent *e.* wandering, found
P. L. 9, 1181. I rue that *e.* now, which is
P. R. 2, 474. saving doctrine, and from *e.* lead
P. R. 3, 212. my *e.* was my *e.*, and my crime
P. R. 4, 235. *e.* by his own arms is best evinced
**Erst.**—P. L. 1, 360. powers that *e.* in heaven
P. L. 2, 470. certain to be refused , what *e.*
P. L. 6, 187. as *e.* thou saidst, from flight
P. L. 6, 308. where *e.* was thickest fight
P. L. 9, 163. O foul descent! that I who *e.*
P. L. 9, 876. opener mine eyes, dim *e.*, dilated
P. L. 9, 1081. of God or angel *e.* with joy
P. L. 11, 868. the heart of Adam, *e.* so sad
P. R. 2, 145. lest I, who *e.* thought none my
S. A. 339. as *e.* in highest, behold him where
S. A. 1543. which *e.* my eyes beheld, and yet
A. 9. seemed *e.* so lavish and profuse
Cir. 2. that *e.* with music and triumphant song
**Eruption.**—P. L. 1, 656. our first *e.* thither
P. L. 8, 235. lest he, incensed at such *e.* bold
**Erymanth.**—A. 100. though *E.* your loss deplore
**Esau.**—P. L. 3, 512. when he from *E.* fled
**Escape.**—P. L. 2, 444. dangers and as hard *e.*
P. L. 10, 339. not hoping to *e.*, but shun
**Escaped.**—P. L. 3, 14. *e.* the Stygian pool
P. L. 4, 794. *e.* the bars of hell
P. L. 4, 824. comest thou, *e.* thy prison and
P. L. 6, 448. as one he stood *e.* from cruel fight
P. L. 11, 777. those few *e.* famine and anguish
**Eshtaol.**—S. A. 181. from *E.* and Zora's fruitful
**Espied.**—P. L. 4, 477. till I *e.* thee, fair, indeed
**Espoused.**—P. L. 4, 710. *e.* Eve decked first
P. L. 5, 18. awake my fairest, my *e.*, my latest
S. 23, 1. methought I saw my late *e.* saint
**Essence.**—P. L. 1, 425. in their *e.* pure
P. L. 2, 215. our purer *e.* then will overcome
P. L. 3, 6. bright effluence of bright *e.* increate
P. L. 9, 166. this *e.* to incarnate and imbrute
C. 462. and turns it by degrees to the soul's *e.*
Cir. 7. your fiery *e.* can distil no tear
**Essences.**—P. L. 1, 138. heavenly *e.* can perish
**Essential.**—P. L. 2, 97. this *e.*,—happier far
P. L. 5, 841. princedoms, virtues, powers, *e.*
**Established.**—P. L. 2, 23. *e.* in a safe unenvied
P. L. 12, 245. thus laws and rites *e.*
**Estate.**—P. L. 12, 351. in mean *e.* live moderate

S. A. 170. for him I reckon not in high *e.*
S. A. 742. once more thy face, and know of thy *e.*
**Esteem.**—P. L. 4, 886. in heaven the *e.* of wise
P. L. 9, 328. his foul *e.* of our integrity
P. L. 9, 329. his foul *e.* sticks no dishonour
P. R. 1, 235. though men *e.* thee low of parentage
P. R. 2, 447. for I *e.* those names of men so poor
P. R. 3, 29. all treasures and all gain *e.* as dross
P. R. 4, 160. on what I offer set as high *e.*
P. R. 4, 207. more honour left and more *e.*
II P. 17. black, but such as in *e.*
F. of C. 10. have been held in high *e.* with Paul
**Esteemed.**—C. 514. so *e.* by shallow ignorance
C. 634. unknown, and like *e.*, and the dull swain
**Estotiland.**—P. L. 10, 686. from cold *E.*
**Estranged.**—P. L. 9, 1132. Adam, *e.* in look
**Eternal.**—P. L. 1, 25. assert *e.* Providence
P. L. 1, 70. such place *e.* justice had prepared
P. L. 1, 121. to wage by force or guile *e.* war
P. L. 1, 154. *e.* being to undergo *e.* punishment
P. L. 1, 318. as this can seize *e.* spirits
P. L. 1, 610. and from *e.* splendours flung
P. L. 2, 46. trust was with the *E.* to be deemed
P. L. 2, 98. happier far than miserable to have *e.*
P. L. 2, 161. reserved and destined to *e.* woe
P. L. 2, 695. condemned to waste *e.* days in woe
P. L. 2, 896. ancestors of nature, hold *e.* anarchy
P. L. 3, 2. or of the *e.* co-eternal beam
P. L. 3, 18. I sung of Chaos and *e.* night
P. L. 3, 127. unchangeable, *e.*, which ordained
P. L. 3, 172. all as my *e.* purpose hath decreed
P. L. 3, 349. loud Hosannas filled the *e.* regions
P. L. 3, 374. immortal, infinite, *e.* king
P. L. 4, 70. or hate to me alike it deals *e.* woe
P. L. 4, 268. led on the *e.* spring
P. L. 4, 996. the *E.*, to prevent such horrid fray
P. L. 5, 173. sound his praise in thy *e.* course
P. L. 5, 246. so spake the *E.* Father
P. L. 5, 711. the *e.* eye whose sight discerns
P. L. 6, 96. hymning the *E.* Father.
P. L. 6, 227. had not the *e.* king omnipotent
P. L. 6, 240. deeds of *e.* fame were done
P. L. 6, 385. therefore *e.* silence be their doom
P. L. 6, 424. and if one day, why not *e.* days
P. L. 6, 630. *e.* might to match with their
P. L. 6, 865. *e.* wrath burned after them
P. L. 6, 904. partake his punishment, *e.* misery
P. L. 7, 9. thou with *e.* wisdom didst converse
P. L. 7, 96. *e.* empire, but the more to magnify
P. L. 7, 137. *E.* Father from his throne beheld
P. L. 7, 226. prepared in God's *e.* store
P. L. 7, 517. the Omnipotent *E.* Father
P. L. 7, 576. led to God's *e.* house direct the way
P. L. 8, 413. height and depth of thy *e.* ways
P. L. 10, 32. *E.* Father, from his secret cloud
P. L. 10, 68. Father *E.*, thine is to decree
P. L. 10, 597. to me, who with *e.* famine pine
P. L. 10, 816. am found *e.*, and incorporate both
P. L. 12, 314. safe to *e.* Paradise of rest
P. L. 12, 551. bring forth fruits, joy, and *e.* bliss
P. R. 1, 168. spake the *E.* Father, and all heaven
P. R. 1, 236. thy Father is the *E.* King who rules
P. R. 1, 281. heaven opened her *e.* doors
P. R. 4, 391. *e.* sure, as without end
S. A. 964. *e.* tempests, never to be calmed
S. A. 1717. to himself and father's house, *e.* fame
C. 596. it shall be in *e.* restless change
C. 988. there *e.* summer dwells
C. 1008. make her his *e.* bride
H. 2. wherein the Son of Heaven's *e.* King
**Eternity.**—P. L. 2, 148. wander through *e.*
P. L. 2, 248. wearisome *e.* so spent in worship
P. L. 3, 5. dwelt from *e.*, dwelt then in thee
P. L. 5, 580. time, though in *e.* applied to motion
P. L. 7, 92. in his holy rest through all *e.*
P. L. 8, 406. who am alone from all *e.*
P. L. 12, 556. *e.*, whose end no eye can reach
C. 14. that opes the palace of *e.*
T. 11. then long *e.* shall greet our bliss
**Eternize.**—P. L. 6, 374. *e.* here on earth
P. L. 11, 60. this other served but to *e.* woe

**Etham.**—S. A. 253. the rock of *E.* was retired
**Ethereal.**—P. L. 1, 45. from the *e.* sky
P. L. 1, 285. ponderous shield, *e.* temper
P. L. 2, 139. the *e.* mould, incapable of stain
P. L. 2, 311. *e.* Virtues! or these titles now must
P. L. 2, 601. to starve in ice their soft *e.* warmth
P. L. 2, 978. the *e.* king
P. L. 3, 7. pure *e.* stream whose fountain who
P. L. 3, 100. such I created all the *e.* powers
P. L. 3, 716. and this *e.* quintessence of heaven
P. L. 5, 267. and through the vast *e.* sky
P. L. 5, 418. the air those fires *e.*, and as lowest
P. L. 5, 499. of time, and winged ascend *e.* as we
P. L. 5, 863. of this our native heaven, *e.* sons
P. L. 6, 60. the loud *e.* trumpet from on high
P. L. 6, 330. the *e.* substance closed, not long
P. L. 7, 244. light *e.*, first of things quintessence
P. L. 7, 356. though of *e.* mould
P. L. 8, 646. to heavenly guest, *e.* messenger
P. L. 10, 27. the *e.* people ran to hear and know
P. L. 12, 577. all the *e.* powers, all secrets of
P. R. 1, 163. that all the angels and *e.* powers
P. R. 2, 121. heaven's ancient sons, *e.* thrones
P. R. 3, 28. most tempered pure *e.*
S. A. 549. with touch *e.* of heaven's fiery rod
P. 1. erewhile of music and *e.* mirth
**Ethereous.**—P. L. 6, 473. of this *e.* mould
**Ethiop.**—P L. 4, 282. the *E.* line by Nilus
Il P. 19. or that starred *E.* queen that strove
**Ethiopian.**—P. L. 2, 641. through the wide *E.*
**Etrurian.**—P. L. 1, 303. where the *E.* shades
**Euboic.**—P. L. 2, 546. into the *E.* sea
**Euclid.**—S. 21, 7. let *E.* rest, and Archimedes
**Euphrasy.**—P. L. 11, 414. purged with *e.*
**Euphrates.**—P. L. 1, 420. flood of old *E.*
P. L. 12, 114. on this side *E.* yet residing
P. R. 3, 272. as far as Indus east, *E.* west
P. R. 3, 384. from Egypt to *E.* and beyond
**Europe.**—P. L. 10, 310. *E.* with Asia joined
P. L. 11, 405. on *E.* thence, and where Rome
S. 15, 1. whose name in arms through *E.* rings
S. 22, 12. of which all *E.* rings from side to side
**Euphrosyne.**—L'A. 12. in heaven yclept *E.*
**Eurotas.**—D.F.I. 25. Hyacinth born on *E.* strand
**Eurus.**—P. L. 10, 705. *E.* and Zephyr
**Eurydice.**—L'A. 150. free his half-regained *E.*
**Eurynome.**—P. L. 10, 581. Ophion, with *E.*
**Evade.**—P. L. 10, 1021. so thinking to *e.* the
P. R. 4, 308. or subtle shifts conviction to *e.*
**Evaded.**—P. L. 6, 596. easily, as spirits, *e.*
**Evangelize.**—P. L. 12, 499. to *e.* the nations
**Evasion.**—P. L. 2, 411. or what *e.* bear him
**Evasions.**—P. L. 10, 829. all my *e.* vain
S. A. 842. or by *e.* thy crime uncoverest more
**Eve.**—P. L. 1, 364. yet among the sons of *E.*
P. L. 4, 324. the fairest of her daughters, *E.*
P. L. 4, 409. first of men to first of women, *E.*
P. L. 4, 440. to whom thus *E.* replied
P. L. 4, 481. return, fair *E.*, whom fliest thou
P. L. 4, 610. when Adam thus to *E.*
P. L. 4, 634. to whom thus *E.*, with perfect
P. L. 4, 660. of God and man, accomplished *E*
P. L. 4, 710. espoused *E.* decked first her
P. L. 4, 742. nor *E.* the rites mysterious
P. L. 4, 800. like a toad, close at the ear of *E.*
P. L. 5, 9. to find unwakened *E.* with tresses
P. L. 5, 38. why sleep'st thou. *E.?* now is the
P. L. 5, 74. here happy creature fair angelic *E.*
P. L. 5, 93 thus *E.* her night related
P. L. 5, 303. and *E.* within, due at her hour
P. L. 5, 308. haste hither, *E.*, and worth thy
P. L. 5, 321. to whom thus *E.:* Adam earth's
P. L. 5, 379. but *E.* undecked, save with herself
P. L. 5, 387. long after to blest Mary, second *E.*
P. L. 5, 443. meanwhile at table *E.* ministered
P. L. 7, 50. he with his consorted *E.* the story
P. L. 8, 40. which *E.* perceiving, where she sat
P. L. 8, 172. this Paradise and thy fair *E.*
P. L. 9, 204. and *E.* first to her husband thus
P. L. 9, 227. sole *E.*, associate sole, to me
P. L. 9, 270. to whom the virgin majesty of *E.*

P. L. 9, 291. of God and man, immortal *E.*
P. L. 9, 319. care and matrimonial love; but *E.*
P. L. 9, 376. *E.* persisted; yet submiss, though
P. L. 9, 404. much failing, hapless *E.*
P. L. 9, 422. but wished his hap might find *E.*
P. L. 9, 424. beyond his hope, *E.* separate
P. L. 9, 438. on each bank, the hand of *E.*
P. L. 9, 456. the sweet recess of *E.* thus early
P. L. 9, 495. and toward *E.* addressed his way
P. L. 9, 517. a wanton wreath in sight of *E.*
P. L. 9, 528. turned at length the eye of *E.*
P. L. 9, 550. into the heart of *E.* his words
P. L. 9, 568. of this fair world, resplendent *E.*
P. L. 9, 613. and *E.*, yet more amazed
P. L. 9, 631. lead then, said *E.* he leading
P. L. 9, 644. into fraud led *E.*, our credulous
P. L. 9, 659. to whom thus *E.* yet sinless
P. L. 9, 785. for *E.*, intent now wholly on her
P. L. 9, 828. and Adam, wedded to another *E.*
P. L. 9, 886. thus *E.*, with countenance blithe
P. L. 9, 889. fatal trespass done by *E.*
P. L. 9, 892. the garland wreathed for *E.*
P. L. 9, 911. should God create another *E.*
P. L. 9, 920. calm mood his words to *E.*
P. L. 9, 921. hast presumed, adventurous *E.*
P. L. 9, 960. so Adam, and thus *E.* to him
P. L. 9, 1005. nor *E.* to iterate her former
P. L. 9, 1013. he on *E.* began to cast
P. L. 9, 1016. Adam thus gan *E.* to dalliance
P. L. 9, 1017. *E.*, now I see thou art exact
P. L. 9, 1036. *E.*, whose eye darted contagious
P. L. 9, 1065. till Adam, though not less than *E.*
P. L. 9, 1067. O *E.*, in evil hour thou didst give
P. L. 9, 1133. speech intermitted thus to *E.*
P. L. 9, 1143. with touch of blame thus *E.*
P. L. 9, 1164. of mine to thee, ingrateful *E.*
P. L. 10, 3. the serpent had perverted *E.*
P. L. 10, 109. and with him *E.*, more loth
P. L. 10, 157. having said, he thus to *E.* in few
P. L. 10, 159. to whom sad *E.*, with shame nigh
P. L. 10, 183. Jesus, son of Mary, second *E.*
P. L. 10, 332. after *E.* seduced, unminded slunk
P. L. 10, 335. his guileful act by *E.*, seconded
P. L. 10, 551. the bait of *E.*, used by the tempter
P. L. 10, 582. the wide-encroaching *E.* perhaps
P. L. 10, 863. thus afflicted, when sad *E.* beheld
P. L. 10, 909. but *E.*, not so repulsed with tears
P. L. 10, 966. thus *E.*, recovering heart, replied
P. L. 10, 1012. to *E.* replied: *E.*, thy contempt
P. L. 10, 1097. nor *E.* felt less remorse
P. L. 11, 136. and first matron *E.* had ended
P. L. 11, 140. which thus to *E.* his welcome
P. L. 11, 141. *E.*, easily may faith admit that all
P. L. 11, 159. hail to thee, *E.* rightly called
P. L. 11, 162. to whom thus *E.*, with sad
P. L. 11, 181. so wished, much-humbled *E.*
P. L. 11, 192. not unmoved to *E.* thus spake
P. L. 11, 193. O *E.*, some farther change awaits
P. L. 11, 224. unperceived of Adam, who to *E.*
P. L. 11, 226. *E.*, now expect great tidings
P. L. 11, 265. *E.*, who unseen yet all had heard
P. L. 11, 287. lament not, *E.*, but patiently resign
P. L. 11, 367. *E.* (for I have drenched her eyes)
P. L. 11, 476. what misery the inabstinence of *E.*
P. L. 11, 519. inductive mainly to the sin of *E.*
P. L. 12, 594. may no longer stay; go, waken *E.*
P. L. 12, 607. the bower where *E.* lay sleeping
P. L. 12, 624. our mother *E.*, and Adam heard
P. R. 1, 51. since Adam and his facile consort *E.*
P. R. 1, 54. shall be inflicted by the seed of *E.*
P. R. 2, 141. my success with *E.* in Paradise
P. R. 2, 349. that crude apple that diverted *E.*
P. R. 4, 5. and won so much on *E.*, so little here
P. R. 4, 6. so little here, nay lost. But *E.* was *E.*
P. R. 4. 180. attempt, bolder than that on *E.*
**Eve.**—P. L. 1, 743. to dewy *e.*, a summer's day
P. L. 4, 185. shepherds pen their flocks at *e.*
P. R. 1, 318. wet returned from field at *e.*
S. 1, 2. warblest at *e.* when all the woods
C. 843. her maiden gentleness, and oft at *e.*
**Even** (sb).—P. L. 3, 42. sweet approach of *e.*

P. L. 4, 555. came Uriel, gliding through the *e.*
P. L. 5, 202. witness if I be silent, morn or *e.*
P. L. 5, 425. and at *e.* sups with the ocean
P. L. 7, 252. thus was the first day *e.* and morn
P. L. 7, 274. so *e.* and morning chorus sung the
P. L. 7, 338. so *e.* and morn recorded the third
P. L. 7, 435. and spread their painted wings till *e.*
P. L. 7, 550. so *e.* and morn accomplished the
P. L. 9, 582. dropping with milk at *e.* unsucked
P. L. 11, 276. early visitation, and my last at *e.*
P. R. 2, 268. food to Elijah bringing *e.* and morn
C. 188. the gray-hooded *e.* like a sad votarist
**Even (adj).**—P. L. 1, 349. in *e.* balance down they
P. L. 3, 179. shall stand on *e.* ground against
P. L. 3, 586. shoots invisible virtue *e.* to the deep
P. L. 6, 245. long time in *e.* scale the battle hung
P. L. 6, 544. his orbed shield borne *e.,* or high
P. L. 8, 165. while she paces *e.,* and bears thee
P. L. 10, 47. her own inclining left in *e.* scale
P. L. 11, 348. to dwell on *e.* ground now with
C. 773. in unsuperfluous *e.* proportion
Il P. 38. with *e.* step and musing gait
**Even (adv).**—P. L. 1, 416. *e.* to that hill of scandal
P. L. 1, 680. for *e.* in heaven his looks and
P. L. 5, 83. *e.* to my mouth of that same fruit
P. L. 5, 837. the Father made all things, *e.* thee
P. L. 9, 1079. *e.* shame, the last of evils
P. L. 10, 191. *e.* He who now foretold his fatal
P. L. 11, 148. upborne *e.* to the seat of God
P. L. 11, 418. *e.* to the inmost seat of mental
P. R 1, 264. many a hard assay, *e.* to the death
**Evening.**—P. L. 1, 289. at *e.* from the top
P. L. 2, 493. farewell sweet extend his *e.* beam
P. L. 4, 151. in fair *e.* cloud, or humid bow
P. L. 4, 355. the stars that usher *e.* rose
P. L. 4, 543. levelled his *e.* rays
P. L. 4, 598. now came still *e.* on, and twilight
P. L. 4, 647. sweet the coming on of grateful *e.*
P. L. 4, 654. nor grateful *e.* mild
P. L. 4, 662. round the earth by morrow *e.*
P. L. 4, 792. this *e.* from the sun's decline
P. L. 5, 115. of our last *e.'s* talk in this thy
P. L. 5, 376. these mid-hours, till *e.* rise
P. L. 5, 627. *e.* now approached
P. L. 5, 628. for we have also our *e.*
P. L. 7, 104. or if the star of *e.* and the moon
P. L. 7, 260. both when first *e.* was and when
P. L. 7, 386. glad *e.* and glad morn crowned
P. L. 7, 448. *e.* and morn solemnized
P. L. 7, 450. arose with *e.* harps and matin
P. L. 7, 582. and now on earth the seventh *e.*
P. L. 8, 246. ere sabbath *e.*; so we had in charge
P. L. 9, 278. returned at shut of *e.* flowers
P. L. 9, 1088. umbrage broad and brown as *e.*
P. L. 10, 95. usher in the *e.* cool, when he
P. L. 11, 588. now of love they treat, till the *e.*
P. L. 12, 629. as *e.* mist risen from a river
S. A. 1692. and as an *e.* dragon came
C. 540. this *e.* late, by then the chewing flocks
A. 54. when *e.* gray doth rise I fetch my round
L. 30. oft till the star that rose at *e.,* bright
**Evening-star.**—P. L. 8, 519. haste the *e.-s.*
**Evenly.**—S. A. 671. not *e.* as thou rulest
**Even-song.**—Il P. 64. I woo, to hear thy *e.-s.*
**Event.**—P. L. 1, 118. of this great *e.*
P. L. 1, 134. too well I see and rue the dire *e.*
P. L. 1, 624. though the *e.* was dire
P. L. 2, 82. ascent is easy, then; the *e.* is feared
P. L. 4, 716. and, O! too like in sad *e.*
P. L. 5, 740. and in *e.* know whether I be
P. L. 9, 334. heaven, our witness, from the *e.*
P. L. 9, 405. thy presumed return, *e.* perverse
P. L. 9, 984. but I feel far otherwise the *e.*
P. L. 10, 969. thence by just *e.* found so
P. L. 11, 593. such happy interview, and fair *e.*
S. A. 737. in the perverse *e.* than I foresaw
S. A. 1551. so in the sad *e.* too much concerned
S. A. 1756. of true experience from this great *e*
C. 411. hope and fear does arbitrate the *e.*
**Events.**—P. L. 4, 1001. now ponders all *e.*
**P. R. 2, 104. laid up, portending strange *e.***

C. 405. fear the dread *e.* that dog them both
V. Ex. 70. that far *e.* full wisely could presage
**Ever.**—P. L. 1, 160. but *e.* to do ill our sole
P. L. 1, 210. nor *e.* thence had risen
P. L. 1. 228. if it were land that *e.* burned
P. L. 1, 250. happy fields where joy for *e.* dwells
P. L. 1, 330. awake, arise, or be for *e.* fallen
P. L. 1, 608. for *e.* now to have their lot in pain
P. L. 1, 630. could *e.* know repulse
P. L. 2, 153. angry foe can give it, or will *e.*
P. L. 2, 182. or for *e.* sunk under yon boiling
P. L. 2, 338. yet *e.* plotting how the conqueror
P. L. 2, 744. nor *e.* saw till now sight more
P. L. 2, 776. to keep these gates for *e.* shut
P. L. 2 914, and which thus must *e.* fight
P. L. 3, 149. shall resound thee *e.* blessed
P. L. 3, 244. me to possess life in myself for *e.*
P. L. 3, 249. for *e.* with corruption there to
P. L. 3, 318. reign for *e.,* and assume thy merits
P. L. 3, 333. thenceforth shall be for *e.* shut
P. L. 3, 366. harps they took, harps *e.* tuned
P. L. 4, 119. such distempers foul are *e.* clear
P. L. 4, 322. *e.* since in love's embraces met
P. L. 4, 436. but let us *e.* praise him and extol
P. L. 5, 19. last best gift my *e.* new delight
P. L. 5, 405, he gives (whose praise be *e.* sung)
P. L. 5, 446. innocence deserving Paradise! if *e.*
P. L. 5, 611. one individual soul for *e.* happy
P. L. 5, 810. no ear *e.* to hear in heaven
P. L. 6, 184. serve in heaven God *e.* blessed
P. L. 6, 733. be all in all, and I in thee for *e.*
P. L. 7, 586. fixed for *e.* firm and sure
P. L. 8, 479. to find her, or for *e.* to deplore her
P. L. 8, 649. honoured *e.* with grateful memory
P. L. 9, 1033. to enjoy thee, fairer now than *e.*
P. L. 10, 71. may'st *e.* rest well pleased
P. L. 10, 637. for *e.,* and seal up his ravenous
P. L. 11, 95. and eat, and live for *e.*
P. L. 11, 96. dream at least to live for *e.*
P. L. 12, 324. regal throne for *e.* shall endure
P. L. 12, 429. in sin for *e.* lost from life
P. L. 12, 563. *e.* to observe his providence
P. L. 12, 573. now acknowledge my Redeemer *e.*
P. R. 1, 324. or caravan? for single none durst *e.*
P. R. 1, 438. who *e.,* by consulting at thy shrine
P. R. 3, 240. unexperienced will be *e.* timorous
P. R. 4, 22. whom repulse upon repulse met *e.*
P. R. 4, 194. that evil one, Satan for *e.* damned
S. A. 446. reproach the most with shame that *e.*
S. A. 510. *e.* more approves, and more accepts
S. A. 761. the penitent, but *e.* to forgive
S. A. 858. priest was ... but *e.* at my ear
S. A. 903. in argument with men a woman *e.*
S. A. 925. may *e.* tend about thee to old age
S. A. 1172. whose ear is *e.* open, and his eye
S. A. 1336. my mind *e.* will condescend to such
S. A. 1735. laurel *e.* green, and branching palm
S. A. 1748. and *e.* best found in the close
C. 211. the virtuous mind, that *e.* walks
C. 368. sweet peace that goodness bosoms *e*
C. 442. fair silver-shafted queen for *e.* chaste-
L'A. 10. in dark Cimmerian desert *e.* dwell
L'A. 135. and *e.,* against eating cares
S. 2, 14. as *e.* in my great task-master's eye
S. 8, 3. if deed of honour did thee *e.* please
S. 14, 8. followed thee up to joy and bliss for *e.*
S. 15, 5. thy firm unshaken virtue *e.* brings
P. 5. but headlong joy is *e.* on the wing
M.W.48. may thy grave peace and quiet *e.* have
L. 181. and wipe the tears for *e.* from his eyes
T. 16. truth, and peace, and love, shall *e.* shine
T. 21. attired with stars, we shall for *e.* sit
**Ever-burning.**—P. L. 1, 69. *e.-b.* sulphur
**Ever-during.**—P. L. 3, 45. and *e.-d.* dark
P. L. 7, 206. her *e.-d.* gates, harmonious sound
**Ever-failing.**—S. A. 348. O *e.-f.* trust in mortal
**Everlasting.**—P. L. 2, 184. with *e.* groans
P. L. 2, 232. when *e.* fate shall yield to fickle
P. L. 3, 395. that shook heaven's *e.* frame
P. L. 7, 565. open ye *e.* gates, they sung
**P. R. 3, 199. when I begin my *e.* kingdom**

C. 199. and filled their lamps with *e*. oil
H. 13. forsook the courts of *e*. day
**Everlastingly.**—S. M. 16. singing *e*.
**Evermore.**—M. W. 50. sweet rest seize thee *e*.
**Ever-threatening.**—P. L. 3, 425. *e.-t*. storms
**Every.**—P. L. 1, 356. forthwith from *e*. squadron
P. L. 1, 758. their summons called from *e*. band
P. L. 2, 877. and *e*. bolt and bar of massy iron
P. L. 3, 638. and to *e*. limb suitable grace
P. L. 5, 8. matin song of birds on *e*. bough
P. L. 5, 194. with *e*. plant, in sign of worship
P. L. 5, 410. within them *e*. lower faculty
P. L. 5, 747. impearls on *e*. leaf and *e*. flower
P. L. 5, 186, *e*. soul in heaven shall bend
P. L. 6, 345. live throughout vital in *e*. part
P. L. 6, 554. *e*. side with shadowing squadrons
P. L. 6, 848. and *e*. eye glared lightning
P. L. 7, 317. then herbs of *e*. leaf, that sudden
P. L. 7, 336. and *e*. herb, before it grew on the
P. L. 7, 357. and *e*. magnitude of stars
P. L. 7, 394. and *e*. bird of wing after his kind
P. L. 7, 523. and *e*. creeping thing that creeps
P. L. 7, 534. and *e*. living thing that moves
P. L. 7, 621. and *e*. star perhaps a world
P. L. 8, 321. of *e*. tree that in the garden grows
P. L. 8, 489. in *e*. gesture, dignity and love
P. L. 9, 84. with inspection deep considered *e*.
P. L. 9, 160. and pry in *e*. bush and brake
P. L. 9, 310. receive access in *e*. virtue
P. L. 9, 459. her graceful innocence, her *e*. air
P. L. 9, 521. from *e*. beast, more duteous at her
P. L. 9, 721. by the sun, producing *e*. kind
P. L. 11, 324. and pile up *e*. stone of lustre
P. L. 11, 337. land, sea, and air, and *e*. kind
P. L. 11, 734. of *e*. beast, and bird, and insect
P. L. 12, 522. by carnal power shall force on *e*.
P. R. 1, 295. looking round, on *e*. side beheld
P. R. 1, 448. his angels president in *e*. province
P. R. 2, 224. at *e*. sudden slighting quite
P. R. 2, 468. which *e*. wise and virtuous man
P. R. 3, 125. his good communicable to *e*. soul
P. R. 3, 348. and not *e*. way secure
S. A. 93. she all in *e*. part
S. A. 97. might look at will through *e*. pore
S. A. 204. sung … for a fool in *e*. street
S. A. 749. and arts of *e*. woman false like thee
S. A. 1323. and *e*. sort of gymnic artists
C. 19. of *e*. salt flood and each ebbing stream
C. 64. offering to *e*. weary traveller
C. 251. at *e*. fall smoothing the raven down
C. 269. forbidding *e*. bleak unkindly fog
C. 311. I know each lane. and *e*. alley green
C. 313. and *e*. bosky bourn from side to side
C. 496. and sweetened *e*. muskrose of the dale
C. 524. and here to *e*. thirsty wanderer
C. 621. in *e*. virtuous plant and healing herb
C. 768. if *e*. just man that now pines with want
A. 59. and visit *e*. sprout with puissant words
L. 93. and questioned *e*. gust of rugged wings
L. 148. and *e*. flower that sad embroidery wears
L'A. 67. and *e*. shepherd tells his tale
Il P. 171. of *e*. star that heaven doth **shew**
Il P. 172. and *e*. herb that sips the dew
T. 14. when *e*. thing that is sincerely good
**Eves.**—L'A.130. on summer *e*. by haunted stream
**Evidence.**—P. L. 9, 962. illustrious *e*.
P. L. 10, 361. which thy looks now also *e*.
**Evident.**—P. L. 9, 1077. in our faces *e*.
**Evil.**—P. L. 1, 163. out of our *e*. seek to bring
P. L. 1, 165. out of good still to find means of *e*.
P. L. 1, 216. while he sought *e*. to others
P. L. 1, 335. nor did they not perceive the *e*.
P. L. 1, 339. in Egypt's *e*. day
P. L. 2, 261. what placesoe'er thrive under *e*.
P. L. 2, 562. of good and *e*. much they argued
P. L. 2, 623. God by curse created *e*., for *e*. only
P. L. 3, 683. the *e*. that walks always invisible .
P. L. 4, 110. all good to me is lost, *e.*. be thou
P. L. 4, 563. no *e*. thing approach or enter in
P. L. 4, 896. but *e*. hast not tried, and wilt
P. L. 5, 98. can I like this uncouth dream, of *e*.

P. L. 5, 99. yet *e*. whence ? in thee can harbour
P. L. 5, 117. *e*. into the mind of God or man
P. L. 5, 207. gathered aught of *e*., or concealed
P. L. 5, 871. and fly, ere *e*. intercept thy flight
P. L. 6, 262. author of *e*., unknown till thy
P. L. 6, 275. hence, then! and *E*. go with thee
P. L. 6, 276. offspring to the place of *e*., hell
P. L. 6, 289. which thou callest *e*., but we style
P. L. 6, 395. to such *e*. brought by sin
P. L. 6, 437. of *e*. then so small, as easy
P. L. 6, 455. from which *e*. ruin must needs
P. L. 7, 25. *e*. days, on *e*. days though fallen
P. L. 7, 56. but the *e*., soon driven back
P. L. 7, 188. had ordained good out of *e*.
P. L. 7, 543. works knowledge of good and *e*.
P. L. 7, 615. his *e*. thou usest and from thence
P. L. 9, 463. that space the *E*. One abstracted
P. L. 9, 464. abstracted stood from his own *e*.
P. L. 9, 638. oft, they say, some *e*. spirit attends
P. L. 9, 697. knowledge of good and *e*.
P. L. 9, 698. of *e*., if what is *e*. be real
P. L. 9, 709. knowing both good and *e*.
P. L. 9, 723. knowledge of good and *e*. in this
P. L. 9, 752. knowledge both of good and *e*.
P. L. 9, 774. under this ignorance of good or *e*.
P. L. 9, 780. her rash hand, in *e*. hour
P. L. 9, 864. nor to *e*. unknown opening the
P. L. 9, 1067. O Eve, in *e*. hour thou didst
P. L. 9, 1072. good and *e*.; good lost, and *e*. got
P. L. 9, 1078. whence *e*. store even shame
P. L. 9, 1180. I thought no *e*. durst attempt
P. L. 9, 1185. left to herself, if *e*. thence ensue
P. L. 10, 125. O heaven! in *e*. strait this day
P. L. 10, 734. feeling the *e*. on him brought
P. L. 10, 849. which to his *e*. conscience
P. L. 10, 963. no sudden, but a slow-paced *e*.
P. L. 11, 85. to know both good and *e*.
P. L. 11, 87. knowledge of good lost, and *e*. got
P. L. 11, 89. known good by itself, and *e*. not
P. L. 11, 373. to the *e*. turn my obvious breast
P. L. 11, 765. my part of *e*. only, each day's lot
P. L. 11, 772. his children ; *e*. he may be sure
P. L. 11, 774. and he the future *e*. shall no less
P. L. 12, 47. regardless whether good or *e*.
P. L. 12, 470. all this good of *e*. shall produce
P. L. 12, 471. and *e*. turn to good
P. L. 12, 566. with good still overcoming *e*.
P. R. 2, 371. knowledge works, at least of *e*.
P. R. 3, 218. rather than aggravate my *e*. state
P. R. 4, 194. *E*. One, Satan for ever damned
S. A. 704. for oft alike both come to *e*. end
S. A. 736. though the fact more *e*. drew
S. A. 967. bid go with *e*. omen, and the brand
S. A. 1523. this *e*. on the Philistines is fallen
S. A. 1538. *e*. news rides post
S.A.1567. lest *e*. tidings, with too rude irruption
C. 432. some say no *e*. thing that walks by night
C. 593. but *e*. on itself shall back recoil
A. 50. and from the boughs brush off the *e*. dew
**Evils.**—P. L. 2, 281. may compose our present *e*.
P. L. 6, 463. is perfect misery, the worst of *e*.
P. L. 9, 1079. last of *e*.; of the first be sure then
P. L. 10, 978. as in our *e*., and of easier choice
P. L. 10, 1080. to *e*. which our own misdeeds
P. L. 12, 604. though sad (with cause) for *e*. past
S.A.105. from worst of other *e*., pains and wrongs
S. A. 194, how many *e*. have inclosed me round
S.A.374. nothing of all these *e*. hath befallen me
S. A. 648. hopeless are all my *e*., all remediless
S. A. 1169. these *e*. I deserve and more
C. 360. to cast the fashion of uncertain *e*.
**Evince.**—P. L. 12, 287. *e*. their natural pravity
**Evinced.**—P. R. 4, 235. his own arms is best *e*.
**Ewe.**—P. L. 9, 582. of *e*. or goat, dropping with
P.R. 1, 315. as seemed, the quest of some stray *e*.
C. 503. on such a trivial toy as a strayed *e*.
**Ewes.**—P. L. 11, 649. *e*. and their bleating
**Exact.**—P. L. 7, 477. and smallest lineaments *e*.
P. L. 8, 539. show elaborate, of inward less *e*.
P. L. 9, 1017. Eve, now I see thou art *e*. of taste
P. L. 12, 402. the law of God *e*. he shall fulfil

S. A. 507. and let another hand, not thine, *e.*
S. A. 788. the gentler, if severely thou *e.* not
S. 19, 7. doth God *e.* day-labour, light denied
**Exactly.**—P. L. 8, 451. *e.* to thy heart's desire
**Exacts.**—P. L. 12, 590. *e.* our parting hence
P. R. 3, 120. his foes pronounced glory he *e.*
**Exalt.**— P. L. 3, 313. humiliation shall *e.* with
P. L. 4, 525. whom knowledge might *e.*
P. L. 5, 829. bent rather to *e.* our happy state
P. L. 7, 150. lest his heart *e.* him in the harm
S. A. 689. lower than thou didst *e.* them high
**Exaltation.**—P. L. 5, 90. to this high *e.*
P. L. 6, 727. this I my glory account, my *e.*
P. R. 2, 92. my *e.* to afflictions high
P. R. 3, 197. my *e.* without change or end
**Exalted.**—P. L. 1, 736. *e.* to such power
P. L. 2, 5. Satan *e.* sat, by merit, raised to that
P. L. 6, 99. high in the midst, *e.* as a God
P. L. 9, 150. and him endow, *e.* from so base
P. L. 12, 457. at God's right hand, *e.* high
P. R. 1, 36. the *e.* man to whom such high attest
P. R. 2, 46. their power unjust they have *e.*
P. R. 2, 206. than Solomon, of more *e.* mind
**Example.**—P. L. 4, 881. transgress by thy *e.*
P. L. 5, 901. nor number, nor *e.*, with him
P. L. 6, 910. by terrible *e.*, the reward
P. L. 7, 42. by dire *e.* to heave apostasy
P. L. 9, 962. illustrious evidence, *e.* high
P. L. 10, 840. beyond all past *e.* and future
P. L. 11, 809. against *e.*, good against allurement
P. L. 12, 572. taught this by his *e.*
P. R. 1, 232. can raise them though above *e.*
S. A. 166. the rarer thy *e.* stands
S. A. 765. as I by thee, to ages an *e.*
S.A.822. I gave, thou say'st, the *e.*, I led the way
**Examples.**—S. A. 290. of such *e.* add me to the
**Exasperate.**—P. L. 2, 143. we must *e.*
S. A. 625. *e.*, exulcerate, and raise
S. A. 1417. may now *e.* them, I know not
**Exceed.**—S. A. 817. all mortals dost *e.*
**Exceeded.**—P. L. 5, 459. so far *e.* human
**Exceeding.**—P. L. 9, 961. trial of *e.* love
Cir. 15. O more *e.* love, or law more just
Cir. 16. just law indeed, but more *e.* love
**Excel.**—P. L. 3, 133. so shall my glory *e.*
P. L. 8, 542. inward faculties, which most *e.*
P. R. 3, 307. in which fight they most *e.*
S. A. 74. of man, or worm, the vilest here *e.* me
**Excelled.**—P. L. 2, 884. to shut *e.* her power
P. L. 4, 490. how beauty is *e.* by manly grace
P. L. 9, 897. creature in whom *e.* whatever
P. L. 10, 150. whose perfection far *e.* hers
S. A. 523. when in strength all mortals I *e.*
**Excellence.**—P. L. 2, 350. in power and *e.*
P. L. 5, 456. whose *e.* he saw transcend
P. L. 6, 637. behold the *e.*, the power
P. L. 6, 821. of other *e.* not emulous, nor care
P. L. 8, 91. that great or bright infers not *e.*
P. L. 10, 1017. refutes that *e.* brought in thee
V. Ex. 79. in worth and *e.* he shall outgo them
**Excellent.**—P. L. 8, 566. to things less *e.*
P. L. 10, 1015. sublime and *e.*
P. R. 1, 381. what I see *e.* in good or fair
**Excelling.**—P. L. 1, 359. and forms *e.* human
P. R. 4, 347. Sion's songs, to all true tastes *e.*
**Excels.**—P. L. 2, 124. when he who most *e.*
P. L. 2, 125. and in what *e.* mistrustful
P. L. 6, 177. who rules is worthiest, and *e.*
P. L. 6, 822. not emulous, nor care who them *e.*
P. L. 8, 456. as with an object that *e.* the sense
C. 63. *e.* his mother at her mighty art
**Except.**—P. L. 2, 300. than whom, Satan *e.*
P. L. 2, 678. God and his Son *e.*, created thing
P. L. 2, 1032. *e.* whom God and good angels
P. L. 3, 684. evil that walks invisible, *e.* to God
P. L. 9, 545. one man *e.*, who sees thee
P. L. 10, 680. in days and nights, *e.* to those
P. L. 11, 808. one man *e.*, the only son of light
P. R. 4, 85. these two thrones *e.*, the rest are
**Excepted.**—P. L. 11, 426. touched the *e.* tree
**Exception.**—P. R. 3, 119. *e.* hath declared

**Excess.**—P. L. 1, 123. and in the *e.* of joy
P. L. 1, 593. and the *e.* of glory obscured
P. L. 3, 696. leads to no *e.* that reaches blame
P. L. 3, 698. merits praise the more it seems *e.*
P. L. 5, 640. where full measure only bounds *e.*
P. L. 9, 648. to me, though fruit be here to *e.*
P. L. 11, 111. and with tears bewailing their *e.*
P. L. 11, 498. till firmer thoughts restrained *e.*
C. 771. now heaps upon some few with vast *e.*
Cir. 24. of vengeful justice bore for our *e.*
**Excessive.**—P. L. 2, 779. and now *e.* grown
P. L. 3, 380. dark with *e.* bright thy skirts
P. L. 6, 463. and, *e.*, overturns all patience
**Excite.**—P. L. 2, 567. and *e.* fallacious hope
P. L. 4, 522. hence I will *e.* their minds with
**Excites.**—P. L. 2, 484. which glory *e.* or close
P. L. 7, 68. liquid murmur heard new thirst *e.*
P. L. 9, 264. no bliss enjoyed by us *e.* his envy
P. L. 9, 472. of mischief, gratulating, thus *e.*
P. R. 1, 397. envy, they say, *e.* me thus to gain
P. R. 1, 423. or pleasure to do ill *e.*
P. R. 3, 26. glory the reward that sole *e.* to
**Exclaimed.**—P. L. 10, 416. Chaos over-built *e.*
**Exclude.**—P. L. 3, 202. such from mercy I *e.*
P. L. 4, 584. it to *e.* spiritual substance
**Excluded.**—P. L. 4, 105. all hope *e.* thus
P. R. 1, 349. hath he *e.* my resort sometimes
S. A. 494. *e.* all friendship and avoided as a blab
**Exclusion.**—P. L. 3, 525. *e.* from the doors
**Exclusive.**—P. L. 8, 625. joint, or limb, *e.* bars
**Excursion.**—P. L. 2, 396. and opportune *e.*
P. L. 8, 231. far on *e.* toward the gates of hell
**Excuse.**—P. L. 5, 447. had the sons of God *e.*
P. L. 9, 853. in her face *e.* came prologue
P. L. 10, 764. of thee that proud *e.*
P. L. 12, 96. though to the tyrant thereby no *e.*
S. A. 734. which to have merited, without *e.*
S. A. 829. weakness is thy *e.*, and I believe it
S. A. 831. if weakness may *e.*, what murderer
L. 18. hence with denial vain and coy *e.*
**Excused.**—P. L. 4, 394. the tyrant's plea, *e.*
**Execrable.**—P. L. 2, 681. art thou, *e.* shape
P. L. 12, 64. O *e.* son! so to aspire above his
**Execrably.**—S. A. 1362. what act more *e.*
**Execration.**—P. L. 10, 737. shall be the *e.*
**Execute.**—P. L. 1, 430. *e.* their aery purposes
P. L. 2, 732. to *e.* whate'er his wrath which he
P. L. 3, 399. to *e.* fierce vengeance on his foes
P. L. 10, 772. to *e.* what his decree fixed on this
**Executes.**—S. A. 1284. He *e.* his errand on the
**Execution.**—P. L. 10, 853. of tardy *e.*
S. A. 506. or the *e.* leave to high disposal
**Exempt.**—P. L. 2, 318. to live *e.* from heaven's
P. L. 3, 370. no voice *e.*, no voice but well
P. L. 9, 486. foe not informidable, *e.* from wound
P. L. 11, 514. and, for his maker's image sake, *e.*
P. L. 11, 709. and the climes of bliss, *e.* from
S. A. 103. buried, yet not *e.*, by privilege
S. A. 310. hath full right to *e.* whom so it pleases
S. A. 918. *e.* from many a care
**Exemption.**—P. R. 3, 115. no difference. no *e.*
**Exempts.**—S. 13, 5. *e.* thee from the throng
**Exercise.**—P. L. 2, 89. must *e.* us. without hope
P. L. 10, 400. thence on the earth dominion *e.*
P. L. 10, 796. how can he *e.* wrath without
P. L. 10, 927. on me *e.* not thy hatred for this
P. R. 1, 156. I mean to *e.* him
S. A. 612. there *e.* all his fierce accidents
S.A.1287. but patience is more oft the *e.* of saints
**Exercised.**—P. L. 4, 551. about him *e.* heroic
**Exhalation.**—P. L. 1, 711. rose like an *e.*
P. L. 10, 694. blast, vapour, and mist, and *e.*
P. L. 11, 741. vapour and *e.*, dusk and moist
**Exhalations.**—P. L. 5, 185. *e.* that now rise
P. L. 5, 425, alimental recompense in humid *e.*
**Exhale.**—P. L. 5, 421. no nourishment *e.*
**Exhaled.**—P. L. 5, 642. night with clouds *e.*
P. L. 9, 1049. powers made err, was now *e.*
**Exhaling.**—P. L. 7, 255. when orient light *e.*
**Exhausted.**—P. L. 6, 852. *e.* spiritless

P. R. 4, 136. e. all by lust and rapine
**Exhilarating.**—P. L. 9, 1047. e. vapour
**Exhorting.**—P. L. 2, 179. e. glorious war
**Exile.**—P. L. 1, 632. e. hath emptied heaven
P. L. 2, 207. to endure e., or ignominy, or bonds
P. L. 10, 484. placed in a paradise, by our e.
**Exiled.**—P. L. 4, 106. e., his new delight
S. A. 98. then had I not been thus e. from light
**Exorbitant.**—P. L. 3, 177. to foul e. desires
**Expanded.**—P. L. 1, 225. then with e. wings
**Expanse.**—P. L. 2, 1014. into the wild e.
P. L. 4, 456. pure as the e. of heaven; I thither
P. L. 7, 264. the firmament, e. of liquid, pure
P. L. 7, 340. high in the e. of heaven, to divide
**Expatiate.**—P. L. 1, 774. e. and confer their
**Expect.**—P. L. 4, 972. thyself e. to feel
P. L. 5, 892. soon e. to feel his thunder on thy
P. L. 6, 186. yet chains in hell, not realms, e.
P. L. 9, 382. the willinger I go, nor much e.
P. L. 11, 226. Eve, now e. great tidings
P. L. 11, 359. good with bad e. to hear
P. L. 12, 384. his capital bruise e. with mortal
P. L. 12, 591. on yonder hill, e. their motion
P. R. 3, 126. of whom what could he less e.
P. R. 4, 181. more blasphemous; which e. to rue
S. A. 1352. e. another message, more imperious
S. A. 1423. e. to hear nothing dishonourable
L. 84. of so much fame in heaven e. thy meed
**Expectance.**—V. Ex. 54. e. calls thee now
**Expectation.**—P. L. 2, 417. and e. held his
P. L. 6, 306. while e. stood in horror
P. L. 9, 789. through e. high of knowledge
P. L. 10, 536. sublime with e. when to see
P. L. 10, 782. would torment me with cruel e.
P. L. 12, 378. why our great E. should be
P. R. 2, 42. and again prolong our e.
P. R. 3, 207. the e. more of worse torments
**Expected.**—P. L. 5, 811. to hear in heaven e.
P. L. 9, 281. may tempt it, I e. not to hear
P. L. 10, 1048. we e. immediate dissolution
P. R. 2, 33. now come, so long e. of our fathers
**Expecting.**—P. L. 10, 439. and now e. each
P. L. 10, 504. he stood e. their universal shout
P. R. 3, 192. suffering, abstaining, quietly e.
**Expedite.**—P. L. 10, 474. to e. your glorious
**Expedition.**—P. L. 2, 342. with dangerous e.
P. L. 6, 86. hasting on with furious e.
P. L. 7, 193. on his great e. now appeared
P. R. 1, 101. sole undertook the dismal e.
S. A. 1283. with winged e. swift as the lightning
**Expel.**—P. L. 2, 140. would soon e. her mischief
P. R. 4, 100. might'st thou e. this monster from
P. R. 4, 127. I shall, thou say'st, e. a brutish
P. R. 4, 129. e. a devil who first made him such
**Expelled.**—P. L. 2, 195. thus e., to suffer here
P. L. 2, 983. all usurpation thence e., reduce
P. L. 8, 332. and this happy state shalt lose, e.
**Experience.**—P. L. 1, 118. e. of this great
P. L. 5, 826. by e. taught, we know how good
P. L. 8, 190. till warned, or by e. taught, she
P. L. 9, 807. E., next, to thee I owe, best guide
P. L. 9, 988. on my e., Adam, freely taste
P. R. 3, 238. best school of best e., quickest
S. A. 188. I learn now of my own e., not by talk
S. A. 382. but warned by oft e.
S. A. 1756. with new acquist of true e.
Il P. 173. till old e. do attain
**Experienced.**—P. L. 1, 568. darts his e. eye
**Experiment.**—P. L. 10, 967. sad e. I know
**Expert.**—P. L. 6, 233. e. when to advance
P. R. 2, 158. e. in amorous arts
S. A. 1044. what pilot so e. but needs must wreck
**Expiate.**—P. L. 3, 207. to e. his treason
S. A. 490. and e., if possible, my crime
S. A. 736. yet if tears may e.
**Expiations.**—P. L. 12, 291. shadowy e. weak
**Expire.**—P. L. 2, 93. be quite abolished and e.
**Expired.**—P. R. 4, 174. the time, till which e.
P. R. 4, 395. he knew his power not yet e.
P. R. 4, 568. at length in the air e. and fell
**Explain.**—S. A. 1583. slaughter, then, or how? e.

**Explained.**—P. L. 2, 518. by herald's voice e.
**Exploded.**—P. L. 11, 669. old and young e.
**Exploding.**—P. L. 10, 546. turned to e. hiss
**Exploit.**—P. L. 2, 111. and high e.
P.. L. 3, 465. with many a vain e.
P. L. 10, 407. to Death exposed by my e.
P. R. 1, 102. and the e. performed successfully
**Exploits.**—P. L. 5, 565. e. of warring spirits
P. L. 11, 790. and great e., but of true virtue
S. A 32. separate to God, designed for great e.
S. A. 525. from heaven foretold, and high e.
S. A. 1492. all those high e. by him achieved
**Explore.**—P. L. 2, 971. with purpose to e.
P. L. 7, 95. what we not to e. the secrets ask
**Explores.**—P. L. 2, 632. e. his solitary flight
P. L. 6, 113. thus his own undaunted heart e.
**Expose.**—P. L. 2, 828. e. with lonely steps
P. L. 10, 130. conceal, and not e. to blame
P. L. 12, 339. and e. their land, their city, his
P. R. 1, 142. henceforth I e. to Satan; let him
**Exposed.**—P. L. 1, 505. e. a matron to avoid
P. L. 2, 360. this place may lie e., the utmost
P. L. 3, 425. starless e., and ever threatening
P. L. 4, 206. to all delight of human sense e.
P. L. 9, 341. and Eden were no Eden, thus e.
P. L. 10, 407. through Sin to Death e.
P. L. 10, 957. to me committed, and by me e.
P. R. 2, 204. thence to the bait of woman lay e.
P. R. 4, 140. beasts, and men to beasts e.
S. A. 75. I, dark in light, e. to daily fraud
**Exposes.**—P. L. 2, 27. the highest place e.
S. A. 919. to which eye-sight e., daily, men abroad
**Express.**—P. L. 2, 480. nor failed they to e.
P. L. 3, 3. may I e. thee unblamed
P. L. 5, 574. to corporal forms, as may e.
P. L. 7, 528. in the image of God e.
P. L. 8, 616. and how their love e. they?
P. L. 10, 926. against a foe by doom e.
P. L. 11, 354. his face e., and of his steps
P. R. 1, 233. matchless deeds e. thy matchless
P. R. 2, 332. nature ashamed, or, better to e.
C. 69. the e. resemblance of the gods is changed
**Expressed.**—P.L. 3, 140. substantially e.
P. L. 6, 720. he all his father full e.
P. L. 9, 554. of brute, and human sense e.
P. L. 9, 1164. e. immutable when thou wert
P. L. 10, 67. all his father manifest e.
P. L. 11, 597. bent of nature; which he thus e.
P. R. 4, 351. unless where moral virtue is e.
A. 12. less than half we find e.
**Expressing.**—P. L. 8, 440. e. the spirit
P. L. 8, 544. and less e. the character of that
P. R. 4, 601. still e. the Son of God
**Expression.**—P. L. 3, 591. beyond e. bright
P. L. 9, 527. gentle dumb e. turned at length
**Expressly.**—P. L. 9, 356. to do what God e.
P. R. 2, 3. so late e. called Jesus Messiah
S. A. 578. which was e. given thee to annoy
**Expulsion.**—P. L. 6, 880. the e. of his foes
P. R. 2, 128. who no less threatens than our e.
**Expunged.**—P. L. 3, 49. to me e. and rased
**Exquisitest.**—P. R. 2, 346. and e. name
**Extend.**—P. L. 2, 326. over hell e. his empire
P. L. 2, 498. sun with farewell sweet e.
P. L. 5, 651. their camp e. by living streams
P. L. 7, 230. and said, Thus far e., thus far thy
P. L. 10, 804. that were to e. his sentence
P. R. 3, 65. when, to e. his fame through heaven
P. R. 4, 222. empire must e., so let e. thy mind
**Extended.**—P. L. 1, 195. e. long and large
P. L. 2, 885. that with e. wings a bannered host
P. L. 10, 1047. e. wide in circuit, undetermined
P. L. 3, 557. canopy of night's e. shade
**Extends.**—P. L. 9, 108. yet e. to all
P. L. 12, 211. Moses once more his potent rod e.
**Extent.**—P. L. 7, 496. of huge e. sometimes
P. L. 10, 808. not to the e. of their own sphere
P. R. 3, 406. and his full sceptre sway to just e.
**Extenuate.**—P. L. 10, 645. who can e. thee
S. A. 767. to lessen or e. my offence
**Exterior.**—P. 9, 336. without e. help

**External.**—P. L. 5, 103. of all *e.* things
**Extinct.**—P. L. 1, 141. though all our glory *e.*
P. L. 9, 829. shall live with her enjoying, I *e.*
S.A.70. light, the prime work of God, to me is *e.*
**Extinguish.**—P. L. 4, 666. and *e.* life
**Extinguished.**—S. A. 1688. and thought *e.*
**Extol.**—P. L. 2. 479. *e.* him equal to the
P. L. 3, 146. both heaven and earth shall high *e.*
P. L. 4, 436. praise him, and *e.* his bounty
P. L. 4, 733. with us *e.* thy goodness infinite
P. L. 5, 164. join all ye creatures to *e.* him first
P. R. 2, 453. *e.* not riches, then, the toil of fools
P. R. 3, 50. rabble, who *e.* things vulgar
**Extolled,**—P. L. 3, 398. acclaim thee only *e.*
P. R. 3, 54. what delight to be by such *e.*
**Extollest.**—P. R. 4, 353. then *e.* as those
**Extolling.**—S. A. 654. *e.* patience as the truest
**Extort.**—P. L. 1, 111. *e.* from me
**Extorts.**—P. R. 1, 423. what thy fear *e.*
**Extracted.**—P. L. 8, 497. name, of man *e.*
**Extracting.**—P. L. 5, 25. *e.* liquid sweet
**Extraordinary.**—S. A. 1383. *e.* my thoughts
**Extravagant.**—P. L. 6, 616. somewhat *e.*
**Extreme.**—S. A. 1342. joined with *e.* contempt
C. 273. not any boast of skill, but *e.* shift
**Extremes.**—P. L. 1, 276. so oft in worst *e.*
P. L. 2, 599. change of fierce *e.*, *e.* by change
P. L. 7, 272. lest fierce *e.* contiguous might
P. L. 10, 976. to some relief of our *e.*, or end
**Extremity.**—C. 643. that this *e.* compelled
**Exulcerate.**—S.A.625.exasperate,*e.*,and raise
**Eye.**—P. L. 1, 456. his *e.* surveyed the dark
P. L. 1, 568. darts his experienced *e.*
P. L. 1, 604. cruel his *e.*. but cast signs of
P. L. 2, 189. whose *e.* views all things at one
P. L. 2, 748. and do I seem now in thine *e.*
P. L. 3, 58. above all height bent down his *e.*
P. L. 2, 193. shall not be slow, mine *e.* not shut
P. L. 3, 534. and his *e.* with choice regard from
P. L. 3, 547. which to his *e.* discovers unaware
P. L. 3, 573. likest heaven allured his *e.*
P. L. 3, 578. his lordly *e.* keep distance due
P. L. 3, 614. far and wide his *e.* commands
P. L. 3, 660. and as his *e.* to visit oft this new
P. L. 4, 117. him counterfeit, if any *e.* beheld
P. L. 4, 125. whose *e,* pursued him down the
P. L. 4, 279. his stepdame Rhea's *e.*
P. L. 4, 300. his fair large front and *e.* sublime
P. L. 4, 572. mine *e.* pursued him still, but
P. L. 5, 26. but with startled *e.* on Adam
P. L. 5, 131. from either *e.* and wiped them
P. R. 5, 171. this great world both *e.* and soul
P. L. 5, 711. eternal *e.*. whose sight discerns
P. L. 6, 149. the grand foe. with scornful *e.*
P. L. 6, 350. they live all head, all *e.*, all ear
P. L. 6, 476. whose *e.* so superficially surveys
P. L. 6, 848. and every *e.* glared lightning
P. L. 8, 307. fruit that hung to the *e.* tempting
P. L. 8, 488. in all her steps, heaven in her *e.*
P. L. 9, 397. with ardent look his *e.* pursued
P. L. 9, 518. in sight of Eve, to lure her *e.*
P. L. 9, 528. turned at length the *e.* of Eve
P. L. 9, 743. solicited her longing *e.;* yet first
P. L. 9, 777. fair to the *e.*, inviting to the taste
P. L. 9, 923. coveting to *e.* that sacred fruit
P. L. 9, 1036. whose *e.* darted contagious fire
P. L. 10, 5. for what can scape the *e.* of God
P. L. 11, 191. and with his *e.* the chase
P. L. 11, 212. fear that day dimmed Adam's *e.*
P. L. 11, 385. his *e.* might there command
P. L. 11, 396. nor could his *e.* not ken
P. L. 11, 620. troll the tongue, and roll the *e.*
P. L. 12, 556. whose end no *e.* can reach
P. R. 1, 319. first with curious *e.* perused him
P. R. 2, 153. set women in his *e.* and in his
P. R. 2, 210. leisure will vouchsafe an *e.*
P. R. 2, 296. and to a superstitious *e.*
P. R. 3, 293. turning with easy *e.*, thou mayst
P. R. 4, 611. to the gates cast round thine *e.*
P. R. 4, 112. of arms before, allure mine *e.*
P. R. 4, 216. slipping from thy mother's *e.*

P. R. 4, 240. Athens, the *e.* of Greece
P. R. 4, 507. seldom have I ceased to *e.*
S. A. 94. to such a tender ball as the *e.* confined
S. A. 459. mine *e.* to harbour sleep or thoughts
S. A. 636. under His special *e.* abstemious I grew
S. A. 690. unseemly falls in human *e.*
S. A. 1172. whose ear is ever open, and his *e.*
S. A. 1625. which without help of *e.* might be
C. 155. to cheat the *e.* with blear illusion
C. 164. when once her *e.* hath met the virtue
C. 329. *e.* me, blest Providence, and square my
C. 395. of dragon-watch with unenchanted *e.*
C. 978. where day never shuts his *e.*
L'A. 69. mine *e.* hath caught new pleasures
Il P. 140. where no profaner *e.* may look
Il P. 141. hide me from day's garish *e.*
S. 1, 5. thy liquid notes that close the *e.* of day
S. 2, 14. as ever in my great task-master's *e.*
H. 59. and kings sat still with awful *e.*
P. 43. mine *e.* hath found that sad sepulchral
**Eyed.**—P. L. 4, 504. *e.* them askance
P. L. 11, 585. the men, though grave, *e.* them
**Eyeless.**—S. A. 41. *e.* in Gaza, at the mill
**Eyelids.**—P. L. 4, 616. inclines our *e.*
P. L. 5, 674. what sleep can close thy *e.*
L. 26. under the opening *e.* of the morn
Il P. 150. softly on my *e.* laid
**Eyes.**—P. L. 1, 56. he throws his baleful *e.*
P. L. 1, 193. and *e.* that sparkling blazed
P. L. 2, 239. with what *e.* could we stand
P. L. 2, 388. and joy sparkled in all their *e.*
P. L. 2, 753. dim thine *e.*, and dizzy swum
P. L. 2, 803. before mine *e.* in opposition
P. L. 2, 890. before their *e.* in sudden view
P. L. 3, 23. not these *e.*, that roll in vain
P. L. 3, 53. there plant *e.*, all mist from thence
P. L. 3, 382. but with both wings veil their *e.*
P. L. 3, 650. and are his *e.* that run through
P. L. 3, 700. to witness with thine *e.*
P. L. 4, 358. O hell! what do mine *e.* with grief
P. L. 4, 466. there I had fixed mine *e.* till now
P. L. 4, 492. and with *e.* of conjugal attraction
P. L. 4, 658. when sleep hath shut all *e.*
P. L. 5, 44. heaven wakes with all his *e.*
P. L. 5, 647. the unsleeping *e.* of God
P. L. 6, 571. which to our *e.* discovered
P. L. 6, 755. set with *e.*; with *e.* the wheels
P. L. 6, 846. distinct with *e.*, and from the
P. L. 6, 847. distinct alike with multitude of *e.*
P. L. 7, 67. still *e.* the current stream
P. L. 7, 446. hue of rainbows and starry *e.*
P. L. 7, 496. brazen *e.* and hairy mane terrific
P. L. 7, 513. heart, and voice, and *e.*, directed
P. L. 8, 63. her shot darts of desire into all *e.*
P. L. 8, 257. my wondering *e.* I turned and
P. L. 8, 310. before mine *e.* all real, as the dream
P. L. 8, 459. nature as in aid, and closed mine *e.*
P. L. 8, 460. mine *e.* he closed, but open left the
P. L. 9, 500. crested aloft, and carbuncle his *e.*
P. L. 9, 706. your *e.* that seem so clear, yet are
P. L. 9, 866. but of divine effect to open *e.*
P. L. 9, 875. opener mine *e.*, dim erst, dilated
P. L. 9, 985. opened *e.*, new hopes, new joys
P. L. 9, 1014. Eve began to cast lascivious *e.*
P. L. 9, 1053. their *e.* how opened, and their
P. L. 9, 1070. our *e.* opened we find indeed
P. L. 9, 1122. nor only tears rained at their *e.*
P. L. 10, 553. their earnest *e.* they fixed
P. L. 11, 130. all their shape spangled with *e.*
P. L. 11, 305. consolation left familiar to our *e.*
P. L. 11, 367. for I have drenched her *e.*
P. L. 11, 412. Michael from Adam's *e.* the film
P. L. 11, 419. Adam, now enforced to close his *e.*
P. L. 11, 423. ope thine *e.*, and first behold
P. L. 11, 429. his *e.* he opened, and beheld
P. L. 11, 478. before his *e.* appeared
P. L. 11, 585. and let their *e.* rove without rein
P. L. 11, 598. true opener of mine *e.*
P. L. 11, 611. direct thine *e.* and soon behold
P. L. 12, 863. with uplifted hands and *e.* devout
P. L. 12, 109. avert his holy *e.*, resolving

P. L. 12, 274. mine *e*. true opening, and my
P. R. 2, 31. our *e*. beheld Messiah certainly
P. R. 2, 180. wanton *e*. on the daughters of men
P. R. 2, 338. Saviour, lifting up his *e*., beheld
P. R. 3, 245. before thine *e*. the monarchies
P. R. 3, 390. before mine *e*. thou hast set
P. R. 4, 38. and groves presented to his *e*.
S. A. 33. captived, and both my *e*. put out
S. A. 124. or do my *e*. misrepresent?
S. A. 584. light again within thy *e*. to spring
S. A. 726. now stands and *e*. thee, fixed
S. A. 1103. I lose, prevented by thy *e*. put out
S. A. 1160. to put out both thine *e*.
S. A. 1490. it shall be my delight to tend his *e*.
S. A. 1543. which erst my *e*. beheld, and yet
S. A. 1637. and *e*. fast fixed, he stood, as one who
S. A. 1689. with inward *e*. illuminated
S. A. 1744. from whence captivity and loss of *e*.
C. 842. or, if our *e*. be barred that happiness
C. 753. love-darting *e*. or tresses like the morn
C. 758. to charm my judgment, as mine *e*.
A. 27. bright honour sparkle through your *e*.

L. 81. spreads aloft by those pure *e*.
L. 139. throw hither all your quaint enamelled *e*.
L. 181. and wipe the tears for ever from his *e*.
L'A. 80. the cynosure of neighbouring *e*.
L'A. 121. with store of ladies, whose bright *e*.
Il P. 40. thy rapt soul sitting in thine *e*.
Il P. 166. and bring all heaven before mine *e*.
S. 22, 1. these *e*. though clear to outward view
H. 43. confounded, that her Maker's *e*.
P. 16. that dropped . . . down his fair *e*.
V. Ex. 66. from *e*. of mortals walk invisible
**Eyesight.**—S. A. 919. to which *e*. exposes
S. A. 1489. older than thy age through *e*. lost
S. A. 1502. his strength with *e*. was not lost
S. A. 1503. God will restore him *e*. to his
S. A. 1527. what if his *e*. by miracle restored
**Eye-witness.**—S. A. 1594. *e.-w*. of what first or
**Eye-witnesses** —P. L. 6, 883. *e.-w*. of his acts
**Eyn.**—H. 223. of Bethlehem blind his dusky *e*.
**Eyries.**—P. L. 7, 424. cedar-tops their *e*. build
**Ezekiel.**—P. L. 1, 455. sacred porch *E*. saw

# F.

**Fable.**—P. L. 1, 580. resounds in *f*. or romance
P. R. 4, 341. in *f*., hymn, or song, so personating
L. 160. sleep'st by the *f*. of Bellerus old
**Fabled.**—P. L. 1, 741. fell from heaven they *f*.
P. L. 9, 30. *f*. knights in battles feigned
P. L. 10, 580. and *f*. how the serpent
P. R. 2, 358. than feigned of old or *f*. since
**Fables.**—P. L. 1, 197. as whom the *f*. name
P. L. 2, 627. and worse than *f*. yet have feigned
P. L. 4, 250. Hesperian *f*. true, if true
P. L. 11, 11. when the ancient pair in *f*. old
C. 800. she *f*. not. I feel that I do fear
**Fablest.**—P. L. 6, 292. into the hell thou *f*.
**Fabling.**—P. R. 4, 295. the next to *f*. fell
**Fabric.**—P. L. 1, 710. out of the earth a *f*. huge
P. L. 8, 76. he his *f*. of the heavens hath left
P.L.10, 482. a *f*. wonderful of absolute perfection
**Fabricius.**—P. R. 2, 446. Quintius, *F*.
**Fabulous.**—C. 513. I'll tell ye; 'tis not vain or *f*.
**Face.**—P. L. 1, 600. but his *f*. deep scars
P. L. 2, 304. and princely counsel in his *f*.
P. L. 2, 490. o'er spread heaven's cheerful *f*.
P. L. 3, 44. or flocks, or herds, or human *f*.
P. L. 3, 140. and in his *f*. divine compassion
P. L. 3, 262. and return, father, to see thy *f*.
P. L. 3, 407. mercy and justice in thy *f*.
P. L. 3, 637. yet such as in his *f*. youth smiled
P. L. 4, 114. each passion dimmed his *f*.
P. L. 5, 30. glad I see thy *f*., and morn returned
P. L. 5, 43. shadowy sets off the *f*. of things
P. L. 5, 644. *f*. of brightest heaven had changed
P. L. 6, 540. settled in his *f*. I see sad resolution
P. L. 6, 681. Son, in whose *f*. invisible
P. L. 6, 721. ineffably into his *f*. received
P. L. 6, 783. heaven his wonted *f*. renewed
P. L. 7, 278. over all the *f*. of earth main ocean
P. L. 7, 316. clad her universal *f*. with pleasant
P. L. 7, 377. with full *f*. borrowing her light
P. L. 7, 636. first this world and *f*. of things
P. L. 9, 853. in her *f*. excuse came prologue
P. L. 9, 1063. silent, and in *f*. confounded long
P. L. 9, 1080. shall I behold the *f*. henceforth
P. L. 10, 205. in the sweat of thy *f*. shalt thou
P. L. 10, 723. hide me from the *f*. of God
P. L. 10, 1064. now the sky with various *f*.
P. L. 11, 316. as from his *f*. I shall be hid
P. L. 11, 353. his *f*. express, and of his steps
P. L. 11, 712. the *f*. of things quite changed
P. L. 11, 843. wrinkled the *f*. of deluge
P. R. 1, 92. in his *f*. the glimpses of his
P. R. 3, 324. against the *f*. of their pursuers
P. R. 4, 433. beams had cheered the *f*. of earth
S. A. 742. desirous to behold once more thy *f*.

S. A. 1749. oft He seems to hide His *f*.
C. 530. reason's mintage charactered in the *f*.
S. 23, 10. her *f*. was veiled; yet to my fancied
S. 23, 12. so clear as in no *f*. with more delight
D.F. I. 34. O no for something in thy *f*. did shine
**Faces.**—P. L. 6, 753. four *f*. each had
P. L. 9, 1076. and in our *f*. evident the signs
P. L. 11, 128. four *f*. each had like a double
P. L. 11, 641. fierce *f*. threatening war
P. L. 12, 644. gate with dreadful *f*. thronged
P. R. 4, 76. dusk *f*. with white silken turbants
**Facile.**—P. L. 4, 967. not to scorn the *f*. gates
P. L. 8, 65. benevolent and *f*. thus replied
P. L. 9, 1158. too *f*. then, thou didst not much
P. R. 1, 51. since Adam and his *f*. consort Eve
**Fact.**—P. L. 2, 124. who most excels in *f*. of arms
P. L. 9, 928. perhaps the *f*. is not so heinous
P. L. 9, 980. *f*. pernicious to thy peace
P. L. 11, 457. but the bloody *f*. will be avenged
S.A.493. heinous had the *f*. been, how deserving
S. A. 736. though the *f*. more evil drew
**Faction.**—P. L. 2, 32. grow up there from *f*.
P. L. 2, 901. they around the flag of each his *f*.
**Factious.**—P. L. 11, 664. soon in *f*. opposition
P. L. 12, 352. and multitude *f*. they grow
**Faculties.**—P. L. 5, 101. many lesser *f*.
P. L. 8, 542. and inward *f*. which most excel
C. 628. telling their strange and vigorous *f*.
**Faculty.**—P. L. 5, 410. them every lower *f*.
**Fade.**—P. L. 3, 360. with these that never *f*.
**Faded.**—P. L. 1, 602. care sat on his *f*. cheek
P. L. 1, 375. curse their frail original and *f*. bliss
P. L. 2, 376. *f*. so soon
P. L. 4, 870. of regal port, but *f*. splendour wan
P. L. 9, 893. and all the *f*. roses shed
**Fading.**—D.F. I. 2. silken primrose *f*. timelessly
**Faeries.**—C. 118. trip the pert *f*., and the dapper
**Faery.**—P. L. 1, 781. *f*. elves whose midnight
P. R. 2, 359. of *f*. damsels met in forest wide
C. 298. I took it for a *f*. vision
C. 436. no goblin or swart *f*. of the mine
L'A. 102. how *f*. Mab the junkets eat
V. Ex. 60. the *f*. ladies danced upon the hearth
**Fail.**—P. L. 1, 117. empyreal substance cannot *f*.
P. L. 1, 167. if I *f*. not
P. L. 1, 633. shall *f*. to re-ascend, self-raised
P. L. 2, 205. if that *f*. then, shrink and fear
P. L. 6, 117. there *f*. where virtue fails
P. L. 7, 38. so *f*. not thou who thee implores
P. L. 9, 942. needs with us must *f*.
P. L. 9, 1142. conclude they then begin to *f*.
P. L. 10, 856. shall truth *f*. to keep her word
P. L. 12, 9. I perceive thy mortal sight to *f*.

P. R. 2, 54. he will not *f.*, nor will withdraw
P. R. 3, 395. and *f.* me of the throne
C. 597. if this *f.*, the firmament is rottenness
L'A. 99. till the livelong daylight *f.*
Il P. 155. but let my due feet never *f.*
H. 171. and, wroth to see his kingdom *f.*
**Failed.**—P. L. 2, 480. nor *f.* they to express
P. L. 3, 101. them who stood, and them who *f.*
P. L. 4, 357. scarce thus at length *f.* speech
P. L. 7, 139. at least our envious foe hath *f.*
P. L. 8, 534. nature *f.* in me, and left some part
P. L. 9, 145. now *f.* more angels to create
P. R. 1, 147. less over-weening since he *f.*
P. R. 4, 612. that seat of earthly bliss be *f.*
U.C.I.10.had not his weekly course of carriage *f.*
**Failing.**—P. L. 2, 931. but that seat soon *f.*
P. L. 9, 404. much *f.*, hapless Eve
P. L. 10, 129. whose *f.*, while her faith to me
S. A. 901. pretexts and varnished colours *f.*
**Fails.**—P. L. 6,117. there fail where virtue *f.*
P. L. 8, 38. describe whose swiftness number *f.*
**Fain**—S. A. 1535. yet hope would *f.* subscribe
C. 783. *f.* would I something say; yet to what
**Faint.**—P. L. 6, 392. through the *f.* Satanic host
P. L. 6, 799. disdaining flight or *f.* retreat
P. L. 11, 108. lest they *f.* at the sad sentence
P. L. 11, 631. or in the midway *f.*
C. 331.unmuffle, ye *f.* stars; and thou, fair moon
S. 23, 4. from death by force, though pale and *f.*
**Fainted.**—P. L. 1, 530. raised their *f.* courage
U. C. II. 16. *f.*, and died, nor would with ale be
**Fainting.**—S. A. 666. and *f.* spirits uphold
**Fair.**—P. L. 1, 445. beguiled by *f.* idolatresses
P. L. 1, 468. delightful seat was *f.* Damascus
P. L. 2, 398. unvisited of heaven's *f.* light
P. L. 2, 650. seemed woman to the waist, and *f.*
P. L. 2, 748. once deemed so *f.* in heaven
P. L. 2, 757. shining heavenly *f.*, a goddess
P. L. 2, 818. and my *f.* son here show'st me
P. L. 3, 47. for the book of knowledge *f.*
P. L. 3, 338. and love triumphing, and *f.* truth
P. L. 3, 554. sight of all this world beheld so *f.*
P. L. 3, 694. *f.* angel, thy desire, which tends
P. L. 3, 727. so called that opposite *f.* star
P. L. 4, 151. his beams than in *f.* evening
P. L. 4, 268. not that *f.* field of Enna where
P. L. 4, 300. his *f.* large front and eye sublime
P. L. 4, 339. dalliance, as beseems *f.* couple
P. L. 4, 379. not please like this *f.* paradise
P. L. 4, 468. thou seest, *f.* creature, is thyself
P. L. 4, 477. till I espied thee, *f.*, indeed, and
P. L. 4, 478. methought, less *f.*, less winning
P. L. 4, 481. return, *f.* Eve, whom fliest thou
P. L. 4, 491. wisdom, which alone is truly *f.*
P. L. 4, 521. O *f.* foundation laid whereon to
P. L. 4, 610. *f.* consort, the hour of night
P. L. 4, 648. her solemn bird, and this *f.* moon
P. L. 4, 718. mankind with her *f.* looks
P. L. 4, 742. I ween, Adam from his *f.* spouse
P. L. 4, 770. sings to his proud *f.*
P. L. 4, 790. where those two of.creatures lodge
P. L. 4, 820. back stepped those two *f.* angels
P. L. 5, 52. *f.* it seemed, much fairer to my
P. L. 5, 58. and, 'O *f.* plant,' said he with fruit
P. L. 5, 74. happy creature, *f.* angelic Eve
P. L. 5, 124. *f.* morning first smiles on the
P. L. 5, 129. so cheered he his *f.* spouse
P. L. 5, 155. thus wondrous *f.*; thyself how
P. L. 5, 380. more lovely *f.* than wood nymph
P. L. 6, 524. when *f.* morn orient in heaven
P. L. 6, 611. entertain them *f.* with open front
P. L. 7, 556. how good, how *f.*, answering his
P. L. 8, 47. and, touched by her *f.* tendance
P. L. 8, 172. this Paradise and thy *f.* Eve
P. L. 8, 221. and outward both, his image *f.*
P. L. 8, 273. 'thou sun' said. I *'f.* light, and thou
P. L. 8, 276. ye that live and move, *f.* creatures
P. L. 8, 338. not only these *f.* bounds, but all
P. L. 8, 471. but different sex, so lovely *f.*
P. L. 8, 472. what seemed *f.* in all the world
P. L. 8, 493. giver of all things *f.*! but fairest

P. L. 8, 568. an outside, *f.* no doubt, and worthy
P. L. 8, 596. neither her outside formed so *f.*
P. L. 9, 443. with his *f.* Egyptian spouse
P. L. 9, 452. with nymph-like step, *f.* virgin
P. L. 9, 489. she *f.*, divinely *f.*, fit love for gods
P. L. 9, 588. fairest resemblance of thy Maker *f.*
P. L. 9, 545. what in thee is *f.*, one man except
P. L. 9, 568. empress of this *f.* world
P. L. 9, 585. I had of tasting those *f.* apples
P. L. 9, 605. all things *f.* and good
P. L. 9, 606. all that *f.* and good in thy divine
P. L. 9, 608. no *f.* to thine equivalent or second
P. L. 9, 661. the fruit of this *f.* tree amidst
P. L. 9, 720. for this *f.* earth I see
P. L. 9, 731. import your need of this *f.* fruit
P. L. 9, 763. in the day we eat of this *f.* fruit
P. L. 9, 777. *f.* to the eye, inviting to the taste
P. L. 9, 798. thy *f.* fruit let hang, as to no end
P. L. 9, 972. if any be, of tasting this *f.* fruit
P. L. 9, 996. gave him of that *f.* enticing fruit
P. L. 9, 1159. permit, approve, and *f.* dismiss
P. L. 10, 352. Sin, his *f.* enchanting daughter
P. L. 10, 384. *f.* daughter, and thou son
P. L. 10, 550. *f.* fruit, like that which grew
P. L. 10, 561. the fruitage *f.* to sight
P. L. 10, 618. which I so *f.* and good created
P. L. 10, 769. for I submit; his doom is *f.*
P. L. 10, 818. *f.* patrimony that I must leave
P. L. 10, 891. this novelty on earth, this *f.*
P. L. 10, 943. creature so *f.* his reconcilement
P. L. 10, 1067. these *f.* spreading trees
P. L. 11, 57. I, at first, with two *f.* gifts
P. L. 11, 582. a bevy of *f.* women, richly gay
P. L. 11, 593. such happy interview and *f.*
P. L. 11, 614. for that *f.* female troop thou
P. L. 11, 625. to the smiles of these *f.* atheists
P. L. 11, 630. entered so *f.*, should turn aside
P. L. 11, 647. of beeves, *f.* oxen and *f.* kine
P. L. 11, 717. where passing *f.* allured them
P. L. 12, 26. who not content with *f.* equality
P. R. 1, 63. in this *f.* empire won of earth
P. R. 1, 381. what I see excellent in good or *f.*
P. R. 2, 155. are in each region passing *f.*
P. R. 2, 200. in his prime youth, the *f.* Iberian
P. R. 2, 301. and with *f.* speech these words
P. R. 3, 257. and left between *f.* champaign
P. R. 3, 351. and show all this *f.* sight
P. R. 4, 55.many a *f.* edifice besides, more like
P. R. 4, 426. morning *f.* came forth with
P. R. 4, 442. would also seem of this *f.* change
P. R. 4, 451. *f.* morning yet betides thee, Son
P. R. 4, 544. till underneath them *f.* Jerusalem
S. A. 217. than of thine own tribe, fairer, or as *f.*
S. A. 533. of *f.* fallacious looks, venereal trains
S. A. 688. which were a *f.* dismission
S. A. 728. like a *f.* flower surcharged with dew
S. A. 934. thy *f.* enchanted cup and warbling
S. A. 1062. *f.* days have oft contracted wind
S. A. 1178. *f.* honour that thou dost thy God
S. A. 1723. nothing but well and *f.*, and what
C. 34. where his *f.* offspring nursed in princely
C. 152. well stocked with as *f.* a herd as grazed
C. 160. I, under *f.* pretence of friendly ends
C. 283. and left your *f.* side all unguarded, lady
C. 331. unmuffle ye faint stars and thou *f.* moon
C. 393. but beauty, like the *f.* Hesperian tree
C. 442. *f.* silver-shafted queen for ever chaste
C. 689. timely rest have wanted, but, *f.* virgin
C. 831. commended her *f.* innocence to the
C. 860. Sabrina *f.*, listen where thou art sitting
C. 880. and *f.* Ligea's golden comb
C. 929. never scorch thy tresses *f.*
C. 969. three *f.* branches of your own
C. 981. all amidst the gardens *f.*
C. 1009. and from her *f.* unspotted side
A. 33 *f.* silver-buskined nymphs as great
A. 45. I am the power of this *f.* wood
L. 22. and bid *f.* peace be to my sable shroud
L. 73. but the *f.* guerdon when we hope to find
L'A. 11. but come, thou goddess *f.* and free
L'A. 23. filled her with thee, a daughter *f.*

H. 37. only, with speeches *f.*
P. 16. dropped with odorous oil down his *f.*eyes
D. F. I. 11. likewise he some *f.* one wedded not
D. F. I. 21. from her *f.* hiding place
S. M. 21. broke the *f.* music that all creatures
M. W. 4. besides what her virtues *f.*
M. W. 41. but the *f.* blossom hangs the head
M. W. 63. that *f.* Syrian shepherdess
V. Ex. 28. fly swiftly to this *f.* assembly's ears
**Fair-appearing.**—P. L. 9, 354. some *f.-a.* good
**Fairer.**—P. L. 2. 110. *f.* person lost not heaven
P. L. 4, 270. herself a *f.* flower, by gloomy Dis
P. L. 5, 53. fair it seemed, much *f.* to my fancy
P. L. 9, 1032. with ardour to enjoy thee, *f.* now
P. R. 2, 352. of *f.* hue than Ganymed or Hylas
P. R. 2, 358. *f.* than feigned of old, or fabled
P. R. 4, 613. a *f.* paradise is founded now
S. A. 217. than of thine own tribe, *f.*, or as fair
**Fairest.**—P. L. 4, 147. loaden with *f.* fruit
P. L. 4, 324. the *f.* of her daughters, Eve
P. L. 5, 18. awake my *f.*, my espoused
P. L. 5, 166. *f.* of stars, last in the train of night
P. L. 5, 381. or the *f.* goddess feigned of three
P. L. 8, 307. tree loaden with *f.* fruit that hung
P. L. 8, 493. giver of all things fair, but *f.* this
P. L. 9, 432. herself, though *f.* unsupported
P. L. 9, 538. *f.* resemblance of thy Maker fair
P. L. 9, 577. loaden with fruit of *f.* colours
P. L. 9, 851. a bough of *f.* fruit that downy
P. L. 9, 896. O *f.* of creation, last and best of all
P. L. 11, 549. I may be quit, *f.* and easiest
P. R. 2, 154. daughters of men the *f.* found
P. R. 3, 341. to win the *f.* of her sex, Angelica
D.F.I. 1.O *f.* flower, no sooner blown but blasted
**Fairfax.**—S. 15, 1. *F.* whose name in arms
**Fairly.**—C. 168. here she comes, I *f.* step aside
P. R. 4, 187. by thee how *f.* is the giver now
**Faith.**—P. L. 2, 36. then to union and firm *f.*
P. L. 2, 690. first broke peace in heaven and *f.*
P. L. 3, 104. true allegiance, constant *f.* or love
P. L. 4, 520. of their obedience and their *f.*
P. L. 4, 954. was this your discipline and *f.*
P. L. 6, 115. where *f.* and realty remain not
P. L. 6, 143. there be who *f.* prefer, and piety
P. L. 8, 325. pledge of thy obedience and thy *f.*
P. L. 9, 286. that my firm *f.* and love
P. L. 9, 298. supposed not incorruptible of *f.*
P. L. 9, 320. thought less attributed to her *f.*
P. L. 9, 335. and what is *f.*, love, virtue
P. L. 9, 411. despoiled of innocence, of *f.*
P. L. 9, 1075. void, of innocence, of *f.*, of purity
P. L. 9, 1141. needless cause to approve the *f.*
P. L. 10, 129. failing while her *f.* to me remains
P. L. 11, 64. refined by *f.* and faithful works
P. L. 11, 141. Eve, easily may *f.* admit that all
P. L. 11, 458. and the other's *f.* approved
P. L. 11, 807. and temperance, truth, and *f.*
P. L. 12, 128. with what *f.* he leaves his gods
P. L. 12, 154. like him in *f.*, in wisdom
P. L. 12, 295. to them by *f.* imputed, they may
P. L. 12, 306. works of law to works of *f.*
P. L. 12, 409. imputed, becomes theirs by *f.*
P. L. 12, 427. and the benefit embrace by *f.*
P. L. 12, 449. but to the sons of Abraham's *f.*
P. L. 12, 488. and the law of *f.*
P. L. 12, 527. built by *f.* to stand, their own *f.*
P. L. 12, 529. for on earth who against *f.*
P. L. 12, 536. works of *f.* rarely be found
P. L. 12, 582. add *f.*, add virtue, patience
P. L. 12, 599. chiefly what may concern her *f.*
P. L. 12, 603. both in one *f.* unanimous
S. A. 388. in this other was there found more *f.*
S. A. 750. to break all *f.*, all vows, deceive
S. A. 986. chose above the *f.* of wedlock-bands
S. A. 1115. breaking her marriage *f.* to
C. 88. of less *f.* And in this office of his mountain
C.213. welcome pure-eyed *F.*, white-handed Hope
C. 971. their *f.*, their patience, and their truth
S. 14, 1. *f.* and love which parted from thee
S. 14, 7. but, as *f.* pointed with her golden rod
S.14, 9. love led them on, and *f.*, who knew them

S.15, 12. and public *f.* cleared from the shameful
S. 16, 3. guided by *f.* and matchless fortitude
F. of C. 9. men whose life, learning, *f.*, and pure
**Faithful.**—P. L. 1, 264. our *f.* friends
P. L. 1, 611. yet *f.* how they stood
P. L. 4, 933. and ill successes past, a *f.* leader
P. L. 4, 950. and couldst thou '*f.*' add
P. L. 4, 952. *f.* to whom? to thy rebellious crew
P. L. 5, 896. *f.* found among the faithless *f.*
P. L. 6, 204. and the *f.* armies rung Hosanna
P. L. 6, 271. once upright and *f.*, now proved
P. L. 6, 803. *f.* hath been your warfare
P. L. 9, 265. or worse, leave not the *f.* side
P. L. 9, 983. like so true, so *f.*, love unequalled
P. L. 11, 64. refined by faith and *f.* works
P. L. 12, 113. nation from one *f.* man to spring
P. L. 12, 152. whom '*f.* Abraham' due time shall
P. L. 12, 462. to reward his *f.*, and receive them
P. L. 12, 481. what will betide the few his *f.*
P. L. 12, 571. to the *f.*, death the gate of life
S. A. 957. among illustrious women, *f.* wives
S. A. 1498. like a camp of *f.* soldiery
S. A. 1751. and to His *f.* champion hath in place
C. 944. I shall be your *f.* guide
L. 121. that to the *f.* herdman's art belongs
**Faithfulness.**—P. L. 4, 951. of *f.* profaned
**Faithless.**—P. L. 3, 96. and his *f.* progeny
P. L. 5, 897. among the *f.* faithful only he
S. A. 380. a Canaanite, my *f.* enemy
**Falerne.**—P. R. 4, 117. Setia, Cales, and *F.*
**Fall.**—P. L. 1, 30. to *f.* off from their Creator
P. L. 1, 76. the companions of his *f.*
P. L. 1, 642. our attempt, and wrought our *f.*
P. L. 2, 16. and more dread than from no *f.*
P. L. 2, 76. descent and *f.* to us is adverse
P. L. 2, 177. threatening hideous *f.* one day
P. L. 2, 203. and so doubtful what might *f.*
P. L. 2, 549. own heroic deeds and hapless *f.*
P. L. 2, 773. and, in the general *f.*, I also
P. L. 3, 95. so will *f.* he and his faithless
P. L. 3, 99. to have stood, though free to *f.*
P. L. 3, 128. they themselves ordained their *f.*
P. L. 3, 152. *f.* circumvented thus by fraud
P. L. 3, 201. may stumble on, and deeper *f.*
P. L. 3, 237. on me let thine anger *f.*
P. L. 3, 619. shadow from body opaque can *f.*
P. L. 4, 91. the lower still I *f.*, only supreme
P. L. 4, 101. to a worse relapse and heavier *f.*
P. L. 4, 260. waters *f.* down the slope hills
P. L. 5, 130. but silently a gentle tear let *f.*
P. L. 5, 241. the *f.* of others from like state
P. L. 5, 540. in this we stand or *f.*
P. L. 5, 542. *f.* from what high state of bliss
P. L. 5, 878. forsaken of all good! I see thy *f.*
P. L. 6, 55. his fiery Chaos to receive their *f.*
P. L. 6, 285. *f.*, but that they rise unvanquished
P. L. 6, 796. or to *f.* in universal ruin last
P. L. 6, 872. felt tenfold confusion in their *f.*
P. L. 6, 898. and the deep *f.* of those too high
P. L. 7, 19. dismounted on the Aleian field I *f.*
P. L. 8, 640. to stand, or *f.*, free in thine own
P. L. 9, 174. since higher I *f.* short
P. L. 9, 362. and *f.* into deception unaware
P. L. 9, 941. which, in our *f.*, for us created
P. L. 9, 1069. true in our *f.*, false in our
P. L. 10, 16. and manifold in sin, deserved to *f.*
P. L. 10, 44. concurring to necessitate his *f.*
P. L. 10, 174. on the serpent thus his curse let *f.*
P. L. 10, 184. saw Satan *f.* like lightning down
P. L. 10, 451. permissive glory since his *f.*
P. L. 10, 1087. prostrate *f.* before him
P. L. 11, 500. O miserable mankind, to what *f.*
P. L. 12, 118. and *f.* to worship their own
P. L. 12, 391. whose *f.* from heaven, a deadlier
P. R. 1, 373. that he might *f.* in Ramoth
P. R. 2, 88. that to the *f.* and rising he should
P. R. 2, 223. admire, and all her plumes *f.* flat
P. R. 3, 201. not that my rising is thy *f.*
P. R. 4, 166. if thou wilt *f.* down and worship
P. R. 4, 192. that I *f.* down and worship thee
P. R. 4, 567. fresh from his *f.*, and fiercer

P. R. 4, 571. he stood to see his victor *f.*
P. R. 4, 620. thou shalt *f.* from heaven
S. A. 55. proudly• secure, yet liable to *f.*
S. A. 456. to waver, or *f.* off and join with idols
S. A.1265. yet so it may *f.* out because their end
C. 251. at every *f.* smoothing the raven down
C. 491. cóme not too near, you *f.* on iron stakes
P. 49. that they would fitly *f.* in ordered
D. F. I. 44. of shaked Olympus by mischance *f.*
M. W. 45. which the sad morn had let *f.*
**Fallacious.**—P. L. 2, 568. and excite *f.* hope
P. L. 9, 1046. soon as the force of that *f.* fruit
P. R. 3, 4. his weak arguing and *f.* drift
S. A. 320. to seek in marriage that *f.* bride
S. A. 533. of fair *f.* looks, venereal trains
**Fallacy.**—P. R. 1, 155. lost by *f.* surprised
**Fallen.**—P. L. 1, 84. O, how *f.!* how changed
P. L. 1, 92. from what height *f.*
P. L. 1, 157. *f.* cherub, to be weak is miserable
P. L. 1, 282. no wonder, *f.* such a pernicious
P. L. 1, 330. awake, arise, or be for ever *f.*
P. L. 2, 13. though oppressed and *f.,* I give
P. L. 2, 457. terror of heaven, though *f*
P. L. 3, 181. know how frail his *f.* condition is
P. L. 3, 400. through their malice *f.*
P. L. 4, 591. downward to the sun, now *f.*
P. L. 5, 240. what enemy, late *f.* himself from
P. L. 5, 541. and some are *f.,* to disobedience *f.*
P. L. 6, 24. that of so many myriads *f.* yet one
P. L. 6, 852. exhausted, spiritless, afflicted, *f.*
P. L. 7, 25. hoarse or mute, though *f.* on evil
P. L. 7, 26. evil days though *f.,* and evil tongues
P. L. 10, 47. but *f.* he is; and now what rests
P. L. 10, 62. man himself to judge man *f.*
P. L. 11, 129. could have produced, ere *f.* from
P. L. 11, 180. live, though in *f.* state, content
P. R. 1, 405. man *f.,* shall be restored, I never
P. R. 2, 31. what relapse unlooked for are we *f.*
S. A. 169. pitch of abject fortune thou art *f.*
S. A. 414. the base degree to which I now am *f.*
S. A. 1523. this evil on the Philistines is *f.*
S. A. 1558. all her sons are *f.,* all in a moment
S. A. 1559. overwhelmed and *f.*
S. A. 1683. *f.* into wrath divine
**Fallest.**—P. L. 5, 174. and when thou *f*
**Fallible.**—P. L. 6, 428. then *f.,* it seems
**Falling.**—P. L. 1, 174. received us *f.*
P. L. 1, 745. dropped from the zenith, like a *f.*
P. L. 2, 925. if this frame of heaven were *f.*
P. L. 2, 935. to this hour down had been *f.*
P. L. 4, 615. the timely dew of sleep, now *f.*
P. L. 5, 190. or wet the thirsty earth with *f.*
P. L. 5, 191. rising or *f.* still advance his praise
P. L. 10, 663. of them rising with the sun or *f.*
C. 30. and all this tract that fronts the *f.* sun
**Fallows.**—L'A. 71. russet lawns and *f.* gray
**Falls.**—P. L. 3, 130. man *f.,* deceived by the
P. L. 4, 731. and uncropt *f.* to the ground
P. L. 5, 613. into utter darkness *f.*
P. L. 8, 551. knowledge in her presence *f.*
P. R. 4, 70. and where the shadow both way *f.*
S. A. 690. unseemly *f.* in human eye
**False.**—P. L. 2, 112. but all was *f.* and hollow
P. L. 2, 522. raised by *f.* presumptuous
P. L. 2, 565. vain wisdom all, and *f.* philosophy
P. L. 2, 700. back to thy punishment, *f.* fugitive
P. L. 3, 92. destroy, or, worse, by some *f.* guile
P. L. 3, 681. so spake the *f.* dissembler
P. L. 5, 694. so spake the *f.* archangel
P. L. 5, 809. O. argument blasphemous, *f.*
P. L. 6, 121. reason I have tried unsound and *f.*
P. L. 6, 271. upright and faithful, now proved *f.*
P. L. 9, 306. his malice and *f.* guile
P. L. 9, 332. gain from his surmise proved *f.*
P. L. 9, 355. dictate *f.,* and misinform the will
P. L. 9, 1011. that *f.* fruit far other operation
P. L. 9, 1068. to that *f.* worm, of whomsoever
P. L. 9, 1070. true in our fall, *f.* in our promised
P. L. 10, 452. since his fall was left him, or *f.*
P. L. 10, 868. leagued, thyself as *f.* and hateful

P. L. 11, 413. which that *f.* fruit that promised
P. L. 12, 122. his kindred and *f.* gods
P. R. 2, 179. *f.* titled sons of God
P. R. 3, 69. where glory is *f.,* glory
P. R. 3, 138. recreant to God, ingrate and *f.*
P. R. 4, 291. but these are *f.,* or little else but
P. R. 4, 320. far worse, her *f.* resemblance
P. R. 4, 491. as *f.* portents, not sent from God
S. A. 227. she proving *f.,* the next I took to wife
S. A. 749. and arts of every woman *f.* like thee
S. A. 824. I to myself was *f.,* ere thou to me
S. A.901. these *f.* pretexts and varnished colours
C.156. and give it *f.* presentments, lest the place
C. 364. or, if they be but *f.* alarms of fear
C. 690. 'twill not, *f.* traitor! 'twill not restore
C. 759. obtruding *f.* rules pranked in reason's
C.799. were shattered into heaps o'er thy *f.* head
C. 814. what! have you let the *f.* enchanter scape
L.153. let our frail thoughts dally with *f.* surmise
S. 11, 7. and some in file stand spelling *f.*
S. 15, 7. and the *f.* North displays her broken
T. 5. which is no more than what is *f.* and vain
**Falsehood.**—P. L. 4, 122. that practised *f.*
P. L. 4, 811. for no *f.* can endure touch of
P. L. 10, 873. to hellish *f.* snare them
P. R. 3, 443. so fares it when with truth *f.*
S. A. 955. bewail thy *f.* and the pious works
·S. A. 979. of *f.* most unconjugal traduced
C. 281. by *f.,* or discourtesy, or why
C. 698. with visored *f.* and base forgery
**False-imagined.**—D. F. I. 72. her *f.-i.* loss cease
**Falsities.**—P. L. 1, 367. by *f.* and lies
**Faltering.**—P. L. 2, 989, with *f.* speech
P. L. 9, 846. he the *f.* measure felt
P. L. 10, 115. whence Adam, *f.* long, thus
**Fame.**—P. L. 1, 651. there went a *f.* in heaven
P. L. 1, 695. their greatest monuments of *f.*
P. L. 2, 346. prophetic *f.* in heaven err not
P. L. 3, 449. fond hopes of glory or lasting *f.*
P. L. 4, 938. whereof in hell *f.* is not silent
P. L. 6, 240. deeds of eternal *f.* were done
P. L. 6, 375. angels contented with their *f.*
P. L. 6, 384. and through infamy seeks *f.*
P. L. 10, 481. which *f.* in heaven long had
P. L. 11, 386. stood city of old or modern *f.*
P. L. 11, 623. all their virtue, all their *f.*
P. L. 11, 698. thus *f.* shall be achieved
P. L. 11, 699. what most merits *f.* in silence
P. L. 11, 793. achieved thereby *f.* in the world
P. L. 12, 47. regardless whether good or evil *f.*
P. R. 1, 334. *f.* also finds us out
P. R. 2, 209. of this age the wonder and the *f.*
P. R. 3, 25. at thy acts, thyself the *f.* and glory
P. R. 3, 47. what is glory but the blaze of *f.*
P. R. 3, 65. when, to extend his *f.* through
P. R. 3, 70. not glorious, men not worthy of *f.*
P. R. 3, 99. lives now equal in *f.* to proudest
P. R. 3, 100. yet, if for *f.* and glory aught be
P. R. 3, 101. for *f.* his wasted country freed
P. R. 3, 289. of later *f.,* built by Emathian
P. R. 4, 371. tended on by glory or *f.*
S.A.971. *f.,* if not double-faced, is double-mouthed
S. A. 1248. though *f.* divulge him father of five
S. A. 1706. though her body die, her *f.* survives
S.A.1717. to himself and father's house, eternal *f.*
A. 8. *f.,* that her high worth to raise
A.41. what shallow-searching *f.* hath left untold
L.70. *f.* is the spur that the clear spirit doth raise
L. 78. *f.* is no plant that grows on mortal soil
L. 84. of so much *f.* in heaven expect thy meed
S. 8, 6. call *f.* on such gentle acts as these
S. 13, 12. Dante shall give *f.* leave to set thee
W. S. 5. dear son of memory, great heir of *f.*
**Famed.**—P. L. 3, 568. gardens *f.* of old¹
P. L. 12, 332. for wealth and wisdom *f.*
P. R. 1, 34. at that assembly *f.* would not be
P. R. 4, 59. carved work, the hand of *f.* artificers
S. A. 1094. where thou art *f.* to have
C. 1004. celestial Cupid, her *f.* son, advanced
**Familiar.**—P. L. 2, 219. will receive *f.* the
P. L. 2, 761. but, *f.* grown, I pleased, and with

P. L. 9, 2. as with his friend, *f.* used to sit
P. L. 11, 305. only consolation left *f.* to our eyes
**Families.**—P. L. 12, 23. peace, by *f.* and tribes
**Family.**—P. L. 10, 216. as father of his *f.*
P. R. 3, 168. by strong hand his *f.* obtained
**Famine.**—P. L. 2, 847. to hear his *f.* should
P. L. 10, 573. worn with *f.*, long and ceaseless
P. L. 10, 597. to me, who with eternal *f.* pine
P. L. 11, 472. fire, flood, *f.*, by intemperance
P. L. 11, 778. those few escaped *f.* and anguish
P. R. 2, 257. from the sting of *f.* fear no harm
**Famish.**—P. L. 12, 78. and *f.* him of breath
**Famished.**—P. R. 2. 311. Israel here had *f.*
**Famous.**—P. L. 4, 234. many a *f.* realm
P. R. 2, 7. Andrew and Simon, *f.* after known
P. R. 3, 68. *f.* he was in heaven, on earth less
P. R. 3, 94. made *f.* in a land and times
P. R. 4, 221. be *f.*, then, by wisdom
P. R. 4, 241. native to *f.* wits
P. R. 4, 267. thence to the *f.* orators repair
S. A. 145. in Ramath-lechi, *f.* to this day
S. A. 528. the sons of Anak, *f.* now and blazed
S. A. 542. which many a *f.* warrior overturns
A. 28. of *f.* Arcady ye are, and sprung
**Famousest.**—S. A. 982. among the *f.* of women
**Fan.**—P. L. 5, 6. Aurora's *f.* lightly dispersed
P. L. 5, 269. then with quick *f.* winnows
P. L. 10, 94. gentle airs due at their hour, to *f.*
**Fanatic.**—P. L. 1, 480. abused *f.* Egypt
P. R. 4, 292. conjectures, *f.*, built on nothing
Il P. 6. and *f.* fond with gaudy shapes possess
**Fancy.**—P. L. 4, 802. the organs of her *f.*
P. L. 5, 53. it seemed much fairer to my *f.*
P. L. 5, 102. among these *f.* next her office
P. L. 5, 110. oft in her absence mimic *f.* wakes
P. L. 5, 486. give both life and sense, *f.*
P. L. 8, 188. but apt the mind or *f.* is to rove
P. L. 8, 294. moved my *f.* to believe I yet had
P. L. 8, 461. but open left the cell of *f.*
P. L. 9, 1009. they swim in mirth, and *f.*
S. A. 601. humours black that mingle with *f.*
S. A. 794. I saw thee mutable of *f.*, feared lest
C. 548. till *f.* had her fill
C. 669. that *f.* can beget on youthful thoughts
L'A. 133. or sweetest Shakespeare, *F.'s* child
H. 134. enwrap our *f.* long
P. 31. and work my flattered *f.* to belief
W. S. 13. then thou our *f.* of itself bereaving
V. Ex. 32. before thou clothe my *f.* in fit sound
**Fanned.**—P. L. 5, 655. where they slept *f.*
P. L. 7, 432. *f.* with unnumbered plumes
P. R. 2. 364. Arabian odours *f.*
**Fanning.**—P. L. 4, 157. now gentle gales, *f.*
L. 44. *f.* their joyous leaves to thy soft lays
**Fans.**—P. L. 7, 476. their limber *f.* for wings
**Fantasies.**—C. 205. thousand *f.* begin to throng
**Fantastic.**—C. 144. in a light *f.* round
L'A. 34. on the light *f.* toe
**Fantastics.**—V. Ex. 20. our late *f.* with delight
**Far.**—P. L. 1, 59. at once, as *f.* as angels ken
P. L. 1, 73. as *f.* removed from God
P. L. 1, 138. as *f.* as Gods and heavenly
P. L. 1, 507. though *f.* renowned
P. L. 1, 587. thus *f.* these beyond compare
P. L. 1, 607. *f.* other once beheld in bliss
P. L. 1, 666. sudden blaze *f.* round illumined
P. L. 1, 670. there stood a hill not *f.* whose
P. L. 1, 792. but *f.* within, and in their own
P. L. 2, 1. on a throne of royal state which *f.*
P. L. 2, 22. this loss, thus *f.* at least recovered
P. L. 2, 97. happier *f.* than miserable to have
P. L. 2, 133. scout *f.* and wide into the realm of
P. L. 2, 211. and perhaps, thus *f.* removed
P. L. 2, 321. though thus *f.* removed, under the
P. L. 2, 519. hollow abyss heard *f.* and wide
P. L. 2, 582. *f.* off from these, a shout and silent
P. L. 2, 791. and, swifter *f.*, me overtook, his
P. L. 2, 1003. your dungeon, stretching *f.* and

P. L. 2, 1007. your walk, you have not *f.*
P. L. 2, 1036. shoots *f.* into the bosom of dim
P. L. 2, 1047. *f.* off the empyreal heaven
P. L. 3, 88. not *f.* off heaven, in the precincts
P. L. 3, 153. that be from thee *f.*
P. L. 3, 154. that *f.* be from thee, father
P. L. 3, 422. a globe *f.* off it seemed, now seems
P. L. 3, 428. though distant *f.* some small
P. L. 3, 476. strayed so *f.* to seek in Golgotha
P. L. 3, 494. the backside of the world *f.* off
P. L. 3, 501. *f.* distant he descries, ascending
P. L. 3, 504. at top whereof, but *f.* more rich
P. L. 3, 529. wider by *f.* than that of after-times
P. L. 3, 559. that bears Andromeda *f.* off
P. L. 3, 579. dispenses light from *f.*,
P. L. 3, 609. sun, so *f.* from us remote
P. L. 3, 614. *f.* and wide-his eye commands
P. L. 3, 621. his visual ray to objects distant *f.*
P. L. 4, 14. though bold *f.* off and fearless
P. L. 4, 103. therefore as *f.* from granting
P. L. 4, 288. of *f.* nobler shape, erect, and tall
P. L. 4, 446. who enjoy so *f.* the happier lot
P. L. 4, 453. not distant *f.* from thence
P. L. 4, 545. up to the clouds conspicuous *f.*
P. L. 4, 579. see *f.* and wide
P. L. 4, 758. *f.* be it that I should write thee
P. L. 5, 213. reached too *f.* their pampered
P. L. 5. 457. he saw transcend his own so *f.*
P. L. 5, 458. whose high power so *f.* exceeded
P. L. 5, 744. Satan with his powers *f.* was
P. L. 5, 757. high on a hill, *f.* blazing, as a mount
P. L. 5, 803. thus *f.* his bold discourse without
P. L. 5, 828. how *f.* from thought to make us
P. L. 6, 79. *f.* in the horizon to the north
P. L. 6, 295. I fly not, but have sought thee *f.*
P. L. 6, 342. so *f.* beneath his confidence
P. L. 6, 398. *f.* otherwise the inviolable saints
P. L. 6, 415. *f.* in the dark dislodged, and, void
P. L. 6. 487. send forth from *f.*, with thundering
P. L. 6, 551. not distant *f.* with heavy pace
P. L. 6, 700. and thus *f.* have suffered, that the
P. L. 6, 743. and from the impure *f.* separate
P. L. 6, 768. he onward came; *f.* off his coming
P. L. 6, 773. illustrious *f.* and wide
P. L. 7, 32. drive *f.* off the barbarous dissonance
P. L. 7, 71. *f.* differing from this world
P. L. 7, 145. yet *f.* the greater part have kept
P. L. 7, 220. *f.* into Chaos and the world unborn
P. L. 7, 230. thus *f.* extend, thus *f.* thy bounds
P. L. 7, 272. and the loud misrule of Chaos *f.*
P. L. 7, 359. by *f.* the greater part he took
P. L. 7, 369. so *f.* remote, with diminution
P. L. 7, 618. from heaven-gate not *f.*
P. L. 8, 102. and his line stretched out so *f.*
P. L. 8, 120. placed heaven from earth so *f.*
P. L. 8, 156. so *f.* down to this habitable
P. L. 8, 177. contented that thus *f.* hath been
P. L. 8, 185. God hath bid dwell *f.* off all
P. L. 8, 231. *f.* on excursion toward the gates of
P. L. 8, 359. surpassest *f.* my naming
P. L. 8, 437. thus *f.* to try thee, Adam, I was
P. L. 8, 481. out of hope, behold her, not *f.* off
P. L. 8, 529. but here *f.* otherwise, transported
P. L. 8, 598. higher of the genial bed by *f.*
P. L. 8, 79. downward as *f.* antarctic
P. L. 9, 433. from her best prop so *f.*
P. L. 9, 482. for I view *f.* round
P. L. 9, 576. a goodly tree *f.* distant to behold
P. L. 9, 617. grows the tree? from hence how *f.*
P. L. 9, 642. and lost, from succour *f.*
P. L. 9, 772. friendly to man, *f.* from deceit
P. L. 10, 104. joy to meet my coming seen *f.* off
P. L. 10, 150. whose perfection *f.* excelled
P. L. 10, 211. that day, removed *f.* off
P. L. 10, 233. belching outrageous flame *f.* into
P. L. 10, 281. sagacious of his quarry from so *f.*
P. L. 10, 370. us empowered to fortify thus *f.*
P. L. 10, 423. the rest were all *f.* to the inland
P. L. 10, 593. not better *f.* than still at hell's
P. L. 10, 686. and south as *f.* beneath Magellan

P. L. 10,1077. sends a comfortable heat from *f.*
P. L. 11, 121. all approach *f.* off to fright
P. L. 11, 171. *f.* other name deserving
P. L. 11, 333. and *f.* off his steps adore
P. L. 11, 727. and removed his tents *f.* off
P. L. 11, 783. I was *f.* deceived, for now I see
P. L. 12, 45. lest *f.* dispersed in foreign lands
P. L. 12, 587. a paradise within thee, happier *f.*
P. R. 1, 191. converse with solitude, till, *f.* from
P. R. 1, 322. so *f.* from path or road of men
P. R. 1, 332. town or village nigh (nighest is *f.*)
P. R. 1, 340. and to drink go *f.*
P. R. 2, 49. but let us wait; thus *f.*, He hath
P. R. 3, 72. to subdue by conquest *f.* and wide
P. R. 3, 272. as *f.* as Indus east, Euphrates
P. R. 3, 303. see, though from *f.*, his thousands
P. R. 4, 7. this *f.* his overmatch, who
P. R. 4, 46. so *f.* renowned, and with the spoils
P. R. 4, 53. gilded battlements, conspicuous *f.*
P. R. 4, 87. shared among petty kings too *f.*
P. R. 4, 122. thou show'st from nations *f.*
P. R. 4, 346. will *f.* be found unworthy
P. R. 4, 547. *f.* off appearing like a mount
S. A. 341. that invincible Samson, *f.* renowned
S. A. 755. how *f.* urged his patience bears
S. A. 1038. *f.* within defensive arms
S. A. 1467. a third more generous *f.* and civil
C. 193. engaged their wandering steps too *f.*
C. 388. *f.* from the cheerful haunt of men
C. 456. driving *f.* off each thing of sin and guilt
C. 481. some *f.*-off halloa break the silent air
C. 668. from these gates sorrow flies *f.*
C. 824. there is a gentle nymph not *f.* from hence
L. 155. wash *f.* away, where'er thy bones
Il P. 74. I hear the *f.*-off curfew sound
Il P. 81. *f.* from all resort of mirth
H. 22. see how from *f.* upon the eastern road
H. 170. not half so *f.* casts his usurped sway
D. F. I. 17. till thee he spied from *f.*
V.Ex.70. that *f.* events full-wisely could presage
S. 12, 13. but from that mark how *f.* they rove
**Far-beaming.**—H. 9. and that *f-b.* blaze of
**Fare.**—P. L. 5, 495. diet, nor too light *f.*
P. L. 9, 1028. after such delicious *f.* ·
P. L. 10, 735. ill *f.* our ancestor impure
P. R. 2, 202. full of honour, wealth, high *f.*
**Fares.**—P. L. 2, 940. on he *f.*, treading the
P. L. 4, 131. so on he *f.*, and to the border
P. R. 3, 443. so *f.* it when with truth falsehood
**Farewell.**—P. L. 1, 249. *f.*, happy fields, where
P. L. 2, 492. if chance the radiant sun with *f.*
P. L. 4, 108. *f.*, hope; and with hope, *f.* fear
P. L. 4, 109. *f.* remorse! all good to me is lost
S. A. 959. gold of matrimonial treason; so *f.*
S. A. 1413. brethren, *f.*; your company along
**Far-fet.**—P. R. 2, 401. earned the *f-f.* spoil
**Farms.**—P. L. 9, 448. pleasant villages and *f.*
**Farthest.**—P. L. 1, 247. *f.* from him is best
P. L. 2, 1038. nature first begins her *f.* verge
P. L. 4, 892. *f.* from pain, where thou mightst
P. L. 11, 401. of Congo, and Angola *f.* south
P. R. 3, 397. time for thee were better *f.* off
P. R. 4, 69. some from *f.* south, Syene
C. 227. such noise as I can make to be heard *f.*
**Fashion.**—C. 360. cast the *f.* of uncertain evils
**Fashioned.**—P. L. 8, 469. *f.* with his hands
**Fast.**—P. L. 1, 12. *f.* by the oracle of God
P. L. 2, 675. moving onward came as *f.*
P. L. 2, 725. that sat *f.* by hell gate, and kept
P. L. 2, 754. flames thick and *f.* threw forth
P. L. 2, 1051. and *f.* by, hanging in a golden
P. L. 3, 354. once in paradise, *f.* by the tree
P. L. 4, 171. post to Egypt, there *f.* bound
P. L. 4, 190. barred and bolted *f.*, fear no assault
P. L. 4, 221. the tree of knowledge grew *f.*
P. L. 4, 796. seize *f.*, and hither bring
P. L. 6, 5. within the mount of God, *f.* by his
P. L. 6, 543. gripe *f.* his orbed shield
P. L. 6, 870. and too *f.* had bound
P. L. 8, 240. *f.* we found, *f.* shut, the dismal
P. L. 8, 640. stand *f.*! to stand or fall free

P. L. 9, 182. him *f.* sleeping soon he found
P. L. 9, 628. *f.* by a fountain, one small thicket
P. L. 10, 319. they made all *f.*, too *f.* they made
P. L. 10, 333. slunk into the wood *f.* by
P. L. 10, 542. spear and shield, down they as *f.*
P. L. 11, 587. till in the amorous net *f.* caught
P. L. 11, 737. and God made *f.* the door
P. L. 11, 851. *f.* on the top of some high
P. L. 12, 631. and gathers ground *f.* at the
P. L. 12, 639. down the cliff as *f.* to the
P. R. 2, 247. that *f.* to virtue I impute not
P. R. 4, 480. of Israel's sceptre get *f.* hold
S. A. 1432. the angel of thy birth, to stand *f.*
S.A. 1637. and eyes *f.* fixed, he stood as one who
C. 816. snatched his wand and bound him *f.*
Il P. 44. thou fix them on the earth as *f.*
Il P. 46. spare *f.*, that oft with gods doth diet
P. 21. *f.* by his brethren's side
**Fastened.**—P. L. 10, 300. they *f.*, and the mole
S. A. 1398. thou wert firmlier *f.* than a rock
**Fasting.**—P. R. 2, 243. after forty days' *f.*
P. R. 2, 284. *f.* he went to sleep, and *f.* waked
**Fat.**—P. L. 11, 439. the inwards and their *f.*
P. L. 11, 648. from a *f.* meadow-ground
S. A. 1671. and *f.* regorged of bulls and goats
**Fatal.**—P. L. 2, 104. inaccessible, his *f.* throne
P. L. 2, 712. their *f.* hands no second stroke
P. L. 2, 725. and kept the *f.* key
P. L. 2, 786. brandishing his *f.* dart made
P. L. 2, 871. from her side the *f.* key
P. L. 4, 349. and of his *f.* guile gave proof
P. L. 4, 514. one *f.* tree there stands
P. L. 5, 861. when *f.* course had circled
P. L. 9, 889. the *f.* trespass done by Eve
P. L. 10, 4. to taste the *f.* fruit
P. L. 10, 191. even he who now foretold his *f.*
P. L. 10, 364. such *f.* consequence unites us
P. L. 12, 99. but justice and some *f.* curse
P. R. 1, 53. attending when that *f.* wound
P. R. 1, 441. and run not sooner to his *f.* snare
P. R. 4, 205. coming is foretold to me most *f.*
P. R. 4, 525. thou art to be my *f.* enemy
S. A. 1024. had shorn the *f.* harvest of thy head
L. 100. it was that *f.* and perfidious bark
S. 10, 7. victory at Chæronea, *f.* to liberty
D. F. I. 14. and then bewailed his *f.* bliss
**Fate.**—P. L. 1, 116. since, by *f.*, the strength
P. L. 1,133. upheld by strength, or chance, or *f.*
P. L. 1, 448. Syrian damsels to lament his *f.*
P. L. 2, 17. themselves to fear no second *f.*
P. L. 2, 197. since *f.* inevitable subdues us
P. L. 2, 232. when everlasting *f.* shall yield
P. L. 2, 393. lift us up, in spite of *f.*, nearer our
P. L. 2, 550. and complain that *f.* free virtue
P. L. 2, 559. foreknowledge, will, and *f.*
P. L. 2, 560. fixed *f.*, free will, foreknowledge
P. L. 2, 610. but *f.* withstands, and to oppose
P. L. 2, 809. *F.* pronounced, but thou, O father
P. L. 3, 33. other two equalled with me in *f.*
P. L. 3, 113. or their making, or their *f.*
P. L. 3, 120. least impulse, or shadow of *f.*
P. L. 5, 527. not overruled by *f.* inextricable
P. L. 6, 869. but strict *f.* had cast too deep
P. L. 7, 173. and what I will is *f.*
P. L. 9, 689. have attained than *f.* meant me
P. L. 9, 885. when *f.* will not permit
P. L. 9, 927. not God omnipotent, nor *f.*! yet so
P. L. 10, 265. go whither *f.* and inclination
P. L. 10, 480. uproar protesting *f.* supreme
P. L. 11, 181. but *f.* subscribed not
P. R. 4, 265. of *f.*, and chance, and change
P. R. 4, 317. under usual names, fortune and *f.*
P. R. 4, 383. or heaven write aught of *f.*
P. R. 4, 470. wilt prolong all to the push of *f.*
A. 67. on which the *f.* of gods and men is
H. 149. but wisest *F.* says No
M. W. 13. nature and *f.* had had no strife
D. F. I. 22. yet art thou not inglorious in thy *f.*
U. C. II. 30. in course reciprocal, and had his *f.*
**Father.**—P. L. 2, 727. O *f.*, what intends thy

P. L. 2, 730. mortal dart against thy *f.'s* head
P. L. 2, 743. thou call'st me *f.*, that phantasm
P. L. 2, 810. but thou, O *f.*, I forewarn thee
P. L. 2, 864. thou art my *f.*, thou my author
P. L. 3, 56. the Almighty *F.* from above
P. L. 3, 139. all his *F.* shone substantially
P. L. 3, 143. thus he to his *F.* spake
P. L. 3, 144. O *F.*, gracious was that word
P. L. 3, 154. *F.*, who art judge of all things
P. L. 3, 227. *F.*, thy word is passed, man shall
P. L. 3, 262. and return, *F.*. to see thy face
P. L. 3, 271. he attends the will of his great *F.*
P. L. 3, 372. thee, *F.*, first they sung
P. L. 3, 386. the Almighty *F.* shines
P. L. 3, 393. that day thy *F.'s* dreadful thunder
P. L. 3, 398. son of thy *F.'s* might
P. L. 3, 401. *F.* of mercy and grace, thou didst
P. L. 4, 495. leaned on our first *f.*
P. L. 4, 757. the charities of *f.*, son, and brother
P. L. 5, 246. spake the eternal *F.*, and fulfilled
P. L. 5, 403. that one celestial *F.* gives to all
P. L. 5, 596. the *F.* infinite, by whom in bliss
P. L. 5, 663. that day honoured by his great *F.*
P. L. 5, 735. mighty *F.!* thou thy foes justly
P. L. 5, 836. by his word, the mighty *F.* made
P. L. 5, 847. incensed *F.* and the incensed Son
P. L. 5, 855. task transferred from *F.* to his Son
P. L. 6, 96. hymning the eternal *F.*
P. L. 6, 671. had not the Almighty *F.*, where he
P. L. 6, 710. thou mightiest, in thy *F.'s* might
P. L. 6, 720. he all his *F.* full expressed
P. L. 6, 723. O *F.*, O supreme of heavenly
P. L. 6, 814. because the *F.*, to whom in heaven
P. L. 6, 890. courts and temple of his mighty *F.*
P. L. 7, 11. presence of the Almighty *F.*
P. L. 7, 137. eternal *F.* from his throne beheld
P. L. 7, 196. and all his *F.* in him shone
P. L. 7, 517. the omnipotent eternal *F.*
P. L. 7, 588. sat him down with his great *F.*
P. L. 8, 298. ordained first *F.*
P. L. 8, 498. for this cause he shall forgo *f.*
P. L. 10, 32. eternal *F.*, from his secret cloud
P. L. 10, 63. so spake the *F.*; and unfolding
P. L. 10, 66. he full resplendent all his *F.*
P. L. 10, 68. *F.* eternal, thine is to decree
P. L. 10, 216. so now as *f.* of his family
P. L. 10, 223. covered from his *F.'s* sight
P. L. 10, 1097. so spake our *f.* penitent
P. L. 11, 20. in sight before the *F.'s* throne
P. L. 11, 22. see, *F.*, what first-fruits on earth
P. L. 11, 45. to whom the *F.*, without cloud
P. L. 11, 760. as when a *f.* mourns his children
P. L. 12, 103. who, for the shame done to his *f.*
P. L. 12, 121. from his *f.'s* house, his kindred
P. L. 12, 487. the promise of the *F.*, who shall
P. L. 12, 546. to be revealed in glory of the *F.*
P. R. 1, 31. while the *F.'s* voice from heaven
P. R. 1, 93. the glimpses of his *F.'s* glory shine
P. R. 1, 168. so spake the eternal *F.*
P. R. 1, 176. the *F.* knows the Son
P. R. 1, 236. *F.* is the eternal king who rules
P. R. 1, 283. last, the sum of all, my *F.'s* voice
P. R. 1, 486. thy *F.*, who is holy, wise, and pure
P. R. 2, 85. from heaven by his *F.'s* voice
P. R. 2, 99. but went about his *F.'s* business
P. R. 2, 259. hungering more to do my *f.'s* will
P. R. 2, 414. a carpenter thy *f.* known
P. R. 3, 110. least resembling thy great *F.*
P. R. 3, 153. to sit upon thy *f.* David's throne
P. R. 3, 154. by mother's side thy *f.*
P. R. 3, 175. zeal of thy *F.'s* house
P. R. 3, 186. the *F.* in his purpose hath decreed
P. R. 3, 219. stand between me and thy *F.'s* ire
P. R. 3, 282. Judah and all thy *f* David's house
P. R. 3, 353. endeavour, as thy *f.* David did
P. R. 4, 552. I to thy *F.'s* house have brought
P. R. 4, 596. true image of the *F.*
P. R. 4, 603. the attempter of thy *F.'s* throne
S. A. 355. who would be now a *f.* in my stead
S. A. 373. appoint not heavenly disposition, *f.*
S. A. 447. have befallen thee and thy *f.'s* house

S. A. 448. *f.*, I do acknowledge and confess
S. A. 487. spare that proposal, *f.*, spare the
S. A. 602. must not omit a *f.'s* timely care
S. A. 1248. fame divulge him *f.* of five sons
S. A. 1432. from thy *f.'s* field rode up in flames
S. A. 1459. supplication prone and *f.'s* tears
S. A. 1506. agreeable to a *f.'s* love
S. A. 1717. to himself and *f.'s* house, eternal fame
S. A. 1733. home to his *f.'s* house
C. 35. are coming to attend their *f.'s* state
C. 57. much like his *f.*, but his mother more
C. 493. O brother, 'tis my *f.'s* shepherd, sure
C. 828. that had the sceptre from his *f.* Brute
C. 947. is your *f.'s* residence, where this night
Il P. 2. the brood of folly without *f.* bred
S. 10, 10. wherein your *f.'s* house, yet by you
S. 20, 1. Lawrence, of virtuous *f.* virtuous son
H. 7. and with his *f.* work us a perpetual peace
**Fatherly.**—P. L. 12, 63. Adam, *f.* displeased
**Fathers.**—P. R. 1, 351. who fed our *f.* here
P. R. 2, 33. so long expected of our *f.*
P. R. 3, 379. their *f.* in the land of Egypt
P. R. 3, 429. to the promised land their *f.*
S. A. 667. God of our *f.!* what is man
S. A. 1485. *f.* are wont to lay up for their sons
S. 18, 4. all our *f.* worshipped stocks and stones
**Fathom.**—P. L. 2, 934. ten thousand *f.* deep
**Fault.**—P. L. 1, 609. spirits for his *f.* amerced
P. L. 3, 96. Whose *f.*?
P. L. 3, 118. no influence on their *f.*
P. L. 10, 823. all mankind, for one man's *f.*
P. L. 10, 938. till peace obtained from *f.*
S. A. 241. that *f.* I take not on me, but transfer
S. A. 431. enough and more, the burden of that *f.*
S. A. 502. be penitent, and for thy *f.* contrite
**Faults.**—P. L. 10, 1089. confess humbly our *f.*
P. L. 10, 1101. both confessed humbly their *f.*
P. L. 12, 337. whose foul idolatries and other *f.*
S. A. 777. both common female *f.*
**Faulty.**—P. L. 11, 509. erect, though *f.* since
**Faun.**—P. R. 2, 191. or *F.*, or Sylvan
**Fauns.**—L. 34. and *F.* with cloven heel
**Faunus.**—P. L. 4, 708. nor nymph nor *F.*
**Favonius.**—S. 20, 6. till *F.* reinspire the frozen
**Favour.**—P. L. 1, 654. should *f.* equal to the
P. L. 3, 664. man, his chief delight and *f.*
P. L. 5, 462. thy *f.* in this honour done to man
P. L. 5, 661. in power, in *f.*, and pre-eminence
P. L. 7, 72. divine interpreter, by *f.* sent
P. L. 8, 202. by sufferance, and thy wonted *f.*
P. L. 9, 334. find peace within, *f.* from heaven
P. L. 10, 1096. what else but *f.*, grace
P. L. 11, 153. that I was heard with *f.*
P. L. 12, 278. *f.* unmerited by me, who sought
P. L. 12, 622. such *f.* I unworthy am
P. R. 2, 430. they whom I *f.* thrive in wealth
S. A. 273. God hath of His special *f.* raised
S. A. 1357. *f.* renewed, and add a greater sin
S. A. 1412. to *f.*, and perhaps to set thee free
C. 184. under the spreading *f.* of these pines
L. 20. with lucky words *f.* my destined urn
**Favourable.**—P. L. 5, 507. O *f.* spirit
P. L. 11, 169. next *f.* thou, who highly thus to
S. A. 921. will intercede, not doubting their *f.* ear
**Favoured.**—P. L. 1, 30. *f.* of heaven so highly
P. L. 2, 350. but *f.* more of him who rules above
P. R. 2, 68. hail, highly *f.*, among women blest
P. R. 2, 91. this is my *f.* lot, my exaltation
S. A. 1046. *f.* of heaven, who finds one virtuous
C. 78. when any *f.* of high Jove
**Favouring.**—S. A. 1720. but *f.* and assisting
**Favourite.**—P. L. 9, 175. new *f.* of heaven
P. R. 4, 95. to a wicked *f.* all public cares
**Favours.**—P. L. 9, 949. whom God most *f.*
S. A. 685. with no regard of highest *f.* past
**Fawned.**—P. L. 4, 959. *f.*, and cringed
**Fawning.**—P. L. 9, 526. *f.*, and licked the ground
P. R. 1, 452. or like a *f.* parasite, obey'st
**Fawns.**—P. L. 4, 404. two gentle *f.* at play
**Fays.**—H. 235. and the yellow-skirted *f.*
**Fealty.**—P. L. 3, 204. breaks his *f.*, and sins

I

P. L. 8, 344. pay thee *f.* with low subjection
P. L. 9, 262. to withdraw our *f.* from God
**Fear.**—P. L. 1, 558. anguish and doubt and *f.*
P. L. 1, 598. and with *f.* of change perplexes
P. L. 1, 788. at once with joy and *f.* his heart
P. L. 2, 17. trust themselves to *f.* no second fate
P. L. 2, 49. with that care lost went all his *f.*
P. L. 2, 85. if there be in hell *f.* to be worse
P. L. 2, 94. what *f.* we then? what doubt
P. L. 2, 205. *f.* what yet they know must follow
P. L. 2, 293. so much the *f.* of thunder
P. L. 2, 343. whose high walls *f.* no assault
P. L. 2, 627. yet have feigned, or *f.* conceived
P. L. 2, 783. that with *f.* and pain distorted
P. L. 4, 108. and with hope farewell *f.*
P. L. 4, 190. and bolted fast, *f.* no assault
P. L. 4, 574. I. *f.* hath ventured from the deep
P. L. 4, 822. yet thus, unmoved with *f.*, accost
P. L. 4, 854. thy *f.*, said Zephon bold, will save
P. L. 5, 98. uncouth dream, of evil sprung I *f.*
P. L. 5, 396. no *f.* lest dinner cool
P. L. 6, 238. unbecoming deed that argued *f.*
P. L. 6, 393. or with pale *f.* surprised
P. L. 6, 394. then first with *f* surprised
P. L. 6, 397. till that hour not liable to *f.*
P. L. 6, 490. they shall *f.* we have disarmed
P. L. 6, 494. abandon *f.*
P. L. 6, 539. this day; *f.* not his flight
P. L. 6, 912. remember! and *f.* to transgress
P. L. 8, 168. to God above; him serve and *f.*
P. L. 8, 322. *f.* here no dearth
P. L. 9, 285. his fraud is then thy *f.*
P. L. 9, 286. thy equal *f.* that my firm faith
P. L. 9, 326. how are we happy, still in *f.*
P. L. 9, 702. *f.* itself of death removes the *f.*
P. L. 9, 773. *f.* I then? rather, what know to *f.*
P. L. 9, 989. *f.* of death deliver to the winds
P. L. 10, 409. of hell no detriment need *f.*.
P. L. 10, 780. no *f.* of worse to me and to my
P. L. 10, 813. that *f.* comes thundering back
P. L. 10, 1000. at once to free from what we *f*
P. L. 10, 1024. much more I *f.* lest death
P. L. 10, 1082. not *f.* to pass commodiously
P. L. 11, 139. joy, but with *f.* yet linked
P. L. 11, 212. and carnal *f.* that day dimmed
P. L. 11, 234. yet not terrible that I should *f.*
P. L. 11, 361. and to temper joy with *f.*
P. L. 11, 799. all virtue lose and *f.* of God
P. L. 12, 218. and *f.* return them back to Egypt
P. L. 12, 305. from servile *f.* to filial
P. L. 12, 562. to obey is best, and love with *f.*
P. R. 1, 66. his birth to our just *f.* gave no
P. R. 1, 69. highest, greatest, multiplies my *f.*
P. R. 1, 223. persuasion do the work of *f.*
P. R. 1, 422. impute to obedience what thy *f.*
P. R. 1, 451. thou, with trembling *f.*, or like
P. R. 2, 47. and behind them cast all *f.* of thee
P. R. 2, 257. and from the sting of famine *f.*
P. R. 3, 206. where no hope is left, is left no *f.*
P. R. 3, 385. and Rome or Cæsar not need *f.*
P. R. 4, 189. wert thou so void of *f.* or shame
P. R. 4, 195. to whom the fiend, with *f.* abashed
P. R. 4, 454. these flaws, though mortals *f.*
P. R. 4, 617. of tempter and temptation without *f.*
S. A. 740. conjugal affection prevailing over *f.*
S. A. 1065. nor *f.* the bait of honied words
S. A. 1234. nothing from thy hand *f.* I incurable
S. A. 1250. he will directly to the lords, I *f.*
S. A. 1374. venturing to displease God for the *f.*
S. A. 1526. other hands we need not much to *f.*
C. 328. cannot be that I should *f.* to change it
C. 364. or, if they be but false alarms of *f.*
C. 405. I *f.* the dread events that dog them both
C. 410. yet were an equal poise of hope and *f.*
C. 412. that I incline to hope rather than *f.*
C. 565. I stood, harrowed with grief and *f.*
C. 800. she fables not, I feel that I do *f.*
Il P. 30. whilst yet there was no *f.* of Jove
V. Ex. 67. something that doth force my *f.*
**Feared.**—P. L. 1, 628. could have *f.* how such
P. L. 2, 82. ascent is easy. then; the event is *f.*

P. L. 2, 470. to be refused, what erst they *f.*
P. L. 2, 678. might be admired; admired not *f.*
P. L. 5, 135. pious awe, that *f.* to have offended
P. L. 5, 905. nor of violence *f.* aught
P. L. 9, 331. wherefore shunned or *f.* by us
P. L. 9, 511. sought access but *f.* to interrupt
P. L. 9, 536. nor have *f.* thy awful brow more
P. L. 9, 701. not God; not *f.* then, nor obeyed
P. L. 9, 1006. to iterate her former trespass *f.*
P. L. 10, 51. because not yet inflicted, as he *f.*
P. L. 10, 119. oft hast heard, and hast not *f.*
P. R. 4, 488. I never *f.* they could
S. A. 794. *f.* lest one day thou wouldst leave me
S. A. 900. to be pleased, obeyed, or *f.*
S. A. 939. when all men loved, honoured, *f.* me
S. A. 1719. God not parted from him, as was *f.*
C. 446. gods and men *f.* her stern frown
**Fearest.**—P. L. 9, 282. his violence thou *f.*
P. L. 10, 838. what thou desirest, and what thou *f.*
**Fearing.**—P. L. 10, 340. *f.* guilty what his wrath
P. L. 12, 15. *f.* the Deity
P. R. 4, 304. as *f.* God nor man
**Fearless.**—P. L. 1, 131. in dreadful deeds *f.*
P. L. 2, 855. *f.* to be o'ermatched by living
P. L. 4, 14. though bold far off and *f.*
P. L. 5, 875. the flaming Seraph *f.*
P. L. 6, 51. with fire and hostile arms *f.* assault
P. L. 6, 804. *f.* in his righteous cause
P. L. 9, 57. *f.* returned
P. L. 9, 187. *f.*, unfeared, he slept
P. L. 11, 811. *f.* of reproach and scorn
S. A. 529. *f.* of danger, like a petty god
S. A. 810. *f.* at home of partners in my love
**Fears.**—P. L. 1, 275. of hope in *f.* and dangers
P. L. 1, 530. and dispelled their *f.*
P. L. 10, 842. conscience! into what abyss of *f.*
P. L. 10, 1003. we longer shivering under *f.*
P. R. 1, 110. for long indulgence to their *f.*
P. R. 2, 53. and all our *f.* lay on his Providence
P. R. 2, 64. motherly cares and *f.* got head
P. R. 2, 70. and *f.* as eminent above the lot of
P. R. 2, 467. rules passions, desires, and *f.*
S. A. 805. while I at home sat full of cares and *f.*
S. A. 1469. their foe to misery beneath their *f.*
C. 355. her unpillowed head, fraught with sad *f.*
C. 511. ay me unhappy! then my *f.* are true
C. 512. what *f.*, good Thyrsis?
H. 45. but he, her *f.* to cease
F. of C. 18. and succour our just *f.*
V. Ex. 27. that so they may without suspect or *f.*
**Feast.**—P. L. 6, 167. trained up in *f.* and song
P. L. 9, 37. then marshalled *f.* served up in hall
P. L. 11, 592. with *f.* and music all the tents
P. L. 11, 715. to luxury and riot, *f.*, and dance
P. L. 12, 21. wine-offerings poured, and sacred *f.*
P. R. 1, 210. at our great *f.* I went into the
P. R. 4, 637. sung victor, and, from heavenly *f.*
S. A. 12. this day a solemn *f.* the people hold
S. A. 434. this day the Philistines a popular *f.*
S. A. 1194. and in your city held my nuptial *f.*
S. A. 1311. this day to Dagon is a solemn *f.*
S. A. 1315. to honour this great *f.* and great
S. A. 1448. play before them at their *f.*
S. A. 1612. the *f.* and noon grew high
C. 102. meanwhile welcome joy and *f.*
C. 479. a perpetual *f.* of nectared sweets
C. 777. looks to heaven amidst his gorgeous *f.*
L. 117. than how to scramble at the shearers' *f.*
L'A. 127. pomp, and *f.*, and revelry
S. 20, 9. what neat repast shall *f.* us
M. W. 18. the god that sits at marriage *f.*
V. Ex. 49. in solemn songs at king Alcinous' *f.*
**Feastful.**—S. A. 1741. also shall on *f.* days
S. 9, 12. when the bridegroom with his *f.* friends
**Feasts.**—P. L. 1, 390. and solemn *f.* profaned
P. L. 5, 467. at heaven's high *f.* to have fed
P. R. 4, 114. gluttonies and gorgeous *f.*
C. 746. in courts, at *f.*, and high solemnities
**Feat.**—L'A. 101. with stories told of many a *f.*
**Feathered.**—P. L. 5, 284. with *f.* mail

P. L. 7, 420. but *f.* soon and fledge they
P. L. 9, 1117. so girt with *f.* cincture
**Feathers.**—C. 378. she plumes her *f.* and lets
**Feathery.**—C.347.night watches to his *f.*dames
**Feats.**—P. L. 2,537. with *f.* of arms from either
  S. A. 1083. prodigious might and *f.* performed
  S. A. 1278. he all their ammunition and *f.* of war
  S. A.1340. to show them *f.* and play before their
  S.A.1602. of his mighty strength in *f.* and games
**Feature.**—P. L. 10, 279. so scented the grim *f.*
**Features.**—C. 748. it is for homely *f.* to keep
**Fed.**—P. L. 1, 68. *f.* with ever-burning sulphur
P. L. 1, 728. blazing cressets, *f.* with naphtha
P. L. 2, 843. there ye shall be *f.* and filled
P. L. 3, 435. on hills where flocks are *f.*
P. L. 4, 240. *f.* flowers worthy of Paradise
P. L. 5, 415. needs to be sustained and *f.*
P. L. 5, 467. at Heaven's high feasts to have *f.*
P. L. 8, 256. and on the reeking moisture *f.*
P. R. 1, 350. who *f.* our fathers here with manna
P. R. 2. 110. sole but with holiest meditations *f.*
P. R. 2,258. nor mind it, *f.* with better thoughts
P. R. 2, 313. was *f.* twice by a voice inviting
P. R. 4, 593. and, as he *f.*, angelic choirs sung
L. 24. *f.* the same flock by fountain, shade
L. 125. the hungry sheep look up and are not *f.*
**Fee.**—S. 10, 3. unstained with gold or *f.*
  S. 12, 7. which after held the sun and moon in *f.*
**Feeble.**—S. A. 455. and doubt in *f.* hearts
  C. 1022. or, if virtue *f.* were, heaven itself would
  P. 45. and here though grief my *f.* hands up lock
**Feed.**—P. L. 2, 863. that on my bowels *f.*
P. L. 3, 37. then *f.* on thoughts that voluntary
P. L. 5, 417. earth and the sea *f.* air
P. L. 9, 597. at *f.* or fountain never had I found
P. L. 9, 779. to reach and *f.* àt once both
P. L. 10, 604. herbs and fruits and flowers *f.*
P. R. 2, 258. fed with better thoughts, that *f.*
P. R. 2, 421. longer than thou canst *f.* them
S. A. 1562. *f.* on that first; there may in grief be
  C. 721. should in a pet of temperance *f.*
**Feeder.**—C. 779. crams, and blasphemes his *f.*
**Feeds.**—P. L. 5, 416. the grosser *f.* the purer
P. L. 7, 490. *f.* her husband drone deliciously
**Feel.**—P. L. 1, 153. *f.* strength undiminished
P. L. 1, 336. or the fierce pains not *f.*
P. L. 2, 101. and by proof we *f.* our power
P. L. 2,216. inured, not *f.*: or changed at length
P. L. 2, 340. what we most in suffering *f.*
P. L. 2, 598. *f.* by turns the bitter change
P. L. 3, 22. and *f.* thy sovran vital lamp
P. L. 4, 972. heavier load thyself expect to *f.*
P. L. 5, 892. for soon expect to *f.* his thunder
P. L. 6, 157. who, while they *f.* vigour divine
P. L. 8, 282. and *f.* that I am happier than I
P. L. 8, 608. what inward thence I *f.*
P. L. 9, 120. so much more I *f.* torment within
P. L. 9, 315. not thou like sense within thee *f.*
P. L. 9, 680. now I *f.* thy power within me
P. L. 9, 913. no, no! I *f.* the link of nature
P. L. 9, 955. I *f.* the bond of nature
P. L. 9, 983. but I *f.* far otherwise the event
P. L. 9, 1009. mirth, and fancy that they *f.*
P. L. 10, 243. methinks I *f.* new strength
P. L. 10, 811. which I *f.* begun both in me
P. L. 11,465. horrid to think, how horrible to *f.*
P. L. 11, 775. in substance *f.* grievous to bear
P. R. 1, 198. what from within I *f.* myself
P. R. 1, 400. I *f.* by proof that fellowship
P. R. 2, 252. but now I *f.* I hunger
S. A. 9. but here I *f.* amends, the breath
S. A. 594. so much I *f.* my genial spirits droop
S. A. 603. unless he *f.* within some source
S. A. 1155. shalt see, or rather to thy sorrow *f.*
S. A. 1381. I begin to *f.* some rousing motions
C. 145. break off, break off! I *f.* the different
C. 800. she fables not. I *f.* that I do fear
**Feelest.**—P. L. 10, 951. thou *f.* as yet least
  P. R. 4, 621. proof, ere this thou *f.* thy wound
**Feeling.**—P. L. 10, 733. but *f.* the evil
  P. R. 3, 208. torments me than the *f.* can

S. A. 96. and not, as *f.*, through all parts diffused
**Feels.**—H. 221. he *f.* from Judah's land
P. 38. my spirit some transporting cherub *f.*
**Feet.**—P. L. 1, 238. the sole of unblest *f.*
P. L. 2, 404. who shall tempt with wandering *f.*
P. L. 2, 949. head, hands, wings, or *f.*, pursues
P. L. 3, 31. that wash thy hallowed *f.*
P. L. 3, 73. with wearied wings and willing *f.*
P. L. 3, 486. heaven's ascent they lift their *f.*
P. L. 4, 183. and sheer within lights on his *f.*
P. L. 4, 866. I hear the tread of nimble *f.*
P. L. 5, 283. his *f.* shadowed from either heel
P. L. 6, 592. none on their *f.* might stand
P. L. 7, 440. rows her state with oary *f.*
P. L. 8, 261. and upright stood on my *f.*
P. L. 8, 315. in adoration at his *f.* I fell submiss
P. L. 10, 190. shall tread at last under our *f.*
P. L. 10, 215. when he washed his servants' *f.*
P. L. 10, 911. tresses all disordered, at his *f.* fell
P. L. 10, 942. now at his *f.* submissive
P. L. 11, 759. on thy *f.* thou stood'st at last
P. R. 3, 224. why move thy *f.* so slow
P. R. 3, 253. at whose verdant *f.* a spacious
P. R. 4, 621. trod down under his *f.*
S. A. 111. I hear the tread of many *f.*
S. A. 336. hither had informed your younger *f.*
S. A. 732. doubtful *f.* and wavering resolution
S. A. 931. to bring my *f.* again into the snare
S. A. 950. whose doors my *f.* shall never enter
C. 180. shall I inform my unacquainted *f.*
C. 310. the sure guess of well-practised *f.*
C. 887. by Thetis' tinsel-slippered *f.*
C. 897. thus I set my printless *f.*
Il P. 155. hath my due *f.* never fail
H. 25. and lay it lowly at his blessed *f.*
H. 146. with radiant *f.* the tissued clouds down
**Feign.**—P. R. 1, 474. say and unsay, *f.*, flatter
  S. A. 150. like whom the Gentiles *f.* to bear up
**Feigned.**—P. L. 2, 627. than fables yet have *f.*
  P. L. 3, 639. grace diffused, so well he *f.*
P. L. 4, 96. how soon unsay what *f.* submission
P. L. 4, 706. in shadier bower... though but *f.*
P. L. 5, 381. or the fairest goddess *f.*
P. L. 9, 31. fabled knights in battles *f.*
P. L. 9, 439. delicious than those gardens *f.*
P. L. 9, 492. under show of love well *f.*
P. L. 11, 799. from whom their piety *f.*
P. R. 2, 358. fairer than *f.* of old or fabled
S. A. 752. reconcilement move with *f.* remorse
S. A. 829. and much rather confess it *f.*
S. A. 872. in *f.* religion, smooth hypocrisy
S. A. 1116. without *f.* shifts, let be assigned
**Feignedst.**—S.A.1135. *f.* at thy birth was given
**Feigning.**—P. L. 12, 517. though *f.* still
  P. R. 4, 397. left him there *f.* to disappear
**Felicity.**—P. R. 4, 297. in virtue placed *f.*
  M. W. 68. through pangs fled to *f.*
**Fell.**—P. L. 1, 75. place from whence they *f.*
P. L. 1, 445. beguiled by fair idolatresses, *f.*
P. L. 1, 461. where he *f.* flat and shamed
P. L. 1, 491. more lewd *f.* not from heaven
P. L. 1, 586. with all his peerage *f.*
P. L. 1, 679. the least erected spirit that *f.*
P. L. 1, 740. and how he *f.* from heaven
P. L. 1, 743. from morn to noon he *f.* from noon
P. L. 1, 748. this rebellious rout *f.* long before
P. L. 2, 539. with vast Typhœan rage, more *f.*
P. L. 2, 771. down they *f.*. driven headlong
P. L. 2, 826. that in our just pretences armed, *f.*
P. L. 2, 1006. from whence your legions *f.*
P. L. 2, 1023. soon after, when man *f.*
P. L. 3, 102. stood who stood, and *f.* who *f.*
P. L. 3, 129. by their own suggestion *f.*
P. L. 4, 39. remembrance from what state I *f.*
P. L. 4, 64. *f.* not, but stand unshaken
P. L. 4, 230. thence united *f.* down the steep
P. L. 4, 331. to their supper-fruits they *f.*
P. L. 4, 905. Satan *f.*, whom folly overthrew
P. L. 5, 92. and *f.* asleep; but oh, how glad
P. L. 5, 133. he ere they *f.* kissed as the
P. L. 5, 434. they sat, and to their viands *f.*

P. L. 6, 190. but so swift with tempest *f.*
P. L. 6, 593. but down they *f.* by thousands
P. L. 6, 614. flew off, and into strange vagaries *f.*
P. L. 6, 844. tempestuous *f.* his arrows
P. L. 6, 871. nine days they *f.*
P. L. 6, 912. firm they might have stood, yet *f.*
P. L. 7, 134. *f.* with his flaming legions
P. L. 8, 315. in adoration at his feet I *f.*
P. L. 8, 458. sleep, which instantly *f.* on me
P. L. 10, 513. supplanted down he *f.*
P. L. 10, 539. horror on them *f.*
P. L. 10, 542. down *f.* both spear and shield
P. L. 10, 570. so oft they *f.* into the same
P. L. 10, 846. not now, as ere man *f.,* wholesome
P. L. 10, 906. wedlock-bound to a *f.* adversary
P. L. 10, 912. all disordered, at his feet *f.*
P. L. 10, 1099. prostrate *f.* before him reverent
P. L. 11, 446. he *f.,* and deadly pale groaned
P. L. 12, 614. wearied I *f.* asleep.
P. R. 1, 443. justly, since they *f.* idolatrous
P. R. 2, 134. Adam by his wife's allurement *f.*
P. R. 2, 150. the dissolutest spirit that *f.*
P. R. 3, 332. to lay hills plain, *f.* woods
P. R. 3, 415. *f.* off from God to worship calves
P. R. 4, 295. the next to fabling *f.* and smooth
P. R. 4, 311. and how man *f.*
P. R. 4, 415. and *f.* on the vexed wilderness
P. R. 4, 562. Satan smitten with amazement *f.*
P. R. 4, 568. in the air expired and *f.*
P. R. 4, 571. *f.* whence he stood to see
P. R. 4, 576. struck with dread and anguish, *f.*
P. R. 4, 581. so Satan *f.;* and straight a fiery
S. A. 144. a thousand foreskins *f.,* the flower
S. A. 532. into the snare I *f.* of fair looks
S. A. 1580. by him *f.,* thou say'st; by whom *f.* he.
S. A. 1582. unwounded of his enemies he *f.*
C. 50. on Circe's island *f.*
C. 53. downward *f.* into a grovelling swine
C. 259. *f.* Charybdis murmured soft applause
**Felled.**—P. L. 6, 250. and *f.* squadrons at once
P. L. 6, 575. in wood or mountain *f.*
S. A. 263. with a trivial weapon *f.* their
**Fellows.**—P. L. 1, 606. the *f.* of his crime
P. L. 2, 428. glory raised above his *f.*
P. L 6, 160. thou com'st before thy *f.*
C. 485. some roving robber calling to his *f.*
**Fellow-servant.**—P. L. 8, 225. of our *f.-s.*
**Fellowship.**—P. L. 8, 389. of *f.* I speak
P. L. 8. 442. whose *f.,* therefore unmeet for thee
P. R. 1, 401. that *f.* in pain divides not smart
**Fellowships.**—P. L. 11, 80. in *f.* of joy
**Felon.**—L. 91. and asked the *f.* winds
**Felonious.**—C. 196. but for some *f.* end
**Felt.**—P. L. 1, 227. that *f.* unusual weight
P. L. 2, 77. who but *f.* of late, when the fierce
P. L. 2, 543. *f.* the envenomed robe, and tore
P. L. 2, 780. prodigious motion *f.* and rueful
P. L. 4, 847. and *f.* how awful goodness is
P. L. 6, 872. confounded Chaos roared and *f.*
P. L. 8, 530. here passion first I *f.,* commotion
P. L. 9, 782. she eat; earth *f.* the wound
P. L. 9, 846. he the faltering measure *f.*
P. L. 9, 859. agony of love till now not *f.*
P. L. 10, 361. I *f.,* though distant from thee
P. L. 10, 511. his visage drawn he *f.* to sharp
P. L. 10, 541. for what they saw they *f.*
P. L. 10, 717. abandoned, but worse *f.* within
P. L. 10, 1098. nor Eve *f.* less remorse
P. R. 1, 89. first-begot we know, and sore have *f.*
P. R. 1, 308. nor tasted human food, nor hunger *f.*
S. A. 1006. without much inward passion *f.*
S. A. 1257. much more affliction than already *f.*
S. A. 1636. which when Samson *f.* in his arms
**Female.**—P. L. 7, 490. next appeared the *f.* bee
P. L. 7, 530. but thy consort *f.,*
P. L. 8, 150. communicating male and *f.* light
P. L. 9, 822. so to add what wants in *f.* sex
P. L. 9, 999. fondly overcome with *f.* charm
P. L. 10, 897. through *f.* snares
P. L. 11, 614. for that fair *f.* troop
P. R. 1, 151. I can produce a man of *f.* seed

P. R. 2, 219. her *f.* pride deject
S. A. 711. *f.* of sex it seems
S. A. 777. both common *f.* faults
S. A. 1055. despotic power over his *f.*
S. A. 1060. not swayed by *f.* usurpation
**Feminine.**—P. L. 1, 423. those male, these *f.*
P. L. 9, 458. angelic, but more soft and *f.*
P. L. 10, 893. with men, as angels, without *f.*
S. A. 403. with blandished parleys, *f.* assaults
**Fen.**—C. 433. by lake, or moorish *f.*
**Fence.**—P. L. 4, 187. leaps o'er the *f.* with ease
S. A. 937. to *f.* my ear against thy sorceries
C. 791. so well been taught her dazzling *f.*
**Fenced.**—P. L. 4, 372. your heaven ill *f.*
P. L. 4, 697. *f.* up the verdant wall
P. L. 9, 1119. thus *f.,* and as they thought
**Fenceless.**—P. L. 10, 303. now *f.* world
**Fennel.**—P. L. 9, 581. smell of sweetest *f.*
**Fens.**—P. L. 2, 621. rocks, caves, lakes, *f.,* bogs
P. L. 7, 417. the tepid caves and *f.*
**Ferment.**—S. A. 619. *f.* and rage
**Fermented.**—P. L. 7, 281. *f.* the great mother
**Ferry**—P. L. 2, 604. they *f.* over this Lethean
**Fertile**—P. L. 1, 468. on the *f.* banks
P. L. 4, 216. out of the *f.* ground he caused
P. L. 4, 645. the *f.* earth after soft showers
P. L. 5, 319. Nature multiplies her *f.* growth
P. L. 7, 454. and straight opening her *f.* womb
P. L. 9, 801. *f.* burden ease of thy full branches
P. R. 3, 259. *f.* of corn the glebe
**Fertility.**—C. 729. strangled with her waste *f.*
**Fervent.**—P. L. 5, 849. so spake the *f.* angel
**Fervently.**—P. L. 9, 342. Adam *f.* replied
P. R. 3, 121. to whom our Saviour *f.* replied
**Fervid.**—P. L. 5, 301. shot down his *f.* rays
P. L. 7, 224. then stayed the *f.* wheels
**Fesole.**—P. L. 1, 289. from the top of *F.*
**Fester.**—S. A. 621. rankle, and *f.,* and gangrene
**Festered.**—S. A. 186. and are as balm to *f.*
**Festival.**—S. A. 1598. trumpets *f.* proclaimed
H. 147. as at some *f.*
**Festivals.**—P. L. 6, 94. *f.* of joy and love
P. L. 11, 723. triumphs or *f.*
S. A. 983. sung at solemn *f.*
C. 848. for which the shepherds at their *f.*
**Fetch.**—P. L. 8, 137. industrious of herself, *f.* day
S. A. 921. I may *f.* thee from forth
S. A. 1731. to *f.* him hence and solemnly attend
C. 708. and *f.* their precepts from the cynic tub
A. 54. I *f.* my round
H. 135. time will run back and *f.* the age
**Fetched.**—P. R. 4, 589. ambrosial fruits *f.*
U. C. II. 18. if I mayn't carry, sure I'll ne'er be *f.*
**Fettered.**—S. A. 1160. and *f.* send thee into
S. A. 1235. my heels are *f.,* but my fist is free
H. 234. each *f.* ghost slips to his several grave
**Fetters.**—S. A. 35. to grind in brazen *f.*
C. 819. in stony *f.* fixed and motionless
**Feverish.**—C. 8. to keep up a *f.* being
**Feverous.**—P. L. 11, 482. all *f.* kinds
**Few.**—P. L. 3, 496. to *f.* unknown long after
P. L. 6, 148. how *f.* sometimes may know
P. L. 7, 31. and fit audience find though *f.*
P. L. 10, 157. having said, he thus to Eve in *f.*
P. L. 11, 777. those *f.* escaped
P. L. 12, 13. *f.,* and while the dread of judgment
P. L. 12, 480. will betide the *f.* his faithful
P. R. 3, 20. though against thy *f.* in arms
P. R. 3, 59. wise are *f.,* and glory scarce of *f.*
P. R. 3, 234. Jerusalem *f.* days' short sojourn
S. A. 1400. which to no *f.* of them would prove
C. 391. his *f.* books, or his beads, or maple dish
C. 771. now heaps upon some *f.* with vast excess
S. 9, 3. and with those *f.* art eminently seen
S. 17, 11. thou hast learned, which *f.* have done
**Fez.**—P. L. 11, 403. of Almansor, *F.* and Sus
**Fickle.**—P. L. 2, 233. shall yield to *f.* chance
P. L. 9, 948. *f.* their state whom God most
S. A. 164. O mirror of our *f.* state
Il P. 10. *f.* pensioners of Morpheus' train
**Fie.**—V. Ex. 53. but *f.,* my wandering muse

**Field.**—P. L. 1, 105. though the *f.* be lost
P. L. 1, 677. to trench a *f.* or cast a rampart
P. L. 1, 763. though like a covered *f.*
P. L. 2, 292. for such another *f.* they dreaded
P. L. 3, 430. the fiend at large in spacious *f.*
P. L. 3, 513. the *f.* of Luz dreaming by night
P. L. 4, 186. in hurdled cotes amid the *f.*
P. L. 4, 245. first warmly smote the open *f.*
P. L. 4, 265. breathing the smell of *f.*
P. L. 4, 268. not that fair *f.* of Enna where
P. L. 4, 980. as when a *f.* of Ceres ripe
P. L. 5, 20. morning shines and the fresh *f.*
P. L. 5, 136. so all was cleared, and to the *f.*
P. L. 5, 292. now is come into the blissful *f.*
P. L. 6, 309. and left large *f.*, unsafe within
P. L. 6, 410. on the foughten *f.* Michael
P. L. 7, 19. dismounted, on the Aleian *f.* I fall
P. L. 7, 322. the corny reed embattled in her *f.*
P. L. 7, 335. and each plant of the *f.*
P. L. 7, 358. with stars the heaven thick as a *f.*
P. L. 7, 495. serpent, subtlest beast of all the *f.*
P. L. 7, 522. beast of the *f.*, and over all the earth
P. L. 9, 86. serpent subtlest beast of all the *f.*
P. L. 9, 417. in bower and *f.* he sought
P. L. 9, 520. before her through the *f.*
P. L. 9, 560. serpent, subtlest beast of all the *f.*
P. L. 9, 575. till on a day, roving the *f.*
P. L. 10, 176. all cattle, each beast of the *f.*
P. L. 10, 204. thou shalt eat the herb of the *f.*
P. L. 10, 275. against the day of battle, to a *f.*
P. L. 10, 533. issuing forth to the open *f.*
P. L. 11, 171. but the *f.* to labour calls us
P. L. 11, 215. *f.* pavilioned with his guardians
P. L. 11, 429. beheld a *f.* part arable
P. L. 11, 654. the ensanguined *f.*
P. R. 1, 9. into the desert, his victorious *f.*
P. R. 1, 318. to warm him wet returned from *f.*
P. R. 3, 73. and in *f.* great battles win
P. R. 3, 268. forest, and *f.*, and flood
P. R. 3, 326. the *f.* all iron cast a gleaming
P. R. 4, 505. the angelic song in Bethlehem *f.*
S. A. 1087. each other's force in camp or listed *f.*.
S. A. 1094. that fortune had brought me to the *f.*
S. A. 1432. from thy father's *f.*
S. 16, 8. Dunbar *f.* resounds thy praises loud

**Fields.**—P. L. 1, 249. farewell, happy *f.*
P. L. 1, 520. over Adria to the Hesperian *f.*
P. L. 2, 493. *f.* revive, the birds .. renew
P. L. 2, 530. Olympian games or Pythian *f.*
P. L. 2, 768. war arose, and *f.* were fought
P. L. 3, 460. those argent *f.* more likely
P. L. 3, 569. *f.* and groves and flowery vales
P. L. 3, 606. what wonder then if *f.*
P. L. 7, 460. the cattle in the *f.* and meadows
P. L. 8, 145. if land be there, *f.* and inhabitants
P. L. 8, 301. and, over *f.* and waters, as in air
P. R. 1, 243. in the *f.* of Bethlehem
C. 60. roving the Celtic and Iberian *f.*
C. 979. up in the broad *f.* of the sky
S. 18, 11. o'er all the Italian *f.* where still doth
S. 20. 2. the *f.* are dank and ways are mire
D. F. I. 40. or in the Elysian *f.*

**Fiend.**—P. L. 1, 283. when the superior *f.*
P. L. 2, 643. so seemed far off the flying *f.*
P. L. 2, 677. the *F.* what this might be admired
P. L. 2, 815. the subtle *f.* his lore soon learned
P. L. 2, 917. the *f.* stood on the brink of hell
P. L. 2, 947. so eagerly the *f.*, o'er bog or steep
P. L. 3, 430. here walked the *f.* at large
P. L. 3, 440. the *f.* walked up and down
P. L. 3, 498. all this dark globe the *f.* found
P. L. 3, 524. let down whether to dare the *f.*
P. L. 3, 588. there lands the *f.*; a spot like which
P. L. 4, 166. those odorous sweets the *f.*
P. L. 4, 285. the *f.* saw undelighted all delight
P. L. 4, 393. so spake the *f.*, and with necessity
P. L. 4, 819. started up in his own shape the *f.*
P. L. 4, 857. the *f.* replied not, overcome
P. L. 4, 924. to which the *f.* thus answered
P. L. 4, 1005. spying thus bespake the *f.*
P. L. 4, 1013. the *f.* looked up, and knew

P. L. 9, 412. since first break of dawn the *f.*
P. L. 10, 20. much wondering how the subtle *f.*
P. L. 10, 233. since the *f.* passed through
P. L. 11, 101. lest the *f.* or in behalf of man
P. R. 1, 465. the subtle *f.*, though inly stung
P. R. 2, 323. thy refusal? said the subtle *f.*
P. R. 3, 345. at sight whereof the *f.*
P. R. 3, 441. and to the *f.* made answer meet
P. R. 4, 195. to whom the *f.*, with fear abashed
P. R. 4, 430. spectres which the *f.* had raised
P. R. 4, 499. the *f.* now swoln with rage replied
P. R. 4, 576. with dread and anguish, fell the *f.*
L'A. 110. then lies him down the lubbar- *f.*

**Fiends.**—P. L. 4, 953. army of *f.*, fit body

**Fierce.**—P. L. 1, 100. to the *f.* contention
P. L. 1, 305. when, with *f.* winds Orion armed
P. L. 1, 336. or the *f.* pains not feel
P. L. 1, 667. and *f.* with grasped arms
P. L. 2, 78. the *f.* foe hung on our broken rear
P. L. 2, 219. familiar the *f.* heat, and void of pain
P. L. 2, 580. *f.* Phlegethon whose waves of
P. L. 2, 599. the bitter change of *f.* extremes
P. L. 2, 599. extremes by change more *f.*
P. L. 2, 671. *f.* as ten furies, terrible as hell
P. L. 2, 898. moist, and dry, four champions *f.*
P. L. 3, 399. execute *f.* vengeance on his foes
P. L. 4, 128. his gestures *f.* he marked
P. L. 4, 509. neither joy nor love, but *f.* desire
P. L. 4, 871. and *f.* demeanour
P. L. 6, 93. and in *f.* hosting meet, who wont
P. L. 6, 201. presage of victory and *f.* desire
P. L. 6, 220. millions of *f.* encountering angels
P. L. 6, 356. and with *f.* ensigns pierced
P. L. 6, 610. erewhile they *f.* were coming
P. L. 6, 765. and from about him *f.* effusion
P. L. 6, 794. stood re-embattled *f.*
P. L. 6, 829. and the orbs of his *f.* chariot rolled
P. L. 7, 272. lest *f.* extremes contiguous
P. L. 9, 462. bereaved his fierceness of the *f.*
P. L. 9, 471. then soon *f.* hate he recollects
P. L. 10, 556. scalding thirst and hunger *f.*
P. L. 10, 703. as *f.* forth rush the Levant
P. L. 10, 709. introduced through *f.* antipathy
P. L. 10, 739. shall with a *f.* reflux on me
P. L. 10, 865. soft words to his *f.* passion
P. L. 11, 483. convulsions, epilepsies, *f.* catarrhs
P. L. 11, 641. concourse in arms, *f.* faces
P. L. 12, 634. before them blazed, *f.* as a comet
P. R. 1, 90. his *f.* thunder drove us to the deep
P. R. 1, 313. the lion and *f.* tiger glared aloof
P. R. 4, 269. wielded at will that *f.* democracy
P. R. 4, 412. abortive poured *f.* rain with
S. A. 612. there exercise all his *f.* accidents
S. A. 952. lest *f.* remembrance wake my sudden
S. A. 985. to save her country from a *f.* destroyer
C. 426. no savage *f.*, bandit or mountaineer
C. 654. *f.* sign of battle make and menace high
S. 17, 4. the *f.* Epirot and the African bold
P. 24. his godlike acts and his temptations *f.*

**Fiercely.**—P. L. 10, 478. *f.* opposed my journey
P. L. 12, 593. in signal of remove, waves *f.*

**Fierceness.**—P. L. 9, 462. bereaved his *f.*

**Fiercer.**—P. L. 2, 45. now *f.* by despair
P. R. 4, 567. and *f.* grapple joined

**Fiercest.**—P. L. 2, 44. and the *f.* spirit
P. L. 4, 927. well thou know'st I stood thy *f.*
P. L. 6, 314. of *f.* opposition in mid sky
S. A. 127. or *f.* wild beast could withstand

**Fiery.**—P. L. 1, 52. rolling in the *f.* gulf
P. L. 1, 68. and a *f.* deluge
P. L. 1, 173. o'erblown hath laid the *f.* surge
P. L. 1, 184. off the tossing of these *f.* waves
P. L. 1, 377. slumber on that *f.* couch
P. L. 2, 180. caught in a *f.* tempest shall be
P. L. 2, 512. a globe of *f.* seraphim enclosed
P. L. 2, 531. part curb their *f.* steed or shun
P. L. 2, 620. over many a frozen, many a *f.* Alp
P. L. 2, 635. up to the *f.* concave, towering high
P. L. 3, 522. rapt in a chariot drawn by *f.* steeds
P. L. 4, 402. a lion now he stalks with *f.* glare
P. L. 4, 978. angelic squadron bright turned *f.*

P. L. 6, 17. flaming arms and *f.* steeds
P. L. 6, 55. opens wide his *f.* Chaos to receive
P. L. 6, 80. from skirt to skirt a *f.* region
P. L. 6,213. over head the dismal hiss of *f.* darts
P. L. 6, 215. so under *f.* cope together rushed
P. L. 6, 304. now waved their *f.* swords
P. L. 6, 391. and *f.* foaming steeds
P. L. 6, 479. of spiritous and *f.* spume
P. L. 12, 208. then through the *f.* pillar
P. L. 12, 257. a *f.* gleam by night
P. L. 12, 492. and quench his *f.* darts
P. L. 12, 644. dreadful faces thronged and *f.* arms
P. R. 1,312. the *f.* serpent fled and noxious worm
P. R. 2, 16. the great Thisbite who on *f.* wheels
P. R. 4, 424. some bent at thee their *f.* darts
P. R. 4, 581. and straight a *f.* globe of angels
S. A. 27. as in a *f.* column charioting
S. A. 549. with touch ethereal of heaven's *f.* rod
S. A. 1690. his *f.* virtue roused
Cir. 7. your *f.* essence can distil no tear
**Fiery-wheeled.**—Il P. 53. the *f.-w.* throne
**Fifth.**—P. L. 7, 448. solemnized the *f.* day
**Fight.**—P. L. 2, 20. in council or in *f.*
P. L. 2, 914. and which thus must ever *f.*
P. L. 4,945. practised distances to cringe not *f.*
P. L. 4, 1003. sequel each of parting and of *f.*
P. L. 6, 30. well hast thou fought the better *f.*
P. L. 6, 48. and by millions ranged for *f.*
P. L. 6, 87. by *f.* or by surprise
P. L. 6, 232. led in *f.,* yet leader seemed
P. L. 6, 243. on firm ground a standing *f.*
P. L. 6, 296. and both addressed for *f.*
P. L. 6, 308. where erst was thickest *f.*
P. L. 6, 403. in *f.* they stood unwearied
P. L. 6, 423. sustained one day in doubtful *f.*
P. L. 6,448. as one he stood escaped from cruel *f.*
P. L. 6, 454. against unequal arms to *f.* in pain
P. L. 6, 531. or if for *f.* in motion or in halt
P. L. 6, 537. arm warriors—arm for *f.!*
P. L. 6, 687. sore hath been their *f.*
P. L. 6, 693. whence in perpetual *f.*
P. L. 6, 786. and to rebellious *f.*
P. L. 10, 278. the following day in bloody *f.*
P. L. 12, 289. stirring up sin against law to *f.*
P. L. 12, 385. say where and when their *f.*
P. L. 12, 386. dream not of their *f.* as of a duel
P. R. 3, 307. in which *f.* they most excel
P. R. 3,328. cuirassiers all in steel for standing *f.*
S.  A. 344. walked their streets, none offering *f.*
S.A.1111.in *f.* with stand me single and unarmed
S. A. 1175. defy thee to the trial of mortal *f.*
S. A. 1222. who now defies thee thrice to single *f.*
S. A. 1226. to *f.* with thee no man of arms
S. A. 1253. and offered *f.* will not dare mention
**Fighting.**—P. L. 2, 1015. of *f.* elements
P. L. 6, 249. the dire attack of *f.* seraphim
P. R. 4, 140. of *f.* beasts, and men to beasts
**Fig-tree.**—P. L. 9, 1101. they chose the *f.-t.*
**Figure.**—P. L. 7, 426. in common, ranged in *f.*
P. L. 12,241. whose high office who Moses in *f.*
**Figures.**—L. 105. inwrought with *f.* dim
**File.**—S. 11, 6. and some in *f.* stand spelling false
**Files.**—P. L. 1, 567. he through the armed *f.*
P. L. 4, 797. so saying, on he led his radiant *f.*
P. L. 5, 651. dispersed in bands and *f.*
P. L. 6, 339. retired from off the *f.* of war·
P. L. 6, 599. nor served it to relax their serried *f.*
**Filial.**—P. L. 3, 269. above which only shone *f.*
P. L. 4, 294. severe but in true *f.* freedom placed
P. L. 6, 722. and thus the *f.* Godhead
P. L. 7, 175. his word, the *f.* Godhead, gave
P. L. 7, 587. the *f.* power arrived and sat him
P. L. 12, 306. from servile fear to *f.*
P. R. 1, 177. ventures his *f.* virtue
S.A.511. pleased with humble and *f.* submission
**Fill.**—P. L. 1, 350. and *f.* all the plain
P. L. 4, 294. shall enjoy their *f.* of bliss on bliss
P. L. 4, 733. a race to *f.* the earth who shall
P. L. 5, 389. whose fruitful womb shall *f.*
P. L. 5, 504. meanwhile enjoy your *f.*
P. L. 7, 168. because I am who *f.* infinitude

P. L. 7, 397. and running streams the waters *f.*
P.L.7,531. be fruitful, multiply, and *f.* the earth
P. L. 8, 104. an edifice too large for him to *f.*
P. L. 8, 214. they satiate and soon *f.*
P. L. 9, 196. his nostrils *f.* with grateful smell
P. L. 9, 595. and eat my *f.* I spared not
P. L. 9, 1005. took no thought, eating his *f.*
P. L. 10, 506. and high applause to *f.* his ear
P. L. 10, 892. and not *f.* the world at once
P. L. 12, 177. lice and flies must all his palace *f.*
P. L. 12, 178. and *f.* all the land
P. L. 12, 558. and have my *f.* of knowledge
P. R. 3, 332. fell woods or valleys *f.*
C. 548. till fancy had her *f.,* but ere a close
C. 931. thy molten crystal *f.* with mud
L. 150. and daffadillies *f.* their cups with tears
·Il P. 4. or *f.* the fixed mind with all your toys
Il P. 128. when the gust hath blown his *f.*
S. 1, 3. with fresh hope the lover's heart dost *f.*
S.9,10. to *f.* thy odorous lamp with deeds of light
S. 14, 14. drink thy *f.* of pure immortal streams
**Filled.**—P. L. 1, 495. who *f.* with lust
P. L. 1, 707. by strange conveyance *f.* each
P. L. 2, 129. the towers of heaven are *f.* with
P.L. 2,284. when such murmur *f.* the assembly
P. L. 2, 843. there ye shall be fed and *f.*
D. L. 2, 847. to hear his famine should be *f.*
P. L. 3, 135. ambrosial fragrance *f.* all heaven
P. L. 3, 348. and loud hosannas *f.* the eternal
P. L. 3, 447. when sin with vanity had *f.*
P. L. 4, 351. and now *f.* with pasture, gazing
P. L. 4, 827. said Satan, *f.* with scorn
P. L. 5, 286. that heavenly fragrance *f.*
P. L. 6, 200. ours joy *f.,* and shout presage
P. L. 7,51. and was *f.* with admiration and deep
P. L. 7, 257. the hollow universal orb they *f.*
P. L. 8, 468. with flesh *f.* up and healed
P. L. 10,570. their jaws with soot and cinders *f.*
P. L. 11, 77. the angelic blast *f.* all the regions
P. L. 11, 888. he saw the whole earth *f.*
P. R. 2, 77. *f.* with infant blood the streets
S. A. 718. sails *f.,* and streamers waving
S. A. 1613. had *f.* their hearts with mirth
C. 198. and *f.* their lamps with everlasting oil
C. 550. and *f.* the air with barbarous dissonance
L'A. 23. *f.* her with thee, a daughter fair
**Filling.**—S. 15. 2. *f* each mouth with envy
**Fills.**—P. L. 3, 731. hence *f.* and empties
P. L. 7, 88. and this which yields or *f.* all space
P. L. 11, 336. his omnipresence *f.* land, sea
S. A. 552. whose beads that turbulent liquor *f.*
**Film.**—P. L. 11, 412. from Adam's eyes the *f.*
**Filth.**—P. L. 10, 630. to lick up the draff and *f.*
**Fin.**—P. R. 2, 345. all fish,... of shell or *f.*
**Final.**—P. L. 2, 142. our *f.* hope is flat despair
P. L. 2, 563. of happiness and *f.* misery
P. L. 3, 458. till *f.* dissolution, wander here
P. L. 6, 798. and now to *f.* battle drew
P. L. 9, 88. of thoughts revolved, his *f.* sentence
P. L. 10, 1085. end in dust, our *f.* rest
P. L. 11, 62. so death becomes his *f.* remedy
P. L. 11, 493. as their chief good and *f.* hope
P. R. 1, 461. into the world to teach his *f.* will
P. R. 3, 211. the end I would attain, my *f.* good
S. A. 1171. yet despair not of his *f.* pardon
**Finally.**—P. L. 3, 150. should man *f.* be lost
S. A. 1296. whom patience *f.* must crown
**Find.**—P. L. 1, 165. and out of good still to *f.*
P. L. 1, 320. for the ease you *f.* to slumber here
P. L. 1, 648. at length from us may *f.*
P. L. 2, 83. some worse way his wrath may *f.*
P. L. 2,344. what if we *f.* some easier enterprize
P. L. 2, 403. whom shall we *f.* sufficient
P. L. 2,406. through the palpable obscure *f.* out
P. L. 2, 525. where he may likeliest *f.*
P. L. 2, 802. that rest or intermission none I *f.*
P. L. 2, 1011. glad that now his sea should *f.*
P. L. 3, 24. *f.* thy piercing ray and *f.* no dawn
P. L. 3, 131. man therefore shall *f.* grace
P. L. 3, 145. that man should *f.* grace
P. L. 3, 213. where shall we *f.* such love

P. L. 3, 227. man shall *f.* grace
P. L. 3, 228. and shall grace not *f.* means
P. L. 3, 453. here *f.* fit retribution
P. L. 3, 631. in hope to *f.* who might direct
P. L. 3, 671. I may *f.* him, and with secret gaze
P. L. 4, 448. to thyself canst nowhere *f.*
P. L. 4, 575. him thy care must be to *f.*
P. L. 4, 796. such where ye *f.* seize fast
P. L. 4, 849. but chiefly to *f.* here observed
P. L. 4, 938. here in hope to *f.* better abode
P. L. 5, 9. his wonder was to *f.* unwakened Eve
P. L. 5, 28. O sole in whom my thoughts *f.*
P. L. 5, 49. to *f.* thee I directed then my walk
P. L. 5, 93. but O how glad I waked to *f.*
P. L. 5, 114. such resemblances, methinks, I *f.*
P. L. 5, 429. and *f.* the ground covered
P. L. 5, 494. and *f.* no inconvenient diet
P. L. 5, 531. finds no acceptance nor can *f.*
P. L. 6, 172. still thou err'st. nor end wilt *f.*
P. L. 6, 341. shame to *f.* himself not matchless
P. L. 6, 433. now we *f.* this our empyreal form
P. L. 6, 453. and too unequal work we *f.*
P. L. 7, 31. and fit audience *f.* though few
P. L. 8, 97. beams, unactive else, their vigour *f.*
P. L. 8, 366. all enjoying, what contentment *f.*
P. L. 8, 875. with these *f.* pastime and bear rule
P. L. 8, 433. nor in their ways complacence *f.*
P. L. 8, 438. *f.* thee knowing not of beasts alone
P. L. 8, 479. to *f.* her, or for ever to deplore
P. L. 8, 523. and must confess to *f.* in all things
P. L. 8, 624. and obstacle *f.* none of membrane
P. L. 9, 119. but I in none of these *f.* place
P. L. 9, 129. for only in destroying I *f.* ease
P. L. 9, 160. hap may *f.* the serpent sleeping
P. L. 9, 181. soonest he might *f.* the serpent
P. L. 9, 219. *f.* what to redress till noon
P. L. 9, 257. with greedy hope to *f.* his wish
P. L. 9, 333. *f.* peace within, favour from heaven
P. L. 9, 370. *f.* us both securer than thus warned
P. L. 9, 381. may *f.* us both perhaps far less
P. L. 9, 414. where likeliest he might *f.*
P. L. 9, 421. but wished his hap might *f.*
P. L. 9, 1071. we *f.* indeed and *f.* we know
P. L. 9, 1176. to meet no danger or to *f.*
P. L. 10, 52. but soon shall *f.* forbearance
P. L. 10, 844. I *f.* no way from deep to deeper
P. L. 10, 894. or *f.* some other way to generate
P. L. 10, 899. he never shall *f.* out fit mate
P. L. 10, 968. my words with thee can *f.*
P. L. 11, 223. *f.* where Adam sheltered
P. L. 11, 890. such grace shall one just man *f.*
P. L. 12, 40. shall *f.* the plain wherein a black
P. L. 12, 273. now first I *f.* mine eyes true
P. L. 12, 295. they may *f.* justification
P. L. 12, 522. laws which none shall *f.* left
P. R. 1, 101. to *f.* out and ruin Adam
P. R. 1, 121. where he might likeliest *f.* this
P. R. 1, 459. for they shall *f.* thee mute
P. R. 1, 471. where easily canst thou *f.* one
P. R. 2, 59. to *f.* whom at the first they found
P. R. 2, 131. but *f.* far other labour
P. R. 2, 208. what woman will you *f.* though
P. R. 2, 388. where no acceptance it can *f.*
P. R. 3, 398. think not thou to *f.* me slack
P. R. 4, 130. tormentor, conscience, *f.* him out
P. R. 4, 333. can I *f.* that solace
P. R. 4, 477. be sure to *f.* what I foretold thee
S. A. 17. I seek this unfrequented place to *f.*
S. A. 40. ask from this great deliverer now and *f.*
S. A. 306. but never *f.* self-satisfying solution
S. A. 423. how thou mightst *f.* some occasion
S. A. 610. secret passage *f.* to the inmost mind
S. A. 771. I may, if possible, thy pardon *f.*
S. A. 1376. shall never unrepented *f.* forgiveness
S. A. 1396. or we shall *f.* such engines to assail
S. A. 1443. supposing here to *f.* his son
S. A. 1716. let but them *f.* courage to lay hold
S. A. 1725. let us go *f.* the body where it lies
C. 204. yet nought but single darkness do I *f.*
C. 304. like the path to heaven, to help you *f.*
C. 307. to out *f.* that, good shepherd, I suppose

C. 500. how couldst thou *f.* this dark sequestered
C. 606. I'll *f.* him out and force him to return
C. 644. but now I *f.* it true, for by this means
A. 12. less than half we *f.* expressed
L. 73. but the fair guerdon when we hope to *f.*
S. 9, 8. no anger *f.* in thee but pity and ruth
V. Ex. 83. to *f.* a foe it shall not be his hap
L'A. 5. *f.* out some uncouth cell
Il P. 168. *f.* out the peaceful hermitage
F. of C. 13. but we do hope to *f.* out all your tricks
**Finding.**—P. L. 4, 889. *f.* way, break loose
S. A. 619. but, *f.* no redress ferment and rage
U. C. 'I. 11. but lately *f.* him so long at home
**Finds.**—P. L. 3, 228. that *f.* her way
P. L. 4, 92. in misery seeks joy ambition *f.*
P. L. 5, 531. such with him *f.* no acceptance
P. R. 1, 334. fame also *f.* us out
P. R. 4, 319. in these true wisdom *f.* her not
S. A. 1046. favoured of heaven, who *f.* one virtuous
**Find'st.**—P. L. 5, 231. thou *f.* him
P. L. 8, 586. what higher in her society thou *f.*
P. R. 1, 495. do as thou *f.* permission
P. R. 4, 486. me worse than wet thou *f.* not
**Fine.**—S. A. 702. in *f.*, just or unjust alike seem
**Finger.**—P. R. 4, 428. who with her radiant *f.*
C. 914. thrice upon thy *f.'s.* tip
H. 95. as never was by mortal *f.* strook
**Fingers.**—L. 4. and with forced *f.* rude
**Finish.**—P. L. 4, 661. to *f.* round the earth
**Finished.**—P. L. 2, 284. he scarce had *f.*
P. L. 2, 815. she *f.*; and the subtle fiend his lore
P. L. 4, 727. appointed work employed have *f.*
P. L. 5, 559. the sun hath *f.* half his journey
P. L. 6, 141. unaided, could have *f.* thee
P. L. 6, 522. secret they *f.* and in order set
P. L. 7, 548. here *f.* he, and all that he had made
S. A. 1710. and heroicly hath *f.* a life heroic
**Finisher.**—P. L. 12, 375. *f.* of utmost hope
**Finite.**—P. L. 10, 802. *f.* to infinite
**Finny.**—C. 115. with all their *f.* drove
**Fins.**—P. L. 7, 401. of fish that with their *f.*
**Fir.**—P. L. 4, 139. cedar and pine and *f.*
P. L. 6, 574. hollowed bodies made of oak or *f.*
P. L. 10, 1076. kindles the gummy bark of *f.*
**Fire.**—P. L. 1, 48. chains and penal *f.*
P. L. 1, 77. whirlwinds of tempestuous *f.*
P. L. 1, 151. in the heart of hell to work in *f.*
P. L. 1, 229. with solid, as the lake with liquid *f.*
P. L. 1, 234. fuelled entrails thence conceiving *f.*
P. L. 1, 280. prostrate on yon lake of *f.*
P. L. 1, 298. vaulted with *f.*
P. L. 1, 395. passed through *f.* to his grim idol
P. L. 1, 612. heaven's *f.* hath scathed
P. L. 1, 671. belched *f.* and rolling smoke
P. L. 1, 701. underneath had veins of liquid *f.*
P. L. 2, 67. *f.* and horror shot with equal rage
P. L. 2, 69. Tartarean sulphur and strange *f.*
P. L. 2, 88. where pain of unextinguishable *f.*
P. L. 2, 141. and purge off the baser *f.*
P. L. 2, 176. should spout her cataracts of *f.*
P. L. 2, 364. either with hell *f.* to waste
P. L. 2, 434. this huge convex of *f.*
P. L. 2, 581. whose waves of torrent *f.* inflame
P. L. 2, 595. and cold performs the effect of *f.*
P. L. 2, 600. from beds of raging *f.* to starve
P. L. 2, 603. of time thence hurried back to *f.*
P. L. 2, 647. impaled with circling *f.*
P. L. 2, 912. nor shore, nor air, nor *f.*
P. L. 2, 937. instinct with *f.* and nitre
P. L. 2, 1013. like a pyramid of *f.*
P. L. 3, 594. as glowing iron with *f.*
P. L. 3, 715. elements, earth, flood, air, *f.*
P. L. 4, 719. who had stole Jove's authentic *f.*
P. L. 5, 439. if by *f.* of sooty coal the empiric
P. L. 5, 893. thunder on thy head, devouring *f.*
P. L. 6, 50. them with *f.* and hostile arms
P. L. 6, 214. flying, vaulted either host with *f.*
P. L. 6, 245. all air seemed then conflicting *f.*
P. L. 6, 485. with touch of *f.* dilated
P. L. 6, 520. pernicious with one touch to *f.*
P. L. 6, 546. storm of arrows barbed with *f.*

P. L. 6,580. a reed stood waving tipped with *f*.
P. L. 6, 849. and shot forth pernicious *f*.
P. L. 6, 876. their fit habitation fraught with *f*.
P. L. 9, 392. as art, yet rude, guiltless of *f*.
P. L. 9, 634. wandering *f*. compact of unctuous
P. L. 9, 1096. whose eye darted contagious *f*.
P. L. 10, 1073. grind the air attrite to *f*.
P. L. 10, 1078. such *f*. to use
P. L. 11, 217. Dothan, covered with a camp of *f*.
P. L. 11, 441. propitious *f*. from heaven
P. L. 11, 472. by *f*., flood, famine
P. L. 11, 566. where casual *f*. had wasted woods
P. L. 11, 658. stones and sulphurous *f*.
P. L. 11, 900. shall hold their course till *f*.
P. L. 12, 182. hail mixed with *f*. must rend
P. L. 12, 202. in a cloud and pillar of *f*.
P. L. 12, 203. by day a cloud, by night a pillar of *f*.
P. R. 2, 124. powers of *f*., air, water, and earth
P. R. 3, 220. whose ire I dread more than the *f*.
P. R. 4, 201. tetrarchs of *f*., air, flood
P. R. 4, 412. water with *f*. in ruin reconciled
S. A. 1435. and be now a shield of *f*.
C. 111. we that are of purer *f*. imitate
C. 433. in fog, or *f*., by lake or moorish fen
L'A. 112. basks at the *f*. his hairy strength
Il P. 94. in *f*., air, flood, or under ground
S. 20, 3. and by the *f*. help waste a sullen day
H. 28. his secret altar touched with hallowed *f*.
H. 159. while the red *f*. and smouldering clouds
D. F. I. 62. thereby to set the hearts of men on *f*.
V. Ex. 40. the spheres of watchful *f*.

**Fired.**—P. L. 4, 557. vapours *f*. impress the air
S. A. 1419. the well-feasted priest then ... *f*.

**Fires.**—P. L. 1, 346. nether and surrounding *f*.
P. L. 2, 170. breath that kindled those grim *f*.
P. L. 2, 213. whence these raging *f*. will slacken
P. L. 2, 275. piercing *f*. as soft as now severe
P. L. 2, 401. to heal the scar of these corrosive *f*.
P. L. 2, 709. like a comet burned, that *f*
P. L. 4, 667. these soft *f*. not only enlighten
P. L. 5, 177. and ye five other wandering *f*.
P. L. 5, 417. the air those *f*. ethereal
P. L. 6, 413. cherubic waving *f*.
P. L. 6, 756. and careering *f*. between
P. L. 7, 87. distant so high, with moving *f*.
P. L. 12, 256. zodiac representing the heavenly *f*.

**Firm.**—P. L. 1, 350. down they light on the *f*.
P. L. 1, 554. *f*. and unmoved with dread
P. L. 2, 36. to union and *f*. faith and *f*. accord
P. L. 2, 497. *f*. concord holds, men only disagree
P. L. 2, 589. which on *f*. land thaws not
P. L. 3, 75. that seemed *f*. land embosomed
P. L. 3, 418. upon the *f*. opacous globe
P. L. 4, 695. and what higher grew of *f*.
P. L. 4, 873. stand *f*., for in his look defiance
P. L. 5, 210. *f*. peace recovered soon
P. L. 5, 502. retain, unalterably *f*. his
P. L. 6, 69. on they move indissolubly *f*.
P. L. 6, 242. on *f*. ground a standing fight
P. L. 6, 399. cubic phalanx *f*., advanced entire
P. L. 6, 534. in slow but *f*. battalion
P. L. 6, 911. *f*. they might have stood, yet fell
P. L. 7, 267. partition *f*. and sure
P. L. 7, 362. *f*. to retain
P. L. 7, 443. others on ground walked *f*.
P. L. 7, 586. fixed for ever *f*. and sure
P. L. 9, 286. thy equal fear that my *f*. faith
P. L. 9, 359. *f*. we subsist, yet possible to swerve
P. L. 9, 1160. hadst thou been *f*. and fixed
P. L. 10, 295. fixed as *f*. as Delos
P. L. 11, 71. and in their state though *f*. stood
P. L. 12, 127. not knowing to what land, yet *f*.
P. R. 1, 4. by one man's *f*. obedience fully tried
P. R. 4, 292. fancies built on nothing *f*.
P. R. 4, 534. rock of adamant, and as a centre, *f*.
C. 588. this I hold *f*.—virtue may be assailed
S. 15, 5. thy *f*. unshaken virtue ever brings
S. 17, 13. therefore on thy *f*. hand religion leans

**Firmament.**—P. L. 2, 175. opened, and this *f*.
P. L. 3, 75. firm land embosomed without *f*.
P. L. 3, 574. through the calm *f*.

P. L. 4, 604. now glowed the *f*. with living
P. L. 6, 757. over their heads a crystal *f*.
P. L. 7, 261. again God said, let there be *f*.
P. L. 7, 264. and God made the *f*., expanse
P. L. 7, 274. and heaven he named the *f*.
P. L. 7, 344. their office in the *f*. of heaven
P. L. 7, 349. and set them in the *f*. of heaven
P. L. 7, 390. displayed on the open *f*. of heaven
P. L. 8, 18. an atom with the *f*. compared
P. L. 11, 206. that draws o'er the blue *f*.
C. 598. if this fail, the pillared *f*. is rottenness

**Firmer.**—P. L. 11, 498. till *f*. thoughts

**Firmest.**—S. A. 796. and hold thee to me *f*.

**Firmlier.**—S. A. 1398. thou wert *f*. fastened

**Firmly.**—P. L. 6, 430. true is, less *f*. armed

**Firmness.**—P. L. 5, 324. by frugal storing *f*.
P. L. 9, 279. but that thou shouldst my *f*.

**First.**—P. L. 1, 1. of man's *f*. disobedience
P. L. 1, 8. that shepherd, who *f*. taught
P. L. 1, 19. thou from the *f*. wast present
P. L. 1, 27. say *f*., for heaven hides nothing
P. L. 1, 28. say *f*., what cause moved our grand
P. L. 1, 33. who *f*. seduced them to that foul
P. L. 1, 376. who *f*., who last, roused from the
P. L. 1, 392. *f*. Moloch, horrid king
P. L. 1, 514. these *f*. in Crete and Ida known
P. L. 1, 656. shall be perhaps our *f*. eruption
P. L. 1, 684. by him *f*. men also
P. L. 2, 19. did *f*. create your leader
P. L. 2, 129. *f*., what revenge?
P. L. 2, 201. this was at *f*. resolved
P. L. 2, 324. still *f*. and last will reign sole king
P. L. 2, 379. counsel *f*. devised by Satan
P. L. 2, 402. but *f*., whom shall we send
P. L. 2, 617. viewed *f*. their lamentable lot
P. L. 2, 680. with disdainful look thus *f*. began
P. L. 2, 690. who *f*. broke peace in heaven
P. L. 2, 740. till *f*. I know of thee what thing
P. L. 2, 742. in this infernal vale *f*. met
P. L. 2, 760. back they recoiled afraid at *f*.
P. L. 2, 1002. *f*. hell, your dungeon stretching
P. L. 2, 1037. here nature *f*. begins
P. L. 3, 64. on earth he *f*. beheld
P. L. 3, 65. our two *f*. parents, yet the only two
P. L. 3, 129. the *f*. sort by their own
P. L. 3, 131. man falls deceived by the other *f*.
P. L. 3, 134. but mercy, *f*. and last
P. L. 3, 356. heaven removed, where *f*. it grew
P. L. 3, 372. thee, father, *f*. they sung
P. L. 3, 383. next they sang, of all creation *f*.
P. L. 3, 419. whose *f*. convex divides
P. L. 3, 464. *f*. from the ancient world
P. L. 3, 483. and that *f*. moved
P. L. 3, 549. of some foreign land *f*. seen
P. L. 3, 562. into the world's *f*. regions
P. L. 3, 634. but *f*. he casts to change
P. L. 3, 656. the *f*. art wont his great
P. L. 4, 6. our *f*. parents had been warned
P. L. 4, 9. for now Satan, now *f*. inflamed
P. L. 4, 12. his loss of that *f*. battle
P. L. 4, 121. was the *f*. that practised
P. L. 4, 192. so clomb this *f*. grand thief
P. L. 4, 244. where the morning sun *f*.
P. L. 4, 352. Satan, still in gaze as *f*. he stood
P. L. 4, 408. Adam, *f*. of men, to *f*. of women, Eve
P. L. 4, 450. when from sleep I *f*. awaked
P. L. 4, 495. half-embracing leaned on our *f*.
P. L. 4, 528. *f*., with narrow search I must walk
P. L. 4, 570. where he *f*. lighted, soon discerned
P. L. 4, 624. the east with *f*. approach of light
P. L. 4, 643. when *f*. on this delightful land
P. L. 4, 710. espoused Eve decked *f*. her
P. L. 4, 757. father, son, and brother, *f*. were
P. L. 4, 921. courageous chief the *f*. in flight
P. L. 4, 935. I therefore, I alone, *f*. undertook
P. L. 4, 947. pretending *f*. wise to fly pain
P. L. 4, 999. wherein all things created *f*.
P. L. 5, 124. when fair morning *f*. smiles
P. L. 5, 137. *f*., from under shady arborous roof
P. L. 5, 165. him *f*., him last, him midst
P. L. 5, 265. Delos or Samos *f*. appearing, kens

P. L. 5, 418. and as lowest, *f.* the moon
P. L. 5, 472. one *f.* matter all
P. L. 5, 659. he of the *f.*, if not the *f.* archangel
P. L. 6, 18. reflecting blaze on blaze *f.* met
P. L. 6, 92. strange to us it seemed at *f.*
P. L. 6, 151. hour of my revenge *f.* sought for
P. L. 6, 153. the *f.* assay of this grief hand
P. L. 6, 154. since *f.* that tongue inspired
P. L. 6, 164. at *f.* I thought that liberty
P. L. 6, 261. visage all inflamed, *f.* thus began
P. L. 6, 327. then Satan *f.* knew pain
P. L. 6, 394. then *f.* with fear surprised
P. L. 6, 661. purest at *f.*, now gross by sinning
P. L. 6, 724. *f.*, highest, holiest, best
P. L. 6, 774. but by his own *f.* seen
P. L. 7, 63. of heaven and earth conspicuous *f.*
P. L. 7, 86. how *f.* began this heaven
P. L. 7, 244. ethereal, *f.* of things, quintessence
P. L. 7, 252. thus was the *f.* day even and morn
P. L. 7, 255. exhaling *f.* from darkness they
P. L. 7, 260. *f.* evening was, and when *f.* morn
P. L. 7, 354. for of celestial bodies *f.* the sun
P. L. 7, 355. unlightsome *f.*, though of ethereal
P. L. 7, 370. *f.* in his east the glorious lamp was
P. L. 7, 384. then *f.* adorned
P. L. 7, 484. *f.* crept the parsimonious emmet
P. L. 7, 501. *f.* wheeled their course.
P. L. 7, 636. how *f.* this world and face
P. L. 8, 90. consider *f.*, that great or bright
L. L. 8, 96. there *f.* received his beams
P. L. 8, 284. I *f.* drew air and *f.* beheld
P. L. 8, 288. there gentle sleep *f.* found
P. L. 8, 297. *f.* man, of men innumerable
P. L. 8, 530. here passion *f.* I felt, commotion
P. L. 8, 555. as one intended *f.*, not after made
P. L. 8, 633. but *f.* of all Him
P. L. 9, 25. since *f.* this subject for heroic song
P. L. 9, 70. though sin, not time, *f.* wrought
P. L. 9, 97. but *f.* from inward grief
P. L. 9, 170. obnoxious, *f.* or last, to basest
P. L. 9, 171. at *f.* though sweet, bitter ere long
P. L. 9, 204. Eve *f.* to her husband thus began
P. L. 9, 213. or hear what to my mind *f.*
P. L. 9, 261. whether his *f.* design be to
P. L. 9, 305. or daring, *f.* on me the assault
P. L. 9, 368. approve *f.* thy obedience
P. L. 9, 383. so proud will *f.* the weaker seek
P. L. 9, 412. since *f.* break of dawn the fiend
P. L. 9, 511. at *f.*, as one who sought access
P. L. 9, 555. the *f.* at least of these I thought
P. L. 9, 571. I was at *f.* as other beasts
P. L. 9, 616. of that fruit in thee *f.* proved
P. L. 9, 718. gods are *f.*, and that advantage
P. L. 9, 743. yet *f.*, pausing awhile
P. L. 9, 747. at *f.* assay gave elocution to the
P. L. 9, 769. which *f.* hath tasted envies not
P. L. 9, 835. but *f.* low reverence done
P. L. 9, 848. that morn when *f.* they parted
P. L. 9, 895. till thus at length *f.* to himself
P. L. 9, 930. *f.* by the serpent, by him *f.*
P. L. 9, 949. me *f.* he ruined, now mankind
P. L. 9, 1012. far other operation *f.* displayed
P. L. 9, 1030. since the day I saw thee *f.*
P. L. 9, 1079. of the *f.* be sure then
P. L. 9, 1115. how unlike to thief *f.* naked glory
P. L. 9, 1162. to whom, then *f.* incensed, Adam
P. L. 9, 1186. she *f.* his weak indulgence
P. L. 10, 39. when *f.* this tempter crossed
P. L. 10, 109. Eve, more loth, though *f.* to offend
P. L. 10, 172. Satan, *f.* in sin, his doom applied
P. L. 10, 316. he *f.* lighted from his wing
P. L. 10, 326. Paradise *f.* tending, when behold
P. L. 10, 402. *f.* make sure your thrall
P. L. 10, 582. had *f.* the rule of high Olympus
P. L. 10, 604. and fruits, and flowers, feed *f.*
P. L. 10, 652. the sun had *f.* his precept so to
P. L. 10, 707. but discord *f.*, daughter of sin
P. L. 10, 831. *f.* and last on me
P. L. 10, 950. bear thine own *f.*
P. L. 11, 55. wrought by sin, that *f.* distempered
P. L. 11, 57. I, at *f.*, with two fair gifts created

P. L. 11, 136. Adam and *f.* matron Eve
P. L. 11, 168. that I, who *f.* brought death
P. L. 11, 182. nature *f.* gave signs, impressed
P. L. 11, 188. *f.* hunter then, pursued a gentle
P. L. 11, 277. from the *f.* opening bud
P. L. 11, 423. ope thine eyes, and *f.* behold
P. L. 11, 467. thou hast seen in his *f.* shape
P. L. 11, 572. he formed *f.* his own tools
P. L. 11, 591. then *f.* to marriage rites invoked
P. L. 11, 789. they *f.* seen in acts of prowess
P. L. 12, 173. but *f.* the lawless tyrant
P. L. 12, 273. now *f.* I find mine eyes true
P. L. 12, 320. by judges *f.*, then under kings
P. L. 12, 331. but *f.* a long succession must
P. L. 12, 350. the house of God they *f.* re-edify
P. L. 12, 353. but *f.* among the priests
P. L. 12, 472. by creation *f.* brought forth light
P. L. 12, 498. spirit, poured *f.* on his apostles
P. R. 1, 114. attempt at *f.* against mankind
P. R. 1, 154. by conquest what the *f.* man lost
P. R. 1, 155. *f.* I mean to exercise him in the
P. R. 1, 157. shall *f.* lay down the rudiments
P. R. 1, 187. which way *f.* publish his godlike
P. R. 1, 221. *f.* by winning words
P. R. 1, 277. and *f.* refused on me his baptism
P. R. 1, 319. who *f.* with curious eye perused
P. R. 1, 399. at *f.* it may be
P. R. 2, 59. to find whom at the *f.* they found
P. R. 2, 107. had passed since *f.* her salutation
P. R. 2, 133. when I dealt with Adam, *f.* of men
P. R. 2, 244. now hungering *f.*
P. R. 2, 328. or offered *f.* to idols
P. R. 2, 427. get riches *f.*, get wealth
P. R. 3, 188. hath decreed that I shall *f.*
P. R. 3, 195. reign who *f.* well hath obeyed
P. R. 3, 277. of that *f.* golden monarchy
P. R. 3, 295. who founded *f.* that empire
P. R. 3, 363. the Parthian *f.* by my advice
P. R. 4, 129. expel a devil who *f.* made him
P. R. 4, 137. *f.* ambitious grown of triumph
P. R. 4, 176. the *f.* of all commandments
P. R. 4, 293. the *f.* and wisest of them all
P. R. 4, 504. with the *f.* I knew
S. A. 151. which shall I *f.* bewail? thy bondage
S. A. 219. the *f.* I saw at Timna and she pleased
S. A. 383. did not she of Timna *f.* betray me
S. A. 773. *f.* granting, as I do, it was a weakness
S. A. 781. to what I did thou showedst me *f.*
S. A. 883. why then didst thou at *f.* receive me
S. A. 1035. seeming at *f.* all heavenly
S. A. 1071. I less conjecture than when *f.* I saw
S. A. 1435. that spirit that *f.* rushed on thee
S. A. 1548. to thee *f.* reverend Manoah
S. A. 1562. feed on that *f.*
S. A. 1578. ere I give the reins to grief, say, *f.*
S. A. 1594. eye-witness of what *f.* or last was
C. 46. Bacchus, that *f.* from out the purple grape
C. 82. but *f.* I must put off these my sky-robes
C. 325. where it *f.* was named, and yet is most
C. 469. the divine property of her *f.* being
C. 672. and *f.* behold this cordial julep here
C. 963. such court guise as Mercury did *f.* devise
L. 48. when *f.* the white-thorn blows
L'A. 114. ere the *f.* cock his matin rings
Il P. 51. but, *f.* and chiefest, with thee bring
S. 1, 6. *f.* heard before the shallow cuckoo's bill
S. 12, 12. for who loves that must *f.* be wise
S. 13, 2. *f.* taught our English music
H. 26. the honour *f.* thy Lord to greet
H. 155. yet *f.*, to those ychained in sleep
Cir. 3. *f.* heard by . . shepherds' ear
Cir. 25. and seals obedience *f.*
S. M. 24. whilst they stood in *f.* obedience
V. Ex. 2. move my *f.* endeavouring tongue
V. Ex. 11. need'st not be ambitious to be *f.*
**First-begot.**—P. R. 1, 89. his *f.-b.* we know
**First-born.**—P. L. 1, 489. both her *f.-b.*
P. L. 1, 510. Titan, heaven's *f.-b.*
P. L. 3, 1. holy light, offspring of heaven *f.-b.*
P. L. 12, 189. one midnight-stroke, all the *f.-b.*
S. A. 391. conceived her spurious *f.-b.*

S. A. 1576. abortive as the *f.-b.* bloom of spring
**First-created.**—S. A. 83. O *f.-c.* beam
**First-fruits.**—P. L. 11, 22. *f.-f.* on earth
P. L. 11, 435. from his tillage brought *f.-f.*
**Firstlings.**—P. L. 11, 437. *f.* of his flock
**First-Mover's.**—P. L. 7, 500. great *F.M.'s* hand
**First-moving.**—D.F.I.39. that high *f.-m.* sphere
**Fish**—P.L.1,463. upward man and downward *f.*
P. L. 7, 401. and shoals of *f.* that with their fins
P. L. 7, 447. the waters thus with *f.* replenished
P. L. 7, 503. by fowl, *f.,* beast, was flown
P. L. 7, 521. over the *f.* and fowl of sea and air
P. L. 7, 533. over *f.* of the sea and fowl of the air
P. L. 8, 341. live in sea, or air, beast, *f.,* and fowl
P. L. 8, 346. the same of *f.* within their watery
P. L. 8, 395. much less can bird with beast, or *f.*
P. L. 10, 604. each beast next and *f.* and fowl
P. L. 10, 711. fowl with fowl and *f.* with *f.*
P. L. 12, 67. he gave us only over beast, *f.*
P. R. 2, 344. all *f.* from sea or shore
**Fishermen.**—P. R. 2, 27. plain *f.*
**Fishy.**—P. L. 4, 168. the *f.* fume that drove
**Fist.**—S. A. 1235. but my *f.* is free
**Fit.**—P. L. 2, 306. *f.* to bear the weight
P. L. 3, 454. here find *f.* retribution
P. L. 3, 643. his habit *f.* for speed succinct
P. L. 4, 816. laid *f.* for the tun, some magazine
P. L. 4, 953. army of fiends, *f.* body to *f.* head
P. L. 5, 69. here, it seems, as only *f.* for gods
P. L. 5, 148. in *f.* strains pronounced or sung
P. L. 5, 315. and pour abundance *f.* to honour
P. L. 5, 348. wants her *f.* vessels pure
P. L. 5, 690. *f.* entertainment to receive our
P. L. 6, 303. *f.* to decide the empire of great
P. L. 6, 543. and each *f.* well his helm
P. L. 6, 636. such hellish mischief *f.* to oppose
P. L. 6, 876. hell, their *f.* habitation,
P. L. 7, 31. and *f.* audience find though few
P. L. 8, 390. *f.* to participate all rational delight
P. L. 8, 448. see how thou couldst judge of *f.*
P. L. 8, 450. thy likeness, thy *f.* help, thy other
P. L. 9, 89. his final sentence chose *f.* vessel
P. L. 9, 489. she fair, divinely fair, *f.* love for
P. L. 10, 139. so good, so *f.,* so acceptable
P. L. 10, 242. can *f.* his punishment
P. L. 10, 626. with some *f.* of passion
P. L. 10, 899. he never shall find out *f.* mate
P. L. 11, 271. *f.* haunt of gods
P. L. 11, 571. ore he drained into *f.* moulds
P. L. 12, 597. at season *f.* let her with thee
P. R. 1, 73. and *f.* them so purified to receive
C. 546. wrapped in a pleasing *f.* of melancholy
C. 700. with liquorish baits *f.* to ensnare a brute
C. 792. thou art not *f.* to hear thyself convinced
Il P. 78. some still removed place will *f.*
P. 42. trance, and anguish, and ecstatic *f.*
D. F. I. 46. took up and in *f.* place did reinstall
V. Ex. 32. thou clothe my fancy in *f.* sound
A. 76. whose lustre leads us and for her most *f.*
**Fitly.**—P. L. 8, 394. so *f.* them in pairs thou hast
P. 49. that they would *f.* fall in ordered
**Fits.**—S. A. 929. condition take no care; it *f.* not
S.A. 1236. this insolence other kind of answer *f.*
S. A. 1318. appear as *f.* before the ... lords
**Fitter.**—P. L. 11, 98. he was taken, *f.* soil
P. L. 11, 262. whence thou wast taken, *f.* soil
**Fittest.**—P. L. 9, 89. *f.* imp of fraud
P. R. 4, 373. the wilderness for thee is *f.* place
**Fitting.**—P. R. 4, 219. *f.* Moses' chair
**Five.**—P. L. 5, 104. the *f.* watchful senses
P. L. 5, 177. and ye *f.* other wandering fires
P. L. 10, 657. to the other *f.* their planetary
S. A. 1248. fame divulge him father of *f.* sons
**Fix.**—P. L. 1, 382. durst *f.* their seats
P. L. 12, 432. and *f.* far deeper in his head
Il P. 44. thou *f.* them on the earth as fast
**Fixed.**—P. L. 1, 97. that *f.* mind
P. L. 1, 206. with *f.* anchor in his scaly rind
P. L. 1, 560. united force with *f.* thought
P. L. 1, 723. stood *f.* her stately height
P. L.2,18. me though just right and the *f.* laws

P. L. 2, 560. *f.* fate, free will, foreknowledge
P. L. 3, 481. planets seven, and pass the *f.*
P. L. 3, 629. or *f.* in cogitation deep
P. L. 3, 669. hath man his *f.* seat, or *f.* seat
P. L. 4, 465. there I had *f.* mine eyes till now
P. L. 5, 176. *f.* stars, *f.* in their orb that flies
P. L. 5, 621. starry sphere of planets and of *f.*
P. L. 7, 586. *f.* for ever firm and sure
P. L. 8, 3. still stood *f.* to hear.
P. L. 9, 735. *f.* on the fruit she gazed
P. L. 9, 952. I with thee have *f.* my lot
P. L. 9, 1160. hadst thou been firm and *f.*
P. L. 10, 295. as with a trident smote and *f.*
P. L. 10, 553. their earnest eyes they *f.*
P. L. 10, 661. taught the *f.* their influence
P. L. 10, 773. to execute what his decree *f.*
P. L. 11, 851. top of some high mountain *f.*
P. L. 12, 555. till time stand *f.*
P. L. 12, 627. to their *f.* station
P.R. 1, 127. purposed counsel, preordained and *f.*
S. A. 726. now stands and eyes thee, *f.*
S.A. 1481. I am *f.* not to part hence without him
S. A. 1637. and eyes fast *f.* he stood
C. 819. in stony fetters *f.* and motionless
Il P. 4. or fill the *f.* mind with all your toys
S. 9, 9. thy care is *f.* and zealously attends
H. 70, stand *f.* in steadfast gaze
H. 241. hath *f.* her polished car
**Fixes.**—P.L. 4, 28. his grieved look he *f.* sad
C. 529. the likeness of a beast *f.* instead
**Flag.**—P. L. 2, 900. they around the *f.* of each
C. 604. under the sooty *f.* of Acheron
**Flail.**—L'A. 108. his shadowy *f.* hath threshed
**Flame.**—P. L. 2, 889. smoke and ruddy *f.*
P. L. 4, 784. as *f.* they part, half wheeling
P. L. 5, 807. and in a *f.* of zeal severe
P. L. 5, 891. raging into sudden *f.* distinguish
P. L. 6, 483. yield us pregnant with infernal *f.*
P. L. 6, 584. immediate in a *f.,* but soon obscured
P. L. 6, 766. of smoke and bickering *f.*
P. L. 9, 637. kindled through agitation to a *f.*
P. L. 10, 232. belching outrageous *f.*
P. L. 11, 1075. slant lightning whose thwart *f.*
P. L. 11, 120. and of a sword the *f.* wide waving
P. R. 3, 26. the *f.* of most erected spirits
S. A. 262. threads touched with the *f.*
S. A. 1351. by adding fuel to the *f.*
S. A. 1691. from under ashes into sudden *f.*
C. 129. dark veiled Cotytto to whom the secret *f.*
C. 795. to such a *f.* of sacred vehemence
H. 81. as his inferior *f.* the new lightened world
M. W. 20. but with a scarce well-lighted *f.*
**Flamed.**—P. L. 1, 62. as one great furnace *f.*
P. L. 10, 562. bituminous lake where Sodom *f.*
P. R. 1, 216. victorious deeds *f.* in my heart
**Flamens.**—H.194. affrights the *f.* at their service
**Flames.**—P. L. 1, 62. from those *f.* no light
P. L. 1, 182. the glimmering of these livid *f.*
P. L. 1, 222. on each hand the *f.*
P. L. 2, 61. with hell *f.* and fury all at once
P. L. 2, 172. and plunge us in the *f.*
P. L. 2, 214. if his breath stir not their *f.*
P. L. 2, 754. thy head *f.* thick and fast
P. L. 3, 470. leaped fondly into Ætna *f.*
P. L. 6, 58. in dusky wreaths, reluctant *f.*
P. L. 6, 510. flashing thick *f.,* wheel within
S. A. 25. all in *f.* ascended from off the altar
S. A. 1433. rode up in *f.* after his message told
C. 673. that *f.* and dances in his crystal bounds
L. 171. *f.* in the forehead of the morning sky
L'A. 61. robed in *f.* and amber light
**Flaming.**—P. L. 1, 45. hurled headlong *f.*
P. L. 1, 664. millions of *f.* swords
P. L. 3, 394. nor stop thy *f.* chariot wheels
P. L. 4, 554. hung high with diamond *f.*
P. L. 5, 598. amidst, as from a *f.* mount
P. L. 5, 875. the *f.* seraph fearless, though alone
P. L. 6, 17. chariots and *f.* arms
P. L. 6, 102. enclosed with *f.* cherubim
P. L. 6, 213. in *f.* volleys flew
P. L. 7, 134. fell with his *f.* legions

P. L. 8, 162. he from the East his f. road begin
P. L. 9,156. and f. ministers to watch and tend
P. L. 11, 101. thy choice of f. warriors
P. L. 11, 216. nor that which on the f. mount
P. L.'12, 592. a f. sword in signal of remove
P. L. 12, 643. waved over by that f. brand
Cir. 1. ye f. powers and winged warriors bright
**Flank.**—P. L. 6, 570. and to either f. retired
**Flaring.**—Il P. L. 132. to fling his f. beams
**Flashing.**—P. L. 6, 751. f. thick flames
**Flashy.**—L. 123. their lean and f. songs
**Flat.**—P. L. 1, 461. where he fell f.
P. L. 2, 143. thus repulsed our final hope is f.
P. L. 9, 627. beyond a row of myrtles on a f.
P. L. 9, 987. f. seems and harsh
P. R. 2, 223. and all her plumes fall f.
P. R. 4, 363. ruins kingdoms and lays cities f.
S. A. 595. my hopes all f.
C. 375. sun and moon were in the f. sea sunk
**Flatly.**—P. L. 5, 819. f. unjust to bind
**Flatter.**—P. R. 1, 474. say and unsay, feign, f.
**Flattered.**—P. L. 10, 42. and f. out of all
P. 31. and work my f. fancy to belief
**Flatteries.**—P. R. 4, 125. outlandish f.
**Flattering.**—P. R. 1, 375. all his f. prophets
S. A. 392. thrice she assayed with f. prayers
Hor. 11. of f. gales unmindful
**Flaunting.**—C. 545. with f. honey-suckle
**Flavour.**—S. A. 544. the f. or the smell or taste
**Flaw.**—P. L. 10, 698. and stormy gust and f.
**Flaws.**—P. R. 4. 454. these f., though mortals
**Fled.**—P. L. 1, 520. f. over Adria to the Hesperian
P. L. 2, 165. what when we f. amain
P. L. 2, 613. as once it f. the lip of Tantalus
P. L. 2, 787. I f. and cried out death
P. L. 2, 790. I f.; but he pursued
P. L. 2, 994. such a numerous host f. not
P. L. 3, 512. when he from Esau f.
P. L. 3, 712. at his second bidding darkness f.
P. L. 4, 919. to them less pain, less to be f.
P. L. 4, 1014. f. murmuring, and with him f.
P. L. 6,362. and uncouth pain f. bellowing
P. L. 6, 395. and sense of pain, f. ignominious
P. L. 6, 531. where lodged or whither f.
P. L. 6, 538. foe at hand, whom f. we thought
P. L. 6, 868. and would have f. affrighted
P. L. 9, 53. who late f. before the threats
P. L. 9, 58. by night he f. and at midnight
P. L. 9, 394. Pomona when she f. Vertumnus
P. L. 10, 339. terrified he f.
P. L. 10, 713. much in awe of man, but f.
P. L. 11,330. though I f. him angry
P. L. 11, 563. f. and pursued transverse
P. L. 11, 841. for the clouds were f.
P. R. 1,312. fiery serpent f and noxious worm
P. R. 2, 270. he saw the prophet also how he f.
S. A. 139. the bold Ascalonite f. from his ramp
S. A. 264. they only lived who f.
C. 662. as Daphne was,root-bound,that f. Apollo
S. 23, 14. I waked, she f., and day brought
H. 205. and sullen Moloch, f.
D. F. I. 48. and thou some goddess f.
M. W. 68. through pangs f. to felicity
**Fledge.**—P. L. 3, 627. on his shoulders f.
**Fledged.**—P. L. 7, 420. feathered soon and f.
**Fledst.**—P. L. 4, 963. thither whence thou f.
**Fleece.**—S. A. 538. all my precious f.
**Fleeced.**—P. L. 7, 472. f. the flocks
**Fleecy.**—P. L. 3. 558. Libra to the f. star
P. L. 5. 187. sun paint your f. skirts with gold
P. L. 11, 648. or f. flock, ewes and their
C. 504. not all the f. wealth that doth enrich
Il P. 72. stooping through a f. cloud
**Fleet.**—P. L. 2, 636. far off at sea a f. descried
P. L. 3, 457. dissolved on earth, f. hither
P. R. 3, 313. in mail their horses clad, yet f.
C. 896. whilst from off the waters f.
**Fleeting.**—P. L. 10, 741. f. joys of Paradise
**Flesh.**—P. L. 1, 428. like cumbrous f.
P. L. 3, 284. made f. when time shall be
P. L. 3, 434. to gorge the f. of lambs

P. L. 4,441. from whom I was formed, f. of thy f.
P. L. 4,483. his f., his bone
P. L. 8, 468. but suddenly with f. filled up
P. L. 8, 495. bone of my bone, f. of my f.
P. L. 8, 499. shall be one f., one heart, one soul
P. L. 8,629. as f. to mix with f., or soul with soul
P. L. 9, 914. f. of f., bone of my bone thou art
P. L. 9, 959. we are one, one f.
P. L. 11, 4. and made new f. regenerate
P. L. 11, 888. all f. corrupting each their way
P. L. 12, 180. blains must all his f. emboss
P. L. 12, 303. from f. to spirit
P. L. 12, 405. endure by coming in the f.
P. R. 1, 162. a mass of sinful f.
**Fleshliest.**—P. R. 2, 152. the f. incubus
**Fleshly.**—P. R. 3, 387. of f. arm
P. R. 4, 599. from heaven enshrined in f.
Il P. 92. her mansion in this f. nook
P. 17. poor f. tabernacle entered
**Flew.**—P. L. 3, 445. like aerial vapours f.
P. L. 3, 521. f. o'er the lake, rapt in a chariot
P. L. 3, 717. f. upward spirited with various
P. L. 4, 194. up he f., and on the tree of life
P. L. 4, 1004. quick up f. and kicked the beam
P. L. 5, 87. up to the clouds with him I f.
P. L. 5, 251. f. through the midst of heaven
P. L. 6, 213. of fiery darts in flaming volleys f.
P. L. 6, 507. from council to the work they f.
P. L. 6, 614. they changed their minds, f. off
P. L. 6, 642. lightning glimpse, they ran, they f.
P. L. 8, 264. lived, and moved, and walked, or f.
P. L. 10, 284. f. diverse
P. L. 11, 15. to heaven their prayers f. up
P. R. 4, 582. angels on full sail of wing f. nigh
S. A. 262. on their whole host I f. unarmed
S. 14, 11. that up they f. so drest
**Flies.**—P. L. 2, 612. and of itself the water f.
P. L. 2, 950. sinks, or wades, or creeps, or f.
P. L. 3, 435. f. toward the springs of Ganges
P. L. 5, 176. fixed stars, fixed in their orb that f.
P. L. 5, 274. to Egyptian Thebes he f.
P. L. 11, 855. from out the ark a raven f.
P. L. 12, 177. and f. must all his palace fill
P. R. 1, 39. f. to his place
P. R. 4, 15. or as a swarm of f. in vintage time
C. 668. from these gates sorrow f. far
**Fliest.**—P.L. 4,482. whom f. thou? Whom thou f.
P. L. 5, 175. meet'st the orient sun, now f.
**Flight.**—P. L. 1, 14. that with no middle f.
P. L. 1, 225. he steers his f. aloft
P. L. 1, 555. to f. or foul retreat
P. L. 2, 80. what compulsion and laborious f.
P. L. 2, 221. the never-ending f. of future days
P. L. 2, 407. or spread his aery f., upborne
P. L. 2, 632. explores his solitary f.
P. L. 2, 928. sail-broad vans he spreads for f.
P. L. 3, 15. while in my f. through utter
P. L. 3, 563. world's first region throws his f.
P. L. 3, 631. might direct his wandering f.
P. L. 3, 741. throws his steep f. in many
P. L. 4, 12. first battle and his f. to hell
P. L. 4, 595. by shorter f. to the east had left
P. L. 4, 913. by flying, meet thy f. sevenfold
P. L. 4, 921. courageous chief! the first in f.
P. L. 4, 922. thy deserted host this cause of f.
P. L. 5, 89. wondering at my f. and change
P. L. 5, 266. down thither prone in f. he speeds
P. L. 5, 871. and fly, ere evil intercept thy f.
P. L. 6, 152. thou return'st from f.
P. L. 6, 187. returned, as erst thou saidst, from f.
P. L. 6, 236. no thought of f., none of retreat
P. L. 6, 285. thou turned the least of these to f.
P. L. 6, 367. meaner thoughts learned in their f.
P. L. 6, 397. not liable to fear, or f., or pain
P. L. 6, 539. fear not his f.,
P. L. 6, 798. to final battle drew, disdaining f.
P. L. 7, 4. above the f. of Pegasean wing
P. L. 7, 294. such f. the ... command impressed
P. L. 7, 430. with mutual wing easing their f.
P. L. 8, 199. let us descend a lower f.
P. L. 10, 83. convict by f., and rebel to all law

P. L. 11, 7. winged for heaven with speedier *f.*
P. L. 11, 190. eastern gate was bent their *f.*
P. L. 11, 202. of *f.,* pursued in the air
P. R. 2, 241. to the desert takes with these his *f.*
P. R. 3, 306. of equal dread in *f.* or in pursuit
P. R. 3, 325. and overcame by *f.*
S. A. 974. greatest names in his wild aery *f.*
S. A. 1118. or rather *f.,* no great advantage
C. 158. and put the damsel to suspicious *f.*
C. 579. into swift *f.,* till I had found you here
C. 832. that stayed her *f.* with his cross-flowing
L'A. 41. to hear the lark begin his *f.*
H. 72. will not take their *f.,* for all the morning
D. F. I. 42. from us . . thou didst take thy *f.*

**Flights.**—P. R. 2, 385. call swift *f.* of angels

**Fling.**—C. 990. about the cedared alleys *f.*
Il P. 131. when the sun begins to *f.*

**Flings.**—L'A. 113. and crop-full out of doors he *f.*

**Float.**—C. 249. how sweetly did they *f.*
L. 12. he must not *f.* upon his watery bier

**Floated.**—P. L. 9. 503. *f.* redundant

**Floating.**—P. L. 1, 196 lay *f.* many a rood
P. L. 1, 310. their *f.* carcases
P. L. 10, 296. and fixed as firm as Delos *f.* once
P. L. 11, 745. the *f.* vessel swum uplifted
P. R. 4, 585. and upbore as on a *f.* couch
S. A. 1072. the sumptuous Dalila *f.* this way

**Floats.**—P. L. 7, 432. the air *f.* as they pass
P. L. 11, 850. the ark no more now *f.*

**Flock.**—P. L. 5, 709. the starry *f.*
P. L. 6, 857. as a herd of goats or timorous *f.*
P. L. 10, 273. as when a *f.* of ravenous fowl
P. L. 11, 437. came with the firstlings of his *f.*
P. L. 11, 648. fleecy *f.,* ewes and their .... lambs
P. L. 12, 19. and from the herd or *f.*
S. A. 1450. city rings and numbers thither *f.*
C. 499. or straggling wether the pent *f.* forsook
L. 24. fed the same *f.* by fountain, shade

**Flocked**—P. R. 1, 21 to his great baptism *f.*
P. R. 4, 511. whither all *f.* to the Baptist

**Flocking.**—P. L. 1, 522. these and more came *f.*
H. 232. the *f.* shadows pale

**Flocks.**—P. L. 3, 44. *f.* or herds, or human
P. L. 3, 435. on hills where *f.* are fed
P. L. 4, 185. where shepherds pen their *f.* at eve
P. L. 4, 252. or level downs, and *f.*
P. L. 7, 461. those rare and solitary, these in *f.*
P. L. 7, 472. fleeced the *f.* and bleating rose
P. L. 12, 132. cumbrous train of herds and *f.*
P. R. 3, 260. with *f.* the hills
C. 175. when for their teeming *f.*
C. 344. the folded *f.* penned in their wattled
C. 531. tending my *f.* hard by in the crofts
C. 540. the chewing *f.* had ta'en their supper
C. 712. covering the earth with . . and *f.*
A. 103. bring your *f.* and live with us
L. 29. battening our *f.* with the fresh dews
L'A. 72. where the nibbling *f.* do stray

**Flood.**—P. L. 1, 195. prone on the *f.,* extended
P. L. 1, 239. to have scaped the Stygian *f.*
P. L. 1, 312. covering the *f.* under amazement
P. L. 1, 324. cherub and seraph rolling in the *f.*
P. L. 1, 419. who from the bordering *f.* of old
P. L. 2, 577. abhorred Styx, the *f.* of deadly hate
P. L. 2, 587. beyond this *f.* a frozen continent
P. L. 2, 640. they on the trading *f.* through the
P. L. 3, 535. Paneas, the fount of Jordan's *f.*
P. L. 3, 715. the cumbrous elements, earth, *f.*
P. L. 4, 231. and met the nether *f.*
P. L. 7, 57. redounded as a *f.* on those from
P. L. 11, 472. fire, *f.,* famine, by intemperance
P. L. 11, 748. all dwellings else *f.* overwhelmed
P. L. 11, 756. another *f.,* of tears and sorrow a *f.*
P. L. 11, 831. pushed by the horned *f.*
P. L. 11, 840. and saw the ark hull on the *f.*
P. L. 11, 893. to destroy the earth again by *f.*
P. L. 12, 117. patriarch lived who scaped the *f.*
P. R. 1, 24. to the *f.* Jordan came
P. R. 2, 178. before the *f.,* thou, with thy lusty
P. R. 3, 268. forest and field and *f.*
P. R. 3, 436. passing cleave the Assyrian *f.*

P. R. 4, 201. tetrarchs of fire, air, *f.*
C. 19. of every salt *f.,* and each ebbing stream
C. 831. commended her fair innocence to the *f.*
C. 930. nor wet October's torrent *f.*
A. 29. of that renowned *f.* so often sung
L. 85. Arethuse, and thou honoured *f.*
L. 185. to all that wander in that perilous *f.*
Il P. 94. in fire, air, *f.* or under ground
P. 37. that whirled the prophet up at Chebar *f.*
T. 13. and joy shall overtake us as a *f.*

**Floods.**—P. L. 1, 77. with *f.* and whirlwinds
P. L. 6, 830. as with the sound of torrent *f.*
P. L. 7, 295. impressed on the swift *f.*

**Floor.**—P. L. 4, 984. lest on the threshing-*f.*
L. 167. sunk though he be beneath the watery *f.*

**Flora.**—P. L. 5, 16. Zephyrus on *F.* breathes
P. R. 2, 365. and *F.'s* earliest smells

**Florid.**—P. L. 4, 278. her *f.* son, young Bacchus
P. L. 7, 90. embracing round this *f.* earth
P. L. 7, 445. with the *f.* hue of rainbows

**Flourished.**—P. L. 4, 699, *f.* heads between
P. L. 7, 320. forth *f.* thick the clustering vine
P. L. 9, 672. where eloquence *f.,* since mute
S. 10, 10. the days wherein your father *f.*

**Flourishing.**—P. R. 3, 80. all the *f.* works

**Flow.**—P. L. 3, 31. and warbling *f.*
P. L. 4, 410. all ear to hear new utterance *f.*
P. L. 5, 195. and ye that warble as ye *f.*
P. L. 8, 601. that daily *f.* from all her words
P. L. 9, 239. for smiles from reason *f.*
W. S. 10. thy easy numbers *f.*

**Flowed.**—P. L. 1, 11. and Siloa's brook that *f.*
P. L. 3, 518. and underneath a bright sea *f.*
P. L. 5, 150. eloquence *f.* from their lips
P. L. 6, 332. nectarous humour issuing *f.*
P. L. 7, 8. the hills appeared or fountain *f.*
P. L. 7, 279. main ocean *f.,* not idle, but with
P. L. 11, 241. a military vest of purple *f.*
P. R. 3, 255. from his side two rivers *f.*
S. A. 547. wherever fountain or fresh current *f.*

**Flower.**—P. L. 1, 316. warriors, the *f.* of heaven
P. L. 3, 353. amarant, a *f.* which once in paradise
P. L. 4, 270. herself a fairer *f.* by gloomy Dis
P. L. 4, 644. on herb, tree, fruit, and *f.*
P. L. 4, 652. nor herb, fruit, *f.,* glistering
P. L. 4, 697. each beauteous *f.,* iris all hues
P. L. 5, 481. last the bright consummate *f.*
P. L. 5, 747. impearls on every leaf and every *f.*
P. L. 6, 475. with plant, fruit, *f.,* ambrosial
P. L. 9, 206. still to tend plant, herb, and *f.*
P. L. 9, 428. oft stooping to support each *f.*
P. L. 9, 432. though fairest unsupported *f.*
P. R. 1, 67. but his growth now to youth's full *f.*
P. R. 3, 314. *f.* and choice of many provinces
S. A. 144. a thousand foreskins fell, the *f.*
S. A. 728. like a fair *f.* surcharged with dew
S. A. 938. if in my *f.* of youth and strength
S. A. 1654. their choice nobility and *f.*
C. 633. bore a bright golden *f.*
L. 106. like to that sanguine *f.*
L. 148. every *f.* that sad embroidery wears
D. F. I. 1. O fairest *f.,* no sooner blown
D. F. I. 27. transformed him to a purple *f.*
M. W. 39. who only thought to crop the *f.*

**Flowered.**—P. L. 7, 317. leaf that sudden *f.*

**Flowerets.**—P. L. 5, 379. with *f.* decked
P. L. 5, 636. on flowers reposed, with fresh *f.*
P. L. 6, 784. with fresh *f.* hill
L. 135. their bells and *f.* of a thousand hues

**Flowering.**—P. L. 5, 293. and *f.* odours

**Flowers.**—P. L. 1, 771. among fresh dews and *f.*
P. L. 2, 245. ambrosial odours and ambrosial *f.*
P. L. 3, 357. *f.* aloft, shading the fount of life
P. L. 3, 359. rolls o'er Elysian *f.* her amber
P. L. 4, 241. and fed *f.* worthy of Paradise
P. L. 4, 256. *f.* of all hue, and without thorn
P. L. 4, 269. where Proserpine gathering *f.*
P. L. 4, 334. downy banks damasked with *f.*
P. L. 4, 438. growing plants and tend these *f.*
P. L. 4, 451. reposed under a shade on *f.*
P. L. 4, 501. the clouds that shed May *f.*

P. L. 4, 709. *f.*, garlands, and sweet-smelling
P. L. 5, 126. the fountains and the *f.*
P. L. 5, 212. among sweet dews and *f.*
P. L. 5, 482. *f.* and their fruit
P. L. 5, 636. on *f.* reposed, and with fresh
P. L. 8, 44. among her fruits and *f.*
F. L. 8, 286. on a shady bank profuse or *f.*
P. L. 8, 527. sight, smell, herbs, fruits, and *f.*
P. L. 9, 193. dawn in Eden on the humid *f.*
P. L. 9, 278. returned at shut of evening *f.*
P. L. 9, 408. hid among sweet *f.* and shades
P. L. 9, 437. thick-woven arborets and *f.*
P. L. 9, 840. had wove of choicest *f.*
P. L. 9, 1089. *f.* were the couch
P. L. 10, 603. and fruits and *f.*
P. L. 10, 679. smiled on earth with vernant *f.*
P. L. 11, 273. O *f.*, that never will in other
P. L. 11, 327. gums and fruits, and *f.*
P. L. 11, 594. youth not lost, songs garlands *f.*
P. R. 2, 356. and *f.* from Amalthea's horn
S. A. 987. with odours visited and annual *f.*
S. A. 1742. visit his tomb with *f.*
C. 994. *f.* of more mingled hue
L. 47. to *f.* that their gay wardrobe wear
L. 141. purple all the ground with vernal *f.*
L'A. 147. on a bed of heaped Elysian *f.*
M. W. 57. and some *f.* and some bays
**Flower-inwoven.**—H. 187. with *f.-i.* tresses
**Flowery.**—P. L. 1, 410. the *f.* dale of Sibma
P. L. 3, 30. chief, thee, Sion, and the *f.* brooks
P. L. 3, 569. field and groves and *f.* vales
P. L. 4, 254. or the *f.* lap of some irriguous
P. L. 4, 626. to reform yon *f.* arbors
P. L. 4, 772. the *f.* roof showered roses
P. L. 8, 254. on the *f.* herb I found me laid
P. L. 9, 456. this *f.* plat, the sweet recess
P. L. 11, 881. or serve they as a *f.* verge
P. R. 4, 247. *f.* hill. Hymettus, with the sound
P. R. 4, 586. then in a *f.* valley set him down
C. 239. Oh, if thou have hid them in some *f.*
Il P. 143. that at her *f.* work doth sing
M. M. 3. the *f.* May, who from her green lap
V. Ex. 84. and peace shall lull him in her *f.* lap
**Flowery-kirtled.**—C. 254. the *f.-k.* Naiades
**Flowing.**—P. L. 3, 640. his *f.* hair in curls
P. L. 4, 496. the *f.* gold of her loose tresses
P. L. 5, 444. and their *f.* cups with pleasant
P. L. 10, 910. with tears that ceased not *f.*
P. L. 11, 846. which made their *f.* shrink
P. R. 2, 436. in height of all their *f.* wealth
Il P. 34. *f.* with majestic train
U. C. II. 31. linked to the mutual *f.* of the seas
**Flown.**—P. L. 1, 502. *f.* with insolence and wine
P. L. 7, 503. by fowl, fish, beast, was *f.*
P. L. 10, 422. *f.* to the upper world
**Flows.**—P. L. 5, 633. nectar *f.* in pearl
P. L. 9, 81. to the land where *f.* Ganges
P. L. 12, 158. where it *f.* disgorging at seven
**Fluctuates.**—P. L. 9, 668. *f.* disturbed
**Fluid.**—P. L. 6, 349. more than can the *f.* air
P. L. 7, 237. throughout the *f.* mass
P. L. 11, 882. the *f* skirts of that same
**Flung.**—P. L. 1, 610. from eternal splendours *f.*
P. L. 6, 654. main promontories *f.*
P. L. 8, 517. from their wings *f.* rose, *f.*
**Flushing.**—P. L. 9. 887. distemper *f.*
**Flute.**—C. 173. such as the jocund *f.*
L. 33. tempered to the oaten *f.*
**Flutes.**—P. L., 1, 551. to the Dorian mood of *f.*
**Fluttered.**—P. L. 3, 491. and *f.* into rags
**Fluttering.**—P. L. 2, 933. unawares *f.*
**Fly.**—P. L. 1, 772. fresh dews and flowers *f.*
P. L. 2, 879. on a sudden open *f.* with
P. L. 3, 494. *f.* o'er the backside of the world
P. L. 4, 22. no more than from himself, can *f.*
P. L. 4, 73. which way shall I *f.*
P. L. 4, 75. which way I *f* is hell
P. L. 4, 859. to strive or *f.* he held it vain
P. L. 4, 910. he judges it to *f.* from pain
P. L. 4, 948. pretending first wise to *f.* pain
P. L. 4, 963. *f.* thither whence thou fledst

P. L. 5, 871. *f.* ere evil intercept thy flight
P. L. 5, 889. not for thy advice or threats I *f.*
P. L. 6, 295. I *f.* not, but have sought thee far
P. L. 7, 389. and let fowl *f.* above the earth
P. L. 11, 547. I *f.* not death
P. L. 11, 650. scarce with life the shepherds *f.*
P. R. 1, 440. to *f.* or follow what
P. R. 2, 75. enforced to *f.* thence into Egypt
P. R. 3, 216. willingly I could *f.* and hope
P. R. 4, 629. shall *f.* and beg to hide them
S. A. 1541. shall I run or which way *f.*
C. 939. let us *f.* this cursed place
C. 976. to the ocean now I *f.* and those happy
C. 1013. I can *f.*, or I can run
S. 2, 3. my hasting days *f.* on with full career
S. 18, 14. early may *f.* the Babylonian woe
H. 236. *f.* after the night steeds
T. 1. *f.*, envious Time, till thou run out
V. Ex. 28. *f.* swiftly to this fair assembly's ears
D. F. I. 60. after short abode *f.* back
**Flying.**—P. L. 2, 574. their *f.* march along
P. L. 2, 643. so seemed far off the *f.* fiend
P. L. 2, 942. half *f.;* behoves him
P. L. 4, 913. which thou incurr'st by *f.*
P. L. 5, 688. homeward with *f.* march
P. L. 6, 214. and, *f.*, vaulted either host
P. L. 6, 536. *f.*, and in mid air aloud cried
P. L. 7, 17. lest from this *f.* steed unreined
P. L. 7, 429. high over seas *f.*, and over lands
P. L. 10, 276. come *f.*, lured with scent
P. R. 3, 323. *f.* behind them, shot, sharp sleet
S. A. 254. not *f.*, but forecasting in what
C. 829. she, guiltless damsel, *f.* the mad pursuit
**Foam.**—P. L. 1, 209. on the Norway *f.*
P. L. 6, 512. sulphurous and nitrous *f.*
**Foaming.**—P. L. 6, 391. and fiery *f.* steeds
P. L. 10, 301. over the *f.* deep high-arched
P. L. 11, 643. part curb the *f.* steed
**Foe.**—P. L. 1, 122. irreconcileable to our *f.*
P. L. 1, 179. satiate fury yield it from our *f.*
P. L. 1, 649. hath overcome but half his *f.*
P. L. 2, 72. upright wing against a higher *f.*
P. L. 2, 78. the fierce *f.* hung on our rear
P. L. 2, 152. whether our angry *f.* can give it
P. L. 2, 202. we were wise against so great a *f.*
P. L. 2, 210. our supreme *f.* in time may much
P. L. 2, 369. may prove their *f.*
P. L. 2, 463. no watch against a wakeful *f.*
P. L. 2, 722. either like to meet so great a *f.*
P. L. 2, 769. to our almighty *f.* clear victory
P. L. 2, 804. grim death, my son and *f.*
P. L. 2, 1039. her outmost works, a broken *f.*
P. L. 3, 179. against his mortal *f.*
P. L. 4, 7. the coming of their secret *f.*
P. L. 4, 372. for heaven to keep out such a *f.*
P. L. 4, 373. now is entered, yet no purposed *f.*
P. L. 4, 749. our destroyer, *f.* to God and man
P. L. 5, 724. a *f.* is rising, who intends to erect
P. L. 6, 129. half-way he met his daring *f.*
P. L. 6, 149. the grand *f.*, with scornful eye
P. L. 6, 363. Uriel and Raphael his vaunting *f.*
P. L. 6, 530. descry the distant *f.*, where lodged
P. L. 6, 537. *f.* at hand, whom fled we thought
P. L. 6, 551. with heavy pace the *f.*
P. L. 7, 139. at least our envious *f.* hath failed
P. L. 9, 15. on his *f.* pursued thrice fugitive
P. L. 9, 253. what malicious *f.*, envying
P. L. 9, 280. because we have a *f.* may tempt
P. L. 9, 295. attempt itself intended by our *f.*
P. L. 9, 323. straitened by a *f.*
P. L. 9, 327. only our *f.*, tempting
P. L. 9, 361. some specious object by the *f.*
P. L. 9, 383. a *f.* so proud will first the weaker
P. L. 9, 486. *f.* not informidable
P. L. 9, 951. of scorn, not to be given the *f.*
P. L. 10, 11. whatever wiles of *f.* or seeming
P. L. 10, 431. the Tartar from his Russian *f.*
P. L. 10, 926. against a *f.* by doom express
P. L. 10, 1033. our grand *f.*, Satan
P. L. 10, 1038. so our *f.* shall scape
P. L. 11, 155. thy seed shall bruise our *f.*

P. R. 1, 10. the spiritual f.
P. R. 1, 387. men generally think me much a f.
S. A. 561. and at another to let in the f.
S. A. 884. thy country's f. professed
S. A. 1193. I chose a wife, which argued me no f.
S. A. 1262. my deadliest f. will prove my
S. A. 1469. reduced their f. to misery beneath
S. A. 1518. slaughter of one f. could not ascend
D. F. I. 66. whom sin hath made our f.
V. Ex. 83. to find a f. it shall not be his hap
**Foes.**—P. L. 1, 437. the spear of despicable f.
P. L. 2, 504. as if man had not hellish f. enow
P. L. 3, 258. by thee raised, I ruin all my f.
P. L. 3, 399. to execute fierce vengeance on his f.
P. L. 3, 677. justly hath driven out his rebel f.
P. L. 5, 735. thou thy f. justly hast in derision
P. L. 5, 876. encompassed round with f.
P. L. 6, 39. back on thy f. more glorious
P. L. 6, 402. innocence gave them above their f.
P. L. 6, 440. to better us, and worse our f.
P. L. 6, 487. among our f. such implements
P. L. 6, 603. to their f. a laughter
P. L. 6, 627. they show us when our f. walk
P. L. 6, 688. when two such f. met armed
P. L. 6, 785. this saw his hapless f., but stood
P. L. 6, 831. on his impious f. right onward drove
P. L. 6, 880. victor, from the expulsion of his f.
P. L. 11, 703. so beset with f. for daring single
P. L. 12, 453. through the air over his f.
P. R. 1, 159. sin and death, the two grand f.
P. R. 3, 120. from us, his f. pronounced
S. A. 109. life in captivity among inhuman f.
S. A. 342. the dread of Israel's f.
S. A. 366. thy f.' derision, captive, poor, and
S. A. 423. find some occasion to infest our f.
S. A. 424. our f. found soon occasion
S. A. 897. and prosecute their f.
S. A. 1529. be dealing dole among his f.
S. A. 1586. at variance.. among his f.
S. A. 1667. with thy slaughtered f.
C. 449. wherewith she freezed her f.
S. 16, 11. new f. arise to bind our souls
**Fog.**—C. 269. forbidding every bleak unkindly f.
C. 433. in f. or fire, by lake or moorish fen
**Foil.**—P. L. 10, 375. and fully avenged our f.
P. L. 12, 389. more strength to f. the enemy
P. R. 4, 569. so, after many a f.. the tempter
L. 79. nor in the glistering f. set off to the world
**Foiled.**—P. L. 1, 273. none could have f.
P. L. 2, 330. and f. with loss irreparable
P. L. 6, 200. but greater rage to see thus f.
P. L. 8, 608. not therefore f.
P. R. 1, 5. the tempter f. in all his wiles
P. R. 4, 565. and oft f. still rose
**Foils.**—P. R. 4, 13. tempting him who f. him still
**Fold.**—P. L. 2, 651. in many a scaly f.
P. L. 4, 187. o'er the fence with ease into the f.
P. L. 4, 192. this first grand thief into God's f.
P. L. 9, 499. folds that towered f. above f.
S. A. 1665. but tangled in the f. of dire necessity
C. 93. the star that bids the shepherd f.
C. 498. hath any ram slipped from the f.
C. 542. and were in f.
L. 115. creep and intrude, and climb into the f.
S. 18, 6. thy sheep, and in their ancient f.
**Folded.**—C. 344. the f. flocks penned in their
H. 172. the scaly horror of his f. tail
**Folds.**—P. L. 1, 724. opening their brazen f.
P. L. 2, 645. three f. were brass, three iron
P. L. 7, 484. involved their snaky f.
P. L. 9, 161. in whose mazy f. to hide me
P. L. 9, 498. circular base of rising f.
P. L. 11, 431. the other part sheep-walks and f.
P. R. 1, 244. to shepherds watching at their f.
**Follow.**—P. L. 2, 206. yet they know must f.
P. L. 2, 662. nor uglier f. the night-hag
P. L. 2, 866. whom should I obey ... whom f.?
P. L. 4, 469. but f. me, and I will bring thee
P. L. 4, 476. what could I do but f. straight
P. L. 8, 611. approve the best and f. what I
P. L. 9, 133. soon f., as to him linked in weal

P. L. 11, 291. him to f. thou art bound
P. L. 11, 371. ascend, I f. thee safe guide
P. L. 12, 335. such f. him as shall be registered
P. R. 1, 440. to fly or f. what concerned him most
P. R. 1, 483. most men admire virtue who f. not
P. R. 3, 430. unreformed, headlong would f.
C. 657. Thyrsis, lead on apace, I'll f. thee
C. 1018. mortals that would f. me
A. 86. f. me as I sing, touch the warbled string
A. 90. f. me, I will bring you where she sits
**Followed.**—P. L. 1, 238. him f. his next mate
P. L. 1, 467. him f. Rimmom, whose delightful
P. L. 6, 598. but now foul dissipation f.
P. L. 7, 222. all his train f. in bright procession
P. L. 7, 558. up he rode, f. with acclamation
P. L. 8, 508. I f. her; she what was honour knew
P. L. 8, 645. Adam thus f. with benediction
P. L. 10, 533. they all him f., issuing forth
P. L. 12, 439. men who in his life still f. him
P. R. 4, 523. and f. thee still on to this waste
S. 14, 8. f. thee up to joy and bliss for ever
**Followers.**—P. L. 1, 606. of his crime, the f.
P. L. 12, 484. worse with his f. than with him
P. R. 2, 419. what f., what retinue canst thou
**Following.**—P. L. 2, 1025. amain f. his track
P. L. 4, 437. f. our delightful task to prune
P. L. 4, 481. f. criedst aloud, return fair Eve
P. L. 7, 3. whose voice divine f.
P. L. 9, 808. not f. thee, I had remained
P. L. 10, 278. designed for death, the f. day
P. L. 10, 314. f. the track of Satan
P. L. 10, 367. detain from f. thy illustrious
P. L. 10, 589. behind her death, close f.
P. L. 11, 352. still f. thee, still compassing thee
P. R. 1, 192. thought f. thought, and step by step
P. R. 1, 315. in rural weeds, f. as seemed
**Follows.**—P. L. 2, 25. which f. dignity
**Folly.**—P. L. 2, 686. retire or taste thy f.
P. L. 3, 153. though joined with his own f.
P. L. 4, 905. since Satan fell, whom f. overthrew
P. L. 4, 1007. f. then to boast what arms can do
P. L. 6, 139. incessant armies to defeat thy f.
P. L. 7, 130. soon turns wisdom to f.
P. L. 8, 553. loses discountenanced, and like f.
P. L. 10, 619. had not the f. of man let in
P. L. 10, 621. who impute f. to me
P. L. 12, 560. beyond which was my f.
S. A. 377. as vile hath been my f.
S. A. 825. such pardon therefore as I give my f.
S. A. 1000. and aggravate my f., who committed
S. A. 1043. to f. and shameful deeds, which ruin
C. 975. o'er sensual f. and intemperance
Il P. 2. the brood of f. without father bred
Il P. 61. sweet bird, that shunn'st the noise of f.
**Foment.**—P. L. 4, 669. various influence f.
P. L. 10, 1071. may with matter sere f.
**Fomented.**—P. L. 11, 338. f. by his virtual
**Fond.**—P. L. 3, 449. built their f. hopes of glory
P. L. 6, 90. their thoughts proved f. and vain
P. L. 8, 195. emptiness or f. impertinence
P. L. 8, 209. f., were it not in hope of thy reply
P. L. 10, 834. f. wish! couldst thou support
P. R. 2, 211. will vouchsafe an eye of f. desire
S. A. 228. O that I never had! f. wish too late
S. A. 812. though f. and reasonless to some
S. A. 1682. f. are mortal men, fallen into wrath
C. 67. taste through f. intemperate thirst
Il P. 6. and fancies f. with gaudy shapes possess
**Fondly.**—P. L. 3, 470. f. into Ætna flames
P. L. 7, 152. my damage f. deemed. I can repair
P. L. 9, 999. f. overcome with female charm
P. L. 10, 564. they, f. thinking to allay
P. L. 11, 59. that f. lost, this other served
L. 56. ay me! I f. dream
S. 19, 8. I f. ask
**Fontarabbia.**—P. L. 1, 587. peerage fell by F.
**Food.**—P. L. 5, 400. for f. and for delight
P. L. 5, 401. unsavoury f. perhaps to spiritual
P. L. 5, 407. no ingrateful f.; and f. alike those
P. L. 5, 465. f. not of angels, yet accepted so
P. L. 5, 633. on a sudden piled with angels' f.

P. L. 7, 126. but knowledge is as *f.*, and needs
P. L. 7, 408. their *f.* in jointed armour watch
P. L. 7, 540. all their pleasant fruit for *f.*
P. L. 9, 237. *f.*, or talk between—*f.* of the mind
P. L. 9, 240. and are of love the *f.*
P. L. 9, 573. my *f.*, nor aught but *f.* discerned
P. L. 9, 717. participating godlike *f.*
P. L. 9, 768. or to us denied this intellectual *f.*
P. L. 10, 986. must be at last *f.* for so foul
P. L. 11, 54. to air as gross, and mortal *f.*
P. L. 12, 74. what *f.* will he convey up thither
P. R. 1, 308. nor tasted human *f.*, nor hunger felt
P. R. 1,345. *f.*, where of we wretched seldom taste
P. R. 1, 353. and forty days Elijah without *f.*
P. R. 1, 429. for lying is thy sustenance, thy *f.*
P. R. 2, 231. hungers where no *f.* is to be found
P. R. 2, 246. and human *f.* nor tasted
P. R. 2, 268. *f.* to Elijah bringing
P. R. 2, 320. tell me, if *f.* were now before thee
P. R. 4, 588. spread a table of celestial *f.*
S. A. 574. or the draff of servile *f.* consume me
S. A. 1366. honest and lawful, to deserve my *f.*
**Fool.**—P. L. 6, 135. *f.!* not to think how vain
S. A. 77. still as a *f.*, in power of others
S. A. 201. for a word, a tear, *f.!* have divulged
S. A. 203. am I not sung and proverbed for a *f.*
S. A. 298. but the heart of the *f.*
S. A. 496. the mark of *f.* set on his front
S. A. 907. I was a *f.*, too rash, and quite mistaken
S. A. 1338. although their drudge, to be their *f.*
C. 662. *f.* do not boast, thou canst not touch
**Fooled.**—P. L. 10, 880. *f.* and beguiled
**Foolish.**—S. A. 198. a *f.* pilot, have shipwrecked
**Foolishness.**—C. 706. O *f.* of men!
**Fools.**—P. L. 3, 496. called the paradise of *f.*
P. R. 2, 453. extol not riches, then, the toil of *f.*
C. 477. not harsh and crabbed as dull *f.* suppose
**Foot.**—P. L. 2, 941. half on *f.*, half flying
P. L. 3, 485. and now at *f.* of heaven's ascent
P. L. 6, 625. had moved from head to *f.* well
P. L. 7, 228. one *f.* he centred, and the other
P. L. 9, 71. where Tigris, at the *f.* of Paradise
P. L. 10, 347. the brink of Chaos, near the *f.*
P. L. 11, 645. horse and *f.*
P. L. 11, 848. that stole with soft *f.* towards
P. L. 11, 858. tree or ground whereon his *f.*
P. R. 3, 327. nor wanted clouds of *f.*
P. R. 4, 559. thou chance to dash thy *f.* against
P. R. 4, 610. never more will dare set *f.*
S. A. 136. whom insupportably his *f.* advanced
S. A. 1618. horse and *f.* before him and behind
**Footing.**—C. 146. of some chaste *f.* near about
L. 103. next Camus, reverend sire, went *f.* slow
**Footstep.**—P. L. 11, 329. appearances or *f.*
**Footsteps.**—P. R. 4, 521. I watched thy *f.*
**Forage.**—P. L. 11, 646. from *f.* drives a herd
**Forbear.**—P. L. 8, 490. could not *f.* aloud
**Forbearance.**—P. L. 10, 53. shall find *f.*
**Forbid.**—P. L. 5, 62. *f.* who will, none shall
P. L. 9, 356. to do what God expressly hath *f.*
P. L. 9, 703. why then was this *f.*?
P. L. 10, 685. which had *f.* the snow from cold
P. R. 1, 495. I bid not, nor *f.*
S. A. 13. and *f.* laborious works
**Forbiddance.**—P. L. 9, 903. the strict *f.*
**Forbidden.**—P. L. 1, 2. fruit of that *f.* tree
P. L. 2, 852. by him *f.* to unlock these
P. L. 4, 515. *f.* them to taste; knowledge *f.*
P. L. 5, 69. *f.* here, it seems, as only fit for gods
P. L. 9, 904. how to violate the sacred fruit *f.*
P. L. 9, 1025. pleasure be in things to us *f.*
P. L. 9, 1026. for this one tree had been *f.* ten
P. L. 10, 554. imagining for one *f.* tree
P. L. 12, 279. sought *f.* knowledge by *f.* means
P. R. 2, 369. these are not fruits *f.*
S. A. 555. when God, with these *f.*, made choice
S. A. 1139. I know no spells, use no *f.* arts
S. A. 1409. scandalous or *f.* in our law
**Forbidder.**—P. L. 9, 815. our great *F.*
**Forbidding;**—P. L. 2, 475. than his voice *f.*
P. L. 9, 753. but his *f.* commends thee more

C. 269. by blest song *f.* every bleak unkindly fog
**Forbids.**—P. L. 4, 82. that word disdain *f.*
P. L. 5, 61. or envy, or what reserve, *f.* to taste
P. L. 9, 750. who *f.* thy use conceals not
P. L. 9, 753. *f.* us then to taste
P. L. 9, 758. what *f.* he but to know
P. L. 9, 759. *f.* us good, *f.* us to be wise?
P. L. 11, 49. the law I gave to nature him *f.*
S. A. 1320. our law *f.* at their religious rites
**Forbore.**—P. L. 2, 736. the hellish pest *f.*
P. L. 9, 1034. so said he, and *f.* not glance
**Forborne.**—P. L. 9, 747. taste, too long *f.*
**Force.**—P. L. 1, 94. the *f.* of those dire arms
P. L. 1, 101. innumerable *f.* of spirits armed
P. L. 1, 121. to wage by *f.* or guile eternal war
P. L. 1, 144. whom I now of *f.* believe
P. L. 1, 145. could have o'erpowered such *f.*
P. L. 1, 230. as when the *f.* of subterranean
P. L. 1, 248. *f.* hath made supreme above his
P. L. 1, 560. breathing united *f.*
P. L. 1, 574. met such embodied *f.*
P. L. 1, 629. how such united *f.* of gods
P. L. 1, 647. what *f.* effected not
P. L. 1, 649. who overcomes by *f.* hath overcome
P. L. 2, 62. o'er heaven's high towers to *f.*
P. L. 2, 135. or could we break our way by *f.*
P. L. 2, 188. for what can *f.* or guile with him
P. L. 2, 250. by *f.* impossible
P. L. 2, 358. how attempted best by *f.*
P. L. 2, 551. free virtue should enthral to *f.*
P. L. 2, 853. against all *f.* death ready stands
P. L. 2, 1012. with fresh alacrity and *f.* renewed
P. L. 3, 91. with purpose to assay if him by *f.*
P. L. 4, 813. but returns of *f.* to its own
P. L. 5, 730. draw with speed what *f.* is left
P. L. 6, 41. subdue by *f.* who reason for their
P. L. 6, 125. when reason hath to deal with *f.*
P. L. 6, 222. and arm him with the *f.* of all
P. L. 6, 293. meanwhile thy utmost *f.*
P. L. 6, 324. with steep *f.* to smite descending
P. L. 6, 622. of hard contents, and full of *f.*
P. L. 6, 794. by *f.* or fraud weening to prosper
P. L. 9, 348. secure from outward *f.*
P. L. 9, 1046. as the *f.* of that fallacious fruit
P. L. 9, 1173. this had been *f.*, and *f.* upon thee
P. L. 10, 246. sympathy, or some connatural *f.*
P. L. 12, 412. seized on by *f.*
P. L. 12, 521. laws by carnal power shall *f.*
P. L. 12, 525. but *f.* the Spirit of grace itself
P. R. 1, 97. not *f.*, but well-couched fraud
P. R. 1, 153. and at length all his vast *f.*
P. R. 1, 347. think'st thou such *f.* in bread
P. R. 2, 479. and oft by *f.*, which to a generous
P. R. 4, 602. with godlike *f.* endued against
S. A. 146. then by main *f.* pulled up
S. A. 935. no more on me have power; their *f.*
S. A. 1087. each other's *f.* in camp or listed field
S. A. 1206. it was the *f.* of conquest, *f.* with *f.*
S. A. 1219. had not disabled me, not all your *f.*
S. A. 1273. brute and boisterous *f.*
S. A. 1369. outward *f.* constrains
S. A. 1397. as thou shalt come of *f.*
S. A. 1627. all with incredible stupendous *f.*
S. A. 1647. with the *f.* of winds and waters pent
C. 590. surprised by unjust *f.*
C. 607. and *f.* him to return his purchase back
C. 906. through the *f.* and through the wile
S. 23, 4. rescued from death by *f.*, though pale
D. F. I. 4. winter's *f.* that made thy blossom dry
F. of C. 6. *f.* our consciences that Christ set free
V. Ex. 67. something that doth *f.* my fear
V. Ex. 89. what *f.*, what mighty spell
**Forced.**—P. L. 2, 243. sing *f.* halleluiahs
P. L. 6, 598. dissipation followed and *f.* rout
P. L. 10, 475. *f.* to ride the untractable abyss
P. L. 10, 829. after all disputes, *f.* I absolve
P. L. 10, 991. *f.* to satisfy his ravenous maw
S. A. 1096. I should have *f.* thee soon
S. A. 1451. lest I should see him *f.* to things
L. 4. and with *f.* fingers rude
**Forces.**—P. R. 3, 337. such *f.* met not

**Forcible.**—P. L. 2, 793. in embraces *f.*
P. L. 6, 465. with what more *f.* we may offend
P. L. 9, 955. so *f.* within my heart I feel
**Forcing.**—P. L. 6, 196. or waters *f.* way
**Ford.**—P. L. 2, 612. terror guards the *f.*
P. L. 12, 130. passing now the *f.* to Haran
P. R. 1, 328. at the *f.* of Jordan honoured so
P. R. 4, 510. till, at the *f.* of Jordan, whither all
**Forecast.**—V. Ex. 13. and if it happen as I did *f.*
**Forecasting.**—S. A. 254. but *f.* in what place
**Forefathers.**—P. R. 3, 422. God óf their *f.*
**Foregoing.**—P. R. 4, 483. as a sure *f.* sign
**Forehead.**—C. 733. imblaze the *f.* of the deep
L. 171. flames in the *f.* of the morning sky
**Foreign.**—P. L. 3, 548. of some *f.* land
P. L. 10, 441. from the search of *f.* worlds
P. L. 12, 46. in *f.* lands, their memory be lost!
C. 265. Hail, *f.* wonder!
**Foreknew.**—P. L. 3, 117. if I *f.*
**Foreknowing.**—P. L. 11, 773. neither his *f.*
**Foreknowledge.**—P. L. 2, 559. *f.* will, and
P. L. 2, 560. fixed fate, free will, *f.* absolute
P. L. 3, 116. by absolute decree, or high *f.*
P. L. 3, 118. if I foreknew, *f.* had no influence
P. L. 11, 768. by my *f.* gaining birth abortive
**Foreland.**—P. L. 9, 514. river's mouth or *f.*
**Forelock.**—P. L. 4, 302. from his parted *f.*
P. R. 3, 173. but on occasion's *f.* watchful wait
**Foremost.**—P. L. 2, 28. *f.* to stand against
**Forerun.**—P. L. 1, 677. *f.* the royal camp
**Forerunners.**—P. L. 11, 195. *f.* of his purpose
**Forerunning.**—P. L. 7, 584. *f.* night
**Foresaw.**—S. A. 737. perverse event than I *f.*
V. Ex. 72. *f.* what future days should bring
**Foreseeing.**—P. L. 1, 627. *f.* or presaging
P. L. 3, 79. thus to his only son *f.* spake
**Foreseen.**—P. L. 3, 121. by me immutably *f.*
P. L. 6, 673. consulting on the sum of things, *f.*
P. L. 11, 763. O visions ill *f.!*
**Foresight.**—P. L. 1, 119. in *f.* much advanced
P. L. 11, 368. while thou to *f.* wakest
**Fore-signify.**—P. R. 4, 464. they oft *f.-s.*
**Foreskins.**—S. A. 144. a thousand *f.* fell
**Forest.**—P. L. 1, 547. a *f.* huge of spears
P. L. 1, 613. hath scathed the *f.* oaks
P. L. 1, 782. whose midnight revels by a *f.* side
P. L. 4, 342. in wood or wilderness, *f.*, or den
P. L. 5, 298. him through the spicy *f.* onward
P. L. 7, 458. the wild beast, where he wons in *f.*
P. L. 9. 117. shores with *f.* crowned
P. L. 11, 189. goodliest of all the *f.*
P. R. 2, 359. of faery damsels met in *f.* wide
P. R. 3, 268. o'er hill and dale, *f.* and field
**Forestall.**—C. 362. what need a man *f.*
**Forestalled.**—P. L. 10, 1024. so to be *f.*
**Forestalling.**—C. 285. perhaps *f.* night
**Forests.**—C. 423. may trace huge *f.*
Il P. 119. of *f.* and enchantments drear
**Foretasted.**—P. L. 9, 929. *f.* fruit
**Foretell.**—P. L. 12, 242. whose day he shall *f.*
P. R. 4, 375. yet remember what I *f.* thee
S. 1, 10. *f.* my hopeless doom
**Foretold.**—P. L. 2, 830. a place *f.* should be
P. L. 9, 1171. I admonished thee, *f.* the danger
P. L. 10, 38. *f.* so lately what would come
P. L. 10, 191. He who now *f.* his fatal bruise
P. L. 10, 482. fame in heaven long had *f.*
P. L. 10, 1051. pains only in child-bearing were *f.*
P. L. 11, 771. let no man seek henceforth to be *f.*
P. L. 12, 327. *f.*, *f.* to Abraham
P. L. 12, 329. to kings *f.*
P. L. 12, 543. obscurely then *f.*
P. R. 1, 238. a messenger from God *f.* thy birth
P. R. 1, 239. he *f.* thou shouldst be great
P. R. 1, 453. to thyself ascribest the truth *f.*
P. R. 2, 87. but trouble, as old Simeon plain *f.*
P. R. 3, 351. though *f.* by prophet or by angel
P. R. 4, 204. whose coming is *f.* to me most
P. R. 4, 478. be sure to find what I *f.* thee
P. R. 4, 502. of the Messiah I have heard *f.*
S. A. 23. was my birth from Heaven *f.*
S. A. 44. what if all *f.* had been fulfilled

S. A. 525. of birth from Heaven *f.*
S. A. 1662. the work for which thou wast *f.*
**Forewarn.**—P. L. 2, 810. O father, I *f.* thee
P. L. 7, 73. to *f.* us timely of what might else
P. L. 12, 507. but in their room, as they *f.*
**Forewarned.**—P. L. 7, 41. archangel had *f.*
P. L. 9, 61. and *f.* the Cherubim that kept
P. L. 9, 378. with thy permission, and thus *f.*
**Forewarning.**—P. L. 10, 876. rejected my *f.*
**Forfeit.**—P. L. 3, 176. *f.* and enthralled
P. L. 10. 304. now fenceless world *f.* to death
S. A. 508. thy penal *f.* from thyself
H. 6. that he our deadly *f.* should release
**Forfeiture.**—P. L. 3, 221. the deadly *f.*
**Forge.**—P. L. 4, 802. with them *f.* illusions
P. L. 11, 564. who at the *f.* labouring
**Forgery.**—S. A. 131. useless the *f.* of brazen
C. 698. with vizored falsehood and base *f.*
**Forget.**—P. L. 3, 32. nor sometimes *f.* those
P. L. 3, 415. never shall my harp thy praise *f.*
P. L. 4, 512. let me not *f.* what I have gained
P. L. 4, 639. with thee conversing I *f.* all time
P. L. 5, 550. yet that we never shall *f.* to love
P. L. 9, 474. to *f.* what hither brought us
P. L. 11, 878. and all his anger to *f.*
C. 76. and all their friends and native home *f.*
Il P. 42. *f.* thyself to marble
S. 18, 5. *f.* not; in thy book record
**Forgetful.**—P. L. 2, 74. of that *f.* lake
P. L. 4, 54. *f.* what from him I still received
**Forgetfulness.**—P. L. 2, 608. in sweet *f.*
**Forgets.**—P. L. 2, 585. *f.*, *f.* both joy and grief
**Forgive.**—S. A. 761. but ever to *f.*
S. A. 787. thine *f.* mine
S. A. 954. at distance I *f.* thee, go with that
**Forgiven.**—P. L. 10, 956. infirmer sex *f.*
**Forgiveness.**—S. A. 909. obtain *f.* of thee
S. A. 1376. shall never, unrepented, find *f.*
**Forgo.**—P. L. 8, 497. for this cause he shall *f.*
P. L. 9, 908. how *f.* thy sweet converse and love
P. L. 11, 541. all taste of pleasure must *f.*
S. A. 940. slight me, sell me, and *f.* me
S. A. 1483. if need be I am ready to *f.*
**Forgoes.**—H. 196. while each peculiar power *f.*
**Forgot.**—P. L. 2, 747. hast thou *f.* me then
P. L. 11, 807. temperance, truth, and faith *f.*
S. A. 479. must not in the meanwhile, here *f.*
S. 22. 3. bereft of light, their seeing have *f.*
H. 67. who now hath quite *f.* to rave
**Forked.**—P. L. 10, 518. *f.* tongue to *f.* tongue
**Forlorn.**—P. L. 1, 180. dreary plain, *f.*
P. L. 2, 615. thus roving on in confused march *f.*
P. L. 4, 374. whom I could pity thus *f.*
P. L. 7, 20. erroneous there to wander and *f.*
P. L. 9, 910. to live again in these wild woods *f.*
P. L. 10, 921. *f.* of thee whither shall I betake
C. 39. threats the *f.* and wandering passenger
L'A. 3. in Stygian cave *f.*
**Form.**—P. L. 1, 591. his *f.* had yet not lost
P. L. 2, 532. or fronted brigads *f.*
P. L. 3, 605. through a limbec to his native *f.*
P. L. 4, 876. how busied, in what *f.* and posture
P. L. 6, 433. we find this our empyreal *f.*
P. L. 9, 457. her heavenly *f.* angelic
P. L. 10, 214. thenceforth the *f.* of servant
P. L. 10, 543. the dire *f.* catched by contagion
P. L. 10, 872. lest that too heavenly *f.*
P. R. 4, 364. best *f.* a king
P. R. 4, 599. fleshly tabernacle and human *f.*
C. 70. into some brutish *f.* of wolf or bear
C. 215. thou unblemished *f.* of Chastity
S. 11, 2. woven close, both matter, *f.*, and style
H. 8. that glorious *f.*, that light unsufferable
**Formed.**—P. L. 1, 705. a third as soon had *f.*
P. L. 3, 124. for so I *f.* them free
P. L. 4, 297. for contemplation he and valour *f.*
P. L. 4, 365. such grace the hand that *f.*
P. L. 4, 441. I was *f.*, flesh of thy flesh
P. L. 5, 516. his love desert, who *f.* us
P. L. 5, 824. and *f.* the powers of heaven
P. L. 5, 853. that we were *f.* then sayest thou
P. L. 6, 690. in their creation they were *f.*

P. L. 7, 276. the earth was *f.*, but, in the womb
P. L. 7, 356. then *f.* the moon globose
P. L. 7, 524. he *f.* thee, Adam, thee, O man
P. L. 8, 469. the rib he *f.* and fashioned
P. L. 8, 596. neither her outside *f.* so fair
P. L. 9, 149. into our room a creature *f.*
P. L. 9, 392. rude, guiltless of fire, had *f.*
P. L. 9, 898. can to sight or thought be *f.*
P. L. 11, 369. while she to life was *f.*
P. L. 11, 571. which he *f.* first his own tools
**Former.**—P. L. 2, 234. the *f.*, vain to hope
P. L. 2, 585. forthwith his *f.* state and being
P. L. 4, 94. by act of grace my *f.* state
P. L. 5, 658. his *f.* name is heard no more
P. L. 8, 290. I then was passing to my *f.* state
P. L. 9, 1006. nor Eve to iterate her *f.* trespass
P. L. 12, 105. thus will this latter, as the *f.*
S. A. 231. I thought it lawful from my *f.* act
S. A. 372. be it but for honour's sake of *f.* deeds
S. A. 416. yet so base as was my *f.* servitude
S. A. 1510. horribly loud, unlike the *f.* shout
P. 25. *f.* sufferings, otherwhere are found
**Formidable.**—P. L. 2, 649. a *f.* shape
**Forming.**—P. L. 8, 470. under his *f.* hands
**Formless.**—P. L. 3, 12. void and *f.* infinite
P. L. 3, 708. when at his word the *f.* mass
**Forms.**—P. L. 1, 301. his legions, angel *f.*
P. L. 1, 358. godlike shapes and *f.* excelling
P. L. 1, 481. disguised in brutish *f.*
P. L. 1, 789. incorporeal spirits to smallest *f.*
P. L. 3, 717. spirited with various *f.*
P. L. 5, 105. she *f.* imaginations, aery shapes
P. L. 5, 457. whose radiant *f.* divine effulgence
P. L. 5, 473. endued with various *f.*
P. L. 5, 573. likening spiritual to corporal *f.*
P. L. 7, 455. living creatures, perfect *f.*
P. L. 8, 223. each word, each motion *f.*
P. L. 12, 534. in outward rites and specious *f.*
P. R. 3, 322. he saw them in their *f.* of battle
C. 605. the monstrous *f.* 'twixt Africa and Ind
**Forsake.**—P. L. 1, 368. to *f.* God their creator
P. L. 10, 914. *f.* me not thus, Adam!
P. L. 12, 118. to *f.* the living God
H. 198. *f.* their temples dim
**Forsaken.**—P. L. 5, 878. *f.* of all good
L. 142. bring the rathe primrose that *f.* dies
**Forsook.**—P. L. 1, 432. race of Israel oft *f.*
P. L. 11, 516. then *f.* them, when themselves
S. A. 629. sleep hath *f.* and given me o'er
C. 499. or straggling wether the pent flock *f.*
Il P. 91. the immortal mind that hath *f.*
H. 13. *f.* the courts of everlasting day
V. Ex. 51. *f.* the hated earth
**Fort.**—S. A. 236. gave up my *f.* of silence to a
S. A. 278. how Succoth and thy *f.* of Penuel
**Forth.**—P. L. 2, 506. and *f.* in order came
P. L. 2, 786. he, my inbred enemy *f.* issued
P. L. 4, 779. *f.* issuing at the accustomed hour
P. L. 5, 712. from *f.* his holy mount
P. L. 6, 749. *f.* rushed with whirlwind sound
P. R. 7, 166. ride *f.*, and bid the deep within
P. L. 7, 320. *f.* flourished thick the clustering
P. L. 11, 135. her rosy progress smiling. Let us *f.*
P. R. 3, 305. martial equipage they issue *f.*
S. A. 922. from *f.* this loathsome prison-house
**Forthwith.**—P. L. 1, 221. *f.* upright he rears
P. L. 1, 356. *f.* from every squadron
P. L. 1, 535. who *f.* from the glittering staff
P. L. 1, 755. a solemn council *f.* to be held
P. L. 2, 585. whereof who drinks *f.* his former
P. L. 2, 874. *f.* the huge portcullis high up
P. L. 3, 326. *f.* from all winds the living
P. L. 3, 327. and *f.* the cited dead
P. L. 5, 86. *f.* up to the clouds with him I flew
P. L. 5, 586. *f.* from all the ends of heaven
P. L. 5, 630. *f.* from dance to sweet repast
P. L. 6, 335. *f.* on all sides to his aid was run
P. L. 6, 507. from council to the work they *f.*
P. L. 6, 637. *f.* behold the excellence the
P. L. 7, 243. let there be light, said God, and *f.*
P. L. 7, 399. *f.* the sounds and seas, each creek

P. L. 8, 271. to speak I tried, and *f.* spake
P. L. 8, 291. insensible, and *f.* to dissolve
P. L. 9, 724. whoso eats thereof. *f.* attains
P. L. 10, 1098. they *f.* to the place repairing
P. L. 11, 855. *f.* from out the ark a raven flies
P. L. 12, 56. *f.* a hideous gabble rises loud
P. R. 2, 236. *f.* to him takes a chosen band
S. A. 329. advise *f.* how thou oughtst
**Fortify.**—P. L. 10, 370. empowered to *f.* thus
**Fortitude.**—P. L. 9, 31. *f.* of patience
P. L. 12, 570. is *f.* to highest victory
S. A. 654. extolling patience as the truest *f.*
S. A. 1288. the trial of their *f.*, making them
S. 16, 3. guided by faith and matchless *f.*
**Fortunate.**—P. L. 3, 569. *f.* fields, and groves
**Fortune.**—P. R. 2, 429. *f.* is in my hand
P. R. 4, 317. under usual names *F.* and Fate
S. A. 169. to lowest pitch of abject *f.*
S. A. 172. or the sphere of *f.* raises
S. A. 1093. that *f.* had brought me to the field
S. A. 1291. victor over all that tyranny or *f.*
S. 16, 5. on the neck of crowned *f.* proud
**Fortunes.**—M. W. 72. like *f.* may her soul
**Forty.**—P. R. 1, 303. full *f.* days he passed
P. R. 1, 352. *f.* days, nor eat nor drank
P. R. 1, 353. and *f.* days Elijah without food
P. R. 2, 243. after *f.* days fasting
P. R. 2, 276. whereof sufficed him *f.* days
P. R. 2, 315. of thee these *f.* days none hath
**Fought.**—P. L. 1, 578. that *f.* at Thebes
P. L. 2, 45. fiercest spirit that *f.* in heaven
P. L. 2, 768. and fields were *f.* in heaven
P. L. 6, 29. well hast thou *f.* the better fight
P. L. 6, 220. of fierce encountering angels *f.*
P. L. 6, 355. where the might of Gabriel *f.*
P. L. 6. 666. that underground they *f.*
P. L. 12, 261. how many battles *f.*
**Foughten.**—P. L. 6, 410. on the *f.* field
**Foul.**—P. L. 1, 33. seduced them to that *f.*
P. L. 1, 135. with sad overthrow and *f.* defeat
P. L. 1, 446. fell to idols *f.*
P. L. 1, 555. to flight or *f.* retreat
P. L. 2, 651. but ended *f.* in many a scaly fold
P. L. 2, 748. I seem now in thine eye so *f.*
P. L. 2, 793. and in embraces forcible and *f.*
P. L. 3, 177. by sin to *f.* exorbitant desires
P. L. 3, 692. to the fraudulent impostor *f.*
P. L. 4, 118. from such distempers *f.*
P. L. 4, 571. with passions *f.* obscured
P. L. 4, 840. and place of doom obscure and *f.*
P. L. 6, 124. though brutish that contest and *f.*
P. L. 6, 388. rout entered, and *f.* disorder
P. L. 6, 588. disgorging *f.* their devilish glut
P. L. 6, 598. but now *f.* dissipation followed
P. L. 9, 6. *f.* distrust and breach disloyal
P. L. 9, 163. O *f.* descent! that I who erst
P. L. 9, 297. the tempted with dishonour *f.*
P. L. 9, 328. affronts us with his *f.* esteem
P. L. 9, 329. his *f.* esteem sticks no dishonour
P. L. 9, 331. but turns *f.* on himself
P. L. 9, 1078. the signs of *f.* concupiscence
P. L. 10, 986. must be at last food for so *f.*
P. L. 11, 51. no unharmonious mixture *f.*
P. L. 11, 124. a receptacle prove to spirits *f.*
P. L. 11, 464. O sight of terror, *f.* and ugly
P. L. 12, 337. *f.* idolatries and other faults
P. R. 3, 161. oft the law, with *f.* affronts
P. R. 4, 426. thus passed the night so *f.*
P. R. 4, 628. demoniac holds, possession *f.*
S. A. 371. subject him to so *f.* indignities
S. A. 410. but *f.* effeminacy held me yoked
S. A. 902. in thy guilt, how *f.* must thou appear
C. 74. not once perceive their *f.* disfigurement
C. 383. hides a dark soul and *f.* thoughts
C. 464. loose gestures, and *f.* talk
C. 608. or drag him by the curls to a *f.* death
C. 645. I knew the *f.* enchanter
C. 696. with thy brewed enchantments. *f.*
L. 127. rot inwardly, and *f.* contagion spread
H. 44. look so near upon her *f.* deformities
D. F. I. 14. a *f.* reproach was held

K

U. C. I. 3. being *f.*, twenty to one
**Found.**—P. L. 1, 237. such resting *f.* the sole
P. L. 1, 333. sleeping *f.* by whom they dread
P. L. 1, 513. Rhea's son, like measure *f.*
P. L. 1, 524. to have *f.* their chief not in despair
P. L. 1, 525. to have *f.* themselves not lost
P. L. 1, 621. words interwove with sighs *f.* out
P. L. 2, 296. and no less desire to *f.* this nether
P. L. 2, 424. champions could be *f.*
P. L. 2, 561. and *f.* no end, in wandering mazes
P. L. 2, 617. and *f.* no rest
P. L. 3, 275. the only peace *f.* out for mankind
P. L. 3, 308. and hast been *f.* by merit more
P. L. 3, 310. *f.* worthiest to be so by being good
P. L. 3, 411. nowhere to be *f.* less than Divine
P. L. 3, 443. living or lifeless, to be *f.* was none
P. L. 3, 498. all this dark globe the fiend *f.*
P. L. 3, 591. the place he *f.* beyond expression
P. L. 3, 615. for sight no obstacle *f.* here
P. L. 4, 174. but farther way *f.* none
P. L. 4, 450. and *f.* myself reposed
P. L. 4, 799. him they *f.* squat like a toad
P. L. 4, 875. whom they brought, where *f.*
P. L. 4, 900. they *f.* me where they say
P. L. 5, 18. my espoused, my latest *f.*
P. L. 5, 48. I rose as at thy call, but *f.* thee not
P. L. 5, 406. may of purest spirits be *f.*
P. L. 5, 501. if ye be *f.* obedient
P. L. 5, 513. that caution joined, if ye be *f.*
P. L. 5, 742. or be *f.* the worst in heaven
P. L. 5, 848. while pardon may be *f.*, in time
P. L. 5, 896. faithful *f.* among the faithless
P. L. 6, 19. and *f.* already known what he
P. L. 6, 420. *f.* worthy not of liberty alone
P. L. 6, 500. once *f.*, which yet unfound
P. L. 6, 513. nitrous foam they *f.*
P. L. 6, 518. whereof to *f.* their engines
P. L. 6, 635. and *f.* them arms
P. L. 6, 694. and no solution will be *f.*
P. L. 7, 298. where way they *f.*
P. L. 7, 302. wandering, *f.* their way
P. L. 8, 240. we *f.*, fast shut the dismal gates
P. L. 8, 254. on the flowery herb I *f.* me laid
P. L. 8, 288. there gentle sleep first *f.* me
P. L. 8, 309. I waked, and *f.* before mine eyes
P. L. 8, 355. I *f.* not what methought
P. L. 8, 416. and in thee is no deficience *f.*
P. L. 8, 435. acceptance *f.* .
P. L. 8, 594. no mate for thee was *f.*
P. L. 9, 69. by stealth *f.* unsuspected way
P. L. 9, 85. and *f.* the serpent subtlest beast
P. L. 9, 182. him fast sleeping soon he *f.*
P. L. 9, 232. nothing lovelier can be *f.*
P. L. 9, 298. how *f.* they harbour in thy breast
P. L. 9, 301. though ineffectual *f.*
P. L. 9, 597. at feed or fountain never had I *f.*
P. L. 9, 874. have also tasted, and have also *f.*
P. L. 9, 982. nor yet on him *f.* deadly
P. L. 9, 1053. soon *f.* their eyes how opened
P. L. 9, 1116. Columbus the American
P. L. 10, 256. to *f.* a path over this main
P. L. 10, 420. and all about *f.* desolate
P. L. 10, 480. thence how I *f.* the new-created
P. L. 10, 816. both Death and I am *f.* eternal
P. L. 10, 888. to my just number *f.*
P. L. 10, 969. *f.* so erroneous
P. L. 10, 970. *f.* so unfortunate
P. L. 10, 1001. he not *f.*, supply with our own
P. L. 11, 137. and *f.* strength added from above
P. L. 11, 350. God is, as here, and will be *f.*
P. L. 11, 456. that his brother's offering *f.*
P. L. 11, 566. whether *f.* where casual fire
P. L. 11, 673. refuge none was *f.*
P. L. 11, 800. in sharp contest of battle *f.*
P. L. 11, 876. for one man *f.* so perfect
P. L. 12, 224. they shall *f.* their government
P. L. 12, 537. works of faith rarely be *f.*
P. L. 12, 608. ran before, but *f.* her waked
P. R. 1, 104. and the way *f.* prosperous once
P. R. 1, 207. the law of God I read, and *f.* it sweet
P. R. 1, 252. whose bright course led on they *f.*

P. R. 1, 256. by vision, *f.* thee in the temple
P. R. 1, 262. and soon *f.* of whom they spake
P. R. 2, 9. now missing him their joy so lately *f.*
P. R. 2, 10. so lately *f.* and so abruptly gone
P. R. 2, 59. to find whom at the first they *f.*
P. R. 2, 97. I lost him but so *f.* as well I saw
P. R. 2, 131. have *f.* him, viewed him
P. R. 2, 154. daughters of men the fairest *f.*
P. R. 2, 232. hungers where no food is to be *f.*
P. R. 2, 273. he *f.* his supper on the coals
P. R. 2, 283. and *f.* all was but a dream
P. R. 2, 309. *f.* he relief by a providing angel
P. R. 3, 230. what of perfection can . . be *f.*
P. R. 3, 242. who, seeking asses, *f.* a kingdom
P. R. 3, 365. of late *f.* able by invasion
P. R. 4, 217. there wast *f.* among the gravest
P. R. 4, 346. will far be *f.* unworthy
P. R. 4, 373. I *f.* thee there, and thither will
P. R. 4, 447. walking on a sunny hill he *f.*
P. R. 4, 532. and confess have *f.* thee proof
P. R. 4, 574. that once *f.* out and solved
S. A. 20. no sooner *f.* alone but rush upon me
S. A. 193. not to be *f.*, though sought
S. A. 301. as to his own edicts *f.* contradicting
S. A. 387. in this other was there *f.* more faith
S. A. 425. I am sure our foes *f.* soon occasion
S. A. 789. strength from me . . . was *f.*
S. A. 1047. *f.* that in domestic good combines
S. A. 1461. averse I *f.* and wondrous harsh
S. A. 1748. and ever best *f.* in the close
C. 323. courtesy which oft is sooner *f.* in
C. 454. that when a soul is *f.* sincerely so
C. 570. till guided by mine ear I *f.* the place
C. 579. till I had *f.* you here
Il P. 93. those demons that are *f.* in fire, air
P. 25. former sufferings otherwhere are *f.*
P. 43. mine eye hath *f.* that sad sepulchral rock
M. W. 16. quickly *f.* a lover meet
**Foundation.**—P. L. 4, 521. O fair *f.* laid
C. 808. against the canon laws of our *f.*
**Foundations.**—P. L. 6, 643. from their *f.*
P. L. 6, 870. had cast too deep her dark *f.*
H. 123. and cast the dark *f.* deep
**Founded.**—P. L. 1, 427. nor *f.* on the brittle
P. L. 1, 703. with wondrous art *f.* the massy ore
P. L. 4, 755. by thee *f.* in reason, loyal, just
P. L. 7, 239. then *f.*, then conglobed
P. L. 7, 618. from Heaven gate not far, *f.*
P. L. 12, 550. *f.* in righteousness and peace
P. R. 3, 295. who *f.* first that empire
P. R. 4, 613. a fairer paradise is *f.* now
**Foundered.**—P. L. 2, 940. nigh *f.* on he fares
**Foundest.**—P. L. 9, 407. *f.* either sweet repast
S. A. 427. temptation *f.* or over-potent charms
**Fount.**—P. L. 3, 357. shading the *f.* of life
P. L. 3, 535. Paneas, the *f.* of Jordan's flood
P. L. 4, 237. how from that sapphire *f.*
P. L. 11, 279. and water from the ambrosial *f.*
P. R. 4, 590. and from the *f.* of life ambrosial
**Fountain.**—P. L. 1, 783. by a forest side or *f.*
P. L. 3, 8. pure ethereal stream whose *f.*
P. L. 3, 375. thee, Author of all being *F.* of light
P. L. 4, 229. rose a fresh *f.* and with many a rill
P. L. 4, 326. by a fresh *f.* side they sat them
P. L. 4, 531. wandering spirits of heaven by *f.*
P. L. 4. 760. perpetual *f.* of domestic sweets
P. L. 5, 203. to hill or valley, *f.*, or fresh shade
P. L. 7, 8. before the hills appeared or *f.* flowed
P. L. 7, 364. hither as to their *f.* other stars
P. L. 9, 73. rose up a *f.* by the tree of life
P. L. 9, 420. by *f.* or by shady rivulet
P. L. 9, 597. at feed or *f.* never had I found
P. L. 9, 628. fast by a *f.* one small thicket past
P. L. 11, 78. of amarantine shade, *f.*, or spring
P. L. 11, 322. here with him at this *f.* talked
P. R. 2, 184. in wood or grove by mossy *f.* side
P. R. 4, 289. light from above, from the *F.*
S. A. 547. wherever *f.* or fresh current flowed
S. A. 581. God who caused a *f.* at thy prayer
C. 912. drops that from my *f.* pure
L. 24. fed the same flock by *f.* shade and rill

L. 85. O *f.* Arethuse, and thou honoured flood
**Fountain-brim.**—C. 119. brook and *f.-b.*
**Fountainless.**—P. R. 3, 264. *f.* and dry
**Fountains.**—P. L. 5, 126. the groves, the *f.*
P. L, 5, 195. *f.* and ye that warble as ye flow
P. L. 10, 860. O woods, O *f.,* hillocks, dales
P. L. 11, 826. all *f.* of the deep broke up
**Fountain-side.**—P. L. 7, 327. and each *f.-s.*
**Four.**—P. L. 2, 516. *f.* winds *f.* speedy cherubim
P. L. 2, 574. *f.* ways their flying march
P. L. 2, 575. of *f.* infernal rivers, that disgorge
P. L. 2, 898. *f.* champions fierce
P. L. 4, 233. now divided into *f.* main streams
P. L. 5, 192. that from *f.* quarters blow
P. L. 6, 753. *f.* cherubic shapes, *f.* faces each
P. L. 6, 827. at once the *f.* spread out their
P. L. 6, 845. from the fourfold-visaged *F.*
P. L. 9, 65. *f.* times crossed the car of night
P. L. 11, 128. *f.* faces each had like a double
P. L. 11, 737. with their *f.* wives
P. R. 2, 245. *f.* times ten days I have passed
P. R. 4, 415. rushed abroad from the *f.* hinges
**Fourfold-visaged.**—P. L. 6, 845. the *f.-v.*
**Four-footed.**—P. L. 4, 397. those *f.-f.* kinds
**Fourth.**—P. L. 7, 386. crowned the *f.* day
S. A. 402. *f.* time when mustering all her wiles
**Fowl.**—P. L. 7, 389. let *f.* fly above the earth
P. L. 7, 398. and let the *f.* be multiplied
P. L. 7, 447. fish replenished and the air with *f.*
P. L. 7, 503. by *f.,* fish, beast, was flown
P. L. 7, 521. over the fish, and *f.* of sea and air
P. L. 7, 533. over fish of the sea and *f.* of the air
P. L. 8, 341. live in sea, or air, beast, fish, and *f.*
P. L. 8, 395. can bird with beast or fish with *f.*
P. L. 10, 274. a flock of ravenous *f.*
P. L. 10, 604. each beast next and fish and *f.*
P. L. 10, 710. beast gan war and *f.* with *f.*
P. L. 12, 67. only over beast, fish, *f.,* dominion
P. R. 2, 342. beasts of chase or *f.* of game
S. A. 1695. of tame villatic *f.*
**Fowls.**—P. L. 5, 271. to all the *f.* he seems
P. R. 1, 501. *f.* in their clay nests were couched
S. A. 694. to dogs and *f.* a prey, or else captived
**Fragile.**—P. R. 3, 388. and *f.* arms
**Fragrance.**—P. L. 3, 135. ambrosial *f.* filled
P. L. 4, 653. nor *f.* after showers;
P. L. 5, 286. that heavenly *f.* filled the circuit
P. L. 8, 266. with *f.* and with joy my heart
P. L. 9, 425. he spies veiled in a cloud of *f.*
**Fragrant.**—P. L. 4, 645. *f.* the fertile earth
P. L. 4, 695. what higher grew of firm and *f.*
P. L. 5, 379. with flowerets decked and *f.* smells
P. R. 2, 351. by the wine that *f.* smell diffused
C. 674. with spirits of balm and *f.* syrups
**Frail.**—P. L. 2, 375. shall curse their *f.* original
P. L. 2, 1030. the utmost orb of this *f.* world
P. L. 3, 180. that he may know how *f.* his
P. L. 3, 404. thee purposed not to doom *f.* man
P. L. 4, 11. to wreak on *f.* man his loss
P. L. 6, 345. not as *f.* man in entrails
P. L. 9, 340. *f.* is our happiness if this be so
S. A. 656. all chances incident to man's *f.* life
C. 8. strive to keep up a *f.* and feverish being
L. 153. let our *f.* thoughts dally with false
Cir. 19. throned in secret bliss, for us *f.* dust
**Frailty.**—P. L. 10, 956. thy *f.* and infirmer sex
P. L. 11, 302. and dejection and despair our *f.*
S. A. 369. if he through *f.* err
S. A. 783. thou have trusted the woman's *f.*
C. 686. by which all mortal *f.* must subsist
**Frame.**—P. L. 2, 924. or less than if this *f.*
P. L. 3, 395. that shook heaven's everlasting *f.*
P. L. 5, 154. this universal *f.* thus wondrous
P. L. 7, 273. might distemper the whole *f.*
P. L. 8, 15. when I behold this goodly *f.*
P. L. 8, 81. how they will wield the mighty *f.*
P. R. 4, 455. as dangerous to the pillared *f.*
**Framed.**—P. L. 4, 691. when he *f.* all things
P. L. 5, 256. divine the sovran Architect had *f.*
P. L. 5, 460. thus to the empyreal minister he *f.*
P. L. 7, 355. a mighty sphere he *f.*

P. L. 12, 249. by his prescript a sanctuary is *f.*
**Frames.**—P. L. 5, 106. joining or disjoining *f.*
**Franciscan.**—P. L. 3, 480. or in *F.* think
**Fraternal.**—P. L. 12, 26. equality *f.* state
**Fraud.**—P. L. 1, 401. he led by *f.* to build
P. L. 1, 646. to work in close design by *f.*
P. L. 3, 152. fall circumvented thus by *f.*
P. L. 4, 121. artificer of *f.* and was the first
P. L. 5, 880. involved in this perfidious *f.*
P. L. 6, 555. squadrons deep to hide the *f.*
P. L. 6, 794. by force or *f.* weening to prosper
P. L. 7, 143. and into *f.* drew many
P. L. 9, 55. now improved in meditated *f.*
P. L. 9, 89. fit vessel, fittest imp of *f.*
P. L. 9, 285. his *f.* is then thy fear
P. L. 9, 287. love can by his *f.* be shaken
P. L. 9, 643. into *f.* led Eve our credulous
P. L. 9, 904. some cursed *f.* of enemy
P. L. 9, 1150. thou couldst not have discerned *f.*
P. L. 10, 485. him by *f.* I have seduced
P. L. 10, 871. may show thy inward *f.*
P. R. 1, 97. not force but well-couched *f.*
P. R. 1, 372. draw the proud king Ahab into *f.*
P. R. 4, 3. discovered in his *f.*
S. A. 76. to daily *f.* contempt, abuse, and wrong
S. 15, 13. from the shameful brand of public *f.*
**Fraudulent.**—P. L. 3, 692. who to the *f.*
P. L. 9, 531. his *f.* temptation thus began
P. R. 4, 609. and frustrated the conquest *f.*
**Fraught.**—P. L. 2, 715. heaven's artillery *f.*
P. L. 2, 1054. thither full *f.* with mischievous
P. L. 5, 661. yet *f.* with envy against the Son
P. L. 6, 876. hell their fit habitation *f.* with fire
P. L. 10, 346. with joy and tidings *f.*
P. L. 11, 207. with something heavenly *f.*
P. R. 1, 38. then with envy *f.* and rage
P. R. 3, 336. and waggons *f.* with utensils
S. A. 1075. his *f.* we soon shall know
C. 355. leans her unpillowed head, *f.* with sad
**Fray.**—P. L. 2, 908. more embroils the *f.*
P. L. 4, 996. eternal to prevent such horrid *f.*
**Freaked.**—L. 144. white pink, and the pansy *f.*
**Free.**—P. L. 1, 259. here at least we shall be *f.*
P. L. 2, 19. did first create your leader, next *f.*
P. L. 2, 255. though in this vast recess *f.*
P. L. 2 551. and complain that Fate *f.* Virtue
P. L. 2, 560. fixed fate, *f.* will, foreknowledge
P. L. 2, 823. but to set *f.* from out this dark
P. L. 3, 99. sufficient to have stood though *f.*
P. L. 3, 103. not *f.,* what proof could they have
P. L. 4, 66. hadst thou the same *f.* will
P. L. 4, 68. but heaven's *f.* love dealt equally
P. L. 4, 415. as liberal and *f.* as infinite
P. L. 4, 434. who enjoy *f.* leave so large to all
P. L. 4, 747. and commands to some leaves *f.*
P. L. 5, 235. happiness in his power left *f.*
P. L. 5, 236. *f.* will, his will though *f.*
P. L. 5, 527. ordained thy will by nature *f.*
P. L. 5, 532. for how can hearts not *f.* be tried
P. L. 5, 791. not equal all, yet *f.,* equally *f.*
P. L. 5, 819. unjust to bind with laws the *f.*
P. L. 6, 181. not *f.* but to thyself enthralled
P. L. 6, 292. to dwell *f.,* if not to reign
P. L. 6, 451. leader to *f.* enjoyment of our right
P. L. 7, 171. my goodness which is *f.*
P. L. 7, 464. the tawny lion pawing to get *f.*
P. L. 8, 440. well the spirit within thee *f.*
P. L. 8, 610. yet still *f.* approve the best
P. L. 8, 636. which else *f.* will would not admit
P. L. 8, 641. to stand or fall *f.* in thine own
P. L. 9, 351. but God left *f.* the will
P. L. 9, 352. reason is *f.,* and reason he made
P. L. 9, 372. go for thy stay not *f.* absents thee
P. L. 9, 671. in Athens or *f.* Rome
P. L. 9, 802. thy full branches offered *f.* to all
P. L. 9, 825. for inferior who is *f.*
P. L. 9, 1174. and force upon *f.* will hath here
P. L. 10, 999. ourselves and seed at once to *f.*
P. L. 11, 513. from such deformities be *f.*

P. L. 12, 71. human left from human *f.*
P. L. 12. 90. reduce man till then *f.*
P. L. 12, 92. unworthy powers to reign over *f.*
P. L. 12, 304. of strict laws to *f.* acceptance
P. R. 2, 48. vindicate thy glory, *f.* thy people
P. R. 3, 175. duty to *f.* thy country
P. R. 3, 284. till Cyrus set them *f.*
P. R. 3, 358. by *f.* consent of all
P. R. 4, 102. victor-people *f.* from servile yoke
P. R. 4, 131. nor yet to *f.* that people
P. R. 4, 143. and valiant man would seek to *f.*
P. R. 4, 145. inward slaves make outward *f.*
S. A. 317. to set His people *f.*
S. A. 1213. to *f.* my country
S. A. 1235. my heels are fettered, but my fist is *f.*
S. A. 1412. to favour and perhaps to set thee *f.*
S. A. 1572. to *f.* him, .. but death who sets all *f.*
C. 818. we cannot *f.* the lady that sits here
C. 1007. till *f.* consent the gods among
C. 1019. love virtue, she alone is *f.*
A. 34. I know this quest of yours and *f.* intent
L'A. 11. but come thou goddess fair and *f.*
L'A. 40. in unreproved pleasures *f.*
L'A. 149. to have quite set *f.* his half-regained
S. 12, 10. revolt when truth would set them *f.*
S. 16, 13. help us to save *f.* consciences
F. of C. 6. our consciences that Christ set *f.*
**Freed.**—P. L. 8, 182. *f.* from intricacies
P. L. 9, 140. in one night *f.* from servitude
P. R. 1, 220. truth were *f.* and equity restored
P. R. 3, 102. his wasted country *f.* from Punic
P. R. 3, 428. *f.* as to their ancient patrimony
S. 15, 11. till truth and right from violence be *f.*
**Freedom.**—P. L. 3, 109. of *f.* both despoiled
P. L. 3, 128. *f.* they themselves ordained
P. L. 4, 294. severe but in true filial *f.* placed
P. L. 5, 797. and splendour less in *f.* equal
P. L. 6, 169. servility with *f.* to contend
P. L. 8, 434. I emboldened spake and *f.* used
P. L. 9, 762. what profits then our inward *f.*
P. L. 11, 580. might preserve *f.* and peace
P. L. 11, 798. with their *f.* lost, lose all virtue
P. L. 12, 95. undeservedly enthral his outward *f.*
P. R. 1, 62. our *f.* . . . in this fair empire
P. R. 3, 77. made captive yet deserving *f.*
S. A. 1715. to Israel honour hath left and *f.*
C. 663. touch the *f.* of my mind
S. 12, 9. that bawl for *f.* in their senseless mood
**Freely.**—P. L. 3, 102. *f.* they stood, who stood
P. L. 3, 175. but grace in me *f* vouchsafed
P. L. 3, 240. this glory next to thee *f.* put off
P. L. 4, 72. will chose *f.* what it now so justly
P. L. 4, 381. he gave it me, which I as *f.* give
P. L. 5, 538. *f.* we serve because we *f.* love
P. L. 6, 565. while we discharge *f.* our part
P. L. 7, 540. and *f.* all their pleasant fruit
P. L. 8, 322. eat *f.* with glad heart
P. L. 8, 443. good reason was thou *f.* shouldst
P. L. 9, 732. reach then, and *f.* taste
P. L. 9, 988. on my experience, Adam, *f.* taste
P. R. 3, 126. communicable to every soul *f.*
S. A. 7. scarce *f.* draw the air, imprisoned
S. A. 1373. if I obey them I do it *f.*
P. 12. which he for us did *f.* undergo
**Free-will.**—P. L. 10, 9. and *f.-w.* armed
P. L. 10, 3. moment of impulse his *f.-w.*
**Freezed.**—C. 449. wherewith she *f.* her foes
**Freezing.**—D. F. I. 16. empire of the *f.* air
**French.**—S. 21, 8. and what the *F.*
**Frequence.**—P. R. 1, 128. who in full *f.* bright
P. R. 2, 130. in full *f.* was empowered
**Frequent.**—P. L. 1, 797. *f.* and full
P. L. 3, 534. his angels to and fro passed *f.*
P. L. 7, 148. and this high temple to *f.*
P. L. 7, 504. was swum, was walked, *f.*
P. L. 7, 571. with *f.* intercourse thither will send
P. L. 11, 317. *f.* with worship place by place
P. L. 11, 838. by men who there *f.* or therein
S. A. 275. how *f.* to desert him
**Frequented.**—P. L. 11, 722. he oft *f.* their
**Frequenting.**— P. L. 10, 1091. the air *f.*

P. L. 10, 1103. and with their sighs the air *f.*
**Fresh.**—P. L. 1, 771. they among *f.* dews.
P. L. 2, 1012. with *f.* alacrity and force renewed
P. L. 4, 229. rose a *f.* fountain and with many
P. L. 4, 326. by a *f.* fountain-side they sat
P. L. 4, 623. to-morrow ere *f.* morning streak
P. L. 5, 20. the morning shines and the *f.* field
P. L. 5, 125. and let us to our *f.* employments
P. L. 5, 203. hill or valley, fountain, or *f.* shade
P. L. 5, 636. with *f.* flowerets crowned
P. L. 6, 784. with *f.* flowerets hill and valley  .
P. L. 7, 274. enlightened earth so *f.* and gay
P. L. 8, 467. life-blood streaming *f.*
P. L. 8, 515. *f.* gales and gentle airs
P. L. 11, 135. with *f.* dews embalmed the earth
P. L. 11, 845. and of the *f.* wave largely drew
P. L. 12, 15. remains *f.* in their minds
P. L. 12, 423. rise out of his grave *f.* as the
P. R. 4, 435. who all things now behold more *f.*
P. R. 4, 567. *f.* from his fall and fiercer grapple
P. R. 4, 570. *f.* assaults amidst his pride
S. A. 10. breath of heaven *f.* blowing pure and
S. A. 547. wherever fountain or *f.* current flowed
S. A. 1317. where I will see thee heartened and *f.*
C. 670. when the *f.* blood grows lively and  ·
L. 29. with the *f.* dews of night
L. 138. on whose *f.* lap the swart-star sparely
L. 193. to-morrow to *f.* woods and pastures new
S. 1, 3. with *f.* hope the lover's heart dost fill
S. 20, 7. and clothe in *f.* attire the lily and
**Fresh-blown.**—L'A. 22. and *f.-b.* roses washed
**Freshest.**—P. L. 9, 1041. earth's *f.,* softest
**Freshet.**—P. R. 2, 345. *f.* or purling brook
**Fret.**—P. L. 7, 597. all sounds on *f.,* by string
S. 9, 7. at thy growing virtues *f.* their spleen
**Fretted.**—P. L. 1, 717. the roof was *f.* gold
**Friar.**—L'A. 104. and he by *f.'s* lantern led
**Friars.**—P. L. 3, 474. eremites and *f.*
**Friend.**—P. L. 5, 229. this day as *f.* with *f.*
P. L. 9, 2. as with his *f.* familiar used
P. L. 10, 11. whatever wiles of foe or seeming *f.*
P. L. 10, 60. man's *f.* his mediator
S. A. 334. towards your once gloried *f.*
S. A. 492. secrets of men the secrets of a *f.*
S. A. 1263. my speediest *f.* by death to rid me
C. 949. many a *f.* to congratulate his presence
S. 22, 10. the conscience, *f.,* to have lost them
**Friendliest.**—P. L. 5, 668. dusky hour *f.*
**Friendly.**—P. L. 4, 36. with no *f.* voice.
P. L. 6, 22. those *f.* powers who him received
P. L. 8, 9. vouchsafed this *f.* condescension
P. L. 8, 651. be good and *f.* still and oft return
P. L. 9, 564. and how to me so *f.* grown above
P. L. 9, 772. author unsuspect *f.* to man
S. A. 1078. though for no *f.* intent
S. A. 1508. I know your *f.* minds
C. 160. I under fair pretence of *f.* ends
C. 282. to seek in the valley some cool *f.* spring
C. 488. if he be *f.* he comes well
C. 678. to life so *f.* or so cool to thirst
**Friends.**—P. L. 1, 264. then our faithful *f.*
P. L. 4, 866. O *f.* I hear the tread of nimble feet
P. L. 6, 378. aided by this host of *f.*
P. L. 6, 609. O *f.* why come not on these victors
P. L. 12, 129. he leaves his gods, his *f.*
P. R. 2, 422. money brings honour, *f.,* conquest
P. R. 2, 425. that got him puissant *f.*
S. A. 180. we come thy *f.* and neighbours
S. A. 187. your coming *f.* revives me
S. A. 189. who *f.* bear in their superscription
S. A. 193. ye see O *f.* how many evils
S. A. 202. tell me *f.* am I not sung and proverbed
S. A. 605. and healing words from these thy *f.*
S. A. 1196. under pretence of bridal *f.* and guests
S. A. 1415. offend them to see me girt with *f.*
S. A. 1730. will send for all my kindred, all my *f.*
C. 76. and all their *f.* and native home forget
S. 9, 12. when the Bridegroom with his feastful *f.*
**Friendship.**—P. L. 11, 796. raise out of *f.*
S. A. 495. excluded all *f.* and avoided as a blab
**Frieze.**—P. L. 1, 716. cornice or *f.*

C. 722. and nothing wear but *f.*
**Fright.**—P. L. 11, 121. approach far off to *f.*
Il P. 138. or *f.* them from their hallowed haunt
**Frighted.**—P. L. 1, 543. beyond *f.* the reign
P. L. 2, 994. fled not in silence through the *f.*
C. 553. gave respite to the drowsy *f.* steeds
**Fringed.**—P. L. 4, 262. that to the *f.* bank
**Frisking.**—P. L. 4, 340. about them *f.*
**Frith.**—P. L. 2, 949. no narrow *f.* he had to cross
**Frivolous.**—C. 445. set at naught the *f.* bolt
**Frizzled.**—P. L. 7, 323. and bush with *f.* hair
**Fro.**—P. L. 2, 605. sound both to and *f.*
P. L. 6, 328. and writhed him to and *f.*
S. A. 1649. with horrible convulsion to and *f.*
**Frock.**—S. A. 133. steel and *f.* of mail
**Frogs.**—P. L. 12, 177. *f.*, lice, and flies
S. 12, 5. those kinds that were transformed to *f.*
**Frolic.**—C. 59. ripe and *f.* of his full-grown age
L'A 18. the *f.* wind that breathes the spring
**Front.**—P. L. 1, 563. a horrid *f.* of dreadful
P. L. 2, 302. deep on his *f.* engraven
P. L. 2, 683. advance thy miscreated *f.*
P. L. 2, 716. then stand *f.* to *f.* hovering
P. L. 4, 300. his fair large *f.* and eye sublime
P. L. 4, 865. their chief Gabriel from the *f.*
P. L. 6, 105. and *f.* to *f.* presented stood
P. L. 6, 558. vanguard to right and left the *f.*
P. L. 6, 569. when to right and left the *f.* divided
P. L. 6, 611. entertain them fair with open *f.*
P. L. 7, 509. and upright with *f.* serene
P. L. 9, 330. sticks no dishonour on our *f.*
P. L. 12, 592. at whose *f.* a flaming sword
P. L. 12, 632. high in *f.* advanced
S. A. 496. the mark of fool set on his *f.*
H. 39. to hide her guilty *f.* with innocent snow
P. 18. his starry *f.* low-roofed beneath
**Fronted.**—P. L. 2, 532. or *f.* brigads form
**Frontier.**—P. L. 1, 466. and Gaza's *f.* bounds
**Frontiers.**—P. L. 2, 998. I upon my *f.* here
**Frontispiece.**—P. L. 3, 506. *f.* of diamond
**Fronts.**—C. 30. this tract that *f.* the falling sun
**Frore.**—P. L. 2, 595. the parching air burns *f.*
**Frost.**—P. L. 11, 899. heat and hoary *f.*
S. A. 1577. with the lagging rear of winter's *f.*
1. 47. or *f.* to flowers that their gay wardrobe
**Froth.**—P. R. 4, 20. and in *f.* or bubbles end
**Frounced.**—Il P. 123. not tricked and *f.*
**Frown.**—P. L. 2, 713. and such a *f.* each cast
P. L. 2, 720. that hell grew darker at their *f.*
P. L. 3, 424. wild under the *f.* of Night
P. L. 6, 260. hostile *f.* and visage all inflamed
S. A. 948. to gloss upon and censuring *f.* or smile
C. 446. gods and men feared her stern *f.*
C. 666. why are you vexed, lady, why do you *f.*
**Frowned.**—P. L. 2, 719. so *f.* the mighty.
**Frowning.**—P. L. 2, 106. he ended *f.*
P. L. 4, 924. which the fiend thus answered *f.*
**Frowns.**—C. 667. here dwell no *f.* nor anger
**Frozen.**—P. L. 1, 352. poured never from her *f.*
P. L. 2, 587. a *f.* continent lies dark and wild
P. L. 2, 602. immovable, infixed, and *f.* round
P. L. 2, 620. o'er many a *f.* many a fiery Alp
S. 20, 7. till Favonius re-inspire the *f.* earth
**Frugal.**—P. L. 5, 324. save what by *f.* storing
P. L. 8, 26. I oft admire how Nature wise and *f.*
P. R. 4, 134. *f.* and mild and temperate
**Fruit.**—P. L. 1, 1. the *f.* of that forbidden tree
P. L. 4, 147. trees loaden with fairest *f.*
P. L. 4, 219. ambrosial *f.* of vegetable gold
P. L. 4, 249. others whose *f.* burnished with
P. L. 4, 422. that bear delicious *f.* so various
P. L. 4, 644. on herb, tree, *f.*, and flower
P. L. 4, 652. nor herb, *f.*, flower, glistering
P. L. 5, 58. O fair plant said he with *f.*
P. L. 5, 67. O *f.* divine, sweet of thyself
P. L. 5, 83. to my mouth of that same *f.*
P. L. 5, 341. *f.* of all kinds,
P. L. 5, 482. flowers and their *f.*
P. L. 5, 635. *f.* of delicious vines
P. L. 6, 475. with plant, *f.*, flower ambrosial
P. L. 7, 311. fruit-tree yielding *f.* after her kind

P. L. 7, 325. their branches hung with copious *f.*
P. L. 7, 540. freely all their pleasant *f.* for food
P. L. 8, 307. each tree loaden with fairest *f.*
P. L. 8, 320. to till and keep and of the *f.* to eat
P. L. 9, 577. loaden with *f.* of fairest colours
P. L. 9, 588. at the scent of that alluring *f.*
P. L. 9, 616. the virtue of that *f.* in thee
P. L. 9, 621. as leaves a greater store of *f.*
P. L. 9, 648. fruitless to me though *f.* be here
P. L. 9, 656. of the *f.* of all these garden trees
P. L. 9, 659. the *f.* of each tree in the garden
P. L. 9, 661. but of the *f.* of this fair tree
P. L. 9, 686. by the *f.*? it gives you life
P. L. 9, 731. import your need of this fair *f.*
P. L. 9, 735. fixed on the *f.* she gazed
P. L. 9, 741. the smell so savoury of that *f.*
P. L. 9, 763. in the day we eat of this fair *f.*
P. L. 9, 776. here grows the cure of all, this *f.*
P. L. 9, 781. in evil hour forth reaching to the *f.*
P. L. 9, 788. as seemed in *f.* she never tasted
P. L. 9, 798. and thy fair *f.* let hang
P. L. 9, 851. a bough of fairest *f.* that downy
P. L. 9, 869. hath eaten of the *f.*
P. L. 9, 904. how to violate the sacred *f.*
P. L. 9, 929. coveting to eye that sacred *f.*
P. L. 9, 929. foretasted *f.* profaned first
P. L. 9, 972. of tasting this fair *f.*
P. L. 9, 996. gave him of that fair enticing *f.*
P. L. 9, 1011. but that false *f.* far other
P. L. 9, 1023. abstained from this delightful *f.*
P. L. 9, 1046. as the force of that fallacious *f.*
P. L. 9, 1073. bad *f.* of knowledge
P. L. 9, 1101. the fig-tree not that kind for *f.*
P. L. 10, 4. to taste the fatal *f.* was known
P. L. 10, 13. high injunction not to taste that *f.*
P. L. 10, 550. with fair *f.* like that which grew
P. L. 10, 565. instead of *f.* chewed bitter ashes
P. L. 10, 687. at that tasted *f.*
P. L. 10, 1053. recompensed with joy, *f.* of thy
P. L. 11, 86. since his taste of that defended *f.*
P. L. 11, 125. stolen *f.* Man once more to delude
P. L. 11, 413. which that false *f.* that promised
P. L. 11, 535. like ripe *f.* thou drop into thy
P. L. 12, 184. devours not herb, or *f.*, or grain
C. 186. to bring me berries or such cooling *f.*
C. 396. to save her blossoms and defend her *f.*
M. W. 30. spoiled at once both *f.* and tree
**Fruitage.**—P. L. 5, 427. ambrosial *f.* bear
P. L. 10, 561. greedily they plucked the *f.*
**Fruitful.**—P. L. 3, 337. see golden days *f.*
P. L. 5, 388. whose *f.* womb shall fill the world
P. L. 7, 396. blessed them saying be *f.*
P. L. 7, 531. blessed mankind and said be *f.*
P. L. 8, 96. in the *f.* earth there first received
S. A. 181. from Eshtaol and Zora's *f.* vale
P. L. 5, 320. by disburdening grows more *f.*
**Fruition.**—P. L. 3, 307. enjoying godlike *f.*
P. L. 4, 767. joyless, unendeared, casual *f.*
**Fruitless.**—P. L. 5, 215. check *f.* embraces
P. L. 9, 648. *f.* to me though fruit be here
P. L. 9, 1188. in mutual accusation spent the *f.*
**Fruits.**—P. L. 3, 67. *f.* of joy and love
P. L. 3, 451. the *f.* of painful superstition
P. L. 4, 148. blossoms and *f.* at once of golden
P. L. 4, 331. supper *f.* they fell, nectarine *f.*
P. L. 5, 304. prepared for dinner savoury *f.*
P. L. 5, 390. these various *f.* the trees of God
P. L. 5, 464. these earthly *f.* to taste
P. L. 8, 44. went forth among her *f.* and flowers
P. L. 8, 147. rain produce *f.* in her softened soil
P. L. 8, 212. than *f.* of palm-tree
P. L. 8, 527. of taste, sight, smell, herbs, *f.*
P. L. 9, 745. thy virtues doubtless best of *f.*
P. L. 10, 603. therefore on these herbs and *f.*
P. L. 11, 26. *f.* of more pleasing savour
P. L. 11, 285. accustomed to immortal *f.*
P. L. 11, 327. offer sweet-smelling gums and *f.*
P. L. 12, 551. bring forth *f.* joy and eternal bliss
P. R. 2, 356. Naiades with *f.* and flowers
P. R. 2, 369. these are not *f.* forbidden
P. R. 4, 30. that screened the *f.* of the earth

P. R. 4, 589. ambrosial *f.* fetched from the tree
C. 712. covering the earth with odours *f.* and
**Fruit-tree.**—P. L. 7, 311. *f.-t* yielding fruit
**Fruit-trees.**—P. L. 5, 213. any row of *f.-t.*
**Frustrate.**—P. L. 2, 193. to *f.* all our plots
P. L. 3, 157. thus obtain his end and *f.* thine
P. L. 9, 944. be *f.* do, undo and labour lose
P. L. 11, 16. winds blown vagabond or *f.*
P. R. 1, 180. be *f.* all ye stratagems of hell
S. A. 589. nor shall his wondrous gifts be *f.* thus
S. A. 1149. to *f.* and dissolve these magic spells
**Frustrated.**—P. R. 4, 609. *f.* the conquest
**Fry.**—P. L. 7, 400. with *f.* innumerable swarm
**Fuel.**—S. A. 1351. by adding *f.* to the flame
**Fuelled.**—P. L. 1, 234. and *f.* entrails thence
**Fugitive.** P. L. 2, 700. false *f.*
P. L. 4, 923. thou surely hadst not come sole *f.*
P. L. 9, 16. pursued thrice *f.* about Troy wall
P. R. 2, 308. the *f.* bond-woman with her son
**Fugitives.**—P. L. 2, 57. here heaven's *f.*
**Fugue.**—P. L. 11, 563. the resonant *f.*
**Fulfil.**—P. L. 1, 431. works of love or enmity *f.*
P. L. 3, 157. shall he *f.* his malice
P. L. 6, 675. his great purpose he might so *f.*
P. L. 6, 729. thy will fulfilled which to *f.*
P. L. 9, 230. how we might best *f.* the work
P. L. 12, 402. the law of God exact he shall *f.*
P. L. 12, 404. by love, though love may *f.*
P. R. 3, 177. so shalt thou best *f.* best verify
**Fulfilled.**—P. L. 5, 246. and *f.* all justice
P. L. 6, 729. thy will *f.* which to fulfil is all
P. L. 7, 635. and thy request think now *f.*
P. L. 8, 491. hath made amends thou hast *f.*
P. L. 11, 602. here nature seems *f.* in all her
P. R. 1, 126. but contrary unweeting he *f.*
P. R. 3, 182. things are best *f.* in their due time
P. R. 4, 381. prophecies of thee are best *f.*
S. A. 45. had been *f.* but through mine own
S. A. 1661. living or dying thou hast *f.*
**Fulfilling.** P. L. 12, 396. but by *f.* that
P. R. 2, 108. meekly composed awaited the *f.*
H. 106. and that her reign had here its last *f.*
**Fulgent.**—P. L. 10, 449. from a cloud his *f.* head
**Full.**—P. L. 1, 372. gay religions *f.* of pomp
P. L. 1, 536. which *f.* high advanced
P. L. 1, 641. and his regal state put forth at *f.*
P. L. 1, 660. but these thoughts *f.* counsel must
P. L. 1, 797. on golden seats frequent and *f.*
P. L. 2, 24. yielded with *f.* consent
P. L. 2, 147. who would lose though *f.* of pain
P. L. 2, 388. with *f.* assent they vote
P. L. 2, 655. wide Cerberean mouths *f.* loud
P. L. 2, 688. to whom the Goblin *f.* of wrath
P. L. 2, 805. me his parent would *f.* soon devour
P. L. 2, 1054. *f.* fraught with mischievous
P. L. 3, 332. hell her numbers *f.* thenceforth
P. L. 3, 378. shadest the *f.* blaze of thy beams
P. L. 4, 687. in *f.* harmonic number joined
P. L. 4, 784. our circuit meets *f.* west
P. L. 5, 517. *f.* to the utmost measure
P. L. 5, 556. the *f.* relation must be strange
P. L. 5, 639. where *f.* measure only bounds
P. L. 5, 720. in *f.* resplendence heir of all
P. L. 5, 862. fatal course had circled his *f.* orb
P. L. 6, 622. of hard contents and *f.* of force
P. L. 6, 720. with rays direct shone *f.*
P. L. 6, 720. he all his Father *f.* expressed
P. L. 6, 826. *f.* of wrath bent on his enemies
P. L. 6, 834. *f.* soon among them he arrived
P. L. 7, 70. great things and *f.* of wonder
P. L. 7, 377. with *f.* face borrowing her light
P. L. 7, 456. perfect forms limbed and *f.* grown
P. L. 8, 232. squared in *f.* legion
P. L. 9, 62. thence *f.* of anguish driven
P. L. 9, 802. fertile burden ease of thy *f.* branches
P. L. 9, 819. give him to partake *f.* happiness
P. L. 9, 1126. calm region once and *f.* of peace
P. L. 10, 65. he *f.* resplendent all his Father
P. L. 10, 503. but up and enter now into *f.* bliss
P. L. 10, 951. ill able to sustain his *f.* wrath
P. L. 11, 675. his guide lamenting turned *f.* sad

P. L. 11, 815. much more safe and *f.* of peace
P. L. 12, 301. with purpose to resign them in *f.*
P. L. 12, 473. *f.* of doubt I stand
P. R. 1, 14. with prosperous wing *f.* summed
P. R. 1, 67. his growth now to youth's *f.* flower
P. R. 1, 128. in *f.* frequence bright of angels
P. R. 1, 267. *f.* weight must be transferred
P. R. 1, 287. now *f.*, that I no more should live
P. R. 1, 303. *f.* forty days he passed
P. R. 2, 34. his words his wisdom *f.* of grace
P. R. 2, 83. but now *f.* grown to man
P. R. 2, 130. consenting in *f.* frequence
P. R. 2, 201. *f.* of honour, wealth, high fare
P. R. 3, 383. on the throne of David in *f.* glory
P. R. 3, 405. his *f.* sceptre sway
P. R. 4, 380. now at *f.* age, fulness of time
P. R. 4, 582. globe of angels on *f.* sail of wing
S. A. 214. who hast of sorrow thy *f.* load
S. A. 310. and hath *f.* right to exempt
S. A. 526. *f.* of divine instinct
S. A. 759. wisest and best men *f.* oft beguiled
S. A. 805. I at home sat *f.* of cares and fears
S. A. 869. took *f.* possession of me
S. A. 1573. paid his ransom and *f.* discharge
C. 175. their teeming flocks and granges *f.*
C. 711. such a *f.* and unwithdrawing hand
C. 772. nature's *f.* blessings...well dispensed
C. 925. their *f.* tribute never miss
A. 42. which I *f.* oft, amidst these shades
S. 7, 3. my hasting days fly on with *f.* career
S. 23, 8. *f.* sight of her in heaven without
H. 132. *f.* consort to the angelic symphony
H. 166. our bliss *f.* and perfect is, but now
Cir. 23. and the *f.* wrath beside
U. C. I. 7. he had any time, this ten years *f.*
**Full-blazing.**—P. L. 4, 29. the *f.-b.* sun
**Full-grown.**—C. 59. frolic of his *f.-g.* age
**Full-orbed.**—P. L. 5. 42. *f.-o.* the moon
**Full-voiced.**—II P. 162, to the *f.-v.* choir below
**Fully.**—P. L. 8, 180. *f.* hast thou satisfied me
P. L. 10, 79. them *f.* satisfied
P. L. 10, 374. and *f.* avenged our foil in heaven
P. R. 1, 4. by one man's firm obedience *f.* tried
S. A. 1712. on his enemies *f.* revenged
**Fulmined.**—P. R. 4, 270. and *f.* over Greece
**Fulness.**—P. L. 3, 225, in whom the *f.* dwells
P. R. 4, 380. at full age *f.* of time
**Fume.**—P. L. 4, 168. the fishy *f.* that drove him
P. L. 8, 194. what is more is *f.*
**Fumed.**—P. L. 11, 18. where the golden altar *f.*
**Fumes.**—P. L. 9, 1050. bred of unkindly *f.*
S. A. 552. that turbulent liquor fills with *f.*
**Fuming.**—P. L. 5, 6. sound of leaves and *f.* rills
P. L. 7, 600. clouds *f.* from golden censers
**Functions.**—S. A. 596. all her *f.* weary of herself
**Funeral.**—S. A. 1732. silent obsequy and *f.*
M. W. 46. morn had let fall on her hastening *f.*
**Fur.**—C. 1. 707. those budge doctors of the Stoic *f.*
**Furies.**—P. L. 2, 596. thither by harpy-footed *f.*
P. L. 2, 671. fierce as ten *f.*, terrible as hell
P. L. 6, 859, pursued with terrors and with *f.*
P. L. 10, 620. let in these wasteful *f.*
P. R. 4, 422, infernal ghosts and hellish *f.*
C. 641. or ghastly *F.'* apparition
**Furious.**—P. L. 4, 4. came *f.* down
P. L. 6, 86. hasting on with *f.* expedition
P. L. 6, 357. the deep array of Moloch *f.* king
P. L. 7, 213. turned by *f.* winds
P. L. 8, 244. and loud lament, and *f.* rage
P. L. 11, 854. the retreating sea their *f.* tide
S. A. 836. call it *f.* rage to satisfy thy lust
**Furlongs.**—C. 946. and not many *f.* thence
**Furnace.**—P. L. 1, 62. as one great *f.* flamed
P. L. 2, 388. so wide they stood and like a *f.*
H. 1. 210, in dismal dance about the *f.* blue.
**Furniture.**—P. L. 9, 34. tilting *f.*
**Furrow.**—C. 292. his loose traces from the *f.*
**Furrowed.**—L'A. 64. whistles o'er the *f.* land
**Further.**—P. L. 4, 174. *f.* way found none
S. A. 2. little *f.* on for yonder bank hath choice
A. 39. to *f.* this night's glad solemnity

**Fury.**—P. L. 1, 179. whether scorn or satiate *f*.
P. L. 1, 235. sublimed with mineral *f*.
P. L. 2, 61. armed with hell-flames and *f*.
P. L. 2, 728. what *f*. O son possesses thee
P. L. 2, 938. that *f*. stayed, quenched in a boggy
P. L. 5, 808. the current of his *f*. thus opposed
P. L. 6, 207. now storming *f*. rose.
P. L. 6, 591. with such impetuous *f*. smote
P. L. 10, 240. ere this he had returned with *f*.
L. 75. comes the blind *F*. with the abhorred
**Fusil.**—P. L. 11, 573. wrought *f*. or graven
**Future.**—P. L. 2, 222. never ending flight of *f*.
P. L. 3, 78. past, present, *f*. he beholds
P. L. 5, 582. durable by present past and *f*.

P. L. 6, 429. fallible of *f*. we may deem him
P. L. 6, 502. yet haply of thy race in *f*. days
P. L. 7, 183. good will to *f*. men
P. L. 7, 486. parsimonious emmet, provident of *f*.
P. L. 10, 345. instant, but of *f*. time
P. L. 10, 840. beyond all past example and *f*.
P. L. 11, 114. to Adam what shall come in *f*.
P. L. 11, 357. show thee what shall come in *f*.
P. L. 11, 764. had I lived ignorant of *f*. days
P. L. 11, 774. and he the *f*. evil shall no less
P. L. 11, 870. thou who *f*.things canst represent
P. R. 1, 396. they may direct their *f*. life
V. Ex. 72. foresaw what *f*. days should bring

# G

**Gabble.**—P. L. 12, 56. a hideous *g*. rises loud
**Gabriel.**—P. L. 4, 549. rocky pillars *G*. sat
P. L. 4, 561. *G*. thy course by lot hath given
P. L. 4, 781. when *G*. to his next in power
P. L. 4, 865. their chief *G*. from the front
P. L. 4, 877. with stern regard thus *G*. spake
P. L. 4, 886. *G*. thou hadst in heaven
P. L. 4, 1005. which *G*. spying thus bespake
P. L. 6, 46. *G*. lead forth to battle these my
P. L. 6, 355. where the might of *G*. fought
P. L. 9, 54. who fled before the threats of *G*.
P. R. 1, 129. to *G*. smiling spake:—*G*. this day
P. R. 4, 504. announced by *G*. with the first
**Gadding.**—L. 40. the *g*. vine o'ergrown
**Gades.**—P. R, 4, 77. Gallia *G*. and the British
**Gadire.**—S. A. 716. the isles of Javan or *G*.
**Gain.**—P. L. 1, 190. we may *g*. from hope
P. L. 2, 1009. spoil and ruin are my *g*.
P. L. 6, 907. thee once to *g*. companion
P. L. 8, 122. too high and no advantage *g*.
P. L. 9, 332. double honour *g*. from his surmise
P. L. 12, 199. till his rescued *g*. their shore
P. L. 12, 223. this also shall they *g*. by their delay
P. R. 1, 397. envy they say excites me thus to *g*
P. R. 2, 419. what retinue canst thou *g*.
P. R. 2, 434. impotent to *g*. dominion
P. R. 2, 486. to *g*. a sceptre oftest better missed
P. R. 3, 29. all treasures and all *g*. esteem
P. R. 4, 211. *g*. them as thou canst or not
S. A. 835. God or man will *g*. thee no
T. 8. so little is thy *g*.
**Gained.**—P. L. 1, 471. a leper once he lost and *g*.
P. L. 4, 512. let me not forget what I have *g*.
P. L. 5, 174. when high noon hast *g*.
P. L. 8, 435. which *g*. this answer
P. L. 9, 529. he glad of her attention *g*.
P. L. 10, 373. they wisdom *g*. with odds
P. L. 10, 902. shall see her *g*. by a far worse
P. R. 1, 391. by them I *g*. what I have *g*.
P. R. 2, 434. to gain dominion or to keep it *g*.
S. A. 353. I *g*. a son and such a son as all men
S. 9, 14. hast *g*. they entrance Virgin wise
**Gaining.**—P. L. 11, 768. *g*. birth abortive
P. R. 4, 471. thy way of *g*. David's throne
S. 20, 119. may be won from the hard season *g*.
**Gains,**—P. L. 3, 428. some small reflection *g*.
P. L. 5, 324. by frugal storing firmness *g*.
P. L. 9, 1003. lives as thou saidst and *g*. to live
**Gainsay.**—P. L. 9, 1158. didst not much *g*.
**Gait.**—P. L. 4, 568. and marked his aery *g*.
P. L. 4, 870. by his *g*. and fierce demeanour
P. L. 7, 411. enormous in their *g*.
P. L. 9, 389. but Delia's self in *g*. surpassed
P. L. 11, 230. by his *g*. none of the meanest
11 P. 38. with even step and musing *g*.
**Galasp.**—S. 11, 9. Colkitto or Macdonald or *G*.
**Galaxy.**—P. L. 7, 579. in the *g*. that milky way
**Gale.**—P. R. 2, 364. and winds of gentlest *g*.
**Gales.**—P. L. 4, 156. no gentle *g*. fanning
P. L. 8, 515. fresh *g*. and gentle airs whispered
Hor. 11. of flattering *g*. unmindful

**Galilean.**—P. R. 3, 233. viewed the *G*. towns
L. 109. the pilot of the *G*. lake
**Galilee.**—P. R. 1, 135. the Virgin pure in *G*.
**Galileo.**—P. L. 5, 262. the glass of *G*.
**Gallaphrone.**—P. R. 3, 340. the city of *G*.
**Gallia.**—P. R. 4, 77. from *G*. Gades and the
**Gambolled.**—P. L. 4, 345. *g*. before them
**Game.**—P. L. 6, 697. war seemed a civil *g*.
P. L. 11, 714. now was turned to jollity and *g*.
P. L. 12, 30. men not beasts shall be his *g*.
P. R. 2, 342. beasts of chase or fowl of *g*.
S. A. 1331. make a *g*. of my calamities
**Games.**—P. L. 2, 530. as at the Olympian *g*.
P. L. 4, 551. about him exercised heroic *g*.
P. L. 9, 33. or to describe races and *g*.
S. A. 1312. sacrifices triumph pomp and *g*.
S. A. 1602. mighty strength in feat and *g*.
**Gamesome.**—P. L. 6, 620. Belial in like *g*. mood
C. 173. the jocund flute, or *g*. pipe
**Gan.**—P. L. 6, 60. from on high *g*. blow
P. L. 9, 1016. Adam thus *g*. Eve to dalliance
P. L. 10, 710. beast now with beast *g*. war
P. R. 4, 410. either tropic now *g*. thunder
**Ganges.**—P. L. 3, 436. the springs of *G*.
P. L. 9, 82. where flows *G*. and Indus
**Gangrene.**—S. A. 621. rankle, and fester, and *g*.
**Ganymed.**—P. R. 2, 353. fairer hue than *G*.
**Gap.**—P. L. 6, 861. a spacious *g*. disclosed
**Gaped.** P. L. 6, 577. hideous orifice *g*. on us.
**Gaping.**—P. L. 2, 440. receives him ... wide *g*.
**Garb.**—P. L. 2, 226. words clothed in reason's *g*.
C. 759. false rules pranked in reason's *g*.
**Garden.**—P. L. 3, 66. in the happy *g*. placed
P. L. 4, 209. paradise of God the *g*. was
P. L. 4, 215. his far more pleasant *g*.
P. L. 4, 226. that mountain as his *g*. mould
P. L. 4, 230. with many a rill watered the *g*.
P. L. 4, 285. Assyrian *g*. where the fiend
P. L. 4, 529. I must walk round this *g*.
P. L. 4, 789. search through this *g*.
P. L. 5, 260. earth and the *g*. of God
P. L. 5, 368. what the *g*. choicest bears
P. L. 5, 752. is no more than what this *g*. is
P. L. 7, 538. this *g*. planted with the trees of God
P. L. 8, 299. I come thy guide to the *g*. of bliss
P. L. 8, 321. of every tree that in the *g*. grows
P. L. 8, 326. amid the *g*. by the tree of life
P. L. 9, 206. may we labour still to dress this *g*.
P. L. 9, 660. of each tree in the *g*. we may eat
P. L. 9, 662. amidst the *g*. God hath said ye
P. L. 10, 98. they heard now walking in the *g*.
P. L. 10, 116. I heard thee in the *g*.
P. L. 10, 746. or here place in this delicious *g*.
P. L. 11, 97. send him from the *g*. forth
P. L. 11, 118. on the east side of the *g*. place
P. L. 11, 222. to seize possession of the *g*.
P. L. 11, 261. and send thee from the *g*. forth
P. R. 1, 1. I who erewhile the happy *g*. sung
**Gardening.**—P. L. 4, 328. their sweet *g*.
P. L. 9, 203. hands' dispatch of two *g*. so
P. L. 9, 391. such *g*. tools
**Garden-plot.**—P. L. 9, 418. grove or *g*.-*p*.

**Gardens.**—P. L. 3, 568. those Hesperian g.
P. L. 9, 439. more delicious than those g.
P. R. 4, 38. presented to his eyes
C. 981. all amidst the g. fair of Hesperus
II P. 50. Leisure that in trim g. takes his
**Garden-trees.**—P. L. 9, 657. all these g.-t.
**Garish.**—II P. 141. hide me from day's g. eye
**Garland.** P. L. 9, 840. of choicest flowers, a g.
P. L. 9, 892. the g. wreathed for Eve
C. 850. throw sweet g. wreaths into her stream
M. W. 21. in his g. as he stood
**Garlands.**—P. L. 3, 352. now in loose g.
P. L. 4, 709. g., and sweet smelling herbs
P. L. 11, 594. songs, g., flowers
**Garrisoned.**—S. A. 1497. g. round about him
**Garrulity.**—S. A. 491. my crime shameful g.
**Gash.**—P. L. 6, 331. from the g. a stream
**Gasp.**—S. 11, 11. Quintilian stare and g.
**Gate.**—P. L. 2, 725. that sat fast by Hell-g.
P.L. 2,746. to whom thus the portress of Hell-g.
P. L. 2, 173. and towards the g. rolling her
P. L. 3, 505. work as of a kingly palace g.
P. L. 3, 515. this is the g. of Heaven
P. L. 3, 541. by steps of gold to Heaven-g.
P. L. 3, 686. Suspicion sleeps at Wisdom's g.
P. L. 4, 178. one g. there only was
P. L. 4, 542. against the eastern g. of Paradise
P. L. 4, 579. in at this g. none pass
P. L. 5, 253. g. of heaven arrived, the g.
P. L. 10, 298. asphaltic slime, broad as the g.
P. L. 10, 418. through the g. wide open
P. L. 11, 190. to the eastern g. was bent
P. L. 12, 571. to the faithful death the g. of life
P. L. 12, 638. to the eastern g. led them
P. L. 12, 643. g. with dreadful faces thronged
S. A. 560. at one g. to make defence
L'A. 59. right against the eastern g.
**Gates.**—P. L. 1, 171. back to the g. of heaven
P. L. 1, 326. Heaven-g. discern the advantage
P. L. 1, 761. the g. and porches wide
P. L. 2, 436. and g. of burning adamant barred
P. L. 2, 631. and toward the g. of hell explores
P. L. 2, 645. and thrice threefold the g.
P. L. 2, 648. before the g.there sat on either side
P. L. 2, 684. athwart my way to yonder g.
P. L. 2, 776. to keep these g. for ever shut
P. L. 2, 853. to unlock these adamantine g.
P. L. 2, 884. the g. wide open stood
P. L. 2, 996. heaven g. poured out by millions
P. L. 4, 382. entertain you two, her widest g.
P. L. 4, 898. let him surer bar his iron g.
P. L. 4, 967. g. of hell too slightly barred
P. L. 6, 4. rosy hand unbarred the g. of light
P. L. 7, 206. heaven opened her ever-during g.
P. L. 7, 565. open ye everlasting g. they sung
P. L. 8, 231. excursion toward the g. of hell
P. L. 8, 241. fast shut the dismal g.
P. L. 10, 230. within the g. of hell sat Sin
P. L. 10, 231. in counterview within the g.
P. L. 10, 282. then both from out hell g.
P. L. 11, 640. cities of men with lofty g.
P. R. 3, 287. Hecatompylos her hundred g.
P. R. 3, 311. numbers numberless the city g.
P. R. 4, 61. to the g. cast round thine eye
P. R. 4, 624. in all her g. Abaddon rues
S. A. 147. on his shoulders bore the g. of Azza
S. A. 1597. as the g. I entered with sunrise
C. 667. from these g. sorrow flies
H. 148. will open wide the g. of her high
**Gath.**—P. L. 1, 465. in G. and Ascalon
S. A. 266. had by this possessed the towers of G
S. A. 981. in Ecron, Gaza, Ashdod, and in G.
S. A. 1068. the giant Harapha of G.
S. A. 1078. I am of G. men call me Harapha
S. A. 1127. thou oft shalt wish thyself at G.
S. A. 1129. but shalt never see G. more
**Gather.**—P. R. 1, 316. withered sticks to g.
**Gathered.**—P. L. 4, 271. gloomy Dis was g.
P. L. 5, 207. if the night have g. aught of evil
P. L. 7, 283. when God said be g.now ye waters
P. L. 7, 363. firm to.retain her g. beams

P. L. 9, 852. fairest fruit,... new g.
P. L. 9, 1111. those leaves they g.
P. L. 10, 299. to the roots of hell the g. beach
P. L. 10, 344. thence g. his own doom
P. L. 10, 1070. how we his g. beams reflected
P. L. 11,537. with ease g., not harshly plucked
P. R. 3, 300. in Ctesiphon hath g. all his host
S. A. 251. the Philistines with g. powers
C. 595. g. like scum settled to itself
**Gathering.**—P. L. 4, 269. Proserpine g.
P. R. 4, 330. as children g. pebbles on the shore
**Gathers.**—P. L. 2, 590. thaws not but g. heap
P. L. 4, 343. she g. tribute large
P. L. 12, 631. g. ground fast at the labourer's
**Gaudy.**—C. 851. pansies, pinks, and g.daffodils
II P. 6. fancies fond with g. shapes possess
H. 33. had doffed her g. trim.
**Gaul.**—Brut. 8. beyond the realm of G.
**Gauntlet.**—S. A. 1121. greaves and g.
**Gave.**—P. L. 1, 736. and g. to rule
P. L. 4, 144.to our general sire g.prospect large
P. L. 4, 350. of his fatal guile g. proof
P. L. 4, 380. he g. it me which I as freely give
P. L. 4, 787. g. them thus in charge
P. L. 4, 969. but Satan to no threats g. heed
P. L. 5, 252. to his speed g. way through all
P. L. 5, 858. while the Maker g. thee being
P. L. 6, 402. their innocence g. them above
P. L. 7, 175. the filial Godhead g. effect
P. L. 7, 541. pleasant fruit for food g. thee
P. L. 8, 514. the earth g. sign of gratulation
P. L. 9, 266. faithful side that g. thee being
P. L. 9, 748. g. elocution to the mute
P. L. 9, 783. through all her works g. signs
P. L. 9, 996. she g. him of that.... fruit
P. L. 9, 1001. nature g. a second groan
P. L. 9, 1066. g. utterance to these words
P. L. 10, 123. whereof I g. thee charge
P. L. 10, 143. she g. me of the tree and I did
P. L. 10, 430. so he departing g. command
P. L. 10, 650. g. them several charge
P. L. 11, 49. the law I g. to Nature
P. L. 11, 72. he ended and the Son g. signal
P. L. 11, 182. Nature first g. signs impressed
P. L. 11, 277. and g. ye names
P. L. 11, 339. all the earth he g. thee to
P. L. 11, 497. g. him up to tears a space
P. L. 12, 67. he g. us only over beast, fish
P. R. 1, 66. to our just fear g. no small cause
P. R. 1, 369. when he g. up into my hands
P. R. 4, 258. and his who g. them breath
S. A. 58. God when he g. me strength to show
S. A. 236. g. up my fort of silence to a woman
S. A. 822. I g. thou sayest the example
S. A. 1054. g. to the man despotic power
S. A. 1140. who g. me this strength
S. A. 1209. as a league-breaker g. up bound
S. A. 1215. to their masters g. me up
S. A. 1581. what glorious hand g. Samson
S. A. 1634. to the arched roof g. main support
C. 419. heaven g. it may be termed her own
C. 553. g. respite to the ... steeds
C. 584. is this the confidence you g. me?
C. 637. Hermes once to wise Ulysses g.
C. 638. called it hæmony and g. it me
C. 676. in Egypt g. to Jove-born Helena
C. 837. and g. her to his daughters
S. 23, 3. Jove's great son to her glad husband g.
U. C. II. 11. all men life g. him his death
**Gavest.**—P. L. 2, 865. thou my being g. me
P. L. 7, 493. and g. them names
P. L. 10, 138. g. me as thy perfect gift so
**Gay.**—P. L. 1, 372. adorned with g. religions
P. L. 4, 149. with g. enamelled colours mixed
P. L. 4, 942. thou and thy g. legions dare
P. L. 7, 318. made g. her bosom smelling
P. L. 7, 444. whose g. train adorns him
P. L. 8, 274. enlightened earth so fresh and g.
P. L. 9, 428. whose head though g. carnation
P. L. 11, 582. fair women richly g. in gems
P. L. 11, 615. so blithe, so smooth, so g. yet

P. L. 11, 866. with three listed colours g.
S. A. 712. so be decked, ornate and g.
C. 299. some g. creatures of the element
C. 790. enjoy your dear wit and g. rhetoric
L. 47. flowers that their g. wardrobe wear
Il P. 8. the g. motes that people the sunbeams
**Gayest.**—P. L. 11, 186. two birds of g. plume
V. Ex. 21. those richest robes and g. attire
**Gaza.**—P. L. 1, 466. Accaron and G.'s frontier
S. A. 41. in G. at the mill with slaves
S. A. 435. popular feast here celebrate in G.
S. A. 981. in Ecron, G., Ashdod and in Gath
S. A. 1558. G. yet stands but all her sons
S. A. 1729. G. is not in plight to say us nay
S. A. 1752. whence G. mourns
**Gaze.**—P. L. 3, 613. new to g. the Devil saw
P. L. 3, 671. secret g. or open admiration
P. L. 4, 356. Satan still in g. as first he stood
P. L. 5, 47. by thy beauty still to g.
P. L. 6, 205. stood at g. the adverse legions
P. L. 9, 524. but as in g. admiring
P. L. 9, 535. approach thee thus and g. insatiate
P. L. 9, 539. thee all things living g. on
P. L. 9, 578. I nearer drew to g.
P. L. 9, 611. to come and g. and worship thee
S. A. 34. of my enemies the scorn and g.
S. A. 567. to visitants a g. or pitied object
C. 736. g. upon the sun with shameless brows
A. 43. sat to wonder at and g. upon
H. 70. stand fixed in steadfast g.
**Gazed.**—P. L. 5, 57. on that tree he also g.
P. L. 5, 272. g. by all as that sole bird
P. L. 8, 258. and g. awhile the ample sky
P. L. 9, 735. fixed on the fruit she g.
P. L. 11, 845. on his wide watery glass g. hot
P. R. 1, 414. emptied, g. unpitied, shunned
C. 54. Nymph that g. upon his clustering locks
**Gazing.**—P. L. 4, 351. filled with pasture g. sat
**Gear.**—C. 167. about his country g.
**Gehenna.**—P. L. 1, 405. and black G. called
**Gemmed.**—P. L. 7, 325. or g. their blossoms
**Gems.**—P. L. 1, 538. with g. and golden lustre
P. L. 2, 271. her hidden lustre g. and gold
P. L. 3, 507. thick with sparkling orient g.
P. L. 4, 649. and these the g. of Heaven
P. L. 6, 475. plant, fruit, flower ambrosial, g.
P. L. 11, 583. gay in g. and wanton dress
P. R. 3, 14. oraculous g. on Aaron's breast
P. R. 4, 119. embossed with g. and studs
C. 22. like to rich and various g. inlay
C. 719. precious g. to store her children with
**General.**—P. L. 1, 337. yet to their g.'s voice
P. L. 1, 421. g. names of Baalim and Ashtaroth
P. L. 2, 481. for the g safety he despised his
P. L. 2, 773. and in the g. fall I also
P. L. 3, 328. to the g. doom shall hasten
P. L. 4, 144. to our g. sire gave prospect
P. L. 4, 492. so spake our g. mother
P. L. 4, 659. to whom our g. ancestor replied
P. L. 11, 76. once more to sound at g. doom
S. A. 1524. could else a g. cry be heard
**Generally.**—P. R. 1, 387. men g. think
**Generate.**—P. L. 7, 387. let the waters g.
P. L. 10, 894. or find some other way to g.
**Generated.**—P. L. 7, 393. the waters g.
**Generation.**—P. L. 1, 653. therein plant a g.
P. L. 7, 102. to hear thee tell his g.
**Generations.**—P. L. 11, 344. spread all g.
**Generous.**—P. R. 2, 479. which to a g. mind
S. A. 1467. a third more g. far and civil
**Genezaret.**—P. R. 2, 23. the broad lake G.
**Genial.**—P. L. 4, 712. what day the g. Angel
P. L. 7, 282. satiate with g. moisture
P. L. 8, 598. higher of the g. bed by far
S. A. 594. I feel my g. spirits droop
**Genius.**—L. 183. thou art the g. of the shore
Il P. 154. or the unseen g. of the wood
H. 186. parting g. is with sighing sent
**Gentiles.**—P. L. 4, 277. G. Ammon call
P. L. 12, 310. Joshua whom the G. Jesus call
P. R. 1, 456. shalt thou . . . abuse the G.

P. R. 3, 425. distinguishable scarce from G.
P. R. 4, 227. the G. also know and write
P. R. 4, 229. with the G...thou must converse
S. A. 150. the G. feign to bear up heaven
S. A. 500. a sin that G. . . . condemn
**Gentle.**—P. L. 3, 585. with g. penetration
P. L. 4, 156. now g. gales fanning their
P. L. 4, 308. but required with g. sway
P. L. 4, 337. nor g. purpose nor endearing
P. L. 4, 366. ah g. pair ye little think how
P. L. 4, 404. in some purlieu two g. fawns
P. L. 4, 488. thy g. hand seized mine
P. L. 4, 806. like g. breaths from rivers pure
P. L. 5, 37. with g. voice I thought it thine
P. L. 5, 130. but silently a g. tear let fall
P. L. 8, 287. there g. sleep first found me
P. L. 8, 515. gales and g. airs whispered it
P. L. 8, 648. g. to me and affable hath been
P. L. 9, 527. his g. dumb expression turned
P. L. 10, 93. and g. airs due at their hour
P. L. 10, 919. whereon I live, thy g. looks
P. L. 11, 188. first hunter then pursued a g.
P. L. 11, 421. but him the g. Angel by the hand
P. L. 12, 435. a g. wafting to immortal life
P. L. 12, 595. I with g. dreams have calmed
P. R. 2, 375. thy g. ministers who come to pay
P. R. 3, 215. though to that g. brow willingly
C. 236. canst thou not tell me of a g. pair
C. 271. nay g. shepherd ill is lost that praise
C. 304. g. villager what readiest way would
C. 337. some g. taper though a rush-candle
C. 681. for g. usage and soft delicacy
C. 824. a g. nymph not far from hence
C. 900. g. swain, at thy request, I am here
A. 26. stay g. swains for though
L. 19. so may some g Muse
L. 92. what mishap hath doomed this g. swain
S. 8, 6. that call fame on such g. acts as
H. 38. she wooes the g. air
P. 52. the g. neighbourhood of grove and
M. W. 47. g. Lady may thy grave
**Gentleness.**—C. 843. retains her maiden g.
**Gentler.**—S. A. 788. may censure thine the g.
**Gentlest.**—P. R. 2, 364. winds of g. gale
**Gently.**—P. L. 1, 529. g. raised fainting courage
P. L. 3, 583. that g. warms the universe
P. L. 4, 259. and g. creeps luxuriant
P. L. 7, 81. g. for our instruction to impart
P. L. 8, 293. whose inward apparition g. moved
P. L. 9, 431. then she upstays g. with myrtle
P. L. 11, 298. g. hast thou told thy message
P. L. 11, 758. till g. reared by the angel
C. 575. who g. asked if he had seen such two
Il P. 60. g. o'er the accustomed oak
**Germans.**—P. R. 4, 78. G. and Scythians
**Geryon's**—P. L. 11, 410. G. sons call El Dorado
**Gesture.**—P. L. 1, 590. in shape and g.
P. L. 8, 489. in every g. dignity and love
P. L. 9, 460. her every air of g. or least action
**Gestures.**—P. L. 4, 128. his g. fierce
C. 464. by unchaste looks, loose g. and
**Get.**—P. L. 7, 464. lion pawing to g. free
P. L. 12, 45. and g. themselves a name
P. R. 2, 427. g. riches first g. wealth
P. R. 4, 193. g. thee behind me
P. R. 4, 480. of Israel's sceptre g. fast hold
S. A. 798. thy secrets g. into my power
**Ghastly.**—P. L. 2, 846. grinned horrible a g.
P. L. 6, 368. mangled with g. wounds
P. L. 11, 481 all maladies of g. spasm
C. 641. or g. furies' apparition
**Ghost.**—C. 434. stubborn unlaid g.
H. 234. each fettered g. slips to his several grave
**Ghosts.**—P. R. 4, 422. infernal g. and hellish
**Giant.**—P. L. 1, 576. though all the g. brood
P. L. 1, 778. to surpass Earth's g. sons
P. L. 7, 605. from the g. Angels
S. A. 1068. I know him ... the g. Harapha
S. A. 1181. tongue-doughty g. how dost thou
S. A. 1247. I dread him not nor all his g. brood
V. Ex. 93. like some earth-born g.

**Giants.**—P. L. 3, 464. those *g.* came
P. L. 11, 642. *g.* of mighty bone and bold
P. L. 11, 688. such were these *g.* men of high
S. A. 148. the hill by Hebron seat of *g.* old
Brut. 9. where *g.* dwelt of old
**Giantship.**—S. A. 1244. his *g.* is gone
**Gibeah.**—P. L. 1, 504. that night in *G.*
**Gibeon.**—P. L. 12, 265. sun in *G.* stand
**Gibraltar.**—P. L. 1, 355. beneath *G.*
**Giddy.**—L'A. 141. wanton heed and *g.* cunning
**Gideon.**—P. R. 2, 439. *G.* and Jephtha
S. A. 280. matchless *G.* in pursuit of Madian
**Gift.**—P. L. 4, 735. thy *g.* of sleep
P. L. 5, 19. heaven's last best *g.* my ever-new
P. L. 5, 366. who yet by sovran *g.* possess this
P. L. 6, 626. not understood this *g.* they had
P. L. 9, 540. gaze on all things thine by *g.*
P. L. 9, 806. had the *g.* been theirs it had not
P. L. 10, 138. and gavest me as thy perfect *g.*
P. L. 11, 340. no despicable *g.*
P. L. 12, 138. there by promise he receives *g.*
P. R. 2, 381. shall I receive by *g.* what of my
P. R. 3, 116. above all sacrifice or hallowed *g.*
P. R. 4, 169. for what can less so great a *g.*
S. A. 47. who this high *g.* of strength
S. A. 59. how slight the *g.* was hung it
S. A. 201. divulged the secret *g.* of God
S. A. 577. serve the Philistines with that *g.*
S. A. 1354. shall I abuse this consecrated *g.*
S. A. 1500. not to sit idle with so great a *g.*
**Gifts.**—P. L. 4, 715. endowed with all their *g.*
P. L. 5, 317. afford our givers their own *g.*
P. L. 8, 220. God on thee abundantly his *g.*
P. L. 8, 494. but fairest this of all thy *g.*
P. L. 10, 153. and her *g.* were such as under
P. L. 11, 57. I at first with two fair *g.* created
P. L. 11, 612. they his *g.* acknowledged none
P. L. 11, 636. and superior *g.* received
P. L. 12, 500. shall them with wondrous *g.* endue
P. R. 2, 137. more than human *g.* from Heaven
P. R. 2, 391. count thy specious *g.*, no *g.*
S. A. 358. why are his *g.* desirable to tempt
S. A. 589. shall his wondrous *g.* be frustrate
S. A. 679. with *g.* and graces ... adorned
S. A. 1026. that inward *g.* were left for haste
C. 754. there was another meaning in these *g*
S. 19, 10. either man's work or his own *g.*
**Gigantic.**—P. L. 11, 659. slaughter and *g.* deeds
S. A. 1249. all of *g.* size, Goliath chief
**Gilded.**—P. R. 4, 53. with *g.* battlements
C. 95. and the *g.* car of day
**Gilds.**—P. L. 3, 551. the rising sun *g.* with his
P. L. 7, 366. and hence the morning planet *g.*
**Gills.**—P. L. 7, 415. and at his *g.* draws in
**Gins.**—S. A. 933. to my cost thy *g.* and toils
**Gird.**—P. L. 6, 542. adamantine coat *g.* well
P. L. 8, 82. how *g.* the sphere with centric
P. L. 9, 1113. to *g.* their waist vain covering
P. L. 6, 714. my almighty arms *g.* on
**Girded.**—P. L. 9, 1096. and *g.* on our loins
P. R. 1, 120. his easy steps *g.* with snaky wiles
**Girt.**—P. L. 4, 276. *g.* with the river Triton
P. L. 5, 281. the middle pair *g.* like a starry
P. L. 7, 194. *g.* with omnipotence
P. L. 9, 1116. so *g.* with feathered cincture
S. A. 846. what sieges *g.* me round ere I
S. A. 1415. perhaps offend them to see me *g.*
C. 214. hovering angel *g.* with golden wings
C. 602. let him be *g.* with all the grisly legions
H. 202. now sits not *g.* with tapers' holy shine
U. C. I., 1. death hath broke his *g.*
**Give.**—P. L. 2, 14. I *g.* not heaven for lost
P. L. 2, 153. whether our angry foe can *g.* it
P. L. 2, 157. to *g.* his enemies their wish
P. L. 3, 318. all power I *g.* thee
P. L. 4, 381. he gave it me which I as freely *g.*
P. L. 4, 483. to *g.* thee being I lent out of my
P. L. 4, 841. shalt *g.* account to him who sent
P. L. 5, 206. he bounteous still to *g.* us only
P. L. 5, 485. *g.* both life and sense
P. L. 5, 693. to pass triumphant and *g.* laws

P. L. 5, 822. shalt thou *g.* law to God
P. L. 7, 345. to *g.* light on the earth
P. L. 8, 319. this paradise I *g.* thee
P. L. 8, 339. earth to thee and to thy race I *g.*
P. L. 9, 805. others envy what they cannot *g.*
P. L. 9, 818. *g.* him to partake full happiness
P. L. 9, 1067. in evil hour thou didst *g.* ear
P. L. 12, 12. thou therefore *g.* due audience
P. L. 12, 392. disabled not to *g.* thee thy
P. R. 1, 449. *g.* thee in command what to the
P. R. 2, 393. that I have also power to *g.*
P. R. 2, 481. besides to *g.* a kingdom hath been
P. R. 3, 10. to thy large heart *g.* utterance
P. R. 4, 104. buy that right I *g.* it thee
P. R. 4, 161. nor what I part with mean to *g.*
P. R. 4, 163. kingdoms of the world to thee I *g.*
P. R. 4, 164. for given to me I *g.* to whom
P. R. 4, 315. all glory arrogate to God *g.* none
P. R. 4, 385. the stars .... *g.* me to spell
P. R. 4, 556. will *g.* command concerning thee
S. A. 302. *g.* the reins to wandering thought
S. A. 825. such pardon therefore as I *g.* my
S. A. 1117. sight may *g.* thee or rather flight
S. A. 1228. and *g.* thy verdict
S. A. 1264. worst that he can *g.* to me the best
S. A. 1453. to *g.* ye part with me
S. A. 1578. I *g.* the reins to grief
S. A. 1593. *g.* us if thou canst ... relation
C. 81. I shoot from heaven to *g.* him safe
C. 156. and *g.* it false presentments
C. 199. with everlasting oil to *g.* due light
C. 243. and *g.* resounding grace to all
C. 276. to *g.* me answer from her mossy couch
C. 648. as I will *g.* you when we go
C. 703. none but such as are good men can *g.*
A. 23. Juno dares not *g.* her odds
A. 101. a better soil shall *g.* ye thanks
L'A. 37. and if I *g.* thee honour due
L'A. 151. these delights if thou canst *g.*
Il P. 175. these pleasures Melancholy *g.*
S. 13, 12. Dante shall *g.* Fame leave to set thee
Cir. 11. now bleeds to *g.* us ease
D. F. I. 76, this if thou do, he will an offspring *g.*
M. W. 51. that, to *g.* the world increase
V. Ex. 65. she heard them *g.* thee this that thou
**Given.**—P. L. 1, 347. till, as a signal *g.*
P. L. 1, 776. till the signal *g.* behold
P. L. 2, 332. for what peace will be *g.* to us
P. L. 2, 775. powerful key into my hand was *g.*
P. L. 3, 103. what proof could they have *g.*
P. L. 3, 243. thou hast *g.* me to possess life
P. L. 4, 430. and dominion *g.* over all other
P. L. 4, 561. to thee thy course by lot hath *g.*
P. L. 4, 1007. neither our own but *g.* what
P. L. 5, 454. not to let the occasion pass *g.* him
P. L. 5, 523. this was that caution *g.* thee
P. L. 5, 740. all regal power *g.* me to quell
P. L. 6, 322. was *g.* him tempered so
P. L. 6, 887. and Lord, to him dominion *g.*
P. L. 8, 386. in proportion due *g.* and received
P. L. 8, 545. dominion *g.* o'er other creatures
P. L. 9, 10. and just rebuke and judgment *g.*
P. L. 9, 951. matter of scorn not to be *g.* the foe
P. L. 10, 224. and dominion *g.* me large beyond
P. L. 10, 385. high proof ye now have *g.*
P. L. 10, 488. your laughter hath *g.* up both
P. L. 11, 255. many days *g.* thee of grace
P. L. 11, 502. why is life *g.* to be thus wrested
P. L. 12, 66. authority usurped from God not *g.*
P. L. 12, 282. many and so various laws are *g.*
P. L. 12, 287. and therefore was law *g.* them
P. L. 12, 300. and but *g.* with purpose to resign
P. L. 12, 519. promised alike and *g.* to all
P. R. 1, 37. to whom such high attest was *g.*
P. R. 1, 431. all oracles by thee are *g.*
P. R. 1, 442. for God hath justly *g.* the nations
P. R. 3, 251. such power was *g.* him then
P. R. 4, 104. to me the power is *g.*
P. R. 4, 164. *g.* to me I give to whom I please
P. R. 4, 182. of the world to thee were *g.*
P. R. 4, 185. if *g.* by whom but by the King of

P. R. 4, 186. if *g.* to thee by thee how fairly
S. A. 359. then *g.* with solemn hand as graces
S. A. 378. the mystery of God *g.* me under pledge
S. A. 578. which was expressly *g.* thee to annoy
S. A. 1135. at thy birth was *g.* thee
S. A. 1697. so Virtue *g.* for lost
S. A. 629. sleep hath forsook and *g.* me o'er
S. A. 121. and by himself *g.* over
H. 78. had *g.* day her room, the sun himself
**Giver.**—P. L. 8, 493. *g.* of all things fair
P. R. 2, 322. as I like the *g.* answered Jesus
P. R. 4, 187. by thee how fairly is the *G.* now
C. 775. and then the *g.* would be better thanked
**Givers.**—P. L. 5, 317. we may afford our *g.*
**Gives.**—P. L. 5, 119. which *g.* me hope that
P. L. 5, 403. that one celestial Father *g.* to all
P. L. 5, 404. therefore what he *g.* whose praise
P. L. 8, 171. joy thou in what he *g.* to thee
P. L. 9, 40. justly *g.* heroic name to person
P. L. 9, 686. it *g.* you life to knowledge
P. R. 4, 23. yet *g.* not o'er though desperate
C. 9. unmindful of the crown that virtue *g.*
C. 26. and *g.* them leave to wear their sapphire
C. 525. by sly enticement *g.* his baneful cup
U. C. II. 11. rest that *g.* all men life gave him his
**Givest.**—P. L. 9, 810. and *g.* access
**Giving.**—P. L. 3, 299. *g.* to death, and dying
P. L. 6, 730. sceptre and power thy *g.* I assume
**M. W.** 14. in *g.* limit to her life
**Glad.**—P. L. 2, 1011. *g.* that now his sea should
P. L. 3, 270. as a sacrifice *g.* to be offered
P. L. 3, 630. *g.* was the spirit impure
P. L. 4, 150. sun more *g.* impressed his beams
P. L. 5, 29. my glory, my perfection *g.* I see
P. L. 5, 92. but O how *g.* I waked to find
P. L. 6, 258. and *g.* as hoping here to end
P. L. 7, 291. they hasted with *g.* precipitance
P. L. 7, 386. *g.* evening and *g.* morn crowned
P. L. 8, 245. *g.* we returned up to the coasts
P. L. 8, 322. eat freely with *g.* heart
P. L. 9, 528. he *g.* of her attention gained
P. L. 9, 625. whom the wily adder blithe and *g.*
P. L. 10, 383. the Prince of Darkness answered *g.*
P. L. 10, 777. how *g.* would lay me down
P. L. 11, 20. them the *g.* son presenting thus
P. L. 11, 507. *g.* to be so dismissed in peace
P. L. 12, 375. O prophet of *g.* tidings
P. R. 1, 477. and *g.* to scape so quit
P. R. 2, 53. let us be *g.* of this
P. R. 4, 441. *g.* would also seem of this fair chance
S. A. 924. with nursing diligence to me *g.* office
S. A. 1444. of him bringing to us some *g.* news
A. 39. to further this night's *g.* solemnity
L. 35. from the *g.* sound not be absent long
S. 23, 3. whom Jove's great son to her *g.* husband
U. C. II. 6. death was half *g.* when he had got
**Glade.**—P. L. 4, 231. fell down the steep *g.*
P. L. 9, 1085. in some *g.* obscured
C. 79. to pass through this adventurous *g.*
C. 532. that brow this bottom *g.*
**Glades.**—Il P. 27. in glimmering bowers and *g.*
**Gladlier.**—P. L. 6, 731. and *g.* shall resign
P. L. 8, 47. touched by her fair tendance *g.* grew
**Gladly.**—P. L. 2, 1044. holds *g.* the port
P. L. 6, 21. *g.* then he mixed among those
P. L. 8, 226. and inquire *g.* into the ways of God
P. L. 9, 966. *g.* of our union hear thee speak
P. L. 10, 775. how *g.* would I meet mortality
P. L. 11, 332. I now *g.* behold though but his
P. L. 12, 366. they *g.* thither haste
S. A. 259. and they as *g.* yield me
C. 413. and *g.* banish squint suspicion
**Glance.**—P. L. 7, 405. sporting with quick *g.*
P. L. 8, 533. the charm of beauty's powerful *g.*
P. L. 9, 1034. so said he and forbore not *g.*
P. L. 11, 442. consumed with nimble *g.*
S. A. 1284. expedition swift as the lightning *g.*
C. 884. upon thy streams with wily *g.*
**Glanced.**—P. L. 10, 1054. *g.* on the ground
**Glancing.**—C. 80. swift as the sparkle of a *g.* star
**Glare.**—P. L. 4, 402. he stalks with fiery *g.*

**Glared.**—P. L. 6, 849. and every eye *g.*
P. L. 10, 714. with countenance grim *g.* on him
P. R. 1, 313. the lion and fierce tiger *g.* aloof
**Glass.**—P. L. 1, 288. through optic *g.*
P. L. 5, 261. as when by night the *g.* of Galilee
P. L. 11, 844. clear sun on his wide watery *g.*
P. R. 4, 41. or *g.* of telescope
C. 65. his orient liquor in a crystal *g.*
C. 651. break his *g.* and shed the luscious liquor
Il P. 113. that owned the virtuous ring and *g.*
V. Ex. 71. in times long and dark prospective *g.*
**Glassy.**—P. L. 7, 619. clear hyaline the *g.* sea
C. 861. under the *g.* cool translucent wave
**Glaucus.**—C. 874. and old soothsaying *G.'* spell
**Glazed.**—P. L. 3, 590. through his *g.* optic
**Gleam.**—P. L. 4, 499. at last a *g.* of dawning
P. L. 4, 461. a shape within the watery *g.*
P. L. 12, 257. a fiery *g.* by night
C. 225. and casts a *g.* over this tufted grove
**Gleaming.**—P. R. 3, 326. cast a *g.* brown
**Glebe.**—P. R. 3, 259. fertile of corn the *g.*
**Glibbed.**—P. R. 1, 375. prophets *g.* with lies
**Glide.**—P. L. 5, 200. ye that in waters *g.*
P. L. 7, 402. *g.* under the green wave
P. L. 9, 159. of midnight vapour *g.* obscure
**Glides.**—P. L. 12, 630. o'er the marish *g.*
**Gliding.**—P. L. 4, 555. came Uriel *g.* through
P. L. 11, 568. *g.* hot to some cave's mouth
P. L. 12, 629. *g.* meteorous as evening-mist
**Glimmering.**—P. L. 1, 182. *g.* of these livid
P. L. 2, 1037. bosom of dim night a *g.* dawn
P. L. 3, 429. of *g.* air less vexed with tempest
Il P. 27. oft in *g.* bowers and glades he met her
H. 75. but in their *g.* orbs did glow
**Glimpse.**—P. L. 1, 524. some *g.* of joy
P. L. 4, 867. and now by *g.* discern Ithuriel
P. L. 6, 642. light as the lightning *g.* they ran
P. L. 8, 156. scarce to contribute each orb a *g.*
L'A. 107. when in one night ere *g.* of morn
**Glimpses.**—P. R. 1, 93. in his face the *g.*
**Glistered.**—P. L. 9, 643. so *g.* the dire snake
**Glistering.**—P. L. 3, 550. with *g.* spires
P. L. 4, 645. fruit and flower *g.* with dew
P. L. 4, 653. nor herb, fruit, flower *g.* with dew
P. L. 8, 93. comparison of heaven so small nor *g.*
P. L. 11, 247. in a *g.* zodiac
C. 219. would send a *g.* guardian if need were
L. 79. nor in the *g.* foil set off to the world
**Glitter.**—P. L. 10, 452. or false *g.*
**Glittering.**—P. L. 1, 535. from the *g.* staff
P. L. 3, 366. harps ever tuned that *g.* by their
P. L. 4, 656. *g.* starlight without thee is sweet
P. L. 5, 291. their *g.* tents he passed
P. L. 5, 592. or in their *g.* tissues bear emblazed
P. R. 4, 54. turrets and terraces and *g.* spires
A. 81. and so attend ye toward her *g.* state
H. 114. are seen in *g.* ranks with wings displayed
**Globe.**—P. L. 1, 291. mountains in her spotty *g.*
P. L. 2, 512. him round a *g.* of fiery seraphim
P. L. 3, 418. meanwhile upon the firm opacous *g.*
P. L. 3, 422. a *g.* far off it seemed.
P. L. 3, 498. all this dark *g.* the fiend found
P. L. 3, 722. look downward on that *g.*
P. L. 4, 723. moon's resplendent *g.* and starry
P. L. 7, 280. prolific humour softening all her *g.*
P. L. 10, 671. pushed oblique the centric *g.*
P. R. 1, 365. I enjoy large liberty to round this *g.*
P. R. 4, 581. a fiery *g.* of angels on full sail
H. 110. a *g.* of circular light
**Globes.**—P. L. 5. 259. to other shining *g.*
P. L. 6, 590. thunderbolts and hail of iron *g.*
**Globose.**—P. L. 5, 753. from one entire *g.*
P. L. 7, 357. then formed the moon *g.*
**Globous.**—P. L. 5, 649. than all this *g.* earth
**Gloom.**—P. L. 1, 244. this mournful *g.* for that
P. L. 1, 544. all in a moment through the *g.*
P. L. 2, 400. orient beam purge off this *g.*
P. L. 2, 858. into this *g.* of Tartarus profound
P. L. 7, 246. to journey through the aery *g.*
P. L. 10, 848. with damps and dreadful *g.*
C. 132. of Stygian darkness spets her thickest *g.*

Il P. 80. teach light to counterfeit a g.
H. 77. and though the shady g.
**Gloomiest.**—P. L. 10, 716. hid in g. shade
**Gloomy.**—P. L. 1, 152. in the g. deep
P. L. 2, 976. where your g. bounds confine
P. L. 3, 242. under his g. power I shall not
P. L. 4, 270. herself a fairer flower by g. Dis
P. L. 6, 832. g. as night under his burning
P. R. 1, 42. a g. consistory
S. A. 161. to incorporate with g. night
C. 470. such are those thick and g. shadows
C. 945. through this g. covert wide
**Gloried.**—S. A. 334. towards your once g. friend
**Glories.**—P. L. 1, 573. in his strength g.
P. L. 1, 719. equalled in all their g.
H. 143. orbed in a rainbow and like g. wearing
**Glorified.**—P. R. 3, 113. by all his angels g.
**Glorify.**—P. L. 3, 695. thereby to g. the great
P. L. 6, 725. always seekest to g. thy son
P. L. 7, 116. best may serve to g. the Maker
H. 154. so both himself and us to g.
**Glorious.**—P. L. 1, 89. in the g. enterprise
P. L. 2, 16. more g. and more dread
P. L. 2, 179. designing or exhorting g. war
P. L. 3, 139. the Son of God was seen most g.
P. L. 3, 376. invisible amidst the g. brightness
P. L. 3, 612. precious things of colour g.
P. L. 3, 622. saw within ken a g. angel stand
P. L. 4, 39. how g. once above thy sphere
P. L. 4, 292. the image of their g. Maker shone
P. L. 4, 658. for whom this g. sight when sleep
P. L. 5, 153. these are thy g. works
P. L. 5, 309. g. shape comes this way moving
P. L. 5, 362. than heaven such g. shape contain
P. L. 5, 567. the ruin of so many g. once
P. L. 5, 833. thyself though great and g.
P. L. 6, 39. back on thy foes more g. to return
P. L. 7, 370. in his east the g. lamp was seen
P. L. 7, 574. so sung the g. train ascending
P. L. 8, 464. and saw the Shape still g.
P. L. 9, 961. O g. trial of exceeding love
P. L. 9, 1177. to find matter of g. trial
P. L. 10, 391. mine with this g. work
P. L. 10, 474. to expedite your g. march
P. L. 10, 537. issuing forth their g. chief
P. L. 10, 721. is this the end of this new g. world
P. L. 11, 211. a g. apparition
P. L. 11, 213. not that more g. when the angels
P. L. 12, 334. shall in a g. temple enshrine
P. R. 1, 8. thou spirit who ledst this g. Eremite
P. R. 1, 242. at thy nativity a g. choir of angels
P. R. 3, 70. attributed to things not g.
P. R. 3, 71. they err who count it g. to subdue
P. R. 4, 45. great and g. Rome
P. R. 4, 546. the g. temple reared her pile
P. R. 4, 634. on thy g. work now enter
S. A. 36. O g. strength put to the labour of a
S. A. 363. g. for a while the miracle of men
S. A. 705. once thy g. champion
S. A. 855. how g. to entrap a common enemy
S. A. 1130. durst not thus disparage g. arms
S. A. 1581. g. hand gave Samson his death's
S. A. 1660. O dearly bought revenge yet g.
S. 14, 12. spake the truth of thee on g. themes
S. 16, 4. to peace and truth thy g. way hast
H. 8. that g. form, that light unsufferable
P. 40. once g. towers, now sunk in guiltless blood
**Gloriously.**—P. L. 3, 323. attended g.
P. L. 3, 655. of God's high throne g. bright
P. R. 4, 127. how easily subdued, how g.
S. A. 200. trusted to me from above, g. rigged
S. A. 1752. hath in place bore witness g.
**Glory.**—P. L. 1, 39. to set himself in g. above
P. L. 1, 110. that g. never shall his wrath
P. L. 1, 141. though all our g. extinct
P. L. 1, 370. the invisible g. of him that made
P. L. 1, 594. and the excess of g. obscured
P. L. 1, 612. how they stood, their g. withered
P. L. 2, 386. but their spite still serves his g.
P. L. 2, 427. Satan whom now transcendent g.
P. L. 2, 484. which g. excites or close ambition

P. L. 2, 564. passion and apathy and g. and
P. L. 3, 63. the radiant image of his g. sat
P. L. 3, 133. so shall my g. excel but mercy first
P. L. 3, 164. what for thy g. thou hast made
P. L. 3, 239. and this g. next to thee freely
P. L. 3, 312. love hath abounded more than g.
P. L. 3, 388. impressed the effulgence of his g.
P. L. 3, 449. built their fond hopes of g.
P. L. 4, 32. O thou that with surpassing g.
P. L. 4, 838. that g. then when thou no more
P. L. 4, 853. more g. will be won or less be lost
P. L. 5, 29. my g., my perfection glad I see
P. L. 5, 719. Son thou in whom my g. I behold
P. L. 5, 738. matter to me of g.
P. L. 5, 839. crowned them with g. and to their g.
P. L. 6, 290. but we style the strife of g.
P. L. 6, 383. yet to g. aspires vain-glorious
P. L. 6, 422. honour, dominion, g., and renown
P. L. 6, 680. effulgence of my g., Son beloved
P. L. 6, 701. that the g. may be thine of ending
P. L. 6, 726. this I my g. account, my exaltation
P. L. 6, 747. the right hand of g. where he sat
P. L. 6, 792. grieving to see his g.
P. L. 6, 815. kingdom and power and g.
P. L. 6, 891. who into g. him received
P. L. 7, 182. g. they sung to the Most High
P. L. 7, 184. g. to him whose just avenging ire
P. L. 7, 187. to him g. and praise whose
P. L. 7, 208. to let forth the King of g.
P. L. 7, 219. uplifted in paternal g. rode
P. L. 7, 499. now heaven in all her g. shone
P. L. 8, 12. g. attributed to the high Creator
P. L. 9, 135. to me shall be the g. sole among
P. L. 9, 1115. how unlike to that first naked g.
P. L. 10, 64. toward the right hand his g.
P. L. 10, 86. of high collateral g.
P. L. 10, 226. blissful bosom re-assumed in g.
P. L. 10, 386. of Satan for I g. in the name
P. L. 10, 451. with what permissive g.
P. L. 10, 722. me so late the g. of that g.
P. L. 11, 333. but his utmost skirts of g.
P. L. 11, 384. all earth's kingdoms and their g.
P. L. 11, 694. and for g. done of triumph
P. L. 11, 694. the highest pitch of human g.
P. L. 12, 172. they return with g. and spoil
P. L. 12, 371. his g. with the heavens
P. L. 12, 456. then enter into g. and resume
P. L. 12, 460. with g. and power to judge both
P. L. 12, 477. to God more g. more good-will
P. L. 12, 546. from heaven to be revealed in g.
P. R. 1, 93. glimpses of his Father's g. shine
P. R. 1, 454. thy g. shall be soon retrenched
P. R. 2, 48. arise and vindicate thy g.
P. R. 2, 227. honour, g. and popular praise
P. R. 2, 386. arrayed in g. on my cup to attend
P. R. 3, 25. the fame and g.—g., the reward
P. R. 3, 38. quench not the thirst of g.
P. R. 3, 41. the more inflamed with g.
P. R. 3, 46. nor empire to affect for g.'s sake
P. R. 3, 47. for what is g. but the blaze of fame
P. R. 3, 59. and g. scarce of few is raised
P. R. 3, 60. this is true g. and renown
P. R. 3, 69. where g. is false g.
P. R. 3, 88. but if there be in g. aught of good
P. R. 3, 100. if for fame and g. aught be done
P. R. 3, 105. shall I seek g. then as vain men seek
P. R. 3, 109. think not so slight of g. therein
P. R. 3, 110. seeks g. and for his g. all things
P. R. 3, 114. requires g. from men, from all men
P. R. 3, 117. g. he requires and g. he receives
P. R. 3, 120. from us his foes pronounced g.
P. R. 3, 123. though chiefly not for g. as prime
P. R. 3, 127. g. and benediction that is thanks
P. R. 3, 134. but why should man seek g.
P. R. 3, 143. who advance his g. not their own
P. R. 3, 144. he himself to g. will advance
P. R. 3, 148. for he himself insatiable of g.
P. R. 3, 150. of g. as thou wilt, said he, so deem
P. R. 3, 236. hast not seen, much less her g.
P. R. 3, 383. on the throne of David in full g.
P. R. 4, 89. kingdoms of the world and all their g.

P. R. 4, 315. and to themselves all *g.* arrogate
P. R. 4, 371. tended on by *g.* or fame
P. R. 4, 536. riches, kingdoms, *g.* have been
S. A. 167. from the top of wondrous *g.*
S. A. 179. the *g.* late of Israel now the grief
S. A. 303. regardless of his *g.'s* diminution
S. A. 475. to vindicate the *g.* of his name
S. A. 597. my race of *g.* run and race of shame
S. A. 680. to some great work thy *g.*
S. A. 1098. the *g.* of prowess been recovered
S. A. 1148. how highly it concerns his *g.*
S. A. 1429. to what may serve his *g.* best
C. 592. shall in the happy trial prove most *g.*
L. 180. sing and singing in their *g.* move
Cir. 20. emptied his *g.* even to nakedness
M. W. 61. thou bright saint high sitt'st in *g.*
**Glorying.**—P. L. 1, 239. both *g.* to have
**Gloss.**—P. L. 5, 435. common *g.* of theologians
S. A. 948. to *g.* upon and censuring frown
**Glossy.**—P. L. 1, 672. shone with a *g.* scurf
**Glow.**—H. 75. in their glimmering orbs did *g.*
**Glowed.**—P. L. 4, 604. now *g.* the firmament
P. L. 8, 618. a smile that *g.* celestial rosy red
P. L. 9, 427. roses blushing round about her *g.*
P. L. 9, 887. in her cheek distemper flushing *g.*
**Glowing.**—P. L. 3, 594. as *g.* iron with fire
P. L. 5, 10. and *g.* cheek as through unquiet
C. 96. gilded car of day his *g.* axle doth allay
L. 145, the *g.* violet, the musk-rose
Il P. 79. *g.* embers through the room
**Glozed.**—P. L. 9, 549. so *g.* the tempter
**Glozing.**—P. L. 1, 93. will hearken to his *g.* lies
C. 161. well-placed words of *g.* courtesy
**Glut.**—P. L. 3, 259. with his carcase *g.* the grave
P. L. 6, 589. disgorging foul their devilish *g.*
P. L. 10, 990. so death shall be deceived his *g.*
T. 4. and *g.* thyself with what thy womb
**Glutinous.**—C. 917. smeared with gums of *g.*
**Glutted.**—P. L. 10, 633. sucked and *g.* offal
**Gluttonies.**—P. R. 4, 114. sumptuous *g.*
**Gluttonous.**—P. L. 11, 533. not *g.* delight
**Gluttony.**—C. 776. *g.* ne'er looks to heaven
**Gnashing.**—P. L. 6, 340. *g.* for anguish
**Gnaw.**—P. L. 2, 799. howl and *g.* my bowels
**Go.**—P. L. 2, 456. *g.* therefore mighty powers
P. L. 2, 826. I *g.* this uncouth errand
P. L. 2, 1008. *g.* and speed!
P. L. 5, 118. God or man may come and *g.*
P. L. 5, 229. *g.* therefore half this day as friend
P. L. 5, 313. *g.* with speed and what thy stores
P. L. 6, 44. *g.* Michael of celestial armies prince
P. L. 6, 275. hence then and evil *g.* with thee
P. L. 6, 710. *g.* then thou mightiest
P. L. 8, 646. *g.* heavenly guest
P. L. 9, 372. *g.* for thy stay not free absents
P. L. 9, 373. *g.* in thy native innocence
P. L. 9, 382. the willinger I *g.* nor much expect
P. L. 9, 1156. command me absolutely not to *g.*
P. L. 10, 71. I *g.* to judge on earth these thy
P. L. 10, 177. on thy belly grovelling thou shalt *g.*
P. L. 10, 265. *g.* whither fate and inclination
P. L. 10, 409. *g.* and be strong
P. L. 12, 201. who shall *g.* before them
P. L. 12, 537. so shall the world *g.* on to good
P. L. 12, 594. no longer stay, *g.* waken Eve
P. L. 12, 615. with thee to *g.* is to stay here
P. L. 12, 617. without thee here to stay is to *g.*
P. R. 1, 340. and to drink *g.* far
S. A. 954. I forgive thee; *g.* with that
S. A. 967. bid *g.* with evil omen and the brand
S. A. 999. so let her *g.*
S. A. 1146. *g.* to his temple, invocate his aid
S. A. 1237. *g.* baffled coward lest I run upon thee
S. A. 1384. I with this messenger will *g.* along
S. A. 1408. like a wild beast I am content to *g.*
S. A. 1427. *g.* and the Holy One of Israel
S. A. 1725. let us *g.* find the body where it lies
C. 648. as I will give you when we *g.*
C. 779. shall I *g.* on? or have I said enough?
A. 78. yet as we *g.* whate'er the skill of lesser
L. 108. last came and last did *g.*

L'A. 33. come and trip it as you *g.*
H. 76. Lord himself bespake and bid them *g.*
**Goal.**—P. L. 2, 531. or shun the *g.* with rapid
C. 100. pacing toward the other *g.*
**Goat.**—P. L. 9, 582. ewe or *g.* dropping with milk
C. 71. or ounce, or tiger, hog, or bearded *g.*
**Goats.**—P. L. 6, 857. and as a herd of *g.*
P. L. 12, 292. the blood of bulls and *g.*
S. A. 1671. and fat regorged of bulls and *g.*
**Goblin.**—P. L. 2, 688. the *g.* full of wrath
C. 436. no *g.* or swart faery of the mine
L'A. 105. tells how the drudging *g.* sweat
**God.**—P. L. 1, 12. fast by the oracle of *G.*
P. L. 1, 26. and justify the ways of *G.* to men
P. L. 1, 42. the throne and monarchy of *G.*
P. L. 1, 73. as far removed from *G.*
P. L. 1, 201. which *G.* of all his works
P. L. 1, 366. through *G.'s* high sufferance
P. L. 1, 369. to forsake *G.* their creator
P. L. 1, 388. long after next the seat of *G.*
P. L. 1, 402. right against the temple of *G.*
P. L. 1, 470. against the house of *G.* was bold
P. L. 1, 473. *G.'s* altar to disparage
P. L. 1, 496. lust and violence the house of *G.*
P. L. 2, 49. of *G.* or hell or worse he recked not
P. L. 2, 368. that their *G.* may prove their foe
P. L. 2, 478. and as a *G.* extol him equal
P. L. 2, 499. and *G.* proclaiming peace
P. L. 2, 622. which *G.* by curse created evil
P. L. 2, 629. meanwhile the adversary of *G.*
P. L. 2, 678. *G.* and his Son except created
P. L. 2, 694. outcast from *G.*
P. L. 2, 1083. whom *G.* and good angels guard
P. L. 3, 3. unblamed since *G.* is light
P. L. 3, 10. at the voice of *G.*
P. L. 3, 77. him *G.* beholding from his prospect
P. L. 3, 135. thus while *G.* spake
P. L. 3, 138. beyond compare the Son of *G.*
P. L. 3, 224. had not the Son of *G.* in whom
P. L. 3, 306. throned in highest bliss equal to *G.*
P. L. 3, 309. more than birthright Son of *G.*
P. L. 3, 316. both *G.* and man, Son both of *G.*
P. L. 3, 341. *G.* shall be all in all
P. L. 3, 412. hail Son of *G.*, Saviour of men
P. L. 3, 470. he who to be deemed a *G.* leaped
P. L. 3, 531. the promised land to *G.* so dear
P. L. 3, 649. of the seven who in *G.'s* presence
P. L. 3, 655. in sight of *G.'s* high throne
P. L. 3, 684. that walks invisible except to *G.*
P. L. 3, 695. tends to know the works of *G.*
P. L. 4, 33. from thy sole dominion like the *g.*
P. L. 4, 152. when *G.* hath showered the earth
P. L. 4, 192. this first grand thief into *G.'s* fold
P. L. 4, 202. so little knows any but *G.* alone
P. L. 4, 209. blissful Paradise of *G.* the garden
P. L. 4, 215. more pleasant garden *G.* ordained
P. L. 4, 225. for *G.* had thrown that mountain
P. L. 4, 299. he for *G.* only, she for *G.* in him
P. L. 4, 320. nor shunned the sight of *G.*
P. L. 4, 427. *G.* hath pronounced it death
P. L. 4, 567. chiefly man *G.'s* latest image
P. L. 4, 612. since *G.* hath set labour and rest
P. L. 4, 622. of their doings *G.* takes no account
P. L. 4, 636. so *G.* ordains, *G.* is thy law
P. L. 4, 660. daughter of *G.* and man
P. L. 4, 676. want spectators, *G.* want praise
P. L. 4, 722. open sky adored the *G.* that made
P. L. 4, 738. adoration pure which *G.* likes best
P. L. 4, 746. as impure what *G.* declares pure
P. L. 4, 749. our destroyer foe to *G.* and man
P. L. 4, 884. whose dwelling *G.* hath planted
P. L. 5, 60. nor *G.* nor man
P. L. 5, 117. evil into the mind of *G.* or man
P. L. 5, 260. garden of *G.* with cedars crowned
P. L. 5, 322. of *G.* inspired
P. L. 5, 330. *G.* hath dispensed his bounties
P. L. 5, 390. these various fruits the trees of *G.*
P. L. 5, 430. *G.* hath here varied his bounty
P. L. 5, 447. then had the sons of *G.* excuse
P. L. 5, 461. inhabitant with *G.* now know I
P. L. 5, 491. wonder not then what *G.* for you

P. L. 5, 512. by steps we may ascend to G.
P. L. 5, 520. that thou art happy owe to G.
P. L. 5, 524. G. made thee perfect
P. L. 5, 536. stand in sight of G. enthroned
P. L. 5, 613. cast out from G. and blessed vision
P. L. 5, 626. that G.'s own ear listens delighted
P. L. 5, 643. from that high mount of G.
P. L. 5, 647. the unsleeping eyes of G.
P. L. 5, 650. such are the courts of G.
P. L. 5, 662. with envy against the Son of G.
P. L. 5, 763. affecting all equality with G.
P. L. 5, 814. the just decree of G. pronounced
P. L. 5, 822. shalt thou give law to G.?
P. L. 5, 877. O alienate from G., O spirit
P. L. 5, 883. to quit the yoke of G.'s Messiah
P. L. 6, 5. is a cave within the mount of G.
P. L. 6, 29. servant of G., well done
P. L. 6, 36. to stand approved in sight of G.
P. L. 6, 52. drive them out from G. and bliss
P. L. 6, 68. in the cause of G. and his Messiah
P. L. 6, 88. by surprise to win the mount of G.
P. L. 6, 99. high in the midst exalted as a G.
P. L. 6, 133. the throne of G. unguarded
P. L. 6, 144. who faith prefer and piety to G.
P. L. 6, 175. to serve whom G. ordains
P. L. 6, 176. G. and nature bid the same
P. L. 6, 184. let me serve in heaven G. ever
P. L. 6, 279. sudden vengeance winged from G.
P. L. 6, 321. from the armoury of G.
P. L. 6, 343. confidence to equal G. in power
P. L. 6, 638. which G. hath in his mighty
P. L. 6, 718. G. and Messiah his anointed king
P. L. 6, 770. chariots of G. half on each hand
P. L. 6, 796. prevail against G. and Messiah
P. L. 6, 799. when the great Son of G.
P. L. 6, 803. and of G. accepted
P. L. 6, 811. G.'s indignation on these godless
P. L. 6, 834. all but the throne itself of G.
P. L. 7, 55. war so near the peace of G. in bliss
P. L. 7, 176. are the acts of G. more swift
P. L. 7, 200. winged from the armoury of G.
P. L. 7, 226. prepared in G.'s eternal store
P. L. 7, 232. thus G. the heaven created
P. L. 7, 235. his brooding wings the spirit of G.
P. L. 7, 243. let there be light said G.
P. L. 7, 249. G. saw the light was good
P. L. 7, 259. hymning praised G. and his works
P. L. 7, 261. G. said let there be firmament
P. L. 7, 263. and G. made the firmament
P. L. 7, 282. with genial moisture when G. said
P. L. 7, 304. easy ere G. had bid the ground
P. L. 7, 331. though G. had yet not rained upon
P. L. 7, 336. ere it was in the earth G. made
P. L. 7, 337. G. saw that it was good
P. L. 7, 346. and G. made two great lights
P. L. 7, 352. G. saw surveying his great work
P. L. 7, 387. G. said let the waters generate
P. L. 7, 391. and G. created the great whales
P. L. 7, 450. G. said let the earth bring forth
P. L. 7, 515. and worship G. supreme
P. L. 7, 527. he created thee in the image of G.
P. L. 7, 538. planted with the trees of G.
P. L. 7, 569. for G. will deign to visit oft
P. L. 7, 576. led to G.'s eternal house direct
P. L. 7, 626. sons of men whom G. hath
P. L. 8, 67. for heaven is as the book of G.
P. L. 8, 112. out from heaven where G. resides
P. L. 8, 119. G. to remove his ways from human
P. L. 8, 168. leave them to G. above
P. L. 8, 185. from which G. hath bid dwell far
P. L. 8, 219. for G. on thee abundantly his gifts
P. L. 8, 226. inquire gladly into the ways of G.
P. L. 8, 227. for G. we see hath honoured thee
P. L. 8, 234. while G. was in his work
P. L. 8, 353. with such knowledge G. endued
P. L. 9, 1. where G. or angel guest with man
P. L. 9, 102. for what G. after better worse
P. L. 9, 107. as G. in heaven is centre
P. L. 9, 231. work which here G. hath assigned
P. L. 9, 262. to withdraw our fealty from G.
P. L. 9, 280. my firmness therefore doubt to G.

P. L. 9, 291. daughter of G. and man
P. L. 9, 344. all things as the will of G. ordained
P. L. 9, 351. but G. left free the will
P. L. 9, 356. do what G. expressly hath forbid
P. L. 9, 375. G. towards thee hath done his part
P. L. 9, 506. or the g. in Epidaurus
P. L. 9, 556. whom g. on their creation-day
P. L. 9, 618. many are the trees of G. that grow
P. L. 9, 652. G. so commanded and left that
P. L. 9, 656. indeed hath G. then said that
P. L. 9, 662. G. hath said ye shall not eat
P. L. 9, 692. or will G. incense his ire for such
P. L. 9, 700. G. therefore cannot hurt ye and be
P. L. 9, 701. not just, not G., not feared then
P. L. 9, 775. of G. or death of law or penalty
P. L. 9, 826. but what if G. have seen
P. L. 9, 897. creation last and best of all G.'s
P. L. 9, 911. should G. create another Eve
P. L. 9, 927. not G. omnipotent nor fate
P. L. 9, 938. I think that G. creator wise
P. L. 9, 943. so G. shall uncreate, be frustrate
P. L. 9, 945. not well conceived of G.
P. L. 9, 948. their state whom G. most favours
P. L. 9, 1081. of G. or angel erst with joy
P. L. 10, 6. for what can scape the eye of G.
P. L. 10, 97. the voice of G. they heard now
P. L. 10, 101. till G. approaching thus to Adam
P. L. 10, 111. not in their looks either to G.
P. L. 10, 145. was she thy G. that her thou
P. L. 10, 149. wherein G. set thee above her
P. L. 10, 163. which when the Lord G. heard
P. L. 10, 171. yet G. at last to Satan first in sin
P. L. 10, 338. descend the Son of G. to judge
P. L. 10, 724. hide me from the face of G.
P. L. 10, 759. though G. made thee without
P. L. 10, 766. G. made thee of choice his own
P. L. 10, 785. spirit of man which G. inspired
P. L. 10, 799. which to G. himself impossible
P. L. 10, 828. acquitted stand in sight of G.
P. L. 10, 888. O why did G. creator wise
P. L. 10, 931. thou against G. only, I against G.
P. L. 10, 1022. doubt not but G. hath wiselier
P. L. 40, 1045. reluctance against G. and his
P. L. 11, 75. when G. descended
P. L. 11, 104. and from the paradise of G.
P. L. 11, 145. as to concern the mind of G.
P. L. 11, 148. upborne even to the seat of G.
P. L. 11, 350. in valley and in plain G. is as here
P. L. 11, 377. so both ascend in the visions of G.
P. L. 11, 508. can thus the image of G. in man
P. L. 11, 521. disfiguring not G.'s likeness
P. L. 11, 525. G.'s image did not reverence
P. L. 11, 578. to worship G. aright and know
P. L. 11, 622. titled them the sons of G.
P. L. 11, 704. G. would come to judge them
P. L. 11, 707. to walk with G. high in salvation
P. L. 11, 737. and G. made fast the door
P. L. 11, 799. all virtue lose and fear of G.
P. L. 11, 817. of G. observed the one just man
P. L. 11, 836. to teach thee that G. attributes
P. L. 11, 867. peace from G. and covenant new
P. L. 11, 877. that G. vouchsafes to raise
P. L. 11, 880. as the brow of G. appeased
P. L. 11, 885. so willingly doth G. remit his ire
P. L. 12, 48. G. who oft descends to visit men
P. L. 12, 66. authority usurped from G.
P. L. 12, 73. to G. his tower intends siege
P. L. 12, 92. G. in judgment just subjects him
P. L. 12, 106. till G. at last wearied with their
P. L. 12, 118. to forsake the living G.
P. L. 12, 120. yet him G. the most High
P. L. 12, 134. trusting all his wealth with G.
P. L. 12, 170. sent from G. to claim his people
P. L. 12, 174. who denies to know their G.
P. L. 12, 200. wondrous power G. to his saint
P. L. 12, 209. G. looking forth will trouble
P. L. 12, 227. from the mount Sinai
P. L. 12, 235. but the voice of G. to mortal ear
P. L. 12, 239. instructed that to G. is no access
P. L. 12, 245. such delight hath G. in men
P. L. 12, 281. among whom G. will deign

P. L. 12, 284. how can *G.* with such reside
P. L. 12, 296. may find justification towards *G.*
P. L. 12, 307. though of *G.* highly beloved
P. L. 12, 318. provoking *G.* to raise them
P. L. 12, 333. the clouded ark of *G.* till then
P. L. 12, 339. so incense *G.* as to leave them
P. L. 12, 349. *G.* disposed, the house of *G.*
P. L. 12, 382. from thy womb the Son of *G.*
P. L. 12, 397. obedience to the law of *G.*
P. L. 12, 402. the law of *G.* exact he shall fulfil
P. L. 12, 457. resume his seat at *G.'s* right hand
P. L. 12, 477. to *G.* more glory
P. L. 12, 478. more good-will to men from *G.*
P. L. 12, 519. appropriating the Spirit of *G.*
P. R. 12, 562. and love with fear the only *G.*
P. L. 12, 579. all nature's works or works of *G.*
P. L. 12, 611. for *G.* is also in sleep
P. L. 12, 633. the brandished sword of *G.*
P. R. 1, 11. by proof the undoubted Son of *G.*
P. R. 1, 122. man of men attested Son of *G.*
P. R. 1, 136. called the Son of *G.*
P. R. 1, 173. and triumph to the Son of *G.*
P. R. 1, 183. meanwhile the Son of *G.* who yet
P. R. 1, 207. the law of *G.* I read
P. R. 1, 238. a messenger from *G.* foretold
P. R. 1, 293. concerns my knowledge *G.* reveals
P. R. 1, 330. and called thee Son of *G.*
P. R. 1, 335. to whom the Son of *G.*
P. R. 1, 342. but if thou be the Son of *G.*
P. R. 1, 346. he ended and the Son of *G.* replied
P. R. 1, 350. proceeding from the mouth of *G.*
P. R. 1, 368. I came among the Sons of *G.*
P. R. 1, 379. lost to be beloved of *G.*
P. R. 1, 385. I know declared the Son of *G.*
P. R. 1, 442. *G.* hath justly given the nations
P. R. 1, 460. *G.* hath now sent his living oracle
P. R. 2, 4. Jesus Messiah Son of *G.* declared
P. R. 2, 14. and for a time caught up to *G.*
P. R. 2, 42. of Israel send thy Messiah forth
P. R. 2, 67. to have conceived of *G.*
P. R. 2, 179. false titled Sons of *G.*
P. R. 2, 242. from shade to shade the Son of *G.*
P. R. 2, 250. or *G.* support nature
P. R. 2, 253. yet *G.* can satisfy that need
P. R. 2, 303. more wonder that the Son of *G.*
P. R. 2, 311. had not *G.* rained from heaven
P. R. 2, 368. what doubts the Son of *G.* to sit
P. R. 2, 377. what doubt'st thou Son of *G.*
P. R. 2, 475. to know and knowing worship *G.*
P. R. 3, 1. so spake the Son of *G.* and Satan
P. R. 3, 60. true glory and renown when *G.*
P. R. 3, 138. turned recreant to *G.*, ingrate
P. R. 3, 141. that which to *G.* alone of right
P. R. 3, 142. yet so much bounty is in *G.*
P. R. 3, 145. so spake the Son of *G.* and here
P. R. 3, 252. he took the Son of *G.* up to a
P. R. 3, 416. fell off from *G.* to worship calves
P. R. 3, 422. the *G.* of their fore-fathers
P. R. 3, 426. and *G.* with idols in their worship
P. R. 3, 432. who serve idols with *G.*
P. R. 4, 109. to whom the Son of *G.* unmoved
P. R. 4, 177. thou shalt worship the Lord thy *G.*
P. R. 4, 178. and darest thou to the Son of *G.*
P. R. 4, 186. king of kings *G.* over all supreme
P. R. 4, 192. I fall down and worship thee as *G.*
P. R. 4, 196. be not so sore offended, Son of God
P. R. 4, 197. though sons of *G.* both angels are
P. R. 4, 203. *G.* of this world invoked
P. R. 4, 303. and all possessing equal to *G.*
P. R. 4, 304. shames not to prefer as fearing *G.*
P. R. 4, 310. ignorant of themselves of *G.* much
P. R. 4, 315. all glory arrogate to *G.* give none
P. R. 4, 348. where *G.* is praised aright
P. R. 4, 350. such are from *G.* inspired
P. R. 4, 491. portents not sent from *G.*
P. R. 4, 495. and wouldst be thought my *G.*
P. R. 4, 520. all men are sons of *G.*
P. R. 4, 561. tempt not the Lord thy *G.* he said
S. A. 31. as of a person separate to *G.*
S. A. 58. *G.* when he gave me strength to show
S. A. 70. the prime work of *G.* to me is extinct

S. A. 201. have divulged the secret gift of *G.*
S. A. 222. that what I motioned was of *G.*
S. A. 243. those great acts which *G.* had done
S. A. 273. *G.* hath of his special favour raised
S. A. 292. *G.'s* proposed deliverance
S. A. 293. just are the ways of *G.*
S. A. 295. unless there be who think not *G.*
S. A. 356. wherefore did *G.* grant me my
S. A. 368. alas methinks whom *G.* hath chosen
S. A. 378. the mystery of *G.* given me under
S. A. 440. Dagon shall be magnified and *G.*
S. A. 441. besides whom is no *g.*
S. A. 451. to *G.* have brought dishonour
S. A. 454. scandal to Israel diffidence of *G.*
S. A. 462. contest is now 'twixt *G.* and Dagon
S. A. 463. overthrown to enter lists with *G.*
S. A. 465. preferring before the *G.* of Abraham
S. A. 473. for *G.* ....will not long defer
S. A. 477. whether *G.* be Lord or Dagon
S. A. 497. but I *G.'s* counsel have not kept
S. A. 509. *G.* will relent and quit thee all
S. A. 515. for self-offence more than for *G.*
S. A. 517. who knows but *G.* hath set before us
S. A. 529. like a petty *g.* I walked about
S. A. 555. when *G.* with these forbidden made
S. A. 581. *G.* who caused a fountain at thy
S. A. 667. *G.* of our fathers what is man
S. A. 835. *G.* or man will gain thee no
S. A. 999. let her go, *G.* sent her to debase
S. A. 1053. therefore *G.'s* universal law
S. A. 1140. my trust in the living *G.* who gave
S. A. 1145. for proof hereof if Dagon be thy *g.*
S. A. 1150. to be the power of Israel's *G.* avow
S. A. 1155. feel whose *G.* is strongest thine or
S. A. 1156. presume not on thy *G.* whate'er he
S. A. 1170. acknowledge them from *G.* inflicted
S. A. 1176. by combat to decide whose *g.* is *G.*
S. A. 1178. fair honour that thou dost thy *G.*
S. A. 1270. *G.* into the hands of their deliverer
S. A. 1340. play before their *g.*
S. A. 1374. to displease *G.* for the fear of man
S. A. 1375. and man prefer set *G.* behind
S. A. 1425. unworthy our *G.*, our law
S. A. 1465. both *G.* and state they easily would
S. A. 1495. I persuade me *G.* had not permitted
S. A. 1508. *G.* will restore him eye-sight
S. A. 1527. for to Israel's *G.* nothing is hard
S. A. 1582. *G.* hath wrought things as incredible
S. A. 1621. clamouring their *G.* with praise
S. A. 1719. with *G.* not parted from him
S. 14, 2. ripened thy just soul to dwell with *G.*
S. 16, 6. hast reared *G.'s* trophies and his work
S. 19, 7. doth *G.* exact day-labour light denied
S. 19, 9. *G.* doth not need either man's work
S. 21, 14. and when *G.* sends a cheerful hour
H. 16. afford a present to the infant *G.*
H. 199. with that twice-battered *g.* of Palestine
M. W. 18. the *g.* that sits at marriage feast
S. M. 26. in tune with heaven till *G.* ere long
D. F. I. 74. what a present thou to *G.* hast sent
Hor. 16. the stern *g.* of sea.

**Goddess.**—P. L. 2, 757. heavenly fair a *g.* armed
P. L. 5, 78. among the gods thyself a *g.*
P. L. 5, 381. or the fairest *g.* feigned of three
P. L. 7, 40. say *g.* what ensued when Raphael
P. L. 9, 547. who shouldst be seen a *g.* among
P. L. 9, 732. *g.* humane reach then and freely
C. 128. hail *g.* of nocturnal sport
C. 267. unless the *g.* that in rural shine
C. 842. made *g.* of the river still she retains
C. 865. *g.* of the silver lake listen and save
C. 902. *g.* dear we implore thy powerful hand
A. 18. sitting like a *g.* bright
L'A. 11. but come thou *g.* fair and free
Il P. 11. but hail thou *g.* sage and holy
Il P. 132. me *g.* bring to arched walks of
D. F. I. 48. and thou some *g.* fled

**Goddesses.**—P. L. 11, 615. that seemed of *g.*
P. R. 2, 156. more like to *g.*
Brut. 1. *G.* of shades and Huntress

**Goddess-like.**—P. L. 8, 59. with *g.-l.* demeanour

P. L. 9, 389. surpassed and *g.-l.* deport
**Godhead.**—P. L. 2, 242. and to his *G.* sing
P. L. 3, 206. affecting *G.* and so losing all
P. L. 6, 722. and thus the filial *G.* answering
P. L. 7, 175. his word the filial *G.* gave effect
P. L. 7, 586. the imperial throne of *G.*
P. L. 9, 790. nor was *G.* from her thought
P. L. 9, 877. ampler heart and growing up to *G.*
P. L. 12, 389. joins the Son manhood to *G.*
S. A. 1153. with the utmost of his *g.* seconded
H. 227. our Babe to show his *G.* true
**Godless.**—P. L. 6, 49. to that *g.* crew
P. L. 6, 811. God's indignation on these *g.*
**Godlike.**—P. L. 1, 358. *g.* shapes and forms
P. L. 2, 511. *g.* imitated state
P. L. 3, 307. and equally enjoying *g.* fruition
P. L. 4, 289. *g.* erect with native honour clad
P. L. 5, 351. to meet his *g.* guest walks forth
P. L. 6, 67. under their *g.* leaders in the cause
P. L. 6, 301. to such height of *g.* power
P. L. 7, 110. thus the *g.* angel answered mild
P. L. 8, 249. so spake the *g.* Power and thus
P. L. 9, 717. participating *g.* food
P. L. 12, 427. this *g.* act annuls thy doom
P. R. 1, 188. first publish his *g.* office
P. R. 1, 386. and behold thy *g.* deeds
P. R. 3, 21. these *g.* virtues wherefore dost
P. R. 4, 348. God is praised aright and *g.* men
P. R. 4, 602. with *g.* force endued
S. A. 28. charioting his *g.* presence
P. 24. his *g.* acts and his temptations fierce
**Gods.**—P. L. 1, 116. by fate the strength of *g.*
P. L. 1, 138. as far as *g.* and heavenly essences
P. L. 1, 240. as *g.* and by their own recovered
P. L. 1, 384. *g.* adored among the nations round
P. L. 1, 435. bowing lowly down to bestial *g.*
P. L. 1, 475. the *g.* whom he had vanquished
P. L. 1, 481. their wandering *g.* disguised
P. L. 1, 489. her first born and all her bleating *g.*
P. L. 1, 508. though far renowned the Ionian *g.*
P. L. 1, 509. of Javan's issue held *g.*
P. L. 1, 570. their visages and stature as of *g.*
P. L. 1, 579. mixed with auxiliar *g.*
P. L. 1, 629. how such united force of *g.*
P. L. 1, 720. Belus or Serapis their *g.*
P. L. 2, 108. battle dangerous to less than *g.*
P. L. 2, 352. his will pronounced among the *g.*
P. L. 2, 391. synod of *g.* and like to what ye are
P. L. 2, 868. of light and bliss among the *g.*
P. L. 3, 341. ye *g.* adore him who to compass
P. L. 4, 526. might exalt equal with *g.*
P. L. 4, 714. whom the *g.* endowed with all
P. L. 5, 70. only fit for *g.* yet able to make *g.*
P. L. 5, 71. and why not *g.* of men since good
P. L. 5, 77. and be henceforth among the *g.*
P. L. 5, 81. and see what life the *g.* live there
P. L. 6, 156. durst oppose a third part of the *g.*
P. L. 6, 301. for likest *g.* they seemed
P. L. 6, 366. that to be less than *g.* disdained
P. L. 6, 452. to free enjoyment of our right as *g.*
P. L. 6, 453. hard for *g.* and to unequal work
P. L. 7, 329. a seat where *g.* might dwell
P. L. 9, 100. seat worthier to of *g.* as built with
P. L. 9, 164. with *g.* to sit the highest
P. L. 9, 489. she fair divinely fair fit love for *g.*
P. L. 9, 547. should be seen a goddess among *g.*
P. L. 9, 708. ye shall be as *g.* knowing both
P. L. 9, 710. ye shall be as *g.* since I as man
P. L. 9, 712. I of brute, human; ye of human *g.*
P. L. 9, 714. by putting off human, to put on *g.*
P. L. 9, 716. and what are *g.* that man may
P. L. 9, 718. *g.* are first and that advantage use
P. L. 9, 804. mature in knowledge, as the *g.*
P. L. 9, 838. sap derived from nectar drink of *g.*
P. L. 9, 866. to open eyes and make them *g.*
P. L. 9, 937. which cannot be but to be *g.*
P. L. 10, 90. the speed of *g.* time counts not
P. L. 10, 502. what remains ye *g.*, but up
P. L. 11, 271. walks and shades, fit haunt of *g.*
P. L. 11, 696. of mankind *g.* and sons of *g.*
P. L. 12, 120. work in wood and stone for *g.*

P. L. 12, 122. his kindred and false *g.*
P. L. 12, 129. he leaves his *g.*, his friends
P. R. 1, 117. potentates and kings, yea *g.*
P. R. 2, 171. made him bow to the *g.* of his
P. R. 3, 81. with pride and must be titled *g.*
P. R. 3, 430. and to their *g.* perhaps of Bethel
P. R. 4, 56. more like houses of *g.*
P. R. 4, 342. personating their *g.* ridiculous
S. A. 545. that cheers the heart of *g.* and men
S. A. 859. how meritorious with the *g.*
S. A. 896. to please thy *g.* thou didst it, *g.*
S. A. 899. *g.* cannot be
C. 11. amongst the enthroned *g.* on sainted seats
C. 24. which he to grace his tributary *g.*
C. 69. resemblance of the *g.* is changed
C. 177. praise the ... Pan and thank the *g.*
C. 445. *g.* and men feared her stern frown
C. 1007. till free consent the *g.* among
A. 22. mother of a hundred *g.*
A. 67. the fate of *g.* and men is wound
A. 79. whate'er the skill of lesser *g.* can show
Il P. 46. spare fast that oft with *g.* doth diet
H. 211. the brutish *g.* of Nile as fast
H. 224. nor all the *g.* beside
D. F. I. 14. which 'mongst the wanton *g.*
Hor. 5. on faith and changed *g.* complain
**Goes.**—P. L. 4, 469. with thee it came and *g.*
P. L. 11, 290. with thee *g.* thy husband
S. A. 904. a woman ever *g.* by the worse
M. W. 25. and now with second hope she *g.*
**Going.**—P. L. 9, 1157. *g.* into such danger
P. L. 11, 290. thy *g.* is not lonely
**Gold.**—P. L. 1, 372. religions full of pomp and *g.*
P. L. 1, 483. borrowed *g.* composed the calf
P. L. 1, 682. of heaven's pavement trodden *g.*
P. L. 1, 690. and digged out ribs of *g.*
P. L. 1. 717. the roof was fretted *g.*
P. L. 2, 4. on her kings barbaric pearl and *g.*
P. L. 2, 271. her hidden lustre gems and *g.*
P. L. 2. 947. purloined the guarded *g.*
P. L. 3, 352. inwove with amarant and *g.*
P. L. 3, 506. frontispiece of diamond and *g.*
P. L. 3, 541. that scaled by steps of *g.*
P. L. 3, 595. metal, part seemed *g.*, part silver
P. L. 3, 608. and rivers run potable *g.*
P. L. 3, 642. coloured plume sprinkled with *g.*
P. L. 4, 220. ambrosial fruit of vegetable *g.*
P. L. 4, 238. on orient pearl and sands of *g.*
P. L. 4, 496. under the flowing *g.* of her loose
P. L. 4, 554. with diamond flaming and with *g.*
P. L. 4, 596. with reflected purple and *g.*
P. L. 5, 187. paint your fleecy skirts with *g.*
P. L. 5, 282. loins and thighs with downy *g.*
P. L. 5, 356. and grooms besmeared with *g.*
P. L. 5, 442. metals of drossiest ore to perfect *g.*
P. L. 5, 634. in pearl, in diamond and massy *g.*
P. L. 5, 759. quarries hewn and rocks of *g.*
P. L. 6, 13. highest heaven arrayed in *g.*
P. L. 6, 110. armed in adamant and *g.*
P. L. 6, 475. flower ambrosial gems and *g.*
P. L. 7, 406. their waved coats dropt with *g.*
P. L. 7, 479. with spots of *g.* and purple azure
P. L. 7, 577. and ample road whose dust is *g.*
P. L. 9, 429. or specked with *g.* hung drooping
P. L. 9, 501. with burnished neck of verdant *g.*
P. L. 9, 578. fairest colours mixed ruddy and *g.*
P. L. 12, 250. of cedar overlaid with *g.* therein
P. L. 12, 253. over these a mercy-seat of *g.*
P. L. 12, 363. to offer incense myrrh and *g.*
P. R. 1, 251. thee with incense myrrh and *g.*
P. R. 2, 425. *g.* that got him puissant friends
P. R. 4, 60. in cedar, marble, ivory, or *g.*
P. R. 4, 118. in *g.* crystal and myrrhine cups
S. A. 389. spousal embraces vitiated with *g.*
S. A. 831. weakness to resist Philistian *g.*
S. A. 849. it was not *g.* as to my charge thou
S. A. 958. with the *g.* of matrimonial treason
S. A. 1114. they had hired a woman with their *g.*
C. 394. Hesperian tree laden with blooming *g.*
S. 10, 3. who lived in both unstained with *g.*
S. 17, 8. her two main nerves iron and *g.*

H. 135. time will ... fetch the age of *g*.
Hor. 9. enjoys thee credulous, all *g*.
**Golden.**—P. L. 1, 538. gems and *g*. lustre rich
P. L. 1, 715. overlaid with *g*. architrave
P. L. 1, 796. a thousand demi-gods on *g*.seats
P. L. 2, 328. with his *g*. those in Heaven
P. L. 2, 1005. my realm linked in a *g*.chain
P. L. 2, 1051. and fast by hanging in a *g*. chain
P. L. 3, 337. see *g*. days fruitful of *g*. deeds
P. L. 3, 365. crowned again their *g* harps
P. L. 3, 572. above them all, the *g*. sun
P. L. 3, 625. of beaming sunny rays a *g*. tiar
P. L. 4, 148.blossoms and fruits at once of *g*.hue
P. L. 4, 249. fruit burnished with *g*.rind hung
P. L. 4, 305. her unadorned *g*. tresses
P. L. 4, 763. here love his *g*. shafts employs
P. L. 4, 997. hung forth in heaven his *g*. scales
P. L. 5, 255. wide on *g*. hinges turning
P. L. 5, 713. and from within the *g*. lamps
P. L. 5, 886. that *g*. sceptre which thou didst
P. L. 6, 28. from midst a *g*. cloud thus mild
P. L. 6, 102. flaming cherubim and *g*. shields
P. L. 6, 527. in arms they stood of *g*. panoply
P. L. 7, 207. on *g*. hinges moving
P. L. 7, 225. he took the *g*.compasses prepared
P. L. 7, 258. and touched their *g*. harps
P. L. 7, 365. in their *g*. urns draw light
P. L. 7, 597. on fret by string or *g*. wire
P. L. 7, 600. clouds fuming from *g*. censers
P. L. 11, 18. where the *g*. altar fumed
P. L. 11, 24. which in this *g*. censer mixed
P. L. 11, 392. down to the *g*. Chersonese
P. R. 2, 459. crown *g*. in show is but a wreath
P. R. 3, 277. of that first *g*. monarchy the seat
P. R. 4, 74. from India and the *g*.Chersonese
P. R. 4, 548. of alabaster topt with *g*. spires
C. 13. lay their just hands on that *g*.key
C. 214. hovering angel girt with *g*. wings
C. 633. bore a bright *g*. flower
C. 880. and fair Ligea's *g*. comb
C. 933. the beryl and the *g*. ore
C. 983. that sing about the *g*. tree
L. 111. the *g*. opes, the iron shuts amain
L'A. 146. from *g*. slumber on a bed
Il P. 52. him that yon soars on *g*. wing
S. 14. 7. as faith pointed with her *g*. rod
S. M. 13. their immortal harps of *g*. wires
Hor. 4. in wreaths thy *g*. hair
V. Ex. 38. to the touch of *g*. wires
**Golden-winged.**—D. F. I.57. of the *g.-w.* host
**Golgotha.**—P. L. 3, 477. to seek in *G*. him dead
**Goliath.**—S. A. 1249. gigantic size *G*. chief
**Gone.**—P. L. 3, 544. desert ways with peril *g*.
P. L. 5, 91. suddenly my guide was *g*.
P. L. 5, 885. decrees against thee are *g*. forth
P. L. 6, 670. now all heaven had *g*. to wrack
P. L. 1, 1055. innocence,... was *g*.
P. L. 11, 781. all would have then *g*. well
P. R. 2, 10. so lately found and so abruptly *g*.
P. R. 2, 39. for whither is he *g*.
P. R. 2, 116. and with speed was *g*.
P. R. 4, 459. and soon are *g*.
P. L. 4, 994. elements at least had *g*. to wrack
S. A. 997. she's *g*., a manifest serpent
S. A. 1244. his giantship is *g*. somewhat
S. A. 1350. he's *g*. and who knows how he
C. 107. rigour now is *g*. to bed
L. 37. but O the heavy change now thou art *g*
U. C. I, 18. has supped and's newly *g*. to bed
U. C. II, 33. his letters are delivered all and *g*.
**Gonfalons.**—P. L. 5, 589. standards and *g*.
**Good.**—P. L. 1, 159. to do aught *g*. never will
P. L. 1, 163. of our evil seek to bring forth *g*.
P. L. 1, 165. and out of *g*. still to find means
P. L. 1, 418. till *g*. Josiah drove them thence
P. L. 2, 30. where there is then no *g*. for which
P. L. 2, 152. and who knows, let this be *g*.
P. L. 2, 253. but rather seek our own *g*.
P. L. 2, 562. of *g*. and evil much they argued
P. L. 2, 623. created evil for evil only *g*.
P. L. 2, 848. destined to that *g*. hour

P. L. 2, 940. neither sea nor *g*. dry land
P. L. 2, 1083. except whom God and *g*. angels
P. L. 3, 310. worthiest to be so by being *g*.
P. L. 4, 44. and with his *g*. upbraided none
P. L. 4, 48. yet all his *g*. proved ill in me
P. L. 4, 109. *g*. to me is lost, evil be thou my *g*.
P. L. 4, 203. to value right the *g*. before him.
P. L. 4, 222. knowledge of *g*. bought dear
P. L. 4, 414. be infinitely *q*. and of his *g*.
P. L. 4, 838. when thou no more wast *g*.
P. L. 4, 895. knowest only *g*. but evil hast
P. L. 5, 63. withhold longer thy offered *g*.
P. L. 5, 71. since *g*. the more communicated
P. L. 5, 153. thy glorious works Parent of *g*.
P. L. 5, 206. bounteous still to give us only *g*.
P. L. 5, 399. from whom all perfect *g*.
P. L. 5, 471. if not depraved from *g*.
P. L. 5, 491. what God for you saw *g*.
P. L. 5, 525. and *g*. he made thee
P. L. 5, 570. yet for thy *g*. this is dispensed
P. L. 5, 826. by experience taught we know *g*.
P. L. 5, 827. and of our *g*. and of our dignity
P. L. 5, 878. forsaken of all *g*. I see thy fall
P. L. 7, 76. which to the infinitely *G*. we owe
P. L. 7, 182. *g*. will to future men
P. L. 7, 188. whose wisdom had ordained *g*.
P. L. 7, 191. and thence diffuse his *g*. to worlds
P. L. 7, 249. God saw the light was *g*.
P. L. 7, 309. and saw that it was *g*. and said
P. L. 7, 337. God saw that it was *g*.
P. L. 7, 353. his great work that it was *g*.
P. L. 7, 395. and saw that it was *g*. and blessed
P. L. 7, 512. to acknowledge whence his *g*.
P. L. 7, 543. tasted, works knowledge of *g*.
P. L. 7, 549. and behold all was entirely *g*.
P. L. 7, 556. how *g*. how fair
P. L. 7, 616. and from thence createst more *g*.
P. L. 8, 93. may of solid *g*. contain more plenty
P. L. 8, 324. brings knowledge of *g*. and ill
P. L. 8, 361. and all this *g*. to man
P. L. 8, 443. *g*. reason was thou freely
P. L. 8, 445. knew it not *g*. for man to be alone
P. L. 8, 651. be *g*. and friendly still and oft
P. L. 9, 122. all *g*. to me becomes bane
P. L. 9, 233. to study household *g*. and *g*. works
P. L. 9, 354. lest by some fair-appearing *g*.
P. L. 9, 465. for the time remained stupidly *g*.
P. L. 9, 605. all things fair and *g*.
P. L. 9, 606. but all that fair and *g*. in thy
P. L. 9, 697. of *G*. and Evil of *g*. how just
P. L. 9, 709. as gods knowing both *g* and evil
P. L. 9, 723. knowledge of *g*. and evil
P. L. 9, 752. knowledge both of *g*. and evil
P. L. 9, 754.infers the *g*.by thee communicated
P. L. 9, 756. for *g*. unknown sure is not had
P. L. 9, 759. forbids us *g*. forbids us to be wise
P. L. 9, 771. brings with joy the *g*. befallen
P. L. 9, 774. under this ignorance of *g*. or evil
P. L. 9, 899. holy, divine, *g*., amiable, or sweet
P. L. 9, 967. whereof *g*. proof this day affords
P. L. 9, 973. for of *g*. still *g*. proceeds direct
P. L. 9, 1072. both *g*.and evil *g*.lost and evil got
P. L. 9, 1139. despoiled of all our *g*.
P. L. 9, 1154. as *g*. have grown there still
P. L. 10, 138. as thy perfect gift so *g*. so fit
P. L. 10, 618. which I so fair and *g*. created
P. L. 10, 752. by which I was to hold the *g*.
P. L. 10, 758. wilt thou enjoy the *g*. then cavil
P. L. 11, 35. works on me, *g*. or not *g*., ingraft
P. L. 11, 85. to know both *g*. and evil
P. L. 11, 87. knowledge of *g*.lost and evil got
P. L. 11, 89. to have known *g*. by itself
P. L. 11, 142. may faith admit that all the *g*.
P. L. 11, 358. *g*. with bad expect to hear
P. L. 11, 493. as their chief *g*. and final hope
P. L. 11, 616. empty of all *g*. wherein consists
P. L. 11, 685. where *g*. with bad were matched
P. L. 11, 710. what reward awaits the *g*.
P. L. 11, 809. example *g*. against allurement
P. L. 12, 47. regardless whether *g*. or evil
P. L. 12, 336. part *g*. part bad

L

P. L. 12, 470. all this *g.* of evil shall produce
P. L. 12, 471. evil turn to *g.* more wonderful
P. L. 12, 476. much more *g.* thereof shall spring
P. L. 12, 538. to *g.* malignant
P. L. 12, 565. with *g.* still overcoming evil
P. L. 12, 596. have calmed, portending *g.*
P. L. 12, 612. some great *g.* presaging
P. R. 1, 204. to do what might be public *g.*
P. R. 1, 381. what I see excellent in *g.* or fair
P. R. 1, 437. and not well understood as *g.*
P. R. 3, 11. thy heart contains of *g.* wise just
P. R. 3, 57. his lot who dares be singularly *g.*
P. R. 3, 88. but if there be in glory aught of *g.*
P. R. 3, 114. from all men *g.* or bad
P. R. 3, 125. his *g.* communicable to every soul
P. R. 3, 133. so much *g.* so much beneficence
P. R. 3, 139. of all true *g.* himself despoiled
P. R. 3, 211. I would attain my final *g.*
P. R. 4, 526. *g.* reason then if I beforehand
P. R. 4, 535. of mere man both wise and *g.*
S. A. 350. what thing *g.* prayed for
S. A. 811. reasons .... have passed for *g.*
S. A. 867. public *g.* private respects must
S. A. 1048. that in domestic *g.* combines
S. A. 1163. as *g.* for nothing else
S. A. 1230. take *g.* heed my hand survey
S. A. 1381. be of *g.* courage I begin to feel
S. A. 1454. with *g.* success to work his
S. A. 1537. of *g.* or bad so great
S. A. 1538. evil news rides post while *g.*news
C. 217. supreme *g.* to whom all things ill
C. 277. what chance *g.* lady hath bereft you
C. 307. to find out that *g.* shepherd
C. 489. defence is a *g.* cause and heaven be
C. 397. how camest thou here *g.* swain?
C. 512. what fears *g.* Thyrsis?
C. 609. alas *g.* venturous youth I love
C. 658. and some *g.* angel bear a shield
C. 665. while heaven sees *g.*
C. 703. such as are *g.* men can give *g.*
C. 704. which is not *g.* is not delicious
C. 740. the *g.* thereof consists in mutual
C. 764. she, *g.* cateress
C. 765. means her provision only to the *g.*
A. 33. nymphs as great and *g.*
L. 184. shalt be *g.* to all that wander
L'A. 46. at my window bid *g.* morrow
Il P. 153. sent by some spirit to mortals *g.*
S. 10, 1. to that *g.* Earl once President
S. 11, 4. numbering *g.* intellects now seldom
S. 12, 12. that must first be wise and *g.*
S. 14, 5. alms and all thy *g.* endeavour
S. 21, 10. toward solid *g.* what leads the
T. 14. every thing that is sincerely *g.*
S. M. 24. their state of *g.*
D. F. I. 56. to do the world some *g.*
V. Ex. 59. *g.* luck befriend thee Son
**Goodliest.**—P. L. 4, 147. of *g.* trees loaden
P. L. 4, 323. Adam the *g.* man of men since
P. L. 8, 304. enclosed with *g.* trees
P. L. 11, 189. *g.* of all the forest
**Goodly.**—P. L. 3, 548. the *g.* prospect of some
P. L. 8, 15. I behold this *g.* frame
P. L. 9, 576. a *g.* tree far distant to behold
P. L. 11, 509. created once so *g.* and erect
C. 968. here behold so *g.* grown
**Goodness**—P. L. 1, 218. bring forth infinite *g.*
P. L. 3, 158. his malice and thy *g.* bring
P. L. 3, 165. thy *g.* and thy greatness both
P. L. 3, 688. while *g.* thinks no ill where
P. L. 4, 734. who shall with us extol thy *g.*
P. L. 4, 847. and felt how awful *g.* is
P. L. 5, 159. declare thy *g.* beyond thought
P. L. 7, 171. and put not forth my *g.*
P. L. 8, 279. in *g.* and in power pre-eminent
P. L. 8, 647. sent from whose sovran *g.* I adore
P. L. 11, 353. compassing thee round with *g.*
P. L. 12, 469. O, *g.* infinite, *g.* immense
P. R. 3, 124. but to show forth his *g.*
S. A. 760. with *g.* principled not to reject
C. 368. sweet peace that *g.* bosoms ever

C. 594. and mix no more with *g.*
C. 849. carol her *g.* loud in rustic lays
S. 23, 11. sweetness *g.* in her person shined
**Good-will.**—P. L. 12, 477. more *g.-w.* to men
**Gordian.**—P. L. 4, 348. wove with *G.* twine
V. Ex. 90. can loose this *G.* knot
**Gordon.**—S. 11, 8. is it harder sirs than *G.*
**Gore.**—P. L. 11, 460. rolling in dust and *g.*
S. A. 1728. wash off the clotted *g.*
**Gored.**—P. L. 6, 387. with many an inroad *g.*
**Gorge.**—P. L. 3, 434. to *g.* the flesh of lambs
**Gorged.**—P. L. 10, 632. crammed and *g.*
**Gorgeous.**—P. L. 2, 3. or where the *g.* east
P. L. 5, 250. veiled with his *g.* wings
P. L. 6, 103. then lighted from his *g.* throne
P. L. 9, *g.* knights at joust and tournament
P. R. 4, 114. sumptuous gluttonies and *g.* feasts
S. A. 1119. then put on all thy *g.* arms
C. 777. ne'er looks to heaven amidst his *g.*
Il P. 97. sometime let *g.* Tragedy
**Gorgon.**—P. L. 10, 527. bedropt with blood of *G.*
C. 447. what was that snaky-headed *G.* shield
**Gorgonian.**—P. L. 2, 611. Medusa with *G.* terror
P. L. 10, 297. bound with *G.* rigour not to move
**Gorgons.**—P. L. 2, 628. *G.* and hydras
**Gory.**—L. 62. his *g.* visage down the stream was
**Goshen.**—P. L. 1, 309. the sojourners of *G.*
**Gospel.**—S. 16, 14. of hireling wolves whose *g.* is
**Got.**—P. L. 1, 365. *g.* them new names
P. L. 9, 594. amid the tree now *g.* where plenty
P. L. 9, 1072. good and evil, good lost and evil *g.*
P. L. 10, 579. the heathen of their purchase *g.*
P. L. 11, 87. knowledge of good lost and evil *g.*
P. R. 2, 28. close in a cottage low together *g.*
P. R. 2, 64. motherly cares and fears *g.* head
P. R. 2, 425. that *g.* him puissant friends
S. 12, 8. but this is *g.* by casting pearl to hogs
P. 56. had *g.* a race of mourners
D. F. I. 9. the Athenian damsel *g.*
V. Ex. 6. half glad when he had *g.* him
**Govern.**—P. L. 5, 802. our being ordained to *g.*
P. L. 7, 30. still *g.* thou my song Urania
P. L. 7, 510. with front serene *g.* the rest
P. L. 7, 546. beware and *g.* well thy appetite
P. R. 4, 135. but *g.* ill the nations under yoke
**Governed**—P. L. 6, 706. commotion *g.* thus
**Government.**—P. L. 10, 154. *g.* well seemed
P. L. 12, 88. and upstart passions catch the *g.*
P. L. 12, 225. there they shall found their *g.*
P. R. 4, 358. the solid rules of civil *g.*
C. 25. by course commits to several *g.*
**Governors.**—S. A. 242. Israel's *g.* and heads
**Governs.**—P. L. 2, 910. arbiter chance *g.* all
P. L. 6, 178. and excels them whom he *g.*
P. R. 2, 477. *g.* the inner man the nobler part
P. R. 3, 112. all things orders and *g.*
**Gourd.**—P. L. 5, 327. each plant and juiciest *g.*
P. L. 7, 321. forth crept the swelling *g.*
**Gown.**—Il P. 169. the hairy *g.* and mossy cell
**Gowns.**—S. 17, 3. when *g.* not arms repelled
**Grace.**—P. L. 1, 111. to bow and sue for *g.*
P. L. 1, 218. *g.* and mercy shown on man by
P. L. 2, 238. he should relent and publish *g.*
P. L. 2, 499. though under hope of heavenly *g.*
P. L. 2, 1033. good angels guard by special *g.*
P. L. 3, 131. man therefore shall find *g.*
P. L. 3, 142. without measure *g.*
P. L. 3, 145. man should find *g.* for which both
P. L. 3, 174. not of will in him, but *g.* in me
P. L. 3, 183. some I have chosen of peculiar *g.*
P. L. 3, 187. while offered *g.* invites
P. L. 3, 198. long sufferance and my day of *g.*
P. L. 3, 227. man shall find *g.*; and shall *g.* not
P. L. 3, 302. when they may, accept not *g.*
P. L. 3, 401. Father of mercy and *g.*
P. L. 3, 639. and to every limb suitable *g.*
P. L. 4, 94. repent and could obtain by act of *g.*
P. L. 4, 298. softness she and sweet attractive *g.*
P. L. 4, 364. and such *g.* the hand that formed
P. L. 4, 490. how beauty is excelled by manly *g.*
P. L. 4, 845. added *g.* invincible

P. L. 6, 703. into thee such virtue and *g.*
P. L. 7, 573. on errands of supernal *g.*
P. L. 8, 43. *g.* that won who saw to wish
P. L. 8, 215. thy words with *g.* divine imbued
P. L. 8, 222. comeliness and *g.* attends thee
P. L. 8, 488. *g.* was in all her steps
P. L. 10, 767. thy reward was of his *g.*
P. L. 10, 1081. praying, and of *g.* beseeching
P. L. 10, 1096. but favour, *g.*, and mercy shone
P. L. 11, 3. prevenient *g.* descending had
P. L. 11, 23. sprung from thy implanted *g.*
P. L. 11, 255. days given thee of *g.*, wherein
P. L. 11, 359. supernal *g.* contending with
P. L. 11, 890. such *g.* shall one just man find
P. L. 12, 305. to free acceptance of large *g.*
P. L. 12, 478. and over wrath *g.* shall abound
P. L. 12, 525. but force the Spirit of *g.* itself
P. R. 1, 68. all virtue, *g.*, and wisdom to achieve
P. R. 2, 34. his words, his wisdom full of *g.*
P. R. 2, 176. their colour, and attractive *g.*
P. R. 3, 142. so much bounty is in God, such *g.*
P. R. 3, 205. hope is lost of my reception into *g.*
P. R. 4, 312. on *g.* depending
C. 24. to *g.* his tributary gods
C. 243. and give resounding *g.* to all Heaven's
C. 451. and noble *g.* that dashed brute violence
C. 938. lady while heaven lends us *g.*
A. 104. here ye shall have greater *g.*
L'A. 124. while both contend to win her *g.*
S. 2, 13. all is if I have *g.* to use it so
V. Ex. 10. my tongue but little *g.* can do thee
**Graced.**—P. L. 11, 168. am *g.* the source of life
**Graceful.**—P. L. 2, 109. Belial in act more *g.*
P. L. 8, 600. much delights me as those *g.* acts
P. L. 9, 459. her *g.* innocence, her every air
P. L. 11, 1066. the *g.* locks of these fair trees
P. R. 2, 157. *g.* and discreet expert in amorous
**Graces.**—P. L. 2, 762. and with attractive *g.*
P. L. 3, 674. on whom hath all these *g.* poured
P. L. 4, 267. knit with the *G.* and the Hours
P. L. 5, 15. shot forth peculiar *g.*
P. L. 8, 61. a pomp of winning *G.* waited still
P. R. 2, 138. perfections absolute, *g.* divine
S. A. 360. given with solemn hand as *g.*
S. A. 679. with gifts and *g.* eminently adorned
C. 986. the *G.* and the rosy-bosomed Hours
L'A. 15. with two sister *G.* more
M. W. 15. her high birth and her *g.* sweet
**Gracious.**—P. L. 3, 144. *g.* was that word
P. L. 5, 134. the *g.* signs of sweet remorse
P. L. 8, 337. and *g.* purpose thus renewed
P. L. 8, 436. this answer from the *g.* voice
P. L. 10, 118. to whom the *g.* judge without
P. L. 10, 1047. with what mild and *g.* temper
P. L. 12. 271. *g.* things thou hast revealed
S. A. 1173. *g.* to readmit the suppliant
**Gradual.**—P. L. 5, 483. by *g.* scale sublimed
P. L. 9, 112. of creatures animate with *g.* life
**Grain.**—P. L. 4, 817. the smutty *g.* with sudden
P. L. 5, 285. feathered mail, sky-tinctured *g.*
P. L. 5, 430. the ground covered with pearly *g.*
P. L. 6, 515. they reduced to blackest *g.*
P. L. 8, 17. this earth a spot, a *g.*, an atom
P. L. 9, 450. the smell of *g.* or tedded grass
P. L. 11, 242. Meliboean or the *g.* of Sarra
P. L. 12, 184. it devours not herb or fruit or *g.*
S. A. 408. with a *g.* of manhood
C. 750. and cheeks of sorry *g.*
Il P. 33. all in a robe of darkest *g.*
**Grand.**—P. L. 1, 29. moved our *g.* parents
P. L. 1, 122. irreconcileable to our *g.* foe
P. L. 2, 507. forth in order came the *g.* infernal
P. L. 4, 192. so clomb this first *g.* thief
P. L. 6, 149. whom the *g.* foe with scornful eye
P. L. 10, 427. while the *G.* in council sat
P. L. 10, 1033. our *g.* foe Satan
P. R. 1, 159. sin and death the two *g.* foes
**Grandchild.**—P. L. 10, 384. son and *g.* both
P. L. 12, 135. and of his son a *g.* leaves
P. L. 12, 155. the *g.* with twelve sons increased
**Grandeur.**—P. R. 4, 110. *g.* and majestic show

**Grandsire.**—S. 21, 1. *g.* on the royal bench
**Granges.**—C. 175. teeming flocks and *g.*
**Grant.**—P. L. 5, 831. but to *g.* it thee unjust
P. R. 2, 235. he ceased and heard their *g.*
S. A. 356. wherefore did God *g.* me my
C. 361. for *g.* they be so while they rest
Il P. 180. made hell *g.* what love did seek
**Granted.**—P. R. 2, 302. with *g.* leave officious
P. R. 4, 290. no other doctrine needs though *g*
**Granting.**—P. L. 4, 104. as far from *g.* he as
S. A. 773. first *g.*, as I do, it was a weakness
**Grants.**—P. L. 12, 238. *g.* what they besought
**Grape.**—P. L. 4, 259. lays forth her purple *g.*
P. L. 5, 307. from milky stream berry or *g.*
P. L. 5, 344. for drink the *g.* she crushes
S. A. 551. nor envied them the *g.*
C. 46. Bacchus that first from out the purple *g.*
**Grapple.**—P. R. 4, 567. his fall and fiercer *g.*
**Grasp.**—P. L. 4, 989. nor wanted in his *g.*
C. 357. the direful *g.* of savage hunger
**Grasped.**—P. L. 1, 667. and fierce with *g.* arms
**Grasping.**—P. L. 6, 836. in his right hand *g.*
**Grass.**—P. L. 4, 350. other on the *g.* couched
P. L. 7, 310. earth put forth her verdant *g.*
P. L. 7, 315. brought forth the tender *g.*
P. L. 9, 450. the smell of grain, or tedded *g.*
P. L. 9, 502. circling spires that on the *g.*
C. 624. he on the tender *g.* would sit
H. 215. trampling the unshowered *g.*
**Grassy.**—P. L. 4, 601. they to their *g.* couch
P. L. 5, 391. raised of *g.* turf their table was
P. L. 7, 463. the *g.* clods now calved
P. L. 9, 186. but on the *g.* herb fearless unfeared
P. L. 11, 324. altars I would rear of *g.* turf
P. L. 11, 433. an altar... rustic of *g.* sord
P. R. 2, 282. lightly from his *g.* couch up rose
C. 280. they left me weary on a *g.* turf
**Grate.**—P. L. 2, 881. hinges *g.* harsh thunder
L. 124. *g.* on their scrannel pipes
**Grateful.**—P. L. 4, 55. a *g.* mind by owing
P. L. 4, 165. cheered with the *g.* smell
P. L. 4, 331. thirst and appetite more *g.*
P. L. 4, 647. the coming on of *g.* evening
P. L. 5, 645. heaven had changed to *g.* twilight
P. L. 6, 8. through Heaven *g.* vicissitude
P. L. 6, 407. inducing darkness *g.* truce imposed
P. L. 7, 512. but *g.* to acknowledge whence
P. L. 8, 55. would intermix *g.* digressions
P. L. 8, 606. more *g.* than harmonious sound
P. L. 8, 650. honoured ever with *g.* memory
P. L. 9, 197. and his nostrils fill with *g.* smell
P. L. 9, 580. savoury odour blown *g.* to appetite
P. L. 11, 442. with nimble glance and *g.* steam
P. L. 11, 864. and eyes devout *g.* to heaven
S. A. 926. with all things *g.* cheered
**Gratefully.**—P. L. 8, 4. thus *g.* replied
P. L. 11, 370. to whom thus Adam *g.* replied
**Gratify.**—P. L. 10, 625. to *g.* my scornful
**Gratitude.**—P. L. 4, 52. of endless *g.*
P. R. 4, 188. but *g.* in thee is lost long since
**Gratulate.**—P. L. 4, 438. to *g.* the sweet
C. 949. many a friend to *g.* his wished
**Gratulating.**—P. L. 9, 472. *g.* thus excites
**Gratulation.**—P. L. 8, 514. gave sign of *g.*
**Grave.**—P. L. 2, 300. with *g.* aspect he rose
P. L. 2, 911. womb of nature and perhaps her *g.*
P. L. 3, 247. leave me in the loathsome *g.*
P. L. 3, 259. and with his carcase glut the *g.*
P. L. 4, 844. his *g.* rebuke severe in youthful
P. L. 10, 185. rising from his *g.*
P. L. 10, 635. sin and death and yawning *g.*
P. L. 10, 786. then in the *g.* or in some other
P. L. 11, 585. the men though *g.* eyed them
P. L. 11, 662. gray-headed men and *g.*
P. L. 12, 423. rise out of his *g.* fresh as the
P. R. 4, 268. what the lofty *g.* tragedians taught
S. A. 102. myself my sepulchre a moving *g.*
S. A. 868. *g.* authority took full possession
C. 110. with their *g.* saws in slumber lie

C. 472. lingering and sitting by a new-made *g.*
C. 870. and Tethys' *g.* majestic pace
S. 14, 6. not behind nor in the *g.* were trod
S. 23, 2. to me like Alcestis from the *g.*
H. 234. slips to his several *g.*
M. W. 47. lady may thy *g.* peace and quiet
**Gravely.**—P. L. 4, 907. *g.* in doubt whether
**Graven.**—P. L. 1, 716. with bossy sculptures *g.*
P. L. 11, 573. might else be wrought fusil or *g.*
**Graver.**—M. 30. service in some *g.* subject
**Gravest.**—P. R. 4, 218. among the *g.* rabbies
**Gray.**—P. L. 3, 475. white, black and *g.*
P. L. 4,598. twilight *g.* had in her sober livery
P. L. 5, 186. hill or steaming lake dusky or *g.*
P. L. 7, 373. *g.* dawn and the Pleiades
P. L. 11, 540. change to withered weak and *g.*
P. L. 12, 227. mount of Sinai whose *g.* top
P. R. 1, 498. his *g.* dissimulation
P. R. 4, 427. with pilgrim steps in amice *g.*
C. 392. or do his *g.* hairs any violence
A. 54. when evening *g.* doth rise
L. 187. still morn went out with sandals *g.*
L'A. 71. russet lawns and fallows *g.*
**Gray-fly.**—L. 28. what time the *g.-f.* winds her
**Gray-headed.**—P. L. 11, 662. anon *g.-h.*
**Gray-hooded.**—C. 188. the *g.-h.* Even
**Graze.**—P. L. 7, 404. *g.* the sea-weed
P. L. 9, 571. was at first as other beasts that *g.*
P. L. 10, 711. to *g.* the herb
L. 46. to the weanling herds that *g.*
**Grazed.**—P. L. 1, 486. his maker to the *g.* ox
C. 152. stocked with as fair a herd as *g.*
**Grazing.**—P. L. 4, 253. flocks *g.* the tender herb
P. L. 11, 558. by some were herds of cattle *g.*
**Great.**—P. L. 1, 24. height of this *g.* argument
P. L. 1, 62. as one *g.* furnace flamed
P. L. 1, 118. through experience of this *g.* event
P. L. 1, 294. to be the mast of some *g.* ammiral
P. L. 1, 348. uplifted spear of their *g.* sultan
P. L. 1, 358. where stood their *g.* Commander
P. L. 1, 378. at their *g.* emperor's call
P. L. 1, 718. not Babylon nor *g.* Alcairo
P. L. 1, 794. the *g.* seraphic lords and cherubim
P. L. 1, 798. and summons read the *g.* consult
P. L. 2, 137. yet our *g.* enemy all incorruptible
P. L. 2, 202. if we were wise against so *g.* a foe
P. L. 2, 258. when *g.* things of small
P. L. 2, 385. done all to spite the *g.* Creator
P. L. 2, 392. *g.* things resolved which from the
P. L. 2, 452. refusing to accept as *g.* a share
P. L. 2, 515. trumpets' regal sound the *g.* result
P. L. 2, 527. the irksome hours till his *g.* chief
P L. 2, 722. now *g.* deeds had been achieved
P. L. 2, 722. was either like to meet so *g.* a foe
P. L. 2, 922. to compare *g.* things with small
P. L. 3, 167. whom the *g.* Creator thus replied
P. L. 3, 271. attends the will of his *g.* Father
P. L. 3, 311. by being good far more than *g.*
P. L. 3, 576. where the *g.* luminary aloof
P. L. 3, 628. on some *g.* charge employed
P. L. 3, 656. his *g.* authentic will
P. L. 3, 673. on whom the *g.* Creator hath
P. L. 3, 696. to glorify the *g.* Work-master
P. L. 4, 62. some other power as *g.*
P. L. 4, 63. but other powers as *g.* fell not
P. L. 4, 212. *g.* Seleucia built by Grecian kings
P. L. 4, 684. singing their *g.* Creator
P. L. 5, 171. thou Sun of this *g.* world both eye
P. L. 5, 184. to our *g.* Maker still new praise
P. L. 5, 188. honour to the world's *g.* author
P. L. 5, 311. some *g.* behest from heaven to us
P. L. 5, 350. meanwhile our primitive *g.* sire
P. L. 5, 454. given him by his *g.* conference
P. L. 5, 544. to whom our *g.* progenitor
P. L. 5, 560. his other half in the *g.* zone
P. L. 5, 583. on such day as heaven's *g.* year
P. L. 5, 609. under his *g.* vicegerent reign abide
P. L. 5, 660. *g.* in power, in favour
P. L. 5, 663. that day honoured by his *g.* father
P. L. 5, 691. the *g.* Messiah
P. L. 5, 701. *g.* hierarchal standard was to move

P. L. 5, 706. *g.* potentate for *g.* indeed his name
P. L. 5, 760. the palace of *g.* Lucifer
P. L. 5, 769. about the *g.* reception of their king
P. L. 5, 833. thyself though *g.* and glorious
P. L. 6, 95. as sons of one *g.* sire hymning
P. L. 6, 257. the *g.* archangel from his warlike
P. L. 6, 303. to decide the empire of *g.* heaven
P. L. 6, 311. to set forth *g.* things by small
P. L. 6, 675. his *g.* purpose he might so fulfil
P. L. 6, 702. of ending this *g.* war
P. L. 6, 775. when the *g.* ensign of Messiah
P. L. 6, 799. when the *g.* Son of God
P. L. 7, 70. *g.* things and full of wonder in our
P. L. 7, 98. and the *g.* light of day yet wants
P. L. 7, 135. and the *g.* Son returned victorious
P. L. 7, 180. *g.* triumph and rejoicing
P. L. 7, 193. on his *g.* expedition now appeared
P. L. 7, 267. uttermost convex of this *g.* round
P. L. 7, 281. fermented the *g.* mother to
P. L. 7, 294. the *g.* command impressed
P. L. 7, 307. *g.* receptacle of congregated waters
P. L. 7, 346. God made two *g.* lights *g.* for their
P. L. 7, 353. God saw surveying his *g.* work
P. L. 7, 363. *g.* palace now of light
P. L. 7, 381. revolved on heaven's *g.* axle
P. L. 7, 391. and God created the *g.* whales
P. L. 7, 500. as the *g.* first Mover's hand
P. L. 7, 557. answering his *g.* idea
P. L. 7, 567. the *g.* Creator from his work
P. L. 7, 588. sat him down with his *g.* Father
P. L. 7, 602. *g.* are thy works, Jehovah
P. L. 8, 72. the *g.* Architect did wisely to conceal
P. L. 8, 90. consider first that *g.* or bright
P. L. 8, 151. which two *g.* sexes animate
P. L. 8, 278. not of myself by some *g.* Maker
P. L. 8, 635. and keep his *g.* command
P. L. 9, 195. from the earth's *g.* altar send up
P. L. 9, 669. as of some *g.* matter
P. L. 9, 672. to some *g.* cause addressed
P. L. 9, 745. *g.* are thy virtues doubtless
P. L. 9, 815. our *g.* Forbidder
P. L. 9, 843. *g.* joy he promised to his thoughts
P. L. 9, 922. and peril *g.* provoked
P. L. 10, 236. our *g.* author thrives in other
P. L. 10, 284. their power was *g.*
P. L. 10, 306. so if *g.* things to small may be
P. L. 10, 350. *g.* joy was at their meeting
P. L. 10, 440. each hour their *g.* adventurer
P. L. 10, 456. the *g.* consulting peers
P. L. 10, 469. my adventure hard with peril *g.*
P. L. 11, 19. by their *g.* intercessor
P. L. 11, 225. while his *g.* visitant approached
P. L. 11, 226. Eve now expect *g.* tidings
P. L. 11, 231. some *g.* potentate
P. L. 11, 314. to his *g.* bidding I submit
P. L. 11, 346. reverence thee their *g.* progenitor
P. L. 11, 391. Agra and Lahor of *g.* Mogul
P. L. 11, 410. whose *g.* city Geryon's sons
P. L. 11, 450. some *g.* mischief hath befallen
P. L. 11, 695. to be styled *g.* conquerors
P. L. 11, 720. and of their doings *g.* dislike
P. L. 11, 790. and *g.* exploits
P. L. 11, 833. down the *g.* river to the opening
P. L. 12, 59. *g.* laughter was in heaven
P. L. 12, 141. east to the *g.* western sea
P. L. 12, 149. is meant thy *g.* deliverer
P. L. 12, 225. their *g.* senate choose through
P. L. 12, 244. of *g.* Messiah shall sing
P. L. 12, 378. our *g.* Expectation
P. L. 12, 467. paused as at the world's *g.* period
P. L. 12, 503. win *g.* numbers of each nation
P. L. 12, 567. by small accomplishing *g.* things
P. L. 12, 600. the *g.* deliverance by her seed
P. L. 12, 612. some *g.* good presaging
P. R. 1, 18. had the *g.* proclaimer with a voice
P. R. 1, 21. to his *g.* baptism flocked with awe
P. R. 1, 70. before him a *g.* prophet to proclaim
P. R. 1, 113. to him their *g.* dictator
P. R. 1, 136. she should bear a son *g.* in renown
P. R. 1, 145. and vaunts of his *g.* cunning
P. R. 1, 158. the rudiments of his *g.* warfare

P. R. 1, 174. entering his *g.* duel not of arms
P.R.1,210. at our *g.* feast I went into the temple
P. R. 1, 240. thou shouldst be *g.* and sit on
P. R. 2, 16. the *g.* Thisbite who on fiery wheels
P. R. 2, 51. to us revealed him by his *g.* prophet
P. R. 2, 86. I looked for some *g.* change
P. R. 2, 95. where delays he now some *g.* intent
P. R. 2, 101. to some *g.* purpose he obscures
P. R. 2, 112. all his *g.* work to come before him
P. R. 2, 412. *g.* acts require *g.* means
P. R. 2, 426. if at *g.* things thou wouldst arrive
P. R. 3, 39. *g.* Julius whom now all the world
P. R. 3, 73. *g.* battles win *g.* cities by assault
P. R. 3, 82. *g.* benefactors of mankind
P. R. 3, 110. least resembling thy *g.* Father
P. R. 3, 295. the *g.* Seleucia
P. R. 3, 295. now some ages past by *g.* Arsaces
P. R. 3, 299. to have a view of his *g.* power
P. R. 4, 45. than *g.* and glorious Rome
P. R. 4, 81. to Rome's *g.* emperor
P. R. 4, 169. for what can less so *g.* a gift
P. R. 4, 252. who bred *g.* Alexander to subdue
S. A. 28. from some *g.* act or benefit revealed
S. A. 32. designed for *g.* exploits
S. A. 40. ask for this *g.* deliverer now
S. A. 83. first-created beam and thou *g.* Word
S. A. 243. those *g.* acts which God had done
S. A. 279. their *g.* deliverer contemned
S. A. 436. proclaim *g.* pomp and sacrifice
S. A. 467. will arise and his *g.* name assert
S. A. 523. *g.* in hopes with youthful courage
S. A. 680. to some *g.* work thy glory
S. A. 1118. no *g.* advantage on me
S. A. 1315. honour this *g.* feast and *g.* assembly
S. A. 1356. after my *g.* trangression
S. A. 1389. some *g.* act or of my days the last
S. A. 1430. spread his name *g.* among the
S. A. 1439. measure of strength so *g.* to mortal
S. A. 1474. their once *g.* dread captive
S. A. 1499. use him farther yet in some *g.* service
S. A. 1500. not to sit idle with so *g.* a gift
S. A. 1537. or bad so *g.* of bad the sooner
S. A. 1638. some *g.* matter in his mind revolved
S. A. 1756. true experience from this *g.* event
C. 522. of Bacchus and of Circe born *g.* Comus
C. 868. in name of *g.* Oceanus
A. 33. silver-buskined nymphs as *g.* and good
A. 36. the *g.* mistress of yon princely shrine
L. 161. the *g.* vision of the guarded mount
L'A. 60. where the *g.* sun begins his state
Il P. 116. and if aught else *g.* bards beside
S. 2, 14. ever in my *g.* Task-Master's eye
S. 8, 10. the *g.* Emathian conqueror bid
S. 23, 3. Jove's *g.* son to her glad husband
H. 4. our *g.* redemption from above
H. 34. with her *g.* master so to sympathize
H. 120. the Creator *g.* his constellations set
Cir. 21. that *g.* convenant which we still
S. M. 22. their *g.* Lord whose love their motion
W. S. 5. dear son of memory, *g.* heir of fame
**Greater.**—P. L. 1, 4. till one *g.* Man restore
P. L. 1, 258. whom thunder hath made *g.*
P. L. 5, 172. acknowledge him thy *g.*
P. L. 6, 199. but *g.* rage to see thus foiled
P. L. 7, 145. yet far the *g.* part have kept
P. L. 7, 347. the *g.* to have rule by day
P. L. 7, 359. of light by far the *g.* part he took
P. L. 7, 604. *g.* now in thy return than from
P. L. 7, 607. but to create is *g.* than created
P. L. 8, 29. *g.* so manifold to this one use
P. L. 8, 87. bodies bright and *g.* should not
P. L. 9, 621. a *g.* store of fruit untouched
P. L. 10, 515. a *g.* power now ruled him
P. L. 12, 242. to introduce one *g.* of whose day
P. L. 12, 533. the rest far *g.* part will deem
P. R. 1, 279. as much his *g.*
P. R. 2, 27. fishermen (no. *g.* men them call)
P. R. 2, 482. *g.* and nobler done
S. A. 1357. and add a *g.* sin
S. A. 1644. to show you of my strength yet *g.*
A. 104. here ye shall have *g.* grace

H. 83. he saw a *g.* sun appear
**Greatest.**—P. L. 1, 367. *g.* part of mankind
P. L. 1, 695. learn how their *g.* monuments
P. L. 2, 29. condemns to *g.* share of endless
P. L. 10, 247. powerful at *g.* distance to unite
P. L. 10, 528. but still *g.* he the midst
P. R. 1, 69. to achieve things highest, *q.*
P. R. 2, 139. and amplitude of mind to *g.* deeds
P. R. 2, 208. the accomplishment of *g.* things
P. R. 2, 228. rocks whereon *g.* men have
P. R. 3, 239. in all things that to *g.* actions lead
P. R. 4, 564. to compare small things with *g.*
S. A. 974. bears *g.* names in his wild aery
S. A. 1131. which *g.* heroes have in battle
C. 28. *g.* and the best of all the main
**Greatly.**—P. L. 10, 193. thy sorrow I will *g.*
P. L. 11, 869. of Adam erst so sad *g.* rejoiced
P. L. 12, 557. *g.* instructed I shall hence depart
P. L. 12, 558. *g.* in peace of thought
**Greatness.**—P. L. 2, 257. our *g.* will appear
P. L. 3, 165. so should thy goodness and thy *g.*
P. L. 8, 557. and to consummate all *g.* of mind
P. R. 2, 418. what hope dost thou aspire to *g.*
**Greaves.**—S. A. 1121. vant-brace and *g.*
**Grecian.**—P. L. 4, 212. built by *G.* kings
**Greece.**—P. L. 1, 739. or unadored in ancient *G.*
P. L. 10, 307. Xerxes the liberty of *G.* to yoke
P. R. 4, 240. Athens the eye of *G.* mother of arts
P. R. 4, 270. and fulmined over *G.*
P. R. 4, 338. that rather *G.* from us these arts
P. R. 4, 360. all the oratory of *G.* and Rome
C. 439. antiquity from the old schools of *G.*
**Greedier.**—P. R. 4, 141. and *g.* still
**Greedily.**—P. L. 9, 791. *g.* she engorged
P. L. 10, 560. *g.* they plucked the fruitage fair
**Greedy.**—P. L. 9, 257. with *g.* hope to find
T. 10. last of all thy *g.* self consumed
**Greek.**—P. L. 9, 19. so long perplexed the *G.*
P. R. 3, 118. from all nations Jew or *G.*
S. 11, 14. Cambridge and king Edward *G.*
**Green.**—P. L. 4, 133. with her enclosure *g.*
P. L. 4, 325. under a tuft of shade that on a *g.*
P. L. 4, 458. laid me down on the *g.* bank
P. L. 4, 626. yon flowery arbours yonder alleys *g.*
P. L. 5, 480. springs lighter the *g.* stalk
P. L. 7, 316. her universal face with pleasant *g.*
P. L. 7, 337. before it grew on the *g.* stem
P. L. 7, 402. glide under the *g.* wave
P. L. 7, 460. cattle in the fields and meadows *g.*
P. L. 7, 479. spots of gold and purple azure and *g*
P. L. 8, 286. a *g.* shady bank profuse of flowers
P. L. 8, 631. beyond the earth's *g.* cape
P. L. 11, 435. the *g.* ear and the yellow sheaf
P. L. 11, 858. to spy *g.* tree or ground
P. L. 12, 186. on the ground leave nothing *g.*
P. R. 2, 185. in valley or *g.* meadow to waylay
P. R. 4, 435. now behold more fresh and *g.*
S. A. 1735. of laurel ever *g.* and branching palm
C. 232. by slow Meander's margent *g.*
C. 294. I saw them under a *g.* mantling vine
C. 311. I know each lane and every alley *g.*
C. 716. in their *g.* shops weave smooth-haired
C. 894. of turkis blue and emerald *g*
C. 1014. quickly to the *g.* earth's end
A. 84. o'er the smooth enamelled *g.*
L. 42. the willows and the hazel copses *g.*
L. 140. that on the *g.* turf suck the honied
L'A. 58. by hedge-row elms on hillocks *g.*
Il P. 66. on the dry smooth-shaven *g.*
S. 9, 2. hast shunned the broad way and the *g.*
H. 47. she crowned with olive *g.* came softly
H. 214. in Memphian grove or *g.*
M. M. 3. May, who from her *g.* lap throws
**Green-eyed.**—V. Ex. 43. *g.-e.* Neptune raves
**Greet.**—P. R. 2, 281. morn's approach and *g.* her
H. 26. the honour first thy lord to *g.*
H. 94. their hearts and ears did *g.*
T. 11. long eternity shall *g.* our bliss
M. W. 24. matrons run to *g.* her of a lovely son
**Greeting.**—P. L. 6, 188. this *g.* on thy

**Grew.**—P. L. 2, 705. and so threatening *g.* tenfold
P. L. 2, 720. that hell *g.* darker at their frown
P. L. 2, 784. nether shape thus *g.* transformed
P. L. 3, 356. heaven removed where first it *g.*
P. L. 4, 137. up *g.* insuperable height of loftiest
P. L. 4, 195. middle tree and highest there that *g.*
P. L. 4, 221. the tree of knowledge *g.* fast by
P. L. 4, 694. what higher *g.* of firm and fragrant
P. L. 7, 336. every herb before it *g.* on the green
P. L. 8, 47. by her fair tendance gladlier *g.*
P. L. 8, 470. under his forming hands a creature *g.*
P. L. 10, 551. like that which *g.* in Paradise
P. L. 10, 561. fair to sight like that which *g.*
P. L. 11, 152. persuasion in me *g.* that I was
P. R. 1, 208. and in it *g.* to such perfection
P. R. 1, 310. they at his sight *g.* mild
P. R. 3, 40. the more he *g.* in years
S. A. 637. abstemious I *g.* up and thrived
S. A. 1612. the feast and noon *g.* high
**Griding.**—P. L. 6, 329. so sore the *g.* sword
**Grief.**—P. L. 2, 586. forgets both joy and *g.*
P. L. 4, 358. what do mine eyes with *g.* behold
P. L. 9, 97. but first from inward *g.*
P. L. 12, 373. as had like *g.* been dewed in tears
P. R. 1, 110. long indulgence to their fears or *g.*
P. R. 4, 574. once found out and solved for *g.*
S. A. 72. which might in part my *g.* have eased
S. A. 179. the glory late of Israel now the *g.*
S. A. 330. ay me, another inward *g.* awaked
S. A. 659. lenient of *g.* and anxious thought
S. A. 1562. there may in *g.* be surfeit
S. A. 1578. ere I give the reins to *g.*, say first
C. 362. need a man forestall his date of *g.*
C. 565. I stood harrowed with *g.* and fear
P. 29. befriend me, Night, best patroness of *g.*
P. 45. though *g.* my feeble hands up lock
P. 54. for *g.* is easily beguiled
**Griefs.**—S. A. 617. my *g.* not only pain me
**Grieve.**—P. L. 1, 167. perhaps shall *g.* him
P. L. 11, 754. how didst thou *g.* then Adam
**Grieved.**—P. L. 4, 28. his *g.* look he fixes sad
P. L. 11, 887. *g.* at his heart when looking
**Grievest.**—P. R. 1, 407. deservedly thou *g.*
**Grieving.**—P. L. 6, 792. *g.* to see his glory
**Grievous.**—P. L. 11. 776. *g.* to bear
P. L. 10, 501. a bruise or much more *g.* pain
P. L. 12, 508. for teachers *g.* wolves
S. A. 691. too *g.* for the trespass or omission
**Grim.**—P. L. 1, 396. though fire to his *g.* idol
P. L. 2, 170. breath that kindled those *g.* fires
P. L. 2, 682. though *g.* and terrible
P. L. 2, 804. *g.* death my son and foe who sets
P. L. 6, 236. when to close the ridges of *g.* war
P. L. 10, 279. so scented the *g.* feature
P. L. 10, 713. or with countenance *g.* glared
P. L. 11, 469. the ways that lead to his *g.* cave
C. 694. what *g.* aspects are these
L. 128. what the *g.* wolf with privy paw
D. F. I. 8. for since *g.* Aquilo his charioteer
**Grind.**—P. L. 10, 1072. two bodies *g.* the air
S. A. 35. to *g.* in brazen fetters under task
S. A. 1161. to *g.* among the slaves and asses
**Grinding.**—S. A. 415. this *g.* is not yet so base
**Grinned.**—P. L. 2, 846. and death *g.* horrible
**Gripe.**—P. L. 6, 543. *g.* fast his orbèd shield
P. L. 11, 264. heart-struck with chilling *g.*
**Griped.**—P. L. 4, 408. *g.* in each paw
**Grisamber-steamed.**—P. R. 2, 344. *g-s.*
**Grisly.**—P. L. 1, 670. whose *g.* top belched fire
P. L. 2, 704. so spake the *g.* terror and in shape
P. L. 4, 821. so sudden to behold the *g.* king
P. R. 4, 430. and *g.* spectres which the fiend
C. 603. with all the *g.* legions that troop
H. 209. they call the *g.* king
**Groan.**—P. L. 4, 88. inwardly I *g.*
P. L. 6, 658. and many a dolorous *g.*
P. L. 9, 1001. and nature gave a second *g.*
S. A. 1, 1511. noise call you it or universal *g.*
**Groaned.**—P. L. 11, 447. *g.* out his soul
**Groaning.**—P. L. 12, 539. *g.* till the day
**Groans.**—P. L. 2, 184. with everlasting *g.*

P. L. 11, 489. dire was the tossing, deep the *g.*
S. 185. record their *g.* who were thy sheep
**Grooms.**—P. L. 5, 356. *g.* besmeared with gold
**Gross.**—P. L. 1, 491. or more *g.* love vice for itself
P. L. 2, 570. in squadrons and *g.* bands
P. L. 6, 552. the foe approaching *g.* and huge
P. L. 6, 661. purest at first now *g.* by sinning
P. L. 11, 53. as a distemper *g.* to air as *g.*
P. L. 12, 76. will pine his entrails *g.* and famish
C. 458. tell her of things that no *g.* ear can hear
A. 73. of human mould with *g.* unpurged ear
**Grosser.**—P. L. 5, 416. the *g.* feeds the purer
P. L. 9, 1049. air and *g.* sleep bred of unkindly
**Grossness.**—T. 20. then all this earthy *g.* quit
**Grotesque.**—P. L. 4, 136. *g.* and wild
**Grots.**—P. L. 4, 257. *g.* and caves of cool recess
C. 429. *g.* and caverns shagged with horrid
**Ground.**—P. L. 1, 421. Egypt from Syrian *g.*
P. L. 1, 705. within the *g.* a various mould
P. L. 1, 767. both on the *g.* and in the air
P. L. 2, 929. uplifted spurns the *g.*
P. L. 3, 179. shall stand on even *g.* against his
P. L. 3, 350. to the *g.* with solemn adoration
P. L. 4, 216. out of the fertile *g.* he caused
P. L. 4, 406. as one who chose his *g.* whence
P. L. 4, 702. with rich inlay broidered the *g.*
P. L. 4, 731. and uncropt falls to the *g.*
P. L. 5, 348. strews the *g.* with rose and odours
P. L. 5, 367. possess this spacious *g.*
P. L. 5, 429. the *g.* covered with pearly grain
P. L. 6, 71. for high above the *g.* their march
P. L. 6, 196. winds under *g.* or waters forcing
P. L. 6, 242. on firm *g.* a standing fight
P. L. 6, 388. all the *g.* with shivered armour
P. L. 6, 478. deep under *g.* materials dark
P. L. 6, 666. under *g.* they fought in dismal
P. L. 7, 210. on heavenly *g.* they stood
P. L. 7, 301. but they or under *g.* or circuit wide
P. L. 7, 304. ere God had bid the *g.* be dry
P. L. 7, 332. and man to till the *g.* none was
P. L. 7, 334. went up and watered all the *g.*
P. L. 7, 422. with clang despised the *g.*
P. L. 7, 442. others on *g.* walked firm
P. L. 7, 456. out of the *g.* up rose as from his
P. L. 7, 469. under *g.* bore up his branching head
P. L. 7, 475. came forth whatever creeps the *g.*
P. L. 7, 481. streaking the *g.* with sinuous trace
P. L. 7, 523. creeping thing that creeps the *g.*
P. L. 7, 525. dust of the *g.* and in thy nostrils
P. L. 9, 497. with intended wave prone on the *g.*
P. L. 9, 526. and licked the *g.* whereon she trod
P. L. 9, 590. for high from *g.* the branches
P. L. 9, 1104. that in the *g.* the bended twigs
P. L. 9, 1151. no *g.* of enmity between us known
P. L. 10, 201. cursed is the *g.* for thy sake
P. L. 10, 206. unto the *g.* for thou out of the *g.*
P. L. 10, 850. *g.* outstretched he lay on the *g.*
P. L. 10, 1054. curse aslope glanced on the *g.*
P. L. 10, 1090. with tears watering the *g.*
P. L. 10, 1102. with tears watering the *g.*
P. L. 11, 98. to till the *g.* whence he was taken
P. L. 11, 106. from hallowed *g.* the unholy
P. L. 11, 202. pursued in the air and o'er the *g.*
P. L. 11, 262. to till the *g.* whence thou wast
P. L. 11, 348. to dwell on even *g.* now with
P. L. 11, 570. washed by stream from under *g.*
P. L. 11, 850. no more now floats but seems on *g.*
P. L. 11, 858. green tree or *g.* whereon his
P. L. 11, 861. dry *g.* appears and from his ark
P. L. 12, 42. boils out from under *g.*
P. L. 12, 186. and on the *g.* leave nothing green
P. L. 12, 628. on the *g.* gliding meteorous
P. L. 12, 631. gathers *g.* fast at the labourer's
S. A. 531. on hostile *g.* none daring my affront
S. A. 582. from the dry *g.* to spring
C. 143. come knit hands and beat the *g.*
C. 146. some chaste footing near about this *g.*
C. 652. and shed the luscious liquor on the *g.*
C. 943. till we come to holier *g.*
C. 1001. in slumber soft and on the *g.*
A. 55. over the mount and all this hallowed *g.*

L. 141. and purple all the *g.* with vernal flowers
Il P. 73. oft on a plat of rising *g.*
Il P. 94. in fire, air, flood, or under *g.*
S. 8, 12. when temple and tower went to the *g.*
H. 168. old dragon under *g.* in straiter limits
**Grounded.**—P. L. 8, 572. self-esteem *g.* on
S. A. 865. that *g.* maxim so rife and celebrated
**Ground-nest.**—P. R. 2, 280. lark left his *g.-n.*
**Grounds.**—P. L. 2, 126. *g.* his courage on despair
P. R. 3, 349. secure on no slight *g.* thy safety
**Grove.**—P. L. 1, 403. and made his *g.*
P. L. 1, 416. by the *g.* of Moloch homicide
P. L. 3, 28. clear spring or shady *g.*
P. L. 4, 265. breathing the smell of field and *g.*
P. L. 4, 272. nor that sweet *g.* of Daphne
P. L. 4, 982. waving bends her bearded *g.*
P. L. 5, 22. how blows the citron *g.*
P. L. 7, 537. brought thee into this delicious *g.*
P. L. 9, 418. of *g.* or garden-plot more pleasant
P. L. 10, 548. there stood a *g.* hard by
P. R. 2, 184. in wood or *g.* by mossy fountain
P. R. 2, 289. only in a bottom saw a pleasant *g.*
P. R. 4, 244. see there the olive-*g.* of Academe
C. 225. and casts a gleam over this tufted *g.*
A. 46. to nurse the saplings tall and curl the *g.*
Il P. 1, 29. secret shades of woody Ida's inmost *g.*
S. 1, 10. my hopeless doom in some *g.* nigh
H. 214. in Memphian *g.* or green.
P. 52. gentle neighbourhood of *g.* and spring
**Grovelling.**—P. L. 1, 280. *g.* and prostrate
P. L. 10, 177. upon thy belly *g.* thou shalt go
S. A. 141. or *g.* soiled their crested helmets
C. 53. downward fell into a *g.* swine
**Groves.**—P. L. 3, 569. fortunate fields and *g.*
P. L. 4, 248. *g.* whose rich trees wept odorous
P. L. 5, 126. among the *g.* the fountains
P. L. 5, 292. through *g.* of myrrh
P. L. 7, 404. and through *g.* of coral stray
P. L. 9, 388. betook her to the *g.*
P. R. 4, 38. gardens and *g.* presented to his eyes
C. 937. with *g.* of myrrh and cinnamon
L. 174. other *g.* and other streams along
Il P. 133. to arched walks of twilight *g.*
M. M. 7. woods and *g.* are of thy dressing
**Grow.**—P. L. 1, 691. that riches *g.* in hell
P. L. 2, 31. no strife can *g.* up there from faction
P. L. 2, 220. this horror will *g.* mild
P. L. 4, 98. for never can true reconcilement *g.*
P. L. 4, 216. the fertile ground he caused to *g.*
P. L. 4, 671. stellar virtue on all kinds that *g.*
P. L. 6, 477. as not to mind from whence they *g.*
P. L. 9, 618. many are the trees of God that *g.*
P. L. 9, 623. till men *g.* up to their provision
P. L. 9, 803. till dieted by thee I *g.* mature
P. L. 9, 1105. daughters *g.* about the mother
P. L. 11, 5. and made new flesh regenerate *g.*
P. L. 11, 274. never will in other climate *g.*
P. L. 12, 352. factious they *g.*
P. L. 12, 400. which out of thine will *g.*
S. A. 676. *g.* up and perish as the summer-fly
S. A. 1496. strength again to *g.* up with his hair
C. 378. she plumes her feathers and lets *g.*
C. 735. below would *g.* inured to light
C. 956. come let us haste the stars *g.* high
S. 11, 10. rugged names to our like mouth *g* sleek
S. 18, 12. that from these may *g.* a hundredfold
**Growing.**—P. L. 2, 315. here a *g.* empire
P. L. 2, 767. my womb conceived a *g.* burden
P. L. 4, 438. to prune these *g.* plants and tend
P. L. 9, 202. may ply their *g.* work
P. L. 9, 877. and *g.* up to godhead
P. L. 10, 244. strength within me rise, wings *g.*
P. L. 10, 715. from without the *g.* miseries
P. L. 12, 164. there he dies and leaves his race *g.*
P. R. 1, 227. these *g.* thoughts my mother soon
S. 9, 7. and at thy *g.* virtues fret their spleen
**Grown.**—P. L. 2, 761. but familiar *g.* I pleased
P. L. 2, 779. and now excessive *g.*
P. L. 6, 661. now gross by sinning *g.*
P. L. 7, 456. perfect forms, limbed and full *g.*
P. L. 9, 564. and how to me so friendly *g.*

P. L. 9, 742. inclinable now *g.* to touch or taste
P. L. 9, 807. it had not here thus *g.*
P. L. 9, 1154. as good have *g.* there still
P. L. 10, 529. now dragon *g.* larger than whom
P. L. 12, 116. that men should be so stupid *g.*
P. L. 12, 164. *g.* suspected to a sequent king
P. L. 12, 351. till *g.* in wealth and multitude
P. R. 2, 83. full *g.* to man acknowledged as I
P. R. 4, 137. ambitious *g.* of triumph
S. A. 268. but what more oft in nations *g.* corrupt
C. 968. here behold so goodly *g.*
**Grows.**—P. L. 3, 356. first it grew there *g.*
P. L. 4, 425. so near *g.* death to life
P. L. 5, 72. communicated more abundant *g.*
P. L. 5, 319. disburdening *g.* more fruitful
P. L. 8, 321. of every tree that in the garden *g.*
P. L. 9, 208. under our labour *g.* luxurious
P. L. 9, 617. but say where *g.* the free
P. L. 9, 776. here *g.* the cure of all
C. 467. the soul *g.* clotted by contagion
C. 670. when the fresh blood *g.* lively and returns
C. 891. where *g.* the willow and the osier dank
L. 78. fame is no plant that *g.* on mortal soil
**Growth.**—P. L. 1, 614. top their stately *g.*
P. L. 4, 629. than ours to lop their wanton *g.*
P. L. 5, 319. nature multiplies her fertile *g.*
P. L. 5, 635. delicious vines the *g.* of heaven
P. L. 9, 113. of *g.*, sense, reason, all summed
P. L. 9, 211. with wanton *g.* derides
P. R. 1, 67. but his *g.* now to youth's full flower
C. 270. to touch the prosperous *g.* of this tall wood
**Grudging.**—C. 725. serve him as a *g.* master
**Grunsel.**—P. L. 1, 460. on the *g.* edge
**Gryphon.**—P. L. 2, 943. as when a *g.*
**Guard.**—P. L. 2, 1033. God and good angels *g.*
P. L. 4, 280. where Abassin kings their issue *g.*
P. L. 6, 412. placed in *g.* their watches round
P. L. 8, 559. an awe about her as a *g.* angelic
P. L. 11, 122. and *g.* all passage to the tree
C. 42. I was despatched for their defence and *g.*
C. 394. had need the *g.* of dragon-watch
C. 487. best draw and stand upon our *g.*
C. 695. Mercy *g.* me!
S. 8, 4. *g.* them, and him within protect
**Guarded.**—P. L. 2, 947. purloined the *g.* gold
L. 161. where the great vision of the *g.* mount
**Guardian.**—C. 219. would send a glistering *g.*
**Guardians.**—P. L. 3, 512. bands of *g.* bright
P. L. 11, 215. the field pavilioned with his *g.*
**Guards.**—P. L. 2, 611. Gorgonian terror *g.* the ford
P. L. 4, 550. Gabriel sat chief of angelic *g.*
P. L. 4, 862. where those half-rounding *g.*
P. L. 9, 269. who *g.* her or with her the worst
P. L. 10, 18. the angelic *g.* ascended mute
P. L. 12, 590. *g.* by me encamped on yonder hill
S. A. 1617. on each side went armed *g.*
**Guendolen.**—C. 830. her enraged stepdame *G.*
**Guerdon.**—L. 73. but the fair *g.* when we hope
**Guess.**—P. L. 8, 85. by thy reasoning this I *g.*
S. A. 1540. an Hebrew as I *g.* and of our tribe
C. 201. this is the place as well as I may *g.*
C. 310. without the sure *g.* of well-practised feet
**Guessed.**—P. L. 5, 290. message high they *g.*
C. 577. but soon I *g.* ye were the two she meant
**Guest.**—P. L. 5, 313. this day to be our *g.*
P. L. 5, 351. to meet his godlike *g.* walks forth
P. L. 5, 383. to entertain her *g.* from heaven
P. L. 5, 507. O favourable spirit, propitious *g.*
P. L. 7, 14. I have presumed an earthly *g.*
P. L. 7, 69. proceeded thus to ask his heavenly *g.*
P. L. 7, 109. Adam his illustrious *g.* besought
P. L. 8, 646. go heavenly *g.* ethereal messenger
P. L. 9, 1. or angel *g.* with man as with his
P. R. 2, 278. or as a *g.* with Daniel at his pulse
L. 118. and shove away the worthy bidden *g.*
**Guests.**—P. L. 12, 166. as inmate *g.*
P. L. 12, 167. of *g.* he makes them slaves
S. A. 1196. under pretence of bridal friends and *g.*
**Guiana.**—P. L. 11, 410. and yet unspoiled *G.*
**Guide.**—P. L. 2, 975. alone and without *g.*
P. L. 3, 194. place within them as a *g.*

P. L. 4, 442. without whom am to no end my *g.*
P. L. 5, 91. suddenly my *g.* was gone
P. L. 6, 711. ascend my chariot, *g.* the rapid
P. L. 8, 298. I come thy *g.* to the garden of bliss
P. L. 8, 312. he who was my *g.* up hither
P. L. 8, 613. to heaven is both the way and *g.*
P. L. 9, 646. thus to her *g.* she spake
P. L. 9, 808. next to thee I owe best *g.*
P. L. 10, 146. or was she made thy *g.* superior
P. L. 11, 371. ascend, I follow thee safe *g.*
P. L. 11, 674. to his *g.* lamenting
P. L. 11, 785. unfold celestial *g.*
P. L. 12, 204. to *g.* them in their journey
P. L. 12, 482. who then shall *g.* his people
P. L. 12, 490. to *g.* them in all truth
P. L. 12, 647. and Providence their *g.*
P. R. 1, 336. no other *g.* I seek
P. R. 2, 473. but to *g.* nations in the way
S. A. 1428. the Holy One of Israel be thy *g.*
S. A. 1630. he his *g.* requested
C. 32. has in his charge with tempered awe to *g.*
C. 171. if mine ear be true my best *g.* now
C. 944. I shall be your faithful *g.*
S. 22, 14. content though blind had I no better *g.*
**Guided.**—P. L. 7, 15. with like safety *g.* down
P. L. 8, 486. *g.* by his voice nor uninformed
P. R. 1, 250. *g.* the wise men thither from the
S. A. 1547. to have *g.* me aright I know not how
C. 570. till *g.* by mine ear I found the place
S. 16, 3. *g.* by faith and matchless fortitude
**Guides.**—P. L. 8, 708. the morning star that *g.*
P. L. 12, 362. *g.* the eastern sages who inquire
C. 279. that divide you from near-ushering *g.*
**Guiding.**—S.A. 1. little inward lend thy *g.* hand
ll P. 53. *g.* the fiery-wheeled throne
**Guile.**—P. L. 1, 34. he it was whose *g.*
P. L. 1, 121. to wage by force or *g.* eternal war
P. L. 1, 646. work in close design by fraud or *g.*
P. L. 2, 41. whether of open war or covert *g.*
P. L. 2, 188. for what can force or *g.*
P. L. 3, 92. destroy or worse by some false *g.*
P. L. 4, 349. and of his fatal *g.* gave proof
P. L. 9, 306. nor thou his malice and false *g.*
P. L. 9, 466. of *g.,* of hate, of envy, of revenge
P. L. 9, 733. and his words replete with *g.*
P. L. 9, 772. friendly to man far from deceit or *g.*
P. L. 10, 114. and obstinacy and hate and *g.*
P. R. 1. 123. temptation and all *g.* on him to try
P. R. 2, 237. of spirits likest to himself in *g.*
S. A. 989. Jael, who with inhospitable *g.* smote
**Guileful.**—P. L. 9, 567. the *g.* Tempter
P. L. 10, 334. saw his *g.* act by Eve
C. 537. yet have they many baits and *g.* spells
**Guilefully.**—P. L. 9, 655. Tempter *g.* replied

**Guiles.**—P. R. 2, 391. no gifts but *g.*
**Guilt.**—P. L. 9, 971. with me one *g.* one crime
P. L. 9, 1043. of their mutual *g.* the seal
P. L. 9, 1114. vain covering if to hide their *g.*
P. L. 10, 112. but apparent *g.* and shame
P. L. 10, 166. unable to transfer the *g.* on him
P. L. 12, 443. sign of washing them from *g.*
P. R. 3, 147. stood struck with *g.* of his own sin
S. A. 902. in thy *g.* how foul must thou appear
C. 456. driving far off each thing of sin and *g.*
**Guiltless.**—P. L. 9, 392. art yet rude *g.* of fire
P. L. 10, 823. thus *g.* be condemned, if *g.*
C. 829. *g.* damsel flying the mad pursuit
P. 40. now sunk in *g.* blood
**Guilty.**—P. L. 3, 290. his crime makes *g.*
P. L. 4, 313. then was not *g.* shame
P. L. 9, 785. to the thicket slunk the *g.* serpent
P. L. 9, 1058. naked left to *g.* shame
P. L. 10, 340. fearing *g.* what his wrath
H. 39. to hide her *g.* front with innocent snow
V. Ex. 96. or Severn swift, *g.* of maiden's death
**Guise.**—P. L. 1, 564. in *g.* of warriors old
P. L. 11, 576. by their *g.* just men they seemed
C. 962. such court *g.* as Mercury did first devise
**Gulf.**—P. L. 1, 52. rolling in the fiery *g.*
P. L. 1, 329. transfix us to the bottom of this *g.*
P. L. 2, 12. no deep within her *g.* can hold
P. L. 2, 441. plunged in that abortive *g.*
P. L. 2, 592. a *g.* profound as that Serbonian bog
P. L. 2, 1027. whose boiling *g.* tamely endured
P. L. 3, 70. he then surveyed hell and the *g.*
P. L. 5, 225. scaped through the darksome *g.*
P. L. 6, 53. the *g.* of Tartarus
P. L. 9, 72. into a *g.* shot underground
P. L. 10, 39. first this Tempter crossed the *g.*
P. L. 10, 253. over this *g.* impassable
P. L. 10, 366. nor this unvoyageable *g.* obscure
P. L. 11, 833. the great river to the opening *g.*
**Gulfy.**—V. Ex. 92. Tweed, or Ouse, or *g.* Dun
**Gummy.**—P. L. 10, 1076. the *g.* bark of fir
**Gums.**—P. L. 4, 248. wept odorous *g.* and balm
P. L. 4, 630. blossoms also and those dropping *g.*
P. L. 11, 327. sweet-smelling *g.* and fruits
C. 917. smeared with *g.* of glutinous heat
**Gurge.**—P. L. 12, 41. a black bituminous *g.*
**Gushing.**—P. L. 11, 447. with *g.* blood effused
L. 137. of shades and wanton winds and *g.* brooks
**Gust.**—P. L. 10, 565. allay their appetite with *g.*
P. L. 10, 698. and snow and hail and stormy *g.*
L. 93. questioned every *g.* of rugged wings
ll P. 128. when the *g.* hath blown his fill
**Gymnic.**—S. A. 1324. and every sort of *g.* artists
**Gyves.**—S. A. 1093. I thought *g.* and the mill

# H

**Habergeon.**—S. A. 1120. thy broad *h.*
**Habit.**—P. L. 3, 643. his *h.* fit for speed succinct
P. R. 4, 601. whatever place, *h.,* or state
S. A. 122. in slavish *h.* ill-fitted weeds
S. A. 1073. his *h.* carries peace, his brow defiance
S. A. 1305. by his *h.* I discern him now
**Habitable.**—P. L. 8, 157. down to this *h.*
**Habitant.**—P. L. 8, 99. to thee earth's *h.*
P. L. 10, 588. and to dwell habitual *h.*
**Habitants.**—P. L. 2, 367. the puny *h.*
P. L. 3, 460. more likely *h.* translated saints
C. 459. till oft converse with heavenly *h.*
**Habitation.**—P. L. 2, 573. easier *h.*
P. L. 6, 876. hell their fit *h.* fraught with fire
P. L. 7, 622. perhaps a world of destined *h.*
P. R. 1, 47. hell our hated *h.*
C. 339. from the wicker hole of some clay *h.*
**Habitations.**—P. L. 7, 186. *h.* of the just
P. L. 12, 49. and through their *h.* walks
**Habits.**—P. L. 3, 490. cowls, hoods, and *h.*
P. R. 4, 68. in various *h.* on the Appian road
C. 157. and my quaint *h.* breed astonishment
**Habitual.**—P. L. 10, 588. dwell *h.* habitant

**Habor.**—P. R. 3, 376. yet serve in *H.*
**Hæmony.**—C. 638. he called it *h.* and gave it me
**Hag.**—C. 435. meagre *h.* or stubborn unlaid ghost
**Hail.**—P. L. 1, 171. the sulphurous *h.* shot after
P. L. 1, 250. *h.* horrors ! *h.* infernal world !
P. L. 2, 589. storms of whirlwind and dire *h.*
P. L. 3, 1. *h.* holy Light, offspring of heaven
P. L. 3, 412. *h.* Son of God, Saviour of men
P. L. 4, 750. *h.* wedded love, mysterious law
P. L. 5, 205. *h.* universal Lord, be bounteous
P. L. 5, 385. on whom the angel *h.* bestowed
P. L. 5, 388. *h.* mother of mankind
P. L. 6, 589. chained thunderbolts and *h.* of iron
P. L. 10, 698. armed with ice and snow and *h.*
P. L. 10, 1063. inclement seasons, rain, ice, *h.*
P. L. 11, 158. *h.* to thee, Eve rightly called
P. L. 12, 181. thunder mixed with *h., h.* mixed
P. L. 12, 379. virgin mother *h.,* high in the love
P. R. 2, 68. *h.* highly favoured among women
P. R. 4, 633. *h.* Son of the Most High
C. 128. *h.* goddess of nocturnal sport
C. 265. *h.* foreign wonder
ll P. 11. but *h.* thou goddess sage and holy

Il P. 12. h. divinest Melancholy
M. M. 5, h. bounteous May that dost inspire
V. Ex. 1. h native language that by sinews weak
**Hailed.**—S. A. 354. and such a Son as all men h.
**Hair.**—P. L. 2, 710. and from his horrid h.
P. L. 3, 640. under a coronet his flowing h.
P. L. 5, 131. and wiped them with her h.
P. L. 7, 323. and bush with frizzled h. implicit
S. A. 59. how slight the gift was, hung it in my h.
S. A. 1135. at thy birth was given thee in thy h.
S. A. 1355. strength again returning with my h.
S. A. 1496. strength again to grow up with his h.
C. 863. loose train of thy amber-dropping h.
L. 69. or with the tangles of Neæra's h.
Hor. 4. in wreaths thy golden h.
**Hairs.**—S. A. 1136. though all thy h. mere bristles
C. 392. or do his gray h. any violence
**Hairy.**—P. L. 4, 135. h. sides with thicket
P. L. 7, 497. with brazen eyes and h. mane
L. 104. his mantle h. and his bonnet sedge
L'A. 112. basks at the fire his h. strength
Il P. 169. the h. gown and mossy cell
**Haled.**—P. L. 2, 596. by harpy-footed furies h.
**Half.**—P. L. 1, 398. twilight sheds on h.
P. L. 1, 617. and h. enclose him round
P. L. 1, 649. hath overcome but h. his foe
P. L. 2, 941. h. on foot h. flying
P. L. 2, 975. without guide h. lost I seek
P. L. 4, 112. and more than h. perhaps
P. L. 4, 488. and thee claim my other h.
P. L. 4, 495. h. her swelling breast naked met
P. L. 4, 782. h. these draw off, and coast
P. L. 4, 785. h. wheeling to the shield h. to the
P. L. 4, 820. those two fair angels h. amazed
P. L. 4, 903. disdainfully h. smiling thus replied
P. L. 5, 95. best image of myself and dearer h.
P. L. 5, 229. go therefore h. this day as friend
P. L. 5, 559. the sun had finished h. his journey
P. L. 5, 560. his other h. in the great zone
P. L. 6, 198. h. sunk with all his pines
P. L. 6, 325. and in h. cut sheer
P. L. 6, 770. chariots of God h. on each hand
P. L. 6, 853. yet h. his strength he put not forth
P. L. 7, 21. h. yet remains unsung
P. L. 7, 463. now h. appeared the tawny lion
P. L. 8, 595. whom thus h. abashed Adam replied
P. L. 9, 141. well nigh h. the angelic name
P. L. 9, 426. where she stood h. spied
P. L. 9, 545. to discern h. what in thee is fair
S. A. 79. scarce h. I. seem to live dead more than h.
S. A. 100. to live a life h. dead a living death
C. 724. not h. his riches known and yet despised
A. 12. less than h. we find expressed
S. 19, 2. h. my days in this dark world and wide
H. 170. not h. so far casts his usurped sway
V. Ex. 4. h. unpronounced slide through my
U. C. I. 6. death was h. glad when he had got him
**Half-embracing.**—P. L. 4, 494. h.-e. leaned
**Half-moons.**—P. R. 3, 309. h.-m. and wings
**Half-raised.**—P. L. 5, 12. leaning h.-r.
**Half-regained.**—L'A. 150. his h.-r. Eurydice
**Half-round.**—S. A. 1606. h.-r. on two main .
**Half-rounding.**—P. L. 4, 862. h.-r. guards
**Half-starved.**—P. L. 10, 595. thyself h.-s.
**Half-told.**—Il P. 109. call up him that left h.-t.
**Half-way.**—P. L. 4, 777. h.-w. up hill this vast
P. L. 6, 128. h.-w. he met his daring foe
**Hall.**—P. L. 1, 762. but chief the spacious h.
P. L. 1, 791. amidst the h. of that infernal court
P. L. 9, 38. marshalled feast served up in h.
P. L. 10, 444. the door of that Plutonian h.
P. L. 10, 522. through the h. thick-swarming
P. L. 10, 667. through the dark aerial h.
C. 45. from old or modern bard in h. or bower
C. 649. boldly assault the necromancer's h.
C. 835. bearing her straight to aged Nereus' h.
H. 148. open the gates of her high palace h.
**Halleluiah.**—P. L. 10, 642. sung h.
**Halleluiahs.**—P. L. 2, 243. sing forced h.
P. L. 6, 744. unfeigned h. to thee sing
P. L. 7, 634. and the empyrean rung with h.

**Halloa.**—C. 226. I cannot h. to my brothers
C. 481. far off h. break the silent air
C. 487. I'll h.
C. 490. that h. I should know
**Hallowed.**—P. L. 3, 31. wash thy h. feet.
P. L. 4, 964. within these h. limits thou appear
P. L. 5, 321. Adam, earth's h. mould
P. L. 7, 592. blessed and h. the seventh day
P. L. 11, 106. from h. ground the unholy
P. R. 3, 116. above all sacrifice or h. gift
S. A. 535. and h. pledge of all my strength
A. 55. the mount and all this h. ground
Il P. 138. fright them from their h. haunt
H. 28. his secret altar touched with h. fire
W. S. 3. that his h. reliques should be hid
V. Ex. 98. or coaly Tyne or ancient h. Dee
**Halls.**—C. 324. in tapestry h. and courts
**Halt.**—P. L. 6, 532. in motion or in h.
P. L. 11, 210. and on a hill made h.
**Hamath.**—P. L. 12, 139. from H. northward
**Hamlets.**—L'A. 92. upland h. will invite
**Hammered.**—S. A. 132. the h. cuirass
**Hammon.**—H. 203. H. shrinks his horn
**Hamper.**—S. A. 1397. to assail and h. thee.
**Hand.**—P. L. 1, 222. on each h. the flames
P. L. 1, 732. his h. was known in Heaven
P. L. 2, 3. the gorgeous East with richest h.
P. L. 2, 174. arm again his red right h. to plague
P. L. 2, 369. and with repenting h. abolish his
P. L. 2, 674. Satan was now at h. and from his
P. L. 2, 727. O father what intends thy h.
P. L. 2, 738. that my sudden h. prevented
P. L. 2, 775. this powerful key into my h.
P. L. 2, 869. where I shall reign at thy right h.
P. L. 3, 279. thee from my bosom and right h.
P. L. 3, 455. unaccomplished works nature's h.
P. L. 3, 566. but nigh h. seemed other worlds
P. L. 4, 365. such grace the h. that formed
P. L. 4, 417. who at his h. have nothing merited
P. L. 4, 488. thy gentle h. seized mine
P. L. 4, 552. but nigh at h. celestial armoury
P. L. 4, 689. h. in h. alone they passed
P. L. 5, 17. her h. soft touching whispered thus
P. L. 5, 353. angelic choirs on each h. parting
P. L. 5, 344. heaps with unsparing h.
P. L. 5, 606. ye now behold at my right h.
P. L. 5, 641. showered with copious h. rejoicing
P. L. 5, 864. our own right h.
P. L. 6, 3. with rosy h. unbarred the gates
P. L. 6, 139. with solitary h. reaching beyond
P. L. 6, 154. the first assay of this right h.
P. L. 6, 231. in strength each armed h. a legion
P. L. 6, 307. from each h. with speed retired
P. L. 6, 537. foe at h. whom fled we thought
P. L. 6, 579. and in his h. a reed stood waving
P. L. 6, 683. and in whose h. what by decree
P. L. 6, 747. from the right h. of glory
P. L. 6, 762. at his right h. Victory sat
P. L. 6, 770. chariots of God half on each h.
P. L. 6, 800. to all his host on either h. thus
P. L. 6, 807. punishment to other h. belongs
P. L. 6, 835. his right h. grasping ten thousand
P. L. 6, 892. where now he sits at the right h.
P. L. 7, 202. harnessed at h. celestial equipage
P. L. 7, 224. and in his h. he took the golden
P. L. 7, 500. as the great first Mover's h.
P. L. 8, 27. with superfluous h. so many nobler
P. L. 8, 199. and speak of things at h. useful
P. L. 8, 300. so saying by the h. he took me
P. L. 9, 256. and somewhere nigh at h. watches
P. L. 9, 344. his creating h. nothing imperfect
P. L. 9, 385. from her husband's h. her h. soft
P. L. 9, 438. on each bank the h. of Eve
P. L. 9, 780. so saying her rash h. in evil hour
P. L. 9, 850. in her h. a bough of fairest fruit
P. L. 9, 892. from his slack h. the garland
P. L. 9, 997. fair enticing fruit with liberal h.
P. L. 9, 1037. her h. he seized and to a shady
P. L. 10, 64. toward the right h. his glory
P. L. 10, 140. that from her h. I could suspect
P. L. 10, 322. and on the left h. Hell with long

P. L. 10, 458. who with *h*. silence, and with
P. L. 10, 772. why delays his *h*. to execute
P. L. 11, 28. his own *h*. manuring
P. L. 11, 93. lest therefore his now bolder *h*.
P. L. 11, 248. and in his *h*. the spear
P. L. 11, 276. which I bred up with tender *h*.
P. L. 11, 372. and to the *h*. of Heaven submit
P. L. 11, 421. but him the gentle angel by the *h*.
P. L. 11, 436. yellow sheaf unculled as came to *h*.
P. L. 11, 659. on each *h*. slaughter and gigantic
P. L. 12, 457. resume his seat at God's right *h*.
P. L. 12, 637. in either *h*. the hastening Angel
P. L. 12, 648. they *h*. in *h*. with wandering
P. R. 1, 20. heaven's kingdom nigh at *h*. to all
P. R. 1, 171. while the *h*. sung with the voice
P. R. 2, 35. now, for sure deliverance is at *h*.
P. R. 2, 144. with *h*. or counsel to assist
P. R. 2, 238. to be at *h*. and at his beck appear
P. R. 2, 429. riches are mine fortune is in my *h*.
P. R. 2, 449. riches though offered from the *h*.
P. R. 3, 168. by strong *h*. his family obtained
P. R. 3, 187. he in whose *h*. all times
P. R. 4, 59. carved work the *h*. of famed
P. R. 4, 256. and numbers hit by voice or *h*.
S. A. 1. a little onward lend thy guiding *h*.
S. A. 142. what trivial weapon came to *h*.
S. A. 359. given with solemn *h*. as graces
S. A. 507. and let another *h*. not thine exact
S. A. 593. yield to double darkness nigh to *h*.
S. A. 668. thou toward him with *h*. so various
S. A. 684. changest thy countenance and thy *h*.
S. A. 951. approach at least and touch thy *h*.
S. A. 1105. thou seest it in thy *h*.
S. A. 1159. and delivered up into thy enemies' *h*.
S. A. 1230. but take good heed my *h*. survey not
S. A. 1233. nothing from thy *h*. fear I incurable
S. A. 1302. in his *h*. a sceptre or quaint staff
S. A. 1306. a public officer and now at *h*.
S. A. 1581. what glorious *h*. gave Samson his
C. 397. from the rash *h*. of bold incontinence
C. 711. with such a full and unwithdrawing *h*.
C. 903. we implore thy powerful *h*.
A. 77. if my inferior *h*. or voice could hit
L'A. 35. and in thy right *h*. lead with thee
L'A. 63. while the ploughman near at *h*.
S. 15, 9. O yet a nobler task awaits thy *h*.
S. 17, 13. therefore on thy firm *h*. Religion leans
S. 22, 7. I argue not against Heaven's *h*. or will
H. 222. the dreaded Infant's *h*.
D. F. I. 23. for so Apollo with unweeting *h*.
**Handed.**—P. L. 4, 739. *h*. they went
**Handling.**—P. R. 1, 489. *h*. holy things
**Handmaid.** H. 242. with *h*. lamp attending
**Handmaids.**—S. 14, 10. knew them best thy *h*.
**Hands.**—P. L. 1, 459. head and *h*. lopped off
P. L. 1, 686. and with impious *h*. rifled
P. L. 1, 699. and *h*. innumerable scarce perform
P. L. 2, 712. their fatal *h*. no second stroke
P. L. 2, 949. head, *h*., wings, or feet pursues
P. L. 4, 629. require more *h*. than ours
P. L. 5, 214. needed *h*. to check fruitless
P. L. 5, 854. the work of secondary *h*.
P. L. 6, 458. makes remiss the *h*. of mightiest
P. L. 6, 508. innumerable *h*. were ready
P. L. 6, 646. uplifting bore them in their *h*.
P. L. 8, 362. so amply and with *h*. so liberal
P. L. 8, 469. formed and fashioned with his *h*.
P. L. 8, 470. under his forming *h*. a creature
P. L. 9, 203. outgrew the *h*.' dispatch of two
P. L. 9, 207. till more *h*. aid us
P. L. 9, 244. doubt not but our joint *h*. will keep
P. L. 9, 246. till younger *h*. ere long assist us
P. L. 9, 623. and more *h*. help to disburden
P. L. 10, 373. hath won what thy *h*. builded not
P. L. 10, 1002. supply with our own *h*. his office
P. L. 10, 1058. and his *h*. clothed us unworthy
P. L. 11, 669. and had seized with violent *h*.
P. L. 11, 863. with uplifted *h*. and eyes devout
P. R. 1, 969. gave up into my *h*. Uzzean Job
P. R. 3, 155. thy right be now in powerful *h*.
P. R. 3, 290. or by Parthian *h*.

P. R. 4, 557. in their *h*. they shall uplift thee
S. A. 259. on some conditions came into their *h*.
S. A. 438. bound and blind into their *h*.
S. A. 1185. and delivered bound into our *h*.
S. A. 1260. work of many *h*. which earns my
S. A. 1270. when God into the *h*. of their
S. A. 1299. more than the working day thy *h*.
S. A. 1526. from other *h*. we need not much to
S. A. 1584. by his own *h*.
C. 13. to lay their just *h*. on that golden key
C. 143. come, knit *h*. and beat the ground
C. 875. by Leucothea's lovely *h*.
P. 45. though grief my feeble *h*. up lock
V. Ex. 90. if not your learned *h*. can loose
**Hang.**—P. L. 5, 323. ripe for use *h*. on the
P. L. 9, 798. thy fair fruit let *h*. as to no end
L. 147. cowslips wan that *h*. the pensive head
L'A. 29. such as *h*. on Hebe's cheek
**Hanging.**—P. L. 2, 1051. *h*. in a golden chain
P. L. 9, 622. untouched still *h*. incorruptible
**Hangs.**—P. L. 2, 637. a fleet descried *h*. in
M. W. 41. but the fair blossom *h*. the head
**Hap.**—P. L. 2, 837. might *h*. to move new broils
P. L. 9, 56. maugre what might *h*. of heavier
P. L. 9, 160. where *h*. may find the serpent
P. L. 9, 421. but wished his *h*. might find Eve
V. Ex. 68. once it was my dismal *h*. to hear
V. Ex. 83. find a foe it shall not be his *h*.
**Hapless.**—P. L. 2, 549. heroic deeds and *h*. fall
P. L. 5, 879. and thy *h*. crew involved in this
P. L. 6, 785. this saw his *h*. foes but stood
P. L. 9, 404. much deceived much failing *h*. Eve
P. L. 10, 342. where the *h*. sat in their sad
P. L. 10, 965. to our seed, O *h*. seed
C. 350. O that *h*. virgin, our lost sister
C. 566. O poor *h*. nightingale thought I
L. 164. O ye dolphins, waft the *h*. youth
M. W. 31. the *h*. babe before his birth
Hor. 12. *h*. they to whom thou untried
**Haply.**—P. L. 1, 203. him *h*. slumbering
P. L. 4, 8. *h*. so scaped his mortal snare
P. L. 4, 378. my dwelling *h*. may not please
P. L. 6, 501. yet *h*. of thy race in future days
P. L. 8, 200. whence *h*. mention may arise
P. L. 11, 196. or to warn us *h*. too secure
S. A. 62. herein *h*. had ends above my reach
**Happen.**—S. A. 1423. *h*. what may
V. Ex. 13. and if it *h*. as I did forecast
**Happened.**—P. L. 9, 1147. might as ill have *h*.
**Happens.**—P. R. 1, 334. to hear what *h*. new
**Happier.**—P. L. 2, 24. the *h*. state in heaven
P. L. 2, 97. *h*. far than miserable to have eternal
P. L. 4, 446. I chiefly who enjoy so far the *h*. lot
P. L. 4, 507. in one another's arms the *h*. Eden
P. L. 4, 775. if ye seek no *h*. state and know
P. L. 5, 76. happy though thou art, *h*. thou
P. L. 7, 117. and infer thee also *h*.
P. L. 8, 282. and feel that I am *h*. than I know
P. L. 9, 697. achieving what might lead to *h*. life
P. L. 10, 237. *h*. seat provides for us his offspring
P. L. 11, 88. *h*. had it sufficed him to have
P. L. 12, 464. far *h*. place than this of Eden
P. L. 12, 465. and far *h*. days
P. L. 12, 587. possess a paradise within thee *h*.
P. R. 3, 179. the *h*. reign the sooner it begins
H. 108. all Heaven and Earth in *h*. union
**Happiest.**—P. L. 4, 317. man's life his *h*. life
P. L. 4, 408. in woman's *h*. knowledge
P. L. 4, 774. O yet *h*. if ye seek no happier state
P. L. 10, 904. his *h*. choice too late shall meet
P. R. 3, 225. thy feet so slow to what is best *h*.
S. A. 1718. and which is best and *h*.
S. 13, 11. tunest thee *h*. lines in hymn or
**Happiness.**—P. L. 1, 55. of lost *h*. and lasting
P. L. 2, 563. of *h*. and final misery
P. L. 3, 450. or *h*. in this or the other life
P. L. 4, 417. and placed us here in all this *h*.
P. L. 5, 235. *h*. in his power left free to will
P. L. 5, 504. what *h*. this happy state can
P. L. 6, 741. whom to obey is *h*. entire
P. L. 6, 903. bereaved of *h*. thou mayst partake

P. L. 7, 632. thrice happy if they know their *h.*
P. L. 8, 365. in solitude what *h.*
P. L. 8, 399. a nice and subtle *h.* I see
P. L. 8, 405. I to thee sufficiently possessed of *h.*
P. L. 8, 621. and without love no *h.*
P. L. 9, 254. envying our *h.*
P. L. 9, 340. frail is our *h.* if this be so
P. L. 9, 819. and give him to partake full *h.*
P. L. 10, 725. to behold was then my height of *h.*
P. L. 11, 58. endowed with *h.* and immortality
P. R. 1, 417. imparts to thee no *h.* no joy
C. 343. or if our eyes be barred that *h.*
C. 789. more *h.* than this thy present lot

**Happy.**—P. L. 1, 29. in that *h.* state
P. L. 1, 85. who in the *h.* realms of light
P. L. 1, 141. and *h.* state here swallowed up
P. L. 1, 249. farewell *h.* fields
P. L. 2, 224. present lot appears for *h.* though
P. L. 2, 347. another world the *h.* seat of some
P. L. 2, 410. ere he arrive the *h.* isle
P. L. 3, 66. in the *h.* garden placed
P. L. 3, 232. *h.* for man
P. L. 3, 417. their *h.* hours in joy and hymning
P. L. 3, 532. by which to visit oft those *h.* tribes
P. L. 3, 567. other worlds they seemed or *h.* isles
P. L. 3, 570. *h.* isles, but who dwelt *h.* there
P. L. 3, 632. to paradise the *h.* seat of man
P. L. 3, 679. created this new *h.* race of men
P. L. 4, 60. I had stood then *h.*
P. L. 4, 128. that could befall spirit of *h.* sort
P. L. 4, 247. thus was this place a *h.* rural seat
P. L. 4, 339. fair couple linked in *h.* nuptial
P. L. 4, 370. *h.,* but for so *h.* ill secured
P. L. 4, 519. is that their *h.* state
P. L. 4, 534. live while ye may yet *h.* pair
P. L. 4, 562. this *h.* place no evil thing approach
P. L. 4, 727. *h.* in our mutual help and mutual
P. L. 5, 74. here *h.* creature fair angelic Eve
P. L. 5, 75. *h.* though thou art, happier thou
P. L. 5, 143. of Paradise and Eden's *h.* plains
P. L. 5, 234. as may advise him of his *h.* state
P. L. 5, 364. those *h.* places thou hast deigned
P. L. 5, 504. what happiness this *h.* state
P. L. 5, 520. that thou art *h.* owe to God
P. L. 5, 536. our *h.* state hold as you yours
P. L. 5, 611. as one individual soul for ever *h.*
P. L. 5, 830. bent rather to exalt our *h.* state
P. L. 6, 226. not destroy their *h.* native seat
P. L. 7, 625. pleasant dwelling-place thrice *h.*
P. L. 7, 631. thrice *h.* if they know their
P. L. 8, 285. and first beheld this *h.* light
P. L. 8, 331. this *h.* state shalt lose expelled
P. L. 8, 512. all heaven and *h.* constellations
P. L. 8, 621. that thou knowest us *h.*
P. L. 8, 633. be strong, live *h.,* and love!
P. L. 9, 326. how are we *h.* still in fear of harm
P. L. 9, 337. let us not then suspect our *h.* state
P. L. 9, 347. aught that might his *h.* state
P. L. 9, 975. presented this *h.* trial of thy love
P. L. 9, 1138. we had then remained still *h.*
P. L. 10, 485. a paradise by our exile made *h.*
P. L. 10, 720. O miserable of *h.*! is this the end
P. L. 10, 874. but for thee I had persisted *h.*
P. L. 11, 270. these *h.* walks and shades
P. L. 11, 303. departure from this *h.* place
P. L. 11, 593. such *h.* interview and fair event
P. L. 11, 782. crowned with length of *h.* days
P. L. 12, 605. with meditation on the *h.* end
P. L. 12, 642. of paradise so late their *h.* seat
P. R. 1, 1. I who erewhile the *h.* garden sung
P. R. 1, 416. the *h.* place imparts to thee
P. R. 4, 362. what makes a nation *h.* and keeps
S. A. 354. such a son as all men hailed me *h.*
S. A. 1049. *h.* that house!
C. 592. shall in the *h.* trial prove most glory
C. 977. and those *h.* climes that lie
H. 1. this is the month and this the *h.* morn
H. 167. for from this *h.* day
Cir. 3. first heard by *h.* watchful shepherds' ear

**Happy-making.**—T. 18. to whose *h.-m.* sight

**Harald,** *see* **Herald, Heralds**

**Haran.**—P. L. 12, 131. now the ford to *H.*
**Harangues.**—P. L. 11, 663. *h.* are heard
**Harapha.**—S. A. 1068. the giant *H.* of Gath
S. A. 1079. I am of Gath men call me *H.*
**Harass.**—S. A. 257. prevent the *h.* of their land
**Harbinger.**—P. L. 9, 13. misery, death's *h.*
P. L. 11, 589. till the evening star, love's *h.*
P. R. 1, 71. to proclaim His coming is sent *h*
P. R. 1, 277. whose *h.* he was
S. A. 721. her *h.* a damsel train
H. 49. ready *h.,* with turtle wing the amorous
M. M. 1. now the bright morning star day's *h.*
**Harbour.**—P. L. 1, 185. if any rest can *h.*
P. L. 5, 99. in thee can *h.* none
P. L. 9, 288. how found they *h.* in thy breast
P. R. 3, 210. my *h.* and my ultimate repose
S. A. 459. suffers not mine eye to *h.* sleep
V. Ex. 88. to *h.* those that are at enmity
**Harboured.**—P. R. 1, 307. or *h.* in one cave
**Hard.**—P. L. 1, 417. lust *h.* by hate
P. L. 2, 256. preferring *h.* liberty before
P. L. 2, 433. long is the way and *h.,* that out
P. L. 2, 444. unknown dangers and as *h.* escape
P. L. 2, 1021. with difficulty and labour *h.*
P. L. 3, 21. and up to re-ascend though *h.*
P. L. 3, 200. *h.* be hardened. blind be blinded
P. L. 3, 575. by centre or eccentric *h.* to tell
P. L. 4, 45. nor was his service *h.*
P. L. 4, 432. then let us not think *h.* one easy
P. L. 4, 584. *h.* thou knowest it to exclude
P. L. 4, 932. what behoves from *h.* assays
P. L. 5, 564. sad task and *h.* for how shall
P. L. 6, 452. yet *h.* for gods and too unequal
P. L. 6, 495. counsel joined think nothing *h.*
P. L. 6, 622. of *h.* contents and full of force
P. L. 8, 251. to tell how human life began is *h.*
P. L. 10, 468. by my adventure *h.*
P. L. 10, 548. there stood a grove *h.* by
P. L. 10, 751. unable to perform thy terms too *h.*
P. L. 10, 992. if thou judge it *h.* and difficult
P. L. 11, 146. *h.* to believe may seem
P. R. 1, 264. through many a *h.* assay
P. R. 1, 343. that out of these *h.* stones be made
P. R. 1, 469. and urged me *h.* with doings
P. R. 1, 478. *h.* are the ways of Truth and rough
P. R. 3, 132. *h.* recompense unsuitable return
P. R. 4, 478. many a *h.* assay of dangers
S. A. 865. with *h.* contest
S. A. 1013. what it is, *h.* is to say, harder to hit ·
S. A. 1528. for to Israel's God nothing is *h.*
C. 531. tending my flocks *h.* by
C. 972. and sent them here through *h.* assays
L. 92. what *h.* mishap hath doomed this gentle
L'A. 81. *h.* by a cottage chimney smokes
S. 17, 6. to drift of hollow states *h.* to be spelled
S. 20, 5. what may be won from the *h.* season
P. 14. labours huge and *h.,* too *h.* for human
**Hard-besetting.**—C. 857. in *h.-b.* need
**Hardened.**—P. L. 3, 200. but hard be *h.*
P. L. 6, 791. they *h.* more by what might
P. L. 12, 194. as ice more *h.* after thaw
**Hardening.**—P. L. 1, 572. *h.* in his strength
**Harder.**—P. L. 2, 1016. *h.* beset and more
S. A. 1014. what it is hard is to say, *h.* to hit
S. 11, 8. why is it *h.,* sirs, than Gordon
**Hardest.**—P. R. 2, 168. magnetic *h.* iron draws
**Hardihood.**—C. 650. with dauntless *h.*
**Hardly.**—P. L. 9, 304. though bold will *h.* dare
P. R. 1, 279. much his greater and was *h.* won
**Hardship.**—P. R. 1, 341. misery and *h.* born
**Hardy.**—S. A. 1274. *h.* and industrious to support
P. L. 4, 920. thou than they less *h.* to endure
P. L. 2, 425. so *h.* as to proffer or accept alone
**Harlot.**—P. L. 9, 1060. from the *h.* lap
P. R. 4, 344. laid as varnish on a *h.'s* cheek
**Harlots.**—P. L. 4, 766. bought smile of *h.*
**Harm.**—P. L. 4, 791. perhaps asleep secure of *h.*
P. L. 4, 843. place inviolable and these from *h.*
P. L. 4, 901. but that implies not violence or *h.*
P. L. 6, 656. their armour helped their *h.*
P. L. 7, 150. lest his heart exalt him in the *h.*

P. L. 9, 251. other doubt possesses me lest *h.*
P. L. 9, 326. how are we happy still in fear of *h.*
P. L. 9, 327. but *h.* precedes not sin
P. L. 9, 350. against his will he can receive no *h.*
P. L. 9, 1152. should mean me ill or seek to *h.*
P. L. 10, 1055. what *h?* idleness had been worse
P. R. 2, 257. from the sting of famine fear no *h.*
P. R. 4, 486. other *h.* those terrors which thou
S. A.486.thee who now no more canst do them *h*
S. A. 1187. at Ascalon, who never did thee *h.*
C. 591. even that which mischief meant most *h.*
Il P. 84. to bless the doors from nightly *h.*

**Harmed.**—P. R. 1, 311. nor waking *h.*
P. R. 1, 407. thou art not to be *h.*

**Harmless.**—P. L. 4, 388. your *h.* innocence
P. R. 4, 458. as inconsiderable and *h.* if not
C. 166. I shall appear some *h.* villager

**Harmonic.**—P. L. 3, 687. in full *h.* number

**Harmonies.**—P. L. 7, 560. tuned angelic *h.*
C. 243. give resounding grace to all heaven's *h.*

**Harmonious.**—P. L. 3, 38. move *h.* numbers
P. L. 7, 206. her ever-during gates *h.* sound
P. L. 8, 606. more grateful than *h.* sound
P. R. 2, 362. all the while *h.* airs were heard
S. M. 2. sphere-born *h.* sisters voice and verse

**Harmony.**—P. L. 2, 552. *h.*... suspended Hell
P. L. 5, 625. and in their motions *h.* divine
P. L. 6, 65. to the sound of instrumental *h.*
P. L. 8, 384. what *h.* or true delight
P. L. 8, 605. *h.* to behold in wedded pair
P. L. 10, 358. my heart which by a secret *h.*
P. R. 4, 255. hear and learn the secret power of *h.*
A. 63. then listen I to the celestial Sirens' *h.*
L'A. 144. chains that tie the hidden soul of *h.*
H. 107. she knew such *h.* alone
H. 131. and with your ninefold *h.*
V. Ex. 51. are held with his melodious *h.*

**Harms.**—A. 51. and heal the *h.* of thwarting
S. 8, 4. them and him within protect from *h.*

**Harnessed.**—P. L. 7, 202. *h.* at hand

**Harp.**—P. L. 2, 548. notes angelical to many a *h.*
P. L. 3, 414. and never shall my *h.* thy praise
P. L. 5, 151. tuneable than needed lute or *h.*
P. L. 7, 37. clamour drowned both *h.* and voice
P. L. 7, 594. the *h.* had work and rested not
P. L. 11. 560. chime was heard of *h.* and organ
P. L. 11, 583. to the *h.* they sung soft amorous
P. 9. and set my *h.* to notes of saddest woe

**Harpies.**—P. R. 2, 403. with sound of *h.*
C.605. *h.* and hydras or all the monstrous forms

**Harping.**—H. 115. *h.* in loud and solemn choir

**Harps.**—P. L. 3, 365. their golden *h.* they took
P. L. 7, 258. and touched their golden *h.*
P. L. 7, 450. arose with evening *h.* and matin
P. L. 7, 559. symphonious of ten thousand *h.*
P. R. 4, 336. Hebrew songs and *h.* in Babylon
S. M.13. touch their immortal *h.* of golden wires

**Harpy-footed.**—P. L. 2, 596. *h-f.* Furies

**Harrowed.**—C. 565. *h.* with grief and fear

**Harry.**—S. 13, 1. *H.* whose tuneful

**Harsh.**—P. L. 2, 882. hinges grate *h.* thunder
P. L. 9, 987. flat seems to this and *h.*
S. A. 662. a tune *h.* and of dissonant mood
S. A.1461. much averse I found and wondrous *h.*
C. 477. not *h.* and crabbed as dull fools suppose
L. 3. I come to pluck your berries *h.* and crude
S. M. 20. and with *h.* din broke the fair music

**Harshly.**—P. L. 11, 537. gathered not *h.*
C. 683. and *h.* deal, like an ill borrower

**Hart.**—P. L. 11, 189. *h.* and hind

**Harvest.**—P. L. 4, 981. of Ceres ripe for *h.*
P. L. 9, 842. as reapers oft are wont their *h.*
P. L. 11, 899. seed-time and *h.*
S. A. 1024. had shorn the fatal *h.* of thy head

**Haste.**—P. L. 1, 357. leaders thither *h.*
P. L. 2, 838. I *h.* to know and this once known
P. L. 3, 500. light turned thither-ward in *h.*
P. L. 4, 560. he thus began in *h.*
P. L. 5, 136. and to the field they *h.*
P. L. 5, 211. morning's rural work they *h.*
P. L. 5, 308. *h.* hither Eve and worth thy sight

P. L. 5, 326. but I will *h.* and from each
P. L. 5, 337. with despatchful looks in *h.*
P. L. 5, 686. I am to *h.* and all who under me
P. L. 5, 777. for whom all this *h.* of midnight
P. L. 7, 105. and the moon *h.* to thy audience
P. L. 7, 294. for *h.*
P. L. 8, 519. and bid *h.* the evening star
P. L. 10, 17. in *h.* the angelic guards ascended
P. L. 10, 29. made *h.* to make appear
P. L. 10, 456. forth rushed in *h.* the great
P. L. 11, 104. *h.* thee and from the Paradise
P. L. 11, 449. and thus in *h.* to the angel cried
P. L. 12, 366. they gladly thither *h.*
P. R. 3, 223. to the worst that can be *h.*
P. R. 3, 303. to her aid he marches now in *h.*
P. R. 3, 437. their native land with joy they *h.*
S. A. 1027. that inward gifts were left for *h.*
S. A.1441. Manoah in such *h* with youthful steps
S. A. 1678. to call in *h.* for their destroyer
C. 568. down the lawns I ran with headlong *h.*
C. 920. and I must *h.* ere morning hour
C. 956. come let us *h.* the stars grow high
A. 58. *h.* I all about number my ranks
L'A. 25. *h.* thee Nymph and bring with thee
L'A. 87. then in *h.* her bower she leaves
H. 23. the star-led wizards *h.* with odours sweet
H. 212. Isis, and Orus, and the dog Anubis *h.*
V. Ex.17. *h.* thee straight to dome once a pleasure

**Hasted.**—P. L. 3, 714. to several quarters *h.*
P. L. 6, 254. destruction to withstand he *h.*
P. L. 7, 291. they *h.* with glad precipitance
P. L. 9, 853. to him she *h.* in her face excuse
P. L. 11, 81. the Sons of Light *h.*

**Hasten.**—P. L. 3, 329. general doom shall *h.*
P. L. 5, 846. but *h.* to appease the incensed
P. L. 10, 857. justice divine not *h.* to be just
S. A. 576. *h.* the welcome end of all my pains

**Hastened.**—P. L. 1, 675. a numerous brigad *h.*
S. A. 958. cherish thy *h.* widowhood
U. C. II. 14. too long vacation *h.* on his term

**Hastening.**—P. L. 12, 637. *h.* angel caught
M. W. 46. sad morn had let fall on her *h.* funeral

**Hasting.**—P. L. 4, 353. sun declined was *h.*
P. L. 4, 867. tread of nimble feet *h.* this way
P. L. 6, 85. the banded powers of Satan *h.* on
P. R. 4, 64. to their provinces *h.*
S. 2, 3. my *h.* days fly on with full career

**Hasty.**—P. L. 1, 730. the *h.* multitude

**Hatch.**—P. L. 7, 418. brood as numerous *h.*

**Hatching.**—P. L. 2, 378. in darkness here *h.*

**Hate.**—P. L. 1, 58. obdurate pride and steadfast *h.*
P. L. 1, 107. immortal *h.* and courage never to
P. L. 1, 417. lust hard by *h.* till good Josiah
P. L. 2, 120. not behind in *h.* if what was urged
P. L. 2, 249. in worship paid to whom we *h.*
P. L. 2, 336. but to our power hostility and *h.*
P. L. 2, 577. abhorred Styx the flood of deadly *h.*
P. L. 3, 298. love shall outdo hellish *h.*
P. L. 3, 300. dearly to redeem what hellish *h*
P. L. 4, 37. to tell thee how I *h.* thy beams
P. L. 4, 69. his love accursed since love or *h.*
P. L. 4, 909. where wounds of deadly *h.* have
P. L. 5, 738. of glory whom their *h.* illustrates
P. L. 6, 559. that all may see who *h.* us
P. L. 6, 734. whom thou hatest I *h.*
P. L. 7, 54. so unimaginable as *h.* in heaven
P. L. 9, 466. of guile, of *h.,* of envy, of revenge
P. L. 9, 471. then soon fierce *h.* he re-collects
P. L. 9, 475. what hither brought us, *h.* not love
P. L. 9, 491. by stronger *h., h.* stronger under
P. L. 9, 1123. anger, *h.,* mistrust, suspicion
P. L. 10, 114. anger, and obstinacy, and *h.*
P. L. 10, 906. a fell adversary his *h.* or shame
P. L. 11, 553. nor love thy life nor *h.*
P. L. 11, 601. those were of *h.* and death
P. R. 4, 386. sorrows and labours opposition *h.*
S. A. 400. was worse than undissembled *h.*
S. A. 790. if love which thou interpret'st *h.*
S. A. 839. the way to raise in me inexpiable *h.*
S. A. 939. thou alone could *h.* me thy husband
S. A. 966. reap nothing but repulse and *h.*

S. A. 1266. because their end is *h*. not help to me
C. 760. I *h*. when Vice can bolt her arguments
S. 1, 9. now timely sing ere the rude bird of *h*.
**Hated.**—P. L. 11, 702. and therefore *h*.
P. L. 12, 411. for this he shall live *h*.
P. R. 1, 47. remember Hell our *h*. habitation
P. R. 4, 97. and yet of him suspicious *h*.
S. 11, 13. *h*. not learning worse than toad or asp
D. F. I. 51. once before forsook the *h*. earth
**Hateful.**—P. L. 1, 626. this dire change *h*.
P. L. 2, 859. to sit in *h*. office here confined
P. L. 4, 505. sight *h*. sight tormenting
P. L. 6, 264. these acts of *h*. strife *h*. to all
P. L. 10, 121. as from the *h*. siege of contraries
P. L. 10, 869. leagued thyself as false and *h*.
C. 92. but I hear the tread of *h*. steps
**Hatefullest.**—P. L. 10, 569. *h*. disrelish
**Hates.**—P. L. 2, 857. his commands above who *h*.
**Hatest.**—P. L. 6, 734. whom thou *h*. I hate
**Hating.**—P. R. 4, 97. hated of all and *h*.
**Hatred.**—P. L. 1, 308. with perfidious *h*.
P. L. 2, 500. yet live in *h*., enmity, and strife
P. L. 10, 928. on me exercise not thy *h*.
S. A. 772. the easier towards me or thy *h*. less
**Have.**—P. L. 4, 485. to *h*. thee by my side
P. L. 10, 501. *h*. the account of my performance
P. L. 10, 1004. and *h*. the power of many ways
P. L. 10, 1030. I *h*. in view calling to mind
P. L. 11, 99. this my behest *h*. thou in charge
P. L. 12, 558. and *h*. my fill of knowledge
P. R. 2, 226. with such as *h*. more show
P. R. 2, 318. I as thou seest *h*. none
P. R. 2, 393. that I *h*. also power to give
P. R. 3, 298. to *h*. a view of his great power
**Haven.**—P. R. 3, 321. to Balsara's *h*.
**Haughty.**—P. L. 4, 858. went *h*. on
P. L. 5, 852. and more *h*. thus replied
P. L. 6, 109. Satan with vast and *h*. strides
P. L. 9, 484. of courage *h*., and of limb heroic
S. A. 1069. his look *h*. as is his pile high-built
C. 33. an old and *h*. nation proud in arms
**Haunt.**—P. L. 3, 27. where the Muses *h*.
P. L. 4, 184. drives to seek new *h*. for prey
P. L. 7, 330. and love to *h*. her sacred shades
P. L. 11, 271. happy walks and shades fit *h*.
P. L. 11, 835. the *h*. of seals and orcs
P. R. 2, 296. *h*. of wood-gods and wood-nymphs
C. 388. far from the cheerful *h*. of men and herds
Il P. 138. or fright them from their hallowed *h*.
**Haunted.**—P. L. 4, 708. nor Faunus *h*.
L'A. 130. on summer eves by *h*. stream
H. 184. from *h*. spring and dale
**Haunts.**—P. R. 2, 191. these *h*. delight
C. 536. in their obscured *h*. of inmost bowers
**Havoc.**—P. L. 2, 1009. *h*. and spoil...are my gain
P. L. 6, 449. his riven arms to *h*. hewn
P. L. 9, 30. with long and tedious *h*.
P. L. 10, 617. to waste and *h*. yonder world
**Hawthorn.**—L'A. 68. under the *h*. in the dale
**Haycock.**—L'A. 90. to the tanned *h* in the mead
**Hazard.**—P. L. 1, 89. equal hope and *h*.
P. L. 2, 453. as great a share of *h*. as of honour
P. L. 2, 455. and so much to him due of *h*.
P. L. 2, 473. he through *h*. huge must earn
P. L. 4, 933. not to *h*. all through ways
P. L. 5, 729. let us advise and to this *h*. draw
P. L. 10, 491. without our *h*. labour or alarm
P. R. 1, 95. on the utmost edge of *h*.
S. A. 1241. to the *h*. of thy brains
**Hazardous.**—P. R. 3, 228. enterprise so *h*.
**Hazel.**—L. 42. the willows and the *h*. copses
**Head.**—P. L. 1, 193. with *h*. uplifted above
P. L. 1, 211. had risen or heaved his *h*.
P. L. 1, 459. *h*. and hands lopped off
P. L. 2, 672. what seemed his *h*. the likeness
P. L. 2, 711. each at the *h*. levelled his deadly
P. L. 2, 730. mortal dart against thy father's *h*.
P. L. 2, 754. thy *h*. flames thick and fast
P. L. 2, 758. a goddess armed out of thy *h*.
P. L. 2, 949. with *h*., hands, wings, or feet
P. L. 3, 86. upon his own rebellious *h*.

P. L. 3, 220. upon his own *h*. draw the deadly
P. L. 3, 286. be thou in Adam's room the *h*.
P. L. 3, 319. under thee, as *h*. supreme
P. L. 3, 626. a golden tiar circled his *h*.
P. L. 4, 134. champaign *h*. of a steep wilderness
P. L. 4, 283. by Nilus' *h*., enclosed with shining
P. L. 4, 443. my guide and *h*.
P. L. 4, 826. at the *h*. of these that sleep
P. L. 4, 953. army of fiends, fit body to fit *h*.
P. L. 5, 606. your *h*. I him appoint
P. L. 5, 830. under one *h*. more near united
P. L. 5, 842. since he the *h*. one of our
P. L. 5, 893. expect to feel his thunder on thy *h*.
P. L. 6, 212. over *h*. the dismal hiss of fiery
P. L. 6, 346. frail man in entrails heart or *h*.
P. L. 6, 350. all heart they live, all *h*., all eye
P. L. 6, 556. suddenly at *h*. appeared Satan
P. L. 2, 992. made *h*. against Heaven's King
P. L. 6, 625. need from *h*. to foot well understand
P. L. 6, 779. under their *h*. embodied all in one
P. L. 7, 470. stag...bore up his branching *h*.
P. L. 8, 292. suddenly stood at my *h*. a dream
P. L. 8, 574. she will acknowledge thee her *h*.
P. L. 9, 184. his *h*. the midst well stored
P. L. 9, 189. and his brutal sense in heart or *h*.
P. L. 9, 428. whose *h*. though gay carnation
P. L. 9, 499. his *h*. crested aloft and carbuncle
P. L. 9, 1155. why didst not thou the *h*. command
P. L. 10, 133. on my *h*. both sin and punishment
P. L. 10, 181. her seed shall bruise thy *h*.
P. L. 10, 449. fulgent *h*. and shape star-bright
P. L. 10, 499. his seed...shall bruise my *h*.
P. L. 10, 523. complicated monsters *h*. and tail
P. L. 10, 732. multiply but curses on my *h*.
P. L. 10, 735. will curse my *h*.
P. L. 10, 815. revolution on my defenceless *h*.
P. L. 10, 934. the sentence from thy *h*. removed
P. L. 10, 955. on my *h*. all might be visited
P. L. 10, 1032. Seed shall bruise the Serpent's *h*.
P. L. 10, 1035. to crush his *h*. would be revenge
P. L. 11, 534. many years over thy *h*. return
P. L. 11, 864. over his *h*. beholds a dewy cloud
P. L. 12, 150. who shall bruise the Serpent's *h*.
P. L. 12, 388. or the local wounds of *h*. or heel
P. L. 12, 430. shall bruise the *h*. of Satan
P. L. 12, 432. and fix far deeper in his *h*.
P. R. 1, 55. by the seed of Eve upon my *h*.
P. R. 1, 60. by the *h*. broken be not intended
P. R. 1, 82. thence on his *h*. a perfect dove
P. R. 1, 98. ere in the *h*. of nations he appear
P. R. 1, 267. must be transferred upon my *h*.
P. R. 2, 64. motherly cares and fears got *h*.
P. R. 4, 48. above the rest lifting his stately *h*.
P. R. 4, 406. damps of night his sheltered *h*.
P. R. 4, 407. for at his *h*. the Tempter watched
S. A. 119. with languished *h*. unpropped
S. A. 192. but in adverse withdraw their *h*.
S. A. 197. could I once look up, or heave the *h*.
S. A. 535. my *h*. and hallowed pledge of all my
S. A. 609. in heart, *h*., breast and reins
S. A. 727. with *h*. declined like a fair flower
S. A. 1024. shorn the fatal harvest of thy *h*.
S. A. 1125. shall not withhold me from thy *h*.
S. A. 1636. with *h*. awhile inclined
S. A. 1639. with *h*. erect thus cried aloud
C. 108. Advice with scrupulous *h*.
C. 355. leans her unpillowed *h*. fraught with
C. 744. on the stalk with languished *h*.
C. 799. shattered into heaps o'er thy false *h*.
C. 836. piteous of her woes reared her lank *h*.
C. 885. rise, rise and heave thy rosy *h*.
C. 898. o'er the cowslip's velvet *h*. that bends
C. 934. may thy lofty *h*. be crowned
L. 51. closed o'er the *h*. of your loved Lycidas
L. 102. that sunk so low that sacred *h*. of thine
L. 147. cowslips wan that hang the pensive *h*.
L. 169. and yet anon repairs his drooping *h*.
L'A. 145. that Orpheus' self may heave his *h*.
Il P. 71. and oft as if her *h*. she bowed
H. 80. and hid his *h*. for shame
P. 15. sovereign Priest stooping his regal *h*.

**M.** W. 41. but the fair blossom hangs the *h.*
D. F. I. 49. to hide thy nectared *h.*
V. Ex. 64. all their blessings on thy sleeping *h.*
**Headlong.**—P. L. 1, 45. hurled *h.* flaming
P. L. 1, 750. was *h.* sent with his industrious
P. L. 2, 374. hurled *h.* to partake with us
P. L. 2, 772. driven *h.* from the pitch of heaven
P. L. 6, 864. *h.* themselves they threw down
P. R. 3, 430. unreformed *h.* would follow
P. R. 4, 575. for grief and spite cast herself *h.*
C. 568. down the lawns I ran with *h.* haste
C. 887. and bridle in thy *h.* wave
P. 5. but *h.* joy is ever on the wing
**Heads.**—P. L. 1, 357. the *h.* and leaders thither
P. L. 1, 435. for which their *h.* as low bowed
P. L. 2, 178. fall one day upon our *h.*
P. L. 4, 35. all the stars hide their diminished *h.*
P. L. 4, 699. reared high their flourished *h.*
P. L. 6, 653. and on their *h.* main promontories
P. L. 6, 757. over their *h,* a crystal firmament
P. L. 6, 840. shields and helms and helmed *h.*
P. L. 10, 1040. shall double ours upon our *h.*
P. R. 4, 463. over whose *h.* they roar
S. A. 242. on Israel's governors and *h.* of tribes
S. A. 552. whose *h.* that turbulent liquor fills
S. A. 677. *h.* without name no more remembered
S. A. 1589. their *h.* and on his own he pulled
S. A. 1652. upon the *h.* of all who sat beneath
S. A. 1696. cloudless thunder bolted on their *h.*
S. 15, 7. new rebellions raise their hydra *h.*
**Headstrong**—P. R. 2, 470. *h.* multitudes
**Heal.**—P. L. 2, 401. to *h.* the scar of these
A. 51. and *h.* the harms of thwarting thunder
**Healed.**—P. L. 6, 344. yet soon he *h.*
P. L. 6, 436. by native vigour *h.*
P. L. 8, 468. suddenly with flesh filled up and *h.*
**Healing.**—P. L. 9, 290. whom with *h.* wounds
S. A. 605. *h.* words from these thy friends
C. 621. in every virtuous plant and *h.* herb
**Heals.**—C. 847. she with precious vialed liquors *h.*
**Health.**—S. A. 554. drinks our chief support of *h.*
**Healthful.**—P. L. 11, 523. Nature's *h.* rules
**Heap.**—P. L. 1, 215. he might *h.* on himself
P. L. 2, 590. on firm land thaws not but gathers *h.*
P. L. 3, 709. world's material mould came to a *h.*
P. L. 4, 815. lights on a *h.* of nitrous powder
P. L. 6, 389. and on a *h.* chariot and charioteer
P. R. 2, 427. first get wealth and treasure *h.*
S. A. 276. to *h.* ingratitude on worthiest deeds
**Heaped.**—P. L. 3, 83. nor all the chains *h.* on
P. L. 5, 391. have *h.* this table raised of grassy
P. L. 6, 668. confusion *h.* upon confusion rose
P. L. 12, 338. and other faults *h.* to the popular
L'A. 147. on a bed of *h.* Elysian flowers
**Heaps.**—P. L. 5, 344. and on the board *h.*
P. L. 5, 558. but on they rolled in *h.*
S. A. 1530. over *h.* of slaughtered walk his way
C. 398. may as well spread out the unsunned *h.*
C. 771. now *h.* upon some few with vast excess
C. 799. were shattered into *h.* o'er thy false head
**Hear.**—P. L. 1, 274. if once they *h.* that voice
P. L. 2, 65. he shall *h.* infernal thunder
P. L. 2, 846. to *h.* his famine should be filled
P. L. 3, 185. the rest shall *h.* me call and oft
P. L. 3, 195. whom if they will *h.* light after
P. L. 3, 701. contented with report *h.* only
P. L. 4, 410. turned him all ear to *h.* new
P. L. 4, 866. O friends I *h.* the tread of nimble
P. L. 5, 411. whereby they *h.,* see, smell, touch
P. L. 5, 555. more desire to *h.* if thou consent
P. L. 5, 600. *h.* all ye angels progeny of light
P. L. 5, 602. *h.* my decree which unrevoked
P. L. 5, 810. no ear ever to *h.* in heaven expected
P. L. 6, 567. and loud that all may *h.*
P. L. 7, 52. to *h.* of things so high and strange
P. L. 7, 101. and longer will delay to *h.* thee tell
P. L. 8, 3. still stood fixed to *h.*
P. L. 8, 204. now *h.* me relate my story
P. L. 8, 208. inviting thee to *h.* while I relate
P. L. 9, 213. *h.* what to my mind first thoughts
P. L. 9, 281. I expected not to *h.*

P. L. 9, 862. strange the cause and wonderful to *h.*
P. L. 9, 966. gladly of our union *h.* thee speak
P. L. 10, 27. ethereal people ran to *h.* and know
P. L. 10, 731. now death to *h.* for what can I
P. L. 11, 31. *h.* his sighs though mute
P. L. 11, 359. good with bad expect to *h.*
P. L. 12, 61. to see the hubbub strange and *h.*
P. L. 12, 367. squadroned Angels *h.* his carol
P. R. 1, 198. and *h.* what from without comes
P. R. 1, 211. to *h.* the teachers of our Law
P. R. 1, 333. aught we *h.* and curious are to *h.*
P. R. 1, 385. to *h.* attent thy wisdom
P. R. 1, 481. what wonder then if I delight to *h.*
P. R. 1, 484. to *h.* thee when I come
P. R. 2, 83. as I *h.* by John the Baptist
P. R. 3, 349. *h.* and mark to what end I have
P. R. 4, 123. tedious waste of time to sit and *h.*
P. R. 4, 254. there thou shalt *h.* and learn
P. R. 4, 500. *h.* O Son of David, virgin-born
S. A. 110. I *h.* the tread of many feet
S. A. 176. I *h.* the sound of words
S. A. 766. *h.* me Samson not that I endeavour
S. A. 845. *h.* what assaults I had
S. A. 1232. ears unused *h.* these dishonours
S. A. 1423. to *h.* nothing dishonourable
S. A. 1456. say reverend sire; we thirst to *h.*
S. A. 1553. yet what it was we *h.* not
C. 91. but I *h.* the tread of hateful steps
C. 343. might we but *h.* the folded flocks
C. 458. of things that no gross ear can *h.*
C. 480. list I *h.* some far-off halloa break
C. 495. huddling brook to *h.* his madrigal
C. 792. thou art not fit to *h.* thyself convinced
A. 72. the heavenly tune which none can *h.*
L. 36. and old Damætas loved to *h.* our song
L'A. 41. to *h.* the lark begin his flight
L'A. 147. *h.* such strains as would have won
Il P. 64. I woo to *h.* thy evensong
Il P. 74. I *h.* the far-off curfew sound
S. 20, 10. whence we may rise to *h.* the lute
D. F. I. 37. that thou these plaints dost *h.*
V. Ex. 68. once it was my dismal hap to *h.*
**Heard.**—P. L. 1, 275. *h.* so oft in worst extremes
P. L. 1, 331. they *h.* and were abashed
P. L. 2, 290. such applause was *h.* as Mammon
P. L. 2, 477. as the sound of thunder *h.*
P. L. 2, 519. the hollow Abyss *h.* far and wide
P. L. 2, 580. lamentation loud *h.* on the rueful
P. L. 2, 993. I saw and *h.* for such a numerous
P. L. 3, 710. confusion *h.* his voice
P. L. 4, 2. *h.* cry in Heaven aloud
P. L. 4, 681. have we *h.* celestial voices
P. L. 5, 546. Divine instructor I have *h.*
P. L. 5, 557. worthy of sacred silence to be *h.*
P. L. 5, 659. his former name is *h.* no more
P. L. 6, 28. voice ... thus mild was *h.*
P. L. 6, 208. such as *h.* in Heaven till now
P. L. 6, 557. and thus was *h.* commanding loud
P. L. 6, 618. if our proposals once again were *h.*
P. L. 6, 769. twenty thousand I their number *h.*
P. L. 6, 782. they *h.* his voice and went
P. L. 6, 867. hell *h.* the insufferable noise
P. L. 6, 909. let it profit thee to have *h.*
P. L. 7, 51. the step *h.* attentive and marvelling
P. L. 7, 68. whose liquid murmur *h.* new thirst
P. L. 7, 181. *h.* declared the Almighty's will
P. L. 7, 221. for Chaos *h.* his voice
P. L. 7, 296. for of armies thou hast *h.*
P. L. 8, 10. now *h.* with wonder
P. L. 8, 203. thee I have *h.* relating what was
P. L. 8, 205. which perhaps thou hast not *h.*
P. L. 8, 242. ere our approaching *h.* within noise
P. L. 8, 452. he ended or I *h.* no more
P. L. 8, 500. she *h.* me thus
P. L. 9, 518. she busied, *h.* the sound of rustling
P. L. 9, 888. soon as he *h.* the fatal trespass
P. L. 9, 1128. and the Will *h.* not
P. L. 10, 23. displeased all were who *h.*
P. L. 10, 97. the voice of God they *h.* now
P. L. 10, 99. they *h.* and from his presence hid
P. L. 10, 116. I *h.* thee in the garden

P. L. 10, 119. my voice thou oft hast *h.*
P. L. 10, 163. which when the Lord God *h.*
P. L. 10, 729. O voice once *h.* delightfully
P. L. 10, 954. speed before thee and be louder *h.*
P. L. 10, 1047. he both *h.* and judged
P. L. 11, 74. his trumpet *h.* in Oreb since
P. L. 11. 153. I was *h.* with favour
P. L. 11, 252. sufficient that thy prayers are *h.*
P. L. 11, 266. Eve who unseen yet all had *h.*
P. L. 11, 322. among these pines his voice I *h.*
P. L. 11, 560. melodious chime was *h.*
P. L. 11, 663. and harangues are *h.*
P. L. 12, 103. the shame done to his father *h.*
P. L. 12, 529. faith and conscience can be *h.*
P. L. 12, 598. thee partake what thou hast *h.*
P. L. 12, 624. and Adam *h.* well pleased
P. R. 1, 33. that *h.* the Adversary who roving
P. R. 1, 84. out of Heaven the sovran voice I *h.*
P. R. 1, 259. this having *h.* straight I again
P. R. 1, 270. of whose birth I oft had *h.* not
P. R. 1,284. audibly *h.* from Heaven pronounced
P. R. 1, 330. I saw and *h.*, for we sometimes
P. R. 2, 33. have *h.* his words his wisdom full
P. R. 2, 107. first her salutation *h.*
P. R. 2, 182. have we not seen or by relation *h.*
P. R. 2, 235. he ceased and *h.* their grant
P. R. 2, 362. while harmonious airs were *h.*
P. R. 2, 403. of harpies' wings and talons *h.*
P. R. 4, 116. I have also *h.* perhaps have read
P. R. 4, 452. I *h.* the wrack as earth and sky
P. R. 4, 502. of the Messiah I have *h.* foretold
P. R. 4, 513. by voice from Heaven *h.* thee
S. A. 215. to say I oft have *h.* men wonder
S. A. 406. might I be *h.* no long petition
S. A. 1082. I have *h.* of thy prodigious might
S. A. 1449. I *h.* all as I came
S. A. 1515. indeed methought I *h.* the noise
S. A. 1524. could else a general cry be *h.*
S. A. 1631. for so from such as nearer stood we *h.*
C. 44. what never yet was *h.* in tale or song
C.227. such noise as I can make to be *h.* farthest
C. 252. I have oft *h.* my mother Circe
C. 264. I never *h.* it till now. I'll speak to her
C. 533. he and his monstrous rout are *h.* to howl
L. 27. we drove afield and both together *h.*
L. 87. that strain I *h.* was of a higher mood
Il P. 137. was never *h.* the Nymphs to daunt
S. 1, 6. first *h.* before the shallow cuckoo's bill
H. 54. was *h.* the world around
H. 101. nature that *h.* such sound beneath
H. 183. a voice of weeping *h.* and loud lament
Cir. 3. first *h.* by happy watchful shepherds' ear
V. Ex. 65. she *h.* them give thee this that thou
**Heard'st.**—P. L. 7, 561. remember'st for thou *h.*
**Hearers.**—U. C. II. 19. cross doctors all stood *h.*
**Hearing.**—P. L. 7, 118. be withheld thy *h.*
**Hearken.**—P. L. 3, 93. for Man will *h.* to his
P. R. 2, 428. not difficult if thou *h.* to me
C. 169. and *h.* if I may her business hear
C. 625. would sit and *h.* even to ecstasy
**Hearkened.**—P. L. 9, 1134. *h.* to my words
P. L. 10, 198. because thou hast *h.* to the voice
**Hears.**—P. L. 7, 100. thy potent voice he *h.*
P. L. 10, 506. *h.* on all sides from innumerable
L. 176, *h.* the unexpressive nuptial song
Il P. 47. and *h.* the Muses in a ring
**Hear'st**—P. L. 3, 7. *h.* thou rather
P. L. 5, 224. thou *h.* what stir on earth
**Heart.**—P. L. 1, 18. the upright *h.* and pure
P. L. 1, 151. in the *h.* of Hell to work in fire
P. L. 1, 400. the wisest *h.* of Solomon he led
P. L. 1, 444. whose *h.* though large
P. L. 1, 571. now his *h.* distends with pride
P. L. 1, 788. with joy and fear his *h.* rebounds
P. L. 4, 154. to the *h.* inspires vernal delight
P. L. 4, 484. of my side to thee nearest my *h.*
P. L. 4, 861. awe from above had quelled his *h.*
P. L. 6, 113. and thus his own undaunted *h.*
P. L. 6, 346. not as frail man in entrails *h.*
P. L. 6, 350. all *h.* they live, all head, all eye
P. L. 7, 60. the doubts that in his *h.*

P. L. 7, 114. *h.* of man suffice to comprehend
P. L. 7, 150. lest his *h.* exalt him in the harm
P. L. 7, 486. in small room large *h.* enclosed
P. L. 7, 513. thither with *h.* and voice and eyes
P. L. 8, 266. with fragrance and with joy my *h.*
P. L. 8, 322. freely with glad *h.* fear here no
P. L. 8, 451. thy wish exactly to thy *h.'s* desire
P. L. 8, 475. sweetness into my *h.* unfelt before
P. L. 8, 499. they shall be one flesh, one *h.*
P. L. 8, 590. love refines the thoughts and *h.*
P. L. 9, 189. his brutal sense in *h.* or head
P. L. 9, 550. into the *h.* of Eve his words made
P. L. 9, 734. into her *h.* too easy entrance won
P. L. 9, 845. yet oft his *h.* divine of something
P. L. 9, 876. ampler *h.* and growing up to
P. L. 9, 913. of thee would never from my *h.*
P. L. 9, 955. so forcible within my *h.* I feel
P. L. 9, 967. one *h.* one soul in both
P. L. 10, 6. or deceive his *h.* omniscient
P. L. 10, 357. for I no sooner in my *h.* divined
P. L. 10, 358. my *h.* which by a secret harmony
P. L. 10, 915. sincere and reverence in my *h.*
P. L. 10, 940. soon his *h.* relented towards her
P. L. 10, 966. to whom thus Eve recovering *h.*
P. L. 10, 973. the sole contentment of my *h.*
P. L. 10, 1061. and his *h.* to pity incline
P. L. 11, 27. sown with contrition in his *h.*
P. L. 11, 92. his *h.* I know how variable
P. L. 11, 150. before him humbled all my *h.*
P. L. 11, 288. not set thy *h.* thus over-fond
P. L. 11, 448. Adam in his *h.* dismayed
P. L. 11, 494. what *h.* of rock could long
P. L. 11, 595. symphonies attached the *h.*
P. L. 11, 868. the *h.* of Adam erst so sad
P. L. 11, 887. grieved at his *h.* when looking
P. L. 12, 25. of proud ambitious *h.*
P. L. 12, 193. and oft humbles his stubborn *h.*
P. L. 12, 274. and my *h.* much eased
P. L. 12, 524. the Spirit within shall on the *h.*
P. L. 12, 613. with sorrow and *h's.* distress
P. R. 1, 216. victorious deeds flamed in my *h.*
P. R. 2, 103. my *h.* hath been a storehouse
P. R. 2, 169. when nothing else beguiled the *h.*
P. R. 2, 410. all thy *h.* is set on high designs
P. R. 3, 10. thy words to thy large *h.* give
P. R. 3, 10. thy *h.* contains of good, wise, just
S. A. 298. was there school but the *h.* of the fool
S. A. 407. I yielded and unlocked her all my *h.*
S. A. 545. that cheers the *h.* of gods and men
S. A. 609. in *h.* head, breast, and reins
S. A. 1368. where the *h.* joins not outward acts
S.1,3.thou with fresh hope the lover's *h.* dost fill
S. 22, 8. nor bate a jot of *h.* or hope
Cir. 28. will pierce more near his *h.*
W. S. 10. easy numbers flow and that each *h.*
**Heart-easing.**—L'A. 13. and by men *h.-e.*
**Heartened.**—S. A. 1317. where I will see thee *h.*
**Heart-grief.**—S. A. 1339. of sorrow and *h.-g.*
**Hearth.**—S. A. 566. sit idle on the household *h.*
Il P. 82. save the cricket on the *h.*
H. 190. on the holy *h.* the Lars and Lemures
V. Ex. 40. her gay ladies danced upon the *h.*
**Hearts.**—P. L. 3, 189. and soften stony *h.*
P. L. 5, 448. in those *h.* love unlibidinous
P. L. 5, 532. for how can *h.* not free be tried
P. L. 10, 1091. frequenting sent from *h.* contrite
P. L. 10, 1103. sent from *h.* contrite in sign
P. L. 11, 4. removed the stony from their *h.*
P. L. 12, 489. love upon their *h.* shall write
P.R. 1,222. winning words to conquer willing *h.*
P. R. 1, 463. henceforth to dwell in pious *h.*
P. R. 2, 162. and in retiring draw *h.* after them
S.A. 455. and doubt in feeble *h.* propense enough
S. A. 792. powerful of sway in human *h.*
S. A. 1613. had filled their *h.* with mirth
S. A. 1669. their *h.* were jocund and sublime
H. 94. their *h.* and ears did greet
D. F. I. 62. thereby to set the *h.* of men on fire
**Heart-sick.**—P. L. 11, 482. of *h.-s.* agony
**Heart-struck.**—P. L. 11, 264. at the news *h.-s.*
**Heat.**—P. L. 1, 453. Sion's daughters with like *h.*

P. L. 2, 219. will receive familiar the fierce *h.*
P. L. 4, 668. with kindly *h.* of various influence
P. L. 5, 231. thou find'st him from the *h.*
P. L. 5, 369. till this meridian *h.* be over
P. L. 5, 437. concoctive *h.* to transubstantiate
P. L. 9, 1108. Indian herdsman shunning *h.*
P. L. 10, 616. see with what *h.* these dogs
P. L. 10, 653. affect the earth with cold and *h.*
P. L. 10, 656. to bring solstitial summer's *h.*
P. L. 10, 691. pinching cold and scorching *h.*
P. L. 10, 1057. lest cold or *h.* should injure us
P. L. 10, 1077. sends a comfortable *h.* from far
P. L. 11, 589. all in *h.* they light the nuptial
P. L. 11, 899. seed-time and harvest *h.*
P. L. 12, 634. as a comet which with torrid *h.*
C. 358. of savage hunger, or of savage *h.*
C. 917. smeared with gums of glutinous *h.*
**Heath.**—P. L. 1, 615. stands on the blasted *h.*
**Heathen.**—P. L. 1, 375. through the *h.* world
P. L. 10, 579. among the *h.* of their purchase
P. R. 2, 443. among the *h.* for throughout
P. R. 3, 176. to free thy country from her *h.*
P. R. 3, 418. and all the idolatries of *h.* round
S. A. 451. high among the *h.* round
S. A. 693. the hostile sword of *h.* and profane
S. A. 1430. great among the *h.* round
**Heathenish.**—P. R. 3, 419. *h.* crimes
**Heaths.**—C. 423. forests and unharboured *h.*
**Heave.**—P. L. 11, 827. shall *h.* the ocean
S. A. 197. could I once look up or *h.* the head
S. A. 1626. *h.* pull, draw, or break
C. 885. rise, rise and *h.* thy rosy head
L'A. 145. that Orpheus' self may *h.* his head
**Heaved.**—P. L. 1, 211. had risen or *h.* his head
P. L. 7, 288. so high as *h.* the tumid hills
Il P. 136. where the rude axe with *h.* stroke
**Heaven.**—P. L. 1, 27. for *h.* hides nothing
P. L. 1, 30. favoured of *h.* so highly
P. L. 1, 37. had cast him out from *h.*
P. L. 1, 43. raised impious war in *h.*
P.L. 1, 73. far removed from God and light of *h.*
P. L. 1, 82. and thence in *h.* called Satan
P. L. 1, 104. dubious battle on the plains of *h.*
P. L. 1, 124. reigning holds the tyranny of *h.*
P. L. 1, 131. endangered *h.'s* perpetual king
P. L. 1, 136. hath lost us *h.* and all this mighty
P. L. 1, 171. back to the gates of *h.*
P. L. 1, 174. that from the precipice of *h.*
P. L. 1, 212. and high permission of all-ruling *h.*
P. L. 1, 244. the seat that we must change for *h.*
P. L. 1, 255. can make a *h.* of hell, a hell of *h.*
P. L. 1, 263. to reign in hell than serve in *h.*
P. L. 1, 270. what may be yet regained in *h.*
P. L. 1, 297. not like those steps on *h.'s* azure
P. L. 1, 316. warriors the flower of *h.*
P. L. 1, 321. to slumber here as in the vales of *h.*
P. L. 1, 326. his swift pursuers from *h.* gates
P. L. 1, 360. and Powers that erst in *h.* sat
P. L. 1, 439. queen of *h.* with crescent horns
P. L. 1, 491. not a Spirit more lewd fell not from *h.*
P. L. 1, 509. yet confessed later than *h.* and earth
P. L. 1, 510. Titan *h.'s* first-born
P.L. 1, 517. ruled the middle air their highest *h.*
P. L. 1, 610. for his fault amerced of *h.*
P. L. 1, 612. as when *h.'s* fire hath scathed
P. L. 1, 633. whose exile hath emptied *h.*
P. L. 1, 635. for me be witness all the host of *h.*
P. L. 1, 638. but he who reigns monarch in *h.*
P. L. 1, 651. so rife there went a fame in *h.*
P.L. 1, 654. should favour equal to the sons of *h.*
P. L. 1, 669. defiance toward the vault of *h.*
P. L. 1, 680. fell from *h.* for even in *h.* his looks
P. L. 1, 682. the riches of *h.'s* pavement
P. L. 1, 733. his hand was known in *h.*
P. L. 1, 741. how he fell from *h.* they fabled
P. L. 1, 749. to have built in *h.* high towers
P. L. 2, 9. insatiate to pursue vain war with *h.*
P. L. 2, 11. powers and dominions deities of *h.*
P. L. 2, 14. oppressed and fallen I give not *h.*
P. L. 2, 18. just right and the fixed laws of *h.*
P.L. 2, 25. the happier state in *h.* which follows

P. L. 2, 37. more than can be in *h.* we now
P. L. 2, 45. the fiercest spirit that fought in *h.*
P. L. 2, 57. sit lingering here *h.'s* fugitives
P. L. 2, 62. o'er *h.'s* high towers to force
P. L. 2, 102. our power sufficient to disturb his *h.*
P. L. 2, 110. a fairer person lost not *h.*
P. L. 2, 137. to confound *h.'s* purest light
P. L. 2, 129. the towers of *h.* are filled with
P. L. 2, 166. and strook with *h.'s* afflicting
P. L. 2, 190. he from *h.'s* height all these our
P. L. 2, 194. vile the race of *h.* thus trampled
P. L. 2, 229. either to disenthrone the king of *h.*
P. L. 2, 236. place can be for us within *h.'s*
P. L. 2, 247. this must be our task in *h.*
P. L. 2, 251. obtained unacceptable though in *h.*
P. L. 2, 264. doth *h.'s* all-ruling Sire choose
P. L. 2, 268. and *h.* resembles hell
P. L. 2, 273. and what can *h.* show more
P. L. 2, 298. in emulation opposite to *h.*
P. L. 2, 310. imperial powers offspring of *h.*
P. L. 2, 316. and know not that the King of *h.*
P. L. 2, 319. exempt from *h.'s* high jurisdiction
P. L. 2, 328. here as with his golden those in *h.*
P. L. 2, 343. *h.* whose high walls fear no assault
P. L. 2, 346. and prophetic fame in *h.* err not
P. L. 2, 353. that shook *h.'s* whole circumference
P. L. 2, 358. *h.* be shut and *h.'s* high Arbitrator
P. L. 2, 397. we may chance re-enter *h.* or else
P. L. 2, 398. dwell not unvisited of *h.'s* fair light
P. L. 2, 430. O Progeny of *h.* empyreal Thrones
P. L. 2, 457. mighty powers terror of *h.*
P. L. 2, 479. him equal to the Highest in *H.*
P. L. 2, 490. o'er-spread *h.'s* cheerful face
P. L. 2, 509. seemed alone the antagonist of *h.*
P. L. 2, 538. from either end of *h.* the welkin
P. L. 2, 687. not to contend with spirits of *h.*
P. L. 2, 690. who first broke peace in *h.*
P. L. 2, 692. the third part of *h.'s* sons
P. L. 2, 696. thou thyself with spirits of *h.*
P. L. 2, 715. with *h.'s* artillery fraught
P. L. 2, 749. once deemed so fair in *h.*
P. L. 2, 751. bold conspiracy against *h.'s* king
P. L. 2, 759. seized all the host of *h.*
P. L. 2, 768. and fields were fought in *h.*
P. L. 2, 772. from the pitch of *h.* down into
P. L. 2, 819. of dalliance had with thee in *h.*
P. L. 2, 833. place of bliss in the purlieus of *h.*
P. L. 2, 836. lest *h.* surcharged with potent
P. L. 2, 851. by command of *h.'s* all-powerful
P. L. 2, 860. inhabitant of *h.* and heavenly-born
P. L. 2, 925. if this frame of *h.* were falling
P. L. 2, 977. gloomy bounds confine with *h.*
P. L. 2, 992. made head against *h.'s* king
P. L. 2, 996. *h.* gates poured out by millions
P. L. 2, 1004. now lately *h.* and earth
P. L. 2, 1006. to that side *h.* from whence
P. L. 2, 1025. such was the will of *h.*
P. L. 2, 1035. and from the walls of *h.* shoots
P. L. 2, 1047. far off the empyreal *h.* extended
P. L. 3, 1. hail, holy light, offspring of *h.*
P. L. 3, 60. about him all the Sanctities of *h.*
P. L. 3, 71. coasting the wall of *h.* on this side
P. L. 3, 88. far off *h.* in the precincts of light
P. L. 3, 133. mercy and justice both through *h.*
P. L. 3, 136. ambrosial fragrance filled all *h.*
P. L. 3, 146. for which both *h.* and earth shall
P. L. 3, 205. against the high supremacy of *h.*
P. L. 3, 216. dwells in all *h.* charity so dear
P. L. 3, 218. silence was in *h.*, on man's behalf
P. L. 3, 257. pleased out of *h.* shalt look down
P. L. 3, 261. enter *h.* long absent and return
P. L. 3, 272. admiration seized all *h.*
P. L. 3, 274. O thou in *h.* and earth the only
P. L. 3, 323. of them that bide in *h.* or earth
P. L. 3, 323. thou attended gloriously from *h.*
P. L. 3, 335. and from her ashes spring new *h.*
P. L. 3, 347. *h.* rung with jubilee and loud
P. L. 3, 356. but soon for man's offence to *h.*
P. L. 3, 358. river of bliss through midst of *h.*
P. L. 3, 371. such concord is in *h.*
P. L. 3, 381. thy skirts appear yet dazzle *h.*

P. L. 3, 390. *h.* of heavens and all the powers
P. L. 3, 395. that shook *h.'s* everlasting frame
P. L. 3, 417. thus they in *h.* above the starry
P. L. 3, 427. which from the wall of *h.*
P. L. 3, 477. him dead who lives in *h.*
P. L. 3, 484. at *h.'s* wicket seems to wait them
P. L. 3, 486. and now at foot of *h.'s* ascent
P. L. 3, 503. up to the wall of *h.* a structure high
P. L. 3, 515. waking cried, this is the gate of *h.*
P. L. 3, 517. but drawn up to *h.* sometimes
P. L. 3, 541. scaled by steps of gold to *h.* gate
P. L. 3, 552. though after *h.* seen
P. L. 3, 572. golden sun in splendour likest *h.*
P. L. 3, 657. interpreter through highest *h.*
P. L. 3, 685. by his permissive will through *h*
P. L. 3, 691. sharpest-sighted spirit of all in *h.*
P. L. 3, 701. with report hear only in *h.*
P. L. 3, 716. quintessence of *h.* flew upward
P. L. 3, 729. still renewing through mid *h.*
P. L. 3, 737. superior spirits is wont in *h.*
P. L. 4, 2. heard cry in *h.* aloud
P. L. 4, 29. towards *h.* and the full-blazing sun
P. L. 4, 41. warring in *h.* against *h.'s* matchless
P. L. 4, 68. but *h.'s* free love dealt equally
P. L. 4, 78. the hell I suffer seems a *h.*
P. L. 4, 111. divided empire with *h.'s* King
P. L. 4, 208. yea more, a *h.* on earth
P. L. 4, 355. and in the ascending scale of *h.*
P. L. 4, 371. and this high seat your *h.*
P. L. 4, 456. pure as the expanse of *h.*
P. L. 4, 531. meet some wandering spirit of *h.*
P. L. 4, 539. where *h.* with earth and ocean
P. L. 4, 552. the unarmed youth of *h.*
P. L. 4, 571. alien from *h.*, with passions foul
P. L. 4, 581. come well known from *h.*
P. L. 4, 620. and the regard of *h.* on all
P. L. 4, 649. and these the gems of *h.* her starry
P. L. 4, 676. that *h.* would want spectators
P. L. 4, 688. and lift our thoughts to *h.*
P. L. 4, 722. both sky, air, earth, and *h.*
P. L. 4, 837. as when thou stood'st in *h.*
P. L. 4, 886. Gabriel! thou hadst in *h.*
P. L. 4, 904. O loss of one in *h.* to judge of wise
P. L. 4, 944. high up in *h.* with songs
P. L. 4, 960. adored *h.'s* awful monarch
P. L. 4, 973. though *h.'s* king ride on thy wings
P. L. 4, 976. through the road of *h.* star-paved
P. L. 4, 993. the starry cope of *h.* perhaps
P. L. 4, 997. hung forth in *h.* his golden scales
P. L. 4, 1009. since thine no more than *h.*
P. L. 5, 19. *h.'s* last best gift
P. L. 5, 44. *h.* wakes with all his eyes
P. L. 5, 55. winged like one of those from *h.*
P. L. 5, 80. ascend to *h.*, by merit thine
P. L. 5, 163. circle his throne rejoicing ye in *h.*
P. L. 5, 220. beheld with pity *h.'s* high king
P. L. 5, 240. late fallen himself from *h.*
P. L. 5, 251. flew through the midst of *h.*
P. L. 5, 254. till at the gate of *h.* arrived
P. L. 5, 283. gold and colours dipped in *h.*
P. L. 5, 311. some great behest from *h.*
P. L. 5, 330. dispensed his bounties as in *h.*
P. L. 5, 362. place none can than *h.* such
P. L. 5, 374. oft invite though spirits of *h.*
P. L. 5, 383. to entertain her guest from *h.*
P. L. 5, 426. though in *h.* the trees of life
P. L. 5, 432. delights as may compare with *h.*
P. L. 5, 456. of their being who dwell in *h.*
P. L. 5, 467. at *h.'s* high feasts to have fed
P. L. 5, 519. to whom the angel: Son of *h.*
P. L. 5, 542. and so from *h.* to deepest hell
P. L. 5, 554. thou tell'st hath passed in *h.*
P. L. 5, 560. other half in the great zone of *h.*
P. L. 5, 575. if earth be but the shadow of *h.*
P. L. 5, 583. on such day as *h.'s* great year
P. L. 5, 586. from all the ends of *h.* appeared
P. L. 5, 608. shall bow all knees in *h.*
P. L. 5, 635. delicious vines the growth of *h.*
P. L. 5, 644. face of brightest *h.* had changed
P. L. 5, 659. name is heard no more in *h.*
P. L. 5, 676. passed the lips of *h.'s* Almighty

P. L. 5, 700. dim night had disencumbered *h.*
P. L. 5, 707. and high was his degree in *h.*
P. L. 5, 710. him the third part of *h.'s* host
P. L. 5, 742. or be found the worst in *h.*
P. L. 5, 765. Messiah was declared in sight of *h.*
P. L. 5, 790. natives and sons of *h.* possessed
P. L. 5, 810. no ear ever to hear in *h.* expected
P. L. 5, 816. every soul in *h.* shall bend
P. L. 5, 824. and formed the powers of *h.*
P. L. 5, 837. the Spirits of *h.* by him created
P. L. 5, 863. birth mature of this our native *h.*
P. L. 6, 2. through *h.'s* wide champaign held
P. L. 6, 7. makes through *h.* grateful vicissitude
P. L. 6, 11. till her hour to veil the *h.*
P. L. 6, 13. in highest *h.* arrayed in gold
P. L. 6, 51. and to the brow of *h.* pursuing
P. L. 6, 62. stood for *h.* in mighty quadrate
P. L. 6, 77. over many a tract of *h.*
P. L. 6, 114. O *h.*, that such resemblance
P. L. 6, 164. I thought that liberty and *h.*
P. L. 6, 168. the minstrelsy of *h.*
P. L. 6, 184. let me serve in *h.* God ever blest
P. L. 6, 203. through the vast of *h.* it sounded
P. L. 6, 208. such as heard in *h.* till now was
P. L. 6, 217. all *h.* resounded, and had earth
P. L. 6, 228. from his stronghold of *h.*
P. L. 6, 259. here to end intestine war in *h.*
P. L. 6, 263. till thy revolt unnamed in *h.*
P. L. 6, 267. thou disturbed *h.'s* blessed peace
P. L. 6, 272. *h.* casts thee out from all her
P. L. 6, 273. *h.* the seat of bliss brooks not
P. L. 6, 291. turn this *h.* itself into the hell
P. L. 6, 303. to decide the empire of great *h.*
P. L. 6, 359. nor from the Holy One of *h.*
P. L. 6, 375. contented with their fame in *h.*
P. L. 6, 379. cancelled from *h.* and sacred
P. L. 6, 406. and over *h.* inducing darkness
P. L. 6, 425. what *h.'s* Lord had powerfullest
P. L. 6, 474. continent of spacious *h.* adorned
P. L. 6, 480. till touched with *h.'s* ray
P. L. 6, 524. now when fair morn orient in *h.*
P. L. 6, 563. that I doubt, however, witness *h.*
P. L. 6, 564. *h.* witness thou anon
P. L. 6, 585. soon obscured with smoke all *h.*
P. L. 6, 640. for earth hath this variety from *h.*
P. L. 6, 669. and now all *h.* had gone to wrack
P. L. 6, 672. shrined in his sanctuary of *h.*
P. L. 6, 685. as we compute the days of *h.*
P. L. 6, 698. which makes wild work in *h.*
P. L. 6, 705. in *h.* and hell thy power above
P. L. 6, 712. rapid wheels that shake *h.'s* basis
P. L. 6, 716. from all *h.'s* bounds into the utter
P. L. 6, 737. armed with thy might rid *h.*
P. L. 6, 749. began to shine dawning through *h.*
P. L. 6, 776. by angels borne, his sign in *h.*
P. L. 6, 783. *h.* his wonted face
P. L. 6, 814. to whom in *h.* supreme
P. L. 6, 855. but root them out of *h.*
P. L. 6, 860. the bounds and crystal wall of *h.*
P. L. 6, 865. down from the verge of *h.*
P. L. 6, 868. hell saw *h.* ruining from *h.*
P. L. 6, 878. disburdened *h.* rejoiced and soon
P. L. 6, 889. rode triumphant through mid *h.*
P. L. 6, 893. thus measuring things in *h.*
P. L. 6, 897. and war in *h.*
P. L. 7, 1. descend from *h.* Urania
P. L. 7, 13. the *h.* of heavens I have presumed
P. L. 7, 43. what befell in *h.* to those apostates
P. L. 7, 54. so unimaginable as hate in *h.*
P. L. 7, 63. *h* and earth conspicuous first began
P. L. 7, 86. first began this *h.* which we behold
P. L. 7, 99. suspense in *h.* held by thy voice
P. L. 7, 124. none communicable in earth or *h.*
P. L. 7, 131. after Lucifer from *h.* fell
P. L. 7, 146. *h.* yet populous retains number
P. L. 7, 151. to have dispeopled *h.*
P. L. 7, 160. be changed to *h.* and *h.* to earth
P. L. 7, 162. inhabit lax ye powers of *h.*
P. L. 7, 167. appointed bounds be *h.* and earth
P. L. 7, 180. triumph and rejoicing was in *h.*
P. L. 7, 205. *h.* opened wide her ever-during

M

P. L. 7, 215. to assault *h.'s* height
P. L. 7, 232. God the *h.* created
P. L. 7, 256. birthday of *h.* and earth
P. L. 7, 274. and *h.* he named the firmament
P. L. 7, 283. ye waters under *h.*
P. L. 7, 329. that earth now seemed like to *h.*
P. L. 7, 340. high in the expanse of *h.* to divide
P. L. 7, 344. their office in the firmament of *h.*
P. L. 7, 349. set them in the firmament of *h.*
P. L. 7, 358. and sowed with stars the *h.*
P. L. 7, 373. through *h.'s* high road
P. L. 7, 381. revolved on *h.'s* great axle
P. L. 7, 390. on the open firmament of *h.*
P. L. 7, 499. now *h.* in all her glory shone
P. L. 7, 511. magnanimous to correspond with *h.*
P. L. 7, 553. to the *h.* of heavens his high abode
P. L. 7, 574. he through *h.* that opened wide
P. L. 7, 585. of *h.'s* high-seated top
P. L. 7, 617. this new-made world another *h.*
P. L. 8, 16. this world of *h.* and earth consisting
P. L. 8, 66. for *h.* is as the book of God
P. L. 8, 70. whether *h.* move or earth
P. L. 8, 79. when they come to model *h.*
P. L. 8, 88. nor *h.* such journeys run
P. L. 8, 92. though in comparison of *h.* so small
P. L. 8, 100. and for the *h.'s* wide circuit
P. L. 8, 111. set out from *h.*
P. L. 8, 120. placed *h.* from earth so far
P. L. 8, 160. whether the sun predominant in *h.*
P. L. 8, 172. *h.* is for thee too high to know
P. L. 8, 178. not of earth only but of highest *h.*
P. L. 8, 181. intelligence of *h.* angel serene
P. L. 8, 210. while I sit with thee I seem in *h.*
P. L. 8, 224. nor less think we in *h.* of thee
P. L. 8, 257. straight toward *h.* my wondering
P. L. 8, 483. with what all earth or *h.* could
P. L. 8, 488. grace in all her steps *h.* in her eye
P. L. 8, 511. all *h.* and happy constellations
P. L. 8, 613. for love thou sayst leads up to *h.*
P. L. 8, 652. so parted they, the angel up to *h.*
P. L. 9, 8. on the part of *h.* now alienated
P. L. 9, 99. O earth how like to *h.*
P. L. 9, 103. terrestrial *h.* danced round by
P. L. 9, 107. as God in *h.* is centre yet extends
P. L. 9, 123. and in *h.* much worse would be
P. L. 9, 124. neither here seek I, no nor in *h.*
P. L. 9, 125. unless by mastering *h.'s* Supreme
P. L. 9, 176. this new favourite of *h.* this man
P. L. 9, 273. offspring of *h.* and earth
P. L. 9, 334. favour from *h.* our witness
P. L. 9, 468. though in mid *h.* soon ended
P. L. 9, 488. enfeebled me to what I was in *h.*
P. L. 9, 534. thy looks the *h.* of mildness
P. L. 9, 604. considered all things visible in *h.*
P. L. 9, 811. and I perhaps am secret; *h.* is high
P. L. 10, 5. the fatal fruit was known in *h.*
P. L. 10, 17. up into *h.* from Paradise in haste
P. L. 10, 57. whether in *h.* or earth or hell
P. L. 10, 69. mine both in *h.* and earth
P. L. 10, 125. O *h.* in evil strait
P. L. 10, 184. fall like lightning down from *h.*
P. L. 10, 321. the confines met of empyrean *h.*
P. L. 10, 375. and fully avenged our foil in *h.*
P. L. 10, 387. antagonist of *h.'s* almighty king
P. L. 10, 389. that so near *h.'s* door triumphal
P. L. 10, 467. to our native *h.* little inferior
P. L. 10, 481. fame in *h.* long had foretold
P. L. 10, 598. alike is hell or paradise, or *h.*
P. L. 10, 638. then *h.* and earth renewed shall
P. L. 10, 647. by whom new *h.* and earth shall
P. L. 10, 648. or down from *h.* descend
P. L. 10, 889. peopled highest *h.* with spirits
P. L. 10, 914. witness *h.* what love sincere
P. L. 10, 933. there with my cries importune *h.*
P. L. 11, 7. winged for *h.* with speedier flight
P. L. 11, 14. to *h.* their prayers flew up
P. L. 11, 66. resigns him up with *h.* and earth
P. L. 11, 68. all the blest through *h.'s* wide
P. L. 11, 142. the good which we enjoy from *h.*
P. L. 11, 143. from us aught should ascend to *h.*
P. L. 11, 194. which *h.* by these mute signs in

P. L. 11, 251. Adam *h.'s* high behest no preface
P. L. 11, 335. Adam thou know'st *h.* his
P. L. 11, 372. and to the hand of *h.* submit
P. L. 11, 441. propitious fire from *h.* consumed
P. L. 11, 457. brother's offering found from *h.*
P. L. 11, 554. how long or short permit to *h.*
P. L. 11, 681. whom had not *h.* rescued
P. L. 11, 740. together drove from under *h.*
P. L. 11, 825. all the cataracts of *h.* set open
P. L. 11, 849. as the *h.* his windows shut
P. L. 11, 864. grateful to *h.* over his head
P. L. 11, 879. those coloured streaks in *h.*
P. L. 11, 901. both *h.* and earth wherein the
P. L. 12, 34. despite of *h.* or from *h.* claiming
P. L. 12, 44. tower whose top may reach to *h.*
P. L. 12, 59. great laughter was in *h.*
P. L. 12, 263. or how the sun shall in mid *h.*
P. L. 12, 270. O sent from *h.* enlightener
P. L. 12, 347. stablished as the days of *h.*
P. L. 12, 361. a star unseen before in *h.*
P. L. 12, 380. hail high in the love of *h.*
P. L. 12, 391. whose fall from *h.* a deadlier
P. L. 12, 451. then to the *h.* of heavens
P. L. 12, 458. high above all names in *h.*
P. L. 12, 463. into bliss whether in *h.* or earth
P. L. 12, 479. if our deliverer up to *h.* must
P. L. 12, 485. but from *h.* he to his own
P. L. 12, 504. the tidings brought from *h.*
P. L. 12, 509. all the sacred mysteries of *h.*
P. L. 12, 545. from *h.* to be revealed in glory
P. L. 12, 579. or works of God in *h.,* air, earth
P. L. 12, 618. thou to me art all things under *h.*
P. R. 1, 20. and *h.'s* kingdom nigh at hand
P. R. 1, 30. on him baptized *h.* opened
P. R. 1, 32. from *h.* pronounced him his beloved
P. R. 1, 55. long the decrees of *h.* delay
P. R. 1, 78. but to receive the testimony of *h.*
P. R. 1, 81. *h.* above the clouds unfold her
P. R. 1, 84. and out of *h.* the sovran voice
P. R. 1, 87. he who obtains the monarchy of *h.*
P. R. 1, 168. and all *h.* admiring stood
P. R. 1, 182. so they in *h.* their odes and vigils
P. R. 1, 237. all *h.* and earth angels and sons
P. R. 1, 249. star not seen before in *h.* appearing
P. R. 1, 253. thy star new-graven in *h.*
P. R. 1, 276. for it was shown him so from *h.*
P. R. 1, 281. *h.* opened her eternal doors
P. R. 1, 284. audibly heard from *h.* pronounced
P. R. 1, 289. authority which I derived from *h.*
P. R. 1, 366. nor from the *h.* of heavens
P. R. 1, 410. to come into the *h.* of heavens
P. R. 1, 416. or of scorn to all the host of *h.*
P. R. 1, 420. never more in hell than when in *h.*
P. R. 1, 421. thou art serviceable to *h.'s* king
P. R. 2, 17. on fiery wheels rode up to *h.*
P. R. 2, 85. Son owned from *h.* by his Father's
P. R. 2, 121. princes *h.'s* ancient sons ethereal
P. R. 2, 137. human sights from *h.* adorned
P. R. 2, 312. God rained from *h.* manna
P. R. 3, 62. and divulges him through *h.*
P. R. 3, 65. to extend his fame through *h.*
P. R. 3, 68. famous he was in *h.* on earth
P. R. 3, 112. not content in *h.*
P. R. 4, 273. from *h.* descended
P. R. 4, 382. if I read aught in *h.*
P. R. 4, 383. or *h.* write aught of fate
P. R. 4, 410. and both ends of *h.*
P. R. 4, 455. to the pillared frame of *h.*
P. R. 4, 512. from *h.* heard thee pronounced
P. R. 4, 539. Son of God by voice from *h.*
P. R. 4, 598. remote from *h.*
P. R. 4, 605. and down from *h.* cast with all
P. R. 4, 620. thou shalt fall from *h.* trod down
S. A. 10. the breath of *h.* fresh blowing pure
S. A. 23. O wherefore was my birth from *h.*
S. A. 150. whom the Gentiles feign to bear up *h.*
S. A. 525. of birth from *h.* foretold
S. A. 549. with touch ethereal of *h.'s* fiery rod
S. A. 565. and the work from *h.* imposed
S. A. 632. and sense of *h.'s* desertion
S. A. 1046. favoured of *h.* who finds one virtuous

S. A. 1134. thou from *h.* feignedst at thy birth
S. A. 1212. command from *h.* to free my country
S.A. 1217. I was to do my part from *h.* assigned
S. A. 1438. for never was from *h.* imparted
S. A. 1509. mercy of *h.* what hideous noise was
C. 81. I shoot from *h.* to give him safe convoy
C. 94. now the top of *h.* doth hold
C. 198. the stars that nature hung in *h.*
C. 243. resounding grace to all *h.'s* harmonies
C. 303. it were a journey like the path to *h.*
C. 417. unless the strength of *h.* if you mean that
C. 419. if *h.* gave it, may be termed her own
C. 453. so dear to *h.* is saintly chastity
C. 486. *h.* keep my sister
C. 489. defence is a good cause and *h.* be for us
C. 600. against the opposing will and arm of *h.*
C. 665. while *h.* sees good
C. 777. for swinish gluttony ne'er looks to *h.*
C. 938. come, lady, while *h.* lends us grace
C. 970. *h.* hath timely tried their youth
C. 1023. *h.* itself would stoop to her
L. 31. toward *h.'s* descent had sloped his
L. 84. of so much fame in *h.* expect thy meed
L'A. 12. in *h.* yclept Euphrosyne
Il P. 70. through the *h.'s* wide pathless way
Il P. 166. and bring all *h.* before mine eyes
Il P. 171. of every star that *h.* doth show
S. 2, 12. which time leads me and the will of *h.*
S. 18, 10. redoubled to the hills and they to *h.*
S. 21, 11. for other things mind *h.* a time ordains
S. 22, 7. yet I argue not against *h.'s* hand or will
S. 23, 8. full sight of her in *h.* without restraint
H. 2. wherein the Son of *h.'s* eternal King
H. 10. at *h.'s* high council-table
H. 19. now while the *h.* by the sun's team untrod
H. 108. could hold all *h.* and earth in happier
H. 116. with unexpressive notes to *h.'s* new born
H. 130. and let the base of *h.'s* deep organ blow
H. 147. and *h.* as at some festival
H. 201. *h.'s* queen and mother both
H. 240. *h.'s* youngest-teemed star
P. 32. *h.* and earth are coloured with my woe
P. 44. that was the casket of *h.'s* richest store
S. M. 1. blest pair of Sirens, pledges of *h.'s* joy
S. M. 26. and keep in tune with *h.*
Cir. 10. he who with all *h.'s* heraldry
D.F.I.33. could *h.* for pity thee so strictly doom
D. F. I. 48. besiege the wall of sheeny *h.*
D. F. I. 61. to show what creatures *h.* doth breed
D. F. I. 63. and unto *h.* aspire
V. Ex. 34. and at *h.'s* door look in
V. Ex. 44. in *h.'s* defiance mustering all his
**Heaven-banished.**—P. L. 10, 437. *h.-b.*
**Heaven-born.**—H. 30. while the *h.-b.* child
**Heaven-fallen.**—P. L. 10, 535. *h.-f.*
**Heaven-gate.**—P. L. 5, 198. to *h.-g.* ascend
P. L. 7, 618. another heaven from *h.-g.* not far
P. L. 10, 22. from earth arrived at *h.-g.*
P. L. 10, 88. ministrant accompanied to *h.-g.*
**Heaven-gifted.**—S. A. 36. *h.-g.* strength
**Heaven-loved.**—D. F. I. 65. thy *h.-l.* innocence
**Heavenly.**—P. L. 1, 6. sing *h.* Muse that on
P. L. 1, 138. as far as gods and *h.* essences
P. L. 1, 361. though of their names in *h.* records
P. L. 2, 499. though under hope of *h.* grace
P. L. 2, 757. shining *h.* fair, a goddess armed
P. L. 2, 813. bright arms though tempered *h.*
P. L. 2, 824. and all the *h.* host of spirits
P. L. 3, 19. taught by the *h.* Muse to venture
P. L. 3, 213. say *h.* powers, where shall we find
P. L. 3, 217. but all the *h.* choir stood mute
P. L. 3, 298. so *h.* love shall outdo hellish hate
P. L. 4, 118. for *h.* minds from such distempers
P. L. 4, 361. to *h.* spirits bright little inferior
P. L. 4, 686. with *h.* touch of instrumental
P. L. 4, 711. and *h.* choirs the hymenæan sing
P. L. 5, 286. that *h.* fragrance filled the circuit
P. L. 5, 316. and receive our *h.* stranger
P. L. 5, 397. *h.* stranger please to taste these
P. L. 5, 500. here or in *h.* Paradises
P. L. 6, 165. to *h.* souls had been all one

P. L. 6, 723. O supreme of *h.* thrones
P. L. 6, 788. in *h.* spirits could such
P. L. 7, 39. thou art *h.,* she an empty dream
P. L. 7, 69. proceeded thus to ask his *h.* guest
P. L. 7, 210. on *h.* ground they stood
P. L. 8, 217. thus Raphael answered *h.* meek
P. L. 8, 356. and to the *h.* vision thus presumed
P. L. 8, 379. let not my words offend thee *h.*
P. L. 8, 453. my earthly by his *h.* overpowered
P. L. 8, 485. led by her *h.* maker though unseen
P. L. 8, 592. by which to *h.* love thou may'st
P. L. 8, 615. love not the *h.* spirits
P. L. 8, 646. go *h.* guest ethereal messenger
P. L. 9, 151. with *h.* spoils, our spoils
P. L. 9, 457. her *h.* form angelic but more soft
P. L. 9, 607. in thy beauty's *h.* ray
P. L. 9, 730. can envy dwell in *h.* breasts
P. L. 9, 1082. those *h.* shapes will dazzle now
P. L. 10, 624. to enter and possess a place so *h.*
P. L. 10, 641. he ended and the *h.* audience
P. L. 10, 872. lest that too *h.* form pretended
P. L. 11, 17. dimensionless through *h.* doors
P. L. 11, 207. slow descends with something *h.*
P. L. 11, 208. by this the *h.* bands ... lighted
P. L. 11, 230. one of the *h.* host and by his gait
P. L. 11, 871. represent as present *h.* instructor
P. L. 12, 256. a zodiac representing the *h.* fires
P. R. 1, 28. have resigned to him his *h.* office
P. R. 1, 221. more humane more *h.*
P. R. 4, 594. sung *h.* anthems of his victory
P. R. 4, 637. sung victor and from *h.* feast
S. A. 373. appoint not *h.* disposition, father
S. A. 1035. seeming at first all *h.* under virgin
C. 459. till oft converse with *h.* habitants
C. 515. the sage poets taught by the *h.* Muse
A. 72. after the *h.* tune which none can hear
S. 9, 4. that labour up the hill of *h.* truth
H. 15. say *h.* Muse, shall not thy sacred vein
H. 100. thousand echoes still prolongs each *h.*
P. 3. joyous news of *h.* infant's birth
D. F. I. 55. or any other of that *h.* brood
**Heavenly-born.**—P. L. 2, 860. and *h.-b.*
P. L. 7, 7. *h.-b.* before the hills appeared
**Heavenly-guided.**—T. 19. our *h.-g.* soul
**Heavens.**—P. L. 1, 9. how the *h.* and earth
P. L. 3, 9. before the sun before the *h.* thou
P. L. 3, 390. he heaven of *h.* and all the powers
P. L. 3, 651. that run through all the *h.*
P. L. 5, 156. who sitt'st above these *h.*
P. L. 5, 578. where these *h.* now roll
P.L. 7, 13. into the heaven of *h.* I have presumed
P. L. 7, 553. up to the heaven of *h.*
P. L. 7, 562. the *h.* and all the constellations
P. L. 7, 566. open ye *h.* your living doors
P. L. 8, 76. he his fabric of the *h.* hath left
P. L. 8, 115. admitting motion in the *h.* to show
P. L. 9, 103. heaven danced round by other *h.*
P. L. 10, 692. changes in the *h.* though slow
P. L. 12, 371. his glory with the *h.*
P. L. 12, 549. new *h.,* new earth
P. R. 1, 366. the heaven of *h.*
P. R. 1, 410. to come into the heaven of *h.*
**Heaven-towers.**—P. L. 12, 52. obstruct *h.-t.*
**Heaven-warring.**—P. L. 2, 424. *h.-w.*
**Heavier.**—P. L. 3, 159. though to his *h.* doom
P. L. 4, 101. lead me to a worse relapse and *h.*
P. L. 4, 972. far *h.* load thyself expect to feel
P. L. 9, 57. what might hap of *h.* on himself
P. L. 10, 835. that burden *h.* than the earth
P. L. 10, 836. than all the world much *h.*
**Heaviest.**—P. L. 6, 265. though *h.*
S. A. 445. of all thy sufferings think the *h.*
P. 13. most perfect hero tried in *h.* plight
**Heaviness.**—U. C. II. 22. he died for *h.*
**Heavy.**—P. L. 2, 902. light armed or *h.*
P. L. 6, 551. not distant far with *h.* pace
P. L. 10, 741. *h.* though in their place
P. L. 12, 103. heard this *h.* curse
P. L. 12, 531. *h.* persecution shall arise
L. 37. but oh the *h.* change now thou art gone

T. 3. whose speed is but the *h.* plummet's pace
**Hebe.**—C. 290. as smooth as *H.'s* their unrazored
L'A. 29. such as hang on *H.'s* cheek
V. Ex. 38. while *H.* brings immortal nectar
**Hebrew.**—P. R. 4, 336. *H.* songs and harps
S. A. 1319. thou knowest I am a *H.* therefore tell
S. A. 1540. a *H.* as I guess and of our tribe
**Hebrews.**—S. A. 1308. *H.*, the prisoner Samson
**Hebrides.**—L. 156. beyond the stormy *H.*
**Hebron.**—S. A. 148. up to the hill by *H.*
**Hebrus.**—L. 63. the swift *H.* to the Lesbian
**Hecate.**—C. 135. wherein thou ridest with *H.*
C. 535. doing abhorred rites to *H.*
**Hecatompylos.**—P. R. 3, 287. and *H.*
**Hedger.**—C. 293. swinked *h.* at his supper sat
**Hedge-row.**—L'A. 58. by *h.-r.* elms
**Heed.**—P. L. 4, 969. Satan to no threats gave *h.*
P. L. 8, 635. take *h.* lest passion sway thy
P. L. 10, 1030. calling to mind with *h.*
S. A. 1230. take good *h.* my hand survey not
L'A. 141. with wanton *h.* and giddy cunning
**Heel.**—P. L. 5, 284. shadowed from either *h.*
P. L. 10, 181. bruise thy head thou bruise his *h.*
P. L. 10, 498. I am to bruise his *h.*
P. L. 12, 385. shall bruise the victor's *h.*
P. L. 12, 388. or the local wounds of head or *h.*
P. L. 12, 433. death shall bruise the victor's *h.*
P. L. 12, 631. fast at the labourer's *h.*
S. A. 140. turned their plated backs under his *h.*
L. 34. and Fauns with cloven *h.*
**Heels.**—P. L. 2, 135. and at our *h.* all hell
P. R. 2, 420. or at thy *h.* the dizzy multitude
S. A. 1235. my *h.* are fettered but my fist is free
**Height**—P. L. 1, 24. the *h.* of this
P. L. 1, 92. from what *h.* fallen
P. L. 1, 282. fallen such a pernicious *h.*
P. L. 1, 552. to *h.* of noblest temper
P. L. 1, 723. stood fixed her stately *h.*
P. L. 2, 95. to the *h.* enraged
P. L. 2, 190. he from heaven's *h.*
P. L. 2, 324. for he be sure in *h.* or depth
P. L. 2, 893. where length breadth and *h.*
P. L. 3, 58. sits high throned above all *h.*
P. L. 4, 95. how soon would *h.* recall high
P. L. 4, 138. insuperable *h* of loftiest shade
P. L. 4, 564. this day at *h.* of noon
P. L. 6, 132. the *h.* of thy aspiring
P. L. 6, 300. lift human imagination to such *h.*
P. L. 6, 793. and aspiring to his *h.*
P. L. 7, 215. to assault heaven's *h.*
P. L. 8, 413. the *h.* and depth of thy eternal ways
P. L. 8, 430. canst raise thy creature to what *h.*
P. L. 8, 454. strained to the *h.*
P. L. 9, 167. that to the *h.* of deity aspired
P. L. 9, 510. Scipio, the *h.* of Rome
P. L. 9, 675. sometimes in *h.* begun
P. L. 9, 677. standing, moving, or to *h.* upgrown
P. L. 10, 724. whom to behold was then my *h.*
P. L. 11, 730. length, and breadth and *h.*
P. R. 1, 13. and bear through *h.* or depth
P. R. 1, 231. to what *h.* sacred virtue
P. R. 2, 45. to what *h.* their power
P. R. 2, 436. in *h.* of all their flowing wealth
P. R. 4, 39. the *h.* of mountains interposed
S. A. 384. in her *h.* of nuptial love professed
S. A. 683. amidst their *h.* of noon
S. A. 1349. up to the *h.*
A. 75. the peerless *h.* of her immortal praise
**Heightened.**—P. L. 6, 629. *h.* in their thoughts
**Heinous.**—P. L. 9, 929. the fact is not so *h.*
P. L. 10, 1. *h.* and despiteful act
S. A. 493. *h.* had the fact been
S. A. 991. nor shall I count it *h.* to enjoy
**Heir.**—P. L. 5, 720. *h.* of all my might
P. L. 6, 707. to manifest thee worthiest to be *h.*
P. L. 6, 708. of all things to be *h.* and to be king
P. L. 6, 887. Son, *H.*, and Lord
P. R. 3, 405. I mean to reign David's true *h.*
P. R. 4, 633. of both worlds queller of Satan
C. 501. O my loved master's *h.* and his next joy
H. 116. to heaven's new-born *h.*

M. W. 3. a viscount's daughter an earl's *h.*
W. S. 5. dear son of memory, great *h.* of fame
**Held.**—P. L. 1, 200. by ancient Tarsus *h.*
P. L. 1, 508. of Javan's issue *h.* gods
P. L. 1, 618. attention *h.* them mute
P. L. 1, 734. sceptred angels *h.* their residence
P. L. 1, 755. a solemn council forthwith to be *h.*
P. L. 2, 417. expectation *h.* his look suspense
P. L. 2, 761. and for a sign portentous *h.* me
P. L. 3, 643. and *h.* before his decent steps
P. L. 3, 690. and *h.* the sharpest-sighted
P. L. 4, 860. to strive or fly he *h.* it vain
P. L. 4, 887. esteem of wise and such I *h.* thee
P. L. 5, 82. he drew nigh, and to me *h.*
P. L. 5, 83. of that same fruit *h.* part
P. L. 5, 771. thus *h.* their ears
P. L. 6, 2. heaven's wide champaign *h.* his way
P. L. 7, 100. *h.* by thy voice thy potent voice
P. L. 9, 180. a black mist low-creeping he *h.*
P. L. 9, 443. king *h.* dalliance with his
P. L. 10, 411. through thickest constellations *h.*
P. L. 10, 800. to God himself impossible is *h.*
P. L. 11, 693. shall be *h.* the highest pitch
P. R. 1, 221. *h.* it more humane more heavenly
P. R. 3, 33. won Asia and the throne of Cyrus *n.*
P. R. 4, 10. man who had been matchless *h.*
S. A. 410. but foul effeminacy *h.* me yoked
S. A. 863. only my love of thee *h.* long debate
S. A. 1081. the Emims old that Kiriathaim *h.*
S. A. 1194. in your city *h.* my nuptial feast
C. 834. *h.* up their pearled wrists and took her in
A. 24. who had thought this clime had *h.*
Il P. 26. such mixture was not *h.* a stain
Il P. 41. there *h.* in holy passion still
S. 12, 7. which after *h.* the sun and moon in fee
S. 17, 2. ne'er *h.* the helm of Rome
D. F. I. 14. a foul reproach was *h.*
F. of C. 10. been *h.* in high esteem with Paul
V. Ex. 51. are *h.* with his melodious harmony
**Helena.**—C. 676. in Egypt gave to Jove-born *H.*
**Helicon.**—M. W. 56. wept for thee in *H.*
**Hell.**—P. L. 1, 28. nor the deep tract of *h.*
P. L. 1, 151. here in the heart of *h.* to work in
P. L. 1, 251. and thou profoundest *h.*
P. L. 1, 255. a heaven of *h.* a *h.* of heaven
P. L. 1, 262. is worth ambition though in *h.*
P. L. 1, 263. better to reign in *h.* than serve
P. L. 1, 270. or what more lost in *h.*
P. L. 1, 315. that all the hollow deep of *h.*
P. L. 1, 381. those who from the pit of *h.*
P. L. 1, 405. black Gehenna called the type of *h.*
P. L. 1, 418. good Josiah drove them thence to *h.*
P. L. 1, 542. a shout that tore *h.'s* concave
P. L. 1, 666. far round illumined *h*
P. L. 1, 691. none admire that riches grow in *h.*
P. L. 1, 751. his industrious crew to build in *h.*
P. L. 2, 32. for none sure will claim in *h.*
P. L. 2, 49. of God or *h.*, or worse he recked not
P. L. 2, 61. armed with *h.* flames and fury
P. L. 2, 84. if there be in *h.* fear to be worse
P. L. 2, 135. at our heels all *h.* should rise
P. L. 2, 167. this *h.* then seemed a refuge from
P. L. 2, 176. this firmament of *h.* should spout
P. L. 2, 268. and heaven resembles *h.*
P. L. 2, 293. they dreaded worse than *h.*
P. L. 2, 313. changing style be called princes of *h.*
P. L. 2, 326. over *h.* extend his empire
P. L. 2, 364. *h.* fire to waste his whole creation
P. L. 2, 383. earth with *h.* to mingle and involve
P. L. 2, 433. that out of *h.* leads up
P. L. 2, 459. render *h.* more tolerable
P. L. 2, 510. nor less than *h.'s* dread emperor
P. L. 2, 519. all the host of *h.* with deafening
P. L. 2, 541. *h.* scarce holds the wild uproar
P. L. 2, 554. the harmony... suspended *h.*
P. L. 2, 631. toward the gates of *h.* explores
P. L. 2, 644. at last appear *h.* bounds
P. L. 2, 671. fierce as ten furies, terrible as *h.*
P. L. 2, 676. *h.* trembled as he strode
P. L. 2, 719. that *h.* grew darker at their frown

P. L. 2, 723. whereof all *h.* had rung
P. L. 2, 788. *h.* trembled at the hideous name
P. L. 2, 918. stood on the brink of *h.* and looked
P. L. 2, 1002. first *h.*, your dungeon
P. L. 2, 1029. from *h.* continued reaching
P. L. 3, 70. he then surveyed *h.* and the gulf
P. L. 3, 82. no bounds prescribed no bars of *h.*
P. L. 3, 160. to *h.* draw after him the whole
P. L. 3, 223. adjudged to death and *h.* by doom
P. L. 3, 255. shall lead *h.* captive, maugre *h.*
P. L. 3, 322. or earth or under earth in *h.*
P. L. 3, 332. *h.* her numbers full thenceforth
P. L. 3, 678. his rebel foes to deepest *h.*
P. L. 4, 12. that first battle and his flight to *h.*
P. L. 4, 20. the *h.* within him, for within him *h.*
P. L. 4, 21. nor from *h.* one step no more
P. L. 4, 75. which way I fly is *h.*, myself am *h.*
P. L. 4, 78. the *h.* I suffer seems a heaven
P. L. 4, 89. they adore me on the throne of *h.*
P. L. 4, 358. O *h.* what do mine eyes with grief
P. L. 4, 381. *h.* shall unfold
P. L. 4, 508. while I to *h.* am thrust
P. L. 4, 795. escaped the bars of *h.*
P. L. 4, 823. those rebel spirits adjudged to *h.*
P. L. 4, 871. seems the prince of *h.*
P. L. 4, 889. finding way break loose from *h.*
P. L. 4, 909. unlicensed from his bounds in *h.*
P. L. 4, 914. scourge that wisdom back to *h.*
P. L. 4, 918. with thee came not all *h.* broke
P. L. 4, 937. whereof in *h.* fame is not silent
P. L. 4, 967. the facile gates of *h.* too slightly
P. L. 5, 225. Satan from *h.* scaped through
P. L. 5, 450. the injured lover's *h.*
P. L. 5, 542. from heaven to deepest *h.*
P. L. 6, 183. reign thou in *h.*, thy kingdom
P. L. 6, 186. yet chains in *h.* not realms expect
P. L. 6, 276. to the place of evil *h.*
P. L. 6, 291. turn this heaven itself into the *h.*
P. L. 6, 705. in heaven and *h.* thy power above
P. L. 6, 867. *h.* heard the … noise; *h.* saw
P. L. 6, 874. *h.* at last yawning received them
P. L. 6, 876. *h.* their fit habitation
P. L. 8, 231. excursion toward the gates of *h.*
P. L. 9, 467. but the hot *h.* that always in him
P. L. 9, 476. nor hope of paradise for *h.*
P. L. 9, 487. so much hath *h.* debased
P. L. 10, 39. crossed the gulf from *h.*
P. L. 10, 57. whether in heaven or earth or *h.*
P. L. 10, 230. within the gates of *h.* sat Sin
P. L. 10, 257. over this main from *h.* to that
P. L. 10, 288. shoaling towards the mouth of *h.*
P. L. 10, 299. to the roots of *h.* the gathered
P. L. 10, 305. easy, inoffensive, down to *h.*
P. L. 10, 322. on the left hand *h.* with long
P. L. 10, 346. and tidings fraught to *h.* he now
P. L. 10, 365. *h.* could no longer hold us in her
P. L. 10, 392. *h.* and this world one realm
P. L. 10, 408. the affairs of *h.* no detriment
P. L. 10, 437. left desert utmost *h.*
P. L. 10, 594. than still at *h.'s* dark threshold
P. L. 10, 598. alike is *h.* or paradise or heaven
P. L. 10, 616. with what heat these dogs of *h.*
P. L. 10, 621. so doth the prince of *h.*
P. L. 10, 636. obstruct the mouth of *h.*
P. L. 12, 42. under ground the mouth of *h.*
P. R. 1, 46. remember *h.* our hated habitation
P. R. 1, 116. march from *h.'s* deep vaulted den
P. R. 1, 153. and drive him back to *h.*
P. R. 1, 180. be frustrate all ye stratagems of *h.*
P. R. 1, 409. who boast'st release from *h.*
P. R. 1, 420. so never more in *h.* than when in
P. R. 2, 128. our expulsion down to *h.*
P. R. 3, 220. I dread more than the fire of *h.*
P. R. 4, 623. and hold'st in *h.* no triumph
C. 518. rifted rocks whose entrance leads to *h.*
C. 581. how are ye joined with *h.* in triple knot
Il P. 108. made *h.* grant what love did seek
H. 189. and *h.* itself will pass away
H. 218. nought but profoundest *h.*
**Hell-born.**—P. L. 2, 687. learn by proof *h.-b.*
**Hell-doomed.**—P. L. 2, 697. of heaven *h.-d.*

**Hell-gate.**—P. L. 2, 725. sat fast by *h.-g.* and kept
P. L. 2, 746. thus the portress of *h.-g.* replied
P. L. 10, 415. down the causey to *h.-g.*
**Hell-gates.**—P. L. 10, 282. from out *h-g*
P. L. 10, 369. confined within *h.-g.*
**Hell-hounds.**—P. L. 2, 654. a cry of *h.-h.*
P. L. 10, 630. my *h.-h.* to lick up the draff
**Hellespont.**—P. L. 10, 309. over *H.*
**Hellish.**—P. L. 2, 504. man had not *h.* foes
P. L. 2, 735. at her words the *h.* pest forbore
P. L. 3, 298. heavenly love shall outdo *h.* hate
P. L. 3, 300. to redeem what *h.* hate so easily
P. L. 6, 636. against such *h.* mischief fit
P. L. 9, 409. waited with *h.* rancour imminent
P. L. 10, 585. in Paradise the *h.* pair
P. L. 10, 873. pretended to *h.* falsehood
P. R. 1, 175. to vanquish by wisdom *h.* wiles
P. R. 4, 422. infernal ghosts and *h.* furies round
C. 613. those that quell the might of *h.* charms
**Helm.**—P. L. 6, 543. each fit well his *h.*
P. L. 11, 245. his starry *h.* unbuckled showed
S. A. 1045. with such a steers-mate at the *h.*
S. 17, 3. ne'er held the *h.* of Rome
**Helmed.**—P. L. 6, 840. helms and *h.* heads
H. 112. the *h.* cherubim, and sworded seraphim
**Helmet.**—S. A. 1119. thy *h.* and brigandine
**Helmets.**—P. L. 6, 83. of rigid spears and *h.*
S. A. 141. soiled their crested *h.*
**Helms.**—P. L. 1, 547. thronging *h.* appeared
P. L. 4, 553. armoury, shields, *h.* and spears
P. L. 6, 840. shields and *h.* and helmed heads
**Help.**—P. L. 4, 727. happy in our mutual *h.*
P. L. 8, 418. by conversation with his like to *h.*
P. L. 8, 450. thy likeness, thy fit *h.*
P. L. 9, 336. without exterior *h.* sustained
P. L. 9, 624. and more hands *h.* to disburden
P. L. 10, 137. whom thou madest to be my *h.*
P. L. 11, 165. for thee ordained a *h.* became
P. R. 4, 103. with my *h.* thou may'st to me
S. A. 1266. because their end is hate not *h.* to me
S. A. 1625. which without *h.* of eye might be
C. 304. to *h.* you find them
C. 909. 'tis my office best to *h.* ensnared chastity
S. 16, 13. *h.* us to save free conscience from the
S. 20, 4. by the fire *h.* waste a sullen day
**Helped.**—P. L. 6, 656. their armour *h.* their harm
**Helpful.**—A. 38. and with all *h.* service
**Helping.**—C. 845. *h.* all urchin blasts and ill-luck
**Helpless.**—S. A. 644. left me all *h.*
S. A. 943. in most things as a child *h.*
C. 402. and let a single *h.* maiden pass
C. 583. weakness of one virgin, alone and *h.*
**Hem.**—P. L. 4, 979. began to *h.* him round
A. 83. approach and kiss her sacred vesture's *h.*
**Hemisphere.**—P. L. 3, 725. as the other *h.*
P. L. 7, 250. light from darkness by the *h.*
P. L. 7, 384. that then appeared spangling the *h.*
P. L. 9, 52. night's *h.* had veiled the horizon
P. L. 11, 379. from whose top the *h.* of earth
**Hence.**—P. L. 1, 260. will not drive us *h.*
P. L. 3, 540. Satan from *h.* now on the lower
P. L. 3, 723. light from *h.* though but reflected
P. L. 3, 731. *h.* fills and empties to enlighten
P. L. 4, 522. *h.* I will excite their minds with
P. L. 4, 872. likely to part *h.* without contest
P. L. 5, 257. from *h.* no cloud or to obstruct
P. L. 6, 275. *h.* then and evil go with thee along
P. L. 6, 288. and with threats to chase me *h.*
P. L. 7, 366. *h.* the morning-planet gilds her
P. L. 8, 332. expelled from *h.* into a world
P. L. 9, 617. from *h.* how far?
P. L. 10, 260. their passage *h.* for intercourse
P. L. 10, 304. from *h.* a passage broad
P. L. 11, 315. departing *h.* as from his face
P. L. 11, 356. confirmed ere thou from *h.* depart
P. L. 12, 557. greatly instructed I shall *h.* depart
P. L. 12, 590. hour precise exacts our parting *h.*
P. L. 12, 617. to go *h.* unwilling
P. L. 12, 619. art banished *h.*
P. L. 12, 621. consolation yet secure I carry *h.*
P. R. 1, 336. will bring me *h.* no other guide

P. R. 2, 56. then snatch him *h.*
P. R. 2, 317. what concludest thou *h.*
S. A. 15. *h.* with leave retiring from the popular
S. A. 224. that by occasion *h.* I might begin
S. A. 1229. come nearer, part not *h.* so slight
S. A. 1263. speediest friend by death to rid me *h.*
S. A. 1447. by order of the lords new-parted *h.*
S. A. 1481. I am fixed not to part *h.* without him
S. A. 1572. all my hopes defeated to free him *h.*
S. A. 1731. to fetch him *h.* and solemnly attend
L. 18. *h.* with denial vain and coy excuse
Il P. 1. *h.* vain deluding joys
**Henceforth.**—P. L. 1, 187. how we may *h.*
P. L. 1, 643. *h.* his might we know
P. L. 3, 414. the copious matter of my song *h.*
P. L. 4, 378. you must dwell or you with me *h.*
P. L. 4, 486. to have thee by my side *h.*
P. L. 4, 966. as *h.* not to scorn the facile gates
P. L. 5, 77. be *h.* among the gods thyself
P. L. 5, 881. *h.* no more be troubled how
P. L. 7, 569. open and *h.* oft
P. L. 9, 799. *h.* my early care not without song
P. L. 9, 1081. how shall I behold the face *h.*
P. L. 9, 1140. let none *h.* seek needless cause
P. L. 10, 379. *h.* monarchy with thee divide
P. L. 10, 872. to warn all creatures from thee *h.*
P. L. 11, 176. I never from thy side *h.* to stray
P. L. 11, 547. *h.* I fly not death nor would
P. L. 11, 771. let no man seek *h.* to be foretold
P. L. 12, 11. *h.* what is to come I will relate
P. L. 12, 561. *h.* I learn that to obey is best
P. R. 1, 142. *h.* I expose
P. R. 1, 456. *h.* oracles are ceased
P. R. 1, 462. Spirit of Truth *h.* to dwell
P. R. 4, 610. he never more *h.* will dare
S. A. 970. I desist *h.*
L. 183. *h.* thou art the genius of the shore
**Herald.**—P. R. 2, 279. now the *h.* lark
L. 89. and listens to the *h.* of the sea
**Heraldry.**—Cir. 10. with all heaven's *h.*
**Heralds or Haralds.**—P. L. 1, 752. winged *h.*
P. L. 11, 660. in other part the sceptred *h.* call
**Herb.**—P. L. 4, 253. flocks grazing the tender *h.*
P. L. 4, 644. spreads his orient beams on *h.*
P. L. 4, 652. nor *h.*, fruit, flower, glistering
P. L. 7, 310. *h.* yielding seed
P. L. 7, 336. every *h.* before it grew on the green
P. L. 8, 254. soft on the flowery *h.*
P. L. 9, 111. productive in *h.*, plant and nobler
P. L. 9, 186. but on the grassy *h.* fearless
P. L. 9, 206. still to tend plant, *h.* and flower
P. L. 9, 572. beasts that graze the trodden *h.*
P. L. 10, 204. thou shalt eat the *h.* of the field
P. L. 10, 711. to graze the *h.* all leaving
P. L. 12, 184. what it devours not *h.*, or fruit
S. A. 626. no cooling *h.* or med'cinal liquor
C. 541. had ta'en their supper on the savoury *h.*
C. 621. in every virtuous plant and healing *h.*
Il P. 172. and every *h.* that sips the dew
**Herbs.**—P. L. 4, 709. and sweet smelling *h.*
P. L. 7, 317. hive *h.* of every leaf
P. L. 8, 527. I mean of taste, sight, smell, *h.*
P. L. 10, 603. thou therefore on these *h.*
S. A. 1727. with lavers pure and cleansing *h.*
C. 255. culling their potent *h.*
L'A. 85. of *h.* and other country messes
**Herculean.**—P. L. 9, 1060. *H.* Samson
**Herd.**—P. L. 4, 396. among the sportful *h.*
P. L. 6, 856. and as a *h.* of goats
P. L. 9, 522. Circæan call the *h.* disguised
P. L. 11, 647. from forage drives a *h.*
P. L. 12, 19. from the *h.* or flock oft sacrificing
P. L. 12, 481. left among the unfaithful *h.*
P. R. 2, 287. were in view sheep-cote or *h.*
P. R. 2, 288. but cottage *h.* or sheep-cote none
P. R. 3, 49. what the people but a *h.* confused
P. R. 4, 630. beg to hide them in a *h.* of swine
C. 152. with as fair a *h.* as grazed
**Herdman.**—L. 121. to the faithful *h.'s* art
**Herds.**—P. L. 2, 494. and bleating *h.* attest
P. L. 3, 44. or flocks or *h.* or human face

P. L. 4, 754. among the bestial *h.* to range
P. L. 7, 462. in broad *h.* upsprung ,
P. L. 9, 1109. tends his pasturing *h.*
P. L. 11, 557. by some were *h.*
P. L. 12, 132. a cumbrous train of *h.* and flocks
P. R. 3, 260. with *h.* the pastures thronged
C. 388. the cheerful haunt of men and *h.*
C. 731. the *h.* would over-multitude their lords
C. 844. visits the *h.* along the twilight meadows
L. 46. the weanling *h.* that graze
**Herdsman.**—P. L. 9, 1108. oft the Indian *h.*
**Here.**—P. L. 1, 71. '*h.* their prison ordained
P. L. 1, 142. *h.* swallowed up in endless misery
P. L. 1, 151. *h.* in the heart of hell to work
P. L. 2, 458. intend at home while *h.* shall be
P. L. 2, 694. are *h.* condemned to waste
P. L. 2, 697. breathest defiance *h.* and scorn
P. L. 2, 777. pensive *h.* I sat alone
P. L. 2, 818. and my fair son *h.* show'st me
P. L. 2, 859. to sit in hateful office *h.* confined
P. L. 2, 861. *h.* in perpetual agony and pain
P. L. 2, 899. strive *h.* for mastery
P. L. 2, 998. I upon my frontiers *h.* keep
P. L. 2, 1037. *h.* nature first begins
P. L. 3, 266. his words *h.* ended
P. L. 3, 315. *h.* shalt thou sit incarnate, *h.* shalt
P. L. 3, 430. *h.* walked the fiend at large
P. L. 3, 453. *h.* find fit retribution
P. L. 3, 458. till final dissolution wander *h.*
P. L. 3, 476. *h.* pilgrims roam that strayed
P. L. 3, 600. like to that which *h.*
P. L. 3, 606. if fields and regions *h.*
P. L. 3, 611. *h.* in the dark
P. L. 3, 613. *h.* matter new to gaze the devil
P. L. 3, 615. for sight no obstacle found *h.*
P. L. 3, 659. and *h.* art likeliest
P. L. 4, 235. whereof *h.* needs no account
P. L. 4, 251. if true, *h.* only
P. L. 4, 416. and placed us *h.*
P. L. 4, 580. none 'pass the vigilance *h.*
P. L. 4, 703. other creature *h.*, bird, beast
P. L. 4, 708. *h.*, in close recess
P. L. 4, 763. *h.* love his golden shafts employs *h.*
P. L. 4, 765. reigns *h.* and revels
P. L. 4, 826. *h.* watching at the head of these
P. L. 4, 849. but chiefly to find *h.*
P. L. 4, 884. God hath planted *h.*
P. L. 4, 938. *h.* in hope to find better abode
P. L. 4, 940. to settle *h.* on earth or in mid air
P. L. 5, 63. why else set *h.*
P. L. 5, 69. forbidden *h.* it seems as only fit
P. L. 5, 74. *h.* happy creature fair angelic Eve
P. L. 5, 294. nature *h.* wantoned at will
P. L. 5, 329. he beholding shall confess that *h.*
P. L. 5, 373. or such place hast *h.* to dwell
P. L. 5, 394. spring and autumn *h.* danced
P. L. 5, 430. yet God hath *h.* varied his bounty
P. L. 5, 500. *h.* or in heavenly paradises
P. L. 5, 516. placed us *h.*
P. L. 5, 778. and hurried meeting *h.*
P. L. 6, 12. there might well seem twilight *h.*
P. L. 6, 258. as hoping *h.* to end intestine war
P. L. 6, 271. think not *h.* to trouble holy rest
P. L. 6, 292. *h.* however to dwell free
P. L. 6, 374. their names eternize *h.* on earth
P. L. 6, 801. *h.* stand ye angels armed
P. L. 7, 144. many whom their place knows *h.*
P. L. 7, 157. there to dwell not *h.*
P. L. 7, 541. all sorts are *h.*
P. L. 7, 548. *h.* finished he
P. L. 8, 118. to thee who hast thy dwelling *h.*
P. L. 8, 277. how came I thus, how *h.*
P. L. 8, 311. the dream had lively shadowed *h.*
P. L. 8, 322. fear *h.* no death
P. L. 8, 381. hast thou not made me *h.*
P. L. 8, 528. but *h.* far otherwise
P. L. 8, 530. *h.* passion first I felt
P. L. 8, 532. *h.* only weak against the charm
P. L. 9, 124. but neither *h.* seek I
P. L. 9, 280. might best fulfil the work which *h.*
P. L. 9, 476. hope *h.* to taste of pleasure

P. L. 9, 542. but *h.* in this enclosure wild
P. L. 9, 648. though fruit be *h.*
P. L. 9, 776. *h.* grows the cure of all
P. L. 9, 806. it had not *h.* thus grown
P. L. 9, 1084. O might I *h.* in solitude live
P. L. 9, 1149. or *h.* the attempt
P. L. 9, 1174. force upon free will hath *h.*
P. L. 10, 104. I miss thee *h.*
P. L. 10, 235. O son, why sit we *h.*
P. L. 10, 375. *h.* thou shalt monarch reign
P. L. 10, 600. which *h.* though plenteous
P. L. 10, 725. well if *h.* would end the misery
P. L. 10, 745. *h.* place in this delicious garden
P. L. 10, 1007. she ended *h.*
P. L. 11, 178. while *h.* we dwell
P. L. 11, 180. *h.* let us live
P. L. 11, 317. *h.* I could frequent with worship
P. L. 11, 322. *h.* with him at this fountain
P. L. 11, 350. in valley and in plain God is as *h.*
P. L. 11, 368. *h.* sleep below while thou
P. L. 11, 459. though *h.* thou see him die
P. L. 11, 502. better end *h.* unborn
P. L. 11, 602. *h.* nature seems fulfilled
P. L. 11, 786. whether *h.* the race of man
P. L. 12, 2. *h.* the archangel paused
P. L. 12, 144. *h.* the double-founted stream
P. L. 12, 270. *h.* Adam interposed
P. L. 12, 616. with thee to go is to stay *h.*
P. R. 1, 324. and dropt not *h.* his carcase
P. R. 1, 338. we *h.* live on tough roots
P. R. 1, 351. who fed our fathers *h.*
P. R. 2, 143. over-sure of like succeeding *h.*
P. R. 2, 249. part of what I suffer *h.*
P. R. 2, 311. all the race of Israel *h.*
P. R. 2, 313. wandering *h.* was fed twice
P. R. 2, 316. forty and more deserted *h.*
P. R. 2, 416. lost in a desert *h.*
P. R. 3, 145. *h.* again Satan had not to answer
P. R. 3, 263. *h.* and there was room
P. R. 3, 269. many a league *h.*
P. R. 3, 275. *h.* Nineveh
P. R. 4, 6. won so much on Eve so little *h.*
P. R. 4, 281. these *h.* revolve
P. R. 4, 466. for only thou *h.* dwell'st
P. R. 4, 531. opportunity I *h.* have had
S. A. 9. but *h.* I feel amends
S. A. 11. *h.* leave me to respire
S. A. 74. the vilest *h.* excel me
S. A. 337. say if he be *h.*
S. A. 488. let me *h.* as I deserve pay
S. A. 807. *h.* I should still enjoy thee
S. A. 1520. stay *h.* or run
S. A. 1552. *h.* before thee
S. A. 1721. nothing is *h.* for tears
H. 239. song should *h.* have ending
**Hereafter.**—P. L. 3, 444. but store *h.*
P. L. 7, 488. of just equality perhaps *h.*
P. L. 8, 79. *h.* when they come to model heaven
P. L. 12, 156. to a land *h.* called Egypt
P. R. 1, 164. men *h.* may discern
P. R. 4, 625. *h.* learn with awe to dread
**Hereby.**—P. L. 4, 672. *h.* apter to receive
S. A. 106. but made *h.* obnoxious
**Hereditary.**—P. L. 12, 370. the throne *h.*
**Herein.**—P. R. 4, 356. but *h.* to our prophets
S. A. 61. *h.* haply had ends above my reach
**Hereof.**—S. A. 1145. for proof *h.* if Dagon be
**Heretics.**—F. of C. 11. named and printed *h.*
**Hermes.**—P. L. 3, 603. they bind volatile *H.*
P. L. 4, 717. son of Japhet brought by *H.*
P. L. 11, 133. pastoral reed of *H.*
C. 637. that *H.* once to wise Ulysses gave
Il P. 88. with thrice-great *H.*
**Hermione.**—P. L. 9, 506. *H.* and Cadmus
**Hermit.**—C. 390. for who would rob a *h.*
**Hermitage.**—Il P. 168. find out the peaceful *h.*
**Hermon.**—P. L. 12, 141. from *H.* east
P. L. 12, 142. mount *H.* yonder
**Hero.**—P. 13. most perfect *H.* tried
**Herod.**—P. R. 2, 424. and his son *H.*
**Heroes.**—P. L. 1, 552. noblest temper *h.* old

P. L. 11, 243. worn by kings and *h.* old
S. A. 1131. which greatest *h.* have in battle worn
V. Ex. 47. last of kings and queens and *h.* old
**Heroic.**—P. L. 1, 577. the *h.* race were joined
P. L. 2, 549. their own *h.* deeds
P. L. 4, 551. about him exercised *h.* games
P. L. 6, 66. breathed *h.* ardour
P. L. 9, 14. argument not less but more *h.*
P. L. 9, 25. since first this subject for *h.* song
P. L. 9, 29. the only argument *h.* deemed
P. L. 9, 32. of patience and *h.* martyrdom
P. L. 9, 40. justly gives *h.* name to person
P. L. 9, 485. and of limb *h.* built
P. L. 11, 690. and valour and *h.* virtue called
P. R. 1, 15. to tell of deeds above *h.*
P. R. 1, 216. deeds flamed in my heart *h.* acts
S. A. 527. after some proof of acts indeed *h.*
S. A. 125. that *h.* that renowned Samson
S. A. 318. have prompted this *h.* Nazarite
S. A. 1279. with plain *h.* magnitude of mind
S. A. 1711. and heroicly hath finished a life *h.*
**Heroicly.**—S. A. 1710. and *h.* hath finished
**Hers.**—P. L. 9, 47. if all be mine not *h.*
P. L. 10, 151. whose perfection far excelled *h.*
**Herse.**—L. 151. to strew the laureate *h.*
M. W. 58. for thy *h.* to strew the ways
**Herself.**—P. L. 2, 875. which but *h.*
P. L. 4, 270. *h.* a fairer flower by gloomy Dis
P. L. 5, 380. undecked save with *h.*
P. L. 7, 312. whose seed is in *h.* upon the earth
P. L. 8, 34. more noble than *h.* attains
P. L. 8, 137. if earth industrious of *h.*
P. L. 8, 506. *h.* though pure of sinful thought
P. L. 8, 548. and in *h.* complete
P. L. 9, 432. mindless the while *h.*
P. L. 9, 744. awhile thus to *h.* she mused
P. L. 9, 794. thus to *h.* she pleasingly began
P. L. 9, 1185. and left to *h.* if evil thence ensue
P. R. 4, 575. for grief and spite cast *h.* headlong
S. A. 596. in all her functions weary of *h.*
C. 857. to aid a virgin such as was *h.*
L. 58. the muse *h.* that Orpheus bore
**Hesebon.**—P. L. 1, 408. in *H* and Horonaim
**Hesperian.**—P. L. 1, 520. to the *H.* fields
P. L. 3, 568. those *H.* gardens
P. L. 4, 250. *H.* fables true
P. L. 8, 632. and vermeil isles *H.* sets my signal
C. 393. but beauty like the fair *H.* tree
**Hesperides.**—P. R. 2, 357. ladies of the *H.*
**Hesperus.**—P. L. 4, 605. *H.* that led
P. L. 9, 49. the star of *H.*
C. 982. all amidst the gardens fair of *H.*
**Hewing.**—P. L. 11, 728. *h.* timber tall
**Hewn.**—P. L. 1, 293. *h.* on Norwegian hills
P. L. 5, 759. diamond quarries *h.* and rocks
P. L. 6, 449. his riven arms to havoc *h.*
**Hid.**—P. L. 1, 673. that in his womb was *h.*
P. L. 1, 688. for treasures better *h.*
P. L. 3, 89. and in shadiest covert *h.*
P. L. 3, 624. but not his brightness *h.*
P. L. 3, 707. but *h.* their causes deep
P. L. 4, 278. *h.* Amalthea and her florid son
P. L. 4, 497. flowing gold of her loose tresses *h.*
P. L. 6, 896. have else to human race been *h.*
P. L. 7, 600. from golden censers *h.*
P. L. 8, 126. now high, now low, then *h.*
P. L. 8, 167. not thy thoughts with matters *h.*
P. L. 9, 76. then sought where to lie *h.*
P. L. 9, 408. *h.* among sweet flowers
P. L. 9, 436. then voluble and bold, now *h.*
P. L. 10, 100. from his presence *h.*
P. L. 10, 117. being naked *h.* myself
P. L. 10, 716. saw already in part though *h.*
P. L. 11, 316. as from his face I shall be *h.*
P. L. 11, 579. and know his works not *h.*
P. L. 11, 699. in silence *h.*
S. A. 89. *h.* in her vacant interlunar cave
C. 239. have *h.* in some flowery cave
C. 571. where that damned wizard *h.*
H. 80. and *h.* his head for shame
D. F. I. 32. *h.* from the world in a .... tomb

W. S. 3. his hallowed reliques should be *h.*
**Hidden.**—P. L. 2, 271. wants not her *h.* lustre
P. L. 6, 442. if other *h.* cause left them superior
P. L. 6, 516. part *h.* veins digged up
C. 248. to testify his *h.* residence
C. 415. she has a *h.* strength
C. 416. what *h.* strength?
C. 418. I mean that too, but yet a *h.* strength
L'A. 144. the *h.* soul of harmony
**Hide.**—P. L. 4, 35. *h.* their diminished heads
P. L. 6, 555. shadowing squadrons deep to *h.*
P. L. 9, 90. and his dark suggestions *h.*
P. L. 9, 162. in whose mazy folds to *h.* me
P. L. 9, 1090. cedars with innumerable boughs *h.*
P. L. 9, 1092. may for the present serve to *h.*
P. L. 9, 1113. vain covering if to *h.* their guilt
P. L. 10, 723. *h.* me from the face of God
P. L. 10, 974. from thee I will not *h.*
P. L. 11, 68. I will not *h.* my judgments
P. L. 11, 111. all terror *h.*
P. R. 3, 21. wherefore dost thou *h.*
P. R. 4, 630. beg to *h.* them in a herd of swine
S. A. 1749. oft he seems to *h.* his face
Il P. 141. *h.* me from day's garish eye
S. 19, 3. that one talent which is death to *h.*
H. 39. to *h.* her guilty front
D. F. I. 49. here below to *h.* thy nectared head
**Hideous.**—P. L. 1, 46. *h.* ruin and combustion
P. L. 1, 313. under amazement of their *h.* change
P. L. 2, 177. threatening *h.* fall
P. L. 2, 656. and rung a *h.* peal
P. L. 2, 726. with *h.* outcry rushed between
P. L. 2, 788. hell trembled at the *h.* name
P. L. 6, 107. in terrible array of *h.* length
P. L. 6, 206. nor less *h.* joined the horrid shock
P. L. 6, 577. with *h.* orifice gaped on us wide
P. L. 12, 56. forthwith a *h.* gabble rises loud
P. R. 1, 362. yet to that *h.* place not so confined
S. A. 1509. what *h.* noise was that
C. 520. within the navel of this *h.* wood
L. 61. the rout that made the *h.* roar
H. 174. no voice or *h.* hum runs through
**Hides.**—P. L. 1, 27. for heaven *h.* nothing
C. 383. he that *h.* a dark soul
**Hierarch.**—P. L. 5, 468. whom the winged *h.*
P. L. 11, 220. princely *h.* in their bright stand
**Hierarchal.**—P. L. 5, 701. *h.* standard
**Hierarchies.**—P. L. 5, 591. of *h.*
P. L. 5, 692. through all the *h.*
P. L. 7, 192. so sang the *h.*
**Hierarchs.**—P. L. 5, 587. under their *h.*
**Hierarchy.**—P. L. 1, 737. each in his *h.*
F. of C. 7. and ride us with a classic *h.*
**Hies.**—P. L. 2, 1055. in a cursed hour he *h.*
**High.**—P. L. 1, 40. to have equalled the Most *H.*
P. L. 1, 98. and *h.* disdain
P. L. 1, 132. and put to proof his *h.* supremacy
P. L. 1, 161. the contrary to his *h.* will
P. L. 1, 212. *h.* permission of all-ruling Heaven
P. L. 1, 304. *h.* over-arched embower
P. L. 1, 366. through God's *h.* sufferance
P. L. 1, 463. yet had his temple *h.*
P. L. 1, 528. with *h.* words that bore semblance
P. L. 1, 536. which full *h.* advanced
P. L. 1, 733. by many a towered structure *h.*
P. L. 1, 749. to have built in heaven *h.* towers
P. L. 1, 756. *h.* capital of Satan and his peers
P. L. 2, 1. *h.* on a throne of royal state
P. L. 2, 7. and from despair thus *h.* uplifted
P. L. 2, 8. aspires beyond thus *h.*
P. L. 2, 62. o'er heaven's *h.* towers to force
P. L. 2, 111. dignity composed and *h.* exploit
P. L. 2, 319. from heaven's *h.* jurisdiction
P. L. 2, 343. whose *h.* walls fear no assault
P. L. 2, 359. and heaven's *h.* arbitrator sit
P. L. 2, 456. above the rest *h.* honoured sits
P. L. 2, 472. winning cheap the *h.* repute
P. L. 2, 558. elevate and reasoned *h.*
P. L. 2, 635. to the fiery concave towering *h.*
P. L. 2, 644. hell bounds *h.* reaching
P. L. 2, 826. fell with us from on *h.*

P. L. 2, 874. forthwith the huge portcullis *h.*
P. L. 2, 909. next him *h.* arbiter chance governs
P. L. 3, 58. sits *h.* throned above all height
P. L. 3, 77. God beholding from his prospect *h.*
P. L. 3, 116. or *h.* foreknowledge
P. L. 3, 126. and revoke the *h.* decree
P. L. 3, 146. heaven and earth shall *h.* extol
P. L. 3, 205. sins against the *h.* supremacy
P. L. 3, 254. the ample air in triumph *h.*
P. L. 3, 311. good far more than great or *h.*
P. L. 3, 369. waken raptures *h.*
P. L. 3, 503. a structure *h.*
P. L. 3, 533. on *h.* behests
P. L. 3, 556. *h.* above the circling canopy
P. L. 3, 655. in sight of God's *h.* throne
P. L. 4, 30. sat *h.* in his meridian tower
P. L. 4, 49. lifted up so *h.* I sdeined subjection
P. L. 4, 90. and sceptre *h.* advanced
P. L. 4, 95. how soon would height recall *h.*
P. L. 4, 181. at one slight bound *h.* overleaped
P. L. 4, 219. *h.* eminent blooming ambrosial
P. L. 4, 226. as his garden mould *h.*
P. L. 4, 284. a whole day's journey *h.*
P. L. 4, 359. our room of bliss thus *h.* advanced
P. L. 4, 371. and this *h.* seat your heaven
P. L. 4, 395. his lofty stand on that *h.* tree
P. L. 4, 546. one entrance *h.*
P. L. 4, 554. hung *h,* with diamond flaming
P. L. 4, 699. reared *h.* their flourished heads
P. L. 4, 809. blown up with *h.* conceits
P. L. 4, 944. *h.* up in heaven
P. L. 5, 90. to this *h.* exaltation
P. L. 5, 174. and when *h.* noon hast gained
P. L. 5, 220. beheld with pity heaven's *h.* king
P. L. 5, 289. to his message *h.* in honour rise
P. L. 5, 290. on some message *h.*
P. L. 5, 458. whose *h.* power so far exceeded
P. L. 5, 467. at heaven's *h.* feasts to have fed
P. L. 5, 543. O fall from what *h.* state of bliss
P. L. 5, 563. *h.* matter thou enjoin'st me
P. L. 5, 588. ten thousand thousand ensigns *h.*
P. L. 5, 643. from that *h.* mount of God
P. L. 5, 699. he was taught that the Most *H.*
P. L. 5, 707. and *h.* was his degree in heaven
P. L. 5, 717. banded to oppose his *h.* throne
P. L. 5, 732. this our *h.* place, our sanctuary
P. L. 5, 757. to his royal seat, *h.* on a hill
P. L. 5, 812. thyself so *h.* above thy peers
P. L. 6, 26. they led him *h.*
P. L. 6, 60. ethereal trumpet from on *h.*
P. L. 6, 71. *h.* above the ground
P. L. 6, 99. *h.* in the midst exalted as a God
P. L. 6, 189. a noble stroke he lifted *h.*
P. L. 6, 228. *h.* over-ruled
P. L. 6, 401. such *h.* advantages
P. L. 6, 544. his orbed shield borne even or *h.*
P. L. 6, 745. hymns of *h.* praise
P. L. 6, 891. his mighty Father throned on *h.*
P. L. 6, 899. the deep fall of those too *h.*
P. L. 6, 906. despite done against the Most *H.*
P. L. 7, 53. of things so *h* and strange
P. L. 7, 87. distant so *h.* with moving fires
P. L. 7, 141. inaccessible *h.* strength
P. L. 7, 148. this *h.* temple to frequent
P. L. 7, 182. glory they sung, to the Most *H.*
P. L. 7, 233. so *h.* as heaved the tumid hills
P. L. 7, 326. *h.* woods the fields were crowned
P. L. 7, 340. *h.* in the expanse of heaven
P. L. 7, 373. through heaven's *h.* road
P. L. 7, 423. *h.* over seas flying
P. L. 7, 553. to the heaven of heavens his *h.*
P. L. 8, 12. attributed to the *h.* Creator
P. L. 8, 50. not capable her ear of what was *h.*
P. L. 8, 55. and solve *h.* dispute
P. L. 8, 101. the maker's *h.* magnificence
P. L. 8, 121. might err in things too *h.*
P. L. 8, 126. now *h.,* now low, then hid
P. L. 8, 172. heaven is for thee too *h.*
P. L. 8, 198. from this *h.* pitch let us
P. L. 8, 233. he sends upon his *h.* behests
P. L. 8, 303. a woody mountain whose *h.* top

P. L. 9, 170. down as low as *h*. he soared
P. L. 9, 574. and apprehended nothing *h*.
P. L. 9, 590. *h*. from ground the branches
P. L. 9, 602. thenceforth to speculations *h*.
P. L. 9, 789. expectation *h*. of knowledge
P. L. 9, 811. heaven is *h*., *h*. and remote to see
P. L. 9, 940. prime creatures dignified so *h*.
P. L. 9, 962. example *h*.
P. L. 9, 1107. a pillared shade *h*. overarched
P. L. 9, 1122. but *h*. winds worse within
P. L. 9, 1123. *h*. passions
P. L. 10, 13. the *h*. injunction not to taste
P. L. 10, 31. the Most *H*. eternal Father
P. L. 10, 86. of *h*. collateral glory
P. L. 10, 259. a monument of merit *h*.
P. L. 10, 308. Susa his Memnonian palace *h*.
P. L. 10, 385. *h*. proof ye now have given
P. L. 10, 445. ascended his *h*. throne
P. L. 10, 505. universal shout and *h*. applause
P. L. 10, 583. had first the rule of *h*. Olympus
P. L. 10, 953. if prayers could alter *h*. decrees
P. L. 11, 72. signal *h*. to the bright minister
P. L. 11, 81. resorting to the summons *h*.
P. L. 11, 251. heaven's *h*. behest
P. L. 11, 562. through all proportions low and *h*.
P. L. 11, 575. from the *h*. neighbouring hills
P. L. 11, 688. giants, men of *h*. renown
P. L. 11, 705. him the Most *H*.
P. L. 11, 708. *h*. in salvation
P. L. 11, 793. in the world *h*. titles
P. L. 11, 851. on the top of some *h*. mountain
P. L. 12, 120. God the Most *H*.
P. L. 12, 240. whose *h*. office now
P. L. 12, 342. whose *h*. walls thou saw'st left
P. L. 12, 369. the power of the Most *H*.
P. L. 12, 380. virgin mother hail, *h*. in the love
P. L. 12, 382. the Son of God Most *H*.
P. L. 12, 401. so only can *h*. justice rest appaid
P. L. 12, 457. exalted *h*. above all names
P. L. 12, 632. *h*. in front advanced
P. R. 1, 37. to whom such *h*. attest was given
P. R. 1, 128. preordained and fixed of the Most *H*.
P. R. 1, 142. birth divine and *h*. prediction
P. R. 1, 229. *h*. are thy thoughts
P. R. 1, 232. above example *h*.
P. R. 1, 370. illustrate his *h*. worth
P. R. 2, 5. and on that *h*. authority
P. R. 2, 30. from what *h*. hope to what relapse
P. R. 2, 66. what avails me now that honour *h*.
P. R. 2, 92. my exaltation to afflictions *h*.
P. R. 2, 114. end of being on earth and mission *h*.
P. R. 2, 202. full of honour wealth *h*. fare
P. R. 2, 280. *h*. towering to descry the morn's
P. R. 2, 286. from whose *h*. top to ken the
P. R. 2, 410. set on *h*. designs. *h*. actions
P. R. 3, 26. that sole excites to *h*. attempts
P. R. 3, 228. enterprise so hazardous and *h*.
P. R. 3, 252. Son of God up to a mountain *h*.
P. R. 3, 265. this *h*. mountain too
P. R. 4, 26. western side of that *h*. mountain
P. R. 4, 51. compass huge and *h*. the structure
P. R. 4, 160. on what I offer set as *h*. esteem
P. R. 4, 266. *h*. actions and *h*. passions
P. R. 4, 417. pines though rooted deep as *h*.
P. R. 4, 545. the holy city lifted *h*. her towers
P. R. 4, 633. hail, Son of the Most *H*.
S. A. 47. this *h*. gift of strength committed
S. A. 170. for him I reckon not in *h*. estate
S. A. 450. his praises *h*. among the heathen
S. A. 506. the execution leave to *h*. disposal
S. A. 525. from heaven foretold and *h*. exploits
S. A. 689. lower than thou didst exalt them *h*.
S. A. 1221. maimed for *h*. attempts
S. A. 1458. at home or through the *h*. street
S. A. 1492. all those *h*. exploits by him achieved
S. A. 1599. proclaimed through each *h*. street
S. A. 1606. on two main pillars vaulted *h*.
S. A. 1612. noon grew *h*. and sacrifice
S. A. 1613. mirth *h*. cheer and wine
S. A. 1740. matchless valour and adventures *h*.
C. 20. 'twixt *h*. and nether Jove

C. 78. when any favoured of *h*. Jove
C. 516. storied of old in *h*. immortal verse
C. 654. sign of battle make and menace *h*.
C. 746. at feasts and *h*. solemnities
C. 785. sublime notion and *h*. mystery
C. 798. thy magic structures reared so *h*.
C. 956. let us haste, the stars grow *h*.
A. 8. her *h*. worth to raise
A. 58. shakes the *h*. thicket
L. 25. ere the *h*. lawns appeared
L. 54. on the shaggy top of Mona *h*.
L. 172. Lycidas sunk low but mounted *h*.
L'A. 56. through the *h*. wood echoing shrill
L'A. 78. bosomed *h*. in tufted trees
L'A. 120. in weeds of peace *h*. triumphs hold
Il P. 86. seen in some *h*. lonely tower
Il P. 157. and love the *h*. embowed roof
Il P. 163. in service *h*. and anthems clear
S. 7, 11. that same lot, however mean or *h*.
H. 10. at heaven's *h*. council-table
H. 55. spear and shield were *h*. up hung
H. 148. the gates of her *h*. palace hall
M. W. 15. her *h*. birth and her graces sweet
Cir. 19. *h*. throned in secret bliss
D. F. I. 39. that *h*. first-moving sphere
M. W. 61. thou bright saint *h*. sit'st in glory
F. of C. 10. have been held in *h*. esteem
**High-arched**—P. L. 10, 301. *h.-a*. a bridge
**High-blest**.—P. L. 11, 145. of God *h.-b*.
**High-built**.—S. A. 1069. *h.-b*. and proud
**High-climbing**.—P. L. 3, 546. *h.-c*. hill
**Higher**.—P. L. 2, 72. against a *h*. foe
P. L. 2, 300. Satan except, none *h*. sat
P. L. 4, 50. thought one step *h*. would set
P. L. 4, 142. *h*. than their tops
P. L. 4, 146. *h*. than that wall
P. L. 4, 694. what *h*. grew of firm
P. L. 5, 422. her moist continent to *h*. orbs
P. L. 8, 358. or aught than mankind *h*.
P. L. 8, 551. all *h*. knowledge in her presence
P. L. 8, 586. what *h*. in her society
P. L. 8, 598. though *h*. of the genial bed
P. L. 9, 42. nor studious *h*. argument
P. L. 9, 174. since *h*. I fall short
P. L. 9, 483. whose *h*. intellectual more I shun
P. L. 9, 690. by venturing *h*. than my lot
P. L. 9, 934. *h*. degree of life
P. L. 11, 381. not *h*. that hill nor wider
P. L. 12, 576. hope no *h*. though all the stars
P. R. 2, 203. aimed not beyond *h*. design
P. R. 4, 198. if I to try whether in *h*. sort
P. R. 4, 258. who gave them breath but *h*. sung
P. R. 4, 521. in some respect far *h*.
P. R. 4, 546. and *h*. yet the glorious temple
C. 1021. *h*. than the sphery chime
L. 87. that strain I heard was of a *h*. mood
Il P. 22. yet thou art *h*. far descended
S. 13, 12. give fame leave to set thee *h*.
**Highest**.—P. L. 1, 517. their *h*. heaven
P. L. 1, 667. they raged against the *H*.
P. L. 2, 27. will envy whom the *h*. place exposes
P. L. 2, 429. conscious of *h*. worth
P. L. 2, 479. equal to the *H*. in heaven
P. L. 2, 630. thoughts inflamed of *h*. design
P. L. 2, 693. conjured against the *H*.
P. L. 3, 305. though throned in *h*. bliss
P. L. 3, 657. interpreter through *h*. heaven
P. L. 4, 51. one step higher would set me *h*.
P. L. 4, 182. all bound of hill or *h*. wall
P. L. 4, 195. the middle tree and *h*. there
P. L. 5, 865. shall teach us *h*. deeds
P. L. 6, 13. such as in *h*. heaven arrayed
P. L. 6, 112. bent on *h*. deeds
P. L. 6, 114. such resemblance of the *H*.
P. L. 6, 205. rung Hosanna to the *H*.
P. L. 6, 724. first, *h*., holiest, best
P. L. 7, 83. as to *h*. wisdom seemed
P. L. 8, 178. not of earth only but of *h*. heaven
P. L. 9, 164. with gods to sit the *h*.
P. L. 9, 683. to trace the ways of *h*. agents
P. L. 9, 1086. where *h*. woods impenetrable

P. L. 10, 889. that peopled *h.* heaven
P. L. 10, 1027. provoke the *H.* to make death
P. L. 11, 297. named of them the *h.*
P. L. 11, 378. it was a hill of paradise the *h.*
P. L. 11, 693. shall be held the *h.* pitch
P. L. 11, 829. till inundation rise above the *h.*
P. L. 12, 570. is fortitude to *h.* victory
P. R. 1, 69. to achieve things *h.*
P. R. 1, 139. the power of the *H.* o'ershadow her
P. R. 2, 438. in lowest poverty to *h.* deeds
P. R. 3, 30. powers all but the *h.*
P. R. 4, 106. at the *h.* without the *h.* attained
P. R. 4, 549. there on the *h.* pinnacle he set
P. R. 4, 553. and *h.* placed *h.* is
S. A. 61. of *h.* dispensation
S. A. 175. crowned with *h.* praises
S. A. 339. as erst in *h.,* behold him where he lies
S. A. 685. with no regard of *h.* favours past
S. A. 1101. bear'st the *h.* name for valiant acts
S. A. 1747. dispose of *h.* wisdom
Il P. 68. riding near her *h.* noon
**Highly.**—P. L. 1, 30. favoured of heaven so *h.*
P. L. 1, 666. *h.* they raged against the Highest
P. L. 2, 387. the bold design pleased *h.*
P. L. 2, 845. for both seemed *h.* pleased
P. L. 11, 170. who *h.* thus to entitle me
P. L. 12, 308. though of God *h.* beloved
S. A. 1333. this will offend them *h.*
S. A. 1148. how *h.* it concerns his glory now
**Highly-favoured**—M. W. 65. *h.-f.* Joseph
P. R. 2, 68. hail, *h.-f.*
**High-raised.**—S. M. 5. to our *h.-r.* phantasy
**High-roofed.**—P. R. 2, 293. the shade *h.-r.*
**High-seated.**—P. L. 7, 585. heaven's *h.-s.* top
**Hightened.**—P. L. 9, 793. *h.* as with wine
**Highth.**—*See* **Height.**
**High-towered.**—P. R. 3, 261. cities and *h-t*
**Hill.**—P. L. 1, 10. if Sion *h.* delight thee
P. L. 1, 231. a *h.* torn from Pelorus
P. L. 1, 403. on that opprobrious *h.*
P. L. 1, 416. even to that *h.* of scandal
P. L. 1, 670. there stood a *h.*
P. L. 1, 689. opened into the *h.* a spacious wound
P. L. 2, 495. that *h.* and valley rings
P. L. 2, 557. others apart sat on a *h.*
P. L. 2, 944. o'er *h.* or moory dale
P. L. 3, 28. or shady grove or sunny *h.*
P. L. 3, 546. brow of some high-climbing *h.*
P. L. 4, 172. the ascent of that steep savage *h.*
P. L. 4, 182. bound of *h.* or highest wall
P. L. 4, 224. through the shaggy *h.*
P. L. 4, 243. poured forth profuse on *h.* and dale
P. L. 4, 538. through waste, o'er *h.,* o'er dale
P. L. 4, 681. the steep of echoing *h.*
P. L. 4, 777. half way up *h.*
P. L. 5, 186. now rise from *h.* or steaming lake
P. L. 5, 203. to *h.* or valley
P. L. 5, 604. on this holy *h.* Him have anointed
P. L. 5, 619. dance about the sacred *h.*
P. L. 5, 732. our sanctuary, our *h.*
P. L. 5, 757. on a *h.* far blazing as a mount
P. L. 6, 25. on to the sacred *h* they led him
P. L. 6, 57. darken all the *h.*
P. L. 6, 69. nor obvious *h.* nor straitening vale
P. L. 6, 784. with fresh flowerets *h.* and valley
P. L. 6, 641. pleasure situate in *h.* and dale
P. L. 7, 3. above the Olympian *h.* I soar
P. L. 7, 300. nor withstood them rock or *h.*
P. L. 8, 262. I saw *h.,* dale and shady woods
P. L. 8, 514. gave sign of gratulation and each *h.*
P. L. 8, 520. his *h.* top to light the bridal lamp
P. L. 9, 116. sweet interchange of *h.* and valley
P. L. 11, 187. from a *h.* the beast that reigns
P. L. 11, 210. and on a *h.* made halt
P. L. 11, 229. blazing cloud that veils the *h.*
P. L. 11, 367. ascend this *h.*
P. L. 11, 377. it was a *h.* of Paradise
P. L. 11, 381. not higher that *h.* nor wider
P. L. 12, 591. on yonder *h.* expect their motion
P. L. 12, 606. and they both descend the *h.*
P. L. 12, 626. and from the other *h.*

P. R. 1, 303. whether on *h.* sometimes
P. R. 2, 217. as on the top of Virtue's *h.*
P. R. 2, 285. up to a *h.* anon his steps he reared
P. R. 3, 267. and o'er *h.* and dale
P. R. 3, 333. or where plain was raise *h.*
P. R. 4, 247. there flowery *h.* Hymettus
P. R. 4, 447. walking on a sunny *h.* he found
S. A. 148. up to the *h.* by Hebron
C. 295. along the side of yon small *h.*
L. 23. for we were nursed upon the selfsame *h.*
L'A. 55. from the side of some hoar *h.*
S. 9, 4. up the *h.* of heavenly truth
M. M. 8. *h.* and dale doth boast thy blessing
**Hillock.**—P. L. 4, 254. or palmy *h.*
**Hillocks.**—P. L. 7, 469. threw in *h.*
P. L. 10, 860. O woods, O fountains, *h.,* dales
L'A. 58. by hedge-row elms, on *h.* green
**Hills.**—P. L. 1, 293. hewn on Norwegian *h.*
P. L. 2. 540. rend up both rocks and *h.*
P. L. 3, 435. on *h.* where flocks are fed
P. L. 4, 261. waters fall down the slope *h.*
P. L. 5, 261. cedars crowned above all *h.*
P. L. 5, 547. by night from neighbouring *h.*
P. L. 6, 528. others from the dawning *h.*
P. L. 6, 639. arms away they threw and to the *h.*
P. L. 6, 644. they plucked the seated *h.*
P. L. 6, 663. the neighbouring *h.* uptore
P. L. 6, 664. so *h.* amid the air encountered *h.*
P. L. 6, 781. at his command the uprooted *h.*
P. L. 7, 8. before the *h.* appeared
P. L. 7, 288. high as heaved the tumid *h.*
P. L. 8, 275. ye *h.* and dales, ye rivers, woods
P. L. 11, 575. from the high neighbouring *h.*
P. L. 11, 740. the *h.* to their supply
P. L. 11, 829. rise above the highest *h.*
P. L. 11, 852. and now the tops of *h.*
P. L. 12, 146. to Senir that long ridge of *h.*
P. R. 3, 260. thronged with flocks the *h.*
P. R. 3, 332. lay *h.* plain, fell woods or valleys
P. R. 4, 29. backed with a ridge of *h.*
P. R. 4, 35. on seven small *h.* with palaces
C. 424. infamous *h.* and sandy perilous wilds
C. 927. tumble down the snowy *h.*
L. 190. the sun had stretched out all the *h.*
S. 18, 9. the vales redoubled to the *h.*
V. Ex. 42. *h.* of snow and lofts of piled thunder
**Hilly.**—C. 531. my flocks hard by i' the *h.* crofts
**Himself.**—P. L. 1, 39. to set *h.* in glory
P. L. 1, 79. one next *h.* in power
P. L. 1, 215. he might heap on *h.* damnation
P. L. 1, 219. but on *h.* treble confusion
P. L. 3, 234. atonement for *h.* or offering meet
P. L. 3, 409. offered *h.* to die for man's offence
P. L. 4, 18. back recoils upon *h.*
P. L. 4, 22. no more than from *h.*
P. L. 4, 397. *h.* now one, now other
P. L. 4, 504. eyed them askance and to *h.* thus
P. L. 4, 934. ways of danger by *h.* untried
P. L. 5, 240. late fallen *h.* from heaven
P. L. 5, 353. in *h.* was all his state
P. L. 5, 665. and thought *h.* impaired
P. L. 5, 775. another now hath to *h.* engrossed
P. L. 6, 238. each on *h.* relied
P. L. 6, 341. shame to find *h.* not matchless
P. L. 7, 140. who thought all like *h.*
P. L. 8, 251. for who *h.* beginning knew
P. L. 9, 57. what might hap of heavier on *h.*
P. L. 9, 331. but turns foul on *h.*
P. L. 9, 348. within *h.* the danger lies
P. L. 9, 673. stood in *h.* collected
P. L. 9, 895. first to *h.* he inward silence broke
P. L. 10, 62. and destined man *h.* to judge
P. L. 10, 510. wondering at *h.*
P. L. 10, 799. which to God *h.* impossible is held
P. L. 10, 845. thus Adam to *h.* lamented loud
P. L. 10, 878. though by the devil *h.*
P. L. 11, 820. to save *h.* and household
P. L. 12, 65. to *h.* assuming authority usurped
P. L. 12, 70. such title to *h.* reserving
P. L. 12, 76. to sustain *h.* and his rash army
P. L. 12, 91. permits within *h.*

P. L. 12, 228. descending will *h.* in thunder
P. R. 1, 76. he *h.* among them was baptized
P. R. 2, 98. well I saw he could not lose *h.*
P. R. 2, 111. into *h.* descended
P. R. 2, 237. band of spirits likest to *h.*
P. R. 2, 244. and to *h.* thus said
P. R. 2, 466. yet he who reigns within *h.*
P. R. 2, 471. subject *h.* to anarchy within
P. R. 3, 139. and so of all true good *h.* despoiled
P. R. 3, 140. yet sacrilegious to *h.*
P. R. 3, 144. he *h.* to glory will advance
P. R. 3, 147. for he *h.* insatiable of glory
P. R. 3, 433. (time to *h.* best known)
P. R. 4, 302. perfect in *h.* and all possessing
P. R. 4, 312. degraded by *h.* on grace depending
P. R. 4, 327. versed in books and shallow in *h.*
S. A. 42. *h.* in bonds under Philistian yoke
S. A. 121. and by *h.* given over
S. A. 130. weaponless *h.* made arms ridiculous
S. A. 299. and no man therein doctor but *h.*
S. A. 309. who made our laws to bind us not *h.*
S. A. 346. *h.* an army
S. A. 347. to save *h.* against a coward armed
S. A. 1585. so soon at variance with *h.*
S. A. 1658. pulled down the destruction on *h.*
S. A. 1709. Samson hath quit *h.* like Samson
S. A. 1717. to *h.* and father's house eternal fame
C. 385. *h.* is his own dungeon
L. 11. *h.* to sing and build the lofty rhyme
**Hind.**—P. L. 11, 189. the forest hart and *h.*
**Hinder.**—P. R. 7, 465. to get free his *h.* parts
**Hindered.**—P. L. 10. 8. wise and just *h.* not
**Hinders.**—P. L. 9, 778. wise what *h.* then
S. A. 1533. what *h.* now?
**Hindmost.**—C. 190. rose from the *h.* wheels
**Hinds.**—C. 174. the loose unlettered *h.*
S. 12, 5. when those *h.* that were transformed
**Hinges.**—P. L. 2, 881. on their *h.* grate
P. L. 5, 255. self-opened wide on golden *h.*
P. L. 7, 207. on golden *h.* moving to let forth
P. R. 4, 415. rushed abroad from the four *h.*
H. 122. and the well-balanced world on *h.* hung
**Hinnom.**—P. L. 1, 404. valley of *H.*
**Hippogrif.**—P. R. 4, 542. wing of *h.*
**Hippotades.**—L. 96. and sage *H.*
**Hired.**—S. A. 1114. till they had *h.* a woman
**Hireling.**—S. 16, 14. of *h.* wolves
**Hirelings.**—P. L. 4. 193. lewd *h.*
**Hispahan.**—P. L. 11, 394. since in *H.*
**Hiss.**—P. L. 1, 768. the *h.* of rustling wings
P. L. 6. 212. the dismal *h.* of fiery darts
P. L. 10, 508. a dismal universal *h.*
P. L. 10, 518. but *h.* for *h.* returned
P. L. 10, 543. and the dire *h.* renewed
P. L. 10, 546. turned to exploding *h.*
P. L. 10, 573. long and ceaseless *h.*
**Hissing.**—P. L. 10, 522. the din of *h.*
**Hist.**—Il P. 55. and the mute silence *h.* along
**Historian.**—P. L. 8, 7. divine *h.*
**Hit.**—P. L. 6, 592. that whom they *h.*
P. R. 4. 255. in tones and numbers *h.* by voice
S. A. 1014. what it is, hard is to say, harder to *h.*
C. 286. how easy my misfortune is to *h.*
A. 77. if my inferior hand or voice could *h.*
Il P. 14. to *h.* the sense of human sight
**Hither.**—P. L. 2, 857. hates me and hath *h.*
P. L. 3, 445. up *h.* like aerial vapours flew
P. L. 3, 457. dissolved on earth fleet *h.*
P. L. 3, 463. *h.* of ill-joined sons
P. L. 3, 698. that led thee *h.*
P. L. 3, 722. whose *h.* side with light
P. L. 4, 796. seize fast and *h.* bring
P. L. 4, 908. what boldness brought him *h.*
P. L. 5, 308. haste *h.* Eve
P. L. 7, 159. at length the way up *h.*
P. L. 7, 364. *h.* as to their fountain
P. L. 8, 313. He who was my guide up *h.*
P. L. 8, 347. not *h.* summoned
P. L. 9, 475. to forget what *h.* brought us
P. L. 9, 647. might have spared our coming *h.*
P. L. 11, 344. had *h.* come from all the ends

P. L. 11, 574. but on the *h.* side
P. R. 1, 335. who brought me *h.*
P. R. 1, 494. thy coming *h.*
P. R. 3, 350. I have brought thee *h.*
S. A. 335. *h.* hath informed your younger feet
S. A. 821. malice not repentance brought thee *h.*
S. A. 1070. what wind hath blown him *h.*
S. A. 1445. my inducement *h.*
S. A. 1536. a little stay will bring some notice *h.*
S. A. 1539. to our wish I see one *h.* speeding
L. 134. and bid them *h.* cast their bells
L. 139. throw *h.* all your quaint enamelled eyes
**Hitherto.**—P. L. 9, 28. *h.* the only argument
P. L. 9. 797. *h.* obscured, infamed
S. A. 1640. *h.* what your commands imposed
**Hitherward.**—P. L. 4, 794. seen *h.* bent
S. A. 1067, a rougher tongue draws *h.*
**Hitting.**—S. A. 1568. *h.* thy aged ear
**Hive.**—P. L. 1, 770. youth about the *h.*
**Hoar.**—A. 98. old Lycæus or Cyllene *h.*
L'A. 55. from the side of some *h.* hill
**Hoarded.**—C. 739. coin must not be *h.*
**Hoarse.**—P. L. 2, 287. with *h.* cadence
P. L. 2, 661. from the *h.* Trinacrian shore
P. L. 5, 873. *h.* murmur echoed to his words
P. L. 7, 25. unchanged to *h.* or mute
P. L. 12, 58. till *h.* and all in rage
**Hoary.**—P. L. 2, 891. secrets of the *h.* deep
P. L. 11, 899. harvest heat and *h.* frost
C. 871. by *h.* Nereus' wrinkled look
**Hobson.**—U. C. I. 1, here lies old *H.*
U. C. I. 18, *H.* has supped, and's newly gone to
**Hog.**—C. 71. or tiger, *h.,* or bearded goat
**Hogs.**—S. 12, 8. got by casting pearl to *h.*
**Hold.**—P. L. 1, 657. infernal pit shall never *h.*
P. L. 2, 12. no deep within her gulf can *h.*
P. L. 2, 362. left to their defence who *h.* it
P. L. 2, 895. *h.* eternal anarchy
P. L. 3, 84. main abyss wide interrupt can *h.*
P. L. 3, 461. or middle spirits *h.*
P. L. 4, 111. empire with heaven's King I *h.*
P. L. 4, 907. in doubt whether to *h.*
P. L. 5, 347. nor these to *h.* wants her fit
P. L. 5, 395. awhile discourse they *h.*
P. L. 5, 537. *h.* as you yours while our obedience
P. L. 5, 723. we mean to *h.* what anciently
P. L. 7, 532. and throughout dominion *h.*
P. L. 8, 408. how have I then with whom to *h.*
P. L. 10, 135. should I *h.* my peace
P. L. 10, 365. hell could no longer *h.* us
P. L. 10, 406. my *h.* of this new kingdom
P. L. 10, 751. by which I was to *h.* the good
P. L. 11, 635. who should better *h.* his place
P. L. 11, 900. shall *h.* their course till fire purge
P. L. 12, 68. that right we *h.* by his dominion
P. R. 2, 125. so may we *h.* our place
P. R. 4, 168. and *h.* them all
P. R. 4, 232. or they with thee *h.* conversation
P. R. 4, 480. thou of Israel's sceptre get fast *h.*
P. R. 4, 494. at least might seem to *h.* all power
S. A. 12. this day a solemn feast the people *h.*
S. A. 719. courted by all the winds that *h.* them
S. A. 796. to endear and *h.* thee to me firmest
S. A. 802. safe custody and *h.*
S. A. 1349. whether to *h.* or break
C. 94. now the top of heaven doth *h.*
C. 588. this I *h.* firm:—virtue may be assailed
C. 919. now the spell hath lost his *h.*
A. 65. and sing to those that *h.* the vital shears
L. 119. that scarce themselves know how to *h.*
L. 162. toward Namancos and Bayona's *h.*
L'A. 120. in weeds of peace high triumphs *h.*
Il P. 90. what worlds or what vast regions *h.*
H. 108. could *h.* all heaven and earth
**Holding.**—L'A. 32. laughter *h.* both his sides
**Holds.**—P. L. 1, 124. *h.* the tyranny
P. L. 2, 497. firm concord. *h.*
P. L. 2, 541. hell scarce *h.* the wild uproar
P. L. 2, 1043. like a weather-beaten vessel *h.*
P. L. 4, 263. her crystal mirror *h.*
P. L. 5, 103. Fancy next her office *h.*

P. L. 5, 441. can turn or *h.* it possible to turn
P. L. 5, 537. while our obedience *h.*
P. L. 7, 382. thousand lesser lights dividual *h.*
P. L. 11, 633. the tenor of man's woe *h.* on
P. R. 3, 296. under his dominion *h.*
P. R. 4, 628. from thy demoniac *h.* possession
S. A. 1369. force constrains the sentence *h.*
C. 1005. *h.* his dear Psyche sweet entranced
**Hold'st.**—P. R. 4, 623. *h.* in hell no triumph
**Hole.**—C. 338. from the wicker *h.* of some clay
**Holiday.**—C. 959. till next sunshine *h.*
L'A. 98. on a sunshine *h.*
**Holier.**—C. 943. till we come to *h.* ground
**Holies.**—P. R. 4, 349. the holiest of *h.*
**Holiest.**—P. L. 4, 759. unbefitting *h.* place
P. L. 6, 724. first highest, *h.,* best
P. R. 2, 110. with *h.* meditations fed
P. R. 4, 349. the *h.* of Holies and his Saints
**Hollow.**—P. L. 1, 314. all the *h.* deep of hell
P. L. 1, 707.by strange conveyance filled each *h.*
P. L. 2, 112. but all was false and *h.*
P. L. 2, 285. as when *h.* rocks retain the sound
P. L. 2, 518. the *h.* abyss heard far and wide
P. L. 6, 484. which into *h.* engines long
P. L. 6, 552. in *h.* cube training his devilish
P. L. 6, 578. portending *h.* truce
P. L. 7, 257. the *h.* universal orb
P. L. 7, 289. down sunk a *h.* bottom broad
P. R. 4, 124. so many *h.* compliments and lies
S. 17, 6. the drift of *h.* states hard to be spelled
H. 102. beneath the *h.* round of Cynthia's seat
H. 178. with *h.* shriek
**Hollowed.**—P. L. 6, 574. or *h.* bodies
**Holocaust.**—S. A. 1702. and lay erewhile a *h.*
**Eoly.**—P. L. 1, 390. his *h.* rites and solemn
P. L. 1, 683. than aught divine or *h.*
P. L. 3, 1. hail *h.* light, offspring of heaven
P. L. 5, 147. various style nor *h.* rapture
P. L. 5, 386. the *h.* salutation used long after
P. L. 5, 593. *h.* memorials acts of zeal and love
P. L. 5, 604. on this *h.* hill Him have anointed
P. L. 5, 712. from forth his *h.* mount
P. L. 6, 272. think not here to trouble *h.* rest
P. L. 6, 359. nor from the *H.* One of heaven
P. L. 6, 743. circling thy *h.* mount
P. L. 7, 91. the Creator in his *h.* rest
P. L. 7, 584. when at the *h.* mount
P. L. 7, 594. but not in silence *h.* kept
P. L. 7, 631. a race of worshippers *h.* and just
P. L. 9, 899. *h.* divine, good, amiable
P. L. 11, 606. *h.* and pure conformity divine
P. L. 12, 109. avert his *h.* eyes
P. L. 12, 248. the *H.* One with mortal men
P. L. 12, 340. his temple and his *h.* ark
P. R. 1, 195. his *h.* meditations thus pursued
P. R. 1, 486.thy Father who is *h.* wise and pure
P. R. 1, 489. handling *h.* things
P. R. 2, 8. though in *H.* writ not named
P. R. 4, 545. the *h.* city lifted high her towers
S. A. 362. ordained thy nurture *h.*
S. A. 497. his *h.* secret have published
S. A. 1358. by prostituting *h.* things
S. A. 1427. and the *H.* One of Israel be thy guide
C. 246. sure something *h.* lodges in that breast
C. 767. and *h.* dictate of spare temperance
Il P. 11. but hail thou goddess sage and *h.*
Il P. 41. there held in *h.* passion
H. 5. for so the *h.* sages once did sing
H. 133. if such *h.* song enwrap our fancy long
H. 190. on the *h.* hearth, the Lars and Lemures
H. 202. not girt with tapers' *h.* shine
P. 41. there doth my soul in *h.* vision sit
S. M. 15. hymns devout and *h.* psalms
**Holy-days.**—S. A. 1421. people on their *h.-d.*
**Holy Ghost.**—P. R. 1, 139. the *H. G.*
**Holy Land.**—P. L. 3, 536. where the *H. L.*
**Homage.**—P. R. 2, 376. come to pay thee *h.*
**Home.**—P. L. 2, 457. intend at *h.* while here
P. L. 6, 622. and full of force urged *h.*
P. L. 10, 1085. our final rest and native *h.*
P. L. 11, 154. peace returned *h.* to my breast

P. L. 11, 692. and bring *h.* spoils
P. R. 2, 79. from Egypt *h.* returned
P. R. 2, 415. in poverty and straits at *h.*
P. R. 3, 233. most part spent at *h.*
P. R. 4, 281. revolve or as thou likest at *h.*
P. R. 4, 639. *h.* to his mother's house
C. 76. and all their friends and native *h.* forget
C. 748. it is for homely features to keep *h.*
S. 15, 6. ever brings victory *h.*
S. A. 518. to return thee *h.* to thy country
S. A. 579. better at *h.* lie bed-rid
S.A. 805. while I at *h.* sat full of cares and fears
S. A. 810. fearless at *h.* of partners in my love
S. A. 917. at *h.* in leisure and domestic ease
S. A. 1458. at *h.* or through the high street
S. A. 1733. *h.* to his father's house
U. C. I. 11. but lately finding him so long at *h.*
**Home-felt.**—C. 262. a sacred and *h.-f.* delight
**Homely.**—P. L. 10, 605. no *h.* morsels
C. 748. it is for *h.* features to keep home
L. 65. to tend the *h.* slighted shepherd's trade
**Homer.**—P. R. 4, 259. Melesigenes thence *H.*
**Homeward.**—P. L. 5, 688. *h.* with flying
P. L. 12, 632. fast at the labourer's heel *h.*
L. 163. look *h.* angel now, and melt with ruth
**Homicide,**—P. L. 1, 417. of Moloch *h.*
**Honest.**—S. A. 1366. by labour *h.* and lawful
C. 322. and trust thy *h.* offered courtesy
**Honesty.**—C. 691. restore the truth and *h.*
**Honey.**—P. L. 7, 492. her waxen cells with *h.*
**Honeysuckle.**—C. 545. with flaunting *h.*
**Honied.**—S. A. 1066. the bait of *h.* words
L. 140. on the green turf suck the *h.* showers
Il P. 142. while the bee with *h.* thigh
**Honour.**—P. L. 1, 533. that proud *h.* claimed
P. L. 2, 453. as great a share of hazard as of *h.*
P. L. 3, 343. adore the Son, and *h.* him as me
P. L. 3, 660. like *h.* to obtain
P. L. 3, 738. where *h.* due and reverence none
P. L. 4, 289. godlike erect with native *h.* clad
P. L. 4, 314. *h.* dishonourable
P. L. 4, 390. just *h.* and empire
P. L. 5, 188. in *h.* to the world's great Author
P. L. 5, 289. to his message high in *h.* rise
P. L. 5, 315. fit to *h.* and receive
P. L. 5, 365. and *h.* these
P. L. 5, 462. thy favour in this *h.* done to man
P. L. 5, 817. and in that *h.* due confess him
P. L. 5, 844. all *h.* to him done
P. L. 6, 422. *h.,* dominion, glory, and renown
P. L. 6, 676. to *h.* his anointed Son
P. L. 8, 58. in love and mutual *h.*
P. L. 8, 508. she what was *h.* knew
P. L. 8, 577. with *h.* thou mayst love thy mate
P. L. 9, 332. rather double *h.* gain
P. L. 9, 1057. and *h.* from about them
P. L. 9, 1074. of *h.* void of innocence of faith
P. L. 11, 617. woman's domestic *h.*
P. R. 1, 75. to do him *h.* as their king
P. R. 1, 251. to *h.* thee with incense
P. R. 2, 66. what avails me now that *h.* high
P. R. 2, 86. to *h.*?
P. R. 2, 202. full of *h.,* wealth, high fare
P. R. 2, 227. of worth, of *h.,* glory
P. R. 2, 336. with *h.* only deign to sit and eat
P. R. 2, 422. money brings *h.,* friends
P. R. 2, 464. his *h.,* virtue, merit
P. R. 3, 95. who names not now with *h.*
P. R. 4, 122. what *h.* that, but tedious waste
P. R. 4, 207. more *h.* left and more esteem
P. R. 4, 368. since neither wealth nor *h.*
S. A. 372. be it but for *h.'s* sake
S. A. 412. O blot to *h.* and religion
S. A. 449. I this *h.* I this pomp have brought
S. A. 992. the public marks of *h.* and reward
S. A. 1101. that *h.* certain to have won
S. A. 1166. so to stain his *h.*
S. A. 1178. fair *h.* that thou dost thy God
S. A. 1276. all such as *h.* truth
S. A. 1315. to *h.* this great feast
S. A. 1360. vaunting my strength in *h.*

S. A. 1715. to Israel *h.* hath left
C. 220. to keep my life and *h.* unassailed
C. 864. listen for dear *h.'s* sake
A. 27. I see bright *h.* sparkle through your eyes
A. 35. was all in *h.* and devotion meant
L'A. 37. and if I give thee *h.* due
S. 8, 3. if deed of *h.* did thee ever please
S. 13, 10. to *h.* thee the priest of Phœbus' choir
H. 26. the *h.* first thy Lord to greet
D. F. I. 3. summer's chief *h.*

**Honourable.**—S. A. 1108, your *h.* lords
S. A. 855. how *h.* how glorious

**Honoured.**—P. L. 2, 456. above the rest high *h.*
P. L. 5, 73. the author not impaired but *h.*
P. L. 5, 663. that day *h.* by his great father
P. L. 6, 816. hath *h.* me according to his will
P. L. 8, 227. for God we see hath *h.* thee
P. L. 8, 649. and shall be *h.* ever
P. R. 1, 329. at the ford of Jordan *h.* so
S. A. 989. when all men hord, *h.*, feared me
L. 85. thou *h.* flood, smooth-sliding Mincius
S. 10, 14. and to possess them *h.* Margaret
M. W. 2. the *h.* wife of Winchester
W. S. 1. what needs my Shaksp. for his *h.* bones
C. 564. my most *h.* lady, your dear sister

**Honouring.**—P. L. 8. 569. thy *h.* and thy love

**Honours.**—P. L. 5, 780. be devised of *h.* new
P. R. 4. 536. for *h.*, riches, kingdoms, glory

**Honour'st**—S. 13, 9. thou *h.* verse

**Hoods.**—P. L. 3, 490. cowls, *h.* and habits

**Hook.**—C. 872. and the Carpathian wizard's *h.*

**Hooked.**—H. 56. the *h.* chariot stood

**Hope.**—P. L. 1, 66. *h.* never comes
P. L. 1, 88. equal *h.* and hazard
P. L. 1, 120. we may with more successful *h.*
P. L. 1, 190. reinforcement we may gain from *h.*
P. L. 1, 275. their liveliest pledge of *h.*
P. L. 2, 7. thus high uplifted beyond *h.*
P. L. 2, 89. exercise us without *h.* of end
P. L. 2, 142. our final *h.* is flat despair
P. L. 2, 221. besides what *h.*
P. L. 2, 232. him to unthrone we then may *h.*
P. L. 2, 234. vain to *h.* argues as vain
P. L. 2, 416. the weight of all and our last *h.*
P. L. 2, 498. under *h.* of heavenly grace
P. L. 2, 522. raised by false presumptuous *h.*
P. L. 2, 568. and excite fallacious *h.*
P. L. 2, 811. neither vainly *h.* to be
P. L. 3, 630. as now in *h.* to find
P. L. 4, 60. no unbounded *h.* had raised
P. L. 4, 105. all *h.* excluded thus
P. L. 4, 108. farewell *h.* and with *h.* farewell
P. L. 4, 160. beyond the Cape of *H.*
P. L. 4, 892. thou mightst *h.* to change
P. L. 4, 938. in *h.* to find better abode
P. L. 4, 960. but in *h.* to dispossess
P. L. 5, 119. gives me *h.*
P. L. 6, 131. thy *h.* was to have reached
P. L. 6, 287. that thou shouldst *h.*
P. L. 6, 497. their languished *h.* revived
P. L. 6, 787. *h.* conceiving from despair
P. L. 7, 121. let thine own inventions *h.* .
P. L. 8, 209. were it not in *h.* of thy reply
P. L. 8, 481. when out of *h.* behold her
P. L. 9, 126. nor *h.* to be myself less miserable
P. L. 9, 257. with greedy *h.* to find his wish
P. L. 9, 422. he wished but not with *h.*
P. L. 9, 424. when to his wish beyond his *h.*
P. L. 9, 475. *h.* of Paradise for hell, *h.* here
P. L. 9, 633. *h.* elevates and joy brightens
P. L. 10, 463. returned successful beyond *h.*
P. L. 10, 838. alike destroys all *h.* of refuge
P. L. 10, 995. desire to languish without *h.*
P. L. 10, 1043. cuts us off from *h.*
P. L. 11, 138. new *h.* to spring out of despair
P. L. 11, 271. where I had *h.*
P. L. 11, 308. by prayer incessant I could *h.*
P. L. 11, 493. as their chief good and final *h.*
P. L. 11, 599. and more *h.* of peaceful days
P. L. 11, 779. I had *h.* when violence was
P. L. 12, 376. finisher of utmost *h.*

P. L. 12, 576. *h.* no higher though all the stars
P. R. 1, 105. best to *h.* of like success
P. R. 2, 30. from what high *h.* to what relapse
P. R. 2, 57. soon we shall see our *h.*
P. R. 2, 58. they out of their plaints new *h.*
P. R. 2, 165. and with voluptuous *h.*
P. R. 2, 417. which way or from what *h.*
P. R. 3, 204. all *h.* is lost of my reception
P. R. 3, 206. where no *h.* is left, is left no fear
P. R. 3, 216. willingly I could fly and *h.*
P. R. 3, 359. couldst thou *h.* long to enjoy
P. R. 4, 3. in his fraud, thrown from his *h.*
S. A. 82. total eclipse without all *h.* of day
S. A. 120. as one past *h.* abandoned
S. A. 460. this only *h.* relieves me
S. A. 472. with cause this *h.* relieves thee
S. A. 647. in the list of them that *h.*
S. A. 838. my love how couldst thou *h.*
S. A. 1453. what *h.* I have
S. A. 1455. *h.* would much rejoice us
S. A. 1535. yet *h.* would fain subscribe
S. A. 1571. all my *h.'s* defeated
C. 213. pure-eyed faith, white-handed *h.*
C. 400. and tell me it is safe as bid me *h.*
C. 410. an equal poise of *h.* and fear
C. 412. I incline to *h.* rather than fear
L. 73. the fair guerdon when we *h.*
S. 1, 3. fresh *h.* the lover's heart dost fill
S. 9, 11. and *h.* that reaps not shame
S. 22, 8. nor bate a jot of heart or *h.*
M. W. 25. and now with second *h.* she goes
F. of C. 13. do *h.* to find out all your tricks

**Hoped.**—P. L. 3, 740. sped with *h.* success
P. R. 4, 578. triumphals of his *h.* success

**Hopeful.**—P. L. 4, 984. his *h.* sheaves
P. L. 10, 972. new acceptance *h.* to regain
P. L. 11, 543. *h.* and cheerful
S. A. 1575. *h.* of his delivery

**Hopeless.**—P. L. 2, 186. ages of *h.* end
P. L. 9. 259. *h.* to circumvent us
S. A. 648. *h.* are all my evils
S. 1, 10. foretell my *h.* doom

**Hopes.**—P. L. 1, 637. have lost our *h.*
P. L. 3, 449. built their fond *h.* of glory
P. L. 4, 808. vain *h.*, vain aims
P. L. 9, 985. new *h.*, new joys
P. L. 10, 1011. to better *h.*
S. A. 523. and great in *h.*
S. A. 595. my *h.* all flat
S. A. 1504. thy *h.* are not ill-founded

**Hoping.**—P. L. 6, 258. as *h.* here to end
P. L. 10, 339. not *h.* to escape

**Horizon.**—P. L. 3, 560. beyond the *h.*
P. L. 6, 79. far in the *h.* to the north
P. L. 7, 371. the *h.* round invested with
P. L. 9, 52. veiled the *h.*
P. L. 10, 684. rounded still the *h.*
P. 23. to this *h.* is my Phœbus bound

**Horizontal.**—P. L. 1, 595. the *h.* misty air

**Horn.**—P. R. 2, 356. from Amalthea's *h.*
P. R. 3, 327. nor on each *h.*
A. 57. tasselled *h.*
L. 28. the gray-fly winds her sultry *h.*
L'A 53. listening how the hounds and *h.*
H. 203. the Lybic Hammon shrinks his *h.*

**Horned.**—P. L. 10, 525. cerastes *h.*
P. L. 11, 831. pushed by the *h.* flood

**Hornets.**—S. A. 20. a deadly swarm of *h.*

**Horns.**—P. L. 1, 439. with crescent *h.*
P. L. 4, 978. sharpening in mooned *h.*
P. L. 7, 366. the morning planet gilds her *h.*
P. L. 10, 433. the *h.* of Turkish crescent

**Horny.**—P. R. 2, 267. with their *h.* beaks

**Horonaim.**—P. L. 1, 409. in Hesebon and *H.*

**Horrent.**—P. L. 2, 513. and *h.* arms

**Horrible.**—P. L. 1, 61. a dungeon *h.*
P. L. 1, 137. in *h.* destruction laid thus low
P. L. 2, 846. and death grinned *h.*
P. L. 6, 210. clashing brayed *h.* discord
P. L. 10, 472. deep of *h.* confusion
P. L. 11, 465. horrid to think, how *h.* to feel

S. A. 1649. with *h.* convulsion
**Horribly.**—S. A .1510. *h.* loud
**Horrid.**—P. L. 1, 51. he with his *h* crew
P. L. 1, 83. breaking the *h.* silence
P. L. 1, 224. leave in the midst a *h.* vale
P. L. 1, 392. first Moloch *h.* king
P. L. 1, 563. a *h.* front of dreadful length
P. L. 2, 63. turning our tortures into *h.* arms
P. L. 2, 644. high reaching to the *h.* roof
P. L. 2, 676. with *h* strides
P. L. 2, 710. from his *h.* hair
P. L. 4, 996. the eternal to prevent such *h.* fray
P. L. 6, 207. joined the *h.* shock
P. L. 6, 252. *h.* edge came down wide-wasting
P. L. 6, 305. and in the air made *h.* circles
P. L. 6. 668. *h.* confusion heaped upon confusion
P. L. 9, 185. not yet in *h.* shade or dismal den
P. L. 10, 540. and *h.* sympathy
P. L. 10, 789. O thought, *h.* if true
P. L. 11, 465. *h.* to think how horrible to feel
P. R. 1, 296. desert, dusk with *h.* shades
P. R. 4, 94. his *h.* lusts in private to enjoy
P. R. 4, 411. the clouds from many a *h.* rift
S. A. 501. to their abyss and *h.* pains confined
C. 429. caverns shagged with *h.* shades
L'A. 4. 'mongst *h.* shapes
H. 157. with such a *h.* clang
S. A. 1542. the sight of this so *h.* spectacle
**Horror.**—P. L. 2, 67. black fire and *h.*
P. L. 2, 220. this *h.* will grow mild
P. L. 2, 616. bands with shuddering *h.* pale
P. L. 2, 703. strange *h.* seize thee
P. L. 4, 18. *h.* and doubt distract
P. L. 4, 989. on his crest sat *h.* plumed
P. L. 5, 65. damp *h.* chilled at such bold words
P. L. 6, 307. while expectation stood in *h.*
P. L. 6, 863. struck them with *h.*
P. L. 9, 890. *h.* chill ran through his veins
P. L. 10, 539. *h.* on them fell
S. A. 1550. some distance from the place of *h.*
C. 38. the nodding *h.* of whose shady brows
H. 172. the scaly *h.* of his folded tail
**Horrors.**—P. L. 1, 250. hail *h.* hail
P. L. 2, 177. impendent *h.* threatening hideous
P. L. 10. 843. into what abyss of fears and *h.*
**Horse.**—P. L. 2, 887. with *h.* and chariots
P. L. 10, 590. not mounted yet on his pale *h.*
P. L. 11, 645. both *h.* and foot
P. R. 4, 66. legions and cohorts turms of *h.*
S. A. 1618. both *h.* and foot before him
Il P. 114. the wondrous *h.* of brass
**Horsemen.**—P. R. 3, 307. all *h.*
**Horses.**—P. L. 5, 356. retinue long of *h.*
P. R. 3, 313. in mail their *h.* clad
**Hosanna.**—P. L. 6, 205. *h.* to the Highest
**Hosannas.**—P. L. 3, 348. loud *h.* filled
**Hospitable.**—P. L. 1, 504. the *h.* door
P. L. 5, 332. on *h.* thoughts intent
P. R. 2, 262. under the *h.* covert nigh
P. R. 4, 242. or *h.* in her sweet recess
C. 187. kind *h.* woods provide
**Host.**—P. L. 1, 37. his *h.* of rebel angels
P. L. 1, 136. and all this mighty *h.*
P. L. 1, 541. the universal *h.* up sent
P. L. 1, 635. witness all the *h.* of heaven
P. L. 1, 754. throughout the *h.* proclaim
P. L. 2, 519. and all the *h.* of hell
P. L. 2, 759. amazement seized all the *h.*
P. L. 2, 824. all the heavenly *h.* of Spirits
P. L. 2, 885. with extended wings a bannered *h.*
P. L. 2, 993. for such a numerous *h.* fled not
P. L. 4, 606. Hesperus, that led the starry *h.*
P. L. 4, 922. alleged to thy deserted *h.*
P. L. 5, 535. myself and all the angelic *h.*
P. L. 5, 583. the empyreal *h.* of angels
P. L. 5, 710. the third part of heaven's *h.*
P. L. 5, 744. an *h.* innumerable as the stars
P. L. 5, 874. applause through the infinite *h.*
P. L. 6, 38. aided by this *h.* of friends
P. L. 6, 104. 'twixt *h.* and *h.*
P. L. 6, 214. vaulted either *h.* with fire

P. L. 6, 231. seemed a numerous *h.*
P. L. 6, 392. through the faint Satanic *h.*
P. L. 6, 527. of golden panoply refulgent *h.*
P. L. 6, 590. which on the victor *h.*
P. L. 6, 633. all his *h.* derided
P. L. 6, 647. terror seized the rebel *h.*
P. L. 6, 800. to all his *h.* on either hand
P. L. 6, 830. or of a numerous *h.*
P. L. 7, 132. amidst the *h.* of angels
P. L. 9, 441. Alcinous, *h.* of old Laertes' son
P. L. 10, 259. to all the infernal *h.*
P. L. 10, 437. the late heaven-banished *h.*
P. L. 11, 230. one of the heavenly *h.*
P. L. 12, 196. the sea swallows him with his *h.*
P. L. 12, 209. forth will trouble all his *h.*
P. R. 1, 416. scorn to all the *h.* of heaven
P. R. 3, 300. Ctesiphon hath gathered all his *h.*
S. A. 262. on their whole *h.* I flew unarmed
H. 21. the spangled *h.* keep watch in squadrons
S. M. 12. the cherubic *h.* in thousand choirs
D. F. I. 57. thou of the golden-winged *h.*
**Hostile.**—P. L. 2, 1040. with less *h.* din
P. L. 5, 904. through *h.* scorn
P. L. 6, 50. with fire and *h.* arms
P. L. 6, 260. *h.* frown and visage all inflamed
P. L. 11, 796. raise out of friendship *h.* deeds
P. L. 12, 31. with war and *h.* snare
S. A. 531. on *h.* ground none daring
S. A. 692. oft leavest them to the *h.* sword
S. A. 893. worse than *h.* deeds
S. A. 1210. and did *h.* acts
S. A. 1561. the desolation of a *h.* city
H. 57. unstained with *h.* blood
**Hostility.**—P. L. 2, 336. *h.* and hate
S. A. 1203. I used *h.* and took their spoil
**Hosting.**—P. L. 6, 93. and in fierce *h.* meet
**Hot.**—P. L. 2, 898. for *h.,* cold, moist, and dry
P. L. 9, 467. but the *h.* hell
P. L. 10, 694. mist and exhalation *h.*
P. L. 11, 568. thence gliding *h.*
P. L. 11, 845. the clear sun .... gazed *h.*
**Hoverest.**—D. F. I. 38. where'er thou *h.*
**Hovering.**—P. L. 1, 345. *h.* on wing
P. L. 2, 717. stand front to front *h.* a space
P. L. 5, 140. yet *h.* o'er the ocean-brim
P. L. 9, 639. *h.* and blazing with delusive light
P. L. 10, 285. *h.* upon the waters
C. 214. thou *h.* angel girt with golden wings
Il P. 9. or likest *h.* dreams
**Hounds.**—L'A. 53. how the *h.* and horn
**Hour.**—P. L. 1, 697. and in an *h.*
P. L. 2, 91. the torturing *h.*
P. L. 2, 848. destined to that good *h.*
P. L. 2, 934. to this *h.* down had been falling
P. L. 2, 1055. accursed and in a cursed *h.*
P. L. 4, 581. and since meridian *h.*
P. L. 4, 610. the *h.* of night
P. L. 4, 779. forth issuing at the accustomed *h.*
P. L. 4, 963. from this *h.*
P. L. 5, 170. while day arises that sweet *h.*
P. L. 5, 303. due at her *h.* prepared
P. L. 5, 667. the dusky *h.* friendliest to sleep
P. L. 6, 10. till her *h.* to veil the heaven
P. L. 6, 150. wished *h.* of my revenge
P. L. 6, 396. till that *h.* not liable to fear
P. L. 8, 213. at the *h.* of sweet repast
P. L. 8, 512. on that *h.* shed their selectest
P. L. 9, 225. the *h.* of supper comes unearned
P. L. 9, 406. never from that *h.* in Paradise
P. L. 9, 596. such pleasure till that *h.*
P. L. 9, 739. meanwhile the *h.* of noon
P. L. 9, 780. her rash hand in evil *h.*
P. L. 9, 1067. O Eve in evil *h.* thou didst give
P. L. 10, 93. gentle airs due at their *h.*
P. L. 10, 440. expecting each *h.*
P. L. 10, 771. O welcome *h.* whenever
P. L. 10, 923. yet we live scarce one short *h.*
P. L. 11, 203. the self-same *h.*
P. L. 12, 589. the *h.* precise
P. R. 2, 260. it was the *h.* of night
P. R. 4, 522. I watched thy footsteps from that *h.*

S. A. 364. then in an *h.* ensnared
S. A. 1056. nor from that right to part an *h.*
C. 920. and I must haste ere morning *h.*
Il P. 85. or let my lamp at midnight *h.*
S. 9, 13. passes to bliss at the mid *h.* of night
S. 21, 14. when God sends a cheerful *h.*
**Hourly.**—P. L. 2. 796. *h.* conceived and *h.* born
**Hours.**—P. L. 2, 527. the irksome *h.*
P. L. 3, 417. happy *h.* in joy and hymning
P. L. 4, 267. knit with the Graces and the *H.*
P. L. 6, 3. waked by the circling *H.*
P. L. 7, 444. whose clarion sounds the silent *h.*
P. L. 8, 69. seasons, *h.*, or days, or months
P. L. 9, 1188. spent the fruitless *h.*
P. R. 1, 57. too soon for us, the circling *h.*
P. R. 4, 331. I would delight my private *h.*
C. 986. the Graces and the rosy-bosomed *H.*
S. 1, 4. the jolly *H.* lead on propitious May
T. 2. the lazy leaden-stepping *H.*
**House.**—P. L. 1, 470. against the *h.* of God
P. L. 1, 496. filled with lust and violence the *h.*
P. L. 2, 823. from out this dark and dismal *h.*
P. L. 6, 877. the *h.* of woe and pain
P. L. 7, 576. led to God's eternal *h.*
P. L. 10, 465. the *h.* of woe
P. L. 12, 121. from his father's *h.*
P. L. 12, 349. the *h.* of God they first re-edify
P. R. 3, 175. zeal of thy father's *h.*
P. R. 3, 282. and all thy father David's *h.*
P. R. 4, 273. descended to the low-roofed *h.*
P. R. 4, 552. I to thy Father's *h.* have brought
P. R. 4, 639. home to his mother's *h.*
S. A. 447. thee and thy father's *h.*
S. A. 518. thy country and his sacred *h.*
S. A. 949. this jail I count the *h.* of liberty
S. A. 1049. happy that *h.*
S. A. 1112. nor in the *h.* with chamber-ambushes
S. A. 1491. and view him sitting in the *h.*
S. A. 1717. to himself and father's *h.* eternal fame
S. A. 1733. home to his father's *h.*
C. 85. to the service of this *h.* belongs
S. 8, 11. bid spare the *h.* of Pindarus
H. 14. a darksome *h.* of mortal clay
M. W. 10. to *h.* with darkness and with death
M. W. 54. that thy noble *h.* doth bring
**Household.**—P. L. 9, 233. to study *h.* good
P. L. 10, 908. and *h.* peace confound
P. L. 11, 820. to save himself and *h.*
S. A. 566. to sit idle on the *h.* hearth
**Houses.**— P. L. 9, 446. *h.* thick and sewers
P. R. 4, 56. more like *h.* of gods
**How.**—P. L. 1, 187. consult *h.* we may henceforth
P. L. 1, 188. our own loss *h.* repair
P. L. 1, 189. *h.* overcome this dire calamity
P. L. 1, 217. *h.* all his malice served but to bring
P. L. 1, 611. yet faithful *h.* they stood
P. L. 1, 629. *h.* such united force of gods *h.* such
P. L. 1, 695. *h.* their greatest monuments
P. L. 1, 740. and *h.* he fell from heaven
P. L. 2, 153. *h.* he can is doubtful
P. L. 2, 280. *h.* in safety best we may compose
P. L. 2, 338. plotting *h.* the conqueror
P. L. 2, 356. *h.* endued and what their power
P. L. 3, 719. and *h.* they move
P. L. 4, 37. add thy name O sun to tell thee *h.*
P. L. 4, 48. and pay him thanks *h.* due
P. L. 4, 236. but rather to tell *h. . . . h.* from
P. L. 4, 315. sin bred *h.* have ye troubled
P. L. 4, 452. whence thither brought and *h.*
P. L. 4, 490. *h.* beauty is excelled
P. L. 4, 876. *h.* busied, in what form
P. L. 5, 21. *h.* spring our tended plants, *h.*
P. L. 5, 24. *h.* nature paints her colours, *h.*
P. L. 5, 226. and *h.* disturbed
P. L. 5, 227. *h.* he designs
P. L. 5, 531. for *h.* can hearts not free be tried
P. L. 5, 564. for *h.* shall I
P. L. 5, 566. *h.* without remorse
P. L. 5, 568. last unfold the secrets
P. L. 5, 678. *h.* then can now thy sleep
P. L. 5, 715. saw in whom, *h.* spread among

P. L. 5, 779. only to consult *h.* we may best
P. L. 5, 783. but double *h.* endured
P. L. 5, 882. no more be troubled *h.* to quit
P. L. 6, 266. *h.* hast thou disturbed heaven's
P. L. 6, 269. *h.* hast thou instilled thy malice
P. L. 6, 498. all admired and each *h.* he
P. L. 6, 559. *h.* we seek peace
P. L. 6, 901. who now is plotting *h.* he may
P. L. 7, 62. *h.* this world of heaven and earth
P. L. 7, 86. *h.* first began this heaven
P. L. 7, 555. *h.* it showed in prospect
P. L. 7, 636. *h.* first this world and face
P. L. 8, 26. I oft admire *h.* nature
P. L. 8, 45. *h.* they prospered bud and bloom
P. L. 8, 80. *h.* they will wield the mighty frame
P. L. 8, 81. *h.* build, unbuild, contrive to save
P. L. 8, 82. *h.* gird the sphere with centric
P. L. 8, 250. to tell *h.* human life began
P. L. 8, 277. tell if ye saw *h.* I came thus *h.*
P. L. 8, 280. tell me *h.* may I know him *h.* adore
P. L. 8, 359. *h.* may I adore thee
P. L. 8, 408. *h.* have I then with whom to hold
P. L. 8, 448. to see *h.* thou couldst judge of fit
P. L. 8, 615. and *h.* their love
P. L. 9, 201. then commune *h.*
P. L. 9, 230. well thy thoughts employed *h.*
P. L. 9, 288. thoughts which *h.* found they
P. L. 9, 326. *h.* are we happy still in fear
P. L. 9, 563. *h.* camest thou . . ., and *h.*
P. L. 9, 563. and *h.* to me so friendly grown
P. L. 9, 686. *h.* should you?
P. L. 9, 764. *h.* dies the serpent?
P. L. 9, 900. *h.* art thou lost, *h.* on a sudden
P. L. 9, 902. rather *h.* hast thou yielded
P. L. 9, 903. *h.* to violate the sacred fruit
P. L. 9, 908. *h.* can I live without thee *h.*
P. L. 9, 964. but short of thy perfection *h.*
P. L. 9, 991. eyes *h.* opened and their minds *h.*
P. L. 9, 1080. *h.* shall I behold the face
P. L. 9, 1114. O *h.* unlike to that
P. L. 10, 2. and *h.* he in the serpent had
P. L. 10, 20. wondering *h.* the subtle fiend
P. L. 10, 28. to hear and know *h.* all befell
P. L. 10, 120. *h.* is it now become so dreadful
P. L. 10, 211. then pitying *h.* they stood
P. L. 10, 480. I found the new-created world
P. L. 10, 580. and fabled *h.* the serpent
P. L. 10, 689. else *h.* had the world inhabited
P. L. 10, 796. *h.* can he exercise wrath
P. L. 10, 821. so disinherited *h.* would you
P. L. 10, 827. *h.* can they then acquitted stand
P. L. 10, 960. *h.* we may lighten
P. L. 10, 1070. *h.* we his gathered beams
P. L. 11, 69. *h.* with mankind I proceed
P. L. 11, 70. *h.* with peccant angels late
P. L. 11, 282. from thee *h.* shall I part
P. L. 11, 284. *h.* shall we breathe in other air
P. L. 11, 528. *h.* we may come to Death
P. L. 11, 548. bent rather *h.* I may be quit
P. L. 11, 554. live well *h.* long or short permit
P. L. 11, 754. *h.* didst thou grieve then
P. L. 11, 785. *h.* comes it thus
P. L. 11, 802. thenceforth shall practise *h.*
P. L. 12, 263. *h.* the sun shall in mid heaven
P. L. 12, 284. *h.* can God with such reside
P. R. 1, 132. *h.* I begin to verify
P. R. 1, 137. toldst her doubting *h.* these
P. R. 1, 186. *h.* best the mighty work he might
P. R. 2, 44. the kings of the earth *h.* they
P. R. 2, 113. *h.* to begin, *h.* to accomplish
P. R. 2, 197. *h.* all the beauties of the east
P. R. 2, 199. *h.* he, surnamed of Africa
P. R. 2, 216. *h.* would one look
P. R. 2, 270. the prophet also, *h.* he fled
P. R. 2, 272. *h.* awaked he found his supper
P. R. 2, 319. *h.* hast thou hunger
P. R. 3, 194. what I can suffer, *h.* obey
P. R. 3, 250. know *h.* best their opposition
P. R. 3, 308. see *h.* in warlike muster
P. R. 3, 359. *h.* couldst thou hope long to enjoy
P. R. 4, 118. and *h.* they quaff in gold

P. R. 4, 231. *h.* wilt thou
P. R. 4, 233. *h.* wilt thou reason with them *h.*
P. R. 4, 311. *h.* the world began and *h.*
P. R. 4, 472. for both the when and *h.*
S. A. 118. *h.* he lies at random carelessly
S. A. 197. *h.* could I once look up
S. A. 422. prompting *h.* thou mightst find
S. A. 604. deliverance by ransom or *h.* else
S. A. 796. *h.* to endear and hold thee to me
S. A. 838. *h.* couldst thou hope who took'st
S. A. 1547. guided me aright I know not *h.*
S. A. 1579. *h.* died he, death to life is crown
**However.**—P. L. 4, 911. to fly from pain *h.*
P. L. 6, 292. here *h.* to dwell free
P. L. 6, 563. I doubt *h.*, witness heaven
P. L. 9, 683. of highest agents deemed *h.*
P. L. 9, 952. *h.* I with thee have fixed my lot
P. L. 10, 134. *h.* insupportable
P. L. 10, 578. *h.*, some tradition they dispersed
P. L. 11, 373. *h.* chastening
P. R. 2, 135. *h.* to this man inferior far
P. R. 4, 321. *h.* many books
S. A. 601. I *h.* must not omit
**Howl.**—P. L. 2, 799. *h.* and gnaw my bowels
C. 533. his monstrous rout are heard to *h.*
**Howled.**—P. L. 2, 658. barked and *h.* within
P. R. 4, 423. some *h.*, some yelled, some shrieked
**Hubbub.**—P. L. 2, 951. a universal *h.* wild
P. L. 12, 60. looking down to see the *h.*
**Huddling.**—C. 495. the *h.* brook to hear his
**Hue.**—P. L. 1, 230. and such appeared in *h.*
P. L. 1, 527. countenance cast like doubtful *h.*
P. L. 4, 148. and fruits at once of golden *h.*
P. L. 4, 256. flowers of all *h.*
P. L. 7, 445. with the florid *h.* of rainbows
P. L. 8, 619. rosy red, love's proper *h.*
P. L. 11, 552. tents of various *h.*
P. R. 2, 352. of fairer *h.* than Ganymed
Il P. 16. o'erlaid with black, staid Wisdom's *h.*
H. 207. his burning idol all of blackest *h.*
C. 994. flowers of more mingled *h.*
**Hues.**—P. L. 4, 698. all *h.* roses and jessamin
L. 135. bells and flowerets of a thousand *h.*
**Hug.**—C. 164. and *h.* him into snares
**Huge.**—P. L. 1, 57. witnessed *h.* affliction
P. L. 1, 196. in bulk as *h.* as whom the fables
P. L. 1, 209. so stretched out *h.* in length
P. L. 1, 547. a forest *h.* of spears
P. L. 1, 710. out of the earth a fabric *h.*
P. L. 2, 434. our prison strong, this *h.* convex
P. L. 2, 473. he through hazard *h.* must earn
P. L. 2, 709. the length of Ophiuchus *h.*
P. L. 2, 874. with the *h.* portcullis high
P. L. 6, 193. ten paces *h.* he back recoiled
P. L. 6, 251. with *h.* two-handed sway
P. L. 6, 364. *h.* and in a rock of diamond
P. L. 6, 552. the foe approaching gross and *h.*
P. L. 6, 873. so *h.* a rout incumbered him
P. L. 7, 285. immediately the mountains *h.*
P. L. 7, 410. part *h.* of bulk, wallowing unwieldy
P. L. 7, 496. of *h.* extent sometimes
P. L. 10, 531. *h.* Python
P. L. 11, 729. to build a vessel of *h.* bulk
P. R. 3, 261. *h.* cities and high-towered
P. R. 4, 51. compass *h.* and high the structure
S. A. 65. so many and so *h.*
C. 423. *h.* forests and unharboured heaths
H. 226. Typhon *h.* ending in snaky twine
P. 14. of labours *h.* and hard
Cir. 27. but O! ere long *h.* pangs
**Hugest**—P. L. 1, 202. created *h.*
P. L. 7, 413. *h.* of living creatures
**Hull.**—P. L. 11, 840. and saw the ark *h.*
**Hum.**—L'A. 118. the busy *h.* of men
H. 174. no voice or hideous *h.*
**Human.**—P. L. 1, 359. forms excelling *h.*
P. L. 1, 393. blood of *h.* sacrifice
P. L. 1, 482. brutish forms rather than *h.*
P. L. 3, 44. flocks or herds, or *h.* face divine
P. L. 3, 462. the angelical and *h.* kind
P. L. 4, 206. to all delight of *h.* sense

P. L. 4, 475. be called mother of *h.* race
P. L. 4, 751. true source of *h.* offspring
P. L. 5, 227. disturbed this night the *h.* pair
P. L. 5, 459. high power so far exceeded *h.*
P. L. 5, 518. *h.* desires can seek or apprehend
P. L. 5, 565. for how shall I relate to *h.* sense
P. L. 5, 572. surmounts the reach of *h.*
P. L. 6, 300. lift *h.* imagination to such height
P. L. 6, 896. might have else to *h.* race
P. L. 7, 75. which *h.* knowledge could
P. L. 7, 177. *h.* ears cannot without process
P. L. 7, 368. though from *h.* sight so far remote
P. L. 7, 640. not surpassing *h.* measure
P. L. 8, 119. God to remove his ways from *h.*
P. L. 8, 250. for man to tell how *h.* life began
P. L. 8, 392. the brute cannot be *h.* consort
P. L. 8, 414. all *h.* thoughts come short
P. L. 8, 587. attractive, *h.*, rational
P. L. 9, 197. forth came the *h.* pair
P. L. 9, 241. not the lowest end of *h.* life
P. L. 9, 554. tongue of brute and *h.* sense
P. L. 9, 561. I knew, but not with *h.* voice
P. L. 9, 712. I, of brute, *h.*, ye of *h.* gods
P. L. 9, 714. by putting off *h.* to put on gods
P. L. 9, 871. with *h.* voice and *h.* sense
P. L. 10, 793. since *h.* reach no farther knows
P. L. 10, 908. calamity shall cause to *h.* life
P. L. 11, 147. or one short sigh of *h.* breath
P. L. 11, 694. the highest pitch of *h.* glory
P. L. 12, 10. impair and weary *h.* sense
P. L. 12, 71. *h.* left from *h.*
P. R. 1, 298. return was difficult by *h.* steps
P. R. 1, 308. nor tasted *h.* food, nor hunger felt
P. R. 2, 137. more than *h.* gifts from heaven
P. R. 2, 246. *h.* food nor tasted
P. R. 3, 231. or *h.* nature can receive
P. R. 3, 402. argument of *h.* weakness
P. R. 4, 265. chance, and change in *h.* life
P. R. 4, 599. fleshly tabernacle and *h.* form
S. A. 690. unseemly falls in *h.* eye
S. A. 792. powerful of sway in *h.* hearts
S. A. 1313. thy strength they know surpassing *h.*
C. 68. works their *h.* countenance
C. 297. their port was more than *h.*
A. 73. of *h.* mould with gross unpurged ear
Il P. 14. to hit the sense of *h.* sight
H. 126. once bless our *h.* ears
P. 14. huge and hard, too hard for *h.* wight
D. F. I. 58. who having clad thyself in *h.* weed
**Humane.**—P. L. 2, 109. more graceful and *h.*
P. L. 9, 732. goddess *h.* reach then
P. R. 1, 221. yet held it more *h.*
**Humber.**—M. 99. or *H.* loud
**Humble.**—P. L. 2, 240. in his presence *h.*
P. L. 7, 322. and the *h.* shrub and bush
P. L. 8, 878. and *h.* deprecation thus replied
P. L. 10, 912. all disordered at his feet fell *h.*
P. L. 11, 295. to Michael thus his *h.* words
P. R. 3, 189. be tried in *h.* state
S. A. 511. pleased with *h.* and filial submission
S. A. 965. why do I *h.* thus myself
H. 24. prevent them with thy *h.* ode
**Humbled.**—P. L. 6, 342. and his pride *h.*
P. L. 11, 150. kneeled and before him *h.*
P. R. 3, 421. *h.* themselves
**Humbles.**—P. L. 12, 193. *h.* his stubborn heart
**Humbling.**—P. L. 10, 576. this annual *h.*
**Humbly.**—P. L. 10, 1089. confess *h.*
P. L. 10, 1101. both confessed *h.* their faults
**Humid.**—P. L. 4, 151. cloud or *h.* bow
P. L. 5, 425. in *h.* exhalations
P. L. 7, 306. perpetual draw their *h.* train
P. L. 9, 193. dawn in Eden on the *h.* flowers
C. 992. Iris there with *h.* bow
**Humiliation.**—P. L. 3, 313. *h.* shall exalt
P. L. 10, 1092. sorrow unfeigned and *h.* meek
P. L. 10, 1104. sorrow unfeigned and *h.* meek
P. R. 1, 160. by *h.* and strong sufferance
**Humming.**—P. R. 4, 17. oft with *h.* sound
**Humour.**—P. L. 3, 610. terrestrial *h.*
P. L. 6, 332. nectarous *h.*

P. L. 7, 280. but with warm prolific *h.*
S. 13, 8. with smooth air couldst *h.* best
**Humours.**—S. A. 600. mind and *h.* black
**Hundred.**—P. R. 1, 428. in four *h.* mouths
P. R. 3, 287. Hecatompylus her *h.* gates
A. 22. Cybele mother of a *h.* gods
S. 18, 13. that from these may grow a *h.* fold
**Hundreds.**—P. L. 1, 760. with *h.*
**Hung.**—P. L. 1, 287. *h.* on his shoulders
P. L. 1, 342. *h* like night
P. L. 2, 78. when the fierce foe *h.* on
P. L. 2, 1005. *h.* o'er my realm
P. L. 3, 367. by their side like quivers *h.*
P. L. 4, 250. with golden rind *h.* amiable
P. L. 4, 302. his parted forelock manly *h.*
P. L. 4, 554. spears *h.* high
P. L. 4, 997. *h.* forth in heaven his golden scales
P. L. 5, 13. looks of cordial love *h.* over her
P. L. 6, 190. which *h.* not
P. L. 6, 246. in even scale the battle *h.*
P. L. 6, 763. beside him *h.* his bow and quiver
P. L. 7, 242. self-balanced on her centre *h.*
P. L. 7, 325. branches *h.* with copious fruit
P. L. 8, 307. loaden with fairest fruit that *h.*
P. L. 9, 430. *h.* drooping
P. L. 9, 594. where plenty *h.* tempting
P. L. 11, 247. *h.* the sword Satan's dire dread
S. A. 59. *h.* it in my hair
S. A. 1736. with all his trophies *h.*
C. 198. stars that nature *h.* in heaven
Il P. 118. of tourneys, and of trophies *h.*
H. 55. spear and shield were high up *h.*
H. 122. the well-balanced world on hinges *h.*
U. C. II. 3. so *h.* his destiny
Hor. 14. to have *h.* my dank
**Hunger.**—P. L. 4, 184. whom *h.* drives
P. L. 5, 437. keen dispatch of real *h.*
P. L. 8, 213. to thirst and *h.* both
P. L. 9, 586. *h.* and thirst at once powerful
P. L. 10, 556. scalding thirst and *h.* fierce
P. L. 10, 568. *h.* and thirst constraining
P. R. 1, 308. tasted human food nor *h.* felt
P. R. 1, 325. pined with *h.* and with drouth
P. R. 2, 252. but now I feel I *h.*
P. R. 2, 255. though *h.* still remain
P. R. 2, 306. well I know not without *h.*
P. R. 2, 319. how hast thou *h.* then
P. R. 2, 333. troubled, that thou shouldst *h.*
P. R. 2, 373. destroys life's enemy, *h.*
P. R. 2, 389. and with my *h.* what hast thou
P. R. 2, 406. by *h.,* that each other creature
P. R. 4, 121. tell who thirst and *h.*
P. R. 4, 592. what *h.* if aught *h.* had impaired
C. 358. the direful grasp of savage *h.*
**Hunger-bit.**—P. R. 2, 416. and *h.-b.*
**Hungered.**—P. R. 1, 309. *h.* then at last
**Hungering.**—P. R. 2, 244. now *h.* first
P. R. 2, 259. *h.* more to do my Father's will
**Hungers.**—P. R. 2, 231. I know her *h.*
**Hungry.**—P. R. 4, 403. *h.* and cold
L. 125. the *h.* sheep look up, and are not fed
**Hunt.**—Il P. 124. with the Attick boy to *h.*
**Hunter.**—P. L. 11, 188. first *h.* then pursued
P. L. 12, 33. a mighty *h.*
**Hunting.**—P. L. 12, 30. *h.,* and men not beasts
**Huntress.**—C. 441. hence had the *h.* Dian
Brut. 1. Goddess of shades, and *h.*
**Hurdled.**—P. L. 4, 186. in *h.* cotes
**Hurl.**—C. 153. I *h.* my dazzling spells
**Hurled.**—P. L. 1, 45. *h.* headlong flaming
P. L. 2, 180. shall be *h.* each on his rock
P. L. 2, 374. *h.* headlong to partake with us
P. L. 6, 665. *h.* to and fro with jaculation

P. L. 10, 636. through Chaos *h.*
L. 155. far away where'er thy bones are *h.*
**Hurling.**—P. L. 1, 669. *h.* defiance
**Hurried.**—P. L. 2, 603. thence *h.* back
P. L. 2, 937. with fire and nitre *h.* him
P. L. 5, 778. and *h.* meeting here
P. R. 4, 402. after his aery jaunt, though *h.*
P. 50. I thence *h.* on viewless wing
**Hurt.**—P. L. 9, 700. God therefore cannot *h.*
P. L. 9, 727. can your knowledge *h.* him
P. L. 12, 418. never to *h.* them more
S. A. 1676. who *h.* their minds and urged them
C. 589. virtue may be assailed but never *h.*
**Hurtful.**—P. L. 2, 259. useful of *h.*
C. 437. hath *h.* power o'er true virginity
A. 53. *h.* worm with cankered venom bites
**Husband.**—P. L. 7, 490. that feeds her *h.*
P. L. 8, 52. her *h.* the relater she preferred
P. L. 9, 204. Eve first to her *h.* thus began
P. L. 9, 234. good works in her *h.* to promote
P. L. 9, 268. seemliest by her *h.* stays
P. L. 9, 385. from her *h.'s* hand
P. L. 9, 482. her *h.* (for I view far round)
P. L. 10, 4. had perverted Eve her *h.*
P. L. 10, 195. and to thy *h.'s* will
P. L. 10, 336. seconded upon her *h.*
P. L. 11, 291. with thee goes thy *h.*
S. A. 755. to try her *h.*
S. A. 883. at first receive me for thy *h.*
S. A. 940. could hate me thy *h.,* slight me
S. 23, 3. Jove's great son to her glad *h.* gave
**Hush.**—C. 88. and *h.* the waving woods
**Husk.**—P. L. 5, 342. smooth rind or bearded *h.*
**Huswife's.**—C. 751. to tease the *h.* wool
**Hutched.**—C. 719. *h.* the all-worshipped ore
**Hyacinth.**—P. L. 4, 701. crocus and *h.*
P. L. 9, 1041. and asphodel and *h.*
C. 998. beds of *h.* and roses
D. F. I. 25. young *H.* born on Eurotas' strand
**Hyacinthine.**—P. L. 4, 301. *h.* locks
**Hyæna.**—S. A. 748. out, out *h.*
**Hyaline.**—P. L. 7, 619. on the clear *h.*
**Hydaspes.**—P. L. 3, 436. of Ganges or *H.*
**Hydra.**—S. 15, 7. raise their *h.* heads
**Hydras.**—P. L. 2, 628. gorgons and *h.*
C. 605. *h.* or all the monstrous forms
**Hydrus.**—P. L. 10, 525. cerastes horned, *h.*
**Hylas.**—P. R. 2, 353. Ganymed or *H.*
**Hymen.**—P. L. 11, 591. and bid invoke *H.*
L'A. 125. there let *H.* oft appear in saffron robe
**Hymenæan.**—P. L. 4, 711. choirs the *h.* sung
**Hymettus.**—P. R. 4, 247. flowery hill *H.*
**Hymn.**—P. L. 4, 944. songs to *h.* his throne
P. R. 4, 341. in fable *h.* or song
S. 13, 11. their happiest lines in *h.*
H. 17. no verse, no *h.* or solemn strain
**Hymning.**—P. L. 3, 417. in joy and *h.* spent
P. L. 6, 96. sons of one great sire *h.* the eternal
P. L. 7, 258. and *h.* praised God and his works
**Hymns.**—P. L. 2, 242. with warbled *h.*
P. L. 3, 148. innumerable sound of *h.*
P. L. 5, 656. melodious *h.* about the sovran
P. L. 6, 745. *h.* of high praise
P. R. 1, 169. then into *h.* burst forth
P. R. 4, 335. our law and story strewed with *h.*
S. M. 15. *h.* devout and holy psalms
**Hypocrisy.**—P. L. 3, 683. can discern *h.*
S. A. 872. in feigned religion, smooth *h.*
**Hypocrite.**—P. L. 4, 957. thou sly *h.*
P. R. 1, 487. suffers the *h.* or atheous priest
**Hypocrites.**—P. L. 4, 744. whatever *h.*
**Hyrcanian.**—P. R. 3, 317 to the *H.* cliffs
**Hyrcanus.**—P. R. 3, 367. old *H.* bound

# I.

**Iambic.**—P. R. 4, 262. in chorus or *i.*
**Iberian.**—P. R. 2, 200. the fair *I.* maid
P. R. 3, 318. and dark *I.* dales

C. 60. roving the Celtic and *I.* fields
**Ice.**—P. L. 2, 591. snow and *i.* a gulf profound
P. L. 2, 600. beds of raging fire to starve in *i.*

N

P. L. 10, 291. mountains of *i*.
P. L. 10, 697. armed with *i*.
P. L. 10, 1063. rain, *i*., hail and snow
P. L. 12, 193. but still as *i*. more hardened
**Icy-pearled.**—D. F. I. 15. in *i.-p.* car
**Ida.**—P. L. 1, 515. first in Crete and *I*.
P. L. 5, 382. three that in mount *I*.
Il P. 29. in secret shades of woody *I.'s* inmost
**Idea.**—P. L. 7, 557. answering his great *i*.
**Idiots.**—P. L. 3, 474. embryos and *i*.
**Idle.**—P. L. 4, 617. all day long rove *i*.
P. L. 6, 839. down their *i*. weapons dropped
P. L. 7, 279. not *i*. but witli warm prolific
S. A. 566.- to sit *i*. on the household hearth
S. A. 579. at home lie bed-rid, not only *i*.
S. A. 1500. not to sit *i*. with so great a gift
Il P. 5. dwell in some *i*. brain
S. 22, 4. nor to their *i*. orbs doth sight appear
H. 55. the *i*. spear and shield
**Idleness.**—P. L. 10, 1055. *i*. had been worse
**Idly.**—P. L. 10, 236. each other viewing *i*.
P. L. 11, 645. nor *i*. mustering stood
**Idol.**—P. L. 1, 396: through fire to his grim *i*.
P. L. 6, 101. *i*. of majesty divine
S. A. 1297. this *i.'s* day hath been to thee no day
S. A. 1672. chanting their *i*.
H. 207. his burning *i*. all of blackest hue
**Idolatresses.**—P. L. 1, 445. by fair *i*.
**Idolatries.**—P. L. 1, 456. the dark *i*.
P. L. 12, 337. foul *i*. and other faults
P. R. 3, 418. the *i*. of heathen round
**Idolatrous.**—P. R. 1, 444. they fell *i*.
S. A. 443. and had in scorn by the *i*. rout
S. A. 1364. the Philistines, *i*., uncircumcised
S. A. 1378. present in temples at *i*. rites
**Idolatry.**—S. A. 1670. drunk with *i*.
**Idolisms.**—P. R. 4, 234. how refute their *i*.
**Idolists.**—S. A. 453. and oped the mouths of *i*.
**Idols.**—P. L. 1, 375. and various *i*.
P. L. 1, 446. fell to *i*. foul
P. R. 2, 329. or offered first to *i*.
P. R. 3, 426. God with *i*. in their worship
P. R. 3, 432. enemies who serve *i*. with God
S. A. 441. compared with *i*., disglorified
S. A. 456. to waver or fall off and join with *i*.
S. A. 1358. by prostituting holy things to *i*.
**Idol-worship.**—P. L. 12, 115. up in *i.-w.*
S. A. 1365. not in their *i.-w.*
**Ignoble.**—P. L. 2, 227. *i*. ease
P. L. 12, 221. to noble and *i*. is more sweet
S. A. 416. as was my former servitude *i*.
**Ignobly.**—P. L. 11, 624. all their fame, *i*.
**Ignominious.**—P. L. 6, 395. fled *i*.
S. A. 417. unmanly, *i*., infamous
**Ignominy.**—P. L. 1, 115. that were an *i*.
P. L. 2, 207. exile, or *i*., or bonds
P. L. 6, 383. dispraise and *i*.
P. R. 3, 136. condemnation, *i*., and shame
**Ignorance.**—P. L. 4, 519. only stand by *i*.
P. L. 9, 774. under this *i*. of good or evil
P. L. 9, 809. I had remained in *i*.
C. 514. though so esteemed by shallow *i*.
**Ignorant.**—P. L. 9, 704. keep ye low and *i*.
P. L. 11, 764. better had I lived *i*.
P. R. 4, 310. *i*. of themselves
**Ilissus.**—P. R. 4, 249. there *I*. rolls
**Ilium.**—P. L. 1, 571. fought at Thebes and *I*.
**Ill.**—P. L. 1, 160. to do *i*. our sole delight
P. L. 2, 224. for happy though but *i*., for *i*.
P. L. 2, 381. from the author of all *i*.
P. L. 2, 445. I should *i*. become this throne
P. L. 2, 462. the pain of this *i*. mansion
P. L. 2, 935. by *i*. chance
P. L. 3, 688. thinks no *i*. where no *i*. seems
P. L. 4, 48. yet all his good proved *i*. in me
P. L. 4, 222. good bought dear by knowing *i*.
P. L. 4, 320. for they thought no *i*.
P. L. 4, 370. for so happy *i*. secured
P. L. 4, 932. hard assays and *i*. successes
P. L. 5, 113. *i*. matching words and deeds
P. L. 6, 150. *i*. for thee

P. L. 6, 738. to their prepared *i*. mansion
P. L. 8, 324. knowledge of good and *i*.
P. L. 9, 845. his heart divine of something *i*.
P. L. 9, 1055. shadowed them from knowing *i*.
P. L. 9, 1147. but might as *i*. have happened
P. L. 9, 1152. why he should mean me *i*.
P. L. 10, 140. I could suspect no *i*.
P. L. 10, 735. *i*. fare our ancestor impure
P. L. 10, 950. bear thine own first, *i*. able
P. L. 10, 952. and my displeasure bear'st so *i*.
P. L. 11, 763. O visions *i*. foreseen
P. R. 1, 64. this *i*. news I bring
P. R. 1, 200. *i*. sorting with my present state
P. R. 1, 321. what *i*. chance hath brought thee
P. R. 1, 423. or pleasure to do *i*. excites
P. R. 2, 469. and who attains not *i*.
P. R. 4, 135. but govern *i*. the nations under
P. R. 4, 339. *i*. imitated while they loudest sing
P. R. 4, 419. *i*. wast thou shrouded then
P. R. 4, 464. oft foresignify and threaten *i*.
S. A. 209. these two, proportioned *i*.
C. 217. things *i*. are but as slavish officers
C. 271. gentle shepherd, *i*. is lost that praise
C. 683. harshly deal like an *i*. borrower
A. 48. all my plants I save from nightly *i*.
**Illaudable.**—P. L. 6, 382. *i*. nought merits
**Ill-boding.**—P. R. 4, 490. signs betokening or *i.-b.*
**Ill-fenced.**—P. L. 4, 372. *i.-f.* for heaven to keep out
**Ill-fitted.**—S. A. 122. in slavish habit *i.-f*
**Ill-founded.**—S. A. 1504. hopes are not *i.-f*.
**Ill-greeting.**—C. 406. some *i.-g.* touch
**Illimitable.**—P. L. 2, 892. dark *i*. ocean
**Ill-joined.**—P. L. 3, 463. of *i.-j.* sons
**Ill-luck.**—C. 845. blasts and *i.-l.* signs
**Ill-managed.**—C. 172. *i.-m.* merriment
**Ill-mated.**—P. L. 11, 684. *i-m.* marriages
**Ill-meaning.**—S. A. 1195. *i.-m.* politician
**Illuminate.**—P. L. 7, 350. heaven to *i*.
**Illuminated.**—S. A. 1689. inward eyes *i*.
**Illumine.**—P. L. 1, 23. what in me is dark *i*.
**Illumined.**—P. L. 1, 666. far round *i*. hell
**Illusion.**—P. L. 10, 571. into the same *i*.
C. 155. to cheat the eye with blear *i*.
**Illusions.**—P. L. 4, 803. forge *i*.
**Illustrate.**—P. L. 10, 78. as may *i*.
P. R. 1, 370. and *i*. his high worth
**Illustrates.**—P. L. 5, 739. their hate *i*.
**Illustrious.**—P. L. 3, 627. *i*. on his shoulders
P. L. 5, 842. obscured but more *i*. made
P. L. 6, 773. *i*. far and wide
P. L. 7, 109. Adam his *i*. guest besought
P. L. 9, 962. *i*. evidence example high
P. L. 10, 367. following thy *i*. track
S. A. 957. *i*. women, faithful wives
S. A. 1318. appear as fits before the *i*. lords
**Ill-worthy.**—P. L. 11, 163. *i.-w.* I such title
**Illyria.**—P. L. 9, 505. in *I*.
**Image.**—P. L. 1, 371. transform oft to the *i*.
P. L. 1, 440. to whose bright *i*. nightly
P. L. 1, 459. maimed his brute *i*.
P. L. 2, 764. thy perfect *i*. viewing
P. L. 3, 63. on his right the radiant *i*.
P. L. 4, 292. the *i*. of their glorious Maker
P. L. 4, 472. he whose *i*. thou art
P. L. 4, 480. that smooth watery *i*.
P. L. 4, 567. man, God's latest *i*.
P. L. 5, 95. *i*. of myself and dearer half
P. L. 5, 784. to his *i*. now proclaimed
P. L. 6, 736. *i*. of thee in all things
P. L. 7, 519. let us make man in our *i*.
P. L. 7, 526. own *i*. he created thee in the *i*.
P. L. 7, 627. created in his *i*. there to dwell
P. L. 8, 221. inward and outward both his *i*.
P. L. 8, 424. his *i*. multiplied
P. L. 8, 441. my *i*. not imparted to the brute
P. L. 8, 544. resembling less his *i*.
P. L. 11, 508. can thus the *i*. of God in man
P. L. 11, 514. and for his Maker's *i*. sake
P. L. 11, 515. their Maker's *i*. answered
P. L. 11, 518. took his *i*. whom they served
P. L. 11, 525. God's *i*. did not reverence

P. R. 4, 596. *i.* of the Father
S. A. 706. the *i.* of thy strength
**Imagination.**—P. L. 6, 300. human *i.*
S. A. 1544. for dire *i.* still pursues me
**Imaginations.**—P. L. 2, 10. proud *i.*
P. L. 5, 105. she forms *i.*, aery shapes
**Imagine.**—C. 415. defenceless left as you *i.*
**Imagined.**—P. L. 3, 599. *i.* rather
P. L. 5, 263. observes *i.* lands and regions
P. L. 10, 291. the *i.* way beyond Pestora
P. L. 10, 881. *i.* wise
**Imagining.**—P. L. 10, 553. *i.* for one
**Imaus.**—P. L. 3, 431. a vulture on *I.* bred
**Imbalmed.**—P. L. 2, 842. the buxom air *i.*
**Imbarked.**—P. L. 11, 753. swum *i.*
S. A. 1045. *i.* with such a steers-mate
**Imbathe.**—C. 837. to *i.* in nectared lavers
**Imbattled.**—P. L. 1, 129. the *i.* Seraphim
**Imbellished.**—P. L. 3, 507. and gold *i.*
**Imblaze.**—C. 733. would so *i.* the forehead
**Imblazed.**—P. L. 1, 538. lustre rich *i.*
P. L. 5, 592. their glittering tissues bear *i.*
**Imblazoned.**—P. L. 9, 34. *i.* shields
**Imblazonry.**—P. L. 2, 513. bright *i.*
**Imbodied.**—P. L. 1, 574. such *i.* force
P. L. 6, 779. *i.* all in one
**Imbodies.**—C. 468. by contagion *i.*
**Imbordered.**—P. L. 9, 438. *i.* on each bank
**Imbosomed.**—P. L. 3, 75. firm land *i.*
P. L. 5, 597. in bliss *i.* sat the Son
**Imbower.**—P. L. 1, 304. over-arched *i.*
**Imbowered.**—C. 62. in thick shelter...*i.*
**Imbreathed.**—S. M. 4. things with *i.* sense
**Imbroiled.**—P. L. 2, 966. confusion all *i.*
**Imbrowned.**—P. L. 4, 246. shade *i.*
**Imbrued.**—S. 16, 7. with blood of.Scots *i.*
**Imbrute.**—P. L. 9, 166. incarnate and *i.*
**Imbrutes.**—C. 468. imbodies and *i.*
**Imbued.**—P. L. 8, 216. with grace divine *i.*
**Imitate.**—P. L. 2, 270. his light *i.*
P. L. 5, 111. mimic Fancy wakes to *i.* her
C. 112. *i.* the starry choir
**Imitated.**—P. L. 2, 511. *i.* state
P. R. 4, 339. ill *i.* while they loudest sing
**Imitation.**—P. L. 5, 764. in *i.* of that mount
P. L. 6, 662. in *i.*, to like arms betook
**Immanacled.**—C. 665. thou hast *i.*
**Immature.**—P. L. 7, 277. embryon, *i.*
**Immeasurable.**—P. L. 1, 549. depth *i.*
P. L. 7, 211. they viewed the vast *i.* abyss
S. A. 206. *i.* strength they might behold
**Immeasurably.**—P. L. 2, 844. filled *i.*
**Immediate.**—P. L. 2, 121. *i.* war
P. L. 6, 584. *i.* in a flame
P. L. 7, 176. *i.* are the acts of God
P. L. 8, 617. irradiance virtual or *i.*
P. L. 10, 52. some *i.* stroke
P. L. 10, 1049. we expected *i.* dissolution
**Immediately.**—P. L. 7, 285. *i.* the mountains
P. L. 11, 477. *i.* a place before his eyes
P. L. 12, 87. *i.* inordinate desires
S. A. 1614. *i.* was Samson brought
**Immedicable.**—S. A. 620. wounds *i.*
**Immense.**—P. L. 1, 790. their shapes *i.*
P. L. 2, 829. the void *i.* to search
P. L. 4, 52. in a moment quit the debt *i.*
P. L. 5, 88. beheld the earth outstretched *i.*
P. L. 6, 704. such virtue and grace *i.*
P. L. 7, 196. sapience and love *i.*
P. L. 7, 620. amplitude almost *i.*
P. L. 10, 300. and the mole *i.*
P. L. 12, 469. goodness *i.*
**Imminent.**—P. L. 6, 317. arm uplifted *i.*
P. L. 9, 409. with hellish rancour *i.*
P. L. 11, 725. in prison under judgments *i.*
**Immixed.**—S. A. 1657. Samson with these *i.*
**Immortal.**—P. L. 1, 53. though *i.*
P. L. 1, 107. *i.* hate
P. L. 1, 559. from mortal or *i.* minds
P. L. 1, 622. O myriads of *i.* spirits
P. L. 2, 13. can hold *i.* vigour

P. L. 2, 553. what could it less when spirits *i.*
P. L. 3, 67. reaping *i.* fruits of joy and love
P. L. 3, 267. yet spake and breathed *i.* love
P. L. 3, 353. *i.* amarant a flower which once
P. L. 3, 373. *i.*, infinite, eternal
P. L. 7, 77. we owe *i.* thanks
P. L. 9, 291. *i.* Eve
P. L. 9, 1166. might have lived and joyed *i.*
P. L. 11, 50. those pure *i.* elements
P. L. 11, 285. accustomed to *i.* fruits
P. L. 12, 435. a gentle wafting to *i.* life
C. 2. my mansion is where those *i.* shapes
C. 463. till all be made *i.*
C. 516. storied of old in high *i.* verse
C. 841. and underwent a quick *i.* change
A. 75. the peerless height of her *i.* praise
L'A. 137. married to *i.* verse
Il P. 91. the *i.* mind that hath forsook
S. 14, 14. and drink thy fill of pure *i.* streams
S. 20, 12. warble *i.* notes and Tuscan air
S. M. 13. touch their *i.* harps of golden wires
U. C. II. 28. he had been an *i.* carrier
V. Ex. 39. Hebe brings *i.* nectar
**Immortality.**—P. L. 4, 201. pledge of *i.*
P. L. 5, 638. in communion sweet quaff *i.*
P. L. 11, 59. with happiness and *i.*
**Immovable.**—P. L. 2, 602. *i.*, infixed
P. L. 10, 303. the wall *i.*
P. L. 10, 938. *i.* till peace obtained
**Immured.**—C. 521. *i.* in cypress shades
**Immures.**—P. L. 2, 435. *i.* us round
**Immutable.**—P. L. 3, 373. *i.*, immortal
P. L. 5, 524. God made thee perfect not *i.*
P. L. 9, 1165. expressed *i.*
**Immutably.**—P. L. 3, 121. *i.* foreseen
P. L. 7, 79. to observe *i.* his sovran will
**Imp.**—P. L. 9, 89. fit vessel fittest *i.* of fraud
S. 15, 8. to *i.* their serpent wings
**Impair.**—P. L. 7, 608. who can *i.* thee
P. L. 12, 10. must needs *i.* and weary
**Impaired.**—P. L. 4, 850. lustre visibly *i.*
P. L. 5, 73. the author not *i.* but honoured
P. L. 5, 665. and thought himself *i.*
P. L. 6, 691. save what sin hath *i.*
P. L. 9, 144. repair his numbers thus *i.*
P. R. 4, 592. if aught hunger had *i.*
C. 380. sometimes *i.*
**Impaled.**—P. L. 2, 647, *i.* with circling fire
P. L. 6, 553. *i.* on every side
**Imparadised.**—P. L. 4, 506. these two *i.*
**Impart.**—P. L. 5, 677. was wont to *i.*
P. L. 7, 81. *i.* things above earthly thought
P. L. 9, 728. or this tree *i.* against his will
P. R. 2, 397. to *i.* to thy apparent need
P. R. 3, 124. *i.* his good communicable
**Imparted.**—P. L. 8, 441. my image not *i.*
S. A. 1438. for never was from heaven *i.*
**Impartial.**—S. A. 827. *i.*, self-severe
**Imparts.**—P. L. 5, 423. sun that light *i.*
P. R. 1, 417. *i.* to thee no happiness
**Impassable.**—P. L. 10, 254. this gulf *i.*
**Impassioned.**—P. L. 9, 678. tempter all *i.*
**Impassive.**—P. L. 6, 455. unpained, *i.*
**Impatience.**—P. L. 10, 1044. *i.* and despite
**Impearls.**—P. L. 5, 747. which the sun *i.*
**Impediment.**—P. L. 6, 548. quit of all *i.*
**Impendent.**—P. L. 2, 177. *i.* horrors
P. L. 5, 891. lest the wrath *i.* raging
**Impenetrable.**—P. L. 2, 647. *i.* impaled
P. L. 9, 1086. where highest woods *i.*
**Impenetrably.**—P. L. 6, 400. *i.* armed
**Impenitence.**—P. L. 11, 816. their *i.*
**Impenitent.**—P. R. 3, 423. died *i.*
**Imperfect.**—P. L. 9, 345. nothing *i.*
P. L. 8, 338. left so *i.* by the Maker wise
P. L. 12, 300. so law appears *i.*
V. Ex. 3. *i.* words with childish trips
**Imperfection.**—P. L. 8, 423. his single *i.*
**Imperial.**—P. L. 1, 536. the *i.* ensign
P. L. 2, 310. thrones and *i.* powers
P. L. 2, 446. this *i.* sovranty

P. L. 5, 584. by *i.* summons called
P. L. 5, 801. to the abuse of those *i.* titles
P. L. 7, 585. the *i.* throne of Godhead
P. R. 4, 33. on each side an *i.* city stood
P. R. 4, 51. *i.* palace compass huge and high
C. 21. *i.* rule of all the sea-girt isles
**Imperious.**—P. L. 6, 287. hope *i.*
S. A. 1352. expect another message more *i.*
**Imperishable.**—P. L. 6, 435. injury *i.*
**Impertinence.**—P. L. 8, 195. fond *i.*
**Impervious.**—P. L. 10, 254. impassable, *i.*
**Impetuous.**—P. L. 1, 175. *i.* rage
P. L. 2, 880. with *i.* recoil
P. L. 4, 560. to beware *i.* winds
P. L. 6, 591. with such *i.* fury smote
P. L. 11, 744. down rushed the rain *i.*
S. A. 1422. *i.*, insolent unquenchable
**Impious.**—P. L. 1, 43. *i.* war in heaven
P. L. 1, 342. o'er the realm of *i.* Pharaoh
P. L. 1, 686. and with *i.* hands
P. L. 5, 813. thou with *i.* obloquy
P. L. 5, 845. cease then this *i.* rage
P. L. 6, 188. on thy *i.* crest receive
P. L. 6, 831. on his *i.* foes right onward
P. R. 4, 173. abominable terms, *i.* condition
S. A. 891. but an *i.* crew of men conspiring
**Impiously.**—P. L. 7, 611. while *i.* they
S. A. 498. *i.* weakly at least and shamefully
**Implacable.**—P. L. 6, 658. pain *i.*
S. A. 960. I see thou art *i.*
**Implanted.**—P. L. 11, 23. *i.* grace
**Implements.**—P. L. 6, 488. *i.* of mischief
**Implicit.**—P. L. 7, 323. frizzled hair *i.*
**Implied.**—P. L. 4, 307. *i.* subjection
**Implies.**—P. L. 4, 901. *i.* not violence
P. L. 10, 1017. and *i.* not thy contempt
**Implore.**—S. A. 521. his pardon I *i.*
C. 903. we *i.* thy powerful hand
**Implored.**—P. L. 8, 377. speech *i.*
**Implores.**—P. L. 7, 38. who thee *i.*
**Imploring.**—S. A. 512. him who *i.* mercy
**Import.**—P. L. 9, 731. *i.* your need
**Important.**—P. L. 11, 9. nor *i.* less seemed
S. A. 1379. *i.* cause thou need'st not doubt
**Imports.**—P. L. 8, 71. *i.* not
C. 287. *i.* their loss beside the present need
**Importune.**—P. L. 9, 610. though *i.*
P. L. 10, 933. with my cries *i.* heaven
P. R. 2, 404. the *i.* tempter still remained
S. A. 775. curiosity, inquisitive. *i.* of secrets
**Importuned.**—S. A. 1680. unweetingly *i.*
**Importuning.**—S. A. 797. by *i.* to learn
**Importunity.**—P. R. 4, 24. vain *i.*
S. A. 51. o'ercome with *i.* and tears
S. A. 397. turned to sport her *i.* each time
S. A. 779. to make known for *i.*
**Impose.**—P. L. 1, 567. mighty chief had to *i.*
P. L. 8, 30. orbs *i.* such restless revolution
P. L. 11, 227. *i.* new laws to be observed
S. A. 1258. they can not well *i.* nor I sustain
**Imposed.**—P. L. 2, 241. strict laws *i.*
P. L. 5, 679. new laws thou seest *i.*
P. L. 6, 407. grateful truce *i.*
P. L. 7, 545. death is the penalty *i.*
P. L. 9, 235. not so strictly hath our Lord *i.*
P. L. 11, 172. now with sweat *i.*
P. L. 12, 397. the law of God *i.*
S. A. 565. and the work from heaven *i.*
S. A. 1343. my message was *i.* on me
S. A. 1640. what your commands *i.*
**Imposition.**—P. L. 12, 304. *i.* of strict laws
**Impossible.**—P. L. 2, 250. by force *i.*
P. L. 4, 548. *i.* to climb
P. L. 6, 501. most would have thought *i.*
P. L. 7, 58. *i.* to mix with blessedness
P. L. 10, 800. to God himself *i.* is held
**Impossibly.**—P. L. 9, 360. reason not *i.*
**Impostor.**—P. L. 3, 692. to the fraudulent *i.*
C. 762. *I.*, do not charge most innocent nature
**Impotence.**—P. L. 2, 156. through *i.*
S. A. 52. O *i.* of mind in body strong

**Impotent.**—P. R. 2, 433. these three is *i.*
**Impowered.**—P. L. 10, 369. us *i.* to fortify
P. R. 2, 130. in full frequence was *i.*
**Impregnable.**—P. L. 2, 131. all access *i.*
P. R. 4, 50. her citadel *i.*
**Impregned.**—P. L. 9, 737. *i.* with reason
**Impregns.**—P. L. 4, 500. *i.* the clouds
**Impress.**—P. L. 4, 558. vapours fired *i.*
**Impressed.**—P. L. 3, 388. *i.* the effulgence
P. L. 4, 150. the sun more glad *i.* his beams
P. L. 7, 294. the great command *i.*
P. L. 11, 182. signs *i.* on bird, beast, air
**Impresses.**—P. L. 9, 35, *i.* quaint
**Impression.**—P. R. 1, 106. words *i.* left
W. S. 12. Delphic lines with deep *i.* took
**Imprisoned.**—S. A. 8. freely draw the air *i.*
S. A. 158. now indeed in real darkness
**Imprisonment.**—S. A. 155. O worst *i.*
**Improve.**—P. R. 1, 213. what might *i.*
**Improved.**—P. L. 5, 498. *i.* by tract of time
P. L. 9, 54. *i.* in meditated fraud and malice
**Imprudence.**—P. L. 11, 686. by *i.* mixed
**Impudence.**—S. A. 398. with what *i.*
**Impudent.**—P. R. 4, 154. the tempter *i.*
**Impulse.**—P. L. 3, 120. without least *i.*
P. L. 9, 530. or *i.* of vocal air
P. L. 10, 45. lightest moment of *i.*
S. A. 223. I knew from intimate *i.*
**Impulsion.**—S. A. 422. plead divine *i.*
**Impure.**—P. L. 3, 630. glad was the spirit *i.*
P. L. 4, 746. defaming as *i.* what God declares
P. L. 6, 742. from the *i.* far separate
P. L. 10, 735. ill fare our ancestor *i.*
S. A. 1424. nothing dishonourable, *i.*, unworthy
**Impurpled.**—P. L. 3, 364. *i.* with celestial
**Impute.**—P. L. 10, 620. furies who *i.*
P. R. 1, 422. wilt thou *i.* to obedience
P. R. 2, 248. that fast to virtue I *i.* not
**Imputed.**—P. L. 3, 291. thy merit *i.* shall
P. L. 12, 295. to them by faith *i.*
P. L. 12, 409. his obedience *i.* becomes theirs
**Imputest.**—P. L. 9, 1145. *i.* thou that
**Inabstinence**—P. L. 11, 476. *i.* of Eve
**Inaccessible.**—P. L. 2, 104. though *i.*
P. L. 3, 377. where thou sitt'st throned *i.*
P. L. 7, 141. this *i.* high strength
P. R. 3, 274. and *i.* the Arabian drouth
**Inbred.**—P. L. 2, 785. but he my *i.* enemy
**Incapable.**—P. L. 2, 140. *i.* of stain
P. L. 5, 505. *i.* of more
P. L. 6, 434. our empyreal form *i.* of mortal
**Incarnate.**—P. L. 3, 315. thou sit *i.* here
P. L. 9, 166. this essence to *i.*
**Incense.**—P. L. 2, 94. to *i.* his utmost ire
P. L. 7, 599. of *i.* clouds
P. L. 9, 194. breathed this morning *i.*
P. L. 9, 692. will God *i.* his ire for such
P. L. 11, 18. clad with *i.* where the golden altar
P. L. 11, 25. this golden censer mixed with *i.*
P. L. 11, 439. with *i.* strewed
P. L. 12, 338. will so *i.* God as to leave them
P. L. 12, 363. to offer *i.*, myrrh and gold
P. R. 1, 251. to honour thee with *i.*
**Incensed.**—P. L. 2, 707. *i.* with indignation
P. L. 3, 187. to appease betimes the *i.* Deity
P. L. 5, 847. the *i.* Father and the *i.* Son
P. L. 6, 130. at this prevention more *i.*
P. L. 8, 235. lest he *i.* at such eruption bold
P. L. 9, 1162. to whom then first *i.* Adam
**Incentive.**—P. L. 6, 519. part *i.* reed
**Incessant.**—P. L. 1, 698. they with *i.* toil
P. L. 6, 138. have raised *i.* armies to defeat
P. L. 11, 308. if by prayer *i.* I could hope
**Incessantly.**—P. R. 4, 323. who reads *i.*
**Incestuous.**—P. L. 10, 602. the *i.* mother
S. A. 833. *i.*, sacrilegious
**Incident.**—S. A. 656. chances *i.* to man's frail
S. A. 774. weakness in me but *i.* to all our sex
**Incited.**—P. L. 8, 125. and their own *i.*
**Inclement.**—P. L. 3, 426. *i.* sky
P. L. 10, 1063. to shun the *i.* seasons

**Inclinable.**—P. L. 9, 742. *i.* now grown
**Inclination.**—P. L. 2, 524. *i.* or sad.choice
P. L. 10, 265. go whither fate and *i.* strong
**Incline.**—P. L. 3, 402. more to pity *i.*
P. L. 10, 1061. and his heart to pity *i.*
P. L. 11, 145. to *i.* his will
C. 412. that I *i.* to hope rather than fear
**Inclined.**—P. L. 3, 405. more to pity *i.*
P. L. 11, 250. he kingly from his state *i.* not
P. L. 11, 596. of Adam soon *i.* to admit delight
P. R. 4, 212. thyself seem'st otherwise *i.*
S. A. 1636. with head awhile *i.*
S. 23, 13. but O as to embrace me she *i.*
**Inclines.**—P. L. 2, 314. the popular vote *i.*
P. L. 4, 615. with soft slumbrous weight *i.*
**Inclining.**—P. L. 10, 46. to her own *i.*
**Inclose.**—P. L. 1, 617. half *i.* him round
**Inclosed.**—P. L. 2, 512. fiery seraphim *i.*
P. L. 3, 420. *i.* from Chaos
S. A. 194. how many evils have *i.* me round
**Included.**—P. L. 9, 416. the whole *i.* race
**Incomposed.**—P. L. 2, 989. visage *i.*
**Incomprehensible.**—P. L. 8, 20. spaces *i.*
**Inconsiderable.**—P. R. 4, 457. as *i.*
**Incontinence.**—C. 397. rash hand of bold *i.*
**Inconvenient.**—P. L. 5, 495. no *i.* diet
**Incorporate.**—P. L. 10, 816. and *i.* both
S. A. 161. to *i.* with gloomy night
**Incorporeal.**—P. L. 1, 789. *i.* spirits
P. L. 5, 413. and corporeal to *i.* turn
P. L. 8, 37. journey brought of *i.* speed
**Incorrupt.**—P. L. 11, 56. of *i.* corrupted
**Incorruptible.**—P. L. 2, 138. all *i.*
P. L. 9, 298. supposed not *i.* of faith
P. L. 9, 622. fruit untouched still hanging *i.*
**Increase.**—P. L. 4, 748. our Maker bids *i.*
P. L. 10, 486. the more to *i.* your wonder
P. L. 10, 730. *i.* and multiply
P. L. 10, 731. for what can I *i.* or multiply
M. W. 51. that to give the world *i.*
U. C. II. 32. strange to think his wain was his *i.*
**Increased.**—P. L. 10, 351. his joy *i.*
P. L. 12, 155. with twelve sons *i.*
P. R. 2, 12. as the days *i.*, *i.* their doubt
**Increate.**—P. L. 3, 6. of bright essence *i.*
**Incredible.**—P. L. 4, 593. *i.* how swift
S. A. 1084. feats performed *i.* to me
S. A. 1627. with *i.* stupendous force
S. A. 1532. God hath wrought things as *i.*
**Incubus.**—P. R. 2, 152. the fleshliest *i.*
**Incumbent.**—P. L. 1, 226. *i.* on the dusky air
**Incumbered.**—P. L. 6, 874. so huge a rout *i.*
**Incur.**—P. L. 8, 336. in my choice not to *i.*
P. L. 9, 992. of choice to *i.* divine displeasure
**Incurable.**—S. A. 1234. nothing ... fear I *i.*
**Incurred.**—P. L. 10, 15. *i.* (what could they less)
**Incurrest.**—P. L. 4, 913. thou *i.* by flying
**Incursions.**—P. R. 3, 301. whose *i.* wild
**Ind.**—P. L. 2, 2. wealth of Ormus and of *I.*
C. 606. 'twixt Africa and *I.*
**Indamaged.**—P. R. 4, 206. trial hath *i.*
**Indebted.**—P. L. 3, 235. *i.* and undone
P. L. 4, 57. pays at once *i.* and discharged
**Indecent.**—P. L. 6, 601. *i.* overthrow
**Indeed.**—P. L. 1, 114. that were low *i.*
P. L. 2, 99. or if our substance be *i.* divine
P. L. 3, 702. wonderful *i.* are all his works
P. L. 4, 444. for we to him *i.* all praises owe
P. L. 4, 477. till I espied thee fair *i.*, and tall
P. L. 5, 706. great *i.* his name
P. L. 8, 524. delight *i.*, but such as used or not
P. L. 9, 650. wondrous *i.* if cause of such effects
P. L. 9, 656. *i.* hath God then said that
P. L. 10, 152. adorned she was *i.* and lovely
P. L. 10, 1036. would be revenge *i.*
P. R. 1, 410. thou comest *i.*
P. R. 2, 316. forty and more deserted here *i.*
P. R. 3, 165. he *i.* retired into the desert
P. R. 4, 354. statists *i.*, and lovers
S. A. 158. imprisoned now *i.* in real darkness
S. A. 291. me easily *i.* mine may neglect

S. A. 527. after some proof of acts *i.* heroic
S. A. 1347. thou shalt have cause to sorrow *i.*
S. A. 1571. the worst *i.* O all my hope's defeated
Cir. 16. just law *i.*
**Indefatigable.**—P. L. 2, 408. *i.* wings
**Indented.**—P. L. 9, 496. not with *i.* wave
V. Ex. 94. thirty arms along the *i.* meads
**India.**—P. L. 5, 339. in *I.* East or West
P. R. 4, 74. *I.* and the golden Chersonese
**Indian.**—P. L. 1, 781. beyond the *I.* mount
P. L. 3, 436. Ganges or Hydaspes *I.* streams
P. L. 9, 1108. oft the *I.* herdsman shunning
P. R. 4, 75. and utmost *I.* isle Taprobane
C. 139. the nice morn on the *I.* steep
**Indians.**—P. L. 9, 1102. to *I.* known
**Indignant.**—P. L. 10, 311. the *i.* waves
**Indignation.**—P. L. 2, 707. with *i.*
P. L. 6, 811. God's *i.* on these godless poured
P. L. 9, 666. zeal and love to man and *i.*
P. L. 10, 418. scorned his *i.*
**Indignities.**—S. A. 371. subject him to so foul *i.*
S. A. 1168. all these *i.* for such they are
S. A. 1341. before their god the worst of all *i.*
**Indignity.**—P. L. 9, 154. and O *i.*
S. A. 411. O *i.*, O blot to honour and religion
**Indirect.**—P. L. 11, 631. to tread paths *i.*
**Indissolubly.**—P. L. 6, 69. move *i.* firm
**Indite.**—P. L. 9, 27. to *i.* wars
**Individual.**— P. L. 4, 486. *i.* solace dear
P. L. 5, 610. united as one *i.* soul for ever
T. 12. shall greet our bliss with an *i.* kiss
**Indorsed.**—P. R. 3, 329. *i.* with towers
**Induce.**—P. L. 2, 503. which might *i.* us
**Induced.**—P. L. 8, 253. longer to converse *i.*
**Inducement.**—P. L. 9, 934. *i.* strong to us
S. A. 1445. my *i.* hither was not at present here
**Induces.**—P. R. 1, 105. *i.* best to hope
**Inducing.**—P. L. 6, 407. *i.* darkness
**Inductive.**—P. L. 11, 519. *i.* mainly to the sin
**Indulgence.**—P. L. 9, 1186. *i.* will accuse
P. R. 1, 110. long *i.* to their fears or grief
**Indulgences.**—P. L. 3, 492. *i.*, dispenses
**Indulgent.**—P. L. 5, 883. those *i.* laws
P. L. 9, 3. familiar used to sit *i.*
**Indus.**—P. L. 9, 82. flows Ganges and *I.*
P. R. 3, 272. as far as *I.* east, Euphrates west
**Industrious.**—P. L. 1, 751. his *i.* crew
P. L. 2, 116. to vice *i.*
P. L. 8, 137. if earth *i.* of herself fetch day
P. R. 4, 248. the sound of bees' *i.* murmur
S. A. 1274. and *i.* to support tyrannic power
**Ineffable.**—P. L. 3, 137. new joy *i.*
P. L. 5, 734. lightning divine, *i.*, serene
**Ineffably.**—P. L. 6, 721. *i.* into his face
**Ineffectual.**—P. L. 9, 301. though *i.* found
**Inelegant.**—P. L. 5, 335. not well joined, *i.*
**Ineloquent.**—P. L. 8, 219. nor tongue *i.*
**Inevitable.**—P. L. 2, 197. since fate *i.*
P. L. 2, 322. far removed under the *i.* curb
S. A. 1586. *i.* cause
**Inevitably.**—P. L. 8, 330. *i.* thou shalt die
S. A. 1657. Samson ... *i.* pulled down
**Inexorable.**—S. A. 827. self-severe, *i.*
**Inexorably.**—P. L. 2, 91. the scourge *i.*
**Inexperience.**—P. L. 4, 931. argue thy *i.*
**Inexpert.**—P. L. 12, 218. terrify them *i.*
**Inexpiable.**—S. A. 839. to raise in me *i.* hate
**Inexplicable.**—P. L. 10, 754. *i.* thy justice
**Inexpressible.**—P. L. 5, 595. of circuit *i.*
P. L. 8, 113. distance *i.* by numbers
**Inextinguishable.**—P. L. 6, 217. *i.* rage
**Inextricable.**—P. L. 5, 528. by fate *i.*
**Infallible.**—P. L. 12, 530. can be heard *i.*
P. R. 3, 16. or tongue of seers old *i.*
**Infamed.**—P. L. 9, 797. obscured, *i.*
**Infamous.**—S. A. 417. ignominious, *i.*
C. 424. *i.* hills and sandy perilous wilds
D. F. I. 12. thereby to wipe away the *i.* blot
**Infamy.**—P. L. 6, 384. through *i.* seeks fame
S. A. 968. the brand of *i.* upon my name
**Infancy.**—P. R. 4, 508. thy *i.*, thy childhood

H. 151. the babe yet lies in smiling *i.*
Cir. 14. his *i.* to seize
**Infant.**—P. L. 2, 664. the smell of *i.* blood
P. L. 12, 168. and kills their *i.* males
P. R. 2, 78. *i.* blood the streets of Bethlehem
S. 18, 8. rolled mother with *i.* down the rocks
H. 16. afford a present to the *i.* God
H. 222. the dreaded *I.'s* hand
P. 3. joyous news of heavenly *I.'s* birth
V. Ex. 4. slide through my *i.* lips
**Infantry.**—P. L. 1, 575. than that small *i.*
**Infect.**—P. L. 10, 608. words, actions, all *i.*
**Infected.**—P. L. 1, 453. *i.* Sion's daughters
**Infection.**—P. L. 1, 483. scape the *i.*
P. 55. might think the *i.* of my sorrows loud
**Infer.**—P. L. 7, 116. and *i.* thee also happier
C. 408. I do not, brother, *i.* as if I thought
**Inferior.**—P. L. 2, 26. envy from each *i.*
P. L. 3, 420. the luminous *i.* orbs
P. L. 4, 59. ordained me some *i.* angel
P. L. 4, 362. heavenly spirits bright little *i.*
P. L. 8, 382. and these *i.* far beneath me set
P. L. 8, 410. which I made and those to me *i.*
P. L. 8, 541. her the *i.*
P. L. 9, 825. for *i.* who is free
P. L. 10, 468. to our native heaven little *i.*
P. R. 2, 135. however to this Man *i.* far
S. A. 73. *i.* to the vilest now become
S. A. 672. and *i.* creatures mute, irrational
A. 77. if my *i.* hand or voice could hit
H. 81. as his *i.* flame the new-enlightened world
**Infernal.**—P. L. 1, 34. the *i.* serpent
P. L. 1, 251. *i.* world!
P. L. 1, 657. for this *i.* pit shall never hold
P. L. 1, 792. amidst the hall of that *i.* court
P. L. 2, 66. he shall hear *i.* thunder
P. L. 2, 387. pleased highly those *i.* states
P. L. 2, 507. came the grand *i.* peers
P. L. 2, 575. banks of four *i.* rivers
P. L. 2, 742. in this *i.* vale first met
P. L. 2, 850. the key of this *i.* pit
P. L. 2, 881. the *i.* doors
P. L. 4, 793. who tells of some *i.* spirit seen
P. L. 4, 965. back to the *i.* pit I drag thee
P. L. 6, 483. yield us pregnant with *i.* flame
P. L. 6, 667. *i.* noise
P. L. 7, 238. black tartareous cold *i.* dregs
P. L. 9, 136. glory sole among the *i.* powers
P. L. 10, 259. of merit high to all the *i.* host
P. L. 10, 389. of all the *i.* empire
P. L. 10, 464. triumphant out of this *i.* pit
P. R. 1, 107. much amazement to the *i.* crew
P. R. 4, 422. *i.* ghosts and hellish furies
P. R. 4, 618. but thou *i.* serpent shalt not
H. 233. to the *i.* jail each fettered ghost slips
**Infers.**—P. L. 8, 91. great or bright *i.* not
P. L. 9, 285. which plain *i.* thy equal fear
P. L. 9, 754. commends thee more which it *i.*
**Infest.**—S.A. 423. find some occasion to *i.* our foes
**Infidel.**—P. L. 1, 582. baptized or *i.*
S. A. 221. I sought to wed the daughter of an *i.*
**Infinite.**—P. L. 1, 218. bring forth *i.* goodness
P. L. 2, 405. the dark unbottomed *i.* abyss
P. L. 2, 797. hourly born with sorrow *i.*
P. L. 3, 12. from the void and formless *i.*
P. L. 3, 373. immutable, immortal, *i.*
P. L. 3, 706. the wisdom *i.* that brought
P. L. 4, 74. which way shall I fly *i.* wrath
P. L. 4, 415. his good as liberal and free as *i.*
P. L. 4, 734. shall with us extol thy goodness *i.*
P. L. 4, 916. that no pain can equal anger *i.*
P. L. 5, 596. the Father *i.* by whom in bliss
P. L. 5, 874. applause through the *i.* host
P. L. 6, 241. deeds of eternal fame ... but *i.*
P. L. 7, 191. his good to worlds and ages *i.*
P. L. 7, 602. Jehovah, *i.* thy power
P. L. 8, 410. *i.* descents
P. L. 8, 420. thou shouldst propagate already *i.*
P. L. 10, 794. for though the Lord of all be *i.*
P. L. 10, 802. finite to *i.*
P. L. 10, 907. which *i.* calamity shall cause

P. L. 11, 167. but *i.* in pardon was my Judge
P. L. 11, 692. with *i.* man-slaughter
P. L. 12, 469. O goodness *i.*
**Infinitely.**—P. L. 4, 414. be *i.* good
P. L. 7, 76. for which to the *i.* Good we owe
**Infinitude.**—P. L. 3, 711. vast *i.* confined
P. L. 7, 169. because I am who fill *i.*
**Infirm.**—P. L. 5, 384. no thought *i.* altered
**Infirmer.**—P. L. 10, 956 *i.* sex.
**Infirmity.**—S. A. 776. with like *i.* to publish
L. 71. that last *i.* of noble mind
**Infixed.**—P. L. 2, 602. immovable, *i.* and frozen
S. A. 1032. of constancy no root *i.*
**Inflame.**—P. L. 2, 581. torrent fire *i.* with rage
P. L. 9, 1081. *i.* my sense with ardour to enjoy
S. A. 1739. and from his memory *i.* their breasts
**Inflamed.**—P. L. 1, 300. beach of that *i.* sea
P. L. 2, 630. Satan with thoughts *i.* of highest
P. L. 2, 791. more it seems *i.* with lust
P. L. 4, 9. now first *i.* with rage
P. L. 6, 261. and visage all *i.*
P. R. 3, 40. the more *i.* with glory
**Inflames.**—P. L. 4, 818. blaze diffused *i.*
P. R. 1, 418. rather *i.* thy torment
**Inflaming.**—P. L. 9, 1013. carnal desire *i.*
**Inflammation.**—S. A. 626. dire *i.* which no
**Inflexible.**—S. A. 816. *i.* as steel
**Inflict.**—P. L. 1, 96. in his rage can else *i.*
P. L. 10, 341. what his wrath might suddenly *i.*
S. A. 1291. over all that tyranny or fortune can *i.*
**Inflicted.**—P. L. 2, 335. punishment *i.*
P. L. 10, 51. because not yet *i.* as he feared
P. R. 1, 54. shall be *i.* by the seed of Eve
S. A. 485. and slaveries worse than death *i.*
S. A. 1170. from God *i.* on me
**Inflictions.**—P. R. 1, 426. with all *i.*
**Influence.**—P. L. 2, 1034. sacred *i.* of light
P. L. 3, 118. foreknowledge had no *i.* on
P. L. 4, 669. with kindly heat of various *i.*
P. L. 5, 695. infused bad *i.* into the unwary
P. L. 7, 375. before him danced shedding sweet *i.*
P. L. 8, 513. on that hour shed their selectest *i.*
P. L. 9, 107. their precious beams of sacred *i.*
P. L. 9, 309. I from the *i.* of thy looks receive
P. L. 10, 662. *i.* malignant when to shower
C. 336. or if your *i.* be quite dammed up
L'A. 122. whose bright eyes rain *i.*
H. 71. bending one way their precious *i.*
**Infolded.**—A. 64. sit upon the nine *i.* spheres
**Inform.**—P. R. 3, 247. introduction to *i.*
C. 180. shall I *i.* my unacquainted feet
**Informed.**—P. L. 3, 593. all alike *i.* with
P. L. 7, 639. that posterity *i.* by thee might
P. L. 9, 275. both by thee *i.* I learn
S. A. 335. hither hath *i.* your younger feet
S. A. 1229. part not hence so slight *i.*
**Informidable.**—P. L. 9, 486. foe not *i.*
**Informing.**—P. L. 12, 232. *i.* them by types
**Infringed.**—P. R. 1, 62. our power to be *i.*
**Infuriate.**—P. L. 6, 486. dilated and *i.*
**Infused.**—P. L. 5, 694. and *i.* bad influence
P. L. 7, 236. vital virtue *i.* and vital warmth
P. L. 8, 474. which from that time *i.* sweetness
P. L. 9, 836. whose presence had *i.* into the
**Ingendered**—P. L. 10, 530. the sun *i.*
**Ingendering.**—P. L. 2, 794. *i.* with me
P. L. 4, 809. blown up with high conceits *i.*
**Inglorious.**—P. L. 1, 624. strife was not *i.*
P. L. 3, 253. stoop *i.*
P. L. 9, 141. one night freed from servitude *i.*
P. L. 12, 220. rather *i.* life
P. R. 3, 42. wept that he had lived so long *i.*
S. A. 580. *i.* unemployed with age outworn
C. 528. the *i.* likeness of a beast
D. F. I. 22. yet art thou not *i.* in thy fate
**Ingorged.**—P. L. 9, 791. greedily she *i.*
**Ingraft.**—P. L. 11, 35. good or not good *i.*
**Ingrate.**—P. L. 3, 97. whose but his own ? *i.*
P. L. 5, 811. expected least of all from thee *i.*
P. R. 3, 138. recreant to God, *i.* and false
**Ingrateful.**—P. L. 5, 407. no *i.* food

P. L. 9, 1164. to thee *i.* Eve
S. A. 282. and how *i.* Ephraim
S. A. 696. and condemnation of the *i.* multitude
**Ingratitude.**—S. A. 276. heap *i.* on worthiest
C. 778. with besotted base *i.*
**Ingredients.**—P. L. 11, 417. these *i.* pierced
**Ingulfed.**—P. L. 4, 225. passed underneath *i.*
  P. L. 5, 614. deep *i.*
**Inhabit.**—P. L. 2, 355. what creatures there *i.*
  P. L. 7, 162. meanwhile *i.* lax, ye powers
**Inhabitant.**—P. L. 2, 860. *i.* of heaven
  P. L. 5, 461. *i.* with God now know I well
**Inhabitants.**—P. L. 4, 5. woe to the *i.*
  P. L. 8, 145. if land be there fields and *i.*
**Inhabitation.**—S. A. 1512. the whole *i.*
**Inhabited.**—P. L. 10, 690. the world *i.*
**Inherit.**—S. A. 1012. can win or long *i.*
**Inheritance.**—P. L. 2, 38. our just *i.* of old
  P. R. 3, 382. thou shalt restore to their *i.*
  S. A. 1476. if my whole *i.* may compass it
**Inhospitable.**—P. L. 11, 306. *i.* appear
  S. A. 989. Jael, who with *i.* guile smote Sisera
**Inhospitably.**—P. L. 12, 168. slaves *i.*
**Inhuman.**—P. L. 11, 511. under *i.* pains
  S. A. 109. life in captivity among *i.* foes
**Inhumanly.**—P. L. 11, 677. *i.* to men
**Inimitable.**—P. L. 3, 508. *i.* on earth
  A. 78. or voice could hit *i.* sounds
**Iniquities.**—P. L. 12, 107. with their *i.*
**Injunction.**—P. L. 10, 13. the high *i.*
**Injure.**—P. L. 10, 1057. heat should *i.* us
**Injured.**—P. L. 5, 460. the *i.* lover's hell
  P. L. 1, 98. from sense of *i.* merit
**Injuries.**—P. L. 10, 925. as joined in *i.*
  P. R. 3, 190. by tribulations, *i.,* insults
  P. L. 4, 387. attend thee scorns reproaches *i.*
**Injurious.**—S. A. 1003. yet beauty though *i.*
**Injury.**—P. L. 1, 500. and *i.* and outrage
  P. L. 6, 434. incapable of mortal *i.* imperishable
**Inlaid.**—P. L. 6, 758. a sapphire throne *i.*
**Inland.**—P. L. 10, 423. far to the *i.* retired
**Inlay.**—P. L. 4, 701. with rich *i.* broidered
  C. 22. that like to rich and various gems *i.*
**Inlet.**—C. 839. the porch and *i.* of each sense
**Inly.**—P. L. 11, 444. whereat he *i.* raged
  P. R. 1, 228. *i.* rejoiced
  P. R. 1, 466. the subtle fiend though *i.* stung
  P. R. 3, 203. to whom the tempter *i.* racked
**Inmate.**—P. L. 9, 495. in serpent *i.* bad
  P. L. 12, 166. as *i.* guests too numerous
**Inmost.**—P. L. 1, 168. his *i.* counsels
  P. L. 4, 738. into their *i.* bower
  P. L. 5, 302. to warm earth's *i.* womb
  P. L. 9, 1048. and *i.* powers made err
  P. L. 11, 418. to the *i.* seat of mental sight
  S. A. 611. secret passage find to the *i.* mind
  C. 536. in their obscured haunts of *i.* bowers
  Il P. 29. of woody Ida's *i.* grove
**Inn.**—P. R. 1, 248. for in the *i.* was left no better
  U. C. I. 13. that he had ta'en up his latest *i.*
**Inner.**—P. R. 2, 477. governs the *i.* man
**Innocence.**—P. L. 4, 318. spotless *i.*
  P. L. 4, 388. your harmless *i.*
  P. L. 4, 745. talk of purity and place and *i.*
  P. L. 5, 445. O *i.,* deserving Paradise
  P. L. 6, 401. such high advantages their *i.*
  P. L. 8, 501. yet *i.* and virgin modesty
  P. L. 9, 373. go in thy native *i.*
  P. L. 9, 411. despoiled of *i.,* of faith, of bliss
  P. L. 9, 459. her graceful *i.* her every air
  P. L. 9, 1054. *i.* that as a veil
  P. L. 9, 1075. of honour void, of *i.,* of faith
  P. L. 11, 30. ere fallen from *i.*
  C. 697. betrayed my credulous *i.*
  C. 831. commended her fair *i.* to the flood
  D. F. I. 65. to bless us with thy heaven-loved *i.*
**Innocent.**—P. L. 4, 11. on *i.* frail man
  P. L. 5, 209. so prayed they *i.*
  C. 574. the aidless *i.* lady his wished prey
  C. 762. do not charge most *i.* nature
  H. 39. to hide her guilty front with *i.* snow

**Innumerable.**—P. L. 1, 101. *i.* force
  P. L. 1, 338. they soon obeyed *i.*
  P. L. 1, 699. and hands *i.* scarce perform
  P. L. 3, 147. with the *i.* sound of hymns
  P. L. 3, 565. amongst *i.* stars that shone
  P. L. 5, 585. *i.* before the Almighty's throne
  P. L. 5, 745. an host *i.* as the stars of night
  P. L. 5, 898. among *i.* false unmoved
  P. L. 6, 82. bristled with upright beams *i.*
  P. L. 6, 508. *i.* hands were ready
  P. L. 7, 88. with moving fires adorned *i.*
  P. L. 7, 156. out of one man a race of men *i.*
  P. L. 7, 400. with fry *i.* swarm
  P. L. 8, 297. of men *i.* ordained first father
  P. L. 9, 1089. ye cedars with *i.* boughs
  P. L. 10, 268. prey *i.*
  P. L. 10, 507. on all sides from *i.* tongues
  P. L. 10, 896. *i.* disturbances on earth
  S. A. 608. with maladies *i.* in heart, head
  C. 713. thronging the seas with spawn *i.*
**Innumerous.**—P. L. 7, 455. *i.* living creatures
  C. 349. in this close dungeon of *i.* boughs
**Inoffensive.**—P. L. 5, 345. *i.* must
  P. L. 8, 164. with *i.* pace
  P. L. 10, 305. smooth, easy, *i.* down to hell
**Inordinate.**—P. L. 4, 808. *i.* desires
  P. L. 12, 87. immediately *i.* desires
**Inquire.**—P. L. 3, 571. he stayed not to *i.*
  P. L. 8, 225. and *i.* gladly into the ways of God
  P. L. 12, 362. guides the eastern sages who *i.*
  P. R. 4, 42. were curious to *i.*
**Inquired.**—P. R. 1, 458. *i.* at Delphos
**Inquisition.**—P. R. 3, 200. what moves thy *i.*
**Inquisitive.**—S. A. 775. curiosity *i.* importune
**Inroad.**—P. L. 3, 421. the *i.* of Darkness
  P. L. 6, 387. with many an *i.* gored
**Inroads.**—P. L. 2, 103. and with perpetual *i.*
**Inrolled.**—P. L. 12, 523. left them *i.*
  S. A. 653. in ancient and in modern books *i.*
  S. A. 1224. a man condemned, a slave *i.*
  S. A. 1736. and acts *i.* in copious legend
**Insatiable.**—P. R. 3, 148. he himself *i.*
**Insatiate.**—P. L. 2, 8. *i.* to pursue vain war
  P. L. 9, 536. approach thee thus and gaze *i.*
**Inscribed.**—P. R. 4, 335. artful terms *i.*
  L. 106. sanguine flower *i.* with woe
**Insect.**—P. L. 4, 704. bird, beast, *i.* or worm
  P. L. 7, 476. creeps the ground, *i.* or worm
  P. L. 11, 734. of every beast, and bird, and *i.*
**Insensate.**—P. L. 6, 787. Powers *i.*
  S. A. 1685. *i.* left or to sense reprobate
**Insensible.**—P. L. 8, 291. my former state *i.*
  P. L. 10, 777. and be earth *i.*
**Insensibly.**—P. L. 6, 692. hath wrought *i.*
  P. L. 8, 130. *i.* three different motions move
**Inseparable.**—P. L. 10, 250. my shade *i.*
**Inseparably.**—P. L. 4, 473. enjoy *i.* thine
  S. A. 154. prison within prison, *i.* dark
**Inshrine.**—P. L. 1, 719, *i.* Belus or Serapis
**Inside.**—P. R. 4, 58. outside and *i.* both
**Insight.**—P. R. 3, 238. quickest *i.*
**Insinuating.**—P. L. 4, 348. serpent sly *i.*
**Insist.**—S. A. 913. nor still *i.* to afflict thyself
**Insisted.**—P. R. 1, 468. sharply thou hast *i.*
**Insolence.**—P. L. 1, 502. flown with *i.*
  S. A. 1236. this *i.* other kind of answer fits
  C. 178. to meet the rudeness and swilled *i.*
**Insolent.**—S. A. 1422. impetuous *i.* unquenchable
**Inspection.**—P. L. 9, 83. and with *i.* deep
**Insphered.**—C. 3. aerial spirits live *i.*
**Inspire.**—P. L. 1, 7. didst *i.* that shepherd
  P. R. 1, 11. *i.* as thou art wont
  M. M. 5. hail bounteous May, that dost *i.*
**Inspired.**—P. L. 4, 273. *i.* Castalian spring
  P. L. 5, 322. earth's hallowed mould of God *i.*
  P. L. 6, 155. that tongue *i.* with contradiction
  P. L. 6, 503. intent on mischief or *i.* with
  P. L. 8, 476. from her air *i.*
  P. L. 9, 189. soon *i.* with act intelligential
  P. L. 10, 785. life the spirit of man which God *i.*
  P. L. 11, 7. which the spirit of prayer *i.*

P. R. 1, 492. a prophet yet *i.*
P. R. 4, 275. his tenement whom well *i.*
P. R. 4, 350. such are from God *i.*
**Inspires.**—P. L. 4, 154. and to the heart *i.*
P. L. 9, 23. dictates to me slumbering or *i.*
H. 180. *i.* the pale-eyed priest
**Inspiring.**—P. L. 4, 804. if *i.* venom
**Instant.**—P. L. 6, 549. *i.* without disturb
P. L. 10, 210. and the *i.* stroke of death
P. L. 10, 345. which understood not *i.*
**Instantly.**—P. L. 8, 458. which *i.* fell on me
**Instead.**—P. L. 1, 553. and *i.* of rage
P. L. 3, 45. but cloud *i.*, and ever-during dark
P. L. 4, 105. behold *i.* of us out-cast exiled
P. L. 4, 316. all mankind with shows *i.*
P. L. 7, 188. *i.* of spirits malign, a better race
P. L. 10, 538. but other sight *i.* a crowd
P. L. 10, 565. *i.* of fruit chewed bitter ashes
P. L. 10, 1040. and we *i.* shall double ours
P. L. 11, 5. new flesh regenerate grow *i.*
P. L. 12, 54. and *i.* to sow a jangling noise
P. R. 3, 131. would likeliest render contempt *i.*
C. 529. inglorious likeness of a beast fixes *i.*
**Instilled.**—P. L. 6, 269. how hast thou *i.*
P. L. 11, 416. the well of life three drops *i.*
**Instinct.**—P. L. 2, 937. cloud *i.* with fire
P. L. 6, 752. itself *i.* with spirit
P. L. 10, 263. by this newfelt attraction and *i.*
P. L. 11, 562. his volant touch *i.* through all
S. A. 526. full of divine *i.* after some proof
S. A. 1545. providence or *i.* of nature
**Instinctive.**—P. L. 8, 259. quick *i.* motion
**Instruct.**—P. L. 1, 19. *i.* me for thou knowest
P. L. 10, 1081. will *i.* us praying
P. R. 1, 439. the more *i.* to fly
**Instructed.**—P. L. 12, 239. *i.* that to God
P. L. 12, 557. greatly *i.* I shall hence depart
S. A. 757. with more cautious and *i.* skill
P. 48. for sure so well *i.* are my tears
**Instructor.**—P. L. 5, 546. divine *i.*
P. L. 11, 871. heavenly *I.*
**Instruction.**—P. L. 7, 81. our *i.* to impart
**Instructs.**—P. L. 5, 320. which *i.* us not
**Instrument.**—P. L. 2, 872. sad *i.* of all our
P. L. 6, 505. might devise like *i.* to plague
P. L. 10, 166. who made him *i.* of mischief
P. R. 3, 388. much *i.* of war
**Instrumental.**—P. L. 4, 686. *i.* sounds
P. L. 6, 65. to the sound of *i.* harmony
**Instruments.**—P. L. 11, 559. sound of *i.*
**Insufferably.**—P. L. 9, 1084. *i.* bright
**Insult.**—S. A. 113. perhaps to *i.*
S. A. 944. how wouldst thou *i.* when I must live
**Insulting.**—P. L. 2, 79. our broken rear *i.*
P. L. 4, 926. *i.* angel well thou know'st I stood
P. R. 4, 138. that *i.* vanity
**Insults.**—P. R. 3, 190. tribulations, injuries, *i.*
**Insuperable.**—P. L. 4, 138. *i.*
**Insupportable.**—P. L. 10, 134. *i.* be all
**Insupportably.**—S. A. 136. when *i.* his foot
**Insurrection.**—P. L. 2, 136. *i.* to confound
**Integrity.**—P. L. 5, 704. to sound or taint *i.*
P. L. 9, 329. with his foul esteem of our *i.*
**Intellect.**—P. L. 6, 351. all ear, all *i.*
**Intellects.**—S. 11, 4. numbering good *i.*
**Intellectual.**—P. L. 2, 147. this *i.* being
P. L. 5, 485. vital spirits aspire to animal to *i.*
P. L. 9, 483. whose higher *i.* more I shun
P. L. 9, 768. or to us denied this *i.* food
**Intelligence.**—P. L. 8, 181. pure *i.* of heaven
**Intelligent.**—P. L. 4, 427. *i.* of seasons
P. R. 3, 58. the *i.* among them and the wise
**Intelligential.**—P. L. 5, 408. pure *i.*
P. L. 9, 190. soon inspired with act *i.*
**Intemperance.**—P. L. 11, 472. by *i.*
C. 975. o'er sensual folly and *i.*
**Intemperate.**—C. 67. fond *i.* thirst
**Intend.**—P. L. 2, 457. *i.* at home while here
P. L. 2, 713. fatal hands no second stroke *i.*
P. L. 5, 867. whether by supplication we *i.*
P. L. 10, 58. I *i.* mercy colleague with justice

S. A. 911. I *i.* for what I have misdone
S. A. 1259. if they *i.* advantage of my labours
**Intended.**—P. L. 1, 652. that he ere long *i.*
P. L. 8, 447. no such company ... *i.* thee
P. L. 8, 555. as one *i.* first not after made
P. L. 9, 45. or years damp my *i.* wing depressed
P. L. 9, 295. the attempt itself *i.* by our foe
P. L. 10, 689. turned his course *i.*
P. R. 1, 61. be not *i.* all our power
**Intends.**—P. L. 1, 14. with no middle flight *i.*
P. L. 2, 727. father what *i.* thy hand she cried
P. L. 2, 740. tell thee yet by deeds what it *i.*
P. L. 4, 898. if he *i.* our stay in that dark
P. L. 5, 693. *i.* to pass triumphant
P. L. 5, 725. who *i.* to erect his throne equal
P. L. 12, 73. to God his tower *i.* siege
S. 21, 8. what the Swede *i.* and what the French
**Intense.**—P. L. 8, 387. the one *i.*
S. A. 615. with answerable pains but more *i.*
**Intent.**—P. L. 1, 787. on their mirth and dance *i.*
P. L. 3, 192. endeavoured with sincere *i.*
P. L. 4, 810. him thus *i.* Ithuriel with his spear
P. L. 5, 332. on hospitable thoughts *i.*
P. L. 6, 503. some one *i.* on mischief
P. L. 9, 162. and the dark *i.* I bring
P. L. 9, 462. the fierce *i.* it brought
P. L. 9, 786. Eve *i.* now wholly on her taste
P. L. 9, 1035. glance or toy of amorous *i.*
P. R. 1, 291. to what *i.* I learn not yet perhaps
P. R. 2, 95. some great *i.* conceals him
P. R. 2, 195. her assaults on worthier things *i.*
P. R. 4, 528. his wisdom, power, *i.*
S. A. 1078. though for no friendly *i.*
S. A. 1754. his uncontrollable *i.*
A. 34. this quest of yours and free *i.*
F. of C. 9. whose life learning faith and pure *i.*
**Inter.**—M. W. 1. this rich marble doth *i.*
**Intercede.**—P. L. 11, 21. thus to *i.* began
S. A. 920. I to the lords will *i.* not doubting
**Intercept.**—P. L. 5, 871. fly ere evil *i.*
P. L. 6, 193. less could his shield such ruin *i.*
P. L. 9, 410. to *i.* thy way or send thee back
P. L. 10, 429. might *i.* their emperor sent so
**Intercession.**—P. L. 10, 228. mixing *i.*
**Intercessor.**—P. L. 3, 219. patron or *i.*
P. L. 10, 96. judge and *I.* both
P. L. 11, 19. by their great *I.*
**Interchange.**—P. L. 9, 115. sweet *i.*
**Intercourse.**—P. L. 2, 1031. with easy *i.*
P. L. 6, 571. and with frequent *i.* thither will
P. L. 9, 238. this sweet *i.* of looks and smiles
P. L. 10, 260. easing their passage hence for *i.*
**Interdict.**—P. R. 2, 369. no *i.* defends
**Interdicted.**—P. L. 5, 52. the tree of *i.*
P. L. 7, 46. charged not to touch the *i.* tree
**Interdiction.**—P. L. 8, 334. the rigid *i.*
**Interfused.**—P. L. 7, 89. ambient air wide *i.*
**Interlunar.**—S. A. 89. hid in her vacant *i.*
**Interminable.**—S. A. 307. would confine the *i.*
**Intermission.**—P. L. 2, 802. that rest or *i.*
P. L. 4, 102. purchase dear short *i.* bought
S. A. 1629. at length for *i.* sake they led him
**Intermit.**—P. L. 2, 462. *i.* no watch against
**Intermits.**—P. L. 9, 223. *i.* our day's work
**Intermitted.**—P. L. 2, 173. *i.* vengeance
P. L. 9, 1133. speech *i.* thus to Eve renewed
**Intermix.**—P. L. 8, 54. *i.* grateful digressions
P. L. 11, 115. *i.* my covenant in the woman's
**Intermixed.**—P. L. 7, 598. soft tunings *i.*
P. L. 9, 218. spring of roses *i.* with myrtle
**Internal.**—P. L. 8, 461. my *i.* sight
P. L. 9, 711. since I as man, *i.* man
S. A. 1334. myself? my conscience and *i.* peace
S. A. 1686. and with blindness *i.* struck
**Interpose.**—P. L. 2, 854. to *i.* his dart
P. L. 12, 4. if Adam aught perhaps might *i.*
L. 152. for so to *i.* a little ease
S. 20, 14. and spare to *i.* them oft is not unwise
**Interposed.**—P. L. 4, 253. were *i.*
P. L. 5, 258. star *i.* however small
P. L. 6, 336. many and strong who *i.* defence

P. L. 10, 323. hell with long reach *i.*
P. L. 12, 270. here Adam *i.,* O sent from heaven
P. R. 4, 39. above the height of mountains *i.*
**Interposes.**—P. L. 3, 728. her aid timely *i.*
**Interposest.**—P. L. 2, 738. strange thou *i.*
**Interposition.**—P. R. 3, 222. cool *i.*
**Interpret.**—P. L. 11, 33. let me *i.* for him
**Interpreted.**—P. L. 5, 762. of men *i.*
**Interpreter.**—P. L. 3, 657. *i.* thro'.... heaven
P. L. 7, 72. divine *i.* by favour sent
**Interpretest.**—S. A. 790. which thou *i.* hate
**Interrupt.**—P. L. 2, 371. and *i.* his joy
P. L. 3, 84. nor yet the main abyss wide *i.*
P. L. 8, 184. nor with perplexing thoughts to *i.*
P. L. 9, 512. who sought access but feared to *i.*
P. L. 12, 317. sins national *i.* their public peace
**Interrupted.**—P. L. 11, 286. the angel *i.*
**Intertwined.**—P. R. 4, 405. thick *i.*
**Interval.**—P. L. 6, 105. left a dreadful *i.*
**Interveined.**—P. R. 3, 257. rivers *i.*
**Intervene.**—P. L. 9, 222. looks *i.*
**Interview.**—P. L. 6, 555. at *i.* both stood
P. L. 11, 593. such happy *i.* and fair event
**Intervolved.**—P. L. 5, 623. eccentric *i.*
**Interwove.**—P. L. 1, 621. words *i.* with
C. 544. and *i.* with flaunting honeysuckle
**Interwoven.**—P. R. 2, 263. trees thick *i.*
**Intestine.**—P. L. 2, 1001. your *i.* broils
P. L. 6, 259. hoping here to end *i.* war
P. L. 11, 484. *i.* stone and ulcer
S. A. 1038. the contrary she proves a thorn *i.*
**Inthrall.**—P. L. 2, 551. should *i.* to force
**Intimate.**—S. A. 223. I knew from *i.* impulse
**Intoxicate.**—P. R. 4, 328. crude or *i.*
**Intoxicated.**—P. L. 9, 1008. with new wine *i.*
**Intranced.**—P. L. 1, 301. forms who lay *i.*
**Intrenched.**—P. L. 1, 601. thunder had *i.*
**Intricacies.**—P. L. 8, 182. freed from *i.*
**Intricate.**—P. L. 2, 877. turns the *i.* wards
P. L. 5, 622. mazes *i.,* eccentric, intervolved
P. L. 9, 632. and made *i.* seem straight
**Introduce.**—P. L. 3, 368. *i.* their sacred song
P. L. 5, 797. or can *i.* law and edict on us
P. L. 12, 241. to *i.* one greater of whose day
**Introduced.**—P. L. 10, 709. death *i.*
**Introduction.**—P. R. 3, 247. sufficient *i.*
**Intrude.**—L. 115. creep and *i.* and climb into
**Intrusion.**—P. L. 12, 178. with loathed *i.*
**Intuitive.**—P. L. 5, 488. discursive or *i.*
**Inundation.**—P. L. 11, 828. till *i.* rise
**Inure.**—P. L. 8, 239. and to *i.* our prompt
**Inured.**—P. L. 2, 216. or *i.* not feel
P. L. 11, 362. equally *i.* by moderation
P. R. 1, 339. to thirst *i.* more than the camel
P. R. 2, 102. I to wait with patience am *i.*
P. R. 4, 139. cruel by their sports to blood *i.*
C. 735. that they below would grow *i.* to light
**Inutterable.**—P. L. 2, 626. *i.* and worse
**Invade.**—P. L. 2, 342. to *i.* heaven
P. L. 3, 726. night would *i.*
P. L. 11, 102. or to *i.* vacant possession
P. R. 2, 127. such an enemy is risen to *i.* us
**Invaded.**—P. L. 6, 653. themselves *i.* next
**Invaders.**—P. L. 11, 801. no aid against *i.*
**Invalid.**—P. L. 8, 116. to show *i.* that which
**Invasion.**—P. R. 3, 365. found able by *i.*
**Inveigle.**—C. 538. *i.* and invite the unwary
**Invent.**—P. L. 6, 464. who therefore can *i.*
P. R. 1, 149. whate'er his cruel malice could *i.*
**Invented.**—P. L. 2, 70. his own *i.* torments
P. L. 4, 524. *i.* with design to keep them low
P. L. 9, 767. for us alone was death *i.*
**Invention.**—P. L. 6, 498. the *i.* all admired
**Inventions.**—P. L. 6, 631. with their *i.*
P. L. 7, 121. nor let thine own *i.* hope things
**Inventor.**—P. L. 6, 499. to be the *i.*
**Inventors.**—P. L. 11, 610. *i.* rare
**Invert.**—C. 682. but you *i.* the covenants
**Invest.**—P. L. 3, 10. with a mantle didst *i.*
**Invested.**—P. L. 7, 372. the horizon round *i.*
**Invests.**—P. L. 1, 208. *i.* the sea

P. L. 11, 233. such majesty *i.* him coming
**Invincible.**—P. L. 1, 140. spirit remains *i.*
P. L. 4, 846. youthful beauty added grace *i.*
P. L. 6, 47. lead forth to battle these my sons *i.*
P. R. 2, 408. thy temperance *i.* besides
S. A. 341. is this the man, that *i.* Samson
S. A. 1271. puts *i.* might to quell the mighty
**Invincibly.**—P. L. 6, 806. so have ye done *i.*
**Inviolable.**—P. L. 4, 843. keep this place *i.*
P. L. 6, 398. far otherwise the *i.* saints
**Invisible.**—P. L. 1, 369. and the *i.* glory
P. L. 3, 55. that I may see and tell of things *i.*
P. L. 3, 375. fountain of light thyself *i.* amidst
P. L. 3, 586. shoots *i.* virtue even to the deep
P. L. 3, 684. evil that walks *i.* except to God
P. L. 5, 157. to us *i.* or dimly seen in these
P. L. 5, 565. the *i.* exploits of warring spirits
P. L. 5, 599. brightness had made *i.*
P. L. 6, 681. *i.* is beheld visibly
P. L. 7, 122. which the *i.* king only omniscient
P. L. 7, 589. for he also went *i.* yet stayed
P. L. 8, 135. *i.* else above all stars
P. L. 10, 444. the door of that Plutonian hall *i.*
V. Ex. 66. from eyes of mortals walk *i.*
**Invisibly.**—P. L. 4, 476. follow straight *i.*
**Invitation.**—P. R. 2, 367. his *i.* earnestly
**Invite.**—P. L. 2, 278. all things *i.* to peaceful
P. L. 5, 374. as may not oft *i.*
P. L. 9, 402. and all things in best order to *i.*
S. A. 1684. as their own ruin on themselves to *i.*
C. 538. to inveigle and *i.* the unwary sense
L'A. 92. the upland hamlets will *i.*
**Invited.**—P. L. 12, 169. comes *i.* by a younger
**Invites.**—P. L. 3, 188. while offered grace *i.*
P. R. 1, 72. who all *i.* and in the consecrated
P. R. 4, 248. oft *i.* to studious musing
**Inviting.**—P. L. 8, 208. *i.* thee to hear
P. L. 9, 777. fair to the eye *i.* to the taste
P. R. 2, 314. fed twice by a voice *i.* him to eat
**Invocate.**—S. A 1146. go to his temple, *i.* his aid
**Invoke.**—P. L. 1, 13. I thence *i.* thy aid
P. L. 11, 590. and bid *i.* Hymen
**Invoked.**—P. L. 11, 492. though oft *i.*
P. L. 11, 591. then first to marriage rites *i.*
P. L. 12, 112. of whom to be *i.*
P. R. 4, 203. God of this world *i.* and world
C. 854. if she be right *i.* in warbled song
**Invoking.**—M. W. 19. he at their *i.* came
**Involve.**—P. L. 2, 384. hell to mingle and *i.*
**Involved.**—P. L. 1, 236. all *i.* with stench
P. L. 2, 807. he knows his end with mine *i.*
P. L. 5, 879. *i.* in this perfidious fraud
P. L. 7, 277. embryon immature *i.*
P. L. 7, 483. *i.* their snaky folds
P. L. 9, 75. with it rose Satan *i.* in rising
P. R. 1, 41. thick clouds and dark tenfold *i.*
S. A. 304. till by their own perplexities *i.*
**Invulnerable.**—P. L. 2, 812. hope to be *i.*
P. L. 6, 400. *i.,* impenetrably armed
**Inward.**—P. L. 3, 52. celestial light shine *i.*
P. L. 3, 584. and to each *i.* part with gentle
P. L. 6, 861. rolled *i.* and a spacious gap
P. L. 8, 221. hath also poured *i.* and outward
P. L. 8, 293. whose *i.* apparition gently moved
P. L. 8, 539. of *i.* less exact
P. L. 8, 542. and *i.* faculties which most excel
P. L. 8, 608. I to thee disclose what *i.* thence
P. L. 9, 97. but first from *i.* grief
P. L. 9, 600. to degree of reason in my *i.*
P. L. 9, 762. what profits then our *i.* freedom
P. L. 9, 895. first to himself he *i.* silence broke
P. L. 9, 1125. and shook sore their *i.* state
P. L. 10, 221. but *i.* nakedness much more
P. L. 10, 871. may show thy *i.* fraud
P. L. 12, 101. outward liberty, their *i.* lost
P. L. 12, 495. with *i.* consolations recompensed
P. R. 1, 463. an *i.* oracle to all truth requisite
P. R. 4, 145. or could of *i.* slaves make outward
S. A. 162. *i.* light alas puts forth no visual beam
S. A. 330. ay me! another *i.* grief awaked
S. A. 1006. without much *i.* passion felt

S. A. 1026. *i.* gifts were left for haste unfinished
S. A. 1689. with *i.* eyes illuminated
C. 466. lets in defilement to the *i.* parts
S. 7, 7. and *i.* ripeness doth much less appear
**Inwardly.**—P. L. 4, 88. *i.* I groan
L. 127. rot *i.* and foul contagion spread
**Inwards.**—P. L. 11, 439. sacrificing laid the *i.*
**Inwove.**—P. L. 3, 352. crowns *i.* with amarant
**Inwoven.**—P. L. 4, 693. covert was *i.* shade
**Inwreathed.**—P. L. 3, 361. *i.* with beams
**Inwrought.**—L. 105. *i.* with figures dim
**Ionian.**—P. L. 1, 508. the *I.* gods
**Irassa.**—P. R. 4, 564. in *I.* strove with Jove's
**Ire.**—P. L. 1, 148. may to rouze his vengeful *i.*
P. L. 2, 95. doubt we to incense his utmost *i.*
P. L. 2, 155. he so wise let loose at once his *i.*
P. L. 4, 115. thrice changed with pale, *i.*, envy
P. L. 6, 843. as a shelter from his *i.*
P. L. 7, 184. glory to him whose just avenging *i.*
P. L. 9, 18. or Neptune's *i.* or Juno's
P. L. 9, 692. will God incense his *i.* for such
P. L. 10, 936. me only just object of his *i.*
P. L. 10, 1023. wiselier armed his vengeful *i.*
P. L. 11, 885. willingly doth God remit his *i.*
P. R. 3, 219. between me and thy Father's *i.*
P. R. 3, 220. whose *i.* I dread more than the fire
S. A. 520. thy offerings to avert his farther *i.*
**Iris.**—P. L. 4, 698. *i.* all hues
P. L. 11, 244. *I.* had dipt the woof
C. 83. these my sky robes spun out of *I.* woof
C. 992. *I.* there with humid bow
**Irksome.**—P. L. 2, 527. entertain the *i.* hours
P. L. 5, 35. knew never till this *i.* night
P. L. 9, 242. not to *i.* toil but to delight
**Iron.**—P. L. 2, 327. with *i.* sceptre rule
P. L. 2, 646. three *i.*, three of adamantine rock
P. L. 2, 878. every bolt and bar of massy *i.*
P. L. 3, 594. with radiant light as glowing *i.*
P. L. 4, 859. champing his *i.* curb
P. L. 4, 898. let him surer bar his *i.* gates
P. L. 5, 887. an *i.* rod to bruise and break
P. L. 6, 576. brass, *i.*, stony mould
P. L. 6, 590. thunderbolts and hail of *i.* globes
P. L. 11, 565. two massy clods of *i.* and gold
P. R. 2, 168. the magnetic hardest *i.* draws
P. R. 3, 326. field all *i.* cast a gleaming brown
S. A. 129. ran on embattled armies clad in *i.*
S. A. 1124. raise such outcries on thy clattered *i.*
C. 491. come not too near, you fall on *i.* stakes
L. 111. the golden opes, the *i.* shuts amain
Il P. 107. drew *i.* tears down Pluto's cheek
S. 17, 8. move by her two main nerves, *i.* and gold
**Irons.**—S. A. 1243. lament these braveries in *i.*
**Irradiance.**—P. L. 8, 617. or do they mix *i.*
**Irradiate.**—P. L. 3, 53. all her powers *i.*
**Irrational.**—P. L. 9, 766. and discerns *i.*
P. L. 10, 708. among the *i.*
S. A. 673. creatures mute, *i.* and brute
**Irreconcileable.**—P. L. 1, 122. *i.* to our
**Irrecoverably.**—S. A. 81. *i.* dark
**Irregular.**—P. L. 5, 624. most *i.*
**Irreligious.**—S. A. 860. an *i.* dishonourer
**Irreparable.**—P. L. 2, 331. with loss *i.*
S. A. 644. with the *i.* loss of sight
**Irresistible.**—P. L. 6, 63. of union *i.*
S. A. 126. that heroic that renowned *i.* Samson
**Irresolute.**—P. L. 9, 87. *i.* of thoughts
P. R. 3, 243. *i.*, unhardy, unadventurous
**Irreverent.**—P. L. 12, 101. *i.* son of him
**Irrevocable.**—P. L. 12, 323. receive *i.*
**Irriguous.**—P. L. 4, 255. some *i.* valley
**Irruption.**—S. A. 1567. with too rude *i.*
**Isaac.**—P. L. 12, 268. Abraham son of *I.*
**Isis.**—P. L. 1, 478. Osiris, *I.*, Orus
H. 212. *I.* and Orus and the dog Anubis haste
**Island.**—P. L. 1, 205. deeming some *i.*
P. L. 11, 834. an *i.* salt and bare
P. R. 4, 92. to Capreæ, an *i.* small but strong
C. 50. on Circe's *i.* fell
**Isle.**—P. L. 1, 746. on Lemnos the Ægean *i.*
P. L. 2, 410. ere he arrive the happy *i.*

P. L. 4, 275. nor that Nyseian *i.*
P. L. 10, 527. or the *i.* Ophiusa
P. R. 4, 251. Meroe, Nilotic *i.*
C. 27. this *i.* the greatest and the best of all
**Isles.**—P. L. 1, 521. roamed the utmost *i.*
P. L. 2, 638. the *i.* of Ternate
P. L. 3, 567. worlds they seemed or happy *i.*
P. L. 3, 570. thrice happy *i.*
P. L. 4, 354. with prone career to the ocean *i.*
P. L. 8, 631. earth's green Cape and Verdant *I.*
P. L. 9, 1118. trees on *i.* and woody shores
S. A. 715. bound for the *i.* of Javan or Gadire
C. 21. imperial rule of all the sea-girt *i.*
C. 517. of dire chimeras and enchanted *i.*
**Ismenian.**—P. R. 4, 576. the *I.* steep
**Israel.**—P. L. 1, 413. when he enticed *I.*
P. L. 1, 432. for those the race of *I.* oft forsook
P. L. 1, 482. nor did *I.* scape the infection
P. L. 12, 267. till *I.* overcome
P. R. 1, 217. to rescue *I.* from the Roman yoke
P. R. 1, 254. they knew thee King of *I.* born
P. R. 2, 36. the kingdom shall to *I.* be restored
P. R. 2, 42. God of *I.* send thy Messiah forth
P. R. 3, 89. of many in *I.*
P. R. 2, 311. the race of *I.* here had famished
P. R. 2, 442. and reign in *I.* without end
P. R. 3, 279. whose success *I.* in long captivity
P. R. 3, 378. lost thus long from *I.*
P. R. 3, 406. to just extent over all *I.*'s sons
P. R. 3, 408. where was it then for *I.*
P. R. 3, 410. to the pride of numbering *I.*
P. R. 3, 413. such was thy zeal to *I.* then
P. R. 3, 441. so spake *I.*'s true king
P. R. 4, 480. ere thou of *I.*'s sceptre get fast
S. A. 39. *I.* from Philistian yoke deliver
S. A. 179. the glory late of *I.* now the grief
S. A. 225. I might begin *I.*'s deliverance
S. A. 233. watching to oppress *I.*'s oppressors
S. A. 240. yet *I.* still serves with all his sons
S. A. 242. on *I.*'s governors and heads of tribes
S. A. 285. defended *I.* from the Ammonite
S. A. 342. the dread of *I.*'s foes
S. A. 454. brought scandal to *I.*
S. A. 1150. to be the power of *I.*'s God avow
S. A. 1177. whom I with *I.*'s sons agree
S. A. 1428. the Holy One of *I.* be thy guide
S. A. 1527. for to *I.*'s God nothing is hard
S. A. 1663. for which thou wast foretold to *I.*
S. A. 1714. to *I.* honour hath left and freedom
**Israelites.**—P. R. 3, 411. ten thousand *I.*
S. A. 1560. sad but thou knowest to *I.* not
**Issue.**—P. L. 2, 508. of Javan's *i.* held Gods
P. L. 4, 280. where Abassin kings their *i.* guard
P. R. 3, 305. martial equipage they *i* forth
**Issued.**—P. L. 2, 786. my inbred enemy forth *i.*
P. L. 4, 454. a murmuring sound of waters *i.*
P. L. 8, 233. see that none thence *i.* forth a spy
P. R. 4, 276. from whose mouth *i.* forth
**Issues.**—P. L. 6, 9. light *i.* forth
**Issuing.**—P. L. 4, 779. *i.* at the accustomed
P. L. 6, 332. nectarous humour *i.* flowed
P. L. 9, 447. forth *i.* on a summer's morn
P. L. 10, 405. of matchless might *i.* from me
P. L. 10, 533. him followed *i.* forth to the open
P. L. 10, 537. in triumph *i.* forth their glorious
P. R. 4, 62. what conflux *i.* forth or entering
**Italian.**—S. 18, 11. o'er all the *I.* fields
**Iterate.**—P. L. 9, 1005. nor Eve to *i.*
**Ithuriel.**— P. L. 4, 788. *I.* and Zephon
**Its.**—P. L. 1, 254. the mind is *i.* own place
P. L. 4, 813. returns of force to *i.* own likeness
H. 106. her reign had here *i.* last fulfilling
**Itself.**—P. L. 1, 254. in *i.* can make a heaven
P. L. 1, 388. within his sanctuary *i.* their
P. L. 1, 492. more gross to love vice for *i.*
P. L. 1, 526. found themselves not lost in loss *i.*
P. L. 2, 68. his throne *i.* mixed with Tartarean
P. L. 2, 612. and of *i.* the water flies all taste
P. L. 6, 291. or turn this heaven *i.* into the hell
P. L. 6, 752. *i.* instinct with spirit
P. L. 6, 834. all but the throne *i.* of God

P. L. 8, 95. whose virtue on *i.* works no effect
P. L. 9, 43. sufficient of *i.* to raise that name
P. L. 9, 172. bitter ere long back on *i.* recoils
P. L. 9, 295. to avoid the attempt *i.* intended
P. L. 9, 702. your fear *i.* of death removes
P. L. 10, 141. whatever in *i.*
P. L. 10, 189. the realm *i.* of Satan
P. L. 11, 89. to have known good by *i.*
P. L. 12, 356. pollution brings upon .. temple *i.*
P. L. 12, 525. the spirit of grace *i.*
P. R. 3, 213. for *i.* condemned
S. A. 91. almost life *i.* if it be true that light
S. A. 769. if it be weighed by *i.*

C. 261. and in sweet madness robbed it of *i.*
C. 474. and linked *i.* by carnal sensualty
C. 593. but evil on *i.* shall back recoil
C. 595. gathered like scum and settled to *i.*
C. 742. unsavoury in the enjoyment of *i.*
C. 1023. heaven *i.* would stoop to her
**Ivory.**—P. L. 4, 778. from their *i.* port
P. R. 4, 60. in cedar, marble, *i.,* or gold
**Ivy.**—P. L. 9, 217. or direct the clasping *i.*
C. 55. with *i.* berries wreathed
C. 544. upon a bank with *i.* canopied
L. 2. ye myrtles brown with *i.* never sere
**Ivy-crowned.**—L'A. 16. to *i.-c.* Bacchus bore

# J.

**Jacob.**—P. L. 3, 510. *J.* saw angels
P. L. 11, 214. when the angels met *J.*
P. R. 3, 377. ten sons of *J.*
**Jaculation.**—P. L. 6, 665. to and fro with *j.*
**Jael.**—S. A. 989. in Mount Ephraim *J.*
**Jail.**—S. A. 949. this *j.* I count the house of
H. 233. troop to the infernal *j.*
**Jangling.**—P. L. 12, 55. to sow a *j.* noise
**Janus.**—P. L. 11, 129. had like a double *J.*
**Japhet.**—P. L. 4, 717. the unwiser son of *J.*
**Jar.**—P. L. 5, 793. *j.* not with liberty
**Jarred.**—S. M. 20. *j.* against nature's chime
**Jarring.**—P. L. 2, 880. recoil and *j.* sound
P. L. 6, 315. and their *j.* spheres confound
**Jasper.**—P. L. 3, 363. like a sea of *j.*
P. L. 3, 519. a bright sea flowed of *j.*
P. L. 11. 209. down from a sky of *j.*
**Jaunt.**—P. R. 4, 402. after his aery *j.*
**Javan.**—P. L. 1, 508. gods of *J.'s* issue
S. A. 716. the isles of *J.* or Gadire
**Javelin.**—P. L. 11, 658. with dart and *j.*
**Jaw.**—S. A. 143. the *j.* of a dead ass
S. A. 1095. wonders with an ass's *j.*
**Jaws.**—P. L. 10, 569. writhed their *j.*
P. L. 10, 637. seal up his ravenous *j.*
**Jealous.**—P. L. 4, 503. with *j.* leer malign
P. L. 10, 478, that *j.* of their secrets
L'A. 6. brooding Darkness spreads his *j.* wings
S. 15, 3. and all her *j.* monarchs
**Jealousies.**—P. L. 5, 703. words and *j.*
**Jealousy.**—P. L. 5, 449. nor *j.* was understood
S. A. 791. the *j.* of love powerful of sway
S. A. 1375. his *j.* shall never unrepented
**Jehovah.**—P. L. 1, 386. and durst abide *J.*
P. L. 1, 487. *J.* who in one night
P. L. 7, 602. great are thy works *J.* infinite
**Jephthah.**—P. R. 2, 439. Gideon and *J.*
S. A. 283. had dealt with *J.* who by argument
**Jericho.**—P. R. 2, 20. nigh to Bethabara in *J.*
**Jerusalem.**—P. R. 3, 234. once a year *J.*
P. R. 3, 283. led captive and *J.* laid waste
P. R. 4, 544. underneath them fair *J.*
**Jessamine.**—P. L. 4, 698. roses and *j.*
L. 143. the tufted crow-toe and pale *j.*
**Jest.**—L'A. 26. *j.* and youthful jollity
**Jester.**—S. A. 1338. to be their fool or *j.*
**Jesus.**—P. L. 10, 183. when *J.* son of Mary
P. L. 12, 310. whom the Gentiles *J.* call
P. R. 2, 4. *J.* Messiah, Son of God
P. R. 2, 317. to whom thus *J.*
P. R. 2, 322. as I like the giver answered *J.*
P. R. 2, 378. to whom thus *J.* temperately
P. R. 2, 432. to whom thus *J.* patiently
P. R. 4, 560. to whom thus *J.* also
**Jet.**—L. 144. and the pansy freaked with *j.*
**Jew.**—P. R. 3, 118. all nations, *J.* or Greek
P. R. 3, 359. none opposite, Samaritan or *J.*
**Jigs.**—C. 952. with *j.* and rural dance
**Job.**—P. R. 1, 147. since he failed in *J.*
P. R. 1, 369. into my hands Uzzean *J.*
P. R. 1, 425. to misdeem of righteous *J.*
P. R. 3, 64. thus he did to *J.*

P. R. 3, 67. hast thou seen my servant *J.* ?
P. R. 3, 95. with honour patient *J.*
**Jocund.**—P. L. 1, 787. with *j.* music
P. L. 7, 372. *j.* to run his longitude
P. L. 9, 793. hightened as with wine *j.* and boon
S. A. 1669. while their hearts were *j.* and sublime
C. 173. such as the *j.* flute or gamesome pipe
C. 985. revels the spruce and *j.* Spring
L'A. 94. and the *j.* rebecks sound
**Jog.**—U.C. II. 4. while he might still *j.* on and keep
**John.**—P. L. 3, 623. the same whom *J.* saw
P. R. 1, 184. Bethabara where *J.* baptized
P. R. 2, 84. as I hear by *J.* the Baptist
**Join.**—P. L. 2, 718. to *j.* their dark encounter
P. L. 3, 282. their nature also to thy nature *j.*
P. L. 3, 370. no voice but well could *j.*
P. L. 5, 164. on earth *j.* all ye creatures
P. L. 5, 197. *j.* voices all ye living souls
P. L. 6, 294. and *j.* him named Almighty
P. L. 9, 882. that equal lot may *j.* us
P. L. 10, 660. when to *j.* in synod unbenign
P. L. 11, 652. cruel tournament the squadrons *j.*
P. L. 11, 686. who of themselves abhor to *j.*
P. L. 12, 516. to *j.* secular power
S. A. 456. to waver or fall off and *j.* with idols
Il P. 45. *j.* with thee calm peace and quiet
H. 27. and *j.* thy voice unto the angel choir
**Joined.**—P. L. 1, 90. *j.* with me once
P. L. 1, 577. with the heroic race were *j.*
P. L. 3, 152. though *j.* with his own folly
P. L. 4, 687. in full, harmonic number *j.*
P. L. 4, 863. closing stood in squadron *j.*
P. L. 5, 335. not to mix tastes not well *j.*
P. L. 5, 513. what meant that caution *j.*
P. L. 5, 834. or all angelic nature *j.* in one
P. L. 6, 62. in mighty quadrate *j.* of union
P. L. 6, 108. the rough edge of battle ere it *j.*
P. L. 6, 206. nor less hideous *j.* the horrid shock
P. L. 6, 494. to strength and counsel *j.*
P. L. 7, 488. *j.* in her popular tribes
P. L. 8, 58. in love and mutual honour *j.*
P. L. 9, 198. and *j.* their vocal worship
P. L. 9, 243. and delight to reason *j.*
P. L. 9, 259. hopeless to circumvent us *j.*
P. L. 9, 909. converse and love so dearly *j.*
P. L. 10, 310. Europe with Asia *j.*
P. L. 10, 925. *j.* in connexion sweet
P. L. 10, 925. both joining as *j.* in injuries
P. R. 3, 258. then meeting *j.* their tribute
P. R. 3, 426. with idols in their worship *j.*
P. R. 4, 284. much more with empire *j.*
P. R. 4, 298. virtue *j.* with riches and long life
P. R. 4. 567. and fiercer grapple *j.*
S. A. 265. had Judah that day *j.*
S. A. 1037. once *j.* the contrary she proves
S. A. 1342. yet on me *j.* with extreme contempt
C. 581. O night and shades, now are ye *j.*
**Joining.**—P. L. 5, 106. *j.* or disjoining
P. L. 10, 302. *j.* to the wall
P. L. 10, 924. both as joined in injuries
**Joins.**—P. L. 12, 38. whom like ambition *j.*
P. L. 12, 388. not therefore *j.* the Son manhood

S. A. 1368. where the heart *j.* not outward acts
**Joint.**—P. L. 1, 426. manacled with *j.* or limb
P. L. 2, 668. in ·member, *j.* or limb
P. L. 8, 625. of membrane, *j.* or limb
P. L. 9, 244. doubt not but our *j.* hands
P. L. 10, 405. on your *j.* vigour now my hold
P. L. 10, 408. if your *j.* power prevail
S. A. 110. with *j.* pace I hear the tread
S. A. 953. my sudden rage to tear thee *j.* by *j.*
**Jointed.**—P. L. 7, 409. in *j.* armour
**Joint-racking.**—P. L. 11, 488. *j.-r.* rheums
**Joints.**—P. L. 8, 269. with supple *j.* as lively
P. L. 9, 891. through his veins and all his *j.*
S. A. 614. as on entrails, *j.*, and limbs
S. A. 1142. through all my sinews, *j.* and bones
C. 614. with his bare wand can unthread thy *j.*
**Jollity.**—P. L. 11, 714. turned to *j.* and game
C. 104. and revelry, tipsy dance, and *j.*
L'A. 26. jest and youthful *j.*, quips and cranks
**Jolly.**—S. 1, 107. while the *j.* Hours lead on
**Jonson.**—L'A. 132. if *J.'s* learned sock be on
**Jordan.**—P. L. 3, 535. the fount of *J.'s* flood
P. L. 12, 145. the double-founted stream *J.*
P. R. 1, 24. to the flood *J.* came
P. R. 1, 119. to the coast of *J.* he directs
P. R. 1, 329. at the ford of *J.* honoured so
P. R. 2, 9. remained at *J.* with the Baptist
P. R. 2, 25. then on the bank of *J.* by a creek
P. R. 2, 62. nor left at *J.* tidings of him none
P. R. 3, 438. as the Red Sea and *J.* once he cleft
P. R. 4, 510. till at the ford of *J.* whither all
**Joseph.**—P. R. 1, 23. the son of *J.*
P. R. 3, 377. ten sons of Jacob, two of *J.*
M. W. 65. the highly-favoured *J.* bore
**Joshua.**—P. L. 12, 310. *J.* whom the Gentiles
**Josiah.**—P. L. 1, 418. till good *J.* drove them
**Jot.**—S. 22. nor bate a *j.* of heart or hope
**Journey.**—P. L. 2, 985. my present *j.*
P. L. 3, 633. *j.'s* end and our beginning woe
P. L. 4, 282. a whole day's *j.* high
P. L. 5, 559. the sun hath finished half his *j.*
P. L. 7, 246. to *j.* through the aery gloom
P. L. 8, 36. such a sunless *j.* brought
P. L. 10, 479. fiercely opposed my *j.* strange
P. L. 12, 1. as one who in his *j.* baits at noon
P. L. 12, 204. guide them in their *j.*
P. L. 12, 258. save when they *j.*
P. R. 3, 276. within her wall several days' *j.*
S. A. 149. no *j.* of a sabbath-day
C. 303. it were a *j.* like the path to heaven
U. C. I. 12. thinking now his *j.'s* end was come
**Journeyed.**—P. L. 4, 173. Satan had *j.* on
**Journeys.**—P. L. 8, 38. such *j.* run
**Joust.**—P. L. 9, 37. gorgeous knights at *j.*
**Jousted.**—P. L. 1, 583. *j.* in Aspramont
**Jove.**—P. L. 1, 198. that warred on *J.*
P. L. 1, 512. he from mightier *J.*
P. L. 1, 514. so *J.* usurping reigned
P. L. 1, 741. thrown by angry *J.*
P. L. 4, 277. Ammon call, and Libyan *J.*
P. L. 4, 719. had stole *J.'s* authentic fire
P. L. 9, 396. virgin of Proserpina from *J.*
P. L. 9, 508. Ammonian *J.* or Capitoline
P. L. 10, 584. ere yet Dictæan *J.* was born
P. R. 2, 215. wrought that effect on *J.*
P. R. 3, 84. one is the son of *J.*
P. R. 4, 565. in Irassa strove with *J.'s* Alcides
C. 1. before the starry threshold of *J.'s* court
C. 20. took in by lot 'twixt high and nether *J.*
C. 41. by quick command from sovran *J.*
C. 78. therefore when any favoured of high *J.*
C. 803. as when the wrath of *J.* speaks thunder
C. 1011. so *J.* hath sworn
A. 44. by lot from *J.* I am the power
L. 16. from beneath the seat of *J.* doth spring
L. 82. and perfect witness of all-judging *J.*
Il P. 30. whilst yet there was no fear of *J.*
Il P. 48. aye round about *J.'s* altar sing
S. 1, 7. O if *J.'s* will
S. 23, 3. *J.'s* great son to her glad husband gave
D. F. I. 45. which careful *J.* in nature's true

**Jove-born.**—C. 676. gave to *J.-b.* Helena
**Joy.**—P. L. 1, 123. and in the excess of *j.*
P. L. 1, 250. farewell happy fields where *j.*
P. L. 1, 524. some glimpse of *j.*
P. L. 1, 788. with *j.* and fear his heart
P. L. 2, 371. his *j.* in our confusion and our *j.*
P. L. 2, 387. and *j.* sparkled in all their eyes
P. L. 2, 495. bleating herds attest their *j.*
P. L. 2, 586. forgets both *j.* and grief
P. L. 2, 765. and such *j.* thou took'st with me
P. L. 3, 67. of *j.* and love, uninterrupted *j.*
P. L. 3, 137. sense of new *j.* ineffable diffused
P. L. 3, 265. but in thy presence *j.* entire
P. L. 3, 338. with *j.* and love triumphing
P. L. 3, 347. as from blest voices uttering *j.*
P. L. 3, 417. happy hours in *j.* and hymning
P. L. 4, 92. such *j.* ambition finds
P. L. 4, 155. inspires vernal delight and *j.*
P. L. 4, 369. the more your taste is now of *j.*
P. L. 4, 509. where neither *j.* nor love
P. L. 5, 46. in whose sight all things *j.*
P. L. 5, 638. quaff immortality and *j.*
P. L. 5, 641. rejoicing in their *j.*
P. L. 6, 23. received with *j.* and acclamations
P. L. 6, 94. meet so oft in festivals of *j.*
P. L. 6, 200. ours *j.* filled and shout
P. L. 6, 617. perhaps for *j.* of offered peace
P. L. 6, 774. them unexpected *j.* surprised
P. L. 7, 161. *j.* and union without end
P. L. 7, 256. with *j.* and shout
P. L. 8, 170. *j.* thou in what he gives to thee
P. L. 8, 266. with fragrance and with *j.*
P. L. 9, 115. if I could *j.* in aught sweet
P. L. 9, 478. other *j.* to me is lost
P. L. 9, 633. hope elevates and *j.* brightens
P. L. 9, 770. but brings with *j.* the good
P. L. 9, 843. great *j.* he promised to his thoughts
P. L. 9, 882. equal lot may join us, equal *j.*
P. L. 9, 990. and for *j.* tenderly wept
P. L. 9, 1081. erst with *j.* and rapture
P. L. 10, 103. wont with *j.* to meet my coming
P. L. 10, 345. with *j.* and tidings fraught
P. L. 10, 350. great *j.* was at their meeting
P. L. 10, 351. his *j.* increased
P. L. 10, 457. and with like *j.* congratulant
P. L. 10, 577. and *j.* for man seduced
P. L. 10, 1052. soon recompensed with *j.*
P. L. 11, 43. all my redeemed may dwell in *j.*
P. L. 11, 80. they sat in fellowship of *j.*
P. L. 11, 139. *j.* but with fear yet linked
P. L. 11, 361. and to temper *j.* with fear
P. L. 11, 625. now swim in *j.*
P. L. 11, 628. of short *j.* bereft
P. L. 11, 869. and thus his *j.* broke forth
P. L. 12, 22. shall spend their days in *j.*
P. L. 12, 372. discerning Adam with such *j.*
P. L. 12, 468. and our sire replete with *j.*
P. L. 12, 504. to receive with *j.* the tidings
P. L. 12, 551. *j.* and eternal bliss
P. R. 1, 417. to thee no happiness, no *j.*
P. R. 2, 9. missing him their *j.* so lately
P. R. 2, 37. thus we rejoiced but soon our *j.*
P. R. 2, 57. soon we shall see our hope, our *j.*
P. R. 2, 119. without sign of boast or sign of *j.*
P. R. 3, 437. to their native land with *j.* they
P. R. 4, 439. amidst this *j.* and brightest
P. R. 4, 638. brought on his way with *j.*
S. A. 1505. thy *j.* thereon conceived agreeable
S. A. 1531. a *j.* presumptuous to be thought
S. A. 1564. and converts it nigh to *j.*
S.A.1574. what windy *j.* this day had I conceived
C. 102. meanwhile welcome *j.* and feast
C. 501. my loved master's heir and his next *j.*
C. 677. of such power to stir up *j.* as this
C. 1011. twins are to be born, youth and *j.*
L.177. in the blest kingdoms meek of *j.* and love
S. 14, 8. followed thee up to *j.* and bliss for ever
P. 5. but headlong *j.* is ever on the wing
S.M.1. blest pair of Sirens, pledges of heaven's *j.*
Cir. 4. so sweetly sung your *j.* the clouds along
T. 13. and *j.* shall overtake us as a flood

**Joyed.**—P. L. 9, 1166. might have lived and *j.*
**Joyless.**—P. L. 4, 766. loveless, *j.*
  P. R. 4, 578. *j.* triumphals or his hoped success
**Joyous.**—P. L. 8, 515. *j.* the birds
  L. 44. fanning their *j.* leaves to thy soft lays
  P. 3. and *j.* news of heavenly Infant's birth
**Joys.**—P. L. 2, 819. *j.* then sweet, now sad
  P. L. 4, 411. sole part of all these *j.*
  P. L. 9, 985. new hopes, new *j.*
  P. L. 10, 741. O fleeting *j.* of Paradise
  Il P. 1. hence vain deluding *j.*
  H. 66. whispering new *j.* to the mild ocean
**Jubilant.**—P. L. 7, 564. pomp ascended *j.*
**Jubilee.**—P. L. 3, 348. heaven rung with *j.*
  P. L. 6, 884. with *j.* advanced
  S. M. 9. with saintly shout and solemn *j.*
**Judæa.**—P. R. 3, 157. *J.* now and all
  S. A. 252. entered *J.* seeking me
**Judah.**—P. L. 1, 457. idolatries of alienated *J.*
  P. R. 2, 424. his son Herod placed on *J.'s* throne
  P. R. 2, 440. whose offspring on the throne of *J.*
  P. R. 3, 282. *J.* and all thy father David's house
  S. A. 256. meanwhile the men of *J.* to prevent
  S. A. 265. had *J.* that day joined or one whole
  S. A. 976. in Dan, in *J.*, and the bordering tribes
  H. 221. he feels from *J.'s* land
**Judge.**—P. L. 2, 233. and Chaos *j.* the strife
  P. L. 3, 123. in all both what they *j.*
  P. L. 3, 154. who art *J.* of all things made
  P. L. 3, 330. thy saints assembled thou shalt *j.*
  P. L. 4, 904. one in heaven to *j.* of wise
  P. L. 4, 912. so *j.* thou still presumptuous
  P. L. 8, 448. to see how thou couldst *j.* of fit
  P. L. 10, 55. but whom send I to *j.* them
  P. L. 10, 62. destined man himself to *j.*
  P. L. 10, 71. I go to *j.* on earth these thy
  P. L. 10, 96. the mild *J.* and Intercessor
  P. L. 10, 118. to whom the gracious *J.* without
  P. L. 10, 126. this day I stand before my *J.*
  P. L. 10, 160. yet not before her *J.* bold
  P. L. 10, 209. both *J.* and Saviour
  P. L. 10, 338. the Son of God to *j.* them
  P. L. 10, 992. if thou *j.* it hard and difficult
  P. L. 11, 167. but infinite in pardon was my *J.*
  P. L. 11, 603. *j.* not what is best by pleasure
  P. L. 11, 705. that God would come to *j.* them
  P. L. 12, 460. to *j.* both quick and dead
  P. L. 12, 46. to *J.* the unfaithful dead
  L'A. 122. rain influence and *j.* the prize
  S. 10, 13. all both *j.* you to relate them true
  S. 14, 13. before the *J.* who thenceforth bid thee
  S. 20, 13. he who of those delights can *j.*
  H. 164. the dreadful *J.* in middle air.
  U. C. II. 21. and to *j.* right
**Judged.**—P. L. 2, 390. well have ye *j.*
  P. L. 2, 448. if aught proposed and *j.* of public
  P. L. 3, 295. be *j.* and die, and dying rise
  P. L. 5, 850. none seconded as out of season *j.*
  P. L. 6, 37. though worlds *j.* thee perverse
  P. L. 6, 426. and *j.* sufficient to subdue us
  P. L. 10, 73. whoever *j.* the worst on me
  P. L. 10, 81. to behold the judgment but the *j.*
  P. L. 10, 173. though in mysterious terms *j.*
  P. L. 10, 209. so *j.* he man, both Judge and
  P. L. 10, 229. thus was sinned and *j.* on earth
  P. L. 10, 494. me also he hath *j.* or rather me
  P. L. 10, 1047. he both heard and *j.* without
  P. L. 10, 1059. us unworthy pitying while he *j.*
  P. L. 10, 1087. place repairing where he *j.* us
  P. L. 10, 1099. place repairing where he *j.* them
  P. L. 12, 412. *j.* and to death condemned
  P. R. 4, 215. as by that early action may be *j.*
  S. A. 882. yet now am *j.* an enemy
  S. A. 994. which to my country I was *j.* to have
**Judges.**—P. L. 4, 910. so wise he *j.* it to fly
  P. L. 12, 320. by *j.* first, then under kings
**Judgest.**—P. L. 3, 155. and *j.* only right
**Judgment.**—P. L. 8, 636. passion sway thy *j.*
  P. L. 9, 10. anger and just rebuke, and *j.* given
  P. L. 10, 57. to thee I have transferred all *j.*
  P. L. 10, 81. where none are to behold the *j.*

P. L. 10, 164. to *j.* he proceeded on the accused
P. L. 10, 197. thus *j.* he pronounced
P. L. 10, 932. to the place of *j.* will return
P. L. 11, 668. truth and peace and *j.* from
P. L. 12, 14. while the dread of *j.* past remains
P. L. 12, 92. God in *j.* just subjects him
P. R. 3, 37. and to ripe years *j.*
P. R. 4, 324. a spirit and *j.* equal or superior
S. A. 1027. *j.* scant, capacity not raised
C. 758. would think to charm my *j.* as mine eyes
**Judgments.**—P. L. 11, 69. not hide my *j.*
  P. L. 11, 725. in prison under *j.* imminent
  P. L. 12, 175. be compelled by signs and *j.*
**Judicious.**—P. L. 8, 591. and is *j.*
  P. L. 9, 1020. and palate call *j.*
**Juggler.**—C. 757. this *j.* would think
**Jugglers.**—S. A. 1325. *j.* and dancers
**Juice.**—S. A. 550. I drank from the clear milky *j.*
**Juiciest.**—P. L. 5, 327. and *j.* gourd
**Julep.**—C. 672. first behold this cordial *j.* here
**Julius.**—P. R. 3, 89. great *J.*
**Juniper.**—P. R. 2, 272. he slept under a *j.*
**Junkets.**— L'A. 102. how faery Mab the *j.* eat
**Juno.**—P. L. 4, 500. as Jupiter on *J.* smiles
  P. L. 9, 18. or Neptune's ire or *J.* that so long
  C. 701. were it a draught for *J.* when she banquets
  A. 23. *J.* dares not give her odds
**Jupiter.**—P. L. 4, 499. as *J.* on Juno smiles
  P. R. 2, 190. Apollo, Neptune, *J.*, or Pan
**Jurisdiction.**—P. L. 2, 319. heaven's high *j.*
**Just.**—P. L. 2, 18. though *j.* right and the fixed
  P. L. 2, 38. return to claim our *j.* inheritance
  P. L. 2, 825. that in our *j.* pretences armed
  P. L. 3, 98. I made him *j.* and right
  P. L. 3, 215. and *j.* the unjust to save
  P. L. 3, 294. so man as is most *j.* shall satisfy
  P. L. 3, 335. wherein the *j.* shall dwell
  P. L. 3, 527. *j.* o'er the blissful seat of paradise
  P. L. 4, 389. yet public reason *j.*
  P. L. 4, 443. what thou hast said is *j.* and right
  P. L. 4, 460. as I bent down to look, *j.* opposite
  P. L. 4, 755. founded in reason, loyal, *j.*
  P. L. 4, 863. those half-rounding guards *j.* met
  P. L. 5, 552. command single is yet so *j.*
  P. L. 5, 814. condemn the *j.* decree of God
  P. L. 6, 121. but *j.* that he who in debate
  P. L. 6, 265. though heaviest by *j.* measure
  P. L. 6, 381. from truth divided and from *j.*
  P. L. 6, 726. as is most *j.*
  P. L. 6, 740. that from thy *j.* obedience could
  P. L. 7, 184. glory to him whose *j.* avenging ire
  P. L. 7, 186. and the habitations of the *j.*
  P. L. 7, 231. this be thy *j.* circumference
  P. L. 7, 487. pattern of *j.* equality perhaps
  P. L. 7, 570. to visit oft the dwellings of *j.* men
  P. L. 7, 631. a race of worshippers holy and *j.*
  P. L. 8, 572. self esteem grounded on *j.*
  P. L. 9, 10. anger and *j.* rebuke
  P. L. 9, 278. *j.* then returned at shut of evening
  P. L. 9, 698. of good how *j.*
  P. L. 9, 700. cannot hurt ye and be *j.*
  P. L. 9, 701. not *j.* not God
  P. L. 9, 1056. *j.* confidence and native
  P. L. 10, 7. who in all things wise and *j.*
  P. L. 10, 535. in station stood or *j.* array
  P. L. 10, 643. *j.* are thy ways
  P. L. 10, 857. justice divine not hasten to be *j.*
  P. L. 10, 888. as supernumerary to my *j.*
  P. L. 10, 936. me, me only, *j.* object of his ire
  P. L. 10, 969. so erroneous thence by *j.* event
  P. L. 10, 1045. against God and his *j.* yoke
  P. L. 11, 65. waked in the renovation of the *j.*
  P. L. 11, 455. the unjust the *j.* hath slain
  P. L. 11, 526. yield it *j.* said Adam and submit
  P. L. 11, 577. by their guise *j.* men they seemed
  P. L. 11, 681. but who was that *j.* man
  P. L. 11, 703. for daring single to be *j.*
  P. L. 11, 818. the one *j.* man alive
  P. L. 11, 876. man found so perfect and so *j.*
  P. L. 11, 890. such grace shall one *j.* man find
  P. L. 11, 901. wherein the *j.* shall dwell

P. L. 12, 16. with some regard to what is *j.*
P. L. 12, 92. God in judgment *j.* subjects him
P. L. 12, 273. which concern *j.* Abraham
P. L. 12, 294. *j.* for unjust
P. L. 12, 540. of respiration to the *j.*
P. R. 1, 66. his birth to our *j.* fear gave no
P. R. 1, 255. *j.* Simeon and prophetic Anna
P. R. 2, 325. by *j.* right
P. R. 3, 11. thy heart contains of good, wise, *j.*
P. R. 3, 62. with approbation marks the *j.* man
P. R. 3, 196. *j.* trial ere I merit my exaltation
P. R. 3, 298. and *j.* in time thou comest
P. R. 3, 406. his full sceptre sway to *j.* extent
P. R. 4, 133. who once *j.* frugal and mild
S. A. 237. in seeking *j.* occasion to provoke
S. A. 293. *j.* are the ways of God
S. A. 300. there be who doubt his ways not *j.*
S. A. 316. nor in respect of the enemy *j.* cause
S. A. 703. *j.* and unjust alike seem miserable
S. A. 770. with *j.* allowance counterpoised
S. A. 854. how *j.* it was, how honourable
S. A. 1269. the spirits of *j.* men long oppressed
C. 13. to lay their *j.* hands on that golden key
C. 601. may never this *j.* sword be lifted up
C. 768. if every *j.* man that now pines with want
S. 13, 3. to span words with *j.* note and accent
S. 14, 2. had featured thy *j.* soul to dwell with God
S.M.14. with those *j.* spirits that wear victorious
Cir. 15. O more exceeding love or law more *j.*
Cir. 16. *j.* law indeed but more exceeding love
D. F. I. 50. or wert thou that *j.* maid who once
F. of C. 18. and succour our *j.* fears
**Justice.**—P. L. 1, 70. such place eternal *j.*
P. L. 2, 733. his wrath which he calls *j.*
P. L. 3, 132. in mercy and *j.* both
P. L. 3, 210. die he or *j.* must
P. L. 3, 407. and end the strife of mercy and *j.*

P. L. 5, 247. and fulfilled all *j.*
P. L. 10, 54. *j.* shall not return
P. L. 10, 59. mercy colleague with *j.*
P. L. 10, 78. I shall temper so *j.* with mercy
P. L. 10, 755. inexplicable thy *j.* seems
P. L. 10, 857. *j.* divine not hasten to be just
P. L. 10, 858. *j.* divine mends not her slowest
P. L. 11, 667. of *j.*, of religion, truth, and peace
P. L. 11, 807. *j.* and temperance, truth
P. L. 12, 99. but *j.* and some fatal curse
P. L. 12, 231. such as appertain to civil *j.*
P. L. 12, 401. so only can high *j.* rest appaid
H. 141. yea truth and *j.* then
Cir. 24. of vengeful *j.* bore for our excess
**Justifiable.**—S. A. 294. and *j.* to men
**Justification.**—P. L. 12, 296. find *j.*
**Justify.**—P. L. 1, 26. and *j.* the ways of God
P. L. 10, 142. her doing seemed to *j.* the deed
**Justling.**—P. L. 2, 1018. betwixt the *j.* rocks
P. L. 10, 1074. as late the clouds *j.* or pushed
**Justly.**—P. L. 3, 112. nor can *j.* accuse
P. L. 3, 677. who *j.* hath driven out his rebel
P. L. 4, 72. chose freely what it now so *j.* rues
P. L. 5, 736. *j.* hast in derision
P. L. 9, 40. not that which *j.* gives heroic name
P. L. 9, 100. if not preferred more *j.*
P. L. 10, 168. *j.* then accursed as vitiated
P. L. 10, 768. thy punishment then *j.* is at his
P. L. 11, 288. patiently resign what *j.* thou
P. L. 12, 79. *j.* thou abhorrest
P. R. 1, 442. for God hath *j.* given the nations
P. R. 1, 443. *j.* since they fell idolatrous
P. R. 4, 84. thou *j.* mayst prefer before
S. A. 375. hath befallen me but *j.* I myself have
S. A. 1171. from God inflicted on me *j.*
A. 10. we may *j.* now accuse of detraction

# K.

**Keen.**—P. L. 5, 436. with *k.* despatch
P. L. 6, 322. neither *k.* nor solid
P. L. 9, 588. that alluring fruit urged me so *k.*
P. L. 10, 1066. the winds blow moist and *k.*
P. L. 11, 842. driven by a *k.* north wind
P. R. 1, 317. a winter's day when winds blow *k.*
C. 422. like a quivered nymph with arrows *k.*
**Keep.**—P. L. 2, 775. to *k.* these gates
P. L. 2, 852. the key, ... I *k.*
P. L. 2, 999. my frontiers here *k.* residence
P. L. 3, 578. that from his lordly eye *k.* distance
P. L. 4, 372. ill-fenced for heaven to *k.* out
P. L. 4, 420. no other service than to *k.* this
P. L. 4, 525. invented with design to *k.* them
P. L. 4, 685. while they *k.* watch or nightly
P. L. 8, 320. count it thine to till and *k.*
P. L. 8, 634. whom to love is to obey and *k.*
P. L. 9, 245. hands will *k.* from wilderness
P. L. 9, 704. why but to *k.* ye low and ignorant
P. L. 9, 820. but *k.* the odds of knowledge
P. L. 10, 856. shall Truth fail to *k.* her word
P. L. 11, 550. which I must *k.* till my appointed
P. R. 2, 434. to gain dominion or to *k.* it gained
S. A. 49. under the seal of silence could not *k.*
S. A. 1521. *k.* together here lest running thither
C. 8. strive to *k.* up a frail and feverish being
C. 121. their merry wakes and pastimes *k.*
C. 220. to *k.* my life and honour unassailed
C. 486. heaven *k.* my sister
C. 584. yes, and *k.* it still
C. 639. and bade me *k.* it as of sovran use
C. 748. it is for homely features to *k.* home
A. 70. and *k.* unsteady Nature to her law
Il P. 37. come, but *k.* thy wonted state
Il P. 145. with such consort as they *k.*
H. 21. the spangled host *k.* watch in squadrons
H. 92. that did their silly thoughts so busy *k.*

H. 124. weltering waves their oozy channel *k.*
S. M. 26. and *k.* in tune with heaven
U. C. II. 4. while he might jog on and *k.* his trot
V. Ex. 56. to *k.* in compass of thy predicament
V. Ex. 78. ungratefully shall strive to *k.* him
**Keeping.**—P. L. 9, 363. not *k.* strictest watch
P. L. 12, 365. to simple shepherds *k.* watch
S. A. 1260. work of many hands which earns *k.*
**Keeps.**—P. L. 7, 379. and still that distance *k.*
P. R. 4, 362. what makes a nation happy and *k.*
C. 167. whom thrift *k.* up about his country gear
**Ken.**—P. L. 1, 59. at once as far as angels *k.*
P. L. 3, 622. saw within *k.* a glorious angel
P. L. 11, 379. hemisphere of earth in clearest *k.*
P. L. 11, 396. nor could his eye not *k.*
P. R. 2, 286. from whose high top to *k.*
**Kennel.**—P. L. 2, 658. into her womb and *k.*
**Kens.**—P. L. 5, 265. *k.* a cloudy spot
**Kept.**—P. L. 2, 725. and *k.* the fatal key
P. L. 5, 128. reserved from night and *k.* for thee
P. L. 5, 900. his loyalty he *k.*, his love, his zeal
P. L. 7, 145. the greater part have *k.*
P. L. 7, 594. but not in silence holy *k.*
P. L. 7, 634. with hallelujahs thus was sabbath *k.*
P. L. 9, 62. forewarned the cherubim that *k.*
P. L. 9, 746. though *k.* from man and worthy
P. L. 10, 427. there *k.* their watch the legions
P. L. 10, 619. and had still *k.* in that state
P. R. 1, 360. *k.* not my station but was driven
S. A. 429. which to have *k.* tacit was in thy power
S. A. 497. but I God's counsel have not *k.*
C. 913. I have *k.* of precious cure
S. 18, 3. them who *k.* thy truth so pure of old
**Kerchiefed.**—Il P. 125. *k.* in a comely cloud
**Kernels.**—P. L. 5, 346. from sweet *k.*
**Key.**—P. L. 2, 725. and kept the fatal *k.*
P. L. 2, 774. at which time this powerful *k.*

P. L. 2, 850. the *k.* of this infernal pit
P. L. 2, 871. from her side the fatal *k.*
S. A. 799. get into my power thy *k.* of strength
C. 13. to lay their just hands on that golden *k.*
**Keyhole.**—P. L. 2, 876. then in the *k.*
**Keys.**—P. L. 3, 485. to wait them with his *k.*
L. 110. two massy *k.* he bore of metals twain
**Kicked.**—P. L. 4, 1004. upflew and *k.* the beam
**Kid.**—P. L. 4, 344. in his paw dandled the *k.*
P. L. 9, 583. unsucked of lamb or *k.*
P. L. 12, 20. oft sacrificing bullock, lamb, or *k.*
S. A. 128. tore the lion as the lion tears the *k.*
C. 498. or young *k.* lost his dam
**Kids.**—P. L. 3, 434. of lambs or yeanling *k.*
**Kill.**—P. L. 10, 402. and lastly *k.*
**Killed.**—S. 10, 8. *k.* with report that old man
D. F. I. 7. thought to kiss but *k.* alas
**Killing.**—L. 45. as *k.* as the canker to the rose
**Kills.**—P. L. 12, 168. *k.* their infant males
**Kind.**—P. L. 1, 704. severing each *k.*
P. L. 3, 462. the angelical and human *k.*
P. L. 4, 217. all trees of noblest *k.* for sight
P. L. 4, 286. all *k.* of living creatures
P. L. 5, 479. in bounds proportioned to each *k.*
P. L. 5, 490. of *k.* the same
P. L. 6, 73. as when the total *k.* of birds
P. L. 7, 311. fruit-tree yielding fruit after her *k.*
P. L. 7, 394. and every bird of wing after his *k.*
P. L. 7, 451. bring forth soul living in her *k.*
P. L. 7, 453. beast of the earth each in their *k.*
P. L. 7, 482. of serpent *k.* wondrous in length
P. L. 8, 393. each with their *k.* lion with lioness
P. L. 9, 565. grown above the rest of brutal *k.*
P. L. 9, 721. by the sun producing every *k.*
P. L. 9, 1101. the fig tree not that *k.* for fruit
P. L. 10, 248. things of like *k.*
P. L. 11, 182. and every *k.* that lives
P. R. 3, 221. a shelter and a *k.* of shading cool
S. A. 786. so near related or the same of *k.*
S. A. 1063. but this another *k.* of tempest brings
S. A. 1236. this insolence other *k.* of answer fits
C. 187. as the *k.* hospitable woods provide
U. C. I. 14. in the *k.* office of a chamberlin
**Kindle.**—C. 794. of this pure cause would *k.*
**Kindled.**—P. L. 2, 170. that *k.* those grim fires
P. L. 9, 637. *k.* through agitation to a flame
**Kindles.**—P. L. 10, 1076. *k.* the gummy bark
**Kindliest.**—P. L. 5, 336. with *k.* change
**Kindly.**—P. L. 4, 228. with *k.* thirst up drawn
P. L. 4, 668. with *k.* heat
P. L. 7, 419. bursting with *k.* rupture
H. 90. was *k.* come to live with them below
**Kindred.**—P. L. 12, 122. his *k.* and false gods
S. A. 1730. will send for all my *k.* all my friends
**Kinds.**—P. L. 4, 397. of those four-footed *k.*
P. L. 4, 671. on all *k.* that grow on earth
P. L. 5, 341. fruit of all *k.* in coat rough
P. L. 7, 393. the waters generated by their *k.*
P. L. 8, 343. bird and beast behold after their *k.*
P. L. 8, 597. in procreation common to all *k.*
P. L. 10, 612. or unimmortal make all *k.*
P. L. 11, 482. all feverous *k.*
**Kine.**—P. L. 9, 450. or tedded grass or *k.*
P. L. 11, 647. fair *k.* from a fat meadow-ground
**King.**—P. L. 1, 131. heaven's perpetual *K.*
P. L. 1, 392. first Moloch horrid *k.*
P. L. 1, 444. built by that uxorious *k.*
P. L. 1, 471. a leper one he lost and gained a *k.*
P. L. 1, 484. and the rebel *k.* doubled that sin
P. L. 1, 735. supreme *k.* exalted to such power
P. L. 2, 43. Moloch sceptred *k.* stood up
P. L. 2, 229. either to disenthrone the *K.*
P. L. 2, 316. know not that the *k.* of heaven
P. L. 2, 325. still first and last will reign sole *k.*
P. L. 2, 698. where I reign *k.*
P. L. 2, 699. to enrage thee more thy *k.*
P. L. 2, 751. conspiracy against heaven's *K.*
P. L. 2, 851. of heaven's all-powerful *K.*
P. L. 2, 978. the ethereal *k.* possesses lately
P. L. 2, 992. made head against heaven's *K.*
P. L. 3, 317. anointed universal *K.*

P. L. 3, 374. infinite eternal *K.*
P. L. 4, 41. against heaven's matchless *K.*
P. L. 4, 111. divided empire with heaven's *K.*
P. L. 4, 821. so sudden to behold the grisly *k.*
P. L. 4, 973. though heaven's *K.* ride on thy
P. L. 5, 220. beheld with pity heaven's high *K.*
P. L. 5, 640. before the all-bounteous *K.*
P. L. 5, 664. proclaimed Messiah *K.* anointed
P. L. 5, 690. fit entertainment to receive our *k.*
P. L. 5, 769. the great reception of their *k.*
P. L. 5, 777. under the name of *K.* anointed
P. L. 5, 818. confess him rightful *K.*
P. L. 5, 870. tidings carry to the anointed *K.*
P. L. 6, 42. and for their *K.* Messiah
P. L. 6, 227. the eternal *K.* Omnipotent
P. L. 6, 357. deep array of Moloch furious *k.*
P. L. 6, 708. all things to be heir and to be *k.*
P. L. 6, 718. God and Messiah his anointed *K.*
P. L. 6, 886. and him sung victorious *k.*
P. L. 7, 122. not revealed which the invisible *k.*
P. L. 7, 208. to let forth the *K.* of glory
P. L. 7, 608. who can impair thee mighty *k.*
P. L. 8, 239. for state as sovran *k.*
P. L. 9, 442. where the sapient *k.* held dalliance
P. L. 10, 387. antagonist of heaven's Almighty *K.*
P. L. 11, 218. against the Syrian *k.*
P. L. 12, 165. grown suspected to a sequent *k.*
P. L. 12, 205. while the obdurate *k.* pursues
P. L. 12, 326. of David (so I name this *k.*)
P. L. 12, 359. the true anointed *K.* Messiah
P. R. 1, 75. to do him honour as their *k.*
P. R. 1, 99. their *k.*, their leader, and supreme
P. R. 1, 236. thy father is the eternal *K.*
P. R. 1, 254. by which they knew thee *k.* of
P. R. 1, 372. to draw the proud *k.* Ahab into
P. R. 1, 421. thou art serviceable to heaven's *k.*
P. R. 2, 76. into Egypt till the murderous *k.*
P. R. 2, 82. little suspicious to any *k.*
P. R. 2, 463. for therein stands the office of a *k.*
P. R. 2, 467. desires and fears is more a *k.*
P. R. 3, 36. Pompey quelled the Pontic *k.*
P. R. 3, 167. o'er a mighty *k.* so oft prevailed
P. R. 3, 226. shouldst be their *k.*
P. R. 3, 299. for now the Parthian *k.*
P. R. 3, 441. so quake Israel's true *K.*
P. R. 4, 185. by whom but by the *K.* of kings
P. R. 4, 283. these rules will render thee a *k.*
P. R. 4, 364. with our law best form a *k.*
Il P. 115. on which the Tartar *k.* did ride
H. 2. the son of heaven's eternal *K.*
H. 209. they call the grisly *k.*
V. Ex. 75. o'er all his brethren he shall reign as *k.*
S. 11, 14. taught'st Cambridge and *K.* Edward
**Kingdom.**—P. L. 2, 325. and of his *k.* lose
P. L. 2, 361. the utmost border of his *k.* left
P. L. 6, 183. reign thou in hell, thy *k.*
P. L. 6, 815. *k.* and power and glory
P. L. 7, 161. one *k.* joy and union without end
P. L. 10, 406. hold of this new *k.* all depends
P. R. 1, 261. heaven's *k.* nigh at hand to all
P. R. 1, 241. of thy *k.* there should be no end
P. R. 1, 265. ere I the promised *k.* can attain
P. R. 2, 36. the *k.* shall to Israel be restored
P. R. 2, 481. besides to give a *k.* hath been
P. R. 3, 152. but to a *k.* thou art born
P. R. 3, 171. if *k.* move thee nor
P. R. 3, 199. when I begin my everlasting *k.*
P. R. 3, 242. he who seeking asses found a *k.*
P. R. 3, 351. thy *k.* though foretold by prophet
P. R. 4, 151. of my *k.* there shall be no end
P. R. 4, 282. time mature thee to a *k.'s* weight
P. R. 4, 369. *k.* nor empire pleases thee
P. R. 4, 389. a *k.* they portend thee but what *k.*
H. 171. and wroth to see his *k.* fail
**Kingdoms.**—P. L. 11, 384. all earth's *k.*
P. L. 11, 403. the *k.* of Almansor, Fez and Sus
P. L. 12, 262. kings destroyed and *k.* won
P. R. 4, 89. *k.* of the world and all their glory
P. R. 4, 163. the *k.* of the world to thee I give
P. R. 4, 182. the *k.* of the world to thee were
P. R. 4, 210. pass as they are transitory the *k.*

P. R. 4, 363. what ruins *k.* and lays cities flat
P. R. 4, 536. riches, *k.*, glory, have been before
L. 177. in the blest *k.* meek of joy and love
**Kingly.**—P. L. 2, 673. likeness of a *k.* crown
P. L. 3, 505. the work as of a *k.* palace gate
P. L. 11, 249. he *k.* from his state inclined not
P. R. 2, 476. yet more *k.* this attracts the soul
S. 19, 12. his state is *k.*
V. Ex. 39. immortal nectar to her *k.* sire
**Kings.**—P. L. 1, 694. works of Memphian *k.*
P. L. 1, 721. or seat their *k.*
P. L. 2, 4. showers on her *k.* barbaric pearl
P. L. 4, 212. Seleucia, bui   by Grecian *k.*
P. L. 4, 280. nor where Abassin *k.* their issue
P. L. 4, 383. and send forth all her *k.*
P. L. 11, 243. worn by *k.* and heroes old
P. L. 11, 390. to Paquin of Sinæan *k.*
P. L. 11, 398. the less maritime *k.* Mombaza
P. L. 12, 262. *k.* destroyed and kingdoms won
P. L. 12, 320. by judges first then under *k.*
P. L. 12, 329. and to *k.* foretold of *k.* the last
P. L. 12, 348. from Babylon by leave of *k.*
P. R. 1, 117. regents and potentates, and *k.*
P. R. 2, 44. the *k.* of the earth how they oppress
P. R. 2, 449. though offered from the hand of *k.*
P. R. 3, 12. should *k.* and nations from thy
P. R. 3, 289. the drink of none but *k.*
P. R. 3, 297. from the luxurious *k.* of Antioch
P. R. 3, 366. and captive lead away her *k.*
P. R. 4, 73. from the Asian *k.* and Parthian
P. R. 4, 87. shared among petty *k.* too far
S. A. 281. of Madian and her vanquished *k.*
S. 15, 4. rumours loud that daunt remotest *k.*
H. 59. and *k.* sat still with awful eye
W. S. 16. *k.* for such a tomb would wish to die
V. Ex. 47. and last of *k.* and queens and heroes old
**Kiriathaim.**—S. A. 1081. Emims old t'at *K.*
**Kiss.**—A. 83. approach and *k.* her sacred vesture's
D. F. I. 6. thought to *k.* but killed
T. 12. with an individual *k.*
**Kissed.**—P. L. 5, 134. he ere they fell *k.*
H. 65. smoothly the waters *k.*
**Kisses.**—P. L. 4, 502. matron lip with *k.* pure
**Knee.**—P. L. 1, 112. with suppliant *k.*
P. L. 5, 788. to bend the supple *k.*
P. L. 5, 817. soul in heaven shall bend the *k.*
P. L. 6, 194. on bended *k.* his nassy spear
**Kneeled.**—P. L. 11, 150. *k.* and before him
**Knees.**—P. L. 3, 321. all *k.* to thee shall bow
P. L. 5, 608. shall bow all *k.* in heaven
P. L. 10, 918. suppliant I beg and clasp thy *k.*
**Knee-tribute.**—P. L. 5, 782. *k.-t.* yet unpaid
**Knew.**—P. L. 1, 93. till then who *k.*
P. L. 4, 828. know ye not me ? ye *k.* me once
P. L. 4, 1013. the fiend looked up and *k.*
P. L. 5, 35. and trouble which my mind *k.*
P. L. 5, 287. straight *k.* him all the bands
P. L. 5, 548. *k.* I not to be both will and deed
P. L. 6, 327. then Satan first *k.* pain
P. L. 8, 4. he, she *k.* would intermix grateful
P. L. 8, 251. for who himself beginning *k.*
P. L. 8, 271. or from what cause *k.* not
P. L. 8, 283. and strayed I *k.* not whither
P. L. 8, 445. *k.* it not good for man to be alone
P. L. 8, 568. she what was honour *k.*
P. L. 9, 561. subtlest beast of all the field I *k.*
P. L. 9, 792. and *k.* not eating death
P. L. 10, 12. for still they *k.* and ought to have
P. L. 10, 19. of his state by this they *k.*
P. L. 10, 170. since he no farther *k.*
P. L. 11, 504. who if we *k.* what we receive
P. R. 1, 254. they *k.* thee king of Israel
P. R. 1, 271. whose birth I oft had heard not *k.*
P. R. 1, 275. straight *k.* me and with loudest
P. R. 1, 286. by which I *k.* the time now full
P. R. 4, 294. this only that he nothing *k.*
P. R. 4, 394. for still he *k.* his power not yet
P. R. 4, 404. with the first I *k.*
S. A. 221. they *k.* not that what I motioned was
S. A. 222. I *k.* from intimate impulse
S. A. 381. this well I *k.* nor was at all surprised

S. A. 803. I *k.* that liberty would draw thee forth
S. A. 1549. my countrymen whom here I *k.*
C. 572. for so by certain signs I *k.*
C. 645. I *k.* the foul enchanter though disguised
L. 10. *k.* himself to sing and build the lofty
L. 95. they *k.* not of his story
S. 14, 9. love led them on and faith who *k.* them
H. 60. as if they surely *k.* their sovran Lord
H. 107. she *k.* such harmony alone
**Knewest.**—P. L. 12, 577. the stars thou *k.*
S. A. 878. loved thee as too well thou *k.*
**Knight.**—S. 8, 1. Colonel or *K.* in arms
**Knights.**—P. L. 1, 581. British and Armoric *k.*
P. L. 2, 536. prick forth the aery *k.* and couch
P. L. 9, 30. fabled *k.* in battles feigned
P. L. 9, 36. gorgeous *k.* at joust and tournament
P. R. 2, 360. by *k.* of Logres or of Lyones
P. R. 3, 342. sought by many prowest *k.*
L'A. 119. where throngs of *k.* and barons bold
**Knit.**—P. L. 4, 267. *k.* with the Graces
C. 143. come *k.* hands and beat the ground
**Knitting.**—C. 862. in twisted braids of lilies *k.*
**Knock.**—S. A. 1722. to wail or *k.* the breast
V. Ex. 24. loudly *k.* to have their passage out
**Knot.**—C. 581. joined with hell in triple *k.*
V. Ex. 90. can loose this Gordian *k.*
**Knot-grass.**—C. 542. of *k.-g.* dew-besprent
**Knots.**—P. L. 4, 242. in beds and curious *k.*
**Know.**—P. L. 1, 630. could ever *k.* repulse
P. L. 1, 643. his might we *k.* and *k.* our own
P. L. 2, 206. shrink and fear what yet they *k.*
P. L. 2, 316. *k.* not that the King of heaven
P. L. 2, 740. till first I *k.* of thee what thing
P. L. 2, 744. I *k.* thee not nor ever saw
P. L. 2, 821. *k.* I come no enemy
P. L. 2, 839. I haste to *k.* and this once known
P. L. 2, 990. I *k.* thee stranger who thou art
P. L. 3, 180. that he may *k.* how frail his fallen
P. L. 3, 662. unspeakable desire to see and *k.*
P. L. 3, 694. thy desire which tends to *k.*
P. L. 3, 703. pleasant to *k.* and worthiest
P. L. 4, 86. they little *k.* how dearly I abide
P. L. 4, 113. and this new world shall *k.*
P. L. 4, 517. can it be sin to *k.* ? can it be death
P. L. 4, 523. with more desire to *k.*
P. L. 4, 565. a spirit zealous as he seemed to *k.*
P. L. 4, 637. to *k.* no more is woman's
P. L. 4, 775. and *k.* to *k.* no more
P. L. 4, 827. *k.* ye not then, said Satan
P. L. 4, 828. *k.* ye not me ?
P. L. 4, 830. not to *k.* me argues yourselves
P. L. 4, 831. if ye *k.* why ask ye
P. L. 4, 1006. Satan I *k.* they strength
P. L. 5, 100. but *k.* that in the soul are many
P. L. 5, 243. this let him *k.*
P. L. 5, 402. only this I *k.* that one celestial
P. L. 5, 414. for *k.* whatever was
P. L. 5, 454. to *k.* of things above his world
P. L. 5, 461. inhabitant with God now *k.* I well
P. L. 5, 741. and in event *k.* whether I be
P. L. 5, 789. if I trust to *k.* ye right or if ye *k.*
P. L. 5, 826. yet by experience taught we *k.*
P. L. 5, 856. doctrine which we would *k.*
P. L. 5, 859. we *k.* no time when we were not
P. L. 5, 860. *k.* none before us self-begot
P. L. 5, 895. can uncreate thee thou shalt *k.*
P. L. 6, 148. how few sometimes may *k.*
T. L. 6, 163. to let thee *k.*
P. L. 6, 704. all may *k.* in heaven and hell
P. L. 7, 61. led or yet sinless with desire to *k.*
P. L. 7, 97. magnify his works the more we *k.*
P. L. 7, 125. is left besides to search and *k.*
P. L. 7, 127. to *k.* in measure what the mind
P. L. 7, 131. *k.* then that after Lucifer
P. L. 7, 631. thrice happy if they *k.* their
P. L. 7, 639. posterity informed by thee might *k.*
P. L. 8, 103. that man may *k.* he dwells not in
P. L. 8, 173. heaven is for thee too high to *k.*
P. L. 8, 191. that not to *k.* at large of things
P. L. 8, 192. but to *k.* that which before us lies

P. L. 8, 280. tell me how may I *k*. him
P. L. 8, 282. feel that I am happier than I *k*.
P. L. 8, 328. for *k*. the day thou eat'st
P. L. 8, 373. they also *k*. and reason not
P. L. 8, 406. for none I *k*. second to me
P. L. 8, 548. so well to *k*. her own
P. L. 9, 368. the other who can *k*.
P. L. 9, 709. both good and evil, as they *k*.
P. L. 9, 726. that man should thus attain to *k*.
P. L. 9, 758. then what forbids he but to *k*.
P. L. 9, 773. what *k*. to fear
P. L. 9, 804. as the gods who all things *k*.
P. L. 9, 1071. we *k*. both good and evil
P. L. 9, 1073. if this be to *k*.
P. L. 9, 1137. I *k*. not whence possessed thee
P. L. 10, 27. to hear and *k*. how all befell
P. L. 10, 169. more to *k*. concerned not man
P. L. 10, 207. *k*. thy birth
P. L. 10, 629. and *k*. not that I called
P. L. 10, 967. Adam, by sad experiment I *k*.
P. L. 11, 50. elements that *k*. no gross
P. L. 11, 85. to *k*. both good and evil
P. L. 11, 92. his heart I *k*. how variable
P. L. 11, 356. *k*. I am sent to show thee
P. L. 11, 475. that thou may'st *k*. what misery
P. L. 11, 578. to worship God aright and *k*.
P. L. 12, 82. yet *k*. withal since thy original
P. L. 12, 174. who denies to *k*. their God
P. L. 12, 599. may concern her faith to *k*.
P. L. 12, 610, and whither went'st I *k*.
P. R. 1, 47. well ye *k*. how many ages
P. R. 1, 89. his first-begot we *k*.
P. R. 1, 150. he now shall *k*. I can produce
P. R. 1, 203. set serious to learn and *k*.
P. R. 1, 234. for *k*. thou art no son of mortal
P. R. 1, 292. not yet perhaps I need not *k*.
P. R. 1, 356. knowing who I am as I *k*. who
P. R. 1, 384. whom I *k*. declared the Son of God
P. R. 1, 464. all truth requisite for men to *k*.
P. R. 1, 494. though I *k*. thy scope
P. R. 2, 231. and now I *k*. he hungers
P. R. 2, 240. each to *k*. his part
P. R. 2, 305. and well I *k*. not without hunger
P. R. 2, 475. to *k*. and knowing worship God
P. R. 3, 7. thou know'st what is of use to *k*.
P. R. 3, 52. they admire they *k*. not what
P. R. 3, 53. and *k*. not whom but as one leads
P. R. 3, 193. that he may *k*. what I can suffer
P. R. 3, 249. that thou mayst *k*. how best
P. R. 3, 347. that thou mayst *k*. I seek not to
P. R. 4, 146. *k*. therefore when my season
P. R. 4, 153. is not for thee to *k*. nor me to tell
P. R. 4, 159. on the other side *k*. also thou
P. R. 4, 227. *k*. and write and teach
P. R. 4, 286. think not but that I *k*. these
P. R. 4, 287. or think I *k*. them not
P. R. 4, 294. *k*. this only that he nothing knew
P. R. 4, 538. therefore to *k*. what more thou
S. A. 62. haply had ends above my reach to *k*.
S. A. 395. what part summed that she might *k*.
S. A. 742. and *k*. of thy estate
S. A. 982. I *k*. thy trains though dearly
S. A. 1067. I *k*. him by his stride the giant
S. A. 1075. his fraught we soon shall *k*.
S. A. 1091. the way to *k*. were not to see but taste
S. A. 1139. I *k*. no spells use no forbidden arts
S. A. 1313. thy strength they *k*. surpassing
S. A. 1418. I *k*. not
S. A. 1508. I *k*. your friendly minds
S. A. 1534. he can I *k*. but doubt to think he will
S. A. 1547. to have guided me aright I *k*. not how
S. A. 1554. thou seest we long to *k*.
S. A. 1556. to *k*. well what I utter
S. A. 1592. more than enough we *k*.
C. 311. I *k*. each lane and every alley green
C. 316. I shall *k*. ere morrow wake
C. 490. that halloa I should *k*.
C. 580. but further *k*. I not
C. 788. thou art worthy that thou shouldst not *k*.
A. 34. I *k*. this quest of yours and free intent
A. 44. for *k*. by lot from Jove I am the power

L. 119. blind mouths that scarce themselves *k*.
S. 17, 9. besides to *k*. both spiritual power
S. 21, 9. to measure life learn thou betimes and *k*.
P. 33. my sorrows are too dark for day to *k*.
V. Ex. 10. I *k*. my tongue but little grace can do

**Knowing.**—P. L. 4, 222. bought dear by *k*. ill
P. L. 7, 83. which yet concerned our *k*.
P. L. 8, 438. find thee *k*. not of beasts alone
P. L. 9, 709. as gods *k*. both good and evil
P. L. 9, 1055. had shadowed them from *k*. ill
P. L. 11, 307. nor *k*. us nor known
P. L. 12, 127. not *k*. to what land
P. R. 1, 356. *k*. who I am as I know who thou
P. R. 2, 475. to know and *k*. worship God
P. R. 4, 288. not therefore am I short of *k*.
P. R. 4, 492. *k*. I shall reign past thy preventing
S. A. 840. *k*. as needs I must by thee betrayed
S. A. 1401. yet *k*. their advantages too many

**Knowledge.**—P. L. 1, 628. the depth of *k*. ill
P. L. 3, 47. and for the book of *k*. fair
P. L. 4, 221. our death the tree of *k*.
P. L. 4, 222. *k*. of good bought dear
P. L. 4, 424. not to taste that only tree of *k*.
P. L. 4, 514. one fatal tree there stands of *k*.
P. L. 4, 515. *k*. forbidden
P. L. 4, 525. to keep them low whom *k*. might
P. L. 4, 638. is woman's happiest *k*.
P. L. 5, 52. the tree of interdicted *k*.
P. L. 5, 60. is *k*. so despised ?
P. L. 5, 108. and call our *k*. or opinion
P. L. 5, 509. the way that might direct our *k*.
P. L. 7, 75. which human *k*. could not reach
P. L. 7, 120. to answer thy desire of *k*.
P. L. 7, 126. but *k*. is as food and needs no less
P. L. 7, 543. works *k*. of good and evil
P. L. 8, 8. allayed the thirst I had of *k*.
P. L. 8, 324. brings *k*. of good and ill
P. L. 8, 353. with such *k*. God endued
P. L. 8, 551. all higher *k*. in her presence falls
P. L. 9, 687. it gives you life to *k*.
P. L. 9, 697. *k*. of good and evil
P. L. 9, 723. who enclosed *k*. of good and evil
P. L. 9, 727. what can your *k*. hurt him
P. L. 9, 752. the Tree of *K*. both of good
P. L. 9, 790. through expectation high of *k*.
P. L. 9, 804. *k*. as the gods who all things know
P. L. 9, 820. keep the odds of *k*. in my power
P. L. 9, 849. the tree of *k*. he must pass
P. L. 9, 998. not to eat against his better *k*.
P. L. 9, 1073. bad fruit of *k*. if this be to know
P. L. 11, 87. his *k*. of good lost and evil got
P. L. 12, 279. who sought forbidden *k*.
P. L. 12, 559. and have my fill of *k*.
P. L. 12, 582. add deeds to thy *k*. answerable
P. R. 1, 213. what might improve my *k*.
P. R. 2, 293. what concerns my *k*. God reveals
P. R. 2, 371. their taste no *k*. works at least
P. R. 4, 224. thy mind o'er all the world in *k*.
P. R. 4, 225. all *k*. is not couched in Moses' law

**Known.**—P. L. 1, 80. long after *k*. in Palestine
P. L. 1, 374. then were they *k*. to men
P. L. 1, 376. say Muse their names then *k*.
P. L. 1, 515. these first in Crete and Ida *k*.
P. L. 1, 732. his hand was *k*. in heaven
P. L. 2, 839. I haste to know and this once *k*.
P. L. 3, 647. was *k*. the archangel
P. L. 4, 581. come well *k*. from heaven
P. L. 4, 757. son and brother first were *k*.
P. L. 4, 836. undiminished brightness to be *k*.
P. L. 6, 20. found already *k*. what he for news
P. L. 6, 418. now *k*. in arms
P. L. 6, 432. till now not *k*. but *k*. as soon
P. L. 7, 85. may no less perhaps avail us *k*.
P. L. 8, 106. ordained for uses to his Lord best *k*.
P. L. 9, 110. all their *k*. virtue
P. L. 9, 699. why not *k*. since easier shunned
P. L. 9, 817. shall I to him make *k*. as yet
P. L. 9, 976. so eminently never had been *k*.
P. L. 9, 1023. nor *k*. till now true relish tasting
P. L. 9, 1102. Indians *k*. in Malabar or Deccan
P. L. 9, 1151. no ground of enmity between us *k*.

P. L. 10, 5. was *k*. in Heaven
P. L. 10, 156. hadst thou *k*. thyself aright
P. L. 10, 684. and not *k*. east or west
P. L. 11, 88. had it sufficed him to have *k*.
P. L. 11, 307. nor knowing us nor *k*.
P. L. 12, 544. now amplier *k*. thy Saviour
P. R. 1, 262. to our scribes *k*. partly and soon
P. R. 1, 437. not well understood as good not *k*.
P. R. 1, 446. his providence to thee not *k*.
P. R. 2, 7. Andrew and Simon famous after *k*.
P. R. 2, 414. a carpenter thy father *k*.
P. R. 3, 68. on earth less *k*.
P. R. 3, 433. time to himself best *k*.
S. A. 641. but now hath cast me off as never *k*.
S. A. 778. was it not weakness also to make *k*.
S. A. 1082. know'st me now if thou at all art *k*.
S. A. 1218. if my *k*. offence had not disabled me
C. 724. not half his riches *k*. and yet despised
S. 10, 9. though later born than to have *k*. the
S. 12, 2. by the *k*. rules of ancient liberty
U. C. I. 5. such a shifter that if truth were *k*.
**Knows.**—P. L. 2, 151. who *k*., let this be good
P. L. 2, 806. he *k*. his end with mine
P. L. 2, 807. *k*. that I should prove a bitter
P. L. 4, 103. this *k*. my punisher
P. L. 4, 201. so little *k*. any but God alone
P. L. 7, 144. drew many whom their place *k*.
P. L. 9, 138. and who *k*. how long before had
P. L. 9, 705. he *k*. that in the day ye eat
P. L. 9, 765. he hath eaten, and knew, and *k*.
P. L. 9, 1146. which who *k*. but might as ill
P. L. 10, 787. who *k*. but I shall die a living
P. L. 10, 793. since human reach no farther *k*.
P. L. 11, 199. what till then our life who *k*.
P. R. 1, 176. the Father *k*. the Son

P. R. 4, 471. no man *k*. when
S. A. 516. who *k*. but God hath set before us
S. A. 1350. he's gone and who *k*. how he may
S. A. 1701. that no second *k*. nor third
C. 50. who *k*. not Circe the daughter of the Sun
C. 87. *k*. to still the wild winds when they roar
S. 8, 5. he can requite thee for he *k*. the charms
**Know'st.**—P. L. 1, 19. instruct me for thou *k*.
P. L. 2, 730. and *k*. for whom
P. L. 3, 276. well thou *k*. how dear to me
P. L. 4, 426. well thou *k*. God hath pronounced
P. L. 4, 584. hard thou *k*. it to exclude spiritual
P. L. 4, 895. who *k*. only good
P. L. 4, 926. well thou *k*., I stood thy fiercest
P. L. 4, 1006. I know thy strength and thou *k*.
P. L. 6, 689. thou *k*. equal in their creation
P. L. 7, 493. thou their natures *k*.
P. L. 7, 536. thence as thou *k*. he brought thee
P. L. 7, 622. but thou *k*. their seasons
P. L. 8, 372. *k*. thou not their language
P. L. 8, 573. of that skill the more thou *k*.
P. L. 8, 620. let it suffice thee that thou *k*. us
P. L. 9, 252. thou *k*. what hath been warned us
P. L. 10, 72. but thou *k*. whoever judged
P. L. 10, 948. of what thou *k*. not
P. L. 11, 335. Adam thou *k*. heaven his
P. R. 3, 7. I see thou *k*. what is of use to know
P. R. 3, 201. *k*. thou not that my rising is thy
S. A. 850. thou *k*. the magistrates and princes
S. A. 1081. thou *k*. me now if thou at all art
S. A. 1319. thou *k*. I am an Hebrew
S. A. 1560. but thou *k*. to Israelites not saddest
V. Ex. 55. thou *k*. it must be now thy only bent
**Ksar.**—P. L. 11, 394. the Russian *k*. in Mosco

# L.

**Laborious.**—P. L. 2, 20. *l*. flight
P. L. 11, 178. enjoined *l*. till day droop
S. A. 14. and forbid *l*. works
L. 72. to scorn delights and live *l*. days
**Labour.**—P. L. 1, 164. our *l*. must be to pervert
P. L. 2, 262. work ease out of pain through *l*.
P. L. 2, 1021. so he with difficulty and *l*. hard
P. L. 2, 1022. with difficulty and *l*. he
P. L. 4, 328. toil of their sweet gardening *l*.
P. L. 4, 613. since God hath set *l*. and rest
P. L. 4, 625. and at our pleasant *l*. to reform
P. L. 6, 492. nor long shall be our *l*.
P. L. 8, 133. or save the sun his *l*.
P. L. 8, 213. from *l*.
P. L. 9, 205. Adam well may we *l*. still
P. L. 9, 208. the work under our *l*. grows
P. L. 9, 236. strictly hath our Lord imposed *l*.
P. L. 9, 302. if such affront I *l*. to avert from
P. L. 9, 944. be frustrate, do, undo, and *l*. lose
P. L. 10, 491. without our hazard *l*. or alarm
P. L. 10, 1054. with *l*. I must earn my bread
P. L. 10, 1056. my *l*. will sustain me
P. L. 11, 172. the field to *l*. calls us now
P. L. 11, 375. and earn rest from *l*. won
P. R. 1, 132. far other *l*. to be undergone
S. A. 37. put to the *l*. of a beast
S. A. 1365. by *l*. honest and lawful
C. 192. is now the *l*. of my thoughts
S. 9, 4. that *l*. up the hill of heavenly truth
.W. S. 2. the *l*. of an age in piled stones
**Laboured.**—C. 291. I saw what time the *l*. ox
**Labourer's.**—P. L. 12, 631. at the *l*. heel
**Labouring.**—P. L. 2, 665. the *l*. moon
P. L. 10, 1012. his more attentive mind *l*. had
P. L. 11, 565. stood one who at the forge *l*.
P. L. 12, 18. *l*. the soil and reaping plenteous
P. R. 3, 330. nor of *l*. pioneers a multitude
S. A. 1298. *l*. thy mind
L'A. 74. the *l*. clouds do often rest
**Labours.**—P. L. 9, 214. let us divide our *l*.

P. L. 9, 841. and her rural *l*. crown
P. R. 4, 486. sorrows and *l*., opposition, hate
S. A. 709. turn his *l*. for thou canst to peaceful
S. A. 1259. if they intend advantage of my *l*.
C. 1006. after her wandering *l*. long
P. 14. heaviest plight of *l*. huge and hard
**Labyrinth.**—P. L. 2, 584. rolls her watery *l*.
P. L. 9, 183. in *l*. of many a round self-rolled
C. 278. dim darkness and this leafy *l*.
**Lack.**—S. A. 905. or *l*. of breath
U. C. II. 24. *l*. of load made his life burdensome
**Lackey.**—C. 455. a thousand liveried angels *l*. her
**Lad.**—P. R. 2, 439. and the shepherd *l*.
C. 619. brought to my mind a certain shepherd *l*.
**Laden.**—S. A. 550. *l*. with fair fruit
C. 394. fair Hesperian tree *l*. with blooming gold
**Ladies.**—P. R. 2, 357. and *l*. of the Hesperides
S. A. 1653. lords, *l*., captains, counsellors
L'A. 121. with store of *l*., whose bright eyes
V. Ex. 60. the faery *l*. danced upon the hearth
**Ladon's.**—A. 97. by sandy *L*.'s lilied banks
**Lady.**—C. 277. what chance good *l*. hath bereft
C. 283. and left your fair side all unguarded *l*.
C. 319. I can conduct you *l*. to a low, but loyal
C. 507. but O my virgin *l*. where is she?
C. 564. my most honoured *l*. your dear sister
C. 574. the aidless innocent *l*. his wished prey
C. 618. how to secure the *l*. from surprisal
C. 659. nay *l*., sit, if I but wave this wand
C. 666. why are you vexed *l*., why do you frown?
C. 737. list *l*., be not coy and be not cozened
C. 818. we cannot free the *l*. that sits here
C. 910. brightest *l*., look on me
C. 938. come *l*., while heaven lends us grace
C. 966. noble lord and *l*. bright
A. 105. to serve the *l*. of this place
S. 9, 1. *l*. that in the prime of earliest youth
M. W. 47. gentle of *l*. may thy grave
**Laertes.**—P. L. 9, 441. host of old *L*. son
**Lag.**—P. L. 10, 266. I shall not *l*. behind
**Lagging.**—S. A. 337. with age came *l*. after

S.A.1577.nipped with the *l.* rear of winter's frost
**Lahor.**—P. L. 11, 391. *L.* of Great Mogul
**Laid.**—P. L. 1, 137. destruction *l.* thus low
P. L. 1, 172. o'erblown hath *l.* the fiery surge
P. L. 4, 457. and *l.* me down on the green bank
P. L. 4, 521. O fair foundation *l.* whereon
P. L. 4, 741. straight side by side were *l.*
P. L. 4, 791. *l.* perhaps asleep secure of harm
P. L. 4, 815. *l.* fit for the tun, some magazine
P. L. 6, 339. they him *l.* gnashing for anguish
P. L. 6, 572. row of pillars *l.* on wheels
P. L. 8, 254. on the flowery herb I found me *l.*
P. L. 10, 1046. his just yoke *l.* on our necks
P. L. 11, 438. sacrificing *l.* the inwards
P. L. 11, 479. wherein were *l.* numbers of all
P. L. 11, 732. and of provisions *l.* in large
P. R. 2, 104. of things and sayings *l.* up
P. R. 2, 261. then *l.* him down
P. R. 3, 283. and Jerusalem *l.* waste
P. R. 4, 343. *l.* as varnish on a harlot's cheek
P. R. 4, 429. chased the clouds and *l.* the winds
Il P. 150. softly on my eyelids *l.*
H. 12. he *l.* aside
H. 238. hath *l.* her Babe to rest
M. W. 32. had burial, yet not *l.* in earth
U. C. I. 2. here alas hath *l.* him in the dirt
**Lair.**—P. L. 7, 457. as from his *l.* the wild beast
**Lake.**—P. L. 1, 210. chained on the burning *l.*
P. L. 1, 229. as the *l.* with liquid fire
P. L. 1, 280. and prostrate on yon *l.*
P. L. 1, 702. liquid fire sluiced from the *l.*
P. L. 2, 74. sleepy drench of that forgetful *l.*
P. L. 2, 169. we lay chained on the burning *l.*
P. L. 2, 576. that disgorge into the burning *l.*
P. L. 3, 521. or flew o'er the *l.* rapt in a chariot
P. L. 4, 261. dispersed or in a *l.*
P. L. 4, 459. to look into the clear smooth *l.*
P. L. 5, 186. now rise from hill or steaming *l.*
P. L. 10, 562. near that bituminous *l.*
P. L. 11, 847. from standing *l.* to tripping ebb
P. R. 2, 23. on this side the broad *l.* Genezaret
P. R. 3, 271. Araxes and the Caspian *l.*
C. 433. in fog or fire by *l.* or moorish fen
C. 865. Goddess of the silver *l.* listen and save
L. 109. the pilot of the Galilean *l.*
**Lakes.**—P. L. 2, 621. rocks, caves, *l.*, fens
P. L. 7, 397. in the seas and *l.*
P. L. 7, 437. others on silver *l.* and rivers
**Lamb.**—P. L. 9, 583. unsucked of *l.* or kid
P. L. 12, 20. oft sacrificing bullock, *l.*, or kid
**Lambs.**—P. L. 3, 434. to gorge the flesh of *l.*
P. L. 11, 649. ewes and their bleating *l.*
**Lament.**—P. L. 1, 448. Syrian damsels to *l.*
P. L. 8, 244. torment and loud *l.* and furious
P. L. 11, 266. with audible *l.* discovered soon
P. L. 11, 287. *l.* not Eve but patiently resign
P. L. 11, 874. far less I now *l.* for one whole
S. A.1242. ere long thou shalt *l.* these braveries
L. 60. whom universal nature did *l.*
H. 183. a voice of weeping heard and loud *l.*
D. F. I. 72. her false-imagined loss cease to *l.*
**Lamentable.**—P. L. 2, 617. their *l.* lot
**Lamentation.**—P. L. 2, 579. named of *l.*
S. A. 1708. no time for *l.* now
S. A. 1713. and *l.* to the sons of Caphtor
**Lamented.**—P. L. 10, 845. to himself *l.* loud
**Lamenting.**—P. L. 5, 894. thee *l.* learn
P. L. 11, 675. and to his guide *l.* turned full sad
**Lamp.**—P. L. 3, 22. and feel thy sovran vital *l.*
P. L. 3, 581. towards his all-cheering *l.*
P. L. 4, 764. here lights his constant *l.*
P. L. 7, 370. first in his east the glorious *l.*
P. L. 8, 520. to light the bridal *l.*
Il P. 85. or let my *l.* at midnight hour
S. 9, 10. to fill thy odorous *l.* with deeds of light
H. 242. with handmaid *l.* attending
**Lamps.**—P. L. 1, 728. many a row of starry *l.*
P. L. 5, 713. and from within the golden *l.*
P. L. 9, 104. yet bear their bright officious *l.*
P. L. 12, 255. before him burn seven *l.*
C. 198. filled their *l.* with everlasting oil

**Lance.**—P. L. 1, 766. combat or career with *l.*
**Lancelot.**—P. R. 2, 361. *L.* or Pelleas
**Land.**—P. L. 1, 227. till on dry *l.* he lights
P. L. 1, 228. if it were *l.* that ever burned
P. L. 1, 343. and darkened all the *l.* of Nile
P. L. 1, 519. through all the bounds of Doric *l.*
P. L. 1, 734. in Ausonian *l.* men call him
P. L. 2, 589. which on firm *l.* thaws not
P. L. 2, 940. neither sea nor good dry *l.*
P. L. 3, 75. that seemed firm *l.* embosomed
P. L. 3, 440. so on this windy sea of *l.*
P. L. 3, 531. the Promised *L.* to God so dear
P. L. 3, 548. goodly prospect of some foreign *l.*
P. L. 3, 653. over moist and dry o'er sea and *l.*
P. L. 4, 643. when first on this delightful *l.*
P. L. 4, 652. nor rising sun on this delightful *l.*
P. L. 4, 662. and from *l.* to *l.* in order
P. L. 7, 284. and let dry *l.* appear
P. L. 7, 307. *l.* earth and the great receptacle
P. L. 7, 415. or swims and seems a moving *l.*
P. L. 7, 473. ambiguous between sea and *l.*
P. L. 8, 144. if *l.* be there
P. L. 9, 76. sea he had searched and *l.* from Eden
P. L. 9, 81. thence to the *l.* where flows Ganges
P. L. 9, 117. now *l.* now sea and shores
P. L. 10, 693. like change on sea and *l.*
P. L. 11, 337. his omnipresence fills *l.*, sea
P. L. 12, 122. into a *l.* which he will show him
P. L. 12, 127. not knowing to what *l.*
P. L. 12, 134. with God who called him in a *l.*
P. L. 12, 138. gift to his progeny of all that *l.*
P. L. 12, 156. to a *l.* hereafter called Egypt
P. L. 12, 159. to sojourn in that *l.* he comes
P. L. 12, 172. back to their promised *l.*
P. L. 12, 178. and fill all the *l.*
P. L. 12, 197. as on dry *l.*
P. L. 12, 259. to the *l.* promised to Abraham
P. L. 12, 339. their *l.*, their city, his temple
P. R. 3, 94. made famous in a *l.* and times
P. R. 3, 157. Judæa now and all the promised *l.*
P. R. 3, 379. their fathers in the *l.* of Egypt
P. R. 3, 420. nor in the *l.* of their captivity
P. R. 3, 437. while to their native *l.* with joy
P. R. 3, 439. when to the Promised *L.*
S. A. 99. as in the *l.* of darkness yet in light
S. A. 257. to prevent the harass of their *l.*
S. A. 710. who is this? what thing of sea or *l.*
L'A. 64. whistles o'er the furrowed *l.*
S. 15, 14. while avarice and rapine share the *l.*
S. 19, 13. and post o'er *l.* and ocean without rest
H. 52. a universal peace through sea and *l.*
D.F.I.26. young Hyacinth the pride of Spartan *l.*
Brut. 8. a *l.* there lies
**Landed.**—P. L. 10, 316. and *l.* safe from out
**Landmark.**—P. L. 11, 432. as the *l.* stood
**Land-pilot's.**—C. 309. the best *l.-p.* art
**Lands.**—P. L. 1, 290. to descry new *l.*
P. L. 3, 588. there *l.* the fiend
P. L. 5, 263. imagined *l.* and regions in the
P. L. 7, 429. high over seas flying and over *l.*
P. L. 12, 46. in foreign *l.* their memory be lost
S. 8, 7. he can spread thy name o'er *l.* and seas
**Landscape.**—P. L. 2, 491. the darkened *l.*
P. L. 4, 153. so lovely seemed that *l.*
P. L. 5, 142. discovering in wide *l.* all the east
L'A. 70. whilst the *l.* round it measures
**Lane.**—C. 311. I know each *l.* and every alley
**Language.**—P. L. 8, 373. know'st thou not *l.*
P. L. 5, 553. what may this mean? *l.* of man
P. L. 12, 54. to rase quite out their native *l.*
P. R. 4, 333. where so soon as in our native *l.*
V. Ex. 1. hail, native *l.*, that by sinews weak
**Languish.**—P. L. 10, 995. to *l.* without hope
**Languished.**—P. L. 6, 497. and their *l.* hope
S. A. 119. with *l.* head unpropped
C. 744. it withers on the stalk with *l.* head
M. W. 33. and the *l.* mother's womb
**Languishing.**—P. L. 10, 996. *l.* with like
**Lank.**—C. 836. reared her *l.* head
**Lantern.**—C. 197. in thy dark *l.* thus close up
L'A. 104. and he by friar's *l.* led

**Lap.**—P. L. 4, 254. the flowery *l.* of some
P. L. 9, 1041. earth's freshest softest *l.*
P. L. 9, 1060. harlot *l.* of Philistean Dalilah
P. L. 10, 778. as in my mother's *l.*
P. L. 11, 536. drop into thy mother's *l.*
S. A. 536. lascivious *l.* of a deceitful concubine
C. 257. take the prisoned soul and *l.* it in Elysium
L. 138. whose fresh *l.* the swart-star sparely
L'A. 136. *l.* me in soft Lydian airs
M. M. 3. flowery May, who from her green *l.*
V. Ex. 84. peace shall lull him in her flowery *l.*
**Lapland.**—P. L. 2, 665. with *L.* witches
**Lapse.**—P. L. 8, 263. *l.* of murmuring streams
P. L. 12, 83. since thy original *l.*
**Lapsed.**—P. L. 3, 176. renew his *l.* powers
P. L. 10, 572. whom they triumphed once *l.*
**Larboard.**—P. L. 2, 1019. on the *l.*
**Large.**—P. L. 1, 195. extended long and *l.*
P. L. 1, 285. massy *l.* and round
P. L. 1, 444. whose heart though *l.*
P. L. 1, 790. and were at *l.*
P. L. 3, 430. here walked the fiend at *l.*
P. L. 3, 495. into a limbo *l.* and broad
P. L. 3, 530. though that were *l.*
P. L. 4, 144. gave prospect *l.* into his nether
P. L. 4, 223. through Eden went a river *l.*
P. L. 4, 300. his fair *l.* front and eye sublime
P. L. 4, 434. who enjoy free leave so *l.* to all
P. L. 4, 730. this delicious place for us too *l.*
P. L. 5, 318. *l.* bestow their *l.* bestowed
P. L. 5, 343. she gathers tribute *l.*
P. L. 6, 309. and left *l.* field unsafe within
P. L. 7, 486. in small room *l.* heart enclosed
P. L. 8, 104. an edifice too *l.* for him to fill
P. L. 8, 191. that not to know at *l.* of things
P. L. 8, 375. thy realm is *l.*
P. L. 10, 244. dominion given me *l.*
P. L. 11, 626. in joy ere long to swim at *l.*
P. L. 11, 732. of provisions laid in *l.* for man
P. L. 12, 21. *l.* wine offerings poured
P. L. 12, 305. to free acceptance of *l.* grace
P. R. 1, 365. enjoy *l.* liberty
P. R. 3, 10. thy words to thy *l.* heart
P. R. 3, 73. to over-run *l.* countries
P. R. 3, 262. and so *l.* the prospect was
L. 184. in thy *l.* recompense
F. of C. 20. new presbyter is but old priest writ *l.*
**Largely.**—P. L. 8, 7. who thus *l.* hast allayed
P. L. 9, 1043. disport took *l.*
P. L. 11, 845. and of the fresh wave *l.* drew
**Larger.**—P. L. 10, 529. *l.* than whom the sun
**Lark.**—P. R. 2, 279. and now the herald *l.*
C. 317. the low-roosted *l.* from her thatched
L'A. 41. to hear the *l.* begin his flight
**Lars.**—H. 191. the *L.* and Lemures moan
**Lascivious.**—P. L. 9, 1014. cast *l.* eyes
P. R. 4, 91. old and *l.*
S. A. 536. in the *l.* lap of a deceitful concubine
**Last.**—P. L. 1, 376. who first who *l.* roused
P. L. 1, 490. Belial came *l.* than whom a spirit
P. L. 1, 571. their number *l.* he sums
P. L. 1, 620. at *l.* words interwove with sighs
P. L. 2, 324. still first and *l.* will reign sole king
P. L. 2, 416. and our *l.* hope relies
P. L. 3, 134. but mercy first and *l.* shall
P. L. 3, 259. death *l.* and with his carcase
P. L. 3, 278. man the least though *l.* created
P. L. 5, 19. heaven's *l.* best gift
P. L. 5, 115. of our *l.* evening's talk
P. L. 5, 165. him first him *l.* him midst
P. L. 5, 166. fairest of stars *l.* in the train
P. L. 5, 481. *l.* the bright consummate flower
P. L. 5, 568. *l.* unfold the secrets of another
P. L. 6, 693. they needs must *l.* endless
P. L. 6, 797. or to fall in universal ruin *l.*
P. L. 7, 323. *l.* rose as in dance the stately trees
P. L. 7, 449. the sixth and of creation *l.* arose
P. L. 8, 302. *l.* led me up a woody mountain
P. L. 9, 170. obnoxious first or *l.* to basest
P. L. 9, 377. yet submiss though *l.* replied

P. L. 9, 379. thy own *l.* reasoning words
P. L. 9, 896. O fairest of creation, *l.* and best
P. L. 9, 1079. even shame the *l.* of evils
P. L. 10, 197. on Adam *l.* thus judgment
P. L. 10, 609. thy *l.* and sweetest prey
P. L. 10, 812. and so *l.* to perpetuity
P. L. 10, 831. first and *l.* on me, me only
P. L. 11, 275. my early visitation and my *l.*
P. L. 11, 545. and *l.* consume the balm of life
P. L. 11, 579. nor those things *l.* which might
P. L. 11, 736. *l.* the sire and his three sons
P. L. 11, 787. those whom *l.* thou saw'st
P. L. 11, 872. I revive at this *l.* sight
P. L. 12, 189. *l.* with one midnight-stroke
P. L. 12, 330. of kings the *l.*
P. L. 12, 545. *l.*, in the clouds
P. L. 12, 552. and thus Adam *l.* replied
P. L. 12, 574. thus also the angel *l.* replied
P. R. 1, 35. would not be *l.*
P. R. 1, 283. and *l.* the sum of all my Father's
P. R. 4, 300. the Stoic *l.* in philosophic pride
P. R. 4, 444. by this his *l.* affront resolved
P. R. 4, 509. thy manhood *l.*
P. R. 4, 622. thy wound yet not thy *l.*
S. A. 944. scorned, and *l.*, neglected
S. A. 1023. nor this *l.* so treacherously had shorn
S. A. 1389. or of my days the *l.*
S. A. 1426. the *l.* of me or no I cannot warrant
S. A. 1594. eye-witness of what first or *l.* was done
L. 71. that *l.* infirmity of noble mind
L. 108. *l.* came, and *l.* did go
H. 106. her reign had here its *l.* fulfilling
H. 163. when at the world's *l.* session
T. 10. and *l.* of all thy greedy self consumed
D. F. I. 77. that till the world's *l.* end
V. Ex. 14. the daintiest dishes .. be served up *l.*
V. Ex. 47. *l.* of kings and queens and heroes
U. C. II. 25. even to his *l.* breath
**Last (at).**—P. L. 2, 426. till at *l.* Satan
P. L. 2, 643. at *l.* appear hell bounds
P. L. 2, 781. at *l.* this odious offspring
P. L. 2, 927. at *l.* his sail broad vans he spreads
P. L. 2, 1034. now at *l.* the sacred influence
P. L. 3, 499. till at *l.* a gleam of dawning light
P. L. 3, 545. at *l.* by break of cheerful dawn
P. L. 4, 79. O then at *l.* relent
P. L. 5, 497. your bodies may at *l.* turn all to
P. L. 6, 78. at *l.* far in the horizon to the north
P. L. 6, 874. hell at *l.* yawning received them
P. L. 10, 171. yet God at *l.* to Satan first in sin
P. L. 10, 190. whom he shall tread at *l.* under
P. L. 10, 449. at *l.* as from a cloud his fulgent
P. L. 10, 635. death and yawning grave at *l.*
P. L. 10, 890. create at *l.* this novelty on earth
P. L. 10, 981. devoured by death at *l.*
P. L. 10, 985. must be at *l.* food for so foul
P. L. 11, 664. till at *l.*
P. L. 11, 759. on thy feet thou stood'st at *l.*
P. L. 11, 778. and anguish will at *l.* consume
P. L. 12, 106. till God at *l.* wearied with their
P. L. 12, 356. at *l.* they seize the sceptre.
P. R. 1, 309. hungered then at *l.* among wild
S. A. 24. who at *l.* in sight of both my parents
S. A. 275. at *l.* to heap ingratitude on worthiest
S. A. 1566. to utter what will come at *l.* too soon
S. A. 1639. at *l.* with head erect thus cried aloud
C. 61. at *l.* betakes him to this ominous wood
C. 555. at *l.* a soft and solemn-breathing sound
C. 594. when at *l.* gathered like scum
C. 735. and come at *l.* to gaze upon the sun
L. 192. at *l.* he rose and twitched his mantle
Il P. 167. and may at *l.* my weary age
H. 109. at *l.* surrounds their sight
H. 165. and then at *l.* our bliss
**Lasted.**—U. C. II. 27. had his doings *l.*
**Lasting.**—P. L. 1, 55. *l.* pain
P. L. 3, 449. fond hopes of glory or *l.* fame
P. L. 10, 742. dear-bought with *l.* woes
Brut. 11. there thou shalt find a *l.* seat
**Lastly.**—P. L. 3, 240. and for him *l.* die
P. L. 10, 402. make sure your thrall and *l.* kill

P. L. 11, 280. thee *l.* nuptial bower
P. R. 4, 888. and *l.* cruel death
S. A. 1590. O *l.* over-strong against thyself
L. 83. as he pronounces *l.* on each deed
**Late.**—P. L. 1, 113. so *l.* doubted his empire
P. L. 3, 151. thy creature *l.* so loved
P. L. 5, 113. words and deeds long past or *l.*
P. L. 5, 240. what enemy *l.* fallen himself
P. L. 9, 26. long choosing and beginning *l.*
P. L. 9, 53. when Satan who *l.* fled before
P. L. 10, 436. the *l.* heaven-banished
P. L. 10, 861. with other echo *l.* I taught
P. L. 10, 941. towards her his life so *l.*
P. L. 10, 1073. *l.* the clouds justling or pushed
P. L. 11, 70. with peccant angels *l.* they saw
P. L. 11, 653. cattle pastured *l.* now scattered
P. L. 11, 751. where luxury *l.* reigned
P. L. 11, 752. of mankind so numerous *l.*
P. L. 11, 886. though *l.* repenting him of man
P. L. 12, 195. pursuing whom he *l.* dismissed
P. R. 1, 65. destined to this is *l.* of woman born
P. R. 1, 133. that solemn message *l.* on which
P. R. 1, 327. thou seem'st the man whom *l.*
S. A. 179. the glory *l.* of Israel now the grief
S. A. 746. though *l.* yet in some part to
C. 179. swilled insolence of such *l.* wassailers
C. 540. this evening *l.*
S. 7, 4. but my *l.* spring no bud or blossom
S. 23, 1. methought I saw my *l.* espoused saint
V. Ex. 20. which takes our *l.* fantastics with
**Late (of).**—P. L. 2, 77. felt of *l.*
P. L. 2, 991. angel who of *l.* made head
P. L. 9, 1115. such of *l.* Columbus found
P. R. 3, 364. of *l.* found able by invasion to
S. 11,1. a book was writ of *l.* called Tetrachordon
D. F. I. 47. or did of *l.* earth's sons besiege the
**Late (so).**—P. L. 5, 675. so *l.* hath passed
P. L. 7, 92. so *l.* to build in Chaos
P. L. 9, 982. so *l.* of thy so true so faithful
P. L. 10, 721. me so *l.* the glory of that glory
P. L. 12, 642. paradise so *l.* their happy seat
P. R. 2, 3. whom they had so *l.* expressly called
**Late (too).**—P. L. 6, 147. learn too *l.*
P. L. 9, 44. unless an age too *l.* or cold climate
P. L. 9, 884. and I then too *l.* renounce deity
P. L. 10, 755. to say truth too *l.* I thus contest
P. L. 10, 904. or his happiest choice too *l.*
P. R. 3, 42. but thou yet art not too *l.*
S. A. 228. O that I never had! fond wish too *l.*
S. 1, 11. from year to year hast sung too *l.*
**Lately.**—P. L. 2, 979. king possesses *l.*
P. L. 2, 1004. now *l.* heaven and earth
P. L. 10, 38. foretold so *l.* what would come
P. L. 12, 542. at return of him so *l.* promised
P. R. 2, 9. missing him their joy so *l.* found
P. R. 2, 10. so *l.* found and so abruptly gone
U. C. I. 11. but *l.* finding him so long at home
**Later.**—P. L. 1, 509. yet confessed *l.*
P. L. 10, 613. to mature sooner or *l.*
P. R. 3, 289. of *l.* fame built by Emathian
Il P. 101. or what though rare of *l.* age
S. 10, 9. though *l.* born than to have known
**Lateral.**—P. L. 10, 705. with their *l.* noise
**Latest.**—P. L. 4, 567. God's *l.* image
P. L. 5, 18. my espoused, my *l.* found
P. 22. these *l.* scenes confine my roving verse
U. C. I. 13. that he had ta'en up his *l.* inn
**Latona.**—A. 20. might she the wise *L.* be
S. 12, 6. railed at *L.'s* twin-born progeny
**Latter.**—P. L. 2, 235. argues as vain the *l.*
P. L. 4, 1004. the *l.* quick upflew and kicked
P. L. 5, 489. the *l.* most is ours
P. L. 9, 558. the *l.* I demur for in their looks
P. L. 12, 105. thus will this *l.* as the former
V. Ex. 8. that now I use thee in my *l.* task
**Laugh.**—P. L. 2, 204. I *l.* when those who
P. L. 10, 626. that *l.* as if transported with
P. L. 11, 626. and *l.*
**Laughs.**—P. L. 2, 731. who sits above and *l.*
**Laugh'st.**—P. L. 5, 737. *l.* at their vain
**Laughter.**—P. L. 6, 603. to their foes a *l.*

P. L. 8, 78. to move his *l.* at their quaint
P. L. 10, 488. worth your *l.*
P. L. 12, 59. great *l.* was in heaven
L'A. 32. and *L.* holding both his sides
**Laureate.**—L. 151. to strew the *l.* hearse
S. 16, 9. and Worcester's *l.* wreath
**Laurel.**—P. L. 4, 694. *l.* and myrtle
S. A. 1735. plant it round with shade of *l.*
**Laurels.**—L. 1. yet once more O ye *l.*
**Lavers.**—S. A. 1727. with *l.* pure and cleansing
C. 838. in nectared *l.* strewed with asphodel
**Laves.**—L. 175. nectar pure his oozy locks he *l.*
**Laving.**—P. R. 1, 280. out of the *l.* stream
**Lavinia.**—P. L. 9, 17. rage of Turnus for *L.*
**Lavish.**—C. 465. but most by lewd and *l.* act
A. 9. seemed erst so *l.* and profuse
**Lavished.**—S. A. 1026. was *l.* on their sex
**Law.**—P. L. 2, 200. nor the *l.* unjust
P. L. 4, 637. God is thy *l.* thou mine
P. L. 4, 750. hail wedded love, mysterious *l.*
P. L. 5, 798. introduce *l.* and edict on us
P. L. 5, 798. who without *l.* err not
P. L. 5, 822. shalt thou give *l.* to God?
P. L. 6, 41. reason for their *l.* refuse
P. L. 6, 42. right reason for their *l.*
P. L. 9, 654. we live *l.* to ourselves
P. L. 9, 775. of God or death, of *l.* or penalty
P. L. 10, 83. convict by flight and rebel to all *l.*
P. L. 10, 805. beyond dust and Nature's *l.*
P. L. 11, 49. the *l.* I gave to Nature him forbids
P. L. 12, 29. quite dispossess concord and *l.*
P. L. 12, 287. and therefore was *l.* given them
P. L. 12, 289. by stirring up sin against *l.*
P. L. 12, 290. when they see *l.* can discover sin
P. L. 12, 297. which the *l.* by ceremonies
P. L. 12, 300. so *l.* appears imperfect
P. L. 12, 306. works of *l.* to works of faith
P. L. 12, 309. being but the minister of *l.*
P. L. 12, 397. obedience to the *l.* of God imposed
P. L. 12, 402. the *l.* of God exact he shall fulfil
P. L. 12, 404. though love alone fulfil the *l.*
P. L. 12, 416. the *l.* that is against thee
P. L. 12, 488. the *l.* of faith working thro' love
P. R. 1, 207. the *L.* of God I read
P. R. 1, 212. to hear the teachers of our *l.*
P. R. 1, 260. straight I again revolved the *l.*
P. R. 2, 328. meats by the *l.* unclean
P. R. 3, 161. violated the temple of the *l.*
P. R. 4, 225. is not couched in Moses' *l.*
P. R. 4, 334. all our *l.* and story
P. R. 4, 364. these only with our *l.* best form
S. A. 890. against the *l.* of nature *l.* of nations
S. A. 1053. God's universal *l.*
S. A. 1225. due by the *l.* to capital punishment
S. A. 1320. our *l.* forbids at their religious rites
S. A. 1386. that may dishonour our *l.* or stain
S. A. 1409. scandalous or forbidden in our *l.*
S. A. 1425. our God our *l.* my nation or myself
S. A. 1666. whose *l.* in death conjoined thee
A. 70. and keep unsteady Nature to her *l.*
S. 23, 6. purification in the old *l.* did save
Cir. 15. O more exceeding love or *l.* more just
Cir. 16. just *l.* indeed but more exceeding love
**Lawful.**—P. L. 5, 570. not *l.* to reveal
P. L. 8, 614. bear with me then if *l.* what I ask
P. R. 2, 230. satisfy *l.* desires of nature
S. A. 231. I thought it *l.* from my former act
S. A. 1366. by labour honest and *l.*
**Lawless.**—P. L. 12, 173. but first the *l.* tyrant
P. R. 2, 472. or *l.* passions in him
**Lawn.**—Il P. 35. and sable stole of cypress *l.*
H. 85. the shepherds on the *l.*
**Lawns.**—P. L. 4, 252. *l.* or level downs
C. 568. then down the *l.* I ran with headlong
C. 965. on the *l.* and on the leas
L. 25. together both ere the high *l.* appeared
L'A. 71. russet *l.* and fallows gray
**Lawrence.**—S. 20, 1. *L.* of virtuous father
**Laws.**—P. L. 2, 18. and the fixed *l.* of heaven
P. L. 2, 241. and receive strict *l.* imposed
P. L. 5, 679. new *l.* thou seest imposed, new *l.*

P. L. 5, 693. to pass triumphant and give *l.*
P. L. 5, 819. flatly unjust to bind with *l.*
P. L. 5, 844. his *l.* our *l.*
P. L. 5, 883. those indulgent *l.* will not
P. L. 11, 228. or impose new *l.* to be observed
P. L. 12, 226. to rule by *l.* ordained
P. L. 12, 230. ordain them *l.*
P. L. 12, 244. thus *l.* and rites established
P. L. 12, 282. so many and so various *l.* are given
P. L. 12, 283. so many *l.* argue so many sins
P. L. 12, 304. from imposition of strict *l.*
P. L. 12, 521. spiritual *l.* by carnal power
P. L. 12, 522. *l.* which none shall find
S. A. 309. who made our *l.* to bind us
S. A. 314. with his own *l.* he can best dispense
C. 766. that live according to her sober *l.*
S. 21, 3. and in his volumes taught our *l.*
**Lax.**—P. L. 7, 162. meanwhile inhabit *l.*
**Lay.**—P. L. 1, 52. he with his horrid crew *l.*
P. L. 1, 196. *l.* floating many a rood
P. L. 1, 209. the arch-fiend *l.* chained
P. L. 1, 301. angel forms who *l.* entranced
P. L. 1, 312. abject and lost *l.* these
P. L. 2, 168. *l.* chained on the burning lake
P. L. 3, 339. thou thy regal sceptre shalt *l.* by
P. L. 3, 628. *l.* waving round
P. L. 4, 28. Eden which now in his view *l.*
P. L. 6, 239. as only in his arm the moment *l.*
P. L. 6, 390. chariot and charioteer *l.*
P. L. 8, 463. I saw though sleeping where I *l.*
P. L. 9, 418. or garden-plot more pleasant *l.*
P. L. 9, 1173. lurking enemy that *l.* in wait
P. L. 10, 89. and all the coast in prospect *l.*
P. L. 10, 777. how glad would *l.* me down
P. L. 10, 851. on the ground outstretched he *l.*
P. L. 11, 380. amplest reach of prospect *l.*
P. L. 11, 506. or soon beg to *l.* it down
P. L. 11, 656. others to a city strong *l.* siege
P. L. 12, 608. Adam to the bower where Eve *l.*
P. R. 1, 157. he shall first *l.* down the rudiments
P. R. 2, 54. all our fears *l.* on his providence
P. R. 2, 204. to the bait of women *l.* exposed
P. R. 2, 482. and nobler done and to *l.* down
P. R. 3, 255. outstretched in circuit wide *l.*
P. R. 3, 332. to. *l.* hills plain, fell woods
S. A. 395. in what part my strength *l.* stored
S. A. 535. at length to *l.* my head
S. A. 1097. where the ass *l.* thrown
S. A. 1239. and with one buffet *l.* thy structure
S. A. 1485. fathers are wont to *l.* up for their
S. A. 1486. for thy son art bent to *l.* out all
S. A. 1702. and *l.* erewhile a holocaust
S. A. 1716. courage to *l.* hold on this occasion
C. 13. to *l.* their just hands on that golden key
L. 189. warbling his Doric *l.*
S. 1, 8. linked that amorous power to thy soft *l.*
H. 25. and *l.* it lowly at his blessed feet
**Lays.**—P. L. 4, 259. mantling vine *l.* forth
P. L. 7, 436. all night tuned her soft *l.*
P. R. 4, 363. ruins kingdoms and *l.* cities flat
C. 849. carol her goodness loud in rustic ... *l.*
L. 44. fanning their joyous leaves to thy soft *l.*
**Lay'st.**—P. R. 1, 247. manger where thou *l.*
P. R. 2, 189. *l.* thy scapes on names adored
S. A. 1149. it was not gold as to my charge *l.*
**Lazar-house.**—P. L. 11, 479. a *l.-h.* it seemed
**Lazy.**—T. 2. call on the *l.* leaden-stepping hours
**Lea.**—V. Ex. 97. rocky Avon or of sedgy *L.*
**Lead.**—P. L. 3, 255. shall *l.* hell captive
P. L. 4, 100. would but *l.* me to a worse
P. L. 4, 530. a chance but chance may *l.*
P. L. 5, 375. *l.* on then where thy bower
P. L. 5, 684. of thy myriads which we *l.*
P. L. 6, 46. Gabriel, *l.* forth to battle these
P. L. 6, 47. *l.* forth my armed saints
P. L. 8, 86. who art to *l.* thy offspring
P. L. 9, 631. *l.* then said Eve, he leading
P. L. 9, 696. what might *l.* to happier life
P. L. 10, 261. as their lot shall *l.*
P. L. 10, 463. to *l.* ye forth triumphant out
P. L. 10, 830. though thro' mazes *l.* me still

P. L. 11, 364. so shalt thou *l.* safest thy life
P. L. 11, 468. many are the ways that *l.*
P. L. 12, 17. shall *l.* their lives and multiply
P. L. 12, 309. his people into Canaan *l.*
P. L. 12, 614. but now *l.* on, in me is no delay
P. R. 2, 166. *l.* at will the manliest
P. R. 2, 474. and from error *l.* to know
P. R. 3, 239. things that to greatest actions *l.*
P. R. 3, 366. and captive *l.* away her kings
C. 114. *l.* in swift round the months and years
C. 330. shepherd, *l.* on
C. 657. Thyrsis, *l.* on apace, I'll follow thee
A. 40. *l.* ye where ye may more near behold
L'A. 35. in thy right hand *l.* with thee
L'A. 89. or if the earlier season *l.*
S. 1, 4. the jolly Hours *l.* on propitious May
S. 22, 13. this thought might *l.* me
**Leaden.**—II P. 43. with a sad *l.* downward cast
**Leaden-stepping.**—T. 2. lazy *l.-s.* Hours
**Leader.**—P. L. 1, 272. *l.* of those armies bright
P. L. 2, 19. did first create your *l.*
P. L. 4, 933. a faithful *l.*
P. L. 4, 949. argues no *l.* but a liar traced
P. L. 6, 232. led in fight, yet *l.* seemed each
P. L. 6, 451. *l.* to free enjoyment of our right
P. L. 6, 621. *l.*, the terms we sent
P. R. 1, 99. their king, their *l.* and supreme
**Leaders.**—P. L. 1, 357. the heads and *l.*
P. L. 6, 67. under their godlike *l.* in the cause
**Leading.**—P. L. 9. 631. he *l.* swiftly
P. L. 10, 267. nor err the way, thou *l.*
P. R. 1, 189. forth walked alone the Spirit *l.*
**Leads.**—P. L. 2, 433. out of hell *l.* up
P. L. 2, 525. as inclination or sad choice *l.*
P. L. 2, 976. I seek what readiest path *l.*
P. L. 3, 696. *l.* to no excess
P. L. 8, 613. love thou say'st *l.* up to heaven
P. L. 9, 215. thou where choice *l.* thee
P. L. 12, 222. arms where rashness *l.* not on
P. R. 3, 53. as one *l.* the other
C. 518. rifted rocks whose entrance *l.* to hell
A. 76. whose lustre *l.* us and for her most fit
S. 7, 12. toward which time *l.* me and the will
S. 21, 10. toward solid good what *l.* the nearest
M. M. 2. *l.* with her the flowery May
**Lead'st.**—P. L. 11, 372. the path thou *l.* me
**Leaf.**—P. L. 4, 695. of firm and fragrant *l.*
P. L. 5, 747. impearls on every *l.* and every
P. L. 7, 317. herbs of every *l.* that sudden
C. 622. that spreads her verdant *l.*
C. 631. the *l.* was darkish and had prickles
**Leafy.**— C. 278. this *l.* labyrinth
**League.**—P. L. 1, 87. he whom mutual *l.*
P. L. 2, 319. in new *l.* banded against
P. L. 2, 929. many a *l.* as in a cloudy chair
P. L. 4, 164. and many a *l.* cheered with
P. L. 4, 339. linked in happy nuptial *l.*
P. L. 4, 375. *l.* with you I seek
P. L. 10, 274. though many a *l.* remote
P. L. 10, 438. many a dark *l.*
P. R. 3, 269. cut shorter many a *l.*
P. R. 3, 370. thou wilt by conquest or by *l.*
S. A. 1139. when thou hadst broke the *l.*
S. 15, 8. the false North displays her broken *l.*
**League-breaker.**—S. A. 1184. thee as a *l-b.*
S. A. 1209. as a *l.-b.* gave up bound
**Leagued.**—P. L. 10, 868. with him *l.*
P. R. 1, 359. who *l.* with millions more
**Leagues.**—P. L. 3, 488. ten thousand *l.*
P. R. 3, 392. of enemies of aids battles and *l.*
**Lean.**—S. A. 1632. as over-tired to let him *l.*
C. 584. yes and keep it still, *l.* on it safely
C. 709. praising the *l.* and sallow abstinence
L. 123. and when they list their *l.* and flashy
**Leaned.**—P. L. 4, 494. *l.* on our first father
**Leaning.**—P. L. 5, 12. he on his side *l.*
**Leans.**—C. 355. *l.* her unpillowed head
S. 17, 13. therefore on thy firm hand religion *l.*
**Leaped.**—P. L. 3, 470. *l.* fondly into Ætna

P. L. 3, 472. *l.* into the sea
**Leaps.**—P. L. 4, 187. *l.* o'er the fence
**Learn.**—P. L. 1, 695. *l.* how their greatest
P. L. 2, 354. to *l.* what creatures there inhabit
P. L. 2, 686. and *l.* by proof
P. L. 4, 400. of their state he more might *l.*
P. L. 5, 894. who created thee lamenting *l.*
P. L. 6, 147. now *l.* too late how few
P. L. 6, 717. there let them *l.* as likes them
P. L. 8, 68. to read his wondrous works and *l.*
P. L. 8, 190. or by experience taught she *l.*
P. L. 9, 275. both by thee informed I *l.*
P. L. 11, 360. thereby to *l.* true patience
P. L. 12, 561. I *l.* that to obey is best
P. R. 1, 91. who this is we must *l.*
P. R. 1, 203. serious to *l.* and know
P. R. 1, 292. I *l.* not yet
P. R. 4, 254. hear and *l.* the secret power
P. R. 4, 515. that I might *l.* in what degree
P. R. 4, 625. hereafter *l.* with awe to dread
S. A. 187. I *l.* now of my own experience
S. A. 798. to *l.* thy secrets
S. 21, 9. to measure life *l.* thou betimes
D. F. I. 73. and wisely *l.* to curb thy sorrows
**Learned.**—P. L. 2, 816. fiend his lore soon *l.*
P. L. 4, 533. what further would be *l.*
P. L. 5, 856. which we would know whence *l.*
P. L. 6, 367. meaner thoughts *l.* in their flight
P. L. 12, 440. what of him they *l.*
P. L. 12, 575. this having *l.* thou hast attained
S. A. 936. of adder's wisdom I have *l.*
C. 530. this have I *l.* tending my flocks
C. 822. which once of Meliboeus old I *l.*
L. 120. or have *l.* aught else the least
S. 17, 11. thou hast *l.* which few have done
S. 18, 13. who having *l.* thy way early may fly
**Learned (adj.)**—L'A. 132. Jonson's *l.* sock
V. Ex. 90. if not your *l.* hands
**Learning.**—P. R. 4, 231. without their *l.*
S. 11, 13. hated not *l.* worse than toad or asp
F. of C. 9. men, whose life, *l.*, faith, and pure
**Learnt.**—P. R. 1, 146. he might have *l.* less
P. R. 4, 361. is plainest taught and easiest *l.*
**Leas.**—C. 965. on the lawns and on the *l.*
**Lease.**—M.W.52.shortened hast thy own life's *l.*
**Least.**—P. L. 1, 679. *l.* erected spirit that fell
P. L. 2, 338. Conqueror *l.* may reap his conquest
P. L. 2, 339. and may *l.* rejoice
P. L. 3, 120. without *l.* impulse or shadow
P. L. 3, 277. man the *l.* though last created
P. L. 4, 510. our other torments not the *l.*
P. L. 4, 855. save us trial what the *l.* can
P. L. 5, 811. expected *l.* of all from thee
P. L. 6, 221. the *l.* of whom could wield these
P. L. 6, 284. hast thou turned the *l.* of these
P. L. 8, 35. attains her end without *l.* motion
P. L. 8, 397. can man with beast and *l.* of all
P. L. 8, 578. who sees when thou art seen *l.*
P. L. 9, 380. our trial when *l.* sought
P. L. 9, 460. every air of gesture or *l.* action
P. L. 10, 875. when *l.* was safe rejected
P. L. 10, 951. thou feel'st as yet *l.* part
P. R. 3, 109. therein *l.* resembling thy great
P. R. 4, 11. over reached where *l.* he thought
S. A. 195. yet that which was the worst now *l.*
S. A. 927. thou hast lost thou *l.* shall miss
S. A. 1058. so shall he *l.* confusion draw
S. A. 1136. thy hair where strength can *l.* abide
L. 120. or have learned aught else the *l.* that to
**Least (at).**—P. L. 1, 258. here at *l.* we shall be
P. L. 2, 22. this loss thus far at *l.* recovered
P. L. 4, 110. evil be thou my good, by thee at *l.*
P. L. 4, 807. raise at *l.* distempered
P. L. 4, 994. all the elements at *l.* had gone
P. L. 7, 139. at *l.* our envious foe hath failed
P. L. 8, 537. at *l.* on her bestowed too much
P. L. 9, 146. if they at *l.* are his created
P. L. 9, 296. at *l.* asperses the tempted
P. L. 9, 555. the first at *l.* of these I thought
P. L. 11, 39. at *l.* his days numbered
P. L. 11, 95. dream at *l.* to live for ever

P. R. 1, 60. at *l.* if so we can
P. R. 1, 224. at *l.* to try and teach the erring
P. R. 1, 380. at *l.* contemplate and admire
P. R. 1, 459. at *l.* in vain
P. R. 1, 485. and talk at *l.* though I despair
P. R. 2, 136. if he be man by mother's side at *l.*
P. R. 2, 371. at *l.* of evil
P. R. 3, 103. the man at *l.*
P. R. 4, 494. at *l.* might seem to hold all power
S. A. 208. should at *l.* have paired
S. A. 218. at *l.* of thy own nation and as noble
S. A. 322. at *l.* vain reasonings down
S. A. 499. weakly at *l.* and shamefully
S. A. 951. let me approach at *l.* and touch
**Leathern.**—C. 626. ope his *l.* scrip
**Leave.**—P. L. 1, 224. *l.* in the midst a horrid
P. L. 1, 236. and *l.* a singed bottom
P. L. 2, 250. by *l.* obtained unacceptable
P. L. 2, 685. that be assured without *l.* asked
P. L. 3, 238. I for his sake will *l.* thy bosom
P. L. 3, 247. thou wilt not *l.* me
P. L. 3, 739. took *l.* and moves toward the coast
P. L. 4, 434. who enjoy free *l.* so large to all
P. L. 4, 529. and no corner *l.* unspied
P. L. 4, 789. *l.* unsearched no nook
P. L. 5, 118. and *l.* no spot or blame behind
P. L. 5, 669. and *l.* unworshipped, unobeyed
P. L. 8, 168. *l.* them to God above
P. L. 8, 237. not that they durst without his *l.*
P. L. 8, 377. I with *l.* of speech implored
P. L. 9, 265. *l.* not the faithful side
P. L. 9, 725. attains wisdom without their *l.*
P. L. 10, 760. God made thee without thy *l.*
P. L. 10, 819. fair patrimony that I must *l.*
P. L. 10, 820. and *l.* ye none
P. L. 10, 1070. diurnal star *l.* cold the night
P. L. 11, 269. thus *l.* thee paradise, thus *l.*
P. L. 11, 804. what their lords shall *l.* them
P. L. 12, 110. to *l.* them to their own
P. L. 12, 186. on the ground *l.* nothing green
P. L. 12, 339. so incense God as to *l.* them
P. L. 12, 348. from Babylon by *l.* of kings
P. L. 12, 439. to them shall *l.* in charge
P. L. 12, 455. and there confounded *l.*
P. L. 12, 586. not be loth to *l.* this Paradise
P. R. 1, 409. and *l.* to come into the heaven
P. R. 2, 302. with granted *l.* officious I return
P. R. 3, 78. who *l.* behind nothing but ruin
P. R. 3, 440. his due time and providence I *l.*
P. R. 4, 236. look once more ere we *l.* this
S. A. 11. here *l.* me to respire
S. A. 15. with *l.* retiring from the popular
S. A. 506. or the execution *l.* to high disposal
S. A. 794. feared lest one day thou wouldst *l.* me
S. A. 885. for me thou wast to *l.* parents
S. A. 996. I *l.* him to his lot and like my own
C. 26. and gives them *l.* to wear their sapphire
C. 473. as loth to *l.* the body that it loved
S. 13, 12. Dante shall give Fame *l.* to set thee
H. 140. *l.* her dolorous mansions to the peering
**Leaves (verb.)**—P. L. 4, 747. *l.* free to all
P. L. 9, 615. thy overpraising *l.* in doubt
P. L. 9, 621. as *l.* a greater store of fruit
P. L. 9, 1074. *l.* us naked thus of honour
P. L. 10, 434. *l.* all waste beyond the realm
P. L. 12, 129. he *l.* his gods, his friends
P. L. 12, 153. and of his son a grandchild *l.*
P. L. 12, 163. there dies and *l.* his race growing
P. R. 4, 306. when he lists he *l.*
L'A. 87. and then in haste her bower she *l.*
**Leaves.**—P. L. 1, 302. thick as autumnal *l.*
P. L. 4, 266. attune the trembling *l.*
P. L. 5, 6. sound of *l.* and fuming rills
P. L. 5, 219. to adorn his barren *l.*
P. L. 5, 480. from thence the *l.* more aery
P. L. 9, 519. heard the sound of rustling *l.*
P. L. 9, 1095. whose broad smooth *l.* together
P. L. 2, 1110. those *l.* they gathered broad as
A. 57. awakes the slumbering *l.*
L. 5. shatter your *l.* before the mellowing year
L. 44. fanning their joyous *l.* to thy soft lays

Il P. 129. ending on the rustling *l.*
P. 34. the *l.* should all be black whereon I write
W. S. 11. hath from the *l.* of thy unvalued book
**Leavest.**—S. A. 692. oft *l.* them to the hostile
**Leaving.**—P. L. 10, 711. the herb all *l.*
P. R. 1, 364. oft *l.* my dolorous prison
H. 178. the steep of Delphos *l.*
H. 236. *l.* their moon-loved maze
**Lebanon.**—P. L. 1, 447. wound in *L.*
**Led.**—P. L. 1, 129. *l.* the embattled seraphim
P. L. 1, 401. wisest heart of Solomon he *l.*
P. L. 1, 455. when by the vision *l.*
P. L. 1, 678. Mammon *l.* them on
P. L. 3, 698. *l.* thee hither from thy empyreal
P. L. 4, 268. *l.* on the eternal spring
P. L. 4, 476. follow straight invisibly thus *l.*
P. L. 4, 605. Hesperus that *l.* the starry host
P. L. 4, 797. on he *l.* his radiant files
P. L. 5, 215. *l.* the vine to wed her elm
P. L. 5, 356. rich retinue long of horses *l.*
P. L. 6, 26. *l.* him high applauded
P. L. 6, 232. *l.* in fight yet leader seemed
P. L. 7, 61. and now *l.* on yet sinless
P. L. 7, 575. *l.* to God's eternal house direct
P. L. 8, 269. as lively vigour *l.*
P. L. 8, 302. last *l.* me up a woody mountain
P. L. 8, 485. *l.* by their heavenly Maker
P. L. 8, 511. to the nuptial bower I *l.* her
P. L. 9, 473. thoughts whither have ye *l.* me
P. L. 9, 644. *l.* Eve our credulous mother
P. L. 9, 1039. he *l.* her nothing loth
P. L. 10, 188. captivity *l.* captive
P. L. 10, 324. to each of these three places *l.*
P. L. 12, 639. to the eastern gate *l.* them
P. R. 1, 115. *l.* their march from hell's deep
P. R. 1, 192. and step by step *l.* on
P. R. 1, 252. by whose bright course *l.* on
P. R. 1, 290. by some strong motion I am *l.*
P. R. 1, 299. and he still on was *l.*
P. R. 2, 222. of weak minds *l.* captive
P. R. 3, 283. David's house *l.* captive
P. R. 3, 295. by great Arsaces *l.*
P. R. 4, 228. *l.* by Nature's light
S. A. 365. assaulted, overcome, *l.* bound
S. A. 638. he *l.* me on to mightiest deeds
S. A. 741. hath *l.* me on desirous to behold
S. A. 823. I *l.* the way
S. A. 1623. but undaunted where they *l.*
S. A. 1629. they *l.* him between the pillars
S. A. 1635. he unsuspicious *l.* him
L'A. 104. and he by friar's lantern *l.*
Il P. 69. like one that had been *l.* astray
S. 14, 9. Love *l.* them on, and Faith
**Ledst.**—P. R. 1, 8. thou Spirit who *l.* this
**Lee.**—P. L. 1, 207. moors by his side under the *l.*
**Leer.**—P. L. 4, 503. yet with jealous *l.* malign
**Lees.**—C. 809. yet 'tis but the *l.* and settlings
**Left.**—P. L. 1, 146. have *l.* us this our spirit
P. L. 1, 213. *l.* him at large to his own dark
P. L. 1, 433. unfrequented *l.* his righteous
P. L. 2, 361. utmost border of his kingdom *l.*
P. L. 2, 633. right hand coast sometimes the *l.*
P. L. 2, 755. on the *l.* side opening wide
P. L. 3, 207. expiate his treason hath nought *l.*
P. L. 4, 80. is there no place *l.* for repentance
P. L. 4, 80. none for pardon *l.*
P. L. 4, 181. but by submission
P. L. 4, 428. only sign of our obedience *l.*
P. L. 4, 595. had *l.* him there arraying with
P. L. 5, 235. happiness in his power *l.* free
P. L. 5, 236. *l.* to his own free will
P. L. 5, 526. to persevere he *l.* it in thy power
P. L. 5, 730. draw with speed what force is *l.*
P. L. 6, 104. but narrow space was *l.*
P. L. 6, 309. and *l.* large field
P. L. 6, 443. if other hidden cause *l.* them
P. L. 6, 558. to right and *l.* the front unfold
P. L. 6, 569. to right and *l.* the front divided
P. L. 6, 689. to themselves I *l.* them
P. L. 6, 851. of their wonted vigour *l.*

P. L. 7, 125. enough is *l.* besides to search
P. L. 8, 2. in Adam's ear so charming *l.*
P. L. 8, 77. his fabric of the heavens hath *l.*
P. L. 8, 460. but open *l.* the cell of fancy
P. L. 8, 465. who stooping opened my *l.* side
P. L. 8, 478. she disappeared and *l.* me dark
P. L. 8, 534. and *l.* some part not proof
P. L. 9, 142. thinner *l.* the throng of his adorers
P. L. 9, 338. our happy state *l.* so imperfect
P. L. 9, 345. nothing imperfect or deficient *l.*
P. L. 9, 351. but God *l.* free the will
P. L. 9, 652. God so commanded and *l.* that
P. L. 9, 1051. now had *l.* them
P. L. 9, 1057. naked *l.* to guilty Shame
P. L. 9, 1185. and *l.* to herself
P. L. 10, 46. to her own inclining *l.*
P. L. 10, 322. and on the *l.* hand held
P. L. 10, 421. had *l.* their charge
P. L. 10, 437. *l.* desert utmost hell
P. L. 10, 452. glory since his fall was *l.* him
P. L. 10, 534. where all yet *l.* of that revolted
P. L. 11, 221. in their bright stand there *l.*
P. L. 11, 304. and only consolation *l.* familiar
P. L. 11, 753. all *l.* in one small bottom
P. L. 12, 61. thus was the building *l.* ridiculous
P. L. 12, 71. human *l.* from human free
P. L. 12, 343. whose high walls thou sawest *l.*
P. L. 12, 481. faithful *l.* among the unfaithful
P. L. 12, 506. and their story written *l.*
P. L. 12, 513. *l.* only in those written records
P. L. 12, 523. laws which none shall find *l.*
P. R. 1, 16. unrecorded *l.* through many
P. R. 1, 106. and his words impression *l.*
P. R. 1, 248. in the inn was *l.* no better room
P. R. 2, 62. nor *l.* at Jordan tidings of him none
P. R. 2, 116. with sly preface to return had *l.*
P. R. 2, 280. and now the herald lark *l.* his
P. R. 3, 206. where no hope is *l.* is *l.* no fear
P. R. 3, 256. *l.* between fair champaign
P. R. 3, 423. died impenitent and *l.* a race
P. R. 4, 207. rather more honour *l.*
P. R. 4, 396. and *l.* him there
S. A. 644. *l.* me all helpless
S. A. 1027. that inward gifts were *l.* for haste
S. A. 1097. or *l.* thy carcase where the ass lay
S. A. 1480. and he in that calamitous prison *l.*
S. A. 1685. insensate *l.* or to sense reprobate
S. A. 1712. hath *l.* them years of mourning
S. A. 1715. to Israel honour hath *l.* and freedom
C. 137. all thy dues be done and none *l.* out
C. 188. they *l.* me then when the gray-hooded
C. 280. they *l.* me weary on a grassy turf
C. 283. and *l.* your fair side all unguarded
C. 414. my sister is not so defenceless *l.*
A. 41. shallow-searching fame hath *l.* untold
L. 9. and hath not *l.* his peer
Il P. 109. or call up him that *l.* half-told
S. 10, 4. *l.* them both more in himself content
H. 206. hath *l.* in shadows dread
**Legal.**—P. L. 12, 410. not their own though *l.*
S. A. 313. without taint of sin or *l.* debt
**Legend.**—S. A. 1737. in copious *l.*
**Legion.**—P. L. 6, 230. as each divided *l.*
P. L. 6, 232. in strength each armed hand a *l.*
P. L. 8, 232. squared in full *l.*
**Legions.**—P. L. 1, 301. and called his *l.*
P. L. 1, 632. that all these puissant *l.*
P. L. 2, 132. the bordering deep encamp their *l.*
P. L. 2, 537. till thickest *l.* close
P. L. 2, 1006. from whence your *l.* fell
P. L. 4, 942. what thou and thy gay *l.* dare
P. L. 5, 669. he resolved with all his *l.*
P. L. 6, 64. moved on in silence their bright *l.*
P. L. 6, 142. whelmed thy *l.* under darkness
P. L. 6, 206. nor stood at gaze the adverse *l.*
P. L. 6, 655. and oppressed would *l.* armed
P. L. 7, 134. fell with his flaming *l.*
P. L. 10, 427. there kept their watch the *l.*
P. R. 4, 66. *l.* and cohorts, turms of horse
P. R. 4, 629. thee and thy *l.* yelling
C. 603. with all the grisly *l.* that troop

**Legs.**—P. L. 10, 512. his *l.* entwining
**Leisure.**—P.L.2,1046. weighs his ... wings at *l.*
P. L. 10, 510. not long had *l.*
P. R. 2, 210. on whom his *l.* will vouchsafe
S. A. 917. at home in *l.* and domestic ease
Il P. 49. and add to these retired *l.*
U.C.II.23. his *l.* told him that his time was come
**Lemnos.**—P. L. 1, 746. on *L.* the Ægean isle
**Lemures.**—H. 191. the Lars and *L.* moan
**Lend.**—P. L. 9, 260. speedy aid might *l.*
P. L. 12, 200. power God to his saint will *l.*
P. R. 1, 393. *l.* them oft my aid
P. R. 4, 272. next *l.* thine ear
S. A. 1. a little onward *l.* thy guiding hand
C. 706. O foolishness of men that *l.* their ears
C. 797. the brute earth would *l.* her nerves
S. 13, 9. and verse must *l.* her wing
**Lends.**—C. 938. while heaven *l.* us grace
**Length.**—P. L. 1, 209. huge in *l.*
P. L. 1, 564. of dreadful *l.* and dazzling arms
P. L. 2, 217. or changed at *l.* and to the place
P. L. 2, 274. may in *l.* of time
P. L. 2, 709. that fires the *l.* of Ophiuchus
P. L. 2, 893. where *l.*, breadth, and height
P. L. 2, 1028. a bridge of wondrous *l.*
P. L. 6, 78. tenfold the *l.* of this terrene
P. L. 6, 107. in terrible array of hideous *l.*
P. L. 7, 483. wondrous in *l.* and corpulence
P. L. 9, 79. in *l.* west from Orontes
P. L. 9, 792. satiate at *l.* and hightened
P. L. 10, 302. of *l.* prodigious
P. L. 11, 730. by cubit, *l.* and breadth
P. L. 11, 782. crowned with *l.* of happy days
P. L. 12, 504. at *l.* their ministry performed
P. R. 3, 275. of *l.* within her wall
P. R. 4, 29. to equal *l.* backed with a ridge
S. A. 348. at one spear's *l.*
S. A. 570. till *l.* of years and sedentary
L'A. 111. stretched out all the chimney's *l.*
**Length(at).**—P. L. 1, 648. at *l.* from us
P. L. 2, 951. at *l.* a universal hubbub wild
P. L. 4, 357. scarce thus at *l.* failed speech
P. L. 4, 607. at *l.* apparent queen unveiled her
P. L. 5, 755. at *l.* into the limits
P. L. 6, 249. at *l.* saw where the sword
P. L. 6, 635. rage prompted them at *l.*
P. L. 6, 795. at *l.* prevail against
P. L. 7, 158. they open to themselves at *l.*
P. L. 9, 527. dumb expression turned at *l.*
P. L. 9, 551. at *l.* not unamazed she thus in
P. L. 9, 598. sated at *l.* ere long I might
P. L. 9, 894. till thus at *l.* first to himself he
P. L. 9, 1066. at *l.* gave utterance to these
P. L. 11, 719. at *l.* a reverend sire among them
P. L. 12, 191. the river-dragon tamed at *l.*
P. L. 12, 258. save when they journey and at *l.*
P. R. 1, 152. and at *l.* all his vast force
P. R. 3, 5. at *l.* collecting all his serpent wiles
P. R. 3, 433. at *l.* (time to himself best known)
P. R. 4, 503. birth at *l.* announced by Gabriel
P. R. 4, 568. throttled at *l.* in the air expired
S. A. 250. till at *l.* their lords the Philistines
S. A. 535. at *l.* to lay my head
S. A. 865. at *l.* that grounded maxim so rife
S. A. 962. yet winds to seas are reconciled at *l.*
S. A. 1629. at *l.* for intermission sake they led
V.Ex.43. may tell at *l.* how green-eyed Neptune
**Lengthened.**—P. L. 10, 774. and *l.* out
**Lenient.**—S. A. 659. *l.* of grief and anxious
**Lent.**—P. L. 4, 483. to give thee being I *l.*
C. 680. to those dainty limbs which nature *l.*
D. F. I. 75. render him with patience what he *l.*
**Leo.**—P. L. 10, 676. by *L.* and the Virgin
**Leper.**—P. L. 1, 471. a *l.* once he lost
**Leprous.**—H. 138. and *l.* sin will melt from
**Lesbian.**—L. 63. swift Hebrus to the *L.* shore
**Less.**—P. L. 1, 144. since no *l.* than such
P. L. 1, 257. all but *l.* than he whom
P. L. 1, 593. nor appeared *l.* than Archangel
P. L. 1, 647. that he no *l.* at length from us
P. L. 1, 779. now *l.* than smallest dwarfs

P. L. 2, 47. rather than be *l.* cared not to be
P. L. 2, 108. battle dangerous to *l.* than gods
P. L. 2, 295. and no *l.* desire to found this
P. L. 2, 349. though *l.* in power and excellence
P. L. 2, 414. we now no *l.* choice in our
P. L. 2. 443. what remains him *l.* than unknown
P. L. 2, 509. nor *l.* than Hell's dread Emperor
P. L. 2, 553. what could it *l.* when spirits
P. L. 2, 659. far *l.* abhorred
P. L. 2, 848. no *l.* rejoiced his mother bad
P. L. 2, 920. nor was his ear *l.* pealed
P. L. 2, 924. or *l.* than if this frame of heaven
P. L. 2, 1040. with tumult *l.* and with *l.* hostile
P. L. 3, 119. which had no *l.* proved certain
P. L. 3, 220. much *l.* that durst upon his
P. L. 3, 411. love nowhere to be found *l.*
P. L. 3, 626. nor *l.* his locks behind illustrious
P. L. 4, 46. what could be *l.* than to afford him
P. L. 4, 478. *l.* fair, *l.* winning soft, *l.* amiably
P. L. 4, 617. unemployed and *l.* need rest
P. L. 4, 854. most glory will be won or *l.* be lost
P. L. 4, 919. to them *l.* pain *l.* to be fled
P. L. 4, 925. not that I *l.* endure or shrink
P. L. 5, 262. the glass of Galileo *l.* assured
P. L. 5, 796. in power and splendour *l.*
P. L. 5, 799. much *l.* for this to be our Lord
P. L. 5, 829. far from thought to make us *l.*
P. L. 5, 874. nor *l.* for that the flaming seraph
P. L. 6, 59. nor with *l.* dread the loud
P. L. 6, 192. *l.* could his shield such ruin
P. L. 6, 366. that to be *l.* than gods disdained
P. L. 6, 468. no *l.* than for deliverance
P. L. 6, 495. much *l.* to be despaired
P. L. 6, 844. nor *l.* on either side tempestuous
P. L. 7, 85. what may no *l.* perhaps avail us
P. L. 7, 126. needs no *l.* her temperance
P. L. 7, 348. the *l.* by night altern
P. L. 8, 33. might with far *l.* compass
P. L. 8, 88. greater should not serve the *l.*
P. L. 8, 224. nor *l.* think we in heaven of thee
P. L. 8, 248. with thy words no *l.* than thou
P. L. 8, 395. much *l.* can bird with beast
P. L. 8, 407. second to me or like, equal much *l.*
P. L. 8, 444. and *l.* expressing the character
P. L. 8, 539. of inward *l.* exact
P. L. 8, 543. her resembling *l.* his image
P. L. 9, 14. argument not *l.* but more heroic
P. L. 9, 320. who thought *l.* attributed to her
P. L. 9, 346. all that he created much *l.* man
P. L. 9, 381. may find us both perhaps far *l.*
P. L. 9, 533. much *l.* arm thy looks
P. L. 9, 1065. till Adam though not *l.* than Eve
P. L. 10, 15. what could they *l.*?
P. L. 10, 107. or come I *l.* conspicuous
P. L. 10, 531. his power no *l.* he seemed
P. L. 10, 998. torment *l.* than none of what
P. L. 10, 1098. nor Eve felt *l.* remorse
P. L. 11, 9. nor important *l.* seemed their
P. L. 11, 774. he the future evil shall no *l.*
P. L. 11, 784. no *l.* than war to waste
P. L. 11, 874. far *l.* I now lament for one
P. R. 1, 147. might have learnt *l.* overweening
P. R. 1, 383. what can be then *l.* in me than
P. R. 1, 404. what can it *l.* ?
P. R. 2, 69. I to sorrows am no *l.* advanced
P. R. 2, 127. who no *l.* threatens than our
P. R. 3, 126. what could he *l.* expect
P. R. 3, 236. much *l.* her glory
P. R. 3, 257. fair champaign with *l.* rivers
P. R. 4, 105. aim therefore at no *l.* than all
P. R. 4, 113. allure mine eye much *l.* my mind
P. R. 4, 169. what can *l.* so great a gift
P. R. 4, 171. I never liked thy talk thy offers *l.*
P. R. 4, 459. a sneeze to man's *l.* universe
S. A. 305. they ravel more still *l.* resolved
S. A. 620. nor *l.* than wounds immedicable
S. A. 772. the easier towards me or thy hatred *l.*
S. A. 792. nor *l.* in mine towards thee
S. A. 900. *l.* therefore to be pleased
S. A. 1071. I *l.* conjecture than when first
S. A. 1142. no *l.* through all my sinews

S. A. 1421. no *l.* the people on their holydays
S. 7, 7. inward ripeness doth much *l.* appear
S. 7, 9. yet be *l.* or more, or soon or slow
S.16,11. peace hath her victories no *l.*renowned
A. 12. *l.* than half we find expressed
C. 88. nor of *l.* faith
C. 288. no *l.* than if I should my brothers lose
**'Less.**—Il P. 56. *'l.* Philomel will deign a song
**Lessen.**—P. L. 3, 304. *l.* or degrade
P. L. 7, 614. who seeks to *l.* thee
S. A. 767. to *l.* or extenuate my offence
**Lessens.**—S. A. 1563. that still *l.* the sorrow
**Lesser.**—P. L. 5, 101. many *l.* faculties
P. L. 7, 382. with thousand *l.* lights dividual
A. 79. whate'er the skill of *l.* gods can show
**Lest.**—P. L. 2, 468. prudent *l. ...* others
P. L. 2, 483. *l.* bad men should boast their
P. L. 2, 701. *l.* with a whip of scorpions
P. L. 2, 836. *l.* heaven surcharged
P. L. 4, 665. *l.* total darkness should
P. L. 4, 984. *l.* on the threshing floor
P. L. 5, 244. *l.* wilfully transgressing
P. L. 5, 396. no fear *l.* dinner cool
P. L. 5, 731. *l.* unawares we lose this
P. L. 5, 890. *l.* the wrath impendent raging
P. L. 6, 163. unanswered *l.* thou boast
P. L. 7, 17. *l.* from this flying steed unreined
P. L. 7, 44. *l.*the like befall in Paradise to Adam
P. L. 7, 150. but *l.* his heart exalt him
P. L. 7, 272. *l.* fierce extremes contiguous
P. L. 7, 546. govern well thy appetite *l.* sin
P. L. 8, 235.*l.* he incensed at such eruption bold
P. L. 8, 635. take heed *l.* passion sway thy
P. L. 9, 251. other doubt possesses me *l.* harm
P. L. 9, 354. *l.* by some fair appearing good
P. L. 9, 663. nor shall ye touch it *l.* ye die
P. L. 9, 883.*l.* thou not tasting different degree
P. L. 9, 947. *l.* the adversary triumph and say
P. L. 10, 133. *l.* on my head both sin
P. L. 10, 252. *l.* the difficulty of passing back
P. L. 10, 783. *l.* all I cannot die
P. L. 10, 784. *l.* that pure breath of life
P. L. 10, 872. *l.* that too heavenly form
P. L. 10, 1024. much more I fear *l.* death
P. L. 10, 1056. *l.* cold or heat should injure
P. L. 11, 93. *l.* therefore his now bolder hand
P. L. 11, 101. *l.* the Fiend
P. L. 11, 108. *l.* they faint at the sad sentence
P. L. 11, 123. *l.* paradise a receptacle prove
P. L. 11, 883. *l.* it again dissolve and shower
P. L. 12, 45. and get themselves a name *l.*
P. L. 12, 217. *l.* entering on
P. R. 2, 140. I am returned *l.* confidence
P. R. 2, 145. *l.* I who erst thought none
P. R. 4, 558. *l.* at any time thou chance
P. R. 4, 631. *l.* he command them down into
S. A. 794. feared *l.* one day thou wouldst
S. A. 952. not for thy life *l.* fierce remembrance
S. A.1237. go baffled coward, *l.* I run upon thee
S. A. 1254. not dare mention *l.* a question
S. A. 1414. I will not wish *l.* it perhaps offend
S. A. 1451. *l.* I should see him forced
S. A. 1521. best keep together here *l.* running
S.A.1567.*l.* evil tidings with too rude irruption
C. 156. give it false presentments *l.* the place
C. 406. *l.* some ill-greeting touch attempt the
C. 940. *l.* the sorcerer us entice
S. 19, 6. *l.* He returning chide
**Lethe.**—P. L. 2, 583. *L.* the river of oblivion
**Lethean.**—P. L. 2, 604. over this *L.* sound
**Lets.**—P. L. 9, 1184. *l.* her will rule
P. L. 12, 196. but them *l.* pass
P. L. 12, 344. in captivity he *l.* them dwell
C. 466. *l.* in defilement to the inward parts
**Letters.**—P. 35. and *l.,* where my tears
U. C. II. 33. his *l.* are delivered all and gone
**Leucothea.**—P. L. 11, 135. *L.* waked
C. 875. by *L.'s* lovely hands
**Levant.**—P. L. 10, 704. *L.* and the Ponent
**Level.**—P. L. 1, 726. *l.* pavement
P. L. 2, 634. shaves with *l.* wing the deep

P. L. 4, 252. lawns or *l.* downs
L. 98. the air was calm and on the *l.* brine
**Levelled.**—P. L. 2, 712. each at the head *l.*
P. L. 4, 543. *l.* his evening rays
P. L. 6, 591. *l.* with such impetuous fury
P. L. 7, 376. opposite in *l.* west was set
**Leviathan.**—P. L. 1, 201. that sea-beast *l.*
P. L. 7, 412. *l.* hugest of living creatures
**Levied.**—P. L. 2, 905. *l.* to side with warring
P. L. 11, 219. had *l.* war, war unproclaimed
**Levity.**—S. A. 880. not out of *l.*
**Levy.**—P. L. 2, 501. and *l.* cruel wars
**Lewd.**—P. L. 1, 490. a spirit more *l.* fell not
P. L. 4, 193. into his church *l.* hirelings
C. 465. but most by *l.* and lavish act of sin
**Lewdly.**—P. L. 6, 182. yet *l.* darest our
**Lewdly-pampered.**—C. 770. *l.-p.* luxury
**Liable.**—P. L. 6, 397. till that hour not *l.*
S. A. 55. proudly secure yet *l.* to fall
**Liar.**—P. L. 4, 949. argues no leader but a *l.*
P. R. 1, 428. a *l.* in four hundred mouths
**Libbard.**—P. L. 7, 467. the *l.* and the tiger
**Libecchio.**—P. L. 10, 706. Sirocco and *L.*
**Liberal.**—P. L. 9, 996. with *l.* hand
P. L. 4, 415. good and of his good as *l.*
P. L. 8, 362. so amply and with hands so *l.*
**Liberty.**—P. L. 2, 256. preferring hard *l.*
P. L. 4, 958. now wouldst seem patron of *l.*
P. L. 5, 793. orders and degrees jar not with *l.*
P. L. 5, 823. dispute with him the points of *l.*
P. L. 6, 164. first I thought that *l.* and heaven
P. L. 6, 420. found worthy not of *l.* alone
P. L. 10, 307. the *l.* of Greece to yoke
P. L. 10, 368. thou hast achieved our *l.*
P. L. 12, 82. affecting to subdue rational *l.*
P. L. 12, 83. true *l.* is lost
P. L. 12, 100. deprives them of their outward *l.*
P. L. 12, 526. and bind his consort *l.*
P. R. 1, 365. I enjoy large *l.* to round this globe
P. R. 3, 427. should I of these the *l.* regard
S. A. 270. to love bondage more than *l.*
S. A. 271. bondage with ease than strenuous *l.*
S. A. 803. I knew that *l.* would draw thee forth
S. A. 949. this jail I count the house of *l.* to
S. A. 1454. with good success to work his *l.*
L'A. 36. the mountain-nymph, sweet *L.*
S. 10, 7. victory at Chæronea, fatal to *l.*
S. 12, 2. by the known rules of ancient *l.*
S. 12, 11. license they mean when they cry *l.*
S. 22, 11. in *l.'s* defence my noble task
**Libra.**—P. L. 3, 558. from eastern point of *L.*
**Libyan.**—P. L. 1, 355. to the *L.* sands
P. L. 4, 277. Gentiles Ammon call and *L.* Jove
P. L. 12, 635. vapour as the *L.* air adust
**Libyc.**—P. L. 2, 532. frogs, *l.,* and flies
**License.**—S. 12, 11. *l.* they mean when thy cry
**Lichas.**—P. L. 2, 545. *L.* from the top of Œta
**Lick.**—P. L. 10, 630. to *l.* up the draff
**Licked.**—P. L. 9, 526. and *l.* the ground
**Lickerish** (or **Liquorish**). C. 700. *l.* baits
**Lictors.**—P. R. 4, 65. *l.* and rods
**Lie.**—P. L. 1, 266. *l.* thus astonished
P. L. 1, 279. though now they *l.* grovelling
P. L. 2, 360. this place may *l.* exposed
P. L. 3, 243. I shall not long *l.* vanquished
P. L. 4, 631. that *l.* bestrown unsightly
P. L. 9, 76. then sought where to *l.* hid
P. L. 10, 276. where armies *l.* encamped
P. L. 12, 190. first-born of Egypt must *l.* dead
P. R. 1, 263. my way must *l.* through many
P. R. 1, 473. may stand him more instead to *l.*
S. A. 480. *l.* in this miserable loathsome plight
S. A. 579. better at home *l.* bed-rid not only idle
C. 110. with their grave saws in slumber *l.*
C. 977. those happy climes that *l.*
A. 68. such sweet compulsion doth in music *l.*
L.53.where your old bards the famous Druids *l.*
S. 18, 2. whose bones *l.* scattered on the Alpine
D. F. I. 31. or that thy beauties *l.* in wormy bed
W. S.15.and so sepulchred in such pomp dost *l.*

V. Ex. 36. before the thunderous throne doth *l.*
V. Ex. 62. to the room where thou didst *l.*
**Lies (noun).** P. L. 1, 367. by falsities and *l.*
P. L. 3, 93. man will hearken to his glozing *l.*
P. L. 5, 243. but by deceit and *l.*
P. L. 5, 709. with *l.* drew after him
P. L. 10, 42. believing *l.* against his Maker
P. R. 1, 375. glibbed with *l.*
P. R. 1, 407. composed of *l.*
P. R. 1, 408. and in *l.* will end
P. R. 4, 124. hollow compliments and *l.*
C. 692. banished from thy tongue with *l.*
**Lies (verb.)** P. L. 2, 588. continent *l.* dark
P. L. 2, 958. the nearest coast of darkness *l.*
P. L. 2, 974. as my way *l.* through your
P. L. 4, 569. the mount that *l.* from Eden
P. L. 8, 193. before us *l.* in daily life
P. L. 8, 641. in thine own arbitrement it *l.*
P. L. 9, 349. the danger *l.,* yet *l.*
P. L. 9, 620. in such abundance *l.* our choice
P. L. 9, 725. wherein *l.* the offence that man
P. L. 10, 987. in thy power int *l.*
P. L. 11, 177. where'er our day's work *l.*
P. L. 11, 653. now scattered *l.*
P. R. 2, 462. each man's burden *l.*
S. A. 118. see how he *l.* at random carelessly
S. A. 339. behold him where he *l.*
S. A. 1725. let us go find the body where it *l.*
C.37. their way *l.* through the perplexed paths
L. 80. nor in broad rumour *l.*
L. 151. the laureate hearse where Lycid *l.*
L'A. 79. where perhaps some beauty *l.*
L'A. 110. then *l.* him down the lubbar fiend
H. 31. all meanly wrapt in the rude manger *l.*
H. 151. the Babe yet *l.* in smiling infancy
P. 21. then *l.* him meekly down
U. C. II. 1. here *l.* old Hobson
**Liest.**—S. A. 1663. now *l.* victorious
**Lieth.**—U. C. II. 1.here *l.*one who did most truly
**Life.**—P. L. 1, 363. from the book of *l.*
P. L. 2, 624. where all *l.* dies, death lives
P. L. 3, 236. me for him, *l.* for *l.,* I offer
P. L. 3, 244. thou hast given me to possess *l.*
P. L. 3, 294. from thee receive new *l.*
P. L. 3, 297. ransomed with his own dear *l.*
P. L. 3, 354. in paradise fast by the tree of *l.*
P. L. 3, 357. flowers aloft shading the fount of *l.*
P. L. 3, 450. happiness in this or the other *l.*
P. L. 4, 194. up he flew and on the tree of *l.*
P. L. 4, 196. yet not true *l.* thereby regained
P. L. 4, 218. all amid them stood the tree of *l.*
P. L. 4, 220. and next to *l.* our death
P. L. 4, 317. from man's *l.* his happiest *l.*
P. L. 4, 424. planted by the Tree of *L.*
P. L. 4, 425. so near grows death to *l.*
P. L. 4, 485. substantial *l.*
P. L. 4, 666. and extinguish *l.* in nature
P. L. 5, 81. see what *l.* the gods live there
P. L. 5, 427. the trees of *l.* ambrosial fruitage
P. L. 5, 474. and in things that live of *l.*
P. L. 5, 485. give both *l.* and sense
P. L. 5, 652. streams among the trees of *l.*
P. L. 6, 460. may well spare out of *l.* perhaps
P. L. 6, 461. content which is the calmest *l.*
P. L. 7, 239. adverse to *l.*
P. L. 7, 526. breathed the breath of *l.*
P. L. 8, 184. to interrupt the sweet of *l.*
P. L. 8, 193. which before us lies in daily *l.*
P. L. 8, 250. to tell how human *l.* began
P. L. 8, 326. amid the garden by the tree of *l.*
P. L. 9, 73. rose up a fountain by the tree of *l.*
P. L. 9, 112. creatures animate with gradual *l.*
P. L. 9, 241. the lowest end of human *l.*
P. L. 9, 686. by the fruit? it gives you *l.*
P. L. 9, 689. yet both live and *l.* more perfect
P. L. 9, 697. what might lead to happier *l.*
P. L. 9, 833. without him live no *l.*
P. L. 9, 934. higher degree of *l.*
P. L. 9, 954. with thee death is to me as *l.*
P. L. 9, 984. not death but *l.* augmented
P. L. 10,128. my other self the partner of my *l.*

P. L. 10, 178. shalt eat all the days of thy *l.*
P. L. 10, 202. eat thereof all the days of thy *l.*
P. L. 10, 784. lest that pure breath of *l.*
P. L. 10, 790. it was but breath of *l.* that sinned
P. L. 10, 790. what dies but what had *l.*
P. L. 10, 908. calamity shall cause to human *l.*
P. L. 10, 941. towards her his *l.* so late
P. L. 10, 985. that after wretched *l.* must be
P. L. 10, 1013. Eve thy contempt of *l.*
P. L. 10, 1019. for loss of *l.* and pleasure
P. L. 10, 1083. to pass commodiously this *l.*
P. L. 11, 42. to better *l.* shall yield him
P. L. 11, 62. after *l.* tried in sharp tribulation
P. L. 11, 64. and faithful works to second *l.*
P. L. 11, 79. by the waters of *l.*
P. L. 11, 94. reach also of the tree of *l.* and eat
P. L. 11, 122. guard all passage to the tree of *l.*
P. L. 11, 169. am graced the source of *l.*
P. L. 11, 198. and what till then our *l.*
P. L. 11, 331. recalled to *l.* prolonged
P. L. 11, 365. so shalt thou lead safest thy *l.*
P. L. 11, 369. while she to *l.* was formed
P. L. 11, 416. from the well of *l.* three drops
P. L. 11, 446. with a stone that beat out *l.*
P. L. 11, 502. why is *l.* given to be thus
P. L. 11, 506. either not accept *l.* offered
P. L. 11, 546. last consume the balm of *l.*
P. L. 11, 548. nor would prolong *l.* much
P. L. 11, 553. nor love thy *l.* nor hate
P. L. 11, 610. arts that polish *l.*
P. L. 11, 650. scarce with *l.* the shepherds fly
P. L. 11, 823. of man and beast select for *l.*
P. L. 12, 220. choosing rather inglorious *l.*
P. L. 12, 220. *l.* to noble and ignoble
P. L. 12, 406. reproachful *l.* and cursed death
P. L. 12, 407. proclaiming *l.* to all who shall
P. L. 12, 414. slain for bringing *l.*
P. L. 12, 425. as offered *l.* neglect not
P. L. 12, 429. for ever lost from *l.*
P. L. 12, 435. a gentle wafting to immortal *l.*
P. L. 12, 438. men who in his *l.* still followed
P. L. 12, 443. from guilt of sin to *l.* pure
P. L. 12, 571. death the gate of *l.*
P. R. 1, 396. they may direct their future *l.*
P. R. 2, 77. who sought his *l.*
P. R. 2, 80. his *l.* private, unactive, calm
P. R. 2, 372. *l.* destroys *l.'s* enemy
P. R. 3, 22. affecting private *l.*
P. R. 3, 232. thy *l.* hath yet been private
P. R. 4, 265. chance and change in human *l.*
P. R. 4, 298. joined with riches and long *l.*
P. R. 4, 305. pain or torment, death and *l.*
P. R. 4, 370. proposed in *l.* contemplative
P. R. 4, 589. fruits fetched from the tree of *l.*
P. R. 4, 590. from the fount of *l.* ambrosial
S. A. 66. each apart would ask a *l.* to wail
S. A. 90. since light so necessary is to *l.*
S. A. 91. almost *l.* itself if it be true that light
S. A. 100. to live a *l.* half dead a living death
S.A.107.obnoxious more to all the miseries of *l.*
S. A. 108. *l.* in captivity among inhuman foes
S. A. 512. who imploring mercy sues for *l.*
S. A. 521. his pardon I implore but as for *l.*
S. A. 534. pleasure and voluptuous *l.*
S. A. 592. nor the other light of *l.* continue long
S. A. 656. all chances incident to man's frail *l.*
S. A. 688. remit to *l.* obscured
S. A. 888. if aught against my *l.* thy country
S. A. 915. *l.* yet hath many solaces
S. A. 952. not for thy *l.* lest fierce remembrance
S. A. 1002. trust of secrecy my safety and my *l.*
S. A.1009. not wedlock treachery endangering *l.*
S. A. 1059. least confusion draw on his whole *l.*
S. A. 1388. this day will be remarkable in my *l.*
S. A. 1406. for a *l.* who will not change his
S. A. 1579. death to *l.* is crown or shame
S. A. 1668. more than all thy *l.* had slain before
S. A.1711. and heroicly hath finished a *l.* heroic
C. 220. to keep my *l.* and honour unassailed
C. 609. to a foul death cursed as his *l.*
C. 678. to *l.* so friendly or so cool to thirst

L. 76. and slits the thin-spun l. but not the praise
S.14,4. death called l. which us from l. doth sever
S. 21, 9. to measure l. learn thou betimes
M. W. 14. in giving limit to her l.
M. W. 52. shortened hast thy own l.'s lease
U. C. II. 11. rest that gives all men l. gave him
U. C.II. 24. lack of load made his l. burdensome
F.of C.9. whose l. learning faith and pure intent
**Life-blood.**—P. L. 8, 467. and l.-b. streaming
**Life-giving.**—P. L. 4, 199. of that l.-g. plant
**Lifeless.**—P. L. 3, 443. living or l.
P. L. 9, 1154. have grown there still a l. rib
P. L. 10, 707. thus began outrage from l. things
**Lift.**—P. L. 2, 393. l. us up in spite of Fate
P. L. 3, 486. they l. their feet
P. L. 4, 688. and l. our thoughts to heaven
P. L. 6, 299. that may l. human imagination
S. 8, 9. l. not thy spear against the Muses' bower
**Lifted.**—P. L. 4, 49. l. up so high I sdeined
P. L. 6, 189. a noble stroke he l. high
P. R. 4, 545. the Holy City l. high her towers
C. 601. may never this just sword be l. up
**Lifting.**—P. R. 2, 338. our Saviour l. up his eyes
P. R. 4, 48. l. his stately head
**Ligea.**—C. 880. and fair L.'s golden comb
**Light.**—P. L. 1, 63. no l. but rather darkness
P. L. 1, 73. as far removed from God and l.
P. L. 1, 85. who in the happy realms of l.
P. L. 1, 181. the seat of desolation void of l.
P. L. 1, 245. mournful gloom for that celestial l.
P. L. 1, 349. in even balance down they l.
P. L. 1, 391. their darkness durst affront his l.
P. L. 1, 729. yielded l. as from a sky
P. L. 2, 137. to confound Heaven's purest l.
P. L. 2, 220. will grow mild, this darkness l.
P. L. 2, 269. as he our darkness, cannot we his l.
P. L. 2, 398. not unvisited of Heaven's fair l.
P. L. 2, 433. that out of Hell leads up to l.
P. L. 2, 867. to that new world of l. and bliss
P. L. 2, 959. of darkness lies bordering on l.
P. L. 2, 974. your spacious empire up to l.
P. L. 2, 1035. last the sacred influence of l.
P. L. 2, 1024. the calmer wave by dubious l.
P. L. 3, 1. hail holy L., offspring of Heaven
P. L. 3, 3. since God is l.
P. L. 3, 4. and never but in unapproached l.
P. L. 3, 51. so much the rather thou, celestial L.
P. L. 3, 88. far off Heaven in the precincts of l.
P. L. 3, 196. l. after l. well used they shall
P. L. 3, 375. Author of all being, fountain of l.
P. L. 3, 439. and wind their cany waggons l.
P. L. 3, 500. till at last a gleam of dawning l.
P. L. 3, 579. dispenses l. from far
P. L. 3, 594. all alike informed with radiant l.
P. L. 3, 713. l. shone, and order from disorder
P. L. 3, 723. l. from hence though but reflected
P. L. 3, 724. that l., his day
P. L. 3, 730. with borrowed l. her countenance
P. L. 4, 608. unveiled her peerless l.
P. L. 4, 624. the east with first approach of l.
P. L. 4, 664. ministering l. prepared, they set
P. L. 4, 1012. and shown how l. how weak
P. L. 5, 42. and with more pleasing l. shadowy
P. L. 5, 160. who best can tell, ye Sons of L.
P. L. 5, 179. who out of darkness called up l.
P. L. 5, 208. disperse it as now l. dispels
P. L. 5, 250. up springing l. flew through
P. L. 5, 423. the sun that l. imparts to all
P. L. 5, 495. no inconvenient diet nor too l.
P. L. 5, 600. hear all ye Angels progeny of l.
P. L. 5, 643. whence l. and shade spring both
P. L. 5, 714. saw without their l. rebellion
P. L. 6, 4. rosy hand unbarred the gates of l.
P. L. 6, 6. where l. and darkness in perpetual
P. L. 6, 9. l. issues forth, and at the other door
P. L. 6, 481. opening to the ambient l.
P. L. 6, 642. l. as the lightning glimpse
P. L. 7, 98. and the great l. of day yet wants
P. L. 7, 243. be L. said God and forthwith L.
P. L. 7, 249. the L. was good and l. from darkness
P. L. 7, 251. L. the Day and Darkness Night

P. L. 7, 254. when orient l. exhaling first
P. L. 7, 345. to give l. on the earth and it was so
P. L. 7, 352. and l. from darkness to divide
P. L. 7, 359. of l. by far the greater part he took
P. L. 7, 362. to receive and drink the liquid l.
P. L. 7, 363. great palace now of l.
P. L. 7, 365. in their golden urns draw l.
P. L. 7, 377. borrowing her l. from him
P. L. 7, 378. for other l. she needed none
P. L. 8, 22. merely to officiate l. round this
P. L. 8, 37. her warmth and l.
P. L. 8, 140. what if that l. sent from her
P. L. 8,150. communicating male and female l.
P. L. 8, 156. contribute each orb a glimpse of l.
P. L. 8, 158. to this habitable which returns l.
P. L. 8, 245. we returned up to the coasts of l.
P. L. 8, 273. thou sun, said I, fair l.
P. L. 8, 285. and first beheld this happy l.
P. L. 8, 520. on his hill top to l. the bridal lamp
P. L. 9, 105. l. above l. for thee alone as seems
P. L. 9, 173. I reck not, so it l. well aimed
P. L. 9, 192. whenas sacred l. began to dawn
P. L. 9, 305. first on me the assault shall l.
P. L. 9, 386. like a Wood-nymph l.
P. L. 9, 639. and blazing with delusive l.
P. L. 10, 73. judged the worst on me must l.
P. L. 10, 740. as on their natural centre l.
P. L. 10, 934. from thy head removed may l.
P. L. 11,80. in fellowships of joy the Sons of L.
P. L. 11, 134. resalute the world with sacred l.
P. L. 11, 590. all in heat they l. the nuptial
P. L. 11, 767. on me l. at once
P. L. 11, 808. the only son of l. in a dark age
P. L. 11, 858. ground whereon his foot may l.
P. L. 12, 421. ere the third dawning l. return
P. L. 12, 423. fresh as the dawning l.
P. L. 12, 473. l. out of darkness
P. R. 1, 116. deep-vaulted den to dwell in l.
P. R. 4, 228. led by Nature's l.
P. R. 4, 239. pure the air and l.
P. R. 4, 289. L. from above from the fountain of L.
P. R. 4, 352. by l. of Nature
P. R. 4, 400. privation mere of l. and absent day
P. R. 4, 460. ofttimes noxious where they l.
P. R. 4, 597. in the bosom of bliss and l. of l.
S.A.70. l. the prime work of God to me is extinct
S. A. 75. I dark in l. exposed to daily fraud
S. A. 84. let there be l., and l. was over all
S. A. 90. since l. so necessary is to life
S.A.92. that l. is in the soul she all in every part
S. A. 98. then had I not been thus exiled from l.
S. A. 99. as in the land of darkness yet in l.
S. A. 160. shut up from outward l.
S. A. 162. for inward l. alas puts forth no visual
S.A.584. cause l. again within thy eyes to spring
S. A. 591. dark orbs no more shall treat with l.
S. A. 592. nor the other l. of life continue long
C. 144. in a l. fantastic round
C. 199. with everlasting oil to give due l.
C.340. with thy long levelled rule of streaming l.
C. 369. as that the single want of l. and noise
C.374. what Virtue would by her own radiant l.
C. 381. he that has l. within his own clear breast
C. 735. that they below would grow inured to l.
A. 19. in the centre of her l.
L'A. 34. on the l. fantastic toe
L'A. 61. robed in flames and amber l.
Il P. 80. teach l. to counterfeit a gloom
Il P. 160. casting a dim religious l.
S. 9, 10. to fill thy odorous lamp with deeds of l.
S. 19, 1. when I consider how my l. is spent
S. 19, 7. doth God exact day-labour l. denied
S. 20, 9. meant repast shall feast us l. and choice
S. 22, 3. bereft of l. their seeing have forgot
H. 8. that glorious form that l. unsufferable
H. 20. hath took no print of the approaching l.
H. 62. wherein the Prince of L.
H. 73. to fetch all the morning l.
H. 110. a globe of circular l.
P. 6. wintry solstice like the shortened l.
S. M. 28. and sing in endless morn of l.

**M. W. 70.** of blazing Majesty and *L.*
**U. C. I. 16.** and took away the *l.*
**U.C.II.22.**died for heaviness that his cart went *l.*
**Light-armed.**—P. L. 2, 902. *l.-a.* or heavy
P. L. 6, 529. and scouts each coast *l.-a.*
P. R. 3, 311. *l.-a.* troops in coats of mail
**Lighted.**—P. L. 4, 570. where he first *l.*
P. L. 6, 103. then *l.* from his gorgeous throne
P. L. 10, 316. where he first *l.* from his wing
P. L. 11, 209. down from a sky of jasper *l.*
**Lighten.**—P. L. 10, 960. *l.* each other's burden
S. A. 744. to *l.* what thou sufferest and appease
**Lightens.**—P. R. 1, 402. nor *l.* aught
**Lighter.**—P. L. 2, 906. poise their *l.* wings
P. L. 5, 480. so from the root springs *l.*
C. 962. other trippings to be trod of *l.* toes
**Lightest.**—P. L. 10, 45. with *l.* moment
**Lightly.**—P. L. 4, 811. his spear touched *l.*
P. L. 5, 7. Aurora's fan *l.* dispersed
P. R. 2, 282. as *l.* from his grassy couch up rose
**Lightning.**—P. L. 1, 175. winged with red *l.*
P. L. 2, 66. hear infernal thunder and for *l.* see
P. L. 5, 734. *l.* divine, ineffable, serene
P. L. 6, 642. light as the *l.* glimpse they ran
P. L. 6, 849. and every eye glared *l.*
P. L. 10, 184. saw Satan fall like *l.* down
P. L. 10, 1075. tine the slant *l.*
P. L. 12, 229. will himself in thunder, *l.*
P. R. 4, 412. poured fierce rain with *l.* mixed
P. R. 4, 620. like an autumnal star or *l.*
S. A. 1284. winged expedition swift as the *l.*
**Lights.**—P. L. 1, 228. till on dry land he *l.*
P. L. 3, 437. but in his way *l.* on the barren
P. L. 3, 742. stayed till on Niphates top he *l.*
P. L. 4, 183. and sheer within *l.* on his feet
P. L. 4, 763. his golden shafts employs here *l.*
P. L. 4, 815. as when a spark *l.* on a heap
P. L. 5, 276. he *l.* and to his proper shape
P. L. 7, 339. the Almighty spake let there be *L.*
P. L. 7, 343. and let them be for *l.* as I ordain
P. L. 7, 346. and God made two great *L.*
P. L. 7, 382. with thousand lesser *l.* dividual
P. L. 10, 833. on me ... all the blame *l.* due
**Like.**—P. L. 1, 287. on his shoulders *l.* the moon
P. L. 1, 296. not *l.* those steps on Heaven's azure
P. L. 1, 343. *l.* night and darkened all the land
P. L. 1, 351. *l.* which the populous North
P. L. 1, 354. came *l.* a deluge on the South
P. L. 1, 428. *l.* cumbrous flesh
P. L. 1, 453. infected Sion's daughters with *l.*
P. L. 1, 513. his own and Rhea's son *l.* measure
P. L. 1, 527. *l.* doubtful hue, but he, his wonted
P. L. 1, 537. shone *l.* a meteor streaming
P. L. 1, 591. stood *l.* a tower
P. L. 1, 630. how such as stood *l.* these
P. L. 1, 711. rose *l.* an exhalation
P. L. 1, 713. built *l.* a temple where pilasters
P. L. 1, 745. *l.* a falling star
P. L. 1, 763. though *l.* a covered field
P. L. 1, 780. *l.* that Pygmæan race beyond
P. L. 1, 793. and in their own dimensions *l.*
P. L. 2, 349. to be created *l.* to us
P. L. 2, 391. sy nod of gods and *l.* to what ye are
P. L. 2, 708. and *l.* a comet burned
P. L. 2, 721. once more was either *l.* to meet
P. L. 2, 888. and *l.* a furnace mouth
P. L. 2, 1013. springs upward *l.* a pyramid of fire
P. L. 2, 1043. and *l.* a weather-beaten vessel
P. L. 3, 363. the bright pavement that *l.* a sea
P. L. 3, 367. glittering by their side *l.* quivers
P. L. 3, 379. round about thee *l.* a radiant
P. L. 3, 445. up hither *l.* aërial vapours flew
P. L. 3, 568. *l.* those Hesperian gardens famed
P. L. 3, 588. a spot *l.* which perhaps
P. L. 3, 593. not all parts *l.* but all alike
P. L. 3, 600 that stone or *l.* to that which here
P. L. 3, 660. *l.* honour to obtain
P. L. 4, 17. and *l.* a devilish engine back
P. L. 4, 33. *l.* the god of this new world
P. L. 4, 196. sat *l.* a cormorant
P. L. 4, 379. may not please *l.* this fair paradise

P. L. 4, 384. not *l.* these narrow limits
P. L. 4, 448. while thou *l.* consort to thyself
P. L. 4, 474. shalt bear multitudes *l.* thyself
P. L. 4, 612. mind us of *l.* repose
P. L. 4, 715. and oh! too *l.* in sad event
P. L. 4, 800. squat *l.* a toad, close at the ear
P. L. 4, 806. *l.* gentle breaths from rivers pure
P. L. 4, 825. why sat'st thou *l.* an enemy
P. L. 4, 833. your message *l.* to end
P. L. 4, 858. but *l.* a proud steed reined went
P. L. 4, 987. *l.* Teneriff or Atlas unremoved
P. L. 5, 55. one shaped and winged *l.* one of
P. L. 5, 97. nor can I *l.* this
P. L. 5, 241. the fall of others from *l.* state of
P. L. 5, 281. the middle pair girt *l.* a starry
P. L. 5, 285. *l.* Maia's son he stood
P. L. 5, 378. that *l.* Pomona's arbour smiled
P. L. 5, 576. things therein each to other *l.*
P. L. 6, 8. grateful vicissitude *l.* day and night
P. L. 6, 354. in other parts *l.* deeds deserved
P. L. 6, 467. or arm ourselves with *l.* defence
P. L. 6, 505. might devise *l.* instrument to
P. L. 6, 561. ready to receive them if they *l.*
P. L. 6, 573. for *l.* to pillars most they seemed
P. L. 6, 620. thus Belial in *l.* gamesome mood
P. L. 6, 662. the rest in imitation to *l.* arms
P. L. 7, 15. with *l.* safety guided down
P. L. 7, 44. lest the *l.* befall in Paradise to Adam
P. L. 7, 140. thought all *l.* himself rebellious
P. L. 7, 240. then conglobed *l.* things to *l.*
P. L. 7, 329. Earth now seemed *l.* to Heaven
P. L. 7, 414. the deep stretched *l.* a promontory
P. L. 8, 407. for none I know second to me or *l.*
P. L. 8, 418. by conversation with his *l.*
P. L. 8, 424. and beget *l.* of his *l.* his image
P. L. 8, 511. I led her blushing *l.* the Morn
P. L. 8, 553. and *l.* Folly shows
P. L. 9, 99. O Earth how *l.* to Heaven
P. L. 9, 180. *l.* a black mist low creeping
P. L. 9, 315. why shouldst not thou *l.* sense
P. L. 9, 325. endued single with *l.* defence
P. L. 9, 386. and *l.* a Wood-nymph light
P. L. 9, 592. with *l.* desire longing and envying
P. L. 9, 953. undergo *l.* doom if death consort
P. L. 10, 184. saw Satan fall *l.* lightning down
P. L. 10, 241. since no place *l.* this can fit
P. L. 10, 248. things of *l.* kind
P. L. 10, 457. their dark divan and with *l.* joy
P. L. 10, 544. *l.* in punishment as in their crime
P. L. 10, 550. with fair fruit *l.* that which grew
P. L. 10, 561. the fruitage fair to sight *l.* that
P. L. 10, 673. *l.* distant breath
P. L. 10, 693. though slow produced *l.* change
P. L. 10, 841. to Satan only *l.* both crime
P. L. 10, 870. wants but that thy shape *l.* his
P. L. 10, 997. present object languishing with *l.*
P. L. 11, 84. O sons *l.* one of us man is before
P. L. 11, 129. four faces each had *l.* a double
P. L. 11, 535. till *l.* ripe fruit thou drop into
P. L. 11, 742. now the thickened sky *l.* a dark
P. L. 12, 88. he with a crew whom *l.* ambition
P. L. 12, 154. leaves, *l.* him in faith, in wisdom
P. L. 12, 324. the *l.* shall sing all prophecy
P. L. 12, 373. had *l.* grief been dewed in tears
P. L. 12, 434. a death *l.* sleep a gentle wafting
P. L. 12, 445. death *l.* that which the Redeemer
P. R. 1, 105. induces best to hope of *l.* success
P. R. 1, 258. *l.* things of thee to all that present
P. R. 1, 282. Spirit descended on me *l.* a dove
P. R. 1, 452. or *l.* a fawning parasite obey'st
P. R. 2, 143. over-sure of *l.* succeeding here
P. R. 2, 156. more *l.* to goddesses than mortal
P. R. 2, 321. thereafter as I *l.* the giver
P. R. 2, 457. what if with *l.* aversion I reject
P. R. 3, 424. left a race behind *l.* to themselves
P. R. 4, 55. more *l.* houses of gods
P. R. 4, 147. it shall be *l.* a tree spreading
P. R. 4, 462. *l.* turbulencies in the affairs
P. R. 4, 547. far off appearing *l.* a mount
P. R. 4, 619. *l.* an autumnal star or lightning
S. A. 19. that *l.* a deadly swarm of hornets armed

S. A. 150. _l._ whom the Gentiles feign to bear up
S.A.198. who _l._ a foolish pilot have ship wrecked
S. A. 529. fearless of danger _l._ a petty god
S. A. 538. who shore me _l._ a tame wether
S. A. 714. comes this way sailing _l._ a stately ship
S. A. 728. _l._ a fair flower surcharged with dew
S. A. 749. and arts of every woman false _l._ thee
S. A. 776. then with _l._ infirmity to publish them
S. A. 996. leave him to his lot and _l._ my own
S. A. 1016. much _l._ thy riddle, Samson
S. A. 1137. were bristles ranged _l._ those that
S. A. 1188. then _l._ a robber stripp'dst them
S. A. 1403. through their streets _l._ a wild beast
S.A.1497. garrisoned round about him _l._ a camp
S. A. 1699. _l._ that self-begotten bird
S. A. 1710. Samson hath quit himself _l._ Samson
C. 22. that _l._ to rich and various gems inlay
C. 57. much _l._ his father but his mother more
C. 189. _l._ a sad votarist in palmer's weed
C. 303. it were a journey _l._ the path to Heaven
C. 393. but Beauty _l._ the fair Hesperian tree
C.422.and _l._ a quivered nymph with arrows keen
C.483. either some one _l._ us night-foundered here
C. 534. _l._ stabled wolves or tigers at their prey
C. 556. rose _l._ a steam of rich distilled perfumes
C. 595. gathered _l._ scum and settled to itself
C. 634. unknown and _l._ esteemed
C. 655. or _l._ the sons of Vulcan vomit smoke
C. 683. and harshly deal _l._ an ill borrower
C.727.and live _l._ Nature's bastards not her sons
C. 743. if you let slip time, _l._ a neglected rose
C. 753. love-darting eyes or tresses _l._ the morn
A. 16. shooting her beams _l._ silver threads
A. 18. sitting _l._ a goddess bright
L. 106. _l._ to that sanguine flower inscribed with
Il P. 69. _l._ one that had been led astray
Il P. 174. to something _l._ prophetic strain
S. 11, 10. those rugged names to our _l._ mouths
S.11,12. thy age _l._ ours O soul of Sir John Cheek
S.23,2. brought to me _l._ Alcestis from the grave
H.143. orbed in a rainbow and _l._ glories wearing
P. 6. in wintry solstice _l._ the shortened light
M. W. 72. _l._ fortunes may her soul acquaint
U. C. II. 9. _l._ an engine moved with wheel
V.Ex.93. or Trent who _l._ some earth-born giant
M. W. 62. next her much _l._ to thee in story
M. W. 67. and at her next birth much _l._ thee
**Liked.**—P. L. 11, 587. fast caught, they _l._
P. R. 4, 171. I never _l._ thy talk thy offers less
**Likelier.**—P. L. 4, 527. what _l._ can ensue
**Likeliest.**—P. L. 2, 525. where he may _l._ find
P. L. 3, 659. and here art _l._ by supreme decree
P. L. 6, 688. as _l._ was when two such foes met
P. L. 9, 414. on his quest where _l._ he might
P. R. 1, 121. he might _l._ find this new-declared
P. R. 3, 130. would _l._ render contempt
C. 90. and in this office of his mountain watch _l._
C. 192. 'tis _l._ they had engaged
**Likely.**—P.L.3,460. more _l._ habitants translated
P. L. 4, 872. nor _l._ to part hence
P. L. 9, 935. as _l._ tasting to attain proportional
P. L. 9, 365. and most _l._ if from me thou sever
**Liken.**—P. L. 6, 299. or to what things _l._
**Likeness.**—P. L. 2, 673. _l._ of a kingly crown
P. L. 4, 813. returns of force to its own _l._
P. L. 8, 450. thy _l._ thy fit help thy other self
P. L. 10, 327. Satan in _l._ of an Angel bright
P. L. 11, 521. disfiguring not God's _l._ but their
P. L. 11, 522. or if his _l._ by themselves defaced
P. R. 1, 30. in _l._ of a dove the Spirit descended
C. 84. and take the weeds and _l._ of a swain
C. 528. and the inglorious _l._ of a beast
**Likening.**—P. L. 1, 486. _l._ his Maker to the
P. L. 5, 573. by _l._ spiritual to corporal forms
**Likes.**—P. L. 4, 738. which God _l._ best
P. L. 6, 353. or size assume as _l._ them best
P. L. 6, 717. there let them learn as _l_ them
P. R. 2, 382. when and where _l._ me best
**Likest.**—P. L. 2, 756. _l._ to thee in shape
P. L. 3, 572. the golden sun in splendour _l._
P. L. 6, 301. for _l._ gods they seemed

P. L. 9. 394. thus adorned _l._ she seemèd
P. R. 2,237. a chosen band of spirits _l._ to himself
P. R. 4, 281. these here revolve or as thou _l._
C. 237. that _l._ thy Narcissus are
Il P. 9. or _l._ hovering dreams
**Likewise.**—D. F. I. 11. if _l._ he some fair one
**Liking.**—P. L. 11, 587. and each his _l._ chose
**Lilied.**—A. 97. by sandy Ladon's _l._ banks
**Lilies.**—C. 862. in twisted braids of _l._ knitting
**Lily.**—S.20,8. clothe in fresh attire the _l._ and rose
**Limb.**—P. L. 1, 426. manacled with joint or _l._
P.L.2,668. distinguishable in member joint or _l._
P. L. 3, 638. and to every _l._ suitable grace
P. L. 6, 352. as they please they _l._ themselves
P. L. 8, 267. myself I then perused and _l._ by _l._
P. L. 8, 625. find none of membrane joint or _l._
P. L. 9, 484. and of _l._ heroic built
S. A. 1089. and each _l._ to survey
**Limbec.**—P. L. 3, 605. drained through a _l._
**Limbed.**—P. L. 7, 456. _l._ and full-grown
**Limber.**—P. L. 7,476. those waved their _l._ fans
**Limbo.**—P. L. 3, 495. into a L. large and broad
**Limbs.**—P. L. 4, 772. and on their naked _l._
P. L. 10, 1069. better warmth to cherish our _l._
S. A. 571. and sedentary numbness craze my _l._
S. A. 614. as on entrails joints and _l._
_C._ 680. and to those dainty _l._ which Nature lent
**Lime-twigs.**—C. 646. the very _l.-t._ of his spells
**Limit.**—P. L. 6, 140. reaching beyond all _l._
P. L. 12, 115. Jordan true _l._ eastward
M. W. 14. in giving _l._ to her life
**Limitary.**—P. L. 4, 971. proud _l._ Cherub
**Limited.**—P. L. 6, 229. and _l._ their might
**Limits.**—P. L. 4, 384. not like these narrow _l._
P. L. 4, 964. within these h allowed _l._
P. L. 5, 755. at length into the _l._ of the north
C. 316. or shroud within these _l._ I shall know
H. 169. in straiter _l._ bound not half so far
**Line.**—P. L. 4, 210. Eden stretched her _l._
P. L. 4, 282. the Ethiop _l._ by Nilus' head
P. L. 7, 480. as a _l._ their long dimension drew
P. L. 8. 102. and his _l._ stretched out so far
P. L. 9, 64. thrice the equinoctial _l._ he circled
C. 923. sprung of old Anchises' _l._
Il P. 99. presenting Thebes or Pelops' _l._
**Lineaments.**—P. L. 5, 278. his _l._ divine
P. L. 7, 477. smallest _l._ exact in all the liveries
P. R. 1, 92. for Man he seems in all his _l._
**Lines.**—S.13,11. tunest their happiest _l._ in hymn
W. S. 12. those Delphic _l._ with deep impression
**Linger.**—S. A. 466. will not connive or _l._ thus
**Lingering.**—P. L. 2, 56. sit _l._ here
P. L. 2, 702. a whip of scorpions I pursue thy _l._
P. L. 12, 638. hastening Angel caught our _l._
S. A. 618. pain me as a _l._ disease
C. 472. _l._ and sitting by a new-made grave
**Lingerest.**—P. R. 3, 227. perhaps thou _l._
**Lining.**—C. 222. her silver _l._ on the night
**Link.**—P. L. 9, 914. no, no! I feel the _l._
**Linked.**—P. L. 1, 328. so with _l._ thunderbolts
P. L. 2, 1005. hung o'er my realm _l._
P. L. 4, 339. fair couple _l._ in happy nuptial
P. L. 9, 133. soon follow as to him _l._ in woal
P. L. 9, 970. shall separate us _l._ in love so dear
P. L. 10, 905. already _l._ and wedlock-bound
P. L. 11, 139. joy but with fear yet _l._
C. 474. and _l._ itself by carnal sensualty
L'A. 140. of _l._ sweetness long drawn out
S. 1, 8. have _l._ that amorous power to thy soft
U. C. II. 31. _l._ to the mutual flowing of the seas
**Links.**—S. A. 1410. doff these _l._
**Lion.**—P. L. 4, 343. sporting the _l._ ramped
P. L. 4, 402. about them round a _l._ now
P. L. 7, 464. the tawny _l._ pawing to get free
P. L.8,393. each with their kind, _l._ with lioness
P. R. 1, 313. the _l._ and fierce tiger glared aloof
S. A. 128. who tore the _l._ as the _l._ tears the kid
S.A.139. the bold Ascalonite fled from his _l._ ramp
**Lioness.**—P. L. 8, 393. lion with _l._
C. 443. wherewith she tamed the brinded _l._
**Lip.**—P. L. 2, 614. once it fled the _l._ of Tantalus

P. L. 4, 501. pressed her matron *l.* with kisses
P. L. 8, 56. from his *l.* not words alone
C. 752.what need a vermeil-tinctured *l.* for that
C. 915. thrice upon thy rubied *l.*
**Lips.**—P. L. 5, 150. flowed from their *l.* in prose
P. L. 5, 675. so late hath passed the *l.*
P. L. 8, 218. nor are thy *l.* ungraceful
P. L. 9, 1144. what words have passed thy *l.*
C. 290. as smooth as Hebe's their unrazored *l.*
C.756.I had not thought to have unlocked my *l.*
V. Ex. 4. slide through my infant *l.*
**Liquid.**—P. L. 1, 229. as the lake with *l.* fire
P. L. 1, 701. underneath had veins of *l.* fire
P. L. 3, 519. of jasper or of *l.* pearl
P. L. 4, 455. and spread into a *l.* plain
P. L. 5, 25.sits on the bloom extracting *l.* sweet
P. L. 6, 348. nor in their *l.* texture
P. L. 7, 68. whose *l.* murmur heard
P. L. 7, 264. the firmament expanse of *l.* pure
P. L. 7, 362. to receive and drink the *l.* light
P. L. 8,263. and *l.* lapse of murmuring streams
P. L. 11, 500. *l.* ore he drained into fit moulds
S. A. 557. whose drink was only from the *l.*
C. 980. there I suck the *l.* air
S. 1, 5. thy *l.* notes that close the eye of day
**Liquor.**—S. A. 552. heads that turbulent *l.* fills
S. A. 627. or med'cinal *l.* can assuage
C. 65. his orient *l.* in a crystal glass
C. 652. and shed the luscious *l.*
**Liquorish.**—C. 700. *l.* baits
**Liquors.**—P.L. 5,445. with pleasant *l.* crowned
C. 847. with precious vialed *l.* heals
**List.**—P. L. 2,656. yet when they *l.* would creep
P. L. 2, 798. for when they *l.* into the womb
P. L. 4, 803. with them forge illusions as he *l.*
P. L. 8, 75. or if they *l.* to try conjecture
S. A. 647. nor am I in the *l.* of them that hope
C. 480. *l.*! *l.*! I hear some far-off halloa break
C. 737. *l.*, lady be not coy and be not cozened
C. 997. *l.*, mortals, if your ears be true
L. 123. and when they *l.* their lean and flashy
**Listed.**—P. L. 11, 866. three *l.* colours gay
S. A. 1087. in camp or *l.* field
C.49.coasting the Tyrrhene shore,as the winds *l.*
**Listen.**—P. L. 6, 908. but *l.* not to his
C. 43. and *l.* why, for I will tell you now
C. 860. Sabrina fair, *l.* where thou art sitting
C. 864. *l.* for dear honour's sake
C. 866. *l.* and save, *l.* and appear to us
A. 62. then *l.* I to the celestial Sirens' harmony
**Listened.**—C. 551. at which I ceased and *l.*
**Listening.**—P. L. 7, 106. Sleep *l.* to thee
P. L. 7,563. the planets in their station *l.* stood
P. L. 10, 342. and *l.* where the hapless pair sat
C. 203. was rife and perfect in my *l.* ear
L'A. 53. oft *l.* how the hounds and horn
Cir. 5. through the soft silence of the *l.* night
V. Ex. 37. *l.* to what unshorn Apollo sings
**Listens.**—P. L. 5, 627. God's own ear *l.*
L. 89. and *l.* to the herald of the sea
**Lists.**—P. R. 4,306. which when he *l.* he leaves
S. A. 463. me overthrown to enter *l.* with God
**Lithe.**—P. L. 4, 347. wreathed his *l.* proboscis
**Litter.**—C. 554. draw the *l.* of close-curtained
**Little.**—P. L. 2, 1000. serve that *l.* which is
P. L. 4, 86. ay me they *l.* know how dearly
P. L. 4, 201. so *l.* knows any but God alone
P. L. 4,362. to heavenly Spirits bright *l.* inferior
P. L. 4, 366. gentle pair, *ye l.* think how nigh
P. L. 9, 224. our day's work brought to *l.*
P. L. 10, 320. now in *l.* space the confines met
P. L. 10, 468. to our native Heaven *l.* inferior
P. L. 10, 600. though plenteous all too *l.* seems
P. L. 10, 968. *l.* weight my words with thee
P. R. 2, 82. *l.* suspicious to any king
P. R. 4, 6. and won so much on Eve so *l.* here
P. R. 4, 291. but these are false or *l.* else
S. A. 1. a *l.* onward lend thy guiding hand
S. A. 2. a *l.* further on
S. A. 661. in his pangs their sound *l.* prevails
S.A.1126.that in a *l.* time while breath remains

S.A.1536.a *l.*stay will bring some notice hither
S.A.1599.*l.* I had despatched when all abroad
C. 27. and wield their *l.* tridents
C. 348. some solace yet, some *l.* cheering
C. 611. but here thy sword can do thee *l.*stead
C. 642. I pursed it up, but *l.* reckoning made
L. 116. of other care they *l.* reckoning make
L. 152. for so to interpose a *l.* ease
V.Ex. 10. I know my tongue but *l.* grace can do
H. 88. full *l.* thought they then
Il P. 3. how *l.* you bested
T. 7. so *l.* is our loss, so *l.* is thy gain
**Liturgy.**—F. of C.2. with vows renounced his *l.*
**Live.**—P. L. 2, 194. shall we then *l.* thus vile
P. L. 2, 254. and from our own *l.* to ourselves
P. L. 2, 318. to *l.* exempt from Heaven's high
P. L. 2, 500. yet *l.* in hatred enmity and strife
P. L. 2, 868. among the gods who *l.* at ease
P. L. 3, 244. by thee I *l.*, though now to Death
P. L. 3, 293. and *l.* in thee transplanted
P. L. 4, 533. *l.* while ye may, yet happy pair
P. L. 5, 81. the gods *l.* there, and such *l.* thou
P. L. 5, 474. in things that *l.*
P. L. 5, 795. monarchy over such as *l.* by right
P. L. 6, 344. for Spirits that *l.* throughout
P. L. 6, 350. all heart they *l.* all head, all eye
P. L. 6, 461. but *l.* content which is the calmest
P. L. 8, 152. each orb perhaps with some that *l.*
P. L. 8, 176. what creatures there *l.*
P. L. 8, 182. taught to *l.* the easiest way
P. L. 8, 276. and ye that *l.* and move
P. L. 8, 281. that thus I move and *l.*
P. L. 8, 340. that therein *l.*, or *l.* in sea or air
P. L. 8, 633. be strong, *l.* happy, and love
P. L. 9, 653. the rest we *l.* law to ourselves
P. L. 9, 688. yet both *l.*, and life more perfect
P. L. 9, 829. shall *l.* with her enjoying
P. L. 9, 833. without him *l.* no life
P. L. 9, 908. how can I *l.* without thee
P. L. 9, 910. to *l.* again in these wild woods
P. L. 9, 933. lives as thou saidst and gains to *l.*
P. L. 9, 1085. Oh might I here in solitude *l.*
P. L. 10, 269. from all things there that *l.*
P. L. 10, 919. bereave me not whereon I *l.*
P. L. 10, 924. while yet we *l.* scarce one short
P. L. 10, 1028. to make death in us *l.*
P. L. 11, 38. let him *l.* before thee reconciled
P. L. 11, 95. and *l.* for ever, dream at least to *l.*
P. L. 11, 161. man is to *l.* and all things *l.*
P. L. 11, 180. here let us *l.* though in fallen
P. L. 11, 535. so may'st thou *l.* till like ripe
P. L. 11, 554. but what thou livest, *l.* well
P. L. 11, 629. shame that they who to *l.* well
P. L. 11, 802. shall practise how to *l.* secure
P. L. 11, 872. assured that man shall *l.*
P. L. 12, 299. and not performing cannot *l.*
P. L. 12, 351. in mean estate *l.* moderate
P. L. 12, 411. for this he shall *l.* hated
P. L. 12, 602. thou may *l.*
P. R. 1, 287. that I no more should *l.* obscure
P. R. 1, 339. for we here *l.* on tough roots
P. R. 3, 55. to *l.* upon their tongues
S. A. 79.scarce half I seem to *l.* dead more than
S. A. 100. to *l.* a life half dead a living death
S. A. 945. when I must *l.* uxorious to thy will
S. A. 1479. to *l.* the poorest in my tribe
C. 3. of bright aerial spirits *l.* insphered
C. 300. that in the colours of the rainbow *l.*
C. 727. and *l.* like nature's bastards not her sons
C. 766. that *l.* according to her sober laws
A. 45. and *l.* in oaken bower
A. 103. bring your flocks and *l.* with us
L. 72. to scorn delights and *l.* laborious days
L'A. 30. and live to *l.* in dimple sleek
L'A. 39. to *l.* with her and *l.* with thee
L'A. 152. mirth with thee I mean to *l.*
Il P. 176. and I with thee will choose to *l.*
H. 90. was kindly come to *l.* with them below
S. M. 28. to *l.* with him and sing in endless morn
D. F. I. 77. shall make thy name to *l.*

V. Ex. 77. that cannot *l.* from him asunder
V. Ex. 85. yet shall he *l.* in strife
**Lived.**—P. L. 4, 198. death to them who *l.*
P. L. 7, 204. for within them Spirit *l.*
P. L. 8, 264. creatures that *l.* and moved
P. L. 8, 295. to believe I· yet had being and *l.*
P. L. 9, 1166. might have *l.* and joyed
P. L. 11, 764. better had I *l.* ignorant of future
P. L. 12, 117. yet the patriarch *l.* who scaped
P. R. 2, 201. for Solomon he *l.* at ease
P. R. 3, 41. that he had *l.* so long inglorious
S. A. 264. they only *l.* who fled
S.10, 3. who *l.* in both unstained with gold or fee
**Livelier.**—P. L. 11, 242. *l.* than Melibœan
S. A. 1442. much *l.* than erewhile he seems
**Liveliest.**—P. L. 1, 274. their *l.* pledge of hope
**Livelong.**—L'A. 99. till the *l.* daylight fail
W. S. 8. hast built thyself a *l.* monument
**Lively.**—P. L. 4, 1. so *l.* shines in them divine
P. L. 8, 269. with supple joints as *l.*
P. L. 8, 311. the dream had *l.* shadowed
C. 670. when the fresh blood grows *l.* and returns
L'A. 49. while the cock with *l.* din
Il P. 149. of *l.* portraiture displayed
P. 47. my plaining verse as *l.* as before
**Liver.**—P. L. 6, 346. heart or head, *l.* or reins
**Liveried.**—C. 455. a thousand *l.* angels lackey
**Liveries.**—P. L. 7, 478. in all the *l.* decked
L'A. 62. the clouds in thousand *l.* dight
**Livery.**—P. L. 4, 599. had in her sober *l.* all
S. A. 1616. in their state *l.* clad
**Lives.**—P. L. 2, 624. where all life dies death *l.*
P. L. 3, 477. seek in Golgotha him dead who *l.*
P. L. 4, 888. *l.* there who loves his pain ?
P. L. 9, 764. he hath eaten and *l.* and knows
P. L. 9, 932. he yet *l.*, *l.* as thou saidst
P. L. 11, 337. sea and air and every kind that *l.*
P. L. 11, 621. whose *l.* religious titled them
P. L. 12, 17. shall lead their *l.* and multiply
P. R. 1, 349. man *l.* not by bread only
P. R. 3, 98. suffering death unjust *l.* now
P. R. 3, 410. *l.* of threescore and ten thousand
S. A. 1707. a secular bird ages of *l.*
L. 81. but *l.* and spreads aloft by those pure eyes
**Livest.**—P. L. 11, 553. but what thou *l.*
C. 230. Echo sweetest Nymph that *l.* unseen
**Livid.**—P. L. 1, 182. *l.* flames
**Living.**—P. L. 1, 439. forsook their *l.* strength
P. L. 2, 613. the water flies all taste of *l.* wight
P. L. 2, 855. to be o'ermatched by *l.* might
P. L. 2, 1050. battlements adorned of *l.* sapphire
P. L. 3, 327. from all winds the *l.*
P. L. 3, 443. *l.* or lifeless to be found was none
P. L. 4, 287. of *l.* creatures new to sight
P. L. 4, 605. now glowed the firmament with *l.*
P. L. 5, 197. join voices all ye *l.* Souls
P. L. 5, 652. their camp extend by *l.* streams
P. L. 6, 846. and from the *l.* wheels distinct
P. L. 7, 388. reptile with spawn abundant *l.* soul
P. L. 7, 392. and each soul *l.*, each that crept
P. L. 7, 413. leviathan hugest of *l.* creatures
P. L. 7, 451. let the earth bring forth soul *l.*
P. L. 7, 455. innumerous *l.* creatures
P. L. 7, 528. and thou becamest a *l.* soul
P. L. 7, 534. and every *l.* thing that moves
P. L. 7, 566. open ye heavens your *l.* doors
P. L. 8, 154. unpossessed by *l.* soul
P. L. 8, 370. with various *l.* creatures
P. L. 9, 228. above all *l.* creatures dear
P. L. 9, 539. thee all things *l.* gaze on
P. L. 10, 277. lured with scent of *l.* carcases
P. L. 10, 788. who knows but I shall die a *l.*
P. L. 10, 974. *l.* or dying from thee I will not hide
P. L. 14, 160. mother of all things *l.*
P. L. 12, 118. to forsake the *l.* God and fall
P. L. 12, 527. *l.* temples built by faith to stand
P. R. 1, 460. God hath now sent his *l.* Oracle
S. A. 100. to live a life half dead, a *l.* death
S. A. 984. *l.* and dead recorded
S.A.1140. my trust is in the *l.* God who gave me
S. A. 1661. *l.* or dying thou hast fulfilled

S. A. 1673. our *L.* Dread who dwells in Silo
S. 10, 11. madam, methinks I see him *l.* yet
M. W. 34. was not long a *l.* tomb
**Lo.**—P. L. 3, 486. when *l.* a violent cross wind
P. L. 10, 1050. when *l.* to thee pains only
P. L. 11, 733. when *l.* a wonder strange
**Load.**—P. L. 4, 972. far heavier *l.* thyself
P. L. 5, 59. deigns none to ease thy *l.* and taste
P. L. 6, 644. the seated hills with all their *l.*
P. R. 1, 402. each man's peculiar *l.*
S. A. 214. who hast of sorrow thy full *l.* besides
S. 14, 3. this earthly *l.* of death called life
U. C. II. 24. lack of *l.* made his life burdensome
**Loaded.**—S. A. 149. of a sabbath-day and *l.* so
**Loaden.**—P. L. 4, 147. trees *l.* with fairest
P. L. 8, 307. each tree *l.* with fairest fruit
P. L. 9, 577. *l.* with fruit of fairest colours
P. R. 4, 418. *l.* with stormy blasts
S. A. 1243. lament these braveries in irons *l.* on
**Loads.**—S. 21, 13. superfluous burden *l.* the day
**Loathed.**—P. L. 12, 178. with *l.* intrusion
L'A. 1. hence *l.* Melancholy
**Loathsome.**—P. L. 3, 247. in the *l.* grave
P. L. 11, 524. healthful rules to *l.* sickness
S. A. 480. lie in this miserable *l.* plight
S. A. 922. this *l.* prison-house
**Local.**—P. L. 12, 387. *l.* wounds of head or heel
**Lock.**—P. L. 45. though grief my feeble hands up *l.*
**Locked.**—A. 62. when drowsiness hath *l.* up
**Locks.**—P. L. 3, 361. bind their resplendent *l.*
P. L. 3, 626. nor less his *l.* behind illustrious
P. L. 4, 301. and hyacinthine *l.*
P. L. 5, 56. his dewy *l.* distilled ambrosia
P. L. 10, 559. than the snaky *l.* that curled
P. L. 10, 1066. shattering the graceful *l.*
S. A. 327. *l.* white as down
S. A. 568. redundant *l.* robustious to no purpose
S. A. 587. miraculous yet remaining in those *l.*
S. A. 1143. while I preserved these *l.* unshorn
S. A. 1164. with those thy boisterous *l.*
S. A. 1493. on his shoulders waving those *l.*
C. 54. Nymph that gazed upon his clustering *l.*
C. 105. braid your *l.* with rosy twine
C. 882. sleeking her soft alluring *l.*
L. 112. he shook his mitred *l.* and stern bespake
L. 175. with nectar pure his oozy *l.* he laves
L'A. 9. as rugged as thy *l.*
**Locrine.**—C. 827. she was the daughter of *L.*
C. 922. virgin daughter of *L.*
**Locusts.**—P. L. 1, 341. a pitchy cloud of *l.*
P. L. 12, 185. a darksome cloud of *l.* swarming
**Lodge.**—P. L. 4, 720. thus at their shady *l.*
P. L. 4, 790. where those two fair creatures *l.*
P. L. 5, 377. so to the sylvan *l.* they came
P. L. 6, 7. in perpetual round *l.* and dislodge
C. 188. here to *l.* under the spreading favour
C. 346. or whistle from the *l.*
U. C. 1. 15. his room where he must *l.*
**Lodged.**—P. L. 6, 531. where *l.* or whither
P. L. 7, 201. between two brazen mountains *l.*
P. L. 8, 105. *l.* in a small partition
P. L. 11, 823. for life shall in the ark be *l.*
P.R.1,184. *l.* in Bethabara where John baptized
P. R. 1, 301. things past and to come *l.* in his
P. R. 2, 6. with him talked and with him *l.*
S. A. 48. in what part *l.* how easily bereft me
C. 315. and if your stray attendance be yet *l.*
S. 19. *l.* with me useless though my soul more
**Lodges.**—C. 246. sure something holy *l.* in that
**Loftiest.**—P. L. 1, 499. above their *l.* towers
P. L. 4, 138. insuperable height of *l.* shade
**Lofts.**—V. Ex. 42. and *l.* of piled thunder
**Lofty.**—P. L. 3, 734. those *l.* shades his bower
P. L. 4, 395. then from his *l.* stand on that
P. L. 11, 640. cities of men with *l.* gates
P. R. 4, 261. thence what the *l.* grave
C. 934. may thy *l.* head be crowned
L. 11. himself to sing and build the *l.* rhyme
**Logres.**—P. R. 2, 360. knights of *L.* of Lyones
**Loins.**—P. L. 1, 352. from her frozen *l.*
P. L. 5, 282. skirted his *l.* and thighs

P. L. 9, 1096. girded on our *l.* may cover
P. L. 10, 983. of our *l.* to bring into this world
P. L. 11, 455. to come out of thy *l.*
P. L. 12, 380. yet from my *l.* thou shalt proceed
P. L. 12, 447. only to the sons of Abraham's *l.*
C. 718. in her own *l.* she hutched the
**Loneliness.**—C.404. of night or *l.* it recks me not
**Lonely.**—P. L. 2, 828. expose with *l.* steps
P. L. 1, 290. thy going is not *l.* with thee goes
C. 200. to the misled and *l.* traveller
Il P. 86. be seen in some high *l.* tower
H. 181. the *l.* mountains o'er
**Long.**—P. L. 1, 80. *l.* after known in Palestine
P. L. 1, 195. extended *l.* and large
P. L. 1, 383. *l.* after next the seat of God
P. L. 1, 507. the rest were *l.* to tell
P. L. 1, 651. that he ere *l.* intended to create
P. L. 1, 659. the Abyss *l.* under darkness cover
P. L. 1, 748. this rebellious rout fell *l.* before
P. L. 2, 286. blustering winds which all night *l.*
P. L. 2, 297. by policy and *l.* process of time
P. L. 2, 390. well have ye judged well ended *l.*
P. L. 2, 432. *l.* is the way and hard
P. L. 2, 778. but *l.* I sat not
P. L. 3, 14. though *l.* detained in that obscure
P. L. 3, 198. this my *l.* sufferance and my day
P. L. 3, 242. I shall not *l.* lie vanquished
P. L. 3, 261. shall enter Heaven *l.* absent
P. L. 3, 336. after all their tribulations *l.*
P. L. 3, 378. thus *l.* from Israel serving as of
P. L. 3, 473. and many more too *l.*
P. L. 3, 497. to few unknown *l.* after
P. L. 3, 499. and *l.* he wandered
P. L. 3, 601. philosophers in vain so *l.* have
P. L. 4, 113. as man ere *l.* and this new world
P. L. 4, 371. ill secured *l.* to continue
P. L. 4, 535. for *l.* woes are to succeed
P. L. 4, 603. she all night *l.* her amorous descant
P. L. 4, 616. other creatures all day *l.* rove idle
P. L. 4, 657. wherefore all night *l.* shine these?
P. L. 5, 113. ill matching words and deeds *l.* past
P. L. 5, 355. when their rich retinue *l.* of horses
P. L. 5, 657. sovran throne alternate all night *l.*
P. L. 5, 762. not *l.* after he affecting all
P. L. 5, 904. *l.* way through hostile scorn
P. L. 6, 245. *l.* time in even scale the battle
P. L. 6, 331. ethereal substance closed not *l.*
P. L. 6, 484. into hollow engines *l.* and round
P. L. 6, 492. nor *l.* shall be our labour
P. L. 6, 538. will save us *l.* pursuit
P. L. 6, 582. not *l.* for sudden all at once
P. L. 6, 634. but they stood not *l.*
P. L. 6, 659. *l.* struggling underneath
P. L. 7, 159. under *l.* obedience tried
P. L. 7, 328. with borders *l.* the rivers
P. L. 7, 480. these as a line their *l.* dimension
P. L. 8, 242. but *l.* ere our approaching heard
P. L. 8, 454. which it had *l.* stood under
P. L. 9, 18. that so *l.* perplexed the Greek
P. L. 9, 26. *l.* choosing and beginning late
P. L. 9, 30. with *l.* and tedious havoc
P. L. 9, 87. him after *l.* debate irresolute
P. L. 9, 138. and who knows how *l.* before had
P. L. 9, 172. bitter ere *l.* back on itself recoils
P. L. 9, 246. till younger hands ere *l.* assist us
P. L. 9, 397. her *l.* with ardent look his eye
P. L. 9, 445. as one who *l.* in populous city
P. L. 9, 598. sated at length ere *l.* I might
P. L. 9, 601. speech wanted not *l.*
P. L. 9, 626. the way is ready and not *l.*
P. L. 9, 747. whose taste too *l.* forborne
P. L. 9, 844. solace in her return so *l.* delayed
P. L. 9, 857. and thought it *l.* deprived
P. L. 9, 949. who can please him *l.*?
P. L. 9, 1064. *l.* they sat as strucken mute
P. L. 9, 1104. arms branching so broad and *l.*
P. L. 10, 115. whence Adam faltering *l.* thus
P. L. 10, 189. realm itself of Satan *l.* usurped
P. L. 10, 323. Hell with *l.* reach interposed
P. L. 10, 352. *l.* he admiring stood till Sin
P. L. 10, 469. *l.* were to tell what I have done

P. L. 10, 482. fame in Heaven *l.* had foretold
P. L. 10, 509. wondered but not *l.* had leisure
P. L. 10, 573. *l.* and ceaseless hiss
P. L. 10, 964. a *l.* day's dying
P. L. 11, 198. how *l.* and what till then our life
P. L. 11, 494. what heart of rock could *l.*
P. L. 11, 554. live well how *l.* or short permit
P. L. 11, 581. they on the plain *l.* had not
P. L. 11, 626. in joy ere *l.* to swim at large
P. L. 11, 627. the world ere *l.* a world of tears
P. L. 12, 23. and dwell *l.* time in peace
P. L. 12, 146. Senir that *l.* ridge of hills
P. L. 12, 261. the rest were *l.* to tell
P. L. 12, 316. *l.* time shall dwell and prosper
P. L. 12, 331. first a *l.* succession must ensue
P. L. 12, 421. Death over him no power shall *l.*
P. R. 1, 17. worthy to have not remained so *l.*
P. R. 1, 28. nor was *l.* his witness unconfirmed
P. R. 1, 55. *l.* the decrees of Heaven delay
P. R. 1, 95. which admits no *l.* debate
P. R. 1, 110. for *l.* indulgence to their fears
P. R. 1, 125. to end his reign on Earth so *l.*
P.R.2,15. Moses was in the mount and missing *l.*
P. R. 2, 32. so *l.* expected
P. R. 2, 101. thus *l.* to some great purpose
P. R. 2, 103. heart hath been a storehouse *l.*
P. R. 2, 189. many more too *l.*
P. R. 2, 304. in this wild solitude so *l.* should
P. R. 3, 41. wept that he had lived so *l.*
P. R. 3, 279. whose success Israel in *l.* captivity
P. R. 3, 360. how couldst thou hope *l.* to enjoy
P. R. 3, 389. instrument of war *l.* in preparing
P. R. 4, 27. *l.* but in breadth not wide
P. R. 4, 84. and *l.* renown thou justly mayst
P. R. 4, 107. will be for thee no sitting or not *l.*
P. R. 4, 246. thick-warbled notes the summer *l.*
P. R. 4, 298. virtue joined with riches and *l.* life
P. R. 4, 604. him *l.* of old thou didst debel
P. R. 4, 618. thou Infernal Serpent shall not *l.*
S. A. 171. whom *l.* descent of birth
S. A. 468. shall ere *l.* receive such a discomfit
S. A. 474. will not *l.* defer
S. A. 476. nor will *l.* endure it doubtful
S. A. 592. nor the other light of life continue *l.*
S. A. 650. might I be heard no *l.* petition
S. A. 863. only my love of thee held *l.* debate
S.A.1012. that woman's love can win or *l.* inherit
S.A.1033. that either they love nothing or not *l.*
S. A. 1125. which *l.* shall not withhold me from
S. A. 1242. by Astaroth ere *l.* thou shalt lament
S. A. 1269. to the spirits of just men *l.* oppressed
S.A.1554. preface needs thou seest we *l.* to know
C. 151. I shall ere *l.* be well stocked with as fair
C. 183. wearied out with this *l.* way
C. 562. but oh, ere *l.* too well I did perceive
C. 1006. after her wandering labours *l.*
L. 35. would not be absent *l.*
L'A. 140. of linked sweetness *l.* drawn out
Il P. 23. thee bright-haired Vesta *l.* of yore
S.13,4. with Midas' ears committing short and *l.*
H.111. that with *l.* beams the shamefaced Night
H. 134. enwrap our fancy *l.*
P. 7. in dark and *l.* out-living night
D. F. I. 17. he wandered *l.* till thee he spied
T. 11. then *l.* Eternity shall greet our bliss
M. M. 34. was not *l.* a living tomb
M. W. 10. and welcome thee and wish thee *l.*
V. Ex. 71. and in Time's *l.* and dark prospective
P.10. which on our dearest Lord did seize ere *l.*
Cir. 26. but O! ere *l.* huge pangs
S.M. 26. keep in tune with heaven till God ere *l.*
U. C. I. 11. but lately finding him so *l.* at home
U.C.11. 14. too *l.* vacation hastened on his term
**Longer.**—P. L. 3, 561. and without *l.* pause
P. L. 5, 63. none shall from me withhold *l.*
P. L. 7, 101. and *l.* will delay to hear thee tell
P. L. 8, 252. desire with thee still *l.* to converse
P. L. 9, 140. not *l.* than since I in one night
P. L. 10, 365. hell could no *l.* hold us in
P. L. 10, 1003. why stand we *l.* shivering
P. L. 11, 48. but *l.* in that Paradise to dwell

P

P. L. 11, 91. my motions in him *l.* than they
P. L. 11, 259. but *l.* in this Paradise to dwell
P. L. 12, 336. part good part bad of bad the *l.*
P. L. 12, 437. *l.* on earth than certain times
P. L. 12, 594. we may no *l.* stay go waken Eve
P. R. 2, 421. *l.* than thou canst feed them
C. 577. *l.* I durst not stay but soon I guessed
H. 225. nor all the gods beside *l.* dare abide
**Longest.**—P. R. 1, 56. *l.* time to him is short
**Longing.**—P. L. 2, 55. *l.* wait the signal
P. L. 4, 511. still unfulfilled with pain of *l.*
P. L. 9, 593. with like desire *l.* and envying
P. L. 9, 743. solicited her *l.* eye
P. L. 10, 877. *l.* to be seen though by the Devil
**Longitude.**—P. L. 3, 576. or *l.*
P. L. 4, 539. meanwhile in utmost *l.*
P. L. 5, 754. entire globose stretched into *l.*
P. L. 7, 373. his *l.* through heaven's high road
**Long-levelled.**—C. 340. with thy *l.-l.* rule
**Long-threatened.**—P. R. 1, 59. *l.-t.* wound
**Long-uncoupled.**—D. F. I. 13. of *l.-u.* bed
**Long-wandered.**—P. L. 12, 313. *l.-w.* man
**Look.**—P. L. 2, 106. his *l.* denounced desperate
P. L. 2, 307. his *l.* drew audience and attention
P. L. 2, 418. expectation held his *l.* suspense
P. L. 2, 680. and with disdainful *l.* thus first
P. L. 3, 257. out of heaven shalt *l.* down
P. L. 3, 722. *l.* downward on that globe
P. L. 4, 28. his grieved *l.* he fixes sad
P. L. 4, 458. to *l.* into the clear smooth lake
P. L. 4, 460. as I bent down to *l.* just opposite
P. L. 4, 462. bending to *l.* on me I started back
P. L. 4, 873. stand firm for in his *l.* defiance
P. L. 4, 1010. for proof *l.* up and read thy lot
P. L. 5, 800. to be our Lord and *l.* for adoration
P. L. 6, 469. whereto with *l.* composed Satan
P. L. 9, 397. her long with ardent *l.* his eye
P. L. 9, 454. she most and in her *l.* sums all
P. L. 9, 687. by the Threatener? *l.* on me
P. L. 9, 1132. Adam estranged in *l.* and altered
P. L. 10, 296. his *l.* bound with Gorgonian rigour
P. L. 10, 1094. in whose *l.* serene
P. L. 11, 897. triple-coloured bow whereon to *l.*
P. R. 2, 216. one *l.* from his majestic brow
P. R. 4, 236. *l.* once more ere we leave this
S. A. 97. she might *l.* at will through every pore
S. A. 197. how could I once *l.* up or heave the head
S. A. 1065. *l.* now for no enchanting voice
S. A. 1068. his *l.* haughty as is his pile high-built
S. A. 1304. comes on amain speed in his *l.*
C. 871. by hoary Nereus' wrinkled *l.*
C. 910. brightest lady, *l.* on me
A. 1. nymphs and shepherds, *l.*
L. 125. the hungry sheep *l.* up and are not fed
L. 163. *l.* homeward Angel now and melt with
Il P. 140. where no profaner eye may *l.*
S. 13, 6. with praise enough for envy to *l.* wan
H. 44. should *l.* so near upon her foul deformities
V. Ex. 35. at heaven's door *l.* in and see each
**Looked.**—P. L. 2, 918. and *l.* a while
P. L. 4, 178. one gate there only was and that *l.*
P. L. 4, 1013. the Fiend *l.* up and knew
P. L. 5, 54. and as I wondering *l.* beside it
P. L. 6, 529. others from the dawning hills *l.*
P. L. 10, 412. the blasted stars *l.* wan
P. L. 11, 556. he *l.* and saw a spacious plain
P. L. 11, 638. he *l.* and saw wide territory
P. L. 11, 712. he *l.* and saw the face of things
P. L. 11, 840. he *l.* and saw the ark hull on
P. R. 2, 86. I *l.* for some great change to honour
P. R. 3, 310. he *l.* and saw what numbers
**Lookest.**—P. L. 4, 33. *l.* from thy sole dominion
**Looking.**—P. L. 9, 312. thou *l.* on
P. L. 10, 993. conversing, *l.* loving
P. L. 11, 381. nor wider *l.* round
P. L. 11, 887. when *l.* down he saw the whole
P. L. 12, 60. laughter was in Heaven and *l.* down
P. L. 12, 209. God *l.* forth will trouble all his host
P. L. 12, 641. they *l.* back all the eastern side
**Looks.**—P. L. 1, 522. but with *l.* downcast
P. L. 1, 595. *l.* through the horizontal misty air

P. L. 1, 680. his *l.* and thoughts were always
P. L. 3, 542. *l.* down with wonder at the sudden
P. L. 4, 291. in their *l.* divine
P. L. 4, 464. with answering *l.* of sympathy
P. L. 4, 570. soon discerned his *l.* alien
P. L. 4, 718. ensnared mankind with her fair *l.*
P. L. 5, 12. with *l.* of cordial love hung over
P. L. 5, 122. nor cloud those *l.*
P. L. 5, 331. so saying with dispatchful *l.*
P. L. 8, 474. and in her *l.*
P. L. 8, 616. how their love express they by *l.*
P. L. 9, 222. what wonder if so near *l.* intervene
P. L. 9, 239. or this sweet intercourse of *l.*
P. L. 9, 309. I from the influence of thy *l.*
P. L. 9, 534. much less arm thy *l.* the heaven
P. L. 9, 558. for in their *l.* much reason and in
P. L. 10, 111. love was not in their *l.*
P. L. 10, 360. which thy *l.* now also evidence
P. L. 10, 608. his thoughts, his *l.*, words, actions
P. L. 10, 919. not whereon I live thy gentle *l.*
P. R. 1, 43. with *l.* aghast and sad he thus bespake
S. A. 533. of fair fallacious *l.* venereal trains
S. A. 1246. and lower *l.* but in a sultry chafe
C. 450. but rigid *l.* of chaste austerity
C. 464. by unchaste *l.* loose gestures and foul talk
C. 777. for swinish Gluttony ne'er *l.* to Heaven
L. 138. on whose fresh lap the swart-star *l.*
L. 162. *l.* toward Namancos and Bayona's hold
Il P. 39. and *l.* commercing with the skies
**Loophole.**—C. 140. from her cabined *l.* peep
**Loopholes.**—P. L. 9, 1110. at *l.* cut
**Loose.**—P. L. 2, 155. will he so wise let *l.* at once
P. L. 2, 887. and chariots ranked in *l.* array
P. L. 3, 87. through all restraint broke *l.*
P. L. 3, 362. now in *l.* garlands thick thrown
P. L. 4, 497. flowing gold of her *l.* tresses hid
P. L. 4, 889. finding way break *l.* from Hell
P. L. 4, 918. with thee came not all Hell broke *l.*
P. L. 6, 696. to disordered rage let *l.* the reins
S. A. 675. that wandering *l.* about
C. 174. stirs up among the *l.* unlettered hinds
C. 292. in his *l.* traces from the furrow came
C. 464. unchaste looks *l.* gestures and foul talk
C. 863. the *l.* train of thy amber-dropping hair
V. Ex. 90. can *l.* this Gordian knot
**Loosely.**—P. L. 7, 425. part *l.* wing the region
S. A. 1022. nor both so *l.* disallied their nuptials
**Loosening.**—P. L. 6, 643. *l.* to and fro
**Lop.**—P. L. 4, 629. to *l.* their wanton growth
P. L. 9, 210. what we by day *l.* overgrown
**Lopped.**—P. L. 1, 459. head and hands *l.* off
P. L. 6, 575. with branches *l.*
**Loquacious.**—P. L. 10, 161. hold or *l.*
**Lord.**—P. L. 2, 236. unless heaven's *L.* supreme
P. L. 2, 699. thy king and *l.*
P. L. 4, 516. why should their *L.* envy them
P. L. 4, 943. business were to serve their *L.*
P. L. 5, 205. hail universal *L.* be bounteous
P. L. 5, 608. and shall confess him *L.*
P. L. 5, 709. to be our *L.* and look for adoration
P. L. 6, 425. what heaven's *L.* had powerfullest
P. L. 6, 887. Son, Heir and *L.* to him dominion
P. L. 7, 205. attendant on their *L.*
P. L. 8, 106. for uses to his *L.* best known
P. L. 8, 376. so spake the universal *L.*
P. L. 9, 154. him *l.* pronounced
P. L. 9, 235. yet not so strictly hath our *L.*
P. L. 9, 273. and Earth and all Earth's *L.*
P. L. 10, 401. chiefly on man sole *l.* of all
P. L. 10, 794. though the *L.* of all be infinite
P. L. 11, 257. well may then thy *L.* appeased
P. L. 12, 34. he shall be styled before the *L.*
P. L. 12, 70. but man over men he made not *l.*
P. L. 12, 502. do all miracles as did their *L.*
P. L. 12, 544. known thy Saviour and thy *L.*
P. R. 1, 475. art placed above me thou art *L.*
P. R. 2, 335. treat thee as beseems and as her *L.*
P. R. 2, 376. and acknowledge thee their *L.*
P. R. 4, 167. worship me as thy superior *l.*
P. R. 4, 177. thou shalt worship the *L.* thy God
P. R. 4, 561. tempt not the *L.* thy God

S. A. 477. whether God be *L.* or Dagon
C. 492. what voice is that, my young *l.*?
C. 966. noble *L.* and Lady bright
S. 18, 1. avenge O *L.* thy slaughtered saints
H. 26. have thou the honour first thy *L.* to greet
H. 60. as if they surely knew their sovereign *L.*
H. 76. until their *L.* himself bespake and bid
H. 242. her sleeping *L.* with handmaid lamp
P. 10. which on our dearest *L.* did seize ere long
S. M. 22. to their great *L.*
F. of C. 1. because you have thrown off your *L.*
**Lorded.**—S. A. 267. and *l.* over them whom now
**Lordliest.**—S. A. 1418. lords are *l.* in their wine
**Lordly.**—P. L. 2, 243. while he *l.* sits our
P. L. 3, 578. that from his *l.* eye keep distance
S. A. 1353. more *l.* thundering than thou well
**Lords.**—P. L. 1, 32. *l.* of the world besides
P. L. 1, 794. the great Seraphic *l.* and Cherubim
P. L. 4, 290. in naked majesty seemed *l.* of all
P. L. 6, 451. deliverer from new *l.*
P. L. 8, 339. as *l.* possess it and all things
P. L. 9, 658. yet *l.* declared of all in earth or air
P. L. 10, 467. now possess as *l.* a spacious world
P. L. 11, 803. on what their *l.* shall leave them
P. L. 12, 93. subjects him from without to *l.*
P. L. 12, 349. by leave of kings their *l.*
S. A. 251. their *l.* the Philistines
S. A. 482. have made way to some Philistian *l.*
S. A. 920. I to the *l.* will intercede not doubting
S. A. 947. bearing my words and doings to the *l.*
S. A. 1108. such usage as your honourable *l.*
S. A. 1182. is not thy nation subject to our *l.*
S. A. 1195. but your ill-meaning politician *l.*
S. A. 1205. my nation was subjected to your *l.*
S. A. 1250. he will directly to the *l.* I fear
S. A. 1310. Samson to thee our *l.* thus bid me say
S. A. 1371. the Philistian *l.* command
S. A. 1391. from our *l.* to thee I am bid say
S. A. 1411. win the *l.* to favour and perhaps to set
S. A. 1418. *l.* are lordliest in their wine
S. A. 1447. by order of the *l.* new-parted hence
S. A. 1457. I have attempted one by one the *l.*
S. A. 1607. with seats where all the *l.* and each
S. A. 1640. hitherto, *l.,* what your commands
S. A. 1653. *l.,* ladies, captains, counsellors
C. 731. the herds would overmultitude their *l.*
**Lore.**—P. L. 2, 815. the subtle Fiend his *l.*
P. L. 9, 1128. the will heard not her *l.*
P. R. 1, 483. who follow not her *l.*
C. 34. where his fair offspring nursed in princely *l.*
**Lose.**—P. L. 2, 146. who would *l.* though full of
P. L. 2, 325. and of his kingdom *l.* no part
P. L. 2, 483. neither do the Spirits damned *l.*
P. L. 2, 607. with one small drop to *l.* in sweet
P. L. 5, 21. we *l.* the prime to mark how
P. L. 5, 731. lest unawares we *l.* this our high
P. L. 7, 153. if such it be to *l.* self-lost
P. L. 8, 332. and this happy state shalt *l.*
P. L. 9, 944. frustrate, do, undo, and labour *l.*
P. L. 9, 959. to *l.* thee were to *l.* myself
P. L. 11, 459. faith approved *l.* no reward
P. L. 11, 798. their freedom lost all virtue *l.*
P. L. 12, 358. then *l.* it to a stranger
P. R. 2, 98. I saw he could not *l.* himself
S. A. 1103. I *l.* prevented by thy eyes put out
S. A. 1286. who surprised *l.* their defence
C. 288. no less than if I should my brothers *l.*
C. 468. till she quite *l.* the divine property
H. 99. the air such pleasure loth to *l.*
**Loses.**—P. L. 8, 553. in discourse with her *l.*
P. R. 3, 104. *l.* though but verbal his reward
**Losing.**—P. L. 3, 206. affecting Godhead and so *l.*
P. L. 3, 280. to save by *l.* thee a while
**Loss.**—P. L. 1, 4. with *l.* of Eden till one greater
P. L. 1, 188. our own *l.* how repair
P. L. 1, 265. associates and co-partners of our *l.*
P. L. 1, 526. themselves not lost in *l.* itself
P. L. 1, 631. who can yet believe though after *l.*
P. L. 2, 21. this *l.* thus far at least recovered
P. L. 2, 330. and foiled with *l.* irreparable
P. L. 2, 440. with utter *l.* of being threatens him

P. L. 2, 770. to our part *l.* and rout through all
P. L. 3, 308. to save a world from utter *l.*
P. L. 3, 678. and to repair that *l.* created
P. L. 4, 11. wreak on innocent frail Man his *l.*
P. L. 4, 849. saw, and pined his *l.*
P. L. 4, 904. O *l.* of one in Heaven to judge
P. L. 7, 74. of what might else have been our *l.*
P. L. 8, 480. or for ever to deplore her *l.*
P. L. 9, 131. to what may work his utter *l.*
P. L. 9, 912. yet *l.* of thee would never from
P. L. 10, 752. to the *l.* of that sufficient penalty
P. L. 10, 1019. for *l.* of life and pleasure
P. R. 2, 29. their unexpected *l.* and plaints
P. R. 4, 366. quite at a *l.*
S. A. 67. O *l.* of sight of thee I most complain
S. A. 644. with the irreparable *l.* of sight
S. A. 1744. from whence captivity and *l.* of eyes
C. 287. imports their *l.* beside the present need
A. 100. though Erymanth your *l.* deplore
L. 49. such Lycidas thy *l.* to shepherd's ear
S. 12. all this waste of wealth and *l.* of blood
H. 153. must redeem our *l.*
T. 7. so little is our *l.* so little is thy gain
D. F. I. 72. her false-imagined *l.* cease to lament
V. Ex. 9. small *l.* it is that thence can come
**Lost.**—P. L. 1, 55. both of *l.* happiness
P. L. 1, 105. though the field be *l.* all is not *l.*
P. L. 1, 136. hath *l.* us Heaven
P. L. 1, 243. said then the *l.* Archangel
P. L. 1, 270. or what more *l.* in Hell
P. L. 1, 312. abject and *l.* lay these
P. L. 1, 316. flower of heaven, once yours now *l.*
P. L. 1, 471. a leper once he *l.* and gained a king
P. L. 1, 525. found themselves not *l.* in loss itself
P. L. 1, 591. his form had yet not *l.* all her
P. L. 1, 637. or dangers shunned by me have *l.*
P. L. 2, 14. I give not Heaven for *l.*
P. L. 2, 48. with that care *l.* went all his fear
P. L. 2, 110. a fairer person *l.* not Heaven
P. L. 2, 149. swallowed up and *l.*
P. L. 2, 231. or to regain our own right *l.*
P. L. 2, 561. no end in wandering mazes *l.*
P. L. 2, 894. and time and place are *l.*
P. L. 2, 975. alone and without guide half *l.*
P. L. 2, 982. if I that region *l.* all usurpation
P. L. 3, 150. for should Man finally be *l.*
P. L. 3, 173. man shall not quite be *l.*
P. L. 3, 223. all mankind must have been *l.*
P. L. 3, 233. once dead in sins and *l.*
P. L. 3, 280. the whole race *l.*
P. L. 4, 109. good to me is *l.* evil be thou my
P. L. 4, 573. but under shade *l.* sight of him
P. L. 4, 854. more glory will be won or less be *l.*
P. L. 6, 25. yet one returned not *l.*
P. L. 6, 838. they astonished all resistance *l.*
P. L. 9, 479. other joy to me is *l.*
P. L. 9, 642. there swallowed up and *l.*
P. L. 9, 784. gave signs of woe that all was *l.*
P. L. 9, 900. how art thou *l.* how on a sudden *l.*
P. L. 9, 1022. much pleasure we have *l.*
P. L. 9, 1072. both good and evil, good *l.*
P. L. 9, 1165. when thou wert *l.* not I
P. L. 10, 374. gained with odds what war hath *l.*
P. L. 10, 574. their *l.* shape
P. L. 10, 929. on me already *l.*
P. L. 10, 945. as one disarmed his anger all he *l.*
P. L. 10, 1036. which will be *l.* by death brought
P. L. 11, 59. that fondly *l.* this other served
P. L. 11, 87. boast his knowledge of good *l.*
P. L. 11, 288. resign what justly thou hast *l.*
P. L. 11, 347. but this pre-eminence thou hast *l.*
P. L. 11, 594. of love and youth not *l.*
P. L. 11, 682. had in his righteousness been *l.*
P. L. 11, 798. shall with their freedom *l.* all
P. L. 12, 84. thy original lapse true liberty is *l.*
P. L. 12, 101. outward liberty their inward *l.*
P. L. 12, 429. in sin for ever *l.*
P. L. 12, 621. though all by me is *l.*
P. R. 1, 2. by one man's disobedience *l.*
P. R. 1, 52. and his facile consort Eve *l.* Paradise

P. R. 1, 154. by conquest what the first man *l*.
P. R. 1, 377. though I have *l*. much lustre
P. R. 1, 378. to be beloved of God, I have not *l*.
P. R. 1, 382. I should so have *l*. all sense
P. R. 1, 390. by them I *l*. not what I *l*.
P. R. 1, 419. representing *l*. bliss
P. R. 2, 19. with care sought *l*. Elijah
P. R. 2, 97. I *l*. him but so found as well I saw
P. R. 2, 416. *l*. in a desert here and hunger-bit
P. R. 3, 148. insatiable of glory had *l*. all
P. R. 3, 204. all hope is *l*. of my reception
P. R. 3, 377. ten sons of Jacob two of Joseph *l*.
P. R. 4, 6. so little here, nay *l*.
P. R. 4, 188. gratitude in thee is *l*. long since
P. R. 4, 352. light of Nature not in all quite *l*.
P. R. 4, 608. hast regained *l*. Paradise
S. A. 152. bewail thy bondage or *l*. sight
S. A. 914. though sight be *l*. life yet hath many
S. A. 927. that what by me thou hast *l*. thou least
S. A. 1489. older than thy age through eye sight *l*.
S. A. 1502. his strength with eyesight was not *l*.
S. A. 1697. so Virtue given for *l*.,
C. 52. whose charmed cup whoever tasted *l*.
C. 271. nay gentle shepherd ill is *l*. that praise
C. 359. but O that hapless virgin our *l*. sister
C. 498. or young kid *l*. his dam
C. 510. we *l*. her as we came
C. 919. now the spell hath *l*. his hold
S. 22, 10. the conscience friend to have *l*. them
Cir. 18. were *l*.in death till He that dwelt above
**Lot.**—P. L. 1, 608. for ever now to have their *l*.
P. L. 2, 223. our present *l*. appears for happy
P. L. 2, 617. viewed first their lamentable *l*.
P. L. 4, 446. enjoy so far the happier *l*.
P. L. 4, 561. Gabriel to thee thy course by *l*.
P. L. 4, 1011. for proof look up and read thy *l*.
P. L. 9, 690. by venturing higher than my *l*.
P. L. 9, 881. that equal *l*. may join us
P. L. 9, 952. however I with thee have fixed my *l*.
P. L. 10, 261. or transmigration as their *l*.
P. L. 11, 765. each day's *l*. enough to bear
P. R. 2, 70. above the *l*. of other women
P. R. 2, 91. this is my favoured *l*.
P. R. 3, 57. his *l*. who dares be singularly good
S. A. 996. I leave him to his *l*. and like my own
S. A. 1292. either of these is in thy *l*., Samson
S. A. 1743. his *l*. unfortunate in nuptial choice
C. 20. took in by *l*. 'twixt high and nether Jove
C. 789. more happiness than this thy present *l*.
A. 44. for know by *l*. from Jove I am the Power
S. 2, 11. to that same *l*. however mean or high
**Loth.**—P. L. 4, 386. *l*. to this revenge
P. L. 9, 946. yet would be *l*. us to abolish
P. L. 9, 1039. he led her nothing *l*.
P. L. 10, 109. with him Eve more *l*.
P. L. 12, 585. then wilt thou not be *l*. to leave
P. R. 3, 241. will be ever timorous and *l*.
C. 177. I should be *l*. to meet the rudeness
C. 473. as *l*. to leave the body that it loved
H. 99. the air such pleasure *l*. to lose
**Loud.**—P. L. 1, 314. he called so *l*.
P. L. 1, 394. drums and timbrels *l*.
P. L. 1, 532. at the warlike sound of trumpets *l*.
P. L. 2, 520. returned them *l*. acclaim
P. L. 2, 579. Cocytus, named of lamentation *l*.
P. L. 2, 655. with wide Cerberean mouths full *l*.
P. L. 2, 921. his ear less pealed with noises *l*.
P. L. 3, 346. with a shout *l*. as from numbers
P. L. 3, 348. and *l*. Hosannas filled the eternal
P. L. 3, 397. with *l*. acclaim thee only extolled
P. L. 3, 429. less vexed with tempest *l*.
P. L. 5, 193. ye Winds breathe soft or *l*.
P. L. 6, 23. with joy and acclamations *l*.
P. L. 6, 59. less dread the *l*. ethereal trumpet
P. L. 6, 557. thus was heard commanding *l*.
P. L. 6, 567. and *l*. that all may hear
P. L. 7, 271. the *l*. misrule of Chaos
P. L. 8, 244. torment and *l*. lament and furious
P. L. 10, 455. *l*. was the acclaim
P. L. 10, 641. and the heavenly audience *l*.
P. L. 10, 699. and Cæcias, and Argestes *l*.

P. L. 10, 845. Adam to himself lamented *l*.
P. L. 12, 56. forthwith a hideous gabble rises *l*.
P. L. 12, 229. lightning and *l*. trumpet sound
P. R. 2, 235. heard their grant in *l*. acclaim
P. R. 2, 290. of tuneful birds resounding *l*.
P. R. 4, 488. noising *l*. and threatening nigh
S.A.248. deeds themselves though mute spoke *l*.
S.A.436. great pomp and sacrifice and praises *l*.
S. A. 1090. if thy appearance answer *l*. report
S. A. 1510. horribly *l*. unlike the former shout
S. A. 1552. the accident was *l*. and here before
C. 202. whence even now the tumult of *l*. mirth
C. 849. carol her goodness *l*. in rustic lays
Il P. 126. while rocking winds are piping *l*.
S. 15, 4. rumours *l*. that daunt remotest kings
S. 16, 8. and Dunbar field resounds thy praises *l*.
H. 115. harping in *l*. and solemn choir
H. 163. a voice of weeping heard and *l*. lament
H. 215. the unshowered' grass with lowings *l*.
P.26.*l*.o'er the rest Cremona's trump doth sound
P.55. might think the infection of my sorrows *l*.
S. M. 11. their *l*. uplifted angel-trumpets blow
V.Ex.99. Humber *l*. that keeps the Scythian's
**Louder.**—P. L. 10, 954. and be *l*. heard
**Loudest.**—P. L. 2, 954. with *l*. vehemence
P. L. 11, 8. with speedier flight than *l*. oratory
P. R. 1, 275. with *l*. voice proclaimed
P. R. 4, 339. ill imitated while they *l*. sing
**Loudly.**—L. 17. begin and somewhat *l*. sweep
V.Ex.24. and *l*.knock to have their passage out
**Lour.**—S. A. 1057. smile she or *l*.
**Loured.**—P. L. 9, 1002. sky *l*. and muttering
**Louring.**—P. L. 2, 490. the *l*. element scowls
P. R. 4, 398. brought in *l*. night
**Lours.**—P. L. 4, 873. in his look defiance *l*.
**Love.**—P. L. 1, 431. works of *l*. or enmity
P. L. 1, 491. or more gross to *l*. vice for itself
P. L. 3, 29. smit with the *l*. of sacred song
P. L. 3, 67. *l*., uninterrupted joy, unrivalled *l*.
P. L. 3, 104. true allegiance, constant faith or *l*.
P. L. 3, 142. *l*. without end
P. L. 3, 213. where shall we find such *l*.
P. L. 3, 225. in whom the fulness dwells of *l*.
P. L. 3, 267. and breathed immortal *l*.
P. L. 3, 298. so heavenly *l*. shall outdo hellish
P. L. 3, 312. because in thee *l*. hath abounded
P. L. 3, 338. of golden deeds with joy and *l*.
P. L. 3, 410. O unexampled *l*. nowhere to be
P. L. 4, 68. but Heaven's free *l*. dealt equally
P. L. 4, 69. be then his *l*. accursed, since *l*.
P. L. 4, 322. in *l*.'s embraces met
P. L. 4, 363. could *l*. so lively shines in them
P. L. 4, 446. looks of sympathy and *l*.
P. L. 4, 499. smiled with superior *l*. as Jupiter
P. L. 4, 509. where neither joy nor *l*. but fierce
P. L. 4, 728. in our mutual help and mutual *l*.
P. L. 4, 743. rites mysterious of connubial *l*.
P. L. 4, 750. hail wedded *l*. mysterious law
P. L. 4, 763. here *l*. his golden shafts employs
P. L. 5, 12. with looks of cordial *l*. hung over
P. L. 5, 449. but in those hearts *l*.
P. L. 5, 502. and retain unalterably firm his *l*.
P. L. 5, 515. possibly his *l*. desert who formed
P. L. 5, 539. freely we serve because we freely *l*.
P. L. 5, 540. we freely *l*. as in our will to *l*.
P. L. 5, 550. yet that we never shall forget to *l*.
P. L. 5, 593. holy memorials acts of zeal and *l*.
P. L. 5, 900. his loyalty he kept, his *l*., his zeal
P. L. 6, 94. in festivals of joy and *l*.
P. L. 7, 195. sapience and *l*. immense
P. L. 7, 330. and *l*. to haunt her sacred shades
P. L. 8, 58. O when meet now such pairs in *l*.
P. L. 8, 228. and set on man his equal *l*.
P. L. 8, 426. requires collateral *l*. a ned darset
P. L. 8, 477. the spirit of *l*. and amorous delight
P. L. 8, 489. in every gesture, dignity and *l*.
P. L. 8, 569. thy honouring and thy *l*.
P. L. 8, 577. that with honour thou mayst *l*.
P. L. 8, 587. attractive, human, rational *l*. still
P. L. 8, 589. wherein true *l*. consists not
P. L. 8, 589. *l*. refines the thoughts

P. L. 8, 592. to heavenly *l*. thou mayst
P. L. 8, 602. with *l*. and sweet compliance
P. L. 8, 612. to *l*. thou blamest me not, for *l*.
P. L. 8, 615. *l*. not the heavenly spirits
P. L. 8, 615. and how their *l*. express they?
P. L. 8, 619. celestial rosy red *l.'s* proper hue
P. L. 8, 621. and without *l*. no happiness
P. L. 8, 633. be strong, live happy, and *l*.
P. L. 8, 634. but first of all him whom to *l*.
P. L. 9, 240. and are of *l*. the food
P. L. 9, 241. *l*.,not the lowest end of human life
P. L. 9, 263. or to disturb conjugal *l*.
P. L. 9, 286. my firm faith and *l*.
P. L. 9, 319. in his care and matrimonial *l*.
P. L. 9, 335. what is faith, *l*., virtue, unassayed
P. L. 9, 357. not then mistrust but tender *l*.
P. L. 9, 475. hate not *l*. nor hope
P. L. 9, 489. she fair, divinely fair, fit *l*. for Gods
P. L. 9, 490. not terrible, though terror be in *l*.
P. L. 9, 492. hate stronger under show of *l*.
P. L. 9, 665. but with show of zeal and *l*. to man
P. L. 9, 822. the more to draw his *l*. and render
P. L. 9, 832. so dear I *l*. him that with him
P. L. 9, 858. agony of *l*. till now not felt
P. L. 9, 882. us equal joy as equal *l*.
P. L. 9, 909. thy sweet converse and *l*. so dearly
P. L. 9, 961. O glorious trial of exceeding *l*.
P. L. 9, 970. shall separate us linked in *l*. so dear
P. L. 9, 975. presented this happy trial of thy *l*.
P. L. 9, 983. so true, so faithful, *l*. unequalled
P. L. 9, 991. much won that he his *l*. had so
P. L. 9, 1042. their fill of *l*. and *l.'s* disport
P. L. 9, 1163. is this the *l*. is this the recompense
P. L. 10, 111. *l*. was not in their looks
P. L. 10, 153. and lovely to attract thy *l*.
P. L. 10, 903. or if she *l*. withheld by parents
P. L. 10, 915. witness Heaven what *l*. sincere
P. L. 10, 960. but strive in offices of *l*.
P. L. 10,973. regain thy *l*. the sole contentment
P. L. 10, 994. to abstain from *l.'s* due rites
P. L. 11, 353. with goodness and paternal *l*.
P. L. 11, 553. nor *l*. thy life nor hate
P. L. 11,588. of *l*. they treat till the evening star
P. L. 11,589. till the evening star *l.'s* harbinger
P. L. 11, 594. fair event of *l*. a youth not lost
P. L. 12, 380. virgin mother hail, high in the *l*.
P. L. 12, 403. and by *l*. though *l*. alone fulfil
P.L. 12, 489. the law of faith working through *l*.
P. L. 12, 550. in righteousness and peace and *l*.
P. L. 12, 562. to obey is best and *l*. with fear
P. L. 12, 583. *l*. by name to come called charity
P. R. 1, 380. I have not lost to *l*.
S. A. 270. to *l*. bondage more than liberty
S. A. 385. in her height of nuptial *l*. professed
S. A. 388. in her prime of *l*., spousal embraces
S. A. 790. and what if *l*. which thou interpret'st
S. A. 791. the jealousy of *l*. powerful of sway
S. A. 808. and *l.'s* prisoner not the Philistines'
S. A. 810. fearless at home of partners in my *l*.
S. A. 811. these reasons in *l.'s* law have passed
S. A. 813. *l*. hath oft well meaning wrought
S. A. 836. *l*.constrained thee! call it furious rage
S. A. 837. *l*. seeks to have *l*.
S. A. 863. my *l*. how couldst thou hope
S. A. 863. only my *l*. of thee held long debate
S. A. 873. but had thy *l*. still odiously pretended
S. A. 923. where my redoubled *l*. and care
S. A. 1005. returning to regain *l*. once possessed
S.A.1012. that woman's *l*.can win or long inherit
S.A.1033. that either they *l*. nothing or not long
S. A. 1506. conceived agreeable to a father's *l*.
C. 124. Venus now wakes and wakens *l*.
C. 332. that wont'st to *l*. the traveller's benison
C. 610. I *l*. thy courage yet and bold emprise
C. 1019. mortals that would follow me *l*. virtue
L. 177. in the blest kingdoms meek of joy and *l*.
L'A. 30. and *l*. to live in dimple sleek
Il P. 108. and made hell grant what *l*. did seek
Il P. 157. and *l*. the high embowed roof
S. 1, 7. portend success in *l*.
S.1, 13. whether the muse or *l*.call thee his mate

S. 14, 1. Faith and *l*. which parted from thee
S.14, 9. *l*. led them on and Faith who knew them
S. 23, 11. yet to my fancied sight, *l*., sweetness
Cir. 15. O more exceeding *l*. or law more just
Cir. 16. just law indeed but more exceeding *l*.
T. 16. with Truth and Peace and *L*. shall ever
S. M. 22. whose *l*. their motion swayed
**Loved.**—P. L. 3, 151. thy creature late so *l*.
P. L. 9, 1007. more to soothe him with her *l*.
S. A. 878. *l*. thee as too well thou knew'st
S. A. 939. when all men *l*., honoured, feared me
C. 473. as loth to leave the body that it *l*.
C. 501. O my *l*. master's heir and his next joy
C. 623. he *l*. me well and oft would beg me sing
L. 36. and old Damœtas *l*. to hear our song
L. 51. closed o'er the head of your *l*. Lycidas
**Love-darting.**—C. 753. *l-d*. eyes
**Love-laboured.**—P. L. 5, 41. his *l-l*. song
**Loveless.**—P. L. 4, 766. of harlots *l*. joyless
**Lovelier.**—P. L. 9, 232. nothing *l*. can
P. L. 9, 505. never since of serpent kind *l*.
**Loveliest.**—P. L. 4, 321. passed the *l*. pair
P. L. 8, 558. build in her *l*. and create an awe
**Loveliness.**—P. L. 8, 547. her *l*. so absolute
**Love-lorn.**—C. 234. where the *l-l*. nightingale
**Lovely.**—P.L.4,152. so *l*. seemed that landscape
P. L. 4, 714. more *l*. than Pandora
P. L. 4, 848. in her shape how *l*.
P. L. 5, 380. more *l*. fair than wood-nymph
P. L. 7, 502. consummate *l*. smiled
P. L. 8,471. manlike but different sex so *l*. fair
P. L. 9, 504. pleasing was his shape and *l*.
P. L. 10, 152. adorned she was indeed and *l*.
C. 875. by Leucothea's *l*. hands
L'A. 14. whom *l*. Venus at a birth
D. F. I. 5. for he being amorous on that *l*. dye
M. W. 24. to greet her of a *l*. son
**Love-quarrels.**—S. A. 1008. *l-q*. oft
**Lover.**—P. L. 4, 769. *l*. sings to his proud fair
P. L. 5, 450. the injured *l.'s* hell
S. 1, 3. with fresh hope the *l.'s* heart dost
M. W. 16. quickly found a *l*. meet
**Lovers.**—P. R. 4, 355. and *l*. of their country
**Loves.**—P. L. 4, 888. lives there who *l*. his pain
P. L. 9, 271. as one who *l*. and some unkindness
C. 856. for maidenhood she *l*. and will be swift
Il P. 134. and shadows brown that Sylvan *l*.
S. 12, 12. for who *l*. that must first be wise
H. 91. perhaps their *l*. or else their sheep
**Lovest.**—P. L. 6, 733. in me all whom thou *l*.
**Love-tale.**—P. L. 1, 452. the *l-t* infected
**Loving.**—P. L. 8, 588. in *l*. thou dost well
P. L. 10, 993. conversing, looking, *l*., to abstain
**Low.**—P. L. 1, 23. what is *l*. raise and support
P. L. 1, 114. that were *l*. indeed
P. L. 1, 137. in horrible destruction laid thus *l*.
P. L. 1, 435. their heads as *l*. bowed down
P. L. 2, 81. and laborious flight we sunk thus *l*.
P. L. 2, 115. for his thoughts were *l*.
P. L. 3, 736. Satan bowing *l*. as to superior
P. L. 4, 525. with design to keep them *l*.
P. L. 5, 360. as to a superior nature bowing *l*.
P. L. 7, 288. so *l*. down sunk a hollow bottom
P. L. 8, 126. now high now *l*. then hid
P. L. 8, 345. pay thee fealty with *l*. subjection
P. L. 8, 350. cowering *l*. with blandishment
P. L. 9, 169. who aspires must down as *l*.
P. L. 9, 572. of abject thoughts and *l*.
P. L. 9, 704. to keep ye *l*. and ignorant
P. L. 9, 835. but first *l*. reverence done
Cir. 10, 92. was the sun in western cadence *l*.
P. L. 10, 682. the *l*. sun to recompense his
P. L. 11, 249. Adam bowed *l*.
P. L. 11, 562. *l*. and high·
P. L. 12, 97. will decline so *l*. from virtue
P. R. 1, 235. though men esteem thee *l*.
P. R. 1, 497. bowing *l*. his gray dissimulation
P. R. 2, 28. close in a cottage *l*. together got
P. R. 2, 413. thou art unknown unfriended *l*.
S. A. 338. as signal now in *l*. dejected state
S. A. 1239. with one buffet lay thy structure *l*.

C.319. conduct you Lady to a *l.*but loyal cottage
A. 37. whom with *l.* reverence I adore as mine
A.71. and the*l.*world in measured motion draw
L. 102. that sunk so *l.* that sacred head of thine
L.136. ye valleys *l.*where the mild whispers use
L. 172. so Lycidas sunk *l.* but mounted high
**Low-browed.**—L'A.8.ebonshades and *l-b.*rocks
**Low-creeping.**—P. L. 9, 180. a black mist *l-c.*
**Low-delved.**—D. F. I. 32. in a *l-d.* tomb
**Lower.**—P. L. 3, 540. now on the *l.* stair
P. L. 4, 76. and in the lowest deep a *l.* deep
P. L. 4, 91. the *l.* still I fall, only supreme in
P. L. 5, 410. every *l.* faculty of sense
P. L. 7, 18. though from a *l.* clime
P. L. 7, 84. deign to descend now *l.* and relate
P. L. 8, 199. let us descend a *l.* flight
P. L. 11, 283. wander down into a *l.* world
S. A. 38. debased *l.* than bondslave
S. A. 689. but throw'st them *l.* than thou didst
S. A. 1246. and *l.* looks but in a sultry chafe
**Lowest.**—P. L. 2, 392. which from the *l.* deep
P. L. 2, 882. that the *l.* bottom shook of Erebus
P. L. 4, 76. and in the *l.* deep a lower deep
P. L. 4, 831. the *l.* of your throng
P. L. 5, 158. dimly seen in these thy *l.* works
P. L. 5, 418. and as *l.* first the moon
P. L. 9, 241. love, not the *l.* end of human life
P.L.10, 443. plebeian Angel militant of *l.* order
P. R. 2, 438. attained in *l.* poverty to highest
S. A. 169. to *l.* pitch of abject fortune thou art
**Lowings.**—H. 215. unshowered grass with *l.*
**Lowliest.**—P. L. 11, 1. thus they in *l.* plight
**Lowliness.**—P. L. 8, 42. with *l.* majestic
**Lowly.**—P. L. 1, 434. bowing *l.* down
P. L. 3, 349. *l.* reverent towards either throne
P. L. 5, 144. *l.* they bowed adoring
P. L. 5, 201. stately tread or *l.* creep
P. L. 5, 463. under whose *l.* roof thou hast
P.L.8,173. be *l.* wise think only what concerns
P.L. 8, 412. he ceased I *l.* answered
P.L.10, 937. she ended weeping and her *l.*plight
C. 323. which oft is sooner found in *l.* sheds
H. 25. and lay it *l.* at his blessed feet
**Low-roofed.**—P. R. 4, 273. to the *l-r.* house
P. 18. his starry front *l-r.* beneath the skies
**Low-roosted**—C. 317. or the *l-r.* lark
**Low-thoughted.**—C. 189. and with *l-t.* care
**Loyal.**—P. L. 4, 755. founded in reason *l.* just
C. 320. a low but *l.* cottage
**Loyalty.**—P. L. 5, 900. his *l.* he kept
**Lubbar-fiend.**—L'A. 110. the *l.-f.*
**Lucent.**—P. L. 3, 589. in the sun's *l.* orb
**Lucid.**—P. L. 1, 469. Abbana and Pharphar *l.*
P. L. 11, 240. over his *l.* arms a military vest
**Lucifer.**—P. L. 5, 760. the palace of great *L.*
P. L. 7, 131. then that after *L.* from heaven
P. L. 10, 425. city and proud seat of *L.*
H. 74. or *L.* that often warned them thence
**Lucina.**—M. W. 26. and calls *L.* to her throes
M. W. 28. Atropos for *L.* came
**Luck.**—V. Ex. 59. good *l.* befriend thee Son
**Lucky.**—L.20. with *l.*words favour my destined
**Lucre.**—P. L. 12, 511. of *l.* of ambition
**Lucrine.**—P. R. 2, 347. Pontus and *L.* bay
**Luggage.**—P.R. 3, 401. cumbersome *l.* of war
**Lull.**—P. L. 2, 287. *l.* sea-faring men
A. 69. to *l.* the daughters of Necessity
V. Ex. 84. peace shall *l.* him in her flowery lap
**Lulled.**—P. L. 4, 771. these *l.* by nightingales
C. 260. yet they in pleasing slumber *l.* the sense

L'A. 116. by whispering winds soon *l.* asleep
**Luminaries.**—P. L. 7, 385. their bright *l.*
P. L. 8, 98. yet not to earth are those bright *l.*
**Luminary.**—P. L. 3, 576. where the great *l.*
**Luminous.**—P. L. 3, 420. the *l.* inferior orbs
P. L. 8, 140. her other part still *l.* by his ray
**Lure.**—P. L. 9, 518. in sight of Eve to *l.* her eye
**Lured.**—P. L. 2, 664. *l.* with the smell of infant
P. L. 10, 276. *l.* with scent of living carcases
**Lures.**—P. R. 2, 194. of beauty and her *l.*
**Lurk.**—P. L. 4, 587. in whatsoever shape he *l.*
**Lurking.**—P. L. 9, 1172. and the *l.* enemy
**Lurks.**—P. L. 9, 267. danger or dishonour *l.*
**Lurk'st.**—P. R. 2, 183. how thou *l.*
**Luscious.**—C. 652. and shed the *l.* liquor
**Lust.**—P. L. 1, 417. *l.* hard by hate
P. L. 1, 496. filled with *l.* and violence
P. L. 2, 791. more inflamed with *l.* than rage
P. L. 4, 753. by thee adulterous *l.* was driven
P. L. 9, 1015. she him as wantonly repaid in *l.*
P. L. 11, 795. ease and sloth surfeit and *l.*
P. R. 4, 137. provinces exhausted all by *l.*
S. A. 837. call it furious rage to satisfy thy *l.*
C. 463. when *l.* by unchaste looks
**Lustful.**—P. L. 1, 415. yet thence his *l.* orgies
P. L. 11, 619. to the taste of *l.* appetence
**Lustre.**—P. L. 1, 97. changed in outward *l.*
P. L. 1, 538. with gems and golden *l.* rich
P. L. 2, 271. desert soil wants not her hidden *l.*
P. L. 4, 850. to find here observed his *l.* visibly
P. L. 10, 447. placed in regal *l.*
P. L. 11, 325. and pile up every stone of *l.*
P. R. 1, 378. lost much *l.* of my native brightness
A. 76. whose *l.* leads us
**Lusts.**—P. R. 4, 94. his horrid *l.* in private
**Lusty.**—P. R. 2, 178. thou with thy *l.* crew
H. 36. to wanton with the sun her *l.* paramour
**Lute.**—P. L. 5, 151. than needed *l.* or harp
C. 478. but musical as is Apollo's *l.*
S. 20, 11. to hear the *l.* well touched
P. 28. and softer strings of *l.* or viol still
**Luxuriant.**—P. L. 4, 260. gently creeps *l.*
**Luxurious.**—P. L. 1, 498. and in *l.* cities
P. L. 9, 209. *l.* restraint
P. L. 11, 788. in triumph and *l.* wealth
P. R. 3, 297. from the *l.* kings of Antioch won
P. R. 4, 141. *l.* by their wealth
**Luxury.**—P. L. 1, 722. strove in wealth and *l.*
P. L. 11, 715. to *l.* and riot, feast and dance
P. L.11,751.in their palaces where *l.*late reigned
P. R. 4, 111. of *l.* though called magnificence
C. 770. lewdly-pampered *L.*
**Luz.**—P. L. 3, 513. in the field of *L.*
**Lycæus.**—A. 98. on old *L.* or Cyllene hoar
**Lyceum.**—P. R. 4, 253. *L.* there
**Lycid.**—L. 151. the laureate hearse where *L.* lies
**Lycidas.**—L. 8. for *L.* is dead, dead ere his prime
L. 9. young *L.* and hath not left his peer
L. 10. who would not sing for *L.*?
L. 49. such *L.* thy loss to shepherd's ear
L. 51. closed o'er the head of your loved *L.*
L. 166. for *L.* your sorrow is not dead
L. 172. so *L.* sunk low but mounted high
L. 182. now *L.* the shepherds weep no more
**Lydian.**—L'A. 136. lap me in soft *L.* airs
**Lying.**—P. R. 1, 429. for *l.* is thy sustenance
**Lyones.**—P. R. 2, 360. knights of Logres or of *L.*
**Lyre.**—P. L. 3, 17. than to the Orphean *l.*
**Lyric.**—P. R. 4, 257. Dorian *l.* odes.
S. A. 1737. in copious legend or sweet *l.* song

# M.

**Mab.**—L'A. 102 how faery *M.* the junkets eat
**Macdonnel.**—S. 11, 9. Colkitto, or *M.*
**Mace.**—P. L. 10, 294. Death with his *m.* petrific
C. 869. by the earth-shaking Neptune's *m.*
**Macedon.**—P. R. 4, 271. *M.* and Artaxerxes'
**Macedonian.**—P. R. 3, 32. *M.* Philip

**Machabeus.**—P. R. 3, 165. so did not *M.*
**Machærus.**—P. R. 2, 22. *M.* and each town
**Machination.**—P. L. 6, 504. devilish *m.*
**Machinations.**—P. R. 1, 181. devilish *m.*
**Mad.**—P. L. 4, 129. and *m.* demeanour
P. R. 4, 446. and *m.* despite to be so oft repelled

S. A. 1677. and urged them on with *m.* desire
C. 829. the guiltless damsel flying the *m.* pursuit
**Madam.**—S. 10. 11. *m.* methinks I see him
**Madding.**—P. L. 6, 210. the *m.* wheels
**Made.**—P. L. 1, 248. force hath *m.* supreme
P. L. 1, 258. whom thunder hath *m.* greater
P. L. 1, 370. invisible glory of him that *m.* them
P. L. 1, 403. and *m.* his grove the pleasant valley
P. L. 2, 238. publish grace to all on promise *m.*
P. L. 2, 787. his fatal dart *m.* to destroy
P. L. 2, 992. *m.* head against Heaven's King
P. L. 3, 98. I *m.* him just and right
P. L. 3, 110. *m.* passive both
P. L. 3, 155. who art Judge of all things *m.*
P. L. 3, 164. what for thy glory thou hast *m.*
P. L. 3, 284. *m.* flesh when time shall be
P. L. 3, 386. without cloud *m.* visible
P. L. 4, 97. ease would recant vows *m.* in pain
P. L. 4, 329. and *m.* ease more easy
P. L. 4, 413. needs must the Power that *m.* us
P. L. 4, 672. *m.* hereby apter to receive
P. L. 4, 722. adored the God that *m.* both
P. L. 4, 928. vollied thunder *m.* all speed
P. L. 5, 204. *m.* vocal by my song
P. L. 5, 524. God *m.* thee perfect not immutable
P. L. 5, 525. good he *m.* thee, but to persevere
P. L. 5, 561. thus Adam *m.* request
P. L. 5, 599. brightness had *m.* invisible
P. L. 5, 735. *m.* answer, Mighty Father
P. L. 5, 823. who *m.* thee what thou art
P. L. 5, 836. the mighty Father *m.* all things
P. L. 5, 842. obscured but more illustrious *m.*
P. L. 6, 305. and in the air *m.* horrid circle
P. L. 6, 441. what between us *m.* the odds
P. L. 6, 514. or hollowed bodies *m.* of oak or fir
P. L. 6, 632. and of his thunder *m.* a scorn
P. L. 7, 263. God *m.* the firmament expanse
P. L. 7, 318. *m.* gay her bosom smelling sweet
P. L. 7, 336. ere it was in the earth God *m.*
P. L. 7, 346. and God *m.* two great lights
P. L. 7, 348. and *m.* the stars
P. L. 7, 361. in the sun's orb *m.* porous to receive
P. L. 7, 515. worship God Supreme who *m.* him
P. L. 7, 548. and all that he had *m.* viewed
P. L. 8, 381. hast thou not *m.* me here
P. L. 8, 409. save with the creatures which I *m.*
P. L. 8, 491. this turn hath *m.* amends
P. L. 8, 544. resembling less his image who *m.*
P. L. 8, 555. as one intended first not after *m.*
P. L. 8, 576. *m.* so adorn for thy delight
P. L. 8, 583. would not be to them *m.* common
P. L. 9, 132. for whom all this was *m.*
P. L. 9, 152. man he *m.* and for him built
P. L. 9, 243. but to delight he *m.* us
P. L. 9, 352. reason is free and reason he *m.* right
P. L. 9, 550. the heart of Eve his words *m.* way
P. L. 9, 632. and *m.* intricate seem straight
P. L. 9, 749. the tongue not *m.* for speech
P. L. 9, 931. by him first *m.* common
P. L. 9, 943. with us must fail dependent *m.*
P. L. 9, 1049. and inmost powers *m.* err
P. L. 10, 29. *m.* haste to make appear
P. L. 10, 146. or was she *m.* thy guide superior
P. L. 10, 149. set thee above her *m.* of thee
P. L. 10, 166. transfer the guilt on him who *m.*
P. L. 10, 319. they *m.* all fast, too fast they *m.*
P. L. 10, 391. and *m.* one realm
P. L. 10, 485. by our exile *m.* happy
P. L. 10, 638. earth renewed shall be *m.* pure
P. L. 10, 760. God *m.* thee without thy leave
P. L. 10, 766. God *m.* thee of choice his own
P. L. 11, 4. and *m.* new flesh regenerate grow
P. L. 11, 44. *m.* one with me as I with thee
P. L. 11, 210. and on a hill *m.* halt
P. L. 11, 559. that *m.* melodious chime
P. L. 11, 737. and God *m.* fast the door
P. L. 11, 846. which *m.* their flowing shrink
P. L. 12, 70. but man over men he *m.* not lord
P. R. 1, 208. *m.* it my whole delight
P. R. 1, 343. of these hard stones be *m.* thee bread
P. R. 2, 170. and *m.* him build and *m.* him bow

P. R. 2, 193. with a smile *m.* small account
P. R. 2, 207. *m.* and set wholly on the
P. R. 3, 77. *m.* captive yet deserving freedom
P. R. 3, 94. *m.* famous in a land and times
P. R. 3, 111. for his glory all things *m.*
P. R. 3, 442. *m.* answer meet that *m.* void all
P. R. 4, 101. from his throne now *m.* a sty
P. R. 4, 129. expel a devil who first *m.* him such
P. R. 4, 133. deservedly *m.* vassal
P. R. 4, 155. I see all offers *m.* by me how slight
S. A. 34. *m.* of my enemies the scorn and gaze
S. A. 56. not *m.* to rule but to subserve
S. A. 106. but *m.* hereby obnoxious more
S. A. 131. weaponless himself *m.* arms ridiculous
S. A. 309. who *m.* our laws to bind us not himself
S. A. 481. have *m.* way to some Philistian lords
S. A. 555. *m.* choice to rear his mighty champion
S. A. 803. that *m.* for me
S. A. 1489. *m.* older than thy age
S. A. 1622. who had *m.* their dreadful enemy
C. 463. till all be *m.* immortal
C. 642. I pursued it up but little reckoning *m.*
C. 842. *m.* Goddess of the river
A. 60. with puissant words and murmurs *m.*
L. 61. by the rout that *m.* the hideous roar
Il P. 108. and *m.* Hell grant what love did seek
S. 11, 11. that would have *m.* Quintilian stare
H. 118. such music before was never *m.*
D. F. I. 4. Winter's force that *m.* thy blossom dry
D. F. I. 66. whom sin hath *m.* our foe
S. M. 21. the fair music that all creatures *m.*
U. C. II. 5. *m.* of sphere-metal never to decay
V. Ex. 16. this same small neglect that I have *m.*
U. C. II. 24. lack of load *m.* his life burdensome
**Madest.**—P. L. 1, 22. and *m.* it pregnant
P. L. 4, 724. thou also *m.* the night
P. L. 10, 137. this woman whom thou *m.*
V. Ex. 3. and *m.* imperfect words with childish
**Madian.**—S. A. 281. in pursuit of *M.*
**Madness.**—P. L. 11, 486. moon-struck *m.*
S. A. 553. O *m.* to think use of strongest wines
C. 261. and in sweet *m.* robbed it of itself
**Madrigal.**—C. 495. brook to hear his *m.*
**Mænalus.**—A. 102. from the stony *M.*
**Mæonides.**—V. L. 3, 35. blind *M.*
**Mæotis.**—P. L. 9, 78. the pool *M.*
**Magazine.**—P. L. 4, 816. some *m.* to store
**Magazines.**—S. A. 1281. their armouries and *m.*
**Magellan.**—P. L. 10, 687. as far beneath *M.*
**Magic.**—P. L. 1, 727. pendent by subtle *m.*
S. A. 1149. and dissolve these *m.* spells
C. 165. hath met the virtue of this *m.* dust
C. 435. that breaks his *m.* chains at curfew time
C. 798. till all thy *m.* structures reared so high
**Magician.**—S. A. 1133. some *m.'s* art
C. 602. but for that damned *m.* let him be girt
**Magistrates.**—S. A. 850. the *m.* and princes
S. A. 1183. *m.* confessed it when they took thee
**Magnanimity.**—S. A. 1470. the rest was *m.*
**Magnanimous.**—P. L. 7, 511. from thence *m.*
P. R. 2, 483. far more *m.* than to assume
S. A. 524. and *m.* thoughts of birth from Heaven
**Magnetic.**—P. L. 3, 583. by his *m.* beam
P. R. 2, 168. as the *m.* hardest iron draws
**Magnific.**—P. L. 5, 773. if these *m.* titles
P. L. 10, 354. O Parent, these are thy *m.* deeds
**Magnificence.**—P. L. 1, 718. such *m.* equalled
P. L. 2, 273. skill or art from whence to raise *m.*
P. L. 8, 101. the maker's high *m.* who built
P. R. 4, 111. of luxury though called *m.*
**Magnificent.**—P. L. 3, 502. by degrees *m.*
P. L. 7, 568. from his work returned *m.*
P. L. 9, 153. and for him built *m.* this world
**Magnified.**—P. L. 7, 606. thy thunders *m.*
S. A. 440. so Dagon shall be *m.*
**Magnify.**—P. L. 7, 97. more to *m.* his works
**Magnitude.**—P. L. 2, 1053. of smallest *m.*
P. L. 7, 357. and every *m.* of stars
S. A. 1279. with plain heroic *m.* of mind
**Magnitudes.**—P. L. 8, 17. compute their *m.*
**Mahanaim.**—P. L. 11, 214. met Jacob in *M.*

**Maia's.**—P. L. 5, 285. like *M.* son he stood
**Maid.**—P. L. 5, 223. the seven-times wedded *m.*
P. R. 2, 200. dismissed ... the fair Iberian *m.*
L'A. 95. to many a youth and many a *m.*
H. 3. of wedded *M.* and Virgin-Mother born
D. F. I. 56. or wert thou that just *M.*
**Maiden.**—C. 402. let a single helpless *m.* pass
C. 843. still she retains her *m.* gentleness
H. 42. the saintly veil of *m.* white to throw
V. Ex. 96. or Severn swift guilty of *m.'s* death
**Maidenhood.**—C. 855. for *m.* she loves
**Maids.**—H. 204. in vain the Tyrian *m.*
**Mail.**—P. L. 5, 284. with feathered *m.*
P. L. 6, 368. wounds through plate and *m.*
P. R. 3, 312. in coats of *m.* and military pride
P. R. 3, 313. in *m.* their horses clad
S. A. 133. and frock of *m.* Adamantean proof
**Maimed.**—P. L. 1, 459. *m.* his brute image
S. A. 1221. though by his blindness *m.* for high
**Main.**—P. L. 2, 121. *m.* reason to persuade
P. L. 3, 83. nor yet the *m.* Abyss wide interrupt
P. L. 4, 233. now divided into four *m.* streams
P. L. 6, 216. together rushed both battles *m.*
P. L. 6, 243. soaring on *m.* wing
P. L. 6, 471. believest so *m.* to our success
P. L. 6, 654. on their heads *m.* promontories
P. L. 6, 698. and dangerous to the *m.*
P. L. 7, 279. over all the face of earth *m.* ocean
P. L. 10, 257. a path over this *m.* from hell
P. L. 12, 431. sin and death his two *m.* arms
P. R. 1, 112. management of this *m.* enterprise
P. R. 4, 457. are to the *m.* as inconsiderable
S. A. 146. then by *m.* force pulled up
S. A. 1606. half-round on two *m.* pillars vaulted
S. A. 1634. to the arched roof gave *m.* support
S. 17, 8. her two *m.* nerves, iron and gold
**Mainly.**—P. L. 11, 519. inductive *m.* to the sin
**Maintained.**—P. L. 6, 30. who single hast *m.*
**Majestic.**—P. L. 2, 305. *m.* though in ruin
P. L. 8, 42. with lowliness *m.* from her seat
P. R. 2, 216. one look from his *m.* brow
P. R. 4, 110. grandeur and *m.* show
P. R. 4, 359. in their *m.* unaffected style
C. 870. and Tethys' grave *m.* pace
Il P. 34. flowing with *m.* train and sable stole
**Majesty.**—P. L. 2, 266. the *m.* of darkness
P. L. 4, 290. in naked *m.* seemed lords of all
P. L. 4, 677. till the Moon rising in clouded *m.*
P. L. 6, 101. idol of *m.* divine
P. L. 7, 195. with radiance crowned *m.* divine
P. L. 8, 509. and with obsequious *m.* approved
P. L. 9, 270. to whom the virgin *m.* of Eve
P. L. 11, 232. such *m.* invests him coming
P. R. 2, 159. virgin *m.* with mild and sweet
C. 430. she may pass on with unblenched *m.*
A. 2. what sudden blaze of *m.*
H. 9. and that far-beaming blaze of, *m.*
M. W. 70. bosom bright of blazing *M.* and Light
**Make.**—P. L. 1, 255. can *m.* a Heaven of Hell
P. L. 2, 113. *m.* the worse appear the better
P. L. 4, 346. to *m.* them mirth used all his
P. L. 5, 70. yet able to *m.* gods of men
P. L. 5, 829. far from thought to *m.* us less
P. L. 7, 519. let us *m.* now Man in our image
P. L. 8, 484. to *m.* her amiable
P. L. 9, 127. but others to *m.* such as I
P. L. 9, 778. of virtue to *m.* wise
P. L. 9, 817. shall I to him *m.* known as yet
P. L. 9, 866. to open eyes and *m.* them Gods
P. L. 10ᵗ 29. made haste to *m.* appear
P. L. 10, 402. him first *m.* sure your thrall
P. L. 10, 611. both to destroy or unimmortal *m.*
P. L. 10, 798. *m.* deathless death that were to *m.*
P. L. 10, 1000. let us *m.* short
P. L. 10, 1028. provoke the Highest to *m.* death
P. L. 11, 680. of whom such massacre *m.* they
P. R. 1, 223. and *m.* persuasion do the work
P. R. 3, 363. one of these thou must *m.* sure
P. R. 4, 145. of inward slaves *m.* outward free
S. A. 401. she sought to *m.* me traitor to myself
S. A. 425. *m.* thee their captive and their triumph

S. A. 560. what boots it at one gate to *m.* defence
S. A. 778. was it not weakness also to *m.* known
S. A. 956. *m.* memorable among illustrious
S. A. 1328. to *m.* them sport with blind activity
S. A. 1331. or *m.* a game of my calamities
C. 227. such noise as I can *m.* to be heard farthest
C. 617. approach so near as to *m.* this relation
C. 654. fierce sign of battle *m.* and menace high
C. 846. the shrewd meddling elf delights to *m.*
C. 1008. *m.* her his eternal bride
L. 116. of other care they little reckoning *m.*
D. F. I. 77. shall *m.* thy name to live
W. S. 14. *m.* us marble with too much conceiving
U.C. II. 20. for one carrier put down to *m.* six
V. Ex. 31. such as may *m.* thee search thy coffers
V. Ex. 76. yet every one shall *m.* him underling
H. 132. *m.* full consort to the angelic symphony
**Maker.**—P. L. 1, 486. likening his *M.* to the
P. L. 2, 915. unless the Almighty *M.*
P. L. 3, 113. nor can justly accuse their *M.*
P. L. 3, 676. the universal *M.* we may praise
P. L. 4, 292. image of their glorious *M.* shone
P. L. 4, 380. yet such accept your *M's.* work
P. L. 4, 725. also madest the night *M.* omnipotent
P. L. 4, 748. our *M.* bids increase
P. L. 5, 148. to praise their *M.*
P. L. 5, 184. vary to our great *M.* still new
P. L. 5, 551. never shall forget to love our *M.*
P. L. 5, 858. while the *M.* gave thee being
P. L. 7, 116. best may serve to glorify the *M.*
P. L. 8, 101. the *M's.* high magnificence
P. L. 8, 278. not of myself, by some great *M.*
P. L. 8, 380. my *M.* be propitious while I speak
P. L. 8, 485. led by her heavenly *M.*
P. L. 9, 177. to spite his *M.* raised from dust
P. L. 9, 338. left so imperfect by the *M.* wise
P. L. 9, 538. fairest resemblance of thy *M.* fair
P. L. 10, 43. believing lies against his *M.*
P. L. 10, 743. did I request thee *M.* from my clay
P. L. 11, 514. and for his *M's.* image sake
P. L. 11, 515. their *M's.* image answered
P. L. 11, 611. unmindful of their *M.*
S. 19, 5. more bent to serve therewith my *M.*
H. 43. confounded that her *M's.* eyes
**Makes.**—P. L. 3, 290. his crime *m.* guilty all
P. L. 6, 7. which *m.* through Heaven grateful
P. L. 6, 458. *m.* remiss the hands of mightiest
P. L. 6, 697. which *m.* wild work in Heaven
P. L. 11, 651. call in aid which *m.* a bloody fray
P. L. 11, 892. *m.* a covenant never to destroy
P. L. 12, 167. of guests he *m.* them slaves
P. R. 4, 362. what *m.* a nation happy and keeps
S. A. 731. but now again she *m.* address to speak
C. 126. 'tis only daylight that *m.* sin
C. 133. and *m.* one blot of all the air
**Making.**—P. L. 3, 113. their Maker or their *m.*
P. L. 5, 858. remember'st thou thy *m.*
P. L. 9, 138. six nights and days continued *m.*
S. A. 1289. *m.* them each his own deliverer
**Malabar.**—P. L. 9, 1103. in *M.* or Deccan
**Maladies.**—P. L. 11, 480. all *m.* of ghastly
S. A. 608. with *m.* innumerable in heart, head
**Malecontent.**—P. R. 2, 392. Satan *m.*
**Male.**—P. L. 1, 422. those *m.* these feminine
P. L. 7, 529. *m.* he created thee but thy consort
P. L. 8, 150. communicating *m.* and female light
**Malediction.**—S. A. 978. with *m.* mentioned
**Males.**—P. L. 12, 168. and kills their infant *m.*
**Malice.**—P. L. 1, 217. how all his *m.* served
P. L. 2, 382. could spring so deep a *m.*
P. L. 3, 158. shall he fulfil his *m.* and thy
P. L. 3, 400. him through their *m.* fallen
P. L. 4, 49. proved ill in me and wrought but *m.*
P. L. 4, 123. deep *m.* to conceal
P. L. 5, 666. deep *m.* thence conceiving
P. L. 6, 270. how hast thou instilled thy *m.*
P. L. 6, 502. in future days if *m.* should abound
P. L. 9, 55. improved in meditated fraud and *m.*
P. L. 9, 306. nor thou his *m.* and false guile
P. L. 9, 461. overawed his *m.* and with rapine
P. R. 1, 149. whate'er his cruel *m.* could invent

P. L. 1, 424. what but thy *m.* moved thee
S. A. 821. that *m.* not repentance brought thee
C. 587. against the threats of *m.* or of sorcery
**Malicious.**—P. L. 9, 253. *m.* foe
S. A. 1251. and with *m.* counsel stir them up
**Malign.**—P. L. 3, 553. the Spirit *m.*
P. L. 4, 503. with jealous leer *m.* eyed them
P. L. 6, 313. rushing from aspect *m.*
P. L. 7, 189. instead of spirits *m.* a better race
**Malignant.**—P. L. 10, 662. influence *m.*
P. L. 12, 538. to good *m.* to bad men benign
**Mammon.**—P. L. 1, 678. *M.* led them on, *M.*
P. L. 2, 228. and after him thus *M.* spake
P. L. 2, 291. applause was heard as *M.* ended
**Man.**—P. L. 1, 1. of *M.'s* first disobedience
P. L. 1, 4. till one greater *M.* restore us
P. L. 1, 219. grace and mercy shown on *m.*
P. L. 1, 366. high sufferance for the trial of *m.*
P. L. 1, 462. upward *m.* and downward fish
P. L. 1, 573. for never since created *m.*
P. L. 2, 348. seat of some new race called *M.*
P. L. 2, 504. as if *m.* had not hellish foes enow
P. L. 2, 629. the adversary of God and *m.*
P. L. 2, 1023. when *m.* fell strange alteration
P. L. 3, 90. and *m.* there placed with purpose
P. L. 3, 93. for *M.* will hearken to his glozing
P. L. 3, 130. *M.* falls deceived by the other first
P. L. 3, 131. *M.* therefore shall find grace
P. L. 3, 145. that *M.* should find grace
P. L. 3, 150. should *M.* finally be lost, should *M.*
P. L. 3, 173. *m.* shall not quite be lost but saved
P. L. 3, 203. *m.* disobeying disloyal breaks
P. L. 3, 215. to redeem *m.'s* mortal crime
P. L. 3, 218. on *M.'s* behalf
P. L. 3, 227. *m.* shall find grace
P. L. 3, 232. happy for *M.* so coming
P. L. 3, 238. account me *M.*
P. L. 3, 277. nor *M.* the least though last
P. L. 3, 283. and be thyself *m.* among men
P. L. 3, 294. so *M.* as is most just
P. L. 3, 295. shall satisfy for *M.*
P. L. 3, 304. descending to assume *m.'s* nature
P. L. 3, 316. *M.* son both of God and *M.*
P. L. 3, 355. for *M.'s* offence to Heaven
P. L. 3, 400. not so on *M.*
P. L. 3, 404. purposed not to doom frail *M.*
P. L. 3, 410. to die for *M.'s* offence
P. L. 3, 632. to Paradise the happy seat of *m.*
P. L. 3, 663. chiefly *M.* his chief delight
P. L. 3, 668. hath *M.* his fixed seat
P. L. 3, 682. neither *M.* nor Angel
P. L. 3, 724. that place is Earth the seat of *M.*
P. L. 4, 11. to wreak on innocent frail *M.*
P. L. 4, 113. as *m.* ere long and this new world
P. L. 4, 177. all path of *m.* or beast that passed
P. L. 4, 317. and banished from *M.'s* life
P. L. 4, 323. Adam the goodliest *m.* of men
P. L. 4, 566. Almighty's works and chiefly *m.*
P. L. 4, 618. *m.* hath his daily work
P. L. 4, 660. daughter of God and *m.*
P. L. 4, 692. all things to *m.'s* delightful use
P. L. 4, 705. such was their awe of *m.*
P. L. 4, 749. our destroyer, foe to God and *m.*
P. L. 5, 60. nor God nor *m.*
P. L. 5, 117. evil into the mind of God or *m.*
P. L. 5, 405. to *m.* in part spiritual
P. L. 5, 462. in this honour done to *m.*
P. L. 5, 483. and their fruit *m.'s* nourishment
P. L. 6, 345. not as frail *m.* in entrails, heart
P. L. 7, 114. heart of *m.* suffice to comprehend
P. L. 7, 155. out of one *m.* a race of men
P. L. 7, 332. and *m.* to till the ground none was
P. L. 7, 347. Lights great for their use to *m.*
P. L. 7, 519. *M.* in our image *M.* in our similitude
P. L. 7, 524. he formed thee Adam, thee O *M.*
P. L. 8, 72. the rest from *M.* or Angel
P. L. 8, 103. that *m.* may know he dwells not
P. L. 8, 226. into the ways of God with *m.*
P. L. 8, 228. and set on *m.* his equal love
P. L. 8, 250. for *m.* to tell how human life began
P. L. 8, 297. first *m.* of men innumerable

P. L. 8, 361. and all this good to *m.*
P. L. 8, 397. worse then can *m.* with beast
P. L. 8, 416. not so is *m.* but in degree
P. L. 8, 422. but *m.* by number is to manifest
P. L. 8, 445. knew it not good for *m.* to be alone
P. L. 8, 496. Woman is her name of *M.* extracted
P. L. 8, 585. subdue the soul of *m.*
P. L. 9, 2. with *m.* as with his friend familiar
P. L. 9, 7. breach disloyal on the part of *m.*
P. L. 9, 56. bent on *m.'s* destruction
P. L. 9, 113. all summed up in *m.*
P. L. 9, 152. *m.* he made and for him built
P. L. 9, 176. new favourite of Heaven, this *m.*
P. L. 9, 291. daughter of God and *m.*
P. L. 9, 346. of all that he created much less *m.*
P. L. 9, 545. one *m.* except, who sees thee?
P. L. 9, 553. language of *m.*
P. L. 9, 666. with show of zeal and love to *m.*
P. L. 9, 691. shall that be shut to *m.*
P. L. 9, 710. since I as *m.*, internal, *m.*
P. L. 9, 716. what are Gods that *m.* may not
P. L. 9, 726. that *m.* should thus attain to know
P. L. 9, 746. best of fruits though kept from *m.*
P. L. 9, 772. friendly to *m.* far from deceit
P. L. 9, 933. and gains to live as *m.*
P. L. 9, 1069. taught to counterfeit *m.'s* voice
P. L. 10, 9. Satan to attempt the mind of *M.*
P. L. 10, 19. mute and sad for *m.*
P. L. 10, 41. *m.* should be seduced and flattered
P. L. 10, 60. *m.'s* friend, his Mediator
P. L. 10, 62. *M.* himself to judge *M.* fallen
P. L. 10, 97. Intercessor both to sentence *M.*
P. L. 10, 101. both *m.* and wife
P. L. 10, 170. more to know concerned not *m.*
P. L. 10, 209. so judged he *M.*, both Judge
P. L. 10, 227. what had passed with *m.* recounted
P. L. 10, 401. chiefly on *M.* sole lord of all
P. L. 10, 483. therein *M.* placed in a Paradise
P. L. 10, 489. given up both his beloved *M.*
P. L. 10, 492. over *M.* to rule as over all
P. L. 10, 496. in whose shape *m.* I deceived
P. L. 10, 571. not as *M.* whom they triumphed
P. L. 10, 577. their pride and joy for *M.* seduced
P. L. 10, 607. till I in *m.* residing
P. L. 10, 619. had not the folly of *m.* let in
P. L. 10, 631. which *M.'s* polluting sin
P. L. 10, 713. nor stood much in awe of *M.*
P. L. 10, 744. from my clay to mould me *m.*
P. L. 10, 784. pure breath of life, the spirit of *M.*
P. L. 10, 795. *M.* is not so but mortal doomed
P. L. 10, 797. exercise wrath without end on *M.*
P. L. 10, 803. punished *m.* to satisfy his rigour
P. L. 10, 823. should all mankind for one *m.'s*
P. L. 10, 846. not now, as ere *m.* fell, wholesome
P. L. 11, 23. from thy implanted grace in *M.*
P. L. 11, 46. all thy request for *M.* accepted
P. L. 11, 84. O sons like one of us *m.* is become
P. L. 11, 102. or in behalf of *m.* or to invade
P. L. 11, 125. with whose stolen fruit *M.* once
P. L. 11, 161. *M.* is to live and all things live for *M.*
P. L. 11, 219. who to surprise one *m.*
P. L. 11, 239. celestial but as *m.* clad to meet *m.*
P. L. 11, 451. to that meek *m.*
P. L. 11, 467. Death ... in his first shape on *m.*
P. L. 11, 497. compassion quelled his best of *m.*
P. L. 11, 508. thus the image of God in *m.*
P. L. 11, 511. why should not *m.* retaining
P. L. 11, 632. I see the tenor of *m.'s* woe
P. L. 11, 634. from *m.'s* effeminate slackness
P. L. 11, 681. but who was that just *m.*
P. L. 11, 733. of provisions laid in large for *m.*
P. L. 11, 770. let no *m.* seek henceforth to be
P. L. 11, 777. *m.* is not whom to warn
P. L. 11, 782. of happy days the race of *m.*
P. L. 11, 786. and whether here the race of *m.*
P. L. 11, 808. one *m.* except, the only son of light
P. L. 11, 818. the one just *m.* alive
P. L. 11, 822. with them of *m.* and beast select
P. L. 11, 872. assured that *m.* shall live
P. L. 11, 876. for one *m.* found so perfect
P. L. 11, 886. though late repenting him of *m.*

P. L. 11, 890. such grace shall one just *m.* find
P. L. 11, 895. to drown the world with *m.*
P. L. 12, 7. and *m.* as from a second stock
P. L. 12, 69. but *m.* over men he made not
P. L. 12, 73. encroachment proud stays not on *m.*
P. L. 12, 74. wretched *m.,* what food will he
P. L. 12, 86. reason in *m.* obscured
P. L. 12, 90. and to servitude reduce *m.*
P. L. 12, 113. a nation from one faithful *m.*
P. L. 12, 265. *m.'s* voice commanding
P. L. 12, 293. must be paid for *m.*
P. L. 12, 298. nor *m.* the moral part perform
P. L. 12, 313. long-wandered *m.*
P. L. 12, 382. so God with *m.* unites
P. L. 12, 424. which *m.* from death redeems
P. L. 12, 425. his death for *m.*
P. L. 12, 493. what *m.* can do against them
P. R. 1, 2. by one *m.'s* disobedience lost
P. R. 1, 4. by one *m.'s* firm obedience
P. R. 1, 36. the exalted *m.* to whom such high
P. R. 1, 91. *M.* he seems in all his lineaments
P. R. 1, 122. this *m.* of men attested Son of God
P. R. 1, 132. conversant on Earth with *m.*
P. R. 1, 140. this *M.* born and now upgrown
P. R. 1, 150. know I can produce a *m.*
P. R. 1, 154. by conquest what the first *m.* lost
P. R. 1, 166. this perfect *m.* by merit called
P. R. 1, 234. thou art no son of mortal *m.*
P. R. 1, 314. but now an aged *m.* in rural weeds
P. R. 1, 327. for that to me thou seem'st the *m.*
P. R. 1, 349. *m.* lives not by bread only
P. R. 1, 402. each *m.'s* peculiar load
P. R. 1, 403. small consolation then were *M.*
P. R. 1, 404. that *M., M.* fallen shall be restored
P. R. 1, 484. when I come (since no *m.* comes)
P. R. 2, 83. full grown to *m.*
P. R. 2, 135. however to this *M.* inferior far
P. R. 2, 136. if he be *M.* by mother's side
P. R. 2, 298. suddenly a *m.* before him stood
P. R. 2, 454. the wise *m.'s* cumbrance if not
P. R. 2, 462. each *m.'s* burden lies
P. R. 2, 468. which every wise and virtuous *m.*
P. R. 2, 477. governs the inner *m.*
P. R. 3, 62. approbation marks the just *m.*
P. R. 3, 103. the *m.* at least
P. R. 3, 134. but why should *m.* seek glory
P. R. 3, 230. what of perfection can in *M.* be
P. R. 4, 10. as a *m.* who had been matchless
P. R. 4, 143. what wise and valiant *m.* would
P. R. 4, 220. childhood shows the *m.* as morning
P. R. 4, 301. and his virtuous *m.,* wise, perfect
P. R. 4, 304. not to prefer as fearing God nor *m.*
P. R. 4, 311. how the world began and how *m.* fell
P. R. 4, 459. as a sneeze to *m.'s* less universe
P. R. 4, 461. on *m.,* beast, plant
P. R. 4, 471. no *m.* knows when for both
P. R. 4, 535. firm to the utmost of mere *m.*
P. R. 4, 538. what more thou art than *m.*
S. A. 74. the vilest now become of *m.* or worm
S. A. 127. whom unarmed no strength of *m.*
S. A. 165. since *m.* on earth unparalleled
S. A. 299. and no *m.* therein doctor but himself
S. A. 340. O miserable change ! is this the *m.*
S. A. 349. O what not in *m.* deceivable and vain
S. A. 656. all chances incident to *m.'s* frail life
S. A. 667. God of our fathers what is *m.*
S. A. 835. with God or *m.* will gain thee
S. A. 844. no plea in *m.* or woman
S. A. 1054. gave to the *m.* despotic power
S. A. 1106. to combat with a blind *m.* I disdain
S. A. 1224. a *m.* condemned, a slave
S. A. 1226. to fight with thee no *m.* of arms will
S. A. 1233. no *m.* withholds thee
S. A. 1374. for the fear of *m.* and *m.* prefer
S. A. 1390. in time thou hast resolved the *m.*
C. 163. wind me into the easy-hearted *m.*
C. 362. what need a *m.* forestall his date of grief
C. 768. if every just *m.* that now pines with want
S. 10, 8. killed with report that old *m.* eloquent
S. 13, 7. to after-age thou shalt be writ the *m.*
S. 19, 10. either *m.'s* work or his own gifts

S. 22, 6. or star throughout the year, or *m.*
**Manacled.**—P. L. 1, 426. not tied or *m.*
**Manacles.**—S. A. 1309. his *m.* remark him
**Managed.**—P. L. 8, 573. and right well *m.*
**Management.**—P. R. 1, 112. and *m.* of this
**Mane.**—P. L. 7, 466. shakes his brinded *m.*
    P. L. 7, 497. with brazen eyes and hairy *m.*
**Manger.**—P. R. 1, 247. directed to the *m.*
    P. R. 2, 75. a stable was our warmth, a *m.* his
    H. 31. all meanly wrapt in the rude *m.* lies
**Mangle.**—S. A. 624. *m.* my apprehensive
**Mangled.**—P. L. 6, 368. *m.* with ghastly
**Manhood.**—P. L. 3, 314. with thee thy *m.*
    P. L. 10, 148. to her thou didst resign thy *m.*
    P. L. 11, 246. prime in *m.* where youth ended
    P. L. 12, 389. not therefore joins the Son *m.*
    P. R. 4, 509. thy *m.* last
    S. A. 408. with a grain of *m.*
    S. 7, 6. that I to *m.* am arrived so near
**Manifest.**—P. L. 6, 707. to *m.* thee worthiest
    P. L. 7, 615. against his purpose serves to *m.*
    P. L. 8, 422. to *m.* his single imperfection
    P. L. 10, 66. all his Father *m.* expressed
    S. A. 997. a *m.* serpent by her sting
**Manifold.**—P. L. 4, 435. of *m.* delights
    P. L. 10, 16. and *m.* in sin deserved to fall
    P. L. 8, 29. greater so *m.*
**Mankind.**—P. L. 1, 36. the mother of *m.*
    P. L. 1, 368. greatest part of *m.* they corrupted
    P. L. 2, 383. to confound the race of *m.* in one
    P. L. 3, 66. only two of *m.* in the happy Garden
    P. L. 3, 161. after him the whole race of *m.*
    P. L. 3, 222. now without redemption all *m.*
    P. L. 3, 275. the only peace found out for *m.*
    P. L. 3, 286. in Adam's room the head of all *m.*
    P. L. 4, 10. the tempter ere the accuser of *m.*
    P. L. 4, 107. his new delight, *m.* created
    P. L. 4, 315. how have ye troubled all *m.*
    P. L. 4, 718. ensnared *m.* with her fair looks
    P. L. 5, 228. in them at once to ruin all *m.*
    P. L. 5, 388. hail mother of *m.* whose fruitful
    P. L. 5, 506. the patriarch of *m.* replied
    P. L. 7, 530. blessed *m.* and said be fruitful
    P. L. 8, 358. above *m.* or aught than *m.* higher
    P. L. 8, 579. if the sense of touch whereby *m.*
    P. L. 8, 650. thou to *m.* be good and friendly
    P. L. 9, 376. so spake the patriarch of *m.*
    P. L. 9, 415. the only two of *m.*
    P. L. 9, 494. Enemy of *m.* enclosed in serpent
    P. L. 9, 950. me first he ruined now *m.*
    P. L. 10, 498. he will put between me and *m.*
    P. L. 10, 646. the Son destined Restorer of *m.*
    P. L. 10, 822. why should all *m.* for one man's
    P. L. 10, 895. some other way to generate *m.*
    P. L. 11, 13. to restore the race of *m.* drowned
    P. L. 11, 38. the smell of peace towards *m.*
    P. L. 11, 69. how with *m.* I proceed
    P. L. 11, 159. rightly called mother of all *m.*
    P. L. 11, 500. O miserable *m.* to what fall
    P. L. 11, 696. great conquerors, patrons of *m.*
    P. L. 11, 752. of *m.* so numerous late
    P. L. 11, 891. not to blot out *m.*
    P. L. 12, 235. achieve *m.'s* deliverance
    P. L. 12, 276. would become of me and all *m.*
    P. L. 12, 417. the sins of all *m.* with him
    P. L. 12, 601. by the Woman's Seed on all *m.*
    P. R. 1, 3. now sing recovered Paradise to all *m.*
    P. R. 1, 114. whose attempt at first against *m.*
    P. R. 1, 187. Saviour to *m.*
    P. R. 1, 266. or work redemption for *m.*
    P. R. 1, 388. think me such a foe to all *m.*
    P. R. 3, 82. Great Benefactors of *m.*
    P. R. 4, 635. now enter and begin to save *M.*
**Manlier.**—P. R. 2, 225. with *m.* objects
**Manliest.**—P. R. 2, 167. *m.* resolutest breast
**Manlike.**—P. L. 8, 471. a creature grew *m.*
**Manly.**—P. L. 4, 302. his parted forelock *m.*
    P. L. 4, 490. how beauty is excelled by *m.* grace
    C. 289. were they of *m.* prime or youthful bloom
**Manna.**—P. L. 2, 113. his tongue dropped *m.*
    P. R. 1, 351. who fed our fathers here with *m.*

P. R. 2, 312. had not God rained from heaven *m.*
**Manner.**—P. R. 1, 50. ruled in *m.* at our will
**Manners.**—P. R. 4, 83. civility of *m.*, arts
**Manoah.**—S. A. 328. old *M.*
  S. A. 1441. old *M.* in such haste with youthful
  S. A. 1548. to thee first, reverend *M.*
  S. A. 1565. ah! *M.*, I refrain too suddenly
**Mansion.**—P. L. 1, 268. in this unhappy *m.*
  P. L. 2, 462. or slack the pain of this ill *m.*
  P. L. 3, 699. from thy empyreal *m.* thus alone
  P. L. 6, 738. to their prepared ill *m.* driven
  P. L. 3, 296. thy *m.* wants thee, Adam
  C. 2. my *m.* is where those immortal shapes
  Il P. 92. forsook her *m.* in this fleshly nook
**Mansions.**—H. 140. and leave her dolorous *m.*
**Man-slaughter.**—P. L. 11, 693. infinite *m.-s.*
**Mantle.**—P. L. 3, 10. as with a *m.* didst invest
  P. L. 4, 609. o'er the dark her silver *m.* threw
  L. 104. his *m.* hairy, and his bonnet sedge
  L. 192. at last he rose and twitched his *m.* blue
  P. 30. over the pole thy thickest *m.* throw
**Mantling.**—P. L. 4, 258. the *m.* vine
  P. L. 5, 279. came *m.* o'er his breast
  P. L. 7, 439. neck between her white wings *m.*
  C. 294. I saw them under a green *m.* vine
**Manuring.**—P. L. 4, 628. mock our scant *m.*
  P. L. 11, 28. those which his own hand *m.*
**Many.**—P.L.1,128. O Chief, of *m.* throned Powers
  P. L. 1, 196. lay floating *m.* a rood
  P. L. 1, 700. on the plain in *m.* cells prepared
  P. L. 1, 709. to *m.* a row of pipes
  P. L. 1, 727. *m.* a row of starry lamps
  P. L. 1, 733. by *m.* a towered structure high
  P. L. 2, 548. with notes angelical to *m.* a harp
  P. L. 2, 618. *m.* a dark and dreary vale
  P. L. 2, 619. and *m.* a region dolorous
  P. L. 2, 620. o'er *m.* a frozen *m.* a fiery Alp
  P. L. 2, 651. but ended foul in *m.* a scaly fold
  P. L. 2, 929. thence *m.* a league as in a cloudy
  P. L. 2, 938. hurried him as *m.* miles aloft
  P. L. 3, 289. as *m.* as are restored
  P. L. 3, 465. with *m.* a vain exploit
  P. L. 3, 473. and *m.* more too long
  P. L. 3, 611. in the dark so *m.* precious things
  P. L. 3, 642. wings he wore of *m.* a coloured
  P. L. 3, 741. in *m.* an aery wheel
  P. L. 4, 164. *m.* a league
  P. L. 4, 229. with *m.* a rill watered the garden
  P. L. 4, 234. wandering in *m.* a famous realm
  P. L. 4, 429. among so *m.* signs of power
  P. L. 5, 101. are *m.* lesser faculties that serve
  P. L. 5, 346. must and meaths from *m.* a berry
  P. L. 5, 567. the ruin of so *m.* glorious once
  P. L. 6, 24. that of so *m.* myriads fallen yet one
  P. L. 6, 76. over *m.* a tract of heaven
  P. L. 6, 77. and *m.* a province wide
  P. L. 6, 336. by angels *m.* and strong
  P. L. 6, 387. with *m.* an inroad gored
  P. L. 6, 624. amused them all and stumbled *m.*
  P. L. 6, 658. and *m.* a dolorous groan
  P. L. 7, 144. into fraud drew *m.*
  P. L. 8, 28. so *m.* nobler bodies to create greater
  P. L. 9, 183. in labyrinth of *m.* a round
  P. L. 9, 434. and *m.* a walk traversed
  P. L. 9, 517. curled *m.* a wanton wreath
  P. L. 9, 618. for *m.* are the trees of God
  P. L. 9, 730. these and *m.* more causes import
  P. L. 10, 274. through *m.* a league remote
  P. L. 10, 311. scourged with *m.* a stroke
  P. L. 10, 438. *m.* a dark league
  P. L. 10, 1005. and have the power of *m.* ways
  P. L. 10, 1084. with *m.* comforts
  P. L. 11, 254. defeated of his seizure *m.* days
  P. L. 11, 256. one bad act with *m.* deeds
  P. L. 11, 323. so *m.* grateful altars I would
  P. L. 11, 351. and of his presence *m.* a sign
  P. L. 11, 467. *m.* shapes of death and *m.* are the
  P. L. 11, 534. till *m.* years over thy head
  P. L. 11, 767. the burden of *m.* ages on me
  P. L. 12, 261. how *m.* battles fought
  P. L. 12, 262. how *m.* kings destroyed

P. L. 12, 282. so *m.* and so various laws
  P. L. 12, 283. so *m.* laws argue so *m.* sins
  P. L. 12, 425. as *m.* as offered life neglect not
  P. L. 12, 530. yet *m.* will presume
  P. L. 12, 602. which will be *m.* days
  P. R. 1, 16. unrecorded left through *m.* an age
  P. R. 1, 48. how *m.* ages as the years of men
  P. R. 1, 118. of *m.* a pleasant realm and province
  P. R. 1, 264. through *m.* a hard assay
  P. R. 2, 11. began to doubt and doubted *m.* days
  P. R. 2, 80. hath been our dwelling *m.* years
  P. R. 2, 89. of *m.* in Israel and to a sign spoken
  P. R. 2, 155. *m.* are in each region passing fair
  P. R. 2, 188. *m.* more too long
  P. R. 2, 193. how *m.* have with a smile made
  P. R. 2, 441. on the throne of Judah sat so *m.* ages
  P. R. 3, 137. who for so *m.* benefits received
  P. R. 3, 269. cut shorter *m.* a league
  P. R. 3, 315. and choice of *m.* provinces
  P. R. 3, 342. sought by *m.* prowest
  P. R. 4, 55. *m.* a fair edifice besides
  P. R. 4, 124. so *m.* hollow compliments and lies
  P. R. 4, 321. *m.* books .... are wearisome
  P. R. 4, 411. the clouds from *m.* a horrid rift
  P. R. 4, 478. *m.* a hard assay of dangers
  P. R. 4, 482. so *m.* terrors, voices, prodigies
  P. R. 4, 569. after *m.* a foil the Tempter proud
  S. A. 65. so *m.* and so huge that each apart
  S. A. 111. I hear the tread of *m.* feet
  S. A. 194. how *m.* evils have inclosed me round
  S. A. 287. in that sore battle when so *m.* died
  S. A. 439. who slew'st them *m.* a slain
  S. A. 542. which *m.* a famous warrior overturns
  S. A. 652. *m.* are the sayings of the wise
  S. A. 915. life yet hath *m.* solaces
  S. A. 918. exempt from *m.* a care and chance
  S. A. 1260. the work of *m.* hands
  S. A. 1401. yet knowing their advantages too *m.*
  C. 526. with *m.* murmurs mixed
  C. 537. yet have they *m.* baits and guileful spells
  C. 935. with *m.* a tower and terrace round
  C. 946. and not *m.* furlongs thence
  C. 949. *m.* a friend to congratulate his wished
  L'A. 95. to *m.* a youth and *m.* a maid
  L'A. 101. with stories told of *m.* a feat
  L'A. 139. with *m.* a winding bout
  V. Ex. 74. shall subject be to *m.* an Accident
**Maple.**—C. 391. his beads or *m.* dish
**Marasmus.**—P. L. 11, 487. *m.* and wide-wasting
**Marble.**—P. L. 3, 564. through the pure *m.*
  P. R. 4, 60. in cedar, *m.*, ivory, or gold
  C. 916. next this *m.* venomed seat
  Il P. 42. forget thyself to *m.*
  H. 195. and the chill *m.* seems to sweat
  M. W. 1. this rich *m.* doth inter the honoured wife
  W. S. 14. make us *m.* with too much conceiving
**March.**—P. L. 1, 413. on their *m.* from Nile
  P. L. 2, 574. their flying *m.* along the banks
  P. L. 2, 615. thus roving on in confused *m.*
  P. L. 5, 688. homeward with flying *m.*
  P. L. 5, 778. all this haste of midnight *m.*
  P. L. 6, 72. for high above the ground their *m.*
  P. L. 10, 474. to expedite your glorious *m.*
  P. R. 1, 115. their *m.* from Hell's deep-vaulted
**Marched.**—P. L. 6, 77. tract of Heaven they *m.*
**Marches.**—P. R. 3, 303. to her aid he *m.*
**Marching.**—P. L. 1, 488. passed from Egypt *m.*
  P. L. 2, 886. under spread ensigns *m.*
  P. L. 12, 40. *m.* from Eden towards the west
**Marchioness.**—M. W. 74. no *M.* but now a queen
**Margaret.**—S. 10, 14. honoured *M.*
**Margent.**—C. 232. by slow Meander's *m.* green
**Margiana.**—P. R. 3, 317. *M.* to the Hyrcanian
**Mariner.**—P. L. 4, 558. and shows the *m.*
**Mariners.**—C. 48. the Tuscan *m.* transformed
**Marish.**—P. L. 12, 630. o'er the *m.* glides
**Maritime.**—P. L. 11, 398. the less *m.* kings
**Mark.**—P. L. 4, 400. unespied to *m.* what
  P. L. 4, 962. but *m.* what I areed thee now
  P. L. 5, 21. we lose the prime to *m.* how spring
  P. L. 9, 92. none would suspicious *m.*

P. L. 9, 528. the eye of Eve to *m.* his play
P. L. 12, 50. to *m.* their doings
P. R. 3, 349. hear and *m.* to what end I have
S. A. 496. the *m.* of fool set on his front
A. 14. *m.* what radiant state she spreads
S. 12, 13. from that *m.* how far they rove we see
**Marked.**—P. L. 4, 129. his gestures fierce he *m.*
P. L. 4, 401. might learn by word or action *m.*
P. L. 4, 568. and *m.* his aery gait
P. R. 1, 297. the way he came not having *m.*
**Marks.**—P. R. 3, 61. with approbation *m.*
S. A. 992. the public *m.* of honour and reward
**Marle.**—P. L. 1, 296.' over the burning *m.*
**Marocco.**—P. L. 1, 584. Damasco or *M.*
P. L. 11, 404. *M.* and Algiers, and Tremisen
**Marred.**—P. L. 4, 116. *m.* his borrowed visage
P. L. 9, 136. in one day to have *m.* what he
**Marriage.**—P. L. 5, 223. secured his *m.*
P. L. 8, 487. of nuptial sanctity and *m.* rites
P. L. 11, 591. hymen then first to *m.* rites
S. A. 224. and therefore urged the *m.* on
S. A. 320. to seek in *m.* that fallacious bride
S. A. 1115. breaking her *m.* faith
M. W. 18. the god that sits at *m.* feast
**Marriageable.**—P. L. 5, 217. her *m.* arms
**Marriage-choices.**—S. A. 420. thy *m.-c.*
**Marriages**—P. L. 11, 684. those ill-mated *m.*
**Married.**—L'A. 137. *m.* to immortal verse
**Marrying.**—P. L. 11, 716. *m.* or prostituting
**Mars.**—P. R. 3, 84. son of Jove of *M.* the other,
**Marshalled.**—P. L. 9, 37. then *m.* feast
**Martial.**—P. L. 1, 540. blowing *m.* sounds
P. R. 3, 304. in what *m.* equipage
**Martyrdom.**—P. L. 9, 32. heroic *m.* unsung
**Martyred.**—S. 18, 10. their *m.* blood and ashes
**Marvelling.**—P. L. 9,551. at the voice much *m.*
**Mary.**—P. L. 5, 387. to blessed *M.* second Eve
P. L. 10, 183. Jesus son of *M.* second Eve
P. R. 2, 60. to his mother *M.* when she saw
P. R. 2, 105. thus *M.* pondering oft
S. 9, 5. the better part with *M.* and with Ruth
**Masculine.**—P. L. 10, 890. with Spirits *m.*
**Mask.**—P. L. 4, 768. mixed dance or wanton *m.*
L'A. 128. with *m.* and antique pageantry
S. 22, 13. lead me through the world's vain *m.*
P. 19. Oh what a *m.* was there, what a disguise
**Mass.**—P. L. 3, 708. the formless *m.*
P. L. 7, 237. throughout the fluid *m.*
P. L. 12, 548. from the conflagrant *m.* purged
P. R. 1, 162. and *m.* of sinful flesh
**Massacre.**—P. L. 11, 679. such *m.* make they
**Massy.**—P. L. 1, 285. *m.*, large and round
P. L. 1, 703. founded the *m.* ore
P. L. 2, 878. and every bolt and bar of *m.* iron
P. L. 5, 634. in pearl, in diamond and *m.* gold
P. L. 6,195. on bended knee his *m.* spear upstayed
P. L. 11, 565. two *m.* clods of iron and brass
S. A. 147. the gates of Azza post and *m.* bar
S. A. 1633. both his arms on those two *m.* pillars
S. A. 1648. those two *m.* pillars
L. 110. two *m.* keys he bore of metals twain
Il P. 158. with antique pillars *m.* proof
**Mast.**—P. L. 1, 293. the *m.* of some great ammiral
**Master.**—C. 501. O my loved *m.'s* heir
C. 725. and we should serve him as a grudging *m.*
H. 34. with her great *M.* so to sympathise
**Mastering.**—P. L. 9, 125. unless by *m.*
**Masters.**—S. A. 1215. but to their *m.* gave me up
S. A. 1404. *ms.'* commands come with a power
**Master-work.**—P. L. 7, 505. the *m.-w.*, the end
**Mastery.**—P. L. 2, 899. strive here for *m.*
P. L. 9, 29. chief *m.* to dissect
**Match.**—P. L. 6, 631. *m.* with their inventions
S. A. 346. himself an army now unequal *m.*
S. A. 1164. no worthy *m.* for valour to assail
**Matched.**—P. L. 2, 720. so *m.* they stood
P. L. 11, 685. where good with bad were *m.*
**Matching.**—P. L. 5, 113. ill *m.* words and deeds
**Matchless.**—P. L. 1, 623. O Powers *m.*
P. L. 2, 487. rejoicing in their *m.* chief
P. L. 4, 41. against heaven's *m.* King

P. L. 6, 341. and shame to find himself not *m.*
P. L. 6, 457. valour or strength though *m.*
P. L. 10, 404. of *m.* might
P. R. 1, 233. by *m.* deeds express thy *m.* Sire
P. R. 4, 10. but as a man who had been *m.*
S. A. 178. *m.* in might, the glory late of Israel
S. A. 280. the *m.* Gideon, in pursuit of Madian
S. A. 1740. to *m.* valour and adventures high
S. 16, 3. guided by faith and *m.* fortitude
**Mate.**—P. L. 1, 192. talking to his nearest *m.*
P. L. 1, 238. him followed his next *m.*
P. L. 4, 828. ye knew me once no *m.* for you
P. L. 7, 403. part single or with *m.* graze
P. L. 8,578. with honour thou mayst love thy *m.*
P. L. 8, 594. among the beasts no *m.* for thee
P. L. 10, 899. he never shall find out fit *m.*
S. A. 173. whose strength while virtue was her *m.*
S. 1, 13. whether the Muse or Love call thee his *m.*
D. F. I. 24. whilom did slay his dearly-loved *m.*
**Material.**—P. L. 3. 709. this world's *m.*
**Materials.**—P. L. 2, 916. ordain his dark *m.*
P. L. 6, 478. *m.* dark and crude
**Mates.**—P. L. 6, 608. and to his *m.* thus
**Matin.**—P. L. 5, 7. and the shrill *m.* song
P. L. 6, 526. and to arms the *m.* trumpet sung
P. L. 7, 450. arose with evening harps and *m.*
L'A. 114. ere the first cock his *m.* rings
**Matrimonial.**—P. L. 9, 319. care and *m.* love
S. A. 959. with the gold of *m.* treason
**Matron.**—P. L. 1, 505. exposed a *m.* to avoid
P. L. 4, 501. pressed her *m.* lip with kisses pure
P. L. 11, 136. when Adam and first *m.* Eve
S. A. 722. some rich Philistian *m.* she may seem
D. F. I. 54. that crowned *M.* sage, white-robed
**Matrons.**—M. W. 23. once had the early *m.* run
**Matter.**—P. L. 1, 256. what *m.* where
P. L. 3, 413. thy name shall be the copious *m.*
P. L. 3, 613. here *m.* new to gaze the Devil met
P. L. 5, 472. one first *m.*
P. L. 5, 563. high *m.* thou enjoin'st me
P. L. 5, 738. *m.* to me of glory
P. L. 7, 233. the earth, *m.* unformed and void
P. L. 9, 669. as of some great *m.*
P. L. 9, 951. *m.* of scorn
P. L. 9, 1177. to find *m.* of glorious trial
P. L. 10, 807. to the reception of their *m.* act
P. L. 10, 1071. may with *m.* sere foment
S. A. 1638. or some great *m.* in his mind revolved
S. 11, 2. woven close both *m.* form and style
**Matters.**—P. L. 8, 167. thoughts with *m.* hid
P. R. 4, 329. toys and trifles for choice *m.*
S. A. 1348. *m.* now are strained up to the height
**Mature.**—P. L. 1, 660. full counsel must *m.*
P. L. 5, 862. birth *m.* of this our native Heaven
P. L. 9, 803. till dieted by thee I grow *m.*
P. L. 10, 612. and for destruction to *m.*
P. L. 10, 882. constant, *m.*, proof against all
P. L. 11, 537. not harshly plucked for death *m.*
P. R. 1, 188. publish his godlike office now *m.*
P. R. 3, 37. and to ripe years judgment *m.*
P. R. 4, 282. till time *m.* thee to a kingdom's
**Maturest.**—P. L. 2. 115. dash *m.* counsels
**Maugre.**—P. L. 3. 255. Hell captive *m.* Hell
P. L. 9, 56. *m.* what might hap
P. R. 3,368. old Hyrcanus bound, *m.* the Roman
**Maw.**—P. L. 2, 847. and blessed his *m.*
P. L. 10, 601. all too little seems to stuff this *m.*
P. L. 10, 991. forced to satisfy his ravenous *m.*
S. 16,14. hireling wolves whose Gospel is their *m.*
**Maxim.**—S. A. 865. that grounded *m.* so rife
**Maxims.**—P. R. 3, 400. to need thy politic *m.*
**May.**—P. L. 4, 501. clouds that shed *M.* flowers
S. 1,4. while the jolly Hours lead on propitious *M.*
M. M. 3. the flowery *M.* who from her green lap
M. M. 5. hail bounteous *M.*, that dost inspire
**Maying.**—L'A. 20. as he met her once a-*M.*
**Maze.**—P. L. 9, 499. fold above fold a surging *m.*
P. R. 2, 246. wandering this woody *m.*
H. 236. leaving their moon-loved *m.*
**Mazes.**—P. L. 2, 561. in wandering *m.* lost
P. L. 5, 622. resembles nearest *m.* intricate

P. L. 10, 830. though through *m.*
C. 181. in the blind *m.* of this tangled wood
L'A. 142. the melting voice through *m.* running
**Mazy.**—P. L. 4, 239. with *m.* error
P. L. 9, 161. in whose *m.* folds to hide me
**Mead.**—L'A. 90. to the tanned haycock in the *m.*
**Meadow.**—P. R. 2, 185. in valley or green *m.*
**Meadow-ground.**—P. L. 11, 648. fat *m.-g.*
**Meadows.**—P. L. 7, 460. the fields and *m.* green
C. 844. visits the herds along the twilight *m.*
L'A. 75. *m.* trim with daisies pied
**Meads.**—V. Ex. 94. arms along the indented *m.*
**Meagre.**—P. L. 10, 264. the *m.* shadow
C. 434. blue *m.* hag, or stubborn unlaid ghost
**Mean.**—P. L. 2, 684. through them I *m.* to pass
P. L. 2, 981. directed no *m.* recompense it brings
P. L. 3, 272. what this might *m.* and whither tend
P. L. 4, 62. me though *m.* drawn to his part
P. L. 4, 632. ask riddance if we *m.* to tread
P. L. 5, 723. we *m.* to hold what anciently
P. L. 6, 120. I *m.* to try
P. L. 6, 290. strife of glory which we *m.* to win
P. L. 6, 421. too *m.* pretence
P. L. 8, 473. seemed now *m.* or in her summed up
P. L. 8, 527. these delicacies I *m.* of taste
P. L. 9, 39. the skill of artifice or office *m.*
P. L. 9, 553. what may this *m.*? language of man
P. L. 9, 860. never more *m.* I to try what rash
P. L. 9, 1152. why *he* should *m.* me ill or seek
P. L. 11, 9. yet their port not of *m.* suitors
P. L. 11, 879. what *m.* those coloured streaks
P. L. 12, 351. and for a while in *m.* estate live
P. R. 1, 155. first I *m.* to exercise him in
P. R. 2, 6. I *m.* Andrew and Simon
P. R. 3, 404. I must deliver if I *m.* to reign
P. R. 4, 161. nor what I part with *m.* to give
S. A. 207. of wisdom nothing more than *m.*
S. A. 1644. I *m.* to show you of my strength yet
C. 417. the strength of Heaven if you *m.* that
C. 418. I *m.* that too but yet a hidden strength
L'A. 152. mirth with thee I *m.* to live
S. 2, 10. to that same lot however *m.* or high
S. 12, 11. licence they *m.* when they cry Liberty
S. 21, 2. with no *m.* applause pronounced
**Meander's.**—C. 232. slow *M.'s* margent green
**Meaner.**—P. L. 6, 367, *m.* thoughts
**Meanest.**—P. L. 4, 204. to their *m.* use
P. L. 11, 231. and by his gait none of the *m.*
P. R. 4, 230. persuasion as thou *m.*
**Meaning.**—P. L. 7, 5. the *m.* not the name
P. L. 9, 1019. since to each *m.* savour we apply
P. R. 4, 516. in what degree or *m.* thou art
S. A. 813. love hath oft well *m.* wrought much
C. 754. there was another *m.* in these gifts
**Meanly.**—H. 31. all *m.* wrapt in the rude manger
**Means.**—P. L. 1, 165. of good still to find *m.*
P. L. 3, 228. shall grace not find *m.* that finds
P. L. 10, 1062. and teach us further by what *m.*
P. L. 12, 234. by what *m.* he shall achieve
P. L. 12, 279. knowledge by forbidden *m.*
P. R. 2, 412. great acts require great *m.*
P. R. 3, 89. may by *m.* far different be attained
P. R. 3, 355. prediction,... supposes *m.*
P. R. 3, 356. without *m.* used what it predicts
P. R. 3, 394. *m.* I must use thou say'st
P. R. 4, 152. *m.* there shall be to this
P. R. 4, 475. but concealing the time and *m.*
S. A. 315. he would not else who never wanted *m.*
S. A. 444. to have come to pass by *m.*
S. A. 516. what offered *m.* who knows but God
S. A. 562. by which *m.* now blind dishearten
S. A. 603. to prosecute the *m.* of thy deliverance
S. A. 795. sought by all *m.*
C. 644. by this *m.* I knew the foul enchanter
C. 765. *m.* her provision only to the good
C. 821. some other *m.* I have which may be used
S. 17, 10. spiritual power and civil, what each *m.*
**Meant.**—P. L. 3, 516. mysteriously was *m.*
P. L. 5, 513. but say what *m.* that caution
P. L. 6, 854. for he *m.* not to destroy
P. L. 9, 690. more perfect.... than fate *m.* me

P. L. 10, 545. the applause they *m.* turned
P. L. 10, 1033. piteous amends unless be *m.*
P. L. 10, 1050. which we thought was *m.* by
P. L. 12, 149. that seed is *m.* thy great Deliverer
P. R. 1, 83. whate'er it *m.*
P. R. 2, 99. what he *m.* I mused
C. 578. soon I guessed ye were the two she *m.*
C. 591. even that which Mischief *m.* most harm
A. 35. was all in honour and devotion *m.*
Il P. 120. where more is *m.* than meets the ear
**Meanwhile.**—P. L. 1, 752. *m.* the winged
P. L. 2, 629. *m.* the adversary of God and man
P. L. 2, 767. *m.* war arose and fields were fought
P. L. 3, 333. *m.* the world shall burn
P. L. 3, 418. *m.* upon the firm opacous globe
P. L. 4, 260. *m.* murmuring waters fall down
P. L. 4, 599. *m.* in utmost longitude
P. L. 4, 633. *m.* as Nature wills, night bids us
P. L. 5, 350. *m.* our primitive great sire to meet
P. L. 5, 443. *m.* at table Eve ministered naked
P. L. 5, 503. *m.* enjoy your fill what happiness
P. L. 5, 711. *m.* the Eternal Eye whose sight
P. L. 6, 186. *m.* from me returned as erst thou
P. L. 6, 293. *m.* thy utmost force.... I fly not
P. L. 6, 354. *m.* in other parts like deeds
P. L. 6, 493. *m.* revive, abandon fear
P. L. 7, 162. *m.* inhabit lax ye Powers of Heaven
P. L. 7, 192. *m.* the Son on his great expedition
P. L. 7, 417. *m.* the tepid caves and fens
P. L. 9, 739. *m.* the hour of noon drew on
P. L. 10, 1. *m.* the heinous and despiteful act
P. L. 10, 229. *m.* ere thus was sinned and judged
P. L. 10, 585. *m.* in Paradise the hellish pair
P. L. 11, 133. *m.* to resalute the world with
P. L. 11, 738. *m.* the south-wind rose
P. L. 12, 315. *m.* they in their earthly Canaan
P. R. 1, 183. *m.* the Son of God
P. R. 2, 1. *m.* the new-baptized
S. A. 256. *m.* the men of Judah to prevent
S. A. 479. thou must not, in the *m.*, here forgot
S. A. 604. *m.* be calm
C. 102. *m.* welcome joy and feast
L. 32. *m.* the rural ditties were not mute
**Measure.**—P. L. 1, 513. Rhea's son like *m.*
P. L. 3, 142. and without *m.* grace
P. L. 5, 517. full to the utmost *m.*
P. L. 5, 639. where full *m.* only bounds excess
P. L. 6, 265. by just *m.*
P. L. 6, 821. since by strength they *m.* all
P. L. 7, 128. to know in *m.* that the mind may
P. L. 7, 603. what thought can *m.* thee
P. L. 7, 640. aught not surpassing human *m.* say
P. L. 9, 846. he the faltering *m.* felt
S. A. 1439. *m.* of strength so great to mortal seed
S. 2, 10. it shall be still in strictest *m.* even
S. 21, 9. to *m.* life learn thou betimes
**Measured.**—P. L. 4, 776. now had night *m.*
P. L. 11, 730. *m.* by cubit length and breadth
P. L. 12, 554. *m.* this transient world
P. R. 1, 210. yet my age had *m.* twice six years
A. 71. and the low world in *m.* motion draw
**Measures.**—P. L. 1, 50. the space that *m.* day
P. L. 5, 581. *m.* all things durable by present
P. R. 1, 170. and in celestial *m.* moved
L'A. 70. whilst the landscape round it *m.*
**Measuring.**—P. L. 6, 893. thus *m.* things
**Meaths.**—P. L. 5, 345. *m.* from many a berry
**Meats.**—P. L. 5, 451. thus when with *m.*
P. L. 11, 473. by intemperance more in *m.*
P. R. 2, 265. *m.* and drinks nuture's refreshment
P. R. 2, 328. *m.* by the law unclean
P. R. 2, 341. dishes piled and *m.* of noblest sort
**Med'cinal.**—S. A. 627. cooling herb or *m.* liquor
C. 636. and yet more *m.* is it than that moly
**Meddling.**—C. 846. that the shrewd *m.* elf
**Medes.**—P. R. 3, 376. among the *M.* dispersed
**Media.**—P. L. 4, 171. vengeance sent from *M.*
P. R. 3, 320. of Adiabene, *M.*, and the south
**Mediation.**—P. L. 3, 226. his dearest *m.*
**Mediator.**—P. L. 10, 60. man's friend, his *M.*
P. L. 12, 240. to God is no access without *M.*

**Meditate.**—C. 547. to *m*. my rural minstrelsy
L. 66. and strictly *m*. the thankless Muse
**Meditated.**—P. L. 9, 55. improved in *m*. fraud
**Meditation.**—P. L. 12, 605. *m*. on the happy
C. 386. that musing *M*. most affects
**Meditations.**—P. R. 1, 195. his holy *m*.
P. R. 2, 110. with holiest *m*. fed
**Medusa.**—P. L. 2, 611. *M*. with Gorgonian
**Medway.**—V.Ex. 100. *M*. smooth
**Meed.**—L.14. without the *m*. of some melodious
L. 84. of so much fame in Heaven expect thy *m*.
**Meek.**—P. L. 3, 266. his *m*. aspect
P. L. 4, 494. and *m*. surrender half-embracing
P.L. 5, 359. submiss approach and reverence *m*.
P.L. 8, 217.thus Raphael answered heavenly *m*.
P. L. 10, 1092. and humiliation *m*.
P. L. 10, 1104. and humiliation *m*.
P. L. 11,162. thus Eve with sad demeanour *m*.
P. L. 11, 437. a shepherd next more *m*. came
P. L. 11, 451. to that *m*. man
P. L. 12, 569. and worldly wise by simply *m*.
P. L. 12, 597. and all her spirits composed to *m*.
P. R. 3, 217. that placid aspect and *m*. regard
P. R. 4, 401. our Saviour *m*.
P. R. 4, 636. our Saviour *m*. sung victor
S. A. 1036. under virgin veil soft modest *m*.
L. 177. in the blest kingdoms *m*. of joy and love
**Meek-eyed.**—H. 46. sent down the *m-e*. Peace
**Meekly.**—P. R. 2, 108. thoughts *m*. composed
S. 14. *m*. thou didst resign this earthly load
P. 21. then lies him *m*. down
**Meet.**—P. L. 2, 64. when to *m*. the noise of his
P. L. 2, 722. was either like to *m*. so great a foe
P. L. 2, 955. undaunted to *m*. there whatever
P.L. 3, 234. atonement for himself or offering *m*.
P. L. 3, 675. and all things as is *m*.
P. L. 4, 530. chance may lead where I may *m*.
P. L. 4, 913. *m*. thy flight sevenfold
P. L. 5, 350. to *m*. his godlike guest walks forth
P. L. 6, 93. in fierce hosting *m*. who wont to *m*.
P. L. 6, 439. when next we *m*.
P. L. 6, 882. to *m*. him all his saints who
P. L. 8, 57. Oh when *m*. now such pairs in love
P. L. 8,139.averse from the sun's beam *m*. night
P. L. 8, 448. thou couldst judge of fit and *m*.
P. L. 8, 609. who *m*. with various objects
P. L. 9, 360. Reason not impossibly may *m*.
P. L. 9, 711. is but proportion *m*.
P. L. 9, 847. and forth to *m*. her went
P. L. 9, 1028. let us play as *m*. is after such
P. L. 9, 1176. either to *m*. no danger
P. L. 10, 103. wont with joy to *m*. my coming
P. L. 10, 349. unhoped met who to *m*. him
P. L. 10, 599. where most with ravin I may *m*.
P. L. 10, 775. how gladly would I *m*. mortality
P. L. 10, 905. happiest choice too late shall *m*.
P. L. 11, 237. with reverence I must *m*.
P. L. 11, 240. but as man clad to *m*. man
P. L. 11, 604. though to Nature seeming *m*.
P. R. 3, 442. to the Fiend made answer *m*.
P. R. 4, 232. with thee hold conversation *m*.
S.A.1123. I only with an oaken staff will *m*.thee
C.178. to *m*. the rudeness and swilled insolence
C.363. and run to *m*. what he would most avoid
A. 31. stole under seas to *m*. his Arethuse
S. 20. where shall we sometimes *m*.
M. W. 16. quickly found a lover *m*.
**Meetest.**—P. L. 5, 175. moon, that now *m*.
**Meeting.**—P. L. 5, 778. and hurried *m*. here
P. L. 10, 350. great joy was at their *m*.
P. L. 10, 879. but with the serpent *m*.
P. R. 3, 258. then *m*. joined their tribute
L'A. 138. such as the *m*. soul may pierce
**Meets.**—P. L. 2, 931. *m*. a vast vacuity
P. L. 4, 154. now purer air *m*. his approach
P. L. 4, 540. heaven with earth and ocean *m*.
P. L. 4, 784. our circuit *m*. full west
P. L. 9, 271. who loves and some unkindness *m*.
P. R. 4, 320. her false resemblance only *m*.
Il P. 120. where more is meant than *m*. the ear
**Megæra.**—P. L. 10, 560. locks that curled *M*.

**Melancholy.**—P. L. 11, 485. moping *M*.
P. L. 11,544. in thy blood will reign a *m*. damp
C. 546. wrapped in a pleasing fit of *m*.
C. 810. and settlings of a *m*. blood
L'A. 1. hence loathed *M*.
Il P. 12. hail' divinest *M*.
Il P. 62. most musical, most *m*.
Il P. 175. these pleasures, *M*., give
**Melesigenes.**—P. R. 4, 259. blind *M*.
**Melibœan.**—P. L. 11, 242. livelier than *M*.
**Melibœus.**—C. 822. which once of *M*. old
**Melind.**—P. L. 11, 399. Quiloa and *M*.
**Mellifluous.**—P. L. 5, 429. *m*. dews
P. R. 4, 277. *m*. streams that watered all
**Mellowing.**—L. 5. before the *m*. year
**Melodious.**—P. L. 3, 371. could join *m*. part
P. L. 5, 196. *m*. murmurs warbling tune his
P. L. 5, 656.*m*.hymns about the sovran throne
P. L. 11, 559. instruments that made *m*.chime
L. 14. without the meed of some *m*. tear
H. 129. let your silver chime move in *m*. time
S. M. 18. may rightly answer that *m*. noise
V. Ex. 51. held with his *m*. harmony
**Melody.**—P. L. 8, 528. and the *m*. of birds
**Melt.**—P. L. 4, 389. harmless innocence *m*.
L. 163. and *m*. with ruth
H.138. leprous Sin will *m*. from earthly mould
**Melted.**—P. L. 11, 566. iron and brass had *m*.
**Melting.**—L'A. 142. the *m*. voice through mazes
**Member.**—P. L. 2, 668. distinguishable in *m*.
**Membrane.**—P. L. 8, 625. find none of *m*.
**Memnon's.**—Il P. 18. Prince *M*.'s sister
**Memnonian.**—P. L. 10, 308. his *M*. palace
**Memorable.**—S. A. 956. to make thee *m*.
P. R. 3, 96. poor Socrates (who next more *m*.)
**Memorial.**—P. L. 1, 362. records now be no *m*.
P. L. 6, 355. like deeds deserved *m*.
P. R. 2, 445. what hath been done worthy of *m*.
**Memorials.**—P. L. 5, 593. holy *m*.
**Memory.**—P. L. 4, 24. wakes the bitter *m*.
P.L. 6, 379.cancelled from heaven and sacred *m*.
P. L. 7, 66. or without was done before his *m*.
P. L. 7, 637. and what before thy *m*. was done
P. L. 8, 650. be honoured ever with grateful *m*.
P. L. 11, 154. and to my *m*. his promise
P. L. 11, 325. in *m*. or monument to ages
P. L. 12, 46. in foreign lands their *m*. be lost
S.A.1739. and from his *m*.inflame their breasts
C. 206. fantasies begin to throng into my *m*.
W. S. 5. dear son of *M*., great heir of fame
**Memphian.**—P. L. 1, 307. and his *M*.chivalry
P. L. 1, 694. and the works of *M*. kings
H. 214. nor is Osiris seen in *M*. grove or green
**Men.**—P. L. 1, 26. justify the ways of God to *m*.
P. L. 1, 51. day and night to mortal *m*.'
P. L. 1, 332. as when *m*. wont to watch on duty
P. L. 1, 374. then were they known to *m*.
P. L. 1, 685. by him first *m*. also
P. L. 1, 740. and in Ausonian land *m*. called him
P. L. 2, 288. hoarse cadence lull sea-faring *m*.
P. L. 2, 483. bad *m*. should boast their specious
P. L. 2, 496. O shame to *m*., devil with devil
P.L. 2, 497. *m*.only disagree of creatures rational
P. L. 3, 46. from the cheerful ways of *m*. cut
P. L. 3, 268. immortal love to mortal *m*.
P. L. 3, 283. be thyself man among *m*. on earth
P. L. 3, 287. as in him perish all *m*. so true
P. L. 3, 331. thou shalt judge bad *m*. and angels
P. L. 3, 412. Saviour of *m*. thy name shall be
P. L. 3, 447. vanity had filled the works of *m*.
P. L. 3, 453. naught seeking but the praise of *m*.
P. L. 3, 679. created this new happy race of *m*.
P. L. 4, 4. furious down to be revenged on *m*.
P. L. 4, 295. whence true authority in *m*.
P. L. 4, 323. Adam, the goodliest man of *m*.
P. L. 4, 408. Adam, first of *m*. to first of women
P. L. 4, 613. and rest as day and night to *m*.
P. L. 4, 675. nor think though *m*. were none
P. L. 4, 753. adulterous lust was driven from *m*.
P. L. 5, 70. yet able to make gods of *m*.
P. L. 5, 71. and why not gods of *m*. since good

P. L. 5,493. time may come when *m*. with angels
P. L. 5, 563. O prime of *m*.
P. L. 5, 761. that structure in the dialect of *m*.
P. L. 6, 376. seek not the praise of *m*.
P. L. 6, 505. instrument to plague the sons of *m*.
P. L. 7, 156. out of one man a race of *m*.
P. L. 7, 183. good-will to future *m*.
P. L. 7, 570. to visit oft the dwellings of just *m*.
P. L. 7, 623. among these the seat of *m*. earth
P. L. 7, 625. thrice happy *m*. and sons of *m*.
P. L. 8, 218. nor are thy lips ungraceful Sire of *M*.
P. L. 8, 297. first man, of *m*. innumerable
P. L. 9, 622. till *m*. grow up to their provision
P. L. 10, 893. fill the world at once with *m*.
P. L. 11, 360. contending with sinfulness of *m*.
P. L. 11, 477. in abstinence of Eve shall bring on *m*.
P. L. 11, 577. just *m*. they seemed
P. L. 11, 580. freedom and peace to *m*.
P. L. 11, 585. the *m*. though grave eyed them
P. L. 11, 621. to these that sober race of *m*.
P. L. 11, 640. cities of *m*. with lofty gates
P. L. 11, 662. gray-headed *m*. and grave
P. L. 11, 676. death's ministers not *m*.
P. L. 11, 677. thus deal death inhumanly to *m*.
P. L. 11, 680. of their brethren, *m*. of *m*.
P. L. 11, 688. such were these giants, *m*. of high
P. L. 11, 697. rightlier called and plagues of *m*.
P. L. 11, 838. *m*. who there frequent
P. L. 12, 13. this second source of *m*.
P. L. 12, 30. *m*. not beasts shall be his game
P. L. 12, 48. God who oft descends to visit *m*.
P. L. 12, 69. man over *m*. he made not lord
P. L. 12, 80. on the quiet state of *m*. such trouble
P. L. 12, 115. Oh that *m*. (canst thou believe)
P. L. 12, 245. such delight hath God in *m*.
P. L. 12, 248. the Holy One with mortal *m*.
P. L. 12, 354. *m*. who attend the altar
P. L. 12, 438. *m*. who in his life still followed
P. L. 12, 477. more glory more good-will to *m*.
P. L. 12, 538. to good malignant to bad *m*. benign
P. R. 1, 48. how many ages as the years of *m*.
P. R. 1, 122. this man of *m*. attested Son of God
P. R. 1, 132. on Earth with man or *m*.'s affairs
P. R. 1, 164. they now and *m*. hereafter
P. R. 1, 167. to earn salvation for the sons of *m*.
P. R. 1, 191. till far from track of *m*.
P. R. 1, 235. though *m*. esteem thee low
P. R. 1, 237. Angels and sons of *m*.
P. R. 1, 250. guided the wise *m*. thither
P. R. 1, 322. so far from path or road of *m*.
P. R. 1, 341. *m*. to much misery and hardship
P. R. 1, 387. *m*. generally think me much a foe
P. R. 1, 464. to all truth requisite for *m*. to know
P. R. 1, 482. most *m*. admire virtue who follow
P. R. 2, 27. fishermen (no greater *m*. them call)
P. R. 2, 133. when I dealt with Adam first of *m*.
P. R. 2, 154. among daughters of *m*. the fairest
P. R. 2, 180. wanton eyes on the daughters of *m*.
P. R. 2, 192. among the sons of *m*.
P. R. 2, 228. rocks whereon greatest *m*. have
P. R. 2, 437. but *m*. endued with these have oft
P. R. 2, 447. for I esteem those names of *m*.
P. R. 2, 470. cities of *m*. or headstrong
P. R. 3, 70. to things not glorious. *m*. not worthy
P. R. 3, 85. discover them scarce *m*.
P. R. 3, 105. as vain *m*. seek, oft not deserved
P. R. 3, 114. glory from *m*., from all *m*.
P. R. 3, 355. in all things and all *m*.
P. R. 4, 30. fruits of the earth and seats of *m*.
P. R. 4, 140. of fighting beasts and *m*. to beasts
P. R. 4, 197. Sons of God both Angels are and *M*.
P. R. 4, 200. what both from *M*. and Angels
P. R. 4, 276. the oracle pronounced wisest of *m*.
P. R. 4, 322. wise *m*. have said
P. R. 4, 348. and godlike *m*.
P. R. 4, 357. as *m*. divinely taught
P. R. 4, 462. turbulencies in the affairs of *m*.
P. R. 4, 466. of *m*. at thee for only thou here
P. R. 4, 520. all *m*. are sons of God
S. A. 157. which *m*. enjoying sight oft without
S. A. 168. strongest of mortal *m*.

S. A. 210. wisest *m*. have erred
S. A. 215. truth to say I oft have heard *m*. wonder
S. A. 256. meanwhile the *m*. of Judah to prevent
S. A. 294. the ways of God and justifiable to *m*.
S. A. 332. brethren and *m*. of Dan
S. A. 354. and such a son as all *m*. hailed me
S. A. 364. glorious for awhile, the miracle of *m*.
S. A. 406. at times when *m*. seek most repose
S. A. 492. to have revealed secrets of *m*.
S. A. 545. that cheers the heart of gods and *m*.
S. A. 674. nor do I name of *m*. the common rout
S. A. 759. wisest and best *m*. full oft beguiled
S. A. 787. that *m*. may censure thine the gentler
S. A. 847. have awed the best resolved of *m*.
S. A. 867. celebrated in the mouths of wisest *m*.
S. A. 892. of *m*. conspiring to uphold their state
S. A. 903. in argument with *m*. a woman ever
S. A. 919. which eyesight exposes daily *m*. abroad
S. A. 938. all *m*. loved, honoured, feared me
S. A. 1015. which way soever *m*. refer it
S. A. 1034. whate'er it be to wisest *m*. and best
S. A. 1079. I am of Gath, *m*. call me Harapha
S. A. 1186. notorious murder on those thirty *m*.
S. A. 1269. to the spirits of just *m*. long oppressed
S. A. 1273. brute and boisterous force of violent *m*.
S. A. 1294. might endued above the sons of *m*.
S. A. 1407. so mutable are all the ways of *m*.
S. A. 1682. so fond are mortal *m*. fallen into wrath
C. 6. of this dim spot which *m*. call earth
C. 208. airy tongues that syllable *m*.'s names
C. 388. far from the cheerful haunt of *m*.
C. 445. good and *m*. feared her stern frown
C. 588. or that power which erring *m*. call Chance
C. 703. none but such as are good *m*. can give
C. 706. O foolishness of *m*. that lend their ears
A. 67. on which the fate of gods and *m*. is wound
L'A. 13. and by *m*. heart-easing Mirth
L'A. 118. and the busy hum of *m*.
S. 16. Cromwell, our chief of *m*.
H. 142. and Justice then will down return to *m*.
D. F. I. 62. thereby to set the hearts of *m*. on fire
F. of C. 9. *m*. whose life, learning, faith
U. C. II. 11. that gives all *m*. life gave him his
**Menace.**—C. 654. sign of battle make and *m*.
**Menaced.**—P. L. 9, 977. I thought death *m*.
**Mends.**—P. L. 10, 859. Justice divine *m*. not
**Mental.**—P. L. 11, 418. inmost seat of *m*. sight
**Mention.**—P. L. 2, 820. now sad to *m*.
P. L. 8, 200. whence haply *m*. may arise
P. R. 1, 45. for much more willingly I *m*. Air
P. R. 2, 327. nor *m*. I meats by the law unclean
P. R. 3, 92. I *m*. still him whom thy wrongs
S. A. 331. *m*. of that name renews the assault
S. A. 1254. and offered fight will not dare *m*.
**Mentioned.**—P. L. 10, 1041. no more be *m*.
S. A. 978. with malediction *m*.
**Merchants.**—P. L. 2, 639. whence *m*. bring
**Merciful.**—P. L. 12, 565. *m*. over all his works
**Mercury.**—C. 963. court guise as *M*. did first
**Mercy.**—P. L. 1, 218. grace and *m*. shown on
P. L. 3, 132. in *m*. and justice both
P. L. 3, 134. but *m*. first and last shall brightest
P. L. 3, 202. none but such from *m*. I exclude
P. L. 3, 401. Father of *m*. and grace
P. L. 3, 407. end the strife of *m*. and justice
P. L. 10, 59. I intend *m*. colleague with justice
P. L. 10, 78. I shall temper so justice with *m*.
P. L. 10. 1096. but favour, grace and *m*. shone
P. L. 12, 346. brings them back remembering *m*.
S. A. 512. him who imploring *m*. sues for life
S. A. 1509. *M*. of Heaven, what hideous noise
C. 695. *M*. guard me
H. 144. *M*. will sit between, throned in celestial
**Mercy-seat.**—P. L. 11, 2. from the *m-s*.
P. L. 19, 253. over these a *m-s*. of gold
**Mere.**—P. L. 4, 316. *m*. shows of seeming pure
P. L. 9, 413. the Fiend, *m*. serpent in appearance
P. R. 4, 400. privation *m*. of light
P. R. 4, 535. to the utmost of *m*. man both wise
C. 807. this is *m*. moral babble
F. of C. 8. taught ye by me. A. S. and Rutherford

**Merely.**—P. L. 5, 774. not *m.* titular
P. L. 8, 22. *m.* to officiate light round this
'  ( and *m.* mortal dross
U.C.II.15.*m.*to drive the time away he sickened
**Meridian.**—P. L. 4, 30. high in his *m.* tower
P. L. 4, 581. and since *m.* hour no creature
P. L. 5, 369. till this *m.* heat be over
**Merit.**—P. L. 1, 98. from sense of injured *m.*
P. L. 1, 575. *m.* more than that small infantry
P. L. 2, 5. by *m.* raised to that bad eminence
P. L. 2, 21. hath been achieved of *m.*
P. L. 3, 290. thy *m.* imputed
P. L. 3, 309. and hast been found by *m.* more
P. L. 5, 80. ascend to Heaven by *m.* thine
P. L. 6, 43. Messiah who by right of *m.* reigns
P. L. 7, 157. till by degrees of *m.* raised they
P. L. 10, 259. a monument of *m.* high to all
P. L. 11, 35. my *m.* those shall perfect
P. R. 1, 166. this perfect man by *m.* called
P. R. 2, 456. prompt her to do aught may *m.*
P. R. 2, 464. his honour virtue *m.* and chief
P. R. 3, 196. just trial ere I *m.* my exaltation
S. A. 1011. comeliness of shape or amplest *m.*
**Merited.**—P. L. 4, 418. have nothing *m.*
P. L. 6, 153. to receive thy *m.* reward
P. L. 10, 888. amply have *m.* of me
S. A. 734. which to have *m.* without excuse
**Meritorious.**—S. A. 859. preaching how *m.*
**Merits.**—P. L. 3, 319. and assume thy *m.*
P. L. 3, 697. but rather *m.* praise the more
P. L. 6, 382. nought *m.* but dispraise
P. L. 9, 995. such recompense best *m.*
P. L. 11, 699. and what most *m.* fame
P. L. 12, 409. his *m.* to save them
**Meroe.**—P. R. 4, 71. *M.,* Nilotic isle
**Merriment.**—C. 172. riot and ill-managed *m.*
**Merry.**—C.121.their *m.*wakes and pastimes keep
L'A. 93. when the *m.* bells ring round
**Message.**—P. L. 4, 833. begin your *m.*
P. L. 5, 289. and to his *m.* high in honour rise
P. L. 5, 290. for on some *m.* high they guessed
P. L. 11, 299. gently hast thou told thy *m.*
P. L. 12, 174. or *m.* to regard
P. R. 1, 133. I begin to verify that solemn *m.*
S. A. 635. promised by heavenly *m.* twice
S. A. 1307. his *m.* will be short and voluble
S.A.1343.my *m.* was imposed on me with speed
S. A. 1345. so take it with what speed thy *m.*
S. A. 1352. expect another *m.* more imperious
S.A.1391. this second *m.* from our lords to thee
S. A. 1433. after his *m.* told of thy conception
**Messenger.**—P. L. 8. 646. ethereal *m.*
P. L. 11, 856. and after him the surer *m.*
P. R. 1, 238. a *m.*from God foretold thy birth
S. A. 1384. I with this *m.* will go along
**Messengers.**—P. L. 3, 229. thy winged *m.*
P. L. 7, 572. winged *m.* on errands of supernal
**Messes.**—L'A. 85. herbs and other country *m.*
**Messiah.**—P. L. 5, 664. proclaimed *M.* King
P. L. 5, 691. great *M.* and his new commands
P. L. 5, 765. *M.* was declared in-sight of Heaven
P. L. 5, 883. how to quit the yoke of God's *M.*
P. L. 6, 43. for their law and for their king *M.*
P. L. 6, 68. in the cause of God and his *M.*
P. L. 6, 718. God and *M.* his anointed King
P. L. 6, 775. when the great ensign of *M.* blazed
P. L. 6, 796. prevail against God and *M.*
P. L. 6, 881. *M.* his triumphal chariot turned
P. L. 12, 244. of great *M.* shall sing
P. L. 12, 359. the true anointed King *M.*
P. R. 1, 245. told them the *M.* now was born
P. R. 1, 261. what was writ concerning the *M.*
P. R. 1, 272. come who was to come before *M.*
P. R. 2, 4. called Jesus *M.,* Son of God declared
P. R. 2, 32. our eyes beheld *M.* certainly now
P. R. 2, 43. God of Israel send thy *M.* forth
P. R. 4, 502. of the *M.* I have heard foretold
**Met.**—P. L. 1, 574. *m.* such embodied force
P. L. 2, 742. why in this infernal vale first *m.*
P. L. 3, 613. matter new to gaze the Devil *m.*
P. L. 4, 231. and *m.* the nether flood

P. L. 4, 322. ever since in love's embraces *m.*
P. L. 4, 496. half her swelling breast naked *m.*
P. L. 4, 863. those half-rounding guards just *m.*
P. L. 6, 18. blaze on blaze first *m.* his view
P. L. 6, 128. half-way *m.* his daring foe
P. L. 6, 131. proud! art thou *m.*?
P. L. 6, 156. in synod *m.* their deities to assert
P. L. 6, 247. and *m.* in arms no equal
P. L. 6, 323. it *m.* the sword of Satan
P. L. 6, 532. him soon they *m.* under spread
P. L. 6, 688. two such foes *m.* armed
P. L. 9, 325. with like defence wherever *m.*
P. L. 9, 449. from each thing *m.* conceives
P. L. 9, 849. there he her *m.*
P. L. 10, 285. what they *m.* solid or slimy
P. L. 10, 321. the confines *m.* of empyrean
P.L. 10, 349. unhoped *m.* who to meet him came
P. L. 10, 390. with triumphal act have *m.*
P. L. 11, 213. more glorious when the angels *m.*
P. L. 11, 722. their assemblies whereso *m.*
P. R. 2, 359. of faery damsels *m.* in forest wide
P. R. 3, 337. such forces *m.* not, nor so wide
P. R. 4, 22. repulse upon repulse *m.* ever
P. R. 4, 385. in their conjunction *m.*
S. A. 1588. the edifice where all were *m.* to see
S. A. 1656. *m.* from all parts to solemnize
C. 165. hath *m.* the virtue of this magic dust
C. 572. had *m.* already ere my best speed could
C. 948. where this night are *m.* in state
L'A. 20. as he *m.* her once a-Maying
L'A. 83. where Corydon and Thyrsis *m.*
Il P.28. in glimmering bowers and glades he *m.*
S. 13, 14. *m.*in the milder shades of Purgatory
**Metal.**—P. L. 1, 540. sonorous *m.*
P. L. 3, 592. *m.* or stone
P. L. 3, 595. if *m.* part seemed gold part silver
P. L. 11, 573. fusil or graven in *m.*
**Metallic.**—P. L. 1, 673. *m.* ore
**Metals.**—P. L. 5, 442. *m.* of drossiest ore
L. 110. two massy keys he bore, of *m.* twain
**Meteor.**—P. L. 1, 537. like a *m.* streaming
**Meteorous.**—P. L. 12, 629. *m.* as evening mist
**Methinks.**—P. L. 5, 114. resemblances *m.*
P. L. 10, 243. *m.* I feel new strength within
P. L. 10, 1029. some safer resolution which *m.*
S. 10, 11. madam, *m.,* I see him living yet
**Method.**—P. R. 4, 540. another *m.* I must
**Methought.**—P. L. 4, 478. yet *m.* less fair
P. L. 5, 35. *m.* close at mine ear one called me
P. L. 5, 50. and on, *m.,* alone I passed through
P. L. 5, 85. so quickened appetite that I *m.*
P. L. 5, 91. and I, *m.,* sunk down and fell asleep
P. L. 8, 295. one came, *m.,* of shape divine
P. L. 8, 355. I found not what, *m.,* I wanted still
P. L. 8, 462. abstract as in a trance, *m.* I saw
P. L. 11, 151. *m.* I saw him placable and mild
S. A. 1515. of ruin indeed, *m.* I heard the noise
C. 171. *m.* it was the sound of riot
C. 482. *m.* so too, what should it be?
S. 23, 1. *m.* I saw my late espoused saint
**Metropolis.**—P. L. 3, 549. some renowned *m.*
P. L. 10, 439. careful watch round their *m.*
**Mexico.**—P. L. 11, 407. he also saw rich *M.*
**Michael.**—P. L. 2, 294. and the sword of *M.*
P. L. 6, 44. go *M.,* of celestial armies prince
P.L. 6, 202. *M.*bid sound the archangel trumpet
P. L. 6, 250. saw where the sword of *M.* smote
P. L. 6, 321. the sword of *M.* from the armoury
P. L. 6, 411. *M.* and his Angels prevalent
P. L. 6, 686. *M.* and his Powers
P. L. 6, 777. whose conduct *M.* soon reduced
P. L. 11, 99. *M.,* this my behest have thou
P. L. 11, 295. to *M.* thus his humble words
P. L. 11, 334. to whom thus *M.,* with regard
P. L. 11, 412. to nobler sights *M.* from Adam's
P. L. 11, 453. to whom *M.* thus, he also moved
P. L. 11, 466. to whom thus *M.*
P. L. 11, 515. their Maker's image, answered *M.*
P. L. 11, 530. there is, said *M.,* if thou well
P. L. 11, 552. *M.* replied, nor love thy life

P. L. 11, 603. to whom thus *M.:* judge not
P. L. 11, 688. to whom thus *M.:* these are
P. L. 11, 787. to whom thus *M.:* those whom
P. L. 12, 79. to whom thus *M.:* justly thou
P. L. 12, 285. to whom thus *M.:* doubt not
P. L. 12, 386. to whom thus *M.:* dream not
P. L. 12, 466. so spake the Archangel *M.*
**Mickle.**—C. 31. noble Peer of *m.* trust and power
**Microscope.**—P. R. 4, 57. disposed my aery *m.*
**Mid.**—P. L. 2, 718. dark encounter in *m.* air
P. L. 3, 729. still renewing through *m.* heaven
P. L. 4, 940. to settle here on earth or in *m.* air
P. L. 6, 91. proved fond and vain in the *m.* way
P. L. 6, 314. of fiercest opposition in *m.* sky
P. L. 6, 536. came flying and in *m.* air aloud
P. L. 6, 854. checked his thunder in *m.* volley
P. L. 6, 889. triumphant through *m.* heaven
P. L. 7, 403. sculls that oft bank the *m.* sea
P. L. 7, 442. tower the *m.* aerial sky
P. L. 9, 468. though in *m.* Heaven
P. L. 12, 263. how the sun shall in *m.* heaven
P. R. 1, 39. but in *m.* air to council summons
C. 957. Night sits monarch yet in the *m.* sky
S. 9, 13. passes to bliss at the *m.* hour of night
**Midas.**—S. 13. with *M.* ears committing short
**Mid-course.**—P. L. 11, 204. ere day's *m.-c.*
**Mid-day.**—P. L. 8, 112. and ere *m.-d.* arrived
C. 384. benighted walks under the *m.-d.* sun
**Middle.**—P. L. 1, 14. that with no *m.* flight
P. L. 1, 516. ruled the *m.* air their highest
P. L. 2, 653. about her *m.* round a cry of Hell
P.L.3,16.through utter and through *m.* darkness
P. L. 3, 461. translated spirits or *m.* spirits
P. L. 4, 195. the *m.* tree and highest there
P. L. 5, 280. the *m.* pair girt like a starry zone
P. L. 5, 339. or *m.* shore in Pontus or the Punic
P. L. 9, 605. visible in heaven or earth, or *m.*
P. L. 9, 1097. may cover round those *m.* parts
P. L. 11, 665. till at last of *m.* age one rising
P. R. 2, 117. up to the *m.* region of thick air
H. 164. in *m.* air shall spread his throne
D. F. I. 16. through *m.* empire of the freezing air
**Mid-hours.**—P. L. 5, 376. for these *m.-h.*
**Midnight.**—P. L. 1, 782. whose *m.* revels
P. L. 4, 682. celestial voices to the *m.* air
P. L. 4, 768. dance or wanton mask or *m.* ball
P. L. 5, 667. soon as *m.* brought on the dusky
P. L. 5, 778. whom all this haste of *m.* march
P. L. 9, 58. by night he fled and at *m.* returned
P. L. 9, 159. wrapt in mist of *m.* vapour
P. L. 9, 181. he held on his *m.* search
C. 103. *m.* shout and revelry
C. 130. the secret flame of *m.* torches burns
L'A. 2. of Cerberus and blackest *M.* born
II P. 85. or let my lamp at *m.* hour
H. 191. Lars and Lemures moan with *m.* plaint
**Midnight-stroke.**—P. L. 12, 189. one *m.-s.*
**Mid-noon.**—P. L. 5, 311. morn risen on *m.-n.*
**Midriff.**—P. L. 11, 445. smote him into the *m.*
**Midst.**—P. L. 1, 224. leave in the *m.* a horrid
P. L. 2, 508. *m.* came their mighty Paramount
P. L. 3, 358. river of bliss through *m.* of heaven
P. L. 5, 165. him first, him last, him *m.*
P. L. 5, 251. light flew through the *m.* of heaven
P. L. 6, 28. from whence a voice from *m.*
P. L. 6, 99. high in the *m.* exalted as a God
P. L. 6, 417. and in the *m.* thus undismayed
P. L. 9, 184. his head the *m.* well stored
P. L. 10, 441. he through the *m.* unmarked
P. L. 10, 528. but still greatest he the *m.*
P. L. 11, 432. the *m.* an altar as the landmark
P. R. 2, 294. that opened in the *m.* a woody
P. R. 4, 31. thence in the *m.* divided by a river
S. A. 1339. in my *m.* of sorrow and heart-grief
H. 11. to sit the *m.* of Trinal Unity
**Midway.**—P. L. 11, 631. or in the *m.* faint
**Might (noun).**—P. L. 1, 110. his wrath or *m.*
P. L. 1, 506. were the prime in order and in *m.*
P. L. 1, 643. henceforth his *m.* we know
P. L. 2, 192. not more almighty to resist our *m.*
P. L. 2, 855. to be o'ermatched by living *m.*

P. L. 3, 170. my wisdom and effectual *m.*
P. L. 3, 398. Son of thy Father's *m.*
P. L. 4, 346. make them mirth used all his *m.*
P. L. 4, 986. collecting all his *m.* dilated stood
P. L. 5, 720. Heir of all my *m.*
P. L. 6, 116. strength and *m.* there fail
P. L. 6, 229. overruled and limited their *m.*
P. L. 6, 320. nor odds appeared in *m.* or swift
P. L. 6, 355. where the *m.* of Gabriel fought
P. L. 6, 377. in *m.* though wondrous
P. L. 6, 630. *m.* to match with their inventions
P. L. 6, 710. thou mightiest in thy Father's *m.*
P. L. 6, 737. armed with thy *m.* rid heaven
P. L. 7, 165. and *m.* with thee I send along
P. L. 7, 223. creation and the wonders of his *m.*
P. L. 7, 615. to manifest the more thy *m.*
P. L. 10, 404. of matchless *m.*
P. L. 11, 689. for in those days *m.* only shall be
P. L. 11, 830. by *m.* of waves be moved out
S. A. 178. matchless in *m.* the glory late of Israel
S. A. 588. his *m.* continues in thee not for nought
S. A. 1083. thy prodigious *m.* and feats performed
S. A. 1271. *m.* to quell the mighty of the earth
S. A. 1293. with *m.* endued above the sons of men
C. 613. those that quell the *m.* of hellish charms
L. 173. through the dear *m.* of Him that walked
Brut. 13. whose dreaded *m.*
**Mightier.**—P. L. 1, 149. or do him *m.* service
P. L. 1, 512. he from *m.* Jove
P. L. 6, 32. in word *m.* than they
**Mightiest.**—P. L. 1, 99. with the *M.*
P. L. 2, 307. bear the weight of *m.* monarchies
P. L. 6, 112. among the *m.* bent on highest
P. L. 6, 200. rage to see thus foiled their *m.*
P. L. 6, 386. now their *m.* quelled the battle
P. L. 6, 459. and makes remiss the hands of *m.*
P. L. 6, 710. go then thou *M.* in thy Father's
P. L. 11, 387. the seat of *m.* empire
P. R. 3, 262. seem the seats of *m.* monarchs
S. A. 638. he led me on to *m.* deeds
**Mighty.**—P. L. 1, 20. and with *m.* wings
P. L. 1, 136. and all this *m.* host
P. L. 1, 222. rears from off the pool his *m.* stature
P. L. 1, 533. be upreared his *m.* standard
P. L. 1, 566. awaiting what command their *m.*
P. L. 1, 665. from the thighs of *m.* Cherubim
P. L. 2, 456. go therefore *m.* Powers
P. L. 2, 508. midst came their *m.* Paramount
P. L. 2, 719. so frowned the *m.* combatants
P. L. 2, 991. that *m.* leading Angel who of late
P. L. 5, 735. *m.* Father thou thy foes justly
P. L. 5, 748. the *m.* regencies of Seraphim
P. L. 5, 836. as by his Word the *m.* Father
P. L. 6, 62. in *m.* quadrate joined
P. L. 6, 638. which God hath in his *m.* Angels
P. L. 6, 841. of Thrones and *m.* Seraphim
P. L. 6, 890. courts and temple of his *m.* Father
P. L. 7, 355. a *m.* sphere he framed unlightsome
P. L. 7, 608. who can impair thee *m.* King
P. L. 8, 81. how they will wield the *m.* frame
P. L. 10, 455. their *m.* Chief returned
P. L. 10, 650. his *m.* Angels
P. L. 11, 642. giants of *m.* bone
P. L. 12, 33. a *m.* hunter thence he shall be
P. L. 12, 124. from him will raise a *m.* nation
P. R. 1, 40. to council summons all his *m.* peers
P. R. 1, 186. how best the *m.* work he might
P. R. 2, 448. who could do *m.* things and could
P. R. 3, 167. and o'er a *m.* king so oft prevailed
S. A. 556. *m.* champion strong above compare
S. A. 706. and *m.* minister
S. A. 1272. to quell the *m.* of the earth
S. A. 1602. his *m.* strength in feats and games
C. 63. excels his mother at her *m.* art
H. 89. that the *m.* Pan was kindly come to live
V. Ex. 89. what power, what force, what *m.* spell
**Mild.**—P. L. 2, 220. this horror will grow *m.*
P. L. 2, 397. or else in some *m.* zone dwell not
P. L. 2, 546. others more *m.* retreated
P. L. 4, 479. less winning soft less amiably *m.*
P. L. 4, 647. grateful evening *m.*

Q

P. L. 4, 654. nor grateful evening *m.*
P. L. 5, 16. *m.* as when Zephyrus on Flora
P. L. 5, 371. the angelic Virtue answered *m.*
P. L. 6, 28. from midst a golden cloud thus *m.*
P. L. 7, 110. the godlike Angel answered *m.*
P. L. 9, 226. *m.* answer Adam thus returned
P. L. 10, 67. and thus divinely answered *m.*
P. L. 10, 96. came the *m.* Judge and Intercessor
P. L. 10, 847. wholesome, and cool, and *m.*
P. L. 10, 1046. remember with what *m.*
P. L. 11, 151. I saw him placable and *m.*
P. L. 11, 234. nor sociably *m.* as Raphael
P. L. 11, 286. thus the Angel interrupted *m.*
P. R. 1, 310. they at his sight grew *m.*
P. R. 2, 125. hold our place and these *m.* seats
P. R. 2, 159. virgin majesty with *m.* and sweet
P. R. 4, 134. frugal and *m.* and temperate
C. 4. in regions *m.* of calm and serene air
L. 136. valleys low where the *m.* whispers use
S. 19, 11. who best bear his *m.* yoke
S. 21, 11. for other things *m.* Heaven a time
H. 66. whispering new joys to the *m.* ocean
P. 53. would soon unbosom all their echoes *m.*
**Milder.**—P. L. 2, 816. *m.* and thus answered
P. L. 6, 98. ended soon each *m.* thought
S. 13, 14. met in the *m.* shades of Purgatory
**Mildew.**—C. 640. *m.* blast, or damp
**Mildly.**—P. L. 8, 317. said *m.:* Author of all
**Mildness**—P. L. 6, 735. as I put thy *m.* on
P. L. 9, 534. arm thy looks the heaven of *m.*
**Mile-End.**—S. 11, 7. might walk to *M.-E.* Green
**Miles.**—P. L. 2, 938. him as many *m.* aloft
**Militant.**—P. L. 6, 61. the Powers *m.*
P. L. 10, 442. show plebeian Angel *m.* of lowest
**Military.**—P. L. 4, 955. your *m.* obedience
P. L. 6, 45. and thou in *m.* prowess next
P. L. 11, 241. a *m.* vest of purple flowed
P. R. 3, 312. in coats of mail and *m.* pride
**Milk.**—P. L. 9, 582. dropping with *m.* at even
**Milkmaid.**—L'A. 65. and the *m.* singeth blithe
**Milky.**—P. L. 5, 306. from *m.* stream
P. L. 7, 579. seen in the galaxy that *m.* way
S. A. 550. from the clear *m.* juice allaying thirst
**Mill.**—S. A. 41. in Gaza at the *m.* with slaves
S.A. 1093. I thought gyves and the *m.* had tamed
S. A. 1327. and overlaboured at their public *m.*
S. A. 1393. at the public *m.* our drudge
**Millions.**—P. L. 1, 609. *m.* of Spirits for his fault
P. L. 1, 664. *m.* of flaming swords
P. L. 2, 55. *m.* that stand in arms and longing
P. L. 2, 997. poured out by *m.* her victorious
P. L. 4, 677. *m.* of spiritual creatures walk
P. L. 6, 48. by thousands and by *m.* ranged
P. L. 6, 220. *m.* of fierce encountering Angels
P. R. 1, 359. who leagued with *m.* more in rash
C. 715. and set to work *m.* of spinning worms
**Mimic.**—P. L. 5, 110. oft in her absence *m.*
**Mimics.**—S. A. 1325. antics, mummers, *m.*
**Mincing.**—C. 964. with the *m.* Dryades
**Mincius.**—L. 86. smooth-sliding *M.*
**Mind.**—P. L. 1, 97. that fixed *m.* and high disdain
P. L. 1, 139. for the *m.* and spirit remains
P. L. 1, 253. a *m.* not to be changed by place
P. L. 1, 254. the *m.* is its own place
P. L. 1, 626. but what power of *m.* foreseeing
P. L. 2, 34. that with ambitious *m.* will covet
P. L. 2, 189. or who deceive his *m.* whose eye
P. L. 2, 212. not *m.* us not offending
P. L. 3, 52. and the *m.* through all her powers
P. L. 3, 705. what created *m.* can comprehend
P. L. 4, 55. understood not that a grateful *m.*
P. L. 4, 612. all things .... *m.* us of like repose
P. L. 4, 618. his daily work of body or *m.*
P. L. 5, 34. trouble which my *m.* knew never
P. L. 5, 117. evil into the *m.* of God or man
P. L. 5, 452. sudden *m.* arose in Adam
P. L. 5, 902. or change his constant *m.*
P. L. 6, 477. not to *m.* from whence they grew
P. L. 7, 128. in measure what the *m.* may well
P. L. 8, 188. but apt the *m.* or fancy is to rove

P. L. 8, 525. works in the *m.* no change
P. L. 8, 541. in the *m.* and inward faculties
P. L. 8, 557. to consummate all greatness of *m.*
P. L. 8, 604. unfeigned union of *m.*
P. L. 9, 213. or hear what to my *m.* first
P. L. 9, 238. talk between,—food of the *m.*
P. L. 9, 358. I should *m.* thee oft and *m.* thou me
P. L. 9, 603. with capacious *m.* considered all
P. L. 9, 779. feed at once both body and *m.*
P. L. 9, 1120. but not at rest or ease of *m.*
P. L. 9, 1125. their inward state of *m.*
P. L. 10, 8. not Satan to attempt the *m.* of Man
P. L. 10, 825. but all corrupt both *m.* and will
P. L. 10, 1011. his more attentive *m.*
P. L. 10, 1015. than what thy *m.* contemns
P. L. 10, 1030. calling to *m.* with heed
P. L. 11, 144. as to concern the *m.* of God
P. L. 11, 687. prodigious births of body or *m.*
P. L. 11, 898. whereon to look and call to *m.*
P. L. 12, 444. and in *m.* prepared it so befall
P. R. 1, 202. all my *m.* was set serious to learn
P. R. 2, 105. and oft to *m.* recalling
P. R. 2, 139. and amplitude of *m.* to greatest
P. R. 2, 206. Solomon of more exalted *m.*
P. R. 2, 258. nor *m.* it, fed with better thoughts
P. R. 2, 479. by force which to a generous *m.*
P. R. 4, 113. allure mine eye much less my *m.*
P. R. 4, 223. extend thy *m.* o'er all the world
P. R. 4, 401. and with untroubled *m.*
S. A. 18. ease to the body some none to the *m.*
S. A. 52. O impotence of *m.* in body strong
S. A. 185. the tumours of a troubled *m.*
S. A. 412. servile *m.* rewarded well with servile
S. A. 600. from anguish of the *m.* and humours
S. A. 611. secret passage find to the inmost *m.*
S.A. 745. and appease thy *m.* with what amends
S.A. 1279. with plain heroic magnitude of *m.*
S. A. 1336. my *m.* ever will condescend to such
S. A. 1387. if there be aught of presage in the *m.*
S.A.1638. or some great matter in his *m.* revolved
S. A. 1758. and calm of *m.* all passion spent
C. 211. but not astound the virtuous *m.*
C. 461. the unpolluted temple of the *m.*
C.619. brought to my *m.* a certain shepherd lad
C.663. thou canst not touch the freedom of my *m.*
L. 71. that last infirmity of noble *m.*
Il P. 4. or fill the fixed *m.* with all your toys
Il P. 91. the immortal *m.* that hath forsook
S. 23, 9. came vested all in white pure as her *m.*
V. Ex. 33. such where the deep transported *m.*
**Minded.**—P. L. 4, 583. Spirit of other sort so *m.*
P. L. 8, 444. and be so *m.* still
P. L. 9, 519. sound of rustling leaves but *m.* not
P. L. 11, 156. which then not *m.* in dismay
S. A. 1603. *m.* not to be absent at that
**Mindless.**—P. L. 9, 431. *m.* the while herself
**Minds.**—P. L. 1, 559. mortal or immortal *m.*
P. L. 2, 521. thence more at ease their *m.*
P. L. 4, 118. for Heavenly *m.* from such
P. L. 4, 522. hence I will excite their *m.*
P. L. 5, 680. new *m.* may raise in us who serve
P. L. 5, 786. erect our *m.* and teach us to cast
P. L. 6, 444. we can preserve unhurt our *m.*
P. L. 6, 613. straight they changed their *m.*
P. L. 9, 1053. and their *m.* how darkened
P. L. 12, 15. remains fresh in their *m.* fearing
P. R. 2, 221. in the admiration only of weak *m.*
S.A.1213. their servile *m.* me their deliverer sent
S. A. 1508. I know your friendly *m.*
S. A. 1676. who hurt their *m.* and urged them on
**Mine*.**—P. L. 5, 443. perfect gold as from the *m.*
P. L. 11, 656. battery scale and *m.* assaulting
C. 436. no goblin or swart faery of the *m.*
**Mineral.**—P. L. 1, 235. sublimed with *m.* fury
P. L. 6, 517. of *m.* and stone whereof to found
**Minerva.**—C. 448. shield that wise *M.* wore
**Mingle.**—P. L. 2, 384. Earth with Hell to *m.*
P. L. 6, 277. there *m.* broils ere this avenging
P. R. 4, 453. as earth and sky would *m.*

*The pronoun *mine* also occurs several times.

S. A. 601. humours black that *m.* with thy fancy
**Mingled.**—P. L. 6, 513. they found, they *m.*
C. 994. flowers of more *m.* hue
**Minims.**—P. L. 7, 482. not all *m.* of nature
**Minister.**—P. L. 5, 460. the empyreal *m.*
  P. L. 11, 73. signal high to the bright *m.*
  P. L. 12, 308. being but the *m.* of law
  P. R. 1, 488. and *m.* about his altar
  S. A. 706. image of thy strength and mighty *m.*
**Ministered.**—P. L. 5, 444. at table Eve *m.*
**Ministeries.**—P. L. 7, 149. with *m.* due
**Ministering.**—P. L. 4, 664. *m.* light
  P. L. 6, 167. *m.* Spirits trained up in feast
  P. L. 6, 182. yet lewdly darest our *m.* upbraid
**Ministers.**—P. L. 1, 170. his *m.* of vengeance
  P. L. 9, 156. and flaming *m.* to watch and tend
  P. L. 11, 676. Oh what are these? death's *m.*
  P. R. 2, 375. thy gentle *m.* who come to pay
**Ministrant.**—P. L. 10, 87. dominations *m.*
  P. R. 2, 385. and call swift flights of Angels *m.*
**Ministry.**—P. L. 12, 505. their *m.* performed
**Minstrelsy.**—P. L. 6, 168. *m.* of Heaven
  C.547. to meditate my rural *m.* till fancy had her
**Mintage.**—C. 529. unmoulding reason's *m.*
**Minute.**—Il P. 130. *m.* drops from off the eaves
**Minutes.**—P. L. 10, 91. with swiftest *m.* winged
**Miracle.**—P. L. 9, 562. redouble then this *m.*
  P. R. 1, 337. by *m.* he may, replied the swain
  S. A. 364. glorious for awhile the *m.* of men
  S. A. 1528. his eyesight . . . by *m.* restored
**Miracles.**—P. L. 12, 501. and do all *m.*
**Miraculous.**—S. A. 587. this strength *m.*
**Mire.**—P. L. 4, 1010. to trample thee as *m.*
  S. 20. the fields are dank and ways are *m.*
**Mires.**—P. L. 9, 641. to bogs and *m.*
**Mirror.**—P. L. 4, 263. her crystal *m.* holds
  P. L. 7, 377. in levelled west was set, his *m.*
  S. A. 164. O *m.* of our fickle state
**Mirth.**—P. L. 1, 786. they on their *m.* and dance
  P. L. 4, 346. to make them *m.* used all his might
  P. L. 9, 1009. they swim in *m.*
  S. A. 1613. had filled their hearts with *m.*
  C. 202. whence even now the tumult of loud *m.*
  C. 955. will double all their *m.* and cheer
  L'A. 13. heart-easing *M.*
  L'A. 38. *M.* admit me of thy crew
  L'A. 152. *M.* with thee I mean to live
  Il P. 81. far from all resort of *m.*
  S. 21. in *m.* that after no repenting draws
  P. 168. erewhile of music and ethereal *m.*
  M. M. 6. *m.* and youth, and warm desire
**Misbecoming.**—C. 372. into *m.* plight
**Miscellaneous.**—P. R. 3, 50. a *m.* rabble
**Mischance.**—M. W. 27. but whether by *m.*
  D. F. I. 44. by *m.* didst fall
**Mischief.**—P. L. 2, 141. soon expel her *m.*
  P. L.6,488. such implements of *m.* as shall dash
  P. L. 6, 503. some one intent on *m.* or inspired
  P. L. 6, 636. against such hellish *m.* fit
  P. L. 9, 472. thoughts of *m.* gratulating thus
  P. L. 9, 633. seem straight to *m.*
  P. L. 10, 167. who made him instrument of *m.*
  P. L. 10, 895. this *m.* had not then befallen
  P. L. 11, 450. O Teacher some great *m.* hath
  P. R. 4, 440. after all his *m.* done
  S. A. 1039. a cleaving *m.*
  C.591. yea even that which *M.* meant most harm
**Mischievous.**—P. L. 2, 1054. *m.* revenge
**Miscreated.**—P. L. 2, 683. advance thy *m.* front
**Misdeed.**—S. A. 747. but more unfortunate *m.*
**Misdeeds.**—P. L. 10, 1080. *m.* have wrought
**Misdeem.**—P. L. 9, 301. *m.* not then
  P. R. 1, 424. but thy malice moved thee to *m.*
**Misdoing.**—P. R. 1, 225. not wilfully *m.*
**Misdone.**—S. A. 911. what I have *m.* misguided
**Miser's.**—C. 399. unsunned heaps of *m.* treasure
**Miserable.**—P. L. 1, 157. to be weak is *m.*
  P. L. 2, 98. happier far than *m.* to have eternal
  P. L. 2, 752. all on a sudden *m.* pain surprised
  P. L. 4, 73. me *m.*! which way shall I fly
  P. L. 9, 126. nor hope to be myself less *m.*

P. L. 9, 1139. shamed, naked, *m.*
P. L. 10, 720. O *m.* of happy! is this the end
P. L. 10, 839. and concludes thee *m.* beyond all
P. L. 10, 930. me than thyself more *m.*
P. L. 10, 981. and *m.* it is to be to others cause
P. L. 11, 500. O *m.* mankind! to what fall
P. R. 1, 411. as a poor *m.* captive thrall
P. R. 1, 471. where easily canst thou find one *m.*
S. A. 340. O *m.* change! is this the man
S. A. 480. in this *m.* loathsome plight
S. A. 703. just or unjust alike seem *m.*
S. A. 762. are drawn to wear out *m.* days
S. A. 101. O yet more *m.*! myself my sepulchre
**Miseries.**—P. L. 10, 715. the growing *m.*
S. A. 64. and proves the source of all my *m.*
S. A. 107. obnoxious more to all the *m.* of life
S. A. 651. the close of all my *m.* and the balm
**Misery.**—P. L. 1, 90. now *m.* hath joined
P. L. 1, 142. here swallowed up in endless *m.*
P. L. 2, 459. what best may ease the present *m.*
P. L. 2, 563. of happiness and final *m.*
P. L. 4, 92. still I fall, only supreme in *m.*
P. L. 6, 268. and into Nature brought *m.*
P. L. 6, 462. but pain is perfect *m.*
P. L. 6, 904. partake his punishment eternal *m.*
P. L. 9, 12. Death and *M.*, Death's harbinger
P. L. 10. 726. yet well if here would end the *m.*
P. L. 10, 810. endless *m.* from this day onward
P. L. 10, 928. thy hatred for this *m.*
P. L. 10, 982. to be to others cause of *m.*
P. L. 10, 997. which would be *m.*
P. L. 10, 1021. covet death as utmost end of *m.*
P. L. 11, 476. what *m.* the inabstinence of Eve
P. R. 1, 341. men to such *m.* and hardship born
P. R. 1, 398. companions of my *m.* and woe
P. R. 1, 470. which not will but *m.* hath wrested
S. A. 1469. reduced their foe to *m.* beneath
C. 73. so perfect is their *m.*
**Misfortune.**—P. L. 10, 900. some *m.* brings
C. 286. how easy my *m.* is to hit
**Misgave.**—P. L. 9, 846. something ill *m.* him
**Misguided.**—S.A. 912. what I have misdone *m.*
**Mishap.**—P. L. 10, 239. if *m.* ere this he had
L. 92. what hard *m.* hath doomed this gentle
**Misinform.**—P. L. 9, 355. *m.* the will
**Misjoining.**—P. L. 5, 111. but *m.* shapes
**Mislead.**—P. R. 4, 309. they teach and not *m.*
**Misleads.**—P. L. 9, 640. *m.* the amazed
**Misled.**—P. R. 1, 226. but unaware *m.*
C. 200. to the *m.* and lonely traveller
**Misrepresent.**—S. A. 124. or do my eyes *m.*?
**Misrule.**—P. L. 7, 271. the loud *m.* of Chaos
P. L. 10, 628. at random yielded up to their *m.*
**Miss.**—P. L. 3, 735. thy way thou canst not *m.*
P. L. 10, 104. I *m.* thee here not pleased
P. L. 10, 262. nor can I *m.* the way so strongly
S.A.927. by me thou hast lost thou least shalt *m.*
C. 925. their full tribute never *m.*
**Missed.**—P. L. 6, 499. he to be the inventor *m.*
P. L. 9, 857. thee I have *m.* and thought it long
P. L. 11, 15. prayers flew up nor *m.* the way
P. R. 2, 486. to gain a sceptre oftest better *m.*
**Missing.**—P. R. 2, 9. now *m.* him their joy
P. R. 2, 15. Moses was in the mount and *m.*
P. R. 2, 77. and *m.* filled with infant blood
P. R. 4, 208. me nought advantaged *m.* what
Il P. 65. and *m.* thee I walk unseen
**Mission.**—P. R. 2, 114. and *m.* high
**Missive.**—P. L. 6, 519. their balls of *m.* ruin
**Mist.**—P. L. 3, 53. all *m.* from thence purge
P. L. 5, 435. nor seemingly the Angel nor in *m.*
P. L. 7, 333. from the earth a dewy *m.* went up
P. L. 9, 75. rose Satan involved in rising *m.*
P. L. 9, 158. wrapt in *m.* of midnight vapour
P. L. 9. 180. like a black *m.* low creeping
P. L. 10, 694. sideral blast vapour and *m.*
L. 126. swoln with wind and the rank *m.*
**Mistake.**—P. L. 10, 900. misfortune . . . or *m.*
**Mistaken.**—S.A.907. quite *m.* in what I thought
**Misthought.**—P. L. 9, 289. Adam *m.* of her
**Mistook.**—C. 815. O ye *m.* ye should have

A. 4. from hence descry too divine to be *m.*
**Mistress.**—P. L. 9, 532. wonder not sovran *m.*
A. 36. to the great *m.* of yon princely shrine
A. 106. though Syrinx your Pan's *m.* were
**Mistrust.**—P. L. 9, 357. not *m.* but tender love
P. L. 9, 1124. anger hate *m.* suspicion discord
**Mistrustful.**—P. L. 2, 126. in what excels *m.*
**Mists.**—P. L. 5, 185. ye *M.* and Exhalations
C.337. with black usurping *m.* some gentle taper
**Misty.**—P. L. 1, 595. the horizontal *m.* air
V. Ex. 41. and *m.* regions of wide air
**Misused.**—C.47. the sweet poison of *m.* wine
**Mitigate.**—P. L. 1, 558. wanting power to *m.*
P. L. 10, 76. that I may *m.* their doom on me
P. L. 11, 41. which I to *m.* thus plead
**Mitred.**—L. 112. he shook his *m.* locks
**Mix.**—P. L. 5, 182. *m.* and nourish all things
P. L. 5, 334. so contrived as not to *m.* tastes
P. L. 7, 58. impossible to *m.* with blessedness
P. L. 7, 215. and with the centre *m.* the pole
P. L. 8, 616. or do they *m.* irradiance
P. L. 8, 627. they *m.* union of pure, with pure
P. L. 8, 629. as flesh to *m.* with flesh or soul
P. L. 11, 529. and *m.* with our connatural dust
S. A. 969. to *m.* with thy concernments I desist
C. 594. and *m.* no more with goodness
**Mixed.**—P. L. 1, 58. *m.* with obdurate pride
P. L. 1, 579. on each side *m.* with auxiliar gods
P. L. 2, 69. his throne itself *m.* with Tartarean
P. L. 2, 913. these in their pregnant causes *m.*
P. L. 3, 456. abortive monstrous or unkindly *m.*
P. L. 3, 610. with terrestrial humour *m.*
P. L. 4, 149. with gay enamelled colours *m.*
P. L. 4, 768. nor in court amours *m.* dance
P. L. 6, 21. gladly then he *m.* among
P. L. 8, 236. with creation might have *m.*
P. L. 8, 602. words and actions *m.* with love
P. L. 9, 165. and *m.* with bestial slime
P. L. 9, 577. with fruit of fairest colours *m.*
P. L. 10, 24. yet *m.* with pity
P. L. 11, 24. which in this golden censer *m.*
P. L. 11, 662. with warriors *m.* assemble
P. L. 11, 686. and by imprudence *m.*
P. L. 12, 181. thunder *m.* with hail, hail *m.*
P. R. 4, 412. fierce rain with lightning *m.*
S. A. 1031. or was too much of self-love' *m.*
C.526. with many murmurs *m.* whose pleasing
C. 674. spirits of balm and fragrant syrups *m.*
S. M. 3. wed your divine sounds and *m.* power
**Mixing**—P. L. 10, 228. *m.* intercession sweet
P. R. 1, 433. by *m.* somewhat true to vent more
**Mixture.**— P. L. 11, 51. no unharmonious *m.*
C. 244. can any mortal *m.* of earth's mould
Il P. 26. such *m.* was not held a stain
**Moab's.**—P. L. 1, 406. dread of *M.* sons
**Moan.**—H. 191. the Lars and Lemures *m.*
M. W. 55. here be tears of perfect *m.*
**Moans.**—S. 18, 8. their *m.* the vales redoubled
**Mock.**—P. L. 4, 628. *m.* our scant manuring
P. R. 2, 56. *m.* us with his blest sight then
**Mocked.**—P.L. 10, 774. why am I *m.* with death
P. L. 12, 59. till hoarse and all in rage as *m.*
**Mode.**—P. L. 1, 474. for one of Syrian race
P. R. 2, 340. a table richly spread in regal *m.*
**Model.**—P. L. 3, 509. by *m.* or by shading pencil
P. L. 8, 79. hereafter when they come to *m.*
**Moderate.**—P. L. 12, 351. in mean estate live *m.*
C. 769. had but a *m.* and beseeming share
S. A. 1464. others more *m.* seeming
**Moderation.**—P. L. 11, 363. inured by *m.*
**Modern.**—P. L. 11, 386. city of old or *m.* fame
S. A. 653. in ancient and in *m.* books enrolled
C. 45. from old or *m.* bard in hall or bower
**Modest.**—P. L. 4, 310. *m.* pride
S A. 1036. under virgin veil soft *m.* meek
**Modesty.**—P.L. 8,501. innocence and virgin *m.*
P. R. 3, 241. timorous and loth with novice *m.*
**Modin.**—P. R. 3, 170. *M.* and her suburbs
**Mogul.**—P. L. 11, 391. and Lahor of great *M.*
**Moist.**—P. L. 2, 898. for Hot, Cold, *M.,* and Dry
P. L. 3, 652. over *m.* and dry o'er sea and land

P. L. 5, 325. and superfluous *m.* consumes
P. L. 5, 422. from her *m.* continent to higher
P. L. 7, 408. attend *m.* nutriment
P. L. 80, 1066. while the winds blow *m.*
P. L. 11, 741. and exhalation dusk and *m.*
C. 825. with *m.* curb sways the smooth Severn
C. 918. I touch with chaste palms *m.* and cold
L. 159. or whether thou to our *m.* vows denied
**Moisture.**—P. L. 7, 282. satiate with genial *m.*
P. L. 8. 256. and on the reeking *m.* fed
**Mole.**—P. L. 7, 467. as the *m.* rising
P. L. 10, 300. and the *m.* immense wrought on
V. Ex. 95. or sullen *M.* that runneth underneath
**Molest.**—P. L. 8, 186. anxious cares and not *m.*
P. R. 4, 498. nor me in vain *m.*
S. A. 1525. the sufferers then will scarce *m.* us
**Moloch.**—P. L. 1, 392. first *M.* horrid king
P. L. 1, 417. by the grove of *M.* homicide
P. L. 2, 43. next him *M.,* sceptred king, stood up
P. L. 6, 357. the deep array of *M.* furious king
H. 205. sullen *M.* fled hath left in shadows dread
**Molten.**—C. 931. thy *m.* crystal fill with mud
**Moly.**—C. 636. more med'cinal is it than that *m.*
**Mombaza.**—P. L. 11, 399. *M.* and Quiloa
**Moment.**—P. L. 1, 544. all in a *m.*
P. L. 2, 448. proposed and judged of public *m.*
P. L. 2, 609. all in one *m.* and so near the brink
P. L. 2, 907. he rules a *m.*
P. L. 4, 51. and in a *m.* quit the debt immense
P. L. 6, 239. as only in his arm the *m.* lay
P. L. 6, 509. in a *m.* up they turned
P. L. 7, 154. and in a *m.* will create another
P. L. 10, 45. touch with lightest *m.* of impulse
P. R. 4, 162. all these which in a *m.* thou
S. A. 1559. but all her sons are fallen all in a *m.*
**Mona.**—L. 54. nor on the shaggy top of *M.* high
**Monarch.**—P. L. 1, 638. but he who reigns *m.*
P. L. 2, 467. saying rose the *M.* and prevented
P. L. 4, 960. servilely adored heaven's awful *m.*
P. L. 5, 832. that equal over equals *m.* reign
P. L. 10, 375. here thou shalt *m.* reign
C. 957. Night sits *m.* yet in the mid sky
**Monarchal.**—P. L. 2, 428. with *m.* pride
**Monarchies.**—P. L. 2, 307. of mightiest *m.*
P. R. 3, 246. and see before thine eyes the *m.*
P. R. 4, 150. shall to pieces dash all *m.* besides
**Monarchs.**—P. L. 1, 599. change perplexes *m.*
P. R. 2, 237. empires and *m.* and their radiant
P. R. 3, 262. seem the seats of mightiest *m.*
S. 15, 3. and all her jealous *m.* with amaze
**Monarchy.**—P. L. 1, 42. throne and *m.* of God
P. L. 5, 795. assume *m.* over such as live by
P. L. 10, 379. and henceforth *m.* with thee
P. R. 1, 87. he who obtains the *m.* of Heaven
P. R. 3, 277. of that first golden *m.* the seat
**Money.**—P. R. 2, 422. *m.* brings honour
**Monster.**—P. L. 1, 462. Dagon his name sea *m.*
P. L. 2, 675. the *m.* moving onward came
P. L. 10, 596. whom thus the Sin-born *M.*
P. L. 10, 986. be at last food for so foul a *m.*
P. R. 4, 100. mightst thou expel this *m.*
P. R. 4, 128. I shall ... expel a brutish *m.*
P. R. 4, 572. Theban *m.* that proposed her
S. A. 220. that specious *m.*
**Monsters.**—P. L. 2, 795. these yelling *m.*
P. L. 10, 523. complicated *m.* head and tail
C. 695. these ugly-headed *m.*
**Monstrous.**—P. L. 1, 197. of *m.* size
P. L. 1, 479. with *m.* shapes and sorceries
P. L. 2, 625. all *m.* all prodigious things
P. L. 3, 456. abortive or unkindly mixed
P. L. 6, 862. *m.* sight struck them with horror
P. L. 10, 514. down he fell a *m.* serpent
P. L. 11, 474. of which a *m.* crew before thee
C. 533. he and his *m.* rout are heard to howl
C. 605. the *m.* forms 'twixt Africa and Ind
L. 158. visit'st the bottom of the *m.* world
**Montalban.**—P. L. 1, 583. Aspramont or of
**Montezume.**—P. L. 11, 407. the seat of *M.*
**Month.**—H. 1. this is the *m.* and this the happy
**Monthly.**—P. L. 3, 728. her *m.* round

**Months.**—P. L. 3, 581. days, *m.*, and years
P. L. 8, 69. his seasons, hours, or days, or *m.*
C. 114. lead in swift round the *m.* and years
**Monument.**—P. L. 10, 258. a *m.* of merit
P. L. 11, 326. in memory or *m.* to ages
S. A. 570. vain *m.* of strength
S. A. 1734. there will I build him a *m.*
W. S. 8. hast built thyself a live-long *m.*
**Monumental.**—Il P. 135. of pine or *m.* oak
**Monuments.**—P. L. 1, 695. their greatest *m.*
**Mood.**—P. L. 1, 550. to the Dorian *m.* of flutes
P. L. 6, 620. thus Belial in like gamesome *m.*
P. L. 9, 920. thus in calm *m.* his words to Eve
P. R. 4, 450. and in a careless *m.* thus to him
S. A. 662. and of dissonant *m.* from his complaint
C. 371. could stir the constant *m.* of her calm
L. 87. that strain I heard was of a higher *m.*
S. 12, 9. for freedom in their senseless *m.*
**Moon.**—P. L. 1, 287. his shoulders like the *m.*
P. L. 1, 440. bright image nightly by the *m.*
P. L. 1, 596. or from behind the *m.*
P. L. 1, 784. overhead the *m.* sits arbitress
P. L. 2, 665. while the labouring *m.* eclipses
P. L. 2, 1053. close by the *m.*
P. L. 3, 459. not in the neighbouring *m.*
P. L. 3, 726. but there the neighbouring *m.*
P. L. 4, 606. the *M.* rising in clouded majesty
P. L. 4, 648. her solemn bird and this fair *m.*
P. L. 4, 655. walk by *m.* or glittering starlight
P. L. 4, 723. the *m.'s* resplendent globe
P. L. 4, 798. radiant files dazzling the *m.*
P. L. 5, 42. now reigns full-orbed the *m.*
P. L. 5, 175. *m.* that now meet'st the orient
P. L. 5, 263. lands and regions in the *m.*
P. L. 5, 418. and as lowest, first the *m.*
P. L. 5, 421. nor doth the *m.* no nourishment
P. L. 7, 104. the star of evening and the *m.*
P. L. 7, 356. then formed the *M.* globose
P. L. 7, 375. less bright the *M.*
P. L. 8, 142. to the terrestrial *m.* be as a star
P. L. 10, 656. to the blanc *m.* her office
P. L. 12, 266. and thou *M.* in the vale of Aialon
S. A. 87. silent as the *m.* when she deserts
C. 116. now to the *m.* in wavering morrice move
C. 331. unmuffle ye faint stars and thou fair *m.*
C. 374. though sun and *m.* were in the flat sea
C. 1017. to the corners of the *m.*
Il P. 67. to behold the wandering *m.*
S. 12, 7. which after held the sun and *m.* in fee
S. 22, 5. of sun, or *m.*, or star
U. C. II. 29. obedient to the *m.* he spent his date
**Mooned.**—P. L. 4, 978. sharpening in *m.* horns
H. 200. and *m.* Ashtaroth, heaven's queen
**Moon-loved.**—H. 236. leaving their *m.-l.* maze
**Moons.**—P. L. 8, 149. with their attendant *m.*
**Moon-struck.**—P. L. 11, 486. *m.-s.* madness
**Moorish.**—C. 433. by lake or *m.* fen
**Moors.**—P. L. 1, 207. *m.* by his side under
**Moory.**—P. L. 2, 944. o'er hill or *m.* dale
**Moping.**—P. L. 11, 485. *m.* melancholy
**Moral.**—P. L. 12, 298. nor man the *m.* part
P. R. 4, 263. teachers best of *m.* prudence
P. R. 4, 351. unless where *m.* virtue is expressed
S. A. 324. that *m.* verdict quits her of unclean
C. 807. this is mere *m.* babble and direct
**Moreh.**—P. L. 12, 137. neighbouring plain of *M.*
**Morn.**—P. L. 1, 208. and wished *m.* delays
P. L. 1, 742. from *m,* to noon he fell
P. L. 3, 42. the sweet approach of even or *m.*
P. L. 4, 641. sweet is the breath of *M.*
P. L. 4, 650. but neither breath of *M.*
P. L. 4, 773. roof showered roses which the *m.*
P. L. 5, 1. now *M.* her rosy steps in the eastern
P. L. 5, 30. glad I see thy face and *m.* returned
P. L. 5, 168. day that crown'st the smiling *m.*
P. L. 5, 202. witness if I be silent *m.* or even
P. L. 5, 310. seems another *m.* risen on
P. L. 5, 428. from off the boughs each *m.*
P. L. 5, 628. have also our evening and our *m.*
P. L. 5, 716. how spread among the sons of *m.*
P. L. 6, 2. till *M.* waked by the circling Hours

P. L. 6, 12. and now went forth the *M.*
P. L. 6, 524. when fair *M.* orient in Heaven
P. L. 6, 748. and the third sacred *m.* began
P. L. 7, 29. when *m.* purples the east
P. L. 7. 252. thus was the first Day even and *m.*
P. L. 7, 260. first evening was and when first *m.*
P. L. 7, 338. even and *m.* recorded the third Day
P. L. 7, 386. glad evening and glad *m.* crowned
P. L. 7, 448. evening and *m.* solemnized
P. L. 7, 550. even and *m.* accomplished the sixth
P. L. 8, 511. I led her blushing like the *M.*
P. L. 9, 191. waiting close the approach of *m.*
P. L. 9, 447. forth issuing on a summer's *m.*
P. L. 9, 848. the way she took that *m.* when
P. L. 9, 1136. of wandering this unhappy *m.*
P. L. 11, 173. the *M.* begin her rosy progress
P. L. 11, 184. after short blush of *M.*
P. L. 12, 422. the stars of *m.* shall see him rise
P. R. 2, 268. food to Elijah bringing even and *m.*
P. R. 2, 281. to descry the *M.'s* approach
P. R. 4, 438. gratulate the sweet return of *m.*
P. R. 4, 439. yet amidst this joy and brightest *m.*
C. 139. the blabbing eastern scout the nice *m.*
C. 753. love-darting eyes or tresses like the *m.*
A. 56. and early ere the odorous breath of *m.*
L. 26. under the opening eyelids of the *m.*
L. 187. while the still *m.* went out with sandals
L'A. 54. cheerly rouse the slumbering *m.*
L'A. 107. in one night ere glimpse of *m.*
Il P. 122. till civil-suited *M.* appear
H. 1. this is the month and this the happy *m.*
S. M. 28. and sing in endless *m.* of light
M. W. 45. which the sad *m.* had let fall
**Morning.**—P. L. 4, 244. where the *m.* sun
P. L. 4, 623. ere fresh *m.* streak the east
P. L. 5, 20. the *m.* shines and the fresh field calls
P. L. 5, 124. fair *M.* first smiles on the world
P. L. 5, 145. their orisons each *m.* duly paid
P. L. 5, 211. on to their *m.'s* rural work
P. L. 5, 746. *m.* dew-drops which the sun
P. L. 7, 108. dismiss thee ere the *m.* shine
P. L. 7, 275. so even and *m.* chorus sung
P. L. 7, 366. and hence the *m.* planet gilds her
P. L. 9, 194. that breathed their *m.* incense
P. L. 9, 800. not without song each *m.*
P. L. 12, 207. defends between till *m.* watch
P. R. 1, 294. spake our *M.* Star then in his rise
P. R. 4, 221. as *m.* shows the day
P. R. 4, 426. till *M.* fair came forth
P. R. 4, 451. fair *m.* yet betides thee Son of
S. A. 1598. the *m.* trumpets festival proclaimed
C. 622. spreads her verdant leaf to the *m.* ray
C. 920. and I must haste ere *m.* hour
L. 171. flames in the forehead of the *m.* sky
H. 73. for all the *m.* light
H. 119. but when of old the Sons of *M.* sung
**Morning-hour.**—P. L. 8, 111. *m.-h.* set out
**Morning-light.**—P. L. 11, 204. and *m.-l.*
**Morning-star.**—P. L. 5, 708. as the *m.-s.*
M. M. 1. now the bright *m-s.* day's harbinger
**Morpheus.**—Il P. 10. pensioners of *M.* train
**Morrice.**—C. 116. in wavering *m.* move
**Morrow.**—P. L. 4, 588. by *m.* dawning
P. L. 4, 662. round the earth by *m.* evening
P. L. 5, 33. works of day past or *m.* next
C. 317. I shall know ere *m.* wake
L'A. 46. and at my window bid good *m.*
**Morrow's.**—P. L. 3, 33. *m.'s* next design
**Morsel.**—P. L. 2, 808. should prove a bitter *m.*
**Morsels.**—P. L. 10, 605. no homely *m.*
**Mortal.**—P. L. 1, 2. whose *m.* taste brought
P. L. 1, 51. measures day and night to *m.* men
P. L. 1, 559. from *m.* or immortal minds
P. L. 1, 588. beyond compare of *m.* prowess
P. L. 1, 693. let those who boast in *m.* things
P. L. 1, 766. to *m.* combat, or career with lance
P. L. 2, 653. a serpent armed with *m.* sting
P. L. 2, 729. bend that *m.* dart against thy
P. L. 2, 813. that *m.* dint
P. L. 3, 55. tell of things invisible to *m.* sight
P. L. 3, 179. on even ground against his *m.* foe

P. L. 3, 214. which of you will be *m.* to redeem
P. L. 3, 253. of his *m.* sting disarmed
P. L. 3, 268. breathed immortal love to *m.* men
P. L. 4, 8. haply so scaped his *m.* snare
P. L. 6, 348. in their liquid texture *m.* wound
P. L. 6, 434. incapable of *m.* injury
P. L. 7, 24. more safe I sing with *m.* voice
P. L. 8, 331. thou shalt die from that day *m.*
P. L. 9, 1003. wept at completing of the *m.* sin
P. L. 10, 48. *m.* sentence pass on his transgression
P. L. 10, 273. the smell of *m.* change on earth
P. L. 10, 796. man is not so but *m.* doomed
P. L. 11, 54. as gross and *m.* food
P. L. 11, 273. of that day that must be *m.* to us
P. L. 11, 366. endure thy *m.* passage
P. L. 12, 9. but I perceive thy *m.* sight to fail ·
P. L. 12, 236. voice of God to *m.* ear is dreadful
P. L. 12, 248. Holy One with *m.* men to dwell
P. L. 12, 384. capital bruise expect with *m.* pain
P. R. 1, 86. his mother then is *m.* but his Sire
P. R. 1, 234. know thou art no son of *m.* man
P. R. 2, 157. more like to goddesses than *m.*
P. R. 4, 318. one regardless quite of *m.* things
S. A. 168. strongest of *m.* men to lowest pitch
S. A. 349. O ever-failing trust in *m.* strength
S. A. 639. above the nerve of *m.* arm
S. A. 1102. certain to have won by *m.* duel
S. A. 1175. defy thee to the trial of *m.* fight
S. A. 1489. strength so great to *m.* seed
S. A. 1682. so fond are *m.* men fallen into wrath
C. 10. after this *m.* change
C. 244. can any *m.* mixture of earth's mould
C. 686. by which all *m.* frailty must subsist
C. 802. though not *m.* yet a cold shuddering dew
A. 62. when drowsiness hath locked up *m.* sense
L. 78. fame is no plant that grows on *m.* soil
H. 14. chose with us a darksome house of *m.* clay
H. 95. as never was by *m.* finger strook
T. 6. and merely *m.* dross so little is our loss
D. F. I. 41. O say me true if thou wert *m.* wight
**Mortality.**—P. L. 10, 776. would I meet *m.*
D. F. I. 35. in thy face did shine above *m.*
**Mortals.**—P. L. 2, 1032. tempt or punish *m.*
P. R. 4, 454. and these flaws though *m.* fear
S. A. 523. when in strength all *m.* I excelled
S. A. 817. if thou in strength all *m.* dost exceed
C. 997. (list *m.* if your ears be true)
C. 1018. *m.* that would follow me love virtue
Il P. 153. sent by some Spirit to *m.* good
V. Ex. 66. from eyes of *m.* walk invisible
**Mortification.**—S. A. 622. to black *m.*
**Mosaic.**—P. L. 4, 700. wrought *M.*
**Mosco.**—P. L. 11, 395. the Russian Ksar in *M.*
**Moses.**—P. L. 12, 170. *M.* and Aaron
P. L. 12, 198. awed by the rod of *M.* so to stand
P. L. 12, 211. *M.* once more his potent rod
P. L. 12, 237. they beseech that *M.* might report
P. L. 12, 241. whose high office now *M.*
P. L. 12, 307. and therefore shall not *M.*
P. R. 1, 352. *M.* was forty days nor eat nor drank
P. R. 2, 15. *M.* was in the Mount and missing
P. R. 4, 219. and questions fitting *M.'s* chair
P. R. 4, 225. knowledge is not couched in *M.'s*
**Mossy.**—P. L. 5, 392. and *m.* seats had round
P. L. 9, 589. about the *m.* trunk I wound
P. R. 2, 184. in wood or grove by *m.* fountain
C. 276. to give me answer from her *m.* couch
Il P. 169. the hairy gown and *m.* cell
**Motes.**—Il P. 8. gay *m.* that people the sunbeams
**Mother.**—P. L. 1, 36. deceived the *m.* of mankind
P. L. 1, 687. rifled the bowels of their *m.* earth
P. L. 2, 792. me overtook his *m.* all dismayed
P. L. 2, 849. no less rejoiced his *m.* bad
P. L. 4, 475. thence be called *m.* of human race
P. L. 4, 492. so spake our general *m.*
P. L. 5, 338. whatever Earth all-bearing *m.*
P. L. 5, 388. hail *m.* of mankind
P. L. 7, 281. fermented the great *m.* to conceive
P. L. 8, 498. he shall forgo father and *m.*
P. L. 9, 644. our credulous *m.*
P. L. 9, 680. wisdom-giving plant *m.* of scienc

P. L. 9, 1106. daughters grow about the *m.* tree
P. L. 10, 602. the incestuous *m.* thus replied
P. L. 10, 778. lay me down as in my *m.'s* lap
P. L. 11, 159. *M.* of all mankind, *M.* of all
P. L. 11, 536. thou drop into thy *M.'s* lap
P. L. 12, 368. a Virgin is his *m.* but his Sire
P. L. 12, 379. virgin *M.* hail! high in the love
P. L. 12, 624. so spake our *m.* Eve
P. R. 1, 86. his *m.* then is mortal
P. R. 1, 227. these growing thoughts my *m.*
P. R. 2, 136. but to his *m.* Mary when she saw
P. R. 2, 136. if he be Man by *m.'s* side at least
P. R. 3, 154. by *m.'s* side thy father
P. R. 4, 216. from thy *m.'s* eye thou went'st
P. R. 4, 240. the eye of Greece, *m.* of arts
P. R. 4, 566. from his *m.* Earth new strength
P. R. 4, 639. home to his *m.'s* house
C. 57. much like his father but his *m.* more
C. 63. excels his *m.* at her mighty art
C. 153. as grazed about my *m.* Circe
C. 253. my *m.* Circe with the Sirens three
C. 523. deep skilled in all his *m.'s* witcheries
A. 22. *m.* of a hundred gods
S. 18, 8. rolled *m.* with infant down the rocks
H. 3. of wedded Maid and Virgin-*M.* born
H. 201. heaven's queen and *m.* both
M. W. 33. the languished *m.'s* womb
D. F. I. 71. the *m.* of so sweet a child
**Motherly.**—P. R. 2, 64. *m.* cares and fears
**Motion.**—P. L. 2, 75. that in our proper *m.*
P. L. 2, 151. devoid of sense and *m.*
P. L. 2. 780. prodigious *m.* felt and rueful throes
P. L. 5, 581. though in eternity applied to *m.*
P. L. 6, 192. no sight nor *m.* of swift thought
P. L. 6, 302. in stature, *m.*, arms
P. L. 6, 532. or if for fight, in *m.* or in halt
P. L. 7, 177. more swift than time or *m.*
P. L. 8, 35. attains her end without least *m.*
P. L. 8, 115. admitting *m.* in the heavens
P. L. 8, 223. and each word each *m.* forms
P. L. 8, 259. raised by quick instinctive *m.*
P. L. 9, 674. each part *m.* each act won
P. L. 12, 592. on yonder hill expect their *m.*
P. R. 1, 290. now by some strong *m.* I am led
P. R. 4, 601. whatever place, habit, or state or *m.*
A. 71. and the low world in measured *m.* draw
S. M. 22. whose love their *m.* swayed
U. C. II. 7. time numbers *m.*
U. C. II. 8. *m.* numbered out his time
**Motioned.**—P. L. 9, 229. well hast thou *m.*
S. A. 222. knew not that what I *m.* was of God
**Motionless.**—C. 819. fetters fixed and *m.*
**Motions.**—P. L. 2, 191. these our *m.* vain sees
P. L. 3, 582. turn swift their various *m.*
P. L. 5, 625. and in their *m.* harmony divine
P. L. 7, 500. her glory shone and rolled her *m.*
P. L. 8, 130. insensibly three different *m.* move
P. L. 10, 658. their planetary *m.*, and aspects
P. L. 11, 91. my *m.* in him longer than they
S. A. 1382. I begin to feel some rousing *m.* in me
**Move.**—P. L. 1, 549. they *m.* in perfect phalanx
P. L. 2, 837. might hap to *m.* new broils
P. L. 3, 37. on thoughts that voluntary *m.*
P. L. 3, 579. as they *m.* their starry dance
P. L. 3, 719. and how they *m.*
P. L. 5, 177. that *m.* in mystic dance
P. L. 5, 554. some doubt within me *m.*
P. L. 5, 701. hierarchal standard was to *m.*
P. L. 6, 68. on they *m.* indissolubly firm
P. L. 6, 550. and onward *m.* embattled
P. L. 6, 790. or wonders in *m.* the obdurate
P. L. 8, 33. might with far less compass *m.*
P. L. 8, 70. whether heaven *m.* or earth
P. L. 8, 77. to *m.* his laughter at their quaint
P. L. 8, 130. three different motions *m.*
P. L. 8, 276. live and *m.* fair creatures
P. L. 8, 281. that thus I *m.* and live
P. L. 8, 585. soul of man or passion in him *m.*
P. L. 9, 1016. thus gan Eve to dalliance *m.*
P. L. 10, 297. with Gorgonian rigour not to *m.*
P. L. 10, 652. sun had first his precept so to *m.*

P. L. 11, 91. in him longer than they *m.*
P. R. 3, 171. if kingdom *m.* thee not, let *m.* thee
P. R. 3, 224. why *m.* thy feet so slow
S. A. 752. and reconcilement *m.* with feigned
C. 116. now to the moon in wavering morrice *m.*
L. 180. that sing and singing in their glory *m.*
S. 17. *m.* by her two main nerves iron and gold
H. 129. *m.* in melodious time
V. Ex. 2. didst *m.* my first endeavouring tongue
U. C. II. 2. he could never die while he could *m.*
**Moved.**—P. L. 1, 29. *m.* our grand parents
P. L. 1, 561. *m.* on in silence to soft pipes
P. L. 2, 876. Stygian Powers could once have *m.*
P. L. 2, 1022. with difficulty and labour *m.* on
P. L. 3, 483. trepidation talked and that first *m.*
P. L. 4, 902. the warlike angel *m.* disdainfully
P. L. 6, 63. *m.* on in silence their bright legions
P. L. 6, 302. gods they seemed stood they or *m.*
P. L. 6, 405. from their place by violence *m.*
P. L. 7, 91. what cause *m.* the Creator in his
P. L. 8, 116. that which thee to doubt it *m.*
P. L. 8, 132. *m.* contrary with thwart obliquities
P. L. 8, 264. creatures that lived and *m.*
P. L. 8, 293. inward apparition gently *m.*
P. L. 9, 667. and as to passion *m.* fluctuates
P. L. 9, 1143. to whom soon *m.* with touch
P. L. 11, 453. to whom Michael thus, he also *m.*
P. L. 11, 560. who *m.* their stops and chords
P. L. 11, 830. by might of waves be *m.* out
P. R. 1, 170. and in celestial measures *m.*
P. R. 1, 424. what but thy malice *m.* thee to
P. R. 2, 407. to be harmed therefore not *m.*
S. A. 895. but zeal *m.* thee to please thy gods
S. A. 1452. but that which *m.* my coming now
C. 796. that dumb things would be *m.*
U. C. II. 9. like an engine *m.* with wheel and
**Mover.**—P. L. 7, 500. the great first *M.'s* hand
**Moves.**—P. L. 7, 534. every living thing that *m.*
P. L. 10, 359. a secret harmony still *m.* with
P. R. 3, 200. what *m.* by inquisition
S. A. 726. yet on she *m.* now stands and eyes
C. 247. and with these raptures *m.* the vocal air
**Moving.**—P. L. 1, 284. was *m.* toward the shore
P. L. 2, 675. the monster *m.* onward came
P. L. 4, 409. to first of women Eve thus *m.* speech
P. L. 5, 310. glorious shape comes this way *m.*
P. L. 6, 533. under spread ensigns *m.* nigh
P. L. 7, 87. distant so high with *m.* fires adorned
P. L. 7, 207. on golden hinges *m.* to let forth
P. L. 7, 415. sleeps or swims and seems a *m.* land
P. L. 9, 677. so standing, *m.* or to height
S. A. 102. myself my sepulchre a *m.* grave
**Mould.**—P. L. 1, 706. a various *m.*
P. L. 2, 139. the ethereal *m.* incapable of stain
P. L. 2, 355. of what *m.* or substance
P. L. 3, 709. this world's material *m.*
P. L. 4, 226. that mountain as his garden *m.*
P. L. 4, 360. creatures of other *m.*, earth-born
P. L. 5, 321. Adam, earth's hallowed *m.*
P. L. 6, 473. of this ethereous *m.* whereon
P. L. 6, 576. brass, iron, stony *m.*
P. L. 7, 356. first though of ethereal *m.*
P. L. 7, 470. scarce from his *m.* Behemoth
P. L. 9, 485. heroic built though of terrestrial *m.*
P. L. 10, 744. from my clay to *m.* me man
C. 17. with the rank vapours of this sin-worn *m.*
C. 244. can any mortal mixture of earth's *m.*
A. 73. of human *m.* with gross unpurged ear
H. 138. leprous Sin will melt from earthly *m.*
**Moulds.**—P. L. 11, 571. he drained into fit *m.*
**Mound.**—P. L. 4, 134. as with a rural *m.*
**Mount.**—P. L. 1, 15. above the Aonian *m.*
P. L. 1, 781. beyond the Indian *m.*
P. L. 3, 530. over *M.* Sion
P. L. 4, 126. and on the Assyrian *m.* saw him
P. L. 4, 281. *m.* Amara, though this by some
P. L. 4, 569. but in the *m.* that lies from Eden
P. L. 5, 382. three that in *M.* Ida naked strove
P. L. 5, 598. as from a flaming *m.*
P. L. 5, 643. from that high *m.* of God
P. L. 5, 712. from forth his holy *m.*

P. L. 5, 757. as a *m.* raised on a *m.*
P. L. 5, 764. in imitation of that *m.* whereon
P. L. 6, 5. there is a cave within the *m.* of God
P. L. 6, 88. fight or by surprise to win the *m.*
P. L. 6, 743. circling thy holy *m.*
P. L. 7, 584. when at the holy *m.* of Heaven's
P. L. 7, 600. from golden censers hid the *m.*
P. L. 11, 216. on the flaming *m.* appeared
P. L. 11, 320. on this *m.* he appeared
P. L. 11, 402. from Niger flood to Atlas *m.*
P. L. 11, 829. then shall this *M.* of Paradise
P. L. 12, 227. the *M.* of Sinai whose gray top
P. R. 1, 351. in the *M.* Moses was forty days
P. R. 2, 15. Moses was in the *M.* and missing
P. R. 4, 236. ere we leave this specular *m.*
P. R. 4, 547. appearing like a *m.* of alabaster
A. 55. over the *m.* and all this hallowed ground
L. 161. the great Vision of the guarded *M.*
**Mountain.**—P. L. 1, 443. on the offensive *m.*
P. L. 1, 613. forest oaks or *m.* pines
P. L. 2, 488. from *m.* tops the dusky clouds
P. L. 4, 226. that *m.* as his garden mould
P. L. 5, 766. the *M.* of the Congregation
P. L. 6, 197. side long had pushed a *m.* from
P. L. 6, 575. lop in wood or *m.* felled
P. L. 8, 303. last led me up a woody *m.*
P. L. 10, 1065. begins to show us in this *m.*
P. L. 11, 567. wasted woods, on *m.* or in vale
P. L. 11, 728. from the *m.* hewing timber tall
P. L. 11, 851. on the top of some high *m.*
P. R. 3, 252. the Son of God up to a *m.* high
P. R. 3, 253. it was a *m.* at whose verdant feet
P. R. 3, 265. to this high *m.* top the Tempter
P. R. 4, 26. western side of that high *m.*
C. 89. and in this office of his *m.* watch
**Mountaineer.**—C. 426. bandit or *m.*
**Mountain-nymph.**—L'A. 36. *m.-n.*
**Mountain-pard.**—C. 444. and spotted *m.-p.*
**Mountains.**—P. L. 1, 291. rivers or *m.* in her
P. L. 6, 649. the bottom of the *m.* upward
P. L. 6, 652. under the weight of *m.* buried
P. L. 6, 697. with *m.* as with weapons armed
P. L. 6, 842. wished the *m.* now might be
P. L. 7, 201. between two brazen *m.* lodged
P. L. 7, 214. and surging waves as *m.* to assault
P. L. 7, 285. immediately the *m.* huge appear
P. L. 10, 291. *m.* of ice that stop the imagined
P. R. 4, 39. above the height of *m.* interposed
S. A. 1648. when *m.* tremble
L'A. 73. *m.* on whose barren breast
S. 18, 2. lie scattered on the Alpine *m.* cold
H. 181. the lonely *m.* o'er
P. 51. take up a weeping on the *m.* wild
**Mounted,**—P. L. 4, 1014. knew his *m.* scale
P. L. 5, 300. while now the *m.* sun shot down
P. L. 6, 572. a triple *m.* row of pillars laid
P. L. 10, 589. not *m.* yet on his pale horse
L. 172. so Lycidas sunk low and *m.* high
**Mounting.**—D. F. I. 15. *m.* up in icy-pearled car
**Mourn.**—L. 41. and all their echoes *m.*
H. 188. in twilight shade of tangled thickets *m.*
H. 204. maids their wounded Thammuz *m.*
Cir. 6. ye flaming Powers, ... now *m.*
**Mourned.**—P. L. 1, 458. who *m.* in earnest
**Mourners.**—P. L. 1, 56. had got a race of *m.*
**Mourneth.**—C. 235. her sad song *m.* well
**Mournful.**—P. L. 1, 244. this *m.* gloom
P. 28. more apt for *m.* things
**Mourning.**—S. A. 1712. left them years of *m.*
**Mourns.**—P. L. 11, 760. as when a father *m.*
P. R. 3, 279. Israel in long captivity still *m.*
S. A. 1752. whence Gaza *m.* and all that band
**Must.**—P. R. 4, 16. wine-press where sweet *m.*
**Mouth.**—P. L. 2, 888. and like a furnace *m.*
P. L. 5, 83. even to my *m.* of that same fruit
P. L. 9, 187. in at his *m.* the Devil entered
P. L. 9, 514. nigh river's *m.* or foreland
P. L. 10, 288. shoaling towards the *m.* of Hell
P. L. 10, 636. obstruct the *m.* of Hell for ever
P. L. 11, 569. gliding hot to some cave's *m.*
P. L. 12, 42. from under ground the *m.* of Hell

P. R. 1, 350. proceeding from the *m.* of God
P. R. 1, 482. to hear her dictates from thy *m.*
P. R. 3, 12. kings and nations from thy *m.*
P. R. 4, 276. whose *m.* issued forth mellifluous
S. A. 1522. we unawares run into danger's *m.*
S. 15, 2. filling each *m.* with envy or with praise
**Mouths.**—P. L. 2, 517. to their *m.* the sounding
P. L. 2. 655. barked with wide Cerberean *m.*
P. L. 2, 967. Discord with a thousand various *m.*
P. L. 4, 513. I have gained from their own *m.*
P. L. 6, 576. had not their *m.* with hideous
P. L. 10, 547. on themselves from their own *m.*
P. L. 12, 158. it flows disgorging at seven *m.*
P. R. 1, 428. to be a liar in four hundred *m.*
S. A. 452. and oped the *m.* of idolist and atheists
S. A. 866. celebrated in the *m.* of wisest men
L. 119. blind *m.* that scarce themselves know
S. 11, 10. those rugged names to our like *m.*
**Mower.**—L'A. 66. and the *m.* whets his scythe
**Mows.**—P. L. 10, 606. scythe of time *m.* down
**Mozambic.**—P. L. 4, 161. now are passed *M.*
**Much-humbled,**—P. L. 11, 181. *m.-h.* Eve
**Mud.**—C. 931. thy molten crystal fill with *m.*
**Mulciber.**—P. L. 1, 740. men called him *M.*
**Mules.**—P. R. 3, 335. *m.* after these
**Multiform.**—P. L. 5, 182. *m.,* and mix
**Multiplied.**—P. L. 7, 398. the fowl be *m.*
P. L. 8, 424. like of his like his image *m.*
P. R. 4, 41. of vision *m.* through air or glass
**Multiplies.**—P. L. 5, 318. where Nature *m.*
P. R. 1, 69. things highest, greatest, *m.* my fear
**Multiply.**—P. L. 7, 396. be fruitful, *m.*
P. L. 7, 531. be fruitful *m.* and fill the earth
P. L. 7, 630. and *m.* a race of worshippers holy
P. L. 10, 193. thy sorrow I will greatly *m.*
P. L. 10, 730. increase and *m.*
P.L.10,732. what can I increase or *m.* but curses
P. L. 11, 677. and *m.* ten thousand-fold
P. L. 12. 17. shall lead their lives and *m.* apace
**Multitude.**—P. L. 1, 351. *m.* like which
P. L. 1, 702. a second *m.* with wondrous art
P. L. 1, 730. the hasty *m.* admiring entered
P. L. 2, 323. reserved his captive *m.*
P. L. 2, 836. surcharged with potent *m.*
P. L. 3, 260. then with the *m.* of my redeemed
P. L. 3, 345. but all the *m.* of angels
P. L. 6, 810. number . . . is not ordained nor *m.*
P. L. 6, 847. distinct alike with *m.* of eyes
P. L. 7, 188. from his throne beheld their *m.*
P. L. 10, 554. for one forbidden tree a *m.*
P. L. 10, 643. through *m.* that sung
P. L. 12, 352. grown in wealth and *m.*
P. R. 1, 196. Oh what a *m.* of thoughts at once
P. R. 2, 420. or at thy heels the dizzy *m.*
P. R. 3, 331. nor of labouring pioneers a *m.*
S. A. 696. and condemnation of the ingrateful *m.*
**Multitudes.**—P. L. 4, 474. bear *m.* like thyself
P. L. 5, 716. what *m.* were banded to oppose
P. L. 6, 31. against revolted *m.* the cause of truth
P. L. 10, 26. about the new-arrived in *m.*
P. R. 2, 470. cities of men or headstrong *m.*
**Mummers.**—S. A. 1325. antics, *m.,* mimics
**Mural.**—P. L. 6, 879. soon repaired her *m.* breach
**Murder.**—S. A. 1186. committed notorious *m.*
**Murderous.**—P. R. 2, 76. till the *m.* king
**Murky.**—P. L. 10, 280. wide into the *m.* air
**Murmur.**—P. L. 2, 284. such *m.* filled assembly
P. L. 5, 873. hoarse *m.* echoed to his words
P. L. 7, 68. whose liquid *m.* heard new thirst
P. R. 4, 248. the sound of bees' industrious *m.*
S. 19, 9. but Patience to prevent that *m.* soon
**Murmured.**—C.259.Charybdis *m.* soft applause
**Murmuring.**—P. L. 4, 260. *m.* waters fall
P.L.4,453.a *m.* sound of waters issued from a cave
P. L. 4, 1015. but fled *m.* and with him fled
P. L. 8, 263. and liquid lapse of *m.* streams
P. R. 3, 108. to whom the Tempter *m.* thus
Il P. 144. and the waters *m.* with such consort
**Murmurs.**—P. L. 5, 196. melodious *m.*
C. 526. with many *m.* mixed
A. 60. with puissant words and *m.* made to bless

**Murrain.**—P. L. 12, 179. of rot and *m.* die
**Murtherer.**—S. A. 832. what *m.* what traitor
S. A. 1180. *m.,* a revolter and a robber
**Musæus.**—Il P. 104. raise *m.* from his
**Muse.**—P. L. 1, 6. sing heavenly *M.* that on the
P. L. 1, 376. say *M.* their names then known
P. L. 3, 19. taught by the heavenly *M.*
P. L. 7, 37. nor could the *M.* defend her son
P. L. 7, 52. filled with admiration and deep *m.*
C. 515. sage poets taught by the heavenly *M.*
L. 19. so may some gentle *M.* with lucky words
L. 58. what could the *M.* herself that Orpheus
L. 66. and strictly meditate the thankless *M.*
L. 133. return Sicilian *M.* and call the vales
S. 1, 13. whether the *M.* or Love call thee his
H. 15. say heavenly *M.* shall not thy sacred vein
P. 4. my *M.* with angels did divide to sing
V. Ex. 53. my wandering *M.* how thou dost stray
**Mused.**—L'A. 9, 744. thus to herself she *m.*
P. R. 2, 99. what he meant I *m.*
**Muses.**—P. L. 3, 27. where the *M.* haunt
P. L. 7, 6. nor of the *M.* nine nor on the top
Il P. 47. and hears the *M.* in a ring
S. 8, 9. lift not thy spear against the *M.'* bower
**Music.**—P. L. 1, 787. jocund *m.* charm his ear
P. L. 5, 548. from neighbouring hills aerial *m.*
P. L. 11, 592. with feast and *m.* all the tents
P. R. 4, 332. with *m.* or with poem
A. 68. such sweet compulsion doth in *m.* lie
A. 74. and yet such *m.* worthiest were to blaze
Il P. 151. and as I wake sweet *m.* breathe
S. 13, 2. first taught our English *m.* how to span
H. 93. *m.* sweet their hearts and ears did greet
H. 117. such *m.* as 'tis said
P. 1. erewhile of *m.* and ethereal mirth
Cir. 2. that erst with *m.* and triumphant song
S. M. 21. broke the fair *m.* that all creatures
**Musical.**—C. 478. but *m.* as is Apollo's lute
Il P. 62. most *m.,* most melancholy
**Musing.**—P. R. 1, 185. *m.* and much revolving
P. R. 4, 249. oft invites to studious *m.*
S. A. 1017. though one should *m.* sit
C. 386. that *m.* Meditation most affects
Il P. 38. with even step and *m.* gait
**Musk-rose.**—C. 496. and sweetened every *m.-r.*
L. 146. the *m.-r.* and the well-attired woodbine
**Musky.**—C. 989. and west winds with *m.* wing
**Muster.**—P. R. 3, 308. see how in warlike *m.*
**Mustering.**—P. L. 2, 268. *m.* their rage
P. L. 11, 645. horse and foot nor idly *m.* stood
S. A. 402. when *m.* all her wiles
V. Ex. 44. in Heaven's defiance *m.* all his waves
**Mutable.**—P. L. 5, 237. though free yet *m.*
S. A. 793. I saw thee *m.* of fancy
S. A. 1407. so *m.* are all the ways of men
**Mute.**—P. L. 1, 618. attention held them *m.*
P. L. 2, 420. but all sat *m.* pondering the danger
P. L. 3, 217. but all the heavenly choir stood *m.*
P. L. 7, 25. voice unchanged to hoarse or *m.*
P. L. 8, 222. speaking or *m.,* all comeliness
P. L. 9, 557. created *m.* to all articulate sound
P. L. 9, 563. how camest thou speakable of *m.*
P. L. 9, 672. eloquence flourished since *m.*
P. L. 9, 748. first assay gave elocution to the *m.*
P. L. 9, 1064. long they sat as stricken *m.*
P. L. 10, 18. ascended *m.* and sad for man
P. L. 11, 31. hear his sighs though *m.*
P. L. 11, 194. which Heaven by these *m.* signs
P. R. 1, 12. my prompted song else *m.*
P. R. 1, 459. in vain for they shall find thee *m.*
P. R. 3, 2. Satan stood a while as *m.* confounded
S.A. 248. the deeds themselves though *m.* spoke
S. A. 672. and inferior creatures *m.* irrational
L. 32. meanwhile the rural ditties were not *m.*
Il P. 55. and the *m.* Silence hist along
**Mutely.**—V. Ex. 6. where he had *m.* sat
**Mutiny.**—P. L. 2, 926. these elements in *m.* had
**Muttering.**—P. L. 9, 1002. and *m.* thunder
**Mutters.**—C. 817. backward *m.* of dissevering
**Mutual.**—P. L. 1, 87. if he whom *m.* league
P. L. 4, 376. and *m.* amity, so strait, so close

P. L. 4, 727. happy in our *m.* help and *m.* love
P. L. 6, 506. on war and *m.* slaughter bent
P. L. 7, 429. with *m.* wing easing their flight
P. L. 8, 58. such pairs in love and *m.* honour
P. L. 8, 385. which must be *m.* in proportion
P. L. 9, 1043. of their *m.* guilt the seal
P. L. 9, 1187. thus they in *m.* accusation spent
C. 741. consists in *m.* and partaken bliss
U. C. II. 31. linked to the *m.* flowing of the seas
**Myriads.**—P. L. 1, 87. didst outshine *m.*
P. L. 1, 622. O *m.* of immortal Spirits
P. L. 5, 684. of all those *m.* which we lead
P. L. 6, 24. that of so many *m.* fallen yet one
P. L. 7, 201. where stand of old *m.*
**Myrrh.**—P. L. 5, 23. what drops the *m.*
P. L. 5, 292. blissful field through groves of *m.*
P. L. 9, 629. thicket past of blowing *m.*
P. L. 12, 363. to offer incense, *m.* and gold
P. R. 1, 251. to honour thee with incense *m.*
C. 937. with groves of *m.* and cinnamon
**Myrrhine.**—P. R. 4, 119. and *m.* cups
**Myrtle.**—P. L. 4, 262. bank with *m.* crowned
P. L. 4, 694. laurel and *m.* and what higher
P. L. 9, 219. spring of roses intermixed with *m.*
P. L. 9, 431. she upstays gently with *m.* band
H. 51. and waving wide her *m.* wand
**Myrtles.**—P. L. 9, 627. beyond a row of *m.*
L. 2. ye *m.* brown with ivy never sere
**Myself.**—P. L. 2, 828. one for all *m.* expose
P. L. 3, 244. me to possess life in *m.* for ever
P. L. 4, 75. which way I fly is Hell *m.* am Hell
P. L. 4, 450. found *m.* reposed under a shade
P. L. 5, 95. best image of *m.* and dearer half
P. L. 5, 535. *m.* and all the angelic host
P. L. 5, 607. and by *m.* have sworn to him

P. L. 7, 170. though I uncircumscribed *m.*
P. L. 8, 267. *m.* I then perused and limb by limb
P. L. 8, 278. not of *m.* by some great Maker
P. L. 8, 495. flesh of my flesh *m.* before me
P. L. 9, 126. nor hope to be *m.* less miserable
P. L. 9, 959. to lose thee were to lose *m.*
P. L. 10, 117. being naked hid *m.*
P. L. 10, 127. either to undergo *m.* the total
P. L. 10, 820. Oh were I able to waste it all *m.*
P. R. 1, 198. consider what from within I feel *m.*
P. R. 1, 204. *m.* I thought born to that end
P. R. 4, 453. but *m.* was distant
S. A. 46. whom have I to complain of but *m.*
S. A. 375. *m.* have brought them on sole author
S. A. 401. she sought to make me traitor to *m.*
S. A. 809. whole to *m.* unhazarded abroad
S. A. 824. I to *m.* was false ere thou to me
S. A. 1334. *m.* my conscience and internal peace
S. A. 1425. our God our law, my nation or *m.*
**Mysteries.**—P. L. 12, 509. sacred *m.* of Heaven
P. R. 3, 249. apt in regal arts and regal *m.*
**Mysterious.**—P. L. 4, 312. those *m.* parts
P. L. 4, 743. nor Eve the rites *m.* of connubial
P. L. 4, 750. hail, wedded love, *m.* law
P. L. 8, 599. and with *m.* reverence I deem
P. L. 10, 173. though in *m.* terms
C. 130. *m.* dame that ne'er art called
Il P. 147. let some strange *m.* dream
**Mysteriously.**—P. L. 3, 516. each stair *m.* was
**Mystery.**—S. A. 378. who have profaned the *m.*
C. 785. apprehend the sublime notion and high *m.*
**Mystic.**—P. L. 5, 178. that move in *m.* dance
P. L. 9, 442. or that not *m.* where the sapient
**Mystical.**—P. L. 5, 620. *m.* dance

# N.

**Naiades.**—P. R. 2, 355. Diana's train and *N.*
C. 254. amidst the flowery-kirtled *N.*
**Nailed.**—P. L. 12, 413. *n.* to the cross
S. A. 990. Sisera sleeping through the temples *n.*
**Nails.**—P. L. 12, 415. to the cross he *n.* thy enemies
**Naked.**—P. L. 4, 290. in *n.* majesty seemed lords
P. L. 4, 319. so passed they *n.* on nor shunned
P. L. 4, 496. half her swelling breast *n.* met
P. L. 4, 713. in *n.* beauty more adorned
P. L. 4, 772. and on their *n.* limbs the flowery
P. L. 5, 382. three that in Mount Ida *n.* strove
P. L. 5, 444. at table Eve ministered *n.*
P. L. 9, 1057. *n.* left to guilty Shame
P. L. 9, 1074. which leaves us *n.* thus
P. L. 9, 1115. how unlike to that first *n.* glory
P. L. 9, 1117. with feathered cincture *n.* else
P. L. 9, 1139. shamed. *n.*, miserable
P. L. 10, 117. and of thy voice afraid being *n.*
P. L. 10, 121. thou art *n.* who hath told thee?
P. L. 10, 212. how they stood before him *n.*
H. 40. and on her *n.* shame
V. Ex. 23. I have some *n.* thoughts that rove
**Nakedness.**—P. L. 10, 217. he clad their *n.*
P. L. 10, 221. inward *n.* much more opprobrious
Cir. 20. emptied his glory even to *n.*
**Namancos.**—L. 162. toward *N.* and Bayona's
**Name.**—P. L. 1, 197. as whom the fables *n.*
P. L. 1, 412. Peor his other *n.* when he enticed
P. L. 1, 462. Dagon his *n.* sea-monster
P. L. 1, 738. nor was his *n.* unheard or unadored
P. L. 2, 788. hell trembled at the hideous *n.*
P. L. 2, 964. the dreaded *n.* of Demogorgon
P. L. 3, 412. thy *n.* shall be the copious matter
P. L. 4, 36. and add thy *n.* O Sun to tell thee
P. L. 4, 950. O *n.* O sacred *n.* of faithfulness
P. L. 5, 658. his former *n.* is heard no more
P. L. 5, 707. great indeed his *n.* and high
P. L. 5, 776. under the *n.* of king anointed
P. L. 6, 174. depravest it with the *n.* servitude
P. L. 7, 1. by that *n.* if rightly thou art called
P. L. 7, 5. the meaning not the *n.* I call
P. L. 7, 536. for no place is yet distinct by *n.*

P. L. 8, 114. inexpressible by numbers that *n.*
P. L. 8, 272. readily could *n.* whate'er I saw
P. L. 8, 357. Oh by what *n.* for thou above all
P. L. 8, 496. Woman is her *n.* of Man extracted
P. L. 9, 40. justly gives heroic *n.* to person
P. L. 9, 44. sufficient of itself to raise that *n.*
P. L. 9, 142. well nigh half the angelic *n.*
P. L. 10, 386. of Satan, for I glory in the *n.*
P. L. 10, 649. the Creator calling forth by *n.*
P. L. 10, 867. serpent that *n.* best befits thee
P. L. 11, 171. far other *n.* deserving
P. L. 12, 36. from rebellion shall derive his *n.*
P. L. 12, 45. and get themselves a *n.*
P. L. 12, 311. his *n.* and office bearing
P. L. 12, 326. of David (so I *n.* this king)
P. L. 12, 577. all the stars thou knew'st by *n.*
P. L. 12, 584. love by *n.* to come called charity
P. R. 2, 346. of shell or fin and exquisitest *n.*
S. A. 331. awaked with mention of that *n.*
S. A. 467. but will arise and His great *n.* assert
S. A. 475. to vindicate the glory of His *n.*
S. A. 674. nor do I *n.* of men the common rout
S. A. 677. heads without *n.* no more remembered
S. A. 894. for which our country is a *n.* so dear
S. A. 968. brand of infamy upon my *n.* denounced
S. A. 975. my *n.* perhaps among the circumcised
S. A. 1101. thou bearest the highest *n.* for valiant
S. A. 1429. spread His *n.* great among the heathen
C. 738. with that same vaunted *n.* Virginity
C. 749. they had their *n.* thence
C. 826. Sabrina is her *n.*, a virgin pure
C. 868. appear to us in *n.* of great Oceanus
S. 8, 7. he can spread thy *n.* o'er lands and seas
S. 15, 1. Fairfax whose *n.* in arms
M. W. 60. devoted to thy virtuous *n.*
D. F. I. 77. shall make thy *n.* to live
W. S. 6. thou such weak witness of thy *n.*
V. Ex. 99. that keeps the Scythian's *n.*
**Named.**—P. L. 1, 80. and *n.* Beelzebub
P. L. 1, 574. as *n.* with these could merit more
P. L. 2, 579. Cocytus *n.* of lamentation loud
P. L. 5, 839. and to their glory *n.* Thrones

P. L. 6, 294. and join him *n*. Almighty
P. L. 7, 252. and Darkness Night he *n*.
P. L. 7, 274. and Heaven he *n*. the Firmament
P. L. 8, 352. I *n*. them as they passed
P. L. 8, 439. which thou hast rightly *n*.
P. L. 11, 296. or *n*. of them the highest
P. L. 12, 62. and the work 'Confusion' *n*.
P. R. 2, 8. others though in Holy Writ not *n*.
S. A. 982. I shall be *n*. among the famousest
C. 58. therefore she brought up and Comus *n*.
C. 325. where it first was *n*. and yet is most
F. of C. 11. be *n*. and printed heretics
**Nameless.**—P. L. 6, 380. *n*. in dark oblivion
**Names.**—P. L. 1, 361. though of their *n*. in
P. L. 1, 365. got them new *n*.
P. L. 1, 374. known to men by various *n*.
P. L. 1, 376. say Muse their *n*. then known
P. L. 1, 421. general *n*. of Baälim and Ashtaroth
P. L. 1, 477. who under *n*. of old renown
P. L. 6, 76. over Eden to receive their *n*.
P. L. 6, 373. and their *n*. eternize here on earth
P. L. 7, 493. gavest them *n*. needless to thee
P. L. 8, 344. to receive from thee their *n*.
P. L. 11, 277. and gave ye *n*.
P. L. 12, 140. things by their *n*. I call
P. L. 12, 458. exalted high above all *n*.
P. L. 12, 515. seek to avail themselves of *n*.
P. R. 2, 189. then lay'st thy scapes on *n*. adored
P. R. 2, 447. I esteem those *n*. of men so poor
P. R. 3, 95. who *n*. not now with honour
P. R. 4, 316. rather accuse him under usual *n*.
S. A. 974. bears greatest *n*. in his wild aery flight
C. 208. and airy tongues that syllable men's *n*.
C. 627. and show me simples of a thousand *n*.
S. 11, 10. those rugged *n*. to our like mouths
**Naming.**—P. L. 8, 359. surpassest far my *n*.
P. L. 9, 751. conceals not from us *n*. thee
P. R. 4, 539. worth *n*. Son of God by voice
**Naphtha.**—P. L. 1, 729. cressets fed with *N*.
**Nipt.**—S. A. 1577. *n*. with the lagging rear
**Narcissus.**—C. 237. that likest thy *N*. are
**Nard.**—P. L. 5, 293. cassia, *n*. and balm
C. 991. *n*. and cassia's balmy smells
**Narrow.**—P. L. 1, 779. in *n*. room throng
P. L. 2, 919. for no *n*. frith he had to cross
P. L. 4, 207. in *n*. room Nature's whole wealth
P. L. 4, 384. room, not like these *n*. limits
P. L. 4, 528. but first with *n*. search I must
P. L. 6, 104. but *n*. space was left
P. L. 6, 583. and to a *n*. vent applied
P. L. 9, 83. the orb he roamed with *n*. search
P. L. 9, 323. in *n*. circuit straitened by a foe
P. L. 11, 341. his presence to these *n*. bounds
S. A. 1117. be assigned some *n*. place enclosed
**Narrower.**—P. L. 7, 21. but *n*. bound within
P. R. 4, 515. my nearer view and *n*. scrutiny
**Nathless.**—P. L. 1, 299. *n*. he so endured
**Nation.**—P. L. 12, 111. one peculiar *n*. to select
P. L. 12, 113. a *n*. from one faithful man
P. L. 12, 124. from him will raise a mighty *n*.
P. L. 12, 164. leaves his race growing into a *n*.
P. L. 12, 414. nailed to the cross by his own *n*.
P. L. 12, 503. they win great numbers of each *n*.
P. R. 4, 362. what makes a *n*. happy and keeps
S. A. 218. at least of thy own *n*. and as noble
S. A. 565. can I be useful? wherein serve my *n*.
S. A. 857. destroyed such numbers of our *n*.
S. A. 877. daughters of my tribe and of my *n*.
S. A. 1182. is not thy *n*. subject to our lords
S. A. 1205. my *n*. was subjected to your lords
S. A. 1425. our God our law, my *n*. or myself
S. A. 1494. of a *n*. armed the strength contained
C. 33. and old and haughty *n*. proud in arms
**National.**—P. L. 12, 317. sins *n*. interrupt
S. A. 312. from *n*. obstriction, without taint of sin
**Nations.**—P. L. 1, 385. adored among the *n*.
P. L. 1, 598. twilight sheds on half the *n*.
P. L. 4, 663. to *n*. yet unborn ministering light
P. L. 11, 692. overcome in battle and subdue *n*.
P. L. 11, 792. subduing *n*. and achieved
P. L. 12, 97. sometimes *n*. will decline so low

P. L. 12, 126. in his seed all *n*. shall be blest
P. L. 12, 147. all *n*. of the earth shall in his seed
P. L. 12, 277. in whom all *n*. shall be blest
P. L. 12, 329. as in whom shall trust all *n*.
P. L. 12, 440. to teach all *n*. what of him
P. L. 12, 446. all *n*. they shall teach
P. L. 12, 450. so in his seed all *n*. shall be blest
P. L. 12, 499. he sends to evangelize the *n*.
P. R. 1, 79. thenceforth the *n*. may not doubt
P. R. 1, 98. ere in the head of *n* he appear
P. R. 1, 432. confessed more true among the *n*.
P. R. 1, 442. God hath justly given the *n*. up
P. R. 2, 473. to guide *n*. in the way of truth
P. R. 3, 12. should kings and *n*. from thy mouth
P. R. 3, 76. enslave peaceable *n*.
P. R. 3, 113. from all *n*. Jew or Greek
P. R. 4, 47. and with the spoils enriched of *n*.
P. R. 4, 80. all *n*. now to Rome obedience pay
P. R. 4, 122. showest from *n*. far and nigh
P. R. 4, 135. but govern ill the *n*. under yoke
P. R. 4, 202. *n*. besides from all the quartered
S. A. 268. but what more oft in *n*. grown corrupt
S. A. 890. against the law of nature, law of *n*.
**Native.**—P. L. 1, 450. Adonis from his *n*. rock
P. L. 1, 634. and repossess their *n*. seat
P. L. 2, 76. we ascend up to our *n*. seat
P. L. 2, 1050. once his *n*. seat and fast by
P. L. 3, 605. through a limbec to his *n*. form
P. L. 4, 158. dispense *n*. perfumes and whisper
P. L. 4, 289. godlike erect with *n*. honour clad
P. L. 5, 361. *N*. of Heaven for other place none
P. L. 5, 863. birth mature of this our *n*. Heaven
P. L. 6, 226. not destroy their happy *n*. seat
P. L. 6, 436. by *n*. vigour healed
P. L. 7, 16. return me to my *n*. element
P. L. 7, 245. and from her *n*. east to journey
P. L. 9, 93. as from his wit and *n*. subtlety
P. L. 9, 373. in thy *n*. innocence rely on what
P. L. 9, 1056. confidence and *n*. righteousness
P. L. 10, 467. to our *n*. Heaven little inferior
P. L. 10, 1085. dust our final rest and *n*. home
P. L. 11, 270. thus leave thee, *n*. soil
P. L. 11, 292. he abides think there thy *n*. soil
P. L. 11, 463. the way I must return to *n*. dust
P. L. 12, 54. to rase quite out their *n*. language
P. L. 12, 129. leaves his gods, his friends, and *n*.
P. R. 1, 378. lost much lustre of my *n*. brightness
P. R. 2, 313. that prophet bold *n*. of Thebez.
P. R. 3, 437. while to their *n*. land with joy
P. R. 4, 241. *n*. to famous wits
P. R. 4, 333. soon as in our *n*. language
C. 76. and all their friends and *n*. home forget
L'A. 134. warble his *n*. wood-notes wild
V. Ex. 1. hail *N*. Language that by sinews weak
**Natives.**—P. L. 5, 790. *n*. and sons of Heaven
**Nativity.**—P. L. 6, 482. these in their dark *n*.
P. R. 1, 242. at thy *n*. a glorious choir of Angels
S. A. 1141. who gave me at my *n*. this strength
**Natural.**—P. L. 10, 740. as on their *n*. centre
P. L. 10, 765. not thy election but *n*. necessity
P. L. 12, 288. to evince their *n*. pravity
P. L. 12, 645. some *n*. tears they dropped
V. Ex. 87. yea it shall be his *n*. property
**Nature.**—P. L. 2, 218. in temper and in *n*.
P. L. 2, 624. death lives and *n*. breeds perverse
P. L. 2, 895. night and Chaos ancestors of *N*.
P. L. 2, 911. womb of *N*. and perhaps her grave
P. L. 2, 1037. here *N*. first begins her farthest
P. L. 3, 49. blank of *N.'s* works to me expunged
P. L. 3, 126. I else must change their *n*.
P. L. 3, 282. their *n*. also to thy *n*. join
P. L. 3, 304. by descending to assume man's *n*.
P. L. 3, 455. unaccomplished works of *N.'s* hand
P. L. 4, 207. in narrow room *N.'s* whole wealth
P. L. 4, 242. but *N*. boon poured forth profuse
P. L. 4, 314. dishonest shame of *n.'s* works
P. L. 4, 633. as *N*. wills night bids us rest
P. L. 4, 667. and extinguish life in *n*. and all
P. L. 5, 24. how *N*. paints her colours
P. L. 5, 45. whom to behold but thee, *N.'s* desire
P. L. 5, 109. into her private cell when *N*. rests

P. L. 5, 181. the eldest birth of *N.'s* womb
P. L. 5, 294. a wilderness of sweets for *N.* here
P. L. 5, 318. *N.* multiplies her fertile growth
P. L. 5, 360. as to a superior *n.* bowing low
P. L. 5, 452. they had sufficed not burdened *n.*
P. L. 5, 509. scale of *n.* set from centre
P. L. 5, 527. ordained thy will by *n.* free
P. L. 5, 834. or all angelic *n.* joined in one
P. L. 6, 176. God and *N.* bid the same
P. L. 6, 176. to serve whom God ordains or *N.*
P. L. 6, 267. and into *N.* brought misery
P. L. 6, 311. if *N.'s* concord broke
P. L. 6, 442. between us made the odds in *n.*
P. L. 6, 511. the originals of *n.* in their crude
P. L. 7, 103. the rising birth of *N.*
P. L. 7, 482. not all minims of *n.*
P. L. 8, 26. reasoning I oft admire how *N.* wise
P. L. 8, 153. such vast room in *n.* unpossessed
P. L. 8, 353. and understood their *n.* with such
P. L. 8, 459. called by *n.* as in aid
P. L. 8, 506. or to say all, *N.* herself
P. L. 8, 534. or *n.* failed in me and left some
P. L. 8, 541. in the prime end of *N.*
P. L. 8, 561. accuse not *N.* she hath done her
P. L. 9, 27. not sedulous by *n.* to ind'te wars
P. L. 9, 624. more hands help to disburden *N.*
P. L. 9, 782. and *n.* from her seat sighing
P. L. 9, 914. I feel the link of *n.* draw me
P. L. 9, 956. I feel the bond of *n.* draw me
P. L. 9, 1001. and *N.* gave a second groan
P. L. 10, 169. then accursed as vitiated in *n.*
P. L. 10, 805. beyond dust and *N.'s* law
P. L. 10, 885. but a rib crooked, by *n.* bent
P. L. 10, 892. on earth this fair defect of *N.*
P. L. 11, 49. the law I gave to *N.* him forbids
P. L. 11, 182. *N.* first gave signs impressed
P. L. 11, 194. Heaven by these mute signs in *n.*
P. L. 11, 523. they pervert pure *N.'s* healthful
P. L. 11, 597. to admit delight the bent of *N.*
P. L. 11, 602. here *N.* seems fulfilled in all
P. L. 11, 604. though to *N.* seeming meet
P. L. 12, 29. dispossess concord and law of *N.*
P. L. 12, 578. all *N.'s* works, or works of God
P. R. 1, 13. height or depth of *N.'s* bounds
P. R. 2, 230. to satisfy lawful desires of *n.*
P. R. 2, 249. if *n.* need not or God support *n.*
P. R. 2, 253. which declares *N.* hath need
P. R. 2, 265. meats and drinks, *n.'s* refreshment
P. R. 2, 295. *N.'s* own work, *N.* taught Art
P. R. 2, 332. behold *N.* ashamed
P. R. 3, 231. or human *n.* can receive
P. P. 4, 228. led by *N.'s* light
P. R. 4, 352. light of *N.* not in all quite lost
S. A. 595. *N.* within me seems
S. A. 890. against the law of *n.* law of nations
S. A. 1545. Providence or instinct of *n.* seems
C. 198. that *N.* hung in heaven
C. 411. my *n.* is that I incline to hope rather
C. 559. and wished she might deny her *n.*
C. 680. to those dainty limbs which *N.* lent
C. 710. wherefore did *N.* pour her bounties forth
C. 727. and live like *N.'s* bastards not her sons
C. 739. beauty is *N.'s* coin must not be hoarded
C. 745. beauty is *N.'s* brag and must be shown
C. 762. impostor do not charge most innocent *N.*
C. 772. *N.'s* blessings would be well dispensed
A. 70. and keep unsteady *N.* to her law
L. 60. whom universal *N.* did lament
H. 32. *N.* in awe to him had doffed her gaudy
H. 101. *N.* that heard such sound
M. W. 13. *N.* and fate had had no strife
S. M. 20. sin jarred against *n.'s* chime
D.F.I. 45. which careful Jove in *n.'s* true behoof
V. Ex. 46. when beldam *N.* in her cradle was
**Natures.**—P. L. 5, 402. perhaps to spiritual *n.*
P. L. 7, 498. and thou their *n.* know'st
**Navel.**—C. 520. the *n.* of this hideous wood
**Nay.**—P. L. 4, 71. *n.*, cursed be thou
P. L. 9, 1159. *n.*, didst permit approve and fair
P. R. 4, 6. won... so little here, *n.* lost
S. A. 350. *n.*, what thing good prayed for but

S. A. 1729. Gaza is not in plight to say us *n.*
C. 271. *n.* gentle shepherd ill is lost that praise
C. 659. *n.* Lady sit, if I but wave this wand
**Nazareth.**—P.R. 1, 23. with them came from *N.*
P. R. 2, 79. in *N.* hath been our dwelling
**Nazarite.**—S. A. 318. prompted this heroic *N.*
S. A. 1359. a *N.* in place abominable
S. A. 1366. or stain my vow of *N*
**Neæra.**—L. 69. or with the tangles of *N.'s* hair
**Near.**—P. L. 4, 787. that *n.* him stood and gave
P. L. 2, 609. and so *n.* the brink
P. L. 4, 425. so *n.* grows death to life
P. L. 5, 830. under one head more *n.* united
P. L. 7, 55. and war so *n.* the peace of God
P. L. 9, 220. while so *n.* each other
P. L. 9, 221. what wonder if so *n.*
P. L. 10, 347. *n.* the foot of this new wondrous
P. L. 10, 389. so *n.* Heaven's door
P. L. 10, 562. *n.* that bituminous lake where
S. A. 725. my traitress! let her not come *n.*
S. A. 786. so *n.* related or the same of kind
C. 486. some chaste footing *n.* about this ground
C. 491. come not too *n.*, you fall on iron
C. 567. how *n.* the deadly snare
C. 616. how durst thou then thyself approach *n.*
L'A. 63. whilst the ploughman *n.* at hand
Il P. 68. riding *n.* her highest noon
D. F. I. 10. it touched his deity full *n.*
A. 40. lead ye where ye may more *n.* behold
Cir. 28. will pierce more *n.* his heart
S. 2, 6. that I to manhood am arrived so *n.*
H. 44. look so *n.* upon her foul deformities
**Nearer.**—P.L. 1, 785. and *n.* to the earth wheels
P. L. 2, 394. in spite of Fate *n.* our ancient seat
P. L. 9, 1008. so much the *n.* danger
P. L. 4, 133. delicious Paradise now *n.*
P. L. 4, 399. served best his end *n.* to view
P. L. 5, 358. *n.* his presence Adam though not
P. L. 5, 476. as *n.* to him placed or *n.* tending
P. L. 6, 81. and *n.* view, bristled with upright
P. L. 7, 62. to know what *n.* might concern him
P. L. 9, 434. *n.* he drew and many a walk
P. L. 9, 578. I *n.* drew to gaze
P. R. 1, 400. but long since with woe *n.*
P. R. 3, 364. as *n.* and of late found able by
P. R. 4, 237. westward much *n.* by south-west
P. R. 4, 514. I thought thee worth my *n.* view
S. A. 723. and now at *n.* view no other certain
S. A. 1229. come *n.*, part not hence so slight
S.A. 1631. for so from such as *n.* stood we heard
**Nearest.**—P. L. 1, 192. talking to his *n.* mate
P. L. 2, 958. which way the *n.* coast of darkness
P. L. 3, 649. *n.* to his throne stand ready
P. L. 4, 484. out of my side to thee, *n.*, my heart
P.L. 5, 622. yonder starry sphere..resembles *n.*
C. 90. likeliest and *n.* to the present aid
S. 21, 10. solid good what leads the *n.* way
**Nearly.**—P. L. 5, 721. *n.* it now concerns
**Near-ushering.**—C. 279. from *n.-u.* guides
**Neat.**—S. 20, 9. what *n.* repast shall feast us
**Neat-handed.**—L'A. 86. the *n.-h.* Phillis
**Nebaioth.**—P. R. 2, 309. her son, outcast *N.*
**Nebo.**—P. L. 1, 407. from Aroer to *N.*
**Necessary.**—S. A. 90. since light so *n.* is to life
**Necessitate.**—P. L. 10, 44. to *n.* his fall
**Necessitated.**—P. L. 5, 530. not our *n.*
**Necessity.**—P. L. 3, 110. had served *n.*
P. L. 4, 393. and with *n.*, the tyrant's plea
P. L. 5, 528. by fate inextricable or strict *n.*
P. L. 7, 172. *n.* and Chance approach not me
P. L. 10, 131. but strict *n.* subdues me
P. L. 10, 765. not thy election but natural *n.*
S. A. 1666. tangled in the fold of dire *n.*
A. 69. to lull the daughters of *N.*
**Neck.**—P. L. 7, 438. the swan with arched *n.*
P. L. 9, 501. with burnished *n.* of verdant gold
P. L. 9, 525. and sleek enamelled *n.*
S. 16, 5. and on the *n.* of crowned Fortune
**Necks.**—P. L. 3, 395. o'er the *n.* thou drovest
P. L. 5, 787. will ye submit your *n.* and

P. L. 10, 1046. his just yoke laid on our *n.*
P. R. 4, 418. sturdiest oaks bowed their stiff *n.*
**Necromancer's.**—C. 649. assault the *n.'s* hall
**Nectar.**—P. L. 4, 240. brooks ... ran *n.*
P. L. 5, 428. fruitage bear and vines yield *n.*
P. L. 5, 633. and rubied *n.* flows in pearl
P. L. 9, 838. sap derived from *n.*, drink of gods
L. 175. with *n.* pure his oozy locks he laves
**Nectared.**—C. 838. in *n.* lavers strewed with
D. F. I. 40. to hide thy *n.* head
C. 479. a perpetual feast of *n.* sweets
**Nectarine.**—P. L. 4, 332. *n.* fruits
**Nectarous.**—P. L. 5, 306. of *n.* draughts
P.L.6,332. from the gash a stream of *n.* humour
**Need.**—P. L. 2, 53. contrive who *n.* or when
P. L. 2, 341. nor shall we *n.* with dangerous
P. L. 2, 413. here he had *n.* all circumspection
P. L. 3, 340. regal sceptre then no more shall *n.*
P. L. 4, 419. perform aught whereof he hath *n*
P. L. 4, 617. unemployed and less *n.* rest
P. L. 5, 629. for change delectable not *n.*
P. L. 6, 318. that might determine and not *n.*
P. L. 6, 625. who receives them right had *n.*
P. L. 8, 419. no *n.* that thou shouldst propagate
P. L. 8, 628. nor restrained conveyance *n.*
P. L. 9, 296. as to debar us when we *n.*
P. L. 9, 246. as wide as we *n.* walk
P. L. 9, 260. other speedy aid might lend at *n.*
P. L. 9, 311. if *n.* were of outward strength
P. L. 9, 731. import your *n.* of this fair fruit
P. L. 10, 80. attendance none shall *n.*
P.L.10,409. affairs of Hell no detriment *n.* fear
P. L. 10,1082. *n.* not fear to pass commodiously
P. R. 1, 292. perhaps I *n.* not know
P. R. 2, 249. if nature *n.* not
P. R. 2, 253. Nature hath *n.* of what
P. R. 2, 254. yet God can satisfy that *n.*
P. R. 2, 318. they all had *n.* of what she asks
P. R. 2, 397. chose to impart to thy apparent *n.*
P. R. 3, 385. Rome or Cæsar not *n.* fear
P. R. 3, 399. or to *n.* politic maxims
S. A. 1107. and thou hast *n.* much washing
S. A. 1437. be efficacious in thee now at *n.*
S. A. 1483. if *n.* be I am ready to forgo
S. A. 1526. from other hands we *n.* not much
C. 219. send a glistering guardian if *n.* were
C. 287. imports their loss beside the present *n.*
C. 362. what *n.* a man forestall his date of grief
C. 394. had *n.* the guard of dragon-watch
C. 752. what *n.* a vermeil-tinctured lip for that
C. 857. such as was herself in hard-besetting *n.*
L. 122. what recks it them ? what *n.* they?
S. 19, 9. God doth not *n.* either man's work
H.82. new-enlightened world no more should *n.*
V. Ex. 81. from others he shall stand in *n.* of
**Needed.**—P. L. 5, 151. more tuneable than *n.*
P. L. 5, 214. and *n.* hands to check fruitless
P. L. 5, 384. no veil she *n.*, virtue-proof
P. L. 7, 378. for other light she *n.* none
**Needing.**—P. R. 2, 251. though *n.*
**Needless.**—P. L. 7, 494. *n.* to thee repeated
P. L. 9, 1140. seek *n.* cause to approve the faith
P. L. 2, 484. riches are *n.* then
C. 942. not a waste or *n.* sound
**Needs.**—P. L. 2, 277. which must *n.* remove
P. L. 3, 105. where only what they *n.* must
P. L. 4, 235. whereof here *n.* no account
P. L. 4, 412. *n.* must the Power that made us
P. L. 5, 302. more warmth than Adam *n.*
P. L. 5, 414. created *n.* to be sustained
P. L. 5, 556. which must *n.* be strange
P. L. 6, 456. from which evil ruin must *n.* ensue
P. L. 6, 693. in perpetual fight they *n.* must
P. L. 7, 126. Knowledge is as food and *n.* no less
P. L. 8, 136. which *n.* not thy belief
P. L. 9, 215. choice leads thee or where most *n.*
P. L. 9, 307. subtle he *n.* must be who
P. L. 9, 942. for us created *n.* with us must fail
P. L. 11,251. heaven's high behest no preface *n.*
P. L. 12, 10. must *n.* impair and weary human
P. L. 12, 383. *n.* must the Serpent now his

P. R. 4, 290. no other doctrine *n.*
P. R. 4, 325. and what he brings what *n.* he
S. A. 840. knowing, as *n.* I must, by thee
S. A. 1044. what pilot so expert but *n.* must
S.A.1345.take it with what speed thy message *n.*
S. A. 1519. some dismal accident it *n.* must be
S. A. 1554. no preface *n.*
W.S.1.what *n.*my Shakspeare for his honoured
**Need'st.**—P. L. 8, 564. most thou *n.* her nigh
S. A. 1379. thou *n.* not doubt
W. S. 6. what *n.*thou such weak witness of thy
V. Ex. 11. thou *n.* not be ambitious to be first
**Ne'er.**—S. A. 212. last pretend they *n.* so wise
C. 127. which these dun shades will *n.* report
C. 131. that *n.* art called but when the dragon
C. 777. for swinish Gluttony *n.* looks to Heaven
U. C. II. 18. I'll *n.* be fetched
**Neglect.**—P. L. 3, 199. they who *n.* and scorn
P. L. 12, 426. as many as offered life *n.* not
S. A. 291. me easily indeed mine may *n.*
C. 510. or our *n.*, we lost her as we came
V.Ex.16. for this same small *n.*that I have made
**Neglected.**—S. A. 481. loathsome plight *n.*
S. A. 944. contemned and scorned and last *n.*
C. 743. if you let slip time, like a *n.* rose
**Neglects.**—P. L. 3, 738. reverence none *n.*
**Negus.**—P. L. 11, 397. the empire of *N.*
**Neighbour.**—C. 484. or else some *n.* woodman
C. 576. supposing him some *n.* villager
**Neighbourhood.**—P. L. 1, 400. audacious *n.*
C. 314. my daily walks and ancient *n.*
P. 52. the gentle *n.* of grove and spring
**Neighbouring.**—P. L. 2, 395. with *n.* arms
P. L. 3, 459. not in the *n.* moon as some have
P. L. 3, 726. but there the *n.* moon
P. L. 4, 145. into his nether empire *n.* round
P. L. 5, 547. songs by night from *n.* hills
P. L. 6, 663. and the *n.* hills uptore
P. L. 11, 575. from the high *n.* hills
P. L. 12, 136. about Sechem and the *n.* plain
P. R. 3, 76. peaceable nations *n.* or remote
P. R. 3, 319. from Atropatia and the *n.* plains
L'A. 80. the Cynosure of *n.* eyes
**Neighbours.**—S. A. 180. thy friends and *n.*
**Nepenthes.**—C. 675. that *n.* which the wife
**Neptune.**—P. L. 9, 18. or *N.'s* ire or Juno's
P. R. 2, 190. Apollo, *N.*, Jupiter or Pan
C. 18. *N.* besides the sway of every salt flood
C. 869. by the earth-shaking *N.'s* mace
L. 90. herald of the sea that came in *N.'s* plea
V. Ex. 43. how green-eyed *N.* raves
**Nereus'.**—C. 835. straight to aged *N.* hall
C. 871. by hoary *N.* wrinkled look
**Nerve.**—P. L. 11, 415. purged ... the visual *n.*
S. A. 639. above the *n.* of mortal arm
**Nerves.**—S. A. 1646. straining all his *n.*
C. 660. your *n.* are all chained up in alabaster
C. 797. the brute Earth would lend her *n.*
S. 17, 8. by her two main *n.*, iron and gold
**Nests.**—P. L. 4, 601. these to their *n.* were slunk
P. R. 1, 501. fowls in their clay *n.* were couched
S. A. 1694. and *n.* in order ranged
**Net.**—P. L. 11, 586. in the amorous *n.* fast caught
**Nether.**—P. L. 1, 346. upper *n.* and surrounding
P. L. 2, 296. to found this *n.* empire
P. L. 2, 784. all my *n.* shape thus grew
P. L. 4, 145. into his *n.* empire neighbouring
P. L. 4, 231. and met the *n.* flood
P. L. 7, 624. earth with her *n.* ocean
P. L. 11, 328. in yonder *n.* world where shall I
C. 20. took in by lot 'twixt high and *n.* Jove
**Nethermost.**—P.L.2,956.Spirit of the *n.* Abyss
P. L. 2, 969. Powers and Spirits of this *n.* Abyss
**Nets.**—P. R. 2, 162. tangled in amorous *n.*
**Never-ending.**—P. L. 2, 221. *n.-e.* flight
**Nevertheless.**—P. L. 10, 970. *n.* restored
**New.**—P. L. 1, 252. receive thy *n.* possessor
P. L. 1, 279. they will soon resume *n.* courage
P. L. 1, 290. or in Valdarno to descry *n.* lands
P. L. 1, 365. got them *n.* names
P. L. 1, 645. or dread *n.* war provoked

P. L. 1, 650. space may produce n. worlds
P. L. 1, 774. n. rubbed with balm
P. L. 2, 239. on promise made of n. subjection
P. L. 2, 319. in n. league banded against his
P. L. 2, 348. the happy seat of some n. race
P. L. 2, 403. we send in search of this n. world
P. L. 2, 837. might hap to move n. broils
P. L. 2, 867. bring me soon to that n. world
P. L. 3, 137. sense of n. joy ineffable diffused
P. L. 3, 294. and from thee receive n. life
P. L. 3, 335. from her ashes spring n. Heaven
P. L. 3, 468. n. Babels had they wherewithal
P. L. 3, 613. matter n. to gaze the Devil met
P. L. 3, 661. to visit oft this n. creation round
P. L. 3, 679. created this n. happy race of Men
P. L. 4, 34. like the God of this n. world
P. L. 4, 106. his n. delight mankind created
P. L. 4, 113. as man ere long and this n. world
P. L. 4, 184. hunger drives to seek n. haunt
P. L. 4, 205. with n. wonder now he views
P. L. 4, 287. of living creatures n. to sight
P. L. 4, 391. by conquering this n. world
P. L. 4, 410. all ear to hear n. utterance flow
P. L. 4, 575. to raise n. troubles
P. L. 5, 19. last best gift my ever n. delight
P. L. 5, 184. to our great Maker still n. praise
P. L. 5, 431. his bounty so with n. delights
P. L. 5, 679. n. laws thou seest imposed
P. L. 5, 680. n. laws from him .. n. minds may
P. L. 5, 681. in us who serve n. counsels
P. L. 5, 691. great Messiah and his n. command
P. L. 5, 780. may be devised of honours n.
P. L. 5, 855. strange point and n.
P. L. 6, 451. deliverer from n. Lords
P. L. 6, 571. to our eyes discovered n. and strange
P. L. 7, 68. whose liquid murmur heard n. thirst
P. L. 7, 209. coming to create n. worlds
P. L. 8, 311. here had n. begun my wandering
P. L. 9, 175. this n. favourite of Heaven
P. L. 9, 222. or object n. casual discourse
P. L. 9, 667. n. part puts on
P. L. 9, 843. and n. solace in her return
P. L. 9, 852. fruit that downy smiled n. gathered
P. L. 9, 985. n. hopes, n. joys
P. L. 9, 1008. now as with n. wine intoxicated
P. L. 9, 1097. this n. comer Shame
P. L. 10, 243. methinks I feel n. strength
P. L. 10, 257. from Hell to that n. world
P. L. 10, 348. foot of this n. wondrous pontifice
P. L. 10, 377. from this n. world retiring by
P. L. 10, 406. my hold of this n. kingdom
P. L. 10, 647. by whom n. Heaven and Earth
P. L. 10, 721. is this the end of this n. glorious
P. L. 10, 972. to place of n. acceptance
P. L. 11, 4. and made n. flesh regenerate grow
P. L. 11, 103. some n. trouble raise
P. L. 11, 138. n. hope to spring out of despair
P. L. 11, 228. or impose n. laws to be observed
P. L. 14, 867. peace from God and covenant n.
P. L. 11, 900. till fire purge all things n.
P. L. 12, 5. n. speech resumes
P. L. 12, 549. n. Heavens, n. earth
P. R. 1, 328. our n. baptizing Prophet
P. R. 1, 334. to hear what happens n.
P. R. 2, 38. into perplexity and n. amaze
P. R. 2, 58. out of their plaints n. hope resume
P. R. 2, 126. these mild seats without n. trouble
P. R. 3, 266. and n. train of words began
P. R. 4, 278. schools of Academics, old and n.
P. R. 4, 443. yet with no n. device
P. R. 4, 566. from his mother Earth n. strength
S. A. 1329. seek occasion of n. quarrels
S. A. 1447. by order of the lords n. parted hence
S. A. 1755. with n. acquist of true experience
C. 941. with some other n. device
C. 967. I have brought ye n. delight
L. 193. to-morrow to fresh woods and pastures n.
S. 11, 3. the subject n. it walked the town
S. 15, 6. n. rebellions raise their hydra heads
S. 16, 11. n. foes arise threatening to bind
H. 18. to welcome him to this his n. abode

H. 66. whispering n. joys to the mild ocean
L'A. 69. straight mine eye hath caught n.
M. W. 40. flower n. shot up from vernal shower
F. of C. 20, n. presbyter is but old Priest writ
**New-arrived.**—P. L. 10, 26. n.-a. in multitudes
**New-baptized.**—P. R. 2, 1. the n.-b. who yet
**New-born.**—H. 116. Heaven's n.-b. Heir
**New-created.**—P. L. 3, 89. the n.-c. world
P. L. 4, 937. and spy this n.-c. world
P. L. 7, 554. thence to behold this n.-c. world
P. L. 10. 481. how I found the n.-c. world
**New-declared.**—P. R. 1, 121. find this n.-d.
**New-enlightened.**—H. 82. the n.-e. world
**New-enlivened.**—C. 228. my n.-e. spirits
**New-entrusted.**—C. 36. and n.-e. sceptre
**New-fangled.**—V. Ex. 19. not those n.-f. toys
**New-felt.**—P. L. 10, 263. n.-f. attraction
**New-graven.**—P. R. 1, 253. n.-g. in heaven
**Newly.**—U. C. I. 18. Hobson has supped and's n.
**New-made.**—P. L. 7, 617. this n.-m. world
C. 472. lingering and sitting by a n.-m. grave
**New-reaped.**—P. L. 11, 431. sheaves n.-r.
**New-risen.**—P. L. 1, 594. when the sun n.-r.
**News.**—P. L. 6, 20. what he for n. had thought
P. L. 10, 21. as the unwelcome n. from earth
P. L. 11, 263. for Adam at the n. heart-struck
P. R. 1, 64. for this ill n. I bring
S. A. 1444. bringing to us some glad n.
S. A. 1538. evil n. rides post while good n. baits
S. A. 1569. suspense in n. is torture
P. 3. and joyous n. of Heavenly Infant's birth
**New-spangled.**—L. 170. with n.-s. ore
**New-waked.**—P. L. 8, 4 then as n.-w. thus
P. L. 8, 253. as n.-w. from soundest sleep
**New-welcome.**—M. W. 71. with thee n.-w. Saint
**Next.**—P. L. 1, 79. one n. himself in power and n.
P. L. 1, 238. him followed his n. mate
P. L. 1, 378. as n. in worth came singly
P. L. 1, 383. long after n. the seat of God
P. L. 1, 406. n. Chemos, the obscene dread
P. L. 1, 446. Thammuz came n. behind
P. L. 1, 457. n. came one who mourned in earnest
P. L. 2, 19. n. free choice
P. L. 2, 43. he ceased and n. him Moloch
P. L. 2, 439. Night receives him n. wide gaping
P. L. 2, 909. n. him, high arbiter, Chance
P. L. 2, 965. Rumour n. and Chance
P. L. 3, 239. this glory n. to thee freely put off
P. L. 3, 383. thee n. they sang, of all creation
P. L. 3, 466. the builders n. of Babel
P. L. 4, 220. and n. to life our death
P. L. 4, 781. when Gabriel to his n. in power
P. L. 4, 864. awaiting n. command
P. L. 4, 948. professing n. the spy
P. L. 5, 33. of day past or morrow's n. design
P. L. 5, 102. among these Fancy n. her office
P. L. 5, 671. and his n. subordinate awakening
P. L. 6, 45. and thou in military prowess n.
P. L. 6, 316. with n. to almighty arms
P. L. 6, 439. when n. we meet may serve
P. L. 6, 446. in the assembly n. upstood Nisroch
P. L. 6, 653. themselves invaded n.
P. L. 7, 489. swarming n. appeared the bee
P. L. 8, 449. what n. I bring shall please thee
P. L. 9, 174. on him who n. provokes my envy
P. L. 9, 807. experience n. to thee I owe
P. L. 9, 950. whom will he n.
P. L. 10, 604. on each beast n. and fish and
P. L. 10, 645. n. to the Son destined restorer
P. L. 11, 169. n. favourable thou who highly
P. L. 11, 436. a shepherd n. more meek came
P. L. 12, 332. and his n. son for wealth
P. R. 3, 96. who n. more memorable?
P. R. 3, 417. the deities of Egypt Baal n. and
P. R. 4, 253. Lyceum there and painted Stoa n.
P. R. 4, 272. to sage philosophy n. lend thine ear
P. R. 4, 295. the n. to fabling fell and smooth
S. A. 227. she proving false, the n. I took to wife
S. A. 1507. in both which we as n. participate
C. 185. stepped as they said to the n. thicket side
C. 501. O my loved master's heir and his n. joy

C. 916. *n.* this marble venomed seat
C. 959. till *n.* sunshine holiday
L. 103. *n.* Camus, reverend sire, went footing
M. W. 62. .*n.* her, much like to thee in story
M. W. 67. and at her *n.* birth much like thee
V. Ex. 41. misty regions of wide air *n.* under
V. Ex. 58. that to the *n.* I may resign my room
**Nibbling.**—L'A. 72. where the *n.* flocks do stray
**Nice.**—P. L. 4, 241. which not *n.* art in beds
P. L. 5, 433. to taste think not I shall be *n.*
P. L. 8, 399. a *n.* and subtle happiness I see
P. R. 4, 157. will please the difficult and *n.*
C. 139. the blabbing eastern scout the *n.* morn
**Nicely.**—P. R. 4, 377. thus *n.* or cautiously
**Nicest.**—P. L. 6, 584. applied with *n.* touch
**Niger.**—P. L. 11, 402. thence from *N.* flood
**Niggard.**—C. 726. as a penurious *n.* of his wealth
**Nigh.**—P. L. 1. 700. *n.* on the plain in many
P. L. 2, 940. *n.* foundered on he fares
P. L. 3, 566. but *n.* hand seemed other worlds
P. L. 3, 645. he drew not *n.* unheard
P. L. 3, 646. the Angel bright ere he drew *n.*
P. L. 4, 15. which *n.* the birth now rolling
P. L. 4, 366. gentle pair *ye* little think how *n.*
P. L. 4, 552. but *n.* at hand celestial armoury
P. L. 4, 861. now drew they *n.* the western
P. L. 5, 82. so saying he drew *n.* and to me
P. L. 6, 295. have sought thee far and *n.*
P. L. 6, 533. under spread ensigns moving *n.*
P. L. 8, 564. when most thou need'st her *n.*
P. L. 9, 141. well *n* half the angelic name
P. L. 9, 256. and somewhere *n.* at hand watches
P. L. 9, 433. best prop so far and storm so *n.*
P. L. 9, 482. her husband . . . not *n.*
P. L. 9, 514. *n.* river's mouth
P. L. 9, 595. where plenty hung tempting so *n.*
P. L. 10, 159. Eve with shame *n.* overwhelmed
P. L. 10, 632. till crammed and gorged *n.* burst
P. L. 10, 864. approaching *n.* soft words to his
P. L. 11, 184. in her sight the bird of Jove
P. L. 11, 193. some farther change awaits us *n.*
P. L. 11, 238. the Archangel soon drew *n.*
P. L. 12, 625. now too *n.* the Archangel stood
P. R. 1, 20. Heaven's kingdom *n.* at hand to all
P. R. 1, 36. the voice divine *n.* thunder-struck
P. R. 1, 332. town or village *n.* (nighest is far)
P. R. 2, 20. *n.* to Bethabara in Jericho
P. R. 2, 262. under the hospitable covert *n.*
P. R. 4, 122. showest from nations far and *n.*
P. R. 4, 489. noising loud and threatening *n.*
P. R. 4, 582. Angels on full sail of wing flew *n.*
S. A. 178. he speaks let us draw *n.*
S. A. 593. but yield to double darkness *n.* at hand
S. A. 1564. lessens the sorrow and converts it *n.*
S. 1, 10. foretell hopeless doom in some grove *n.*
**Nighest.**— P. R. 1, 332. village nigh (*n.* is far)
**Night.**—P. L. 1, 50. that measures day and *n.*
P. L. 1, 207. while *n.* invests the sea
P. L. 1, 343. like *n.* and darkened all the land
P. L. 1, 487. who in one *n.* when he passed
P. L. 1, 500. and when *n.* darkens the streets
P. L. 1, 503. and that *n.* in Gibeah
P. L. 1, 543. the reign of Chaos and old *N.*
P. L. 2, 133. far and wide into the realm of *N.*
P. L. 2, 150. in the wide womb of uncreated *n.*
P. L. 2, 286. blustering winds which all *n.* long
P. L. 2, 308. audience and attention still as *n.*
P. L. 2, 439. void profound of unessential *N.*
P. L. 2, 505. that day and *n.* for his destruction
P. L. 2, 670. black it stood as *N.*
P. L. 2, 894. where eldest *N.* and Chaos
P. L. 2, 962. sable-vested *N.* eldest of things
P. L. 2, 970. Chaos and ancient *N.* I come
P. L. 2, 986. the standard there of ancient *N.*
P. L. 2, 1002. weakening the sceptre of old *N.*
P. L. 2, 1036. far into the bosom of dim *N.*
P. L. 3, 18. I sung of Chaos and eternal *N.*
P. L. 3, 71. the wall of Heaven on this side *N.*
P. L. 3, 424. under the frown of *N.*
P. L. 3, 514. dreaming by *n.* under the open
P. L. 3, 545. a scout . . . with peril gone all *n.*

P. L. 3, 557. the circling canopy of *n.'s*
P. L. 3, 726. *n.* would invade
P. L. 3, 732. her pale dominion checks the *n*
P. L. 4, 550. the angelic guards awaiting *n.*
P. L. 4, 557. star in autumn thwarts the *n.*
P. L. 4, 603. she all *n.* long her amorous
P. L. 4, 611. fair consort, the hour of *n.*
P. L. 4, 613. labour and rest as day and *n.* to men
P. L. 4, 633. as Nature wills, *n.* bids us rest
P. L. 4, 647. silent *n.* with this her solemn bird
P. L. 4, 654. nor silent *n.* with this her solemn
P. L. 4, 657. wherefore all *n.* long shine these
P. L. 4, 665. total darkness should by *n.* regain
P. L. 5, 674. though unbeheld in deep of *n.*
P. L. 4, 680. works behold both day and *n.*
P. L. 4, 688. their songs divide the *n.*
P. L. 4, 724. thou also madest the *n.* Maker
P. L. 4, 776. now had *N.* measured with her
P. L. 4, 1015. with him fled the shades of *n.*
P. L. 5, 30. this *n.* such *n.* till this I never passed
P. L. 5, 35. knew never till this irksome *n.*
P. L. 5, 93. thus Eve her *n.* related
P. L. 5, 96. of thy thoughts this *n.* in sleep
P. L. 5, 128. reserved from *n.* and kept for
P. L. 5, 162. choral symphonies day without *n.*
P. L. 5, 166. last in the train of *n.*
P. L. 5, 206. and if the *n.* have gathered aught
P. L. 5, 227. disturbed this *n.* the human pair
P. L. 5, 261. as when by *n.* the glass of Galileo
P. L. 5, 547. than when cherubic songs by *n.*
P. L. 5, 642. now when ambrosial *n.*
P. L. 5, 645. for *n.* comes not there in darker
P. L. 5, 657. the sovran throne alternate all *n.*
P. L. 5, 685. yet dim *N.* her shadowy cloud
P. L. 5, 699. now ere *n.* now ere dim *n.*
P. L. 5, 745. innumerable as the stars of *n.*
P. L. 6, 1. all *n.* the dreadless Angel unpursued
P. L. 6, 8. grateful vicissitude like day and *n.*
P. L. 6, 14. from before her vanished *N.*
P. L. 6, 406. now *N.* her course began
P. L. 6, 416. Potentates to council called by *n.*
P. L. 6, 521. ere day-spring, under conscious *n.*
P. L. 6, 832. onward drove gloomy as *n.*
P. L. 7, 105. *N.* with her will bring silence
P. L. 7, 123. hath suppressed in *n.*
P. L. 7, 251. and Darkness *N.* he named
P. L. 7, 341. to divide the day from *n.*
P. L. 7, 348. the less by *n.* altern
P. L. 7, 351. in their vicissitude, and rule the *n.*
P. L. 7, 380. and still that distance keeps till *n.*
P. L. 7, 436. but all *n.* tuned her soft lays
P. L. 7, 584. twilight . . . came on forerunning *n.*
P. L. 8, 24. one day and *n.*, in all their vast survey
P. L. 8, 136. the wheel of day and *n.*
P. L. 8, 139. averse from the sun's beam meet *n.*
P. L. 8, 143. her by day as she by *n.* this earth
P. L. 8, 518. the amorous bird of *n.* sung sponsal
P. L. 9, 51. short arbiter 'twixt day and *n.*
P. L. 9, 52. *n.'s* hemisphere had veiled the horizon
P. L. 9, 58. by *n.* he fled and at midnight
P. L. 9, 65. four times crossed the car of *N.*
P. L. 9, 140. in one *n.* freed from servitude
P. L. 9, 211. one *n.* or two with wanton growth
P. L. 9, 635. the *n.* condenses and the cold
P. L. 10, 342. returned by *n.* and listening
P. L. 10, 477. in the womb of unoriginal *N.*
P. L. 10, 846. lamented loud through the still *n.*
P. L. 10, 1070. diurnal star leave cold the *n.*
P. L. 11, 173. though after sleepless *n.*
P. L. 11, 826. shall pour rain day and *n.*
P. L. 11, 898. day and *n.*, seed-time and harvest
P. L. 12, 203. by day a cloud, by *n.* a pillar of fire
P. L. 12, 206. all *n.* he will pursue
P. L. 12, 257. a fiery gleam by *n.*
P. L. 12, 264. and *n.'s* due course adjourn
P. L. 12, 365. shepherds keeping watch by *n.*
P. R. 1, 244. watching at their folds by *n.*
P. R. 1, 304. each *n.* under the covert of some
P. R. 1, 500. now began *N.* with her sullen wing
P. R. 2, 260. it was the hour of *n.* when thus
P. R. 2, 279. thus wore out *n.*

P. R. 4, 398. brought in louring *N.*
P. R. 4, 406. from dews and damps of *n.*
P. R. 4, 426. thus passed the *n.* so foul
P. R. 4, 436. after a *n.* of storm so ruinous
P. R. 4, 452. fair morning ... after a dismal *n.*
P. R. 4, 481. this ominous *n.* that closed
S. A. 98. the moon when she deserts the *n.*
S. A. 161. to incorporate with gloomy *n.*
S. A. 404. surceased not day nor *n.* to storm
S. A. 807. I should still enjoy thee day and *n.*
C. 122. what hath *n.* to do with sleep
C. 128. *n.* hath better sweets to prove
C. 195. else O thievish *N.* why shouldst thou
C 222. turn forth her silver lining on the *n.*
C. 250. through the empty-vaulted *n.*
C. 285. perhaps forestalling *n.* prevented them
C. 335. in double *n.* of darkness and of shades
C. 404. of *n.* or loneliness it recks me not
C. 432. some say no evil thing that walks by *n.*
C. 532. *n.* by *n.* he and his monstrous rout
C. 580. O *N.* and shades how are ye joined
C. 948. where this *n.* are met in state
C. 957. but *N.* sits monarch yet in the mid sky
A. 39. to further this *n.'s* glad solemnity
A. 61. but else in deep of *n.* when drowsiness
L. 29. our flocks with the fresh dews of *n.*
L'A. and singing startle the dull *n.*
L'A. 107. when in one *n.* ere glimpse of morn
Il P. 58. smoothing the rugged brow of *n.*
Il P. 121. thus *n.* oft see me in thy pale career
S. 9, 13. passes to bliss at the mid-hour of *n.*
S. 23, 14. she fled, and day brought back my *n.*
H. 61. peaceful was the *n,* wherein the Prince
H. 111. that with long beams the shamefaced *N.*
P. 7. in dark and long out-living *n.*
P. 29. befriend me *N.* best patroness of grief
Cir. 5. through the soft silence of the listening *n.*
U. C. I. 15. his room where he must lodge that *n.*
**Night-foundered.**—P. L. 1, 204. *n.-f.* skiff
C. 483. either some one like us *n.-f.* here
**Night-hag.**—P. L. 2, 662. follow the *n.-h.*
**Nightingale.**—P. L. 4, 602. the wakeful *n.*
P. L. 7, 435. nor then the solemn *n.* ceased
C. 234. where the love-lorn *n.*
C. 566. and O poor hapless *n.* thought I
S. 1, 1. O *n.* that on yon bloomy spray
**Nightingales.**—P. L. 4, 771. lulled by *n.*
**Nightly.**—P. L. 1, 440. *n.* by the moon
P. L. 1, 642. stemming *n.* toward the pole
P. L. 3, 32. *n.* I visit nor sometimes forget
P. L. 4, 685. or *n.* rounding walk
P. L. 5, 714. lamps that burn *n.* before him
P. L. 7, 29. while thou visit'st my slumbers *n.*
P. L. 7, 580. which *n.* as a circling zone
P. L. 9, 22. who deigns her *n.* visitation
P. L. 9, 47. who brings it *n.* to my ear
C. 113. who in their *n.* watchful spheres
C. 235. *n.* to thee her sad song mourneth well
C. 883. by all the nymphs that *n.* dance
A. 48. and all my plants I save from *n.* ill
Il P. 84. to bless the doors from *n.* harm
H. 179. no *n.* trance or breathed spell
**Night-raven.**—L'A. 7. and the *n.-r.* sings
**Nights.**—P. L. 9, 63. space of seven continued *n.*
P. L. 9, 137. six *n.* and days continued making
P. L. 10, 680. equal in days and *n.*
P. R. 2, 460. troubles, cares and sleepless *n.*
**Night-steeds.**—H. 236. fly after the *n.-s.*
**Night-wanderer.**—P. L. 9, 640. *n.w.*
**Night-warbling.**—P. L. 5, 40. the *n.-w.* bird
**Night-watches.**—P. L. 4, 780. their *n.-w.*
C. 347. count the *n.-w.* to his feathery dames
**Nile.**—P. L. 1, 343. darkened all the land of *N.*
P. L. 1, 413. on their march from *N.*
P. L. 12, 157. Egypt divided by the river *N.*
H. 211. the brutish gods of *N.*
**Nilotic.**—P. R. 4, 71. Meroë *N.* isle
**Nilus.**—P. L. 4, 283. Ethiop line by *N.* head
**Nimble.**—P. L. 4, 866. I hear the tread of *n.* feet
P. L. 6, 73. passive air upbore their *n.* tread
P. L. 11, 442. consumed with *n.* glance

**Nine.**—P. L. 1, 50. *n.* times the space that
P. L. 6, 871. *n.* days they fell confounded
P. L. 7, 6. nor of the Muses *N.*
A. 64. that sit upon the *n.* enfolded spheres
**Ninefold.**—P. L. 2, 436. immures us round *n.*
H. 131. and with your *n.* harmony
**Nineveh.**—P. R. 3, 275. *N.* of length within
**Ninus.**—P. R. 3, 276. built by *N.* old
**Nip.**—M. W. 36. saved with care from winter's *n.*
**Niphates.**—P. L. 3, 742. till on *N.* top he lights
**Nisibis.**—P. R. 3, 291. Seleucia, *N.*
**Nisroch.**—P. L. 6, 447. next upstood *N.*
**Nitre.**—P. L. 2, 937. instinct with fire and *n.*
**Nitrous.**—P. L. 4, 815. a heap of *n.* powder
P. L. 6, 512. sulphurous and *n.* foam they found
**Nobility.**—S. A. 1654. their choice *n.* and flower
**Noble.**—P. L. 6, 189. a *n.* stroke he lifted
P. L. 8, 34. served by more *n.* than herself
P. L. 12, 221. for life to *n.* and ignoble is more
P. R. 4, 99. appearing and beginning *n.* deeds
S. A. 218. at least of thy own nation and as *n.*
S. A. 1166. nor by the sword of *n.* warrior
S. A. 1724. what may quiet us in a death so *n.*
C. 31. a *n.* Peer of mickle trust and power
C. 451. and *n.* grace that dashed brute violence
C. 966. *n.* Lord and Lady bright
A. 82. where ye may all that are of *n.* stem
L. 71. that last infirmity of *n.* mind
S. 10, 12. so well your words his *n.* virtues praise
S. 22, 11. in Liberty's defence my *n.* task
M. W. 5. her virtues fair added to her *n.* birth
M. W. 54. that thy *n.* house doth bring
**Nobleness.**—P. L. 8, 557. and *n.*
**Nobler.**—P. L. 2, 116. to *n.* deeds timorous
P. L. 4, 288. two of far *n.* shape erect and tall
P. L. 8, 28. so many *n.* bodies to create greater
P. L. 9, 111. in herb, plant and *n.* birth
P. L. 11, 411. but to *n.* sights Michael
P. L. 11, 605. created as thou art to *n.* end
P. R. 2, 477. governs the inner man the *n.* part
P. R. 2, 482. thought greater and *n.* done
S. 15, 9. O yet a *n.* task awaits thy hand
**Noblest.**—P. L. 1, 552. to height of *n.* temper
P. L. 4, 217. all trees of *n.* kind for sight
P. R. 2, 341. dishes piled and meats of *n.* sort
P. R. 4, 52. skill of *n.* architects
**Nobly.**—P. R. 4, 239. a city stands built *n.*
**Nocent.**—P. L. 9, 186. nor *n.* yet
**Nocturnal.**—P. L. 3, 40. tunes her *n.* note
P. L. 8, 134. *n.* and diurnal rhomb supposed
C. 128. hail! Goddess of *n.* sport
**Nod.**—C. 960. here be without duck or *n.*
**Nodding.**—C. 38. the *n.* horror of whose shady
**Nods.**—L'A. 28. *N.* Becks and wreathed Smiles
**Noise.**—P. L. 1, 394. though for the *n.* of drums
P. L. 1, 498. where the *n.* of riot ascends
P. L. 2, 64. when to meet the *n.* of his almighty
P. L. 2, 657. if aught disturbed their *n.*
P. L. 2, 896. amidst the *n.* of endless wars
P. L. 2, 957. might in that *n.* reside
P. L. 6, 211. dire was the *n.* of conflict
P. L. 6, 487. forth from far with thundering *n.*
P. L. 6, 587. embowelled with outrageous *n.*
P. L. 6, 667. infernal *n.,* war seemed a civil game
P. L. 6, 867. heard the insufferable *n.*
P. L. 8, 243. *n.,* other than the sound of dance
P. L. 10, 567. with spattering *n.* rejected
P. L. 10, 705. and Zephyr with their lateral *n.*
P. L. 12, 55. to sow a jangling *n.* of words
S. A. 16. with leave retiring from the popular *n.*
S. A. 1088. of whom such *n.* hath walked about
S. A. 1472. what *n.* or shout was that
S. A. 1508. what *n.,* mercy of Heaven, what *n.*
S. A. 1511. *n.* call you it or universal groan
S. A. 1513. death and deathful deeds are in that *n.*
S. A. 1515. ruin indeed methought I heard the *n.*
C. 170. this way the *n.* was if mine ear be true
C. 227. such *n.* as I can make to be heard farthest
C. 369. as that the single want of light and *n.*
Il P. 61. sweet bird that shunnest the *n.* of folly
S. 12. when straight a barbarous *n.* environs me

H. 97. answering the stringed *n.*
S. M. 18. may rightly answer that melodious *n.*
**Noises.**—P. L. 2, 921. pealed with *n.* loud
**Noising.**—P. R. 4, 488. though *n.* loud
**Noisome.**—P. L. 11, 478. sad *n.* dark
A. 49. of *n.* winds and blasting vapours chill
**None.**—P. L. 1, 273. *n.* could have foiled
P. L. 1, 690. let *n.* admire that riches grow
P. L. 2, 32. for *n.* sure will claim in Hell
P. L. 2, 33. *n.* whose portion is so small
P. L. 2, 255. free and to *n.* accountable
P. L. 2, 300. Satan except, *n.* higher sat
P. L. 2, 331. terms of peace yet *n.* vouchsafed
P. L. 2, 423. *n.* among the choice and prime
P. L. 2, 466. this enterprise *n.* shall partake
P. L. 2, 667. might be called that shape had *n.*
P. L. 2, 776. *n.* can pass without my opening
P. L. 2, 802. that rest or intermission *n.* I find
P. L. 2, 814. save he who reigns above *n.* can
P. L. 3, 132. shall find grace the other *n.*
P. L. 3, 182. to me owe all ... and to *n.* but me
P. L. 3, 202. *n.* but such from mercy I exclude
P. L. 3, 219. patron or intercessor *n.* appeared
P. L. 3, 235. and undone hath *n.* to bring
P. L. 3, 289. as are restored without thee *n.*
P. L. 3, 443. living or lifeless to be found was *n.*
P. L. 3, 444. *n.* yet, but store hereafter
P. L. 3, 669. his fixed seat or fixed seat hath *n.*
P. L. 3, 738. where honour due and reverence *n.*
P. L. 4, 45. and with his good upbraided *n.*
P. L. 4, 80. *n.* for pardon left
P. L. 4, 81. *n.* left but by submission
P. L. 4, 174. but further way found *n.*
P. L. 4, 579. at this gate *n.* pass the vigilance
P. L. 4, 675. nor think though men were *n.*
P. L. 4, 704. insect or worm durst enter *n.*
P. L. 4, 737. and other rites observing *n.* but
P. L. 5, 44. in vain if *n.* regard
P. L. 5, 59. deigns *n.* to ease thy load
P. L. 5, 62. forbid who will *n.* shall from me
P. L. 5, 99. evil whence? in thee can harbour *n.*
P. L. 5, 362. other place *n.* can than Heaven
P. L. 5, 538. on other surety *n.*
P. L. 5, 791. of heaven possessed before by *n.*
P. L. 5, 805. Abdiel than whom *n.* with more
P. L. 5, 850. his zeal *n.* seconded as out of season
P. L. 5, 860. know *n.* before us, self-begot
P. L. 6, 159. can allow omnipotence to *n.*
P. L. 6, 237. no thought of flight *n.* of retreat
P. L. 6, 442. made the odds, in nature *n.*
P. L. 6, 508. *n.* arguing stood
P. L. 6, 592. whom they hit *n.* on their feet
P. L. 6, 702. since *n.* but thou can end it
P. L. 7, 124. to *n.* communicate in earth
P. L. 7, 333. and man to till the ground *n.* was
P. L. 7, 378. for other light she needed *n.*
P. L. 8, 233. to see that *n.* thence issued forth
P. L. 8, 285. when answer *n.* returned
P. L. 8, 406. for *n.* I know second to me
P. L. 8, 624. and obstacle find *n.* of membrane
P. L. 9, 92. whatever sleights *n.* would
P. L. 9, 118. I in *n.* of these find place or refuge
P. L. 9, 1140. let *n.* henceforth seek needless
P. L. 10, 80. attendance *n.* shall need
P. L. 10, 84. conviction to the Serpent *n.*
P. L. 10, 820. waste it all myself and leave ye *n.*
P. L. 10, 998. torment less than *n.* of what
P. L. 11, 231. and by his gait *n.* of the meanest
P. L. 11, 612. but they his gifts acknowledged *n.*
P. L. 11, 673. and refuge *n.* was found
P. L. 11, 837. if *n.* be thither brought
P. L. 12, 522. laws which *n.* shall find left
P. R. 1, 323. for single *n.* durst ever
P. R. 2, 62. nor left at Jordan tidings of him *n.*
P. R. 2, 146. who erst thought *n.* my equal
P. R. 2, 177. *n.* are, thou think'st but taken
P. R. 2, 288. herd or sheep-cote *n.* he saw
P. R. 2, 315. these forty days *n.* hath regard
P. R. 2, 318. I as thou seest have *n.*
P. R. 3, 289. the drink of *n.* but kings
P. R. 3, 358. by free consent of all, *n.* opposite

P. R. 4, 184. other donation *n.* thou canst
P. R. 4, 315. all glory arrogate, to God give *n.*
P. R. 4, 487. which thou speak'st of did me *n.*
S. A. 18. ease to the body some, *n.* to the mind
S. A. 344. walked their streets *n.* offering fight
S. A. 531. on hostile ground *n.* daring my affront.
S. A. 1628. *n.* daring to appear antagonist
C. 137. of all thy due be done and *n.* left out
C. 702. *n.* but such as are good men can give good
A. 72. after the heavenly tune which *n.* can hear
**Nook.**—P. L. 1, 707. filled each hollow *n.*
P. L. 4, 789. leave unsearched no *n.*
P. L. 9, 277. as in a shady *n.* I stood behind
C. 500. couldst thou find this dark sequestered *n.*
Il P. 92. her mansion in this fleshly *n.*
**Noon.**—P. L. 1, 734. morn to *n.* he fell, from *n.*
P. L. 3, 616. his beams at *n.* culminate
P. L. 4, 564. this day at height of *n.*
P. L. 4, 627. our walk at *n.* with branches
P. L. 5, 174. and when high *n.* hast gained
P. L. 5, 231. thou findest him from the heat of *n.*
P. L. 9, 219. find what to redress till *n.*
P. L. 9, 401. returned by *n.* amid the bower
P. L. 9, 739. meanwhile the hour of *n.* drew on
P. L. 10, 93. sun in western cadence low from *n.*
P. L. 12, 1. one who in his journey baits at *n.*
P. R. 2, 156. passing fair as the *n.* sky
P. R. 2, 292. determined there to rest at *n.*
S. A. 80. O dark, dark, dark, amid the blaze of *n.*
S. A. 683. amidst their height of *n.*
S. A. 1612. feast and *n.* grew high and sacrifice
Il P. 68. riding near her highest *n.*
**Noontide.**—P. L. 2, 309. summer's *n.* air
P. L. 4, 246. shade imbrowned the *n.* bowers
P. L. 9, 405. in best order to invite *n.* repast
**North.**—P. L. 1, 351. the populous *N.*
P. L. 2, 489. while the *N.* wind sleeps
P. L. 4, 569. the mount that lies from Eden *n.*
P. L. 4, 783. these other wheel the *n.*
P. L. 5, 689. we possess the quarters of the *n.*
P. L. 5, 726. throughout the spacious *n.*
P. L. 5, 755. at length into the limits of the *N.*
P. L. 6, 79. far in the horizon to the *n.* appeared
P. L. 10, 654. and from the *n.* to call decrepit
P. L. 10, 695. now from the *n.* of Norumbega
P. L. 11, 842. driven by a keen *n.* wind
P. R. 4, 28. and on the *n.* to equal length
P. R. 4, 78. Scythians and Sarmatians *n.*
P. R. 4, 448. backed on the *n.* and west
S. 15, 7. the false *N.* displays her broken league
**North-east.**—P. L. 4, 161. off at sea *n-e.* winds
**Northern.**—P. R. 3, 338. all his *n.* powers
**Northward.**—P. L. 12, 139. from Hamath *n.*
**Norumbega.**—P. L. 10, 696. the north of *N.*
**Norway.**—P. L. 1, 203. slumbering on the *N.*
**Norwegian.**—P. L. 1, 293. hewn on *N.* hills
**Nostril.**—P. L. 10, 280. upturned his *n.* wide
**Nostrils.**—P. L. 7, 525. and in thy *n.* breathed
P. L. 9, 196. his *n.* fill with grateful smell
**Note.**—P. L. 3, 40. tunes her nocturnal *n.*
P. L. 4, 683. or responsive each to other's *n.*
P. R. 2, 306. others of some *n.* as story tells
S. 13, 3. how to span words with just *n.*
**Notes.**—P. L. 2, 494. the birds their *n.* renew
P. L. 2, 548. sing with *n.* angelical to many
P. L. 3, 17. with other *n.* than to the Orphean
P. L. 5, 199. bear on your wings and in your *n.*
P. L. 9, 6. I now must change those *n.* to tragic
P. R. 4, 246. trills her thick-warbled *n.*
P. R. 4, 437. cleared up their choicest *n.*
L'A. 139. in *n.* with many a winding bout
Il P. 106. such *n.* as warbled to the string
S. 1, 5. thy liquid *n.* that close the eye of day
S. 20, 12. warble immortal *n.* and Tuscan air
H. 116. unexpressive *n.* to Heaven's new-born
P. 9. and set my harp to *n.* of saddest woe
**Nothing.**—P. L. 1, 27. for Heaven hides *n.*
P. L. 2, 97. and reduce to *n.* this essential
P. L. 2, 101. we are at worst on this side *n.*
P. L. 4, 418. who at his hand have *n.* merited
P. L. 6, 495. and counsel joined think *n.* hard

P. L. 8, 571. n. profits more than self-esteem
P. L. 9, 232. for n. lovelier can be found
P. L. 9, 345. his creating hand n. imperfect
P. L. 9, 574. and apprehended n. high
P. L. 9, 722. producing every kind, them n.
P. L. 9, 1039. he led her n. loth
P. L. 10, 869. n. wants but that thy shape
P. L. 10, 1010. Adam with such counsel n. swayed
P. L. 12, 186. on the ground leave n. green
P. R. 2, 169. women when n. else beguiled
P. R. 3, 79, who leave behind n. but ruin
P. R. 3, 129. them who could return him n.
P. R. 3, 135. of his own hath n. and to whom n.
P. R. 3, 389. soon to n. brought
P. R. 4, 157. n. will please the difficult
P. R. 4, 158. or n. more than still to contradict
P. R. 4, 292. conjectures fancies built on n.
P. R. 4, 294. to know this only that he n. knew
S. A. 207. of wisdom n. more than mean
S. A. 374. n. of all these evils hath befallen me
S. A. 474. for God, n. more certain, will not
S. A. 801. n. was designed against thee but
S. A. 881. who could deny thee n.
S. A. 966. reap n. but repulse and hate
S. A. 1033. that either they love n. or not long
S. A. 1163. as good for n. else, no better service
S. A. 1233. n. from thy hand fear I incurable
S. A. 1385. n. to do be sure that may dishonour
S. A. 1408. yet this be sure in n. to comply
S. A. 1424. me expect to hear n. dishonourable.
S. A. 1484. not wanting him I shall want n.
S. A. 1528. for to Israel's God n. is hard
S. A. 1721. n. is here for tears, n. to wail
S. A. 1723. n. but well and fair
C. 722. and n. wear but frieze
L. 129. daily devours apace and n. said
V. Ex. 81. from others he shall stand in need of n.
**Notice.**—S. A. 250. count them things worth n.
S. A. 1536. a little stay will bring some n. hither
**Notion.**—P. L. 7, 179. as earthly n. can receive
C. 785. the sublime n. and high mystery
**Notions.**—P. L. 8, 187. thoughts and n. vain
**Notorious.**—S. A. 1186. committed n. murder
**Notus.**—P. L. 10, 702. N. and Afer black
**Nought.**—P. L. 2, 679. created thing n. valued
P. L. 3, 158. and thy goodness bring to n.
P. L. 3, 207. to expiate his treason hath n. left
P. L. 3, 453. n. seeking but the praise of men
P. L. 6, 382. illaudable n. merits but dispraise
P. L. 9, 786. n. else regarded
P. R. 1, 181. devilish machinations come to n.
P. R. 3, 393. plausible to the world .. worth n.
P. R. 4, 161. nor .. mean to give for n.
P. R. 4, 208. me n. advantaged matures what
S. A. 588. his might continues in thee not for n.
S. A. 779. for importunity, that is for n.
S. A. 1215. to their masters gave me up for n.
C. 204. yet n. but single darkness do I find
C. 445. but set at n. the frivolous bolt of Cupid
H. 218. n. but profoundest hell
**Nourish.**—P. L. 4, 670. n. or in part shed
P. L. 5, 183. mix and n. all things
P. L. 5, 325. frugal storing firmness gains to n.
P. R. 1, 230. but n. them and let them soar
**Nourisher.**—P. L. 5, 398. bounties which our N.
**Nourishment.**—P. L. 5, 421. no n. exhale
P. L. 5, 483. flowers and their fruit man's n.
P. L. 7, 130. wisdom to folly as n. to wind
P. L. 11, 533. thence due n. not gluttonous
**Novelty.**—P. L. 10, 891. this n. on earth
**Novice.**—P. R. 3, 241. with n. modesty
**Noxious.**—P. L. 2, 216. overcome their n.
P. L. 7, 498. though to thee not n. but obedient
P. L. 10, 660. of n. efficacy
P. R. 1, 312. the fiery serpent fled and n. worm
P. R. 4, 460. yet as being ofttimes n. where
**Nulled.**—S. A. 935. their force is n.
**Number.**—P. L. 1, 571. their n. last he sums
P. L. 1, 791. though without n. still amidst
P. L. 3, 346. loud as from numbers without n.
P. L. 3, 706. comprehend their n.

P. L. 4, 687. in full harmonic n. joined
P. L. 5, 843. he the head one of our n. thus
P. L. 5, 901. nor n. nor example with him
P. L. 6, 49. equal in n. to that godless crew
P. L. 6, 769. I their n. heard
P. L. 6, 809. n. to this day's work is not
P. L. 7, 147. n. sufficient to possess her realms
P. L. 7, 613. and from thee withdraw the n.
P. L. 8, 38. to describe whose swiftness n. fails
P. L. 8, 422. but man by n. is to manifest
P. L. 10, 888. as supernumerary to my just n.
S. A. 1295. may chance to n. thee with those
S. A. 1667. in n. more than all thy life had slain
C. 148. our n. may affright
A. 59. n. my ranks and visit every sprout
M. W. 11. had the n. of her days
**Numbered.**—P. L. 6, 229. though n. such
P. L. 8, 19. and all her n. stars that seem to roll
P. L. 10, 576. annual humbling certain n. days
P. L. 11, 40. at least his days n. though sad
S. A. 1478. shall willingly be paid and n. down
U. C. II. 8. motion n. out his time
**Numbering.**—P. R. 3, 410. pride of n. Israel
S. 11, 4. n. good intellects now seldom pored on
**Numberless.**—P. L. 1, 344. so n. were those
P. L. 1, 780. in narrow room throng n.
P. L. 3, 719. turned to stars n. as thou seest
P. L. 5, 653. pavilions n. and sudden reared
P. L. 6, 224. army against army n. to raise
P. L. 7, 197. about his chariot n. were poured
P. L. 7, 492. the rest are n.
P. L. 8, 108. though n. to his omnipotence
P. L. 9, 548. by Angels n. thy daily train
P. R. 3, 310. looked and saw what numbers n.
Il P. 7. as thick and n. as the gay motes
**Numbers.**—P. L. 3, 38. move harmonious n.
P. L. 3, 332. Hell her n. full thenceforth shall
P. L. 3, 346. loud as from n. without number
P. L. 3, 580. move their starry dance in n.
P. L. 8, 114. inexpressible by n.
P. L. 8, 421. and through all n. absolute
P. L. 9, 144. to repair his n. thus impaired
P. L. 11, 480. wherein were laid n. of all
P. L. 12, 503. great n. of each nation to receive
P. R. 3, 310. he looked and saw what n.
P. R. 4, 255. in tones and n. hit by voice
S. A. 857. had destroyed such n. of our nation
S. H. 1450. the city rings and n. thither flock
W. S. 10. thy easy n. flow
U. C. II. 7. time n. motion
**Numbness.**—S. A. 571. and sedentary n. craze
**Numerous.**—P. L. 1, 675. a n. brigad hastened
P. L. 2, 993. such a n. host fled not in silence
P. L. 4, 385. to receive your n. offspring
P. L. 5, 150. in prose or n. verse
P. L. 5, 389. shall fill the world more n.
P. L. 6, 231. might have seemed a n. host
P. L. 6, 830. of torrent floods or of a n. host
P. L. 7, 418. their brood as n. hatch
P. L. 7, 621. with stars n.
P. L. 10, 397. among these n. orbs all yours
P. L. 11, 130. spangled with eyes more n.
P. L. 11, 752. of mankind so n. late all left
P. L. 12, 132. herds and flocks and n. servitude
P. L. 12, 167. as inmate guests too n.
P. R. 3, 344. such and so n. was their chivalry
**Numbing.**—C. 853. and thaw the n. spell
**Nun.**—Il P. 31. come pensive N. devout and pure
**Nuptial.**—P. L. 4, 339. linked in happy n.
P. L. 4, 710. espoused Eve decked first her n.
P. L. 8, 487. nor uninformed of n. sanctity
P. L. 8, 510. to the n. bower I led her blushing
P. L. 10, 994. from love's due rites n. embraces
P. L. 11, 280. thee lastly n. bower
P. L. 11, 590. all in heat they light the n. torch
S. A. 385. in her height of n. love
S. A. 1194. and in your city held my n. feast
S. A. 1734. his lot unfortunate in n. choice
L. 176. and hears the unexpressive n. song
**Nuptials.**—S. A. 1023. loosely disallied their n.
**Nurse.**—S. A. 1487. sons wont to n. their parents

R

S. A. 1488. thou in old age carest how to n.
C. 377. wherewith her best n. contemplation
A. 46. to n. thy saplings tall and curl the grove
V. Ex. 61. thy drowsy n. hath sworn she did
**Nursed.**—C. 34. where his fair offspring n.
L. 23. for we were n. upon the self-same hill
**Nursery.**—P. L. 8, 46. bud and bloom, her n.
**Nursing.**—S. A. 924. with n. diligence
**Nursling.**—S. A. 633. I was his n. once
**Nurture.**—S. A. 362. ordained thy n. holy
**Nut-brown.**—L'A. 100. to the spicy n.-b. ale
**Nutriment.**—P. L. 7, 408. attend moist n.
**Nutriments.**—P. L. 5, 496. these corporal n.
**Nymph.**—P. L. 4, 707. nor n. nor Faunus haunted
C. 54. this n. that gazed upon his clustering locks

C. 230. sweet Echo, sweetest N.
C. 422. like a quivered n. with arrows keen
C. 824. there is a gentle n. not far from hence
L'A. 25. haste thee n. and bring with thee
**Nymph-like.**—P. L. 9. 452. with n.-l. step
**Nymphs.**—P. R. 2, 355. n. of Diana's train
C. 833. the water n. that in the bottom played
C. 883. by all the n. the nightly dance
A. 1. look n. and shepherds look
A. 33. fair silverbuskined n. as great and good
A. 96. n. and shepherds dance no more
L. 50. where were ye n. when the remorseless
Il P. 137. was never heard the n. to daunt
H. 188. the n. in twilight shade
**Nyseian.**—P. L. 4, 275. nor that N. isle

# O.

**Oak.**—P. L. 6, 574. bodies made of o. or fir
P. R. 1, 305. the covert of some ancient o.
Il P. 60. gently o'er the accustomed o.
Il P. 135. pine or monumental o.
**Oaken.**—S. A. 1123. I only with an o. staff
A. 45. of this fair wood, and live in o. bower
**Oaks.**—P. L. 1, 613. hath scathed the forest o.
P. R. 4, 417. sturdiest o. bowed their stiff
L. 186. sang the uncouth swain to the o. and rills
L'A. 82. from betwixt two aged o.
**Oar.**—P. L. 2, 942. behoves him now both o.
**Oary.**—P. L. 7, 440. rows her state with o. feet
**Oat.**—L. 88. but now my o. proceeds and listens
**Oaten.**—C. 345. or sound of pastoral reed with o.
L. 33. tempered to the o. flute
**Oath.**—P. L. 2, 352. an o. that shook heaven's
**Ob.**—P. L. 9, 78. up beyond the river O.
**Obdurate.**—P. L. 1, 58. mixed with o. pride
P. L. 6, 790. or wonders m ove the o. to relent
P. L. 12, 205. while the o. king pursues
**Obdured.**—P. L. 2, 568. or arm the o. breast
P. L. 6, 785. saw his hapless foes but stood o.
**Obedience.**—P. L. 3, 95. sole pledge of his o.
P. L. 3, 107. what pleasure I from such o. paid
P. L. 3, 190. to pray, repent and bring o. due
P. L. 3, 191. to prayer repentance and o. due
P. L. 3, 269. above which only shone filial o.
P. L. 4, 428. the only sign of our o. left
P. L. 4, 520. proof of their o. and their faith
P. L. 4, 955. military o. to dissolve allegiance
P. L. 5, 514. can we want o. then to him
P. L. 5, 522. to thyself that is to thy o.
P. L. 5, 537. while our o. holds
P. L. 6, 740. that from thy just o. could revolt
P. L. 6, 902. he may seduce thee also from o.
P. L. 7, 159. under long o. tried
P. L. 8, 240. and to inure our prompt o.
P. L. 8, 325. I have set the pledge of thy o.
P. L. 9, 368. approve first thy o.
P. L. 12, 397. o. to the law of God imposed
P. L. 12, 403. both by o. and by love
P. L. 12, 408. and that his o. imputed becomes
P. R. 1, 4. by one man's firm o. fully tried
P. R. 1, 422. wilt thou impute to o. what thy
P. R. 4, 80. all nations now to Rome o. pay
S. M. 24. whilst they stood in first o.
Cir. 25. and seals o. first with wounding smart
**Obedient.**—P. L. 5, 501. if he be found o.
P. L. 5, 514. caution joined if ye be found o.
P. L. 7, 498. not noxious but o. at thy call
P. L. 12, 246. such delight hath God in men o.
U. C. II. 29. o. to the moon he spent his date
**Obey.**—P. L. 2, 865. whom should I o. but thee
P. L. 4, 636. what thou biddest unargued I o.
P. L. 5, 551. and o. him whose command single
P. L. 6, 185. behests o. worthiest to be obeyed
P. L. 6, 741. whom to o. is happiness entire
P. L. 8, 634. him whom to love is to o.
P. L. 10, 145. that her thou didst o.
P. L. 11, 112. if patiently thy bidding they o.

P. L. 12, 561. I learn that to o. is best
P. R. 3, 194. know what I can suffer, how o.
S. A. 1372. if I o. them I do it freely
**Obeyed.**—P. L. 1, 337. they soon o. innumerable
P. L. 5, 704. but all o. the wonted signal
P. L. 5, 806. and divine commands o.
P. L. 6, 185. behests obey worthiest to be o.
P. L. 7, 48. so easily o. amid the choice of all
P. L. 7, 453. the earth o. and straight opening
P. L. 8, 272. my tongue o. and readily could
P. L. 9, 570. and right thou shouldst be o.
P. L. 9, 701. not God, not feared then nor o.
P. L. 12, 86. reason in man obscured or not o.
P. R. 3, 196. best reign who first well hath o.
S. A. 895. not therefore to be o.
S. A. 900. less therefore to be pleased o. or feared
**Obeying.**—P. L. 9, 868. as we are not o.
P. L. 10, 14. which they not o. incurred
S. A. 1641. I have performed as reason was o.
**Obeys.**—P. L. 9, 351. what o. reason is free
P. L. 12, 126. he straight o. not knowing
P. L. 12, 212. the sea his rod o.
P. R. 3, 159. a province under Roman yoke o.
**Obey'st.**—P. R. 1, 452. a fawning parasite o.
**Object.**—P. L. 4, 896. and wilt o. his will
P. L. 8, 456. as with an o. that excels the sense
P. L. 8, 535. not proof enough such o. to sustain
P. L. 9, 222. or o. new casual discourse draw on
P. L. 9, 361. meet some specious o. by the foe
P. L. 10, 936. me only just o. of his ire
P. L. 10, 996. before the present o.
P. L. 11, 201. why else this double o.
P. R. 2, 163. such o. hath the power to soften
S. A. 559. against another o. more enticing
S. A. 568. to visitants a gaze or pitied o.
**Objects.**—P. L. 3, 621. to o. distant far
P. L. 8, 609. who meet with various o.
P. L. 12, 9. o. divine must needs impair
P. R. 2, 225. therefore with manlier o. we must
S. A. 71. and all her various o. of delight
**Oblige.**—P. L. 9, 980. than o. thee with a fact
**Oblique.**—P. L. 3, 564. marble air his o. way
P. L. 9, 510. with tract o. at first
P. L. 10, 671. they with labour pushed o.
**Obliquities.**—P. L. 8, 132. with thwart o.
**Oblivion.**—P. L. 2, 583. Lethe the river of o.
P. L. 6, 380. nameless in dark o. let them dwell
**Oblivious.**—P. L. 1, 266. on the o. pool
**Obloquy.**—P. L. 5, 813. impious o. condemn
P. R. 3, 131. contempt instead dishonour o.
S. A. 452. to God have brought dishonour o.
**Obnoxious.**—P. L. 9, 170. o. first or last
P. L. 9, 1094. most to shame o. and unseemliest
S. A. 106. but made hereby o. more to all
**Obscene.**—P. L. 1, 406. the o. dread of Moab's
**Obscure.**—P. L. 1, 429. bright or o.
P. L. 1, 524. appeared o. some glimpse of joy
P. L. 2, 132. or with o. wing scout far and wide
P. L. 2, 406. and through the palpable o. find
P. L. 3, 15. long detained in that o. sojourn

P. L. 4, 840. now thy sin and place of doom o.
P. L. 7, 229. through the vast profundity o.
P. L. 8, 192. of things remote from use o.
P. L. 8, 230. bound on a voyage uncouth and o.
P. L. 9, 159. in mist of midnight vapour glide o.
P. L. 10, 366. nor this unvoyageable gulf o.
P. L. 11, 283. into a lower world to this o.
P. R. 1, 24. came as then o. unmarked
P. R. 1, 287. that I no more should live o.
P. R. 3, 22. more o. in savage wilderness
P. R. 3, 94. made famous in a land and times o.
S. A. 296. if any be they walk o.
S. A. 572. to a contemptible old age o.
**Obscured.**—P. L. 1, 594. the excess of glory o.
P. L. 4, 571. with passions foul o.
P. L. 5, 841. nor by his reign o. but more
P. L. 6, 585. soon o. with smoke
P. L. 9, 797. hitherto o. infamed
P. L. 9, 1086. in some glade o.
P. L. 12, 86. reason in man o. or not obeyed
S. A. 688. to life o. which were a fair dismission
C. 536. in their o. haunts of inmost bowers
**Obscurely.**—P. L. 12, 543. o. then foretold
S. A. 1611. I among these aloof o. stood
**Obscures.**—P. R. 2, 101. great purpose he o.
**Obsequious.**—P. L. 6, 10. the other door o.
P. L. 6, 783. they heard his voice and went o.
P. L. 8, 509. and with o. majesty approved
**Obsequy.**—S. A. 1732. silent o. and funeral train
**Observe.**—P. L. 7, 78. to o...his will
P. L. 10, 334. to o. the sequel
P. L. 11, 530. well o. the rule of not too much
P. L. 12, 563. ever to o. his providence
P. R. 3, 235. and what thence couldst thou o.
P. R. 4, 477. if thou o. not this be sure to find
**Observed.**—P. L. 1, 588. yet o. their dread
P. L. 4, 849. his loss but chiefly to find here o.
P. L. 9, 94. in other beasts o.
P. L. 10, 430. gave command and they o.
P. L. 11, 191. Adam o. and with his eye
P. L. 11, 228. or impose new laws to be o.
P. L. 11, 817. of them derided but of God o.
**Observes.**—P. L. 5, 262. o. imagined lands
**Observing.**—P. L. 4, 737. other rites o. none
**Obstacle.**—P. L. 3, 615. for sight no o. found
P. L. 8, 824. and o. find none of membrane
**Obstinacy.**—P. L. 10, 114. anger and o. and
**Obstriction.**—S. A. 312. from national o.
**Obstruct.**—P. L. 5, 257. or to o. his sight
P. L. 10, 636. o. the mouth of hell
P. L. 12, 52. ere the tower o. heaven-towers
**Obtain.**—P. L. 3, 156. thus o. his end
P. L. 3, 660. by supreme decree like honor to o.
P. L. 4, 93. I could repent and could o. by act
P. L. 7, 112. with caution asked o.
P. L. 9, 20. if answerable style I can o.
P. L. 10, 75. and not repenting this o. of right
P. L. 11, 47. request for man, accepted Son, o.
P. R. 3, 354. thou never shalt o
S. A. 909. let me o. forgiveness of thee Samson
**Obtained.**—P. L. 2, 250. impossible by leave o.
P. L. 10, '938. immoveable till peace o.
P. R. 2, 73. could be o. to shelter him or me
P. R. 3, 168. that by strong hand his family o.
S. A. 814. yet always pity or pardon hath o.
**Obtains.**—P. L. 3, 546. o. the brow of some
P. R. 1, 87. he who o. the monarchy of heaven
**Obtrude.**—P. R. 2, 387. o. this diligence
**Obtruded.**—P. L. 11, 504. why o. on us
**Obtrudest.**—P. R. 4, 493. o. thy offered aid
**Obtruding.**—C. 759. o. false rules
**Obtrusive.**—P. L. 8, 504. not o., but retired
**Obtuse.**—P. L. 11, 541. thy senses then o.
**Obvious.**—P. L. 6, 69. nor o. hill
P. L. 8, 158. is o. to dispute
P. L. 8, 504. not o. not obtrusive but retired
P. L. 10, 106. where o. duty erewhile appeared
P. L. 11, 374. to the evil turn my o. breast
S. A. 95. so o. and so easy to be quenched
**Occasion.**—P. L. 1, 178. let us not slip the o.
P. L. 2, 341. nor will o. want, nor shall we need

P. L. 5, 453. not to let the o. pass
P. L. 9, 480. let me not let pass o. which now
P. L. 9, 974. still good proceeds direct or by o.
P. R. 3, 173. but on o.'s forelock watchful wait
P. R. 3, 174. they themselves rather are o. best
S. A. 224. that by o. hence I might begin
S. A. 237. in seeking just o. to provoke
S. A. 423. find some o. to infest our foes
S. A. 425. this I am sure our foes found soon o.
S. A. 1329. do they not seek o. of new quarrels
S. A. 1716. find courage to lay hold on this o.
C. 91. and nearest to the present aid of this o.
L. 6. bitter constraint and sad o. dear
**Occasionally.**—P. L. 8, 556. after made o.
**Occasioned.**—P. L. 12. 475. by me done and o.
**Occasions.**—S. A. 1596. o. drew me early to this
**Ocean.**—P. L. 1, 202. that swim the o. stream
P. L. 2, 183. under yon boiling o. wrapped in
P. L. 2, 892. dark illimitable o. without bound
P. L. 3, 76. uncertain which in o. or in air
P. L. 3, 539. such as bound the o. wave
P. L. 4, 165. with the grateful smell old o.
P. L. 4, 354. with prone career to the o. isles
P. L. 4, 540. where heaven with earth and o.
P. L. 5, 426. and at even sups with the o.
P. L. 7, 271. in wide crystalline o.
P. L. 7, 279. main o. flowed not idle
P. L. 7, 412. tempest the o.
P. L. 7, 624. earth with her nether o.
P. L. 9, 80. to the o. barred at Darien
P. L. 11, 827. shall heave the o. to usurp
C. 976. to the o. now I fly
L. 168. so sinks the day-star in the o. bed
S. 19, 13. and post o'er land and o. without rest
H. 66. whispering new joys to the mild o.
**Ocean-brim.**—P. L. 5, 140. o'er the o.-b.
**Oceanus.**—C. 868. in name of great O.
**October's.**—C. 930. nor wet O.'s torrent flood
**Odds.**—P. L. 4, 447. pre-eminent by so much o.
P. L. 6, 319. nor o. appeared in might or swift
P. L. 6, 441. what between us made the o.
P. L. 9, 820. but keep the o. of knowledge
P. L. 10, 374. thy wisdom gained, with o.
A. 23. Juno dares not give her o.
**Ode.**—H. 24. prevent them with thy humble o.
**Odes.**—P. R. 1, 182. their o. and vigils tuned
P. R. 4, 257. Æolian charms and Dorian lyric o.
**Odious.**—P. L. 1, 475. to burn his o. offerings
P. L. 2, 781. at last this o. offspring whom
P. L. 6, 408. the o. din of war
P. L. 9, 880. tedious unshared with thee and o.
P. L. 11, 704. utter o. truth that God would come
**Odiously.**—S. A. 873. thy love still o. pretended
**Odoriferous.**—P. L. 4, 157. their o. wings
**Odorous.**—P. L. 4, 166. those o. sweets
P. L. 4, 248. whose rich trees wept o. gums
P. L. 4, 696. and each bushy shrub
P. L. 5, 482. consummate flower, spirits o.
S. A. 720. an amber scent of o. perfume
C. 993. waters the o. banks that blow
A. 56. and early ere the o. breath of morn
S. 9, 10. to fill thy o. lamp with deeds of light
P. 16. that dropt with o. oil down his fair eyes
**Odour.**—P. L. 9, 579. a savoury o.
**Odours.**—P. L. 2, 245. o. and ambrosial flowers
P. L. 2, 843. the buxom air embalmed with o.
P. L. 4, 162. north-east winds blow Sabæan o.
P. L. 5, 293. and flowering o.
P. L. 5, 349. with rose and o. from the shrub
P. L. 8, 517. flung rose flung o. from the spicy
P. R. 2, 364. gentlest gale Arabian o. fanned
S. A. 987. with o. visited and annual flowers
C. 106. dropping o. dropping wine
C. 712. covering the earth with o.
H. 23. the star-led wizards haste with o. sweet
**Œchalia.**—P. L. 2, 542. from Œ. crowned with
**Œta.**—P. L. 2, 545. from the top of Œ. threw
**O'er.**—P. L. 1, 365. till wandering o. the earth
P. L. 1, 562. o. the burnt soil
P. L. 1, 725. o. the smooth and level pavement
P. L. 1, 742. sheer o. the crystal battlements

P. L. 2, 62. *o.* heaven's high towers
P. L. 2, 485. ambition varnished *o.* with zeal
P. L. 2, 491. *o.* the darkened landscape
P. L. 2, 620. *o.* many a frozen, many a fiery Alp
P. L. 2, 944. *o.* hill or moory dale pursues the
P. L. 2, 948. *o.* bog or steep through strait
P. L. 2, 1005. hung *o.* my realm linked in a
P. L. 3, 359. rolls *o.* Elysian flowers her amber
P. L. 3, 395. while *o.* the necks thou drovest
P. L. 3, 494. fly *o.* the backside of the world
P. L. 3, 521. or flew *o.* the lake
P. L. 3, 527. just *o.* the blissful seat of paradise
P. L. 3, 653. over moist and dry *o.* sea and
P. L. 4, 187. leaps *o.* the fence with ease into
P. L. 4, 191. or *o.* the tiles
P. L. 4, 258. *o.* which the mantling vine lays
P. L. 4, 538. through waste, *o.* hill, *o.* dale
P. L. 4, 609. and *o.* the dark her silver mantle
P. L. 5, 140. yet hovering *o.* the ocean-brim
P. L. 5, 279. came mantling *o.* his breast
P. L. 6, 746. so said he *o.* his sceptre bowing
P. L. 6, 840. *o.* shields and helms and helmed
P. L. 8, 83. centric and eccentric scribbled *o.*
P. L. 8, 546. of that dominion given *o.* other
P. L. 11, 202. in the air and *o.* the ground
P. L. 11, 206. that draws *o.* the blue firmament
P. L. 11, 747. rode tilting *o.* the waves
P. L. 12, 630. from a river *o.* the marish glides
P. R. 1, 218. to subdue and quell *o.* all the earth
P. R. 3, 267. well have we speeded and *o.* hill
P. R. 4, 223. so let extend thy mind *o.* all the
**O'erblown.**—P. L. 1, 172. *o.* hath laid the
**O'ercome.**—P. R. 1, 161. his weakness shall *o.*
S. A. 51. *o.* with importunity and tears
**O'erflowed.**—P. L. 8, 266. with joy my heart *o.*
**O'erfraught.**—C. 732. the sea *o.* would swell
**O'ergrown.**—L. 40. and the gadding vine *o.*
**O'erlaid.**—Il P. 16. *o.* with black staid wisdom's
**O'erleaped.**—P. L. 4, 583. *o.* these earthly
**O'ermatched.**—P. L. 2, 855. fearless to be *o.*
**O'erpowered.**—P. L. 1, 145. could have *o.*
**O'ershades.**—P. L. 5, 376. thy bower *o.*
**O'ershadow.**—P. R. 1, 140. Highest *o.* her
**O'erspread.**—P. L. 2, 489. *o.* heaven's
**O'erthrew.**—P. L. 1, 306. whose waves *o.*
**O'erwatched.**—P. L. 2, 288. sea-faring men *o.*
**O'erwearied.**—P. L. 6, 392. stood recoiled *o.*
**O'erwhelm.**—P. L. 6, 489. and *o.* whatever
S. A. 370. he should not so *o.* and as a thrall
**O'erwhelmed.**—P. L. 1, 76. *o.* with floods
**O'erworn.**—S. A. 123. ill-fitted weeds *o.*
**Off.**—P. L. 1, 184. from *o.* the tossing of these
P. L. 1, 221. upright he rears from *o.* the pool
P. L. 2, 582. far *o.* from these a slow and silent
P. L. 2, 636. as when far *o.* at sea a fleet
P. L. 2, 643. so seemed far *o.* the flying fiend
P. L. 3, 559. that bears Andromeda far *o.*
P. L. 4, 17. beat *o.* returns as oft
P. L. 4, 161. *o.* at sea north-east winds blow
P. L. 5, 428. though from *o.* the boughs each
P. L. 6, 339. it stood retired from *o.* the files
P. R. 3, 397. for there were better farthest *o.*
S. A. 26. all in flames ascended from *o.* the altar
C. 229. and they perhaps are not far *o.*
**Offal.**—P. L. 10, 633. sucked and glutted *o.*
**Offence.**—P. L. 3, 355. but soon for man's *o.*
P. L. 3, 410. offered himself to die for man's *o.*
P. L. 5, 34. but of *o.* and trouble
P. L. 9, 726. the *o.* that man should thus attain
P. L. 10, 171. nor altered his *o.*
P. L. 10, 854. denounced the day of his *o.*
S. A. 515. for self *o.* more than for God offended
S. A. 767. to lessen or extenuate my *o.*
S. A. 1004. after *o.* returning to regain love once
S. A. 1218. if my known *o.* had not disabled me
**Offend.**—P. L. 1. 187. may henceforth most *o.*
P. L. 6, 465. with what more forcible we may *o.*
P. L. 8, 379. let not my words *o.* thee heavenly
P. L. 10, 110. Eve more loth though first to *o.*
P. L. 11, 236. whom not to *o.* with reverence
S. A. 1333. regard thyself, this will *o.* them highly

S. A. 1414. perhaps *o.* them to see me girt with
**Offended.**—P. L. 5, 135. feared to have *o.*
P. L. 10, 488. thereat *o.*, worth your laughter
P. L. 10, 566. which the *o.* taste with spattering
P. L. 10, 916. and unweeting have *o.*
P. L. 11, 149. by prayer the *o.* Deity to appease
P. L. 11, 811. allurement custom and a world *o.*.
P. R. 4, 196. be not so sore *o.* Son of God
S. A. 515. for self offence more than for God *o.*.
Il P. 21. the sea-nymphs and their powers *o.*
**Offending.**—P. L. 2, 212. not mind us not *o.*
**Offensive.**—P. L. 1, 443. on the *o.* mountain
**Offer.**—P. L. 2, 469. the chief might *o.* now
P. L. 3, 237. life for life I *o.*, on me let thine
P. L. 11, 327. thereon *o.* sweet smelling gums
P. L. 12, 363. to *o.* incense, myrrh and gold
P. R. 2, 399. but I see what I can do or *o.*
P. R. 3, 380. this *o.* sets before thee to deliver
P. R. 4, 160. on what I *o.* set as high esteem
P. R. 4, 190. as *o.* them to me the Son of God
S. A. 1255. whether he durst accept the *o.* or not
C. 702. I would not taste thy treasonous *o.*
**Offered.**—P. L. 3, 187. while *o.* grace invites
P. L. 3, 270. as a sacrifice glad to be *o.*
P. L. 3, 409. *o.* himself to die for man's offence
P. L. 5, 63. from me withhold longer thy *o.* good
P. L. 6, 617. perhaps for joy of *o.* peace
P. L. 9, 300. anger would resent the *o.* wrong
P. L. 9, 802. of thy full branches *o.* free to all
P. L. 11, 506. would either not accept life *o.*.
P. L. 12, 425. as many as *o.* life neglect not
P. R. 2, 328. or *o.* first to idols
P. R. 2, 449. contemn riches though *o.*
P. R. 4, 156. how slight thou valuest because *o.*
P. R. 4, 377. thus nicely or cautiously my *o.* aid
P. R. 4, 468. the perfect season *o.* with my aid
P. R. 4, 493. obtrudest thy *o.* aid
S. A. 390. vitiated with gold though *o.* only
S. A. 516. what *o.* means who knows but God
S. A. 1253. and *o.* fight will not dare mention
C. 322. and trust thy honest *o.* courtesy
**Offering.**—P. L. 3, 234. or *o.* meet
P. L. 11, 441. his *o.* soon propitious fire
P. L. 11, 456. for envy that his brother's *o.*
S. A. 26. from off the altar where an *o.* burned
S. A. 344. walked their streets none *o.* fight
S. A. 1152. *o.* to combat thee his champion bold
C. 64. *o.* to every weary traveller
**Offerings.**—P. L. 1, 475. to burn his odious *o.*
P. L. 2, 246. ambrosial flowers our servile *o.*
S. A. 519. where thou mayst bring thy *o.* to avert
**Offers.**—P. R. 4, 155. I see all *o.* made by me
P. R. 4, 171. I never liked thy talk thy *o.* less
**Office.**—P. L. 2, 859. to sit in hateful *o.* here
P. L. 5, 103. among these Fancy next her *o.*
P. L. 7, 344. their *o.* in the firmament of heaven
P. L. 9, 39. the skill of artifice or *o.* mean
P. L. 9, 49. the star of Hesperus whose *o.* is
P. L. 10, 657. to the blanc moon her *o.* they
P. L. 10, 1002. with our own hands his *o.*
P. L. 12, 240. whose high *o.* now Moses
P. L. 12, 311. his name and *o.* bearing
P. R. 1, 28. resigned to him his heavenly *o.*
P. R. 1, 188. publish his godlike *o.* now mature
P. R. 1, 374. they demurring I undertook that *o.*
P. R. 2, 463. for therein stands the *o.* of a king
S. A. 924. with nursing diligence to me glad *o.*
C. 389. and in this *o.* of his mountain watch
C. 908. my *o.* best to help ensnared chastity
D. F. I. 70. best perform that *o.* where thou
U. C. I. 14. in the kind *o.* of a chamberlin
**Officer.**—S. A. 1306. a public *o.* and now at
**Officers.**—C. 218. but as slavish *o.* of vengeance
**Offices.**—P. L. 10, 960. but strive in *o.* of
**Officiate.**—P. L. 8, 22. merely to *o.* light
**Officious.**—P. L. 8, 99. bright luminaries *o.*
P. L. 9, 104. yet bear their bright *o.* lamps
P. R. 2, 302. with granted leave *o.* I return
**Offspring.**—P. L. 2, 310. *o.* of heaven
P. L. 2, 781. at last this odious *o.* whom thou
P. L. 3, 1. hail holy light *o.* of heaven firstborn

P. L. 4, 385. to receive your numerous *o.*
P. L. 4, 751. true source of human *o.* sole
P. L. 6, 276. thy *o.*, to the place of evil
P. L. 8, 86. who art to lead thy *o.*
P. L. 9, 273. *o.* of heaven and earth and all
P. L. 10, 238. happier seat provides for us his *o.*
P. L. 10, 349. who to meet him came his *o.*
P. L. 10, 781. fear of worse to me and to my *o.*
P. L. 11, 358. future days to thee and to thy *o.*
P. L. 11, 613. a beauteous *o.* shall beget
P. L. 11, 755. to behold the end of all thy *o.*
P. R. 2, 440. whose *o.* on the throne of Judah
P. R. 3, 375. whose *o.* in his territory yet serve
P. R. 4, 399. louring night her shadowy *o.*
C. 34. where his fair *o.* nursed in princely lore
D. F. I. 76. this if thou do he will an *o.* give
**Oft.**—P. L. 1, 205. deeming some island, *o.*
P. L. 1, 275. heard so *o.* in worst extremes
P. L. 1, 371. to transform *o.* to the image of
P. L. 1, 432. for those the race of Israel *o.*
P. L. 1, 493. who more *o.* than he in temples
P. L. 2, 131. *o.* on the bordering deep encamp
P. L. 2, 263. how *o.* amidst thick clouds
P. L. 2, 763. thee chiefly who full *o.*
P. L. 3, 185. shall hear me call and *o.* be warned
P. L. 3, 599. imagined rather *o.* than
P. L. 3, 661. to visit *o.* this new creation
P. L. 3, 686. and *o.* though wisdom wake
P. L. 4, 405. rising changes *o.* his couchant
P. L. 4, 449. that day I *o.* remember when
P. L. 4, 684. *o.* in bands while they keep watch
P. L. 5, 32. if dreamed not as I *o.* am wont
P. L. 5, 56. one of those from heaven by us *o.*
P. L. 5, 110. *o.* in her absence mimic fancy
P. L. 5, 112. wild work produces *o.*
P. L. 5, 374. as may not *o.* invite
P. L. 6, 94. who wont to meet so *o.* in festivals
P. L. 7, 402. sculls that *o.* bank the mid sea
P. L. 7, 440. yet *o.* they quit the dank and rising
P. L. 7, 569. open and henceforth *o.*
P. L. 7, 570. will deign to visit *o.* the dwellings
P. L. 8, 25. reasoning I *o.* admire how nature
P. L. 8, 651. and friendly still and *o.* return
P. L. 9, 358. that I should mind thee *o.*
P. L. 9, 399. *o.* he to her his charge of quick
P. L. 9, 400. she to him as *o.* engaged to be
P. L. 9, 427. about her glowed *o.* stooping
P. L. 9, 515. the wind veers *o.* as *o.* so steers
P. L. 9, 524. *o.* he bowed his turret neck
P. L. 9, 559. in their actions *o.* appears
P. L. 9, 638. which *o.* they say some evil spirit
P. L. 9, 641. to bogs and mires and *o.* through
P. L. 9, 842. reapers *o.* are wont their harvest
P. L. 9, 845. *o.* his heart divine of something ill
P. L. 9, 1082. with joy and rapture so *o.* beheld
P. L. 9, 1108. there *o.* the Indian herdsman
P. L. 10, 119. my voice thou *o.* hast heard
P. L. 10, 567. *o.* they assayed
P. L. 10, 568. drugged as *o.* with hatefullest
P. L. 10, 570. so *o.* they fell into the same
P. L. 10, 851. *o.* cursed his creation, death as *o.*
P. L. 11, 492. though *o.* invoked
P. L. 11, 721. he *o.* frequented their assemblies
P. L. 12, 20. *o.* sacrificing bullock
P. L. 12, 48. but God who *o.* descends to visit
P. L. 12, 94. who *o.* as undeservedly enthral
P. L. 12, 192. and *o.* humbles his stubborn
P. L. 12, 319. from whom as *o.* he saves them
P. L. 12, 377. what *o.* my steadiest thoughts
P. L. 12, 496. *o.* supported so as shall amaze
P. R. 1, 270. of whose birth I *o.* had heard
P. R. 1, 363. but that *o.* leaving my dolorous
P. R. 1, 393. lend them *o.* my aid *o.* my advice
P. R. 2, 105. pondering *o.* and *o.* to mind
P. R. 2, 234. and his strength as *o.* assay
P. R. 2, 437. men endued with these have *o.*
P. R. 2, 479. *o.* by force which to a generous
P. R. 3, 106. as vain men seek *o.* not deserved
P. R. 3, 160. *o.* have they violated the temple *o.*
P. R. 3, 167. and o'er a mighty king so *o.*
P. R. 3, 273. *o.* beyond to south the Persian

P. R. 4, 4. thrown from his hope so *o.*
P. R. 4, 17. beat off returns as *o.* with
P. R. 4, 248. of bees' industrious murmur *o.*
P. R. 4, 303. *o.* shames not to prefer
P. R. 4, 446. mad despite to be so *o.* repelled
P. R. 4, 464. they *o.* foresignify and threaten
P. R. 4, 565. *o.* foiled still rose receiving
S. A. 157. men enjoying sight *o.* without cause
S. A. 215. yet truth to say I *o.* have heard men
S. A. 268. but what more *o.* in nations grown
S. A. 382. but warned by *o.* experience
S. A. 682. thou *o.* amidst their height of noon
S. A. 692. *o.* leavest them to the hostile sword
S. A. 704. for *o.* alike both come to evil end
S. A. 759. wisest and best, men full *o.* beguiled
S. A. 813. love hath *o.* well meaning wrought
S. A. 1008. love-quarrels *o.* in pleasing concord
S. A. 1062. fair days have *o.* contracted wind
S. A. 1127. thou *o.* shalt wish thyself at Gath
S. A. 1287. but patience is more *o.* the exercise
S. A. 1745. all is best though we *o.* doubt
S. A. 1749. *o.* he seems to hide his face
C. 252. I have *o.* heard my mother Circe with
C. 323. which *o.* is sooner found in lowly sheds
C. 376. wisdom's self *o.* seeks to sweet retired
C. 459. till *o.* converse with heavenly habitants
C. 471. *o.* seen in charnel vaults and sepulchres
C. 494. Thyrsis whose artful strains have *o.*
C. 623. he loved me well and *o.* would beg me
C. 843. and *o.* at eve visits the herds
C. 999. where young Adonis *o.* reposes
L. 30. *o.* till the star that rose at evening bright
L'A. 53. *o.* listening how the hounds and horn
L'A. 125. there let Hymen *o.* appear
Il P. 27. *o.* in glimmering bowers and glades
Il P. 46. spare fast that *o.* with gods doth diet
Il P. 63. thee chauntress *o.* the woods among
Il P. 71. and *o.* as if her head she bowed
Il P. 73. *o.* on a plat of rising ground
Il P. 87. where I may *o.* outwatch the Bear
Il P. 121. thus *o.* see me in thy pale career
A. 42. which I full *o.* amidst these shades alone
S. 20, 14. and spare to interpose them *o.*
**Often.**—P. L. 1, 387. yea *o.* placed within his
P. L. 4, 680. how *o.* from the steep of echoing
P. R. 1, 199. from without comes *o.* to my ears
S. A. 351. but *o.* proves our woe, our bane
C. 569. paths and turnings *o.* trod by day
L'A. 74. the labouring clouds do *o.* rest
H. 74. or Lucifer that *o.* warned them thence
A. 29. of that renowned flood so *o.* sung
S. 21, 4. which others at their bar so *o.* wrench
**Oftest.**—P. L. 5, 489. discourse is *o.* yours
P. R. 2, 228. greatest men have *o.* wrecked
P. R. 2, 486. to gain a sceptre *o.* better missed
S. A. 1080. but *o.* to affect the wrong
**Oft-invocated.**—S. A. 575. and *o.-i.* death hasten
**Oft-times.**—P. L. 1, 166. which *o.-t.* may
P. L. 8, 571. *o.-t.* nothing profits more
P. R. 1, 472. and not enforced *o.-t.* to part from
P. R. 4, 460. yet as being *o.-t.* noxious where
**Og.**—S. A. 1080. of stock renowned as *O.* or Anak
**Oil.**—P. L. 12, 89. corn, wine and *o.*
P. R. 3, 259. of corn the glebe of *o.* and wine
C. 199. and filled their lamps with everlasting *o.*
**Oils.**—C. 840. dropped in ambrosial *o.*
**Old.**—P. L. 1, 420. flood of *o.* Euphrates
P. L. 1, 477. who under names of *o.* renown
P. L. 1, 519. or who with Saturn *o.*
P. L. 1, 543. the reign of Chaos and *o.* Night
P. L. 1, 552. heroes *o.* arming to battle
P. L. 1, 565. in guise of warriors *o.*
P. L. 1, 639. upheld by *o.* repute
P. L. 2, 38. to claim our just inheritance of *o.*
P. L. 2, 593. Damiata and mount Casius *o.*
P. L. 2, 988. and him thus the Anarch *o.*
P. L. 2, 1002. the sceptre of *o.* Night
P. L. 3, 36. Tiresias and Phineus prophets *o.*
P. L. 3, 421. the inroad of darkness *o.*
P. L. 3, 568. Hesperian gardens famed of *o.*
P. L. 3, 604. in various shapes *o.* Proteus

P. L. 4, 165. with the grateful smell o. Ocean
P. L. 4, 276. where o. Cham whom Gentiles
P. L. 4, 666. by night regain her o. possession
P. L. 7, 7. nor on the top of o. Olympus dwell'st
P. L. 7, 200. where stand of o. myriads
P. L. 9, 101. reforming what was o.
P. L. 9, 145. virtue spent of o. now failed
P. L. 9, 441. Alcinous host of o. Laertes' son
P. L. 9, 670. when of o. some orator renowned
P. L. 10, 226. reassumed in glory as of o.
P. L. 11, 11. when the ancient pair in fables o.
P. L. 11, 243. worn by kings and heroes o.
P. L. 11, 386. city of o. or modern fame
P. L. 11, 588. this is o. age
P. L. 11, 668. him o. and young exploded
P. R. 1, 46. this our o. conquest
P. R. 2, 21. city of palms, Ænon, and Salem o.
P. R. 2, 87. but trouble as o. Simeon plain
P. R. 2, 147. so spake the o. serpent doubting
P. R. 2, 174. because of o. thou thyself doat'st
P. R. 2, 358. fairer than feigned of o. or fabled
P. R. 3, 15. or tongue of seers o., infallible
P. R. 3, 178. the prophets o. who sung
P. R. 3, 276. built by Ninus o.
P. R. 3, 367. Antigonus and o. Hyrcanus
P. R. 3, 378. serving as of o.
P. R. 4, 90. and now is o., o. and lascivious
P. R. 4, 278. of Academics o. and new
P. R. 4, 604. him long of o. thou didst debel
S. A. 139. o. warriors turned their plated backs
S. A. 148. to the hill by Hebron seat of giants o.
S. A. 328. here comes ... o. Manoah
S. A. 333. if o. respect as I suppose
S. A. 572. to a contemptible o. age obscure
S. A. 700. diseases and deformed in crude o. age
S. A. 925. may ever tend about thee to o. age
S. A. 1080. and the Emims o. that Kiriathaim
S. A. 1441. comes o. Manoah in such haste
S. A. 1487. wont to nurse their parents in o. age
S. A. 1488. thou in o. age carest how to nurse
S. A. 1533. things as incredible for his people o.
C. 33. an o. and haughty nation proud in arms
C. 45. from o. or modern bard
C. 439. antiquity from the o. schools of Greece
C. 516. storied of o. in high immortal verse
C. 822. which once of Meliboeus o. I learned
C. 852. and as the o. swain said she can unlock
C. 874. and o. soothsaying Glaucus' spell
C. 923. sprung of o. Anchises' line
A. 98. on o. Lycæus or Cyllene hoar
L. 36. and o. Damœtas loved to hear our song
L. 53. where your o. bards the famous Druids
L. 160. sleep'st by the fable of Bellerus o.
L'A. 97. and young and o. come forth to play
Il P. 173. till o. experience do attain
S. 10, 8. killed with report that o. man eloquent
S. 17, 1. young in years but in sage counsel o.
S. 18, 3. them who kept thy truth so pure of o.
S. 23, 6. purification in the o. law did save
H. 119. but when of o. the sons of morning sung
H. 168. the o. dragon under ground
U. C. I. 1. here lies o. Hobson death hath broke
U. C. II. 8. 'gainst o. truth motion numbered out
F. of C. 20. new presbyter is but o. priest writ
V. Ex. 47. last of kings and queens and heroes o.
V. Ex. 69. a sibyl o. bow-bent with crooked age
**Older.**—S. A. 1489. made o. than thy age through
**Olive.**—P. R. 4, 244. see there the o. grove of
H. 47. she crowned with o. green came softly
**Olive-leaf.**—P. L. 11, 860. in his bill an o-l.
**Olympian.**—P. L. 2, 530. at the O. games
P. L. 7, 3. above the O. hill I soar
**Olympias.**—P. L. 9, 509. he with 'O.
**Olympus.**—P. L. 1, 516. snowy top of cold O.
P. L. 7, 7. nor on the top of old O. dwell'st
P. L. 10, 583. had first the rule of high O.
D. F. I. 44. of shaked O. by mischance didst fall
**Omen.**—S. A. 967. bid go with evil o.
**Ominous.**—P. R. 4, 481. whereof this o. night
C. 61. at last betakes him to this o. wood

**Omission.**—S. A. 691. for the trespass or o.
**Omit.**—S. A. 602. must not o. a father's timely
**Omnific.**—P. L. 7, 217. said then the o. Word
**Omnipotence.**—P. L. 5, 722. sure of our o.
P. L. 6, 159. can allow o. to none
P. L. 6, 684. second O.
P.L. 7, 194. girt with o., with radiance crowned
P. L. 8, 108. though numberless to his o.
**Omnipotent.**—P. L. 1, 49. durst defy the O.
P. L. 1, 273. which but the O. none could have
P. L. 2, 198. subdues us and o. decree
P. L. 3, 372. thee father first they sung o.
P. L. 4, 86. boasting I could subdue the O.
P. L. 4, 725. madest the night, Maker O.
P. L. 5, 616. so spake the O. and with his
P. L. 6, 136. against the O. to rise in arms
P. L. 6, 227. had not the eternal king O.
P. L. 7, 136. the O. eternal Father from his
P. L. 7, 516. therefore the O. eternal Father
P. L. 9, 927. not God o., nor fate
**Omnipresence.**—P. L. 7, 590. hath o.
P. L. 11, 336. his o. fills land sea and air
**Omniscient.**—P. L. 6, 430. till now o.
P. L. 7, 123. the invisible king only O.
P. L. 10, 7. or deceive his heart o.
**Once.**—P. L. 1, 90. joined with me o.
P. L. 1, 59. at o. as far as angels ken
P. L. 1, 268. or o. more with rallied arms to try
P. L. 1, 274. if o. they hear that voice
P. L. 1, 316. the flower of heaven o. yours now
P. L. 1, 471. a leper o. he lost and gained a king
P. L. 1, 607. (far other o. beheld in bliss)
P. L. 1, 788. at o. with joy and fear his heart
P. L. 2, 61. with hell flames and fury all at o.
P. L. 2, 155. he so wise let loose at o. his ire
P. L. 2, 475. and at o. with him they rose
P. L. 2, 476. their rising all at o. was as the
P. L. 2, 613. as o. it fled the lip of Tantalus
P. L. 2, 748. o. deemed so fair in heaven
P. L. 2, 839. I haste to know and this o. known
P. L. 2, 876. not all the Stygian powers could o.
P. L. 2, 1023. but he o. past, soon after when
P. L. 2, 1050. o. his native seat
P. L. 3, 59. and their works at o. to view
P. L. 3, 233. he her aid can never seek o. dead
P. L. 3, 353. a flower which o. in paradise
P. L. 3, 543. view of all this world at o.
P. L. 3, 689. which now for o. beguiled Uriel
P. L. 4, 39. how glorious o. above thy sphere
P. L. 4, 56. at o. indebted and discharged
P. L. 4, 125. to deceive Uriel o. warned
P. L. 4, 148. blossoms and fruits at o. of golden
P. L. 4, 828. ye knew me o. no mate for you
P. L. 4, 853. or all at o. more glory will be won
P. L. 4, 959. who more than thou o. fawned
P. L. 5, 228. in them at o. to ruin all mankind
P. L. 5, 275. at o. on the eastern cliff
P. L. 5, 567. glorious o. and perfect while they
P. L. 6, 251. and felled squadrons at o.
P. L. 6, 270. o. upright and faithful
P. L. 6, 319. as not of power at o.
P. L. 6, 500. so easy it seemed o. found
P. L. 6, 582. for sudden all at o. their reeds
P. L. 6, 618. if our proposals o. again were
P. L. 6, 625. at o. the four spread out their
P. L. 6, 907. thee o. to gain companion of his
P. L. 7, 17. o. Bellerophon, though from a lower
P. L. 7, 132. brighter o. amidst the host of angels
P. L. 7, 462. at o. and in broad herds upsprung
P. L. 7, 475. at o. came forth whatever creeps
P. L. 9, 303. which on us both at o. the enemy
P. L. 9, 586. hunger and thirst at o. powerful
P. L. 9, 779. feed at o. both body and mind
P. L. 9, 1125. calm region o. and full of peace
P. L. 10, 296. fixed as firm as Delos floating o.
P. L. 10, 526. not so thick swarmed o. the soil
P. L. 10, 572. as man whom they triumphed o.
P. L. 10, 587. in power before o. actual
P. L. 10, 729. O voice o. heard delightfully
P. L. 10, 892. and not fill the world at o.
P. L. 10, 999. then both ourselves and seed at o.

P. L. 11, 75. and perhaps *o*. more to sound
P. L. 11, 125. with whoso stolen fruit man *o*.
P. L. 11, 369. as *o*. thou slept'st while she
P. L. 11, 508. created *o*. so goodly and erect
P. L. 11, 761. children all in view destroyed at *o*.
P. L. 11, 768. of many ages on me light at *o*.
P. L. 11, 857. sent forth *o*. and again to spy
P. L. 12, 211. Moses *o*. more his potent rod
P. R. 1, 104. and the way found prosperous *o*.
P. R. 1, 196. a multitude of thoughts at *o*.
P. R. 2, 14. as *o*. Moses was in the Mount
P. R. 2, 17. rode up to heaven yet *o*. again
P. R. 2, 111. and at *o*. all his great work to
P. R. 2, 214. as the zone of Venus *o*. wrought
P. R. 3, 162. as did *o*. Antiochus
P. R. 3, 170. with Modin and her suburbs *o*.
P. R. 3, 234. and *o*. a year Jerusalem
P. R. 3, 438. as the Red Sea and Jordan *o*.
P. R. 4, 132. that people victor *o*. now vile
P. R. 4, 133. who *o*. just frugal and mild
P. R. 4, 574. that *o*. found out and solved
S. A. 22. what *o*. I was
S. A. 197. how could I *o*. look up
S. A. 334. as I suppose towards your *o*. gloried
S. A. 368. methinks whom God hath chosen *o*.
S. A. 633. I was his nursling *o*. and choice
S. A. 705. so deal not with this *o*. thy glorious
S. A. 742. desirous to behold *o*. more thy face
S. A. 885. *o*. a wife for me thou wast to leave
S. A. 932. into the snare where *o*. I have been
S. A. 1005. returning to regain love *o*. possessed
S. A. 1087. *o*. joined the contrary she proves
S. A. 1174. in confidence whereof I *o*. again
S. A. 1417. so dreaded *o*. may now exasperate
S. A. 1474. their *o*. great dread captive and blind
S. A. 1587. at *o*. both to destroy and be destroyed
C. 74. not *o*. perceive their foul disfigurement
C. 164. when *o*. her eye hath met the virtue
C. 637. that Hermes *o*. to wise Ulysses gave
C. 822. which *o*. of Melibœus old I learned
L. 131. ready to smite *o*. and smite no more
L'A. 20. as he met her *o*. a-Maying
H. 5. for so the holy sages *o*. did sing
P. 40. *o*. glorious towers now sunk in guiltless
T. 19. when *o*. our heavenly-guided soul
S. M. 19. as *o*. we did till disproportioned sin
M. W. 23. *o*. had the early matrons run
M. W. 30. spoiled at *o*. both fruit and tree
D. F. I. 50. or wert thou that just maid who *o*.
V. Ex. 17. haste thee straight to do me *o*.
**One.**—P. L. 1, 4. till *o*. greater Man restore us
P. L. 1, 32. for *o*. restraint, lords of the world
P. L. 1, 62. as *o*. great furnace flamed
P. L. 1, 79. *o*. next himself in power and next
P. L. 1, 252. *o*. who brings a mind not to be
P. L. 1, 474. and displace for *o*. of Syrian mode
P. L. 1, 487. who in *o*. night when he passed
P. L. 1, 488. equalled with *o*. stroke
P. L. 1, 638. till then as *o*. secure
P. L. 1, 708. as in an organ from *o*. blast of
P. L. 2, 178. fall *o*. day upon our heads
P. L. 2, 190. eye views all things at *o*. view
P. L. 2, 383. the race of mankind in *o*. root
P. L. 2, 607. with *o*. small drop to lose in sweet
P. L. 2, 609. all pain and woe all in *o*. moment
P. L. 2, 650. the *o*. seemed woman to the waist
P. L. 2, 702. or with *o*. stroke of this dart
P. L. 2, 734. his wrath which *o*. day will
P. L. 2, 827. and *o*. for all myself expose
P. L. 3, 50. wisdom at *o*. entrance quite shut
P. L. 3, 608. when with *o*. virtuous touch
P. L. 3, 648. *o*. of the seven who in God's
P. L. 4, 22. nor from hell *o*. step no more
P. L. 4, 50. *o*. step higher would set me highest
P. L. 4, 175. entwined as *o*. continued brake
P. L. 4, 178. *o*. gate there only was, and that
P. L. 4, 181. at *o*. slight bound high overleaped
P. L. 4, 597. himself now *o*. now other
P. L. 4, 406. as *o*. who chose his ground
P. L. 4, 421. no other service than to keep this *o*.
P. L. 4, 433. then let us not think hard *o*. easy

P. L. 4, 506. these two imparadised in *o*.
P. L. 4, 514. *o*. fatal tree there stands
P. L. 4, 545. winding with *o*. ascent accessible
P. L. 4, 546. accessible from earth *o*. entrance
P. L. 4, 573. *o*. of the banished crew
P. L. 4, 904. O loss of *o*. in heaven to judge
P. L. 5, 36. close at mine ear *o*. called me forth
P. L. 5, 55. *o*. shaped and winged liked *o*.
P. L. 5, 403. only this I know that *o*. celestial
P. L. 5, 469. O Adam *o*. Almighty is from whom
P. L. 5, 472. *o*. first matter all
P. L. 5, 610. united as *o*. individual soul
P. L. 5, 678. both waking we were *o*. how then
P. L. 5, 697. or several *o*. by *o*.
P. L. 5, 753. from *o*. entire globose stretched
P. L. 5, 783. too much to *o*. but double how
P. L. 5, 784. to *o*. and to his image now
P. L. 5, 821. *o*. over all with unsucceeded power
P. L. 5, 830. under *o*. head more near united
P. L. 5, 834. or all angelic nature joined in *o*.
P. L. 5, 843. since he the head *o*. of our number
P. L. 6, 23. that *o*. that of so many myriads fallen
P. L. 6, 24. yet *o*. returned not lost
P. L. 6, 95. as sons of *o*. great Sire hymning
P. L. 6, 140. at *o*. blow unaided could have
P. L. 6, 165. to heavenly souls had been all *o*.
P. L. 6, 317. *o*. stroke they aimed that might
P. L. 6, 359. nor from the Holy *O*. of heaven
P. L. 6, 423. who have sustained *o*. day
P. L. 6, 424. and if *o*. day why not eternal days
P. L. 6, 448. as *o*. he stood escaped from cruel
P. L. 6, 503. some *o*. intent on mischief
P. L. 6, 520. pernicious with *o*. touch to fire
P. L. 6, 779. under their head embodied all in *o*.
P. L. 6, 848. *o*. spirit in them ruled
P. L. 7, 66. as *o*. whose drouth yet scarce
P. L. 7, 155. out of *o*. man a race of men
P. L. 7, 228. *o*. foot he centred and the other
P. L. 7, 284. into *o*. place and let dry land appear
P. L. 8, 24. *o*. day and night in all their vast
P. L. 8, 29. to this *o*. use for aught appears
P. L. 8, 295. *o*. came methought of shape divine
P. L. 8, 387. the *o*. intense, the other still remiss
P. L. 8, 421. all numbers absolute though *o*.
P. L. 8, 499. they shall be *o*. flesh, *o*. heart *o*. soul
P. L. 8, 555. as *o*. intended first not after made
P. L. 8, 604. union of mind or in us both *o*. soul
P. L. 9, 136. in *o*. day to have marred what
P. L. 9, 140. since I in *o*. night
P. L. 9, 211. *o*. night or two with wanton
P. L. 9, 271. as *o*. who loves
P. L. 9, 445. as *o*. who long in populous city
P. L. 9, 463. the Evil *O*. abstracted stood
P. L. 9, 511. as *o*. who sought access but feared
P. L. 9, 545. *o*. man except
P. L. 9, 628. *o*. small thicket past of blowing
P. L. 9, 769. yet that *o*. beast which first hath
P. L. 9, 917. as *o*. from sad dismay recomforted
P. L. 9, 958. we are *o*., *o*. flesh
P. L. 9, 967. *o*. heart *o*. soul in both whereof
P. L. 9, 971. undergo with me *o*. guilt, *o*. crime
P. L. 9, 1026. for this *o*. tree
P. L. 10, 391. *o*. realm, hell and this world
P. L. 10, 392. *o*. continent
P. L. 10, 554. for *o*. forbidden tree
P. L. 10, 633. at *o*. sling of thy victorious arms
P. L. 10, 782. yet *o*. doubt pursues me still
P. L. 10, 809. say that death be not *o*. stroke
P. L. 10, 823. why should all mankind for *o*.
P. L. 10, 855. with *o*. thrice acceptable stroke
P. L. 10, 923. yet we live scarce *o*. short hour
P. L. 10, 925. *o*. enmity against a foe by doom
P. L. 10, 945. as *o*. disarmed his anger all
P. L. 11, 44. *o*. with me as I with thee am *o*.
P. L. 11, 84. O sons like *o*. of us man is become
P. L. 11, 147. or *o*. short sigh of human breath
P. L. 11, 203. *o*. way the self-same hour
P. L. 11, 219. who to surprise *o*. man
P. L. 11, 230. *o*. of the heavenly host
P. L. 11, 256. and *o*. bad act with many deeds

P. L. 11, 564. in other part stood o. who at the
P. L. 11, 646. o. way a band select from forage
P. L. 11, 753. all left in o. small bottom swum
P. L. 11, 808. o. man except the only son of
P. L. 11, 818. the o. just man alive
P. L. 11, 874. for o. whole world of wicked
P. L. 11, 876. than I rejoice for o. man found
P. L. 11, 890. such grace shall o. just man find
P. L. 12, 1. as o. who in his journey baits at
P. L. 12, 6. thus thou hast seen o. world begin
P. L. 12, 24. till o. shall rise of proud ambitious
P. L. 12, 111. and o. peculiar nation to select
P. L. 12, 113. a nation from o. faithful man
P. L. 12, 189. last with o. midnight-stroke all
P. L. 12, 242. to introduce o. greater of whose
P. L. 12, 248. the Holy O. with mortal men
P. L. 12, 581. and all the rule, o. empire
P. L. 12, 603. both in o. faith unanimous
P. R. 1, 2. by o. man's disobedience lost
P. R. 1, 4. by o. man's firm obedience fully
P. R. 1, 189. o. day forth walked alone the
P. R. 1, 216. o. while to rescue Israel from the
P. R. 1, 307. or harboured in o. cave
P. R. 1, 471. where easily canst thou find o.
P. R. 2, 216. how would o. look from his
P. R. 2, 300. as o. in city or court or palace
P. R. 3, 53. but as o. leads the other
P. R. 3, 84. o. is the son of Jove
P. R. 3, 256. the o. winding the other straight
P. R. 3, 362. therefore o. of these thou must
P. R. 4, 194. that Evil O. Satan for ever damned
P. R. 4, 317. as o. regardless quite of mortal
S. A. 120. as o. past hope abandoned
S. A. 265. Judah that day joined, or o. whole tribe
S. A. 348. at o. spear's length
S. A. 650. boots it at o. gate to make defence
S. A. 649. this o. prayer yet remains
S. A. 794. feared lest o. day thou wouldst leave
S. A. 974. on both his wings o. black the other
S. A. 1016. o. or seven though o. should musing
S. A. 1047. who finds o.' virtuous
S. A. 1239. with o. buffet lay thy structure low
S. A. 1427. the Holy O. of Israel be thy guide
S. A. 1457. I have attempted o. by o. the lords
S. A. 1518. from slaughter of o. foe could not
S. A. 1539. and to our wish I see o. higher
S. A. 1637. fast fixed he stood as o. who prayed
C. 133. and makes o. blot of all the air
C. 483. either some o. like us night-foundered
C. 582. against the unarmed weakness of o.
C. 811. o. sip of this will bathe the drooping
L'A. 107. when in o. night ere glimpse of morn
Il P. 69. like o. that had been led astray
S. 11, 7. while o. might walk to Mile-End Green
S. 19, 3. that o. talent which is death to hide
H. 71. bending o. way their precious influence
M. W. 7. summers three times eight save o.
D.F.I.11. if likewise he some fair o. wedded not
U.C.II.1. here lieth o. who did most truly prove
U.C.I.3. the ways being foul, twenty to o.
U.C.II.20. o. carrier put down to make six bearers
V. Ex. 76. yet every o. shall make him underling
**Only.**—P. L. 1, 64. served o. to discover sights
P. L. 2, 497. men o. disagree of creatures
P. L. 2, 623. created evil, for evil o. good
P. L. 2, 728. against thy o. son
P. L. 3, 64. image of his glory sat his o. Son
P. L. 3, 65. our two first parents yet the o. two
P. L. 3, 79. thus to his o. Son foreseeing spake
P. L. 3, 105. where o. what they needs must
P. L. 3, 155. and judgest o. right
P. L. 3, 268. above which o. shone filial
P. L. 3, 274. the o. peace found out for mankind
P. L. 3, 281. thou therefore whom thou o.
P. L. 3, 398. powers with loud acclaim thee o.
P. L. 3, 403. no sooner did thy dear and o. Son
P. L. 3, 683. the o. evil that walks invisible
P. L. 3, 701. hear o. in Heaven
P. L. 4, 91. o. supreme in misery
P. L. 4, 178. one gate there o. was
P. L. 4, 199. but o. used for prospect

P. L. 4, 251. Hesperian fables true if true here o
P. L. 4, 299. he for God o. she for God in him
P. L. 4, 423. not to taste that o. tree
P. L. 4, 428. the o. sign of our obedience left
P. L. 4, 518. and do they o. stand by ignorance
P. L. 4, 668. these soft fires not o. enlighten
P. L. 4, 895. who know'st o. good
P. L. 4, 991. nor o. paradise in this commotion
P. L. 5, 5. which the o. sound of leaves
P. L. 5, 69. here it seems as o. fit for gods
P. L. 5, 206. bounteous still to give us o. good
P. L. 5, 366. with us two o. who yet by sovran
P. L. 5, 402. o. this I know that one celestial
P. L. 5, 604. whom I declare my o. son
P. L. 5, 639. full measure o. bounds excess
P. L. 5, 718. and smiling to his o. Son
P. L. 5, 779. this o. to consult how we may
P. L. 5, 815. that to his o. Son by right endued
P. L. 5, 897. among the faithless faithful o. he
P. L. 6, 239. as o. in his arm the moment lay
P. L. 6, 491. his o. dreaded bolt
P. L. 6, 810. stand o. & behold God's indignation
P. L. 7, 123. invisible King o. omniscient
P. L. 8, 14. doubt remains which o. thy solution
P. L. 8, 155. o. to shine yet scarce contribute
P. L. 8, 174. think o. what concerns thee
P. L. 8, 178. not of earth o. but of highest
P. L. 8, 338. not o. these fair bounds but all
P. L. 8, 447. for trial o. brought to see how
P. L. 8, 532. here o. weak against the charm
P. L. 8, 616. by looks o.?
P. L. 9, 28. hitherto the o. argument heroic
P. L. 9, 129. for o. in destroying I find ease
P. L. 9, 327. o. our foe tempting
P. L. 9, 380. last reasoning words touched o.
P. L. 9, 415. the o. two of mankind
P. L. 9, 681. not o. to discern things in their
P. L. 9, 923. had it been o. coveting to eye
P. L. 9, 1121. nor o. tears rained
P. L. 10, 220. nor he their outward o. with
P. L. 10, 461. such not o. of right
P. L. 10, 826. not to do o. but to will the same
P. L. 10, 832. on me, me o. as the source and
P. L. 10, 841. to Satan o. like
P. L. 10, 921. in this uttermost distress my o.
P. L. 10, 931. thou against God o.
P. L. 10, 936. me, me o. just object of his ire
P. L. 10, 1043. and savours o. rancour and pride
P. L. 10, 1051. pains o. in child-bearing
P. L. 11, 304. and o. consolation left familiar
P. L. 11, 336. and all the earth not this rock o.
P. L. 11, 618. bred o. and completed to the taste
P. L. 11, 689. might o. shall be admired
P. L. 11, 701. the o. righteous in a world
P. L. 11, 765. so had borne my part of evil o.
P. L. 11, 808. the o. son of light in a dark age
P. L. 12, 67. he gave us o. over beast, fish, fowl
P. L. 12, 401. so o. can high justice rest appaid
P. L. 12, 447. not o. to the sons of Abraham's
P. L. 12, 513. left o. in those written records
P. L. 12, 562. and love with fear the o. God
P. L. 12, 581. and all the rule one empire o.
P. R. 1, 226. the stubborn o. to subdue
P. R. 1, 349. man lives not by bread o. but each
P. R. 2, 13. they thought he might be o. shown
P. R. 2, 221. beauty stands in the admiration o.
P. R. 2, 229. or that which o. seems to satisfy
P. R. 2, 289. o. in a bottom saw a pleasant grove
P. R. 2, 336. with honour o. deign to sit
P. R. 2, 404. o. the importune Tempter still
P. R. 2, 478. that other o'er the body o. reigns
P. R. 4, 177. the Lord thy God and o. him
P. R. 4, 294. to know this o. that he nothing
P. R. 4, 320. her false resemblance o. meets
P. R. 4, 364. these o. with our law best
P. R. 4, 420. yet o. stood'st unshaken
P. R. 4, 466. for o. thou here dwell'st
S. A. 264. they o. lived who fled
S. A. 390. vitiated with gold though offered o.
S. A. 460. this o. hope relieves me that the
S. A. 557. whose drink was o. from the liquid

S. A. 579. at home lie bed-rid not *o*. idle
S. A. 617. my griefs not *o*. pain me
S. A. 630. benumbing opium as my *o*. cure
S. A. 687. nor *o*. dost degrade them or remit
S. A. 863. *o*. my love of thee held long debate
S. A. 912. *o*. what remains past cure
S. A. 1123. I *o*. with an oaken staff will meet
S. A. 1190. with armed powers thee *o*. seeking
S. A. 1654. not *o*. of this but each Philistian
S. A. 1679. they *o*. set on sport and play
S. A. 1742. *o*. bewailing his lot
C. 126. 'tis *o*. daylight that makes sin
C. 765. means her provision *o*. to the good
S. 16, 2. not of war *o*. but detractions rude
S. 19, 14. they also serve who *o*. stand and wait
H.37.*o*.with speeches fair she wooes the gentle
M. W. 39. who *o*. thought to crop the flower
V. Ex. 25. and weary of their place do *o*. stay
V. Ex. 55. it must be now thy *o*. bent
U. C. II. 34. *o*. remains this superscription
**Only-begotten.**—P. L. 3, 80. *o.-b*. Son
**Onset.**—P. L. 2, 364. achieved by sudden *o*.
P. L. 6, 98. sound of *o*. ended soon each milder
**Onward.**—P. L. 2, 675. moving *o*. came as fast
P. L. 5, 298. through the spicy forest *o*. come
P. L. 6, 550. and *o*. moved embattled
P. L. 6, 768. he *o*. came
P. L. 6, 831. his impious foes right *o*. drove
P. L. 10, 811. endless misery from th**is** day *o*.
S. A. 1. a little *o*. lend thy guiding hand
S. 22, 9. but still bear up and steer right *o*.
**Ooze.**—P. L. 7, 303. and on the washy *o*. deep
**Oozy.**—L. 175. with nectar pure his *o*. locks he
H. 124. their *o*. channel keep
**Opacous.**—P. L. 3, 418. upon the firm *o*. globe
P. L. 8, 23. to officiate light round this *o*. earth
**Opal.**—P. L. 2, 1049. *o*. towers and battlements
**Opaque.**—P. L. 3, 619. from body *o*. can fall
**Ope.**—P. L. 11, 423. Adam now *o*. thine eyes
C. 626. and in requital *o*. his leathern scrip
**Oped.**—S. A. 452. the mouths of idolists
**Open.**—P. L. 1, 662. war *o*. or understood
P. L. 2, 41. whether of *o*. war or covert guile
P. L. 2, 51. my sentence is for *o*. war
P. L. 2, 119. I should be much for *o*. war
P. L. 2, 187. war therefore *o*. or concealed alike
P. L. 2, 879. on a sudden *o*. fly with impetuous
P. L. 2, 884. the gates wide *o*. stood
P. L. 3, 514. dreaming by night under the *o*.
P. L. 3, 672. with secret gaze or *o*. admiration
P. L. 4, 245. first warmly smote the *o*. field
P. L. 4, 721. and under *o*. sky adored the God
P. L. 5, 127. that *o*. now their choicest bosomed
P. L. 5, 188. they forth were come to *o*.sight
P. L. 6, 235. *o*. when and when to close
P. L. 6, 560. and with *o*. breast stand ready
P. L. 6, 611. to entertain them fair with *o*. front
P. L. 7, 158. they *o*. to themselves at length
P. L. 7, 390. displayed on the *o*. firmament
P. L. 7, 565. *o*. ye everlasting gates they sung
P. L. 7, 569. *o*. and henceforth oft
P. L. 8, 460. but *o*. left the cell of fancy
P. L. 9, 692. which to the beast is *o*.
P. L. 9, 866. but of divine effect to *o*. eyes
P. L. 10, 187. triumphed in *o*. show
P. L. 10, 232. the gates that now stood *o*. wide
P. L. 10, 419. wide *o*. and unguarded Satan
P. L. 10, 533. issuing forth to the *o*. field
P. L. 10, 1061. if we pray him will his ear be *o*.
P. L. 11, 825. the cataracts of heaven set *o*.
S. A. 1172. whose ear is ever *o*. and his eye
S. A. 1609. other side was *o*. where the throng
H. 148. will *o*. wide the gates of her high palace
**Opened.**—P. L. 1, 689. *o*. into the hill a spacious
P. L. 2, 175. what if all her stores were *o*.
P. L. 2, 883. she *o*. but to shut excelled her
P. L. 3, 526. direct against which *o*. from
P. L. 7, 205. heaven *o*. wide his ever-during
P. L. 7, 575. he through heaven that *o*. wide
P. L. 8, 465. stooping *o*. my left side and took
P. L. 9, 708. perfectly be then *o*. and cleared

P. L. 9, 985. life augmented *o*. eyes, new hopes
P. L. 9, 1053. their eyes how *o*. and their minds
P. L. 9, 1071. our eyes *o*. we find indeed
P. L. 11, 429. his eyes he *o*. and beheld a field
P. R. 1, 30. heaven *o*. and in likeness of a dove
P. R. 1, 281. heaven *o*. her eternal doors
P. R. 2, 294. that *o*. in the midst a woody scene
**Opener.**—P. L. 9, 875. *o*. mine eyes
P. L. 11, 598. true *o*. of mine eyes prime angel
**Opening.**—P. L. 1, 724. *o*. their brazen folds
P. L. 2, 755. till on the left side *o*. wide
P. L. 2, 777. which none can pass without *o*.
P. L. 3, 538. so wide the *o*. seemed
P. L. 6, 481. so beauteous *o*. to the ambient
P. L. 6, 860. crystal wall of heaven which *o*.
P. L. 7, 318. *o*. their various colours
P. L. 7, 454. and straight *o*. her fertile womb
P. L. 9, 865. nor to evil unknown *o*. the way
P. L. 10, 234. the fiend passed through, Sin *o*.
P. L. 11, 277. from the first *o*. bud
P. L. 11, 833. down ... to the *o*. gulf
P. L. 12, 274. l find mine eyes true *o*.
L. 26. under the *o*. eyelids of the morn
**Openly.**—P. R. 1, 288. but *o*. begin as best
S. A. 398. how *o*. and with what impudence
**Opens.**—P. L. 4, 77. threatening to devour me *o*.
P. L. 6, 54. which ready *o*. wide his fiery
**Open'st.**—P. L. 9, 809. thou *o*. wisdom's way
**Operation.**—P. L. 8, 323. tree whose *o*. brings
P. L. 9, 796. of *o*. blest to sapience
P. L. 9, 1012. that false fruit far other *o*. first
**Opes.**—C. 14. that *o*. the palace of Eternity
L. 111. the golden *o*. the iron shuts amain
**Ophion.**—P. L. 10, 581. *O*. with Eurynome
**Ophir.**—P. L. 11, 400. Sofala thought *O*.
**Ophiuchus.**—P. L. 2, 709. the length of *O*.
**Ophiusa.**—P. L. 10, 528. or the isle *O*.
**Opiate.**—P. L. 11, 133. Hermes or his *o*. rod
**Opinion.**—P. L. 2, 471. refused might in *o*.
P. L. 5, 108. and call our knowledge or *o*.
**Opinions.**—P. L. 8, 78. at their quaint *o*. wide
**Opium.**—S. A. 630. to death's benumbing *o*.
**Opportune.**—P. L. 2, 396. and *o*. excursion
P. L. 9, 481. alone the woman *o*. to all attempts
P. L. 9, 85. which of all most *o*. mightserve
**Opportunely.**—P. R. 2, 396. rather *o*.
**Opportunity.**—P. R. 4, 531. and *o*. I here
C. 401. as bid me hope danger will wink on *o*.
**Oppose.**—P. L. 2, 419. second or *o*. or undertake
P. L. 2, 610. but fate withstands and to *o*.
P. L. 5, 717. were banded to *o*. his high decree
P. L. 6, 155. durst *o*. a third part of the gods
P. L. 6, 636. such hellish mischief fit to *o*.
S. A. 862. to *o*. against such powerful arguments
**Opposed.**—P. L. 1, 41. the Most High if he *o*.
P. L. 1, 103. utmost power with adverse power *o*.
P. L. 5, 808. the current of his fury thus *o*.
P. L. 6, 254. and *o*. the rocky orb of tenfold
P. L. 10, 478. jealous of their secrets fiercely *o*.
P. R. 1, 96. must with something sudden be *o*.
**Opposing.**—C. 600. against the *o*. will and arm
**Opposite.**—P. L. 2, 298. emulation *o*. to heaven
P. L. 3, 727. so call that *o*. fair star
P. L. 4, 460. as I bent down to look just *o*.
P. L. 6, 128. forth stepping *o*. half-way he met
P. L. 6, 306. broad suns their shields blazed *o*.
P. L. 7, 376. but *o*. in levelled west was set
P. L. 10, 659. sextile square, and trine, and *o*.
P. R. 3, 358. by free consent of all none *o*.
**Opposition.**—P. L. 2, 803. mine eyes in *o*.
P. L. 6, 314. of fiercest *o*. in mid sky
P. L. 11, 664. but soon in factious *o*. till at last
P. R. 3, 250. how best their *o*. to withstand
P. R. 4, 386. sorrows and labours *o*. hate
S. A. 1050. but virtue which breaks through *o*.
**Oppress.**—P. R. 2, 44. of the earth how they *o*.
S. A. 232. still watching *o*. Israel's oppressors
**Oppressed.**—P. L. 2, 13. though *o*. and fallen
P. L. 6, 655. and *o*. whole legions armed
P. L. 9, 1045. till dewy sleep *o*. them wearied
P. R. 2, 331. would scruple that with want *o*.

S. A. 1269. to the spirits of just men long *o*.
**Oppresses.**—P. L. 7, 129. *o*. else with surfeit
**Oppression.**—P. L. 8, 288. and with soft *o*.
P. L. 11, 672. violence proceeded and *o*.
**Oppressor.**—S. A. 1272. of the earth the *o*.
**Oppressors.**—S. A. 233. to oppress Israel's *o*.
**Opprobrious.**—P. L. 1, 403. on that *o*. hill
P. L. 2. 58. accept this dark *o*. den of shame
P. L. 10, 222. inward nakedness much more *o*.
**Ops.**—P. L. 10, 584. by Saturn driven and *O*.
**Optic.**—P. L. 1,288. through *o*. glass the Tuscan
P. L. 3, 590. through his glazed *o*. tube
P. R. 4, 40. *o*. skill of vision multiplied
**Oracle.**—P. L. 1, 12. fast by the *o*. of God
P. L. 10, 182. so spake this *o*. then verified
P. R. 1, 460. God hath now sent his living *o*.
P. R. 1, 463. an inward *o*. to all truth requisite
P. R. 3, 13. thy counsel would be as the *o*.
P. R. 4, 275. well inspired the *o*. pronounced
**Oracles.**—P. R. 1, 395. and answers *o*. portents
P. R. 1, 430. all *o*. by thee are given
P. R. 1, 456. henceforth *o*. are ceased
H. 173. the *o*. are dumb no voice or hideous
**Oracling.**—P. R. 1, 455. thou by *o*. abuse
**Oraculous.**—P. R. 3, 14. those *o*. gems
**Orator.**—P. L. 9, 670. when of old some *o*.
**Orators.**—P. R. 4, 267. the famous *o*. repair
P. R. 4, 353. their *o*. thou then extoll'st
**Oratory.**—P. L. 11, 8. than loudest *o*.
P. R. 4, 360. all the *o*. of Greece and Rome
**Orb.**—P. L. 1, 287. whose *o*. through optic glass
P. L. 2, 1029. reaching the utmost *o*. of this
P. L. 3, 589. astronomer in the sun's lucent *o*.
P. L. 4, 592. whether the prime *o*.
P. L. 5, 176. the fixed stars fixed in their *o*.
P. L. 5, 596. they stood *o*. within *o*.
P. L. 5, 862. fatal course had circled his full *o*.
P. L. 6, 254. and opposed the rocky *o*.
P. L. 7, 257. the hollow universal *o*. they filled
P. L. 7, 361. the sun's *o*. made porous to receive
P. L. 8, 84. cycle and epicycle *o*. in *o*.
P. L. 8, 152. stored in each *o*.
P. L. 8, 156. scarce to contribute each *o*.
P. L. 9, 82. thus the *o*. he roamed with narrow
**Orbed.**—P. L. 6, 543. gripe fast his *o*. shield
H. 143. down return to men *o*. in a rainbow
**Orbicular.**—P. L. 3, 718. that rolled *o*.
P. L. 10, 381. his quadrature from thy *o*. world
**Orbs.**—P. L. 3, 25. hath quenched their *o*.
P. L. 3, 420. the luminous inferior *o*. enclosed
P. L. 3, 668. which of all these shining *o*. hath
P. L. 3, 670. but all these shining *o*.
P. L. 5, 422. her moist continent to higher *o*.
P. L. 5, 594. when in *o*. of circuit inexpressible
P. L. 6, 828. and the *o* of his fierce chariot
P. L. 8, 30. on their *o*. impose such restless
P. L. 9, 109. centring receivest from all those *o*.
P. L. 10, 397. among these numerous *o*. all
S. A. 591. that these dark *o*. no more shall treat
S. 22. nor to their idle *o*. doth sight appear
H. 75. but in their glimmering *o*. did glow
**Orcs.**—P. L. 11, 835. haunts of seals and *o*.
**Orcus.**—P. L. 2, 946. and by them stood *O*.
**Ordain.**—P. L. 2, 915. them *o*. his dark
P. L. 7, 343. and let them be for lights as I *o*.
P. L. 12, 230. and loud trumpet's sound *o*.
**Ordained.**—P. L. 1, 71. here their prison *o*.
P. L. 2, 732. at thee *o*. his drudge to execute
P. L. 3, 127. their freedom they themselves *o*.
P. L. 3, 665. these his works so wondrous he *o*.
P. L. 4, 58. had his powerful destiny *o*. me
P. L. 4, 215. far more pleasant garden God *o*.
P. L. 4, 729. crown of all our bliss *o*. by thee
P. L. 5, 526. *o*. thy will by nature free
P. L. 5, 615. his place *o*. without redemption
P. L. 5, 802. our being *o*. to govern not to serve
P. L. 6, 700. for thee I have *o*. and thus far
P. L. 6, 809. number to this day's work is not *o*.
P. L. 7, 187. whose wisdom had *o*. good
P. L. 7, 590. the work *o*. author and end of all
P. L. 8, 106. the rest *o*. for uses to his Lord

P. L. 8, 297. first man of men innumerable *o*.
P. L. 9, 344. all things as the will of God *o*.
P. L. 9, 470. he sees of pleasure not for him *o*.
P. L. 10, 1039. shall scape his punishment *o*.
P. L. 11, 164. who for thee *o*. a help became
P. L. 12, 226. to rule by laws *o*.
P. R. 3, 152. *o*. to sit upon thy father David's
P. R. 4, 473. thou shalt be what thou art *o*.
S.A.362. for this *o*. thy nurture holy as of a plant
**Ordains.**—P. L. 2, 201. law unjust that so *o*.
P. L. 4, 636. unargued I obey, so God *o*.
P. L. 6, 175. to serve whom God *o*. or nature
S. 21, 11. for other things mild heaven a time *o*.
**Order.**—P. L. 1, 506. these were the prime in *o*.
P. L. 1, 569. their *o*. due, their visages
P. L. 2, 280. the settled state of *o*.
P. L. 2, 507. and forth in *o*. came the grand
P. L. 3, 713. light shone and *o*. from disorder
P. L. 4, 663. and from land to land in *o*.
P. L. 5, 334. what *o*. so contrived as not to mix
P. L. 6, 522. secret they finished and in *o*. set
P. L. 6, 548. soon in *o*. quit of all impediment
P. L. 6, 855. with branching palm each *o*.
P. L. 9, 402. and all things in best *o*. to invite
P. L. 10, 443. angel militant of lowest *o*. passed
P. L. 11, 736. and entered in as taught their *o*.
P. R. 2, 351. in *o*. stood tall stripling youths
S. A. 1447. by *o*. of the lords new parted hence
S. A. 1608. might sit in *o*. to behold
S. A. 1694. and nests in *o*. ranged
H. 244. bright-harnessed angels sit in *o*.
**Ordered.**—P. L. 1, 565. with *o*. spear and shield
S. A. 30. my breeding *o*. and prescribed
P. 49. that they would fitly fall in *o*. characters.
**Ordering.**—P. L. 8, 377. and seemed so *o*.
**Orderly.**—P. L. 6, 74. birds in *o*. array
**Orders.**—P. L. 1, 737. the *o*. bright
P. L. 5, 587. under their hierarchs in *o*. bright
P. L. 5, 591. of hierarchies of *o*. and degrees
P. L. 5, 792. *o*. and degrees jar not with liberty
P. L. 10, 615. to those bright *o*. uttered thus
P. R. 3, 112. all things made all things *o*.
S.A.672. not evenly as thou rulest the angelic *o*.
**Ore.**—P. L. 1, 673. his womb was hid metallic *o*.
P. L. 1, 703. founded the massy *o*.
P. L. 5, 442. metals of drossiest *o*. to perfect,
P. L. 11, 570. the liquid *o*. he drained into fit
C. 719. she hutched the all-worshipped *o*.
C. 933. the beryl and the golden *o*.
L. 170. his beams and with new-spangled *o*.
**Oread.**—P. L. 9, 387. *O*. or Dryad
**Oreb.**—P. L. 1, 7. that on the secret top of *O*.
P. L. 1, 484. composed the calf in *O*.
P. L. 11, 74. his trumpet heard in *O*. since
**Organ.**—P. L. 1, 708. as in an *o*. from one blast
P. L. 11, 560. of harp and *o*. and who moved
Il P. 161. there let the pealing *o*. blow
H.130. and let the bass of heaven's deep *o*. blow
**Organic.**—P. L. 9, 530. with serpent-tongue *o*.
**Organs.**—P. L. 4. 802. the *o*. of her fancy
P. L. 7, 596. and dulcimer all *o*. of sweet stops
**Orgies.**—P. L. 1, 415. yet thence his lustful *o*.
**Orient.**—P. L. 1, 546. with *o*. colours waving
P. L. 2, 399. and at the brightening *o*. beam
P. L. 2, 507. thick with sparkling *o*. gems
P. L. 4, 238. on *o*. pearl and sands of gold
P. L. 4, 644. he spreads his *o*. beams on herb
P. L. 5, 2. advancing sowed the earth with *o*.
P. L. 5, 175. moon that now meet'st the *o*. sun
P. L. 6, 15. shot through with *o*. beams
P. L. 6, 524. now when fair morn *o*. in heaven
P. L. 7, 254. when *o*. light exhaling first
P. L. 11, 205. morning-light more *o*.
C. 65. his *o*. liquor in a crystal glass
H. 231. pillows his chin upon an *o*. wave
**Orifice.**—P. L. 6, 577. with hideous *o*. gaped
**Original.**—P. L. 1, 592. all her *o*. brightness
P. L. 2, 375. curse their frail *o*. and faded bliss
P. L. 2, 984. reduce to her *o*. darkness
P. L. 9, 150. him endow exalted from so base *o*.
P. L. 9, 1004. at completing of the mortal sin *o*.

P. L. 11, 424. the effects which thy *o.* crime
P. L. 12, 83. since thy *o.* lapse true liberty
**Originals.**—P. L. 6, 511. the *o.* of nature
**Orion.**—P. L. 1, 305. with fierce winds *O.* armed
**Orisons.**—P. L. 5, 145. and began their *o.*
P. L. 11, 137. had ended now their *o.* and found
**Ormus.**—P. L. 2, 2. outshone the wealth of *O.*
**Ornament.**—P. L. 5, 280. with regal *o.*
P. L. 8, 538. on her bestowed too much of *o.*
S. A. 1025. is it for that such outward *o.*
S. A. 1132. their *o.* and safety
**Ornaments.**—P. L. 9, 1076. our wonted *o.*
**Ornate.**—S. A. 712. that so bedecked *o.* and gay
**Orontes.**—P. L. 4, 273. of Daphne by *O.*
P. L. 9, 80. west from *O.* to the ocean barred
**Orphean.**—P. L. 3, 17. than to the *O.* lyre
**Orpheus.**—L. 58. muse herself that *O.* bore
L'A. 145. that *O.* self may heave his head
Il P. 105. or bid the soul of *O.* sing
**Orus.**—P. L. 1, 478. Osiris, Isis. *O.* and their
H. 212. Isis, and *O.* and the dog Anubis haste
**Osier.**—C. 891. grows the willow and the *o.* dank
**Osiers.**—P. R. 2, 26. winds with reeds and *o.*
**Osiris.**—P. L. 1, 478. *O.*, Isis, Orus and their
H. 213. nor is *O.* seen in Memphian grove
**Ostentation.**—P. R. 3, 387. much *o.* vain
**Other.**—P. L. 1, 194. his *o.* parts besides prone
P. L. 1, 412. Peor his *o.* name
P. L. 1, 607. (far *o.* once beheld in bliss)
P. L. 2, 108. on the *o.* side up rose Belial
P. L. 2, 422. each in *o.'s* countenance read
P. L. 2, 502. wasting the earth each *o.* to destroy
P. L. 2, 666. the *o.* shape, if shape it might be
P. L. 2, 706. on the *o.* side incensed
P. L. 2, 714. such a frown each cast at the *o.*
P. L. 2, 806. devour for want of *o.* prey
P. L. 2, 977. or if some *o.* place from your
P. L. 2, 1020. by the *o.* whirlpool steered
P. L. 3, 17. with *o.* notes than to the Orphean
P. L. 3, 83. those *o.* two equalled with me
P. L. 3, 131. man falls deceived by the *o.* first
P. L. 3, 132. shall find grace the *o.* none
P. L. 3, 211. some *o.* able and as willing pay
P. L. 3, 442. for *o.* creature in this place living
P. L. 3, 450. or happiness in this or the *o.* life
P. L. 3, 566. seemed *o.* worlds, or *o.* worlds
P. L. 3, 725. which else as the *o.* hemisphere
P. L. 4, 61. some *o.* power as great might have
P. L. 4, 63. but *o.* powers as great fell not
P. L. 4, 84. with *o.* promises and *o.* vaunts
P. L. 4, 179. and that looked east on the *o.* side
P. L. 4, 360. creatures of *o.* mould earth-born
P. L. 4, 398. himself now one now *o.* as their
P. L. 4, 420. no *o.* service than to keep this one
P. L. 4, 431. over all *o.* creatures that possess
P. L. 4, 488. and thee claim my *o.* half
P. L. 4, 510. among our *o.* torments
P. L. 4, 582. if Spirit of *o.* sort so minded have
P. L. 4, 616. *o.* creatures all day long rove idle
P. L. 4, 621. while *o.* animals unactive range
P. L. 4, 683. sole or responsive each to *o.'s* note
P. L. 4, 703. *o.* creature here bird, beast, insect
P. L. 4, 736. and *o.* rites observing none
P. L. 4, 783. these *o.* wheel the north
P. L. 4, 985. on the *o.* side Satan alarmed
P. L. 5, 132. two *o.* precious drops that ready
P. L. 5, 177. and ye five *o.* wandering fires
P. L. 5, 259. not unconform to *o.* shining globes
P. L. 5, 361. native of heaven, for *o.* place none
P. L. 5, 534. and can no *o.* choose
P. L. 5, 538. on *o.* surety none
P. L. 5, 560. his *o.* half in the great zone
P. L. 5, 576. and things therein each to *o.* like
P. L. 5, 618. that day as *o.* solemn days
P. L. 5, 884. *o.* decrees against thee are gone
P. L. 6, 9. at the *o.* door obsequious darkness
P. L. 6, 354. meanwhile in *o.* sort in might though wondrous
P. L. 6, 376. *o.* sort in might though wondrous
P. L. 6, 413. on the *o.* part Satan with his
P. L. 6, 442. if *o.* hidden cause left them
P. L. 6, 807. the punishment to *o.* hand belongs

P. L. 6, 821. of *o.* excellence not emulous
P. L. 6, 823. nor *o.* strife with them do I
P. L. 7, 228. one foot he centred as the *o.* turned
P. L. 7, 364. hither as to their fountain *o.* stars
P. L. 7, 378. for *o.* light she needed none
P. L. 7, 444. and the *o.* whose gay train adorns
P. L. 7, 507. not prone and brute as *o.* creatures
P. L. 8, 123. *o.* stars by his attractive virtue
P. L. 8, 139. her *o.* part still luminous by his ray
P. L. 8, 148. and *o.* suns perhaps with their
P. L. 8, 169. of *o.* creatures as him pleases best
P. L. 8, 175. not of *o.* worlds what creatures
P. L. 8, 243. noise *o.* than the sound of dance
P. L. 8, 387. the one intense the *o.* still remiss
P. L. 8, 411. beneath what *o.* creatures are
P. L. 8, 450. thy fit help, thy *o.* self
P. L. 8, 480. and *o.* pleasures all abjure
P. L. 8, 546. given o'er *o.* creatures
P. L. 8, 581. such dear delight beyond all *o.*
P. L. 9, 94. in *o.* beasts observed
P. L. 9, 103. danced round by *o.* heavens
P. L. 9, 220. for while so near each *o.* thus
P. L. 9, 251. *o.* doubt possesses me lest harm
P. L. 9, 260. each to *o.* speedy aid might lend
P. L. 9, 368. the *o.* who can know
P. L. 9, 478. *o.* joy to me is lost
P. L. 9, 571. I was at first as *o.* beasts
P. L. 9, 592. all *o.* beasts that saw
P. L. 9, 813. and *o.* care perhaps may have
P. L. 9, 888. on the *o.* side Adam soon as he
P. L. 9, 1012. that false fruit far *o.* operation
P. L. 9, 1052. and each the *o.* viewing
P. L. 9, 1093. the parts of each from *o.*
P. L. 10, 128. to accuse my *o.* self the partner
P. L. 10, 235. why sit we here each *o.* viewing
P. L. 10, 237. thrives in *o.* worlds and happier
P. L. 10, 414. the *o.* way Satan went 'down
P. L. 10, 513. his legs entwining each *o.*
P. L. 10, 538. but *o.* sight instead
P. L. 10, 657. to the *o.* five their planetary
P. L. 10, 712. herb all leaving devoured each *o.*
P. L. 10, 787. or in some *o.* dismal place
P. L. 10, 861. *o.* echo late I taught
P. L. 10, 894. or find some *o.* way to generate
P. L. 10, 959. nor blame each *o.* blamed enough
P. L. 10, 862. and resound far *o.* song
P. L. 10, 961. lighten each *o.'s* burden in our
P. L. 11, 60. that fondly lost this *o.* served
P. L. 11, 171. far *o.* name deserving
P. L. 11, 274. flowers that never will in *o.* climate
P. L. 11, 284. how shall we breathe in *o.* air
P. L. 11, 431. the *o.* part sheep-walks and folds
P. L. 11, 443. the *o.'s* not for his was not sincere
P. L. 11, 458. and the *o.'s* faith approved
P. L. 11, 527. but is there yet no *o.* way besides
P. L. 11, 564. in *o.* part stood one who at the
P. L. 11, 660. in *o.* part the sceptred heralds
P. L. 12, 57. each to *o.* calls not understood
P. L. 12, 337. whose foul idolatries and *o.* faults
P. L. 12, 626. and from the *o.* hill to their fixed
P. R. 1, 100. I when no *o.* durst, sole undertook
P. R. 1, 336. will bring me hence no *o.* guide
P. R. 1, 338. what *o.* way I see not for we here
P. R. 1, 348. for I discern thee *o.* than thou
P. R. 1, 427. the *o.* service was thy chosen task
P. R. 2, 71. above the lot of *o.* women
P. R. 2, 132. far *o.* labour to be undergone
P. R. 2, 254. satisfy that need some *o.* way
P. R. 2, 406. by hunger that each *o.* creature
P. R. 2, 478. that *o.* o'er the body only reigns
P. R. 3, 53. but as one leads the *o.*
P. R. 3, 84. one is the son of Jove, of Mars the *o.*
P. R. 3, 256. the one winding, the *o.* straight
P. R. 3, 419. their *o.* worse than heathenish
P. R. 4, 44. the city which thou seest no *o.*
P. R. 4, 159. on the *o.* side know also thou
P. R. 4, 184. *o.* donation none thou canst
P. R. 4, 290. no *o.* doctrine needs
P. R. 4, 486. *o.* harm those terrors which thou
S. A. 105. from worst of *o.* evils, pains and wrongs
S. A. 208. this with the *o.* should at least have

S. A. 246. I on the *o.* side used no ambition
S. A. 387. in this *o.* was there found more faith
S. A. 592. nor the *o.* light of life continue long
S. A. 723. and now at nearer view no *o.* certain
S. A. 768. but that on the *o.* side if it be weighed
S. A. 875. taught thee far *o.* reasonings
S. A. 916. where *o.* senses want not their delights
S. A. 974. on both his wings one black the *o.* white
S. A. 1087. each *o.'s* force in camp or listed field
S. A. 1096. forced thee soon with *o.* arms
S. A. 1236. this insolence *o.* kind of answer fits
S. A. 1252. some way or *o.* yet farther to afflict
S. A. 1302. I descry this way some *o.* tending
S. A. 1526. from *o.* hands we need not much to fear
S. A. 1609. the *o.* side was open where the throng
S. A. 1643. now of my own accord such *o.* trial
C. 72. all *o.* parts remaining as they were
C. 100. pacing toward the *o.* goal
C. 612. far *o.* arms and *o.* weapons must
C. 684. with that which you received on *o.* terms
C. 821. some *o.* means I have which may be used
C. 941. with some *o.* new device
C. 961. *o.* trippings to be trod of lighter toes
L. 116. of *o.* care they little reckoning make
L. 174. where *o.* groves and *o.* streams along
L'A. 85. of herbs and *o.* country messes
S. 21, 11. for *o.* things mild heaven a time ordains
P. 25. and former sufferings *o.* where are found
D. F. I. 55. or any *o.* of that heavenly brood
**Others.**—P. L. 1, 216. while he sought evil to *o.*
P. L. 2, 469. lest from his resolution raised *o.*
P. L. 2, 539. with vast Typhœan rage
P. L. 2, 546. *o.* more mild retreated in a silent
P. L. 2, 557. *o.* apart sat on a hill retired
P. L. 3, 469. *o.* came single
P. L. 4, 249. *o.* whose fruit burnished with
P. L. 4, 350. *o.* on the grass couched
P. L. 4, 880. and disturbed the charge of *o.*
P. L. 5, 241. fall of *o.* from like state of bliss
P. L. 6, 337. while *o.* bore him on their shields
P. L. 6, 528. *o.* from the dawning hills looked
P. L. 7, 437. *o.* on silver lakes and rivers bathed
P. L. 7, 442. *o.* on ground walked firm
P. L. 9, 127. but *o.* to make
P. L. 9, 308. nor think superfluous *o.*' aid
P. L. 9, 805. though *o.* envy what they cannot
P. L. 10, 982. miserable it is to be to *o.* cause
P. L. 11, 558. *o.* whence the sound
P. L. 11, 655. *o.* to a city strong lay siege
P. L. 11, 657. *o.* from the wall defend
P. L. 12, 37. though of rebellion *o.* he accuse
P. R. 1, 273. I as all *o.* to his baptism came
P. R. 2, 8. with *o.* though in holy writ
P. R. 2, 61. saw *o.* returned from baptism
P. R. 2, 174. thou all *o.* by thyself
P. R. 2, 306. *o.* of some note as story tells
P. R. 2, 400. of these things *o.* quickly will
P. R. 4, 297. *o.* in virtue placed felicity
S. A. 78. in power of *o.* never in my own
S. A. 815. be not unlike all *o.* not austere
S. A. 1191. to *o.* did no violence nor spoil
S. A. 1464. *o.* more moderate seeming but their
L. 67. were it not better done as *o.* use
S. 21, 4. which *o.* at their bar so often wrench
V. Ex. 81. from *o.* he shall stand in need
**Otherwise.**—P. L. 8, 529. but here far *o.*
P. L. 6, 398. far *o.* the inviolable saints
P. L. 9, 984. I feel far *o.* the event
P. R. 4, 212. and thou thyself seem'st *o.*
S. A. 590. all *o.* to me my thoughts portend
C. 318. if *o.* I can conduct you lady to a low
**Ought.**—P. L. 8, 74. scanned by them who *o.*
P. L. 10, 12. for still they knew and *o.* to have
P. R. 4, 288. am I short of knowing what I *o.*
**Oughtst.**—S. A. 329. how thou *o.* to receive
**Ounce.**—P. L. 7, 466. the *o.*, the libbard
C. 71. or *o.* or tiger, hog, or bearded goat
**Ounces.**—P. L. 4, 344. bears, tigers, *o.*, pards
**Ours.**—P. L. 4, 629. more hands than *o.* to lop
P. L. 5, 489. the latter most is *o.*
P. L. 5, 629. we *o.* for change delectable not

P. L. 5, 726. to erect his throne equal to *o.*
P. L. 6, 200. *o.* joy filled and shout
P. L. 10, 1040. and we instead shall double *o.*
**Ourselves.**—P. L. 2, 225. we procure not to *o.*
P. L. 2, 253. seek our own good from *o.*
P. L. 6, 467. or arm *o.* with like defence
P. L. 8, 186. we *o.* seek them with wandering
P. L. 9, 654. we live law to *o.*
P. L. 10, 999. then both *o.* and seed at once
P. L. 10, 1002. our own hands his office on *o.*
P. L. 10, 1037. be lost by death brought on *o.*
P. L. 10, 1042. against *o.* and wilful barrenness
**Ouse.**—V. Ex. 92. of utmost Tweed or *O.*
**Outbrake.**—H. 159. smouldering clouds *o.*
**Outbreathed.**—P. R. 2, 29. and plaints *o.*
**Outcast.**—P. L. 2, 694. *o.* from God
P. L. 4, 106. behold instead of us *o.* exiled
P. R. 2, 309. with her son *o.* Nebaioth
**Outcries.**—S. A. 1124. and raise such *o.* on thy
**Outcry.**—P. L. 2, 726. with hideous *o.*
P. L. 2, 737. so strange thy *o.* and thy words
S. A. 1517. that *o.* from slaughter of one foe
**Outdo.**—P. L. 3, 298. so heavenly love shall *o.*
**Out-done.**—P. L. 1, 696. easily *o.-d.* by spirits
**Out-flew.**—P. L. 1, 663. *o.-f.* millions
**Outgo.**—V. Ex. 79. he shall *o.* them
**Outgrew.**—P. L. 9, 202. much their work *o.*
**Outlandish.**—P. R. 4, 125. *o.* flatteries
**Out-lasted.**—D. F. I. 3. if thou hadst *o.-l* bleak
**Outlaw's.**—C. 399. treasure by an *o.* den
**Outlive.**—P. L. 11, 538. then thou must *o.*
**Out-living.**—P. 7. and long *o.-l.* night
**Out-poured.**—P. R. 3, 311. the city gates *o.-p.*
S. A. 544. the dancing ruby sparkling *o.-p.*
**Outmost.**—P. L. 2, 1039. as from her *o.* works
**Outrage.**—P. L. 1, 500. injury and *o.*
P. L. 10, 707. thus began *o.* from lifeless things
**Outrageous.**—P. L. 2, 435. fire *o.* to devour
P. L. 6, 587. embowelled with *o* noise the air
P. L. 7, 212. *o.* as a sea dark wasteful wild
P. L. 10, 232. belching *o.* flame far into Chaos
**Outshine.**—P. L. 1, 86. brightness didst *o.*
**Outshone.**—P. L. 2, 2. which far *o.* the wealth
**Outside.**—P. L. 3, 74. the bare *o.* of this world
P. L. 8, 568. what transports thee so? an *o.*
P. L. 8, 596. neither her *o.* formed so fair
P. L. 10, 317. the *o.* bare of this round world
P. R. 4, 58. thou mayst behold *o.* and inside
**Outspread.**—P. L. 1, 20. mighty wings *o.*
P. L. 5, 649. all this globous earth in plain *o.*
P. L. 7, 235. brooding wings the spirit God *o.*
**Outstretched.**—P. L. 5, 88. the earth *o.*
P. L. 10, 851. on the ground *o.* he lay
P. R. 3, 254. a spacious plain *o.* in circuit
U. C. II. 17. on his swooning bed *o.*
**Outwatch.**—Il P. 87. I may oft *o.* the Bear
**Outward.**—P. L. 1, 97. changed in *o.* lustre
P. L. 4, 120. smoothed with *o.* calm
P. L. 8, 221. inward and *o.* both his image
P. L. 8, 538. in *o.* show elaborate of inward less
P. L. 8, 543. in *o.* also her resembling less
P. L. 8, 642. perfect within no *o.* aid require
P. L. 9, 312. stronger if need were *o.* strength
P. L. 9, 348. secure from *o.* force
P. L. 10, 220. nor he their *o.* only with the
P. L. 12, 95. undeservedly enthral *o.* freedom
P. L. 12, 100. deprives them of their *o.* liberty
P. L. 12, 534. will deem in *o.* rites and specious
P. R. 4, 145. of inward slaves make *o.* free
S. A. 160. shut up from *o.* light to incorporate
S. A. 1025. is it for that such *o.* ornament
S. A. 1368. *o.* acts defile not
S. A. 1369. *o.* force constrains
C. 460. begin to cast a beam on the *o.* shape
S. 22, 2. to *o.* view of blemish or of spot
**Outworn.**—S. A. 580. with age *o.*
**Over-arched.**—P. L. 1, 304. high *o.-a.* embower
P. L. 9, 1107. high *o.-a.* and echoing walks
**Overawed.**—P. L. 9, 460. *o.* his malice
**Overbuilt.**—P. L. 10, 416. Chaos *o.*
**Overcame.**—P. R. 1, 148. perseverance *o.*

P. R. 3, 325. and *o.* by flight
**Overcome.**—P. L. 1, 109. else not to be *o.*
P. L. 1, 189. how *o.* this dire calamity
P. L. 1, 649. who overcomes by force hath *o.*
P. L. 2, 215. our purer essence then will *o.*
P. L. 4, 857. the fiend replied not *o.* with rage
P. L. 6, 126. so most reason is that reason *o.*
P. L. 9, 313. shame to be *o.* or over-reached
P. L. 9, 999. not deceived but fondly *o.*
P. L. 11, 374. arming to *o.* by suffering
P. L. 11, 691. *o.* in battle and subdue nations
P. L. 12, 267. till Israel *o.* so call the third
P. L. 12, 390. nor so is *o.* Satan
S. A. 365. ensnared, assaulted, *o.*, led bound
**Overcomes.**—P. L. 1, 648. who *o.* by force
**Overcoming.**—P. L. 12, 566. good still *o.* evil
**Over-exquisite.**—C. 359. brother be not *o.-e.*
**Over-fond.**—P. L. 11, 289. thy heart thus *o.-f.*
**Overgrown.**—P. L. 4, 136. with thicket *o.*
P. L. 4, 627. walk at noon with branches *o.*
P. L. 9, 210. lop *o.* or prune, or prop, or bind
**Overgrowth.**—P. L. 12, 166. stop their *o.*
**Over-head.**—P. L. 1, 784. *o.-h.* the moon sits
P. L. 4, 137. and *o.-h.* up grew insuperable
P. L. 9, 1038. thick *o.-h.* with verdant roof
**Overheard.**—P. L. 9, 276. parting angel *o.*
**Overhung.**—P. L. 4, 547. cliff that *o.*
**Overjoyed.**—P. L. 5, 67. but he thus *o.*
P. L. 8, 490. I *o.*, could not forbear aloud
**Over-just.**—S. A. 514. *o.-j.* and self-displeased
**Over-laboured.**—S. A. 1327. and *o.-l.* at their
**Overlaid.**—P. L. 1, 714. and Doric pillars *o.*
P. L. 12, 250. of cedar *o.* with gold therein
**Overlay.**—P. L. 10, 370. and *o.* with this
P. R. 3, 333. or *o.* with bridges rivers proud
**Overleaped.**—P. L. 4, 181. high *o.*
**Overlive.**—P. L. 10, 773. why do I *o.*?
**Overloved.**—P. L. 10, 1019. pleasure *o.*
**Over-match.**—P. R. 4, 7. this far his *o.-m.*
**Over-matched.**—P. R. 2, 146. now be *o.-m.*
**Overmuch.**—P. L. 8, 565. by attributing *o.*
P. L. 9, 1178. I also erred in *o.* admiring
S. A. 213. deject not then so *o.* thyself
**Over-multitude.**—C. 731. herds would *o.-m.*
**Overpassed.**—P. R. 2, 198. and slightly *o.*
**Overplied.**—S. 22, 10. to have lost them *o.*
**Over-potent.**—S. A. 427. or *o.-p.* charms
**Overpower.**—P. L. 2, 237. supreme we *o.*
**Overpowered.**—P. L. 6, 419. not to be *o.*
P. L. 8, 453. my earthly by his heavenly *o.*
S. A. 880. not out of levity but *o.* by request
**Overpraising.**—P. L. 9, 615. serpent, thy *o.*
**Over-reach.**—P. L. 10, 879. over-weening too *o.-r.*
**Over-reached.**—P. L. 9, 313. overcome or *o.-r.*
P. R. 4, 11. *o.-r.* where least he thought
**Over-ripe.**—P. R. 3, 31. years are ripe and *o.-r.*
**Over-ruled.**—P. L. 3, 114. *o.-r.* their will
P. L. 5, 527. not *o.-r.* by fate inextricable
P. L. 6, 228. stronghold of heaven high *o.-r.*
**Overrun.**—P. R. 3, 72. to *o.* large countries
**Overshadow.**—P. L. 12, 187. must *o.* all
**Overshadowing.**—P. L. 7, 165. my *o.* Spirit
P. R. 4, 148. spreading and *o.* all the earth
**Overspread.**—P. L. 6, 670. with ruin *o.*
**Over-strong.**—S. A. 1590. O soul's *o.-s.* against
**Over-sure.**—P. R. 2, 142. to persuasion *o.-s.*
**Overtake.**—T. 13. and joy shall *o.* us as a flood
**Overtask.**—C. 309. *o.* the best land-pilot's art
**Overthrew.**—P. L. 4, 905. whom folly *o.*
P. L. 6, 372. of Ramiel scorched and blasted *o.*
**Overthrow.**—P. L. 1, 135. that with sad *o.*
P. L. 6, 601. repeated and indecent *o.* doubled
P. R. 1, 115. so well had thrived in Adam's *o.*
**Overthrown.**—P. L. 2, 992. though *o.*
P. L. 6, 856. the *o.* he raised and as a herd
S. A. 463. Dagon hath presumed me *o.* to enter
S. A. 1698. depressed and *o.* as seemed
U. C. 1, 4. he's here stuck in a slough and *o.*
**Over-tired.**—S. A. 1632. as *o.-t.* to let him lean
**Overtook.**—P. L. 2, 792. me *o.*
**Overtrusting.**—P. L. 9, 1183. in women *o.*

**Overture.**—P. L. 6, 562. if they like our *o.*
**Overturned.**—P. L. 6, 390. charioteer lay *o.*
**Overturns.**—P. L. 6, 463. and excessive *o.*
S. A. 542. which many a famous warrior *o.*
**Overwatched.**—S. A. 405. *o.* and wearied out
**Overween.**—S. 9, 6. they that *o.*
**Overweening.**—P. L. 10, 878. *o.* to over-reach
P. R. 1, 147. he might have learnt less *o.*
**Overwhelm.**—P. L. 12, 214. return and *o.*
**Overwhelmed.**—P. L. 10, 159. shame nigh *o.*
P. L. 11, 748. all dwellings else flood *o.*
S. A. 1559. all in a moment *o.* and fallen
**Over-woody.**—P. L. 5, 213. fruit-trees *o.-w.*
**Owe.**—P. L. 2, 856. what *o.* I to his commands
P. L. 3, 181. and to me *o.* all his deliverance
P. L. 4, 53. still paying still to *o.*
P. L. 4, 444. to him indeed all praises *o.*
P. L. 5, 520. that thou art happy *o.* to God
P. L. 5, 521. that thou continuest such *o.* to
P. L. 6, 468. for deliverance what we *o.*
P. L. 7, 76. to the infinitely Good we *o.*
P. L. 9, 807. experience next to thine I *o.*
P. L. 9, 1141. to approve the faith they *o.*
P. R. 2, 325. *o.* not all creatures by just right
S. A. 1405. such as *o.* them absolute subjection
S. 17, 12. bounds of either sword to thee we *o.*
**Owes.**—P. L. 4, 56. by owing *o.* not
**Owing.**—P. L. 4, 56. a grateful mind by *o.*
**Owls.**—S. 12, 4. of *o.* and cuckoos, asses, apes
**Own.**—P. L. 1, 188. our *o.* loss how repair
P. L. 1, 213. at large to his *o.* dark designs
P. L. 1, 240. and their *o.* recovered strength
P. L. 1, 254. the mind is its *o.* place
P. L. 1, 460. lopped off in his *o.* temple
P. L. 1, 513. his *o.* and Rhea's son
P. L. 1, 643. his might we know & know our *o.*
P. L. 1, 793. and in their *o.* dimensions
P. L. 2, 70. his *o.* invented torments
P. L. 2, 231. if war be best or to regain our *o.*
P. L. 2, 253. seek our *o.* good from ourselves
P. L. 2, 360. sit secure in his *o.* strength
P. L. 2, 366. or possess all as our *o.* and drive
P. L. 2, 370. repenting hand abolish his *o.* works
P. L. 2, 422. read his *o.* dismay
P. L. 2, 482. general safety he despised his *o.*
P. L. 2, 549. their *o.* heroic deeds
P. L. 2, 782. thine *o.* begotten
P. L. 2, 863. mine *o.* brood that on my bowels
P. L. 3, 59. his *o.* works and their works
P. L. 3, 86. upon his *o.* rebellious head
P. L. 3, 117. themselves decreed their *o.* revolt
P. L. 3, 129. by their *o.* suggestion fell
P. L. 3, 153. though joined with his *o.* folly
P. L. 3, 220. upon his *o.* head draw deadly
P. L. 3, 292. their *o.* both righteous and
P. L. 3, 297. ransomed with his *o.* dear life
L. L. 3, 304. lessen or degrade thine *o.*
P. L. 4, 513. have gained from their *o.* mouths
P. L. 4, 813. but returns of force to its *o.*
P. L. 4, 819. so started up in his *o.* shape
P. L. 4, 1007. neither our *o.* but given
P. L. 5, 236. left to his *o.* free will
P. L. 5, 317. afford our givers their *o.* gifts
P. L. 5, 352. with his *o.* complete perfections
P. L. 5, 457. excellence he saw transcend his *o.*
P. L. 5, 626. that God's *o.* ear listens
P. L. 5, 845. honour to him done returns our *o.*
P. L. 5, 861. self-begot, self-raised by our *o.*
P. L. 5, 864. our puissance is our *o.*
P. L. 5, 864. our *o.* right hand shall teach us
P. L. 6, 113. and thus his *o.* undaunted heart
P. L. 6, 773. but by his *o.* first seen
P. L. 7, 121. nor let thine *o.* inventions hope
P. L. 7, 526. in his *o.* image he created thee
P. L. 8, 103. may know the dwells not in his *o.*
P. L. 8, 124. his attractive virtue and their *o.*
P. L. 8, 549. so well to know her *o.*
P. L. 8, 641. in thine *o.* arbitrement it lies
P. L. 9, 254. and of his *o.* despairing
P. L. 9, 379. chiefly by what thy *o.* reasoning

P. L. 9, 464. abstracted stood from his *o*. evil
P. L. 9, 956. bond of nature draw me to my *o*.
P. L. 9, 957. my *o*. in thee for what thou art
P. L. 10, 344. thence gathered his *o*. doom
P. L. 10, 355. which thou view'st as thine *o*.
P. L. 10, 547. cast on themselves from their *o*.
P. L. 10, 727. and would bear my *o*. deservings
P. L. 10, 738. so besides mine *o*. that bide upon
P. L. 10. 766. God made thee ot choice his *o*.
P. L. 10, 808. not the extent of their *o*. sphere
P. L. 10, 831. lead me still but to my *o*.
P. L. 10, 950. bear thine *o*. first
P. L. 10, 983. our *o*. begotten and of our loins
P. L. 10, 1002. with our *o*. hands
P. L. 10, 1080. to evils which our *o*. misdeeds
P. L. 11, 28. than those which his *o*. hand
P. L. 11, 521. not God's likeness but their *o*.
P. L. 11, 572. from which he formed first his *o*.
P. L. 12, 110. to leave them to their *o*. polluted
P. L. 12, 119. to worship their *o*. work in wood
P. L. 12, 410. merits to save them not their *o*.
P. L. 12, 414. nailed to the cross by his *o*. nation
P. L. 12, 486. he to his *o*. a comforter will send
P. L. 12, 510. to their *o*. vile advantages shall
P. L. 12, 528. by faith to stand, their *o*. faith
P. L. 12, 539. under her *o*. weight groaning
P. R. 1, 213. improve my knowledge or their *o*.
P. R. 2, 295. nature's *o*. work it seemed
P. R. 2, 381. I receive by gift what of my *o*.
P. R. 3, 134. who of his *o*. hath nothing
P. R. 3, 143. who advance his glory not their *o*.
P. R. 3, 147. stood struck with guilt of his *o*.
P. R. 3, 363. these thou must make sure thy *o*.
P. R. 3, 415. were they who wrought their *o*.
P. R. 4, 9. to cope with or his *o*.
P. R. 4, 191. to me my *o*.
P. R. 4, 235. error by his *o*. arms is best
P. R. 4, 260. Phœbus challenged for his *o*.
P. R. 4, 340. vices of their deities and their *o*.
S. A. 45. fulfilled but through mine *o*. default

S. A. 78. in power of others never in my *o*.
S. A. 188. I learn now of my *o*. experience
S. A. 217. of thine *o*. tribe fairer or as fair
S. A. 218. at least of thy *o*. nation and as noble
S. A. 301. as to his *o*. edicts found contradicting
S. A. 304. till by their *o*. perplexities involved
S. A. 308. and tie him to his *o*. prescript
S. A. 314. for with his *o*. laws he can dispense
S. A. 503. but act not in thy *o*. affliction son
S. A. 844. though to thy *o*. condemning
S. A. 887. nor under their protection but my *o*.
S. A. 899. the contradiction of their *o*. deity
S. A. 970. nor too much disapprove my *o*.
S. A. 996. I leave him to his lot and like my *o*.
S. A. 1267. draw their *o*. ruin who attempt the
S. A. 1289. making them each his *o*. deliverer
S. A. 1584. by his *o*. hands
S. A. 1589. upon their heads and on his *o*. he
S. A. 1643. now of my *o*. accord such other
S. A. 1681. unweetingly importuned their *o*.
S. A. 1684. as their *o*. ruin on themselves to
C. 374. virtue would by her *o*. radiant light
C. 381. he that has light within his *o*. clear
C. 385. himself is his *o*. dungeon
C. 419. if heaven gave it may be termed her *o*.
C. 718. *o*. loins she hutched the all-worshipped
C. 728. quite surcharged with her *o*. weight
C. 969. three fair branches of your *o*.
**Own(verb).**—M.W.6.more than she could *o*.from
**Owned.**—P. R. 2, 85. Son *o*. from heaven by his
Il·P. 113. that *o*. the virtuous ring and glass
**Owners.**—S. A. 1261. small profit daily to my *o*.
**Owns.**—S. A. 1157. thee he regards not, *o*. not
**Ox.**—P. L. 1, 486. his maker to the grazed *o*.
P. L. 8, 396. nor with the *o*. the ape
C.291.two such I saw what time the laboured *o*.
**Oxen.**—P. L. 11, 389. fair *o*. and fair kine
**Oxus.**—P. L. 11, 389. Samarchand by *O*.

# P.

**Pace.**—P. L. 6, 551. with heavy *p*. the foe
P. L. 8, 164. with inoffensive *p*. that spinning
P. L. 10, 589. her death close following *p*. for *p*.
P. L. 10, 859. mends not her slowest *p*.
S. A. 110. with joint *p*.I hear the tread of many
C. 145. I feel the different *p*. of some chaste
C. 870. and Tethys' grave majestic *p*.
T.3. whose speed is but the heavy plummet's *p*.
**Paces.**—P. L. 6, 193. ten *p*. huge
P. L. 8, 165. while she *p*. even and bears thee
**Pacific.**—P. L. 11, 860. he brings *p*. sign
**Pacing.**—C. 100. *p*. toward the other goal
**Packed.**—V. Ex. 12. I have thither *p*. the worst
**Packing.**—F. of C. 14. your plots and *p*.
**Pact.**—P. R. 4, 191. on such abhorred *p*.
**Padan-Aram.**—P. L. 3, 513. fled to *P.-A.*
**Pageantry.**—L'A. 128. mask and antique *p*.
**Paid.**—P. L. 1, 441. virgins *p*. their vows
P. L. 2, 248. eternity so spent in worship *p*.
P. L. 3, 107. from such obedience *p*.
P. L. 3, 246. yet that debt *p*. thou wilt not
P. L. 5, 145. their orisons each morning duly *p*.
P. L. 11, 452. is pity thus and pure devotion *p*.
P. L. 12, 293. blood more precious must be *p*.
P. L. 12, 424. thy ramson *p*.
S. A. 432. bitterly hast thou *p*. and still art
S. A. 1477. shall willingly be *p*. and numbered
S. A. 1573. hath *p*. his ramsom now and full
C.776.would be better thanked his praise due *p*.
**Pain.**—P. L. 1, 55. lost happiness and lasting *p*.
P. L. 1, 125. though in *p*. vaunting aloud
P. L. 1, 558. and *p*. from mortal or immortal
P. L. 1, 608. for ever now to have their lot in *p*.
P. L. 2, 30. to greatest share of endless *p*.
P.L.2,34. whose portion is so small of present *p*.

P. L. 2, 88. where *p*. of unextinguishable fire
P. L. 2, 147. who would lose though full of *p*.
P. L. 2, 207. exile or ignominy, or bonds, or *p*.
P. L. 2, 219. and void of *p*.
P. L. 2, 261. work ease out of *p*.
P. L. 2, 278. needs remove the sensible of *p*.
P. L. 2, 461. or deceive or slack the *p*. of this
P. L. 2, 544. and tore through *p*.
P. L. 2, 567. a pleasing sorcery could charm *p*.
P. L. 2, 586. both joy and grief pleasure and *p*.
P. L. 2, 608. sweet forgetfulness all *p*. and woe
P. L. 2, 695. waste eternal days in woe and *p*.
P. L. 2, 752. all on a sudden miserable *p*.
P. L. 2, 783. that with fear and *p*. distorted
P. L. 2, 823. this dark and dismal house of *p*.
P. L. 2, 861. here in perpetual agony and *p*.
P. L. 4, 97. ease would recant vows made in *p*.
P. L. 4, 271. which cost Ceres all that *p*.
P. L. 4, 511. still unfulfilled with *p*. of longing
P. L. 4, 888. lives there who loves his *p*.
P. L. 4, 892. farthest from *p*. where thou
P. L. 4, 910. so wise he judges it to fly from *p*.
P. L. 4, 915. that no *p*. can equal anger
P. L. 4, 918. is *p*. to them less, *p*. less to be fled
P. L. 4, 921. the first in flight from *p*.
P. L. 4, 925. I less endure or shrink from *p*.
P. L. 4, 948. pretending first wise to fly *p*.
P. L. 6, 280. precipitate thee with augmented *p*.
P. L. 6, 327. then Satan first knew *p*.
P. L. 6, 362. shattered arms and uncouth *p*.
P. L. 6, 394. with fear surprised and sense of *p*.
P. L. 6, 397. not liable to fear, or flight, or *p*.
P. L. 6, 431. disadvantage we endured and *p*.
P. L. 6, 454. against unequal arms to fight in *p*.
P. L. 6, 457. quelled with *p*. which all subdues

P. L. 6, 462. p. is perfect misery
P. L. 6, 657. wrought them p. implacable
P. L. 6, 877. the house of woe and p.
P. L. 9, 283. not capable of death or p.
P. L. 9, 487. hell debased and p. enfeebled me
P. L. 9, 694. whom the p. of death denounced
P. L. 9, 861. the p. of absence
P. L. 10, 470. with what p. voyaged the unreal
P. L. 10, 501. bruise or much more grievous p.
P. L. 10, 775. lengthened out to deathless p.
P. L. 10, 964. to augment our p.
P. L. 10, 1025. will not exempt us from the p.
P. L. 11, 601. hate and death or p. much worse
P. L. 12, 384. bruise expect with mortal p.
P. R. 1, 401. fellowship in p. divides not smart
P. R. 4, 305. contemning all wealth, pleasure p.
S.A.617.my griefs not only p. me as a lingering
C. 687. refreshment after toil, ease after p.
**Pained.**—P. L. 6, 404. unobnoxious to be p.
**Painful.**—P. L. 1, 562. charmed their p. steps
P. L. 3, 452. fruit of p. superstition and blind
P. L. 11, 528. besides these p. passages
S. A. 699. p. diseases and deformed in crude old
**Pains.**—P. L. 1, 147. suffer and support our p.
P. L. 1, 336. or the fierce p. not feel
P. L. 10, 1051. p. only in child-bearing
P. L. 11, 511. be debased under inhuman p.
P. R. 2, 401. whose p. have earned the far-fet
P. R. 4, 479. of dangers and adversities, and p.
S.A.105.from worst of other evils p.and wrongs
S. A. 485. by p. and slaveries worse than death
S. A. 501. to their abyss and horrid p. confined
S. A. 576. hasten the welcome end of all my p.
S. A. 615. with answerable p. but more intense
**Paint.**—P. L. 5, 187. till the sun p. your fleecy
**Painted.**—P. L. 7, 434. spread their p. wings
P. R. 4, 253. Lyceum there and p. Stoa next
**Paints.**—P. L. 5, 24. how nature p. her colours
**Pair.**—P. L. 4, 321. they passed the loveliest p.
P. L. 4, 336. ah gentle p. ye little think how
P. L. 4, 534. live while we may, yet happy p.
P. L. 4, 774. blest p. and O yet happiest if ye
P. L. 5, 227. disturbed this night the human p.
P. L. 5, 278. the p. that clad each shoulder
P. L. 5, 280. the middle p. girt like a starry
P. L. 8, 605. harmony to behold in wedded p.
P. L. 9, 197. forth came the human p.
P. L. 10, 342. where the hapless p. sat in
P. L. 10, 585. in Paradise the hellish p.
P. L. 11, 10. than when the ancient p. in fables
P. L. 11, 105. remorse drive out the sinful p.
C. 236. canst thou not tell me of a gentle p.
S.M.1.blest p. of Sirens pledges of Heaven's joy
**Paired.**—S. A. 208. should at least have p.
**Pairs.**—P. L. 7, 459. among the trees in p.
P. L. 8, 58. O when meet now such p. in love
P. L. 8, 394. fitly them in p. thou hast combined
P. L. 11, 735. came sevens and p. and entered
**Palace.**—P. L. 3, 505. as of a kingly p. gate
P. L. 5, 760. the p. of great Lucifer
P. L. 7, 363. great p. now of light
P. L. 10, 308. from Susa his Memnonian p.
P. L. 12, 177. lice and flies must all his p. fill
P. R. 2, 300. as one in city, or court, or p. bred
P. R. 4, 51. the imperial p. compass huge
C. 14. that opes the p. of eternity
H. 148. will open wide the gates of her high p.
**Palaces.**—P. L. 1, 497. in courts and p.
P. L. 11, 750. and in their p. where luxury
P. R. 4, 35. on seven small hills with p.
**Palate.**—P. R. 4, 50. and there Mount P.
**Palatine.**—P. R. 4, 50. and there Mount P.
**Pale.**—P. L. 1, 183. casts p. and dreadful
P. L. 1, 786. to the earth wheels her p. course
P. L. 2, 616. with shuddering horror p.
P. L. 3, 732. and in her p. dominion checks
P. L. 4, 115. thrice changed with p.
P. L. 6, 393. or with p. fear surprised
P. L. 9, 894. speechless he stood and p. till thus
P. L. 10, 590. not mounted yet on his p. horse
P. L. 10, 1009. as dyed her cheeks with p.

P. L. 11. 446. deadly p. groaned out his soul
C. 333. stoop thy p. visage though an amber
L. 143. the tufted crow-toe and p. jessamine
Il P. 121, thus night oft see me in thy p. career
Il P. 156. to walk the studious cloisters p.
S. 23, 4. rescued from death by force though p.
H. 185. edged with poplar p.
H. 232. the flocking shadows p.
M. M.4. the yellow cowslip and the p. primrose
**Pale-eyed.**—H. 180. inspires the p.-e. priest
**Pales.**—P. L. 9, 393. to P or Pomona
**Palestine.**—P. L. 1, 80. after known in P.
P. L. 1, 465. dreaded through the coast of P.
S. A.144. thousand foreskins fell the flower of P.
S. A.1099. glory of prowess been recovered to P.
H. 199. with that twice-battered god of P.
**Pall.**—Il P. 98. in sceptred p. come sweeping by
**Pallet.**—C. 318. lark from her thatched p. rouse
**Palm.**—P. L. 4, 139. fir and branching p.
P. L. 6, 885. shaded with branching p.
P. L. 9, 435. stateliest covert cedar pine or p.
S. A.1735. of laurel ever green and branching p.
**Palmer's.**—C. 189. like a sad votarist in p. weed
**Palms.**—P. R. 2, 21. in Jericho the city of p.
C. 918. I touch with chaste p. moist and cold
S.M.14. those spirits just that wear victorious p.
**Palm-tree.**—P. L. 8, 212. than fruits of p.-t.
**Palmy.**—P. L. 4, 254. p. hillock or the flowery
**Palpable.**—P. L. 2, 406. through the p. obscure
P. L. 12, 188. p. darkness
**Pampered.**—P. L. 5, 214. their p. boughs
**Pan.**—P. L. 4, 266. while universal P. knit
P. L. 4, 707. P. or Sylvanus never slept
P. R. 2, 190. Apollo, Neptune, Jupiter or P.
C. 176. they praise the bounteous P.
C. 268. dwell'st here with P. or Sylvan
A. 106. though Syrinx your P.'s mistress were
H. 89. the mighty P. was kindly come to live
**Pandemonium.**—P. L. 1, 756. beheld at P.
P. L. 10, 424. P. city and proud seat of Lucifer
**Pandora.**—P. L. 4, 714. more lovely than P.
**Paneas.**—P. L. 3, 535. from P. the fount
**Pangs.**—P. L. 2, 703. and p. unfelt before
P. L. 9, 1001. from her entrails as again in p.
P. L. 11, 484. intestine stone and ulcer colic p.
S. A. 660. with the afflicted in his p.
Cir. 27. but O! ere long huge p. and strong
M. W. 68. through p. fled to felicity
**Panim.**—P. L. 1, 765. the best of P. chivalry
**Panope.**—L. 99. sleek P. with all her sisters
**Panoply.**—P. L. 6, 527. of golden p. refulgent
P. L. 6, 760. he in celestial p. all armed
**Pansies.**—P. L. 9, 1040. p. and violets
C. 851. of p. pinks and gaudy daffodils
**Pansy.**—L.144.violets and the p.freaked with jet
**Paquin.**—P. L. 11, 390. to P. of Sinæan kings
**Parables.**—S. A. 500. that Gentiles in their p.
**Parade.**—P. L. 4, 780. watches in warlike p.
**Paradise.**—P. L. 3, 354. which once in p.
P. L. 3, 478. and they who to be sure of p.
P. L. 3, 496. since called the p. of fools
P. L. 3, 527. just o'er the blissful seat of p.
P. L. 3, 632. to p. the happy seat of man
P. L. 3, 733. that spot to which I point is p.
P. L. 4, 132. where delicious p. now nearer
P. L. 4, 143. the verdurous wall of p. upsprung
P. L. 4, 208. blissful p. of God the garden was
P. L. 4, 241. and fed flowers worthy of p.
P. L. 4, 274. might with this p. of Eden strive
P. L. 4, 282. this by some supposed true p.
P. L. 4, 379. may not please like this fair p.
P. L. 4, 422. of all the trees in p. that bear
P. L. 4, 542. against the eastern gate of p.
P. L. 4, 752. sole propriety in p.
P. L. 4, 991. nor only p. in this commotion
P. L. 5, 143. of p. and Eden's happy plains
P. L. 5, 226. hath raised in p.
P. L. 5, 275. on the eastern cliff of p.
P. L. 5, 446. O innocence deserving p.
P. L. 7, 45. the like befall in p. to Adam
P. L. 8, 171. gives to thee this p.

P. L. 8, 319. this *p*. I give thee count it thine
P. L. 9, 71. where Tigris at the foot of *p*.
P. L. 9, 406. thou never from that hour in *p*.
P. L. 9, 476. nor hope of *p*. for hell
P. L. 9, 619. the trees of God that grow in *p*.
P. L. 9, 796. precious of all trees in *p*.
P. L. 10, 2. despiteful act of Satan done in *p*.
P. L. 10, 17. up into heaven from *p*. in haste
P. L. 10, 326. to *p*. first tending
P. L. 10, 398. all yours right down to *p*.
P. L. 10, 484. placed in a *p*.
P. L. 10, 551. fruit like that which grew in *p*.
P. L. 10, 585. meanwhile in *p*. the hellish pair
P. L. 10, 598. alike is hell or *p*. or heaven
P. L. 10, 742. joys of *p*. dear-bought with
P. L. 11, 29. all the trees of *p*. could have
P. L. 11, 48. longer in that *p*. to dwell
P. L. 11, 104. haste thee and from the *p*. of God
P. L. 11, 123. lest *p*. a receptable prove
P. L. 11, 210. lighted now in *p*.
P. L. 11, 259. but longer in this *p*. to dwell
P. L. 11, 269. must I thus leave thee *p*.
P. L. 11, 342. narrow bounds confined of *p*.
P. L. 11, 378. it was a hill of *p*. the highest
P. L. 11, 830. then shall this mount of *p*.
P. L. 12, 314. safe to eternal *p*. of rest
P. L. 12, 464. for then the earth shall all be *p*.
P. L. 12, 586. not be loth to leave this *p*.
P. L. 12, 587. shalt possess a *p*. within thee
P. L. 12, 642. all the eastern side beheld of *p*.
P. R. 1, 3. now sing recovered *p*. to all mankind
P. R. 1, 52. and his facile consort Eve lost *p*.
P. R. 2, 141. of my success with Eve in *p*.
P. R. 4, 604. and thief of *p*.
P. R. 4, 608. hast regained lost *p*.
P. R. 4, 611. will dare set foot in *p*. to tempt
P. R. 4, 613. a fairer *p*. is founded now
**Paradises.**—P. L. 5, 500. in heavenly *p*. dwell
**Paradoxes.**—P. L. 4, 234. traditions, *p*.
**Paragoned.**—P. L. 10, 426. star to Satan *p*.
**Parallax.**—P. R. 4, 40. by what strange *p*.
**Parallel.**—P. L. 5, 141. shot *p*. to the earth
**Paramount.**—P. L. 2, 508. their mighty *p*.
**Paramour.**—H. 36. the sun her lusty *p*.
**Paranymph.**—S. A. 1020. thy *p*. worthless
**Parasite.**—P. R. 1, 452. a fawning *p*. obey'st
**Parch.**—P. L. 12, 636. to *p*. that temperate
**Parched.**—P. L. 10, 556. yet *p*. with scalding
**Parching.**—P. L. 2, 594. the *p*. air burns frore
L. 13. unwept and welter to the *p*. wind
**Pardon.**—P. L. 4, 80. none for *p*. left
P. L. 5, 848. while *p*. may be found in time
P.L.10, 1089. confess humbly our faults &*p*. beg
P. L. 10, 1101. and *p*. begged
P. L. 11, 167. but infinite in *p*. was my judge
S. A. 521. his *p*. I implore
S. A. 738. though my *p*. no way assured
S. A. 771. I may if possible thy *p*. find
S. A. 814. yet always pity or *p*. hath obtained
S. A. 825. such *p*. therefore as I give my folly
S. A. 1171. yet despair not of his final *p*.
V. Ex. 7. here I salute thee and thy *p*. ask
**Pardons.**—P. L. 3, 492. dispenses, *p*., bulls
**Pards.**—P. L. 4, 344. bears, tigers, ounces, *p*.
**Parent.**—P. L. 2, 805. me his *p*. works
P. L. 5, 153. these are thy glorious works, P.
P. L. 10, 331. their *p*. soon discerned
P. L. 10, 354. O *p*. these are thy magnific deeds
**Parentage.**—P. R. 1, 234. thee low of *p*.
**Parents.**—P. L. 1, 29. moved our grand *p*.
P. L. 1, 393. of human sacrifice and *p*. tears
P. L. 1, 510. heaven and earth their boasted *p*.
P. L. 3, 65. our two first *p*. yet the only two
P. L. 4, 6. our first *p*. had been warned
P. L. 10, 904. or if she love withheld by *p*.
P. L. 12, 638. angel caught our lingering *p*.
S. A. 25. who at last in sight of both my *p*.
S. A. 220. she pleased me, met my *p*.
S.A.886.for me thou wast to leave *p*.and country
S.A.1487.sons wont to nurse their *p*. in old age
**Parle.**—P. L. 6, 296. they ended *p*. and both

P. R. 4. 529. by *p*. or composition
S. A. 785. then with weakness come to *p*.
**Parliament.**—S. 10. the breaking of that *p*.
F. of C. 15. that so the *P*. may
**Parley.**—C. 241. sweet queen of *p*., daughter
**Parleys.**—S.A.403. with blandished *p*. feminine
**Parricide.**—S. A. 832. what traitor *p*.
**Parsimonious.**—P. L. 7, 485. the *p*. emmet
**Part.**—P. L. 1, 267. not to share with us their *p*.
P. L. 1, 367. the greatest *p*. of mankind
P. L. 1, 645. our better *p*. remains
P. L. 2, 325. and of his kingdom lose no *p*.
P. L. 2, 380. first devised by Satan and in *p*.
P. L. 2, 528. *p*. on the plain or in the air
P. L. 2, 531. *p*. curb their fiery steeds or shun
P. L. 2, 570. another *p*. in squadrons and gross
P. L. 2, 692. drew after him the third *p*.
P. L. 2, 770. to our *p*. loss and rout
P. L. 3, 371. but well could join melodious *p*.
P. L. 3, 584. to each inward *p*. with gentle
P. L. 3, 595. if metal, *p*. seemed gold *p*. silver
P. L. 4, 63. me though mean drawn to his *p*.
P. L. 4, 411. sole partner and sole *p*. of all
P. L. 4, 487. *p*. of my soul I seek thee
P. L. 4, 670. or in *p*. shed down their stellar
P. L. 4, 784. as flame they *p*. half wheeling
P. L. 4, 872. nor likely to *p*. hence without
P. L. 5, 83. of that same fruit held *p*.
P. L. 5, 405. to man in *p*. spiritual
P. L. 5, 710. drew after him the third *p*.
P. L. 6, 156. durst oppose a third *p*. of the
P. L. 6, 345. live throughout vital in every *p*.
P. L. 6, 413. on the other *p*. Satan with his
P. L. 6, 516. *p*. hidden veins digged up
P. L. 6, 519. of missive ruin *p*. incentive reed
P. L. 6, 565. while we discharge freely our *p*.
P. L. 7, 145. yet far the greater *p*. have kept
P. L. 7, 293. *p*. rise in crystal wall or ridge
P. L. 7, 359. of light by far the greater *p*.
P. L. 7, 403. bank the mid sea *p*. single
P. L. 7, 410. *p*. of bulk wallowing unwieldy
P. L. 7, 425. *p*. loosely wing the region *p*. more
P. L. 8, 138. with her *p*. averse from the sun's
P. L. 8, 189. her other *p*. still luminous
P. L. 8, 534. nature failed in me and left some *p*.
P. L. 8, 561. not nature, she hath done her *p*.
P. L. 8, 645. show us *p*., go heavenly guest
P. L. 9, 7. breach disloyal on the *p*. of man
P. L. 9, 8. on the *p*. of heaven now alienated
P. L. 9, 72. till *p*. rose up a fountain by the tree
P. L. 9, 375. God towards thee hath done his *p*.
P. L. 9, 667. new *p*. puts on
P. L. 9, 673. each *p*. motion each act won
P. L. 9, 879. as thou hast *p*., to me is bliss
P. L. 9, 1018. of sapience no small *p*.
P. L. 9, 1119. to bear rule which was thy *p*
P. L. 10, 155. their shame in *p*. covered
P. L. 10, 716. saw already in *p*. though hid
P. L. 10, 817. nor I on my *p*. single
P. L. 10, 886. more to the *p*. sinister
P. L. 10, 951. whose thou feel'st as yet least *p*.
P. L. 10, 1031. with heed *p*. of our sentence
P. L. 11, 282. from thee how shall I *p*.
P. L. 11, 430. and beheld a field, *p*. arable
P. L. 11, 431. other *p*. sheep-walks and folds
P. L. 11, 513. still divine similitude in *p*.
P. L. 11, 564. in other *p*. stood one
P. L. 11, 643. *p*. wield their arms *p*. curb
P. L. 11, 660. in other *p*. the sceptred heralds
P. L. 11, 765. so had borne my *p*. of evil only
P. L. 12, 230. *p*. such as appertain to civil
P. L. 12, 298. nor man the moral *p*. perform
P. L. 12, 336. registered *p*. good *p*. bad
P. L. 12, 533. the rest far greater *p*. will deem
P. R. 1, 472. and not enforced ofttimes to *p*.
P. R. 2, 240. each to know his *p*.
P. R. 2, 248. virtue I impute not or count *p*.
P. R. 2, 477. the inner man the nobler *p*.
P. R. 3, 155. will not *p*. easily from possession
P. R. 3, 232. most *p*. spent at home
P. R. 3, 399. on my *p*. aught endeavouring

P. R. 4, 161. nor what I *p.* with mean to give
S. A. 48. in what *p.* lodged how easily bereft
S. A. 72. which might in *p.* my grief have eased
S. A. 93. light is in the soul she all in every *p.*
S. A. 394. *p.* my strength lay stored in what *p.*
S. A. 681. which in *p.* they effect
S. A. 746. late yet in some *p.* to recompense
S. A. 1056. nor from that right to *p.* an hour
S. A. 1217. to do my *p.* from heaven assigned
S. A. 1229. *p.* not hence so slight informed
S. A. 1453. to give ye *p.* with me what hope I
S. A. 1463. that *p.* most reverenced Dagon
S. A. 1481. I am fixed not to *p.* hence without
S. 9, 5. the better *p.* with Mary and with Ruth
H. 105. to think her *p.* was done
**Partake.**—P. L. 2, 374. hurled headlong to *p.*
P. L. 2, 466. enterprize none shall *p.* with me
P. L. 5, 75. fair angelic Eve *p.* thou also
P. L. 6, 903. thou mayst *p.* his punishment
P. L. 9, 3. with him *p.* rural repast
P. L. 9, 199. the season prime for sweetest
P. L. 9, 818. and give him to *p.* full happiness
P. L. 12, 598. let her with thee *p.* what thou
S. A. 1455. that hope would much rejoice us *p.*
**Partaken.**—C. 741. in mutual and *p.* bliss
**Partakers.**—P. L. 4, 731. abundance wants *p.*
**Partakes.**—P. L. 8, 364. me I see not who *p.*
**Parted.**—P. L. 4, 302. from his *p.* forelock
P. L. 8, 652. so *p.* they the angel up to heaven
P. L. 9, 848. took that morn when first they *p.*
P. L. 9, 916. never shall be *p.* bliss or woe
P. L. 9, 1153. I to have never *p.* from thy side
P. L. 10, 380. of all things *p.* by the empyreal
S. A. 1447. by order of the lords new *p.* hence
S. A. 1719. with God not *p.* from him as was
C. 56. had by him ere he *p.* thence a son
S. 14. 1. faith and love which *p.* from thee never
**Parthenope.**—C. 879. by dead *P.'s* dear tomb
**Parthian.**—P. R. 3, 290. or by *P.* hands
P. R. 3, 294. all these the *P.* now some ages
P. R. 3, 299. for now the *P.* king
P. R. 3, 362. enclosing enemies Roman and *P.*
P. R. 3, 363. *P* first by my advice as nearer
P. R. 3, 369. be my task to render thee the *P.*
P. R. 4, 73. the Asian kings and *P.* among
P. R. 4, 85. justly mayst prefer before the *P.*
**Partial.**—P. L. 2, 552. their song was *p.*
**Participate.**—P. L. 5, 494. angels may *p.*
P. L. 8, 390. fit to *p.* all rational delight
S. A. 1507. in both which we as next *p.*
**Participating.**—P. L. 9, 717. as they *p.*
**Particular.**—S. A. 1595. relation more *p.*
**Parting.**—P. L. 4, 1003. sequel each of *p.*
P. L. 5, 252. angelic choirs on each hand *p.*
P. L. 8, 630. the *p.* sun beyond the earth's green
P. L. 9, 276. and from the *p.* angel overheard
P. L. 12, 590. hour precise exacts our *p.* hence
H. 186. the *p.* Genius is with sighing sent
**Partition.**—P. L. 7, 267. *p.* firm and sure
P. L. 8, 105. lodged in a small *p.*
**Partly.**—P. R. 1, 262. known *p.* and soon
**Partner.**—P. L. 4, 411. sole *p.* and sole part
P. L. 10, 128. my other self the *p.* of my life
**Partners.**—S. A. 810. fearless at home of *p.*
**Partook.**—P. R. 2, 277. that with Elijah he *p.*
**Parts.**—P. L. 1, 194. his other *p.* besides prone
P. L. 1, 420. to the brook that *p.* Egypt
P. L. 2, 660. in the sea that *p.* Calabria
P. L. 3, 593. not all *p.* like, but all alike
P. L. 4, 312. nor those mysterious *p.* were then
P. L. 6, 354. meanwhile in other *p.* like deeds
P. L. 7, 465. lion pawing to get free his hinder *p.*
P. L. 9, 1093. the *p.* of each from other
P. P. 9, 1097. may cover round those middle *p.*
S. A. 96. and not as feeling through all *p.*
S. A. 624. mangle my apprehensive tenderest *p.*
S. A. 1656. met from all *p.* to solemnize this feast
C. 72. all other *p.* remaining as they were
C. 466. lets in defilement to the inward *p.*
**Party.**—P. L. 2, 368. seduce them to our *p.*
**Pass.**—P. L. 1, 352. to *p.* Rhene or the Danaw

P. L. 2, 438. these passed, if any *p.* the void
P. L. 2, 606. wish and struggle as they *p.*
P. L. 2, 684. through them I mean to *p.* that
P. L. 2, 776. which none can *p.* without
P. L. 2, 886. marching might *p.* through
P. L. 2, 1031. with easy intercourse *p.* to and fro
P. L. 3, 480. or in Franciscan think to *p.*
P. L. 3, 481. they *p.* the planets seven and *p.*
P. L. 4, 579. in at this gate none *p.* vigilance
P. L. 5, 453. Adam not to let the occasion *p.*
P. L. 5, 693. intends to *p.* triumphant and give
P. L. 7, 432. the air floats as they *p.* fanned
P. L. 9, 231. nor of me shalt *p.* unpraised
P. L. 9, 452. with nymph-like step fair virgin *p.*
P. L. 9, 479. then let me not let *p.* occasion
P. L. 9, 849. the tree of knowledge he must *p.*
P. L. 10, 38. so lately what would come to *p.*
P. L. 10, 48. but that the mortal sentence *p.*
P. L. 10, 1083. to *p.* commodiously this life
P. L. 12, 196. but them lets *p.*
P. R. 1, 322. who *p.* in troop or caravan
P. R. 2, 233. I shall let *p.* no advantage
P. R. 3, 151. not worth the seeking, let it *p.*
P. R. 4, 209. therefore let *p.* as they are
S. A. 444. which to have come to *p.* by means
C. 79. chances to *p.* through this adventurous
C. 402. and let a single helpless maiden *p.*
C. 539. of them that *p.* unweeting by the way
V. Ex. 45. then sing of secret things that to *p.*
V. Ex. 72. what future days should bring to *p.*
H. 139. and hell itself will *p.* away
C. 430. she may *p.* on with unblenched majesty
**Passage.**—P. L. 3, 528. *p.* down to the earth a *p.*
P. L. 4, 232. which from his darksome *p.* now
P. L. 10, 260. easing their *p.* hence
P. L. 10, 304. from hence a *p.* broad smooth
P. L. 10, 475. but I toiled out my uncouth *p.*
P. L. 11, 122. guard all *p.* to the tree of life
P. L. 11, 366. endure thy mortal *p.* when
S. A. 610. but must secret *p.* find to the inmost
V. Ex. 24. and loudly knock to have their *p.*
**Passages.**—P. L. 11, 528. these painful *p.*
**Passed.**—P. L. 1, 395. that *p.* through fire
P. L. 1, 487. when he *p.* from Egypt marching
P. L. 2, 438. these *p.* if any pass the void
P. L. 2, 619. many a dark and dreary vale *p.*
P. L. 2, 1017. than when Argo *p.* through
P. L. 3, 227. Father thy word is *p.* man shall
P. L. 3, 498. the fiend found as he *p.*
P. L. 3, 534. behests his angels to and fro *p.*
P. L. 4, 160. and now are *p.* Mozambic
P. L. 4, 177. all path of man or beast that *p.*
P. L. 4, 225. *p.* underneath ingulfed
P. L. 4, 319. so *p.* they naked on nor shunned
P. L. 4, 321. hand in hand they *p.* the loveliest
P. L. 4, 689. hand in hand alone they *p.* on
P. L. 5, 31. (such night till this I never *p.*)
P. L. 5, 50. and on methought alone I *p.*
P. L. 5, 291. their glittering tents he *p.*
P. L. 5, 554. though what thou tell'st hath *p.*
P. L. 5, 675. so late hath *p.* the lips of heaven's
P. L. 5, 748. regions they *p.* the mighty
P. L. 5, 754. having *p.* at length into the limits
P. L. 5, 903. from amidst them forth he *p.*
P. L. 6, 330. with discontinuous wound *p.*
P. L. 6, 699. two days are therefore *p.* the third
P. L. 7, 253. nor *p.* uncelebrated nor unsung
P. L. 8, 352. I named them as they *p.*
P. L. 9, 1144. what words have *p.* thy lips
P. L. 10, 227. what had *p.* with man recounted
P. L. 10, 233. since the fiend *p.* through sin
P. L. 10, 419. Satan *p.* and all about found
P. L. 10, 443. angel militant of lowest order *p.*
P. L. 11, 16. in they *p.* dimensionless
P. R. 1, 303. full forty days he *p.*
P. R. 2, 245. four times ten days I've *p.*
P. R. 3, 439. Promised Land their fathers *p.*
P. R. 4, 426. *p.* the night so foul till morning
S. A. 811. these reasons in love's law have *p.*
C. 302. and as I *p.* I worshipped
**Passenger.**—C. 39. forlorn and wandering *p.*

**Passes.**—P. L. 8, 173. to know what *p.* there
　L. 21. and as he *p.* turn and bid fair peace
　S. 9, 13. *p.* to bliss at the mid hour of night
**Passing.**—P. L. 8, 290. I then was *p.* to my
　P. L. 10, 252. but lest the difficulty of *p.* back
　P. L. 10, 714. countenance grim glared him *p.*
　P. L. 11, 717. where *p.* fair allured them
　P. L. 12, 130. *p.* now the ford to Haran
　P. R. 2, 155. many are in each region *p.* fair
　P. R. 3, 436. at their *p.* cleave the Assyrian
　S. A. 1458. at home or through the high street *p.*
　V. Ex. 40. then *p.* through the spheres
**Passion.**—P. L. 1, 605. signs of remorse and *p.*
　P. L. 2, 564. of happiness and final misery *p.*
　P. L. 4, 114. thus while he spake each *p.*
　P. L. 8, 530. here *p.* first I felt, commotion
　P. L. 8, 585. soul of man or *p.* in him move
　P. L. 8, 588. in loving thou dost well in *p.* not
　P. L. 8, 635. heed lest *p.* sway thy judgment
　P. L. 9, 98. his bursting *p.* into plaints thus
　P. L. 9, 667. and as to *p.* moved fluctuates
　P. L. 10, 627. transported with some fit of *p.*
　P. L. 10, 718. and in a troubled sea of *p.* tost
　P. L. 10, 865. soft words to his fierce *p.*
　S. A. 1006. without much inward *p.* felt
　S. A. 1758. and calm of mind all *p.* spent
　Il P. 41. there held in holy *p.* still
**Passions.**—P. L. 1, 454. whose wanton *p.*
　P. L. 4, 571. alien from heaven with *p.* foul
　P. L. 9, 1123. high *p.* anger hate mistrust
　P. L. 12, 88. inordinate desires and upstart *p.*
　P. R. 2, 467. and rules *p.,* desires and fears
　P. R. 2, 472. lawless *p.* in him which he serves
　P. R. 4, 266. high actions and high *p.* best
**Passive.**—P. L. 3, 110. made *p.* both
　P. L. 6, 72. and the *p.* air upbore their nimble
**Past.**—P. L. 1, 628. the depth of knowledge *p.*
　P. L. 2, 1023. but he once *p.* soon after when
　P. L. 3, 62. received beatitude *p.* utterance
　P. L.. 3, 78. wherein *p.,* present, future
　P. L. 3, 328. the cited dead of all *p.* ages
　P. L. 4, 762. or *p.* as saints and patriarchs used
　P. L. 4, 932. hard assays and ill successes *p.*
　P. L. 5, 33. works of day *p.* or morrow's next
　P. L. 5, 113. matching words and deeds long *p.*
　P. L. 5, 582. by present *p.* and future
　P. L. 6, 895. thou mayst beware by what is *p.*
　P. L. 7, 253. nor *p.* uncelebrated nor unsung
　P. L. 9, 628. one small thicket *p.* of blowing
　P. L. 9, 926. but *p.* who can recall or done undo
　P. L. 10, 341. that *p.* returned by night
　P. L. 10, 840. beyond all *p.* example and future
　P. L. 11, 158. the bitterness of death is *p.*
　P. L. 11, 600. days portends than those two *p.*
　P. L. 11, 776. but that care now is *p.*
　P. L. 12, 14. while the dread of judgment *p.*
　P. L. 12, 604. though sad with cause for evils *p.*
　P. R. 1, 300. thoughts accompanied of things *p.*
　P. R. 2, 106. recalling what remarkably had *p.*
　P. R. 3, 294. now some ages *p.* by great Arsaces
　P. R. 4, 342. and themselves *p.* shame
　P. R. 4, 492. I shall reign *p.* thy preventing
　S. A. 22. present, times *p.,* what once I was
　S. A. 120. as one *p.* hope abandoned
　S. A. 685. with no regard of highest favours *p.*
　S. A. 912. remains *p.* cure bear not too sensibly
　S. A. 1064. no less abstruse my riddling days *p.*
　L. 132. return Alpheus the dread voice is *p.*
**Pastime.**—P. L. 8, 375. with these find *p.*
**Pastimes.**—C. 121. their merry wakes and *p.*
**Pastoral.**—P. L. 11, 132. *p.* reed of Hermes
　C. 345. or sound of *p.* reed with oaten stops
**Pastry.**—P. R. 2, 343. *p.* built or from the spit
**Pasture.**—P. L. 4, 351. and now filled with *p.*
　P. L. 7, 404. graze the sea-weed their *p.*
**Pastured.**—P. L. 11, 653. where cattle *p.*
**Pastures.**—P. R. 3, 260. with herds the *p.*
　L. 193. to-morrow to fresh woods and *p.* new
**Pasturing.**—P. L. 7. 462. flocks *p.* at once
　P. L. 9, 1109. tends his *p.* herds at loop-holes
**Paternal.**—P. L. 6, 750. chariot of *p.* Deity

P. L. 7, 219. uplifted in *p.* glory rode
P. L. 11, 353. with goodness and *p.* love his
P. L. 12, 24. by families and tribes under *p.*
**Path.**—P. L. 2, 976. I seek what readiest *p.*
P. L. 4, 177. all *p.* of man or beast that passed
P. L. 6, 173. from the *p.* of truth remote
P. L. 10, 256. to found a *p.* over this main
P. L. 11, 371. I follow thee safe guide the *p.*
P. R. 1, 322. so far from *p.* or road of men
C. 303. it were a journey like the *p.* to heaven
**Pathless.**—P. R. 1, 296. a *p.* desert dusk
Il P. 70. through the heaven's wide *p.* way
**Paths.**—P. L. 9, 244. these *p.* and bowers
P. L. 11, 631. should turn aside to tread *p.*
P. L. 11, 814. and before them set the *p.*
C. 37. lies through the perplexed *p.* of this
C. 569. through *p.* and turnings often trod by
**Patience.**—P. L. 2, 569. with stubborn *p.*
P. L. 6, 464. and excessive overturns all *p.*
P. L. 9, 32. better fortitude of *p.* and heroic
P. L. 11, 361. to learn true *p.*
P. L. 12, 583. add virtue *p.* temperance
P. R. 1, 426. but his *p.* won
P. R. 2, 102. but I to wait with *p.* am inured
P. R. 3, 92. by *p.* temperance
P. R. 3, 93. thy wrongs with saintly *p.* borne
S. A. 654. extolling *p.* as the truest fortitude
S. A. 755. how far urged his *p.* bears
S. A. 1287. but *p.* is more oft the exercise of saints
S. A. 1296. whom *p.* finally must crown
C. 971. their faith their *p.* and their truth
S. 19, 8. but *P.* to prevent that murmur soon
D. F. I. 75. and render him with *p.* what he lent
**Patient.**—P. R. 3, 95. whom *p.* with honour *p.* Job
P. R. 4, 420. O *p.* Son of God
S. A. 1623. he *p.* but undaunted where they led
**Patiently.**—P. L. 11, 112. if *p.* thy bidding
P. L. 11, 287. but *p.* resign what justly thou
P. L. 11, 551. and *p.* attend my dissolution
P. R. 2, 432. to whom thus Jesus *p.* replied
**Patriarch.**—P. L. 5, 506. to whom the *p.*
P. L. 9, 376. so spake the *p.* of mankind
P. L. 12, 117. while yet the *p.* lived who scaped
P. L. 12, 151. this *p.* blest whom faithful
**Patriarchs.**—P. L. 4, 762. as Saints and *p.*
**Patrimony.**—P. L. 10, 818. fair *p.* that I
P. R. 3, 428. who freed as to their ancient *p.*
S. A. 1482. for his redemption all my *p.*
**Patron.**—P. L. 3, 219. *p.* or intercessor none
P. L. 4, 958. now wouldst seem *p.* of liberty
**Patroness.**—P. L. 9, 21. of my celestial *p.*
P. 29. befriend me Night best *p.* of grief
**Patrons.**—P. L. 11, 696. great conquerors *p.*
**Pattern.**—P. L. 7, 487. *p.* of just equality
**Paul.**—F. of C. 10. been held in high esteem with *P.*
**Pause.**—P. L. 3, 561. and without longer *p.*
P. L. 5, 562. after short *p.* assenting thus began
P. L. 6, 162. this *p.* between, unanswered lest
S. 21, 7. let Euclid rest and Archimedes *p.*
**Paused.**—P. L. 5, 64. this said he *p.* not
P. L. 12, 2. so here the archangel *p.*
P. L. 12, 466. *p.* as at the world's great period
**Pausing.**—P. L. 9, 744. yet first *p.* awhile
**Paved.**—P. L. 2, 1026. *p.* after him a broad
P. L. 10, 473. and death a broad way now is *p.*
**Pavement.**—P. L. 1, 682. riches of heaven's *p.*
P. L. 1, 726. o'er the smooth and level *p.*
P. L. 3, 363. the bright *p.* that like a sea
P. L. 7, 578. whose dust is gold and *p.* stars
**Pavilion.**—P. L. 2, 960. and his dark *p.*
**Pavilioned.**—P L. 11, 215. field *p.* with his
**Pavilions.**—P. L. 5, 653. *p.* numberless
**Paw.**—P. L. 4, 343. in his *p.* dandled the kid
P. L. 4, 408. seize them both griped in each *p.*
L. 128. besides what the grim wolf with privy *p.*
S. 16, 13. from the *p.* of hireling wolves
**Pawing.**—P. L. 7, 464. the tawny lion *p.* to get
**Pay.**—P. L. 3, 211. able and as willing *p.*
P. L. 4, 47. and *p.* him thanks how due
P. L. 8, 344. *p.* thee fealty with low subjection
P. L. 10, 1026. the pain we are by doom to *p.*

P. L. 11, 36. and for these my death shall *p.*
P. R. 2, 375. thy gentle ministers who come to *p.*
P. R. 4, 80. nations now to Rome obedience *p.*
S. A. 489. as I deserve *p.* on my punishment
S. A. 1204. to *p.* my underminers in their coin
**Paying.**—P. L. 4, 53. so burdensome still *p.*
S. A. 432. bitterly hast thou paid and still art *p.*
**Paynim.**—P. R. 3, 343. both *P.* and the peers
**Pays.**—P. L. 4, 56. owing owes not but still *p.*
**Peace.**—P. L. 1, 65. where *p.* and rest can
P. L. 1, 660. *p.* is despaired for who can think
P. L. 2, 228. ease and peaceful sloth not *p.*
P. L. 2, 292. and his sentence pleased advising *p.*
P. L. 2, 329. what sit we then projecting *p.*
P. L. 2, 331. irreparable terms of *p.* yet none
P. L. 2, 332. for what *p.* will be given
P. L. 2, 499. God proclaiming *p.* yet live in hatred
P. L. 2, 690. who first broke *p.* in heaven
P. L. 3, 263. but *p.* assured and reconcilement
P. L. 3, 274. the only *p.* found out for mankind
P. L. 4, 104. granting he as I from begging *p.*
P. L. 5, 210. firm *p.* recovered soon and wonted
P. L. 6, 267. thou disturbed heaven's blessed *p.*
P. L. 6, 560. how we seek *p.* and composure
P. L. 6, 617. perhaps for joy of offered *p.*
P. L. 7, 55. and war so near the *p.* of God in bliss
P. L. 7, 183. future men and in their dwellings *p.*
P. L. 7, 216. ye troubled waves and thou deep *p.*
P. L. 9, 333. *p.* within favour from heaven
P. L. 9, 981. with a fact pernicious to thy *p.*
P. L. 9, 1126. calm region once and full of *p.*
P. L. 10, 135. should I hold my *p.* yet thou
P. L. 10, 908. and household *p.* confound
P. L. 10, 913. embracing them besought his *p.*
P. L. 10, 924. between us two let there be *p.*
P. L. 10, 938. immovable till *p.* obtained
P. L. 11, 38. the smell of *p.* toward mankind
P. L. 11, 117. though sorrowing yet in *p.*
P. L. 11, 153. *p.* returned home to my breast
P. L. 11, 507. glad to be so dismissed in *p.*
P. L. 11, 580. might preserve freedom and *p.*
P. L. 11, 667. of religion, truth and *p.*
P. L. 11, 781. *p.* would have crowned
P. L. 11, 784. *p.* to corrupt no less than war
P. L. 11, 796. of friendship hostile deeds in *p.*
P. L. 11, 815. much more safe and full of *p.*
P. L. 11, 867. betokening *p.* from God
P. L. 12, 23. long time in *p.* by families
P. L. 12, 296. *p.* of conscience which the law
P. L. 12, 317. interrupt their public *p.*
P. L. 12, 355. and should most endeavour *p.*
P. L. 12, 550. founded in righteousness and *p.*
P. L. 12, 558. greatly in *p.* of thought
P. R. 3, 80. and all the flourishing works of *p.*
P. R. 3, 91. by deeds of *p.* by wisdom eminent
P. R. 4, 425. unappalled in calm and sinless *p.*
S. A. 60. but *p.* I must not quarrel with the will
S. A. 966. and suing for *p.* reap nothing
S. A. 1049. his way to *p.* is smooth
S. A. 1070. comes he in *p.* what wind hath blown
S. A. 1073. his habit carries *p.* his brow defiance
S. A. 1074. or *p.* or not, alike to me he comes
S. A. 1334. my conscience and internal *p.*
S. A. 1445. *p.* with you brethren, my inducement
S. A. 1757. with *p.* and consolation... dismissed
C. 359. *p.,* brother be not over exquisite
C. 368. and the sweet *p.* be to my sable shroud
L. 22. and bid fair *p.* be to my sable shroud
L'A. 120. in weeds or *p.* high triumphs hold
Il P. 45. and join with thee calm *p.* and quiet
S. 16, 4. to *p.* and truth thy glorious way hast
S. 16, 10. *p.* hath her victories no less renowned
S. 17, 117. whether to settle *p.* or to unfold
S. 17, 14. on thy firm hand Religion leans in *p.*
H. 7. and with his Father work us a perpetual *p.*
H. 46. sent down the meek-eyed *p.*
H. 52. she strikes a universal *p.* through sea
H. 63. his reign of *p.* upon the earth began
T. 16. with truth and *p.* and love shall ever shine
M. W. 48. may thy grave *p.* and quiet ever have
V. Ex. 84. and *p.* shall lull him in her flowery lap

**Peaceable.**—P. R. 3, 76. and enslave *p.*
**Peaceful.**—P. L. 2, 227. ease and *p.* sloth
P. L. 2, 279. all things invite to *p.* counsels
P. L. 10, 946. and thus with *p.* words upraised
P. L. 11, 600. more hope of *p.* days portends
S. A. 709. turn his labours for thou canst to *p.* end
Il P. 168. my weary age find out the *p.* hermitage
H. 61. but *p.* was the night wherein the Prince
**Peal.**—P. L. 2, 656. and rung a hideous *p.*
P. L. 3, 329. such a *p.* shall rouse their sleep
S. A. 235. who vanquished with a *p.* of words
**Pealed.**—P. L. 2, 920. nor was his ear less *p.*
**Pealing.**—Il P. 161. there let the *p.* organ blow
**Peals.**—S. A. 906. when I was worried with thy *p.*
**Pearl.**—P. L. 2, 4. on her kings barbaric *p.*
P. L. 3, 519. of jasper or of liquid *p.* whereon
P. L. 4, 238. rolling on orient *p.* and sands
P. L. 5, 2. sowed the earth with orient *p.*
P. L. 5, 634. in *p.,* in diamond, and massy gold
P. R. 4, 120. embossed with gems and studs of *p.*
S. 12, 8. but this is got by casting *p.* to hogs
**Pearled.**—C. 834. held up their *p.* wrists
**Pearls.**—M. W. 43. and those *p.* of dew she wears
**Pearly.**—P. L. 5, 430. covered with *p.* grain.
P. L. 7, 407. or in their *p.* shells at ease attend
**Peasant.**—P. L. 1, 783. some belated *p.* sees
**Pebbles.**—P. R. 4, 330. children gathering *p.*
**Peccant.**—P. L. 11, 70. as how with *p.* angels
**Peculiar.**—P. L. 3, 183. chosen of *p.* grace
P. L. 5, 15. beauty,... shot forth *p.* graces
P. L. 7, 368. they augment their small *p.*
P. L. 12, 111. and one *p.* nation to select
P. R. 1, 402. nor lightens aught each man's *p.*
H. 196. while each *p.* power foregoes
**Peeling.**—P. R. 4, 136. *p.* their provinces
**Peep.**—C. 140. from her cabined loop-hole *p.*
**Peer.**—C. 31. a noble *p.* of mickle trust and power
L. 9. young Lycidas and hath not left his *p.*
**Peerage.**—P. L. 1, 586. with all his *p.* fell
**Peering.**—H. 140. to the *p.* day
**Peerless.**—P. L. 4, 608. unveiled her *p.* light
A. 75. the *p.* height of her immortal praise
**Peers.**—P. L. 1, 39. in glory above his *p.*
P. L. 1, 618. inclose him round with all his *p.*
P. L. 1, 757. high capital of Satan and his *p.*
P. L. 2, 119. should be much for open war O *p.*
P. L. 2, 445. I should ill become this throne O *p.*
P. L. 2, 507. in order came the grand infernal *p.*
P. L. 5, 812. place thyself so high above thy *p.*
P. L. 6, 127. from his armed *p.* forth stepping
P. L. 10, 456. in haste the great consulting *p.*
P. R. 1, 40. to council summons all his mighty *p.*
P. R. 3, 343. both Paynim, and the *p.* of
**Pegasean.**—P. L. 7, 4. above the flight of *P.* wing
**Pellean.**—P. R. 2, 196. remember that *P.*
**Pelleas.**—P. R. 2, 361. Lancelot or *P.* or
**Pellenore.**—P. R. 2, 361. or Pelleas or *P.*
**Pelops.**—Il P. 99. presenting Thebes or *P.'* line
**Pelorus.**—P. L. 1, 232. a hill torn from *P.*
**Pen.**—P. L. 4, 185. where shepherds *p.* their
**Penal.**—P. L. 1, 48. chains and *p.* fire
S. A. 508. thy *p.* forfeit from thyself
**Penalty.**—P. L. 7, 545. death is the *p.*
P. L. 9, 775. of God or death of law or *p.*
P. L. 10, 15. incurred,... the *p.*
P. L. 10, 753. to the loss of that sufficient *p.*
P. L. 10, 1022. so thinking to evade the *p.*
P. L. 11, 197. secure of our discharge from *p.*
P. L. 12, 398. imposed on *p.* of death
P. L. 12, 399. the *p.* to thy transgression due
**Penance**—P. L. 2, 92. hour calls us to *p.*
P. L. 10, 550. reigns above to aggravate their *p.*
S. A. 738. my *p.* hath not slackened though my
**Pencil.**—P. L. 3, 509. or by shading *p.* drawn
**Pendent.**—P. L. 1, 727. *p.* by subtle magic
P. L. 2, 1052. this *p.* world in bigness as a star
P. L. 4, 239. with mazy error under *p.* shade
P. L. 10, 313. a ridge of *p.* rock
**Pendulous.**—P. L. 4, 1000. the *p.* round
**Penetration.**—P. L. 3, 585. gentle *p.*
**Penitent.**—P. L. 10, 1097. our father *p.*

P. L. 12, 319. whom as oft he saves them *p.*
P. R. 3, 421. humbled themselves or *p.*
S. A. 502. be *p.* and for thy fault contrite
S.A.754.not truly *p.*but chief to try her husband
S. A. 761. not to reject the *p.*but ever to forgive
**Penned.**—C. 344. flocks *p.* in their wattled cotes
**Pennons.**—P. L. 2, 933. fluttering his *p.* vain
P. L. 7, 441. and rising on stiff *p.* tower
**Pens.**—P. L. 7, 421. they summed their *p.*
**Pensioners.**—Il P. 10. fickle *p.* of Morpheus'
**Pensive.**—P. L. 2, 777. *p.* here I sat alone
P. L. 4, 173. Satan had journeyed on *p.* and
P. L. 8, 287. profuse of flowers *p.* I sat me down
C. 387. the *p.* secrecy of desert cell
L.147.with cowslips wan that hang the *p.*head
Il P. 31. come *p.* Nun, devout and pure
P. 42. in *p.* trance and anguish and ecstatic fit
**Pent.**—P. L. 6, 657. their substance *p.* which
P. L. 9, 445. one who long in populous city *p.*
S.A.1647.with the force of winds and waters *p.*
C. 499. or straggling wether the *p.*flock forsook
**Pentateuch.**—P. R. 4, 226. the *P.* or what
**Penuel.**—S. A. 278. Succoth and the fort of *P.*
**Penurious.**—C. 726. a *p.* niggard of his wealth
**People.**—P. L. 10, 27. the ethereal *p.* ran
P. L. 12, 171. sent from God to claim his *p.*
P. L. 12, 181. all his flesh emboss and all his *p.*
P. L. 12, 309. his *p.* into Canaan lead
P. L. 12, 483. who then shall guide his *p.*
P. R. 2, 48. free thy *p.* from their yoke
P. R. 3, 48. *p.'s* praise if always praise unmixed
P. R. 3, 49. what the *p.* but a herd confused
P. R. 4, 102. *p.* free from servile yoke
P. R. 4, 132. that *p.* victor once now vile
S. A. 12. this day a solemn feast the *p.* hold
S. A. 317. to set his *p.* free have prompted this
S.A.681. and *p.'s*safety which in part they effect
S. A. 1158. hath cut off quite from his *p.*
S. A. 1421. no less the *p.* on their holy days
S. A. 1473. doubtless the *p.* shouting to behold
S. A.1533. wrought things as incredible for his *p.*
S. A.1601. should be brought forth to show the *p.*
S. A. 1620. at sight of him the *p.* with a shout
Il P. 8. as the gay motes that *p.* the sunbeams
**Peopled.**—P. L. 10, 889. *p.* highest heaven
**Peor.**—P. L. 1, 412. *P.* his other name
H. 197. *P.* and Baalim forsake their temples dim
**Peræa.**—P. R. 2, 24. or in *p.*
**Perceive.**—P. L. 1, 335. nor did they not *p.*
P. L. 3, 404. *p.* thee purposed not to doom
P. L. 6, 623. such as we might *p.* amused
P. L. 9, 598. ere long I might *p.* strange
P. L. 12, 8. but I *p.* thy mortal sight to fail
C. 74. not once *p.* their foul disfigurement
C. 563. too well I did *p.* it was the voice
**Perceived.**—P. L. 299. when Beelzebub *p.*
P. L. 6, 19. war he *p.* war in procinct
S. A. 1201. when I *p.* all set on enmity
**Perceivest.**—P. L. 8, 566. as thou thyself *p.*
**Perceiving.**—P. L. 8, 41. which Eve *p.*
P.R.1,227.growing thoughts my mother soon *p.*
S. A. 397. each time *p.* how openly
**Perched.**—S. A. 1693. on the *p.* roosts
**Perdition.**—P. L. 1, 47. to bottomless *p.*
D.F.I. 67. to turn swift-rushing black *p.* hence
**Perfect.**—P. L. 1, 550. in *p.* phalanx
P. L. 2, 764. who full oft thyself in me thy *p.*
P. L. 4, 577. Uriel no wonder if thy *p.* sight
P. L. 4, 634. to whom thus Eve with *p.* beauty
P. L. 5, 399. whom all *p.* good unmeasured out
P. L. 5, 442. metals of drossiest ore to *p.* gold
P. L. 5, 524. God made thee *p.* not immutable
P. L. 5, 568. glorious once and *p.* while
P. L. 6, 71. nor stream divides their *p.* ranks
P. L. 6, 462. but pain is *p.* misery
P. L. 7, 455. living creatures *p.* forms
P. L. 8, 415. thou in thyself art *p.* and in thee
P. L. 8, 642. *p.* within no outward aid require
P. L. 9, 689. and life more *p.* have attained
P. L. 9, 1179. what seemed in thee so *p.*
P. L. 10, 138. and gavest me as thy *p.* gift

P. L. 11, 36. merit those shall *p.* and for these
P. L. 11, 876. for one man found so *p.* and so
P. R. 1, 83. thence on his head a *p.* dove descend
P. R. 1, 166. I have chose this *p.* man
P. R. 3, 11. of good wise just the *p.* shape
P. R. 4, 302. *p.* in himself and all possessing
P. R. 4, 468. the *p.* season offered with my aid
S. A. 946. uxorious to thy will in *p.* thraldom
C. 203. was rife and *p.* in my listening ear
L. 82. and *p.* witness of all judging Jove
H. 166. full and *p.* is but now begins
S. M. 23. their motion swayed in *p.* diapason
M. W. 55. here be tears of *p.* moan
P. 13. most *p.* hero tried in heaviest plight
C. 73. and they so *p.* is their misery
**Perfection.**—P. L. 4, 673. to receive *p.*
P. L. 5, 29. my glory my *p.* glad I see thy face
P. L. 5, 472. all such to *p.* one first matter
P. L. 9, 964. but short of thy *p.* how shall I
P. L. 10, 150. whose *p.* far excelled hers in all
P. L. 10, 483. fabric wonderful of absolute *p.*
P. R. 1, 209. and in it grew to such *p.* that ere
P. R. 3, 230. what of *p.* can in man be found
**Perfections.**—P. L. 5, 353. complete *p.*
P. L. 9, 1031. wedded thee adorned with all *p.*
P. R. 2, 138. *p.* absolute, graces divine
**Perfectly.**—P. L. 9, 707. shall *p.* be then
T. I5. that is sincerely good and *p.* divine
**Perfidious.**—P. L. 1, 308. with *p.* hatred
P. L. 5, 880. involved in this *p.* fraud
L. 100. it was that fatal and *p.* bark
**Perform.**—P. L. 1, 699. innumerable scarce *p.*
P. L. 4, 418. have nothing merited nor can *p.*
P. L. 7, 164. this I *p.* speak thou and be it done
P. L. 10, 750. unable to *p.* thy terms too hard
P. L. 12, 299. nor man the moral part *p.*
D. F. I. 70. thou canst best *p.* that office
**Performance.**—P. L. 10, 502. of my *p.*
**Performed.**—P. L. 6, 695. that *p.* what war
P. L. 11, 440. and all due rites *p.*
P. L. 12, 505. their ministry *p.* and race well
P. R. 1, 102. and the exploit *p.* successfully
P. R. 2, 49. let us wait thus far He hath *p.*
S. A. 1083. of thy prodigious might and feats *p.*
S. A. 1218. and had *p.* it if my known offence
S.A.1626.to heave pull draw or break he still *p.*
S. A. 1641. I have *p.* as reason was obeying
**Performing.**—P. L. 11, 300. and in *p.* end
P. L. 12, 299. and not *p.* cannot live
**Performs.**—P. L. 2, 595. and cold *p.* the
**Perfume.**—S. A. 720. amber scent of odorous *p.*
**Perfumes.**—P. L. 4, 158. native *p.*
C. 556. rose like a steam of rich distilled *p.*
**Perhaps.**—P. L. 1, 166. so as *p.* shall grieve
P. L. 1, 176. *p.* hath spent his shafts
P. L. 1, 655. shall be *p.* our first eruption
P. L. 2, 70. but *p.* the way seems difficult
P. L. 2, 178. while we *p.* designing or exhorting
P. L. 2, 211. and *p.* thus far removed not
P. L. 2, 362. here *p.* some advantageous act
P. L. 2, 394. *p.* in view of those bright confines
P. L. 2, 572. *p.* might yield them easier
P. L. 2, 835. to supply *p.* our vacant room
P. L. 2, 911. womb of nature and *p.* her grave
P. L. 3, 588. a spot like which *p.* astronomer
P. L. 3, 700. with thine eyes what some *p.*
P. L. 4, 112. by thee and more than half *p.*
P. L. 4, 360. of other mould, earth-born *p.*
P. L. 4, 791. now laid *p.* asleep secure of harm
P. L. 4, 993. but the starry cope of heaven *p.*
P. L. 5, 312. great behest from heaven to us *p.*
P. L. 5, 401. unsavoury food *p.* to spiritual
P. L. 5, 496. from these corporal nutriments *p.*
P. L. 5, 569. the secrets of another world *p.*
P. L. 6, 438. *p.* more valid arms weapons more
S. A. 460. we may well spare out of life *p.*
P. L. 6, 616. extravagant and wild *p.* for joy
P. L. 7, 85. what may no less *p.* avail us know*n*.
P. L. 7, 437. pattern of just equality *p.* hereafter
P. L. 7, 621. every star *p.* a world of destined
P. L. 8, 77. *p.* to move his laughter at their

P. L. 8, 148. other suns p. with their attendant
P. L. 8, 152. stored in each orb p. with some
P. L. 8, 205. my story which p. thou hast not
P. L. 8, 536. or from my side subducting took p.
P. L. 9, 139. though p. not longer than since I
P. L. 9, 247. but if much converse p. thee
P. L. 9, 263. conjugal love than which p.
P. L. 9, 381. may find us, both p. far less
P. L. 9, 532. wonder not sovran mistress if p.
P. L. 9, 610. though importune p. to come
P. L. 9, 713. so ye shall die p. by putting off
P. L. 9, 811. and I p. am secret, heaven is high
P. L. 9, 813. and other care p. may have
P. L. 9, 823. and p. a thing not undesirable
P. L. 9, 928. yet so p. thou shalt not die p.
P. L. 9, 1148. thou being by or to thyself p.
P. L. 9, 1177. and p. I also erred in overmuch
P. L. 10, 253. stay his return p. over this gulf
P. L. 10, 582. the wide-encroaching Eve p.
P. L. 10, 923. we live scarce one short hour p.
P. L. 11, 74. trumpet heard in Oreb since p.
P. L. 11, 75. and p. once more to sound
P. L. 11. 226. now expect great tidings which p.
P. L. 11, 343. this had been p. thy capital seat
P. L. 11, 406. in spirit p. he also saw rich Mexico
P. L. 12, 4. if Adam aught p. might interpose
P. R. 1, 292. I learn not yet p. I need not
P. R. 2, 452. soon accomplish what they did p.
P. R. 3, 227. p. thou lingerst in deep thoughts
P. R. 3, 430. and to their gods p. of Bethel
P. R. 4, 116. (for I have also heard p. have read)
S. A. 112. p. my enemies who come to stare
S. A. 113. to stare at my affliction and p. to insult
S. A. 508. p. God will relent and quit thee all
S. A. 697. if these they scape p. in poverty
S. A. 812. though fond and reasonless to some p.
S. A. 1077. as these p. yet wish it had not been
S. A. 1300. and yet p. more trouble is behind
S. A. 1347. p. thou shalt have cause to sorrow
S. A. 1412. to favour and p. to set thee free
S. A. 1414. lest it p. offend them to see
C. 229. prompt me and they p. are not far off
C. 285. p. forestalling night prevented them
C. 353. p. some cold bank is her bolster now
L'A. 79. where p. some beauty lies
H. 91. p. their loves or else their sheep
**Peril.**—P. L. 3, 544. desert ways with p. gone
P. L. 9, 922. and p. great provoked who thus
P. L. 10, 469. adventure hard with p. great
C. 40. and there their tender age might suffer p.
**Perilous.**—P. L. 1, 276. and on the p. edge of
P. L. 2, 420. or oppose or undertake the p.
S. A. 804. would draw thee forth to p. enterprises
C. 424. infamous hills and sandy p. wilds
L. 185. to all that wander in that p. flood
**Period.**—P. L. 12, 467. the world's great p.
C. 585. not a p. shall be unsaid for me
**Periods.**—P. L. 2, 603. p. of time thence
**Peripatetics.**—P. R. 4, 279. surnamed P.
**Perish.**—P. L. 1, 139. heavenly essences can p.
P. L. 2, 149. to p. rather swallowed up and lost
P. L. 3, 287. as in him p. all men so in thee
P. L. 10, 785. cannot together p. with this
S. A. 676. grow up and p. as the summer fly
**Perished.**—S. A. 1512. the whole inhabitation p.
**Permission.**—P. L. 1, 212. high p. of all-ruling
P. L. 9, 378. with thy p. then and thus
P. R. 1, 496. do as thou findest p. from above
P. R. 4, 175. which expired thou hast p. on one
**Permissive.**—P. L. 3, 685. by his p. will
P. L. 8, 435. freedom used p. and acceptance
P. L. 10, 451. with what p. glory since his fall
**Permit.**—P. L. 9, 885. when fate will not p.
P. L. 9, 1159. nay didst p. approve and fair
P. L. 11, 554. how long or short p. to heaven
P. R. 1, 483. p. me to hear thee when I come
Il P. 77. or if the air will not p.
**Permits.**—P. L. 4, 1009. than heaven p. nor
P. L. 11, 260. in this paradise to dwell p. not
P. L. 12, 90. since he p. within himself
**Permitted.**—P. L. 6, 674. and p. all advised

P. L. 10, 574. lost shape p. they resumed
P. R. 4, 183. p. rather and by thee usurped
S. A. 1159. into thy enemies' hand, p. them
S. A. 1495 and I persuade me God had not p.
**Permitting.**—P. L. 9, 4. rural repast p. him
**Pernicious.**—P. L. 1, 282. such a p. height
P. L. 6, 520. p. with one touch to fire
P. L. 6, 849. lightning and shot forth p. fire
P. L. 9, 981. with a fact p. to thy peace
S. A. 1400. to no few of them would prove p.
**Perpetual.**—P. L. 1, 131. heaven's p. king
P. L. 2, 103. and with p. inroads to alarm
P. L. 2, 588. beat with p. storms of whirlwind
P. L. 2, 861. here in p. agony and pain
P. L. 4, 760. p. fountain of domestic sweets
P. L. 6, 182. p. circle, multiform, and mix
P. L. 6, 693. where light and darkness in p.
P. L. 6, 693. whence in p. fight they needs
P. L. 7, 306. and p. draw their humid train
P. L. 10, 679. else had the spring p. smiled
P. L. 11, 108. from thence p. banishment
C. 479. and a p. feast of nectared sweets
H. 7. and with his Father work us a p. peace
**Perpetuity.**—P. L. 10, 813. and so last to p.
**Perplex.**—P. L. 2, 114. to p. and dash
P. L. 10, 979. if care of our descent p. us most
**Perplexed.**—P. L. 2, 525. choice leads him p.
P. L. 4, 176. had p. all path of man or beast
P. L. 9, 19. that so long p. the Greek
P. L. 12, 275. ere while p. with thoughts
P. R. 4, 1. p. and troubled at his bad success
C. 37. lies through the p. paths of this drear
**Perplexes.**—P. L. 1, 599. fear of change p.
**Perplexing.**—P. L. 8, 183. with p. thoughts
**Perplexities.**—S. A. 304. by their own p.
**Perplexity.**—P. R. 2, 38. into p. and new
**Persecution.**—P. L. 12, 531. heavy p. shall
**Persecutors.**—P. L. 12, 497. proudest p.
**Persepolis.**—P. R. 3, 284. P. his city
**Perseverance.**——P. R. 1, 148. p. overcame
**Persevere.**—P. L. 5, 525. but to p. he left
P. L. 7, 632. and p. upright
P. L. 12, 532. on all who in the worship p.
**Persevering.**—P. L. 8, 639. I in thy p. shall
**Persian.**—P. L. 11, 393. or where the P.
P. R. 3, 273. to south the P. bay
**Persisted.**—P. L. 9, 377. Eve p. yet submiss
P. L. 10, 874. but for thee I had p. happy
S. A. 249. but they p. deaf and would not seem
**Persisting.**—P. L. 3, 197. to the end p. safe
**Person.**—P. L. 2, 110. a fairer p. lost not heaven
P. L. 3, 41. justly gives heroic name to p. or to
P. L. 9, 444. the place admired the p. more
P. L. 10, 156. thy part and p. hadst thou
S. A. 31. as of a p. separate to God
S. A. 851. and princes of my country came in p.
S. A. 1208. but I a private p. whom my country
S. A. 1211. a p. raised with strength sufficient
C. 406. attempt the p. of our unowned sister
S. 23. love sweetness goodness in her p. shined
**Personating.**—P. R. 4, 341. or song so p.
**Persons.**—P. R. 2, 240. of various p. each to
**Persuade.**—P. L. 2, 121. reason to p.
P. L. 9, 979. sustain alone the worst and not p.
P. R. 3, 44. thou neither dost p. me to seek
S. A. 586. and I p. me so why else this strength
S. A. 1495. and I p. me God had not permitted
D. F. I. 29. yet can I not p. me thou art dead
**Persuaders.**—P. L. 9, 587. once powerful p.
**Persuasion.**—P. L. 11, 152. p. in me grew
P. R. 1, 223. and make p. do the work of fear
P. R. 2, 142. deceive ye to p. over-sure of like
P. R. 4, 230. ruling them by p. as thou mean'st
S. A. 658. studied argument and much p. sought
**Persuasive.**—P. L. 2, 118. and with p.
P. L. 9, 737. the sound yet rung of his p. words
P. R. 2, 159. arts enchanting tongues p.
P. R. 4, 4. and the p. rhetoric that sleeked
**Persuasively.**—P. R. 3, 373. with me p.
**Pert.**—C. 118. trip the p. faeries and the dapper
**Perturbation.**—P. L. 4, 120. each p.

P. L. 10, 113. and shame and p. and despair
**Peru.**—P. L. 11, 408. in P. the richer seat
**Perused.**—P. L. 8, 267. myself I then p.
P. R. 1, 320. who first with curious eye p. him
**Perverse.**—P. L. 2, 625. p. all monstrous
P. L. 2, 1030. spirits p. with easy intercourse
P. L. 6, 37. though worlds judged thee p.
P. L. 6, 562. and turn not back p.
P. L. 6, 706. and this p. commotion governed
P. L. 9, 405. of thy presumed return event p.
P. L. 11, 701. the only righteous in a world p.
S. A. 737. in the p. event than I foresaw
**Perverseness.**—P. L. 6, 788. such p. dwell
P. L. 10, 902. seldom gain through her p.
**Pervert.**—P. L. 1, 164. must be to p. that end
P. L. 3, 92. by some false guile p. and shall p.
P. L. 11, 523. they p. pure nature's healthful
**Perverted.**—P. L. 10, 3. serpent had p. Eve
P. L. 12. 547. dissolve Satan with his p. world
**Perverts.**—P. L. 4, 203. before him but p.
**Pest.**—P. L. 2, 735. her words the hellish p.
**Pestered.**—C. 7. confined and p. in this pinfold
**Pestilence.**—P. L. 2, 711. hair shakes p.
P. L. 11, 487. marasmus and wide wasting p.
P. R. 3, 412. by three days' p. such was thy zeal
D. F. I. 68. or drive away the slaughtering p.
**Pestilent.**—P. L. 10, 695. hot corrupt and p.
**Pet.**—C. 721. should in a p. of temperance feed
**Petition.**—P. L. 11, 10. less seemed their p.
S. A. 650. might I be-heard no long p.
**Petrific.**—P. L. 10, 294. his mace p. cold
**Petsora.**—P. L. 10, 292. beyond P. eastward
**Petty.**—P. L. 9, 693. ire for such a p. trespass
P. R. 4, 87. shared among p. kings too far
S. A. 529. like a p. god I walked about admired
S. A. 1223. as a p. enterprise of small enforce
C. 926. from a thousand p. rills
**Phalanx.**—P. L. 1, 550. in perfect p. to the
P. L. 4,979. sharpening in mooned horns their p.
P. L. 6, 399. in cubic p. firm advanced entire
**Phantasm.**—P. L. 2, 743. and that p. call'st
**Phantasms.**—P. L. 4, 803. as he list p.
**Phantasy.**—S. M. 5. and to our high-raised p.
**Pharaoh.**—P. L. 1, 342. of impious P.
P. L. 12, 163. be the second in that realm of P.
**Pharphar.**—P. L. 1, 469. of Abbana and P.
**Philasters.**—P. L. 1, 713. where p. round
**Philip.**—P. R. 3, 32. Macedonian P. had
**Philistean.**—P. L. 9, 1061. harlot lap of P.
**Philistian.**—S. A. 39. Israel from P. yoke
S. A. 42. himself in bonds under P. yoke
S. A. 216. why thou shouldst wed P. women
S. A. 482. have made way to some P. lords
S. A. 722. some rich P. matron she may seem
S. A. 831. weakness to resist P. gold
S. A. 1371. the P. lords command
S.A.1655. not only of this but each P. city round
S. A. 1714. through all P. bounds
**Philistine.**—S. A. 238. the P. thy country's
S. A. 1099. won by a P. from the unforeskinned
**Philistines.**—S. A. 251. their lords the P.
S. A. 434. this day the P. a popular feast
S. A. 808. mine and love's prisoner not the P.
S.A.1189. P. when thou hadst broke the league
S. A. 1192. among the daughters of the P.
S.A.1363.with thy strength thou servest the P.
S. A. 1523. this evil on the P. is fallen
**Phillis.**—L'A. 86. the neat-handed P. dresses
**Philomel.**—Il P. 56. 'less P. will deign a song
**Philosophers.**—P. L. 3, 601. p. in vain so
**Philosophic.**—P. R. 4, 300. in p. pride
**Philosophy.**—P. L. 2, 565. and false p.
P. R. 4, 272. to sage p. next lend thine ear
C. 476. how charming is divine p.
**Phineus.**—P. L. 3, 36. and P. prophets old
**Phlegethon.**—P. L. 2, 580. fierce P. whose
**Phlegra.**—P. L. 1, 577. the giant brood of P.
**Phœbus.**—P. R. 4, 260. whose poem P.
C. 66. to quench the drouth of P.
C.190.rose from the hindmost wheels of P.wain

L. 77. but not the praise, P. replied
S. 13, 10. to honour thee the priest of P.' choir
P. 23. to this horizon is my P. bound
**Phœnicians.**—P. L. 1, 438. the P. called
**Phœnix.**—P. L. 5, 272. he seems a p.
**Phrenzy.**—P. L. 11, 485. demoniac p.
S. A. 1675. them he a spirit of p. sent
**Phylacteries.**—F. of C. 17. clip your p.
**Pick.**—S. A. 1326. but they must p. me out
**Pick-axe.**—P. L. 1, 676. with spade and p.-a.
**Picture.**—Hor. 14. me in my vowed p.
**Pied.**—L'A. 75. meadows trim with daisies p.
**Pieces.**—P. L. 6, 489. as shall dash to p.
P. R. 4, 149. or as a stone that shall to p. dash
**Piemontese.**—S. 18, 7. slain by the bloody P.
**Pierce.**—P. R. 2, 91. a sword shall p.
S.A.1568.hitting thy aged ear should p.too deep
L'A. 138. such as the meeting soul may p.
S.M.4. things with imbreathed sense able to p.
Cir. 28. will p. more near his heart
**Pierced.**—P. L. 4, 99. hate have p. so deep
P. L. 6,356. and with fierce ensigns p. the deep
P. L. 6, 435. and though p. with wound soon
P. L. 11, 417. the power of these ingredients p.
**Piercing.**—P. L. 2, 275. these p. fires as soft
P. L. 3, 24. roll in vain to find thy p. ray
**Piety.**—P. L. 6, 144. faith prefer and p. to God
P. L. 11, 452. is p. thus and pure devotion paid
P. L. 11, 799. from whom their p. feigned
P. L. 12, 321. the second both for p. renowned
S. A. 993. conferred upon me for the p.
**Pile.**—P. L. 1, 722. the ascending p. stood fixed
P. L. 2, 591. and ruin seems of ancient p.
P. L. 11, 324. and p. up every stone of lustre
P. R. 4, 547. the glorious temple reared her p.
S. A. 1069. as is his p. high-built and proud
**Piled.**—P. L. 4, 544. a rock of alabaster p. up
P. L. 5, 394. to side all autumn p.
P. L. 5, 632. on a sudden p. with angel's food
P. R. 2, 341. with dishes p. and meats
W. S. 2. the labour of an age in p. stones
V.Ex.42.and hills of snow and lofts of p.thunder
**Pilfering.**—C. 504. the stealth of p. wolf
**Pilgrim.**—L. R. 4,427. came forth with p. steps
**Pilgrims.**—P. L. 3, 476. here p. roam that
**Pillar.**—P. L. 2, 302. seemed a p. of state
P. L. 12, 202. go before them in a cloud and p.
P. L. 12, 203. by day a cloud by night a p. of fire
P. L. 12, 208. then through the fiery p.
**Pillared.**—P. L. 9, 1106. a p. shade high
P. R. 4, 455. as dangerous to the p. frame
C.598.if this fail the p. firmament is rottenness
**Pillars.**—P. L. 1, 714. and Doric p. overlaid
P. L. 4, 549. betwixt rocky p. Gabriel sat
P. L. 6, 572. mounted row of p. laid on wheels
P. L. 6, 573. for like to p. most they seemed
P. R. 4, 58. outside and inside both p. and
S. A. 1630. they led him between the p.
S.A.1633. both his arms on those two massy p.
S. A. 1648. those two massy p.
Il P. 158. with antique p. massy proof
**Pillows.**—H. 231. p. his chin upon an orient
**Pilot.**—P. L. 1, 204. the p. of some small
P. L. 5, 264. or p. from amidst the Cyclades
S.A.198.who like a foolish p. have shipwrecked
S. A. 1044. must p. so expert but needs must
L. 109. the p. of the Galilian lake
**Pinched.**—L'A. 103. she was p. and pulled she
**Pinching.**—P. L. 10, 691. avoided p. cold and
**Pindarus.**—S. 8, 11. bid spare the house of P.
**Pine.**—P. L. 1, 292. to equal which the tallest p.
P. L. 2, 601. and there to p. immovable infixed
P. L. 4, 139. cedar, and p., and fir
P. L. 9, 435. stateliest covert, cedar p. palm
P. L. 10, 597. who with eternal famine p.
P. L. 10, 1076. the gummy bark of fir or p.
P. L. 12, 77. the clouds will p. his entrails
Il P. 135. of p. or monumental oak
**Pined.**—P. L. 4, 466. and p. with vain desire
P. L. 4, 848. her shape how lovely saw and p.

P. R. 1, 325. not here his carcass *p.* with hunger
**Pines.**—P. L. 1, 613. or mountain *p.*
P. L. 2, 544. pull up by roots Thessalian *p.*
P. L. 4, 511. unfulfilled with pain of longing *p.*
P. L. 5, 193. and wave your tops ye *p.*
P. L. 6, 198. his seat half sunk with all his *p.*
P. L. 9, 1088. cover me ye *p.*
P. L 11, 321. among these *p.* his voice I heard
P. R. 4, 416. whose tallest *p.* though rooted
C. 184. under the spreading favour of these *p.*
C. 768. if every just man that now *p.* with want
**Pinfold.**—C. 7. confined and pestered in this *p.*
**Pining.**—P. L. 11, 486. *p.* atrophy
**Pink.**—L. 144. the white *p.* and the pansy
**Pinks.**—C. 851. pansies *p.* and gaudy daffodils
**Pinnace.**—P. L. 2, 289. or *p.* anchors in
**Pinnacle.**—P. R. 4, 549. the highest *p.*
**Pinnacles.**—P. L. 3, 550. and *p.* adorned
**Pins.**—P. L. 10, 318. with *p.* of adamant
**Pioneers.**—P. L. 1, 676. as when bands of *p.*
P. R. 3, 330. nor of labouring *p.* multitude
**Pious.**—P. L. 5, 135. and *p.* awe that feared to
P. L. 11, 362. joy with fear and *p.* sorrow
P. R. 1, 463. truth henceforth to dwell in *p.*
S. A. 955. bewail thy falsehood and *p.* works
**Pipe.**—P. L. 7, 595. rested not the solemn *p.*
P. L. 11, 132. Arcadian *p.* the pastoral reed
P. R. 1, 480. and tunable as sylvan *p.* song
C. 86. who with his soft *p.* and smooth-dittied
C. 173. such as the jocund flute gamesome *p.*
**Piped.**—C. 823. shepherd that e'er *p.* on plains
**Pipes.**—P. L. 1, 561. in silence to soft *p.*
P. L. 1, 709. many a row of *p.* the sound board
P. R. 2, 363. chiming strings or charming *p.*
S. A. 1616. before him *p.* and timbrels
L. 124. grate on their scrannel *p.* of wretched
**Piping.**—Il P. 126. while rocking winds are *p.*
**Pit.**—P. L. 1, 91. into what *p.* thou seest
P. L. 1, 381. chief were those who from the *p.*
P. L. 1, 657. for this infernal *p.* shall never
P. L. 2, 850. the key of this infernal *p.* by due
P. L. 4, 965. back to the infernal *p.* I drag
P. L. 6, 866. after them to the bottomless *p.*
P. L. 10, 464. triumphant out of this infernal *p.*
**Pitch.**—P. L. 2, 772. from the *p.* of heaven
P. L. 8, 198. therefore from this high *p.* let us
P. L. 11, 693. shall be held the highest *p.* of
P. L. 11, 731. smeared round with *p.* and
S. A. 169. to lowest *p.* of abject fortune
**Pitched.**—P. L. 12, 136. his tents *p.* about
**Pitchy.**—P. L. 1, 340. a *p.* cloud of locusts
**Piteous.**—P. L. 10, 1032. *p.* amends ! unless
C. 836. who *p.* of her woes reared her lank
**Pitied.**—S. A. 568. a gaze or *p.* object
**Pity.**—P. L. 3, 402. but much more to *p.*
P. L. 3, 405. but much more to *p.* inclined
P. L. 4, 374. whom I could *p.* thus forlorn
P. L. 5, 220. beheld with *p.* heaven's high
P. L. 10, 25. yet mixed with *p.* violated not
P. L. 10, 1061. and his heart to *p.* incline
P. L. 11, 629. O *p.* and shame that they who
S. A. 814. yet always *p.* pardon hath obtained
S. 9, 8. no anger find in thee but *p.* and ruth
D. F. I. 33. could heaven for *p.* thee so strictly
**Pitying.**—P. L. 10, 211. then *p.* how they
P. L. 10, 1059. us unworthy *p.* while he judged
**Placable.**—P. L. 11, 151. I saw him *p.* and
**Place.**—P. L. 1, 70. such *p.* eternal justice had
P. L. 1, 75. O how unlike the *p.* from whence
P. L. 1, 253. not to be changed by *p.* or time
P. L. 1, 254. the mind is its own *p.*
P. L. 1, 318. or have ye chosen this *p.*
P. L. 1, 625. as this *p.* testifies
P. L. 1, 759. by *p.* or choice the worthiest
P. L. 2, 27. will envy whom the highest *p.*
P. L. 2, 57. and for their dwelling *p.* accept
P. L. 2, 217. and to the *p.* conformed in temper
P. L. 2, 235. what *p.* can be for us within
P. L. 2, 260. and in what *p.* soe'er thrive
P. L. 2, 317. hath doomed this *p.* our dungeon
P. L. 2, 345. there is a *p.* if ancient and

P. L. 2, 360. this *p.* may lie exposed
P. L. 2, 830. wandering quest a *p.* foretold
P. L. 2, 832. a *p.* of bliss in the purlieus of
P. L. 2, 840. and bring ye to the *p.* where
P. L. 2, 894. and time and *p.* are lost where
P. L. 2, 977. or if some other *p.* from your
P. L. 3, 194. and I will *p.* within them as
P. L. 3, 591. the *p.* he found beyond expression
P. L. 3, 720. each had his *p.* appointed
P. L. 3, 724. that *p.* is earth the seat of man
P. L. 4, 23. can fly by change of *p.* now
P. L. 4, 79. is there no *p.* left for repentance
P. L. 4, 246. thus was this *p.* a happy rural
P. L. 4, 385. if no better *p.* thank him who
P. L. 4, 442. for other creature in this *p.* living
P. L. 4, 562. that to this happy *p.* no evil
P. L. 4, 690. it was a *p.* chosen by the sovran
P. L. 4, 729. and this delicious *p.* for us too
P. L. 4, 745. austerely talk of purity and *p.*
P. L. 4, 759. think thee unbefitting holiest *p.*
P. L. 4, 840. now thy sin and *p.* of doom
P. L. 4, 843. to keep this *p.* inviolable
P. L. 4, 882. thy bold entrance on this *p.*
P. L. 4, 891. and boldly venture to whatever *p.*
P. L. 4, 894. with delight which in this *p.*
P. L. 5, 361. native of heaven for other *p.*
P. L. 5, 373. or such *p.* hast here to dwell
P. L. 5, 614. his *p.* ordained without redemption
P. L. 5, 682. more in this *p.* to utter is not safe
P. L. 5, 732. this our high *p.* our sanctuary
P. L. 5, 812. in *p.* thyself so high above
P. L. 6, 53. into their *p.* of punishment
P. L. 6, 276. thy offspring to the *p.* of evil
P. L. 6, 405. though from their *p.* by violence
P. L. 6, 782. each to his *p.*
P. L. 7, 135. through the deep into his *p.*
P. L. 7, 144. drew many whom their *p.* knows
P. L. 7, 240. things to like the rest several *p.*
P. L. 7, 284. into one *p.* and let dry land appear
P. L. 7, 535. for no *p.* is yet distinct by name
P. L. 9, 69. there was a *p.* now not
P. L. 9, 119. but I in none of these find *p.*
P. L. 9, 444. much he the *p.* admired
P. L. 9, 1174. upon free will hath here no *p.*
P. L. 10, 148. and the *p.* wherein God set thee
P. L. 10, 241. since no *p.* like this can fit his
P. L. 10, 315. to the self-same *p.* where he first
P. L. 10, 624. them to enter and possess a *p.*
P. L. 10, 741. heavy though in their *p.*
P. L. 10, 745. or here *p.* in this delicious garden
P. L. 10, 787. or in some other dismal *p.*
P. L. 10, 932. to the *p.* of judgment will return
P. L. 10, 953. I to that *p.* would speed before
P. L. 10, 971. restored by thee vile as I am to *p.*
P. L. 10, 1086. than to the *p.* repairing where
P. L. 10, 1098. forthwith to the *p.* repairing
P. L. 11, 118. on the east side of the garden *p.*
P. L. 11, 267. discovered soon the *p.* of her
P. L. 11, 303. departure from this happy *p.*
P. L. 11, 318. *p.* by *p.* where he vouchsafed
P. L. 11, 477. a *p.* before his eyes appeared
P. L. 11, 635. hold his *p.* by wisdom
P. L. 11, 831. be moved out of his *p.*
P. L. 11, 836. God attributes to *p.* no sanctity
P. L. 12, 142. each *p.* behold in prospect as I
P. L. 12, 363. inquire his *p.* to offer incense
P. L. 12, 364. his *p.* of birth a solemn angel tells
P. L. 12, 464. far happier *p.* than this of Eden
P. L. 12, 647. where to choose their *p.* of rest
P. R. 1, 39. envy fraught and rage flies to his *p.*
P. R. 1, 252. course led on they found the *p.*
P. R. 1, 321. chance hath brought thee to this *p.*
P. R. 1, 362. to that hideous *p.* not so confined
P. R. 1, 412. comes to the *p.* where he before
P. R. 1, 416. the happy *p.* imparts to thee
P. R. 2, 19. sought lost Elijah so in each *p.*
P. R. 2, 125. so may we hold our *p.* and these
P. R. 2, 396. and rather opportunely in this *p.*
P. R. 4, 101. and in his *p.* ascending
P. R. 4, 373. the wilderness for thee is fittest *p.*
P. R. 4, 600. whatever *p.*, habit or state

S. A. 17. I seek this unfrequented *p.* to find
S. A. 254. in what *p.* to set upon them what
S. A. 333. ye seem though in this uncouth *p.*
S. A. 910. afford me *p.* to show what recompense
S. A. 1085. that I was never present on the *p.*
S. A. 1117. assigned some narrow *p.* enclosed
S. A. 1359. a Nazarite in *p.* abominable
S. A. 1550. some distance from the *p.* of horror
S. A. 1624. to the *p.* and what was set before
S. A. 1751. hath in *p.* bore witness gloriously
C. 156. give it false presentments lest the *p.*
C. 201. this is the *p.* as well as I may guess
C. 305. readiest way would bring me to that *p.*
C. 326. in a *p.* less warranted than this or less
C. 570. guided by mine ear I found the *p.*
C. 939. let us fly this cursed *p.*
A. 105. to serve the lady of this *p.*
Il P. 78. some still removed *p.* will fit
D. F. I. 46. took up and in fit *p.* did reinstall
V. Ex. 25. and weary of their *p.* do only stay
**Placed.**—P. L. 1, 387. yea often *p.* within his
P. L. 2, 833. and therein *p.* a race of upstart
P. L. 3, 66. in the happy garden *p.* reaping
P. L. 3, 90. and man there *p.* with purpose to
P. L. 4, 294. but in true filial freedom *p.*
P. L. 4, 416. raised us from the dust and *p.*
P. L. 4, 580. none pass the vigilance here *p.*
P. L. 5, 476. and pure as nearer to him *p.*
P. L. 5, 516. us from the dust and *p.* us here
P. L. 6, 412. *p.* in guard their watches round
P. L. 6, 638. God hath in his mighty angels *p.*
P. L. 7, 360. from her cloudy shrine and *p.*
P. L. 8, 120. *p.* heaven from earth so far that
P. L. 8, 170. best wherever *p.* let him dispose
P. L. 8, 559. about her as a guard angelic *p.*
P. L. 8, 638. the weal or woe in thee is *p.*
P. L. 10, 447. at the upper end was *p.* in regal
P. L. 10, 484. therein man *p.* in a paradise
P. L. 12, 315. they in their earthly Canaan *p.*
P. R. 1, 475. but thou art. *p.* above me thou
P. R. 2, 424. and his son Herod *p.* on Judah's
P. R. 4, 297. others in virtue *p.* felicity
P. R. 4, 553. and highest is best
**Places.**—P. L. 5, 364. those happy *p.* thou
P. L. 10, 324. in sight to each of these three *p.*
P. L. 11, 305. all *p.* else inhospitable appear
P. L. 12, 516. avail themselves of names *p.* and
P. L. 12, 618. all things under heaven, all *p.*
**Placid.**—P. R. 3, 217. from that *p.* aspect and
**Plague.**—P. L. 2, 174. right hand to *p.* us
P. L. 6, 505. like instrument to *p.* the sons of
**Plagued.**—P. L. 10, 572. thus were they *p.*
**Plagues.**—P. L. 6, 838. their souls infixed *p.*
P. L. 11, 697. rightlier called and *p.* of men
**Plain.**—P. L. 1, 180. seest thou yon dreary *p.*
P. L. 1, 350. and fill all the *p.*
P. L. 1, 397. in Rabba and her watery *p.*
P. L. 1, 700. nigh on the *p.* in many cells
P. L. 2, 528. part on the *p.* or in the air
P. L. 3, 466. builders next of Babel on the *p.*
P. L. 4, 243. profuse on hill and dale and *p.*
P. L. 4, 455. and spread into a liquid *p.*
P. L. 5, 648. wide over all the *p.* and wider
P. L. 5, 649. than all this globous earth in *p.*
P. L. 6, 15. when all the *p.* covered with thick
P. L. 7, 299. if through *p.* soft ebbing
P. L. 8, 303. mountain whose high top was *p.*
P. L. 9, 285. which *p.* infers thy equal fear
P. L. 9, 758. in *p.* then what forbids he but
P. L. 11, 349. in valley and in *p.* God is here
P. L. 11, 556. and saw a spacious *p.* whereon
P. L. 11, 576. down to the *p.* descended
P. L. 11, 580. they on the *p.* long had not
P. L. 11, 649. their bleating lambs over the *p.*
P. L. 11, 673. through all the *p.* and refuge
P. L. 12, 41. shall find the *p.* wherein a black
P. L. 12, 136. Sechem and the neighbouring *p.*
P. L. 12, 640. the cliff as fast to the subjected *p.*
P. R. 2, 27. fishermen, no greater men
P. R. 2, 87. trouble as old Simeon *p.* foretold
P R. 3, 254. a spacious *p.* outstretched in

P. R. 3, 332. lay hills *p.*, fell woods or valleys
P. R. 3, 333. where *p.* was raise hill or overlay
P. R. 4, 27. another *p.* long but in breadth not
P. R. 4, 193. get thee behind me *p.* thou now
P. R. 4, 296. doubted all things though *p.*
P. R. 4, 543. over the wilderness and o'er the *p.*
S. A. 1279. with *p.* heroic magnitude of mind
S. A. 1256. that he durst not *p.* enough appeared
Hor. 5. *p.* in thy neatness.
**Plained.**—P. L. 4, 504. and to himself thus *p.*
**Plainest.**—P. R. 4, 361. in them is *p.* taught
**Plaining.**—P. 47. my *p.* verse as lively as before
**Plainlier.**—P. L. 12, 151. to thee anon *p.*
**Plains.**—P. L. 1, 104. battle on the *p.* of heaven
P. L. 3, 437. lights on the barren *p.* of Sericana
P. L. 5, 143. Paradise and Eden's happy *p.*
P. L. 8, 262. and shady woods and sunny *p.*
P. L. 8, 275. ye rivers woods and *p.*
P. L. 9, 116. hill and valley, rivers, woods, *p.*
P. L. 10, 432. by Astracan over the snowy *p.*
P. R. 3, 319. Atropatia and neighbouring *p.*
C. 823. the soothest shepherd that e'er on *p.*
**Plaint.**—P. L. 10, 343. discourse and various *p.*
P. L. 10, 913. and thus proceeded in her *p.*
P. L. 11, 499. scarce recovering words his *p.*
P. L. 11, 762. to the angel utteredst thus thy *p.*
H. 191. moan with midnight *p.*
**Plaints.**—P. L. 9, 98. bursting passion into *p.*
P. R. 2, 29. unexpected loss and *p.* outbreathed
P. R. 2, 58. thus they out of their *p.* new hope
D. F. I. 37. if so it be that thou these *p.* dost
**Planet.**—P. L. 7, 366. hence the morning *p.*
P. L. 8, 129. the *p.* earth so steadfast though
A. 52. or what the cross dire-looking *p.* smites
Il P. 96. with *p.* or with element
**Planetary.**—P. L. 10, 658. other five their *p.*
**Planets.**—P. L. 3, 481. they pass the *p.*
P. L. 5, 621. yonder starry sphere of *p.*
P. L. 6, 313. two *p.* rushing from aspect malign
P. L. 7, 563. *p.* in their station listening stood
P. L. 10, 413. and *p.* planet-struck real eclipse
**Planet-struck.**—P. L. 10, 413. planets *p.*-*s.*
**Plank.**—P. L. 1, 772. or on the smoothed *p.*
**Plant.**—P. L. 1, 652. therein *p.* a generation
P. L. 3, 53. there *p.* eyes all mist from thence
P. L. 4, 199. virtue thought of that life-giving *p.*
P. L. 4, 240. visiting each *p.* and fed flowers
P. L. 5, 58. add O fair *p.*, said he, with fruit
P. L. 5, 193. with every *p.* in sign of worship
P. L. 5, 327. each *p.* and juiciest gourd
P. L. 6, 475. with *p.*, fruit, flower, ambrosial
P. L. 7, 335. all the ground and each *p.*
P. L. 9, 111. productive in herb, *p.* and nobler
P. L. 9, 206. still to tend *p.*, herb, and flower
P. L. 9, 679. sacred wise and wisdom-giving *p.*
P. L. 9, 837. infused into the *p.* sciential sap
P. R. 4, 434. dried the wet from drooping *p.*
P. R. 4, 461. on man, beast, *p.* wasteful
S. A. 362. as of a *p.* select and sacred glorious
S. A. 1734. a monument, and *p.* it round with
C. 621. in every virtuous *p.* and healing herb
L. 78. fame is no *p.* that grows on mortal soil
**Plantation.**—P. L. 9, 419. tendance or *p.*
**Planted.**—P. L. 4, 210. the east of Eden *p.*
P. L. 4, 424. that only tree of knowledge *p.* by
P. L. 4, 884. whose dwelling God hath *p.* here
P. L. 7, 538. garden *p.* with the trees of God
P. L. 8, 305. enclosed with goodliest trees *p.*
**Planter.**—P. L. 4, 691. by the sovran *p.*
**Plants.**—P. L. 4, 438. prune these growing *p.*
P. L. 5, 22. how spring our tended *p.*
P. L. 7, 473. the flocks and bleating rose as *p.*
A. 48. and all my *p.* I save from nightly ill
**Plat.**—P. L. 9, 456. this flowery *p.* the sweet
Il P. 73. off on a *p.* of rising ground
**Platane.**—P. L. 4, 478. and tall under a *p.*
**Plate.**—P. R. 6, 368. wounds through *p.*
**Plated.**—S. A. 140. warriors turned their *p.* backs
**Plato.**—P. L. 3, 472. who to enjoy *P.'s* Elysium
P. R. 4, 245. grove of Academe *P.'s* retirement
Il P. 89. or unsphere the spirit of *P.*

**Plausible.**—P. R. 3, 393. *p.* to the world
**Play.**—P. L. 4, 404. two gentle fawns at *p.*
 P. L. 7, 10. thy sister and with her didst *p.*
 P. L. 7, 410. and bended dolphins *p.*
 P. L. 8, 372. at thy command to come and *p.*
 P. L. 9, 528. the eye of Eve to mark his *p.*
 P. L. 9, 583. of lamb or kid that tend their *p.*
 P. L. 9, 1027. so well refreshed now let us *p.*
 P. L. 9, 1045. wearied with their amorous *p.*
 P. R. 1, 201. no childish *p.* to me was pleasing
 P. R. 2, 26. with reeds and osiers whispering *p.*
 S. A. 719. by all the winds that hold them *p.*
 S. A. 1340. them feats and *p.* before their god
 S.A.1448.come and *p.* before them at their feast
 S. A. 1679. they only set on sport and *p.*
 C. 301. and *p.* in the plighted clouds
 C. 958. back shepherds back enough your *p.*
 L'A. 97. and young and old come forth to *p.*
**Played.**—P. L. 3, 641. curls on either cheek *p.*
 P. L. 4, 340. about them frisking *p.* all beasts
 P. L. 5, 295. and *p.* at will her virgin fancies
 P. L. 9, 1048. about their spirits had *p.*
 C.833. the water nymphs that in the bottom *p.*
 L. 99. sleek Panope with all her sisters *p.*
**Playing.**—P. L. 8, 510. neither were ye *p.* on the steep
 L. A. 19. Zephyr with Aurora *p.*
**Plea.**—P. L. 4, 394. with necessity the tyrants *p.*
 P. L. 10, 30. with righteous *p.* their utmost
 P. R. 3, 149. yet of another *p.* bethought him
 S. A. 834. all wickedness is weakness that *p.*
 S. A. 843. thou determinest weakness for no *p.*
 L. 90. that came in Neptune's *p.*
**Plead.**—P. L. 11, 41. I to mitigate thus *p.*
 S. A. 421. but thou didst *p.* divine impulsion
 S.A.833. incestuous sacrilegious but may *p.* it?
**Pleaded.**—P. L. 2, 379. thus Beelzebub *p.*
 P. L. 8, 510. approved my *p.* reason
**Pleasant.**—P. L. 1, 404. the *p.* valley of
 P. L. 3, 703. *p.* to know and worthiest to be
 P. L. 4, 28. which now in his view lay *p.*
 P. L. 4, 214. this *p.* soil his far more *p* garden
 P. L. 4, 625. and at our *p.* labour, to reform
 P. L. 4, 642. *p.* the sun when first on this
 P. L. 5, 38. now is the *p.* time, the cool the
 P. L. 5, 84. the *p.* savoury smell so quickened
 P. L. 5, 445. flowing cups with *p.* liquors
 P. L. 6, 628. they among themselves in *p.* vein
 P. L. 7, 316. her universal face with *p.* green
 P. L. 7, 540. and freely all their *p.* fruit for food
 P. L. 7, 625. their *p.* dwelling place
 P. L. 8, 215. they satiate and soon fill though *p.*
 P. L. 8, 306. of earth before scarce *p.* seemed
 P. L. 9, 207. herb and flower our *p.* task
 P. L. 9, 418. of grove or garden-plot more *p.*
 P. L. 9, 448. among the *p.* villages and farms
 P. L. 11, 179. can be toilsome in these *p.* walks
 P. L. 11, 607. those tents thou sawest so *p.*
 P. R. 1, 118. of many a *p.* realm and province
 P. R. 2, 289. in a bottom saw a *p.* grove
 P. R. 3, 255. lay *p.* from his side two rivers
 Hor. 2. on roses in some *p.* cave
**Pleasantest.**—P. L. 8, 212. palm tree *p.* to
**Please.**—P. L. 1, 423. spirits when they *p.*
 P. L. 2, 270. we his light imitate when we *p.*
 P. L. 4, 378. haply may not *p.* like this fair
 P. L. 4, 640. all *p.* alike
 P. L. 5, 304. of taste to *p.* true appetite
 P. L. 5, 397. stranger, *p.* to taste these bounties
 P. L. 6, 351. and as they *p.* they limb
 P. L. 7, 49. of all tastes else to *p.* their appetite
 P. L. 8, 449. what next I bring shall *p.* thee
 P. L. 9, 949. who can *p.* him long me first
 P. R. 4, 157. nothing will *p.* the difficult
 P. R. 4, 164. given to me, I give to whom I *p.*
 S. A. 896. to *p.* thy gods thou didst it
 C. 174. to *p.* and sate the curious taste
 L'A. 116. towered cities *p.* us then
 S. 8, 3. if deed of honour did thee ever *p.*
**Pleased.**—P. L. 2, 117. yet he *p.* the ear and
 P. L. 2, 291. and his sentence *p.* advising peace
 P. L. 2, 387. the bold design *p.* highly those

 P. L. 2, 395. might have bestowed on whom I *p.*
 P. L. 2, 762. but familiar grown I *p.* and with
 P. L. 2, 845. for both seemed highly *p.*
 P. L. 3, 241. and for him lastly die well *p.*
 P. L. 3, 257. *p.* out of heaven shalt look down
 P. L. 4, 164. with such delay well *p.* they
 P. L. 4, 167. better *p.* than Asmodeus with
 P. L. 4, 337. that *p.* so well our victors' ear
 P. L. 4, 463. but *p.* I soon returned *p.* it
 P. L. 4, 604. silence was *p.* now glowed the
 P. L. 5, 617. all seemed well *p.* all seemed but
 P. L. 5, 825. powers of heaven such as he *p.*
 P. L. 6, 728. delight that thou in me well *p.*
 P. L. 7, 11. of the Almighty Father *p.*
 P. L. 8, 57. his lip not words alone *p.* her
 P. L. 8, 248. *p.* with thy words no less than
 P. L. 8, 429. yet so *p.* canst raise thy creature
 P. L. 8, 437. to try thee Adam I was *p.*
 P. L. 9, 26. this subject for heroic song *p.*
 P. L. 9, 580. more *p.* my sense than smell of
 P. L. 10, 71. mayst ever rest well *p.*
 P. L. 10, 105. not *p.* thus entertained with
 L. L. 12, 625. Adam heard well *p.* but answered
 P.R.1, 85. this is my Son beloved—in him am *p.*
 P.R.1, 286. beloved Son in whom he was well *p.*
 S. A. 219. and she *p.* me not my parents
 S. A. 511. (*p.* with humble and filial submission)
 S.A.900. less therefore to be *p.* obeyed or feared
**Pleases.**—P. L. 8, 169. creatures as him *p.* best
 P. L. 9, 453. pleasing seemed for her now *p.*
 P. R. 4, 369. kingdom nor empire *p.* thee
 S.A.311.full right to exempt whom so it *p.* him
**Pleasing.**—P. L. 2, 566. yet with a *p.* sorcery
 P. L. 5, 42. and with more *p.* light shadowy
 P. L. 9, 453. what *p.* seemed for her now pleases
 P. L. 9, 503. *p.* was his shape and lovely
 P. L. 11, 26. fruits of more *p.* savour from thy
 P. R. 1, 202. no childish play to me was *p.*
 P. R. 1, 479. smooth on the tongue discoursed *p.*
 S. A. 1008. love-quarrels oft in *p.* concord end
 C. 260. yet they in *p.* slumber lulled the sense
 C. 526. *p.* poison the visage quite transforms
 C. 546. wrapped in a *p.* fit of melancholy
**Pleasingly.**—P. L. 9, 794. she *p.* began
**Pleasure.**—P. L. 2, 586. joy and grief, *p.*
 P. L. 3, 107. what *p.* I from such obedience
 P. L. 6, 459. sense of *p.* we may well spare out
 P. L. 6, 641. of *p.* situate in hill and dale
 P. L. 8, 50. such *p.* she reserved Adam relating
 P. L. 8, 402. taste no *p.* though in *p.* solitary
 P. L. 8, 593. not sunk in carnal *p.* for which
 P. L. 9, 455. such *p.* took the serpent to behold
 P. L. 9, 470. the more he sees of *p.* not for him
 P. L. 9, 477. hope here to taste of *p.*
 P. L. 9, 447. all *p.* to destroy save what is in
 P. L. 9, 596. for such *p.* till that hour
 P. L. 9, 1022. much *p.* we have lost while we
 P. L. 9, 1024. if such *p.* be in things to us
 P. L. 10, 1013. contempt of life and *p.* seems
 P. L. 10, 1019. for loss of life and *p.* overloved
 P. L. 11, 541. all taste of *p.* must forego
 P. L. 11, 604. judge not what is best by *p.*
 P. L. 11, 794. their course to *p.* ease and sloth
 P. R. 1, 423. or *p.* to do ill excites
 P. R. 4, 299. in corporal *p.* he and careless ease
 P. R. 4, 305. all wealth, *p.*, pain, or torment
 S. A. 534. softened with *p.* and voluptuous life
 C. 77. to roll with *p.* in a sensual sty
 Il P. 50. that in trim gardens takes his *p.*
 H. 99. the air such *p.* loth to lose
 V. Ex. 17.haste thee straight to do me once a *p.*
**Pleasures.**—P. L. 4, 535. short *p.* for long
 P. L. 8, 480. and other *p.* all abjure
 P. L. 9, 120. and the more I see *p.* about me
 P. R. 3, 28. who all *p.* else despise
 C. 668. all the *p.* that fancy can beget
 L'A. 40. in unreproved *p.* free
 L'A. 69. straight mine eye hath caught new *p.*
 Il P. 175. these *p.*, Melancholy, give
**Plebeian.**—P. L. 10, 442. in show *p.* angel
**Pledge.**—P. L. 1, 274. their liveliest *p.* of hope

P. L. 2, 818. dear *p*. of dalliance had with thee
P. L. 3, 95. transgress the sole command sole *p*.
P. L. 5, 168. sure *p*. of day that crownest
P. L. 5, 200. what well used had been the *p*.
P. L. 8, 325. I have set the *p*. of thy obedience
S.A. 378. the mystery of God given me under *p*.
S. A. 535. and hallowed *p*. of all my strength
S. A. 1144. the *p*. of my unviolated vow
L.107.ah who hath reft, quoth he, my dearest *p*.
**Pledges.**—S. M. 1. *p*. of heaven's joy
**Pleiades.**—P. L. 7, 374. dawn and the *P*.
**Plenipotent.**—P. L. 10, 404. *p*. on earth
**Plenteous.**—P. L. 6, 263. now *p*. as thou
P. L. 10, 600. which here though *p*. all too little
P. L. 12, 18. and reaping *p*. crop, corn, wine
**Plenteously.**—P. L. 7, 392. *p*. the waters
**Plenty.**—P. L. 8, 94. contain more *p*.
P. L. 9, 594. where *p*. hung tempting so nigh
C. 718. that no corner might be vacant of her *p*.
**Plies.**—P. L. 2, 954. thither he *p*. undaunted
**Plight.**—P. L. 1, 335. the evil *p*. in which
P. L. 6, 607. Satan beheld their *p*. and to his
P. L. 9, 1091. but let us now as in bad *p*. divise
P. L. 10, 937. ended weeping and her lowly *p*.
P. L. 11, 1. thus they in lowliest *p*. repentant
S. A. 480. lie in this miserable loathsome *p*.
S. A. 1729. (Gaza is not in *p*. to say us nay)
C. 372. and put them into misbecoming *p*.
Il P. 57. in her sweetest saddest *p*.
P. 13. most perfect hero tried in heaviest *p*.
**Plighted.**—C. 301. and play in the *p*. clouds
**Plots.**—P. L. 2, 193. wise to frustrate all our *p*.
F. of C.14. your *p*. and packing worse than those
**Plotting.**—P. L. 2, 338. *p*. how the conqueror
P. L. 5, 240. *p*. now the fall of others from like
P. L. 6, 901. who now is *p*. how he may seduce
**Ploughed.**—S. 16, 4. thy glorious way hast *p*.
**Ploughman.**—P. L. 4, 983. careful *p*. doubting
L'A. 63. while the *p*. near at hand
**Pluck.**—P. L. 5, 327. will *p*. such choice
P. L. 8, 309. stirred in me sudden appetite to *p*.
P. L. 9, 595. to *p*. and eat my fill I spared not
L. 3. I come to *p*. your berries harsh and crude
**Plucked.**—P. L. 5, 65. venturous arm he *p*.
P. L. 5, 84. fruit held part which he had *p*.
P. L. 6, 644. they *p*. the seated hills with all
P. L. 9, 781. she *p*. she eat earth felt the wound
P. L. 10, 560. greedily they *p*. the fruitage fair
P. L. 11, 537. gathered not harshly *p*. for death
M. W. 38. *p*. up by some unheedy swain
**Plucking.**—C. 296. *p*. ripe clusters from the
**Plumb.**—P. L. 2, 933. *p*. down he drops
**Plume.**—P. L. 3, 642. of many a coloured *p*.
P. L. 6, 161. ambitious to win from me some *p*.
P. L. 11, 186. two birds of gayest *p*. before him
**Plumed.**—P. L. 4, 989. sat Horror *p*.
**Plumes.**—P. L. 5, 286. and shook his *p*. that
P. L. 7, 432. fanned with unnumbered *p*.
P. R. 2, 222. cease to admire and all her *p*. fall
C. 378. she *p*. her feathers and lets grow her
C. 730. and the winged air darked with *p*.
**Plummet.**—T.3. speed is but the heavy *p*.'s pace
**Plumy.**—P. L. 4, 583. who on their *p*. vans
**Plunge.**—P. L. 2, 172. and *p*. us in the flames
**Plunged.**—P. L. 2, 441. *p*. in that abortive
P. L. 10, 476. untractable abyss *p*. in the womb
P. L. 10, 844. no way from deep to deeper *p*.
**Plurality.**—F. of C.3. seize the widowed whore *p*.
**Pluto.**—L'A. 149. would have won the ear of *P*.
Il P. 107. drew iron tears down *P*.'s cheek
**Plutonian.**—P. L. 10, 444. door of that *P*. hall
**Ply.**—P. L. 2, 642. *p*. stemming nightly toward
P. L. 9, 201. that day they best may *p*. their
C. 750. will serve to *p*. the sampler and to tease
**Poem.**—P. L. 9, 41. to person or to *p*.
P. R. 4, 260. whose *p*. Phœbus challenged for
P. R. 4, 332. with music or with *p*. where so
**Poet.**—S. 8, 13. repeated air of sad Electra's *p*.
**Poets.**—C. 515. what the sage *p*. taught by the
L'A. 129. such sights as youthful *p*. dream
**Point.**—P. L. 3, 557. from eastern *p*. of Libra

P. L. 3, 733. that spot of which I *p*. is paradise
P. L. 4, 559. from what *p*. of his compass to
P. L. 4, 590. whose *p*. now raised bore
P. L. 4, 862. drew they nigh the western *p*.
P. L. 5, 855. strange *p*. and new !
P. L. 12, 143. behold in prospect as I *p*. them
P. R. 4, 463. they roar and seem to *p*.
S. A. 1514. ruin destruction at the utmost *p*.
C. 306. due west it rises from this shrubby *p*.
H. 86. or o'er the *p*. of dawn
**Pointed.**—S. 14, 7. Faith *p*. upward with her
P. R. 2, 51. *p*. at and shown in public
**Pointing.**—P. L. 1, 223. slope their *p*. spires
**Points.**—P. L. 5, 823. with him the *p*. of
P. R. 4, 219. on *p*. and questions fitting Moses'
**Poise.**—P. L. 2, 905. and *p*. their lighter wings
C. 410. yet where an equal *p*. of hope and fear
**Poised.**—P. L. 5, 579. rests upon her centre *p*.
**Poison.**—C. 47. crushed the sweet *p*. of misused
C. 526. whose pleasing *p*. the visage quite
**Poisonous.**—S. A. 763. with a *p*. bosom snake
**Polar.**—P. L. 5, 269. now on the *p*. winds
P. L. 10, 289. as when two *p*. winds blowing
P. L. 10, 681. except to those beyond the *p*.
**Pole.**—P. L. 1, 74. thrice to the utmost *p*.
P.L.2,642. ply stemming nightly toward the *p*.
P. L. 3, 560. then from *p*. to *p*. he views in
P. L. 4, 724. resplendent globe and starry *p*.
P. L. 7, 23. on earth not rapt above the *p*.
P. L. 7, 215. and with the centre mix the *p*.
P. L. 9, 66. crossed the car of night from *p*. to *p*.
C. 99. shoots against the dusky *p*.
P. 30. over the *p*. thy thickest mantle throw
**Poles.**—P. L. 10, 669. the *p*. of earth twice
V.Ex.34.above the wheeling *p*. and at heaven's
**Policy.**—P. L. 2, 297. might rise by *p*. and
P. R. 3, 391. and in my ear vented much *p*.
**Polish.**—P. L. 11, 610. of arts that *p*. life
**Polished.**—H. 241. hath fixed her *p*. car
**Politician.**—S. A. 1195. but your ill-meaning *p*.
**Politic.**—P. R. 3, 400. thy *p*. maxims
**Pollute.**—H. 41. *p*. with sinful blame
**Polluted.**—P. L. 10, 167. and *p*. from the
P. L. 12, 110. to leave them to their own *p*.
**Polluting.**—P. L. 10, 631. man's *p*. sins
**Pollution.**—P. L. 12, 355. their strife *p*.
**Pomona.**—P. L. 5, 378. that like *P*.'s arbour
P. L. 9, 393. to Pales or *P*. thus adorned
P. L. 9, 394. *P*. when she fled Vertumnus
**Pomp.**—P. L. 1, 372. full of *p*. and gold
P. L. 2, 257. before the easy yoke of servile *p*.
P. L. 2, 510. hell's dread emperor with *p*.
P. L. 5, 354. solemn than the tedious *p*. that
P. L. 7, 564. while the bright *p*. ascended
P. L. 8, 61. for on her, as queen, a *p*. of winning
P. L. 11, 748. with all their *p*. deep under
P. R. 1, 457. thou no more with *p*. or sacrifice
P. R. 3, 246. monarchies of the earth their *p*.
S.A.357. and as a blessing with such *p*. adorned
S. A. 436. great *p*. and sacrifice and praises loud
S. A. 449. I this honour, I this *p*. have brought
S.A.1312. with sacrifices triumph *p*. and games
L'A. 127. and *p*. and feast and revelry
W. S. 15. and so sepulchred in such *p*. dost lie
**Pompey.**—P. R. 3, 35. young *P*. quelled the
**Pompous.**—P. R. 2, 390. thy *p*. delicacies
**Pond.**—P. L. 9, 641. and oft through *p*. or
**Ponder.**—P. L. 12, 147. this *p*. that all
**Pondering.**—P. L. 2, 421. *p*. the danger with
P. L. 2, 919. brink of hell and looked a while *p*.
P. L. 6, 127. so *p*. and from his armed peers
P. R. 2, 105. thus Mary *p*. oft, and oft to mind
**Ponderous.**—P. L. 1, 284. his *p*. shield
**Ponders.**—P. L. 4, 1001. now *p*. all events
**Ponent.**—P. L. 10, 704. Levant and the *P*.
**Pontic.**—P. R. 3, 36. Pompey quelled the *P*.
**Pontifical.**—P. L. 10, 313. wondrous art *p*.
**Pontifice.**—P. L. 10, 348. wondrous *p*.
**Pontus.**—P. L. 5, 340. in *P*. or the Punic
P. L. 9, 77. over *P*. and the pool Mæotis
P. R. 2, 347. *P*. and Lucrine bay, and Afric

**Pool.**—P. L. 1, 221. rears from off the *p*.
P. L. 1, 266. thus astonished on the oblivious *p*.
P. L. 1, 411. and Eleale to the Asphaltic *p*.
P. L. 3, 14. escaped the Stygian *p*.
P. L. 9, 77. over Pontus and the *p*. Mæotis
P.L.9,641.and mires and oft through pond or *p*.
P. R. 4, 79. Danubius to the Tauric *p*.
**Poor.**—P. L. 12, 133. not wandering *p*.
P. R. 1, 411. as a *p*. miserable captive thrall
P. R. 2, 447. esteem those names of men so *p*.
P. R. 3, 96. *p*. Socrates
S. A. 366. thy foes' derision captive,*p*.and blind
C. 566. and O *p*. hapless nightingale thought I
P. 17. *p*. fleshly tabernacle entered
**Poorest.**—S. A. 1479. to live the *p*.in my tribe
**Poplar.**—H. 185. edged with *p*. pale
**Popular.**—P. L. 2, 313. for so the *p*. vote
P.L. 7,488.joined in her *p*.tribes of commonalty
P. L. 12, 338. and other faults heaped to the *p*.
P. R. 2, 227. of honour, glory and *p*. praise
S. A. 16. with leave retiring from the*p*.noise
S. A. 434. this day the Philistines a *p*. feast
**Populous.**—P. L. 1,351.like which the *p*.North
P. L. 1, 770. pour forth their *p*. youth
P. L. 2, 903. swarm *p*. unnumbered as the sands
P. L. 7, 146. heaven yet *p*. retains number
P. L. 9, 445. as one who long in *p*. city pent
**Porch.**—P. L. 1, 454. passions in the sacred *p*.
C. 839. and through the *p*. and inlet of each
**Porches.**—P. L. 1, 762. the gates and *p*. wide
P. R. 4, 36. *p*. and theatres, baths, aqueducts
**Porcupines.**—S. A. 1138. wild boars or ruffled *p*.
**Pore.**—S. A. 97. every look at will through *p*.
**Pored.**—S. 11, 4. good intellects now seldom *p*.
**Porous.**—P. L. 4, 228. veins of *p*. earth
P. L. 7, 361. in the sun's orb made *p*. to receive
**Port.**—P. L. 2, 1044. holds gladly the *p*. though
P. L. 4, 778. and from their ivory *p*. the
P. L. 4, 868. them comes a third of regal *p*.
P. L. 11, 8. yet their *p*. not of mean suitors
P. L. 11, 397. empire of Negus to his utmost *p*.
R. R. 3, 209. worst is my *p*.
C. 297. their *p*. was more than human, as they
**Portal.**—P. L. 3, 508. orient gems the *p*. shone
V.Ex. 5. driving dumb silence from the *p*. door
**Portals.**—P. L. 7,575. opened wide her blazing *p*.
**Portcullis.**—P. L. 2, 874. the huge *p*. high
**Ported.**—P. L. 4, 980. round with *p*. spears
**Fortend.**—P. R. 4, 389. a kingdom they *p*.
S. A. 590. all otherwise to me my thoughts *p*.
S. 1, 7. *p*. success in love
**Portending.**—P. L. 6, 578. *p*. hollow truce
P. L. 12, 596. dreams have calmed *p*. good
P. R. 2, 104. sayings laid up *p*. strange events
**Portends.**—P. L. 11, 600. peaceful days *p*.
**Portentous.**—P. L. 2, 761. sign *p*. held me
P. L. 10, 371. and overlay with this *p*. bridge
**Portents.**—P. R. 1, 395. answers oracles *p*.
P. R. 4, 491. as false *p*. not sent from God, but
**Portion.**—P. L. 1, 72. and their *p*. set
P. L. 2, 33. none whose *p*. is so small of present
**Portraiture.**—Il P. 149. of lively *p*. displayed
**Portrayed.**—P. L. 6, 84. argument *p*.
**Portress.**—P. L. 2, 746. the *p*. of hell-gate
**Possess.**—P. L. 2, 365. or *p*.all as our own and
P. L. 3, 243. thou hast given me to *p*. life in
P. L. 4, 431. all other creatures that *p*. earth
**P.** L. 5, 366. who yet by sovran gift *p*. this
P. L. 5, 688. with flying march where we *p*.
P. L. 7, 147. number sufficient to *p*. her realms
P. L. 8, 340. as lords *p*. it and all things that
P. L. 10, 466. now *p*. as lords a spacious world
P. L. 10, 623. I suffer them to enter and *p*.
P. L. 11, 339. all the earth he gave thee to *p*.
P. L. 12, 586. but shalt *p*. a paradise within
Il P. 6. and fancies fond with gaudy shapes *p*.
S. 10, 14. and to *p*. them, honoured Margaret
**Possessed.**—P. L. 5, 790. sons of heaven *p*.
P. L. 8, 404. sufficiently *p*. of happiness
P. L. 9, 1137. I know not whence *p*. thee
P. R. 1, 49. this universe we have *p*. and ruled

P. R. 3, 357. but say thou wert *p*. of David's
S. A. 266. they had by this *p*. the towers of Gath
S. A. 1005. returning to regain love once *p*.
**Possesses.**—P. L. 2, 729. *p*. thee to bend
P. L. 2, 979. the ethereal king *p*. lately
P. L. 9, 251. but other doubt *p*. me lest harm
**Possessing.**—P. L. 9, 189. heart or head *p*.
P. R. 4, 302. and all *p*. equal to God
**Possession.**—P. L. 4, 666. regain her old *p*.
P. L. 4, 941. though for *p*. put to try once
P. L. 10, 461. for in *p*. such not
P. L. 11, 103. or to invade vacant *p*.
P. L. 11, 222. to seize *p*. of the garden he alone
P. R. 3, 156. not part easily from *p*. won with
P. R. 4, 628. from thy demoniac holds *p*.
S. A. 869. took full *p*. of me and prevailed
**Possessor.**—P. L. 1, 252. receive thy new *p*.
**Possible.**—P. L. 5, 441. turn or holds it *p*.
P. L. 9, 359. firm we subsist yet *p*. to swerve
S. A. 490. and expiate if *p*. my crime
S. A. 771. I may if *p*. thy pardon find
**Possibly.**—P. L. 5, 515. or *p*. his love desert
**Post.**—P. L. 4, 171. from Media *p*. to Egypt
S. A. 147. the gates of Azza *p*. and massy bar
S. A. 1538. evil news rides *p*. while good news
S. 19, 13. and *p*. o'er land and ocean without rest
D.F.I. 59. to earth from thy prefixed seat didst *p*.
**Posterity.**—P. L. 3, 209. with his whole *p*.
P. L. 7, 638. that *p*. informed by thee might
P. L. 10, 818. in me all *p*. stands cursed
S. A. 977. to all *p*. may stand defamed
**Posture.**—P. L. 1, 322. or in this abject *p*.
P. L. 4, 876. how busied in what form and *p*.
P. L. 6, 605. in *p*. to displode their second tire
**Potable.**—P. L. 3, 608. and rivers run *p*. gold
**Potent.**—P. L. 1, 95. nor what the *p*. victor
P. L. 1, 338. as when the *p*. rod of Amram's son
P. L. 2, 318. not our safe retreat beyond his *p*.
P. L. 2, 836. lest heaven surcharged with *p*.
P. L. 4, 673. from the sun's more *p*. ray
P. L. 6, 135. terror of thy power or *p*. tongue
P. L. 6, 366. two *p*. thrones that to be less
P. L. 7, 100. held by thy voice thy *p*. voice
P. L. 12, 211. Moses once more his *p*. rod
C. 255. culling their *p*. herbs and baleful drugs
**Potentate.**—P. L. 5, 706. of their great *p*.
P. L. 11, 231. some great *p*. or of the thrones
**Potentates.**—P. L. 1, 315. princes *p*. warriors
P. L. 5, 749. regencies of Seraphim and *p*.
P. L. 6, 416. his *p*. to council called by night
P. L. 7, 198. Cherub and Seraph *p*. and thrones
P. R. 1, 117. regents and *p*. and kings yea gods
P. R. 2, 118. where all his *p*. in council sat
**Potion.**—C. 68. soon as the *p*. works their human
**Poverty.**—P. R. 2, 415. thyself bred up in *p*.
P. R. 2, 438. attained in lowest *p*. to highest
P. R. 2, 451. may also in this *p*. as soon
S. A. 697. if these they escape perhaps in *p*.
**Pour.**—P. L. 5, 314. and *p*. abundance fit
P. L. 1, 770. *p*. forth their populous youth
P. L. 6, 544. for this day will *p*. down if I
P. L. 11, 825. on the earth shalt *p*. rain
C. 710. wherefore did nature *p*. her bounties forth
**Poured.**—P. L. 1, 220. wrath and vengeance *p*.
P. L. 1, 352. never from her frozen loins
P. L. 2, 997. *p*. out by millions her victorious
P. L. 3, 674. on whom hath all these graces *p*.
P. L. 4, 243. *p*. forth profuse on hill and dale
P. L. 4, 365. on their shape hath *p*.
P. L. 6, 811. indignation on these godless *p*.
P.L.7,197.about his chariot numberless were *p*.
P. L. 1, 220. abundantly his gifts hath also *p*.
P. L. 9, 98. bursting passion into plaints thus *p*.
P. L. 12, 21. with large wine-offerings *p*.
P. L. 12, 498. the Spirit *p*. first on his apostles
P. R. 4, 16. wine-press where sweet must is *p*.
P. R. 4, 411. abortive *p*. fierce rain
**Pouring.**—P. L. 5, 296. virgin fancies *p*. forth
**Powder.**—P. L. 4, 815. on a heap of nitrous *p*.
**Powdered.**—P. L. 7, 581. *p*. with stars
**Power.**—P. L. 1, 44. him the almighty *p*. hurled

P. L. 1, 79. one next himself in *p.* and next in
P. L. 1, 103. his utmost *p.* with adverse *p.*
P. L. 1, 112. and deify his *p.*
P. L. 1, 241. by the sufferance of supernal *p.*
P. L. 1, 556. nor wanting *p.* to mitigate and
P. L. 1, 626. but what *p.* of mind foreseeing or
P. L. 1, 736. exalted to such *p.* and gave to
P. L. 1, 753. by command of sovran *p.*
P. L. 2, 102. we feel our *p.* sufficient to disturb
P. L. 2, 336. but to our *p.* hostility and hate
P. L. 2, 350. though less in *p.* and excellence
P. L. 2, 356. and what their *p.* and where their
P. L. 2, 447. with splendour armed with *p.*
P. L. 2, 884. opened but to shut excelled her *p.*
P. L. 2, 955. meet there whatever *p.*
P. L. 3, 242. under his gloomy *p.* I shall not
P. L. 3, 317. all *p.* I give thee, reign for ever
P. L. 4, 61. some other *p.* as great might
P. L. 4, 66. the same free will and *p.* to stand
P. L. 4, 412. must the *P.* that made us and for
P. L. 4, 429. among so many signs of *p.* and
P. L. 4, 781. when Gabriel to his next in *p.* thus
P. L. 4, 881. but have *p.* and right to question
P. L. 4, 956. allegiance to the acknowledged *P.*
P. L. 5, 159. beyond thought and *p.* divine
P. L. 5, 235. happiness in his *p.* left free to will
P. L. 5, 458. whose high *p.* so far exceeded
P. L. 5, 526. to persevere he left it in thy *p.*
P. L. 5, 660. in *p.* in favour and pre-eminence
P. L. 5, 728. in battle what our *p.* is or our
P. L. 5, 739. when they see all regal *p.* given me
P. L. 5, 776. hath to himself engrossed all *p.*
P. L. 5, 796. if in *p.* and splendour less
P. L. 5, 821. one over all with unsucceeded *p.*
P. L. 5, 861. by our own quickening *p.*
P. L. 6, 134. abandoned at the terror of thy *p.*
P. L. 6, 223. how much more of *p.* army against
P. L. 6, 247. prodigious *p.* had shown and met
P. L. 6, 301. to such height of Godlike *p.*
P. L. 6, 319. as not of *p.* at once
P. L. 6, 343. his confidence to equal God in *p.*
P. L. 6, 637. behold the excellence the *p.*
P. L. 6, 678. and to declare all *p.* on him
P. L. 6, 705. in heaven and hell thy *p.* above
P. L. 6, 730. sceptre and *p.* thy giving I assume
P. L. 6, 780. before him *p.* divine his way
P. L. 6, 815. kingdom and *p.* and glory
P. L. 7, 587. the filial *p.* arrived and sat him
P. L. 7, 603. thy works Jehovah! infinite thy *p.*
P. L. 8, 249. so spake the godlike *p.* and thus
P. L. 8, 279. in goodness and in *p.* pre-eminent
P. L. 8, 379. my words offend thee heavenly *p.*
P. L. 9, 95. might beget of diabolic *p.*
P. L. 9, 349. yet lies within his *p.*
P. L. 9, 680. now I feel thy *p.* within me clear
P. L. 9, 820. the odds of knowledge in my *p.*
P. L. 9, 835. first low reverence done as to the *p.*
P. L. 9, 945. who though his *p.* creation could
P. L. 10, 251. death from sin no *p.* can separate
P. L. 10, 255. yet to thy *p.* and mine not
P. L. 10, 284. and with *p.* (their *p.* was great)
P. L. 10, 408. if your joint *p.* prevail the affairs
P. L. 10, 515. a greater *p.* now ruled him
P. L. 10, 531. and his *p.* no less he seemed
P. L. 10, 586. sin there in *p.* before once actual
P. L. 10, 801. argument of weakness not of *p.*
P. L. 10, 986. in thy *p.* it lies yet ere conception
P. L. 10, 1004. and have the *p.* of many ways
P. L. 11, 126. the archangelic *p.* prepared
P. L. 11, 338. fomented by his virtual *p.*
P. L. 11, 417. deep the *p.* of these ingredients
P. L. 12, 200. wondrous *p.* God to his saint
P. L. 12, 369. his sire the *p.* of the Most High
P. L. 12, 420. death over him no *p.* shall long
P. L. 12, 460. with glory and *p.* to judge both
P. L. 12, 517. and with these to join secular *p.*
P. L. 12, 521. Spiritual laws by carnal *p.*
P. R. 1, 61. be not intended all our *p.* to be
P. R. 1, 139. the *p.* of the Highest o'ershadow
P. R. 1, 219. violence and proud tyrannic *p.*
P. R. 2, 45. to what height their *p.* unjust

P. R. 2, 163. such object hath the *p.* to soften
P. R. 2, 327. stay till bid but tender all their *p.*
P. R. 2, 380. and who withholds my *p.* that
P. R. 2, 393. I have also *p.* to give thou seest
P. R. 2, 394. of that *p.* I bring thee voluntary
P. R. 3, 251. such *p.* was given him then
P. R. 3, 299. to have a view of his great *p.*
P. R. 4, 65. and rods the ensigns of their *p.*
P. R. 4, 82. in ample territory wealth and *p.*
P. R. 4, 103. my help thou mayst to me the *p.*
P. R. 4, 254. hear and learn the secret *p.*
P. R. 4, 394. for still he knew his *p.* not yet
P. R. 4, 494. at least might seem to hold all *p.*
P. R. 4, 528. who and what he is, his wisdom, *p.*
S. A. 78. in *p.* of others never in my own
S. A. 184. apt words have *p.* to swage
S. A. 534. which to have kept tacit was in thy *p.*
S. A. 745. with what amends is in my *p.*
S. A. 798. into my *p.* thy key of strength
S. A. 935. no more on me have *p.*, their force is
S. A. 1003. beauty.... hath strange *p.*
S. A. 1054. despotic *p.* over his female in due awe
S. A. 1150. which I to be the *p.* of Israel's God
S. A. 1275. and industrious to support tyrannic *p.*
S. A. 1367. of those who have me in their civil *p.*
S. A. 1404. masters' commands come with a *p.*
C. 31. a noble peer of mickle trust and *p.*
C. 155. of *p.* to cheat the eye with blear illusion
C. 437. hath hurtful *p.* o'er true virginity
C. 587. or that *p.* which erring men call chance
C. 677. is of such *p.* to stir up joy as this
C. 782. against the sun-clad *p.* of chastity
C. 801. her words set off by some superior *p.*
C. 817. and backward mutters of dissevering *p.*
C. 858. and add the *p.* of some adjuring verse
A. 44. for know by lot from Jove I am the *p.*
Il P. 95. whose *p.* hath a true consent
Il P. 103. but O sad virgin that thy *p.*
S. 1, 8. have linked that amorous *p.* to thy soft
S. 8, 13. had the *p.* to save the Athenian walls
S. 17, 10. both spiritual *p.* and civil what each
H. 127. if ye have *p.* to touch our senses so
H. 196. while each peculiar *p.* foregoes
S. M. 3. wed your divine sounds and mixed *p.*
D. F. I. 28. so to change thee winter had no *p.*
V. Ex. 89. what *p.*, what force, what mighty spell
**Powerful.**—P. L. 2, 774. time this *p.* key
P. L. 3, 602. though by their *p.* art they bind
P. L. 4, 58. O had his *p.* destiny ordained me
P. L. 7, 208. in his *p.* word and spirit
P. L. 8, 533. against the charm of beauty's *p.*
P. L. 9, 587. hunger and thirst at once *p.*
P. L. 10, 247. *p.* at greatest distance to unite
P. R. 3, 155. though thy right be now in *p.*
S. A. 791. the jealousy of love *p.* of sway
S. A. 862. to oppose against such *p.* arguments
C. 903. we implore thy *p.* hand
**Powerfullest.**—P. L. 6, 425. had *p.* to send
**Powers.**—P. L. 1, 128. of many throned *p.*
P. L. 1, 186. and re-assembling our afflicted *p.*
P. L. 1, 360. and *p.* that erst in heaven sat on
P. L. 1, 622. O *p.* matchless but with the
P. L. 2, 11. *p.* and dominions, deities of heaven
P. L. 2, 310. thrones and imperial *p.* offspring of
P. L. 2, 456. go therefore mighty *p.* terror of
P. L. 2, 522. the ranged *p.* disband
P. L. 2, 825. herself not all the Stygian *p.*
P. L. 2, 968. ye *p.* and spirits of this
P. L. 3, 52. and the mind through all her *p.*
P. L. 3, 100. I created all the ethereal *p.*
P. L. 3, 176. more I will renew his lapsed *p.*
P. L. 3, 213. say heavenly *p.* where shall we
P. L. 3, 256. and show the *p.* of darkness
P. L. 3, 320. princedoms, *p.* dominions I reduce
P. L. 3, 390. and all the *p.* therein by thee
P. L. 3, 397. thy *p.* with loud acclaim thee
P. L. 4, 63. but other *p.* as great fell not
P. L. 4, 939. and my afflicted *p.* to settle here
P. L. 5, 601. dominations, princedoms virtues *p.*
P. L. 5, 697. several one by one the regent *p.*
P. L. 5, 743. but Satan with his *p.* far was

P. L. 5, 772. dominations princedoms virtues *p.*
P. L. 5, 824. and formed the *p.* of heaven such
P. L. 5, 840. princedoms, virtues. *p.* essential *p.*
P. L. 6, 22. among those friendly *p.* who him
P. L. 6, 61. at which command the *p.* militant
P. L. 6, 85. the banded *p.* of Satan hasting on
P. L. 6, 686. since Michael and his *p.* went
P. L. 6, 786. to rebellious fight rallied their *p.*
P. L. 6, 898. in heaven among the angelic *p.*
P. L. 7, 162. inhabit lax ye *p.* of heaven
P. L. 9, 136. glory sole among the infernal *p.*
P. L. 9, 600. degree of reason in my inward *p.*
P. L. 9, 1048. and inmost *p.* made err
P. L. 10, 34. assembled angels and ye *p.*
P. L. 10, 86. and *p.* princedoms and dominations
P. L. 10, 186. principalities and *p.* triumphed
P. L. 10, 395. to my associate *p.*
P. L. 10, 460. dominations princedoms virtues *p.*
P. L. 11, 221. bright stand there left his *p.*
P. L. 12, 91. within himself unworthy *p.* to
P. L. 12, 577. and all the ethereal *p.*, all secrets
P. R. 1, 44. O ancient *p.* of air and this wide
P. R. 1, 163. angels and ethereal *p.*
P. R. 2, 124. called *p.* of fire air water earth
P. R. 3, 30. and dignities and *p.* all but the
P. R. 3, 338. Agrican with all his northern *p.*
S. A. 251. the Philistines with gathered *p.*
S. A. 1110. not with their whole united *p.*
S. A. 1190. went up with armed *p.* thee only
Il P. 21. the sea-nymphs and their *p.* offended
Cir. 1. flaming *p.* and winged warriors bright
**Practice.**—S. A. 114. their daily *p.* to afflict.
**Practise.**—P. L. 11, 802. shall *p.* how to live
**Practised.**—P. L. 4, 122. *p.* falsehood under
P. L. 4, 124. yet not enough had *p.* to deceive
P. L. 4, 945. and *p.* distances to cringe not
**Prætors.**—P. R. 4, 63. *p.*, proconsuls
**Praise.**—P. L. 1, 731. and the work some *p.*
P. L. 3, 106. what *p.* could they receive
P. L. 3, 414. and never shall my harp thy *p.*
P. L. 3, 415. nor from thy father's *p.* disjoin
P. L. 3, 453. naught seeking but the *p.* of men
P. L. 3, 676. the universal maker we may *p.*
P. L. 3, 697. but rather merits *p.* the more
P. L. 4, 46. could be less than to afford him *p.*
P. L. 4, 436. but let us ever *p.* him and extol
P. L. 4, 638. happiest knowledge and her *p.*
P. L. 4, 676. want spectators God want *p.*
P. L. 4, 679. all these with ceaseless *p.* his
P. L. 5, 147. holy rapture wanted they to *p.*
P. L. 5, 169. *p.* him in thy sphere while day
P. L. 5, 172. him thy greater sound his *p.*
P. L. 5, 179. resound his *p.* who out of darkness
P. L. 5, 184. to our great Maker still new *p.*
P. L. 5, 191. or falling still advance his *p.*
P. L. 5, 192. his *p.* ye winds that from four
P. L. 5, 196. murmurs warbling tune his *p.*
P. L. 5, 199. your wings and in your notes *p.*
P. L. 5, 204. vocal by my song and taught his *p.*
P. L. 5, 405. what he gives whose *p.* be ever
P. L. 6, 376. seek not the *p.* of men
P. L. 6, 745. hymns of high *p.* and I among
P. L. 7, 187. him glory and *p.* whose wisdom
P. L. 9, 195. earth's great altar send up silent *p.*
P. L. 9, 693. and not *p.* rather your dauntless
P. L. 9, 749. to speak thy *p.* thy *p.* he also
P. L. 9, 800. song each morning and due *p.*
P. L. 9, 1020. I the *p.* yield thee so well this
P. L. 11, 617. domestic honour and chief *p.*
P. R. 2, 227. of honour, glory and popular *p.*
P. R. 2, 251. though needing what *p.* is it
P. R. 2, 456. her to do aught may merit *p.*
P. R. 2, 464. honour, virtue, merit and *p.*
P. R. 3, 48. people's *p.* if always *p.* unmixed
P. R. 3, 51. well weighed scarce worth the *p.*
P. R. 3, 52. they *p.* and they admire, they know
P. R. 3, 56. to be dispraised were no small *p.*
S. A. 420. I cannot *p.* thy marriage choices
S. A. 1410. I *p.* thy resolution doff these links
S. A. 1621. clamouring their god with *p.*
C. 176. in wanton dance they *p.* the bounteous

C. 271. nay gentle shepherd ill is lost that *p.*
C. 776. would be better thanked his *p.* due paid
C. 973. with a crown of deathless *p.*
A. 11. of detraction from her *p.*
A. 75. the peerless height of her immortal *p.*
L. 76. slits the thin-spun life. But not the *p.*
Il P. 20. her beauty's *p.* above the sea-nymphs
S. 10, 12. well your words his noble virtues *p.*
S. 13, 6. with *p.* enough for envy to look wan
S. 15, 2. filling each mouth with envy or with *p.*
M. W. 12. been as complete as was her *p.*
**Praised.**—P. L. 2, 480. how much they *p.*
P. L. 7, 258. hymning *p.* God and his works
P. R. 4, 348. God is *p.* aright and godlike
**Praises.**—P. L. 3, 147. shall high extol thy *p.*
P. L. 4, 444. for we to him indeed all *p.* owe
P. R. 3, 64. with true applause recount his *p.*
S. A. 175. universally crowned with highest *p.*
S. A. 436. great pomp and sacrifice and *p.* loud
S. A. 450. advanced his *p.* high among the
S. 16, 8. and Dunbar field resounds thy *p.* loud
**Praising.**—C. 709. *p.* the lean and sallow
**Pranked.**—C. 759. false rules *p.* in reason's garb
**Pravity.**—P. L. 12, 288. their natural *p.* by
**Prancing.**—P. R. 3, 314. *p.* their riders bore
**Pray.**—P. L. 3, 790. to *p.* repent and bring
P. L. 10, 1060. if we *p.* him will his ear
P. L. 11, 32. with what words to *p.* let me
V. Ex. 15. I *p.* thee then deny me not thy aid
**Prayed.**—P. L. 5, 209. so *p.* they innocent
S. A. 351. thing good *p.* for but often proves
S. A. 352. I *p.* for children and thought
S. A. 1637. eyes fast fixed he stood as one who *p.*
**Prayer.**—P. L. 3, 191. to *p.* repentance
P. L. 11, 6. which the spirit of *p.* inspired
P. L. 11, 146. belief may seem yet this will *p.*
P. L. 11, 149. for since I sought by *p.* the
P. L. 11, 307. and if by *p.* incessant I could
P. L. 11, 311. but *p.* against his absolute
S. A. 581. God who caused a fountain at thy *p.*
S. A. 649. this one *p.* yet remains might I be
**Prayers.**—P. L. 10, 859. for *p.* or cries
P. L. 10, 952. if *p.* could alter high decrees
P. L. 11, 14. to heaven their *p.* flew up
P. L. 11, 24. these sighs and *p.* which in this
P. L. 11, 252. sufficient that thy *p.* are heard
S. A. 359. tempt our earnest *p.* then given with
S. A. 392. thrice she assayed with flattering *p.*
S. A. 520. with *p.* and vows renewed
S. A. 961. more deaf to *p.* than winds and seas
**Praying.**—P. L. 10, 1081. instruct us *p.* and
P. L. 11, 2. lowliest plight repentant stood *p.*
P. R. 1, 490. handling holy things *p.* vowing
**Prays.**—P. L. 11, 90. now repents and *p.*
**Preached.**—P. L. 11, 723. and to them *p.*
P. L. 12, 448. salvation shall be *p.* but to the
**Preaching.**—S. A. 859. *p.* how meritorious
**Preamble.**—P. L. 3, 367. and with *p.* sweet
**Precedence.**—P. L. 2, 33. claim in hell *p.*
**Precedes.**—P. L. 9, 327. but harm *p.* not
P. L. 10, 640. curse pronounced on both *p.*
**Precept.**—P. L. 10, 652. had first his *p.* so to
**Precepts.**—P. R. 4, 264. brief sententious *p.*
C. 708. and fetch their *p.* from the cynic tub
**Predestination.**—P. L. 3, 114. *p.* overruled
**Precincts.**—P. L. 3, 88. in the *p.* of light
**Precious.**—P. L. 1, 692. deserve the *p.* bane
P. L. 3, 611. in the dark so many *p.* things
P. L. 5, 132. two other *p.* drops that ready
P. L. 9, 106. in thee concentring all their *p.*
P. L. 9, 795. O sovran virtuous *p.* of all trees
P. L. 12, 293. some blood more *p.* must be
S. A. 533. like a tame wether, all my *p.* fleece
C. 719. and *p.* gems to store her children with
C. 847. which she with *p.* vialed liquors heals
C. 913. I have kept of *p.* cure
H. 71. bending one way their *p.* influence
**Precipice.**—P. L. 1, 173. that from the *p.*
**Precipitance.**—P. L. 7, 291. with glad *p.*
**Precipitant.**—P. L. 3, 563. his flight *p.*
**Precipitate.**—P. L. 6, 280. *p.* thee with

**Precise.**—P. L. 12, 589. for the hour *p.* exacts
**Predicament.**—M. 56. in compass of thy *p.*
**Prediction.**—P. L. 12, 553. hath thy *p.* seer
　P. R. 1, 142. of his birth divine and high *p.*
　P. R. 3, 354. *p.* still in all things and all men
　P. R. 3, 394. *p.* else will unpredict
　S. A. 44. me not rashly call in doubt divine *p.*
**Predicts.**—P. R. 3, 356. what it *p.*
**Predominant.**—P. L. 8, 160. the sun *p.* in
**Pre-eminence.**—P. L. 5, 661. favour and *p.-e.*
　P. L. 11, 347. but this *p.-e* thou hast lost
**Pre-eminent.**—P. L. 5, 447. thee *p.-e.*
　P. L. 8, 279. in goodness and in power *p.-e.*
**Preface.**—P. L. 9, 676. as no delay of *p.*
　P. L. 11, 251. Adam heaven's high behest no *p.*
　P. R. 2, 115. for Satan with sly *p.* to return
　S. A. 1554. no *p.* needs thou seest we long to
**Prefer.**—P. L. 1, 17. O Spirit that dost *p.*
　P. L. 6, 144. there be who faith *p.* and piety
　P. R. 4, 84. justly mayst *p.* before the Parthian
　P. R. 4, 303. oft shames not to *p.*
　S. A. 1374. and man *p.* set God behind
**Preferred.**—P. L. 8, 52. the relater she *p.*
　P. L. 9, 99. how like to heaven if not *p.*
　S. A. 1019. had not so soon *p.* thy paranymph
**Preferring.**—P. L. 1, 102. and me *p.*
　P. L. 2, 255. *p.* hard liberty before the easy
　S. A. 464. and *p.* before the God of Abraham
　S. A. 1672. chanting their idol and *p.*
**Prefixed.**—P. R. 1, 269. the time *p.* I waited
　P. R. 4, 392. for no date *p.* directs
　D. F. I. 59. to earth from thy *p.* seat didst
**Pregnant.**—P. L. 1, 22. and madest it *p.*
　P. L. 2, 779. my womb *p.* by thee and now
　P. L. 2, 913. but all these in their *p.* causes
　P. L. 6, 483. shall yield us *p.* with infernal
　P. 56. on some *p.* cloud
**Prelate.**—F. of C. 1. have thrown off your *p.*
**Preordained.**—P. R. 1, 127. counsel *p.*
**Prepare.**—P. L. 5, 689. *p.* fit entertainment
　P. L. 11, 555. and now *p.* thee for another
　P. L. 11, 637. but now *p.* thee for another
　P. R. 1, 272. before Messiah and his way *p.*
**Prepared.**—P. L. 1, 70. eternal justice had *p.*
　P. L. 1, 615. he now *p.* to speak
　P. L. 1, 700. nigh on the plain in many cells *p.*
　P. L. 4, 664. light *p.* they set and rise
　P. L. 5, 303. due at her hour *p.* for dinner
　P. L. 6, 738. to their *p.* ill mansion driven
　P. L. 6, 780. him power divine his way *p.*
　P. L. 7, 225. he took the golden compasses *p.*
　P. L. 8, 299. to the garden of bliss thy seat *p.*
　P. L. 9, 381. find us both perhaps far less *p.*
　P. L. 11, 126. the archangelic power *p.* for
　P. L. 11, 365. and best *p.* endure thy mortal
　P. L. 11, 571. he drained into fit moulds *p.*
　P. L. 12, 444. and in mind *p.* if so befall
　P. R. 2, 273. found his supper on the coals *p.*
**Preparing.**—P. R. 3, 389. long in *p.* soon
**Presage.**—P. L. 6, 201. and shout *p.* of
　S. A. 1387. if there be aught of *p.* in the mind
　V. Ex. 70. that far events full wisely could *p.*
**Presages.**—P. R. 1, 394. my advice by *p.* and
**Presaging.**—P. L. 1, 627. foreseeing or *p.*
　P. L. 12, 613. some great good *p.* since with
　M. W. 44. prove to be *p.* tears
**Presbyter.**—F. of C. 20. new *p.* is but old priest
**Prescribed.**—P. L. 3, 82. *p.* no bars of hell
　P. L. 4, 878. Satan broke the bounds *p.*
　P. L. 4, 909. from his bounds in hell *p.*
　P. L. 10, 657. blanc moon her office they *p.*
　S. A. 30. why was my breeding ordered and *p.*
**Prescript.**—P. L. 12, 249. by his *p.*
　S. A. 308. and tie him to his own *p.*
**Presence.**—P. L. 2, 240. we stand in his *p.*
　P. L. 3, 265. but in thy *p.* joy entire
　P. L. 3, 649. one of the seven who in God's *p.*
　P. L. 5, 358. nearer his *p.* Adam though not
　P. L. 7, 11. in *p.* of the Almighty Father
　P. L. 8, 314. *P.* divine
　P. L. 8, 551. knowledge in her *p.* falls degraded

　P. L. 9, 836. whose *p.* had infused into the
　P. L. 9, 858. thought it long deprived thy *p.*
　P. L. 10, 100. from his *p.* hid themselves
　P. L. 10, 144. to whom the Sovran *P.* thus
　P. L. 11, 319. where he vouchsafed *P.* divine
　P. L. 11, 341. his *p.* to these narrow bounds
　P. L. 11, 351. and of his *p.* many a sign still
　P. L. 12, 108. withdraw his *p.* from among
　P. L. 12, 563. to walk as in his *p.* ever to
　S. A. 28. charioting his godlike *p.*
　S. A. 1321. forbids at their religious rites *p.*
　C. 950. many a friend to gratulate wished *p.*
**Present.**—P. L. 1, 20. from the first wast *p.*
　P. L. 1, 628. the depth of knowledge past *p.*
　P. L. 2, 34. none whose portion is so small *p.*
　P. L. 2, 223. since our *p.* lot appears happy
　P. L. 2, 281. best we may compose our *p.*
　P. L. 2, 459. what best may ease the *p.* misery
　P. L. 2, 985. which is my *p.* journey and once
　P. L. 3, 78. wherein past *p.* future he beholds
　P. L. 4, 762. *p.* or past as saints and patriarchs
　P. L. 5, 582. all things durable by *p.* past and
　P. L. 6, 26. led him high applauded and *p.*
　P. L. 7, 518. for where is not he *p.* thus to
　P. L. 9, 213. to my mind first thoughts *p.*
　P. L. 9, 316. within thee feel when I am *p.*
　P. L. 9, 1092. what best may for the *p.* serve
　P. L. 10, 340. hoping to escape but shun the *p.*
　P. L. 10, 651. as sorted best with *p.* things
　P. L. 10, 996. before the *p.* object languishing
　P. L. 11, 351. here and will be found alike *p.*
　P. L. 11, 871. things canst represent as *p.*
　P. L. 12, 201. though *p.* in his angel who shall
　P. R. 1, 200. ill sorting with my *p.* state
　P. R. 1, 258. to all that *p.* stood
　S. A. 21. and *p.* times past what once I was
　S. A. 1085. in this displeased that I never *p.*
　S. A. 1378. *p.* in temples at idolatrous rites
　S. A. 1446. was not at *p.* here to find my son
　C. 90. likeliest and nearest to the *p.* aid
　C. 287. imports their loss beside the *p.* need
　C. 789. more happiness than this thy *p.* lot
　S. 19, 5. and *p.* my true account lest He
　H. 16. afford a *p.* to the infant God
　S. M. 5. to our high-raised phantasy *p.*
　D. F. I. 74. what a *p.* thou to God hast sent
**Presented.**—P. L. 3, 48. *p.* with a universal
　P. L. 6, 106. *p.* stood in terrible array
　P. L. 9, 974. hath *p.* this happy trial of thy
　P. R. 4, 38. gardens and groves *p.* to his eyes
**Presenting.**—P. L. 11, 21. the glad Son *p.*
　Il P. 99. *p.* Thebes or Pelops' line
**Presentments.**—C. 156. give it false *p.*
**Preserve.**—P. L. 6, 443. we can *p.* unhurt
　P. L. 11, 579. which might *p.* freedom and
　P. L. 11, 873. the creatures and their seed *p.*
**Preserved.**—S. A. 1143. while I *p.* these
**Preserves.**—P. R. 2, 372. but life *p.*
**President.**—P. R. 1, 447. his angels *p.* in
　S. 10, 1. once *p.* of England's council
**Pressed.**—P. L. 4, 501. and *p.* her matron
　P. L. 5, 346. and from sweet kernels *p.* she
　S. A. 854. and of religion *p.* how just it was
　U. C. II. 26. were *p.* to death he cried more
**Presume.**—P. L. 8, 121. if it *p.* might err in
　P. L. 12, 530. yet many will *p.* whence heavy
　S. A. 1156. *p.* not on thy God whate'er he be
**Presumed.**—P. L. 6, 631. inventions they *p.*
　P. L. 7, 13. into the heaven of heavens I *p.*
　P. L. 8, 356. and to the heavenly vision thus *p.*
　P. L. 9, 405. of thy *p.* return event perverse
　P. L. 9, 921. bold deed thou hast *p.* adventurous
　P. R. 3, 345. whereof the fiend yet more *p.*
　S. A. 462. Dagon hath *p.* me overthrown to
　S. A. 1209. *p.* single rebellion and did hostile
**Presumes.**—P. L. 10, 50. which he *p.* already
**Presumption.**—C. 431. not done in pride or in *p.*
**Presumptuous.**—P. L. 2, 522. false *p.* hope
　P. L. 4, 912. so judge thou still *p.* till the
　P. L. 8, 367. thus I *p.* and the vision bright
　S. A. 1531. that were a joy *p.* to be thought

**Presumptuously.**—S.A.498.his holy secret *p.*
**Pretence.**—P. L. 6, 421. too mean *p.*
P. L. 12, 520. and from that *p.* spiritual laws
S. A. 1196. under *p.* of bridal friends and guests
C. 160. I under fair *p.* of friendly ends
**Pretences.**—P. L. 2, 825. that in our just *p.*
**Pretend.**—P. L. 5, 244. transgressing he *p.*
S. A. 212. and shall again *p.* they ne'er so wise
**Pretended.**—P. L. 10. 872. *p.* to hellish
S. A. 873. but had thy love still odiously *p.*
C. 326. it first was named and yet is most *p.*
**Pretending.**—P. L. 4, 947. *p.* first wise to
P. L. 5, 768. *p.* so commanded to consult
**Pretends.**—P. R. 1, 73. *p.* to wash off sin
**Pretend'st.**—P. R. 1, 430. yet thou *p.* to truth
**Pretexts.**—S. A. 901. these false *p.* varnished
**Prevail.**—P. L. 6, 795. and at length *p.*
P. L. 10, 40. I told ye then he should *p.*
P. L. 10, 408. if your joint power *p.* the affairs
**Prevailed.**—P. L. 9, 873. hath so *p.* that I
P. R. 3, 167. and o'er a mighty king so oft *p.*
S. A. 869. took full possession of me and *p.*
M. 9. and surely death could never have *p.*
**Prevailing.**—P. L. 4, 973. from my *p.* arm
S. A. 740. but conjugal affection *p.* over fear
**Prevails.**—P. L. 10, 258. Satan now *p.*
S. A. 661. in his pangs their sound little *p.*
**Prevalent.**—P. L. 6, 411. his angels *p.*
P. L. 11, 144. so *p.* as to concern the mind of
**Prevenient.**—P. L. 11, 3. above *p.* grace
**Prevent.**—P. L. 4, 996. the eternal to *p.*
P. L. 10, 37. your sincerest care could not *p.*
P. L. 10, 987. yet ere conception to *p.* the race
P. L. 11, 773. neither his foreknowing can *p.*
S. A. 256. meanwhile the men of Judah to *p.*
C. 573. already ere my best speed could *p.*
S.19,8. Patience to *p.* that murmur soon replies
H. 24. O run, *p.* them with thy humble ode
V. Ex. 73. nor can you it *p.*
**Prevented.**—P. L. 2, 467. and *p.* all reply
P. L. 2, 739. *p.* spares to tell thee yet by deeds
S. A. 1103. I lose *p.* by thy eyes put out
C. 285. perhaps forestalling night *p.* them
**Preventing.**—P. L. 4, 492. reign past thy *p.*
**Prevention.**—P. L. 6, 129. at this *p.* more
P. L. 6,320. odds appeared in might or swift *p.*
**Preventive.**—M. 16. their wholesome and *p.*
**Prey.**—P. L. 1, 382. roaming to seek their *p.*
P. L. 2,181. sport and *p.* of racking whirlwinds
P. L. 2, 806. soon devour for want of other *p.*
P. L. 2, 844. all things shall be your *p.*
P. L. 3, 248. in the loathsome grave his *p.*
P.L.3,433. dislodging from a region scarce of *p.*
P. L. 3, 441. and down alone bent on his *p.*
P. L. 4, 184. drives to seek new haunt for *p.*
P. L. 4, 399. nearer to view his *p.* and unespied
P.L. 9,416. whole included race his purposed *p.*
P. L. 10, 268. *p.* innumerable
P. L. 10, 490. to sin and death a *p.*
P. L. 10, 609. him thy last and sweetest *p.*
P. L. 11, 124. and all my trees their *p.*
P. L. 11, 798. the world high titles and rich *p.*
P. L.12,341. all his sacred things a scorn and *p.*
S. A. 260. to the uncircumcised a welcome *p.*
S. A. 613. and on her purest spirits *p*
S. A. 694. to dogs and fowls a *p.* or else captived
C. 534. like stabled wolves or tigers at their *p.*
C. 574. the aidless innocent lady his wished *p.*
**Prick.**—P. L. 2, 536. *p.* forth the aery knights
**Prickles.**—C. 631. leaf was darkish and had *p.*
**Pride.**—P. L. 1, 36. what time his *p.*
P. L. 1, 58. mixed with obdurate *p.*
P. L. 1,527. he, his wonted *p.* soon recollecting
P. L. 1, 572. and now his heart distends with *p.*
P. L.1,603. and considerate *p.* waiting revenge
P. L. 2, 40. till *p.* and worse ambition threw
P. L. 2, 428. with monarchal *p.* conscious
P. L. 4, 310. with coy submission modest *p.*
P. L. 4, 809. with high conceits engendering *p.*
P. L. 5,665. could not bear through *p.* that sight
P. L. 5, 740. power given me to quell their *p.*

P. L. 6, 341. himself not matchless and his *p.*
P. L. 7, 478. the liveries decked of summer's *p.*
P. L. 10, 577. to dash their *p.* and joy for man
P. L. 10, 874. had not thy *p.* and wandering
P. L. 10, 1044. and savours only rancour and *p.*
P. L. 11, 795. till wantonness and *p.* raise out
P. R. 2, 219. her female *p.* deject or turn
P. R. 3, 35. brought down the Carthaginian *p.*
P. R. 3, 81. then swell with *p.*
P. R. 3, 312. in coats of mail and military *p.*
P. R. 3, 409. to the *p.* of numbering Israel
P. R. 4, 300. in philosophic *p.* by him called
P. R. 4, 570. fresh assaults amidst his *p.*
S. A. 286. had not his prowess quelled their *p.*
S. A. 532. then swollen with *p.* into the snare
C. 431. be it not done in *p.* or in presumption
C. 761. and virtue has no tongue to check her *p.*
D.F.I.26. young Hyacinth the *p.* of Spartan land
M. W. 37. the *p.* of her carnation train
**Priest.**—P. L. 1, 494. when the *p.* turns atheist
P. L. 11, 25. I thy *p.* before thee bring
P. R. 1, 257. before the altar and the vested *p.*
P. R. 1,487. suffers the hypocrite or atheous *p.*
P. R. 3, 83. worshipped with temple *p.* and
S. A.857. and the *p.* was not behind but ever at
S. A. 1419. and the well feasted *p.* then soonest
S. 13, 10. to honour thee, the *p.* of Phœbus'
H. 180. inspires the pale-eyed *p.*
P. 15. he sovran *p.* stooping his regal head
F. of C.20. new presbyter is but old *p.* writ large
**Priests.**—P. L. 1, 480. Egypt and her *p.*
P. L. 12, 353. but first among the *p.* dissension
P. R. 3, 169. his family obtained though *p.*
S. A. 1463. most reverenced Dagon and his *p.*
S.A.1653.lords,ladies,captains,counsellors or *p.*
C. 136. and befriend us thy vowed *p.*
**Prime.**—P. L. 1, 506. the *p.* in order and in
P. L. 2, 423. none among the choice and *p.* of
P. L. 3, 637. not of the *p.* yet such as in his
P. L. 4,592. whether the *p.* orb, incredible how
P. L. 5, 21. we lose the *p.* to mark how spring
P. L. 5, 170. day arises that sweet hour of *p.*
P. L. 5, 295. Nature here wantoned as in her *p.*
P. L. 5, 563. matter thou enjoin'st me O *p.* of
P. L. 6, 447. Nisroch of principalities the *p.*
P. L. 8, 194. is the *p.* wisdom what is more is
P. L. 8, 540. for well I understand in the *p.*
P. L. 9, 200. the season *p.* for sweetest scents
P. L. 9, 395. or to Ceres in her *p.* yet virgin of
P. L. 9, 940. destroy us his *p.* creatures
P. L. 10, 356. their author and *p.* architect
P. L. 11, 245. he¹m unbuckled showed him *p.*
P. L. 11, 598. *p.* angel blest
P. R. 1, 413. among the *p.* in splendour now
P. R. 2, 200. dismissed in his *p.* youth the fair
P. R. 3, 123. though chiefly not for glory as *p.*
S. A. 70. the *p.* work of God to me extinct
S. A.85. why am I thus bereaved thy ·*p.* decree
S. A. 234. she was not the *p.* cause but I myself
C. 289. were they of manly *p.* or youthful bloom
L. 8. for Lycidas is dead, dead ere his *p.*
S. 9, 1. lady that in the *p.* of earliest youth
**Primitive.**—P. L. 5, 350. meanwhile our *p.*
**Primrose.**—L. 142. bring the rathe *p.* that
D. F. I. 2. soft silken *p.* fading timelessly
M. M. 4. the yellow cowslip and the pale *p.*·
**Primrose-season.**—C. 671. April buds in *p.-s.*
**Prince.**—P. L. 1, 128. O *p.* O chief of many
P. L. 4, 871. seems the *p.* of hell
P. L. 6, 44. go Michael of celestial armies *p.*
P. L. 6,281. so spake the *p.* of angels to whom
P. L. 10, 185. down from heaven *p.* of the air
P. L. 10, 383. whom thus the *p.* of darkness
P. L. 10, 621. so doth the *p.* of hell
P. L. 11, 298. may seem *p.* above princes
P. L. 12, 454. surprise the serpent, *p.* of air
P. R. 4, 441. the *p.* of darkness
Il P. 18. *p.* Memnon's sister might beseem
H. 62. wherein the *P.* of light his reign of peace
**Princedoms.**—P. L. 3, 320. thrones, *p.*

P. L. 5, 601. thrones, dominations, *p.*. virtues
P. L. 5, 772. thrones, dominations, *p.*, virtues
P. L. 5, 840. thrones, dominations, *p.*, virtues
P. L. 10, 87. *p.* and dominations ministrant
P. L. 10, 460. thrones, dominations, *p.*, virtues
**Princely.**—P. L. 1, 359. *p.* dignities, and
P. L. 2, 304. and *p.* counsel in his face
P. L. 11, 220. the *p.* hierarch in their bright
C. 34. where his fair offspring nursed in *p.* lore
A. 36. to the great mistress of yon *p.* shrine
**Princes.**—P. L. 1, 315. *p.*, potentates, warriors
P. L. 1, 735. and sat as *p.*.
P. L. 2, 313. changing style be called *p.* of hell
P. L. 5, 355. the tedious pomp that waits on *p.*
P. L. 11, 298. of shape may seem prince above *p.*
P. R. 2, 121. *p.* heaven's ancient sons, ethereal
S. A. 851. and *p.* of my country came in person
C. 325. than in tapestry halls and courts of *p.*
**Principalities.**—P. L. 6, 447. Nisroch of *p.*
P. L. 10, 186. spoiled *p.* and powers triumphed
**Principled.**—S. A. 760. with goodness *p.*
**Principles.**—M. 10. his *p.* being ceased
**Print.**—A. 85. where no *p.* of step hath been
H. 20. hath took no *p.* of the approaching light
**Printed.**—F. of C. 11. must now be named and *p.*
**Printless.**—C. 897. thus I set my *p.* feet
**Prison.**—P. L. 1, 71. here their *p.* ordained
P. L. 2, 59. the *p.* of his tyranny who reigns
P. L. 2, 434. our *p.* strong this huge convex
P. L. 4, 824. comest thou escaped thy *p.*
P. L. 4, 906. and now returns him from his *p.*
P. L. 6, 660. ere they could wind out of such *p.*
P. L. 11, 725. as to souls in *p.* under judgments
P. R. 1, 364. but that oft leaving my dolorous *p.*
S.A.6. daily in the common *p.* else enjoined me
S. A. 153. thy bondage or lost sight *p.* within *p.*
S.A.1161. fettered send thee into the common *p.*
S. A. 1480. he in that calamitous *p.* left
**Prisoned.**—C. 256. would take the *p.* soul
**Prisoner.**—S. A. 7. where I a *p.* chained scarce
S. A.808. mine and love's *p.* not the Philistines'
S. A. 1308. Hebrews, the *p.* Samson here I seek
S.A.1460. to accept of ransom for my son their *p.*
**Prison-house.**—S. A. 922. this lonesome *p.-h.*
**Prithee.**—C. 512. what fears, good Thyssis? *p.*
C. 615. why *p.*, shepherd
**Private.**—P. L. 5, 109. retires into her *p.* cell
P. R. 2, 81. his life *p.* unactive calm
P. R. 3, 22. affecting *p.* life
P. R. 3, 232. life hath yet been *p.*
P. R. 4, 94. his horrid lusts in *p.* to enjoy
P. R. 4, 331. or if I would delight my *p.* hours
P. R. 4, 509. thy manhood last though yet in *p.*
P. R. 4, 639. home to his mother's house *p.*
S.A. 868. the public good *p.* respects must yield
S. A. 1208. but I a *p.* person whom my country
S. A. 1211. I was no *p.* but a person raised
S. A. 1465. but their aim *p.* reward
**Privation.**—P. R. 4, 400. *p.* mere of light
**Privilege.**—P. L. 7. 589. *p.* hath omnipresence
S. A. 104. by *p.* of death and burial
**Privy.**—L. 128. what the grim wolf with *p.* paw
**Prize.**—L'A. 122. rain influence and judge the *p.*
**Proboscis.**—P. L. 4, 347. his lithe *p.*
**Proceed.**—P. L. 5, 470. all things *p.* and up
P. L. 10, 824. what can *p.* but all corrupt
P. L. 11, 69. I *p.* as how with peccant angels
P. L. 12, 7. and man as from a second stock *p.*
P. L. 12, 381. from my loins thou shalt *p.*
S.A.599. believe not these suggestions which *p.*
**Proceeded.**—P. L. 7, 69. *p.* thus to ask his
P. L. 10, 164. to judgment he *p.* on the accused
P. L. 10, 913. and thus *p.* in her plaint
P. L. 11, 672. violence *p.* and oppression
**Proceeding.**—P. L. 9, 94. native subtlety *p.*
P. R. 1, 350. but each word *p.* from the mouth
**Proceeds.**—P. L.9, 719. all from them *p.*
P. L. 9, 973. still good *p.*, direct or by occasion
L. 88. but now my oat *p.*
**Proceed'st.**—P. R. 4, 125. then *p.* to talk
**Process.**—P. L. 2. 297. and long *p.* of time

P. L. 7, 178. cannot without *p.* of speech be
**Procession.**—P. L. 7, 222. in bright *p.*
**Procinct.**—P. L. 6, 19. war in *p.*
**Proclaim.**—P. L. 1, 754. the host *p.* a solemn
P. L. 3, 325. archangels to *p.* thy dread
P. R. 1, 70. before him a great prophet to *p.*
S. A. 435. and *p.* great pomp and sacrifice
**Proclaimed.**—P. L. 5, 663. and *p.* Messiah
P. L. 5, 784. to one and to his image now *p.*
P. R. 1, 275. and with loudest voice *p.* me him
P. R. 4, 474. angels have *p.* it but concealing
S. A. 1598. the morning trumpets festival *p.*
**Proclaimer.**—P. R. 1, 18. had the great *p.*
**Proclaiming.**—P. L. 2, 499. and God *p.*
P. L. 12, 407. *p.* life to all who shall believe
**Proclaims.**—P. L. 12, 361. heaven *p.* him
S. A. 972. and with contrary blast *p.* most
**Proconsuls.**—P. R. 4, 63. *p.* to their
**Procreation.**—P. L. 8, 597. in *p.* common
**Procure.**—P. L. 2, 225. worst if we *p.* not to
**Prodigies.**—P. R. 4, 482. terrors, voices, *p.*
**Prodigious.**—P. L. 2, 625. all *p.* things
P. L. 2, 780. *p.* motion felt and rueful throes
P. L. 6, 247. *p.* power had shown and met in
P. L. 10, 302. a bridge of length *p.*
P. L.11,687. produce *p.* births of body or mind
S. A.1083. of thy *p.* might and feats performed
**Produce.**—P. L. 1, 650. space may *p.* new
P. L. 8, 146. and rain *p.* fruits in her softened
P. L. 11, 687. *p.* prodigious births of body
P. L. 12, 470. that all this of evil shall *p.*
P. R. 1, 150. he now shall know I can *p.* a man
P. R. 4, 184. donation none thou canst *p.*
S. A. 1346. I am sorry what this stoutness .. *p.*
**Produced.**—P. L. 10, 692. though slow *p.*
P. L. 11, 29. the trees of paradise could have *p.*
P. R. 3, 122. reason since his word all things *p.*
**Produces.**—P. L. 3, 610. *p.* with terrestrial
P. L. 5, 112. wild work *p.* oft
**Producing.**—P. L. 9, 721. by the sun *p.*
P. L. 11, 683. these are the *p.* of
**Product.**—P. L. 9, 111. *p.* in herb plant
**Productive.**—P. L. 9, 111. *p.* in herb plant
**Proem.**—P. L. 9, 549. and his *p.* tuned
**Profane.**—S. A. 693. sword of heathen and *p.*
S. A. 1362. what act more execrably unclean *p.*
C. 781. arm his *p.* tongue with contemptuous
**Profaned.**—P. L. 1, 390. and solemn feasts *p.*
P. L. 4, 951. O sacred name of faithfulness *p.*
P.L.9, 930. foretasted fruit *p.* first by the serpent
S. A. 377. who have *p.* the mystery of God
**Profaner.**—Il P. 140. where no *p.* eye may look
**Professed.**—P. R. 4, 293. wisest of them all *p.*
S. A. 385. in her height of nuptial love *p.*
S. A. 884. then thy country's foe *p.*
**Professing.**—P. L. 4, 948. *p.* next the spy
**Proffer.**—P. L. 2, 425. so hardy as to *p.*
**Proffered.**—P. R. 2, 330. nor *p.* by an enemy
**Profit.**—P. L. 6, 909. let it *p.* thee to have
P. R. 4, 345. thin sown with aught of *p.*
S.A.1261. with no small *p.* daily to my owners
**Profits.**—P. L. 8, 571. oft-times nothing *p.*
P. L. 9, 761. what *p.* then our inward freedom
**Profluent.**—P. L. 12, 442. baptizing in the *p.*
**Profound.**—P. L. 2, 438. *p.* of unessential
P. L. 2, 592. all else deep snow and ice a gulf *p.*
P. L. 2, 858. into this gloom of Tartarus *p.*
P. L. 2, 980. thither to arrive I travel this *p.*
P. L. 7, 233. darkness *p.* covered the abyss
P. R. 4, 214. to contemplation and *p.* dispute
**Profoundest.**—P. L. 1, 251. and thou *p.* Hell
H. 218. nought but *p.* hell can be his shroud
**Profundity.**—P. L. 7, 229. the vast *p.* obscure
**Profuse.**—P. L. 4, 243. poured forth *p.* on hill
P. L. 8, 286. a green shady bank *p.* of flowers
A. 9. seemed erst so lavish and *p.*
**Progenitor.**—P. L. 5, 544. our great *p.*
P. L. 11,346. and reverence thee their great *p.*
**Progeny.**—P. L. 2, 430. O *p.* of heaven
P. L. 3, 96. so will fall he and his faithless *p.*
P. L. 5, 503. his love entire whose *p.* you are
P. L. 5, 600. hear all ye angels *p.* of light

P. L. 11, 107. denounce to them and to their *p*.
P. L. 12, 138. promise he receives gift to his *p*.
P. R. 4, 554. now show thy *p*.if not to stand
S. 12, 6. railed at Latona's twin-born *p*.
**Progress.**—P. L. 4, 976. *p*. through the road
P. L. 11, 175. begins her rosy *p*. smiling
**Progressive.**—P. L. 8, 127. *p*. retrograde
**Prohibit.**—P. L. 2, 437. barred over us *p*. all
**Prohibition.**—P. L. 4, 433. one easy *p*.
P. L. 9, 645. to the tree of *p*. root of all our
**Prohibitions.**—P. L. 9, 760. such *p*. bind
**Projecting.**—P. L. 2, 329. sit we then *p*.
**Projects.**—P. L. 3, 391. *p*. deep of enemies
**Prolific.**—P. L. 7, 280. with warm *p*. humour
**Prologue.**—P. L. 9, 854. came *p*. and apology
**Prolong.**—P. L. 11, 547. nor would *p*. life
P. R. 2, 41. and again *p*. our expectation
P. R. 4, 469. but wilt *p*.all to the push of fate
**Prolonged.**—P. L. 11, 331. recalled to life *p*.
**Prolongs.**—H. 100. thousand echoes still *p*.
**Promiscuous.**—P. L. 1, 380. *p*. crowd stood
P. R. 3, 118. *p*. from all nations Jew or Greek
**Promise.**—P. L. 2, 238. grace to all on *p*. made
P. L. 11, 155. and to my memory his *p*.
P. L. 12, 137. there by *p*. he receives gift to his
P. L. 12, 322. a *p*. shall receive irrevocable
P. L. 12, 487. *p*. of the Father who shall dwell
S. A. 38.*p*. was that I should Israel..Philistian
S. A. 753. confess and *p*. wonders in her change
**Promised.**—P. L. 3, 531. over the *p*. Land
P. L. 4, 589. so *p*. he and Uriel to his charge
P. L. 4, 732. but thou hast *p*. from us two
P. L. 9, 843. great joy he *p*. to his thoughts
P. L. 9, 1070. true in our fall false in our *p*.
P. L. 11, 331. recalled to life prolonged and *p*.
P. L. 11, 413. that *p*. clearer sight had bred
P. L. 12, 172. and spoil back to their *p*. land
P. L. 12, 260. land *p*. to Abraham and his seed
P. L. 12, 519.*p*. alike and given to all believers
P. L. 12, 542. at return of him so lately *p*.
P. L. 12, 623. by me the *p*. seed shall all restore
P. R. 1, 265. ere I the *p*. kingdom can attain
P. R. 3, 157. Judæa now and all the *P*. land
P. R. 3, 439. when to the *P*. Land their fathers
S. A. 635. *p*. by heavenly message twice
**Promises.**—P. L. 4, 84. seduced with other *p*.
**Promontories.**—P. L. 6, 654. main *p*. flung
**Promontory.**—P. L. 7, 414. stretched like a *p*.
L. 94. that blows from off each beaked *p*.
**Promote.**—P. L. 9, 234. in her husband to *p*.
P. L. 10, 745. I solicit thee from darkness to *p*.
P. R. 1, 205. born to that end born to *p*. all
**Promotion.**—P. R. 3, 202. and my *p*. will be
**Prompt.**—P. L. 5, 149. such *p*. eloquence
P. L. 8, 240. and to inure our *p*. obedience
P. L. 2, 456. *p*. her to do aught may merit
C. 229. my new-enlivened spirits *p*. me
S. 12, 1. I did but *p*. the age to quit
P. L. 9, 854. came prologue and apology to *p*.
**Prompted.**—P. L. 6, 635. rage *p*. them
P. R. 1, 12. inspire as thou art wont my *p*. song
S. A. 318. have *p*. this heroic Nazarite
**Prompting.**—S.A. 422. divine impulsion *p*. how
**Prone.**—P. L. 1, 195. *p*. on the flood
P. L. 2, 478. they bend with awful reverence *p*.
P. L. 4, 353. was hasting now with *p*. career
P. L. 5, 266. down thither *p*. in flight he speeds
P. L. 7, 506. a creature who not *p*.
P.L.8,433. conversing cannot these erect from *p*.
P. L. 9, 497. *p*. on the ground
P. L. 10. 514. on his belly *p*. reluctant
S. A. 1459. with supplication *p*. and father's tears
**Pronounced.**—P. L. 2, 352. so was his will *p*.
P. L. 2, 809. so fate *p*. but thou O father
P. L. 4, 761. bed is undefiled and chaste *p*.
P. L. 4, 427. God hath *p*. it death to taste that
P. L. 5, 148. fit strains *p*. or sung unmeditated
P. L. 5, 814. just decree of God *p*. and sworn
P. L. 8, 333. sternly he *p*. the rigid interdiction
P. L. 9, 154. him lord *p*. and O indignity !
P. L. 9,553. may this mean language of man *p*.

P. L. 10, 197. on Adam last thus judgment he *p*.
P. L. 10, 640. till then the curse *p*. on both
P. L. 10, 1022. thinking to evade the penalty *p*.
P. L. 11, 83. the Almighty thus *p*. his sovran
P. R. 1, 32. from heaven *p*. him his beloved Son
P. R. 1, 284. audibly heard from heaven *p*. me
P. R. 3, 120. from us his foes *p*. glory he exacts
P. R. 4, 275. whom well inspired the oracle *p*.
P. R. 4, 513. heard thee *p*. the Son of God
S. 21, 3. with no mean applause *p*.
**Pronouncing.**—S. A. 289. for want of well *p*.
**Proof.**—P. L. 1, 132. and put to *p*. his high
P. L. 2, 101. and by *p*. we feel our power
P. L. 2, 686. or taste thy folly and learn by *p*.
P. L. 3, 103. not free what *p*. could they have
P. L. 4, 350. his fatal guile gave *p*. unheeded
P. L. 4, 520. the *p*. of their obedience and
P. L. 4, 1010. for *p*. look up and read thy lot
P. L. 5, 865. by *p*. to try who is our equal
P. L. 8, 535. not *p*. enough such object to
P. L. 9, 298. not *p*. against temptation
P. L. 9, 967. one soul in both whereof good *p*.
P. L. 9,1142. when earnestly they seek such *p*.
P. L. 10, 385. high *p*. ye now have given to be
P. L. 10, 882. constant, mature, *p*. against all
P. R. 1, 11. by *p*. the undoubted Son of God
P. R. 1, 130. Gabriel this day by *p*. thou shalt
P. R. 1, 400. I feel by *p*. that fellowship in
P. R. 4, 533. have found thee *p*. against all
P. R. 4, 621. for *p*. ere this thou feel'st thy
S. A. 134. and frock of mail Adamantean *p*.
S. A. 526. after some *p*. of acts indeed heroic
S. A. 1145. for *p*. hereof if Dagon be thy god
S. A. 1314. and now some public *p*. thereof
S. A. 1475. or at some *p*. of strength before them
S. A. 1602. *p*. of his mighty strength in feats and
**Prop.**—P. L. 9, 210. or prune, or *p*. or bind
P. L. 9, 433. from her best *p*. so far and storm
**Propagate.**—P. L. 8, 420. thou shouldst *p*.
**Propagated.**—P. L. 8, 580. mankind is *p*.
P. L. 10, 729. or shall beget is *p*. curse
**Propense.**—S.A. 455. in feeble hearts *p*. enough
**Proper.**—P. L. 2, 75. that in our *p*. motion
P. L. 3, 634. he casts to change his *p*. shape
P. L. 5, 276. he lights and to his *p*. shape
P. R. 5, 493. but convert as you to *p*. substance
P. L. 8, 619. celestial rosy red love's *p*. hue
**Properly.**—P. L. 10, 791. the body *p*. hath
**Property.**—C. 469. the divine *p*. of her first
V. Ex. 87. yea it shall be his natural *p*.
**Prophecies.**—P. R. 4, 381. when *p*. of thee
**Prophecy.**—P. L. 12, 325. shall sing all *p*.
S. A. 473. and these words I as a *p*. receive
**Prophesied.**—P. R. 4, 108. be *p*. what
**Prophet.**—P. L. 12, 357. O *p*. of glad tidings
P. R. 1, 70. before him a great *p*. to proclaim
P. R. 1, 80. I saw the *p*. do him reverence
P. R. 1, 328. our new baptizing *p*. at the ford
P. R. 1, 491. a *p*. yet inspired
P. R. 2, 51. by his great *p*. pointed out
P. R. 2, 270. he saw the *p*. also
P. R. 2, 312. and that *p*. bold, native of Thebez
P. R. 3, 352. though foretold by *p*. or by
P. 37. that whirled the *p*. up at Chebar flood
**Prophetic.**—P. L. 2, 346. and *p*. fame in
P. R. 1, 255. just Simeon and *p*. Anna warned
P. R. 3, 184. if of my reign *p*. writ hath
H. 180. from the *p*. cell
Il P. 174. to something like *p*. strain
**Prophets.**—P. L. 3, 36. and Phineus *p*. old
P. L. 12, 243. and all the *p*. in their age the
P. R. 1, 260. I again revolved the law and *p*.
P. R. 1, 375. of all his flattering *p*. glibbed with
P. R. 2, 18. therefore as those young *p*. then
P. R. 3, 178. the *p*. old who sung thy endless
P. R. 4, 226. the Pentateuch or what the *p*.
P. R. 4, 356. but herein to our *p*. far beneath
P. R. 4, 503. I have heard foretold by all the *p*.
**Propitiation.**—P. L. 11, 34. advocate and *p*.
**Propitious.**—P. L. 5, 507. *p*. guest
P. L. 8, 380. my maker be *p*. while I speak

T

P. L. 11, 441. offering soon *p.* fire from heaven
P. L. 12, 612. which he hath sent *p.* some great
S. 1, 4. while the jolly Hours lead on *p.* May
**Proportion.**—P. L. 8, 385. mutual in *p.* due
P. L. 9, 711. is but *p.* meet
C. 773. in unsuperfluous even *p.*
**Proportional.**—P. L. 9, 936. *p.* ascent
**Proportioned.**—P. L. 5, 479. in bounds *p.*
S. A. 209. these two *p.* ill drove me transverse
C. 330. and square my trial to my *p.* strength
**Proportions.**—P. L. 11, 562. through all *p.*
**Proposal.**—S. A. 487. spare that *p.* father spare
**Proposals.**—P. L. 6, 618. I suppose if our *p.*
**Propose.**—P. R. 1, 212. and to *p.* what might
**Proposed.**—P. L. 2, 380. and in part *p.*
P. L. 2, 447. if aught *p.* and judged of public
P. L. 8, 64. and Raphael now to Adam's doubt *p.*
P. L. 10, 757. whatever when they were *p.*
P. R. 1, 371. and when to all his angels he *p.*
P. R. 4, 199. have *p.* what both from men
P. R. 4, 370. by me *p.* in life contemplative
P. R. 4, 572. Theban monster that *p.* her riddle
S. A. 292. but God's *p.* deliverance not so
S. A. 1200. that solved the riddle which I had *p.*
S. A. 1471. if some convenient ransom were *p.*
**Proposest.**—P. L. 8, 400. see thou to thyself *p.*
P. L. 10, 1038. childless days resolved as thou *p.*
**Propound.**—P. L. 6, 567. touch what we *p.*
P. R. 4, 178. darest thou to the Son of God *p.*
**Propounded.**—P. L. 6, 612. *p.* terms
**Propriety.**—P. L. 4, 751. sole *p.* in paradise
**Prose.**—P. L. 1, 16. things unattempted yet in *p.*
P. L. 5, 150. in *p.* or numerous verse
**Prosecute.**—S. A. 603. to *p.* the means of thy
S. A. 897. to acquit themselves and *p.* their foes
**Proserpina.**—P. L. 9, 396. yet virgin of *P.*
**Proserpine.**—P. L. 4, 269. *P.* gathering
**Prospect.**—P. L. 3, 77. from his *p.* high
P. L. 3, 548. the goodly *p.* of some foreign land
P. L. 4, 144. gave *p.* large into his nether
P. L. 4, 200. plant but only used for *p.*
P. L. 5, 88. a *p.* wide and various
P. L. 7, 423. the ground under a cloud in *p.*
P. L. 7, 556. how it showed in *p.* from his throne
P. L. 10, 89. Eden and all the coast in *p.* lay
P. L. 10, 552. on that *p.* strange their earnest
P. L. 11, 380. out to the amplest reach of *p.*
P. L. 12, 143. each place behold in *p.* as I point
P. R. 2, 286. whose high top to ken the *p.*
P. R. 3, 263. so large the *p.* was that here
**Prospective.**—V. Ex. 71, long and dark *p.* glass
**Prosper.**—P. L. 2, 39. to *p.* than prosperity
P. L. 6, 795. by force or fraud weening to *p.*
P. L. 12, 316. long time shall dwell and *p.*
**Prospered.**—P. L. 8, 45. to visit how they *p.*
P. L. 10, 360. that thou on earth hadst *p.*
**Prosperity.**—P. L. 2, 39. to prosper than *p.*
**Prosperous.**—P. L. 2, 259. useful of hurtful *p.*
P. L. 11, 364. either state to bear *p.* or adverse
P. R. 1, 14. with *p.* wing full summed to tell of
P. R. 1, 104. and the way found *p.* once
S. A. 191, in *p.* days they swarm but in adverse
C. 270. to touch the *p.* growth of this tall wood
**Prostituting.**—P. L. 11, 716. or *p.* as befell
S. A. 1358. greater sin by *p.* holy things to idols
**Prostrate.**—P. L. 1, 280. and *p.* on yon lake
P. L. 6, 841. thrones and mighty seraphim *p.*
P. L. 10, 1087. *p.* fall before him reverent
P. L. 10, 1099. *p.* fell before him reverent
**Prostration.**—P. L. 5, 782. unpaid *p.* vile
**Protect.**—S. 8, 4. and him within *p.* from
**Protection.**—S. A. 887. nor under their *p.* but
**Protects.**—P. L. 9, 266. shades thee and *p.*
**Protesting.**—P. L. 10, 480. *p.* fate supreme
**Proteus.**—P. L. 3, 604. old *P.* from the sea
**Proud.**—P. L. 1, 43. war in heaven and battle *p.*
P. L. 1, 533. that *p.* honour claimed Azazel
P. L. 2, 10. his *p.* imaginations thus displayed
P. L. 2, 533. as when to warn *p.* cities war
P. L. 2, 691. and in *p.* rebellious arms drew
P. L. 3, 159. or *p.* return though to his

P. L. 4, 536. so saying his *p.* step he scornful
P. L. 4, 770. starved lover sings to his *p.* fair
P. L. 4, 858. but like a *p.* steed reined, went
P. L. 4, 971. *p.* limitary cherub
P. L. 5, 809. argument blasphemous false and *p.*
P. L. 5, 907. on those *p.* towers to swift
P. L. 6, 89. the envier of his state the *p.* aspirer
P. L. 6, 131. *p.* art thou met thy hope was to
P. L. 6, 191. on the *p.* crest of Satan that no:
P. L. 6, 609. why come not on these victors *p.*
P. L. 6, 789. but to convince the *p.* what
P. L. 7, 609. easily the *p.* attempt of spirits
P. L. 9, 383. a foe so *p.* will first the weaker
P. L. 10, 424. city and *p.* seat of Lucifer
P. L. 10, 764. for his contempt of thee that *p.*
P. L. 12, 25. till one shall rise of *p.* ambitious
P. L. 12, 72. his encroachment *p.* stays not on
P. L. 12, 342. a scorn and prey to that *p.* city
P. R. 1, 219. brute violence and *p.* tyrannic
P. R. 1, 372. draw the *p.* king Ahab into fraud
P. R. 3, 334. overlay with bridges rivers *p.* as
P. R. 4, 569. after many a foil the tempter *p.*
P. R. 4, 595. temptation and the tempter *p.*
S. A. 137. in scorn of their *p.* arms and warlike
S. A. 345. their armies ranked in *p.* array
S. A. 1069. as is his pile high-built and *p.*
S. A. 1462. contemptuous *p.* set on revenge
C. 33. an old and haughty nation *p.* in arms
S. 16, 5. and on the neck of crowned fortune *p.*
**Proudest.**—P. L. 12, 497. amaze their *p.*
P. R. 3, 99. lives now equal in fame to *p.*
**Proudly.**—P. L. 1, 590. shape and gesture *p.*
P. L. 7, 439. her white wings mantling *p.* rows
P. R. 4, 34. with towers and temples *p.* elevate
P. R. 4, 580. who durst so *p.* tempt the Son of
S. A. 55. *p.* secure yet liable to fall
**Prove.**—P. L. 2, 369. may *p.* their foe, and
P. L. 2, 808. and knows that I should *p.*
P. L. 4, 985. his hopeful sheaves *p.* chaff
P. L. 6, 170. or weakest *p.* where boldest
P. L. 6, 170. deeds compared this day shall *p.*
P. L. 8, 388. but soon *p.* tedious alike
P. L. 10, 664. or falling should *p.* tempestuous
P. L. 10, 761. what if thy Son *p.* disobedient
P. L. 10, 963. *p.* no sudden but a slow-paced
P. L. 11, 123. lest paradise a receptacle *p.*
P. R. 1, 370. to *p.* him and illustrate his high
S. A. 1181. tongue-doughty giant how dost thou
S. A. 1262. my deadliest foe will *p.* my speediest
S. A. 1400. which to no few of them would *p.*
C. 123. night hath better sweets to *p.*
C. 592. shall in the happy trial *p.* most glory
M. W. 44. *p.* to be presaging tears
U. C. II. 1. here lieth one who did most truly *p.*
**Proved.**—P. L. 1, 92. so much the stronger *p.*
P. L. 3, 119. which had no less *p.* certain
P. L. 4, 48. yet all his good *p.* ill in me
P. L. 6, 90. their thoughts *p.* fond and vain
P. L. 6, 271. once upright and faithful now *p.*
P. L. 9, 333. gain from his surmise *p.* false
P. L. 9, 616. virtue of that fruit in thee first *p.*
**Proverbed.**—S. A. 203. sung and *p.* for a fool
**Proves.**—P. L. 6, 428. but *p.* not so then
P. L. 6, 819. in battle which the stronger *p.*
S. A. 64. and *p.* the source of all my miseries
S. A. 351. but often *p.* our woe our bane
S. A. 1037. joined the contrary she *p.*, a thorn
S. A. 1575. which now *p.* abortive
**Provide.**—P. L. 6, 520. part incentive reed *p.*
C. 187. as the kind hospitable woods *p.*
**Provided.**—P. L. 8, 363. thou hast *p.* all
P. L. 10, 1058. timely care hath unbesought *p.*
P. L. 11, 61. till I *p.* death
**Providence.**—P. L. 1, 25. assert eternal *p.*
P. L. 1, 162. if then his *p.* out of our evil seek
P. L. 2, 559. of *p.* foreknowledge will and fate
P. L. 12, 564. ever to observe his *p.* and on him
P. L. 12, 647. choose their place of rest and *p.*
P. R. 1, 445. among them to declare his *p.*
P. R. 2, 54. and all our fears lay on his *p.*
P. R. 3, 440. to his due time and *p.* I leave

S. A. 670. temper'st thy *p.* through his short
S. A. 1545. but *p.* or instinct of nature seems
C. 329. eye me blessed *P.* and square my trial
**Provident.**—P. L. 7, 485. emmet *p.* of future
P. L. 5, 828. good and of our dignity how *p.*
**Provides.**—P. L. 10, 237. happier seat *p.*
**Providing.**—P. R. 2, 310. relief by a *p.*
**Province.**—P. L. 6, 77. and many a *p.* wide
P. R. 1, 118. of many a pleasant realm and *p.*
P. R. 1, 448. or his angels president in every *p.*
P. R. 3, 158. reduced a *p.* under Roman yoke
**Provinces.**—P. R. 3, 315. choice of many *p.*
P. R. 4, 63. prætors, proconsuls to their *p.*
P. R. 4, 136. peeling their *p.* exhausted all
**Proving.**—S. A. 227. she *p.* false the next I took
**Provision.**—P. L. 9, 623. grow up to their *p.*
P. R. 2, 402. both table and *p.* vanished quite
C. 765. mean her *p.* only to the good
**Provisions.**—P. L. 11, 732. and of *p.* laid in
**Provoke.**—P. L. 1, 644. so as not either to *p.*
P. L. 2, 82. should we again *p.* our stronger
P. L. 10, 1027. such acts of contumacy will *p.*
S. A. 237. in seeking just occasion to *p.*
**Provoked.**—P. L. 1, 645. dread new war *p.*
P. L. 4, 916. pain can equal anger infinite *p.*
P. L. 6, 154. first assay of this right hand *p.*
P. L. 9, 922. and peril great *p.* who thus hast
S. A. 466. will not connive or linger thus *p.*
S. A. 643. whom I by his appointment had *p.*
**Provokes.**—P. L. 9, 175. who next *p.* my
**Provoking.**—P. L. 12, 318. *p.* God to raise
**Prow.**—P. L. 11, 746. with beaked *p.* rode
**Prowess.**—P. L. 1, 588. compare of mortal *p.*
P. L. 6, 45. and thou in military *p.* next
P. L. 11, 789. they first seen in acts of *p.*
P. R. 3, 19. the world could not sustain thy *p.*
S. A. 286. had not his *p.* quelled their pride
S. A. 1098. so had the glory of *p.* been recovered
**Prowest.**—P. R. 3, 342. sought by many *p.*
**Prowling.**—P. L. 4, 183. as when a *p.* wolf
**Prudence.**—P. R. 4, 263. teachers of moral *p.*
**Prudent.**—P. L. 2, 468. *p.* lest from his
P. L. 7, 430. so steers the *p.* crane her annual
**Prune.**—P. L. 4, 438. to *p.* these growing
P. L. 9, 210. lop overgrown or *p.* or prop
**Pry.**—P. L. 1, 655. thither if but to *p.*
P. L. 9, 159. and *p.* in every bush and brake
**Psalms.**—P. R. 4, 335. our *p.* with artful
S. M. 15. hymns devout and holy *p.*
**Psyche.**—C. 1005. holds his dear *P.* sweet
**Public.**—P. L. 2, 303. and *p.* care
P. L. 2, 448. proposed and judged of *p.* moment
P. L. 6, 389. yet *p.* reason just honour and
P. L. 10, 508. universal hiss the sound of *p.*
P. L. 12, 317. national interrupt their *p.* peace
P. R. 1, 204. thence to do what might be *p.*
P. R. 2, 52. pointed at and shown in *p.*
P. R. 2, 84. and in *p.* shown Son
P. R. 2, 465. that for the *p.* all this weight
P. R. 4, 96. to a wicked favourite all *p.* cares
S. A. 867. to the *p.* good private respects must
S. A. 992. the *p.* marks of honour and reward
S. A. 1306. a *p.* officer and now at hand
S. A. 1314. now some *p.* proof thereof require
S. A. 1327. and overlaboured at their *p.* mill
S. A. 1393. at the *p.* mill our drudge
S. A. 1615. was Samson as a *p.* servant brought
S. 15, 12. and *p.* faith cleared from the shameful
**Publish.**—P. L. 2, 238. should relent and *p.*
P. R. 1, 188. and which way first *p.* his godlike
S. A. 777. with like infirmity to *p.*
**Published.**—S. A. 498. presumptuously have *p.*
**Puissance.**—P. L. 5, 864. our *p.* is our own
P. L. 6, 119. his *p.* trusting in the Almighty's
**Puissant.**—P. L. 1, 632. all these *p.* legions
P. L. 6, 714. and sword upon thy *p.* thigh
P. L. 12, 322. for piety renowned and *p.* deeds
P. R. 2, 425. that got him *p.* friends
A. 60. *p.* words and murmurs made to bless
**Pull.**—S. A. 1626. to heave, *p.*, draw, or break
**Pulled.**—S. A. 1589. and on his own he *p.*

L'A. 103. she was pinched and *p.* she said
S. A. 146. then by main force *p.* up and on his
S. A. 1658. *p.* down the same destruction on
U. C. I. 16. *p.* off his boots and took away
**Pulp.**—P. L. 4, 335. the savoury *p.* they chew
**Pulse.**—P. L. 2, 278. with Daniel at his *p.*
C. 721. should in a pet of temperance feed on *p.*
**Punctual.**—P. L. 8, 23. earth this *p.* spot
**Punic.**—P. L. 5, 340. in Pontus or the *P.* coast
P. R. 3, 102. his wasted country freed from *P.*
**Punish.**—P. L. 2, 159. his anger saves to *p.*
P. L. 2, 1032. to tempt or *p.* mortals except
**Punished.**—P. L. 2, 213. satisfied with what is *p.*
P. L. 10, 516. now ruled him *p.* in the shape
P. L. 10, 803. in *p.* man to satisfy his rigour
P. R. 3, 214. whether thou reign
**Punisher.**—P. L. 4, 103. this knows my *p.*
**Punishment.**—P. L. 1, 155. eternal *p.*
P. L. 2, 334. stripes, and arbitrary *p.* inflicted
P. L. 2, 699. back to thy *p.* false fugitive
P. L. 4, 911. and to scape his *p.*
P. L. 5, 881. both of thy crime and *p.*
P. L. 6, 53. into their place of *p.* the gulf
P. L. 6, 807. the *p.* to other hand belongs
P. L. 6, 904. partake his *p.* eternal misery
P. L. 10, 133. lest on my head both sin and *p.*
P. L. 10, 242. can fit his *p.* or their revenge
P. L. 10, 544. like in *p.* as in their crime
P. L. 10, 768. thy *p.* then justly is at his will
P. L. 10, 949. who desirest the *p.* all thyself
P. L. 10, 1039. shall scape his *p.* ordained
P. L. 11, 520. therefore so abject is their *p.*
P. L. 11, 710. awaits the good the rest what *p.*
P. L. 12, 404. thy *p.* he shall endure by coming
S. A. 413. rewarded well with servile *p.*
S. A. 489. as I deserve pay on my *p.*
S. A. 504. but if the *p.* thou canst avoid
S. A. 702. causeless suffering the *p.* of dissolute
S. A. 1225. down by the law to capital *p.*
**Puny.**—P. L. 2, 367. as we were driven the *p.*
**Purchase.**—P. L. 4, 101. so should I *p.* dear
P. L. 10, 500. a world who would not *p.* with
P. L. 10, 579. among the heathen of their *p.*
C. 607. and force him to return his *p.* back
**Pure.**—P. L. 1, 18. the upright heart and *p.*
P. L. 1, 425. uncompounded is their essence *p.*
P. L. 3, 7. *p.* ethereal stream whose fountain
P. L. 3, 57. from the *p.* Empyrean
P. L. 3, 564. through the *p.* marble air
P. L. 3, 607. breathe forth Elixir *p.* and rivers
P. L. 4, 153. and of *p.* now purer air meets
P. L. 4, 293. wisdom sanctitude severe and *p.*
P. L. 4, 316. instead, mere shows of seeming *p.*
P. L. 4, 456. *p.* as the expanse of heaven
P. L. 4, 502. her matron lip with kisses *p.*
P. L. 4, 737. but adoration *p.* which God likes
P. L. 4, 747. as impure what God declares *p.*
P. L. 4, 755. founded in reason loyal, just, and *p.*
P. L. 4, 805. the animal spirits that from *p.*
P. L. 4, 806. like gentle breaths from rivers *p.*
P. L. 4, 837. stood'st in heaven upright and *p.*
P. L. 5, 4. sleep was aery-light from *p.* digestion
P. L. 5, 100. can harbour none created *p.*
P. L. 5, 348. wants her fit vessels *p.*
P. L. 5, 407. food alike those *p.* intelligential
P. L. 5, 475. more refined more spirituous and *p.*
P. L. 6, 758. sapphire throne inlaid with *p.* amber
P. L. 7, 244. first of things quintessence *p.*
P. L. 7, 264. the firmament expanse of liquid *p.*
P. L. 8, 180. thou satisfied me *p.* intelligence
P. L. 8, 506. nature herself though *p.* of sinful
P. L. 8, 622. whatever *p.* thou in the body
P. L. 8, 623. and *p.* thou wert created
P. L. 8, 627. total they mix union of *p.* with *p.*
P. L. 10, 632. hath shed on what was *p.*
P. L. 10, 638. earth renewed shall be made *p.*
P. L. 10, 784. lest that *p.* breath of life
P. L. 11, 50. those *p.* immortal elements that
P. L. 11, 285. we breathe in other air less *p.*
P. L. 11, 452. is piety thus and *p.* devotion
P. L. 11, 523. while they pervert *p.* nature's

P. L. 11, 606. holy and *p.* conformity divine
P. L. 12, 444. them from guilt of sin to life *p.*
P. L. 12, 513. only in those written records *p.*
P. R. 1, 74. them so purified to receive him *p.*
P. R. 1, 77. not thence to be more *p.* but to
P. R. 1, 134. which I sent thee to the Virgin *p.*
P. R. 1, 486. Father who is holy, wise, and *p.*
P. R. 2, 63. though calm her breast though *p.*
P. R. 2, 370. the touching of these viands *p.*
P. R. 3, 27. most tempered *p.* ethereal
P. R. 4, 239. built nobly *p.* the air and light
S. A. 10. of heaven fresh blowing *p.* and sweet
S. A. 548. against the eastern ray translucent *p.*
S. A. 1727. with lavers *p.* and cleansing herbs
C. 16. I would not soil these *p.* ambrosial weeds
C. 794. the uncontrolled worth of this *p.* cause
C. 826. Sabrina is her name a virgin *p.*
C. 912. drops that from my fountain *p.*
L. 81. but lives and spreads aloft by those *p.*
L. 175. with nectar *p.* his oozy locks he laves
Il P. 31. come pensive nun devout and *p.*
S. 9. 14. gained thy entrance virgin wise and *p.*
S. 14, 14. and drink thy fill of *p.* immortal
S. 18, 3. who kept thy truth so *p.* of old
S. 23, 9. came vested all in white *p.* as her
S. M. 6. that undisturbed song of *p.* concent
F. of C. 9. men, whose life, learning, faith, and *p.*
S. 18, 3. who kept thy truth so *p.* of old
**Pure-eyed.**—C. 213. O welcome *p.-e.* faith
**Purer.**—P. L. 2, 215. our *p.* essence then will
P. L. 4, 153. and of pure now *p.* air meets his
P. L. 5, 416. elements the grosser feeds the *p.*
C. 111. we that are of *p.* fire
**Purest.**—P. L. 2, 137. to confound Heaven's *p.*
P. L. 5, 406. may of *p.* spirits be found no
P. L. 6, 660. though spirits of *p.* light *p.* at
S. A. 613. and on her *p.* spirits prey
**Purfled.**—C. 995. than her *p.* scarf can show
**Purgatory.**—S. 13, 14. the milder shades of *p.*
**Purge.**—P. L. 3, 54. from thence *p.* and
P. L. 2, 141. and *p.* off the baser fire victorious
P. L. 2, 400. at the brightening orient beam *p.*
P. L. 11, 52. and *p.* him off as a distemper
P. L. 11, 900. till fire *p.* all things new both
**Purged.**—P. L. 7, 237. but downward *p.* the
P. L. 11, 414. *p.* with euphrasy and rue
P. L. 12, 548. the conflagrant mass *p.* and
**Purification.**—S. 23, 6. *p.* in the old law did
**Purified.**—P. R. 1, 74. and fit them so *p.* to
**Purity.**—P. L. 4, 745. talk of *p.* and place
P. L. 9, 1075. void of innocence of faith of *p.*
S. A. 319. against his vow of strictest *p.*
C. 427. will dare to soil her virgin *p.*
**Purlieu.**—P. L. 4, 404. hath spied in some *p.*
**Purlieus.**—P. L. 2, 833. in the *p.* of heaven
**Purling.**—P. R. 2, 345. freshet or *p.* brook
**Purloined.**—P. L. 2, 946. wakeful custody *p.*
**Purple.**—P. L. 1, 451. ran *p.* to the sea
P. L. 4, 259. vine lays forth her *p.* grape
P. L. 4, 596. arraying with reflected *p.*
P. L. 4, 764. and waves his *p.* wings reigns
P. L. 7, 479. with spots of gold and *p.* azure
P. L. 9, 429. carnation *p.* azure or specked
P. L. 11, 241. a military vest of *p.* flowed
C. 46. Bacchus that first from out the *p.* grape
L. 141. and *p.* all the ground with vernal flowers
S. 14, 10. clad them o'er with *p.* beams
D. F. I. 27. then transformed him to a *p.* flower
**Purples.**—P. L. 7, 30. when morn *p.* the east
**Purpose.**—P. L. 2, 971. with *p.* to explore
P. L. 3, 90. with *p.* to assay if him by force
P. L. 3, 172. all as my eternal *p.* hath decreed
P. L. 4, 337. nor gentle *p.* nor endearing smiles
P. L. 4, 584. these earthly bounds on *p.*
P. L. 6, 675. that his great *p.* he might so fulfil
P. L. 7, 78. with solemn *p.* to observe immutably
P. L. 7, 614. seeks to lessen thee against his *p.*
P. L. 8, 337. and gracious *p.* thus renewed
P. L. 11, 195. nature shows forerunners of his *p.*
P. L. 12, 301. and but given with *p.*
P. R. 1, 444. but when his *p.* is among them

P. R. 2, 101. thus long to some great *p.* he
P. R. 3, 186. the Father in his *p.* hath decreed
P. R. 4, 93. with *p.* there his horrid lusts
S. A. 569. redundant locks robustious to no *p.*
S. A. 1406. for a life who will not change his *p.*
S. A. 1498. were not his *p.* to use him farther yet
**Purposed.**—P. L. 3, 404. perceive thee *p.*
P. L. 4, 373. now is entered yet no *p.* foe to you
P. L. 9, 416. the whole included race his *p.*
P. R. 1, 127. unweeting he fulfilled the *p.*
S. A. 399. what impudence she *p.* to betray me
C. 284. they were but twain and *p.* quick return
V. Ex. 57. then quick about thy *p.* business come
**Purposes.**—P. L. 1, 430. execute their aery *p.*
**Pursed.**—C. 642. I *p.* it up but little reckoning
**Pursue.**—P. L. 2, 8. insatiate to *p.* vain war
P. L. 2, 249. us not then *p.* by force impossible
P. L. 2, 701. lest with a whip of scorpions I *p.*
P. L. 4, 362. whom my thoughts *p.* with wonder
P. L. 6, 715. *p.* these sons of darkness
P. L. 12, 206. all night he will *p.* but his approach
P. R. 4, 470. *p.* thy way of gaining David's
S. A. 1275. but raging to *p.* the righteous
C. 503. or to *p.* the stealth of pilfering wolf
**Pursued.**—P. L. 1, 308. perfidious hatred they *p.*
P. L. 2, 79. and *p.* us through the deep
P. L. 2, 165. *p.* and struck with heaven's
P. L. 2, 790. I fled, but he *p.* though more
P. L. 4, 125. whose eye *p.* him down the way
P. L. 4, 572. mine eye *p.* him still
P. L. 6, 858. them before him thunder struck *p.*
P. L. 9, 15. on his foe *p.* thrice fugitive about
P. L. 9, 397. long with ardent look his eye *p.*
P. L. 11, 188. first hunter then *p.* a gentle brace
P. L. 11, 202. of flight *p.* in the air and o'er
P. L. 11, 563. fled and *p.* transverse the
P. R. 1, 195. his holy meditations thus *p.*
P. R. 2, 405. with these words his temptation *p.*
S. 16, 6. reared God's trophies and his work *p.*
**Pursuers.**—P. L. 1, 326. his swift *p.* from
P. R. 3, 325. against the face of their *p.* and
**Pursues.**—P. L. 1, 15. while it *p.* things
P. L. 2, 524. wandering each his several way *p.*
P. L. 2, 945. *p.* the Arimaspian who by stealth
P. L. 2, 949. hands, wings or feet *p.* his way
P. L. 10, 783. yet one doubt *p.* me still
P. L. 12, 205. them while the obdurate king *p.*
P. R. 4, 24. and his vain importunity *p.*
S. A. 1544. for dire imagination still *p.* me
**Pursuing.**—P. L. 2, 998. victorious bands *p.*
P. L. 6, 52. and to the brow of heaven *p.*
P. L. 11, 192. and with his eye the chase *p.*
P. L. 12, 195. till in his rage *p.* whom he late
**Pursuit.**—P. L. 1, 170. of vengeance and *p.*
P. L. 3, 397. back from *p.* thy powers
P. L. 6, 538. we thought well save us long *p.*
P. R. 3, 306. of equal dread in flight or in *p.*
S. A. 280. in *p.* of Madian and her vanquished
C. 829. guiltless damsel flying the mad *p.*
**Purveyed.**—P. L. 9, 1021. this day thou hast *p.*
P. R. 2, 333. hath *p.* from all the elements her
**Push.**—P. R. 4, 470. all to the *p.* of fate
**Pushed.**—P. L. 6, 197. side long had *p.*
P. L. 10, 670. they with labour *p.* oblique the
P. L. 10, 1074. justling or *p.* with winds rude
P. L. 11, 831. moved out of his place *p.* by the
**Put.**—P. L. 1, 132. *p.* to proof his high supremacy
P. L. 1, 641. and his regal state *p.* forth at full
P. L. 2, 517. *p.* to their mouths the sounding
P. L. 3, 240. glory next to thee freely *p.* off
P. L. 3, 479. dying *p.* on the weeds of Dominic
P. L. 4, 3. the dragon *p.* to second rout
P. L. 4, 941. though for possession *p.* to try
P. L. 4, 1002. in these he *p.* two weights
P. L. 6, 583. all at once their reeds *p.* forth
P. L. 6, 734. and can *p.* on thy terrors as I *p.*
P. L. 6, 853. yet half his strength he *p.* not
P. L. 7, 171. and *p.* not forth my goodness
P. L. 7, 310. and said let the earth *p.* forth the
P. L. 9, 714. by putting off human to *p.* on
P. L. 10, 179. thee and the woman I will *p.*

P. L. 10, 497. enmity which he will *p*. between
P. R. 2, 218. and *p*. to rout all her array
S. A. 33. captived and both my eyes *p*. out
S. A. 37. O glorious strength *p*. to the labour of a
S. A. 1103. I lose prevented by thy eyes *p*. out
S. A. 1119. then *p*. on all thy gorgeous arms
S. A. 1160. permitted them to *p*. out both thine
C. 82. first I must *p*. off these my sky-robes
C. 158. and *p*. the damsel to suspicious flight
C. 372. and *p*. them into misbecoming plight
U. C. II. 12. and too much breathing *p*. him out
U. C. II. 20. for one carrier *p*. down to make six

**Puts.**—P. L. 2, 631. *p*. on swift wings and toward
P. L. 4, 386. thank him who *p*. me
P. L. 4, 888. but this question asked *p*. me in

P. L. 9, 667. at his wrong new part *p*. on
S. A. 163. for inward light alas *p*. forth no visual
S. A. 1271. *p*. invincible might to quell the
**Putting.**—P. L. 4, 739. and eased the *p*. off
P. L. 9, 713. by *p*. off human to put on gods
**Pygmean.**—P. L. 1, 780. like that *P*. race
**Pyramid.**—P. L. 2, 1013. upward like a *p*.
W. S. 4. under a star-ypointing *p*.
**Pyramids.**—P. L. 5, 758. with *p*. and towers
**Pyrrha.**—P. L. 11, 12. Deucalion and chaste *P*.
Hor. 3. in some pleasant cave *P*.
**Pythian.**—P. L. 2, 530. Olympian games or *P*.
P. L. 10, 530. engendered in the *P*. vale on slime
**Python.**—P. L. 10, 531. on slime huge *P*.

# Q.

**Quadrate.**—P. L. 6, 62. in mighty *q*. joined
**Quadrature.**—P. L. 10, 381. his *q*. from thy
**Quaff.**—P. L. 5, 638. *q*. immortality and joy
P. R. 4, 118. how they *q*. in gold, crystal
**Quaint.**—P. L. 8, 78. laughter at their *q*. opinions
P. L. 9, 35. impresses *q*. caparisons and steeds
S. A. 1303. in his hand a sceptre or *q*. staff
C. 157. and my *q*. habits breed astonishment
A. 47. with ringlets *q*. and wanton windings
L. 139. throw hither all your *q*. enamelled eyes
H. 194. affrights the flamens at their service *q*.
**Qualms.**—P. L. 11, 481. *q*. of heart-sick agony
**Quarrel.**—S. A. 60. I must not *q*. with the will
**Quarrels.**—S. A. 1329. seek occasion of new *q*.
**Quarries.**—P. L. 5, 759. from diamond *q*.
**Quarry.**—P. L. 10, 281. sagacious of his *q*.
P. 46. yet on the softened *q*. would I score
**Quarter.**—P. L. 6, 530. scour each *q*.
**Quartered.**—P. R. 4, 202. all the *q*. winds
**Quarters.**—P. L. 3, 714. to their several *q*.
P. L. 5, 192. ye winds that from four *q*. blow
P. L. 5, 689. where we possess the *q*. of the north
C. 29. he *q*. to his blue-haired deities
**Quaternion.**—P. L. 5, 181. that in *q*. run
**Queen.**—P. L. 1, 439. *q*. of heaven with crescent
P. L. 4, 608. Moon, at length apparent *q*.
P. L. 8, 60. for on her as *q*. a pomp of winning
P. L. 9, 684. *q*. of this universe do not believe
P. L. 9, 842. reapers oft are wont their harvest *q*.
P. R. 2, 212. as sitting *q*. adored on beauty's
P. R. 4, 45. and glorious Rome *q*. of the earth
C. 241. tell me but where sweet *q*. of parley
C. 265. and she shall be my *q*.
C. 442. fair silver-shafted *q*. for ever chaste
C. 446. and she was *q*. of the woods
C. 1002. sadly sits the Assyrian *q*.
A. 94. such a rural *q*. all Arcadia hath not seen
Il P. 19. or that starred Ethiop *q*. that strove
H. 201. heaven's *q*. and mother both
M. W. 74. no marchioness but now a *q*.
**Queens.**—M. 47. and last of kings and *q*.
**Quell.**—P. L. 5, 740. power given me to *q*.
P. L. 12, 311. shall *q*. the adversary serpent
P. R. 1, 218. then to subdue and *q*. o'er all
S. A. 1272. to *q*. the mighty of the earth
C. 613. be those that *q*. the might of hellish
**Quelled.**—P. L. 4, 860. from above had *q*.
P. L. 6, 386. their mightiest *q*. the battle
P. L. 6, 457. *q*. with pain which all subdues
P. L. 11, 496. compassion *q*. his best of man
P. R. 3, 35. young Pompey *q*.
S. A. 286. had not his prowess *q*. their pride
S. A. 563. dishonoured, *q*., to what .. be useful?
**Queller.**—P. R. 4, 634. *q*. of Satan
**Quench.**—P. L. 12, 492. and *q*. his fiery darts
P. R. 3, 38. *q*. not the thirst of glory
C. 66. to *q*. the drouth of Phœbus
**Quenched.**—P. L. 2, 939. *q*. in a boggy Syrtis
P. L. 3, 25. so thick a drop serene hath *q*.
S. A. 95. so obvious and so easy to be *q*.
**Quest.**—P. L. 2, 830. search with wandering *q*.

P. L. 9, 414. and on his *q*. where likeliest he
P. R. 1, 315. following as seemed the *q*. of some
C. 321. where you may be safe till farther *q*.
A. 34. I know this *q*. of yours and free intent
D. F. I. 18. there ended was his *q*.
**Question.**—P. L. 4, 882. to *q*. thy bold entrance
P. L. 4, 887. but this *q*. asked puts me in doubt
P. L. 9, 720. I *q* it for this fair earth I see
S. A. 1254. lest a *q*. rise whether he durst accept
**Questioned.**—P. L. 3, 166. be *q*. and blasphemed
L. 93. and *q*. every gust of rugged wings
**Questions.**—P. R. 4, 219. on points and *q*.
**Quick.**—P. L. 4, 1004. the latter *q*. upflew and
P. L. 5, 269. then with *q*. fan winnows the
P. L. 6, 597. by *q*. contraction or remove
P. L. 6, 619. compel them to a *q*. result
P. L. 7, 405. or sporting with *q*. glance show
P. L. 8, 259. till raised by *q*. instinctive motion
P. L. 9, 399. he to her his charge of *q*. return
P. L. 12, 460. to judge both *q*. and dead
P. R. 2, 172. to whom *q*. answer Satan thus
P. R. 3, 323. how *q*. they wheeled and flying
S. A. 764. if not by *q*. destruction soon cut off
C. 41. but that by *q*. command from sovran Jove
C. 284. they were but twain and purposed *q*.
C. 841. and underwent a *q*. immortal change
V. Ex. 57. then *q*. about thy purposed business
**Quickened.**—P. L. 5, 85. so *q*. appetite that
P. L. 9, 587. powerful persuaders *q*. at the
U. C. II. 16 died nor would with ale be *q*.
**Quickening.**—P. L. 5, 861. our own *q*.
**Quickest.**—P. R. 3, 238. experience *q*. in sight
**Quickly.**—P. R. 2, 400. others *q*. will dispose
C. 1014. *q*. to the green earth's end
M. W. 16. *q*. found a lover meet
D. F. I. 42. *q*. thou didst take thy flight
**Quiet.**—P. L. 11, 272. hope to spend *q*. though
P. L. 12, 80. on the *q*. state of men such
P. R. 3, 360. thou hope long to enjoy it *q*.
S. A. 1724. and what may *q*. us in a death so
Il P. 45. and join with thee calm peace and *q*.
M. W. 48. may thy grave peace and *q*. ever have
**Quietly.**—P. R. 3, 192. abstaining *q*.
**Quills.**—L. 188. the tender stops of various *q*.
**Quiloa.**—P. L. 11, 399. Mombaza and *Q*. and
**Quintessence.**—P. L. 3, 716. *q*. of heaven
P. L. 7, 244. ethereal first of things *q*. pure
**Quintilian.**—S. 11, 11. made *Q*. stare and gasp
**Quintius.**—P. R. 2, 446. *Q*. Fabricius, Curius
**Quips.**—L'A. 27. *q*. and cranks and wanton wiles
**Quire.** *
**Quit.**—P. L. 4, 51. in a moment *q*. the debt
P. L. 5, 882. no more be troubled how to *q*.
P. L. 6, 548. *q*. of all impediment
P. L. 7, 440. yet oft they *q*. the dank and rising
P. L. 11, 548. bent rather how I may be *q*.
P. R. 1, 477. or reproof and glad to 'scape so *q*.
P. R. 3, 244. bring thee where thou soon shalt *q*.

* For **Quire, Quires** etc. see **Choir.**
**Choirs,** etc.

S. A. 509. God will relent and q. thee all his debt
S.A. 1484. if need be I am ready to forego and q.
S.A. 1709. Samson hath q. himself like Samson
S. 12, 1. I did but prompt the age to q. their clogs
T. 20. then all this earthly grossness q.
**Quite.**—P. L. 2, 93. we should be q. abolished
P. L. 2, 96. to the height enraged will either q.
P. L. 2, 282. dismissing q. all thoughts of war
P. L. 3, 50. wisdom at one entrance q. shut out
P. L. 3, 173. man shall not q. be lost but saved
P. L. 11, 258. redeem thee q. from death's
P. L. 11, 712. and saw the face of things q.
P. L. 12, 28. and q. dispossess concord and law
P. L. 12, 54. to rase q. out their native language
P. L. 2, 224. at every sudden slighting q.
P. R. 2, 402. table and provision vanished q.
P. R. 4, 317. as one regardless q. of mortal
P. R. 4, 352. not in all q. lost
P. R. 4, 366. q. at a loss for all his darts were
S. A. 469. as shall q. despoil him of all these

S. A. 907. I was a fool too rash and q. mistaken
S. A. 1158. hath cut off q. from his people
S.A. 1688. despised and thought extinguished q.
C. 336. or if your influence be q. dammed up
C. 468. she q. lose the divine property of her first
C. 527. whose pleasing poison the visage q.
C. 728. who would be q. surcharged with her
L'A. 149. to have q. set free his half-regained
H. 67. who now hath q. forgot to rave
**Quits.**—S. A. 324. that moral verdict q. her
**Quitted.**—P. L. 3, 307. q. all to save a world
P. L. 4, 770. sings to his proud fair best q.
P. L. 10, 627. I to them had q. all
**Quiver.**—P. L. 6, 764. hung his bow and q.
P. L. 9, 390. though not as she with bow and q.
**Quivered.**—C. 422. like a q. nymph with arrows
**Quivers.**—P. L. 3, 367. by their side like q. hung
**Quoth.**—L. 107. ah who hath reft q. he my dearest
U. C. II. 17. nay q. he on his swooning bed

# R.

**Rabba.**—P. L. 1, 397. R. and her watery plain
**Rabbies.**—P. R. 4, 218. among the gravest r.
**Rabble.**—P. R. 3, 50. a miscellaneous r.
**Race.**—P. L. 1, 432. for those the r. of Israel
P. L. 1, 577. with the heroic r. were joined
P. L. 1, 780. like that Pygmean r.
P. L. 2, 194. shall we then live thus vile, the r.
P. L. 2, 348. the happy seat of some new r.
P. L. 2, 382. to confound the r. of mankind
P. L. 2, 529. upon the wing or in swift r.
P. L. 2, 834. and therein placed a r. of upstart
P. L. 3, 161. draw after him the whole r. of
P. L. 3, 280. by losing thee awhile the whole r.
P. L. 3, 679. created this new happy r. of men
P. L. 4, 475. be called mother of human r.
P. L. 4, 732. a r. to fill the earth who shall
P. L. 6, 501. yet haply of thy r. in future days
P. L. 8, 896. might have else to human r. been
P. L. 7, 33. of Bacchus and his revellers the r.
P. L. 7, 45. in Paradise to Adam or his r.
P. L. 7, 99. yet wants to run much of his r.
P. L. 7, 155. out of one man a r. of men
P. L. 7, 189. instead of spirits malign a better r.
P. L. 7, 530. but thy consort female for r.
P. L. 7, 630. multiply a r. of worshippers holy
P. L. 8, 339. the earth to thee and to thy r. I
P. L. 9, 416. in them the whole included r. his
P. L. 10, 385. ye now have given to be the r.
P. L. 10, 607. through the r. his thoughts his
P. L. 10, 984. into this cursed world a woful r.
P. L. 10, 988. to prevent the r. unblest to being
P. L. 11, 13. to restore the r. of mankind
P. L. 11, 331. to life prolonged and promised r.
P. L. 11, 608. dwell his r. who slew his brother
P. L. 11, 621. to these that sober r. of men
P. L. 11, 782. length of happy days the r. of man
P. L. 11, 786. and whether here the r. of man
P. L. 12, 104. curse ... on his vicious r.
P. L. 12, 163. dies and leaves his r.
P. L. 12, 214. the r. elect safe towards Canaan
P. L. 12, 505. ministry performed and r. well run
P. L. 12, 554. this transient world the r. of
P. R. 2, 181. coupled with them and begot a r.
P. R. 2, 310. all the r. of Israel here had
P. R. 3, 423. and left a r. behind like to
S. A. 29. or benefit revealed to Abraham's r.
S. A. 597. my r. of glory run and r. of shame
S. A. 1100. from the unforeskinned r. of whom
P. 56. had got a r. of mourners
T. 1. Fly envious Time, till thou run out thy r.
**Races.**—P. L. 9, 33. or to describe r. and games
**Racked.**—P. L. 1, 126. but r. with deep despair
P. R. 3, 203. whom the tempter inly r. replied
**Racking.**—P. L. 2, 182. sport and prey of r.
P. L. 11, 481. ghastly spasm or r. torture
**Radiance.**—P. L. 7, 194. with r. crowned

**Radiant.**—P. L. 2, 492. if chance the r. sun
P. L. 3, 63. on his right the r. image of his
P. L. 3, 379. round about thee like a r. shrine
P. L. 3, 594. all alike informed with r. light
P. L. 3, 646. his r. visage turned admonished
P. L. 4, 797. so saying on he led his r. files
P. L. 5, 457. whose r. forms divine effulgence
P. L. 6, 761. of r. Urim work divinely wrought
P. L. 7, 247. sphered in a r. cloud
P. L. 10, 85. thus saying from his r. seat he rose
P. L. 11, 206. draws o'er the blue firmament a r.
P. R. 3, 237. empires and monarchs and their r.
P. R. 4, 428. who with her r. finger stilled
C. 374. what virtue would by her own r. light
A. 14. mark what r. state she spreads
H. 146. r. feet the tissued clouds down steering
M. W. 73. with thee there clad in r. sheen
**Rafters.**—C. 324. in lowly sheds with smoky r.
**Rage.**—P. L. 1, 95. the potent victor in his r.
P. L. 1, 175. with red lightning and impetuous r.
P. L. 1, 553. and instead of r. deliberate valor
P. L. 2, 67. fire and horror shot with equal r.
P. L. 2, 144. Almighty victor to spend all his r.
P. L. 2, 171. should blow them into sevenfold r.
P. L. 2, 268. thunders roar mustering their r.
P. L. 2, 539. others with vast Typhoean r. more
P. L. 2, 581. waves of torrent fire inflame with r.
P. L. 2, 791. it seems inflamed with lust than r.
P. L. 3, 80. Only begotten Son seest thou what r.
P. L. 3, 241. on me let death wreak all his r.
P. L. 4, 9. now first inflamed with r.
P. L. 4, 857. replied not overcome with r.
P. L. 4, 969. but waxing more in r. replied
P. L. 5, 845. cease then this impious r.
P. L. 6, 199. but greater r. to see thus foiled
P. L. 6, 217. assault and inextinguishable r.
P. L. 6, 635. r. prompted them at length
P. L. 6, 696. and to disordered r. let loose
P. L. 6, 813. against me is all their r.
P. L. 8, 244. and loud lament and furious r.
P. L. 9, 16. r. of Turnus for Lavinia disespoused
P. L. 12, 58. till hoarse and all in r. as mocked
P. L. 12, 194. till in his r. pursuing whom
P. R. 1, 38. then with envy fraught and r.
P. R. 3, 102. country freed from Punic r.
P. R. 4, 445. of better course to vent his r.
P. R. 4, 499. the fiend now swoln with r.
S. A. 619. but finding no redress ferment and r.
S. A. 836. call it furious r. to satisfy thy lust
S.A. 953. fierce remembrance wake my sudden r.
**Raged.**—P. L. 1, 277. edge of battle when it r.
P. L. 1, 666. highly they r. against the Highest
P. L. 6, 211. wheels of brazen chariots r.
P. L. 11, 444. whereat he inly r. and as they
**Rages.**—S. A. 963. thy anger unappeasable .. r.
**Ragged.**—L'A. 9. as r. as thy locks

**Raging.**—P. L. 2, 213. whence these r. fires
P. L. 2, 600. from beds of r. fire to starve in ice
P. L. 5, 891. r. into sudden flame distinguish
P. L. 10, 286. as in r. sea tost up and down
S. A. 1275. but r. to pursue the righteous
**Rags.**—P. L. 3, 491. tossed and fluttered into r.
S.A. 415. these r. this grinding is not yet so base
**Railed.**—S. 12, 6. r. at Latona's twin-born
**Rain.**—P. L. 8, 146. as clouds and clouds may r.
P. L. 8, 146. and r. produce fruits in her
P. L. 10, 1063. the inclement seasons r. ice
P. L. 11, 743. rushed the :r. impetuous
P. L. 11, 826. on the earth shall pour r.
P. L. 11, 894. nor r. to drown the world with
P. R. 4, 412. abortive poured fierce r. with
S. A. 1062. fair days have oft contracted .. and r.
L'A. 122. whose bright eyes r. influence
**Rainbow.**—C. 300. in the colours of the r. live
H. 143. will down return to men orbed in a r.
**Rainbows.**—P. L. 7, 446. of r. and starry eyes
**Rained.**—P. L. 7, 331. not r. upon the earth
P. L. 9,1122. nor only tears r. at their eyes but
P. R. 2, 312. had not God r. from heaven
**Raise.**—P. L. 1, 23. what is low r. and support
P. L. 2, 272. from whence to r. magnificence
P. L. 3, 296. rising with him r. his brethren
P. L. 4, 574. from the deep to r. new troubles
P. L. 4, 806. thence r. at least distempered
P. L. 5,680. new minds may r. in us who serve
P. L. 6, 224. against army numberless to r.
P. L. 8, 430. canst r. thy creature to what
P. L. 9, 43. sufficient of itself to r. that name
P. L. 9, 314. utmost vigour r. and raised unite
P. L. 11, 103. some new trouble r.
P. L. 11, 796. till wantonness and pride r.
P. L. 11, 877. that God vouchsafes to r.
P. L. 12, 123. and from him will r. a mighty
P. L. 12, 162. whose worthy deeds r. him to be
P. L. 12, 318. provoking God to r. them
P. L. 12, 547. then r. from the conflagrant
P. R. 1, 232. can r. then though above example
P. R. 3, 333. or where pain was r. hill
S. A. 625. exasperate exulcerate and r.
S. A. 839. the way to r. in me inexpiable hate
S. A. 1124. and r. such outcries on thy clattered
A. 8. fame that her high worth to r.
L. 70. Fame is the spur that the clear spirit .. r.
Il P. 104. might r. Musœus from his bower
S. 15. though new rebellions r. their hydra
**Raised.**—P. L. 1, 43. r. impious war in heaven
P. L. 1, 99. that with the Mightiest r. me to
P. L. 1, 529. gently r. their fainted courage
P. L. 1, 551. such as r. to height of
P. L. 2, 5. by merit r. to that bad eminence
P. L. 2, 427. whom now transcendent glory r.
P. L. 2, 468. lest from his resolution r. others
P. L. 2, 521. and somewhat r. by false
P. L. 3, 258. while by thee r. I ruin all my foes
P. L. 4, 60. unbounded hope had r. ambition
P. L. 4, 226. as his garden mould high r.
P. L. 4, 416. that r. us from the dust and
P. L. 4, 590. whose point now r. bore him
P. L. 5, 926. hath r. in paradise
P. L. 5, 391. r. of grassy turf their table was
P. L. 5, 758. as a mount r. on a mount
P. L. 6, 138. have r. incessant armies to defeat
P. L. 6, 856. the overthrown he r.
P. L. 7, 157. till by degrees of merit r.
P. L. 8, 258. till r. by quick instinctive motion
P. L. 8, 300. saying by the hand he took me r.
P. L. 9, 177. to spite, his Maker r. from dust
P. L. 9, 314. utmost vigour raise and r. unite
P. L. 9, 667. in act r. as of some great matter
P. L. 9, 740. an eager appetite r. by the smell
P. L. 10, 457. r. from their dark divan
P. L. 10, 1012. attentive mind labouring had r.
P. L. 11, 422. gentle angel by the hand soon r.
P. R. 1, 7. and Eden r. in the waste wilderness
P. R. 1, 124. so to subvert whom he suspected r.
P. R. 2, 64. cares and fears got head and r.
P. R. 2, 423. what r. Antipater the Edomite

P. R. 3, 59. and glory scarce of few is r.
P. R. 4, 430. had r. to tempt the Son of God
S.A.273. whom God hath of his special favour r.
S. A. 1028. capacity not r. to apprehend or value
S. A. 1211. a person r. with strength sufficient
**Raises.**—S. A. 172. or the sphere of fortune r.
**Rallied.**—P. L. 1, 269. with r. arms to try
P. L. 6, 786. to rebellious flight r. their powers
**Ram**—C. 497. hath any r. slipped from the fold
**Ramath-lechi.**—S. A. 145. in R.-l. famous
**Ramiel.**—P. L. 6, 372. and the violence of R.
**Ramoth.**—P. R. 1, 373. that he might fall in R.
**Ramp.**—S.A.139. A scalonite fled from his lion r.
**Rampant.**—P. L. 7, 466. and r. shakes his
**Rampart.**—P. L. 1, 678. trench a field or cast a r.
**Ramped.**—P. L. 4, 343. the lion r. and in his
**Ran**—P. L. 1, 451. r. purple to the sea
P. L. 4, 240. under pendent shades r. nectar
P. L. 6, 642. the lightning glimpse they r.
P. L. 8, 268. sometimes went and sometimes r.
P. L. 9, 891. while horror chill r. through
P. L. 10, 27. the ethereal people r. to hear
P. L. 12, 608. where 'Eve lay sleeping r.
S. A. 129. r. on embattled armies clad in iron
C. 568. then down the lawns I r. with headlong
**Rancour.**—P. L. 9, 409. with hellish r.
P. L. 10, 1044. only r. and pride, impatience
**Random.**—S. A. 118. see how he lies at r.
P. L. 4, 930. but still thy words at r. as before
P. L. 10, 628. at r. yielded up to their misrule
**Rang.**—H. 158. as on Mount Sinai r.
**Range.**—P. L. 4, 621. animals unactive r.
P. L. 4, 754. among the bestial herds to r.
P. L. 9, 134. that destruction wide may r.
P. L. 10, 492. to r. in and to dwell
P. R. 1, 366. this globe of earth or r. in the air
**Ranged.**—P. L. 2, 522. the r. powers disband
P. L. 6, 48. by thousands and by millions r. for
P. L. 7, 426. r. in figure wedge their way
P. L. 11, 644. single or in array of battle r.
P. R. 3, 322. them in their forms of battle r.
S. A. 1137. were bristles r. like those that ridge
S. A. 1694. and nests in order r.
**Ranging.**—P. L. 6, 248. r. through the dire
P. L. 11, 278. or r. your tribes and
C. 17. with the r. vapours of this sin-worn
L. 546. swoln with wind and the r. mist they
**Ranked.**—P. L. 2, 887. chariots r. in loose
P. L. 6, 604. in view stood r. of seraphim
S. A. 345. duelled their armies r. in proud array
**Rankle.**—S. A. 621. wounds immedicable r.
**Ranks.**—P. L. 1, 616. where at their doubled r.
P. L. 4, 140. and as the r. ascend shade above
P. L. 6, 71. nor stream divides their perfect r.
P. L. 12, 213. on their embattled r. the waves
A. 59. number my r. and visit every sprout
A. 99. trip no more in twilight r.
H. 114. are seen in glittering r. with wings
**Ransacked.**—P. L. 1, 686. r. the centre and
**Ransom.**—P. L. 3, 221. forfeiture and r. set
P. L. 10, 61. both r. and Redeemer voluntary
P. L. 12, 424. thy r. paid which man from
S. A. 483. with whom to treat about thy r.
S. A. 604. of thy deliverance by r. or how else
S. A. 1460. accept of r. for my son their prisoner
S. A. 1471. if some convenient r. were proposed
S. A. 1476. his r. if my whole inheritance
S. A. 1573. paid his r. now and full discharge
**Ransomed.**—P. L. 3, 297. raise his brethren r.
**Rapacious.**—P. L. 11, 258. death's r. claim
**Rape.**—P. L. 1, 505. matron to avoid worse r.
P. L. 2, 794. of that r. begot these yelling
P. L. 11, 717. r. or adultery
D. F. I. 9. by boisterous r. the Athenian damsel
**Raphael.**—P. L. 5, 221. and to him called R.
P. L. 5, 224. R. said he thou hearest what stir
P. L. 5, 561. and R. after short pause assenting
P. L. 6, 363. Uriel and R. his vaunting foe
P. L. 7, 40. what ensued when R. the affable
P. L. 8, 64. R. now to Adam's doubt proposed
P. L. 8, 217. to whom thus R. answered

P. L. 11, 235. nor sociably mild as *R.*
**Rapid.**—P. L. 2, 532. or shun the goal with *r.*
P. L. 4, 227. upon the *r.* current which
P. L. 6, 711. guide the *r.* wheels that shake
P. L. 11, 853. thence the *r.* currents drive
**Rapine.**—P. L. 9, 461. and with *r.* sweet
P. R. 4, 137. exhausted all by lust and *r.*
S. 15, 14. while avarice and *r.* share the land
**Rapt.**—P. L. 3, 522. *r.* in a chariot drawn
P. L. 7, 23. standing on earth not *r.* above the
P. L. 11, 706. *r.* in a balmy cloud with winged
P. R. 2, 40. what accident hath *r.* him from us
C.794. would kindle my *r.* spirits to such a flame
Il P. 40. thy *r.* soul sitting in thine eyes
**Rapture.**—P. L. 5, 147. style nor holy *r.*
P. L. 7, 36. where woods and rocks had ears to *r.*
P. L. 7, 299. if steep with torrent *r.*
P. L. 9, 1082. erst with joy and *r.* so oft beheld
H. 98. as all their souls in blissful *r.* took
**Raptures.**—P. L. 3, 369. and waken *r.* high
C. 247. and with these *r.* moves the vocal air
**Rare.**—P. L. 2, 948. strait, rough, dense or *r.*
P. L. 3, 21. to reascend though hard and *r.*
P. L. 3, 612. of colour glorious and effect so *r.*
P. L. 6, 353. as likes them best condense or *r.*
P. L. 7, 461. those *r.* and solitary these in flocks
P. L. 11, 610. arts that polish life inventors *r.*
P. R. 2, 186. to waylay some beauty *r.*, Calisto
Il P. 101. or what though *r.* of later age
**Rarely.**—P. L. 12, 537. works of faith *r.*
S. A.1047. one virtuous *r.* found that in domestic
**Rarer.**—S. A. 166. the *r.* thy example stands
**Rase.**—P. L. 2, 923. bent to *r.* some capital city
P. L. 12, 53. to *r.* quite out their native
**Rased.**—P. L. 1, 362. blotted out and *r.* by their
P. L. 3, 49. to me expunged and *r.*
**Rash.**—P. L. 5, 851. or singular and *r.*
P. L. 9, 780. so saying her *r.* hand in evil hour
P. L. 9, 860. never more mean I to try what *r.*
P. L. 12, 76. to sustain himself and his *r.* army
P. R. 1, 359. leagued with millions more in *r.*
P. R. 4, 8. and *r.* beforehand had no better
S. A. 747. my *r.* but more unfortunate misdeed
C. 397. from the *r.* hand of bold incontinence
S. A. 907. I was a fool too *r.* and quite mistaken
**Rashly.**—S. A. 43. let me not *r.* call in doubt
**Rashness.**—P. L. 12, 222. in arms where *r.*
**Rate.**—S. A. 1313. surpassing human *r.*
**Rathe.**—L. 142. bring the *r.* primrose that
**Rather.**—P. L. 1, 63. no light but *r.* darkness
P. L. 1, 482. in brutish forms *r.* than human
P. L. 1, 606. of his crime the followers *r.*
P. L. 2, 47. and *r.* than be less cared not to be
P. L. 2, 60. no let us *r.* choose armed with hell
P. L. 2, 149. to perish *r.* swallowed up and lost
P. L. 2, 252. but *r.* seek our own good from
P. L. 3, 7. or hearest thou *r.* pure ethereal
P. L. 3, 51. so much the *r.* thou celestial light
P. L. 3, 599. imagined *r.* oft than elsewhere
P. L. 3, 697. but *r.* merits praise the more it
P. L. 4, 236. but *r.* to tell how if art could tell
P. L. 5, 829. bent *r.* to exalt our happy state
P. L. 6, 166. most through sloth had *r.* serve
P. L. 8, 54. and of him to ask chose *r.*
P. L. 8, 75. by them who ought *r.* admire
P. L. 9, 332. who *r.* double honour gain from
P. L. 9, 694. and not praise *r.* your dauntless
P. L. 9, 773. what fear I then *r.* what know
P. L. 9, 819. or *r.* not but keep the odds
P. L. 9, 902. *r.* how hast thou yielded to
P. L. 9, 969. *r.* than death or aught than death
P. L. 9, 979. *r.* die deserted than oblige thee
P. L. 9, 1167. yet willingly chose *r.* death with
P. L. 10, 494. or *r.* me not, but the brute
P. L. 10, 884. all was but a show *r.* than solid
P. L. 10, 1026. *r.* such acts of contumacy
P. L. 11, 166. to me reproach *r.* belongs
P. L. 11, 503. *r.* why obtruded on us thus
P. L. 11, 548. bent *r.* how I may be quit
P. L. 12, 219. choosing *r.* inglorious life with
P. R. 1, 74. or *r.* to do him honour as their

P. R. 1, 326. I ask the *r.* and the more admire
P. R. 1, 390. I lost not what I lost *r.* by them
P. R. 1, 418. no joy—*r.* inflames thy torment
P. R. 2, 144. I summon all *r.* to be in readiness
P. R. 2, 396. and *r.* opportunely in this place
P. R. 3, 162. with foul affronts abominations *r.*
P. R. 3, 174. they themselves *r.* are occasion
P. R. 3, 218. *r.* than aggravate my evil state
P. R. 3, 402. of human weakness *r.* than of
P. R. 4, 183. permitted *r.* and by thee
P. R. 4, 207. *r.* more honour left and more
P. R. 4, 316. *r.* accuse him under usual names
P. R. 4, 338. that *r.* Greece from us these arts
P. R. 4, 444. *r.* by this his last affront resolved
S.A.216. thou shouldst wed Philistian woman *r.*
S. A. 421. *r.* approved them not but thou didst
S. A. 573. here *r.* let me drudge and earn my
S. A. 661. or *r.* seems a tune harsh and of
S. A. 828. and much *r.* confess it feigned
S. A. 1118. or *r.* flight no great advantage on me
S. A.1154. shalt see or *r.* to thy sorrow soon feel
S. A. 1478. much *r.* I shall choose to
S. A. 1517. thy son is *r.* slaying them
C. 412. that I incline to hope *r.* than fear
V. Ex. 29. yet I had *r.* if I were to choose
**Rational.**—P. L. 2, 498. of creatures *r.*
P. L. 5, 409. substances require as doth your *r.*
P. L. 8, 391. fit to participate all *r.* delight
P. L. 8, 587. attractive human *r.* love still
P. L. 12, 82. affecting to subdue *r.* liberty
**Rattling.**—P. L. 2, 715. clouds... come *r.* on
P. L. 6, 546. but *r.* storm of arrows barbed
**Rave.**—H. 67. who now hath quite forgot to *r.*
**Ravel.**—S.A. 305. they *r.* more still less resolved
**Raven.**—P. L. 11, 855. from out the ark a *r.* flies
C. 251. at every fall smoothing the *r.* down
**Ravenous.**—P. L. 10, 274. a flock of *r.* fowl
P. L. 10, 637. for ever and seal up his *r.* jaws
P. L. 10, 991. be forced to satisfy his *r.* maw
P. R. 2, 269. though *r.* taught to abstain
**Ravens.**—P. R. 2, 267. and saw the *r.* with
**Raves.**—V. Ex. 43. how green-eyed Neptune *r.*
**Ravin.**—P. L. 10, 599. where most with *r.*
**Ravishment.**—P. L. 2, 554. and took with *r.*
P. L. 5, 46. with *r.* attracted by thy beauty
P. L. 9, 541. thy celestial beauty adore with *r.*
C. 245. breathe such divine enchanting *r.*
**Ray.**—P. L. 3, 24. vain to find thy visual *r.*
P. L. 3, 620. sharpened his visual *r.* to objects
P. L. 4, 673. from the sun's more potent *r.*
P. L. 5, 141. parallel to the earth his dewy *r.*
P. L. 6, 480. till touched with heaven's *r.*
P. L. 8, 140. other part still luminous by his *r.*
P. L. 9, 607. and in thy beauty's heavenly *r.*
S. A. 548. against the eastern *r.* translucent
C.622. spreads her verdant leaf to the morning *r.*
**Rays.**—P. L. 3, 625. of beaming sunny *r.*
P. L. 4, 543. levelled his evening *r.*
P. L. 5, 301. shot down direct his fervid *r.*
P. L. 6, 719. and on his Son with *r.* direct
P. L. 7, 372. round invested with bright *r.*
C. 425. where through the sacred *r.* of chastity
H. 223. the *r.* of Bethlehem blind his dusky eyn
**Razor.**—S. A. 1167. but by the barbar's *r.* best
**Reach.**—P. L. 2,606. struggle as they pass to *r.*
P. L. 4, 801. assaying by his devilish art to *r.*
P. L. 5, 571. and what surmounts the *r.*
P. L. 7, 75. which human knowledge could not *r.*
P. L. 9, 591. would require thy utmost *r.*
P. L. 9, 593. and envying stood but could not *r.*
P. L. 9, 732. goddess humane *r.* then and freely
P. L. 9, 779. what hinders then to *r.*
P. L. 10, 323. hell with long *r.* interposed
P. L. 10, 793. since human *r.* no farther knows
P. L. 11, 94. *r.* also of the tree of life and eat
P. L. 11, 380. stretched out to the amplest *r.*
P. L. 12,44. a city and tower whose top may *r.*
P. L. 12, 556. eternity whose end no eye can *r.*
S. A. 62. haply had ends above my *r.* to know
S. A. 177. dissolves unjointed ere it *r.* my ear
S. A. 1380. wilt here come off surmounts my *r.*

**Reached.**—P. L. 4, 988. his stature *r.* the sky
P. L. 5, 213. *r.* too far their pampered boughs
P. L. 6, 131. thy hope was to have *r.* the height
**Reaches.**—P. L. 3, 697. to no excess that *r.*
**Reaching.**—P. L. 2, 644. hell bounds high *r.*
P. L. 2, 1029. *r.* the utmost orb of this frail
P. L. 6, 140. or with solitary hand *r.* beyond
P. L. 9, 781. her rash hand in evil hour forth *r.*
**Read.**—P. L. 1, 798. and summons *r.* the great
P. L. 2, 422. in other's countenance *r.* his own
P. L. 4, 1011. for proof look up and *r.* thy lot
P. L. 8, 68. wherein to *r.* his wondrous works
P. R. 1, 207. above my years the law of God I *r.*
P. R. 4, 116. I have also heard perhaps have *r.*
P. R. 4, 382. contrary if I *r.* aught in heaven
F. of C. 19. when they shall *r.* this clearly
**Readiest.**—P. L. 2, 976. I seek what *r.* path
P. L. 12. 216. not the *r.* way lest entering on
P. R. 3, 128. thanks the slightest, easiest, *r.*
C. 305. what *r.* way would bring me to that
**Readily.**—P. L. 8, 272. and *r.* could name
**Readiness.**—P. L. R. 2, 144. rather to be in *r.*
**Reading.**—P. R. 4, 323. and to his *r.* brings
**Re-admit.**—S. A. 1173. gracious to *r.-a.* the
**Reads.**—P. R. 4, 322. who *r.* incessantly and to
**Ready.**—P. L. 2, 854. death *r.* stands to interpose
P. L. 3, 72. and *r.* now to stoop with wearied
P. L. 3, 650. stand *r.* at command and are his
P. L. 5, 132. *r.* stood each in crystal sluice
P. L. 6, 54. which *r.* opens wide his fiery Chaos
P. L. 6, 509. innumerable hands were *r.*
P. L. 6, 561. with open breast stand *r.*
P. L. 9, 626. Empress the way is *r.* and not long
S. A. 1483. if need be I am *r.* to forgo
L. 131. stands *r.* to smite once and smite no
H. 49. his *r.* harbinger with turtle wing
**Real.**—P. L. 5, 437. dispatch of *r.* hunger
P. L. 8, 310. before mine eyes all *r.* as the dream
P. L. 9, 699. what is evil be *r.* why not known
P. L. 10, 151. far excelled hers in all *r.* dignity
P. L. 10, 413. planets, planet-struck *r.* eclipse
P. R. 4, 390. but what kingdom *r.* or allegoric
S. A. 159. in *r.* darkness of the body dwells
**Realities.**—P. L. 8, 575. and to *r.* yield all
**Realm.**—P. L. 1, 342. that o'er the *r.* of impious
P. L. 1, 409. in Hesebon and Horonáim Seon's *r.*
P. L. 2, 133. scout far and wide into the *r.*
P. L. 2, 972. to disturb the secrets of your *r.*
P. L. 2, 1005. hung o'er my *r.* linked in
P. L. 4, 234. wandering many a famous *r.*
P. L. 8, 375. thy *r.* is large
P. L. 10, 189. the *r.* itself of Satan long usurped
P. L. 10, 391. glorious work and made one *r.*
P. L. 10, 392. hell and this world one *r.*
P. L. 10, 435. leaves all waste beyond the *r.*
P. L. 11, 400. to the *r.* of Congo and Angola
P. L. 12, 162. him to be the second in that *r.*
P. L. 12, 455. drag in chains through all his *r.*
P. R. 1, 118. of many a pleasant *r.* and province
P. R. 4, 72. *r.* of Bocchus to the Blackmoor
**Realms.**—P. L. 1, 85. who in the happy *r.*
P. L. 4, 1002. ponders all events battles and *r.*
P. L. 6, 186. yet chains in hell not *r.* expect
P. L. 7, 147. number sufficient to possess her *r.*
P. R. 2, 422. honour, friends, conquest and *r.*
P. R. 2, 458. like aversion I reject riches and *r.*
**Realty.**—P. L. 6, 115. where faith and *r.*
**Reap.**—P. L. 2, 339. the conqueror least may *r.*
S. A. 966. *r.* nothing but repulse and hate
**Reaper.**—P. L. 11, 434. a sweaty *r.* from his
**Reapers.**—P. L. 9, 842. as *r.* oft are wont
**Reaping.**—P. L. 3, 67. *r.* immortal fruits
P. L. 12, 18. and *r.* plenteous crop corn wine
**Reaps.**—S. 9, 11. and hope that *r.* not shame
**Rear.**—P. L. 2, 78. hung on our broken *r.*
P. L. 5, 589. and gonfalons 'twixt van and *r.*
P. L. 9, 497. but on his *r.* circular base
P. L. 11, 278. who now shall *r.* ye to the sun
P. L. 11, 323. many grateful altars I would *r.*
S. A. 555. *r.* his mighty champion strong above
S. A. 1577. nipped with the lagging *r.* of winter's

L'A. 50. scatters the *r.* of darkness thin
**Reared.**—P. L. 1, 464. his temple high *r.* in
P. L. 4, 699. and jessamine *r.* high their
P. L. 5, 653. numberless and sudden *r.*
P. L. 8, 316. he *r.* me and whom thou sought'st
P. L. 11, 758. till gently *r.* by the angel on thy
P. R. 2, 285. up to a hill anon his steps he *r.*
P. R. 4, 546. the glorious temple *r.* her pile
C. 798. till all thy magic structures *r.* so high
C. 836. who piteous of her woes *r.* her lank head
S. 16, 6. hast *r.* God's trophies and his work
**Rears.**—P. L. 1, 221. upright he *r.* from off
**Reascend.**—P. L. 1, 633. fail to *r.* self-raised
P. L. 3, 20. the dark descent and up to *r.*
P. L. 12, 480. deliverer up to heaven must *r.*
**Reason.**—P. L. 1, 248. whom *r.* hath equalled
P. L. 2, 114. the worse appear the better *r.*
P. L. 2, 121. main *r.* to persuade immediate
P. L. 2, 226. with words clothed in *r.'s* garb
P. L. 2, 431. with *r.* hath deep silence
P. L. 3, 108. when will and *r.* (*r.* also his choice)
P. L. 4, 389. yet public *r.* just honour and
P. L. 4, 755. founded in *r.* loyal just and pure
P. L. 4, 895. to thee no *r.* who knowest only
P. L. 5, 102. lesser faculties that serve *r.* as
P. L. 5, 106. which *r.* joining or disjoining
P. L. 5, 487. whence the soul *r.* receives and *r.*
P. L. 5, 794. who can in *r.* then or right
P. L. 6, 41. *r.* for their law refuse right *r.*
P. L. 6, 120. whose *r.* I have tried unsound
P. L. 6, 125. when *r.* hath to deal with force
P. L. 6, 126. yet so most *r.* is that *r.* overcome
P. L. 7, 508. endued with sanctity of *r.*
P. L. 8, 374. and *r.* not contemptibly
P. L. 8, 443. good *r.* was thou freely shouldst
P. L. 8, 510. approved my pleaded *r.*
P. L. 8, 554. authority and *r.* on her wait as one
P. L. 8, 591. hath his seat in *r.* and is judicious
P. L. 9, 113. of growth sense *r.* all summed up
P. L. 9, 239. smiles from *r.* flow to brute denied
P. L. 9, 243. and delight to *r.* joined
P. L. 9, 352. what obeys *r.* is free and *r.* he
P. L. 9, 360. since *r.* not impossibly may
P. L. 9, 559. for in their looks much *r.* and in
P. L. 9, 600. to degree of *r.* in my inward
P. L. 9, 654. law to ourselves our *r.* is our law
P. L. 9, 738. with *r.* to her seeming and with
P. L. 9, 1130. over sovran *r.* claimed superior
P. L. 12, 84. which always with right *r.* dwells
P. L. 12, 86. *r.* in man obscured or not obeyed
P. L. 12, 89. catch the government from *r.*
P. L. 12, 92. powers to reign over free *r.*
P. L. 12, 98. so low from virtue which is *r.*
P. R. 2, 485. and for thy *r.* why they should be
P. R. 3, 122. and *r.* since his word all things
P. R. 4, 233. how wilt thou *r.* with them how
P. R. 4, 526. good *r.* then if I beforehand seek
S. A. 322. down *r.* then at least vain reasonings
S. A. 323. though *r.* here aver
S. A. 1641. I have performed as *r.* was obeying
C. 529. unmoulding *r.'s* mintage charactered in
C. 759. obtruding false rules pranked in *r.'s* garb
S. 1, 12. for my relief yet hadst no *r.* why
**Reasoned.**—P. L. 2, 558. more elevate and *r.*
**Reasoning.**—P. L. 8, 25. *r.* I oft admire how
P. L. 8, 85. already by thy *r.* this I guess
P. L. 9, 379. chiefly by what thy own last *r.*
P. L. 9, 872. human voice and human sense *r.*
**Reasonings.**—P. L. 10, 830. evasions vain and *r.*
S. A. 322. at least vain *r.* down
S. A. 875. it would have taught thee far other *r.*
**Reasonless.**—P. L. 4, 516. suspicious *r.*
S. A. 812. though fond and *r.* to some perhaps
**Reasons.**—P. L. 9, 765. and speaks, and *r.*
S. A. 811. these *r.* in love's law have passed for
S. A. 864. and combated in silence all these *r.*
C. 162. baited with *r.* not unplausible
**Reassembling.**—P. L. 1, 186. *r.* our afflicted
**Reassumed.**—P. L. 10, 225. blissful bosom *r.*
**Rebecks.**—L'A. 94. and the jocund *r.* sound

**Rebel.**—P. L. 1, 38. all his host of r. angels
P. L. 1, 484. and the r. king doubled that sin
P. L. 3, 677. who justly hath driven out his r.
P. L. 4, 823. which of those r. spirits adjudged
P. L. 6, 199. amazement seized the r. thrones
P. L. 6, 647. and terror seized the r. host
P. L. 10, 83. convict by flight and r. to all law
**Rebelled.**—P. L. 6, 179. or him who hath r.
P. L. 6, 737. thy might rid heaven of these r.
P. L. 6, 899. of those too high aspiring who r.
**Rebellion.**—P. L. 1, 363. razed by their r.
P. L. 5, 715. saw without their light r. rising
P. L. 6, 269. uncreated till the crime of thy r.
P. L. 12, 36. and from r. shall derive his name
P. L. 12, 37. though of r. others he accuse
S.A.1210. presumed single r. and did hostile acts
**Rebellions.**—S. 15, 6. new r. raise their hydra
**Rebellious.**—P. L. 1, 71. prepared for those r.
P. L. 1, 747. for he with this r. rout
P. L. 2, 691. and in proud r. arms drew after
P. L. 3, 86. shall redound upon his own r. head
P. L. 4, 952. faithful to whom? to thy r. crew
P. L. 6, 50. in number to that godless crew r.
P. L. 6, 414. Satan with his r. disappeared
P. L. 6, 786. to r. fight rallied their Powers
P. L. 7, 140. who thought all like himself r.
**Rebels.**—P. L. 5, 742. dextrous to subdue thy r.
**Rebound.**—P. L. 10, 739. fierce reflux on me r.
**Rebounding.**—P. L. 10, 417. and with r.
**Rebounds.**—P. L. 1, 788. his heart r.
**Rebuff.**—P. L. 2, 936. chance the strong r.
**Rebuilt.**—P. R. 3, 281. as ancient but r.
**Rebuke.**—P. L. 4, 844. his grave r. severe in
P. L. 6, 342. his pride humbled by such r.
P. L. 9, 10. and distaste anger and just r.
P. R. 1, 468. sharply thou hast insisted on r.
**Recall.**—P. L. 4, 95. soon would height r.
P. L. 5, 885. thee are gone forth without r.
P. L. 9, 926. but past who can r. or done undo
P. R. 2, 55. will withdraw him now nor will r.
**Recalled.**—P. L. 1, 169. angry victor hath r.
P. L. 11, 330. r. to life prolonged and promised
P. L. 11, 422. and his attention thus r.
**Recalling.**—P. R. 2, 106. and oft to mind r.
**Recant.**—P. L. 4, 96. would r. vows made in
**Receive.**—P. L. 1, 252. r. thy new possessor
P. L. 2, 218. will r. familiar the fierce heat
P. L. 2, 240. and r. strict laws imposed to
P. L. 3, 106. what praise could they r. what
P. L. 3, 252. his death's wound shall then r.
P. L. 3, 294. transplanted from thee r. new
P. L. 4, 384. to r. your numerous offspring
P. L. 4, 672. made hereby apter to r. perfection
P. L. 5, 315. abundance fit to honour and r.
P. L. 5, 690. fit entertainment to r. our king
P. L. 5, 781. r. him coming to r. from us
P. L. 6, 55. his fiery Chaos to r. their fall
P. L. 6, 75. came summoned over Eden to r.
P. L. 6, 152. to r. thy merited reward
P. L. 6, 188. greeting on thy impious crest r.
P. L. 6, 349. liquid texture mortal wound r.
P. L. 6, 561. open breast stand ready to r. them
P. L. 7, 78. his admonishment r. with solemn
P. L. 7, 179. so told as earthly notion can r.
P. L. 7, 361. to r. and drink the liquid light
P. L. 8, 343. I bring them to r. from these their
P. L. 9, 284. can either not r. or can repel
P. L. 9, 309. influence of thy looks r. access
P. L. 9, 350. against his will he can r. no harm
P. L. 10, 639. to sanctity that shall r. no stain
P. L. 11, 37. and in me from these r. the
P. L. 11, 505. who if we knew what we r.
P. L. 11, 707. did as thou saw'st r. to walk
P. L. 12, 322. a promise shall r. irrevocable
P. L. 12, 462. to reward his faithful and r.
P. L. 12, 503. to r. with joy the tidings
P. R. 1, 74. them so purified to r. him pure
P. R. 1, 77. but to r. the testimony of heaven
P. R. 2, 381. shall I r. by gift what of my own
P. R. 3, 231. or human nature can r. consider
P. R. 4, 200. both from men and angels I r.

S. A. 329. how thou oughtst to r. him.
S. A. 468. shall ere long r. such a discomfit
S. A. 473. and these words I as a prophecy r.
S. A. 883. why then didst thou at first r. me
S. A. 1214. me their deliverer sent would not r.
**Received.**—P. L. 1, 174. r. us falling
P. L. 3, 61. and from his sight r. beatitude
P. L. 4, 54. forgetful what from him I still r.
P. L. 4, 309. and by her yielded by him best r.
P. L. 5, 248. winged saint after his charge r.
P. L. 6, 22. those friendly Powers who him r.
P. L. 6, 721. ineffably into his face r.
P. L. 6, 805. and as ye have r. so have ye done
P. L. 6, 875. hell at last yawning r. them
P. L. 6, 891. on high who into glory him r.
P. L. 7, 119. commission from above I have r.
P. L. 8, 96. the fruitful earth there first r.
P. L. 8, 386. in proportion due given and r.
P. L. 10, 750. resign and render back all I r.
P. L. 11, 636. by wisdom and superior gifts r.
P. L. 12, 609. with words not sad she him r.
P. R. 3, 137. who for so many benefits r.
P. R. 4, 263. with delight r. in brief
P. R. 4, 583. on their plumy vans r. him soft
P. R. 4, 623. by this repulse r. and hold'st in
C. 684. with that which you r. on other terms
**Receives.**—P. L. 2, 439. of unessential night r.
P. L. 5, 423. the sun that light imparts to all r.
P. L. 5, 487. the soul reason r. and reason is
P. L. 6, 624. who r. them right had need
P. L. 8, 35. and r. as tribute such a sumless
P. L. 8, 89. when she alone r. the benefit
P. L. 12, 137. there by promise he r. gift to his
P. R. 3, 117. glory he requires and glory he r.
P. R. 4, 288. he who r. light from above
**Receivest.**—P. L. 9, 109. so thou centring r.
**Receiving.**—P. R. 4, 566. still rose r. from
**Receptacle.**—P. L. 7, 807. and the great r.
P. L. 11, 123. lest paradise a r. prove to spirits
**Reception.**—P. L. 5, 769. about the great r.
P. L. 10, 807. according still to the r.
P. R. 3, 205. all hope is lost of my r. into grace
**Recess.**—P. L. 1, 795. in close r. and secret
P. L. 2, 254. though in this vast r. free and to
P. L. 4, 258. grots and caves of cool r.
P. L. 4, 708. here in close r. with flowers
P. L. 9, 456. the sweet r. of Eve thus early
P. L. 11, 304. this happy place our sweet r.
P. L. 4, 242. or hospitable in her sweet r.
**Reciprocal.**—P. L. 8, 144. r. if land be there
U. C. II. 30. in course r. and had his fate
**Reck.**—P. L. 9, 173. let it; I r. not so it light
**Recked.**—P. L. 2, 50. or hell or worse he r. not
**Reckon.**—P. L. 8, 71. imports not if thou r.
S. A. 170. for him I r. not in high estate
**Reckoning.**—C. 642. I pursed it up but little r.
L. 116. of other care they little r. make
**Reckons.**—S. 17, 14. r. thee her eldest son
**Reckon'st.**—P. L. 2, 696. and r. thou thyself
**Recks.**—C. 404. of night or loneliness it r. me
L. 122. what r. it them? what need they?
**Reclaim.**—P. L. 6, 791. what might most r.
**Recline.**—P. L. 4, 333. r. on the soft downy
**Recoil.**—P. L. 2, 880. with impetuous r.
C. 593. but evil on itself shall back r.
**Recoiled.**—P. L. 6, 194. huge he back r.
P. L. 6, 391. what stood r. o'erwearied
P. L. 2, 759. back they r. afraid at first
**Recoils.**—P. L. 4, 17. devilish engine back r.
P. L. 9, 172. bitter ere long back on itself r.
**Recollecting.**—P. L. 1, 528. pride soon r.
**Recollects.**—P. L. 9, 471. fierce hate he r.
**Recomforted.**—P. L. 9, 918. sad dismay r.
**Recommend.**—P. L. 4, 329. sufficed to r. cool
P. R. 1, 301. as well might r. such solitude
**Recompense.**—P. L. 2, 981. no mean r. it
P. L. 4, 47. afford him praise the easiest r.
P. L. 4, 893. and soonest r. dole with delight
P. L. 5, 424. from all his alimental r. in humid
P. L. 8, 5. what thanks sufficient or what r.
P. L. 9, 994. r. for such compliance bad such r.

P. L. 9, 1163. is this the love is this the *r.*
P. L. 10, 683. while the low sun to *r.* his
P. R. 3, 128. slightest, easiest, readiest *r.*
P. R. 3, 132. hard *r.* unsuitable return
S. A. 746. though late yet in some part to *r.*
S. A. 910. afford me place to show what *r.*
L. 184. in thy large *r.* and shalt be good
**Recompensed.**—P. L. 10, 1052. soon *r.* with
P. L. 12, 495. with inward consolations *r.*
**Reconciled.**—P. L. 11, 39. before thee *r.*
P. R. 4, 413. water with fire in ruin *r.*
S. A. 962. yet winds to seas are *r.* at length
**Reconcilement.**—P. L. 3, 264. and *r.*
P. L. 4, 98. for never can true *r.* grow
P. L. 10, 943. creature so fair his *r.* seeking
S. A. 752. and *r.* move with feigned remorse
**Record.**—S. 18, 5. *r.* their groans who were
**Recorded.**—P. L. 5, 594. zeal and love *r.*
P. L. 7, 338. so even and morn *r.* the third day
S. A. 984. living and dead *r.*
**Recorders.**—P. L. 1, 551. flutes and soft *r.*
**Records.**—P. L. 1, 361. names in heavenly *r.*
P. L. 12, 252. the *r.* of his covenant over these
P. L. 12, 513. left only in those written *r.* pure
**Recount.**—P. L. 7, 112. though to *r.* Almighty
P. R. 3, 64. who with true applause *r.* his
**Recounted.**—P. L. 10, 228. with man *r.*
**Recover.**—S. A. 1555. but I *r.* breath
**Recovered.**—P. L. 1, 240. and by their own *r.*
P. L. 2, 22. yet this loss thus far at least *r.*
P. L. 4, 357. at length failed speech *r.* sad
P. L. 5, 210. firm peace *r.* soon and wonted
P. R. 1, 3. now sing *r.* paradise to all mankind
S. A. 1098. so had the glory of prowess been *r.*
**Recovering.**—P. L. 10, 966. thus Eve *r.*
P. L. 11, 294. from the cold sudden damp *r.*
P. L. 11, 499. and scarce *r.* words his plaint
**Recreant.**—P. R. 3, 138. turned *r.* to God
**Recure.**—P. L. 12, 393. thy Saviour shall *r.*
**Red.**—P. L. 1, 175. winged with *r.* lightning
P. L. 1. 306. hath vexed the *R.* sea coast
P. L. 2, 174. arm again his *r.* right hand to
P. L. 4, 978. squadron bright turned fiery *r.*
P. L. 8, 619. celestial rosy *r.* love's proper hue
H. 159. while the *r.* fire
H. 230. curtained with cloudy *r.*
**Redeem.**—P. L. 3, 214. be mortal to *r.* man's
P. L. 3, 281. therefore whom thou only canst *r.*
P. L. 3, 299. and dying to *r.* so dearly to *r.*
P. L. 11, 258. *r.* thee quite from death's
H. 153. must *r.* our loss
**Redeemed.**—P. L. 3, 260. multitude of my *r.*
P. L. 11, 43. all my *r.* may dwell in joy and
**Redeemer.**—P. L. 10, 61. and *r.* voluntary
P. L. 12, 445. like that which the *R.* died
P. L. 12, 573. I now acknowledge my *R.* ever
**Redeems.**—P. L. 12, 424. man from death *r.*
P. L. 12, 434. or theirs whom he *r.* a death
**Redemption.**—P. L. 3, 222. without *r.* all
P. L. 5, 615. ordained without *r.* without end
P. L. 12, 408. all who shall believe in his *r.*
P. R. 1, 266. or work *r.* for mankind whose
S. A. 1482. for his *r.* all my patrimony
H. 4. our great *r.* from above did bring
**Redouble.**—P. L. 9, 562. *r.* then this
**Redoubled.**—P. L. 6, 370. but with *r.* blow
S. A. 923. where my *r.* love and care
S. 18, 9. the vales *r.* to the hills and they to
**Redound.**—P. L. 3, 85. that shall *r.* upon
P. L. 9, 128. though thereby worse to me *r.*
**Redounded.**—P. L. 7, 57. *r.* as a flood on
**Redounding.**—P. L. 2, 889. cast forth *r.*
**Redounds.**—P. L. 5, 438. what *r.* transpires
**Redress.**—P. L. 9, 219. find what to *r.* till
S. A. 619. but finding no *r.* ferment and rage
**Reduce.**—P. L. 2, 96. and *r.* to nothing this
P. L. 2, 983. *r.* to her original darkness and
P. L. 3, 320. powers dominions I *r.*
P. L. 10, 748. but right and equal to *r.* me
P. L. 12, 89. and to servitude *r.* man till then
**Reduced.**—P. L. 1, 790. *r.* their shapes

P. L. 5, 843. our number thus *r.* becomes
P. L. 6, 514. they *r.* to blackest grain and into
P. L. 6, 777. whose conduct Michael soon *r.*
P. L. 10, 438. *r.* in careful watch round their
P. R. 3, 158. *r.* a province under Roman yoke
S. A. 1468. having *r.* their foe to misery beneath
**Redundant.**—P. L. 9, 503. floated *r.*
S. A. 568. these *r.* locks robustious to no purpose
**Reed.**—P. L. 5, 23. and what the balmy *r.*
P. L. 6, 519. ruin part incentive *r.* provide
P. L. 6, 579. in his hand a *r.* stood waving
P. L. 7, 321. up stood the corny *r.* embattled
P. L. 11, 132. the pastoral *r.* of Hermes
C. 345. or sound of pastoral *r.* with oaten stops
**Re-edify.**—P. L. 12, 350. they first *r.-e.*
**Reeds.**—P. L. 6, 582. all at once their *r.* put
P., R. 2, 26. where winds with *r.* and osiers
L. 86. Mincius, crowned with vocal *r.*
**Reeking.**—P. L. 8, 256. and on the *r.* moisture
**Re-embattled.**—P. L. 6, 794. stood *r.-e.*
**Re-enter.**—P. L. 2, 397. we may chance *r.-e.*
**Refer.**—S. A. 1015. which way soever men *r.* it
**Refined.**—P. L. 11, 63. and *r.* by faith and
P. L. 12, 548. conflagrant mass purged and *r.*
P. L. 5, 475. but more *r.* more spirituous
**Refines.**—P. L. 8, 589. love *r.* the thoughts
**Reflected.**—P. L. 3, 723. though but *r.*
P. L. 4, 596. with *r.* purple and gold the
P. L. 10, 1071. his gathered beams *r.* may
**Reflecting.**—P. L. 6, 18. *r.* blaze on blaze
**Reflection.**—P. L. 3, 428. some small *r.*
P. L. 7, 367. by tincture or *r.* they augment
**Reflourishes.**—S. A. 1704. revives *r.* then
**Reflux.**—P. L. 10, 739. a fierce *r.* on man
**Reform.**—P. L. 4, 625. to *r.* yon flowery
**Reforming.**—P. L. 9, 101. *r.* what was
**Refrain.**—S. A. 1565. Manoah I *r.* too suddenly
**Refrained.**—P. L. 6, 360. *r.* his tongue
**Refrains.**—S. 21, 14. sends a cheerful hour *r.*
**Refreshed.**—P. L. 9, 1027. so well *r.* now let
P. R. 4, 591. that soon *r.* him wearied and
P. R. 4, 637. from heavenly feast *r.* brought
S. A. 551. allaying thirst and *r.*
**Refreshings.**—S. A. 665. secret *r.* that repair
**Refreshment.**—P. L. 9, 237. we need *r.*
P. R. 2, 265. of meats and drinks nature's *r.*
C. 687. *r.* after toil ease after pain
**Reft.**—L. 107. ah who hath *r.* quoth he my dearest
**Refuge.**—P. L. 2, 168. a *r.* from those wounds
P. L. 9, 119. I in none of these find place or *r.*
P. L. 10, 839. alike destroys all hope of *r.*
P. L. 11, 673. through all the plain and *r.*
**Refulgent.**—P. L. 6, 527. panoply *r.*
**Refusal**—P. R. 2, 323. that cause thy *r.*
S. A. 1330. on my *r.* to distress me more
**Refuse.**—P. L. 2, 451. and not *r.* to reign
P. L. 5, 492. if I *r.* not but convert as you
P. L. 6, 41. who reason for their law. *r.*
P. L. 12, 31. such as *r.* subjection to his empire
P. R. 2, 329. those young Daniel could *r.*
**Refused.**—P. L. 2, 470. now certain to be *r.*
P. L. 2, 471. and so *r.* might in opinion stand
P. L. 4, 743. mysterious of connubial love *r.*
P. L. 10, 756. then should have been *r.* those
P. R. 1, 278. and first *r.* on me his baptism
P. R. 4, 496. and storm'st *r.* thinking to terrify
**Refusing.**—P. L. 2, 452. *r.* to accept as great
**Refute.**—P. R. 4, 233. how *r.* their idolisms
**Refuted.**—S. A. 1220. these shifts *r.* answer
**Refutes.**—P. L. 10, 1016. *r.* that excellence
**Regain.**—P. L. 1, 5. and *r.* the blissful seat
P. L. 2, 230. if war be best or to *r.* our own
P. L. 4, 665. total darkness should by night *r.*
P. L. 10, 972. hopeful to *r.* thy love the sole
P. R. 2, 441. many ages and shall yet *r.*
P. R. 3, 163. think'st thou to *r.* thy right
P. R. 3, 371. by him thou shalt *r.* without him
S. A. 1004. after offence returning to *r.* love once
C. 274. how to *r.* my severed company
**Regained.**—P. L. 1, 270. *r.* in heaven or what
P. L. 4, 197. yet not true life thereby *r.* but sat

P. R. 4, 608. by vanquishing temptation hast r.
**Regal.**—P. L. 1, 640. and his r. state put forth
P. L. 2, 515. with trumpet's r. sound the great
P. L. 3, 339. then thou thy r. sceptre shalt lay
P. L. 4, 869. and with them comes a third of r.
P. L. 5, 280. mantling o'er his breast with r.
P. L. 5, 739. when they see all r. power given
P. L. 5, 816. by right endued with r. sceptre
P. L. 10, 447. upper end was placed in r. lustre
P. L. 12, 323. that his r. throne for ever shall
P. R. 2, 183. in courts and r. chambers how
P. R. 2, 340. a table richly spread in r. mode
P. R. 2, 461. to him who wears the r. diadem
P. R. 3, 248. in r. arts and r. mysteries
P. R. 4, 98. endued with r. virtues as thou art
P. 15. he sovran priest stooping his r. head
**Regard.**—P. L. 1, 653. whom his choice r.
P. L. 2, 281. with r. of what we are, and where
P. L. 3, 534. and his eye with choice r.
P. L. 4, 620. and the r. of heaven on all his
P. L. 4, 877. whom with stern r. thus Gabriel
P. L. 5, 44. the face of things in vain if none r.
P. L. 10, 866. but her with stern r. he thus
P. L. 11, 334. to whom thus Michael with r.
P. L. 12, 16. with some r. to what is just
P. L. 12, 174. know their God or message to r.
P. L. 12, 357. r. not David's sons
P. R. 2, 315. thee these forty days none hath r.
P. R. 3, 217. that placid aspect and meek r.
P. R. 3, 427. should I of these the liberty r.
S. A. 684. with no r. of highest favours past
S. A. 1333. r. thyself. this will offend them
C. 620. of small r. to see to yet well skilled
**Regarded.**—P. L. 9, 787. taste naught else r.
**Regardless.**—P. L. 3, 408. r. of the bliss
P. L. 12, 47. r. whether good or evil fame
P. R. 4, 317. as one r. quite of mortal things
S. A. 303. r. of his glory's diminution
**Regards.**—S. A. 1157. thee he r. not, owns not
**Regencies.**—P. L. 5, 748. the mighty r. of
**Regenerate.**—P. L. 11, 5. new flesh r.
**Regent.**—P. L. 3, 690. Uriel through r. of the
P. L. 5, 697. or several one by one the r.
P. L. 7, 371. the glorious lamp was seen r. of day
P. L. 9, 60. cautious of day since Uriel r. of the sun
**Regents.**—P. R. 1, 117. r. and potentates and
**Regiment.**—P. L. 1, 758. and squared r.
**Region.**—P. L. 1, 242. is this the r. this the soil
P. L. 2, 443. or unknown r. what remains him
P. L. 2, 619. and many a r. dolorous
P. L. 2, 982. if I that r. lost all usurpation
P. L. 3, 433. dislodging form a r. scarce of
P. L. 3, 562. into the world's first r.
P. L. 6, 80. from skirt to skirt a fiery r.
P. L. 7, 425. part loosely wing the r. part more
P. L. 9, 1125. calm r. once and full of peace
P. R. 2, 117. up to the middle r. of thick air
P. R. 2, 155. many are in each r. passing fair
H. 103. the airy r. thrilling
**Regions.**—P. L. 1, 65. r. of sorrow, doleful
P. L. 3, 349. Hosannas filled the eternal r.
P. L. 3, 606. wonder then if fields and r. here
P. L. 5, 263. imagined lands and r. in the moon
P. L. 5, 748. r. they passed the mighty
P. L. 5, 750. r. to which all thy dominion
P. L. 6, 223. him with the force of all their r.
P. L. 11, 77. the angelic blast filled all the r.
P. R. 1, 22. flocked with awe the r. round
P. R. 1, 392. copartner in these r. of the world
P. R. 4, 67. or embassies from r. far remote
C. 4. in r. mild of calm and serene air
Il P. 90. what worlds or what vast r. hold
V. Ex. 41. and misty r. of wide air next under
**Registered.**—P. L. 12, 335. shall be r. part
**Regorged.**—S. A. 1671. fat r. of bulls and goats
**Regret.**—P. L. 10, 1018. but anguish and r.
**Regular.**—P. L. 5, 623. yet r. then most
**Regulus.**—P. R. 2, 446. Fabricius, Curius, R.
**Reject.**—P. L. 4, 523. and to r. envious
P. L. 5, 886. golden sceptre which thou didst r.
P. R. 2, 457. what if with like aversion I r.

P. R. 4, 467. not tell thee if thou didst r.
S. A. 516. r. not then what offered means
S. A. 760. with goodness principled not to r.
**Rejected.**—P. L. 10, 567. spattering noise r.
P. L. 10, 876. when least was safe r. my
P. R. 4, 376. cause to wish thou never hadst r.
**Reject'st.**—P. R. 4, 156. offered and r.
**Reign.**—P. L. 1, 102. that durst dislike his r.
P. L. 1, 261. we may r. secure and in my choice
P. L. 1, 262. to r. is worth ambition tho' in hell
P. L. 1, 263. better to r. in hell than serve in
P. L. 1, 543. frighted the r. of Chaos and old
P. L. 2, 324. still first and last will r. sole king
P. L. 2, 451. and not refuse to r. refusing to
P. L. 2, 698. defiance here and scorn where I r.
P. L. 2, 868. where I shall r. at thy right hand
P. L. 2, 963. of things the consort of his r.
P. L. 3, 315. thou sit incarnate here shalt r.
P. L. 3, 318. r. for ever and assume thy merits
P. L. 4, 112. more than half perhaps will r.
P. L. 4, 961. to dispossess him and thyself to r.
P. L. 5, 609. his great vicegerent r. abide
P. L. 5, 820. and equal over equals to let r.
P. L. 5, 832. that equal over equals monarch r.
P. L. 5, 841. nor by his r. obscured but more
P. L. 6, 183. r. thou in hell thy kingdom
P. L. 6, 293. however to dwell free if not to r.
P. L. 6, 888. him dominion given worthiest to r.
P. L. 7, 381. and her r. with thousand lesser
P. L. 10, 375. here thou shalt monarch r.
P. L. 10, 399. there dwell and r. in bliss
P. L. 11, 543. in thy blood will r. a melancholy
P. L. 12, 91. unworthy powers to r. over free
P. L. 12, 286. doubt not but that sin will r.
P. L. 12, 330. the last for of his r. shall be
P. L. 12, 370. and bound his r. with earth's
P. R. 1, 125. to end his r. on earth so long
P. R. 2, 123. from the element each of his r.
P. R. 2, 442. and r. in Israel without end
P. R. 3, 178. old who sung thy endless r.
P. R. 3, 179. the happier r. the sooner it begins
P. R. 3, 180. r. then what canst thou better do
P. R. 3, 184. if of my r. prophetic writ hath
P. R. 3, 195. best r. who first well hath obeyed
P. R. 3, 215. be punished whether thou r. or r.
P. R. 3, 216. I could fly and hope thy r.
P. R. 3, 385. on the throne of David .. shalt r.
P. R. 3, 404. I must deliver if I mean to r.
P. R. 4, 492. I shall r. past the presenting
Il P. 25. in Saturn's r. such mixture was not
H. 63. his r. of peace upon the earth began
H. 106. and that her r. had here its last fulfilling
V. Ex. 75. o'er all his brethren he shall r. as king
**Reigned.**—P. L. 1, 514. so Jove usurping r.
P. L. 5, 341. or where Alcinous r.
P. L. 5, 449. in those hearts love unlibidinous r.
P. L. 5, 578. r. where these heavens
P. L. 11, 751. where luxury late r. sea-monsters
**Reigning.**—P. L. 1, 124. sole r. holds
P. R. 2, 480. so r. can be no sincere delight
**Reigns.**—P. L. 1, 497. and palaces he also r.
P. L. 1, 637. but he who r. monarch in heaven
P. L. 2, 59. the prison of his tyranny who r.
P. L. 2, 454. due alike to him who r.
P. L. 2, 814. save he who r. above, none can
P. L. 2, 909. embroils the fray by which he r.
P. L. 4, 765. r. here and revels not in the
P. L. 5, 41. now r. full orbed the moon
P. L. 5, 680. new laws from him who r. new
P. L. 6, 43. Messiah who by right of merit r.
P. L. 10, 549. his will who r. above to aggravate
P. L. 11, 187. down from a hill the beast that r.
P. R. 2, 466. yet he who r. within himself
P. R. 2, 478. that other o'er the body only r.
C. 334. and disinherit Chaos that r. here
C. 480. where no crude surfeit r.
**Rein.**—P. L. 11, 586. their eyes rove without r.
**Reined.**—P. L. 4, 858. like a proud steed r.
**Reinforcement.**—P. L. 1, 190. what r. we
**Reins.**—P. L. 6, 346. heart or head, liver or r.
P. L. 6, 696. to disordered rage let loose the r.

P. L. 10, 672. the sun was bid turn r. from the
S.A. 302. then give the r. to wandering thought
S. A. 609. in heart, head, breast and r.
S. A. 1578. yet ere I give the r. to grief say first
**Reinspire.**—S. 20, 6. till Favonius r. the frozen
**Reinstall.**—P. R. 3, 372. can truly r. thee
P. R. 4, 615. thou a Saviour art come down to r.
D. F. I. 46. took up and in fit place did r.
**Rejoice.**—P. L. 2, 339. and may least r. in
P. L. 8, 392. they r. each with their kind
P. L. 8, 639. I in thy persevering shall r. and
P. L. 10, 396. these successes and with them r.
P. L. 11, 875. than I r. for one man found so
P. L. 12, 475. or r. much more that much
S.A.1455.that hope would much r. us to partake
**Rejoiced.**—P. L. 2, 848. no less r. his mother
P. L. 5, 851. whereat r. the Apostate and more
P. L. 6, 878. heaven r. and soon repaired
P. L. 10, 120. but still r. how is it now become
P. L. 11, 869. greatly r. and thus his joy broke
P. R. 1, 228. by words at times cast forth inly r.
P. R. 2, 37. thus we r. but soon our joy is
**Rejoicing.**—P. L. 2, 487. r. in their matchless
P. L. 4, 13. yet not r. in his speed though
P. L. 5, 163. without night circle his throne r.
P. L. 5, 641. showered with copious hand r.
P. L. 7, 180. great triumph and r. was in
P. L. 8, 314. presence divine r. but with awe
**Reiterated.**—P. L. 1, 214. that with r.
**Relapse.**—P. L. 4, 100. me to a worse r.
P. R. 2, 30. to what r. unlooked for are we
**Relate.**—P. L. 1, 746. thus they r. erring
P. L. 5, 564. for how shall I r. to human sense
P. L. 6, 298. with the tongue of angels can r.
P. L. 6, 373. I might r. of thousands and their
P. L. 7, 84. and r. what may no less perhaps
P. L. 7, 604. can measure thee or tongue r. thee
P. L. 8, 9. this friendly condescension to r.
P. L. 8, 204. my remembrance now hear me r.
P. L. 8, 208. inviting thee to hear while I r.
P. L. 11, 319. and to my sons r. on this mount
P. L. 12, 11. henceforth what is to come I will r.
S. A. 1563. r. by whom. By Samson
S. 10, 13. that all both judge you to r. them true
**Related.**—P. L. 4, 875. and brief r. whom
P. L. 5, 94. thus Eve her night r. and thus
S. A. 786. so near r. or the same of kind
**Relater.**—P. L. 8, 52. her husband the r.
**Relating.**—P. L. 8, 51. Adam r. she sole
P. L. 8, 203. thee I have heard r. what was
**Relation.**—P. L. 5, 556. the full r. which
P. L. 8, 247. but thy r. now for I attend
P. R. 2, 182. have we not seen or by r. heard
P. R. 4, 519. and if I was I am, r. stands
S. A. 1595. r. more particular and distinct
C. 617. approach so near as to make this r.
**Relations.**—P. L. 4, 756. r. dear and all the
**Relax.**—P. L. 6, 599. to r. their serried files
**Relaxed.**—P. L. 9, 891. and all his joints r.
**Release.**—P. R. 1, 409. who boast'st r. from
H. 6. he our deadly forfeit should r.
**Released.**—P. L. 11, 197. from death r.
**Relent.**—P. L. 2, 237. he should r. and
P. L. 4, 79. O then at last r. is there no place
P. L. 6, 790. wonders move the obdurate to r.
P. L. 10, 1093. he will r. and turn from his
S. A. 509. God will r. and quit thee all his debt
**Relented.**—P. L. 10, 940. soon his heart r.
**Relentless.**—P. L. 9, 130. to my r. thoughts
**Relents.**—P. L. 11, 891. that he r. not to
**Relied.**—P. L. 6, 238. each on himself r.
**Relief.**—P. L. 10, 976. tending to some r.
P. R. 2, 309. yet found he r. by a providing
S. 1, 12. for my r. yet hadst no reason why
**Relies.**—P. L. 2, 416. and our last hope r.
**Relieve.**—P. R. 1, 344. save thyself and us r.
**Relieves.**—S. A. 5. when any chance r. me
S. A. 460. this only hope r. me that the strife
S. A. 472. with cause this hope r. thee
**Religion.**—P. L. 11, 667. of justice of r.
P. L. 12, 535. rites and specious forms r. satisfied

S. A. 412. O indignity, O blot to honour and r
S. A. 854. and of r. pressed how just it was
S. A. 872. in feigned r. smooth hypocrisy
S. A. 1420. if aught r. seem concerned
S. 17, 13. therefore on thy firm hand r. leans
**Religions.**—P. L. 1, 372. adorned with gay r.
**Religious.**—P. L. 11, 622. whose lives r.
P. L. 12, 231. part r. rites of sacrifice informing
S.A.1320.law forbids at their r.rites my presence
Il P. 160. casting a dim r. light
**Reliques.**—P. L. 3, 491. r. beads indulgences
P. L. 5, 273. to enshrine his r. in the sun's
W. S. 3. or that his hallowed r. should be hid
**Relish.**—P. L. 9, 1024. till now true r. tasting
**Reluctance.**—P. L. 2, 337. untamed r. and
P. L. 10, 1045. r. against God and his just yoke
**Reluctant.**—P. L. 4, 311. and sweet r.
P. L. 6, 58. in dusky wreaths r. flames
P. L. 10, 515. on his belly prone r. but in vain
**Rely.**—P. L. 9, 373. in thy native innocence r.
**Remain.**—P. L. 2, 320. but to r. in strictest
P. L. 3, 124. them free and free they must r.
P. L. 3, 263. wherein no cloud of anger shall r.
P. L. 5, 773. if these magnific titles yet r.
P. L. 6, 115. yet r. where faith and realty r.
P. L. 10, 989. childless thou art childless r.
P. R. 2, 255. though hunger still r. so it r.
**Remained.**—P. L. 2, 768. r. (for what could else)
P. L. 7, 504. and of the sixth day yet r.
P. L. 9, 464. and for the time r. stupidly good
P. L. 9, 808. not following thee I had r. in
P. L. 9, 1138. we had then r. still happy
P. R. 1, 17. worthy to have not r. so long
P. R. 2, 243. after forty days fasting had r.
P. R. 2, 404. only the importune tempter still r.
**Remaining.**—S.A.587.strength miraculous..r.
S.A.1549.my countrymen whom here I knew r.
C. 72. all other parts r. as they were
**Remains.**—P. L. 1, 139. the mind and spirit r.
P. L. 1, 645. our better part r.
P. L. 2, 443. what r. him less than unknown
P. L. 6, 38. the easier conquest now r. thee
P. L. 7, 21. half yet r. unsung but narrower
P. L. 8, 13. something yet of doubt r. which
P. L. 9, 43. r. sufficient of itself to raise that
P. L. 10, 129. failing while her faith to me r.
P. L. 10, 502. what r. ye gods but get up and enter
P. L. 12, 14. the dread of judgment past r.
P. R. 4, 326. uncertain and unsettled still r.
S. A. 483. a worse thing yet r.
S. A.649. this one prayer yet r.might I be heard
S. A. 912. what r. past cure bear not too sensibly
S. A. 1126. that in a little time while breath r.
S. 16. 9. yet much r. to conquer still
U. C. II. 34. only r. this superscription
**Remark.**—S. A. 1309. his manacles r. him there
**Remarkable.**—S. A. 1388. this day will be r. in
**Remarkably.**—P. L. 9, 982. r. so late of thy
P. R. 2, 106. recalling what r. had passed
**Remediless.**—P. L. 9, 919. to what seemed r.
S. A. 648. hopeless are all my evils all r.
D. F. I. 17. for we by rightful doom r.
**Remedy.**—P. L. 6, 438. as easy think the r.
P. L. 10, 1079. what may else be r.
P. L. 11, 62. his final r. and after life tried in
**Remember.**—P. L. 4, 449. that day I oft r.
P. L. 6, 912. r. and fear to transgress
P. L. 8, 327. what I warn thee shun to taste
P. L. 10, 1046. r. with what mild and gracious
P. R. 1, 46. than r. hell our hated habitation
P. R. 2, 196. r. that Pellean conqueror
P. R. 2, 445. canst thou not r. Quintius
P. R. 3, 66. thou to thy reproach mayst well r.
P. R. 4, 374. yet r. what I foretell thee
C. 416. has a hidden strength which you r. not
**Remembered.**—P. L. 10, 12. to have still r.
S. A. 677. heads without name no more r.
**Remembering.**—P. L. 12, 346. r. mercy
P. R. 3, 434. r. Abraham by some wondrous
**Remember'st.**—P. L. 5, 674. and r. what

P. L. 5, 857. *r.* thou thy making while the
P. L. 7, 561. (thou *r.* for thou heard'st)
**Remembrance.**—P. L. 3, 704. had in *r.*
P. L. 4, 38. that bring to my *r.* from what
P. L. 8, 204. what was done ere my *r.*
S. A. 277. thy words to my *r.* bring
S. A. 952. lest fierce *r.* wake my sudden rage
**Remiss.**—P. L. 6, 458. and makes *r.* the hands
P. L. 8, 387. the one intense the other still *r.*
S.A. 239. thou never wast *r.* I bear thee witness
**Remission.**—S. A. 835. man will gain thee no *r.*
**Remit.**—P. L. 2, 210. in time may much *r.* his
P. L. 11, 885. so willingly doth God *r.* his ire
S. A. 687. or *r.* to life obscured which were a
S. A. 1470. the rest was magnanimity to *r.*
**Remorse.**—P. L. 1, 605. but cast signs of *r.*
P. L. 4, 109. farewell fear farewell *r.*
P. L. 5, 134. as the gracious signs of sweet *r.*
P. L. 5, 566. how without *r.* the ruin of so
P. L. 10, 1098. nor Eve felt less *r.*
P. L. 11, 105. without *r.* drive out the sinful
S. A. 752. reconcilement move with feigned *r.*
S. A. 1007. and secret sting of amorous *r.*
**Remorseless.**—L. 50. when the *r.* deep
M. W. 29. and with *r.* cruelty
**Remote.**—P. L. 2, 477. of thunder heard *r.*
P. L. 3, 609. arch-chemic sun so far from us *r.*
P. L. 4, 284. but wide *r.* from this Assyrian
P. L. 6, 173. from the path of truth *r.*
P. L. 7, 369. so far *r.* with diminution seen
P. L. 8, 191. not to know at large of things *r.*
P. L. 9, 812. and *r.* to see from thence distinct
P. L. 10, 274. though many a league *r.*
P. R. 3, 76. peaceable nations neighbouring or *r.*
P. R. 4, 598. or *r.* from heaven enshrined in
P. R. 4, 67. or embassies from regions far *r.*
**Remotest.**—S. 15, 4. loud that daunt *r.* kings
**Remove.**—P. L. 2, 277. which must needs *r.*
P. L. 6, 597. by quick contraction or *r.* but
P. L. 8, 119. God to *r.* his ways from human
P. L. 11, 96. to *r.* him I decree and send him
P. L. 11, 260. to *r.* thee I am come
P. L. 12, 204. guide them in their journey and *r.*
P. L. 12, 290. law can discover sin but not *r.*
P. L. 12, 593. in signal of *r.* waves fiercely
P. R. 4, 343. *r.* their swelling epithets thick
S. A. 1051. and all temptation can *r.*
**Removed.**—P. L. 1, 73. as far *r.* from God
P. L. 2, 211. and perhaps thus far *r.* not mind
P. L. 2, 321. though thus far *r.* under the
P. L. 2, 835. our vacant room though more *r.*
P. L. 3, 356. for man's offence to heaven *r.*
P. L. 7, 272. the loud misrule of Chaos far *r.*
P. L. 10, 211. of death denounced that day *r.*
P. L. 10, 934. all the sentence from thy head *r.*
P. L. 11, 3. had *r.* the stony from their hearts
P. L. 11, 412. from Adam's eyes the film *r.*
P. L. 11, 727. and *r.* his tents far off
P. L. 11, 889. yet those *r.* such grace shall one
P. R. 4, 87. shared among petty kings too far *r.*
Il P. 78. some still *r.* place will fit
**Removes.**—P. L. 9, 702. fear of death *r.* the fear
**Rend.**—P. L. 2, 540. *r.* up both rocks and hills,
P. L. 10, 700. Thrascias *r.* the woods
P. L. 12, 182. hail mixed with fire must *r.*
**Render.**—P. L. 2, 130. armed watch that *r.*
P. L. 2, 459. easé the present misery and *r.* hell
P. L. 6, 602. would *r.* them yet more
P. L. 8, 6. or what recompense equal have I to *r.*
P. L. 9, 823. and *r.* me more equal and perhaps
P. L. 10, 749. desirous to resign and *r.* back
P. R. 3, 130. would likest *r.* contempt instead
P. R. 3, 369. it shall be my task to *r.* thee
P. R. 4, 283. these rules will *r.* thee a king
S.A. 1232. hear these dishonours and not *r.* death
D. F. I. 75. and *r.* him with patience what he
**Rendering.**—P. L. 11, 551. day of *r.* up
**Renders.**—P. L. 8, 196. and *r.* us in things
S.A. 1282. magazines contemns, *r.* them useless
**Renew.**—P. L. 2, 494. the birds their notes *r.*
P. L. 3, 175. once more I will *r.* his lapsed

P. R. 4, 19. all to shivers dashed the assault *r.*
S. M. 25. O may we soon again *r.* that song
**Renewed.**—P. L. 2, 1012. alacrity and force *r.*
P. L. 3, 226. his dearest mediation thus *r.*
P. L. 6, 783. heaven his wonted face *r.*
P. L. 8, 337. and gracious purpose thus *r.*
P. L. 9, 321. thus her reply with accent sweet *r.*
P. L. 9, 1133. speech intermitted thus to Eve *r.*
P. L. 10, 543. and the dire hiss *r.* and the dire
P. L. 10, 638. then heaven and earth *r.* shall be
P. L. 11, 66. him up with heaven and earth *r.*
P. L. 11, 116. covenant in the woman's seed *r.*
P. L. 11, 140. thus to Eve his welcome words *r.*
P. L. 11, 499. recovering words his plaint *r.*
P. R. 2, 367. his invitation earnestly *r.*
P. R. 3, 6. with soothing words *r.* him thus
P. R. 3, 346. to our Saviour thus his words *r.*
S. A. 520. with prayers and vows *r.*
S.A. 1357. so requite favour *r.* and add a greater
**Renewing.**—P. L. 3, 729. still ending still *r.*
P. R. 4, 570. *r.* fresh assaults amidst his pride
**Renews.**—P. L. 2, 389. his speech he thus *r.*
S. A. 331. with mention of that name *r.* the
**Renounce.**—P. L. 2, 312. titles now must we *r.*
P. L. 3, 291. imputed shall absolve them who *r.*
P. L. 9, 884. I then too late *r.* deity for thee
S. A. 828. thou wilt *r.* thy seeking and much
**Renounced.**—F. of C. 2. and with stiff vows *r.*
**Renovation.**—P. L. 11, 65. waked in the *r.*
**Renown.**—P. L. 1, 477. under names of old *r.*
P. L. 3, 34. so were I equalled with them in *r.*
P. L. 6, 378. nor of *r.* less eager yet by doom
P. L. 6, 422. honour, dominion, glory and *r.*
P. L. 11, 688. were these giants men of high *r.*
P. L. 11, 698. fame shall be achieved, *r.* on earth
P. L. 12, 154. like him in faith in wisdom and *r.*
P. R. 1, 136. she should bear a son great in *r.*
P. R. 3, 60. this is true glory and *r.* when God
P. R. 4, 84. and long *r.* thou justly mayst prefer
**Renowned.**—P. L. 1, 507. though far *r.* the
P. L. 3, 465. a vain exploit though then *r.*
P. L. 3, 549. or some *r.* metropolis
P. L. 9, 440. or of revived Adonis or *r.* Alcinous
P. L. 9, 670. as when of old some orator *r.*
P. L. 9, 1101. not that kind for fruit *r.*
P. L. 12, 321. the second both for piety *r.*
P. R. 4, 46. so far *r.* and with the spoils enriched
S. A. 125. that heroic that *r.* irresistible Samson
S. A. 341. that invincible Samson far *r.*
S. A. 988. less *r.* than in mount Ephraim Jael
S. A. 1079. of stock *r.* as Og, or Anak
A. 29. of that *r.* flood so often sung
S. 16, 11. Peace hath her victories no less *r.*
**Repaid.**—P. L. 9, 178. with spite is best *r.*
P. L. 9, 1015. she him as wantonly *r.* in lust
P. L. 10, 218. as the snake with youthful coat *r.*
P. R. 4, 188. how fairly is the giver now *r.*
**Repair.**—P. L. 1, 188. our own loss how *r.*
P. L. 3, 678. and to *r.* that loss created this new
P. L. 7, 152. I can *r.* that detriment if such it be
P. L. 8, 457. sunk down and sought *r.* of sleep
P. L. 9, 144. to *r.* his numbers thus impaired
P. R. 4, 267. thence to the famous orators *r.*
S. A. 665. secret refreshings that *r.* his strength
**Repaired.**—P. L. 4, 773. which the morn *r.*
P. L. 6, 878. heaven rejoiced and soon *r.*
P. R. 4, 591. soon refreshed him wearied and *r.*
**Repairing.**—P. L. 7, 365. other stars *r.*
P. L. 10, 1087. than to the place *r.* where he
P. L. 10, 1099. they forthwith to the place *r.*
**Repairs.**—L. 169. anon *r.* his drooping beams
**Repast.**—P. L. 2, 800. my bowels their *r.*
P. L. 5, 232. to respite his day-labour with *r.*
P. L. 5, 630. forthwith from dance to sweet *r.*
P. L. 8, 214. at the hour of sweet *r.* they satiate
P. L. 9, 4. and with him partake rural *r.*
P. L. 9, 403. invite noontide *r.* or afternoon's
P. L. 9, 407. foundest either sweet *r.* or sound
P. R. 2, 250. or God support nature without *r.*
C. 688. that have been tired all day without *r.*
S. 20, 9. what neat *r.* shall feast us light and

**Repealed.**—P. L. 7, 59. soon *r.* the doubts
**Repeat.**—P. L. 6, 318. and not need *r.*
P. L. 9, 946. though his power creation could *r.*
**Repeated.**—P. L. 6, 601. repulse *r.*
P. L. 7, 494. needless to thee *r.* nor unknown
P. L. 8, 32. restless revolution day by day *r.*
P. L. 9, 400. her his charge of quick return *r.*
S. A. 504. to be *r.* the subject of their cruelty
S. 8, 12. and the *r.* air of sad Electra's poet
**Repel.**—P. L. 8, 643. to transgress *r.*
P. L. 9, 284. can either not receive or can *r.*
**Repelled.**—P. L. 7, 611. vain thou hast *r.*
P. L. 10, 866. with stern regard he thus *r.*
P. R. 4, 446. and mad despite to be so oft *r.*
S. 17, 3. when gowns not arms *r.* the fierce
**Repent.**—P. L. 1, 96. do I *r.* or change
P. L. 3, 190. to pray *r.* and bring obedience
P. L. 4, 93. but say I could *r.* and could obtain
P. L. 11, 255. of grace wherein thou mayst *r.*
P. L. 12, 474. I stand whether I should *r.* me
S. A. 504. *r.* the sin, but if the punishment
**Repentance.**—P. L. 3, 191. to prayer *r.*
P. L. 4, 80. is there no place left for *r.* none
P. L. 11, 724. preached conversion and *r.*
P. R. 1, 20. than the sound of trumpet cried *r.*
S.A. 821. that malice not *r.* brought thee hither
**Repentant.**—P. L. 11, 1. *r.* stood
P. R. 3, 435. may bring them back *r.* and
S. A. 751. then as *r.* to submit beseech
**Repenting.**—P. L. 2, 369. and with *r.* hand
P. L. 10, 75. and not *r.* this obtain of right
P. L. 11, 886. though late *r.* him of man
S. 21, 6. in mirth that after no *r.* draws
**Repents.**—P. L. 11, 90. he sorrows now *r.*
**Repine.**—P. L. 6, 460. and not *r.* but live
P. R. 2, 94. I will not argue that nor will *r.*
**Repines.**—S. A. 995. at this whoever envies or *r.*
**Replenished.**—P. L. 7, 447. with fish *r.* and
P. L. 8, 371. and the air *r.* and all these at thy
**Replete.**—P. L. 9, 733. and his words *r.*
P. L. 12, 468. and our sire *r.* with joy
**Replied.**—P. L. 1, 156. arch-fiend *r.*
P. L. 2, 688. whom the goblin full of wrath *r.*
P. L. 2, 746. thus the portress of Hell gate *r.*
P. L. 3, 167. to whom the great Creator thus *r.*
P. L. 3, 273. but soon the Almighty thus *r.*
P. L. 4, 440. to whom thus Eve *r.* O thou for
P. L. 4, 659. to whom our general ancestor *r.*
P. L. 4, 857. the fiend *r.* not overcome with
P. L. 4, 903. disdainfully half smiling thus *r.*
P. L. 4, 946. whom the warrior angel soon *r.*
P. L. 4, 969. but waxing more in rage *r.*
P. L. 5, 468. whom the winged hierarch *r.*
P. L. 5, 506. the patriarch of mankind *r.*
P. L. 5, 852. apostate and more haughty thus *r.*
P. L. 6, 171. in brief thus Abdiel stern *r.*
P. L. 6, 469. with look composed Satan *r.*
P. L. 8, 4. new-waked thus gratefully *r.*
P. L. 8, 65. benevolent and facile thus *r.*
P. L. 8, 179. thus Adam cleared of doubt *r.*
P. L. 8, 368. a smile more brightened thus *r.*
P. L. 8, 378. and humble deprecation thus *r.*
P. L. 8, 595. whom thus half abashed Adam *r.*
P. L. 9, 272. sweet austere composure thus *r.*
P. L. 9, 290. with healing words Adam *r.*
P. L. 9, 342. to whom thus Adam fervently *r.*
P. L. 9, 377. yet submiss though last *r.*
P. L. 9, 567. whom the guileful tempter thus *r.*
P. L. 9, 614. yet more amazed unwary thus *r.*
P. L. 9, 655. to whom the tempter guilefully *r.*
P. L. 9, 960. so Adam and thus Eve to him *r.*
P. L. 9, 1162. then first incensed Adam *r.*
P. L. 10, 118. gracious judge without revile *r.*
P. L. 10, 124. to whom thus Adam sore beset *r.*
P. L. 10, 144. the Sovran Presence thus *r.*
P. L. 10, 161. thus abashed *r.*
P. L. 10, 602. the incestuous mother thus *r.*
P. L. 10, 966. thus Eve recovering heart *r.*
P. L. 10, 1012. and thus to Eve *r.*
P. L. 11, 370. whom thus Adam gratefully *r.*
P. L. 11, 453. Michael thus he also moved *r.*

P. L. 11, 552. Michael *r.*, nor love thy life
P. L. 12, 468. with joy and wonder thus *r.*
P. L. 12, 552. he ended and thus Adam last *r.*
P. L. 12, 574. whom thus also the angel last *r.*
P. R. 1, 337. by miracle he may, *r.* the swain
P. R. 1, 346. he ended and the Son of God *r.*
P. R. 1, 406. whom our Saviour sternly thus *r.*
P. R. 2, 319. hast thou hunger then Satan *r.*
P. R. 2, 378. to whom thus Jesus temperately *r.*
P. R. 2, 432. to whom thus Jesus patiently *r.*
P. R. 3, 43. whom our Saviour calmly thus *r.*
P. R. 3, 108. the tempter murmuring thus *r.*
P. R. 3, 121. to whom our Saviour fervently *r.*
P. R. 3, 203. whom the tempter inly racked *r.*
P. R. 4, 109. whom the Son of God unmoved *r.*
P. R. 4, 154. to whom the tempter impudent *r.*
P. R. 4, 195. the fiend with fear abashed *r.*
P. R. 4, 285. to whom our Saviour sagely thus *r.*
P. R. 4, 367. to our Saviour with stern brow *r.*
P. R. 4, 499. the fiend now swoln with rage *r.*
L. 77. but not the praise, Phœbus *r.*
**Replies.**—S. 19, 9. that murmur soon *r.*
**Reply.**—P. L. 2, 467. and prevented all *r.*
P. L. 2, 1010. ceased and Satan stayed not to *r.*
P. L. 8, 209. fond were it not in hope of thy *r.*
P. L. 9, 321. thus her *r.* with accent sweet
P. R. 3, 3. confounded what to say what to *r.*
P. R. 4, 2. the tempter stood nor had what to *r.*
**Report.**—P. L. 3, 701. contented with *r.* hear
P. L. 5, 869. this *r.* these tidings carry to the
P. L. 12, 237. they beseech that Moses might *r.*
S. A. 117. O change beyond *r.* thought or belief
S. A. 1090. if thy appearance answer loud *r.*
S. A. 1350. gone and who knows how he may *r.*
C. 127. which these dun shades will ne'er *r.*
S. 10, 8. killed with *r.* that old man eloquent
**Reported.**—P. L. 6, 21. thought to have *r.*
**Repose.**—P. L. 1, 319. *r.* your wearied virtue
P. L. 4, 612. mind us of like *r.* since God hath
P. L. 5, 28. sole in whom my thoughts find all *r.*
P. L. 5, 233. day-labour with repast or with *r.*
P. L. 9, 403. noontide repast or afternoon's *r.*
P. L. 9, 407. either sweet repast or sound *r.*
P. R. 2, 275. and eat the second time after *r.*
S. A. 406. at times when men seek most *r.* and
**Reposed.**—P. L. 4, 450. and found myself *r.*
P. L. 5, 636. on flowers *r.* and with fresh
**Reposes.**—C. 999. where young Adonis oft *r.*
**Repossess.**—P. L. 1, 634. and *r.* their native
**Represent.**—P. L. 5, 104. watchful senses *r.*
P. L. 11, 870. future things canst *r.* as present
**Represented.**—P. L. 10, 849. conscience *r.*
**Representing.**—P. L. 8, 610. variously *r.*
P. L. 12, 255. as in a zodiac *r.* the heavenly
P. R. 1, 418. inflames thy torment *r.* lost bliss
**Repress.**—S. A. 543. thou couldst *r.* nor did the
**Reprieve.**—S. A. 288. without *r.* adjudged to
**Reproach.**—P. L. 6, 34. universal *r.* fear
P. L. 9, 1098. there sit not and *r.* us as
P. L. 11, 165. to me *r.* rather belongs
P. L. 11, 811. fearless of *r.* and scorn or
P. R. 3, 66. as thou to thy *r.* mayst well
S. A. 353. thought barrenness in wedlock a *r.*
S. A. 446. of all *r.* the most with shame that ever
S. A. 823. I led the way bitter *r.* but true
D. F. I. 14. a foul *r.* was held
**Reproaches.**—P. R. 4, 387. thee scorns *r.*
S. A. 393. prayers and sighs and amorous *r.*
**Reproachful.**—P. L. 12, 406. to a *r.* life
**Reprobate.**—P. L. 1, 697. by spirits *r.*
P. R. 1, 491. vouchsafed his voice to Balaam *r.*
S. A. 1685. insensate left or to sense *r.*
**Reproof.**—P. R. 1, 477. endure check or *r.*
**Reproved.**—P. L. 10, 761. and *r.* retort
**Reptile.**—P. L. 7, 388. *r.* with spawn
**Repulse,**—P. L. 1, 630. could ever know *r.*
P. L. 6, 600. if on they rushed *r.* repeated
P. L. 9, 384. the more shall shame him his *r.*
P. R. 4, 21. *r.* upon *r.*
P. R. 4, 623. by this *r.* received and hold'st

S. A. 966. reap nothing but r. and hate
**Repulsed.**—P. L. 2, 142. thus r. our final
P. L. 10, 10. complete to have discovered and r.
P. L. 10, 910. but Eve not so r. with tears that
P. R. 1, 6. foiled in all his wiles defeated and r.
S. A. 1006. nor can be easily r. without much
**Repute.**—P. L. 1, 639. by old r. consent
P. L. 2, 472. winning cheap the high r. which
**Request.**—P. L. 5, 561. thus Adam made r.
P. L. 6, 894. at thy r. and that thou. mayst
P. L. 7, 111. this also thy r. with caution asked
P. L. 7, 635. and thy r. think now fulfilled
P. L. 10, 743. did I r. thee Maker from my
P. L. 11, 46. all thy r. for man accepted son
P. L. 11, 47. all thy r. was my decree
S. A. 356. O wherefore did God grant me my r.
S. A. 881. out of levity but overpowered by thy r.
C. 900. gentle swain at thy r. I am here
M. W. 17. the virgin choir for her r.
**Requested.**—S. A. 1630. he his guide r.
**Require.**—P. L. 4, 628. r. more hands than ours
P. L. 5, 408. pure intelligential substances r.
P. L. 8, 642. perfect within no outward aid r.
P. L. 9, 590. the branches would r. thy utmost
P. R. 2, 412. great acts r. great means of
P. R. 3, 17. to deeds that might r. the array of
S. A. 1314. and now some public proof thereof r.
**Required.**—P. L. 4, 308. but r. with gentle
**Requires.**—P. L. 3, 735. me mine r.
P. L. 4, 419. he who r. from us no other
P. L. 5, 529. he r. not our necessitated
P. L. 8, 425. which r. collateral love and
P. R. 3, 113. by all his angels glorified r.
P. R. 3, 117. glory he r. and glory he receives
**Requisite.**—P. R. 1, 464. to all truth r. for
**Requital.**—C. 626. and in r. ope his leathern
**Requite.**—S. A. 1356. so r. favour renewed and
S. 8, 5. he can r. thee for he knows the charms
**Resalute.**—P. L. 11, 134. meanwhile to r.
**Rescue.**—P. R. 1, 217. one while to r. Israel
**Rescued.**—P. L. 11, 682. had not heaven r.
P. L. 12, 199. divided till his r. gain their shore
S. 23, 4. r. from death by force though pale
**Resemblance.**—P. L. 4, 364. them divine r.
P. L. 6, 114. O heaven that such r. of the
P. L. 9, 588. fairest r. of thy Maker fair
P. R. 4, 320. delusion far worse her false r.
C. 69. the express r. of the gods is changed
**Resemblances.**—P. L. 5, 114. some such r.
**Resembles.**—P. L. 2, 268. and heaven r. hell
P. L. 5, 622. in all her wheels r. nearest
**Resemblest.**—P. L. 4, 839. and thou r. now
**Resembling.**—P. L. 2, 1045. waste r. air
P. L. 8, 543. in outward also her r. less his image
P. R. 3, 110. therein least r. thy great Father
**Resent.**—P. L. 9, 300. and anger wouldst r.
**Reserve.**—P. L. 5, 61. or envy or what r.
P. R. 4, 165. yet with this r. not else
**Reserved.**—P. L. 1, 54. r. him to more wrath
P. L. 2, 161. we are decreed r. and destined
P. L. 2, 322. r. his captive multitude
P. L. 5, 128. r. from night and kept for thee
P. L. 8, 50. such pleasure she r. Adam relating
P. L. 9, 768. for beasts r. for beasts it seems
P. L. 11, 501. to what wretched state r.
S. A. 645. r. alive to be repeated the subject
**Reserving.**—P. L. 12, 71. title to himself r.
**Reside.**—P. L. 2, 265. all-ruling Sire choose to r.
P. L. 2, 957. abyss might in that noise r,
P. L. 12, 284. how can God with such r.
**Residence.**—P. L. 1, 734. angels held their r.
P. L. 2, 999. I upon my frontiers here keep r.
P. L. 8, 346. of fish within their watery r.
C. 248. to testify his hidden r.
C. 947. is your father's r.
**Resides.**—P. L. 8, 112. heaven where God r.
**Residing.**—P. L. 10, 607. till I in man r.
P. L. 12, 114. him on this side Euphrates yet r.
**Resign.**—P. L. 6, 731. and gladlier shall r.
P. L. 10, 148. that to her thou didst r.
P. L. 10, 749. desirous to r. and render back

P. L. 11, 287. but patiently r. what justly thou
P. L. 12, 301. and but given with purpose to r.
S. 14, 3. meekly thou didst r. this
V. Ex. 58. to the next I may r. my room
**Resigned.**—P. R. 1, 27. and would have r.
**Resigns.**—P. L. 3, 688. and to simplicity r.
P. L. 11, 66. r. him up with heaven and earth
**Resist.**—P. L. 1, 162. high will whom we r.
P. L. 2, 192. not more almighty to r. our might
P. L. 2, 814. he who reigns above none can r.
P. L. 4, 1013. how light how weak if thou r.
P. L. 6, 323. keen nor solid might r. that edge
P. L. 12, 491. with spiritual armour able to r.
P. R. 1, 151. far abler to r. all his solicitations
S. A. 830. weakness to r. Philistian gold
S. A. 1753. and all that band them to r.
**Resistance.**—P. L. 6, 838. astonished all r.
**Resistless.**—P. L. 2, 62. to force r. way
P. R. 4, 268. those ancient whose r. eloquence
S. A. 1404. commands come with a power r.
**Resolve.**—P. L. 1, 120. more successful hope r.
P. L. 8, 14. which only thy solution can r.
P. L. 9, 830. death to think confirmed then I r.
S. 21, 5. to-day deep thoughts r. with me to
D. F. I. 36. r. me then O soul most surely blest
**Resolved.**—P. L. 1, 662. understood must be r.
P. L. 2, 201. this was at first r. if we were wise
P. L. 2, 392. great things r. which from the
P. L. 5, 668. he r. with all his legions to
P. L. 9, 97. thus he r. but first from inward
P. L. 9, 585. of tasting those fair apples I r.
P. L. 9, 968. this day affords declaring thee r.
P. L. 10, 1088. or childless days r. as thou
P. R. 4, 444. rather by this his last affront r.
S. A. 305. they ravel more still less r.
S. A. 408. who with a grain of manhood well r.
S. A. 1390. in time thou hast r. the man returns
**Resolving.**—P. L. 12, 109. his holy eyes r.
C. 183. r. here to lodge under the spreading
**Resolutest.**—P. R. 2, 167. the manliest r.
**Resolution.**—P. L. 1, 191. if not what r.
P. L. 2, 468. prudent lest from his r. raised
P. L. 6, 541. in his face I see sad r. and secure
P. L. 9, 907. for with thee certain my r. is to
P. L. 10, 1029. then let us seek some safer r.
S. A. 732. with doubtful feet and wavering r.
S. A. 1344. is this thy r.?
S. A. 1410. I praise thy r. doff these links
**Resonant.**—P. L. 11, 563. the r. fugue
**Resort.**—P. R. 1, 367. hath he excluded my r.
S. A. 1738. thither shall all the valiant youth r.
C. 379. that in the various bustle of r.
C. 952. with jigs and rural dance r.
Il P. 81. far from all r. of mirth
**Resorting.**—P. L. 11, 81. r. to the summons
**Resound.**—P. L. 3, 149. shall r. thee ever
P. L. 5, 178. r. his praise who out of darkness
P. L. 10, 862. and r. far other song
P. L. 11, 592. with feast and music all the tents r.
**Resounded.**—P. L. 1, 315. deep of hell r.
P. L. 2, 789. her caves and back r. death
P. L. 6, 218. all heaven r. and had earth been
P. L. 7, 561. harmonies the earth, the air r.
**Resounding.**—P. R. 2, 290. birds r. loud
C. 243. and give r. grace to all heaven's harmonies
H. 182. and the r. shore
**Resounds.**—P. L. 1, 579. and what r. in fable
P. L. 8, 334. which r. yet dreadful in mine ear
S. 16, 8. and Dunbar field r. thy praises loud
**Respect.**—P. R. 4, 521. in some r. far higher
S. A. 316. nor in r. of the enemy just cause
S. A. 333. if old r. as I suppose towards my once
**Respects.**—S. A. 868. the public good private r.
**Respiration.**—P. L. 12, 540. of r. to the
**Respire.**—S. A. 11. born here leave me to r.
**Respite.**—P. L. 2, 461. or charm to r. or
P. L. 5, 232. to r. his day-labour with repast
P. L. 11, 272. the r. of that day that must be
C. 553. gave r. to the drowsy frighted steeds
**Resplendence.**—P. L. 5, 720. in full r. heir
**Resplendent.**—P. L. 3, 361. bind their r.

P. L. 4, 723. the moon's *r*. globe and starry
P. L. 9, 568. empress of this fair world *r*. Eve
P. L. 10, 66. he full *r*. all his father manifest
**Responsive.**—P. L. 4, 683. sole or *r*. each to
**Rest.**—P. L. 1, 66. where peace and *r*. can never
P. L. 1, 185. there *r*. if any *r*. can harbour there
P. L. 1, 507. the *r*. were long to tell
P. L. 1, 589. he above the *r*. in shape and gesture
P. L. 1, 671. the *r*. entire shone with a glossy
P. L. 2, 54. while they sit contriving shall the *r*.
P. L. 2, 415. as he above the *r*. high honoured
P. L. 2, 618. lamentable lot and found no *r*.
P. L. 2, 802. that *r*. or intermission none I find
P. L. 3, 184. peculiar grace elect above the *r*.
P. L. 3, 185. above the *r*. so is my will the *r*.
P. L. 3, 721. the *r*. in circuit walls this
P. L. 4, 547. *r*. was craggy cliff that overhung
P. L. 4, 611. and all things now retired to *r*.
P. L. 4, 613. since God hath set labour and *r*.
P. L. 4, 617. idle unemployed and less need *r*.
P. L. 4, 633. as nature wills night bids us *r*.
P. L. 4, 900. the *r*. is true they found me where
P. L. 5, 11. glowing cheek as through unquiet *r*.
P. L. 5, 368. in yonder shady bower to *r*.
P. L. 5, 647. the unsleeping eyes of God to *r*.
P. L. 6, 162. may show destruction to the *r*.
P. L. 6, 272. think not here to trouble holy *r*.
P. L. 6, 415. the dark dislodged and void of *r*.
P. L. 6, 662. the *r*. in imitation to like arms
P. L. 6, 802. this day from battle *r*.
P. L. 7, 91. in his holy *r*. through all eternity
P. L. 7, 240. like things to like the *r*. to several
P. L. 7, 492. the *r*. are numberless and thou
P. L. 7, 510. with front serene govern the *r*.
P. L. 8, 71. the *r*. from man or angel the great
P. L. 8, 105. the *r*. ordained for uses to his Lord
P. L. 9, 564. me so friendly grown above the *r*.
P. L. 9, 649. the credit of whose virtue *r*.
P. L. 9, 653. sole daughter of his voice the *r*.
P. L. 9, 1120. but not at *r*. or ease of mind
P. L. 10, 71. mayst ever *r*. well pleased
P. L. 10, 296. the *r*. his look bound with
P. L. 10, 422. the *r*. were all far to the inland
P. L. 10, 532. seemed above the *r*. still to retain
P. L. 10, 778. there I should *r*. and sleep secure
P. L. 10, 1008. vehement despair broke off the *r*.
P. L. 11, 1085. end in dust our final *r*.
P. L. 11, 375. and earn *r*. from labour won
P. L. 11, 710. reward awaits the good the *r*.
P. L. 12, 112. nation to select from all the *r*.
P. L. 12, 257. a cloud shall *r*. by day a fiery
P. L. 12, 260. the *r*. were long to tell
P. L. 12, 314. safe to eternal paradise of *r*.
P. L. 12, 401. so only can high justice *r*. appaid
P. L. 12, 533. the *r*. far greater part will deem
P. L. 12, 585. called charity the soul of ail the *r*.
P. L. 12, 647. where to choose their place of *r*.
P. R. 2, 233. the *r*. commit to me I shall let
P. R. 2, 292. determined there to *r*. at noon
P. R. 4, 48. above the *r*. lifting his stately head
P. R. 4, 86. these two thrones except the *r*.
P. R. 4, 344. the *r*. thin sown with aught
P. R. 4, 403. and cold betook him to his *r*.
P. R. 4, 511. flocked to the Baptist I among the *r*.
S. A. 14. unwillingly this *r*. their superstition
S. A. 406. when men seek most repose and *r*.
S. A. 459. eye to harbour sleep or thoughts to *r*.
S. A. 598. and I shall shortly be with them that *r*.
S. A. 1297. day hath been to thee no day of *r*.
S. A. 1470. the *r*. was magnanimity to remit
C. 361. while they *r*. unknown what need a man
C. 629. amongst the *r*. a small unsightly root
C. 689. and timely *r*. have wanted
A. 13. envy bid conceal the *r*.
L'A. 74. the labouring clouds do often *r*.
S. 14, 13. who thenceforth bid thee *r*. and drink
S. 19, 13. and post o'er land and ocean without *r*.
S. 21, 7. let Euclid *r*. and Archimedes pause
H. 216. nor can he be at *r*.
H. 238. hath laid her Babe to *r*.
P. 26. loud o'er the *r*. Cremona's trump doth

M. W. 50. sweet *r*. seize thee evermore
U. C. II. 11. *r*. that gives all men life, gave him his
V. Ex. 50. while sad Ulysses' soul and all the *r*.
**Rested.**—P. L. 7, 595. had work and *r*.
**Resting.**—P. L. 1, 237. such *r*. found the sole
P. L. 7, 592. now *r*. blessed and hallowed the
P. L. 7, 593. as *r*. on that day from all his work
**Restless.**—P. L. 2, 526. to his *r*. thoughts
P. L. 8, 31. such *r*. revolution day by day
S. A. 19. none to the mind from *r*. thoughts
C. 596. it shall be in eternal *r*.
**Restorative.**—P. R. 2, 373. with sweet *r*.
**Restore.**—P. L. 1, 5. one greater Man *r*. us
P. L. 11, 12. to *r*. the race of mankind drowned
P. L. 12, 623. me the promised seed shall all *r*.
P. R. 3, 381. it from servitude thou shalt *r*.
S. A. 1503. God will *r*. eyesight to his strength
C. 690. but fair virgin this will *r*. all soon
C. 691. 'twill not *r*. the truth and honesty
**Restored.**—P. L. 3, 288. *r*. as many as are *r*.
P. L. 10, 971. nevertheless *r*. by thee vile as I
P. L. 12, 3. the world destroyed and world *r*.
P. R. 1, 220. till truth were freed and equity *r*.
P. R. 1, 405. man fallen shall be *r*. I never
P. R. 2, 36. the kingdom shall to Israel be *r*.
S. A. 1528. by miracle *r*. he now be dealing dole
**Restorer.**—P. L. 10, 646. *r*. of mankind
**Restrained.**—P. L. 8, 628. nor *r*. conveyance
P. L. 9, 868. or not *r*. as we or not obeying
P. L. 11, 498. till firmer thoughts *r*. excess
**Restraint.**—P. L. 1, 32. for one *r*.
P. L. 3, 87. through all *r*. broke loose he
P. L. 9, 209. labour grows luxurious by *r*.
P. L. 9, 791. greedily she ingorged without *r*.
P. L. 9, 1170. enough severe it seems in thy *r*.
P. L. 9, 1184. *r*. she will not brook and left
S. 23. full sight of her in heaven without *r*.
**Rests.**—P. L. 3, 389. on thee his ample spirit *r*.
P. L. 5, 109. her private cell when nature *r*.
P. L. 5, 578. where earth now *r*. upon her
P. L. 10, 48. what *r*. but that the mortal
P. R. 1, 39. flies to his place nor *r*. but in mid
**Result.**—P. L. 2, 515. sound the great *r*.
P. L. 6, 619. should compel them to a quick *r*.
**Resume.**—P. L. 1, 278. they will soon *r*. new
P. L. 12, 456. and *r*. his seat at God's right
P. R. 2, 58. they out of their plaints new hope *r*.
**Resumed.**—P. L. 10, 574. permitted they *r*.
**Resumes.**—P. L. 12, 5. new speech *r*.
**Resurrection.**—P. L. 12, 436. nor after *r*.
**Retain.**—P. L. 2, 285. as when hollow rocks *r*.
P. L. 5, 501. and *r*. unalterably firm his love
P. L. 7, 362. firm to *r*. her gathered beams
P. L. 10, 532. he seemed above the rest still to *r*.
**Retained.**—P. L. 9, 601. to this shape *r*.
**Retaining.**—P. L. 11, 512. not man *r*. still
**Retains.**—P. L. 7, 146. heaven yet populous *r*.
C. 842. still she *r*. her maiden gentleness
**Retinue.**—P. L. 5, 355. when their rich *r*.
P. R. 2, 419. what followers what *r*. canst thou
**Retire.**—P. L. 2, 686. *r*. or taste thy folly
P. L. 2, 1038. and Chaos to *r*. as from her
P. L. 7, 170. though I uncircumscribed myself *r*.
P. L. 9, 810. givest access though secret she *r*.
P. L. 11, 237. reverence I must meet and thou *r*.
P. L. 11, 267. discovered soon the place of her *r*.
P. L. 12, 535. truth shall *r*. bestuck with
P. R. 2, 40. will he now *r*. after appearance
P. R. 2, 161. skilled to *r*. and in retiring draw
S. A. 1061. but had we best *r*.? I see a storm
C. 656. yet will they soon *r*. if he but shrink
**Retired.**—P. L. 2, 556. apart sat on a hill *r*.
P. L. 4, 532. fountain side or in thick shade *r*.
P. L. 4, 611. hour of night and all things now *r*.
P. L. 5, 231. him from the heat of noon *r*.
P. L. 6, 306. from each hand with speed *r*.
P. L. 6, 338. where it stood *r*. from off the files
P. L. 6, 409. under her cloudy covert both *r*.
P. L. 6, 570. and to either flank *r*.
P. L. 6, 781. his command the uprooted hills *r*.
P. L. 8, 41. perceiving where she sat *r*. in sight

U

P. L. 8, 504. not obvious, not obtrusive but *r*.
P. L. 9, 537. thy awful brow more awful thus *r*.
P. L. 10, 423. rest were all far to the inland *r*.
P. R. 3, 166. he indeed *r*. into the desert
P. R. 4, 91. and from Rome *r*. to Capreæ
S. A. 253. safe to the rock of Elham was *r*.
C. 376. oft seeks to sweet *r*. solitude
Il P. 49. and add to these *r*. leisure
**Retirement.**—P. L. 9, 250. and short *r*.
 P. R. 4, 245. olive grove of Academe Plato's *r*.
**Retires.**—P. L. 5, 108. *r*. into her private cell
P.L.10,433.by Astracan over the snowy plains *r*.
**Retiring.**—P. L. 10, 378. this new world *r*.
 P. R. 2, 161. skilled to retire and in *r*. draw
 P. R. 3, 164. sitting still or thus *r*.
 S. A. 16. hence with leave *r*.from the popular
**Retort.**—P. L. 10, 761. reproved *r*.
**Retorted.**—P. L. 5, 906. and with *r*. scorn
**Retreat.**—P. L. 1, 555. to flight or foul *r*.
 P. L. 2, 317. not our safe *r*. beyond his potent
 P. L. 6, 237. no thought of flight none of *r*.
 P. L. 6, 799. disdaining flight or faint *r*.
 P. L. 10, 435. in his *r*. to Tauris or Casbeen
**Retreated.**—P. L. 2, 547. others more mild *r*.
**Retreating.**—P. L. 11, 854. towards the *r*.
**Retrenched.**—P. R. 1, 454. shall be soon *r*.
**Retribution.**—P. L. 3, 454. here find fit *r*.
**Retrograde.**—P. L. 8, 127. progressive *r*.
**Return.**—P. L. 2, 37. we now *r*. to claim
 P. L. 2, 335. and what peace can we *r*.
 P. L. 2, 527. hours till his great chief *r*.
 P. L. 2, 799. womb that bred them they *r*.
 P. L. 2, 889. and this once known shall soon *r*.
 P. L. 3, 41. thus with the year seasons *r*.
 P. L. 3, 159. or proud *r*. though to his heavier
 P. L. 3, 261. and *r*. father to see thy face
 P. L. 4, 42. ah wherefore he deserved no such *r*.
 P. L. 4, 481. *r*. fair Eve whom fliest thou
 P. L. 4, 534. enjoy till I *r*. short pleasures
 P. L. 5, 470. things proceed and up to him *r*.
 P. L. 6, 39. back on thy foes more glorious to *r*.
 P. L. 6, 606. back defeated to *r*. they worse
 P. L. 7, 16. *r*. me to my native element
 P. L. 7, 604. greater now in thy *r*. than from
 P. L. 8, 21. and their swift *r*. diurnal
 P. L. 8, 651. be good and friendly still and oft *r*.
 P. L. 9, 250. short retirement urges sweet *r*.
 P. L. 9, 399. oft he to her his charge of quick *r*.
 P. L. 9, 405. of thy presumed *r*. event perverse
 P. L. 9, 839. waiting desirous her *r*. had wove
 P. L. 9, 844. and new solace in her *r*. so long
 P. L. 10, 54. justice shall not *r*. as bounty
 P. L. 10, 206. till thou *r*. unto the ground
 P. L. 10, 208. then dust art and shalt to dust *r*.
 P. L. 10, 253. stay his *r*. perhaps over this gulf
 P. L. 10, 770. dust I am and shall to dust *r*.
 P. L. 10, 932. to the place of judgment will *r*.
 P. L. 11, 200. thither must *r*. and be no more
 P. L. 11, 463. is this the way I must *r*. to native
 P. L. 11, 534. till many years over thy head *r*.
 P. L. 11, 816. and shall *r*. of them derived
 P. L. 12, 171. they *r*. with glory and spoil
 P. L. 12, 213. embattled ranks the waves *r*.
 P. L. 12, 219. and fear *r*. them back to Egypt
 P. L. 12, 422. ere the third dawning light *r*.
 P. L. 12, 541. at *r*. of him so lately promised
 P. R. 1, 297. way he came not having marked *r*.
 P. R. 2, 57. we shall see our hope our joy *r*.
 P. R. 2, 115. *r*. to Satan with sly preface to *r*.
 P. R. 2, 302. with granted leave officious I *r*.
 P. R. 3, 129. from them who could *r*. him
 P. R. 3, 132. hard recompense unsuitable *r*.
 P. R. 4, 64. or on *r*. in robes of state
 P. R. 4,374. found thee there and tnither will *r*.
 P. R. 4, 438. to gratulate the sweet *r*. of morn
 S. A. 517. to *r*. thee home to thy country
 S. A. 1332. *r*. the way thou camest I will not
 C. 194. and envious darkness ere they could *r*.
 C. 284. were but twain and purposed quick *r*.
 C. 607. and force him to *r*. his purchase back
 L. 38. now thou art gone and never must *r*.

L. 132. *r*. Alpheus the dread voice is past
L. 133. *r*. Sicilian muse and call the vales
H. 142. will down *r*. to men
**Returned.**—P. L. 2, 520. deafening shout *r*.
 P. L. 2, 736. then these to her Satan *r*.
 P. L. 3, 693. in his uprightness answer thus *r*.
 P. L. 4, 463. but pleased I soon *r*. pleased it *r*.
 P. L. 4, 576. the winged warrior thus *r*.
 P. L. 4, 590. and Uriel to his charge *r*. on that
 P. L. 5, 30. glad I see thy face and morn *r*.
 P. L. 6, 25. yet one *r*. not lost
 P. L. 6, 187. from me *r*. as erst thou saidst
 P. L. 7, 135. and the great son *r*. victorious
 P. L. 7, 552. desisting though unwearied up *r*.
 P. L. 7, 567. *r*. magnificent his six days' work
 P. L. 8, 245. glad we *r*. up to the coasts of light
 P. L. 8, 285. when answer none *r*.
 P. L. 8, 337. but soon his clear aspect *r*.
 P. L. 9, 57. of heavier on himself fearless *r*.
 P. L. 9, 58. and at midnight *r*.
 P. L. 9, 67. on the eighth *r*. and on the coast
 P. L. 9, 226. whom mild answer Adam thus *r*.
 P. L. 9, 401. as oft engaged to be *r*. by noon
 P. L. 10, 34. ye powers *r*. from unsuccessful
 P. L. 10, 224. to him with swift ascent he up *r*.
 P. L. 10, 240. if mishap ere this he had *r*.
 P. L. 10, 341. that past, *r*. by night, and
 P. L. 10, 346. tidings fraught to hell he now *r*.
 P. L. 10, 455. their mighty chief *r*. loud was
 P. L. 10, 462. *r*. successful beyond hope
 P. L. 10, 518. but hiss for hiss *r*. with forked
 P. L. 11, 153. peace *r*. home to my breast
 P. L. 11, 294. and his scattered spirits *r*.
 P. L. 12, 348. *r*. from Babylon by leave of
 P. R. 1, 318. to warn him wet *r*. from field at
 P. R. 1, 324. *r*. and dropt not here his carcass
 P. R. 1, 439. *r*. the wiser or the more instruct
 P. R. 1, 467. and this answer smooth *r*.
 P. R. 2, 24. or in Peræa but *r*. in vain
 P. R. 2, 61. others *r*. from baptism not her son
 P. R. 2, 79. from Egypt home *r*. in Nazareth
 P. R. 2, 140. therefore I am *r*. lest confidence
 P. R. 2, 172. whom quick answer Satan thus *r*.
 P. R. 3, 181. whom our Saviour answer thus *r*.
 P. R. 4, 639. to his mother's house private *r*.
**Returning.**—P. L. 6, 879. *r*. whence it
 P. L. 9, 850. her met scarce from the tree *r*.
 P. L. 11, 859. the second time *r*. in his bill an
 P. L. 12, 632. the labourer's heel homeward *r*.
 P. R. 3, 130. and not *r*. that would likeliest
 S.A.1004. offence *r*.to regain love once possessed
 S.A. 1355. again *r*. with my hair after my great
 S. 19. my true account lest He *r*. chide
**Returns.**—P. L. 1, 140. and vigour soon *r*.
 P. L. 3, 41. seasons return but not to me *r*.
 P. L. 4, 812. but *r*. of force to its own likeness
 P. L. 4, 906. and now *r*. him from his prison
 P. L. 5, 276. lights and to his proper shape *r*.
 P. L. 5, 845. all honour to him done *r*. our
 P. L. 8, 157. habitable which *r*. light back
 P. R. 4, 17. beat oft *r*. as oft with humming
 S.A.1390. in time thou hast resolved: the man *r*.
 S. A. 1750. to hide his face but unexpectedly *r*.
 C. 670. when the fresh blood grows lively and *r*.
**Return'st.**—P. L. 6, 151. thou *r*. from flight
 P. L. 12, 610. whence thou *r*. and whither
**Reveal.**—P, L. 5, 570. not lawful to *r*.
 P. L. 11, 115. *r*. to Adam what shall come
 S. A. 50. but weakly to a woman must *r*. it
 S. A. 383. and *r*. the secret wrested from me
**Revealed.**—P. L. 6, 895. to thee I have *r*.
 P.L.7,71. differing from this world thou hast *r*.
 P.L.7,122. own inventions hope things not *r*.
 P. L. 8, 177. that thus far hath been *r*.
 P. L. 12, 151. to thee anon plainlier shall be *r*.
 P. L. 12, 272. gracious things thou hast *r*.
 P. L. 12, 545. from heaven to be *r*. in glory of
 P. R. 1, 307. or harboured in one cave is not *r*.
 P. R. 2, 50. sent his anointed and to us *r*. him
 S. A. 29. or benefit *r*. to Abraham's race

S. A. 491. to have *r.* secrets of men the secrets
S. A. 782. but I to enemies *r.* and should not
S. A. 800. 'thou wilt say why then *r.*
**Reveals.**—P. R. 1, 293. my knowledge God *r.*
**Revellers.**—P. L. 7, 33. of Bacchus and his *r.*
**Revelry.**—C. 103. midnight shout and *r.*
L'A. 127. and pomp, and feast, and *r.*
**Revels.**—P. L. 1, 782. whose midnight *r.*
P. L. 4, 765. here and *r.* not in the bought
C. 985. *r.* the spruce and jocund spring
**Revenge.**—P. L. 1, 35. with envy and *r.*
P. L. 1, 107. and study of *r.*
P. L. 1, 604. and considerate pride waiting *r.*
P. L. 2, 105. which if not victory is yet *r.*
P. L. 2, 107. and his look denounced desperate *r.*
P. L. 2, 128. scope of all his aim after some dire *r.*
P. L. 2, 129. first what *r.* the towers of heaven
P. L. 2, 337. untamed reluctance and *r.* though
P. L. 2, 371. this would surpass common *r.*
P. L. 2, 987. be the advantage all mine the *r.*
P. L. 2, 1054. full fraught with mischievous *r.*
P. L. 3, 85. so bent he seems on desperate *r.*
P. L. 3, 160. with *r.* accomplished
P. L. 4, 123. malice to conceal couched with *r.*
P. L. 4, 386. him who puts me loth to this *r.*
P. L. 4, 390. honour and empire with *r.* enlarged
P. L. 6, 151. but in wished hour of my *r.* first
P. L. 6, 905. would be all his solace and *r.*
P. L. 9, 168. what will not ambition and *r.*
P. L. 9, 171. *r.* at first though sweet bitter . . long
P. L. 9, 466. of guile, of hate, of envy. of *r.*
P. L. 10, 242. can fit his punishment or their *r.*
P. L. 10, 1036. to crush his head would be *r.*
S. A. 484. have satisfied their utmost of *r.*
S. A. 1462. contemptuous proud set on *r.*
S. A. 1591. dreadful way thou took'st to thy *r.*
S. A. 1660. O dearly-bought *r.* yet glorious
**Revenged.**—P. L. 4, 4. furious down to be *r.*
S. A. 1468. who confessed they had enough *r.*
S. A. 1712. on his enemies fully *r.*
**Reverence.**—P. L. 2, 478. bend with awful *r.*
P. L. 3, 738. where honour due and *r.* none
P. L. 5, 359. yet with submiss approach and *r.*
P. L. 8, 599. and with mysterious *r.* I deem
P. L. 9, 835. first low *r.* done as to the power
P. L. 10, 915. what love sincere and *r.* in my
P. L. 11, 237. with *r.* I must meet and thou
P. L. 11, 346. to celebrate and *r.* thee their
P. L. 11, 525. God's image did not *r.* in
P. R. 1, 80. I saw the prophet do him *r.*
A. 37. whom with low *r.* I adore as mine
**Reverenced.**—S. A. 1463. that part most *r.*
**Reverend.**—P. L. 11, 719. at length a *r.* sire
S. A. 326. but see here comes thy *r.* sire
S. A. 1456. say *r.* Sire we thirst to hear
S. A. 1548. to thee first *r.* Manoah and to these
L. 103. next Camus *r.* sire went footing slow
**Reverent.**—P. L. 3, 349. lowly *r.* towards
P. L. 10, 1088. prostrate fall before him *r.*
P. L. 10, 1100. prostrate fall before him *r.*
P. R. 2, 220. or turn to *r.* awe for beauty stands
**Reverse.**—P. L. 6, 326. with swift wheel *r.*
P. L. 11, 41. I to mitigate thus plead not to *r.*
**Reversed.**—C. 816. without his rod *r.* and
**Revile.**—P. L. 10, 118. judge without *r.*
**Reviling.**—P. L. 10, 1048. without wrath or *r.*
**Revisit.**—P. L. 3, 13. thee I *r.* now with
P. L. 3, 21. thee I *r.* safe and feel thy sovran
**Revisit'st.**—P. L. 3, 23. but thou *r.* not
**Revive.**—P. L. 1, 279. new courage and *r.*
P. L. 2, 493. the fields *r.* the birds their notes
P. L. 6, 493. meanwhile *r.* abandon fear
P. L. 11, 871. heavenly instructor I *r.* at this
**Revived.**—P. L. 6, 497. languished hope *r.*
P. L. 9, 440. or of *r.* Adonis or renowned
C. 840. dropped in ambrosial oils till she *r.*
**Revives.**—P. L. 12, 420. he dies but soon *r.*
S. A. 187. your coming friends *r.* me
S. A. 1704. *r.* reflourishes then vigorous most
**Reviving.**—S. A. 1268. comely it is and how *r.*
**Revoke.**—P. L. 3, 126. and *r.* the high decree

**Revokes.**—P. R. 3, 356. what it predicts *r.*
**Revolt.**—P. L. 1, 33. to that foul *r.*
P. L. 1, 611. eternal splendours flung for his *r.*
P. L. 2, 326. his kingdom lose no part by our *r.*
P. L. 3, 117. themselves decreed their own *r.*
P. L. 6, 262. of evil unknown till thy *r.*
P. L. 6, 740. from thy just obedience could *r.*
P. L. 9, 7. the part of man *r.* and disobedience
P. R. 1, 359. with millions more in rash *r.*
S. 12, 10. still *r.* when truth would set them
**Revolted.**—P. L. 4, 835. think not *r.* spirit
P. L. 6, 31. against *r.* multitudes the cause
P. L. 10, 534. where all yet left of that *r.*
**Revolter.**—S. A. 1180. a murderer a *r.* and a
**Revolve.**—P. R. 4, 281. these here *r.* or as
**Revolved.**—P. L. 7, 381. *r.* on heaven's
P. L. 9, 88. of thoughts *r.* his final sentence
P. R. 1, 259. I again *r.* the Law and Prophets
S. A. 1638. or some great matter in his mind *r.*
**Revolving.**—P. L. 4, 31. then much *r.* thus
P. R. 1, 185. musing and much *r.* in his breast
**Revolution.**—P. L. 8, 31. restless *r.* day by
P. L. 10, 814. back with dreadful *r.* on my
U. C. II. 6. until his *r.* was at stay
**Revolutions.**—P. L. 2, 597. at certain *r.* all
**Reward.**—P. L. 3, 451. their *r.* on earth
P. L. 6, 153. receive thy merited *r.*
P. L. 6, 910. by terrible example the *r.* of
P. L. 7, 628. and in *r.* to rule over his works
P. L. 10, 767. to serve him thy *r.* was of his
P. L. 11, 459. other's faith approved lose no *r.*
P. L. 11, 709. what *r.* awaits the good the rest
P. L. 12, 461. but to *r.* his faithful and receive
P. R. 3, 25. glory the *r.* that sole excites to
P. R. 3, 87. or shameful death their due *r.*
P. R. 3, 104. and loses, though but verbal, his *r.*
S. A. 992. the public marks of honour and *r.*
S. A. 1465. but their aim private *r.*
**Rewarded.**—S. A. 413. *r.* well with servile
**Rhea.**—P. L. 1, 513. his own and *R.'s* son like
P. L. 4, 279. from his stepdame *R.'s* eye
**Rhene.**—P. L. 1, 353. to pass *R.* or the Danaw
**Rhetoric.**—P. R. 4, 4. *r.* that sleeked his
C. 790. enjoy your dear wit and gay *r.*
**Rheums.**—P. L. 11, 488. and joint-racking *r.*
**Rhodope.**—P. L. 7, 35. in *R.* where woods and
**Rhomb.**—P. L. 8, 134. nocturnal and diurnal *r.*
**Rhombs.**—P. R. 3, 309. in *r.* and wedges
**Rhyme.**—P. L. 1, 16. unattempted yet in . . *r.*
L. 11. himself to sing and build the lofty *r.*
P. L. 8, 466. took from thence a *r.* with
P. L. 8, 469. the *r.* he formed and fashioned
P. L. 9, 912. and I another *r.* afford yet loss
P. L. 10, 884. all but a *r.* crooked by nature
**Ribs.**—P. L. 1, 690. and digged out *r.* of gold
P. L. 10, 512. his arms clung to his *r.* his legs
C. 562. create a soul under the *r.* of death
**Rich.**—P. L. 1, 538. golden lustre *r.* imblazed
P. L. 3, 504. whereof but far more *r.* appeared
P. L. 4, 189. the cash of some *r.* burgher whose
P. L. 4, 248. groves whose *r.* trees wept odorous
P. L. 4, 701. with *r.* inlay broidered the ground
P. L. 5, 355. their *r.* retinue long of horses led
P. L. 7, 501. earth in her *r.* attire consummate
P. L. 10, 292. to the *r.* Cathaian coast
P. L. 11, 407. perhaps he also saw *r.* Mexico
P. L. 11, 793. high titles and *r.* prey
S. A. 722. some *r.* Philistian matron she may
C. 22. that like to *r.* and various gems inlay
C. 556. rose like a steam of *r.* distilled perfumes
M. W. 1. this *r.* marble doth inter
**Rich-clad.**—P. R. 2, 352. stripling youths *r.-c.*
**Richer.**—P. L. 11, 408. in Peru the *r.* seat
**Riches.**—P. L. 1, 682. more the *r.* of heavens
P. L. 1, 691. let none admire that *r.* grow in
P. L. 12, 580. and all the *r.* of this world
P. R. 2, 427. get *r.* first get wealth and
P. R. 2, 429. *r.* are mine fortune is in my hand
P. R. 2, 449. things and could contemn *r.*
P. R. 2, 453. extol not *r.* then the toil of fools

P. R. 2, 458. with like aversion I reject *r.*
P. R. 2, 484. *r.* are needless then both for
P. R. 4, 298. but virtue joined with *r.*
P. R. 4, 536. honours, *r.*, kingdoms, glory have
C. 724. not half his *r.* known and yet despised
**Richest.**—P. L. 2, 3. gorgeous east with *r.* hand
P. L. 10, 446. under state of *r.* texture
S. A. 1479.to live the poorest in my tribe than *r.*
P. 44. that was the casket of heaven's *r.* store
V. Ex. 21. cull those *r.* robes and gayest attire
**Richly.**—P. L. 11, 582. women *r.* gay in gems
P. R. 2, 340. a table *r.* spread in regal mode
Il P. 159. and storied windows *r.* dight
**Rid.**—P. L. 6, 737. thy might *r.* heaven of these
S. A. 1263. friend by death to *r.* me hence
**Riddance.**—P. L. 4, 632. ask *r.* if we mean
**Riddle.**—P. R. 4, 573. proposed her *r.* and
S. A. 1016. much like thy *r.* Samson in one day
S. A. 1200. solved the *r.* which I had proposed
**Riddling.**—S. A. 1064. my *r.* days are past
**Ride.**—P. L. 1, 764. champions bold wont *r.* in
P. L. 2, 540. both rocks and hills and *r.* the air
P. L. 4, 974. though heaven's king *r.* on thy
P. L. 7, 166. I send along *r.* forth and bid
P. L. 10, 475. forced to *r.* the untractable abyss
Il P. 115. on which the Tartar king did *r.*
F. of C. 7. and *r.* us with a classic hierarchy
**Riders.**—P. R. 3, 314. prancing their *r.* bore
S. A. 1324. gymnic artists, wrestlers, *r.*,runners
**Rides.**—P. L. 1, 769. the sun with Taurus *r.*
P. L. 2, 930. ascending *r.* audacious
S. A. 1538. evil news *r.* post...good news baits
**Ridest.**—C. 135. thou *r.* with Hecate
**Ridge.**—P. L. 2, 432. whose snowy *r.* the roving
P. L. 7, 293. part rise in crystal wall or *r.* direct
P. L. 10, 313. by wondrous art pontifical a *r.*
P. L. 12, 146. shall dwell to Senir that long *r.*
P. R. 4, 29. to equal length backed with a *r.*
S. A. 1137. that *r.* the back of chafed wild boars
**Ridges.**—P. L. 6, 236. and when to close the *r.*
**Ridiculous.**—P. L. 12, 62. building left *r.*
P. R. 4, 342. their gods *r.* and themselves past
S. A. 131. and weaponless himself made arms *r.*
S. A. 539. then turned me out *r.* despoiled
S. A. 1361. besides how vile contemptible *r.*
S. A. 1501. useless and thence *r.* about him
**Riding.**—P.L. 2, 663. *r.* through the air she comes
Il P. 68. *r.* near her highest noon
**Rife.**—P. L. 1, 650. whereof so *r.* there went a fame
S. A. 866. so *r.* and celebrated in the mouths
C. 203. was *r.* and perfect in my listening
**Rifled.**—P. L. 1, 687, *r.* the bowels of their
**Rift.**—P. R. 4, 411. from many a horrid *r.*
**Rifted.**—S. A. 1621. the people with a shout *r.*
C. 518. and *r.* rocks whose entrance leads to hell
**Rigged.**—S. A. 200. from above gloriously *r.*
L. 101. built in the eclipse and *r.* with curses
**Right.**—P. L. 1, 150. as his thralls by *r.* of war
P. L. 1, 247. can dispose and bid what shall be *r.*
P. L. 1, 402. *r.* against the temple of God
P. L. 1, 534. claimed Azazel as his *r.*
P. L. 2, 18. me though just *r.* and the fixed laws
P. L. 2, 174. arm again his red *r.* hand to plague
P. L. 2, 231. war be best or to regain our own *r.*
P. L. 2, 869. where I shall reign at thy *r.* hand
P. L. 3, 62. on his *r.* the radiant image of his
P. L. 3, 98. I made him just and *r.* sufficient
P. L. 3, 111. they therefore as to *r.* belonged
P. L. 3, 155. all things made and judgest only *r.*
P. L. 3, 279. I spare thee from my bosom and *r.*
P. L. 4, 202. any but God alone to value *r.*
P. L. 4, 443. what thou hast said is just and *r.*
P. L. 4, 541. with *r.* aspect against the eastern
P. L. 4, 881. but have power and *r.* to question
P. L. 5, 606. whom ye now behold at my *r.* hand
P. L. 5, 728. what our power is or our *r.*
P. L. 5, 789. if I trust to know ye *r.* or if ye
P. L. 5, 794. can in reason then or *r.* assume
P. L. 5, 795. monarchy over such as live by *r.*
P. L. 5, 815. by *r.* endued with regal sceptre
P. L. 5, 864. puissance is our own our own. *r.*

P. L. 6, 42. who reason for their law refuse *r.*
P. L. 6, 43. Messiah who by *r.* of merit reigns
P. L. 6, 154. the first assay of this *r.* hand
P. L. 6, 327. deep entering shared all his *r.* side
P. L. 6, 452. leader to free enjoyment of our *r.*
P. L. 6, 558. vanguard to *r.* and left the front
P. L. 6, 569. when to *r.* and left the front
P. L. 6, 624. who receives them *r.* had need
P. L. 6, 709. by sacred unction thy deserved *r.*
P. L. 6, 747. from the *r.* hand of glory where
P. L. 6, 762. at his *r.* hand Victory sat
P. L. 6, 831. he on his impious foes *r.* onward
P. L. 6, 835. his *r.* hand grasping ten thousand
P. L. 6, 892. where now he sits at the *r.* hand
P. L. 8, 71. imports not if thou reckon *r.*
P. L. 8, 572. on just and *r.* well managed
P. L. 9, 352. is free and reason he made *r.*
P. L. 9, 570. and *r.* thou shouldst be obeyed
P. L. 9, 611. and worship thee of *r.* declared
P. L. 9, 676. brooking through his zeal of *r.*
P. L. 10, 64. unfolding bright toward the *r.*
P. L. 10, 76. of *r.* that I may mitigate their
P. L. 10, 398. all yours *r.* down to paradise
P. L. 10, 461. possession such not only of *r.*
P. L. 10, 747. were but *r.* and equal to reduce
P. L. 11, 666. spake much of *r.* and wrong
P. L. 12, 16. some regard to what is just and *r.*
P. L. 12, 68. that *r.* we hold by his dominion
P. L. 12, 84. which always with *r.* reason
P. L. 12, 360. might be born barred of his *r.*
P. L. 12, 457. resume his seat at God's *r.* hand
P. R. 2, 324. hast thou not *r.* to all created
P. R. 2, 325. all creatures by just *r.* to thee
P. R. 2, 379. not that to all things I had *r.*
P. R. 2, 390. withholds my power that *r.* to use
P. R. 3, 141. that which to God alone of *r.*
P. R. 3, 154. though thy *r.* be now in powerful
P. R. 3, 164. thou to regain thy *r.* by
P. R. 4, 104. is given, and by that *r.* I give it
S. A. 310. and hath full *r.* to exempt whom so it
S. A. 1056. nor from that *r.* to part an hour
C. 854. if she be *r.* invoked in warbled song
L'A. 35. and in thy *r.* hand lead with thee
L'A. 59. *r.* against the eastern gate
S. 22. 9. but still bear up and steer *r.* onward
S. 15, 11. till truth and *r.* from violence be freed
U. C. II. 21. his chief disease and to judge *r.*
**Righteous.**—P. L. 1, 434. left his *r.* altar
P. L. 3, 292. their own both *r.* and unrighteous
P. L. 6, 804. accepted fearless in his *r.* cause
P. L. 10, 30. with *r.* plea their utmost vigilance
P. L. 10, 644. just are thy ways *r.* are thy
P. L. 1, 701. the only *r.* in a world perverse
P. R. 1, 206. to promote all truth all *r.* things
P. R. 1, 425. moved thee to misdeem of *r.* Job
S. A. 1276. but raging to pursue the *r.*
**Righteousness.**—P. L. 9. 1056. native *r.*
P. L. 10, 222. with his robe of *r.* arraying
P. L. 11, 682. heaven rescued had in his *r.*
P. L. 11, 814. before them set the paths of *r.*
P. L. 12, 294. just for unjust that in such *r.*
P. L. 12, 550. founded in *r.* and peace and love
**Rightful.**—P. L. 5, 818. confess him *r.* king
Cir. 17. for we by *r.* doom remediless
**Right-hand.**—P. L. 2, 633. the *r.-h.* coast
**Rightlier.**—P. L. 11, 697. destroyers *r.*
P. R. 2, 123. *r.* called powers of fire air water
**Rightliest.**—P. R. 4, 475. each act is *r.* done
**Rightly.**—P. L. 7, 2. by that name if *r.* thou
P. L. 8, 439. thou hast *r.* named but of thyself
P. L. 11, 159. Eve *r.* called mother of all
P. L. 12, 418. to hurt them more who *r.* trust
Il P. 170. where I may sit and *r.* spell
S. M. 18. may *r.* answer that melodious
**Rigid.**—P. L. 3, 212. and as willing pay the *r.*
P. L. 6, 83. of *r.* spears and helmets thronged
P. L. 8, 334. sternly he pronounced the *r.*
P. L. 9, 685. do not believe those *r.* threats
S. A. 1493. and still art paving that *r.* score
C. 450. but *r.* looks of chaste austerity
**Rigorously.**—P. L. 11, 109. sentence *r.*

**Rigour.**—P. L. 10, 297. with Gorgonian *r.*
  P. L. 10, 803. in punished man to satisfy his *r.*
  P. R. 1, 363. not so confined by *r.* unconniving
  C. 107. *r.* now is gone to bed
**Rill.**—P. L. 4, 229. and with many a *r.* watered
  L. 24. fed the same flock by fountain shade & *r.*
**Rills.**—P. L. 5, 6. sound of leaves and fuming *r.*
  C. 926. from a thousand petty *r.*
  L. 186. sang the uncouth swain to the oaks and *r.*
**Rimmon.**—P. L. 1, 467. him followed *R.*
**Rind.**—P. L. 1, 206. fixed anchor in his scaly *r.*
  P. L. 4, 249. fruit burnished with golden *r.*
  P. L. 4, 335. and in the *r.* still as they thirsted
  P. L. 5, 342. coat rough or smooth *r.* or bearded
  C. 664. although this corporal *r.* thou hast
**Ring.**—L'A. 93, when the merry bells *r.* round
  Il P. 47. and hears the Muses in a *r.*
  U P. 113. that owned the virtuous *r.* and glass
  H. 208. in vain with cymbals' *r.*
  H. 125. *r.* out ye crystal spheres
  P. 2. wherewith the stage of air and earth did *r.*
**Ringlets.**—P. L. 4, 306. but in wanton *r.*
  A. 47. with *r.* quaint and wanton windings wove
**Rings.**—P. L. 2, 495. that hill and valley *r.*
  S. A. 1449. the city *r.* and numbers thither flock
  L'A. 114. ere the first cock his matin *r.*
  S. 15, 1. whose name in arms through Europe *r.*
  S. 22, 12. of which all Europe *r.* from side to side
**Riot.**—P. L. 1, 499. where the noise of *r.* ascends
  P. L. 10, 521. as accessories to his bold *r.*
  P. L. 11, 715. to luxury and *r.* feast and dance
  C. 172. of *r.* and ill-managed merriment
**Riotous.**—C. 763. her children should be *r.*
**Ripe.**—P. L. 4, 981. as when a field of Ceres *r.*
  P. L. 5, 323. where store all seasons *r.* for use
  P. L. 11, 535. till like *r.* fruit thou drop into
  P. L. 12, 459. world's dissolution shall be *r.*
  P. R. 3, 31. thy years are *r.* and over ripe
  C. 59. who *r.* and frolics of his full-grown
  C. 296. *r.* clusters from the tender shoots
**Ripened.**—S. 14, 2. had *r.* thy soul to dwell
**Ripeness.**—S. 2, 7. and inward *r.* doth much
**Rise.**—P. L. 1, 545. ten thousand banners *r.*
  P. L. 2, 135. all hell should *r.* with blackest
  P. L. 2, 296. which might *r.* by policy, and long
  P. L. 3, 250. but I shall *r.* victorious and subdue
  P. L. 3, 296. and dying *r.* and rising with him
  P. L. 4, 664. light prepared they set and *r.*
  P. L. 5, 125. let us to our fresh employments *r.*
  P. L. 5, 185. mists and exhalations that now *r.*
  P. L. 5, 188. to the world's great author *r.*
  P. L. 5, 289. to his message high in honour *r.*
  P. L. 5, 376. these mid-hours till evening *r.*
  P. L. 6, 136. against the Omnipotent to *r.* in
  P. L. 6, 285. but that they *r.* unvanquished
  P. L. 7, 293. part *r.* in crystal wall or ridge
  P. L. 8, 161. predominant in heaven *r.* on the
  P. L. 8, 161. *r.* on the earth or earth *r.* on the
  P. L. 8, 296. thy mansion wants thee Adam *r.*
  P. L. 9, 1123. winds worse within began to *r.*
  P. L. 10, 243. feel new strength within me *r.*
  P. L. 10, 647. and earth shall to the ages *r.*
  P. L. 10, 958. but *r.* let us no more contend
  P. L. 11, 828. till inundation *r.* above
  P. L. 12, 24. till one shall *r.* of proud ambitious
  P. L. 12, 326. shall *r.* a Son, the woman's seed
  P. L. 12, 422. the stars of morn shall see him *r.*
  P. R. 1, 294. our Morning star then in his *r.*
  P. R. 2, 274. by the angel was bid *r.* and eat
  S. A. 1254. lest a question *r.* whether he durst
  S. A. 1316. *r.* therefore with all speed and come
  C. 885. *r.*, *r.* and heave thy rosy head
  A. 54. when evening gray doth *r.* I fetch my
  L'A. 44. till the dappled dawn doth *r.*
  S. 20. 10. whence we may *r.* to hear the lute well
**Risen.**—P. L. 1, 211. nor ever thence had *r.* or
  P. L. 2, 726. *r.* and with hideous outcry
  P. L. 4, 624. we must be *r.* and at our pleasant
  P. L. 5, 311. seems another morn *r.* on
  P. L. 10, 555. forbidden tree a multitude now *r.*
  P. L. 10, 975. in my unquiet breast are *r.*

P. L. 12, 630. as evening-mist *r.* from a river
P. R. 2, 127. such an enemy is *r.* to invade us
**Rises.**—P. L. 12, 56. a hideous gabble *r.* loud
  C. 306. due west it *r.* from this shrubby point
**Rising.**—P. L. 2, 15. descent celestial virtues *r.*
  P. L. 2, 301. and in his *r.* seemed a pillar of
  P. L. 2, 476. their *r.* all at once was as the
  P. L. 3, 11. the *r.* world of waters dark and
  P. L. 3, 296. and dying rise and *r.* with him
  P. L. 3, 551. which now the *r.* sun gilds with
  P. L. 4, 405. then *r.* changes oft his couchant
  P. L. 5, 607. till the moon *r.* in clouded
  P. L. 4, 641. her *r.* sweet with charm of
  P. L. 4, 651. nor *r.* sun on this delightful
  P. L. 5, 191. *r.* or falling still advance his
  P. L. 5, 715. without their light rebellion *r.*
  P. L. 5, 725. is *r.* who intends to erect his
  P. L. 7, 102. his generation and the *r.* birth of
  P. L. 7, 441. and *r.* on stiff pennons tower
  P. L. 7, 468. *r.* the crumbled earth above them
  P. L. 9, 75. rose Satan involved in *r.* mist
  P. L. 9, 498. circular base of *r.* folds that
  P. L. 9, 1070. false in our promised *r.*
  P. L. 10, 185. *r.* from his grave spoiled
  P. L. 10, 663. which of them *r.* with the sun
  P. L. 11, 665. till at last of middle age one *r.*
  P. R. 1, 80. on him *r.* out of the water
  P. R. 2, 88. that to the fall and *r.* he should be
  P. R. 3, 201. knowest thou not that my *r.*
  Il P. 73. oft on a plat of *r.* ground
**Rites.**—P. L. 1, 390. his holy *r.* and solemn
  P. L. 1, 414. to do him wanton *r.* which cost
  P. L. 4, 736. and other *r.* observing none but
  P. L. 4, 742. nor Eve the *r.* mysterious of
  P. L. 7, 149. with ministeries due and solemn *r.*
  P. L. 8, 487. of nuptial sanctity and marriage *r.*
  P. L. 10, 994. from love's due *r.* nuptial embraces
  P. L. 11, 440. and all due *r.* performed
  P. L. 11, 591. then first to marriage *r.* invoked
  P. L. 12, 231. part religious *r.* of sacrifice
  P. L. 12, 244. thus laws and *r.* established
  P. L. 12, 534. in outward *r.* and specious forms
  S. A. 1320. their religious *r.* my presence
  S. A. 1378. present in temples at idolatrous *r.*
  C. 125. come let us our *r.* begin
  C. 535. doing abhorred *r.* to Hecate
**Rivals.**—P. L. 2, 472. in opinion stand his *r.*
  S. A. 387. had corrupted her my spies and *r.*
**Riven.**—P. L. 6, 449. sore toiled his *r.* arms
**River.**—P. L. 2, 583. Lethe the *r.* of oblivion
  P. L. 3, 358. and where the *r.* of bliss through
  P. L. 4, 223. southward through Eden went a *r.*
  P. L. 4, 276. girt with the *r.* Triton
  P. L. 9, 74. in with the *r.* sunk and with it rose
  P. L. 9, 78. up beyond the *r.* Ob
  P. L. 9, 514. nigh *r.'s* mouth or foreland
  P. L. 11, 833. down the great *r.* to the opening
  P. L. 12, 157. Egypt divided by the *r.* Nile
  P. L. 12, 630. as evening-mist risen from a *r.*
  P. R. 4, 32. thence in the midst divided she by a *r.*
  C. 842. made goddess of the *r.* still she retains
**River-dragon.**—P. L. 12. 191. *r.-d* tamed
**River-horse.**—P. L. 7, 474. the *r.-h.* and scaly
**Rivers.**—P. L. 1, 291. *r.* or mountains in her
  P. L. 2, 575. along the banks of four infernal *r.*
  P. L. 3, 607. breathe forth elixir pure and *r.*
  P. L. 4, 806. like gentle breaths from *r.* pure
  P. L. 7, 305. where *r.* now stream, and perpetual
  P. L. 7, 328. with borders long the *r.* that earth
  P. L. 7, 437. others on silver lakes and *r.* bathed
  P. L. 8, 275. ye hills and dales, ye *r.*, woods
  P. L. 9, 116. interchange of hill and valley *r.*
  P. L. 12, 176. to blood unshed the *r.* must be
  P. R. 3, 255. lay pleasant, from his side two *r.*
  P. R. 3, 257. champaign with less *r.* intervened
  P. R. 3, 334. overlay with bridges, *r.*, proud
  L'A. 76. shallow brooks and *r.* wide
  V. Ex. 91. *R.* arise whether thou be the son
**Rivulet.**—P. L. 9, 420. or by shady *r.*
**Road.**—P. L. 4, 976. in progress though the *r.*
  P. L. 5, 253. through all the empyreal *r.*

P. L. 7, 373. longitude through heaven's high *r.*
P. L. 7, 577. a broad and ample *r.* whose dust
P. L. 8, 162. he from the east his flaming *r.*
P. L. 10, 394. through darkness on your *r.*
P. L. 10, 672. turn reins from the equinoctial *r.*
P. R. 1, 322. so far from path or *r.* of men who
P. R. 4, 68. in various habits on the Appian *r.*
H. 22. see, how from far, upon the eastern *r.*
**Roam.**—P. L. 3, 476. here pilgrims *r.* that
P. L. 4, 538. waste o'er hill o'er dale his *r.*
P. R. 1, 502. beasts came forth the woods to *r.*
**Roamed**—P. L. 1, 521. *r.* the utmost isles
P. L. 9, 82. thus the orb he *r.* with narrow
**Roaming.**—P. L. 1, 382. *r.* to seek their prey
P. R. 2, 179. false titled sons of God *r.*
**Roar.**—P. L. 2, 267. whence deep thunders *r.*
P. L. 6, 586. *r.* embowelled with outrageous
P. L. 11, 713. throat of war had ceased to *r.*
P. R. 4, 428. her radiant finger stilled the *r.*
P. R. 4, 463. over whose heads they *r.* and seem
C. 87. knows to still the wild winds when they *r.*
C. 549. the wonted *r.* was up amidst the woods
L. 61. by the rout that made the hideous *r.*
Il P. 76. swinging slow with sullen *r.*
V. Ex. 86. devouring war shall never cease to *r.*
**Roared.**—P. L. 6, 871. confounded Chaos *r.*
**Rob.**—P. R. 3, 75. *r.* and spoil, burn, slaughter
C. 390. for who would *r.* a hermit of his weeds
**Robbed.**—C. 261. and in sweet madness *r.* it
**Robber.**—S. A. 1180. a revolter and a *r.*
S. A. 1188. then like a *r.* stripp'dst them of their
C. 485. some roving *r.* calling to his fellows
**Robe.**—P. L. 2, 543. felt the envenomed *r.*, and
P. L. 9, 1058. he covered but his *r.* uncovered
P. L. 10, 222. with his *r.* of righteousness
L'A. 126. in saffron *r.* with taper clear
Il P. 33, all in a *r.* of darkest grain
**Robed.**—L'A. 61. *r.* in flames and amber light
**Robes.**—P. R. 4, 64. return in *r.* of state
V. Ex. 21. those richest *r.* and gayest attire
**Robustious.**—S. A. 569. redundant locks *r.* to
**Rock.**—P. L. 1, 450. Adonis from his native *r.*
P. L. 2, 181. each on his *r.* transfixed, the sport
P. L. 2, 646. three iron three of adamantine *r.*
P. L. 2, 878. of massy iron or solid *r.* with ease
P. L. 4, 283. enclosed with shining *r.*
P. L. 4, 543. it was a *r.* of alabaster
P. L. 6, 364. though huge and in a *r.* of
P. L. 7, 300. nor withstood them *r.* or hill
P. L. 10, 313. pontifical a ridge of pendent *r.*
P. L. 11, 336. and all the earth not this *r.* only
P. L. 11, 494. what heart of *r.* could long
P. R. 4, 18. or surging waves against a solid *r.*
P. R. 4, 49. on the Tarpeian *r.* her citadel
P. R. 4, 533. as a *r.* of adamant and as a centre
S. A. 253. who then safe to the *r.* of Etham was
S. A. 1398. wert firmlier fastened than a *r.*
P. 43. mine eye hath found that sad sepulchral *r.*
**Rocking.**—Il P. 126. while *r.* winds are piping
**Rocks.**—P. L. 2, 285. as when hollow *r.* retain
P. L. 2, 540. rend up both *r.* and hills
P. L. 2, 621. *r.* caves, lakes, fens, bogs, dens
P. L. 2, 1018. betwixt the justling *r.*
P. L. 5, 759. diamond quarries hewn and *r.* of
P. L. 6, 63. though standing else as *r.* but
P. L. 6, 645. *r.* waters woods
P. L. 7, 35. where woods and *r.* had ears to
P. L. 7, 408. or under *r.* their food in joined
P. L. 9, 118. shores with forest crowned *r.* dens
P. L. 11, 832. and now the tops of hills as *r.*
P. R. 1, 194. and with dark shades and *r.*
P. R. 2, 228. *r.* whereon greatest men have
C. 518. rifted *r.* whose entrance leads to hell
C. 881. wherewith she sits on diamond *r.*
L'A. 8. under ebon shades and low-browed *r.*
S. 18, 8. rolled mother with infant down the *r.*
**Rocky.**—P. L. 4, 549. betwixt these *r.* pillars
P. L. 6, 254. and opposed the *r.* orb of tenfold
V. Ex. 97. or *r.* Avon or of sedgy Lea
**Rod.**—P. L. 1, 338. the potent *r.* of Amram's son

P. L. 5, 887. is now an iron *r.* to bruise and
P. L. 11, 133. reed of Hermes or his opiate *r.*
P. L. 12, 198. awed by the *r.* of Moses so to
P. L. 12, 211. Moses once more his potent *r.*
P. L. 12, 212. extends over the sea, the sea his *r.*
S. A. 549. touch ethereal of Heaven's fiery *r.*
C. 816. without his *r.* reversed and backward
S. 14, 7. but as faith pointed with her golden *r.*
**Rode.**—P. L. 4, 606. led the starry host *r.*
P. L. 6, 771. he on the wings of Cherub *r.*
P. L. 6, 840. helms and helmed heads he *r.*
P. L. 6, 888. he celebrated *r.* triumphant
P. L. 7, 219. uplifted in paternal glory *r.*
P. L. 7, 557. up he *r.* followed with acclamation
P. L. 9, 63. space of seven continued nights he *r.*
P. L. 11, 747. with beaked prow *r.* tilting o'er
P. R. 2, 17. who on fiery wheels *r.* up to heaven
P. R. 3, 36. and in triumph had *r.*
S. A. 1423. who from thy father's field *r.* up
**Rods.**—P. R. 4, 65. lictors and *r.* the ensigns
**Roll.**—P. L. 3, 23. not these eyes that *r.* in vain
P. L. 5, 578. where these heavens now *r.*
P. L. 6, 57. and smoke to *r.* in dusky wreaths
P. L. 8, 19. her numbered stars that seem to *r.*
P. L. 10, 666. thunder when to *r.* with terror
P. L. 11, 620. dress and troll the tongue and *r.*
P. R. 3, 187. hand all times and seasons *r.*
S. A. 290. of such examples add me to the *r.*
C. 77. to *r.* with pleasure in a sensual sty
C. 932. may thy billows *r.* ashore
**Rolled.**—P. L. 1, 223. and *r.* in billows
P. L. 3, 718. that *r.* orbicular and turned
P. L. 4, 593. incredible how swift had thither *r.*
P. L. 6, 594. by thousands angel on archangel *r.*
P. L. 6, 765. from about him fierce effusion *r.*
P. L. 6, 829. and the orbs of his fierce chariot *r.*
P. L. 6, 861. *r.* inward and a spacious gap
P. L. 6, 879. returning whence it *r.*
P. L. 7, 499. in all her glory shone and *r.* her
P. L. 9, 631. he leading swiftly *r.* in tangles
P. L. 10, 553. but on they *r.* in heaps and up
P. L. 11, 749. their pomp deep under water *r.*
S. 18, 7. that *r.* mother . . down the rocks
**Rolling.**—P. L. 1, 52. *r.* in the fiery gulf
P. L. 1, 324. cherub and seraph *r.* in the flood
P. L. 1, 671. belched fire and *r.* smoke
P. L. 2, 873. and towards the gate *r.* her bestial
P. L. 4, 16. which nigh the birth now *r.* boils
P. L. 4, 238. *r.* on orient pearl and sands of gold
P. L. 7, 298. watery throng wave *r.* after wave
P. L. 11, 460. see him die *r.* in dust and gore
P. R. 3, 86. scarce men *r.* in brutish vices
**Rolls.**—P. L. 2, 583. river of oblivion *r.* her
P. L. 3, 359. *r.* o'er Elysian flowers her amber
P. L. 12, 183. on the earth devouring where it *r.*
P. R. 4, 249. there Ilissus *r.* his whispering
**Roman**—P. R. 1, 217. Israel from the *R.* yoke
P. R. 3, 158. reduced a province under *R.* yoke
P. R. 3, 362. such enclosing enemies *R.*
P. R. 3, 368. Hyrcanus bound maugre the *R.*
**Romance.**—P. L. 1, 580. in fable or *r.*
**Romances.**—P. R. 3, 339. Albracca as *r.* tell
**Rome.**—P. L. 9, 510. Scipio the height of *R.*
P. L. 9, 671. Athens or free *R.* where eloquence
P. L. 11, 405. where *R.* was to sway the world
P. R. 3, 385. and *R.* or Cæsar need not fear
P. R. 4, 45. great and glorious *R.* Queen of the
P. R. 4, 80. all nations now to *R.* obedience
P. R. 4, 81. to *R.*'s great emperor
P. R. 4, 91. and from *R.* retired to Capreæ
P. R. 4, 360. all the oratory of Greece and *R.*
S. 17, 3. ne'er held the helm of *R.*
**Rood.**—P. L. 1, 196. lay floating many a *r.*
**Roof.**—P. L. 1, 717. the *r.* was fretted gold
P. L. 1, 726. the arched *r.* pendent by subtle
P. L. 2, 644. high reaching to the horrid *r.*
P. L. 4, 692. the *r.* of thickest covert was
P. L. 4, 772. the flowery *r.* showered roses
P. L. 5, 137. from under shady arborous *r.*
P. L. 5, 463. under whose lowly *r.* thou hast
P. L. 9, 1038. thick overhead with verdant *r.*

S. A. 1634. that to the arched *r.* gave main
S. A. 1651. the whole *r.* after them with burst of
A. 88. under the shady *r.* ot branching elm
Il P. 157. and love the high-embowed *r.*
H. 175. runs though the arched *r.*
D. F. I. 43. some star which from the ruined *r.*
**Roofed**—P. R. 2, 293. high *r.* and walks
**Roofs.**—P. R. 4, 58. inside both pillars and *r.*
**Room.**—P. L. 1, 779. in narrow *r.* throng
P. L. 2, 835. to supply perhaps our vacant *r.*
P. L. 3, 285. be thou in Adam's *r.* the head
P. L. 4, 207. in narrow *r.* nature's whole
P. L. 4, 359. into our *r.* of bliss thus high
P. L. 4, 383. there will be *r.* not like these
P. L. 7, 190. race to bring into their vacant *r.*
P. L. 7, 486. in small *r.* large heart enclosed
P. L. 8, 153. for such vast *r.* in nature
P. L. 9, 148. to advance into our *r.* a creature
P. L. 12, 507. but in their *r.*, as they forewarn
R. R. 1, 248. for in the inn was left no better *r.*
P. R. 3, 263. that here and there was *r.* for
Il P. 79, where glowing embers through the *r.*
H. 78. had given day her *r.*
U. C. I. 15. showed him his *r.* where he must lodge
V. Ex. 58. that to the next I may resign my *r.*
V. Ex. 62. come tripping to the *r.* where thou
**Roosts.**—S. A. 1693. assailant on the perched *r.*
**Root.**—P. L. 2, 383. race of mankind in one *r.*
P. L. 3, 288. so in thee as from a second *r.*
P. L. 5, 479. so from the *r.* springs lighter the
P. L. 6, 855. not to destroy but *r.* them out of
P. L. 9, 645. to the tree of prohibition *r.* of all
P. L. 9, 1105. the bended twigs take *r.*
P. L. 11, 834. and there take *r.* an island salt
S. A. 1032. of constancy no *r.* infixed
C. 629. amongst the rest a small unsightly *r.*
**Root-bound.**—C. 662. as Daphne was *r.-b.*
**Rooted.**—P. R. 4, 417. though *r.* deep as high
**Roots.**—P. L. 2, 544. though pain up by the *r.*
P. L. 10, 299. deep to the *r.* of hell the gathered
P. R. 1, 339. for we here live on tough *r.* and
**Rose.**—P. L. 1, 10. the Heavens and Earth *r.* out
P. L. 1, 546. with them *r.* a forest huge of
P. L. 1, 711. *r.* like an exhalation
P. L. 2, 108. on the other side up *r.* Belial in
P. L. 2, 301. with grave aspect he *r.* and in his
P. L. 2, 466. thus saying *r.* the monarch and
P. L. 2, 475. and at once with him they *r.*
P. L. 4, 229. *r.* a fresh fountain, and with
P. L. 4, 355. the stars that usher evening *r.*
P. L. 4, 548. still as it *r.* impossible to
P. L. 5, 48. I *r.* as at thy call but found thee
P. L. 6, 207. now storming fury *r.*
P. L. 6, 525. up *r.* the victor-angels and to
P. L. 6, 669. heaped upon confusion *r.*
P. L. 6, 746. he o'er his sceptre bowing *r.*
P. L. 7, 324. *r.* as in dance the stately trees
P. L. 7, 385. bright luminaries that set and *r.*
P. L. 7, 456. out of the ground up *r.* as from his
P. L. 7, 459. among the trees in pairs they *r.*
P. L. 7, 472. fleeced the flocks and bleating *r.*
P. L. 8, 44. *r.* and went forth among her fruits
P. L. 9, 73. till part *r.* up a fountain by the tree
P. L. 9, 74. in with the river sunk with it *r.*
P. L. 9, 1051. up they *r.* as from unrest
P. L. 9, 1059. *r.* the Danite strong Herculean
P. L. 10, 85. from his radiant seat he *r.* of high
P. L. 10, 329. while the sun in Aries *r.*
P. L. 11, 738. the south wind *r.* and with black
P. R. 1, 280. but as I *r.* out ot the laving stream
P. R. 2, 149. when from amidst them *r.* Belial
P. R. 2, 282. lightly from his grassy couch up *r.*
P. R. 4, 397. darkness now *r.* as day-light sunk
P. R. 4, 565. still *r.* receiving from his mother
C. 190. *r.* from the hindmost wheels of Phœbus'
C. 556. *r.* like a steam of rich distilled perfumes
L. 30. oft till the star that *r.* at evening bright
L. 192. at last he *r.* and twitched his mantle
**Rose** (*noun*).—P. L. 3, 43. bloom or summer's *r.*
P. L. 4, 256. all hue and without thorn the *r.*
P. L. 5, 349. with *r.* and odours from

P. L. 8, 517. and from their wings flung *r.*
C. 743. if you let slip time like a neglected *r.*
L. 45. as killing as the canker to the *r.*
S. 20, 8. clothe in fresh attire the lily and *r.*
**Roseate.**—P. L. 5, 646. and *r.* dews disposed
**Roses.**—P. L. 3, 364. impurpled with celestial *r.*
P. L. 4, 698. iris all hues, *r.* and jessamine
P. L. 4, 773. the flowery roof showered *r.*
P. L. 9, 218. while I in yonder spring of *r.*
P. L. 9, 426. so thick the *r.* blushing round
P. L. 9, 893. and all the faded *r.* shed
C. 998. beds of hyacinth and *r.*
A. 32. and ye the beathing *r.* of the wood
L'A. 22. and fresh-blown *r.* washed in dew
Hor. 2. courts thee on *r.* in some pleasant
**Rosy**—P. L. 5, 1. now morn her *r.* steps in
P. L. 6, 3. with *r.* hand unbarred the gates
P. L. 8, 619. celestial *r.* red love's proper hue
P. L. 11, 175. begins her *r.* progress smiling
C. 105. braid your locks with *r.* twine
C. 885. rise, rise and heave thy *r.* head
**Rosy-bosomed.**—C. 986. Graces and the *r.-b.*
**Rot.**—P. L. 12, 179. his cattle must of *r.*
L. 127. *r.* inwardly and foul contagion spread
U. C. II 3. so hung his destiny never to *r.*
**Rotherford.**—F. of C. 8. ye by mere A. S. and *R.*
**Rottenness.**—C. 598. pillared firmament is *r.*
**Rove.**—P. L. 4, 617. creatures all day long *r.*
P. L. 8. 188. but apt the mind or fancy is to *r.*
P. L. 11, 586. eyed them and let their eyes *r.*
P. R. 3, 79. nothing but ruin wheresoe'er they *r.*
S. 22, 13. from that mark how far they *r.* we see
M. 23. I have some naked thoughts that *r.*
**Rough.**—P. L. 2. 948. through strait *r.* dense
P. L. 5, 342. in coat *r.* or smooth rind or
P. L. 6, 108. on the *r.* edge of battle ere it joined
P. R. 1, 478. hard are the ways of truth and *r.*
C. 266. whom certain these *r.* shades did never
L. 34. *r.* Satyrs danced and Fauns
Hor. 7. seas *r.* with black winds
**Rougher.**—S. A. 1066. a *r.* tongue draws
**Roving**—P. L. 2, 614. thus *r.* on in confused
P. L. 3, 432. whose snowy ridge the *r.* Tartar
P. L. 8, 189. and of her *r.* is no end
P. L. 9, 575. till on a day *r.* the field I chanced
P. R. 1, 33. who *r.* still about the world at that
C. 60. *r.* the Celtic and Iberian fields
C. 485. some *r.* robber calling to his fellows
P. 22. these latest scenes confine my *r.* verse
**Round**—P. L. 1, 56. *r.* he throws his baleful
P. L. 1, 61. a dungeon horrible on all sides *r.*
P. L. 1, 285. massy, large, and *r.*
P. L. 1, 340. waved *r.* the coast
P. L. 1, 385. gods adored among the nations *r.*
P. L. 1, 617. and half enclose him *r.* with all
P. L. 1, 666. far *r.* illumined hell
P. L. 1, 713. where pilasters *r.* were set
P. L. 2, 266. the majesty of darkness *r.* covers
P. L. 2, 413. stations thick of angels watching *r.*
P. L. 2, 435. us *r.* ninefold, and gates of burning
P. L. 2, 511. him *r.* a globe of fiery
P. L. 2, 602. infixed and frozen *r.*
P. L. 2, 653. about her middle *r.* a cry
P. L. 2, 801. with conscious terrors vex me *r.*
P. L. 2, 832. vast and *r.* a place of bliss in the
P. L. 2, 1015. on all sides *r.* environed
P. L. 2, 1048. undetermined square or *r.*
P. L. 3, 379. a cloud drawn *r.* about thee like
P. L. 3, 419. the firm opacous globe of this *r.*
P. L. 3, 426. of Chaos blustering *r.* inclement
P. L. 3, 555. *r.* he surveys, and well might
P. L. 3, 618. whence no way *r.* shadow from
P. L. 3, 661. to visit oft this new creation *r.*
P. L. 3, 728. and her monthly *r.* still ending
P. L. 4, 21. within him hell he brings and *r.*
P. L. 4, 145. his nether empire neighbouring *r.*
P. L. 4, 302. *r.* from his parted forelock manly
P. L. 4, 401. about them *r.* a lion now he
P. L. 4, 528. narrow search I must walk *r.*
P. L. 4, 661. those have their course to finish *r.*
P. L. 4, 979. and began to hem him *r.*

P. L. 4, 1000. *r.* earth with balanced air
P. L. 5, 281. and *r.* skirted his loins
P. L. 5, 392. and mossy seat had *r.*
P. L. 5, 419. whence in her visage *r.* those
P. L. 5, 876. encompassed *r.* with foes thus
P. L. 6, 6. light and darkness in perpetual *r.*
P. L. 6, 412. placed in guard their watches *r.*
P. L. 6, 484. hollow engines long and *r.*
P. L. 6, 529. from the dawning hills looked *r.*
P. L. 7, 27. with dangers compassed *r.* and
P. L. 7, 90. embracing *r.* this florid earth
P. L. 7, 229. *r.* the vast profundity obscure
P. L. 7, 267. uttermost convex of this great *r.*
P. L. 7, 371. the horizon *r.* invested with
P. L. 8, 23. merely to officiate light *r.* this
P. L. 8, 261. about me *r.* I saw hill dale and
P. L. 8, 318. above or *r.* about thee or beneath
P. L. 9, 52. had veiled the horizon *r.*
P. L. 9, 103. terrestrial heaven danced *r.*
P. L. 9, 114. could I have walked thee *r.*
P. L. 9, 183. in labyrinth ·of many a *r.*
P. L. 9, 216. whether to wind the woodbine *r.*
P. L. 9, 426. so thick the roses blushing *r.*
P. L. 9, 482. her husband (for I view far *r.*)
P. L. 9, 591. *r.* the tree all other beasts that saw
P. L. 9, 636. and the cold environs *r.*
P. L. 9, 1096. may cover *r.* those middle parts
P. L. 10, 318. the outside bare of this *r.* world
P. L. 10, 439. careful watch *r.* their metropolis
P. L. 10, 448. he sat and *r.* about him saw
P. L. 11, 352. still compassing thee *r.*
P. L. 11, 381. nor wider looking *r.*
P. L. 11, 731. smeared *r.* with pitch and in
P. L. 11, 824. the ark be lodged and sheltered *r.*
P. L. 12, 593. signal of remove waves fiercely *r.*
P. R. 1, 22. flocked with awe the regions *r.*
P. R. 1, 194. dark shades and rocks environed *r.*
P. R. 1, 295. and looking *r.* on every side
P. R. 1, 365. I enjoy large liberty to *r.* this globe
P. R. 2, 286. to ken the prospect *r.*
P. R. 2, 297. he viewed it *r.* when suddenly
P. R. 3, 418. all the idolatries of heathen *r.*
P. R. 4, 422. and hellish furies *r.* environed
P. R. 4, 481. that closed thee *r.* so many
S. A. 194. how many evils have inclosed me *r.*
S. A. 257. the harass of their land beset me *r.*
S. A. 451. high among the heathen *r.*
S.A. 846. what sieges girt me *r.* ere I consented
S. A. 1430. great among the heathen *r.*
S. A. 1655. only of this but each Philistian city *r.*
S. A. 1734. plant it *r.* with shade of laurel ever
C. 114. lead in swift *r.* the months and years
C. 144. in a light fantastic *r.*
A. 15. in circle *r.* her shining throne
A. 54. evening gray doth rise I fetch my *r.*
L'A. 70. whilst the landscape *r.* it measures
L'A. 93. when the merry bells ring *r.*
Il P. 48. aye *r.* about Jove's altar sing
H. 102. beneath the hollow *r.*
H. 192. in urns and altars *r.*
M. 31. as may make thee search thy coffers *r.*
S. A. 1497. garrisoned *r.* about him like a camp
V. Ex. 63. and sweetly singing *r.* about thy bed
**Rounded.**—P. L. 10, 684. their sight had *r.*
**Rounding.**—P. L. 4. 685. or nightly *r.* walk
**Rounds.**—P. L. 8, 125. about him various *r.*
**Rouse.**—P. L. 1, 334. *r.* and bestir themselves
P. L. 3, 329. such a peal shall *r.* their sleep
C. 318. lark from her thatched pallet *r.*
L'A. 54. cheerly *r.* the slumbering morn
**Roused.**— P. L. 1, 377. *r.* from the slumber
P. L. 2, 287. which all night long had *r.* the sea
S. A. 1690. his fiery virtue *r.*
**Rousing.**— S. A. 1382. I begin to feel some *r.*
**Rout.**—P. L. 1, 747. he with this rebellious *r.*
P. L. 2, 770. to our part loss and *r.* through all
P. L. 2, 995. *r.* on *r.* confusion worse confounded
P. L. 4, 3. when the dragon put to second *r.*
P. L. 6, 387. deformed *r.* entered
P. L. 6, 598. dissipation followed and forced *r.*
P. L. 6, 873. so huge a *r.* incumbered him with

P. L. 7, 34. of that vile *r.* that tore the Thracian
P. L. 10, 534. all yet left of that revolted *r.*
P. R. 2, 218. and put to *r.* all her array
S. A. 443. by the idolatrous *r.* amidst their wine
S. A. 674. nor do I name of men the common *r.*
C. 533. he and his monstrous *r.* are heard to
L. 61. by the *r.* that made the hideous roar
**Row.**—P. L. 1, 709. to many a *r.* of pipes
P. L. 1, 727. many a *r.* of starry lamps
P. L. 4, 146. a circling *r.* of goodliest trees
P. L. 5, 212. dews and flowers where any *r.*
P. L. 6, 572. a triple mounted *r.* of pillars laid
P. L. 6, 604 stood ranked of Seraphim another *r.*
P. L. 6, 650. those cursed engines triple *r.*
P. L. 9, 627. beyond a *r.* of myrtles on a flat
H. 87. sat simply chatting in a rustic *r.*
S. M. 10. the bright Seraphim in burning *r.*
**Rows.**—P. L. 7, 439. wings mantling proudly *r.*
**Royal.**—P. L. 1, 677. fore-run the *r.* camp
P. L. 2, 1. high on a throne of *r.* state which far
P. L. 4, 211. Auran eastward to the *r.* towers
P. L. 5, 756. Satan to his *r.* seat high on a hill
P. L. 12, 325. that of the *r.* stock of David
P. R. 3, 373. in David's *r.* seat his true
S. 21, 1. Cyriack whose grandsire on the *r.* bench
**Royalties.**—P. L. 2, 451. do I assume these *r.*
**Royal-towered.**—V. Ex. 100. or *r.-t.* Thame
**Rubbed.**—P. L. 1, 774. new *r.* with balm
**Rubied.**—P. L. 5, 633. and *r.* nectar flows
C. 915. thrice upon thy *r.* lip
**Rubric.**—P. R. 4, 393. in the starry *r.* set
**Ruby.**—P. L. 3, 597. or chrysolite *r.* or topaz
S. A. 543. the dancing *r.* sparkling out-poured
**Ruddy.**—P. L. 2, 889. smoke and *r.* flame
P. L. 9, 578. fairest colours mixed *r.* and gold
**Rude.**—P. L. 9, 391. as art yet *r.* guiltless of fire
P. L. 9, 544. beholders *r.* and shallow to discern
P. L. 10, 1074. justling or pushed with winds *r.*
C. 352. from the chill dew among *r.* burs
L. 4. and with forced fingers *r.*
Il P. 136. where the *r.* axe with heaved stroke
S. 1, 9. now timely sing ere the *r.* bird of hate
S. 16, 2. not of war only but detractions *r.*
H. 31. all meanly wrapt in the *r.* manger lies
S. A. 1567. lest evil tidings with too *r.* irruption
**Rudeness.**—C. 178. to meet the *r.* and swilled
**Rudiments.**—P. R. 1, 157. first lay down the *r.*
P. R. 3, 245. those *r.* and see before thine eyes
**Rue.**—P. L. 1, 134. I see and *r.* the dire event
P. L. 9, 1180. but I *r.* that error now which is
P. L. 11, 414. purged with euphrasy and *r.*
P. R. 4, 181. blasphemous which expect to *r.*
**Rueful.**—P. L. 2, 580. loud heard on the *r.*
P. L. 2, 780. prodigious motion felt and *r.*
S. A. 1553. with *r.* cry yet what it was we hear
**Rues.**—P. L. 4, 72. what it now so justly *r.*
P. R. 4, 624. in all her gates Abaddon *r.* thy
**Ruffled.**—S. A. 1138. wild boars or *r.* porcupines
C. 380. were all to *r.* and sometimes impaired
**Rugged.**—C. 354. or 'gainst the *r.* bark of some
L. 93. and questioned every gust of *r.* wings
Il P. 58. smoothing the *r.* brow of night
S. 11, 10. those *r.* names to our like mouths grow
**Rugged'st.**—P. R. 2, 164. smooth the *r.*
**Ruin.**—P. L. 1, 46. hideous *r.* and combustion
P. L. 1, 91. now misery hath joined in equal *r.*
P. L. 2, 305. yet shone majestic though in *r.*
P. L. 2, 590. and *r.* seems of ancient pile
P. L. 2, 995. *r.* upon *r.* rout on rout.
P. L. 2, 1009. havoc and spoil, and *r.* are
P. L. 3, 258. while by thee raised I *r.* all my
P. L. 4, 522. laid whereon to build their *r.*
P. L. 5, 228. in them at once to *r.* all mankind
P. L. 5, 567. the *r.* of so many glorious once
P. L. 6, 193. could his shield such *r.* intercept
P. L. 6, 456. from which evil *r.* must needs
P. L. 6, 519. and their balls of missive *r.*
P. L. 6, 670. had gone to rack with *r.*
P. L. 6, 797. or to fall in universal *r.* last
P. L. 6, 874. rout incumbered him with *r.*
P. L. 9, 275. enemy we have who seeks our *r.*

P. L. 9, 493. the way which to her *r.* now I
P. R. 1, 102. to find out and *r.* Adam
P. R. 1, 415. a spectacle of *r.* or of scorn
P. R. 3, 79. nothing but *r.* wheresoe'er they
P. R. 4, 413. water with fire in *r.* reconciled
P. R. 4, 579. *r.* and desperation and dismay
S. A. 1043. and shameful deeds which *r.* ends
S. A. 1267. draw their own *r.* who attempt the
S. A. 1514. *r.* destruction at the utmost point
S. A. 1515. of *r.* indeed methought I heard the
S. A. 1684. their own *r.* on themselves to invite
S. 8, 14. the Athenian walls from *r.* bare
**Ruined.**—P. L. 1, 593. less than arch-angel *r.*
P. L. 9, 906. and me with thee hath *r.* for
P. L. 9, 950. me first he *r.* now mankind
D. F. I. 43. some star which from the *r.* roof
**Ruining.**—P. L. 6, 868. hell saw heaven *r.*
**Ruinous.**—P. L. 2, 921. noises loud and *r.* to
P. L. 6, 216. *r.* assault and inextinguishable
P. R. 4, 436. after a night of storm so *r.*
**Ruins.**—P. R. 4. 363. what *r.* kingdoms and
**Rule.**—P. L. 1, 736. to such power and gave to *r.*
P. L. 2, 327. and with iron sceptre *r.* us here
P. L. 4, 301. eye sublime declared absolute *r.*
P. L. 4, 429. so many signs of power and *r.*
P. L. 5, 297. wild above *r.* or art enormous
P. L. 7, 347. the greater to have *r.* by day
P. L. 7, 350. *r.* the day in their vicissitude and *r.*
P. L. 7, 520. and let them *r.* over the fish and
P. L. 7, 628. and in reward to *r.* over his works
P. L. 8, 375. find pastime and bear *r.* thy
P. L. 9, 1184. overtrusting lets her will *r.*
P. L. 10, 155. unseemly to bear *r.* which was
P. L. 10, 196. he over thee shall *r.*
P. L. 10, 493. over man to *r.* as over all
P. L. 10, 582. had first the *r.* of high Olympus
P. L. 11, 339. he gave thee to possess and *r.*
P. L. 11, 531. observe the *r.* of not too much
P. L. 12, 24. and tribes under paternal *r.*
P. L. 12, 226. to *r.* by laws ordained
P. L. 12, 581. and all the *r.* one empire only
P. R. 2, 469. who attains not, ill aspires to *r.*
P. R. 4, 619. shalt not long *r.* in the clouds
S. A. 56. not made to *r.* but to subserve where
C. 21. imperial *r.* of all the sea-girt isles
C. 340. thy long-levelled *r.* of streaming light
**Ruled.**—P. L. 1, 516. *r.* the middle air their
P. L. 3, 711. and wild uproar stood *r.*
P. L. 6, 848. one spirit in them *r.* and every
P. L. 9, 1127. for understanding *r.* not
P. L. 10, 493. as over all he should have *r.*
P. L. 10, 516. a greater power now *r.* him
P. R. 1, 49. universe we have possessed and *r.*
P. R. 3, 159. nor is always *r.* with temperate
**Rules.**—P. L. 2, 351. more of Him who *r.* above
P. L. 2, 907. to whom these most adhere he *r.*
P. L. 6, 177. when he who *r.* is worthiest
P. L. 11, 523. pervert pure nature's healthful *r*
P. R. 1, 236. father is the eternal king who *r.*
P. R. 2, 466. and *r.* passions desires and fears
P. R. 4, 283. these *r.* will render thee a king
P. R. 4, 358. the solid *r.* of civil government
C.759.obtruding false *r.* pranked in reason's garb
C. 876. and her son that *r.* the strands
S. 12, 1. by the known *r.* of ancient liberty
**Rulest.**—S. A. 671. not evenly as thou *r.*
**Ruling.**—P. R. 4, 230. *r.* them by persuasion
**Ruminating.**—P. L. 4, 352. or bedward *r.*
**Rumour.**—P. L. 2, 965. *R.* next and Chance
L. 80. nor in broad *r.* lies
**Rumoured.**—P. L. 4, 817. to store against a *r.*
S. A. 1600, when all abroad was *r.* that this day
**Rumours.**—S. 15, 4. and *r.* loud that daunt
**Run.**—P. L. 3, 607. and rivers *r.* potable gold
P. L. 3, 651. that *r.* through all the heavens
P. L. 5, 181. that in quaternion *r.* perpetual
P. L. 6, 335. on all sides to his aid was *r.*
P. L. 7, 98. yet wants to *r.* much of his race
P. L. 7, 372. jocund to *r.* his longitude through
P. L. 8, 88. nor heaven such journeys *r.*
P.L.12, 505. ministry performed and race well *r.*

P. R. 1, 441. and *r.* not sooner to his fatal snare
S. A. 597. my race of glory *r.* and race of shame
S. A. 1237. go baffled coward lest I *r.* upon thee
S. A. 1520. what shall we do stay here or *r.*
S. A. 1522. we unawares *r.* into danger's mouth
S. A. 1541. whither shall I *r.* or which way fly
C. 147. *r.* to your shrouds within these brakes
C. 363. *r.* to meet what he would most avoid
C. 1013. I can fly or I can *r.*
S. 20,·5. time will *r.* on smoother
H. 24. O *r.* prevent them with thy humble ode
M. W. 23. once had the early matrons *r.*
H. 135. time will *r.* back and fetch the age
T. 1. fly envious Time till thou *r.* out thy race
**Rung.**—P. L. 2, 655. and *r.* a hideous peal yet
P. L. 2, 723. whereof all hell had *r.*
P. L. 3, 347. heaven *r.* with jubilee and loud
P. L. 6, 204. faithful armies *r.* Hosanna
P. L. 7, 562. and all the constellations *r.*
P. L. 7, 633. so sung they and the empyrean *r.*
P. L. 9, 737. in her ears the sound yet *r.* of his
**Runners.**—S.A.1324.artists,wrestlers,riders,*r.*
**Runneth.**—V. Ex. 95. or sullen Mole, that *r.*
**Running.**—P. L. 7, 397. lakes and *r.* streams
S. A. 1521. keep together here lest *r.* thither
L'A. 142. the melting voice through mazes *r.*
**Runs.**—P. L. 4, 234. *r.* diverse wandering many
H. 175. *r.* through the arched roof
**Rupture.**—P. L. 7, 419. with kindly *r.*
**Rural.**—P. L. 4, 134. as with a *r.* mound
P. L. 4, 247. thus was this place a happy *r.*
P. L. 5, 211. on to their morning's *r.* work
P. L. 9, 4. with him partake *r.* repast
P. L. 9, 451. dairy each *r.* sight each *r.* sound
P. L. 9, 841. and her *r.* labours crown
P. L. 11, 639. towns and *r.* works between
C. 267. the goddess that in *r.* shrine
C. 547. to meditate my *r.* minstrelsy
C. 952. with jigs and *r.* dance resort
A. 94. such a *r.* queen
L. 32. meanwhile the *r.* ditties were not mute
**Rush.**—P. L. 2, 534. and armies *r.* to battle
S. A. 21. but *r.* upon me thronging and present
C. 651. *r.* on him break his glass and shed the
P. L. 10, 704. forth *r.* the Levant and
**Rush-candle.**—C. 338. though a *r.-c.* from the
**Rushed.**—P. L. 2, 726. hideous outcry *r.*
P. L. 6, 215. together *r.* both battles main
P. L. 6, 600. if on they *r.* repulse repeated
P. L. 6, 749. forth *r.* with whirlwind sound
P. L. 10, 456. forth *r.* in haste the great
P. L. 11, 743. down *r.* the rain impetuous and
P. R. 4, 414. but *r.* abroad from the four
S. A. 1435. that spirit that first *r.* on thee
**Rushing.**—P. L. 4, 407. whence *r.* he might
P. L. 6, 97. and *r.* sound of onset ended soon
P. L. 6, 313. two planets *r.* from aspect malign
P. 36. see the chariot and those *r.* wheels
**Rushy-fringed.**—C. 890. by the *r.-f.* bank
**Russet.**—L'A. 71. *r.* lawns and fallows gray
**Russian.**—P. L. 10, 431. from his *R.* foe
P. L. 11, 394. or where the *R.* Ksar in Mosco
**Rustic.**—P. L. 11, 433. *r.* of grassy
P. R. 2, 299. not *r.* as before but
C. 849. carol her goodness loud in *r.* lays
H. 87. sat simply chatting in a *r.* row
**Rustling.**—P. L. 1, 768. the hiss of *r.* wings
P. L. 9, 519. the sound of *r.*
Il P. 129. ending on the *r.* leaves
**Ruth.**—L. 163. angel now and melt with *R.*
S. 9, 5. the better part with Mary and with *R.*
S. 9, 8. no anger find in thee but pity and *r.*
**Sabæan.**—P. L. 4, 162. winds blow *S.* odours
**Sabbath.**—P. L. 7, 634. thus was *S.* kept
P. L. 8, 246. up to the coasts of light ere *S.*
**Sabbath-day.**—S. A. 149. no journey of a *s.-d.*
**Sable.**—C. 221. was I deceived or did a *s.* cloud
L. 22. and bid fair peace be to my *s.* shroud
Il. P. 35. and *s.* stole of cypress lawn
**Sable-stoled.**—H. 220. the *s.-s.* sorcerers bear

**Sable-vested.**—P. L. 2, 962. sat *s.-v.* night
**Sabrina.**— C. 826. *S.* is her name a virgin pure
C. 859. *S.* fair listen where thou art sitting
**Sacred.**—P. L. 1, 454. passions in the *s.* porch
P. L. 2, 1034. but now at last the *s.* influence
P. L. 3, 29. smit with the love of *s.* song
P. L. 3,148. innumerable sound of hymns and *s.*
P. L. 3, 208. but to destructions *s.* and devote
P. L. 3, 369. they introduce their *s.* song
P. L. 4, 706. in shadier bower more *s.*
P. L. 4, 951. 0 name 0 *s.* name of faithfulness
P. L. 5, 557. worthy of *s.* silence to be heard
P. L. 5, 619. in song and dance about the *s.* hill
P. L. 6, 25. on to the *s.* hill they led him high
P. L. 6, 379. cancelled from heaven and *s.*
P. L. 6, 709. by *s.* unction thy deserved right
P. L. 6, 748. and the third *s.* morn began
P. L. 7, 331. and love to haunt her *s.* shades
P. L. 9, 107. all their precious beams of *s.*
P. L. 9, 192. now when as *s.* light began
P. L. 9, 679. 0 *s.* wise and wisdom-giving plant
P. L. 9, 904. how to violate the *s.* fruit
P. L. 9, 924. only coveting to eye that *s.* fruit *s.*
P. L. 11,134. to resalute the world with *s.* light
P. L. 12, 21. large wine-offerings poured and *s.*
P. L. 12, 341. with all his *s.* things a scorn
P. L. 12,509. who all the *s.* mysteries of heaven
P. R. 1, 231. to what height is *s.* virtue and true
P. R. 1, 488. to tread his *s.* courts and minister
S. A. 363. as of a plant select and *s.* glorious
S. A. 428. to violate the *s.* trust of silence
S. A.518. home to thy country and his *s.* house
S. A. 1001. to such a viper his most *s.* trust
C. 262. but such a *s.* and home-felt delight
C. 425. through the *s.* rays of chastity
C. 795. to such a flame of *s.* vehemence
A. 83. approach and kiss her *s.* vesture's hem
L. 15. begin then sisters of the *s.* well
L. 102. that sunk so low that *s.* head of thine
H. 15. say heavenly muse shall not thy *s.* vein
H. 217. within his *s.* chest
Hor. 14. the *s.* wall declares to have hung
**Sacrifice.**—P. L. 1, 393. blood of human *s.*
P. L. 3, 269. as a *s.* glad to be offered
P. L. 12,232. part religious rites of *s.* informing
P. R. 1, 457. and thou no more with pomp or *s.*
P. R. 3,83. worshipped with temple priest and *s.*
P. R. 3, 116. above all *s.* or hallowed gift
S. A. 436. great pomp and *s.* and praises loud
S. A. 1612. the feast and noon grew high and *s.*
**Sacrificed.**—P. L. 11, 451. who well had *s.*
**Sacrifices.**—S. A. 1312. with *s.* triumph pomp
**Sacrificing.**—P. L. 11, 438. then *s.* laid
P. L. 12, 20. oft *s.* bullock, lamb or kid
**Sacrilegious.**—P. R. 3, 140. *s.* to himself
S. A. 833. incestuous *s.* but may plead it
**Sad.**—P. L. 1, 135. that with *s.* overthrow
P. L. 2, 146. be our cure to be no more *s.* cure
P. L. 2, 524. as inclination or *s.* choice leads
P. L. 2, 578. *s.* Acheron of sorrow black and
P. L. 2, 820. and joys then sweet now *s.* to
P. L. 2, 872. the fatal key *s.* instrument of all
P. L. 3, 525. or aggravate his *s.* exclusion from
P. L. 4, 28. his grieved look he fixes *s.*
P. L. 4, 357. length failed speech recovered *s.*
P. L. 4, 716. and 0 too like in *s.* event
P. L. 5, 94. and thus Adam answered *s.*
P. L. 5, 116. addition strange yet be not *s.*
P. L. 5, 564. 0 prime of men *s.* task and hard
P. L. 6, 541. in his face I see *s.* resolution and
P. L. 9, 13. *s.* task yet argument not less
P. L. 9,917. as one from *s.* dismay recomforted
P. L. 9,1002. some *s.* drops wept at completing
P. L. 10, 18. guards ascended mute and *s.*
P. L. 10, 159. to whom *s.* Eve with shame
P. L. 10, 343. sat in their *s.* discourse and
P. L. 10, 719. to disburden sought with *s.*
P. L. 10, 863. whom thus afflicted when *s.* Eve
P. L. 10, 967. Adam by *s.* experiment I know
P. L. 10, 977. though sharp and *s.* yet
P. L. 11, 40. his days numbered though *s.*

P. L. 11, 109. lest they faint at the *s.* sentence
P. L. 11, 162. thus Eve with *s.* demeanour
P. L. 11, 272. hope to spend quiet though *s.*
P. L. 11,478. a place before his eyes appeared *s.*
P. L. 11, 675. guide lamenting turned full *s.*
P. L. 11, 755. of all thy offspring end so *s.*
P. L. 11, 868. the heart of Adam erst so *s.*
P. L. 12, 603. though *s.* with cause for evils
P. L. 12, 609. and thus with words not *s.* she
P. R. 1, 43, with looks aghast and *s.* he thus
P. R. 1, 109. with deep dismay at these *s.*
S.A.1551. s**à** in the *s.* event too much concerned
S. A. 1560. *s.* but thou know'st to Israelites not
C. 189. like a *s.* votarist in palmer's weed
C. 235. nightly to thee her *s.* song mourneth
C. 355. unpillowed head fraught with *s.* fears
L. 6. bitter constraint and *s.* occasion dear
L. 148. every flower that *s.* embroidery wears
Il P. 43. with a *s.* leaden downward cast
Il P. 103. but 0 *s.* virgin that thy power
S. 8, 13. the repeated air of *s.* Electra's poet
S. 10, 5. the sad breaking of that Parliament
P. 43. mine eye hath found that *s.* ... rock
Cir. 6. mourn, and if *s.* share with us to bear
M. W. 45. which the *s.* morn had let fall
V. Ex. 50. while *s.* Ulysses' soul and all the rest
**Saddest.**—S. A. 1560. to Israelites not *s.*
Il P. 57. in her sweetest *s.* plight
P. 9. and set my harp to notes of *s.* woe ·
**Sadly.**—C. 509. to tell thee *s.* shepherd without
C. 1002. *s.* sits the Assyrian queen
**Sadness.**—P. L. 4, 156. to drive all *s.* but
P. L. 10, 23. dim *s.* did not spare that time
**Safe.**—P. L. 1, 310. beheld from the *s.* shore
P. L. 2, 23. established in a *s.* unenvied throne
P. L. 2, 317. this place our dungeon, not our *s.*
P. L. 2, 411. or what evasion bear him *s.*
P. L. 3, 21. thee I revisit *s.* and feel thy sovran
P. L. 3, 197. and to the end persisting *s.* arrive
P. L. 5, 683. in this place to utter is not *s.*
P. L. 7, 24. more *s.* I sing with mortal voice
P. L. 9, 815. our great forbidder *s.* with, all
P. L. 10, 316. from his wing and landed *s.*
P. L. 10, 875. when least was *s.* rejected my
P. L. 11, 371. ascend I follow thee *s.* guide
P. L. 11, 814. how much more *s.* and full
P. L. 12, 215. the race elect *s.* towards Canaan
P. L. 12, 314. *s.* to eternal Paradise of rest
S. A.253. who then *s.* to the rock of Etham was
S. A. 802. against thee but *s.* custody and hold
C.81. I shoot from heaven to give him *s.* convoy
C. 320. where you may be *s.* till farther quest
C. 400. and tell me it is *s.* as bid me hope
C. 693. was this the cottage and the *s.* abode
C. 389. and sits as *s.* as in a senate house
**Safely.**—P. R. 4, 555. down *s.* if Son of God
C. 585. yes and keep it still; lean on it *s.*
**Safer.**—P. L. 10, 1029. seek some *s.* resolution
**Safest.**—P. L. 9, 268. or dishonour lurks *s.*
P. L. 11, 365. so shalt thou lead *s.* thy life
S. A. 135. but *s.* he who stood aloof
**Safety.**—P. L. 2, 280. how in *s.* best we may
P. L. 2, 481. that for the general *s.* he despised
P. L. 7, 15. with like *s.* guided down
P. R. 3, 349. secure on no slight grounds thy *s.*
S. A. 681. people's *s.* which in part they effect
S. A. 780. wherein consisted all thy .. *s.*
S. A. 799. thy key of strength and *s.*
S. A. 1002. trust of secrecy my *s.* and my life
S. A.1128. boast again in *s.* what thou wouldst
S. A.1132. in battle worn their ornament and *s.*
**Saffron.**—L'A. 126. in *s.* robe with taper clear
**Sagacious.**—P. L. 10, 281. *s.* of his quarry
**Sage.**—P. L. 2, 305. *s.* he stood with Atlantean
P. R. 4, 272. to *s.* philosophy next lend thine
C.515. what the *s.* poets taught by the heavenly
C. 786, the *s.* and serious doctrine of virginity
L. 96. *s.* Hippotades their answer brings
Il P. 11. but hail thou goddess *s.* and holy
Il P. 117. in *s.* and solemn tunes have sung
S. 17, 1. Vane .... in *s.* counsel old

D.F.I. 54. crowned Matron, s. white-robed Truth
**Sagely.**—P. R. 4, 285. to whom our Saviour s.
**Sager.**—L'A. 17. or whether as some s. sing
**Sages.**—P. L. 12, 362. and guides the eastern s.
P. R. 4, 251. then view the schools of ancient s.
H. 5. for so the holy s. once did sing
**Said.**—P. L. 1, 243. s. then the lost archangel
P. L. 2, 417. this s. he sat, and expectation held
P. L. 3, 736. s. he turned and Satan bowing low
P. L. 4, 443. what thou hast s. is just and right
P. L. 4, 736. this s. unanimous and other rites
P. L. 4, 827. know ye not then s. Satan filled
P. L. 4, 851. if I must contend s. he best
P. L. 4, 854. thy fear s. Zephon bold will save
P. L. 5, 37. it s. why sleep'st thou Eve?
P. L. 5, 58. O fair plant s. he with fruit
P. L. 5, 64. s. he paused not but with venturous
P. L. 5, 224. Raphael s. he thou hear'st what
P. L. 5, 361. thus s. native of heaven for other
P. L. 5, 718. and smiling to his only son thus s.
P. L. 5, 872. he s. and as the sound of waters
P. L. 6, 719. he s. and on his son with rays
P. L. 6, 746. so s. o'er his sceptre bowing rose
P. L. 7, 217. s. then the omnific word your
P. L. 7, 230. and s. thus far extend thus far thy
P. L. 7, 243. let there be light s. God and
P. L. 7, 261. again God s. let there be firmament
P. L. 7, 282. with genial moisture when God s.
P. L. 7, 309. and s. let the earth put forth the
P. L. 7, 313. he scarce had s. when the bare
P. L. 7, 387. and God s. let the waters generate
P. L. 7, 450. when God s. let the earth bring
P. L. 7, 524. this s. he formed thee Adam thee
P. L. 7, 530. then blessed mankind and s. be
P. L. 8, 273. s. I fair light and thou enlightened
P. L. 8, 296. methought of shape divine and s.
P. L. 8, 317. s. mildly author of all this thou
P. L. 9, 631. lead then s. Eve he leading
P. L. 9, 656. indeed hath God then s. that of
P. L. 9, 662. God hath s. ye shall not eat
P. L. 9, 664. she scarce had s. though brief
P. L. 9, 917. so having s. as one from sad
P. L. 9, 1034. so s. he and forbore not glance
P. L. 10, 157. so having s. he thus to Eve in
P. L. 10, 504. so having s. awhile he stood
P. L. 10, 610. this s. they both betook them
P. L. 10, 855. why comes not death s. he with
P. L. 11, 526. I yield it just s. Adam and
P. L. 11, 530. there is s. Michael if thou well
P. L. 11, 635. s. the angel, who should better
P. L. 12, 485. be sure they will s. the angel
P. R. 1, 229. inly rejoiced and s. to me apart
P. R. 2, 244. first and to himself thus s.
P. R. 2, 323. s. the subtle fiend
P. R. 3, 150. of glory as thou wilt s. he so deem
P. R. 3, 183. is for all things truth hath s.
P. R. 4, 322. wise men have s. are wearisome
P. R. 4, 450. in a careless mood thus to him s.
P. R. 4, 561. He s, and stood but Satan
C. 185. stepped as they s. to the next thicket side
C. 632. but in another country as he s.
C. 780. shall I go on or have I s. enow
C. 852. and as the old swain s. she can unlock
L. 129. daily devours apace and nothing s.
L'A. 103. she was pinched and pulled she s.
H. 117. such music as 'tis s.
U. C. I. 17. if any ask for him it shall be s.
V. Ex. 73. your son, s. she, shall subject be
**Saidst.**—P. L. 6, 187. thou s. from flight
P. L. 9, 933. lives as thou s. and gains to live
P. L. 9, 1157. into such danger as thou s.
P. R. 2, 379. s. thou not that to all things I
**Sail.**—P. L. 2, 942. him now both oar and s.
P. L. 4, 159. as when to them who s. beyond
P. L. 6, 534. back with speediest s.
P. L. 9, 515. as oft so steers and shifts her s.
P. R. 4, 582. globe of angels on full s. of
**Sail-broad.**—P. L. 2, 927. at last his s.-b.
**Sailing.**—P. L. 2, 638. close s. from Bengala or
P. L. 3, 520. s. arrived wafted by angels
S. A. 713. comes this way s. like a stately ship

**Sails.**—P. L. 3, 439. drive with s. and wind
P. L. 5, 268. s. between worlds and worlds
S. A. 718. s. filled and streamers waving
**Saint.**—P. L. 3, 484. now S. Peter at heaven's
P. L. 5, 247. nor delayed the winged s. after
P. L. 12, 200. wondrous power God to his s.
S. 23, 1. methought I saw my late espoused s.
M. W. 61. thou bright s. high sitst in glory
M. W. 71. there with thee new welcome s.
**Sainted.**—C. 11. enthroned gods on s. seats
**Saintly.**—P. L. 4, 122. falsehood under s.
P. R. 3, 93. him whom thy wrongs with s.
C. 453. so dear to heaven is s. chastity
Il P. 13. whose s. visage is too bright
H. 42. the s. veil of maiden white to throw
S. M. 9. with s. shout and solemn Jubilee
**Saints.**—P. L. 3, 330. then all thy s. assembled
P. L. 3, 461. more likely habitants translated s.
P. L. 4, 762. present or past as s. and patriarchs
P. L. 6, 47. lead forth my armed s.
P. L. 6, 398. far otherwise the inviolable s.
P. L. 6, 742. then shall thy s. unmixed
P. L. 6, 767. with ten thousand, thousand s.
P. L. 6, 801. stand still in bright array ye s.
P. L. 6, 882. to meet him all his s. who silent
P. L. 7, 136. returned victorious with his s.
P. L. 10, 614. from his transcendent seat the s.
P. L. 11, 705. come to judge them with his s.
P. R. 4, 349. the holiest of holies and his s.
S. A. 1288. patience is more oft the exercise of s.
L. 178. there entertain him all the s. above
S. 18, 1. avenge O Lord thy slaughtered s. whose
**Sake.**—P. L. 3, 238. I for his s. will leave thy
P. L. 9, 993. incur divine displeasure for her s.
P. L. 10, 201. cursed is the ground for thy s.
P. L. 10, 802. draw out for anger's s. finite
P. L. 11, 514. and for his maker's image s.
P. L. 12, 569. that suffering for truth's s.
P. R. 3, 45. me to seek wealth for empire's s.
P. R. 3, 46. nor empire to affect for glory's s.
P. R. 3, 98. for truth's s. suffering death
S. A. 372. be it but for honour's s.
S. A. 1629. at length for intermission s.
C. 864. listen for dear honour's s.
L. 114. enow of such as for their bellies' s.
**Sale.**—S. A. 1466. they easily would set to s.
**Salem.**—P. R. 2, 21. of palms Œnon and S. old
P. 39. to bear me where the towers of S. stood
**Sallow.**—C. 709. the lean and s. abstinence
**Salmanassar.**—P. R. 3, 278. and seat of S.
**Salt.**—P. L. 11. 834. an island s. and bare
C. 19. of every s. flood and each ebbing stream
**Salvation.**—P. L. 11, 708. high in s.
P. L. 12, 441. of him they learned and his s.
P. L. 12, 448. s. shall be preached but to the
P. R. 1, 167. to earn s. for the sons of men
**Salve.**—P. R. 4, 12. to s. his credit and for
S. A. 184. s. to thy sores apt words have power
**Salutation.**—P. L. 5, 386. the holy s. used
P. R. 2, 107. had passed since first her s. heard
**Salute.**—P. R. 2, 67. conceived of God or that s.
M. M. 9. thus we s. thee with our early song
V. Ex. 7. here I s. thee and thy pardon ask
**Samarchand.**—P. L. 11, 389. S. by Oxus
**Samaritan.**—P. R. 3, 359. S. or Jew
**Same.**—P. L. 1, 256. if I be still the s.
P. L. 3, 623. the s. whom John saw also
P. L. 4, 66. hadst thou the s. free will and
P. L. 4, 835. not revolted spirit thy shape the s.
P. L. 5, 83. ev'n to my mouth of that s. fruit
P. L. 5, 490. but in degree of kind the s.
P. L. 6, 176. God and nature bid the s.
P. L. 8, 345. understand the s. of fish within
P. L. 8, 581. think the s. vouchsafed to cattle
P. L. 10, 571. so oft they fell into the s.
P. L. 10, 826. only but to with the s. with me
P. L. 11, 633. holds on the s. from woman to
P. L. 11, 882. skirts of that s. watery cloud
P. R. 1, 354. wondered this barren waste the s.
P. R. 3, 413. thy zeal to Israel then the s. that
S. A. 232. from my former act and the s. end

S. A. 786. so near related or the s. of kind
S. A. 1658. pulled down the s. destruction on
C. 738. with that s. vaunted name virginity
L. 24. fed the s. flock by fountain shade and rill
S. 2, 10. to that s. lot however mean or high
V. Ex. 16. this s. small neglect that I have made
**Samoed.**—P. L. 10, 696. and the S. shore
**Samos.**—P. L. 5, 265. Delos or S. first
**Sampler.**—C. 751. to ply the s. and to tease
**Samson.**—P. L. 9, 1060. Herculean S. from the
S. A. 126. heroic that renowned irresistible S.
S. A. 341. that invincible S. far renowned
S. A. 488. who hath delivered thee S. bound
S. A. 445. come to pass by means of thee S.
S. A. 733. still dreading thy displeasure S.
S. A. 766. yet hear me S. not that I endeavour
S. A. 909. let me obtain forgiveness of thee S.
S. A. 1016. much like thy riddle S. in one day
S. A. 1076. I come not S. to condole thy chance
S. A. 1129. what thou wouldst have done to S.
S. A. 1293. either of these is in thy lot S.
S. A. 1308. Hebrews the prisoner S. here I seek
S. A. 1310. S. to thee our lords thus bid me say
S. A. 1348. consider S. matters now are strained
S. A. 1391. S. this second message from our lords
S. A. 1570. take then the worst in brief S. is dead
S. A. 1601. S. should be brought forth to show
S. A. 1615. was S. as a public servant brought
S. A. 1635. which when S. felt in his arms
S. A. 1657. S. with these immixed inevitably
S. A. 1709. S. hath quit himself like S.
**Sanctities.**—P. L. 3, 60. about him all the s.
**Sanctitude.**—P. L. 4, 293. truth, wisdom, s.
**Sanctity.**—P. L. 7, 508. but endued with s.
P. L. 8, 487. nor uninformed of nuptial s.
P. L. 10, 639. to s. that shall receive no stain
P. L. 11, 837. to place no s. if none be thither
**Sanctuary.**—P. L. 1, 388. within his s. itself
P. L. 5, 732. this our high place our s. our hill
P. L. 6, 672. shrined in his s. of heaven secure
P. L. 12, 249. by his prescript a s. is framed
S. A. 1674. who dwells in Silo his bright s.
**Sandals.**—L. 187. morn went out with s. gray
**Sands.**—P. L. 1, 355. Gibraltar to the Libyan s.
P. L. 2, 903. unnumbered as the s. of Barca
P. L. 4, 238. rolling on orient pearl and s.
C. 117. and on the tawny s. and shelves
C. 209. on s. and shores and desert wildernesses
**Sandy.**—C. 424. infamous hills and s. perilous
A. 97. by s. Ladon's lilied banks
**Sang.**—P. L. 3, 383. thee next they s. of all
P. L. 7, 192. so s. the hierarchies
L. 186. thus s. the uncouth swain to the oaks
**Sanguine.**—P. L. 6, 333. issuing flowed s.
L. 106. like to that s. flower inscribed with woe
**Sap.**—P. L. 9, 837. sciential s. derived from
**Sapience.**—P. L. 7, 195. s. and love immense
P. L. 9, 797. of operation blest to s.
P. L. 9, 1018. exact of taste and elegant of s.
**Sapient.**—P. L. 9, 442. where the s. king
**Saplings.**—A. 46. to nurse the s. tall and
**Sapphire.**—P. L. 2, 1050. adorned of living s.
P. L. 4, 237. how from that s. fount the
P. L. 6, 758. whereon a s. throne inlaid with
P. L. 6, 772. the crystalline sky in s. throned
C. 26. gives them leave to wear their s. crowns
**Sapphire-coloured.**—S. M. 7. before thee s.-c.
**Sapphires.**—P. L. 4, 605. with living s.
**Sarmatians.**—P. R. 4, 78. and S. north
**Sarra.**—P. L. 11, 243. or the grain of S.
**Sat.**—P. L. 1, 360. erst in heaven s. on thrones
P. L. 1, 602. and care s. on his faded cheek
P. L. 1, 634. s. on his throne, upheld by old
P. L. 1, 735. and s. as princes
P. L. 1, 795. in close recess and secret conclave s.
P. L. 2, 5. Satan exalted s. by merit raised to
P. L. 2, 300. Satan except none higher s.
P. L. 2, 303. deliberation s. and public care
P. L. 2, 417. this said he s. and expectation
P. L. 2, 420. but all s. mute pondering the
P. L. 3, 557. others apart s. on a hill retired

P. L. 2, 648. before the gates, there s. on either
P. L. 2, 724. pulled down the snaky sorceress that s. fast
P. L. 2, 777. here I s. alone but long I s. not
P. L. 2, 962. with him enthroned s. sable vested
P. L. 3, 63. the radiant image of his glory s.
P. L. 3, 408. bliss wherein he s. second to thee
P. L. 4, 30. which now s. high in his meridian
P. L. 4, 196. s. like a cormorant
P. L. 4, 197. but s. devising death to them
P. L. 4, 327. by a fresh fountain side they s.
P. L. 4, 333. sidelong as they s. recline on the
P. L. 4, 351. filled with pasture gazing s.
P. L. 4, 549. rocky pillars Gabriel s.
P. L. 4, 989. and on his crest s. horror plumed
P. L. 5, 299. in the door he s. of his cool bower
P. L. 5, 433. so down they s. and to their
P. L. 5, 597. by whom in bliss imbosomed s.
P. L. 6, 100. apostate in his sunbright chariot s.
P. L. 6, 446. he s. and in the assembly next
P. L. 6, 747. right hand of glory where he s.
P. L. 6, 763. at his right hand Victory s.
P. L. 7, 587. and s. him down with his great
P. L. 8, 41. perceiving where she s. retired in
P. L. 8, 287. pensive I s. me down there gentle
P. L. 9, 1064. long they s. as stricken mute
P. L. 9, 1121. they s. them down to weep, nor
P. L. 10, 230. within the gates of hell s. Sin
P. L. 10, 343. where the hapless pair s. in
P. L. 10, 428. in council s. solicitous what
P. L. 10, 448. down awhile he s. and round
P. L. 10, 559. s. thicker than the snaky locks
P. L. 10, 594. dark threshold to have s. watch
P. L. 10, 864. desolate where she s. approaching
P. L. 11, 79. where'er they s. in fellowships
P. L. 11, 393. where the Persian in Ecbatan s.
P. R. 1, 412. the place where he before had s.
P. R. 2, 118. all his potentates in council s.
P. R. 2, 440. on the throne of Judah s.
P. R. 4, 577. and to his crew that s. consulting
S. A. 805. I at home s. full of cares and fears
S. A. 1652. upon the heads of all who s. beneath
C. 293. and the swinked hedger at his supper s.
C. 543. I s. me down to watch upon a bank
A. 43. have s. to wonder at and gaze upon
H. 59. and kings s. still with awful eye
H. 87. s. simply chatting in a rustic row
V. Ex. 6. where he had mutely s. two years
**Satan.**—P. L. 1, 82. thence in heaven called S.
P. L. 1, 192. thus S. talking to his nearest
P. L. 1, 271. so S. spake
P. L. 1, 757. the high capital of S. and his peers
P. L. 2, 5. S. exalted sat by merit raised to that
P. L. 2, 300. than whom S. except, none higher
P. L. 2, 380. counsel first devised by S. and in
P. L. 2, 427. S. whom now transcendent glory
P. L. 2, 630. S. with thoughts inflamed of
P. L. 2, 674. S. was now at hand and from his
P. L. 2, 707. incensed with indignation S.
P. L. 2, 736. then these to her S. returned
P. L. 2, 968. to whom S. turning boldly thus
P. L. 2, 988. thus S. and him thus the Anarch
P. L. 2, 1010. he ceased and S. stayed not to
P. L. 2, 1041. that S. with less toil, and now
P. L. 3, 70. and S. there coasting the wall of
P. L. 3, 422. S. alighted walks, a globe far off
P. L. 3, 540. S. from hence, now on the lower
P. L. 3, 653. him S. thus accosts
P. L. 3, 736. and S. bowing low as to superior
P. L. 4, 9. for now S. now first inflamed with
P. L. 4, 173. S. had journeyed on pensive and
P. L. 4, 356. when S. still in gaze as first he
P. L. 4, 827. know ye not then said S. filled
P. L. 4, 878. why hast thou S. broke the
P. L. 4, 885. whom thus S. with contemptuous
P. L. 4, 905. since S. fell whom folly overthrew
P. L. 4, 950. S. and couldst thou faithful add
P. L. 4, 968. so threatened he but S. to no
P. L. 4, 985. on the other side S. alarmed
P. L. 5, 225. S. from hell 'scaped through the
P. L. 5, 658. but not so waked S. so call him

P. L. 5, 743. but *S.* with his powers far was
P. L. 5, 756. and *S.* to his royal seat, high on
P. L. 6, 85. the banded powers of *S.* hasting
P. L. 6, 109. *S.* with vast and haughty strides
P. L. 6, 191. on the proud crest of *S.*
P. L. 6, 246. till *S.* who that day prodigious
P. L. 6, 324. it met the sword of *S.*
P. L. 6, 327. then *S.* first knew pain
P. L. 6, 414. *S.* with his rebellious disappeared
P. L. 6, 469. whereto with look composed *S.*
P. L. 6, 557. suddenly at head appeared *S.*
P. L. 6, 607. *S.* beheld their plight and to his
P. L. 6, 900. aspiring who rebelled with *S.*
P. L. 9, 53. when *S.* who late fled before the
P. L. 9, 75. and with it rose *S.* involved in
P. L. 10, 2. despiteful act of *S.* done in
P. L. 10, 8. wise and just hindered not *S.*
P. L. 10, 172. to *S.* first in sin his doom applied
P. L. 10, 184. saw *S.* fall like lightning down
P. L. 10, 189. the realm itself of *S.* long
P. L. 10, 236. while *S.* our great author
P. L. 10, 258. to that new world where *S.* now
P. L. 10, 315. the track of *S.* to the selfsame
P. L. 10, 327. behold *S.* in likeness of an angel
P. L. 10, 386. have given to be the race of *S.*
P. L. 10, 414. the other way *S.* went down
P. L. 10, 419. *S.* passed and all about found
P. L. 10, 426. of that bright star to *S.* paragoned
P. L. 10, 591. of *S.* sprung all conquering death
P. L. 10, 841. to *S.* only like both crime
P. L. 10, 1034. grand foe *S.* who in the serpent.
P. L. 11, 248. hung the sword *S.'s* dire dread
P. L. 12, 391. nor so is overcome *S.* whose fall
P. L. 12, 394. not by destroying *S.* but his
P. L. 12, 430. this act shall bruise the head of *S.*
P. L. 12, 492. able to resist *S.'s* assaults
P. L. 12, 547. to dissolve *S.* with his perverted
P. R. 1, 143. henceforth I expose to *S.* let him
P. R. 1, 497. he added not and *S.* bowing low
P. R. 2, 115. for *S.* with sly preface to return
P. R. 2, 172. to whom quick answer *S.* thus
P. R. 2, 319. how hast thou hunger then *S.*
P. R. 2, 392. to whom thus answered *S.*
P. R. 3, 1. and *S.* stood awhile as mute
P. R. 3, 146. and here again *S.* had not to
P. R. 4, 21. so *S.* whom repulse upon repulse
P. R. 4, 194. that evil one *S.* for ever damned
P. R. 4, 365. so spake the Son of God but *S.*
P. R. 4, 562. but *S.* smitten with amazement
P. R. 4, 581. so *S.* fell and straight a fiery globe
P. R. 4, 634. heir of both worlds queller of *S.*
**Satanic.**—P. L. 6, 392. through the faint *S.*
P. R. 1, 161. his weakness shall o'ercome *S.*
**Sate.**—C. 714. but all to please and *s.* the curious
**Sated.**—P. L. 9, 598. *s.* at length ere long
**Satiate.**—P. L. 1, 179. whether scorn or *s.*
P. L. 7, 282. to conceive *s.* with genial moisture
P. L. 8, 214. they *s.* and soon fill though pleasant
P. L. 9, 248. if much converse perhaps thee *s.*
P. L. 9, 792. knew not eating death *s.* at length
**Satiety.**—P. L. 8, 216. to their sweetness no *s.*
**Satisfaction.**—P. L. 3, 212. the rigid *s.*
P. L. 12, 419. who rightly trust in this his *s.*
**Satisfied.**—P. L. 2, 212. *s.* with what is
P. L. 8, 180. how fully hast thou *s.* me pure
P. L. 10, 79. may illustrate most them fully *s.*
P. L. 10, 804. man to satisfy his rigour *s.* never
P. L. 12, 535. and specious forms religion *s.*
S. A. 484. have *s.* their utmost of revenge
Cir. 22. which we still transgress entirely *s.*
**Satisfy.**—P. L. 3, 295. most just shall *s.* for
P. L. 9, 584. to *s.* the sharp desire I had
P. L. 10, 803. in punished man to his rigour
P. L. 10, 991. be forced to *s.* his ravenous maw
P. R. 2, 229. or that which only seems to *s.*
P. R. 2, 254. yet God can *s.* that need
S. A. 837. call it furious rage to *s.* thy lust
**Sat'st.**—P. L. 1, 21. dove-like *s.* brooding on
P. L. 4, 825. why *s.* thou like an enemy in wait
P. R. 4, 425. *s.* unappalled in calm and sinless
**Saturn.**—P. L. 1, 512. seized by younger *S.*

P. L. 1, 519. or who with *S.* old
P. L. 10, 583. thence by *S.* driven and Ops
C. 805. to some of *S.'s* crew
Il P. 24. to solitary *S.* bore
Il P. 25. in *S.'s* reign such mixture was not held
**Satyr.**—P. R. 2, 191. or Pan, *S.*, or Faun
**Satyrs.**—L. 34. rough *S.* danced and Fauns
**Savage.**—P. L. 4, 172. of that steep *s.* hill
P. L. 7, 36. the *s.* clamour drowned both harp.
P. L. 9, 1085. O might I here in solitude live *s.*
P. R. 3, 23. or more obscure in *s.* wilderness
C. 358. direful grasp of *s.* hunger or of *s.* heat
C. 426. no *s.* fierce bandit or mountaineer
**Save.**—P. L. 1, 182. *s.* what the glimmering
P. L. 2, 814. *s.* he who reigns above none can
P. L. 3, 215. and just the unjust to *s.*
P. L. 3, 279. to *s.* by losing thee awhile
P. L. 3, 307. quitted all to *s.* a world from utter
P. L. 3, 427. *s.* on that side which from the wall
P. L. 4, 855. Zephon bold will *s.* us
P. L. 5, 39. the silent *s.* where silence yields
P. L. 5, 324. *s.* what by frugal storing firmness
P. L. 5, 380. but Eve undecked *s.* with herself
P. L. 5, 655. *s.* those who in their course
P. L. 6, 538. whom fled we thought will *s.* us
P. L. 6, 691. *s.* what sin hath impaired which
P. L. 8, 82. how build unbuild contrive to *s.*
P. L. 8, 133. or *s.* the sun his labour and that
P. L. 8, 409. *s.* with the creatures which I made
P. L. 9, 478. all pleasure to destroy *s.* what is in
P. L. 11, 820. to *s.* himself and household
P. L. 12, 258. *s.* when they journey and at
P. L. 12, 291. *s.* by those shadowy expiations
P. L. 12, 410. his merits to *s.* them not their
P. R. 1, 344. so shalt thou *s.* thyself and us
P. R. 4, 635. now enter and begin to *s.* mankind
S. A. 347. to *s.* himself against a coward armed
S. A. 984. who to *s.* her country from a fierce
C. 396. to *s.* her blossoms and defend her fruit.
C. 866. listen and *s.*, listen and appear to us
A. 48. and all my plants I *s.* from nightly ill
Il P. 82. *s.* the cricket on the hearth
S. 8, 14. had the power to *s.* the Athenian walls.
S. 16, 13. help us to *s.* free conscience
S. 23. 6. purification in the old law did *s.*
M. W. 7. summers three times eight *s.* one
**Saved.**—P. L. 3, 173. be *s.* who will, yet not
M. W. 36. *s.* with care from winter's nip
**Saves.**—P. L. 2, 158. anger whom his anger *s.*
P. L. 12, 319. from whom as oft he *s.* them
**Saving.**—P. R. 2, 474. by *s.* doctrine and from
**Saviour.**—P. L. 3, 412. *S.* of men thy name
P. L. 10, 209. judged he man both judge and *S.*
P. L. 12, 393. which he who comes thy *S.* shall
P. L. 12, 544. now amplier known thy *S.*
P. R. 1, 187. of *S.* to mankind and which way
P. R. 1, 406. to whom our *S.* sternly thus replied
P. R. 1, 465. so spake our *S.* but the subtle
P. R. 1, 493. to whom our *S.* with unaltered
P. R. 2, 283. up rose our *S.* and found all was
P. R. 2, 338. our *S.* lifting up his eyes beheld
P. R. 3, 43. to whom our *S.* calmly thus replied
P. R. 3, 121. to whom our *S.* fervently replied
P. R. 3, 181. to whom our *S.* answer thus
P. R. 3, 266. brought our *S.* and new train
P. R. 3, 346. and to our *S.* thus his words
P. R. 3, 386. to whom our *S.* answered thus.
P. R. 4, 25. he brought our *S.* to the western
P. R. 4, 170. whom thus our *S.* answered
P. R. 4, 285. to whom our *S.* sagely thus
P. R. 4, 367. thus to our *S.* with stern brow
P. R. 4, 401. our *S.* meek and with untroubled
P. R. 4, 442. and to our *S.* came yet with no
P. R. 4, 506. that sung thee *S.* born
P. R. 4, 615. whom thou a *S.* art come down
P. R. 4, 636. our *S.* meek sung victor
**Savour.**—P. L. 9, 1019. meaning *s.* we apply
P. L. 10, 269. and taste the *s.* of death from all
P. L. 11, 26. fruits of more pleasing *s.* from thy
P. R. 2, 342. and meats of noblest sort and *s.*
**Savours.**—P. L. 10, 1043. and *s.* only rancour

**Savoury.**—P. L. 4, 335. the *s.* pulp they chew
P. L. 5, 84. the pleasant *s.* smell so quickened
P. L. 5, 304. prepared for dinner *s.* fruits
P. L. 9, 579. from the boughs a *s.* odour blown
P. L. 9, 741. by the smell so *s.* of that fruit
C. 541. had ta'en their supper on the *s.* herb
L'A. 84. are at their *s.* dinner set

**Saw.**—P. L. 1, 455. the sacred porch Ezekiel *s.*
P. L. 2, 744. nor ever *s.* till now sight more
P. L. 2, 993. *s.* and heard for such a numerous
P. L. 3, 510. as whereon Jacob *s.* angels
P. L. 3, 590. his glazed optic tube yet never *s.*
P. L. 3, 622. whereby he soon *s.* within ken a
P. L. 3, 623. whom John *s.* also in the sun
P. L. 3, 708. I *s.* when at his word the formless
P. L. 4, 1. which he, who *s.* the Apocalypse
P. L. 4, 127. and on the Assyrian mount *s.* him
P. L. 4, 179. which when the arch-felon *s.* due
P. L. 4, 286. where the fiend *s.* undelighted all
P. L. 4, 847. and *s.* virtue in her shape how
P. L. 5, 456. whose excellence he *s.* transcend
P. L. 5, 491. not then what God for you *s.* good
P. L. 5, 714. *s.* without their light
P. L. 5, 715. *s.* in whom
P. L. 5, 856. who *s.* when this creation was
P. L. 6, 250. at length *s.* where the sword of
P. L. 6, 510. and *s.* beneath the originals of
P. L. 6, 651. they *s.* them whelmed and all their
P. L. 6, 648. towards them so dread they *s.*
P. L. 6, 785. this *s.* his hapless foes but stood
P. L. 6, 867. hell *s.* heaven ruining from heaven
P. L. 7, 249. God *s.* the light was good
P. L. 7, 809. and *s.* that it was good and said let
P. L. 7, 337. God *s.* that it was good
P. L. 7, 352. God *s.* surveying his great work
P. L. 7, 395. and *s.* that it was good and blessed
P. L. 8, 43. and grace that won who *s.* to wish
P. L. 8, 261. I *s.* hill dale and shady woods
P. L. 8, 273. readily could name whate'er I *s.*
P. L. 8, 277. tell if ye *s.* how I came thus how
P. L. 8, 305. that what I *s.* of earth before
P. L. 8, 462. methought I *s.* though sleeping
P. L. 8, 463. and *s.* the shape still glorious
P. L. 8, 482. such as I *s.* her in my dream
P. L. 9, 592. all other beasts that *s.* with like
P. L. 9, 646. which when she *s.* thus to her
P. L. 9, 1030. since the day I *s.* thee first and
P. L. 10, 184. *s.* Satan fall like lightning
P. L. 10, 334. *s.* his guileful act
P. L. 10, 336. *s.* their shame that sought vain
P. L. 10, 337. but when he *s.* descend the Son
P. L. 10, 448. he sat and round about him *s.*
P. L. 10, 538. they *s.* but other sight instead
P. L. 10, 540. for what they *s.* they felt
P. L. 10, 715. miseries which Adam *s.* already
P. L. 11, 70. with peccant angels late they *s.*
P. L. 11, 151. methought I *s.* him placable and
P. L. 11, 214. *s.* the field pavilioned with his
P. L. 11, 406. in spirit perhaps he also *s.* rich
P. L. 11, 556. he looked and *s.* a spacious plain
P. L. 11, 638. he looked and *s.* wide territory
P. L. 11, 712. he looked and *s.* the face
P. L. 11, 726. which when he *s.* he ceased
P. L. 11, 840. he looked and *s.* the ark hull
P. L. 11, 887. he *s.* the whole earth filled
P. R. 1, 79. I *s.* the prophet do him reverence
P. R. 1, 319. he *s.* approach who first with
P. R. 1, 330. I *s.* and heard for we sometimes
P. R. 2, 60. but to his mother Mary when she *s.*
P. R. 2, 97. so found as well I *s.* he could not
P. R. 2, 267. and *s.* the ravens with their horny
P. R. 2, 270. he saw the prophet also how he
P. R. 2, 288. herd or sheep-cote none he *s.*
P. R. 2, 289. only in a bottom *s.* a pleasant
P. R. 3, 310. he looked and *s.* what numbers
P. R. 3, 322. he *s.* them in their forms of battle
S. A. 219. the first I *s.* at Timna and she pleased
S. A. 419. that *s.* not how degenerately I served
S. A. 793. I *s.* thee mutable of fancy
S. A. 797. no better way I *s.*
S. A. 1071. I less conjecture than when first I *s.*

C. 182. my brothers when they *s.* me wearied
C. 291. two such I *s.* what time the laboured ox
C. 294. I *s.* them under a green mantling vine
S. 23, 1. methought I *s.* my late espoused saint
H. 83. he *s.* a greater sun appear

**Saws.**—C. 110. with their grave *s.* in slumber lie

**Saw'st.**—P. L. 2, 796. surround me as thou *s.*
P. L. 8, 446. no such company as then thou *s.*
P. L. 11, 471. some as thou *s.* by violent stroke
P. L. 11, 607. those tents thou *s.* so pleasant
P. L. 11, 614. for that fair female troop thou *s.*
P. L. 11, 684. those ill-mated marriages thou *s.*
P. L. 11, 707. did as thou *s.* receive to walk
P. L. 11, 787. whom last thou, *s.* in triumph
P. L. 12, 342. whose high walls thou *s.* left in

**Say.**—P. L. 1, 27. *s.* first for Heaven hides nothing
P. L. 1, 28. *s.* first what cause
P. L. 1, 376. *s.* Muse their names then known
P. L. 2, 160. wherefore cease we then *s.* they
P. L. 3, 213. *s.* heavenly powers where shall we
P. L. 4, 93. but *s.* I could repent and could
P. L. 4, 900. true they found me where they *s.*
P. L. 4, 947. to *s.* and straight unsay pretending
P. L. 5, 512. but *s.* what meant that caution
P. L. 7, 40. *s.* goddess what ensued when Raphael
P. L. 7, 640. not surpassing human measure *s.*
P. L. 8, 228. on man is equal love *s.* therefore
P. L. 8, 505. or to *s.* all nature herself
P. L. 8, 549. that what she wills to do or *s.*
P. L. 9, 562. redouble then this miracle and *s.*
P. L. 9, 566. *s.* for such wonder claims attention
P. L. 9, 617. but *s.* where grows the tree
P. L. 9, 638. which oft they *s.* some evil spirit
P. L. 9, 948. and *s.* fickle their state whom God
P. L. 10, 158. *s.* woman what is this which
P. L. 10, 575. yearly enjoined some *s.* to
P. L. 10, 668. some *s.* he bid his angels turn
P. L. 10, 671. some *s.* the sun was bid turn
P. L. 10, 755. thy justice seems yet to *s.* truth
P. L. 10, 808. but *s.* that death be not one
P. L. 11, 879. but *s.* what mean those coloured
P. L. 12, 384. *s.* where and when their fight
P. L. 12, 479. but *s.* if our deliverer up to
P. R. 1, 397. envy they *s.* excites me thus
P. R. 1, 450. to the smallest tittle thou shalt *s.*
P. R. 1, 474. *s.* and unsay feign flatter or abjure
P. R. 3, 2. confounded what to *s.* what to reply
P. R. 3, 8. what best to *s.* canst *s.* to do canst do
P. R. 3, 357. but *s.* thou wert possessed of
S. A. 204. do they not *s.* how well are come upon
S. A. 215. yet truth to *s.* I oft have heard men
S. A. 337. *s.* if he be here
S. A. 669. so various or might I *s.* contrarious
S. A. 799. thou wilt *s.* why then revealed
S. A. 1013. but what it is, hard is to *s.* harder to
S. A. 1310. to thee our lords thus bid me *s.*
S. A. 1392. to thee I am bid *s.* art thou our slave
S. A. 1456. *s.* reverend sire we thirst to hear
S. A. 1578. yet ere I give the reins to grief *s.*
S. A. 1729. (Gaza is not in plight to *s.* us nay)
C. 432. some *s.* no evil thing that walks by
C. 783. would I something *s.* yet to what end
H. 15. *s.* heavenly muse shall not thy
D. F. I. 41. O *s.* me true if thou wert mortal
U.C. II 25. ev'n to his last breath there be that *s.*

**Saying.**—P. L. 2, 466. thus *s.* rose the monarch
P. L. 2, 871. thus *s.* from her side the fatal
P. L. 4, 536. so *s.* his proud step he scornful
P. L. 4, 797. so *s.* on he led his radiant files
P. L. 5, 82. so *s.* he drew nigh and to me held
P. L. 5, 331. so *s.* with dispatchful looks in
P. L. 6, 189. so *s.* a noble stroke he lifted high
P. L. 7, 395. and blessed them *s.* be fruitful
P. L. 8, 300. so *s.* by the hand he took me
P. L. 8, 644. so *s.* he arose whom Adam thus
P. L. 9, 179. so *s.* through each thicket dank
P. L. 9, 385. thus *s.* from her husband's hand
P. L. 9, 780. so *s.* her rash hand in evil hour
P. L. 9, 834. so *s.* from the tree her step she
P. L. 9, 990. so *s.* she embraced him and for joy
P. L. 10, 85. thus *s.* from his radiant seat he

P. L. 10, 200. I charged thee *s.* thou shalt not
P. L. 10, 272. so *s.* with delight he snuffed the
P. L. 10, 410. so *s.* he dismissed them they
P. R. 4, 394. so *s.* he took for still he knew his
P. R. 4, 541. so *s.* he caught him up
**Sayings.**—P. R. 2, 104. of things and *s.* laid up
S. A. 652. many are the *s.* of the wise
**Says.**—H. 149. but wisest fate *s.* no
**Say'st.**—P. L. 5, 818. unjust thou *s.* flatly
P. L. 5, 853. that we were formed then *s.* thou
P. L. 8, 612. for love thou *s.* leads up to heaven
P. R. 3, 394. means I must use thou *s.*
P. R. 4, 127. I shall thou *s.* expel a brutish
S. A. 822. I gave thou *s.* the example
S. A. 1580. all by him fell thou *s.* by whom fell
**Scaffolds.**—S. A. 1610. on banks and *s.* under
**Scalding.**—P. L. 10, 556. with *s.* thirst and
**Scale.**—P. L. 2, 71. difficult and steep to *s.*
P. L. 4, 354. and in the ascending *s.* of heaven
P. L. 4, 1014. up and knew his mounted *s.*
P. L. 5, 483. nourishment by gradual *s.*
P. L. 5, 509. and the *s.* of nature set
P. L. 6, 245. long time in even *s.* the battle
P. L. 8, 591. is the *s.* by which to heavenly
P. L. 10, 47. her own inclining left in even *s.*
P. L. 11, 656. by battery *s.* and mine assaulting
P. R. 2, 173. Belial in much uneven *s.* thou
**Scaled.**—P. L. 3, 541. that *s.* by steps of gold
**Scales.**—P. L. 4, 997. in heaven his golden *s.*
P. L. 7, 401. and shining *s.* glide under the green
P. L. 10, 676. Leo and the Virgin and the *S.*
**Scaly.**—P. L. 1, 206. fixed anchor in his *s.* rind
P. L. 2, 651. ended foul in many a *s.* fold
P. L. 7, 474. the river-horse and *s.* crocodile
C. 873. by *s.* Triton's winding shell
H. 172. swindges the *s.* horror of his tail
**Scan.**—S. 13, 3. not to *s.* with Midas' ears
**Scandal.**—P. L. 1, 416. ev'n to that hill of *s.*
S. A. 453. brought *s.* to Israel diffidence of God
**Scandalous.**—S. A. 1409. *s.* or forbidden in our
**Scanned.**—P. L. 8, 74. to be *s.* by them who
**Scant.**—P. L. 4, 628. mock our *s,* manuring
S. A. 1027. judgment *s.* capacity not raised
C. 308. in such a *s.* allowance of star-light
**Scape.**—P. L. 1, 482. did Israel *s.* the infection
P. L. 1, 749. nor did he *s.* by all his engines
P. L. 2, 442. if thence he *s.* into whatever world
P. L. 4, 911. and to *s.* his punishment
P. L. 10, 5. for what can *s.* the eye of God
P. L. 10, 1039. shall *s.* his punishment ordained
P. R. 1, 477. check or reproof and glad to *s.*
S. A. 697. if these they *s.* perhaps in poverty
C. 814. what have you let the false enchanter *s.*
**Scaped.**—P. L. 1, 239. both glorying to have *s.*
P. L. 4, 7. and *s.* haply so *s.* his mortal snare
P. L. 4, 906. now returns him from his prison *s.*
P. L. 5, 225. from hell *s.* through the darksome
P. L. 12, 117. yet the patriarch lived who *s.*
S. A. 1659. the vulgar only *s.* who stood without
**Scapes.**—P. R. 2, 189. then lay'st thy *s.* on
**Scar.**—P. L. 2. 401. to heal the *s.* of these
**Scarce.**—P. L. 1, 483. he *s.* had ceased
P. L. 1, 699. and hands innumerable *s.* perform
P. L. 2, 284. he *s.* had finished when such
P. L. 2, 541. hell *s.* holds the wild uproar
P. L. 3, 433. dislodging from a region *s.* of prey
P. L. 4, 357. *s.* thus at length failed speech
P. L. 4, 874. he *s.* had ended when those two
P. L. 5, 139. and the sun who *s.* up-risen
P. L. 5, 558. for *s.* the sun hath finished half
P. L. 5, 559. and *s.* begins his other half in
P. L. 6, 393. the faint Satanic host defensive *s.*
P. L. 6, 568. in ambiguous words he *s.* had
P. L. 7, 67. yet *s.* allayed still eyes the current
P. L. 7, 313. he *s.* had said when the bare earth
P. L. 7, 319. and these *s.* blown forth flourished
P. L. 7, 470. *s.* from his mould Behemoth
P. L. 8, 155. only to shine yet *s.* to contribute
P. L. 8, 306. what I saw of earth before *s.*
P. L. 9, 664. she *s.* had said though brief
P. L. 9, 850. there he her met *s.* from the tree

P. L. 10, 654. earth with cold & heat *s.* tolerable
P. L. 10, 923. while yet we live *s.* one short hour
P. L. 11, 499. and *s.* recovering words his
P. L. 11, 650. *s.* with life the shepherds fly
P. L. 11, 762. and *s.* to the angel utter'dst thus
P. R. 2, 72. when *s.* a shed could be obtained
P. R. 2, 96. when twelve years he *s.* had seen
P. R. 3, 51. and well weighed *s.* worth the
P. R. 3, 59. glory *s.* of few is raised
P. R. 3, 85. death discover them *s.* men
P. R. 3, 233. *s.* viewed the Galilean towns
P. R. 3, 424. distinguishable *s.* from Gentiles
P. R. 4, 86. the rest are barbarous and *s.* worth
S. A. 7. chained *s.* freely draw the air
S. A. 79. *s.* half I seem to live dead more than
S. A. 1525. the sufferers then will *s.* molest
S. A. 1546. though disturbed and *s.* consulted
L. 119. blind mouths that *s.* themselves know
M. W. 20. but with a *s.* well lighted flame
**Scarf.**—C. 995. than her purfled *s.* can shew
**Scars.**— P. L. 1, 601. his face deep *s.* of thunder
**Scathed.**—P. L. 1, 613. hath *s.* the forest oak
**Scattered.**—P. L. 1, 304. or *s.* sedge afloat
P. L. 1, 325. with *s.* arms and ensigns
P. L. 11, 294. and his *s.* spirits returned
P. L. 11, 653. cattle pastured late now *s.* lies
S. 18, 2. lie *s.* on the Alpine mountains
**Scatters.**—L'A. 50. *s.* the rear of darkness
**Scene.**—P. L. 4, 140. a sylvan *s.*
P. L. 11, 637. now prepare thee for another *s.*
P. R. 2, 239. were to unfold some active *s.*
P. R. 2, 294. opened in the midst a woody *s.*
P. R. 4, 142. and from the daily *s.* effeminate
**Scenes.**—P. 22. these latest *s.* confine my roving
**Scent.**—P. L. 9, 587, quickened at the *s.* of
P. L. 10, 267. such a *s.* I draw of carnage
P. L. 10, 277. flying lured with *s.* of
S. A. 390. the *s.* conceived her . . . first-born
S. A. 720. an amber *s.* of odorous perfume
**Scented.**—P. L. 10, 279. so *s.* the grim feature
**Scents.**—P. L. 9, 200. prime for sweetest *s.*
**Sceptre.**—P. L. 2, 327. and with iron *s.* rule
P. L. 2, 1002. weakening the *s.* of old Night
P. L. 3, 339. then thou thy regal *s.* shalt lay
P. L. 4, 90. with diadem and *s.* high advanced
P. L. 5, 816. by right endued with regal *s.*
P. L. 5, 886. that golden *s.* which thou didst
P. L. 6, 730. *s.* and power thy giving I assume
P. L. 6, 746. so said he o'er his *s.* bowing rose
P. L. 12, 357. seize the *s.* and regard not
P. R. 2, 486. to gain a *s.* oftest better missed
P. R. 3, 405. and his full *s.* sway to just extent
P. R. 4. 480. ere thou of Israel's *s.* get fast
S. A. 1303. in his hand a *s.* or quaint staff
C. 36. and new-entrusted *s.* But their way
C. 828. that had the *s.* from his father Brute
**Sceptred.**—P. L. 2, 43. him Moloch *s.* king
P. L. 1, 734. where *s.* angels held their residence
P. L. 11, 660. in other part the *s.* heralds call
Il P. 98. in *s.* pall come sweeping by
**School.**—P. R. 3, 238. best *s.* of best experience
S. A. 297. for of such doctrine never was there *s.*
**Schools.**—P. R. 4, 251. then view the *s.* of
P. R. 4, 277. that watered all the *s.*
C. 439. antiquity from the old *s.* of Greece
**Science.**—P. L. 9, 680. mother of *s.* now I
**Sciential.**—P. L. 9, 837. into the plant *s.*
**Scipio.**—P. L. 9. 510. with her who bore *S.*
P. R. 3, 34. young *S.* had brought down the
**Scoffing.**—P. L. 6, 568. *s.* in ambiguous
P. L. 6, 629. in pleasant vein stood *s.*
**Scoop.**—P. L. 4, 336. still as they thirsted *s.* the
**Scope.**—P. L. 2, 127. as the *s.* of all his aim
P. R. 1, 494. coming hither though I know thy *s.*
**Scorch.**—C. 929. never *s.* thy tresses fair
**Scorched.**—P. L. 6, 372. violence of Ramiel *s.*
**Scorching.**—P. L. 10, 691. cold and *s.* heat
**Score.**—S. A. 433. still act paying that rigid *s.*
P. 46. yet on the softened quarry would I *s.*
**Scorn.**—P. L. 1, 178. whether *s.* or satiate fury
P. L. 1, 619. he assayed and thrice in spite of *s.*

P. L. 2, 697. and breathest defiance here and s.
P. L. 3, 199. they who neglect and s. shall
P. L. 4, 827. then said Satan filled with s.
P. L. 4, 834. thus Zephon answering s. with s.
P. L. 4, 902. thus he in s. the warlike angel
P. L. 4, 966. not to s. the facile gates of hell
P. L. 5, 904. long way through hostile s.¹
P. L. 5, 906. and with retorted s. his back
P. L. 6, 632. and of his thunder made a s.
P. L. 9, 299. thou thyself with s. and anger
P. L. 9, 951. matter of s. not to be given the foe
P. L. 9, 1011. breeding wings wherewith to s.
P. L. 10, 509. universal hiss the sound of public s.
P. L. 11,-811. fearless of reproach and s.
P. L. 12, 341. with all his sacred things a s.
P. R. 1, 415. a spectacle of ruin or of s.
P. R. 4, 550. and added thus in s. there stand
S. A. 34. made of my enemies the s. and gaze
S. A. 137. in s. of their proud arms and warlike
S. A. 442. and had in s. by the idolatrous rout
S. A. 494. how deserving contempt and s. of all
S. A. 646. the subject of their cruelty or s.
L. 72. to s. delights and live laborious days
D. F. I. 63. to s. the sordid world
**Scorned.**—P. L. 6, 40. glorious to return than s.
P. L. 10, 54. justice shall not return as bounty s.
P. L. 10, 418. the bars assailed that s. his
P. R. 2, 194. easily s. all her assaults on worthier
S. A. 943. thence easily contemned and s.
**Scornful.**—P. L. 4, 536. proud step he s.
P. L. 6, 149. whom the grand foe with s. eye
P. L. 10, 625. conniving seem to gratify my s.
**Scorning.**—P. L. 2, 134. the realm of night s.
C. 685. s. the unexempt condition
**Scorns.**—P. R. 3, 191. contempts and s.
P. R. 4, 387. attend thee s. reproaches injuries
**Scorpion.**—P. L. 4, 998. Astrea and the S.
P. L. 10, 328. betwixt the Centaur and the S.
P. L. 10, 524. S. and Asp and Amphisbæna dire
S. A. 360. draw a s.'s tail behind
**Scorpions.**—P. L.' 2, 701. with a whip of s.
**Scotch.**— F. of C. 12. and S. What-d'ye-call
**Scots.**—S. 16, 7. Darwen stream with blood of S.
**Scour.**—P. L. 6, 529. each coast light-armed s.
**Scourge.**—P. L. 2, 90. when the s. inexorably
P. L. 4, 914. and s. that wisdom back to hell
**Scourged.**—P. L. 10, 311. and s. with many
**Scours.**—P. L. 2, 633. sometimes he s. the right
**Scout.**—P. L. 2, 133. s. far and wide into
P. L. 3, 543. as when a s. through dark
C. 138. ere the blabbing eastern s.
**Scouts.**—P. L. 6, 529. and s. each coast
**Scowls.**—P. L. 2, 491. s. o'er the darkened
**Scramble.**—L. 117. how to s. at the ... feast
**Scrannel.**—L. 124. grate on their s. pipes
**Screened.**—P. R. 4, 30. that s. the fruits
**Scribbled.**—P. L. 8, 83. and eccentric s. o'er
**Scribes.**—P. R. 1, 261. to our s. known partly
**Scrip.**—C. 626. in requital ope his leathern s.
**Scroll.**—P. L. 12, 336. of bad the longer s.
**Scruple.**—P. R. 2, 331. who would s. that
**Scrupled.**—P. L. 9, 997. he s. not to eat
**Scrupulous.**—C. 108. and advice with s. head
**Scrutiny.**—P. R. 4, 515. view and narrower s.
**Sculls.**—P. L. 7, 402. wave in s. that oft
**Sculptures.**—P. L. 1, 716. with bossy s.
**Scum.**—C. 595. gathered like s. and settled to
**Scummed.**—P. L. 1, 704. and s. the bullion
**Scurf.**—P. L. 1, 672. shone with a glossy s.
**Scylla.**—P. L. 2, 660. vexed S. bathing in the
C. 257. S. wept and chid her barking waves
**Scythe.**—P. L. 10, 606. the s. of time mows
L'A. 66. and the mower whets his s.
**Scythian.**—P. R. 3, 301. against the S. whose
V. Ex. 99. or Humber loud that keeps the S.'s.
**Scythians.**—P. R. 4, 78. Germans and S.
**Sdeined**—P. L. 4, 50. lifted up so high I s.
**Sea.**—P. L. 1, 208. invests the s. and wished
P. L. 1, 300. on the beach of that inflamed s.
P. L. 1, 451. ran purple to the s.
P. L. 1, 462. Dagon his name s.-monster

P. L. 2, 287. all night long had roused the s.
P. L. 2, 546. Œta threw into the Euboic s.
P. L. 2, 636. as when far off at s. a fleet
P. L. 2, 660. vexed Scylla bathing in the s.
R. L. 2, 912. of neither s. nor shore nor air
P. L. 2, 939. neither s. nor good dry land
P. L. 2, 1011. that now his s. should find a
P. L. 3, 363. that like a s. of jasper shone
P. L. 3, 440. so on this windy s. of land
P. L. 3, 472. Plato's Elysium, leaped into the s
P. L. 3, 518. and underneath a bright s.
P. L. 3, 604. old Proteus from the s.
P. L. 3, 653. over moist and dry o'er s. and land
P. L. 4, 161. off at s. north-east winds blow
P. L. 4, 432. that possess earth air and s.
P. L. 5, 416. earth the s. earth and the s.
P. L. 5, 753. is to all the earth and all the s.
P. L. 7, 212. outrageous, as a s. dark wasteful
P. L. 7, 403. bank the mid s. part single
P. L. 7, 416. and at his trunk spouts out a s.
P. L. 7, 473. ambiguous between s. and land
P. L. 7, 521. over the fish and fowl of s. and air
P. L. 7, 533. over fish of the s. and fowl
P. L. 7, 619. on the clear hyaline the glassy s.
P. L. 7, 629. on earth in s. or air and multiply
P. L. 8, 341. or live in s. or air beast, fish
P. L. 9, 76. s. he had searched and land
P. L. 9, 117. now land, now s. and shores
P. L. 10, 286. as in raging s. tost up and down
P. L. 10, 290. upon the Cronian s. together
P. L. 10, 309. to the s. and over Hellespont
P. L. 10, 666. when with bluster to confound s.
P. L. 10, 693. slow produced like change on s.
P. L. 10, 718. and in a troubled s. of passion
P. L. 11, 337. land, s. and air and every kind
P. L. 11, 749. s. covered s., s. without shore
P. L. 11, 854. towards the retreating s. their
P. L. 11, 883. nor let the s. surpass his bounds
P. L. 12, 141. east to the great western s.
P. L. 12, 142. yonder s. each place behold
P. L. 12, 159. at seven months into the s.
P. L. 12, 195. the s. swallows him with his
P. L. 12, 212. extends over the s. the s. his rod
P. L. 12, 579. of God in heaven air earth or s.
P. R. 2, 344. all fish from s. or shore
P. R. 3, 258. joined their tribute to the s.
P. R. 3, 438. as the Red S. and Jordan once
P. R. 4, 28. washed by the southern s. and on
P. R. 4, 72. of Bocchus to the Blackmoor s.
S. A. 710. who is this? what thing of s. or land
S. A. 962. reconciled at length and s. to shore
C. 375. though sun and moon were in the flat s.
C. 732. the s. o'erfraught would swell
L. 89. and listens to the herald of the s.
H. 52. she strikes a universal peace through s.
Hor. 16. the stern god of s.
**Sea-beast.**— P. L. 1, 200. or that s.-b.
**Sea-faring,**—P. L. 2, 288. s.-f. men o'erwatched
**Sea-girt.**—C. 21. imperial rule of all the s.-g. isles
**Sea-idol.**—S. A. 13. Dagon their s.-i. and forbid
**Seal.**—P. L. 4, 966. and s. thee so as henceforth
P. L. 7, 409. the s. and bended dolphins play
P. L. 9, 1043. of their mutual guilt the s.
P. L. 10, 637. for ever and s. up his ravenous
S. A. 49. under the s. of silence could not keep
**Seals.**—P. L. 11, 835. the haunt of s. and orcs
Cir. 25. s. obedience first with wounding smart
**Seamen.**—P. L. 1, 205. island oft as s. tell
**Sea-mews.**—P. L. 11, 835. orcs and s.-m.' clang
**Sea-monsters.**— P. L. 11, 751. s.-m. whelped
**Sea-nymphs.**—Il P. 21. praise above the s.-n.
**Search.**— P. L. 2, 403. s. of this new world
P. L. 2, 830. through the void immense to s.
P. L. 4, 528. but first with narrow s. I must
P. L. 4, 789. with winged speed s. through
P. L. 4, 799. in s. of whom they sought
P. L. 6, 445. due s. and consultation will
P. L. 7, 125. enough is left besides to s.
P. L. 8, 66. to ask or s. I blame thee not
P. L. 9, 83. the orb he roamed with narrow s.
P. L. 9, 181. he held on his midnight s. where

P. L. 10, 440. their great adventurer from the *s.*
A. 7. here our solemn *s.* hath end
V. Ex. 31. as may make thee *s.* thy coffers round
**Searched.**—P. L. 9, 76. sea he had *s.* and land
P. L. 12, 377. my steadiest thoughts have *s.*
**Searching.**—P. R. 1, 260. *s.* what was writ.
**Seas.**—P L. 3, 559. far off Atlantic *s.*
P. L. 7, 308. of congregated waters he called *s.*
P. L. 7, 396. in the *s.* and lakes and running
P. L. 7, 399. forthwith the sounds and *s.* each
P. L. 7, 428. high over *s.* flying and over lands
P. L. 10, 642. sung halleluiah as the sound of *s.*
P. L. 10, 700. Thrascias rend the woods and *s.*
S. A. 961. winds to *s.* are reconciled at length
S. A. 961. deaf to prayers than winds and *s.*
C. 115. sounds and *s.* with all their finny drove
C. 713. thronging the *s.* with spawn
A. 31. stole under *s.* to meet his Arethuse
L. 154. whilst thee the shores and sounding *s.*
S. 8, 7. spread thy name o'er lands and *s.*
Cir. 9. *s.* wept from our deep sorrow
U. C. II. 31. linked to the mutual flowing of the *s.*
Hor. 6. *s.* rough with black winds
**Season.**—P. L. 5, 850. seconded as out of *s.*
P. L. 9, 200. partake the *s.* prime for sweetest
P. L. 10, 609. *s.* him thy last and sweetest prey
P. L. 12, 597. thou at *s.* fit let her with thee
P. R. 2, 72. in such a *s.* born when scarce
P. R. 4, 146. know therefore when my *s.* comes
P. R. 4, 380. at full age fulness of time thy *s.*
P. R. 4, 468. the perfect *s.* offered with my aid
L. 7. compels me to disturb your *s.* due
L'A. 89. or if the earlier *s.* lead
S. 20, 5. may be won from the hard *s.* gaining
H. 35. it was no *s.* then for her
**Seasons.**—P. L. 3, 41. thus with the year *s.*
P. L. 4, 640. all *s.* and their change all please
P. L. 5, 323. where store all *s.* ripe for use
P. L. 7, 242. for *s.* and for days and circling
P. L. 7, 427. intelligent of *s.* and set forth their
P. L. 7, 623. then know'st their *s.* among
P. L. 8, 69. his *s.* hours or days or months or
P. L. 10, 678. to bring in change of *s.* to each
P. L. 10, 1063. the inclement *s.* rain ice hail
P. R. 3, 187. he in whose hand all times and *s.*
**Seat.**—P. L. 1, 5. and regain the blissful *s.*
P. L. 1, 181. the *s.* of desolation, void of light
P. L. 1, 243. this the *s.* that we must change
P. L. 1, 383. long after next the *s.* of God
P. L. 1, 467. whose delightful *s.* was fair
P. L. 1, 634. and repossess their native *s.*
P. L. 1, 720. or *s.* their kings
P. L. 2, 76. ascend up to our native *s.*
P. L. 2, 347. another world the happy seat of
P. L. 2, 394. spite of fate nearer our ancient *s.*
P. L. 2, 674. was now at hand and from his *s.*
P. L. 2, 931. but that *s.* soon failing meets
P. L. 2, 1050. once his native *s.* and fast by
P. L. 3, 527. just o'er the blissful *s.* of
P. L. 3, 632. to paradise the happy *s.* of man
P. L. 3, 669. hath man his fixed *s.*, or fixed *s.*
P. L. 3, 724. that place is earth the *s.* of man
P. L. 4, 247. a happy rural *s.* of various view
P. L. 4, 371. and this high *s.* your heaven
P. L. 5, 756. Satan to his royal *s.* high on
P. L. 6, 27. and present before the *s.* supreme
P. L. 6, 197. pushed a mountain from his *s.*
P. L. 6, 226. not destroy their happy native *s.*
P. L. 6, 273. heaven the *s.* of bliss brooks not
P. L. 7, 141. the *s.* of Deity supreme
P. L. 7, 329. a *s.* where Gods might dwell or
P. L. 7, 623. among these the *s.* of men earth
P. L. 8, 42. with lowliness majestic from her *s.*
P. L. 8, 299. the garden of bliss thy *s.* prepared
P. L. 8, 557. and nobleness their *s.* build in her
P. L. 8, 590. hath his *s.* in reason and is
P. L. 9, 100. if not preferred justly *s.*
P. L. 9, 153. this world and earth his *s.*
P. L. 9, 782. nature from her *s.* sighing
P. L. 10, 85. from his radiant *s.* he rose of
P. L. 10, 237. and happier *s.* provides for us
P. L. 10, 424. city and proud *s.* of Lucifer

P. L. 10, 614. seeing from his transcendent *s.*
P. L. 11, 148. upborne even to the *s.* of God
P. L. 11, 343. had been perhaps thy capital *s.*
P. L. 11, 386. the *s.* of mightiest empire
P. L. 11, 388. of Cambalu *s.* of Cathaian Can
P. L. 11, 407. rich Mexico the *s.* of Montezume
P. L. 11, 408. Cusco in Peru the richer *s.*
P. L. 11, 418. ev'n to the inmost *s.* of mental
P. L. 11, 575. which was their *s.* down to the
P. L. 12, 457. and resume his *s.* at God's
P. L. 12, 642. of paradise so late their happy *s.*
P. R. 2, 442. ages and shall yet regain that *s.*
P. R. 3, 277. golden monarchy the *s.* and
P. R. 3, 373. in David's royal *s.* his true
P. R. 4, 469. with my aid to win thy destined *s.*
P. R. 4, 612. for though that *s.* of earthly bliss
S. A. 148. the hill by Hebron *s.* of giants old
C. 916. next this marble venoméd *s.*
L. 16. that from beneath the *s.* of Jove doth
H. 103. Cynthia's *s.* the aery region thrilling
H. 196. foregoes his wonted *s.*
D. F. I. 59. earth from thy prefixed *s.* didst post
**Seated.**—P. L. 6, 644. they plucked the *s.*
P. R. 2, 217. *s.* as on the top of virtue's hill
**Seats.**—P. L. 1, 383. durst fix their *s.*
P. L. 1, 796. a thousand demi-gods on golden *s.*
P. L. 5, 892. and mossy *s.* had round
P. L. 11, 82. and took their *s.* till from his
P. R. 2, 125. hold our place and these mild *s.*
P. R. 3, 262. well might seem the *s.* of
P. R. 4, 30. screened the fruits of the earth and *s.*
S. A. 1607. with *s.* where all the lords and each
C. 11. amongst the enthroned gods on sainted *s.*
**Sea-weed.**—P. L. 7, 404. mate graze the *s.-w.*
**Sechem.**—P. L. 12, 135. pitched about S.
**Second.**—P. L. 1, 702. a *s.* multitude with
P. L. 2, 17. trust themselves to fear no *s.* fate
P. L. 2, 419. awaiting who appeared to *s.* or
P. L. 2, 713. their fatal hands no *s.* stroke
P. L. 3, 288. so in thee as from a *s.* root shall
P. L. 3, 409. the bliss wherein he sat *s.* to thee
P. L. 3, 712. till at his *s.* bidding darkness fled
P. L. 4, 3. then when the dragon put to *s.* rout
P. L. 5, 387. long after to blest Mary *s.* Eve
P. L. 6, 605. in posture to displode their *s.* tire
P. L. 6, 684. *s.* Omnipotence two days are
P. L. 7, 275. morning chorus sung the *s.* day
P. L. 8, 407. for none I know *s.* to me or like
P. L. 9, 101. as built with *s.* thoughts reforming
P. L. 9, 609. no fair to thine equivalent or *s.*
P. L. 9, 1001. and nature gave a *s.* groan
P. L. 10, 183. when Jesus Son of Mary *s.* Eve
P. L. 10, 591. *s.* of Satan sprung all-conquering
P. L. 11, 64. by faith and faithful works to *s.*
P. L. 11, 383. the tempter set our *s.* Adam
P. L. 11, 859. the *s.* time returning, in his bill
P. L. 12, 7. and man as from a *s.* stock proceed
P. L. 12, 13. this *s.* source of men while yet
P. L. 12, 35. from heaven claiming *s.* sovranty
P. L. 12, 162. raise him to be the *s.* in that
P. L. 12, 321. the *s.* both for piety renowned
P. R. 2, 275. and eat the *s.* time after repose
S. A. 1391. this *s.* message from our lords
S. A. 1701. that no *s.* knows nor third
M. W. 25. and now with *s.* hope she goes
**Secondary.**—P. L. 5, 854. the work of *s.*
**Seconded.**—P. L. 4, 929. and *s.* thy else not
P. L. 5, 850. his zeal none *s.* as out of season
P. L. 10, 335. by Eve though all unweeting *s.*
S. A. 1153. with the utmost of his godhead *s.*
**Secrecy.**—P. L. 8, 427. thou in thy *s.* although
S. A. 1002. trust of *s.* my safety and my life
C. 387. the pensive *s.* of desert cell
**Secret.**—P. L. 1, 6. that on the *s.* top of Oreb
P. L. 1, 795. in close recess and *s.* conclave sat
P. L. 2, 663. the night hag when called in *s.*
P. L. 2, 766. thou took'st with me in *s.*
P. L. 2, 838. than this more *s.* now designed
P. L. 3, 671. with *s.* gaze or open admiratino
P. L. 4, 7. the coming of their *s.* foe, and
P. L. 5, 672. thus to him in *s.* spake

▼

P. L. 6, 522. *s.* they finished and in order set
P. L. 9, 810. and givest access though *s.* she
P. L. 9, 811. and I perhaps am *s.* heaven is
P. L. 10, 32. from his *s.* cloud amidst
P. L. 10, 248. to unite with *s.* amity things of
P. L. 10, 358. my heart which by a *s.* harmony
P. R. 1, 15. deeds above heroic though in *s.*
P. R. 4, 254. hear and learn the *s.* power of
S. A. 201. have divulged the *s.* gift of God
S. A. 384. the *s.* wrested from me in her height
S. A. 394. to win from me my capital *s.*
S. A. 497. his holy *s.* presumptuously have
S. A. 610. must *s.* passage find to the inmost
S. A. 665. *s.* refreshings that repair his strength
S. A. 1007. and *s.* sting of amorous remorse
S. A. 1199. wring from me and tell to them my *s.*
C. 129. dark-veiled Cotytto to whom the *s.* flame
A. 30. divine Alpheus who by *s.* sluice
Il P. 28. and in *s.* shades of woody Ida's inmost
H. 28. from out his *s.* altar touched
Cir. 19. high throned in *s.* bliss
V. Ex. 45. then sing of *s.* things that came
**Secretest.**—P. L. 10, 249. of like kind by *s.*
**Secrets.**—P. L. 2, 891. the *s.* of the hoary
P. L. 2, 972. to disturb the *s.* of your realm
P. L. 5, 569. how last unfold the *s.* of another
P. L. 7, 95. what we not to explore the *s.* ask
P. L. 8, 74. and not divulge his *s.* to be
P. L. 10, 478. that jealous of their *s.* fiercely
P. L. 12, 578. all *s.* of the deep all nature's
S. A. 492. to have revealed *s.* of men the *s.* of a
S. A. 776. curiosity inquisitive importune of *s.*
S. A. 798. to learn thy *s.* get into my power
S. A. 879. unbosomed all my *s.* to thee
**Sect.**—P. L. 6, 147. my *s.* thou seest now learn
P. R. 4, 279. and the *s.* Epicurean
**Secular.**—P. L. 12, 517. to join *s.* power
S. A. 1707. a *s.* bird ages of lives
S. 16, 12. to bind our souls with *s.* chains
**Secure.**—P. L. 1, 261. here we may reign *s.*
P. L. 2, 638. till then as one *s.*
P. L. 2, 359. high arbitrator sit *s.*
P. L. 2, 399. unvisited of heaven's fair light *s.*
P. L. 4, 186. in hurdled cotes amid the field *s.*
P. L. 4, 791. now laid perhaps asleep *s.* of harm
P. L. 5, 238. to beware he swerve not too *s.*
P. L. 5, 638. quaff immortality and joy *s.*
P. L. 5, 736. and *s.* laugh'st at their vain
P. L. 6, 541. face I see sad resolution and *s.*
P. L. 6, 672. in his sanctuary of heaven *s.*
P. L. 9, 339. as not *s.* to single or combined
P. L. 9, 347. happy state *s.*, *s.* from outward force
P. L. 9, 1175. but confidence then bore thee on *s.*
P. L. 10, 779. there I should rest and sleep *s.*
P. L. 11, 196. haply too *s.* of our discharge
P. L. 11, 746. and *s.* with beaked prow
P. L. 11, 803. shall practise how to live *s.*
P. L. 12, 620. consolation yet *s.* I carry hence
P. R. 1, 176. therefore *s.* ventures his filial
P. R. 3, 348. *s.* on no slight grounds thy safety
P. R. 3, 360. to enjoy it quiet and *s.*
P. R. 4, 616. where they shall dwell *s.* when
S. A. 55. proudly *s.* yet liable to fall
C. 409. infer as if I thought my sister's state *s.*
C. 618. how to *s.* the lady from surprisal
L'A. 91. sometimes with *s.* delight
C. 327. a place less warranted than this or less *s.*
**Secured.**—P. L. 4, 370. for so happy ill *s.*
P. L. 5, 222. man *s.* his marriage with the
**Securely.**—P. L. 6, 130. thus *s.* him defied
**Securer.**—P. L. 9, 371. may find us both *s.*
**Sedentary.**—P. L. 8, 32. while the *s.* earth
S. A. 571. till length of years and *s.* numbness
**Sedge.**—P. L. 1, 304. or scattered *s.* afloat
L. 104. his mantle hairy and his bonnet *s.*
**Sedgy.**—V. Ex. 97. or rocky Avon or of *s.* Lee
**Seditious.**—P. L. 6, 152. from flight *s.* angel
**Seduce.**—P. L. 2, 368. or if not drive *s.* them
P. L. 6, 901. now is plotting how he may *s.*
P. L. 9, 307. needs must be who could *s.* angels
P. R. 1, 178. whate'er may tempt whate'er *s.*

**Seduced.**—P. L. 1, 33. who first *s.* them to
P. L. 1, 219. mercy shown on man by him *s.*
P. L. 4, 83. whom I *s.* with other promises
P. L. 9, 287. can by his fraud be shaken or *s.*
P. L. 10, 41. man should be *s.* and flattered out
P. L. 10, 332. he after Eve *s.* unminded slunk
P. L. 10, 485. him by fraud I have *s.* from his
P. L. 10, 577. their pride and joy for man *s.*
**Sedulous.**—P. L. 9, 27. not *s.* by nature
**See.**—P. L. 1, 134. too well I *s.* and rue the dire
P. L. 1, 169. but *s.* the angry victor hath
P. L. 1, 216. and enraged might *s.*
P. L. 2, 66. infernal thunder and for lightning *s.*
P. L. 3, 54. that I may *s.* and tell of things
P. L. 3, 262. and return father to *s.* thy face
P. L. 3, 337. *s.* golden days fruitful of golden
P. L. 3, 489. then might ye *s.* cowls, hoods
P. L. 3, 662. unspeakable desire to *s.* and know
P. L. 4, 489. and from that time *s.* how beauty
P. L. 4, 579. *s.* far and wide, in at this gate
P. L. 5, 29. my glory, my perfection glad I *s.*
P. L. 5, 80. and *s.* what life the gods live there
P. L. 5, 411. whereby they hear *s.*, smell, touch
P. L. 5, 739. when they *s.* all regal power
P. L. 5, 878. forsaken of all good I *s.* thy fall
P. L. 6, 166. but now I *s.* that most through
P. L. 6, 199. but greater rage to *s.* thus foiled
P. L. 6, 540. and settled in his face I *s.* sad
P. L. 6, 559. that all may *s.* who hate us how
P. L. 6, 792. grieving to *s.* his glory at the
P. L. 7, 145. far the greater part have kept I *s.*
P. L. 8, 227. for God we *s.* hath honoured thee
P. L. 8, 233. to *s.* that none thence issued forth
P. L. 8, 364. but with me I. *s.* not who partakes
P. L. 8, 399. a nice and subtle happiness I *s.*
P. L. 8, 448. to *s.* how thou couldst judge
P. L. 8, 494. I now *s.* bone of my bone
P. L. 9, 119. and the more I *s.* pleasures about
P. L. 9, 720. I question it for this fair earth I *s.*
P. L. 9, 812. and remote to *s.* from thence
P. L. 9, 1017. Eve now I *s.* thou art exact of
P. L. 9, 1090. hide me where I may never *s.*
P. L. 10, 536. with expectation when to *s.*
P. L. 10, 616. *s.* with what heat these dogs of
P. L. 10, 902. but shall *s.* her gained by a far
P. L. 10, 962. if aught I *s.* will prove no
P. L. 11, 22. *s.* Father what first fruits on
P. L. 11, 173. for *s.* the morn all unconcerned
P. L. 11, 415. for he had much to *s.*
P. L. 11, 459. though here thou *s.* him die
P. L. 11, 462. but still I *s.* the tenor of man's
P. L. 11, 783. I was far deceived for now I *s.*
P. L. 12, 8. much thou hast yet to *s.* but I
P. L. 12, 51. comes down to *s.* their city ere
P. L. 12, 60. and looking down to *s.* the
P. L. 12, 128. I *s.* him but thou canst not with
P. L. 12, 135. I *s.* his tents pitched about
P. L. 12, 158. river Nile *s.* where it flows
P. L. 12, 276. but now I *s.* his day in whom
P. L. 12, 289. that when they *s.* law can
P. L. 12, 422. the stars of morn shall *s.*
P. L. 12, 590. *s.* the guards by me encamped
P. R. 1, 94. ye *s.* our danger on the utmost
P. R. 1, 246. where they mark *s.* him and to
P. R. 1, 338. what other way I *s.* not for we here
P. R. 1, 381. what I *s.* excellent in good or fair
P. R. 1, 384. to *s.* thee and approach thee whom
P. R. 2, 57. soon we shall *s.* our hope our joy
P. R. 2, 398. but I *s.* what I can do or offer is
P. R. 3, 7. I *s.* thou know'st what is of use t o
P. R. 3, 245. and *s.* before thine eyes the
P. R. 3, 303. *s.* though from far his thousands
P. R. 3, 308. *s.* how in warlike muster they
P. R. 4, 61. and *s.* what conflux issuing forth
P. R. 4, 155. I *s.* all offers made by me how
P. R. 4, 244. *s.* there the olive grove of
P. R. 4, 274. *s.* there his tenement whom well
P. R. 4, 571. fell whence he stood to *s.* his
S. A. 75. they creep yet *s.* I dark in light exposed
S. A. 118. *s.* how he lies at random, carelessly
S. A. 193. ye *s.* O friends how many evils have

S. A. 326. but s. here comes thy reverend sire
S. A. 960. I s. thou art implacable more deaf to
S.A.1061. but had we best retire I s. a storm
S. A. 1088. and now am come to s. of whom
S. A. 1091. the way to know were not to s. but
S. A. 1129. but shalt never s. Gath more
S. A. 1154. then thou shalt s. or rather to thy
S. A. 1317. where I will s. thee heartened and
S. A. 1415. perhaps offend them to s. me girt
S. A. 1451. lest I should s. him forced to things
S. A. 1520. shall we do stay here or run and s.
S. A. 1539. and to our wish I s. one hither
S. A. 1588. edifice where all were met to s. him
C. 216. I s. ye visibly and now believe
C. 373. virtue could s. to do what virtue would
C. 620. of small regard to s. to yet well skilled
C. 668. s. here be all the pleasures that fancy
A. 27. I s. bright honour sparkle through your
Il P. 121. thus Night, oft s. me in thy pale career
S. 10, 11. Madam methinks I s. him living yet
S.12, 13. from that mark how far they rove we s.
H. 22. s. how from far upon the eastern road
H. 171. and wroth to s. his kingdom fail
H. 237. but s., the Virgin blest
P. 36. s. the chariot and those rushing wheels
V. Ex. 35. look in and s. each blissful deity
**Seed.**—P. L. 1, 8. first taught the chosen s.
P. L. 3, 284. flesh when time shall be of virgin s.
P. L. 7, 310. herb yielding s., and fruit-tree
P. L. 7, 312. whose s. is in herself upon the earth
P. L. 10, 180. between thine and her s., her s.
P. L. 10, 499. his s., when is not set, shall bruise*
P. L. 10, 965. and to our s. (O hapless s.)
P. L. 10, 999. then both ourselves and s. at once
P. L. 10, 1031. that thy s. shall bruise
P. L. 11, 26. from thy s. sown with contrition
P. L. 11, 116. my covenant in the woman's s.
P. L. 11, 155. his promise that thy s. shall bruise
P. L. 11, 873. all the creatures and their s.
P. L. 12, 125. so that in his s. all nations shall
P. L. 12, 148. nations of the earth shall in his s.
P. L. 12, 148. by that s. is meant thy great
P. L. 12, 233. of that destined s. to bruise
P. L. 12, 260. promised to Abraham and his s.
P. L. 12, 273. concern just Abraham and his s.
P. L. 12, 327. a son the woman's s. to thee
P. L. 12, 379. should be called the s. of woman
P. L. 12, 395. but his works in thee and in thy s.
P. L. 12, 450. so in his s. all nations shall be
P. L. 12, 543. the woman's s. obscurely then
P. L. 12, 600. s. to come (for by the woman's s.)
P. L. 12, 623. by me the promised s. shall all
P. R. 1, 54. shall be inflicted by the s. of Eve
P. R. 1, 64. the woman's s. destined to this
P. R. 1, 151. I can produce a man of female s.
S. A. 1439. strength so great to mortal s.
**Seed-time.**—P. L. 11, 899. s.-t. and harvest
**Seeing.**—P. L. 8, 507. wrought in her so that s.
P. L. 9, 369. not s. thee attempted who attest
P. L. 10, 613. which the Almighty s. from his
S. A. 243. who s. those great acts which God had
S. 22, 3. bereft of light their s. have forgot
**Seek.**—P. L. 1, 163. out of our evil s. to bring
P. L. 1, 382. roaming to s. their prey on earth
P. L. 1, 480. to s. their wandering gods
P. L. 2, 252. but rather s. our own good from
P. L. 2, 464. s. deliverance for us all
P. L. 2, 975. I s. what readiest path leads
P. L. 3, 233. so coming he her aid can never s.
P. L. 3, 476. to s. in Golgotha him dead who
P. L. 4, 184. whom hunger drives to s. new
P. L. 4, 272. all that pain to s. her through the
P. L. 4, 375. league with you I s. and mutual
P. L. 4, 735. and when we s. as now thy gift
P. L. 4, 774. if ye s. no happier state and know
P. L. 5, 518. human desires can s. or apprehend
P. L. 6, 376. s. not the praise of men
P. L. 6, 559. may see when we have us how we s.
P. L. 8, 187. unless we ourselves s. them with
P. L. 8, 197. unprepared and still to s.
P. L. 8, 390. of fellowship I speak such as I s.

P. L. 9, 124. but neither here s. I no nor in
P. L. 9, 127. myself less miserable by what I s.
P. L. 9, 364. s. not temptation then, which to
P. L. 9, 383. so proud will first the weaker s.
P. L. 9, 1140. let none henceforth s. needless
P. L. 9, 1141. when earnestly they s. such
P. L. 9, 1152. should mean me ill or s. to harm
P. L. 10, 1001. let us s. death or he not found
P. L. 10, 1028. then let us s. some safer
P. L. 10, 1067. which bids us s. some better
P. L. 11, 328. nether world where shall I s.
P. L. 11, 770. let no man s. henceforth to be
P. L. 12, 515. then shall they s. to avail
P. R. 1, 336. me hence no other guide I s.
P. R. 3, 44. dost persuade me to s. wealth
P. R. 3, 105. I s. glory then as vain men s.
P. R. 3, 106. I s. not mine but his who sent me
P. R. 3, 134. but why should man s. glory
P. R. 3, 347. mayst know I s. not to engage
P. R. 4, 143. wise and valiant man would s. to
P. R. 4, 314. and in themselves s. virtue
P. R. 4, 325. what needs he elsewhere s.
P. R. 4, 526. if I beforehand s. to understand
S. A. 16. I s. this unfrequented place to find
S. A. 320. to s. in marriage that fallacious
S. A. 406. times when men s. most repose
S. A. 522. to what end should I s. it
S. A. 1308. the prisoner Samson here I s.
S. A. 1329. do they not s. occasion of new
C. 282. to s. in the valley some cool friendly
C. 302. if those you s. it were a journey
C. 366. I do not think my sister so to s.
C. 699. wouldst thou s. again to trap me here
Il P. 108. made hell grant what love did s.
**Seeking.**—P. L. 3, 453. naught s. but the
P. L. 10, 943. so fair his reconcilement s.
P. L. 11, 532. what thou eat'st and drink'st s.
P. R. 3, 151. worth or not worth the s. let it
P. R. 3, 242. as he who s. asses found a
S. A. 237. in s. just occasion to provoke
S. A. 252. entered Judea s. me who then
S. A. 828. thou wilt renounce thy s. and much
S. A. 1190. up with armed powers thee only s.
**Seeks.**—P. L. 6, 384. and through infamy s.
P. L. 7, 613. who s. to lessen thee against his
P. L. 9, 255. s. to work us woe and shame by
P. L. 9, 274. such an enemy we have who s.
P. L. 12, 165. who s. to stop their overgrowth
P. R. 3, 110. he s. glory and for his glory all
P. R. 4, 318. who therefore s. in these true
S. A. 837. love s. to have love
C. 376. oft s. to sweet retired solitude
**Seek'st.**—P. L. 6, 724. always s. to glorify
P. L. 7, 639. if else thou s. aught not surpassing
P. L. 8, 428. best with thyself accompanied s.
**Seem.**—P. L. 2, 122. dissuade me most and s. to
P. L. 2, 747. and do I s. now in thine eye so
P. L. 4, 957. who now wouldst s. patron of
P. L. 5, 466. more willingly thou couldst not s.
P. L. 5, 624. most when most irregular they s.
P. L. 6, 12. darkness there might well s.
P. L. 8, 19. her numbered stars that s. to roll
P. L. 8, 117. not that I so affirm though so it s.
P. L. 8, 129. earth so steadfast though she s.
P. L. 8, 210. I sit with thee I s. in heaven
P. L. 8, 404. s. I to thee sufficiently possessed of
P. L. 8, 580. s. such dear delight
P. L. 9, 632. made intricate s. straight to
P. L. 9, 706. your eyes that s. so clear
P. L. 9, 1093. that s. most to shame obnoxious
P. L. 10, 624. and conniving s. to gratify
P. L. 11, 146. his will hard to believe may s.
P. L. 11, 297. for such of shape may s. prince
P. R. 3, 261. well might s. the seats of mightiest
P. R. 4, 355. lovers of their country as may s.
P. R. 4, 441. would also s. of this fair change
P. R. 4, 463. over whose heads they roar and s.
P. R. 4, 494. at least might s. to hold all power
S. A. 79. scarce half I s. to live dead more than
S.A. 249. and would not s. to count them things
S. A. 332. for such ye s. though in this uncouth

S. A. 376. aught s. vile as vile hath been my folly
S. A. 703. just or unjust alike s. miserable
S. A. 722. some rich Philistian matron she may s.
S. A. 1420. if aught religion s. concerned
S. A. 1504. thy hopes are not ill-founded nor s.
**Seemed.**—P. L. 1, 777. they but now who s. in
P. L. 2, 110. he s. for dignity composed
P. L. 2, 167. this hell then s. a refuge from those
P. L. 2, 301. and in his rising s. a pillar of state
P. L. 2, 508. and s. alone the antagonist
P. L. 2, 642. so s. far off the flying fiend
P. L. 2, 650. the one s. woman to the waist
P. L. 2, 669. might be called that shadow s.
P. L. 2, 670. for each s. either black it stood
P. L. 2, 672. what s. his head the likeness
P. L. 2, 845. for both s. highly pleased
P. L. 3, 74. that s. firm land imbosomed
P. L. 3, 423. a globe far off it s. now seems
P. L. 3, 538. so wide the opening s. where
P. L. 3, 566. but nigh hand s. other worlds
P. L. 3, 567. or other worlds they s. or happy
P. L. 3, 595. if metal part s. gold, part silver
P. L. 3, 629. on some great charge employed he s.
P. L. 4, 152. so lovely s. that landscape
P. L. 4, 290. majesty s. lords of all and worthy s.
P. L. 4, 296. not equal as their sex not equal s.
P. L. 4, 459. that to me s. another sky
P. L. 4, 565. a spirit zealous as he s. to know
P. L. 4, 850. his lustre visibly impaired yet s.
P. L. 4, 990. nor wanted in his grasp what s.
P. L. 5, 52. fair it s. much fairer to my fancy
P. L. 5, 617. all s. well pleased all s. but were
P. L. 6, 91. though strange to us it s. at first
P. L. 6, 146. when I alone s. in thy world
P. L. 6, 230. each divided legion might have s.
P. L. 6, 232. led in fight yet leader s. each
P. L. 6, 244. tormented all the air all air s.
P. L. 6, 301. for likest gods they s. stood
P. L. 6, 499. so easy it s. once found which
P. L. 6, 573. for like to-pillars most they s.
P. L. 6, 615. for a dance they s. somewhat
P. L. 6, 667. war s. a civil game to this uproar
P. L. 7, 83. as to highest wisdom s.
P. L. 7, 329. that earth now s. like to heaven
P. L. 8, 39. and by his countenance s. entering
P. L. 8, 306. of earth before scarce pleasant s.
P. L. 8, 376. and s. so ordering I with leave
P. L. 8, 475. that what s. fair in all the world
P. L. 9, 394. Pomona thus adorned likest she s.
P. L. 9, 453. what pleasing s. for her now
P. L. 9, 787. such delight till then as s. in fruit
P. L. 9, 919. submitting to what s. remediless
P. L. 9, 1179. admiring what s. in thee so perfect
P. L. 10, 142. her doing s. to justify the deed
P. L. 10, 154. such as under government well s.
P. L. 10, 531. power no less he s. above the rest
P. L. 10, 1095. when angry most he s. and most
P. L. 11, 10. nor important less s. their petition
P. L. 11, 479. a lazar house it s. wherein were
P. L. 11, 577. their guise just men they s.
P. L. 11, 614. that s. of goddesses so blithe
P. R. 1, 315. following as s. the quest of some
P. R. 2, 295. own work it s. (nature taught art)
P. R. 2, 357. and ladies of the Hesperides that s.
S. A. 1698. depressed and overthrown as s.
A. 9. s. erst so lavish and profuse
**Seeming.**—P. L. 4, 316. mere shows of s. pure
P. L. 9, 738. impregned with reason to her s.
P. L. 10, 11. whatever wiles of foe or s. friend
P. L. 11, 604. pleasure though to nature s.
S. A. 1635. s. at first all heavenly
S. A. 1464. others more moderate s.
**Seemingly.**—P. L. 5, 434. nor s. the angel
**Seemlier.**—P. R. 2, 299. as before but s. clad
**Seemliest.**—P. L. 9, 268. safest and s. by her
**Seems.**—P. L. 2, 71. perhaps the way s. difficult
P. R. 2, 590. and ruin s. of ancient pile
P. L. 2, 790. though more it s. inflamed with
P. L. 3, 84. so bent he s. on desperate revenge
P. L. 3, 423. now s. a boundless continent
P. L. 3, 484. at heaven's wicket s. to wait them

P. L. 3, 689. thinks no ill where no ill s.
P. L. 3, 698. merits praise the more it s. excess
P. L. 4, 78. the hell I suffer s. a heaven
P. L. 4, 513. all is not theirs it s.
P. L. 4, 871. and fierce demeanour s. the prince
P. L. 4, 883. employed it s. to violate sleep
P. L. 5, 69. forbidden here it s. as only fit
P. L. 5, 271. to all the fowls he s. a phœnix
P. L. 5, 310. s. another morn risen on mid-noon
P. L. 6, 428. then fallible it s. of future we
P. L. 7, 415. sleeps or swims and s. a moving
P. L. 8, 547. so absolute she s. and in herself
P. L. 8, 550. she wills to do or say s. wisest
P. L. 9, 105. above light for thee alone as s.
P. L. 9, 769. for beasts it s. yet that one beast
P. L. 9, 287. flat s. to this and harsh
P. L. 9, 1170. not enough severe it s. in thy
P. L. 10, 600. though plenteous all too little s.
P. L. 10, 755. inexplicable thy justice s. yet to
P. L. 10, 1013. contempt of life and pleasure s.
P. L. 11, 599. much better s. this vision and
P. L. 11, 602. here nature s. fulfilled in all her
P. L. 11, 850. no more now floats but s. on
P. R. 1, 91. for man he s. in all his lineaments
P. R. 2, 93. afflicted I may be it s. and blest
P. R. 2, 229. or that which only s. to satisfy
P. R. 2, 450. and what in me s. wanting but
S. A. 595. my hopes all flat nature within me s.
S. A. 661. or rather s. a tune harsh
S. A. 711. female of sex it s.
S. A. 1443. much livelier than erewhile he s.
S. A. 1545. providence or instinct of nature s.
S. A. 1749. oft he s. to hide his face
H. 195. and the chill marble s. to sweat
**Seem'st.**—P. L. 9, 371. thus warned thou s.
P. R. 1, 327. for that to me thou s. the man
P. R. 1, 348. I discern thee other than thou s.
P. R. 4, 212. and thou thyself s. otherwise
**Seen.**—P. L. 1, 344. were those bad angels s.
P. L. 1, 544. were s. ten thousand banners
P. L. 3, 138. the son of God was s. most
P. L. 3, 549. of some foreign land first s.
P. L. 3, 552. though after heaven s.
P. L. 3, 599. rather oft than elsewhere s.
P. L. 4, 793. who tells of some infernal spirit s.
P. L. 4, 997. yet s. betwixt Astrea and the
P. L. 5, 56. of those from heaven by us oft s.
P. L. 5, 157. to us invisible or dimly s. in these
P. L. 6, 770. half on each hand were s.
P. L. 6, 774. but by his own first s.
P. L. 7, 369. so far remote with diminution s.
P. L. 7, 370. in his east the glorious lamp was s.
P. L. 7, 579. s. in the galaxy that milky way
P. L. 8, 578. thy mate who sees when thou art s.
P. L. 9, 436. voluble and bold now hid, now s.
P. L. 9, 508. Jove or Capitoline was s.
P. L. 9, 546. who shouldst be s. a goddess
P. L. 9, 826. be well but what if God have s.
P. L. 9, 1094. obnoxious and unseemliest s.
P. L. 10, 58. easy it may be s. that I intend mercy
P. L. 10, 104. with joy to meet my coming s.
P. L. 10, 877. longing to be s. though by the
P. L. 11, 462. but have I now s. death is this
P. L. 11, 466. death thou hast s. in his first
P. L. 11, 561. their stops and chords was s.
P. L. 11, 745. till the earth no more was s.
P. L. 11, 789. are they first s. in acts of prowess
P. L. 12, 6. thus thou hast s. one world begin
P. R. 1, 249. a star not s. before in heaven
P. R. 2, 2. and had s. him whom they had so
P. R. 2, 96. when twelve years he scarce had s.
P. R. 2, 182. have we not s. or by relation
P. R. 3, 67. he asked thee hast thou s. my
P. R. 3, 236. the world thou hast not s. much
S. A. 1440. in thy wondrous actions hath been s.
C. 471. oft s. in charnel vaults, and sepulchres
C. 575. who gently asked if he had s. such
A. 95. all Arcadia hath not s.
L. 43. shall now no more be s.
Il P. 86. be s. in some high lonely tower
S. 9, 3. and with those few art eminently s.

H. 114. are s. in glittering ranks with wings
H. 213. nor is Osiris s.
M. W. 35. so have I s. some tender slip
**Seer.**—P. L. 12, 553. thy prediction s. blest
**Seers.**—P. R. 3, 15. tongue of s. old infallible
**Sees.**—P. L. 1, 783. peasant s. or dreams he s.
P. L. 2, 191. all these our motions vain s. and
P. L. 5, 258. interposed however small he s.
P. L. 8, 578. thy mate who s. when thou art
P. L. 9, 469. the more he s. of pleasure
P. L. 9, 546. who s. thee? (and what is one?)
C. 665. while heaven s. good
L'A. 77. towers and battlements it s.
**Seest.**—P. L. 1, 91. into what pit thou s.
P. L. 1, 180. s. thou yon dreary plain
P. L. 2, 781. this odious offspring whom thou s.
P. L. 3, 80. only begotten Son, s. thou what
P. L. 3, 719. numberless as thou s. and how
P. L. 4, 467. a voice thus warned me what thou s.
P. L. 4, 468. what there thou s. fair creature
P. L. 5, 679. new laws thou s. imposed new
P. L. 6, 142. but thou s. all are not of thy train
P. L. 6, 147. my sect thou s. now learn too late
P. L. 6, 263. now plenteous as thou s. these
P. L. 7, 580. nightly as a circling zone thou s.
P. L. 8, 128. in six thou s. and what if seventh
P. L. 8, 145. her spots thou s. as clouds
P. L. 8, 206. till then thou s. how subtly
P. L. 8, 317. author of all this thou s. above
P. R. 2, 318. they all had need I as thou s.
P. R. 2, 393. have also power to give thou s.
P. R. 3, 285. his city there thou s. and Bactra
P. R. 4, 44. the city which thou s. no other
P. R. 4, 47. there the Capitol thou s. above
S. A. 826. which when thou s. impartial
S. A. 1105. thou s. it in thy hand
S. A. 1554. thou s. we long to know
**Seize.**—P. L. 1, 317. astonishment as this can s.
P. L. 2, 703. strange horror s. thee and pangs
P. L. 4, 407. whence rushing he might surest s.
P. L. 4, 796. such where ye find s. fast
P. L. 11, 221 to s. possession of the garden
P. L. 12, 356. at last they s. the sceptre
C. 653. but s. his wand though he and his cursed
S. 8, 2. chance on these defenceless doors may s.
P. 10. which on our dearest Lord did s. ere long
Cir. 14. our sin sore doth begin his infancy to s.
M. W. 50. sweet rest s. thee evermore
F. of C. 3. to s. the widowed whore plurality
**Seized.**—P. L. 1, 511. birthright s. by younger
P. L. 2, 432. hath deep silence and demur s.
P. L. 2, 758. amazement s. all the host
P. L. 3, 271. admiration s. all heaven what
P. L. 3, 552. such wonder s. though after
P. L. 3, 553. malign but much more envy s.
P. L. 4, 489. with that thy gentle hand
P. L. 6, 198. amazement s. the rebel thrones
P. L. 6, 647. terror s. the rebel host
P. L. 7, 143. he trusted to have s. and into
P. L. 8, 288. and with soft oppression s. my
P. L. 9, 1037. her hand he s. and to a shady
P. L. 11, 669. exploded and had s. with violent
P. L. 12, 412. s. on by force
**Seizure.**—P. L. 11, 254. defeated of his s.
**Seldom.**—P. L. 9, 423. with hope of what so s.
P. L. 10, 901. wishes most shall s. gain
P. R. 1, 345. with food whereof we wretched s.
P. R. 1, 436. which they who asked have s.
P. R. 4, 507. from that time s. have I ceased
S. 11, 4. numbering good intellects now s. pored
**Select.**—P. L. 11, 646. one way a band s. from
P. L. 11, 823. with them of man and beast s.
P. L. 12, 111. and one peculiar nation to s.
S. A. 363. as of a plant s. and sacred glorious
**Selectest.**—P. L. 8, 513. shed their s. influence
**Seleucia.**—P. L. 4, 212. S., built by Grecian kings
P. R. 3, 291. the great S., Nisibis
**Self.**—P. L. 8, 450. thy fit help thy other s.
P. L. 9, 388. but Delia's s. in gait surpassed
P. L. 10, 128. to accuse my other s. the partner
S. A. 102. my s. my sepulchre a moving grave

S. A. 234. she was not the cause but I my s.
C. 375. wisdom's s. oft seeks to sweet retired
L'A. 145. that Orpheus s. may heave his head
T. 10. and last of all thy greedy s. consumed
**Self-balanced.**—P. L. 7, 242. earth s.-b. on her
**Self-begot.**—P. L. 5, 860. us s.-b. self raised
**Self-begotten.**—S. A. 1699. like that s.-b. bird
**Self-condemning.**—P. L. 9, 1188. neither s.-c.
**Self-consumed.**—C. 597. self-fed and s.-c.
**Self-deceived.**—P. R. 4, 7. who s.-d. and
**Self-delusion.**—C. 365. bitter is such s.-d.
**Self-depraved.**—P. L. 3, 130. self-tempted s.-d.
**Self-destruction.**—P. L. 10, 1016. s.-d.
**Self-displeased.**—S. A. 514. over-just and s.-d.
**Self-esteem.**—P. L. 8, 572. more than s.-e.
**Self-fed.**—C. 597. s.-f. and self-consumed
**Self-killed.**—S. A. 1664. s.-k. not willingly
**Self-knowing.**—P. L. 7, 510. the rest s.-k.
**Self-left.**—P. L. 11, 93. and vain s.-l.
**Self-lost.**—P. L. 7, 154. such it be to lose s.-l.
**Self-love.**—S. A. 1031. too much of s.-l. mixed
**Self-offence.**—S. A. 515. for s.-o. more
**Self-opened.**—P. L. 5, 254. the gate s.-o. wide
**Self-preservation.**—S. A. 505. avoid s.-p.
**Self-raised.**—P. L. 1, 634. to reascend s.-r.
P. L. 5, 860. s.-r. by our own quickening power
**Self-rigorous.**—S. A. 513. than who s.-r.
**Self-rolled.**—P. L. 9, 183. many a round s.-r.
**Self-same.**—P. L. 6, 87. that s.-s. day by
P. L. 10, 315. to the s.-s. place where he first
P. L. 11, 203. one way the s.-s. hour
L. 23. for we were nursed upon the s.-s. hill
**Self-satisfying.**—S. A. 306. s.-s. solution
**Self-severe.**—S. A. 827. impartial s.-s.
**Self-tempted.**—P. L. 3, 130. fell s.-t.
**Self-violence.**—S. A. 1584. s.-v.? what cause
**Sell.**—S. A. 940. slight me s. me and forgo me
**Semblance.**—P. L. 1, 529. that bore s. of worth
P. L. 9, 607. in thy divine s. and in thy
S. 2, 5. perhaps my s. might deceive the truth
**Semele.**—P. R. 2, 187. Daphne or S. Antiopa
**Sennaar.**—P. L. 3, 467. on the plain of S.
**Senate.**—P. L. 12, 225. their great s. choose
**Senate-house.**—C. 389. as safe as in a s.-h.
**Senator.**—S. 17, 2. than whom a better s. ne'er
**Send.**—P. L. 2, 402. whom shall we s. in search
P. L. 2, 415. for on whom we s. the weight of
P. L. 3, 324. and from thee s. the summoning
P. L. 4, 383. and s. forth all her kings
P. L. 5, 548. neighbouring hills aereal music s.
P. L. 6, 425. Lord had powerfullest to s.
P. L. 6, 486. shall s. forth from far
P. L. 7, 166. I s. along ride forth and bid
P. L. 7, 572. will s. his winged messengers
P. L. 9, 195. great altar s. up silent praise
P. L. 9, 410. to intercept thy way or s. thee
P. L. 10, 55. but whom s. I to judge them
P. L. 10, 403. my substitutes I s. ye and
P. L. 11, 97. and s. him from the garden forth
P. L. 11, 117. s. them forth though sorrowing
P. L. 11, 261. and s. thee from the garden
P. L. 12, 486. to his own a comforter will s.
P. R. 1, 158. ere I s. him forth to conquer sin
P. R. 2, 43. God of Israel s. thy Messiah forth
S. A. 1160. and fettered s. thee into the common
S. A. 1431. s. thee the angel of thy birth
S. A. 1730. will s. for all my kindred all my
C. 219. would s. a glistering guardian if need
**Sender.**—P. L. 4, 852. best the s. not the sent
**Sending.**—P. L. 10, 59. with justice s. thee
S. A. 1394. darest thou at our s. and command
**Sends.**—P. L. 8, 238. but us he s. upon his
P. L. 10, 1077. and s. a comfortable heat
P. L. 12, 498. whom he s. to evangelize
P. R. 1, 462. and s. his Spirit of truth henceforth
S. 21, 14. when God s. a cheerful hour refrains
**Seneschals.**—P. L. 9, 38. with sewers and s.
**Senir.**—P. L. 12, 146. sons shall dwell to S.
**Sense.**—P. L. 1, 98. from s. of injured merit
P. L. 2, 151. devoid of s. and motion
P. L. 2, 556. song charms the s.

P. L. 3, 137. s. of new joy ineffable diffused
P. L. 4, 206. to all delight of human s. exposed
P. L. 4, 379. please like this fair paradise your s.
P. L. 5, 411. every lower faculty of s.
P. L. 5, 485. give both life and s.
P. L. 5, 565. for how shall I relate to human s.
P. L. 5, 572. surmounts the reach of human s.
P. L. 6, 351. all eye, all ear, all intellect, all s.
P. L. 6, 394. then first with fear surprised and s.
P. L. 6, 459. s. of pleasure we may well spare
P. L. 8, 119. remove his ways from human s.
P. L. 8, 289. oppression seized my drowsed s.
P. L. 8, 456. as with an object that excels the s.
P. L. 8, 579. but if the s. of touch whereby
P. L. 8, 609. from the s. variously representing
P. L. 9, 96. power active within beyond the s.
P. L. 9, 113. of growth s. reason all summed
P. L. 9, 188. and his brutal s. in heart or head
P. L. 9, 315. why shouldst not thou like s.
P. L. 9, 554. by tongue of brute and human s.
P. L. 9, 580. more pleased my s. than smell
P. L. 9, 871. with human voice and human s.
P. L. 9, 987. of sweet before had touched my s.
P. L. 9, 1031. so inflame my s. with ardour
P. L. 10, 754. why hast thou added the s.
P. L. 10, 810. stroke as I supposed bereaving s.
P. L. 11, 469. to s. more terrible at the entrance
P. L. 12, 10. impair and weary human s.
P. R. 1, 382. I should so have lost all s.
P. R. 1, 435. dark ambiguous and with double s.
P. L. 4, 296. doubted all things though plain s.
P. R. 4, 517. which bears no single s.
S. A. 176. their s. the air dissolves unjointed
S. A. 616. though void of corporal s.
S. A. 632. and s. of heaven's desertion
S. A. 1042. his s. depraved to folly and shameful
S. A. 1556. s. distract to know well what I utter
S. A. 1685. insensate left or to s. reprobate
C. 260. yet they in pleasing slumber lulled the s.
C. 538. to inveigle and invite the unwary s.
C. 839. and through the porch and inlet of each s.
A. 62. when drowsiness hath locked up mortal s.
Il P. 14. to hit the s. of human sight
S. M. 4. dead things with inbreathed s.
**Senseless.**—S. 12, 9. freedom in their s. mood
**Senses.**—P. L. 3, 188. I will clear their s.
P. L. 5, 104. the five watchful s. represent
P. L. 11, 265. that all his s. bound
P. L. 11, 540. thy s. then obtuse all taste
S. A. 916. where other s. want not their delights
H. 127. if ye have power to touch our s. so
**Sensible.**—P. L. 2, 278. remove the s. of pain
**Sensibly.**—S. A. 913. past cure bear not too s.
**Sensual.**—P. L. 9, 1129. now to s. appetite
C. 77. to roll with pleasure in a s. sty
C. 975. o'er s. folly and intemperance
**Sensualest.**—P. R. 2, 151. that fell the s.
**Sensuality.**—C. 474. linked itself by carnal s.
**Sent.**—P. L. 1, 541. up s. a shout that tore Hell's
P. L. 1, 585. or whom Biserta s. from
P. L. 1, 750. but was headlong s.
P. L. 4, 170. and with a vengeance s. from
P. L. 4, 842. give account to him who s. us
P. L. 4, 852. the sender not the s. or all at once
P. L. 6, 621. the terms we s. were terms of force
P. L. 6, 836. thunders which he s. before him
P. L. 7, 72. divine interpreter by favour s.
P. L. 8, 141. what if that light s. from her
P. L. 8, 647. s. from whose sovran goodness I
P. L. 10, 209. man both judge and Saviour s.
P. L. 10, 429. intercept their emperor s.
P. L. 10, 557. though to delude them s. could
P. L. 10, 1091. air frequenting s. from hearts
P. L. 10, 1103. s. from hearts contrite in sign of
P. L. 11, 356. I am s. to show thee what shall
P. L. 11, 742. exhalation dusk and moist s. up
P. L. 11, 857. the surer messenger a dove s.
P. L. 12, 170. s. from God to claim his people
P. L. 12, 270. O s. from heaven enlightener
P. L. 12, 612. which he hath s. propitious
P. R. 1, 71. to proclaim his coming is s.

P. R. 1, 134. message late on which I s. thee
P. R. 1, 460. God hath now s. his living oracle
P. R. 2, 50. s. his Anointed and to us revealed
P. R. 3, 107. seek not mine but his who s. me
P. R. 4, 131. for him I was not s. nor yet to
P. R. 4, 491. as false portents not s. from God
P. R. 4, 632. bound and to torment s. before
S. A. 999. so let her go God s. her to debase me
S. A. 1214. me their deliverer s. would not receive
S. A. 1675. among them he a spirit of phrenzy s.
C. 972. and s. them here through hard assays
L. 62. gory visage down the stream was s.
Il P. 153. s. by some spirit to mortals good
H. 186. the parting genius is with sighing s.
M. W. 59. s. thee from the banks of Came
D. F. I. 74. what a present thou to God hast s.
H. 46. s. down the meek-eyed peace
**Sentence.**—P. L. 2, 51. my s. is for open war
P. L. 2, 208. or bonds or pain the s. of their
P. L. 2, 291. and his s. pleased advising peace
P. L. 3, 145. word which closed thy sovran s.
P. L. 3, 332. arraigned shall sink beneath thy s.
P. L. 9, 88. of thoughts revolved his final s.
P. L. 10, 48. but that the mortal s. pass on his
P. L. 10, 97. and intercessor both to s. man
P. L. 10, 192. and to the woman thus his s.
P. L. 10, 776. would I meet mortality my s.
P. L. 10, 805. that were to extend his s.
P. L. 10, 934. that all the s. from thy head
P. L. 10, 1031. to mind with heed part of our s.
P. L. 11, 109. lest they faint at the sad s.
P. L. 11, 253. then due by s. when thou didst
S. A. 1369. outward force constrains the s. holds
**Sententious.**—P. R. 4, 264. in brief s.
**Senteries.**—P. L. 2, 412. the strict s.
**Seon.**—P. L. 1, 409. and Horonaim S.'s realm
**Separate.**—P. L. 6, 743. the impure far s.
P. L. 9, 422. wished his hap might find Eve s.
P. L. 9, 424. to his wish beyond his hope Eve s.
P. L. 9, 970. shall s. us linked in love so dear
P. L. 10, 251. death from sin no power can s.
S. A. 31. as of a person s. to God.
**Septentrion.**—P. R. 4, 31. from cold S.
**Sepulchral.**—P. 43. that sad s. rock.
**Sepulchre.**—S. A. 102. myself my s. a moving
**Sepulchred.**—W. S. 15. so s. in such pomp dost
**Sepulchres.**—C. 471. in charnel vaults and s.
**Sequel.**—P. L. 4, 1003. the s. each of parting
P. L. 10, 334. changing shape to observe the s.
**Sequent.**—P. L. 12, 165. suspected to a s. king
**Sequestered.**—P. L. 4, 706. sacred and s.
C. 500. how couldst thou find this dark s. nook
**Seraph.**—P. L. 1, 324. cherub and s. rolling
P. L. 3, 667. brightest s. tell in which of all
P. L. 5, 277. a s. winged six wings he wore
P. L. 5, 875. the flaming s. fearless though
P. L. 5, 896. so spake the s. Abdiel faithful
P. L. 6, 579. at each behind a s. stood
P. L. 7, 113. what words or tongue of s. can
P. L. 7, 198. cherub and s. potentates and
**Seraphic.**—P. L. 1, 539. s. arms and trophies
P. L. 1, 794. the great s. lords and cherubim
**Seraphim.**—P. L. 1, 129. led the embattled s.
P. L. 2, 512. him round a globe of fiery s.
P. L. 2, 750. and in sight of all the s. with thee
P. L. 3, 381. that brightest s. approach not
P. L. 5, 749. the mighty regencies of s.
P. L. 5, 804. when among the s. Abdiel
P. L. 6, 249. attack of fighting s. confused
P. L. 6, 604. view stood ranked of s. another row
P. L. 6, 841. of thrones and mighty s. prostrate
H. 113. the helmed cherubim, and sworded s.
S. M. 10. where the bright S. in burning row
**Serapis.**—P. L. 1, 720. Belus or S. their gods
**Serbonian.**—P. L. 2, 592. profound as that S.
**Sere.**—P. L. 10, 1071. may with matter s.
L. 2. myrtles brown with ivy never s.
**Serenate.**—P. L. 4, 769. s. which the starved
**Serene.**—P. L. 3, 25. so thick a drop s. hath
P. L. 5, 123. wont to be more cheerful and s.
P. L. 5, 734. lightning divine ineffable s.

P. L. 7, 509. and upright with front s. govern
P. L. 8, 181. intelligence of heaven, angel s.
P. L. 10, 1094. in whose look s. when angry
P. L. 11, 45. whom the father without cloud s.
C. 4. in regions mild of calm and s. air
**Sericana.**—P. L. 3, 438. barren plains of S.
**Serious.**—P. R. 1, 203, all my mind was set s.
C. 787. the sage and s. doctrine of virginity
**Serpent.**—P. L. 1, 34. the infernal s.
P. L. 2, 652. a s. armed with mortal sting
P. L. 4, 347. close the s. sly insinuating
P. L. 7, 302. with s. error wandering
P. L. 7, 482. some of s. kind wondrous in length
P. L. 7, 495. the s. subtlest beast of all the field
P. L. 9, 86. the s. subtlest beast of all the field
P. L. 9, 160. where hap may find the s. sleeping
P. L. 9, 182. where soonest he might find the s.
P. L. 9, 413. mere s. in appearance
P. L. 9, 455. such pleasure took the s. to behold
P. L. 9, 495. enclosed in s. inmate bad
P. L. 9, 560. thee s. subtlest beast of all the field
P. L. 9, 615. s. thy overpraising leaves in
P. L. 9, 647. s. we might have spared our
P. L. 9, 764. how dies the s. he hath eaten and
P. L. 9, 785. slunk the guilty s. and well
P. L. 9, 867. the s. wise or not restrained
P. L. 9, 930. profaned first by the s. by him
P. L. 9, 1150. have discerned fraud in the s.
P. L. 10, 3. and how he in the s. had perverted
P. L. 10, 84. conviction to the s. none belongs
P. L. 10, 162. the s. me beguiled and I did eat
P. L. 10, 165. he proceeded on the accused s.
P. L. 10, 174. on the s. thus his curse let fall
P. L. 10, 495. the brute s. in whose shape man
P. L. 10, 514. down he fell a montrous s.
P. L. 10, 580. and fabled how the s. whom
P. L. 10, 867. of my sight thou s. that name
P. L. 10, 879. with the s. meeting, fooled
P. L. 10, 927. that cruel s. on me exercise not
P. L. 10, 1032. that thy seed shall bruise the s.'s
P. L. 10, 1034. who in the s. hath contrived
P. L. 12, 150. who shall bruise the s.'s head
P. L. 12, 234. destined seed to bruise the s.
P. L. 12, 383. needs must the s. now his
P. L. 12, 454. there shall surprise the s. prince
P. P. 1, 312. the fiery s. fled and noxious worm
P. R. 2, 147. so spake the old s. doubting
P. R. 3, 5. at length collecting all his s. wiles
P. R. 4, 618. but thou infernal s. shalt not
S. A. 997. she's gone a manifest s. by her sting
S. 15, 8. to imp their s. wings
**Serpentine.**—P. L. 10, 870. and colour s.
**Serpent-kind.**—P. L. 9, 504. s.-k. lovelier
**Serpents.**—P. L. 10, 520. alike to s. all
P. L. 10, 539. instead a crowd of ugly s.
**Serpent-tongue.**—P. L. 9, 529. with s.-t.
**Serraliona.**—P. L. 10, 703. clouds from S.
**Serried.**—P. L. 1, 548. and s. shields in thick
P. L. 6, 599. served it to relax their s. files
**Servant.**—P. L. 6, 29. s. of God well done
P. L. 10, 215. thenceforth the form of s. to
P. L. 12, 104. this heavy curse s. of servants
P. R. 3, 67. hast thou seen my s. Job
S. A. 1615. was Samson as a public s. brought
**Servants**—P. L. 10, 214. his s.' feet so now
P. L. 12, 104. this heavy curse servant of s.
S. A. 1755. his s. he with new acquist of true
C. 10. after this mortal change to her true s.
**Serve.**—P. L. 1, 263. in hell than s. in heaven
P. L. 2, 999. if all I can will s. that little
P. L. 3, 680. new happy race of men to s. him
P. L. 4, 943. easier business were to s. their
P. L. 5, 101. lesser faculties that s. reason as
P. L. 5, 322. small store will s. where store all
P. L. 5, 532. be tried whether they s. willing
P. L. 5, 538. freely we s. because we freely love
P. L. 5, 590. for distinction s. of hierarchies
P. L. 5, 681. new minds may raise in us who s.
P. L. 5, 802. being ordained to govern not to s.
P. L. 6, 166. most through sloth had rather s.
P. L. 6, 175. to s. whom God ordains or nature

P. L. 6, 179. this is servitude to s. the unwise
P. L. 6, 180. as thine now s. thee
P. L. 6, 183. let me s. in heaven God ever blest
P. L. 6, 440. may s. to better us and worse our
P. L. 7, 115. which best may s. to glorify
P. L. 8, 87. bright and greater should not s.
P. L. 8, 168. leave them to God above him s.
P. L. 9, 85. of all most opportune might s. his
P. L. 9, 1092. what best may for the present s.
P. L. 10, 727. own deservings but this will not s.
P. L. 10, 767. to s. him thy reward was of his
P. L. 11, 517. when themselves they vilified to s.
P. L. 11, 881. or s. they as a flowery verge
P. R. 1, 316. which might s. against a winter's
P. R. 3, 375. offspring in his territory yet s.
P. R. 3, 431. s. their enemies who s.
P. R. 4, 177. Lord thy God and only him shalt s.
S. A. 267. lorded over them whom now they s.
S. A. 564. to what can I be useful wherein s.
S. A. 577. wilt thou then s. the Philistines
S. A. 585. wherewith to s. him better than thou
S. A. 743. if aught in my ability may s.
S. A. 1216. whence to this day they s.
S. A. 1429. to what may s. his glory best
C. 725. we should s. him as a grudging master
C. 750. will s. to ply the sampler and to tease
A. 105. to s. the lady of this place
S. 1, 14. both them I s. and of their train am I
S. 19, 5. more bent to s. therewith my Maker
S. 19, 11. who best bear his mild yoke they s.
S. 19, 14. they also s. who only stand and wait
**Served.**—P. L. 1, 64. s. only to discover sights
P. L. 1, 217. how all his malice s. but to bring
P. L. 3, 110. had s. necessity not me?
P. L. 4, 398. as their shape s. best his end
P. L. 6, 599. nor s. it to relax their serried files
P. L. 8, 34. s. by more noble than herself attains
P. L. 9, 38. then marshalled feast s. up in hall
P. L. 9, 547. adored and s. by angels numberless
P. L. 11, 60. that fondly lost this other s.
P. L. 11, 518. and took his image whom they s.
P. R. 3, 379. fathers in the land of Egypt s.
S. A. 419. that saw not how degenerately I s.
M. W. 66. to him that s. for her before
V. Ex. 14. the daintiest dishes shall be s. up last
**Serves.**—P. L. 2, 385. but their spite still s.
P. L. 7, 614. against his purpose s. to manifest
P. R. 2, 472. lawless passions in him which he s.
S. A. 240. yet Israel still s. with all his sons
**Servest.**—S. A. 1363. with this strength thou s.
**Service.**—P. L. 1, 149. or do him mightier s.
P. L. 4, 45. nor was his s. hard
P. L. 4, 420. no other s. than to keep this one
P. L. 5, 529. our voluntary s. he requires not
P. L. 9, 155. subjected to his s. angel-wings
P. R. 1, 427. the other s. was thy chosen task
P. R. 2, 326. duty and s. nor to stay till bid
S. A. 686. thee on them, or them to thee of s.
S. A. 1163. s. with those thy boisterous locks
S. A. 1499. to use him further yet in some s.
C. 85. that to the s. of this house belongs
A. 38. and with all helpful s. will comply
Il P. 163. in s. high and anthems clear
H. 194. affrights the flamens at their s. quaint
V. Ex. 30. thy s. in some graver subject use
**Serviceable.**—P. R. 1, 421. but thou art s.
H. 244. bright harnessed angels sit in order s.
**Servile.**—P. L. 2, 246. flowers our s. offerings
P. L. 2, 257. the easy yoke of s. pomp
P. L. 12, 305. from s. fear to filial
P. R. 4, 102. a victor people free from s. yoke
S. A. 5. relieves me from my task of s. toil
S. A. 412. s. mind rewarded well with s.
S. A. 574. or the draff of s. food consume me
S. A. 1213. if their s. minds me their deliverer
**Servilely.**—P. L. 4, 959. and s. adored
**Servility.**—P. L. 6, 169. s. with freedom to
**Serving.**—P. R. 3, 378. long from Israel s. as
**Servitude.**—P. L. 6, 175. the name of s.
P. L. 6, 178. this is s. to serve the unwise
P. L. 9, 141. in one night freed from s.

P. L. 12. 89. and to s. reduce man till then
P. L. 12, 132. herds and flocks and numerous s.
P. L. 12, 220. rather inglorious life with s.
P. R. 3, 176. thy country from her heathen s.
P. R. 3, 381. these if from s. thou shalt restore
S. A. 269. and by their vices brought to s.
S. A. 416. is not yet so base as was my former s.
S. A. 1336. so debased with corporal s. that my
**Session.**—P. L. 2, 514. then of their s. ended
H. 163. when at the world's last s.
**Set.**—P L. 1, 39. to s. himself in glory above his
P. L. 1, 72. darkness and their portion s.
P. L. 1, 714. where pilasters round were s.
P. L. 2, 822. but to s. free from out this dark
P. L. 3, 221. deadly forfeiture and ransom s.
P. L. 3, 538. where bounds were s. to darkness
P. L. 3, 587. so wondrously was s. his station
P. L. 4, 51. one step higher would s. me
P. L. 4, 612. God hath s. labour and rest
P. L. 4, 664. light prepared they s. and rise
P. L. 5, 63. why else s. here
P. L. 5, 509. scale of nature s. from
P. L. 5, 632. tables are s. and piled
P. L. 6, 89. and on his throne to s. the envier
P. L. 6, 310. such as to s. forth great things
P. L. 6, 522. they finished and in order s.
P. L. 6, 755. and wings were s. with eyes with
P. L. 7, 349. and s. them in the firmament of
P. L. 7, 376. but opposite in levelled west was s.
P. L. 7, 385. bright luminaries that s. and rose
P. L. 7, 427. intelligent of seasons and s. forth
P. L. 7, 583. the sun was s. and twilight from
P. L. 8, 67. is as the book of God before thee s.
P. L. 8, 111. who since the morning hour s. out
P. L. 8, 227. and s. on man his equal love
P. L. 8, 324. which I have s. the pledge of thy
P. L. 8, 382. these inferior far beneath me s.
P. L. 9, 941. dignified so high s. over all his
P. L. 10, 149. wherein God s. thee above her
P. L. 10, 499. his seed when is not s. shall
P. L. 10, 664. to the winds they s. their
P. L. 11, 288. nor s. thy heart thus overfond
P. L. 11, 382. for different cause the tempter s.
P. L. 11, 813. and before them s. the paths of
P. L. 11, 825. the cataracts of heaven s. open
P. L. 11, 896. will therein s. his triple-coloured
P. L. 12, 247. vouchsafes among them to s. up
P. R. 1, 202. all my mind was s. serious to learn
P. R. 2, 112. great work to come before him s.
P. R. 2, 153. s. women in his eye and in his
P. R. 2, 207. made and s. wholly on the
P. R. 2, 320. if food were now before thee s.
P. R. 2, 410. and all thy heart is s. on high
P. R. 3, 284. till Cyrus s. them free
P. R. 3, 390. before mine eyes thou hast s. and
P. R. 4, 160. on what I offer s. as high esteem
P. R. 4, 378. which would have s. thee in short
P. R. 4, 393. directs me in the starry rubric s.
P. R. 4, 549. there on the highest pinnacle he s.
P. R. 4, 586. in a flowery valley s. him down
P. R. 4, 587. and s. before him spread a table
P. R. 4, 610. never more henceforth will dare s.
S. A. 255. in what place to s. upon them what
S. A. 317. to s. his people free
S. A. 496. the mark of fool s. on his front
S. A. 517. who knows but God hath s. before us
S. A. 1201. when I perceived all s. on enmity
S. A. 1375. and man prefer s. God behind
S. A. 1412. to favour and perhaps to s. thee free
S. A. 1462. contemptuous proud s. on revenge
S. A. 1466. God and state they easily would s.
S. A. 1624. came to the place and what was s.
S. A. 1679. the only s. on sport and play
C. 444. but s. at naught the frivolous bolt
C. 715. s. to work millions of spinning worms
C. 801. her words s. off by some superior power
C. 893. thick s. with agate and the azure sheen
C. 897. thus I s. my printless feet
L'A. 84. are at their savoury dinner s.
L'A. 106. to earn his cream-bowl duly s.
L'A. 149. to have quite s. free his half-regained

Il P. 20. to s. her beauty's praise above
S. 12, 10. and still revolt when truth would s.
S. 13, 12. Dante shall give Fame leave to s. thee
H. 121. his constellations s.
P. 9. and s. my harp to notes of saddest woe
D. F. I. 62. to s. the hearts of men on fire
F. of C. 6. force our consciences that Christ s. free
L. 80 nor in the glistering foil s. off to the world
**Setia.**—P. R. 4, 117. their wines of S. Cales
**Sets.**—P. L. 2, 804. my son and foe who s. them
P. L. 5, 43. shadowy s. off the face of things
P. L. 5, 357. dazzles the crowd and s. them
P. L. 8, 632. isles Hesperian s. my signal
P. L. 12, 52. and in derision s. upon their
P. R. 3, 380. this offer s. before thee to deliver
S. A. 1572. but death who s. all free hath paid
**Setting.**—P L. 1, 744. and with the s. sun
P. L. 4, 540. the s. sun slowly descended
**Settle.**—P. L. 4, 940. to s. here on earth
S. 17. 5. whether to s. peace or to unfold
**Settled.**—P. L. 2, 279. counsels and the s.
P. R. 6, 540. and s. in his face I see sad
C. 595. gathered like scum and s. to itself
**Settlings.**—C. 800. and s. of a melancholy
**Seven.**—P. L. 3, 481. they pass the planets s.
P. L. 3, 648. one of the s. who in God's
P. L. 3, 654. for thou of those s. spirits that
P. L. 9, 63. the space of s. continued nights
P. L. 10, 673. with the s. Atlantic Sisters
P. L. 12, 158. disgorging at s. mouths
P. L. 12, 255. before him burn s. lamps
P. R. 4, 35. on s. small hills with palaces
S. A. 1017. in one day or s. though one should
**Sevenfold.**—P. L. 2, 171. them into s. rage
P. L. 4, 1914. meet thy flight s. and scourge
**Sevens.**—P. L. 11, 735. came s. and pairs
**Seventh.**—P. L. 7, 581. now on earth the s.
P. L. 7, 592. blessed and hallowed the s. day
P. L. 8, 128. what if s. to these the planet earth
P. L. 11, 700. but he the s. from thee whom
**Seven-times-folded.**—S. A. 1122, and s.-t-f.
**Seven-times-wedded.**—P. L. 5, 223. s.-t.-w.
**Seventy.**—P. L. 12, 345. the space of s. years
**Sever.**—P. L. 9, 366. if from me thou s. not
S. 14, 4. which us from life doth s.
**Several.**—P. L. 2, 523. his s. way pursues
P. L. 2, 901. in their s. clans
P. L. 3, 714. swift to their s. quarters hasted
P. L. 5, 477. each in their s. active spheres
P. L. 5, 697. or s. one by one the regent
P. L. 7, 240. things to like the rest to s. place
P. L. 8, 131. which else to s. spheres thou must
P. L. 10, 323. three s. ways in sight to each of
P. L. 10, 610. they both betook them s. ways
P. L. 10, 650. gave them s. charge assorted
P. R. 3, 276. within her wall s. days' journey
C. 25. by course commits to s. government
H. 234. slips to his s. grave
**Severe.**—P. L. 2, 276. fires as soft as now s.
P. L. 2, 333. given to us enslaved but custody s.
P. L. 3, 224. to death and hell by doom s.
P. L. 4, 293. wisdom, sanctitude s. and pure
P. L. 4, 294. s., but in true filial freedom placed
P. L. 4, 845. his grave rebuke s. in youthful
P. L. 5, 807. and in a flame of zeal s.
P. L. 6, 825. too s. to be beheld and full
P. L. 9, 1144. have passed thy lips Adam s.
P. L. 9, 1169. not enough s. it seems in thy
P. L. 10, 1095. most he seemed and most s.
P. R. 4, 280. sect Epicurean and the Stoic s.
**Severed.**—P. L. 9, 252. harm befall thee s.
P. L. 9, 958. our state cannot be s.; we are one
C. 274. how to regain my s. company
**Severely.**—S. A. 788. the gentler if s. thou
**Severest.**— P. R. 2, 164. tame s. temper
**Severing.**—P. L. 1, 704. s. each kind
**Severity.**—C. 109. strict age and sour s.
**Severn.**—C. 825. sways the smooth S. stream
V. Ex. 96. or S. swift guilty of maiden's death
**Severs.**—S. 17, 11. each means what s. each
**Sewed.**—P. L. 9, 1095. leaves together s.

P. L. 9, 1112, together s. to gird their waist
**Sewers.**—P. L. 9, 38. up in hall with s. and
P. L. 9, 446. where houses thick and s. annoy
**Sex.**—P. L. 1, 424. can either s. assume or both
P. L. 4, 296. though both not equal as their s.
P. L. 8, 471. manlike but different s. so lovely
P. L. 9, 574. nor aught but food discerned or s.·
P. L. 9, 822. so to add what wants in female s.
P. L. 10, 898. and strait conjunction with this s.
P. L. 10, 956. frailty and infirmer s. forgiven
P. R. 3, 341. to win the fairest of her s.
S. A. 711. female of s. it seems
S. A. 774. weakness … incident to all our s.
S. A. 1026. was lavished on their s. that inward
**Sexes.**—P. L. 8, 151. which two great s.
**Sextile.**—P. L. 10, 659. in s. square, and
**Shackles.**—S. A. 1326. me out with s. tired
**Shade.**—P. L. 3, 557. of night's extended s.
P. L. 3, 615. sight no obstacle found here nor s.
P. L. 4, 138. insuperable height of loftiest s.
P. L. 4, 141. s. above s. a woody theatre
P. L. 4, 245. and where the unpierced s.
P. L. 4, 325. under a tuft of s. that on a green
P. L. 4, 451. found myself reposed under a s.
P. L. 4, 532. by fountain side or in thick s.
P. L. 4, 572. but under s. lost sight of him
P. L. 4, 693. of thickest covert was inwoven s.
P. L. 4, 868. Ithuriel and Zephon through the s.
P. L. 5, 203. fountain or fresh s.
P. L. 5, 230. in what bower or s. thou find'st
P. L. 5, 277. six wings he wore to s. his
P. L. 5, 643. whence light and s. spring both ·
P. L. 6, 666. ground they fought in dismal s.
P. L. 6, 828. with dreadful s. contiguous and
P. L. 8, 653. up to heaven from the thick s.
P. L. 9, 185. not yet in horrid s. or dismal den
P. L. 9, 1106. a pillared s. high overarched
P. L. 9, 1110. loop-holes cut through thickest s.
P. L. 10, 249. thou my s. inseparable must
P. L. 10, 716. in part though hid in gloomiest s.
P. L. 11, 78. blissful bowers of amaranthine s.
P. R. 2, 242. where still from s. to s. the Son of
P. R. 2, 292. and entered soon the s. high
P. R. 2, 339. space under the broadest s.
S. A. 3. for yonder bank hath choice of sun or s.
S. A. 1734. and plant it round with s. of laurel
L. 24. fed the same flock by fountain, s. and rill
L. 68. to sport with Amaryllis in the s.    ·
L'A. 96. dancing in the chequered s.
H. 188. the nymphs in twilight s.
**Shaded.**—P. L. 6, 885. s. with branching palm
**Shades.**—P. L. 1, 65. of sorrow, doleful s.
P. L. 1, 303. where the Etrurian s.
P. L. 2, 621. fens, bogs, dens, and s. of death
P. L. 3, 734. Adam's abode those lofty s. his
P. L. 4, 239. mazy error under pendent s.
P. L. 4, 1015. with him fled the s. of night
P. L. 7, 331. and love to haunt her sacred s.
P. L. 9, 266. that gave thee being still s. thee
P. L. 9, 408. hid among sweet flowers and s.
P. L. 10, 861. other echo late I taught your s.
P. L. 11, 270. these happy walks and s. fit
P. R. 1, 194. and with dark s. and rocks ·
P. R. 1, 296. pathless desert dusk with horrid s.
P. R. 4, 243. suburban, studious walks and s.
P. R. 4, 404. under some concourse of s.
C. 62. and in thick shelter of black s. embowered
C. 127. which these dun s. will ne'er report
C. 266. whom certain these rough s. did never
C. 335. in double night of darkness and of s.
C. 429. grots and caverns shagged with horrid s.
C. 521. immured in cypress s. a sorcerer dwells
C. 580. O night, and s.! how are ye joined
C. 984. along the crisped s. and bowers
A. 42. which I full oft amidst these s. alone
L. 137. s. and wanton winds and gushing brooks
L'A. 8. under ebon s. and low-browed rocks
Il P. 28. and in secret s. of woody Ida's inmost
S. 13, 14. met in the milder s. of purgatory
**Shadest.**—P. L. 3, 377. but when thou s. the
**Shadier.**—P. L. 4, 705. in s. bower more

**Shadiest.**—P. L. 3, 39. and in s. covert hid
**Shading.**—P. L. 3, 357. s. the fount of life
P. L. 3, 509. by model or by s. pencil drawn
P. R. 3, 221. a kind of s. cool interposition
**Shadow.**—P. L. 2, 669. might be called that s.
P. L. 3, 120. so without least impulse or s.
P. L. 3, 619. s. from body opaque can fall
P. L. 4, 470. where no s. stays thy coming
P. L. 5, 575. though what if earth be but the s.
P. L. 9, 12. sin and her s. death and misery
P. L. 10, 264. whom thus the meagre s. answered
P. R. 4, 70. where the s. both way falls
**Shadowed.**—P. L. 5, 284. s. from either heel
P. L. 8, 311. all real as the dream had lively s.
P. L. 9, 1055. a veil had s. them from knowing
**Shadowing.**—P. L. 6, 554. every side with s.
P. L. 6, 655. s. and oppressed whole legions
**Shadows.**—P. L. 12, 233. by types and s.
C. 207. of calling shapes and beckoning s. dire
C. 470. such are those thick and gloomy s. damp
Il P. 134. and s. brown that Sylvan loves
H. 206. hath left in s. dread
H. 232. the flocking· s. pale
**Shadowy.**—P. L. 4, 776. with her s. cone
P. L. 5, 43. s. sets off the face of things
P. L. 5, 686. ere yet dim night her s. cloud
P. L. 12, 291. save by those s. expiations weak
P. L. 12, 303. disciplined from s. types to truth
P. R. 4, 399. brought in lowering night her s.
L'A. 108. his s. flail hath threshed the corn
**Shady.**—P. L. 3, 28. clear spring or s. grove
P. L. 4, 720. thus at their s. lodge arrived both
P. L. 5, 137. from under s. arborous roof
P. L. 5, 367. in yonder s. bower to rest
P. L. 8, 262. hill, dale and s. woods and sunny
P. L. 8, 286. green s. bank profuse of flowers
P. L. 9, 277. as in a s. nook I stood behind
P. L. 9, 420. by fountain or by s. rivulet
P. L. 9, 1037. her hand he seized and to a s.
P. R. 1, 304. on hill sometimes anon on s. vale
C. 38. the nodding horror of whose s. brows
A. 88. under the s. roof of branching elm
H. 77. and though the s. gloom
**Shafts.**—P. L. 1, 176. hath spent his s.
P. R. 3, 305. they issue forth steel bows and s.
**Shagged.**—C. 429. caverns s. with horrid shades
**Shaggy.**—P. L. 4, 224. but through the s. hill
P. L. 6, 645. waters, woods and by the s. tops
L. 54. nor on the s. top of Mona high
**Shake.**—P. L. 6, 712. the rapid wheels that s.
C. 797. and s. till all thy magic structures
H. 162. shall from the surface to the centre s.
**Shaked.**—D.F.I. 44. of s. Olympus by mischance
**Shaken.**—P. L. 9, 287. can by his fraud be s.
**Shakes.**—P. L. 2, 711. from his horrid hair s.
P. L. 7, 466. and rampant s. his brinded mane
A. 58. or tasselled horn s. the high thicket
**Shakespeare.**—L'A. 133. or sweetest S. fancy's
W. S. 1. what needs my S. for his bones
**Shallow.**—P. L. 9, 544. and s. to discern half
P. R. 4, 327. versed in books and s. in himself
C. 514. though so esteemed by s. ignorance
L'A. 76. s. brooks and rivers wide
S. 1, 6. first heard before the s. cuckoo's bill
F. of C. 12. s. Edwards and Scotch What-d'ye-call
**Shallow-searching.**—A. 41. s.-s. fame hath
**Shame.**—P. L. 1, 115. an ignominy and s.
P. L. 2, 58. accept this dark opprobrious den of s.
P. L. 2, 496. O s. to men, devil with devil damned
P. L. 2, 564. apathy and glory and s.
P. L. 4, 82. my dread of s. among the spirits
P. L. 4, 313. guilty s. dishonest s. of nature's
P. L. 6, 340. for anguish and despite and s.
P. L. 9, 255. seeks to work us woe and s. by sly
P. L. 9, 312. while s. thou looking on s. to be
P. L. 9, 384. so bent the more shall s. him
P. L. 9, 1058. naked left to guilty s.
P. L. 9, 1079. whence evil store even s. the last
P. L. 9, 1094. to s. obnoxious and unseemliest
P. L. 9, 1097. that this new-comer s. there sit
P. L. 9, 1114. to hide their guilt and dreaded s.

P. L. 9, 1119. and as they thought their *s*.
P. L. 10, 113. but apparent guilt and *s*.
P. L. 10, 159. to whom sad Eve with *s*.
P. L. 10, 336. saw their *s*. that sought vain
P. L. 10, 546. triumph to *s*. cast on themselves
P. L. 10, 555. to work them farther woe or *s*.
P. L. 10, 906. to a fell adversary his hate or *s*.
P. L. 11, 629. O pity and *s*. that they who
P. L. 12, 102. who for the *s*. done to his father
P. R. 3, 136. but condemnation ignominy and *s*.
P. R. 4, 14. and never cease though to his *s*.
P. R. 4, 189. wert thou so void of fear or *s*.
P. R. 4, 342. ridiculous and themselves past *s*.
S. A. 196. confused with *s*. how could I once look
S. A. 446. of all reproach the most with *s*.
S. A. 457. which is my chief affliction *s*.
S. A. 597. my race of glory run and race of *s*.
S. A. 841. in vain thou strivest to cover *s*. with *s*.
S. A. 1579. death to life is crown or *s*.
S. 9, 11. and hope that reaps not *s*.
H. 40. and on her naked *s*.
H. 80. and hid his head for *s*.
W. S. 9. to the *s*. of slow-endeavouring art
**Shamed.**—P. L. 1, 461. where he fell flat and *s*.
P. L. 9, 1139. of all our good *s*. naked miserable
S.A. 563. now blind disheartened *s*. dishonoured
**Shamefaced.**—H. 111. the *s*. night arrayed
**Shameful.**—P. L. 12, 413. a *s*. and accursed
P. R. 3, 87. violent or *s*. death their due reward
P. R. 4, 22. and to *s*. silence brought
S. A. 491. expiate . . . my crime *s*. garrulity
S. A. 1043. to folly and *s*. deeds which ruin ends
S. 15, 12. public faith cleared from the *s*. brand
**Shamefully.**—S. A. 499. weakly at least and *s*.
**Shameless.**—C. 736. upon the sun with *s*. brows
**Shames.**—P. R. 4, 303. oft *s*. not to prefer
**Shape.**—P. L. 1, 428. but in what *s*. they choose
P. L. 1, 590. in *s*. and gesture proudly eminent
P. L. 2, 448. in the *s*. of difficulty or danger
P. L. 2, 649. on either side a formidable *s*.
P. L. 2, 666. the other *s*. if *s*. it might be
P. L. 2, 681. who and what art thou execrable *s*.
P. L. 2, 704. and in *s*. so speaking and so
P. L. 2, 756. to thee in *s*. and countenance
P. L. 2, 784. all my nether *s*. thus grew
P. L. 3, 634. he casts to change his proper *s*.
P. L. 4, 288. two of far nobler *s*. erect and tall
P. L. 4, 365. hand that formed them on their *s*.
P. L. 4, 398. as their *s*. served best his end
P. L. 4, 461. a *s*. within the watery gleam
P. L. 4, 587. in whatsoever *s*. he lurk of whom
P. L. 4, 819. so started up in his own *s*. the fiend
P. L. 4, 835. think not revolted spirit thy *s*.
P. L. 4, 848. and saw virtue in her *s*. how
P. L. 5, 276. he lights and to his proper *s*.
P. L. 5, 309. what glorious *s*. comes this way
P. L. 5, 362. heaven such glorious *s*. contain
P. L. 6, 352. and colour *s*. or size assume as
P. L. 8, 295. one came methought of *s*. divine
P. L. 8, 463. and saw the *s*. still glorious before
P. L. 9, 503. pleasing was his *s*. and lovely
P. L. 9, 601. not long though to this *s*. retained
P. L. 10, 333. and changing *s*. to observe the
P. L. 10, 450. and *s*. star-bright appeared or
P. L. 10, 495. the brute serpent in whose *s*.
P. L. 10, 516. him punished in the *s*. he sinned
P. L. 10, 574. till their lost *s*. permitted they
P. L. 10, 869. nothing wants but that thy *s*.
P. L. 11, 129. all their *s*. spangled with eyes
P. L. 11, 297. for such of *s*. may seem prince
P. L. 11, 467. thou hast seen in his first *s*. on
P. R. 2, 176. admiring their *s*. their colour
P. R. 3, 11. of good, wise, just the perfect *s*.
P. R. 4, 449. he starts in wonted *s*.
S. A. 1011. strength comeliness of *s*. or amplest
C. 52. who ever tasted, lost his upright *s*.
C. 460. begin to cast a beam on the outward *s*.
**Shaped.**—P. L. 5, 55. one *s*. and winged like
**Shapes.**—P. L. 1, 358. godlike *s*. and forms
P. L. 1, 479. with monstrous *s*. and sorceries

P. L. 1, 790. reduced their *s*. immense and
P. L. 3, 604. in various *s*. old Proteus from
P. L. 5, 105. she forms imaginations aery *s*.
P. L. 5, 111. but misjoining *s*. wild work ensues
P. L. 6, 753. by four cherubic *s*. four faces each
P. L. 9, 1082. those heavenly *s*. will dazzle
P. L. 11, 467. but many *s*. of death and many
C. 2. my mansion is where those immortal *s*.
C. 207. of calling *s*. and beckoning shadows dire
L'A. 4. 'mongst horrid *s*. and shrieks and sights
Il P. 6. and fancies fond with gaudy *s*. possess
**Share.**—P. L. 1, 267. call them not to *s*. with
P. L. 2, 29. and condemns to greatest *s*. of
P. L. 2, 452. refusing to accept as great a *s*. of
P. L. 9, 831. Adam shall *s*. with me in bliss or
P. L. 10, 961. each others burden in our *s*. of
S. A. 53. without a double *s*. of wisdom
C. 769. had but a moderate and beseeming *s*.
S. 15, 14. while avarice and rapine *s*. the land
Cir. 6. now mourn and if sad *s*. with us to bear
**Shared.**—P. L. 6, 326. deep entering *s*. all
P. R. 4, 87. *s*. among petty kings too far
**Sharp.**—P. L. 2, 902. or heavy *s*. smooth
P. L. 9, 584. to satisfy the *s*. desire I had of
P. L. 10, 511. his visage drawn he felt to *s*..
P. L. 10, 977. though *s*. and sad yet tolerable
P. L. 11, 63. after life tried in *s*. tribulation
P. L. 11, 800. in *s*. contest of battle found no
P. R. 3, 324. behind them shot *s*. sleet of
**Sharpened.**—P. L. 3, 620. *s*. his visual
**Sharpening.**—P. L. 4, 978. *s*. in mooned
**Sharpest.**—P. L. 9, 91. hide from *s*. sight
**Sharpest-sighted.**—P. L. 3, 691. *s*.-*s*.
**Sharply.**—P. R. 1, 468. *s*. thou hast insisted
**Shatter.**—L. 5. *s*. your leaves
**Shattered.**—P. L. 1, 232. or the *s*. side of
P. L. 6, 361. with *s*. arms and uncouth pain
S.A. 1241. to the hazard of thy brains and *s*. sides
C. 799. were *s*. into heaps over thy false head
**Shattering.**—P. L. 10, 1066. *s*. the graceful
**Shaven.**—S. A. 540. ridiculous despoiled *s*.
**Shaves.**—P. L. 2, 634. now *s*. with level wing
**Sheaf.**—P. L. 11, 435. ear and the yellow *s*.
**Shearers.**—L. 117. to scramble at the *s*.'s feast
**Shears.**—A. 65. to those that hold the vital *s*.
L.75. comes the blind Fury with the abhorred *s*.
F. of C. 16. their wholesome and preventive *s*.
**Sheaves.**—P. L. 4, 984. his hopeful *s*. prove
P. L. 11, 430. whereon were *s*. new-reaped
L'A. 88. with Thestylis to bind the *s*.
**Shed.**—P. L. 4, 501. impregns the clouds that *s*.
P. L. 4, 670. in part *s*. down their stellar
P. L. 8, 513. on that hour *s*. their selectest
P. L. 9, 893. and all the faded roses *s*.
P. L. 10, 631. polluting sin with taint hath *s*.
P. R. 2, 72. when scarce a *s*. could be obtained
C. 652. and *s*. the luscious liquor on the ground
L. 149. bid Amaranthus all his beauty *s*.
**Shedding.**—P. L. 7, 375. *s*. sweet influence
**Sheds.**—P. L. 1, 597. disastrous twilight *s*.
C. 323. which oft is sooner found in lowly *s*.
**Sheen.**—C. 893. set with agate and the azure *s*.
C. 1003. but far above in spangled *s*.
H. 145. throned in celestial *s*.
M. W. 73. with thee there clad in radiant *s*.
**Sheeny.**—D.F.I.48. besiege the wall of *s*. heaven
**Sheep.**—L. 125. the hungry *s*. look up and are
S. 18, 6. record their groans who were thy *s*.
H. 91. perhaps their loves or else their *s*.
**Sheep-cote.**—P. R. 2, 287. view *s*.-*c*. or herd
P. R. 2, 288. but cottage herd or *s*.-*c*. none he
**Sheep-hook.**—L. 120. know how to hold a *s*.-*h*.
**Sheep-walks.**—P. L. 11, 431. other part *s*.-*w*.
**Sheer.**—P. L. 1, 742. *s*. o'er the crystal
P. L. 4, 182. and *s*. within lights on his feet
P. L. 6, 325. and in half cut *s*.
P. R. 4, 419. torn up *s*.
**Shell.**—P. L. 5, 342. or bearded husk or *s*.
P. R. 2, 345. or purling brook, of *s*. or fin
C. 231. that livest unseen within thy aery *s*.
C. 873. by scaly Triton's winding *s*.

**Shells.**—P. L. 7, 407. or in their pearly *s.*
**Shelter.**—P. L. 2, 167. besought the deep to *s.*
  P. L. 6, 843. thrown on them as a *s.* from his
  P. R. 2, 73. could be obtained to *s.* him or me
  P. R. 3, 221. a *s.* and a kind of shading cool
  C. 62. and in thick *s.* of black shades embowered
**Sheltered.**—P. L. 11, 223. where Adam *s.*  ̄
  P. L. 11, 824. in the ark be lodged and *s.* round
  P. R. 4, 406. dews and damps of night his *s.*
  P. R. 4, 407. but, *s.,* slept in vain
**Shelters.**—P. L. 9, 1109. *s.* in cool
**Shelves.**—C. 117. and on the tawny sands and *s.*
**Shepherd.**—P. L. 1, 8. that *s.* who first
  P. L. 11, 436. a *s.* next more meek came with
  P. R. 2, 439. Gideon and Jephthah and the *s.*
  C. 93. the star that bids the *s.* fold
  C. 271. nay gentle *s.* ill is lost that praise
  C. 307. to find out that good *s.* I suppose
  C. 321. *s.* I take thy word and trust thy honest
  C. 330. to my proportioned strength! *s.* lead on
  C. 493. O brother 'tis my father's *s.* sure
  C. 509. to tell thee sadly *s.* without blame
  C. 615. why prithee *s.* how durst thou then
  C. 619. brought to my mind a certain *s.* lad
  C. 823. the soothest *s.* that e'er piped on plains
  C. 908. *s.* 'tis my office best to help ensnared
  L. 39. thee *s.,* thee the woods and desert caves
  L. 49. such Lycidas thy loss to *s.'s* ear
  L. 65. to tend the homely slighted *s.'s* trade
  L'A. 67. and every *s.* tells his tale
**Shepherdess.**—M. W. 63. that fair Syrian *s.*
**Shepherds.**—P. L. 4, 185. watching where *s.*
  P. L. 11, 650. scarce with life the *s.* fly but call
  P. L. 12, 365. to simple *s.* keeping watch
  P. R. 1, 244. in the fields of Bethlehem sung to *s.*
  C. 848. for which the *s.* at their festivals
  C. 958. back *s.* back enough your play
  A. 1. look nymphs and *s.* look
  A. 96. nymphs and *s.* dance no more
  L. 165. weep no more woful *s.* weep no more
  L. 182. now Lycidas the *s.* weep no more
  H. 85. the *s.* on the lawn or e'er the point
  Cir. 3. first heard by happy watchful *s.'* ear
**Shew.**—C. 512. good Thyrsis? prithee briefly *s.*
  C. 995. that her purfled scarf can *s.*
  Il P. 171. of every star that heaven doth *s.*
**Sheweth.**—S. 2, 4. spring no bud or blossom *s.*
**Shibboleth.**—S. A. 289. of well pronouncing *s.*
**Shield.**—P. L. 1, 284. his ponderous *s.*
  P. L. 1, 565. with ordered spear and *s.*
  P. L. 4, 785. they part half wheeling to the *s.*
  P. L. 4, 990. what seemed both spear and *s.*
  P.·L. 6, 192. less could his *s.* such ruin
  P. L. 6, 255. of tenfold adamant his ample *s.*
  P. L. 6, 543. gripe fast his orbed *s.* borne even
  P. L. 10, 542. down fell both spear and *s.* down
  P. R. 4, 405. arms thick intertwined might *s.*
  S. A. 132. useless the forgery of brazen *s.*
  S. A. 284. not worse than by his *s.* and spear
  S. A. 1122. beam and seven-times-folded *s.*
  S. A. 1434. and be now a *s.* of fire
  C. 447. what was that snaky-headed Gorgon *s.*
  C. 658. and some good angel bear a *s.* before us
  H. 55. the idle spear and *s.* were high up hung
**Shields.**—P. L. 1, 548. and serried *s.* in thick
  P. L. 1, 668. clashed on their sounding *s.*
  P. L. 4, 553. celestial armoury *s.,* helms
  P. L. 6, 83. *s.* various with boastful argument
  P. L. 6, 102. flaming cherubim and golden *s.*
  P. L. 6, 305. two broad suns their *s.*
  P. L. 6, 337. while others bore him on their *s.*
  P. L. 6, 840. o'er *s.* and helms and helmed
  P. L. 9, 34. or tilting furniture emblazoned *s.*
**Shift.**—C. 273. any boast of skill but extreme *s.*
**Shifter.**—U. C. I. 5. 'twas such a *s.* that if truth
**Shifts.**—U. P. L. 9, 515. so steers and *s.* her sail
  P. R. 4, 308. or subtle *s.* conviction to evade
  S. A. 1116. therefore without feigned *s.* let be
  S. A. 1220. these *s.* refuted answer thy appellant
  C. 617. care and utmost *s.* how to secure
**Shine.**—P. L. 3, 52. celestial light *s.* inward

  P. L. 3, 134. first and last shall brightest *s.*
  P. L. 4, 657. but wherefore all night long *s.*
  P. L. 4, 675. in deep of night *s.* not in vain
  P. L. 6, 748. third sacred morn began to *s.*
  P. L. 7, 108. dismiss thee ere the morning *s.*
  P. L. 8, 155. only to *s.* yet scarce to contribute
  P. L. 9, 104. that *s.* yet bear their bright
  P. L. 10, 652. first his precept so to move so *s.*
  P. R. 1, 93. glimpses of his Father's glory *s.*
  H. 202. now sits not girt with taper's holy *s.*
  T. 16. truth and peace and love shall ever *s.*
  D. F. I. 34. O no for something in thy face did *s.*
**Shined.**—S. 23, 11. goodness in her person *s.*
**Shines.**—P. L. 3, 386. the Almighty Father *s.*
  P. L. 3, 723. from hence though but reflected *s.*
  P. L. 4, 363. and could love so lively *s.* in them
  P. L. 5, 20. awake the morning *s.* and the
  P. L. 7, 380. then in the east her turn she *s.*
  P. L. 8, 94. plenty than the sun that barren *s.*
  S. A. 1052. most *s.* and most is acceptable above
**Shining.**—P. L. 2, 757. then *s.* heavenly fair
  P. L. 4, 668. in which of all these *s.* orbs hath
  P. L. 3, 670. but all these *s.* orbs his choice to
  P. L. 4, 283. enclosed with *s.* rock
  P. L. 5, 259. not unconform to other *s.* globes
  P. L. 7, 401. of fish that with their fins and *s.*
  A. 15. in circle round her *s.* throne
**Ship.**—P. L. 9, 513. as when a *s.* by skilful
  S. A. 714. comes this way sailing like a stately *s.*
**Shipwrecked.**—S.·A. 198. have *s.* my vessel
**Shivered.**—P. L. 6, 389. all the ground with *s.*
**Shivering.**—P. L. 10, 1003. longer *s.* under
**Shivers.**—P. R. 4, 19. though all to *s.* dashed
**Shoaling.**—P. L. 10, 288. from each side *s.*
**Shoals.**—P. L. 7, 400. and *s.* of fish that with
**Shock.**—P. L. 2, 1014. through the *s.* of
  P. L. 6, 207. less hideous joined the horrid *s.*
  P. L. 10, 1074. with winds rude in their *s.*
**Shone.**—P. L. 1, 537. *s.* like a meteor
  P. L. 1, 599. darkened so yet *s.* above them all
  P. L. 1, 672. the rest entire *s.* with a glossy
  P. L. 2, 304. princely counsel in his face yet *s.*
  P. L. 3, 139. in him all his father *s.*
  P. L. 3, 268. which only *s.* filial obedience
  P. L. 3, 363. that like a sea of jasper *s.*
  P. L. 3, 508. sparkling orient gems the portal *s.*
  P. L. 3, 565. innumerable stars that *s.* stars
  P. L. 3, 597. twelve that *s.* in Aaron's
  P. L. 3, 713. light *s.* and order from disorder
  P. L. 4, 292. image of their glorious maker *s.*
  P. L. 6, 720. on his Son with rays direct *s.* full
  P. L. 6, 768. came far off his coming *s.*
  P. L. 7, 196. and all his Father in him *s.*
  P. L. 7, 499. now heaven in all her glory *s.*
  P. L. 10, 682. to them day had unbenighted *s.*
  P. L. 10, 1096. but favour grace and mercy *s.*
**Shook.**—P. L. 1, 105. and *s.* his throne
  P. L. 2, 353. *s.* heaven's whole circumference
  P. L. 2, 672. and *s.* a dreadful dart  ·
  P. L. 2, 882. that the lowest bottom *s.* of
  P. L. 3, 394. thy flaming chariot wheels that *s.*
  P. L. 5, 286. and *s.* his plumes that heavenly
  P. L. 6, 219. all earth had to her centre *s.*
  P. L. 6, 833. the steadfast empyrean *s.*
  P. L. 9, 1124. and *s.* sore their inward state of
  P. L. 11, 492. triumphant death his dart *s.*
  P. R. 4, 270. *s.* the arsenal and fulmined
  S. A. 1650. he tugged he *s.* till down they
  L. 112. he *s.* his mitred locks and stern bespake
  S. A. 409. might easily have *s.* off all her snares
**Shoon.**—C. 635. treads on it daily with his ... *s.*
**Shoot.**—P. L. 6, 480. they *s.* forth so beauteous.
  C. 81. I. *s.* from heaven to give him
**Shooting.**—P. L. 4, 556. swift as a *s.* star
  A. 16. *s.* her beams like silver threads
**Shoots.**—P. L. 2, 1036. *s.* far into the bosom
  P. L. 3, 586. *s.* invisible virtue even to the
  C. 99. *s.* against the dusky pole
  C. 296. plucking ripe clusters from the tender *s*
**Shops.**—C. 716. that in their green *s.* weave the
**Shore.**—P. L. 1, 284. moving toward the *s.*

P. L. 1, 310. who beheld from the safe *s.*
P. L. 1, 585. or whom Biserta sent from Afric *s.*
P. L. 2, 661. from the hoarse Trinacrian *s.*
P. L. 2, 912. of neither sea nor *s.* nor air nor
P. L. 2, 1011. now his sea should find a *s.*
P. L. 3, 537. on Egypt and the Arabian *s.*
P. L. 4, 162. from the spicy *s.* of Araby the Blest
P. L. 5, 339. or middle *s.* in Pontus
P. L. 7, 210. and from the *s.* they viewed the
P. L. 10, 666. to confound sea air and *s.*
P. L. 10, 696. Norumbega and the Samoed *s.*
P. L. 11, 750. sea without *s.*
P. L. 12, 143. on the *s.*, Mount Carmel
P. L. 12, 199. till his rescued gain their *s.*
P. L. 12, 215. safe towards Canaan from the *s.*
P. R. 2, 344. all fish from sea or *s.*
P. R. 4, 93. but strong, on the Campanian *s.*
P. R. 4, 238. where on the Ægean *s.* a city
P. R. 4, 330. gathering pebbles on the *s.*
S. A. 537. who *s.* me like a tame wether
S. A. 962. are reconciled at length and sea to *s.*
C. 49. coasting the Tyrrhene *s.* as the winds
L. 63. down the swift Hebrus to the Lesbian *s.*
L. 183. henceforth thou art the genius of the *s.*
Il P. 75. over some wide-watered *s.*
H. 182. and the resounding *s.*
**Shores.**—P. L. 7, 417. caves and fens and *s.*
P. L. 9, 117. now land now sea and *s.* with
P. L. 9, 1118, the trees on isles and woody *s.*
C. 209. on sands and *s.* and desert wildernesses
L. 154. Ay me! whilst thee the *s.* and sounding
**Shorn.**—P. L. 1, 596. *s.* of his beams
P. L. 9, 1062. and waked *s.* of his strength
S. A. 1024. had *s.* the fatal harvest of thy head
**Short.**—P. L. 1, 797. after *s.* silence then and
P. L. 4, 102. *s.* intermission bought with
P. L. 4, 535. enjoy till I return *s.* pleasures for
P. L. 5, 562. after *s.* pause assenting thus
P. L. 8, 414. all human thoughts come *s.*
P. L. 9, 50. twilight upon the earth *s.* arbiter
P. L. 9, 174. since higher I fall *s.* on him who
P. L. 9, 248. to *s.* absence I could yield
P. L. 9, 250. and *s.* retirement urges sweet
P. L. 9, 963. but *s.* of thy perfection how shall
P. L. 10, 923. while yet we live scarce one *s.* hour
P. L. 10, 1000. let us make *s.*, let us seek death
P. L. 11, 147. or one *s.* sigh of human breath
P. L. 11, 184. after *s.* blush of morn
P. L. 11, 554. how long or *s.* permit to heaven
P. L. 11, 628. to whom thus Adam of *s.* joy
P. R. 1, 56. for longest time to him is *s.*
P. R. 3, 235. few days' *s.* sojourn and what
P. R. 4, 287. not therefore am I *s.* of knowing
P. R. 4, 378. set thee in *s.* time with ease on
S. A. 670. thy providence through his *s.* course
S. A. 1307. his message will be *s.* and voluble
S. 13, 4. with Midas' ears committing *s.* and long
D.F.I. 60. and after *s.* abode fly back with speed
M. W. 9. after so *s.* time of breath
**Shortened.**—P. 6. wintry solstice like the *s.* light
M. W. 52. *s.* hast thy own life's lease
**Shorter.**—P. L. 4, 595. by *s.* flight to the east
P. R. 3, 269. cut *s.* many a league
**Shortest.**—P. L. 10, 1005. ways to die the *s.*
**Shortly.**—S. A. 598. and I shall *s.* be with them
**Shot.**—P. L. 1, 172. the sulphurous hail *s.* after
P. L. 2, 67. black fire and horror *s.* with equal
P. L. 3, 618. as they now *s.* upward still direct
P. L. 5, 141. *s.* parallel to the earth his dewy
P. L. 8, 62. and from about her *s.* darts of desire
P. L. 9, 72. into a gulf *s.* underground.
P. R. 3, 323. behind them *s.* sharp sleet
P. L. 5, 301. *s.* down direct his fervid rays
P. L. 5, 15. whether waking or asleep *s.* forth
P. L. 15. *s.* through with orient beams
P. L. 6, 849. glared lightning and *s.* forth
M. W. 40. new *s.* up from vernal shower
**Shove.**—L. 118. *s.* away the worthy bidden guest
**Shoulder.**—P. L. 5, 279. that clad each *s.*
**Shoulders.**—P. L. 1, 287. hung on his *s.*
P. L. 2, 306. with Atlantean *s.* fit to bear

P. L. 3, 627. illustrious on his *s.* fledge with
P. L. 4, 303. but not beneath his *s.* broad
P. R. 2, 462. when on his *s.* each man's burden
S. A. 146. and on his *s.* bore the gates of Azza
S. A. 1493. on his *s.* waving down those locks
Il P. 36. over thy decent *s.* drawn
**Shout.**—P. L. 1, 542. a *s.* that tore hell's concave
P. L. 2, 520. the host of hell with deafening *s.*
P. L. 3, 345. the multitude of angels with a *s.*
P. L. 6, 96. but the *s.* of battle now began
P. L. 6, 200. ours joy filled and *s.* presage
P. L. 7, 256. with joy and *s.* the hollow universal
P. L. 10, 505. expecting their universal *s.*
S. A. 1472. what noise or *s.* was that?
S. A. 1510. horribly loud unlike the former *s.*
S. A. 1620. at sight of him the people with a *s.*
C. 103. midnight *s.* and revelry
S. M. 9. with saintly *s.* and solemn jubilee
**Shouting.**—S. A. 1473. doubtless the people *s.*
**Show.**—P. L. 2, 273. what can heaven *s.* more
P. L. 3, 255. and *s.* the powers of darkness
P. L. 4, 122. practised falsehood under saintly *s.*
P. L. 4, 558. and *s.* the mariner from what
P. L. 6, 161. that thy success may *s.* destruction
P. L. 6, 627. they *s.* us when our foes walk
P. L. 7, 406. with quick glance *s.* to the sun
P. L. 8, 115. to *s.* invalid that which thee to
P. L. 8, 538. in outward *s.* elaborate of inward
P. L. 9, 492. hate stronger under *s.* of love
P. L. 9, 665. but with *s.* of zeal and love to
P. L. 10, 187. triumphed in open *s.* and with
P. L. 10, 442. in *s.* plebeian angel militant of
P. L. 10, 870. and colour serpentine may *s.* thy
P. L. 10, 883. understood not all was but a *s.*
P. L. 10, 1004. shivering under fears that *s.*
P. L. 10, 1065. with various face begins to *s.*
P. L. 11, 357. to *s.* thee what shall come in
P. L. 11, 384. to *s.* him all earth's kingdoms
P. L. 11, 709. to *s.* thee what reward awaits
P. L. 12, 123. into a land which he will *s.*
P. R. 1, 141. to *s.* him worthy of his birth
P. R. 2, 226. with such as have more *s.* of
P. R. 2, 459. a crown golden in *s.* is but a
P. R. 3, 124. to *s.* forth his goodness and impart
P. R. 4, 110. this grandeur and majestic *s.*
P. R. 4, 554. now *s.* thy progeny if not to
S. A. 58. to *s.* withal how slight the gift was
S. A. 910. afford me place to *s.* what recompense
S. A. 1340. to *s.* them feats and play before their
S. A. 1601. should be brought forth to *s.* the
S. A. 1644. I mean to *s.* you of my strength yet
C. 627. and *s.* me simples of a thousand names
A. 79. whate'er the skill of lesser gods can *s.*
S. 21, 12. disapproves that care though wise in *s.*
H. 227. our Babe to *s.* his Godhead true
D.F.I. 61. as if to *s.* what creatures heaven doth
**Showed.**—P. L. 7, 555. how it *s.* in prospect
P. L. 11, 245. his starry helm unbuckled *s.*
D. F. I. 35. above mortality that *s.* thou
U. C. I. 15. *s.* him his room where he must lodge
**Show'dst.**—S. A. 781. thou *s.* me first the way
**Shower.**—P. L. 2, 491. landscape snow or *s.*
P. L. 6, 545. no drizzling *s.* but rattling storm
P. L. 10, 662. influence malignant when to *s.*
P. L. 11, 883. again dissolve and *s.* the earth
P. L. 12, 124. and upon him *s.* his benediction
Il P. 127. or ushered with a *s.* still
M. W. 40. new shot up from vernal *s.*
**Showered.**—P. L. 4, 152. when God hath *s.*
P. L. 4, 773. the flowery roof *s.* roses which
P. L. 5, 640. the all bounteous king who *s.*
**Showers.**—P. L. 2, 4. *s.* on her kings
P. L. 4, 646. the fertile earth after soft *s.*
P. L. 4, 653. nor fragrance after *s.* nor
P. L. 5, 190. the thirsty earth with falling *s.*
P. R. 3, 324. shot sharp sleet of arrowy *s.*
L. 140. that on the green turf suck the honied *s.*
**Showery.**—P. L. 6, 759. colours of the *s.* arch
**Shown.**—P. L. 1, 218. grace and mercy *s.* on
P. L. 4, 1012. and *s.* how light how weak if
P. L. 6, 247. prodigious power had *s.* and met

P. R. 1, 276. for it was *s.* him so from heaven
P. R. 2, 13. they thought he might be only *s.*
P. R. 2, 51. pointed at and *s.* in public
P. R. 2, 84. and in public *s.*
P. R. 3, 350. and *s.* all this fair sight
P. R. 3, 401. luggage of war there *s.* me
P. R. 4, 88. having *s.* thee I have *s.*
S. A. 994. my country I was judged to have *s.*
S.A.1475. some proof of strength before them *s.*
C. 745. beauty is nature's brag and must be *s.*
**Shows.**—P. L. 4, 316. with *s.* instead mere *s.*
P. L. 8, 553. discountenanced and like folly *s.*
P. L. 8, 575. and to realities yield all her *s.*
P. L. 11, 194. by these mute signs in nature *s.*
P. R. 3,286.Ecbatana her structure vast there *s.*
P. R. 4, 220. *s.* the man as morning *s.* the day
**Show'st.**—P. L. 2, 818. my fair son here *s.* me
P. R. 4, 121. embassies thou *s.* from nations
**Shrewd.**—C. 846. the *s.* meddling elf delights
**Shriek.**—H. 178. with hollow *s.* the steep
**Shrieked.**—P. R. 4, 423. some yelled some *s.*
**Shrieks.**—L'A. 4. 'mongst horrid shapes and *s*
**Shrill.**—P. L. 5, 7. and the *s.* matin song
L'A. 56. through the high wood echoing *s.*
**Shrine.**—P. L. 3, 379. thee like a radiant *s.*
P. L. 7, 360. transplanted from her cloudy *s.*
P. L. 11, 13. before the *s.* of Themis stood
P. R. 1, 438. who ever by consulting at thy *s.*
C. 267. unless the goddess that in rural *s.*
A. 36. to the great mistress of yon princely *s.*
H. 176. Apollo from his *s.*
**Shrined.**—P. L. 6, 672. *s.* in his sanctuary
**Shrines.**—P. L. 1, 388. sanctuary itself their *s.*
**Shrink.**—P. L. 2, 205. *s.* and fear what yet
P. L. 4, 925. not that I less endure or *s.*
P. L. 11, 846. which made their flowing *s.*
P. R. 2, 223. her plumes fall flat and *s.* into
C. 656. yet will they soon retire if he but *s.*
**Shrinks.**—H. 203. Lybic Hammon *s.* his horn
**Shroud.**—P. L. 10, 1068. some better *s.*
C. 316. or *s.* within these limits I shall know
L. 22. and bid fair peace be to my sable *s.*
H.218.nought but profoundest hell can be his *s.*
**Shrouded.**—P. R. 4, 419. ill wast thou *s.*
**Shrouds.**—P. L. 2, 1044. the port though *s.*
C. 147. to your *s.* within these brakes and trees
**Shrub.**—P. L. 4, 696. each odorous bushy *s.*
P. L. 5, 349. with rose and odours from the *s.*
P. L. 7, 322. and the humble *s.* and bush with
P. L. 8,517. rose flung odours from the spicy *s.*
**Shrubby.**—C. 306. west it rises from this *s.*
**Shrubs.**—P. L. 4, 176. undergrowth of *s.* and
**Shrunk.**—L.133.voice is past that *s.* thy streams
**Shuddering.**—P. L. 2, 616. *s.* horror pale
C. 802. yet a cold *s.* dew dips me all o'er
**Shun.**—P. L. 2, 581. or *s.* the goal with rapid
P. L. 2, 810. I forewarn thee *s.* his deadly
P. L. 8, 327. *s.* to taste
P. L. 8, 828. *s.* the bitter consequence
P. L. 9, 483. higher intellectual more I *s.*
P. L. 10, 339. not hoping to escape but *s.* the
P. L. 10, 1062. by what means to *s.*
**Shunned.**—P. L. 1, 636. or dangers *s.* by me
P. L. 2, 679. thing nought valued he nor *s.*
P. L. 2, 1019. when Ulysses on the larboard *s.*
P. L. 4, 319. nor *s.* the sight of God or angel
P. L. 9, 331. then wherefore *s.* or feared by us
P. L. 9, 699. why not known since easier *s.*
P. R. 1, 414. ejected emptied gazed unpitied *s.*
S. 9, 2. hast *s.* the broad way and the green
**Shunning.**—P. L. 9, 1108, herdsman *s.* heat
**Shunn'st.**—II P. 61. sweet bird that *s.* the noise
**Shut.**—P. L. 2, 358. though heaven be *s.* and
P. L. 2, 776. to keep these gates for ever *s.*
P. L. 2,883. she opened but to *s.* excelled her
P. L. 3, 193. shall not be slow mine eye not *s.*
P. L. 3,333. full thenceforth shall be for ever *s.*
P. L. 4, 658. glorious sight when sleep hath *s.*
P. L. 8, 240. we found fast *s.* the dismal gates
P. L. 9, 691. shall that be *s.* to man which to
P. L. 11, 849. as the heaven his windows *s.*

P. L. 9, 278. returned at *s.* of evening flowers
P. L. 3, 50. wisdom at one entrance quite *s.* out
S. A. 160. *s.* up from outward light
**Shuts.**—C. 978. where day never *s.* his eye
L. 111 the golden opes the iron *s.* amain
**Sibyl.**—V. Ex. 69. a *s.* old bow bent with ... age
**Sicilian.**—L. 133. return *S.* muse and call
**Sick.**—P. L. 11, 490. despair tended the *s.*
**Sicken.**—H. 137. will *s.* soon and die
**Sickened.**—U. C. II. 15. the time away he *s.*
**Sickness.**—P. L. 11, 524, to loathsome *s.*
S. A. 698. with *s.* and disease thou bowest them
**Side.**—P. L. 1, 78. and weltering by his *s.*
P. L. 1, 207. moors by his *s.* under the lee
P. L. 1, 232. or the shattered *s.* of thundering
P. L. 1,578. on each *s.* mixed with auxiliar gods
P. L. 1,782. whose midnight revels by a forest *s.*
P. L. 2, 101. we are at worst on this *s.* nothing
P. L. 2,108. on the other *s.* up rose Belial
P. L. 2, 649. on either *s.* a formidable shape
P. L. 2, 706. on the other *s.* incensed with
P. L. 2, 755. till on the left *s.* opening wide
P. L. 2, 871. thus saying from her *s.* the fatal
P. L. 2, 905. levied to *s.* with warring winds
P. L. 2, 1006. to that *s.* heaven from whence
P. L. 3, 71. the wall of heaven on this *s.* night
P. L. 3, 366. tuned that glittering by their *s.*
P. L. 3,427. save on that *s.* which from the wall
P. L. 3, 722. whose hither *s.* with light from
P. L. 4, 179. that looked east on the other *s.*
P. L. 4, 257. another *s.* umbrageous grots
P. L. 4, 326. by a fresh fountain-*s.* they sat
P. L. 4, 484. out of my *s.* to thee nearest my
P. L. 4, 485. to have thee by my *s.* henceforth
P. L. 4, 531. by fountain *s.* or in thick shade
P. L. 4, 695. on either *s.* acanthus and each
P. L. 4, 741. straight *s.* by *s.* were laid
P. L. 4, 985. on the other *s.* Satan alarmed
P. L. 5, 11. he on his *s.* leaning half-raised
P. L. 5, 393. on her ample square from *s.* to *s.*
P. L. 6, 133. and his *s.* abandoned at the terror
P. L. 6, 221. angels fought on either *s.*
P. L. 6, 327. entering shared all his right *s.*
P. L. 6,554. every *s.* with shadowing squadrons
P. L. 6. 844. nor less on either *s.* tempestuous
P. L. 8, 465. who stooping opened my left *s.*
P. L. 8, 536. or from my *s.* subducting took
P. L. 9, 265. or worse leave not the faithful *s.*
P. L. 9, 888. on the other *s.* Adam soon as he
P. L. 9, 965. from whose dear *s.* I boast me
P. L. 9,1153. I to have never parted from thy *s.*
P. L. 10, 288. from each *s.* shoaling towards
P. L. 10, 415. on either *s.* disparted Chaos
P. L. 10,881. to thrust thee from my *s.* imagined
P. L. 11, 118. and on the east *s.* of the garden
P. L. 11, 176. I never from thy *s.* henceforth
P. L. 11, 246. by his *s.* as in a glistering Zodiac
P. L. 11, 574. but on the hither *s.* a different
P. L. 11, 731. and in the *s.* a door contrived
P. L. 12, 114. him on this *s.* Euphrates yet
P. L. 12, 641. looking back all the eastern *s.*
P. R. 1, 295. looking round on every *s.* beheld
P. R. 2, 23. on this *s.* the broad lake Genezaret
P. R. 2, 136. if he be man by mother's *s.* at
P. R. 2, 184. or grove by mossy fountain-*s.*
P. R. 3, 154. by mother's *s.* thy father
P. R. 3, 255. from his *s.* two rivers flowed
P. R. 4, 25. our Saviour to the western *s.*
P. R. 4, 33. on each *s.* an imperial city stood
P. R. 4, 159. on the other *s.* know also thou
S. A. 246. I on the other *s.* used no ambition to
S. A. 768. but that on the other *s.* if it be weighed
S. A. 1432. to stand fast by thy *s.*
S. A. 1609. the other *s.* was open where the
S. A. 1617. on each *s.* went armed guards
C. 283. and left your fair *s.* all unguarded lady
C. 295. that crawls along the *s.* of yon small hill
C. 313. and every bosky bourn from *s.* to *s.*
C. 1009. and from her fair unspotted *s.*
L'A. 55. from the *s.* of some hoar hill
S. 22, 15, of which all Europe rings from *s.* to *s*

P. 21. fast by his brethren's *s*.
**Sideboard.**—P. R. 2, 350. and at a stately *s*.
**Sidelong.**—P. L. 4, 333. *s*. as they sat
P. L. 6, 197. *s*. had pushed a mountain from
P. L. 9, 512. *s*. he works his way
**Sideral.**—P. L. 10, 693. *s*. blast vapour and
**Sides.**—P. L. 1, 61. a dungeon horrible on all *s*.
P. L. 2, 1015. on all *s*. round environed wins
P. L. 4, 135. whose hairy *s*. with thicket
P. L. 6, 335. forthwith on all *s*. to his aid was
P. L. 10, 507. on all *s*. from innumerable
S. A. 1241. hazard of thy brains and shattered *s*.
L'A. 32. and laughter holding both his *s*.
**Sideways.**—M. W. 42. *s*. as on a dying bed
**Sidonian.**—P. L. 1, 441. *S*. Virgins paid their
**Siege.**—P. L. 2. 343. walls fear no assault or *s*.
P. L. 9, 121. as from the hateful *s*. of contraries
P. L. 11, 656. others to a city strong lay *s*.
P. L. 12, 74. to God his tower intends *s*. and
**Sieges.**—S. A. 846. what *s*. girt me round ere I
**Sift.**—P. R. 4, 532. to try thee *s*. thee and
**Sigh.**—P. L. 11, 147. or one short *s*. of human
**Sighed.**—P. L. 2, 788. and *s*. from all her caves
**Sighing.**—P. L. 9, 783. from her seat *s*.
H. 186. the parting genius is with *s*. sent
**Sighs.**—P. L. 1, 621. interwove with *s*. found
P. L. 4, 31. much revolving thus in *s*. began
P. L. 10, 1090. and with our *s*. the air
P. L. 10, 1102. with their *s*. the air frequenting
P. L. 11, 5. that *s*. now breathed unutterable
P. L. 11, 23. these *s*. and prayers which in
P. L. 11, 31. hear his *s*. though mute
P. R. 2, 65. thoughts which she in *s*. thus clad
S. A. 392. with flattering prayers and *s*. and
Cir. 8. burn in your *s*. and borrow
**Sight.**—P. L. 2, 745. saw till now *s*. more
P. L. 2, 749. when at the assembly and in *s*. of
P. L. 3, 43. or *s*. of vernal bloom or summer's
P. L. 3, 55. tell of things invisible to mortal *s*.
P. L. 3, 61. from his *s*. received beatitude
P. L. 3, 256. thou at the *s*. pleased out of
P. L. 3, 554. at *s*. of all this world beheld
P. L. 3, 615. for *s*. no obstacle found here
P. L. 3, 655. in *s*. of God's high throne
P. L. 4, 34. at whose *s*. all the stars hide
P. L. 4, 217. all trees of noblest kind for *s*.
P. L. 4, 287. living creatures new to *s*.
P. L. 4, 319. nor shunned the *s*. of God or angel
P. L. 4, 505. *s*. hateful, *s*. tormenting
P. L. 4, 573. but under shade lost *s*. of him
P. L. 4, 577. Uriel no wonder if thy perfect *s*.
P. L. 4, 658. for whom this glorious *s*. when
P. L. 5, 46. in whose *s*. all things joy
P. L. 5, 138. as they forth were come to open *s*.
P. L. 5, 257. or to obstruct his *s*. star interposed
P. L. 4, 308. haste hither Eve and worth thy *s*.
P. L. 5, 448. to have been enamoured at that *s*.
P. L. 5, 536. that stand in *s*. of God enthroned
P. L. 5, 665. not bear through pride that *s*.
P. L. 5, 711. whose *s*. discerns abstrusest
P. L. 5, 765. Messiah was declared in *s*.
P. L. 6, 36. all thy care to stand approved in *s*.
P. L. 6, 111. Abdiel that *s*. endured not
P. L. 6, 118. though to *s*. unconquerable
P. L. 6, 191. that no *s*. nor motion of swift
P. L. 6, 792. grieving to see his glory at the *s*.
P. L. 6, 862. the montrous *s*. struck them
P. L. 7, 185. driven out the ungodly from his *s*.
P. L. 7, 368. though from human *s*. so far
P. L. 8, 41. where she sat retired in *s*.
P. L. 8, 63. into all eyes to wish her still in *s*.
P. L. 8, 120. that earthly *s*. if it presume might
P. L. 8, 461. left the cell of fancy my internal *s*.
P. L. 8, 527. these delicacies I mean of taste *s*.
P. L. 9, 91. suggestions hide from sharpest *s*.
P. L. 9, 294. I dissuade thy absence from my *s*.
P. L. 9, 310. in thy *s*. more wise more watchful
P. L. 9, 517. many a wanton wreath in *s*. of Eve
P. L. 9, 565. of brutal kind that daily are in *s*.
P. L. 9, 861. the pain of absence from thy *s*.
P. L. 9, 898. whatever can to *s*. or thought be

P. L. 10, 223. covered from his Father's *s*.
P. L. 10, 324. in *s*. to each of these three places
P. L. 10, 350. at *s*. of that stupendous bridge
P. L. 10, 538. saw but other *s*. instead a crowd
P. L. 10, 561. the fruitage fair to *s*. like that
P. L. 10, 683. in their *s*. had rounded still
P. L. 10, 828. then acquitted stand in *s*. of God
P. L. 10, 867. out of my *s*. thou serpent that
P. L. 11, 19. came in *s*. before the Father's
P. L. 11, 184. nigh in her *s*. the bird of Jove
P. L. 11, 201. else this double object in our *s*.
P. L. 11, 281. with what to *s*. or smell was sweet
P. L. 11, 413. that promised clearer *s*. had bred
P. L. 11, 418. to the inmost seat of mental *s*.
P. L. 11, 448. at that *s*. was Adam in his heart
P. L. 11, 463. O *s*. of terror foul and ugly
P. L. 11, 494. *s*. so deform what heart of rock
P. L. 11, 555. now prepare thee for another *s*.
P. L. 11, 872. I revive at this last *s*. assured
P. L. 11, 890. shall one just man find in his *s*.
P. L. 12, 9. but I perceive thy mortal *s*. to fail
P. R. 1, 271. I oft had heard not knew by *s*.
P. R. 1, 310. they at his *s*. grew mild nor
P. R. 2, 56. mock us with his blest *s*. then
P. R. 3, 345. at *s*. whereof the fiend yet more
P. R. 3, 351. and show all this fair *s*.
P. R. 4, 86. barbarous and scarce worth the *s*.
S. A. 24. who at last in *s*. of both my parents
S. A. 67. O loss of *s*. of thee I most complain
S. A. 93. why was the *s*. to such a tender ball as
S. A. 152. thy bondage or lost *s*. prison within
S. A. 157. which men enjoying *s*. oft without
S. A. 196. for had I *s*. confused with shame
S. A. 645. with the irreparable loss of *s*.
S. A. 914. though *s*. be lost life yet hath many
S. A. 1117. where *s*. may give thee or rather flight
S. A. 1294. but *s*. bereaved may chance
S. A. 1415. and how the *s*. of me as of a common
S. A. 1542. the *s*. of this so horrid spectacle
S. A. 1620. at *s*. of him the people with a shout
S. A. 1687. but he though blind of *s*.
Il P. 14. to hit the sense of human *s*.
S. 22, 4. nor to their idle orbs doth *s*. appear
S. 23, 8. full *s*. of her in heaven without restraint
S. 23, 10. her face was veiled yet to my fancied *s*.
H. 109. at last surrounds their *s*.
T. 18. of him to whose happy-making *s*. alone
**Sights.**—P. L. 1, 64. served only to discover *s*.
P. L. 11, 411. but to nobler *s*. Michael from
L'A. 4. horrid shapes and shrieks and *s*. unholy
L'A. 129. such *s*. as youthful poets dream
**Sign.**—P. L. 1, 672. undoubted *s*. that in his
P. L. 2, 760. and called me Sin, and for a *s*.
P. L. 4, 428. the only *s*. of our obedience left
P. L. 4, 998. betwixt Astrea and the Scorpion *s*.
P. L. 4, 1011. and read thy lot in yon celestial *s*.
P. L. 5, 194. with every plant in *s*. of worship
P. L. 6, 58. reluctant flames the *s*. of wrath
P. L. 6, 776. by angels borne his *s*. in heaven
P. L. 8, 342. in *s*. whereof each bird and beast
P. L. 8, 514. the earth gave *s*. of gratulation
P. L. 10, 1091. in *s*. of sorrow unfeigned and
P. L. 10, 1103. in *s*. of sorrow unfeigned and
P. L. 11, 351. and of his presence many a *s*.
P. L. 11, 860. an olive-leaf he brings pacific *s*.
P. L. 12, 442. the *s*. of washing them from
P. R. 2, 89. and to a *s*. spoken against
P. R. 2, 119. there without *s*. of boast or *s*. of
P. R. 4, 483. warn thee as a sure foregoing *s*.
C. 654. fierce *s*. of battle make and menace high
**Signal.**—P. L. 1, 278. assaults their surest *s*.
P. L. 1, 347. till as a *s*. given
P. L. 1, 776. till the *s*. given behold a wonder
P. L. 2, 56. and longing wait the *s*. to
P. L. 2, 717. till winds the *s*. blow to join
P. L. 5, 705. but all obeyed the wonted *s*.
P. L. 8, 632. my *s*. to depart
P. L. 11, 72. *s*. high to the bright minister
P. L. 12, 593. in *s*. of remove waves fiercely
S. A. 338. as *s*. now in low dejected state
**Signs.**—P. L. 1, 605. but cast *s*. of remorse and

P. L. 2, 831. and by concurring s. ere now
P. L. 4, 429. among so many s. of power and
P. L. 5, 134. kissed as the gracious s. of sweet
P. L. 6, 789. but to convince the proud what s.
P. L. 7, 341. for s. for seasons and for days and
P. L. 9, 783. though all her works gave s.
P. L. 9, 1077. in our faces evident the s. of foul
P. L. 11, 182. gave s. impressed on bird beast
P. L. 11, 194. which heaven by the mute s.
P. L. 12, 175. be compelled by s. and judgments
P. R. 1, 394. oft my advice by presages and s.
P. R. 4, 489. as s. betokening or illboding
C. 573. (for so by certain s. I knew)
C. 845. and ill-luck s. that the shrewd meddling
**Silence.**—P. L. 1, 83. breaking the horrid s.
P. L. 1, 561. moved on in s. to soft pipes
P. L. 1, 797. after short s. then and summons
P. L. 2, 431. with reason hath deep s.
P. L. 2, 994. fled not in s. through the frighted
P. L. 3, 218. and s. was in heaven
P. L. 4, 600. s. accompanied for beast and bird
P. L. 4, 604. descant sung; s. was pleased
P. L. 5, 39. s. yields to the night-warbling
P. L. 5, 557. worthy of sacred s. to be heard
P. L. 5, 668. hour friendliest to sleep and s.
P. L. 6, 64. moved on in s. their bright legions
P. L. 6, 385. therefore eternal s. be their doom
P. L. 6, 408. and s. on the odious din of war
P. L. 7, 106. night with her will bring s.
P. L. 7, 216. s. ye troubled waves and thou
P. L. 7, 594. but not in s. holy kept
P. L. 9, 895. first to himself he inward s. broke
P. L. 10, 353. enchanting daughter thus the s.
P. L. 10, 459. with hand s. and with these words
P. L. 11, 699. and what most merits fame in s.
P. R. 4, 22. and to shameful s. brought
P. R. 4, 43. and now the tempter thus his s. broke
S. A. 49. under the seal of s. could not keep
S. A. 236. gave up my fort of s. to a woman
S. A. 428. to violate the sacred trust of s.
S. A. 864. and combated in s. all these reasons
C. 250. did they float upon the wings of s.
C. 552. till an unusual stop of sudden s.
C. 557. that even s. was took ere she was ware
Il P. 55. and the mute s. hist along
Cir. 5. through the soft s. of the listening night
V. Ex. 5. driving dumb s. from the portal door
**Silent.**—P. L. 2, 547. retreated in a s. valley
P. L. 2, 582. a slow and s. stream Lethe the river
P. L. 3, 267. but his meek aspect s. yet spake
P. L. 4, 647. then s. Night with this her solemn
P. L. 4, 654. nor s. Night with this her solemn
P. L. 4, 938. whereof in hell fame is not s.
P. L. 5, 39. the pleasant time the cool the s.
P. L. 5, 202. witness if I be s. morn or even
P. L. 6, 523. with s. circumspection unespied
P. L. 6, 882. who s. stood eye-witnesses
P. L. 7, 444. whose clarion sounds the s. hours
P. L. 8, 163. or she from west her s. course
P. L. 9, 195. earth's great altar send up s. praise
P. L. 9, 1063. bare of all their virtue s.
P. R. 2, 261. when thus the Son communed in s.
S. A. 87. and s. as the moon when she deserts
S. A. 1732. with s. obsequy and funeral train
C. 481. some far-off halloa break the s. air
**Silently.**—P. L. 2, 842. wing s. the buxom air
P. L. 5, 130. but s. a gentle tear let fall
**Silk.**—C. 716. weave the smooth-haired s. to deck
**Silken.**—P. R. 4, 76. with white s. turbants
S. A. 730. the borders of her s. veil
D. F. I. 2. soft s. primrose fading timelessly
**Silly.**—P. L. 9, 92. was all that did their s. thoughts
**Silo.**—S. A. 1674. in S. his bright sanctuary
**Siloa.**—P. L. 1, 11. and S.'s brook that flowed
**Silver.**—P. L. 3, 595. seemed gold part s.
P. L. 3, 644. before his decent steps a s. wand
P. L. 4, 605. over the dark her s. mantle
P. L. 7, 437. others on s. lakes
C. 222. turn forth her s. lining on the night
C. 865. goddess of the s. lake listen and save
A. 16. shooting her beams like s. threads

H. 128. and let your s. chime
**Silver-buskined.**—A. 33. fair s.-b. nymphs as
**Silver-shafted.**—C. 442. fair s.-s. queen
**Simeon.**—P. R. 1, 255. just S. and prophetic
P. R. 2, 87. but trouble as old S. plain foretold
**Similitude.**—P. L. 3, 384. Son, divine s.
P. L. 7, 520. man in our image man in our s.
P. L. 11, 512. retaining still divine s. in part
**Simon.**—P. R. 2, 7. I mean Andrew and S.
**Simple.**—P. L. 12, 365. to s. shepherds
P. R. 2, 348. how s. to these cates compared
**Simples.**—C. 627. and show me s. of a thousand
**Simplicity.**—P. L. 3, 687. and to s. resigns
P. L. 4, 318. s. and spotless innocence
**Simply.**—P. L. 12, 569. worldly wise by s. meek
H. 87. sat s. chatting in a rustic row
**Sin.**—P. L. 1, 485. doubled that s. in Bethel and
P. L. 2, 760. and called me s. and for a sign
P. L. 2, 1024. s. and death amain following
P. L. 3, 177. and enthralled by s. to foul
P. L. 3, 446. when s. with vanity had filled the
P. L. 4, 517. can it be s. to know?
P. L. 4, 758. I should write thee s. or blame
P. L. 4, 840. resemblest now thy s. and place
P. L. 6, 396. by s. of disobedience
P. L. 6, 506. to plague the sons of men for s.
P. L. 6, 691. save what s. hath impaired which
P. L. 7, 546. lest s. surprise thee and her black
P. L. 9, 12. s. and her shadow death and misery
P. L. 9, 70. though s. not time first wrought
P. L. ?, 292. for such thou art from s. and
P. L. 9, 327. but harm precedes not s. only our
P. L. 9, 1003. at completing of the mortal s.
P. L. 9, 1044. the seal the solace of their s.
P. L. 10, 16. and manifold in s. deserved to
P. L. 10, 133. lost on my head both s. and
P. L. 10, 172. to Satan first in s. his doom
P. L. 10, 230. within the gates of hell sat S.
P. L. 10, 234. S. opening
P. L. 10, 251. for death from s. no power can
P. L. 10, 352. long he admiring stood till s.
P. L. 10, 407. through s. to death exposed by
P. L. 10, 473. by s. and death a broad way
P. L. 10, 490. to s. and death a prey and so to
P. L. 10, 586. s. there in power before
P. L. 10, 590. to whom s. thus began
P. L. 10, 631. which man's polluting s. with
P. L. 10, 635. both s. and death and yawning
P. L. 10, 708. but discord first daughter of s.
P. L. 10, 791. what dies but what had life and s.?
P. L. 11, 55. wrought by s. that first
P. L. 11, 427. nor sinned thy s. yet from that s.
P. L. 11, 519. inductive mainly to the s. of
P. L. 11, 678. ten thousand-fold the s. of him
P. L. 12, 285. doubt not but that s. will reign
P. L. 12, 289. by stirring up s. against law
P. L. 12, 290. when they see law can discover s.
P. L. 12, 429. in s. for ever lost from life
P. L. 12, 431. defeating s. and death his two
P. L. 12, 443. of washing them from guilt of s.
P. L. 12, 474. repent me now of s. by me done
P. R. 1, 73. pretends to wash off s.
P. R. 1, 579. to conquer s. and death the two
P. R. 3, 147. stood struck with guilt of his own s.
S. A. 313. without taint of s. or legal debt
S. A. 499. a s. that Gentiles in their parables
S. A. 504. repent the s. but if the punishment
S. A. 1357. favour renewed and add a greater s.
C. 126. 'tis only day-light that makes s.
C. 456. driving far off each thing of s. and guilt
C. 465. but most by lewd and lavish act of s.
H. 138. and leprous s. will melt from earthly
Cir. 12. alas how soon our s. sore doth begin
S. M. 19. as once we did till disproportioned s.
D. F. I. 66. to slake his wrath whom s. hath made
F. of C. 4. from them whose s. ye envied
**Sinæan.**—P. L. 11, 390. to Paquin of S. kings
**Sinai.**—P. L. 1, 7. the secret top of Oreb or of S.
P. L. 12, 227. God from the mount of S. whose
H. 158. as on Mount S. rang
**Sin-born.**—P. L. 10, 596. whom thus the s.-b.

**Sin-bred.**—P. L. 4, 315. *s.-b.* how have ye
**Since.**—P. L. 1, 116. *s.* by fate the strength
  P. L. 1, 118. *s.* through experience of this great
  P. L. 1, 144. *s.* no less than such
  P. L. 1, 245. *s.* he who now is sovran can dispose
  P. L. 1, 573. for never *s.* created man
  P. L. 1, 582. and all who *s.* baptized or infidel
  P. L. 2, 12. for *s.* no deep within her gulf can
  P. L. 2, 197. *s.* fate inevitable subdues us
  P. L. 2, 223. *s.* our present lot appears for happy
  P. L. 2, 817. dear daughter *s.* thou claimest me
  P. L. 3, 3. I express thee unblamed *s.* God is
  P. L. 3, 495. *s.* called the Paradise of fools
  P. L. 4, 69. his love accursed *s.* love or hate
  P. L. 4, 71. *s.* against his thy will chose freely
  P. L. 4, 193. so *s.* into his church lewd hirelings
  P. L. 4, 322. that ever *s.* in love's embraces met
  P. L. 4, 323. Adam the goodliest man of men *s.*
  P. L. 4, 341. all beasts of the earth *s.* wild
  P. L. 4, 581. and *s.* meridian hour no creature
  P. L. 4, 612. mind us of like repose *s.* God hath
  P. L. 4, 905. *s.* Satan fell whom folly overthrew
  P. L. 4, 1008. *s.* thine no more than heaven
  P. L. 5, 71. and why not gods of men *s.* good
  P. L. 5, 363. *s.* by descending from the thrones
  P. L. 5, 774. not merely titular *s.* by decree
  P. L. 5, 842. *s.* he the head one of our number
  P. L. 6, 154. *s.* first that tongue inspired
  P. L. 6, 433. *s.* now we find this our empyreal
  P. L. 6, 686. *s.* Michael and his powers went
  P. L. 6, 702. of ending this great war *s.* none
  P. L. 6, 820. or I alone against them *s.* by
  P. L. 7, 80. but *s.* thou hast vouchsafed gently
  P. L. 8, 111. who *s.* the morning-hour set out
  P. L. 8, 347. not hither summoned *s.* they
  P. L. 8, 645. *s.* to part go heavenly guest
  P. L. 9, 25. *s.* first this subject for heroic song
  P. L. 9, 60. cautious of day *s.* Uriel regent
  P. L. 9, 140. perhaps not longer than *s.* I in
  P. L. 9, 174. *s.* higher I fall short
  P. L. 9, 360. *s.* reason not impossibly may meet
  P. L. 9, 412. for now and *s.* first break of dawn
  P. L. 9, 497. not ... prone on the ground as *s.*
  P. L. 9, 504. and lovely never *s.* of serpent-kind
  P. L. 9, 672. where eloquence flourished *s.* mute
  P. L. 9, 699. why not known *s.* easier shunned
  P. L. 9, 710. that ye shall be as gods *s.* I as man
  P. L. 9, 1019. *s.* to each meaning savour we
  P. L. 9, 1029. for never did thy beauty *s.* the
  P. L. 9, 1070. *s.* our eyes opened we find indeed
  P. L. 10, 170. (*s.* he no farther knew)
  P. L. 10, 233. far into Chaos *s.* the fiend passed
  P. L. 10, 241. *s.* no place like this can fit his
  P. L. 10, 451. with what permissive glory *s.*
  P. L. 10, 793. let this appease the doubt *s.*
  P. L. 10, 853. *s.* denounced the day of his
  P. L. 10, 962. *s.* this day's death denounced
  P. L. 11, 74. his trumpet heard in Oreb *s.*
  P. L. 11, 85. *s.* his taste of that defended fruit
  P. L. 11, 148. for *s.* I sought by prayer the
  P. L. 11, 160. mother of all things living *s.* by
  P. L. 11, 393. in Ecbatan sat or *s.* in Hispahan
  P. L. 11, 509. goodly and erect, though faulty *s.*
  P. L. 12, 83. *s.* thy original lapse true liberty
  P. L. 12, 90. therefore *s.* he permits within
  P. L. 12, 613. good presaging *s.* with sorrow
  P. R. 1, 51. *s.* Adam and his facile consort Eve
  P. R. 1, 52. though *s.* with dread attending
  P. R. 1, 147. less overweening *s.* he failed in Job
  P. R. 1, 399. but long *s.* with woe nearer
  P. R. 1, 443. justly *s.* they fell idolatrous
  P. R. 1, 484. when I come (*s.* no man comes)
  P. R. 2, 100. he meant I mused, *s.* understand
  P. R. 2, 107. had passed *s.* first her salutation
  P. R. 2, 358. than feigned of old or fabled *s.*
  P. R. 3, 122. and reason *s.* his word all things
  P. R. 4, 172. now both abhor *s.* thou hast dared
  P. R. 4, 189. gratitude in thee is lost long *s.*
  P. R. 4, 368. *s.* neither wealth nor honour arms
  S. A. 90. *s.* light so necessary is to life

S. A. 165. *s.* man on earth unparalleled
S. A. 843. *s.* thou determinest weakness
S. A. 929. thou and I long *s.* are twain
S. A. 1502. and *s.* his strength with eye-sight
**Sincere.**—P. L. 3, 103. they have given *s.*
  P. L. 3, 192. though but endeavoured with *s.*
  P. L. 9, 320. less attributed to her faith *s.*
  P. L. 10, 915. what love *s.* and reverence in my
  P. L. 11, 443. the other's not for his was not *s.*
  P. R. 2, 480. so reigning can be no *s.* delight
  P. R. 3, 435. bring them back repentant and *s.*
  S. A. 874. as it ought *s.* it would have taught
**Sincerely.**—C. 454. when a soul is found *s.* so
  T. 14. when everything that is *s.* good
**Sincerest.**—P. L. 10, 37. which your *s.* care
**Sinews.**—S. A. 1142. less through all my *s.* joints
  C. 615. unthread thy joints and crumble all thy *s.*
  V. Ex. 1. hail native language that by *s.* weak
**Sinful.**—P. L. 3, 186. oft be warned their *s.* state
  P. L. 8, 506. nature herself tho' pure of *s.* thought
  P. L. 11, 105. drive out the *s.* pair
  P. R. 1, 162. all the world and mass of *s.* flesh
  H. 41. pollute with *s.* blame
**Sinfulness.**—P. L. 11. 360. with *s.* of men
**Sing.**—P. L. 1, 6. *s.* heavenly Muse, that on the
  P. L. 2, 242. and to his Godhead *s.* forced
  P. L. 2, 547. retreated in a silent valley *s.* with
  P. L. 2, 553. when spirits immortal *s.*
  P. L. 6, 744. unfeigned hallelujahs to thee *s.*
  P. L. 7, 24. more safe I *s.* with mortal voice
  P. L. 11, 619. of lustful appetence to *s.* to
  P. L. 12, 244. of great Messiah shall *s.*
  P. L. 12, 324. the like shall *s.* all prophecy
  P. R. 1, 2. now *s.* recovered paradise to all
  P. R. 4, 339. imitated while they loudest *s.*
  C. 623. he loved me well and oft would beg me *s.*
  C. 983. that *s.* about the golden tree
  A. 65. and *s.* to those that hold the vital shears
  A. 86. follow me as I *s.*
  L. 10. who would not *s.* for Lycidas?
  L. 11. knew himself to *s.* & build the lofty rhyme
  L. 180. that *s.* and singing in their glory move
  L'A. 17. or whether (as some sager *s.*)
  Il P. 48. aye round about Jove's altar *s.*
  Il P. 105. or bid the soul of Orpheus *s.*
  Il P. 143. that at her flowery work doth *s.*
  S. 1, 9. timely *s.* ere the rude bird of hate
  S. 13, 13. than his Casella whom he wooed to *s.*
  H. 5. for so the holy sages once did *s.*
  P. 4. my muse with angels did divide to *s.*
  S. M. 28. and *s.* in endless morn of light
  V. Ex. 45. *s.* of secret things that came to pass
**Singed.**—P. L. 1, 236. and leave a *s.* bottom
  P. L. 1, 614. with *s.* top their stately growth
  C. 928. summer drouth or *s.* air
**Singeth.**—L'A. 65. and the milk-maid *s.* blithe
**Singing.**—P. L. 4, 684. to other's note *s.*
  P. L. 5, 198. that *s.* up to heaven-gate ascend
  P. R. 1, 171. circling the throne and *s.* while
  L. 180. that sing and *s.* in their glory move
  L'A. 42. and *s.* startle the dull night
  S. M. 16. *s.* everlastingly
  V. Ex. 63. and sweetly *s.* round about thy bed
**Single.**—P. L. 3, 469. others came *s.*
  P. L. 4, 856. can do *s.* against thee wicked and
  P. L. 5, 552. whose command *s.* is yet so just
  P. L. 5, 903. his constant mind though *s.*
  P. L. 6, 30. who *s.* hast maintained against
  P. L. 6, 233. seemed each warrior *s.* as in
  P. L. 7, 403. bank the mid sea part *s.* or with
  P. L. 8, 423. is to manifest his *s.* imperfection
  P. L. 9, 325. we not endued *s.* with like defence
  P. L. 9, 339. as not secure to *s.* or combined
  P. L. 9, 536. and gaze insatiate I thus *s.*
  P. L. 10, 817. nor I on my part *s.* in me all
  P. L. 11, 644. *s.* or in array of battle ranged
  P. L. 11, 703. beset with foes for daring *s.* to
  P. R. 1, 323. in troop or caravan for *s.* none
  P. R. 4, 384. the stars voluminous or *s.*
  P. R. 4, 517. which bears no *s.* sense
  S. A. 344. who *s.* combatant duelled their armies

S. A. 1092. dost thou already s. me? I thought
S. A. 1111. in fight withstand me s. and unarmed
S. A. 1210. presumed s. rebellion and did
S. A. 1222. who no defies thee thrice to s. fight
C. 204. yet naught but s. darkness do I find
C. 369. as that the s. want of light and noise
C. 402. and let a s. helpless maiden pass
**Singly.**—P. L. 1, 379. came s. where he stood
S. A. 244. s. by me against their conquerors
**Sings.**—P. L. 3, 39. as the wakeful bird s. darkling
P. L. 4, 769. serenate which the starved lover s.
L'A. 7. and the night-raven s.
V. Ex. 37. listening to what unshorn Apollo s.
**Sing'st.**—C. 567. how sweet thou s. how near
**Singular.**—P. L. 5, 851. or s. or rash
**Singularly.**—P. R. 3, 57. dares be s. good
**Sinister.**—P. L. 10, 886. more to the part s.
**Sink.**—P. L. 3, 331. they arraigned shall s.
**Sinks.**—P. L. 2, 950. and swims, or s., or wades
L. 168. so s. the day-star in the ocean bed
**Sinless.**—P. L. 7, 61. and now led on yet s. with
P. L. 9, 659. to whom thus Eve yet s. of the
P. L. 10, 690. the world inhabited though s.
P. R. 4, 425. unappalled in calm and s. peace
**Sinned.**—P. L. 6, 402. not to have s. not to
P. L. 10, 229. meanwhile ere thus was s.
P. L. 10, 516. punished in the shape he s.
P. L. 10, 790. it was but breath of life that s.
P. L. 10, 930. both have s. but thou against
P. L. 11, 427. nor s. thy sin yet from that sin
**Sinning.**—P. L. 6, 661. now gross by s. grown
**Sins.**—P. L. 3, 204. and s. against the high
P. L. 3, 233. aid can never seek once dead in s.
P. L. 12, 283. so many laws argue so many s.
P. L. 12, 316. but when s. national interrupt
P. L. 12, 416. law that is against thee and the s.
P. R. 1, 266. redemption for mankind whose s.
**Sinuous.**—P. L. 7, 481. with s. trace
**Sin-worn.**—C. 17. vapours of the s.-w. mould
**Sion.**—P. L. 1, 10. or if S. hill delight thee
P. L. 1, 386. Jehovah thundering out of S.
P. L. 1, 442. in S. also not unsung
P. L. 1, 453. infected S.'s daughters with like
P. L. 3, 30. but chief thee S. and the flowery
P. L. 3, 530. over mount S. and though that
P. R. 4, 347. with S.'s songs to all true tastes
**Sip.**—C. 811. s. of this will bathe the drooping
**Sips.**—Il P. 172. and every herb that s. the dew
**Sir.**—P. R. 1, 321. S. what ill chance hath
**Sire.**—P. L. 2, 264. doth heaven's all-ruling S.
P. L. 2, 817. thou claimest me for thy s.
P. L. 2, 849. and thus bespake her s.
P. L. 4, 144. which to our general s. gave
P. L. 4, 712. what day the genial angel to our s.
P. L. 5, 350. meanwhile our primitive great s.
P. L. 6, 95. as sons of one great s. hymning
P. L. 8, 39. spake our s. and by his countenance
P. L. 8, 218. nor are thy lips ungraceful, s.
P. L. 8, 249. the godlike power and thus our s.
P. L. 11, 460. to which our s. alas both
P. L. 11, 719. at length a reverend s. among
P. L. 11, 736. last the s. and his three sons
P. L. 11, 862. the ancient s. descends with all
P. L. 12, 368. his s. the power of the Most High
P. L. 12, 467. and our s. replete with joy
P. R. 1, 86. his mother then is mortal but his S.
P. R. 1, 233. deeds express thy matchless S.
S. A. 326. but see here comes thy reverend s.
S. A. 1456. say reverend s. we thirst to hear
L. 103. next Camus reverend s. went footing
V. Ex. 39. immortal nectar to her kingly s.
**Sirens.**—C. 253. my mother Circe with the S.
C. 878. and the songs of s. sweet
A. 63. then listen I to the celestial S.' harmony
S. M. 1. blest pair of s.
**Sirocco.**—P. L. 10, 706. S. and Libecchio
**Sisera.**—S. A. 990. smote S. sleeping through
**Sister.**—P. L. 7, 10. wisdom thy s. and with her
C. 350. but O that hapless virgin our lost s.
C. 366. I do not think my s. so to seek
C. 407. attempt the person of our unowned s.

C. 408. infer as if I thought my s.'s. state secure
C. 414. my s. is not so defenceless left
C. 486. heaven keep my s.
C. 564. of my most honoured lady your dear s.
L'A. 15. with two s. Graces more
Il P. 18. prince Memnon's s. might beseem
**Sisters.**—P. L. 10, 674. Atlantic S. and the
L. 15. begin then S. of the sacred well
L. 99. sleek Panope with all her s. played
S. M. 2. sphere-born harmonious s. Voice
**Sit.**—P. L. 2, 54. for while they s. contriving
P. L. 2, 56. the signal to ascend s. lingering
P. L. 2, 139. on his throne s. unpolluted
P. L. 2, 329. what s. we then projecting peace
P. L. 2, 359. heaven's high Arbitrator s. secure
P. L. 2, 377. s. in darkness here hatching vain
P. L. 2, 859. to s. in hateful office here confined
P. L. 3, 315. here shalt thou s. incarnate here
P. L. 5, 369. the garden choicest bears to s.
P. L. 8, 210. for while I s. with thee I seem in
P. L. 9, 3. with his friend familiar used to s.
P. L. 9, 164. with gods to s. the highest am
P. L. 9, 1098. this new-comer shame there s.
P. L. 10, 235. O son why s. we here each other
P. L. 10, 421. appointed to s. there had left
P. R. 1, 240. thou shouldst be great and s. on
P. R. 2, 336. with honour. Only deign to s.
P. R. 2, 368. what doubts the Son of God to s.
P. R. 2, 377. doubtest thou Son of God s. down
P. R. 2, 431. virtue valour wisdom s. in want
P. R. 3, 153. ordained to s. upon thy father
P. R. 4, 123. but tedious waste of time to s.
P. R. 4, 146. when my season comes to s.
S. A. 4. there I am wont to s. when any chance
S. A. 566. but to s. idle on the household hearth
S. A. 1017. or seven though one should musing s.
S. A. 1500. not to s. idle with so great a gift
S. A. 1608. of sort might s. in order to behold
C. 382. may s. in the centre and enjoy bright day
C. 625. would s. and hearken even to ecstasy
C. 659. nay lady s. if I but wave this wand
A. 64. that s. upon the nine enfolded spheres
Il P. 170. where I may s. and rightly spell
H. 11. to s. the midst of Trinal Unity
H. 68. while birds of calm s. brooding on the
H. 144. mercy will s. between
H. 244. bright-harnessed angels s. in order
P. 41. there doth my soul in holy vision s.
T. 21. attired with stars we shall for ever s.
**Sits.**—P. L. 1, 785. over-head the moon s. arbitress
P. L. 2, 243. while he lordly s. our envied
P. L. 2, 456. he above the rest high honoured s.
P. L. 2, 731. for him who s. above and laughs
P. L. 2, 803. before mine eyes in opposition s.
P. L. 2, 907. Chaos umpire s. and by decision
P. L. 3, 57. the pure empyrean where he s.
P. L. 5, 25. s. on the bloom extracting liquid
P. L. 6, 671. he s. shrined in his sanctuary
P. L. 6, 892. where now he s. at the right hand
S. A. 1309. his manacles remark him there he s.
C. 389. and s. as safe as in a senate-house
C. 818. we cannot free the lady that s. here
C. 881. wherewith she s. on diamond rocks
C. 957. but night s. monarch yet in the mid sky
C. 1002. sadly s. the Assyrian queen
A. 91. I will bring you where she s.
H. 202. now s. not girt with taper's holy shine
S. M. 8. to Him that s. thereon
M. W. 18. the god that s. at marriage feast
**Sittim.**—P. L. 1, 413. he enticed Israel in S.
**Sitting.** P. L. 2, 164. is this then worst thus s.
P. L. 4, 829. there s. where ye durst not soar
P. L. 8, 89. heaven such journeys run earth s.
P. R. 2, 212. as s. queen adored on beauty's
P. R. 3, 164. thou to regain thy right by s. still
P. R. 4, 107. will be for thee no s. or not long
S. A. 1491. view him s. in the house ennobled
C. 472. lingering and s. by a new-made grave
C. 860. Sabrina fair listen where thou art s.
A. 18. s. like a goddess bright
Il P. 40. thy rapt soul s. in thine eyes

w

**Sitt'st.**—P. L. 3, 376. where thou s. throned
P. L. 4, 578. sun's bright circle where thou s.
P. L. 5, 156. unspeakable who s. above these
M. W. 61. whilst thou bright saint high s.
**Situate.**—P. L. 6, 641. of pleasure s. in hill
**Situation.**—P. L. 1, 60. the dismal s. waste
**Six.**—P. L. 5, 277. a seraph winged s. wings
P. L. 7, 568. magnificent his s. days' work
P. L. 7, 601. creation and the s. days' acts they
P. L. 8, 128. in s. thou seest and what if seventh
P. L. 9, 137. what he Almighty styled s. nights
P. R. 1, 210. my age had measured twice s. years
U.C.II.20.one carrier put down to make s.bearers
**Sixth.**—P. L. 7, 449. the s. and of creation last
P. L. 7, 504. and of the s. day yet remained
P. L. 7, 550. morn accomplished the s. day
**Size.**—P. L. 1, 197. fables name of monstrous s.
P. L. 6, 352. colour shape or s. assume as likes
S. A. 1249. all of gigantic s. Goliath chief
**Skies.**—C.242.mayst thou be translated to the s.
L'A. 43. from his watch-tower ·in the s.
Il P. 39. and looks commercing with the s.
P. 18. his starry front low-roofed beneath the s.
**Skiff.**—P. L. 1, 204. small night foundered s.
**Skilful.**—P. L. 9, 515. a ship by s. steersman
**Skill.**—P. L. 2, 272. nor want we s. or art
P. L. 8, 573. of that s. the more thou know'st
P. L. 9, 39. the s. of artifice or office mean
P. L. 9, 1112. and with what s. they had
P. R. 3, 17. thy s. of conduct would be such
P. R. 4, 40. or optic s. of vision multiplied
P. R. 4, 52. high the structure s. of noblest
P. R. 4, 552. to stand upright will ask thee s.
S. A.757. with more cautious and instructed s.
C. 273. not any boast of s. but extreme shift
A. 79. whate'er the s. of lesser gods can show
S.13,5. thy worth and s. exempts thee from the
**Skilled.**—P. L. 9, 42. me of these nor s. nor
P. R. 2, 161. s. to retire and in retiring draw
C. 523. deep s. in all his mother's witcheries
C. 620. yet well s. in every virtuous plant
**Skins.**—P. L. 10, 217. with s. of beasts
P. L. 10, 220. with the s. of beasts
**Skirt.**—P. L. 6, 80. from s. to s. fiery region
**Skirted.**—P. L. 5, 282. s. his loins and thighs
**Skirts.**—P.L.3,380. with excessive bright thy s.
P. L. 5, 187. till the sun paint your fleecy s.
P. L. 11,332. though but his utmost s. of glory
P. L. 11, 882. the fluid s. of that same watery
**Sky.**—P. L. 1, 45. from the ethereal s.
P. L. 1, 730. yielded light as from a s.
P. L. 2, 534. appears waged in the troubled s.
P. L. 2, 710. Ophiuchus huge in the arctic s.
P. L. 3, 324. shalt in the s. appear and from
P. L. 3, 426. blustering round inclement s.
P. L. 3, 514. by night under the open s.
P. L. 4, 459. that to me seemed another s.
P. L. 4, 721. under open s. adored the God
P. L. 4, 722. both s., air, earth and heaven
P. L. 4, 988. his stature reached the s. and on
P. L. 5, 189. with clouds the uncoloured s.
P. L. 5, 267. and through the vast ethereal s.
P. L.6.314. opposition in mid s. should combat
P. L. 6, 772. on the crystalline s. in sapphire
P. L. 7, 287. their tops ascend the s.
P. L. 7, 442. tower the mid aereal s.
P. L. 8, 258. and gazed awhile the ample s.
P. L. 9, 1002. gave a second groan, s. loured
P. L. 10, 1064. which now the s. with various
P. L. 11, 209. down from a s. of jasper
P. L. 11, 742. and now the thickened s. like
P. L. 12, 182. fire must rend the Egyptian s.
P. R. 2, 156. passing fair as the noon s.
P. R. 4, 453. heard the wrack as earth and s.
S. A.1472. noise or shout was that? it tore the s.
S. A. 1610. and scaffolds under s. might stand
C. 957. night sits monarch yet in the mid s.
C. 979. up in the broad fields of the s.
L.171. flames in the forehead of the morning s.
**Sky-robes.**—C. 83. these my s.-r. spun out of
**Sky-tinctured.**—P. L. 5, 285. s.-t. grain

**Slack.**—P. L. 2, 461. or deceive, or s. the pain
P. L. 4, 164. well pleased they s. their course
P. L. 9, 892. from his s. hand the garland
P. R. 3, 398. think not thou to find me s.
**Slacken.**— P. L. 2, 214. will s. if his breath
P. R. 2, 455. more apt to s. virtue and abate
**Slackened.**—S. A. 738. hath not s. though my
**Slackness.**—P. L. 11, 634. s. it begins
**Slain.**—P. L. 10, 217. or s. or as the snake
P. L. 11, 455. the unjust the just hath s.
P. L. 12, 414. by his own nation s. for bringing
S. A. 439. who slewest them many a s.
S. A. 1516. O it continues they have s. my son
S. A.1664.and now liest victorious among thy s.
S. A. 1668. more than all thy life had s. before.
S. 18, 7. s. by the bloody Piemontese that
**Slake.**—D.F.I.66.to s. his wrath whom sin hath
**Slanderous.**—P. L. 12, 536. with s. darts
**Slant.**—P. L. 10, 1075. tine the s. lightning
**Slave.**—S. A. 38. debased lower than bond s.
S. A. 1224. with thee? a man condemned a s.
S. A. 1392. art thou our s. our captive
**Slaveries.**—S. A. 485. by pains and s. worse
**Slavery.**—S.A.418.ignominious infamous true s.
**Slaves.**—P. L. 12, 167. guests he makes them s:
P. R. 4, 145. or could of inward s. make
S. A. 41. eyeless in Gaza at the mill with s.
S. A.367. into a dungeon thrust to work with s.
S. A.1162.among the s. and asses thy comrades
**Slaughter.**—P. L. 6, 506. mutual s. bent
P. L. 11, 659. on each hand s. and gigantic
P. R. 3, 75. but rob and spoil, burn, s.
S. A. 1518. from s. of one foe could not ascend
S. A.1583. wearied with s. then or how explain
**Slaughtered.**—S. A. 1530. over heaps of s.
S. A. 1667. conjoined thee with thy s. foes
S.18,1. avenge O Lord thy s.saints whose bones
**Slaughtering.**—D. F. I. 62. the s. pestilence
**Slavish.**—S. A. 122. in s. habit ill-fitted weeds
C. 218. are but as s. officers of vengeance
**Slay.**—D. F. I. 24. did s. his dearly-loved mate
**Slaying.**—S. A. 1517. thy son is rather s. them
**Sleek.**—P. L. 9, 525. and s. enamelled neck
L. 99. s. Panope with all her sisters played
L'A. 30. and love to live in dimple s.
S. 11, 10. names to our like mouths grow s.
**Sleeked.**—P. R. 4, 5. rhetoric that s. his
**Sleeking.**—C. 882. s. her soft alluring locks
**Sleep.**—P. L. 3, 329. peal shall rouse their s.
P. L. 4, 449. I oft remember when from s.
P. L. 4, 614. and the timely dew of s. now
P. L. 4, 658. whom this glorious sight when s.
P. L. 4, 678. when we wake and when we s.
P. L. 4, 735. when we seek as now thy gift of s.
P. L. 4, 773. s. on blest pair and O yet happiest
P.L.4,826.watching at the head of these that s.
P. L. 4, 988. employed it seems to violate s.
P. L. 5, 3. his s. was aerylight, from pure
P. L. 5, 96. of thy thoughts this night in s.
P. L. 5, 120. that what is s. thou didst abhor
P. L. 5, 668. the dusky hour friendliest to s.
P. L. 5, 679. how then can now thy s. dissent
P. L. 7, 106. and s. listening to thee will watch
P. L. 8, 253. as new waked from soundest s.
P. L. 8, 287. there gentle s. first found me
P. L. 8, 458. sunk down and sought repair of s.
P. L. 9, 190. but his s. disturbed not waiting
P. L. 9, 1044. till dewy s. oppressed them
P. L. 9, 1049. and grosser s. bred of unkindly
P. L. 10, 779. there I should rest and s. secure
P. L. 11, 368. here s. below while thou to
P. L. 12, 434. a death like s. a gentle wafting
P. R. 2, 284. fasting he went to s. and fasting
P. R. 4, 409. with ugly dreams disturbed his s.
S. A. 459. mine eye to harbour s. or thoughts
S. A. 629. s. hath forsook and given me o'er
C. 122. what hath night to do with s.
C.554. that draw the litter of close-curtained s.
Il P. 146. entice the dewy-feathered S.
H. 155. yet first to those ychained in s.

**Sleeping.**—P. L. 1, 333. *s.* found by whom
P. L. 8, 463. methought I saw though *s.* where
P. L. 9, 161. where hap may find the serpent *s.*
P. L. 9, 182. him fast *s.* soon he found
P. L. 12, 608. to the bower where Eve lay *s.*
P. R. 1, 311. nor *s.* him nor waking harmed
S. A. 990. smote Sisera *s.* through the temples
S.A.1113.close-banded durst attack me,no,not *s.*
H. 242. her *s.* Lord with…lamp attending
V.Ex.64.strew all their blessings on thy *s.* head
**Sleepless.**—P. L. 11, 173. though after *s.* night
P. R. 2, 460. troubles, cares and *s.* nights
**Sleeps.**—P. L. 2, 489. while the north wind *s.*
P. L. 3, 686. though wisdom wake suspicion *s.*
P. L. 7, 414. stretched like a promontory *s.*
P. L. 8, 164. that spinning *s.* on her soft axle
**Sleep'st**—P. L. 5, 38. it said why *s.* thou
P. L. 5, 673. *s.* thou companion dear what sleep
L. 160. *s.* by the fable of Bellerus old
**Sleepy.**—P. L. 2, 73. if the *s.* drench of that
**Sleet.**—P. R. 3, 324. shot sharp *s.* of arrowy
**Sleights.**—P. L. 9, 92. whatever *s.* none
**Slender.**—P. L. 4, 304. veil down to the *s.* waist
Hor. 1. what *s.* youth, bedewed with
**Slept.**—P. L. 4, 707. Pan or Sylvanus never *s.*
P. L. 4, 771. lulled by nightingales embracing *s.*
P. L. 5, 654. where they *s.* fanned with cool
P. L. 9, 187. fearless unfeared he *s.*
P. R. 2, 263. he *s.* and dreamed as appetite
P. R. 2, 271. there he *s.* under a juniper
P. R. 4, 407. but sheltered *s.* in vain for at his
P. R. 4, 413. nor *s.* the winds within their stony
**Slept'st.**—P. L. 11, 369. as once thou *s.*
**Slew.**—P. L. 11, 609. dwell his race who *s.*
P. L. 11, 678. the sin of him who *s.* his brother
**Slew'st.**—S. A. 439. who *s.* them many a slain
**Slide.**—V. Ex. 4. half unpronounced *s.* through
**Sliding.**—P. L. 8, 302. as in air smooth *s.*
C. 892. my *s.* chariot stays
H. 47. crowned with olive green came softly *s.*
**Slight.**—P. L. 4, 181. at one *s.* bound high
P. L. 7, 47. if they transgress and *s.* that sole
P. R. 3, 109. think not so *s.* of glory therein
P. R. 3, 349. secure on no *s.* grounds thy safety
P. R. 4, 155. how *s.* thou valuest because offered
S. A. 59. how *s.* the gift was hung it in my hair
S.A.940.thy husband *s.* me, sell me and forgo me
S. A. 1229. nearer part not hence so *s.* informed
V. Ex. 19. new-fangled toys and trimming *s.*
**Slighted.**—L. 65.tend the homely *s.* shepherd's
**Slightest.**—P. R. 3, 128. thanks the *s.* easiest
**Slighting.**—P. R. 2, 224. at every sudden *s.*
**Slightly.**—P. R. 2, 198. he *s.* viewed and *s.*
P. L. 4, 967. the facile gates of hell too *s.* barred
**Slime.**—P. L. 9, 165. and mixed with bestial *s.*
P. L. 10, 298. and with asphaltic *s.* broad
P. L. 10, 530. in the Pythian vale on *s.*
**Slimy.**—P. L. 10, 286. solid or *s.* as in raging
**Sling.**—P. L. 10, 633. at one *s.* of thy victorious
**Slingers.**—S. A.1619. archers and *s.* cataphracts
**Slip.**—P. L. 1, 178. let us not *s.* the occasion
C. 743. if you let *s.* time like a neglected rose
M. W. 35. so have I seen some tender *s.*
**Slipped.**—C. 498. hath any ram *s.* from the fold
**Slipping.**—P. R. 4, 216. when *s.* from thy
**Slips.**—H. 234. *s.* to his several grave
**Slits.**—L. 76. and *s.* the thin spun life
**Slope.**—P. L. 1, 223. *s.* their pointing spires
P. L. 4, 261. water's fall down the *s.* hills
P. L. 4, 591. bore him *s.* downward to the sun
C. 98. and the *s.* sun his upward beam
**Sloped.**—L. 31. toward heaven's descent had *s.*
**Sloth.**—P. L. 2, 227. ease and peaceful *s.* not
P. L. 6, 166. I see that most through *s.* had
P. L. 11, 794. to pleasure ease and *s.*
**Slothful.**—P. L. 2, 117. timorous and *s.*
**Slough.**—U. C. I. 4. he's here stuck in a *s.* and
**Slow.**—P. L. 2, 337. and revenge though *s.*
P. L. 2, 582. a *s.* and silent stream Lethe the
P. L. 2, 902. sharp smooth swift or *s.*
P. L. 3, 193. mine ear shall not be *s.*

P. L. 4, 173. had journeyed on pensive and *s.*
P. L. 6, 533. in *s.* but firm battalion
P. L. 8, 110. me thou thinkst not *s.* who since
P. L. 10, 692. changes in the heavens though *s.*
P. L. 11, 207. and *s.* descends with
P. L. 12, 648. with wandering steps and *s.*
P. R. 3, 172. zeal and duty are not *s.* but
P. R. 3, 224. why move thy feet so *s.* to what
C. 232. by *s.* Meander's margent green
C. 1015. where the bowed welkin *s.* doth bend
L. 103. Camus reverend sire went footing *s.*
Il P. 76. swinging *s.* with sullen roar
S. 7, 9. yet be it less or more or soon or *s.*
**Slow-endeavouring.**—W. S. 9. of *s.-e.* art
**Slowest.**—P. L. 10, 859. mends not her *s.* pace
**Slowly.**—P. L. 4, 541. the setting sun *s.*
**Slow-paced.**—P. L. 10, 963. but a *s.-p.* evil
**Sluice.**—P. L. 5, 133. each in their crystal *s.*
A. 30. divine Alpheus who by secret *s.*
**Sluiced.**—P. L. 1, 702. fire *s.* from the lake
**Sluices.**—P. L. 11, 849. now had stopt his *s.*
**Slumber.**—P. L. 1, 321. to *s.* here as in the
P. L. 1, 377. roused from the *s.* on that fiery
C. 110. with their grave saws in *s.* lie
C. 260. yet they in pleasing *s.* lulled the sense
C. 1001. in *s.* soft and on the ground
L'A. 146. from golden *s.* on a bed
**Slumbered.**—P. L. 4, 24. despair that *s.*
**Slumbering.**—P. L. 1, 203. him haply *s.* on
P. L. 9, 23. and dictates to me *s.* or inspires
A. 57. awakes the *s.* leaves or tasselled horn
L'A. 54. cheerly rouse the *s.* morn
**Slumbers.**—P. L. 7, 29. thou visit'st my *s.*
**Slumbrous.**—P. L. 4, 615. soft *s.* weight
**Slunk.**—P. L. 4, 602. to their nests were *s.*
P. L. 9, 784. back to the thicket *s.* the guilty
P. L. 10, 332. seduced unminded *s.*
**Sly.**—P. L. 4, 347. the serpent *s.* insinuating
P. L. 4, 537. turned but with *s.* circumspection
P. L. 4, 957. and thou *s.* hypocrite who now
P. L. 9, 256. us woe and shame by *s.* assault
P. L. 9, 613. the spirited *s.* snake
P. R. 2, 115. for Satan with *s.* preface to return
C. 525. by *s.* enticement gives his baneful cup
C. 571. that damned wizard hid in *s.* disguise
**Small.**—P. L.1,204. some *s.* night-foundered skiff
P. L. 1, 575. could merit more than that *s.*
P. L. 2, 33. none whose portion is so *s.* of present
P. L. 2, 258. when great things of *s.*
P. L. 2, 607. with one *s.* drop to lose in sweet
P. L. 2, 922. to compare great things with *s.*
P. L. 3, 428. reflection gains of glimmering
P. L. 5, 258. star interposed however *s.* he sees
P. L. 5, 322. *s.* store will serve where store all
P. L. 6, 311. as to set forth great things by *s.*
P. L. 6, 437. of evil then so *s.* as easy think
P. L. 7, 368. they augment their *s.* peculiar
P. L. 7, 486. in *s.* room large heart enclosed
P. L. 8, 92. though in comparison of heaven so *s.*
P. L. 8, 105. lodged in a *s.* partition
P. L. 9, 628. one *s.* thicket past of blowing
P. L. 9, 1018. sapience no *s.* part
P. L. 10, 306. great things to *s.* may be compared
P. L. 11, 734. every beast and bird and insect *s.*
P. L. 11, 753. all left in one *s.* bottom swum
P. L. 12, 566. and by *s.* accomplishing great
P. R. 1, 66. to our just fear gave no *s.* cause
P. R. 2, 403. *s.* consolation then were man
P. R. 2, 193. made *s.* account of beauty and her
P. R. 3, 56, of whom to be dispraised were no *s.*
P. R. 4, 35. on seven *s.* hills with palaces
P. R. 4, 92. to Capreæ an island *s.* but strong
P. R. 4, 564. to compare *s.* things with greatest
S. A. 1223. as a petty enterprise of *s.* enforce
S. A. 1261. with no *s.* profit daily to my owners
C. 295. that crawls along the side of yon *s.* hill
C. 620. of *s.* regard to see to yet well skilled
C.. 629. amongst the rest a *s.* unsightly root
V Ex. 9. *s.* loss it is that thence can come
V. Ex. 16. this same *s.* neglect that I have made
**Smaller.**—P. L. 7, 433. the *s.* birds with song

**Smallest.**—P. L. 1, 779. now less than s.
P. L. 1, 789. thus incorporeal spirits to s. forms
P. L. 2, 1053. as a star of s. magnitude close
P. L. 6, 137. who out of s. things could without
P. L. 7, 477. and s. lineaments exact
P. R. 1, 450. what'to the s. tittle thou shaltsay
**Smart.**—P. L. 4, 102. bought with double s.
P. R. 1, 401. fellowship in pain divides not s.
Cir. 25. seals obedience first with wounding s.
D. F. I. 69. to stand 'twixt us and our deserved s.
**Smeared.**—P. L. 1, 731. s. round with pitch
C. 917. s. with gums of glutinous heat
**Smell.**—P. L. 2, 664. lured with the s. of infant
P. L. 4, 165. cheered with the grateful s. old
P. L. 4, 217. all trees of noblest kind for sight s.
P. L. 4, 265. breathing the s. of field and grove
P. L. 5, 84. the pleasant savoury s. so quickened
P. L. 5, 411. whereby they hear, see, s.. touch
P. L. 8, 527. delicacies I mean of taste, sight s.
P. L. 9, 197. his nostrils fill with grateful s.
P. L. 9, 450. s. of grain or tedded grass or kine
P. L. 9, 581. more pleased my sense than s.
P. L. 9, 740. raised by the s. so savoury of that
P. L. 9, 852. new gathered and ambrosial s.
P. L. 10, 272. he snuffed the s. of mortal change
P. L. 11, 38. from these receive the s. of peace
P. L. 11. 281. with what to sight or s. was sweet
P. R. 2, 351. by the wine that fragrant s.
S. A. 544. the s. or taste that cheers the heart
**Smelling.**—P. L. 7, 319. s. sweet
**Smells.**—P. L. 5, 127. choicest bosomed s.
P. L. 5, 379. flowerets decked and fragrant s.
P. R. 2, 365. and Flora's earliest s.
C. 991. nard and Cassia's balmy s.
**Smile.**—P. L. 2, 146. grinned . . . a ghastly s.
P. L. 3, 257. shalt look down and s.
P. L. 4, 765. not in the bought s. of harlots
P. L. 8, 368. the vision bright as with a s.
P. L. 8, 618. with a s. that glowed celestial
P. R. 2, 198. how many have with a s. made
S. A. 948. gloss upon and censuring frown or s.
S. A. 1057. s. she or lour
**Smiled.**—P. L. 3, 364. with celestial roses s.
P. L. 3, 638. as in his face youth s. celestial
P. L. 4, 499. and submissive charms s. with
P. L. 5, 378. that like Pomona's arbour s.
P. L. 6, 784. fresh flowerets hill and valley s.
P. L. 7, 502. rich attire consummate lovely s.
P. L. 8, 265. the branches warbling all things s.
P. L. 9, 851. of fairest fruit that downy s.
P. L. 10, 679. the spring perpetual s. on earth
C. 252. the raven down of darkness till it s.
**Smiles.**—P. L. 4, 165. old ocean s.
P. L. 4, 337. purpose nor endearing s. wanted
P. L. 4, 500. love as Jupiter on Juno s.
P. L. 5, 124. fair morning first s. on the world
P. L. 9, 222. near looks intervene and s.
P. L. 9, 239. intercourse of looks and s. for s.
P. L. 9, 480. let pass occasion which now s.
P. L. 11, 624. to the trains and to the s. of
L'A. 28. nods and becks and wreathed s.
**Smiling.**—P. L. 4, 903. half s. thus replied
P. L. 5, 68. of day that crown'st the s. morn
P. L. 5, 718. and s. to his only Son thus said
P. L. 11, 175. Morn begins her rosy progress s.
P. R. 1, 129. thus to Gabriel s. spake
H. 151. the Babe yet lies in s. infancy
**Smit.**—P. L. 3, 29. s. with the love of sacred
**Smite.**—P. L. 6, 324. to s. descending
L. 131. stands ready to s. once and s. no more
**Smites.**—A. 52. the cross dire-looking planet s.
**Smitten.**—P. R. 4, 562. but Satan s. with
**Smoke.**—P. L. 1, 537. with stench and s.
P. L. 1, 671. belched fire and rolling s.
P. L. 2, 889. redounding s. and ruddy flame
P. L. 2, 928. and in the surging s. uplifted
P. L. 6, 57. and s. to roll in dusky wreaths
P. L. 6, 585. but soon obscured with s. all
P. L. 6, 766. of s. and bickering flame and
C. 5. above the s. and stir of this dim spot
C. 655. or like the sons of Vulcan vomit s.

**Smoked.**—P. L. 1, 493. temple stood or altar s.
**Smokes.**—L'A. 81. hard by a cottage chimney s.
**Smoky.**—C. 324. in lowly sheds with s. rafters
**Smooth.**—P. L. 1, 450. while s. Adonis from his
P. L. 1, 725. o'er the s. and level pavement
P. L. 2, 816. thus answered s., dear daughter
P. L. 2, 902. sharp, s., swift or slow
P. L. 4, 459. to look into the clear s. lake
P. L. 4, 480. mild than that s. watery image
P. L. 5, 342. in coat rough or s. rind or
P. L. 7, 409. on s. the seal and bended dolphins
P. L. 8, 166. and bears thee soft with the s. air
P. L. 8, 302. as in air s. sliding without step
P. L. 9, 1095. whose broad s. leaves together
P. L. 10, 305. a passage broad s. easy inoffensive
P. L. 11, 615. so blithe so s. so gay yet empty
P. R. 1, 467. and this answer s. returned
P. R. 1, 479. s. on the tongue discoursed pleasing
P. R. 2, 164. s. the rugged'st brow
P. R. 4, 295. the next to fabling fell and s.
S. A. 872. in feigned religion s. hypocrisy
S.A. 1049. his way to peace is s.
C. 825. with moist curb sways the s. Severn
A. 84. the s. enamelled green
S. 13, 8. that with s. air couldst humour best
V.Ex.100. or Medway s.or royal-towered Thame
C. 290. as s. as Thebes their unrazored lips
**Smooth-dittied.**—C. 86. pipe and s.-d. song
**Smoothed.**—P. L. 1, 772. or on the s. plank
P. L. 4, 120. each perturbation s. with outward
**Smoother.**—S. 20, 6. time will run on s.
**Smooth-haired.**—C. 716. weave the s.-h. silk
**Smoothing.**—C. 251. fall s. the raven-down
Il P. 58. s. the rugged brow of night
**Smoothly.**—C. 1012. but now my task is s. done
H. 65. s. the waters kissed
**Smooths.**—P. L. 5, 626. so s. her charming
**Smooth-shaven.**—Il P. 66. the dry s.-s. green
**Smooth-sliding.**—L. 86. s.-s. Mincius crowned
**Smote.**—P. L. 4, 244. the morning sun first warmly s.
P. L. 6, 250. saw where the sword of Michael s.
P. L. 6, 591. with such impetuous fury s.
P. L. 10, 295. as with a trident s. and fixed
P. L. 11, 445. and as they talked s. him into
S. A. 990. who with inhospitable guile s. Sisera
**Smouldering.**—H. 159. and s. clouds outbrake
**Smutty.**—P. L. 4, 817. the s. grain with sudden
**Snake.**—P. L. 9, 91. for in the wily s. whatever
P. L. 9, 613. so talked the spirited sly s.
P. L. 9, 643. so glistered the dire s. and into
P. L. 10, 218. or slain or as the s. with youthful
P. L. 11, 426. nor with the s. conspired
S. A. 763. entangled with a poisonous bosom s.
**Snaky.**—P. L. 2, 724. had not the s. sorceress
P. L. 7, 484. involved their s. folds and added
P. L. 10, 559. than the s. locks that curled
P. R. 1, 120. his easy steps girded with s. wiles
H. 226. not Typhon huge ending in s. twine
**Snaky-headed.**—C. 447. what was that s.-h.
**Snare.**—P. L. 4, 8. so 'scaped his mortal s.
P. L. 10, 873. to hellish falsehood s. them
P. L. 11, 165. thee ordained a help became thy s.
P. L. 12, 31. with war and hostile s. such
P. R. 1, 441. and run not sooner to his fatal s.
P. R. 2, 454. wise man's cumbrance if not s.
S. A. 230. specious monster my accomplished s.
S. A. 532. into the s. I fell of fair fallacious looks
S. A. 931. to bring my feet again into the s.
C. 567. sweet thou sing'st how near the deadly s.
**Snares.**—P. L. 10, 897. through female s.
P. R. 1, 97. but well-couched fraud well-woven s.
P. R. 3, 191. contempts and scorns and s.
P. R. 4, 611. foot in paradise to tempt his s.
S. A. 409. might easily have shook off all her s.
S. A. 845. hear what assaults I had what s.
C. 164. and hug him into s.
P. 11. dangers and s. and wrongs and worse
**Snatch.**—P. R. 2, 56. then s. him hence
**Snatched.**—P. L. 10, 1025. lest death so s.
P. L. 11, 670. not a cloud descending s. him

C. 815. ye should have *s.* his wand
**Sneeze.**—P. R. 4, 458. not wholesome as a *s.*
**Snow.**—P. L. 2, 491. *s.* or shower
P. L. 2, 591. all else deep *s.* and ice a gulf
P. L. 10, 685. which had forbid the *s.* from
P. L. 10, 698. armed with ice and *s.* and hail
P. L. 10, 1063. seasons rain ice hail and *s.*
H. 39. to hide her guilty front with innocent *s.*
V. Ex. 42. hills of *s.* and lofts of piled thunder
**Snow-soft.**—D. F. I. 19. descended from his *s.-s.*
**Snowy.**—P. L. 1, 515. thence on the *s.* top of
P. L. 3, 432. whose *s.* ridge the roving Tartar
P. L. 10, 432. over the *s.* plains retires
S. A. 628. nor breath of vernal air from *s.* Alp
C. 927. that tumble down the *s.* hills
**Snuffed.**—P. L. 10, 272. he *s.* the smell
**Soaked.**—S. A. 1726. it lies *s.* in his enemies
**Soar.**—P. L. 1, 1 4. no middle flight intends to *s.*
P. L. 4, 829. there sitting where ye durst
P. L. 5, 270. till within *s.* of towering eagles
P. L. 7, 3. above the Olympian hill I *s.*
P. R. 1, 230. but nourish them and let them *s.*
C. 1016, and from thence can *s.* as soon
V. Ex. 33. the deep transported mind may *s.*
**Soared.**—P. L. 9, 170. as low as high he *s.*
**Soaring.**—P. L. 6, 243. then, *s.* on main
P. L. 7, 421. and *s.* the air sublime
**Soars.**—P. L. 2, 634. then *s.* up to the fiery
Il P. 52. him that yon *s.* on golden wing
**Sober.**—P. L. 4, 599. had in her *s.* livery all
P. L. 11, 621. to these that *s.* race of men
C. 263. such *s.* certainty of waking bliss
C. 766. that live according to her *s.* laws
Il P. 32. *s.* steadfast and demure
**Sociable.**—P. L. 5, 221. Raphael the *s.* spirit
**Sociably.**—P. L. 11, 234. nor *s.* mild as
**Social.**—P. L. 8, 429. accompanied seek'st not *s.*
**Societies.**—P. L. 179. solemn troops and sweet *s.*
**Society.**—P. L. 8, 383. what *s.* can sort
P. L. 8, 586. what higher in her *s.*
P. L. 9, 249. for solitude sometimes is best *s.*
P. L. 9, 1007. to soothe him with her loved *s.*
P. R. 1, 302. such solitude before choicest *s.*
**Sock.**—L'A. 132. if Jonson's learned *s.* be on
**Socrates.**—P. R. 3, 96. poor *S.* who next
P. R. 4, 274. to the low-roofed house of *S.*
**Sodom.**—P. L. 1, 503. witness the streets of *S.*
P. L. 10, 562. bituminous lake where *S.* flamed
**Soe'er.**—P. L. 2, 260. and in what place *s.*
**Soever.**—S. A. 1015. which way *s.* men refer it
**Sofala.**—P. L. 11, 400. and *S.* thought Ophir
**Soft.**—P.L.1,424. so *s.* and uncompounded is their
P. L. 1, 551. of flutes and *s.* recorders
P. L. 1, 561. moved on in silence to *s.* pipes
P. L. 2, 276. these piercing fires as *s.* as now
P. L. 2, 400. the *s.* delicious air
P. L. 2, 601. to starve in ice their *s.* ethereal
P. L. 4, 326. stood whispering *s.* by a fresh
P. L. 4, 334. recline on the *s.* downy bank
P. L. 4, 471. thy coming and thy *s.* embraces
P. L. 4, 479. less winning *s.* less amiably mild
P. L. 4, 615. now falling with *s.* slumbrous
P. L. 4, 646. the fertile earth after *s.* showers
P. L. 4, 667. which these *s.* fires not only
P. L. 5, 17. her hand *s.* touching whispered
P. L. 5, 193. breathe *s.* or loud and wave
P. L. 7, 300. if through plain, *s.* ebbing
P. L. 7, 436. but all night tuned her *s.* lays
P. L. 7, 598. tempered *s.* tunings intermixed
P. L. 8, 165. that spinning sleeps on her *s.* axle
P. L. 8, 166. and bears thee *s.* with the smooth
P. L. 8, 254. *s.* on the flowery herb I found me
P. L. 8, 288. and with *s.* oppression seized
P. L. 9, 386. her hand *s.* she withdrew
P. L. 9, 458. heavenly form angelic but more *s.*
P. L. 10, 98. by *s.* winds brought to their ears
P. L. 10, 865. *s.* words to his fierce passion she
P. L. 11, 584. they sung *s.* amorous ditties
P. L. 11, 848. that stole with *s.* foot towards
P. R. 2, 365. odours fanned from their *s.* wings
P. R. 4, 583. their plumy vans received him *s.*

S. A. 1036. modest, meek, demure
C. 86. with his *s.* pipe and smooth dittied song
C. 259. and fell Charybdis murmured *s.* applause
C. 555. at last a *s.* and solemn-breathing sourd
C. 681. for gentle usage and *s.* delicacy
C. 882. sleeking her *s.* alluring locks
C. 1001. in slumber *s.* and on the ground
L. 44. fanning their joyous leaves to thy *s.* lays
L'A. 136. lap me in *s.* Lydian airs
S. 1, 8. linked that amorous power to thy *s.* lay
D. F. I. 2. *s.* silken primrose fading timelessly
Cir. 5. the *s.* silence of the listening night
**Soften.**—P. L. 3, 189. and *s.* stony hearts
P. R. 2, 163. such object hath the power to *s.*
**Softened.**—P. L. 4, 147. fruits in her *s.* soil
P. L. 11, 110, I behold them *s.* and with tears
S. A. 534. *s.* with pleasure and voluptuous life
P. 46. yet on the *s.* quarry would I score
**Softening.**—P. L. 7, 280. prolific humour *s.*,
**Softer.**—P. 27. me *s.* airs befit and *s.* strings
**Softest.**—P. L. 9, 1041. earth's freshest, *s.* lap
**Softly.**— S. A. 115. this, this is he *s.* awhile
Il P. 150. *s.* on my eyelids laid
H. 47. crowned with olive green came *s.* sliding
**Softness.**—P. L. 4, 298. for *s.* she and sweet
**Sogdiana.**—P. R. 3, 302. have wasted *S.*
**Soil.**—P. L. 1, 242. is this the region this the *s.*
P. L. 1, 562. o'er the burnt *s.*
P. L. 1, 691. *s.* may best deserve the precious
P. L. 2, 270. this desert *s.* wants not her hidden
P. L. 2, 904. sands of Barca or Cyrene's torrid *s.*
P. L. 4, 214. in this pleasant *s.* his far more
P. L. 6, 510. up they turned wide the celestial *s.*
P. L. 8, 147. rain produce fruits in her softened *s.*
P. L. 10, 293. the aggregated *s.* death with his
P. L. 10, 526. the *s.* bedropt with blood
P. L. 11, 98. whence he was taken fitter *s.*
P. L. 11, 262. whence thou wast taken fitter *s.*
P. L. 11, 270. thus leave thee native *s.* these
P. L. 11, 292. he abides think there thy native *s.*
P. L. 42, 18. labouring the *s.* and reaping
P. L. 12, 129. his gods, his friends and native *s.*
P. R. 4, 239. pure the air and light the *s.*
C. 16. I would not *s.* these pure ambrosial
C. 427. will dare to *s.* her virgin purity
C. 633. a bright golden flower but not in this *s.*
A. 101. a better *s.* shall give ye thanks
L. 78. fame is no plant that grows on mortal *s.*
**Soiled.**—P. L. 9, 1076. ornaments now *s.* and
S. A. 123. ill-fitted weeds overworn and *s.*
S. A. 141. or grovelling *s.* their crested helmets
**Sojourn.**—P. L. 3, 15. in that obscure *s.*
P. L. 12, 159. to *s.* in that land he comes
P. R. 3, 235. short *s.* and what thence
**Sojourned.**—P. L. 7, 249. cloudy tabernacle *s.*
**Sojourners.**—P. L. 1, 309. the *s.* of Goshen
P. L. 12, 192. submits to let his *s.* depart
**Solace.**—P. L. 4, 486. an individual *s.* dear
P. L. 6, 905. which would be all his *s.* and
P. L. 8, 419. to help or *s.* his defects
P. L. 9, 844. and new *s.* in her return so long
P. L. 9, 1044. guilt the seal the *s.* of their sin
P. R. 4, 334. native language can I find that *s.*
C. 348. be some *s.* yet some little cheering
**Solaced.**—P. L. 7, 434. with song *s.* the woods
**Solaces.**—S. A. 915. life yet hath many *s.*
**Soldan.**—P. L. 1, 764. and at the *S.'s* chair
**Soldiery.**—S. A. 1498. a camp of faithful *s.*
**Sole.**—P. L. 1, 124. *s.* reigning holds the
P. L. 1, 160. but ever to do ill our *s.* delight
P. L. 1, 237. such resting found the *s.* of unblest
P. L. 2, 325. first and last will reign *s.* king
P. L. 2, 827. them I go this uncouth errand *s.*
P. L. 3, 94. transgress the *s.* command, *s.* pledge
P. L. 3, 276. O thou my *s.* complacence
P. L. 4, 33. look'st from thy *s.* dominion like
P. L. 4, 411. *s.* partner and *s.* part of all these
P. L. 4, 683. *s.* or responsive each to others
P. L. 4, 751. *s.* propriety in paradise of all
P. L. 4, 923. thou surely hadst not come *s.*
P. L. 5, 28. O *s.* in whom my thoughts find

P. L. 5, 272. a phœnix gazed by all as that *s*. bird
P. L. 6, 808. vengeance is his or whose he *s*.
P. L. 6, 880. *s*. victor from the expulsion of his
L. L. 7, 47. trangress and slight that *s*. command
P. L. 8, 51. Adam relating she *s*. auditress
P. L. 8, 329. my *s*. command transgressed
P. L. 9, 135. to me shall be the glory *s*. among
P. L. 9, 227. *s*. Eve associate *s*. to me beyond
P. L. 9, 533. if perhaps thou canst who art *s*.
P. L. 9, 653. and left that command *s*. daughter
P. L. 10, 401. chiefly on man *s*. lord of all
P. L. 10, 935. on me *s*. cause to thee of all this
P. L. 10, 941. towards her his life so late and *s*.
P. L. 10, 973. regain ... the *s*. contentment
P. L. 12, 564. and on him *s*. depend
P. R. 1, 100. I when no other durst *s*. undertook
P. R. 2, 110.·*s*. but with holiest meditations fed
P. R. 3, 26. glory the reward that *s*. excites
S. A. 376. *s*. author I. *s*. cause
**Solemn.** — P. L. 1, 390. his holy rites and *s*. feasts
P. L. 1, 557. and swage with *s*. touches troubled
P. L. 1, 755. a *s*. council forthwith to be held
P. L. 3, 351. with *s*. adoration down they cast
P. L. 4, 648. with this her *s*. bird and this fair
P. L. 4, 655. nor silent night with this her *s*.
P. L. 5, 354. more *s*. than the tedious pomp
P. L. 5, 618. that day as other *s*. days they spent
P. L. 7, 78. with *s*. purpose to observe immutably
P. L. 7, 149. with ministeries due and *s*. rites
P. L. 7, 202. against a *s*. day harnessed at hand
P. L. 7, 435. nor then the *s*. nightingale ceased
P. L. 7, 595. had work and rested not the *s*. pipe
P. L. 11, 236. but *s*. and sublime whom not
P. L. 12, 364. his place of birth a *s*. angel tells
P. R. 1, 133. I begin to verify that *s*. message
P. R. 2, 354. under the trees now tripped now *s*.
S. A. 12. a *s*. feast the people hold
S. A. 359. then given with *s*. hand as graces
S. A. 983. sung at *s*. festivals
S. A. 1311. this day to Dagon is a *s*. feast
C. 457. and in clear dream and *s*. vision
A. 7. here our *s*. search hath end
L. 179. in *s*. troops and sweet societies
Il P. 117. in sage and *s*. tunes have sung
H. 17. hast thou no verse no hymn or *s*. strain
H. 115. harping in loud and *s*. choir
S. M. 9. with saintly shout and *s*. jubilee
V. Ex. 49. in *s*. songs at king Alcinous' feast
**Solemn-breathing.** — C. 555. and *s.-b*. sound
**Solemnest.** — S. A. 1147. with *s*. devotion spread
**Solemnities.** — C. 746. at feasts and high *s*.
**Solemnity.** — C. 142. our concealed *s*.
A. 39. to further this night's glad *s*.
**Solemnize.** — S. A. 1656. met from all parts to *s*.
**Solemnized.** — P. L. 7, 448. *s*. the fifth day
**Solemnly.** — S. A. 678. but such as thou hast *s*.
S. A. 1731. to fetch him hence and *s*. attend
**Solicit.** — P. L. 8, 167. *s*. not thy thoughts
P. L. 10, 744. did I *s*. thee from darkness
**Solicitation.** — S. A. 488. the trouble of that's.
**Solicitations.** — P. R. 1, 152. all his *s*. and
**Solicited.** — P. L. 9, 743. *s*. her longing eye
S. A. 852 *s*. commanded threatened urged
**Solicitous.** — P. L. 10, 428. sat *s*. what
P. R. 2, 120. and blank he thus began
P. R. 3, 200. why art thou *s*. what moves thy
**Solid.** — P. L. 1, 229. burned with *s*., as the lake
P. L. 2, 878. of massy iron or *s*. rock with ease
P. L. 6, 323. so that neither keen nor *s*. might
P. L. 8, 93. may of *s*. good contain more plenty
P. L. 10, 286. or slimy as in raging sea
P. L. 10, 884. a show rather than *s*. virtue
P. R. 4, 18. or surging waves against a *s*. rock
P. R. 4, 358. the *s*. rules of civil government
S. 21, 10. toward *s*. good what leads the nearest
**Solitary.** — P. L. 2, 632. explores his *s*. flight
P. L. 6, 139. or with *s*. hand reaching beyond
P. L. 7, 461. those rare and *s*. these in flocks
P. L. 8, 402. no pleasure though in pleasure *s*.
P. L. 12, 649. through Eden took their *s*. way
Il P. 24. to *s*. Saturn bore

**Solitude.** — P. L. 3, 69. love in blissful *s*.
P. L. 7, 28. dangers compassed round and *s*.
P. L. 8, 364. in *s*. what happiness who can
P. L. 8, 369. what call'st thou *s*. is not the earth
P. L. 9, 249. for *s*. sometimes is best society
P. L. 9, 1085. O might I here in *s*. live savage
P. L. 10, 105. pleased thus entertained with *s*.
P. R. 1, 191. the better to converse with *s*.
P. R. 1, 302. such *s*. before choicest society
P. R. 2, 304. in this wild *s*. so long should bide
C. 376. oft seeks to sweet retired *s*.
**Solomon.** — P. L. 1, 401. heart of *S*. he led
P. R. 2, 170. beguiled the heart of wisest *S*.
P. R. 2, 201. for *S*. he lived at ease and full of
P. R. 2, 206. is wiser far than *S*.
**Solstice.** — P. 6. in wintry *s*. like the shortened
**Solstitial.** — P. L. 10, 656. south to bring *s*.
**Solve.** — P. L. 8, 55. and *s*. high dispute
**Solved.** — P. R. 4, 573. and him who *s*. it not
P. R. 4, 574. once found out and *s*. for grief
S. A. 1200. *s*. the riddle which I had proposed
**Solution.** — P. L. 6, 694. and no *s*. will be
P. L. 8, 14. remains which only thy *s*. can
S. A. 306. but never find self-satisfying *s*.
**Some.** — P. L. 1, 204. the pilot of *s*. small
P. L. 1, 205. deeming *s*. island, oft, as seamen
P. L. 1, 294. to be the mast of *s*. great ammiral
P. L. 1, 524. appeared obscure *s*. glimpse of joy
P. L. 1, 731. work *s*. praise and *s*. the architect
P. L. 1, 783. *s*. belated peasant sees or dreams
P. L. 2, 83. *s*. worse way his wrath may find
P. L. 2, 128. as the scope of all his aim after *s*.
P. L. 2, 345. what if we find *s*. easier enterprise
P. L. 2, 348. the happy seat of *s*. new race
P. L. 2, 363. *s*. advantageous act may be
P. L. 2, 397. or else in *s*. mild zone dwell not
P. L. 2, 924. bent to rase *s*. capital city
P. L. 2, 936. of *s*. tumultuous cloud instinct
P. L. 2, 977. or if *s*. other place from your
P. L. 3, 92. destroy or worse by *s*. false guile
P. L. 3, 183. *s*. I have chosen of peculiar grace
P. L. 3, 211. unless for him *s*. other able .
P. L. 3, 428. *s*. small reflection gains of
P. L. 3, 459. not in the neighbouring moon as *s*.
P. L. 3, 546. the brow of *s*. high-climbing hill
P. L. 3, 548. goodly prospect of *s*. foreign land
P. L. 3, 549. or *s*. renowned metropolis
P. L. 3, 628. on *s*. great charge employed
P. L. 3, 700. with thine eyes what *s*. perhaps
P. L. 4, 59. his powerful destiny ordained me *s*.
P. L. 4, 61. *s*. other power as great might have
P. L. 4, 189. unhoard the cash of *s*. rich
P. L. 4, 255. or the flowery lap of *s*. irriguous
P. L. 4, 281. though this by *s*. supposed true
P. L. 4, 404. hath spied in *s*. purlieu two gentle
P. L. 4, 426. *s*. dreadful thing no doubt
P. L. 4, 531. where I may meet *s*. wandering
P. L. 4, 747. commands to *s*. leaves free to all
P. L. 4, 793. who tells of *s*. infernal spirit seen
P. L. 5, 114. *s*. such resemblances methinks
P. L. 5, 290. for on *s*. message high they guessed
P. L. 5, 311. *s*. great behest from heaven
P. L. 5, 541. in this we stand or fall and *s*. are
P. L. 5, 554. *s*. doubt within me move
P. L. 6, 161. ambitious to win from me *s*. plume
P. L. 6, 279. or *s*. more sudden vengeance
P. L. 6, 431. is less firmly armed *s*. disadvantage
P. L. 6, 503. *s*. one intent on mischief or
P. L. 7, 482. all minims of nature *s*. of serpent
P. L. 8, 147. for *s*. to eat allotted there
P. L. 8, 152. perhaps with *s*. that live
P. L. 8, 278. not of myself by *s*. great maker
P. L. 8, 534. nature failed in me and left *s*. part
P. L. 9, 271. one who loves and *s*. unkindness
P. L. 9, 354. lest by *s*. fair-appearing good
P. L. 9, 361. may meet *s*. specious object by
P. L. 9, 638. which oft they say *s*. evil spirit
P. L. 9, 669. raised as of *s*. great matter to
P. L. 9, 670. as when of old *s*. orator renowned
P. L. 9, 672. to *s*. great cause addressed stood

P. L. 9, 904. s. cursed fraud of enemy hath
P. L. 9, 1002. muttering thunder s. sad drops
P. L. 9, 1085. in s. glade obscured
P. L. 9,1095. s. tree whose broad smooth leaves
P. L. 10, 52. by s. immediate stroke but soon
P. L. 10, 246. or sympathy or s. connatural
P. L. 10, 575. yearly enjoined s. say to undergo
P. L. 10, 578. however s. tradition they
P. L. 10, 626. transported with s. fit of passion
P. L. 10, 668. s. say he bid his angels turn
P. L. 10, 671. s. say the sun was bid turn reins
P. L. 10, 787. then in the grave or in s. other
P. L. 10, 894. or find s. other way to generate
P. L. 10, 900. but such as s. misfortune brings
P. L. 10, 976. tending to s. relief of our
P. L. 10, 1029. let us seek s. safer resolution
P. L. 10,1068. s. better shroud s. better warmth
P. L. 11, 103. invade vacant possession s. new
P. L. 11, 193. O Eve s. farther change awaits
P. L. 11, 198. from death released s. days
P. L. 11, 231. s. great potentate
P. L. 11, 425. original crime hath wrought in s.
P. L. 11, 450. O teacher s. great mischief hath
P. L. 11, 471. s. as thou sawest by violent
P. L. 11, 557. by s., were herds of cattle
P. L. 11, 569. thence gliding hot to s. cave's
P. L. 11,851. fast on the top of s. high mountain
P. L. 12, 16. with some regard to what is just
P. L. 12, 99. but justice and s. fatal curse
P. L. 12, 293. they may conclude s. blood more
P. L. 12, 612. he hath sent propitious s. great
P. L. 12, 645. s. natural tears they dropped
P. R. 1, 183. yet s. days lodged in Bethabara
P. R. 1, 290. and now by s. stong motion I am
P. R. 1, 305. under the covert of s. ancient
P. R. 1,315. as seemed the quest of s. stray ewe
P. R. 2, 65. s. troubled thoughts which she in
P. R. 2, 86. I looked for s. great change
P. R. 2,95. where delay he now? s. great intent
P. R. 2, 101. thus long to s. great purpose he
P. R. 2, 186. to way-lay s. beauty rare Calisto
P. R. 2, 239. if cause were to unfold s. active
P. R. 2, 254. can satisfy that need s. other way
P. R. 2, 306. others of s. note as story tells
P. R. 3, 294. now s. ages past by great
P. R. 3, 434. remembering Abraham by s.
P. R. 4, 69. s. from farthest south Syene
P. R. 4, 404. wherever under s. concourse of
P. R. 4, 423. s. yelled s. shrieked
P. R. 4, 521. in s. respect far higher so declared
S. A. 17. this unfrequented place to find s. ease
S. A. 18. ease to the body s. none to the mind
S. A. 28. from s. great act or benefit revealed
S. A. 258. I willingly on s. conditions came
S. A. 423. find s. occasion to infest our foes
S. A. 482. have made way to s. Philistian
S. A. 526. after s. proof of acts indeed heroic
S. A. 664. s. source of consolation from above
S. A. 680. to s. great work thy glory
S. A. 722. s. rich Philistian matron
S. A. 746. late yet in s. part to recompense
S. A. 812. though fond and reasonless to s.
S. A. 1117. let be assigned s. narrow place
S.A.1133. black enchantments s. magician's art
S. A. 1252. s. way or other yet farther to afflict
S. A. 1253. he must allege s. cause
S. A. 1314. and now s. public proof thereof
S. A. 1379. for s. important cause thou need'st
S. A. 1382. I begin to feel rousing motions
S. A.1389. by s. great act or of my days the last
S. A. 1444. or of him bringing to us s. glad news
S. A.1461. s. much averse I found and wondrous
S. A. 1471. s. convenient ransom were proposed
S. A. 1475. or at s. proof of strength before them
S. A. 1499. to use him further yet in s. great
S. A. 1519. s. dismal accident it needs must be
S. A. 1536. a little stay will bring s. notice
S. A. 1550. as at s. distance from the place of
S. A. 1638. s. great matter in his mind revolved
C. 12. yet s. there be that by due steps aspire
C. 70. into s. brutish form of wolf or bear

C. 146. s. chaste footing near about this ground
C. 148. s. virgin sure
C. 166. I shall appear s. harmless villager
C. 196. shouldst thou but for s. felonious end
C. 239. if thou have hid them in s. flowery cave
C. 282. in the valley s. cool friendly spring
C. 299. of s. gay creatures of the element
C. 337. s. gentle taper though a rush candle
C. 339. the wicker hole of s. clay habitation
C. 348. 'twould be s. solace yet s. little cheering
C. 353. perhaps s. cold bank is her bolster now
C. 354. 'gainst the rugged bark of s. broad elm
C. 406. lest some ill-greeting touch attempt
C. 432. s. say no evil thing that walks by night
C. 481. s. far-off halloa break the silent air
C.483. either s. one like us night-foundered here
C. 484. or else s. neighbour woodman
C. 485. s. roving robber calling to his fellows
C. 576. supposing him s. neighbour villager
C. 658. and s. good angel bear a shield before us
C. 771. now heaps uppn s. few with fast excess
C. 801. her words set off by s. superior power
C. 805. to s. of Saturn's crew I must dissemble
C.821. s. other means I have which may be used
C. 859. and add the power of s. adjuring verse
C. 941. with s. other new device
L. 14. without the meed of s. melodious tear
L. 19. so may s. gentle Muse with lucky words
L'A. 5. find out s. uncouth cell
L'A. 17. or whether as s. sager sing
L'A. 55. from the side of s. hoar hill
L'A. 79. where perhaps s. beauty lies
Il P. 5. dwell in s. idle brain and fancies fond
Il P. 75. over s. wide-watered shore
Il P. 78. s. still removed place will fit
Il P. 86. be seen in s. high lonely tower
Il P. 139. there in close covert by s. brook
Il P. 147. and let s. strange mysterious dream
Il P. 153. sent by s. spirit to mortals good
S. 1, 10. my hopeless doom in s. grove nigh
S. 2, 8. that s. timely-happy spirits endueth
S. 11, 6. and s. in file stand spelling false
H. 147. and· heaven as at s. festival
P. 38. my spirit s. transporting cherub feels
P. 56. a race of mourners on s. pregnant cloud
D. F. I. 11. if likewise he s. fair one wedded not
D. F. I. 43. s. star which from the ruined
D. F. I. 48. and thou s. goddess fled
D. F. I. 56. to do the world s. good
M. W. 35. so have I seen s. tender slip
M. W. 38. plucked up by s. unheedy swain
M. W. 57. and s. flowers and s. bays
V. Ex. 23. I have s. naked thoughts that rove
V. Ex. 30. thy service in s. graver subject use
V. Ex. 93. who like s. earth-born giant
**Something.**—P. L. 8, 13. s. yet of doubt
P. L. 8, 201. of s. not unseasonable to ask
P. L. 9, 845. yet oft his heart divine of s.ill
P. L. 10, 1014. argue in thee s. more sublime
P. L. 11, 207. with s. heavenly fraught
P. R.1,96. but must with s. sudden be opposed
S. A. 1383. dispose to s. extraordinary
C. 246. sure s. holy lodges in that breast
C. 783. fain would I s. say yet to what end
Il P. 174. to s. like prophetic strain
D. F. I. 34. O no, for s. in thy face did shine
V. Ex. 67. there is s. that doth force my fear
**Sometime.**—P. L. 9, 824. s. superior
L'A. 57. s. walking not unseen
**Sometimes.**—P. L. 2,632. s. he scours the right
P. L. 2, 633. s. the left
P. L. 3, 32. nor s. forget those other two
P. L. 3, 517. but drawn up to heaven s.
P. L. 4, 27. s. towards Eden which now in his
P. L. 4, 29. s. towards heaven and the
P. L. 5, 79. but s. in the air as we s. ascend
P. L. 6, 148. how few s. may know when
P. L. 6, 242. s. on firm ground a standing fight
P. L. 7, 496. of huge extent s.
P. L. 8, 268. and s. went and s. ran with supple
P. L. 9, 249. for solitude s. is best society

P. L. 9, 675. s. in height began as no delay of
P. L. 12, 97. yet s. nations will decline so low
P. R. 1, 304. whether on hill s
P. R. 1, 330. for we s. who dwell this wild
P. R. 1, 367. hath he excluded my resort s.
P. R. 2, 13. s. they thought he might be only
P. R. 2, 277. s. that with Elijah he partook
C. 380. were all to-ruffled and s. impaired
L'A. 91. s. with secure delight
Il P. 97. s. let gorgeous Tragedy
S. 20, 3. where shall we s. meet and by the fire
**Somewhat.**—P. L. 2, 521. and s. raised by
P. L. 6, 615. they seemed s. extravagant and
P. R. 1, 433. by mixing s. true to vent more
S. A. 1244. his giantship is gone s. crestfallen
L. 17. begin and s. loudly sweep the string
**Somewhere.**—P. L. 9, 256. s. nigh at hand
**Son.**— P. L. I, 339. the potent rod of Amram's s.
P. L. 1, 513. his own and Rhea's s. like measure
P. L. 1, 580. in fable or romance of Uther's s.
P. L. 2, 678. God and his S. except created
P. L. 2, 728. thy only s.? what fury O S. possesses
P. L. 2, 743. and that phantasm call'st my s.
P. L. 2, 804. grim Death, my s. and foe who
P. L. 2, 818. and my fair s. here show'st me
P. L. 3, 64. image of his glory sat his only S.
P. L. 3, 79. thus to his only S. foreseeing
P. L. 3, 138. beyond compare the S. of God
P. L. 3, 151. late so loved thy youngest s.
P. L. 3, 168. O. S. in whom my soul hath chief
P. L. 3, 169. S. of my bosom S. who art alone
P. L. 3, 224. had not the S. of God in whom
P. L. 3, 286. of all mankind though Adam's s.
P. L. 3, 309. more than birthright S. of God
P. L. 3, 316. both God, and man, S. both of
P. L. 3, 343. adore the S. and honour him as
P. L. 3, 384. begotten S. divine similitude
P. L. 3, 398. S. of thy Father's might
P. L. 3, 403. thy dear and only S. perceive
P. L. 3, 412. hail S. of God Saviour of men
P. L. 4, 170. from the spouse of Tobit's s.
P. L. 4, 278. and her florid o. young Bacchus
P. L. 4, 716. when to the unwiser s. of Japhet
P. L. 4, 757. all the charities of father, s. and
P. L. 5, 285. like Maia's s. he stood
P. L. 5, 519. to whom the angel: S. of heaven
P. L. 5, 597. in bliss embosomed sat the S.
P. L. 5, 604. whom I declare my only S.
P. L. 5, 662. with envy against the S. of God
P. L. 5, 718. smiling to his only S. thus said:
P. L. 5, 719. S. thou in whom my glory I behold
P. L. 5, 733. to whom the S. with calm aspect
P. L. 5, 743. so spake the S. but Satan with
P. L. 5, 815. that to his only S. by right endued
P. L. 5, 835. equal to him begotten S.? by whom
P. L. 5, 847. incensed Father and the incensed S.
P. L. 5, 855. transferred from Father to his S.
P. L. 6, 676. to honour his anointed S. avenged
P. L. 6, 678. whence to his S. the assessor
P. L. 6, 680. effulgence of my glory S. beloved S.
P. L. 6, 719. and on his S. with rays direct
P. L. 6, 725. always seek'st to glorify thy S.
P. L. 6, 799. when the great S. of God
P. L. 6, 824. so spake the S. and into terror
P. L. 6, 887. S. heir and Lord
P. L. 7, 38. nor could the Muse defend her s.
P. L. 7, 135. and the great S. returned victorious
P. L. 7, 138. and to his S. thus spake
P. L. 7, 163. and thou my Word, begotten S.
P. L. 7, 192. meanwhile the S. on his great
P. L. 7, 518. thus to his S. audibly spake
P. L. 9, 19. perplexed the Greek and Cytherea's s.
P. L. 9, 176. this man of clay, s. of despite
P. L. 9, 441. Alcinous host of old Laertes' s.
P. L. 10, 56. vicegerent S. to thee I have
P. L. 10, 64. on the S. blazed forth unclouded
P. L. 10, 70. that thou in me thy S. beloved
P. L. 10, 183. Jesus S. of Mary second Eve
P. L. 10, 235. O s., why sit we here each other
P. L. 10, 338. saw descend the S. of God to judge
P. L. 10, 363. I must after thee with this thy s.

P. L. 10, 384. fair daughter and thou s.
P. L. 10, 634. well-pleasing S.
P. L. 10, 645. next to the S. destined restorer
P. L. 10, 760. what if thy s. prove disobedient
P. L. 11, 20. the glad S. presenting thus to
P. L. 11, 46. request for man accepted S. obtain
P. L. 11, 72. he ended and the S. gave signal
P. L. 11, 808. the only s. of light in a dark age
P. L. 12, 64. O execrable s.! so to aspire above
P. L. 12, 80. that s. who on the quiet state of
P. L. 12, 101. witness the irreverent s. of him
P. L. 12, 153. a s. and of his s. a grand child
P. L. 12, 160. comes invited by a younger s.
P. L. 12, 161. in time of dearth a s. whose
P. L. 12, 268. third from Abraham, s. of Isaac
P. L. 12, 327. a S. the woman's seed to thee
P. L. 12, 332. and his next s. for wealth and
P. L. 12, 381. from thy womb the S. of God
P. L. 12, 388. not therefore joins the S.
P. R. 1, 11. by proof the undoubted S. of God
P. R. 1, 23. from Nazareth the s. of Joseph
P. R. 1, 32. pronounced him his beloved S.
P. R. 1, 85. this is my S. beloved
P. R. 1, 88. will he not do to advance his S.
P. R. 1, 122. this man of men attested S. of God
P. R. 1, 135. that she should bear a s. great in
P. R. 1, 136. renown, and called the S. of God
P. R. 1, 166. perfect man by merit called my S.
P. R. 1, 173. and triumph to the S. of God
P. R. 1, 176. the Father knows the S. therefore
P. R. 1, 183. meanwhile the S. of God who yet
P. R. 1, 230. are thy thoughts O S. but nourish
P. R. 1, 234. for know thou art no s. of mortal
P. R. 1, 285. me his beloved S. in whom alone
P. R. 1, 329. honoured so and called thee S. of God
P. R. 1, 335. to whom the S. of God who brought
P. R. 1, 342. if thou be the S. of God command
P. R. 1, 346. he ended and the S. of God replied
P. R. 1, 385. I know declared the S. of God
P. R. 2, 4. called Jesus Messiah S. of God
P. R. 2, 61. returned from baptism not her S.
P. R. 2, 85. S. owned from heaven by his Father's
P. R. 2, 109. the while her S. tracing the desert
P. R. 2, 242. from shade to shade the S. of God
P. R. 2, 260. the hour of night when thus the S.
P. R. 2, 303. more wonder that the S. of God.
P. R. 2, 308. the fugitive bondwoman with her s.
P. R. 2, 368. what doubts the S. of God to sit
P. R. 2, 377. what doubtest thou S. of God?
P. R. 2, 424. and his s. Herod placed on Judah's
P. R. 3, 1. so spake the S. of God and Satan
P. R. 3, 31. the s. of Macedonian Philip had
P. R. 3, 84. one is the s. of Jove of Mars the
P. R. 3, 145. so spake the S. of God
P. R. 3, 252. he took the S. of God up to a
P. R. 4, 90. this emperor hath no s. and now
P. R. 4, 109. to whom the S. of God unmoved
P. R. 4, 178. and darest thou to the S. of God
P. R. 4, 190. as offer them to me the S. of God
P. R. 4, 196. be not so sore offended S. of God
P. R. 4, 365. so spake the S. of God but Satan
P. R. 4, 396. brought back the S. of God and
P. R. 4, 420. shrouded then O patient S. of God
P. R. 4, 431. had raised to tempt the S. of God
P. R. 4, 451. morning yet betides thee S. of God
P. R. 4, 484. so talked he while the S. of God
P. R. 4, 500. hear O S. of David, virgin-born
P. R. 4, 501. for S. of God to me is yet in doubt
P. R. 4, 513. pronounced the S. of God beloved
P. R. 4, 517. S. of God which bears no single
P. R. 4, 518. the S. of God I also am or was
P. R. 4, 539. worth naming of S. of God by voice
P. R. 4, 550. pinnacle he set the S. of God
P. R. 4, 555. thyself down. Safely if S. of God
P. R. 4, 580. so proudly tempt the S. of God
P. R. 4, 602. the S. of God with godlike force
P. R. 4, 626. with awe to dread the S. of God
P. R. 4, 633. hail S. of the most High heir of
P. R. 4, 636. thus they the S. of God
S. A. 335. your once gloried friend my s.
S. A. 353. I gained a s. and such a s. as all men

S. A. 420. I cannot praise thy marriage choices *s*.
S. A. 503. but act not in thy own affliction *s*.
S. A. 1443. supposing here to find his *s*.
S. A. 1460. to accept of ransom for my *s*.
S. A. 1486. thou for thy *s*. art bent to lay out all
S. A. 1488. in old age carest how to nurse thy *s*.
S. A. 1516. they have slain my *s*.
S. A. 1517. thy *s*. is rather slaying them
C. 56. had by him ere he parted thence a *s*.
C. 876. and her *s*. that rules the strands
C. 1004. celestial Cupid her famed *s*. advanced
L. 59. the Muse herself for her enchanting *s*.
S. 17, 14. in peace and reckons thee her eldest *s*.
S. 20, 1. Lawrence of virtuous father virtuous *s*.
S. 23, 3. Jove's great *s*. to her glad husband gave
H. 2. wherein the *S*. of heaven's eternal king
M. W. 24. to greet her of a lovely *s*.
W. S. 5. dear *s*. of memory great heir of fame
V. Ex. 59. good luck befriend thee, *S*.; for
V. Ex. 73. your *s*. said she nor can you it prevent
V. Ex. 91. Rivers arise whether thou be the *s*.
**Song.**—P. L. 1, 13. to my adventurous *s*.
P. L. 2, 552. their *s*. was partial; but the
P. L. 2, 556. eloquence the soul *s*. charms the sense
P. L. 3, 29. smit with the love of sacred *s*.
P. L. 3, 369. they introduce their sacred *s*.
P. L. 3, 413. be the copious matter of my *s*.
P. L. 5, 7. the shrill matin *s*. of birds on every
P. L. 5, 41. tunes sweetest his lovelaboured *s*.
P. L. 5, 178. in mystic dance not without *s*.
P. L. 5, 204. made vocal by my *s*. and taught
P. L. 5, 619. in *s*. and dance about the sacred
P. L. 6, 167. spirits trained up in feast and *s*.
P. L. 7, 12. pleased with thy celestial *s*.
P. L. 7, 30. still govern thou my *s*. Urania
P. L. 7, 107. bid his absence till thy *s*. end
P. L. 7, 433. the smaller birds with *s*. solaced
P. L. 8, 243. than the sound of dance or *s*.
P. L. 9, 25. first this subject for heroic *s*.
P. L. 9, 800. not without *s*. each morning
P. L. 10, 648. such was their *s*.
P. L. 10, 862. and resound far other *s*.
P. R. 1, 12. as thou wront my prompted *s*.
P. R. 1, 480. and tunable as sylvan pipe or *s*.
P. R. 2, 281. approach and greet her with his *s*.
P. R. 4, 341. in fable hymn or *s*.
P. R. 4, 505. of the angelic *s*. in Bethlehem
S. A. 1737. in copious legend or sweet lyric *s*.
C. 44. what never yet was heard in tale or *s*.
C. 86. with his soft pipe, and smooth-dittied *s*.
C. 235. nightly to thee her sad *s*. mourneth well
C. 268. by blest *s*. forbidding every bleak
C. 854. if she be right invoked in warbled *s*.
L. 36. and old Damœtas loved to hear our *s*.
L. 176. and hears the unexpressive nuptial *s*.
Il P. 56. 'less Philomel will deign a *s*.
S. 13, 1. whose tuneful and well measured *s*.
H. 133. for if such holy *s*.
H. 239. time is our tedious *s*. have ending
P. 8. for now to sorrow must I tune my *s*.
Cir. 2. that erst with music and triumphant *s*.
S. M. 6. that undisturbed *s*. of pure concent
S. M. 25. O may we soon again renew that *s*.
M. M. 9. thus we salute thee with our early *s*.
**Songs.**—P. L. 1, 441. paid their vows and *s*.
P. L. 3, 148. sound of hymns and sacred *s*.
P. L. 4, 687. their *s*. divide the night
P. L. 4, 944. with *s*. to hymn his throne
P. L. 5, 161. with *s*. and choral symphonies
P. L. 5, 547. than when cherubic *s*. by night
P. L. 11, 594. *s*. garlands, flowers
P. R. 4. 346. our Hebrew *s*. and harps
P. R. 4, 347. unworthy to compare with Sion's *s*.
C. 878. and the *s*. of Sirens sweet
L. 123. and when they list their lean and flashy *s*.
V. Ex. 49. in solemn *s*. at king Alcinous' feast
**Sonorous.**—P. L. 1, 540. all the while *s*. metal
**Sons.**—P. L. 2, 353. when her barbarous *s*.
P. L. 1, 364. nor ... yet among the *s*. of Eve
P. L. 1, 406. the obscene dread of Moab's *s*.
P. L. 1, 495. as did Eli's *s*. who filled with lust

P. L. 1, 501. then wander forth the *s*. of Belial
P. L. 1, 654. favour equal to the *s*. of heaven
P. L. 1, 778. in bigness to surpass earth's giant *s*.
P. L. 2. 373. when his darling *s*. hurled headlong
P. L. 2, 692. the third part of heaven's *s*.
P. L. 3, 290. his crime makes guilty all his *s*.
P. L. 3, 463. of ill-joined *s*. and daughters born
P. L. 3, 658. where all his *s*. thy embassy attend
P. L. 4, 213. or where the *s*. of Eden long
P. L. 4, 324. of men since born his *s*.
P. L. 5, 160. ye who best can tell ye *s*. of light
P. L. 5, 389. world more numerous with thy *s*.
P. L. 5, 447. then had the *s*. of God excuse
P. L. 5, 716. how spread among the *s*. of morn
P. L. 5, 790. natives and *s*. of heaven possessed
P. L. 5, 863. this our native heaven ethereal *s*.
P. L. 6, 46. lead forth to battle these my *s*.
P. L. 6, 95. as *s*. of one great Sire hymning
P. L. 6, 505. instrument to plague the *s*. of men
P. L. 6, 715. pursue these *s*. of darkness
P. L. 7, 626. and *s*. of men whom God hath thus
P. L. 8, 637. and of all thy *s*. the weal or woe
P. L. 10, 819. patrimony that I must leave ye *s*.
P. L. 11, 84. O *s*. like one of us man is become
P. L. 11, 319. and to my *s*. relate on this
P. L. 11, 348. on even ground now with thy *s*.
P. L. 11, 410. city Geryon's *s*. call El Dorado
P. L. 11, 622. titled them the *s*. of God
P. L. 11, 696. of mankind gods and *s*. of gods
P. L. 11, 736. his three *s*. with their four wives
P. L. 11, 758. drowned and sunk thee as thy *s*.
P. L. 11, 875. world of wicked *s*. destroyed
P. L. 12, 145. but his *s*. shall dwell to Senir
P. L. 12, 155. the grandchild with twelve *s*.
P. L. 12, 357. sceptre and regard not David's *s*.
P. L. 12, 447. not only to the *s*. of Abraham's
P. L. 12, 448. but to the *s*. of Abraham's faith
P. R. 1, 167. to earn salvation for the *s*. of men
P. R. 1, 237. angels and *s*. of men
P. R. 1, 368. came among the *s*. of God when
P. R. 2, 121. heaven's ancient *s*. ethereal thrones
P. R. 2, 179. false titled *s*. of God roaming the
P. R. 2, 192. among the *s*. of men how many
P. R. 3, 377. ten *s*. of Jacob two of Joseph lost
P. R. 3, 406. to just extent over all Israel's *s*.
P. R. 4, 197. though *s*. of God both angels are
P. R. 4, 520. all men are *s*. of God
P. R. 4, 614. now for Adam and his chosen *s*.
S. A. 240. yet Israel still serves with all his *s*.
S. A. 528. far beyond the *s*. of Anak famous now
S. A. 1177. thine or whom I with Israel's *s*. adore
S. A. 1248. fame divulge him father of five *s*.
S. A. 1294. might endued above the *s*. of men
S. A. 1485. fathers are wont to lay up for their *s*
S. A. 1487. *s*. wont to nurse their parents in old
S. A. 1558. but all her *s*. are fallen all in a moment
S. A. 1713. and lamentation to the *s*. of Caphtor
C. 655. or like the *s*. of Vulcan vomit smoke
C. 717. weave the ... silk to deck her *s*.
C. 727. and live like nature's bastards not her *s*.
H. 119. but when of old the *s*. of morning sung
D. F. I. 47. or did of late earth's *s*. besiege the wall
**Soon.**—P. L. 1, 78. he *s*. discerns
P. L. 1, 127. and him thus answered *s*. his bold
P. L. 1, 140. and vigour *s*. returns
P. L. 1, 278. they will *s*. resume new courage
P. L. 1, 337. they *s*. obeyed innumerable
P. L. 1, 528. his wonted pride *s*. recollecting
P. L. 1, 568. and *s*. traverse the whole battalion
P. L. 1, 688. *s*. had his crew opened into the
P. L. 1, 705. a third as *s*. had formed
P. L. 2, 140. of stain would *s*. expel her mischief
P. L. 2, 376. and faded bliss, faded so *s*.!
P. L. 2, 805. and me his parent would full *s*.
P. L. 2, 816. the subtle fiend his lore *s*. learned
P. L. 2, 839. once known shall *s*. return
P. L. 2, 866. thou wilt bring me *s*. to that new
P. L. 2, 931. but that seat *s*. failing meets
P. L. 3, 273. but *s*. the Almighty thus replied
P. L. 3, 355. but *s*. for man's offence to heaven

P. L. 3, 621. whereby he *s*. saw within ken a
P. L. 4, 94. of grace my former state; how *s*.
P. L. 4, 95. height recall high thoughts, how *s*.
P. L. 4, 119. whereof he *s*. aware each
P. L. 4, 463. but pleased I *s*. returned
P. L. 4, 464. *s*. returned pleased it returned as *s*.
P. L. 4, 570. *s*. discerned his looks alien from
P. L. 4, 822. unmoved with fear accost him *s*.
P. L. 4, 946. to whom the warrior angel *s*.
P. L. 4, 995. had not *s*. the Eternal, to prevent
P. L. 5, 138. *s*. as they forth were come
P. L. 5, 210. firm peace recovered *s*. and wonted
P. L. 5, 667. *s*. as midnight brought on the
P. L. 5, 892. for *s*. expect to feel his thunder
P. L. 6, 98. sound of onset ended *s*. each
P. L. 6, 344. yet *s*. he healed for spirits that
P. L. 6, 432. till now not known but known as *s*.
P. L. 6, 436. pierced with wound *s*. closing
P. L. 6, 528. refulgent host *s*. banded
P. L. 6, 532. him *s*. they met under spread
P. L. 6, 547. and *s*. in order, quit of all
P. L. 6, 585. in a flame but *s*. obscured with
P. L. 6, 736. of thee in all things and shall *s*.
P. L. 6, 777. under whose conduct Michael *s*.
P. L. 6, 834. full *s*. among them he arrived
P. L. 6, 878. heaven rejoiced and *s*. repaired
P. L. 7, 56. but the evil *s*. driven back redounded
P. L. 7, 59. whence Adam *s*. repealed the doubts
P. L. 7, 93. and the work begun how *s*. absolved
P. L. 7, 129. *s*. turns wisdom to folly
P. L. 7, 418, from the egg that *s*. bursting with
P. L. 8, 214. they satiate and *s*. fill
P. L. 8, 256. with his beams the sun *s*. dried
P. L. 8, 336. but *s*. his clear aspect returned
P. L. 8, 388. but *s*. prove tedious alike
P. L. 9, 132. all this will *s*. follow as to him
P. L. 9, 182. him fast sleeping *s*. he found
P. L. 9, 189. *s*. inspired with act intelligential
P. L. 9, 468. though in mid heaven *s*. ended
P. L. 9, 470. then *s*. fierce hate he recollects
P. L. 9, 589. the mossy trunk I wound me *s*.
P. L. 9, 630. I can bring thee thither *s*.
P. L. 9, 880. unshared with thee and odious *s*.
P. L. 9, 888. *s*. as he heard the fatal trespass
P. L. 9, 1046. *s*. as the force of that fallacious
P. L. 9, 1053. the other viewing *s*. found their
P. L. 9, 1100. there *s*. they chose the fig-tree
P. L. 9, 1143. to whom *s*. moved with touch of
P. L. 10, 21. *s*. as the unwelcome news from
P. L. 10, 52. but *s*. shall find forbearance
P. L. 10, 160. nigh overwhelmed confessing *s*.
P. L. 10, 264. the meagre shadow answered *s*.
P. L. 10, 331. their parent *s*. discerned
P. L. 10, 586. the hellish pair too *s*. arrived
P. L. 10, 596. the sin-born monster answered *s*.
P. L. 10, 940. *s*. his heart relented towards her
P. L. 10, 946. peaceful words upraised her *s*.
P. L. 10, 1052. *s*. recompensed with joy
P. L. 11, 227. perhaps of us will *s*. determine
P. L. 11, 238. he ended and the archangel *s*.
P. L. 11, 267. discovered *s*. the place of her
P. L. 11, 422. gentle angel by the hand *s*. raised
P. L. 11, 441. his offering *s*. propitious fire
P. L. 11, 506. or *s*. beg to lay it down
P. L. 11, 596. inclined to admit delight
P. L. 11, 663. but *s*. in factious opposition
P. L. 11, 711. which now direct thine eyes and *s*.
P. L. 12, 50. them beholding *s*. comes down
P. L. 12, 420. so he dies but *s*. revives
P. L. 12, 553. how *s*. hath thy prediction seer
P. L. 12, 645. tears they dropt but wiped them *s*.
P. R. 1, 25. but him the Baptist *s*. descried
P. R. 1, 57. and now too *s*. for us the circling
P. R. 1, 227. thoughts my mother *s*. perceiving
P. R. 1, 262. and *s*. found of whom they spake
P. R. 1, 454. this thy glory shall be *s*. retrenched
P. R. 2, 37. thus we rejoiced but *s*. our joy is
P. R. 2, 57. we shall see our hope our joy
P. R. 2, 75. *s*. enforced to fly thence into Egypt
P. R. 2, 292. and entered *s*. the shade high
P. R. 2, 383. I can at will, doubt not, as *s*. as

P. R. 2, 451. as *s*. accomplish what they did
P. R. 3, 149. of another plea bethought him *s*.
P. R. 3, 244. I will bring thee where thou *s*.
P. R. 3, 389. long in preparing *s*. to nothing
P. R. 4, 332. where so *s*. as in our native,
P. R. 4, 375. remember what I foretell thee *s*.
P. R. 4, 408. and *s*. with ugly dreams disturbed
P. R. 4, 459. and *s*. are gone
P. R. 4, 591. that *s*. refreshed him wearied
S. A. 425. I am sure our foes found *s*. occasion
S. A. 764. if not by quick destruction *s*. cut off
S. A. 1019. not so *s*. preferred thy paranymph
S. A. 1075. his fraught we *s*. shall know
S. A. 1096. I should have forced thee *s*.
S. A. 1155. or rather to thy sorrow *s*. feel
S. A. 1566. what will come at last too *s*.
S. A. 1585. brought him so *s*. at variance with
C. 68. *s*. as the potion works their human
C. 577. but *s*. I guessed ye were the two
C. 656. yet will they *s*. retire if he but shrink
C. 690. fair virgin this will restore all *s*.
C. 1016. and from thence can soar as *s*.
L'A. 116. by whispering winds *s*. lulled asleep
S. 2, 1. *s*. hath time the subtle thief of youth
S. 2, 9. yet be it less or more, or *s*. or slow
S. 19, 9. but Patience to prevent that murmur *s*.
P. 7. *s*. swallowed up in dark and long out-living
P. 53. would *s*. unbosom all their echoes mild
M. W. 8. alas too *s*. after so short time
Cir. 12. alas! how *s*. our sin sore doth begin
S. M. 25. O may we *s*. again renew that song
**Sooner.**—P. L. 3, 344. no *s*. had the Almighty
P. L. 3, 403. no *s*. did thy dear and only Son
P. L. 6, 595. the *s*. for their arms
P. L. 10, 357. for I no *s*. in my heart divined
P. L. 10, 613. and for destruction to mature *s*.
P. L. 11, 822. no *s*. he with them of man
P. R. 1, 441. and run not *s*. to his fatal snare
P. R. 3, 179. the happier reign the *s*. it begins
S. A. 20. no *s*. found alone but rush upon me
S. A. 426. thou the *s*. temptation found'st
S. A. 1537. of good or bad so great of bad the *s*.
C. 323. which oft is *s*. found in lowly sheds
D. F. I. 1. O fairest flower no *s*. blown but blasted
**Soonest.**—P. L. 4, 893. and *s*. recompense
P. L. 9, 181. where *s*. he might find the serpent
S. A. 1419. and the well-feasted priest then *s*.
**Soot.**—P. L. 10. 570. writhed their jaws with *s*.
**Sooth.**—D. F. I. 51. the hated earth O tell me *s*.
**Soothe.**—P. L. 9, 1006. the more to *s*. him
**Soothest.**—C. 823. the *s*. shepherd that e'er
**Soothing.**—P. R. 3, 6. with *s*. words renewed
**Soothsaying.**—C. 874. and old *s*. Glaucus' spell
**Sooty.**—P. L. 5. 440. if by fire of *s*. coal
C. 604. under the *s*. flag of Acheron
**Sophi.**—P. L. 10, 433. or Bactrian *S*. from the
**Sorcerer.**—C. 521. cypress shades a *s*. dwells
C. 940. lest the *s*. us entice
**Sorcerers.**—H. 220. the sable-stoled *s*. bear
**Sorceress.**—P. L. 2, 724. not the snaky *s*.
S. A. 819. how cunningly the *s*. displays
**Sorceries.**—P. L. 1, 479. *s*. abused
S. A. 937. to fence my ear against thy *s*.
**Sorcery.**—P. L. 2, 566. yet with a pleasing *s*.
C. 587. against the threats of malice or of *s*.
**Sord.**—P. L. 11, 433. rustic of grassy *s*. thither
**Sordid.**—D. F. I. 63. to scorn the *s*. world
**Sore.**—P. L. 1, 298. smote on him *s*. besides
P. L. 6, 328. so *s*. the griding sword with
P. L. 6, 449. *s*. toiled his riven arms to havoc
P. L. 6, 687. *s*. hath been their fight as likeliest
P. L. 9, 1124. and shook *s*. their inward state
P. L. 10, 124. to whom thus Adam *s*. beset
P. R. 1, 89. his first-begot we know and *s*. have
P. R. 4, 196. be not so *s*. offended Son of God
P. R. 4, 402. his aery jaunt though hurried *s*.
S. A. 287. in that *s*. battle when so many died
Cir. 13. *s*. doth begin his infancy to seize
M. W. 49. after this thy travail *s*.
**Sorec.**—S. A. 229. was in the vale of *S*. Dalila
**Sores.**—S. A. 184. salve to thy *s*. apt words have

S. A. 607. to the body's wounds and *s.*
**Sorrow.**—P. L. 1, 65. regions of *s.* doleful
P. L. 1, 558. *s.* and pain from mortal
P. L. 2, 578. sad Acheron of *s.* black and deep
P. L. 2, 605. their *s.* to augment and wish
P. L. 2, 797. conceived and hourly born with *s.*
P. L. 8, 333. hence into a world of woe and *s.*
P. L. 10, 193. thy *s.* I will greatly multiply by
P. L. 10, 195. children thou shalt bring in *s.*
P. L. 10, 201. thou in *s.* shalt eat thereof all
P. L. 10, 717. to *s.* abandoned but worse felt
P. L. 10, 1092. in sign of *s.* unfeigned and
P. L. 10, 1104. of *s.* unfeigned and humiliation
P. L. 11, 264. with chilling gripe of *s.* stood
P. L. 11, 301. what besides of *s.* and dejection
P. L. 11, 362. temper joy with fear and pious *s.*
P. L. 11, 757. another flood, of tears and *s.*
P. L. 12, 613. since with *s.* and heart's distress
S. A. 214. who hast of *s.* thy full load besides
S. A. 457. is my chief affliction shame and *s.*
S. A. 1154. shalt see or rather to thy *s.* soon feel
S. A. 1339. in my midst of *s.* and heart grief
S. A. 1347. thou shalt have cause to *s.* indeed
S. A. 1564. lessens the *s.* and converts it nigh to
C. 668. from these gates *s.* flies far
L. 166. for Lycidas your *s.* is not dead
L'A. 45. then to come in spite of *s.*
P. 8. for now to *s.* must I tune my song
Cir. 9. seas wept from our deep *s.*
**Sorrowed.**—S. A. 1603. I *s.* at his captive state
**Sorrowing.** P. L. 11, 117. *s.* yet in peace
M. W. 53. the *s.* that thy noble house doth bring
**Sorrows.**—P. L. 11, 90. he *s.* now repents
P. R. 2, 69. while I to *s.* am no less advanced
P. R. 4, 386. *s.* and labours opposition hate
P. 33. my *s.* are too dark for day to know
P. 55. might think the infection of my *s.* loud
D. F. I. 73. and wisely learn to curb thy *s.* wild
**Sorry.**—S. A. 1346. I am *s.* what this stoutness
C. 750. coarse complexions and cheeks of *s.* grain
**Sort.**—P. L. 3, 129. the first *s.* by their own
P. L. 4, 128. than could befall spirit of happy *s.*
P. L. 4, 582. if spirit of other *s.* so minded
P. L. 6, 376. the other *s.* in might though
P. L. 8, 384. what society can *s.* what harmony
P. L. 9, 816. but to Adam in what *s.* shall I
P. L. 11, 574. a different *s.* from the high
P. R. 2, 341. piled and masters of noblest *s.*
P. R. 4, 198. if I to try whether in higher *s.*
P. R. 4, 296. a third *s.* doubted all things
S. A. 1323. and every *s.* of gymnic artists
S. A. 1608. lack degree of *s.* might sit in order
**Sorted.**—P. L. 10, 651. as *s.* best with
**Sorting.**—P. R. 1, 200. ill *s.* with my present
**Sorts.**—P. L. 7, 541. all *s.* are here that all the
**Sottish.**—P. L. 1, 472. Ahaz his *s.* conqueror
**Sought.**—P. L. 1, 215. while he *s.* evil to
P. L. 2, 332. of peace yet none vouchsafed or *s.*
P. L. 3, 601. in vain so long have *s.*
P. L. 4, 799. in search of whom they *s.*
P. L. 4, 894. delight which in this place I *s.*
P. L. 6, 151. hour of my revenge first *s.* for
P. L. 6, 295. I fly not but have *s.* thee far
P. L. 8, 457. sunk down and *s.* repair of sleep
P. L. 9, 75. then *s.* where to lie hid
P. L. 9, 380. that our trial when least *s.* may
P. L. 9, 417. in bower and field he *s.* where
P. L. 9, 421. he *s.* them both but wished his
P. L. 9, 511. as one who *s.* access but feared to
P. L. 9, 860. mean I to try what rash untried I *s.*
P. L. 9, 878. for thee chiefly I *s.*
P. L. 10, 336. saw their shame that *s.* vain
P. L. 10, 719. thus to disburden *s.* with sad
P. L. 10, 752. which I was to hold the good I *s.*
P. L. 10, 762. didst thou beget me I *s.* it not
P. L. 10, 1016. therefore *s.* refutes that
P. L. 11, 148. since I *s.* by prayer the offended
P. L. 12, 278. favour unmerited by me who *s.*
P. R. 2, 19. then with care *s.* lost Elijah
P. R. 2, 77. who *s.* his life and missing filled
P. R. 2, 485. thy reason why they should be *s.*

P. R. 3, 16. or wert thou *s.* to deeds that might
P. R. 3, 342. his daughter *s.* by many prowest
S. A. 193. not to be found though *s.*
S. A. 220. I *s.* to wed the daughter of an infidel
S. A. 401. she *s.* to make me traitor to myself
S. A. 658. argument and much persuasion *s.*
S. A. 795. *s.* by all means therefore how
S. A. 889. thy country *s.* of thee it *s.* unjustly
**Sought'st.**—P. L. 8, 316. and whom thou *s.*
**Soul.**—P. L. 2, 556. for eloquence the *s.* song
P. L. 3, 168. O Son in whom my *s.* hath chief
P. L. 4, 487. nor suffer my unspotted *s.* for ever
P. L. 4, 487. part of my *s.* I seek thee
P. L. 5, 100. but know that in the *s.* are many
P. L. 5, 171. of this great world both eye and *s.*
P. L. 5, 486. whence the *s.* reason receives
P. L. 5, 610. united as one individual *s.*
P. L. 5, 816. every *s.* in heaven shall bend
P. L. 7, 388. with spawn abundant living *s.*
P. L. 7, 392. and each *s.* living each that crept
P. L. 7, 451. let the earth bring forth *s.* living
P. L. 7, 528. and thou becamest a living *s.*
P. L. 8, 154. by living *s.* desert and desolate
P. L. 8, 499. shall be one flesh, one heart, one *s.*
P. L. 8, 585. worthy to subdue the *s.* of man
P. L. 8, 604. union of mind or in us both one *s.*
P. L. 8, 629. flesh to mix with flesh or *s.* with *s.*
P. L. 9, 967. one heart, one *s.* in both whereof
P. L. 11, 447. deadly pale, groaned out his *s.*
P. L. 12, 584. called charity the *s.* of all the rest
P. R. 1, 224. least to try and teach the erring *s.*
P. R. 2, 90. that through my very *s.* a sword
P. R. 2, 476. attracts the *s.* governs the inner
P. R. 3, 125. his good communicable to every *s.*
P. R. 4, 313. much of the *s.* they talk but all
S. A. 92. that light is in the *s.*
S. A. 156. thy *s.* which men enjoying sight oft
S. A. 458. the anguish of my *s.* that suffers not
C. 256. would take the prisoned *s.* and lap it in
C. 383. but he that hides a dark *s.* and foul
C. 454. that when a *s.* is found sincerely so
C. 462. turns it by degrees to the *s.'s* essence
C. 467. the *s.* grows clotted by contagion
C. 561. that might create a *s.* under the ribs
C. 784. thou hast, nor ear, nor *s.* to apprehend
L'A. 138. such as the meeting *s.* may pierce
L'A. 144. the hidden *s.* of harmony
Il P. 40. thy rapt *s.* sitting in thine eyes
Il P. 105. or bid the *s.* of Orpheus sing
S. 14, 2. had ripened thy just *s.* to dwell
S. 11, 12. O *s.* of Sir John Cheek
S. 19, 4. though my *s.* more bent to serve
P. 41. there doth my *s.* in holy vision sit
T. 19. once our heavenly-guided *s.* shall
D. F. I. 21. unhoused thy virgin *s.*
D. F. I. 36. resolve me then O *s.* most surely blest
M. W. 72. like fortunes may her *s.* acquaint
V. Ex. 50. while sad Ulysses' *s.* and all the rest
**Souls.**—P. L. 5, 197. all ye living *s.* ye birds
P. L. 6, 165. to heavenly *s.* had been all one
P. L. 6, 837. such as in their *s.* infixed plagues
P. L. 11, 724. conversion and repentance as to *s.*
S. 16, 12. threatening to bind our *s.* with secular
H. 98. as all their *s.* in blissful rapture took
**Sound.**—P. L. 1, 531. at the warlike *s.*
P. L. 1, 711. with the *s.* of dulcet symphonies
P. L. 1, 754. and trumpet's *s.*
P. L. 2, 286. as when hollow rocks retain the *s.*
P. L. 2, 476. was as the *s.* of thunder heard
P. L. 2, 515. with trumpets' regal *s.* the great
P. L. 2, 604. this Lethean *s.* both to and fro
P. L. 2, 880. impetuous recoil and jarring *s.*
P. L. 3, 147. with the innumerable *s.* of
P. L. 4, 453. far from thence a murmuring *s.*
P. L. 5, 5. which the only *s.* of leaves and
P. L. 5, 172. *s.* his praise
P. L. 5, 703. and jealousies to *s.* or taint
P. L. 5, 872. and as the *s.* of waters deep
P. L. 6, 64. to the *s.* of instrumental harmony
P. L. 6, 97. and rushing *s.* of onset ended soon
P. L. 6, 202. Michael bid *s.* the archangel

P. L. 6, 444. our minds and understanding *s.*
P. L. 6, 749. with whirlwind *s.* the chariot of
P. L. 6, 829. as with the *s.* of torrent floods
P. L. 7, 206. harmonious *s.* on golden hinges
P. L. 7, 558. and the *s.* symphonious of ten
P. L. 8, 243. noise other than the *s.* of dance
P. L. 8, 606. grateful than harmonious *s.* to the
P. L. 9, 407. found'st either sweet repast or *s.*
P. L. 9, 451. each rural sight each rural *s.*
P. L. 9, 518. she busied heard the *s.* of rustling
P. L. 9, 557. mute to all articulate *s.*
P. L. 9, 736. in her ears the *s.* yet rung of his
P. L. 10, 508. universal hiss the *s.* of public
P. L. 10, 642. sung halleluiah as the *s.* of seas
P. L. 11, 76. once more to *s.* at general doom
P. L. 11, 558. the *s.* of instruments that made
P. L. 12, 229. and loud trumpets *s.*
P. R. 1, 19. more awful than the *s.* of trumpet
P. R. 2, 403. with *s.* of harpies' wings
P. R. 4, 17. returns as oft with humming *s.*
P. R. 4, 247. with the *s.* of bees'. industrious
S. A. 176. the *s.* of words their sense the air
S. A. 660. with the afflicted in his pangs their *s.*
C. 171. methought it was the *s.* of riot
C. 345. or *s.* of pastoral reed with oaten stops
C. 555. last a soft and solemn-breathing *s.*
C. 942. not a waste or needless *s.*
L. 35. from the glad *s.* would not be absent long
L'A. 94. and the jocund rebecks *s.*
Il P. 74. 1 hear the far-off curfew *s.*
H. 53. no war or battle's *s.*
H. 101. Nature that heard such *s.*
H. 193. a drear and dying *s.*
P. 26. o'er the rest Cremona's trump doth *s.*
V. Ex. 32. before thou clothe my fancy in fit *s.*
**Sound-board.**—P. L. 1, 709. the *s.-b.* breathes
**Sounded.**—P. L. 6, 204. vast of heaven it *s.*
**Soundest.**—P. L. 8, 253. waked from *s.* sleep
**Sounding.**—P.L.1,668.clashed on their *s.* shields
P. L. 2,517. put to their mouths the *s.* alchymy
L. 154. ay me! whilst thee the shores and *s.* seas
**Sounds.**—P. L. 1,540. metal blowing martial *s.*
P. L. 2, 952. of stunning *s.* and voices all
P. L. 4, 686. heavenly touch or instrumental *s.*
P. L. 7,399. forthwith the *s.* and seas each creek
P. L. 7, 443. the crested cock whose clarion *s.*
P. L. 7, 597. all *s.* on fret by string or golden
C. 115. the *s.* and seas with all their finny drove
A. 78. or voice could hit inimitable *s.*
S. M. 3. wed your divine *s.*
**Sour.**—C. 109. strict age and *s.* severity
**Source.**—P. L. 4, 750. *s.* of human offspring
P. L. 10, 832. me, me only as the *s.* and spring
P. L. 11, 169. am graced the *s.* of life
P. L. 12, 13. this second *s.* of men while ye
S. A. 64. and proves the *s.* of all my miseries
S. A. 664. some *s.* of consolation from above
**South.**—P. L. 1. 354. came like a deluge on the *s.*
P. L. 4, 782. these draw off and coast the *s.*
P. L. 10, 655. from the *s.* to bring solstitial
P. L. 10, 686. and *s.* far beneath Magellan
P. L. 10, 701. blast upturns them from the *s.*
P. L. 11, 401. of Congo and Angola farthest *s.*
P. L. 11, 738. meanwhile the *s.* wind rose
P. L. 12, 139. Hamath northward to the deserts.
P. R. 3, 273. to *s.* the Persian bay
P. R. 3, 320. of Adiabene, Media and the *s.*
P. R. 4, 69. some from farthest *s.* Syene
**Southern.**—P. R. 4, 28. washed by the *s.* sea
**Southmost.**—P. L. 1, 408, and the wild of *s.*
**Southward.**—P. L. 4, 223. *s.* through Eden
**South-west.**—P. R. 4, 237. nearer by *s.-w.*
**Sovran.**—P. L. 1,246. who now is *s.* can dispose
P. L. 1, 753. by command of *s.* power
P. L. 2, 244. while he lordly sits our envied *s.*
P. L. 3, 22. and feel thy *s.* vital lamp
P. L. 3, 145. was that word which closed thy *s.*
P. L. 4, 691. it was a place chosen by the *s.*
P. L. 5, 256. by work divine the *s.* architect
P. L. 5, 366. who yet by *s.* gift possess this
P. L. 5, 656. about the *s.* throne alternate all

P. L. 6, 56. so spake the *s.* voice and clouds
P. L. 7, 79. to observe immutably his *s.* will
P. L. 8, 239. for state as *s.* King
P. L. 8, 647. sent from whose *s.* goodness I adore
P. L. 9,532. wonder not *s.* mistress if perhaps
P. L. 9. 612. of right declared *s.* of creatures
P. L. 9, 795. O *s.* virtuous precious of all trees
P. L. 9, 1130. over *s.* reason claimed superior
P. L. 10, 144. to whom the *S.* Presence thus
P. L. 11, 83. Almighty thus pronounced his *s.*
P. R. 1, 84, and out of heaven the *s.* voice
C. 41. but that by quick command from *s.* Jove
C. 639. and bade me keep it as of *s.* use
H. 60. as if they surely knew their *s.* Lord was
P. 15. he *s.* Priest stooping his regal head
**Sovranty.**—P. L. 2, 446. and this imperial *s.*
P. L. 12, 35. from heaven claiming second *s.*
**Sow.**—P. L. 12, 55. and instead to *s.* a jangling
S. 18, 10. their martyred blood and ashes *s.*
**Sowed.**—P. L. 5, 2. advancing *s.* the earth
P. L. 7, 358. and *s.* with stars the heaven thick
S. 20, 8. the lily and rose that neither *s.* nor
**Sown.**—P. L. 11, 27. from thy seed *s.* with
P. R. 4, 345. thin *s.* with aught of profit or
**Space.**—P. L. 1, 40. nine times the *s.* that
P. L. 1, 650. *s.* may produce new worlds
P. L. 2, 717. stand front to front hovering a *s.*
P. L. 6, 104. host and host but narrow *s.* was
P. L. 7, 89. and this which yields or fills all *s.*
P. L. 7, 169. nor vacuous the *s.* though I
P. L. 9, 63. the *s.* of seven continued nights he
P. L. 9, 463. that *s.* the evil one abstracted
P. L. 10, 320. and now in little *s.* the confines
P. L. 11, 498. and gave him up to tears a *s.*
P. L. 12, 345. the *s.* of seventy years then
P. R. 1, 169. all heaven admiring stood a *s.*
P. R. 2, 339. in ample *s.* under the broadest
**Spaces.**—P. L. 7, 725. wide within her ample *s.*
P. L. 8, 20. that seem to roll *s.* incomprehensible
**Spacious.**—P. L. 1, 689. into the hill a *s.*
P. L. 1, 762. but chief the *s.* hall
P. L. 2, 974. lies through your *s.* empire up to
P. L. 3, 430. walked the fiend at large in *s.* field
P. L. 5, 367. by sovran gift possess this *s.* ground
P. L. 5, 726. throughout the *s.* north
P. L. 6, 474. this continent of *s.* heaven adorned
P. L. 6, 861. and a *s.* gap disclosed into the
P. L. 8, 102. building was a *s.* theatre
P. L. 10, 467. now possess as lords a *s.* world
P. L. 11, 556. and saw a *s.* plain whereon
P. R. 3, 254. a *s.* plain outstretched in circuit
S. A. 1605. the building was a *s.* theatre
**Spade.**—P. L. 1,676. with *s.* and pick axe armed
**Spades.**—P. R. 3, 331. with *s.* and axes armed
**Spake.**—P. L. 1, 125. so *s.* the apostate angel
P. L. 1,271. so Satan *s.* and him Beëlzebub thus
P. L. 1, 663. he *s.* and, to confirm his words
P. L. 2, 50. and these words thereafter *s.*
P. L. 2, 228. and after him thus Mammon *s.*
P. L. 2, 309. while thus he *s.*
P. L. 2, 429. of highest worth unmoved thus *s.*
P. L. 2, 704. so *s.* the grisly terror and in shape
P. L. 2, 735. she *s.* and at her words the
P. L. 3, 79. thus to his only son foreseeing *s.*
P. L. 3, 135. thus while God *s.* ambrosial
P. L. 3, 143. uttering thus He to his Father *s.*
P. L. 3, 267. his meek aspect silent yet *s.* and
P. L. 3, 681. so *s.* the false dissembler
P. L. 4, 114. thus while he *s.* each passion
P. L. 4, 393. so *s.* the fiend and with necessity
P. L. 4. 492. so *s.* our general mother
P. L. 4, 781. to his next in power thus *s.*
P. L. 4, 844. so *s.* the Cherub and his grave
P. L. 4, 877. with stern regard thus Gabriel *s.*
P. L. 4, 977. while thus he *s.* the angelic
P. L. 5, 27. Adam whom embracing thus she *s.*
P. L. 4, 246. so *s.* the eternal Father and
P. L. 5, 599. had made invisible thus *s.*
P. L. 5, 616. so *s.* the Omnipotent and
P. L. 5, 672. thus to him in secret *s.*
P. L. 5, 694. so *s.* the false arch-angel and

P. L. 5, 743. so s. the Son, but Satan with
P. L. 5, 849. so s. the fervent angel but his zeal
P. L. 5, 896. so s. the Seraph Abdiel faithful
P. L. 6, 56. so s. the sovran voice and clouds
P. L. 6, 281. so s. the prince of angels to whom
P. L. 6, 450. cloudy in aspect thus answering s.
P. L. 6, 722. the filial Godhead answering s.
P. L. 6, 800. his host on either hand thus s.
P. L. 6, 824. so s. the Son and into terror
P. L. 7, 138. and to his Son thus s.
P. L. 7, 174. so s. the Almighty and to what he s.
P. L. 7, 339. again the Almighty s. let there be
P. L. 7. 518. thus to his Son audibly s.
P. L. 8, 39. so s. our sire and by his countenance
P. L. 8, 249. so s. the godlike power and thus
P. L. 8, 271. to speak I tried and forthwith s.
P. L. 8, 349. as thus he s. each bird and beast
P. L. 8, 376. so s. the universal Lord and seemed
P. L. 8, 434. thus I emboldened s.
P. L. 9, 318. so s. domestic Adam in his care
P. L. 9, 376. so s. the patriarch of mankind
P. L. 9, 494. so s. the enemy of mankind
P. L. 9, 552. unamazed she thus in answer s.
P. L. 9, 646. thus to her guide she s.
P. L. 9, 1150. in the serpent speaking as he s.
P. L. 10, 63. so s. the Father and unfolding
P. L. 10, 182. so s. this oracle then verified
P. L. 10, 1097. so s. our father penitent
P. L. 11, 181. so s. so wished much-humbled Eve
P. L. 11, 192. not unmoved to Eve thus s.
P. L. 11, 225. great visitant approached thus s.
P. L. 11, 666. s. much of right and wrong
P. L. 12, 466. so s. the archangel Michael
P. L. 12, 624. so s. our mother Eve and Adam
P. R. 1, 129. thus to Gabriel smiling s.
P. R. 1, 168. so s. the eternal Father and all
P. R. 1, 256. found thee in the temple and s.
P. R. 1, 262. and soon found of whom they s.
P. R. 1, 294. so s. our morning star then in his
P. R. 1, 320. then with words thus uttered s.
P. R. 1, 465. so s. our Saviour but the subtle
P. R. 2, 147. so s. the old serpent doubting
P. R. 2, 337. he s. no dream for as his word
P. R. 3, 1. so s. the Son of God and Satan stood
P. R. 3, 145. so s. the Son of God and here
P. R. 3, 441. so s. Israel's true king
P. R. 4, 365. so s. the Son of God but Satan
S. 14, 12. s. the truth of thee on glorious themes
H. 58. the trumpet s. not to the armed throng
**Spakest.**—P. L. 8, 444. I ere thou s. knew it
**Span.**—S. 13, 2. our English music how to s.
**Spangled.**—P. L. 11, 130. all their shape s.
C. 1003. but far above in s. sheen
H. 21. all the s. host keep watch in squadrons
**Spangling.**—P. L. 7, 384. s. the hemisphere
**Spare.** —P. L. 3, 278. that for him I s. thee
P. L. 3, 393. dreadful thunder didst not s.
P. L. 5, 320. which instructs us not to s.
P. L. 6, 460. sense of pleasure we may well s.
P. L. 10, 23. dim sadness did not s. that time
P. L. 10, 511. drawn he felt to sharp and s.
S. A. 487. s. that proposal father s. the trouble
C. 767. and holy dictate of s. temperance
Il P. 46. fast that oft with gods doth diet
S. 8, 10. bid s. the house of Pindarus
S. 20, 13. of those delights can judge and s.
**Spared.**—P. L. 9, 596. my fill I s. not
P. L. 9, 647. we might have s. our coming
L. 113. how well could I have s. for thee young
**Sparely.**—L. 138. the swart-star s. looks
**Spares.**—P. L. 2, 139. s. to tell thee yet by
**Spark.**—P. L. 4, 814. as when a s. lights on a
**Sparkle.**—C. 80. swift as the s. of a glancing
A. 27. I see bright honour s. through your eyes
**Sparkled.**—P. L. 2, 388. and joy s. in all
**Sparkles.**—P. L. 6, 766. flame and s. dire
**Sparkling.**—P. L. 1, 194. eyes that s. blazed
P. L. 3, 507. thick with s. orient gems
S. A. 544. s. out-poured the flavour or the smell
**Spartan.**—P. L. 10, 674. and the S. twins
D. F. I. 26. Hyacinth the pride of S. land

**Spasm.**—P. L. 11, 481 maladies of ghastly s.
**Spattering**—P. L. 10, 567. taste with s. noise
**Spawn.**—P. L. 7, 388. reptile with s. abundant
C. 713. thronging the seas with s. innumerable
**Speak.**—P. L. 1, 616. he now prepared to s.
P. L. 2, 42. who can advise may s.
P. L. 5, 160. s. ye who best can tell
P. L. 7, 164. this I perform s. thou and be it
P. L. 8, 100. the heaven's wide circuit let it s.
P. L. 8, 199. and s. of things at hand
P. L. 8, 271. to s. I tried and forthwith spake
P. L. 8, 380. my maker be propitious while I s.
P. L. 8, 389. of fellowship I s. such as I seek
P. L. 9, 749. not made for speech to s. thy praise
P. L. 9, 966. gladly of our union. hear thee s.
P. L. 12, 501. to s. all tongues and do all
S. A. 731. now again she makes address to s.
S. A. 1569. suspense in news is torture s.
C. 264. I'll s. to her she shall be my queen
C. 357. or while we s. within the direful grasp
C. 490. that halloa I should know what are you s.
C. 592. what voice is that? my young lord? s.
V. Ex. 2. move my first endeavouring tongue to s.
**Speakable.**—P. L. 9, 563. how camest thou s.
**Speaking.**—P. L. 2, 705. s. and so threatening
P. L. 8, 3. thought him still s. still stood fixed
P. L. 8, 222. s. or mute all comeliness and grace
P. L. 9, 1150. fraud in the serpent s. as he spake
**Speaks.**—P. L. 9, 765. and knows and s.
S. A. 178. he s. let us draw nigh
C. 804. as when the wrath of love s. thunder
**Speak'st**—P. L. 4, 487. terrors which thou s.
**Spear.**—P. L. 1, 292. his s. to equal which the
P. L. 1, 347. the up-lifted s. of their great
P. L. 1, 436. sunk before s. of despicable
P. L. 1, 565. with ordered s. and shield
P. L. 2, 204. I laugh when those who at the s.
P. L. 4, 785. wheeling to the shield half to the s.
P. L. 4, 810. Ithuriel with his s. touched
P. L. 4, 929. seconded thy else not dreaded s.
P. L. 4, 990. what seemed both s. and shield
P. L. 6, 195. his massy s. upstayed
P. L. 10, 542. down fell both s. and shield
P. L. 11, 248. and in his hand the s.
S. A. 132. the forgery of brazen shield and s.
S. A. 284. not worse than by his shield and s.
S. A. 348. a coward armed at one s.'-s length
S. A. 1121. and thy s. a weaver's beam
S. 8, 9. lift not thy s. against the Muses' bower
H. 55. the idle s. and shield were high up hung
**Spears.**—P. L. 1, 547. a forest huge of s.
P. L. 2, 536. the aery knights and couch their s.
P. L. 4, 553. shields, helms and s.
P. L. 4, 980. to hem him round with ported s.
P. L. 6, 83. or rigid s. and helmets thronged
S. A. 1619. archers and slingers cataphracts and s.
**Special.**—P. L. 2, 1033. angels guard by s.
S. A. 273. whom God hath of his s. favour raised
S. A. 636. under his s. eye abstemious I grew up
**Specious.**—P. L. 2, 484. boast their s. deeds
P. L. 9, 361. meet some s. object by the foe
P. L. 12, 534. in outward rites and s. forms
P. R. 2, 391. and count thy s. gifts no gifts
S. A. 230. that s. monster my accomplished snare
**Specked.**—P. L. 9, 429. or s. with gold
**Speckled.**—H. 136. and s. vanity
**Spectacle.**—P. R. 1, 415. a s. of ruin
S. A. 1542. the sight of this so horrid s.
S. A. 1604. not to be absent at that s.
**Spectators.**—P. L. 4, 676. would want s.
**Spectres.**—P. R. 4, 430. and grisly s. which
**Specular.**—P. R. 4, 236. we leave this s. mount
**Speculation.**—P. L. 12, 589. this top of s.
**Speculations.**—P. L. 9, 602. to s. high
**Sped.**—P. L. 3, 740. down from the ecliptic s.
L. 122. what need they? they are s.
**Speech.**—P. L. 2, 389. his s. he thus renews
P. L. 2, 989. with faltering s. and visage
P. L. 4, 357. at length failed s. recovered sad
P. L. 4, 409. first of women Eve thus moving s.
P. L. 5, 459. his wary s. thus to the empyreal

P. L. 7, 178. cannot without process of *s*. be told
P. L. 8, 377. I with leave of *s*. implored
P. L. 9, 600. and *s*. wanted not long
P. L. 9, 749. taught the tongue not made for *s*.
P. L. 9, 1133. *s*. intermitted thus to Eve renewed
P. L. 12, 5. with transition sweet new *s*. resumes
P. R. 2, 301. and with fair *s*. these words
**Speeches.**—H. 37. only with *s*. fair
**Speechless.**—P. L. 9, 894. *s*. he stood
**Speed.**—P. L. 1, 674. thither winged with *s*.
P. L. 2, 700. and to thy *s*. add wings
P. L. 2, 1008. much the nearer danger go and *s*.
P. L. 3, 643. his habit fit for *s*. succinct
P. L. 4, 13. yet not rejoicing in his *s*. though
P. L. 4, 568. described his way bent all on *s*.
P. L. 4, 788. with winged *s*. search through
P. L. 4, 928. blasting vollied thunder made all *s*.
P. L. 5, 252. to his *s*. gave way through all
P. L. 5, 313. but go with *s*. and what thy stores
P. L. 5, 730. draw with *s*. what force is left
P. L. 5, 744. far was advanced on winged *s*.
P. L. 6, 307. from each hand with *s*. retired
P. L. 8, 37. journey brought of incorporeal *s*.
P. L. 8, 38. *s*. to describe whose swiftness
P. L. 8, 110. could add *s*. almost spiritual
P. L. 10, 40. then he should prevail and *s*.
P. L. 10, 90. the *s*. of Gods time counts not
P. L. 10, 410. they with *s*. their course
P. L. 10, 954. I to that place would *s*. before
P. L. 12, 2. baits at noon though bent on *s*.
P. R. 2, 116. with *s*. was gone up to the middle
S. A. 1304. comes on amain *s*. in his look
S. A. 1316. rise therefore with all *s*.
S. A. 1343. message was imposed on me with *s*.
S. A. 1345. so take it with what *s*. thy message
S. A. 1728. I with what *s*. the while
C. 573. already ere my best *s*. could prevent
S. 19, 12. thousands at his bidding *s*.
H. 79. the sun himself withheld his wonted *s*.
T. 3. whose *s*. is but the heavy plummet's pace
D. F. I. 60. and after short abode fly back with *s*.
**Speeded.**—P. R. 3, 267. well have we *s*.
**Speedier.**—P. L. 11, 7. heaven with *s*. flight
**Speediest.**—P. L. 3, 229. the *s*. of thy winged
P. L. 6, 534. with *s*. sail Zophiel of cherubim
S. A. 1263. my *s*. friend by death to rid me hence
**Speedily.**—P. L. 5, 692. who *s*. through all
**Speeding.**—S. A. 1539. I see one hither *s*.
**Speeds.**—P. L. 5, 267. prone in flight he *s*.
**Speedy.**—P. L. 1, 156. whereto with *s*. words
P. L. 2, 516. four *s*. cherubim put to their mouths
P. L. 9, 260. where each to other *s*. aid might
S. A. 650. *s*. death the close of all my miseries
S. A. 1681. their own destruction to come *s*. upon
**Spell.**—P. R. 4, 385. met give me to *s*.
C. 853. and thaw the numbing *s*.
C. 874. and old soothsàying Glaucus' *s*.
C. 919. now the *s*. hath lost his hold
Il P. 170. where I may sit and rightly *s*.
H. 79. no nightly trance or breathed *s*.
V. Ex. 89. what power what force what might *s*.
**Spelled.**—S. 17, 6. hollow states hard to be *s*.
**Spelling.**—S. 11, 7. some in file stand *s*. false
**Spells.**—S. A. 1132. not *s*. and black enchantments
S. A. 1139. I know no *s*. use no forbidden arts
S. A. 1149. to frustrate and dissolve these magics.
C. 154. my dazzling *s*. into the spongy air
C. 537. yet have they many baits and guileful *s*.
C. 646. entered the very lime-twigs of his *s*.
**Spend.**—P. L. 2, 144. to *s*. all his rage
P. L. 11, 271. where I had hope to *s*. quiet
P. L. 12, 22. shall *s*. their days in joy unblamed
**Spent.**—P. L. 1, 176. perhaps hath *s*. his shafts
P. L. 2, 248. how wearisome eternity so *s*.
P. L. 3, 417. happy hours in joy and hymning *s*.
P. L. 5, 618. day as other solemn days they *s*.
P. L. 8, 206. and day is not yet *s*. till then thou
P. L. 8, 457. dazzled and *s*., sunk down
P. L. 9, 145. virtue *s*. of old now failed more
P. L. 9, 1187. thus they in mutual accusation *s*.
P. R. 3, 232. hath yet been private most part *s*.

P. R. 4, 366. at a loss (for all his darts were *s*.)
P. R. 4, 443. no new device (they all were *s*.)
S. A. 1758. and calm of mind all passion *s*.
S. 19, 1. when I consider how my light is *s*.
U. C. II. 29. obedient to the moon he *s*. his date
**Spets.**—C. 132. darkness *s*. her thickest gloom
**Sphere.**—P. L. 3, 416. above the starry *s*.
P. L. 3, 482. and that crystalline *s*. whose
P. L. 4, 39. how glorious once above thy *s*.
P. L. 4, 564. at height of noon came to my *s*.
P. L. 5, 169. praise him in thy *s*. while day
P. L. 5, 620. dance which yonder starry *s*.
P. L. 7, 22. within the visible diurnal *s*.
P. L. 7, 355. a mighty *s*. he framed unlightsome
P. L. 8, 82. how gird the *s*. with centric and
P. L. 10, 808. to the extent of their own *s*.
S. A. 172. or the *s*. of fortune raises
C. 241. sweet queen of parley, daughter of the *s*.
H. 48. down through the turning *s*.
D. F. I. 39. above that high first-moving *s*.
**Sphere-born.**—S. M. 2. *s.-b*. harmonious sisters
**Sphered.**—P. L. 7, 247. *s*. in a radiant cloud
**Sphere-metal.**—U. C. II. 5. made of *s.-m*. never to
**Spheres.**—P. L. 5, 477. their several active *s*.
P. L. 6, 315. and their jarring *s*. confound
P. L. 8, 131. which else to several *s*. thou must
C. 113. who in their nightly watchful *s*.
A. 64. that sit upon the nine enfolded *s*.
V. Ex. 40. then passing through the *s*.
**Sphery.**—C. 1021. higher than the *s*. chime
**Spicy.**—P. L. 2, 640. bring their *s*. drugs
P. L. 4, 162. Sabæan odours from the *s*. shore
P. L. 5, 298. him through the *s*. forest onward
P. L. 8, 517. flung odours from the *s*. shrub
L'A. 100. then to the *s*. nut-brown ale
**Spied.**—P. L. 4, 403. who by chance hath *s*.
P. L. 9, 426. where she stood half *s*. so thick
D. F. I. 17. he wandered long till thee he *s*. from far
**Spies.**—P. L. 9, 424. Eve separate he *s*.
P. L. 9, 815. safe with all his *s*. about him
S. A. 386. to them who had corrupted her my *s*.
S. A. 1197. appointed to await me thirty *s*.
**Spilt.**—P. L. 11, 791. having *s*. much blood
**Spindle.**—A. 66. turn the adamantine *s*. round
**Spinning.**—P. L. 8, 164. that *s*. sleeps
C. 715. and set to work millions of *s*. worms
**Spires.**—P. L. 1, 223. slope their pointing *s*.
P. L. 3, 550. with glistering *s*. and pinnacles
P. L. 9, 502. amidst his circling *s*. that on the
P. R. 4, 54. and terraces, and glittering *s*.
P. R. 4, 548. topt with golden *s*.
**Spirit.**—P. L. 1, 17. thou O *S*. that dost prefer
P. L. 1, 139. for the mind and *s*. remains
P. L. 1, 146. have left us this our *s*. and
P. L. 1, 490. than whom a *s*. more lewd fell not
P. L. 1, 679. the least erected *s*. that fell
P. L. 2, 44. the strongest and the fiercest *s*.
P. L. 2, 956. whatever power or *s*. of the
P. L. 3, 389. transfused on thee his ample *S*.
P. L. 3, 553. the *s*. malign but much more
P. L. 3, 630. glad was the *s*. impure
P. L. 3, 691. the sharpest-sighted *s*. of all in
P. L. 4, 128. could befall *s*. of happy sort
P. L. 4, 531. I may meet some wandering *s*. of
P. L. 4, 565. a *s*. zealous, as he seemed, to
P. L. 4, 582. *s*. of other sort so minded have
P. L. 4, 793. tells of some infernal *s*. seen
P. L. 4, 835. think not, revolted *s*., thy shape
P. L. 5, 221. Raphael the sociable *s*. that
P. L. 5, 478. till body up to *s*. work
P. L. 5, 497. bodies may at last turn all to *s*.
P. L. 5, 507. O favourable *s*., propitious guest
P. L. 5, 877. O alienate from God O *s*. accursed
P. L. 6, 752. itself instinct with *s*.
P. L. 6, 848. one *s*. in them ruled and every
P. L. 7, 165. my over-shadowing *S*. and might
P. L. 7, 204. for within them *s*. lived
P. L. 7, 209. in his powerful word and *S*.
P. L. 7, 235. his brooding wings the *S*. of God
P. L. 8, 440. expressing well the *s*. within thee

P. L. 8, 477. the *s.* of love and amorous delight
P. L. 9, 638. which oft they say some evil *s.*
P. L. 10, 754. lest that pure breath of life the *s.*
P. L. 11, 6. which the *S.* of prayer inspired
P. L. 11, 406. in *s.* perhaps he also saw rich
P. L. 11, 611. of their Maker, though his *S.*
P. L. 12, 53. upon their tongues a various *s.*
P. L. 12, 303. types to truth from flesh to *s.*
P. L. 12, 488. shall dwell, his *S.* within them
P. L. 12, 497. the *S.* poured first on his Apostles
P. L. 12, 514. not but by the *S.* understood
P. L. 12, 519. appropriating the *S.* of God
P. L. 12, 523. or what the *S.* within shall on
P. L. 12, 525. but force the *S.* of grace itself
P. L. 12, 533. in the worship persevere of *S.*
P. R. 1, 8. thou *S.* who led'st this glorious
P. R. 1, 31. and in likeness of a dove the *S.*
P. R. 1, 189. one day forth walked alone the *S.*
P. R. 1, 215. yet this not all to which my *S.*
P. R. 1, 282. the *S.* descended on me like a
P. R. 1, 358. 'tis true I am that *s.* unfortunate
P. R. 1, 462. and sends his *S.* of truth henceforth
P. R. 2, 150. the dissolutest *s.* that fell the
P. R. 4, 324. brings not a *s.* and judgment
P. R. 4, 495. ambitious *s.* and wouldst be
S. A. 1238. bulk without *s.* vast
S. A. 1435. that *s.* that first rushed on thee
S. A. 1675. among them he a *s.* of frenzy sent
L. 70. fame is the spur that the clear *s.* doth raise
Il P. 89. or unsphere the *s.* of Plato
Il P. 153. sent by some *s.* to mortals good
P. 38. my *s.* some transporting cherub feels
D. F. I. 38. tell me bright *s.*
**Spirited.**—P. L. 3, 717. *s.* with various forms
P. L. 9, 613. so talked the *s.* sly snake and Eve
**Spiritless.**—P. L. 6, 852. exhausted *s.*
**Spiritous.**—P. L. 5, 475. more refined more *s.*
P. L. 6, 479. of *s.* and fiery
**Spirits.**—P. L. 1, 101. force of *s.* armed
P. L. 1, 318. can seize eternal *s.*
P. L. 1, 423. for *s.* when they please
P. L. 1, 609. millions of *s.* for his fault amerced
P. L. 1, 622. O myriads of immortal *s.*
P. L. 1, 658. never hold celestial *s.* in bondage
P. L. 1, 697. are easily outdone by *s.* reprobate
P. L. 1, 789. thus incorporeal *s.* to smallest
P. L. 2, 482. for neither do the *s.* damned lose
P. L. 2, 553. what could it less when *s.*
P. L. 2, 687. not to contend with *s.* of heaven
P. L. 2, 696. thou thyself with *s.* of heaven
P. L. 2, 825. and all the heavenly host of *s.*
P. L. 2, 969. ye powers and *s.* of this
P. L. 2, 1030. by which the *s.* perverse with
P. L. 3, 101. all the ethereal powers and *s.*
P. L. 3, 136. and in the blessed *s.* elect sense
P. L. 3, 360. the *s.* elect bind their resplendent
P. L. 3, 461. or middle *s.* hold betwixt
P. L. 3, 654. thou of those seven *s.* that stand
P. L. 3, 737. as to superior *s.* is wont
P. L. 4, 83. and my dread of shame among the *s.*
P. L. 4, 361. not *s.* yet to heavenly *s.* bright
P. L. 4, 786. from these two strong and subtle *s.*
P. L. 4, 805. the animal *s.* that from pure blood
P. L. 4, 823. which of those rebel *s.* adjudged
P. L. 5, 374. as may not oft invite though *s.*
P. L. 5, 406. may of purest *s.* be found
P. L. 5, 439. what redounds transpires through *s.*
P. L. 5, 482. the bright consummate flower *s.*
P. L. 5, 484. to vital *s.* aspire
P. L. 5, 566. the invisible exploits of warring *s.*
P. L. 5, 837. and all the *s.* of heaven by him
P. L. 6, 167. ministering *s.* trained up in feast
P. L. 6, 333. such as celestial *s.* may bleed
P. L. 6, 344. for *s.* that live throughout vital in
P. L. 6, 596. have easily as *s.* evaded swift
P. L. 6, 660. though *s.* of purest light purest
P. L. 6, 788. heavenly *s.* could such perverseness
P. L. 7, 189. instead of *s.* malign a better race
P. L. 7, 199. winged *s.* and chariots winged
P. L. 7, 610. easily the proud attempt of *s.*
P. L. 8, 466. from thence a rib with cordial *s.*

P. L. 8, 615. love not the heavenly *s.* and how
P. L. 8, 626. if *s.* embrace total they mix
P. L. 9, 876. opener mine eyes dim erst dilated *s.*
P. L. 9, 1048. about their *s.* had played
P. L. 10, 890. peopled highest heaven with *s.*
P. L. 11, 124. a receptacle prove to *s.* foul
P. L. 11, 294. and his scattered *s.* returned
P. L. 11, 420. sunk down and all his *s.* became
P. L. 11, 545. of cold and dry to weigh thy *s.*
P. L. 11, 596. and all her *s.* composed to meek
P. R. 2, 122. demonian *s.* now
P. R. 2, 237. chosen band of *s.* likest to himself
P. R. 2, 374. all these are *s.* of air and woods
P. R. 3, 27. the flame of most erected *s.*
S. A. 594. so much I feel my genial *s.* droop
S. A. 613. and on her purest *s.* prey
S. A. 666. and fainting *s.* uphold
S. A. 1269. to the *s.* of just men long oppressed
C. 3. of bright aerial *s.* live insphered
C. 228. for my new-enlivened *s.* prompt me
C. 674. with *s.* of balm and fragrant syrups mixed
C. 794. would kindle my rapt *s.* to such a flame
C. 812. will bathe the drooping *s.* in delight
S. 7, 8. that some more timely-happy *s.* endueth
S. M. 14. those just *s.* that wear victorious palms
V. Ex. 22. deepest *s.* and choicest wits desire
**Spiritual.**—P. L. 4, 585. exclude *s.* substance
P. L. 4, 677. millions of *s.* creatures walk
P. L. 5, 402. unsavoury food perhaps to *s.*
P. L. 5, 406. to man in part *s.*
P. L. 5, 573. by likening *s.* to corporal forms
P. L. 8, 110. could add speed almost *s.*
P. L. 12, 491. and also arm with *s.* armour
P. L. 12, 518. though feigning still to act by *s.*
P. L. 12, 521. *s.* laws by carnal power
P. R. 1, 10. against the *s.* foe and brought'st
S. 17, 10. both *s.* power and civil what each means
**Spit.**—P. R. 2, 343. in pastry built or from the *s.*
**Spite.**—P. L. 1, 619. thrice in *s.* of scorn
P. L. 2, 384. done all to *s.* the great Creator
P. L. 2, 385. but their *s.* still serves his glory
P. L. 2, 293. lift us up in *s.* of fate nearer our
P. L. 9, 147. or to *s.* us more
P. L. 9, 177. whom the more to *s.*
P. L. 9, 178. *s.* then with *s.* is best repaid
P. R. 4, 12. to salve his credit and for very *s.*
P. R. 4, 574. for grief and *s.* cast herself headlong
S. A. 1462. proud set on revenge and *s.*
L'A. 45. then to come in *s.* of sorrow
**Spleen.**—S. 9, 7. thy growing virtues fret their *s.*
**Splendid.**—P. L. 2, 252. state of *s.* vassalage
**Splendour.**—P. L. 2, 447. adorned with *s.*
P. L. 3, 572. the golden sun in *s.* likest heaven
P. L. 4, 870. of regal port but faded *s.* wan
P. L. 5, 796. if in power and *s.* less in freedom
P. R. 1, 413. among the prime in *s.*
P. R. 2, 366. such was the *s.*
A. 92. clad in *s.* as befits her deity
**Splendours.**—P. L. 1, 610. from eternal *s.*
**Spoil.**—P. L. 2, 1009. havoc and *s.* and ruin
P. L. 3, 251. vanquisher spoiled of his vaunted *s.*
P. L. 12, 172. they return with glory and *s.*
P. R. 2, 401. pains have earned the far-fet *s.*
P. R. 3, 75. but rob and *s.* burn, slaughter
S. A. 1191. to others did no violence nor *s.*
S. A. 1203. I used hostility and took their *s.*
**Spoiled.**—P. L. 3, 251. subdue my vanquisher *s.*
P. L. 10, 186. from his grave *s.* principalities
P. L. 11, 832. with all his verdure *s.* and trees
M. W. 30. *s.* at once both fruit and tree
**Spoils.**—P. L. 4, 159. they stole those balmy *s.*
P. L. 9, 151. with heavenly *s.* our *s.*
P. L. 11, 692. and bring home *s.* with infinite
P. R. 4, 46. with the *s.* enriched of nations
**Spoke.**—P. L. 10, 517. he would have *s.* but
S. A. 248. the deeds themselves though mute *s.*
S. A. 727. about to have *s.* but now with head
**Spoken.**—P. L. 3, 171. all hast thou *s.* as my
P. R. 2, 90. and to a sign *s.* against
**Sponge.**—P. R. 4, 329. matters worth a *s.*
**Spongy.**—C. 154. my dazzling spells into the *s*

**Spontaneous.**—P. L. 7, 204. now came forth s.
**Sport.**—P. L. 2, 181. the s. and prey of racking
　P. L. 3, 493. the s. of winds
　S. A. 396. and turned to s. her importunity
　S. A. 1328. to make them s. with blind activity
　S. A. 1679. they only set on s. and play
　C. 128. hail goddess of nocturnal s..
　C. 953. we shall catch them at their s.
　L. 68. to s. with Amaryllis in the shade
　L'A. 31. s. that wrinkled care derides
**Sportful.**—P. L. 4, 396. among the s. herd
**Sporting.**—P. L. 4, 343. s. the lion ramped
　P. L. 7, 405. or s. with quick glance show to
**Sports.**—P. R. 4, 139. their s. to blood inured
　S. A. 1614. when to their s. they turned
**Spot.**—P. L. 3, 588. s. like which perhaps
　P. L. 3, 733. that s to which I point is paradise
　P. L. 5, 119. and leave no s. or blame behind
　P. L. 5, 266. kens a cloudy s.
　P. L. 8, 17. this earth a s. a grain an atom
　P. L. 8, 23. earth this punctual s.
　P. L. 9, 439. s. more delicious than those
　C. 5. above the smoke and stir of this dim s.
　S. 22, 2. to outward view of blemish or of s.
　S. 23, 5. mine as whom washed from s. of
**Spotless.**—P. L. 4, 318. and s. innocence
**Spots.**—P. L. 5, 419. her visage round those s.
　P. L. 7, 479. with s. of gold and purple
　P. L. 8, 145. her s. thou seest as clouds
**Spotted.**—C. 444. and s. mountain-pard
**Spotty.**—P. L. 1, 291. mountains in her s. globe
**Spousal.**—P. L. 8, 519. bird of night sung s.
　S. A. 389. also in her prime of love s. embraces
**Spouse.**—P. L. 4, 169. enamoured from the s.
　P. L. 4, 742. I ween Adam from his fair s.
　P. L. 5, 129. so cheered he his fair s. and she
　P. L. 9, 443. dalliance with his fair Egyptian s.
**Spoused.**—P. L. 5, 216. she s. about him
**Spout.**—P. L. 2, 176. hell should s. her cataracts
**Spouts.**—P. L. 7, 416. at his trunk s. out a sea
**Spray.**—P. R. 4, 437. notes in bush and s.
　S. 1, 1. O nightingale that on yon bloomy s.
**Spread.**—P. L. 1, 354. and s. beneath Gibraltar
　P. L. 2, 407. or s. his aery flight upborne with
　P. L. 2, 886. under s. ensigns marching
　P. L. 2, 960. and his dark pavilion s.
　P. L. 2, 1046. weighs his s. wings at leisure
　P. L. 4, 255. lap of some irriguous valley s.
　P. L. 4, 454. and s. into a liquid plain
　P. L. 5, 715. how s. among the sons of morn
　P. L. 5, 880. contagion s. both of thy crime
　P. L. 6, 241. wide was s. that war and various
　P. L. 6, 533. under s. ensigns moving nigh
　P. L. 6, 827. at once the four s. out their starry
　P. L. 7, 324. and s. their branches hung with
　P. L. 7, 434. and s. their painted wings
　P. L. 9, 1087. s. their umbrage broad
　P. L. 10, 446. under state of richest texture s.
　P. L. 11, 343. whence had s. all generations
　P. L. 11, 638. and saw wide territory s. before
　P. R. 2, 340. a table richly s. in regal mode
　P. R. 4, 587. set before him s. a table of celestial
　S. A. 1147. s. before him how highly it concerns
　S. A. 1429. s. his name great among the heathen
　L. 127. rot inwardly and foul contagion s.
　S. 8, 7. he can s. thy name o'er lands and seas
　H. 164. in middle air shall s. his throne
　C. 398. you may as well s. out the unsunned
**Spreading.**—P. L. 10, 412. s. their bane
　P. R. 4, 148. it shall be like a tree s. and
　C. 184. under the s. favour of these pines
**Spreads.**—P. L. 2, 928. vans he s. for flight
　P. L. 4, 643. he s. his orient beams on herb
　P. L. 9, 1103. in Malabar or Deccan s. her arms
　C. 622. s. her verdant leaf to the morning ray
　A. 14. mark what radiant state she s.
　L. 55. nor yet where Deva s. her wizard stream
　L. 81. but lives and s. aloft by those pure eyes
　L'A. 6. where brooding darkness s. his jealous
　V. Ex. 93. some earth-born giant s. his ... arms
**Spring.**—P. L. 1, 769. as bees in s. time

　P. L. 2, 381. from the author of all ill could s.
　P. L. 3, 23. clear s. or shady grove, or sunny
　P. L. 3, 334. and from her ashes s. new heaven
　P. L. 4, 268. led on the eternal s.
　P. L. 4, 274. and the inspired Castalian s.
　P. L. 5, 21. to mark how s. our tended plants
　P. L. 5, 394. s. and autumn here danced hand
　P. L. 5, 644. whence light and shade s. both
　P. L. 9, 218. while I in yonder s. of roses
　P. L. 10, 678. else had the s. perpetual smiled
　P. L. 10, 832. me only as the source and s.
　P. L. 11, 78. amaranthine shade fountain or s.
　P. L. 11, 138. new hope to s. out of despair
　P. L. 11, 425. hath wrought in some to s. from
　P. L. 12, 113. from one faithful man to s.
　P. L. 12, 476. much more good thereof shall s.
　S. A. 582. from the dry ground to s. thy thirst to
　S. A. 584. cause light again within thy eyes to s.
　S. A. 1576. abortive as the first-born bloom of s.
　C. 282. seek in the valley some cool friendly s.
　C. 985. revels the spruce and jocund s.
　L. 16. from beneath the seat of Jove doth s.
　L'A. 18. the frolic wind that breathes the s.
　S. 2, 4. but my late s. no bud or blossom sheweth
　H. 184. from haunted s. and dale
　P. 52. the gentle neighbourhood of grove and s.
**Springing.**—P. L. 5, 250. up s. light flew
**Springs.**—P. L. 2, 1013. s. upward like a
　P. L. 3, 425. flies toward the s. of Ganges or
　P. L. 5, 480. so from the root s. lighter the
　P. L. 7, 465. then s. as broke from bonds
　P. L. 12, 353. among the priests dissension s.
　P. R. 2, 374. are spirits of air and woods and s.
**Sprinkle.**—C. 911. thus I s. on thy breast drops
**Sprinkled.**—P. L. 3, 642. s. with gold
**Sprout.**—A. 59. and visit every s. with puissant
**Sprung.**—P. L. 1, 331. up they s. upon the wing
　P. L. 2, 758. goddess armed out of thy head I s.
　P. L. 3, 713. order from disorder s.
　P. L. 5, 98. this uncouth dream of evil s. I fear
　P. L. 6, 312. the constellations war were s.
　P. L. 7, 58. as a flood on those from whom it s.
　P. L. 7, 245. s. from the deep
　P. L. 8, 46. they at her coming s. and touched
　P. L. 8, 259. quick instinctive motion up I s.
　P. L. 9, 965. from whose dear side I beat me s.
　P. L. 10, 548. a grove hard by s. up with this
　P. L. 10, 591. of Satan s. all-conquering Death
　P. L. 11, 22. s. from thy implanted grace
　C. 578. with that I s. into swift flight till I had
　C. 923. s. of old Anchises' line
　A. 28. of famous Arcady ye are and s.
**Spume.**—P. L. 6, 479. of spirituous and fiery s.
**Spun.**—P. L. 7, 241. and between s. out the air
　S. 20, 8. rose that neither sowed nor s.
　C. 83. these my sky-robes s. out of Iris' woof
**Spur.**—L. 70. fame in the s. that the clear spirit
**Spurious.**—S. A. 391. conceived her s. first-born
**Spurned.**—S. A. 138. s. them to death by troops
**Spurns.**—P. L. 2, 929. uplifted s. the ground
**Spy.**—P. L. 2, 970. I come no s. with purpose
　P. L. 4, 936. and s. this new-created world
　P. L. 4, 948. to fly pain professing next the s.
　P. L. 8, 233. that none thence issued forth a s.
　P. L. 11, 857. once and again to s. green tree
　V. Ex. 61. the drowsy nurse ... did them s.
**Spying.**—P. L. 4, 1005. which Gabriel s. thus
**Squadron.**—P. L. 1, 356. from every s. and
　P. L. 4, 863. and closing stood in s. joined
　P. L. 4, 977. while thus he spake the angelic s.
**Squadroned.**—P. L. 12, 367. choir of s. angels
**Squadrons.**—P. L. 2, 570. another part in s.
　P. L. 6, 16. covered with thick embattled s.
　P. L. 6, 251. and felled s. at once
　P. L. 6, 554. on every side with shadowing s.
　P. L. 11, 652. with cruel tournament the s.
　H. 21. all the spangled host keep watch in s.
**Square.**—P. L. 2, 1048. undetermined s. or
　P. L. 5, 393. on her ample s. from side to side
　P. L. 10, 659. in sextile s. and trine and opposite
　C. 329. s. my trial to my proportioned strength

P. L. 10, 659 in sextile s. and trine and opposite
C. 329. s. my trial to my proportioned strength
**Squared.**—P. L. 1, 758. and s. regiment
P. L. 8, 232. s. in full legion
**Squat.**—P. L. 4, 800. s. at the ear of Eve
**Squint.**—C. 413. and gladly banish s. suspicion
**Stable.**—P. R. 2, 74. a s. was our warmth
H. 243. and all about the courtly s.
**Stabled.**—P. L. 11, 752. whelped and s.
C. 534. like s. wolves or tigers at their prey
**Stablished.**—P. L. 12, 347. s. as the days
**Stack.**—L'A. 51. and to the s. or the barn-door
**Staff.**—P. L. 1, 535. from the glittering s.
S. A. 1123. I only with an oaken s.will meet thee
S. A. 1303. a sceptre or quaint s. he bears
**Stag.**—P. L. 7, 469. the swift s. from under
**Stage.**—L'A. 131. then to the well-trod s. anon
Il P. 102. ennobled hath the buskined s.
P. 2. wherewith the s. of air and earth did ring
**Staid.**—Il P. 16. with black, s. Wisdom's hue
**Stain.**—P. L. 2, 140. mould incapable of s.
P. L. 10, 689. to sanctity that shall receive no s.
S.A. 325. unchaste was subsequent her s. not his
S.A. 1166. so to s. his honour, but by the barber
S. A. 1386. or s. my vow of Nazarite
Il P. 26. such mixture was not held a s.
**Stained.**—P. L. 6, 334. and all his armour s.
P. L. 9, 1076. ornaments now soiled and s.
**Stair.**—P. L. 3, 516. each s. mysteriously was
P. L. 3, 540. now on the lower s. that scaled
**Stairs.**—P. L. 3, 510. the s. were such as
P. L. 3, 523. the s. were then let down
**Stakes.**—C. 491. not too near you fall on iron s.
**Stalk.**—P. L. 5, 323. for use hangs on the s.
P. L. 5, 337. and from each tender s.
P. L. 5, 480. root springs lighter the green s.
P. L. 9, 428. to support each flower of tender s.
C. 744. it withers on the s.
**Stalking.**—S. A. 1245. s. with unconscionable
**Stalks.**—P. L. 4, 402. a lion now he s.
**Stall-reader.**—S. 11, 5. cries the s.-r. Bless us
**Stand.**—P. L. 1, 563. advanced in view they s.
P.L.2,28. foremost to s. against the thunderer's
P. L. 2, 55. millions that s. in arms and longing
P. L. 2, 240. with what eyes could we s. in his
P. L. 2, 471. and so refused might in opinion s.
P. L. 2, 716. then s. front to front hovering
P. L. 2, 897. of endless wars and by confusion s.
P. L. 3, 178. yet once more he shall s. on even
P. L. 3, 622. within ken a glorious angel s.
P. L. 3, 650. s. ready at command
P. L. 3, 654. s. in sight of God's high throne
P. L. 4, 64. but s. unshaken from within
P. L. 4, 66. the same free will and power to s.
P. L. 4, 395. then from his lofty s. on that high
P. L. 4, 518. and do they only s. by ignorance
P. L. 4, 873. s. firm for in his look defiance
P. L. 5, 522. that is to thy obedience therein s.
P. L. 5, 535. and all the angelic host that s.
P. L. 5, 540. in this we s. or fall
P.L.5, 602. my decree which unrevoked shall s.
P. L. 6, 36. this was all thy care to s. approved
P. L. 6, 234. expert when to advance or s.
P. L. 6, 473. ethereous mould whereon we s.
P. L. 6, 561. with open breast s. ready to receive
P. L. 6, 565. ye who appointed s. do as you
P. L. 6, 592. none on their feet might s.
P.L.6,801. s. still in bright array ye saints here s.
P.L.6,810. s. only and behold God's indignation
P. L. 7, 200. where s. of old myriads
P. L. 8, 640 s. fast! to s. or fall, free in thine
P. L. 10, 125. in evil strait this day I s.
P. L. 10, 827. how can they then acquitted s.
P. L. 10, 1003. why s. we longer shivering
P. L. 11, 221. in their bright s. there left his
P. L. 12, 198. awed by the rod of Moses so to s.
P. L. 12, 263. shall in mid heaven s. still a day
P. L. 12, 265. sun in Gibeon s. and thou moon
P. L. 12, 473. full of doubt I s. whether I
P. L. 12, 527. built by faith to s.
P. L. 12, 555. till time s. fixed

P. R. 1, 473. if it may s. him more in stead to lie
P. R. 3, 219. would s. between me and thy
P. R. 4, 551. there s. if thou wilt s. to s. upright
P. R. 4, 554. if not to s. cast thyself down safely
S. A. 977. to all posterity may s. defamed
S.A.1431. send thee the angel of thy birth to s.
S.A.1610. banks and scaffolds under sky might s.
C. 487. best draw and s. upon our guard
S. 11, 7. and some in file s. spelling false
S. 19, 14. they also serve who only s. and wait
H. 70. s. fixed in steadfast gaze
D.F.I.69. to s. 'twixt us and our deserved smart
V. Ex. 81. from others he shall s. in need
**Standard.**—P. L. 1, 533. upreared his mighty s.
P. L. 2, 986. erect the s. there of ancient Night
P. L. 5, 701. great hierarchal s. was to move
P. L. 7, 297. troop to their s. so the watery
**Standards.**—P. L. 5, 589. s. and gonfalons
**Standing.**—P. L. 6, 243. on firm ground a s.
P. L. 6, 593. though s. else as rocks but down
P. L. 7, 23. s. on earth not rapt above the pole
P. L. 8, 127. progressive retrograde or s. still
P. L. 9, 677. s., moving or to height upgrown
P. L. 11, 847. from s. lake to tripping ebb
P. R. 3, 328. cuirassiers all in steel for s. fight
**Stands.**—P. L. 1, 615. s. on the blasted heath
P. L. 2, 854. death ready s. to interpose his
P. L. 4, 514. one fatal tree there s. of knowledge
P. L. 4, 983. the careful ploughman doubting s.
P. L. 6, 489. o'erwhelm whatever s. adverse
P. L. 10, 818. in me all posterity s. cursed
P. R. 2, 220. beauty s. in the admiration only
P. R. 2, 463. for therein s. the office of a king
P. R. 4, 238. on the Ægean shore a city s.
P. R. 4, 519. and if I was, I am, relation s.
S. A. 166. the rarer thy example s.
S. A. 726. now s. and eyes thee fixed
S.A. 1558. Gaza yet s. but all her sons are fallen
L. 131. s. ready to smite once and smite no more
**Star.**—P. L. 1, 745. zenith like a falling s.
P. L. 2, 1052. in bigness as a s. of smallest
P. L. 3, 558. point of Libra to the fleecy s.
P. L. 3, 727. so call that opposite fair s.
P. L. 4, 556. sunbeam swift as a shooting s.
P. L. 5, 258. s. interposed, however small
P. L. 7, 104. or if the s. of evening and the
P. L. 7, 133. of angels than that s. the stars
P. L. 7, 621. every s. perhaps a world of
P. L. 8, 142. the terrestrial moon be as a s.
P. L. 8, 519. and bid haste the evening s.
P. L. 9, 48. the s. of Hesperus whose office is to
P. L. 9, 1087. woods inpenetrable to s. or
P. L. 10, 426. bright s. to Satan paragoned
P. L. 10, 1069. ere this diurnal s. leave cold
P. L. 11, 588. the evening s. love's harbinger
P. L. 12, 360. yet at his birth a s. unseen
P. R. 1, 249. a s. not seen before in heaven
P. R. 1, 253. affirming it thy s. new-graven in
P. R. 1, 294. so spake our Morning S. then in
P. R. 4, 619. like an autumnal s. or lightning
C. 80. swift as the sparkle of a glancing s.
C. 93. the s. that bids the shepherd fold
C. 341. and thou shalt be our s. of Arcady
L. 30. oft till the s. that rose at evening bright
Il P. 171. of every s. that heaven doth shew
S. 22, 5. of sun or moon or s. throughout
H. 240. heaven's youngest-teemed s.
D. F. I. 43. some s. which from the ruined
**Star-bright.**—P. L. 10, 450. s.-b. appeared
**Stare.**—S.A. 112. who come to s. at my affliction
S. 11, 11. would have made Quintilian s. and
**Star-led.**—H. 23. the s.-l. wizards haste with
**Starless.**—P. L. 3, 425. s. exposed and
**Starlight.**—P. L. 4, 656. or glittering s.
C. 308. in such a scant allowance of s.
**Star-paved.**—P. L. 4, 976. of heaven s.-p.
**Star-proof.**—A. 89. of branching elm s.-p.
**Starred.**—Il P. 19. or that s. Ethiop queen
**Starry.**—P. L. 1, 728. many a row of s. lamps
P. L. 3, 416. in heaven above the s. sphere
P. L. 3, 580. as they move their s. dance

x

P. ·L. 4, 606. that led the s. host rode brightest
P. L. 4, 649. the gems of heaven her s. train
P. L. 4, 724. resplendent globe and s. pole
P. L. 4, 992. but the s. cope of heaven perhaps
P. L. 5, 281. the middle pair girt like a s. zone
P. L. 5, 620. dance which yonder s. sphere
P. L. 5, 709. morning-star that guides the s.
P. L. 6, 827. the four spread out their s. wings
P. L. 7, 446. the florid hue of rainbows and s.
P. L. 11, 245. his s. helm unbuckled showed
P. R. 4, 393. directs me in the s. rubric set
C. 1. before the s. threshold of Jove's court
C. 112. of purer fire imitate the s. choir
P. 18. his s. front low-roofed beneath the skies
**Stars.**—P. L. 3, 61. stood thick as s. and from
P. L. 3, 565. innumerable s. that shone s.
P. L. 3, 718. rolled orbicular and turned to s.
P. L. 4, 34. at whose sight all the s. hide their
P. L. 4, 355. the s. that usher evening rose
P. L. 5, 166. fairest of s. last in the train
P. L. 5, 176. with the fixed s. fixed in their orb
P. L. 5, 745. an host innumerable as the s.
P. L. 5, 746. or s. of morning, dew-drops
P. L. 6, 754. with s. their bodies all and wings
P. L. 7, 133. than that star the s. among
P. L. 7, 348. by night altern and made the s.
P. L. 7, 357. and every magnitude of s.
P. L. 7, 358. and sowed with s. the heaven
P. L. 7, 364. hither as to their fountain other s.
P. L. 7, 383. with thousand thousand s. that
P. L. 7, 578. and pavement s. as s. to thee appear
P. L. 7, 581. thou seest powdered with s.
P. L. 7, 620. amplitude almost immense with s.
P. L. 8, 19. and all her numbered s. that seem
P. L. 8, 80. model heaven and calculate the s.
P. L. 8, 123. and other s. by his attractive virtue
P. L. 8, 135. above all s. the wheel of day
P. L. 10, 412. spreading their bane the blasted s.
P. L. 12, 422. the s. of morn shall see him rise
P. L. 12, 576. hope no higher though all the s.
P. R. 4, 383. s. voluminous or single characters
C. 197. in thy dark lantern thus close up the s.
C. 331. unmuffle ye faint s. and thou fair moon
C. 734. and so bestud with s. that they below
C. 956. come let us haste the s. grow high
H. 69. the s. with deep amaze stand fixed in
T. 21. attired with s. we shall for ever sit
**Started.**—P. L. 4, 462. I s. back, it s. back
P. L. 4, 819. so s. up in his own shape the fiend
**Startle.**—C. 210. these thoughts may s. well
L'A. 42. and singing s. the dull night
**Startled.**—P. L. 5, 26. but with s. eye on
**Starts.**—P. L. 4, 813. up he s. discovered
P. R. 4, 449. out of the wood he s. in wonted
**Starve.**—P. L. 2, 600. raging fire to s. in ice
**Starved.**—P. L. 4, 769. which the s. lover
**Star-ypointing.**—W.S.4. under a s.-y. pyramid
**State.**—P. L. 1, 29. in that happy s.
P. L. 1, 141. and happy s. here swallowed up
P. L. 1, 640. and his regal s. put forth
P. L. 1, 775. expatiate and confer their s. affairs
P. L. 2, 1. high on a throne of royal s. which far
P. L. 2, 24. the happier s. in heaven
P. L. 2, 251. our s. of splendid vassalage
P. L. 2, 279. peaceful counsels and the settled s.
P. L. 2, 302. and in his rising seemed a pillar of s.
P. L. 2, 511. and God-like imitated s.
P. L. 2, 585. who drinks forth with his former s.
P. L. 3, 186. and oft be warned their sinful s.
P. L. 4, 38. tò my remembrance from what s.
P. L. 4, 94. obtain by act of grace my former s.
P. L. 4, 400. what of their s. he more might
P. L. 4, 519. is that their happy s.
P. L. 4, 775. if ye seek no happier s. and know
P. L. 5, 234. may advise him of his happy s.
P. L. 5, 241. fall of others from like s. of bliss
P. L. 5, 288. and to his s. and to his message
P. L. 5, 353. in himself was all his s.
P. L. 5, 504. what happiness this happy s. can
P. L. 5, 536. our happy s. hold as you yours
P. L. 5, 543. O fall from what high s. of bliss

P. L. 5, 830. bent rather to exalt our happy s.
P. L. 6, 89. throne to set the envier of his s.
P. L. 6, 900. he who envies now thy s. who
P. L. 7, 440. rows her s. with oary feet
P. L. 8, 176. in what s. condition or degree
P. L. 8, 239. for s. as sovran king
P. L. 8, 290. I then was passing to my former s.
P. L. 8, 331. this happy s. shalt lose expelled
P. L. 8, 403. thou then of me and this my s.
P. L. 8, 521. thus have I told thee all my s.
P. L. 9, 123. much worse would be my s.
P. L. 9, 337. let us not then suspect our happy s.
P. L. 9, 347. or aught that might his happy s.
P. L. 9, 915. and from thy s. mine never shall
P. L. 9, 948. and say fickle their s. whom God
P. L. 9, 958. our s. cannot be severed we are
P. L. 9, 1125. their inward s. of mind calm
P. L. 10, 19. for of his s. by this they knew
P. L. 10, 445. throne which under s. of richest
P. L. 10, 619. and had still kept in that s. had
P. L. 11, 71. and in their s. though firm stood
P. L. 11, 180. here let us live though in fallen s.
P. L. 11, 249. he kingly from his s. inclined
P. L. 11, 363. inured by moderation either s.
P. L. 11, 501. to what wretched s. reserved
P. L. 12, 26. with fair equality fraternal s.
P. L. 12, 80. on the quiet s. of men such trouble
P. R. 1, 200. ill sorting with my present s.
P. R. 2, 203. higher design than to enjoy his s.
P. R. 3, 189. be tried in humble s. and things
P. R. 3, 218. rather than aggravate my evil s.
P. R. 3, 246. of the earth their pomp and s.
P. R. 4, 64. or on return in robes of s.
P. R. 4, 601. whatever place, habit, or s. or
S. A. 164. O mirror of our fickle s.
S. A. 338. as signal now in low dejected s.
S. A. 424. I s. not that, this I am sure
S. A. 708. behold him in this s. calamitous
S. A. 892. of men conspiring to uphold their s.
S. A. 1465. both God and s. they easily would set
S. A. 1603. sorrowed at his captive s. but minded
S. A. 1616. in their s. livery clad
C. 35. are coming to attend their father's s.
C. 408. infer as if I thought my sister's s. secure
C. 475. to a degenerate and degraded s.
C. 948. where this night are met in s.
A. 14. mark what radiant s. she spreads .
A. 81. and so attend ye toward her glittering s.
L'A. 60. where the great sun begins his s.
Il P. 37. come but keep thy wonted s.
S. 19, 11. his s. is kingly
S. M. 24. in first obedience and their s. of good
**Stateliest.**—P. L. 4, 142. theatre of s. view
P. L. 9, 435. of s. covert cedar pine or palm
**Stately.**—P. L. 1, 614. with singed top their s.
P. L. 1, 723. stood fixed her s. height
P. L. 5, 201. and s. tread or lowly creep
P. L. 7, 324. rose as in dance the s. trees
P. R. 2, 350. and at a s. sideboard
P. R. 4, 48. above the rest lifting his s. head
S. A. 714. comes this way sailing like a s. ship
**States.**—P. L. 2, 387. highly those infernal s.
S. 17, 6. the drift of hollow s. hard to be spelled
**Station.**—P. L. 3, 587. was set his s. bright
P. L. 7, 146. part have kept I see their s.
P. L. 7, 563. the planets in their s. listening
P. L. 10, 535. heaven-fallen in s. stood
P. L. 12, 627. from the other hill to their fixed s.
P. R. 1, 360. not my happy s. but was driven
P. R. 4, 584. from his uneasy s. and upbore
**Stations.**—P. L. 2, 412. sentries and s. thick
**Statists.**—P. R. 4, 354. top of eloquence s.
**Statue.**—C. 661. and you a s. or as Daphne
**Statues.**—P. R. 4, 37. s. and trophies
**Stature.**—P. L. 1, 222. his mighty s.
P. L. 1, 570. their visages and s. as of gods
P. L. 4, 988. his s. reached the sky
P. L. 6, 302. in s. motion arms
P. L. 7, 509. might erect his s. and upright
**Stay.**—P. L. 4, 898. if he intends our s.
P. L. 8, 43. that won who saw to wish her s.

P. L. 9, 372. go for thy *s.* not free absents thee
P. L. 9, 398. delighted but desiring more her *s.*
P. L. 9, 856. thou not wondered Adam at my *s.*
P. L. 10, 253. *s.* his return perhaps over this
P. L. 10, 921. my only strength and *s.*
P. L. 12, 436. nor after resurrection shall he *s.*
P. L. 12, 594. we may no longer *s.* go waken
P. L. 12, 616. with thee too go is to *s.* here
P. R. 2, 326. nor to *s.* till bid
S. A. 43. yet *s.* let me not rashly call in doubt
S. A. 1520. what shall we do? *s.* here or run
S. A. 1536. a little *s.* will bring some notice
C. 134. *s.* thy cloudy ebon day
C. 577. longer I durst not *s.* but soon I guessed
C. 820. yet *s.* be not disturbed now I bethink me
A. 26. *s.* gentle swains for
D. F. I. 64. O why didst thou not *s.* here below
U. C. II. 6. until his revolution was at *s.*
V. Ex. 25. and weary of their place do only *s.*
**Stayed.**—P. L. 2, 938. that fury *s.* quenched in
P. L. 2, 1010. ceased and Satan *s.* not to reply
P. L. 3, 571. he *s.* not to enquire
P. L. 3, 742. nor *s.* till on Niphates' top he
P. L. 6, 325. nor *s.* but with swift wheel
P. L. 7, 218. nor *s.* but on the wings
P. L. 7, 224. then *s.* the fervid wheels and in his
P. L. 7, 589. for he also went invisible yet *s.*
P. L. 9, 1134. hearkened to my words and *s.*
P. R. 4, 421. nor yet *s.* the terror there
P. R. 4, 485. Son of God went on and *s.* not
S. 14, 6. *s.* not behind nor in the grave were trod
C. 832. that *s.* her flight with his
**Stays.**—P. L. 4, 470. no shadow *s.* thy coming
P. L. 9, 268. and seemliest by her husband *s.*
P. L. 12, 73. his encroachment proud *s.* not on
C. 892. my sliding chariot, *s.*
**Stead.**—P. R. 1, 473. may stand him more in *s.*
S. A. 355. who would be now a father in my *s.*
C. 611. but here thy sword can do thee little *s.*
**Steadfast.**—P. L. 1, 58. obdurate pride and *s.*
P. L. 2, 927. had from her axle torn the *s.* earth
P. L. 6, 833. the *s.* empyrean shook throughout
P. L. 8, 129. the planet earth so *s.* though she
Il P. 32. sober *s.* and demure all in a robe
H. 70. stand fixed in *s.* gaze
**Steadiest.**—P. L. 12, 377. my *s.* thoughts
**Steady.**—P. L. 5, 268. worlds with *s.* wing
**Stealth.**—P. L. 2, 945. Arimaspian who by *s.*
P. L. 9, 68. by *s.* found unsuspected way
C. 503. or to pursue the *s.* of pilfering wolf
**Steam.**—P. L. 11, 442. glance and grateful *s.*
C. 556. rose like a *s.* of rich distilled perfumes
**Steaming.**—P. L. 5, 186. from hill or *s.* lake
**Steed**—P. L. 4, 858. but like a proud *s.* reined
P. L. 7, 17, lest from this flying *s.* unreined
P. L. 11, 643. their arms past curb the foaming *s.*
**Steeds.**—P. L. 2, 531. part curb their fiery *s.*
P. L. 3, 522. rapt in a chariot drawn by fiery *s.*
P. L. 6, 17. and flaming arms and fiery *s.*
P. L. 6, 391. and fiery foaming *s.*
P. L. 9, 35. impresses quaint, caparisons and *s.*
P. L. 11, 706. in a balmy cloud with winged *s.*
C. 553. gave respite to the drowsy frighted *s.*
**Steel.**—P. L. 2, 569. patience as with triple *s.*
P. R. 3, 305. they issue forth *s.* bows and shafts
P. R. 3, 328 cuirassiers all in *s.* for standing
S. A. 133. Chalybean-tempered *s.* and frock
S. A. 816. thou art strong inflexible as *s.*
C. 421. she that has that is clad in complete *s.*
**Steep.**—P. L. 2, 71. seems difficult and *s.* to scale
P. L. 2, 948. o'er bog or *s.* through strait rough
P. L. 3, 741. throws his *s.* flight in many
P. L. 4, 135. champaign head of a *s.* wilderness
P. L. 4, 172. to the ascent of that *s.* savage hill
P. L. 4, 231. thence united fell down the *s.*
P. L. 4, 680. how often from the *s.* of echoing
P. L. 6, 324. with *s.* force to smite descending
P. L. 7, 99. to run much of his race though *s.*
P. L. 7, 299. if *s.* with torrent rapture
P. R. 4, 575. headlong from the Ismenian *s.*
C. 97. in the *s.* Atlantic stream

C. 139. the nice morn on the Indian *s.*
L. 52. for neither were ye playing on the *s.*
H. 178. the *s.* of Delphos leaving
**Steer.**—S. 22, 8. still bear up and *s.* right onward
**Steered.**—P. L. 2, 1020. the other whirlpool *s.*
**Steering.**—P. L. 10, 328. *s.* his zenith
S. A. 111. the tread of many feet *s.* this way
H. 146. radiant feet the tissued clouds down *s.*
**Steers.**—P. L. 1, 225. he *s.* his flight aloft
P. L. 7, 430. so *s.* the prudent crane her annual
P. L. 9, 515. as oft so *s.* and shifts her sail
**Steersman.**—P. L. 9, 513. ship by skilful *s.*
**Steers-mate.**—S. A. 1045. with such a *s.-m.*
**Stellar.**—P. L. 4, 671. shed down their *s.*
**Stem.**—P. L. 7, 337. it grew on the green *s.*
A. 82. where ye may all that are of noble *s.*
**Stemming.**—P. L. 2, 642. *s.* nightly toward
**Stench.**—P. L. 1, 237. all involved with *s.*
**Step.**—P. L. 4, 22. nor from hell one *s.* no more
P. L. 4, 50. and thought one *s.* higher would
P. L. 4, 536. so saying his proud *s.* he scornful
P. L. 8, 302. as in air smooth sliding without *s.*
P. L. 9, 452. if chance with nymph-like *s.* fair
P. L. 9, 834. so saying from the tree her *s.*
P. R. 1, 192. and *s.* by *s.* led on
S. A. 327. with careful *s.*
C. 168. but here she comes, I fairly *s.* aside
A. 85. where no print of *s.* hath been
Il P. 38. with even *s.* and musing gait
**Stepdame.**—P. L. 4, 279. his *s.* Rhea's son
C. 830. of her enraged *s.* Guendolen
**Stepped.**— P. L. 4, 820. back *s.* those two fair
C. 185. *s.* as they said to the next thicket side
**Stepping.**—P. L. 6, 128. *s.* opposite half way
**Steps.**—P. L. 1, 295. to support uneasy *s.*
P. L. 1, 296. not like those *s.* on heaven's azure
P. L. 1, 562. that charmed their painful *s.*
P. L. 2, 828. with lonely *s.* to tread the
P. L. 3, 501. thitherward in haste his travelled *s.*
P. L. 3, 541. that scaled by *s.* of gold to
P. L. 3, 644. before his decent *s.* a silver wand
P. L. 5, 1. now morn her rosy *s.* in the eastern
P. L. 5, 512. by *s.* we may ascend to God
P. L. 8, 488. grace was in all her *s.* heaven in
P. L. 11, 333. and far off his *s.* adore
P. L. 11, 354. and of his *s.* the track divine
P. L. 12, 648. hand in hand with wandering *s.*
P. R. 1, 120. he directs his easy *s.* girded with
P. R. 1, 298. by human *s.* untrod
P. R. 2, 285. up to a hill anon his *s.* he reared
P. R. 4, 427. came forth with pilgrim *s.*
S. A. 2. lend thy guiding hand to these dark *s.*
S. A. 1442. Manoah in such haste with youthful *s.*
C. 12. yet some there be that by due *s.* aspire
C. 92. but I hear the tread of hateful *s.*
C. 193. they had engaged their wandering *s.* too
**Stern.**—P. L. 4, 877. to whom with *s.* regard
P. L. 4, 924. fiend thus answered frowning *s.*
P. L. 6, 171 whom in brief thus Abdiel *s.*
P. L. 9, 15. than the wrath of *s.* Achilles
P. L. 10, 866. but her with *s.* regard he thus
P. R. 4, 367. thus to our Saviour with *s.* brow
C. 446. gods and men feared her *s.* frown
L. 112. he shook his mitred locks and *s.* bespake
**Sternly.**—P. L. 8, 333. woe and sorrow *s.*
P. R. 1, 406. to whom our Saviour *s.* thus replied
**Sticks.**—P. L. 9, 330. his foul esteem *s.* no
P. R. 1, 316. or withered *s.* to gather
**Stiff.**—P. L. 7, 441. and rising on *s.* pennons
P. R. 4, 418 sturdiest oaks bowed their *s.* necks
F. of C. 2. with *s.* vows renounced his liturgy
**Stifling.**—P. L. 11, 313. blown *s.* back on
**Still.**—P. L. 1, 68. torture without end *s.* urges
P. L. 1, 165. and out of good *s.* to find means of
P. L. 1, 256. what matter where if I be *s.* the
P. L. 1, 641. but *s.* his strength concealed
P. L. 1, 791. *s.* amidst the hall of that infernal
P. L. 2, 74. that forgetful lake benumb not *s.*
P. L. 2, 295. sword of Michael wrought *s.*
P. L. 2, 308. audience and attention *s.* as night
P. L. 2, 324. *s.* first and last will reign sole king

P. L. 2, 385. but their spite *s.* serves his glory
P. L. 2, 658. yet there *s.* barked and howled
P. L. 2, 1001. encroached on *s.* through your
P. L. 3, 301. and *s.* destroys in those who when
P. L. 3, 467. and *s.* with vain design new Babels
P. L. 3, 618. as they now shot upward *s.* direct
P. L. 3, 729. and her monthly round *s.* ending
P. L. 4, 53. so burdensome, *s.* paving *s.* to owe
P. L. 4, 54. forgetful what from him I *s.* received
P. L. 4, 565. by owing owes not but *s.* pays
P. L. 4, 77. *s.* threatening to devour me opens
P. L. 4, 91. the lower *s.* I fall only supreme
P. L. 4, 336. *s.* as they thirsted scoop the
P. L. 4, 356. when Satan *s.* in gaze as first he
P. L. 4, 511. *s.* unfulfilled with pain of longing
P. L. 4, 548. *s.* as it rose impossible
P. L. 4, 572. mine eye pursued him *s.*
P. L. 4, 598. now came *s.* evening on
P. L. 4, 912. so judge thou *s.* presumptuous
P. L. 4, 930. *s.* thy words at random as before
P. L. 5, 47. ravishment attracted by thy beauty *s.*
P. L. 5, 184. vary to our great Maker *s.* new
P. L. 5, 191. rising or falling *s.* advance his
P. L. 5, 205. universal Lord be bounteous *s.*
P. L. 5, 553. thoughts assured me and *s.* assure
P. L. 6, 172. *s.* thou errest nor end wilt find
P. L. 6, 801. stand *s.* in bright array ye saints
P. L. 7, 30. *s.* govern thou my song Urania
P. L. 7, 67. yet scarce allayed *s.* eyes the current
P. L. 7, 379. and *s.* that distance keeps till night
P. L. 8, 3. thought him *s.* speaking *s.* stood
P. L. 8, 61. a pomp of winning graces waited *s.*
P. L. 8, 63. desire into all eyes to wish her *s.* in
P. L. 8, 89. such journeys run earth sitting *s.*
P. L. 8, 127. progressive retrograde or standing *s.*
P. L. 8, 140. her other part *s.* luminous by his
P. L. 8, 197. unprepared and *s.* to seek
P. L. 8, 355. not what .methought I wanted *s.*
P. L. 8, 387. the one intense the other *s.* remiss
P. L. 8, 444. and be so minded *s.*
P. L. 8, 464. and saw the shape *s.* glorious before
P. L. 8, 587. attractive human rational love *s.*
P. L. 8, 610. *s.* free approve the best and follow
P. L. 8, 651. be good and friendly *s.* and oft
P. L. 9, 205. Adam well may we labour *s.*
P. L. 9, 206. *s.* to tend plant, herb and flower
P. L. 9, 266. that gave thee being *s.* shades
P. L. 9, 326. how are we happy *s.* in fear
P. L. 9, 353. bid her well beware and *s.* erect
P. L. 9, 622. fruit untouched *s.* hanging
P. L. 9, 1138. we had then remained *s.* happy
P. L. 9, 1154. as good have grown there *s.*
P. L. 10, 12. *s.* they knew and ought to have *s.*
P. L. 10, 120. and hast not feared but *s.* rejoiced
P. L. 10, 359. by a secret harmony *s.* moves
P. L. 10, 376. there let him *s.* Victor sway
P. L. 10, 528. but *s.* greatest he the midst
P. L. 10, 532. above the rest *s.* to retain
P. L. 10, 594. than *s.* at hell's dark threshold
P. L. 10, 618. and had *s.* kept in that state
P. L. 10, 684. in their sight had rounded *s.*
P. L. 10, 783. yet one doubt pursues me *s.*
P. L. 10, 806. according *s.* to the reception
P. L. 10, 830. lead me *s.* but to my own
P. L. 10, 846. lamented loud thro' the *s.* night
P. L. 11, 352. many a sign *s.* following thee *s.*
P. L. 11, 512. retaining *s.* divine similitude
P. L. 11, 632. *s.* I see the tenor of man's woe
P. L. 12, 106. *s.* tend from bad to worse
P. L. 12, 193. but *s.* as ice more hardened after
P. L. 12, 263. shall in mid heaven stand *s.*
P. L. 12, 439. men who in his life *s.* followed
P. L. 12, 517. though feigning *s.* to act by
P. L. 12, 566. with good *s.* overcoming evil
P. R. 1, 33. who roving *s.* about the world
P. R. 1, 299. and *s.* on was led but with such
P. R. 2, 242. where *s.* from shade to shade
P. R. 2, 255. though hunger *s.* remain
P. R. 2, 404. only the importune tempter *s.*
P. R. 3, 92. I mention *s.* him whom thy wrongs
P. R. 3, 164. to regain thy right by sitting *s.*

P. R. 3, 279. Israel in long captivity *s.* mourns
P. R. 3, 354. prediction *s.* in all things and all
P. R. 4, 13. *s.* will be tempting him who foils
P. R. 4, 121. tell who thirst and hunger *s.*
P. R. 4, 141. by their wealth and greedier *s.*
P. R. 4, 158. nothing more than *s.* to contradict
P. R. 4, 326. uncertain and unsettled *s.*
P. R. 4, 394. for *s.* he knew his power not yet
P. R. 4, 523. and followed thee *s.* on to this
P. R. 4, 565. and oft foiled *s.* rose receiving
P. R. 4, 601. *s.* expressing the Son of God
S. A. 77. *s.* as a fool in power of others never in
S. A. 232. *s.* .... to oppress Israel's oppressors
S. A. 240. yet Israel *s.* serves with all his sons
S. A. 432. hast thou paid and *s.* art paying
S. A. 733. I came *s.* dreading thy displeasure
S. A. 807. here I should *s.* enjoy thee day
S. A. 873. but had thy love *s.* odiously pretended
S. A. 913. nor *s.* insist to afflict thyself in vain
S. A. 963. thy anger unappeasable *s.* rages
S. A. 1544. for dire imagination *s.* pursues me
S. A. 1563. that *s.* lessens the sorrow and converts
S. A. 1626. pull draw or break he *s.* performed
C. 87. well knows to *s.* the wild winds
C. 560. *s.* to be so displaced
C. 584. yes and keep it *s.*, lean on it safely
C. 842. made goddess of the river *s.* she retains
L. 187. while the *s.* morn went out with sandals
Il P. 41. there held in holy passion *s.*
Il P. 78. some *s.* removed place will fit
Il P. 127. or ushered with a shower *s.*
S. I. 2. warblest at eve when all the woods are *s.*
S. 22, 8. but *s.* bear up and steer right onward
H. 59. and kings sat *s.* with awful eye
P. 28. line or viol *s.* more apt

**Stilled.**—P. R. 4, 428. her radiant finger *s.*
**Sting.**—P. L. 2, 653. armed with mortal *s.*
P. L. 3, 253. of his mortal *s.* disarmed
P. R. 2, 257. and from the *s.* of famine fear
S. A. 997. she's gone a manifest serpent by her *s.*
S. A. 1007. and secret *s.* of amorous remorse
**Stings.**—P. L. 12, 432. in his head their *s.*
S. A. 623. my tormentors armed with deadly *s.*
**Stir.**—P. L. 2, 214. his breath *s.* not their flames
P. L. 4, 19. and from the bottom *s.* the hell
P. L. 5, 224. thou hear'st what *s.* on earth
S. A. 1251. and with malicious counsel *s.* them up
C. 5. above the smoke and *s.* of this dim spot
C. 371. could *s.* the constant mood of her calm
C. 677. is of such power to *s.* up joy as this
**Stirred.**—P. L. 8, 308. *s.* in me sudden
P. L. 1, 35. *s.* up with envy and revenge
**Stirring.**—P. L. 12, 288. by *s.* up sin against
**Stirs.**—C. 174. *s.* up among the loose unlettered
**Stoa.**—P. R. 4, 253. there and pointed S.
**Stock.**—P. L. 12, 7. man as from a second *s.*
P. L. 12, 325. that of the royal *s.* of David
S. A. 1079. of *s.* renowned as Og or Anak
**Stocked.**—C. 152. be well *s.* with as fair a herd
**Stocks.**—S. 18, 4. our fathers worshipped *s.* and
**Stoic.**—P. R. 4, 280. Epicurean and the S.
P. R. 4, 300. the S. last in philosophic pride
C. 707. to those budge doctors of the S. fur
**Stole.**—P. L. 4, 158. whisper whence they *s.*
P. L. 4, 719. who had *s.* Jove's authentic fire
P. L. 11, 847. that *s.* with soft foot towards the
C. 195. darkness ere they could return had *s.*
C. 557. and *s.* upon the air that even silence
A. 31. *s.* under seas to meet his Arethuse
Il P. 35. and sable *s.* of cypress lawn
**Stolen.**—P. L. 10, 20. the subtle fiend had *s.*
P. L. 11, 125. with whose *s.* fruit man once
S. 2, 3. *s.* on his wing my three and twentieth
**Stone.**—P. L. 3, 592. on earth metal or *s.*
P. L. 3, 596. if *s.* carbuncle most or chrysolite
P. L. 3, 598. and a *s.* besides imagined rather
P. L. 3, 600. that *s.* or like to that which here
P. L. 4, 702. than with *s.* of costliest emblem
P. L. 6, 517. of mineral and *s.* whereof to
P. L. 11, 324. and pile up every *s.* of lustre
P. L. 11, 445. smote him into the midriff...*s.*

P. L. 11, 484. intestine *s.* and ulcer colic pangs
P. L. 12, 119. their own work in wood and *s.*
P. R. 4, 115. on citron tables or Atlantic *s.*
P. R. 4, 149. or as a *s.* that shall to pieces
P. R. 4, 559. to dash thy foot against a *s.*
C. 449 she freezed her foes to congealed *s.*
**Stones.**—P. L. 11, 658. dart and javelin *s.* and
P. R. 1, 343. that out of these hard *s.* be made
S.18,4. all our fathers worshipped stocks and *s.*
W. S. 2. the labour of an age in piled *s.*
**Stony.**—P. L. 3, 189. and soften *s.* hearts to
P. L. 6, 576. brass iron *s.* mould
P. L. 11, 4. removed the *s.* from their hearts
P. R. 4, 414. the winds within their *s.* caves
C. 819. in *s.* fetters fixed and motionless
A. 102. from the *s.* Mænalus
**Stood.**—P. L. 1, 300. of that inflamed sea he *s.*
P. L. 1, 357. where *s.* their great commander
P. L. 1, 379. came singly where he *s.*
P. L. 1, 442. the promiscuous crowd *s.* yet aloof
P. L. 1, 442. where *s.* her temple
P. L. 1,492. to him no temple *s.* or altar smoked
P. L. 1, 591. *s.* like a tower
P. L. 1, 611. yet faithful how they *s.*
P. L. 1, 630. how such as *s.* like these
P. L. 1, 670. there *s.* a hill not far whose grisly
P. L. 1, 723. the ascending pile *s.* fixed her
P. L. 2, 44. Moloch sceptred king *s.* up
P. L. 2, 305. sage he *s.* with Atlantean
P. L. 2, 670. black it *s.* as night
P. L. 2, 707. with indignation Satan *s.*
P. L. 2, 720. they *s.* for never but once more
P. L. 2, 884. the gates wide open *s.*
P. L. 2, 888. so wide they *s.* and like a furnace
P. L. 2, 918. *s.* on the brink of hell and looked
P. L. 2, 963. and by them *s.* Orcus and Ades
P. L. 3, 61. *s.* thick as stars
P. L. 3, 99. sufficient to have *s.* though free to
P. L. 3, 101. both them who *s.* and them who
P. L. 3, 102. freely they *s.* who *s.* and fell who
P. L. 3, 217. but all the heavenly choir *s.* mute
P. L. 3, 516. nor *s.* there always but drawn up
P. L. 3, 555. and well might, where he *s.*
P. L. 3, 711. and wild uproar *s.* ruled, *s.* vast
P. L. 4, 59. I had *s.* then happy
P. L. 4, 218. all amid them *s.* the tree of life
P. L. 4, 326. *s.* whispering soft
P. L. 4, 356. Satan still in gaze as first he *s.*
P. L. 4, 455. then *s.* unmoved pure as the
P. L. 4, 720. their shady lodge arrived both *s.*
P. L. 4, 779. *s.* armed to their night watches
P. L. 4, 787. that near him *s.*
P. L. 4, 846. the devil *s.* and felt how awful
P. L. 4, 863. and closing *s.* in squadron
P. L. 4, 926. thou know'st I *s.* thy fiercest
P. L. 4, 986. collecting all his might dilated *s.*
P. L. 5, 54. beside it *s.* one shaped and winged
P. L. 5, 132. that ready *s.* each in their
P. L. 5, 249. where he *s.* veiled with his
P. L. 5, 285. like Maia's son he *s.*
P. L. 5, 383. *s.* to entertain her guest from
P. L. 5, 568. and perfect while they *s.*
P. L. 5, 595. of circuit inexpressible they *s.*
P. L. 5, 631. all in circles as they *s.* tables are
P. L. 5. 807. Abdiel...*s.* up and in a flame of zeal
P. L. 6, 62. that *s.* for heaven in mighty
P. L. 6, 106. presented *s.* in terrible array
P. L. 6, 111. he *s.* among the mightiest
P. L. 6, 205. nor *s.* at gaze the adverse legions
P. L. 6,302. for likest gods they seemed *s.* they
P. L. 6, 306. while expectation *s.* in horror
P. L. 6, 338. where it *s.* retired from off the
P. L. 6, 369. nor *s.* unmindful Abdiel to annoy
P. L. 6, 391. what *s.* recoiled o'erwearied
P. L. 6, 403. in fight they *s.* unwearied
P. L. 6, 448. as one he *s.* escaped from cruel
P. L. 6, 508. none arguing *s.*
P. L. 6, 526. in arms they *s.* of golden panoply
P. L. 6, 555. at interview both *s.* awhile
P. L. 6, 579. a seraph *s.*
P. L. 6, 580. a reed *s.* waving

P. L. 6, 581. while we, suspense, collected *s.*
P. L. 6, 604. in view *s.* ranked of seraphim
P. L. 6, 629. themselves in pleasant vein *s.*
P. L. 6, 633. *s.* awhile in trouble but they *s.*
P. L. 6, 785. this saw his hapless foes but *s.*
P. L. 6, 794. *s.* re-embattled fierce
P. L. 6, 882. silent *s.* eye-witnesses of
P. L. 6, 911. firm they might have *s.* yet fell
P. L. 7, 321. up *s.* the corny reed embattled in
P. L. 7, 210. on heavenly ground they *s.*
P. L. 7,563. planets in their station listening *s.*
P. L. 8, 3. thought him still speaking still *s.*
P. L. 8, 261. and upright *s.* on my feet
P. L. 8, 292. suddenly *s.* at my head a dream
P. L. 8, 454. which it had long *s.* under
P. L. 8, 464. before whom awake I *s.*
P. L. 9, 277. as in a shady nook I *s.* behind
P. L. 9, 425. a cloud of fragrance where she *s.*
P. L. 9, 463. abstracted *s.* from his own evil
P. L. 9, 523. uncalled before her *s.*
P. L. 9, 593. longing and envying *s.*
P. L. 9, 673. to some great cause addressed *s.* in
P. L. 9, 890. amazed, astonied *s.* and blank
P. L. 9, 894. speechless he *s.* and pale
P. L. 10, 211. then pitying how they *s.* before
P. L. 10,232. within the gates that now *s.* open
P. L. 10, 352. long he admiring *s.* till sin
P. L. 10, 504. awhile he *s.* expecting their
P. L. 10,535. heaven-fallen in station *s.* or just
P. L. 10, 547. there *s.* a grove hard by
P. L. 10, 712. nor *s.* much in awe of man
P. L. 11, 1. they in lowliest plight repentant *s.*
P. L. 11, 14. before the shrine of Themis *s.*
P. L. 11, 71. and in their state though firm *s.*
P. L. 11, 264. with chilling gripe of sorrow *s.*
P. L. 11, 321. under this tree *s.* visible
P. L. 11, 385. wherever *s.* city of old or modern
P. L. 11, 432. an altar as the landmark *s.*
P. L. 11, 564. in other part *s.* one who at
P. L. 11, 645. and foot nor idly mustering *s.*
P.L. 11, 743. thickened sky like a dark ceiling *s.*
P. L. 12, 626. for now too nigh the archangel *s.*
P. R. 1,169. and all heaven admiring *s.* a space
P. R. 1,258. things of thee to all that presents *s.*
P. R. 2, 266. he by the brook of Cherith *s.*
P.R. 2, 298. when suddenly a man before him *s.*
P. R. 2, 351. in order *s.* tall stripling youths
P. R. 2, 354. trees now tripped now solemn *s.*
P. R. 3, 1. Satan *s.* awhile as mute confounded
P. R. 3, 146. but *s.* struck with guilt of his own
P. R. 4, 33. on each side an imperial city *s.*
P. R. 4, 561. he said and *s.* but Satan smitten
P. R. 4. 571. fell whence he *s.* to see his victor
S. A. 135. but safest he who *s.* aloof
S. A. 1611. I among these aloof obscurely *s.*
S.A.1631.(for so from such as nearer *s.* we heard)
S. A. 1637. and eyes fast fixed he *s.* as one
S.A.1659.the vulgar only 'scaped who *s.*without
C. 297. port was more than human as they *s.*
C. 565. amazed I *s.* harrowed with grief
H. 56. the hooked chariot *s.* unstained
P. 39. to bear me where the towers of Salem *s.*
M. W..21. and in his garland as he *s.*
S. M. 23. whilst they *s.* in first obedience
U.C.II.19.but vow though the cross doctors all *s.*
**Stood'st.**—P. L. 4, 837. as when thou *s.* in
P. L. 11, 759. on thy feet thou *s.* at last
P. R. 4, 420. yet only *s.* unshaken
P. R. 3, 409. when thou *s.* up his tempter
**Stoop.**—P. L. 3, 73. and ready now to *s.* with
P. L. 3, 252. wound shall then receive and *s.*
S. A. 468. Dagon must *s.* and shall...receive
C. 333. *s.* thy pale visage
C. 1023. heaven itself would *s.* to her
**Stooped.**—P. L. 8, 351. each bird *s.* on his wing
P. L. 11, 185. the bird of Jove *s.* from his aery
**Stooping.**—P. L. 8, 465. who *s.* opened my left
P. L. 9, 427. oft *s.* to support each flower
Il P. 72. *s.* through a fleecy cloud
P. 15. he sovran priest *s.* his regal head

**Stop.**—P. L. 3, 394. nor *s.* thy flaming
P. L. 7, 596. and dulcimer all organs of sweet *s.*
P. L. 10, 291. mountains of ice that *s.* the
P. L. 12, 166. who seeks to *s.* their overgrowth
C. 552. till an unusual *s.* of sudden silence
**Stops.**—P. L. 11, 561. who moved their *s.* and
C. 345. sound of pastoral reed with oaten *s.*
L. 188. he touched the tender *s.* of various quills
**Stopt.**—P. L. 11, 848. who now had *s.* his sluices
**Store.**—P. L. 3, 444. none yet but *s.* hereafter
P. L. 4, 255. some irriguous valley spread her *s.*
P. L. 4, 816. for the tun, some magazine to *s.*
P. L. 5, 128. from night and kept for thee in *s.*
P. L. 5, 322. small *s.* will serve where *s.* all
P. L. 6, 515. blackest grain and into *s.* conveyed
P L. 7, 226. prepared in God's eternal *s.*
P. L. 9, 621. as leaves a greater *s.* of fruit
P. L. 9, 1078. whence evil *s.* even shame
P. R. 2, 334. all the elements her choicest *s.*
C. 720. and precious gems to *s.* her children
C. 774. and she no wit encumbered with her *s.*
L'A. 121. with *s.* of ladies whose bright eyes
P. 44. that was the casket of heaven's richest *s.*
**Stored.**—P. L. 6, 764. three-bolted thunder *s.*
P. L. 7, 492. builds her waxen cells with honey *s.*
P. L. 8, 152. *s.* in each orb perhaps with some
P. L. 9, 184. well *s.* with subtle wiles
S. A. 395. in what part my strength lay *s.*
**Storehouse.**—P. R. 2, 103. been a *s.* long
**Stores.**—P. L. 2, 175. what if all her *s.* were
P. L. 5, 314. and what thy *s.* contain bring
**Storied.**—C. 516. *s.* of old in high immortal
Il P. 159. and *s.* windows richly dight
**Stories.**—L'A. 101. with *s.* told of many a feat
**Storing.**—P. L. 5. 324. save what by frugal *s.*
**Stork.**—P. L. 7, 423. there the eagle and the *s.*
**Storm.**—P. L. 1, 172. hail shot after us in *s.*
P. L. 6, 546. but rattling *s.* of arrows barbed
P. L. 9, 433. from her best prop so far and *s.*
P. L. 12, 59. and all in rage as mocked they *s.*
P. R. 4, 436. after a night of *s.* so ruinous
S. A. 405. to *s.* me overwatched and wearied out
S. A. 1061. but had we best retire I see a *s.*
**Storming.**—P. L. 6, 207. now *s.* fury rose
**Storms.**—P. L. 2, 588. beat with perpetual *s.*
P. L. 2, 922. than when Bellona *s.* with all
P. L. 3, 425. and ever-threatening *s.* of Chaos
Hor 7. and *s.* unwonted, shall admire
**Storm'st.**—P. R. 4, 496. *s.* refused thinking
**Stormy.**—P. L. 10, 698. bail and *s.* gust
P. R. 4, 418. stiff necks loaden with *s.* blasts
L. 156. whether beyond the *s.* Hebrides
**Story.**—P. L. 7, 51. the *s.* heard attentive and
P. L. 8, 205. my *s.* which perhaps thou hast
P. L. 8, 522. and brought my *s.* to the sum
P. L. 9, 886. Eve with countenance blithe her *s.*
P. L. 12, 506. their doctrine and their *s.* written
P. R. 2, 307. others of some note as *s.* tells
P. R. 4, 334. our law and *s.* strewed with hymns
L. 95. they knew not of his *s.*
Il P. 110. left half-told the *s.* of Cambuscan bold
S. 13, 11. tunest their happiest lines in hymn or *s.*
M. W. 62. next her much like to thee in *s.*
**Stoutly.**—L'A. 52. *s.* struts his dames before
**Stoutness.**—S. A. 1346. what this *s.* will
**Straggling.**—C. 499. or *s.* wether the pent
**Straight.**—P. L. 1, 531. then *s.* commands that
P. L. 1, 723. and *s.* the doors opening
P. L. 2, 948. through *s.* rough dense or rare
P. L. 2, 959. when *s.* behold the throne
P.L.3,647.and *s.* was known the arch-angel
P. L. 4, 376. so *s.* so close that I with
P. L. 4, 405. *s.* couches close then rising
P. L. 4, 476. what could I do but follow *s.*
P. L. 4, 741. *s.* side by side were laid
P. L. 4, 947. to say and *s.* unsay pretending
P. L. 5, 287. *s.* knew him all the bands of
P. L. 6, 613. terms of composition *s.* they
P. L. 7, 453. and *s.* opening her fertile womb
P. L. 8, 257. *s.* toward heaven my wondering
P. L. 9, 632. made intricate seem *s.*

P. L. 10, 90. down he descended *s.*
P. L. 10, 361. but *s.* I felt though distant
P. L. 12, 126. he *s.* obeys not knowing to what
P. R. 1, 259. this having heard *s.* I again
P. R. 1, 275. he *s.* knew me and with loudest
P. R. 3, 256. the one winding the other *s.*
P. R. 4, 581. and *s.* a fiery globe of angels
S. A. 385. carrying it *s.* to them who had
C. 811. but this will cure all *s.* one sip of this
C. 835. bearing her *s.* to aged Nereus' hall
L'A. 69. *s.* mine eye hath caught new pleasures
S. 12, 3. when *s.* a barbarous noise environs me
U.C.II.10. his principles being ceased he ended *s.*
V. Ex. 17. haste thee *s.* to do me once a pleasure
**Strain.**—L. 87. that *s.* I heard was of a higher
Il. P. 174. to something like prophetic *s.*
H.17. hast thou no verse, no hymn, or solemn *s.*
**Strained.**—P. L. 8, 454. *s.* to the height in
**Straining.**—S. A. 1646. *s.* all his nerves
**Strains.**—P. L. 5, 148. in fit *s.* pronounced
C.494. Thyrsis? whose artful *s.* have oft delayed
C. 561. and took in *s.* that might create a soul
L'A. 148. such *s.* as would have won the ear of
**Strait.**—P. L. 4, 376. so *s.* so close that I with
P. L. 10, 125. O heaven in evil *s.* this day I
P. L. 10, 898. and *s.* conjunction with this sea
**Straitened.**—P. L. 1, 776. swarmed and were *s.*
P. L. 9, 323. in narrow circuit *s.* by a foe
**Straitening.**—P. L. 6, 70. nor *s.* vale nor
**Straiter.**—H. 169. in *s.* limits bound
**Straits.**—P. R. 2, 415. in poverty and *s.*
**Strand.**—P. L. 1, 379. stood on the bare *s.*
D. F. I. 25. young Hyacinth born on Eurotas' *s.*
**Strands.**—C. 876. and her son that rules the *s.*
**Strange.**—P. L. 1, 707. by *s.* conveyance
P. L. 2, 69. with Tartarean sulphur and *s.* fire
P. L. 2, 703. *s.* horror seize thee and pangs
P. L. 2, 737. so *s.* thy outcry and thy words so *s.*
P. L. 2, 1024. *s.* alteration! sin and death
P. L. 4, 287. creatures new to sight and *s.*
P. L. 5, 116. but with addition *s.*
P. L. 5, 556. relation which must needs be *s.*
P. L. 5, 855. *s.* point and new
P. L. 6, 91. though *s.* to us it seemed at first
P. L. 6, 571. to our eyes discovered new and *s.*
P. L. 6, 614. and into *s.* vagaries fell
P. L. 7, 53. of things so high and *s.*
P. L. 8, 531. passion first I felt commotion *s.*
P. L. 9, 599. ere long I might perceive *s.*
P. L. 9, 861. *s.* hath been the cause
P. L. 9, 1135. when that *s.* desire of wandering
P. L. 10, 479. fiercely opposed my journey *s.*
P. L. 10, 552. on that prospect *s.* their earnest
P. L. 10, 799. that were to make *s.* contradiction
P. L. 11, 733. when lo a wonder *s.*
P. L. 12, 60. to see the hubbub *s.* and hear
P.R.2,104. sayings laid up portending *s.* events
P. R. 4, 40. by what *s.* parallax or optic skill
S. A. 1003. beauty ... hath *s.* power
C. 628. telling their *s.* and vigorous faculties
Il P. 147. and let some *s.* mysterious dream
U. C. II. 32. *s.* to think his wain was his increase
**Stranger.**—P. L. 2, 990. I know thee *s.*
P. L. 5, 316. honour and receive our heavenly *s.*
P. L. 5, 397. heavenly *s.* please to taste these
P. L. 12, 358. then lose it to a *s.* that the true
**Strangled.**—C. 729. and *s.* with her waste
**Stratagems.**—P. R. 1, 180. all ye *s.* of hell
**Straw.**—L. 124. scrannel pipes of wretched *s.*
**Straw-built.**—P. L. 1, 773. their *s.-b.* citadel
**Stray.**—P. L. 7, 405. through groves of coral *s.*
P. L. 11, 176. from thy side henceforth to *s.*
P. R. 1, 315. as seemed the quest of some *s.* ewe
C. 315. and if your *s.* attendance be yet lodged
L'A. 72. where the nibbling flocks do *s.*
V.Ex.53.my wandering muse how thou dost *s.*
**Strayed.**—P. L. 3, 476. that *s.* so far to seek
P. L. 8, 283. while thus I called and *s.* I knew
C. 503. on such a trivial toy as a *s.* ewe
L. 97. that not a blast was from his dungeon *s.*
**Strays.**—C. 895. that in the channel *s.*

**Streak.**—P. L. 4, 623. ere fresh morning *s.*
**Streaking.**—P. L. 7, 481. *s.* the ground with
**Streaks.**—P. L. 11, 879. those coloured *s.*
**Stream.**—P. L. 1, 202. that swim the ocean *s.*
P. L. 1, 398. to the *s.* of utmost Arnon
P. L. 2, 580. loud heard on the rueful *s.*
P. L. 2, 582. a slow and silent *s.* Lethe the river
P. L. 2, 607. as they pass to reach the tempting *s.*
P. L. 3, 7. pure ethereal *s.* whose fountain
P. L. 3, 359. o'er Elysian flowers her amber *s.*
P. L. 4, 336. they thirsted scoop the brimming *s.*
P. L. 5, 306. from milky *s.* berry or grape
P. L. 5, 590. *s.* in the air and for distinction
P. L. 6, 70. wood nor *s.* divides their perfect
P. L. 6, 332. from the gash a *s.* of nectarous
P. L. 7, 67. scarce allayed still eyes the current *s.*
P. L. 7, 306. where rivers now *s.* and perpetual
P. L. 11, 569. or whether washed by *s.* from
P. L. 12, 144. the double-founted *s.*
P. L. 12, 442. baptizing in the profluent *s.*
P. R. 1, 72. and in the consecrated *s.* pretends
P. R. 1, 280. but as I rose out of the laving *s.*
P. R. 3, 288. there Susa by Choaspes amber *s.*
P. R. 4, 250. there Ilissus rolls his whispering *s.*
S. A. 546. allure thee from the cool crystalline *s.*
S. A. 1726. and from the *s.* with lavers pure
C. 19. of every salt flood and each ebbing *s.*
C. 97. in the steep Atlantic *s.*
C. 722. feed on pulse drink the clear *s.*
C. 825. moist curb sways the smooth Severn *s.*
C. 850. throw sweet garland wreaths into her *s.*
L. 55. nor yet where Deva spreads her wizard *s.*
L. 62. his gory visage down the *s.* was sent
L'A. 130. on summer eves by haunted *s.*
Il P. 148. wave at his wings in aery *s.*
S. 16, 7. while Darwen *s.* with blood of Scots
**Streamers.**—S. A. 718. sails filled and *s.* waving
**Streaming.**—P. L. 1, 537. *s.* to the wind
P. L. 8, 467. and life-blood *s.* fresh
C. 340. with thy long-levelled rule of *s.* light
**Streams.**—P. L. 1, 469. Pharphar, lucid *s.*
P. L. 2, 576. the burning lake their baleful *s.*
P. L. 3, 436. of Ganges or Hydaspes Indian *s.*
P. L. 4, 233. and now divided into four main *s.*
P. L. 4, 263. or in a lake,... unite their *s.*
P. L. 5, 652. their camp extend by living *s.*
P. L. 7, 397. and lakes and running *s.*
P. L. 8, 263. and liquid lapse of murmuring *s.*
P. R. 4, 277. mellifluous *s.* that watered all the
C. 884. upon thy *s.* with wily glance
L. 133. the dread voice is past that shrunk thy *s.*
L. 174. where other groves and other *s.* along
S. 14, 14. and drink thy fill of pure immortal *s.*
**Street.**—S. A. 204. proverbed for a fool in every *s.*
S. A. 1458. through the high *s.* passing
S. A. 1599. proclaimed through each high s.
**Streets.**—P. L. 1, 501. night darkens the *s.*
P. L. 1, 503. witness the *s.* of Sodom
P. R. 2, 78. with infant blood the *s.* of Bethlehem
S. A. 343. equivalent to angels walked their *s.*
S. A. 1402. they shall not trail me through their *s.*
**Strength.**—P. L. 1, 116. since by fate the *s.* of
P. L. 1, 133. whether upheld by *s.* or chance or
P. L. 1, 146. have left us this our spirit and *s.*
P. L. 1, 154. though yet we feel *s.* undiminished
P. L. 1, 240. and by their own recovered *s.*
P. L. 1, 427. nor founded on the brittle *s.* of
P. L. 1, 433. oft forsook their living *s.*
P. L. 1, 572. and hardening in his *s.* glories
P. L. 1, 641. but still his *s.* concealed
P. L. 1, 696. and *s.* and art are easily out-done
P. L. 2, 47. to be deemed equal in *s.*
P. L. 2, 200. to suffer as to do our *s.* is equal
P. L. 2, 360. sit secure in his own *s.*
P. L. 2, 410. what *s.* what art can then suffice
P. L. 4, 1006. Satan I know thy *s.* and thou
P. L. 6, 116. *s.* and might there fail where
P. L. 6, 231. in *s.* each armed hand a legion
P. L. 6, 381. for *s.* from truth divided and
P. L. 6, 457. for what avails valour or *s.*
P. L. 6, 494. to *s.* and counsel joined think

P. L. 6, 820. since by *s.* they measure all of
P. L. 6, 850. that withered all their *s.*
P. L. 6, 853. yet half his *s.* he put not forth
P. L. 7, 141. this inaccessible high *s.* the seat
P. L. 9, 312. if need were of outward *s.*
P. L. 9, 484. and *s.* of courage haughty and of
P. L. 9, 1062. and waked shorn of his *s.*
P. L. 10, 9. with *s.* entire and free will armed
P. L. 10, 243. methinks I feel new *s.* within
P. L. 10, 921. uttermost distress my only *s.*
P. L. 11, 138. and found *s.* added from above
P. L. 11, 539. outlive thy youth thy *s.* thy
P. L. 12, 389. with more *s.* to foil thy enemy
P. L. 12, 430. the head of Satan crush his *s.*
P. R. 1, 161. weakness shall o'ercome Satanic *s.*
P. R. 2, 234. and his *s.* as oft assay
P. R. 2, 276. *s.* whereof sufficed him forty days
P. R. 3, 402. human weakness rather than of *s.*
P. R. 4, 9. the *s.* he was to cope with
P. R. 4, 566. from his mother earth new *s.*
S. A. 36. with this heaven-gifted *s.* O glorious *s.*
S. A. 47. who this high gift of *s.* committed
S. A. 53. what is *s.* without a double share
S. A. 58. God when he gave me *s.* to show withal
S. A. 63. suffices that to me *s.* is my bane
S. A. 127. whom unarmed no *s.* of man
S. A. 173. but thee whose *s.* while virtue was her
S. A. 206. immeasurable *s.* they might behold
S. A. 342. who with a *s.* equivalent to angels
S. A. 349. O ever-failing trust in mortal *s.*
S. A. 394. in what part my *s.* lay stored
S. A. 522. when in *s.* all mortals I excelled
S. A. 536. and hallowed pledge of all my *s.*
S. A. 570. clustering down vain monument of *s.*
S. A. 586. this *s.* miraculous yet remaining
S. A. 665. secret refreshings that repair his *s.*
S. A. 706. the image of thy *s.* and mighty minister
S. A. 780. wherein consisted all thy *s.* and safety
S. A. 789. more *s.* from me than in thyself was
S. A. 799. get into my power thy key of *s.*
S. A. 817. if thou in *s.* all mortals dost exceed
S. A. 938. if in my flower of youth and *s.*
S. A. 1011. *s.* comeliness of shape
S. A. 1136. in thy hair where *s.* can least abide
S. A. 1141. who gave me at my nativity this *s.*
S. A. 1212. *s.* sufficient and command from heaven
S. A. 1228. to descant on my *s.*
S. A. 1313. thy *s.* they know surpassing human
S. A. 1355. shall I abuse this consecrated gift of *s.*
S. A. 1360. vaunting my *s.* in honour to... Dagon
S. A. 1363. with *s.* thou servest the Philistines
S. A. 1439. measure of *s.* so great to mortal seed
S. A. 1475. or at some proof of *s.* before them
S. A. 1494. that of a nation armed the *s.* contained
S. A. 1496. his *s.* again to grow up with his hair
S. A. 1502. since his *s.* with eye-sight was not lost
S. A. 1503. God will restore him eye-sight to his *s.*
S. A. 1602. proof of his mighty *s.* in feats
S. A. 1644. I mean to show you of my *s.*
C. 330. and square my trial to my proportioned *s.*
C. 415. she has a hidden *s.* which you remember
C. 416. what hidden *s.* unless the *s.* of heaven
C. 418. I mean that too but yet a hidden *s.*
L'A. 112. basks at the fire his hairy *s.*
**Strenuous.**—S. A. 271. than *s.* liberty
**Stretched.**—P. L. 4, 210. Eden *s.* her line
P. L. 5, 754. from one entire globose *s.* into
P. L. 6, 80. from skirt to skirt a fiery region *s.*
P. L. 7, 414. on the deep *s.* like a promontory
P. L. 1, 209. so *s.* out huge in length
P. L. 8, 102. and his line *s.* out so far
P. L. 11, 380. *s.* out to the amplest reach
L. 190. and now the sun had *s.* out all the hills
L'A. 111. and *s.* out all the chimney's length
**Stretching.**—P. L. 2, 1003. your dungeon *s.*
**Strew.**—L. 151. *s.* the laureate hearse where Lycid
V. Ex. 64. *s.* all their blessings on thy sleeping
M. W. 58. for thy hearse to *s.* the ways
**Strewed.**—P. L. 11, 439. fat with incense *s.*
P. R. 4, 334. story *s.* with hymns
C. 838. in nectared lavers *s.* with asphodel

**Strews.**—P. L. 5, 348. then *s.* the ground
**Strict.**—P. L. 2, 241. and receive *s.* laws
P. L. 2, 412. through the *s.* senteries
P. L. 4, 562. by lot hath given charge and *s.*
P. L. 5, 528. by fate inextricable or *s.* necessity
P. L. 6, 869. but *s.* fate had cast too deep
P. L. 9, 903. yielded to transgress the *s.*
P. L. 10, 131. but *s.* necessity subdues me
P. L. 12, 304. from imposition of *s.* laws to free
C. 109. *s.* age and sour severity
**Strictest.**—P. L. 2, 321. but to remain in *s.*
P. L. 4, 783. and coast the south with *s.* watch
P. L. 9, 363. not keeping *s.* watch as she was
S. A. 319. against his vow of *s.* purity
S. 2, 10, it shall be still in *s.* measure even
**Strictly.**—P. L. 3, 402. thou didst not doom so *s.*
P. L. 3, 405. not to doom frail man so *s.*
P. L. 9, 235. yet not so *s.* hath our Lord
L. 66. *s.* meditate the thankless muse
D.F. I. 33. could heaven for pity thee so *s.* doom
**Stride.**—S. A. 1067. I know him by his *s.* the
**Strides.**—P. L. 2. 676. with horrid *s.* hell
P. L. 6, 109. Satan, with vast and haughty *s.*
S. A. 1245. stalking with less unconscionable *s.*
**Strife.**—P. L. 1, 623. and that *s.* was not
P. L. 2, 31. no good for which to strive no *s.*
P. L. 2, 233. and chaos judge the *s.*
P. L. 2, 500. yet live in hatred enmity and *s.*
P. L. 3, 406. and end the *s.* of mercy and
P. L. 6, 264. these acts of hateful *s.*
P. L. 6, 289. the *s.* which thou call'st evil but
P. L. 6, 823. nor other *s.* with them do I
P. L. 12, 355. their *s.* pollution brings upon
S. A. 460. this only hope relieves me that the *s.*
M. W. 13. nature and fate had had no *s.*
V. Ex. 85. yet shall he live in *s.* and at his door
**Strike.**—P. L. 11, 492. but delayed to *s.*
S.A.1645.as with amaze shall *s.* all who behold
**Strikes.**—H. 52. *s.* a universal peace through
**String.**—P. L. 7, 597. by *s.* or golden wire
A. 87. and touch the warbled *s.*
L. 17. begin and somewhat loudly sweep the *s.*
Il P. 106. such notes as warbled to the *s.*
**Stringed.**—H. 97. answering the *s.* noise
**Strings.**—P. R. 2, 363. heard of chiming *s.* or
P. 27. me softer airs befit and softer *s.*
**Stripes.**—P. L. 2, 334. and *s.* and arbitrary
P. R. 4, 388. violence and *s.* and lastly cruel
**Stripling.**—P. L. 3, 636. and now a *s.*
P. R. 2, 352. tall *s.* youths rich clad of fairer
**Stripp'dst.**—S. A. 1188. then like a robber *s.*
**Strive.**—P. L. 2, 31. no good for which to *s.*
P. L. 2, 899. *s.* here for mastery and to battle
P. L. 4, 275. with this Paradise of Eden *s.*
P. L. 4, 859. to *s.* or fly he held it vain
P. L. 10, 959. but *s.* in offices of love how we
C. 8. *s.* to keep up a frail and feverish being
V. Ex. 78. ungratefully shall *s.* to keep him
**Strivest.**—S. A. 841. in vain thou *s.* to cover
**Strode.**—P. L. 2, 676. hell trembled as he *s.*
**Stroke.**—P. L. 1, 488. equalled with one *s.*
P. L. 2, 702. or with one *s.* of this dart
P. L. 2, 713. their fatal hands no second *s.*
P. L. 6, 189. so saying a noble *s.* he lifted high
P. L. 6, 317. one *s.* they aimed that might
P. L. 10, 52. by some immediate *s.* but soon
P. L. 10, 210. and the instant *s.* of death
P. L. 10, 311. and scourged with many a *s.*
P. L. 10, 809. not one *s.* as I supposed bereaving
P. L. 10, 855. with one thrice-acceptable *s.*
P. L. 11, 268. O unexpected *s.* worse than
P. L. 11, 471. some as thou sawest by violent *s.*
P. L. 12, 385. what *s.* shall bruise the victor's
P. R. 1, 59. bide the *s.* of that long-threatened
Il P. 136. where the rude axe with heaved *s.*
P. 20. yet more the *s.* of death he must abide
**Strong.**—P. L. 2, 434. our prison *s.* this huge
P. L. 2, 936. had not by ill chance the *s.* rebuff
P. L. 4, 786. from these two *s.* and subtle spirits
P. L. 6, 336. by angels many and *s.* who
P. L. 8, 241. the dismal gates and barricadoed *s.*

P. L. 8, 633. be *s.*, live happy and love
P. L. 9, 934. inducement *s.* to us as likely tasting
P. L. 9, 1059. So rose the Danite *s.* Herculean
P. L. 10, 265. go whither fate and inclination *s.*
P. L. 10, 409. detriment need fear go and be *s.*
P. L. 11, 655. others to a city *s.* lay siege
P.L.12,568. deemed weak subverting worldly *s.*
P. R. 1, 160. by humiliation and *s.* sufferance
P. R. 1, 290. and now by some *s.* motion I am
P.R. 3, 168. that by *s.* hand his family obtained
P. R. 3, 313. their horses clad yet fleet and *s.*
P. R. 4, 92. to Caprea, an island small but *s.*
S. A. 52. O impotence of mind in body *s.*
S. A. 556. his mighty champion *s.* above
S. A. 816. not austere as thou art *s.* inflexible
S. A. 1134. art armed thee or charmed thee *s.*
Cir. 27. but O ere long huge pangs and *s.*
**Stronger.**—P. L. 1, 92. so much the *s.* proved
P.L.2,83. should we again provoke our *s.* some
P. L. 6, 819. in battle which the *s.* proves
P. L. 9, 311. more watchful *s.* if need were
P. R. 9, 491. not approached by *s.* hate, hate *s.*
**Strongest.**—P. L. 2, 44. the *s.* and the fiercest
S. A. 168. *s.* of mortal men to lowest pitch
S. A. 553. O madness to think use of *s.* wines
S. A. 554. *s.* drinks our chief support of health
S. A. 1155. soon feel whose God is *s.*
**Stronghold.**—P. L. 6, 228. from his *s.* of heaven
**Strongly.**—P. L. 1, 147. *s.* to suffer and support
P. L. 10,262. nor can I miss the way so *s.* drawn
C. 806. I must dissemble and try her yet more *s.*
**Strong-siding.**—C. 212. by a *s.-s.* champion
**Strook.**—P. L. 2, 165. pursued and *s.* with
H. 95. never was by mortal finger *s.*
**Strove.**—P. L. 1, 721. Egypt with Assyria *s.*
P. L. 5, 382. three that in Mount Ida naked *s.*
P. R. 4, 564. in Irassa. *s.* with Jove's Alcides
Il P. 19. or that starred Ethiop queen that *s.*
**Strow.**—P. L. 1, 302. *s.* the brooks in
**Strown.**—P. L. 6, 389. with shivered armour *s.*
**Struck.**—P. L. 6, 863. monstrous sight *s.* them
P. R. 3, 146. stood *s.* with guilt of his own sin
P. R. 4, 576. so *s.* with dread and anguish fell
S. A. 1686. and with blindness internal *s.*
**Strucken.**—P. L. 9, 1064. they sat as *s.* mute
**Structure.**—P. L. 1, 733. a towered *s.* high
P. L. 3, 503. up to the wall of heaven a *s.*
P. L. 5, 761. so call that *s.* in the dialect of
P. R. 3, 286. Ecbatana her *s.* vast there shows
S. A. 1239. and with one buffet lay thy *s.* low
**Structures.**—C. 798. till all thy magic *s.*
**Struggle.**—P. L. 2, 606. *s.* as they pass to
**Struggling.**—P. L. 6, 659. *s.* underneath
**Struts.**—L'A. 52. stoutly *s.* his dames before
**Stubble.**—C. 599. and earth's base built on *s.*
**Stubborn.**—P. L. 2, 569. with *s.* patience
P. L. 12, 193. and oft humbles his *s.* heart
P. R. 1, 226. the *s.* only to subdue
C. 434. blue meagre hag or *s.* unlaid ghost
**Stubs.**—P. R. 1, 339. on tough roots and *s.*
**Stuck.**—U. C. I. 4. he's here *s.* in a slough and
**Studied.**—S. A. 658. writ with *s.* argument
**Studious.**—P. L. 8, 40. entering on *s.* thoughts
P. L. 9, 42. me of these nor skilled nor *s.*
P. L. 11, 609. *s.* they appear of arts
P. R. 4, 243. city or suburban *s.* walks and
P. R. 4, 249. oft invites to *s.* musing
Il P. 162. to walk the *s.* cloister's pale
**Studs**—P. R. 4, 120. gems and *s.* of pearl
**Study.**—P. L. 1, 107. and *s.* of revenge
P. L. 9, 233. than to *s.* household good
P. L. 11, 577, and all their *s.* bent to worship
**Stuff.**—P. L. 10, 601. seems to *s.* this maw
P. L. 12, 43. and of that *s.* they cast
**Stumble.**—P. L. 3, 201. that they may *s.* on
**Stumbled.**—P. L. 6, 624. and *s.* many
**Stung.**—P. R. 1, 466. though inly *s.* with
**Stunning.**—P. L. 2, 952. of *s.* sounds and
**Stupendous.**—P. L. 10, 351. that *s.* bridge
S. A. 1627. all with incredible *s.* force
**Stupid.**—P. L. 12, 116. should be so *s.*

**Stupidly.**—P. L. 9, 465. remained s. good
**Sturdiest.**—P. R. 4, 417. and s. oaks bowed
**Sty.**—P. R. 4, 101. his throne now made a s.
  C. 77. to roll with pleasure in a sensual s.
**Stygian.**—P. L. 1, 239. scaped the S. flood
  P. L. 2, 506. the S. council thus dissolved
  P. L. 2, 875. which but herself not all the S.
  P. L. 3, 14. escaped the S. pool
  P. L. 10, 453. the S. throng bent their aspect
  C. 132. of S. darkness spets her thickest gloom
  L'A. 3. in S. cave forlorn
**Style**—P. L. 2, 312. and changing s. be called
  P. L. 5, 146, morning duly paid in various s.
  P. L. 5, 146. for neither various s. nor holy
  P. L. 6, 289. but we s. the strife of glory
  P. L. 9, 20. if answerable s. I can obtain
  P. L. 9, 1132. estranged in look and altered s.
  P. R. 4, 359. their majestic unaffected s.
  S. 11, 2. and woven close both matter form and s.
**Styled.**—P. L. 9, 137. what he Almighty s.
  P. L. 11, 695. to be s. great conquerors
  P. L. 12, 33. hunter thence he shall be s.
**Styx.**—P. L. 2, 577. abhorred S. the flood
**Subducting.**—P. L. 8, 536. or from my side s.
**Subdue.**—P. L. 3, 250. rise victorious and s.
  P. L. 4, 85. boasting I could s. the omnipotent
  P. L. 5, 741. know whether I be dextrous to s.
  P. L. 6, 40. and to s. by force who reason for
  P. L. 6, 427. judged sufficient to s. us to his will
  P. L. 7, 532. s. it and throughout dominion hold
  P. L. 8, 584. therein enjoyed were worthy to s.
  P. L. 11, 691. to overcome in battle and s.
  P. L. 12, 81. affecting to s. rational
  P. R. 1, 218. then to s. and quell o'er all the earth
  P. R. 1, 226. the stubborn only to s.
  P. R. 3, 71. they err who count it glorious to s.
  P. R. 4, 252. bred great Alexander to s. the
**Subdued.**—P. L. 6, 259. arch-foe s. or captive
  P. R. 4, 126. of the emperor how easily s.
  S.A.174. while virtue was her mate might have s.
  S. A. 1167. but by the barber's razor best s.
**Subdues.**—P. L. 2, 198. since, fate inevitable s.
  P. L. 6, 458. quelled with pain which all s.
  P. L. 10, 132. necessity s. me and calamitous
**Subduing.**—P. L. 11, 792. s. nations
**Subject.**—P. L. 8, 607. yet these s not
  P. L. 9, 25. since first this s. for heroic song
  P. R. 2, 471. s. himself to anarchy within
  S. A. 371. s. him to so foul indignities
  S. A. 646. the s. of their cruelty and scorn
  S.A.886. was I their s. nor under their protection
  S. A. 1182. is not thy nation s. to our lords
  S. 11, 3. the s. new it walked the town awhile
  V. Ex. 30. thy service in some graver s. use
  V. Ex. 74. shall s. be to many an accident
**Subjected.**—P. L. 9, 155. and O indignity s.
  P. L. 12, 640. down the cliff as fast to the s. plain
  S. A. 1205. my nation was s. to your lords
**Subjection.**—P. L. 2, 239. made of new s.
  P. L. 4, 50. lifted up so high I sdeined s.
  P. L. 4, 308. which implied s. but required
  P. L. 8, 345. and pay thee fealty with low s.
  P. L. 8, 570. thy love not thy s.
  P. L. 9, 1128. both in s. now to sensual appetite
  P. L. 10, 153. lovely to attract thy love not thy s.
  P. L. 12, 32. as refuse s. to his empire tyrannous
  S. A. 1405. to such as owe them absolute s.
**Subjects.**—P. L. 12, 93. in judgment just s.
**Sublime.**—P. L. 2, 528. or in the air s.
  P. L. 3, 72. in the dun air s. and ready now
  P. L. 4, 300. his fair large front and eye s.
  P. L. 6, 771. he on the wings of cherub rode s.
  P. L. 7, 421. and soaring the air s. with clang
  P. L. 8, 455. in that celestial colloquy s.
  P. L. 10, 536. s. with expectation when to see
  P. L. 10, 1014. argue in thee something more s.
  P. L. 11, 236. but solemn and s. whom not
  P. R. 4, 542. bore through the air s.
  S.A. 1669. while their hearts were jocund and s.
  C. 785. to apprehend the s. notion and high
**Sublimed.**—P. L. 1, 235. s. with mineral fury

---

  P. L. 5, 483. nourishment by gradual scale s.
**Sublunar**—P. L. 4, 777. this vast s. vault
**Submiss.**—P. L. 5, 359. not awed yet with s.
  P. L. 8, 316. in adoration at his feet I fell s.
  P. L. 9, 377. yet s. though last replied
  P. R. 1, 476. from thee I can and must s. endure
**Submission.**—P. L. 1, 661. who can think s.
  P. L. 4, 81. left but by s. and that word disdain
  P. L. 4, 96. soon unsay what feigned s. swore
  P. L. 4, 310. yielded with coy s. modest pride
  P. L. 12, 597. her spirits composed to meek s.
  S. A. 511. best pleased with humble and filial s.
**Submissive.**—P. L. 4, 498. and s. charms
  P. L. 10, 942. now at his feet s. in distress
**Submit.**—P. L. 1, 108. and courage never to s.
  P. L. 4, 85. promises and other vaunts than to s.
  P. L. 5, 787. will ye s. your necks and choose
  P. L. 10, 196 to thy husband's will thine shall s.
  P. L. 10, 769. be it so for I s. his doom is fair
  P. L. 11, 314. therefore to his great bidding I s.
  P. L. 11, 372. and to the hand of heaven s.
  P. L. 11, 526. yield it just said Adam and s.
  S. A. 751. then as repentant to s. beseech
**Submits.**—P. L. 12, 191. tamed at length s.
  S. A. 758. again transgresses and again s.
**Submitting.**—P. L. 9, 919. s. to what
**Subordinate.**—P. L. 5, 671. and his next s.
**Suborned.**—P. L. 9, 361. object by the foe s.
**Subscribe.**—S. A. 1535. yet hope would fain s.
**Subscribed.**—P. L. 11, 182. but fate s. not
**Subsequent.**—S. A. 325. s. her stain not his
**Subserve.**—S. A. 57. but to s. where wisdom
**Subsist.**—P. L. 9, 359. firm we s. yet possible
  P. L. 10, 922. whither shall I betake me where s.
  P. R. 3, 19. or s. in battle though against thy
  C. 686. by which all mortal frailty must s.
**Substance.**—P. L. 1, 117. this empyreal s.
  P. L. 1, 529. that bore semblance of worth not s.
  P. L. 2, 99. or if our s. be indeed divine
  P. L. 2, 356. of what mould, or s.
  P. L. 2, 669. or s. might be called that shadow
  P. L. 4, 585. to exclude spiritual s. with
  P. L. 5, 420. vapours not yet into her s.
  P. L. 5, 474. various forms various degrees of s.
  P. L. 5, 493. but convert as you to proper s.
  P. L. 6, 330. but the ethereal s. closed not
  P. L. 6, 657. into their s. pent, which wrought
  P. L. 11, 775. in apprehension than in s. feel
**Substances.**—P. L. 5, 408. intelligential s.
  P. L. 8, 109. that to corporeal s. could add speed
**Substantial.**—P. L. 4, 189. whose s. doors
  P. L. 4, 485. nearest my heart s. life
**Substantially.**—P. L. 3, 140. s. expressed
**Substitute.**—P. L. 8, 881. mo here thy s.
**Substitutes.**—P. L. 10, 403. my s. I send
**Subterranean.**—P. L. 1, 231. of s. wind
**Subtle.**—P. L. 1, 727. pendent by s. magic
  P. L. 2, 815. the s. fiend his lore soon learned
  P. L. 4, 786. strong and s. spirits he called
  P. L. 6, 513. and with s. art concocted
  P. L. 8, 192. remote from use obscure and s.
  P. L. 8, 399. a nice and s. happiness I see
  P. L. 9, 184. the midst well stored with s.
  P. L. 9, 307. s. he needs must be who could
  P. L. 9, 324. straitened by a foe s. or violent
  P. L. 10, 20. much wondering how the s. fiend
  P. R. 1, 465. but the s. fiend though only stung
  P. R. 2, 323. thy refusal? said the s. fiend
  P. R. 4, 308. or s. shifts conviction to evade
  S. 2, 1. how soon hath time the s. thief of youth
**Subtlest.**—P. L. 7, 495. the serpent s. beast
  P. L. 9, 86. the serpent s. beast of all the field
  P. L. 9, 560. thee serpent s. beast of all the field
**Subtleties.**—S. A. 56. to fall by weakest s.
**Subtlety.**—P. L. 2, 358. best by force or s.
  P. L. 9, 93. as from his wit and native s.
  P. R. 1, 144. and now assay his utmost s.
**Subtly.**—P. L. 8, 207. how s. to detain thee
**Subvert.**—P. R. 1, 124. so to s. whom he
**Subverting.**—P. L. 12, 568. deemed weak s.
**Suburb.**—P. L. 1, 773. s. of their straw-built

**Suburban.**—P. R. 4, 243. city or *s.*
**Suburbs.**—P. R. 3, 170. with Modin and her *s.*
**Succeed.**—P. L. 1, 166. which oft-times may *s.*
P. L. 4, 535. pleasures for long woes are to *s.*
P. L. 10, 733. who of all ages to *s.* but feeling
P. L. 12, 508. wolves shall *s.* for teachers
**Succeeded.**—S. A. 908. would have *s.* best
**Succeeding.**—P. R. 2, 143. of like *s.* here
**Success.**—P. L. 2, 9. and by *s.* untaught
P. L. 2, 123. ominous conjecture on the whole *s.*
P. L. 3, 740. the ecliptic sped with hoped *s.*
P. L. 6, 161. that thy *s.* may show destruction
P. L. 6, 471. believest so main to our *s.* I bring
P. L. 10, 239. it cannot be but that *s.* attends
P. R. 1, 105. induces best to hope of like *s.*
P. R. 2, 141. lest confidence of my *s.* with Eve
P. R. 3, 278. whose *s.* Israel in long captivity
P. R. 4, 1. perplexed and troubled at his bad *s.*
P. R. 4, 23. gives not o'er though desperate of *s.*
P. R. 4, 578. joyless triumphals of his hoped *s.*
S. A. 1454. with good *s.* to work his liberty
S. 1, 7. portend *s.* in love
**Successes.**—P. L. 4, 932. assays and ill *s.* past
P. L. 10, 396. them to acquaint with these *s.*
**Successful.**—P. L. 1, 120. with more *s.* hope
P. L. 10. 463. returned *s.* beyond hope
**Successfully.**—P. R. 1, 103. performed *s.*
**Succession.**—P. L. 12, 331. but first a long *s.*
**Successive.**—P. L. 4, 614. night to men *s.*
**Successor.**—P. R. 3, 373. his true *s.*
S. A. 1021. worthless to thee compared *s.* in thy
**Succinct.**—P. L. 3, 643. habit fit for speed *s.*
**Succoth.**—S. A. 278. *S.* and the fort of Penuel
**Succour.**—P. L. 9, 642. and lost from *s.* far
F. of C. 18. and *s.* our just fears
**Such.**—P. L. 1, 70. *s.* place eternal justice had
P. L. 1, 145. than *s.* could have o'erpowered *s.*
P. L. 1, 230. and *s.* appeared in hue
P. L. 1, 237. *s.* resting found the sole of unblest
P. L. 1, 282. no wonder fallen *s.* a pernicious
P. L. 1, 317. if *s.* astonishment as this can
P. L. 1, 399. nor content with *s.* audacious
P. L. 1, 523. yet *s.* wherein appeared
P. L. 1, 551. *s.* as raised to height of noblest
P. L. 1, 574. met *s.* embodied force
P. L. 1, 620. tears *s.* as angels weep burst forth
P. L. 1, 629. how *s.* united force of gods how *s.*
P. L. 1, 718. *s.* magnificence equalled
P. L. 1, 736. exalted to *s.* power and gave to rule
P. L. 2, 73. let *s.* bethink them if the sleepy
P. L. 2, 284. he scarce had finished when *s.*
P. L. 2, 290. *s.* applause was heard as Mammon
P. L. 2, 292. for *s.* another field they dreaded
P. L. 2, 713. *s.* a frown each cast at the other
P. L. 2, 765. and *s.* joy thou took'st with me
P. L. 2, 993. for *s.* a numerous host fled not
P. L. 2, 1025. *s.* was the will of heaven
P. L. 3, 100. *s.* I created all the ethereal powers
P. L. 3, 107. what pleasure I from *s.* obedience
P. L. 3, 202. and none but *s.* from mercy
P. L. 3, 213. where shall we find *s.* love
P. L. 3, 329. *s.* a peal shall rouse their sleep
P. L. 3, 371. *s.* concord is in heaven
P. L. 3, 510. the stairs were *s.* as whereon Jacob
P. L. 3, 539. *s.* as bound the ocean wave
P. L. 3, 552. *s.* wonder seized though after
P. L. 3, 637. not of the prime yet *s.* as in his
P. L. 4, 42. ah wherefore he deserved no *s.*
P. L. 4, 92. *s.* joy ambition finds
P. L. 4, 118. heavenly minds from *s.* distempers
P. L. 4, 163. with *s.* delay well pleased they
P. L. 4, 364. and *s.* grace the hand that
P. L. 4, 372. for heaven to keep out *s.* a foe as
P. L. 4, 379. yet *s.* accept your maker's work
P. L. 4, 526. aspiring to be *s.* they taste
P. L. 4, 580. but *s.* as come well known from
P. L. 4, 705. *s.* was their awe of man
P. L. 4, 796. *s.* where ye find seize fast
P. L. 4, 887. and *s.* I held thee
P. L. 4, 996. the Eternal to prevent *s.* horrid fray
P. L. 5, 26. *s.* whispering waked her but with

P. L. 5, 31. *s.* night till this I never passed
P. L. 5, 66. at *s.* bold words vouched with
P. L. 5, 81. the gods live there and *s.* live thou
P. L. 5, 114. some *s.* resemblance methinks
P. L. 5, 149. *s.* prompt eloquence flowed
P. L. 5, 233. and *s.* discourse bring on as may
P. L. 5, 327. will pluck *s.* choice to entertain
P. L. 5, 362. none can than heaven *s.* glorious
P. L. 5, 372. nor art thou *s.* created
P. L. 5, 373. or *s.* place hast here to dwell
P. L. 5, 472. created all *s.* to perfection
P. L. 5, 521. that thou continuest *s.* owe to
P. L. 5, 530. *s.* with him finds no acceptance
P. L. 5, 582. on *s.* day as heaven's great year
P. L. 5, 650. *s.* are the courts of God
P. L. 5, 724. *s.* a foe is rising who intends to
P. L. 5, 795. over *s.* as live by right his equals
P. L. 5, 825. the powers of heaven *s.* as he
P. L. 6, 13. went forth the morn *s.* as in
P. L. 6, 114. O heaven that *s.* resemblance
P. L. 6, 168. *s.* hast thou armed the minstrelsy
P. L. 6, 193. less could his shield *s.* ruin
P. L. 6, 208. *s.* as heard in heaven till now was
P. L. 6, 229. though numbered *s.* as each
P. L. 6, 253. *s.* destruction to withstand
P. L. 6, 300. lift human imagination to *s.*
P. L. 6, 310. unsafe within the wind of *s.*
P. L. 6, 310. *s.* as, to set forth great things by
P. L. 6, 333. *s.* as celestial spirits may bleed
P. L. 6, 342. and his pride humbled by *s.*
P. L. 6, 395. to *s.* evil brought by sin
P. L. 6, 401. *s.* high advantages their innocence
P. L. 6, 488. among our foes *s.* implements
P. L. 6, 591. with *s.* impetuous fury smote
P. L. 6, 623. *s.* as we might perceive amused
P. L. 6, 660. ere they could wind out of *s.*
P. L. 6, 688. as likeliest was when two *s.* foes
P. L. 6, 703. into thee *s.* virtue and grace
P. L. 6, 788. in heavenly spirits could *s.*
P. L. 6, 837. *s.* as in their souls infixed plagues
P. L. 7, 56. with *s.* confusion
P. L. 7, 118. *s.* commission from above I have
P. L. 7, 153. if *s.* it be to lose self-lost
P. L. 7, 181. when *s.* was heard declared the
P. L. 7, 294. *s.* flight the great command
P. L. 7, 589. *s.* privilege hath Omnipresence
P. L. 8, 20. for *s.* their distance argues
P. L. 8, 27. could commit *s.* disproportions
P. L. 8, 31. on their orbs impose *s.* restless
P. L. 8, 36. as tribute *s.* a sumless journey
P. L. 8, 48. as not with *s.* discourse delighted
P. L. 8, 50. *s.* pleasure she reserved
P. L. 8, 58. O when meet now *s.* pairs in love
P. L. 8, 88. nor heaven *s.* journeys run
P. L. 8, 153. *s.* vast room in nature unpossessed
P. L. 8, 232. *s.* command we had
P. L. 8, 235. lest he incensed at *s.* eruption bold
P. L. 8, 353. with *s.* knowledge God endued
P. L. 8, 390. of fellowship I speak *s.* as I seek
P. L. 8, 446. and no *s.* company as then
P.L. 8, 482. *s.* as I saw her in my dream adorned
P. L. 8, 502. but *s.* as used or not works in the
P. L. 8, 535. not proof enough *s.* object to sustain
P. L. 8, 580. seem *s.* dear delight beyond all
P. L. 9, 127. but others to make *s.* as I
P. L. 9, 145. whether *s.* virtue spent of old
P. L. 9, 274. that *s.* an enemy we have who
P. L. 9, 282. thou fearest not being *s.* as we
P. L. 9, 292. for *s.* thou art from sin and blame
P. L. 9, 302. if *s.* affront I labour to avert
P. L. 9, 391. but with *s.* gardening tools as art
P. L. 9, 408. *s.* ambush hid among sweet flowers
P. L. 9, 455. *s.* pleasure took the serpent
P. L. 9, 520. as used to *s.* disport before her
P. L. 9, 566. say for *s.* wonder claims attention
P. L. 9, 596. for *s.* pleasure till that hour
P. L. 9, 620. in *s.* abundance lies our choice
P. L. 9, 650. wondrous indeed if cause of *s.*
P. L. 9, 693. will God incense his ire for *s.*
P. L. 9, 760. *s.* prohibitions bind not but if
P. L. 9, 787. *s.* delight till then as seemed

P. L. 9, 867. hath been tasted s. the serpent
P. L. 9, 994. s. compliance bad s. recompense
P. L. 3, 1024. if s. pleasure be in things to us
P. L. 9, 1028. as meet is after s. delicious fare
P. L. 9, 1102. but s. as at this day to Indians
P. L. 9, 1115. s. of late Columbus found
P. L. 9, 1142. when earnestly they seek s. proof
P. L. 9, 1157. going into s. danger as thou
P. L. 10, 154. her gifts were s. as under
P. L. 10, 267. s. a scent I draw of carnage
P. L. 10, 364. s. fatal consequence unites us
P. L. 10, 461. in possession s., not only of right
P. L. 10, 648. s. was their song
P. L. 10, 899. but s. as some misfortune brings
P. L. 10, 1010. but Adam with s. counsel
P. L. 10, 1026. rather s. acts of contumacy will
P. L. 10, 1078. s. fire to use and what may else
P. L. 11, 163. ill-worthy I s. title should belong
P. L. 11, 232. or of the thrones above s. majesty
P. L. 11, 297. for s. of shape may seem prince
P. L. 11, 510. to s. unsightly sufferings be
P. L. 11, 513. from s. deformities be free
P. L. 11, 593. s. happy interview and fair event
P. L. 11, 679. s. massacre make they but of
P. L. 11, 688. s. were these giants men of high
P. L. 11, 890. yet those removed s. grace shall
P. L. 12, 31. s. as refuse subjection to his
P. L. 12, 70. he made not lord s. title to himself
P. L. 12, 81. quiet state of men s. trouble brought
P. L. 12, 200. s. wondrous power God to his
P. L. 12, 230. part s. appertain to civil
P. L. 12, 245. s. delight hath God in men
P. L. 12, 284. how can God with s. reside
P. L. 12, 294. that in s. righteousness
P. L. 12, 335. s. follow him as shall be registered
P. L. 12, 372. Adam with s. joy surcharged
P. L. 12, 494. against s. cruelties with inward
P. L. 12, 622. s. favour I unworthy am
P. R. 1, 37. to whom s. high attest was given
P. R. 1, 209. and in it grew to s. perfection
P. R. 1, 299. but with s. thoughts accompanied
P. R. 1, 302. recommend s. solitude before
P. R. 1, 347. thinkest thou s. force in bread
P. R. 1, 492. disdain not s. access to me
P. R. 2, 72. in s. a season born when scarce
P. R. 2, 126. s an enemy is risen to invade us
P. R. 2, 163. s. object hath the power to soften
P. R. 2, 177. thinkest but taken with s. toys
P. R. 2, 226. with s. as have more show of
P. R. 2, 366. s. was the splendour and the
P. R. 3, 18. thy skill of conduct would be s.
P. R. 3, 54. and what delight to be by s. extolled
P. R. 3, 142. so much bounty is in God s. grace
P. R. 3, 251. s. power was given him then
P. R. 3, 337. s. forces met nor so wide
P. R. 3, 344. s. and so numerous was their
P. R. 3, 361. between two s. enclosing enemies
P. R. 3, 412. s. was thy zeal to Israel then
P. R. 4, 129. expel a devil who first made him s.
P. R. 4, 191. to me my own on s. abhorred
P. R. 4, 350. s. are from God inspired not s.
S. A. 94. to s. a tender ball as the eye confined
S. A. 290. of s. examples add me to the roll
S. A. 297. for of s. doctrine never was there school
S. A. 332. for s. ye seem though in this uncouth
S. A. 354. s. a son as all men hailed me happy
S. A. 357. and as a blessing with s. pomp adorned
S. A. 469. shall ere long receive s. a discomfit
S. A. 678. but s. as thou hast solemnly elected
S. A. 825. s. pardon therefore as I give my folly
S. A. 857. who had destroyed s. numbers of our
S. A. 862. oppose against s. powerful arguments
S. A. 1001. to s. a viper his most sacred trust
S. A. 1025. is it for that s. outward ornament
S. A. 1045. embarked with s. a steers-mate at
S. A. 1088. of whom s. noise hath walked about
S. A. 1095. wrought s. wonders with an ass's jaw
S. A. 1108. s. usage as your honourable lords
S. A. 1124. and raise s. outcries on thy clattered
S. A. 1168. all these indignities for s. they are
S. A. 1276. the righteous and all s. as honour

S. A. 1396. or we shall find s. engines to assail
S. A. 1405. s. as owe them absolute subjection
S. A. 1441. old Monoah in s. haste with youthful
S. A. 1631. for so from s. as nearer stood
S. A. 1643. now of my own accord s. other trial
C. 15. to s. my errand is and but for s.
C. 173. s. as the jocund flute or gamesome pipe
C. 186. to bring me berries or s. cooling fruit
C. 227. s. noise as I can make to be heard
C. 262. but s. a sacred and home-felt delight
C. 263. s. sober certainty of waking bliss
C. 245. breathe s. divine enchanting ravishment
C. 291. two s. I saw what time the laboured ox
C. 365. how bitter is s. self-delusion
C. 470. s. are those thick and gloomy shadows
C. 502. I came not here on s. a trivial toy
C. 519. for s. there be but unbelief is blind
C. 575. who gently asked if he had seen s. two
C. 677. is of s. power to stir up joy as this
C. 703. none but s. as are good men can give good
C. 711. with s. a full and unwithdrawing hand
C. 795. to s. a flame of sacred vehemence
C. 856. to aid a virgin s. as was herself
C. 962. and s. court guise as Mercury did first
A. 68. s. sweet compulsion doth in music lie
A. 74. and yet s. music worthiest were to blaze
A. 94. s. a rural queen
L. 49. s. Lycidas thy loss to shepherd's ear
L. 114. enow of s. as for their bellies' sake
L'A. 29. s. hang on Hebe's cheek
L'A. 129. s. sights as youthful poets dream
L'A. 138. s. as the meeting soul may pierce
L'A. 148. s. strains as would have won the ear
Il P. 17. black but s. as in esteem
Il P. 26. s. mixture was not held a stain
Il P. 106. s. notes as warbled to the string
Il P. 145. with s. consort as they keep
S. 23, 7. and s. as yet once more I trust to have
H. 93. when s. music sweet
H. 99. the air s. pleasure loth to lose
H. 101. nature that heard s. sound
H. 107. she knew s. harmony alone
H. 117. s. music as 'tis said
D. F. I. 40. in the Elysian fields (if s. there were)
U. C. I. 5. s. a shifter that if truth were known
W. S. 15. and so sepulchred in s. pomp dost lie
W. S. 16. kings for s. a tomb would wish to die
V. Ex. 33. s. where the deep transported mind
Suck.—C. 980. there I s. the liquid air
L. 140. that on the green turf s. the honied
Sucked.—P. L. 10, 633. with s. and glutted offal
Sudden.—P. L. 1, 665. the s. blaze far round
P. L. 2, 364. be achieved by s. onset
P. L. 2, 738. that my s. hand prevented
P. L. 2, 752. all on a s. miserable pain surprised
P. L. 2, 879. on a s. open fly with impetuous
P. L. 2, 890. before their eyes in s. view
P. L. 3, 542. looks down with wonder at the s.
P. L. 4, 818. with s. blaze diffused
P. L. 4, 821. so s. to behold the grisly king
P. L. 5, 51. that brought me on a s. to the tree
P. L. 5, 452. s. mind arose in Adam not to let
P. L. 5, 632. and on a s. piled with angels
P. L. 5, 653. pavilions numberless and s. reared
P. L. 5, 891. raging into s. flame
P. L. 6, 279. or some more s. vengeance winged
P. L. 6, 582. for s. all at once their reeds put
P. L. 7, 317. herbs of every leaf that s. flowered
P. L. 8, 308. stirred in me s. appetite to pluck
P. L. 8, 354. God endued my s. apprehension
P. L. 9, 900. how art thou lost how on a s. lost
P. L. 10, 453. all amazed at that so s. blaze
P. L. 10, 963. will prove no s. but a slow-paced
P. L. 11, 293. Adam by this from the cold s. damp
P. R. 1, 96. but must with something s. be
P. R. 2, 224. at every s. slighting quite abashed
S. A. 953. fierce remembrance wake my s. rage
S. A. 1691. from under ashes into s. flame
C. 452. with s. adoration and blank awe
C. 552. till an unusual stop of s. silence
C. 954. and our s. coming there

A. 2. what *s.* blaze of majesty
L. 74. and think to burst out into *s.* blaze
**Suddenly.**—P. L. 5, 90. *s.* my guide was
P. L. 6, 556. but *s.* at head appeared Satan
P. L. 8, 292. when *s.* stood at my head a dream
P. L. 8, 468. wide was the wound but *s.* with
P. L. 10, 341. guilty what his wrath might *s.*
P. L. 11, 183. air *s.* eclipsed after short blush
P. R. 2, 298. when *s.* a man before him stood
S. A. 1565. I refrain too *s.* to utter what will come
**Sue.**—P. L. 1, 111. to bow and *s.* for grace
**Sues.**—S. A. 512. him who imploring mercy *s.*
**Suffer.**—P. L. 1, 147. strongly to *s.* and
P. L. 2, 162. what can we *s.* more
P. L. 2, 163. what can we *s.* worse?
P. L. 2, 195. thus expelled to *s.* here chains
P. L. 2, 199. to *s.* as to do our strength is equal
P. L. 3, 248. nor *s.* my unspotted soul for ever
P. L. 4, 78. to which the hell I *s.* seems
P. L. 10, 213. that now must *s.* change
P. L. 10, 623. I *s.* them to enter and possess
P. R. 2, 249. or count part of what I *s.* here
P. R. 3, 194. that he may know what I can *s.*
P. R. 3, 195. who best can *s.* best can do
S.A. 233. of what now I *s.* she was not the prime
C. 40. and here their tender age might *s.* peril
C. 809. I must not *s.* this
**Sufferance.**—P. L. 1, 241. not by the *s.*
P. L. 1, 366. through God's high *s.*
P. L. 3, 198. this my long *s.* and my day of grace
P. L. 8, 202. by *s.* and thy wonted favour deigned
P. R. 1, 160. by humiliation and strong *s.*
**Suffered.**—P. L. 6, 701. and thus far have *s.*
P. L. 10, 414. planet-struck real eclipse then *s.*
P. L. 10, 470. what *s.* with what pain voyaged
P. R. 3, 97. by what he taught and *s.* for
P. R. 3, 101. and glory aught be done aught *s.*
**Sufferers.**—S. A. 1525. the *s.* then will scarce
**Suffering.**—P. L. 1, 158. miserable doing or *s.*
P. L. 2, 340. in doing what we most in *s.* feel
P. L. 11, 375. arming to overcome by *s.*
P. L. 12, 398. and *s.* death the penalty to thy
P. L. 12, 569. that *s.* for truth's sake is fortitude
P. R. 3, 98. for truth's sake *s.* death unjust
P. R. 3, 192. *s.*, abstaining quietly expecting
S. A. 701. causeless *s.* the punishment
**Sufferings.**—P. L. 4, 26. worse *s.*
P. L. 11. 510. to such unsightly *s.* be debased
S. A. 445. of all thy *s.* think the heaviest
P. 25. and former *s.* otherwhere are found
**Suffers.**—P. R. 1, 487. *s.* the hypocrite or
S. A. 458. the anguish of my soul that *s.* not
**Suffer'st.**—S. A. 744. to lighten what thou *s.*
**Suffice.**—P. L. 1, 148. that we may so *s.* his
P. L. 2, 411. what strength what art can then *s.*
P.L. 3, 189. what may *s.* and soften stony hearts
P. L. 7, 113. words or tongue of seraph can *s.*
P. L. 7, 114. or heart of man *s.* to
P. L. 8, 620. let it *s.* thee that thou know'st
**Sufficed.**—P. L. 4, 328. than *s.* to recommend
P. L. 5, 451. with meats and drinks they had *s.*
P. L. 11, 88. happier had it *s.* him to have
P. R. 2, 276. the strength whereof *s.* him forty
**Suffices.**—S. A. 63. *s.* that to me strength is
**Sufficient.**—P. L. 2, 102. feel our power *s.*
P. L. 2, 404. whom shall we find *s.* who shall
P. L. 3, 99. *s.* to have stood though free to fall
P. L. 6, 427. judged *s.* to subdue us to his will
P. L. 7, 147. number *s.* to possess her realms
P. L. 8, 5. what thanks *s.* or what recompense
P. L. 9, 43. *s.* of itself to raise that name unless
P. L. 10, 753. to the loss of that *s.* penalty why
P. L. 11, 252. *s.* that thy prayers are heard
P. R. 3, 247. *s.* introduction to inform thee
S. A. 1212. with strength *s.* and command
**Sufficiently.**—P. L. 8, 404. I to thee *s.*
**Suffrage.**—P. L. 2, 415. less choice in our *s.*
**Suffusion.**—P. L. 3, 26. orbs or dim *s* veiled
**Suggest.**—P. R. 1, 355. why dost thou then *s.*
**Suggested.**—P. L. 5. 702. tells the *s.* cause
**Suggestion.**—P. L. 1, 685. and by his *s.*

P. L. 3, 129. the first sort by their own *s.* fell
**Suggestions.**—P. L. 9, 90. and his dark *s.*
S. A. 599. believe not these *s.* which proceed
**Suing.**—S. A. 965. and *s.* for peace reap nothing
**Suit.**—P. L. 8, 388. cannot well *s.* with either
**Suitable.**—P. L. 3, 639. and to every limb *s.*
**Suitors.**—P. L. 11, 9. not of mean *s.*
**Sullen.**—P. R. 1, 500. night with her *s.* wing
II P. 76. swinging slow with *s.* roar
S. 20, 4. and by the fire help waste a *s.* day
H. 205. and *s.* Moloch fled hath left in shadows
V. Ex. 95. or *s.* Mole that runneth underneath
**Sulphur.**—P. L. 1, 69. with ever-burning *s.*
P. L. 1, 674. metallic ore the work of *s.*
P.L.2, 69. throne itself mixed with Tartarean *s.*
**Sulphurous.**—P. L. 1, 171. the *s.* hail shot
P. L. 6, 512. *s.* and nitrous foam they found
P. L. 11, 658. dart and javelin stones and *s.*
**Sultan.**—P. L. 1, 348. spear of their great *S.*
P. L. 11, 395. the *S.* in Bizance Turchestan-born
**Sultry.**—S. A. 1246. lower looks but in a *s.* chafe
L. 28. what time the gray-fly winds her *s.* horn
**Sum.**—P. L. 6, 673. consulting on the *s.* of things
P. L. 8. 522. and brought my story to the *s.*
P. L. 12, 338. faults heaped to the popular *s.*
P. L. 12, 575. thou hast attained the *s.*
P. R. 1, 283. and last the *s.* of all my Father's
S. A. 1557. tell us the *s.* the circumstance defer
**Sumless.**—P. L. 8, 36. such a *s.* journey brought
**Summed.**—P. L. 7, 421. they *s.* their pens
P. L. 8, 473. or in her *s.* up, in her contained
P. L. 9, 113. of growth sense reason all *s.* up
P. R. 1, 14. with prosperous wing full *s.* to tell
S. A. 395. in what part *s.* that she might know
**Summer.**—P. L. 1, 449. all a *s.'s* day
P. L. 1, 744. from noon to dewy eve a *s.'s* day
P. L. 2, 309. still as night or *s.'s* noontide air
P. L. 3, 43. or sight of vernal bloom or *s.'s* rose
P. L. 7, 478. all the liveries decked of *s.'s* pride
P. L. 9, 447. forth issuing on a *s.'s* morn
P. L. 10, 656. to bring solstitial *s.'s* heat
P. R. 3, 222. cool interposition as a *s.'s* cloud
P. R. 4, 246. thick-warbled notes the *s.* long
C. 923. *s.* drouth or singed air
C. 988. there eternal *s.* dwells
L'A. 130. on *s.* eves by haunted stream
D. F. I. 3. *s.'s* chief honour if thou hadst
**Summer-fly.**—S. A. 676. and perish as the *s.-f.*
**Summers.**—M. W. 7. *s.* three times eight save
**Summon.**—P. L. 9, 374. *s.* all
P. R. 2, 143. I *s.* all rather to be in readiness
**Summoned.**—P. L. 6, 75. came *s.* over Eden
P. L. 8, 347. not hither *s.* since they cannot
**Summoning.**—P. L. 3, 325. the *s.* archangels
**Summons.**—P. L. 1, 757. their *s.* called from
P. L. 1, 798. and *s.* read the great consult began
P. L. 5, 584. by imperial *s.* called
P. L. 11, 81. of light hasted resorting to the *s.*
P. R. 1, 40. to council *s.* all his mighty peers
C. 988. till thou our *s.* answered have
**Sumptuous.**—P. R. 4, 114. their *s.* gluttonies
S. A. 1072. the *s.* Dalila floating
**Sums.**—P. L. 1, 571. their number last he *s.*
P. L. 9, 454. and in her look *s.* all delight
**Sun.**—P. L. 1, 594. as when the *s.* new risen
P. L. 1, 744. and with the setting *s.*
P. L. 1, 769. when the *s.* with Taurus rides
P. L. 2, 492. if chance the radiant *s.* with
P. L. 3, 8. before the *s.* before the heavens
P. L. 3, 551. which now the rising *s.* gilds with
P. L. 3, 572. above them all the golden *s.*
P. L. 3, 589. in the *s.'s* lucent orb
P. L. 3, 609. the arch-chemic *s.* so far from us
P. L. 3, 623. same whom John saw also in the *s.*
P. L. 3, 690. Uriel though regent of the *s.*
P. L. 4, 29. and the full-blazing *s.*
P. L. 4, 37. and add thy name O *s.* to tell thee
P. L. 4, 150. which the *s.* more glad impressed
P. L. 4, 244. where the morning *s.* first warmly
P. L. 4, 352. for the *s.* declined was hasting
P. L. 4, 540. the setting *s.* slowly descended

P. L. 4, 578. amid the *s.'s* bright circle where
P. L. 4, 591. bore him slope downward to the *s.*
P. L. 4, 642. pleasant the *s.* when first on this
P. L. 4, 651. nor rising *s.* on this delightful
P. L. 4, 673. to receive perfection from the *s.*
P. L. 4, 792. this evening from the *s.'s* decline
P. L. 5, 139. the *s.* who scarce uprisen
P. L. 5, 171. thou *s.* of this great world
P. L. 5, 175. moon that now meet'st the orient *s.*
P. L. 5, 187. till the *s.* paint your fleecy skirts
P. L. 5, 273. to enshrine his reliques in the *s.'s*
P. L. 5, 300. while now the mounted *s.* shot
P. L. 5, 370. and the *s.* more cool decline
P. L. 5, 423. the *s.* that light imparts to all
P. L. 5, 558. scarce the *s.* hath finished half
P. L. 5, 746. morning dew-drops which the *s.*
P. L. 7, 247. radiant cloud for yet the *s.* was
P. L. 7, 354. for of celestial bodies first the *s.*
P. L. 7, 361. and placed in the *s.'s* orb made
P. L. 7, 406. show to the *s.* their waved coats
P. L. 7, 582. the *s.* was set and twilight from
P. L. 8, 94. contain more plenty than the *s.*
P. L. 8, 122. what if the *s.* be centre to the
P. L. 8, 133. or save the *s.* his labour
P. L. 8, 139. her part averse from the *s.'s* beam
P. L. 8, 160. whether the *s.* ... . rise on the earth
P. L. 8, 161. or earth rise on the *s.*
P. L. 8, 255. with his beams the *s.* soon dried
P. L. 8, 273. thou *s.* said I fair light and thou
P. L. 8, 630. the parting *s.* beyond the earth's
P. L. 9, 48. the *s.* was sunk and after him the
P. L. 9, 60. since Uriel, regent of the *s.*
P. L. 9, 721. warmed by the *s.* producing
P. L. 10, 92. now was the *s.* in western
P. L. 10, 329. while the *s.* in Aries rose
P. L. 10, 529. than whom the *s.* engendered
P. L. 10, 651. the *s.* had first his precept so to
P. L. 10, 663. of them rising with the *s.* or
P. L. 10, 670. and more from the *s.'s* axle
P. L. 10, 671. some say the *s.* was bid
P. L. 10, 682. shone while the low *s.*
P. L. 10, 688. the *s.* as from Thyestean
P. L. 10, 1078. which might supply the *s.*
P. L. 11, 278. who now shall rear ye to the *s.*
P. L. 11, 844. and the clear *s.* on his wide
P. L. 12, 263. or how the *s.* shall in mid
P. L. 12, 265. commanding *s.* in Gibeon stand
P. R. 4, 432. and now the *s.* with more
S. A. 3. yonder bank hath choice of *s.* or shade
S. A. 86. the *s.* to me is dark
C. 30. all this tract that fronts the falling *s.*
C. 51. knows not Circe the daughter of the *s.*
C. 98. and the slope *s.* his upward beam
C. 141. and to the tell-tale *s.* descry
C. 374. though *s.* and moon were in the flat sea
C. 384. benighted walks under the mid-day *s.*
C. 736. gaze upon the *s.* with shameless brows
L. 190. now the *s.* had stretched out all the hills
L'A. 60. where the great *s.* begins his state
Il P. 131. and when the *s.* begins to fling
S. 8, 8. whatever clime the *s.'s* bright circle
S. 12, 7. which after held the *s.* and moon in fee
S. 22, 5. of *s.* or moon or star throughout the
H. 19. while the heaven by the *s.'s* team untrod
H. 36. to wanton with the *s.* her lusty paramour
H. 79. the *s.* himself withheld his wonted speed
H. 83. he saw a greater *s.* appear
H. 229. so when the *s.* in bed
**Sun-beam.**—P. L. 4, 556. gliding on a *s.-b.*
**Sun-beams.**—Il P. 8. motes that people the *s.-b.*
**Sun-bright.**—P. L. 6, 100. in his *s.-b.* chariot
**Sun-clad.**—C. 782. against the *s.-c.* power of
**Sung.**—P. L. 3, 18. I *s.* of Chaos and eternal
P. L. 3, 372. thee father first they *s.*
P. L. 4, 603. night long her amorous descant *s.*
P. L. 4, 711. heavenly choirs the hymenæan *s.*
P. L. 5, 148. in fit strains pronounced or *s.*
P. L. 5, 405. he gives whose praise be ever *s.*
P. L. 6, 526. and to arms the matin trumpet *s.*
P. L. 6, 886. *s.* triumph and him *s.* victorious
P. L. 7, 182. glory they *s.* to the Most High

P. L. 7, 259. and his works Creator him they *s.*
P. L. 7, 275. so even and morning chorus *s.*
P. L. 7, 565. open ye everlasting gates they *s.*
P. L. 7, 573. on errands of supernal grace so *s.*
P. L. 7, 601. the six days' acts they *s.*
P. L. 7, 633. so *s.* they and the empyrean rung
P. L. 8, 519. till the amorous bird of night *s.*
P. L. 10, 642. *s.* halleluiah as the sound of seas
P. L. 10, 643. through multitude that *s.*
P. L. 11, 583. to the harp they *s.* soft amorous
P. L. 12, 367. squadroned angels hear his carol *s.*
P. R. 1, 1. I who erewhile the happy garden *s.*
P. R. 1, 172. while the hand *s.* with the voice
P. R. 1, 243. in the fields of Bethlehem *s.*
P. R. 3, 178. the prophets old who *s.* thy endless
P. R. 4, 258. who gave them breath but higher *s.*
P. R. 4, 506. on thy birth-night that *s.* thee
P. R. 4, 594. angelic choirs *s.* heavenly anthems
P. R. 4, 637. *s.* victor and from heavenly feast
S. A. 203. am I not *s.* and proverbed for a fool
S. A. 983. *s.* at solemn festivals
C. 256. who as they *s.* would take the prisoned
A. 29. of that renowned flood so often *s.*
Il P. 117. in sage and solemn tunes have *s.*
S. 1, 11. as thou from year to year hast *s.*
H. 119. but when of old the sons of morning *s.*
Cir. 4. so sweetly *s.* your joy the clouds along
S. M. 7. aye *s.* before the sapphire-coloured
**Sunk.**—P. L. 1, 436. *s.* before the spear
P. L. 2, 81. compulsion and laborious flight we *s.*
P. L. 2, 182. or for ever *s.* under yon boiling
P. L. 2, 594. where armies whole have *s.*
P. L. 5, 91. and I methought *s.* down
P. L. 6, 198. a mountain from his seat half *s.*
P. L. 7, 289. down *s.* a hollow bottom
P. L. 8, 457. and spent *s.* down
P. L. 8, 593. not *s.* in carnal pleasure
P. L. 9, 48. the sun was *s.* and after him the star
P. L. 9, 74. in with the river *s.* and with it rose
P. L. 11, 420. *s.* down and all his spirits became
P. L. 11, 758. drowned and *s.* thee as thy sons
P. R. 4, 398. darkness now rose as daylight *s.*
C. 375. sun and moon were in the flat sea *s.*
L. 102. that *s.* so low that sacred head of thine
L. 167. *s.* though he be beneath the watery floor
L. 172. so Lycidas *s.* low but mounted high
P. 40. now *s.* in guiltless blood
**Sun-light.**—P. L. 9, 1087. to star or *s.-l.*
**Sunny.**—P. L. 3, 28. shady grove or *s.* hill
P. L. 3, 625. of beaming *s.* rays a golden tiar
P. L. 8, 262. and shady woods and *s.* plains
P. R. 4, 447. him walking on a *s.* hill he found
**Sunrise.**—S. A. 1597. the gates I entered with *s.*
**Suns.**—P. L. 6, 305. two broad *s.* their shields
P. L. 8, 148. and other *s.* perhaps with their
**Sunshine.**—P. L. 3, 616. nor shade but all *s.*
C. 959. enough your play, till next *s.* holiday
L'A. 98. on a *s.* holiday
**Superficially.**—P. L. 6, 476. eye so *s.*
**Superfluous.**—P. L. 4, 832. and *s.* begin
P. L. 5, 325. and *s.* moist consumes
P. L. 8, 27. with *s.* hand so many nobler bodies
P. L. 9, 308. nor think *s.* others' aid
S. 21, 13. that with *s.* burden loads the day
**Superior.**—P. L. 1, 283. when the *s.* fiend
P. L. 3, 737. as to *s.* spirits is wont in heaven
P. L. 4, 499. submissive charms smiled with *s.*
P. L. 5, 360. as to a *s.* nature bowing low
P. L. 5, 705. the wonted signal and *s.* voice
P. L. 5, 905. which he sustained *s.*
P. L. 6, 443. other hidden cause left them *s.*
P. L. 8, 532. *s.* and unmoved
P. L. 9, 825. sometime *s.*
P. L. 9, 1131. sovran reason claimed *s.* sway
P. L. 10, 147. was she made thy guide *s.*
P. L. 11, 636. his place by wisdom and *s.* gifts
P. R. 4, 167. and worship me as thy *s.* lord
P. R. 4, 324. and judgment equal or *s.*
C. 801. her words set off by some *s.* power
**Supernal.**—P. L. 1, 241. the sufferance of *s.*
P. L. 7, 573. messengers on errands of *s.* grace

P. L. 11,359. s. grace contending with sinfulness
**Supernumerary.**—P. L. 10, 887. s. to my
**Superscription.**—S. A. 190. bear in their s.
U. C. II. 34. only remains this s.
**Superstition.**—P. L. 3, 452. of painful s.
S. A.15. unwillingly this rest their s. yields me
**Superstitions.**—P. L. 12, 512. with s. and
**Superstitious.**—P. R. 2, 296. and to a s.
**Supped.**—U. C. I. 18. Hobson has s. and's
**Supper.**—P. L. 4, 331. to their s. fruits they
P. L. 9, 225. the hour of s. comes unearned
P. R. 2, 273. he found his s. on the coals
C. 293. and the swinked hedger at his s. sat
C. 541. had ta'en their s. on the savoury herb
**Supplanted.**—P. L. 10, 513. till s. down he
P. R. 4, 607. now thou hast avenged s. Adam
**Supple.**—P. L. 5, 788. to bend the s. knee
P. L. 8, 269. with s. joints as lively vigour led
**Suppliant.**—P. L. 1, 112. for grace with s.
P. L. 10, 917. thy s. I beg and clasp thy knees
S. A. 1173. gracious to re-admit the s.
**Supplication.**—P. L. 5, 867. whether by s.
P L. 11, 31. therefore bend thine ear to s.
S. A. 1459. with s. prone and father's tears
**Supplied.**—S. A. 926. cheered and so s.
**Supply.**—P. L. 2, 834. upstart creatures to s.
P. L. 10, 1001. s. with our own hands
P. L. 10, 1078. which might s. the sun
P. L. 11, 740. the hills to their s. vapour and
**Support.**—P. L. 1, 23. what is low raise and s.
P. L. 1, 147. strongly to suffer and s. our pains
P. L. 1, 295. to s. uneasy steps
P. L. 9, 427. oft stooping to s. each flower
P. L. 10, 834. couldst thou s. that burden
P. R. 2, 250. or God s. nature without repast
S. A. 554. and strongest drinks our chief s.
S. A. 1274. and industrious to s. tyrannic power
S. A. 1634. that to the arched roof gave main s.
**Supported.**—P. L. 12, 496. and oft s.
**Supports.**—S. 22, 9. what s. me dost thou ask?
**Suppose.**—P. L. 2, 237. s. he should relent
P. L. 6,617. but I s. if our proposals once again
S. A.334. as I s. towards your once gloried friend
C. 307. to find out that good shepherd I s.
C. 477. not harsh and crabbed as dull fools s.
**Supposed.**—P. L. 1, 451. s. with blood of
P. L. 4, 130. then alone as he s. all unobserved
P. L. 4, 281. by some s. true Paradise
P. L. 8, 134. nocturnal and diurnal rhomb s.
P. L. 9, 297. s. not incorruptible
P. L. 10, 809. not one stroke as I s. bereaving
**Supposes.**—P. R. 3, 355. s. means
**Supposest.**—P. L. 8, 86. and s. that bodies
**Supposing.**—S. A. 1443. s. here to find his son
C. 576. s. him some neighbour villager
**Suppressed.**—P. L. 7, 123. hath s. in night
**Supremacy.**—P. L. 1, 132. his high s.
P. L. 3, 205. sins against the high s. of heaven
**Supreme.**— P. L. 1, 248. force hath made s.
P. L. 1, 735. whom the s. king exalted to such
P. L. 2, 210. our s. foe in time may much remit
P.L.2,236. unless heaven's Lord s. we over-power
P. L. 2, 510. dread emperor with pomp s.
P. L. 3, 319. under thee as head s.
P. L. 3, 659. and here art likeliest by s. decree
P. L. 4. 91. the lower still I fall only s. in misery
P. L. 4, 956. to the acknowledged Power s.
P. L. 5, 670. unobeyed the throne s.
P. L. 6, 27. and present before the seat s.
P. L. 6,723. O Father O S. of heavenly thrones
P. L. 6, 814. to whom in heaven s. kingdom
P. L. 7, 142. the seat of Deity s.
P. L. 7,515. and worship God s. who made him
P. L. 8, 414. thoughts come short, S. of things
P. L. 9, 125. unless by mastering heaven's S.
P. L. 10, 28. towards the throne s. accountable
P. L. 10, 70. heaven and earth to do thy will s.
P.L.10,480. clamorous uproar protesting fate s.
P. L. 11, 82. till from his throne s.
P. R. 1, 99. their king their leader and s.
P. R. 4, 186. king of kings God over all s.

C. 217. that He the S. Good to whom all things
T. 17. about the s. throne of him to whose
**Sups.**—P. L. 5, 426. at even s. with the ocean
**Surceased.**—P. L. 6, 258. his warlike toil s.
S. A. 404. she s. not day nor night to storm me
**Surcharged.**—P. L. 2, 836. lest heaven s.
P. L. 5, 58. fair plant, said he, with fruit s.
P. L. 12, 373. with such joy s. as had like grief
S.A.728.like a fair flower s. with dew she weeps
S. A. 769. by itself with aggravations not s.
C. 728. would be quite s. with her own weight
**Sure.**—P. L. 1, 158. but of this be s.
P. L. 2, 32. for none s. will claim in hell
P. L. 2, 154. that he never will is s.
P. L. 2, 169. that s. was worse
P. L. 2, 323. for he be s. in height or depth
P. L. 3, 478. and they who to be s. of Paradise
P. L. 4, 841. for thou be s. shalt give account
P. L. 5, 168. s. pledge of day that crown'st
P. L. 5, 721. nearly it now concerns us to be s.
P. L. 6, 647. amaze be s. and terror seized
P. L. 7, 267. partition firm and s. the waters
P. L. 7, 586. fixed for ever firm and s.
P. L. 9, 756. for good unknown s. is not had
P. L. 9, 1080. of the first be s.
P. L. 10, 402. him first make s. your thrall
P. L. 11, 772. evil he may be s. which neither
P. L. 12, 485. be s. they will said the angel
P. R. 2, 35. for s. deliverance is at hand
P. R. 3, 363. one of these thou must make s.
P. R. 4, 391. eternal s. as without end
P. R. 4, 477. if thou observe not this be s. to
P. R. 4, 483. may warn thee as a s. foregoing
S. A. 424. this I am s. our foes found soon
S. A. 465. he be s. will not connive or linger
S. A. 1385. nothing to do be s.
S. A. 1408. yet this be s. in nothing to comply
C. 148. some virgin s. for so I can distinguish
C. 246. s. something holy lodges in that breast
C. 310. without the s. guess of well practised
C. 493. O brother 'tis my father's shepherd s.
S. 9, 11. that reaps not shame therefore be s.
P. 48. for s. so well instructed are my tears
U. C. II. 18. s. I'll ne'er be fetched
**Surely.**—P. L. 4, 923. thou s. hadst not
H. 60. they s. knew their sovran Lord was by
U.C.I.9 and s. death could never have prevailed
D. F. I. 36. resolve me then O soul most s. blest
**Surer.**—P. L. 2, 39. s. to prosper than
P. L. 4, 897. let him s. bar his iron gates
P. L. 11, 856. and after him the s. messenger
**Surest.**—P. L.1,278. in all assaults their s. signal
P. L. 4, 407. whence rushing he might s.
**Surety.**—P. L. 5, 538. on other s. none
**Surface.**—P. L. 6, 472. beholds the bright s.
H. 162. shall from the s. to the centre shake
**Surfeit.**—P. L. 5, 639. and joy secure of s.
P. L. 7, 129. oppresses else with s. and soon
P. L. 11, 795. ease and sloth s. and lust
S. A. 1562. there may in grief be s.
C. 480. where no crude s. reigns
**Surge.**—P. L. 1, 173. hath laid the fiery s.
P. L. 10, 417. and with rebounding s. the bars
**Surging.**—P. L. 2, 928. and in the s. smoke
P. L. 7, 214. and s. waves as mountains
P. L. 9, 499. fold above fold a s. maze
P. R. 4, 18. or s. waves against a solid rock
**Surmise.**—P. L. 9, 333. gain from his s.
P. L. 11, 340. s. not then his presence to these
L. 153. let our frail thoughts dally with false s.
**Surmounts.**—P. L. 5, 571. and what s. the
S. A. 1380. how thou wilt come off s. my reach
**Surnamed.**—P. R. 2, 199. how he s. of Africa
P. R. 4, 279. with those s. Peripatetics
**Surpass.**—P. L. 1, 778. in bigness to s. earth's
P. L. 2, 370. this would s. common revenge
P. L. 11, 894. nor let the sea s. his bounds
**Surpassed.**—P. L. 9, 389. Delia's self in gait s.
**Surpassest.**—P. L. 8, 359. s. far my naming
**Surpassing.**—P. L. 4, 32. with s. glory
P. L. 7, 640. aught not s. human measure say

S.A.1313.thy strength they know *s*.human rate
**Surprisal.**—P. L. 5, 245. he pretend *s*.
C. 618. how to secure the lady from *s*.
**Surprise.**—P. L. 2, 134. scorning *s*.
P. L. 6, 87. that self-same day by fight or by *s*.
P. L. 7, 547. lest sin *s*. thee and her black
P. L. 11, 218. who to *s*. one man assassin like
P. L. 12, 453. there shall *s*. the serpent
**Surprised.**—P. L. 2, 753. pain *s*. thee
P. L. 4, 814. up he starts discovered and *s*.
P. L. 6, 393. with fear *s*., then first with fear *s*.
P. L. 6, 774. them unexpected joy *s*.
P. L. 9, 354. lest by some fair appearing good *s*.
P. R. 1, 108. distracted and *s*. with deep dismay
P. R. 1, 155. the first man lost by fallacy *s*.
S. A. 881. this well I knew nor was at all *s*.
S. A. 1285. who *s*. lose their defence
C. 590. *s*. by unjust force but not enthralled
**Surrender.**—P. L. 4, 494. with meek *s*.
**Surround.**—P. L. 2, 796. *s*. me as thou sawest
**Surrounding.**—P. L. 1, 346. and *s*. fires
C. 403. uninjured in this wild *s*. waste
**Surrounds.**—P. L. 3, 46. ever-during dark *s*.
H. 109. at last *s*. their sight
**Survey.**—P. L. 8, 24. in all their vast *s*.
S. A. 1089. and each limb to *s*. if thy appearance
S. A. 1227. camest thou for this vain boaster to *s*.
S. A. 1230. take good heed my hand *s*. not thee
**Surveyed.**—P. L. 1, 456. his eye *s*. the dark
P. L. 3, 69. he then *s*. hell and the gulf
P. L. 8, 268. I then perused and limb by limb *s*.
P. R. 1, 37. awhile *s*. with wonder
**Surveying.**—P. L. 7, 353. God saw *s*.
**Surveys.**—P. L. 3, 555. round he *s*.
P. L. 6, 476. whose eye so superficially *s*. these
**Survives.**—S. A. 1706. her body die her fame *s*.
**Sus.**—P. L. 11, 403. of Almansor, Fez and *S*.
**Susa.**—P. L. 10, 308. from *S*., his Memnonian
P. R. 3, 288. there *S*. by Choaspes amber
**Susiana.**—P. R. 3, 321. of *S*. to Balsara's
**Suspect.**—P. L. 9, 337. let us not then *s*. our
P. L. 10, 140. from her hand I could *s*. no ill
P. R. 2, 399. I see what I can do or offer is *s*.
S. A. 272. and to despise or envy or *s*.
V. Ex. 27. that so they may without *s*. or fears
**Suspected.**—P. L. 12, 165. and now grown *s*.
P. R. 1, 124. so to subvert whom he *s*. raised
**Suspend.**—P. L. 6, 692. for I *s*. their doom
**Suspended.**—P. L. 2, 554. harmony *s*. hell
**Suspense.**—P. L. 2, 418. held his look *s*.
P. L. 6, 580. while we *s*. collected stood
P. L. 7, 99. *s*. in heaven held by thy voice thy
S. A. 1569. *s*. in news is torture speak them out
**Suspicion.**—P. L. 3, 686. *s*. sleeps at wisdom's
P. L. 9, 1124. anger hate mistrust *s*. discord
C. 413. and gladly banish squint *s*.
**Suspicious.**—P. L. 4, 516. *s*. reasonless
P. L. 9, 92. whatever sleights none would *s*.
P. R. 2, 82. little *s*. to any king
P. R. 4, 96. public cares and yet of him *s*.
C. 158. and put the damsel to *s*. flight
**Sustain.**—P. L. 2, 209. which if we can *s*. and
P. L. 8, 535. not proof enough such object to *s*.
P. L. 9, 978. I would *s*. alone the worst and
P. L. 10, 950. ill able to *s*. his full wrath
P. L. 10, 1056. my labour will *s*. me
P. L. 11, 302. our frailty can *s*.
P. L. 12, 75. will he convey up thither to *s*.
P. R. 3, 19. the world could not *s*. thy prowess
S. A. 1258. they cannot well impose nor I *s*.
**Sustained.**—P. L. 5, 415. needs to be *s*. and fed
P. L. 5, 904. which he *s*. superior nor of
P. L. 6, 423. who have *s*. one day in doubtful
P. L. 9, 336. alone without exterior help *s*.
P. L. 10, 1083. commodiously this life *s*. by
**Sustenance.**—P. R. 1, 429. is thy *s*. thy food
**Swaddling.**—H. 228. can in his *s*. bands
**Swage.**—P. L. 1, 556. power to mitigate and *s*.
S. A. 184. apt words have power to *s*.
**Swain.**—P. R. 1, 337. he may replied the *s*.
C. 84. and take the weeds and likeness of a *s*.

C. 497. how camest thou here good *s*.?
C. 634. and the dull *s*. treads on it daily
C. 852. and as the old *s*. said she can unlock
C. 900. gentle *s*. at thy request I am here
L. 92. hard mishap hath doomed this gentle *s*.
L. 113.well could I have spared for thee young *s*.
L. 186. thus sang the uncouth *s*. to the oaks
M. W. 38. plucked up by some unheedy *s*.
**Swains.**—C. 951. all the *s*. that there abide
A. 26. stay gentle *s*. for though in this disguise
**Swallowed.**—P. L. 1, 142. here *s*. up in
P. L. 2, 149. to perish rather *s*. up and lost
P. L. 9, 642. there *s*. up and lost from succour
P. 7. soon *s*. up in dark
**Swallows.**—P. L. 12, 196. the sea *s*. him
**Swan.**—P. L. 7, 438. the *s*. with arched neck
**Swarm.**—P. L. 2, 903. *s*. populous unnumbered
P. L. 7, 400. fry innumerable *s*. and shoals of
P. R. 1, 197. at once awakened in me *s*.
P. R. 4, 15. or as a *s*. of flies in vintage time
S. A. 19. that like a deadly *s*. of hornets
S. A. 192. in prosperous days they *s*.
**Swarmed.**—P. L. 1, 767. thick *s*. both on the
P. L. 1, 776. the aery crowd *s*. and were
P. L. 10, 526. not so thick *s*. once the soil
**Swarming.**—P. L. 7, 489. *s*. next the female bee
P. L. 21, 185. a darksome cloud of locusts *s*.
**Swart.**—C. 436. no goblin or *s*. faery of the
**Swart-star.**—L. 138. fresh lap the *s*.-*s*. sparely
**Sway**—P. L. 2, 984. darkness and your *s*.
P. L. 4, 308. but required with gentle *s*.
P. L. 6, 234. or turn the *s*. of battle
P. L. 6, 251. with huge two-handed *s*.
P. L. 8, 635. take heed lest passion *s*. thy
P. L. 9, 1131. reason claimed superior *s*.
P. L. 10, 376. there let him still victor *s*.
P. L. 11, 405. where Rome was to *s*. the world
P. R. 3, 160. is always ruled with temperate *s*.
P. R. 3, 405. and his full sceptre *s*. to just
S. A. 791. the jealousy of love powerful of *s*.
C. 18. Neptune besides the *s*. of every salt flood
S. 18, 11. the Italian fields where still doth *s*.
H. 170. casts his usurped *s*.
**Swayed.**—P. L. 10, 1010. counsel nothing *s*.
S. A. 1059. not *s*. by female usurpation
S. M. 22. whose love their motion *s*.
**Sways.**—P. L. 4, 983. which way the wind *s*.
C. 825. with moist curb *s*. the smooth Severn
**Sweat.**—P. L. 8, 255. in balmy *s*.
P. L. 10, 205. in the *s*. of thy face shalt thou
P. L. 11, 172. calls us now with *s*. imposed
L'A. 105. how the drudging goblin *s*.
H. 195. and the chill marble seems to *s*.
**Sweaty.**—P. L. 11, 434. a *s*. reaper from his
**Swede.**—S. 21, 8. and what the *S*. intend
**Sweep.**—L. 17. somewhat loudly *s*. the string
**Sweeping.**—Il P. 98. sceptred pall come *s*. by
**Sweet.**—P. L. 1, 712. symphonies and voices *s*.
P. L. 2, 492. the radiant sun with farewell *s*.
P. L. 2, 555. in discourse more *s*.
P. L. 2, 608. to lose in *s*. forgetfulness all pain
P. L. 2, 820. joys then *s*. now sad to mention
P. L. 3, 42. the *s*. approach of even or morn
P. L. 3, 346. *s*. as from blest voices
P. L. 3, 367. and with preamble *s*. of charming
P. L. 4, 272. nor that *s*. grove of Daphne
P. L. 4, 298. softness she and *s*. attractive grace
P. L. 4, 311. and *s*. reluctant amorous delay
P. L. 4, 328. their *s*. gardening labour
P. L. 4, 439. toilsome yet with thee were *s*.
P. L. 4, 641. *s*. is the breath of morn her rising
P. L. 4, 646. *s*. the coming on of grateful evening
P. L. 4, 656. without thee is *s*.
P. L. 5, 25. on the bloom extracting liquid *s*.
P. L. 5, 59. to ease thy load and taste thy *s*.
P. L. 5, 68. *s*. of thyself but much more *s*. thus
P. L. 5, 134. the gracious signs of *s*. remorse
P. L. 5, 170. day arises that *s*. hour of prime
P. L. 5, 212. among *s*. dews and flowers where
P. L. 5, 296. fancies pouring forth more *s*.
P. L. 5, 346. and from *s*. kernels pressed

P. L. 5, 630. forthwith from dance to s. repast
P. L. 5, 637. and in communion s. quaff
P. L. 7, 319. made gay her bosom smelling s.
P. L. 7, 375. danced shedding s. influence
P. L. 7, 596. and dulcimer all organs of s. stop
P. L. 8, 184. thoughts to interrupt the s. of life
P. L. 8, 214. at the hour of s. repast they satiate
P. L. 8, 603. with love and s. compliance
P. L. 9, 115. s. interchange of hill and
P. L. 9, 171. revenge at first though s. bitter
P. L. 9, 238. or this s. intercourse of looks and
P. L. 9, 250. short retirement urges s. return
P. L. 9, 272. with s. austere composure thus
P. L. 9, 321. her reply with accent s. renewed
P. L. 9, 407. either s. repast or sound repose
P. L. 9, 408. such ambush hid among s. flowers
P. L. 9, 456. this flowery plat, the s. recess of
P. L. 9, 461. with rapine s. bereaved his
P. L. 9, 473. with what s. compulsion
P. L. 9, 899. holy divine good amiable or s.
P. L. 9, 909. thy s. converse and love so dearly
P. L. 9, 986. that what of s. before hath
P. L. 10, 228. recounted mixing intercession s.
P. L. 10, 359. with thine joined in connexion s.
P. L. 10, 994. due rites nuptial embraces s.
P. L. 11, 281. what to sight or smell was s.
P. L. 11, 303. this happy place our s. recess
P. L. 12, 5. then with transition s. new speech
P. L. 12, 221. life to noble and ignoble is more s.
P. R. 1, 207. and found it s. made it my whole
P. R. 2, 160. majesty with mild and s. allayed
P. R. 2, 265. and drink nature's refreshment s.
P. R. 2, 373. with s. restorative delight
P. R. 4, 16. the wine-press where s. must is
P. R. 4, 242. or hospitable in her s. recess
P. R. 4, 438. to gratulate the s. return of morn
S. A. 10. of heaven fresh blowing pure and s.
S. A. 1737. in copious legend or s. lyric song
C. 47. crushed the s. poison of misused wine
C. 230. s. Echo, sweetest nymph that livest
C. 241. tell me but where s. queen of parley
C. 261. and in s. madness robbed it of itself
C. 368. the s. peace that goodness bosoms ever
C. 567. how s. thou singest how near the deadly
C. 850. throw s. garland wreaths into her stream
C. 878. and the song of Sirens s.
C. 1005. holds his dear Psyche s. entranced
A. 68. such s. compulsion doth in music lie
L. 179. in solemn troops and s. societies
L'A. 36. the mountain-nymph s. liberty
Il P. 61. s. bird that shunnest the noise of folly
Il P. 151. and as I wake s. music breathe
H. 23. the star-led wizards haste with odours s.
H. 93. when such music s.
M. W. 15. her high birth and her graces s.
M. W. 50. s. rest seize thee evermore
V. Ex. 52. in willing chains and s. captivity
D. F. I. 71. then thou the mother of so s. a child
**Sweet-briar.**—L'A. 47. the s.-b. or the vine
**Sweetened.**—C. 496. and s. every muskrose
**Sweeter.**—P. L. 8, 211. and s. thy discourse
**Sweetest.**—P. L. 5, 41. now awake tunes s.
P. L. 9, 200. the season prime for s. scents
P. L. 9, 581. than smell of s. fennel
P. L. 10, 609. season him thy last and s. prey
C. 230. sweet Echo s. nymph that livest unseen
L'A. 133. or s. Shakespeare, Fancy's child
Il P. 57. in her s., saddest plight
**Sweetly.**—V. Ex. 63. and s. singing round about
C. 249. how s. did they float upon the wings
Cir. 4. so s. sung your joy the clouds along
**Sweetness.**—P. L. 5, 152. to add more s.
P. L. 8, 216. bring to their s. no satiety
P. L. 8, 475. infused s. into my heart unfelt
L'A. 140. of linked s. long drawn out
Il P. 164. as may with s. through mine ear
S. 23. 11. love s. goodness in her person shined
**Sweets.**—P. L. 4, 166. odorous s. the fiend
P. L. 4, 760. perpetual fountain of domestic s.
P. L. 5, 294. a wilderness of s.

C. 123. night hath better s. to prove
C. 479. and a perpetual feast of nectared s.
**Sweet-smelling.**—P. L. 4, 709. s.-s. herbs
P. L. 11, 327. thereon offer s.-s. gums and
**Sweet-smiling.** D. F. I. 53. thou that s.-s. youth
**Swell.**—P. R. 3, 81. then s. with pride
C. 732. the sea o'erfraught would s.
**Swelling.**—P. L. 4, 495. half her s. breast
P. L. 7, 321. forth crept the s. gourd
P. R. 4, 343. remove their s. epithets thick laid
**Swerve.**—P. L. 5, 238. to beware he s. not
P. L. 5, 902. to s. from truth or change his
P. L. 9, 359. firm we subsist yet possible to s.
**Swerved.**—P. L. 6, 386. the battle s.
**Swift.**—P. L. 1, 326. his s. pursuers from heaven
P. L. 2, 529. upon the wing or in s. race
P. L. 2, 631. puts on s. wings and toward the
P. L. 2, 902. heavy, sharp, smooth, s. or slow
P. L. 3, 582. his all-cheering lamp turn s.
P. L. 3, 652. or down to the earth bear his s.
P. L. 3, 714. s. to their several quarters hasted
P. L. 4, 556. on a sun-beam s. as a shooting star
P. L. 4, 593. the prime orb incredible how s.
P. L. 5, 907. proud towers to s. destruction
P. L. 6, 190. which hung not but so s. with
P. L. 6, 192. that no sight nor motion of s.
P. L. 6, 320. nor odds appeared in might or s.
P. L. 6, 326. but with s. wheel reverse
P. L. 6, 596. have easily as spirits evaded s.
P. L. 7, 176. more s. than time or motion
P. L. 7, 295. command impressed on the s. flood
P. L. 7, 469. the s. stag from under ground bore
P. L. 8, 21. and their s. return diurnal
P. L. 8, 133. that s. nocturnal
P. L. 9, 633. intricate seem straight to mischief s.
P. L. 10, 224. to him with s. ascent he up
P. L. 11, 127. archangelic power prepared for s.
P. R. 2, 385. and call s. flights of angels
S. A. 1284. winged expedition s. as the lightning
C. 80. s. as the sparkle of a glancing star
C. 114. lead in s. round the months and years
C. 579. into s. flight till I had found you here
C. 856. and will be s. to aid a virgin
L. 63. down the s. Hebrus to the Lesbian shore
V. Ex. 96. or Severn s. guilty of maiden's death
**Swifter.**—P. L. 2, 791. and s. far we overtook
**Swiftest.**—P. L. 6, 535. cherubim the s. wing
P. L. 10, 91. with s. minutes winged
**Swiftly.**—P. L. 9, 631. he leading s. rolled
V. Ex. 28. fly s. to this fair assembly's ears
**Swiftness.**—P. L. 8, 38. whose s. number fails
P. L. 8, 107. the s. of those circles attribute
**Swift-rushing.**—D. F. I. 67. s.-r. black perdition
**Swilled.**—C. 178. to meet the rudeness and s.
**Swim.**—P. L. 1, 202. that s. the ocean stream
P. L. 9, 1009. they s. in mirth and fancy
P. L. 11, 626. now s. in joy ere long to s. at
**Swims.**—P. L. 2, 950. and s. or sinks, or wades
P. L. 7, 414. like a promontory sleeps or s.
**Swindges.**—H. 172. s. the scaly horror
**Swine.**—P. R. 4, 630. hide them in a herd of s.
C. 53. and downward fell into a grovelling s.
**Swing.**—S. A. 1240. or s. thee in the air then dash
**Swinging.**—Il P. 76. s. slow with sullen roar
**Swinish.**—C. 776. for s. gluttony ne'er looks
**Swinked.**—C. 293. and the s. hedger at his supper
**Swoln.**—P. R. 4, 499. the fiend now s. with rage
S. A. 532. then s. with pride
L. 126. but s. with wind and the rank mist they
**Swooning.**—U. C. II. 17. nay quoth he on his s.
**Swoonings.**—S. A. 631. thence faintings s.
**Sword.**—P. L. 2, 294. and the s. of Michael
P. L. 6, 250. saw where the s. of Michael smote
P. L. 6, 278. ere this avenging s. begin thy
P. L. 6, 320. but the s. of Michael from the
P. L. 6, 324. it met the s. of Satan
P. L. 6, 329. the griding s. with discontinuous
P. L. 6, 714. and s. upon thy puissant thigh
P. L. 11, 120. and of a s. the flame wide-waving
P. L. 11, 247. hung the s. Satan's dire dread
P. L. 12, 592. a flaming s. in signal of remove

P. L. 12, 633. the brandished *s*. of God
P. R. 2, 91. my very soul a *s*. shall pierce
S. A. 143. the jaw of a dead ass his *s*. of bone
S. A. 692. oft leavest them to the hostile *s*.
S. A. 1165. nor by the *s*. of noble warrior
C. 601. may never this just *s*. be lifted up
C. 611. but here thy *s*. can do thee little stead
S. 17, 12. the bounds of either *s*. to thee we owe
F. of C. 5. ye for this adjure the civil *s*.
**Sworded.**—H. 113. and *s*. seraphim
**Sword-law.**—P. L. 11, 672. oppression and *s.-l.*
**Sword-players.**—S. A.1323. have they not *s.-p.*
**Swords.**—P. L. 1, 664. millions of flaming *s*.
P. L. 6, 304. now waved their fiery *s*.
**Swore.**—P. L. 4, 96. feigned submission *s*.
**Sworn.**—P. L. 1, 322. have ye *s*. to adore
P. L. 5, 607. and by myself have *s*. to him
P. L. 5, 814. decree of God pronounced and *s*.
P. L. 12, 346 and his covenant *s*
C. 1011. so Jove hath *s*.
V. Ex. 61. nurse hath *s*. she did them spy
**Swum.**—P. L. 2, 753. and dizzy *s*. in darkness
P. L. 7, 503. was flown was *s*. was walked
P. L. 11, 745. the floating vessel *s*. uplifted
P. L. 11, 753. in one small bottom *s*. embarked
**Syene.**—P. R. 4, 70. *S*. and where the shadow
**Syllable.**—C. 208. tongues that *s*. men's names
**Sylvan.**—P. L. 4, 140. a *s*. scene
P. L. 5, 377. so to the *s*. lodge they came
P. R. 1, 480. and tunable as *s*. pipe or song

P. R. 2, 191. or Faun, or *s*.? but these haunts
C. 268. dwell'st here with Pan or *S*.
Il P. 134. and shadows brown that *S*. loves
**Sylvanus.**—P. L. 4, 707. Pan or *S*. never
**Sympathize.**—C. 796. would be moved to *s*.
H. 34. with her great master so to *s*.
**Sympathy.**—P. L. 4, 465. looks of *s*. and love
P. L. 10, 246. whatever draws me on or *s*.
P. L. 10, 540. on them fell and horrid *s*.
**Symphonies.**—P. L. 1, 712. of dulcet *s*. and
P. L. 5, 162. and choral *s*. day without night
P. L. 11, 595. and charming *s*. attached the
**Symphonious.**—P. L. 7, 559. the sound *s*.
**Symphony.**—P. L. 3, 368. of charming *s*.
H. 132. full consort to the angelic *s*.
**Synod.**—P. L. 2, 391. *s*. of gods and like to
P. L. 6, 156. in *s*. met their deities to assert
P. L. 10, 661. and when to join in *s*. unbenign
P. L. 11, 67. but let us call to *s*. all the blessed
**Syrian.**—P. L. 1, 421. parts Egypt from *S*.
P. L. 1, 448. the *S*. damsels to lament his fate
P. L. 1, 474. and displace for one of *S*. mode
P. L. 11, 218. against the *S*. king
M. W. 63. that fair *S*. shepherdess
**Syrinx.**—P. R. 2, 188. Amymone, *S*., many
A. 106. though *S*. your Pan's mistress were
A. 107. yet *S*. well might wait on her
**Syrtis.**—P. L. 2, 939. a boggy *s*. neither sea
**Syrups.**—C. 674. of balm and fragrant *s*. mixed

# T.

**Tabernacle.**—P. L. 7, 248. she in a cloudy *t*.
P. L. 12, 247. among them to set up his *t*.
P. R. 4, 599. from heaven enshrined in fleshly *t*.
P. 17. poor fleshly *t*. entered
**Tabernacles.**—P. L. 5, 654. celestial *t*.
**Table.**—P. L. 5, 391. have heaped this *t*. raised
P. L. 5, 443. meanwhile at *t*. Eve ministered
P. R. 2, 340. a *t*. richly spread in regal mode
P. R. 2, 384. command a *t*. this wilderness
P. R. 2, 402. both *t*. and provision vanished
P. R. 4, 588. before him spread a *t*. of celestial
**Tables.**—P. L. 5, 632. they stood *t*. are set
P. R. 4, 115. on citron *t*. or Atlantic stone
**Tacit.**—S. A. 430. which to have kept *t*. was in
**Tackle.**—P. L. 2, 1044. shrouds and *t*. torn
S. A. 717. with all her bravery on and *t*. trim
**Ta'en.**—C.541. had *t*. their supper on the savoury
U. C. I. 13. and that he had *t*. up his latest inn
**Tail.**—P. L. 10, 523. monsters head and *t*.
S. A. 360. draw a scorpion's *t*. behind
H. 172. the scaly horror of his folded *t*.
**Taint.**—P. L. 4, 804. venom he might *t*.
P. L. 5, 704. and jealousies to sound or *t*.
P. L. 10, 631. polluting sin with *t*. hath shed
P. L. 12, 512. superstitions and traditions *t*.
S. A. 312. without *t*. of sin or legal debt
S. 23, 5. washed from spot of child-bed *t*.
**Tainted.**—P. L. 11, 52. eject him *t*. now
**Taint-worm.**—L. 46. or *t.-w.* to the weanling
**Take.**—P. L. 8, 635. *t*. heed lest passion
P. L. 9, 1105. the bended twigs *t*. root
P. L. 11, 100. *t*. to thee from among the
P. L. 11, 834. and there *t*. root an island salt
P. R. 3, 140. yet sacrilegious to himself would *t*.
S. A. 241. that fault I *t*. not on me but transfer
S. A. 826. *t*. to thy wicked deed
S. A. 928. no, no, of my condition *t*. no care
S. A. 1230. but *t*. good heed my hand survey not
S.A. 1345. so *t*. it with what speed thy message
S. A. 1570. *t*. then the worst in brief
C. 84. and *t*. the weeds and likeness of a swain
C. 256. who as they sung would *t*. the prisoned
C. 321. shepherd I *t*. thy word and trust thy

H. 72. and will not *t*. their flight
P. 51. *t*. up a weeping on the mountains wild
D. F. I. 42. why from us so quickly thou didst *t*.
**Taken.**—P. L. 10, 207. of the ground wast *t*.
P. L. 11, 98. to till the ground whence he was *t*.
P.L. 11, 262. till the ground whence thou wast *t*.
P. R. 2, 177. none are thou thinkest but *t*. with
**Takes.**—P. L. 4, 622. God *t*. no account
P. R. 2, 236. forthwith to him *t*. a chosen band
P. R. 2, 241. then to the desert *t*. with these
Il P. 50. that in trim gardens *t*. his pleasure
V. Ex. 20. *t*. our late fantastics with delight
**Tale.**—C. 44. what never yet was heard in *t*.
L'A. 67. and every shepherd tells his *t*.
Il P. 100. or the *t*. of Troy divine
**Talent.**—S. 19, 3. and that one *t*. which is death
**Tales.**—L'A. 115. thus done the *t*. to bed they
**Talk.**—P. L. 4, 744. austerely *t*. of purity
P. L. 4, 970. when I am thy captive's *t*. in this thy
P. L. 5, 115. of our last evening's *t*. in this thy
P. L. 9, 1. no more of *t*. where God or angel
P. L. 9, 237. or *t*. between food of the mind
P. R. 1, 485. and *t*. at least though I despair to
P. R. 3, 55. upon their tongues and be their *t*.
P. R. 4, 125. then proceed'st to *t*. of the
P. R. 4, 171. I never liked thy *t*. thy offers less
P. R. 4, 307. for all his tedious *t*. is but vain
P. R. 4, 313. much of the soul they *t*.
S. A. 188. of my own experience not by *t*.
C.464. unchaste looks loose gestures and foul *t*.
**Talked.**—P. L. 3, 483. *t*. and that first moved
P. L. 9, 613. so *t*. the spirited sly snake
P. L. 11, 322. with him at this fountain *t*.
P. L. 11, 444. he inly raged and as they *t*.
P. R.2, 6. and with him *t*. and with him lodged
P. R. 4, 484. so *t*. he while the Son of God
**Talking.**—P. L. 1, 192. thus Satan *t*. to his
P. L. 4, 689. thus *t*. hand in hand alone they
**Tall.**—P. L. 1, 534. as his right, a cherub *t*.
P. L. 4, 288. far nobler shape erect and *t*.
P. L. 4, 477. thee fair indeed and *t*. under
P. L. 11, 728. the mountain hewing timber *t*.
P. R. 2, 352. in order stood *t*. stripling youths

Y

C. 270. the prosperous growth of this *t*. wood
A. 46. to nurse the saplings *t*. and curl the grove
**Tallest.**—P. L. 1, 292. equal which the *t*. pine
P. R. 4, 416. whose *t*. pines though rooted
**Talons.**—P. R. 2, 403. wings and *t*. heard
**Tame.**—P. L. 6, 686. went forth to *t*. these
P. R. 2, 163. hath the power to soften and *t*.
S. A. 538. who shore me like a *t*. wether
S. A. 1695. of *t*. villatic fowl
**Tamed.**—P. L. 12, 191. *t*. at length submits
S. A. 1093. I thought gyves and the mill had *t*.
C. 443. wherewith she *t*. the brinded lioness
**Tamely.**—P. L. 2, 1028. *t*. endured a bridge
**Tames.**—P. R. 2, 406. each other creature *t*.
**Tangled.**—P. R. 2, 162. after them *t*. in
S. A. 1665. but *t*. in the fold of dire necessity
C. 181. in the blind mazes of this *t*. wood
H. 188. in twilight shade of *t*. thickets mourn
**Tangles.**—P. L. 9, 632. in *t*. and made
L. 69. or with the *t*. of Neæra's hair
**Tangling.**—P. L. 4, 176. of shrubs and *t*.
**Tanned.**—L'A. 90. to the *t*. haycock in the mead
**Tantalus.**—P. L. 2, 614. fled the lip of *T*.
**Taper.**—C. 337. gentle *t*. though a rush-candle
L'A. 126. in saffron robe with *t*. clear
**Tapers.**—H. 202. now sits not girt with *t*. holy
**Tapestry.**—C. 324. than in *t*. halls and courts
**Taprobane.**—P. R. 4, 75. utmost Indian isle *T*.
**Tardy.**—P. L. 10, 853. accused of *t*. execution
**Targe.**—P. L. 9, 1111. as Amazonian *t*.
**Tarpeian.**—P. R. 4, 49. on the *T*. rock
**Tarsus.**—P. L. 1, 200. by ancient *T*. held
S. A. 715. like a stately ship of *T*.
**Tartar.**—P. L. 3, 432. the roving *T*. bounds
P. L. 10, 431. as when the *T*. from his Russian
Il P. 115. on which the *T*. king did ride
**Tartarean.**—P. L. 2, 69. with *T*. sulphur
**Tartareous.**—P. L. 7, 238. the black *t*.... dregs
**Tartarus.**—P. L. 2, 858. this gloom of *T*.
P. L. 6, 54. of punishment the gulf of *T*.
**Task.**—P. L. 1, 159. good never will be our *t*.
P. L. 2, 246. this must be our *t*. in heaven this
P. L. 4, 437. following our delightful *t*. to prune
P. L. 5, 564. sad *t*. and hard for how shall I
P. L. 5, 854. by *t*. transferred from Father
P. L. 9, 13. sad *t*. yet argument not less but
P. L. 9, 207. our pleasant *t*. enjoined
P. L. 9, 221. our *t*. we choose
P. R. 1, 427. the other service was thy chosen *t*.
P. R. 3, 368. it shall be my *t*. to render thee
S. A. 5. relieves me from my *t*. of servile toil
S. A. 35. to grind in brazen fetters under *t*.
C. 18. but to my *t*.
C. 1012. but now my *t*. is smoothly done
S. 15, 9. O yet a nobler *t*. awaits thy hand
S. 22, 11. in liberty's defence my noble *t*.
V. Ex. 8. that now I use thee in my latter *t*.
**Task-master.**—S. 2, 14. my great *t.-m.'s* eye
**Tasselled.**—A. 57. slumbering leaves or *t*. horn
**Taste.**—P. L. 1, 2. whose mortal *t*. brought
P. L. 2, 613. and of itself the water flies all *t*.
P. L. 2, 686. retire or *t*. thy folly and learn by
P. L. 3, 199. who neglect and scorn shall never *t*.
P. L. 4, 217. of noblest kind for sight, smell, *t*.
P. L. 4, 251. if true here only and of delicious *t*.
P. L. 4, 369. more woe the more your *t*. is now
P. L. 4, 423. not to *t*. that only tree of knowledge
P. L. 4, 427. God hath pronounced it death to *t*.
P. L. 4, 515. forbidden them to *t*. knowledge
P. L. 4, 527. aspiring to be such they *t*. and die
P. L. 5, 59. deigns none to ease thy load and *t*.
P. L. 5, 61. envy or what reserve forbids to *t*.
P. L. 5, 77. *t*. this and be henceforth among
P. L. 5, 86. that I methought could not but *t*.
P. L. 5, 304. savoury fruits of *t*. to please true
P. L. 5, 336. bring *t*. after *t*. upheld with
P. L. 5, 369. garden choicest bears to sit and *t*.
P. L. 5, 397. heavenly stranger please to *t*.
P. L. 5, 411. they hear, see, smell, touch, *t*.
P. L. 5, 432. and to *t*. think not I shall be nice
P. L. 5, 464. enter and these earthly fruits to *t*.

P. L. 7, 539. delectable both to behold and *t*.
P. L. 8, 327. what I warn thee shun to *t*.
P. L. 8, 401. and wilt *t*. no pleasure though in
P. L. 8, 527. these delicacies I mean of *t*., sight
P. L. 9, 476. hope here to *t*. of pleasure
P. L. 9, 651. but of this tree we may not *t*.
P. L. 9, 732. reach then and freely *t*.
P. L. 9, 742. inclinable now grown to touch or *t*.
P. L. 9, 747. whose *t*. too long forborne at first
P. L. 9, 753. forbids us then to *t*. but his
P. L. 9, 777. fair to the eye inviting to the *t*.
P. L. 9, 786. intent now wholly on her *t*.
P. L. 9, 866. eyes and make them gods who *t*.
P. L. 9, 881. thou therefore also *t*. that equal
P. L. 9, 925. much more to *t*. it under ban
P. L. 9, 931. common and unhallowed ere our *t*.
P. L. 9, 986. *t*. so divine that what of sweet
P. L. 9, 988. on my experience Adam freely *t*.
P. L. 9, 1017. Eve now I see thou art exact of *t*.
P. L. 10, 4. to *t*. the fatal fruit was known in
P. L. 10, 13. the high injunction not to *t*. that
P. L. 10, 268. and *t* the savour of death
P. L. 10, 563. more delusive not the touch but *t*.
P. L. 10, 566. which the offended *t*. with
P. L. 11, 85. since his *t*. of that defended fruit
P. L. 11, 541. all *t*. of pleasure must forgo
P. L. 11, 618. bred only and completed to the *t*.
P. R. 1, 345. food whereof we wretched seldom *t*.
P. R. 2, 371. their *t*. no knowledge works
S. A. 545. *t*. that cheers the heart of gods
S. A. 1091. the way ... were not to see but *t*.
C. 66. which as they *t*. for most do *t*. through
C. 702. I would not *t*. thy treasonous offer
C. 714. but all to please and sate the curious *t*.
C. 813. the bliss of dreams be wise and *t*.
S. 20, 10. light and choice of Attic *t*. with wine
**Tasted.**—P. L. 5, 65. he plucked he *t*.
P. L. 7, 543. which *t*. works knowledge of good
P. L. 9, 688. on me, me who have touched and *t*.
P. L. 9, 770. which first hath *t*. envies not
P. L. 9, 788. such delight in fruit she never *t*.
P. L. 9, 864. as we are told a tree of danger *t*.
P. L. 9, 867. and hath been *t*. such
P. L. 9, 874. have also *t*. and have also found
P. L. 10, 687. at that *t*. fruit the sun as from
P. R. 1, 308. nor *t*. human food nor hunger felt
P. R. 2, 131. have found him viewed him *t*.
P. R. 2, 247. human food nor *t*. nor had appetite
C. 52. whose charmed cup whoever *t*. lost his
**Tastes.**—P. L. 5, 335. not to mix *t*. not well
P. L. 7, 49. easily obeyed amid the choice of all *t*.
P. R. 4, 347. with Sion's songs to all true *t*.
**Tasting.**—P. L. 5, 412. *t*. concoct digest
P. L. 9, 585. sharp desire I had of *t*. those fair
P. L. 9, 883. lest thou not *t*. different degree
P. L. 9, 935. as likely *t*. to attain proportional
P. L. 9, 972. one guilt, one crime if any be of *t*.
P. L. 9, 1024. nor known till now true relish *t*.
**Taught.**—P. L. 1, 8. that shepherd who first *t*.
P. L. 1, 685. and by his suggestion *t*.
P. L. 3, 19. *t* by the heavenly muse to venture
P. L. 4, 915. which *t*. thee yet no better
P. L. 5, 204. made vocal by my song and *t*.
P. L. 5, 508. well hast thou *t*. the way that
P. L. 5, 698. tells as he was *t*. that the Most
P. L. 5, 826. yet by experience *t*. we know how
P. L. 8, 182. *t*. to live the easiest way
P. L. 8, 190. till warned or by experience *t*.
P. L. 9, 748. *t*. the tongue not made for speech
P. L. 9, 1068. of whomsoever *t*. to counterfeit
P. L. 10, 661. and *t*. the fixed their influence
P. L. 10, 861. with other echo late I *t*. your
P. L. 11, 531. of not too much by temperance *t*.
P. L. 11, 612. though his Spirit *t*. them
P. L. 11, 735. and entered in as *t*. their order
P. L. 12, 572. *t*. this by his example whom
P. R. 2, 269. though ravenous *t*. to abstain
P. R. 2, 295. nature *t*. art
P. R. 3, 97. by what he *t*. and suffered for
P. R. 4, 220. teaching not *t*.
P. R. 4, 261. what the lofty grave tragedians *t*.

P. R. 4, 357. as men divinely *t.*
P. R. 4, 361. in them is plainest *t.* and easiest
S. A. 874. have *t.* thee far other reasonings
C. 515. what the sage poets *t.* by the heavenly
C. 791. hath so well been *t.* her dazzling fence
S. 13, 2. first *t.* our English music how to span
S. 21, 3. and in his volumes *t.* our laws
F. of C. 8. *t.* ye by mere A. S. and Rutherford
**Taught'st.**—S. 11, 14. when thou *t.* Cambridge
**Tauric.**—P. R. 4, 79. to the *T.* pool
**Tauris.**—P. L. 10, 436. his retreat to *T.* or
**Taurus.**—P. L. 1, 769. the sun with *T.* rides
P. L. 10, 673. like-distant breadth to *T.* with
**Tawny.**—P. L. 7, 464. the *t.* lion pawing to get
C. 117. and on the *t.* sands and shelves
**Tax.**—S. A. 210. *t.* not divine disposal
**Teach.**—P. L. 5, 786. *t.* us to cast off
P. L. 5, 865. our own right hand shall *t.* us
P. L. 10, 1062.. and *t.* us farther by what
P. L. 11, 836. to *t.* thee that God attributes to
P. L. 12, 440. them shall leave in charge to *t.*
P. L. 12, 446. all nations they shall *t.* for from
P. R. 1, 224. at least to try and *t.* the erring
P. R. 1, 461. into the world to *t.* his final will
P. R. 4, 227. write and *t.* to admiration
P. R. 4, 309. alas what can they *t.* and not
C. 1020. she can *t.* ye how to climb
Il P. 80. *t.* light to counterfeit a gloom
**Teacher.**—P. L. 11, 450. O *t.* some great
**Teachers.**—P. L. 12, 508. for *t.* grievous
P. R. 1, 212. there to hear the *t.* of our law
P. R. 4, 262. *t.* best of moral prudence
**Teaching.**—P. R. 4, 220. *t.* not taught the
P. R. 4, 357. divinely taught and better *t.*
**Team.**—H. 19. heaven by the sun's *t.* untrod
**Tear** (verb) S. A. 953. to *t.* thee joint by joint
**Tear.**—P. L. 5, 130. but silently a gentle *t.* let
S.A. 200. and for a word, a *t.*, fool! have divulged
L. 14. the meed of some melodious *t.*
Cir. 7. your fiery essence can distil no *t.*
**Tears** (verb).—S. A. 128. as the lion *t.* the kid
**Tears.**—P. L. 1, 393. and parent's *t.*
P. L. 1, 620. *t.* such as angels weep, burst forth
P. L. 9, 1121. them down to weep; nor only *t.*
P. L. 10, 910. with *t.* that ceased not flowing
P. L. 10, 1089. with *t.* watering the ground
P. L. 10, 1101. with *t.* watering the ground
P. L. 11, 110. and with *t.* bewailing their
P. L. 11, 497. and gave him up to *t.* a space
P. L. 11, 627. ere long a world of *t.* must weep
P. L. 11, 674. Adam was all in *t.*, and to his
P. L. 11, 757. thee another flood, of *t.* and
P. L. 12, 373. like grief been dewed in *t.*
P. L. 12, 645. some natural *t.* they dropped
S. A. 51. o'ercome with importunity and *t.*
S. A. 735. yet if *t.* may expiate
S. A. 1459. supplication prone and father's *t.*
S. A. 1721. nothing is here for *t.*
L. 150. and daffadillies fill their cups with *t.*
L. 181. and wipe the *t.* for ever from his eyes
Il P. 107. drew iron *t.* down Pluto's cheek
P. 35. where my *t.* have washed
P. 48. for sure so well instructed are my *t.*
M. W. 44. prove to be presaging *t.*
M. W. 55. here be *t.* of perfect moan
**Tease.**—C. 751. and to *t.* the housewife's wool
**Teats.**—P. L. 9, 581. or the *t.* of ewe or goat
**Tedded.**—P. L. 9, 450. or *t.* grass
**Tedious.**—P. L. 5, 354. than the *t.* pomp
P. L. 8, 389. but soon prove *t.* alike
P. L. 9, 30. with long and *t.* havoc fabled
P. L. 9, 880. *t.* unshared with thee and odious
P. R. 4, 123. but *t.* waste of time to sit
P. R. 4, 307. for all his *t.* talk is but vain boast
H.239.time is our *t.*song should here have ending
**Teemed.**—P. L. 7, 454. fertile womb *t.* at a birth
S. A. 1703. from out her ashy womb now *t.*
**Teeming.**—C. 175. when from their *t.* flocks
**Telassar.**—P. L. 4, 214. before dwelt in *T.*
**Telescope.**—P. L. 4, 42. or glass of *t.*
**Tell.**—P. L. 1, 205. some island oft as seamen *t.*

P. L. 1, 507. the rest were long to *t.*
P. L. 1, 693. and wondering *t.* of Babel
P. L. 2, 739. spares to *t.* thee yet by deeds
P. L. 3, 8. stream whose fountain who shall *t.*
P. L. 3, 54. that I may see and *t.* of things
P. L. 3, 575. by centre or eccentric hard to *t.*
P. L. 3, 667. brightest seraph *t.* in which of all
P. L. 4, 37. and add thy name O sun to *t.* thee
P. L. 4, 236. but rather to *t.* how if art could *t.*
P. L. 5, 160. speak ye who best can *t.* ye sons
P. L. 5, 238. *t.* him withal his danger
P. L. 5, 685. *t.* them that by command ere yet
P. L. 7, 101. longer will delay to hear thee *t.*
P. L. 8, 250. for man to *t.* how human life began
P. L. 8, 276. that live and move fair creatures *t.*
P. L. 8, 280. *t.* me how may I know him how
P. L. 9, 569. easy to me it is to *t.* thee all what
P. L. 10, 469. long were to *t.* what I have done
P. L. 12, 261. the rest were long to *t.*
P. R. 1, 14. to *t.* of deeds above heroic
P. R. 2, 215. that effect on Jove so fables *t.*
P. R. 2, 320. *t.* me if food were now before
P. R. 3, 339. besieged Albracca as romances *t.*
P. R. 4, 113. to *t.* their sumptuous gluttonies
P. R. 4, 120. to me shouldst *t.* who thirst
P. R. 4, 153. nor for thee to know nor me to *t.*
P. R. 4, 467. did I not *t.* thee if thou didst
S. A. 202. *t.* me friends am I not sung
S. A. 1199. and *t.* to them my secret
S. A. 1319. knowest I am an Hebrew therefore *t.*
S. A. 1557. *t.* us the sum the circumstance defer.
C. 43. and listen why for I will *t.* you now
C. 236. canst thou not *t.* me of a gentle pair
C. 240. *t.* me but where sweet queen of parley
C. 400. and *t.* me it is safe as bid me hope
C. 458. *t.* her of things that no gross ear can hear
C. 509. *t.* thee sadly shepherd without blame
C. 513. I'll *t.* ye 'tis not vain or fabulous
D. F. I. 38. *t.* me bright spirit
D. F. I. 51. O *t.* me sooth
V. Ex. 43. *t.* at length how green-eyed Neptune
**Telling.**—P. L. 11, 299. might else in *t.*
C. 628. *t.* their strange and vigorous
**Tells.**—P. L. 4, 793. who *t.* of some infernal
P. L. 5, 698. *t.* as he was taught
P. L. 5, 702. *t.* the suggested cause and casts
P. L. 12, 364. place of birth a solemn angel *t.*
P. R. 2, 307. others of some note as story *t.*
L'A. 67. and every shepherd *t.* his tale
L'A. 105. *t.* how the drudging goblin sweat
**Tell'st.**—P. L. 4, 588. he lurk of whom thou *t.*
P. L. 5, 553. what thou *t.* hath passed
**Tell-tale.**—C. 141. and to the *t.-t.* sun descry
**Temir.**—P. L. 11, 389. by Oxus *T.'s* throne
**Temper.**—P. L. 1, 285. ethereal *t.*
P. L. 1, 552. to height of noblest *t.* heroes old
P. L. 2, 218. and to the place conformed in *t.*
P. L. 2, 276. our *t.* changed into their *t.* which
P. L. 4, 670. *t.* or nourish or in part shed down
P. L. 4, 812. can endure touch of celestial *t.*
P. L. 10, 77. yet I shall *t.* so justice with
P. L. 10, 1047. with what mild and gracious *t.*
P. L. 11, 361. and to joy with fear and pious
P. R. 2, 164. to soften and tame severest *t.*
**Temperance.**—P. L. 7, 127. no less her *t.*
P. L. 11, 531. rule of not too much, by *t.* taught
P. L. 11, 805. more than enough, that *t.* may
P. L. 11, 807. justice and *t.*, truth and faith
P. L. 12, 583. add virtue patience, *t.*, add love
P. R. 2, 408. thy *t.* invincible besides
P. R. 3, 92. by patience *t.* I mention still
S. A. 558. but what availed this *t.* not complete
C. 721. should in a pet of *t.* feed on pulse
C. 767. and holy dictate of spare *t.*
**Temperate.**—P. L. 5, 5. and *t.* vapours
P. L. 12, 636. began to parch that *t.* clime
P. R. 3, 160. nor is always ruled with *t.* sway
P. R. 4, 134. frugal and mild and *t.*
**Temperately.**—P. R. 2, 378. *t.* replied
**Tempered.**—P. L. 2, 813. though *t.* heavenly
P. L. 6, 322. was given him *t.* so that neither

P. L. 6, 480. touched with heaven's ray and *t.*
P. L. 7, 598. *t.* soft tunings intermixed with
P. R. 3, 27. most *t.* pure ethereal
S. A. 133. Chalybean *t.* steel, and frock of mail
C. 32. has in his charge with *t.* awe to guide
L. 33. *t.* to the oaten flute
**Tempering.**—P. L. 7, 15. empyreal air thy *t.*
**Tempers.**—P. L. 5, 347. she *t.* dulcet creams
**Temper'st.**—S. A. 670. *t.* thy providence
**Tempest.**—P. L. 2, 180. caught in a fiery *t.*
P. L. 2, 290. anchors in a craggy bay after the *t.*
P. L. 3, 429. less vexed with *t.*
P. L. 6, 190. hung not but so swift with *t.* fell
P. L. 7, 412. *t.* the ocean
P. R. 4, 465. this *t.* at this desert most was bent
S. A. 964. eternal *t.* never to be calmed
S. A. 1063. but this another kind of *t.* brings
**Tempestuous.**—P. L. 1, 77. whirlwinds of *t.* fire
P. L. 6, 844. nor less on either side *t.* fell
P. L. 10, 664. should prove *t.*
**Temple.**—P. L. 1, 402. *t.* right against the *t.* of
P. L. 1, 443. where stood her *t.*
P. L. 1, 460. and hands lopped off in his own *t.*
P. L. 1, 463. yet had his *t.* high
P. L. 1, 492. to him no *t.* stood or altar smoked
P. L. 1, 713. built like a *t.*
P. L. 5, 274. his reliques in the sun's bright *t.*
P. L. 6, 890. into the courts and *t.* of his
P. L. 7, 148. and this high *t.* to frequent
P. L. 12, 334. shall in a glorious *t.* enshrine
P. L. 12, 356. pullution brings upon the *t.*
P. R. 1, 211. I went into the *t.* there to hear the
P. R. 1, 256. by vision found thee in the *t.*
P. R. 3, 83. worshipped with *t.,* priest, and
P. R. 3, 161. oft have they violated the *t.*
P. R. 4, 217. thou went'st alone into the *t.*
P. R. 4, 546. the glorious *t.* reared her pile
S. A. 1146. go to his *t.* invocate his aid
S. A. 1370. but who constrains me to the *t.* of
C. 461. the unpolluted *t.* of the mind
S. 8. 11. when *t.* and tower went to the ground
**Temples.**—P. L. 1, 18. before all *t.* the upright
P. L. 1, 494. yet who more oft than he in *t.*
P. L. 12, 527. living *t.* built by faith to stand
P. R. 1, 449. disdaining to approach thy *t.*
P. R. 3, 268. field and flood, *t.* and towers
P. R. 4, 34. with towers and *t.*
S. A. 990. smote Sisera sleeping through the *t.*
S. A. 1378. present in *t.* at idolatrous rites
H. 198. Peor and Baälim forsake their *t.* dim
**Temporal.**—P. L. 12, 433. than *t.* death
**Tempt.**—P. L. 2, 404. shall *t.* with wandering
P. L. 2, 1032. to *t.* or punish mortals
P. L. 5, 846. and *t.* not these but hasten
P. L. 9, 281. because we have a foe may *t.* it
P. L. 9, 736. which to behold might *t.* alone
P. R. 1, 143. let him *t.* and now assay his utmost
P. R. 1, 178. against whate'er may *t.* whate'er
P. R. 4, 481. the fiend had raised to *t.* the Son
P. R. 4, 561. *t.* not the Lord thy God
P. R. 4, 580. who durst so proudly *t.* the Son
P. R. 4, 611. will dare set foot in paradise to *t.*
S. A. 358. why are his gifts desirable to *t.*
**Temptation.**—P. L. 8, 643. all *t.* to transgress
P. L. 9, 299. not proof against *t.* thou thyself
P. L. 9, 364. seek not *t.* then which to avoid
P. L. 9, 531. his fraudulent *t.* thus began
P. R. 1, 5. obedience fully tried through all *t.*
P. R. 1, 123. *t* and all guile on him to try
P. R. 2, 405. and with these words his *t.*
P. R. 4, 533. have found thee proof against all *t.*
P. R. 4, 595. victory over *t.* and the tempter
P. R. 4, 608. and by vanquishing *t.* hast regained
P. R. 4, 617. secure .... of tempter and *t.*
S. A. 427. thou the sooner *t.* found'st
S. A. 1051. and all *t.* can remove
**Temptations.**—P. L. 4, 65. to all *t.* armed
P. L. 6, 908. but listen not to his *t.* warn thy
P. 24. his godlike acts and his *t.* fierce
**Tempted.**—P. L. 1, 642. which *t.* our attempt
P. L. 9, 297. asperses the *t.* with dishonour foul

P. L. 10, 14. not to taste that fruit whoever *t.*
S. A. 801. I was assured by those who *t.*
**Tempter.**—P. L. 4, 10. the *t.* ere the accuser
P. L. 9, 549. so glozed the *t.* and his proem
P. L. 9, 567. to whom the guileful *t.* thus
P. L. 9, 655. to whom the *t.* guilefully replied
P. L. 9, 665. when now more bold the *t.*
P. L. 9, 678. the *t.* all impassioned thus began
P. L. 10, 39. when first this *t.* crossed the gulf
P. L. 10, 552. the bait of Eve used by the *t.*
P. L. 11, 382. whereon for different cause the *t.*
P. R. 1, 5. the *t.* foiled in all his wiles
P. R. 2, 366. and the *t.* now his invitation
P. R. 2, 404. only the importune *t.* still
P. R. 3, 108. to whom the *t.* murmuring thus
P. R. 3, 203. to whom the *t.* inly racked
P. R. 3, 265. to this high mountain too the *t.*
P. R. 3, 409. when thou stood'st up his *t.*
P. R. 4, 2. the *t.* stood nor had what to reply
P. R. 4, 43. and now the *t.* thus his silence
P. R. 4, 154. to whom the *t.* impudent replied
P. R. 4, 408. for at his head the *t.* watched
P. R. 4, 569. after many a foil the *t.* proud
P. R. 4, 595. over temptation and the *t.* proud
P. R. 4, 617. of *t.* and temptation without fear
**Tempting.**—P. L. 2, 607. to reach the *t.* stream
P. L. 8, 324. fairest fruit that hung to the eye *t.*
P. L. 9, 328. only our foe *t.* affronts us with
P. L. 9, 595. where plenty hung *t.* so nigh
P. R. 4, 13. still will be *t.* him who foils him
**Tempts.**—P. L. 9, 296. for he who *t.* though in
S. A. 1535. hope would fain subscribe and *t.* belief
**Ten.**—P. L. 2, 671. fierce as *t.* furies
P. L. 6, 193. *t.* paces huge he back recoiled
P. L. 6, 767. attended with *t.* thousand
P. L. 9, 1026. for one tree had been forbidden *t.*
P. L. 10, 669. the poles of earth twice *t.* degrees
P. L. 11, 678. and multiply *t.* thousand-fold
P. L. 12, 190. with *t.* wounds the river-dragon
P. R. 2, 245. four times *t.* days I've passed
P. R. 3, 374. of thy brethren those *t.* tribes
P. R. 3, 377. *t.* sons of Jacob two of Joseph
P. R. 3, 403. as thou call'st them those *t.* tribes
L'A. 109. that *t.* day-labourers could not end
U. C. I. 7. for he had any time this *t.* years full
**Tend.**—P. L. 1, 183. thither let us *t.*
P. L. 3, 272. what this might mean and whither *t.*
P. L. 4, 438. and *t.* these flowers
P. L. 9, 156. watch and *t.* their earthly charge
P. L. 9, 206. still to *t.* plant herb and flower
P. L. 9, 493. which to her ruin now I *t.*
P. L. 9, 583. lamb or kid that *t.* their play
P. L. 9, 801. my early care, ... shall *t.* thee
P. L. 12, 106. still *t.* from bad to worse
S. A. 925. may ever *t.* about thee to old age
S. A. 1490. it shall be my delight to *t.* his eyes
L. 65. to *t.* the homely slighted shepherd's trade
**Tendance.**—P. L. 8, 47. by her fair *t.* gladlier
P. L. 9, 419. their *t.* or plantation for delight
**Tended.**—P. L. 5, 22. how spring our *t.* plants
P. L. 11, 490. despair *t.* the sick
P. R. 4, 371. *t.* on by glory or fame
**Tender.**—P. L. 4, 253. grazing the *t.* herb
P. L. 5, 337. and from each *t.* stalk
P. L. 7, 315. brought forth the *t.* grass
P. L. 9, 357. not then mistrust but *t.* love
P. L. 9, 428. to support each flower of *t.* stalk
P. L. 11, 276. which I bred up with *t.* hand
P. R. 2, 327. but *t.* all their power
S. A. 94. to such a *t.* ball as the eye confined
C. 40. and here their *t.* age might suffer peril
C. 296. plucking ripe clusters from the *t.* shoots
C. 624. he on the *t.* grass would sit
L. 188. he touched the *t.* stops of various quills
M. W. 35. so have I seen some *t.* slip
**Tenderest.**—S. A. 624. my apprehensive *t.* parts
**Tenderly.**—P. L. 9, 991. and for joy *t.* wept
**Tending.**—P. L. 5, 476. or nearer *t.*
P. L. 9, 212. wanton growth derides *t.* to wild
P. L. 10, 326. to Paradise first *t.* when behold
P. L. 10, 976. *t.* to some relief of our extremes

S. A. 1302. for I descry this way some other *t*.
C. 531. *t*. my flocks hard by i' the hilly crofts
**Tendrils.**—P. L. 4, 307. the vine curls her *t*.
**Tends.**—P. L. 3, 694. desire which *t*. to know
P. L. 9, 1109. and *t*. his pasturing herds
**Tenement.**—P. R. 4, 274. see there his *t*.
**Teneriff.**—P. L. 4, 987. like *T*. or Atlas
**Tenfold.**—P. L. 2, 705. grew *t*. more dreadful
P. L. 6, 78. *t*. the length of this terrene
P. L. 6, 255. of *t*. adamant his ample shield
P. L. 6, 872. and felt *t*. confusion in their fall
P. R. 1, 41. thick clouds and dark *t*. involved
**Tenor.**—P. L. 11, 632. but still I see the *t*.
**Tent.**—P. L. 12, 256. over the *t*. a cloud shall
**Tenth.**—P. L. 6, 194. the *t*. on bended knee
**Tents.**—P. L. 5, 291. their glittering *t*.
P. L. 5, 890. I fly these wicked *t*. devoted
P. L. 11, 557. a spacious plain whereon were *t*.
P. L. 11, 581. when from the *t*. behold a bevy
P. L. 11, 592. feast and music all the *t*. resound
P. L. 11, 607. *t*. saw'st so pleasant were the *t*.
P. L. 11, 727. removed his *t*. far off
P. L. 12, 135. I see his *t*. pitched about Sechem
P. L. 12, 333. till then in *t*. wandering
**Tepid.**—P. L. 7, 417. meanwhile the *t*. caves
**Teredon.**—P. R. 3, 292. Artaxata *T*.
**Term.**—U. C. II. 14. vacation hastened on his *t*.
**Termed.**—C. 419. it may be *t*. her own
**Terms.**—P. L. 2. 331. *t*. of peace yet none
P. L. 6, 612. propounded *t*. of composition
P. L. 6, 621. leader the *t*. we sent were *t*.
P. L. 10, 173. though in mysterious *t*. judged
P. L. 10, 751. unable to perform thy *t*. too hard
P. L. 10, 757. should have been refused those *t*.
P. R. 4, 173. abominable *t*. impious condition
P. R. 4, 335. our psalms with artful *t*. inscribed
C. 684. which you received on other *t*.
**Ternate.**—P. L. 2, 639. or the isles of *T*.
**Terrace.**—C. 935. with many a tower and *t*.
**Terraces.**—P. R. 4, 54. turrets and *t*. and
**Terrene.**—P. L. 6, 78. the length of this *t*.
**Terrestrial.**—P. L. 3, 610. produces with *t*.
P. L. 8, 142. to the *t*. moon be as a star
P. L. 9, 103. *t*. heaven danced round by other
P. L. 9, 485. of limb heroic built though of *t*.
**Terrible.**—P. L. 2, 671. ten furies *t*. as hell
P. L. 2, 682. that dar'st though grim and *t*.
P. L. 6, 106. presented stood in *t*. array
P. L. 6, 910. by *t*. example the reward
P. L. 9, 490. not *t*. though terror be in love
P. L. 11, 233. yet not *t*. that I should fear
P. L. 11, 470. more *t*. at the entrance than
P. R. 2, 160. with mild and sweet allayed yet *t*.
**Terrific.**—P. L. 7, 497. eyes and hairy mane *t*.
**Terrified.**—P. L. 10, 338. *t*. he fled
**Terrify.**—P. L. 12, 218. war *t*. them inexpert
P. R. 1, 179. allure or *t*. or undermine
P. R. 4, 496. thinking to *t*. me to thy will
**Territory.**—P. L. 11, 638. and saw wide *t*.
P. R. 3, 375. whose offspring in his *t*. yet serve
P. R. 4, 82. in ample *t*. wealth and power
**Terror.**—P. L. 1, 113. from the *t*. of this arm
P. L. 2, 457. mighty powers *t*. of Heaven
P. L. 2, 611. Medusa with Gorgonian *t*. guards
P. L. 2, 704. so spake the grisly *t*. and in shape
P. L. 6, 134. abandoned at the *t*. of thy power
P. L. 6, 647. and *t*. seized the rebel host
P. L. 6, 824. into *t*. changed his countenance
P. L. 9, 490. not terrible though *t*. be in love
P. L. 10, 667. with *t*. through the dark aëreal
P. L. 10, 850. all things with double *t*.
P. L. 11, 111. all *t*. hide
P. L. 11, 464. O sight of *t*. foul and ugly
P. L. 12, 238. report to them his will and *t*. cease
P. R. 4, 421. nor yet stayed the *t*. there
P. R. 4, 627. shall chase thee with the *t*. of his
H. 161. with *t*. of that blast
**Terrors.**—P. L. 2, 801. with conscious *t*.
P. L. 2, 862. with *t*. and with clamours compassed
P. L. 6, 735. put on thy *t*. as I put thy mildness
P. L. 6, 859. pursued with *t*. and with furies

P. R. 4, 431. to tempt the Son of God with *t*.
P. R. 4, 482. so many *t*. voices prodigies
P. R. 4, 487. those *t*. which thou speak'st of
**Test.**—S. A. 1151. and challenge Dagon to the *t*.
**Testified.**—P. L. 11, 721. and *t*. against their
**Testifies.**—P. L. 1, 625. as this place *t*.
**Testify.**—C. 248. to *t*. his hidden residence
C. 440. to *t*. the arms of chastity
**Testimony.**—P. L. 6, 33. and for the *t*.
P. L. 12, 251. an ark and in the ark his *t*.
P. R. 1, 78. but to receive the *t*. of heaven
**Tethy's.**—C. 870, and *T*. grave majestic pace
**Tetrachordon.**—S. 11, 1. of late called *T*.
**Tetrarchs.**—P. R. 4, 201. *t*. of fire, air, flood
**Texture**—P. L. 6, 348. nor in their liquid *t*.
P. L. 10, 446. which under state of chastity
**Thame.**—V. Ex. 100. smooth or royal-towered *T*.
**Thammuz.**—P. L. 1, 446. *T*. came next
P. L. 1, 452. with blood of *T*. yearly wounded
H. 204. their wounded *T*. mourn
**Thamyris.**—P. L. 3, 35. blind *T*. and blind
**Thank.**—P. L. 4, 386. *t*. him who puts me
P. L. 10, 736. for this we may *t*. Adam
C. 177. praise the bounteous Pan and *t*. the gods
**Thanked.**—C. 775. the giver would be better *t*
**Thankless.**—L. 66. strictly meditate the *t*. Muse
**Thanks.**—P. L. 4, 47. and pay him *t*. how due
P. L. 4, 445. all praises owe and daily *t*.
P. L. 7, 77. we owe immortal *t*.
P. L. 8, 5. what *t*. sufficient or what recompense
P. L. 10, 736. but his *t*. shall be the execration
P. R. 3, 127. glory and benediction that is *t*.
A. 101. a better soil shall give ye *t*.
**Thatched.**—C. 318. from her *t*. pallet rouse
**Thaw.**—P. L. 12, 194. more hardened after *t*.
C. 853. and *t*. the numbing spell
**Thaws.**—P. L. 2, 590. which on firm land *t*.
**Theatre.**—P. L. 4, 141. a woody *t*.
S. A. 1605. the building was a spacious *t*.
**Theatres.**—P. R. 4, 36. porches and *t*. baths
**Theban.**—P. R. 4, 572. and as that *T*. monster
**Thebes.**—P. L. 1, 578. fought at *T*. and Ilium
P. L. 5, 274. to Egyptian *T*. he flies
Il P. 99. presenting *T*. or Pelops' line
**Thebez.**—P. R. 2, 313. native of *T*. wandering
**Theirs.**—P. L. 4, 513. all is not *t*. it seems
P. L. 9, 806. had the gift been *t*. it had not
P. L. 12, 400. and due to *t*. which out of thine
P. L. 12, 409. his obedience imputed becomes
P. L. 12, 434. or *t*. whom he redeems
**Themes.**—S. 14, 12. truth of thee on glorious *t*.
**Themis.**—P. L. 11, 14. the shrine of *T*. stood
S. 21, 2. on the royal bench of British *T*.
**Themselves.**—P. L. 1, 334. *t*. ere well awake
P. L. 1, 525. to have found *t*. not lost in loss
P. L. 1, 793. and in their own dimensions like *t*.
P. L. 2, 17. and trust *t*. to fear no second fate
P. L. 2, 501. hatred enmity and strife among *t*.
P. L. 3, 116. they *t*. decreed
P. L. 3, 122. authors to *t*. in all both what
P. L. 3, 125. must remain till they enthrall *t*.
P. L. 3, 128. they *t*. ordained their fall
P. L. 6, 352. and as they please they limb *t*.
P. L. 6, 547. so warned he them aware *t*.
P. L. 6, 628. so they among *t*. in pleasant vein
P. L. 6, 653. *t*. invaded next and on their
P. L. 6, 689. for to *t*. I left them
P. L. 6, 864. headlong *t*. they threw down
P. L. 7, 158. they open to *t*. at length the way
P. L. 9, 110. in thee not in *t*. all their known
P. L. 10, 100. and from his presence hid *t*.
P. L. 10, 541. what they saw they felt *t*. now
P. L. 10, 547. cast on *t*. from their own mouths
P. L. 11, 516. then forsook them when *t*. they
P. L. 11, 522. or if his likeness by *t*. defaced
P. L. 11, 525. image did not reverence in *t*.
P. L. 11, 685. who of *t*. abhor to join and by
P. L. 12, 45. and get *t*. a name lest far
P. L. 12, 515. then shall they seek to avail *t*.
P. L. 12, 518. to *t*. appropriating the Spirit of
P. R. 1, 448. who *t*. disdaining to approach thy

P. R. 2, 484. are needless then both for *t.*
P. R. 3, 174. they *t.* rather are occasion best
P. R. 3, 414. *t.* were they who wrought their
P. R. 3, 421. humbled *t.* or penitent besought
P. R. 3, 424. and left a race behind like to *t.*
P. R. 4, 144. these thus degenerate by *t.*
P. R. 4, 310. ignorant of *t.* of God much more
P. R. 4, 314. and in *t.* seek virtue and to *t.* all
P. R. 4, 342. their gods ridiculous and *t.* past
S. A. 248. the deeds *t.* though mute spoke loud
S. A. 897. to acquit *t.* and prosecute their foes
S. A. 1684. as their own ruin on *t.* invite
C. 75. but boast *t.* more comely than before
L. 119. that scarce *t.* know how to hold
**Thence.**—P. L. 1, 12. I *t.* invoke thy aid
P. L. 1, 82. and *t.* in heaven called Satan
P. L. 1, 210. nor ever *t.* had risen
P. L. 1, 234. and fuelled entrails *t.*
P. L. 1, 404. Tophet *t.* and black Gehenna
P. L. 1, 415. yet *t.* his lustful orgies he enlarged
P. L. 1, 418. till good Josiah drove them *t.* to hell
P. L. 1, 515 *t.* on the snowy top of cold Olympus
P. L. 2, 442. if *t.* he scape into whatever world
P. L. 2, 521. *t.* more at ease their minds
P. L. 2, 603. periods of time *t.* hurried back
P. L. 2, 929. *t.* many a league as in a cloudy
P. L. 2, 983. all usurpation *t.* expelled reduce
P. L. 3, 53. all mist from *t.* purge and disperse
P. L. 4, 194. *t.* up he flew and on the tree of
P. L. 4, 230. *t.* united fell down the steep glade
P. L. 4, 453. not distant far from *t.*
P. L. 4, 474. and *t.* be called mother of human
P. L. 4, 582. since meridian hour no creature *t.*
P. L. 4, 806. *t.* raise at least distempered
P. L. 4, 856. against thee wicked and *t.* weak
P. L. 5, 480. the green stalk from *t.* the leaves
P. L. 5, 666. deep malice *t.* conceiving
P. L. 7, 190. and *t.* diffuse his good to worlds
P. L. 7, 510. from *t.* magnanimous to correspond
P. L. 7, 536. *t.* as thou know'st he brought thee
P. L. 7, 554. *t.* to behold this new created
P. L. 7, 616. and from *t.* createst more
P. L. 8, 233. to see that none *t.* issued forth
P. L. 8, 466. and took from *t.* a rib
P. L. 8, 608. to thee disclose what inward *t.* I feel
P. L. 9, 62. *t.* full of anguish driven the space of
P. L. 9, 81. *t.* to the land where flows
P. L. 9, 812. to see from *t.* distinct each thing
P. L. 9, 1185. left to herself if evil *t.* ensue
P. L. 10, 344. *t.* gathered his own doom which
P. L. 10, 399. *t.* on the earth dominion
P. L. 10, 480. *t.* how I found the new created
P. L. 10, 583. *t.* by Saturn driven and Ops
P. L. 10, 675. *t.* down amain by Leo and the
P. L. 10, 969. *t.* by just event found so
P. L. 11, 107. from *t.* perpetual banishment
P. L. 11, 390. and *t.* to Agra and Lahor
P. L. 11, 402. or *t.* from Niger flood to Atlas
P. L. 11, 405. on Europe *t.* and where Rome
P. L. 11, 532. seeking from *t.* due nourishment
P. L. 11, 568. *t.* gliding hot to some cave's
P. L. 11, 670. cloud descending snatched him *t.*
P. L. 11, 718. *t.* from cups to civil broils
P. L. 11, 853. *t.* the rapid currents drive
P. L. 12, 33. mighty hunter *t.* he shall be called
P. L. 12, 343. Babylon *t.* called
P. L. 12, 458. and *t.* shall come when this
P. R. 1, 10. brought'st him *t.* by proof the
P. R. 1, 77. not *t.* to be more pure
P. R. 1, 82. *t.* on his head a perfect dove descend
P. R. 1, 203 to learn and know and *t.* to do
P. R. 2, 76. soon enforced to fly *t.* into Egypt
P. R. 2, 204. *t.* to the bait of women lay exposed
P. R. 3, 235. and what *t.* couldst thou observe
P. R. 3, 271. *t.* on as far as Indus
P. R. 3, 340. from *t.* to win the fairest of her sex
P. R. 4, 31. *t.* in the midst divided by a river
P. R. 4, 61. *t.* to the gates cast round thine eye
P. R. 4, 259. blind Melesigenes *t.* Homer called
P. R. 4, 261. *t.* what the lofty grave tragedians
P. R. 4, 267. *t.* to the famous orators repair

S. A. 631. *t.* faintings swoonings of despair
S. A. 943. helpless *t.* easily contemned
S. A. 1501. useless and *t.* ridiculous about him
C. 56. had by him ere he parted *t.* a son
C. 749. they had their name *t.*
**Thenceforth.**—P. L. 3, 265. no more *t.*
P. L. 3, 333. hell her numbers full *t.* shall be
P. L. 9, 602. *t.* to speculations high or deep
P. L. 9, 870. but *t.* endued with human voice
P. L. 10, 214. *t.* the form of servant to assume
P. L. 11, 802. *t.* shall practise how to live
P. L. 12, 109. resolving from *t.* to leave them
P. R. 1, 79. that who he is *t.* the nations may
P. R. 4, 514. *t.* I thought thee worth
S. 14, 13. who *t.* bid thee rest and drink thy fill
**Theologians.**—P. L. 5, 436. gloss of *t.*
**Thereafter.**—P. L. 2, 50. and these words *t.*
P. R. 2, 321. wouldst thou not eat? *t.* as I like
**Thereat.**—P. L. 10, 487. he *t.* offended
**Thereby.**—P. L. 3, 695. *t.* to glorify
P. L. 4, 197. yet not true life *t.* regained
P. L. 9, 128. though *t.* worse to me redound
P. L. 11, 360. *t.* to learn true patience and to
P. L. 11, 792. and achieved *t.* fame in the
P. L. 12, 96. though to the tyrant *t.* no excuse
P. R. 3, 107. and *t.* witness whence I am
S. A. 425. found soon occasion *t.* to make thee
S. A. 941. blind and *t.* deceivable
D. F. I. 12. *t.* to wipe away the infamous blot
D. F. I. 62. *t.* to set the hearts of men on fire
**Therefore.**—P. L. 2, 187. war *t.* open or
P. L. 2, 456. go *t.* mighty Powers terror of
P. L. 3, 111. they *t.* as to right belonged
P. L. 3, 131. man *t.* shall find grace
P. L. 3, 281. thou *t.* whom thou only canst
P. L. 3, 313. *t.* thy humiliation shall exalt
P. L. 4, 103. *t.* as far from granting he as I
P. L. 5, 935. I *t.* I alone first undertook
P. L. 5, 229. go *t.* half this day as friend with
P. L. 5, 372. Adam I *t.* came nor art thou such
P. L. 5, 404. *t.* what he gives whose praise
P. L. 6, 385. *t.* eternal silence be their doom
P. L. 6, 464. he who *t.* can invent with what
P. L. 6, 699. two days are *t.* passed the third
P. L. 6, 817. *t.* to me their doom he hath
P. L. 7, 516. *t.* the omnipotent Eternal Father
P. L. 8, 198. *t.* from this high pitch let us
P. L. 8, 228. say *t.* on
P. L. 8, 442. whose fellowship *t.* unmeet for
P. L. 8, 608. not *t.* foiled
P. L. 9, 212. thou *t.* now advise or hear what
P. L. 9, 279. that thou shouldst my firmness *t.*
P. L. 9, 700. God *t.* cannot hurt ye and be just
P. L. 9, 881. thou *t.* also taste that equal lot
P. L. 10, 393. I *t.* while I descend through
P. L. 10, 603. thou *t.* on these herbs and fruits
P. L. 10, 1016. but self-destruction *t.* sought
P. L. 11, 30. *t.* bend thine ear to supplication
P. L. 11, 93. lest *t.* his now bolder hand
P. L. 11, 314. *t.* to his great bidding I submit
P. L. 11, 520. *t.* so abject is their punishment
P. L. 11, 702. and *t.* hated *t.* so beset with foes
P. L. 11, 801. *t.* cooled in zeal
P. L. 12, 12. thou *t.* give due audience
P. L. 12, 90. *t.* since he permits within himself
P. L. 12, 287. and *t.* was law given them
P. L. 12, 307. *t.* shall not Moses
P. L. 12, 388. not *t.* joins the Son manhood
P. L. 1, 588. let us descend now *t.* from this
P. R. 1, 176 *t.* secure ventures his filial virtue
P. R. 1, 206. *t.* above my years the law of God
P. R. 2, 18. *t.* as those young prophets then
P. R. 2, 140. *t.* I am returned lest confidence
P. R. 2, 225. *t.* with manlier objects we must
P. R. 2, 407. not to be harmed *t.* not moved
P. R. 2, 426. *t.* if at great things thou wouldst
P. R. 3, 362. *t.* one of these thou must make
P. R. 4, 105. aim *t.* at no less than all the
P. R. 4, 146. know *t.* when my season comes
P. R. 4, 209. *t.* let pass as they are transitory
P. R. 4, 287. not *t.* am I short of knowing what

P. R. 4, 318. who *t*. seeks in these true wisdom
P. R. 4, 522. *t*. I watched thy footsteps from
P. R. 4, 538. *t*. to know what more thou art
S. A. 223. and *t*. urged the marriage on
S. A.795. sought by all means *t*. how to endear
S. A. 825. such pardon *t*. as I give my folly
S.A. 834. all wickedness is weakness that plea*t*.
S.A.895. not *t*. to be obeyed but zeal moved thee
S. A. 900. less *t*. to be pleased obeyed or feared
S. A.1319. thou know'st I am an Hebrew *t*. tell
C. 58. whom *t*. she brought up and Comus named
**Therein.**—P. L. 1, 652. *t*. plant a generation
P. L. 2, 883. and *t*. placed a race of upstart
P. L. 3, 390. and all the Powers *t*. by thee
P. L. 5, 522. thyself that is to thy obedience *t*.
P. L. 5, 575. and things *t*. each to other like
P. L. 8, 340. and all things that *t*. live
P. L. 8,·584. if aught *t*. enjoyed were worthy
P. L. 10, 483. of absolute perfection *t*. man
P. L. 11, 838. by men who there frequent or *t*.
P. L. 11, 895. to drown the world with man *t*.
P. L. 11, 896. will *t*. set his triple-coloured bow
P. L. 12, 250. *t*. an ark
P. R. 2, 463. for *t*. stands the office of a king
P. R. 3, 109. *t*. least resembling thy great
S. A. 299. and no man *t*. doctor but himself
**Thereof.**—P. L. 8, 329. the day thou eat'st *t*.
P. L. 9, 663. God hath said ye shall not eat *t*.
P. L. 9, 706. ye eat *t*. your eyes that seem so
P. L. 9, 724. that whoso eats *t*. forthwith
P. L. 10,200. thee saying thou shalt not eat *t*.
P. L. 10, 202. thou in sorrow shalt eat *t*. all
P. L. 12, 476. that much more good *t*. shall
S. A.1314. and now some public proof *t*. require
C. 740. and the good *t*. consists in mutual
**Thereon.**—P. L. 11,326. *t*. offer sweet-smelling
S. A. 1505. and thy joy *t*. conceived agreeable
**Thessalian.**—P. L. 2, 544. *T*. pines
**Thestylis.**—L'A. 88. with *T*. to bind the sheaves
**Thetis.**—C. 877. by *T*.' tinsel-slippered feet
**Thick.**—P. L. 1, 302. *t*. as autumnal leaves
P. L. 1, 311. so *t*. bestrown
P. L. 1, 548. and serried shields in *t*. array
P. L. 1, 767. *t*. swarmed both on the ground
P. L. 1, 775. so *t*. the aery crowd swarmed
P. L. 2, 264. how oft amidst *t*. clouds and dark
P. L. 2, 412. the strict senteries and stations *t*.
P. L. 2, 754. thy head flames *t*. and fast threw
P. L. 3, 25. so *t*. a drop serene hath quenched
P. L. 3, 61. stood *t*. as stars and from his sight
P. L. 3, 362. in loose garlands *t*. thrown off
P. L. 3, 507. *t*. with sparkling orient gems
P. L. 3, 577. aloof the vulgar constellations *t*.
P. L. 4,174. *t*. entwined as one continued brake
P. L. 4, 532. by fountain side or in *t*. shade
P. L. 4, 980. as *t*. as when a field of Ceres, ripe
P. L. 6, 16, with *t*. embattled squadrons
P. L. 6, 539. so *t*. a cloud he comes
P. L. 6, 751. flashing *t*. flames wheel within
P. L. 7, 320. forth flourished *t*. the clustering
P. L. 7, 358. with stars the heaven *t*. as a field
P. L. 8, 653. up to heaven from the *t*. shade
P. L. 9, 426. so *t*. the roses blushing round
P. L. 9, 446. where houses *t*. and sewers
P. L. 9, 1038. *t*. overhead with verdant roof
P. L. 10, 526. not so *t*. swarmed once the soil
P. R. 1, 41. within *t*. clouds and dark tenfold
P. R. 2, 117. up to the middle region of *t*. air
P. R. 2, 263. of trees *t*. interwoven there he
P. R. 4, 343. their swelling epithets *t*. laid as
P. R. 4, 405. whose branching arms *t*.
P. R. 4, 448. on the north and west by a *t*.
C. 62. and in *t*. shelter of black shades
C. 432. those *t*. and gloomy shadows damp
C. 893. *t*. set with agate and the azure sheen
Il P. 7, as *t*. and numberless as the gay motes
**Thickened.**—P. L. 11, 742. the *t*. sky like a
**Thicker.**—P. L. 10, 559. sat *t*. than the
**Thickest.**—P. L. 2, 537. till *t*. legions close
P. L. 4, 693. the roof of *t*. covert was in woven
P. L. 6, 308. where erst was *t*. fight

P. L. 9, 1100. together went into the *t*. wood
P. L. 9, 1110. loop-holes cut through *t*. shade
P. L. 10, 101. among the *t*. trees
P. L. 10, 411. course through *t*. constellations
C. 132. of Stygian darkness spets her *t*. gloom
P. 30. over the pole thy *t*. mantle throw
**Thicket.**—P. L. 4, 136. with *t*. overgrown
P. L. 4, 681. from the steep of echoing hill or *t*.
P. L. 7, 458. in forest wild in *t*., brake or den
P. L. 9, 179. through each *t*. dank or dry
P. L. 9,628. one small *t*. past of blowing myrrh
P. L. 9, 784. back to the *t*. slunk the guilty
A. 58. or tasselled horn shakes the high *t*.
**Thickets.**—H. 188. twilight shade of tangled *t*.
**Thicket-side.**—C. 185. said to the next *t.-s*.
**Thick-rammed.**—P. L. 6, 485. round *t.-r*.
**Thick-swarming.**—P. L. 10, 522. *t.-s*.
**Thick-warbled.**—P. L. 4, 246. her *t.-w*.
**Thick-woven.**—P. L. 9, 437. among *t.-w*.
**Thief.**—P. L. 4, 188. or as a *t*. bent to unhoard
P. L. 4, 192, clomb this first grand *t*. into God
P. R. 4, 604. and *t*. of Paradise
S. 2,1. how soon hath time the subtle *t*. of youth
**Thievish.**—C. 195. O *t*. night why shouldst
**Thigh.**—P. L. 6, 714. upon thy puissant *t*.
Il P. 142. while the bee with honied *t*.
**Thighs.**—P. L. 1,664. the *t*. of mighty cherubim
P. L. 5,282. skirted his loins and *t*. with downy
**Thin.**—P. L. 12, 76. where *t*. air above the
P. R. 1, 499. disappeared into *t*. air diffused
P. R. 4, 345. the rest *t*. sown with aught of
L'A. 50. scatters the rear of darkness *t*.
**Thine.**—P. R. 2, 748. and do I seem now in *t*.
P. L. 2, 753. dim *t*. eyes and dizzy swum
**Thing.**—P. L. 2, 679. created *t*. naught valued
P. L. 2, 741. till first I know of thee what *t*.
P. L. 4, 426. some dreadful *t*. no doubt
P. L. 4, 563. no evil *t*. approach or enter in
P. L. 7, 523. and every creeping *t*. that creeps
P. L. 7, 534. and every living *t*. that moves
P. L. 9,449. from each *t*. met conceives delight
P. L. 9, 695. of death denounced whatever *t*.
P. L. 9, 813. to see from thence distinct each *t*.
P. L. 9, 824. and perhaps a *t*. not undesirable
P. L. 10, 605. whatever *t*. the scythe of Time
S. A. 350. nay what *t*. good prayed for but often
S. A. 433. a worse *t*. yet remains
S. A. 710. but who is this what *t*. of sea or land
C. 432. some say no evil *t*. that walks by night
C. 456. driving far off each *t*. of sin and guilt
T. 9. for when as each *t*. bad thou hast entombed
T. 14. when every *t*. that is sincerely good
**Things.**—P. L. 1, 16. *t*. unattempted yet in prose
P. L. 1, 389. and with cursed *t*.
P.L. 1,693. here let those who boast in mortal *t*.
P. L. 2, 190. his mind whose eye views all *t*.
P. L. 2, 258. when great *t*. of small useful
P. L. 2, 278. all *t*. invite to peaceful counsels
P. L. 2, 392. great *t*. resolved which from the
P. L. 2, 625. all monstrous all prodigious *t*.
P. L. 2, 844. all *t*. shall be your prey
P, L. 2, 922. to compare great *t*. with small
P. L. 2, 962. night eldest of *t*. the consort of
P. L. 3, 55. that I may see and tell of *t*.
P. L. 3, 155. who art judge of all *t*. made
P. L. 3, 446. of all *t*. transitory and vain
P. L. 3, 448. all *t*. vain and all who in vain *t*.
P. L. 3, 611. in the dark so many precious *t*.
P. L. 3, 675. that both in him and all *t*. as is
P. L. 4,203. but perverts best *t*. to worst abuse
P. L. 4, 434. enjoy free leave so large to all *t*.
P. L. 4, 599. had in her sober livery all *t*. clad
P. L. 4, 611. the hour of night and all *t*. now
P. L. 4, 667. extinguish life in nature and all *t*.
P. L. 4, 692. when he framed all *t*.
P. L. 4, 752. sole propriety in Paradise of all *t*.
P. L. 4, 999. wherein all *t*. created first he
P. L. 5, 43. shadowy sets off the face of *t*.
P. L. 5, 46. in whose sight all *t*. joy with
P. L. 5, 103. external *t*. which the five
P. L. 5, 183. and mix and nourish all *t*.

P. L. 5, 455. to know of *t.* above his world
P. L. 5, 470. all *t.* proceed and up to him return
P. L. 5, 474. and in *t.* that live of life
P. L. 5, 511. in contemplation of created *t.*
P. L. 5, 575. and *t.* therein each to other like
P. L. 5, 581. all *t.* durable by present past
P. L. 5, 837. the mighty Father made all *t.*
P. L. 6, 137. who out of smallest *t.* could
P. L. 6, 298. or to what *t.* liken on earth
P. L. 6, 311. as to set forth great *t.* by small
P. L. 6, 477. so superficially surveys these *t.*
P. L. 6, 673. consulting on the sum of *t.* foreseen
P. L. 6, 708. of all *t.* to be heir and to be king
P. L. 6, 736. image of thee in all *t.*
P. L. 6, 893. thus measuring *t.* in heaven by *t.*
P. L. 7, 53. to hear of *t.* so high and strange *t.*
P. L. 7, 70. great *t.* and full of wonder in our ears
P. L. 7, 82. to impart *t.* above earthly thought
P. L. 7, 122. nor let thine own inventions hope *t.*
P. L. 7, 227. this universe and all created *t.*
P. L. 7, 240. then conglobed like *t.* to like
P. L. 7, 244. light ethereal first of *t.*
P. L. 7, 452. cattle and creeping *t.* and beast
P. L. 7, 591. author and end of all *t.*
P. L. 7, 636. how first this world and face of *t.*
P. L. 8, 10. to relate *t.* else by me unsearchable
P. L. 8, 121. if it presume might err in *t.* too
P. L. 8, 159. but whether thus these *t.*
P. L. 8, 191. not to know at large of *t.* remote
P. L. 8, 196. renders us in *t.* that most concern
P. L. 8, 199. and speak of *t.* at hand
P. L. 8, 265. all *t.* smiled
P. L. 8, 340. and all *t.* that therein live
P. L. 8, 363. thou hast provided all *t.* but with
P. L. 8, 414. thoughts come short supreme of *t.*
P. L. 8, 476. and into all *t.* from her air inspired
P. L. 8, 493. giver of all *t.* fair but fairest this
P. L. 8, 524. find in all *t.* else delight indeed
P. L. 8, 565. by attributing over much to *t.* less
P. L. 9, 171. obnoxious first or last to basest *t.*
P. L. 9, 194. all *t.* that breathe from the earth's
P. L. 9, 343. best are all *t.* as the will of
P. L. 9, 402. and all *t.* in best order to invite
P. L. 9, 539. thee all *t.* living gaze on all *t.*
P. L. 9, 604. considered all *t.* visible in heaven
P. L. 9, 605. all *t.* fair and good but all that
P. L. 9, 682. not only to discern *t.* in their
P. L. 9, 722. if they all *t.* who enclosed
P. L. 9, 804. as the gods who all *t.* know
P. L. 9, 1025. if such pleasure be in *t.* to us
P. L. 10, 7. who in all *t.* wise and just hindered
P. L. 10, 248. to unite with secret amity *t.*
P. L. 10, 269. from all *t.* there that live
P. L. 10, 306. so if great *t.* to small may be
P. L. 10, 380. monarchy with thee divide of all *t.*
P. L. 10, 651. as sorted best with present *t.*
P. L. 10, 707. thus began outrage from lifeless *t.*
P. L. 10, 850. represented all *t.* with double
P. L. 11, 56. distempered all *t.* and of incorrupt
P. L. 11, 160. mother of all *t.* living
P. L. 11, 161. by thee man is to live and all *t.*
P. L. 11, 308. change the will of him who all *t.*
P. L. 11, 579. nor those *t.* last which might
P. L. 11, 712. and saw the face of *t.* quite
P. L. 11, 870. O thou who future *t.* canst
P. L. 11, 900. till fire purge all *t.* new
P. L. 12, 140. *t.* by their names I call though
P. L. 12, 271. gracious *t.* thou hast revealed
P. L. 12, 341. with all his sacred *t.*
P. L. 12, 567. by small accomplishing great *t.*
P. L. 12, 618. thou to me art all *t.* under
P. R. 1, 69. to achieve *t.* highest greatest
P. R. 1, 137. doubting how these *t.* could be
P. R. 1, 206. promote all truth all righteous *t.*
P. R. 1, 258. like *t.* of thee to all that present
P. R. 1, 300. thoughts accompanied of *t.* past
P. R. 1, 489. about his altar, handling holy *t.*
P. R. 2, 103. storehouse long of *t.* and sayings
P. R. 2, 195. all her assaults on worthier *t.*
P. R. 2, 208. the accomplishment of greatest *t.*
P. R. 2, 305. so long should bide of all *t.*

P. R. 2, 324. hast thou not right to all created *t.?*
P. R. 2, 379. said'st thou not that to all *t.*
P. R. 2, 400. of these *t.* others quickly will
P. R. 2, 426. therefore if at great *t.* thou
P. R. 2, 448. who could do mighty *t.*
P. R. 3, 51. who extol *t.* vulgar
P. R. 3, 70. to *t.* not glorious men not worthy
P. R. 3, 111. all *t.* made, all *t.* orders
P. R. 3, 122. since his word all *t.* produced
P. R. 3, 182. all *t.* are best fulfilled in their due
P. R. 3, 183. and time there is for all *t.*
P. R. 3, 189. tried in humble state and *t.* adverse
P. R. 3, 239. in all *t.* that to greatest actions
P. R. 3, 355. in all *t.* and all men supposes
P. R. 4, 244. all *t.* in it comprehend
P. R. 4, 286. think not but that I know these *t.*
P. R. 4, 296. a third sort doubted all *t.* though
P. R. 4, 318. as one regardless quite of mortal *t.*
P. R. 4, 435. who all *t.* now behold more fresh
P. R. 4, 564. to compare small *t.* with greatest
S. A. 250. to count them *t.* worth notice
S. A. 926. with all *t.* grateful cheered
S. A. 942. in most *t.* as a child helpless
S. A. 1358. by prostituting holy *t.* to idols
S. A. 1451. lest I should see him forced to *t.*
S. A. 1532. yet God hath wrought *t.* as incredible
S. A. 1592. but while *t.* yet are in confusion
C. 217. *t.* ill are as slavish officers of vengeance
C. 458. tell her of *t.* that no gross ear can hear
C. 703. none but ... good men can give good *t.*
C. 796. dumb *t.* would be moved to sympathize
S. 21, 11. for other *t.* mild heaven a time ordains
P. 28. more apt for mournful *t.*
S. M. 4. dead *t.* with inbreathed sense
V. Ex. 45. then sing of secret *t.* that came to pass
**Think.**—P. L. 1, 661. who can *t.* submission
P. L. 3, 480. or in Franciscan *t.* to pass
P. L. 4, 432. then let us not *t.* hard one easy
P. L. 4, 675. nor *t.* though men were none
P. L. 4, 759. or *t.* thee unbefitting holiest place
P. L. 4, 835. *t.* not revolted spirit thy shape
P. L. 5, 433. and to taste *t.* not I shall be nice
P. L. 6, 135. fool not to *t.* how vain
P. L. 6, 271. but *t.* not here to trouble holy rest
P. L. 6, 282. nor *t.* thou with wind of aery
P. L. 6, 437. as easy *t.* the remedy
P. L. 6, 495. *t.* nothing hard
P. L. 7, 635. and thy request *t.* now fulfilled
P. L. 8, 174. be lowly wise *t.* only what concerns
P. L. 8, 224. nor less *t.* we in heaven of thee
P. L. 8, 581. *t.* the same vouchsafed to cattle
P. L. 9, 308. nor *t.* superfluous others' aid
P. L. 9, 370. but if thou *t.* trial unsought
P. L. 9, 380. a death to *t.*
P. L. 9, 938. nor can I *t.* that God creator wise
P. L. 11, 292. where he abides *t.* there thy
P. L. 11, 465. horrid to *t.* how horrible to feel
P. R. 1, 387. men generally *t.* me such a foe
P. R. 3, 109. *t.* not so slight of glory therein
P. R. 3, 398. *t.* not thou to find me slack
P. R. 4, 286. *t.* not but that I know these things
S. A. 295. unless there be who *t.* not God at all
S. A. 445. of all thy sufferings *t.* the heaviest
S. A. 553. O madness to *t.* use of strongest wines
S. A. 930. nor *t.* me so unwary or accursed
S. A. 1335. can they *t.* me so broken so debased
S. A. 1534. he can I know but doubt to *t.* he will
C. 366. I do not *t.* my sister so to seek
C. 755. *t.* what and be advised
C. 758. would *t.* to charm my judgment
L. 74. and *t.* to burst out into sudden blaze
H. 105. to *t.* her part was done
P. 55. might *t.* the infection of my sorrows loud
D. F. I. 74. *t.* what a present thou .. hast sent
U. C. II. 32. to *t.* his wain was his increase
**Thinking.**—P. L. 10, 564. they fondly *t.* to
P. L. 10, 1021. so *t.* to evade the penalty
P. R. 4, 496. *t.* to terrify me to thy will
U. C. I. 12. and *t.* now his journey's end was come
**Thinks.**—P. L. 3, 688. goodness *t.* no ill
**Think'st.**—P. L. 8, 110. me thou *t.* not slow

P. L. 8, 403. what *t.* thou then of me
P. L. 10, 592. what *t.* thou of our empire now
P. R. 1, 347. *t.* thou such force in bread
P. R. 2, 177. none are thou *t.* but taken with
P. R. 3, 163. and *t.* thou to regain thy right
**Thinner.**—P. L. 8. 348. to draw the *t.* air
P. L. 9, 142. *t.* left the throng of his adorers
**Thin-spun.**—L. 76. and slits the *t.-s.* life
**Third.**—P. L. 1, 705. a *t.* as soon had formed
P. L. 2, 692. after him the *t.* part of heaven's
P. L. 4, 869. and with them comes a *t.* of regal
P. L. 5, 283. the *t.* his feet shadowed
P. L. 5, 710. drew after him the *t.* part of
P. L. 6, 156. durst oppose a *t.* part of the gods
P. L. 6, 699. days are therefore passed the *t.* is
P. L. 6, 748. and the *t.* sacred morn began to
P. L. 7, 338. so even and morn recorded the *t.*
P. L. 10, 82. the *t.* best absent is
P. L. 12, 267. so call the *t.* from Abraham
P. L. 12, 421. ere the *t.* dawning light return
P. R. 4, 296. a *t.* sort doubted all things
S. A. 1466. a *t.* more generous far and civil
S. A. 1701. that no second knows nor *t.*
**Thirst.**—P. L. 4, 228. with kindly *t.* updrawn
P. L. 4, 330. ease more easy wholesome *t.* and
P. L. 5, 305. and not disrelish *t.* of nectarous
P. L. 7, 68. whose liquid murmur heard new *t.*
P. L. 8, 8. allayed the *t.* I had of knowledge
P. L. 8, 212. of palm tree pleasantest to *t.*
P. L. 9, 586. hunger and *t.* at once powerful
P. L. 10, 556. yet parched with scalding *t.* and
P. L. 10, 568. oft they assayed hunger and *t.*
P. L. 11, 846. wave largely drew as after *t.*
P. R. 1, 339. to *t.* inured more than the camel
P. R. 3, 88. quench not the *t.* of glory but
P. R. 4, 120. to me shouldst tell who *t.* and
P. R. 4. 593. if aught hunger had impaired or *t.*
S. A. 551. from the clear milky juice allaying *t.*
S. A. 582. thy *t.* to allay after the brunt of battle
S. A. 1456. say reverend sire, we *t.* to hear
C. 67. through fond intemperate *t.*
C. 678. to life so friendly or so cool to *t.*
**Thirsted.**—P. L. 4, 336. still as they *t.* scoop
**Thirsty.**—P. L. 5, 190. or wet the *t.* earth
C. 524. and here to every *t.* wanderer
**Thirty.**—S. A. 1186. murder on those *t.* men
S. A. 1197. appointed to await me *t.* spies
V. Ex. 94. his *t.* arms along the indented meads
**Thisbite.**—P. R. 2, 16. and the great *T.*
**Thistles.**—P. L. 10, 203. thorns also and *t.*
C. 352. the chill dew amongst rude burs and *t.*
**Thither.**—P. L. 1, 183. *t.* let us tend
P. L. 1, 357. the heads and leaders *t.* haste
P. L. 1, 655. *t.* if but to pry
P. L. 1, 656. our first eruption *t.* or elsewhere
P. L. 1, 674. *t.* winged with speed
P. L. 2, 354. *t.* let us bend all our thoughts
P. L. 2, 596. *t.* by harpy-footed furies haled
P. L. 2, 954. *t.* he plies undaunted to meet
P. L. 2, 979. *t.* to arrive I travel this profound
P. L. 2, 1054. *t.* full fraught with mischievous
P. L. 3, 573. *t.* his course he bends through
P. L. 4, 452. whence *t.* brought and how
P. L. 4, 456. I *t.* went with unexperienced
P. L. 4, 555. *t.* came Uriel gliding through
P. L. 4, 593. incredible how swift had *t.* rolled
P. L. 4, 890. break loose from hell though *t.*
P. L. 4, 963. fly *t.* whence thou fledst
P. L. 5, 266. down *t.* prone in flight he speeds
P. L. 5, 767. for *t.* he assembled all his train
P. L. 5, 770. *t.* to come and with calumnious
P. L. 7, 290. *t.* they hasted
P. L. 7, 513. *t.* with heart and voice and eyes
P. L. 7, 572. with ... intercourse *t.* will send
P. L. 9, 630. I can bring thee *t.*
P. L. 10, 629. not that I called and drew them *t.*
P. L. 11, 200. *t.* must return and be no more
P. L. 11, 433. *t.* anon a sweaty reaper
P. L. 11, 837. to place no sanctity if none be *t.*
P. L. 12, 75. what food will he convey up *t.*
P. L. 12, 366. they gladly *t.* haste and by

P. R. 1, 250. guided the wise men *t.* from the
P. R. 2, 291. *t.* he bent his way determined
P. R. 4, 374. I found thee there and *t.* will
S. A. 1450. the city rings and numbers *t.* flock
S. A. 1521. lest running *t.* we unawares
S. A. 1738. *t.* shall all the valiant youth resort
V. Ex. 12. believe me I have *t.* packed the worst
**Thitherward.**—P. L. 3, 500. turned *t.*
P. L. 8, 260. up I sprung as *t.* endeavouring
**Thone.**—C. 675. nepenthes which the wife of *T.*
**Thorn.**—P. L. 4, 256. and without *t.* the rose
S. A. 1037. the contrary she proves, a *t.* intestine
**Thorns.**—P. L. 10, 203. *t.* also and thistles
P. R. 2, 459. golden in show, is but a wreath of *t.*
**Thoroughfare.**—P. L. 10. 393. of easy *t.*
**Though.**—P. L. 1, 53. confounded *t.* immortal
P. L. 1, 87. didst outshine myriads *t.* bright
P. L. 1, 97. *t.* changed in outward lustre
P. L. 1, 105. what *t.* the field be lost
P. L. 1, 125. *t.* in pain vaunting aloud
P. L. 1, 141. *t.* all our glory extinct
P. L. 1, 153. *t.* yet we feel strength undiminished
P. L. 1, 262. to reign is worth ambition *t.* in hell
P. L. 1, 361. *t.* of their names in heavenly records
P. L. 1, 394. *t.* for the noise of drums
P. L. 1, 444. whose heart *t.* large
P. L. 1, 507. *t.* far renowned, the Ionian gods
P. L. 1, 576. *t.* all the giant brood of Phlegra
P. L. 1, 614. their stately growth *t.* bare
P. L. 1, 624. *t.* the event was dire
P. L. 1, 631. *t.* after loss
P. L. 1, 763. *t.* like a covered field
P. L. 1, 791. *t.* without number still
P. L. 2, 13. *t.* oppressed and fallen
P. L. 2, 18. me *t.* just right and the fixed laws
P. L. 2, 104. to alarm *t.* inaccessible
P. L. 2, 112. *t.* his tongue dropped manna
P. L. 2, 147. for who would lose *t.* full of pain
P. L. 2, 224. for happy *t.* but ill
P. L. 2, 251. unacceptable *t.* in heaven
P. L. 2, 254. *t.* in this vast recess free
P. L. 2, 305. yet shone majestic *t.* in ruin
P. L. 2, 321. *t.* thus far removed under the
P. L. 2, 337. reluctance and revenge *t.* slow
P. L. 2, 349. *t.* less in power and excellence
P. L. 2, 432. seized us *t.* undismayed
P. L. 2, 457. terror of Heaven *t.* fallen
P. L. 2, 498. *t.* under hope of heavenly grace
P. L. 2, 682. that darest, *t.* grim and terrible
P. L. 2, 790. he pursued, *t.* more, it seems
P. L. 2, 813. in those bright arms *t.* tempered
P. L. 2, 835. our vacant room *t.* more removed
P. L. 2, 1044. holds gladly the port *t.* shrouds
P. L. 3, 14. *t.* long detained in that obscure
P. L. 3, 21. to reascend *t.* hard and rare
P. L. 3, 99. sufficient to have stood *t.* free to
P. L. 3, 152. *t.* joined with his own folly
P. L. 3, 159. or proud return *t.* to his heavier
P. L. 3, 176. *t.* forfeit and enthralled by sin
P. L. 3, 192. *t.* but endeavoured with sincere
P. L. 3, 245. *t.* now to death I yield and am
P. L. 3, 278. nor man the least *t.* last created
P. L. 3, 286. head of all mankind *t.* Adam's son
P. L. 3, 305. *t.* throned in highest bliss equal
P. L. 3, 428. *t.* distant far
P. L. 3, 465. vain exploit *t.* then renowned
P. L. 3, 530. and *t.* that were large
P. L. 3, 552. *t.* after heaven seen
P. L. 3, 585. with gentle penetration *t.* unseen
P. L. 3, 602. *t.* by their powerful art
P. L. 3, 686. and oft *t.* wisdom wake suspicion
P. L. 3, 690. beguiled Uriel *t.* regent of the sun
P. L. 3, 723. with light from hence *t.* but
P. L. 4, 13. *t.* bold far off and fearless
P. L. 4, 62. and me *t.* mean drawn to his part
P. L. 4, 167. *t.* with them better pleased
P. L. 4, 169. that drove him *t.* enamoured
P. L. 4, 281. *t.* this by some supposed true
P. L. 4, 295. *t.* both not equal as their sex
P. L. 4, 375. pity thus forlorn *t.* I unpitied

P. L. 4, 392. to do what else *t.* damned
P. L. 4, 663. in order *t.* to nations yet unborn
P. L. 4, 674. *t.* unbeheld in deep of night
P. L. 4, 675. nor think *t.* men were none that
P. L. 4, 706. and sequestered *t.* but feigned
P. L. 4, 890. loose from hell *t.* thither doomed
P. L. 4, 941. *t.* for possession put to try once
P. L. 4, 973. *t.* Heaven's King ride on thy wings
P. L. 4, 1009. *t.* doubled now to trample thee
P. L. 5, 75. happy *t.* thou art
P. L. 5, 236. his own free will his will *t.* free
P. L. 5, 358. Adam, not awed yet
P. L. 5, 374. as may not oft invite *t.* spirits
P. L. 5, 394. *t.* spring and autumn here danced
P. L. 5, 426. *t.* in heaven the trees of life
P. L. 5, 428. *t.* from off the boughs each morn
P. L. 5, 553. *t.* what thou tell'st hath passed
P. L. 5, 574. *t.* what if earth be but the shadow
P. L. 5, 580. for time *t.* in eternity applied
P. L. 5, 875. the flaming Seraph fearless *t.* alone
P. L. 5, 903. change his constant mind *t.* single
P. L. 6, 11. *t.* darkness there might well seem
P. L. 6, 36. worlds judged thee perverse
P. L. 6, 91. *t.* strange to us it seemed at first
P. L. 6, 118. *t.* to sight unconquerable
P. L. 6, 124. *t.* brutish that contest and foul
P. L. 6, 144. *t.* then to thee not visible when
P. L. 6, 226. and disturb *t.* not destroy their
P. L. 6, 229. *t.* numbered such as each divided
P. L. 6, 265. *t.* heaviest .... on thyself
P. L. 6, 297. who *t.* with the tongue of angels
P. L. 6, 364. *t.* huge and in a rock of diamond
P. L. 6, 377. in might *t.* wondrous and in acts
P. L. 6, 405. *t.* from their place by violence
P. L. 6, 429. *t.* till now omniscient thought
P. L. 6, 435. and *t.* pierced with wound soon
P. L. 6, 457. valour or strength *t.* matchless
P. L. 6, 593. none on their feet might stand *t.*
P. L. 6, 660. *t.* spirits of purest light
P. L. 7, 18. once Bellerophon *t.* from a lower
P. L. 7, 25. on evil days *t.* fallen
P. L. 7, 31. and fit audience find *t.* few
P. L. 7, 50. to please their appetite *t.* wandering
P. L. 7, 99. to run much of his race *t.* steep
P. L. 7, 112. *t.* to recount almighty works
P. L. 7, 148. to possess her realm *t.* wide
P. L. 7, 170. *t.* I uncircumscribed myself retire
P. L. 7, 331. *t.* God had yet not rained upon
P. L. 7, 356. unlightsome first *t.* of ethereal
P. L. 7, 368. *t.* from human sight so far remote
P. L. 7, 497. *t.* to thee not noxious but obedient
P. L. 7, 552. desisting *t.* unwearied up returned
P. L. 8, 92. *t.* in comparison of heaven so small
P. L. 8, 108. *t.* numberless to his
P. L. 8, 117. not that I so affirm *t.* so it seem
P. L. 8, 129. the planet earth so steadfast *t.* she
P. L. 8, 215. they satiate and soon fill *t.* pleasant
P. L. 8, 289. untroubled *t.* I thought I then was
P. L. 8, 335. dreadful in mine ear *t.* in my
P. L. 8, 402. taste no pleasure *t.* in pleasure
P. L. 8, 421. through all numbers absolute *t.* one
P. L. 8, 463. methought I saw *t.* sleeping where
P. L. 8, 485. by her heavenly maker *t.* unseen
P. L. 8, 500. and *t.* divinely brought
P. L. 8, 506. nature herself *t.* pure of sinful
P. L. 8, 598. *t.* higher of the genial bed by far
P. L. 9, 70. now not, *t.* sin not time first
P. L. 9, 128. *t.* thereby worse to me redound
P. L. 9, 139. *t.* perhaps not longer than since I
P. L. 9, 171. revenge at first *t.* sweet
P. L. 9, 224. brought to little *t.* begun early
P. L. 9, 296. for he who tempts *t.* in vain
P. L. 9, 301. the offered wrong *t.* ineffectual
P. L. 9, 304. the enemy *t.* bold will hardly
P. L. 9, 377. yet submiss *t.* last replied
P. L. 9, 390. *t.* not as she with bow and
P. L. 9, 428. whose head, *t.* gay carnation
P. L. 9, 432. herself *t.* fairest unsupported
P. L. 9, 468. burns *t.* in mid Heaven
P. L. 9, 485. of limb heroic built *t.* of
P. L. 9, 490. not terrible, *t.* terror be in love

P. L. 9, 551. his words made way, *t.* at the
P. L. 9, 601. speech wanted not long *t.* to
P. L. 9, 610. *t.* importune perhaps
P. L. 9, 648. fruitless to me *t.* fruit be here
P. L. 9, 664. she scarce had said *t.* brief when
P. L. 9, 715. death to be wished *t.* threatened
P. L. 9, 746. best of fruits *t.* kept from man
P. L. 9, 805. *t.* others envy what they cannot
P. L. 9, 810. givest access *t.* secret she retire
P. L. 9, 939. Creator wise *t.* threatening
P. L. 9, 945. who *t.* his power creation could
P. L. 9, 1065. till Adam *t.* not less than Eve
P. L. 10, 91. time counts not *t.* with swiftest
P. L. 10, 109. with him Eve more loth *t.* first
P. L. 10, 135. *t.* should I hold my peace yet
P. L. 10, 165. serpent *t.* brute unable to transfer
P. L. 10, 173. *t.* in mysterious terms
P. L. 10, 227. all. *t.* all knowing
P. L. 10, 274. *t.* many a league remote
P. L. 10, 331. soon discerned *t.* in disguise
P. L. 10, 335. by Eve, *t.* all unweeting
P. L. 10, 362. I felt *t.* distant from thee worlds
P. L. 10, 557. *t.* to delude them sent could not
P. L. 10, 592. our empire now *t.* earned with
P. L. 10, 600. which here *t.* plenteous
P. L. 10, 690. the world inhabited *t.* sinless
P. L. 10, 692. in the heavens *t.* slow produced
P. L. 10, 716. in part *t.* hid in gloomiest shade
P. L. 10, 741. heavy *t.* in their place
P. L. 10, 759. and *t.* God made thee without
P. L. 10, 794. for *t.* the Lord of all be infinite
P. L. 10, 830. *t.* through mazes
P. L. 10, 836. *t.* divided with that bad woman
P. L. 10, 878. longing to be seen *t.* by the Devil
P. L. 10, 977. *t.* sharp and sad yet tolerable
P. L. 11, 31. hear his sighs *t.* mute
P. L. 11, 40. at least his days numbered *t.* sad
P. L. 11, 71. and in their state *t.* firm stood
P. L. 11, 117. *t.* sorrowing yet in peace
P. L. 11, 173. *t.* after sleepless night
P. L. 11, 177. *t.* now enjoined laborious
P. L. 11, 180. here let us live *t.* in fallen state
P. L. 11, 272. I had hope to spend quiet *t.* sad
P. L. 11, 330. for *t.* I fled him angry
P. L. 11, 332. gladly behold *t.* but his utmost
P. L. 11, 459. *t.* here thou see him die
P. L. 11, 492. delayed to strike, *t.* oft invoked
P. L. 11, 496. *t.* not of woman born
P. L. 11, 509. goodly and erect *t.* faulty since
P. L. 11, 585. the men *t.* grave eyed then and
P. L. 11, 604. by pleasure *t.* to nature seeming
P. L. 11, 611. *t.* his spirit taught them
P. L. 11, 760. on thy feet thou stood'st at last *t.*
P. L. 11, 886. *t.* late repenting him of man
P. L. 12, 2. baits at noon *t.* bent on speed
P. L. 12, 37. *t.* of rebellion others he accuse
P. L. 12, 96. tyranny must be *t.* to the tyrant
P. L. 12, 140. names I call *t.* yet unnamed
P. L. 12, 201. *t.* present in his angel
P. L. 12, 307. *t.* of God highly beloved
P. L. 12, 403. and by love *t.* love alone fulfil
P. L. 12, 410. not their own, *t.* legal works
P. L. 12, 494. not afraid *t.* to the death
P. L. 12, 514. *t.* not but by the Spirit
P. L. 12, 517. *t.* feigning still to act by spiritual
P. L. 12, 576. hope no higher *t.* all the stars
P. L. 12, 603. in one faith unanimous *t.* sad
P. L. 12, 621. I carry hence *t.* all by me is lost
P. R. 1, 15. deeds above heroic *t.* in secret done
P. R. 1, 52. *t.* since with dread attending
P. R. 1, 92. *t.* in his face the glimpses of his
P. R. 1, 177. ventures his filial virtue *t.* untried
P. R. 1, 232. can raise them *t.* above example
P. R. 1, 235. *t.* men esteem thee low of parentage
P. R. 1, 377. I have lost much lustre of my
P. R. 1, 466. but the subtle fiend *t.* inly stung
P. R. 1, 485. and talk at least *t.* I despair to
P. R. 1, 494. thy coming hither *t.* I know thy
P. R. 2, 8. others *t.* in Holy Writ not named
P. R. 2, 63. her breast *t.* calm her breast *t.* pure
P. R. 2, 134. *t.* Adam by his wife's allurement

P. R. 2, 209. what woman will you find *t*.
P. R. 2, 251. *t*. needing, what praise is it to
P. R. 2, 255. *t*. hunger still remain so it remain
P. R. 2, 269. *t*.ravenous taught to abstain from
P. R. 2, 330. *t*. who would scruple that with
P. R. 2, 449. contemn riches *t*. offered from the
P. R. 3, 20. subsist in battle *t*. against thy few
P. R. 3, 104. and loses *t*. but verbal his reward
P. R. 3, 123. *t*. chiefly not for glory as prime
P. R. 3, 154. *t*. thy right be now in powerful
P. R. 3, 169. his family obtained *t*. priests
P. R. 3, 215. *t*. to that gentle brow willingly
P. R. 3, 229. for *t*. in thee be united what
P. R. 3, 303. see *t*. from far his
P. R. 3, 351. thy kingdom *t*.foretold by prophet
P. R. 4, 14. and never cease *t*. to his shame
P. R. 4, 19. *t*. all to shivers dashed
P. R. 4, 23. yet gives not o'er *t*. desperate
P. R. 4, 111. of luxury *t*. called magnificence
P. R. 4, 113. *t*. thou shouldst add to tell their
P. R. 4, 197. *t*. sons of God both angels are
P. R. 4, 290. no other doctrine needs *t*. granted
P. R. 4, 296. doubted all things *t*. plain sense
P. R. 4, 402. after his aery jaunt *t*. hurried
P. R. 4, 417. whose tallest pines *t*. rooted deep
P. R. 4, 454. and these flaws *t*. mortals fear
P. R. 4, 488. *t*. noising loud and threatening
P. R. 4, 509. thy manhood last *t*. yet in private
P. R. 4, 512. the rest (*t*. not to be baptized)
P. R. 4, 612. for *t*. that seat of earthly bliss
S. A. 193. not to be found *t*. sought
S. A. 248. deeds themselves *t*.mute spoke loud
S. A. 323. *t*.reason here aver, that moral verdict
S. A. 333. such ye seem *t*. in this uncouth place
S. A. 390. vitiated with gold *t*. offered only
S. A. 736. *t*. the fact more evil drew
S. A. 733. *t*. my pardon no way assured
S. A. 746. *t*.late yet in some part to recompense
S. A. 812. *t*.fond and reasonless to some perhaps
S. A. 844. in man or woman *t*. to thy own
S. A. 914. *t*. sight be lost life yet hath many
S.A. 983. I know thy trains *t*. dearly to my cost
S. A. 1003. yet beauty *t*. injurious hath strange
S. A. 1546. or reason *t*. disturbed
S.A.1706. and *t*. her body die her fame survives
**Thought.**—P. L. 1, 54. for now the *t*.
P. L. 1, 560. breathing united force with fixed *t*.
P. L. 4, 50. and *t*. one step higher would set
P. L. 4, 198. on the virtue *t*. of that life-giving
P. L. 4, 320. for they *t*. no ill
P. L. 4, 457. thither went with unexperienced *t*.
P. L. 4, 794. (who could have *t*.)
P. L. 5, 37. with gentle voice, I *t*. it thine it
P. L. 5, 159. thy goodness beyond *t*.
P. L. 5, 384. no *t*. infirm altered her cheek
P. L. 5, 576. like more than on earth is *t*.
P. L. 5, 665. and *t*. himself impaired
P. L. 5, 727. hath in his *t*. to try in battle
P. L. 5, 828. how far from *t*. to make us less
P. L. 6, 20. known what he for news had *t*.
P. L. 6, 98. ended soon each milder *t*.
P. L. 6, 164. at first I *t*. that liberty and heaven
P. L. 6, 192. no sight nor motion of swift *t*.
P. L. 6, 236. no *t*. of flight none of retreat
P. L. 6, 430. though till now omniscient *t*.
P. L. 6, 500. most would have *t*. impossible
P. L. 6, 538. the foe at hand whom fled we *t*.
P. L. 7, 53. things to their *t*. so unimaginable
P. L. 7, 82. to impart things above earthly *t*.
P. L. 7, 139. who *t*. all like himself rebellious
P. L. 7, 603. what *t*. can measure thee
P. L. 7, 611. they *t*. thee to diminish
P. L. 8, 3. that he awhile *t*. him still speaking
P. L. 8, 289. though I *t*. I then was passing
P. L. 8, 506. though pure of sinful *t*.
P. L. 9, 319. who *t*. less attributed to her faith
P. L. 9, 555. the first at least of these I *t*.
P. L. 9, 790. nor was godhead from her *t*.
P. L. 9, 857. and *t*. it long deprived thy presence
P. L. 9, 898. whatever can to sight or *t*. be
P. L. 9, 977. were it I *t*. death menaced

P. L. 9, 1004. Adam took no *t*. eating his fill
P. L. 9, 1119. and as they *t*. their shame in
P. L. 9, 1179. that I *t*. no evil durst attempt
P. L. 10, 219. and *t*. not much to clothe his
P. L. 10, 788. O. *t*. horrid, if true
P. L. 10, 1017. that excellence *t*. in thee
P. L. 10, 1049. which we *t*. was meant by death
P. L. 11, 400. and Sofala *t*. Ophir
P. L. 11, 770. with *t*. that they must be
P. L. 12, 558. greatly in peace of *t*.
P. R. 1, 192. from track of men *t*. following *t*.
P. R. 1, 204. myself I *t*. born to that end
P. R. 2, 13. sometimes they *t*. he might be only
P. R. 2, 146. lest I who erst *t*. none my equal
P. R. 2, 266. him *t*. he by the brook of Cherith
P. R. 2, 481. to give a kingdom hath been *t*.
P. R. 4, 11. overreached where least he *t*.
P. R. 4, 495. wouldst be *t*. my God
P. R. 4, 514. thenceforth I *t*. thee worth my
P. R. 4, 520. yet thee I *t*. in some respect far
S. A. 117. O change beyond report *t*. or belief
S. A. 231. I *t*. it lawful from my former act
S. A. 302. then give the reins to wandering *t*.
S. A. 352. *t*. barrenness in wedlock a reproach
S. A. 659. lenient of grief and anxious *t*.
S. A. 870. virtue as I *t*. truth duty so enjoining
S.A. 871. I *t*. where all thy circling wiles would
S. A. 908. in what I *t*. would have succeeded best
S. A. 1092. *t*. gyves and the mill had tamed thee
S.A. 1531. that were a joy presumptuous to be *t*.
S. A. 1688. despised and *t*. extinguished quite
C. 408. infer as if I *t*. my sister's state secure
C. 505. is worth a *t*. to this my errand
C. 566. and O poor hapless nightingale *t*. I
C. 756. I had not *t*. to have unlocked my lips
A. 24. who had *t*. this clime had held
L. 189. with eager *t*. warbling his Doric lay
S. 22, 13. this *t*. might lead me through
H. 88. full little *t*. they then
D.F.I. 6. that did thy cheek envermeil *t*. *to* kiss
D. F. I. 10. he *t*. it touched his deity full near
M. W. 39. who only *t*. to crop the flower
**Thoughts.**—P. L. 1, 88. united *t*. and
P. L. 1, 557. with solemn touches troubled *t*.
P. L. 1, 659. but these *t*. full counsel must
P. L. 1, 680. his looks and *t*. were always
P. L. 2, 115. for his *t*. were low
P. L. 2, 148. those *t*. that wander through
P. L. 2, 283. dismissing quite all *t*. of war
P. L. 2, 354. thither let us bend all our *t*.
P. L. 2, 421. pondering the danger with deep *t*.
P. L. 2, 526. find truce to his restless *t*.
P. L. 2, 558. in *t*. more elevate
P. L. 2, 630. Satan with *t*. inflamed of highest
P. L. 3, 37. then feed on *t*. that voluntary
P. L. 3, 171. spoken as my *t*. are
P. L. 4, 19. and doubt distract his troubled *t*.
P. L. 4, 95. soon would height recall high *t*.
P. L. 4, 362. whom my *t*. pursue with wonder
P. L. 4, 688. divide the night and lift our *t*.
P. L. 4, 807. least distempered discontented *t*.
P. L. 5, 28. O sole in whom my *t*. find all
P. L. 5, 96. the trouble of thy *t*. this night in
P. L. 5, 209. and to their *t*. firm peace recovered
P. L. 5, 332. on hospitable *t*. intent
P. L. 5, 552. my constant *t*. assured me
P. L. 5, 676. thou to me thy *t*. wast wont I
P. L. 5, 712. whose sight discerns abstrusest *t*.
P. L. 6, 90. their *t*. proved fond and vain in
P. L. 6, 367. but meaner *t*. learned in their
P. L. 6, 581. collected stood within our *t*.
P. L. 6, 629. heightened in their *t*. beyond all
P. L. 8, 40. seemed entering on studious *t*.
P. L. 8, 167. solicit not thy *t*. with matters hid
P. L. 8, 183. nor with perplexing *t*. to interrupt
P. L. 8, 187. seek them with wandering *t*.
P. L. 8, 414. all human *t*. come short
P.L. 8, 590. love refines the *t*. and heart enlarges
P. L. 9, 88. of *t*. revolved his final sentence
P. L. 9, 101. built with second *t*. reforming
P. L. 9, 130. I find ease to my relentless *t*.

P. L. 9, 213. or hear what to my mind first *t.*
P. L. 9, 229. well thy *t.* employed how we
P. L. 9, 288. *t.* which how found they harbour
P. L. 9, 471. all his *t.* of mischief
P. L. 9, 473. *t.* whither have ye led me with
P. L. 9, 572. of abject *t.* and low as was my
P. L. 9, 603. I turned my *t.* and with capacious
P. L. 9, 843. great joy he promised to his *t.*
P. L. 9, 918. and after *t.* disturbed submitting
P. L. 10, 608. his *t.*, his looks, words, actions
P. L. 10, 975. what *t.* in my unquiet breast
P. L. 10, 1008. so much of death her *t.* had
P. L. 11, 498. till firmer *t.* restrained excess
P. L. 12, 275. erewhile perplexed with *t.*
P. L. 12, 377. what oft my steadiest *t.* have
P. R. 1, 190. his deep *t.* the better to converse
P. R. 1, 196. O what a multitude of *t.* at once
P. R. 1, 227. these growing *t.* my mother soon
P. R. 1, 229. high are thy *t.* O son
P. R. 1, 299. but with such *t.* accompanied
P. R. 2, 65. some troubled *t.* which she in sighs
P. R. 2, 107. with *t.* meekly composed
P. R. 2, 258. fed with better *t.* that feed me
P. R. 3, 227. perhaps thou linger'st in deep *t.*
S. A. 19. none to the mind from restless *t.*
S. A. 459. eye to harbour sleep or *t.* to rest
S. A. 524. *t.* of birth from heaven foretold
S. A. 590. all otherwise to me my *t.* portend
S. A. 623. *t.* my tormentors armed with deadly
S. A. 1383. dispose to something.... my *t.*
C. 192. is now the labour of my *t.* 'tis likeliest
C. 210. these *t.* may startle well but not astound
C. 371. could stir the constant mood of her calm *t.*
C. 383. but he that hides a dark soul and foul *t.*
C. 669. that fancy can beget on youthful *t.*
L. 153. let our frail *t.* dally with false surmise
S. 21,5. to-day deep *t.* resolve with me to drench
H. 92. was all that did their silly *t.* so busy keep
V. Ex. 23. I have some naked *t.* that rove about
**Thousand.**—P. L. 1, 545. ten *t.* banners rise
P. L. 1, 796. a *t.* demi-gods on golden seats
P. L. 2, 967. discord with a *t.* various mouths
P. L. 2, 934. ten *t.* fathom deep and to this
P. L. 3, 488. them transverse ten *t.* leagues
P. L. 5, 249. but from among *t.* celestial ardours
P. L. 5, 588. ten *t. t.* ensigns high advanced
P. L. 6, 767. attended with ten *t. t.* saints
P. L. 6, 769. twenty *t.* (I their number heard)
P. L. 6, 836. grasping ten *t.* thunders
P. L. 7, 382. and her reign with *t.* lesser lights
P. L. 7, 383. with *t. t.* stars that then appeared
P. L. 7,559. the sound symphonious of ten *t.* harps
P. L. 8,601. those graceful acts those *t.* decencies
P. R. 3, 411. the lives of threescore and ten *t.*
S. A. 144. a *t.* foreskins fell the flower
C. 205. a *t.* fantasies begin to throng into my
C. 455. a *t.* liveried angels lackey her
C. 627. and show me simples of a *t.* names
C. 926. from a *t.* petty rills
L. 135. their bells and flowerets of a *t.* hues
L'A. 62. the clouds in *t.* liveries dight
H. 100. with *t.* echoes still prolongs each
S. M. 12. and the cherubic host in *t.* choirs
**Thousand-fold.**—P. L. 11, 678. ten *t.-f.*
**Thousands.**—P. L. 1, 760. *t.* trooping came
P. L. 6, 48. by *t.* and by millions ranged
P. L. 6,148. few sometimes may know when *t.* err
P. L. 6, 270. thou instilled thy malice into *t.*
P. L. 6,373. relate of *t.* and their names eternize
P. L. 6, 594. but down they fell by *t.*
P. R. 3, 304. see though from far his *t.*
S. 19, 12. *t.* at his bidding speed
**Thracian.**—P. L. 7, 34. that tore the *T.* bard
**Thraldom.**—S. A. 946. to thy will in perfect *t.*
**Thrall.**—P. L. 10, 402. make sure your *t.*
P. R. 1, 411. as a poor miserable captive *t.*
S. A. 370. and as a *t.* subject him to so foul
S. A. 1622. made their dreadful enemy their *t.*
**Thralls.**—P. L. 1, 149. his *t.* by right of war
**Thrascias.**—P. L. 10, 700. and *T.* rend the
**Threads.**—S. A. 261. but cords to me were *t.*

A. 16. shooting her beams like silver *t.*
**Threaten.**—P. R. 4, 464. fore-signify and *t.*
**Threatened.**—P. L. 4, 968. so *t.* he but
P. L. 6,359. chariot wheels to drag him bound *t.*
P. L. 9, 715. death to be wished though *t.*
P. L. 9, 870. is become not dead as we are *t.*
S. A. 852. solicited, commanded, *t.* urged
**Threatener.**— P. L. 9, 687. by the *t.?*
**Threatening.**—P. L. 2, 177. *t.* hideous fall
P. L. 2, 705. so *t.* grew tenfold more dreadful
P. L. 4, 77. still *t.* to devour me opens wide
P. L. 9, 989. though *t.* will in earnest so destroy
P. L. 11, 641. concourse in arms fierce faces *t.*
P. R. 4, 489. though noising loud and *t.* nigh
S. 16,12. *t.* to bind our souls with secular chains
**Threatens.**—P. L. 2, 441. loss of being *t.* him
P. R. 2, 128. who no less *t.* than our expulsion
**Threats.**—P. L. 4, 968. but Satan to no *t.*
P. L. 5, 889. yet not for thy advice or *t.* I fly
P. L. 6, 283. think thou with wind of aery *t.*
P. L. 6, 287. and with *t.* to chase me hence
P. L. 9,53. who late fled before the *t.* of Gabriel
P. L. 9, 685. not believe those rigid *t.* of death
C. 39. *t.* the forlorn and wandering passenger
C. 586. against the *t.* of malice or of
**Three.**—P. L. 2, 645. *t.* folds were brass, *t.* iron *t.*
P. L. 5, 382. *t.* that in mount Ida naked strove
P. L. 8,130. insensibly *t.* different motions move
P. L. 10, 323. *t.* several ways
P. L. 10, 324. to each of these *t.* places led
P. L. 10, 364. fatal consequence unites us *t.*
P. L. 11, 416. and from the well of life *t.* drops
P. L. 11, 736. the sire and his *t.* sons with their
P. L. 11,866. conspicuous with *t.* listed colours
P. L. 12, 188. and blot out *t.* days
P. R. 2, 433. yet wealth without these *t.* is
P. R. 3, 412. by *t.* days' pestilence such was
C. 253. my mother Circe with the Sirens *t.*
C. 969. *t.* fair branches of your own
C. 982. and his daughters *t.* that sing about the
S. 22, 1. Cyriac this *t.* years' day these eyes
M. W. 7. summers *t.* times eight save one
**Three-bolted.**—P. L. 6, 764. *t.-b.* thunder
**Threefold.**—P. L. 2, 645. and thrice *t.* the
**Threescore.**—P. R. 3, 411. cost the lives of *t.*
**Threshed.**—L'A. 108. flail hath *t.* the corn
**Threshing-floor.**—P. L. 4,984. lest on the *t.-f.*
**Threshold.**—P. L. 10, 594. hell's dark *t.* to
C. 1. before the starry *t.* of Jove's
**Threw.**—P. L. 2,545. Lichas from the top of Œta *t.*
P. L. 2, 755. flames thick and fast *t.* forth
P. L. 3, 391. thee created and by thee *t.* down
P. L. 4, 40. and worse ambition *t.* me down
P. L. 4, 609. o'er the dark her silver mantle *t.*
P. L. 6,639. their arms away they *t.* and to the
P. L. 6, 864. headlong themselves they *t.*
P. L. 7, 468. the crumbled earth above them *t.*
**Thrice.**—P. L. 1, 74. as from the centre *t.* to
P. L. 1, 619. *t.* he assayed and *t.* in spite of scorn
P. L. 2, 645. and *t.* three-fold the gates
P. L. 3, 570. *t.* happy isles but who dwelt
P. L. 4, 115. *t.* changed with pale ire envy and
P. L. 7, 625. *t.* happy men
P. L. 7, 631. *t.* happy if they know their
P. R. 9, 16. pursued *t.* fugitive about Troy wall
P. R. 9, 64. *t.* the equinoctial line he circled
S. A. 392. *t.* she assayed with flattering prayers
S. A. 396. *t.* I deluded her and turned to sport
S. A.1222. who now defies thee *t.* to single fight
C. 914. *t.* upon thy finger's tip *t.* upon thy
**Thrice-acceptable.**—P. L. 10, 855. *t.-a.*
**Thrice-great.**—Il P. 88. with *t.-g.* Hermes
**Thrift.**—C. 167. whom *t.* keeps up about his
**Thrilling.**—H. 103. the aery region *t.*
**Thrive.**—P. L. 2, 261. in what place soe'er *t.*
P. R. 2, 430. they whom I favour *t.* in wealth
**Thrived.**—P. R. 1, 114. so well had *t.*
S. A. 637. abstemious I grew up and *t.* amain
**Thrives.**—P. L. 10, 236. *t.* in other worlds
**Throat.**—P. L. 11, 713. the brazen *t.* of war

**Throes.**—P. L. 2, 780. motion felt and rueful *t.*
M. W. 26. and calls Lucina to her *t.*
**Throne.**—P. L. 1, 42. against the *t.*
P. L. 1, 105. and shook his *t.*
P. L. 1, 639. sat on his *t.* upheld by old repute
P. L. 2, 1. high on a *t.* of royal state
P. L. 2, 23. established in a safe unenvied *t.*
P. L. 2, 68. and his *t.* itself mixed with
P. L. 2, 104. though inaccessible his fatal *t.*
P. L. 2, 138. all incorruptible would on his *t.*
P. L. 2, 241. to celebrate his *t.* with warbled
P. L. 2, 267. darkness round covers his *t.*
P. L. 2, 320. league banded against his *t.*
P. L. 2, 445. but I should ill become this *t.*
P. L. 2, 959. straight behold the *t.* of Chaos
P. L. 3, 148. wherewith thy *t.* encompassed
P. L. 3, 314. thee thy manhood also to this *t.*
P. L. 3, 350. lowly reverent towards either *t.*
P. L. 3, 649. nearest to his *t.* stand ready at
P. L. 3, 655. in sight of God's high *t.*
P. L. 4, 89. they adore me on the *t.* of hell
P. L. 4, 597. that on his western *t.* attend
P. L. 4, 944. with songs to hymn his *t.*
P. L. 5, 163. day without night circle his *t.*
P. L. 5, 585. before the Almighty's *t.*
P. L. 5, 656. about the sovran *t.* alternate all
P. L. 5, 670. unworshipped unobeyed the *t.*
P. L. 5, 725. who intends to erect his *t.* equal
P. L. 5, 868. begirt the Almighty *t.* beseeching
P. L. 6, 5. the mount of God fast by his *t.*
P. L. 6, 88. and on his *t.* to set the envier
P. L. 6, 103. then lighted from his gorgeous *t.*
P. L. 6, 133. the *t.* of God unguarded
P. L. 6, 426. send against us from about his *t.*
P. L. 6, 679. to his son the Assessor of his *t.*
P. L. 6, 758. a sapphire *t.* inlaid with pure
P. L. 6, 834. all but the *t.* itself of God
P. L. 7, 137. from his *t.* beheld their multitude
P. L. 7, 556. it showed in prospect from his *t.*
P. L. 7, 585. the imperial *t.* of Godhead
P. L. 10, 28. they towards the *t.* supreme
P. L. 10, 382. thee now more dangerous to his *t.*
P. L. 10, 445. his high *t.* which under state
P. L. 11, 20. came in sight before the Father's *t.*
P. L. 11, 82. till from his *t.* supreme
P. L. 11, 389. Samarchand by Oxus Temir's *t.*
P. L. 12, 323. that his regal *t.* for ever shall
P. L. 12, 370. he shall ascend the *t.* hereditary
P. R. 1, 171. circling the *t.* and singing while
P. R. 1, 240. be great and sit on David's *t.*
P. R. 2, 212. sitting queen adored on beauty's *t.*
P. R. 2, 424. placed on Judah's *t.* (thy *t.*)
P. R. 2, 440. whose offspring on the *t.* of Judah
P. R. 3, 33. won Asia and the *t.* of Cyrus held
P. R. 3, 153. thy father David's *t.*
P. R. 3, 169. crown and David's *t.* usurped
P. R. 3, 357. thou wert possessed of David's *t.*
P. R. 3, 383. thou on the *t.* of David
P. R. 3, 395. will unpredict and fail me of the *t.*
P. R. 3, 408. for Israel on David or his *t.*
P. R. 4, 100. expel this monster from his *t.*
P. R. 4, 108. on David's *t.* be prophesied what
P. R. 4, 147. to sit on David's *t.*
P. R. 4, 271. to Macedon and Artaxerxes' *t.*
P. R. 4, 379. on David's *t.* or *t.* of all the world
P. R. 4, 471. thy way of gaining David's *t.*
P. R. 4, 603. the attempter of thy Father's *t.*
A. 15. in circle round her shining *t.*
Il P. 53. guiding the fiery-wheeled *t.*
H. 84. than his bright *t.* or burning axle-tree
H. 164. in middle air shall spread his *t.*
S. M. 7. aye sung before the sapphire-coloured *t.*
T. 17. about the supreme *t.* of him to whose
D.F.I. 56. let down in cloudy *t.* to do the world
V. Ex. 36. how he before the *t.* . . . . doth lie
**Throned.**—P. L. 1, 128. O chief of many *t.*
P. L. 1, 386. *t.* between the Cherubim
P. L. 3, 58. sits high *t.* above all height bent
P. L. 3, 305. though *t.* in highest bliss equal
P. L. 3, 377. where thou sittest *t.* inaccessible
P. L. 6, 772. the crystalline sky in sapphire *t.*

P. L. 6, 890. temple of his mighty Father *t.*
P. R. 4, 596. image of the Father whether *t.*
H. 145. *t.* in celestial sheen with radiant feet
Cir. 19. high *t.* in secret bliss for us frail dust
**Thrones.**—P. L. 1, 360. in heaven sat on *t.*
P. L. 2, 310. *t.* and imperial powers offspring
P. L. 2, 430. O progeny of heaven empyreal *t.*
P. L. 3, 320. *t.* princedoms, powers
P. L. 5, 363. since by descending from the *t.*
P. L. 5, 601. *t.* dominations princedoms virtues
P. L. 5, 749. of seraphim and potentates and *t.*
P. L. 5, 772. *t.* dominations princedoms virtues
P. L. 5, 840. *t.* dominations princedoms virtues
P. L. 6, 199. amazement seized the rebel *t.*
P. L. 6, 366. two potent *t.* that to be less than
P. L. 6, 723. O Supreme of heavenly *t.*
P. L. 6, 841. of *t.* and mighty seraphim
P. L. 7, 198. potentates and *t.*
P. L. 10, 86. him *t.* and powers princedoms
P. L. 10, 460. *t.* dominations princedoms
P. L. 11, 232. or of the *t.* above such majesty
P. L. 11, 296. among the *t.* or named of them
P. R. 2, 121. heaven's ancient sons ethereal *t.*
P. R. 4, 85. these two *t.* except
**Throng.**—P. L. 1, 780. in narrow room *t.*
P. L. 4, 831. the lowest of your *t.* or if ye
P. L. 5, 650. the angelic *t.* dispersed in bands
P. L. 6, 308. the angelic *t.*
P. L. 7, 297. so the watery *t.* wave rolling after
P. L. 9, 142. thinner left the *t.* of his adorers
P. L. 10, 453. Stygian *t.* bent their aspect
P. L. 11, 671. him thence unseen amid the *t.*
P. R. 1, 145. vaunts of his great cunning to the *t.*
S. A. 1069. the other side was open where the *t.*
C. 206. thousand fantasies begin to *t.* into my
S. 13, 5. and skill exempts thee from the *t.*
H. 58. the trumpet spake not to the armed *t.*
**Thronged.**—P. L. 1, 761. all access was *t.*
P. L. 6, 83. of rigid spears and helmets *t.*
P. L. 6, 857. or timorous flock together *t.*
P. L. 12, 644. dreadful faces *t.* and fiery arms
P. R. 3, 260. with herds the pastures *t.*
**Thronging.**—P. L. 1, 547. and *t.* helms
P. L. 2, 555. with ravishment the *t.* audience
S. A. 21. but rush upon me *t.*
C. 713. *t.* the seas with spawn innumerable
**Throngs.**—L'A. 119. where *t.* of knights
**Throttled.**—P. R. 4, 568. *t.* at length
**Through.**—P. L. 1, 118. *t.* experience of this
P. L. 1, 177. *t.* the vast and boundless deep
P. L. 1, 288. *t.* optic glass the Tuscan artist
P. L. 1, 366. *t.* God's high sufferance
P. L. 1, 375. various idols *t.* the heathen world
P. L. 1, 395. that passed *t.* fire to his grim idol
P. L. 1, 464. dreaded *t.* the coast of Palestine
P. L. 1, 518. *t.* all the bounds of Doric land
P. L. 1, 544. all in a moment *t.* the gloom were
P. L. 1, 567. he *t.* the armed files darts
P. L. 1, 595. looks *t.* the horizontal misty air
P. L. 2, 79. and pursued us *t.* the deep
P. L. 2, 148. thoughts that wander *t.* eternity
P. L. 2, 156. belike *t.* impotence or unaware
P. L. 2, 262. out of pain *t.* labour and endurance
P. L. 2, 406. and *t.* the palpable obscure find
P. L. 2, 412. *t.* the strict senteries and stations
P. L. 2, 464. *t.* all the coasts of dark destruction
P. L. 2, 473. which he *t.* hazard huge must earn
P. L. 2, 544. and tore *t.* pain up by the roots
P. L. 2, 618. *t.* many a dark and dreary vale
P. L. 2, 641. the wide Ethiopian to the Cape
P. L. 2, 663. riding *t.* the air she comes
P. L. 2, 684. *t.* them I mean to pass
P. L. 2, 771. loss and rout *t.* all the empyrean
P. L. 2, 820. *t.* dire change befallen us
P. L. 2, 829. and *t.* the void immense to search
P. L. 2, 943. when a gryphon *t.* the wilderness
P. L. 2, 948. o'er bog or steep *t.* strait, rough
P. L. 2, 953. borne *t.* the hollow dark
P. L. 2, 974. lies *t.* your spacious empire up
P. L. 2, 994. fled not in silence *t.* the frighted
P. L. 2, 1001. encroached on still *t.* your

P. L. 2, 1014. and *t.* the shock of fighting
P. L. 2, 1018. when Argo passed *t.* Bosporus
P. L. 3, 16. *t.* utter and *t.* middle darkness
P. L. 3, 52. and the mind *t.* all her powers
P. L. 3, 87. and now *t.* all restraint broke loose
P. L. 3, 133. *t.* heaven and earth
P. L. 3, 254. *t.* the ample air in triumph high
P. L. 3, 358. the river of bliss *t.* midst of heaven
P. L. 3, 378. and *t.* a cloud drawn round about
P. L. 3, 400. him *t.* their malice fallen
P. L. 3, 544. *t.* dark and desert ways
P. L. 3, 564. *t.* the pure marble air his oblique
P. L. 3. 574. *t.* the calm firmament
P. L. 3, 590. *t.* his glazed optic tube
P. L. 3, 605. drained *t.* a limbec to his native
P. L. 3, 657. interpreter *t.* highest heaven
P. L. 3, 685. by his permissive will *t.* heaven
P. L. 3, 729. still renewing *t.* mid heaven
P. L. 4, 223. southward *t.* Eden went a river
P. L. 4, 224. but *t.* the shaggy hill
P. L. 4, 227. which *t.* veins of porous earth
P.L.4,272. all that pain to seek her *t.* the world
P. L. 4, 538. *t.* wood, *t.* waste o'er hill
P. L. 4, 555. came Uriel gliding *t.* the even
P. L. 4, 789. search *t.* this garden
P. L. 4, 868. Ithuriel and Zephon *t.* the shade
P. L. 4, 934. not to hazard all *t.* ways of danger
P. L. 4, 976. in progress *t.* the road of heaven
P. L. 5, 11. and glowing cheek as *t.* unquiet
P. L. 5, 50. methought alone I passed *t.* ways
P. L. 5, 225. from hell scaped *t.* the darksome
P. L.5,251. up springing light flew *t.* the midst
P. L. 5, 253. to his speed gave way *t.* all
P. L. 5, 267. and *t.* the vast ethereal sky
P. L. 5, 292. into the blissful field *t.* groves
P. L. 5, 298. him *t.* the spicy forest onward
P. L.5,439. what redounds transpires *t.* spirits
P. L. 5, 665. could not bear *t.* pride
P. L. 5, 692. who speedily *t.* all the hierarchies
P. L. 5, 874. applause *t.* the infinite host
P. L. 5, 904. long way *t.* hostile scorn
P. L. 6, 2. *t.* heaven's wide champaign held
P. L. 6, 7. makes *t.* heaven grateful vicissitude
P. L. 6, 15. shot *t.* with orient beams
P. L. 6, 166. I see that most *t.* sloth had
P. L. 6, 203. *t.* the vast of heaven it sounded
P. L. 6, 248. ranging *t.* the dire attack
P.L.6,330. with discontinuous wound passed *t.*
P. L. 6, 368. ghastly wounds *t.* plate and mail
P. L. 6, 384. and *t.* infamy seeks fame
P. L. 6, 392. *t.* the faint Satanic host
P. L. 6, 749. dawning *t.* heaven
P. L. 6, 873. *t.* his veil of anarchy
P. L. 6, 889. rode triumphant *t.* mid heaven
P. L. 7, 92. in his holy rest *t.* all eternity
P. L. 7, 134. fell with his flaming legions *t.* the
P. L. 7, 229. round *t.* the vast profundity
P. L. 7,246. to journey *t.* the aery gloom began
P. L. 7, 299. it *t.* plain, soft ebbing
P. L. 7, 373. his longitude *t.* heaven's high
P. L. 7. 404. and *t.* groves of coral stray
P. L. 7,574, he *t.* heaven that opened wide her
P. L. 8, 141. *t.* the wide transpicuous air
P. L. 8, 421. and *t.* all numbers absolute
P. L. 9, 179. so saying *t.* each thicket dank
P. L. 9, 520. before her *t.* the field
P. L. 9, 637. kindled *t.* agitation to a flame
P. L. 9, 641. to bogs and mires and oft *t.* pond
P. L. 9, 676. *t.* his zeal of right
P. L. 9, 783. sighing *t.* all her works
P. L. 9, 789. fancied so *t.* expectation high
P. L. 9, 891. ran *t.* his veins and all his joints
P. L. 9, 1110. at loop-holes cut *t.* thickest
P. L. 10, 188. captivity led captive *t.* the air
P. L. 10, 394. descend *t.* darkness on your
P. L. 10, 407. *t.* sin to death exposed by my
P. L. 10, 411. their course *t.* thickest
P. L. 10, 418. the gate wide open
P. L. 10, 441. he *t.* the midst unmarked
P. L. 10, 522. *t.* the hall thick-swarming now
P. L. 10, 607. *t.* the race his thoughts

P. L. 10, 636. *t.* Chaos hurled obstruct the
P. L. 10, 643. as the sound of seas *t.* multitude
P. L. 10, 667. with terror *t.* the dark aëreal
P. L. 10, 709. introduced *t.* fierce antipathy
P. L. 10, 830. and reasonings though *t.* mazes
P. L. 10, 846. lamented loud *t.* the still night
P. L. 10, 897. *t.* female snares
P. L. 10, 902. *t.* her perverseness
P. L. 11, 17. in they passed *t.* heavenly doors
P. L. 11, 68. all the blessed *t.* heaven's wide
P. L. 11, 562. instinct *t.* all proportions low
P. L. 11, 673. and sword-law *t.* all the plain
P. L. 12, 49. and *t.* their habitations walks
P. L. 12, 208. then *t.* the fiery pillar and the
P. L. 12, 216. from the shore advance *t.* the
P. L. 12, 226. their great senate choose *t.* the
P. L. 12, 313. and bring back *t.* the world's
P. L. 12, 449. wherever *t.* the world
P. L. 12, 452. triumphing *t.* the air over his
P. L. 12, 455. drag in chains *t.* all his realm
P. L. 12,489. working *t.* love upon their hearts
P. L. 12, 649. *t.* Eden took their solitary way
P. R. 1. 5. obedience fully tried *t.* all temptation
P. R. 1, 13. and bear *t.* height or depth of
P. R. 1, 16. unrecorded left *t.* many an age
P. R. 1. 264. my way must lie *t.* many a hard
P. R. 2, 90. that *t.* my very soul a sword shall
P. R. 3, 62. and divulges him *t.* heaven to all
P. R. 3, 65. when to extend his fame *t.* heaven
P. R. 4, 41. of vision multiplied *t.* air or glass
P. R. 4, 542. bore *t.* the air sublime
P. R. 4, 585. as on a floating couch *t.* the
S. A. 45. had been fulfilled but *t.* mine own
S. A. 96. and not as feeling *t.* all parts diffused
S.A.97. that she might look at will *t.* every pore
S. A. 369. to worthliest deeds if he *t.* frailty err
S. A. 1489. older than thy age *t.* eye-sight lost
C. 37. lies *t.* the perplexed paths of this drear
C.67.for most do taste *t.* fond intemperate thirst
C. 425. where *t.* the sacred rays of chastity
M. W. 68. *t.* pangs fled to felicity
**Throughout.**—P. L. 1, 754. *t.* the host
P. L. 5, 726. equal to ours *t.* the spacious north
P. L. 6, 344. for spirits that live *t.* vital
P. L. 6, 833. steadfast empyrean shock *t.*
P. L. 7, 237. *t.* the fluid mass
P. L. 7, 532. subdue it and *t.* dominion hold
P. R. 2, 443. *t.* the world to me is not unknown
P. R. 4, 150. all monarchies besides *t.* the
S. 22, 5. of sun or moon, or star *t.* the year
**Throw** —C. 850. and *t.* sweet garland wreaths
L. 139. *t.* hither all your quaint enamelled eyes
H. 42. the saintly veil of maiden white to *t.*
P. 30. over the pole thy thickest mantle *t.*
**Thrown.**—P. L. 1, 741, *t.* by angry Jove
P. L. 3, 362. now in loose garlands thick *t.* off
P. L. 4, 225. *t.* that mountain as his garden
P. L. 6, 843. might be again *t.* on them
P. L. 10, 887. well if *t.* out as supernumerary
P. R. 4, 3. *t.* from his hope so oft
S.A.1097. or left thy carcass where the ass lay *t.*
F.ofC.1.because you have *t.* off your prelate lord
**Throws.**—P. L. 1, 56. round he *t.* his baleful
P. L. 3, 562. into the world's first region *t.*
P. L. 3, 741. *t.* his steep flight in many an aery
M. M. 3. May who from her green lap *t.*
**Throw'st.**—S. A. 689. but *t.* them lower than
**Thrust.**—P. L. 2, 857. hath hither *t.* me down
P. L. 4, 508. while I to hell am *t.*
S. A. 367. into a dungeon *t.* to work with slaves
**Thummim.**—P. R. 3, 14. Urim and *T.*
**Thunder.**—P. L. 1, 93. proved he with his *t.*
P. L. 1, 174. the *t.* winged with red lightning
P. L. 1, 258. whom *t.* hath made greater
P. L. 1, 601. but his face deep scars of *t.* had
P. L. 2, 66. he shall hear infernal *t.*
P. L. 2, 166. struck with heaven's afflicting *t.*
P. L. 2. 294. fear of *t.* and the sword of Michael
P. L.2,477. was as the sound of *t.* heard remote
P. L. 2, 882. and on their hinges grate harsh *t.*
P. L. 3, 393. thy Father's dreadful *t.* didst

P. L. 4, 928. to thy aid the blasting vollied *t*.
P. L. 5, 893. for soon expect to feel his *t*.
P. L. 6, 606. to displode their second tire of *t*.
P. L. 6, 632. and of his *t*. made a scorn
P. L. 6, 713. all my war, my bow and *t*.,
P. L. 6, 764. with three-bolted *t*. stored
P. L. 6, 854. but checked his *t*. in mid volley
P. L. 9, 1002 and muttering *t*. some sad drops
P. L. 10, 33. in *t*. uttered thus his voice
P. L. 10, 666. the *t*. when to roll with terror
P. L. 10, 780. dreadful voice no more would *t*.
P. L. 12, 181. *t*. mixed with hail
P. L. 12, 229. he descending will himself in *t*.
P. R. 1, 90. when his fierce *t*. drove us to the
P. R. 4, 410. and either tropic now gan *t*.
P. R. 4, 429. stilled the roar of *t*. chased
S.A.1651.whole roof after them with burst of *t*.
S.A.1696.his cloudless *t*. bolted on their heads
C. 804. as when the wrath of Jove speaks *t*.
A. 51. and heal the harms of thwarting *t*. blue
H. 156. must *t*. through the deep
V. Ex. 42. and hills of snow and lofts of piled *t*.
**Thunderbolts.**—P. L. 1, 328. linked *t*.
P. L. 6, 589. chained *t*. and hail of iron globes
**Thunderer.**—P..L. 6, 491. disarmed the *T*.
**Thunderer's.**—P. L. 2, 28. against the *T.'s*
**Thundering.**—P. L. 1, 233. of *t*. Ætna
P. L. 1, 386. Jehovah *t*. out of Sion
P. L. 6, 487. send forth from far with *t*. noise
P. L. 10, 814. that fear comes *t*. back with
S.A.1353.more lordly *t*. than thou well wilt bear
**Thunderous.**—P. L. 10, 702. with *t*. clouds
V. Ex. 36. how he before the *t*. throne doth lie
**Thunders.**—P. L. 2, 267. from whence deep *t*.
P. L. 6, 836. grasping ten thousand *t*.
P. L. 7, 606. thee that day thy *t*. magnified .
**Thunderstruck.**—P. L. 6, 858. him *t*.
P. R. 1, 36. and with the voice divine nigh *t*.
**Thwart.**—P. L. 8, 132. moved contrary with *t*.
P. L. 10, 703. *t*. of these as fierce forth rush
P.L.10,1075.whose *t*. flame driven down kindles
**Thwarting.**—A.51.heal the harms of *t*. thunder
**Thwarts.**—P. L. 4, 557. star in autumn *t*.
**Thyestean.**—P. L. 10, 688. from *T*. banquet
**Thyme.**—L.40. with wild *t*. and the gadding vine
**Thyrsis.**—C. 494. *T*. whose artful strains have
C. 512. what fears good *T*. prithee briefly shew
C. 657. *T*. lead on apace I'll follow thee
L'A. 83. where Corydon and *T*. met
**Thyself.**—P. L. 2, 696. and reckon'st thou *t*.
P. L. 2, 764. who full oft *t*. in me thy perfect
P. L. 3,162. or wilt thou *t*. abolish thy creation
P. L. 3,283. and be *t*. man among men on earth
P. L. 3, 375. fountain of light *t*. invisible
P. L. 4, 412. of all these joys dearer *t*. than all
P. L. 4, 448. while thou like consort to *t*. canst
P. L. 4, 468. thou seest fair creature is *t*.
P. L. 4, 474. him shalt bear multitudes like *t*.
P. L. 4, 890. wouldst *t*. no doubt and boldly
P. L. 4, 961. to dispossess him and *t*. to reign
P. L. 4, 972. far heavier load *t*. expect to feel
P. L. 5, 68. sweet of *t*. but much more sweet
P. L. 5, 78. among the gods *t*. a goddess
P. L. 5, 155. *t*. how wondrous then
P. L. 5, 521. thou continuest such owe to *t*.
P. L. 5, 812. in place *t*. so high above thy
P. L. 5, 833. *t*. though great and glorious dost
P. L. 6, 181. *t*. not free, but to *t*. enthralled
P. L. 6, 265. heaviest by just measure on *t*
P. L. 8, 400. subtle happiness I see thou to *t*.
P. L. 8, 415. thou in *t*. art perfect
P. L. 8, 428. although alone best with *t*.
P. L. 8,439. thou hast rightly named but of *t*.
P. L. 8,566. less excellent as thou *t*. perceivest
P. L. 8, 570. weigh with her *t*. then value
P. L. 9, 299. thou *t*. with scorn and anger ·
P. L. 9, 1148. thou being by or to *t*. perhaps
P. L. 10, 156. hadst thou known *t*. aright
P. L. 10, 595. undreaded and *t*. half-starved
P. L. 10, 868. with him leagued *t*. as false and
P. L. 10, 929. me than *t*. more miserable

P. L. 10, 949. desirest the punishment all on *t*.
P. R. 1, 344. so shalt thou save *t*. and us
P. R. 1, 453. then to *t*. ascribest the truth
P. R. 2, 174. thou weigh'st all others by *t*.
P. R. 2, 175. because of old thou *t*. doatst on
P. R. 2, 414. *t*. bred up in poverty and straits
P. R. 3, 24. earth her wonder at thy acts *t*.
P. R. 3, 225. happiest both to *t*. and all
P. L. 3, 248. of *t*. so apt in regal arts and regal
R. R. 4, 212. and thou *t*. seem'st otherwise
P. R. 4, 284. within *t*. much more with
P. R. 4, 555. cast *t*. down safely if Son of God
S. A. 156, the dungeon of *t*.
S. A. 213. deject not then so overmuch *t*.
S. A. 508. thy penal forfeit from *t*.
S. A. 784. I to thee thou to *t*. wast cruel
S. A. 789. strength from me than in *t*. was found
S. A. 914. nor still insist to afflict *t*. in vain
S. A. 1127. oft shalt wish *t*. at Gath to boast
S. A. 1333. regard *t*. this will offend them
S. A. 1590. O lastly over-strong against *t*.
C. 616. how durst thou then *t*. approach so near
C. 792. thou art npt fit to hear *t*. convinced
**Tiberius.**—P. R. 3, 159. Roman yoke obeys *T*.
**Tide.**—P. L. 11, 854. their furious *t*.
L. 157. thou perhaps under the whelming *t*.
**Tidings.**—P. L. 5, 870. this report these *t*.
P. L. 10, 36. nor troubled at these *t*.
P. L. 10, 346. with joy and *t*. fraught to hell
P. L. 11, 226. Eve now expect great *t*. which
P. L. 11, 302. our frailty can sustain thy *t*.
P. L. 12, 375. O prophet of glad *t*.
P. L. 12,504. to receive with joy the *t*. brought
P. R. 1, 109. with deep dismay at these sad *t*.
P. R. 2, 62. nor left at Jordan *t*. of him none
S. A. 1567. lest evil *t*. with too rude irruption
**Tidore.**—P. L. 2, 639. the isles of Ternate or *T*.
**Tie.**—S. A.308. and *t*. him to his own prescript
L'A. 143. untwisting all the chains that *t*.
**Tied.**—P. L. 1, 426. not *t*. or manacled with
**Tiger.**—P. L. 4, 403. then as a *t*. who by
P. L. 7, 467. the ounce, the libbard and the *t*.
P. R. 1, 313. the lion and fierce *t*. glared aloof
C. 71. or ounce or *t*. hog or bearded goat
**Tigers.**—P. L. 4, 344. bears *t*. ounces pards
C. 534. like stabled wolves or *t*. at their prey
**Tigris.**—P. L. 9, 71. where *T*. at the foot of
**Tiles.**—P. L. 4, 191. climbs or o'er the *t*.
**Tillage.**—P. L. 11, 434. from his *t*. brought
**Tilth.**—P. L. 11, 430. field part arable and *t*.
**Tilting.**—P. L. 9, 34. *t*. furniture emblazoned
P. L. 11,747. beaked prow rode *t*. o'er the waves
**Timber.**—P. L. 11, 728. hewing *t*. tall
**Timbreled.**—P. L. 219. in vain with *t*. anthems
**Timbrels.**—P. L. 1, 394. noise of drums and *t*.
S. A. 1617. before him pipes and *t*.
**Time.**—P. L. 1, 36. what *t*. his pride
P. L. 1, 253. not to be changed by place or *t*.
P. L. 1, 769. as bees in spring *t*.
P. L. 2, 210. our supreme foe in *t*. may much
P. L. 2, 274. torments also may in length of *t*.
P. L. 2, 297. by policy and long process of *t*.
P. L. 2, 348. about this *t*. to be created
P. L. 2,603. periods of *t*. thence hurried back to
P. L. 2, 774. at which *t*. this powerful key
P. L. 2, 894. and *t*. and place are lost
P. L. 3, 284. made flesh when *t*. shall be
P. L. 4, 6. that now while *t*. was our first
P. L. 4, 489. and from that *t*. see how beauty
P. L. 4, 639. with thee conversing I forget all *t*.
P. L. 5, 38. now is the pleasant *t*., the cool
P. L. 5, 493. *t*. may come when men
P. L. 5, 498. improved by tract of *t*.
P. L. 5, 580. for *t*. though in eternity applied
P. L. 5, 848. while pardon may be found in *t*.
P. L. 5, 859. we know no *t*. when we were not
P. L. 6, 245. long *t*. in even scale the battle
P. L. 7, 177. more swift than *t*. or motion
P. L. 8, 474. which from that *t*. infused
P. L. 9, 70. sin not *t*. first wrought the change
P. L. 9, 464. and for the *t*. remained stupidly

P. L. 10, 24. sadness did not spare that *t.*
P. L. 10, 74. on me must light when *t.* shall be
P. L. 10, 91. the speed of gods *t.* counts not
P. L. 10, 345. not instant but of future *t.*
P. L. 10, 606. whatever thing the scythe of *t.*
P. L. 11, 244. in *t.* of truce Iris had dipt
P. L. 11, 859. the second *t.* returning in his bill
P. L. 11, 899. seed *t.* and harvest heat and
P. L. 12, 23. and dwell long *t.* in peace
P. L. 12, 152. faithful Abraham due *t.* shall call
P. L. 12, 161. in *t.* of dearth a son
P. L. 12, 301. purpose to resign them in full *t.*
P. L. 12, 316. long *t.* shall dwell and prosper
P. L. 12, 554. this transient world the race of *t.*
P. L. 12, 555. till *t.* stand fixed
P. R. 1, 56. for longest *t.* to him is short
P. R. 1, 58. the circling hours this dreaded *t.*
P. R. 1, 109. no *t.* was then for long indulgence
P. R. 1, 269. the *t.* prefixed I waited
P. R. 1, 286. by which I knew the *t.* now full
P. R. 2, 14. for a *t.* caught up to God
P. R. 2, 43. send thy Messiah forth the *t.* is come
P. R. 2, 275. and eat the second *t.* after repose
P. R. 3, 182. are best fulfilled in their due *t.*
P. R. 3, 183. and *t.* there is for all things
P. R. 3, 298. and just in *t.* thou comest to have
P. R. 3, 396. my *t.* I told thee and that *t.* for
P. R. 3, 433. (*t.* to himself best known)
P. R. 3, 440. to his due *t.* and providence
P. R. 4, 15. or as a swarm of flies in vintage *t.*
P. R. 4, 123. tedious waste of *t.* to sit and hear
P. R. 4, 174. but I endure the *t.* till which
P. R. 4, 282. till *t.* mature thee to a kingdom's
P. R. 4, 378. set thee in short *t.* with ease on
P. R. 4, 380. now at full age fulness of *t.*
P. R. 4, 475. but concealing the *t.* and means
P. R. 4, 507. from that *t.* seldom have I ceased
P. R. 4, 558. lest at any *t.* thou chance to dash
P. R. 4, 616. shall dwell secure when *t.* shall be
P. R. 4, 632. and to torment sent before their *t.*
S. A. 397. each *t.* perceiving how openly
S. A. 402. the fourth *t.* when mustering all her
S. A. 1126. in a little *t.* while breath remains
S. A. 1390. in *t.* thou hast resolved
S. A. 1708. come, no *t.* for lamentation now
C. 291. two such I saw what *t.* the laboured ox
C. 435. that breaks his magic chains at curfew *t.*
C. 743. if you let slip *t.* like a neglected rose
L. 28. what *t.* the gray-fly winds his sultry horn
S. 2. 1. how soon hath *t.* the subtle thief of youth
S. 2, 12. toward which *t.* leads me and the will
S. 20, 5. *t.* will run on smoother
S. 21, 11. mild heaven a *t.* ordains
H. 129. move in melodious *t.*
H. 135. *t.* will run back and fetch the age of gold
H. 239. *t.* is our tedious song
M. W. 9. after so short *t.* of breath
T. 1. fly envious *t.* till thou run out thy race
T. 22. over death and chance, and thee O *t.*
U. C. I. 7. for he had any *t.* this ten years full
U. C. II. 7. *t.* numbers motion yet without a crime
U. C. II. 8. truth motion numbered out his *t.*
U. C. II. 15. to drive the *t.* away he sickened
U. C. II. 23. leisure told him that his *t.* was come
V. Ex. 71. in *t.'s* long and dark prospective glass
**Timelessly.**—D. F. I. 2. primrose fading *t.*
**Timely.**—P. L. 3, 728. her aid *t.* interposes
P. L. 4, 614. and the *t.* dew of sleep, now
P. L. 7, 74. to forewarn us *t.* of what might else
P. L. 10, 1057. his *t.* care hath unbesought
S. A. 602. must not omit a father's *t.* care
C. 689. and *t.* rest have wanted but fair virgin
C. 970. heaven hath *t.* tried their youth
S. 1, 9. now *t.* sing ere the rude bird of hate
**Timely-happy.**—S. 2, 8. some more *t.-h.* spirits
**Times.**—P. L. 1, 50. nine *t.* the space that
P. L. 9, 65. four *t.* crossed the car of night
P. L. 12, 243. the *t.* of great Messiah shall sing
P. L. 12, 437. than certain *t.* to appear to his
P. R. 1, 228. by words at *t.* cast forth inly
P. R. 2, 245. four *t.* ten days I've passed

P. R. 3, 94. famous in a land and *t.* obscure
P. R. 3, 187. he in whose hand all *t.* and
S. A. 22. present *t.* past what once I was
S. A. 406. at *t.* when men seek most repose and
S. A. 695. unjust tribunals under change of *t.*
M. W. 7. summers three *t.* eight save one
**Timna.**—S. A. 219. the first I saw at *T.*
S. A. 383. did not she of *T.* first betray me
S. A. 795. wouldst leave me as her at *T.*
**Timnian.**—S.A.1018. the *T.* bride had not so soon
**Timorous.**—P. L. 2, 117. but to nobler deeds *t.*
P. L. 6, 857. and as a herd of goats or *t.* flock
P. R. 3, 241. unexperienced will be ever *t.*
S. A. 740. prevailing over fear and *t.* doubt
**Tincture.**—P. L. 7, 367. by *t.* or reflection
**Tine.**—P. L. 10, 1075. *t.* the slant lightning
**Tinsel.**—P. L. 9, 36. bases and *t.* trappings
**Tinsel-slippered.**—C. 877. by Thetis' *t.-s.*
**Tip.**—C. 914. thrice upon thy finger's *t.*
**Tipped.**—P. L. 6, 580. waving *t.* with fire
**Tipsy.**—C. 104. *t.* dance and jollity
**Tire.**—P. L. 6, 605. displode their second *t.*
**Tired.**—S. A. 1326. pick me out with shackles *t.*
C. 688. that have been *t.* all day without repast
**Tiresias.**—P. L. 3, 36. and *T.* and Phineus
**Tissued.**—H. 146. with radiant feet the *t.* clouds
**Tissues.**—P. L. 5, 592. their glittering *t.*
**Titan.**—P. L. 1, 510. *T.* heaven's first-born
**Titanian.**—P. L. 1, 198. *T.* or earth-born
**Title.**—P. L. 11, 163. ill-worthy I such *t.*
P. L. 12, 70. such *t.* to himself reserving
P. R. 4, 199. than these thou bear'st that *t.*
**Titled.**—P. L. 11, 622. lives religious *t.* them
P. R. 2, 179. false *t.* sons of God roaming the
P. R. 3, 81. with pride and must be *t.* gods
**Title-page.**—S. 11, 6. what a word on a *t.-p.* is
**Titles.**—P. L. 2, 311. or these *t.* now must we
P. L. 5, 773. if these magnific *t.* yet remain
P. L. 5, 801. of those imperial *t.* which assert
P. L. 11, 793. fame in the world high *t.*
P. L. 12, 516. places and *t.* and with these to
**Tittle.**—P. R. 1, 450. to the smallest *t.*
**Titular.**—P. L. 5, 774. not merely *t.*
**Toad.**—P. L. 4, 800. like a *t.* close at the ear of
S. 11, 13. not learning worse than *t.* or asp
**To and fro.**—P. L. 1, 772. fly *t.*
P. L. 2, 1031. with easy intercourse pass *t.*
P. L. 3, 533. on high behests his angels *t.*
P. L. 6, 328. and writhed him *t.*
P. L. 6, 643. foundations loosening *t.*
P. L. 6, 665. hurled *t.* with jaculation
**Tobias.**—P. L. 5, 222. to travel with *T.* and
**Tobit.**—P. L. 4, 170. from the spouse of *T.'s*
**To-day.**—S. 21, 5. *t.-d.* deep thoughts resolve
**Toe.**—L'A. 34. on the light fantastic *t.*
**Toes.**—C. 962. trippings to be trod of lighter *t.*
**Together.**—P. L. 5, 696. he *t.* calls or several
P. L. 6, 215. so under fiery cope *t.* rushed
P. L. 6, 316. *t.* both with next to Almighty arm
P. L. 6, 857. of goats or timorous flock *t.*
P. L. 9, 1095. whose broad smooth leaves *t.*
P. L. 9, 1099. so counselled he and both *t.* went
P. L. 9, 1112. *t.* sewed to gird their waist
P. L. 10, 287. tost up and down, *t.* crowded drove
P. L. 10, 290. *t.* drive mountains of ice
P. L. 10, 785. cannot *t.* perish with this
P. L. 11, 739. all the clouds *t.* drove from under
P. R. 2, 28. close in a cottage low *t.* got
S. A. 1521. best keep *t.* here lest running thither
L. 25. *t.* both ere the high lawns appeared
L. 27. we drove afield and both *t.* heard
**Toil.**—P. L. 1, 319. after the *t.* of battle to repose
P. L. 1, 698. in an age they with incessant *t.*
P. L. 2, 1041. that Satan with less *t.* and now
P. L. 4, 327. and after no more *t.* of their sweet
P. L. 6, 257. archangel from his warlike *t.*
P. L. 9, 242. for not to irksome *t.* but to delight
P. R. 2, 453. extol not riches then the *t.* of fools
S. A. 5. relieves me from my task of servile *t.*
C. 687. refreshment after *t.* ease after pain
**Toiled.**—P. L. 6, 449. sore *t.*

P. L. 10, 475. but I *t.* out my uncouth passage
**Toils.**—S.A. 933. dearly to my cost thy gins and *t.*
**Toilsome.**—P. L. 4, 439. which were it *t.*
 P. L. 11, 179. what can be *t.* in these pleasant
**Toil'st.**—P. R. 4, 498. and *t.* in vain
**Told.**—P. L. 7, 178. process of speech be *t.* so *t.*
 P. L. 8, 521. thus have I *t.* thee all my state
 P. L. 9, 863. is not as we are *t.* a tree of danger
 P. L. 9,886. with countenance blithe her story *t.*
 P. L. 10, 40. I *t.* ye then he should prevail
 P. L. 10, 122. that thou art naked who hath *t.*
 P. L. 11, 298. gently hast thou *t.* thy message
 P. R. 1, 245. them the Messiah now was born
 P. R. 3,184. of my reign prophetic Writ hath *t.*
 P. R. 3, 396. my time I *t.* thee and that time
 P. R. 4, 472. when and how is nowhere *t.*
 S. A. 1433. after his message *t.* of thy conception
 L'A. 101. with stories *t.* of many a feat
 M. W. 8. she had *t.* alas too soon
 U. C. II. 23. his leisure, *t.* him that his time
 V. Ex. 48. such as the wise Demodocus once *t.*
**Told'st.**—P. R. 1, 137. then *t.* her doubting
 C. 694. and the safe abode thou *t.* me of
**Tolerable.**—P. L. 2, 460. render hell more *t.*
 P. L. 10, 654. earth with cold and heat scarce *t.*
 P. L. 10, 977. though sharp and sad yet *t.*
**Tomb.**—S. A. 986. my *t.* with odours visited
 S. A. 1742. shall on feastful days visit his *t.* with
 C. 879. by dead Parthenope's dear *t.*
 D. F. I. 32. hid from the world in a low-delved *t.*
 M. W. 34. was not long a living *t.*
 W. S. 16. kings for such a *t.* would wish to die
**To-morrow.**—P. L. 4, 623. *t.-m.* ere fresh morning
 L. 193. *t.-m.* to fresh woods and pastures new
**Tones.**—P. L. 5, 626. her charming *t.* that
 P. R. 4, 255. in *t.* and numbers hit by voice or
**Tongue.**—P. L. 2, 112. though his *t.* dropped
 P. L. 6, 135. terror of thy power or potent *t.*
 P. L. 6, 154. since first that *t.* inspired with
 P. L. 6, 297. who though with the *t.* of angels
 P. L. 6, 360. refrained his *t.* blasphemous but
 P. L. 7, 113. what words or *t.* of seraph
 P. L. 7, 603. can measure thee or *t.* relate thee
 P. L. 8, 219. nor *t.* ineloquent
 P. L. 8, 272. my *t.* obeyed and readily could
 P. L. 9, 554. language of man pronounced by *t.*
 P. L. 9, 674. each act won audience ere the *t.*
 P. L. 9, 749. taught the *t.* not made for speech
 P. L. 10, 518. with forked *t.* to forked *t.*
 P. L. 11, 620. to dress and troll the *t.* and roll
 P. R. 1, 479. smooth on the *t.* discoursed
 P. R. 3, 15. or *t.* of seers old infallible
 P. R. 4, 5. persuasive rhetoric that sleeked his *t.*
 S. A. 1066. a rougher *t.* draws hitherward
 C. 692. thou hast banished from thy *t.* with lies
 C. 761. and virtue has no *t.* to cheek her pride
 C. 781. arm his profane *t.* with contemptuous
 S. 13, 8. smooth air couldst humour best our *t.*
 V. Ex. 2. move my first endeavouring *t.* to speak
 V. Ex. 10. my *t.* but little grace can do thee
**Tongue-batteries.**—S. A. 404. assaults *t.-b.*
**Tongue-doughty.**—S. A. 1181. *t.-d.* giant
**Tongues.**—P. L. 7, 26. though fallen and evil *t.*
 P. L. 10, 507. on all sides from innumerable *t.*
 P. L. 12, 53. sets upon their *t.* a various spirit
 P. L. 12, 501. to speak all *t.* and do all miracles
 P. R. 1, 374. and the *t.* of all his flattering
 P. R. 2, 158. in amorous arts enchanting *t.*
 P. R. 3, 55. to live upon their *t.* and be their
 P. R. 3, 280. there Babylon the wonder of all *t.*
 C. 208. and aery *t.* that syllable men's names
**Took.**—P. L. 2, 554. and *t.* with ravishment the
 P. L. 2, 872. sad instrument of all our woe she *t.*
 P. L. 3, 365. their golden harps they *t.*
 P. L. 3, 739. *t.* leave and toward the coast
 P. L. 6, 549. without disturb they *t.* alarm
 P. L. 6, 793. his glory at the sight *t.* envy
 P. L. 7, 225. he *t.* the golden compasses
 P. L. 7, 359. of light by far the greater part he *t.*
 P. L. 8, 300. so saying by the hand he *t.* me
 P. L. 8, 465. stooping opened my left side and *t.*

P. L. 8, 536. or from my side subducting *t.*
 P. L. 9, 455. such pleasure *t.* the serpent
 P. L. 9, 847. the way she *t.* that morn
 P. L. 9, 1004. while Adam *t.* no thought
 P. L. 9, 1043. love and love's disport *t.* largely
 P. L. 11, 82. and *t.* their seats till from his
 P. L. 11, 223. where Adam sheltered *t.* his way
 P. L. 11, 517. and *t.* his image
 P. L. 12, 649. through Eden *t.* their solitary
 P. R. 3, 251. he *t.* the Son of God up to
 P. R. 4, 394. so saying he *t.*
 S. A. 227. she proving false the next I *t.* to wife
 S. A. 869. *t.* full possession of me and prevailed
 S. A. 1183. magistrates confessed it when they *t.*
 S. A. 1203. I used hostility and *t.* their spoil
 C. 20. *t.* in by lot 'twixt high and nether Jove
 C. 298. I *t.* it for a faery vision
 C. 558. was *t.* ere she was ware and wished she
 C. 834. held up their pearled wrists and *t.* her in
 H. 20. hath *t.* no print of the approaching light
 H. 98. as all their souls in blissful rapture *t.*
 W. S. 12. Delphic lines with deep impression *t.*
 U. C. I. 16. pulled off his boots and *t.* ... the light
 C. 561. and *t.* in strains that might create a soul
 D. F. I. 46. *t.* up and in fit place did reinstall
**Took'st**—P. L. 2, 765. and such joy thou *t.*
 S. A. 838. who *t.* the way to raise in me
 S. A. 1591. a dreadful way thou *t.* to thy revenge
**Tools.**—P. L. 11, 572. he formed first his own *t.*
 S. A. 137. their proud arms and warlike *t.*
**Top.**—P. L. 1, 6. that on the secret *t.* of Oreb
 P. L. 1, 289. from the *t.* of Fesolé
 P. L. 1, 515. on the snowy *t.* of cold Olympus
 P. L. 1, 614. with singed *t.* their stately growth
 P. L. 1, 670. whose grisly *t.* belched fire
 P. L. 2, 545. Lichas from the *t.* of Œta threw
 P. L. 3, 504. at *t.* whereof but far more rich
 P. L. 3, 742. till on Niphate's *t.* he lights
 P. L. 5, 598. whose *t.* brightness had made
 P. L. 7, 6. nor on the *t.* of old Olympus
 P. L. 7, 585. heaven's high-seated *t.*
 P. L. 8, 303. a woody mountain whose high *t.*
 P. L. 8, 520. on his hill *t.* to light the bridal
 P. L. 11, 378. from whose *t.* the hemisphere
 P. L. 11, 851. on the *t.* of some high mountain
 P. L. 12, 44. a city and tower whose gray *t.*
 P. L. 12, 227. the mount of Sinai whose gray *t.*
 P. L. 12, 588. descend now therefore from this *t.*
 P. R. 2, 217. seated as on the *t.* of virtue's hill
 P. R. 2, 286. from whose high *t.* to ken
 P. R. 4, 354. extoll'st as those the *t.* of eloquence
 S. A. 167. by how much from the *t.* of wondrous
 C. 94. now the *t.* of heaven doth hold
 L. 54. nor on the shaggy *t.* of Mona high
**Topaz.**—P. L. 3, 597. chrysollite ruby or *t.*
**Tophet.**—P. L. 1, 404. *T.* thence and black
**Tops.**—P. L. 2, 488. as when from mountain *t.*
 P. L. 4, 142. higher than their *t.* the verdurous
 P. L. 5, 193. and wave your *t.* ye pines
 P. L. 6, 654. and by the shaggy *t.* uplifting
 P. L. 7, 287. their *t.* ascend the sky
 P. L. 11, 852. and now the *t.* of hills as rocks
**Topt.**—P. R. 4, 548. of alabaster *t.* with golden
**Torch.**—P. L. 11, 590. they light the nuptial *t.*
**Torches.**—C. 130. the secret flame of midnight *t.*
**Tore.**—P. L. 1, 542. shout that *t.* Hell's concave
 P. L. 2, 543. and *t.* through pain up by the roots
 P. L. 2, 783. *t.* through my entrails
 P. L. 6, 588. and all her entrails *t.*
 P. L. 7, 34. of that vile rout that *t.* the Thracian
 S. A. 128. who *t.* the lion as the lion tears the kid
 S. A. 1472. what ... shout was that? it *t.* the sky
**Torment.**—P. L. 4, 893. change *t.* with ease
 P. L. 8, 244. *t.* and loud lament and furious
 P. L. 9, 121. so much more I feel *t.* within me
 P. L. 10, 781. would *t.* me with cruel
 P. L. 10, 998. and *t.* less than none of what we
 P. L. 11, 769. gaining birth abortive to *t.* me
 P. R. 1, 418. rather inflames thy *t.* representing
 P. R. 4, 305. all wealth pleasure pain or *t.*
 P. R. 4, 632. bound and to *t.* sent before their

S. A. 606. O that *t.* should not be confined
**Tormented.**—P. L. 6. 244. *t.* all the air
**Tormenting.**—P. L. 4, 505. sight *t.* thus
**Tormentor.**—P. R. 4, 130. his *t.* conscience
**Tormentors.**—S. A. 623. thoughts my *t.* armed
**Torments.**—P. L. 1, 56. and lasting pain *t.*
  P. L. 2, 70. strange fire his own invented *t.*
  P. L. 2. 196. to suffer here chains and these *t.*
  P. L. 2, 274. our *t.* also may in length of time
  P. L. 4, 88. under what *t.* inwardly I groan
  P. L. 4, 510. among our other *t.* not the least
  P. R. 3, 208. expectation more of worse *t.*
**Torn.**—P.L.1,232. transports a hill *t.*fromPelorus
  P. L. 2, 926. in mutiny had from her axle *t.*
  P. L. 2, 1044. though shrouds and tackle *t.*
  P. L. 4, 994. disturbed and *t.* with violence of
  P. R. 4, 419. or *t.* up sheer
  H. 187. with flower-inwoven tresses *t.*
**Torrent.**—P. L. 2, 581. whose waves of *t.* fire
  P. L. 6, 830. as with the sound of *t.* floods
  P. L. 7, 299. if steep with *t.* rapture
  C. 930. nor wet October's *t.* flood
**Torrid.**—P. L. 1, 297. and the *t.* clime
  P. L. 2, 904. of Barca of Cyrene's *t.* soil
  P. L. 12, 634. as a comet which with *t.* heat
**Tortuous.**—P. L. 9, 516. and of his *t.* train
**Torture.**—P. L. 1, 67. but *t.* without. end
  P. L. 11, 481. or racking *t.*
  S. A. 1569. suspense in news is *t.*, speak
**Torturer.**—P. L. 2, 64. against the *t.*
**Tortures.**—P. L. 2, 63. *t.* into horrid arms
  P. L. 9, 469. and *t.* him now more
**Torturing.**—P. L. 2, 91. and the *t.* hour
**Tossing.**—P. L. 1,'184. the *t.* of these fiery waves
  P. L. 11, 489. dire was the *t.* deep the groans
**Tost.**—P. L. 3, 490. with their wearers *t.*
  P. L. 9, 1126. now *t.* and turbulent for
  P. L. 10, 287. as in raging sea *t.* up and down
  P. L. 10, 718. in a troubled sea of passion *t.*
**Total.**—P. L. 4, 665. lest *t.* darkness should
  P. L. 6, 73. as when the *t.* kind of birds
  P. L. 8, 627. if spirits embrace *t.* they mix
  P.L.10,127. either to undergo myself the *t.*crime
  S. A. 81. irrecoverably dark *t.* eclipse
**Touch.**—P. L. 3, 608. with one virtuous *t.*
  P. L. 4, 686. with heavenly *t.* of instrumental
  P. L. 4, 812. can endure *t.* of celestial temper
  P. L. 5, 411. they hear see smell *t.* taste
  P. L. 6, 485. with *t.* of fire dilated
  P. L. 6, 520. pernicious with one *t.* to fire
  P. L. 6, 566. and briefly *t.* what we propound
  P. L. 6, 584. narrow vent applied with nicest *t.*
  P. L. 7. 46. charged not to *t.* the interdicted tree
  P. L. 8, 530. transported *t.*
  P. L. 8, 579. but if the sense of *t.* whereby
  P. L. 8, 617. irradiance, virtual or immediate *t.*
  P. L. 9, 651. of this tree we may not.taste nor *t.*
  P. L. 9, 663. nor shall ye *t.* it lest ye die
  P. L. 9, 742. inclinable now grown to *t.* or taste
  P. L. 9, 925. more to taste it under ban to *t.*
  P. L. 9. 1143. to whom soon moved with *t.*
  P. L. 10, 45. or *t.* with lightest moment
  P. L. 10, 563. not the *t.* but taste deceived
  P. L. 11, 561. his volant *t.* instinct through all
  S. A. 549. *t.* ethereal of heaven's fiery rod
  S. A. 951. let me approach . . . and *t.* thy hand
  C. 270. to *t.* the prosperous growth of this tall
  C. 406. lest some ill-greeting *t.* attempt the
  C. 663. thou canst not *t.* the freedom
  C. 918. I *t.* with chaste palms moist and cold
  A. 87. and *t.* the warbled string
  H. 127. if ye have power to *t.* our senses so
  S. M. 13. *t.* their immortal harps of golden wires
  V. Ex. 38. to the *t.* of golden wires
**Touched.**—P. L. 4, 811. with his spear *t.*
  P. L 6, 479. *t.* with heaven's ray and tempered
  P. L. 7, 258. *t.* their golden harps and hymning
  P. L. 8, 47. and *t.* by her fair tendance
  P. L. 9,380. thy own last reasoning words *t.* only
  P. L. 9, 688. look on me, me who have *t.*
  P. L. 9, 987. that what of sweet before hath *t.*

P. L. 11, 425. who never *t.* the excepted tree
S. A. 262. cords to me were threads *t.* with flame
S. A. 1107, thou hast need much washing to be *t.*
L. 77. Phœbus replied and *t.* my trembling ears
L. 188. he *t.* the tender stops of various quills
S. 20, 11. to hear the lute well *t.* or artful voice
H. 28. from out his secret altar *t.* with hallowed
D. F. I. 10. he thought it *t.* his deity full near
**Touches.**—P. L. 1, 557. with solemn *t.* troubled
**Touching.**—P. L. 5, 17. her hand soft *t.*
  P. R. 2, 370. defends the *t.* of these viands pure
**Tough.**—P. R. 1, 339. for we here live on *t.*
**Tour.**—P. L. 11, 185. stooped from his aery *t.*
**Tournament.**—P. L. 9, 37. at joust and *t.*
  P. L. 11, 652. with cruel *t.* the squadrons join
**Tourney.**—[l P. L. 118. of *t.* and of trophies hung
**Toward.**—P. L. 1, 284. moving *t.* the shore
  P. L. 1, 669. hurling defiance *t* the vault
  P. L. 2, 516. the four winds four speedy
  P. L. 2, 631. and *t.* the gates of hell explores
  P. L. 2, 642, ply stemming nightly *t.* the pole
  P. L. 3, 435. flies *t.* the springs of Ganges
  P. L. 2, 739. took leave and *t.* the coast of earth
  P. L. 8, 257. straight *t.* heaven my wondering
  P. L. 9, 495. and *t.* Eve addressed his way
  P. L. 10, 64. unfolding bright *t.* the right hand
  P. L.11,38. receive the smell of peace *t.* mankind
  S. A. 668. that thou *t.* him with hand so various
  S. A. 682. yet *t.* these thus dignified thou oft
  C. 100. pacing *t.* the other goal
  A. 81. and so attend ye *t.* her glittering state
  L. 31. *t.* heaven's descent had sloped
  S. 21, 10. *t.* solid good what leads the nearest
**Towards.**—P. L. 2, 477. *t.* him they bend
  P. L. 2, 873. *t.* the gate rolling her bestial
  P. L. 3, 89. directly *t.* the new created world
  P. L. 3, 350. lowly reverent *t.* either throne
  P. L. 3, 581. *t.* his all-cheering lamp turn
  P. L. 4, 27. sometimes *t.* Eden which now in
  P. L. 4, 29. sometimes *t.* heaven and the
  P. L. 6, 648. when coming *t.* them so dread
  P. L. 9, 375. for God *t.* thee hath done his
  P. L. 10, 23. they *t.* the throne supreme
  P. L. 10, 288. shoaling *t.* the mouth of hell
  P. L. 10, 941. soon his heart relented *t.* her
  P. L. 11, 848. that stole with soft foot *t.* the
  P. L. 11, 854. *t.* the retreating sea their
  P. L. 12, 40. marching from Eden *t.* the west
  P. L. 12, 215.. safe *t.* Canaan from the shore
  P. L. 12, 296. they may find justification *t.*
  S. A.334. as I suppose *t.* your once gloried friend
  S. A. 772. the easier *t.* me or thy hatred less
  S. A. 792. nor less in mine *t.* thee
  S. A. 911. *t.* thee I intend for what I have
**Tower.**—P. L. 1, 591. stood like a *t.*
  P. L. 4, 30. now sat high in his meridian *t.*
  P. L. 7, 441. and rising on stiff pennons *t.*
  P. L. 12, 44. a city and *t.* whose top may
  P. L. 12, 51. down to see their city ere the *t.*
  P. L. 12, 73. to God his *t.* intends siege
  C. 935. with many a *t.* and terrace round
  Il P. 86. be seen in some high lonely *t.*
  S. 8, 11. when temple and *t.* went to the ground
**Towered.**—P. L. 1, 733, by many a *t.* structure
  P. L. 9, 498. that *t.* fold above fold a surging
  A. 21, or the *t.* Cybele
  L'A. 117. *t.* cities please us then
**Towering.**—P. L. 2, 635. concave *t.* high
  P. L. 5, 271. till within soar of *t.* eagles
  P. L. 6, 110. came *t.* armed in adamant
  P. R. 2, 280. high *t.* to descry the Morn's
**Towers.**—P. L. 1, 499. above their loftiest *t.*
  P. L. 1, 749. to have built in heaven high *t.*
  P. L. 2, 62. o'er heaven's high *t.* to force
  P. L. 2, 129. the *t.* of heaven are filled with
  P. L. 2. 1049. with opal *t.* and battlements
  P. L. 4, 211. from Auran eastward to the royal *t.*
  P. L. 5, 758. with pyramids and *t.*
  P. L. 5, 907. on those proud *t.* to swift
  P. L. 11, 640. of men with lofty gates and *t.*
  P. R. 3, 268. field and flood temples and *t.*

P. R. 3, 329. or elephants indorsed with *t.*
P. R. 4, 34, with *t.* and temples proudly elevate
P. R. 4, 545. the holy city lifted high her *t.*
S. A. 266. had by this possessed the *t.* of Gath
L'A. 77. *t.* and battlements it sees
P. 39. to bear me where the *t.* of Salem stood
**Town.**—P. R. 1, 332. to *t.* or village nigh
P. R. 2, 22. and each *t.* or city walled
S. 11, 3. the subject new it walked the *t.* awhile
**Towns.**—P. L. 11, 639. *t.* and rural works
P. R. 3, 233. scarce viewed the Galilean *t.*
**Toy.**—P. L. 9, 1034. and forbore not glance or *t.*
P. R. 2, 223. flat and shrink into a trivial *t.*
C. 502. I came not here on such a trivial *t.*
**Toys.**—P. R. 2, 177. but taken with such *t.*
P. R. 4, 328. collecting *t.* and trifles for choice
Il P. 4. or fill the fixed mind with all your *t.*
V. Ex.19.not those new-fangled *t.* and trimming
**Trace.**—P. L. 7, 481. with sinuous *t.*
P. L. 9, 682. but to *t.* the ways of highest agents
P. L. 11, 329. bright appearances or footstep *t.*
C. 423. *t.* huge forests and unharboured heaths
**Traced.**—P. L. 4, 949. no leader but a liar *t.*
**Traces.**—C. 292. the laboured ox in his loose *t.*
**Tracing.**—P. R. 2, 109. the while her Son *t.*
**Track.**—P. L. 2, 1025. amain following his *t.*
P. L. 10, 314. following the *t.* of Satan
P. L. 10, 367. from following thy illustrious *t.*
P. L. 11, 354. and of his steps the *t.* divine
P. R. 1, 191. till far from *t.* of men
**Tract.**—P. L. 1, 28. nor the deep *t.*-of Hell
P. L. 5, 498. improved by *t.* of time
P. L. 6, 76. so over many a *t.* of heaven
P. L. 9, 510. with *t.* oblique at first as one
C. 30. and all this *t.* that fronts the falling sun
**Trade.**—L. 65. the homely slighted shepherd's *t.*
**Trading.**—P. L. 2, 640. they on the *t.* flood
**Tradition.**—P. L. 10, 578. however some *l.*
**Traditions.**—P. L. 12, 512. and *t.* taint
P. R. 4, 234. their idolisms *t.* paradoxes
**Traduced.**—S. A. 979. most unconjugal *t.*
**Tragedians.**—P. R. 4, 261. lofty grave *t.*
**Tragedy.**—Il P. 97. sometimes let gorgeous *T.*
**Tragic.**—P. L. 9, 6. change those notes to *t.*
**Trail.**—S. A. 1402. because they shall not *t.* me
**Train.**—P. L. 1, 478. Isis, Orus and their *t.*
P. L. 2, 873. rolling her bestial *t.*
P. L. 4, 349. with Gordian twine his braided *t.*
P. L. 4, 649. the gems of heaven her starry *t.*
P. L. 5. 166. fairest of stars last in the *t.* of night
P. L. 5, 351. without more *t.* accompanied
P. L. 5, 767. for thither he assembled all his *t.*
P. L. 6, 143. thou seest all are not of thy *t.*
P. L. 7, 221. him all his *t.* followed in bright
P. L. 7, 306. and perpetual draw their humid *t.*
P. L. 7, 444. and the other whose gay *t.* adorns
P. L. 7, 574. so sung the glorious *t.* ascending
P. L. 9, 387. Oread or Dryad or of Delia's *t.*
P. L. 9, 516. and of his tortuous *t.* curled many
P. L. 9, 548. by angels numberless thy daily *t.*
P. L. 10, 80. attendance none shall need nor *t.*
P. L. 11. 862. sire descends with all his *t.*
P. L. 12, 131. him a cumbrous *t.* of herds
P. R. 2, 355. nymphs of Diana's *t.* and Naiades
P. R. 3. 266. and new *t.* of words began
S. A. 721. a damsel *t.* behind
S. A. 1732. with silent obsequy and funeral *t.*
C. 863. the loose *t.* of thy amber-dropping hair
Il P. 10. the fickle pensioners of Morpheus' *t.*
Il P. 34. flowing with majestic *t.*
M. W. 37. the pride of her carnation *t.*
**Trained.**—P. L. 6, 167. ministering spirits *t.* up
**Training.**—P. L. 6, 553. *t.* his devilish enginery
**Trains.**—P. L. 11, 624. to the *t.* and to the smiles
S. A. 533. of fair fallacious looks venereal *t.*
S. A. 932. I know thy *t.* though dearly to my cost
C. 151. now to my charms and to my wily *t.*
**Traitor.**—P. L. 2, 689. art thou that *t.*
S. A. 401. she sought to make me *t.* to myself
S. A. 83.. what murderer, what *t.* parricide
C. 690. 'twill not false *t.* 'twill not restore

**Traitress.**—S. A. 725. my wife! my *t.* let her not
**Trample.**—P. L. 4, 1010. to *t.* thee as mire
**Trampled.**—P. L. 2, 195. race of heaven thus *t.*
**Trampling.**—H. 215. *t.* the unshowered grass
**Trance.**—P. L. 8, 462. abstract as in a *t.*
H. 179. no nightly *t.* or breathed spell
P. 42. in pensive *t.* and anguish
**Transact.**—P. L. 6, 286. easier to *t.* with me
**Transcend.**—P. L. 5. 457. he saw *t.* his own
**Transcendent.**—P. L. 1, 86. *t.* brightness
P. L. 2, 427. Satan whom now *t.* glory raised
P. L. 10, 614. from his *t.* seat
**Transfer.**—P. L. 10, 165. unable to *t.* the
S. A. 241. that fault I take not on me but *t.*
**Transferred.**—P. L. 5, 854. by task *t.* from
P. L. 6, 678. and to declare all power on him *t.*
P. L. 10, 56. vicegerent son to thee I have *t.*
P. R. 1, 267. full weight must be *t.* upon my
**Transfix.**—P. L. 1, 329. *t.* us to the bottom
**Transfixed.**—P. L. 2, 181. each on his rock *t.*
**Transform.**—P. L. 1, 370. to *t.* oft to the
**Transformed.**—P. L. 2, 785. thus grew *t.*
P. L. 4, 824. and *t.* why sat'st thou
P. L. 9, 507. nor to which *t.* Ammonian Jove
P. L. 10, 519. all *t.* alike to serpents
C. 48. after the Tuscan mariners *t.*
S. 12, 5. as when those hinds that were *t.* to frogs
D. F. I. 27. but then *t.* him to a purple flower
**Transforms.**—C. 527. the visage quite *t.*
**Transfused.**—P. L. 3, 389. *t.* on thee his
P. L. 6, 704. and grace immense I have *t.*
**Transgress.**—P. L. 1, 31. and *t.* his
P. L. 3, 94. and easily *t.* the sole command
P. L. 4, 880. who approve not to *t.* by thy
P. L. 6, 912. remember and fear to *t.*
P. L. 7, 47. if they *t.* and slight that sole
P. L. 8, 643. and all temptation to *t.* repel
P. L. 9, 902. rather how hast thou yielded to *t.*
P. L. 11, 253. by sentence when thou didst *t.*
Cir. 21. that great covenant which we still *t.*
**Transgressed.**—P. L. 8, 330. sole command *t.*
P. L. 9. 1161. neither had I *t.* nor thou
**Transgresses.**—S. A. 758. again *t.* and again
**Transgressing.**—P. L. 5, 244. wilfully *t.*
P. L. 9, 1169. upbraided as the cause of thy *t.*
**Transgression.**—P. L. 10, 49. pass on his *t.*
P. L. 12. 399. the penalty to thy *t.* due
S. A. 1356. returning ... after my great *t.*
**Transgressions.**—P. L. 4, 879. to thy *t.*
S. A. 820. displays her own *t.* to upbraid me
**Transgressor.**—P. L. 11, 164. to me *t.*
**Transgressors.**—P. L. 10. 72. thy *t.*
**Transient.**—P. L. 12, 554. this *t.* world
**Transition.**—P. L. 12, 5. with *t.* sweet
**Transitory.**—P. L. 3, 446. of all things *t.*
P. R. 4, 209. therefore let pass as they are *t.*
**Translated.**—P. L. 3, 461. habitants *t.*
C. 242. so mayst thou be *t.* to the skies
**Translucent.**—S. A. 548. eastern ray *t.* pure
C. 861. under the glassy cool *t.* wave
**Transmigration.**—P. L. 10, 261. or *t.*
**Transparent.**—P. L. 7, 265. *t.* elemental air
**Transpicuous.**—P. L. 8, 141. the wide *t.*
**Transpires.**—P. L. 5, 438. *t.* through Spirits
**Transplanted.**—P. L. 3, 298. *t.* and from
P. L. 7, 360. *t.* from her cloudy shrine
**Transported.**—P. L. 8, 529. otherwise *t.*
P. L. 9, 474. what sweet compulsion thus *t.*
P. L. 10, 626. as if *t.* with some fit of passion
V. Ex. 33. such where the deep *t.* mind may soar
**Transporting.**—P. 38. some *t.* cherub
**Transports.**—P. L. 1, 231. *t.* a hill torn
P. L. 3, 81. seest thou what rage *t.* our
P. L. 8, 567. what admirest thou what *t.* thee so?
**Transubstantiate.**—P. L. 5, 438. to *t.*
**Transverse.**—P. L. 3, 488. blows them *t.*
P. L. 11, 563. fled and pursued *t.* the resonant
S. A. 209. ill drove me *t.*
**Trap.**—C. 699. and wouldst thou seek again to *t.*
**Trappings.**—P. L. 9, 36. bases and tinsel *t.*
**Travail.**—P. L. 10, 593. earned with *t.* difficult

**M. W.** 49. thy *t.* sore sweet rest seize thee
**Travel.**—P. L. 2, 980. thither to arrive I *t.*
P. L. 5, 222. to *t.* with Tobias and secured
**Travelled.**—P. L. 3, 501. in haste his *t.* steps
**Traveller.**—C. 64. offering to every weary *t.*
C. 200. to the misled and lonely *t.*
C. 332. that wont'st to love the *t.'s* benison
**Travelling.**—P. L. 8, 138. fetch day *t.* east
**Traverse.**—P. L. 1, 568. and soon *t.* the whole
**Traversed.**—P. L. 9, 434. many a walk *t.*
**Traversing.**—P. L. 9, 66. pole to pole *t.* each
**Treacherously.**—S. A. 1023. so *t.* had shorn
**Treachery.**—S.A.1009. wedlock *t.* endangering
P. L. 1, 327. descending *t.* us down
P. L. 2, 828. with lonely steps to *t.*
P. L. 4, 632. if we mean to *t.* with ease
P. L. 4, 866. O friends I hear the *t.* of nimble
P. L. 5, 201. and stately *t.* or lowly creep
P. L. 6. 73. passive air upbore their nimble *t.*
P. L. 10, 190. shall *t.* at last under his feet
P. L. 11, 630. turn aside to *t.* paths indirect
P. R. 1, 488. to *t.* his sacred courts and minister
S. A.111.for with joint pace I hear the *t.* of many
C. 91. but I hear the *t.* of hateful steps
C. 899. that bends not as I *t.*
**Treading.**—P. L. 2, 941. *t.* crude consistence
**Treads.**—C.635.and the dull swain *t.* on it daily
**Treason.**—P. L. 3, 207. to expiate his *t.* hath
S. A. 391. her spurious first-born *t.* against me
S. A. 459. with the gold of matrimonial *t.*
**Treasonous.**—C. 702. not taste thy *t.* offer
**Treasure.**—P. R. 2, 427. get wealth and *t.*
C. 399. the unsunned heaps of miser's *t.*
V.Ex.18.from thy wardrobe bring thy chiefest *t.*
**Treasures.**—P. L. 1, 688. for *t.* better hid
P. R. 2, 29. all *t.* and all gain esteem as dross
**Treasury.**—S. 10,2. England's council and her *t.*
**Treat.**—P. L. 11, 588. now of love they *t.*
P. R. 2, 335. to *t.* thee as beseems
P. R. 4, 264. while they *t.* of fate and chance
S. A. 482. with whom to *t.* about thy ransom
S. A. 591. that these dark orbs no more shall *t.*
**Trebisond.**—P. L. 1, 584. Marocco or *T.*
**Treble.**—P. L. 1, 220. on himself *t.* confusion
**Tree.**—P. L. 1, 2. the fruit of that forbidden *t.*
P. L. 3, 354. in paradise fast by the *t.* of life
P. L. 4, 194. up he flew and on the *t.* of life
P. L. 4, 195. the middle *t.* and highest there
P. L. 4, 218. all amid them stood the *t.* of life
P. L. 4, 221. our death the *t.* of knowledge
P. L. 4. 395. from his lofty stand on that high *t.*
P.L.4,423. not to taste that only *t.* of knowledge
P. L. 4, 424. planted by the *t.* of life so near
P. L. 4, 427. pronounced it death to taste that *t.*
P. L. 4, 514. fatal *t.* there stands of knowledge
P. L. 4, 644. spreads his orient beams on herb *t.*
P. L. 5, 51. brought me on a sudden to the *t.*
P. L. 5, 57. on that *t.* he also gazed
P. L. 7, 46. not to touch the interdicted *t.*
P. L. 7,542. *t.* which tasted works knowledge
P. L. 8, 306. each *t.* loaden with fairest fruit
P. L. 8, 321. every *t.* that in the garden grows
P.L.8,323. *t.*whose operation brings knowledge
P. L. 8, 326. amid the garden by the *t.* of life
P. L. 9, 73. rose up a fountain by the *t.* of life
P. L. 9, 576. a goodly *t.* far distant to behold
P. L. 9, 591. round the *t.* all other beasts that
P. L. 9,594.amid the *t.* now got where plenty
P. L. 9, 617. but say where grows the *t.* from
P. L. 9, 644. to the *t.* of prohibition root of all
P. L. 9, 651. but of this *t.* we may not taste
P. L. 9,660. of each *t.* in the garden we may eat
P. L. 9, 661. but of the fruit of this fair *t.*
P. L. 9, 723. knowledge of good and evil in this *t.*
P. L. 9, 727. or this *t.* impart against his will
P. L. 9, 751. naming thee the *t.* of knowledge
P. L. 9, 884. so saying from the *t.* her step she
P. L. 9, 848. the *t.* of knowledge he must pass
P. L. 9,850. there he her met scarce from the *t.*
P. L. 9, 863. this *t.* is not as we are told a *t.*
P. L. 9,1026. it might be wished for this one *t.*

P. L. 9, 1033. bounty of this virtuous *t.*
P. L.9,1095. some *t.* whose broad smooth leaves
P.L.9,1106. daughters grow about the mother *t.*
P. L. 10, 122. of the *t.* whereof I gave thee
P. L. 10, 143. she gave me of the *t.* and I did eat
P. L. 10. 199. and eaten of the *t.* concerning
P. L. 10, 554. imagining for one forbidden *t.*
P. L. 11, 94. reach also of the *t.* of life and eat
P. L. 11, 122. and guard all passage to the *t.*
P. L. 11, 320. under this *t.* stood visible
P. L. 11,426.who never touched the excepted *t.*
P. L. 11, 858. green *t.* or ground whereon his
P. R. 4. 147. it shall be like a *t.* spreading
P.R.4,434. from drooping plant or dropping *t.*
P. R. 4, 589. ambrosial fruits fetched from the *t.*
C. 393. but beauty like the fair Hesperian *t.*
C. 983. that sing about the golden *t.*
M. W. 30. spoiled at once both fruit and *t.*
**Trees.**—P. L. 4, 147. of goodliest *t.* loaden
P. L. 4, 217. all *t.* of noblest kind for sight
P. L. 4, 248. whose rich *t.* wept odorous gums
P. L. 4, 421. of all the *t.* in paradise that bear
P. L. 5, 309. eastward among those *t.* what
P. L.5,390. with these various fruits the *t.*of God
P. L. 5, 426. though in heaven the *t.* of life
P. L. 5, 652. by living streams among the *t.*
P. L. 7, 324. rose as in dance the stately *t.*
P. L. 7, 459. among the *t.* in pairs they rose
P. L. 7, 538. this garden planted with the *t.*
P. L. 8, 304. enclosed with goodliest *t.* planted
P.L.8,313.from among the *t.*appeared presence
P. L. 9, 618. for many are the *t.* of God that
P. L. 9,795. O Sovran virtuous, precious of all *t.*
P. L. 9, 1118. among the *t.* on isles and woody
P.L.10,101.hid themselves among the thickest *t.*
P. L. 10, 558. and up the *t.* climbing
P. L. 10, 1067. locks of these fair spreading *t.*
P. L. 11, 28. all the *t.* of paradise could have
P. L. 11, 124. and all my *t.* their prey
P. L. 11, 832. his verdure spoiled and *t.* adrift
P. R. 2, 263. *t.* thick interwoven there he slept
P. R. 2, 354. under the *t.* now tripped now
C. 147. your shrouds within these brakes and *t.*
L'A. 78. bosomed high in tufted *t.*
**Tremble.**—P. L. 12, 228. gray top shall *t.*
S. A. 1648. when mountains *t.* those two massy
**Trembled.**—P. L. 2, 676. hell *t.* as he strode
P. L. 2, 788. hell *t.* at the hideous name
P. L. 9,1000. earth *t.* from her entrails as again
**Trembling.**—P. L. 4, 266. the *t.* leaves
P. R. 1, 451. *t.* fear or like a fawning parasite
L. 77. Phœbus replied and touched my *t.* ears
**Tremisen.**—P. L. 11, 404. Algiers and *T.*
**Trench.**—P. L. 1, 677. to *t.* a field
**Trent.**—F.of C.14. packing worse than those of *T.*
V. Ex.93. or *T.* who like some earth-born giant
**Trepidation.**—P. L. 3, 483. the *t.* talked
**Trespass.**—P. L. 3, 122. foreseen they *t.*
P. L. 9, 693. incense his ire for such a petty *t.*
P. L. 9, 889. the fatal *t.* done by Eve
P. L. 9, 1006. nor Eve to iterate her former *t.*
S. A. 691. too grievous for the *t.* or omission
**Tresses.**—P. L. 4, 305. unadorned golden *t.*
P. L. 4, 497. the flowing gold of her loose *t.* hid
P. L. 5, 10. Eve with *t.* discomposed
P. L. 9, 841. flowers a garland to adorn her *t.*
P. L. 10, 911. and *t.* all disordered at his feet
C. 753. love-darting eyes or *t.* like the morn
C. 929. never scorch thy *t.* fair
H. 187. with flower-inwoven *t.* torn
**Trial**—P. L. 1, 366. sufferance for the *t.* of man
P. L. 4, 855. said Zephon bold will save us *t.*
P. L.8,447. for *t.* only brought to see how thou
P. L. 9, 316. and thy *t.* choose with me best
P. L. 9, 366. *t.* will come unsought
P. L. 9, 370. but if thou think *t.* unsought
P. L. 9, 380. that our *t.* when least sought
P. L. 9, 961. O glorious *t.* of exceeding love
P. L. 9, 975. hath presented this happy *t.*
P. L. 9, 1177. or to find matter of glorious *t.*
P. R. 3, 196. just *t.* ere I merit my exaltation

P. R. 4, 206. the *t.* hath indamaged thee no way
S. A. 1175. defy thee to the *t.* of mortal fight
S. A. 1288. the *t.* of their fortitude making them
S. A. 1643. now of my own accord such other *t.*
C. 329. square my *t.* to my proportioned strength
C. 592. shall in the happy *t.* prove most glory
**Tribe.**—S. A. 217. than of thine own *t.* fairer
S. A. 265. had Judah ... joined or one whole *t.*
S. A. 876. I before all the daughters of my *t.*
S. A. 1479. live the poorest in my *t.* than richest
S. A. 1540. an Hebrew as I guess and of our *t.*
**Tribes.**—P. L. 3, 532. oft those happy *t.*
P. L. 7, 488. in her popular *t.* of commonalty
P. L. 11, 279. rear ye to the sun or rank your *t.*
P. L. 12, 23. by families and *t.*
P. L. 12, 226. through the twelve *t.*
P. R. 2, 374. of thy brethren those ten *t.*
P. R. 3, 403. as thou callest them those ten *t.*
P. R. 3, 414. as for those captive *t.* themselves
S. A. 242. on Israel's governors and heads of *t.*
S. A. 976. in Judah and the bordering *t.*
**Tribulation.**—P. L. 11, 63. in sharp *t.*
**Tribulations.**—P. L. 3, 336. all their *t.*
P. R. 3, 190. by *t.* injuries insults
**Tribunal.**—P. L. 3, 326. thy dread *t.*
**Tribunals.**—S. A. 695. or to the unjust *t.*
**Tributary.**—C. 24. he to grace his *t.* gods
**Tribute.**—P. L. 5, 343. she gathers *t.* large
P. L. 8. 36. as *t.* such a sumless journey brought
P. R. 3, 258. then meeting joined their *t.* to
C. 925. their full *t.* never miss
**Tricked.**—Il P. 123. not *t.* and frounced
**Tricks.**—L. 170. and *t.* his beams and with
F. of C. 13. but we do hope to find out all your *t.*
**Trident.**—P. L. 10, 295. as with a *t.* smote
**Tridents.**—C. 27. wield their little *t.* but this
**Tried.**—P. L. 4, 896. but evil hast not *t.*
P. L. 5, 532. for how can hearts not free be *t.*
P. L. 6, 120. whose reason I have *t.* unsound
P. L. 6, 418. O now in danger *t.* now known
P. L. 7, 159. under long obedience *t.*
P. L. 8, 271. to speak I *t.* and forthwith spake
P. L. 9, 317. best witness of thy virtue *t.*
P. L. 11, 63. after life *t.* in sharp tribulation
P. L. 11, 805. that temperance may be *t.*
P. R. 1, 4. obedience fully *t.* through all
P. R. 3, 189. be *t.* in humble state and things
S. A. 1086. we might have *t.* each other's force
C. 970. heaven hath timely *t.* their youth
P. 13. most perfect Hero *t.* in heaviest plight
**Trifle.**—P. R. 4, 165. no *t.*
**Trifles.**—P. R. 4, 329. collecting toys and *t.*
**Triform.**—P. L. 3, 730. her countenance *t.*
**Trills.**—P. R. 4, 246. *t.* her thick-warbled notes
**Trim.**—S. A. 717. her bravery on and tackle *t.*
C. 120. wood-nymphs decked with daisies *t.*
L'A. 75. meadows *t.* with daisies pied
Il P. 50. that in *t.* gardens takes his pleasure
H. 33. had doffed her gaudy *t.*
**Trimming.**—V. Ex. 19. and *t.* slight
**Trinacrian.**—P. L. 2, 661. the hoarse *T.* shore
**Trine.**—P. L. 10, 659. square and *t.*
**Trip.**—C. 118. *t.* the pert fairies and the dapper
A. 99. *t.* no more in twilight ranks
L'A. 33. come and *t.* it as you go
**Triple.**—P. L. 2, 569. patience as with *t.* steel
P. L. 5, 750. and thrones in their *t.* degrees
P. L. 6, 650. *t.*ill on those cursed engines' *t.* row
C. 581. how are ye joined with hell in *t.* knot
S. 18, 12. where still doth sway the *t.* tyrant
**Triple-coloured.**—P. L. 11, 897. *t.-c.* bow
**Triple-mounted.**—P. L. 6, 572. a *t.-m.* row
**Tripping.**—P. L. 11, 847. standing lake to *t.*
V. Ex. 62. *t.* to the room where thou didst lie
**Trippings.**—C. 961. other *t.* to be trod
**Trips.**—V. Ex. 3. imperfect words with childish *t.*
**Triton.**—P. L. 4, 276. girt with the river *T.*
C. 873. by scaly *T.'s* winding shell
**Trinal.**—H. 11. to sit the midst of *T.* unity
**Trivial.**—P. R. 2, 223. shrink into a *t.* toy
S. A. 142. with what *t.* weapon came to hand

S. A. 263. with a *t.* weapon felled their choicest
C. 502. I came not here on such a *t.* toy
**Triumph.**—P. L. 3, 254. ample air in *t.* high
P. L. 6, 886. sung *t.* and him sung victorious
P. L. 7, 180. great *t.* and rejoicing was in heaven
P. L. 9. 948. lest the adversary *t.* and say
P. L. 10, 537. in *t.* issuing forth their glorious
P. L. 10, 546. *t.* to shame cast on themselves
P. L. 11, 695. for glory done of *t.*
P. L. 11, 788. thou saw'st in *t.* and luxurious
P. R. 1, 173. victory and *t.* to the Son of God
P. R. 3, 36. quelled the Pontic king and in *t.*
P. R. 4, 138. ambitious grown of *t.*
P. R. 4, 624. and hold'st in hell no *t.*
S. A. 426. make thee their captive and their *t.*
S. A. 1312. with sacrifices *t.* pomp and games
C. 974. to *t.* in victorious dance
**Triumphal.**—P. L. 6, 881. his *t.* chariot
P. L. 10, 390. *t.* with *t.* act have met
P. R. 4, 37. statues and trophies, and *t.* arcs
**Triumphals.**—P. R. 4, 578. joyless *t.*
**Triumphant.**—P. L. 4, 975. draw'st his *t.*
P. L. 5, 693. intends to pass *t.* and give laws
P. L. 6, 889. he celebrated rode *t.* through mid
P. L. 10, 464. to lead ye forth *t.* out of this
P. L. 11, 491. and over them *t.* death his dart
Cir. 2. that erst with music and *t.* song
**Triumphed.**—P. L. 10, 186. *t.* in open show
P. L. 10, 572. not as man whom they *t.* once
**Triumphing.**—P. L. 3, 338. joy and love *t.*
P. L. 12, 452. *t.* through the air over his foes
T. 22. *t.* over death and chance and thee O time
**Triumphs.**—P. L. 1, 123. who now *t.*
P. L. 11, 723. *t.* or festivals
L'A. 120. in weeds of peace high *t.* hold
**Trod.**—P. L. 9, 526. the ground whereon she *t.*
P. R. 2, 307. have *t.* this wilderness
P. R. 4, 620. *t.* down under his feet
C. 569. through paths and turnings often *t.*
C. 961. other trippings to be *t.*
S. 14, 6. not behind nor in the grave were *t.*
**Trodden.**—P. L. 1, 682. pavement *t.* gold
P. L. 9, 572. beasts that graze the *t.* herb
**Troll**—P. L. 11, 620. and *t.* the tongue
**Troop.**—P. L. 1, 437. with these in *t.* came
P. L. 7, 297. *t.* to their standard so the watery
P. L. 11, 614. for that fair female *t.* thou saw'st
P. R. 1, 323. in *t.* or caravan for single none
C. 603. with all the grisly legions that *t.*
H. 233. *t.* to the infernal jail
**Trooping.**—P. L. 1, 760. with thousands *t.*
**Troops.**—P. R. 3, 311. *t.* in coats of mail
S. A. 138. spurned them to death by *t.*
L. 179. in solemn *t.* and sweet societies
**Trophies.**—P. L. 1, 539. seraphic arms and *t.*
P. L. 10, 355. are thy magnific deeds thy *t.*
P. R. 4, 37. statues and *t.* and triumphal
S. A. 470. despoil him of all these boasted *t.*
S. A. 1736. with all his *t.* hung and acts enrolled
Il P. 118. of tourneys and of *t.* hung
S. 16, 6. hast reared God's *t.* and his work
**Tropic.**—P. L. 10, 675. up to the *t.* Crab
P. R. 4, 409. and either *t.* now
**Trot.**—U. C. II. 4. might still jog on and keep his *t.*
**Trouble.**—P. L. 5, 34. of offence and *t.*
P. L. 5, 96. the *t.* of thy thoughts this night
P. L. 6, 272. think not here to *t.* holy rest
P. L. 6, 634. they stood awhile in *t.*
P. L. 11, 103. some new *t.* raise
P. L. 12, 81. on the quiet state of men such *t.*
P. L. 12, 209. God looking forth will *t.* all his
P. R. 2, 87. but *t.* as old Simeon plain foretold
P. R. 2, 126. these mild seats without new *t.*
S. A. 487. spare the *t.* of that solicitation
S. A. 1300. and yet perhaps more *t.* is behind
**Troubled.**—P. L. 1, 557. *t.* thoughts
P. L. 2, 534. war appears waged in the *t.* sky
P. L. 4, 19. and doubt distract his *t.* thoughts
P. L. 4, 315. how have ye *t.* all mankind
P. L. 5, 882. no more be *t.* how to quit the
P. L. 7, 216. silence ye *t.* waves and thou deep

P. L. 10, 36. nor *t.* at these tidings from the
P. L. 10, 718. and in a *t.* sea of passion tost
P. R. 2, 65. some *t.* thoughts which she
P. R. 2, 333. ashamed or better to express *t.*
P. R. 4, 1. perplexed and *t.* at his bad success
S. A. 185. the tumours of a *t.* mind

**Troubles.**—P. L. 4, 575. deep to raise new *t.*
P. R. 2, 460. brings dangers *t.* cares and

**Troublesome.**—P. L. 4, 740. these *t.* disguises

**Troy.**—P. L. 9, 16. fugitive about *T.* wall
Il P. 100. or the tale of *T.* divine

**Truce.**—P. L. 2, 526. *t.* to his restless thoughts
P. L. 6, 407. grateful *t.* imposed
P. L. 6, 578. portending hollow *t.*
P. L. 11, 244. heroes old in time of *t.*
P. R. 4, 529. by parle or composition, *t.* or

**True.**—P. L. 3, 104. *t.* allegiance constant faith
P. L. 4, 98. for never can *t.* reconcilement
P. L. 4, 196. yet not *t.* life thereby regained
P. L. 4, 250. Hesperian fables *t.* if *t.* here only
P. L. 4, 282. by some supposed *t.* Paradise
P. L. 4, 294. severe but in *t.* filial freedom
P. L. 4, 295. whence *t.* authority in men
P. L. 4, 750. mysterious law *t.* source of
P. L. 4, 900. the rest is *t.* they found me
P. L. 5, 305. fruits of taste to please *t.* appetite
P. L. 6, 430. *t.* is less firmly armed
P. L. 8, 384. what harmony or *t.* delight
P. L. 8, 589. in passion not wherein *t.* love
P. L. 9, 788. whether *t.* or fancied so
P. L. 9, 982. of thy so *t.* so faithful love
P. L. 9, 1024. nor known till now *t.* relish
P. L. 9, 1069. *t.* in our fall false in our promised
P. L. 10, 494. *t.* is me also he hath judged
P. L. 10, 789. O thought horrid if *t.* yet why
P. L. 11, 361. thereby to learn *t.* patience
P. L. 11, 598. *t.* opener of mine eyes
P. L. 11, 790. but of *t.* virtue
P. L. 12, 83. since thy original lapse *t.* liberty
P. L. 12, 145. Jordan *t.* limit eastward
P. L. 12, 274. mine eyes *t.* opening
P. L. 12, 358. the *t.* anointed king Messiah
P. R. 1, 231. height sacred virtue and *t.* worth
P. R. 1, 358. 'tis *t.* I am that spirit unfortunate
P. R. 1, 431. and what confessed more *t.* among
P. R. 1, 433. by mixing somewhat *t.* to vent
P. R. 3, 60. this is *t.* glory and renown when
P. R. 3, 63. who with *t.* applause recount his
P. R. 3, 139. of all *t.* good himself despoiled
P. R. 3, 373. David's royal seat his *t.* successor
P· R. 3, 405. if I mean to reign David's *t.* heir
P. R. 3, 441. so spake Israel's *t.* king
P. R. 4, 290. though granted *t.*
P. R. 4, 319. therefore seeks in these *t.* wisdom
P. R. 4, 347. with Sion's songs to all *t.* tastes
P. R. 4, 596. *t.* image of the Father whether
S. A. 91. if it be *t.* that light is in the soul
S. A. 418. ignominious, infamous, *t.* slavery
S. A. 430. *t.* and thou bear'st enough and more
S. A. 823. I led the way, bitter reproach but *t.*
S. A. 1756. with new acquist of *t.* experience
C. 10. after this mortal change to her *t.* servants
C. 170. this way the noise was if mine ear be *t.*
C. 385. 'tis most *t.* that musing meditation
C. 437. hath hurtful power o'er *t.* virginity
C. 511. ay me unhappy then my fears are *t.*
C 644. but now I find it *t.* for by this means
C. 905. of *t.* virgin here distressed
C. 997. list mortals if your ears be *t.*
Il P. 95. whose power hath a *t.* consent
S. 10, 13. that all both judge you to relate them *t.*
S. 19, 6. my *t.* account lest he returning chide
H. 227. our Babe to show his Godhead *t.*
D. F. I. 41. O say me *t.* if thou wert mortal wight
D. F. I. 45. careful Jove in nature's *t.* behoof

**Truest.**—S. A. 654. patience as thee *t.* fortitude

**Truly.**—P. L. 4, 491. which alone is *t.* fair
P. R. 3, 372. that which alone can *t.* re-install
S. A. 754. *t.* penitent but . . . to try her husband
U. C. II. 1. here lieth one who did most *t.* prove

**Trump.**—H. 156. the wakeful *t.* of doom must .

P. 26. loud o'er the rest Cremona's *t.* doth sound

**Trumpery.**—P. L. 3, 475. with all their *t.*

**Trumpet.**—P. L. 1, 754. and *t.'s* sound
P. L. 6, 60. the loud ethereal *t.* from on high
P. L. 6, 203. Michael bid sound the archangel .
P. L. 6, 526. and to arms the matin *t.* sung
P. L. 11, 74. he blew his *t.*
P. L. 12, 229. lightning and loud *t.'s* sound
P. R. 1, 19. voice more awful than the sound of *t.*
H. 58. the *t.* spake not to the armed throng

**Trumpets.**—P. L. 1, 532. sound of *t.* loud
P. L. 2, 515. with *t.s'* regal sound the great
P. L. 7, 296. as armies at the call of *t.*
S. A. 1598. the morning *t.* festival proclaimed
S. M. 11. their loud uplifted angel-*t.* blow

**Trunk.**—P. L. 7, 416. and at his *t.* spouts out
P. L. 9, 589. about the mossy *t.* I wound me

**Trust.**—P. L. 2, 17. and *t.* themselves to fear
P. L. 2, 46. his *t.* was with the eternal to be
P. L. 5, 788. if I *t.* to know ye right
P. L. 10, 881. to *t.* thee from my side imagined
P. L. 12, 328. as in whom shall *t.* all nations
P. L. 12, 418. to hurt them more who rightly *t.*
S. A. 348. O ever failing *t.* in mortal strength
S. A. 428. to violate the sacred *t.* of silence
S. A. 1001. to such a viper his most sacred *t.*
S. A. 1140. my *t.* is in the living God who gave
C. 31. a noble peer of mickle *t.* and power
C. 322. and *t.* thy honest offered courtesy
C. 370. (not being in danger ,as I *t.* she is not)
C. 682. but you invert the covenants of her *t.*
S. 23, 7. and such as yet once more I *t.* to have

**Trusted.**—P. L. 1, 40. he *t.* to have equalled
P. L. 7. 143. he *t.* to have seized and into fraud
P. L. 10, 877. disdained not to be *t.* longing to
S. A. 199. my vessel *t.* to me from above
S. A. 783. nor shouldst thou have *t.* that to

**Trusting.**—P. L. 6, 119. *t.* in the Almighty's
P. L. 12, 133. but *t.* all his wealth with God
S. A. 1178. in *t.* he will accept thee

**Truth.**—P. L. 3, 338. and fair *t.*
P. L. 4, 293. *t.* wisdom sanctitude severe and
P. L. 5, 771. calumnious art of counterfeited *t.*
P. L. 5, 902. to swerve from *t.*
P. L. 6, 32. revolted multitudes the cause of *t.*
P. L. 6, 33. and for the testimony of *t.* hast
P. L. 6, 122. who in debate of *t.* hath won
P. L. 6, 173. from the path of *t.* remote
P. L. 6, 381. for strength from *t.* divided
P. L. 9, 738. reason to her seeming and with *t.*
P. L. 10, 755. yet to say *t.*
P. L. 10, 856. shall *t.* fail to keep her word
P. L. 11, 667. of justice of religion *t.* and peace
P. L. 11, 704. and utter odious *t.* that God would
P. L. 11, 807. justice and temperance *t.* and faith
P. L. 12, 303. from shadowy types to *t.*
P. L. 12, 482. unfaithful herd the enemies of *t.*
P. L. 12, 490. to guide them in all *t.*
P. L. 12, 511. and the *t.* with superstitions
P. L. 12, 533. worship persevere of spirit and *t.*
P. L. 12, 535. *t.* shall retire bestuck with
P. L. 12, 569. that suffering for *t.'s* sake
P. R. 1, 205. to promote all *t.* all righteous
P. R. 1, 220. till *t.* were freed and equity
P. R. 1, 430. yet thou pretend'st to *t.* all oracles
P. R. 1, 446. whence hast thou then thy *t.* but
P. R. 1, 453. to thyself ascribest the *t.* foretold
P. R. 1, 462. and sends his spirit of *t.* henceforth
P. R. 1, 464. to all *t.* requisite for men to know
P. R. 1, 472. enforced ofttimes to part from *t.*
P. R. 1, 478. hard are the ways of *t.* and rough
P. R. 2, 34. his wisdom full of grace and *t.*
P. R. 2, 473. guide nations in the way of *t.*
P. R. 3, 98. for *t.'s* sake suffering death
P. R. 3, 183. *T.* hath said
P. R. 3, 443. so fares it when with *t.* falsehood
S. A. 215. yet *t.* to say I oft have heard men
S. A. 870. virtue as I thought *t.* duty so enjoining
S. A. 1276. the righteous and all such as honour *t.*
C. 691. 'twill not restore the *t.* and honesty
C. 971. their faith their patience and their *t*

S. 2, 5. my semblance might deceive the *t.*
S. 9, 4. that labour up the hill of heavenly *t.*
S. 12, 10. still revolt when *t.* would set them free
S. 14, 12. spake the *t.* of thee on glorious themes
S. 15, 11. till *t.* and right from violence be freed
S. 16, 4. to peace and *t.* thy glorious way hast
S. 18, 3. them who kept thy *t.* so pure of old
H. 141. yea *t.* and justice then
T. 16. *t.* and peace and love shall ever shine
D. F. I. 54. crowned matron sage white-robed *t.*
U. C. I. 5. such a shifter that if *t.* were known
U. C. II. 8. old *t.* motion numbered out his time
**Try.**—P. L. 1, 269. with rallied arms to *t.* what
P. L. 4, 941. though for possession put to *t.*
P. L. 5, 727. hath in his thought to *t.* in battle
P. L. 5, 865. by proof to *t.* who is our equal
P. L. 6, 120. I mean to *t.*
P. L. 6, 818. to *t.* with me in battle
P. L. 8, 75. or if they list to *t.* conjecture
P. L. 8, 437. thus far to *t.* thee Adam I was
P. L. 9, 860. never more mean I to *t.*
P. L. 10, 254. let us *t.*—adventurous work
P. L. 10, 382. *t.* thee now more dangerous
P. R. 1, 123. temptation and all guile on him to *t.*
P. R. 1, 224. at least to *t.* and teach the erring
P. R. 2, 225. with manlier objects we must *t.*
P. R. 4, 198. if I to *t.* whether in higher sort
P. R. 4, 532. to *t.* thee sift thee and confess
S. A. 754. not truly penitent but chief to *t.* her
S. A. 1399. I could be well content to *t.* their art
C. 793. yet should I *t.* the uncontrolled worth
C. 806. I must dissemble and *t.* her yet more
C. 858. this will I *t.* and add the power
**Tub.**—C. 708. their precepts from the Cynic *t.*
**Tube.**—P. L. 3, 590. through his glazed optic *t.*
**Tuft.**—P. L. 4, 325. under a *t.* of shade that
P. L. 9, 417. and field he sought where any *t.*
**Tufted.**—C. 225. casts a gleam over this *t.* grove
L. 143. the *t.* crow-toe and pale jessamine
L'A. 78. bosomed high in *t.* trees
**Tufts.**—P. L. 7, 327. with *t.* the valleys
**Tugged.**—S. A. 1650. he *t.* he shook till down
**Tumble.**—C. 927. that *t.* down the snowy hills
**Tumid.**—P. L. 7, 288 so high as heaved the *t.*
**Tumours.**—S. A. 185. the *t.* of a troubled mind
**Tumult.**—P. L. 2, 966. and *t.* and confusion
P. L. 2, 1040. with *t.* less and with less hostile
P. L. 6, 674. foreseen this *t.* and permitted
C. 202. whence even now the *t.* of loud mirth
**Tumults.**—P. L. 5, 737. vain designs and *t.*
**Tumultuous.**—P. L. 2, 936. of some *t.*
P. L. 4, 16. boils in his *t.* breast
**Tun.**—P. L. 4, 816. fit for the *t.* some magazine
**Tunable.**—P. R. 1, 480. and *t.* as sylvan pipe
**Tune.**—P. L. 5, 196. warbling *t.* his praise
S. A. 661. or rather seems a *t.* harsh
A. 72. after the heavenly *t.* which none can hear
P. 8. for now to sorrow must I *t.* my song
S. M. 26. and keep in *t.* with heaven
**Tuneable.**—P. L. 5, 151. more *t.* than
**Tuned.**—P. L. 3, 366. took harps ever *t.* that
P. L. 7, 436. but all night *t.* her soft lays
P. L. 7, 559. harps that *t.* angelic harmonies
P. L. 9, 549. tempter and his proem *t.*
P. R. 1, 182. heaven their odes and vigils *t.*
**Tuneful.**—P. R. 2, 290. of *t.* birds resounding
S. 13, 1. Harry whose *t.* and well-measured song
**Tunes.**—P. L. 3, 40. *t.* her nocturnal note
P. L. 5, 41. *t.* sweetest his love-laboured song
Il P. 117. in sage and solemn *t.* have sung
**Tunest.**—S. 13, 11. that *t.* their happiest lines in
**Tunings.**—P. L. 7, 598. tempered soft *t.*
**Turbants.**—P. R. 4, 76. silken *t.* wreathed
**Turbulencies.**—P. R. 4, 462. like *t.* in the
**Turbulent.**—P. L. 9, 1126. and *t.* for
P. R. 4, 461. on man beast plant wasteful and *t.*
S. A. 552. whose heads that *t.* liquor fills with
S. A. 1040. in his way to virtue adverse and *t.*
**Turchestan-born.**—P. L. 11, 396. *T.-b.*
**Turf.**—P. L. 5, 391. raised of grassy *t.* their
P. L. 11, 324. I would rear of grassy *t.*

C. 280. they left me weary on a grassy *t.*
L. 140. on the green *t.* suck the honied showers
**Turkis.**—C. 894. of *t.* blue and emerald green
**Turkish.**—P. L. 10, 434. the horns of *T.* crescent
**Turms.**—P. R. 4, 66. *t.* of horse and wings
**Turn.**—P. L. 3, 582. *t.* swift their various motions
P. L. 5, 413. and corporeal to incorporeal *t.*
P. L. 5, 441. can *t.* or holds it possible to *t.*
P. L. 5, 497. your bodies may at last *t.* all to
P. L. 5, 630. from dance to sweet repast they *t.*
P. L. 6, 234. or *t.* the sway of battle
P. L. 6, 291. or *t.* this heaven itself into the
P. L. 6, 562. and *t.* not back perverse
P. L. 7, 380. then in the east her *t.* she shines
P. L. 8, 491. this *t.* hath made amends
P. L. 10, 668. say he bid his angels *t.* askance
P. L. 10, 672. was bid to *t.* reins from the
P. L. 10, 1093. he will relent and *t.* from his
P. L. 11, 373. to the evil *t.* my obvious breast
P. L. 11, 630. should *t.* aside to tread paths
P. L. 11, 806. so all shall *t.* degenerate
P. L. 12, 471. and evil *t.* to good more
P. L. 12, 510. own vile advantages shall *t.*
P. R. 2, 220. her female pride deject or *t.* to
S. A. 708. and *t.* his labours, for thou canst to
L. 21. and as he passes *t.* and bid fair peace
D. F. I. 67. to *t.* swift-rushing black perdition
C. 222. *t.* forth her silver lining on the night
A. 66. and *t.* the adamantine spindle round
**Turned.**—P. L. 3, 500. *t.* thitherward in haste
P. L. 3, 582. or are *t.* by his magnetic beam
P. L. 3, 624. his back was *t.*
P. L. 3, 646. his radiant visage *t.*
P. L. 3, 718. that rolled orbicular and *t.* to
P. L. 3, 736. thus said, he *t.* and Satan bowing
P. L. 4, 410. *t.* him all ear to hear new
P. L. 4, 480. back I *t.* thou following criedst
P. L. 4, 502. aside the devil *t.* for envy
P. L. 4, 536. his proud step he scornful *t.*
P. L. 4, 721. both *t.* and under open sky adored
P. L. 4, 741. nor I *t.* I ween Adam from his fair
P. L. 4, 978. the angelic squadron bright *t.*
P. L. 5, 420. not yet into her substance *t.*
P. L. 5, 906. with retorted scorn his back he *t.*
P. L. 6, 284. hast thou *t.* the least of these
P. L. 6, 509. in a moment up they *t.*
P. L. 6, 881. Messiah his triumphal chariot *t.*
P. L. 7, 213. up from the bottom *t.* by furious
P. L. 7, 228. one foot he centred and the other *t.*
P. L. 8, 257. my wondering eyes I *t.* and gazed
P. L. 8, 507. in her so that seeing me she *t.*
P. L. 9, 527. his gentle dumb expression *t.*
P. L. 9, 603. I *t.* my thoughts and with
P. L. 9, 834. from the tree her step she *t.*
P. L. 9, 920. calm mood his words to Eve he *t.*
P. L. 10, 192. to the woman thus his sentence *t.*
P. L. 10, 546. the applause they meant *t.*
P. L. 10, 688. *t.* his course intended
P. L. 10, 909. he added not and from her *t.*
P. L. 11, 675. and to his guide lamenting *t.*
P. L. 11, 714. all now was *t.* to jollity and game
P. L. 12, 176. to blood unshed the rivers must be *t.*
P. R. 2, 37. we rejoiced but soon our joy is *t.*
P. R. 3, 138. *t.* recreant to God ingrate and false
S. A. 139. old warriors *t.* their plated backs
S. A. 396. and *t.* to sport her importunity
S. A. 539. then *t.* me out ridiculous despoiled
S. A. 1614. to their sports they *t.* immediately
**Turning.**—P. L. 2, 63. *t.* our tortures into
P. L. 2, 968. to whom Satan *t.* boldly thus
P. L. 5, 255. self-opened wide on golden hinges *t.*
P. R. 3, 293. *t.* with easy eye thou mayst behold
H. 48. down through the *t.* sphere
**Turnings.**—C. 569. through paths and *t.* often
**Turns.**—P. L. 1, 495. when the priest *t.* atheist
P. L. 2, 598. and feel by *t.* the bitter change
P. L. 2, 876. then in the key-hole *t.* the intricate
P. L. 5, 332. despachful looks in haste she *t.*
P. L. 6, 7. round lodge and dislodge by *t.*
P. L. 7, 129. *t.* wisdom to folly as nourishment

P. L. 9, 330. no dishonour on our front but *t*.
C. 462. and *t*. it by degrees to the soul's essence
**Turnus.**—P. L. 9, 17. or rage of *T*.
**Turret.**—P. L. 9, 525. his *t*. crest and sleek
**Turrets.**—P. R. 4, 54. *t*. and terraces
**Turtle.**—H. 50. with *t*. wing the amorous clouds
**Tuscan.**—P. L. 1, 288. optic glass the *T*.
C. 48. after the *T*. mariners transformed
S. 20, 12. warble immortal notes and *T*. air
**Twain.**—S. A. 929. thou and I long since are *t*.
C. 284. they were but *t*. and purposed quick
L. 110. two massy keys he bore of metals *t*.
**Tweed.**—V. Ex. 92. of utmost *T*. or Ouse
**Twelve.**—P. L. 3, 597. to the *t*. that shone
P. L. 12, 155. the grandchild with *t*. sons
P. L. 12, 226. through the *t*. tribes to rule
P. R. 2, 96. when *t*. years he scarce had seen
**Twentieth.**—S. 2, 2. my three and *t*. year
**Twenty.**—U. C. I. 3. the ways being foul *t*. to one
**Twice.**—P. L. 9, 859. nor shall be *t*.
P. L. 10, 669. the poles of earth *t*. ten degrees
P. R. 1, 210. my age had measured *t*. six years
P. R. 2, 314. fed *t*. by a voice inviting him to
P. R. 3, 281. ancient but rebuilt by him who *t*.
S. A. 24. from heaven foretold *t*. by an angel
S. A. 361. for this did the angel *t*. descend
S. A. 635. by heavenly message *t*. descending
**Twice-battered.**—H. 199. with that *t.-b*. god
**Twigs.**—P. L. 9, 1105. the bended *t*. take root
**Twilight.**—P." L. 1, 597. disastrous *t*. sheds
P. L. 4, 598. *t*. gray had in her sober livery
P. L. 5, 645. had changed to grateful *t*.
P. L. 6, 12. darkness there might .. seem *t*. here
P. L. 7, 583. the sun was set and *t*. from the
P. L. 9, 50. Hesperus whose office is to bring *t*.
C. 844. visits the herds along the *t*. meadows
A. 99. trip no more in *t*. ranks
Il P. 133. to arched walks of *t*. groves
H. 188. the nymphs in *t*. shade
**Twin-born.**—S. 12, 6. at Latona's *t.-b*. progeny
**Twine.**—P. L. 4. 348. *t*. his braided train
C. 105. braid your locks with rosy *t*.
H. 226. not Typhon huge ending in snaky *t*.
**Twines.**—P. L. 5, 216. about him *t*. her
**Twinned.**—P.L.12,85.with right reason dwells *t*.
**Twins.**—P. L. 10, 674. and the Spartan *T*.
C. 1010. two blissful *t*. are to be born
**Twisted.**—C. 862. in *t*. braids of lilies knitting
L'A. 48. or the *t*. eglantine
**Twitched**—L. 192. and *t*. his mantle blue
**'Twixt.**—P. L. 1, 346. *'t*. upper nether and
P. L. 5, 589. standards & gonfalons *t*. van & rear
P. L. 6, 104. *'t*. host and host but narrow
P. L. 9, 51. short arbiter *'t*. day and night
S. A. 462. all the contest is now *'t*. God and Dagon
C. 20. took in by lot *'t*. high and nether Jove
C. 606. *'t*. Africa and Ind, I'll help him out
D. F. I. 69. to stand *'t*. us and our deserved smart
**Two.**—P. L. 2, 714. as when *t*. black clouds
P. L. 3, 33. those other *t*. equalled with me in
P. L. 3, 65. our *t*. first parents yet the only *t*.
P. L. 4, 288. *t*. of far nobler shape erect and tall
P. L. 4, 382. to entertain you *t*. her widest
P. L. 4, 404. in some purlieu *t*. gentle fawns
P. L. 4, 505. thus these *t*. imparadised in one
P. L. 4, 732. but thou hast promised from us *t*.
P. L. 4, 786. from these *t*. strong and subtle
P. L. 4, 790. where those *t*. fair creatures
P. L. 4, 820. back stepped those *t*. fair angels
P. L. 4, 874. he scarce had ended when those *t*.
P. L. 4, 1002, in these he put *t*. weights
P. L. 5, 132. *t*. other precious drops
P. L. 5, 366. with us *t*. only who yet by

P. L. 6, 305. *t*. broad suns their shields blazed
P. L. 6, 313. *t*. planets rushing from aspect
P. L. 6, 366. *t*. potent thrones, that to be less
P. L. 6, 684. *t*. days are passed, *t*. days, as we
P. L. 6, 688. as likeliest was when *t*. such foes
P. L. 6, 699. *t*. days are therefore passed
P. L. 7, 201. between *t*. brazen mountains
P. L. 7, 346. and God made *t*. great lights
P. L. 8, 151. *t*. great sexes animate the world
P. L. 8, 350. approaching *t*. and *t*. these
P. L. 9, 203. outgrew the hands' dispatch of *t*.
P. L. 9, 211. one night or *t*. with wanton
P. L. 9, 415. the only *t*. of mankind
P. L. 10, 82. those *t*. the third best absent is
P. L. 10, 289. when *t*. polar winds blowing
P. L. 10, 397. you *t*. this way
P. L. 10, 924. between us *t*. let there be peace
P. L. 10, 990. and with us *t*. be forced to satisfy
P. L. 10, 1072. or by collision of *t*. bodies grind
P. L. 11, 57. I at first with *t*. fair gifts created
P. L. 11, 186. *t*. birds of gayest plume
P. L. 11, 454. these *t*. are brethren Adam
P. L. 11. 565. *t*. massy clods of iron and brass
P. L. 11,600. peaceful days portends than those *t*.
P. L. 12, 169. by *t* brethren (these *t*. brethren
P. L. 12, 197. between *t*. crystal walls
P. L. 12, 254. the wings of *t*. bright cherubim
P. L. 12, 431. sin and death his *t*. main arms
P. R. 1, 159. sin and death the *t*. grand foes
P. R. 3, 255. from his side *t*.
P. R. 3, 361. between *t*. such enclosing enemies
P. R. 3, 377. ten sons of Jacob *t*. of Joseph lost
P. R. 4, 85. these *t*. thrones except the rest
S. A. 209. these *t*. proportioned ill
S. A. 261. bound with *t*. cords but cords to me
S. A. 1606. half round on *t*. main pillars vaulted
S. A. 1633. his arms on those *t*. massy pillars
S. A. 1648. when mountains tremble those *t*.
C. 291. *t*. such I saw what time the laboured ox
C. 575. who gently asked if he had seen such *t*.
C. 578. soon I guessed ye were the *t*. she meant
C. 1010. *t*. blissful twins are to be born
L. 110. *t*. massy keys he bore of metals twain
L'A. 15. with *t*. sister Graces more
L'A. 82. from betwixt *t*. aged oaks
S.17,8. move by her *t*. main nerves iron and gold
V. Ex. 6. where he had mutely sat *t*. years before
**Two-handed.**—P. L. 6, 251. huge *t.-h*. sway
L. 130. but that *t.-h*. engine at the door
**Tyne.**—V. Ex. 98. coaly *T*. or ancient hallowed Dee
**Type.**—P. L. 1, 405. the *t*. of Hell
**Types.**—P. L. 12, 232. informing them by *t*.
P. L. 12, 303. disciplined from shadowy *t*.
**Typhœan.**—P. L. 2, 539. with vast *T*. rage
**Typhon.**—P. L. 1, 199. Briareos or *T*.
H. 226. nor *T*. huge ending in snaky twine
**Tyrannic.**—P. R. 1, 219. and proud *t*. power
S. A. 1275. and industrious to support *t*. power
**Tyrannize.**—P. L. 12, 39. or under him to *t*.
**Tyrannous.**—P. L. 12, 32. to his empire *t*.
**Tyranny.**—P. L. 1, 124. holds the *t*. of heaven
P. L. 2, 59. the prison of his *t*. who reigns
P. L. 12, 95. *t*. must be though to the tyrant
S. A. 1291. victor over all that *t*. or fortune can
**Tyrant.**—P. L. 4, 394. necessity the *t.'s* plea
P. L. 10, 466. and dungeon of our *t*.
P. L. 12, 96. though to the *t*. thereby no excuse
P. L. 12, 173. but first the lawless *t*. who
S. 18, 12. where still doth sway the triple *t*.
**Tyrian.**—C. 342. star of Arcady or *T*. Cynosure
H. 204. in vain the *T*. maids
**Tyrrhene.**—C. 49. coasting the *T*. shore

# U.

**Uglier.**—P. L. 2, 662. nor *u.* follow the night-hag
**Ugly.**—P. L. 10, 539. a crowd of *u.* serpents
   P. L. 11, 464. of terror foul and *u.*
   P. R. 4, 408. soon with *u.* dreams
**Ugly-headed.**—C. 695. these *u.-h.* monsters
**Ulcer.**—P. L. 11, 484. intestine stone and *u.*
**Ultimate.**—P. R. 3, 210. and my *u.* repose
**Ulysses.**—P. L. 2, 1019. or when *U.* on the
   C. 637. that Hermes once to wise *U.* gave
   V. Ex. 50. while sad *U.'* soul and all the rest
**Umbrage.**—P. L. 9, 1087. spread their *u.*
**Umbrageous.**—P. L. 4, 257. *u.* grots
**Umpire.**—P. L. 2, 907. Chaos *u.* sits
   P. L. 3, 195. as a guide my *u.* conscience
**Unable.**—P. L. 10, 165. *u.* to transfer the
   P. L. 10, 750. *u.* to perform thy terms too hard
   S. A. 896. gods *u.* to acquit themselves
**Unacceptable.**—P. L. 2, 251. obtained *u.*
**Unaccomplished.**—P. L. 3, 455. *u.* works
**Unacquainted.**—C. 180. inform my *u.* feet
**Unactive.**—P. L. 4, 621. animals *u.* range
   P. L. 8, 97. his beams *u.* else
   P. R. 2, 81. private *u.* calm contemplative
   S. A. 1705. then vigorous most when most *u.*
**Unadmonished.**—P. L. 5, 245. surprisal *u.*
**Unadored.**—P. L. 1, 738. unheard or *u.*
**Unadorned.**—P. L. 4, 305. her *u.* golden tresses
   P. L. 7, 814. bare unsightly *u.*
   C. 23. the *u.* bosom of the deep
**Unadventurous.**—P. R. 3, 243. unhardy *u.*
**Unaffected.**—P. R. 4, 359. majestic *u.*
**Unagreeable.**—P. L. 10, 256. mine not *u.*
**Unaided.**—P. L. 6, 141. *u* could have
**Unalterably.**—P. L. 5, 502. and retain *u.*
**Unaltered.**—P. R. 1, 493. Saviour with *u.* brow
**Unamazed.**—P. L. 9, 552. at length not *u.*
**Unanimous.**—P. L. 4, 736. this said *u.*
   P. L. 6, 95. so oft in festivals of joy and love *u.*
   P. L. 12, 603. both in one faith *u.* though sad
   P. R. 1, 111. *u.* they all commit the care
**Unanswered.**—P. L. 6, 163 *u.* lest thou boast
**Unappalled.**—P. R. 4, 425. sat'st in calm
**Unapparent.**—P. L. 7, 103. the *u.* deep
**Unappeasable.**—S. A. 963. thy anger *u.* still
**Unapproached.**—P. L. 3, 4. in *u.* light
**Unapproved.**—P. L. 5, 118. and go so *v.*
**Unargued.**—P. L. 4, 636. *u.* I obey
**Unarmed.**—P. L. 4, 552. *u.* youth of heaven
   P. L. 6, 595. *u.* they might have
   P. R. 4. 626. he all *u.* shall chase thee
   S. A. 126. whom *u.* no strength of man
   S. A. 263. on their whole host I flew *u.*
   S. A. 1111. in fight withstand me single and *u.*
   C. 582. against the *u.* weakness of one virgin
**Unassailed.**—C. 230. my life and honour *u.*
**Unassayed.**—P. L. 9, 335. love, virtue, *u.*
**Unattempted.**—P. L. 1, 16. things *u.* yet.
**Unattended.**—P. L. 8, 60. not *u* for on her
**Unattending.**—C. 272. is addressed to *u* ears
**Unaware.**—P. L. 2, 156. impotence or *u.*
   P. L. 3, 547. which to his eye discovers *u.*
   P. L. 9, 362. and fall into deception *u.*
   P. R. 1. 225. not wilfully misdoing but *u.*
**Unawares.**—P. L. 2, 932. all *u* fluttering
   P. L. 5, 731. lest *u.* we lose this our high
   S. A. 1522. we *u.* run into danger's mouth
**Unbarred.**—P. L. 6, 4. *u.* the gates of light
**Unbecoming.**—P. L. 6, 237. no *u.* deed that
**Unbefitting.**—P. L. 4, 759. think thee *u.*
**Unbegot.**—P. L. 10, 988. yet *u.*
**Unbeheld.**—P. L. 4, 674. *u.* in deep of night
**Unbelief.**—C. 519. *u.* is blind
**Unbenighted.**—P. L. 10, 682. day had *u.*
**Unbenign.**—P. L. 10, 661. join in synod *u.*
**Unbesought.**—P. L. 10, 1058. care hath *u.*
**Unbid.**—P. L. 10, 204. bring thee forth *u.*

**Unblamed.**—P. L. 3, 3. express thee *u.*
   P. L. 9, 5. him the while venial discourse *u.*
   P. L. 12, 22. shall spend their days in joy *u.*
**Unblemished.**—C. 215. and thou *u.* form of
**Unblenched.**—C. 430. with *u.* majesty
**Unblest.**—P. L. 1, 238. found the sole of *u.*
   P. L. 10, 988. to prevent the race *u.* to being
   C. 907. of *u.* enchanter vile
**Unborn.**—P. L. 4, 663. to nations yet *u.*
   P. L. 7, 220. far into Chaos and the world *u.*
   P. L. 11, 502. better end here *u.*
**Unbosom.**—P. 53. would soon *u.* all their
**Unbosomed.**—S. A. 879. *u.* all my secrets to thee
**Unbottomed.**—P. L. 2, 405. the dark *u.*
**Unbound.**—P. L. 3, 603. and call up *u.*
**Unbounded.**—P. L. 4, 60. no *u.* hope had
   P. L. 10, 471. voyaged the unreal vast *u.*
**Unbroken.**—P. L. 2, 691. faith, till then *u.*
**Unbuckled.**—P. L. 11, 245. starry helm *u.*
**Unbuild.**—P. L. 8, 81. how build *u.* contrive
   P. L. 12, 526. what but *u.* his living temples
**Uncalled.**—P. L. 9, 523. he bolder now *u.*
**Uncelebrated.**—P. L. 7, 253, nor passed *u.*
**Uncertain.**—P. L. 3, 76. *u.* which in ocean
   P. R. 4, 326. *u.* and unsettled still remains
   C. 360. to cast the fashion of *u.* evils
**Uncessant** (or *incessant*).—L. 64. with *u.* care
**Unchangeable.**—P. L. 3, 127. *u.* eternal
**Unchanged.**—P. L. 7, 24. mortal voice *u.*
**Unchaste.**—S. A. 321. bride unclean *u.*
   S. A. 325. *u.* was subsequent
   C. 464. by *u.* looks loose gestures and foul talk
**Unchecked.**—P. L. 8, 189. fancy is to rove *u.*
**Uncircumcised.**—S. A. 260. to the *u.*
   S. A. 640. against the *u.* our enemies
   S. A. 1364. the Philistines idolatrous *u.* unclean
**Uncircumscribed.**—P. L. 7, 170. *u.* myself
**Unclean.**—P. L. 9, 1098. reproach us as *u.*
   P. R. 2, 328. nor mention I meats by the law
   S. A. 321. that fallacious bride *u.* unchaste
   S. A. 324. that moral verdict quits her of *u.*
   S. A. 1362. what act more execrably *u.* profane
   S. A. 1364. idolatrous uncircumcised *u.*
**Unclouded.**—P. L. 10, 65. *u.* deity
**Uncoloured.**—P. L. 5, 189. clouds the *u.* sky
**Uncompassionate.**—S. A. 818. in *u.* anger
**Uncompounded.**—P. L. 1, 425. soft and *u.*
**Unconcerned.**—P. L. 11, 174. morn all *u.*
**Unconfirmed.**—P. R. 1, 29. his witness *u.*
**Unconform.**—P. L. 5, 259. not *u.* to other
**Unconjugal.**—S. A. 979. falsehood most *u.*
**Unconniving.**—P. R. 1, 363. by rigour *u.*
**Unconquerable.**—P. L. 1, 106. *u* will
   P. L. 6, 118. though to sight *u.*
**Unconquered.**—C. 448. wore *u.* virgin
**Unconscionable.**—S. A. 1245. less *u.* strides
**Unconsumed.**—P. L. 1, 69. sulphur *u.*
   P. L. 2, 648. impaled with circling fire yet *u.*
**Uncontrollable.**—S. A. 1754. his *u.* intent
**Uncontrolled.**—C. 793. the *u.* worth of this
**Uncovered.**—P. L. 9, 1059. his robe *u.* more
**Uncover'st.**—S. A. 842. thy crime *u.* more
**Uncouth.**—P. L. 2, 407. find out his *u.* way
   P. L. 2, 827. from them I go this *u.* errand
   P. L. 5, 98. nor can I like this *u* dream
   P. L. 6, 362. with shattered arms and *u.* pain
   P. L. 8, 230. bound on a voyage *u.* and obscure
   P. L. 10, 475. but I toiled out my *u.* passage
   S. A. 333. such ye seem though in this *u.* place
   L. 186. thus sang the *u.* swain to the oaks
   L'A. 5. find out some *u.* cell
**Uncreate.**—P. L. 5, 895. when who can *u.*
   P. L. 9, 943. so God shall *u.* be frustrate
**Uncreated.**—P. L. 2, 150. womb of *u.* night
   P. L. 6, 268. misery *u.* till the crime of thy
**Uncropt.**—P. L. 4, 731. *u.* falls to the ground

**Unction.**—P. L. 6, 709. by sacred *u.*
**Unctuous.**—P. L. 9,635. compact of *u.* vapour
**Unculled.**—P. L. 11, 436. yellow sheaf *u.*
**Undaunted.**—P. L. 2, 677. the *u.* fiend
 P. L. 2, 955. *u.* to meet there whatever power
 P. L. 4, 851. visibly impaired yet seemed *u.*
 P. L. 6,113. and thus his own *u.* heart explores
 S. A. 1623. he patient but *u.* where they led him
**Undazzled.**—P. L. 3, 614. devil met *u.*
**Undecked.**—P. L. 5, 380. *u.* save with herself
**Undefiled.**—P. L. 4, 761. whose bed is *u.*
**Undelighted.**—P. L. 4, 286. saw *u.* all
**Under.**—P. L. 1, 130. *u.* thy conduct
 P. L. 1, 207. moors by his side *u.* the lee
 P. L. 1, 313. *u.* amazement of their hideous
 P. L. 1, 345. hovering on wing *u.* the cope
 P. L. 1, 477. who *u.* names of old renown
 P. L. 1, 602. but *u.* brows of dauntless courage
 P. L. 1, 65 *l.* nor the abyss long *u.* darkness
 P. L. 2, 261. in what place soe'er thrive *u.* evil
 P. L. 2, 322. *u.* the inevitable curb
 P. L. 2, 498. though *u.* hope of heavenly grace
 P. L. 2, 886. *u.* spread ensigns marching
 P. L. 3, 242. *u.* his gloomy power I shall not
 P. L. 3, 275. found out for mankind *u.* wrath
 P. L. 3, 319. *u.* thee as head Supreme thrones
 P. L. 3, 322. in heaven or earth or *u.* earth
 P. L. 3, 424. dark waste and wild *u.* the frown
 P. L. 3, 514. dreaming by night *u.* the open sky
 P. L. 3, 640. *u.* a coronet his flowing hair
 P. L. 4, 88. *u.* what torments inwardly I groan
 P. L. 4, 122. practised falsehood *u.* saintly show
 P. L. 4, 239. mazy error *u.* pendent shades
 P. L. 4, 282. *u.* the Ethiop line by Nilus
 P. L. 4, 325. *u.* a tuft of shade that on a green
 P. L. 4, 451. found myself reposed *u.* a shade
 P. L. 4, 478. fair indeed and tall *u.* a platane
 P. L. 4, 496. *u.* the flowing gold of her loose
 P. L. 4, 572. eye pursued him still but *u.* shade
 P. L. 4, 721. and *u.* open sky adored
 P. L. 5, 137. but first from *u.* shady arborous
 P. L. 5, 288. all the bands of angel *u.* watch
 P. L. 5, 463. *u.* whose lowly roof thou hast
 P. L. 5, 587. *u.* their hierarchs in orders bright
 P. L. 5, 609. *u.* his great vicegerent reign abide
 P. L. 5, 687. and all who *u.* me their banners
 P. L. 5, 698. the regent powers *u.* him regent
 P. L. 5, 776. and us eclipsed *u.* the name of king
 P. L. 5, 880. *u.* one head more near united
 P. L. 6, 67. *u.* their godlike leaders in the cause
 P. L. 6, 142. whelmed thy legions *u.* darkness
 P. L. 6, 196. winds *u.* ground or waters
 P. L. 6, 215. so *u.* fiery cope together rushed
 P. L. 6, 409. *u.* her cloudy covert both retired
 P. L. 6, 478. deep *u.* ground materials dark
 P. L. 6, 521. ere dayspring *u.* conscious night
 P. L. 6, 533. *u.* spread ensigns moving nigh
 P. L. 6, 652. *u.* the weight of mountains buried
 P. L. 6, 666. that *u.* ground they fought
 P. L. 6, 777. *u.* whose conduct Michael soon
 P. L. 6, 779. *u.* their head embodied all in one
 P. L. 6, 832. *u.* his burning
 P. L. 7, 159. *u.* long obedience tried
 P. L. 7, 283. be gathered now ye waters *u.*
 P. L. 7, 301. but they or *u.* ground or circuit
 P. L. 7, 408. or *u.* rocks their food in jointed
 P. L. 7, 422. *u.* a cloud in prospect
 P. L. 7, 469. the swift stag from *u.* ground
 P. L. 8, 454. which it had long stood *u.*
 P. L. 8, 470. *u.* his forming hands a creature
 P. L. 9, 72. into a gulf shot *u.* ground
 P. L. 9, 208. the work *u.* our labour grows
 P. L. 9, 492. hate stronger *u.* show of love
 P. L. 9, 774. *u.* this ignorance of good or evil
 P. L. 9, 925. to taste it *u.* ban to touch
 P. L. 10, 154. such as *u.* government
 P. L. 10, 190. tread at last *u.* our feet
 P. L. 10, 445. throne which *u.* state of richest
 P. L. 10,1003. stand we longer shivering *u.* fears
 P. L. 11, 320. *u.* this tree stood visible
 P. L. 11, 511. be debased *u.* inhuman pains

 P. L. 11, 570. stream from *u.* ground
 P. L. 11, 725. in prison *u.* judgment
 P. L. 11, 740. clouds drove from *u.* heaven
 P. L. 11, 749. with all their pomp deep *u.* water
 P. L. 12, 24. and tribes *u.* paternal rule
 P. L. 12, 39. with him or *u.* him to tyrannize
 P. L. 12, 42. boils out from *u.* ground
 P. L. 12, 320. by judges first then *u.* kings of
 P. L. 12, 539. *u.* her own weight groaning till
 P. L. 12, 618. to me art all things *u.* heaven
 P. R. 1, 305. each night *u.* the covert of some
 P. R. 2, 262. *u.* the hospitable covert nigh
 P. R. 2, 272. there he slept *u.* a juniper
 P. R. 2, 339. in ample space *u.* the broadest
 P. R. 2, 354. *u.* the trees now tripped over
 P. R. 3, 158. reduced a province *u.* Roman yoke
 P. R. 4, 316. rather accuse him *u.* usual names
 P. R. 4, 404. *u.* some concourse of shades
 P. R. 4, 621. fall from heaven trod down *u.* his
 S. A. 49. *u.* the seal of silence could not keep
 S. A. 887. their subject nor *u.* their protection
 S. A. 1035. at first all heavenly *u.* virgin veil
 S. A. 1691. from *u.* ashes into sudden flame
**Under-foot.**—P. L. 4, 700. Mosaic ; *u.-f.* the
**Undergo.**—P. L. 1, 155. being to *u.* eternal
 P. L. 9, 953. certain to *u.* like doom if death
 P. L. 9, 971. to *u.* with me one guilt one crime
 P. L. 10, 126. either to *u.* myself the total
 P. L. 10, 575. to *u.* this annual humbling
 L. 12. which he for us did freely *u.*
**Undergone.**—P. R. 2, 132. labour to be *u.*
**Undergrowth.**—P. L. 4, 175. the *u.* of
**Underling.**—V. Ex. 76. one shall make him *u.*
**Undermine.**—P. R. 1, 179. or terrify or *u.*
**Underminers.**—S. A. 1204. to pay my *u.* in
**Underneath.**—P. L. 1, 701. that *u.* had
 P. L. 3, 518. and *u.* a bright sea flowed of
 P. L. 4, 225. passed *u.* engulfed
 P. L. 5, 87. and *u.* beheld the earth outstretched
 P. L. 6, 659. long struggling *u.* ere they
 P. L. 7, 268. the waters *u.* from those above
 P. R. 4, 456. to the earth's dark basis *u.*
 P. R. 4, 544. till *u.* them fair Jerusalem
 Il P. 152. above about *or u.*
 V. Ex. 95. or sullen Mole that runneth *u.*
**Understand.**—P. L. 6,625. head to foot well *u.*
 P. L. 8, 345. *u.* the same of fish within their
 P. L. 8, 540. for well I *u.*
 P. L. 12, 376. I *u.* what oft my steadiest
 P. R. 2, 100. what he meant I mused since *u.*
 P. R. 4, 527. to *u.* my adversary who and what
**Understanding.**—P. L. 5, 486. and *u.*
 P. L. 6, 444. unhurt our minds and *u.* sound
 P. L. 9. 1127. for *u.* ruled not
**Understood.**—P. L. 1, 662. war open or *u.*
 P. L. 4, 55. and *u.* not that a grateful mind
 P. L. 5, 450. nor jealousy was *u.* the injured
 P. L. 6, 626. not *u.* this gift they had besides
 P. L. 8, 352. named them as they passed and *u.*
 P. L. 9, 1035. of amorous intent well *u.* of Eve
 P. L. 10, 344. *u.* not instant but of future
 P. L. 10, 883. and *u.* not all was but a show
 P. L. 12, 58. each to other calls not *u.*
 P. L. 12, 514. though not but by the Spirit *u.*
 P. R. 1, 436. they who asked have seldom *u.*
 P. R. 1,437. and not well *u.* as good not known
 S. A. 191. of the most I would be *u.*
**Undertake.**—P. L. 2, 419. or *u.* the perilous
**Undertook.**—P. L. 4, 935. I alone first *u.*
 P. L. 10, 74. for so I *u.* before thee
 P. R. 1, 100. I, when no other durst, sole *u.*
 P. R. 1, 374. they demurring, I *u.* that office
 P. R. 2, 129. I. as I *u.* and with the vote
**Underwent.**—C. 841. and *u.* a quick immortal
**Undeserved.**—P. L. 12, 27. dominion *u.*
**Undeservedly.**—P. L. 12, 94. oft as *u.*
**Undesirable.**—P. L. 9, 824. a thing not *u.*
**Undetermined.**—P. L. 2, 1048. *u.* square
**Undiminished.**—P. L. 1, 154. feel strength *u.*
 P. L. 4, 836. or *u.* brightness to be known
**Undiscording.**—S. M. 17. earth with *u.* voice

**Undisguised.**—P. R. 1, 357. arch-fiend now *u.*
**Undismayed.**—P. L. 2, 432. seized us though *u.*
P. L. 6, 417. and in the midst thus *u.* began
**Undissembled.**—S. A. 400. worse than *u.* hate
**Undisturbed.**—S. M. 6. that *u.* song of pure
**Undo.**—P. L. 9, 926. who can recall or done *u.*
P. L. 9, 944. uncreate be frustrate do *u.* and
C. 904. to *u.* the charmed band
**Undone.**—P. L. 3, 235. indebted and *u.* hath
**Undoubted.**—P. L. 1, 672. *u.* sign that in his
P. R. 1, 11. by proof the *u.* Son of God
**Undoubtedly.**—P. L. 10, 1093. *u.* he will
**Undrawn.**—P. L. 6, 751. wheel within wheel *u.*
**Undreaded.**—P. L. 10, 595. unnamed, *u.*
**Undying.**—P. L. 6, 739. and the *u.* worm
**Unearned.**—P. L. 9, 225. supper comes *u.*
**Uneasy.**—P. L. 1, 295. to support *u.* steps
P. R. 4, 584. from his *u.* station and upbore
**Unemployed.**—P. L. 4, 617. rove idle *u.*
S. A. 580. inglorious, *u.* with age outworn
**Unenchanted.**—C. 395. with *u.* eye
**Unendeared.**—P. L. 4, 766. joyless *u.*
**Unenvied.**—P. L. 2, 23. in a safe *u.* throne
**Unequal.**—P. L. 6, 453. too *u.* work we find
P. L. 6, 454. against *u.* arms to fight
S. A. 346. himself an army now *u.* match
**Unequalled.**—P. L. 9, 983. so faithful love *u.*
**Unequals.**—P. L. 8, 383. among *u.* what society
**Unespied**—P. L. 4, 399. and *u.* to mark
P. L. 6, 523. with silent circumspection *u.*
**Unessential.**—P. L. 2, 439. of *u.* night
**Uneven.**—P. R. 2, 173. in much *u.* scale
**Unexampled.**—P. L. 3, 410. O *u.* love
**Unexempt.**—C. 685. scorning the *u.* condition
**Unexpected.**—P. L. 6, 774. them *u.* joy
P. L. 11, 268. O *u.* stroke worse than of death
P. R. 2, 29. their *u.* loss and plaints outbreathed
**Unexpectedly.**—S. A. 1750. his face but *u.*
**Unexperienced.**—P. L. 4, 457. with *u.*
P. R. 3, 240. the wisest *u.* will be ever
**Unexpert.**—P. L. 2, 52. of wiles more *u.*
**Unexpressive.**—L. 176. and hears the *u.*
H. 116. with *u.* notes to heaven's new-born heir
**Unextinguishable.**—P. L. 2, 88. pain of *u.*
**Unfaithful.**—P. L. 12, 461. the *u.* dead
P. L. 12, 481. faithful left among the *u.* herd
**Unfastens.**—P. L. 2, 879. with ease *u.*
**Unfeared.**—P. L. 9, 187. fearless *u.* he slept
**Unfeigned.**—P. L. 6, 744. *u.* hallelujahs
P. L. 8, 603. which declare *u.* union of mind
P. L. 10, 1092. of sorrow *u.* and humiliation
P. L. 10, 1104. in sign of sorrow *u.* and
**Unfelt.**—P. L. 2, 703. and pangs *u.* before
P. L. 8, 475. sweetness into my heart *u.* before
**Unfinished.**—S. A. 1027. were left for haste *u.*
**Unfold.**—P. L. 4, 381. hell shall *u.*
P. L. 5, 568. how last *u.* the secrets of another
P. L. 6, 558. to right and left the front *u.*
P. L. 7, 94. if unforbid thou mayst *u.* what we
P. L. 11, 785. how comes it thus ? *u.* celestial.
P. R. 1, 82. heaven above the clouds *u.* her
P. R. 2, 239. if cause were to *u.* some active
C. 786. that must be uttered to *u.* the sage
Il P. 89. to *u.* what worlds or what vast regions
S. 17, 5. whether to settle peace or to *u.*
**Unfolding.**—P. L. 10, 63. and *u.* bright
**Unforbid.**—P. L. 7, 94. if *u.* thou mayst
**Unforeknown.**—P. L. 3, 119. certain *u.*
**Unforeseen.**—P. L. 2, 821. befallen us *u.*
**Unforeskinned.**—S. A. 1100. from the *u.* race
**Unforewarned.**—P. L. 5, 245. unadmonished *u.*
**Unformed.**—P. L. 7, 233. matter *u.* and void
**Unfortunate.**—P. L. 10, 970. thence ... found so *u.*
P. R. 1, 358. that spirit *u.*
S. A. 747. my rash but more *u.* misdeed
S. A. 1743. his lot *u.* in nuptial choice
**Unfound**—P. L. 6, 500. which yet *u.* most
**Unfounded.**—P. L. 2, 829. tread the *u.* deep
**Unfrequented.**—P. L. 1, 433. and *u.* left
S. A. 17. I seek this *u.* place to find some ease
**Unfriended.**—P. R. 2, 413. unknown, *u.*

**Unfulfilled.**—P. L. 4, 511. still *u.* with pain
**Unfumed.**—P. L. 5, 349. from the shrub *u.*
**Unfurled.**—P. L. 1, 535. the glittering staff *u.*
**Ungodly.**—P. L. 7, 185. had driven out the *u.*
S. A. 898. but by *u.* deeds the contradiction
**Ungoverned.**—P. L. 11, 517. to serve *u.*
**Ungraceful.**—P. L. 8, 218. are thy lips *u.*
**Ungratefully.**—V. Ex. 78. *u.* shall strive to
**Unguarded.**—P. L. 6, 133. throne of God *u.*
P. L. 10. 419. the gate wide open and *u.*
C. 283. and left your fair side all *u.*
**Unhallowed.**—P. L. 9, 931. and *u.* ere our
C. 757. to have unlocked my lips in this *u.* air
**Unhappily.**—P. L. 10, 917. *u.* deceived
**Unhappy.**—P. L. 1, 268. in this *u.* mansion
P. L. 9, 1136. desire of wandering this *u.* morn
C. 511. ay me *u.* then my fears are true
**Unharboured.**—C. 423. forests and *u.* heaths
**Unhardy.**—P. R. 3, 243. *u.* unadventurous
**Unharmonious.**—P. L. 11, 51. gross no *u.*
**Unhazarded.**—S. A. 809. to myself *u.* abroad
**Unheard.**—P. L. 1, 395. children's cries *u.*
P. L. 1, 738. nor was his name *u.* or unadored
P. L. 3, 645. he drew not nigh *u.*
**Unheeded.** P. L. 4, 350. gave proof *u.*
**Unheedy.**—M. W. 38. plucked .. by some *u.* swain
**Unhidebound.**—P. L. 10, 601. this vast *u.*
**Unhoard.**—P. L. 4, 188. bent to *u.* the cash
**Unholy.**—P. L. 7, 106. hollowed ground the *u.*
L'A. 4. horrid shapes and shrieks and sights *u.*
**Unhoped.**—P. L. 10, 348. *u.* met who to meet
**Unhoused.**—D. F. I. 21. *u.* thy virgin soul
**Unhumbled.**—P. R. 3, 429. *u.* unrepentant
**Unhurt.**—P. L. 6, 444. can preserve *u.* our
**Unimaginable.**—P. L. 7, 54. so *u.* as hate
**Unimmortal.**—P. L. 10, 611. or *u.* make
**Unimplored.**—P. L. 3, 231. unprevented *u.*
P. L. 7, 22. who deigns her nightly visitation *u.*
**Uninformed.**—P. L. 8, 486. nor *u.* of nuptial
**Uninjured.**—C. 403. *u.* in this wild surrounding
**Uninterrupted.**—P. L. 3, 68. *u.* joy
**Uninvented.**—P. L. 6, 470. not *u.* that
**Union.**—P. L. 2, 36. this advantage then to *u.*
P. L. 5, 612. disobeys me, disobeys breaks *u.*
P. L. 6, 63. in mighty quadrate joined of *u.*
P. L. 7, 161. one kingdom joy and *u.* without
P. L. 8, 431. to what height thou wilt of *u.*
P. L. 8, 604. which declare unfeigned *u.* of mind
P. L. 8, 627. total they mix *u.* of pure with pure
P. L. 9, 966. gladly of our *u.* hear thee speak
H. 108. hold all heaven and earth in happier *u.*
**Unjointed.**—S. A. 177. dissolves *u.* ere it reach
**Unison.**—P. L. 7, 599. with voice choral or *u.*
**Unite.**—P. L. 4, 263. *u.* their streams
P. L. 9, 314. utmost vigour raise and raised *u.*
P. L. 10, 247. at greatest distance to *u.* with
S. M. 27. to his celestial consort us *u.*
**United.**—P. L. 1, 88. *u.* thoughts and counsels
P. L. 1, 560. breathing *u.* force with fixed thought
P. L. 1, 629. how such *u.* force of gods
P. L. 4, 230. thence *u.* fell down the steep
P. L. 5, 610. *u.* as one individual soul for ever
P. L. 5, 831. under one head more near *u.*
P. L. 9, 608. beauty's heavenly ray *u.* I beheld
P. R. 3, 229. though in thee be *u.* what
S. A. 1110. durst not with their whole *u.* powers
**Unites.**—P. L. 10, 364. fatal consequence *u.* us
P. L. 12. 382. so God with man *u.*
**Unity.**—P. L. 8, 425. in *u.* defective
H. 11. to sit the midst of Trinal *u.*
**Universal.**—P. L. 1, 541. at which the *u.* host
P. L. 2, 951. at length a *u.* hubbub wild
P. L. 3, 48. presented with a *u.* blank of
P. L. 3, 317. anointed *u.* king
P. L. 3, 676. the *u.* Maker we may praise
P. L. 4, 266. while *u.* Pan, knit with the
P. L. 5, 154. thine this *u.* frame
P. L. 5, 205. hail *u.* Lord be bounteous still
P. L. 6, 34. hast borne *u.* reproach
P. L. 6, 797. or to fall in *u.* ruin last
P. L. 7, 257. the hollow *u.* orb they filled

P. L. 7, 316. clad her *u.* face with pleasant green
P. L. 8, 376. so spake the *u.* Lord and seemed
P. L. 9, 612. Sovran of creatures *u.* dame
P. L. 10, 505. expecting their *u.* shout and high
P. L. 10, 508. a dismal *u.* hiss
P. L. 11, 821. a world devote to *u.* wrack
S. A. 1053. God's *u.* law gave to the man
S. A. 1511. noise call you it or *u.* groan
L. 60. whom *u.* nature did lament
H 52. strikes a *u.* peace through sea and land
**Universally.**—P. L. 9, 542. *u.* admired
S. A. 175. *u.* crowned with highest praises
**Universe.**—P. L. 2, 622. a *u.* of death
P. L. 3, 584. that gently warms the *u.*
P. L. 3, 721. the rest in circuit walls this *u.*
P. L. 7, 227. to circumscribe this *u.*
P. L. 8. 360. may I adore thee Author of this *u.*
P. L. 9, 684. queen of this *u.* do not believe
P. R. 1, 49. this *u.* we have possessed and ruled
P. R. 4, 459. as a sneeze to man's less *u.*
**Unjust.**—P. L. 2, 200. nor the law *u.* that so
P. L. 3, 215. and just the *u.* to save
P. L. 5, 818. *u.* thou say'st. flatly *u.* to bind
P. L. 5, 831. but to grant it thee *u.*
P. L. 11, 455. *u.* the just hath slain
P. L. 12, 294. just for *u.* that in such
P. R. 2, 45. to what height their power *u.*
P. R. 3, 98. for truth's sake suffering death *u.*
S. A. 695. or to the *u.* tribunals
S. A. 703. just or *u.* alike seem miserable
C. 590. surprised by *u.* force but not enthralled
**Unjustly.**—P. L. 6, 174. *u.* thou depravest
S. A. 889. thy country sought of thee .... *u.*
**Unkindly.**—P. L. 3, 456. or *u.* mixed
P. L. 9, 1050. and grosser sleep bred of *u.* fumes
C. 269. forbidding every bleak *u.* fog
**Unkindness.**—P. L. 9, 271. some *u.* meets
**Unknown**—P. L. 2, 443. or *u.* region
P. L. 2, 444. than *u.* dangers and as hard escape
P. L. 3, 496. to few *u.* long after
P. L. 4, 830. not to know me argues yourselves *u.*
P. L. 6, 262. author of evil *u.* till thy revolt
P. L. 7, 75. *u.* which human knowledge could
P. L. 7, 494. nor *u.* the serpent, subtlest beast
P. L. 9, 619. and various yet *u.* to us
P. L. 9, 756. *u.* sure is not had or had and yet *u.*
P. L. 9, 864. nor to evil *u.* opening the way
P. L. 9, 905. of enemy hath beguiled thee yet *u.*
P. L. 12, 55. sow a jangling noise of words *u.*
P. L. 12, 134. God who called him in a land *u.*
P. R. 1, 25. came as then obscure unmarked *u.*
P. R. 2, 413. thou art *u.*, unfriended low of birth
P. R. 2, 444. to me is not *u.* what hath been
S. A. 180. come thy friends and neighbours not *u.*
C. 361. while they rest *u.*, what need a man
C. 634. *u.* and like esteemed and the dull swain
**Unlaid.**—C. 434. hag or stubborn *u.* ghost
**Unless.**—P. L. 2, 236. *u.* heaven's Lord
P. L. 2, 915. *u.* the Almighty Maker them ordain
P. L. 3, 210. *u.* for him some other able and as
P. L. 8, 186. *u.* we ourselves seek them
P. L. 9, 44. *u.* an age too late
P. L. 9, 125. *u.* by mastering heaven's Supreme
P. L. 10, 1032. *u.* be meant whom I conjecture
P. R. 3, 352. *u.* thou endeavour as thy father
P. R. 4, 351. *u.* where moral virtue is expressed
S. A. 295. *u.* there be who think not God at all
S. A. 663. *u.* he feel some source of consolation
C. 267. *u.* the goddess that in rural shrine
**Unlettered.**—C. 174. among the loose *u.* hinds
**Unlibidinous.**—P. L. 5, 449. love *u.* reigned
**Unlicensed.**—P. L. 4, 909. *u.* from his bounds
**Unlightsome.**—P. L. 7, 355. *u.* first
**Unlike.**—P. L. 1, 75. how *u.* the place
P. L. 6, 517. nor hath this earth entrails *u.*
P. L. 9, 1114. how *u.* to that first naked glory
S. A. 815. be not *u.* all others not austere
S. A. 1510. horribly loud *u.* the former shout
**Unlimited.**—P. L. 4, 435. and choice *u.*
**Unlock.**—P. L. 2, 852. forbidden to *u.* these
G. 852. she can *u.* the clasping charm

**Unlocked.**—S. A. 407. and *u.* her all my heart
C. 756. I had not thought to have *u.* my lips
**Unlooked.**—P. R. 2, 31. to what relapse *u.* for
**Unmake.**—P. L. 3, 163. and *u.* for him what
**Unmanly.**—S. A. 417. *u.* ignominious infamous
**Unmarked.**—P. L. 10, 441. the midst *u.* in
P. R. 1, 25. came as then obscure *u.* unknown
**Unmeasured.**—P. L. 5, 399. good *u.* out
**Unmeditated.**—P. L. 5, 149. or sung *u.*
**Unmeet.**—P. L. 8, 442. therefore *u.* for thee
**Unmerited.**—P. L. 12, 278. favour *u.* by me
**Unminded.**—P. L. 10, 332, *u.* slunk into the wood
**Unmindful.**—P. L. 6, 369. nor stood *u.*
P. L. 11, 611. *u.* of their Maker
C. 9. *u.* of the crown that virtue gives
Hor. 12. of flattering gales *u.*
**Unmixed.**—P. L. 6, 742. thy saints *u.* and
P. R. 3, 48. people's praise if always praise *u.*
**Unmoved.**—P. L. 1, 554. firm and *u.* with
P. L. 2, 429. conscious of highest worth *u.* thus
P. L. 4, 455. then stood *u.* pure as the expanse
P. L. 4, 822. yet thus *u.* with fear accost him
P. L. 5, 898. among innumerable false *u.*
P. L. 8, 532. in all enjoyments else superior and *u.*
P. L. 11, 192. not *u.* to Eve thus spake
P. R. 4, 109. to whom the Son of God *u.*
P. R. 3, 386. answered thus *u.*
**Unmoulding.**—C. 529. *u.* reason's mintage
**Unmuffle.**—C. 331. *u.* ye faint stars
**Unnamed.**—P. L. 6, 263. thy revolt *u.* in
P. L. 10, 595. *u.* and thyself half-starved
P. L. 12, 140. their names I call though yet *u.*
**Unnumbered.**—P. L. 2, 903. *u.* as the sands
P. L. 7, 432. fanned with *u.* plumes
**Unobeyed.**—P. L. 5, 670. *u.* the throne
**Unobnoxious.**—P. L. 6, 404. *u.* to be pained
**Unobscured.**—P. L. 2, 265. his glory *u.*
**Unobserved.**—P. L. 4, 130. all *u.* unseen
P. R. 4, 638. he *u.* home to his mother's house
**Unopposed.**—P. L. 6, 132. thy aspiring *u.*
**Unoriginal.**—P. L. 10, 477. womb of *u.* Night
**Unowned.**—C. 407. the person of our *u.* sister
**Unpaid**—P. L. 5, 782. knee-tribute yet *u.*
**Unpained.**—P. L. 6, 455. against *u.* impassive
**Unparalleled.**—S. A. 165. man on earth *u.*
A. 25. this clime had held a deity so *u.*
**Unpeopled.**—P. L. 3, 497. now *u.* and
**Unperceived.**—P. L. 3, 681, dissembler *u.*
P. L. 11, 224. not *u.* of Adam who to Eve
**Unpierced.**—P. L. 4, 245. the *u.* shade
**Unpillowed.**—C. 355. leans her *u.* head
**Unpitied.**—P. L. 2, 185. unrespited, *u.*
P. L. 4, 375. pity thus forlorn though I *u.*
P. R. 1, 414. ejected emptied gazed *u.* shunned
**Unplausible.**—C. 162. with reasons not *u.*
**Unpolluted.**—P. L. 2, 139. his throne sit *u.*
C. 461. the *u.* temple of the mind
**Unpossessed.**—P. L. 8, 153. room in nature *u.*
**Unpractised.**—P. L. 8, 197. *u.* unprepared
**Unpraised.**—P. L. 9, 232. nor of me shalt pass *u.*
P. R. 3, 103. the deed becomes *u.*
C. 723. would be unthanked, would be *u.*
**Unpredict.**—P. R. 3, 395. prediction else will *u.*
**Unpremeditated**—P. L. 9, 24. *u.* verse
**Unprepared.**—P. L. 8, 197. unpractised *u.*
**Unprevented.**—P. L. 3, 231 comes *u.*
**Unprincipled.**—C. 367. *u.* in virtue's book
**Unproclaimed.**—P. L. 11, 220. war, war *u.*
**Unpronounced.**—V. Ex. 4. half *u.* slide through
**Unpropt.**—S. A. 119. with languished head *u.*
**Unpurged.**—P. L. 5, 419. *u.* vapours
A. 73. of human mould with gross *u.* ear
**Unpursued.**—P. L. 6, 1. dreadless angel *u.*
**Unquenchable.**—P. L. 6, 877. with fire *u.*
S. A. 1422. impetuous insolent *u.*
**Unquiet.**—P. L. 5, 11. as through *u.* rest
P. L. 10, 975. what thoughts in my *u.* breast
**Unrazored.**—C. 290. as Hebe's their *u.* lips
**Unreal.**—P. L. 10, 471 voyaged the *u.* vast
**Unrecorded.**—P. R. 1, 16. *u.* left
**Unreformed.**—P. R. 3, 429. unrepentant *u.*

**Unreined.**—P. L. 7, 17. from this flying steed *u.*
**Unremoved.**—P. L. 4, 987. or Atlas *u.*
**Unrepentant.**—P. R. 3, 429. unhumbled *u.*
**Unrepented.**—S. A. 1376. shall never *u.* find
**Unreprieved.**—P. L. 2, 185. unpitied *u.*
**Unreproved.**—P. L. 4, 493. attraction *u.*
L'A. 40. in *u.* pleasures free
**Unrest.**—P. L. 9, 1052. rose as from *u.*
P. L. 11, 174. all unconcerned with our *u.*
**Unrevoked.**—P. L. 5, 602. decree which *u.*
**Unrighteous.**—P. L. 3, 292. and *u.* deeds
**Unrivalled.**—P.L.3,68.uninterruptedjoy *u.*love
**Unsafe.**—P. L. 6, 309. *u.* within the wind
**Unsaid.**—C. 586. not a period and be *u.* for me
**Unsavoury.**—P. L. 5, 401. *u.* food perhaps
C. 742. *u.* in the enjoyment of itself
**Unsay.**—P. L. 4, 95. how soon *u.* what feigned
P. L. 4, 947. to say and straight *u.* pretending
P. R. 1, 474. say and *u.* feign flatter or abjure
**Unsearchable.**—P. L. 8, 10. else by me *u.*
S.A.1746.what the *u.*dispose of Highest wisdom
**Unsearched.**—P. L. 4, 789. leave *u.* no nook
**Unseasonable.**—P. L. 8, 201. not *u.* to ask
**Unseemliest.**—P. L. 9, 1094. and *u.* seen
**Unseemly.**—P. L. 10, 155. *u.* to bear rule
S. A. 690. *u.* falls in human eye
S. A.1451. I should see him forced to things *u.*
**Unseen.**—P. L. 2, 659. and howled within *u.*
P. L. 2, 841. and up and down *u.* wing silently
P. L. 3, 585. with gentle penetration though *u.*
P. L. 4, 130. as he supposed all unobserved *u.*
P. L. 4, 678. spiritual creatures walk the earth *u.*
P. L. 8, 485. by her heavenly maker though *u.*
P. L. 10, 21. subtle fiend had stolen entrance *u.*
P. L. 10, 448. sat and round about him saw *u.*
P. L. 11, 265. Eve who *u.* yet all had heard
P. L. 11, 671. snatched him thence *u.* amid
P. L. 12, 49. who oft descends to visit men *u.*
P. L. 12, 361. yet at his birth a star *u.* before
C.230.sweet Echo sweetest nymph that lives *u.*
L'A. 57. sometime walking not *u.*
Il P. 65. and missing thee I walk *u.* on the dry
Il P. 154. or the *u.* Genius of the wood
**Unsettled.**—P. R. 4, 326. *u.* still remains
**Unshaken.**—P. L. 4, 64. fell not but stand *u.*
P. L. 5, 899. *u.* unseduced, unterrified
P. R. 4, 421. yet only stood'st *u.*
S. 15, 5. thy firm *u.* virtue ever brings victory
**Unshared.**—P. L. 9, 880. tedious *u.* with thee
**Unshed.**—P. L. 12, 176. to blood *u.* the rivers
**Unshorn.**—S. A. 1143. preserved these locks *u.*
V. Ex. 37. listening to what *u.* Apollo sings
**Unshowered.**—H. 215. trampling the *u.* grass
**Unsightly.**—P. L. 4, 631. *u.* and unsmooth
P. L. 7, 314. desert and bare *u.* unadorned
P. L. 11, 510. to such *u.* sufferings be debased
C. 629. amongst the rest a small *u.* root
**Unskilful.**—P. L. 11, 32. *u.* with what words
**Unsleeping.**—P. L. 5, 647. the *u.* eyes of God
**Unsmooth.**—P. L. 4, 631. unsightly and *u.*
**Unsought.**—P. L. 3, 231. unimplored *u.*
P.L.8,503.that would be wooed and not *u.* be won
P. L. 9, 866. trial will come *u.*
P. L. 9, 370. if thou think trial *u.* may find us
P. L. 10, 106. duty erewhile appeared *u.*
P. R. 2, 59. whom at the first they found *u.*
C. 732. and the *u.* diamonds would so emblaze
**Unsound.**—P. L. 6, 121. reason I have tried *u.*
**Unspared.**—P. L. 10, 606. devour *u.*
**Unsparing.**—P. L. 5, 344. with *u.* hand
**Unspeakable.**—P. L. 3, 662. *u.* desire to
P. L. 5, 156. *u.* who sitt'st above these heavens
P. L. 6, 297. and both addressed for fight *u.*
**Unsphere.**—Il P. 88. or *u.* the spirit of Plato
**Unspied.**—P. L. 4, 529. no corner leave *u.*
**Unspoiled.**—P. L. 11, 409. and yet *u.*
**Unspotted.**—P. L. 3, 248. suffer my *u.* soul
C. 1009. and from her fair *u.* side
**Unstained.**—S. 10, 3. *u.* with gold or fee
H. 57. *u.* with hostile blood
**Unsteady.**—A. 70. and keep *u.* nature to her

**Unsubstantial.**—P. R. 4, 399. *u.* both
**Unsucceeded.**—P. R. 5, 821. *u.* power
**Unsuccessful.**—P. L. 10, 35. *u.* charge
**Unsucked.**—P. L. 9, 583. at even *u.* of lamb
**Unsufferable.**—P. L. 6, 867. the *u.* noise
H. 8. that glorious form that light *u.*
**Unsuitable.**—P. R. 3, 132. *u.* return
**Unsung.**—P. L. 1, 442. in Sion also not *u.*
P. L. 7, 21. half yet remains *u.* but narrower
P. L. 7, 253. nor *u.* by the celestial choirs
P. L. 9, 33. patience and heroic martyrdom *u.*
P. R. 1, 17. to have not remained so long *u.*
**Unsunned.**—C. 398. *u.* heaps of miser's treasure
**Unsuperfluous.**—C. 773. in *u.* even
**Unsupported.**—P. L. 9, 432. *u.* flower
**Unsuspect.**—P. L. 9, 771. author *u.*
**Unsuspected.**—P. L. 9, 69. found *u.* way
**Unsuspicious.**—S. A. 1635. he *u.* led him
**Unsustained.**—P. L. 9, 430. drooping *u.*
**Untamed.**—P. L. 2, 337. *u.* reluctance
**Untaught.**—P. L. 2, 9. by success *u.*
**Unterrified.**—P. L. 2, 708. Satan stood *u.*
P. L. 5, 899. unshaken unseduced *u.*
**Unthanked.**—C. 723. the all-giver would be *u.*
**Unthought.**—P. L. 2, 821. unforeseen *u.* of
**Unthread.**—C. 614. bare wand can *u.* thy joints
**Unthrone.**—P. L. 2, 231. him to *u.* we hope
**Untold.**—A. 41. fame hath left *u.*
**Untouched.**—P. L. 9, 621. store of fruit *u.*
**Untractable.**—P. L. 10, 476. to ride the *u.*
**Untrained.**—P. L. 12, 222. is more sweet *u.*
**Untried.**—P. L. 4, 934. danger by himself *u.*
P. L. 9, 860. what rash *u.* I sought
P. R. 1, 177. ventures his filial virtue though *u.*
Hor. 13. to whom thou, *u.* seem'st fair
**Untrod.**—P. L. 3, 497. now unpeopled and *u.*
P. R. 1, 298. was difficult by human steps *u.*
H. 19. while the heaven by the sun's team *u.*
**Untroubled.**—P. L. 8, 289. *u.* though I
P. R. 4, 401. Saviour meek and with *u.* mind
**Untwisting.**—L'A.143.*u.*all the chains that tie
**Unvalued.**—W. S. 11. the leaves of thy *u.* book
**Unvanquished.**—P. L. 6, 286. they rise *u.*
**Unveiled.**—P. L. 4, 608. *u.* her peerless light
**Unviolated.**—S. A. 1144. pledge of my *u.* vow
**Unvisited.**—P. L. 2, 398. dwell not *u.* of
**Unvoyageable.**—P. L. 10, 366. nor this *u.*
**Unused.**—S.A.1231.O Baal-zebub can my ears *u.*
**Unusual.**—P. L. 1, 227. that felt *u.* weight
C. 552. till an *u.* stop of sudden silence
**Unutterable.**—P. L. 11, 6. breathed *u.*
**Unwakened.**—P. L. 5, 9. to find *u.* Eve with
**Unwares.**—D.F.I.20.but all *u.*with his cold-kind
**Unwary.**—P. L. 6, 695. into the *u.* breast
P. L. 9, 614. yet more amazed *u.* thus replied
P. L. 10, 947. *u.* and too desirous as before
C. 538. to inveigle and invite the *u.* sense
S. A. 930. nor think me so *u.* or accursed
**Unwearied.**—P. L. 6, 404. in fight they stood *u.*
P. L. 7, 552. from his work desisting though *u.*
**Unweeting.**—P. L. 10, 335. Eve though all *u.*
P. L. 10, 916. and *u.* have offended
P. R. 1, 126. but contrary *u.* he fulfilled
C. 539. of them that pass *u.* by the way
D. F. 1. 23. for so Apollo with *u.* hand
**Unweetingly.**—S. A.1680. *u.*importuned their
**Unwelcome.**—P. L. 10, 21. the *u.* news
**Unwept.**—L. 13. upon his watery bier *u.*
**Unwholesome.**—S. A. 9. *u.* draught
**Unwieldy.**—P. L. 4, 345. the *u.* elephant
P. L. 7, 411. part huge of bulk wallowing *u.*
S. A. 54. vast *u.* burdensome proudly secure
**Unwilling.**—P. L. 12, 617. to go hence *u.*
**Unwillingly.**—S. A. 14. *u.* this rest their
**Unwise.**—P. L. 6, 179. to serve the *u.*
P. R. 3, 115, wise or *u.* no difference
S. 20, 14. spare to interpose them oft is not *u.*
**Unwiser.**—P. L. 4, 716. when to the *u.* son
**Unwithdrawing.**—C. 711. such a full and *u.*
**Unwonted.**—Hor. 8. storms *u.* shall admire
**Unworshipped.**—P. L. 5, 670. and leave *u.*

**Unworthier.**—S. A. 1216. for naught the *u.*
**Unworthy.**—P. L. 10, 1059. clothed us *u.*
  P. L. 12, 91. permits within himself *u.* powers
  P. L. 12, 622. such favour I *u.* am vouchsafed
  P. R. 4, 346. will far be found *u.* to compare
  S. A. 1424. nothing dishonourable impure *u.*
**Unwounded.**—P. L. 6, 466. our yet *u.*
  S. A. 1582. *u.* of his enemies he fell
**Upbore.**—P. L. 6, 72. and the passive air *u.*
  P. R. 4, 584. and *u.* as on a floating couch
**Upborne.**—P. L. 2, 408. *u.* with indefatigable
  P. L. 11, 147. short sigh of human breath *u.*
**Upbraid**—P. L. 6, 182. our ministering *u.*
  S. A. 820. her own transgressions to *u.* me
**Upbraided.**—P. L. 4, 45. his good *u.* none
  P. L. 9, 1168. and am I now *u.* as the cause
**Upgrown.**—P. L. 9, 677. or to height *u.*
  P. R. 1, 140. this man born and now *u.*
**Upheave.**—P. L. 7, 286. broad bare backs *u.*
**Upheaved.**—P. L. 7, 471. born of earth *u.*
**Upheld.**—P. L. 1, 133. whether *u.* by strength
  P. L. 1, 639. *u.* by old repute consent or custom
  P. L. 3, 178. *u.* by me yet once more he shall
  P. L. 3, 180. by me *u.* that he may know how
  P. L. 5, 336. taste after taste *u.* with kindliest
  S. 17, 7. how war may best *u.* move by her two
**Uphold.**—S. A. 666. and fainting spirits *u.*
  S. A. 892. of men conspiring to *u.* their state
**Upland.**—L'A. 92. the *u.* hamlets will invite
**Upled.**—P. L. 7, 12. *u.* by thee into the heaven
**Uplift.**—P. L. 1, 193. with head *u.* above
  P. R. 4, 558. in their hands they shall *u.* thee
**Uplifted.**—P. L. 1, 347. the *u.* spear of their
  P. L. 2, 7. from despair thus high *u.* beyond
  P. L. 9, 929. and in the surging smoke *u.* beyond
  P. L. 6, 317. with next to almighty arm *u.*
  P. L. 7, 219. *u.* in paternal glory rode
  P. L. 11, 746. the floating vessel swum *u.*
  P. L. 11, 863. then with *u.* hands and eyes
  S. M. 11. their loud *u.* angel-trumpets blow
**Uplifting.**—P. L. 6, 646. the shaggy tops *u.*
**Upper.**—P. L. 1, 346. twixt *u.* nether
  P. L. 10, 422. flown to the *u.* world
  P. L. 10, 446. at the *u.* end was placed in regal
**Upraise.**—P. L. 2, 372. and our joy *u.* in his
**Upraised.**—P. L. 10, 946. peaceful words *u.*
**Upreared**—P. L. 1, 532. be *u.* his mighty
**Upright.**—P. L. 1, 18. all temples the *u.*
  P. L. 1, 221. forthwith *u.* he rears from off
  P. L. 2, 112. steep to scale with *u.* wing against
  P. L. 4, 837. as when thou stoodst in heaven *u.*
  P. L. 6, 82. bristled with *u.* beams innumerable
  P. L. 6, 270. once *u.* and faithful now proved
  P. L. 6, 627. show us when our foes walk not *u.*
  P. L. 7, 509. and *u.* with front serene govern
  P. L. 7, 632. and persevere *u.*
  P. L. 8, 260. and *u.* stood on my feet
  P. R. 4, 551. to stand *u.* will ask thee skill
  C. 52. cup whoever tasted lost his *u.* shape
**Uprightness.**—P. L. 3, 683. in his *u.*
**Uprisen.**—P. L. 5, 139. the sun who scarce *u.*
**Uproar.**—P. L. 2, 541. holds the wild *u.*
  P. L. 3, 710. and wild *u.* stood ruled
  P. L. 6, 668. seemed a civil game to this *u.*
  P. L. 10, 479. with clamorous *u.* protesting
**Uprolled.**—P. L. 7, 291. glad precipitance *u.*
**Uprooted.**—P. L. 6, 781. the *u.* hills retired
**Upsprung.**—P. L. 4, 143. wall of paradise *u.*
  P. L. 7, 462. in broad herd *u.*
**Upstart.**—P. L. 2, 834. a race of *u.* creatures
  P. L. 12. 88. inordinate desires and *u.* passions
**Upstayed.**—P. L. 6, 195. his massy spear *u.*
**Upstays.**—P. L. 9, 430. them she *u.* gently
**Upstood**—P. L. 6, 446. the assembly next *u.*
**Uptore.**— P. L. 6, 663. neighbouring hills *u.*
**Upturn.**—P. L. 10, 700. the woods and seas *u.*
**Upturned.**—P. L. 10, 279. *u.* his nostril
**Upturns.**—P. L. 10, 701. *u.* them from the
**Upward.**—P. L. 1, 462. *u.* man and downward
  P. L. 2, 1013. spring *u.* like a pyramid of fire
  P. L. 3, 717. flew *u.* spirited with various forms

**Unworthier.**—S. A. 1216. for naught the *u.*
  P. L. 6, 649. bottom of the mountains *u.* turned
  C. 98. and the slope sun his *u.* beam
**Upwhirled.**—P. L. 3, 493. all these *u.* aloft
**Uw.**—P. L. 12, 130. *U.* of Chaldæa
**Urania.**—P. L. 7, 1. *U.*, by that name
  P. L. 7, 31. still govern thou my song, *U.*
**Urchin.**—C. 845. helping all *u.* blasts
**Urge.**—P. L. 8, 114. but this I *u.* admitting
**Urged.**—P. L. 2. 120. what was *u.* main reason
  P. L. 6, 622. and full of force *u.* home
  P. L. 7, 864. but for worse *u.* them behind
  P. L. 9, 588. of that alluring fruit *u.* me so
  P. L. 11, 109. at the sad sentence rigorously *u.*
  P. R. 1, 469. and *u.* me hard with doings which
  S. A. 223. and therefore *u.* the marriage on
  S. A. 755. how far *u.* his patience bears
  S. A. 852. solicited commanded threatened *u.*
  S. A. 1677. and *u.* them on with mad desire
**Urges.**—P. L. 1, 68. without end still *u.*
  P. L. 9, 250. and short retirement *u.* sweet
**Uriel.**—P. L. 3, 648. the arch-angel *U.*
  P. L. 3, 654. *U.*, for thou of those seven spirits
  P. L. 3, 690. which now for once beguiled *U.*
  P. L. 4, 125. had practised to deceive *U.*
  P. L. 4, 555. thither came *U.* gliding through
  P. L. 4, 577. *U.* no wonder if thy perfect
  P. L. 4, 589. and *U.* to his charge returned
  P. L. 6, 363. *U.* and Raphael his vaunting foe
  P. L. 9, 60. since *U.* regent of the sun
**Urim.**—P. L. 6, 761. of radiant *U.*
  P. R. 3, 14. *U.* and Thummim those oraculous
**Urn.**—L. 20. with lucky words favour my ... *u.*
**Urns.**—P. L. 7, 365. in their golden *u.* draw
  H. 192. in *u.* and altars round
**Usage.**—S. A. 1108. such *u.* as your honourable
  C. 681. for gentle *u.* and soft delicacy
**Use.**—P. L. 4, 204. abuse or to their meanest *u.*
  P. L. 4, 692. things to man's delightful *u.*
  P. L. 5, 323. all seasons ripe for *u.* hang on the
  P. L. 7, 346. great for their *u.* to man
  P. L. 8, 29. to this one *u.* for aught appears
  P. L. 8. 192. of things remote from *u.* obscure
  P. L. 9, 718. and that advantage *u.* on our
  P. L. 9, 750. who forbids thy *u.* conceals not
  P. L. 10, 1078. such fire to *u.* and what may
  P. R. 2, 380. withholds my power that right to *u.*
  P. R. 3. 7. I see thou know'st what is of *u.*
  P. R. 3, 394. means I must *u.* thou sayest
  S. A. 553. O madness to think *u.* of ... wines
  S. A. 941. how wouldst thou *u.* me now blind
  S. A. 1139. I know no spells *u.* no forbidden arts
  S. A. 1499. not his purpose to *u.* him farther
  C. 639. and bade me keep it as of sovran *u.*
  L. 67. were it not better done as others *u.*
  L. 136. valleys low where the mild whispers *u.*
  S. 2, 13. all is if I have grace to *u.* it so
  V. Ex. 8. that now I *u.* thee in my latter task
  V. Ex. 30. thy service in some graver subject *u.*
**Used.**—P. L. 3, 196. light after light well *u.*
  P. L. 4, 199. but only *u.* for prospect
  P. L. 4, 200. what well *u.* had been the pledge
  P. L. 4, 346. to make them mirth *u.* all his might
  P. L. 4, 762. as saints and patriarchs *u.*
  P. L. 4, 975. with thy compeers *u.* to the yoke
  P. L. 5, 386. *u.* long after to blest Mary
  P. L. 8, 434. and freedom *u.* permissive
  P. L. 8, 525. but such as *u.* or not works in
  P. L. 9, 2. as with his friend familiar *u.* to sit
  P. L. 9, 519. as *u.* to such disport before her
  P. L. 10, 552. the bait of Eve *u.* by the tempter
  P. R. 3, 356. without means *u.*
  S. A. 247. *u.* no ambition to commend my deeds
  S. A. 1203. I *u.* hostility and took their spoil
  C. 821. other means I have which may be *u.*
**Useful.**—P. L. 2, 259. *u.* of hurtful prosperous
  P. L. 8. 200. and speak of things at hand *u.*
  S. A. 564. to what can I be *u.* wherein serve
**Useless.**—P. L. 3, 109. *u.* and vain of freedom
  P. L. 8, 25. in all their vast survey *u.* besides
  S. A. 131. the forgery of brazen shield and spear
  S. A. 1282. magazines contemns renders them *u.*

S. A.,1501. not to sit idle with so great a gift *u*.
S. 19, 4. lodged with me *u*.
**Uses**—P. L. 8, 106. ordained for *u*. to his Lord
**Usest**—P. L. 7, 616. his evil thou *u*. and from
**Usher**.—P. L. 4, 355. the stars that *u*. evening
P. L. 10, 94. and *u*. in the evening cool
**Ushered**.—Il P. 127. or *u*. with a shower still
**Usual**.—P. R. 4, 316. accuse him under *u*.
**Usurp**.—P. L. 11, 827. the ocean to *u*. beyond
P. L. 12, 421. over him no power shall long *u*.
**Usurpation**.—P. L. 2, 983. all *u*. thence
S. A. 1060. swayed by female *u*. nor dismayed
**Usurped**.—P. L. 10, 189. of Satan long *u*.
P. L. 12, 66. to himself assuming authority *u*.
P. R. 3, 169. the crown and David's throne *u*.
P. R. 4, 183. permitted rather and by thee *u*.
H. 170. casts his *u*. sway
**Usurper**.—P. L. 12, 72. this *u*.
**Usurping**.—P. L. 1, 514. so Jove *u*. reigned
P. L. 9, 1130. *u*. over Sovran reason claimed
C. 337. with black *u*. mists some gentle taper
**Utensils**.—P. R. 3, 336. with *u*. of war
**Uther**.—P. L. 1, 580. or romance of *U.'s* son
**Utmost**.—P. L. 1, 74. thrice to the *u*. pole
P. L. 1, 103. his *u*. power with adverse power
P. L. 1, 399. to the stream of *u*. Arnon
P. L. 1, 521. roamed the *u*. isles
P. L. 2, 95. what doubt we to incense his *u*. ire
P. L. 2, 361. the *u*. border of his kingdom left
P. L. 2, 1029. reaching the *u*. orb of this frail
P. L. 4, 539. meanwhile in *u*. longitude where
P. L. 5, 517. full to the *u*. measure of what
P. L. 6, 293. meanwhile thy *u*. force
P. L. 9, 314. would *u*. vigour raise
P. L. 9, 591. would require thy *u*. reach
P. L. 10, 30. their *u*. vigilance
P. L. 10, 437. left desert *u*. hell many a dark
P. L. 10, 1020. or if thou covet death as *u*. end
P. L. 11, 332. gladly behold though but his *u*.
P. L. 11, 397. the empire of Negus to his *u*. port
P. L. 12, 376. finisher of *u*. hope
P. R. 1, 94. ye see our danger on the *u*. edge

P. R. 1, 144. and now assay his *u*. subtlety
P. R. 2, 148. was assured their *u*. aid
P. R. 4, 75. and *u*. Indian isle Taprobane
P. R. 4, 535. to the *u*. of mere man both wise
S. A. 484. have satisfied their *u*. of revenge
S. A. 1153. with the *u*. of his godhead seconded
S. A. 1514. ruin destruction at the *u*. point
C. 136. till *u*. end of all thy dues be done
C. 617. care and *u*. shifts how to secure
**Utter**.—P. L. 1, 72. in *u*. darkness
P. L. 1, 626. and this dire change hateful to *u*.
P. L. 2, 87. in this abhorred deep to *u*. woe
P. L. 2, 127. despair and *u*. dissolution
P. L. 2, 440. and with *u*. loss of being threatens
P. L. 3, 16. through *u*. and through middle
P. L.3.308.quitted all to save a world from *u*.loss
P. L. 5, 614. falls into *u*. darkness deep engulfed
P. L. 5, 683. more in this place to *u*. is not safe
P. L. 6, 716. all heaven's bounds into the *u*. deep
P. L. 9, 131. or won to what may work his *u*. loss
P. L. 11, 704. and *u*. odious truth that God
P. R. 4, 172. dared to *u*. the abominable terms
S. A. 1556. sense distract to know well what I *u*.
S. A. 1566. to *u*. what will come at last too soon
**Utterance**.—P. L. 3, 62. beatitude past *u*.
P. L. 4, 410. turned him all ear to hear new *u*.
P. L. 9, 1066. at length gave *u*. to these words
P. R. 3, 10. thy words to thy large heart give *u*.
**Uttered**.—P. L. 10, 33. in thunder *u*. thus his
P. L. 10, 615. to those bright orders *u*. thus his
P. R. 1, 320. then with words thus *u*. spake
S. A. 1646. *u*. straining all his nerves he bowed
C. 786. that must be *u*. to unfold the sage
**Utteredst**.—P. L. 11, 762. to the angel *u*. thus
**Uttering**.—P. L. 3, 143 which *u*. thus he
P. L. 3, 347. sweet as from blest voices *u*. joy
**Uttermost**.—P. L. 7, 266. in circuit to the *u*.
P. L. 10, 920. in this *u*. distress
**Uxorious**.—P. L. 1, 444. built by that *u*. king
S. A. 945. when I must live *u*. to thy will
**Uzzean**.—P. R. 1, 369. into my hands *U*. Job
**Uzziel**.—P. L. 4, 782. *U*. half these draw off

# V.

**Vacant**.—P. L. 2, 835. perhaps our *v*. room
P. L. 7, 190. to bring into their *v*. room
P. L. 11, 103. or to invade *v*. possession
P. R. 2, 116. sly preface to return had left him *v*.
S. A. 89. hid in her *v*. interlunar cave
C. 718. that no corner might be *v*. of her plenty
Hor. 10. always *v*. always amiable
**Vacation**.—U. C. 11, 14. long *v*. hastened on his
**Vacuity**.—P. L. 2, 932. meets a vast *v*.
**Vacuous**.—P. L. 7, 169. nor *v*. the space
**Vagabond**.—P. L. 11, 16. winds blown *v*.
**Vagaries**.—P. L. 6, 614. into strange *v*. fell
**Vain**.—P. L. 1, 44. battle proud with *v*. attempt
P. L.2,9.insatiate to pursue *v*. war with heaven
P. L. 2, 191. our motions *v*. sees and derides
P. L. 2, 234. the former *v*. to hope argues as *v*.
P. L. 2, 378. darkness here hatching *v*. empires
P. L. 2,565. *v*. wisdom all and false philosophy
P. L. 2,933. unawares fluttering his pennons *v*.
P. L. 3, 23. not these eyes that *u*. in *v*.
P. L. 3, 109. useless and *v*. of freedom both
P. L. 3, 446. of all things transitory and *v*.
P. L. 3.448. all things *v*. and all who in *v*. things
P. L. 3, 457. fleet hither and in *v*.
P. L. 3, 465. with many a *v*. exploit
P. L. 3, 467. with *v*. design new Babels
P. L. 3, 601. in *v*. so long have sought in *v*.
P. L. 4, 87. how dearly I abide that boast so *v*.
P. L. 4, 466. and pined with *v*. desire
P. L. 4, 675. in deep of night shine not in *v*.
P. L. 4,808. *c*. hopes, *v*. aims, inordinate desires

P. L. 4, 833. like to end as much in *v*.
P. L. 4, 860. to strive or fly he held it *v*.
P. L. 5, 43. sets off the face of things in *v*.
P. L. 5, 737. their *v*. designs and tumults *v*.
P. L. 6, 90. their thoughts proved fond and *v*.
P. L. 6, 135. fool not to think *v*.
P. L. 7, 610. and their counsels *v*. thou hast
P. L. 8, 187. wandering thoughts and notions *v*.
P. L. 9, 296. for he who tempts though in *v*.
P. L. 9, 1113. *v*. covering if to hide their guilt
P. L. 9, 1189. and of their *v*. contest appeared
P. L. 10, 50. which he presumes already *v*.
P. L. 10, 337. shame that sought *v*. covertures
P. L. 10,515. his belly prone reluctant but in *v*.
P. L. 10,829. all my evasions *v*. and reasonings
P. L. 11, 92. heart I know how variable and *v*.
P. L. 11, 726. but all in *v*. which when he saw
P. L. 12, 377. thoughts have searched in *v*.
P. R. 1, 459. at least in *v*. for they shall find
P. R. 2, 24. but returned in *v*.
P. R. 2, 388. in *v*. where no acceptance it can
P. R. 3, 105. as *v*. men seek oft not deserved
P. R. 3,387. much ostentation *v*. of fleshly arm
P. R. 3, 425. but by circumcision *v*.
P. R. 4, 20. (*v*. battery)
P. R. 4, 24. and his *v*. importunity pursues
P. R. 4, 307. his tedious talk is but *v*. boast
P. R. 4, 407. but sheltered slept in *v*.
P. R. 4,498. thou art discerned and toil'st in *v*.
S. A. 322. at least, *v*. reasonings, down
S. A. 350. O what not in man deceivable and *v*.

S. A. 570. *v.* monument of strength
S. A. 841. *v.* thou strivest to cover shame with
S. A. 914. nor still insist to afflict thyself in *v.*
S. A. 1227. camest thou for this *v.* boaster
S. A. 1504. nor seem *v.* of his delivery
C. 513. 'tis not *v.* or fabulous
L. 18. hence with denial *v.* and coy excuse
Il P. 1. hence *v.* deluding joys
S. 15, 13. in *v.* doth valour bleed while avarice
S. 22, 13. might lead me through the world's *v.*
T. 5. which is no more than what is false and *v.*
H. 204. in *v.* the Tyrian maids
H. 208. in *v.* with cymbals' ring
H. 219. in *v.* with timbreled anthems dark
**Vain-glorious.**—P. L. 6, 384. aspires *v.-g.*
**Vainly.**—P. L. 2, 811. neither *v.* hope to be
**Valdarno.**—P.L.1,290. in *V.* to descry new lands
**Vale.**—P. L. 1, 224. in the midst a horrid *v.*
P. L. 2, 618. through many a dark and dreary *v.*
P. L. 2. 742. in this infernal *v.* first met, thou
P. L. 6. 70. nor straitening *v.* nor wood nor
P. L. 10, 530. engendered in the Pythian *v.* on
P. L. 11, 567. wasted woods on mountain or in *v.*
P. L. 12, 266. thou moon in the *v.* of Aialon
P. R. 1, 304. on hill sometimes anon on shady *v.*
S. A. 181. from Eshtaol and Zora's fruitful *v.*
S. A. 229. was in the *v.* of Sorec Dalila
C. 233. and in the violet-embroidered *v.*
**Vales.**—P. L. 1, 321. slumber here as in the *v.*
P. L. 3, 569. fields and groves and flowery *v.*
L. 134. and call the *v.* and bid them hither cast
S. 18, 9. the *v.* redoubled to the hills and they to
**Valiant.**—P. R. 4, 143. what wise and *v.* man
S. A. 1101. the highest name for *v.* acts
S. A. 1738. thither shall all the *v.* youth resort
**Valid.**—P. L. 6, 438. perhaps more *v.* arms
**Valley.**—P. L. 1, 404. the pleasant *v.* of Hinnom
P. L. 2, 495. that hill and *v.* rings
P. L. 2, 547. retreated in a silent *v.*, sing with
P. L. 4, 255. of some irriguous *v.* spread her
P. L. 5, 203. to hill or *v.* fountain or fresh
P. L. 6, 784. and with fresh flowerets hill and *v.*
P. L. 9, 116. sweet interchange of hill and *v.*
P. L. 11, 349. in *v.* and in plain God is
P. R. 2, 185. in *v.* or green meadow to way-lay
P. R. 4, 586. then in a flowery *v.* set him
C. 282. seek in the *v.* some cool friendly spring
**Valleys.**—P. L. 7, 327. with tufts the *v.*
P. R. 3, 332. hills plain fell woods or *v.* fill
L. 136. low where the mild whispers use
**Vallombrosa.**—P. L. 1, 303. brooks in *V.*
**Valour.**—P. L. 1, 554. deliberate *v.* breathed
P. L. 4, 297. for contemplation he and *v.* formed
P. L. 6, 457. for what avails *v.* or strength
P. L. 11, 690. and *v.* and heroic virtue called
P. R. 2, 431. while virtue *v.* wisdom sit in
S. A. 1010. it is not virtue wisdom *v.* wit
S. A. 1165. no worthy match for *v.* to assail
S. A. 1740. to matchless *v.* and adventures high
S. 15, 13 in vain doth *v.* bleed while avarice
**Value.**—P. L. 4, 202. but God alone to *v.*
P. L. 8, 571. weigh with her thyself then *v.*
S. A. 1029. to apprehend or *v.* what is best in
**Valued.**—P. L. 2, 679. created thing naught *v.*
**Valuest.**—P. R. 4, 156. how slight thou *v.*
**Van.**—P. L. 2, 535. before each *v.* prick forth
P. L. 5, 589. and gonfalons 'twixt *v.* and rear
P. L. 6, 107. before the cloudy *v.*
S. A. 1234. bring up thy *v.*
**Vane.**—S. 17, 1. *V.* young in years but in sage
**Vanguard.**—P. L. 6, 558. *v.* to right and left
**Vanish.**—P. L. 4, 368. these delights will *v.*
**Vanished.**—P. L. 6, 14. from before her *v.*
P. R. 2, 402. both table and provision *v.* quite
**Vanity.**—P. L. 3, 447. when sin with *v.* had
P. L. 10, 875. not thy pride and wandering *v.*
P. R. 4, 138. grown of triumph that insulting *v.*
H. 136. and speckled *v.* will sicken soon and die
**Vanquish.**—P. R. 1, 175. but to *v.* by wisdom
**Vanquished.**—P. L. 1, 52. horrid crew lay *v.*
P. L. 1, 476. the gods whom he had *v.*

P. L. 3, 243. I shall not long lie *v.*
P. L. 6, 365. *v.* Adramelech and Asmadai
P. L. 6, 410. both retired victor and *v.*
S. A. 235. *v.* with a peal of words
S. A. 281. in pursuit of Madian and her *v.* kings
S. A. 562. to let in the foe effeminately *v.*
**Vanquisher.**—P. L. 3, 251. subdue my *v.*
**Vanquishing.**—P. R. 4, 607. *v.* temptation
**Vans.**—P. L. 2, 927. his sail-broad *v.* he spreads
P. R. 4, 583. who on their plumy *v.* received
**Vant-brace.**—S. A. 1121. *v.-b.* and greaves
**Vapour.**—P.L.2,216. overcome their noxious *v.*
P. L. 9, 159. wrapped in mist of midnight *v.*
P. L. 9, 635. compact of unctuous *v.* which
P. L. 9, 1047. that with exhilarating *v.* bland
P. L. 10, 694. sideral blast *v.* and mist
P. L. 11, 741 the hills to their supply *v.*
P. L. 12, 635. and *v.* as the Libyan air adust
**Vapours.**—P. L. 3, 445. like aerial *v.* flew
P. L. 4, 557. when *v.* fired impress the air
P. L. 5, 5. and temperate *v.* bland
P. L. 5, 420. unpurged *v.*
C. 17. with the rank *v.* of this sin-worn mould
A. 49. of noisome winds and blasting *v.* chill
**Variable.**—P. L. 11, 92. how *v.* and vain
**Variance.**—S. A. 1585. brought him so soon at *v.*
**Varied.**—P. L. 5, 431. yet God hath here *v.*
P. L 9, 516. oft so steers and shifts her sail so *v.*
**Variety.**—P. L. 6, 640. for earth hath this *v.*
P. L. 7, 542. that all the earth yields *v.* without
**Various.**—P. L. 1, 374. known to men by *v.*
P. L. 1, 706 within the ground a *v.* mould
P. L. 2, 967. discord with a thousand *v.* mouths
P. L. 3, 582. turn swift their *v.* motions
P. L. 3. 604. *v.* shapes old Proteus from the sea
P. L. 3, 717. flew upward spirited with *v.* forms
P. L. 4, 247. a happy rural seat of *v.* view
P. L. 4, 423. that bear delicious fruit so *v.*
P. L. 4, 669. but with kindly heat of *v.* influence
P. L. 5, 89. a prospect wide and *v.*
P. L. 5, 146. each morning duly paid in *v.* style
P. L. 5, 146. for neither *v.* style nor holy
P. L. 5, 390. than with these *v.* fruits the trees
P. L. 5, 473. endued with *v.* forms *v.* degrees
P. L. 6, 84. shields *v.* with boastful argument
P. L. 6, 242. wide was spread that war and *v.*
P. L. 7, 318. opening their *v.* colours
P. L. 8, 125. dance about him *v.* rounds
P. L. 8, 370. is not the earth with *v.* living
P. L. 8, 609. who meet with *v.* objects
L. 9, 619. and *v.* yet unknown to us
P. L. 10, 343. in their sad discourse and *v.* plaint
P. L. 10, 1064. now the sky with *v.* face
P. L. 11, 557. whereon were tents of *v.* hue
P. L. 12, 53. sets upon their tongues a *v.* spirit
P. L. 12, 282. so many and so *v.* laws are given
P. R. 2, 240. of *v.* persons, each to know his
P. R. 4, 68. in *v.* habits on the Appian road
S. A. 71. and all her *v.* objects of delight
S. A. 668. hand so *v.* or might I say contrarious
C. 22. that like to rich and *v.* gems inlay
C. 379. that in the *v.* bustle of resort
L. 188. he touched the tender stops of *v.* quills
**Variously.**—P. L. 8, 610. from the sense *v.*
**Various-measured.**—P. R. 4. 256. *v.-m.* verse
**Varnish.**—P. R. 4, 344. *v.* on a harlot's cheek
**Varnished.**—P. L. 2, 485. or close ambition *v.*
S. A. 901. these false pretexts and *v.* colours
**Vary.**—P. L. 5, 184. your ceaseless change *v.*
**Vassal.**—P. R. 4, 133. deservedly made *v.*
**Vassalage.**—P. L. 2, 252. state of splendid *v.*
**Vassals.**—P. L. 2, 90. the *v.* of his anger
**Vast.**—P. L. 1, 21. sat'st brooding on the *v.* abyss
P. L. 1, 177. through the *v.* and boundless deep
P. L. 2, 254. though in this *v.* recess
P. L. 2, 409. wings over the *v.* abrupt
P. L. 2, 539. others with *v.* Typhœan rage
P. L. 2, 652. a scaly fold, voluminous and *v.*
P. L. 2, 832. ere now created *v.* and round
P. L. 2, 932. soon failing meets a *v.* vacuity
P. L. 3, 711. stood *v.* infinitude confined

P. L. 4, 777. half way up hill this *v.* sublunar
P. L. 5, 267. and through the *v.* ethereal sky
P. L. 6, 109. Satan with *v.* and haughty
P. L. 6, 203. through the *v.* of heaven
P. L. 6, 256. his ample shield a *v.* circumference
P. L. 7, 211. they viewed the *v.* immeasurable
P. L. 7, 229. round through the *v.* profundity
P. L. 8, 24. in all their *v.* survey useless besides
P. L. 8, 153. for such *v.* room in nature
P. L. 10, 471. voyaged the unreal *v.* unbounded
P. L. 10, 601. this *v.* unhidebound corpse
P. R. 1, 153. and at length all his *v.* force
P. R. 3, 286. her structure *v.* there shows
S A. 54. *v.* unwieldy burdensome proudly secure
S. A. 1238. bulk without spirit *v.*
C. 771. now heaps upon some few with *v.* excess
Il P. 90, what worlds or what *v.* regions hold
**Vastness.**—P. L. 7, 472. upheaved his *v.*
**Vault.**—P. L. 1, 669. toward the *v.* of heaven
P. L. 4, 777. up hill this vast sublunar *v.*
**Vaulted.**—P. L. 1, 298. *v.* with fire
P. L. 6, 214. and flying *v.* either host with fire
S. A. 1606. half round on two main pillars *v.* high
**Vaults.**—C. 471. oft seen in charnel *v.*
**Vaunted.**—P. L. 3, 251. of his *v.* spoil
C. 738. with that same *v.* name virginity
**Vaunting.**—P. L. 1, 126. *v.* aloud but racked
P. L. 6, 363. Uriel and Raphael his *v.* foe
S. A. 1360. in place abominable *v.* my strength
**Vaunts.**—P. L. 4, 84. promises and other *v.*
P. R. 1, 145. and *v.* of his great cunning
**Veers.**—P. L. 9, 515. where the wind *v.* oft
**Vegetable.**—P. L. 4, 220. fruit of *v.* gold
**Vehemence.**—P. L. 2, 954. with loudest *v.*
C. 795. to such a flame of sacred *v.*
**Vehement.**—P. L. 8, 526. nor *v.* desire
P. L. 10, 1007. or *v.* despair broke off the rest
**Veil.**—P. L. 3, 382. with both wings *v.* their eyes
P. L. 4, 304. as a *v.* down to the slender waist
P. L. 5, 383. no *v.* she needed virtue proof
P. L. 5, 646. night comes not there in darker *v.*
P. L. 6, 11. till her hour to *v.* the heaven
P. L. 9, 1054. innocence that as a *v.* had
S. A. 730. wetting the borders of her silken *v.*
S. A. 1035. at first all heavenly under virgin *v.*
H. 42. the saintly *v.* of maiden white to throw
**Veiled.**—P. L. 3, 26. orbs or dim suffusion *v.*
P. L. 5, 250. *v.* with his gorgeous wings
P. L. 9, 52. night's hemisphere had *v.*
P. L. 9, 425. Eve separate he spies *v.* in cloud
S. 23. her face was *v.* yet to my fancied sight
**Veils.**—P. L. 11, 229. cloud that *v.* the hill
**Vein.**—P. L. 6, 628. themselves in pleasant *v.*
H. 15. say heavenly muse shall not thy sacred *v.*
**Veins.**—P. L. 1, 701. that underneath had *v.*
P. L. 4, 227. which through *v.* of porous earth
P. L. 6, 516. part hidden *v.* digged up
P. L. 9, 891. horror chill ran through his *v.*
P. L. 11, 568. down to the *v.* of earth
**Velvet.**—C. 898. o'er the cowslip's *v.* head
**Venereal.**—S. A. 533. of fair fallacious looks *v.*
**Vengeance.**—P. L. 1, 170. his ministers of *v.*
P. L. 1, 220. wrath and *v.* poured
P. L. 2, 173. or from above should intermitted *v.*
P. L. 3, 399. to execute fierce *v.* on his foes
P. L. 4, 170. and with a *v.* sent from Media
P. L. 6, 279. or some more sudden *v.* winged
P. L. 6, 808. *v.* is his or whose he sole appoints
P. L. 12, 541. and *v.* to the wicked at return
C. 218. are but as slavish officers of *v.*
**Vengeful.**—P. L. 1, 148. so suffice his *v.* ire
P. L. 10, 1023. hath wiselier armed his *v.* ire
Cir. 24. of *v.* justice bore for our excess
**Venial.**—P. L. 9, 5. permitting him... *v.* discourse
**Venom.**—P. L. 4, 804. or if inspiring *v.*
A. 53. or hurtful worm with cankered *v.* bites
**Venomed.**—C. 916. next this marble *v.* seat
**Vent.**—P. L. 6, 583. and to a narrow *v.* applied
P. L. 12, 374. in tears without the *v.* of words
P. R. 1, 433. mixing somewhat true to *v.* more lies
P. R. 4, 445. desperate of better course to *v.*

**Vented.**—P. R. 3, 391. in my ear *v.* much policy
**Venture.**—P. L. 3, 19. *v.* down the dark descent
P. L. 4, 891. and boldly *v.* to whatever place
C. 228. to be heard farthest I'll *v.*
**Ventured.**—P. L. 4, 574. hath *v.* from the deep
**Ventures.**—P. R. 1, 177. therefore secure *v.*
**Venturing.**—P. L. 9, 690. by *v.* higher than
S. A. 1373. I do it freely *v.* to displease God
**Venturous.**—P. L. 2, 205. are bold and *v.*
P. L. 5, 64. with *v.* arm he plucked, he tasted
C. 609. alas good *v.* youth I love thy courage
**Venus.**—P. R. 2, 214. as the zone of *V.*
C. 124. *V.* now wakes and wakens love
L'A. 14. whom lovely *V.* at a birth
**Verbal.**—P. R. 3, 104. and loses though but *v.*
**Verdant.**—P. L. 4, 697. fenced up the *v.* wall
P. L. 7, 310. let the earth put forth the *v.* grass
P. L. 8, 631. the earth's green Cape and *V.* Isles
P. L. 9, 501. with burnished neck of *v.* gold
P. L. 9, 1038. thick overhead with *v.* roof
P. R. 3, 253. at whose *v.* feet a spacious plain
C. 622. that spreads her *v.* leaf to the morning
**Verdict.**—S. A. 324. that moral *v.* quits her of
S. A. 1228. on my strength and give thy *v.*
**Verdure.**—P. L. 7, 315. whose *v.* clad her
P. L. 11, 832. with all his *v.* spoiled and trees
**Verdurous.**—P. L. 4, 143. the *v.* wall of
**Verge.**—P. L. 2, 1038. begins her farthest *v.*
P. L. 6, 865. down from the *v.* of heaven
P. L. 11, 881. or serve they as a flowery *v.*
**Verified.**—P. L. 10, 182. this oracle then *v.*
**Verify.**—P. R. 1, 133. how I begin to *v.* that
P. R. 3, 177. best fulfil best *v.* the Prophets old
**Vermeil-tinctured.**—C. 752. a *v.-t.* lip
**Vermin.**—S. A. 574. till *v.* or the draff of servile
**Vernal.**—P. L. 2, 43. or sight of *v.* bloom
P. L. 4, 155. and to the heart inspires *v.* delight
P. L. 4, 264. airs, *v.* airs breathing the smell
S. A. 628. nor breath of *v.* air from snowy Alp
L. 141. and purple all the ground with *v.* flowers
M. W. 40. new shot up from *v.* shower
**Vernant.**—P. L. 10, 679. with *v.* flowers
**Verse.**—P. L. 5, 150. prose or numerous *v.*
P. L. 9, 24. inspires easy my unpremeditated *v.*
P. R. 4, 256. and various-measured *v.*
C. 516. storied of old in high immortal *v.*
C. 859. and add the power of some adjuring *v.*
L'A. 137. married to immortal *v.*
S. 13, 9. thou honour'st *v.* and *v.* must lend her
P. 22. these latest scenes confine my roving *v.*
H. 17. hast thou no *v.* no hymn or solemn strain
H. 47. my plaining *v.* as lively as before
S. M. 2. harmonious sisters Voice and *V.*
**Versed.**—P. R. 4, 327. deep *v.* in books
**Vertumnus.**—P. L. 9, 395. when she fled *V.*
**Very.**—P. R. 2, 90. that through my *v.* soul
P. R. 4, 12. to salve his credit and for *v.* spite
C. 428. yea there where *v.* desolation dwells
C. 646. entered the *v.* lime-twigs of his spells
**Vessel.**—P. L. 2, 1043. *v.* holds gladly the port
P. L. 9, 89. *v.* fittest imp of fraud in whom
P. L. 11, 729. began to build a *v.* of huge bulk
P. L. 11, 745. the floating *v.* swum uplifted
P. L. 12, 559. what this *v.* can contain
S. A. 199. a foolish pilot have shipwrecked my *v.*
**Vessels.**—P. L. 5, 348. wants her fit *v.* pure
**Vest.**—P. L. 11, 241. a military *v.* of purple
**Vesta.**—Il P. 23. thee bright-haired *V.*
**Vested.**—P. R. 1, 257. the altar and the *v.* priest
S. 23, 9. came *v.* all in white pure as her mind
**Vesture.**—A. 83. kiss her sacred *v.'s* hem
**Vex.**—P. L. 2, 801. terrors *v.* me round
**Vexed.**—P. L. 1, 306. hath *v.* the Red-sea coast
P. L. 2, 660. *v.* Scylla, bathing in the sea
P. L. 3, 429. less *v.* with tempest loud
P. L. 10, 314. over the *v.* abyss following
P. R. 4, 416. and fell on the *v.* wilderness
C. 666. why are you *v.* lady why do you frown
**Vialed.**—C. 847. with precious *v.* liquors heals
**Viands.**—P. L. 5, 434. and to their *v.* fell
P. R. 2, 370. defends the touching of these *v.*

**Vice.**—P. L. 1, 492. more gross to love *v.* for itself
P. L. 2, 116. to *v.* industrious but to nobler deeds
P. L. 11, 518. whom they served a brutish *v.*
C. 760. I hate when *v.* can bolt her arguments
**Vicegerent.**—P. L. 5, 609. his great *v.*
P. L. 10, 56. whom but thee *v.* Son?
**Vices.**—P. R. 3, 86. rolling in brutish *v.*
P. R. 4, 340. the *v.* of their deities and their
S. A. 269. and by their *v.* brought to servitude
**Vicious.**—P. L. 12, 104. servants on his *v.* race
**Vicissitude.**—P. L. 6, 8. grateful *v.*
P. L. 7, 351. rule the day in their *v.* and rule
**Victor.**—P. L. 1, 95. nor what the potent *v.*
P. L. 1, 169. but see the angry *v.* hath recalled
P. L. 2, 144. we must exasperate the Almighty *v.*
P. L. 2, 199. and omnipotent decree the *v.'s* will
P. L. 6, 124. in both disputes alike *v.*
P. L. 6, 410. both retired *v.* and vanquished
P. L. 6, 590. which on the *v.* host levelled with
P. L. 6, 880. sole *v.* from the expulsion of his
P. L. 10, 376. there let him still *v.* sway
P. L. 12, 385. what stroke shall bruise the *v.'s*
P. L. 12, 433. temporal death shall bruise the *v.'s*
P. R. 4, 102. a *v.* people free from servile yoke
P. R. 4, 132. that people *v.* once now vile
P. R. 4, 571. fell whence he stood to see his *v.*
P. R. 4, 637. sung *v.* and from heavenly feast
S. A. 1290. each his own deliverer and *v.* over all
**Victor-angels.**—P. L. 6, 525. rose the *v.-a.*
**Victories.**—S. 16, 10. peace hath her *v.* no less
**Victorious.**—P. L. 2, 142. the baser fire *v.*
P. L. 2, 997. poured out by millions her *v.* bands
P. L. 3, 250. but I shall rise *v.* and subdue
P. L. 6, 886. sung triumph and him sung *v.*
P. L. 7, 136. returned *v.* with his saints
P. L. 10, 634. at one sling of thy *v.* arm
P. R. 1, 9. into the desert his *v.* field
P. R. 1. 215. to which my spirit aspired *v.* deeds
S. A. 1663. and now liest *v.* among thy slain
C. 974. to triumph in *v.* dance
S. M. 14. those just spirits that wear *v.* palms
**Victors.**—P. L. 6, 609. come not on these *v.*
P. R. 4, 337. that pleased so well our *v.'s* ear
**Victory.**—P. L. 2, 105. which if not *v.* is yet
P. L. 2, 770. to our Almighty foe clear *v.*
P. L. 6, 201. joy filled and shout presage of *v.*
P. L. 6, 240. in his arm the moment lay of *v.*
P. L. 6, 630. thoughts beyond all doubt of *v.*
P. L. 6, 762. his right hand sat *v.* eagle-winged
P. L. 12, 452. he shall ascend with *v.*
P. L. 12, 570. is fortitude to highest *v.*
P. R. 1, 173. *v.* and triumph to the Son of God
P. R. 4, 594. sung heavenly anthems of his *v.*
S. 10, 6. as that dishonest *v.* at Chæronea
S. 15, 6. unshaken virtue ever brings *v.* home
**View.**—P. L. 1, 27. hides nothing from thy *v.*
P. L. 1, 563. advanced in *v.* they stand
P. L. 2, 190. eye views all things at one *v.*
P. L. 2, 394. perhaps in *v.* of those bright
P. L. 2, 890. before their eyes in sudden *v.*
P. L. 3, 59. and their works at once to *v.*
P. L. 3, 542. with wonder at the sudden *v.*
P. L. 4, 27. Eden now in his *v.* lay pleasant
P. L. 4, 142. a woody theatre of stateliest *v.*
P. L. 4, 247. a happy rural seat of various *v.*
P. L. 4, 399. served best his end nearer to *v.*
P. L. 6, 18. blaze on blaze first met his *v.*
P. L. 6, 81. and nearer *v.* bristled with upright
P. L. 6, 603. in *v.* stood ranked of seraphim
P. L. 7, 618. founded in *v.* on the clear
P. L. 9, 482. (for I *v.* far round)
P. L. 10, 1030. which methinks I have in *v.*
P. L. 11, 761. mourns his children all in *v.*
P. R. 2, 287. if cottage were in *v.* sheepcote or
P. R. 3, 298. to have a *v.* of his great power
P. R. 4, 250. then *v.* the schools of ancient Greece
P. R. 4, 514. I thought thee worth my nearer *v.*
S. A. 723. and now at nearer *v.* no other certain
S. A. 1491. and *v.* him sitting in the house
Il P. 15. and therefore to our weaker *v.*
S. 22, 2. to outward *v.* of blemish or of spot

**Viewed.**—P. L. 2, 617. *v.* first their lamentable
P. L. 7, 211. they *v.* the vast immeasurable
P. L. 7, 548. and 'll that he had made *v.*
P. R. 2, 131. have found him *v.* him tasted him
P. R. 2, 198. he slightly *v.* and slightly
P. R. 2, 297. he *v.* it round then with
P. R. 3, 233. scarce *v.* the Gallilean towns
**Viewing.**—P. L. 2, 764. thy perfect image *v.*
P. L. 9, 1052. unrest and each the other *v.*
P. L. 10, 235. why sit we here each other *v.*
**Viewless.**—P. L. 3, 518. heaven sometimes *v.*
C. 92. I must be *v.* now
P. 50. or should I thence hurried on *v.* wing
**Views.**—P. L. 1, 59. as far as angels ken, he *v.*
P. L. 1, 288. optic glass the Tuscan artist *v.*
P. L. 1, 569. the whole battalion *v.*
P. L. 2, 190. whose eye *v.* all things at one view
P. L. 3, 561. then from pole to pole he *v.*
P. L. 4, 205. him with new wonder now he *v.*
**Viewest.**—P. L. 10, 355. which thou *v.* as not
**Vigilance.**—P. L. 4, 580. the *v.* here placed
P. L. 9, 157. of these the *v.* I dread and to
P. L. 10, 30. with righteous plea their utmost *v.*
**Vigils.**—P. R. 1, 182. their odes and *v.* tuned
**Vigorous.**—C. 628. telling their strange and *v.*
S. A. 1704, then *v.* most when most unactive
**Vigour.**—P. L. 1, 140. and *v.* soon returns
P. L. 2, 13. gulf can hold immortal *v.*
P. L. 6, 158. who while they feel *v.* divine
P. L. 6, 436. soon closing and by native *v.*
P. L. 6, 851. and of their wonted *v.* left them
P. L. 8, 97. beams unactive else their *v.* found
P. L. 8, 269. with supple joints as lively *v.* led
P. L. 9, 314. would utmost *v.* raise and raised
P. L. 10, 405. on your joint *v.* now my hold
S. A. 1280. and celestial *v.* armed
**Vile.**—P. L. 2, 194. shall we then live thus *v.*
P. L. 5, 782. yet unpaid prostration *v.*
P. L. 7, 34. of that *v.* rout that tore the Thracian
P. L. 10, 971. restored by thee *v.* as I am to
P. L. 12, 510. to their own *v.* advantages
P. R. 4, 132. victor one now *v.* and base
S. A. 376. aught seem *v.* as *v.* hath been my folly
S. A. 1361. besides how *v.* contemptible ridiculous
C. 907. of unblessed enchanter *v.*
**Vilest.**—S. A. 73. inferior to the *v.* now become
S. A. 74. of man or worm the *v.* here excel me
**Vilified.**—P. L. 11. 516. themselves they *v.*
**Village.**—P. R. 1, 332. to town or *v.* nigh
C. 346. or whistle from the lodge or *v.* cock
**Villager.**—C. 166. appear some harmless *v.*
C. 304. gentle *v.* what readiest way would bring
C. 576. supposing him some neighbour *v.*
**Villages.**—P. L. 9, 448. among the pleasant *v.*
**Villatic.**—S. A. 1695. of tame *v.* fowl
**Vindicate.**—P. R. 2, 47. arise and *v.* thy
S. A. 475. to *v.* the glory of his name
**Vine.**—P. L. 4, 258. the mantling *v.* lays forth
P. L. 4, 307. as the *v.* curls her tendrils
P. L. 5, 215. or they led the *v.* to wed her
P. L. 7, 320. flourished thick the clustering *v.*
C. 294. I saw them under a green mantling *v.*
L. 40. wild thyme and the gadding *v.* o'ergrown
L'A. 47. through the sweet-briar or the *v.*
**Vines.**—P. L. 1, 410. of Sibma clad with *v.*
P. L. 5, 427. ambrosial fruitage bear and *v.*
P. L. 5, 635. fruit of delicious *v.* the growth
**Vintage.**—P. R. 4, 15. as a swarm of flies in *v.*
**Viol.**—P. 28. of lute or *v.* still
**Violate.**—P. L. 4, 883. to *v.* sleep
P. L. 9, 903. to *v.* the sacred fruit
S. A. 428. to *v.* the sacred trust of silence
**Violated.**—P. L. 10, 25. *v.* not their bliss
P. R. 3, 160. oft have they *v.* the temple oft
**Violating.**—S. A. 893. hostile deeds *v.* the end
**Violence.**—P. L. 1, 496. with lust and *v.*
P. L. 4, 901. but that implies not *v.* or harm
P. L. 4, 995. disturbed and torn with *v.*
P. L. 5, 242. by *v?* no for that shall be
P. L. 5, 905. nor of *v.* feared aught
P. L. 6, 35. far worse to bear than *v.*

P. L. 6, 274. brooks not the works of v.
P. L. 6, 371. and the v. of Ramiel scorched
P. L. 6, 405. their place by v.
P. L. 9, 282. his v. thou fearest not being such
P. L. 10, 1041. no more be mentioned then of v.
P. L. 11, 671. so v. proceeded and oppression
P. L. 11, 780. I had hope when v. was ceased
P. L. 11, 812. fearless of reproach and scorn or v.
P. L. 11, 888. saw the whole earth filled with v.
P. R. 1, 219. brute v. and proud tyrannic power
P. R. 1, 389. they to me never did wrong or v.
P. R. 3, 90. without ambition war or v.
P. R. 3, 191. and scorns, and snares, and v.
P. R. 4, 388. v. and stripes and lastly cruel death
S. A. 1191. to others did no v. nor spoil
C. 392. or do his gray hairs any v.
C. 451. and noble grace that dashed brute v.
S. 15, 11. till truth and right from v. be freed
**Violent.**—P. L. 2, 782. breaking v. way
P. L. 3, 487. when lo! a v. cross wind
P. L. 4, 97. vows made in pain as v. and void
P. L. 6, 439. more valid arms weapons more v.
P. L. 9, 324. straitened by a foe subtle or v.
P. L. 11, 428. to bring forth more v. deeds
P. L. 11, 471. some as thou sawest by v. stroke
P. L. 11, 669. exploded and had seized with v.
P. L. 12, 93. subjects him from without to v.
P. R. 3, 87. v. or shameful death their due
S. A. 1273. the brute and boisterous force of v.
**Violet.**—P. L. 4, 700. underfoot the v. crocus
L. 145. the glowing v. the musk-rose
**Violet-embroidered.**—C. 233. the v.-e. vale
**Violets.**—P. L. 9, 1040. pansies and v.
L'A. 21. there on beds of v. blue
**Viper.**—S. A. 1001. to such a v. his most sacred
**Virgin.**—P. L. 3, 284. time shall be of v. seed
P. L. 5, 296. and played at will her v. fancies
P. L. 8, 501. yet innocence and v. modesty
P. L. 9, 270. to whom the v. majesty of Eve
P. L. 9, 396. or to Ceres in her prime yet v.
P. L. 9, 452. chance with nymph-like step fair v.
P. L. 10, 676. by Leo and the V. and the Scales
P. L. 12, 368. a v. is his mother but his Sire
P. L. 12, 379. v. mother hail high in the love
P. R. 1, 134. on which I sent thee to the V.
P. R. 1, 138. these things could be to her a v.
P. R. 1, 239. thy birth conceived in me a v.
P. R. 2, 159. v. majesty with mild and sweet
S. A. 1035. seeming at first all heavenly under v.
C. 148. some v. sure for so I can distinguish by
C. 350. but O that hapless v. our lost sister
C. 427. will dare to soil her v. purity
C. 448. that wise Minerva wore unconquered v.
C. 507. but O my v. lady where is she
C. 582. against the unarmed weakness of one v.
C. 689. and timely rest have wanted but fair v.
C. 826. Sabrina is her name a v. pure
C. 856. to aid a v. such as was herself
C. 905. of true v. here distressed
C. 922. v. daughter of Locrine
Il P. 103. but O sad v. that thy power
S. 9, 14. gained thy entrance v. wise and pure
H. 3. of wedded maid and v. mother born
H. 237. but see the v. blest
M. W. 17. the v. choir for her request
D. F. I. 21. unhoused thy v. soul
**Virgin-born.**—P. R. 4, 500. of David v.-b.
**Virginity.**—C. 347. hurtful power o'er true v.
C. 738. with that same vaunted name v.
C. 787. the sage and serious doctrine of v.
**Virgins.**—P. L. 1, 441. Sidonian v. paid their
S. A. 1741 the v. also shall on feastful days
**Virtual.**—P. L. 8, 617. v. or immediate touch
P. L. 11, 338. fomented by his v. power and
**Virtue.**—P. L. 1, 320. repose your wearied v.
P. L. 2, 483. the Spirits damned lose all their v.
P. L. 2, 551. that fate free v. should enthrall
P. L. 3, 586. shoots invisible v. even to the deep
P. L. 4, 198. nor on the v. thought of that
P. L. 4, 671. shed down their stellar v. on all
P. L. 4, 848. how awful goodness is and saw v.

P. L. 5, 371. whom thus the angelic v. answered
P. L. 6, 117. might there fail where v. fails
P. L. 6, 703. into thee such v. and grace
P. L. 7, 236. vital v. infused and vital warmth
P. L. 8, 95. whose v. on itself work no effect
P. L. 8, 124. by his attractive v. and their own
P. L. 8, 502. her v. and the conscience
P. L. 9, 110. in themselves all their known v.
P. L. 9, 145. whether such v. spent of old
P. L. 9, 310. receive access in every v.
P. L. 9, 317. with me best witness of thy v.
P. L. 9, 335. and what is faith love v. unassayed
P. L. 9, 374. rely on what thou hast of v.
P. L. 9, 616. overpraising leaves in doubt the v.
P. L. 9, 649. the credit of whose v. rest with
P. L. 9, 694. not praise rather your dauntless v.
P. L. 9, 778. of v. to make wise what hinders
P. L. 9, 973. of tasting this fair fruit whose v.
P. L. 9, 1063. destitute and bare of all their v.
P. L. 10, 372. thy v. hath won what thy hands
P. L. 10, 884. was but a show rather than solid v.
P. L. 11, 623. shall yield up all their v.
P. L. 11, 690. and valour and heroic v. called
P. L. 11, 790. and great exploits but of true v.
P. L. 11, 798. shall with their freedom lost all v.
P. L. 12, 98. will decline so low from v.
P. L. 12, 583. add v. patience, temperance
P. R. 1, 68. displaying all v., grace and wisdom
P. R. 1, 165. from what consummate v. I have
P. R. 1, 177. ventures his filial v. though untried
P. R. 1, 231. to what height sacred v. and true
P. R. 1, 483. most men admire v. who follow not
P. R. 2, 217. seated as on the top of v.'s hill
P. R. 2, 248. that fast to v. I impute not
P. R. 2, 431. while v. valour wisdom sit in
P. R. 2, 455. more apt to slacken v. and abate
P. R. 2, 464. his honour v. merit and chief
P. R. 3, 348. know I seek not to engage thy v.
P. R. 4, 297. others in v. placed felicity
P. R. 4, 298. but v. joined with riches and long
P. R. 4, 301. philosophic pride by him called v.
P. R. 4, 314. and in themselves seek v.
P. R. 4, 351. unless where moral v. is expressed
S. A. 173. but thee whose strength while v. was
S. A. 756. his v. or weakness which way to assail
S. A. 870. v. as I thought truth duty so enjoining
S. A. 1010. it is not v., wisdom, valour, wit
S. A. 1039. in his way to v. adverse and turbulent
S. A. 1050. but v. which breaks through all
S. A. 1690. his fiery v. roused
S. A. 1697. so v. given for lost
C. 9. unmindful of the crown that v. gives
C. 165. hath met the v. of this magic dust
C. 367. or so unprincipled in v.'s book
C. 373. v. could see to do what v. would
C. 589. v. may be assailed but never hurt
C. 761. and v. has no tongue to check her pride
C. 1019. love v., she alone is free
C. 1022. or if v. feeble were
S. 15, 5. thy firm unshaken v. ever brings
**Virtue-proof.**—P. L. 5, 384. v.-p.
**Virtues.**—P. L. 2, 15. celestial v. rising
P. L. 2, 311. ethereal v. or these titles now must
P. L. 5, 601. dominations, princedoms, v. powers
P. L. 5, 773. princedoms, v., powers if these
P. L. 5, 840. dominations, princedoms, v., powers
P. L. 7, 199. and v. winged, spirits and chariots
P. L. 9, 745. great are thy v. doubtless best
P. L. 10, 460. dominations, princedoms, v.
P. R. 3, 21. godlike v. wherefore dost thou hide
P. R. 4, 98. endued with regal v. as thou art
S. 9, 7. and at thy growing v. fret their spleen
S. 10, 12. so well your words his noble v. praise
M. W. 4. what her v. fair added to her noble
**Virtuous.**—P. L. 3, 608. with one v. touch
P. L. 9, 795. O Sovran v., precious of all trees
P. L. 9, 1033. bounty of this v. tree
P. R. 1, 382. I see excellent in good or fair or v.
P. R. 2, 468. which every wise and v. man
P. R. 4, 301. and his v. man wise
S. A. 1047. favoured of heaven who finds one v.

C. 211. but not astound the v. mind
C. 621. in every v. plant and healing herb
Il P. 113. that owned the v. ring and glass
S. 9, 1. lady that in the prime of v. youth
S. 20, 1. Lawrence of v. father v. son
M. W. 60. devoted to thy v. name
**Virtuousest.**—P. L. 8, 550. seems wisest, v.
**Visage.**—P. L. 2, 989. and v. incomposed
P. L. 3, 646. his radiant v. turned admonished
P. L. 4, 116. which marred his borrowed v.
P. L. 5, 419. whence in her v. round
P. L. 6, 261. hostile frown and v. all inflamed
P. L. 10, 511. his v. drawn he felt to sharp
C. 333. stoop thy pale v. through an amber cloud
C. 527. whose pleasing poison the v. quite
L. 62. his gory v. down the stream was sent
Il P. 13. whose saintly v. is too bright
**Visages.**—P. L. 1, 570. their v. and stature
P. L. 10, 24. did not spare that time celestial v.
**Viscount.**—M.W. 3. a v.'s daughter an earl's heir
**Visible.**—P. L. 1, 63. but rather darkness v.
P. L. 3, 386. without cloud made v.
P. L. 6, 145. though then to thee not v. when
P. L. 7, 22. within the v. diurnal sphere
P. L. 9, 604. considered all things v. in heaven
P. L. 11, 321. under this tree stood v.
**Visibly.**—P. L. 3, 141. compassion v. appeared
P. L. 4, 850. here observed his lustre v.
P. L. 6, 682. in whose face invisible is beheld v.
C. 216. I see ye v. and now believe
**Vision.**—P. L. 1, 455. when by the v. led
P. L. 1, 684. enjoyed in v. beatific
P. L. 5, 613. cast out from God and blessed v.
P. L. 8, 356. to the heavenly v. thus presumed
P. L. 8, 367. the v.,... replied
P. L. 11, 599. much better seems this v.
P. L. 12, 121. most High vouchsafes to call by v.
P. R. 1, 256. and prophetic Anna warned by v.
P. R. 4, 41. of v. multiplied through air or glass
C. 298. I took it for a faery v.
C. 457. and in clear dream and solemn v.
L. 161. where the great v. of the guarded mount
P. 41. there doth my soul in holy v. sit
**Visions.**—P. L. 11, 377. ascend in the v. of God
P. L. 11, 763. O v. ill foreseen better had I
**Visit.**—P. L. 3, 32. nightly I v. nor sometimes
P. L. 3, 230. to v. all thy creatures and to all
P. L. 3, 532. by which to v. oft those happy
P. L. 3, 661. to v. oft this new creation round
P. L. 5, 375. though spirits of heaven to v. thee
P. L. 7, 570. will deign to v. oft the dwellings
P. L. 8, 45. to v. how they prospered
P. L. 12, 48. God who oft descends to v. men
S. A. 182. to v. or bewail thee or if better
S.A. 1742. shall on feastful days v. his tomb with
C. 339. v. us with thy long levelled rule
A. 59. number my ranks and v. every sprout
D. F. I. 52. and camest again to v. us once more
**Visitant.**—P. L. 11, 225. while the great v.
**Visitants.**—S. A. 567. to v. a gaze or pitied
**Visitation.**—P. L. 9, 22. her nightly v.
P. L. 11, 275. my early v. and my last at even
**Visited.**—P.L. 10, 955. on my head all might be v.
S. A. 987. my tomb with odours v. and annual
**Visiting.**—P. L. 4, 240. v. each plant, and fed
**Visits.**—C. 844. and oft at eve v. the herds
**Visit'st.**—P. L. 7, 29. while thou v. my slumbers
L. 158. v. the bottom of the monstrous world
**Visored.**—C. 698. with v. falsehood
**Visual.**—P. L. 3, 620. sharpened his v. ray
P. L. 11, 415. then purged ... the v. nerve
S. A. 163. inward light alas puts forth no v. beam
**Vital.**—P. L. 3, 22. feel thy sovran v. lamp
P. L. 5, 484. to v. spirits aspire to animal
P. L. 6, 345. for spirits that live throughout v.
P. L. 7, 236. v. virtue infused and v. warmth
A. 65. and sing to those that held the v. shears
**Vitiated.**—P. L. 10, 169. accursed as v.
S. A. 389. spousal embraces v. with gold
**Vocal.**—P. L. 5, 204. made v. by my song
P. L. 9, 198. and joined their v. worship to the

P. L. 9, 530. impulse of v. air his fraululent
C. 247. and with these raptures moves the v. air
L. 86. smooth-sliding Mincius crowned with v.
**Voice.**—P. L. 1, 274. if once they hear that v.
P. L. 1, 337. yet to their general's v. they soon
P. L. 2, 188. open or concealed alike my v.
P. L. 2, 474. not more the adventure than his v.
P. L. 2, 518. the sounding alchymy by herald's v.
P. L. 3, 9. at the v. of God as with a mantle
P. L. 3, 370. no v. exempt, no v. but well could
P. L. 3, 710. confusion heard his v.
P. L. 4, 1. O for that warning v. which he
P. L. 4, 36. to thee I call but with no friendly v.
P. L. 4, 467. had not a v. thus warned me
P. L. 5, 15. then with v. mild as when
P. L. 5, 37. with gentle v., I thought it thine
P. L. 5, 705. the wonted signal and superior v.
P. L. 6, 27. from whence a v. from midst a
P. L. 6, 56. so spake the Sovran v. and clouds
P. L. 6, 782. each to his place they heard his v.
P. L. 7, 2. whose v. divine following
P. L. 7, 24. more safe I sing with mortal v.
P. L. 7, 37. clamour drowned both harp and v.
P. L. 7, 100. held by thy v., thy potent v., he
P. L. 7, 221. for Chaos heard his v.
P. L. 7, 513. thither with heart and v. and eyes
P. L. 7, 598. soft tunings intermixed with v.
P. L. 8, 2. in Adam's ear so charming left his v.
P. L. 8, 436. this answer from the gracious v.
P. L. 8, 486. and guided by his v. nor uninformed
P. L. 9, 199. the choir of creatures wanting v.
P. L. 9, 551. though at the v. much marvelling
P. L. 9, 561. not with human v. endued
P. L. 9, 653. sole daughter of his v.
P. L. 9, 871. endued with human v. and
P. L. 9, 1069. taught to counterfeit man's v.
P. L. 10, 33. in thunder uttered thus his v.
P. L. 10, 97. the v. of God they heard
P. L. 10, 116. and of thy v. afraid
P. L. 10, 119. my v. thou oft hast heard
P. L. 10, 146. didst obey before his v.
P. L. 10, 198. hearkened to the v. of thy wife
P. L. 10, 615. uttered thus his v.
P. L. 10, 729. O v. once heard delightfully
P. L. 10, 779. his dreadful v. no more would
P. L. 11, 321. among these pines his v. I heard
P. L. 12, 235. but the v. of God to mortal ear
P. L. 12, 265. man's v. commanding
P. R. 1, 18. with a v. more awful than the
P. R. 1, 31. while the Father's v. from heaven
P. R. 1, 35. and with the v. divine
P. R. 1, 84. the Sovran v. I heard
P. R. 1, 172. sung with the v.
P. R. 1, 275. and with loudest v. proclaimed
P. R. 1, 283. the sum of all my Father's v.
P. R. 1, 490. and vouchsafed his v. to Balaam
P. R. 2, 85. from heaven by his Father's v.
P. R. 2, 314. fed twice by a v. inviting him to
P. R. 4, 256. and numbers hit by v. or hand
P. R. 4, 512 by v. from heaven heard thee
P. R. 4, 539. Son of God by v. from heaven
P. R. 4, 627. thee with the terror of his v.
S.A. 1065. look now for no enchanting v. nor fear
C. 492. what v. is that?
C. 563. too well I did perceive it was the v.
A. 77. if my inferior hand or v. could hit
L. 132. return Alpheus the dread v. is past
L'A. 142. the melting v. through mazes running
S. 20, 11. hear the lute well touched or artful v.
H. 27. and join thy v. unto the Angel choir
H. 96. divinely-warbled v.
H. 174. no v. or hideous hum
H. 183. a v. of weeping heard and loud lament
S. M. 2. harmonious sisters V. and Verse
S. M. 17. that we on earth with undiscording v.
**Voices.**—P. L. 1, 712. symphonies and v. sweet
P. L. 2, 952. of stunning sounds and v. all
P. L. 3, 347. sweet as from blest v. uttering joy
P. L. 4, 682. have we heard celestial v.
P. L. 5, 197. join v. all ye living souls ye birds
P. R. 4, 482. so many terrors, v., prodigies

**Void.**—P. L. 1, 181. the seat of desolation *v.*
P. L. 2, 219. the fierce heat and *v.* of pain
P. L. 2, 438. the *v.* profound of unessential night
P. L. 2, 829. and through the *v.* immense
P. L. 3, 12. from the *v.* and formless infinite
P. L. 4, 97. vows made in pain as violent and *v.*
P. L. 6, 415. the dark dislodged and *v.* of rest
P. L. 7, 233. matter unformed and *v.*
P. L. 9, 1074. of honour *v.*, of innocence, of faith
P. L. 10, 50. he presumes already vain and *v.*
P. L. 11, 790. great exploits but of true virtue *v.*
P. L. 12, 427. embrace by faith not *v.* of works
P. R. 3, 442. that made *v.* all his wiles
P. R. 4, 189. wert thou so *v.* of fear or shame
S. A. 616. though *v.* of corporal sense
**Volant.**—P. L. 11, 561. his *v.* touch instinct
**Volatile.**—P. L. 3, 603. they bind *v.* Hermes
**Volley.**—P. L. 6, 854. his thunder in mid *v.*
**Volleys.**—P. L. 6, 213. in flaming *v.*
**Vollied.**—P. L. 4, 928. the blasting *v.* thunder
**Voluble.**—P. L. 4, 594. or this less *v.* earth
P. L. 9, 436. then *v.* and bold now
S. A. 1307. his message will be short and *v.*
**Volumes.**—S. 21, 3. in his *v.* taught our laws
**Voluminous.**—P. L. 2, 652. fold *v.* and vast
P. R. 4, 384. by what the stars *v.* or single
**Voluntary.**—P. L. 3, 37. on thoughts that *v*
P. L. 5, 529. our *v.* service he requires not
P. L. 10, 61. both ransom and Redeemer *v.*
P. R. 2, 394. if of that power I bring thee *v.*
**Voluptuous.**—P. L. 2, 869. right hand *v.*
P. R. 2, 165. enerve and with *v* hope dissolve
S. A. 534. softened with pleasure and *v.* life
**Vomit.**—C. 655. like the sons of Vulcan *v.* smoke
**Votarist.**—C. 189. like a sad *v.* in palmer's weed
**Vote.**—P. L. 2, 313. for so the popular *v.* inclines
P. L. 2, 389. with full assent they *v.*
P. R. 2, 129. I as I undertook and with the *v.*
**Vouched.**—P. L. 5, 66. words *v.* with a deed
**Vouchsafe.**—P. L. 5, 312. and will *v.* this
P. L. 5, 365. *v.* with us two only
P. L. 6, 823. other strife with them do I *v.*

P. R. 2, 210. leisure will *v.* an eye of fond
**Vouchsafed.**—P. L. 2, 332. none *v.* or sought
P. L. 3, 175. in him but grace in me freely *v.*
P. L. 5, 463. lowly roof thou hast *v.* to enter
P. L. 5, 884. indulgent laws will not be now *v.*
P. L. 7, 80. but since thou hast *v.* gently
P. L. 8, 8. and *v.* this friendly condescension to
P. L. 8, 581. think the same *v.* to cattle and
P. L. 11, 318. where he *v.* presence Divine
P. L. 12, 622. such favour I unworthy am *v.*
P. R. 1, 490. and *v.* his voice to Balaam
**Vouchsafes.**—P. L. 11, 877. that God *v.* to
P. L. 12, 120. God the Most High *v.* to call
P. L. 12, 246. that he *v.* among them to set up
**Vouchsafest.**—P. L. 11, 170. to entitle me *v.*
**Vow.**—S. A. 319. against his *v.* of stictest purity
S. A. 379. under pledge of *v.* and have betrayed
S. A. 1144. the pledge of my unviolated *v.*
S. A. 1386. or stain my *v.* of Nazarite
U. C. II. 19. *v.* though the cross doctors all stood
**Vowed.**—C. 136. and befriend us thy *v.* priests
Hor. 13. me in my *v.* picture
**Vowing.**—P. R. 1, 490. praying or *v.*
**Vows.**—P. L. 1, 441. paid their *v.* and songs
P. L. 4, 97. ease would recant *v.* made in pain
P. L. 11, 493. though oft invoked with *v.*
S. A. 520. with prayers and *v.* renewed
S. A. 750. to break all faith all *v.* deceive betray
A. 6. this, this is she to whom our *v.* and wishes
L. 159. or whether thou to our moist *v.* denied
F. of C. 2. and with stiff *v.* renounced his liturgy
**Voyage.**—P. L. 2, 426. alone the dreadful *v.*
P. L. 2, 919. and looked awhile pondering his *v.*
P. L. 7, 431. the prudent crane her annual *v.*
P. L. 8, 230. bound on a *v.* uncouth and obscure
P. R. 1, 103. a calmer *v.* now will waft me
**Voyaged.**—P. L. 10, 471. *v.* the unreal
**Vulcan.**—C. 655 like the sons of *V.* vomit smoke
**Vulgar.**—P. L. 3, 577. the *v.* constellation
P. R. 3, 51. who extol things *v.*
S. A. 1659. the *v.* only scaped who stood without
**Vulture.**—P. L. 3, 431. when a *v.* on Imaus

# W.

**Wades.**—P. L. 2, 950. or sinks or *w.* or creeps
**Waft.**—P. R. 1, 104. calmer voyage now will *w.* me
L. 164. and O ye dolphins *w.* the hapless youth
**Wafted.**—P. L. 3, 521. arrived *w.* by angels
**Wafting.**—P. L. 12, 435. a gentle *w.* to
**Wafts.**—P. L. 2, 1042. and now with ease *w.* on
**Wage.**—P. L. 1, 121. to *w.* by force or guile
**Waged.**—P. L. 2, 534. war appears *w.* in the
**Waggons.**—P. L. 3, 439. their cany *w.* light
P. R. 3, 336. and *w.* fraught with utensils
**Wail.**—S. A. 66. each apart would ask a life to *w.*
S. A. 1721. nothing is here for tears, nothing to *w.*
**Wailing.**—S. A. 806. *w.* thy absence in my
**Wain.**—C. 190. hindmost wheels of Phœbus' *w.*
U. C. II, 32. strange . . . his *w.* was his increase
**Waist.**—P. L. 2, 650. woman to the *w.* and fair
P. L. 4, 304. as a veil down to the slender *w.*
P. L. 5, 281. pair girt like a starry zone his *w.*
P. L. 6, 361. but anon down cloven to the *w.*
P. L. 9, 1113. to gird their *w.* vain covering
**Wait.**—P. L. 2, 55. stand in arms and longing *w.*
P. L. 2, 505. and night for his destruction *w.*
P. L. 3, 485. at heaven's wicket seems to *w.*
P. L. 4, 825. sat'st thou like an enemy in *w.*
P. L. 8, 554. authority and reason on her *w.*
P. L. 9, 1173. the lurking enemy that lay in *w.*
P. R. 2, 49. but let us *w.*
P. R. 2, 102. but I to *w.* with patience am
P. R. 3, 173. on occasion's forelock watchful *w.*
C. 921. to *w.* in Amphitrite's bower
A. 107. yet Syrinx well might *w.* on her
S. 19, 14. they also serve who only stand and *w.*
**Waited.**—P. L. 8, 61. winning graces *w.* still

P. L. 9, 409. *w.* with hellish rancour imminent
P. R. 1, 269. the time prefixed I *w.* when
**Waiting.**—P. L. 1, 604. pride *w.* revenge
P. L. 2, 223. what chance what change worth *w.*
P. L. 9, 191. his sleep disturbed not *w.* close
P. L. 9, 839. Adam the while *w.*
**Waits.**—P. L. 5, 354. pomp that *w.* on princes
**Wake.**—P. L. 4, 678. both when we *w.* and
P. L. 4, 734. when we *w.* and when we seek
S. A. 952. lest fierce remembrance *w.* my sudden
C. 317. I shall know ere morrow *w.*
Il P. 151. and as I *w.* sweet music breathe
**Waked.**—P. L. 5, 3. when Adam *w.*
P. L. 5, 26. such whispering *w.* her but with
P. L. 5, 92. but O how glad I *w.* to find this
P. L. 5, 657. but not so *w.* Satan so call him
P. L. 6, 3. till morn *w.* by the circling hours
P. L. 8, 253. as new *w.* from soundest sleep
P. L. 8, 309. whereat I *w.* and found before
P. L. 8, 478. I *w.* to find her
P. L. 9, 789. and *w.* an eager appetite raised by
P. L. 9, 1061. and *w.* shorn of his strength
P. L. 10, 94. now *w.* and usher in the evening
P. L. 11, 65. in the renovation of the just
P. L. 11, 135. *w.* and with fresh dews embalmed
P. L. 12, 608. ran before but found her *w.*
P. R. 2, 284. he went to sleep and fasting *w.*
S. 23, 14. I *w.* she fled and day brought back my
**Wakeful.**—P. L. 2, 946. against a *w.* foe
P. L. 2, 946. had from his *w.* custody
P. L. 3, 38. as the *w.* bird sings darkling
P. L. 4, 602. all but the *w.* nightingale
P. L. 11, 131. and more *w.* than to drowse

H. 156. the _w._ trump of doom must thunder
**Waken.**—P. L. 3, 369. _w._ raptures high
P. L. 12,594. we may no longer stay, go _w._ Eve
**Wakens.**—C. 124. Venus now wakes and _w._ love
**Wakes.**—P. L. 4, 23._w._ despair that slumbered, _w._
P. L. 5, 44. heaven _w._ with all his eyes
P. L. 5, 110. oft in her absence mimic fancy _w._
C. 121. their merry _w._ and pastimes keep
C. 124. Venus now _w._ and wakens love
**Wakest.**—P. L. 11, 368. thou to foresight _w._
**Waking.**—P. L. 3, 515. and _w._ cried this is
P. L. 5, 14. beheld beauty which whether _w._
P. L. 5, 121. _w._ thou never wilt consent to do
P. L. 5, 678. both _w._ we were one how then
P. R. 1, 311. nor sleeping him nor _w._ harmed
C. 263. such sober certainty of _w._ bliss
**Walk.**—P. L. 2, 1007. if that way be your _w._
P. L. 4, 528. first with narrow search I must _w._
P. L. 4, 627. our _w._ at noon
P. L. 4, 655. _w._ by moon or glittering starlight
P. L. 4, 677. millions of spiritual creatures _w._
P. L. 4, 685. or nightly rounding _w._
P. L. 5, 36. at mine ear one called me forth to _w._
P. L. 5, 49. to find thee I directed then my _w._
P. L. 5, 200. in waters glide and ye that _w._
P. L. 6, 627. they show us when our foes _w._
P. L. 9, 246. as wide as we need _w._ till younger
P. L. 9, 434. nearer he drew and many a _w._
P. L. 11, 707. to _w._ with God high in salvation
P. L. 12, 562. to _w._ as in his presence ever
P. R. 1, 311. his _w._ the fiery serpent fled
P. R. 1, 478. the ways of truth and rough to _w._
P. R. 2, 153. set women in his eye and in his _w._
P. R. 2, 261. the Son communed in silent _w._
S. A. 296. if any be they _w._ obscure
S. A. 1530. over heaps of slaughtered _w._ his way
Il P. 65. and missing thee I _w._ unseen
Il P. 156. to _w._ the studious cloisters pale
S. 11, 7. while one might _w._ to Mile-End Green
V. Ex. 66. from eyes of mortals _w._ invisible
**Walked.**—P. L. 1, 295. his spear he _w._ with
P. L. 3, 430. here _w._ the fiend at large
P. L. 3, 441. the fiend _w._ up and down alone
P. L. 7, 443. others on ground _w._ firm
P. L. 7, 459. in pairs they rose they _w._
P. L. 7,503. beast was flown, was swum, was _w._
P. L. 8, 264. that lived and moved and _w._
P. L. 9, 114. with what delight could I have _w._
P. L. 11,581. they on the plain long had not _w._
P. R. 1, 189. one day forth _w._ alone the Spirit
S. A. 343. equivalent to angels _w._ their streets
S. A. 530. like a petty god I _w._ about admired
S. A. 1089. of whom such noise hath _w._ about
L. 173. the dear might of him that _w._ the waves
S. 11, 3. the subject new it _w._ the town awhile
**Walking.**—P. L. 10, 98. they heard now _w._
P. R. 4, 447. him _w._ on a sunny hill he found
L'A. 57. some time _w._ not unseen
**Walks.**—P. L. 3, 422. Satan alighted _w._
P. L. 3, 683. the only evil that _w._ invisible
P. L. 4, 586. but if within the circuit of these _w._
P. L. 5, 351. meet his godlike guest _w._ forth
P. L. 8, 305. with goodliest trees planted with _w._
P. L. 8,528. herbs fruits and flowers _w._ and the
P. L. 9, 1107. and echoing _w._ between
P. L. 11, 11. be toilsome in these pleasant _w._
P. L. 11, 270. these happy _w._ and shades
P. L. 12, 49. and through their habitations _w._
P. R. 2, 293. high-roofed and _w._ beneath
P. R. 4, 243. or suburban studious _w._
C. 211. the virtuous mind that ever _w._ attended
C. 314. my daily _w._ and ancient neighbourhood
C. 384. benighted _w._ under the mid-day sun
C. 432. some say no evil thing that _w._ by night
Il P. 133. bring to arched _w._ of twilight groves
**Wall.**—P. L. 3, 71. the _w._ of heaven on this
P. L. 3, 427. which from the _w._ of heaven
P. L. 3, 503. up to the _w._ of heaven
P. L. 4, 143. _w._ of paradise up-sprung
P. L. 4, 146. and higher than that _w._ a circling
P. L. 4, 182. all bound of hill or highest _w._

P. L. 4, 697. fenced up the verdant _w._ each
P. L. 6, 860. to the bounds and crystal _w._ of
P. L. 7, 293. part rise in crystal _w._ or ridge
P. L. 9, 16. thrice fugitive about Troy _w._
P. L. 10, 302. joining to the _w._
P. L. 11, 657. from the _w._ defend with dart
P. R. 3, 275. of length within her _w._ several
D. F. I. 47. did of late earth's sons besiege the _w._
Hor. 14. the sacred _w._ declares to have hung
**Walled.**—P. R. 2, 22. and each town or city _w._
**Wallowing.**—P. L. 7, 411. _w._ unwieldy
**Walls.**—P. L. 2, 343. whose high _w._ fear no
P. L. 2, 1035. and from the _w._ of heaven shoots
P. L. 3, 721. the rest in circuit _w._ this universe
P. L. 10, 423. retired about the _w._ of
P. L. 11, 387. the destined _w._ Cambalu
P. L. 12, 197. dry land between two crystal _w._
P. L. 12, 342. whose high _w._ thou saw'st left
P. R. 4, 250. within the _w._ then view the
S. 8, 14. the power to save the Athenian _w._
**Wan.**—P. L. 4, 870. but faded splendour _w._
P. L. 10, 412. the blasted stars looked _w._
L. 147. cowslips _w._ that hang the pensive head
S. 13, 6. with praise enough for envy to look _w._
**Wand.**—P. L. 1, 294. were but a _w._
P. L. 3, 644. before his decent steps a silver _w._
C. 614. he with his bare _w._ can unthread thy
C. 653. but seize his _w._ though he and his cursed
C. 659. nay lady sit; if I but wave this _w._
C. 815. should have snatched his _w._ and bound
H. 51. and waving wide her myrtle _w._
**Wander.**—P. L. 1, 501. then _w._ forth the sons
P. L. 2, 148. those thoughts that _w._
P. L. 3, 27. not the more cease I to _w._ where the
P. L. 3, 458. till final dissolution _w._ here
P. L. 7, 20. erroneous there to _w._ and forlorn
P. L. 7, 330. where gods might dwell or _w._
P. L. 11, 282. and whither _w._ down into a
C. 351. may she _w._ now whither betake her
L. 185. to all that _w._ in that perilous flood
**Wandered.**—P. L. 3, 499. _w._ till at last a
P. R. 1, 354. without food _w._ this barren waste
D. F. I. 17. he _w._ long till thee he spied from far
**Wanderer.**—C. 524. here to every thirsty _w._
**Wandering.**—P. L. 1, 365. till _w._ o'er the
P. L. 1, 481. their _w._ gods disguised in brutish
P. L. 2, 404. who shall tempt with _w._ feet
P. L. 2, 523. and _w._ each his several way pursues
P. L. 2, 561. and found no end in _w._ mazes
P. L. 2, 830. to search with _w._ quest a place
P. L. 2, 973. but by constraint _w._ this darksome
P. L. 3, 631. to find who might direct his _w._
P. L. 3, 667. choirs of cherubim alone thus _w._
P. L. 4, 234. _w._ many a famous realm
P. L. 4, 531. where I may meet some _w._ spirit
P. L. 5, 177. and ye fire other _w._ fires
P. L. 7, 50. to please their appetite though _w._
P. L. 7, 302. with serpent error _w._ found
P. L. 8, 126. their _w._ course now high now low
P. L. 8, 187. we ourselves seek them with _w._
P. L. 8, 312. here had new begun my _w._
P. L. 9, 634. _w._ fire compact of unctuous vapour
P. L. 9, 1136. desire of _w._ this unhappy morn
P. L. 9, 1146. or will of _w._ as thou call'st it
P. L. 10, 875. had not thy pride and _w._ vanity
P. L. 11, 779. _w._ that watery desert
P. L. 12, 133. not _w._ poor but trusting all his
P. L. 12, 334. till then in tents _w._
P. L. 12, 648. they hand in hand with _w._ steps
P. R. 2, 246. _w._ this woody maze
P. R. 2, 313. native of Thebez _w._ here was fed
P. R. 4, 600. and human form _w._ the wilderness
S. A. 302. then give the reins to _w._ thought
S. A. 675. that _w._ loose about
C. 39. threats the forlorn and _w._ passenger
C. 193. they had engaged their _w._ steps too far
C. 1006. after her _w._ labours long
Il P. 67. to behold the _w._ moon
V.Ex.53. but fie my _w._ muse how thou dost stray
**Wannish.**—P. 35. a _w._ white
**Want.**—P. L. 1, 715. nor did there _w._ cornice

P. L. 2, 272. nor w. we skill or art from whence
P. L. 2, 341. nor will occasion w. nor shall we
P. L. 2, 806. would full soon devour for w. of
P. L. 4, 676. heaven would w. spectators God w.
P. L. 5, 365. places thou hast deigned a while to w.
P. L. 5, 514. can we w. obedience then to him
P. L. 9, 755. by thee communicated and our w.
P. L. 12, 396. fulfilling that which thou didst w.
P. R. 1, 331. constrained by w. come forth to town
P. R. 2, 331. who would scruple that with w.
P. R. 2. 431. virtue valour wisdom sit in w.
S. A. 289. for w. of well pronouncing Shibboleth
S. A. 905. w. of words no doubt or lack of breath
S. A. 916. other senses w. not their delights
S. A. 1484. not wanting him I shall w. nothing
C. 369. as that the single w. of light and noise
C. 768. if every just man that now pines with w.
**Wanted.**—P. L. 4, 338. endearing smiles w.
P. L. 4, 989. nor w. in his grasp what seemed
P. L. 5, 147. nor holy rapture w.
P. L. 7, 505. there w. yet the master-work
P. L. 8, 355. I found not what methought I w.
P. L. 9, 601. and speech w. not long though
P. R. 3, 327. nor w. clouds of foot nor on each
S. A. 315. he would not else who never w. means
C. 689. and timely rest have w. but fair virgin
**Wanting.**—P. L. 1, 556. w. power to mitigate
P. L. 9, 199. to the choir of creatures w. voice
P. L. 10, 271. nor shall I to the work,.. be w.
P. R. 2, 450. and what in me seems w.
S. A. 1484. not w. him I shall want nothing
**Wanton.**—P. L. 1, 414. to do him w. rites
P. L. 1, 454. whose w. passions in the sacred
P. L. 4, 306. but in w. ringlets waved as the
P. L. 4, 629. to lop their w. growth
P. L. 4, 768. mixed dance or w. mask
P. L. 9, 211, one night or two with w. growth
P. L. 9, 517. many a w. wreath in sight of Eve
P. L. 11, 583. richly gay in gems and w. dress
P. R. 2, 180. cast w. eyes on the daughters of men
C. 176. in w. dance they praise ... Pan
A. 47. with ringlets quaint and w. windings
L. 137. of shades and w. winds and gushing
L'A. 27. quips and cranks and w. wiles
L'A. 141. with w. heed and giddy cunning
H. 36. to w. with the sun her lusty paramour
D. F. I. 14. which, 'mongst the w. gods
**Wantoned.**—P. L. 5, 295. here w. as in her prime
**Wantonly.**—P. L. 9, 1015. she him as w.
**Wantonness.**—P. L. 11, 795. till w. and
**Wants.**—P. L. 2, 271. this desert soil w. not
P. L. 4, 730. where thy abundance w.
P. L. 5, 348. nor these to hold w. her fit
P. L. 7, 98. yet w. to run much of his race
P. L. 8, 296. thy mansion w. thee Adam rise
P. L. 9, 821. so to add what w. in female sex
P. L. 10, 869. nothing w. but that thy shape
**War.**—P. L. 1, 43. raised impious w. in heaven
P. L. 1, 121. wage by force or guile eternal w.
P. L. 1, 129. led the embattled seraphim to w.
P. L. 1, 150. as his thralls by right of w.
P. L. 1, 645. or dread new w. provoked
P. L. 1, 661. then w. open or understood must
P. L. 1, 668. their sounding shields the din of w.
P. L. 2, 9. to pursue vain w. with heaven
P. L. 2, 41. of open w. or covert guile
P. L. 2, 51. my sentence is for open w. covert guile
P. L. 2, 119. I should be much for open w.
P. L. 2, 121. reason to persuade immediate w.
P. L. 2, 160. say they who counsel w.
P. L. 2, 179. designing or exhorting glorious w.
P. L. 2, 187. therefore open or concealed
P. L. 2, 230. the King of heaven we w., if w.
P. L. 2, 283. dismissing quite all thoughts of w.
P. L. 2, 329. projecting peace and w.? w. hath
P. L. 2, 533. as when to warn proud cities w.
P. L. 2, 711. hair shakes pestilence and w.
P. L. 2, 767. w. arose and fields were fought in
P. L. 4, 817. to store against a rumoured w.
P. L. 6, 19. w. he perceived w. in procinct
P. L. 6, 92. that angel should with angel w.

P. L. 6, 236. to close the ridges of grim w.
P. L. 6, 242. was spread that w. and various
P. L. 6, 259. as hoping here to end intestine w.
P. L. 6, 274. not the works of violence and w.
P. L. 6, 312. among the constellations w. were
P. L. 6, 339. stood retired from off the files of w.
P. L. 6, 377. though wondrous and in acts of w.
P. L. 6, 408. on the odious din of w.
P. L. 6, 506. on w. and mutual slaughter bent
P. L. 6, 667. w. seemed a civil game to this
P. L. 6, 695. w. wearied hath performed what w.
P. L. 6, 702. of ending this great w.
P. L. 6, 712. bring forth all my w. my bow
P. L. 6, 897. the discord which befell and w.
P. L. 7, 55. and w. so near the peace of God
P. L. 10, 374. wisdom gained with odds what w.
P. L. 10, 710. beast now with beast gan w.
P. L. 11, 219. had levied w., w. unproclaimed
P. L. 11, 641. fierce faces threatening w.
P. L. 11, 713. the brazen throat of w. had ceased
P. L. 11, 780. when violence was ceased and w.
P. L. 11, 784. peace to corrupt no less than w.
P. L. 11, 797. conquered also and enslaved by w.
P. L. 12, 31. with w. and hostile snare
P. L. 12, 214, return and overwhelm their w.
P. L. 12, 218. w. terrify them inexpert
P. R. 3, 17. that might require the array of w.
P. R. 3, 90. without ambition w. or violence
P. R. 3, 336. fraught with utensils of w.
P. R. 3, 388. much instrument of w.
P. R. 3, 401. or that cumbersome luggage of w.
S. A. 1278. and feats of w. defeats with plain
S. 15, 10. for what can w. but endless w. still breed
S. 16, 2. not of w. only but detractions rude
S. 16, 11. her victories no less renowned than w.
S. 17, 7. then to advise how w. may best upheld
H. 53. now w. or battle's sound
V. Ex. 86. devouring w. shall never cease
**Warble.**—P. L. 5, 195. and ye that w. as ye
L'A. 134, w. his native wood-notes wild
S. 20, 12. w. immortal notes and Tuscan air
**Warbled.**—P. L. 2, 242. throne with w. hymns
C. 855. if she be right invoked in w. song
A. 87. and touch the w. string
Il P. 106. such notes as w. to the string
**Warblest.**—S. 1, 2. w. at eve when all the
**Warbling.**—P. L. 3, 31. and w. flow
P. L. 5, 196. melodious murmurs w. tune his
P. L. 7, 436. ceased w. but all night tuned her
P. L. 8, 265. birds on the branches w. all things
S. A. 934. thy fair enchanted cup and w. charms
L. 189. with eager thought w. his Doric lay
**Wardrobe.**—L. 47. flowers that their gay w.
V. Ex. 18. and from thy w. bring ... treasure
**Wards.**—P. L. 2, 877. turns the intricate w.
**Ware.**—P. L. 9, 353. her well be w. and still
C. 558. was took ere she was w. and wished
**Warfare.**—P. L. 6, 803. hath been your w.
P. R. 1, 158. down the rudiments of his great w.
**Warlike.**—P. L. 1, 531. at the w. sound of
P. L. 4, 780. armed to their night watches in w.
P. L. 4, 902. the w. angel moved disdainfully
P. L. 6, 257. from his w. toil surceased
P. R. 3, 308. see how in w. muster they appear
S. A. 137. in scorn of their proud arms and w. tools
**Warm.**—P. L. 4, 669. influence foment and w.
P. L. 5, 301. to w. earth's inmost womb
P. L. 7, 279. not idle but with w. prolific humour
P. L. 8, 466. thence a rib with cordial spirits w.
P. R. 1, 318. to w. him wet returned from field
M. M. 6. mirth and youth and w. desire
**Warmed.**—P. L. 9, 721. this fair earth I see w.
P. L. 11, 338. by his virtual power and w.
**Warmly.**—P. L. 4, 244. sun first w. smote
**Warms.**—P. L. 3, 583. that gently w. the
S. 8, 8. clime the sun's bright circle w.
**Warmth.**—P. L. 2, 601. their soft ethereal w.
P. L. 5, 302. more w. than Adam needs
P. L. 7, 236. vital virtue infused and vital w.
P. L. 8, 37. incorporeal speed her w. and light
P. L. 10, 1068. some better w. to cherish our

P. R. 2, 74. a stable was our *w.* a manger his
**Warn.**—P. L. 2, 533. when to *w.* proud cities
P. L. 5, 237. whence *w.* him to beware
P. L. 6, 908. *w.* thy weaker
P. L. 8, 327. remember what I *w.* thee
P. L. 10, 871. to *w.* all creatures from thee
P. L. 11, 195. or to *w.* us haply too secure of
P. L. 11, 777. man is not whom to *w.*
P. R. 4, 483. may *w.* thee as a sure foregoing
**Warned.**—P. L. 3, 185. oft be *w.* their sinful
P. L. 4, 6. our first parents had been *w.* the
P. L. 4, 125. to deceive Uriel once *w.*
P. L. 4, 467. had not a voice thus *w.* me what
P. L. 6, 547. so *w.* he them aware themselves
P. L. 8, 190. till *w.* or by experience taught
P. L. 9, 253. know'st what hath been *w.* us
P. L. 9, 363. strictest watch as she was *w.*
P. L. 9, 371. find us both securer than thus *w.*
P. L. 9, 1171. what could I more I *w.* thee
P. R. 1, 26. Baptist soon descried divinely *w.*
P. R. 1, 255. Simeon and prophetic Anna *w.*
S. A. 382. but *w.* by oft experience
H. 74. or Lucifer that often *w.* them thence
**Warning.**—P. L. 4, 1. O for that *w.* voice
**Warping.**—P. L. 1, 341. *w.* on the eastern
**Warrant.**—S. A. 1426. I cannot *w.*
**Warranted.**—C. 327. in a place less *w.* than this
**Warred**—P. L. 1, 198. thus *w.* on Jove
P. L. 1, 576. small infantry *w.* on by cranes
**Warring.**—P. L. 2, 905. to side with *w.* winds
P. L. 3, 396. the necks drov'st of *w.* angels
P. L. 4, 41. *w.* in heaven against heaven's
P. L. 5, 566. the invisible exploits of *w.* spirits
P. L. 6, 225. to raise dreadful combustion *w.*
**Warrior.** P. L. 4, 576. *w.* thus returned
P. L. 4, 946. to whom the *w.* angel soon
P. L. 6, 233. yet leader seemed each *w.* single
S. A. 542. which many a famous *w.* overturns
S. A. 1166. nor by the sword of noble *w.*
**Warriors.**—P. L. 1, 316. *w.* the flower of heaven
P. L. 1, 565. in guise of *w.* old with ordered spear
P. L. 6, 537. arm *w.*, arm for fight
P. L. 11, 101. thy choice of flaming *w.* lest the
P. L. 11, 662. men and grave with *w.* mixed
S. A. 139. old *w.* turned their plated backs
Cir. 1. and winged *w.* bright
**Wars.**—P. L. 2, 501. cruel *w.* wasting the earth
P. L. 2, 897. of endless *w.* and by confusion
P. L. 9, 28. not sedulous by nature to indite *w.*
**Wary.**—P. L. 2, 917. the *w.* fiend stood on the
P. L. 5, 159. and his *w.* speech thus to the
**Wash.**—P. L. 3, 31. that *w.* thy hallowed feet
L.155. *w.* far away where'er thy bones are buried
P. R. 1, 73. consecrated stream pretends to *w.* off
S. A. 1727. *w.* off the clotted gore
**Washed.**—P. L. 10, 215. as when he *w.* his
P. L. 11, 569. or whether *w.* by stream from
P. R. 4, 28. *w.* by the southern sea and on the
L'A. 22. and fresh-blown roses *w.* in dew
S. 23, 5. mine as whom *w.* from spot of child-bed
P. 35. and letters where my tears have *w.*
**Washing.**—P. L. 12, 443. the sign of *w.* them
S. A. 1107. thou hast need much *w.* to be touched
**Washy.**—P. L. 7, 303. and on the *w.* ooze
**Wassailers.**—C. 179. insolence of such late *w.*
**Waste.**—P. L. 1, 60. the dismal situation *w.*
P. L. 2, 365. either with hell fire to *w.* his whole
P. L. 2, 695. are here condemned to *w.* eternal
P. L. 2, 1045. or in the emptier *w.* resembling
P. L. 3, 424, dark *w.* and wild under the frown
P. L. 4, 538. began through wood, through *w.*
P. L. 10, 282. into the *w.* wide anarchy of Chaos
P. L. 10, 434. leaves all *w.* beyond the realm
P. L. 10, 617. to *w.* and havoc yonder world
P. L. 10, 820. O were I able to *w.* it all myself
P. L. 11, 784. to corrupt no less than war to *w.*
P. L. 11, 791. and done much *w.* subduing
P. R. 1, 7. and Eden raised in the *w.* wilderness
P. R. 1, 354. wandered this barren *w.* the same
P. R. 3, 283. led captive and Jerusalem laid *w.*
P. R. 4, 123. but tedious *w.* of time to sit

P. R. 4, 523. and followed thee still on to this *w.*
C. 403. uninjured in this wild surrounding *w.*
C. 729. and strangled with her *w.* fertility
C. 942. not a *w.* or needless sound
S. 12, 14. for all this *w.* of wealth and loss of blood
S. 20, 4. and by the fire help *w.* a sullen day
**Wasted.**—P. L. 11, 567. fire had *w.* woods
P. R. 3, 102. his *w.* country freed from Punic
P. R. 3, 302. whose incursions wild have *w.*
**Wasteful.**—P. L. 2, 961. on the *w.* deep
P. L. 6, 862. gap disclosed into the *w.* deep
P. L. 7, 212. outrageous as a sea dark *w.* wild
P. L. 10, 620. the folly of man let in these *w.*
P. R. 4, 461. on man, beast, plant. *w.* and
**Wasting.**—P. L. 2, 502. *w.* the earth, each
P. L. 11, 487. marasmus and wide *w.* pestilence
P. R. 2, 256. without this body's *w.* I content
**Watch.**—P. L. 1, 332. men wont to *w.* on duty
P. L. 2, 130. of heaven are filled with armed *w.*
P. L. 2, 462. intermit no *w.* against a wakeful
P. L. 4, 406. rising changes oft his couchant *w.*
P. L. 4, 562. lot hath given charge and strict *w.*
P. L. 4, 685. while they keep *w.* or nightly
P. L. 4, 783. coast the south with strictest *w.*
P. L. 5, 288. all the bands of angels under *w.*
P. L. 7, 106. and sleep listening to thee will *w.*
P. L. 7, 409. in jointed armour *w.*
P. L. 9, 62. the cherubim that kept their *w.*
P. L. 9, 68. or cherubic *w.* by stealth found
P. L. 9, 156. and flaming ministers to *w.* and
P. L. 9, 363. not keeping strictest *w.* as she
P. L. 9, 814. from continual *w.*
P. L. 10, 427. there kept their *w.* the legions
P. L. 10, 438. reduced in careful *w.* round
P. L. 10, 594. dark threshold to have sat *w.*
P. L. 11, 120. cherubic *w.*
P. L. 12, 207. defends between till morning *w.*
P. L. 12, 365. shepherds keeping *w.* by night
C. 89. and in this office of his mountain *w.*
C. 543. I sat me down to *w.* upon a bank
H. 21. and all the spangled host keep *w.*
**Watched.**—P. L. 11, 73. minister that *w.*
P. R. 4, 408. for at his head the tempter *w.*
P. R. 4, 522. therefore I *w.* thy footsteps from
**Watches.**—P. L. 4, 780. to their night *w.*
P. L. 6, 412. placed in guard their *w.* round
P. L. 9, 257. where nigh at hand *w.* no doubt
C. 347. count the night *w.* to his feathery dames
**Watchful.**—P. L. 5, 104. the five *w.* senses
P. L. 9, 311. in thy sight more wise more *w.*
P. L. 11, 128. with him the cohort bright of *w.*
P. R. 3, 173. but on occasion's forelock *w.*
C. 113. who in their nightly *w.* spheres
Cir. 3. first heard by happy *w.* shepherds' ear
V. Ex. 40. the spheres of *w.* fire
**Watching.**—P. L. 2, 413. of angels *w.* round
P. L. 4, 185. *w.* where shepherds pen their
P. L. 4, 826. here *w.* at the head of these that
P. R. 1, 244. to shepherds *w.* at their folds by
S. A. 232. still *w.* to oppress Israel's oppressors
**Watch-tower.**—L'A. 43. from his *w.-t* in the
**Water.**—P. L. 2, 612. the *w.* flies all taste of
P. L. 7, 502. air *w.* earth by fowl fish beast
P. L. 11, 279. and *w.* from the ambrosial fount
P. L. 11, 749. their pomp deep under *w.* rolled
P. R. 1, 81. on him rising out of the *w.*
P. R. 2, 124. powers of fire air *w.* and earth
P. R. 4, 412. *w.* with fire in ruin reconciled
C. 833. the *w.* nymphs that in the bottom played
**Watered.**—P. L. 4, 230. many a rill *w.* the
P. L. 7, 334. a dewy mist went up and *w.* all
P. R. 4, 277. streams that *w.* all the schools
**Watering.**—P. L. 10, 1090. with tears *w.*
P. L. 10, 1102. with tears *w.* the ground
**Waters.**—P. L. 3, 11. of *w.* dark and deep
P. L. 4, 260. *w.* fall down the slope hills
P. L. 4, 454. sound of *w.* issued from a cave
P. L. 5, 200. ye that in *w.* glide, and ye that
P. L. 5, 872. and as the sound of *w.* deep
P. L. 6, 196. winds under ground or *w.* forcing
P. L. 6, 645. rocks *w.* woods

P. L. 7, 262. there be firmament amid the w.
P. L. 7, 263. let it divide the w. from the w.
P. L. 7, 268. the w. underneath from those
P. L. 7, 270. built on circumfluous w. calm
P. L. 7, 277. but in the womb as yet of w.
P. L. 7, 283. be gathered now ye w. under
P. L. 7, 290. and deep capacious bed of w.
P. L. 7, 308. of congregated w. he called seas
P. L. 7, 387. and God said let the w. generate
P. L. 7, 393. the w. generated by their kinds
P. L. 7, 397. lakes and running streams the w.
P. L. 7, 446. the w. thus with fish replenished
P. L. 8, 301. and over fields and w. as in air
P. L. 10, 285. hovering upon the w. what
P. L. 11, 79. by the w. of life where'er they
S. A. 1647. as with the force of winds and w. pent
C. 896. whilst from off the w. fleet
C. 993. w. the odorous banks that blow
Il P. 144. and the w. murmuring
H. 65. smoothly the w. kissed
**Watery.**—P. L. 1, 397, Rabba and her w.
P. L. 2, 584. of oblivion rolls her w. labyrinth
P. L. 4, 461. a shape within the w. gleam
P. L. 4, 480. amiably mild than that smooth w.
P. L. 7, 234. but on the w. calm his brooding
P. L. 7, 297. so the w. throng wave rolling after
P. L. 8, 346. of fish within their w. residence
P. L. 11, 779. wandering that w. desert
P. L. 11, 844. the clear sun on his wide w. glass
P. L. 11, 882. the fluid skirts of that same w.
L. 12. he must not float upon his w. bier
L. 167. sunk though he be beneath the w. floor
**Wattled.**—C. 344. flocks penned in their w. cotes
**Wave.**—P. L. 1, 193. head uplift above the w.
P. L. 2, 1042. wafts on the calmer w.
P. L. 3, 539. as bound the ocean w.
P. L. 5, 193. and w. your tops ye pines
P. L. 5, 194. every plant in sign of worship w.
P. L. 5, 687. all who under me their banners w.
P. L. 7, 298. watery throng, w. rolling after w.
P. L. 7, 402. glide under the green w.
P. L. 9, 496. not with indented w.
P. L. 11, 845. and of the fresh w. largely drew
C. 659. nay lady sit if I but w. this wand
C. 861. under the glassy cool translucent w.
C. 887. and bridle in thy headlong w.
Il P. 148. w. at his wings in aery stream
H. 68. of calm sit brooding on the charmed w.
H. 231. pillows his chin upon an orient w.
**Waved.**—P. L. 1, 340. w. round the coast
P. L. 4, 306. but in wanton ringlets w.
P. L. 6, 304. now w. their fiery swords and in
P. L. 7, 406. show to the sun their w. coats
P. L. 7, 476. those w. their limber fans for
P. L. 12, 643. their happy seat w. over by that
**Waver.**—S. A. 456. to w. or fall off and join with
**Wavering.**—S. A. 732. and w. resolution
C. 116. now to the moon in w. morrice move
**Waves.**—P. L. 1, 184. tossing of these fiery w.
P. L. 1, 306. whose w. o'erthrew Busiris
P. L. 2, 581. whose w. of torrent fire inflame
P. L. 4, 764. and w. his purple wings
P. L. 7, 214. and surging w. as mountains
P. L. 7, 216. silence ye troubled w.
P. L. 10, 311. many a stroke the indignant w.
P. L. 11, 747. rode tilting o'er the w.
P. L. 11, 830. by might of w. be moved out of
P. L. 12, 213. on their embattled ranks the w.
P. L. 12, 593. in signal of remove w. fiercely
P. R. 4, 18. or surging w. against a solid rock
C. 258. and chid her barking w. into attention
C. 924. may thy brimmed w. for this
L. 91. he asked the w. and asked the felon winds
L. 173. the dear might of him that walked the w.
H. 124. and bid the weltering w.
V. Ex. 44. heaven's defiance mustering all his w.
**Waving.**—P. L. 1, 348. w. to direct their course
P. L. 1, 546. with orient colours w.
P. L. 3, 628. lay w. round
P. L. 4, 981. ripe for harvest w. bends her
P. L. 6, 413. cherubic w. fires

P. L. 6, 580. in his hand a reed stood w.
S. A. 718. sails filled and streamers w.
S. A. 1493. on his shoulders w. down those locks
C. 88. and hush the w. woods
H. 51. and w. wide her myrtle wand
**Waxen.**—P. L. 7, 491. and builds her w. cells
**Waying.**—P. L. 4, 969. but w. more in rage
C. 1000. w. well of his deep wound
**Way.**—P. L. 1, 621. with sighs found out their w.
P. L. 2, 40. and by what best w. whether of open
P. L. 2, 62. high towers to force resistless w.
P. L. 2, 71. but perhaps the w. seems difficult
P. L. 2, 83. some worse w. his wrath may find
P. L. 2, 134. or could we break our w. by force
P. L. 2, 407. find out his uncouth w. or spread
P. L. 2, 432. long is the w. and hard that out
P. L. 2, 523. and wandering each his several w.
P. L. 2, 683. thy miscreated front athwart my w.
P. L. 2, 782. breaking violent w.
P. L. 2, 949. wings or feet pursues his w.
P. L. 2, 958. which w. the nearest coast of
P. L. 2, 973. as my w. lies through your
P. L. 2, 1007. if that w. be your walk you have
P. L. 2, 1016. sides round environed wins his w.
P. L. 2, 1026. after him a broad and beaten w.
P. L. 3, 87. restraint broke loose he wings his w.
P. L. 3, 228. not find means that finds her w.
P. L. 3, 437. but in his w. lights on the barren
P. L. 3, 564. pure marble air his oblique w.
P. L. 3, 618. whence no w. round shadow from
P. L. 3, 735. thy w. thou canst not miss me
P. L. 4, 73. me miserable which w. shall I fly
P. L. 4, 75. which w. I fly is hell myself am
P. L. 4, 126. whose eye pursued him down the w.
P. L. 4, 174. but further w. found none so thick
P. L. 4, 177. of man or beast that passed that w.
P. L. 4, 567. I described his w. bent all on speed
P. L. 4, 777. half w. up hill this vast sublunar
P. L. 4, 867. tread of nimble feet hasting this w.
P. L. 4, 889. who would not finding w.
P. L. 4, 982. which w. the wind sways them
P. L. 5, 252. to his speed gave w. through all
P. L. 5, 310. what glorious shape comes this w.
P. L. 5, 508. well hast thou taught the w. that
P. L. 5, 904. long w. through hostile scorn
P. L. 6, 2. heaven's wide champaign held his w.
P. L. 6, 91. proved fond and vain in the mid w.
P. L. 6, 196. under ground or waters forcing w.
P. L. 6, 780. power divine his w. prepared
P. L. 7, 158. open to themselves at length the w.
P. L. 7, 298. wave rolling after wave where w.
P. L. 7, 302. error wandering found their w.
P. L. 7, 426. ranged in figure wedge their w.
P. L. 7, 576. to God's eternal house direct the w.
P. L. 7, 579. seen in the galaxy that milky w.
P. L. 8, 183. taught to live the easiest w.
P. L. 8, 613. leads up to heaven is both the w.
P. L. 9, 69. by stealth found unsuspected w.
P. L. 9, 410. to intercept thy w. or send thee
P. L. 9, 493. the w. which to her ruin now I
P. L. 9, 496. and toward Eve addressed his w.
P. L. 9, 512. sidelong he works his w.
P. L. 9, 550. heart of Eve his words made w.
P. L. 9, 626. empress the w. is ready and not
P. L. 9, 640. night-wanderer from his w.
P. L. 9, 809. thou open'st wisdom's w. and
P. L. 9, 847. the w. she took that morn when
P. L. 9, 853. evil unknown opening the w.
P. L. 10, 262. nor can I miss the w. so strongly
P. L. 10, 267. nor err the w. thou leading
P. L. 10, 291. that stop the imagined w.
P. L. 10, 310. over Hellespont bridging his w.
P. L. 10, 325. and now their w. to earth they
P. L. 10, 397. you two this w. among these
P. L. 10, 414. the other w. Satan went down
P. L. 10, 473. by sin and death a broad w. now
P. L. 10, 844. I find no w. from deep to deeper
P. L. 10, 894. or find some other w. to
P. L. 11, 15. prayers flew up nor missed the w.
P. L. 11, 203. one w. the self-same hour
P. L. 11, 223. where Adam sheltered took his w.

P. L. 11, 462. is this the *w.* I must return
P. L. 11, 527. but is there yet no other *w.*
P. L. 11, 646. one *w.* a band select from forage
P. L. 11, 889. flesh corrupting each their *w.*
P. L. 12, 216. not the readiest *w.*
P. L. 12, 649. Eden took their solitary *w.*
P. R. 1, 104. and the *w.* found prosperous once
P. R. 1, 187. and which *w.* first publish his
P. R. 1, 263. this chiefly that my *w.* must lie
P. R. 1, 272. before Messiah and his *w.* prepare
P. R. 1, 297. the *w.* he came not having marked
P. R. 1, 338. what other *w.* I see not
P. R. 1, 254. satisfy that need some other *w.*
P. R. 2, 291. thither he bent his *w.* determined
P. R. 2, 417. which *w.* or from what hope
P. R. 2, 473. to guide nations in the *w.* of truth
P. R. 3, 348. and not every *w.* secure
P. R. 4, 70. where the shadow both *w.* falls
P. R. 4, 206. trial hath indamaged thee no *w.*
P. R. 4, 470. pursue thy *w.* of gaining David's
P. R. 4, 638. brought on his *w.* with joy
S. A. 111. the tread of many feet steering this *w.*
S. A. 481. have made *w.* to some Philistian lords
S. A. 713. comes this *w.* sailing like a stately ship
S. A. 739. though my pardon no *w.* assured
S. A. 756. virtue or weakness which *w.* to assail
S. A. 781. thou showedst me first the *w.*
S. A. 797. no better *w.* I saw than by importuning
S. A. 823. I led the *w.* bitter reproach but true
S. A. 838. the *w.* to raise in me inexpiable hate
S. A. 1015. which *w.* soever men refer it
S. A. 1039. in his *w.* to virtue adverse
S. A. 1049. his *w.* to peace is smooth
S. A. 1072. sumptuous Dalila floating this *w.*
S. A. 1091. the *w.* to know were not to see but
S. A. 1252. some *w.* or other yet farther to afflict
S. A. 1301. for I descry this *w.* some other tending
S. A. 1382. return the *w.* thou camest
S. A. 1530. over heaps of slaughtered walk his *w.*
S. A. 1541. O whither shall I run or which *w.* fly
S. A. 1591. dreadful *w.* thou took'st to thy revenge
C. 36. but their *w.* lies through the perplexed
C. 170. this *w.* the noise was if mine ear be true
C. 183. wearied out with this long *w.*
C. 305. what readiest *w.* would bring me to that
C. 589. of them that pass unweeting by the *w.*
Il P. 70. through the heaven's wide pathless *w.*
S. 9, 2. wisely hast shunned the broad *w.* and the
S. 16, 4. to peace and truth thy glorious *w.* hast
S. 18, 13. who having learned thy *w.* early may fly
S. 21, 10. solid good what leads the nearest *w.*
H. 71. bending one *w.* their precious influence
V. Ex. 54. expectance calls thee now another *w.*
**Way-lay.**—P. R. 2, 185. to *w.-l.* some beauty
**Ways.**—P. L. 1, 26. and justify the *w.* of God
P. L. 2, 574. four *w.* their flying march along
P. L. 3, 46. from the cheerful *w.* of men cut off
P. L. 3, 544. through dark and desert *w.* with
P. L. 3, 680. wise are all his *w.*
P. L. 4, 620. the regard of heaven on all his *w.*
P. L. 4, 934. through *w.* of danger by himself
P. L. 5, 50. methought alone I passed through *w.*
P. L. 8, 119. God to remove his *w.* from human
P. L. 8, 226. inquire gladly into the *w.*
P. L. 8, 373. not their language and their *w.*
P. L. 8, 413. height and depth of thy eternal *w.*
P. L. 8, 433. nor in their *w.* complacence find
P. L. 9, 682. but to trace the *w.* of highest
P. L. 10, 323. three several *w.* in sight to each
P. L. 10, 610. they both betook them several *w.*
P. L. 10, 643. just are thy *w.* righteous are thy
P. L. 10, 1005. and have the power of many *w.*
P. L. 11, 468. of death and many are the *w.*
P. L. 11, 721. and testified against their *w.*
P. L. 11, 812. he of their wicked *w.* shall them
P. L. 12, 110. them to their own polluted *w.*
P. R. 1, 478. hard are the *w.* of truth and rough
S. A. 293. just are the *w.* of God
S. A. 300. yet more there be who doubt his *w.* not
S. A. 1407. so mutable are all the *w.* of men
S. 20, 2. that the fields are dank and *w.* are mire

M. W. 58. for thy hearse to strew the *w.*
U. C. I. 3. or else the *w.* being foul twenty to one
**Weak.**—P. L. 1, 157. to be *w.* is miserable
P. L. 4, 856. against thee, wicked and thence *w.*
P. L. 8, 532. here only *w.* against the charm
P. L. 4, 1012. and shown how light how *w.*
P. L. 9, 1186. she first his *w.* indulgence will
P. L. 11, 540. which will change to withered *w.*
P. L. 12, 291. by those shadowy expiations *w.*
P. L. 12, 567. by things deemed *w.* subverting
P. R. 2, 221. in the admiration only of *w.* minds
P. R. 3, 4. convinced of his *w.* arguing and
V. Ex. 1. hail native language that by sinews *w.*
W. S. 6. what needst thou such *w.* witness of thy
**Weakening.**—P. L. 2, 1002. *w.* the sceptre
**Weaker.**—P. L. 6, 909. warn thy *w.*
P. L. 9, 383. a foe so proud will first the *w.*
Il P. 15. and therefore to our *w.* view
**Weakest.**—P. L. 6, 117. or *w.* prove where
S. A. 56. yet liable to fall by *w.* subtleties
**Weakly.**—S. A. 50. but *w.* to a woman must
S. A. 499. impiously *w.* at least and shamefully
**Weakness.**—P. L. 2, 357. and where their *w.*
P. L. 10, 801. as argument of *w.* not of power
P. R. 1, 161. his *w.* shall overcome Satanic
P. R. 3, 402. argument of human *w.* rather
S. A. 235. vanquished with a peal of words (O *w.*)
S. A. 756. his virtue or *w.* which way to assail
S. A. 773. first granting, as I do, it was a *w.*
S. A. 778. was it not *w.* also to make known
S. A. 785. let *w.* then with *w.* come to parle
S. A. 829. *w.* is thy excuse and I believe it
S. A. 830. *w.* to resist Philistian gold
S. A. 831. if *w.* may excuse what murderer
S. A. 834. all wickedness is *w.* that plea therefore
S. A. 843. since thou determinest *w.* for no plea
S. A. 1722. no *w.* no contempt dispraise or blame
C. 582. against the unarmed *w.* of one virgin
**Weal.**—P. L. 8, 638. the *w.* or woe in thee is
P. L. 9, 133. as to him linked in *w.* or woe
**Wealth.**—P. L. 1, 722. strove in *w.* and
P. L. 2, 2. outshone the *w.* of Ormus and of Ind
P. L. 4, 207. nature's whole *w.*, yea, more
P. L. 11, 788. in triumph and luxurious *w.*
P. L. 12, 133. but trusting all his *w.* with God
P. L. 12, 332. his next son for *w.* and wisdom
P. L. 12, 352. grown in *w.* and multitude
P. R. 2, 202. and full of honour *w.* high fare
P. R. 2, 427. get riches first get *w.* and
R. R. 2, 430. they whom I favour thrive in *w.*
P. R. 2, 433. *w.* without these three is impotent
P. R. 2, 436. of all their flowing *w.* dissolved
P. R. 3, 44. dost persuade me to seek *w.*
P. R. 4, 82. in ample territory *w.* and power
P. R. 4, 305. contemning all *w.* pleasure pain
P. R. 4, 368. since neither *w.* nor honour arms
C. 504. not all the fleecy *w.* that doth enrich
C. 726. as a penurious niggard of his *w.*
S. 12, 14. for all this waste of *w.* and loss of blood
**Weanling.**—L. 46. or taint-worm to the *w.* herds
**Weapon.**—S. A. 142. what trivial *w.* came to hand
S. A. 263. with a trivial *w.* felled their choicest
**Weaponless.**—S. A. 130. and *w.* himself made
**Weapons.**—P. L. 6, 697. *w.* more violent
P. L. 6, 697. with mountains, as with *w.*
P. L. 6, 839. down their idle *w.* dropped
C. 612. far other arms and other *w.* must
**Wear.**—P. L. 4, 740. disguises which we *w.*
C. 26. and gives them leave to *w.* their sapphire
C. 722. and nothing *w.* but frieze
L. 47. frost to flowers that their gay wardrobe *w.*
S. M. 14. with those just spirits that *w.* victorious
S. A. 762. are drawn to *w.* out miserable days
**Wearers.**—P. L. 3, 490. with their *w.* tossed
**Wearied.**—P. L. 1, 320. to repose your *w.* virtue
P. L. 3, 73. ready now to stoop with *w.* wings
P. L. 6, 695. war *w.* hath performed what war
P. L. 9, 1045. oppressed them *w.* with their
P. L. 12, 107. till God at last *w.* with their
P. L. 12, 614. *w.* I fell asleep

P. R. 4, 591. that soon refreshed him *w*.
S. A. 1588. *w*. with slaughter then or how
S. A. 405. to storm me overwatched and *w*. out
C. 182. my brothers when they saw me *w*. out
**Wearing.**—H. 143. rainbow and like glories *w*.
**Wearisome.**—P. R. 4, 322. many books are *w*.
P. L. 2, 247. how *w*. eternity so spent in worship
**Wears.**—P. R. 2, 461. to him who *w*. the regal
L. 148. and every flower that sad embroidery *w*.
M. W. 43. and those pearls of dew she *w*.
**Weary.**—P. L. 11, 310. to *w*. him with my
P. L. 12, 10. must needs impair and *w*. human
S. A. 596. in all her functions *w*. of herself
C. 64. offering to every *w*. traveller
C. 280. they left me *w*. on a grassy turf
Il P. 167. and may at last my *w*. age
V. Ex. 25. and *w*. of their place do only stay
**Weather-beaten.**—P. L. 2, 1043. a *w.-b*.
**Weave.**—C. 716. that in their green shops *w*.
**Weaver.**—S. A. 1122. add thy spear a *w.'s* beam
**Wed.**—P. L. 5, 216. or they led the vine to *w*.
S. A. 216. thou shouldst *w*. Philistian women
S.A. 220. I sought to *w*. the daughter of an infidel
S. M. 3. *w*. your divine sounds and mixed power
**Wedded.**—P. L. 4, 750. hail *w*. love mysterious
P. L. 8, 605. harmony to behold in *w*. pair
P. L. 9, 828. and Adam *w*. to another Eve
P. L. 9, 1030. the day I saw thee first and *w*.
H. 3. of *w*. maid and virgin mother born
D. F. I. 11. if likewise he some fair one *w*. not
**Wedge.**—P. L. 7, 426. ranged in figure *w*. their
**Wedges.**—P. R. 3, 309. in rhombs and *w*.
**Wedlock.**—S. A. 353. thought barrenness in *w*.
S. A. 1009. not *w*. treachery endangering life
**Wedlock-bands.**—S. A. 986. the faith of *w.-b*.
**Wedlock-bound.**—P. L. 10, 905. and *w*.-*b*.
**Weed.**—C. 189. like a sad votarist in palmer's *w*.
D. F. I. 58. who having clad thyself in human *w*.
**Weeds.**—P. L. 3, 479. dying put on the *w*.
P. R. 1, 314. but now an aged man in rural *w*.
S. A. 122. in slavish habit ill-fitted *w*.
C. 16. l would not soil these pure ambrosial *w*.
C. 84. and take the *w*. and likeness of a swain
C. 390. for who would rob a hermit of his *w*.
L'A. 120. in *w*. of peace high triumphs hold
Hor. 15. my dank and dropping *w*.
**Weekly.**—U.C. I. 10. not his *w*. course of carriage
**Ween.**—P. L. 4, 741. nor turned I *w*. Adam
**Weened.**—P. L. 6, 86. they *w*. that selfsame
**Weening.**—P. L. 6, 795. by force or fraud *w*.
**Weep.**—P. L. 1, 620. tears such as angels *w*.
P. L. 9, 1121. they sat them down to *w*.
P. L. 11, 627. a world of tears must *w*.
L. 165. *w*. no more woful shepherds *w*. no more
L. 182. now Lycidas the shepherds *w*. no more
**Weeping.**—P. L. 10, 937. she ended *w*. and her
H. 183. a voice of *w*. heard and loud lament
P. 51. take up a *w*. on the mountains wild
**Weeps.**—S. A. 728. surcharged with dew she *w*.
**Weigh.**—P. L. 8, 570. *w*. with her thyself then
P. L. 11, 545. of cold and dry to *w*. thy spirits
**Weighed.**—P. L. 4, 999. created first he *w*.
P. L. 4, 1012. where thou art *w*. and shown
P. R. 3, 51. well *w*. scarce worth the praise
P. R. 4, 8. had no better *w*. the strength
S. A. 768. if it be *w*. by itself with aggravations
**Weighs.**—P. L. 2, 1046. *w*. his spread wings
P. L. 3, 482. whose balance *w*. the trepidation
**Weigh'st.**—P. R. 2, 173. uneven scale thou *w*.
**Weight.**—P. L. 1, 227. that felt unusual *w*.
P. L. 2, 307. fit to bear the *w*. of mightiest
P. L. 2, 416. the *w*. of all and our last hope
P. L. 4, 615. with soft slumberous *w*. inclines
P. L. 6, 621. terms we sent were terms of *w*.
P. L. 10, 968. how little *w*. my words with
P. L. 12, 539. under her own *w*. groaning
P. R. 1, 267. full *w*. must be transferred upon
P. R. 2, 465. for the public all this *w*. he bears
P. R. 4, 282. mature thee to a kingdom's *w*.
C. 728. be quite surcharged with her own *w*.
U. C. II. 9. engine moved with wheel and *w*.

U. C. II. 26. pressed to death he cried more *w*.
**Weights.**—P. L. 4, 1002. in these he put two *w*.
**Welcome.**—P. L. 10, 771. O *w*. hour
P. L. 11, 140. which thus to Eve his *w*. words
S. A. 260. to the uncircumcised a *w*. prey
S. A. 576. hasten the *w*. end of all my pains
C. 102. meanwhile *w*. joy and feast
C. 213. O *w*. pure-eyed faith white-handed hope
H. 18. to *w*. him to this his new abode
M. M. 10. and *w*. thee and wish thee long
M. W. 71. there with thee new-*w*. saint
**Welkin.**—P. L. 2, 538. the *w*. burns
C. 1015. where the bowed *w*. slow doth bend
**Well.**—P. L. 1, 134. too *w*. I see and rue the dire
P. L. 1, 334. themselves ere *w*. awake
P. L. 2, 390. *w*. have ye judged, *w*. ended long
P. L. 3, 196. light after light *w*. used they
P. L. 3, 241. and for him lastly die *w*. pleased
P. L. 3, 276. *w*. thou know'st how dear to me
P. L. 3, 370. no voice but *w*. could join
P. L. 3, 555. round he surveys and *w*. might
P. L. 3, 639. grace diffused so *w*. he feigned
P. L. 4, 164. with such delay *w*. pleased they
P. L. 4, 200. what *w*. used had been the pledge
P. L. 4, 426. for *w*. thou know'st God hath
P. L. 4, 581. but such as come *w*. known from,
P. L. 4, 926. *w*. thou know'st I stood thy
P. L. 5, 316. *w*. we may afford our givers
P. L. 5, 335. not to mix tastes not *w*. joined
P. L. 5, 461. now know I *w*. thy favour
P. L. 5, 508. *w*. hast thou taught the way
P. L. 5, 617. all seemed *w*. pleased
P. L. 5, 793. jar not with liberty but *w*. consist
P. L. 5, 888. *w*. thou didst advise yet not for
P. L. 6, 11. though darkness there might *w*.
P. L. 6, 29. servant of God *w*. done *w*. hast
P. L. 6, 159. but *w*. thou comest before thy
P. L. 6, 459. sense of pleasure we may *w*. spare
P. L. 6, 542. gird *w*. and each fit *w*. his helm
P. L. 6, 625. from head to foot *w*. understand
P. L. 6, 728. that thou in me *w*. pleased
P. L. 7, 128. what the mind may *w*. contain
P. L. 7, 546. beware and govern *w*. thy appetite
P. L. 8, 388. cannot *w*. suit with either
P. L. 8, 396. so *w*. converse
P. L. 8, 440. expressing *w*. the spirit within
P. L. 8, 540. for *w*. I understand in the prime
P. L. 8, 548. in herself complete so *w*. to know
P. L. 8, 568. worthy *w*. thy cherishing
P. L. 8, 573. on just and right, *w*. managed
P. L. 8, 588. in loving thou dost *w*. in passion not
P. L. 9, 141. *w*. nigh half the angelic name
P. L. 9, 173. I reck not so it light *w*. aimed
P. L. 9, 184. his head the midst *w*. stored
P. L. 9, 205. Adam *w*. may we labour still
P. L. 9, 229. *w*. thou motioned *w*. thy thoughts
P. L. 9, 353. but bid her *w*. beware and still
P. L. 9, 492. stronger under show of love *w*.
P. L. 9, 785. the guilty serpent and *w*. might
P. L. 9, 826. this may be *w*. but what if God
P. L. 9, 945. not *w*. conceived of God
P. L. 9, 1021. praise yield thee so *w*. this day
P. L. 9, 1027. but come so *w*. refreshed
P. L. 9, 1035. *w*. understood of Eve
P. L. 10, 71. mayst ever rest *w*. pleased
P. L. 10, 154. under government *w*. seemed
P. L. 10, 725. *w*. if here would end the misery
P. L. 10, 887. *w*. if thrown out as supernumerary
P. L. 11, 256. with many deeds *w*. done
P. L. 11, 257. *w*. may then thy Lord appeased
P. L. 11, 416. and from the *w*. of life
P. L. 11, 451. to that meek man who *w*. had
P. L. 11, 530. if thou *w*. observe the rule
P. L. 11, 554. live *w*. how long or short permit
P. L. 11, 629. shame that they who to live *w*.
P. L. 11, 781. all would have then gone *w*.
P. L. 12, 505. ministry performed and race *w*. run
P. L. 12, 625. Adam heard *w*. pleased but
P. R. 1, 47. *w*. ye know how many ages as the
P. R. 4, 56. so *w*. I have disposed my aery
P. R. 1, 114. so *w*. had thrived in Adam's

P. R. 1, 286. in whom alone he was w. pleased
P. R. 1, 301. as w. might recommend such
P. R. 1, 437. and not w. understood as good
P. R. 2, 97. so found as w. I saw he could not
P. R. 2, 305. and w. I know not without hunger
P. R. 3, 51. things vulgar and w. weighed
P. R. 3, 66. as thou to thy reproach mayst w.
P. R. 3, 196. best reign who first w. hath obeyed
P. R. 3, 261. that w. might seem the seats
P. R. 3, 267. w. have we speeded and o'er hill
P. R. 4, 56. so w. I have disposed my aery
P. R. 4, 134. mild and temperate conquered w.
P. R. 4, 337. that pleased so w. our victor's ear
P. R. 4, 275. whom w. inspired the oracle
S. A. 204. how w. are come upon him his deserts
S. A. 289. for want of w. pronouncing Shibboleth
S. A. 381. this w. I knew nor was at all surprised
S. A. 408. who with a grain of manhood w.
S. A. 413. rewarded w. with servile punishment
S. A. 483. w. they may by this have satisfied
S. A. 655. and to the hearing w. of all calamities
S. A. 813. and love hath oft w. meaning wrought
S. A. 878. loved thee as too w. thou knew'st, too w.
S. A. 1207. force with force is w. ejected
S. A. 1258. they cannot w. impose nor I sustain
S. A. 1353. than thou w. wilt bear
S. A. 1399. I could be w. content to try their art
S. A. 1556. and sense distract to know w. what I
S. A. 1723. nothing but w. and fair
C. 87. w. knows to still the wild winds when
C. 152. be w. stocked with as fair a herd as
C. 201. this is the place as w. as I may guess
C. 210. these thoughts may startle w. but not
C. 235. nightly to thee her sad song mourneth w.
C. 398. you may as w. spread out the unsunned
C. 438. if he be friendly he comes w. if not
C. 563. too w. I did perceive it was the voice
C. 620. of small regard to see to, yet w. skilled
C. 623. he loved me w. and oft would beg me sing
C. 772. nature's full blessings would be w.
C. 791. that hath so w. been taught her dazzling
C. 1000. waxing w. of his deep wound
A. 107. yet Syrinx w. might wait on her
L. 15. begin then sisters of the sacred w.
L. 113. how w. could I have spared for thee
S. 10, 12. so w. your words his noble virtues
S. 20, 11. to hear the lute w. touched or artful
**Well-attired.**—L. 146. the w.-a. woodbine
**Well-balanced.**—H. 122. and the w.-b.
**Well-being.**—P. L. 8, 361. for whose w.-b.
**Well-couched.**—P. R. 1, 97. force but w.-c.
**Well-feasted.**—S. A. 1419. and the w.-f. priest
**Well-governed.**—C. 705. to a w.-g. and wise
**Well-lighted.**—M. W. 186. but with a scarce w.-l.
**Well-measured.**—S. 13. add w.-m. song
**Well-placed.**—C. 161. and w.-p. words of
**Well-pleasing.**—P. L. 10, 634. w.-p. son
**Well-practised.**—C. 310. of w.-p. feet
**Well-trod.**—L'A. 131. then to the w.-t. stage
**Well-woven.**—P. R. 1, 97. fraud w.-w. snares
**Welter.**—L. 13. unwept and w. to the parching
**Weltering.**—P. L. 1, 78. and w. by his side
H. 124. and bid the w. waves their oozy channel
**Went.**—P. L. 1, 651. there w. a fame in heaven
P. L. 2, 49. with that care lost w. all his fear
P. L. 4, 126. him down the way he w.
P. L. 4, 223. through Eden w. a river large
P. L. 4, 456. thither w. with unexperienced
P. L. 4, 739. inmost bower handed they w.
P. L. 4, 858. like a proud steed reined w.
P. L. 6, 12. and now w. forth the morn
P. L. 6, 686. Michael and his powers w. forth
P. L. 6, 782. they heard his voice and w.
P. L. 6, 884. and as they w. shaded with
P. L. 7, 334. a dewy mist w. up and watered all
P. L. 7, 588. for he also w. invisible
P. L. 8, 44. and w. forth among her fruits and
P. L. 8, 48. yet w. she not as not with such
P. L. 8, 59. goddess-like demeanour forth she w.
P. L. 8, 268. and sometimes w. and sometimes
P. L. 9, 847. and forth to meet her w. the way

P. L. 9, 1099. counselled he and both together w.
P. L. 10, 414. the other way Satan w. down
P. R. 1, 211. 'I w. into the temple there to hear
P. R. 2, 98. but w. about his Father's business
P. R. 2, 284. fasting he w. to sleep and fasting
P. R. 4, 484. while the Son of God w. on
S. A. 1190. w. up with armed powers the only
S. A. 1617. on each side w. armed guards
L. 103. Camus reverend sire w. footing slow
L. 187. while the still morn w. out with sandals
S. 8, 12. when temple and tower w. to the ground
U. C. II. 22. died for heaviness that his cart w. light
**Went'st.**—P. L. 12, 610. and whither w.
P. R. 4, 216. thou w. alone into the temple
**Wept.**—P. L. 4, 248. rich trees w. odorous
P. L. 9, 991. him and for joy tenderly w.
P. L. 9, 1003. sad drops w. at completing of the
P. L. 11, 495. Adam could not but w.
P. R. 3, 41. w. that he had lived so long
C. 257. Scylla w. and chid her barking waves
Cir. 9. seas w. from our deep sorrow
M. W. 56. w. for thee in Helicon
**Wert.**—P. L. 3, 9. before the heavens thou w.
**West.**—P. L. 4, 784. our circuit meets full w.
P. L. 5, 339. in India east or w. or middle shore
P. L. 7, 376. but opposite in levelled w. was set
P. L. 8, 163. or she from w. her silent course
P. L. 9, 80. w. from Orontes to the ocean barred
P. L. 10, 685. and not known or east or w.
P. L. 12, 40. from Eden towards the w.
P. R. 3, 272. as far as Indus east Euphrates w.
P. R. 4, 71. and more to w. the realm of
P. R. 4, 77. from Gallia Gades and the British w.
P. R. 4, 448. backed on the north and w. by
C. 306. due w. it rises from this shrubby point
C. 989. and w. winds with musky wing
**Westering.**—L. 31. had sloped his w. wheel
**Western.**—P. L. 4, 597. clouds that on his w.
P. L. 4, 862. now drew they nigh the w. point
P. L. 10, 92. now was the sun in w. cadence
P. L. 11, 205. more orient in yon w.
P. L. 12, 141. Hermon east to the great w. sea
P. R. 4, 25. he brought our Saviour to the w.
L. 191. and now was dropt into the w. bay
**Westward.**—P. R. 4, 237. w. much nearer
**Wet.**—P. L. 5, 190. or w. the thirsty earth
P. R. 1, 318. to warm him w. returned from field
P. R. 4, 433. and dried the w. from drooping
P. R. 4, 486. me worse than w. thou find'st not
C. 930. nor w. October's torrent flood
**Wether.**—S. A. 538. who shore me like a tame w.
C. 499. or straggling w. the pent flock forsook
**Wetting.**—S. A. 730. w. the borders of her silken
**Whales**—P. L. 7, 391. created the great w.
**Whate'er.**—P. L. 1, 150. w. his business be
P. L. 2, 162. w. doing what can we suffer more
P. L. 2, 733. to execute w. his wrath
P. L. 4, 425. w. death is some dreadful thing
P. L. 8, 273. and readily could name w. I saw
P. R. 1, 83. dove descend (w. it meant)
P. R. 1, 149. w. his cruel malice could invent
P. R. 1, 178. against w. may tempt w. seduce
S. A. 1034. w. it be to wisest men and best
S. A. 1156. presume not on thy God w. he be
**Whatever.**—P. L. 2, 442. scape into w. world
P. L. 2, 955. undaunted to meet there w. power
P. L. 4, 744. w. hypocrites austerely talk of
P. L. 4, 891. and boldly venture to w. place
P. L. 5, 338. w. earth all-bearing mother yields
P. L. 5, 414. for know w. was created needs
P. L. 6, 489. and o'erwhelm w. stands adverse
P. L. 7, 475. at once came forth w. creeps the
P. L. 8, 622. w. pure thou in the body enjoy'st
P. L. 9, 92. for in the wily snake w. sleights
P. L. 9, 695. of death denounced w. thing
P. L. 9, 898. w. can to sight or thought be
P. L. 10, 11. and repulsed w. wiles of foe or
P. L. 10, 141. and what she did w. in itself
P. L. 10, 245. w. draws me on or sympathy or
P. L. 10, 605. and w. thing the scythe of time
P. L. 10, 757. have been refused those terms w.

P. R. 3, 213. *w.* for itself condemned
P. R. 4, 600. *w.* place habit or state or motion
S. A. 904. goes by the worse *w.* be her cause
S. 8, 8. *w.* clime the sun's bright circle warms
**Whatsoever.**—P. L. 4, 587. in *w.* shape he
**Wheel.**—P. L. 3, 741. in many an aery *w*,
P. L. 4, 783. these other *w.* the north
P. L. 6, 326. but with swift *w.* reverse deep
P. L. 6, 751. flashing thick flames *w.* within *w.*
P. L. 8, 135. above all stars the *w.* of day
P. L. 12, 183. and *w.* on the earth devouring
L. 31. descent had sloped his westering *w.*
U.C.II. 9. an engine moved with *w.* and weight
**Wheeled.**—P. L. 7, 501. first *w.* their course
P. R. 3, 323. how quick they *w.* and flying
**Wheeling.**—P. L. 4, 785. half *w.* to the
V. Ex. 34. above the *w.* poles and at heaven's
**Wheels.**—P. L. 1, 311. broken chariot *w.*
P. L. 1, 786. and nearer to the earth *w.* her
P. L. 2, 532. shun the goal with rapid *w.*
P. L. 3, 394. nor stop thy flaming chariot *w.*
P. L. 4, 975. draw'st his triumphant *w.* in
P. L. 5, 140. with *w.* yet hovering o'er the
P. L. 5, 621. in all her *w.* resembles nearest
P. L. 6, 210. and the madding *w.* of brazen
P. L. 6, 573. mounted row of pillars laid on *w.*
P. L. 6, 711. guide the rapid *w.* that shake
P. L. 6, 755. with eyes the *w.* of beryl
P. L. 6, 882. night under his burning *w.*
P. L. 6, 846. and from the living *w.* distinct
P. L. 7, 224. then stayed the fervid *w.* and in
P. R. 2, 16. who on fiery *w.* rode up to heaven •
C. 190. rose from the hindmost *w.* of Phœbus
P. 36. see the chariot and those rushing *w.*
**Whelmed.**—P. L. 6, 141. and *w.* thy legions
P. L. 6, 651. they saw them *w.* and all their
**Whelming.**—L. 157. perhaps under the *w.* tide
**Whelped.**—P. L. 11, 751. sea-monsters *w.*
**Whenever.**—P. L. 2, 809. *w.* that shall be
P. L. 10, 771. O welcome hour *w.*
**Whereat.**—P. L. 1, 616. *w.* their doubled
P. L. 2, 389. *w.* his speech he thus renews
P. L. 5, 851. *w.* rejoiced the apostate
P. L. 6, 202. *w.* Michael bid sound the
P. L. 8, 309. appetite to pluck and eat *w.*
P. L. 11, 444. *w.* he inly raged and as they
P. L. 11, 868. *w.* the heart of Adam erst so sad
P. L. 12, 636. *w.* in either hand the hastening
**Whereby.**—P. L. 3, 621. *w.* he soon saw
P. L. 5, 411. faculty of sense *w.* they hear see
P. L. 8, 579. but if the sense of touch *w.* mankind
P. R. 1, 396. *w.* they may direct their future life
**Where'er.**—P. L. 11, 79. the waters of life *w.*
P. L. 11, 177. *w.* our day's work lies
L. 155. far away *w.* thy bones are hurled
**Wherefore.**—P. L. 1, 264. but *w.* let we then
P. L. 2, 159. *w.* cease we then say they who
P. L. 2, 450. *w.* do I assume these royalties
P. L. 4, 42. ah *w*? he deserved no such return
P. L. 4, 657. but *w.* all night long shine these
P. L. 4, 917. but *w.* thou alone? *w.* with these
P. L. 4, 960. *w.* but in hope to dispossess him
P. L. 6, 116. *w.* should not strength and might
P. L. 9, 331. then *w.* shunned or feared by us
P. L. 10, 762. reproved retort *w.* didst thou
P. R. 3, 21. these godlike virtues *w.* dost thou
P. R. 3, 23. *w.* deprive all earth her wonder at
S.A.23. O *w.* was my birth from heaven foretold
S. A. 356. O *w.* did God grant
S.A.1441. but *w.* comes old Manoah in such haste
C. 710. *w.* did nature pour her bounties forth
**Wherein.**—P. L. 1, 523. yet such *w.* appeared
P. L. 2, 768. *w.* remained (for what could else)
P. L. 3, 78. *w.* past, present, future, he beholds
P. L. 3, 262. thy face *w.* no cloud of anger
P. L. 3, 335. *w.* the just shall dwell and after
P. L. 3, 408. regardless of the bliss *w.* he sat
P. L. 4, 999. *w.* all things created first he
P. L. 8, 68. the book of God before thee set *w.*
P. L. 8, 391. *w.* the brute cannot be human
P. L. 8, 589. in passion not *w.* true love consists

P. L. 9, 725. and *w.* lies the offence that man
P. L. 10, 149. *w.* God set thee above her made
P. L. 11, 255. of grace *w.* thou mayst repent
P. L. 11, 479. a lazar-house it seemed *w.* were
P. L. 11, 608. the tents of wickedness *w.* shall
P. L. 11, 616. yet empty of all good *w.* consists
P. L. 11, 901. both heaven and earth *w.* the
P. L. 12, 41. the plain *w.* a black bituminous
P. R. 1, 58. *w.* we must bide the stroke of that
S. A. 564. to what can I be useful *w.* serve
S.A.780. *w.* consisted all thy strength and safety
C. 135. *w.* thou ridest with Hecate
H. 2. *w.* the Son of heaven's eternal King
**Whereof.**—P. L. 1, 650. *w.* so rife there went
P. L. 2, 584. *w.* who drinks forth with his
P. L. 2, 723. *w.* all hell had rung
P. L. 3, 504. at top *w.* but far more rich
P. L. 4, 119. *w.* he soon aware each perturbation
P. L. 4, 235. *w.* here needs no account
P. L. 4, 419. nor can perform aught *w.* he hath
P. L. 4, 937. this new created world *w.* in hell
P. L. 6, 518. *w.* to found their engines
P. L. 7, 64. when and *w.* created for what cause
P. L. 8, 342. in sign *w.* each bird and beast
P. L. 9, 967. one heart one soul in both *w.* good
P. L. 10, 123. *w.* I gave thee charge thou
P. L. 12, 150. *w.* to thee anon plainlier shall
P. R. 1, 345. with food *w.* we wretched seldom
P. R. 2, 276. the strength *w.* sufficed him
P. R. 3, 345. at sight *w.* the fiend yet more
P. R. 4, 481. *w.* this ominous night that closed
S. A. 1174. confidence *w.* I once again
**Whereon.**—P. L. 1, 474. *w.* to burn his odious
P. L. 3, 510. the stairs were such as *w.* Jacob
P. L. 3, 519. *w.* who after came from earth
P. L. 4, 521. O fair foundation laid *w.* to build
P. L. 5, 510. *w.* in contemplation of created
P. L. 5, 764. in imitation of that mount *w.*
P. L. 6, 758. *w.* a sapphire throne inlaid with
P. L. 6, 473. of this ethereous mould *w.* we
P. L. 9, 526. and licked the ground *w.* she trod
P. L. 10, 919. bereave me not *w.* I live thy
P. L. 11, 382. *w.* for different cause the tempter
P. L. 11, 430. *w.* were sheaves new-reaped
P. L. 11, 556. and saw a spacious plain *w.* were
P. L. 11, 858. green tree or ground *w.* his foot
P. L. 11, 897. his triple-coloured bow *w.* to look
P. R. 2, 228. rocks *w.* greatest men have
P. 34. the leaves should all be black *w.* I write
**Whereso.**—P. L. 11, 722. assemblies *w.* met
**Wheresoe'er.**—P. R. 3, 79. *w.* they rove
**Whereto.**—P. L. 1, 156. *w.* with speedy words
P. L. 6, 469. *w.* with look composed Satan
P. L. 8, 398. *w.* the Almighty answered not
P. L. 12, 63. *w.* thus Adam fatherly displeased
**Wherever.**—P. L. 7, 535. *w.* thus created for
P. L. 8, 170. as him pleases best *w.* pleased let
P. L. 9, 325. single with like defence *w.* met
P. L. 11, 385. his eye might there command *w.*
P. L. 12, 449. of Abraham's faith *w.* through
P. R. 4, 404. *w.* under some concourse of shades
S. A. 547. *w.* fountain or fresh current flowed
S. A. 1202. as on my enemies *w.* chanced
**Wherewith.**—P. L. 3, 148. *w.* thy throne
P. L. 9, 1011. breeding wings *w.* to scorn the
P. R. 2, 411. high actions but *w.* to be achieved
S.A.585. *w.* to serve him better than thou hast
C. 443. *w.* she tamed the brinded lioness
C.449. *w.* she freezed her foes to congealed stone
P. 2. *w.* the stage of air and earth did ring
**Wherewithal.**—P. L. 3, 468. had they *w.*
**Whether.**—P. L. 1, 132. *w.* upheld by
P. L. 1, 178. *w.* scorn or satiate fury
P. L. 2, 41. by what best way *w.*
P. L. 2, 152. *w.* our angry Foe can give it
P. L. 3, 523. the stairs were then let down *w.* to
P. L. 4, 592. *w.* the prime orb incredible how
P. L. 4, 907. gravely in doubt *w.* to hold
P. L. 5, 14. beheld beauty which *w.* waking or
P. L. 5, 189. *w.* to deck with clouds the
P. L. 5, 532. be tried *w.* they serve wiillng

P. L. 5, 741. know  w. I be dextrous to subdue
P. L. 5, 867. then thou shalt behold w. by
P. L. 8, 70. this to attain w. heaven move or
P. L. 8, 159. but w. thus these things or w. not
P. L. 8, 160. w. the sun predominant in heaven
P. L. 9, 145. w. such virtue spent of old now
P. L. 9, 215. w. to wind the woodbine
P. L. 9, 237. w. food or talk between
P. L. 9, 261. w. his first design be to withdraw
P. L. 9, 788. w. true or fancied so
P. L. 10, 57. all judgment w. in heaven or
P. L. 11, 296. celestial w. among the thrones
P. L. 11, 566. w. found where casual fire had
P. L. 11, 569. or w. washed by stream from
P. L. 11, 786. and w. here the race of man will
P. L. 12, 47. regardless w. good or evil fame
P. L. 12, 463. receive them into bliss w. in
P. L. 12, 474. full of doubt I stand w. I should
P. R. 1, 303. full forty days he passed w. on hill
P. R. 3, 214. alike be punished w. thou reign or
P. R. 4, 198. if I to try w. in higher sort
P. R. 4, 596. w. throned in the bosom of bliss
S. A. 477. w. God be Lord or Dagon
S. A. 1255. lest a question rise w. he durst accept
S. A. 1349. up to the height w. to hold or break
**Whets.**—L'A. 66. and the mower w. his scythe
**Whilere.**—Cir. 10. all heaven's heraldry w.
**Whilom.**—C. 827. w. she was the daughter
D. F. I. 24. w. did slay his dearly-loved mate
**Whip.**—P. L. 2, 701. lest with a w. of scorpions
**Whirled.**—P. 37. that w. the prophet up
**Whirlpool.**—P. L. 2, 1020. other w. steered
**Whirlwind.**—P. L. 2, 541. ride the air in w.
P. L. 2, 589. beat with perpetual storms of w.
P. L. 6, 749. with w. sound the chariot of
**Whirlwinds.**—P. L. 1, 77. floods and w.
P. L. 2, 182. the sport and prey of racking w.
**Whisper.**—P. L. 4, 158. and w. whence
**Whispered.**—P. L. 5, 17. touching w. thus
P. L. 8, 516. fresh gales and gentle airs w. it
**Whispering.**—P. L. 4, 326. stood w. soft by
P. L. 5, 26. such w. waked her but with startled
P. R. 2, 26. winds with reeds and osiers w. play
P. R. 4, 250. there Ilissus rolls his w. stream
L'A. 116. by w. winds soon lulled asleep
H. 66. w. new joys to the mild ocean
**Whispers.**—L. 136. low where the mild w. use
**Whist.**—H. 64. the winds with wonder w.
**Whistle.**—C. 346. or w. from the lodge
**Whistles.**—L'A. 64. w. o'er the furrowed land
**Whit.**—C. 774. and she no w. encumbered with
**White.**—P. L. 3, 475. w., black and gray
P. L. 7, 439. between her w. wings mantling
P. L. 11, 206. the blue firmament a radiant w.
P. R. 4, 76. dusk faces with w. silken turbants
S. A. 327. locks w. as down
S.A. 974. on both his wings one black the other w.
L. 144. the w. pink and the pansy freaked with jet
S. 23, 9. came vested all in w. pure as her mind
H. 42. the saintly veil of maiden w. to throw
P. 35. where my tears have, washed a wannish w.
**White-handed.**—C. 213. w.-h. hope
**White-robed.**—D. F. I. 54. sage w.-r. truth
**White-thorn.**—L. 48. when first the w.-t. blows
**Whither.**—P. L. 3, 272. and w. tend
P. L. 6, 531. where lodged or w. fled
P. L. 8, 283. I called and strayed I knew not w.
P. L. 9, 473. thoughts w. have ye led me with
P. L. 10, 265. go w. fate and inclination strong
P. L. 10, 922. of thee w. shall I betake me
P. L. 11, 282. and w. wander down into a
P. L. 12, 610. thou return'st and w. went'st
P. R. 2, 39. for w. is he gone what accident
P. R. 4, 510. till at the ford of Jordan w. all
S. A. 1541. O w. shall I run or which way fly
C. 351. where may she wander now w. betake her
**Whoever.**—P. L. 10, 14. w. tempted
P. L. 10, 73. w. judged the worst
S. A. 995. at this w. envies or repines
C. 52. whose charmed cup w. tasted lost his
**Whole.**—P. L. 1, 569. the w. battalion views

P. L. 2, 123. cast ominous conjecture on the w.
P. L. 2, 353. shook heaven's w. circumference
P. L. 2, 365. hell fire to waste his w. creation
P. L. 2, 594. where armies w. have sunk
P. L. 3, 161. after him the w. race of mankind
P. L. 3, 209. he with his w. posterity must die
P. L. 3, 280. losing thee awhile the w. race
P. L. 4, 207. in narrow room, nature's w.
P. L. 4, 284. a w. day's journey high
P. L. 6, 655. and oppressed w. legions armed
P. L. 6, 727. account my exaltation and my w.
P. L. 6, 875. yawning received them w. and on
P. L. 7, 273. might distemper the w. frame
P. L. 9, 416. in them the w. included race
P. L. 11, 874. for one w. world of wicked sons
P. L. 11, 888. he saw the w. earth filled with
P. L. 12, 269. and from him his w. descent
P. R. 1, 208. made it my w. delight
S. A. 262. on their w. host I flew unarmed
S. A. 265. or one w. tribe
S. A. 809. w. to myself unhazarded abroad
S. A. 1059. least confusion draw on his w. life
S. A. 1110. who durst not with their w. united
S. A. 1476. his ransom if my w. inheritance
S. A. 1512. as if the w. inhabitation perished
S. A. 1651. the w. roof after them with burst of
**Wholesome.**—P. L. 4, 330. more easy w.
P. L. 10. 847. now as ere man fell w. and cool
P. R. 4, 458. and harmless if not w. as a
F. of C. 16. with their w. and preventive shears
**Wholly.**—P. L. 9, 786. intent now w. on her
P. R. 2, 207. set w. on the accomplishment of
**Whomsoever.**—P. L. 9, 1068. of w. taught
**Whoso.**—P. L. 9, 724. that w. eats thereof
**Wicked.**—P. L. 4, 856. single against thee w.
P. L. 5, 890. I fly these w. tents devoted
P. L. 6, 277. thou and thy w. crew there mingle
P. L. 11, 812. he of their w. ways shall them
P. L. 11, 875. for one whole world of w. sons
P. L. 12, 541. and vengeance to the w.
P. R. 4, 95. committing to a w. favourite all
S. A. 826. as I give my folly take to thy w. deed
S. A. 1285. he executes his errand on' the w.
**Wickedness.**—P. L. 11, 608. the tents of w.
S. A. 834. all w. is weakness that plea therefore
**Wicker.**—C. 338. from the w. hole of some clay
**Wicket.**—P. L. 3, 484. at heaven's w.
**Wide.**—P. L. 1, 724. discover w. within her
P. L. 1, 762. the gates and porches w.
P. L. 2, 133. scout far and w. into the realm
P. L. 2, 150. in the w. womb of uncreated time
P. L. 2, 440. receives him next w. gaping
P. L. 2, 519. the hollow abyss heard far and w.
P. L. 2, 571. on bold adventure to discover w.
P. L. 2, 641. through the w. Æthiopian
P. L. 2, 655. barked with w. Cerberean mouths
P. L. 2, 755. till on the left side opening w.
P. L. 2, 884. the gates w. open stood
P. L. 2, 888. so w. they stood and like a furnace
P. L. 2, 961. spread w. on the wasteful deep
P. L. 2, 1003. dungeon stretching far and w.
P. L. 2, 1047. w. in circuit undetermined
P. L. 3, 84. nor yet the main abyss w. interrupt
P. L. 3, 528. down to the earth a passage w.
P. L. 3, 538. so w. the opening seemed where
P. L. 3, 614. far and w. his eye commands
P. L. 4, 77. threatening to devour me opens w.
P. L. 4, 284. but w. remote from this Assyrian
P. L. 4, 579. see far and w. in at this gate
P. L. 5, 88. a prospect w. and various
P. L. 5, 142. discovering in w. landscape all
P. L. 5, 254. the gate self opened w. on golden
P. L. 5, 287. fragrance filled the circuit w.
P. L. 5, 648. w. over all the plain and wider
P. L. 6, 2. through heaven's w. champaign held
P. L. 6, 54. opens w. his fiery chaos to receive
P. L. 6, 241. for w. was spread that war
P. L. 6, 510. in a moment up they turned w.
P. L. 6, 577. hideous orifice gaped on us w.
P. L. 6, 773. illustrious far and w.

P. L. 6, 860. wall of heaven which opening *w.*
P. L. 7, 89. the ambient air *w.* interfused
P. L. 7, 148. to possess her realms though *w.*
P. L. 7, 205. heaven opened *w.* her ever-during
P. L. 7, 270. in *w.* crystalline ocean
P. L. 7, 301. they or under ground or circuit *w.*
P. L. 7, 575. that opened *w.* her blazing portals
P. L. 8, 78. laughter at their quaint opinions *w.*
P. L. 8, 100. and for the heaven's *w.* circuit let
P. L. 8, 141. sent from her through the *w.*
P. L. 8, 304. a circuit *w.* enclosed with goodliest
P. L. 8, 467. *w.* was the wound but suddenly
P. L. 9, 134. in woe then that destruction *w.*
P. L. 9, 203. dispatch of two gardening so *w.*
P. L. 9, 245. with ease as *w.* as we need walk
P. L. 10, 232. the gates that now stood open *w.*
P. L. 10, 280. upturned his nostril *w.* into the
P. L. 10, 283. into the waste *w.* anarchy of
P. L. 10, 419. through the gate *w.* open
P. L. 11, 68. the blessed through heaven's *w.*
P. L. 11, 638. he looked and saw *w.* territory
P. L. 11, 844. and the clear sun on his *w.*
P. L. 12, 224. delay in the *w.* wilderness
P. L. 12, 371. bound his reign with earth's *w.*
P. R. 1, 44. O ancient powers of air and this *w.*
P. R. 1, 118. a pleasant realm and province *w.*
P. R. 2, 232. no food is to be found in the *w.*
P. R. 2, 359. of faery damsels met in forest *w.*
P. R. 3, 72. to subdue by conquest far and *w.*
P. R. 3, 254. outstretched in circuit *w.* lay
P. R. 3, 337. such forces met not nor so *w.*
P. R. 4, 27. plain long but in breadth not *w.*
P. R. 4, 81. to Rome's great emperor whose *w.*
C. 945. through this gloomy covert *w.*
L'A. 76. shallow brooks and rivers *w.*
Il P. 70. through the heaven's *w.* pathless way
S. 19, 2. half my days in this dark world and *w.*
H. 51. and waving *w.* her myrtle wand
H. 148. will open *w.* the gates of her high palace
V. Ex. 41. and misty regions of *w.* air next under
**Wide-encroaching.**—P. L. 10, 581. *w.-e.*
**Wide-hovering.**—P. L. 11, 739. wings *w.-h.*
**Wider.**—P. L. 3, 529. *w.* by far than that of
P. L. 5, 648. wide over all the plain and *w.* far
P. L. 11, 381. not higher that hill nor *w.*
**Widest.**—P. L. 4, 382. her *w.* gates
**Wide-wasting.**—P. L. 6, 253. down *w.-w.*
P. L. 11, 487. *w.* wasting pestilence
**Wide-watered.**—Il P. 75. some *w.-w.* shore
**Wide-waving.**—P. L. 11, 121. flame *w.-w.*
**Widowed.**—S. A. 806. thy absence in my *w.* bed
F. of C. 3. to seize the *w.* whore Plurality
**Widowhood.**—S. A. 958. thy hastened *w.*
**Wield.**—P. L. 6, 221. least of whom could *w.*
P. L. 8, 80. how they will *w.* the mighty frame
P. L. 11, 643. part *w.* their arms part curb the
C. 27. and *w.* their little tridents
**Wielded.**—P. R. 4, 269. *w.* at will that fierce
**Wife.**—P. L. 8, 498. and to his *w.* adhere
P. L. 9, 267. the *w.* where danger or dishonour
P. L. 10, 101. both man and *w.*
P. L. 10, 198. hearkened to the voice of thy *w.*
P. R. 2, 134. Adam by his *w.'s* allurement
S. A. 227. she proving false the next I took to *w.*
S. A. 724. other certain than Dalila thy *w.*
S. A. 725. my *w.*! my traitress
S. A. 885. being once a *w.* for me thou wast to
S. A. 1193. I chose a *w.* which argued me no foe
C. 675. not that nepenthes which the *w.*
Il P. 112. and who had Canace to *w.*
M. W. 2. the honoured *w.* of Winchester
**Wight.**—P. L. 2, 613. all taste of living *w.*
P. 14. too hard for human *w.*
D. F. I. 41. O say me true if thou wert mortal *w.*
**Wild.**—P. L. 1, 60. situation waste and *w.*
P. L. 1, 180. yon dreary plain forlorn and *w.*
P. L. 1, 407. and the *w.* of southmost Abarim
P. L. 2, 541. hell scarce holds the *w.* uproar
P. L. 2, 588. a frozen continent lies dark and *w.*
P. L. 2, 910. into this *w.* abyss the womb of
P. L. 2, 917. into this *w.* abyss the wary fiend

P. L. 2, 951. at length a universal hubbub *w.*
P. L. 2, 1014. like a pyramid of fire into the *w.*
P. L. 3, 424. dark waste and *w.*
P. L. 3, 710. and *w.* uproar stood ruled
P. L. 4, 136. grotesque and *w.* access denied
P. L. 4, 341. all beasts of the earth since *w.*
P. L. 5, 112. but misjoining shapes *w.* work
P. L. 5, 297. *w.* above rule or art enormous
P. L. 5, 577. this world was not and Chaos *w.*
P. L. 6, 616. somewhat extravagant and *w.*
P. L. 6, 698. which makes *w.* work in heaven
P. L. 6, 873. in their fall through his *w.*
P. L. 7, 212. as a sea dark wasteful *w.*
P. L. 7, 457. the *w.* beast where he wons in forest
P. L. 7, 458. in forest *w.* in thicket brake or
P. L. 9, 212. growth derides tending to *w.*
P. L. 9, 543. in this enclosure *w.* these beasts
P. L. 9, 910. to live again in these *w.* woods
P. L. 9, 1117. and *w.* among the trees on isles
P. L. 10, 477. unoriginal night and Chaos *w.*
P. L. 11, 284. to this obscure and *w.*
P. L. 12, 216. advance through the *w.* desert
P. R. 1, 193. now the bordering desert *w.*
P. R. 1, 310. then at last among *w.* beasts
P. R. 1, 331. for we sometimes who dwell this *w.*
P. R. 1, 502. and now *w.* beasts came forth
P. R. 2, 109. her son tracing the desert *w.*
P. R. 2, 304. in this *w.* solitude so long should
P. R. 3, 301. whose incursions *w.* have wasted
P. R. 4, 523. thee still on to this waste *w.*
S. A. 127. or fiercest *w.* beast could withstand
S. A. 975. bears greatest names in his *w.* aery
S. A. 1138. that ridge the back of chafed *w.* boars
S. A. 1403. trail me through their streets like *w.*
C. 87. well knows to still the *w.* winds when
C. 312. dingle or bushy dell of this *w.* wood
C. 356. what if in *w.* amazement and affright
C. 403. uninjured in this *w.* surrounding waste
L. 40. with *w.* thyme and the gadding vine
L'A. 134. warble his native wood notes *w.*
H. 29. it was the winter *w.*
P. 51. take up a weeping on the mountains *w.*
D. F. I. 73. wisely learn to curb thy sorrows *w.*
**Wilderness.**—P. L. 2, 943. through the *w.*
P. L. 4, 135. the champaign head of a steep *w.*
P. L. 4, 342. in wood or *w.*, forest or den
P. L. 5, 294. a *w.* of sweets
P. L. 9, 245. will keep from *w.* with ease
P. L. 11, 383. set our second Adam in the *w.*
P. L. 12, 224. gain by their delay in the wide *w.*
P. L. 12, 313. world's *w.* long wandered man
P. R. 1, 7. and Eden raised in the waste *w.*
P. R. 1, 156. I mean to exercise him in the *w.*
P. R. 1, 291. strong motion I am led into this *w.*
P. R. 2, 232. food is to be found in the wide *w.*
P. R. 2, 307. have trod this *w.*
P. R. 2, 384. command a table in this *w.*
P. R. 3, 23. or more obscure in savage *w.*
P. R. 4, 372. the *w.* for thee is fittest place
P. R. 4, 395. and to the *w.* brought back
P. R. 4, 416. and fell on the vexed *w.*
P. R. 4, 543. over the *w.* and over the plain
P. R. 4, 600. and human form wandering the *w.*
**Wildernesses.**—C. 209. shores and desert *w.*
**Wilds.**—C. 424. hills and sandy perilous *w.*
**Wile.**—C. 906. through the *w.* of unblest enchanter
**Wiles.**—P. L. 2, 51. of *w.* more unexpert
P. L. 2, 193. to frustrate all our plots and *w.*
P. L. 9, 85. most opportune might serve his *w.*
P. L. 9, 184. well stored with subtle *w.*
P. L. 10, 11. whatever *w.* of foe or seeming
P. R. 1, 6. foiled in all his *w.*
P. R. 1, 120. easy steps girded with snaky *w.*
P. R. 1, 175. vanquish by wisdom hellish *w.*
P. R. 3, 5. length collecting all his serpent *w.*
P. R. 3, 442. meet that made void all his *w.*
S. A. 402. fourth time when mustering all her *w.*
S. A. 871. I thought where all thy circling *w.*
L'A. 27. quips and cranks and wanton *w.*
**Wilful.**—P. L. 10, 1042. and *w.* barrenness
P. L. 12, 619. who for my *w.* crime art banished

**Wilfully.**—P. L. 5, 244. w. transgressing
P. R. 1, 225. not w. misdoing but unaware
**Will.**—P. L. 1, 31. and trangress his w.
P. L. 1, 106. the unconquerable w.
P. L. 1, 161. as being the contrary to his high w.
P. L. 1, 211. but that the w. and high permission
P. L. 2, 199. omnipotent decree the victor's w.
P. L. 2, 351. so was his w. pronounced
P. L. 2, 559. w. and fate fixed fate free w.
P. L. 2, 1025. (such was the w. of heaven)
P. L. 3, 108. w. and reason (reason also is choice)
P. L. 3, 115. predestination overruled their w.
P. L. 3, 174. saved who w., yet not of w. in him
P. L. 3, 184. elect above the rest so is my w.
P. L. 3, 270. he attends the w. of his great
P. L. 3, 656. art wont his great authentic w.
P. L. 3, 685. by his permissive w. through
P. L. 4, 66. hadst thou the same free w. and
P. L. 4, 71. since against his thy w. chose freely
P. L. 4, 182. wilt object his w. who bound us
P. L. 5, 235. in his power left free to w.
P. L. 5, 236. his own free w. his w. though free
P. L. 5, 295. and played at w. her virgin fancies
P. L. 5, 377. till evening rise I have at w.
P. L. 5, 526. ordained thy w. by nature free
P. L. 5, 533. who w. but what they must
P. L. 5, 539. because we freely love as in our w.
P. L. 5, 549. to be both w. and deed created
P. L. 6, 427. sufficient to subdue us to his w.
P. L. 6, 728. declarest thy w. fulfilled
P. L. 6, 816. honoured me according to his w.
P. L. 7, 79. to observe immutably his sovran w.
P. L. 7, 173. and what I w. is fate
P. L. 7, 181. heard declared the Almighty's w.
P. L. 7, 182. they sung to the Most High good w.
P. L. 8, 636. to do aught which else free w.
P. L. 9, 343. best are all things as the w.
P. L. 9, 350. against his w. he can receive
P. L. 9, 351. God left free the w.
P. L. 9, 355. dictate false, and misinform the w.
P. L. 9, 728. or this tree impart against his w.
P. L. 9, 855. which with bland words at w. she
P. L. 9, 1127. and the w. heard not
P. L. 9, 1145. my default or w.
P. L. 9, 1174. and force upon free w. hath here
P. L. 9, 1184. in woman overtrusting lets her w.
P. L. 10, 69. in heaven and earth to do thy w.
P. L. 10, 195. to thy husband's w. thine
P. L. 10, 549. his w. who reigns above to
P. L. 10, 746. as my w. concurred not to my
P. L. 10, 768. punishment then justly is at his w.
P. L. 10, 825. but all corrupt both mind and w.
P. L. 10, 826. not to do only but to w. the same
P. L. 11, 83. thus pronounced his sovran w.
P. L. 11, 145. or to incline his w. hard to believe
P. L. 11, 308. to change the w. of Him who all
P. L. 12, 237. Moses might report to them his w.
P. L. 12, 246. God in men obedient to his w.
P. R. 1, 50. in manner at our w. the affairs
P. R. 1, 461. into the world to teach his final w.
P. R. 1, 469. which not w. but misery
P. R. 2, 167. lead at w. the manliest resolutest
P. R. 2, 259. more to do my Father's w.
P. R. 2, 383. I can at w. doubt not as soon as
P. R. 4, 269. wielded at w. that fierce democraty
P. R. 4, 497. thinking to terrify me to thy w.
S. A. 60. I must not quarrel with the w. of
S. A. 97. that she might look at w. through every
S. A. 945. when I must live uxorious to thy w.
S. A. 1450. I had no w. lest I should see him forced
S. 1, 7. O if Jove's w. have linked
S. 2, 12. toward which time leads me and the w.
S. 22, 7. argue not against heaven's hand or w.
C. 600. against the opposing w. and arm
**Willing.**—P. L. 3, 73. and w. feet on the bare
P. L. 3, 211. some other able, and as w. pay
P. L. 5, 533. whether they serve w. or no
P. R. 1, 226. winning words to conquer w. hearts
V. Ex. 52. in w. chains and sweet captivity
**Willinger,**—P. L. 9, 382. the w. I go nor
**Willingly.**—P. L. 9, 1167. yet w. chose

P. L. 5, 466. as that more w. thou couldst not
P. L. 11, 885. so w. doth God remit his ire
P. R. 1, 45. for much more w. I mention air
P. R. 3, 216. though to that gentle brow w. I
S. A. 258. I w. on some conditions came
S. A. 1477. shall w. be paid and numbered down
S. A. 1665. among thy slain self-killed not w.
**Willow.**—C. 891. where grows the w. and the
**Willows.**—L. 42. the w. and the hazel copses
**Wills.**—P. L. 4, 633. as nature w. night bids
P. L. 8, 549. that what she w. to do or say
**Wily.**—P. L. 9, 91. for in the w. snake
P. L. 9, 625. to whom the w. adder blithe
C. 151. now to my charms and to my w. trains
C. 884. upon thy streams with w. glance
**Win.**—P. L. 6, 88. by fight or by surprise to w.
P. L. 6, 123. should w. in arms
P. L. 6, 160. ambitious to w. from me some
P. L. 6, 290. of glory which we mean to w.
P. L. 12, 269. descent who thus shall Canaan w.
P. L. 12, 502. thus they w. great numbers of
P. R. 3, 73. in field great battles w.
P. R. 3, 340. from thence to w. the fairest of
P. R. 4, 469. with my aid to w. thy destined
P. R. 4, 530. to w. him or w. from him what
S. A. 393. to w. from me my capital secret
S. A. 1012. that woman's love can w. or long
S. A. 1411. by this compliance thou wilt w. the
L'A. 124. both contend to w. her grace
**Winchester.**—M. W. 2. honoured wife of W.
**Wind.**—P. L. 1, 231. force of subterranean w.
P. L. 1, 341. warping on the eastern w.
P. L. 1, 537. like a meteor streaming to the w.
P. L. 1, 708. as in an organ from one blast of w.
P. L. 2, 489. while the north w. sleeps
P. L. 3, 439. drive with sails and w. their cany
P. L. 3, 487. a violent cross w. from either
P. L. 4, 982. which way the w. sways them
P. L. 6, 282. nor think thou with w. of aery
P. L. 6, 309. unsafe within the w. of such
P. L. 6, 659. ere they could w. out of such
P. L. 7, 130. as nourishment to w.
P. L. 9, 215. whether to w. the woodbine
P. L. 9, 514. where the w. veers oft
P. L. 11, 312. than breath against the w.
P. L. 11, 738. the south w. rose and with
P. L. 11, 842. driven by a keen north w.
S. A. 1062. fair days have oft contracted w.
S. A. 1070. what w. hath blown him hither
C. 163. w. me into the easy-hearted man
L. 13. unwept and welter to the parching w.
L. 126. but swoln with w. and the rank mist they
L'A. 18. the frolic w. that breathes the spring
**Winding.**—P. L. 4, 545. w. with one ascent
P. R. 3, 256. the one w. the other straight
C. 873. by scaly Triton's w. shell
L'A. 139. in notes with many a w. bout
**Windings.**—A. 47. quaint and wanton w. wove
**Window.**—P. L. 4, 191. in at the w. climbs
L'A. 46. and at my w. bid good morrow
**Windows.**—P. L. 11, 849. heaven his w. shut
Il P. 159. and storied w. richly dight
**Winds.**—P. L. 1, 235. mineral fury aid the w.
P. L. 1, 305. when with fierce w.
P. L. 2, 286. the sound of blustering w.
P. L. 2, 516. toward the four w. four speedy
P. L. 2, 637. by equinoctial w. close sailing from
P. L. 2, 717. till w. the signal blow to join their
P. L. 2, 905. to side with warring w. and poise
P. L. 3, 326. from all w. the living
P. L. 3, 493. the sport of w. all these upwhirled
P. L. 3, 563. and w. with ease through the pure
P. L. 4, 161. off at sea north-east w. blow
P. L. 4, 560. to beware impetuous w.
P. L. 5, 192. his praise ye w. that from four
P. L. 5, 269. now on the polar w.
P. L. 5, 655. they slept fanned with cool w.
P. L. 6, 196. as if on earth w. underground
P. L. 7, 213. the bottom turned by furious w.
P. L. 7, 431. her annual voyage borne on w.
P. L. 9, 989. fear of death deliver to the w.

P. L. 9, 1122. but high *w.* worse within began
P. L. 10, 98. by soft *w.* brought to their ears
P. L. 10, 289. as when two polar *w.* blowing
P. L. 10, 664. to the *w.* they set their corners
P. L. 10, 704. the Levant and the Ponent *w.*
P. L. 10, 1065. while the *w.* blow moist and
P. L. 10, 1074. pushed with *w.* rude in their
P. L. 11, 15. by envious *w.* blown vagabond
P. R. 1, 317. a winter's day when *w.* blow keen
P. R. 2, 26. where *w.* with reeds and osiers
P. R. 2, 363. and *w.* of gentlest gale
P. R. 4, 202. besides from all the quartered *w.*
P. R. 4, 413. nor slept the *w.* within their
P. R. 4, 429. and laid the *w.*
S. A. 719. courted by all the *w.* that hold them
S. A. 961. more deaf to prayers than *w.* and seas
S. A. 961. yet *w.* to seas are reconciled at length
S. A. 1647. as with the force of *w.* and waters
C. 49. coasting the .... shore as the *w.* listed
C. 87. well knows to still the wild *w.*
C. 989. and west *w.* with musky wing
A. 49. of noisome *w.* and blasting vapours chill
L. 28. what time the gray-fly *w.* her sultry horn
L. 91. he asked the waves and asked the felon *w.*
L. 137. shades and wanton *w.* and gushing brooks
L'A. 116. by whispering *w.* soon lulled asleep
Il P. 126. while rocking *w.* are piping loud
H. 64. the *w.* with wonder whist
**Windy.**—P. L. 3, 440. so on this *w.* sea of land
S. A. 1574. what *w.* joy this day had I conceived
**Wine.**—P. L. 1, 502. with insolence and *w.*
P. L. 9, 793. heightened as with *w.*
P. L. 9, 1008. that now as with new *w.*
P. L. 12, 19. plenteous crop corn *w.* and oil
P. R. 2, 350. *w.* that fragrant smell diffused
P. R. 3, 259. of corn the glebe of oil and *w.*
S. A. 443. by the idolatrous rout amidst their *w.*
S. A. 541. desire of *w.* and all delicious drinks
S. A. 1418. lords are lordliest in their *w.*
S. A. 1613. hearts with mirth high cheer and *w.*
S. A. 1670. drunk with idolatry drunk with *w.*
C. 47. crushed the sweet poison of misused *w.*
C. 106. dropping odours dropping *w.*
S. 20. light and choice of Attic taste with *w.*
**Wine-offerings.**—P. L. 12, 21. large *w.-o.*
**Wine-press.**—P. R. 4, 16. about the *w.-p.*
**Wines.**—P. R. 4, 117. their *w.* of Setia Cales
S. A. 553. O madness to think use of strongest *w.*
**Wing.**—P. L. 1, 332. they sprung upon the *w.*
P. L. 1, 345. hovering on *w.* under the cope of
P. L. 1, 617. ranks they bend from *w.* to *w.*
P. L. 2, 72. steep to scale with upright *w.*
P. L. 2, 132. with obscure *w.* scout far and wide
P. L. 2, 529. upon the *w.* or in swift race
P. L. 2, 634. now shaves with level *w.* the deep
P. L. 2, 842. and up and down unseen *w.*
P. L. 3, 13. thee I revisit now with bolder *w.*
P. L. 5, 268. worlds and worlds with steady *w.*
P. L. 6, 74. of birds in orderly array on *w.*
P. L. 6, 243. then soaring on main *w.* tormented
P. L. 6, 362. on each *w.* Uriel and Raphael
P. L. 6, 535. of cherubim the swiftest *w.*
P. L. 6, 778. army circumfused on either *w.*
P. L. 7, 4. above the flight of Pegasean *w.*
P. L. 7, 394. and every bird of *w.* after his kind
P. L. 7, 425. part loosely *w.* the region
P. L. 7, 429. with mutual *w.* easing their
P. L. 8, 351. each bird stooped on his *w.*
P. L. 9, 45. or years damp my intended *w.*
P. L. 10, 316. first lighted from his *w.* and
P. R. 1, 14. with prosperous *w.* full summed to
P. R. 1, 500. night with her sullen *w.* to
P. R. 4, 541. and without *w.* of hippogrif
P. R. 4. 582. angels on full sail of *w.*
C. 989. and west winds with musky *w.*
Il P. 52. him that yon soars on golden *w.*
S. 2, 2. stolen on his *w.* my three and twentieth
S. 13, 9. and verse must lend her *w.*
H. 50. turtle *w.* the amorous clouds dividing
P. 5, but headlong joy is ever on the *w.*

P. 50. or should I thence hurried on viewless *w.*
**Winged.**—P. L. 1, 175. *w.* with red lightning
P. L. 1, 674. thither *w.* with speed
P. L. 1, 752. meanwhile the *w.* heralds
P. L. 2, 944. with *w.* course o'er hill or moory
P. L. 3, 299. the speediest of thy *w.* messengers
P. L. 4, 576. to whom the *w.* warrior thus
P. L. 4, 788. Ithuriel and Zephon with *w.*
P. L. 5, 55. one shaped and *w.* like one of those
P. L. 5, 247. nor delayed the *w.* saint after his
P. L. 5, 277. a seraph *w.* six wings he wore
P. L. 5, 498. improved by tract of time and *w.*
P. L. 5, 468. whom the *w.* hierarch replied
P. L. 5, 744. far was advanced on *w.* speed
P. L. 6, 279. sudden vengeance *w.* from God
P. L. 7, 199. virtues *w.* spirits and chariots *w.*
P. L. 7, 572. his *w.* messengers on errands
P. L. 10, 91. though with swiftest minutes *w.*
P. L. 11, 7. and *w.* for heaven with speedier
P. L. 11, 706. rapt in a balmy cloud with *w.*
S. A. 1283. with *w.* expedition swift as the
C. 730. the earth cumbered and *w.* air darked
Cir. 179 and *w.* warriors bright
**Wings.**—P. L. 1, 20. with mighty *w.* outspread
P. L. 1, 225. then with expanded *w.*
P. L. 1, 768. brushed with the hiss of rustling *w.*
P. L. 2, 408. upborne with undefatigable *w.*
P. L. 2, 631. puts on swift *w.* and toward the
P. L. 2, 700. and to thy speed add *w.*
P. L. 2, 885. with extended *w.* a bannered host
P. L. 2, 906. and poise their lighter *w.*
P. L. 2, 949. with head, hands, *w.* or feet
P. L. 2, 1046. weighs his spread *w.* at leisure
P. L. 3, 73. ready now to stoop with wearied *w.*
P. L. 3, 87. all restraint broke loose he *w.* his
P. L. 3, 382. but with both *w.* veil their eyes
P. L. 3, 627. shoulders fledge with *w.*
P. L. 3, 641. *w.* he wore of many a coloured
P. L. 4, 157. gales fanning their odoriferous *w.*
P. L. 4, 764. Love waves his purple *w.*
P. L. 4, 974. heaven's King ride on thy *w.*
P. L. 5, 199. bear on your *w.* and in your notes
P. L. 5, 250. veiled with his gorgeous *w.*
P. L. 5, 277. a seraph winged six *w.* he wore
P. L. 6, 755. and *w.* were set with eyes
P. L. 6, 771. he on the *w.* of cherub rode
P. L. 6, 897. the four spread out their starry *w.*
P. L. 7, 218. on the *w.* of cherubim
P. L. 7, 235. on the *w.* the Spirit of God
P. L. 7, 389. fowl fly above the earth with *w.*
P. L. 7, 434. and spread their painted *w.*
P. L. 7, 439. between her white *w.* mantling
P. L. 7, 477. those waved their limber fans for *w.*
P. L. 7, 484. their snaky folds and added *w.*
P. L. 8, 516. and from their *w.* flung rose
P. L. 9, 1010. divinity within them breeding *w.*
P. L. 10, 244. *w.* growing
P. L. 11, 738. south wind rose and with black *w.*
P. L. 15, 253. the *w.* of two bright Cherubim
P. R. 2, 365. odours fanned from their soft *w.*
P. R. 2, 403. with sound of harpies *w.*
P. R. 3, 309. wedges and half-moons and *w.*
P. R. 4, 66. and cohorts turms of horse and *w.*
S. A. 973. both his *w.* one black the other white
C. 214. thou hovering angel girt with golden *w.*
C. 249. how sweetly did they float upon the *w.*
C, 378. plumes her feathers and lets grow her *w.*
L. 93. and questioned every gust of rugged *w.*
L'A. 6. brooding darkness spreads his jealous *w.*
Il P. 148. wave at his *w.* in aery stream
S. 14, 11. with purple beams and azure *w.*
S. 15. 8. to imp their serpent *w.*
H. 114. seen in glittering ranks with *w.* displayed
**Wink.**—C. 401. as bid me hope danger will *w.*
**Winning**—P. L. 2, 472. *w.* cheap the high
P. L. 4, 479. less *w.* soft less amiably mild
P. L. 8, 61. lent her as queen a pomp of *w.* graces
P. R. 1, 154. *w.* by conquest what the first man
P. R. 1, 222. by *w.* words to conquer willing
P. R. 213. descend with all her *w.* charms
**Winnows.**—P. L. 5, 270. with quick fan *w.*

BB

**Wins.**—P. L. 2. 1016. his way *w.*
**Winter.**—P. L. 10, 655. to call decrepit *w.*
  P. R. 1, 317. against a *w.'s* day when wind*s*
  S. A. 1577. nipt with the lagging rear of *w.'s*
  H. 29. it was the *w.* wild while the heaven-born
  D. F. I. 4, *w.'s* force that made thy blossom dry
  D. F. I. 28. to change thee *w.* had no power
  M. W. 36. saved with care from *w.'s* nip
**Wintry.**—P. 6. in *w.* solstice like the shortened
**Wipe.**—L.181. *w.* the tears for ever from his eyes
  D. F. I. 12. thereby to *w.* away the infamous blot
**Wiped.**—P. L. 5, 131. *w.* them with her hair
  P. L. 12, 645. natural tears they dropped but *w.*
**Wire.**—P. L. 7, 597. by string or golden *w.*
**Wires.**—S. M. 13. their immortal harps of ... *w.*
  V. Ex. 38. to the touch of golden *w.*
**Wisdom.**—P. L. 2, 565. vain *w.* all and false
  P. L. 3, 50. and *w.* at one entrance quite shut
  P. L. 3, 170. Son who art alone my word my *w.*
  P. L. 3, 686. *w.* wake, suspicion sleeps at *w.'s.*
  P. L. 3, 706. or the *w.* infinite that brought
  P. L. 4, 293. truth *w.* sanctitude severe
  P. L. 4, 491. *w.* which alone is truly fair
  P. L. 4, 914. and scourge that *w.* back to hell
  P. L. 7, 9. thou with eternal *w.* didst converse
  P. L. 7, 10. *w.* thy sister
  P. L. 7, 83. as to highest *w.* seemed
  P. L. 7, 187. to him glory and praise whose *w.*
  P. L. 7, 930. turns *w.* to folly
  P. L. 8, 194. is the prime *w.* what is more is
  P. L. 8, 552. *w.* in discourse with her loses
  P. L. 8, 563. but thine and be not diffident of *w.*
  P. L. 9, 725. forthwith attains *w.* without their
  P. L. 9, 809. thou open'st *w.'s* way and givest
  P. L. 10, 373. thy *w.* gained with odds what
  P. L. 11, 636. should better hold his place by *w.*
  P. L. 12, 154. him in faith, in *w.* and renown
  P. L. 12, 332. his next son for wealth and *w.*
  P. L. 12, 576. thou hast attained the sum of *w,*
  P. R. 1, 68. displaying all virtue grace and *w.*
  P. R. 1, 175. but to vanquish by *w.* hellish wiles
  P. R. 1, 386. to hear attent thy *w.* and behold
  P. R. 2, 34. his words his *w.* full of grace and
  P. R. 2, 431, while virtue valour *w.* sit in want
  P. R. 3, 91. by deeds of peace by *w.* eminent
  P. R. 4, 222. the day be famous then by *w.*
  P. R. 4, 319. therefore seeks in these true *w.*
  P. R. 4, 528. who and what he is his *w.* power
  S. A. 54. without a double share of *w.*
  S. A. 57. to subserve where *w.* bears command
  S. A. 207. of *w.* nothing more than mean
  S. A. 936. so much of adder's *w.* I have learned
  S. A. 1010. it is not virtue *w.* valour wit
  S. A. 1747. dispose of Highest *W.* brings about
  C. 375. and *w.'s* self oft seeks to sweet retired
**Wisdom-giving.**—P. L. 9, 679. *w.-g.* plant
**Wise.**—P. L. 2, 155. *w.* let loose at once his
  P. L. 2, 193. than *w.* to frustrate all our
  P. L. 2, 202. if we were *w.* against so great a foe
  P. L. 3, 680. *w.* are all his ways
  P. L. 4, 886. hadst in heaven the esteem of *w.*
  P. L. 4, 904. of one in heaven to judge of *w.*
  P. L. 4, 907. in doubt whether to hold them *w.*
  P. L. 4, 910. so *w.* he judges it to fly from pain
  P. L. 4, 948. pretending first *w.* to fly pain
  P. L. 7, 425. part more *w.* in common ranged in
  P. L. 8, 26. I oft admire how nature *w.* and
  P.L.8,173. be lowly *w.* think only what concerns
  P. L. 8, 578. sees when thou art seen least *w.*
  P. L. 9, 311. in thy sight more *w.*
  P. L. 9, 338. left so imperfect by the Maker *w.*
  P. L. 9, 679. O sacred *w.* and wisdom-giving
  P. L. 9, 683. highest agents deemed however *w.*
  P. L. 9, 759. forbids us good forbids us to be *w.*
  P. L. 9, 778. of virtue to make *w.* what hinders
  P. L. 9, 867. serpent *w.* or not restrained as we
  P. L. 9, 938. Creator *w.* though threatening
  P. L. 10, 7. who in all things *w.* and just
  P. L. 10, 881. thee from my side imagined *w.*
  P. L. 10, 889. creator *w.* that peopled highest
  P. L. 11, 666. eminent in *w.* deport

P. L. 12, 568. and worldly *w.* by simply meek
P. R. 1, 250. guided the *w.* men thither from
P. R. 1, 486. thy Father who is holy *w.* and pure
P. R. 2, 454. *w.* man's cumbrance if not snare
P. R. 2, 468. which every *w.* and virtuous man
P. R. 3, 11. thy heart contains of good *w.* just
P. R. 3, 58. and the *w.* are few
P. R. 3, 115. *w.* or unwise no difference no
P. R. 4, 143. what *w.* and valiant man would
P. R. 4, 302. and his virtuous man *w.* perfect
P. R. 4, 322. however many books *w.* men
P. R. 4, 535. of mere man both *w.* and good
S. A. 212. shall again pretend they ne'er so *w.*
S. A. 652. many are the sayings of the *w.*
C. 448. *w.* Minerva wore unconquered virgin
C. 637. that Hermes once to *w.* Ulysses gave
C. 705. to a well-governed and *w.* appetite
C. 813. be *w.* and taste
A. 20. might she the *w.* Latona be
S. 9, 14. hast gained thy entrance virgin *w.* and
S. 12, 12. for who loves that must first be *w.* and
S. 21, 12. and disapproves that care though *w.* in
V. Ex. 48. such as the *w.* Demodocus once told
**Wiselier.**—P. L. 10, 1023. God hath *w.* armed
**Wisely.**—P. L. 8, 73. great Architect did *w.*
  S. 9, 2. *w.* hast shunned the broad way and the
  D.F.I. 73. and *w.* learn to curb thy sorrows wild
  V. Ex. 70. that far events full *w.* could presage
**Wiser.**—P. R. 1, 439. returned the *w.* or the
  P. R. 2, 205. he whom we attempt is *w.* far
**Wisest.**—P. L. 1, 400. the *w.* heart of Solomon
  P. L. 8, 550. seems *w.* virtuousest discreetest
  P. R. 2, 170. beguiled the heart of *w.* Solomon
  P. R. 3, 240. the *w.* unexperienced will be ever
  P. R. 4, 276. the oracle pronounced *w.* of men
  P. R. 4, 293. the first and *w.* of them all
  S. A. 210. tax not divine disposal *w.* men
  S. A. 759. that *w.* and best men full oft beguiled
  S. A. 867. celebrated in the mouths of *w.* men
  S. A. 1034. whate'er it be to *w.* men and best
  H. 149. but *w.* fate says no, this must not yet be
**Wish.**—P. L. 2, 157. to give his enemies their *w.*
  P. L. 2, 606. their sorrow to augment and *w.*
  P. L. 6, 493. ere dawn effect shall end our *w.*
  P. L. 6, 818. that they may have their *w.*
  P. L. 8, 43. and grace that won who saw to *w.*
  P. L. 8, 63. desire into all eyes to *w.* her still
  P. L. 8, 451. thy *w.* exactly to thy heart's desire
  P. L. 9, 258. with greedy hope to find his *w.*
  P. L. 9, 423. when to his *w.* beyond his hope
  P. L. 10, 834. fond *w.*! couldst thou support
  P. R. 4, 376. cause to *w.* thou never hadst
  S. A. 228. O that I never had fond *w.* too late
  S. A. 1077. yet *w.* it had not been
  S. A. 1127. thou oft shalt *w.* thyself at Gath
  S. A. 1414. your company along I will not *w.*
  S.A.1539. and to our *w.* I see one hither speeding
  M. M. 10. and welcome thee and *w.* thee long
  W. S. 16. kings for such a tomb would *w.* to die
**Wished.**—P. L. 1, 208. and *w.* morn delays
  P. L. 6, 150. but in *w.* hour of my revenge
  P. L. 6, 842. that *w.* the mountains now might
  P. L. 9, 421. he sought them both but *w.* his
  P. L. 9, 422. he *w.* but not with hope of what
  P. L. 9, 714. death to be *w.* though threatened
  P. L. 9, 1025. it might be *w.* for this one tree
  P. L. 10, 454. and whom they *w.*
  P. L. 11, 181. so spake so *w.* much-humbled Eve
  C. 558. and *w.* she might deny her nature
  C. 574. the aidless innocent lady his *w.* prey
  C. 950. many a friend to gratulate his *w.* presence
**Wishes.**—P. L. 10, 901. or whom he *w.* most
  A. 6. to whom our vows and *w.* bend
**Wit.**—P. L. 9, 93. as from his *w.* and native
  S. A. 1010. it is not virtue wisdom valour *w.*
  C. 790. enjoy your dear *w.* and gay rhetoric
  L'A. 123. and judge the prize of *w.* or arms
**Witcheries.**—C. 523. skilled in his mother's *w.*
**Witches.**—P. L. 2, 665. dance with Lapland *w.*
**Withal.**—P. L. 5, 238. tell him *w.* his danger
  P. L. 12, 82. yet know *w.* since thy original

P. R. 4, 128. what if I *w*. expel a devil
S. A. 58. to show *w*. how slight the gift was
**Withdraw.**—P. L. 7, 612. and from thee *w*.
P. L. 9, 261. his first design be to *w*. our fealty
P. L. 12, 107. wearied with their iniquities *w*.
P. R. 2, 55. nor will *w*. him now nor will recall
S. A. 192. but in adverse *w* their head
**Withdraws.**—P. L. 5, 686. shadowy cloud *w*.
**Withdrew.**—P. L. 9, 386. her hand soft she *w*.
**Withered.**—P. L. 1, 612. their glory *w*.
P. L. 6, 850. that *w*. all their strength
P. L. 11, 540. which will change to *w*. weak
P. R. 1, 316. or *w*. sticks to gather which might
**Withers.**—C. 744. it *w*. on the stalk
**Withheld.**—P. L. 7, 117. shall not be *w*. thy
P. L. 10, 903. or if she love *w*. by parents
H. 79. the sun himself *w*. his wonted speed
**Withhold.**—P. L. 5, 62. shall from me *w*.
S. A. 1125. which long shall not *w*. me from thy
**Withholds.**—P. R. 2, 380. and who *w*. my
S. A. 1233. no man *w*. thee
**Within.**—P. L. 1, 388. yea often placed *w*.'his
P. L. 1, 705. *w*. the ground a various mould
P. L. 1, 725. discover wide *w*. her ample spaces
P. L. 1, 792. but far *w*. and in their own
P. L. 2, 12. for since no deep *w*. her gulf can
P. L. 2, 236. *w*. heaven's bound
P. L. 2, 295. wrought still *w*. them
P. L. 2, 659. still barked and howled *w*. unseen
P. L. 3, 194. and I will place *w*. them
P. L. 3, 622. whereby he soon saw *w*. ken
P. L. 4, 20. stir the hell *w*. him for *w*. him
P. L. 4, 64. from *w*. or from without to all
P. L. 4, 182. and sheer *w*. lights on his feet
P. L. 4, 461. a shape *w*. the watery gleam
P. L. 4, 586. but if *w*. the circuit of these walks
P. L. 4, 964. if from this hour *w*. these hallowed
P. L. 5, 270. till *w*. soar of towering eagles
P. L. 5, 303. and Eve *w*., due at her hour
F. L. 5, 410. contain *w*. them every lower
P. L. 5, 554. some doubt *w*. me move
P. L. 5, 596. they stood orb *w*. orb
P. L. 5, 713. and from *w*. the golden lamps
P. L. 6, 5. there is a cave *w*. the mount of God
P. L. 6, 158. they feel vigour divine *w*. them
P. L. 6, 309. unsafe *w*. the wind of such
P. L. 6, 581. collected stood *w*. our thoughts
P. L. 6, 751. wheel *w*. wheel undrawn
P. L. 7, 22. *w*. the visible diurnal sphere
P. L. 7, 65. what *w*. Eden or without was done
P. L. 7, 120. thy desire of knowledge *w*. bounds
P. L. 7, 167. and bid the deep *w*. appointed
P. L. 7, 204. for *w*. them spirit lived
P. L. 7, 305. all but *w*. those banks where rivers
P. L. 8, 242. long ere our approaching heard *w*.
P. L. 8, 346. of fish *w*. their watery residence
P. L. 8, 440. expressing well the spirit *w*. thee
P. L. 8, 642. perfect *w*. no outward aid require
P. L. 9, 96. power active *w*. beyond the sense
P. L. 9, 121. so much more I feel torment *w*.
P. L. 9, 315. like sense *w*. thee feel
P. L. 9, 353. find peace *w*. favour from heaven
P. L. 9, 348. *w*. himself the danger lies, yet lies *w*.
P. L. 9, 681. now I feel thy power *w*. me
P. L. 9, 836. done as to the power that dwelt *w*.
P. L. 9, 955. so forcible *w*. my heart I feel the
P. L. 9, 1010. feel divinity *w* them breeding
P. L. 9, 1122. but high winds worse *w*. began
P. L. 10, 230. *w*. the gates of hell sat sin and
P. L. 10, 231. in counterview *w*. the gates
P. L. 10, 243. methinks I feel new strength *w*.
P. L. 10, 369. confined *w*. hell-gates till now
P. L. 10, 717. but worse felt *w*.
P. L. 11, 470. terrible at the entrance than *w*.
P. L. 12, 91. since he permits *w*. himself
P. L. 12, 488. who shall dwell his spirit *w*.
P. L. 12, 523. the spirit *w*. shall on the heart
P. L. 12, 587. a paradise *w*. thee happier far
P. R. 1, 41. *w*. thick clouds and dark
P. R. 1, 198. while I consider what from *w*.
P. R. 2, 63. *w*. her breast though calm

P. R. 2, 466. yet he who reigns *w*. himself
P. R. 2, 471. subject himself to anarchy *w*.
P. R. 3, 275. of length *w*. her wall several
P. R. 4, 250. *w*. the walls then view the schools
P. R. 4, 284. *w*. thyself much more with empire
P. R. 4, 414. nor slept the winds *w*. their stony
S. A. 77. *w*. doors or without still as a fool
S. A. 153. bondage or lost sight prison *w*. prison
S. A. 429. sacred trust of silence deposited *w*. thee
S. A. 584. cause light again *w*. thy eyes to spring
S. A. 595. nature *w*. me seems
S. A. 663. feel *w*. some source of consolation
S. A. 1038. far *w*. defensive arms a cleaving
C. 147. run to your shrouds *w*. these brakes
C. 231. that livest unseen *w*. thy aery shell
C. 357. or while we speak *w*. the direful grasp
C. 381. he that has light *w*. his own clear breast
C. 520. *w*. the navel of this hideous wood
**Without.**—P. L. 1, 67. but torture *w*. end still
P. L. 1, 791. though *w*. number still amidst
P. L. 2, 89. must exercise us *w*. hope of end
P. L. 2, 685. that be assured *w*. leave asked
P. L. 2, 777. none can pass *w*. my opening
P. L. 2, 870. thy daughter and thy darling *w*. end
P. L. 2, 892. ocean *w*. bound *w*. dimension
P. L. 2, 975. alone and *w*. guide half lost I seek
P. L. 3, 75. *w*. firmament uncertain which
P. L. 3, 120. so *w*. least impulse or shadow
P. L. 3, 142. love *w*. end and *w*. measure grace
P. L. 3, 166. and blasphemed *w*. defence
P. L. 3, 222. and now *w*. redemption all
P. L. 3, 289. *w*. thee none
P. L. 3, 346. shout…as from numbers *w*. number
P. L. 3, 385. conspicuous countenance *w*. cloud
P. L. 3, 561. and *w*. longer pause downright
P. L. 4, 65. from within or from *w*. to all
P. L. 4, 265. and *w*. thorn the rose
P. L. 4, 442. and *w*. whom am to no end
P. L. 4, 656. or glittering starlight *w*. thee
P. L. 4, 872. not likely to part hence *w*. contest
P. L. 5, 162. and choral symphonies day *w*. night
P. L. 5, 165. him last him midst and *w*. end
P. L. 5, 178. move in mystic dance not *w*. song
P. L. 5, 351. more train accompanied than
P. L. 5, 566. how *w*. remorse the ruin of so
P. L. 5, 615. ordained *w*. redemption *w*. end
P. L. 5, 714. saw *w*. their light rebellion rising
P. L. 5, 798. who *w* law err not
P. L. 5, 803. thus far his bold discourse *w*. control
P. L. 5, 885. are gone forth *w*. recall
P. L. 6, 137. out of smallest things could *w*. end
P. L. 6, 549. instant *w*. disturb they took alarm
P. L. 7, 65. what within Eden or *w*. was done
P. L. 7, 161. one kingdom joy and union *w*. end
P. L. 7, 178. cannot *w*. process of speech be
P. L. 7, 542. all the earth yields variety *w*. end
P. L. 8, 35. attains her end *w*. least motion
P. L. 8, 237. not that they durst *w*. his leave
P. L. 8, 302. as in air smooth sliding *w*. step
P. L. 8, 621. and *w*. love no happiness
P. L. 9, 336. alone *w*. exterior help sustained
P. L. 9, 725. forthwith attains wisdom *w*. their
P. L. 9, 791. greedily she engorged *w*. restraint
P. L. 9, 800. not *w*. song each morning and due
P. L. 9, 821. in my power *w*. copartner
P. L. 9, 883. *w*. him live no life
P. L. 9, 878. *w*. thee can despise
P. L. 9, 908. how can I live *w*. thee how forego
P. L. 10, 118. the gracious Judge *w*. revile
P. L. 10, 163. when the Lord God heard *w*. delay
P. L. 10, 491. *w*. our hazard labour or alarm
P. L. 10, 714. these were from *w*. the growing
P. L. 10, 760. though God made thee *w*. thy
P. L. 10, 797. he exercise wrath *w*. end on man
P. L. 10, 812. begun both in me and *w*. me
P. L. 10, 893. with men as angels *w*. feminine
P. L. 10, 995. with desire to languish *w*. hope
P. L. 10, 1048. both heard and judged *w*. wrath
P. L. 11, 45. to whom the Father *w*. cloud
P. L. 11, 105. *w*. remorse drive out the sinful
P. L. 11, 586. and let their eyes rove *w*. rein

P. L. 11, 750. sea *w.* shore
P. L. 12, 93. subjects him from *w.*
P. L. 12, 240. to God is no access *w.* Mediator
P. L. 12, 374. dewed in tears *w.* the vent of
P. L. 12, 616. *w.* thee here to stay is to go
P. R. 1, 199. what from *w.* comes often to my
P. R. 1, 353. and forty days Elijah *w.* food
P. R. 2, 119. there *w.* sign of boast or sign of joy
P. R. 2, 126. these mild seats *w.* new trouble
P. R. 2, 250. or God support nature *w.* repast
P. R. 2, 256. remain *w.* this body's wasting
P. R. 2, 306. and well I know not *w.* hunger
P. R. 2, 433. yet wealth *w.* these three is
P. R. 2, 442. and reign in Israel *w.* end
P. R. 3, 90. *w.* ambition war or violence
P. R. 3, 193. *w.* distrust or doubt that he may
P. R. 3, 197. my exaltation *w.* change or end
P. R. 3, 356. *w.* means used what it predicts
P. R. 3, 371. thou shalt regain *w.* him not
P. R. 4, 231. *w.* their learning how wilt thou
P. R. 4, 391. as *w.* end *w.* beginning
P. R. 4, 541. and *w.* wing of hippogrif bore
P. R. 4, 617. of tempter and temptation *w.* fear
S. A. 53. but what is strength *w.* a double share
S. A. 77. within doors or *w.* still as a fool
S. A. 82. total eclipse *w.* all hope of day
S. A. 157. which men enjoying sight oft *w.* cause
S. A. 288. *w.* reprieve adjudged to death
S. A. 677. heads *w.* name no more remembered
S. A. 734. which to have merited *w.* excuse
S. A. 848. to have yielded *w.* blame
S. A. 1006. *w.* much inward passion felt
S. A. 1238. bulk *w.* spirit vast
S. A. 1395. come *w.* delay
S. A. 1481. I am fixed not to part hence *w.* him
S. A. 1625. which *w.* help of eye might be assayed
S. A. 1659. the vulgar only scaped who stood *w.*
C. 310. *w.* the sure guess of well practised feet
C. 409. secure *w.* all doubt or controversy
C. 816. *w.* his rod reversed and backward mutters
L. 14. *w.* the meed of some melodious tear
**Withstand.**—P. L. 6, 253. to *w.* he hasted
P. R. 3, 250. how best their opposition to *w.*
S. A. 127. or fiercest wild beast could *w.*
S. A. 1111. in fight *w.* me single and unarmed
**Withstands.**—P. L. 2, 610. but fate *w.*
**Withstood.**—P. L. 5, 242. that shall be *w.*
P. L. 7, 300. nor *w.* them rock or hill
**Witness.**—P. L. 1, 503. *w.* the streets of Sodom
P. L. 1, 635. for me be *w.* all the host of heaven
P. L. 3, 700. to *w.* with thine eyes what some
P. L. 5, 202. *w.* if I be silent morn or even
P. L. 6, 563. but that I doubt however *w.*
P. L. 6, 564. heaven *w.* thou anon while we
P. L. 7, 617. *w.* this new-made world another
P. L. 9, 317. with me best *w.* of thy virtue
P. L. 9, 334. favour from heaven our *w.*
P. L. 10, 914. *w.* heaven what love sincere
P. L. 12, 101. *w.* the irreverent son of him
P. R. 1, 26. and *w.* bore as to his worthier
P. R. 1, 29. nor was long his *w.* unconfirmed
P. R. 2, 435. *w.* those ancient empires
P. R. 3, 107. and thereby *w.* whence I am
S. A. 239. thou never wast remiss I bear thee *w.*
S. A. 906. *w.* when I was worried with thy peals
S. A. 1752. hath in place bore *w.* gloriously
L. 82. and perfect *w.* of all-judging Jove
W. S. 6. needst thou such weak *w.* of thy name
**Witnessed.**—P. L. 1, 57. that *w.* huge affliction
**Wits.**—P. R. 4, 241. native to famous *w.*
V. Ex. 22. which deepest spirits and choices *w.*
**Wives.**—P. L. 11, 737. with their four *w.*
P. R. 2, 171. made him bow to the gods of his *w.*
S. A. 957. among illustrious women faithful *w.*
**Wizard**—C. 571. where that damned *w.* hid in sly
C. 872. and the Carpathian *w.'s* hook
L. 55. nor yet where Deva spreads her *w.* stream
**Wizards.**—H. 23. the star-led *w.* haste with
**Woe.**—P. L. 1, 3. the world and all our *w.*
P. L. 1, 64. served only to discover sights of *w.*

P. L. 1, 414. wanton rites which cost them *w.*
P. L. 2, 87. in this abhorred deep to utter *w.*
P. L. 2, 161. reserved and destined to eternal *w.*
P. L. 2, 225. we procure not to ourselves more *w.*
P. L. 2, 608. all pain and *w.*
P. L. 2, 695. to waste eternal days in *w.* and pain
P. L. 2, 872. sad instrument of all our *w.*
P. L. 3, 633. journey's end and our beginning *w.*
P. L. 4, 5. *w.* to the inhabitants on earth
P. L. 4, 70. to me alike it deals eternal *w.*
P. L. 4, 368. deliver ye to *w.*
P. L. 4, 369. more *w.* the more your taste is
P. L. 5, 543. high state of bliss into what *w.*
P. L. 6, 877. the house of *w.* and pain
P. L. 6, 907. once to gain companion of his *w.*
P. L. 8, 333. from hence into a world of *w.*
P. L. 8, 638. the weal or *w.* in thee is placed
P. L. 9, 11. brought into this world a world of .
P. L. 9, 133. linked in weal or *w.*; in *w.* then
P. L. 9, 255. seeks to work us *w.* and shame
P. L. 9, 645. tree of prohibition root of all our *w.*
P. L. 9, 783. gave signs of *w.* that all was lost
P. L. 9, 831. share with me in bliss or *w.*
P. L. 9, 916. never shall be parted bliss or *w.*
P. L. 10, 465. accursed the house of *w.*
P. L. 10, 555. work them farther *w.* or shame
P. L. 10, 935. sole cause to thee of all this *w.*
P. L. 10, 961. other's burden in our share of *w.*
P. L. 10, 980. which must be born to certain *w.*
P. L. 11, 60. this other served but to eternize *w.*
P. L. 11, 632. still I see the tenor of man's *w.*
P. R. 1, 398. companions of my misery and *w.*
P. R. 1, 399. but long since with *w.* nearer
S. A. 351. but often proves our *w.* our bane
S. A. 813. oft well meaning wrought much *w.*
L. 106. to that sanguine flower inscribed with *w*
S. 18. 14. early may fly the Babylonian *w.*
P. 9. and set my harp to notes of saddest *w.*
P. 32. heaven and earth are coloured with my *w.*
**Woes.**—P. L. 4, 535. for long *w.* are to succeed
P. L. 10, 742. dear-bought with lasting *w.*
P. L. 10, 754. thou added the sense of endless *w.*
C. 836. piteous of her *w.* reared her lank head
**Woeful.**—P. L. 10, 984. this cursed world a *w.*
L. 165. weep no more *w.* shepherds weep no more
**Wolf.**—P. L. 4, 183. as when a prowling *w.*
C. 70. into some brutish form of *w.* or bear
C. 504. or to pursue the stealth of pilfering *w.*
L. 128. besides what the grim *w.* with privy paw
**Wolves.**—P. L. 12, 508. *w.* .... grievous *w.*
C. 534. like stabled *w.*
S. 16, 14. of hireling *w.* whose gospel is their
**Woman.**—P. L. 2, 650. the one seemed *w.* to the
P. L. 4, 638. is *w.'s* happiest knowledge
P. L. 8, 496. *w.* is her name of man extracted
P. L. 9, 233. lovelier can be found in *w.*
P. L. 9, 343. O *w.* best are all things
P. L. 9, 481. alone the *w.* opportune to all
P. L. 9, 1183. who to worth in *w.* overtrusting
P. L. 10, 137. this *w.* whom thou madest to be
P. L. 10, 158. say *w.* what is this which thou
P. L. 10, 179. between thee and the *w.* I will
P. L. 10, 192. and to the *w.* thus his sentence
P. L. 10, 837. divided with that bad *w.*
P. L. 11, 116. my covenant in the *w.'s.* seed
P. L. 11, 496. though not of *w.* born
P. L. 11, 617. wherein consists *w.'s* domestic
P. L. 11, 633. holds on the same from *w.* to
P. L. 12, 327. Son the *w.'s* seed to thee foretold
P. L. 12, 379. should be called the seed of *w.*
P. L. 12, 543. the *w.'s* seed obscurely then
P. L. 12, 601. by the *w.'s* seed
P. R. 1, 64. *w.'s* seed destined to this is late of *w.*
P. R. 2, 208. what *w.* will you find though
S. A. 50. but weakly to a *w.* must reveal it
S. A. 202. the secret gift of God to a deceitful *w.*
S. A. 236. gave my fort of silence to a *w.*
S. A. 379. and have betrayed it to a *w.*
S. A. 749. and arts of every *w.* false like thee
S. A. 783. trusted that to *w.'s* frailty
S. A. 844. no plea in man or *w.*

S. A. 903. in argument with men a *w.* ever goes
S. A. 1012. that *w.'s* love can win or long inherit
S. A. 1114. till they had hired a *w.* with their gold
S. 22, 6. or star throughout the year or man or *w.*
**Womankind.**—P. R. 2, 175. on *w.* admiring
**Womb.**—P. L. 1, 673. that in his *w.* was hid
P. L. 2, 150. in the wide *w.* of uncreated night
P. L. 2, 657. into her *w.* and kennel there
P. L. 2, 766. my *w.* conceived a growing burden
P. L. 2, 778. till my *w.* pregnant by thee
P. L. 2, 793. when they list into the *w.* they creep
P. L. 2, 911. *w.* of nature and perhaps her grave
P. L. 5, 181. the eldest birth of nature's *w.*
P. L. 5, 302. to warm earth's inmost *w.*
P. L. 5, 388. whose fruitful *w.* shall fill the
P. L. 7, 276. but in the *w.* as yet of
P. L. 7, 454. and straight opening her fertile *w.*
P. L. 10, 476. plunged in the *w.* of unoriginal
P. L. 10, 1053. with joy, fruit of thy *w.*
P. L. 12, 381. and from thy *w.* the Son of God
S. A. 634. his destined from the *w.*
S. A. 1703. from out her ashy *w.* now teemed
C. 131. when the dragon *w.* of Stygian
T. 4. and glut thyself with what thy *w.* devours
D. F. I. 30. thy corse corrupts in earth's dark *w.*
M. W. 33. and the languished mother's *w.*
**Women.**—P. L. 4, 409. to first of *w.* Eve
P. L. 11, 582. behold a bevy of fair *w.*
P. R. 2, 68. highly favoured among *w.*
P. R. 2, 71. above the lot of other *w.*
P. R. 2, 153. set *w.* in his eye and in his walk
P. R. 2, 169. *w.* when nothing else beguiled
P. R. 2, 204. thence to the bait of *w.*
S. A. 211. have erred and by bad *w.* been deceived
S. A. 216. why thou shouldst wed Philistian *w.*
S. A. 957. among illustrious *w.* faithful wives
S. A. 983. named among the famousest of *w.*
**Won.**—P. L. 2, 762. with attractive graces *w.*
P. L. 2, 978. place from your dominion *w.*
P. L. 3, 12. *w.* from the void and formless
P. L. 4, 853. more glory will be *w.* or less be
P. L. 6, 122. who in debate of truth hath *w.*
P. L. 8, 43. and grace that *w.* who saw to wish
P. L. 8, 503. be wooed and not unsought be *w.*
P. L. 9, 131. *w.* to what may work his utter loss
P. L. 9, 674. each act *w.* audience
P. L. 9, 734. into her heart too easy entrance *w.*
P. L. 9, 991. much *w.* that he his love had
P. L. 10, 372. thy virtue hath *w.* what thy
P. L. 10, 459. and with these words attention *w.*
P. L. 11, 375. and earn rest from labour *w.*
P. L. 12, 262. kings distroyed and kingdoms *w.*
P. R. 1, 63. in this fair empire *w.* of earth
P. R. 1, 279. his greater and was hardly *w.*
P. R. 1, 426. all inflictions but his patience *w.*
P. R. 3, 33. had ere these *w.* Asia
P. R. 3, 156. not part easily from possession *w.*
P. R. 3, 297. the luxurious kings of Antioch *w.*
P. R. 4, 5. and *w.* so much on Eve so little here
S. A. 470. of all these boasted trophies *w.* on me
S. A. 1099. *w.* by a Philistine ... unforeskinned
S. A. 1102. that honour certain to have *w.* by
L'A. 148. such strains as would have *w.* the ear
S. 20, 4. what may be *w.* from the hard season
H. 104. now was almost *w.* to think her part was
**Wonder.**—P. L. 1, 282. no *w.* fallen such
P. L. 1, 777. till the signal given behold a *w.*
P. L. 3, 542. looks down with *w.* at the
P. L. 3, 552. such *w.* seized, though after
P. L. 3, 606. what *w.* then if fields and regions
P. L. 4, 205. beneath him with new *w.* now he
P. L. 4, 363. my thoughts pursue with *w.*
P. L. 4, 577. Uriel no *w.* if thy perfect sight
P. L. 5, 9. his *w.* was to find unwakened Eve
P. L. 5, 439. nor *w.* if by fire
P. L. 5, 491. *w.* not then what God for you
P. L. 6, 219. what *w.* when millions of fierce
P. L. 7, 70. great things and full of *w.* in our ears
P. L. 8, 11. now heard with *w.* but delight
P. L. 9, 221. what *w.* if so near looks intervene
P. L. 9, 532. *w.* not sovran mistress if perhaps

P. L. 9, 533. who art sole *w.* much less arm thy
P. L. 9, 566. say for such *w.* claims attention
P. L. 10, 487. the more to increase your *w.*
P. L. 11, 733. when lo a *w.* strange
P. L. 12, 468. our sire replete with joy and *w.*
P. R. 1, 38. awhile surveyed with *w.*
P. R. 1, 481. what *w.* then if I delight to hear
P. R. 2, 209. though of this age the *w.* and the
P. R. 3, 24. wherefore deprive all earth her *w.*
P. R. 3, 229. no *w.* for though in thee be united
P. R. 3, 280. there Babylon the *w.* of all
S. A. 215. truth to say I oft have heard men *w.*
S. A. 1642. not without *w.* or delight beheld
C. 265. hail foreign *w.*
C. 747. where most may *w.* at the workmanship
A. 43. have sat to *w.* at and gaze upon
H. 64. the winds with *w.* whist
W. S. 7. thou in our *w.* and astonishment
**Wondered.**—P. L. 9, 856. hast thou not *w.*
P. L. 10, 509. he *w.* but not long had leisure
**Wonderful.**—P. L. 3, 702. for *w.* indeed
P. L. 9, 862. strange hath been the cause and *w.*
P. L. 10, 482. a fabric *w.* of absolute perfection
P. L. 12, 471. and evil turn to good more *w.*
**Wondering.**—P. L. 1, 693. and *w.* tell of Babel
P. L. 3, 273. might mean and whither tend *w.*
P. L. 4, 451. much *w.* where and what I was
P. L. 5, 54. and as I *w.* looked beside it stood
P. L. 5, 89. *w.* at my flight and change to this
P. L. 8, 257. my *w.* eyes I turned and gazed
P. L. 10, 20. much *w.* how the subtle fiend had
P. L. 10, 510. *w.* at himself now more
**Wonders.**—P. L. 6, 790. or *w.* move the
P. L. 7, 223. creation and the *w.* of his might
S. A. 753. confess and promise *w.* in her change
S. A. 1095. to have wrought such *w.* with an ass's
**Wondrous.**—P. L. 1, 703. multitude with *w.*
P. L. 2, 1028. a bridge of *w.* length from hell
P. L. 3, 285. shall be of virgin seed by *w.* birth
P. L. 3, 663. to see and know all these his *w.*
P. L. 3, 665. all these his works so *w.* he
P. L. 5, 155. frame thus *w.* fair thyself how *w.*
P. L. 6, 377. in might though *w.* and in acts of
P. L. 6, 754. four faces each had *w.*
P. L. 7, 483. *w.* in length and corpulence
P. L. 8, 68. wherein to read his *w.* works and
P. L. 9, 650. *w.* indeed if cause of such effects
P. L. 10, 312. by *w.* art pontifical a ridge of
P. L. 10, 348. this new *w.* pontifice
P. L. 11, 819. shall build a *w.* ark as thou
P. L. 12, 200. such *w.* power God to his saint
P. L. 12, 500. shall them with *w.* gifts endue
P. R. 3, 434. by some *w.* call may bring them
S. A. 167. by how much from the top of *w.* glory
S. A. 589. nor shall his *w.* gifts be frustrate thus
S. A. 1440. as in thy *w.* actions hath been seen
S. A. 1461. much averse I found and *w.* harsh
Il P. 114. and of the *w.* horse of brass
**Wondrously.**—P. L. 3, 587. so *w.* was set
**Wons.**—P. L. 7, 457. wild beast where he *w.*
**Wont.**—P. L. 1, 332. as when men *w.* to watch
P. L. 1, 764. where champions bold *w.* ride in
P. L. 3, 656. the first art *w.* his great authentic
P. L. 3, 737. as to superior spirits is *w.* in
P. L. 5, 32. if dreamed not as I oft am *w.* of
P. L. 5, 123. looks that *w.* to be more cheerful
P. L. 5, 677. wast *w.* I mine to thee was *w.*
P. L. 6, 93. who *w.* to meet so oft in festivals
P. L. 9, 842. as reapers oft are *w.* their harvest
P. L. 10, 103. *w.* with joy to meet my coming
P. R. 1, 12. inspire as thou art *w.* my prompted
P. R. 2, 264. slept and dreamed as appetite is *w.*
S. A. 4. there I am *w.* to sit when any chance
S. A. 1485. fathers are *w.* to lay up for their sons
S. A. 1487. sons *w.* to nurse their parents in old
Il P. 123. not tricked and frounced as she was *w.*
H. 10. wherewith he *w.* at heaven's high
**Wonted.**—P. L. 1, 527. but he his *w.* pride
P. L. 5, 210. peace recovered soon and *w.* calm
P. L. 5, 705. but all obeyed the *w.* signal
P. L. 6, 783. heaven his *w.* face renewed

P. L. 6, 851. and of their *w.* vigour left them
P. L. 8, 202. by sufferance and thy *w.* favour
P. L. 9, 1076. our *w.* ornaments now soiled
P. R. 4, 449. he starts in *w.* shape
S. A. 748. these are thy *w.* arts and arts of every
C. 549. the *w.* roar was up amidst the woods
Il P. 37. come but keep thy *w.* state
H. 79. the sun himself withheld his *w.* speed
H. 196. foregoes his *w.* seat

**Wont'st.**—C. 332. that *w.* to love the traveller's

**Woo.**—Il P. 64. I *w.* to hear thy even-song

**Wood.**—P. L. 4, 342. chase in *w.* or wilderness
P. L. 4, 538. began through *w.* through waste
P. L. 6, 70. nor *w.* nor stream divides their
P. L. 6, 575. with branches lopped in *w.*
P. L. 9, 1100. together went into the thickest *w.*
P. L. 10, 333. unminded slunk into the *w.*
P. L. 11, 440. on the cleft *w.* and all due rites
P. L. 12, 119. worship their own work in *w.* and
P. R. 2, 184. in *w.* or grove by mossy fountain
P. R. 4, 448. on the north and west by a thick *w.*
P. R. 4, 449. out of the *w.* he starts in wonted
C. 37. through the ... paths of this drear *w.*
C. 61. at last betakes him to this ominous *w.*
C. 181. the blind mazes of this tangled *w.*
C. 270. touch the prosperous growth of this tall *w.*
C. 312. dingle or bushy dell of this wild *w.*
C. 520. within the navel of this hideous *w.*
A. 32. and ye the breathing roses of the *w.*
A. 45. I am the power of this fair *w.*
L'A. 56. through the high *w.* echoing shrill
Il P. 154. or the unseen Genius of the *w.*

**Woodbine.**—P. L. 9, 216. to wind the *w.*
L. 146. the musk-rose and the well-attired *w.*

**Wood-gods.**—P. R. 2, 297. the haunt of *w.-g.*

**Woodman.**—C. 484. or else some neighbour *w.*

**Wood-notes.**—L'A. 134. warble his native *w.-n.*

**Wood-nymph.**—P. L. 5, 381. fair than *w.-n.*
P. L. 9, 386. and like a *w.-n.* light Oread or

**Wood-nymphs.**—P. R. 2, 297. and *w.-n.*
C. 120. the *w.-n.* decked with daisies trim

**Woods.**—P. L. 6, 645. rocks, waters *w.*
P. L. 7, 35. where *w.* and rocks had ears to
P. L. 7, 326. with high *w.* the fields were crowned
P. L. 7, 434. birds with song solaced the *w.*
P. L. 8, 262. hill, dale, and shady *w.*
P. L. 8, 275. ye hills and dales, ye rivers, *w.*
P. L. 8, 516. whispered it to the *w.*
P. L. 9, 116. of hill and valley, rivers, *w.* and
P. L. 9, 910. to live again in these wild *w.*
P. L. 9, 1086. where highest *w.* impenetrable
P. L. 10, 700. and Thrascias rend the *w.*
P. L. 10, 860. O *w.*, O fountains, hillocks dales
P. L. 11, 187. the beast that reigns in *w.*
P. L. 11, 567. had wasted *w.* on mountain or in
P. R. 1, 502. now wild beasts came forth the *w.*
P. R. 2, 374. all these are spirits of air and *w.*
P. R. 3, 332. to lay hills plain fell *w.* or valleys
S. A. 1700. in the Arabian *w.* embost
C. 88. and hush the waving *w.*
C. 150. benighted in these *w.*
C. 187. as the kind hospitable *w.* provide
C. 446. she was queen of the *w.*
C. 549. the wonted roar was up amidst the *w.*
L. 39. thee shepherd, thee the *w.* and desert caves
L. 193. to-morrow to fresh *w.* and pastures new
Il P. 63. thee chauntress oft the *w.* among
S. 1, 2. warblest at eve when all the *w.* are still
M. M. 7. *w.* and groves are of thy dressing

**Woody.**—P. L. 4, 141. shade above shade a *w.*
P. L. 8, 303. led me up a *w.* mountain
P. L. 9, 1118. among the trees on isles and *w.*
P. R. 2, 246. wandering this *w.* maze and
P. R. 2, 294. that opened in the midst a *w.*
Il P. 29. in secret shades of *w.* Ida's inmost grove

**Wooed.**—P. L. 8, 503. that would be *w.* and not
S. 13, 13. than his Casella whom he *w.* to sing

**Wooes.**—H. 38. she *w.* the gentle air

**Woof.**—P. L. 11, 244. Iris had dipt the *w.*
C. 83. these my sky robes spun out of Iris' *w.*

**Wool.**—C. 751. and to tease the housewife's *w.*

**Worcester.**—S. 16, 9. *W.'s* laureate wreath

**Word.**—P. L. 3, 144. gracious was that *w.*
P. L. 3, 170. Son who art alone my *w.*
P. L. 3, 227. Father thy *w.* is passed man shall
P. L. 3, 708. I saw when at his *w.* the
P. L. 4, 81. and that *w.* disdain forbids me
P. L. 4, 401. might learn by *w.* or action
P. L. 5, 836. by whom as by his *w.* the mighty
P. L. 6, 32. in *w.* mightier than they
P. L. 7, 163. and thou my *w.* begotten Son by
P. L. 7, 175. his *w.* the filial Godhead gave effect
P. L. 7, 208. in his powerful *w.* and spirit
P. L. 7, 217. said then the omnific *W.*
P. L. 8, 223. and each *w.* each motion forms
P. L. 10, 856. shall truth fail to keep her *w.*
P. R. 1, 349. but each *w.* proceeding from the
P. R. 3, 122. and reason since his *w.* all things
S. A. 83. O first-created beam and thou great *w.*
S. A. 200. and for a *w.* a tear, fool! have divulged
C. 321. I take thy *w.* and trust thy honest offered
S. 11, 5. what a *w.* on a title-page is this

**Words.**—P. L. 1, 82. with bold *w.*
P. L. 1, 156. whereto with speedy *w.*
P. L. 1, 528. with high *w.* that bore semblance
P. L. 1, 663. *w.* interwove with sighs found out
P. L. 1, 663. and to confirm his *w.*
P. L. 2, 50. and these *w.* thereafter spake
P. L. 2, 226. with *w.* clothed in reason's garb
P. L. 2, 735. at her *w.* the hellish pest forbore
P. L. 2, 737. thy outcry and thy *w.* so strange
P. L. 3, 266. his *w.* here ended
P. L. 4, 930. but still thy *w.* at random
P. L. 5, 66. chilled at such bold *w.*
P. L. 5, 113. ill matching *w.* and deeds
P. L. 5, 544. thy *w.* attentive and with more
P. L. 5, 616. with his *w.* all seemed well pleased
P. L. 5, 703. and casts between ambiguous *w.*
P. L. 5, 810. *w.* which no ear ever to hear
P. L. 5, 873. hoarse murmur echoed to his *w.*
P. L. 6, 496. and his *w.* their drooping cheer
P. L. 6, 568. so scoffing in ambiguous *w.*
P. L. 7, 113. what *w.* or tongue of Seraph
P. L. 8, 57. from his lip not *w.* alone pleased her
P. L. 8, 215. but thy *w.* with grace divine
P. L. 8, 248. pleased with thy *w.* no less than
P. L. 8, 379. let not my *w.* offend these
P. L. 8, 492. thou hast fufilled thy *w.* Creator
P. L. 8, 602. that daily flow from all her *w.*
P. L. 9, 290. with healing *w.* Adam replied
P. L. 9, 379. by what thy own last reasoning *w.*
P. L. 9, 550. into the heart of Eve his *w.* made
P. L. 9, 733. his *w.* replete with guile
P. L. 9, 737. persuasive *w.* impregned with
P. L. 9, 855. with bland *w.* at will
P. L. 9, 920. thus in calm mood his *w.* to Eve
P. L. 9, 1066. gave utterance to these *w.*
P. L. 9, 1134. thou hadst hearkened to my *w.*
P. L. 9, 1144. what *w.* have passed thy lips
P. L. 10, 459. with these *w.* attention won
P. L. 10, 865. soft *w.* to his fierce passion
P. L. 10, 946. with peaceful *w.* upraised her
P. L. 10, 968. how little weight my *w.* with thee
P. L. 11, 32. unskilful with that *w.* to pray
P. L. 11, 140. to Eve his welcome *w.* renewed
P. L. 11, 295. thus his humble *w.* addressed
P. L. 11, 499. scarce recovering *w.*
P. L. 12, 55. to sow a jangling noise of *w.*
P. L. 12, 374. tears without the vent of *w.*
P. L. 12, 609. with *w.* not sad she him received
P. R. 1, 106. and his *w.* impression left
P. R. 1, 222. by winning *w.* to conquer willing
P. R. 1, 228. by *w.* at times cast forth inly
P. R. 1, 320. then with *w.* thus uttered spake
P. R. 2, 34. his *w.* his wisdom full of grace
P. R. 2, 301. and with fair speech these *w.* to
P. R. 2, 337. as his *w.* had end
P. R. 2, 405. and with these *w.* his temptation
P. R. 3, 6. with soothing *w.* renewed
P. R. 3, 9. thy actions to thy *w.* accord
P. R. 3, 9. thy *w.* to thy large heart give

P. R. 3, 266. new train of *w.* began
P. R. 3, 346. and to our Saviour thus his *w.*
S. A. 176. I hear the sound of *w.*
S. A. 184. apt *w.* have power to swage the
S. A. 235. vanquished with a peal of *w.*
S. A. 277. thy *w.* to my remembrance bring
S. A. 472. and these *w.* I as a prophecy receive
S. A. 605. and healing *w.* from these thy friends
S. A. 729. and *w.* addressed seem into tears
S. A. 905. for want of *w.* no doubt or lack of
S. A. 947. bearing my *w.* and doings to
S. A. 1066. nor fear the bait of honied *w.*
S. A. 1351. knows how he may report thy *w.*
C. 161. and well-placed *w.* of glozing courtesy
C. 781. profane tongue with contemptuous *w.*
C. 801. her *w.* set off by some superior power
A. 60. with puissant *w.* and murmurs made
L. 20. with lucky *w.* favour my destined urn
S.10, 12. so well your *w.* his noble virtues praise
S.13, 3. how to span *w.* with just note and accent
H. 175. through the arched roof in *w.* deceiving
V. Ex.3. and madest imperfect *w.* with childish
**Wore.**—P. L. 3. 641. wings he *w.* of many
P. L. 4, 305. her unadorned golden tresses *w.*
P. L. 5, 277. six wings he *w.* to shade his
P.L. 7,303. on the washy ooze deep channels *w.*
P. R. 2, 279. thus *w.* out night
C.448.that wise Minerva *w.* unconquered virgin
**Work.**—P. L. 1, 151. in the heart of hell to *w.*
P. L. 1, 646. to' *w.* in close design by fraud
P. L. 1, 674. metallic ore the *w.* of sulphur
P. L. 1, 731. the *w.* some praise
P. L. 2, 261. and *w.* ease out of pain
P. L. 3, 505. the *w.* as of a kingly palace gate
P. L. 3, 635. which else might *w.* him danger
P. L. 4, 380. yet such accept your Maker's *w.*
P. L. 4, 618. man hath his daily *w.* of body
P. L. 4, 726 which we in our appointed *w.*
P. L. 5, 112. misjoining shapes wild *w.* produces
P. L. 5, 211. on to their morning's rural *w.*
P. L. 5, 255. by *w.* divine the sovran architect
P. L. 5, 478. till body up to spirit *w.*
P. L. 5, 853. the *w.* of secondary hand
P. L. 6, 453. hard for gods and too unequal *w.*
P. L. 6, 507. forthwith from council to the *w.*
P. L. 6, 698. which makes wild *w.* in heaven
P. L. 6, 761. of radiant Urim *w.* divinely
P. L. 6, 809. number to this day's *w.* is not
P.L. 7,98. and the *w.* begun how soon absolved
P. L. 7, 353. surveying his great *w.* that it was
P. L. 7,551. yet not till the Creator from his *w.*
P. L. 7, 567. great Creator from his *w.* returned
P. L. 7, 568. his six days' *w.*
P. L. 7, 590. and the *w.* ordained
P. L. 7, 591. and from *w.* now resting blessed
P. L. 7,593. resting on that day from all his *w.*
P. L. 7, 595. the harp had *w.* and rested not
P. L. 8, 234. while God was in his *w.*
P. L. 9, 131. to what may *w.* his utter loss
P. L. 9, 202. their growing *w.* for much their *w.*
P. L. 9, 208. the *w.* under our labour grows
P. L. 9, 224. which intermits our day's *w.*
P. L. 9, 230. how we might best fulfil the *w.*
P. L. 9, 255. seeks to *w.* us woe and shame
P. L. 10, 255. adventurous *w.*
P. L. 10, 270. nor shall I to the *w.* be wanting
P. L. 10, 312. now had they brought the *w.*
P. L. 10, 391. mine with this glorious *w.*
P. L. 10, 555. to *w.* them further woe or shame
P. L. 11, 177. where'er our day's *w.* lies
P. L. 12, 62. and the *w.* confusion named
P. L. 12, 119. to worship their own *w.* in wood
P. R. 1, 186. how best the mighty *w.* he might
P. R. 1, 223. make persuasion do the *w.* of fear
P. R. 1, 266. or *w.* redemption for mankind
P. R.2,112. all his great *w.* to come before him
P. R. 2, 295. nature's own *w.* it seemed
P. R. 4, 59. carved *w.* the hand of famed
P. R. 4, 634. on thy glorious *w.* now enter and
S.A.70.light the prime *w.* of God to me is extinct
S. A. 226. the *w.* to which I was divinely called

S.A.367.into a dungeon thrust to *w.* with slaves
S. A. 565. and the *w.* from heaven imposed
S. A. 680. to some great *w.* thy glory
S. A. 1260. the *w.* of many hands
S. A. 1454. with good success to *w.* his liberty
S. A. 1662. the *w.* for which thou wast foretold
C. 715. and set to *w.* millions of spinning worms
Il P. 143. that at her flowery *w.* doth sing
S. 16, 6. hast reared God's trophies and his *w.*
S. 19, 10. doth not need either man's *w.* or his
H. 7. with his Father *w.* us a perpetual peace
P. 31. and *w.* my flattered fancy to belief
**Working.**—P. L. 12, 489. law of faith *w.*
S. A. 1299. more than the *w.* day thy hands
**Workmanship.**—C. 747. may wonder at the *w.*
**Work-master.**—P. L. 3, 696. the great *w.-m.*
**Works.**—P. L. 1, 201. which God of all his *w.*
P. L. 1, 431. and *w.* of love or enmity fulfil
P. L. 1, 694. and the *w.* of Memphian kings
P. L. 2, 370. repenting hand abolish his own *w.*
P. L. 2, 1039. as from her outmost *w.*, a broken
P. L. 3, 49. universal blank of nature's *w.*
P. L. 3, 59. his own *w.* and their *w.* at once
P. L. 3, 277. how dear to me are all my *w.*
P. L. 3, 447. sin with vanity had filled the *w.*
P. L. 3,455. the unaccomplished *w.* of nature's
P. L. 3, 663. know all these his wondrous *w.*
P. L. 3, 665. all these his *w.* so wondrous he
P. L. 3, 695. which tends to know the *w.* of
P. L. 3, 702. wonderful indeed are all his *w.*
P. L. 4, 314. dishonest shame of nature's *w.*
P. L. 4, 566. to know more of the Almighty's *w.*
P. L. 4, 679. with ceaseless praise his *w.* behold
P. L. 5, 33. *w.* of day past or morrow's next
P. L. 5, 153. these are thy glorious *w.*, Parent
P. L. 5, 158. dimly seen in these thy lowest *w.*
P. L. 6, 274. brooks not the *w.* of violence
P. L. 7, 97. the more to magnify his *w.*
P. L. 7, 112. though to recount almighty *w.*
P. L. 7, 259. hymning praised God and his *w.*
P. L. 7, 516. who made him chief of all his *w.*
P. L. 7,543. which tasted *w.* knowledge of good
P. L. 7, 602. great are thy *w.* Jehovah infinite
P. L. 7, 629. and in reward to rule over his *w.*
P. L. 8, 68. to read his wondrous *w.* and learn
P. L. 8, 95. whose virtue on itself *w.* no effect
P. L. 8, 525. but such as used or not *w.* in the
P. L. 9, 234. and good *w.* in her husband
P. L. 9, 512. feared to interrupt sidelong he *w.*
P. L. 9, 783. sighing through all her *w.* gave
P. L. 9, 897. last and best of all God's *w.*
P. L. 9,941. dignified so high set over all his *w.*
P. L. 10, 644. are thy decrees on all thy *w.*
P. L. 11, 34. all his *w.* on me good or not good
P. L. 11, 64. refined by faith and faithful *w.*
P. L. 11, 578. and know his *w.* not hid
P. L. 11, 639. towns and rural *w.* between
P. L. 12, 306. *w.* of law to *w.* of faith
P. L. 12,394. not by destroying Satan but his *w.*
P. L. 12, 410. not their own though legal *w.*
P. L. 12, 427. embrace by faith not void of *w.*
P. L. 12, 536. *w.* of faith rarely be found
P. L. 12, 565. merciful over all his *w.*
P. L. 12, 578. all nature's *w.*, or *w.* of God
P. R. 2, 371. their taste no knowledge *w.*
P. R. 3, 80. and all the flourishing *w.* of peace
S. A. 14. and forbid laborious *w.*
S.A. 955. bewail thy falsehood and the pious *w.*
C. 68. soon as the potion *w.* their human
S. 14, 5. thy *w.* and alms and all thy good
**World.**—P. L. 1, 3. brought death into the *w.*
P. L. 1, 32. lords of the *w.* besides
P. L. 1,251. infernal *w.*! and thou, profoundest
P.L.1,375. various idols through the heathen *w.*
P. L. 2, 262. this deep *w.* of darkness do we
P. L. 2,347. another *w.* the happy seat of some
P. L. 2, 403. we send in search of this new *w.*
P. L. 2, 442. if thence he scape into whatever *w.*
P. L. 2, 572. to discover wide that dismal *w.*
P. L. 2, 867. wilt bring me soon to that new *w.*
P. L. 2, 1004. heaven and earth another *w.*

P. L. 2, 1030. the utmost orb of this frail *w.*
P. L. 2, 1052. this pendent *w.* in bigness as
P. L. 3, 11. rising *w.* of waters dark and deep
P. L. 3, 74. on the bare outside of this *w.*
P. L. 3, 89. directly towards the new-created *w.*
P. L. 3, 308. to save a *w.* from utter loss
P. L. 3, 334. meanwhile the *w.* shall burn
P. L. 3, 419. opacous globe of this round *w.*
P. L. 3, 464. first from the ancient *w.* those
P. L. 3, 494. fly o'er the backside of the *w.*
P. L. 3, 543. the sudden view of all this *w.* at
P. L. 3, 554. at sight of all this *w.* beheld so fair
P. L. 3, 562. into the *w.'s* first regions
P. L. 3, 709. this *w.'s* material mould
P. L. 4, 34. like the god of this new *w.*
P. L. 4, 107. created and for him this *w.*
P. L. 4, 113. as man ere long and this new *w.*
P. L. 4, 272. to seek her through the *w.*
P. L. 4, 391. conquering this new *w.*
P. L. 4, 413. made us and for us this ample *w.*
P. L. 4, 937. and spy this new-created *w.*
P. L. 5, 124. fair morning first smiles on the *w.*
P. L. 5, 171. thou sun of this great *w.* both eye
P. L. 5, 188. in honour to the *w.'s* great Author
P. L. 5, 389. shall fill the *w.* more numerous
P. L. 5, 455. to know of things above his *w.*
P. L. 5, 569. the secrets of another *w.* perhaps
P. L. 5, 577. as yet this *w.* was not and Chaos
P. L. 6, 146. when I alone seemed in thy *w.*
P. L. 7, 62. how this *w.* of heaven and earth
P. L. 7, 71. far differing from this *w.* thou hast
P. L. 7, 155. in a moment will create another *w.*
P. L. 7, 220. far into Chaos and the *w.* unborn
P. L. 7, 231. this be thy just circumference O *w.*
P. L. 7, 269. for as earth so he the *w.* built
P. L. 7, 554. to behold this new-created *w.*
P. L. 7, 568. his six days' work, a *w.*
P. L. 7, 617. witness this new-made *w.* another
P. L. 7, 621. every star perhaps a *w.*
P. L. 7, 636. how first this *w.* and face of things
P. L. 8, 15. behold this goodly frame this *w.*
P. L. 8, 123, if the sun be centre to the *w.*
P. L. 8, 151. two great sexes animate the *w.*
P. L. 8, 332. expelled from hence into a *w.* of woe
P. L. 8, 472. what seemed fair in all the *w.*
P. L. 9, 11. brought into this *w.* a *w.* of woe
P. L. 9, 153. built magnificent this *w.*
P. L. 9, 568. empress of this fair *w.* resplendent
P. L. 10, 257. to that new *w.* where Satan now
P. L. 10, 303. of this now fenceless *w.*
P. L. 10, 318. outside bare of this round *w.*
P. L. 10, 322. empyrean heaven and of this *w.*
P. L. 10, 372. thine now is all this *w.*
P. L. 10, 377. from this new *w.* retiring
P. L. 10, 381. from thy orbicular *w.*
P. L. 10, 392. hell and this *w.* one realm one
P. L. 10, 422. flown to the upper *w.*
P. L. 10, 467. possess as lords a spacious *w.*
P. L. 10, 481. how I found the new-created *w.*
P. L. 10, 489. his beloved man and all his *w.*
P. L. 10, 500. a *w.* who would not purchase
P. L. 10, 617. yonder *w.* which I so fair
P. L. 10, 689. else how had the *w.* inhabited
P. L. 10, 721. the end of this new glorious *w.*
P. L. 10, 836. than all the *w.* much heavier
P. L. 10, 892. and not fill the *w.* at once with
P. L. 10, 984. to bring into this cursed *w.* a
P. L. 11, 134. to resalute the *w.* with sacred
P. L. 11, 283. into a lower *w.* to this obscure
P. L. 11, 328, in yonder nether *w.* where shall
P. L. 11, 406. where Rome was to sway the *w.*
P. L. 11, 627. the *w.* ere long a *w.* of tears
P. L. 11, 701. the only righteous in a *w.* perverse
P. L. 11, 793. achieved thereby fame in the *w.*
P. L. 11, 810. custom and a *w.* offended
P. L. 11, 821. a *w.* devote to universal wrack
P. L. 11, 874. for one whole *w.* of wicked sons
P. L. 11, 877. to raise another *w.* from him
P. L. 11, 894. nor rain to drown the *w.*
P. L. 12, 3. the *w.* destroyed and *w.* restored
P. L. 12, 6. hast seen one *w.* begin and end

P. L. 12, 105. will this latter as the former *w.*
P. L. 12, 313. through the *w.'s* wilderness
P. L. 12, 449. faith wherever through the *w.*
P. L. 12, 459. when this *w.'s* dissolution shall
P. L. 12, 467. then paused as at the *w.'s* great
P. L. 12, 537. so shall the *w.* go on to good
P. L. 12, 547. Satan with his perverted *w.*
P. L. 12, 554. this transient *w.* the race of
P. L. 12, 580. all the riches of this *w.* enjoyedst
P. L. 12, 646. the *w.* was all before them
P. R. 1, 34. still about the *w.* at that assembly
P. R. 1, 44. powers of air and this wide *w.*
P. R. 1, 162. and all the *w.* a'nd mass of sinful
P. R. 1, 392. copartner in these regions of the *w.*
P. R. 1, 461. into the *w.* to teach his final will
P. R. 2, 443. for throughout the *w.* to me is
P. R. 3, 18. that all the *w.* could not sustain
P. R. 3, 39. great Julius whom now all the *w.*
P. R. 3, 225. both to thyself and all the *w.*
P. R. 3, 236. the *w.* thou hast not seen
P. R. 3, 393. plausible to the *w.*
P. R. 4, 89. the kingdoms of the *w.*
P. R. 4, 105. at no less than all the *w.*
P. R. 4, 150. besides throughout the *w.*
P. R. 4, 163. the kingdoms of the *w.* to thee
P. R. 4, 182. the kingdoms of the *w.* to thee were
P. R. 4, 203. God of this *w.* invoked and *w.*
P. R. 4, 210. transitory the kingdoms of this *w.*
P. R. 4, 223. extend thy mind o'er all the *w.*
P. R. 4, 252. Alexander to subdue the *w.*
P. R. 4, 311. and how the *w.* began and how
P. R. 4, 372. what dost thou in this *w.*
P. R. 4, 429. or throne of all the *w.*
P. R. 4, 415. from the four hinges of the *w.*
C. 720. if all the *w.* should in a pet of temperance
A. 71. and the low *w.* in measured motion draw
L. 80. nor in the glistening foil set off to the *w.*
L. 158. visit'st the bottom of the monstrous *w.*
S. 19, 2. ere half my days in this dark *w.* and wide
S. 22, 13. thought might lead me thro ugh the *w's*
H. 54. was heard the *w.* around
H. 82. the new-enlightened *w.* no more should
H. 122. and the well-balanced *w.* on hinges hung
H. 163, when at the *w.'s* last session
Cir. 11. entered the *w.* now bleeds to give us ease
M. W. 51. that to give the *w.* increase
D. F. I. 32. hid from the *w.* in a low-delved tomb
D. F. I. 56. to do the *w.* some good
D. F. I. 63. to scorn the sordid *w.*
D. F. I. 77. that till the *w.'s* last end
**Worldly.**—P. L. 11, 803. *w.* or dissolute
P. L. 12, 568. subverting *w.* strong and *w.* wise
P. R. 4, 213. otherwise inclined than to a *w.* crown
**Worlds.**—P. L. 1. 650, may produce new *w.*
P. L. 2, 916. dark materials to create more *w.*
P. L. 3, 566. seemed other *w.*
P. L. 3, 567. or other *w.* they seemed
P. L. 3, 674. the great Creator hath bestowed *w.*
P. L. 5, 268. sails between *w.* and *w.*
P. L. 6, 36. though *w.* judged thee perverse
P. L. 7, 191. and thence diffuse his good to *w.*
P. L. 7, 209. coming to create new *w.*
P. L. 8, 175. dream not of other *w.*
P. L. 10, 237. thrives in other *w.* and happier
P. L. 10, 362. though distant from thee *w.*
P. L. 10, 441. from the search of foreign *w.*
P. R. 4, 633. heir of both *w.* queller of Satan
Il P. 90. what *w.* or what vast regions hold
**Worm.**—P. L. 4, 704. or *w.* durst enter none
P. L. 6, 739. of darkness and the undying *w.*
P. L. 7, 476. creeps the ground insect or *w.*
P. L. 9, 1068. to that false *w.* of whomsoever
P. R. 1, 312. fiery serpent fled and noxious *w.*
S. A. 74. of man or *w.* the vilest here excel me
A. 53. or hurtful *w.* with cankered venom bites
**Worms.**—C. 715. millions of spinning *w.*
**Wormy.**—D. F. I. 31. or that thy beauties lie in *w.*
**Worn.**—P. L. 10, 573. were they plagued and *w.*
P. L. 11, 243. *w.* by kings and heroes old
S. A. 1131. which greatest heroes have in battle *w.*
**Worried.**—S. A. 906. witness when I was *w.*

**Worse.**—P. L. 1, 119. in arms not *w.*
P. L. 1, 505. exposed a matron to avoid *w.* rape
P. L. 2, 49. of God or hell or *w.* he recked not
P. L. 2, 83. some *w.* way his wrath may find to
P. L. 2, 85. to be *w.* destroyed what can be *w.*
P. L. 2, 113. and could make the *w.* appear the
P. L. 2, 163. suffer more what can we suffer *w.*
P. L. 2, 169. the burning lake, that sure was *w.*
P. L. 2, 186. this would be *w.*, war therefore
P. L. 2, 196. better these than *w.* by my advice
P. L. 2, 298. they dreaded *w.* than hell
P. L. 2, 626. and *w.* than fables yet have feigned
P. L. 2, 996. confusion *w.* confounded
P. L. 3, 91. by force he can destoy or *w.*
P. L. 4, 26. *w.*; of *w.* deeds *w.* sufferings
P. L. 4, 40. till pride and *w.* ambition
P. L. 4, 100. but lead me to a *w.* relapse
P. L. 6, 34. reproach far *w.* to bear than
P. L. 6, 440. serve to better us and *w.* our foes
P. L. 6, 607. to return they *w.* abhorred
P. L. 6, 863. but far *w.* urged them behind
P. L. 8, 397. *w.* then can man with beast
P. L. 9, 102. what God after better *w.* would build
P. L. 9, 123. and in heaven much *w.* would be
P. L. 9, 128. though thereby *w.* to me redound
P. L. 9, 265. or this or *w.*, leave not the faithful
P. L. 9, 715. which no *w.* than this can bring
P. L. 9, 1122. but high winds *w.* within began
P. L. 10, 717. to sorrow abandoned but *w.* felt
P. L. 10, 780. no fear of *w.* to me and to my
P. L. 10, 903. shall see her gained by a far *w.*
P. L. 10, 1055. idleness had been *w.*
P. L. 11, 268. stroke *w.* than of death
P. L. 11, 601. and death or pain much *w.*
P. L. 12, 106. still tend from bad to *w.*
P. L. 12, 484. will they not deal *w.* with his
P. R. 3, 205. my reception into grace, what *w.*
P. R. 3, 207. if there be *w.*
P. R. 3, 208. the expectation more of *w.*
P. R. 3, 419. besides their other *w.* than
P. R. 4, 320. or by delusion far *w.*
P. R. 4, 486. me *w.* than wet thou find'st not
S. A. 68. blind among enemies O *w.* than chains
S. A. 284. not *w.* than by his shield and spear
S. A. 399. (which was *w.* than undissembled hate)
S. A. 418. and that blindness *w.* than this
S. A. 433. a *w.* thing yet remains
S. A. 485. by pains and slaveries *w.* than death
S. A. 893. by *w.* than hostile deeds
S. A. 904. a woman ever goes by the *w.*
S. 11, 13. hated not learning *w.* than toad or asp
P. 11. snares and wrongs and *w.* than so
F. of C. 14. and packing *w.* than those of Trent
**Worship.**—P. L. 2, 248. eternity so spent in *w.*
P. L. 5, 194. with every plant in sign of *w.*
P. L. 7, 515. and *w.* God Supreme who made
P. L. 7, 628. image there to dwell and *w.* him
P. L. 9, 198. joined their vocal *w.* to the choir
P. L. 9, 611. and gaze and *w.* thee of right
P. L. 11, 318. frequent with *w.* place by place
P. L. 11, 578. to *w.* God aright and know his
P. L. 12, 119. to *w.* their own work in wood
P. L. 12, 532. on all who in the *w.* persevere
P. R. 2, 475. to know and knowing *w.* God
P. R. 3, 416. fell off from God to *w.* calves
P. R. 3, 426. God with idols in the *w.* joined
P. R. 4, 167. and *w.* me as thy superior lord
P. R. 4, 176. thou shalt *w.* the Lord thy God
P. R. 4, 179. to *w.* thee accursed
P. R. 4, 192. that I fall down and *w.* thee
H. 220. sorcerers bear his *w.* ark
S. 18, 4. when all our fathers *w.* stocks and stones
**Worshipped.**—P. L. 1, 397. *w.* in Rabba
P. R. 3, 83. *w.* with temple priest and sacrifice
C. 302. and as I passed I *w.*
**Worshippers.**—P. L. 1, 461. shamed his *w.*
P. L. 7, 613. withdrew the number of thy *w.*
P. L. 7, 630. multiply a race of *w.* holy and just
P. L. 9, 705. keep ye low and ignorant his *w.*
S. A. 471. and with confusion blank his *w.*
**Worst.**—P. L. 1, 276. heard so oft in *w.* extremes

P. L. 2, 100. we are at *w.* on this side nothing
P. L. 2, 163. is this then *w.* thus sitting thus
P. L. 2, 224. happy though but ill for ill not *w.*
P. L. 4, 204. perverts best things to *w.* abuse
P. L. 5, 742. or be found the *w.* in heaven
P. L. 6, 462. pain is perfect misery the *w.* of evils
P. L. 9, 269. or with her the *w.* endures
P. L. 9, 979. I would sustain alone the *w.* and
P. L. 10, 73. the *w.* on me must light
P. R. 3, 209. I would be at the *w.w* is my port
P. R. 3, 223. if I then to the *w.* that can be
S. A. 105. from *w.* of other evils pains and wrongs
S. A. 155. O *w.* imprisonment
S. A. 195. yet that which was the *w.* now least
S. A. 1264. the *w.* that he can give to me the best
S. A. 1341. the *w.* of all indignities
S. A. 1570. take then the *w.* in brief
S. A. 1571. the *w.* indeed O all my hopes defeated
C. 484. or at *w.* some roving robber
V. Ex. 12. believe me I have thither packed the *w.*
**Worth.**—P. L. 1, 272. to reign is *w.* ambition
P. L. 1, 378. as next in *w.* came singly
P. L. 1, 529. words that bore semblance of *w.*
P. L. 2, 223. what change *w.* waiting
P. L. 2, 376. advise if this be *w.* attempting
P. L. 2, 429. conscious of highest *w.*
P. L. 5, 308. haste hither Eve and *w.* thy sight
P. L. 8, 502. and the conscience of her *w.*
P. L. 9, 1183. who to *w.* in woman overtrusting
P. L. 10, 488. thereat offended *w.* your laughter
P. R. 1, 231. sacred virtue and true *w.*
P. R. 1, 370. and illustrate his high *w.*
P. R. 2, 227. more show of *w.* of honour glory
P. R. 3, 51. vulgar and well weighed scarce *w.*
P. R. 3, 151. *w.* or not *w.* the seeking
P. R. 3, 393. plausible to the world to me *w.*
P. R. 4, 86. the rest are barbarous and scarce *w.*
P. R. 4, 329. and trifles for choice matters *w.*
P. R. 4, 514. thenceforth I thought thee *w.*
P. R. 4, 539. *w.* naming Son of God
S. A. 250. would not seem to count them things *w.*
C. 505. is *w.* a thought to this my errand
C. 793. the uncontrolled *w.* of this pure cause
A. 8. fame that her high *w.* to raise
A. 80. I will assay her *w.* to celebrate
S. 13, 5. thy *w.* and skill exempts thee
V. Ex. 79. *w.* and excellence he shall outgo them
**Worthier.**—P. L. 5, 76. thou mayst be *w.*
P. L. 6, 180. who hath rebelled against his *w.*
P. L. 9, 100. seat *w.* of gods
P. R. 1, 27. and witness bore as to his *w.*
P. R. 2, 195. on *w.* things
**Worthies.**—P. R. 3, 74. what do these *w.*
**Worthiest.**—P. L. 1, 759. or choice the *w.*
P. L. 3, 310. found *w.* to be so by being good
P. L. 3, 703. *w.* to be all had in remembrance
P. L. 6, 177. when he who rules is *w.* and excels
P. L. 6, 185. *w.* to be obeyed
P. L. 6, 707. to manifest thee *w.* to be heir
P. L. 6, 888. to him dominion given *w.* to reign
P. R. 3, 226. that thou who *w.* art shouldst be
S. A. 276. to heap ingratitude on *w.* deeds
S. A. 369. whom God hath chosen once to *w.* deeds
A. 74. and yet such music *w.* were to blaze
**Worthily.**—P. L. 11, 524. *w.* since they
**Worthless.**—S. A. 1020. thy paranymph *w.*
**Worthy.**—P. L. 4, 241. and fed flowers *w.*
P. L. 4, 291. seemed lords of all and *w.* seemed
P. L. 5, 557. or of sacred silence to be heard
P. L. 6, 420. found *w.* not of liberty alone
P. L. 8, 568. an outside fair no doubt and *w.* well
P. L. 8, 584. if aught therein enjoyed were *w.*
P. L. 9, 746. though kept from man and *w.*
P. L. 12, 161. a son whose *w.* deeds raise him
P. R. 1, 17. *w.* to have not remained so long
P. R. 1, 141. to show him *w.* of his birth divine
P. R. 2, 445. hath been done *w.* of memorial
P. R. 3, 70. to things not glorious men not *w.*
S. A. 1164. no *w.* match for valour to assail
C. 788. and thou art *w.* that thou shouldst not
L. 118. and shove away the *w.* bidden guest

**Wove.**—P. L. 4, 348. serpent sly insinuating *w.*
  P. L. 9, 839. had *w* of choicest flowers a garland
  A. 47. ringlets quaint and wanton windings *w.*
**Woven.**—S. 11, 2. and *w.* close both matter form
**Wound.**—P. L. 1, 447. whose annual *w.* in
  P. L. 1, 689. opened into the hill a spacious *w.*
  P. L. 3, 252. death his death's *w.* shall then
  P. L. 6, 329. with discontinuous *w.* passed
  P. L. 6, 348. in their liquid texture mortal *w*
  P. L. 6, 405. unobnoxious to be pained by *w.*
  P. L. 6, 435. and though pierced with *w.* soon
  P. L. 8, 467. wide was the *w.* but suddenly with
  P. L. 9, 486. exempt from *w.* I not so much
  P. L. 9, 589. about the mossy trunk I *w.* me
  P. L. 9, 782. earth felt the *w.* and nature from
  P. L. 11, 299. which might else in telling *w.*
  P. L. 12, 392. not to give thee thy death's *w.*
  P. R. 1, 53. attending when that fatal *w.*
  P. R. 1, 59. the stroke of that long-threatened *w.*
  P. R. 4, 622. *w.* yet not thy last and deadliest *w.*
  S.A.1581. what hand gave Samson his death's *w.*
  C. 1000. waxing well of his deep *w.*
  A. 67. on which the fate of gods and men is *w.*
**Wounded.**—P. L. 1, 452. Thammuz yearly *w.*
  H. 204. their *w.* Thammuz mourn
**Wounding.**—Cir. 25. obedience first with *w.*
**Wounds.**—P. L. 2, 168. a refuge from those *w.*
  P. L. 4, 99. where *w.* of deadly hate have
  P. L. 6, 368. mangled with ghastly *w.* through
  P. L. 12, 190. thus with ten *w.* the river-dragon
  P. L. 12, 387. or the local *w.* of head or heel
  P. R. 1, 404. this *w.* me most what can it less
  S. A. 186. and are as balm to festered *w.*
  S. A. 607. to the body's *w.* and sores
  S. A. 620. nor less than *w.* immedicable
**Wrack.**—P. L. 4, 994. at least had gone to *w.*
  P. L. 6, 670. and now all heaven had gone to *w.*
  P. L. 11, 821. a world devote to universal *w.*
  P. R. 4, 452. I heard the *w.* as earth and sky
**Wrapped.**—P. L. 2, 183. *w.* in chains
  P. L. 9, 158. thus *w.* in mist of midnight
  C 546. *w.* in a pleasing fit of melancholy
**Wrapt.**—H. 31. meanly *w.* in the rude manger
**Wrath.**—P. L. 1, 54. reserved him to more *w.*
  P. L. 1, 110. that glory never shall his *w.* or
  P. L. 1, 220. *w.* and vengeance poured
  P. L. 2, 83. some worse way his *w.* may find
  P. L. 2, 688. to whom the goblin full of *w.*
  P. L. 2, 733. to execute whate'er his *w.*
  P. L. 2, 734. *w.* which one day will destroy ye
  P. L. 3, 264. *w.* shall be no more thenceforth
  P. L. 3, 275. found out for mankind under *w.*
  P. L. 4, 74. he to appease thy *w.* and end
  P. L. 4, 912. till the *w.* which thou incurr'st
  P. L. 5, 890. lest the *w.*
  P. L. 6, 59. reluctant flames the sign of *w.*
  P. L. 6, 826. and full of *w.* bent on his enemies
  P. L. 6, 865. eternal *w.* burned after them
  P. L. 9, 14. than the *w.* of stern Achilles on his
  P. L. 10, 95. when he from *w.* more cool
  P. L. 10, 340. fearing guilty what is *w.*
  P. L. 10, 795. is his *w.* also
  P. L. 10, 797. how can he exercise *w.* without end
  P. L. 10, 834. so might the *w.*
  P. L. 10, 951. ill able to sustain his full *w.*
  P. L. 10, 1048. heard and judged without *w.*
  P. L. 11, 815. denouncing *w.* to come on their
  P. L. 12, 478. and over *w.* grace shall abound
  S. A. 1683. fallen into *w.* divine
  C. 803. as when the *w.* of Jove speaks thunder
  Cir. 23. and the full *w.* beside
  D. F. I. 66. to slake his *w.* whom sin hath made
**Wreak.**—P. L. 3, 241. death *w.* all his rage
  P. L. 4, 11. to *w.* on innocent frail man his loss
**Wreath.**—P. L. 9, 517. many a wanton *w.* in
  P. R. 2, 459. in show is but a *w.* of thorns
**Wreathed.**—P. L. 4, 346. *w.* his lithe proboscis
  P. L. 9, 892. the garland *w.* for Eve
  P. R. 4, 76. faces with white silken turbants *w.*

C..55. with ivy berries *w.* and his blithe youth
L'A. 28. nods and becks and *w.* smiles
**Wreaths.**—P. L. 6, 58. to roll in dusky *w.*
  C. 850. and throw sweet garland *w.* into her
  Hor. 4. for whom bind'st thou in *w.*
**Wreck.**—S. A. 1044. but needs must *w.*
**Wrecked.**—P. R. 2, 228. men have oftest *w.*
**Wrench.**—S. 21, 4. at their bar so often *w.*
**Wrested.**—P. L. 11, 503. given to be thus *w.*
  P. R. 1, 470. but misery hath *w.* from me
  S. A. 384. the secret *w.* from me in her height
**Wrestlers.**—S. A. 1324. of gymnic artists, *w.*
**Wretched.**—P. L. 10, 985. that after *w.* life
  P. L. 11, 501. to what *w.* state reserved
  P. L. 12, 74. *w.* man what food will he convey
  P. R. 1, 345. with food whereof we *w.* seldom
  L. 124. grate on their scrannel pipes of *w.* straw
**Wring.**—S. A. 1199. to *w.* from me and tell to
**Wrinkled.**—P. L. 11, 843. *w.* the face of deluge
  C. 871. by hoary Nereus' *w.* look
  L'A. 31. sport that *w.* care derides
**Wrists.**—C. 834. held up their pearled *w.*
**Writ.**—P. R. 1, 260. searching what was *w.*
  P. R. 2, 8. with others though in Holy *W.*
  P. R. 3, 184. if of my reign Prophetic *W.* hath
  S.A.657.consolatories *w.* with studied argument
  S.11,1.a book was *w.* of late called 'Tetrachordon'
  S. 13, 7. to after age thou shalt be *w.* the man
  F. of C. 20, new Presbyter is but Old Priest *w.*
**Write.**—P. L. 4, 758. far be it that I should *w.*
  P. L. 12, 489. love upon their hearts shall *w.*
  P. R. 4, 227. and *w.* and teach to admiration
  P. R. 4, 383. or heaven *w.* aught of fate
  P.34. the leaves should all be black whereon I *w.*
**Writhed.**—P. L. 6, 328. *w.* him to and fro
  P. L. 10, 569. with hatefullest disrelish *w.*
**Written.**—P. L. 12, 506. their story *w.* left
  P. L. 12, 513. left only in those *w.* records pure
  P. R. 1, 347. such force in bread is it not *w.*
  P. R. 4, 175. *w.* the first of all commandments
  P. R. 4, 556. for it is *w.* He will give command
  P. R. 4, 560. also it is *w.* tempt not the Lord
**Wrong.**—P. L. 4, 387. revenge on you who *w.*
  P. L. 9, 300. anger wouldst resent the offered *w.*
  P. L. 9, 666. to man and indignation at his *w.*
  P. L. 11, 666. spake much of right and *w.*
  P. L. 12, 98. virtue which is reason that no *w.*
  P. R. 1, 389. they to me never did *w.* or violence
  S. A. 76. to daily fraud contempt abuse and *w.*
  S. A. 1080. but oftest to affect the *w.*
**Wronged.**—P. L. 4, 387. not for him who *w.*
**Wrongs.**—P. R. 3, 93. him whom thy *w.* with
  S. A.105. from worst of other evils, pains and *w.*
  P. 11. dangers and snares and *w.* and worse
**Wrote.**—P. R. 4, 226. what the prophets *w.*
**Wroth.**—H. 171. and *w.* to see his kingdom fail
**Wrought.**—P. L. 1, 642. and *w.* our fall
  P. L. 2, 295. and the sword of Michael *w.* still
  P. L. 4, 49. proved ill in me and *w.* but malice
  P. L. 4, 699. and *w.* mosaic
  P. L. 5, 901. number nor example with him *w.*
  P. L. 6, 657. which *w.* them pain implacable
  P. L. 6, 691. which yet hath *w.* insensibly
  P. L. 6, 761. work divinely *w.*
  P. L. 8, 507. Nature herself *w.* in her so
  P. L. 9, 70. sin not time first *w.* the change
  P. L. 9, 513. when a ship by .. steersman *w.*
  P. L. 10, 300. the mole immense *w.* on
  P. L. 10, 939. in Adam *w.* commiseration
  P. L.10,1080. which our own misdeeds have *w.*
  P. L. 11, 55. for dissolution *w.* by sin
  P. L. 11,424. which thy original crime hath *w.*
  P. L. 11, 572. then what might else be *w.*
  P. R. 2, 215. the zone of Venus once *w.*
  P. R. 3, 415. they who *w.* their own captivity
  S.A.813.love hath oft well-meaning *w.* much woe
  S. A. 850. it was not gold that *w.* with me
  S. A. 1095. have *w.* such wonders with an ass's
  S. A. 1532. yet God hath *w.* things as incredible

# X.

**Xerxes.**—P. L. 10, 307. _X._ the liberty of Greece to yoke.

# Y.

**Yawning.**—P. L. 6, 875. Hell at last _y._ received
P. L. 10, 635. both sin and death and _y._ grave
**Ychained.**—H. 155. first to those _y._ in sleep
**Yclept.**—L'A. 12. in heaven _y._ Euphrosyne
**Yea.**—P. L. 387. _y._, often placed within his
P. L. 4, 207. nature's whole wealth _y._ more
P. R. 1, 117. potentates and kings _y._ gods
C. 428. _y._ there where very desolation dwells
C. 591. _y._ even that which mischief meant most
V. Ex. 87. _y._ it shall be his natural property
**Yeanling.**—P. L. 3, 434. lambs or _y._ kids
**Year.**—P. L. 3, 40. with the _y._ seasons return
P. L. 5, 583. as heaven's great _y._ brings forth
P. R. 3, 234. and once a _y._ Jerusalem
L.5.shatter your leaves before the mellowing _y._
S. 1, 11. as thou from _y._ to _y._ hast sung too late
S. 2, 2. my three and twentieth _y._
S. 22, 5. sun or moon or star throughout the _y._
**Yearly.**—P. L. 1, 452. Thammuz _y._ wounded
P. L. 10, 575. _y._ enjoined some say to undergo
**Years.**—P. L. 3, 581. days months and _y._
P. L. 7, 342. days and circling _y._
P. L. 8, 69. or days or months or _y._
P. L. 9, 45. age too late or cold climate or _y._
P. L. 11, 534. till many _y._ over thy head
P. L. 12, 345. the space of seventy _y._
P. R. 1, 48. how many ages as the _y._ of men
P. R. 1, 206. therefore above my _y._ the law of
P. R. 1, 210. my age had measured twice six _y._
P. R. 2, 80. hath been our dwelling many _y._
P. R. 2, 96. when twelve _y._ he scarce had seen
P. R. 3, 31. thy _y._ are ripe and over-ripe
P. R. 3, 37. yet _y._ and to ripe _y._ judgment
P. R. 3, 40. the more he grew in _y._ the more
S. A. 570. till length of _y._ and sedentary
S. A. 1712. hath left them _y._ of mourning
C. 114. lead in swift round the months and _y._
S. 17. young in _y._ but in sage counsel old
S. 22, 1. Cyriack this three _y._ day these eyes
M. W. 64. who after _y._ of barrenness
V. Ex. 6. where he had mutely sat two _y._
**Yelled.**—P. R. 4, 423. some howled some _y._
**Yelling.**—P. L. 2, 795. these _y._ monsters
P. R. 4, 629. _y._ they shall fly and beg to hide
**Yellow.**—P. L. 11, 435. and the _y._ sheaf
M. M. 4. the _y._ cowslip and the pale primrose
**Yellow-skirted.**—H. 235. and the _y.-s._ fays
**Yes.**—C. 584. _y._ and keep it still
**Yesterday.**—P. L. 5, 675. what decree of _y._
**Yield.**—P. L. 1, 108. never to submit or _y._
P. L. 1, 179. whether scorn or satiate fury _y._ it
P. L. 2, 232. when everlasting fate shall _y._ to
P. L. 2, 573. if any clime perhaps might _y._ them
P. L. 3, 245. though now to death I _y._ and am
P. L. 5, 401. delight hath caused the earth to _y._
P. L. 5, 428. and vines _y._ nectar
P. L. 6, 488. shall _y._ us pregnant with infernal
P. L. 8, 575. and to realities _y._ all her shows
P. L. 9, 248. to short absence I could _y._
P. L. 9, 1021. I the praise _y._ thee
P. L. 11, 42. better life shall _y._ him wherewith
P. L. 11, 526. I _y._ it just said Adam and submit
P. L. 11, 623. shall _y._ up all their virtue
S. A. 259. and they as gladly _y._ me
S. A. 593. but _y._ to double darkness night at hand
S. A. 868. the public good private respects must _y._
**Yielded.**—P. L. 1, 729. _y._ light as from a sky
P. L. 2, 24. throne _y._ with full consent
P. L. 4, 309. by her _y._ by him best received
P. L. 4, 310. _y._ with coy submission

P. L. 4, 333. which the compliant boughs _y._
P. L. 4, 489. I _y._ and from that time see how
P. L. 9, 902. how hast thou _y._ to transgress
P. L. 10, 628. at random _y._ up to their misrule
S. A. 407. I _y._ and unlocked her all my heart
S. A. 848. to have _y._ without blame
**Yielding.**—P. L. 7, 310. herb _y._ seed
**Yields.**—P. L. 5, 39. save where silence _y._
P. L. 5, 338. earth all-bearing mother _y._
P. L. 7, 88. and this which _y._ or fills all space
P. L. 7, 541. sorts are here that all the earth _y._
P. R. 2, 409. for no allurement _y._ to appetite
S. A. 15. this rest their superstition _y._ me
**Yoke.**—P. L. 2, 256. liberty before the easy _y._
P. L. 4, 975. with thy compeers used to the _y._
P. L. 5, 786. and teach us to cast off this _y._
P. L. 5, 882. more be troubled how to quit the _y._
P. L. 10, 307. Xerxes the liberty of Greece to _y._
P. L. 10, 1045. against God and his just _y._
P. R. 1, 217. to rescue Israel from the Roman _y._
P. R. 2, 48. free thy people from their _y._
P. R. 3, 158. reduced a province under Roman _y._
P. R. 3, 334. bridges rivers proud, as with a _y._
P. R. 4, 102. a victor people free from servile _y._
P. R. 4, 135. but govern ill the nations under _y._
S. A. 39. should Israel from Philistian _y._ deliver
S. A. 42. himself in bonds under Philistian _y._
Il P. 59. while Cynthia checks her dragon _y._
S. 19, 11. who best bear his mild _y._ they serve
**Yoked.**—S. A. 410. held me _y._ her bondslave
**Yon.**—P. L. 1, 180. seest thou _y._ dreary plain
P. L. 1, 280. grovelling and prostrate on _y._ lake
P. L. 2, 183. under _y._ boiling ocean wrapped
P. L. 4, 626. to reform _y_ flowery arbours
P. L. 4, 1011. read thy lot in _y._ celestial sign
C. 295. that crawls under the side of _y._ small hill
A. 36. to the great mistress of _y._ princely shrine
Il P. 52. him that _y._ soars on golden wing
S. 1, 1. O nightingale that on _y._ bloomy spray
**Yonder.**—P. L. 2, 684. athwart my way to _y._ gates
P. L. 4, 626. to reform yon flowery arbours _y._
P. L. 5, 367. in _y._ shady bower to rest
P. L. 5, 620. mystical dance which _y._ starry
P. L. 9, 218. while I in _y._ spring of roses
P. L. 10, 617. and havoc _y._ world
P. L. 11, 229. I descry from _y._ blazing cloud
P. L. 11, 328. in _y_ nether world
P. L. 12, 142. mount Hermon _y._
P. L. 12, 591. on _y._ hill expect their motion
S. A. 3. for _y._ bank hath choice of sun or shade
**Yore.**—Il P. 23. thee bright haired Vesta long of _y._
**Young.**—P. L. 4, 279. her florid son _y._ Bacchus
P. L. 7, 420. disclosed their callow _y._
P. L. 11, 668. him old and _y._ exploded
P. R. 2, 18. therefore as those _y._ prophets then
P. R. 2, 329. those _y._ Daniel could refuse
P. R. 3, 34. _y._ Scipio had brought down the
P. R. 3, 35. _y._ Pompey quelled the Pontic
P. R. 3, 101. if _y._ African for fame his wasted
C. 492. what voice is that? my _y._ lord?
C. 498. or _y._ kid lost his dam
C. 755. be advised you are but _y._ yet
C. 999. where _y._ Adonis oft reposes
L. 9. _y._ Lycidas and hath not left his peer
L. 113. how well could I have spared for thee _y._
L'A. 97. and _y._ and old come forth to play
S. 17, 1. Vane _y._ in years but in sage counsel old
D. F. I. 25. _y._ Hyacinth born on Eurotas' strand
**Younger.**—P. L. 1, 512. seized by _y._ Saturn

P. L. 9, 246. till *y.* hands ere long assist us
P. L. 12, 160. he comes invited by a *y.* son
S. A. 336. hither hath informed your *y.* feet
**Youngest.**—P. L. 3, 151. loved thy *y.* son
**Youngest-teemed.**—H. 240. heaven's *y.-t.* star
**Yours.**—P. L. 1, 316. heaven once *y.* now lost
P. L. 2, 987. *y.* be the advantage
P. L. 5, 489. discourse is oftest *y.*
P. L. 5, 537. as you *y.* while our obedience
P. L. 10, 398. among these numerous orbs all *y.*
**Yourself.**—C. 679. should you be so cruel to *y.*
**Yourselves.**—P. L. 4, 830. argues *y.*
P. L. 5, 789. know ye right or if ye know *y.*
**Youth.**—P. L. 1, 770. populous *y.* about the
P. L. 3, 638. yet such as in his face *y.* smiled
P. L. 4, 552. the unarmed *y.* of heaven
P. L. 11, 246. in manhood where *y.* ended
P. L. 11, 539. outlive thy *y.* thy strength thy
P. L. 11, 542. and for the air of *y.* hopeful and
P. L. 11, 594. and fair event of love and *y.* not
P. R. 1, 67. but his growth now to *y.'s* full
P. R. 2, 197. that Pellean conqueror a *y.*
P. R. 2, 200. dismissed in his prime *y.* the fair
P. R. 4, 508. thy childhood and thy *y.*

S. A. 264. a trivial weapon felled their choicest *y.*
S. A. 938. if in my flower of *y.* and strength
S. A. 1738. thither shall all the valiant *y.* resort
C. 55. and his blithe *y.*
C. 609. alas good venturous *y.* I love thy courage
C. 970. heaven hath timely tried their *y.*
C. 1011. two blissful twins are to be born *y.* and
L. 164. and O ye dolphins waft the hapless *y.*
L'A. 95. to many a *y.* and many a maid
S. 7, 1. how soon hath time the subtle thief of *y.*
S. 9, 1. lady that in the prime of earliest *y.*
M. M. 6. mirth and *y.* and warm desire
D. F. I. 53. or wert thou that sweet smiling *y.*
Hor. 1. what slender *y.* bedewed with liquid
**Youthful.**—P. L. 4, 338. nor *y.* dalliance
P. L. 4, 845. severe in *y.* beauty
P. L. 10, 218. or as the snake with *y.* coat
S. A. 524. and great in hopes with *y.* courage
S. A. 1442. old Manoah in such haste with *y.* steps
C. 289. were they of manly prime or *y.* bloom
C. 669. that fancy can beget on *y.* thoughts
L'A. 26. jest and *y.* jollity
L'A. 129. such sights as *y.* poets dream
**Youths.**—P. R. 2, 352. tall stripling *y.* rich-clad

# Z.

**Zeal.**—P. L. 2, 485. varnished o'er with *z.*
P. L. 3, 452. painful superstition and blind *z.*
P. L. 5, 593. holy memorials acts of *z.* and love
P. L. 5, 805. whom none with more *z.* adored
P. L. 5, 807. and in a flame of *z.* severe
P. L. 5, 849. but his *z.* none seconded
P. L. 5, 900. his loyalty he kept his love his *z.*
P. L. 9, 665. but with show of *z.*
P. L. 9, 676. preface brooking through his *z.*
P. L. 11, 801. therefore cooled in *z.* thenceforth
P. R. 3, 171. let move thee *z.* and duty,—*z.* and
P. R. 3, 175. *z.* of thy father's house
P. R. 3, 407. but whence to thee this *z.*
P. R. 3, 412. such was thy *z.* to Israel
S. A. 895. but *z.* moved thee: to please thy gods
S. A. 1420. priest then soonest fired with *z.*
**Zealous.**—P. L. 4, 565. a spirit *z.* as he
**Zealously.**—S. 9, 9. is fixed and *z.* attends
**Zenith.**—P. L. 1, 745. dropped from the *z.* like

P. L. 10, 329. the Scorpion steering his *z.*
**Zephon.**—P. L. 4, 788. Ithuriel and *Z.* with
P. L. 4, 834. to whom thus *Z.* answering scorn
P. L. 4, 854. thy fear said *Z.* bold will save us
P. L. 4, 868. by glimpse discern Ithuriel and *Z.*
**Zephyr.**—P. L. 4, 329. to recommend cool *z.*
P. L. 10, 705. Eurus and *Z.* with their lateral
L'A. 19. *Z.* with Aurora playing as he met her
**Zephyrus.**—P. L. 5, 16. *Z.* on Flora breathes
**Zodiac.**—P. L. 11, 247. as in a glistering *z.*
P. L. 12, 255. him burn seven lamps as in a *z.*
**Zone.**—P. L. 2, 397. or else in some mild *z.*
P. L. 5, 281. the middle pair girt like a starry *z.*
P. L. 5, 560. his other half in the great *z.* of
P. L. 7, 580. which nightly as a circling *z.* thou
P. R. 2, 214. as the *z.* of Venus once wrought
**Zophiel.**—P. L. 6, 535. *Z.* of cherubim the
**Zora.**—S. A. 181. from Eshtaol and *Z.'s* fruitful

THE END.